PENGUIN BOOKS

THE PENGUIN WEBSTER
HANDY COLLEGE DICTIONARY

Philip Morehead is a lexicographer, an authority on games, and Head of Music Staff of the Lyric Opera of Chicago and the Lyric Opera Center for American Artists. His books include *Hoyle's Rules of Games* and *The New International Dictionary of Music*. He lives in Chicago.

THE PENGUIN
WEBSTER

HANDY COLLEGE

DICTIONARY

Albert and Loy Morehead

EDITORS

Third Edition prepared by
Philip D. Morehead

PENGUIN BOOKS

PENGUIN BOOKS

Published by the Penguin Group
Penguin Putnam Inc., 375 Hudson Street,
New York, New York 10014, U.S.A.
Penguin Books Ltd, 80 Strand, London WC2R 0RL, England
Penguin Books Australia Ltd, 250 Camberwell Road,
Camberwell, Victoria 3124, Australia
Penguin Books Canada Ltd, 10 Alcorn Avenue,
Toronto, Ontario, Canada M4V 3B2
Penguin Books India (P) Ltd, 11 Community Centre,
Panchsheel Park, New Delhi – 110 017, India
Penguin Books (N.Z.) Ltd, Cnr Rosedale and Airborne Roads,
Albany, Auckland, New Zealand
Penguin Books (South Africa) (Pty) Ltd, 24 Sturdee Avenue,
Rosebank, Johannesburg 2196, South Africa

Penguin Books Ltd, Registered Offices:
Harmondsworth, Middlesex, England

First published in the United States of America by Signet,
an imprint of New American Library, a division of Penguin Putnam Inc. 1995
Published in Penguin Books 2003

10 9 8 7 6 5 4 3 2 1

ISBN 0 14 20.0314 X

Printed in the United States of America

CONTENTS

HOW TO USE THIS DICTIONARY

This dictionary supplies the spelling, syllabication, pronunciation, and meaning of the most useful words of the English language as it is spoken in the United States. Abbreviations, foreign words and phrases, and the names and descriptions of places may be found in the pages following the main vocabulary.

Words are not listed separately when they are identical in spelling and pronunciation and differ only in etymology.

SPELLING

Where a word may correctly be spelled in more than one way, we have generally preferred the simplest way. Space does not permit us to include every spelling for which there is authority. The user of this dictionary may rely upon finding a correct way to spell his word, but it will not necessarily be *the only* correct way.

SYLLABICATION

Each word in its first spelling is divided into syllables, either by stress marks or by dots. The syllable preceding the mark (′) is primarily stressed; a syllable preceding the mark (″) receives secondary stress. The dots should not be confused with hyphens. When a word is to be hyphenated in spelling, it is marked with a bold, long hyphen (-).

It is not conventionally proper to divide a word, at the end of a line, at any place except where a stress mark, dot or hyphen appears. Even where the dictionary shows a division into syllables, it is not good style to leave a single letter of a word on one line; for example, words like *abound, alike, glossy,* should not be divided between lines.

GUIDE TO PRONUNCIATION

a	as in fat	û	as in pull	ngg	as in finger
ā	as in fate	ə	as in comma,	nk	as in ink (pro-
ä	as in far		label,		nounced
â	as in fall		pupil,		*ingk*)
ȧ	as in ask		censor,	p	as in pen
ã	as in dare		focus	r	as in rat
e	as in met	b	as in but	s	as in sit, this
ē	as in mete	ch	as in chair	sh	as in she
ẽ	as in her	d	as in day	t	as in to
ė	as in maybe	f	as in fill	th	as in thin
i	as in pin	g	as in go	*th*	as in then
ī	as in pine	h	as in hat	v	as in van
o	as in not	hw	as in when	w	as in win
ō	as in note	j	as in joke	y	as in yet
oo	as in spoon	k	as in keep	z	as in zone, quiz
ô	as in or	kt	as in act	zh	as in azure
oi	as in oil	l	as in late	ö	as in Ger. *schön*
ow	as in owl	m	as in man	ü	as in Fr. *tu*
u	as in tub	n	as in nod	ṅ	as in Fr. *bon*
ū	as in mute	ng	as in sing	kh	as in blockhouse

The criterion for pronunciation is the best usage in regions where there is no marked peculiarity of speech and in normal conversation rather than in formal speech.

Where the respelling of a word for pronunciation would be in all respects the same as the original spelling, the word is not respelled.

Most of the diacritical marks are self-explanatory, but some suggest comment:

ə (the upside-down e, called the schwa) marks the **a** in comma **e** in label **i** in pupil **o** in censor **u** in focus	Any unaccented vowel tends to become an "uh" sound. The use of the ə does not mean you must not pronounce the actual vowel; with meticulous speakers the original vowel sound remains recognizable. Say *char-i-ty* if you wish, but with equal confidence—and much more company—you may say *char-ə-ty.* The schwa is also used to indicate certain "lost" vowel sounds, as in the word *garden,* where the *n* is merely a nasal utterance following the gard-.
à as in ask	However you pronounce *ask, laugh, aunt*—with the *a* as in *cat,* or as in *father,* or somewhere in between—that is how you should render this à.
ô as in corn; horn, torn	Traditionally, dictionaries say that the sound of *o* in *corn, horn, morn* is different from the sound of *o* in *worn, torn, sworn;* that *horse* and *hoarse, border* and *boarder, born* and *borne,* are not pronounced the same. We do not make this distinction. In the few regions where it is made, the *r* is not pronounced.
ė to represent the *y* in story	The terminal *y* is rendered as short *i* in other dictionaries. Along with the writers of popular songs, we hear it, from coast to coast, as an unstressed long *e.*
nk as in ink	This is actually pronounced *ngk;* but since it is never pronounced any other way, it seems unnecessary to respell a word each time *nk* occurs.

Compound words are not respelled for pronunciation if each element is pronounced elsewhere in the dictionary. A derivative form is respelled for pronunciation only to the extent necessary: *odd'i·ty* (-ə-tė).

INFLECTIONAL FORMS

In the formation of plurals, inflection of verbs, and comparison of adjectives and adverbs, only irregular forms are specified in the dictionary. In the absence of specific exception, it should be assumed that the following rules apply.

PLURAL FORMS OF NOUNS

1. Usually, form the plural by adding *-s* to the singular noun. The *-s* is pronounced *z,* unless *s* is easier.

2. Usually add *-es* to a singular noun ending in a sibilant sound. The *-es* then forms a new syllable, pronounced *-iz.* Thus: *dresses* (dres'iz), *matches* (mach'iz).

If the singular noun ends in a sibilant but has a silent terminal *e,* add only *-s,* but the new syllable still occurs: *base, bases* (bā′siz).

3. When a noun ends in *y* preceded by a consonant, the plural form is *-ies: dairy, dairies* (dār′ēz). But when the terminal *y* is preceded by a vowel, add merely *-s: day, days.*

4. The plural form of a noun ending in a consonant and *o* is *-oes: hero, heroes* (hir′ōz). But when a vowel precedes the terminal *o* add merely *-s: radio, radios* (rā′dė-ōz″).

POSSESSIVE FORMS

1. To form the possessive, add *'s* to a singular noun or to a plural noun not ending in *s:* a *man's* voice, the *horse's* mouth, the *fish's* tail, *men's* lives. The pronunciation follows the rules for regular plurals: *fish's* is the same as *fishes* (fish′iz).

2. To form the possessive of a plural noun ending in *s,* add the apostrophe (') alone: the *workers'* wages.

3. The foregoing rules apply also to proper names: *John's* book, John *Harris's* house, the *Smiths'* party. It is incorrect to write *the Harris' ages* instead of *Harrises'.*

4. The possessive forms of pronouns are usually irregular and are given in the dictionary.

INFLECTION OF REGULAR VERBS

1. The present indicative tense uses the infinitive in all cases except third person singular, which is regularly formed the same as the plurals of nouns (see preceding paragraphs). Thus: *to like, I like, you like, we like, they like,* but *he, she,* or *it likes.*

2. The past tense (preterit) is formed by adding *-d* or *-ed* to the infinitive, according as the latter does or does not end with *e.* The *-ed* forms a new syllable after *d* or *t,* and is pronounced *-id*: to want, *wanted* (wont′id); to end, *ended* (en′did). In other cases the *-d* or *-ed* does not form a new syllable and is pronounced *d* or *t,* whichever is easier: to play, *played* (plād); to match, *matched* (macht). A terminal *y* preceded by a consonant changes to *-ied*: to bury, *bur′ied.*

3. The past participle is the same as the preterit.

4. The present participle is formed by adding *-ing* to the infinitive, from which the terminal *e* (if any) is dropped. Thus: to jump, *jump′ing*; to hate, *hat′ing*; to grapple, *grap′pling*; to bury, *bur′y-ing.*

5. A consonant preceded by a short vowel is doubled: to can, *canned* (kand), *can′ning.* (These forms are regularly given in the dictionary.)

6. Many of the fundamental verbs are irregular, as *be, have, go, run, make,* etc. All forms of the auxiliary verbs *be* and *have* are given in the text under the infinitives. The forms of the other irregular verbs are given after the infinitive, in square brackets [ ], in the order: preterit, past participle, present participle. When the preterit and past participle are the same form, it is not repeated. When only one syllable is shown, it replaces the last syllable only of the word previously spelled out: *fit* [fit′ted, -ting].

7. Regular and irregular verbs alike form their other tenses as follows. *Present perfect:* add the past participle to the present indicative of *have.* (Thus: to go, I have gone.) *Past perfect, or pluperfect:* add the past participle to the preterit of *have.* (Thus: to go, I had gone.) *Present progressive:* add the present participle to the present indicative of *be.* (Thus: to go, I am going.) *Past progressive;* add the present participle to the preterit of *be.* (Thus: to go, I was going.) *Passive voice:* add the past participle to the appropriate tense of *be.* (Thus: to call, I am called, I was called, I have been called, I had been called, etc.) *Future tense:* add the infinitive to the appropriate tense of *will* or *shall.* (Thus: to call, I will call, I shall call, I shall be called, etc.) *Subjunctive mood:* add the infinitive to *would* or *should* (active voice) or the past participle to the subjunctive form of *be* (passive voice). (Thus: to call, if I should call, if I should be called.) *Imperative mood:* use the infinitive. (Thus: to go, Go!)

COMPARISON OF ADJECTIVES AND ADVERBS

1. The main vocabulary lists only the positive forms of adjectives and adverbs. The regular formation of the comparative is to add *-r* or *-er* to the positive; of the superlative, to add *-st* or *-est* (according as the positive does or does not end in *e*). A consonant preceded by a short vowel is doubled: *mad, mad'der, mad'dest.* For words ending in *y,* the forms are *-ier, -iest.* Often the regular formation makes for awkward pronunciation; in such a case, for the comparative, precede the positive by *more;* for the superlative, precede it by *most.* In general, this alternative is followed for words of three of more syllables.

2. For adjectives and adverbs compared irregularly, the text appends the comparative and superlative in square brackets [ ]: good [bet'ter, best].

THE FORMATION OF ADDITIONAL WORDS

1. This dictionary lists hundreds of prefixes, suffixes, and other word elements from which additional words can be formed and the meanings of other words can be inferred.

2. The adjectival forms ending in *-ful, -some, -like,* and *-less* are generally omitted from the dictionary.

3. Adverbs are regularly formed from adjectives by the addition of *-ly:* bright, *bright'ly.* When the adjective ends in *-y,* this letter regularly changes to *i,* making the terminal *-ily:* heavy, *heav'i·ly.* When the adjective ends in *-le* preceded by a consonant, the adverb is formed by changing the final *e* to *y:* idle, *i'dly.* Virtually all regular adverbial forms are omitted from the dictionary.

4. Nouns of agency are regularly formed by adding *-er* to a verb: *to pound, pound'er,* one who or that which pounds. The rules follow those for forming the comparatives of adjectives: *to bury, bur'i·er; to pine, pin'er; to dig, dig'ger.* Most of the regular forms are omitted from the dictionary. Such nouns when formed by adding *-or, -ist, -eer,* etc. are given in the dictionary.

AMERICAN, BRITISH AND CANADIAN SPELLINGS

The preferred spellings in this dictionary follow American usage. In the following cases British (and, when indicated, Canadian) usage differs:

1. Many nouns such as *honor, armor* (U.S.) are spelled *honour, armour* (Brit. & Can.). Similar variation between *o* and *ou* occurs in a few other words, as *molt* (U.S.), *moult* (Brit. & Can.); *smolder* (U.S.), *smoulder* (Brit. & Can.).

2. Most verbs ending in *-ize* (U.S. & Can.) are spelled *-ise* (Brit.): *realize* (U.S. & Can.), *realise* (Brit.).

3. Many words ending in *-er* (U.S.) are spelled *-re* (Brit. & Can.): *center, fiber* (U.S.), *centre, fibre* (Brit. & Can.).

4. In forms of verbs ending in *l* preceded by a short vowel, the *l* is not usually doubled (U.S.) and is usually doubled (Brit. & Can.): *traveled, traveling, traveler* (U.S.), *travelled, travelling, traveller* (Brit. & Can.).

MASCULINE AND FEMININE ENTRIES

When separate forms of a word are commonly used to refer to men and women, signalled by the suffixes **-man** and **-or** or **-er** (masculine) and **-woman** and **-ess** (feminine), these forms are often entered sequentially, as:

> **gen′tle·man** (mən) [*pl.* **-men**], **gen′tle·wom″an** n.
> **wait′er** (-ər), **wait′ress** *n.*

BOXES

Boxes are used for word origins (etymologies), usage notes, and grammatical notes. In the boxes, etymologies are signaled by the symbol ↔; usage notes are usually signaled by the symbol ☛; and grammatical notes are indicated by the label (*Gram.*). The sign ❏ followed by a word at the end of an entry means that information about the word can be found in a box under the word referred to. Derivations are given for some of the entries in this dictionary, when the history of the word is of special interest. For a list and brief description of languages cited in the boxes, please see p. 756. In boxes, an asterisk (*) indicates a source word that is assumed to have existed but which has not been found in any written sources.

A

A, a (ā) first letter of the English alphabet. —*adj., indef. art.* one; any. —*prep.* (*Informal*) per (def. 2).

a- *pref.* **1,** not. **2,** in, on. **3,** an intensive, as in *arouse.*

---
a, an
(*Gram.*) Pronunciation is the guide: Before a consonant sound (including a pronounced *h* and the sound *ū*), use *a.* Before a vowel sound (including silent *h*), use *an.*

AA (ā'ā') *n.* antiaircraft fire.

aard'vark" (ärd'värk") *n.* an African ant-eating mammal; groundhog.

ab-, abs- *pref.* away from; off.

a·ba' (ə-bä') *n.* a fabric made of goat's or camel's hair; an Arab outer garment made of this fabric.

a"ba·cá' (ä"bä-kä') *n.* a Philippine palm; its fiber, used in making hemp.

a·back' (ə-bak') *adv.* toward the rear. —**taken aback,** disconcerted.

ab'a·cus (ab'ə-kəs) *n.* a calculating device consisting of beads strung on rods in a frame.

a·baft' (ə-baft') *adv. & prep.* (*Naut.*) toward the stern; behind.

ab"a·lo'ne (ab"-ə-lō'nė) *n.* a large snail abundant on the Pacific coast.

a·ban'don (ə-ban'dən) *v.t.* give up; leave; forsake; cast away. —*n.* freedom from restraint. —**a·ban'doned,** *adj.* reckless; dissolute. —**a·ban'don·ment,** *n.*

a·base' (ə-bās') *v.t.* reduce in rank or estimation. —**a·base'ment,** *n.*

a·bash' (ə-bash') *v.t.* make ashamed or dispirited; embarrass.

a·bate' (ə-bāt') *v.t.* beat down; reduce; moderate. —*v.i.* diminish; lessen. —**a·bate'ment,** *n.*

ab"at·toir' (ab"ə-twär') *n.* slaughterhouse.

ab·bé' (à-bā') *n.* a French ecclesiastic.

ab'bess (ab'es) *n.* the head of a convent.

ab'bey (ab'ė) *n.* a monastery or convent.

ab'bot (ab'ət) *n.* the head of a monastery. —**ab'ba·cy** (ab'ə-sė) *n.*

ab·bre'vi·ate" (ə-brē'vė-āt") *v.t.* shorten by omission of some parts.

ab·bre"vi·a'tion (-ā'shən) *n.* **1,** abridgment. **2,** a shortened form, esp. of a word.

ABC's (ā"bē"sēz') *n.pl.* **1,** the alphabet. **2,** (often *sing.*) the basic facts or principles of a subject.

---
abbreviation, contraction, acronym, initialism
An *abbreviation* is a shortened form of a word, formed by eliminating one or more letters. An abbreviation ends with a period. A *contraction* omits one or more letters from within a word, replacing them with an apostrophe, and does not end with a period. Two special types of abbreviation are *acronym* and *initialism.* Both are made up of the initial letters of the words of a phrase; an acronym is pronounced as a word (*ZIP* Code), whereas an initialism is read letter by letter (*GNP*). Note however that in common usage, *acronym* is used to refer to both acronyms and initialisms.

---

ab'di·cate" (ab'də-kāt") *v.i. & t.* renounce or relinquish an office, power, or right. —**ab"di·ca'tion,** *n.* —**ab'di·ca"tor,** *n.*

ab'do·men (ab'də-mən) *n.* the lower part of the human body, between thorax and pelvis. —**ab·dom'i·nal** (ab-dom'i-nəl) *adj.*

ab·duct' (ab-dukt') *v.t.* carry away by force; kidnap. —**ab·duc'tion,** *n.* —**abduc'-tor,** *n.*

a·beam' (ə-bēm') *adv.* at right angles to the keel of a ship; in a sideward direction.

a"be·ce·dar'i·an (ā"bē-sē-dār'ė-ən) *n.* a beginner. —*adj.* elementary; primary.

a·bed' (ə-bed') *adv.* in bed.

a·bele' (ə-bēl') *n.* the white poplar tree.

Ab'er·deen" An'gus (ab'ər-dēn" ang'gəs) one of a breed of hornless beef cattle.

ab·er'rant (ab-er'ənt) *adj.* straying from the right course; wandering. —**ab·er'-rance, ab·er'ran·cy,** *n.*

ab"er·ra'tion (ab"ə-rā'shən) *n.* **1,** departure from a normal course. **2,** deviation from truth or moral rectitude. **3,** apparent displacement of a heavenly body, due to its motion relative to the earth. **4,** any disturbance of light rays that prevents accurate focusing.

a·bet' (ə-bet') *v.t.* [**a·bet'ted, -ting**] encourage; aid by approval, esp. in bad conduct. —**a·bet'ment,** *n.* —**a·bet'ter, a·bet'tor,** *n.*

a·bey'ance (ə-bā'əns) *n.* temporary suspension or inactivity.

ab·hor' (ab-hôr') *v.t.* [**-horred', -hor'-**

---

ring] regard with extreme repugnance; detest.

ab·hor'rence (ab-hor'əns) *n.* strong hatred; detestation. **—ab·hor'rent,** *adj.* detestable; disgusting.

a·bide' (ə-bīd') *v.i.* [*pret. & p.p.* **a·bode'**] **1,** remain; continue. **2,** dwell. **3,** (with *by*) stand firm. **—v.i. & t.** [**a·bid'ed**] put up with; tolerate.

ab'i·gail" (ab'ə-gāl") *n.* a lady's maid.

> **abigail**
> ↔ The word comes from the name of a character in the play *The Scornful Lady* (1610) by Beaumont and Fletcher.

a·bil'i·ty (ə-bil'ə-tē) *n.* **1,** state of being able; possession of qualities necessary. **2,** competence; skill; a particular talent.

> **ability, capability, capacity, power, skill, talent, gift, genius, faculty, aptitude, know-how, art, craft**
> *Ability*, *capability*, and *capacity* imply both the *power* to do something and the *skill* required for its accomplishment. The ability may be innate, as implied by *talent*, *gift*, *genius*, *faculty*, or *aptitude*; or it may be acquired by practice, as implied by *skill*, *know-how*, *art*, or *craft*.

-a·bil'i·ty *suf.* marking noun forms of adjectives ending in *-able*.

ab'ject (ab'jekt) *adj.* **1,** low in condition or estimation; hopeless. **2,** servile; despicable. **—ab·ject'ness,** *n.*

ab·jure' (ab-jûr') *v.t.* renounce solemnly or on oath; repudiate; forswear. **—ab"ju·ra'tion** (ab"jə-rā'shən) *n.*

ab·la·tive (ab'lə-tiv) *n. & adj.* a grammatical case denoting agency, place, etc., in certain inflected languages, as Latin.

a·blaze' (ə-blāz') *adj.* **1,** on fire. **2,** brilliantly lighted up. **3,** very excited; angry.

a'ble (ā'bəl) *adj.* [**a'bler, a'blest**] **1,** having the means or power to be or act. **2,** having marked intellectual qualifications; talented. **—a'ble-bod"ied,** *adj.* of strong body; physically competent. **—able-bodied seaman,** a fully qualified merchant seaman.

-a·ble (ə-bəl) *suf.* denoting ability, liability, tendency.

a'bled (ā'bəld) *adj.* possessed of certain capabilities, as *differently abled*.

a·bloom' (ə-bloom') *adj.* in blossom.

ab·lu'tion (ab-loo'shən) *n.* washing; cleansing, esp. ceremonial.

ab'ne·gate" (ab'nə-gāt") *v.t.* renounce or

deny oneself (own rights or powers). **—ab"ne·ga'tion,** *n.*

ab·nor'mal (ab-nôr'məl) *adj.* not ordinary; unusual; deviating from a type or standard. **—ab"normal'i·ty** (ab"nôr-mal'ə-tē) *n.* the state or an instance of being abnormal.

a·board' (ə-bôrd') *adv. & prep.* on board (a ship, train, or other conveyance).

a·bode' (ə-bōd') *n.* **1,** dwelling place. **2,** sojourn; continuance. **—v.** pret. & p.p. of *abide.*

a·bol'ish (ə-bol'ish) *v.t.* put an end to; annul; destroy. **—a·bol'ish·ment,** *n.*

ab"o·li'tion (ab"ə-lish'ən) *n.* **1,** destruction; annulment. **2,** the extinction of Negro slavery. **—ab"o·li'tion·ism,** *n.* advocation of abolition, esp. of Negro slavery. **—ab"o·li'tion·ist,** *n.*

A-'bomb" (ā'bom") *n.* atom bomb.

a·bom'i·na·ble (ə-bom'i-nə-bəl) *adj.* detestable; abhorrent. **—Abominable Snowman,** yeti.

a·bom'i·nate" (ə-bom'ə-nāt") *v.t.* hate extremely; abhor; detest.

a·bom"i·na'tion (-nā'shən) *n.* **1,** intense aversion. **2,** a detestable quality, act, or condition.

ab"o·rig'i·nal (ab"ə-rij'i-nəl) *adj.* **1,** pert. to earliest times or conditions; primitive. **2,** indigenous.

ab"o·rig'i·nes (-nēz) *n.pl.* [*sing.* **-ne** (-nē)] earliest inhabitants.

a·bort' (ə-bôrt') *v.i.* **1,** miscarry in giving birth. **2,** remain rudimentary; fail to develop. **—v.t.** cause to miscarry or to fail. **—a·bor'tive,** *adj.*

a·bor'tion (ə-bôr'shən) *n.* **1,** untimely birth; miscarriage. **2,** expulsion or removal of the human fetus. **3,** any fruit or product in a state of arrested development. **—a·bor'tion·ist,** *n.* one who induces abortions.

a·bound' (ə-bownd') *v.i.* be plentiful or prevalent; be filled (with).

> **above, greater, more, over**
> ☞ *Above* means higher in space or rank. *Greater than* means larger in size, bulk, degree, or extent. *More than* means larger in number or quantity. *Over* is the most general (and most vague) term and can be used in all contexts, but it is preferable to choose a more specific word.

a·bout' (ə-bowt') *adv.* **1,** in every direction; all around. **2,** near in time or place; approximately. **3,** on the point of; in readiness. **4,** at work; astir. **—prep. 1,** in regard to. **2,** near to. **3,** on the outside of; surrounding. —**a·bout-"face',** *n.* reversal of attitude or position.

a·bove' (ə-buv') *adv. & prep.* **1,** in a higher place than; superior to. **2,** greater in quantity or degree (than). —*adj.* forementioned.

a·bove'board" *adj. & adv.* without deceit.

> **aboveboard**
> ↔ From a rule in many card games to keep the hands visible above the table.

ab"ra·ca·dab'ra (ab"rə-kə-dab'rə) *n.* **1,** a cabalistic word-charm. **2,** mumbo-jumbo.

a·brade' (ə-brād') *v.i. & t.* wear away by friction.

a·bra'sion (ə-brā'zhən) *n.* **1,** act or result of abrading. **2,** a scraped spot.

a·bra'sive (-siv) *n.* any material for abrading, grinding, or polishing. —*adj.* tending to wear down; rough.

a·breast' (ə-brest') *adj. & adv.* side by side; to the same degree.

a·bridge' (ə-brij') *v.t.* **1,** shorten, as by omission or condensation. **2,** cut off; curtail. —**a·bridg'ment,** *n.*

a·broad' (ə-brâd') *adv.* **1,** in a foreign country; absent. **2,** in circulation; astir.

ab'ro·gate" (ab'rə-gāt") *v.t.* repeal or annul by authoritative act. —**ab"ro·ga'·tion,** *n.*

> **abrogate, arrogate**
> ☛ Do not confuse *abrogate*, to renounce, and *arrogate*, to seize.

ab·rupt' (ə-brupt') *adj.* **1,** changing or terminating suddenly; discontinuous. **2,** precipitous. —**ab·rupt'ness,** *n.*

ab'scess (ab'ses) *n.* localized collection of pus in the body tissues. —*v.i.* form an abscess.

ab·scis'sa (ab-sis'ə) *n.* (*Geom.*) the distance of a point from a vertical line of reference.

ab·scond' (ab-skond') *v.i.* hide or depart suddenly, esp. to avoid legal process.

ab'sence (ab'səns) *n.* **1,** state or period of being away. **2,** lack.

ab'sent (ab'sənt) *adj.* not present; not in a certain place; away. —*v.t.* (ab-sent') keep (oneself) away; withdraw.

ab"sen·tee' (ab"sən-tē') *n.* one who is absent, as from his or her job. —*adj.* not present or in residence. —**ab"sen·tee'·ism,** *n.*

ab'sent·mind"ed *adj.* preoccupied; forgetful. —**ab'sent·mind"ed·ness,** *n.*

ab'sinthe (ab'sinth) *n.* a liqueur made from wormwood and brandy.

ab'so·lute" (ab'sə-loot") *adj.* **1,** unqualified; unlimited. **2,** perfect; complete. **3,** positive; fixed; entirely determined; irrevocable. —*n.* something absolute. —**ab'so·lute"ness,** *n.* —**absolute pitch,** the ability to identify or reproduce any given pitch. —**absolute zero,** the temperature at which (in theory) all molecular motion ceases, about -459.6°F, -273.2°C. —**the Absolute,** God.

ab"so·lu'tion (ab"sə-loo'shən) *n.* **1,** act of absolving. **2,** forgiveness of sins; remission of punishment for sins.

ab'so·lut"ism (ab'sə-loo"tiz-əm) *n.* **1,** advocacy of autocratic government. **2,** any doctrine held without reservations. —**ab"-so·lut'ist,** *adj. & n.*

ab·solve' (ab-zolv') *v.t.* **1,** pardon; free from penalty. **2,** release from an obligation.

ab·sorb' (ab-sôrb') *v.t.* **1,** suck up a liquid; take in; assimilate. **2,** swallow, engulf, or engross completely. —**ab·sorbed',** *adj.* preoccupied.

> **absorb, adsorb**
> ☛ Do not confuse *absorb*, to suck up, with *adsorb*, to cause to condense on the surface.

ab·sorb'ent (-ənt) *adj.* readily sucking up. —**ab·sorb'en·cy,** *n.*

ab·sorb'ing *adj.* very interesting.

ab·sorp'tion (ab-sôrp'shən) *n.* **1,** act of absorbing; assimilation. **2,** preoccupation. —**ab·sorp'tive,** *adj.*

ab·stain' (ab-stān') *v.i.* refrain (usually, from pleasurable action).

ab·ste'mi·ous (ab-stē'mė-əs) *adj.* moderate, temperate, esp. as to food and drink. —**ab·ste'mi·ous·ness,** *n.*

ab·sten'tion (ab-sten'shən) *n.* act of abstaining. —**ab·sten'tious,** *adj.*

ab'sti·nence (ab'sti-nəns) *n.* self-restraint in satisfaction of appetite. —**ab'sti·nent,** *adj.*

ab·stract' (ab-strakt') *v.t.* **1,** consider in general terms. **2,** take away; steal. **3,** (ab'-strakt) reduce to a summary; epitomize. —*n.* (ab'strakt) **1,** a summary or inventory. **2,** the essential aspects of a subject. —*adj.* (ab'strakt) conceived in general or theoretical terms. —**ab·stract'ed,** *adj.* inattentive; preoccupied. —**Abstract Expressionism,** ◻ an American style of abstract painting. ◻ *excerpt*

ab·strac'tion (ab-strak'shən) *n.* **1,** act of abstracting. **2,** state of being preoccupied or inattentive. **3,** an abstract idea, concept, etc.

ab·struse' (ab-stroos') *adj.* **1,** difficult to comprehend. **2,** profound. **—ab·struse'-ness,** *n.*

ab·surd' (ab-sērd') *adj.* contrary to common sense or sound judgment; logically impossible; ridiculous. **—***n.* man's existence as meaningless and without purpose. **—theater of the absurd,** theater which ignores or distorts the usual conventions of character, plot, etc.

ab·surd'i·ty (-ə-tē) *n.* quality of being absurd; something that is absurd.

a·bun'dance (ə-bun'dəns) *n.* copious supply or quantity; plenteousness. **—a·bun'dant,** *adj.*

a·buse' (ə-būz') *v.t.* **1,** put to a wrong or bad use; misapply. **2,** do wrong to; injure; violate; defile. **3,** attack with contumelious language; revile. **4,** assault sexually. **—***n.* (-būs') **1,** improper use; injury; insult. **2,** sexual assault. **—a·bu'sive** (-bū'siv) *adj.*

> **abuse, misuse**
> ☛ Both words mean to use wrongly or incorrectly, but *abuse* often carries the added sense of injury or harm, esp. sexual.

a·but' (ə-but') *v.t.* **[a·but'ted, -ting]** rest against; be contiguous to. **—***v.i.* (with *against*) touch. **—a·but'tal** (-əl), *n.*

a·but'ment (-mənt) *n.* **1,** a junction. **2,** a supporting base.

a·bys'mal (ə-biz'məl) *adj.* **1,** like an abyss; immeasurably deep or low. **2,** (*Informal*) of poor quality.

> **abysmal, abyssal**
> ☛ Both of these words mean immeasurably low. *Abysmal* also has the figurative, colloquial sense of very deep or very bad.

a·byss' (ə-bis') *n.* bottomless pit; gulf; any deep, immeasurable space. Also, **a·bysm'** (a-biz'əm). **—a·bys'sal** (-əl) *adj.* ❑ *abysmal*

a·ca'cia (ə-kā'shə) *n.* **1,** (*cap.*) a genus of shrubby plants. **2,** gum arabic. **3,** the locust tree.

ac'a·deme" (ak'ə-dēm") *n.* **1,** [*also,* **ac"a·de'mi·a** (ak"ə-dē'mē-ə) academic environment. **2,** a scholarly person; pedant.

a·ca"de·mese' (ə-kad"ə-mēz') *n.* a jargon found in academic circles.

ac"a·dem'ic (ak"ə-dem'ik) *adj.* **1,** conforming to set rules or traditions; conventional. **2,** pert. to a college or other institution of higher learning. **3,** theoreti-

cal. **—ac"a·dem'i·cal·ly,** *adv.* **—ac"a·dem'-i·cism** (-ə-siz-əm) *n.*

a·cad"e·mi'cian (ə-kad"ə-mish'ən) *n.* a member of a society for the promotion of an art or science.

a·cad'e·my (ə-kad'ə-mē) *n.* **1,** a school for instruction in a particular art or science. **2,** a private college-preparatory school. **3,** an association of adepts for the promotion of an art or science.

> **academy**
> ↔ The word derives from the name of the park in Athens where the philosopher Plato taught. The park was named after the Greek mythological hero Akademos.

a·can'thus (ə-kan'thəs) *n.* **1,** a spiny shrub of Europe and Africa. **2,** a conventionalized representation of its leaf, used as an ornament in architecture.

a cap·pel'la (ä-kə-pel'ə) (*It., Music*) without accompaniment; lit., in chapel style.

ac'a·rid (ak'ə-rid) *n.* a mite or tick.

ac·cede' (ak-sēd') *v.i.* (with *to*) **1,** give assent; yield. **2,** come into possession of; attain.

ac·cel"er·an'do (ak-sel"ə-rän'dō) (*It., Music*) *adj. & adv.* gradually increasing in speed. **—***n.* a speeding up.

ac·cel'er·ate" (ak-sel'ə-rāt") *v.i.* increase in speed. **—***v.t.* cause to move or develop faster.

ac·cel"er·a'tion (ak-sel"ə-rā'shən) *n.* **1,** act of accelerating. **2,** increase in speed; the rate of such increase.

ac·cel'er·a"tor (ak-sel'ə-rā"tər) *n.* **1,** a pedal for opening and closing the throttle of an automobile. **2,** a substance for hastening a chemical reaction. **3,** a device for producing high-energy atomic particles.

ac'cent (ak'sent) *n.* **1,** special emphasis; stress placed on a particular syllable in uttering a word. **2,** manner of utterance; peculiarity of pronunciation, as *a foreign accent.* **3,** a mark attached to a letter, syllable, or musical note, to show pronunciation, stress, octave, etc. **—***v.t.* (also ak-sent') **1,** utter with emphasis. **2,** mark to show stress, etc.

ac·cen'tu·ate" (ak-sen'choo-āt") *v.t.* stress; emphasize. **—ac·cen"tu·a'tion,** *n.*

ac·cept' (ak-sept') *v.t. & i.* **1,** receive with approval; take in a formal way. **2,** agree to; give credence to. **—ac·cept'a·ble,** *adj.* worthy of approval.

ac·cept'ance (ak-sep'təns) *n.* **1,** act of

accepting; approval. **2,** (*Com.*) a bill one has agreed to pay later.

---
accept, except
☛ Do not confuse *accept*, meaning to receive with approval, and *except*, to leave out or exclude.

---

ac″cep·ta′tion (ak″sep-tā′shən) *n.* meaning; sense.

ac′cess (ak′ses) *n.* **1,** means of approach or admission. **2,** condition of being approachable. —*v.t.* **1,** make contact with. **2,** locate (as data) for transfer. —**ac·ces′si·ble,** *adj.*

ac·ces′sion (ak-sesh′ən) *n.* **1,** attainment of a right or office. **2,** something added; increment. **3,** agreement; consent.

ac·ces′so·ry (ak-ses′ə-rē) *n.* **1,** an added and subordinate part. **2,** (*Law*) one who aids or abets a felony without being present at its commission. —*adj.* **1,** belonging to. **2,** contributory. —**ac·ces′sor·ize** (-īz) *v.t.* supply with accessories; use as an accessory.

ac·ciac″ca·tu′ra (ät-chäk″kə-too′rə) *n.* (*It.*, a crushing) (*Music*) a grace note half a step below its principal.

ac′ci·dent (ak′si-dənt) *n.* **1,** an unfortunate occurrence; mishap; catastrophe. **2,** any chance or fortuitous event.

ac″ci·den′tal (-den′təl) *adj.* **1,** happening by chance. **2,** subsidiary. —*n.* (*Music*) a sign placed before a note indicating the chromatic alteration from its previously understood pitch.

ac·cip′i·ter (ak-sip′ə-tər) *n.* a long-tailed hawk.

ac·claim′ (ə-klām′) *v.t.* **1,** applaud. **2,** proclaim with general approval.

ac″cla·ma′tion (ak″lə-mā′shən) *n.* a demonstration of joy or approval; election by such a demonstration. —**ac·clam′a·to·ry** (ə-klam′ə-tôr-ē) *adj.*

ac′cli·mate″ (ak′lə-māt″) *v.t. & i.* accustom or become accustomed to a new climate or environment. Also, **ac·cli′ma·tize″** (-klī-mə-tīz″). —**ac″cli·ma′tion, ac·cli″ma·ti·za′tion,** *n.*

ac·cliv′i·ty (ə-kliv′ə-tē) *n.* an upward slope.

---
acclivity, proclivity
☛ Do not confuse *acclivity*, a slope, and *proclivity*, a tendency. Both derive from the Latin word for slope.

---

ac′co·lade″ (ak′ə-lād″) *n.* **1,** a ceremony conferring honor, as knighthood. **2,** (*Music*) a brace.

ac·com′mo·date″ (ə-kom′ə-dāt″) *v.t.* **1,**

make suitable; adapt. **2,** do a kindness to; serve; furnish. —*v.i.* come into adjustment or conformance. —**ac·com″mo·dat″ing,** *adj.* obliging; considerate.

ac·com″mo·da′tion (ə-kom″ə-dā′shən) *n.* **1,** adaptation. **2,** readiness to serve. **3,** anything that supplies a want. **4,** (*pl.*) lodgings.

ac·com′pa·ni·ment (ə-kum′pə-nė-mənt) *n.* **1,** something subordinate added to a principal thing. **2,** (*Music*) harmony supplied to support voices, solo instruments, etc.

ac·com′pa·ny (ə-kum′pə-nė) *v.t.* **1,** go with; be associated with. **2,** (*Music*) provide accompaniment for (a voice, etc.). —**ac·com′pa·nist,** *n.*

ac·com′plice (ə-kom′plis) *n.* an associate in a crime.

ac·com′plish (ə-kom′plish) *v.t.* **1,** bring to pass; do; complete. **2,** achieve; gain. —**ac·com′plished,** *adj.* talented; skillful. —**ac·com′plish·ment,** *n.* performance; attainment.

ac·cord′ (ə-kôrd′) *v.i.* be in harmony; agree. —*v.t.* **1,** bring into agreement; adjust. **2,** render; concede. —*n.* agreement. —**ac·cord′ance,** *n.* —**ac·cord′ant,** *adj.*

ac·cord′ing (ə-kôr′ding) *adv.* **1,** (with *to* or *as*) in conformance with; in proportion to. **2,** (with *to*) as said by. —**ac·cord′ing·ly,** *adv.* so; hence; consequently. —**according to Hoyle,** following the rules, esp. in card games.

---
according to Hoyle
↔ The phrase refers to Edmund *Hoyle*, British authority on card games, whose book *Hoyle's Games* (1746) was a model for later games books, much as Noah Webster's dictionary (1828) was a model for later English dictionaries.

---

ac·cor′di·on (ə-kôr′dė-ən) *n.* a handheld keyboard wind instrument with metal reeds, operated by a bellows. —*adj.* pleated like the bellows of an accordion. —**ac·cor′di·on·ist,** *n.*

ac·cost′ (ə-kâst′) *v.t.* approach and speak to; address.

ac·count′ (ə-kownt′) *n.* **1,** a record of pecuniary transactions. **2,** enumeration. **3,** explanatory statement; recital of facts. **4,** advantage. —*v.i.* **1,** keep records, esp. of money. **2,** give explanation. —*v.t.* impute. —**on account,** in part payment. —**on account of,** because of.

ac·count′a·ble (-ə-bəl) *adj.* **1,** able to be explained. **2,** liable. **3,** responsible. —**ac·count″a·bil′i·ty,** *n.*

ac·count′ant (-ənt) *n.* one who practices accounting. —**ac·count′an·cy,** *n.*

ac·count′ing *n.* **1,** the keeping and auditing of financial records. **2,** a statement of transactions; account.

ac·cout′er (ə-koo′tər) *v.t.* equip, esp. for military service; attire. —**ac·cou′ter·ments** (-mənts) *n.pl.* personal clothing; equipment.

ac·cred′it (ə-kred′it) *v.t.* **1,** accept as true; believe. **2,** ascribe or attribute to. **3,** confer authority upon; certify.

ac·crete′ (ə-krēt′) *v.i.* grow together; adhere. —*v.t.* add to.

ac·cre′tion (ə-krē′shən) *n.* act or result of accreting; increase; an added part.

ac·cru′al (ə-kroo′əl) *n.* that which accrues; in accounting, an amount entered on the books but payable or receivable in the future.

ac·crue′ (ə-kroo′) *v.i.* happen in due course; result from natural growth.

ac·cul″tur·a′tion (ə-kul″chə-rā′shən) *n.* the process of adopting the characteristics of another culture.

ac·cu′mu·late″ (ə-kū′myə-lāt″) *v.t.* collect or bring together; amass. —*v.i.* increase in size, quantity, or number. —**ac·cu″mu·la′tion,** *n.* —**ac·cu′mu·la″tive,** *adj.*

ac′cu·ra·cy (ak′yə-rə-sē) *n.* correctness; precision.

ac′cu·rate (ak′yə-rət) *adj.* correct; true; in exact conformity with a standard. —**ac′·cu·rate·ness,** *n.*

ac·curs′ed (ə-kėr′sid) *adj.* doomed to misfortune; detestable. Also, **ac·curst′.** —**ac·curs′ed·ness,** *n.*

ac″cu·sa′tion (ak″yə-zā′shən) *n.* **1,** act of accusing. **2,** a charge of wrongdoing. Also, **ac·cu′sal** (ə-kū′zəl).

ac·cu′sa·tive (ə-kū′zə-tiv) *n.* & *adj.* a grammatical case denoting the direct object of a verb.

ac·cuse′ (ə-kūz′) *v.t.* charge with guilt or blame.

ac·cus′tom (ə-kus′təm) *v.t.* familiarize by custom or use. —**ac·cus′tomed,** *adj.* **1,** customary; usual. **2,** wonted.

AC/DC (a′sē-dē′sē) *adj.* (*Slang*) bisexual.

ace (ās) *n.* **1,** a playing card or face of a die marked with a single pip. **2,** a point won without contest, as in tennis. **3,** an expert; adept. **4,** a very small quantity or degree. **5,** a fighter pilot who has downed five or more enemy planes. —*v.t.* **1,** win a point from (an opponent) without contest. **2,** (*Slang*) (often with *out*) get a high grade or point score on (as a test); complete successfully. —*adj.* of highest rank

or proficiency; excellent. —**ace in the hole, 1,** a card dealt face down. **2,** (*Informal*) a concealed advantage.

a·cerb′ (ə-sėrb′) *adj.* acerbic.

ac′er·bate″ (as′ər-bāt″) *v.t.* embitter; exasperate.

a·cerb′ic (ə-sėr′bik) *adj.* **1,** bitter. **2,** harsh; severe.

a·cerb′i·ty (ə-sėr′bə-tė) *n.* **1,** sourness of taste. **2,** harshness of temper or expression.

ac′er·ose″ (as′ə-rōs″) *adj.* shaped like a needle.

ac·et″a·min′o·phen (a-set″ə-min′ə-fən) *n.* a drug used to relieve pain and reduce fever.

ac″et·an′i·lide (as″i-tan′ə-lid) *n.* a compound formerly used to reduce fever or relieve pain.

ac′e·tate″ (as′ə-tāt″) *n.* (*Chem.*) a salt of acetic acid. —**cellulose acetate,** a thermoplastic compound.

a·ce′tic (ə-sē′tik) *adj.* pert. to vinegar.

a·ce′ti·fy (a-sē′tə-fī) *v.t.* convert to acid or vinegar.

a·ce′to- (ə-sē′tə) *pref.* acetic acid; vinegar.

ac′e·tone″ (as′ə-tōn″) *n.* a distillate of acetates, used as a solvent.

a·ce′tyl (ə-sē′təl) *adj.* containing acetic acid.

a·cet′y·lene (ə-set′ə-lin) *n.* a gas used as an illuminant and to produce a very hot flame.

ache (āk) *n.* continued pain. —*v.i.* **1,** suffer enduring pain. **2,** (*Informal*) yearn. —**ach′y** (-ē) *adj.*

a·chieve′ (ə-chēv′) *v.t.* & *i.* execute successfully; accomplish.

a·chieve′ment (-mənt) *n.* act or result of achieving; consummation; a notable deed.

A·chil′les′ heel (ə-kil′ēz) a vulnerable spot.

Achilles′ heel
↔ From the legend that the Greek hero Achilles was made invulnerable by being dipped in the river Styx by his mother. However, his heel, by which his mother held him when she dipped him, was unprotected.

ach″ro·mat′ic (ak″rə-mat′ik) *adj.* free from coloration, as *achromatic lens,* one that transmits light without decomposing it. —**ach″ro·mat′i·cal·ly,** *adv.*

Ach″ro·my′cin (ak″rə-mī′sin) *n.* (*T.N.*) an antibiotic drug.

ac′id (as′id) *n.* **1,** any substance with a

sour taste. **2,** (*Chem.*) a compound in which hydrogen can be replaced by a metal. **3,** (*Slang*) LSD, a drug producing hallucinations. —*adj.* **1,** having the nature or taste of an acid. **2,** sharp or biting in nature, as *an acid wit.* —**a·cid′i·ty,** *n.* —**a·cid′i·fy,** *v.t.* acetify. —**acid house** *or* **rock,** a style of loud rock music usu. accompanied by lighting designed to produce a hallucinogenic effect. —**acid rain,** rain containing harmful acids. —**acid test,** a definitive test of quality, value, etc.

ac″i·doph′i·lus milk (as″i-dof′ə-ləs) a fermented milk used medicinally.

ac″i·do′sis (as″i-dō′sis) *n.* excess acidity of the blood.

a·cid′u·lous (a-sid′yə-ləs) *adj.* somewhat acid; slightly sour.

-a·cious (ā-shəs) *suf.* forming adjectives from nouns ending in *-acity.*

-a·ci·ty (as-ə-tė) *suf.* the quality of being, or a tendency to be.

ack (ak) *n.* (*Brit.*) the letter A. —**ack′-ack″,** *n.* **1,** antiaircraft fire. **2,** antiaircraft guns.

ac·knowl′edge (ak-nol′ij) *v.t.* **1,** admit the existence or truth of. **2,** give evidence of recognizing or realizing; certify the receipt of. —**ac·knowl′edg·ment,** *n.*

> **acknowledge, allow, admit, concede, confess, own up**
> ☞ *Acknowledge* and *allow* imply simple admission of a truth. *Admit* and *concede* imply a reluctance to acknowledge that truth. *Confess* and *own up* imply criminal or other improper action is being acknowledged.

ac′me (ak′mė) *n.* the top or highest point.

ac′ne (ak′nė) *n.* a disease characterized by pimply skin eruption.

ac′o·lyte″ (ak′ə-līt″) *n.* **1,** a novice, esp. in a religious order. **2,** an attendant; assistant.

ac′o·nite″ (ak′ə-nīt″) *n.* **1,** a plant of genus *Aconitum,* such as monkshood or wolfsbane. **2,** a medicinal tincture of monkshood.

a′corn (ā′kôrn) *n.* the nut of the oak tree.

a·cous′tic (ə-koos′tik) *adj.* pert. to sound, hearing, or acoustics. —*n.* acoustics (def. 2). —**a·cous′ti·cal·ly,** *adv.*

a·cous′tics (-tiks) *n.* **1,** (*sing.*) the science of sound. **2,** (*pl.*) the sound-reflecting properties (of a structure, etc.).

ac·quaint′ (ə-kwānt′) *v.t.* make familiar with; inform.

ac·quaint′ance (-əns) *n.* **1,** personal

knowledge. **2,** a person known only slightly. —**ac·quaint′ance·ship,** *n.*

ac″qui·esce′ (ak″wė-es′) *v.i.* consent; agree. —**ac·qui·es′cence,** *n.* —**ac·qui·es′cent,** *adj.* yielding; submissive.

ac·quire′ (ə-kwīr′) *v.t.* obtain; gain. —**ac·quire′ment,** *n.*

acquired immune deficiency syndrome a condition caused by a virus (HIV) which destroys the body's ability to fight infections. Also, **AIDS.**

ac″qui·si′tion (ak″wə-zish′ən) *n.* **1,** the act of acquiring. **2,** something acquired.

ac·quis′i·tive (ə-kwiz′ə-tiv) *adj.* tending to acquire; avaricious; grasping. —**ac·quis′i·tive·ness,** *n.*

ac·quit′ (ə-kwit′) *v.t.* [**ac·quit′ted, -ting**] **1,** pronounce not guilty; release, as from an obligation. **2,** discharge or pay, as a debt. —**acquit oneself,** behave.

ac·quit′tal (-əl) *n.* act or result of acquitting; exoneration.

a′cre (ā′kər) *n.* a measure of area, 43,560 sq. ft. —**a′cre·age,** *n.*

ac′rid (ak′rid) *adj.* sharp or biting to the tongue; pungent; severe. —**a·crid′i·ty,** **ac′rid·ness,** *n.*

ac′ri·mo″ny (ak′rə-mō″nė) *n.* bitterness of temper or expression. —**ac″ri·mo′ni·ous,** *adj.*

ac′ro- (ak′rə) *pref.* height, highest point.

ac′ro·bat (ak′rə-bat) *n.* a gymnastic performer. —**ac″ro·bat′ic,** *adj.* —**ac″ro·bat′i·cal·ly,** *adv.*

ac″ro·bat′ics (-iks) *n.sing. & pl.* the feats of an acrobat; agility.

ac′ro·nym″ (ak′rə-nim″) *n.* a word made from the initial letters of a term or phrase, as *WAC* (*Women's Army Corps*). ◻ *abbreviation*

ac″ro·pho′bi·a (ak″rə-fō′bė-ə) *n.* fear of high places.

a·crop′o·lis (ə-krop′ə-lis) *n.* **1,** a settlement located on an eminence. **2,** (*cap.*) the citadel of Athens.

a·cross′ (ə-krâs′) *prep.* from side to side of; transverse to; on the other side of. —*adv.* from side to side; crosswise. —**come across, 1,** encounter by chance. **2,** (*Informal*) pay up; tell the truth.

across-the-board, *adj.* all-inclusive.

a·cros′tic (ə-krâs′tik) *n. & adj.* a composition in which the initial letters of lines form a word or phrase.

a·cryl′ic (ə-kril′ik) *adj.* pert. to an acid used in certain plastics, as Lucite and Plexiglas, and in paints. —*n.* **1,** a painting done with acrylic paint. **2,** (*pl.*) acrylic paints.

---

tub, cūte; pûll; labəl; oil, owl, go, chip, she, thin, *th*en, sing, ink; *see p. 6*

act (akt) *v.i.* **1,** do something; exert energy or force in any way. **2,** exert influence; operate. **3,** perform on the stage. **4,** (with *up*) be unruly; behave eccentrically. —*v.t.* (often with *out*) do; perform; transact; represent by action. —*n.* **1,** anything done; an exertion of energy or force; deed. **2,** a law, ordinance, decree, or judgment, etc. **3,** individual performance in a varied program. **4,** a main division of a play. —**act of God,** an unforeseeable or unpreventable natural event.

ACTH *n.* a pituitary derivative used in combating rheumatic fever, arthritis, etc.: *a*(dreno)*c*(ortico)*t*(ropic) *h*(ormone).

act′ing *adj.* **1,** functioning. **2,** serving temporarily.

ac·tin′ic (ak-tin′ik) *adj.* pert. to chemical reactions caused by radiant energy, as in a photographic emulsion by sunlight. —**ac·tin′i·cal·ly,** *adv.*

ac′tin·ide″ (ak′tin-īd″) *adj.* any of a series of radioactive elements similar to actinium.

ac·tin′i·um (ak-tin′ē-əm) *n.* a radioactive chemical element resembling the rare earths, no. 89, symbol Ac.

ac′tion (ak′shən) *n.* **1,** something done; an exertion of energy or force; act. **2,** state of being active; continued influence; behavior; conduct. **3,** a sequence of events; the main story of a play or narrative; a battle. **4,** an operating mechanism, as of a watch. **5,** a legal proceeding. **6,** (*Slang*) the profits or spoils of some activity. —**ac′tion·a·ble,** *adj.* giving ground for a lawsuit.

ac′ti·vate″ (ak′tə-vāt″) *v.t.* make active; hasten action; put into operation. —**activated charcoal,** a highly absorbent form of carbon. —**ac″ti·va′tion,** *n.* —**ac′ti·va″tor,** *n.*

activate, actuate
☛ Both words mean to put into operation; however, *actuate* has the additional sense of inciting to action.

ac′tive (ak′tiv) *adj.* **1,** engaged in action; busy; brisk; agile. **2,** having the power to function, operate, or influence. **3,** (*Gram.*) denoting the verb-form of action performed by the subject. —**ac′tive·ness,** *n.*

ac′tiv·ism (ak′tiv-iz-əm) *n.* a doctrine advocating active involvement or the use of force. —**ac′ti·vist,** *n.*

ac·tiv′i·ty (ak-tiv′ə-tē) *n.* **1,** state of being active. **2,** a function; event.

ac′tor (ak′tər) *n.* one who acts, esp. a stage-player. —**ac′tress,** *n.fem.*

ac′tu·al (ak′choo-əl) *adj.* **1,** of real exis-

tence. **2,** now existing; present. —**ac′tu·al·ize″,** *v.t.*

ac″tu·al′i·ty (ak″choo-al′ə-tē) *n.* **1,** real existence. **2,** something real. **3,** (*pl.*) actual circumstances; realities.

ac′tu·ar·y (ak′choo-er-ē) *n.* one who calculates insurance risks. —**ac″tu·ar′i·al,** *adj.*

ac′tu·ate″ (ak′choo-āt″) *v.t.* put or incite into action. —**ac″tu·a′tion,** *n.* ❏ *activate*

a·cu′men (ə-kū′mən) *n.* mental acuteness; keenness of perception or insight.

a′cu·pres″sure (ak′yû-presh″ər) *n.* therapy in which pressure is applied to specific points on the body for the relief of pain, stress, etc.

ac′u·punc″ture (ak′yû-punk″chər) *n.* an ancient method of therapy and pain relief by puncturing the body with needles at specific points.

a·cute′ (ə-kūt′) *adj.* **1,** sharp-pointed; intense; shrill. **2,** keen in perception or penetration; susceptible of slight impressions; discriminating. —**acute accent,** the mark (′), as in the French é. —**acute angle** (*Geom.*) one of less than 90°. —**a·cute′-ness, a·cu′i·ty** (a-kū′ə-tē) *n.*

acute, chronic
☛ *Acute* refers to something that is sharp, sudden, of short duration; *chronic* refers to something that is continued or of long duration.

-a·cy (ə-sē) *suf.* forming nouns denoting quality or state.

ad *n.* (*Informal*) advertisement.

ad- *pref.* denoting addition, direction, or tendency.

A′da (ā′də) *n.* (*Computers*) a programming language designed for defense-related work.

Ada
↔ Named in honor of 19th-c. English mathematician Augusta *Ada*, Countess of Lovelace, possibly the first computer programmer, who assisted Charles Babbage in the development of an early ancestor of the modern computer.

ad′age (ad′ij) *n.* a pithy saying; proverb; old saying.

a·da′gio (ə-dä′zhō) *adj. & adv.* (*It., Music*) slow. —*n.* a movement in slow time. —**adagio dance,** a dance, usually for two, characterized by much posturing.

ad′a·mant (ad′ə-mənt) *adj.* hard; hard-hearted; unyielding. —*n.* any extremely hard mineral, as diamond. —**ad″a·man′-tine** (ad″ə-man′tīn) *adj.*

---

fat, fāte, fär, fâre, fâll, àsk; met, hē, hēr, maybè; pin, pīne; not, nōte, ôr, tool

Ad′am's apple the prominent formation of thyroid cartilage at the front of a man's throat.

a·dapt′ (ə-dapt′) *v.t.* make suitable; alter to fit. —**a·dapt′a·ble,** *adj.* easy to adapt; readily able to conform. —**ad″ap·ta′tion** (ad″əp-tā′shən) *n.*

> **adapt, adopt**
> ☛ Do not confuse *adapt*, to make suitable, and *adopt*, to receive as one's own.

add (ad) *v.t.* **1,** increase by attaching more; annex. **2,** unite in one sum or aggregate. —*v.i.* **1,** serve as an addition. **2,** perform arithmetical addition. —**add-′on,** *n.* an attachment to a device, etc.

ad′dax (ad′aks) *n.* an Afr. antelope having spirally twisted horns.

ad′dend (ad′end) *n.* a number to be added.

ad·den′dum (ə-den′dəm) *n.* [*pl.* **-da** (-də)] something that is added, as the appendix of a book.

ad′der (ad′ər) *n.* any of several common vipers.

> **adder**
> ↔ From Middle English *nadder*; the phrase *a nadder* was mistakenly thought to be *an adder*.

ad′dict (ad′ikt) *n.* one who has a confirmed habit, as the overuse of drugs. —*v.t.* (ə-dikt′) (fol. by *to*) **1,** cause addiction in. **2,** devote or give (oneself). —**addict′ed,** *adj.* —**ad·dic′tion,** *n.*

ad·di′tion (ə-dish′ən) *n.* **1,** the act or process of adding or uniting. **2,** the arithmetical operation of finding a sum, expressed by the symbol +. **3,** anything added. —**ad·di′tion·al,** *adj.* added; extra.

ad′di·tive (ad′ə-tiv) *n.* a substance, often a chemical, added to a product, as food. —*adj.* produced by addition; cumulative.

ad′dle (ad′əl) *v.t. & i.* make or become muddled or confused. —**ad′dle·pa″ted** (-pā″təd) *adj.* confused; mixed up.

ad·dress′ (ə-dres′) *v.t.* **1,** speak or write to. **2,** direct attention to. **3,** direct for transmission. **4,** pay court to as a lover. —*n.* **1,** a formal utterance in speech or writing directed to a body of persons. **2,** the place where a person lives or may be reached. **3,** personal bearing; manner of speech. **4,** (*Computers*) the location in memory where certain data are stored. —**ad·dress′ee** (-ē) *n.*

ad·duce′ (ə-dūs′) *v.t.* bring forward as a reason or explanation; cite as evidence.

-ade (ād) *suf.* denoting **1,** action or result of action. **2,** a drink.

ad′e·noid″ (ad′ə-noid″) *n.* (usually *pl.*) a swollen lymphatic tissue in the pharynx that often impedes breathing. —**ad″e·noid′-al,** *adj.*

ad′ept (ad′ept) *n.* one who has attained proficiency. —*adj.* (ə-dept′) skillful; expert. —**a·dept′ness,** *n.*

ad′e·quate (ad′i-kwət) *adj.* equal to requirement or occasion; sufficient; suitable. —**ad′e·qua·cy** (-kwə-sē) *n.*

ad·here′ (ad-hir′) *v.i.* **1,** stick fast; become joined. **2,** hold closely, as to an idea or course; be devoted. —**ad·her′ence,** *n.*

ad·her′ent (-ənt) *n.* one who follows a leader or supports a cause.

ad·he′sion (ad-hē′zhən) *n.* adherence, esp. (*Physics*) between unlike particles.

ad·he′sive (ad-hē′siv) *adj.* sticky; tenacious; adhering. —*n.* that which sticks. —**ad·he′sive·ness,** *n.*

ad hoc (ad′ hok′) (*Lat.*) relating exclusively to the subject in question.

a·dieu′ (ə-dū′) *interj. & n.* [*pl.* **-dieus′** or **-dieux′** (-dūz′)] (*Fr.*) farewell; good-bye.

a·dios′ (ä-dyōs′) (*Sp.*) *interj.* good-bye.

ad′i·pose″ (ad′i-pōs″) *adj.* fatty. —*n.* body fat, esp. on the kidneys. —**ad″i·pos′i·ty** (-pos′ə-tē) *n.*

ad′it *n.* an entrance or passageway.

ad·ja′cent (ə-jā′sənt) *adj.* lying near, close, or contiguous; adjoining. —**ad·ja′cen·cy** (-sən-sē) *n.*

> **adjacent, adjoining**
> ☛ Both words mean lying near, but objects that are *adjoining* are actually touching or connected.

ad′jec·tive (aj′ek-tiv) *n.* (*Gram.*) a word used to qualify, limit, or define a noun, as: a *large* book.

ad·join′ (ə-join′) *v.t. & i.* be adjacent; be in contact; abut. ❑ *adjacent*

ad·journ′ (ə-jērn′) *v.t. & i.* **1,** suspend a sitting till another day, as of a legislature or court. **2,** defer; postpone. —**ad·journ′ment,** *n.*

ad·judge′ (ə-juj′) *v.t.* **1,** decide by judicial opinion; pronounce, decree, or award formally. **2,** judge; deem.

ad·ju′di·cate″ (ə-joo′di-kāt″) *v.t. & i.* adjudge; determine judicially. —**ad·ju″di·ca′-tion,** *n.* —**ad·ju′di·ca″tor,** *n.*

ad′junct (a′junkt) *n.* something added to another. —*adj.* additional, esp. in a subordinate sense.

ad·jure′ (ə-jûr′) *v.t.* command, charge, or

bind earnestly and solemnly. **—ad″jur·a′-tion** (aj″ə-rā′shən) *n.*

ad·just′ (ə-just′) *v.t.* **1,** make to fit or conform; adapt. **2,** put in order; regulate. **3,** bring to a satisfactory result; settle. **—adjust′a·ble,** *adj.* **—ad·just′ment,** *n.* **—adjustable rate mortgage,** a mortgage whose interest rate fluctuates based on market conditions.

ad′ju·tant (aj′ə-tənt) *n.* **1,** a military executive officer or aide. **2,** an assistant. **3,** an East Indian stork.

ad-lib′ *v.t. & i.* **[-libbed′, -lib′bing]** *(Informal)* improvise (lines or action not in the script, etc.). **—n.** something improvised.

ad lib′i·tum (ad lib′ə-təm) *(Lat.)* at one's pleasure.

ad·min·is·ter (ad-min′əs-tər) *v.t.* **1,** manage as an agent; conduct; superintend. **2,** make application of; supply; dispense. **—v.i.** (with *to*) bring aid. Also, **ad·min′is·trate″** (-trāt″) administer (def. 1).

ad·min″is·tra′tion (-strā′shən) *n.* **1,** conduct. **2,** any body of men entrusted with ultimate executive powers. **—ad·min′is·tra″tive,** *adj.* ❑ *government*

ad·min′is·tra″tor (ad-min′i-strā″tər) *n.* one who administers; executor. **—ad·min′-is·tra″trix** (-triks) *n.fem.*

ad′mi·ra·ble (ad′mə-rə-bəl) *adj.* worthy of admiration; excellent. **—ad′mi·ra·ble-ness, ad″mi·ra·bil′i·ty,** *n.*

ad′mi·ral (ad′mə-rəl) *n.* **1,** a naval officer of highest rank. **2,** the commander of a fleet. ❑ *emir*

> **admiral**
> ↔ The word comes from Arabic, probably from the phrase *amir-al-*, chief of the ——.

ad′mi·ral·ty (ad′mə-rəl-tė) *n.* **1,** the office of admiral. **2,** the administration of a navy. **3,** maritime law.

ad″mi·ra′tion (ad″mə-rā′shən) *n.* act of admiring; approval.

ad·mire′ (ad-mīr′) *v.t.* regard with approbation, esteem, or affection. **—v.i.** *(Dial.)* wish (to). **—ad·mir′er,** *n.* one who admires, esp., a suitor.

ad·mis′si·ble (ad-mis′ə-bəl) *adj.* that may be conceded or allowed. **—ad·mis″si-bil′i·ty,** *n.*

ad·mis′sion (ad-mish′ən) *n.* **1,** the act of entering or admitting, or being allowed to enter. **2,** entrance fee. **3,** an acknowledgment or confession that something is true.

ad·mit′ *v.t. & i.* **[-mit′ted, -ting] 1,** allow to enter; give means or right of entry. **2,** concede as valid; acknowledge to be true.

—ad·mit′tance (-əns) *n.* permission or right to enter; admission (def. 1). ❑ *acknowledge, admission*

> **admission, admittance**
> ☞ In the sense of being allowed to enter the two words are synonymous, though *admittance* is more formal and stresses the physical act of entering.

ad·mix′ture (ad-miks′chər) *n.* **1,** the act of mixing or mingling, esp. of different substances. **2,** something added; ingredient. **—ad′mix,** *v. & n.*

ad·mon′ish *v.t.* **1,** reprove mildly. **2,** warn against something; exhort; guide. **—ad·mon′ish·ment,** *n.*

ad″mo·ni′tion (ad″mə-nish′ən) *n.* reproof; advice; warning. **—ad·mon′i·to·ry** (ad-mon′ə-tôr-ė) *adj.*

ad nau′se·am (ad-nâ′zė-əm) *(Lat.)* to the extent of causing disgust or boredom.

a·do′ (ə-doo′) *n.* action; bustle; trouble.

a·do′be (ə-dō′bė) *n.* a sun-dried block of mud used in building.

> **adobe**
> ↔ *Adobe* comes to English from Spanish. It derives ultimately from Egyptian, through Coptic and Arabic.

ad″o·les′cence (ad″ə-les′əns) *n.* **1,** the age of human life between puberty and adulthood, from about 14 to 25 (men) or 12 to 21 (women). **2,** the process or stage of development leading to maturity.

ad″o·les′cent (-ənt) *adj.* of or characteristic of adolescence. **—n.** an adolescent boy or girl.

a·dopt′ (ə-dopt′) **1,** take or receive as one's own. **2,** (of a council or legislature) vote to accept. **—a·dop′tion,** *n.* **—a·dop′-tive,** *adj.* ❑ *adapt*

> **adopted, adoptive**
> ☞ In common usage, children are *adopted*, parents are *adoptive* (they do the adopting).

a·dor′a·ble (ə-dôr′ə-bəl) *adj.* worthy of the utmost love or admiration. **—a·dor′a-ble·ness, a·dor″a·bil′i·ty,** *n.*

ad″o·ra′tion (ad″ə-rā′shən) *n.* act of adoring or worshiping.

a·dore′ (ə-dôr′) *v.t.* **1,** regard with utmost love, esteem, or respect. **2,** worship as divine.

a·dorn′ (ə-dôrn′) *v.t.* decorate; dress with ornaments; embellish. **—a·dorn′ment,** *n.*

ad rem (äd rem) *(Lat., Law)* to the point; relevant.

---

fat, fāte, fär, fāre, fâll, ȧsk; met, hē, hėr, maybė; pin, pīne; not, nōte, ôr, tool

ad·re′nal (ə-drē′nəl) *adj.* near or on the kidneys; of the adrenal glands.

ad·ren′a·line (ə-dren′ə-lin) *n.* a hormone that stimulates heart action; epinephrine.

a·drift′ (ə-drift′) *adv. & adj.* floating at random; not moored; swayed by any chance impulse.

a·droit′ (ə-droit′) *adj.* dextrous; skillful; ingenious. **—a·droit′ness,** *n.*

ad·sorp′tion (ad-sôrp′shən) *n.* condensation of a gas on the surface of a solid. **—ad·sorb′,** *v.t.* **—ad·sor′bate** (-bāt) *n.* a substance that is adsorbed. ❑ *absorb*

ad′u·late (ad′yə-lāt″) *v.t.* show feigned devotion to; flatter servilely. **—ad″u·la′tion,** *n.* **—ad′u·la·to·ry** (-lə-tôr-ē) *adj.*

ad′ult *n.* a person or animal grown to full size and strength. **—adj.** (ə-dult′) **1,** full-grown; mature; legally of age. **2,** (*Informal*) pornographic. **—a·dult′hood,** *n.*

a·dul′ter·ant (ə-dul′tər-ənt) *n.* a baser ingredient. **—adj.** serving to adulterate.

a·dul′ter·ate″ (ə-dul′tə-rāt″) *v.t.* debase by addition or substitution of inferior ingredients; make impure. **—a·dul″ter·a′tion,** *n.*

a·dul′ter·er (ə-dul′tər-ər) *n.* one who commits adultery. **—a·dul′ter·ess** (-əs) *n.fem.*

a·dul′ter·y (ə-dul′tə-rē) *n.* illicit relations between a married person and another than her or his lawful spouse. **—a·dul′ter·ous,** *adj.*

ad·um′brate (ad-um′brāt) *v.t.* give a faint shadow or outline of; foreshadow. **—ad″um·bra′tion,** *n.*

ad·vance′ (ad-váns′) *v.t.* **1,** bring forward; raise; enhance; promote. **2,** supply beforehand; furnish on credit. **—v.i. 1,** move forward. **2,** make progress; improve; increase in quantity or price. **—n. 1,** forward movement; a step forward; an improvement. **2,** money or goods supplied beforehand or on credit. **3,** the foremost part, as of an army. **—ad·vance′ment,** *n.* **—advance agent,** someone sent ahead to make arrangements, etc. (as for a tour).

ad·van′tage (ad-ván′tij) *n.* **1,** any favorable circumstance. **2,** benefit; gain; profit. **3,** superiority. **—ad″van·ta′geous** (ad″vən·tā′jəs) *adj.*

ad′vent *n.* **1,** arrival. **2,** (*cap.*) the coming of Christ into the world.

ad″ven·ti′tious (ad″vən-tish′əs) *adj.* not intrinsic to the subject; accidentally or casually acquired; foreign.

ad·ven′ture (ad-ven′chər) *n.* **1,** a remarkable occurrence; a noteworthy event.

2, activity of a hazardous or exciting nature. **—v.t. & i.** embark upon; take the risk of; dare. **—ad·ven′tur·ous,** *adj.* **1,** risky. **2,** daring.

ad·ven′tur·er, *n.* **1,** a bold person; explorer; soldier of fortune. **2,** a social climber.

ad′verb (ad′vērb) *n.* (*Gram.*) a word used to qualify, clarify, limit or extend a verb or adjective, or another adverb. **—ad·ver′bi·al,** *adj.*

ad′ver·sar·y (ad′vər-ser-ē) *n.* an opponent in a contest; enemy.

ad·verse′ (ad-vērs′) *adj.* **1,** contrary in purpose or effect; opposite. **2,** harmful to one's interests; unfortunate.

---

adverse, averse
☛ Do not confuse *adverse*, harmful to one's interests, with *averse*, disposed against.

---

ad·ver′si·ty (ad-vēr′sə-tē) *n.* ill fortune; an unfortunate happening.

ad·vert′ (ad-vērt′) *v.i.* (with *to*) refer; turn attention. **—n.** (ad′vērt) (*Informal*) advertisement.

ad′ver·tise″ (ad′vər-tīz″) *v.t. & i.* **1,** make public announcement of; give information concerning. **2,** praise or otherwise promote, as in selling wares.

ad″ver·tise′ment (-mənt; also, ad·vēr′tis-mənt) *n.* a notice (esp. paid) in a publication, etc.

ad′ver·tis″ing (ad′vər-tī″zing) *n.* the art and practice of promoting enterprises, esp. by paid public notices.

ad″ver·tor′i·al (ad″vər-tôr′ē-əl) *n.* an extended advertisement written in the manner and style of an editorial.

ad·vice′ (ad-vīs′) *n.* **1,** counsel as to a course of action; suggestion. **2,** information; communication of news.

---

advice, advise
☛ Do not confuse the noun *advice* (ad-vīs′) with the verb *advise* (ad-vīz′).

---

ad·vis′a·ble (ad-vī′zə-bəl) *adj.* wise to do. **—ad·vis″a·bil′i·ty,** *n.*

ad·vise′ (ad-vīz′) *v.t.* **1,** give counsel to; offer an opinion to. **2,** urge as wise or prudent; recommend. **3,** give information to. **—v.i.** take or offer advice. **—ad·vised′,** *adj.* considered, as in *ill-advised.* **—ad·vi′sed·ly** (ad-vī′zid-lē) *adv.* with good reason; deliberately. **—ad·vise′ment,** *n.* consideration. ❑ *advice*

ad·vi′so·ry (ad-vī′zə-rē) *adj.* giving advice; consultative.

ad'vo·ca·cy (ad'və-kə-sė) *n.* act of advocating; espousal; support.

ad'vo·cate" (ad'və-kāt") *v.t.* plead in favor of; defend in argument; support. —*n.* (-kət) one who pleads or espouses a cause. ❏ *avocado*

a'dy·tum (ad'ə-təm) *n.* the innermost shrine of a temple.

adz *n.* a cutting tool, comprising a blade fixed at right angles to a handle, used for rough trimming.

ae- see *e-* or *ai-*.

ae'gis (ē'jis) *n.* protection; sponsorship. Also, **e'gis**.

Ae·o'li·an harp (ė-ō'lė-ən) a boxlike stringed instrument sounded by the wind.

a'er·ate" (ā'ər-āt") *v.t.* **1,** expose freely to air. **2,** charge with air, carbon dioxide, or other gas. —**a"er·a'tion,** *n.* —**a'er·a"tor,** *n.*

aer'i·al (er'ė-əl) *adj.* **1,** of, produced by, or inhabiting air. **2,** high in the air. **3,** light in weight or substance; visionary. **4,** graceful; ethereal. —*n.* a radio antenna. —**aer'i·al·ist,** *n.* a trapeze acrobat.

aer'ie (ãr'ė; ir'ė) *n.* **1,** an eagle's nest. **2,** a dwelling on a height. Also, **ey'rie**.

aer'o- (ãr-ə) *pref.* pert. to **1,** air; **2,** gas; **3,** aircraft or aviation.

aer"o·bat'ics (-bat'iks) *n.sing.* or *pl.* the performance of aerial stunts with an airplane or glider; those stunts.

aer'obe (ãr'ōb) *n.* a bacterium requiring oxygen for life.

aer·o'bic (ãr-ō'bik) *adj.* **1,** requiring oxygen for life. **2,** pert. to or employing the techniques of aerobics. —**aer·o'bic·al·ly,** *adv.*

aer·o'bics (ãr-ō'biks) *n.* a type of physical exercise designed to increase heart rate and oxygen intake.

aer'o·drome" *n.* airdrome.

aer"o·dy·nam'ics *n.sing.* a branch of mechanics treating of air and other gases in motion.

aer'o·gram" *n.* a lightweight piece of stationery designed to be folded and mailed by airmail without the use of an envelope.

aer'o·naut" (ãr'ə-nât") *n.* one who flies in the air; a balloonist.

aer"o·nau'tics (-nâ'tiks) *n.* **1,** flight in aircraft. **2,** the art or science of flying. —**aer"o·nau'tic,** *adj.* —**aer"o·nau'ti·cal·ly,** *adv.*

aer'o·sol" (-sol) *n.* **1,** a gas bearing another substance. **2,** a container that discharges such a gas.

aer'o·space" *n.* the area including the earth's atmosphere and space beyond.

—*adj.* pert. to aerospace, or vehicles or travel therein.

aer'o·stat *n.* lighter-than-air aircraft.

aer'o·train *n.* a propeller-driven vehicle supported by a cushion of air over a single rail.

aes'thete (es'thēt) *n.* one who cultivates appreciation of the beautiful. Also, **es'thete**.

aes·thet'ic (es-thet'ik) *adj.* pert. to beauty. —*n.* a philosophy of beauty and good taste. Also, **es·thet'ic.** —**aes·thet'i·cal·ly,** *adv.*

aes·thet'ics (-iks) *n., construed as sing.* the philosophy of beauty and good taste. Also, **es·thet'ics**.

ae·ta'tis (ī-tä'tis) (*Lat.*) aged. Abbr., **aet., aetat.**

a·far' (ə-fär') *adv.* from a distance; far away.

af'fa·ble (af'ə-bəl) *adj.* easy to approach (esp. of one in high station); courteous; gracious. —**af"fa·bil'i·ty,** *n.*

af·fair' (ə-fãr') *n.* **1,** a matter, action, business, or concern requiring attention and effort. **2,** a particular event or performance. **3,** an involvement of love. **4,** (*pl.*) pecuniary interests or relations.

af·fect' (ə-fekt') *v.t.* **1,** produce an effect or change on; influence. **2,** impress deeply. **3,** make a show of; feign; imitate; adopt; assume the character of. —*n.* (af'ekt) feeling; emotion.

---

affect, effect
☞ These two verbs have a wide range of meanings, many of which overlap. For clarity, use *affect* to mean influence or imitate, *effect* to mean bring about. The noun *affect* has the specialized and rarely used meaning of feeling or emotion.

---

af"fec·ta'tion (af"ek-tā'shən) *n.* artificiality of manner; pretension to qualities not actually possessed.

af·fect'ed *adj.* **1,** influenced; impaired. **2,** artificial in manner or conduct. **3,** moved by emotion.

af·fect'ing *adj.* pitiful.

af·fec'tion (ə-fek'shən) *n.* **1,** goodwill; love. **2,** the result, act, or state of being influenced. —**af·fec'tion·ate** (-ət) *adj.* loving; warm-hearted.

af'fer·ent (af'ər-ənt) *adj.* leading inward to a central organ or nerve.

af·fi'ance (ə-fī'əns) *v.t.* bind in promise of marriage; betroth.

af"fi·da'vit (af"i-dā'vit) *n.* (*Law*) a written and sworn declaration of alleged facts.

af·fil′i·ate″ (ə-fil′ė-āt″) *v.i. & t.* bring into association; unite in action and interest; join with. —*n.* (-ė-ət) an associate; a branch organization. —**af·fil″i·a′tion,** *n.*

af·fin′i·ty (ə-fin′ə-tė) *n.* **1,** a natural liking for, or attraction to, a person or thing. **2,** inherent likeness or agreement between things. —**affinity card,** a credit card issued to the members of a special group or the patrons of a particular company.

af·firm′ (ə-fėrm′) *v.t.* **1,** assert positively; declare to be a fact. **2,** confirm; ratify. —*v.i.* (*Law*) declare solemnly, in lieu of swearing upon oath. —**af″fir·ma′tion** (af″ər-mā′shən) *n.*

af·firm′a·tive (ə-fėr′mə-tiv) *adj.* positive in form, not negative. —*n.* **1,** a word or phrase expressing assent, agreement, or affirmation. **2,** the side favoring a proposition. —**affirmative action,** an effort made by an employer to hire members of minority groups.

af·fix′ (ə-fix′) *v.t.* **1,** add or append. **2,** fasten or attach. —*n.* (af′iks) that which is added or attached.

af·fla′tus (ə-flā′təs) *n.* mental force or inspiration, evinced by religious, poetical, or oratorical expression.

af·flict′ (ə-flikt′) *v.t.* distress with mental or bodily pain; torment.

af·flic′tion (ə-flik′shən) *n.* **1,** distress; pain. **2,** a cause of distress; an ill or disease. —**af·flic′tive,** *adj.*

af·flu·ence (af′loo-əns) *n.* **1,** an abundant supply, as of material wealth. **2,** a flowing toward, as of a tributary watercourse.

af·flu·ent (af′loo-ənt) *adj.* **1,** flowing freely. **2,** rich; wealthy.

---
affluent, effluent
☛ Both words refer to flowing, but the common use of *affluent* is as an adjective meaning wealthy; the common use of *effluent* is as a noun meaning liquid waste.
---

af·ford′ (ə-fôrd′) *v.t.* **1,** be able; have the means. **2,** yield; produce; furnish.

af·for′est (ə-for′əst) *v.* to plant with trees.

af·fray′ (ə-frā′) *n.* a noisy quarrel; brawl; disturbance.

af·front′ (ə-frunt′) *n.* a personally offensive act or word; an open manifestation of disrespect or contumely. —*v.t.* insult openly; make ashamed or confused.

Af′ghan (af′gan) *n.* **1,** a native of Afghanistan. **2,** a breed of hound. **3,** (*l.c.*) a kind of woolen blanket or shawl.

a·fi″cio·na′do (ə-fē″shə-nä′dō) *n.* (*Sp.*) enthusiast; devotee.

a·field′ (ə-fēld′) *adv.* abroad; off the beaten track; away from home.

a·fire′ (ə-fīr′) *adv. & adj.* burning.

a·flame′ (ə-flām′) *adv. & adj.* on fire.

a·float′ (ə-flōt′) *adv. & adj.* **1,** borne on the water. **2,** moving about; in circulation.

a·flut′ter (ə-flut′ər) *adj.* **1,** fluttering. **2,** mildly excited; agitated.

a·foot′ (ə-fût′) *adv. & adj.* **1,** walking. **2,** in progress.

a·fore′said (ə-fôr′sed) *adj.* which was mentioned previously. Also, **a·fore′-men″tioned.**

a·fore′thought″ (ə-fôr′thât″) *adj.* premeditated.

a·foul′ (ə-fowl′) *adv. & adj.* in a state of collision or entanglement.

a·fraid′ (ə-frād′) *adj.* filled with fear or apprehension.

A-′frame″ (ā′-) *n.* a building having triangular front and rear walls and a long peaked roof descending nearly to the ground.

Af′ri·can (af′ri-kən) *adj.* pert. to Africa, its inhabitants, or their languages. —*n.* a native of Africa.

African
↔ The word comes from the Latin *Afer,* name for an ancient N. African people.

Af′ri·can-A·mer′i·can *adj. & n.* pert. to American blacks. Also, **Af′ro-A·mer′i·can.**

African-American, black, colored, Negro
☛ The term preferred by the American black community has changed over the years. *Colored* and *Negro,* once commonly accepted, have lost favor. Currently, Black, Afro-American, and African-American are all in use, with the last perhaps the most widely preferred. In this dictionary, for contexts not restricted to the United States *black* is used.

Af′ri·kaans′ (af″ri-kans′) *n.* one of the two official languages of the Republic of So. Africa.

Af′ri·kan′der (af″ri-kan′dər) *n.* Boer. Also, **Af′ri·ka′ner** (-kä′nər).

Af′ro (af′rō) *n.* (*Informal*) **1,** a short, round, bushy hairstyle. **2,** African style of dress; esp., dashiki. —*adj.* (*Informal*) African-American.

aft *adv.* (*Naut.*) in, near, or toward the stern of a ship.

af′ter (áf′tər) *prep.* **1,** later in time; subsequent to. **2,** behind in place; in the rear of; below in rank. **3,** in pursuit of; with desire for. **4,** according to; in proportion to; in imitation of. —*adv. & adj.* **1,** later in time. **2,** behind or below in place. **3,** (*Naut.*) aft.

af′ter·birth″ *n.* the placenta.

af′ter·burn″er *n.* a device for burning fuel in the hot exhaust gases of a turbojet engine to provide extra thrust.

af′ter·math″ *n.* what comes after; the consequences.

af′ter·most″ *adj.* nearest the stern of a vessel; hence, nearest the rear; last.

af″ter·noon′ *n. & adj.* the part of the day from noon to night.

af′ter·thought″ *n.* a belated idea or act.

af′ter·ward (-wərd) *adv.* later in time; subsequently. Also, **af′ter·wards.**

a·gain′ (ə-gen′) *adv.* **1,** once more; another time; anew. **2,** in addition; moreover. **3,** back; in the opposite direction.

a·gainst′ (ə-genst′) *prep.* **1,** in an opposite direction to. **2,** in contact with; toward; upon. **3,** adverse or hostile to. **4,** in provision for; in exchange for.

a·gape′ (ə-gāp′; ə-gap′) *adv. & adj.* with the mouth wide open.

a′ga·pe″ (ä′gä-pā″) *n.* (*Gk.*) Christian brotherly love.

a′gar (ä′gär) *n.* a gelatinous culture medium made from certain seaweeds.

ag′ate (ag′ət) *n.* **1,** a variety of quartz. **2,** a child's marble made of agate or of glass in imitation of agate. **3,** (*Printing*), 5-point type.

a·ga′ve (ə-gä′vē) *n.* a genus of plants found chiefly in Mexico; the century plant.

---

agave
↔ The word comes from the Greek name for the mythological daughter of Cadmus and Harmonia.

---

age (āj) *n.* **1,** the length of time during which a being or thing has existed. **2,** the lifetime of an individual; duration of existence. **3,** a particular period of history; the people and events of an era. **4,** (*Informal*) a long time. —*v.i.* grow old. —*v.t.* **1,** bring to maturity. **2,** make old. —**age′less,** *adj.* unchanging. —**of age,** having reached legal majority.

-age (ij) *suf.* forming nouns denoting condition, effect, result, etc.

a′ged (ā′jəd) *adj.* **1,** old; having lived a long time. **2,** (ājd) having the age of, as *aged twenty years.*

age′ism (āj′iz-əm) *n.* bias or discrimination based on age, usu. old age.

age′less (-ləs) *adj.* never growing old; unchanging.

a′gen·cy (ā′jən-sē) *n.* **1,** a means of producing effects or exerting power; an instrument. **2,** the office and duties of an agent. **3,** a commercial or government office furnishing a particular public service.

a·gen′da (ə-jen′də) *n.pl.* [*sing.* **-dum**] **1,** items of business to be brought before a council, etc. **2,** (*construed as sing.*) [*pl.* **-das**] a list of such items.

a′gent (ā′jənt) *n.* **1,** a person acting on behalf of another. **2,** a representative, as of a commercial firm or government bureau; an official. **3,** an active cause, as (*Chem.*) a substance that produces a reaction. —**Agent Orange,** a herbicide and defoliant containing dioxin.

ag·glom′er·ate″ (ə-glom′ə-rāt″) *v.i. & t.* collect in a mass. —*adj.* (-ət) piled together; in a dense cluster. —*n.* a cluster, as of rock fragments. —**ag·glom″er·a′tion,** *n.*

ag·glu′ti·nate″ (ə-gloo′tə-nāt″) *v.i. & t.* unite or cause to adhere, as with glue. —*adj.* adhering by or as by glue. —**ag·glu″ti·na′tion,** *n.*

ag·glu′ti·nin (ə-gloo′tin-ən) *n.* any organic substance which causes red blood cells or bacteria to agglutinate.

ag·gran′dize (ə-gràn′dīz) *v.t.* **1,** make greater in power, wealth, or rank; widen in scope; extend. **2,** magnify; exaggerate. —**ag·gran′dize·ment** (ə-gràn′diz-mənt) *n.*

ag′gra·vate″ (ag′rə-vāt″) *v.t.* **1,** intensify; make more serious or troublesome; worsen. **2,** (*Informal*) irritate; provoke. —**ag″gra·va′tion,** *n.*

---

aggravate, irritate
☞ In formal writing, do not use *aggravate,* meaning to intensify or worsen, for *irritate,* meaning to vex or annoy.

---

ag′gre·gate″ (ag′ri-gāt″) *v.t.* **1,** collect into a sum, mass, or body. **2,** amount to (a number). —*v.i.* come together. —*n.* (ag′rə-gət) **1,** gross amount. **2,** (*Geol.*) rock formed of a mixture of different minerals. —*adj.* (-gət) total; combined. —**ag″gre·ga′tion,** *n.*

ag·gress′ (ə-gres′) *v.i.* begin a quarrel.

ag·gres′sion (ə-gresh′ən) *n.* **1,** an act of hostility; an assault or encroachment. **2,** offensive action in general.

ag·gres′sive (ə-gres′iv) *adj.* **1,** tending to

attack or be hostile. **2,** vigorous. —**ag·gres'sive·ness,** *n.*

ag·gres'sor (ə-gres'ər) *n.* one who begins a quarrel or starts a war without adequate provocation.

ag·grieved' (ə-grēvd') *adj.* offended; having cause to feel vexed. —**ag·grieve',** *v.t.*

a·ghast' (ə-gȧst') *adj.* struck with amazement; filled with sudden fright and horror.

ag'ile (aj'əl) *adj.* able to move quickly; active; nimble.

a·gil'i·ty (ə-jil'ə-tė) *n.* ability to move quickly; nimbleness.

a'gio (ä'jō) *n.* a premium paid for exchanging one currency for another. —**a''gio·tage'** (-täzh') *n.* speculative buying and selling of stocks.

ag'i·tate'' (aj'ə-tāt'') *v.t.* **1,** force into violent motion; shake briskly; perturb. **2,** call attention to by speech or writing. —*v.i.* engage in discussion or debate. —**ag''i·ta'tion,** *n.* —**ag'i·ta''tor,** *n.*

a·glow' (ə-glō') *adj.* glowing.

ag'nate (ag'nāt) *adj.* related on the father's side. —*n.* a kinsman on the father's side.

ag·nos'tic (ag-nos'tik) *n.* one who holds that ultimate causes (as God) are unknowable. —*adj.* holding this view. —**ag·nos'ti·cal·ly,** *adv.* —**ag·nos'ti·cism** (agnos'ti-siz-əm) *n.*

> **agnostic, atheist**
> ☞ The *agnostic* believes that we do not have enough evidence to say whether or not God exists. The *atheist* is certain that God does not exist. ↔ *Agnostic* was coined by the English biologist T. H. Huxley (1825-95) in opposition to the views of the gnostics, members of an early Christian sect.

a·go' (ə-gō') *adv. & adj.* in past time.

a·gog' (ə-gog') *adj. & adv.* in a state of excitement, curiosity, or eager desire.

> **agog, a gogo**
> ↔ *Agog* derives from the Old French phrase *en gogue*, enjoying oneself. *Gogo* probably also comes from *gogue*, merriment.

a go'go'' (ä gō'gō') *adj.* go-go.

-a·gon (ə-gon) *suf.* denoting a plane geometrical figure, as *pentagon.*

a·gon'ic (ə-gon'ik) *adj.* not forming an angle.

ag'o·nize'' (ag'ə-nīz'') *v.i.* suffer violent anguish. —*v.t.* distress with extreme pain.

ag'o·ny (ag'ə-nė) *n.* **1,** extreme and prolonged mental or bodily pain. **2,** the death struggle.

ag''o·ra·pho'bi·a (ag''ə-rə-fō'bė-ə) *n.* morbid fear of open spaces.

> **agoraphobia**
> ↔ Coined in German in the late 19th c. from Greek *agorā*, marketplace, + *phobiā*, fear.

a·gou'ti (ə-goo'tė) *n.* a rabbitlike rodent of Central and So. Amer.

a·grar'i·an (ə-grār'ė-ən) *adj.* **1,** pert. to land or property rights in land. **2,** agricultural; rural. —*n.* one who favors an equal division of landed property.

a·gree' (ə-grē') *v.i.* **1,** give assent; consent. **2,** be of one opinion or mind; arrive at a settlement. **3,** be consistent; harmonize. **4,** be similar; correspond; coincide. —*v.t.* concede.

a·gree'a·ble (-ə-bəl) *adj.* **1,** pleasing to the mind or senses. **2,** conformable; willing to consent. —**a·gree''a·bil'i·ty,** *n.*

a·gree'ment (-mənt) *n.* **1,** concord; harmony. **2,** a contract; bargain.

ag''ri·cul'ture (ag'ri-kul''chər) *n.* the cultivation of the ground to raise food; husbandry; farming. —**ag''ri·cul'tur·al,** *adj.* —**ag''ri·cul'tur·ist,** *n.*

ag·ro- (ag-rə) *pref.* soil; field.

a·gron'o·my (ə-gron'ə-mė) *n.* the science of crop production and soil management. —**a·gron'o·mist,** *n.*

a·ground' (ə-grownd') *adj. & adv.* on the ground; stranded.

a'gue (ā'gū) *n.* a malarial fever marked by intermittent paroxysms of chills and sweating.

ah (ä) *interj.* of understanding, agreement, or almost any emotion.

a·ha' (ä-hä') *interj.* of surprise, triumph, or contempt.

a·head' (ə-hed') *adv.* **1,** in or to the front; in advance. **2,** forward; onward.

a·hem' (ə-hem') *interj.* to attract attention, as by an affected cough.

-a·hol'ic (-ə-hol'ik) *suf.* addicted to.

a·hoy' (ə-hoi') *interj.* used to attract attention of persons at a distance.

AI (ā'ī') *abbr.* artificial intelligence.

aid (ād) *v.t.* **1,** give support or relief to; help. **2,** promote the accomplishment of; facilitate. —*n.* **1,** assistance; support. **2,** the person who or that which gives help.

aide (ād) *n.* an assistant; esp. (*Mil.*) a secretarial assistant to an officer. Also, **aide'de-camp'** (-də-kamp'). ❏ *aid*

aid, aide
☛ An *aide* is a person who assists another person; an *aid* can be a person or, more often, an object which helps to accomplish something.

AIDS (ādz) *abbr.* a(cquired) i(mmune) d(eficiency) s(yndrome).

ai′grette (ā′gret) *n.* a plume of feathers worn on the head.

ai′ki·do′ (ī′kē-dō′) *n.* (*Jap.*) a Jap. art of self-defense.

ail (āl) *v.t.* affect with pain. —*v.i.* feel pain; be unwell.

ai′ler·on (ā′lə-ron) *n.* a hinged flap in the wing of an airplane, controlling its horizontal position.

ail′ment (-mənt) *n.* illness; malady.

ai·lur′o·phile″ (ī-loor′ə-fīl″) *n.* lover of cats.

aim (ām) *v.t.* point at something; fix in a certain direction, as *aim a gun.* —*v.i.* (with an infinitive) strive toward; intend. —*n.* **1,** the direction in which something is aimed. **2,** the act of aiming. **3,** the thing aimed at; target; intention; purpose. —**aim′less,** *adj.* without purpose or direction.

ain't (ānt) nonstandard form of am not, is not, are not, has not, have not.

Ai′nu (ī′noo) *n.* one of an aboriginal race of Japan; their language.

air (âr) *n.* **1,** the earth's atmosphere; the particular mixture of nitrogen, oxygen, etc., of which it is composed. **2,** a light breeze. **3,** space; scope. **4,** utterance abroad; publication. **5,** outward appearance; personal mien or bearing. **6,** (*pl.*) affected manners. **7,** a tune; a principal melody. —*v.t.* **1,** expose to the air; let air into; ventilate. **2,** bring to public notice; proclaim. **3,** broadcast; put on the air. —*adj.* **1,** operated by compressed air, as *air brake.* **2,** for or by aircraft, as *air base, air raid.* —**air cavalry,** an army unit transported by air for the purpose of reconnaissance or for ground action elsewhere. —**air curtain, air door,** a stream of compressed air, usu. heated or cooled, directed across an opening and replacing a door. —**air cushion, 1,** an inflated cushion. **2,** [also, **air bag**] a device for cushioning shock or equalizing pressure. —**air force,** the branch of the military forces controlling aircraft. —**air lock,** an airtight compartment used as a passageway into a compressed-air chamber. —**air pocket,** a downward current of air. —**get the air,** (*Slang*) be dismissed. —**in the air, 1,** rumored. **2,** uncertain.

air′borne″ (-bôrn″) *adj.* supported by the air; in flight.

air′brush″ *n.* an atomizer for applying liquid paint. —*v.t.* to paint using an airbrush.

air′bus″ *n.* a large, luxurious, short-range airliner.

air′coach″ *n.* a low-priced air passenger transport service.

air-″con·di′tion·ing *n.* a system of indoor ventilation and temperature control. Also, **air cooling.** —**air-″con·di′tion,** *v.t.*

air′craft″ *n.* any type of machine that flies in the air, whether lighter or heavier than air.

air′drome″ (-drōm″) *n.* airport. Also, **aer′o·drome″.**

air′drop″ *v.t.* deliver (personnel or supplies) by dropping from an aircraft with the aid of a parachute. —*n.* such delivery.

Aire′dale″ (âr′dāl″) *n.* a breed of large terriers, named for a district in Yorkshire, England.

air′field″ *n.* a place leveled and surfaced on which aircraft alight; an airport.

air′foil″ *n.* any surface on an aircraft used for steering, lifting, etc., by the flow of air upon it.

air′head *n.* (*Slang*) a stupid person.

air′lift″ *n.* use of aircraft as the sole means of transportation to a place when other means are unavailable.

air′line″ *n.* a company furnishing air transport on fixed schedules.

air′lin″er *n.* a passenger airplane.

air′mail″ *n.* **1,** a postal system for transporting mail by air. **2,** a letter, etc., sent via airmail. —*v.t.* send via airmail. —*adj.* sent via airmail.

air′man (-mən) *n.* [*pl.* **-men**] **1,** aviator. **2,** a rank in the U.S. Air Force.

air′plane″ (âr′plān″) *n.* an engine-driven aircraft heavier than air.

air′play *n.* the playing of recorded material on the radio or TV.

air′port″ (âr′pôrt″) *n.* an airfield having some attendant facilities for handling aircraft, passengers, and freight.

air′ship″ (âr′ship″) *n.* an engine-driven aircraft lighter than air.

air′tight″ *adj.* **1,** sealed against air. **2,** (of an argument, etc.) flawless.

air′time″ *n.* (*Radio & TV*) **1,** the time at which a broadcast is to take place. **2,** the length of a broadcast.

air′waves″ *n.pl.* the media.

air′wor″thy (âr′wẽr″thė) *adj.* of aircraft, safe to fly.

---

fat, fāte, fär, fâre, fâll, ȧsk; met, hē, hẽr, maybė; pin, pīne; not, nōte, ôr, tool

air′y (âr′ė) *adj.* **1,** like air; unsubstantial. **2,** open to a free current of air; well ventilated. **3,** flimsy; unreal; visionary. **4,** light in manner or movement; sprightly. **5,** affectedly lofty; pretentious. —**air′i·ness,** *n.*

aisle (īl) *n.* a passageway giving access, as to the seats in a church or theater.

a·jar′ (ə-jär′) *adv.* & *adj.* **1,** partly open (said of a door). **2,** out of tune.

a·kim′bo (ə-kim′bō) *adv.* & *adj.* in a sharp bend (said of the arms when the hands are placed on the hips and the elbows are extended sideward).

a·kin′ (ə-kin′) *adj.* **1,** related by blood. **2,** similar in nature.

-al (əl) *suf.* pertaining to.

à la (ä′lä) (*Fr.*) in the fashion of; according to. —**à la carte** (kärt) from the bill of fare; not on the dinner. —**à la king,** cooked in a cream sauce. —**à la mode,** served with ice cream.

al′a·bas″ter (al′ə-bas″tər) *n.* a marblelike mineral, often white, used for ornamental purposes. —*adj.* like alabaster; white.

a·lack′ (ə-lak′) *interj.* alas.

a·lac′ri·ty (ə-lak′rə-tė) *n.* cheerful willingness; eager promptitude.

a′lar (ā′lər) *adj.* having wings; pert. to wings.

a·larm′ (ə-lärm′) *n.* **1,** a warning of approaching danger; an urgent summons; a signal for attention. **2,** any mechanical device for giving such a signal. **3,** sudden fear; apprehension of danger. —*v.t.* **1,** fill with anxiety or apprehension; frighten. **2,** give notice of danger to; rouse.

a·larm′ist (-ist) *n.* one disposed to expect or prophesy calamity.

a·lar′um (ə-lär′əm) *n.* (*Archaic*) alarm.

a·las′ (ə-làs′) *interj.* of sorrow or pity.

a′late (ā′lāt) *adj.* having wings or membranes like wings.

alb *n.* a white robe worn by a priest.

al′ba·core″ (al′bə-kôr″) *n.* a food fish of the mackerel family.

al′ba·tross″ (al′bə-trâs″) *n.* a web-footed seabird of the petrel family.

---

albacore, albatross

↔ Both words are of Arabic origin (as are many words beginning with *al-*, which in Arabic means "the"). *Albacore* comes from *al-bakūra,* young camel; the reason for the derivation is unknown. *Albatross* is from *al-ghattās,* sea eagle.

---

al·be′it (âl-bē′it) *conj.* although; notwithstanding that.

al·bi′no (al-bī′nō) *n.* [*pl.* **-nos**] a person or animal having a whitish coloring. —**al′-bi·nism** (al′bə-niz-əm) *n.*

al′bum (al′bəm) *n.* **1,** a book of blank leaves for the insertion of photographs, stamps, or the like. **2,** a phonograph record or a set of records enclosed in an album.

al·bu′men (al-bū′mən) *n.* the white of an egg.

al·bu′min (al-bū′min) *n.* a protein occurring in the body.

al·cal′de (al-kal′dē) *n.* an official of a Spanish or Spanish-American town. Also, **al·cade′** (al-kād′).

al′che·my (al′kə-mė) *n.* the doctrines and processes of early and medieval chemists. —**al′che·mist,** *n.*

al′co·hol″ (al′kə-hâl″) *n.* **1,** a liquid, ethyl hydrate derived by fermentation or distillation from organic substances. **2,** any intoxicating liquor containing alcohol.

al′co·hol′ic (-hol′ik) *adj.* **1,** of or containing alcohol. **2,** suffering from alcoholism. —*n.* one suffering from alcoholism. —**al″co·hol′i·cal·ly,** *adv.*

al′co·hol·ism (-iz-əm) *n.* addiction to excessive drinking of alcoholic liquors; dipsomania.

al′cove (al′kōv) *n.* a covered recess, bay, or niche.

al′de·hyde″ (al′də-hīd″) *n.* a fluid resulting from the oxidation of alcohol.

al den′te (äl den′tā) *adj.* (*It.*) of pasta, chewy; cooked to the right consistency.

al′der (âl′dər) *n.* any of numerous shrubs and trees abundant in temperate climates.

al′der·man (âl′dər-mən) [*pl.* **-men**], **al′der·wom″an,** *n.* a municipal official, in the U.S. usually representing a ward in a legislative body.

Al′der·ney (âl′dər-nė) *n.* one of a breed of dairy cattle, named for a Channel Island.

ale (āl) *n.* a beverage made from malt, similar to beer but containing more alcohol.

a′le·a·tor″y (a′lė-ə-tôr′ė) *adj.* pert. to or governed by chance. Also, **a″le·a·tor′ic.**

a·lem′bic (ə-lem′bik) *n.* a beaker.

a·lert′ (ə-lėrt′) *adj.* **1,** vigilantly attentive; watchful. **2,** brisk, nimble. —*v.t.* warn of or activate for impending danger. —*n.* **1,** a warning signal. **2,** a state of vigilant readiness. —**a·lert′ness,** *n.*

ale′wife (āl′wīf) *n.* a No. Amer. fish similar to the shad.

al″ex·an′drine (al″ək-san′drin) *n.* **1,** a line of French verse having 12 syllables.

2, a line of English verse in iambic pentameter.

alexandrine
↔ Middle French, orig. describing the meter of an Old French poem about Alexander the Great.

a·lex'i·a (ə-lek'sē-ə) *n.* loss of the faculty of understanding written language.
al·fal'fa (al-fal'fə) *n.* a forage plant extensively cultivated in the U.S.; lucerne.
Al″ Fa·tah' (äl″ fä-tä') (*Arabic*) a guerrilla branch of the Palestine Liberation Organization.
al'ga (al'gə) *n.* [*pl.* **al'gae** (-jē)] any of a numerous class of plants that grow in sea and fresh water.
al'ge·bra (al'jə-brə) *n.* **1,** a branch of mathematics concerned with generalizing the arithmetic operations and analyzing equations. **2,** any system of compact notation for dealing with generalizations. —**al″-ge·bra'ic** (-brā'ik) *adj.* —**al″ge·bra'i·cal·ly,** *adv.*

algebra
↔ The word comes from the Arabic term *al jebr*, the reuniting of broken parts. The word was first used in English in reference to the setting of broken bones. Many *al-* words are derived from Arabic words; the *al-* in Arabic means "the."

-al'gi·a (al'jə) *suf.* pain.
AL'GOL *n.* a computer programming language: *algo(rithmic) l(anguage).*
al'go·rism (al'gə-riz-əm) *n.* **1,** the system of Arabic numbers. **2,** calculation; arithmetic.

algorism, algorithm
↔ The word *algorism* comes from the name of an Arab mathematician, *al-Khuwarizmi,* the man of Khuwarizm. *Algorithm* arose in the 17th c. as an alternative spelling.

al'go·rithm (al'gə-rith-əm) *n.* a method of computation. ❏ *algorism*
al·gua·zil' (al-gwä-zēl') *n.* (*Sp.*) **1,** a judicial official in Spain. **2,** a sheriff in Latin America.
a'li·as (ā'lē-əs) *n.* an assumed name. —*adv.* also known as. —**a'li·as·ing,** *n.* (*Computers*) the jagged edges of a computer graphic image or character. Also, **jag'gies.**
al'i·bi'' (al'ə-bī″) *n.* (*Law*) a plea of having been elsewhere at the time an offense is alleged to have been committed; (*Infor-*

mal) any excuse. —**alibi Ike,** (*Slang*) a person always having an excuse.
al'i·dade'' (al'ə-dād″) *n.* a straightedge attached to a telescope or a graduated circle, for sighting or measured angles.
al'ien (āl'yən) *adj.* **1,** not residing in the country of one's citizenship. **2,** different in nature; foreign; adverse or hostile. —*n.* one who is estranged or excluded; a foreigner.
al'ien·a·ble (āl'yə-nə-bəl) *adj.* capable of being sold or transferred.
al'ien·ate'' (āl'yə-nāt″) *v.t.* **1,** repel or turn away in feeling; estrange. **2,** (*Law*) transfer title or property to another.
al''ien·a'tion (āl''yə-nā'shən) *n.* **1,** the act of alienating or being alienated. **2,** derangement; insanity.
al'ien·ist (āl'yən-ist) *n.* a psychiatrist, esp. one who pronounces upon legal insanity.
a·light' (ə-līt') *v.i.* **1,** dismount. **2,** disembark after a flight. —*adv. & adj.* glowing with light or fire.
a·lign' (ə-līn') *v.t. & i.* form into a line; straighten. Also, **a·line'.** —**a·lign'ment,** *n.*
a·like' (ə-līk') *adv.* in the same manner, form, or degree; in common; equally. —*adj.* having resemblance; similar; having no marked difference.
al'i·ment (al'ə-mənt) *n.* anything that nourishes or sustains; food; support. —**al''i·men'ta·ry canal** (al''ə-men'tə-rē) the entire food passage.
al''i·men·ta'tion (al''i-men-tā'shən) *n.* **1,** act of nourishing or being nourished. **2,** maintenance; sustenance.
al'i·mo''ny (al'ə-mō″nē) *n.* an allowance directed to be paid by a person to a former spouse after divorce.
al'i·quant (al'i-kwənt) *adj.* (*Math.*) contained in another number but not dividing it evenly.
al'i·quot (al'i-kwot) *adj.* (*Math.*) of a divisor, not leaving a remainder.
a·lit'e·rate (ā-lit'ə-rət) *adj.* preferring to obtain information through means (such as television) other than reading.
a·live' (ə-līv') *adj.* **1,** living; existent. **2,** active; animated. **3,** open to impressions; susceptible. **4,** filled with living things.
al'ka·li'' (al'kə-lī″) *n.* (*Chem.*) any of numerous substances that have the power of neutralizing acids and forming salts; a base. —**al''ka·line** (-līn) *adj.* —**al''ka·lin'i·ty** (-lin'ə-tē) *n.*
al'ka·loid (al'kə-loid) *n.* any of certain compounds of nitrogen.

al·kyd (al'kīd) *n.* a resin made from fatty acids and glycerol.

all (âl) *adj. & pron.* the whole quantity or number of (as to substance, extent, degree, duration, etc.). —*adj.* every; any. —*adv.* wholly; entirely. —*n.* a totality of things or qualities. —**all in,** (*Informal*) worn out; exhausted. —**all that,** (*Informal*) to that extent. —**all told,** in total. —**all wet,** (*Slang*) wrong; mistaken.

Al'lah (ä'lä) *n.* (*Arabic*) God.

all-″A·mer′i·can *adj.* **1,** the best or one of the best in the U.S. **2,** composed wholly of Americans. **3,** typically American. —*n.* an all-American person, esp. in sports.

all-″a·round′ *adj.* versatile; complete. Also, **all-″round′.**

al·lay′ (a-lā′) *v.t.* **1,** make quiet or calm; pacify. **2,** make less violent; mitigate.

al′le·ga′tion (al″ə-gā′shən) *n.* **1,** act of alleging. **2,** an assertion or plea.

al·lege′ (ə-lej′) *v.t.* **1,** declare positively. **2,** assert without proof.—**al·leged′** (-lejd) *adj.* **1,** asserted. **2,** doubtful. —**al·leg′ed·ly** (ə-lej′əd-lė) *adv.* according to allegation.

al·le′giance (ə-lē′jəns) *n.* **1,** the obligation of a person to his or her state or government. **2,** fidelity to a person or principle; devotion.

al′le·go″ry (al′ə-gôr″ė) *n.* the discussion or representation of a subject, not directly stated, through another analogous to it. —**al″le·gor′i·cal** (al″ə-gor′i-kəl) *adj.*

al″le·gret′to (al″ə-gret′ō) (*It., Music*) *adv. & adj.* quicker than andante, but not so quick as allegro. —*n.* an allegretto movement or work.

al·le′gro (ə-leg′rō) (*It., Music*) *adj.* brisk; lively. —*n.* an allegro movement or work.

al″le·lu′ia (al″ə-loo′yə) *n. & interj.* (*Heb.*) praise ye the Lord.

al′ler·gen (al′ər-jən) *n.* a substance that causes an allergenic reaction.

al·ler′gic (ə-lėr′jik) *adj.* having an allergy (to something); (*Informal*) averse.

al′ler·gy (al′ər-jė) *n.* abnormal sensitivity to certain foods or substances. —**al′ler·gist,** *n.*

al·le′vi·ate″ (ə-lē′vė-āt″) *v.t.* remove in part; lessen; mitigate. —**al·le″vi·a′tion,** *n.*

al′ley (al′ė) *n.* **1,** [also, **al′ley·way″**] a narrow passageway; a back street. **2,** a long, narrow rink for sports, as bowling. **3,** a large playing-marble.

all-′fired″ (âl′fīrd″) *adv.* (*Informal*) greatly; very.

al·li′ance (ə-lī′əns) *n.* **1,** state of being allied or joined together, as in marriage or political confederation. **2,** the aggregate of persons or parties allied. **3,** the instrument of an alliance, as a treaty. **4,** kinship; similarity.

al·lied′ (ə-līd′) *adj.* **1,** joined together by compact or treaty. **2,** similar or related.

al′li·ga″tor (al′ə-gā″tər) *n.* a large lizardlike reptile, akin to the crocodile. —**alligator pear,** avocado.

> **alligator**
> ↔ From Spanish *el lagarto (de Indias),* the lizard of the Indies, from Latin *lacertus,* lizard.

al·lit″er·a′tion (ə-lit″ə-rā′shən) *n.* repetition of the same initial letter or sound in two or more nearby words, as *foolish fancy.* —**al·lit′er·ate,** *v.i.*

al·lo- (al-lō) *pref.* indicating difference or opposition.

al′lo·cate″ (al′ə-kāt″) *v.t.* set apart for a particular purpose; allot; assign. —**al″loca′tion,** *n.*

al″lo·cu′tion (al″ə-kū′shən) *n.* a formal address.

al·lop′a·thy (ə-lop′ə-thė) *n.* treatment of disease by the agents that produce effects different from the symptoms of the disease. —**al′lo·path″,** *n.* —**al″lo·path′ic,** *adj.* —**al″lo·path′i·cal·ly,** *adv.*

al″lo·pe′cia (al″ə-pē′shė-ə) *n.* baldness.

al·lot′ (ə-lot′) *v.t.* [**al·lot′ted, al·lot′ting**] **1,** distribute as by lot; parcel out; apportion. **2,** set apart; appoint; assign for a particular purpose.

al·lot′ment (-mənt) *n.* **1,** act of allotting; distribution. **2,** a portion or share; an assigned quantity.

al′lo·trope″ (al′ə-trōp″) *n.* any of several different physical forms in which a chemical element may occur, as coal or diamond, both carbon. —**al″lo·trop′ic,** *adj.* —**al″lo·trop′i·cal·ly,** *adv.* —**al·lot′ro·py** (ə-lot′rə-pė), **al·lot′ro·pism** (-piz-əm) *n.*

all-″out′ *adj.* with full vigor.

al·low′ (ə-low′) *v.t.* **1,** permit; grant; yield; assign. **2,** admit; concede. **3,** make provision (for); take into account. **4,** (*Dial.*) aver; believe.

al·low′ance (ə-low′əns) *n.* **1,** a share or allotment, esp. of money granted to defray expenses. **2,** an addition or deduction, as the allowable difference from prescribed dimensions in machining. **3,** admission or acceptance; sanction.

al′loy (al′oi) *n.* **1,** a mixture of two or more metals, intimately fused. **2,** an admixture; a deleterious component; taint.

—*v.t.* (ə-loi′) **1,** mix. **2,** debase by admixture.

all right 1, in good condition; correct; correctly; unharmed. **2,** expression of assent or agreement; very well; yes.

---

all right, alright

☞ In written English, *all right* is the preferred form for the sense "correct."

---

all-'round″ *adj.* all-around.

all'spice″ (âl′spīs″) *n.* the berry of a West Indian tree; pimento.

all-'star″ *adj.* **1,** comprising outstanding examples of a certain field. **2,** pert. to a member of such a group. —*n.* a member of an all-star group.

all'-time″ *adj.* for all time; never equaled.

al·lude' (ə-lood′) *v.i.* (with *to*) refer casually or indirectly.

---

allude, refer

☞ To *allude* to something is to *refer* to it *indirectly*, that is, without actually naming it.

---

al·lure' (ə-lûr′) *v.t.* attract by some proposed pleasure or advantage; entice. —*n.* charm. —**al·lure'ment,** *n.* —**al·lur'ing,** *adj.* tempting; charming.

al·lu'sion (ə-loo′zhən) *n.* a casual reference; a slight or incidental mention. —**al·lu'sive** (-siv) *adj.*

---

allusion, delusion, illusion

☞ These three words are sometimes confused. An *allusion* is a casual reference. *Delusion* and *illusion* are both mistaken beliefs, but a *delusion* is stronger and more difficult to dispel.

---

al·lu'vi·um (ə-loo′vē-əm) *n.* [*pl.* **-a** (-ə)] a deposit of sand formed by flowing water. —**al·lu'vi·al,** *adj.*

al·ly' (ə-lī′) *v.t. & i.* join together; combine with; associate. —*n.* (also, a′lī) one joined with another in a common enterprise; a confederate.

al'ma ma'ter (äl′mə mä′tər) (*Lat.*) one's school or college.

al'ma·nac″ (âl′mə-nak″) *n.* a yearly calendar showing the times of certain events, as the rising and setting of the sun and moon, the changes of the moon, the tides, dates of holidays, etc.

al·might'y (âl-mī′tē) *adj.* **1,** supremely powerful; of boundless sufficiency. **2,** (*Informal*) extreme. —*n.* (*cap.*) God.

al'mond (ä′mənd) *n.* **1,** a tree found in subtropical climates. **2,** the edible kernel

of its fruit. **3,** the color of the kernel, light brown. **4,** anything shaped like an almond kernel.

al'mon·er (al′mən-ər) *n.* a giver of alms. —**al'mon·ry** (-rē) *n.*

al'most (âl′mōst) *adv.* nearly all; for the most part; very nearly; all but.

alms (ämz) *n.pl.* what is given to the poor or needy; anything bestowed in charity. —**alms'house″,** *n.* poorhouse.

al'oe (al′ō) *n.* **1,** an African plant used in making drugs and fiber. **2,** the American century plant. **3,** (*pl.*) a bitter purgative drug made from the juice of the aloe.

a·loft' (ə-lâft′) *adv. & adj.* in the air; above the ground; (*Naut.*) in the upper rigging.

a·lo'ha (ə-lō′hä; *Hawaiian* ə-lō′ə) *interj.* of well-wishing, used as both a greeting and a farewell.

---

aloha

↔ This word of courtesy is the Hawaiian word for "love."

---

a·lone' (ə-lōn′) *adj.* apart from or to the exclusion of other persons or things; solitary; single. —*adv.* solely; only.

a·long' (ə-lâng′) *prep.* in a longitudinal direction through, over, or by the side of. —*adv.* **1,** lengthwise. **2,** onward. **3,** in company; together.

a·long'side *adv. & prep.* along or by the side of; beside.

a·loof' (ə-loof′) *adv.* at a distance, but within view; hence, withdrawn. —*adj.* reserved; indifferent. —**a·loof'ness,** *n.*

a·loud' (ə-lowd′) *adv.* audibly; with the natural tone of the voice as distinguished from whispering.

alp *n.* a high mountain.

al·pac'a (al-pak′ə) *n.* **1,** a domesticated sheeplike ruminant of S. Amer. **2,** its hair; a fabric made from the hair. **3,** any glossy fabric made in imitation of alpaca.

al'pen·stock″ (al′pən-) *n.* a long, strong staff with a sharp iron point.

al'pha (al′fə) *n.* **1,** the first letter of the Greek alphabet (A, α), corresponding to English a. **2,** (*Communications*) the letter *a*. —**alpha particle,** a positively charged particle. —**alpha ray,** a stream of alpha particles.

al'pha·bet″ (al′fə-bet″) *n.* the letters of a language in their customary order. —**al″pha·bet'i·cal** (-i-kəl) *adj.* in that order. —**al'pha·bet·ize″** (-bə-tīz″) *v.t.* put into alphabetical order.

al″pha·nu·mer'ic (al″fə-noo-mer′ik) *adj.* consisting of or utilizing letters and numerals.

---

fat, fāte, fär, fāre, fâll, ȧsk; met, hē, hėr, maybė; pin, pīne; not, nōte, ôr, tool

al'pine (al'pīn) *adj.* **1,** mountainous; high; elevated. **2,** (*cap.*) pert. to the Alps.

al·read'y (âl-red'ē) *adv.* previously to the present or a specified time.

al·right' *adj. & adv.* (*Informal*) all right. ❑ *all right*

al'so (âl'sō) *adv.* in addition; too; likewise; further.

al'so-ran" *n.* **1,** in a horse race, a horse not finishing 1st, 2nd, or 3rd. **2,** an unsuccessful contestant. **3,** a person of small importance; a failure.

al'tar (âl'tər) *n.* a structure, as a block of stone or a table, at which religious rites are performed.

al'tar·piece" *n.* a reredos.

al'ter (âl'tər) *v.t.* **1,** make some change in; cause to vary; modify. **2,** to castrate or spay. —*v.i.* become different; change. —**al"ter·a'tion,** *n.*

al"ter·ca'tion (âl"tər-kā'shən) *n.* an angry or noisy dispute; wrangle. —**al'-ter·cate",** *v.i.*

al'ter e'go (âl"tər ē'gō) (*Lat.*) one's other self; an inseparable companion.

al'ter·nate" (âl'tər-nāt") *v.i.* **1,** follow one another in time or place reciprocally. **2,** move or change in turn from one place or condition to another. —*v.t.* do or perform in turns, or in succession. —*adj.* (-nət) **1,** following by turns, recurrently or in succession. **2,** every other one of a series. —*n.* (-nət) a person authorized to take the place of another in his absence. —**al"ter·na'tion,** *n.*

> **alternate, alternative**
> ☛ In current usage, these two adjectives are interchangeable, though strictly speaking there is a distinction between *alternate*, meaning "following by turns," and *alternative*, meaning "affording a choice."

alternating current electric current that reverses its direction of flow, usually 120 times per second.

al·ter'na·tive (âl-tėr'nə-tiv) *n.* one of a set of mutually exclusive choices or possibilities. —*adj.* **1,** affording a choice. **2,** mutually exclusive. **3,** differing from the conventional or established, as *an alternative lifestyle.* ❑ *alternate*

al'ter·na"tor (âl'tər-nā"tər) *n.* an electric generator for producing alternating current.

al·though' (âl-thō') *conj.* in spite of the fact that; even admitting that. Also (*Informal*) **al·tho'.**

> **although, while**
> ☛ In the sense of "in spite of the fact that," *although* is preferred.

al·tim'e·ter (al-tim'ə-tər) *n.* an instrument for measuring altitudes.

al'ti·tude" (al'ti-tood") *n.* the distance upward, esp. from sea level to a point in the atmosphere; height.

al'to (al'tō) (*Music*) *adj.* higher than tenor. —*n.* [*pl.* **-tos**] **1,** a high male or low female voice. **2,** a part in the range of such a voice. **3,** any of several instruments.

al"to·geth'er (âl"tə-ge*th*'ər) *adv.* wholly; entirely. —**in the altogether,** (*Informal*) nude.

> **altogether, all together**
> ☛ *Altogether* means wholly, entirely. *All together* means at the same time, united.

al'tru·ism (al'troo-iz-əm) *n.* regard for the welfare of others; benevolent practices. —**al"tru·ist,** *n.* —**al"tru·is'tic,** *adj.* —**al"tru·is'ti·cal·ly,** *adv.*

al'um (al'əm) *n.* any of numerous bitter, astringent compounds used in drugs and dyes.

a·lu'mi·num (ə-loo'mə-nəm) *n.* a metallic chemical element, much used in alloys because of its light weight, no. 13, symbol Al. Also (*Brit.*) **al"u·min'i·um** (al"ū-min'ē-əm).

a·lum'nus (ə-lum'nəs) *n.masc.* [*pl.* **-ni** (-nī)], **a·lum'na** (-nə) [*pl.* **-nae** (-nē)] *n.fem.* a graduate or former student of a school or college. Also (*Informal*) **a·lum'.**

al·ve'o·lus (al-vē'ə-ləs) *n.* a small cavity. —**al·ve'o·lar** (-lər) *adj.*

al'ways (âl'wāz) *adv.* **1,** throughout all time; uninterruptedly. **2,** at every recurring time.

Alz'heim·er's disease (älts'hī-mərz) a form of dementia of unknown cause, named for the German neurologist Alois Alzheimer, who first described the disease.

am *v.* 1st person sing. of *be.*

am'a·dou (am'ə-doo) *n.* tinder.

> **amadou, amateur**
> ↔ Both words derive from Latin *amator*, lover. In the case of *amadou*, the derivation stems presumably from the perceived parallel between love and combustion.

a·main' (ə-mān') *adv.* **1,** with force, strength, or violence. **2,** full speed; hastily. **3,** exceedingly.

a·mal'gam (ə-mal'gəm) *n.* **1,** an alloy of

mercury with another metal. **2,** any mixture or compound.

a·mal'ga·mate" (ə-mal'gə-māt") *v.t. & i.* **1,** mix or come together; blend; unite. **2,** combine with a metal. **—a·mal"ga·ma'-tion,** *n.*

a·man"u·en'sis (ə-man"ū-en'sis) *n.* [*pl.* -**ses** (sēz)] a person who writes what another dictates; a secretary.

> **amanuensis**
> ↔ From the Latin phrase *servus a manu,* hand servant, i.e., secretary.

am'a·ranth (am'ə-ranth) *n.* any of various flowering plants.

am"a·ryl'lis (am"ə-ril'is) *n.* **1,** a bulbous plant, the belladonna lily. **2,** (*cap.*) a shepherdess.

> **amaryllis**
> ↔ From Greek *Amaryllis,* the name of a shepherdess in Virgil's *Eclogues* and other rustic literature of ancient Greece and Rome.

a·mass' (ə-mas') *v.t.* collect in a mass or heap; bring together in great amount.

am'a·teur" (am'ə-chûr") *n.* **1,** one who pursues an activity for pleasure instead of for material gain. **2,** one who is unskillful; a dilettante. —*adj.* not professional. **—am"a·teur'ish,** *adj.* unskillful. **—am'a·teur·ism,** *n.* ❑ *amadou*

am'a·tive (am'ə-tiv) *adj.* loving.

am'a·to"ry (am'ə-tôr"ē) *adj.* pert. to lovemaking.

a·maze' (ə-māz') *v.t.* cause to feel great astonishment, surprise, or wonder. **—a·maze'ment,** *n.*

am'a·zon" (am'ə-zon") *n.* **1,** (*cap.*) one of a mythological race of female warriors. **2,** a large and strong woman.

am·bas'sa·dor (am-bas'ə-dər) *n.* a diplomatic agent of highest rank. **—am·bas"-sa·dor'i·al** (-dôr'ē-əl) *adj.*

am'ber (am'bər) *n.* **1,** a mineralized resin on which rubbing produces a negative electric charge. **2,** the pale yellow color of amber. —*adj.* like amber; yellow.

am'ber·gris" (am'bər-grēs") *n.* a morbid secretion of the sperm whale, prized for making perfume.

am·bi- *pref.* meaning both, or on both sides. Also, **am·phi-.**

am'bi·ance (am'bē-əns) *n.* **1,** mood; atmosphere. **2,** environment. Also, **am'bi·ence.**

am"bi·dex'trous (am"bi-deks'trəs) *adj.* apt with both hands. Also, **am"bi·dex'ter** (-tər). **—am"bi·dex·ter'i·ty,** *n.*

am'bi·ent (am'bē-ənt) *adj.* surrounding; circling about.

am'bi·gram" *n.* a word so written that it can be read from more than one vantage point, as upside-down or backward.

am·bi·gu'i·ty (am-bi-gū'ə-tē) *n.* state of being ambiguous; double meaning.

am·big'u·ous (am-big'ū-əs) *adj.* of doubtful purport; open to various interpretations; having a double meaning.

am'bit *n.* boundary; compass.

am·bi'tion (am-bish'ən) *n.* eager desire for distinction, power, or fame.

am·bi'tious (am-bish'əs) *adj.* having much ambition; eager for success.

am·biv'a·lence (am-biv'ə-ləns) *n.* mixed or conflicting feelings. **—am·biv'a·lent,** *adj.*

am'ble (am'bəl) *v.i.* move easily and gently, like a walking horse.

am·bro'sia (am-brō'zhə) *n.* **1,** in Greek legend, the food of the gods. **2,** a fruit dessert topped with coconut. **—am·bro'sial** (-zhəl) *adj.*

ambs'ace" (amz'ās") *n.* the lowest throw at dice, double aces.

am'bu·lance (am'bū-ləns) *n.* a vehicle for carrying the sick or wounded. **—ambulance chaser,** a lawyer who unethically solicits as clients the victims of an accident.

> **ambulance**
> ↔ The word developed in the early 19th c. from the French word for field hospital, originally *hôpital ambulant,* "walking hospital."

am'bu·late" (am'bū-lāt") *v.i.* move about from place to place. **—am"bu·la'tion,** *n.* **—am'bu·lant, am'bu·la·to"ry** (-tôr"ē) *adj.*

am"bus·cade' (am"bəs-kād') *n. & v.* ambush.

am'bush (am'bûsh) *v.t.* attack unexpectedly from a hidden position. —*n.* **1,** the act of lying concealed for a surprise attack. **2,** a place of concealment.

a·me'ba (ə-mē'bə) *n.* a one-celled animal that continually changes shape to engulf and absorb its food. Also, **a·moe'ba.**

a·mel'io·rate" (ə-mēl'yə-rāt") *v.t. & i.* make or become better, more satisfactory, or more tolerable. **—a·mel"io·ra'tion,** *n.* **—a·mel'io·ra·tive,** *adj.*

a'men' (ā'men') (*Heb.*) *interj. & adv.* be it so (an expression of invocation or endorsement at the end of a prayer). —*n.* an expression of fervent assent.

a·me'na·ble (ə-mē'nə-bəl) *adj.* **1,** disposed to yield; submissive. **2,** liable, as to

---

fat, fāte, fär, fāre, fåll, åsk; met, hē, hėr, maybė; pin, pīne; not, nōte, ôr, tool

control or claim. **—a·me″na·bil′i·ty, a-me′na·ble·ness,** *n.*

a·mend′ (ə-mend′) *v.t.* **1,** make better; correct; improve. **2,** alter. *—v.i.* become better; reform. *—n.* *(pl.)* compensation for loss or injury; recompense. **—a·mend′-a·to·ry** (-ə-tôr-ė) *adj.*

---

amend, emend
☞ *Amend* is the more general term for "to correct"; *emend* usu. refers only to the correcting of written matter.

---

a·mend′ment (-mənt) *n.* **1,** correction; improvement. **2,** a change, as in a law; *(cap.)* a change in the Constitution of the U.S.

a·men′i·ty (ə-men′ə-tė) *n.* **1,** the quality of being pleasant or agreeable. **2,** *(pl.)* pleasant aspects; conveniences; social courtesies.

a·merce′ (ə-mẽrs′) *v.t.* punish by a fine or by any arbitrary penalty.

Am″er·a′sian (am″ə-rā′zhən) *n.* the offspring of an American and an Asian parent.

A·mer′i·can (ə-mer′i-kən) *adj. & n.* pert. to any country of the Western Hemisphere, esp. the U.S., its people, customs, etc. **—American cheese,** a mild cheddar cheese. **—American plan,** a system whereby a hotel's charge includes room and meals.

American
☞ The word is widely used to refer to inhabitants of the United States of America, although strictly speaking it can refer to any inhabitant of the Western Hemisphere. ↔ From the Latin form of the name of the 15th-c. Italian navigator, *Amerigo* Vespucci.

A·mer″i·ca′na (ə-mer″i-ka′nə) *n.pl.* materials (documents, antiques, etc.) bearing on Amer. history.

A·mer′i·can·ism (-iz-əm) *n.* something peculiarly American, esp. of the United States.

am″er·i′ci·um (am″ə-ris(h)′ė-əm) *n.* a radioactive chemical element, no. 95, symbol Am, produced artificially from plutonium.

Am′er·ind (am′ər-ind) *n.* an Amer. Indian or Eskimo; Native American.

am′e·thyst (am′ə-thist) *n.* **1,** a bluish variety of quartz used in making ornaments. **2,** a violet sapphire. **3,** a light purple or violet color.

a′mi·a·ble (ā′mė-ə-bəl) *adj.* **1,** pleasing;

lovable. **2,** friendly; kindly. **—a″mi·a·bil′-i·ty, a′mi·a·ble·ness,** *n.*

am″i·an′thus (am″ė-an′thəs) *n.* a type of asbestos.

am′i·ca·ble (am′i-kə-bəl) *adj.* exhibiting friendliness; peaceable; harmonious. **—am″i·ca·bil′i·ty,** *n.*

am′ice (am′is) *n.* **1,** a priestly vestment worn at Mass. **2,** a furred hood or cape.

a·mid′ (ə-mid′) *prep.* in the midst of or surrounded by. Also, **a·midst′.**

a·mid′ships″ *adv.* midway of the length of a ship.

a·mi′no acid (ə-mē′nō) any of a large group of organic compounds which are basic constituents of proteins.

Am′ish (äm′ish) *adj.* of a certain sect of Mennonites.

Amish
↔ From the German form of the name Jacob *Amman,* 19th-c. Swiss Mennonite bishop.

---

a·miss′ (ə-mis′) *adv.* in a faulty manner; out of proper course or order. *—adj.* improper; faulty.

am′i·ty (am′ə-tė) *n.* friendship; pleasant relations, esp. between nations.

am′me″ter (am′mē″tər) *n.* an instrument for measuring amperes.

am′mo (am′ō) *n.* *(Slang)* ammunition.

am·mo′ni·a (ə-mōn′yə) *n.* **1,** a gaseous compound of nitrogen and hydrogen. **2,** a solution of this gas in water. **—am·mo′ni·ate″** (-āt″) *v.t.*

am″mu·ni′tion (am″ū-nish′ən) *n.* **1,** materials used in discharging firearms, etc., as bullets, explosives, etc. **2,** means for retaliation or defense, as evidence, etc.

am·ne′sia (am-nē′zhə) *n.* loss of memory. **—am·ne′sic** (-zik) *adj.*

am′nes·ty (am′nəs-tė) *n.* a general pardon for a whole class of offenses against a government.

am″ni·o·cen·te′sis (am″nė-ō-sen-tē′sis) *n.* a surgical procedure for obtaining amniotic fluid from the uterus for diagnosis.

am′ni·on (am′nė-ən) *n.* *(Anat.)* the sac in which an embryo is suspended. **—am·ni-ot′ic** (am-nė-ot′ik) *adj.*

a·moe′ba (ə-mē′bə) *n.* ameba.

a·mok′ (ə-mok′) *adv.* in a frenzied manner. **—run amok,** indiscriminately attack everyone encountered. Also, **a·muck′.**

---

amok
↔ From the Malay adjective *amoq,* "fighting frenziedly."

---

a·mong' (ə-mung') *prep.* **1,** in the midst of; in association with; in the class or group of. **2,** with or by the whole of. **3,** to each of. Also, **a·mongst'** (ə-mungst').

---

among, between
(*Gram.*) The schoolbook rule is to use *between* for two persons or objects and *among* for three or more. However, a more practical and subtle approach is to use *between* for the relationships between individual members of a set, however many, and *among* for a more vague relationship to the group collectively.

---

a·mon″til·la'do (ə-mon″tə-lä'dō) *n.* a dry sherry named after Montilla, a town in Spain.

a·mor'al (ā-môr'əl) *adj.* **1,** neither moral nor immoral; nonmoral. **2,** having no sense of moral responsibility. —**a″mo·ral'i·ty,** *n.*

---

amoral, immoral
☛ *Amoral* means having no morals; *immoral* means violating or not conforming to moral law.

---

am'o·rous (am'ə-rəs) *adj.* **1,** inclined to love; loving. **2,** indicating or conveying love. —**am'o·rous·ness,** *n.*

a·mor'phous (ə-môr'fəs) *adj.* **1,** having no determinate form; of irregular shape. **2,** of no particular kind; heterogeneous. —**a·mor'phous·ness, a·mor'phism** (-fiz-əm) *n.*

am'or·tize″ (am'ər-tīz″) *v.t.* extinguish (a debt) by means of a sinking fund. —**am″or·ti·za'tion,** *n.*

a·mount' (ə-mownt') *n.* **1,** the sum of two or more quantities. **2,** a sum quantity, value, or import, viewed as a whole. —*v.i.* (with *to*) add up; reach in quantity or degree.

---

amount, number, quantity
☛ *Quantity* is the general term, referring either to mass or number of items. *Number* refers to the sum of the individual items and usually takes a plural noun; *amount* refers to the mass of the items and therefore takes a singular noun.

---

a·mour' (ä-mûr') *n.* a love affair.

am'per·age (am'pir-ij) *n.* the measure of a current in amperes.

am'pere (am'pir) *n.* a unit of electromotive force, one volt acting against the resistance of one ohm.

---

ampere
↔ Named after the 19th-c. French physicist André Marie *Ampère*.

---

am'per·sand″ (am'pər-sand″) *n.* the character &: and.

---

ampersand
↔ From the phrase *and per se and*, "and, by itself, and." The symbol is a printed version of the Latin scribes' abbreviation for Latin *et*, and.

---

am·phet'a·mine (am-fet'ə-mēn) *n.* a drug used to relieve nasal congestion and as a stimulant.

am·phib'i·an (am-fib'ē-ən) *n.* an amphibious animal, plant, or airplane.

am·phib'i·ous (am-fib'ē-əs) *adj.* capable of living or operating both on land and in water.

am'phi·the″a·ter (am'fə-thē″ə-tər) *n.* a circular or oval arena, usu. for sports, surrounded by tiers of seats on a sloping gallery.

am'pho·ra (am'fə-rə) *n.* [*pl.* **-rae** (-rē)] a two-handled vessel.

am″pi·cil'lin (am″pə-sil'ən) *n.* an antibiotic drug.

am'ple (am'pəl) *adj.* **1,** large in extent or amount; copious. **2,** plentifully sufficient. —**am'ple·ness,** *n.*

am'pli·fi″er (am'plə-fī″ər) *n.* a device for increasing the amplitude of electrical impulses.

am'pli·fy″ (am'plə-fī″) *v.t.* make larger in extent or importance; enlarge. —**am″pli·fi·ca'tion,** *n.*

am'pli·tude″ (am'pli-tood″) *n.* **1,** extension in space; largeness. **2,** (of a wave) the distance or magnitude of a crest or trough from the mean value. —**amplitude modulation,** a system of radio transmission.

am'poule (am'pool) *n.* a sealed glass bulb holding one or more doses of a hypodermic injection. Also, **am'pule** (-pūl).

am'pu·tate″ (am'pū-tāt″) *v.t.* cut off (a limb). —**am″pu·ta'tion,** *n.* —**am″pu·tee',** *n.*

Am'trak *n.* a nationwide system of passenger railroad service in the U.S.: *Am(erican) Tra(vel on Trac)k.*

a·muck' (ə-muk') *adv.* amok.

am'u·let (am'ū-let) *n.* an object superstitiously worn to bring good luck, avert illness, etc.

a·muse' (ə-mūz') *v.t.* excite pleasure or mirth in; entertain; divert.

a·muse'ment (-mənt) *n.* **1,** pleasurable interest; mirth. **2,** that which amuses; a pastime. —**amusement park,** a commercial park for entertainment, usu. having rides and booths.

an *adj.* indefinite article, used before a word beginning with a vowel sound. ❏ *a*

---

an'a (an'ə) *n.* a collection of writings by or about a person.

-an·a (an·ə) *suf.* denoting an assembly of items.

a·nab'a·sis (ə-nab'ə-sis) *n.* [*pl.* **-ses** (-sēz)] a long march by a military force.

an'a·bol"ic steroid (an'ə-bol"ik) a synthetic hormone used by athletes to increase strength and weight.

a·nach'ro·nism (ə-nak'rə-niz-əm) *n.* an error in respect to dates or the order of historical events. —**a·nach"ro·nis'tic** (-nis'-tik) *adj.* —**a·nach"ro·nis'ti·cal·ly,** *adv.*

an'a·con'da (an"ə-kon'də) *n.* any large snake; boa constrictor.

a·na"cre·on'tic (ə-nak"rē-on'tik) *adj.* amatory.

---

anacreontic
↔ From *Anakreōn*, a Greek writer of love poems.

---

an'a·gram" (an'ə-gram") *n.* a word or phrase formed from another by transposition of the letters.

a'nal (ā'nəl) *adj.* pert. to the anus.—**anal retentive,** (*Psychol.*) rigid; compulsive.

an"al·ge'sia (an"əl-jē'zhə) *n.* inability of a part to feel pain.

an"al·ge'sic (an"əl-jē'zik) *n.* a remedy to relieve pain. —*adj.* relieving pain.

an'a·log" (an'ə-lâg") *adj.* employing measurement along scales rather than by numerical counting. —*n.* **analogue.** —**analog computer,** a computer that represents data as voltages rather than as numbers.

a·nal'o·gous (ə-nal'ə-gəs) *adj.* corresponding; similar.

an'a·logue (an'ə-log) *n.* something analogous to another.

a·nal'o·gy (ə-nal'ə-jē) *n.* similarity or agreement between one thing and another; resemblance; comparison.

a·nal'y·sand (ə-nal'ə-sand) *n.* a client of an analyst.

a·nal'y·sis (ə-nal'ə-sis) *n.* [*pl.* **-ses** (-sēz)] **1,** the separation of a complex material or conception into its elements. **2,** determination of causes from results; induction. **3,** an abstract; summary.

an'a·lyst (an'ə-list) *n.* **1,** one who analyzes. **2,** a psychoanalyst.

an·a·lyt'i·cal (an-ə-lit'i-kəl) *adj.* being or pert. to analysis. Also, **an·a·lyt'ic.**

an'a·lyze" (an'ə-līz") *v.t.* **1,** separate into its elements; determine the constituents of. **2,** examine critically. —**an"a·ly·za'-tion,** *n.*

an'a·pest" (an'ə-pest") *n.* (*Poetry*) a met-

rical foot of two unstressed syllables followed by a stressed one. —**an"a·pes'tic,** *adj.*

an'arch·ism (an'ər-kiz-əm) *n.* the political doctrine that all governments should be abolished.

an'arch·ist (an'ər-kist) *n.* **1,** a social rebel; insurrectionist. **2,** a believer in anarchism. —**an"ar·chis'tic,** *adj.*

an'ar·chy (an'ər-kē) *n.* **1,** general disorder from lack of government. **2,** anarchism. —**an·ar'chic** (an-ärk'ik), **an·ar'chi·cal,** *adj.*

a·nath'e·ma (ə-nath'ə-mə) *n.* **1,** a denunciation, accompanied by excommunication, by an ecclesiastical authority. **2,** any solemn execration or curse. **3,** something accursed. —**a·nath'e·ma·tize",** *v.t.* curse.

a·nat'o·my (ə-nat'ə-mē) *n.* **1,** the structure of an animal or plant body. **2,** the science of structure; the art of dissecting bodies to determine their structure. —**an"-a·tom'i·cal,** *adj.* —**a·nat'o·mize,** *v.t.* dissect.

-ance (əns) *suf.* same as **-ence.**

an'ces·tor (an'ses-tər) *n.* a foregoing person or organism (usually deceased) from whom one is descended; forebear; progenitor.

an·ces'tral (an-ses'trəl) *adj.* pert. to ancestry or an ancestor.

an'ces·try (an'ses-trē) *n.* a series of ancestors; line of descent.

an'chor (ang'kər) *n.* **1,** a device for securing a vessel to the ground under water by means of a cable. **2,** any device that holds in place, gives security or stability. **3,** (*also,* **an'chor·per"son**) the principal newscaster of a news broadcast. **4,** the moderator of a panel, discussion group, etc. **5,** (*Sports*) the last contestant in a relay race. —*v.t.* fix firmly in place. —*v.i.* drop anchor.

an'chor·age (-ij) *n.* a place suitable for anchoring.

an'cho·rite" (ang'kə-rīt") *n.* a recluse; hermit. Also, **an'cho·ret"** (-ret").

an'chor·man", an'chor·wo"man *n.* anchor (def. 3, 4, 5).

an'cho·vy (an'chō-vē) *n.* a small fish similar to the herring.

an·cien' ré·gime' (äṅ-syaṅ'rā-zhēm') (*Fr.*) **1,** in France, the political and social system before the Revolution of 1789. **2,** any old or former system.

an'cient (ān'shənt) *adj.* **1,** having existed in the remote past. **2,** very old. —**Ancient of Days,** God.

an'cil·lar"y (an'sə-ler"ē) *adj.* **1,** serving in a subordinate or auxiliary capacity. **2,** (*In-*

formal) related. —*n.* (*pl.*) (*Mil.*) auxiliary forces, as of supply, transport, etc.

-an·cy (ən-sė) *suf.* same as **-ence, -ency.**

and *conj.* in addition; also; too.

an·dan'te (an-dan'tė) (*It., Music*) *adj.* & *adv.* moderately slow. —*n.* an andante movement or work. —**an·dan·ti'no** (-tē'-nō), *adj., adv.* & *n.* somewhat faster than andante.

and'i"ron (and'ī"ərn) *n.* one of a pair of iron stands used to support wood burned in an open hearth.

and/or *conj.* implying that either or both of the alternatives mentioned may be involved.

> **and/or**
> (*Gram.*) This combination, useful in certain business and technical situations, is best avoided in general writing. It can easily be replaced by rewording.

an'dro- *pref.* man; male.

an'dro·gen (an'drə-jən) *n.* a substance, such as male sex hormones, that enhances masculinity.

an·drog'y·nous (an-droj'ə-nəs) *adj.* **1,** hermaphroditic. **2,** having both male and female characteristics. —**an'dro·gyne"** (an'drə-jin") *n.*

an'droid *n.* an automaton in human form.

an·dros'ter·one" (an-dros'tə-rōn") *n.* a male sex hormone.

an'ec·dote" (an'ek-dōt") *n.* a short narrative of an occurrence. —**an"ec·do'tal,** *adj.*

a·ne'mi·a (ə-nē'mė-ə) *n.* **1,** quantitative deficiency of hemoglobin. **2,** a lack of vigor. —**a·ne'mic,** *adj.* —**a·ne'mi·cal·ly,** *adv.*

an"e·mom'e·ter (an"ə-mom'ə-tər) *n.* a device for measuring the velocity of the wind.

a·nem'o·ne (ə-nem'ə-nė) *n.* **1,** a wild flower. **2,** a small sea animal.

a·nent' (ə-nent') *prep.* (*Archaic*) in regard to; concerning.

an'er·oid" (an'ər-oid") *adj.* using no fluid.

an"es·the'sia (an"əs-thē'zhə) *n.* (*Med.*) loss of feeling, esp. as induced by certain drugs.

an"es·the"si·ol'o·gist (an"əs-thē"zė-ol'ə-jist) *n.* a physician specializing in the administering of anesthetics; anesthetist. —**an"es·the"si·ol'o·gy,** *n.*

an"es·thet'ic (-thet'ik) *n.* a drug that induces anesthesia.

an·es'the·tist (ə-nes'thə-tist) *n.* one who administers an anesthetic.

an·es'the·tize" (ə-nes'thə-tīz") *v.t.* administer an anesthetic to.

an'eu·rysm (an'yə-riz-əm) *n.* a permanent dilation of a blood vessel.

a·new' (ə-nū') *adv.* once more; again; in a new form.

an'gel (ān'jəl) *n.* **1,** an attendant of God, esp. a messenger. **2,** a kindly woman. **3,** (*Informal*) a financial backer. —**an·gel'ic** (an-jel'ik) *adj.* —**an·gel'i·cal·ly,** *adv.* —**angel dust,** (*Slang*) a hallucinogenic drug, phencyclidine hydrochloride. Also, **PCP.** —**angel food cake,** a light white cake made with flour, sugar, and egg whites.

an'gel·fish" *n.* **1,** a shark of the N. Atlantic. **2,** any of several beautifully colored tropical fish.

an·gel'i·ca (an-jel'i-kə) *n.* **1,** a plant of the carrot family. **2,** a wine or liqueur flavored with angelica.

an'ger (ang'gər) *n.* a strong emotion of displeasure and resentment; wrath. —*v.t.* excite to anger.

an·gi'na pec'to·ris (an-jī'nə pek'tə-ris; *Med.* an'jə-nə) a spasm in the chest, symptom of a heart disease.

an'gle (ang'gəl) *n.* **1,** an enclosure or space formed by two intersecting lines or planes. **2,** (*Geom.*) that proportion of a circular arc intercepted by such lines. **3,** an angular projection; a corner. **4,** a point of view; an aspect or phase. —*v.t.* & *i.* form into an angle. —*v.i.* **1,** fish with hook and line. **2,** try to obtain by artful means. —**an'gler,** *n.* a fisherman. —**an'gling,** *n.* the art of fishing. —**angle iron,** a metal support, usu. in the form of a right angle.

an'gle·worm" *n.* an earthworm.

An'gli·can (ang'gli-kən) *adj.* pert. to the Church of England.

An'gli·cism (ang'glə-siz-əm) *n.* something peculiarly English.

an'gli·cize" (ang'gli-sīz") *v.t.* adapt to English form or custom.

An'glo- (ang'glō) *pref.* pert. to England or the English.

An'glo (ang'glō) *n.* & *adj.* (of) a person of English ethnic or English-speaking background. —*n.* (*Slang*) a white person.

An'glo-Sax'on (-sak'sən) *adj.* & *n.* pertaining to the early Germanic inhabitants of England, their language, or their descendants.

An·go'ra (ang-gôr'ə) *n.* **1,** a long-haired domestic cat. **2,** a breed of long-haired goat. **3,** a fabric (usually called mohair) woven from the hair of a goat.

an"gos·tu'ra (ang"gəs-tyûr'ə) *n.* the bitter bark of a tropical Amer. shrub, used medicinally. —**Angostura Bitters,** (*T.N.*) a bitter aromatic tonic (not containing angostura bark).

angostura
↔ Named after a town, now called Ciudad Bolívar, on the Orinoco River in Venezuela.

an′gry (ang′grė) *adj.* **1,** feeling anger; expressive of anger; tempestuous. **2,** sore; inflamed.

Angst (ängst) *n.* (*Ger.*) anxiety; suffering.

ang′strom (ang′strəm) *n.* a unit in measuring wavelength, named for 19th-c. Swedish physicist Anders Jonas Ångström.

an′guish (ang′gwish) *n.* acute bodily or mental distress; extreme pain. —*v.t. & i.* afflict with pain; suffer anguish.

an′gu·lar (ang′gū-lər) *adj.* **1,** having or forming angles, corners, or projections. **2,** bony; gaunt. **3,** stiff in manner. —**an·gu·lar′i·ty** (-lar′ə-tė) *n.*

an·hy′drous (an-hī′drəs) *adj.* (*Chem.*) having lost all water. —**an·hy′dride** (-drid), *n.*

an′il *n.* a W. I. shrub that yields indigo.

an′i·line (an′ə-lin) *n.* a liquid used in making dyes, perfumes, etc.

an″i·mad·ver′sion (an″ə-mad-vėr′zhən) *n.* **1,** a slurring remark; blame. **2,** unfavorable bias. —**an″i·mad·vert′,** *v.i.*

an′i·mal (an′ə-məl) *n.* **1,** any living thing not a plant. **2,** any animal other than man. **3,** a brutish person. —*adj.* **1,** belonging to the realm or nature of animals. **2,** pert. to the bodily appetites or functions of man. —**animal companion,** pet. —**animal rights,** the concept of fair and humane treatment for animals. —**an′i·mal·ism,** *n.* —**an″i·mal′i·ty** (-mal′ə-tė) *n.*

an″i·mal′cule″ (an″i-mal′kūl″) *n.* a minute animal.

an′i·mate″ (an′ə-māt″) *v.t.* **1,** give life to. **2,** infuse with vigor or liveliness. **3,** incite to action. **4,** produce in the manner of an animated cartoon. —*adj.* (-mət) having life; lively. —**an′i·mat″ed,** *adj.* full of spirit; vigorous. —**an″i·ma′tion,** *n.* —**animated cartoon,** a series of cartoons photographed in sequence to give the illusion of motion.

an′i·mism (an′i-miz-əm) *n.* belief in the existence of the soul; general belief in spiritual beings. —**an′i·mist,** *n.*

an″i·mos′i·ty (an″ə-mos′ə-tė) *n.* active enmity; hatred; ill will.

an′i·mus (an′ə-məs) *n.* **1,** animosity. **2,** a grudge.

an′i″on (an′ī″ən) *n.* a negatively charged ion.

an′ise (an′is) *n.* a Mediterranean plant whose seed (*aniseed*) is used in making drugs, perfumes, and liqueurs.

an″i·sette′ (an″i-set′) *n.* an anise-flavored liqueur.

ankh (angk) *n.* in Egyptian art, the symbol of eternal life, a cross with a loop at the top (♀).

an′kle (ang′kəl) *n.* the joint connecting the foot with the leg.

ank′let (ang′klet) *n.* **1,** a low sock that reaches just above the ankle. **2,** a bracelet or other ornament worn on the lower leg.

an′nals (an′əlz) *n.pl.* **1,** a history of events recorded year by year. **2,** historical records generally. —**an′nal·ist,** *n.*

an·neal′ (ə-nēl′) *v.t.* treat (glass, metals, etc.) by heating and gradually cooling, which toughens the substance and removes brittleness.

an·ne·lid (an′ə-lid) *n. & adj.* a segmented worm or leech.

an·nex′ (ə-neks′) *v.t.* **1,** attach at the end; affix. **2,** unite or join, esp. a smaller thing to a larger. —*n.* (an′eks) something annexed, as a subsidiary building; a supplement. —**an″nex·a′tion,** *n.*

An′nie Oak′ley (an′ė ōk′lė) (*Slang*) a free ticket or pass, as to the theater.

Annie Oakley
↔ From the U.S. sharpshooter Annie Oakley, probably from the similarity of the free tickets, punched to prevent resale, to the playing cards Oakley would shoot holes in during her act.

an·ni′hi·late″ (ə-nī′ə-lāt″) *v.t.* destroy utterly; reduce to nothing. —**an·ni″hi·la′tion,** *n.*

an″ni·ver′sa·ry (an″ə-vėr′sə-rė) *n.* **1,** the annually recurring date of a past event. **2,** the celebration of such a date. —*adj.* annual.

an′no Do′mi·ni (an′ō dom′ə-nī) (*Lat.*) in the year of our Lord. *Abbr.,* **A.D.**

an′no·tate″ (an′ō-tāt″) *v.t. & i.* furnish with explanatory or critical notes; comment upon in notes. —**an″no·ta′tion,** *n.*

an·nounce′ (ə-nowns′) *v.t.* make known formally; give notice of; publish; proclaim.

an·nounce′ment (-mənt) *n.* **1,** act of announcing. **2,** what is announced; a formal notice.

an·noun′cer (ə-nown′sər) *n.* one who announces, esp. commercials, news, etc. on radio, television, etc.

an·noy′ (ə-noi′) *v.t. & i.* be troublesome or vexatious to; irk and harass. —**an·noy′-ance,** *n.*

an′nu·al (an′ū-əl) *adj.* **1,** occurring or returning once a year. **2,** lasting or continuing one year. —*n.* **1,** a plant or animal whose natural term of life is one year or season. **2,** a book published once a year, or covering the events of a year.

---

annual, biennial, perennial
☛ An *annual* is a plant that lasts for one year or season; a *biennial* lasts for two years or seasons; a *perennial* lasts for several years or seasons.

---

an·nu′ity (ə-nū′ə-tē) *n.* a periodical payment of money, usually a fixed amount in each year. —**an·nu′i·tant** (-tənt) *n.* one receiving an annuity.

an·nul′ (ə-nul′) *v.t.* [**-nulled′, -nul′ling**] make null or void; abolish. —**an·nul′-ment,** *n.*

an′nu·lar (an′ū-lər) *adj.* having the form of a ring.

an·nun″ci·a′tion (ə-nun″sē-ā′shən) *n.* (usually *cap.*) **1,** the announcement by Gabriel to Mary that she would bear Jesus. **2,** a feast day commemorating this, March 25. —**an·nun′ci·ate,** *v.t.* announce.

an′ode (an′ōd) *n.* the positive pole of a battery; an electrode that emits positive ions.

an′od·ize (-īz) *v.t.* to coat (a metal) with a protective film by electrolysis.

an′o·dyne″ (an′ə-dīn″) *n. & adj.* **1,** a drug that relieves pain. **2,** anything that relieves mental pain or distress.

a·noint′ (ə-noint′) *v.t.* pour oil upon, as in a religious ceremony. —**a·noint′ment,** *n.*

a·nom′a·ly (ə-nom′ə-lē) *n.* deviation from the common rule; something abnormal or irregular. —**a·nom′a·lous,** *adj.*

an′o·mie (an′ə-mē) *n.* **1,** a collapse of social structure. **2,** personal alienation resulting from such collapse.

a·non′ (ə-non′) *adv.* (*Archaic*) in a short time; soon.

an″o·nym′i·ty (an″ə-nim′ə-tē) *n.* state of being anonymous.

a·non′y·mous (ə-non′ə-məs) *adj.* lacking the name of the author, composer, contributor, etc.; from an unacknowledged source. Abbr., **anon.**

a·noph′e·les″ (ə-nof′ə-lēz″) *n.* [*pl.* **-les″**] the mosquito that carries malaria.

an′o·rak (an′ə-rok) *n.* a windproof arctic jacket with an attached hood.

an″o·rex′i·a (an″ə-rek′sē-ə) *n.* loss of appetite, resulting in severe emaciation.

an·oth′er (ə-nu*th*′ər) *adj.* **1,** one more; an additional. **2,** a different; of distinct kind. —*pron.* one additional, or a different, person or thing.

an′ser·ine (an′sər-in) *adj.* gooselike.

an′swer (an′sər) *n.* **1,** a reply or response. **2,** the solution of a problem. —*v.t. & i.* **1,** make a reply or response (to). **2,** serve or suit. **3,** atone (for). —**answering machine,** *n.* a machine for answering a telephone automatically.

an′swer·a·ble *adj.* **1,** capable of being answered. **2,** (with *for*) liable.

ant *n.* a small insect that lives in communities.

-ant (ənt) *suf.* **1,** denoting a doer. **2,** forming participial adjectives: equivalent to **-ing.**

ant·ac′id (ant-as′id) *n. & adj.* a drug or reagent for neutralizing acids.

an·tag′o·nism (an-tag′ə-niz-əm) *n.* mutual resistance or opposition of two forces in action.

an·tag′o·nist (an-tag′ə-nist) *n.* an active opponent. —**an·tag″o·nis′tic,** *adj.* opposed; unfriendly; hostile. —**an·tag″o·nist′ical·ly,** *adv.*

an·tag′o·nize″ (an-tag′ə-nīz″) *v.t.* incur the ill will of; make hostile.

ant·arc′tic (an-tärk′tik) *adj.* near or at the South Pole. —*n.* (*cap.*) the South Polar regions.

an′te (an′tē) *n.* a compulsory bet made by a card player before seeing his cards. —*v.i. & t.* [**-ted** (-tēd), **-te·ing**] make such a bet.

an·te- (an-tē) *pref.* meaning before.

ant′eat″er *n.* a toothless mammal of tropical Amer. that feeds on ants or termites.

an″te·bel′lum (an″tē-bel′əm) *adj.* preceding the war, esp. the U.S. Civil War.

an″te·ce′dent (an″tə-sē′dənt) *adj.* existing or going before, in time or place. —*n.* **1,** (*Gram.*) the noun or phrase for which a pronoun stands. **2,** (*Math., Logic*) the first of two correlative parts, as the first term of a ratio. **3,** (*pl.*) one's origin, previous associations, or avowed principles. —**an″te·ce′dence,** *n.*

an′te·cham″ber *n.* a room leading into another; waiting room.

an′te·date″ *v.t.* **1,** precede in time. **2,** date before the true time. **3,** ascribe to an earlier time.

an″te·di·lu′vi·an (an″tē-di-loo′vē-ən) *adj.* dating from before the Flood; hence, very old.

an′te·lope″ (an′tə-lōp″) *n.* a horned ruminant related to cattle.

---

fat, fāte, fär, fāre, fåll, ȧsk; met, hē, hėr, maybė; pin, pīne; not, nōte, ôr, tool

an·te me·ri′di·em (an′tē mə-rid′ē-əm) (*Lat.*) before noon.

an·ten′na (an-ten′ə) *n.* **1,** a conducting wire from which radio waves are sent or received. **2,** [*pl.* **-nae** (-ē)] one of the appendages occurring in pairs on the head of an insect, also called *feelers.*

an·te′ri·or (an-tir′ē-ər) *adj.* **1,** situated at the front; placed before. **2,** (of a human or animal body) toward the front; toward the head.

an′te·room″ *n.* a smaller room giving access to a larger; waiting room; reception room.

ant·he′li·on (ant-hē′lē-ən) *adj.* a luminous ring caused by the sun's rays.

an′them (an′thəm) *n.* **1,** a sacred hymn. **2,** a song of devotion or patriotism.

an′ther (an′thər) *n.* (*Bot.*) the part of a stamen bearing pollen.

an·thol′o·gist (an-thol′ə-jist) *n.* the compiler of an anthology.

an·thol′o·gy (an-thol′ə-jè) *n.* a collection in one volume of writings of various authors.

> **anthology**
> ↔ From Greek *anthologia*, collection of flowers, hence, of poems.

an′thra·cite (an′thrə-sīt) *n.* hard coal. —*adj.* coal-black.

an′thrax (an′thraks) *n.* a malignant bacterial disease of cattle and man.

an′thro·po- (an′thrə-pō) *pref.* pert. to a human being; man.

an′thro·poid″ (an′thrə-poid″) *adj.* resembling man.

an″thro·pol′o·gy (an″thrə-pol′ə-jè) *n.* **1,** the general science of human beings. **2,** the science of the origin, early development, and culture of humankind. —**an″-thro·pol′o·gist,** *n.*

an·ti- (an-tè) *pref.* against; opposed to.

an″ti·bi·ot′ic (an″ti-bī-ot′ik) *n.* a substance derived from certain organisms that tends to destroy harmful organisms.

an′ti·bod″y (an′ti-bod″ē) *n.* an immunizing agent within the human body that counteracts malignant bacteria.

an′tic (an′tik) *n.* (chiefly *pl.*) escapade; (*pl.*) ludicrous behavior; capers.

An′ti·christ″ (an′tē-krīst″) *n.* the personification of the force of evil.

an·tic′i·pate″ (an-tis′ə-pāt″) *v.t.* **1,** expect; foresee. **2,** realize beforehand. **3,** be ahead of time or of another; forestall. —**an·tic″i·pa′tion,** *n.* —**an·tic′i·pa·to″ry** (-ə-pə-tôr″ē) *adj.*

an″ti·cli′max (an″ti-klī′maks) *n.* an abrupt descent in style or subject from lofty ideas or expression; ludicrous contrast with what has preceded. —**an″ti·cli·mac′tic** (-klī-mak′tik) *adj.*

an′ti·dote″ (an′ti-dōt″) *n.* **1,** a drug that counteracts the effect of a poison. **2,** any remedy against disease or injurious influence.

an″ti·fem′in·ist *adj.* **1,** nonsexist. **2,** opposed to the aims of the feminist movement.

an′ti·freeze″ *n.* a substance that reduces the freezing point of water.

an′ti·gen (an′ti-jən) *n.* any substance or organism, such as bacteria, that stimulates the production of an antibody.

an′ti·he″ro *n.* a protagonist lacking the qualities usu. associated with a hero.

an″ti·his′ta·mine″ (an″tē-his′tə-mēn″) *n.* a medicine used in treatment of allergic reactions.

an′ti·lock″ *adj.* of a brake in a vehicle, designed not to lock or skid when applied suddenly.

an″ti·log′a·rithm *n.* the number of which a given number is the logarithm.

an″ti·ma·cas′sar (an″tē-mə-kas′ər) *n.* an ornamental protective covering for the arm or back of a chair, sofa, etc.

> **antimacassar**
> ↔ From the name of a 19th-c. brand of hair oil, allegedly made from ingredients from Makassar, a region of an island in Indonesia.

an′ti·mat″ter *n.* a hypothetical form of matter with properties the reverse of those of ordinary matter.

an′ti·mo″ny (an′tə-mō″nè) *n.* a metallic chemical element, no. 51, symbol Sb.

an′ti·nov″el *n.* a literary work similar in length to a novel, but lacking the usual character and plot development.

an′ti·par″ti·cle *n.* a particle of antimatter.

an″ti·pas′to (àn″tè-pàs′tō) *n.* (*It.*) an appetizer; hors d'oeuvres.

an·tip′a·thy (an-tip′ə-thè) *n.* dislike. —**an″ti·pa·thet′ic** (an″tè-pə-thet′ik) *adj.* —**an″ti·pa·thet′i·cal·ly,** *adv.*

an′ti·phon (an′ti-fon) *n.* **1,** a psalm, hymn, or prayer sung responsively. **2,** a prelude or conclusion to some part of a service.

an·tiph′o·ny (an-tif′ə-nè) *n.* **1,** alternate singing by two parts of a choir. **2,** a composition arranged to be so chanted. —**an·tiph′o·nal,** *adj.*

an·tip′o·des (an-tip′ə-dèz) *n.pl.* places

diametrically opposite each other on the earth. —**an·tip′o·dal,** *adj.*

an′ti·pope″ *n.* a usurper of the papal office.

an′ti·quar″y (an′ti-kwär″ė) *n.* a collector of or expert on antiques or matters ancient. —**an″ti·quar′i·an** (-kwär′ė-ən) *n. & adj.*

an′ti·quat·ed (an′ti-kwā-tid) *adj.* grown old; obsolete.

an·tique′ (an-tēk′) *adj.* belonging to former times; old-fashioned. —*n.* a relic of antiquity. —*v.t.* so treat (a piece of furniture, etc.) as to make it appear to be an antique.

an·tiq′ui·ty (an-tik′wə-tė) *n.* **1,** ancient times; former ages. **2,** the quality of being ancient.

an″ti-Sem′i·tism (-sem′i-tiz-əm) *n.* prejudice against the Jewish people. —**an″ti-Sem′ite** (-sem′īt), *n.* —**an″ti-Se·mit′ic** (-sə-mit′ik) *adj.*

an″ti·sep′tic (an″ti-sep′tik) *adj. & n.* destructive of microorganisms that cause disease. —**an″ti·sep′ti·cal·ly,** *adv.* —**an″ti·sep′sis,** *n.*

an″ti·so′cial *adj.* not inclined to seek or enjoy the company of others.

an·tith′e·sis (an-tith′ə-sis) *n.* [*pl.* **-ses** (-sėz)] **1,** direct opposition; marked contrast. **2,** what is directly opposite. —**an″ti·thet′i·cal** (an″ti-thet′i-kəl) *adj.*

an″ti·tox′in (an″ti-tok′sin) *n.* a substance that counteracts a toxin or poison.

an″ti·trust′ *adj.* opposed to combinations or trusts that result in monopoly.

an″ti·ven′in *n.* an antidote to poison injected by a snake bite or scorpion sting.

ant′ler (ant′lər) *n.* one of the branching horns of an animal of the deer family.

an′to·nym (an′tə-nim) *n.* a word meaning exactly the opposite of a given word. ❏ *homograph*

an′trum (an′trəm) *n.* a cavity; hole.

a′nus (ā′nəs) *n.* the posterior opening of the alimentary canal.

an′vil (an′vəl) *n.* **1,** a heavy iron block on which metalwork is laid for beating. **2,** a bone of the ear.

anx·i′e·ty (ang-zī′ə-tė) *n.* **1,** uneasiness of mind from care or apprehension. **2,** concern or solicitude.

anx′ious (ank′shəs) *adj.* **1,** full of anxiety; worried. **2,** earnestly desirous. —**anx′ious·ness,** *n.*

an′y (en′ė) *adj. & pron.* one, or some, indiscriminately from a larger number. —*adv.* to whatever extent; in whatever degree; at all. ❏ *either*

an′y·bod″y *pron.* any person. ❏ *anyone*

an′y·how″ *adv.* **1,** in any way. **2,** in any case.

an″y·more′ *adv.* any longer.

an′y·one″ *pron.* any person. ❏ *either*

---

anyone, anybody, everyone, everybody

(*Gram.*) *Anyone, anybody, everyone,* and *everybody* are collective pronouns using a singular verb. However, in current usage, in order to avoid gender-specific references, it is becoming increasingly more acceptable to use the plural *their* as opposed to *his* or *her.* Note that the two-word forms of these words—*any one, every one,* etc.—imply each person or object of the group individually, rather than referring to the whole group collectively.

---

an′y·thing″ *pron.* any thing, fact, or deed.

an′y·way″ *adv.* **1,** in any way. **2,** in any case; nevertheless.

an′y·where″ *adv.* in or to any place.

ao′ dai′ (ou′ dī′) *n.* traditional Vietnamese woman's dress.

A′-OK′ (ā′ō-kā′) *adj.* (*Informal*) all right; in good condition.

A′-one′ (ā′wun′) *adj.* (*Informal*) excellent; first-class.

a·or′ta (ā-ôr′tə) *n.* the chief artery of the human body, issuing from the heart.

a′ou·dad (ä′oo-däd) *n.* a wild sheep of N. Afr.

a·pace′ (ə-pās′) *adv.* speedily.

a·pache′ *n.* **1,** (ə-päsh′) (*Fr.*) a Parisian rowdy or gangster. **2,** (ə-pach′ė) (*cap.*) an Amer. Indian tribe or member of it. —**apache dance** (ə-päsh′) a violent dance originating in the Parisian underworld.

a·part′ (ə-pärt′) *adv.* **1,** with parts separated; in pieces. **2,** at one side; separately from; aside from.

a·part′heid″ (ə-pärt′hāt″) *n.* institutional segregation of races formerly practiced in South Africa.

a·part′ment (ə-pärt′mənt) *n.* **1,** a set of rooms designed for tenancy as a unit. **2,** a single room.

ap″a·thet′ic (ap″ə-thet′ik) *adj.* lacking feeling; expressing or being apathy. —**ap″a·thet′i·cal·ly,** *adv.*

ap′a·thy (ap′ə-thė) *n.* lack of feeling; absence of emotion; indifference.

ape (āp) *n.* **1,** any of several anthropoid animals, the gorilla, chimpanzee, orangutan, or gibbon. **2,** an imitator; a mimic.

---

fat, fāte, fär, fāre, fåll, ȧsk; met, hē, hėr, maybė; pin, pīne; not, nōte, ôr, tool

—v.t. imitate. **—go ape,** (*Slang*) get excited.

a·pé·ri·tif′ (ə-per-i-tēf′) *n.* (*Fr.*) an alcoholic drink taken before a meal.

ap′er·ture (ap′ər-chûr) *n.* an opening; hole; gap.

a′pex (ā′peks) *n.* the highest point of anything; top; peak; climax.

a·pha′sia (ə-fā′zhə) *n.* loss of the faculty of understanding written or spoken language. **—a·pha′sic,** *adj.*

a·phe′li·on (ə-fē′lē-ən) *n.* the point in the orbit of a planet or comet farthest from the sun.

a·pher′e·sis (ə-fer′ə-sis) *n.* the omission of letters or sounds from the beginning of a word, as *squire* for *esquire*.

a′phid (ā′fid) *n.* a plant louse.

aph′o·rism (af′ə-riz-əm) *n.* a concise statement of a principle. **—aph′o·rist,** *n.* **—aph″o·ris′tic,** *adj.* **—aph′o·rize,** *v.t.*

aph″ro·dis′i·ac (af″rə-diz′ē-ak) *adj. & n.* (a substance) stimulating sexual desire.

---

aphrodisiac
↔ From Greek *aphrodisiakós*, sexual, from *Aphrodītē*, Aphrodite, the Greek goddess of love.

---

a′pi·ar″y (ā′pē-ār″ē) *n.* a place where bees are kept.

ap′i·cal (ap′ə-kəl) *adj.* being or pert. to an apex.

a′pi·cul″ture (ā′pi-kul″chər) *n.* the science and art of raising bees.

a·piece′ (ə-pēs′) *adv.* for each.

ap′ish (ā′pish) *adj.* apelike.

a·plomb′ (ə-plom′) *n.* self-confidence; assurance of manner.

---

aplomb
↔ From French *à plomb*, according to the plumb line.

---

ap′o- (ap′ə) *pref.* from; away from.

a·poc′a·lypse (ə-pok′ə-lips) *n.* 1, a revelation. 2, (*cap.*) the book Revelation in the New Testament of the Bible. **—a·poc″a·lyp′tic** (-lip′tik) *adj.* **—a·poc″a·lyp′ti·cal·ly,** *adv.*

a·poc′o·pe (ə-pok′ə-pē) *n.* the cutting of the end of a word.

ap′o·crine (ap′ə-krin) *adj.* pert. to certain glands whose secretions when acted on by bacteria produce the odor of sweat.

A·poc′ry·pha (ə-pok′rə-fə) *n.pl.* certain books of the Old Testament whose canonicity is disputed.

a·poc′ry·phal (ə-pok′rə-fəl) *adj.* 1, of

doubtful authorship or authenticity. 2, spurious.

ap′o·gee (ap′ə-jē) *n.* the point of greatest distance from the earth, in an orbit.

a·pol″o·get′ic (ə-pol″ə-jet′ik) *adj.* expressing regret; constituting an apology. **—a·pol″o·get′i·cal·ly,** *adv.*

a·pol′o·gist (ə-pol′ə-jist) *n.* one who seeks to justify a cause.

a·pol′o·gize″ (ə-pol′ə-jīz″) *v.i.* offer an excuse; express regret.

ap′o·logue (ap′ə-log) *n.* a moral tale; allegory.

a·pol′o·gy (ə-pol′ə-jē) *n.* 1, an expression of regret for a slight or injury. 2, something said or written in defense or vindication.

ap′o·plex″y (ap′ə-plek″sē) *n.* sudden loss of consciousness or mobility from rupture of a blood vessel in the brain. **—ap″o·plec′tic,** *adj.* **—ap″o·plec′ti·cal·ly,** *adv.*

a·pos′ta·sy (ə-pos′tə-sē) *n.* total desertion of one's professed principles, faith, or party. **—a·pos′tate″** (-tāt″) *n. & adj.* **—a·pos′ta·tize,** *v.i.*

a pos·te′ri·o′ri (ā′ pos-tir″ē-ôr′ē) (*Lat.*) from later; after observing what has occurred.

a·pos′tle (ə-pos′əl) *n.* 1, (*cap.*) one of the twelve disciples chosen by Christ to preach the gospel. 2, a pioneer of any great moral reform. **—ap″os·tol′ic** (ap″ə-stol′ik) *adj.* **—ap″os·tol′i·cal·ly,** *adv.*

a·pos′tro·phe (ə-pos′trə-fē) *n.* 1, a mark of punctuation (') indicating the omission of one or more letters. 2, a direct address to a person or persons, interpolated in a speech or writing. **—a·pos′tro·phize″** (-fīz″) *v.t.*

---

apostrophe
(*Gram.*) The apostrophe is used to indicate omission of one or more letters and to indicate possessives, but only in certain limited circumstances to indicate plurals, as of alphabetical letters, numbers, and symbols. It should not be used for the plurals of nouns.

---

a·poth′e·car″y (ə-poth′ə-ker″ē) *n.* one who deals in drugs; pharmacist.

ap′o·thegm (ap′ə-them) *n.* a short, pithy, instructive saying; a maxim.

a·poth″e·o′sis (ə-poth″ē-ō′sis) *n.* [*pl.* **-ses** (-sēz)] glorified personification of a principle or idea. **—ap″o·the′o·size″** (ap″ə-thē′ə-sīz″) *v.t.* deify; exalt.

ap·pall′ (ə-pâl′) *v.t.* fill with fear or horror. Also, **ap·pal′.**

Ap·pa·loo′sa (ap-ə-loo′sə) *n.* a breed of horse having a spotted rump.

ap′pa·nage (ap′ə-nij) *n.* **1,** land or other source of support given to a member of a royal family. **2,** perquisite.

ap″pa·rat′ (ap″ə-rat′) *n.* (*Rus.*) a political organization. **—ap″pa·rat′chik** (-chik) *n.* (*Rus.*) a party functionary or bureaucrat, esp. in a Communist country.

ap″pa·ra′tus (ap″ə-rā′təs) *n.* all the equipment used for some purpose.

ap·par′el (ə-par′əl) *n.* **1,** clothing, esp. outer garments. **2,** outward aspect; guise. **—v.t.** clothe.

ap·par′ent (ə-par′ənt) *adj.* **1,** in plain view; capable of being clearly perceived; obvious. **2,** seeming in appearance, not necessarily real.

---

apparently, evidently
☛ Both words mean according to appearance. However, *apparently* implies a doubt of the truth of the statement, a sense which is missing from *evidently*.

---

ap″pa·ri′tion (ap″ə-rish′ən) *n.* a ghostly appearance; specter; phantom.

ap·peal′ (ə-pēl′) *v.i.* **1,** call for aid, sympathy, or mercy; make an earnest entreaty. **2,** resort. **3,** be attractive; excite interest. **—v.i. & t.** (*Law*) apply for review to a higher court. **—n.** **1,** a call or entreaty for aid, etc. **2,** attractiveness. **3,** (*Law*) application for review. **—ap·peal′ing,** *adj.* arousing admiration or sympathy.

ap·pear′ (ə-pir′) *v.i.* **1,** become visible. **2,** seem to be. **3,** be known; be obvious. **4,** come into public view; be published. **5,** (*Law*) come formally before a tribunal.

ap·pear′ance (-əns) *n.* **1,** act of appearing. **2,** outward look; aspect; semblance. **3,** a coming to a place; presence. **4,** (*pl.*) indications; circumstances.

ap·pease′ (ə-pēz′) *v.t.* **1,** allay (anger or strife); placate, esp. by concession **2,** satisfy (an appetite or demand). **—ap·pease′-ment,** *n.* act of appeasing; partial submission to a threatening nation.

ap·pel′lant (ə-pel′ənt) *n.* one who appeals. **—adj.** appellate.

ap·pel′late (-ət) *adj.* (*Law*) **1,** concerned with an appeal. **2,** having the duty to hear appeals.

ap″pel·la′tion (ap″ə-lā′shən) *n.* **1,** the word by which a thing or person is called; name; title. **2,** the act of naming.

ap·pend′ (ə-pend′) *v.t.* add; attach; subjoin. **—ap·pend′age** (-ij) *n.* an added and subordinate part.

ap″pen·dec′to·my (ap″ən-dek′tə-mē) *n.* removal of the vermiform appendix.

ap·pen″di·ci′tis (a-pen″də-sī′tis) *n.* (*Pathol.*) inflammation of the vermiform appendix.

ap·pen′dix (ə-pen′diks) *n.* [*pl.* **-dix·es, -di·ces″** (-də-sēz″)] a section added but not essential to a document or book. **—vermiform appendix,** a sac attached to the human intestine.

ap″per·tain′ (ap″ər-tān′) *v.i.* belong as a part or member; belong by association or normal relation.

ap′pe·tite″ (ap′ə-tīt″) *n.* **1,** craving for food. **2,** any strong desire. **3,** inclination to satisfy a want.

ap′pe·tiz″er (ap′ə-tīz″ər) *n.* a snack to whet the appetite.

ap′pe·tiz″ing *adj.* appealing to the appetite or taste.

ap·plaud′ (ə-plâd′) *v.t. & i.* **1,** show approval of; commend; praise. **2,** acclaim by clapping the hands.

ap·plause′ (ə-plâz′) *n.* **1,** act of applauding. **2,** a loud expression of approval, as by handclapping.

ap′ple (ap′əl) *n.* an edible fruit, or the tree on which it grows. **—apple butter,** a thick spiced applesauce used as jam. **—the Big Apple,** (*Informal*) New York City.

ap′ple·jack″ *n.* a strong alcoholic liquor or brandy made from cider.

ap′ple-pie″ *adj.* **1,** perfect; ideal: *apple-pie order.* **2,** all-American.

ap′ple·sauce″ *n.* **1,** a sauce of boiled apples. **2,** (*Slang*) nonsense.

ap·pli′ance (ə-plī′əns) *n.* **1,** a tool or utensil for a particular use. **2,** act of applying or putting to use.

ap′pli·ca·ble (ap′li-kə-bəl) *adj.* capable of being applied; suitable; relevant. **—ap″-pli·ca·bil′i·ty,** *n.*

ap′pli·cant (ap′li-kənt) *n.* one who applies, as for a job.

ap″pli·ca′tion (ap″li-kā′shən) *n.* **1,** the act of applying. **2,** something applied, as a salve. **3,** relevance; bearing. **4,** a request or petition. **5,** close attention; diligence. **6,** (*Computers*) a program designed to perform a certain task, as word processing.

ap′pli·ca″tor (ap′li-kā″tər) *n.* a utensil for applying something.

ap″pli·qué′ (ap″li-kā′) *adj.* added by sewing, pasting, cementing, etc. **—n.** ornamentation so added.

ap·ply′ (ə-plī′) *v.t.* **1,** bring into physical contact; lay on. **2,** put to use; bring into operation. **3,** devote to a particular purpose. **4,** give earnestly. —*v.i.* **1,** be applicable or pertinent. **2,** request or appeal. —**ap·plied′,** *adj.* put to practical use.

ap·pog″gia·tu′ra (ə-poj″ə-tûr′ə) (*It., Music*) *n.* a grace note preceding its principal and taking a portion of its time.

ap·point′ (ə-point′) *v.t.* **1,** nominate or assign; designate. **2,** fix by decree; prescribe. **3,** provide with necessary equipment; rig. —**ap·poin′tive,** *adj.* done or filled by appointment.

ap·point′ment (ə-point′mənt) *n.* **1,** the act of appointing. **2,** an office held by a person appointed. **3,** an agreement to meet at a stipulated time. **4,** (*pl.*) furnishings; equipment.

ap·por′tion (ə-pôr′shən) *v.t.* divide and allot proportionally. —**ap·por′tion·ment,** *n.*

ap·pose′ (ə-pōz′) *v.t.* put near together. —**ap″po·si′tion** (ap″ə-zish′ən) *n.*

ap′po·site (ap′ə-zit) *adj.* applicable; suitable; well-adapted. ❏ *opposite*

ap·prais′al (ə-prā′zəl) *n.* act or result of appraising; estimate.

ap·praise′ (ə-prāz′) *v.t.* estimate the quality or value of, esp. in money. —**ap·prais′er,** *n.* one who estimates the value of property.

ap·pre′ci·a·ble (ə-prē′shē-ə-bəl) *adj.* capable of being estimated; large or intense enough to be perceived.

ap·pre′ci·ate″ (ə-prē′shē-āt″) *v.t.* **1,** recognize the worth of; esteem duly. **2,** be fully conscious of. **3,** raise in value. —*v.i.* rise in value. —**ap·pre″ci·a′tion,** *n.* —**ap·pre′ci·a·tive** (-ə-tiv) *adj.* duly grateful.

ap″pre·hend′ (ap″rė-hend′) *v.t.* **1,** seize physically; take into custody; arrest. **2,** grasp mentally; understand. **3,** have fear of; anticipate. —**ap″pre·hen′si·ble** (-hen′sə-bal) *adj.*

ap″pre·hen′sion (ap″rė-hen′shən) *n.* **1,** act of apprehending. **2,** result of apprehending; arrest; understanding.

ap″pre·hen′sive (-siv) *adj.* uneasy or fearful about future events. —**ap″pre·hen′sive·ness,** *n.*

ap·pren′tice (ə-pren′tis) *n.* one who works under tutelage to learn a trade. —**ap·pren′tice·ship,** *n.*

ap·prise′ (ə-prīz′) *v.t.* give notice; inform.

ap·proach′ (ə-prōch′) *v.t. & i.* **1,** draw near to; advance toward. **2,** be similar to in quality or degree. **3,** make advances or proposals to. —*n.* **1,** the act of approaching. **2,** method or means of access; avenue. **3,** nearness; proximity.

ap″pro·ba′tion (ap″rə-bā′shən) *n.* approval; commendation.

ap·pro′pri·ate″ (ə-prō′prė-āt″) *v.t.* **1,** allot (money) for a specific use. **2,** take possession of. —*adj.* (-ət) suitable; applicable. —**ap·pro′pri·ate·ness,** *n.*

ap·pro″pri·a′tion (-ā′shən) *n.* **1,** money set aside for a specific purpose. **2,** act of appropriating.

ap·prov′al (ə-proov′əl) *n.* act or effect of approving; commendation; approbation. —**on approval,** without obligation to buy.

ap·prove′ (ə-proov′) *v.t.* **1,** pronounce good; admit the propriety or excellence of. **2,** sanction officially; ratify. —*v.i.* judge favorably; be pleased.

ap·prox′i·mate (ə-prok′sə-mət) *adj.* **1,** nearly correct or precise. **2,** close together; very similar in form or degree. —*v.i.* (-māt″) be nearly like. —**ap·prox′i·mate·ly,** *adv.* nearly; about. —**ap·prox″i·ma′tion,** *n.*

ap·pur′te·nance (ə-pēr′tə-nəns) *n.* **1,** (*Law*) a right or privilege belonging to a property. **2,** an accessory part; appendage. **3,** (*pl.*) furnishings; apparatus. —**ap·pur′te·nant,** *adj.*

a′pri·cot″ (ā′prə-kot″) *n.* **1,** the fruit of a tree resembling the plum and peach. **2,** the apricot tree. **3,** a light orange color.

A′pril (ā′prəl) *n.* the fourth month of the year.

April
↔ From the Latin *Aprilis*, April, perhaps derived from the name for the Greek god of love, *Aphrodite*.

a pri·o′ri (ā ′prē-ôr′ē) (*Lat.*) from before; before knowing what will occur.

a′pron (ā′prən) *n.* **1,** an outer garment worn to protect the clothing. **2,** any protective shield or flange.

apron
↔ From Middle French *naperon* through Middle English *a napron,* misconstrued as *an apron.*

ap″ro·pos′ (ap″rə-pō′) *adv.* **1,** to the purpose; opportunely. **2,** (with *of*) in reference to. —*adj.* appropriate.

apse (aps) *n.* an alcove or recess, usually semicircular and vaulted.

apt *adj.* **1,** suited to its purpose. **2,** quick in learning. **3,** having a tendency; inclined. —**apt′ness,** *n.*

ap′te·ryx (ap′tə-riks) *n.* the kiwi (def. 1).

ap′ti·tude (ap′ti-tood) *n.* fitness; innate ability. ❑ *ability*

aq′ua- (ak′wə) *pref.* water.

aq′ua·cade″ (-kād″) *n.* a spectacular musical entertainment, with feats performed in the water.

aq′ua·cul″ture *n.* the cultivation of fish or produce in water.

Aq′ua-Lung″ (ak′wə-lung″) *n.* (*T.N.*) an underwater breathing apparatus using compressed-air cylinders.

aq″ua·ma·rine′ (ak″wə-mə-rēn′) *n.* **1,** a bluish-green color. **2,** semiprecious stone.

aq′ua·naut″ (-nât″) *n.* a diver who spends extended periods of time underwater.

aq′ua·plane″ (ak′wə-plān″) *n.* a board towed behind a motorboat for carrying a surf-rider. —*v.i.* **1,** ride on such a board. **2,** hydroplane.

a·quar′i·um (ə-kwār′ē-əm) *n.* a tank, building, etc. in which are kept living aquatic animals and plants.

A·quar′i·us (ə-kwār′ē-əs) *n.* a constellation, the Water Bearer (see *zodiac*).

a·quat′ic (ə-kwat′ik) *adj.* **1,** pert. to water. **2,** living or done in water. —**a·quat′i·cal·ly,** *adv.*

aq′ua·tint″ (ak′wə-tint″) *n.* **1,** a method of engraving. **2,** a print so made.

aq′ua·vit″ (ä′kwə-vēt″) *n.* a strong alcoholic liquor; schnapps. Also, **a′qua vi′tae** (vī′tē).

aq′ue·duct″ (ak′wi-dukt″) *n.* an artificial channel or conduit for conducting water from one place to another.

a′que·ous (ā′kwē-əs) *adj.* like water; containing or formed by water.

aq′ui·fer (ak′wi-fər) *n.* an underground layer of porous rock, sand, etc. containing water.

aq′ui·line (ak′wə-lin) *adj.* **1,** pert. to the eagle. **2,** (of a nose) like an eagle's beak.

ar″a·besque′ (ar″ə-besk′) *n.* **1,** style of fanciful decoration. **2,** a posture in ballet.

Ar′a·bic (ar′ə-bik) *adj.* pert. to Arabia, or its language, or to *Arabic numerals:* 0, 1, 2, 3, etc.

Arabic numerals
↔ Arabic numerals are more properly called Hindu-Arabic numerals; most of our numeral forms were first used in India.

---

ar′a·ble (ar′ə-bəl) *adj.* fit for plowing and tillage. —**ar″a·bil′i·ty,** *n.*

a·rach′nid (ə-rak′nid) *n.* any of a class of arthropods, as the spider.

Ar·a·ma′ic (ar-ə-mā′ik) *n. & adj.* a Semitic language, used by Jesus.

ar′ba·lest (är′bə-lest) *n.* a type of crossbow.

ar′bi·ter (är′bi-tər) *n.* **1,** one who has power to judge and decide. **2,** arbitrator; umpire. ❑ *arbitrate*

ar′bi·trage (är′bi-trij) *n.* simultaneous purchase and sale of commodities in different markets to profit from unequal prices.

ar″bi·trar″y (är′bə-trär″ē) *adj.* **1,** not regulated by fixed rule or law. **2,** despotic. **3,** capricious; unreasonable. —**ar″bi·trar″i·ness,** *n.*

ar′bi·trate″ (är′bi-trāt″) *v.t.* **1,** act as a formal umpire between contestants. **2,** submit to arbitration. —**ar″bi·tra′tion,** *n.* settlement of a dispute by lay judges, out of court. —**ar″bi·tra′tor,** *n.*

---

arbitrate, mediate, arbiter
☛ *Mediate* is the broader term, meaning to serve as intermediary in a dispute to help others reconcile their differences. To *arbitrate* a dispute is to settle it through legal and binding means. An *arbiter* may be an *arbitrator*, but the more frequent use of the word is to mean a person with absolute power of decision.

---

ar′bor (är′bər) *n.* **1,** a bower formed by foliage trained over a lattice. **2,** a shaft or supporting bar in a machine. Also, **ar′bour.** —**ar·bo′re·al** (-bôr′ē-əl) *adj.* pert. to or living in trees.

ar″bo·re′tum (är″bə-rē′təm) *n.* a park in which trees or shrubs are cultivated, usu. for scientific purposes.

ar″bor·vi′tae (-vī′tē) *n.* an evergreen tree; the red cedar.

ar·bu′tus (är-bū′təs) *n.* **1,** any of several evergreen shrubs with scarlet berries. **2,** a creeping vine with fragrant white and pink flowers.

arc (ärk) *n.* **1,** a segment of a circle. **2,** any bow-shaped curve. **3,** a spark or luminescence caused by a flow of current across a gap between two electrical terminals. —*v.i.* form an arc; travel in a curved path.

ar·cade′ (är-kād′) *n.* **1,** a roofed passageway; a covered avenue lined with shops. **2,** an amusement center.

ar·ca′na (är-kä′nä) *n.pl.* secrets; mysteries.

ar·cane′ (är-kān′) *adj.* secret.

arch (ärch) *n.* **1,** a building structure in the shape of a curve concave from below,

---

fat, fāte, fär, fâre, fâll, àsk; met, hē, hêr, maybè; pin, pīne; nŏt, nōte, ôr, tool supported at its extremities. **2,** anything that resembles an arch. —*v.t.* **1,** span with an arch. **2,** curve like an arch. —*adj.* **1,** chief; preeminent. **2,** sly; roguish.

arch- (ärch; ärk) *pref.* first; chief.

-arch (ärk) *suf.* ruler.

ar″chae·ol′o·gy (är″kė-ol′ə-jē) *n.* the study of past cultures through their surviving relics. —**ar″chae·o·log′i·cal,** *adj.* —**ar″chae·ol′o·gist,** *n.*

ar·cha′ic (är-kā′ik) *adj.* **1,** of an earlier period; antiquated. **2,** (*Lexic.*) not in current usage, but familiar in surviving earlier literature. —**ar′cha·ism** (-iz-əm) *n.*

arch′an″gel (ärk′-) *n.* a chief angel.

arch′bish″op (ärch′-) *n.* a bishop of highest rank.

arch″di′o·cese (ärch″-) *n.* the diocese or see of an archbishop. —**arch″di·oc′e·san,** *adj.*

arch′duke″ (ärch′-) *n.* title of former Austrian royal princes.

arch′er (är′chər) *n.* **1,** one who uses a bow and arrow. **2,** (*cap.*) the constellation of Sagittarius. —**arch′er·y** (-ē) *n.*

ar′che·type″ (är′ki-tīp″) *n.* an original model; prototype.

arch″fiend′ (ärch″-) *n.* **1,** a vicious person. **2,** (often *cap.*) the devil; Satan.

ar″chi·pel′a·go (är″kə-pel′ə-gō″) *n.* a group of many islands.

ar′chi·tect″ (är′kə-tekt″) *n.* **1,** one who designs buildings. **2,** the planner or maker of anything.

ar″chi·tec·ton′ics (är″ki-tek-ton′iks) *n.* **1,** the science of construction or structure. **2,** the science of systematizing knowledge. —**ar″chi·tec·ton′ic,** *adj.*

ar″chi·tec′ture (-tek′chər) *n.* **1,** the designing of buildings. **2,** style of building. **3,** the interior design of a computer. —**ar″-chi·tec′tur·al,** *adj.*

ar′chi·trave″ (är′ki-trāv″) *n.* **1,** the lowest layer of a structure supported by columns, resting immediately on the head of the column. **2,** a molding.

ar′chive (är′kīv) *n.* (*often pl.*) **1,** documents preserved for their political or historical value. **2,** the place where such documents are kept. —*v.t. & i.* (*Computers*) to store copies of files for protection. —**ar′chi·vist** (-kə-vist) *n.*

arch′way (ärch′wā) *n.* an entrance or passage under an arch.

-arch·y (är-kē) *suf.* government; rule.

arc-′jet″ *adj.* pert. to an engine in which gases are heated by an electric arc.

arc′light″ *n.* a lamp producing light by means of an electric arc.

arc′tic (ärk′tik) *adj.* near or at the North Pole. —*n.* (*cap.*) the North Polar regions.

ar′dent (är′dənt) *adj.* **1,** fervent in feeling; intense; passionate. **2,** burning; fiery; glowing. —**ar′den·cy,** *n.*

ar′dor (är′dər) *n.* **1,** intensity of feeling; zeal; passion. **2,** fiery heat. Also, **ar′dour.**

ar′du·ous (är′dū-əs) *adj.* requiring prolonged effort. —**ar′du·ous·ness,** *n.*

are (är) *v.* 1st person pl. of *be.*

are (âr; är) *n.* a unit of surface measure, 100 sq. meters.

ar′e·a (âr′ē-ə) *n.* **1,** amount of surface; extent in general; scope. **2,** a region or tract. **3,** field of study. —**area code,** any of a series of 3-digit call numbers used to designate various telephone calling areas in the U.S. and Canada.

a·re′na (ə-rē′nə) *n.* the enclosure in which an athletic contest is held.

aren't (ärnt) *contraction* are not.

a·rête′ (ä-ret′) *n.* a sharp, rocky, mountain ridge.

ar′gent (är′jənt) *adj.* like silver, esp. in color.

ar′gon (är′gon) *n.* a colorless, odorless, inert gaseous element present in air, no. 18, symbol A.

ar′go·sy (är′gə-sė) *n.* a merchant vessel or fleet carrying a rich cargo.

---

argosy
↔ Unrelated to Jason and the Argonauts, the word comes from the Italian word *ragusea,* vessel from Ragusa (an early name for Dubrovnik).

---

ar′got (är′gət) *n.* the slang or cant of a particular class, as of thieves.

---

argot, cant, colloquialism, dialect, jargon, patois, slang
☛ Terms for nonstandard English. *Dialect* and *patois* are the modified language of a region, often including words and expressions not part of the general language. *Colloquialisms* are words or expressions accepted in speech but considered not acceptable in formal writing (labeled *informal* in this dictionary). *Slang* refers to words that are considered substandard even in everyday speech. *Jargon* is the specialized language of science, the arts, etc. *Argot* and *cant* refer to the jargon of the underworld.

---

ar′gue (är′gū) *v.i.* engage in intellectual dispute. —*v.t.* **1,** state reasons for and against; discuss. **2,** maintain; seek to prove. **—ar′gu·a·ble,** *adj.* **—ar′gu·a·bly,** *adv.*

ar′gu·ment (är′gū-mənt) *n.* **1,** discussion of a controversial nature; debate. **2,** a statement or chain of reasoning tending to induce belief. **3,** an abstract or summary of a writing or speech. **—ar″gu·men·ta′tion,** *n.*

ar·gu·men′ta·tive (är-gyə-men′tə-tiv) *adj.* disposed to argue; contentious.

ar′gyle (är′gīl) *adj.* having a diamond-shaped pattern. **—***n.* such a pattern.

> **argyle**
> ↔ Named for *Argyll*, Scotland, because the pattern was based on the tartan of the clan.

Ar′gy·rol″ (är′ji-rōl″) *n.* (*T.N.*) an antiseptic containing silver.

a′ri·a (ä′rē-ə) *n.* **1,** a vocal solo, with or without accompaniment. **2,** any tune.

ar′id *adj.* **1,** lacking moisture; parched with heat. **2,** uninteresting. **—a·rid′i·ty** (ə-rid′ə-tē) *n.*

Ar′ies (âr′ēz) *n.* a northern constellation, the Ram (see *zodiac*).

a·rise′ (ə-rīz′) *v.i.* [**a·rose′, a·ris′en** (-riz′ən)] **1,** come into being or action. **2,** get up; move upward.

ar″is·toc′ra·cy (ar″is-tok′rə-sē) *n.* **1,** government by a privileged upper class. **2,** any class having special privileges or considered superior.

a·ris′to·crat (ə-ris′tə-krat) *n.* a member of the aristocracy, or one who behaves like a nobleman. **—a·ris″to·crat′ic,** *adj.* **—a·ris″to·crat′i·cal·ly,** *adv.*

a·rith′me·tic (ə-rith′mə-tik) *n.* the art of computation, the most elementary branch of mathematics. **—***adj.* (ar″ith-met′ik) of or by arithmetic. **—a·rith″me·ti′cian** (-tish′ən) *n.* **—arithmetic progression,** a sequence of numbers, each different from the number preceding it by the same amount, as 1, 3, 5, 7, etc.

> **arithmetic progression**
> ↔ The three basic mathematical progressions: *arithmetic*, in which a constant number is *added* to each number in the series (plus 2= 1,3,5,7,...); *geometric*, in which each number is *multiplied* by the constant (times 2=1,2,4,8,16,...); and *exponential*, in which each member is increased by the value of the *exponent* (to the 2nd power: 2,4,16,256,...).

ar″ith·met′i·cal (ar″ith-met′i-kəl) *adj.* arithmetic.

ark (ärk) *n.* **1,** the vessel built by Noah to save those chosen from the Flood; a large boat or building. **2,** the chest containing the Covenant (between God and the Jews).

ARM *abbr.* adjustable rate mortgage.

arm (ärm) *n.* **1,** the upper limb of the human body, extending from shoulder to hand. **2,** anything like an arm in form or position. **3,** range of authority; power. **4,** a branch, esp. of military forces. **5,** (usually *pl.*) a weapon. **—***v.t. & i.* equip with arms; provide what is necessary for security or defense. **—at arm's length,** at a distance; on unfriendly terms.

ar·ma′da (är-mä′də) *n.* a fleet of warships.

ar″ma·dil′lo (är″mə-dil′ō) *n.* [*pl.* **-los**] a So. and Central Amer. mammal having hard scales.

Ar″ma·ged′don (är″mə-ged′ən) *n.* **1,** the place of the final battle between good and evil. **2,** any battle or struggle of a decisive nature.

> **Armageddon**
> ↔ From Hebrew *har megiddōn,* the mountain region of Megiddo, site of a great battle (Rev. 16:16).

ar′ma·ment (är′mə-mənt) *n.* **1,** the totality of weapons with which a military unit is armed. **2,** the act of arming.

ar′ma·ture (är′mə-chûr) *n.* **1,** defensive armor; protective covering. **2,** a supporting or connecting member.

arm′chair″ *n.* a chair with side arms.

arm′ful″ *n.* **1,** as much as the arms can hold. **2,** (*Informal*) a stout or shapely girl.

ar′mi·stice (är′mi-stis) *n.* a temporary suspension of hostilities; truce. **—Armistice Day,** Veterans Day.

arm′let (-lət) *n.* **1,** an ornamental band or bracelet worn around the upper arm. **2,** a small inlet of the sea.

ar·moire′ (är-mwär′) *n.* a large cupboard or wardrobe.

ar′mor (är′mər) *n.* **1,** any covering worn for protection against offensive weapons. **2,** anything that protects.

ar·mor′i·al (är-môr′ē-əl) *adj.* pert. to heraldic bearings.

ar′mor·y (är′mə-rē) *n.* a place for storing or manufacturing weapons.

arm′pit″ *n.* the hollow under the arm at the shoulder.

arm-′twist″ing *n.* (*Informal*) persuasion.

ar′my (är′mē) *n.* **1,** a large body of men trained for war on land, excluding naval and (usually) air forces. **2,** any large body of persons.

ar′ni·ca (är′ni-kə) *n.* a medicinal tincture used on wounds and bruises.

a·ro′ma (ə-rō′mə) *n.* an agreeable odor; fragrance. —**ar″o·mat′ic** (ar″ə-mat′ik) *adj.* —**ar″o·mat′i·cal·ly,** *adv.*

a·round′ (ə-rownd′) *prep. & adv.* **1,** on all sides; encircling. **2,** from place to place; here and there. **3,** (*Informal*) near at hand; approximately. **4,** rotating.

a·rouse′ (ə-rowz′) *v.t.* excite into action; awaken; put in motion.

ar·peg′gi·o (är-pej′yō) *n.* (*Music*) the sounding of the notes of a chord in succession instead of simultaneously.

ar′rack (ar′ək) *n.* an Asian liquor made from rice, molasses, or other materials.

ar·raign′ (ə-rān′) *v.t.* **1,** (*Law*) call into court to answer a charge. **2,** accuse. —**arraign′ment,** *n.*

ar·range′ (ə-rānj′) *v.t.* **1,** put in proper order. **2,** come to an agreement; settle. **3,** make preparation; plan. **4,** (*Music*) adapt for performance by particular voices or instruments. —**ar·range′ment,** *n.*

ar′rant (ar′ənt) *adj.* **1,** manifest; notorious. **2,** downright; thorough.

---

arrant, errant
☛Do not confuse *arrant*, meaning notorious or thorough, with *errant*, meaning wandering or erring. In fact, *arrant* was originally a variant spelling of *errant*, but the meanings have diverged.

---

ar′ras (ar′əs) *n.* a tapestry.

---

arras
↔ The word comes from the name of a city in France, a center of tapestry weaving.

---

ar·ray′ (ə-rā′) *n.* **1,** regular order or arrangement; an orderly assemblage. **2,** a display. **3,** raiment or apparel. —*v.t.* **1,** place in order or in a display. **2,** dress; bedeck.

ar·rears′ (ə-rirz′) *n.pl.* that which is overdue, as an unpaid debt.

ar·rest′ (ə-rest′) *v.t.* **1,** take (a person) into custody; seize; capture. **2,** stop forcibly; check or hinder. **3,** catch the attention of. —*n.* **1,** detention under legal warrant. **2,** capture; restraint; stoppage. —**ar·rest′ing,** *adj.* striking.

ar·riv′al (ə-rī′vəl) *n.* **1,** the act, fact, or time of arriving at a place. **2,** a person or thing that arrives.

ar·rive′ (ə-rīv′) *v.i.* **1,** reach a certain point. **2,** come; occur. **3,** attain a position of eminence or success.

ar·ri·viste′ (a-rē-vēst′) *n.* (*Fr.*) social climber.

ar′ro·gant (ar′ə-gənt) *adj.* aggressively haughty. —**ar′ro·gance,** *n.*

ar′ro·gate″ (ar′ə-gāt″) *v.t.* assume, demand, or appropriate unduly or presumptuously. —**ar″ro·ga′tion,** *n.* ❑ *abrogate*

ar′row (ar′ō) *n.* **1,** a rodlike missile weapon made to be shot from a bow. **2,** an angular sign, like the head of an arrow, used to point direction.

ar′row·head″ (-hed″) *n.* **1,** a hard, pointed tip for an arrow. **2,** a wedge-shaped mark.

ar′row·root″ *n.* **1,** a tropical Amer. plant; the starch obtained from it. **2,** any similar starch used in food products.

ar·roy′o (ə-roi′ō) *n.* (*Sp.*) a small gulch or ravine.

arse (ärs) *n.* rump.

ar′se·nal (är′sə-nəl) *n.* a manufactory or storehouse for military arms and supplies.

ar′se·nic (är′sə-nik) *n.* **1,** a volatile chemical element, no. 33, symbol As. **2,** a poison derived therefrom. —**ar·sen′i·cal** (-sen′i-kəl) *adj.*

ar′son (är′sən) *n.* the malicious burning of a building.

art (ärt) *n.* **1,** any system of rules and traditional methods for the practice of a craft, trade, or profession; the application of knowledge and skill. **2,** works designed to give intellectual pleasure, as music, sculpture, and esp. pictorial representation. **3,** skillful workmanship. **4,** cunning; guile. —**Art Dec′o** (dek′ō) a style of decorative art popular in the 1920s and 1930s. —**Art Nou·veau′** (noo-vō′) a style of decorative and architectural art of the late 19th c. ❑ *ability*

ar·te″ri·o·scle·ro′sis (är-tir″ē-ō-skle-rō′sis) *n.* a thickening of the blood vessels.

ar′ter·y (är′tə-rē) *n.* **1,** any of the large vessels that convey blood from the heart to another part of the body. **2,** a main channel of conveyance or transportation. —**ar·te′ri·al** (-tir′ē-əl) *adj.*

ar·te′sian well (är-tē′zhən) a deep well in which water rises by subsurface pressure.

---

artesian well
↔ Named for the Fr. province of Artois, where such wells were drilled in the 18th c.

---

art′ful (ärt′fəl) *adj.* **1,** crafty; wily. **2,** skillful. —**art′ful·ness,** *n.*

---

artful, arty

☛ *Artful* means crafty, skillful. *Arty* refers to something or someone that affects the manner or look of the artist but with questionable taste.

---

ar·thri'tis (är-thrī'tis) *n.* inflammation of a joint. —**ar·thrit'ic** (-thrit'ik) *adj.*

ar'ti·choke" (är'ti-chōk") *n.* a thistlelike plant with an edible head.

ar'ti·cle (är'tə-kəl) *n.* **1,** a separate item; a separate portion of anything. **2,** a literary composition on a specific topic. **3,** (*Gram.*) a word used before a noun, marking its application. —**definite article,** the. —**indefinite article,** a or an.

ar·tic'u·late" (är-tik'ū-lāt") *v.t. & i.* **1,** say or speak distinctly, with clear separation of syllables. **2,** unite by joints. —*adj.* (-lət) **1,** able to speak; expressive. **2,** having joints; segmented. **3,** clear; distinct. —**ar·tic"u·la'tion,** *n.*

ar'ti·fact" (är'ti-fakt") *n.* a man-made object, esp. from prehistoric times.

ar'ti·fice (är'tə-fis) *n.* **1,** a crafty device. **2,** trickery. —**ar·tif'i·cer** (är-tif'ə-sər) *n.*

ar"ti·fi'cial (är"tə-fish'əl) *adj.* **1,** man-made; contrived by human skill. **2,** assumed; pretended; fictitious. **3,** full of affectation. —**ar"ti·fi"ci·al'i·ty** (är"ti-fish"ē-al'ə-tē) *n.* —**artificial horizon,** an instrument showing the position of an aircraft relative to the surface of the earth. —**artificial intelligence,** the use of computers to simulate human intelligence. —**artificial respiration,** expansion and contraction of the lungs by hand or machine, to restore or maintain breathing. —**artificial satellite,** any man-made object caused to revolve in an orbit.

ar·til'ler·y (är-til'ə-rē) *n.* **1,** all heavy, mounted firearms; cannons. **2,** troops servicing such firearms. **3,** (*Slang*) a handgun or other weapon.

ar'ti·san (är'tə-zən) *n.* one skilled in an industrial craft.

art'ist (är'tist) **1,** one who pursues a pictorial art, esp. a painter. **2,** [also, **ar·tiste'** (-tēst')] a performer in an art of entertainment. **3,** a person of special skill. —**ar·tis'-tic,** *adj.* —**ar·tis'ti·cal·ly,** *adv.* —**art'ist·ry** (-rē) *n.*

art'less (ärt'ləs) *adj.* simple and natural; free from guile; sincere. —**art'less·ness,** *n.*

art'y (är'tē) *adj.* (*Informal*) affectedly or superficially interested in the fine arts. Also, **art'sy** (ärt'sē). ❑ *artful*

-ar·y (er-ē) *suf.* forming adjectives: pertaining to.

Ar'yan (är'yən) *adj. & n.* **1,** European or Asiatic (in race). **2,** (*incorrectly*) gentile; Nordic. Also, **Ar'i·an** (ar'ē-ən).

as (az) *adv.* in that degree; to that extent; so far. —*conj.* **1,** to the same degree or extent; in similar manner. **2,** at the same time. **3,** because. **4,** for example. —*pron.* that or who. —**as good as,** (*Informal*) nearly, virtually. —**as per,** according to. —**as such,** in itself; in that capacity. —**as the crow flies,** in a straight and horizontal line; directly.

---

as, like

(*Gram.*) The often-ignored rule for use of these words is to use the conjunction *as* to introduce a clause (a group of words containing a verb) and to use the preposition *like* when comparing nouns.

---

as"a·fet'i·da (as"ə-fet'i-də) *n.* an herb or a pungent drug made from it.

as·bes'tos (az-bes'təs) *n.* a mineral used for fireproofing.

as·cend' (ə-send') *v.i.* go upward; rise. —*v.t.* climb; mount.

as·cend'ant (ə-sen'dənt) *adj.* **1,** rising. **2,** dominant. —*n.* (with *the*) position of superiority. —**as·cend'an·cy,** *n.*

as·cen'sion (ə-sen'shən) *n.* a rising, esp. (*cap.*) of Christ into heaven.

as·cent' (ə-sent') *n.* **1,** act of ascending; a climbing or moving upward; rise. **2,** an upward slope.

as"cer·tain' (as"ər-tān') *v.t.* find out by examination; determine. —**as"cer·tain'-ment,** *n.*

as·cet'ic (ə-set'ik) *adj.* extreme in self-restraint or self-denial. —*n.* a recluse or hermit. —**as·cet'i·cal·ly,** *adv.* —**as·cet'i·cism** (-i-siz-əm) *n.*

ASCII (as'kē) *n.* a code for representing letters and numbers in computers, etc.: *A(merican) S(tandard) C(ode for) I(nformation) I(nterchange).*

a·scor'bic acid (ə-skôr'bik) vitamin C, used to combat scurvy.

as'cot (as'kət) *n.* a broad necktie folded like a scarf.

as·cribe (ə-skrīb') *v.t.* attribute to a cause or source; impute. —**as·crip'tion** (ə-skrip'shən) *n.*

a·sep'tic (ə-sep'tik) *adj.* free of germs that cause disease or decay. —**a·sep'ti·cal·ly,** *adv.*

a·sex'u·al (ā-sek'shoo-əl) *adj.* not having or involving sex.

ash *n.* **1,** the incombustible residue that remains after burning. **2,** (*pl.*) human remains. **3,** a hardwood tree. —**ashtray,** a

---

dish for tobacco ashes. —**Ash Wednesday,** the Wednesday on which Lent begins.

a·shamed′ (ə-shāmd′) *adj.* feeling guilty; abashed.

ash′en (ash′ən) *adj.* **1,** pale; gray. **2,** pert. to the ash tree.

ash′lar (ash′lər) *n.* a block of building stone; such stones collectively. Also, **ash′ler.**

a·shore′ (ə-shôr′) *adj.* to or on land, not water.

ash′y (ash′ē) *adj.* pale as ashes. —**ash′i·ness,** *n.*

A′sian (ā′zhən) *adj.* pert. to Asia or its inhabitants. —*n.* a native of Asia. Also, **A″si·at′ic** (ā″zhē-at′ik). —**Asian flu** or **Asiatic flu,** a mild form of influenza, usually lasting 5 days.

> ### Asian, Asiatic, Oriental
> *Oriental* has traditionally been the term used by Westerners to refer to people and objects from or related to Asia. However, it is vague and ethnocentric, because of its implied establishment of Western as the norm. It is better to use more specific terms, such as *Asian, Chinese,* etc. Avoid *Asiatic,* because it is often considered mildly offensive.

a·side′ (ə-sīd′) *adv.* **1,** on or to one side; apart or separately. **2,** out of consideration or regard. —*n.* (*Theater*) a private remark to the audience.

as′i·nine″ (as′ə-nīn″) *adj.* obtrusively silly; stupid. —**as″i·nin′i·ty** (-nin′ə-tē) *n.*

ask (àsk) *v.t. & i.* **1,** put a question (to); interrogate. **2,** seek to obtain; request. **3,** inquire (about). **4,** invite.

> ### ask
> ↔ This word of Old English origin once had two forms, one of which was *axe,* which through a process of consonant reversal became our *ask.*

a·skance′ (ə-skans′) *adv.* distrustfully; from the side, as a glance.

a·skew′ (ə-skū′) *adv.* in an oblique position; out of line; awry.

a·slant′ (ə-slánt′) *adj. & adv.* slanting; oblique.

a·sleep′ (ə-slēp′) *adv. & adj.* **1,** sleeping; numb. **2,** inactive.

asp *n.* a poisonous snake.

as·par′a·gus (ə-spar′ə-gəs) *n.* a plant having edible shoots.

as′pect (as′pekt) *n.* **1,** one of the ways in which a thing may be viewed or contem-

plated. **2,** outward appearance; facial expression. **3,** view.

> ### asparagus
> ↔ Although this word derives from Greek *asparagos,* for two centuries it was called *sparrowgrass* in English.

as′pen (as′pən) *adj.* tremulous; quivering. —*n.* a poplar tree.

as·per′i·ty (as-per′ə-tē) *n.* harshness of temper; severity.

as·perse′ (ə-spērs′) *v.t.* make false or foul charges against; slander. —**as·per′sion** (-zhən) *n.*

as′phalt (as′fâlt) *n.* a bituminous substance used for paving, etc. —**asphalt jungle,** a large city, esp. its high crime areas.

as′pho·del (as′fə-del) *n.* a plant of the lily family.

as·phyx′i·a (as-fik′sē-ə) *n.* extreme lack of oxygen; suffocation.

as·phyx′i·ate″ (as-fiks′ē-āt″) *v.t. & i.* kill or die by deprivation of oxygen; suffocate. —**as·phyx″i·a′tion,** *n.*

as′pic (as′pik) *n.* a clear jelly made of meat or vegetables.

as′pi·rate″ (as′pə-rāt″) *v.t.* pronounce with an audible emission of breath. —*n. & adj.* (-rət) the sound represented by *h.*

as″pi·ra′tion (as″pə-rā′shən) *n.* **1,** desire; ambition. **2,** breathing.

as·pire′ (ə-spīr′) *v.i.* be ardently desirous, esp. for something spiritual. —**as·pir′ant,** *n.*

as′pi·rin (as′pə-rin) *n.* a drug used to relieve pain and reduce fever.

> ### aspirin
> ↔ Coined in German in 1899 by Heinrich Dreser. The word is derived from the German term for spiraeic acid (a former term for salicylic acid, from which drug aspirin is derived).

ass (as) *n.* **1,** a horselike beast of burden; the donkey. **2,** a stupid person; a fool.

as·sail′ (ə-sāl′) *v.t.* attack; belabor with entreaties or abuse. —**as·sail′ant,** *n.* attacker.

as·sas′sin (ə-sas′in) *n.* one who kills another by secret assault.

> ### assassin
> ↔ From the Arabic word for hashish-eater, referring to a fanatical Muslim sect active at the time of the Crusades.

as·sas′si·nate″ (ə-sas′ə-nāt″) *v.t.* kill violently and treacherously. —**as·sas″si·na′tion,** *n.*

as·sault′ (ə-sâlt′) *v.t.* attack by physical means; assail with argument, abuse. —*n.* an attack. —**assault and battery,** (*Law*) assault with offensive or violent touching of another.

as·say′ (ə-sā′) *v.t.* test; analyze, esp. metallic ore.

> **assay, essay**
> ☛ *Assay* means to analyze or test; *essay* means to try.

as′se·gai″ (as′ə-gī″) *n.* **1,** a So. Afr. hardwood tree, similar to the dogwood. **2,** a slender spear or javelin. —*v.t.* strike or kill with an assegai. Also, **as′sa·gai″.**

as·sem′blage (ə-sem′blij) *n.* persons or things assembled.

as·sem′ble (ə-sem′bəl) *v.t.* **1,** bring together in one place. **2,** fit together. —*v.i.* come together; congregate.

as·sem′bler (-blər) *n.* a computer program which translates instructions into machine language.

as·sem′bly (ə-sem′blē) *n.* **1,** act of bringing or coming together. **2,** a group; congregation. **3,** a legislative body. —**assembly line,** a line of workers and machinery in a factory which assembles a product in consecutive steps.

as·sent′ (ə-sent′) *v.i.* express agreement or approval; concur. —*n.* (as′ent) agreement; acquiescence.

as·sert′ (ə-sẽrt′) *v.t.* **1,** state as true; declare; aver. **2,** claim and defend.

as·ser′tion (ə-sẽr′shən) *n.* **1,** act of asserting. **2,** statement; claim; affirmation.

as·ser′tive (-tiv) *adj.* positive; overbearing. —**as·ser′tive·ness,** *n.*

as·sess′ (ə-ses′) *v.t.* **1,** estimate the value of (property) as a basis for taxation. **2,** impose a tax, charge, or fine. —**as·sess′-ment,** *n.* —**as·ses′sor,** *n.*

as′set (as′et) *n.* **1,** anything advantageous. **2,** (usually *pl.*) items of property available; total resources.

> **asset**
> ↔ The word comes from the Anglo-French phrase *aver asetz,* to have enough (as enough money to pay one's debts).

as·sev′er·ate″ (ə-sev′ə-rāt″) *v.t.* aver solemnly and positively. —**as·sev″er·a′tion,** *n.*

as″si·du′i·ty (as″i-dū′ə-tē) *n.* quality of being assiduous; diligence.

as·sid′u·ous (ə-sij′oo-əs) *adj.* diligent; attentive; unremitting. —**as·sid′u·ous·ness,** *n.*

as·sign′ (ə-sīn′) *v.t.* **1,** set apart; allot;

transfer. **2,** appoint, as to office or duties. **3,** specify; designate; ascribe; refer. —*n.* (*Law*) [also, **as″sign·ee′** (as″ə-nē′)] one to whom property is transferred.

as″sig·na′tion (as″ig-nā′shən) *n.* an appointment for an illicit love meeting.

as·sign′ment (-mənt) *n.* **1,** act of assigning. **2,** something assigned to be done; task; mission. **3,** a document attesting to a transfer of interest.

as·sim′i·late″ (ə-sim′ə-lāt″) *v.t.* **1,** take in and incorporate; absorb and digest. **2,** make similar; bring into conformity; adapt. —*v.i.* assimilate something. —**as·sim″i·la′tion,** *n.*

as·sist′ (ə-sist′) *v.t.* give help; aid. —*v.i.* be present; attend.

as·sist′ance (-əns) *n.* act of assisting; help; aid.

as·sist′ant (-ənt) *n.* a helper.

as·size′ (ə-sīz′) *n.* **1,** a session of a legislature. **2,** (*pl.*) a term of sittings of an English court.

as·so′ci·ate″ (ə-sō′shē-āt″) *v.t.* **1,** link together in some conceptual relationship. **2,** join in partnership; combine in a union. —*v.i.* consort together; unite. —*n.* (-ət) **1,** a partner, confederate, or companion. **2,** anything that usually accompanies another. —*adj.* (-ət) **1,** allied; concomitant. **2,** having subordinate membership.

as·so″ci·a′tion (ə-sō″sē-ā′shən) *n.* **1,** act of associating. **2,** state of being associated; partnership; combination. **3,** a society, league, etc.

as′so·nance (as′ə-nəns) *n.* resemblance in spoken sound, without strict rhyme. —**as′so·nant,** *adj.*

as·sort′ (ə-sôrt′) *v.t.* separate and distribute according to kind; classify; arrange.

as·sort′ment (-mənt) *n.* **1,** act of assorting. **2,** a diversified group or collection.

as·suage′ (ə-swāj′) *v.t.* lessen; mitigate; pacify. —**as·suage′ment,** *n.* —**as·sua′sive** (ə-swā′siv) *adj.*

as·sume′ (ə-soom′) *v.t.* **1,** take for granted without proof. **2,** take upon oneself; undertake. **3,** take the appearance of; pretend to possess. **4,** take for oneself; appropriate.

as·sump′tion (ə-sum′shən) *n.* **1,** act of assuming. **2,** a supposition or hypothesis. **3,** (*cap.*) bodily acceptance into heaven, esp. of the Virgin Mary.

as·sur′ance (ə-shûr′əns) *n.* **1,** an earnest statement intended to give confidence. **2,** freedom from doubt. **3,** boldness; impudence. **4,** a promise or pledge; surety. **5,** insurance.

as·sure' (ə-shûr') *v.t.* **1,** make sure or certain; make secure or stable. **2,** make confident; convince.

---

assure, ensure, insure
☞ *Assure* means to convince a person of something. *Ensure* and *insure* both mean to make certain that something happens, or to obtain insurance on. However, *ensure* is more commonly used in the former sense, *insure* in the latter.

---

as·ta·tine'' (as'tə-tēn'') *n.* an unstable radioactive chemical element, one of the halogens, no. 85, symbol At, a product of radioactive decay.

as'ter (as'tər) *n.* any of many species of common flowers having colored petals around a yellow disk.

as'ter·isk (as'tər-isk) *n.* a symbol (*) used in printing.

a·stern' (ə-stĕrn') *adv. & adj. (Naut.)* to the rear; behind.

as'ter·oid'' (as'tər-oid'') *n.* any of the many planetoids and other small objects located chiefly between Mars and Jupiter.

as·the'ni·a (as-thē'nė-ə) *n.* loss of strength; bodily weakness.

asth'ma (az'mə) *n.* a disorder of respiration, marked by labored breathing. **—asth·mat'ic** (-mat'ik) *adj.* **—asth·mat'i·cal·ly,** *adv.*

a·stig'ma·tism (ə-stig'mə-tiz-əm) *n.* defect of the eye producing imperfect focus. **—as''tig·mat'ic** (as''tig-mat'ik) *adj.*

a·stir' (ə-stēr') *adv. & adj.* on the move; active; out of bed.

as·ton'ish (ə-ston'ish) *v.t.* strike with wonder; surprise; amaze. **—as·ton'ish·ment,** *n.*

as·tound' (ə-stownd') *v.t.* strike with amazement; astonish greatly.

as·tra·khan (as'trə-kən) *n.* **1,** the fur of the Karakul lamb. **2,** a fabric resembling it.

as'tral (as'trəl) *adj.* **1,** pert. to the stars; stellar. **2,** star-shaped.

a·stray' (ə-strā') *adv. & adj.* away from the proper path; wandering.

a·stride' (ə-strīd') *prep.* with one leg on each side of. Also, **a·strad'dle** (ə-strad'əl) *adj.*

as·tringe' (ə-strinj') *v.t.* contract; draw together. **—as·trin'gen·cy,** *n.*

as·trin'gent (ə-strin'jənt) *n.* a substance used to contract the bodily tissues and so

diminish discharge, as of blood. **—adj. 1,** tending to constrict. **2,** severe; austere.

as·tro- (as-trō) *pref.* star.

as'tro·labe'' (as'trə-lāb'') *n.* an astronomical instrument.

as·trol'o·gy (ə-strol'ə-jė) *n.* the study of the supposed influence of the stars and planets on human affairs. **—as·trol'o·ger** (-jər) *n.*

as'tro·naut (as'trə-nât) *n.* the pilot of or a traveler in a space ship. **—as''tro·nau'tics,** *n.sing.* the science of space travel.

as''tro·nom'i·cal (as''trə-nom'i-kəl) *adj.* **1,** pert. to astronomy. **2,** huge.

as·tron'o·my (ə-stron'ə-mė) *n.* the general science of all celestial bodies. **—as·tron'o·mer,** *n.*

as''tro·phys'ics *n.* the branch of astronomy dealing with the physical properties of heavenly bodies; astronomical physics. **—as''tro·phys'i·cal,** *adj.*

As'tro·Turf'' *n. (T.N.)* a brand of artificial grass used in stadiums, etc.

as·tute' (ə-stoot') *adj.* keen in discernment; sagacious; cunning. **—as·tute'ness,** *n.*

a·sun'der (ə-sun'dər) *adv. & adj.* into separate parts; in a position apart.

a·sy'lum (ə-sī'ləm) *n.* **1,** an institution for the care of the insane or afflicted. **2,** any place of refuge or retreat.

---

asylum
↔ Derived from Greek, this word originally meant a refuge for hunted persons; its use for mental hospitals came in the 18th c.

---

a'symp·tote'' (as'im-tōt'') *n.* a straight line considered as tangent to a curve but that does not meet the curve at any distance less than infinity. **—a''symp·tot'ic** (-tot'ik) *adj.*

at *prep.* used in many idiomatic phrases to imply local or relative position, direction of motion or activity, time, order, condition, circumstance, etc.

At'a·brine'' (at'ə-brin) *n. (T.N.)* a drug used against malaria.

at'a·vism (at'ə-viz-əm) *n.* reversion to distant hereditary traits or characteristics. **—at''a·vis'tic** (-vis'tik) *adj.* **—at''a·vis'ti·cal·ly,** *adv.*

a·tax'i·a (ə-tak'sė-ə) *n.* loss of muscle coordination.

ate (āt) *v.* pret. of *eat.*

-ate (āt; ət) *suf.* **1,** forming adjectives or verbs: *salivate, separate.* **2,** *(Chem.)* indicating the salt of an acid: *nitrate.* **3,** denoting function or office: *consulate.*

---

at″el·ier′ (at″əl-yā′) *n.* a studio; workshop.

a′the·ism (ā′thė-iz-əm) *n.* the doctrine that there is no God. —**a′the·ist,** *n* —**a″the·is′tic** (-is′tik) *adj.* —**a″the·is′ti·cal·ly,** *adv.* ❑ *agnostic*

ath″e·nae′um (ath″ə-nē′əm) *n.* an institution of learning; a library.

> **athenaeum**
> ↔ From the Greek temple of Athena in Athens, a place where poets read their works.

a·the′ni·um (a-thē′nė-əm) *n.* einsteinium.

ath′lete (ath′lēt) *n.* one who engages in sports or other exercises, esp. those requiring physical agility and strength. —**athlete's foot,** a fungous skin disease.

ath·let′ic (ath-let′ik) *adj.* **1,** like an athlete; strong. **2,** pert. to athletics. —**ath·let′-i·cal·ly,** *adv.*

ath·let′ics (-iks) *n.pl.* sports requiring physical prowess.

-a·thon (ə-thon) *suf.* denoting an extended event.

a·thwart′ (ə-thwôrt′) *adv. & prep.* **1,** from side to side; crosswise. **2,** perversely.

-a′tion (ā′shən) *suf.* forming nouns denoting the act, process, result, effect, or cause (of the root word).

at′las (at′ləs) *n.* a bound collection of maps.

> **atlas**
> ↔ *Atlas* was a Titan in Greek mythology who bore the world on his shoulders; hence, the association with the world or its representation.

ATM (a′tē′em′) a machine for performing certain banking transactions automatically without a teller: *a(utomated) t(eller) m(achine).*

at′mos·phere′ (at′məs-fir″) *n.* **1,** the entire gaseous envelope of the earth; the air. **2,** a unit of pressure, about 15 pounds per square inch. **3,** environment; predominant aspect or mood. —**at″mos·pher′ic** (-fer′ik) *adj.* —**at″mos·pher′i·cal·ly,** *adv.* —**at″mos·pher′ics,** *n.pl.* (*Radio & TV*) static.

at′oll (at′ol; ə-tol′) *n.* an island enclosing a lagoon.

> **atoll**
> ↔ From a native Maldive name for one of the islands in the Maldive atolls.

at′om (at′əm) *n.* **1,** the smallest particle having the properties of a specific chemical element. **2,** anything extremely small.

—**a·tom′ic** (ə-tom′ik) *adj.* —**a·tom′i·cal·ly,** *adv.* —**atomic clock,** an extremely accurate clock regulated by discharge of atoms. —**atomic number,** the number of protons in the nucleus of a certain atom. —**atomic pile,** an installation consisting of a mass of radioactive matter and apparatus permitting controlled nuclear fission. —**atomic weight,** the average weight of the atoms of a given element.

atom bomb a bomb caused to explode by fission of the nuclei of its atoms. Also, **atomic bomb.**

at′om·ize″ (at′ə-mīz″) *v.t.* reduce to bits, esp. to spray. —**at′om·iz″er,** *n.* a device for reducing liquid to a fine spray.

a·ton′al (ā-tō′nəl) *adj.* (*Music*) having no key. —**a″to·nal′i·ty** (a″tō-nal′ə-tė) *n.*

a·tone′ (ə-tōn′) *v.i.* make amends for sin or error. —**a·tone′ment,** *n.*

a·top′ (ə-top′) *adv. & prep.* on top of.

a′tri·um (ā′trė-əm) *n.* [*pl.* -**a** (-ə)] the main room of an ancient Roman house.

a·tro′cious (ə-trō′shəs) *adj.* **1,** extremely wicked, criminal, or cruel; heinous. **2,** (*Informal*) of poor quality. —**a·tro′cious·ness,** *n.*

a·troc′i·ty (ə-tros′ə-tė) *n.* an atrocious act; wickedness.

at′ro·phy (at′rə-fė) *n.* a wasting away or arrested development, from defective nutrition or lack of use. —*v.i.* waste away.

at′ro·pine (at′rə-pin) *n.* a medicinal drug derived from belladonna.

at·tach′ (ə-tach′) *v.t.* **1,** fasten; affix. **2,** appoint; assign. **3,** (*Law*) seize by legal authority. **4,** bind by ties of affection or interest.

at″ta·ché′ (at″ə-shā′) *n.* **1,** a minor diplomatic officer. **2,** [*also,* **attaché case**] a slim, flat briefcase.

at·tach′ment (ə-tach′mənt) *n.* **1,** act of attaching; state of being attached. **2,** something added, as a part to a machine.

at·tack′ (ə-tak′) *v.t.* **1,** fall upon with force or violence; assault; assail. **2,** begin to work upon; begin to affect. —*n.* **1,** a violent onset or assault. **2,** the offensive in a military conflict. **3,** a seizure or illness.

at·tain′ (ə-tān′) *v.t.* reach or achieve; accomplish.

at·tain′der (-dər) *n.* nullification of civil rights of one convicted of a high crime.

at·tain′ment (-mənt) *n.* **1,** act of attaining. **2,** an acquired personal ability, honor, etc.

at·taint′ (ə-tānt′) *v.t.* disgrace; taint.

at′tar (at′ər) *n.* an essential oil of roses.

at·tempt′ (ə-tempt′) *v.t.* make an effort

to do; endeavor; undertake. —*n.* **1,** an effort to do something. **2,** attack; assault.

at·tend′ (ə-tend′) *v.t. & i.* **1,** be present at. **2,** go with; accompany. **3,** take care of; minister to; serve. **4,** listen to; heed. —**at·tend′ance,** *n.*

at·tend′ant (-ənt) *n.* one who attends another. —*adj.* attending.

at·ten′tion (ə-ten′shən) *n.* **1,** direction of the mind to an object of sense or thought. **2,** observant care; notice. **3,** an act of care, civility, or courtesy. **4,** (*Mil.*) a certain prescribed erect posture.

at·ten′tive (-tiv) *adj.* **1,** observant; intent. **2,** polite; (*Informal*) wooing. —**at·ten′tive·ness,** *n.*

at·ten′u·ate″ (ə-ten′ū-āt″) *v.t. & i.* **1,** make or become thin. **2,** weaken in force; lessen in quantity, value, or degree. —**at·ten″u·a′tion,** *n.*

at·test′ (ə-test′) *v.t.* **1,** bear witness to; declare to be true or genuine. **2,** give proof or evidence of. —**at″tes·ta′tion** (at″es-tā′shən) *n.*

at′tic (at′ik) *n.* a room directly under the roof; a garret. —*adj.* (*cap.*) pert. to Athens or Greece.

---

attic
↔ The name refers to the Attic columns used to support a low story placed above the main facade of a building, called the *attic story.* Over time, the second word disappeared.

---

at·tire′ (ə-tīr′) *v.t.* dress; clothe; adorn. —*n.* clothing; apparel.

at′ti·tude″ (at′ə-tood″) *n.* **1,** a position or manner indicative of feeling, opinion, or intention toward a person or thing. **2,** a bodily posture; position. **3,** (*Slang*) a negative, defensive, etc., posture; *to have an attitude.*

at·ti·tu′di·nize″ (at-i-too′di-nīz″) *v.i.* assume an attitude, esp. affectedly.

at·tor′ney (ə-tër′nė) *n.* **1,** [also, **attorney-at-law**] a lawyer. **2,** one empowered to transact business for another; an agent. —**attorney general,** the chief law officer of a state or nation.

---

attorney, lawyer
☛ A *lawyer* (in England, *solicitor*) is a person who is licensed to practice law. Technically, an *attorney* is someone authorized to act on behalf of another, hence, an agent. The *attorney* may or may not be a *lawyer.* However, this distinction is rarely observed. In England, a *barrister* is a solicitor who tries cases in court.

---

at·tract′ (ə-trakt′) *v.t.* **1,** draw toward (itself) by inherent physical force; cause to cohere with. **2,** invite; allure.

at·trac′tion (ə-trak′shən) *n.* **1,** act of attracting; power to attract. **2,** (*Theater*) an act, motion picture, etc.

at·trac′tive (-tiv) *adj.* appealing; likable; good-looking. —**at·trac′tive·ness,** *n.*

at·trib′ute (ə-trib′yût) *v.t.* consider as belonging, as a possession, quality, or cause; ascribe; impute. —*n.* (at′ri-būt″) characteristic; anything attributed, as a property, quality, or cause. —**at″tri·bu′tion** (at″rə-bū′shən) *n.*

at·tri′tion (ə-trish′ən) *n.* **1,** the act of wearing away, or of being worn down, by friction; abrasion. **2,** loss of personnel due to causes other than dismissal, as death or retirement.

at·tune′ (ə-toon′) *v.t.* make harmonious.

au·bade′ (ō-bäd′) *n.* a serenade performed at dawn.

au′burn (â′bërn) *n.* a reddish-brown color.

auc′tion (âk′shən) *n.* a public sale in which goods are sold to the highest bidder. —*v.t.* sell by auction. —**auc″tion·eer′** (-ir′) *n.*

au·da′cious (â-dā′shəs) *adj.* **1,** bold; daring; intrepid. **2,** unrestrained; impudent.

au·dac′i·ty (â-das′ə-tė) *n.* boldness; impudence.

au′di·ble (â′də-bəl) *adj.* loud enough to be heard. —**au″di·bil′i·ty,** *n.*

au′di·ence (â′dė-əns) *n.* **1,** an assembly of hearers or spectators; the persons reached by a publication, radio, etc. **2,** a formal interview; a hearing. **3,** liberty or opportunity to be heard.

au′di·o″ (â′dė-ō″) *adj.* pert. to audible sound waves. —*n.* the audio or radio portion of a broadcast.

au·di·o- (â-dė-ō) *pref.* hearing.

au′di·o·phile″ *n.* one interested in sound and sound reproduction.

au′dit (â′dit) *n.* an official examination and verification of accounts or dealings. —*v.t. & i.* examine and certify accounts. —**audit trail,** in accounting, a series of cross-references allowing easy checking of information.

au·di′tion (â-dish′ən) *n.* **1,** the sense or act of hearing. **2,** a hearing or performance for test purposes, as by a musician. —*v.i. & t.* perform, or cause to perform, as a test.

au′di·tor (â′di-tər) *n.* **1,** a hearer; listener. **2,** one who audits accounts.

au″di·to′ri·um (â″də-tôr′ė-əm) *n.* a large

---

room, space, or building for containing an audience or spectators.

au'di·to''ry (â'də-tôr''ė) *adj.* pert. to the sense or organs of hearing. Also, **au'di·tive.**

au'ger (â'gər) *n.* a tool for boring holes.

aught (ât) *n.* **1,** anything whatever. **2,** naught. —*adv.* in any respect; at all.

aug·ment' (âg-ment') *v.t.* cause to increase; add to. —*v.i.* increase. —**aug''men·ta'tion,** *n.*

au'gur (â'gər) *v.t. & i.* **1,** predict from omens; foretell. **2,** be a sign of; presage. —*n.* a prophet.

au'gu·ry (â'gyû-rė) *n.* **1,** prophecy divination. **2,** an omen.

au·gust' (â-gust') *adj.* highly dignified; imposing; eminent.

Au'gust (â'gəst) *n.* the eighth month of the year.

> ### August
> ↔ From the Roman emperor Caius Julius Caesar Octavian, to whom the Senate granted the title *Augustus* in 27 B.C. The adjective *august* derives from the same source.

auk (âk) *n.* a diving bird found in northern regions.

auld (ōld) *adj.* (*Scot.*) old.

aunt (ánt) *n.* **1,** the sister of one's father or mother. **2,** the wife of one's uncle.

au pair' (ō per') (*Fr.*) pert. to a young person (usu. foreign) who does domestic duties in exchange for room and board.

au'ra (â'rə) *n.* **1,** a supposed force or imponderable matter emanating from a body and surrounding it like an atmosphere. **2,** a distinctive character or quality.

au'ral (â'rəl) *adj.* pert. to the ear or to hearing.

au're·ole'' (ôr'ė-ōl'') *n.* a halo or nimbus.

Au''re·o·my'cin (ôr''ė-ō-mī'sin) *n.* (*T.N.*) an antibiotic used in treatment of certain virus diseases.

au'ri·cle (â'rə-kəl) *n.* **1,** the outer ear. **2,** one of the chambers of the heart. —**au·ric'u·lar** (â-rik'yə-lər) *adj.*

au·rif'er·ous (â-rif'ər-əs) *adj.* containing gold.

au'rochs (ôr'oks) *n.* [*pl.* **-ochs**] a European wild ox.

au·ro'ra (â-rôr'ə) *n.* **1,** morning twilight; the dawn of anything. **2,** an atmospheric phenomenon causing night lights in polar regions, **aurora bo''re·al'is** (bôr''ė-al'is) in the north, **aurora aus·tra'lis** (â-strā'lis) in the south. —**au·ro'ral,** *adj.*

aus·cul·ta'tion (âs-kəl-tā'shən) *n.* diagnostic listening to the sounds of the body.

aus'pice (â'spis) *n.* **1,** (*pl.*) favoring influence; protection or patronage. **2,** a favorable circumstance.

aus·pi'cious (â-spish'əs) *adj.* well-omened; betokening success. —**aus·pi'cious·ness,** *n.*

> ### auspicious, propitious
> ☞ *Propitious* is the more general term, meaning favorable. *Auspicious* refers specifically to a favorable omen observed before the start of something.

aus·tere' (â-stir') *adj.* **1,** severely simple; unadorned. **2,** serious; morally strict. **3,** harsh; stern; rigorous.

aus·ter'i·ty (âs-ter'ə-tė) *n.* **1,** state of being austere; harshness. **2,** simplicity in living.

au·teur' (ō-tėr') *n.* (*Fr.*) a filmmaker who has a unique and very personal style.

aus'tral (â'strəl) *adj.* southern; lying in the southern hemisphere.

au'tar·chy (â'tär-kė) *n.* **1,** absolute power; autocracy. **2,** self-government. **3,** economic self-sufficiency (of a country). —**au·tar'chic** (â-tär'kik) *adj.*

au·then'tic (â-then'tik) *adj.* **1,** actually of the ascribed authorship or origin; genuine. **2,** duly authorized. —**au·then'ti·cal·ly,** *adv.* —**au·then·tic'i·ty** (-tis'ə-tė) *n.*

au·then'ti·cate'' (â-then'ti-kāt'') *v.t.* make valid; attest to the genuineness of. —**au·then''ti·ca'tion,** *n.*

au'thor (â'thər) *n.* **1,** the originator or creator of anything. **2,** one who writes literary works. —*v.t.* (*Informal*) write. —**au'thor·ship,** *n.*

au·thor''i·tar'i·an (ə-thor''ə-tār'ė-ən) *adj.* favoring rule by absolute authority. —*n.* an advocate of such rule.

> ### authoritarian, authoritative
> ☞ *Authoritarian* refers to rule by absolute authority. *Authoritative* refers to knowledge based on authority.

au·thor'i·ta''tive (-tā''tiv) *adj.* based on authority; authentic. ❏ *authoritarian*

au·thor'i·ty (ə-thor'ə-tė) *n.* **1,** the right to govern, control, or command. **2,** a person or group having such right. **3,** power or influence derived from reputation. **4,** an expert on a subject; an accepted source of information or counsel.

au''thor·i·za'tion (â''thə-ri-zā'shən) *n.* act or result of authorizing; authority to act.

au'thor·ize" (â'thə-rīz") *v.t.* give authority, warrant, or legal power to; empower (a person).

au'tism (â'tiz-əm) *n.* (*Psychol.*) excessive involvement in oneself. —**au·tis'tic**, *adj.*

au'to (â'tō) *n.* automobile.

au·to- (â-tō) *pref.* meaning self.

au"to·bi·og'ra·phy (â"tə-bī-og'rə-fè) *n.* a biography of a person written by himself or herself. —**au"to·bi"o·graph'i·cal**, *adj.*

au'to·clave" (â'tə-klāv") *n.* a pressure cooker.

au·toc'ra·cy (â-tok'rə-sè) *n.* government by an absolute monarch.

au'to·crat" (â'tə-krat") *n.* one who rules by inherent right, subject to no restrictions. —**au"to·crat'ic**, *adj.* —**au"to·crat'i·cal·ly**, *adv.*

au'to·cross" *n.* an automobile race testing endurance.

au"to·da·fé' (â"tō-də-fā') *n.* (*Port.*) a public declaration of judgment, under the Inquisition; lit., an act of faith.

au"to·gi'ro (â"tə-jī'rō) *n.* a propeller-driven aircraft supported in flight by a freely rotating windmill-like rotor.

au'to·graph" (â'tə-gráf") *n.* **1,** one's own signature. **2,** one's own handwriting. **3,** an original handwritten manuscript.

au"to·im·mune' *adj.* pert. to the immune response of an organism against its own components.

Au'to·mat" (â'tə-mat") *n.* (*T.N.*) a restaurant where food is vended by automatic coin machines.

au"to·mat'ic (â"tə-mat'ik) *adj.* **1,** having the power of self-motion. **2,** operated by self-acting machinery. **3,** following inevitably as a consequence. **4,** done without volition; reflex; habitual. —*n.* an automatic pistol. —**au"to·mat'i·cal·ly**, *adv.*

au"to·ma'tion (â"tə-mā'shən) *n.* the handling and fabrication of materials by automatic machinery, esp. when no part of the process is done by hand. —**au'to·mate"**, *v.t. & i.*

au·tom'a·ton" (â-tom'ə-ton") *n.* [*pl.* **-ta** (-tä)] **1,** a machine actuated to operate for some time without external guidance; a mechanical figure actuated by concealed machinery. **2,** a person who acts in a monotonous routine manner. —**au·tom'a·tism**, *n.*

au'to·mo·bile" (â'tə-mə-bēl") *n.* a vehicle propelled by a self-contained engine and designed to travel on ordinary roads. —*adj.* (-mō'bəl) self-propelled. —**au"to·mo·bil'ist**, *n.*

au"to·mo'tive (â"tə-mō'tiv) *adj.* **1,** pert. to self-propelled vehicles, esp. automobiles. **2,** self-propelling.

au·ton'o·my (â-ton'ə-mè) *n.* self-government; independence. —**au·ton'o·mous**, *adj.*

au'to·pi"lot *n.* an automatic guidance system for ships and aircraft; automatic pilot.

au'top·sy (â'top-sè) *n.* dissection and inspection of a dead body to discover the cause of death.

au"to·sug·ges'tion *n.* an effort to produce physical effects on oneself by thinking they will occur.

au'tumn (â'təm) *n.* (*often cap.*) the third season of the year, between summer and winter; also called *fall.* —**au·tum'nal** (â-tum'nəl) *adj.*

aux·il'ia·ry (âg-zil'yə-rè) *adj.* **1,** giving help or support. **2,** subordinate; additional. —*n.* **1,** a support organization affiliated with a larger organization, often as a fund-raising unit. **2,** (*pl.*) foreign troops in the service of a nation at war.

a·vail' (ə-vāl') *v.i. & t.* have force or efficacy; serve. —*n.* efficacy; advantage. —**avail oneself of,** make use of.

a·vail'a·ble (-ə-bəl) *adj.* obtainable; at one's disposal. —**a·vail"a·bil'i·ty**, *n.*

av'a·lanche" (av'ə-lanch") *n.* the sudden fall of a mass of ice and debris down the side of a mountain.

a'vant-garde' (av'änt-gärd') *n. & adj.* (*Fr.*) (in the) vanguard.

av'a·rice (av'ə-ris) *n.* inordinate desire for wealth; greed; covetousness. —**av"a·ri'cious** (-rish'əs) *adj.*

a·vast' (ə-vást') *interj.* (*Naut.*) stop! hold!

av'a·tar" (av'ə-tär") *n.* (*Hindu*) incarnation of a deity.

A've Ma·ri'a (ä'vä mä-rē'ə) a prayer, the Hail Mary, from Luke 1:28 and 1:42 and other sources.

a·venge' (ə-venj') *v.t.* exact satisfaction or vengeance for or on behalf of.

> **avenge, revenge**
> ☛ Though these two words used to be synonymous, a distinction is now often made: one *avenges* wrongs done to someone else, but one *revenges* wrongs done to oneself.

av'e·nue" (av'ə-nū") *n.* **1,** a wide street. **2,** any roadway of approach, passageway, or means of access.

a·ver' (ə-vēr') *v.t.* [**a·verred', a·ver'ring**] declare in a positive manner; affirm with confidence.

av'er·age (av'ər-ij) *n.* **1,** the mean value of a series of quantities, determined by dividing their sum by their number. **2,** any mean, typical, or normal number, quantity, degree, quality, etc. —*adj.* intermediate, typical, or normal. —*v.i.* **1,** determine an average of. **2,** result in an average of.

---

average, mean, median

☛ *Average, arithmetic mean,* or *mean* is the sum of a set of numbers divided by the number of numbers in the set. The *median* is that number that has the same number of values larger than it as there are values smaller than it. ↔ The word *average* derives from an Arabic term for "damaged goods." It later acquired the sense of financial loss for damaged goods, then the sense of the sharing of such a loss, then its present sense of "mean."

---

a·verse' (ə-vērs') *adj.* **1,** disposed against; reluctant. **2,** turned away from in position. ❏ *adverse.*

a·ver'sion (ə-vēr'zhən) *n.* **1,** dislike. **2,** that which is disliked. —**aversion therapy,** a therapy designed to change behavior by use of unpleasant stimulus.

a·vert' (ə-vērt') *v.t.* **1,** ward off; prevent. **2,** turn away.

a'vi·ar"y (ā'vē-er"ē) *n.* an enclosure in which birds are kept.

a"vi·a'tion (ā"vē-ā'shən) *n.* the art or science of flying in the air, esp. in heavier-than-air aircraft.

a'vi·a"tor (ā'vē-ā"tər) *n.* a member of an aircraft's operating crew, esp. a pilot. —**a'vi·ate,** *v.i.*

av'id *adj.* eager. —**a·vid'i·ty** (ə-vid'ə-tē) *n.* eagerness.

a"vi·on'ics (ā"vē-on'iks) *n.* the use of electronic devices in aviation. —**a"vi·on'ic,** *adj.*

av"o·ca'do (av"ə-kä'dō) *n.* [*pl.* **-dos**] *n.* a tropical American fruit: the alligator pear.

---

avocado, advocate

☛ *Avocado* is derived from Nahuatl *ahuacatl,* testicle, and comes to English through Spanish. It is not related to *advocate,* or its French equivalent *avocat,* which derive from Latin *advocatus,* called as a witness, from *vocare,* to call.

---

av"o·ca'tion (av"ə-kā'shən) *n.* an occupation pursued for pleasure or diversion; a hobby.

a·void' (ə-void') *v.t.* keep away from; shun; refrain from. —**a·void'ance,** *n.*

av"oir·du·pois' (av"ər-də-poiz') *n.* **1,** the system of weights in which the ounce, pound, and ton are used. **2,** (*Informal*) body weight.

a·vouch' (ə-vowch') *v.t.* **1,** vouch for; guarantee. **2,** acknowledge frankly.

a·vow' (ə-vow') *n.* declare openly; admit or confess frankly; acknowledge. —**a·vow'al** (əl) *n.*

a·vun'cu·lar (ə-vung'kū-lər) *adj.* like or pert. to an uncle.

AWAC (ā'wak) *n.* an aircraft equipped for sophisticated airborne reconnaisance: *a*(ircraft) *w*(arning) *a*(nd) *c*(ontrol).

a·wait' (ə-wāt') *v.t.* **1,** wait for; look for and expect. **2,** lie in store for.

a·wake' (ə-wāk') *v.i. & t.* [**-woke',** **-waked', -wak'ing**] **1,** wake up. **2,** call into being or action; bestir. —*adj.* **1,** not sleeping. **2,** alert; vigilant.

a·wak'en (ə-wā'kən) *v.i. & t.* awake. —**a·wak'en·ing,** *n.* a sudden awareness or excitement.

a·ward' (ə-wôrd') *v.t.* bestow as a prize or reward, or as something due. —*n.* **1,** anything awarded. **2,** a decision of a judge or arbiter.

---

award, reward

☛ An *award* is a prize given for achievement, often as the result of a judging. A *reward* is a prize given in appreciation for a deed, usu. a good deed.

---

a·ware' (ə-wār') *adj.* conscious (of); informed; cognizant.

a·wash' (ə-wosh') *adv. & adj.* (*Naut.*) just at water level.

a·way' (ə-wā') *adv.* **1,** from this place; off; apart; aside. **2,** out of one's presence, possession, or attention. —*adj.* **1,** absent. **2,** distant.

awe (â) *n.* fear mingled with admiration or reverence. —*v.t.* inspire with awe.

a·weigh' (ə-wā') *adj.* of an anchor, raised so that a ship may sail.

awe'some (-səm) *adj.* **1,** inspiring awe. **2,** (*Slang*) excellent. —**awe'some·ness,** *n.*

awe'struck" *adj.* feeling awe.

aw'ful (â'fəl) *adj.* **1,** inspiring reverential fear. **2,** (*Informal*) extremely bad or unpleasant. —*adv.* [also, **aw'ful·ly**] (*Informal*) very. —**aw'ful·ness,** *n.*

a·while' (ə-hwīl') *adv.* for a short time.

awk'ward (âk'wərd) *adj.* **1,** lacking dexterity or skill; clumsy. **2,** ungraceful; uncouth. **3,** ill-adapted for use. **4,** difficult to handle or deal with; requiring caution. **5,** embarrassing. —**awk'ward·ness,** *n.*

---

awkward
↔ Derived from the Middle English *awk*, meaning "wrong way round," *awkward* originally meant "turned in the wrong direction."

---

awl (âl) *n.* a tool for punching small holes in leather, wood, etc.

awn'ing (â'ning) *n.* a cloth or metal covering, usu. movable, placed above a door or window; a sunshade.

a·woke' (ə-wōk') *v.* pret. of *awake.*

a·wry' (ə-rī') *adv. & adj.* away from a true direction or position; askew; perverse.

ax (aks) *n.* **1,** a cutting tool or weapon, comprising a heavy-bladed head fixed to a handle. **2,** (*Slang*) a musical instrument. —*v.t.* **1,** trim with an ax. **2,** (*Slang*) discharge from employment; injure. Also, **axe.** —**get the ax,** (*Slang*) be discharged or fired.

ax'el (aks'əl) *n.* a type of jump in figure-skating, named for Norwegian figure skater Axel Paulsen, who developed the maneuver.

ax'i·om (ak'sē-əm) *n.* **1,** a proposition deemed to be self-evident and assumed without proof. **2,** a universal proposition, amply proved, easily verifiable, or generally accepted. —**ax'i·o·mat'ic** (-mat'ik) *adj.* —**ax''i·o·mat'i·cal·ly,** *adv.*

ax'is (ak'sis) *n.* [*pl.* **-es** (-sēz)] **1,** the line about which a rotating body turns. **2,** the line with respect to which a body or structure is symmetrical. **3,** a principal supporting member. **4,** (*cap.*) the military alliance of Germany and Italy in World War II. —**ax'i·al** (ak'sē-əl) *adj.*

ax'le (ak'səl) *n.* the pin or shaft on which a wheel turns, or which turns with it on a bearing.

ax'o·lotl'' (ak'sə-lot''əl) *n.* a salamander of the U.S. and Mexico.

ax'on (aks'on) *n.* the branch of a neuron that carries impulses away from the cell body.

a'yah (ä'yə) *n.* a Hindu nurse or maid.

a''yah·tol'lah (ä''yə-tō'lə) *n.* (*Persian*) a Muslim religious leader of the Shiite sect.

aye (ī) *adv. & n.* **1,** yes. **2,** always. Also, **ay.**

aye'-aye' (ī'-ī') *n.* a Madagascan lemur.

Ayr'shire (âr'shər) *n.* one of a breed of dairy cattle.

a·zal'ea (ə-zāl'yə) *n.* a plant bearing brightly colored flowers.

az'i·muth (az'ə-məth) *n.* **1,** an angle measured clockwise from north to south.

2, (*Astron.*) this angle measured on a horizon circle.

AZT *n.* an antiviral drug, azidothymidine, used in the treatment of AIDS.

Az'tec (az'tek) *adj.* pert. to an aboriginal Native American group.

az'ure (azh'ər) *adj. & n.* sky blue.

B

B, b (bē) second letter of the English alphabet.

baa (bä) *v.i.* [**baaed, baa'ing**] *& n.* bleat.

ba'ba (bä'bä) *n.* a type of sponge cake usually soaked with rum.

bab'bitt (bab'it) *n.* **1,** [also, **Babbitt metal**] an alloy of tin, lead, copper and antimony. **2,** (*cap.*) a smug, conformist, middle-class Amer. businessman.

---

babbitt
↔ The metal is named for its inventor, Isaac *Babbitt*. Def. 2 is from the title character of Sinclair Lewis's novel *Babbitt.*

---

bab'ble (bab'əl) *v.i.* **1,** talk idly; chatter. **2,** utter words imperfectly; prattle. —*v.t.* utter incoherently. —*n.* chatter; prattle.

babe (bāb) *n.* **1,** baby. **2,** (*Slang*) girl.

ba'bel (bā'bəl) *n.* confused and overpowering sound; discord.

---

babel
↔ From the ancient city of Babel (Gen. 11:4-9), where a tower was built to reach Heaven. The word comes from Assyrian *bab-ilu*, gate of god.

---

ba'bies'-breath'' (bā'bēz-) *n.* a plant with small white or pink flowers.

ba·boon' *n.* any of several large monkeys.

ba·bush'ka (bə-boosh'kə) *n.* a woman's scarf worn over the head and tied under the chin.

ba'by (bā'bē) *n.* **1,** a very young child; infant. **2,** a childish person. **3,** the youngest child. **4,** (*Slang*) pet (term of endearment). —*adj.* **1,** suited for a baby; infantile. **2,** small. —*v.t.* pamper. —**baby boom,** an increase in population rate in the U.S. in the decade following the end of World War II. —**baby boomer,** a child born during the baby boom. Also, **boom'er.** —**ba'by·hood,** *n.*

ba'by-sit'' *v.i.* act as a temporary nurse for a child. —**ba'by-sit''ter,** *n.*

bac″ca·lau′re·ate (bak″ə-lôr′ĕ-ət) *adj.* pert. to or designating an address given before a graduating class. —*n.* a college or university bachelor's degree.

bac″ca·rat′ (bäk″ä-rä′) *n.* a gambling game played with cards.

bac′cha·nal″ (bäk′ə-nal″) *n.* **1,** a drunken orgy. **2,** a reveler; carouser. —**bac″cha·na′li·an** (-nā′lĕ-ən) *adj. & n.*

Bac′chic (bak′ik) *adj.* **1,** pert. to Bacchus or bacchanalian rites. **2,** (*l.c.*) jovially or riotously intoxicated.

bach′e·lor (bach′ə-lər) *n.* **1,** an unmarried man. **2,** recipient of a college degree. —**bach′e·lor·hood″,** *n.*

> **bachelor**
> ↔ Of obscure origin, the word came to English from French *bacheler*, squire.

bach″e·lor·ette′ (bach″ə-lər-et′) *n.* a young unmarried woman.

ba·cil′lus (bə-sil′əs) *n.* [*pl.* **-li** (-lī)] a rod-shaped bacterium.

back (bak) *n.* **1,** the spinal, posterior, or dorsal side or surface of an animal. **2,** the rear or hind part of anything. **3,** support or stiffening in general. **4,** a player and his position in certain athletic games, as football. —*v.t.* **1,** furnish with a back; support or favor. **2,** cause to move backward. —*v.i.* **1,** (often with *up*) go backward. **2,** (with *down*) retreat; surrender. **3,** (with *off*) relent; soften. **4,** (with *out*) renege (on an arrangement). —*adv.* **1,** toward the rear. **2,** toward the past. —**back′er,** *n.* a financial sponsor, as of a person or enterprise. —**back and fill,** shilly-shally. —**back talk,** an insolent or argumentative reply. —**back up, 1,** reinforce; support. **2,** (*Computers*) make a copy of (as a computer file) for storage and preservation.

back′beat″ *n.* the characteristic driving beat of rock music.

back′bite″ (bak′bīt″) *v.t. & i.* speak evil of (an absent person).

back′board″ *n.* a board or rigid sheet used as backing or reinforcement; esp. the board placed behind the basket on a basketball court.

back′bone″ (bak′bōn″) *n.* **1,** the human spine or vertebral column; any similar supporting or stiffening member. **2,** firmness; resolution.

back′date″ *v.t.* antedate.

back′fire″ *n.* **1,** a premature explosion in a gasoline engine. **2,** a fire set to check a forest fire. **3,** a result opposite to what was intended. —*v.i.* produce a backfire.

back-′for·ma″tion *n.* the creation of a word from what appears to be an inflected form by dropping the apparent prefix or suffix: *in-law* from *mother-in-law.*

back′gam″mon (bak′gam″ən) *n.* a game played by moving pieces (*stones*) on a board in accordance with casts of dice. Also, **gam′mon.**

back′ground″ *n.* **1,** the more distant objects and planes of sight in a view or picture. **2,** antecedent events and circumstances, in relation to a person or later event.

back′hand″ *n.* **1,** writing that slopes to the left. **2,** in tennis, a backhand stroke. —*adj.* performed with the hand turned back outward, as a backhand stroke in tennis.

back′hand″ed *adj.* **1,** backhand. **2,** oblique in meaning; ironic.

back′lash″ *n.* **1,** jarring recoil of badly fitted or worn parts, as in a machine. **2,** a snarl of a fishing line in the reel. **3,** a strong reaction, esp. to social change.

back-′list″ *n.* a publisher's list of previously published books which are kept in stock.

back′log″ (bak′lâg″) *n.* something in reserve; unfilled orders on hand.

back′lot″ *adj.* an outdoor area connected with a motion picture studio used for shooting exterior scenes.

back·or′der *v.t.* hold an order for (merchandise temporarily out of stock) to be filled at some later date. —*n.* an order so held.

back′slash″ *n.* a character consisting of a line with its top angling toward the left (\).

back′slide″ (bak′slīd″) *v.i.* relapse into evil ways; retrogress.

back′stairs″ *adj.* indirect; underhand; secret.

back′stop″ *n.* **1,** a screen. **2,** (*Baseball*) the catcher.

back′track″ *v.i.* **1,** return over the same course; retreat. **2,** withdraw from an agreement, project, etc.

back′up″ *n.* **1,** a substitute or alternative. **2,** one or more singers or musicians accompanying a soloist. **3,** (*Computers*) a copy of a file, usu. made for preservation.

back′ward (bak′wərd) *adv.* [*also,* **back′wards**] *& adj.* **1,** toward the back or rear. **2,** with back foremost; reverse. **3,** in reverse order. **4,** toward or in past time. —*adj.* **1,** late in time; slow; unprogressive. **2,** reluctant; shy.

back′wash″ *n.* **1,** water or air thrown back by an oar, propeller, etc. **2,** aftermath.

---

back′wa″ter *n.* **1,** a pool of water, often stagnant, held back by a dam, etc. **2,** a situation or place considered stagnant or backward. —*adj.* (*Informal*) rustic; lacking culture.

back′woods″ (bak′wûdz″) *adj.* primitive; uncultivated. —*n.* an isolated or unsettled area.

ba′con (bā′kən) *n.* meat from the back and sides of the hog, salted and dried.

bac·te′ri·a (bak-tir′ē-ə) *n.pl.* [*sing.* -**um**] vegetable microörganisms that cause fermentation, decay, disease, etc. —**bac·te′ri·al,** *adj.*

bac·te′ri·cide (bak-tir′ə-sīd) *n.* an agent that destroys bacteria. —**bac″te″ri·ci′dal,** *adj.*

bac·te″ri·ol′o·gy (bak-tir″ē-ol′ə-jē) *n.* the science dealing with bacteria. —**bac·te″ri·o·log′i·cal** (-ə-loj′i-kəl) *adj.* —**bac″te″ri·ol′o·gist,** *n.*

bad *adj.* [**worse, worst**] **1,** wicked; vicious. **2,** not good; defective; not valid. **3,** hurtful; noxious. **4,** unfavorable; unfortunate. **5,** sick. **6,** (*Slang*) excellent; very good. —*n.* any thing or condition that is bad. —**bad′ness,** *n.* —**bad actor,** (*Slang*) a malicious or ill-tempered person. —**bad blood,** a feeling of enmity. —**bad egg,** (*Slang*) a scoundrel. —**bad news,** (*Informal*) (*construed as sing.*) a troublesome person or situation.

> **bad**
> ↔ The origins of *bad* appear to be in Old English words for homosexual, *baeddel* and *baedling*.

bade (bad) *v.* pret. of **bid.**

badge (baj) *n.* a token, mark, or device worn to show allegiance, honors, etc.

badg′er (baj′ər) *n.* a carnivorous mammal prized for its fur. —*v.t.* pester; harass.

bad″i·nage′ (bad″ə-näzh′) *n.* playful banter; raillery.

bad′lands″ *n.pl.* a barren region with eroded rock formations.

bad′ly (-lē) *adv.* **1,** with bad effect. **2,** (*Informal*) very much.

bad′min·ton (bad′min-tən) *n.* an outdoor game similar to tennis played with rackets (*battledores*) and shuttlecocks.

> **badminton**
> ↔ The game is named for the country seat of the Duke of Beaufort in Gloucestershire, England, where it was presumably first played.

bad′mouth″ *v.t.* (*Slang*) speak ill of.

baf′fle (baf′əl) *v.t.* disconcert by interposing obstacles; frustrate; confuse.

—*n.* **1,** an obstacle. **2,** a device or structure for deflecting light, sound, etc. —**baf′fle·ment,** *n.*

bag *n.* **1,** a portable receptacle made of a flexible material, capable of being closed at the mouth. **2,** a suitcase. **3,** anything formed like or serving the purpose of a bag. **4,** the contents of a bag; an amount taken or collected. **5,** (*Slang*) an old woman. **6,** (*Slang*) function or purpose in life. —*v.t.* [**bagged, bag′ging**] capture. —*v.i.* **1,** swell out; bulge. **2,** hang loosely. —**bag person (man, woman), 1,** a street person. **2,** (*Slang*) a go-between; a collector of illicit goods.

ba·gasse′ (bə-gas′) *n.* crushed refuse from sugar making; paper made from the fibers of this refuse.

bag″a·telle′ (bag″ə-tel′) *n.* **1,** anything trifling. **2,** a game played by striking balls with a cue.

ba′gel (bā′gəl) *n.* a ring-shaped roll.

bag′gage (bag′ij) *n.* **1,** containers, as trunks, suitcases, etc., used by a traveler. **2,** (*Offensive*) a saucy young woman.

bag′gy (bag′ē) *adj.* bulging; hanging loosely. —**bag′gi·ness,** *n.*

bag′pipe″ (bag′pīp″) *n.* a musical instrument with several reed pipes, one melodic and the rest drones, actuated by a wind bag.

ba·guette′ (ba-get′) *n.* **1,** a gem cut oblong. **2,** a narrow oblong shape.

bah (bä) *interj.* of disgust or contempt.

bail (bāl) *n.* (*Law*) security given to obtain the temporary release of a prisoner. —*v.t.* **1,** grant or obtain release of a prisoner in bail. **2,** (often with *out*) remove (water) from a boat with a bucket or pump. —**bails′man,** *n.* one who gives or guarantees bail. —**bail out, 1,** bail (def. 2). **2,** jump from an airplane with a parachute. **3,** assist, esp. financially.

> **bail, bale**
> ☞ Do not confuse *bail*, to remove water from, with *bale*, pack into bundles.

bai′ley (bā′lē) *n.* [*pl.* -**leys**] the outermost fortification of a castle. —**Old Bailey,** the English criminal court.

bail′iff (bā′lif) *n.* a deputy officer of a court of law.

bail′i·wick (bāl′ə-wik) *n.* an area of jurisdiction, activity, or influence.

bail′out″ *n.* **1,** act of parachuting. **2,** case of rescuing, especially financially.

bain-′ma·rie′ (bān′mə-rē′) [*pl.* **bains**-

(bān′-)] *n.* a cooking pot used for steaming.

> **bain-marie**
> ↔ From an alchemical device belonging, according to legend, to Mary, sister of Moses, and named, after her, *kaminos Marias*, Mary's furnace.

bait (bāt) *n.* **1,** a lure placed on a fishhook or in a trap. **2,** any device of allurement. —*v.t.* **1,** place bait on or in. **2,** torment; tease. —**bait-and-switch,** *adj.* pert. to an unethical sales method involving advertisement of an item, often nonexistent, at a very low price to lure customers, with the intent to induce them subsequently to purchase a different, higher-priced item.

baize (bāz) *n.* a feltlike woolen fabric.

bake (bāk) *v.t. & i.* **1,** cook by dry heat. **2,** harden by heat. —*v.i.* become baked. —**baked Alaska,** a dessert of cake and ice cream, topped with meringue, and quickly browned in an oven. —**baking powder,** a preparation of baking soda and an acid, used for leavening. —**baking soda,** sodium bicarbonate.

Ba′ke·lite″ (bā′kə-līt″) *n.* (*T.N.*) a thermosetting plastic made of phenol and formaldehyde.

> **Bakelite**
> ↔ From the name of its Belgian inventor, L. H. Baekeland.

bak′er (bā′kər) *n.* one whose business is baking bread. —**baker's dozen,** thirteen.

> **baker's dozen**
> ↔ From a practice of giving 13 to the dozen to avoid the risk of penalties for short weights.

bak′er·y (bā′kə-rė) *n.* a baker's shop or plant.

bak′la·va (bak′lə-və) *n.* a layered pastry filled with nuts and honey.

bak·sheesh′ (bäk-shēsh′) *n.* tip; gratuity.

bal″a·lai′ka (bal′ə-lī′kə) *n.* a Russian musical instrument of the guitar type.

bal′ance (bal′əns) *n.* **1,** an instrument for weighing. **2,** equal distribution of weight; a state of equilibrium; harmonious arrangement of parts. **3,** mental stability; good judgment. **4,** equality between two sides of an account. **5,** an excess or remainder. —*v.t.* **1,** bring into balance or equilibrium. **2,** arrange in harmonious form. **3,** weigh; estimate; compare. **4,** equalize two sides of an account. —*v.i.* come into equilibrium; be harmonious.

—**balance of payments,** the difference in value between a country's exports and imports. —**balance of power,** an equilibrium of power (between states).

bal·bo′a (bal-bō′ə) *n.* the monetary unit of Panama.

> **balboa**
> ↔ Named for the 16th-c. Spanish explorer Vasco Núñez de *Balboa*, who discovered the Pacific Ocean.

bal·brig′gan (bal-brig′ən) *n.* unbleached cotton, used chiefly for underwear, first made in Balbriggan, Ireland.

bal′co·ny (bal′kə-nē) *n.* **1,** a platform projecting from a wall, having an outer railing or parapet. **2,** an elevated tier of seats in a theater.

bald (bâld) *adj.* **1,** destitute of hair or other natural covering. **2,** bare; unadorned. **3,** undisguised. —**bald′ing,** *adj.* becoming bald. —**bald′ness,** *n.*

bal′da·chin (bal′də-kin) *n.* **1,** a canopy over an altar, throne, etc. **2,** a heavy, ornate silk fabric.

bal′der·dash″ (bâl′dər-dash″) *n.* a nonsensical jumble of words.

bald-′faced″ (-fāst″) *adj.* barefaced.

bal′dric (bâl′drik) *n.* an ornamented belt, worn diagonally over one shoulder.

bale (bāl) *n.* **1,** a large bundle of merchandise, closely compressed and bound. **2,** (sorrow; woe. —*v.t.* pack into bales. ❑ *bail*

ba·leen′ (bə-lēn′) *n.* a flexible, bony substance from a whale; whalebone.

bale′ful (bāl′fəl) *adj.* menacing; malign. —**bale′ful·ness,** *n.*

balk (bâk) *n.* **1,** an obstacle; a check or defeat. **2,** a blunder or failure. **3,** (*Baseball*) a penalizable feint by the pitcher. **4,** a heavy wooden timber. —*v.t.* hinder; thwart. —*v.i.* stop at an obstacle; refuse to act or continue. —**balk′y,** *adj.*

ball (bâl) *n.* **1,** any round or roundish body; sphere; globe. **2,** any of various games played with balls, as *football, baseball.* **3,** (*Baseball*) a pitch not struck at by the batter and ruled to be too high, low, or wide. **4,** a solid projectile fired from a gun. **5,** a social assembly for dancing. **6,** (*Slang*) a highball. —*v.t.* (with *up*) (*Slang*) disarrange; confuse. —**ball bearing, 1,** a bearing composed of hard balls moving in grooves. **2,** a ball used in a bearing. —**ball game, 1,** a game or sport involving use of a ball, as baseball. **2,** (*Informal*) set of conditions or circumstances. —**ball park,** (*Informal*) approximate. —**on the ball,** (*Slang*) alert.

bal′lad (bal′əd) *n.* a simple narrative poem; a sentimental song.

bal·lade′ (bə-läd′) *n.* **1,** a poem of three stanzas and an envoy. **2,** (*Music*) a composition in a romantic mood.

bal′last (bal′əst) *n.* **1,** heavy material carried to increase stability or decrease buoyancy. **2,** crushed stone, etc., forming the bed of a railroad.

ball′boy, ball′girl *n.* (*Baseball, Tennis*) a person, usually a youth, who retrieves balls, etc.

bal″le·ri′na (bal″ə-rē′nə) *n.* a female ballet dancer.

bal′let (bal′ā) *n.* **1,** a theatrical pantomime of dancing and music. **2,** a stylized form of solo and group dancing. **3,** a troupe of professional dancers.

bal·let′o·mane (ba-let′ō-mān) *n.* an enthusiastic spectator of ballet dancing.

bal·lis′tics (bə-lis′tiks) *n.* the science of the motion of projectiles.

bal·loon′ (bə-loon′) *n.* **1,** an airship that derives its lift from a large bag inflated with a gas lighter than air. **2,** an inflated rubber bag, used as a child's toy. **3,** (in cartoons) a loop enclosing words represented as issuing from the mouth of a speaker. —*v.i.* swell out. —*adj.* of a loan, having a final payment much larger than the preceding payments. —**bal·loon′ist,** *n.*

bal′lot (bal′ət) *n.* **1,** a ticket or other device for marking an individual vote. **2,** the casting of ballots; the whole number of votes recorded. —*v.i.* **1,** vote by ballot. **2,** draw lots.

ball′point″ pen a fountain pen with a minute ball for a point.

ball′room″ *n.* a room for dancing.

bal′ly·hoo″ (bal′ē-hoo″) *n.* crude or blatant advertising. —*v.t.* promote by ballyhoo.

balm (bäm) *n.* **1,** any of various aromatic resinous substances. **2,** anything that soothes or mitigates pain.

balm′y *adj.* **1,** mild. **2,** fragrant. **3,** (*Slang*) mildly insane. —**balm′i·ness,** *n.*

ba·lo′ney (bə-lō′nē) *n.* **1,** (*Informal*) bologna. **2,** (*Slang*) nonsense; humbug.

bal′sa (bâl′sə) *n.* a tree having exceedingly light wood.

bal′sam (bâl′səm) *n.* **1,** balm. **2,** transparent turpentine. **3,** any plant or tree yielding balsam.

bal′us·ter (bal′ə-stər) *n.* an ornamental upright post giving support to a rail.

bal″us·trade′ (bal″ə-strād′) *n.* a row of balusters topped by a rail.

bam·boo′ *n.* **1,** a woody tropical grass.

2, its hollow stem. —**bamboo curtain,** an ideological and political barrier in the Far East.

> **bamboo**
> ↔ Of Malay origin, the first form of the word was *mambu,* which over time was transformed into the present form.

bam·boo′zle (bam-boo′zəl) *v.t.* deceive by trickery; mystify.

bam·bou′la (bam-boo′lə) *n.* a traditional dance of New Orleans Creoles.

ban *v.t.* [**banned, ban′ning**] forbid; prohibit. —*n.* **1,** prohibition. **2,** denunciation.

ba′nal (bā′nəl; bə-nal′) *adj.* commonplace; trite. —**ba·nal′i·ty** (bə-nal′ə-tē) *n.*

ba·nan′a (bə-nan′ə) *n.* a tropical fruit. —**bananas,** *adj.* (*Slang*) crazy. —**banana seat,** a long, slim bicycle saddle with an upward-curving back.

band *n.* **1,** a flat strip of flexible material, used to bind, confine, trim, or ornament. **2,** a stripe; a zone marked off from adjacent areas. **3,** a company of persons traveling or acting together. **4,** a group of musicians playing together, esp. a group not including stringed instruments. —*v.t.* & *i.* unite.

band′age (ban′dij) *n.* cloth used to bind up a wound.

Band-′Aid″ **1,** (*T.N.*) a brand of adhesive bandage. **2,** (*Informal*) a temporary, makeshift remedy.

ban·dan′na (ban-dan′ə) *n.* a large colored handkerchief.

> **bandanna**
> ↔ From Hindi *badhnu,* tie-dyeing.

band′box″ (band′boks″) *n.* a hat box; a small compartment or room.

ban·deau′ (ban-dō′) *n.* a band worn on the head.

ban′de·role″ (ban′də-rōl″) *n.* a ribbon, streamer, or small flag.

ban′di·coot″ (ban′di-koot″) *n.* **1,** a large E. Indian rat. **2,** a small marsupial of Australia.

ban′dit *n.* a robber, esp. one of a band of marauders. —**ban′dit·ry,** *n.*

ban″do·leer′ (ban″də-lir′) *n.* a cartridge belt worn over the shoulders. Also, **ban″do·lier′.**

band′stand″ *n.* a platform on which a musical band plays.

band′wag″on *n.* **1,** a vehicle carrying a musical band in a parade. **2,** (*Slang*) the successful side, as in an election.

band′width″ *n.* **1,** (*Radio & TV*) the

smallest frequency range within which a signal can be transmitted without distortion. **2,** (*Computers*) the amount of information that can pass between two devices in a certain period of time.

ban′dy (ban′dė) *v.t.* strike, throw, or pass back and forth; give and take. —*adj.* crooked. —**ban′dy-leg″ged**, *adj.* having bowlegs.

bane (bān) *n.* **1,** a deadly poison. **2,** anything that destroys or spoils. —**bane′ful,** *adj.* harmful.

bang *n.* **1,** a loud, explosive noise, of a gun, etc. **2,** (*Informal*) energy; spirit. **3,** (*Slang*) thrill. **4,** (usu. *pl.*) a fringe of short, evenly cut hairs over the forehead. **5,** exclamation point. —*v.t.* **1,** knock about; drub; slam. **2,** (with *up*) (*Slang*) smash; damage. —*v.i.* **1,** strike violently. **2,** make a sudden, loud noise. —*adv.* suddenly; loudly.

bang′er *n.* (*Brit.*) sausage.

ban′gle (bang′gəl) *n.* an ornamental bracelet without a clasp.

bang-′up″ *adj.* (*Slang*) first-rate.

ban′ish *v.t.* put in exile; drive away; dismiss. —**ban′ish·ment,** *n.*

ban′is·ter (ban′is-tər) *n.* **1,** baluster. **2,** the handrail of a staircase.

ban′jo (ban′jō) *n.* [*pl.* **-jos**] a musical stringed instrument with a circular head. —**ban′jo·ist,** *n.*

bank *n.* **1,** a long pile or ridge, as of earth. **2,** a slope; the border of a watercourse. **3,** an elevated plateau in the sea or a river; a shoal. **4,** lateral inclination. **5,** a tier, as of keys on an organ. **6,** an institution for receiving and lending money; the quarters of such an institution. **7,** a store, fund, reserve, or depository. —*v.t.* **1,** provide with or form into a bank. **2,** give a lateral inclination to. **3,** cover up (a fire). **4,** deposit in a bank. —*v.i.* **1,** act as a banker. **2,** depend or rely (on).—**bank card,** a plastic card issued by a bank for identification or for use in automated teller machines.

---

bank
↔ All senses derive from the idea of a bench of some sort. The sense of pile is from Old English *hobanca*, a couch. The institution is traced back to Old High German *bank*, bench. The sense of a tier is also Germanic, through Old French *banc*, bench.

---

bank′a·ble, *adj.* of a business venture, etc., certain to produce a profit.

bank′er (-ər) *n.* one who conducts or works in a bank. —**bank′ing,** *n.*

bank′note″ *n.* a piece of paper money.

bank′roll″ *n.* money supply; funds. —*v.t.* (*Slang*) supply the capital for (a venture).

bank′rupt *n.* (*Law*) one who is adjudged insolvent. —*adj.* unable to pay debts; bereft. —*v.t.* make bankrupt. —**bank′rupt·cy** (-sė) *n.*

ban′ner (ban′ər) *n.* **1,** a flag, pennant, or other device emblematic of a country, faith, etc. **2,** anything displayed as a profession of principles. **3,** a headline extending across the full width of a newspaper. —*adj.* foremost; leading.

banns (banz) *n.pl.* notice of an intended marriage.

ban′quet (bang′kwit) *n.* a sumptuous meal, esp. one given in honor of a person or an occasion.

ban·quette′ (bang-ket′) *n.* **1,** a ledge along the inside of a parapet. **2,** a bench; shelf.

ban′shee″ (ban′shē″) *n.* a wailing spirit that heralds death.

---

banshee
↔ From Gaelic *bean sidhe*, woman of the fairy mound.

---

ban′tam (ban′təm) *n.* **1,** a small variety of chicken. **2,** any small animal. —*adj.* very small.

ban′tam·weight″ *n.* a boxer of 112 to 118 pounds.

ban′ter (ban′tər) *n.* playful talk; good-humored raillery. —*v.t. & i.* make fun of; chaff.

Ban′tu (ban′too) *n. & adj.* pert. to a large family of African tribes.

Bantu
☛ This word may be considered offensive by Africans and should be used with care.

---

ban′yan (ban′yən) *n.* an E. Ind. fig tree.

ban′zai″ (bän′zī″) *interj.* (*Jap.*) may he (it) live 10,000 years!

---

banzai, bonsai
☛ Do not confuse the interjection *banzai* with the horticultural technique of *bonsai*. Both are Japanese.

---

ba′o·bab″ (bā′ō-bab″) *n.* a tropical Afr. tree which bears a gourdlike fruit.

bap′tism (bap′tiz-əm) *n.* a sacrament of the Christian church, signalized by sprinkling with or immersion in water. —**baptis′mal** (-tiz′məl) *adj.*

Bap′tist *n.* a member of a certain Christian denomination.

---

bap′tis·ter·y (bǎp′tis-trē) *n.* a place, font, or tank used in baptism.

bap′tize″ (-tīz″) *v.t.* **1,** administer baptism to. **2,** christen; name. **3,** cleanse spiritually.

bar (bär) *n.* **1,** a rod used as an obstruction or guard. **2,** anything that obstructs. **3,** a band or stripe; anything of oblong shape. **4,** a room where liquors are sold: *barroom.* **5,** lawyers as a whole; the legal profession. **6,** any tribunal. **7,** (*Music*) a vertical line marking the division between measures; a measure. —*v.t.* [**barred, bar′-ring**] **1,** shut out; exclude. **2,** block; close. —*prep.* except. —**bar code,** a machine-readable code composed of vertical bars of differing widths, used for marking merchandise.

barb (bärb) *n.* **1,** a pointed part projecting backward, as on a fishhook. **2,** a beardlike growth or member. **3,** a spiteful remark. —**barbed,** *adj.* **1,** having a hooked point. **2,** spiteful.

bar·bar′i·an (bär-bâr′ē-ən) *n.* a man in a primitive, savage, or uncivilized state. —*adj.* uncivilized.

bar·bar′ic (bär-bar′ik) *adj.* **1,** of or like barbarians. **2,** magnificent but crude. —**bar·bar′i·cal·ly,** *adv.*

bar′ba·rism (bär′bə-riz-əm) *n.* **1,** lack of civilization. **2,** something barbarous. **3,** a word, phrase, form, etc., alien to accepted usage.

bar·bar′i·ty (bär-bar′ə-tē) *n.* **1,** brutality; cruelty. **2,** crudeness.

bar′bar·ous (bär′bə-rəs) *adj.* **1,** uncultured; crude. **2,** brutal; cruel. —**bar′bar·ous·ness,** *n.*

bar′be·cue″ (bär′bə-kū″) *n.* **1,** a social gathering where animal carcasses are roasted whole; any cookout. **2,** a large grille or frame for roasting. —*v.t.* **1,** broil or roast (a carcass) whole. **2,** cook (meat or fish) in a highly seasoned sauce.

---

barbecue
↔ From Sp. *barbacoa,* a type of cooking frame.

---

bar′bell″ *n.* a bar with removable weights used in weightlifting.

bar′ber (bär′bər) *n.* one whose occupation is to shave the beard, cut and dress the hair. —*v.t.* trim or dress the facial hair of.

bar′ber″ry (bär′be″rē) *n.* a shrub whose roots yield a bitter tonic.

bar·bette′ (bär-bet′) *n.* (*Mil.*) a gun platform or housing.

bar′bi·can (bär′bi-kən) *n.* an outpost, usu. a tower, defending the approach to a castle, bridge, etc.

bar′bi·tal″ (bär′bə-tâl″) *n.* a sleep-producing drug.

bar·bit′u·rate″ (bär-bit′yû-rāt″) *n.* one of various sedative drugs.

bar′ca·role″ (bär′kə-rōl″) *n.* a boating song.

bard (bärd) *n.* poet; minstrel.

bare (bâr) *adj.* **1,** without clothing or covering; naked; nude. **2,** without usual furniture or equipment. **3,** bald; unadorned. **4,** open to view; not concealed. **5,** scarcely or just sufficient. —*v.t.* lay open to view; denude; strip. —**bare′ness,** *n.*

bare′back″ *adv. & adj.* without a saddle.

bare′faced″ (-fāst″) *adj.* **1,** boldly open; undisguised. **2,** shameless.

bare′foot″ *adj.* with bare feet.

bare′ly (-lē) *adv.* **1,** only; just. **2,** openly; nakedly.

barf (bärf) *v.i.* (*Slang*) vomit.

bar′fly″ *n.* (*Informal*) one who frequents barrooms.

bar′gain (bär′gən) *n.* **1,** an agreement as to sale or exchange of goods. **2,** an advantageous purchase. —*v.i.* discuss terms of sale; haggle.

barge (bärj) *n.* **1,** an unpowered boat for transporting goods. **2,** any capacious, slow-moving, or ceremonial vessel. —*v.i.* **1,** move in a slow, heavy manner. **2,** (with *in*) (*Informal*) intrude in a rude manner. **3,** (with *into*) (*Informal*) collide with.

bar·gel′lo (bär-jel′ō) *n.* a type of straight stitch used in needlepoint work.

bar′girl″ *n.* (*Offensive*) **1,** a barmaid, esp. one employed to entice men to buy drinks. **2,** a promiscuous woman; prostitute. Also, **B-′girl″.**

bar′i·tone″ (bar′ə-tōn″) *n. & adj.* **1,** a male voice intermediate between bass and tenor. **2,** a musical instrument having analogous range.

bar′i·um (bâr′ē-əm) *n.* a chemical element, no. 56, symbol Ba.

bark (bärk) *n.* **1,** the abrupt cry of a dog. **2,** any similar cry or sound by an animal or person. **3,** the outer covering of the stems of woody plants. **4,** a small three-masted ship. —*v.i.* **1,** utter a harsh sound like the bark of a dog. **2,** speak gruffly; make a clamor. —*v.t.* remove bark from; rub off the skin of.

bark′er (bär′kər) *n.* (*Informal*) a person who urges passersby to enter a theater, etc.

bar′ley (bär′lē) *n.* a cereal plant widely cultivated for food and the making of li-

---

quors. —**barley wine,** (*Brit.*) a strong, dark beer.

bar′maid, bar′man [*pl.* **-men**] *n.* bartender; a waitperson in a bar.

bar mitz′vah (bär mitz′və) *n.* **1,** a Jewish boy who has attained his 13th birthday. **2,** the ceremony recognizing that attainment.

barn (bärn) *n.* an outbuilding of a farm, used for storing grain and housing cattle and horses.

bar′na·cle (bär′nə-kəl) *n.* a small marine crustacean that attaches itself tenaciously to rocks and ships.

barn′storm″ (bärn′stôrm″) *v.i.* (*Informal*) tour rural areas, lecturing or performing publicly.

bar·o- (bär-ə) *pref.* pressure; weight.

ba·rom′e·ter (bə-rom′ə-tər) *n.* an instrument for measuring atmospheric pressure.

bar′on (bar′ən) *n.* **1,** a nobleman in the lower rank of peerage. **2,** a powerful person in industry, business, or finance. —**ba·ro′ni·al** (bə-rō′nē-əl), *adj.*

bar′on·age (-ij) *n.* **1,** the whole body of barons. **2,** a baron's rank.

bar′on·ess *n.* the wife of a baron (def. 1).

bar′on·et″ (bar′ə-net″) *n.* a hereditary noble below a baron and above a knight. —**bar′on·et·cy** (-sē) *n.* his rank.

bar′o·ny (bar′ə-nē) *n.* the estate or rank of a baron.

ba·roque′ (bə-rōk′) *adj.* **1,** in or pert. to a style of art and ornamentation characterized by grotesque or exaggerated forms. **2,** fantastic; grotesque. —*n.* baroque art or style.

bar′rack (bar′ək) *n.* (usually *pl.*) a large building for lodging soldiers.

bar″ra·cu′da (bar″ə-koo′də) *n.* a large, fierce tropical game fish.

bar·rage′ (bə-räzh′) *n.* **1,** (*Mil.*) a barrier of sustained artillery fire. **2,** a sustained flow.

bar′ra·try (bar′ə-trē) *n.* **1,** (*Law*) the defrauding of the owners of a ship by its master or crew. **2,** purchase or sale of offices of church or state. **3,** persistent instigation of litigation.

bar′rel (bar′əl) *n.* **1,** a cylindrical vessel of wooden staves bound together with hoops. **2,** any similar container or part, as the tube of a gun. —**barrel organ,** a hand organ.

bar′ren (bar′ən) *adj.* **1,** incapable of producing offspring; sterile. **2,** unproductive; unprofitable. **3,** destitute of interest or attraction. —**bar′ren·ness,** *n.*

bar·rette′ (bə-ret′) *n.* a clasp for a woman's hair.

bar″ri·cade′ (bar″ə-kād′) *n.* **1,** a hastily made fortification against the advance of any enemy. **2,** any temporary barrier. —*v.t.* block.

bar′ri·er (bar′ē-ər) *n.* **1,** any fence or structure erected to bar passage. **2,** any natural obstacle to passage or communication. **3,** anything that hinders or prevents progress, access, etc. **4,** a limit or boundary. —**barrier reef,** a coral reef parallel to the shore, separated from it by a lagoon.

bar′ri·o (bä′rē-ō) *n.* (*Sp.*) neighborhood; community.

bar′ris·ter (bar′is-tər) *n.* (*Brit.*) a lawyer who tries cases in court. ❑ *attorney.*

bar′row (bar′ō) *n.* **1,** a frame with handles, for carrying a load; a wheelbarrow. **2,** a heap, esp. a burial mound.

bar′tend″er *n.* one who mixes and serves drinks at a bar.

bar′ter (bär′tər) *v.i. & t.* exchange goods without the use of money. —*n.* this method of exchange.

bas′al (bā′səl) *adj.* basic. —**basal metabolism,** rate of expenditure of energy by the body at rest.

ba·salt′ (bə-sâlt′) *n.* a dark, dense, igneous rock.

base (bās) *n.* **1,** the bottom of anything, considered as its support. **2,** a fundamental principle; foundation. **3,** the starting point of action or reckoning; the first ingredient of a concoction. **4,** a principal seat of direction or supply; a depot. **5,** (*Baseball*) one of the four corners of a playing diamond. —*v.t.* **1,** place on a foundation; found. **2,** establish as a fact or conclusion. —*adj.* **1,** morally low; mean in spirit. **2,** low in rank; inferior in value. —**base metal,** a metal that is not a precious metal, as copper or tin. —**base′-ness,** *n.*

base′ball″ *n.* an athletic game in which a ball is batted to advance runners around a circuit of bases; the ball used in this game.

base′board″ *n.* boarding that lines the interior wall of a room, next to the floor.

base′born″ *adj.* **1,** of low or mean parentage. **2,** born out of wedlock; illegitimate.

base′man (-mən) [*pl.* **-men**] *n.* a baseball player who guards one of the bases.

base′ment (bās′mənt) *n.* a story of a building below the entrance level, usually underground.

ba·sen′ji (bə-sen′jē) *n.* a So. African breed of hound.

bash *v.t.* strike with crushing force. —*n.* **1,** a smashing blow. **2,** (*Slang*) a good time; a wild party.

bash′ful (bash′fəl) *adj.* timorous in approach to other persons; diffident; shy. —**bash′ful·ness,** *n.*

bas′ic (bā′sik) *adj.* **1,** pert. to a base or standard. **2,** fundamental. —*n.* (*all cap.*) a computer programming language: *B(eginner's) A(ll-purpose) S(ymbolic) I(nstruction) C(ode).* —**bas′i·cal·ly,** *adv.*

bas′il (baz′əl) *n.* an herb used as flavoring.

ba·sil′i·ca (bə-sil′i-kə) *n.* a church or other building with a broad nave flanked by rows of columns.

bas′i·lisk (bas′ə-lisk) *n.* **1,** a fabulous creature supposed to kill by its breath or look. **2,** a tropical lizard.

ba′sin (bā′sən) *n.* **1,** a shallow, circular vessel for holding liquids. **2,** a lowland.

ba′sis (bā′sis) *n.* [*pl.* **-ses** (-sēz)] **1,** a fundamental principle; foundation; groundwork. **2,** principal ingredient. —**basis point,** one hundredth of one percent.

bask (bȧsk) *v.i.* thrive as the object of benign influence, as warmth, etc.

bas′ket (bas′kit) *n.* **1,** a container woven of pliable reeds, etc. **2,** the contents or capacity of a basket. **3,** (*Basketball*) a wire hoop supporting an open net, fixed to a backboard; the act of throwing the ball through the hoop. —**basket case,** (*Slang*) one who has had all four limbs amputated; hence, a totally ineffectual person. —**basket weave,** a crisscross weave.

bas′ket·ball″ *n.* an indoor athletic game in which the object is to throw an inflated leather ball through a hoop or basket; the ball used in this game.

Basque (bȧsk) *n.* **1,** a people of No. Spain, or their language. **2,** (*l.c.*) a tight blouse.

bas-′re·lief″ (bä′rə-lēf″) *n.* sculpture with the figures projecting only slightly from the surface; low relief.

bass (bās) *adj.* (*Music*) low in pitch or range. —*n.* **1,** [also, **bas′so**] a man who sings bass. **2,** a bass instrument, esp. the bass viol. —**bass′ist,** *n.* one who plays the bass viol.

bass (bas) *n.* **1,** a perchlike food fish. **2,** a tree, the basswood or linden.

bas′set (bas′it) *n.* a hound dog with short legs and long body.

bas′set horn (bas′it) a tenor clarinet.

bas″si·net′ (bas″i-net′) *n.* a hooded basket used as a baby's cradle.

bas′so (bäs′ō) *n.* bass.

bas·soon′ (bə-soon′) *n.* a musical instrument, the baritone of the double-reed wind family.

bast *n.* the fibrous inner bark of certain trees, used for making matting.

bas′ta (bäs′tä) *n.* (*Sp., It.*) enough.

bas′tard (bas′tərd) *n.* an illegitimate child. —*adj.* **1,** of illegitimate birth. **2,** spurious; impure.

bas′tard·ize″ (-īz″) *v.t.* **1,** make a bastard of. **2,** adulterate; debase.

bas′tar·dy (-dē) *n.* **1,** act of begetting a bastard. **2,** illegitimacy.

baste (bāst) *v.t.* **1,** sew with temporary stitches. **2,** moisten (meat) while cooking. **3,** beat with a stick.

bas·tille′ (bas-tēl′) *n.* a prison, esp. one conducted oppressively.

bas″ti·na′do (bas″ti-nā′dō) *n.* punishment by beating the feet with a stick; the stick used.

bas′tion (bas′chən) *n.* **1,** a walled fortification projecting from a main rampart. **2,** a fortified sector.

bat *n.* **1,** a heavy club or cudgel. **2,** the club used to strike the ball in certain games. **3,** a nocturnal flying mammal. **4,** (*Slang*) a spree. —*v.t. & i.* [**bat′ted, -ting**] strike with a bat; have a turn at batting. —**bat a thousand,** (*Informal*) achieve a perfect record. —**batting average,** (*Informal*) record of accomplishment.

bat′boy, bat′girl *n.* (*Baseball*) a person, usu. a youth, who handles the bats for the batters.

batch (bach) *n.* **1,** a quantity prepared for, or produced by, one operation. **2,** a quantity or group from a larger aggregation. —**batch file,** (*Computers*) a file containing a series of commands to be carried out sequentially by an operating system. —**batch processing,** (*Computers*) data processing combining projects in one run.

bate (bāt) *v.t.* lessen or restrain. —**with bated breath,** in suspense.

bath (bȧth) *n.* **1,** a washing of the body in water. **2,** equipment for a bath: the fluid or a bathtub. —**bath chair,** a wheelchair, esp. hooded, used for invalids.

---

bath, bathe

☛ In Amer. English, *bath* is used only as a noun, *bathe* as a verb. In Brit. English, *bath* as a verb has the sense "to wash in a bath." However, the bath chair is named after the town in England where it was first used.

---

bathe (bā*th*) *v.t. & i.* **1,** take or administer a bath. **2,** immerse or be immersed in a liquid. ❏ *bath*

bath'house" *n.* a seaside building where bathers disrobe.

ba·thom'e·ter (bə-thom'i-tər) *n.* an instrument for measuring ocean depths.

ba'thos (bā'thos) *n.* **1,** a ludicrous descent from the elevated to the commonplace. **2,** mawkish pathos.

---
bathos, pathos
☛ *Pathos* is a quality (as of a work of art) that evokes sadness. *Bathos,* in addition to its fundamental meaning of a striking contrast between dignity and baseness, is often used to indicate a false or insincere *pathos.*

---

bath'robe" *n.* a loose robe worn instead of clothing; dressing gown.

bath'room" *n.* a room containing bathing and often other toilet facilities. ❏ *toilet*

bath'tub" *n.* a tub in which a person lies to bathe.

bath'y·scaphe" (-skāf") *n.* a bathysphere having a separate gas-filled chamber overhead for buoyancy.

bath'y·sphere" (bath'is-fir") *n.* an apparatus lowered into deep waters for observation from a spherical compartment.

ba·tik' (bə-tēk') *n.* a method of printing colors on cloth, by covering with wax portions to be unprinted.

ba·tiste' (bə-tēst') *n.* a plain, thin cotton fabric.

bat'man *n.* (*Brit.*) a soldier assigned as personal servant to a military officer.

bat mitz'vah (bäth mits'və) *n.* **1,** a Jewish girl who has attained her 13th birthday. **2,** the ceremony recognizing that attainment. Also, **bath** *or* **bas mitzvah.**

ba·ton' *n.* **1,** a staff or club carried as a symbol of authority. **2,** a wand used in conducting an orchestra.

bat·tal'ion (bə-tal'yən) *n.* (*Mil.*) a body of troops, of variable number but usually less than a regiment.

bat'ten (bat'ən) *v.i.* feed gluttonously; grow fat; thrive. —*v.t.* **1,** fatten. **2,** furnish with battens. **3,** (*Naut.*) cover with tarpaulins secured by battens. —*n.* a light strip of wood; slat.

bat'ter (bat'ər) *v.t. & i.* beat persistently; pound violently. —*n.* **1,** a mixture of flour, eggs, etc. for making bread or pastry; any mixture of similar consistency. **2,** one who wields a bat, as in baseball.

bat'ter·y (bat'ə-rē) *n.* **1,** a device for producing an electric current or storing elec-

tricity. **2,** a unit of artillery; a group of guns. **3,** a set of similar machines or devices. **4,** (*Baseball*) the pitcher and catcher together. **5,** (*Law*) the unlawful beating of another.

bat'ting (bat'ing) *n.* cotton or wool in matted sheets for quilts or bedcovers.

bat'tle (bat'əl) *n.* a fight, hostile encounter, or engagement between opposing forces. —*v.t. & i.* engage in battle; struggle; contest. —**battle fatigue,** a neurosis affecting soldiers in active warfare. —**battle royal,** a fight in which each of several contestants opposes each other.

bat'tle-ax" *n.* **1,** an ax used as a weapon. **2,** (*Slang*) a shrewish old woman.

bat'tle·dore" (-dôr") *n.* the racket used in badminton.

bat'tle·field" *n.* the field or place where a battle is fought. Also, **bat'tle·ground".**

bat'tle·ment (-mənt) *n.* a parapet on a fort, castle, etc. having openings for shooting through.

bat'tle·ship" (bat'əl-ship") *n.* the most heavily armed type of warship.

bat'ty (bat'ē) *adj.* (*Slang*) foolish or crazy. Also, **bats.**

bau'ble (bâ'bəl) *n.* a trinket of little value.

baud (bâd) *n.* a unit of data transmission, usu. one dot or one bit per second, named for 19th-c. French inventor J. M. E. Baudot.

Bau'haus (bow'hows) *adj.* of or pert. to an influential school of design founded in 1919 by German architect Walter Gropius.

baux'ite (bâk'sīt) *n.* the ore from which aluminum is derived.

bawd (bâd) *n.* a prostitute.

bawd'y (bâ'dē) *adj.* lewd; indecent. —**bawd'i·ness,** *n.*

bawl (bâl) *v.i. & t.* shout clamorously; cry vehemently; wail. —**bawl out,** (*Informal*) scold.

bay (bā) *n.* **1,** a recess in a shore; an inlet; a large cove or small gulf. **2,** a turret projecting outward from a wall; a niche or alcove. **3,** a compartment of space. **4,** any of several trees, as laurel. **5,** the deep-toned bark of a hunting dog. **6,** a horse of reddish-brown color. —*v.i.* bark with a deep, prolonged sound. —**at bay,** trapped, as by hunting dogs. —**bay rum,** a fragrant skin and hair lotion. —**bay window, 1,** a group of windows projecting from a room in a floor-level recess. **2,** (*Slang*) a fat belly.

bay'ber·ry (bā'ber-ē) *n.* **1,** a shrub or

tree of the myrtle family; its berry. **2,** a W. Indian tree; its oil, used in *bay rum.*

bay′o·net (bā′ə-net) *n.* a steel weapon for stabbing or slashing, attached to the barrel of a rifle. —*v.t.* stab with a bayonet.

> **bayonet**
> ↔ Named for the city of *Bayonne,* France, where the weapon was first made.

bay′ou (bī′oo) *n.* a cove of a lake; a sluggish watercourse.

ba·zaar′ (bə-zär′) *n.* **1,** a marketplace. **2,** a sale of miscellaneous goods for charitable purposes. ❑ *bizarre*

ba·zoo′ka (bə-zoo′kə) *n.* (*Mil.*) a tubular rocket launcher portable by one or two persons.

> **bazooka**
> ↔ So named for its similarity to an instrument invented and played by American comedian Bob Burns.

BB (bē′bē) *n.* **1,** a size of lead shot used in a type of air rifle (*BB gun*). **2,** a pellet of BB shot.

be (bē) *v.i.* [*present indicative:* **I am; you are** (*Archaic,* **thou art**); **he is; we, you, they are;** *pret.* **I, he was; we, you, they were;** *p.p.* **been** (bin); **be′ing**] **1,** (as substantive) exist; live; have reality; occur; take place; remain in a condition. **2,** (as copulative) a link between a subject and a predicate, as I *am* here; an element in participial and infinitive phrases, as it is *being* done; we wish to *be* informed. **3,** (as auxiliary) used with a participle to form a progressive, as he *is* reading; we *have been* waiting; used to indicate passive voice, as it *was* repaired.

be- (bè) *pref.* **1,** affect with, as *becloud.* **2,** take off or away, as *behead.*

beach (bēch) *n.* the part of a shore washed by the tide or waves. —*v.t.* run or haul (a boat) upon a beach. —**beach buggy,** a motor vehicle with oversize tires for use on sand beaches. —**beach wagon,** a station wagon.

beach′comb″er (-kō″mər) *n.* an outcast living on a tropical beach.

beach′head″ *n.* a military position on an enemy shore.

bea′con (bē′kən) *n.* **1,** a lighthouse, signal buoy, or other fixed marker that guides ships or aircraft. **2,** anything that warns or guides.

bead (bēd) *n.* **1,** a small ball pierced with a hole for stringing with others. **2,** (*pl.*) a necklace or rosary. **3,** a drop of liquid; a

bubble, as in froth. **4,** any small globular body or mass. —*v.t.* ornament with beads. —**bead′y,** *adj.* like or containing beads.

> **bead**
> ↔ From Old English *gebed,* prayer. From the use of the rosary beads to count prayers, the word gradually shifted from the prayer to the object used to count it.

bea′dle (bē′dəl) *n.* a minor official having disciplinary duties.

beads′man (-mən) [*pl.* **-men**], **beads′-wom″an,** *n.* **1,** a person paid to pray for another. **2,** an inmate of a poorhouse.

bea′gle (bē′gəl) *n.* a small, long-eared hunting dog.

beak (bēk) *n.* **1,** the horny bill of a bird. **2,** the snout, jaws, or similar part of any animal.

beak′er (bē′kər) *n.* a glass vessel.

beam (bēm) *n.* **1,** a horizontal supporting member. **2,** a lever or piston. **3,** the greatest width of a ship. **4,** a bundle of parallel rays of light; a focused train of electronic waves. —*v.t. & i.* **1,** emit rays; form like a beam of light. **2,** smile radiantly.

bean (bēn) *n.* **1,** the edible seed of a leguminous plant. **2,** any oval or roundish seed, berry, nut, or lump. **3,** a plant producing seed in the shape of beans. **4,** (*Slang*) head; (*pl.*) money; spirit. —*v.t.* (*Slang*) strike on the head. —**bean counter,** (*Slang*) a statistician, accountant, etc. —**bean curd,** tofu.

bean′er·y (bēn′ə-rė) *n.* a cheap restaurant.

bean′ie (bē′nė) *n.* a child's skullcap.

bean′o (bē′nō) *n.* a form of bingo.

bear (bâr) *v.t.* [**bore, borne, born**] **1,** hold up; support; carry; convey. **2,** put up with; accept; endure; sustain. **3,** bring forward; render. **4,** possess; show; exercise. **5,** give birth to. **6,** produce by natural growth. —*v.i.* **1,** remain firm; be patient. **2,** (with *on*) press; have effect or reference. **3,** move or tend in a specific direction; be situated. **4,** produce offspring, fruit, etc. —*n.* **1,** a large, omnivorous mammal, covered with heavy fur. **2,** a person likened to a bear, as gruff, clumsy, predatory, etc. **3,** a trader in financial stocks who sells short in the belief prices will go down. —*adj.* characterized by declining stock prices: *bear market.* —**Great Bear, Little Bear,** two constellations.

beard (bird) *n.* **1,** the growth of hair on the face of a man, esp. the chin. **2,** a tuft of hair, bristle, etc.

---

tub, cūte, pûll; labəl; oil, owl, go, chip, she, thin, then, sing, ink; *see p. 6*

bear
(*Gram.*) The past participle of *bear* is in almost all cases *borne*. However, *born* is used, in the passive mode, in senses referring to physical birth or a birthlike process and when the focus is on the offspring, as, *A child was born on Christmas day. The idea was born of inspiration.*

bear·ing (bâr′ing) *n.* **1**, the manner in which a person bears or comports himself; carriage; behavior. **2**, the act or capability of producing offspring, fruit, etc. **3**, a supporting member of a structure or machine; a fixed part supporting a moving part. **4**, the relation of parts; mode of connection; implication. **5**, the compass direction of one object from another. **6**, (*pl.*) position; orientation.

bear·ish *adj.* **1**, surly. **2**, pessimistic. —**bear′ish·ness,** *n.*

bé·ar·naise′ (ber-nāz′) *n.* (*Fr.*) a sauce of egg yolks, butter, vinegar, and herbs, named for the Béarn district of France.

beast (bēst) *n.* **1**, any animal, excluding humans; esp., any four-footed animal. **2**, a brutal, coarse, or otherwise beastlike human. —**beast′ly** (-lē) *adj.* very unpleasant.

beat (bēt) *v.t.* [**beat, beat′en, beat′ing**] **1**, strike repeatedly. **2**, move repeatedly; flutter; (*Music*) mark time by strokes. **3**, dash with force. **4**, overcome; vanquish; surpass; baffle. **5**, (*Slang*) swindle. **6**, (with *up*) give a beating to. —*v.i.* **1**, strike repeated blows; strike (against). **2**, throb; pulsate. —*n.* **1**, a stroke, blow, or throb. **2**, a series of regular strokes, as the ticking of a watch. **3**, accent or stress. **4**, an assigned or habitual course of travel. **5**, (*Slang*) publication of a news story in advance of rival newspapers. **6**, (*Slang*) beatnik. —*adj.* **1**, exhausted. **2**, of or pert. to the Beat Generation. —**beat box,** (*Slang*) drum machine. —**Beat Generation,** a youth culture of the 1940s to the 1960s characterized by rock music and the use of drugs.

be·at′i·fy″ (bê-at′ə-fī″) *v.t.* **1**, make supremely happy. **2**, (*Rom. Cath. Ch.*) declare to be blessed and therefore worthy of certain honors. —**be″a·tif′ic** (bē″ə-tif′ik) *adj.* —**be·at′i·fi·ca′tion,** *n.*

be·at′i·tude″ (bê-at′ə-tūd″) *n.* **1**, blessedness; bliss. **2**, (*cap.*) any of Jesus' statements on blessedness in the Sermon on the Mount.

beat′nik (bēt′nik) *n.* a member of the Beat Generation.

beat-′up″ *adj.* (*Slang*) dilapidated; broken down.

beau (bō) *n.* **1**, a male lover; swain. **2**, a man fussy of his dress; a fop.

Beau′fort scale (bō′fərt) a scale of wind velocities, ranging from 0 (calm) to 12 (hurricane), named for its inventor, 19th-c. British admiral Sir Francis Beaufort.

beau′te·ous (bū′tē-əs) *adj.* beautiful. —**beau′te·ous·ness,** *n.*

beau·ti′cian (bū-tish′ən) *n.* one who owns or works in a beauty parlor; cosmetologist.

beau′ti·ful (bū′ti-fəl) *adj.* having beauty; lovely.

beau′ti·fy″ (bū′ti-fī″) *v.t. & i.* make or become beautiful. —**beau″ti·fi·ca′tion,** *n.*

beau′ty (bū′tē) *n.* **1**, the quality of an object of sense or thought that arouses admiration, approval, or pleasure. **2**, a particular trait, grace, or charm that pleases. **3**, a person or object possessing beauty. —**beauty parlor** *or* **salon,** an establishment where hairdressing, manicuring, etc., are performed.

beaux-arts′ (bō-zärts′; *Fr.* -zär′) *n.pl.* (*Fr.*) the fine arts.

bea′ver (bē′vər) *n.* **1**, an amphibious rodent prized for its fur. **2**, a hat made of beaver fur; a man's high silk hat. **3**, a heavy woolen cloth.

bea′ver·board″ *n.* a light sheathing material of wood fiber.

be′bop (bē′bop) *n.* (*Slang*) bop.

be·calm′ (bē-käm′) *v.t.* make calm or still. —**be·calmed′,** *adj.* (*Naut.*) motionless, by lack of wind.

be·cause′ (bē-kâz′) *conj.* for the reason that; since. —*adv.* (with *of*) by reason; on account.

because, since, owing to, due to
(*Gram.*) Although *since* can mean the same as *because*, it is best to reserve *since* for situations relating to time, and use *because* for causal situations. The phrase *the reason is because* is redundant: *because* means "the reason is." The phrases *because of*, *owing to*, and *due to* have the same meaning. However, the adjectival phrases *due to* and *owing to* are best used to modify nouns and noun phrases, not verbal phrases, which can be handled by *because of*: *an economic slump due to market forces*, but *he became sick because of a flu epidemic.*

bêche-′de-mer′ (besh′də-mer′) *n.* (*Fr.*) trepang.

beck (bek) *n.* a beckoning gesture, as in *beck and call.*

beck'on (bek'ən) *v.i. & t.* **1,** signal to approach by a gesture of the hand or head. **2,** lure; entice.

be·cloud' (bė-klowd') *v.t.* obscure; make unclear.

be·come' (bė-kum') *v.i.* [**-came', -com'-ing**] change (into a state or condition); come into being as. —*v.t.* befit in appearance; grace. —**be·com'ing,** *adj.* attractive; appropriate.

bed *n.* **1,** an article of furniture, on which one sleeps. **2,** any place of rest or repose. **3,** any bottom layer or foundation; the ground in which plants are grown; the bottom of a body of water; the lowest layer of a road. —*v.t.* [**bed'ded, bed'ding**] **1,** shelter. **2,** seat firmly in a substance. —*v.i.* go to bed.

bed'bug" *n.* a small blood-sucking insect that infests beds.

bed'cham"ber *n.* a room for sleeping.

bed'clothes" *n.pl.* the sheets, covers, etc. placed on a bed.

bed'ding *n.* bedclothes.

be·deck' (bė-dek') *v.t.* decorate; hang ornaments on.

be·dev'il (bė-dev'əl) *v.t.* torment maliciously; confuse. —**be·dev'il·ment,** *n.*

be·diz'en (be-dī'zən) *v.t.* dress gaudily. —**be·diz'en·ment,** *n.*

bed'lam (bed'ləm) *n.* **1,** wild uproar and confusion. **2,** a lunatic asylum. —**bed'-lam·ite,** *n.*

> **bedlam**
> ↔ From the Hospital of St. Mary of Bethlehem (Old English *Bedleem*), a London lunatic asylum.

Bed'ou·in (bed'û-win) *n.* **1,** one of the Arabs of the Asian and Afr. desert. **2,** any nomad or wanderer.

bed'pan" *n.* **1,** a pan containing hot coals, used for warming a bed. **2,** a toilet pan for use of one confined to bed.

be·drag'gled (bė-drag'əld) *adj.* untidy or soiled, as clothes; unkempt.

bed'rid"den (bed'rid"ən) *adj.* not strong or well enough to rise from bed.

bed'rock" *n.* **1,** the solid rock beneath the surface soil. **2,** the lowest stratum. **3,** any firm foundation.

bed'room" *n.* a room designed to be slept in.

bed'spread" *n.* an outer cover for a bed, usually decorative.

bed'stead" *n.* the framework of a bed.

bee (bē) *n.* **1,** any of a family of insects that live in colonies and gather honey. **2,** a social gathering.

beech (bēch) *n.* a smooth-barked tree found in temperate regions. —**beech'en,** *adj.* —**beech'nut",** *n.* the nut of the beech tree.

beef (bēf) *n.* **1,** the meat of a bovine animal. **2,** [*pl.* **beeves**] a steer, bull, or cow. **3,** (*Informal*) muscle; flesh. **4,** (*Informal*) a complaint. —*v.i.* (*Informal*) complain. —**beef'burg'er,** *n.* an all-beef hamburger. —**beef'eat"er,** *n.* (*Slang*) an English soldier. —**beef'steak",** *n.* a slice from the best cuts of beef. —**beef'y** (-ė) *adj.* brawny.

beef'a·lo" (bē'fə-lō") *n.* a crossbreed of a cow and a buffalo.

bee'hive" *n.* **1,** a dwelling for bees. **2,** something that resembles a beehive, as a hairdo.

bee'line" (bē'līn") *n.* a direct line.

been (bin) *v.* p.p. of *be.*

beep (bēp) *n.* a short, usu. high-pitched, sound. —*v.i.* make this sound. —**beep'er,** *n.* pager.

beer (bir) *n.* **1,** an alcoholic beverage made from grain. **2,** any fermented nonalcoholic beverage.

bees'wax" (bēz'waks") *n.* wax secreted by bees to make honeycomb.

beet (bēt) *n.* a plant with a dark red fleshy root, used as food or to produce sugar.

bee'tle (bē'təl) *n.* **1,** any of an order of insects. **2,** a heavy mallet or pestle. **3,** (*Slang*) a slow racehorse. —*v.t.* beat; ram. —*v.i.* **1,** jut out. **2,** move swiftly; scamper.

bee'tle-browed" (-browd") *adj.* **1,** having projecting eyebrows. **2,** scowling; sullen or menacing.

beeves (bēvz) *n.* pl. of *beef.*

be·fall' (bė-fâl') *v.i.* happen; occur. —*v.t.* happen to.

be·fit' (bė-fit') *v.t.* [**-fit'ted, -ting**] be suitable for; be appropriate to.

be·fogged' (bė-fogd') *adj.* in a fog; bewildered or muddled.

be·fore' (bė-fôr') *prep.* **1,** earlier than; previous to. **2,** in the future. **3,** ahead of in position; in front of. **4,** in precedence of; in preference to. **5,** in the presence of. —*conj.* **1,** previous to the time when. **2,** rather than. —*adv.* **1,** ahead; in advance. **2,** previously; sooner. —**be·fore'hand",** *adv.* in advance of a usual or appointed time.

be·foul' (bė-fowl') *v.t.* make foul.

be·friend' (bė-frend') *v.t.* act as a friend to; aid; favor.

befriend
☞ Note that *befriend* does not mean to make friends with, but to act as a friend to.

be·fud′dle (bė-fud′əl) *v.t.* stupefy with liquor; muddle; confuse.

beg *v.t. & i.* [**begged, beg′ging**] **1,** ask as alms; live by asking alms. **2,** ask as a favor. —**beg the question, 1,** attempt to prove one assertion by means of another (unproved) assertion. **2,** evade the issue at hand.

be·get′ (bė-get′) *v.t.* [**-got′, get′ting**] **1,** procreate; generate (of the male parent). **2,** produce as an effect. —**be·got′ten,** *adj.* sired; fathered.

beg′gar (beg′ər) *n.* **1,** one who begs. **2,** one who is very poor. **3,** fellow; rogue. —*v.t.* **1,** make a beggar of; impoverish. **2,** exhaust the resources of. —**beg′gar·ly,** *adj.* —**beg′gar·y,** *n.*

be·gin′ (bė-gin′) *v.t. & i.* [**-gan′, -gin′ning**] **1,** take the first step in an action; commence; start. **2,** come into existence; arise. —**be·gin′ner,** *n.* one just beginning to learn or do something; a novice.

be·gin′ning *n.* **1,** a start or starting point; an early stage. **2,** origin; source.

be·gone′ (bė-gân′) *interj. & v.* go away!

be·go′ni·a (bi-gō′nė-ə) *n.* a tropical plant having showy flowers, named for 17th-c. French patron of science Michel Bégon.

be·grime′ (bė-grīm′) *v.t.* soil.

be·grudge′ (bė-gruj′) *v.t.* **1,** be disinclined to give or allow. **2,** be envious of another's possession of.

be·guile′ (bė-gīl′) *v.t.* **1,** delude with guile; deceive. **2,** amuse; divert; pass (time). —**be·guile′ment,** *n.*

be·guine′ (bə-gēn′) *n.* a So. Amer. dance; its music.

be·half′ (bė-hàf′) *n.* interest; favor.

be·have′ (bė-hāv′) *v.i.* **1,** conduct oneself or itself; act or operate. **2,** comport oneself properly.

be·hav′ior (bė-hāv′yər) *n.* **1,** manner of behaving; deportment; habits or tendencies. **2,** (*usu. pl.*) pattern of behavior.

be·head′ (bė-hed′) *v.t.* cut off the head of.

be·he′moth (bə-hē′məth; bē′ə-) *n.* a huge, powerful person or animal.

be·hest′ (bė-hest′) *n.* (*Archaic*) a command.

be·hind′ (bė-hīnd′) *prep.* **1,** at the back of; in the rear of; on the farther side of; beyond. **2,** less advanced than; inferior to. **3,** later than. —*adv.* **1,** toward the back or

rear. **2,** in arrears; slow. —*n.* (*Informal*) posterior; buttocks.

be·hind′hand″ *adv.* late; in arrears.

be·hold′ (bė-hōld′) *v.t.* [**-held′, -hold′ing**] observe with care; look at; see. —*interj.* look!

be·hold′en (bė-hōl′dən) *adj.* held by an obligation; grateful.

be·hoof′ (bė-hoof′) *n.* advantage.

be·hoove′ (bė-hoov′) *v.t.* (with expletive *it*) be fitting or necessary.

beige (bāzh) *n.* a light tan color.

be′ing (bē′ing) *n.* **1,** existence; life. **2,** a creature; a human.

be·jew′el (bė-joo′əl) *v.t.* adorn with jewels; spangle.

bel *n.* a unit equal to 10 decibels.

bel
↔ Named for U.S. inventor Alexander Graham *Bell*, inventor of the telephone.

be·la′bor (bė-lā′bər) *v.t.* **1,** beat soundly; thump. **2,** assail persistently, as with criticism.

be·lat′ed (bė-lā′tid) *adj.* coming late or too late.

be·lay′ (bė-lā′) *v.t.* fasten (a rope) by winding it around a pin or cleat. —*interj.* stop! desist!

bel can′to (bel kän′tō) (*It.*) a style of operatic singing emphasizing beautiful tone and line.

belch *v.i.* **1,** eject wind noisily from the stomach through the mouth; eructate. **2,** issue in spurts. —*v.t.* eject violently; emit spasmodically. —*n.* an eructation; a burst, as of smoke, etc.

bel′dam (bel′dəm) *n.* an old woman; a hag.

be·lea′guer (bė-lē′gər) *v.t.* surround, as in laying siege to.

bel′fry (bel′frė) *n.* **1,** a tower for a bell. **2,** the part of a steeple or other structure in which a bell is hung.

belfry
↔ Derived, through French, from Germanic words for refuge and safety; it is unrelated to *bell.*

be·lie′ (bė-lī′) *v.t.* **1,** give a false representation of. **2,** show to be false; contradict.

be·lief′ (bė-lēf′) *n.* **1,** the act of believing; faith. **2,** an accepted opinion.

be·lieve′ (bė-lēv′) *v.t.* **1,** accept as true. **2,** give credence to. **3,** (*Informal*) think. —**be·liev′er,** *n.*

be·lit′tle (bė-lit′əl) *v.t.* make lower in importance; disparage.

bell (bel) *n.* **1,** a hollow metal device giving forth a resonant or tinkling sound when struck. **2,** a cup-shaped object suggesting a bell. **3,** a nautical unit of time. **4,** a flared part, as the mouth of a horn, etc. **5,** (*pl.*) bell-bottom trousers. —*v.i.* swell out. —*v.t.* attach a bell to. —**bell jar,** a bell-shaped glass cover. —**bell metal,** a hard alloy of copper and tin. —**bells and whistles,** (*Informal*) gimmicks (used esp. in computer jargon). —**bell the cat,** to contend with a greatly superior adversary.

bel″la·don′na (bel″ə-don′ə) *n.* a medicinal herb.

bell-′bot″tom *adj.* of trousers, having legs with flared bottoms. —**bell-′bot″-toms,** *n.pl.*

bell′boy″ *n.* bellhop.

belle (bel) *n.* a beautiful woman, a favorite of admirers.

Belle É·poque′, La (bel ā-pâk′, lä) (*Fr.*) the period (1871-1914) between the Franco-Prussian War and the First World War: lit., the beautiful epoch.

belles-″lettres′ (bel-letr′) *n.* (*Fr.*) the fine art of literature.

bell′hop″ *n.* an attendant in a hotel. Also, **bell′boy″, bell′man″.**

bel′li·cose″ (bel′ə-kōs″) *adj.* warlike; pugnacious. —**bel·li·cos′i·ty** (-kos′ə-tė) *n.*

> **bellicose, belligerent**
> ☛ Both adjectives mean warlike, but only *belligerent* has the sense "at war." *Bellicose* is the milder of the two and may even suggest an element of comic bluster.

bel·lig′er·ent (bə-lij′ər-ənt) *adj.* **1,** pert. to war. **2,** given to waging war; bellicose. **3,** at war. —*n.* a country at war. —**bel·lig′-er·ence,** *n.* ❏ *bellicose*

bell′man″ *n.* **1,** bellhop. **2,** a town crier.

bel′low (bel′ō) *v.i. & t.* make a loud, hollow noise; roar. —*n.* a loud outcry.

bel′lows (bel′ōz) *n. sing.* **1,** an instrument for producing a current of air, a kind of box with collapsible sides. **2,** something resembling a bellows.

bell′weth″er (-we*th*″ər) *n.* a sheep (usually wearing a bell) that leads the flock; hence, a leader.

bel′ly (bel′ė) *n.* **1,** the part of a vertebrate animal between its breast and groin; the abdomen; the stomach. **2,** the inside of anything. —*v.i. & t.* bulge. —**belly flop,** a dive resulting in a landing flat on the

belly. —**belly laugh,** a deep, raucous laugh; guffaw.

bel′ly·ache″ *n.* colic. —*v.i.* (*Slang*) complain; gripe.

bel′ly·but″ton *n.* (*Informal*) navel.

bel′ly dance″ *n.* a dance, usually performed by a woman, characterized by gyrating motions of the abdominal area.

be·long′ (bi-lâng′) *v.i.* **1,** (with *to*) be a property or concern (of). **2,** have place (in).

be·long′ing (bi-lâng′ing) *n.* **1,** the state of being a member, part, adjunct, etc. **2,** a possession.

be·lov′ed (bė-luv′id) *adj.* greatly loved. —*n.* one greatly loved.

be·low′ (bė-lō′) *adv.* **1,** in a lower place; beneath. **2,** at a later point in a document. —*prep.* **1,** lower than, in position or direction; under; beneath. **2,** inferior to.

> **below, beneath, under, underneath**
> (*Gram.*) These words of position are functionally synonymous, meaning lower than something else; however, small distinctions can be made. *Below* is the most general. *Beneath* emphasizes the fact of being covered. *Under* and *underneath* imply a position directly below and in a line with something.

belt *n.* **1,** a flexible band worn around the waist. **2,** a similar endless loop. **3,** a stripe; a .zone. —*v.t.* **1,** gird. **2,** beat, as with a belt. **3,** (*Slang*) hit with a fist. —**black, brown,** *etc.,* **belt,** levels of proficiency in certain martial arts.

be·lu′ga (bə-loo′gə) *n.* **1,** a white sturgeon of the Black Sea; its roe, made into caviar. **2,** the white whale.

bel″ve·dere′ (bel″və-dir′) *n.* an upper story of a building that has a fine view.

be·mused′ (bė-mūzd′) *adj.* **1,** confused. **2,** lost in thought.

Ben′a·dryl (ben′ə-dril) *n.* (*T.N.*) a drug for the relief of hay fever.

bench *n.* **1,** a long seat. **2,** the office of judge; the judiciary. **3,** a stout table; workbench. **4,** a shelf.

bench′mark″ *n.* a point of reference for making measurements.

bend *v.t.* [*pret. & p.p.* **bent** or (*Archaic*) **bend′ed**] **1,** put a curve or crook in. **2,** turn in a different direction. **3,** force into submission. —*v.i.* **1,** become curved or crooked. —*n.* **1,** a curve or crook. **2,** a knot. **3,** (*pl.*) a disease caused by rapid emergence from compression. —**bend′er,**

n. (Slang) a drinking spree. **—on bended knee,** kneeling.

be·neath′ (bė-nēth′) *adv.* in a lower place, condition, rank, etc; underneath. *—prep.* below. ❏ *below.*

ben′e·dict (ben′ə-dikt) *n.* a bridegroom.

> **benedict**
> ↔ From the character *Benedick* in Shakespeare's *Much Ado About Nothing* who successfully courts Beatrice.

Ben″e·dic′tine (ben″ə-dik′tēn) *n.* **1,** a monk of the order of St. Benedict. **2,** a liqueur. *—adj.* pert. to St. Benedict or the Benedictines.

ben″e·dic′tion (ben″ə-dik′shən) *n.* **1,** the act of pronouncing a blessing. **2,** a blessing.

ben″e·fac′tion (ben″ə-fak′shən) *n.* **1,** the doing of good. **2,** a benefit conferred, esp. a charitable donation. **—ben′e·fac″tor,** *n.*

ben′e·fice (ben′ə-fis) *n.* an ecclesiastical position providing a living.

be·nef′i·cent (bə-nef′i-sənt) *adj.* conferring benefit; charitable. **—be·nef′i·cence,** *n.*

ben″e·fi′cial (ben″ə-fish′əl) *adj.* **1,** helpful; profitable. **2,** pert. to a benefit.

ben″e·fi′ci·ar·y (ben″ə-fish′ė-er-ė) *n.* a recipient of benefits.

ben′e·fit (ben′ə-fit) *n.* **1,** advantage; profit. **2,** an act of kindness. **3,** an activity, as a theatrical performance, to raise money for a charitable purpose. *—v.i.* **[-fit′ted, -ting]** derive a benefit (from). *—v.t.* be beneficial to.

be·nev′o·lent (bə-nev′ə-lənt) *adj.* manifesting a desire to do good; kind. **—be·nev′o·lence,** *n.*

be·night′ed (bė-nī′tid) *adj.* in a state of mental darkness; in deep ignorance.

be·nign′ (bė-nīn′) *adj.* **1,** of a kind disposition; gracious. **2,** favorable; propitious. **—be·nig′ni·ty** (bė-nig′nə-tė) *n.*

be·nig′nant (bė-nig′nənt) *adj.* kindly; benign. **—be·nig′nan·cy,** *n.*

ben′i·son (ben′i-sən) *n.* a blessing.

ben′ja·min (ben′jə-mən) *n.* **1,** a plant of the laurel family. **2,** the youngest or favorite son.

> **benjamin**
> ↔ The reference is to the youngest son of Jacob and Rachel in Gen. 35:18.

ben′ny (ben′ė) *n. (Slang)* **1,** an overcoat. **2,** an amphetamine tablet.

bent *adj.* **1,** curved or crooked. **2,** deter-

mined; resolved. *—n.* tendency; inclination. *—v. pret. & p.p.* of *bend.*

Ben′ze·drine″ (ben′zə-drēn″) *n. (T.N.)* a type of amphetamine.

ben′zene (ben′zēn) *n.* a volatile liquid derived from coal, used as a solvent and fuel.

> **benzene**
> ↔ Orig. coined as *benzine* in 1933 by German chemist Eilhardt Mitscherlich on the model of *benzoic acid.*

ben′zine (ben′zēn) *n.* a volatile liquid obtained from petroleum, used in cleaning, etc.

ben′zo·ate (ben′zō-ət) *n.* a salt obtained from benzoin, used as a food preservative.

ben′zo·caine″ (ben′zə-kān) *n.* a local anesthetic.

ben′zo·in (ben′zō-in) *n.* a fragrant resin used in perfumes and drugs. **—ben·zo′ic** (-ik) *adj.*

ben′zol (ben′zâl) *n.* a form of benzene used as a motor fuel, etc.

be·queath′ (bė-kwēth′) *v.t.* dispose of (property) by will. **—be·queath′al** (-kwē′thəl) *n.*

be·quest′ (bė-kwest′) *n.* a legacy.

be·rate′ (bė-rāt′) *v.t.* scold.

Ber′ber (bėr′bėr) *n. & adj.* pert. to a No. Afr. people inhabiting Barbary and the Sahara, or their language.

ber′ceuse′ (ber-söz′) *n.* a lullaby.

be·reave′ (bė-rēv′) *v.t.* [*pret. & p.p.* often **be·reft′**] take away from, esp. by death. **—be·reave′ment,** *n.*

> **bereaved, bereft**
> ☛ Both words mean deprived of, but *bereaved* is commonly used only in the sense deprived by death.

be·reft′ (bė-reft′) *adj.* deprived; destitute.; *p.p.* of *bereave.* ❏ *bereaved*

be·ret′ (bə-rā′) *n.* a round, soft, visorless cap.

ber′i·ber′i (ber′ė-) *n.* a vitamin-deficiency disease.

ber·ke′li·um (bėr-kē′lė-əm) *n.* an unstable, radioactive, metallic element, no. 97, symbol Bk, produced artificially from americium.

ber·lin′ (bər-lin′) *n.* **1,** a large, four-wheeled, closed carriage. **2,** [also, **ber·line′**] a type of limousine.

Bermuda onion a large, mild variety of Spanish onion.

---

fat, fāte, fär, fāre, fâll, ȧsk; met, hē, hėr, maybė; pin, pīne; not, nōte, ôr, tool

Bermuda shorts short pants reaching almost to the knees.

ber′ry (ber′ē) *n.* **1,** any small pulpy fruit. **2,** a dry kernel, as of coffee. —*v.i.* **1,** produce berries. **2,** gather berries.

ber·serk′ (bēr·sērk′) *adj.* in a frenzy; amuck.

---
berserk
↔ Originally adapted by Sir Walter Scott from the Icelandic word *berserkr*, frenzied Norse warrior. The adjective form arose in the late 19th c.
---

berth (bērth) *n.* **1,** a sleeping compartment; bunk. **2,** a storage space; a dock. **3,** a job. **4,** a position, as in a competition. —*v.i. & t.* enter or place in a berth.

ber′tha (bēr′thə) *n.* a short cape or collar worn by women.

---
bertha
↔ After the wife of King Pepin the Short of the Franks, known for her modesty.
---

ber′yl (ber′əl) *n.* **1,** a mineral occurring in many colors, prized as a gem. **2,** a bluegreen color.

be·ryl′li·um (bə-ril′ē-əm) *n.* a metallic chemical element, no. 4, symbol Be.

be·seech′ (bē-sēch′) *v.t.* ask urgently; entreat; implore; solicit.

be·seem′ (bē-sēm′) *v.t.* be fit for or worthy of.

be·set′ (bē-set′) *v.t.* [**be·set′, -set′ting**] attack from all sides; assail; harass.

be·shrew′ (bē-shroo′) *v.t.* put a curse on.

be·side′ (bē-sīd′) *prep.* **1,** at the side of; near. **2,** in addition to. **3,** apart from; not connected with. —*adv.* besides.

be·sides′ (bē-sīdz′) *adv.* **1,** moreover; further. **2,** in addition. **3,** otherwise; else. —*prep.* beside.

be·siege′ (bē-sēj′) *v.t.* **1,** lay siege to. **2,** harass, as with demands, etc.

be·smirch′ (bē-smērch′) *v.t.* soil; sully the honor of.

be′som (bē′zəm) *n.* a broom of twigs.

be·sot′ted (bē-sot′id) *adj.* **1,** stupefied, as with drink. **2,** addicted to drink. —**be·sot′,** *v.t.*

be·speak′ (bē-spēk′) *v.t.* [**be·spoke′, be·spo′ken**] **1,** show; indicate. **2,** order in advance.

best *adj.* **1,** superlative of *good.* **2,** largest. —*adv.* **1,** superlative of *well.* **2,** with most advantage or success. **3,** most fully. —*n.* the utmost; the highest quality. —*v.t.* defeat; surpass. —**best boy,** in motion pictures and television, the first assistant (male or female) to the head electrician. —**best man,** chief attendant of the bridegroom at a wedding. —**best woman,** the chief attendant of a bride.

bes′tial (bes′chəl) *adj.* **1,** like a beast; brutal. **2,** pert. to beasts. —**bes·tial′i·ty** (-chal′ə-tē) *n.*

be·stir′ (bē-stēr′) *v.t. & i.* [**-stirred′, -stir′-ring**] agitate; rouse.

be·stow′ (bē-stō′) *v.t.* **1,** give; confer as a gift. **2,** deposit; consign. —**be·stow′al,** *n.*

be·stride′ (bē-strīd′) *v.t.* [**be·strode′, be·strid′den**] **1,** sit astride of; straddle. **2,** step over or across.

bet *v.t. & i.* [**bet, bet′ting**] pledge as forfeit upon some contingency; wager. —*n.* **1,** a wager. **2,** the stake.

be′ta (bā′tə) *n.* the second letter of the Greek alphabet (B, β). —**beta blocker,** a drug used in the treatment of hypertension and other heart irregularities. —**beta particle,** an electron emitted by a radioactive substance. —**beta ray,** a stream of beta particles. —**beta test,** a test of an experimental product, usu. conducted by an organization other than the manufacturer.

be·take′ (bē-tāk′) *v.t.* [**-took′, -tak′ing**] take (oneself) to a place; go.

be′ta·tron″ (bā′tə-tron″) *n.* a device for accelerating electrons to high velocity.

bête″ noire′ (bet″ nwär′) [*pl.* **bêtes noires** (bet″ nwär′)] (*Fr.*) an object of aversion or dislike.

be·think′ (bē-think′) (*Archaic*) *v.t.* [*pret. & p.p.* **-thought′**] remind (oneself); recall.

be·tide′ (bē-tīd′) *v.i. & t.* come to pass; happen (to).

be·times′ (bē-tīmz′) *adv.* (*Archaic*) early; soon.

be·to′ken (bē-tō′kən) *v.t.* be a token or visible sign of; indicate.

be·tray′ (bē-trā′) *v.t.* **1,** deliver treacherously to an enemy. **2,** be unfaithful in (a trust). **3,** reveal unconsciously. —**betray′al,** *n.*

be·troth′ (bē-trâth′) *v.t.* engage to take or give in marriage. —**be·troth′al,** *n.*

bet′ter (bet′ər) *adj.* **1,** comparative of *good.* **2,** larger. **3,** improved in health. —*adv.* comparative of *well.* —*v.t.* **1,** improve. **2,** surpass. —*n.* **1,** something or someone superior. **2,** [also, **bet′tor**] one who bets. —**better half,** (*Derog.*) spouse. —**bet′ter·ment,** *n.* act or effect of bettering; improvement. —**better than,** (*Informal*) more than.

be·tween′ (bē-twēn′) *prep.* **1,** in the

space that separates (two things). **2,** intermediate in time, quantity, or degree. **3,** in joint interest or action of. **4,** involving; concerning. —*adv.* intermediate in space, time, etc. ❑ *among*

be·twixt′ (bė-twikst′) *prep.* (*Archaic*) between.

bev′a·tron″ (bev′ə-tron″) *n.* a device for accelerating electrons, protons, etc.

bev′el (bev′əl) *n.* **1,** an angle other than a right angle between two lines or surfaces. **2,** an instrument for measuring or cutting a bevel. —*v.t. & i.* cut or slant obliquely. —*adj.* oblique.

bev′er·age (bev′ər-ij) *n.* any liquid fit for drinking.

bev′y (bev′ė) *n.* a flock of birds or persons.

be·wail′ (bė-wāl′) *v.t. & i.* mourn aloud (for).

be·ware′ (bė-wâr′) *v.i. & t.* be wary (of), cautious, or vigilant.

be·wil′der (bė-wil′dər) *v.t.* lead into perplexity; confuse. —**be·wil′der·ment,** *n.*

be·witch′ (bė-wich′) *v.t.* **1,** please extremely; charm; fascinate. **2,** cast a spell upon. —**be·witch′ing,** *adj.*

be·yond′ (bė-yond′) *prep. & adv.* **1,** on the other side of; farther on than. **2,** more than; superior to. **3,** outside the reach or limits of.

bez′el (bez′əl) *n.* a beveled face or part.

Bé·zier′ curve (bā-zyā′) (*Computers*) a curved line or line segment generated mathematically and controlled by control handles at its endpoints, named for French mathematician Pierre Bézier.

bhang (bang) *n.* **1,** an E. Indian hemp plant. **2,** a narcotic obtained from it.

bi- (bī) *pref.* two; twice; once in every two.

> **bi-, semi-**
> ☛ As the meaning of these prefixes used with weekly, monthly, annually, is ambiguous at best, it is preferable to specify exactly what one means, as *twice a week* or *once every two years.*

bi·al′y (bė-al′ė) *n.* a flat, onion-flavored breakfast roll.

bi·an′nu·al (bī-an′ū-əl) *adj.* occurring twice a year. ❑ *bi-*

bi′as (bī′əs) *n.* **1,** an oblique line or direction. **2,** prejudice. —*v.t.* prejudice; warp. —*adj. & adv.* oblique; unbalanced.

bi·ath′lon (bī-ath′lon) *n.* an athletic competition combining cross-country skiing and marksmanship.

bib *n.* a cloth worn over the breast to protect the clothing.

bib′e·lot (bib′ə-lō) *n.* any small article prized for beauty or rarity.

Bi′ble (bī′bəl) *n.* **1,** the collection of sacred writings, comprising the Old and New Testaments. **2,** (*l.c.*) any book regarded as authoritative. —**Bible Belt,** (*Informal*) areas of the southern and midwestern U.S. where religious fundamentalism is widely found. —**Bible paper,** extremely thin paper, used for printing bibles, reference works, etc. —**Bib′li·cal** (bib′li-kəl) *adj.*

> **Bible**
> ↔ From Greek *biblia,* books, perhaps from *Bublos,* an ancient Phoenician port and source of papyrus.

bib′li·o- (bib′lė-ō) *pref.* **1,** book. **2,** Bible.

bib″li·og′ra·phy (bib″lė-og′rə-fė) *n.* **1,** classification of books. **2,** a list of books. —**bib″li·o·graph′i·cal,** *adj.*

bib′li·o·phile″ (bib′lė-ō-fīl″) *n.* a lover of books.

bib′u·lous (bib′yə-ləs) *adj.* addicted to drinking liquor. —**bib′u·lous·ness,** *n.*

bi·cam′er·al (bī-kam′ər-əl) *adj.* (of a legislature) comprising two houses.

bi·car′bon·ate of soda (bī-kär′bə-nət) a white, crystalline, alkaline substance, commonly called *baking soda.*

bi″cen·ten′ni·al *adj.* the 200th anniversary.

bi′ceps (bī′seps) *n.sing.* a muscle having a double origin at one end, esp. that on the upper arm.

bi·chlor′ide (bī-klôr′īd) *n.* a compound in which each molecule contains two atoms of chlorine.

bick′er (bik′ər) *v.i. & n.* engage in a petulant quarrel; wrangle.

bi′con·cave″ *adj.* concave on both sides.

bi′con·vex″ *adj.* convex on both sides.

bi′cron (bī′kron) *n.* one billionth of a meter.

bi·cus′pid (bī-kus′pid) *adj.* having two cusps or points. —*n.* a double-pointed tooth.

bi′cy·cle (bī′sik-əl) *n.* a vehicle having two wheels in line. —**bi′cy·clist,** *n.*

bid *v.t.* **1,** [**bade, bid′den, -ding**] command; invite. **2,** [*pret. & p.p.* **bid**] offer a price of. —*v.i.* make an offer. —*n.* **1,** an amount or thing offered. **2,** an effort. **3,** an invitation. —**bid′der,** *n.* —**bid fair,** appear likely.

bid′dy (bid′ė) *n.* **1,** a chicken, esp. a hen. **2,** (*Offensive*) a cackling woman.

bide (bīd) *v.t. & i.* pause; await.

bi·det' (bi-det'; *Fr.* bē-dā') *n.* **1,** a small horse. **2,** a low basin used for bathing the genital area.

bi·en'ni·al (bī-en'ė-əl) *adj.* happening every two years. —*n.* a plant that blooms every two years. ❏ *annual*

bier (bir) *n.* a framework on which a coffin is laid before burial.

biff (bif) *v.t.* (*Informal*) strike sharply. —*n.* a blow.

bi·fo'cal (bī-fō'kəl) *adj.* having two focal points. —*n.* (*pl.*) eyeglasses having a bifocal lens for near and far vision.

bi'fur·cate" (bī'fər-kāt") *v.* divide into two branches. —*adj.* two-branched.

big *adj.* [**big'ger, -gest**] **1,** large in size, extent, degree, etc. **2,** important. **3,** generous, tolerant. —**big bang,** describing a theory that the universe resulted from a single explosion. —**big brother,** (*Slang*) government, esp. oppressive government. —**big shot,** bigwig. —**big ticket,** (*Slang*) expensive. —**big top,** the circus.

big'a·my (big'ə-mė) *n.* the crime of having two wives or husbands at the same time. —**big'a·mist,** *n.* —**big'a·mous,** *adj.*

Big'foot" *n.* sasquatch.

big'horn" *n.* a wild sheep of the Rocky Mountains.

bight (bīt) *n.* **1,** a bend, as of a coastline; a bay. **2,** a loop in rope.

big'ot (big'ət) *n.* a person intolerant of creeds, opinions, etc. other than his own. —**big'ot·ry** (-rė) *n.*

big'wig" *n.* (*Informal*) a high-ranking person.

bike (bīk) *n.* (*Informal*) **1,** bicycle. **2,** motorcycle. —**bik'er,** *n.* (*Informal*) a member of a motorcycle club or gang.

bi·ki'ni (bi-kē'nė) *n.* a woman's scanty two-piece bathing suit.

---

bikini
↔ Named by a French newspaper after the Bikini atoll, test site for an atomic bomb in 1946, apparently because of the explosive effect of the swimsuit on observers.

---

bi·lat'er·al (bī-lat'ər-əl) *adj.* having two sides.

bil'ber"ry (bil'ber"ė) *n.* a flowering shrub; its berry.

Bil'dungs·ro·man" (bil'dungs-rō-män") *n.* (*Ger.*) a novel showing the educational and romantic development of a character.

bile (bīl) *n.* **1,** a secretion of the liver. **2,** ill nature; peevishness.

bilge (bilj) *n.* **1,** the bulging or broadest part, as of a ship or barrel. **2,** (*Slang*) buncombe; obscenity. —**bilge water,** evil-smelling water that collects in the hold of a ship.

bi·lin'gual (bī-ling'gwəl) *adj.* **1,** able to speak two languages. **2,** expressed in two languages. —**bi·lin'gual·ism,** *n.* —**bi·lin'guist,** *n.*

bil'ious (bil'yəs) *adj.* having an excess of bile. —**bil'ious·ness,** *n.*

-bil'i·ty (bil'ə-tė) *suf.* forming nouns of adjectives ending in *-able* and *-ible*.

bilk *v.t.* defraud; swindle.

bill (bil) *n.* **1,** an account of money owed. **2,** a written order to pay money. **3,** a piece of paper money. **4,** a proposed law. **5,** a list or public notice: *handbill.* **6,** the horny beak of a bird. —*v.t.* **1,** enter on a bill; send a bill to. **2,** engage or schedule on a theatrical program. —**bill and coo,** make love sentimentally. —**bill of fare,** a list of dishes available in a restaurant. —**bill of lading,** a list of goods received for transportation. —**Bill of Rights,** constitutional law guaranteeing civil liberties. —**bill of sale,** a document transferring possession.

bil'la·bong" (bil'ə-bong") *n.* (*Australian*) **1,** a branch of a river. **2,** a stagnant backwater.

bill'board" *n.* a large board for posting of advertisements.

bil'let (bil'it) *n.* **1,** a sleeping space or lodging, esp. for a soldier or sailor. **2,** assignment; job. **3,** (also, bi-lā') a ticket; a written note. **4,** a stick of wood, esp. for fuel. —*v.t.* assign to a lodging or place.

bil'let-doux' (bil"ā-doo') *n.* (*Fr.*) a love letter.

bill'fold" *n.* a wallet.

bil'liards (bil'yərdz) *n.* (*construed as sing.*) a game played with balls driven by cues on a rectangular table. —**bil'liard,** *n.* a scoring shot in this game; carom.

bill'ing *n.* **1,** act of sending or listing on a bill. **2,** advertisement of a performer's name on a program.

bil'lings·gate" (bil'ingz-gāt") *n.* coarse and abusive language.

bil'lion (bil'yən) *n.* **1,** (*U.S.*) a thousand millions; also (*Brit.*) **mil'liard. 2,** (*Brit.*) a million millions.

bil'low (bil'ō) *n.* a large sea wave; any similar surging mass. —*v.i.* surge like a sea wave. —**bil'low·y,** *adj.*

bil'ly (bil'ė) *n.* a small bludgeon, esp. a policeman's club.

bil'ly·goat" *n.* a male goat.

bim'bo (bim'bō) *n.* (*Slang, Derog.*) **1,** a

---

tub, cūte, pŭll; labəl; oil, owl, go, chip, she, thin, *th*en, sing, ink; *see p. 6* beautiful young person. **2,** a disreputable person.

bi·met'al·lism (bī-met'ə-liz-əm) *n.* use of both gold and silver as a monetary standard.

bi·month'ly *adj.* **1,** every two months. **2,** twice a month. ❏ *bi-*

bin *n.* a storage compartment.

bi'na·ry (bī'nə-rē) *adj.* **1,** having two parts or components. **2,** based on the radix 2.

bin·au'ral (bī-nôr'əl) *adj.* pert. to, involving, or designed for the use of both ears.

bind (bīnd) *v.t.* [*pret. & p.p.* **bound**] **1,** make fast with a band; fasten; cause to cohere. **2,** form a border on. **3,** obligate; compel. —*v.i.* **1,** stick fast; cohere. **2,** be obligatory. **3,** chafe; restrict.

bind'er (bīn'dər) *n.* **1,** one who binds. **2,** a device for binding; a cover in which loose pages are held. **3,** an adhesive; cement. —**bind'er·y,** *n.* a place where books are bound.

bin'di (bin'dē) *n.* a cosmetic dot worn on the forehead by some women of India, formerly indicating marital status.

bind'ing (bīn'ding) *n.* that which binds: the cover of a bound book, a reinforcing strip, etc.

bindle stiff (*Slang*) a hobo.

binge (binj) *n.* (*Slang*) spree.

bin'go (bing'gō) *n.* a game based on lotto. —*interj.* a cry of triumph.

bin'na·cle (bin'ə-kəl) *n.* the stand that holds a ship's compass.

bi·noc'u·lar (bə-nok'yə-lər) *adj.* having or requiring two eyes. —*n.* (*pl.*) a telescope or microscope with two eyepieces.

bi·no'mi·al (bī-nō'mē-əl) *adj.* having two parts. —*n.* an algebraic expression, as *a* + *b*.

bi'o (bī'ō) *n.* (*Informal*) a biography.

bi·o- (bī-ō, bī-ə) *pref.* **1,** life; living things. **2,** biological.

bi'o·chem'is·try *n.* the chemistry of life and living things.

bi'o·clean'' *adj.* free or almost free from harmful organisms.

bi''o·de·grad'a·ble (-dē-grād'ə-bəl) *adj.* able to be decomposed by bacterial action.

bi''o·feed'back *n.* the monitoring of one's own bodily functions; the data so obtained.

bi·og'ra·phy (bī-og'rə-fē) *n.* **1,** a history of the life of a person. **2,** such histories collectively. —**bi''o·graph'i·cal,** *adj.*

bi·ol'o·gy (bī-ol'ə-jē) *n.* the general science of the structure and processes of living organisms. —**bi''o·log'i·cal,** *adj.* —**bi·ol'o·gist,** *n.*

bi'ome (bī'ōm) *n.* any community of plants and animals.

bi''o·med'i·cine *n.* a branch of medicine concerned with human survival under stress.

bi·on'ic (bī-on'ik) *adj.* relating biological functions and engineering.

bi''o·phys'ics *n.* the physics of life and living things.

bi'op·sy (bī'op-sē) *n.* the removal of tissue or fluids from the body for examination.

bi'o·rhythm (bī'ō-ri*th*-əm) *n.* an innately controlled biological or physical process, such as the sleep cycle. —**bi''orhyth'mic,** *adj.*

bi''o·tech·nol'o·gy *n.* the branch of technology dealing with living organisms.

bi·ot'ic (bī-ot'ik) *adj.* pert. to life.

bi'o·tin (bī'ə-tin) *n.* vitamin H, found in liver, egg yolk, etc.

bi'o·tron'' (bī'ə-tron'') *n.* a chamber for study of the effects of environment on living organisms.

bi'o·type'' (bī'ə-tīp'') *n.* a group of organisms having the same hereditary constitution. —**bi''o·typ'ic** (-tip'ik) *adj.*

bi·par'ti·san (bī-pär'ti-zən) *adj.* representing or involving two parties.

bi·par'tite (bī-pär'tīt) *adj.* having or divided into two corresponding parts.

bi'ped (bī'ped) *n.* a two-footed animal.

bi'plane'' (bī'plān'') *n.* an airplane with two wings in tier.

birch (bėrch) *n.* a tree having smooth bark, often white; its wood.

Birch'er (bėr'chər) *n.* (*Slang*) a member of the John Birch Society, a reactionary political organization.

bird (bėrd) *n.* **1,** any feather-covered vertebrate animal whose forelimbs form wings. **2,** (*Brit. slang*) an attractive young girl. —**bird's-'eye'',** *adj.* general; cursory, as a view from above. —**bird of paradise,** a bird with brilliant plumage, found in New Guinea.

---

bird

↔ In Old English, *bird* meant nestling, and only in the 14th c. did it become the general term. It is of unknown origin.

---

bird'ie (bėr'dē) *n.* (*Golf*) a score on a hole of one under par.

bird′man *n.* **1,** ornithologist. **2,** (*Informal*) aviator.

bi′reme (bī′rēm) *n.* an ancient galley having two banks of oars on each side.

bi·ret′ta (bə-ret′ə) *n.* a stiff cap worn by Roman Catholic priests.

birth (bērth) *n.* **1,** act of being born. **2,** the bringing forth of offspring. **3,** lineage; descent. **4,** the origin or inception of anything.

birth′day″ *n.* the day of one's birth, or any anniversary of it. —**birthday suit,** (*Informal*) the unclothed body.

birth′mark″ *n.* a congenital blemish on the body.

birth′place″ *n.* the place where one was born.

birth′right″ *n.* inheritance.

birth′stone″ *n.* a gem associated with a certain month or period.

bis′cuit (bis′kit) *n.* **1,** (*U.S.*) a small, soft cake made from leavened dough. **2,** (*Brit.*) a flat, hard cake made from unleavened dough; a cracker. **3,** anything in the shape of a biscuit. **4,** plastic material in process of shaping, molding, or baking.

---

biscuit
↔ From Old French *biscut,* twice-cooked, a method of cooking biscuits designed to assure their crispness.

---

bi·sect′ (bī-sekt′) *v.t.* **1,** cut into two parts. **2,** divide into two equal parts. —**bi·sec′tion,** *n.*

bi·sex′u·al (bī-sek′shoo-əl) *adj.* **1,** combining both sexes; hermaphroditic. **2,** applying to both sexes. **3,** attracted sexually to persons of both sexes. —*n.* a person both homo- and heterosexual. —**bi″sex·u·al′i·ty,** *n.*

bish′op (bish′əp) *n.* **1,** a high officer of a church. **2,** a chess piece. —**bish′op·ric** (-rik) *n.* the diocese or office of a bishop; see.

---

bishop
↔ From Greek *episkopos,* overseer (there was no suggestion of a clergy).

---

bis′muth (biz′məth) *n.* a metallic element, no. 83, symbol Bi.

bi′son (bī′sən) *n.* a large animal of the ox family; the buffalo.

bisque (bisk) *n.* **1,** a thickened soup. **2,** unglazed porcelain. **3,** a handicap allowed a weaker player.

bis·sex′tile (bī-seks′til) *adj.* pert. to the extra day of leap year. —*n.* a leap year.

bis′tro (bis′trō) *n.* a small café.

bit *n.* **1,** a small piece or quantity of any-

thing. **2,** any small coin; a money value of 12 cents. **3,** the mouthpiece of a horse's bridle. **4,** the essential part of a cutting tool. **5,** (*Informal*) a routine or pattern of behavior; specialty. **6,** a unit of memory capacity, as in a computer: *bi(nary) (digi)t.* **7,** a unit of information, the result of a choice between two alternatives: in a binary computer, between 0 and 1. —*v.* pret. of *bite.*

bitch (bich) *n.* **1,** a female of the dog family. **2,** (*Slang, Offensive*) a malicious woman. **3,** (*Slang*) a complaint. —*v.i.* (*Slang*) complain. —*v.t.* (with *up*) (*Slang*) bungle; spoil.

bite (bīt) *v.t.* [**bit** (bit), **bit′ten** (bit′ən), **bit′ing**] **1,** grip or pierce with the teeth. **2,** sting. **3,** take firm hold of. **4,** eat into; corrode. —*v.i.* **1,** take a bait; accept something deceptive. **2,** take hold; act with effect. —*n.* **1,** the act of biting. **2,** a piece bitten off. **3,** a small quantity of food.

bit′map″ *n.* (*Computers*) a file describing a digital image as a series of dots and spaces.

bit′stock″ *n.* a handle for a bit or drill; brace.

bit′ten (bit′ən) *v.* p.p. of *bite.*

bit′ter (bit′ər) *adj.* **1,** having a harsh taste. **2,** hard to bear; disagreeable. **3,** cruel; sarcastic. —*n.* (*pl.*) a liquor having a bitter taste. —**bitter end,** the final resolution of a difficult situation. —**bit′ter·ness,** *n.*

---

bitter
↔ The *bitter* in *bitter end* probably comes from *bitt,* a type of post on a ship. The *bitter end* is the inboard end of a mooring line. The adjective *bitter* comes from Old English *biter,* biting.

---

bit′tern (bit′ərn) *n.* a No. Amer. heron.

bi·tu′men (bi-tū′mən) *n.* any of a class of natural substances such as petroleum and asphalt. —**bi·tu′mi·nous,** *adj.*

bi′valve″ (bī′valv″) *n.* a mollusk having two shells, as the oyster. —*adj.* two-shelled.

biv′ou·ac″ (biv′oo-ak″) *n.* an unsheltered encampment or camp. —*v.i.* [**biv′ou·acked″, -ack″ing**] encamp without shelter.

bi·week′ly *adj.* **1,** every two weeks. **2,** twice a week. ❑ *bi-*

bi·zarre′ (bi-zär′) *adj.* odd; whimsical; grotesque. —**bi·zarre′ness,** *n.*

blab *v.t.* [**blabbed, blab′bing**] utter thoughtlessly; disclose. —*v.i.* talk indiscreetly.

---

bizarre, bazaar

☛ Do not confuse *bazaar*, a market, and *bizarre*, strange. ↔ Originally, *bizarre* is derived from Basque *bizarra*, beard; how it acquired its present sense is conjectural. *Bazaar* is Persian for market.

blab'ber (blab'ər) *v.i.* **1,** mumble. **2,** blab; talk idly.

black (blak) *n.* **1,** the color of coal; strictly, the absence of all color or of all illumination. **2,** a Negro. —*adj.* **1,** entirely or relatively dark. **2,** dismal; wicked; evil; calamitous. **3,** Negro. —*v.t.* put blacking on. —**black belt,** a degree of attainment in judo, karate, etc.; the belt conferred to indicate it. —**black box, 1,** a device whose function is known, but whose components and method of operation are concealed. **2,** a recording device installed in an aircraft to record the output from critical instruments and insulated to survive a crash. —**Black Death,** bubonic plague. —**black eye, 1,** a bruise near the eye. **2,** (*Informal*) disgrace. —**black fly,** a very small fly or gnat with a venomous bite. —**black gold,** (*Informal*) oil. —**black hole,** (*Astron.*) a theoretical celestial body considered to be a collapsed star. —**black humor** *or* **comedy,** humor characterized by a cynical, ironic, often grotesque view of the human condition. —**black letter,** a style of type. —**black light,** invisible ultraviolet or infrared light. —**black lung,** a disease caused by breathing coal dust. —**black magic,** magic used malevolently. —**Black Maria** (mə-rī'ə) (*Slang*) a police patrol wagon used to transport prisoners. —**black market,** the selling of goods in violation of legal restrictions.—**black mar'-ket·eer',** one who sells goods on the black market. —**Black Muslim** (mus'ləm) a member of a Negro religious organization following the tenets of Islam. —**Black Nationalism,** an African-American movement advocating political separation of blacks and whites by formation of a black nation either within the boundaries of the U.S. or abroad. —**black out,** lose consciousness. —**Black Power,** a movement among African-Americans to achieve political and economic power without integration. —**black sheep,** a disgraceful member of a family or group. —**Black Shirt,** a member of the Fascist party of Italy. —**Black Studies,** the study of black history and culture. —**black tie,** semiformal evening wear for men. —**black widow,** a kind of poisonous spider. ❑ *African-American*

black'a·moor (blak'ə-mûr) *n.* a black.

black-"and-blue' *adj.* discolored by bruising.

black'ball" *v.t.* reject; ostracize.

black'ber"ry *n.* a thorny vine, or its fruit.

black'bird" *n.* any of various birds having dark plumage.

black'bird"er (-bēr"ər) *n.* (*Hist.*) a trader in black slaves.

black'board" *n.* a slate bulletin board. —**blackboard jungle,** (*Slang*) an urban school whose students are unusually disorderly or destructive.

black'en (-ən) *v.t. & i.* make or become black.

black'face" *n.* an entertainer made up to portray a black person; the makeup used for this purpose. —**black'faced"** (-fāst") *adj.*

black'guard (blag'ərd) *n.* a scoundrel. —**black'guard·ly,** *adj.*

black'head" *n.* **1,** a secretion of fatty matter in a skin follicle. **2,** a disease of poultry.

black'ing *n.* shoe polish.

black'jack" (blak'jak") *n.* **1,** a club with a heavy head and a short elastic shaft. **2,** card game: *twenty-one.* —*v.t.* **1,** hit with a blackjack. **2,** coerce.

black'leg" *n.* **1,** a disease of cattle. **2,** a strikebreaker; scab. **3,** a swindler; a crooked gambler.

black'list" *n.* a list of persons in disfavor. —*v.t.* **1,** vote against (a candidate for club membership). **2,** put on a blacklist.

black'mail" *n.* extortion of a bribe for silence. —*v.t.* threaten exposure unless paid.

black'out" *n.* **1,** the extinguishing of lights, as for protection against enemy airplanes or as a result of an electrical failure. **2,** unconsciousness; a faint. **3,** loss of memory.

black'smith" (blak'smith") *n.* a worker in iron, esp. a horseshoer.

black'thorn" *n.* a prickly shrub.

black'top" *n.* a bituminous substance for paving roads, etc. —*v.t.* pave with blacktop.

blad'der (blad'ər) *n.* **1,** a body sac in which urine is retained. **2,** any elastic sac or bag.

blade (blād) *n.* **1,** the sharpened part of a cutting or piercing weapon or tool; the weapon or tool itself, esp. a sword. **2,** the leaf of a plant; the broad part of a leaf. **3,** any broad thin part, as of an oar. **4,** a gay or rakish fellow. —*v.i.* to skate using a Rollerblade.

blah (blä) *adj.* **1,** listless; debilitated. **2,** dull; uninteresting. **—the blahs,** (*Slang*) boredom; listlessness.

blain (blān) *n.* an inflammatory swelling; a blister.

blame (blām) *v.t.* charge with an error or fault. *—n.* imputation of error or fault; censure. **—blame'wor"thy,** *adj.* culpable.

blanch (blanch) *v.t.* make white or pale. *—v.i.* become pale.

blanc·mange' (bläń-mäńj') *n.* a sweet, almond-flavored pudding containing gelatine.

bland *adj.* **1,** suave. **2,** affable; kindly. **3,** mild; balmy. **4,** oily; nonirritating or nonstimulating (of foods or medicines). **—bland'ness,** *n.*

blan'dish *v.t.* coax or cajole with flattery or caresses. **—blan'dish·ment,** *n.*

blank *adj.* **1,** empty; bare; void of something usual or necessary to completeness. **2,** not written or printed on. **3,** showing no emotion; unresponsive. **4,** complete; unmitigated. **5,** white or pale. *—n.* **1,** a space from which something is absent or omitted; a vacancy. **2,** a printed form or space not filled out by writing. **3,** a rough-fashioned wood or metal part to be finished by tooling. *—v.t.* **1,** (with *out*) make blank. **2,** (*Informal*) keep an opponent in a game from scoring. **—blank'ness,** *n.* **—blank check,** (*Informal*) unlimited authority. **—blank verse,** unrhymed but metrical verse.

blan'ket (blang'kit) *n.* **1,** a large piece of heavy cloth, used as a bedcovering. **2,** any extensive or close covering, as of snow. *—adj.* widespread; comprehensive. *—v.t.* cover with or as with a blanket.

blare (blâr) *v.i.* give out a brazen sound; bellow. *—v.t.* sound loudly; proclaim. *—n.* **1,** a trumpet's sound. **2,** blatancy in sound, color, etc.

blar'ney (blär'nė) *n.* wheedling talk; cajolery. *—v.t. & i.* flatter; cajole.

> **blarney**
> ↔ From the *Blarney Stone*, at Blarney Castle, near Cork, Ireland, which is reputed to impart skill in flattery to one who kisses it.

bla·sé' (blä-zā') *adj.* satiated with pleasure; bored.

blas·pheme' (blas-fēm') *v.i.* speak irreverently of God or sacred things. *—v.t.* **1,** speak impiously of (God, etc.). **2,** speak evil of; revile. **—blas'phe·mous** (-fə-məs), *adj.* **—blas'phe·my** (-fə-mė) *n.*

blast (blåst) *n.* **1,** a forceful stream or sudden gust of air. **2,** the blowing of a horn, whistle, etc.; the sound of a wind

instrument. **3,** an explosion; a charge of explosives. **4,** a blight. *—v.t.* **1,** shatter with explosives. **2,** ruin; destroy; cause to shrivel. **—blast furnace,** a smelting furnace in which fuel is burned under a forced draft of air. **—blast off,** take off (said·esp. of rockets).

blat (blat) *v.i.* bleat *—v.t.* (*Informal*) blurt; blab.

bla'tant (blā'tənt) *adj.* **1,** offensively loud-voiced; noisy. **2,** obtrusive. **—bla'-tan·cy** (-tən-sė) *n.*

> **blatant, flagrant**
> ☛ These words are often misused. *Blatant* means noisy, offensive. *Flagrant* means overtly outrageous, notorious. ↔ *Blatant* was apparently coined by the poet Edmund Spenser in the *Faerie Queene* (1596).

blath'er (bla*th*'ər) *v.* talk or say foolishly. *—n.* foolish talk.

blath'er·skite" (-skīt") *n.* a voluble, foolish talker.

blaze (blāz) *n.* **1,** flame or fire. **2,** any dazzling display, brilliant sunlight; a bright flame; a hot glow. **3,** a sudden outburst of fire, passion, etc. **4,** a white spot on the face of a horse, cow, etc. **5,** a mark made on a tree to indicate a path or boundary. **6,** (*pl.*) (*Slang*) hell. *—v.i.* burst into flame; burn brightly; shine. *—v.t.* **1,** exhibit vividly; proclaim. **2,** mark with a blaze.

> **blaze, blazon**
> ☛ These two words are sometimes confused. Both words can mean to proclaim, but *blaze* more often means to find new ways ("blaze a trail"), whereas *blazon* means to display, trumpet forth.

blaz'er (blā'zər) *n.* **1,** coat for sports wear, usu. brightly colored or navy blue. **2,** a pan for use over a flame. **3,** (*Informal*) anything intensely hot or bright.

bla'zon (blā'zən) *v.t.* **1,** depict or describe in heraldic terms. **2,** adorn. **3,** display; proclaim. *—n.* **1,** a coat of arms. **2,** pompous display. **—bla'zon·ry,** *n.* ❑ *blaze*

bleach (blēch) *v.t. & i.* make or become white, pale, or colorless. *—n.* a bleaching agent.

bleach'ers (blē'chərz) *n.pl.* unsheltered seats on a playing field.

bleak (blēk) *adj.* **1,** desolate and windswept. **2,** cold; piercing. **3,** cheerless; dreary. **—bleak'ness,** *n.*

blear (blir) *v.t.* dim (the eyes) with tears, etc. *—adj.* (of the eyes) sore or dimmed. **—blear'y,** *adj.*

bleat (blēt) *n.* the cry of a sheep, goat, or calf. —*v.i.* utter such a cry.

bled *v.* pret. & p.p. of *bleed.*

bleed (blēd) *v.i.* [**bled**] **1,** emit blood. **2,** exude fluid. **3,** flow out; run together. **4,** feel pity, sorrow, or anguish. —*v.t.* **1,** cause to lose blood, sap, etc.; make flow; drain out. **2,** (*Informal*) extract money from, as by overcharge or blackmail. **3,** (*Printing*) allow (a picture) to run off the page; trim (a page) so as to cut into the printing. —**bleed′er,** *n.* a hemophiliac. —**bleeding heart,** (*Slang*) a person considered unduly softhearted or sympathetic.

bleep (blēp) *n.* a short, high-pitched sound; beep. —*v.t.* blip.

blem′ish *v.t.* deface; mar; damage. —*n.* defect; flaw; stain.

blench *v.i.* draw back; flinch; quail.

blend *v.t.* **1,** mix inseparably. **2,** mix so as to obtain a desired combination of qualities. —*v.i.* **1,** combine into a harmonious whole. **2,** pass imperceptibly into one another. —*n.* **1,** the act of blending. **2,** something formed by blending; a smooth mixture; a harmonious whole.

bless (bles) *v.t.* **1,** consecrate by a religious rite. **2,** invoke God's favor upon. **3,** make happy, fortunate, or prosperous. **4,** praise; extol. —**bless′ed** (-ed), **blessed,** or **blest,** *adj.* —**bless′ed event,** the birth of a child.

> **bless**
> ↔ The original sense of the word was "mark with blood."

bless′ing *n.* **1,** a short prayer for divine approval. **2,** a fortunate occurrence. **3,** benediction; approval.

blew (bloo) *v.* pret. of *blow.*

blight (blīt) *n.* **1,** any widespread disease of plants. **2,** any similar malignant and destructive influence. —*v.t.* **1,** cause to wither or decay. **2,** ruin; frustrate.

blimp *n.* **1,** an airship with a nonrigid gas bag. **2,** (*Informal*) an obese person.

blind (blīnd) *adj.* **1,** lacking or having lost the sense of sight. **2,** lacking in discernment; unable to understand or judge. **3,** irrational; undiscriminating; heedless. **4,** out of sight; hidden; unlighted. **5,** having no opening or outlet. **6,** done without seeing. —*v.t.* **1,** deprive of sight. **2,** make obscure; conceal. **3,** impair the perception or judgment of. —*n.* **1,** something that obstructs vision or excludes light. **2,** something that masks a purpose or action. **3,** a rude shelter for hunters. —**blind′ness,** *n.* —**blind alley,** a street blocked at one end; an impasse. —**blind date,** an engagement

with a stranger. —**blindman's buff,** a game of tag in which the person searching is blindfolded. —**blind spot, 1,** an area of poor visibility, reception, etc. **2,** a part of the retina not sensitive to light. **3,** an area of impaired judgment. —**blind trust,** a trust controlling the assets of a public official and administered by a trustee to avoid conflict of interest.

blind′fold″ *n.* a bandage over the eyes. —*v.t.* put a blindfold on.

blink *v.i.* **1,** wink rapidly and repeatedly. **2,** shine unsteadily; glimmer. —*v.t.* **1,** catch sight of. **2,** regard with indifference; ignore. —*n.* **1,** a wink or gleam. **2,** a glance or glimpse.

blink′er *n.* **1,** an intermittent signal light; flasher. **2,** (*pl.*) [also, **blind′ers**] shades for horses' eyes.

blintz (blints) *n.* a thin rolled pancake with a filling.

blip *n.* **1,** an image on a radar screen. **2,** a temporary adjustment or problem, as in statistics. —*v.t.* censor part of a recording by recording a tone over it.

bliss (blis) *n.* **1,** supreme happiness; spiritual joy. **2,** gladness. —**bliss′ful,** *adj.*

blis′ter (blis′tər) *n.* **1,** a vesicle on the skin. **2,** any similar swelling, as in a coat of paint; an air bubble in a metal casting. —*v.t.* **1,** raise a blister on. **2,** vituperate; mortify. —*v.i.* become blistered.

blithe (blīth) *adj.* merry; joyous; glad; lighthearted. —**blithe′ness,** *n.* —**blithe′some** (-səm) *adj.* merry; gay.

blith′er·ing (blith′ə-ring) *adj.* talking foolishly.

blitz (blits) *n.* **1,** a violent and highly mobile attack by combined military forces of different types. **2,** any sudden or overwhelming onslaught. —*v.t.* attack with a blitz.

blitz′krieg″ (blits′krēg″) *n.* (*Ger.*) lightning warfare; blitz.

bliz′zard (bliz′ərd) *n.* **1,** a heavy fall of snow. **2,** a violent windstorm with sleet or dry snow.

bloat (blōt) *v.t.* **1,** cause to swell or distend. **2,** make vain or conceited. **3,** cure (fish) by smoking. —*v.i.* puff up; dilate. —*n.* a dietary ailment of cattle, sheep, and horses.

bloat′er (-ər) *n.* a fish cured by salting and smoking, like herring.

blob *n.* a small globe of liquid; a drop, bubble, or lump.

bloc (blok) *n.* a group of persons acting together for a particular interest.

block (blok) *n.* **1,** a solid mass of stone,

wood, metal, etc. **2,** a solid mass used as a table for heavy work; a form on which something is molded or shaped. **3,** a base on which an engraving is mounted for printing. **4,** a platform, as that mounted by an auctioneer. **5,** a case containing one or more pulleys, for rigging rope tackles. **6,** an obstruction; the condition of being obstructed. **7,** the area of a town bounded by two intersecting pairs of two adjacent streets. **8,** a portion or section treated as a unit. **9,** a section of a railway, divided for signaling purposes. **10,** (*Computers*) a section of text that has been selected for editing, printing, etc. —*v.i.* **1,** mount on or fit with a block. **2,** (usually with *out*) plan or sketch roughly. **3,** obstruct; check. —*v.t.* (*Theat.*) establish the stage movement (of a play, opera, etc.). —**block′age** (-ij) *n.* an obstruction. —**block′ing,** *n.* (*Theat.*) the stage movements (of a play, opera, etc.).

block·ade′ (blok-ād′) *n.* **1,** the barring of entrance to and exit from a place, esp. a port or coast. **2,** any obstruction of passage or progress. —*v.t.* shut up or obstruct by a blockade.

block′bust″er *n.* **1,** a large explosive aerial bomb. **2,** something large or effective. **3,** a real estate operator.

block′head″ (blok′hed″) *n.* a stupid person.

block′house″ *n.* a house of heavy timber used as a fort.

bloke (blōk) *n.* (*Brit. slang*) a fellow.

blond *adj.* light-colored, esp. as to hair and skin. —*n.* a person with light hair and fair skin. Also, **blonde** (blond) *n.fem.* —**blond′ness,** *n.*

blood (blud) *n.* **1,** the fluid that circulates in the arteries and veins of animals. **2,** any vital fluid; the sap or juice of plants. **3,** descent; lineage; racial heritage. **4,** a person of high spirit; a rake. —**blood′ed,** *adj.* having a good pedigree; purebred. —**bad blood,** enmity. —**blood bank,** a supply of whole blood or plasma. —**blood count,** a count of red and white blood cells per unit of volume. —**blood group,** all persons having the same blood type. —**blood relation,** a person related by birth. —**blood sister** *or* **brother,** **1,** sister (brother) by birth. **2,** a person bound to another by friendship or other bond, as the mixing of blood. **3,** something associated closely with another. —**blood type,** the class of blood determined by agglutination. —**blood vessel,** any vein or artery. —**in cold blood,** deliberately.

blood′hound″ *n.* a keen-scented tracking dog.

blood′less *adj.* **1,** done without bloodshed. **2,** pale. **3,** lacking courage.

blood′let″ting (-let″ing) *n.* **1,** removal of blood from the body, as by opening a vein. **2,** bloodshed.

blood′mo·bile″ (blud′mə-bēl″) *n.* a vehicle equipped as a mobile blood donation center.

blood′shed″ *n.* slaughter.

blood′shot″ *adj.* (of eyes) streaked with red.

blood′stone″ *n.* a variety of chalcedony, green with spots of red.

blood′stream″ *n.* the blood flowing in a circulatory system.

blood′suck″er *n.* **1,** a leech. **2,** an extortioner. —**blood′suck″ing,** *adj.*

blood′thirst″y *adj.* eager to kill. —**blood′thirst″i·ness,** *n.*

blood′y (blud′ē) *adj.* **1,** covered with blood; gory. **2,** marked by great bloodshed. **3,** (*Brit.*) a vulgar expletive. —**blood′i·ness,** *n.* —**Bloody Mary,** a beverage made from vodka and tomato juice.

bloom *n.* **1,** the flower of a plant. **2,** the state of blossoming; a flourishing condition. **3,** a rosy glow or other evidence of youth or good health. **4,** a powdery deposit or coating, as on plums, cabbage leaves, etc. **5,** a rough-rolled ingot of steel. —*v.i.* **1,** produce blossoms. **2,** flourish; be in good health. **3,** glow with color. —**bloom′er,** *n.* a blunder.

bloom′ers (bloo′mərz) *n.pl.* loose trousers gathered at the knees, for women.

---

bloomers

↔ The use of *bloomers* was advocated in the 1850s by feminist Amelia Jenks Bloomer, whose name also spawned the term *bloomerism* for a clothing reform movement.

---

bloom′ing *adj.* (*Slang*) confounded: an expletive of little or no meaning.

bloop′er (bloo′pər) *n.* a blunder, esp. one on radio or television.

blos′som (blos′əm) *n.* **1,** the flower of a plant. **2,** the state of bearing flowers. —*v.i.* **1,** produce blossoms. **2,** become mature; develop.

blot *n.* **1,** a spot or stain, as of ink on paper. **2,** an erasure or obliteration. **3,** a blemish, as upon character or reputation. **4,** in backgammon, a piece exposed to being hit. —*v.t.* [**blot′ted, -ting**] **1,** stain; spatter. **2,** efface; obliterate. **3,** dry with a blotter. —*v.i.* form a stain; become stained.

---

tub, cūte, pûll; labəl; oil, owl, go, chip, she, thin, *th*en, sing, ink; *see p. 6*

blotch (bloch) *n.* a large irregular spot or blot. —*v.t.* blot; blur.

blot′ter (blot′ər) *n.* **1,** a piece of absorbent paper used to remove excess ink. **2,** a journal book, esp. as used in a police station.

blot′to (blot′ō) *adj.* (*Slang*) drunk.

blouse (blows) *n.* **1,** a loose garment worn on the upper body, esp. by women and children. **2,** an outer garment reaching to the knees, often belted, worn by both sexes in Russia and elsewhere.

blou′son (blow′zən) *n.* a woman's garment with a closed waistband.

blow (blō) *v.i.* [**blew, blown** (blōn), **blow′-ing**] **1,** produce a current of air. **2,** be carried about by or as by wind. **3,** make a whistling sound; give out sound. **4,** breathe hard; pant. **5,** (with *up* or *out*) explode. **6,** (with *over*) subside. **7,** (*Informal*) boast. **8,** produce flowers; blossom. **9,** (with *off*) (*Slang*) shirk; avoid. —*v.t.* **1,** drive by a current of air. **2,** force air into or through, in order to clear, cause to sound, inflate, etc. **3,** scatter or shatter, as by exploding. **4,** (with *up*) inflate; enlarge. **5,** (*Slang*) squander. —*n.* **1,** a blast of air; a gale of wind. **2,** a stroke with the hand; a thump. **3,** a sudden shock or calamity. —**blow away,** (*Slang*) **1,** kill. **2,** defeat decisively. **3,** impress; overwhelm.

blow-′dry″ *v.t.* dry (esp. hair) with a hot air blower. —**blow-′dry″er,** *n.*

blow′gun″ *n.* a weapon from which missiles are expelled by one's blowing.

blow′hard″ *n.* (*Informal*) a braggart.

blow′out″ *n.* **1,** a sudden escape of air or liquid, as from a ruptured tire, steam pipe, etc. **2,** (*Informal*) a spree.

blow′pipe″ *n.* a pipe through which air is forced.

blow′torch″ *n.* a portable gas heating appliance, used for welding, soldering, etc.

blow′up″ *n.* **1,** an explosion; outburst. **2,** a photographic enlargement.

blowz′y (blow′zē) *adj.* **1,** disheveled; untidy. **2,** fat and ruddy; red-faced.

blub′ber (blub′ər) *n.* the fat of whales. —*v.i.* weep with a contorted face. —*v.t.* say tearfully.

blu′cher (bloo′kər) *n.* **1,** a shoe in which tongue and upper are cut from one piece. **2,** a short boot.

---

blucher
↔ Named for Prussian field marshal Gebhart von *Blucher.*

---

bludg′eon (bluj′ən) *n.* a heavy-headed club. —*v.t.* **1,** hit with a bludgeon. **2,** bully; coerce.

blue (bloo) *n.* **1,** the color of the clear sky; a hue between green and violet in the spectrum. **2,** (*Poetic*) the sky; the sea. —*adj.* **1,** of blue color; azure. **2,** (of the skin) livid, as from cold or fear. **3,** depressed; despondent. **4,** dismal; unpromising. **5,** strict in morals; puritanic. **6,** risqué; profane. —*v.t.* make blue; dye blue. —**blue baby,** a baby born with an oxygen deficiency. —**blue cheese,** a strong cheese streaked with blue mold, as Roquefort. —**blue law,** a law forbidding or regulating certain activities on Sunday. —**blue ribbon,** first prize.

blue′bell″ (bloo′bel″) *n.* any of various plants having blue bell-shaped flowers.

blue′ber″ry *n.* the small, bluish, edible fruit of various shrubs.

blue′bird″ *n.* a blue songbird of eastern U.S.

blue′ blood″ *n.* (*Informal*) an aristocrat.

blue′bon″net *n.* **1,** the cornflower. **2,** the blue state flower of Texas.

blue′ book″ *n.* **1,** a directory of socially prominent persons. **2,** an examination book.

blue′bot″tle (bloo′bot″əl) *n.* **1,** a large fly of blue-green color. **2,** any of several plants with blue flowers; the cornflower.

blue′-chip″ *adj.* considered among the most successful or profitable in its field.

blue′coat″ *n.* (*Slang*) a police officer.

blue′-col″lar *adj.* pert. to those workers whose employment entails the wearing of work clothes or protective gear.

blue′fish″ *n.* any of various edible fishes, esp. the *Pomatomus saltatrix*, an Atlantic coastal fish.

blue′grass″ *n.* **1,** a variety of grass. **2,** a kind of country music.

blue′jack″et *n.* a sailor.

blue′ jeans″ *n.* jeans.

blue-′pen″cil *v.t.* edit; cancel.

blue′print″ (bloo′print″) *n.* **1,** a photographic process that produces a print with white lines on a blue field. **2,** such a print. **3,** any detailed plan. —*v.t.* make a blueprint of.

blue-″rib′bon, *adj.* **1,** prize-winning. **2,** of a jury, composed of prominent citizens.

blues (blooz) *n.* **1,** a style of mournful jazz music. **2,** a feeling of despondency.

blue′stock″ing *n.* a woman of considerable learning or intellectual tastes.

---

bluestocking
↔ From the informal attire of those attending certain 18th-century literary gatherings. The original "bluestocking" was a man, but the term gradually came to be applied to women only.

bluff (bluf) *v.t. & i.* mislead by a pretense of strength, influence, etc. —*n.* **1,** the act of bluffing. **2,** a broad, steep face of a hill or headland. —*adj.* **1,** somewhat abrupt in manner; rough and hearty; frank. **2,** having a broad front or face.

blu'ing (bloo'ing) *n.* a bluish dye used to whiten clothes after washing.

blun'der (blun'dər) *n.* a gross or stupid mistake. —*v.i.* **1,** make such a mistake. **2,** move blindly or clumsily. —*v.t.* confuse; bungle.

blun'der·buss'' (-bus'') *n.* a musket with flaring mouth.

blunt *adj.* **1,** having a rounded or thick point or edge; not sharp. **2,** rough in manner or speech; abrupt; plain-spoken. —*v.t.* make blunt; impair the force or keenness of. —**blunt'ness,** *n.*

blur (blēr) *v.t.* **[blurred, blur'ring] 1,** make indistinct; obscure without effacing. **2,** sully; stain. **3,** dim the perception or susceptibility of. —*v.i.* become indistinct. —*n.* **1,** a blot, smudge, or smear. **2,** a confused appearance. —**blur'ry,** *adj.* —**blur'ri·ness,** *n.*

blurb (blērb) *n.* a laudatory advertisement, esp. of a book.

blurb
↔ Apparently coined by American author F. Gelett Burgess to promote one of his books: The jacket featured a scantily clad young woman named Miss Belinda *Blurb*, meant to satirize the exaggerated cover material on book jackets.

blurt (blērt) *v.t.* utter suddenly; divulge inadvertently.

blush *v.i.* **1,** become red in the face from shame or embarrassment. **2,** be ashamed. **3,** become red or rosy. —*n.* **1,** a reddening of the face. **2,** a pink tinge. —**blush'er,** *n.* a cosmetic applied to the face. —**blush wine,** rosé.

blus'ter (blus'tər) *v.i.* **1,** be loud and boastful; swagger; utter empty menaces. **2,** roar. —*n.* boastful utterance.

bo'a (bō'ə) *n.* **1,** any of various large snakes that kill by constricting, as *boa constrictor.* **2,** a long neckpiece worn by women.

boar (bôr) *n.* **1,** the wild hog. **2,** an uncastrated domesticated hog.

board (bôrd) *n.* **1,** a long, thin cut of timber. **2,** a flat slab of wood used for some specific purpose, as for ironing, posting notices, playing games. **3,** a table, esp. for food. **4,** provision for daily meals. **5,** a group of officials acting together. **6,** border; edge. —*v.t.* **1,** cover with boards. **2,** furnish with daily meals. **3,** go on or into (a ship, train, vehicle). —*v.i.* be supplied with daily meals. —**board'er,** *n.* a person who boards, as in a boardinghouse. —**board'inghouse,** a lodging house where meals are served.

boast (bōst) *v.i.* **1,** speak vaingloriously or exaggeratedly of one's own worth, property, deeds, etc. **2,** speak with laudable pride. —*v.t.* **1,** speak of with vanity or exultation. **2,** take pride in possessing. —*n.* **1,** something boasted of. **2,** bragging speech. —**boast'ful,** *adj.*

boat (bōt) *n.* **1,** a vessel for transport on water, esp. a small one moved by oars. **2,** an open dish, as for gravy. —*v.i. & t.* go or transport by boat. —**boat'er,** *n.* one who boats. —**boat'ing,** *n.* the sport of going in boats. —**boat people,** *n.pl.* (*Informal*) refugees who attempt to emigrate by means of a boat.

boat'swain (bō'sən; bōt'swān'') *n.* a superior seaman in charge of anchors, cables, etc.

bob *n.* **1,** a jerk; jerking motion. **2,** any small dangling object; a weight on a plumb line; a float on a fishing line. **3,** a style of short haircut. **4,** a kind of sled. **5,** (*Brit.*) a shilling. —*v.i.* **[bobbed, bob'bing]** move jerkily; go up and down quickly. —*v.t.* **1,** cut short. **2,** hit lightly.

bob'bin (bob'in) *n.* a reel or spool for holding thread, yarn, or wire.

bob'ble (bob'əl) *v.t.* fumble. —*v.i.* bob; move jerkily. —*n.* fumble.

bob'by (bob'ē) *n.* (*Brit.*) a police officer.

bobby
↔ Affectionately named for Sir *Robert* Peel, founder of London's Metropolitan Police.

bobby pin a clip for the hair.

bobby socks ankle-length socks. Also, **bobby sox.** —**bobby sox'er** (sok'sər) a teenage girl.

bob'cat'' *n.* an Amer. wildcat.

bob'o·link'' (bob'ə-link'') *n.* an American songbird.

bob'sled'' *n.* a long sled with two sets of runners turning independently.

bob'white'' (bob'hwīt'') *n.* an American quail or partridge.

bock (bok) *n.* a dark beer, usually the first brew of the spring season.

bo·da′cious (bō-dā′shəs) *adj.* (*Dial.*) **1,** excellent. **2,** impudent.

bode (bōd) *v.t. & i.* be an omen (of); portend; betoken.

bo·de′ga (bō-dā′gə) *n.* (*Sp.*) a grocery store.

bod′ice (bod′is) *n.* **1,** a laced outer garment covering the upper body, worn by women. **2,** a close-fitting waist or body of a gown.

> **bodice**
> ↔ Originally this was a variant of *bodies*, the plural of *body*, and referred to the upper part of a woman's dress.

bod′i·ly (bod′ə-lē) *adj.* pert. to the body; corporeal.

bod′kin *n.* **1,** a blunt needle for drawing tape through a hem or loop. **2,** an awl for making holes in cloth, etc. **3,** (*Obs.*) a dagger.

bod′y (bod′ē) *n.* **1,** the physical structure of an animal. **2,** the main portion of this structure, excluding the head, appendages, etc. **3,** the main part of anything; a vehicle exclusive of wheels, etc.; a speech or treatise exclusive of introduction, appendix, etc. **4,** anything existing in three-dimensional space; a solid; anything having inertia or mass. **5,** weight, density, consistency, or other attribute of a solid. **6,** a group of persons or things collectively. —**body English,** in sports, a twisting motion of the body in an attempt to influence the direction of a ball already hit or thrown. —**body language,** physical gestures and signals, often unconscious. —**body politic,** a people, their government, and form of government collectively. —**body shirt, 1,** a close-fitting shirt. **2,** a woman's garment having a snap crotch. —**body stocking,** a closefitting one-piece garment.

bod′y·guard″ *n.* a private guard; an escort.

bod′y·suit″ *n.* a close-fitting one-piece garment, esp. for women.

Boer (bôr) *n.* a So. Afr. native of Dutch descent.

bof′fo (bof′ō) (*Slang*) a hit show. —*adj.* praising; laudatory.

bog *n.* an area of wet and spongy ground; marsh. —*v.t. & i.* [**bogged, bog′ging**] sink in a bog; flounder among obstacles.

bo′gey (bō′gē) *n.* **1,** (*Golf*) a score of par on a hole (*Brit.*) or one over par (*U.S.*).

2, bogy. **3,** (*Slang*) nasal mucus. **4,** (*Brit. slang*) police officer.

bog′gle (bog′əl) *v.i.* **1,** draw back in fright or alarm; shy; shrink. **2,** be clumsy or bungling. —*v.t.* amaze; astound.

bo′gie (bō′gē) *n.* bogy.

bo′gus (bō′gəs) *adj.* counterfeit; spurious; sham.

bo′gy (bō′gē) *n.* a troublesome imp; hobgoblin; anything that annoys. Also, **bo′gie.**

Bo·he′mi·an (bō-hē′mē-ən) *adj.* pert. to Bohemia or Bohemians, or the Czech language. —*n.* (*l.c.*) one who lives a cheerful, unconventional life.

boil *v.i.* **1,** change from liquid to gas under the influence of heat. **2,** be agitated, as by bubbles of gas rising to the surface of a heated liquid; be excited, esp. by anger. —*v.t.* **1,** cause to boil. **2,** cook by boiling. **3,** (with *down*) abridge; condense. —*n.* **1,** the act or condition of boiling. **2,** an inflammatory and suppurating sore on the skin. —**boil′er,** *n.* a vessel in which a liquid is boiled, esp. a tank in which water is converted to steam to operate an engine or furnish heat. —**boil′ing point,** the point at which a liquid will boil; of water, 212° F., 100° C.

boil′er·mak″er *n.* (*Slang*) a mixture of whiskey and beer.

boil′er·plate″ *n.* (*Informal*) phrases of text or model documents used repeatedly with different added information.

bois′ter·ous (boi′stər-əs) *adj.* **1,** noisy and violent; clamorous. **2,** coarse and unrestrained. —**bois′ter·ous·ness,** *n.*

bok′ choy′ (bok′ choi′) an Asian plant cooked as a vegetable.

bo′la (bō′lə) *n.* **1,** a So. Amer. missile weapon, comprising two heavy balls connected by a cord. **2,** bolo tie.

bold (bōld) *adj.* **1,** daring; brave; courageous. **2,** overstepping usual bounds; forward; impudent. **3,** requiring or exhibiting courage. **4,** standing out to view; conspicuous. **5,** steep; abrupt. —**bold′ness,** *n.*

bold′face″ (*Printing*) *n.* a typeface with thick lines. —*adj.* **1,** being, or set in, boldface. **2,** [also, **bold′faced″**] bold; impudent.

bole (bōl) *n.* the trunk of a tree.

bo·le′ro (bō-lār′ō) *n.* [*pl.* **-ros**] **1,** a lively Spanish dance in triple time. **2,** a short close-fitting jacket reaching only to the waist.

bo·li·var′ (bō-lē-vär′) *n.* the monetary unit of Venezuela, named for Venezuelan statesman Simón Bolívar.

boll (bōl) *n.* a pod or seed vessel of cotton, flax, and other plants. **—boll weevil,** a beetle infesting cotton bolls.

bol′lix (bol′iks) *v.t.* (*Informal*) **1,** frustrate; defeat. **2,** baffle. **3,** (often with *up*) mix up; botch.

bo′lo (bō′lō) *n.* a heavy single-edged knife. **—bolo tie,** a string tie with a clasp.

bo·lo′gna (bə-lōn′yə) *n.* a variety of sausage, named for Bologna, Italy.

Bol′she·vik (bol′shə-vik) *n.* a member of the controlling Communist party in the former Soviet Union. **—Bol′she·vism,** *n.* the doctrines of this party. **—Bol′she·vist,** *n.*

> **Bolshevik**
> ↔ Derived from Russian *bolshii*, greater, referring originally to the larger and more radical Bolshevik party as opposed to the Menshevik party (from Russian *menshii*, lesser).

bol′ster (bōl′stər) *n.* **1,** a long cylindrical pillow. **2,** anything resembling a bolster, used to pad or prop. **—v.t.** prop up; support.

bolt (bōlt) *n.* **1,** a metal pin, usually threaded at one end to receive a nut. **2,** the movable pin or bar of a lock that engages the fixed socket or frame. **3,** an arrow used in a crossbow. **4,** a bundle or roll, as of cloth or wallpaper. **5,** a streak of lightning; thunderbolt. **6,** a sudden spring; the act of running away; desertion of a political party or candidate. **—v.t. & i. 1,** fasten with a bolt. **2,** run away from; desert. **3,** swallow (food) hastily. **—adv.** abruptly; stiffly.

bo′lus (bō′ləs) *n.* a large pill or lump of medicine.

bomb (bom) *n.* **1,** an explosive missile, not fired from a gun. **2,** a mass of lava ejected from a volcano. **3,** (*Slang*) an unsuccessful play, etc.; (*Brit. slang*) a smashing success. **4,** (*Slang*) something inferior. **—v.t. & i.** hurl bombs at or on.

bom·bard′ (bom-bärd′) *v.t.* **1,** attack with bombs. **2,** attack with artillery. **3,** assail violently. **4,** attack (a molecule, etc.) with a stream of particles. **—n.** the earliest type of cannon. **—bom″bar·dier′** (bom″bər-dir′) *n.*

bom′bast *n.* high-sounding, extravagant, or stilted words. **—bom·bas′tic,** *adj.* **—bom·bas′ti·cal·ly,** *adv.*

bombe (bâmb) *n.* a layered ice cream dessert.

bombed (bomd) *adj.* (*Slang*) drunk.

bomb′er (bom′ər) *n.* an airplane used to drop bombs.

bomb′shell″. *n.* **1,** a bomb. **2,** a sudden and devastating event.

bomb′sight″ *n.* a device for aiming bombs dropped by aircraft.

bo′na fide″ (bō′nə fīd″) (*Lat.*) **1,** in good faith; without fraud. **2,** made in good faith; genuine.

bo·nan′za (bō-nan′zə) *n.* **1,** a rich mass of ore. **2,** any lucky find or profitable enterprise.

bon′bon″ *n.* a piece of candy.

bond *n.* **1,** anything that binds, fastens, or confines. **2,** something that unites people; a cause of union. **3,** something that constrains action; an obligation or duty. **4,** a written promise or obligation to pay money, perform a duty, etc.; an insurance agreement. **5,** an interest-bearing certificate of indebtedness of a corporation or government. **6,** a substance for compacting particles into a solid mass. **7,** a close-compacted variety of paper. **—v.t. 1,** put under bond. **2,** place a bonded debt upon. **3,** form into a compact mass. **—v.i.** hold together; adhere solidly. **—bond′ing,** *n.* a close psychological relationship between people, as between a parent and child.

bond′age (bon′dij) *n.* **1,** involuntary servitude; slavery. **2,** the state of being under obligation, restraint, or captivity.

bond′man (-mən) [*pl.* **-men**], **bond′-wom″an** *n.* a slave.

bonds′man (bondz′mən) *n.* [*pl.* **-men**] a person who posts a bond as surety for another.

bone (bōn) *n.* **1,** any of the pieces of which the skeleton of a vertebrate is composed. **2,** the hard tissue of which the skeleton is made. **3,** any of various similar hard substances, as ivory. **4,** something made of bone or the like; a domino; a die; a strip of whalebone or metal for stiffening a corset. **—v.t. 1,** remove the bones from. **2,** put bone or bones into. **—v.i.** (with *up*) (*Slang*) study hard; cram.

bone′black″ *n.* a substance made of burned bones used for coloring and as a filter for coloring matter.

bone-′dry″ *adj.* completely dry.

bone′head″ *n.* a stupid person.

bon′er (bō′nər) *n.* (*Informal*) a foolish mistake; a blunder.

bone′yard *n.* (*Slang*) cemetery.

bon′fire″ (bon′fīr″) *n.* a fire built in the open.

> **bonfire**
> ↔ From Middle English *bone fire*, a fire fueled with bones, i.e., a funeral pyre.

bong *n.* the sound of a bell; any similar sound. —*v.* ring or cause to ring like a bell.

bon′go (bong′gō) *n.* **1,** large African antelope. **2,** a small tuned drum played with the fingers.

bon″ho·mie′ (bon″ə-mē′) *n.* friendliness; geniality.

bon′i·face″ (bon′i-fās″) *n.* the keeper of an inn.

> **boniface**
> ↔ A character in the play *The Beaux' Stratagem* (1707) by George Farquhar.

bo·ni′to (bə-nē′tō) *n.* an Atlantic food fish like the mackerel.

bon′kers (bong′kərz) *adj.* (*Slang*) crazy.

bon′net (bon′it) *n.* **1,** a covering for the head worn by women and children, usually tied with ribbons under the chin. **2,** protective cover; the hood of an automobile.

bon′ny (bon′ē) *adj.* pretty.

bon·sai′ (bon-sī′) *n.* (*Jap.*) technique for growing miniaturized trees in pots; a tree so grown. ❑ *banzai*

bo′nus (bō′nəs) *n.* a sum of money given over and above what is required to be paid.

bon′y (bō′nē) *adj.* **1,** of, like, or full of bones. **2,** thin. —**bon′i·ness,** *n.*

boo *interj.* expressing contempt or disapproval, or used to frighten. —*v.t.* show contempt for; disapprove. —*v.i.* utter a boo.

boob *n.* (*Slang*) a fool. —**boob tube,** (*Slang*) television.

boo-'boo *n.* (*Informal*) error; faux pas.

boo′by (boo′bē) *n.* **1,** [also, **boob**] a stupid person. **2,** the contestant who finishes lowest or last in a game. **3,** any of various gannets. —**booby hatch,** (*Informal*) a mental institution. —**booby prize,** an award for the worst performance in a competition. —**booby trap,** a stratagem to deceive the unwary; a hidden explosive or mine. —**boo′by·trap″,** *v.t.*

boo′dle (boo′dəl) *n.* money fraudulently obtained in public service. —*v.t.* obtain money by corruption.

boo′ga·loo (boo′gə-loo) *n.* boogie-woogie.

boo′gie-woo′gie (bû′gē-wû′gē) *n.* a form of jazz music.

book (bûk) *n.* **1,** a written or printed composition of considerable length. **2,** a number of sheets of paper bound together. **3,** a similar bundle of tickets, stamps, tobacco leaves, etc. **4,** (*cap.*) the Bible. **5,** a written record; the script of a play; the libretto of an opera. —*v.t.* **1,** enter in a book; record. **2,** engage place for; engage the services of; schedule. **3,** charge (with a criminal offense). —**by the book,** (*Informal*) according to the rules, correct procedures, etc.

book′case″ *n.* a set of shelves for books.

book′ie (-ē) *n.* (*Slang*) bookmaker.

book′ish (bûk′ish) *adj.* **1,** given to reading. **2,** formal or stilted.

book′keep″ing (bûk′kē″ping) *n.* the theory and practice of keeping records of money transactions.

book′let (-lət) *n.* a small, often coverless book; pamphlet.

book′mak″er *n.* one who accepts bets, esp. on horse races.

book′mark″ *n.* a strip of paper, ribbon, etc. placed between the pages of a book to mark the reader's place.

book′mo·bile″ *n.* a mobile lending library or bookstore.

book′plate″ *n.* a label pasted in a book, bearing the owner's name.

book′worm″ *n.* **1,** an insect larva that feeds on bookbindings. **2,** a person devoted to books and reading.

Bool′e·an algebra (bool′ē-ən) a system of algebra that proceeds deductively from a set of unproved axioms concerning the use of certain undefined symbols.

> **Boolean algebra**
> ↔ Named for 19th-c. English mathematician George *Boole*, who devised it.

boom *n.* **1,** a prolonged hollow sound. **2,** a rapid heightening or increase of interest, activity, popularity, prices, etc. **3,** a spar used to extend the foot of certain kinds of sails. **4,** the movable arm of a derrick. **5,** a barrier set up in water, of logs, chains, etc. —*v.t.* **1,** say or give forth with a prolonged resonant sound. **2,** promote vigorously. —*v.i.* **1,** make a booming sound. **2,** swell in magnitude; flourish. —**boom box,** (*Slang*) a large, portable stereo system.

boom′er·ang″ (boo′mə-rang″) *n.* **1,** a missile weapon of the Australian aborigines, which returns to the thrower if it misses the target. **2,** a scheme or enterprise that recoils with injurious effect. —*v.i.* **1,** to come back, like a boomerang. **2,** backfire.

boon *n.* **1,** a benefit enjoyed; something to be thankful for. **2,** a favor asked. —*adj.* convivial.

boon'docks" (boon'doks") *n.* **1,** the jungle. **2,** (*Slang*) rural regions; the sticks. Also (*Informal*) **boon'ies** (boo'nēz).

boon'dog"gle (boon'dog"əl) *v.i.* (*Slang*) do useless, unproductive work. —*n.* such work.

boor (bûr) *n.* **1,** one who is rude, unmannerly, or clownish. **2,** a rustic. —**boor'ish,** *adj.*

boost *v.t.* **1,** shove upward; lift from below; raise. **2,** aid by speaking well of; promote. **3,** (*Slang*) steal; shoplift. —*n.* **1,** an upward shove. **2,** an act of assistance or promotion.

boost'er (-ər) *n.* **1,** a device to increase applied power. **2,** a zealous supporter.

boot *n.* **1,** a foot covering that reaches high above the ankle, usually to the knee. **2,** (*Brit.*) a shoe that covers the ankle. **3,** any of several kinds of protective covering; a footband for a horse; an apron for the driver's seat of a vehicle. **4,** (*Brit.*) the trunk (of an automobile). **5,** a blow with the foot; a kick. **6,** (*Slang*) dismissal. **7,** [*also,* **Denver boot**] a device attached to the wheel of an automobile to keep it from being driven. —*v.t.* **1,** kick. **2,** (*Slang*) dismiss. **3,** (*Informal*) bungle. **4,** put boots on. —*v.t. & i.* to start (as a computer) by loading its operating system. —**boot'er·y,** *n.* —**boot camp,** a military basic training camp. —**to boot,** in addition.

boot'black" *n.* one who shines shoes.

boot'ee (boo'tè) *n.* **1,** a baby's knitted foot-covering. **2,** a woman's soft overshoe. Also, **boot'ie.**

booth *n.* **1,** a temporary structure as for the display of wares, for voting, etc. **2,** a small room or compartment, as for projecting motion pictures.

boot'jack" *n.* a device for pulling off boots.

boot'leg" *n.* liquor transported or sold illegally. —*v.t. & i.* [**-legged", -leg"ging**] deal in (liquor or other commodity) unlawfully. —*adj.* made, transported or sold illegally. —**boot'leg"ger,** *n.*

boot'less (boot'ləs) *adj.* of no advantage; useless; futile.

boot'lick" *v.t.* (*Slang*) toady to; fawn upon.

boot'strap" *n.* a set of software routines for booting a computer.

boo'ty (boo'tè) *n.* **1,** spoil taken from an enemy in war; anything seized by violence. **2,** any prize or gain.

booze (booz) *n.* (*Informal*) intoxicating liquor. —*v.i.* drink immoderately. —**booz'y,** *adj.*

bop *n.* **1,** a type of jazz music. **2,** (*Slang*) hit.

bo·rac'ic acid (bə-ras'ik) boric acid.

bor'age (bôr'ij) *n.* a plant used in medicines and in salads.

bo'rax (bôr'aks) *n.* **1,** a white crystalline mineral used as a flux and cleansing agent. **2,** (*Slang*) inferior merchandise.

bor·del'lo (bôr-del'o) *n.* a brothel. Also, **bor'del** (bôr'dəl).

bor'der (bôr'dər) *n.* **1,** a side or edge; limit or boundary. **2,** a line separating two countries, etc.; the area near such a line; frontier. **3,** something marking a boundary; an ornamental strip; a frame of lines. —*v.t.* **1,** enclose or adorn with a border. **2,** be a boundary to. **3,** lie at the boundary of; adjoin. —*v.i.* touch upon; abut; approach closely.

bore (bôr) *v.t.* **1,** pierce or gouge out with an auger or drill. **2,** penetrate forcibly. **3,** weary or annoy by tedious iteration, dullness, etc. —*v.i.* **1,** make a hole with a rotary cutting instrument. **2,** advance by persistent thrusting. —*n.* **1,** a hole made by or as if by boring. **2,** the internal diameter of a circular hole or a hollow cylinder; the caliber of a gun. **3,** a tiresome or annoying person. **4,** a cause of ennui. **5,** a periodic and forceful flow of tidal water through a narrow channel. —**bore'some,** *adj.*

bo're·al (bôr'è-əl) *adj.* **1,** pert. to the north wind. **2,** northern.

bore'dom (-dəm) *n.* state of being bored; ennui.

bor'ic (bôr'ik) *adj.* containing boron. —**boric acid,** a substance obtained from borax, used in solution as a mild antiseptic and eyewash.

born (bôrn) *adj.* **1,** brought forth by birth. **2,** congenital. —**born'-a·gain",** *adj.* newly converted to a religious faith, esp. Christianity; having had one's faith revived. ❏ *bear*

borne (bôrn) *v.* p.p. of *bear*. —*adj.* **1,** carried. **2,** endured. ❏ *bear*

bo'ron (bôr'on) *n.* a chemical element, no. 5, symbol B.

bor'ough (bēr'ō) *n.* **1,** an incorporated municipality. **2,** one of the administrative divisions of a city, as in New York.

bor'row (bor'ō) *v.t.* **1,** obtain temporary possession or use of; take (a thing) on pledge to return it or an equivalent. **2,** take and adopt (words, ideas) from a foreign source. **3,** transfer (units) in arithmetical subtraction. —*v.i.* receive a loan.

borsch (bôrsh) *n.* a beet soup. Also, **borsht** (bôrscht).

bor′stal (bôr′stəl) *n.* (*Brit.*) a school for delinquent boys.

bor′zoi (bôr′zoi) *n.* a Russian wolf-hound.

bosh *n.* utter nonsense; nothing.

bosk *n.* a thicket. —**bosk′y** (-ė) *adj.* over-grown with bushes; shady.

bo′′s′n (bō′sən) *n.* boatswain.

bos′om (bûz′əm) *n.* **1,** the human breast. **2,** the enclosure formed by the breast and arms; embrace. **3,** the breast as the supposed seat of tender emotions. **4,** the part of a garment that covers the breast. —*adj.* intimate; familiar. —*v.t.* embrace; cherish.

boss (bâs) *n.* **1,** an overseer of workmen; superintendent; manager. **2,** one who controls a political party. **3,** a rounded protuberance, knob, stud, or enlarged part. —*v.t.* be the boss of; manage; direct. —*v.i.* **1,** be boss. **2,** be domineering. —*adj.* chief; master. —**boss′ism,** *n.* —**boss′y,** *adj.*

bos′′sa no′va (bâs′′ə nō′və) *n.* a Brazilian dance.

Boston terrier (bâs′tən) a small short-haired dog, a cross between the bulldog and the bull terrier. Also, **Boston bull.**

bot′a·ny (bot′ə-nė) *n.* **1,** the general science of plant life. **2,** the plants of a region. —**bo·tan′i·cal** (bə-tan′i-kəl) *adj.*—**bot′-an·ist** (bot′ə-nist) *n.*

botch (boch) *v.t.* spoil by unskillful work; bungle. —*n.* a poorly done piece of work. —**botch′y,** *adj.*

both (bōth) *adj. & pron.* the one and the other (of two); the pair or couple together. —*adv. & conj.* including the two; equally; alike.

---

both, each
☛ Do not confuse *both*, which refers to two things collectively, and *each*, which refers to two (or more) items individually: *Both men went to the game. Each man went to a different game.* (See also *each*.)

---

both′er (bo*th*′ər) *v.t. & i.* give trouble to; annoy; pester; bewilder. —*n.* **1,** someone or something that bothers. **2,** the state of being annoyed or worried. —*interj.* [also (*Informal*) **both′′er·a′tion**] expressing mild vexation or perplexity. —**both′er·some** (-səm) *adj.* causing trouble; perplexing.

bot′tle (bot′əl) *n.* **1,** a vessel for holding liquids, usually of glass. **2,** the contents or capacity of a bottle. **3,** intoxicating liquor. —*v.t.* **1,** put in a bottle. **2,** (often with *up*) shut in; restrain forcibly. —**bot′tle·neck′′,** *n.* a point at which progress is retarded by congestion.

bot′tom (bot′əm) *n.* **1,** the lowest or deepest part of anything; the base, foundation, or root; the underside. **2,** the ground under any body of water. **3,** the hull of a ship; the part of the hull below the wales; a ship generally. **4,** the buttocks. **5,** the fundamental aspect; basic principles. **6,** the lowland along a watercourse. —*adj.* **1,** [also, **bot′′tom·most′′**] lowest; undermost. **2,** fundamental. —*v.t.* **1,** furnish with a bottom. **2,** use as a base. **3,** get to the bottom of; fathom. —*v.i.* **1,** be based; rest. **2,** run aground. **3,** (with *out*) reach the lowest point. —**bottom line,** (*Informal*) the final result, esp. the ultimate cost, of a project, etc.

bot′u·lism (boch′ə-liz-əm) *n.* poisoning due to a toxin produced by certain bacteria in preserved foods.

bou·clé′ (boo-klā′) *adj.* woven with looped yarn to produce a knitted effect.

bou′doir (boo′dwär) *n.* a woman's bedroom or private sitting room.

bouf·fant′ (boo-fän′) *adj.* puffed out; flared.

bou′′gain·vil′le·a (boo′′gən-vil′ė-ə) *n.* a tropical woody vine with red or purple flowers, named for French navigator Louis Antoine de Bougainville.

bough (bow) *n.* a branch of a tree.

bought (bât) *v.* pret. & p.p. of *buy.*

bouil′′la·baisse′ (boo′′yə-bās′) *n.* a highly seasoned fish stew.

bouil′lon (bûl′yən) *n.* a clear soup, the liquid from boiling meat, etc.

boul′der (bōl′dər) *n.* a large detached rock.

boul′e·vard′′ (bûl′ə-värd′′) *n.* a broad street, esp. one shaded by trees or used as a promenade. —**boul′′e·vard·ier′** (-värdyā′) *n.* man about town.

---

boulevard
↔ A French word from Middle Dutch *bolwerc*, fortification, because walkways were constructed along the tops of destroyed bulwarks.

---

bounce (bowns) *v.i.* **1,** spring back like an elastic ball; recoil. **2,** move with a spring or leap. —*v.t.* **1,** cause to spring or rebound. **2,** (*Slang*) eject or dismiss summarily. —*n.* **1,** a rebound; a sudden leap. **2,** elasticity or resilience. **3,** (*Slang*) expulsion or dismissal. **4,** bluster; impudence. —**boun′cer,** *n.* (*Slang*) one employed to eject disorderly patrons. —**boun′cing,** *adj.* vigorous; big.

bound (bownd) *v.i.* **1,** jump; move by leaps. **2,** bounce back; rebound. —*v.t.* **1,** cause to bounce or leap. **2,** be the bound-

---

ary of; limit. **3,** name the boundaries of. **—n. 1,** a jump, leap, or rebound. **2,** a limiting line or boundary. **3,** something that binds or restrains. **4,** (*pl.*) territory near a boundary, or enclosed by it. **—adj. 1,** p.p. of *bind*. **2,** destined; determined; resolved. **3,** traveling (to); destined (for).

bound'a·ry (bown'də-rè) *n.* a bounding line; something that marks a limit.

bound'er (bown'dər) *n.* (*Informal*) a vulgar, ill-bred person; an upstart.

boun'te·ous (bown'tè-əs) *adj.* bountiful. **—boun'te·ous·ness,** *n.*

boun'ti·ful (bown'ti-fəl) *adj.* **1,** generous in giving. **2,** plentiful; abundant. **—boun'-ti·ful·ness,** *n.*

boun'ty (bown'tè) *n.* **1,** liberality in giving; generosity. **2,** a favor given benevolently. **3,** a premium offered by a government to encourage a certain activity, as the destruction of pests.

bou·quet' (bō-kā'; boo-) *n.* **1,** a bunch of flowers. **2,** the characteristic aroma of a wine.

Bour'bon (bûr'bən) *n.* **1,** name of a French royal family. **2,** (*l.c.*) (bēr'bən) a whiskey made from corn.

bour·geois' (bûr-zhwä') *n.* a person of the middle class; a tradesman, or one owning property. **—adj.** middle-class. **—bour″geoi·sie'** (-zē) *n.*

bourne (bûrn) *n.* **1,** boundary; limit. **2,** goal; destination. Also, **bourn.**

bout (bowt) *n.* **1,** a contest between two persons, esp. of physical strength or endurance. **2,** a period of struggle, as against illness. **3,** a turn or round, as of work.

bou·tique' (boo-tēk') *n.* a small store, esp. one specializing in fashionable clothing or accessories.

bou″ton·nière' (boo″tən-yär') *n.* a flower in the buttonhole.

bo'vine (bō'vīn) *adj.* **1,** of the family that includes cattle and the buffalo. **2,** stolid; dull. **—n.** a bovine animal.

bow *v.i.* **1,** bend; curve; stoop. **2,** tend; turn; yield; submit. **3,** bend the body or head in salutation, worship, etc. **4,** make a debut. **5,** (with *out*) resign; retire. **—v.t. 1,** cause (the head, neck, or body) to bend, stoop, or turn. **2,** force to submit; subdue. **—n. 1,** a bend of the body or head in salutation, etc. **2,** the forward end of a ship.

bow (bō) *n.* **1,** a weapon for shooting arrows, comprising a long elastic stick bent in a curve by a string attached to both ends. **2,** a device in similar form, for playing a musical stringed instrument. **3,** a knot in cord or ribbon having one or

more prominent loops. **4,** a bend or curve. **5,** something curved; a rainbow; an earpiece to hold eyeglasses in place. **—adj.** bent like a bow; curved. **—v.t. & i. 1,** bend; curve. **2,** use a bow (in playing an instrument). **—bow window,** a curved bay window.

bowd'ler·ize″ (bowd'lər-īz″) *v.t.* expurgate or paraphrase prudishly.

> **bowdlerize**
> ↔ For Dr. Thomas Bowdler, a 19th-c. English editor who in 1818 published an expurgated edition of Shakespeare's plays. It was his sister Harriet, however, who produced the first edition in 1810.

bow'el (bow'əl) *n.* **1,** the intestine of an animal; (*pl.*) the entire alimentary canal below the stomach. **2,** (*pl.*) the inner parts of anything.

bow'er (bow'ər) *n.* **1,** a shelter made with boughs or vines. **2,** (*Poetic*) a rustic cottage; a boudoir. **3,** a playing-card jack.

bow'ie knife (bō'è) a daggerlike hunting knife.

> **bowie knife**
> ↔ Named for pioneer James *Bowie*, for whom the knife was designed.

bowl (bōl) *n.* **1,** a deep dish or basin; a large drinking-cup. **2,** something bowl-shaped; a rounded hollow in the ground; the container of a spoon or tobacco pipe. **3,** a stadium for athletic contests, etc. **4,** a ball used in bowls or bowling. **—v.i. 1,** play at bowls or bowling. **2,** move with rapid easy motion. **—v.t. 1,** roll or trundle. **2,** (with *over* or *down*) knock down; upset; disconcert. **—bowl'ing,** *n.* a game of knocking down pins with a ball.

bowl'der (bōl'dər) *n.* boulder.

bow'leg″ (bō'leg″) *n.* **1,** an outward curvature of the leg. **2,** a leg so curved. **—bow'leg″ged,** *adj.*

bowl'er (bō'lər) *n.* (*Brit.*) a derby hat.

bowls (bōlz) *n.sing.* an outdoor game of rolling balls toward a goal.

bow'man (bō'mən) *n.* [*pl.* **-men**] **1,** a soldier armed with a bow and arrows; an archer. **2,** (bow'-) a boater.

bow'sprit″ (bow'-) *n.* a large, forward spar.

box (boks) *n.* **1,** a container, case, or receptacle, esp. one that is rectangular. **2,** a compartment or cell of a larger enclosure; a space in a theater barred off by curtains or rails. **3,** a small shelter; a country house for temporary use; a booth for sentries, railroad workers, etc. **4,** a housing or casing; a protective part. **5,** a socket, pit, or hollow part. **6,** an area marked out by a border, esp. rectangular; a bordered section of printed matter on a newspaper; a place where the batter stands in baseball. **7,** a blow with the hand. **8,** an evergreen shrub; its wood. —*v.t.* **1,** put in a box. **2,** enclose; confine; house. **3,** strike with the hand, esp. the ear. **4,** engage in a fistfight or boxing match. —*v.i.* **1,** fight with the fists. **2,** fight cautiously; spar. —**box office, 1,** a ticket booth in a theater. **2,** (*Slang*) receipts from sale of tickets. —**box spring,** a box containing many springs, used as a support for a mattress.

box′car *n.* **1,** a closed railroad freight car. **2,** (*pl.*) in dice games, a throw of two sixes.

box′er (bok′sər) *n.* **1,** one who fights with his fists; a pugilist. **2,** a large smooth-coated dog.

box′ing (bok′sing) *n.* fighting with the fists; pugilism. —**Boxing Day,** the first weekday after Christmas, a holiday in some countries.

boy (boi) *n.* **1,** a male child, esp. before the beginning of youth. **2,** any male person, regarded familiarly or as immature. **3,** a male servant. **4,** (*Slang*) heroin. —**boy′hood″,** *n.* —**boy′ish,** *adj.* like a boy, in manner or appearance.

boy′cott (boi′kot) *v.t.* combine with others to abstain from buying, using, patronizing, etc. (a business, product, etc.), as a means of coercing or intimidating. —*n.* **1,** the act of boycotting. **2,** an instance of boycotting.

> **boycott**
> ↔ From Captain Charles Boycott, a 19th-c. British estate manager ostracized by the Irish Land League because he disagreed with its aims.

Boy Scout a member of the Boy Scouts, an association of boys 8 to about 18 years old.

boy′sen·ber″ry (boi′zən·ber″ē) *n.* a large fruit like a blackberry.

> **boysenberry**
> ↔ Named for the man who bred it, American botanist R. *Boysen.*

bo′zo (bō′zō) *n.* (*Slang*) a man, esp. one who is strong, stupid, and obnoxious.

bra (brä) *n.* brassiere. —**bra′less,** *adj.*

brace (brās) *n.* **1,** something that holds parts together or in place. **2,** something that makes strong, rigid, firm, or steady. **3,** a piece of timber strengthening a

framework; a wire band to straighten the teeth; a truss or support for weak body joints; a bitstock for holding bits or drills. **4,** (*pl.*) trouser suspenders. **5,** a symbol [{ }] for joining printed lines or musical staves; bracket. **6,** a pair or couple. —*v.t.* **1,** join, fix, or strengthen with a brace. **2,** make steady, firm, or tight; increase the tension of. **3,** stimulate; fortify in resolution. —*v.i.* (with *up*) fortify one's resolution or vigor.

brace′let (brās′lət) *n.* **1,** an ornamental band worn on the arm. **2,** any similar circlet or shackle; a handcuff.

bra·ce′ro (brə-se′rō) *n.* (*Sp.*) a Mexican laborer admitted to the U.S. for seasonal work.

bra′chi·al (brā′kē-əl) *adj.* **1,** pert. to the arm, foreleg, wing, or other forelimb of a vertebrate. **2,** like an arm.

brack′en (brak′ən) *n.* **1,** a large fern. **2,** a tract overgrown with ferns.

brack′et (brak′it) *n.* **1,** a supporting piece for a shelf; a small shelf on such a piece. **2,** one of a pair of marks ([ ]) used like a parenthesis; a mark ({) grouping several items. **3,** a group of persons of similar condition, esp. taxpayers. —*v.t.* **1,** support by a bracket. **2,** enclose in brackets. **3,** group persons in or as in a bracket. **4,** (of gunfire) straddle.

brack′ish (brak′ish) *adj.* (of water) salty; stale. —**brack′ish·ness,** *n.*

brad *n.* a small, slender nail.

brae (brā) *n.* (*Scot.*) a slope; hillside.

brag *v.i.* [**bragged, brag′ging**] boast; swagger. —*n.* a boast.

brag″ga·do′ci·o″ (brag″ə-dō′shē-ō″) *n.* [*pl.* **-os″** (-ōz″)] **1,** vain boasting. **2,** a braggart.

> **braggadocio**
> ↔ After *Braggadocchio,* a character in Edmund Spenser's verse romance *The Faerie Queene* (1590-96).

brag′gart (brag′ərt) *n.* a boastful person.

brah′ma (brä′mə) *n.* a large Asiatic domestic fowl, widely bred in the U.S.

Brah′man (brä′mən) *n.* [*pl.* **-mans**] **1,** a member of the priestly and highest caste of Hindus. **2,** a breed of cattle. —**Brah′-man·ism,** *n.*

Brah′min (brä′min) *n.* (*Informal*) a member of an old and prominent family in Boston.

braid (brād) *v.t.* **1,** interlace three strands, as of hair; plait. **2,** weave, as a rug, by braiding. —*n.* **1,** ornamental tape. **2,** a length of braided hair.

Braille (brāl) *n.* a system of raised print-ing, read by touch, for the blind.

Braille
↔ Named after the early-19th-c. French teacher Louis *Braille*, who in-vented the system.

brain (brān) *n.* **1,** a mass of nerve matter in the skull; the organ of thought, con-sciousness, and body control. **2,** (often *pl.*) intelligence. —*v.t.* kill by beating out the brain. —**brain death,** cessation of activity in the central nervous system. —**brain drain,** (*Informal*) the loss of scientists, philosophers, etc., from one country to another. —**brain wave,** (*Informal*) a sud-den inspiration.

brain′child″ *n.* a product of the cre-ative imagination.

brain′sick″ *adj.* crazy. —**brain′sick″ness,** *n.*

brain′storm″ *n.* a sudden aberration or inspiration.

brain trust a group of expert advisers. —**brain′trust″er,** *n.*

brain′wash″ing *n.* intense and pro-longed indoctrination to change one's be-liefs. —**brain′wash″,** *v.t.*

brain′y (brā′nē) *adj.* intelligent. —**brain′-i·ness,** *n.*

braise (brāz) *v.t.* of meat, brown and stew slowly.

brake (brāk) *n.* **1,** a device for slowing or stopping a vehicle or machine. **2,** fig., a retarding influence. **3,** a thicket. —*v.t.* apply a brake.

brake′man (-mən) *n.* [*pl.* -**men**] an assis-tant to a railroad conductor.

bram′ble (bram′bəl) *n.* a thorny shrub. —**bram′bly,** *adj.*

bran *n.* the outer coat of wheat or other grains, used as a breakfast cereal and flour.

branch (branch) *n.* **1,** a limb; a bough. **2,** an offshoot or subdivision. **3,** a stream or small river. **4,** a subordinate office. —*v.t.* put forth branches; diverge. —**branch water,** (*Informal*) tap water.

brand *n.* **1,** a piece of burning wood; an ember. **2,** an identifying mark made with a hot iron; the iron implement so used. **3,** any identifying mark. **4,** an article identi-fied by a brand. **5,** quality as indicated by a brand. **6,** a mark of infamy; stigma. —*v.t.* mark with, or as with, a brand; stigmatize. —**brand-′new″,** *adj.* unused.

bran′dish *v.t.* flourish; wave.

bran′dy (bran′dē) *n.* an alcoholic liquor distilled from wine, cider, etc. —*v.t.* flavor

with or steep in brandy. —**bran′died** (-dĕd) *adj.*

brandy
↔ From *brandy wine*, a translation of the Dutch *brandewijn*, a type of dis-tilled spirit.

brash *adj.* **1,** reckless; impetuous. **2,** im-pudent. —**brash′ness,** *n.*

brass (brás) *n.* **1,** an alloy of copper and zinc. **2,** a brass wind instrument; such in-struments collectively. **3,** (*Informal*) as-surance; impudence. **4,** (*Slang*) persons in authority. —**brass hats,** (*Mil.*) brass (def. 4). —**brass tacks,** (*Informal*) precise facts or details.

bras′sard (bras′ärd) *n.* **1,** a mourning band on the sleeve. **2,** a badge or identi-fying mark worn on the arm.

bras″se·rie′ (bras″ə-rē′) *n.* a restaurant serving beer and food; a tavern.

brass″ie (-ē) *n.* a brass-soled golf club (No. 2 wood).

bras·siere′ (brə-zir′) *n.* a woman's un-dergarment, a band having cups to sup-port the breasts.

brass′y (-ē) *adj.* **1,** having a metallic sound. **2,** (*Informal*) impudent. —**brass′i-ness,** *n.*

brat *n.* **1,** an unruly or spoiled child. **2,** bratwurst.

brat′wurst″ (brat′wĕrst″) *n.* a type of sausage.

bra·va′do (brə-vä′dō) *n.* **1,** swaggering defiance; boastful truculence. **2,** a bully.

brave (brāv) *adj.* **1,** courageous. **2,** splen-did; handsome. —*n.* an American Native warrior. —*v.t.* face with courage; defy. —**brave′ness,** *n.* —**brav′er·y,** *n.* courage.

bra′vo (brä′vō) *interj.* well done! —*n.* **1,** a thug; assassin. **2,** (*Communications*) the letter *b*.

bra·vu′ra (brə-vyūr′ə) *n.* **1,** (*Music*) a passage requiring great skill or spirit of the performer. **2,** daring; bravery.

brawl (brâl) *n.* **1,** a noisy quarrel. **2,** a wild, noisy party. —*v.i.* **1,** quarrel noisily. **2,** carouse.

brawn (brân) *n.* **1,** powerful muscles; muscular strength. **2,** flesh of the boar. —**brawn′y,** *adj.*

bray (brā) *n.* the harsh cry of an ass, or a sound resembling it. —*v.i.* make such a sound. —*v.t.* pound; crush to powder.

braze (brāz) *v.t.* **1,** join with a solder con-taining brass. **2,** make of or cover with brass.

bra′zen (brā′zən) *adj.* **1,** made of brass. **2,** giving forth the sound of vibrating brass. **3,** impudent; shameless. —*v.t.* (with *out*) face with impudence. —**bra'-zen·ness,** *n.*

bra'zier (brā'zhər) *n.* **1,** a worker in brass. **2,** a vessel in which coal or charcoal is burned.

bra·zil' (brə-zil') *n.* a red dye from various tropical trees. —**Brazil nut,** a So. Amer. tree; its nut.

breach (brēch) *n.* **1,** a break or separation; a violation, as of a law; a quarrel. **2,** a gap broken in a wall or the like. **3,** an interruption. —*v.t.* make a break in.

> **breach, breech**
> ☞ These two words are unrelated. A *breach* is a break; the *breech* is the rear of a thing.

bread (bred) *n.* **1,** a food made of flour or meal and generally leavening, baked in loaves. **2,** food in general. **3,** (*Slang*) money. —*v.t.* cover with bread crumbs. —**break bread,** dine.

> **bread**
> ↔ Originally meaning "food," this word is of Germanic origin.

bread'board" *n.* **1,** a board, usu. wooden, on which to knead or slice bread. **2,** a thin board, usu. fiberglass, with predrilled holes, used for making prototypes of circuit boards.

bread'fruit" *n.* a pulpy fruit of a tree found in the So. Seas, baked for food.

bread'stuff" *n.* grain, flour, or meal used to make bread.

breadth (bredth) *n.* **1,** the measure of an object from side to side; width. **2,** liberality; freedom from narrowness. **3,** wide extent; broadness.

bread'win"ner (bred'win"ər) *n.* the principal working member and supporter of a family.

break (brāk) *v.t.* [**broke, bro'ken, break'-ing**] **1,** shatter violently; rupture; crack. **2,** interrupt; destroy the continuity of. **3,** destroy the integrity of; change into smaller units, as *break* a dollar bill. **4,** tame; train. **5,** violate, as a law. **6,** be first to tell, as news. **7,** demote, as an officer. **8,** weaken; soften, as a fall. **9,** exceed or surpass, as a record. **10,** render bankrupt or penniless. **11,** (often with *off*) discontinue. —*v.i.* **1,** be shattered, ruptured, or cracked. **2,** change gait (of a horse), tone (of a voice), etc. **3,** discharge, as a sore. **4,** begin suddenly, as day. **5,** (with *in*) force one's way. **6,** (often with *down*) succumb to illness or emotion. **7,** (often with *up*) disband; separate. —*n.* **1,** a breach; a fracture. **2,**

an interruption; a gap; a suspension. **3,** a sudden change. **4,** an instrumental solo in a jazz performance. —*v.t. & i.* (with *up*) (*Informal*) laugh or cause to laugh uncontrollably. —**break'age,** *n.* —**break down, 1,** separate into component parts; analyze. **2,** to decompose. —**break into, 1,** (*Law*) enter by force with criminal intent. **2,** interrupt. **3,** begin (an activity). —**break out, 1,** to arise. **2,** to develop skin eruptions. **3,** to escape. —**break wind,** expel gas through the anus.

break'a·way" *adj.* **1,** made to break easily. **2,** rebellious.

break-'danc"ing *n.* an acrobatic type of dancing performed to rock or rap music. —**break-'dance",** *v.i.*

break'down" *n.* **1,** a collapse, as from illness. **2,** an analysis.

break'er *n.* a breaking wave.

break'fast (brek'fəst) *n.* the first meal of the day.

> **breakfast**
> ↔ Being the first meal of the day, *breakfast* breaks the night's fast.

break'front" *n.* a large, high cabinet with recessed center or sides.

break'neck" (brāk'nek") *adj.* dangerously fast.

break'through" *n.* **1,** a penetration, as by military forces. **2,** an important development or discovery.

break'up" *n.* disintegration; ruin.

break'wa"ter (brāk'wâ"tər) *n.* a wall to protect a harbor, swimming area, etc., from the effects of the sea.

bream (brēm) *n.* [*pl.* **bream**] any of several American food fishes.

breast (brest) *n.* **1,** the front of the upper body, enclosing the lungs; the chest. **2,** a mammary gland or the flesh covering it. **3,** the chest regarded as the seat of human emotion. —*v.t.* **1,** push against with the breast. **2,** face courageously.

breast'pin" *n.* a brooch.

breast'work" *n.* a protective wall, as of earth.

breath (breth) *n.* **1,** the air inhaled or exhaled in a respiration. **2,** a respiration. **3,** a light breeze. **4,** ability to breathe. **5,** a faint scent. **6,** a trifle; a trivial speech. —**breath'y,** *adj.*

Breath'a·lyz"er (breth'ə-lī"zər) *n.* (*T.N.*) a machine for analyzing the breath of a person, usu. to determine the level of alcohol content. Also, **breath analyzer.**

breathe (brēth) *v.i.* **1,** draw air into and expel it from the lungs; live. **2,** pause; rest.

—*v.t.* **1,** inhale and exhale. **2,** speak softly; whisper. **3,** allow to rest. —**breath'er** (brē'*thər*) *n.* a short rest.

breath'less (breth'ləs) *adj.* **1,** panting. **2,** in suspense; thrilled; astounded. —**breath'-less·ness,** *n.*

breath'tak"ing (breth'tā"king) *adj.* rendering one breathless, as from astonishment, fright, etc.

breech (brēch) *n.* the rear part of anything, esp. a gun; the buttocks. ❏ *breach* **breech'cloth"** *n.* a garment wrapped around the hips.

breech'es (brich'iz) *n.* **1,** short pants, reaching from waist to knee. **2,** (*Informal*) trousers. —**breeches buoy,** a lifesaving apparatus for transporting a person to safety, as from a sinking ship.

breed (brēd) *v.t.* [*pret. & p.p.* **bred**] **1,** beget; produce offspring. **2,** cause to produce offspring; mate. **3,** bring up; rear. —*v.i.* beget; produce; be produced. —*n.* a distinctive race or kind. —**breeder reactor,** a nuclear reactor in which fissionable material is produced.

breed'ing *n.* **1,** genetic strain or background. **2,** gentility.

breeze (brēz) *n.* a light wind. —*v.i.* **1,** blow lightly. **2,** (*Informal*) travel fast without great effort.

breeze'way" *n.* a covered passageway, usu. connecting two buildings.

breez'y (brē'zè) *adj.* **1,** mildly windy. **2,** fresh; airy; (*Informal*) pert. —**breez'i-ness,** *n.*

breth'ren (bre*th*'rin) *n.pl.* **1,** brothers. **2,** associates.

breve (brēv) *n.* **1,** (*Music*) a double whole note (see *note*). **2,** (*Print.*) a diacritical mark (˘).

bre·vet' (brə-vet') *n.* formerly, a temporary promotion to higher military rank. —*v.t.* [**bre·vet'ted, -vet'ting**] promote by brevet.

bre'vi·a·ry (brē'vè-er-è) *n.* a book of daily prayers.

bre·vier' (brə-vēr') *n.* (*Obs., Printing*) 8-point type.

brev'i·ty (brev'ə-tè) *n.* shortness; terseness.

brew (broo) *v.t.* **1,** produce by fermenting grains, as ale. **2,** steep, as tea. —*n.* the beverage so produced.

brew'er (-ər) *n.* a maker of beer. —**brew'er·y** (broo'ə-rè) *n.* a place where beer or ale is brewed. —**brew'mas"ter,** *n.* chief brewer.

bri'ar (brī'ər) *n.* brier.

bri·ard' (brè-ärd') *n.* a breed of French working dog.

bribe (brīb) *n.* a gift or promise given unethically in return for a favor. —*v.t.* make or offer a bribe. —**brib'er·y** (brī'bə-rè) *n.*

> **bribe**
> ↔ From Old French *bribe*, meaning a piece of bread given as alms.

bric-'a-brac" (brik'ə-brak") *n.* unusual small objects of art; knickknacks.

> **bric-a-brac**
> ↔ From a French phrase *à bric et à brac,* a piece and a piece, or "at random."

brick (brik) *n.* **1,** a rectangular block of molded and baked, or dried, clay. **2,** any solid resembling a brick. **3,** (*Informal*) a good fellow. —*adj.* made of brick. —*v.t.* (often with *up*) build with bricks. —**brick'lay"er,** *n.* one who builds with brick.

brick'bat" *n.* **1,** a brick or piece of a brick. **2,** an insulting remark. —*v.t.* [**-bat'-ted, -bat'ting**] throw a brickbat at.

brid'al (brī'dəl) *adj.* pert. to a bride, her wedding, attendants, etc.

bride (brīd) *n.* a woman at, or immediately before or after, her wedding.

bride'groom" *n.* groom (def. 2).

brides'maid" (brīdz'-) *n.* a bride's attendant, usu. unmarried.

bridge (brij) *n.* **1,** a pathway spanning a stream, valley, or road; anything that spans a gap. **2,** the bony structure of the nose. **3,** a raised platform on a ship. **4,** a device for raising the strings of a stringed instrument from the sounding board. **5,** a device for measuring electrical resistance. **6,** a card game. **7,** a device for holding false teeth in place. —*v.t.* build a bridge across; cross; span. —**bridge'head",** *n.* a position held on the enemy's shore of a river. —**bridge'a·ble** (-ə-bəl) *adj.*

bri'dle (brī'dəl) *n.* **1,** the head part of a harness for a horse, etc. **2,** a restraint. —*v.t.* restrain; check. —*v.i.* toss the head, in contempt, deprecation, annoyance, etc. —**bridle path,** a road reserved for horseback riders.

Brie (brē) *n.* a soft white cheese, named for the Brie region of France.

brief (brēf) *adj.* short; terse; succinct. —*n.* a concise summary. —*v.t.* **1,** condense. **2,** give brief instructions to. —**brief"ness,** *n.*

brief'case" *n.* a leather bag for carrying documents; portfolio.

bri'er (brī'ər) *n.* **1,** a thorny shrub. **2,** a root used for making pipes for smoking.

brig *n.* **1,** a square-rigged sailing ship. **2,** a ship's jail.

bri·gade' (bri-gād') *n.* **1,** a military unit, two or more regiments. **2,** an organized body of persons.

brig″a·dier' (brig″ə-dir') *n.* [in the U.S. Army, **brigadier general**] an officer ranking next above colonel.

brig'and (brig'ənd) *n.* a robber; bandit.

brig'an·tine (brig'an-tēn; -tīn) *n.* a type of two-masted sailing vessel.

bright (brīt) *adj.* **1,** having the quality of reflecting light; shining; glowing; clear. **2,** sunny; fair. **3,** clever; mentally alert. **4,** vivacious; happy. **—bright'en** (-ən) *v.t. & i.* make or become bright. **—bright'ness,** *n.*

bril'liance (bril'yəns) *n.* **1,** sparkling appearance; luster; magnificence. **2,** outstanding mental superiority; vivacity.

bril'liant (bril'yənt) *adj.* **1,** lustrous; glittering; sparkling. **2,** marked by high intelligence, ability, or achievement. **—n. 1,** a many-faceted gem. **2,** (*Printing*) 4-point type.

bril'lian·tine″ (bril'yən-tēn″) *n.* **1,** an oily preparation for the hair. **2,** a glossy dress fabric.

brim *n.* the edge; a projecting rim. **—brim'ful″,** *adj.* as full as can be.

brim'stone″ (brim'stōn″) *n.* sulfur. **—adj.** greenish yellow.

brin'dled (brin'dəld) *adj.* gray or brownish streaked with darker colors.

brine (brīn) *n.* **1,** a strong solution of salt in water. **2,** the sea. **—brin'y,** *adj.*

bring *v.t.* [*pret. & p.p.* **brought** (brât)] **1,** carry or conduct to where the speaker is (so distinguished from *take*); fetch. **2,** produce; yield. **3,** (often with *around*) induce; persuade. **4,** command as a price. **5,** (with *up*) rear, as a child.

> **bring, take**
> ☛ It may be a subtle distinction, but *bring* represents movement toward the subject (speaker or writer); *take* is movement away from the subject.

brink *n.* an edge, as of a cliff or the like; verge.

brink'man·ship″ *n.* the policy or practice of pursuing a dangerous course of action almost to the limit.

bri·oche' (brē-osh') *n.* [*pl.* **-oches'** (-osh')] (*Fr.*) a sweet roll or bun.

bri·quette' (bri-ket') *n.* a compacted block of loose material, esp. of coal dust used for fuel.

brisk *adj.* **1,** lively; quick; swift; vivacious. **2,** sharp; stimulating. **—brisk'ness,** *n.*

bris'ket (bris'kit) *n.* a cut of meat from the breast of an animal, esp. beef.

bris'ling *n.* a small herring; a size or grade of sardine.

bris'tle (bris'əl) *n.* a stiff hair. **—v.i.** stand erect, as fur on a frightened cat; evince resentment. **—bris'tly,** *adj.*

bris'tling (bris'ling) *adj.* **1,** stubbly; prickly. **2,** showing resentment.

Bris'tol board (bris'təl) a fine pasteboard used in drawing and printing.

Brit *n.* Briton.

britch'es (brich'əz) *n.* breeches.

Brit'ish *adj.* pert. to Great Britain, its people, customs, etc. **—Brit'ish·er,** *n.*

British thermal unit a unit of heat, the quantity required to raise 1 lb. of water 1° F. Also, **BTU.**

Brit'on (brit'ən) (*Hist.*) *n.* a native of Great Britain.

brit'tle (brit'əl) *adj.* **1,** fragile; easily snapped apart; crisp. **2,** high-strung; lacking strength. **—n.** a hard, brittle candy. **—brit'tle·ness,** *n.*

broach (brōch) *n.* **1,** a tool for piercing. **2,** a brooch. **—v.t. 1,** pierce; open. **2,** introduce, as a subject.

broad (brâd) *adj.* **1,** wide. **2,** of great extent; widespread. **3,** liberal; inclusive. **4,** indelicate; plainspoken. **5,** pronounced openly and sustained, as the *broad a* in *father.* **—n.** (*Offensive*) a woman. **—broad'en,** *v.t. & i.* **—broad jump,** long jump.

broad'cast″ (brâd'kåst″) *adj.* widely published, disseminated, or scattered. **—n.** a widely disseminated radio program. **—v.t. & i.** [*pret. & p.p.* **-cast″** or **-cast″ed**] publish or spread widely.

broad'cloth″ (brâd'klâth″) *n.* **1,** a fine, smooth-finish woolen cloth. **2,** a cotton material with a silky luster.

broad'loom″ *n.* carpeting fabric woven on a wide loom.

broad'mind″ed *adj.* free from prejudice or bigotry; liberal.

broad'side″ *n.* **1,** the side of a ship above the waterline. **2,** a simultaneous discharge of all guns on one side of a warship; fig., any concerted attack. **3,** a large printed sheet.

broad'sword″ *n.* a sword with a broad blade.

bro·cade' (brō-kād') *n.* a rich silken fabric with a raised pattern.

broc'co·li (brok'ə-lē) *n.* a vegetable with edible stalks and flower heads.

bro·chette' (brō-shet') *n.* a small spit or skewer.

bro·chure' (brō-shûr') *n.* a pamphlet.

bro'gan (brō'gən) *n.* a heavy leather boot.

brogue (brōg) *n.* **1,** a dialectal pronunciation of English, esp. that of the Irish. **2,** a low shoe.

broil *v.t. & i.* **1,** cook by direct exposure to an open fire, as on a grill. **2,** subject to great heat. **3,** fret; stew. —*n.* a portion of meat, esp. mixed meats, cooked by broiling.

broil'er (-ər) *n.* **1,** a pan, oven, or stove holding a grill for broiling. **2,** a young fowl to be broiled.

broke (brōk) *v.* pret. of *break.* —*adj.* (*Slang*) without money; penniless.

bro'ken (brō'kən) *adj.* **1,** rough or hilly, as terrain. **2,** shattered; cracked; not in repair. **3,** imperfectly spoken, as a language. **4,** infirm; in poor health. **5,** violated, as a vow. **6,** tamed to obedience; crushed in spirit. —*v.* p.p. of *break.* —**broken home,** a family of which the parents have separated or divorced.

bro"ken-down' *adj.* in bad repair; not operating; decrepit.

bro'ken-heart'ed (här'tid) *adj.* disappointed to the point of despair.

bro'ker (brō'kər) *n.* an agent who buys or sells insurance or property, esp. stocks and bonds on commission.

bro'ker·age (-ij) *n.* **1,** a broker's business or office. **2,** a commission paid to a broker.

bro'mide (brō'mīd) *n.* **1,** a compound of bromine, used as a sedative. **2,** (*Informal*) a trite remark. —**bro·mid'ic** (brō-mid'ik) *adj.*

bro'mine (brō'mēn) *n.* a reddish-brown chemical element, no. 35, symbol Br.

bron'chi (brong'kī) *n.* [*sing.* **-chus** (-kəs)] the two main branches of the windpipe. —**bron'chi·al** (brong'kē-əl) *adj.*

bron·chi'tis (brong-kī'təs) *n.* inflammation in the bronchial tubes.

bron'cho·scope" (brong'kə-skōp") *n.* a tubular instrument that can penetrate to the bronchi or lungs, for inspection or treatment.

bron'co (brong'kō) *n.* in the western U.S., a small wild or unbroken horse. Also, **bron'cho.**

bron"to·sau'rus (bron"tə-sôr'əs) *n.* a prehistoric gigantic reptile of the dinosaur group.

Bronx cheer (*Slang*) raspberry (def. 2).

bronze (bronz) *n.* **1,** an alloy of copper and tin. **2,** the color brown with tinges of red and yellow. —*v.t. & i.* make or become this color, esp. (of persons) by suntanning. —*adj.* of this color. —**Bronze Age,** a period when bronze implements were first used, about 3,500 B.C.

brooch (brōch) *n.* an ornamental pin.

brood *n.* the young hatched in one nest or of one mother. —*v.t. & i.* **1,** sit (on eggs). **2,** ponder moodily. —**brood'er,** *n.* **1,** a heated device for raising baby chicks. **2,** a moody person. —**brood'y,** *adj.* preoccupied.

brook (brûk) *n.* a small stream. —*v.t.* bear; put up with.

broom *n.* **1,** a brush for sweeping. **2,** a shrub of the pea family. —**broom'stick",** *n.* the handle of a broom.

broth (brâth) *n.* a thin soup.

broth'el (broth'əl) *n.* a house of prostitution.

> **brothel**
> ↔ Orig. a term for a despicable person, the word developed from the Middle English phrase *brothel-house* to its present meaning. The word is originally of Germanic origin.

broth'er (bruth'ər) *n.* **1,** a male relative having the same parents as another. **2,** a fellow man. **3,** a member of a religious order, club, society, etc. **4,** [also, **soul brother**] a fellow black. **5,** (*Slang*) heroin.

broth'er·hood" (bruth'ər-hûd") *n.* **1,** fellowship. **2,** a fraternity of men; its members collectively.

broth'er-in-law" *n.* [*pl.* **broth'ers-**] **1,** the brother of one's spouse. **2,** the husband of one's sister.

broth'er·ly (-lė) *adj.* befitting a brother. —**broth'er·li·ness,** *n.*

brough'am (broo'əm) *n.* **1,** a carriage with a straight front. **2,** a similar body for a chauffeur-driven automobile.

> **brougham**
> ↔ After Lord *Brougham,* 19th-c. English statesman.

brought (brât) *v.* pret. & p.p. of *bring.*

brou'ha·ha (broo'hä-hä) *n.* hubbub; uproar; hullabaloo.

brow *n.* **1,** the forehead. **2,** the edge of the top of a cliff or hill.

brow'beat" (brow'bēt") *v.t.* bully; intimidate.

brown *n.* a shade between orange and black. —*adj.* of this color. —*v.t. & i.* make or become brown. —**brown betty,** a baked fruit pudding. —**brown lung,** a disease caused by inhalation of cotton dust. —**brown study,** a reverie.

brown-'bag″ *v.i. & t.* bring one's own food, liquor, etc., to a restaurant, work, etc.

brown'ie (brow'nē) *n.* **1,** a good-natured elf supposed to do chores at night. **2,** a kind of cookie. **3,** (*cap.*) a junior Girl Scout. —**brownie point,** (*Informal*) a fancied mark of favor, as with a superior.

brown'out″ *n.* a partial blackout, to save electricity or to protect against air raids.

brown'shirt″ *n.* a Nazi.

brown'stone″ *n.* a reddish-brown sandstone; a house faced with it.

browse (browz) *n.* twigs, tender shoots, etc., as food for animals. —*v.i.* **1,** feed on or crop twigs, leaves, etc. **2,** read idly here and there, as in a book or library.

bru'in (broo'in) *n.* a bear.

> **bruin**
> ↔ From Middle Dutch *bruin*, brown, the name given the bear in the Dutch version of the fable *Reynard the Fox.*

bruise (brooz) *n.* an injury caused by a blow that discolors but does not break the skin. —*v.t.* inflict such an injury upon. —**bruis'er,** *n.* a fight; a powerful-looking man.

bruit (broot) *v.t.* make known publicly, as by rumor.

brum'ma·gem (brum'ə-jəm) *adj.* cheap; spurious.

> **brummagem**
> ↔ Derived from *Birmingham*, England, apparently because of the counterfeit coins produced there in the 17th c.

brunch *n.* (*Informal*) breakfast eaten at or near lunch time.

bru·net' (broo-net') *adj.* having dark eyes and hair. —*n.* a brunet person. Also, **bru·nette'.**

brunt *n.* the main force of an attack or shock; the principal burden.

brush *n.* **1,** a thicket; scrub. **2,** lopped-off branches of trees. **3,** an implement with hair bristles, wire, etc., attached to a handle or back, for painting, scrubbing, etc. **4,** a bushy tail. **5,** a light touch; a graze. **6,** a minor conflict; a skirmish. —*v.t.* **1,** sweep, rub, clean, etc., with a brush. **2,** remove with or as with a brush. **3,** touch lightly in passing. **4,** (with *off*) dismiss brusquely. —*v.i.* **1,** (with *by*) sweep past. **2,** (with *up*) practice; refresh one's mem-

ory. —**brush'off″,** *n.* a brusque refusal or dismissal.

brusque (brusk) *adj.* abrupt; curt. —**brusque'ness,** *n.*

Brus'sels sprout (brus'əlz) a vegetable whose edible buds resemble miniature cabbage heads.

brut (broot; *Fr.* brü) *adj.* (*Fr.*) of wine, very dry.

bru'tal (broo'təl) *adj.* cruel. —**bru·tal'i·ty** (-tal'ə-tē) *n.*

bru'tal·ize″ (broo'tə-līz″) *v.t. & i.* **1,** make or become brutal. **2,** to treat brutally. —**bru″tal·i·za'tion,** *n.*

brute (broot) *n.* **1,** a beast. **2,** a savage, cruel person. —*adj.* like a beast; not sensitive or reasoning.

brut'ish (broo'tish) *adj.* like an animal; stupid; savage. —**brut'ish·ness,** *n.*

bry'o·ny (brī'ə-nē) *n.* a vine of the gourd family.

bub'ble (bub'əl) *n.* **1,** a thin film of liquid holding gas or air. **2,** a small bead of gas or air in a liquid. **3,** an unsound project or idea. —*v.i.* give forth bubbles; boil; effervesce; be aerated, esp. with a gurgling sound, as a brook. —**bubble gum,** chewing gum that stretches to a strong film. —**bubble memory,** (*Computers*) a type of data storage employing bubble-shaped magnetized regions in a magnetic material.

bub'ble·top″ *adj.* of a car, having a transparent plastic covering (usu. bulletproof).

bu'bo (bū'bō) *n.* an inflammatory swelling of a lymph gland, esp. in the groin. —**bu·bon'ic** (-bon'ik), *adj.* —**bubonic plague,** a deadly, epidemic disease, marked by inflammation of the lymphatic glands.

buc″ca·neer' (buk″ə-nir') *n.* a pirate.

> **buccaneer**
> ↔ This unusual word comes from the Tupi language of the Caribbean islands and originally meant a person who dries meat on a wooden frame over a fire.

buck (buk) *n.* **1,** the male of various animals. **2,** a fop. **3,** (*Slang*) a dollar. **4,** a sawhorse. —*v.i.* **1,** make a sudden, twisting leap, said of a horse. **2,** (*Informal*) demur; suddenly object. **3,** strive, as for a promotion. —*v.t.* **1,** throw off by bucking. **2,** (*Informal*) go against. **3,** in Amer. football, charge into (the opponents' line). —**pass the buck,** (*Slang*) shift the responsibility to another.

buck'a·roo" (buk'ə-roo") *n.* a cowboy.
buck'board" (buk'bôrd") *n.* a light horse-drawn wagon.
buck'et (buk'it) *n.* **1,** a vessel for carrying water or other fluids, usually in the shape of an inverted truncated cone; a pail. **2,** a scoop, as on a dredge. —**bucket seat,** a seat with a rounded back, for one person. —**bucket shop,** a fraudulent stockbroker's office. —**kick the bucket** (*Slang*) die.
buck'eye" (buk'ī") *n.* **1,** a tree or its inedible nutlike seed. **2,** (*cap.*) a native of Ohio.
buck fever the fear of an inexperienced hunter facing approaching game; hence, any fear or excitement preceding a new experience.
buck'le (buk'əl) *n.* **1,** a clasp for joining loose ends, as of a belt or strap. **2,** a bend or kink in metal. —*v.t.* **1,** fasten with a buckle. **2,** crumple; bend. —*v.i.* **1,** (often with *down*) apply oneself with vigor. **2,** crumple; warp.
buck'ler (buk'lər) *n.* a round shield carried on the arm.
buck'ram (buk'rəm) *n.* a coarse, stiffened fabric, used in bookbinding, millinery, etc.
buck'saw" *n.* a saw blade set in a large quadrangular frame.
buck'shot" *n.* a large size of shot used in hunting.
buck'skin" *n.* **1,** leather made of deer or sheepskin. **2,** (*pl.*) garments made of buckskin.
buck'thorn" *n.* any of various shrubs and trees with prickly branches.
buck'tooth" *n.* a tooth that sticks out. —**buck'toothed",** *adj.*
buck'wheat" *n.* a cereal plant whose seeds are ground into flour; this flour.
bu·col'ic (bū-kol'ik) *adj.* pastoral; rustic. —*n.* a poem dealing with simple country life. —**bu·col'i·cal·ly,** *adv.*
bud *n.* **1,** an undeveloped swelling on a plant that may open into a leaf or flower. **2,** a person or thing in an early stage of development. **3,** a debutante. —*v.i.* [**bud'ded, -ding**] sprout.
Bud'dha (bûd'ə) *n.* **1,** the title of saint, in Buddhism. **2,** a conventionalized statue of Gautama Buddha, founder of Buddhism.
Bud'dhism (bûd'iz-əm) *n.* an Asiatic religion that teaches self-denial. —**Bud'dhist** (-ist) *n. & adj.*
bud'dy (bud'ē) *n.* (*Informal*) a friend; pal.

budge (buj) *v.t. & i.* move; stir.
budg'er·i·gar" (buj'ə-rē-gär") *n.* a parakeet. Also, **budg'ie** (-ē).

> **budgerigar**
> ↔ A colorful word of Australian Aborigine derivation, formed of the words for "good cockatoo."

budg'et (buj'it) *n.* an estimate of future financial income and outgo. —*v.t.* plan (expenditures) by making a budget. —**budg'et·ar·y** (-er-ē) *adj.*
buff (buf) *n.* **1,** a dull-yellow leather; a military coat made of it. **2,** a dull-yellowish color. —*v.t.* polish by vigorous rubbing with a soft substance.
buf'fa·lo" (buf'ə-lō") *n.* a kind of wild ox, esp. the Amer. bison. —*v.t.* (*Slang*) **1,** baffle; hoodwink. **2,** overawe; intimidate.
buff'er (buf'ər) *n.* **1,** a polisher. **2,** anything that serves to deaden the shock of striking forces. **3,** (*Computers*) a temporary holding area in memory for data. —**buffer state,** a small neutral nation situated between larger, potentially hostile nations. —**buffer zone,** a demilitarized area between hostile forces.
buf'fet (buf'it) *n.* a slap; any blow. —*v.t.* **1,** beat. **2,** contend against.
buf·fet' (bə-fā') *n.* **1,** a sideboard; a public refreshment counter. **2,** food set out for guests to help themselves. —*adj.* served informally.
buf'fo (bûf'ō) *n.* [*pl.* **-fi** (-fē)] a male singer of comic operatic roles.
buf·foon' (bə-foon') *n.* a clownish jester. —**buf·foon'e·ry** (-ə-rē) *n.* the pranks or behavior of a buffoon.
bug *n.* **1,** one of an order of insects that suck vital fluids. **2,** (*Informal*) any crawling insect. **3,** (*Slang*) a disease germ. **4,** (*Slang*) a fanatic; a zealot. **5,** (*Slang*) a small microphone for secretly transmitting conversations. **6,** (*Slang*) defect. **7,** a mistake in a computer program. —*v.t.* **1,** (*Slang*) install a microphone in (a room, etc.) for secretly transmitting conversations. **2,** (*Informal*) bother; annoy.
bug'a·boo" (bug'ə-boo") *n.* a fancied object of terror. Also, **bug'bear".**
bug'eye" *n.* **1,** a staring or protruding eye. **2,** a small sailboat. —**bug'eyed",** *adj.*

> **bugeye**
> ↔ The sailboat is so called because of the practice of painting an eye on each side of the bow.

bug'ger (bug'ər) *n.* **1,** fellow; lad. **2,** (*Vulgar*) a sodomite. **3,** (*Brit.*) a troublesome

thing or person. **4,** (*Slang*) nasal mucus.
—bugger off, (*Brit.*) (*Slang*) leave.

> **bugger**
> ↔ From Medieval Latin *Bulgarus*,
> Bulgarian or heretic.

bug′gy (bug′ė) *n.* a single-seated, horse-drawn vehicle for two persons, open but with a folding top.
bug′house″ *n.* (*Slang*) an insane asylum.
bu′gle (bū′gəl) *n.* a trumpetlike, valveless brass wind instrument. **—***v.i.* **1,** blow a bugle. **2,** of the elk, utter a cry. **—bu′-gler,** *n.*

> **bugle**
> ↔ This word meant bull in Old French, and refers to the use of a bull's horn as a hunting horn.

build (bild) *v.t.* [*pret. & p.p.* **built** (bilt)] **1,** construct; fashion; erect. **2,** found. **3,** increase and strengthen. **4,** (with *in*) install. **—***v.i.* construct something, esp. a house. **—***n.* bodily figure or shape; form; make or brand of manufacture. **—build′ing,** *n.* any architectural structure, as a house.
bulb *n.* **1,** the rounded underground stem of certain plants, as the lily, onion, etc. **2,** anything shaped like a bulb, as the lamp of an electric light. **—bulb′ous,** *adj.*
bulge (bulj) *n.* an outward swelling; a rounded protuberance. **—***v.t. & i.* swell outward.
bu·lim′i·a (boo-lē′mē-ə) *n.* **1,** an excessively voracious appetite. **2,** an eating disorder consisting of cycles of gorging oneself followed by self-induced vomiting. **—bu·lim′ic,** *adj.*
bulk *n.* **1,** extent or volume, as of massed substance. **2,** an aggregate; a large quantity. **3,** the major part. **4,** massed food fiber that promotes intestinal activity. **—***v.i.* loom large. **—bulk′y,** *adj.*
bulk′head″ (bulk′hed″) *n.* a wall or compartment protruding from a main body, as to protect it.
bull (bûl) *n.* **1,** the male of any animal of the ox family, and of various other large animals. **2,** one who expects the price of stocks to rise. **3,** a papal edict. **4,** a ludicrous blunder in language. **5,** (*Slang*) pompous talk; buncombe. **—bull session,** (*Slang*) an informal conversation.
bull′dog″ (bûl′dâg″) *n.* a powerful shorthaired dog. **—***adj.* tenacious; stubborn. **—***v.t. & i.* in western U. S., throw (a calf steer) by twisting its neck. **—bulldog edition,** the earliest edition of a morning newspaper.

bull′doze″ (bûl′dōz″) *v.t.* coerce; bully; frighten. **—bull′doz″er,** *n.* a tractor having a blade for clearing land, building roads, etc.
bul′let (bûl′ət) *n.* **1,** a small missile to be fired from a firearm; shot. **2,** a large dot, square, etc., used as an ornament in printing.
bul′le·tin (bûl′ə-tən) *n.* **1,** a short, official news report. **2,** a periodical journal, as of an organization. **—bulletin board, 1,** a board of cork or other material for posting notices. **2,** an electronic system maintained on a computer· where users can leave and receive messages by telephone.
bull′fight″ *n.* a combat between a man and a bull, held in an arena for spectators' amusement.
bull′finch″ *n.* any of various finches.
bull′frog″ *n.* an Amer. frog with a bellowing croak.
bull′head″ed (bûl′hed″id) *adj.* obstinate. **—bull′head″ed·ness,** *n.*
bull′horn″ *n.* a loudspeaker.
bul′lion (bûl′yən) *n.* uncoined gold or silver.
bull′ish *adj.* (*Informal*) having a positive attitude; optimistic.
bull market a rising trend in stock prices.
bull′ock (bûl′ək) *n.* an ox; steer.
bull′pen″ *n.* (*Baseball*) a place where relief pitchers warm up.
bull's-′eye″ (bûlz′ī″) *n.* **1,** a thick disk of glass in a deck, roof, etc. **2,** a convex lens for concentrating rays of light. **3,** the center of a target; a shot that reaches it.
bul′ly (bûl′ē) *n.* a tormentor of those smaller or weaker. **—***v.t.* hector with threats and bluster. **—***adj. & interj.* (*Informal*) fine; first-rate. **—bully beef,** canned corned beef.
bul′rush″ (bûl′rush″) *n.* **1,** any of various rushes or reedy plants. **2,** (*Bib.*) the papyrus plant.
bul′wark (bûl′wərk) *n.* **1,** a wall for defense; rampart. **2,** any means of protection.
bum (*Slang*) *v.i.* **[bummed, bum′ming]** loaf; beg. **—***v.t.* get by sponging or begging. **—***n.* **1,** a worthless person; a beggar. **2,** the buttocks. **—***adj.* worthless. **—bum bag,** (*Informal*) a small bag or wallet worn around the waist.
bum′ble (bum′bəl) *v.i. & t.* blunder; bungle.
bum′ble·bee″ (-bē″) *n.* a large, hairy, humming bee.

---

fat, fāte, fär, fāre, fâll, ȧsk; met, hē, hēr, maybė; pin, pīne; not, nōte, ôr, tool

bum′mer (bum′ər) *n.* (*Slang*) something bad or unpleasant; a bad drug trip.

bump *n.* **1,** a thump; collision. **2,** a swelling caused by a blow; any rounded elevation or protuberance. —*v.t.* **1,** strike together or against. **2,** (*Slang*) cancel a passenger's reservation on a flight because of overbooking. —*v.i.* **1,** collide heavily. **2,** jolt along. —**bump′y,** *adj.* —**bump off,** (*Slang*) kill; murder.

bump′er (bum′pər) *n.* **1,** a device, as a protective bar or pad, to deaden the shock of a collision. **2,** a glass filled to the top. —*adj.* (*Informal*) very large.

bump′kin *n.* an awkward fellow.

bump′tious (bump′shəs) *adj.* (*Informal*) ebullient; brash.

bun *n.* **1,** a sweetened biscuit. **2,** a wad of coiled hair as part of a hairdress. **3,** (*pl.*) buttocks.

Bu′na (boo′nə) *n.* (*T.N.*) a synthetic rubber.

bunch *n.* a cluster of things of the same kind growing, grouped, or fastened together. —*v.t. & i.* make into or form a bunch.

bun′co (bung′ko) *n.* (*Informal*) a swindle; confidence game.

bun′combe (bung′kəm) *n.* (*Informal*) humbug; nonsense. Also, **bunk′um.**

> **buncombe**
> ↔ Named after a county in North Carolina and its representative in Congress in the early 1800s who made a particularly long and fatuous speech.

bun′dle (bun′dəl) *n.* **1,** articles packed together; a pack; a package. **2,** (*Informal*) a large quantity. —*v.t.* **1,** tie in a package. **2,** (with *off*) dispose of hurriedly. —*v.i.* **1,** (often with *off*) depart hurriedly. **2,** lie in the same bed without undressing.

bung *n.* a stopper for the hole in a cask; the hole itself: *bunghole.*

bun′ga·low″ (bung′gə-lō″) *n.* a one-story house. —**bun′ga·loid″,** *adj.*

> **bungalow**
> ↔ This type of house originated in India, and its name comes from Bengali *bangla,* Bengali.

bun′gee (bun′jē) *n.* a type of spring. —**bungee cord,** a strong, elastic cord used for securing luggage, etc. —**bungee jumping,** (*Informal*) a sport involving jumping from a high place attached to a bungee cord.

bun′gle (bung′gəl) *v.t. & i.* perform clumsily. —**bung′ler,** *n.*

bun′ion (bun′yən) *n.* a chronic enlargement of the first joint of the big toe.

bunk *n.* **1,** a frame built against a wall for use as a bed. **2,** buncombe. —*v.i.* (with *together*) share the same bed.

bunk′er (bung′kər) *n.* **1,** a bin for storage, esp. a ship's coal bin. **2,** in golf, a sand pit.

bun′ny (bun′ē) *n.* a rabbit.

Bun′sen burner (bun′sən) a burner producing a single jet of hot flame produced by mixture of gas with air, named for 19th-c. German chemist Robert W. Bunsen.

bunt *v.t. & i.* **1,** butt. **2,** (*Baseball*) tap (the ball) without swinging the bat. —*n.* a hit so made.

bun′ting *n.* **1,** a light fabric, esp. used for flags, streamers, etc. **2,** a small songbird. **3,** an infant's outer garment.

buoy (boi) *n.* **1,** an anchored float to guide navigation. **2,** a life-saving device. —*v.t.* (often with *up*) keep from sinking; hence, sustain morally; encourage.

buoy′an·cy (boi′ən-sē) *n.* **1,** ability to float. **2,** lightheartedness. —**buoy′ant,** *adj.*

bur (bėr) *n.* any rough, prickly seed covering. Also, **burr.**

Bur′a·ku″min (bûr′ə-koo″min) *n.pl.* an outcast social caste in Japan.

bur′ble (bėr′bəl) *n.* **1,** a bubbling noise. **2,** excited or confused speech. —*v.i.* **1,** bubble; gush. **2,** make a burbling noise.

bur′den (bėr′dən) *n.* **1,** something carried; a load. **2,** something borne with difficulty, as care, grief, etc. **3,** an encumbrance. **4,** a main theme; a refrain. —*v.t.* **1,** load. **2,** encumber; tax. Also, **bur′then** (bėr′thən). —**bur′den·some,** *adj.*

bur′dock (bėr′dok) *n.* a common bur-bearing weed.

bu′reau (byûr′ō) *n.* **1,** a chest of drawers; a dresser. **2,** an executive branch or office of a government or business.

> **bureau**
> ↔ This word has weaved its way from a color (dark brown), to a cloth of that color, to the use of that cloth in covering a desk, to the desk itself.

bu·reauc′ra·cy (byû-rok′rə-sē) *n.* **1,** the body of administrators in a government; esp., an excessive concentration of such administrators. **2,** control or great influence in government by minor officials.

bu′reau·crat″ (byûr′ə-krat″) *n.* a job-holder in a bureaucracy. —**bu″-**

reau·crat′ic, *adj.* —bu″reau·crat′i·cal·ly, *adv.*

bu·rette′ (byû-ret′) *n.* a graduated measuring tube with a stopcock. Also, bu·ret′.

burg (bĕrg) *n.* (*Informal*) a town.

bur′geon (bĕr′jən) *v.i.* sprout buds.

burg′er (bĕr′gər) *n.* hamburger. ❏ *hamburger*

-burg·er *suf.* patty of ground meat or other food, usu. served on a round bun.

bur′gess (bĕr′jis) *n.* 1, a municipal official or councilman. 2, a full voting citizen.

burgh (bĕrg) *n.* town; borough. —burgh′-er, *n.* townsman.

bur′glar (bĕr′glər) *n.* one who breaks into a house with intent to rob. —bur′-glar·ize″ (-īz″) [also, *Informal*, bur′gle (-gəl)] *v.t.* break into and rob. —bur′-gla·ry, *n.* ❏ *rob*

bur′go·mas″ter (bĕr′gə-) *n.* a mayor, in Ger. and Dutch towns.

Bur′gun·dy (bĕr′gən-dė) *n.* any of various wines from the Burgundy region of France.

bur′i·al (ber′ė-əl) *n.* interment; the act of burying or of being buried.

bu′rin (byûr′in) *n.* an engraving tool for cutting furrows in metal.

burke (bĕrk) *v.t.* 1, murder, esp. by suffocation. 2, suppress.

> **burke**
> ↔ After a murderer named *Burke*, hanged in Scotland for murdering people by suffocation.

bur′lap (bĕr′lap) *n.* a coarse fabric of hemp or jute, used for bags, etc.

bur·lesque′ (bĕr-lesk′) *n.* 1, an imitation of a literary or dramatic work for comic effect; a parody. 2, a theatrical entertainment characterized by coarse comedy. —*v.t.* caricature; parody.

bur′ly (bĕr′lė) *adj.* stout; brawny. —bur′-li·ness, *n.*

burn (bĕrn) *v.t.* [burned or burnt, burn′-ing] 1, destroy by fire. 2, scorch; injure by heat or radiation. 3, produce by fire. 4, consume as fuel. 5, inflame. —*v.i.* 1, be on fire. 2, become charred or scorched. 3, suffer from too much heat or radiation. 4, become inflamed, as with emotion. 5, (*Slang*) be electrocuted. —*n.* 1, an injury caused by fire, heat, or radiation. 2, the firing of an engine.

bur′nish (bĕr′nish) *v.t.* make bright by polishing, esp. metal.

bur·noose′ (bĕr-noos′) *n.* a hooded cloak worn by Arabs.

burn′out (bĕrn′owt) *n.* 1, cessation of

operation of a jet or rocket engine. 2, physical or emotional exhaustion, often a result of stress.

burp (bĕrp) (*Informal*) *n.* a belch. —*v.i.* belch. —*v.t.* hold (a baby) so it will belch gas from the stomach. —burp gun, an automatic pistol.

burr (bĕr) *n.* 1, a roughness left by a tool in cutting metal, wood, etc. 2, a bur. 3, a guttural pronunciation of the letter *r.* 4, a dentist's drill. —*v.t.* 1, make rough or jagged. 2, pronounce with a burr.

bur·ri′to (boo-rē′tō) *n.* (*Sp.*) a tortilla folded and filled, as with meat.

bur′ro (bĕr′ō) *n.* [*pl.* -ros] a small donkey.

bur′row (bĕr′ō) *n.* a hole dug in the ground by an animal. —*v.i.* dig into the ground.

bur′sa (bĕr′sə) *n.* a sac between body joints.

bur′sar (bĕr′sər) *n.* a treasurer.

bur′sa·ry (bĕr′sə-rė) *n.* 1, a treasury. 2, a scholarship.

bur·si′tis (bĕr-sī′tis) *n.* inflammation of a bursa.

burst (bĕrst) *v.i.* [burst, burst′ing] 1, break from internal pressure; explode. 2, break or give way. 3, (with a prep.) display (sudden emotion). 4, appear or go suddenly. —*v.t.* rupture. —*n.* 1, an outburst. 2, an explosion. 3, a rush; a spurt.

bur′y (ber′ė) *v.t.* 1, put underground; inter; entomb. 2, cover or conceal from sight or attention. 3, wholly engage (oneself), as in thought.

bus *n.* 1, a large public motor vehicle: omnibus. 2, (*Slang*) any automobile. —*v.t.* (*Informal*) transport by bus.

bus′boy″ *n.* a waiter's male assistant in a restaurant.

bush (bûsh) *n.* 1, a low, woody shrub. 2, uncleared land; scrub. 3, brush. —*adj.* (*Slang*) amateur; inferior. —bushed, *adj.* (*Informal*) fatigued; worn out. —bush league, (*Informal*) 1, a minor league. 2, of inferior quality. —bush leaguer, (*Informal*) an incompetent amateur.

bush′el (bûsh′əl) *n.* a unit of dry measure; four pecks.

bu′shi·do″ (boo′shė-dō″) *n.* (*Jap.*) the chivalric code of the Jap. gentry and officer class.

bush′ing (bûsh′ing) *n.* 1, a metal lining in which an axle or shaft turns. 2, an insulating lining for a hole.

bush′man (bûsh′mən) *n.* [*pl.* -men] a member of a savage aboriginal tribe in Australia.

---

fat, fāte, fär, fāre, fâll, åsk; met, hē, hėr, maybė; pin, pīne; not, nōte, ôr, tool

bush′mas″ter *n.* a poisonous snake of tropical Amer.

bush′wa (bûsh′wä) *n.* nonsense.

bush′whack″er (bûsh′hwak″ər) *n.* (*Informal*) a backwoodsman; a hillbilly. **—bush′whack″,** *v.t.* ambush.

bush′y (-ė) *adj.* formed like a bush; dense in growth, as a beard. **—bush′iness,** *n.*

busi′ness (biz′nəs) *n.* **1,** occupation; calling. **2,** a commercial enterprise; a company. **3,** commercial pursuits in general; capital engaged in trade or industry. **4,** industrial activity; the activity of businessmen collectively. **5,** duty; aim. **6,** affair; a matter of interest or concern. **7,** (*Theat.*) action illustrative of the script.

busi′ness·like″ *adj.* methodical; efficient; attentive to the business at hand.

busi′ness·man″, busi′ness·wom″an *n.* a person engaged in business. Also, **busi′ness·per″son,** *n.*

bus′kin *n.* a short soft boot.

bus′man (-mən) *n.* a male bus driver. **—busman's holiday,** a holiday spent in activity similar to one's regular work.

bus′per″son *n.* a waiter's assistant in a restaurant.

buss (bus) *v.t.* kiss.

bust *n.* **1,** a sculptured likeness of the head and shoulders of a person. **2,** the human chest or bosom. **3,** (*Informal*) a failure; in cards, a worthless hand. **4,** (*Informal*) a spree. **—v.i.** (*Informal*) burst; fail. **—v.t.** (*Slang*) arrest. **—bust′ed,** *adj.* (*Informal*) out of money.

bus′tard (bus′tərd) *n.* a large cranelike bird.

bus′ter (bus′tər) *n.* (*Informal*) a boy or man (a patronizing term).

Buster Brown a boy's costume comprising a short jacket and knee-length pants.

bus·tier′ (bus-tyä′) *n.* a short bodice worn by women.

bus′tle (bus′əl) *v.i.* be fussily busy. **—n. 1,** stir; ado. **2,** a pad under the back of a woman's skirt.

bus′y (biz′ė) *adj.* **1,** actively occupied. **2,** crowded with activity, as a *busy day.* **—v.t.** keep occupied. **—bus′y·ness,** *n.*

bus′y·bod″y (biz′ė-bod″ė) *n.* a prying or meddling person.

but *adv.* only. **—prep.** except; besides. **—conj. 1,** unless. **2,** nevertheless; though. **3,** on the contrary. **4,** whether.

bu′tane (bū′tān) *n.* a flammable petroleum derivative, used as a fuel, etc.

butch (bûch) *adj.* (*Slang*) **1,** very masculine in appearance or behavior. **2,** pert.

to the male role in a homosexual relationship.

butch′er (bûch′ər) *n.* **1,** one who slaughters animals for food and dresses meat for market; a seller of meat. **2,** one who kills brutally. **—v.t. 1,** kill and dress for food. **2,** murder wantonly. **3,** botch, spoil. **—butch′er·y,** *n.* slaughter.

but′ler (but′lər) *n.* a manservant, usually the head servant of a large household.

butt (but) *n.* **1,** a wine cask. **2,** the thicker end of anything, as of a tool, log, etc. **3,** a target; the object of criticism, a joke, etc. **4,** a push with the head. **—v.i. 1,** strike something with the head. **2,** collide. **3,** abut. **—v.t.** strike with the head.

butte (būt) *n.* a steep-sided hill.

but′ter (but′ər) *n.* **1,** a fatty substance made by churning cream. **2,** any butterlike substance. **—v.t. 1,** spread with butter. **2,** (*Informal*) (with *up*) flatter; ingratiate oneself with.

but′ter·cup″ (but′ər-kup″) *n.* a meadow plant with yellow flowers.

but′ter·fat″ *n.* the fat in milk.

but′ter·fin″gers *n.* (*Informal*) a fumbler; a person who drops things.

but′ter·fly″ (but′ər-flī″) *n.* **1,** an insect with broad, brilliantly colored wings. **2,** (*Informal*) a gay, fickle woman. **3,** (*pl.*) flutters in the stomach caused by nervousness.

but′ter·milk″ *n.* the mildly acid liquid left after butter is churned.

but′ter·nut″ *n.* the Amer. white walnut; the tree; its oily fruit.

but′ter·scotch″ *n.* a hard candy made of brown sugar, corn syrup, and water.

but′ter·y (but′ər-ė) *adj.* like or containing butter. **—n.** a room, esp. in a Brit. college or university, used as a dispensary for food and drink.

---

buttery
↔ The room is not named after butter, but is related to Fr. *boterie*, wine cask or butt.

---

but′tocks (but′əks) *n.pl.* the fleshy part of the hips; the rump.

but′ton (but′ən) *n.* **1,** a knob or disk used on clothes as an ornament or a fastener. **2,** any buttonlike object or device. **—v.t. & i.** fasten with buttons. **—button man,** (*Slang*) a Mafia member of low rank.

but′ton-down″ *adj.* **1,** of a shirt, having collars held down by buttons. **2,** (*Slang*) lacking originality. **3,** (*Slang*) prim; conservative.

but'ton·hole'' (but'ən-hōl'') *n.* the loop or slit for a button. —*v.t.* **1,** make such a slit in. **2,** (*Informal*) detain in conversation.

> **buttonhole**
> ↔ This word was originally, the much more logical *buttonhold*, later modified by repeated mispronunciation.

but'tress (but'ris) *n.* **1,** masonry built against a wall or building for strength and support. **2,** any prop. —*v.t.* prop; brace.

bux'om (buk'səm) *adj.* plump; healthy. —**bux'om·ness,** *n.*

buy (bī) *v.t.* [**bought** (bât), **buy'ing**] **1,** obtain in exchange for money; purchase. **2,** obtain by any sacrifice. **3,** bribe. **4,** (*Slang*) accept; believe.—*n.* (*Informal*) something purchased. —**buy'er,** *n.* a purchaser; a departmental manager in a store. —**buyer's market,** a business condition in which supply exceeds demand. —**buy the farm,** (*Slang*) be killed; die.

buy'out *n.* the purchase of the controlling interest in a company.

buzz (buz) *n.* **1,** a humming sound, as of bees. **2,** a confused murmur. **3,** (*Slang*) a telephone call. —*v.t.* **1,** (*Slang*) swoop down upon in an airplane, as a prank. **2,** enlighten privately. **3,** (with *off*) leave. **4,** (*Informal*) telephone to. —*v.i.* **1,** make a humming sound. **2,** (*Informal*) be very active. —**buzz bomb,** a bomb self-propelled by a rocket or jet engine.

buz'zard (buz'ərd) *n.* **1,** a hawklike bird. **2,** an Amer. vulture.

buzz'saw'' *n.* a circular saw.

buzz'word *n.* a technical term enjoying ephemeral popularity, often used chiefly for effect.

bwa'na (bwä'nə) *n.* master.

by (bī) *prep.* **1,** beside; near. **2,** along; over. **3,** past and beyond. **4,** through the action or agency of. **5,** in or to the amount of. **6,** before; no later than. —*adv.* **1,** near; beside. **2,** aside. **3,** past.

by- (bī) *pref.* **1,** secondary. **2,** out of the way. **3,** near.

by-'and-by' (bī'ən-bī') *adv.* in the near future. —*n.* the future.

bye (bī) *n.* **1,** in a tournament, an idle round in which a competitor nevertheless advances. **2,** good-bye.

by-'e·lec''tion *n.* a special election held between regular elections, as to fill a vacancy.

by'gone'' (bī'gân'') *adj.* of times past; former. —*n.* (*pl.*) deeds done in the past.

by'law'' *n.* a regulation or rule adopted by a corporation or organization.

> **bylaw**
> ↔ Probably from an early Germanic or Norse word for town law.

by'line'' *n.* the line naming the author of a story or article.

by'pass'' *n.* **1,** an alternative route, as a road or pipe. **2,** an operation providing an alternate path for an artery or other blood vessel. —*v.t.* avoid and progress beyond.

by'path'' *n.* **1,** a side or private road. **2,** an indirect route or course; a detour.

by'play'' *n.* a diversion; secondary action.

by-'prod''uct *n.* a secondary product, produced incidentally to the manufacture of something else.

by'stand''er (bī'stan''dər) *n.* a spectator.

byte (bīt) *n.* a group of (usu. eight) binary digits or bits processed by a computer as a unit.

by'way'' *n.* a side road.

by'word'' *n.* **1,** a proverb; a motto or slogan. **2,** a pet expression.

By·zan'tine (bi-zan'tin; biz'ən-tēn'', -tīn'') *adj.* **1,** pert. to Byzantium. **2,** ornate; elaborate. **3,** characterized by intrigue and scheming.

C

C, c (sē) **1,** the third letter of the English alphabet. **2,** (often *cap.*) the Roman numeral for 100. **3,** (*cap.*) a computer programming language. **4,** [also, **C-note**] (*Slang*) a $100 bill.

cab (kab) *n.* **1,** a horse-drawn or motor vehicle for public hire. **2,** the driver's compartment of a truck or locomotive.

ca·bal' (kə-bal') *n.* **1,** a secret scheme or intrigue. **2,** a group of secret plotters.

cab'a·la (kab'ə-lə) *n.* any occult science. —**cab''a·lis'tic,** *adj.*

ca·ba·let'ta (kä-bä-let'ə) *n.* (*It.*) a short melody, usu. ending an aria or duet in Italian opera.

ca·bal·le'ro (kä-bä-yā'rō) *n.* (*Sp.*) horseman.

ca·ba'ña (kə-bä'nyə) *n.* **1,** a small cabin. **2,** a private bathhouse.

cab''a·ret' (kab'ə-rā') *n.* a restaurant that provides entertainment.

cab'bage (kab'ij) *n.* a vegetable plant

---

fat, fāte, fär, fāre, fâll, ȧsk; met, hē, hêr, maybė; pin, pīne; not, nōte, ôr, tool having edible leaves formed into a thick compact head.

cab'by (kab'ē) *n.* (*Informal*) taxicab driver. Also, **cab'bie.**

cab'in (kab'in) *n.* **1,** cottage; hut. **2,** a room in a ship or airplane.

cab'i·net (kab'i-nət) *n.* **1,** a piece of furniture used as a cupboard. **2,** a small meeting room. **3,** an advisory council. —*adj.* **1,** pert. to a council. **2,** of a certain small size.

ca'ble (kā'bəl) *n.* **1,** a thick, strong rope or chain. **2,** a number of wires for conducting electricity, bound together in a cylindrical sheath. **3,** [also, **ca'ble·gram"**] a telegram sent by submarine cable. **4,** (*Naut.*) a unit of length. —*v.t. & i.* furnish with cables; communicate by cable. —**cable-ready,** *adj.* capable of receiving and converting cable TV signals.

ca'ble·cast" *v.t. & n.* broadcast by cable TV.

cab'o·chon" (kab'ə-shon") *n.* a gem polished but not cut in facets.

ca·boo'dle (kə-boo'dəl) *n.* (*Informal*) crowd or collection.

ca·boose' (kə-boos') *n.* a car on a freight train fitted for use of the crew.

cab"ri·o·let' (kab"rē-ə-lā') *n.* **1,** a light two-wheeled carriage. **2,** an automobile with a folding top.

> **cabriolet, cab**
> ↔ From the Italian *capriolare*, leap in the air: the carriage had a very springy suspension. The word *cab* comes from cabriolet.

ca·ca'o (kə-kä'ō) *n.* a tropical evergreen tree whose seeds are the source of cocoa and chocolate.

cac"cia·to're (kach"ə-tôr'ē) *adj.* simmered with herbs and seasonings.

> **cacciatore**
> ↔ From the Italian phrase *alla cacciatora*, in the hunter's manner, from *cacciatore*, hunter.

cache (kash) *n.* **1,** a place of storage or concealment, esp. underground. **2,** a store of provisions, treasure, etc. so concealed. **3,** (*Computers*) a buffer for data read from a storage medium. —*v.t.* hide.

ca·chet' (ka-shā') *n.* **1,** a seal, as on a letter. **2,** a mark of distinction or authentication; a special postmark.

ca·chou' (kə-shoo') *n.* a breath sweetener.

cack'le (kak'əl) *n.* **1,** the shrill repeated cry of a goose or hen. **2,** silly chatter; noisy laughter. —*v.i.* chatter; laugh noisily.

ca·coph'o·ny (kə-kof'ə-nē) *n.* a combination of discordant sounds; dissonance. —**ca·coph'o·nous,** *adj.*

cac'tus (kak'təs) *n.* [*pl.* **-ti** (-tī)] a leafless spiny desert plant.

cad (kad) *n.* an ill-bred or contemptible person. —**cad'dish,** *adj.*

ca·dav'er (kə-dav'ər) *n.* a dead body; corpse. —**ca·dav'er·ous,** *adj.*

cad'die (kad'ē) *n.* a person engaged to carry the clubs of a golf player. —*v.i.* act as a caddie. Also, **cad'dy.**

> **caddie, caddy**
> ↔ These two words, in their senses of golfing assistant and tea chest respectively, have quite different origins. The former comes from a Scottish variant of the French *cadet*, young person (which also came into English as *cadet*); the latter comes from a Malay weight.

cad'dy (kad'ē) *n.* **1,** a small can or chest for holding tea, etc. **2,** caddie. ❑ *caddie*

ca'dence (kā'dəns) *n.* **1,** rhythmic flow. **2,** a fall in pitch or tempo. **3,** (*Music*) a sequence of chords expressing conclusion, finality, or repose. **4,** the beat or rate of a rhythm.

ca·den'za (kə-den'zə) *n.* a passage in showy style for a soloist, as in a concerto.

ca·det' (kə-det') *n.* **1,** a young person in training for army service. **2,** a younger son.

cadge (kaj) *v.t.* beg.

cad'mi·um (kad'mē-əm) *n.* a metallic chemical element, no. 48, symbol Cd.

ca'dre (kåd'rē) *n.* a permanently organized group of persons forming the framework of a larger organization.

ca·du'ce·us (kə-doo'sē-əs) *n.* [*pl.* **-i"** (-ī")] a winged staff: symbol of the medical profession.

cae'cum (sē'kəm) *n.* the inner end of the large intestine to which the vermiform appendix is attached.

> **caecum**
> ↔ From the Latin phrase *intestinum caecum*, blind gut.

Cae'sar salad (sē'zər) a type of mixed salad with a dressing of garlic, anchovy, egg yolk, lemon juice, and cheeses, named for a restaurant in Tijuana, Mexico.

Cae·sar'e·an (si-zâr'ē-ən) *adj.* Cesarean.

cae·su′ra (sĕ-zhûr′ə) *n.* a natural break or pause, due to sense, in a line of poetry.

ca·fé′ (ka-fā′) *n.* a restaurant or barroom.

caf″e·te′ri·a (kaf″ə-tir′ė-ə) *n.* a self-service restaurant.

caf′feine (kaf′ēn) *n.* a bitter alkaloid having a stimulating effect.

caf′tan (kaf′tən) *n.* a long garment with long sleeves worn in the Near East.

cage (kāj) *n.* an enclosure made of wires or bars. —*v.t.* put in a cage. —**cage′ling,** *n.* a caged animal; a prisoner. —**cag′er,** *n.* (*Informal*) a basketball player.

cag′ey (kā′jė) *adj.* (*Informal*) wary; shrewd. Also, **cag′y.**

ca·hoots″ (kə-hoots′) *n.pl.* (*Informal*) secret partnership.

cai′man (kā′mən) *n.* [*pl.* -**mans**] a So. Amer. alligator. Also, **cay′man.**

cairn (kārn) *n.* a heap of stones, erected as a monument. —**cairn terrier,** a small dog of a terrier breed.

cais′son (kā′sən) *n.* **1,** a large boxlike structure with an open bottom, used in underwater excavation. **2,** a floating structure used as a dock, etc. **3,** a wagon for ammunition. —**caisson disease,** the bends.

cai′tiff (kā′tif) *n.* (*Archaic*) a wicked or mean person.

ca·jole′ (kə-jōl′) *v.t.* & *i.* persuade by flattery; wheedle. —**ca·jol′er·y,** *n.*

Ca′jun (kā′jən) *n.* & *adj.* pert. to a group of people descended from French ancestors driven from Acadia (Canada) who settled in Louisiana and Maine.

> **Cajun**
> ↔ The word is a spelling out of a spoken version of *Acadian.*

cake (kāk) *n.* **1,** a sweet food baked from dough. **2,** any loaflike mass, as of soap. —*v.* form or become formed into a compact mass; cohere.

cake′walk″ *n.* **1,** a dance. **2,** (*Informal*) something easy; cinch.

cal′a·bash″ (kal′ə-bash″) *n.* any of various gourds or gourd trees.

cal′a·boose″ (kal′ə-boos″) *n.* (*Slang*) a jail.

cal′a·mine″ (kal′ə-mīn″) *n.* a white mineral, an ore of zinc, used medicinally.

ca·lam′i·ty (kə-lam′ə-tė) *n.* a great misfortune or cause of distress; disaster. —**ca·lam′i·tous,** *adj.*

cal·car′e·ous (kal-kār′ė-əs) *adj.* containing calcium carbonate; chalky.

cal′ci·fy″ (kal′sə-fī″) *v.t.* & *i.* harden or become hard by deposit of calcium. —**cal″ci·fi·ca′tion,** *n.*

cal′ci·mine″ (kal′sə-mīn″) *n.* a thin water-soluble paint, usually white. —*v.t.* whitewash. Also, **kal′so·mine″.**

cal′cine (kal′sīn) *v.t.* heat in order to fuse, crumble, oxidize, etc. —**cal″ci·na′tion,** *n.*

cal′cite (kal′sīt) *n.* calcium carbonate.

cal′ci·um (kal′sė-əm) *n.* a chemical element, no. 20, symbol Ca, found in bone, chalk, lime, etc.

> **calcium**
> ↔ Coined by the 19th-c. English chemist Sir Humphry Davy from Latin *calx*, limestone.

cal′cu·late″ (kal′kū-lāt″) *v.t.* **1,** ascertain by mathematics; compute. **2,** plan. **3,** (*Informal*) intend; guess. —*v.i.* reckon. —**cal′cu·la·ble,** *adj.* —**cal′cu·lat·ed,** *adj.* planned; carefully thought out. —**cal″cu·lat″ing,** *adj.* shrewd; scheming. —**cal″cu·la′tion,** *n.* —**cal″cu·la″tor,** *n.*

> **calculate**
> ↔ From Latin *calculus*, pebble, presumably from its use as a counting stone.

cal′cu·lus (kal′kyə-ləs) *n.* **1,** (*Math.*) any system of computation or analysis by a specialized algebraic notation, esp. differential or integral calculus. **2,** a small stone, as a gallstone.

cal′dron (kâl′drən) *n.* cauldron.

cal″e·fac′tion (kal″ə-fak′shən) *n.* heating. —**cal″e·fac′to·ry** (-tə-rė) *adj.*

cal′en·dar (kal′ən-dər) *n.* **1,** any system of division of time. **2,** a table of days, weeks, and months. **3,** a list, register, or catalog; a list of cases to be tried in a court. —*v.t.* enter in a calendar; register.

cal′en·der (kal′ən-dər) *n.* a machine for pressing, drying or glazing paper, cloth, etc. —*v.t.* treat in a calender.

cal′ends (kal′əndz) *n.pl.* in ancient Rome, the first day of the month.

ca·len′du·la (kə-len′jə-lə) *n.* any of various flowering plants including the marigold.

calf (kǎf) *n.* [*pl.* **calves** (kǎvz)] **1,** the young of certain animals, as cow, elephant, seal, whale. **2,** calfskin leather. **3,** the thick fleshy part of the human leg, below the knee.

cal′i·ber (kal′ə-bər) *n.* **1,** diameter, esp. of the hollow inside of a cylinder. **2,** capacity of mind; degree of importance. Also, **cal′i·bre.**

cal′i·brate″ (kal′ə-brāt″) *v.t.* mark (a measuring instrument) with graduations; verify or rectify. —**cal″i·bra′tion,** *n.*

cal′i·co″ (kal′ə-kō″) *n.* a printed cotton cloth.

> **calico**
> ↔ From *Calicut,* the former name of Kazhikode, India, where the cloth originated.

cal″i·for′ni·um (kal″ə-fôr′nē-əm) *n.* an unstable, radioactive chemical element, no. 98, symbol Cf, produced artificially from curium.

cal′i·per (kal′ə-pər) *n.* **1,** (usually *pl.*) a measuring instrument for determining diameters. **2,** a device used in some brake systems. —*v.t. & i.* measure with calipers.

ca′liph (kā′lif) *n.* title of a sovereign in Mohammedan countries. —**cal′iph·ate** (-āt) *n.*

cal″is·then′ics (kal″əs-then′iks) *n.pl.* light gymnastics.

calk (kâk) *v.t. & n.* caulk.

call (kâl) *v.t.* **1,** utter loudly; announce; proclaim. **2,** attract or demand the attention of; summon. **3,** give a name to; designate; characterize. **4,** telephone to. —*v.i.* **1,** shout. **2,** make a short visit. —*n.* **1,** a cry or shout. **2,** the characteristic cry of an animal or bird; the note of a bugle or horn. **3,** a notice, summons, or invitation. **4,** a short visit. —**call forwarding,** a feature in telephone systems which transfers one's calls to another programmed telephone number. —**call girl,** a prostitute. —**call waiting,** a feature in telephone systems which allows more than one call to be received on the same line.

cal′la (kal′ə) *n.* [also, **calla lily**] a plant with a large white flower and bright yellow spadix.

cal″la·loo′ (kal″ə-loo′) *n.* a thick crab-meat soup of Jamaican origin.

call′back″ *n.* a recall, as of a product for repair of defects, a candidate for another hearing, etc.

cal·lig′ra·phy (kə-lig′rə-fē) *n.* fancy handwriting.

call′ing *n.* **1,** profession or vocation. **2,** act of summoning, etc. —**calling card,** a card bearing one's name.

cal·li′o·pe (kə-lī′ə-pē) *n.* a musical instrument employing steam whistles.

cal·los′i·ty (kə-los′ə-tē) *n.* **1,** a hardened part; a callus. **2,** a callous condition.

cal′lous (kal′əs) *adj.* **1,** hard; hardened. **2,** unfeeling; unkind. —*n.* callus. —*v.t. & i.* to form a callus (on). —**cal′lous·ness,** *n.*

> **callous, callus**
> ☞ Both of these words can refer to hardened skin. Only *callous,* however, is also an adjective, meaning, literally, hardened, or figuratively, unfeeling.

cal′low (kal′ō) *adj.* very immature. —**cal′low·ness,** *n.*

cal′lus (kal′əs) *n.* a hardened or thickened part of the skin. —*v.t. & i.* to form a callus (on). ❑ *callous*

calm (käm) *adj.* **1,** quiet; still. **2,** serene; tranquil. —*n.* the state of being calm. —*v.t. & i.* (often with *down*) quiet. —**calm′ness,** *n.*

cal′o·mel″ (kal′ə-mel″) *n.* a medicine, mercurous chloride, used as a purgative.

cal′o·rie (kal′ə-rē) *n.* a measure of heat, and of the energy-producing property of food. —**ca·lor′ic** (kə-lôr′ik) *adj.* —**cal″o·rif′ic** (kal″ə-rif′ik) *adj.* producing heat.

cal′u·met″ (kal′ū-met″) *n.* a Native American ceremonial tobacco pipe.

ca·lum′ni·ate″ (kə-lum′nē-āt″) *v.t.* slander. —**ca·lum″ni·a′tion,** *n.*

cal′um·ny (kal′əm-nē) *n.* a false accusation of crime or misconduct; slander. —**ca·lum′ni·ous,** *adj.*

cal′va·ry (kal′və-rē) *n.* **1,** a picture or sculpture of the scene of the Crucifixion. **2,** (*cap.*) the place where Christ was crucified.

> **Calvary, cavalry**
> ☞ Do not confuse *Calvary,* the hill where Jesus was crucified, with *cavalry,* a part of an army mounted on horseback (or in motorized vehicles).

calve (kav) *v.i.* bear a calf.

calves (kavz) *n.pl.* of *calf.*

Cal′vin·ism (kal′vin-iz-əm) *n.* the theological doctrines of John Calvin; Presbyterianism. —**Cal′vin·ist,** *n.* —**Cal″vin·is′tic,** *adj.*

cal·vi′ti·es″ (kal-vish′ē-ēz″) *n.* baldness.

ca·lyp′so (kə-lip′sō) *n.* a style of song of the Brit. W. Indies.

ca′lyx (kā′liks) *n.* the outermost envelope of a flower; the sepals.

cal·zo′ne (kal-zō′nä) *n.* a turnover filled with meat and cheese.

cam (kam) *n.* an eccentric wheel or part for converting rotary motion into linear or irregular motion.

ca″ma·ra′de·rie (kä″mə-rä′də-rē) *n.* comradeship.

cam′ber (kam′bər) *n.* a slight curve or arch.

cam′bi·um (kam′bė-əm) *n.* a layer of tissue between bark and wood.

cam′bric (kām′brik) *n.* a closely woven fabric of cotton or linen. **—cambric tea,** hot water, cream, and sugar.

> **cambric**
> ↔ From Dutch *Kameryk*, Cambrai, a city in France.

cam′cord″er (kam′kôr-dər) *n.* a lightweight, handheld video camera and recorder.

came (kām) *v.* pret. of *come.*

cam′el (kam′əl) *n.* **1,** a large ruminant quadruped with two humps, used in Asia and Afr. as a beast of burden; Bactrian camel. **2,** dromedary. **—cam″el·eer′** (kam″ə-lir′) *n.* a camel driver.

ca·mel′lia (kə-mēl′yə) *n.* an evergreen plant bearing red or white flowers.

> **camellia**
> ↔ Named for G. J. *Camellus,* the 17th-c. Jesuit missionary who imported the plant.

ca·mel′o·pard″ (kə-mel′ə-pärd″) *n.* the giraffe.

Cam′em·bert″ (kam′əm-bār″) *n.* a soft-ripening cheese.

cam′e·o″ (kam′ė-ō″) *n.* **1,** a stone or shell decorated with raised carving. **2,** a brief story or play. **3,** a small role performed by a well-known personality.

cam′er·a (kam′ər-ə) *n.* **1,** a photographic apparatus for recording an image on a sensitized surface. **2,** the private chamber of a judge. **—cam′er·a·man″,** *n.* a camera operator. **—in camera,** in private.

> **camera**
> ↔ From the Latin word for a vaulted room. Its photographic sense comes from *camera obscura,* dark chamber, a 17th-c. optical instrument.

camera lu′ci·da (loo′si-də) an optical instrument for projecting an image to be traced or copied on paper.

camera ob·scu′ra (ob-skyûr′ə) a darkened room or box in which a real image of an external object is projected and viewed.

cam′i·on (kam′ė-ən) *n.* **1,** a cart for heavy loads. **2,** a military truck.

cam′i·sole″ (kam′ə-sōl″) *n.* **1,** a woman's blouse. **2,** a straitjacket.

cam′o·mile″ (kam′ə-mīl″) *n.* an herb used to make a medicinal tea.

cam′ou·flage″ (kam′ə-fläzh″) *n.* **1,** (*Mil.*) disguise of objects that cannot be wholly concealed. **2,** any disguise; false pretense. **—v.t.** disguise. **—cam″ou·fleur′** (-flēr′) *n.* one who camouflages.

camp (kamp) *n.* **1,** a place for the erection of temporary shelters. **2,** a group of temporary lodgings, as for lumber workers. **3,** a cabin in the wilderness. **4,** fig., a group or sect. **5,** something interesting or entertaining because of its banality or archaism. **—v.i. 1,** live in a camp. **2,** (with *on*) follow persistently; haunt. **—adj.** campy. **—camp′er,** *n.* motor home; caravan. **—camp chair,** a folding chair. **—camp follower, 1,** a prostitute. **2,** an observer who is not a member, as of a movement. **3,** a politician who switches parties for personal gain.

cam·paign′ (kam-pān′) *n.* **1,** military operations during one season or in a definite enterprise. **2,** a series of activities directed to a single purpose, as for election to public office.

cam″pa·ni′le (kam″pə-nē′lė) *n.* a bell tower.

cam·pan′u·la (kam-pan′yə-lə) *n.* the bellflower.

cam″pe·si′no (käm″pə-sē′nō) *n.* (*Sp.*) a rustic.

cam′phor (kam′fər) *n.* **1,** a vegetable or synthetic gum used in medicine, plastics, etc. **2,** an oriental tree. **—cam′phor·ate″** (-āt″) *v.i.* **—cam′phor·at″ed** (-ā″tid) *adj.*

cam′pus (kam′pəs) *n.* the grounds of a school, esp. a college or university.

camp′y (cam′pė) *adj.* characterized by camp (def. 5).

can (kan) *aux. v.* [pret. **could**] **1,** have the ability or power to; be able to. **2,** (*Informal*) may; have permission to. **—n. 1,** a metal container or receptacle. **2,** (*Slang*) a jail. **3,** (*Vulgar*) toilet. **—v.t.** [**canned** (kand), **can′ning**] **1,** seal in a container. **2,** (*Informal*) dismiss from employment. **3,** record, as on film or tape. **4,** (*Slang*) cease.

> **can, may**
> ☞ (*Gram.*) The person who is able to do something *can* do something; the person who has permission to do something *may* do it. *May* has the additional sense of uncertainty: that person *may* or *may not* do it.

Can′a·da goose (kan′ə-də) a wild goose of No. Amer.

Ca·na′di·an bacon (kə-nā′dė-ən) bacon from the pork loin.

ca·nail′le (ka-nä′yə) *n.* (*Fr.*) riffraff.

ca·nal′ (kə-nal′) *n.* **1,** an artificial waterway for navigation or irrigation. **2,** any channel, duct, or passage conveying or containing a fluid.

can′a·pé (kan′ə-pē) *n.* a small piece of bread or toast bearing a morsel of appetizing food.

ca·nard′ (kə-närd′) *n.* a false story; a hoax.

ca·nar′y (kə-nār′ė) *n.* **1,** a songbird, widely domesticated as a household pet. **2,** a light yellow color.

> **canary**
> ↔ From the Canary Islands, from where they were introduced to the West. The islands' name came from Latin *canarius*, of dogs, because a breed of large dogs was discovered there.

ca·nas′ta (kə-nás′tə) *n.* a card game based on rummy.

can′can (kan′kán) *n.* a posturing dance with high kicking.

can′cel (kan′səl) *v.t.* **1,** draw lines across (something written) so as to deface. **2,** make void; annul. **3,** compensate for; offset; neutralize. —**can″cel·la′tion,** *n.*

can′cer (kan′sər) *n.* a malignant tumor; any evil that grows and spreads. —**can′-cer·ous,** *adj.*

> **cancer**
> ↔ From the Latin word for crab, apparently because of the pattern formed by the blood vessels around an affected area.

Can′cer (kan′sər) *n.* a northern constellation, the Crab (see *zodiac*).

can″de·la′bra (kan″də-lä′brə) *n.* [*pl.* -bras] candelabrum.

can″de·la′brum (kan″də-lä′brəm) *n.* [*pl.* -bra (-brə), -brums] an ornamental branched candlestick.

can·des′cent (kan-des′ənt) *adj.* glowing. —**can·des′cence,** *n.*

can′did (kan′did) *adj.* outspoken; frank. —**can′did·ness,** *n.*

can′di·date″ (kan′də-dāt″) *n.* one who seeks an office or honor. —**can′di·da·cy** (-də-sė) *n.*

can′dle (kan′dəl) *n.* a rod of wax, tallow, or paraffin with an embedded wick, burned to give sustained light. —*v.t.* examine (esp. eggs) by holding between the eye and a light. —**candlepower,** a measure of illumination.

Can′dle·mas (-məs) *n.* a Christian religious festival, Feb. 2, commemorating the purification of the Virgin Mary.

can′dle·pin″ (kan′dəl-pin″) *n.* a nearly cylindrical bowling pin, tapering in at top

and bottom. —**can′dle·pins″,** *n.pl., construed as sing.* a bowling game using candlepins and a small round ball.

can′dle·stick″ *n.* a holder for a candle.

can′dle·wick″ *n.* **1,** the wick of a candle. **2,** a kind of twisted yarn, usu. cotton.

can-′do′ (kan′doo′) *adj.* (*Informal*) resolute; determined.

can′dor (kan′dər) *n.* frankness; sincerity. Also, **can′dour.**

can′dy (kan′dė) *n.* any of a variety of confections containing sugar. —*v.t.* **1,** cook with much sugar or syrup. **2,** make agreeable. —**candy strip′er** (strī′pər) (*Slang*) a teenage volunteer nurses' aide.

cane (kān) *n.* **1,** a walking stick. **2,** the woody stem of certain plants, as sugarcane, bamboo. **3,** pliable woody fibers. —*v.t.* **1,** flog with a cane. **2,** make or weave with cane. —**cane′brake″,** *n.* a thicket of canes.

ca′nine (kā′nīn) *adj.* pert. to dogs. —*n.* **1,** any dog or member of the dog family. **2,** a long, pointed tooth.

can′is·ter (kan′is-tər) *n.* a small can or box; a caddy (def. 1).

can′ker (kang′kər) *n.* an ulcerous sore, esp. in the mouth. —*v.t. & i.* infect or become infected with canker; fig., poison or corrupt slowly. —**can′ker·ous,** *adj.*

can′na (kan′ə) *n.* a tropical flowering plant.

can′na·bis (kan′ə-bis) *n.* hemp. ❑ *hemp*

can′nel coal (kan′əl) a variety of coal that ignites readily and burns brightly.

can′ner (kan′ər) *n.* one who cans food for preservation. —**can′ner·y,** *n.* a place where foods are canned.

can′ni·bal (kan′ə-bəl) *n.* **1,** a person who eats human flesh. **2,** any animal that eats the flesh of its own kind. —**can′ni·bal·ism,** *n.* —**can″ni·bal·is′tic,** *adj.* —**can″ni·bal·is′-ti·cal·ly,** *adv.*

> **cannibal**
> ↔ From Spanish *caríbal*, Carib, from the notion that West Indian natives ate human flesh.

can′ni·bal·ize″ *v.t.* **1,** eat the flesh of. **2,** remove parts of (a machine, etc.) to use in another place.

can′non (kan′ən) *n.* **1,** [*pl. also* **can′non**] a large, mounted gun for hurling projectiles. **2,** (*Brit.*) a carom in billiards. —*v.i.* discharge cannons. —**can″non·eer′** (-ə-nir′) *n.* —**cannon fodder,** young and poorly trained soldiers. —**can′non·ry** (-rė) *n.*

---

tub, cūte, pûll; labəl; oil, owl, go, chip, she, thin, *th*en, sing, ink; *see p. 6*

cannon, canon
☞ Do not confuse the two-*n* form, meaning a piece of artillery, and the one-*n* form, meaning a rule or a church official.

can″non·ade′ (kan″ə-nād′) *n.* concentrated cannon fire. —*v.t. & i.* bombard.

can′not (kan′ot; kə-not′) *v.* can not.

can′ny (kan′ē) *adj.* wary; prudent; sagacious. —**can′ni·ness,** *n.*

ca·noe′ (kə-noo′) *n.* a light, round-bottomed boat pointed at both ends, propelled by paddling. —*v.i.* go in a canoe. —**ca·noe′ist,** *n.*

can′on (kan′ən) *n.* **1,** any rule, law, or body of law, esp. ecclesiastical. **2,** a group of books considered authentic, esp. books of the Bible. **3,** a church officer. —**ca·non′-i·cal** (kə-non′i-kəl) *adj.* —**can″on·ic′i·ty** (-nis′ə-tē) *n.* —**can′on·ize″** (-īz″) *v.t.* designate as a saint. ❏ *cannon*

ca′ñon (kan′yən) (*Sp.*) *n.* canyon.

can′on·ess (kan′ən-is) *n.* a woman who lives in a convent, but has not taken a nun's vows.

can′o·py (kan′ə-pē) *n.* a suspended covering over a bed, entrance, etc.

cant (kant) *n.* **1,** insincere speech or writing, esp. conventional pretense to high ideals or aims. **2,** the special vocabulary or speech of a profession or class, as the whine of beggars; argot. **3,** a tilt, slant, or obliquity. **4,** a salient angle. —*v.i.* **1,** utter cant. **2,** tilt; list. —*v.t.* **1,** make oblique; bevel. **2,** tip; upset. ❏ *argot*

can′t (kånt) *contraction* cannot.

can·ta′bi·le (kan-tä′bə-lē) *n., adj. & adv.* (*It., Music*) (in) a flowing or songlike manner.

can′ta·loupe″ (kan′tə-lōp″) *n.* a variety of muskmelon.

can·tan′ker·ous (kan-tang′kər-əs) *adj.* perverse in disposition; cross; ill-natured. —**can·tan′ker·ous·ness,** *n.*

can·ta′ta (kən-tä′tə) *n.* a choral composition, sacred or secular.

can·teen′ (kan-tēn′) *n.* **1,** a shop, bar, or recreation hall in a military camp, barracks, etc. **2,** a portable container for water.

can′ter (kan′tər) *n.* a gait of a horse; an easy gallop. —*v.i.* ride at a canter.

canter
↔ A shortened form of *Canterbury gallop, trot,* or *pace,* paces used by the pilgrims riding to Canterbury.

can′thus (kan′thəs) *n.* the corner of the eye.

can′ti·lev″er (kan′tə-lev″ər; -lē″vər) *n.* a rigid structure supported at one end. —*v.i.* project like a cantilever. —*v.t.* construct like a cantilever.

can′tle (kan′təl) *n.* the upward curve at the rear of a saddle.

can′to (kan′tō) *n.* a main division of a long poem.

can′ton (kan′tən) *n.* a subdivision of a country; a small district.

can·ton′ment (kan-ton′mənt) *n.* a military camp, esp. a large one.

can′tor (kan′tər) *n.* the singing leader in a cathedral or synagogue.

ca·nuck′ (kə-nûk′) *n. & adj.* (*Slang, offensive*) French Canadian.

can′vas (kan′vəs) *n.* **1,** a heavy cloth of hemp or flax. **2,** something made of canvas, esp. a sail, a tent, or an oil painting. ❏ *hemp*

canvas, canvass
☞ Do not confuse the one-*s* form, meaning heavy cloth, and the two-*s* form, meaning, among other things, a solicitation campaign (though the two words were originally spelled the same, with one *s*).

can′vas·back″ *n.* a No. Amer. wild duck.

can′vass (kan′vəs) *v.t.* **1,** traverse (a district) for purposes of questioning or solicitation. **2,** examine; discuss. —*v.i.* solicit votes, opinions, etc. —*n.* **1,** a campaign of soliciting votes, opinions, etc. **2,** examination; investigation; discussion. ❏ *canvas*

can′yon (kan′yən) *n.* a narrow valley with steep sides; a ravine. Also, **ca′ñon.**

cap (kap) *n.* **1,** a covering for the head. **2,** something resembling a cap, esp. a covering for an opening. **3,** the head or top; the acme. **4,** a noise-making or explosive device. **5,** a capital letter. —*v.t.* [**capped, cap′ping**] **1,** cover with a cap. **2,** complete; bring to a climax; surpass.

ca′pa·ble (kā′pə-bəl) *adj.* **1,** (with *of*) having the ability, capacity, inclination, etc. **2,** competent; efficient. —**ca″pa·bil′i·ty,** *n.*

ca·pa′cious (kə-pā′shəs) *adj.* capable of holding much; roomy. —**ca·pa′cious·ness,** *n.*

ca·pac′i·tance (kə-pas′ə-təns) *n.* the ability of a condenser to store an electrical charge.

ca·pac′i·tate″ (kə-pas′ə-tāt″) *v.t.* make

capable; give legal powers to. —**ca·pac′i·ta″tion**, *n.*

ca·pac′i·tor (kə-pas′ə-tər) *n.* an electrical condenser.

ca·pac′i·ty (kə-pas′ə-tè) *n.* **1,** the power of receiving or containing. **2,** cubic contents; volume. **3,** ability; power to act. **4,** function; role. ❑ *ability*

cap-″a-pie′ (kap″ə-pē′) *adv.* from head to foot.

ca·par′i·son (kə-par′i-sən) *n.* **1,** an ornamental covering for a horse. **2,** equipment; clothing. —*v.t.* equip; bedeck.

cape (kāp) *n.* **1,** a loose outer garment, covering the shoulders. **2,** a piece of land jutting from the coast into a sea or lake. **3,** a small one-story house.

ca′per (kā′pər) *v.i.* leap or skip about; frolic. —*n.* **1,** a leap or skip. **2,** a prank. **3,** a plant whose bud is used for seasoning; the pickled bud.

cap″er·cail′lie (kap″ər-kāl′yė) *n.* a large grouse.

cap′il·lar″y (kap′ə-ler′ė) *adj.* **1,** pert. to a tube of small bore. **2,** pert. to the surface tension of a liquid. **3,** resembling hair. —*n.* a minute tube or vessel. —**cap″il·lar′i·ty,** *n.*

cap′i·tal (kap′ə-təl) *n.* **1,** the city that is the official seat of the government of a country or of a subdivision. **2,** a capital letter. **3,** the head of a pillar. **4,** wealth used in trade; the net worth of a business. **5,** the owners of capital wealth, collectively. —*adj.* **1,** principal; most important. **2,** excellent. **3,** pert. to the seat of government. **4,** (of letters) of the form used at the beginnings of sentences. **5,** (of a crime) punishable by death. —**capital gains,** profit from the sale of assets. —**capital goods,** facilities or goods used to produce other goods. —**capital punishment,** the death penalty. —**capital ship,** a warship of largest size. ❑ *cattle*

---
capital, capitol
☞ Do not confuse *capitol*, a building, with *capital*, a seat of government (and many other things as well).
---

cap′i·tal·ism (-iz-əm) *n.* the economic system in which the ownership and exploitation of wealth are left largely in private hands.

cap′i·tal·ist *n.* **1,** one with wealth invested for profit. **2,** one who favors capitalism. —**cap″i·tal·is′tic,** *adj.* —**cap″·i·tal·is′ti·cal·ly,** *adv.*

cap′i·tal·ize (-īz″) *v.t.* **1,** provide capital for; use as capital on. **2,** use to advantage.

3, begin with a capital letter. —**cap″i·tal·i·za′tion,** *n.*

cap″i·ta′tion (kap″ə-tā′shən) *n.* **1,** a census. **2,** a poll tax.

cap′i·tol (kap′ə-təl) *n.* the chief office building of a government; statehouse. ❑ *capital*

ca·pit′u·late″ (kə-pich′ə-lāt″) *v.i.* surrender on stipulated terms. —**ca·pit″u·la′-tion,** *n.*

ca′po (kä′pō) *n.* (*It.*) the head of a local branch of a crime syndicate.

ca′pon (kā′pon) *n.* a castrated rooster.

cap′o·ral (kap′ə-rəl) *n.* a kind of tobacco.

cap″puc·ci′no (ka″pə-chē′nō) *n.* espresso coffee and steamed milk topped with whipped cream.

---
cappuccino
↔ Italian for Capuchin, from the supposed resemblance in color to a Capuchin's habit.
---

ca·price′ (kə-prēs′) *n.* **1,** a sudden change of mind or humor; a whim. **2,** fickleness. —**ca·pri′cious** (-prē′shəs) *adj.*

ca·pric′ci·o (ka-prēt′chō) *n.* **1,** (*Music*) a free, whimsical composition. **2,** a caprice.

Cap′ri·corn″ (kap′ri-kôrn″) *n.* a constellation, the Goat (see *zodiac*).

cap′ri·ole (kap′rē-ōl) *n.* a leap or caper.

cap·size′ (kap-sīz′) *v.i. & t.* overturn; upset (esp. of a boat).

cap′stan (kap′stən) *n.* a type of windlass, a drum rotating on an upright axle, manually operated.

cap′sule (kap′səl) *n.* **1,** a gelatin case enclosing a dose of medicine. **2,** a small casing or envelope. **3,** the crew compartment of a spacecraft.

cap′tain (kap′tən) *n.* **1,** one in authority; chief; leader. **2,** (*Mil.*) a rank between lieutenant and major. **3,** (*Naval*) a rank between commander and commodore or admiral. **4,** the master of any ship. —*v.t.* command.

cap′tion (kap′shən) *n.* a headline or title. —*v.t.* supply a caption for.

cap′tious (kap′shəs) *adj.* faultfinding; hypercritical. —**cap′tious·ness,** *n.*

cap′ti·vate″ (kap′ti-vāt″) *v.t.* enthrall by charm; fascinate. —**cap″ti·va′tion,** *n.*

cap′tive (kap′tiv) *n.* a prisoner. —*adj.* captured; held prisoner. —**cap·tiv′i·ty** (kap·tiv′ə-tè) *n.*

cap′tor (kap′tər) *n.* one who captures.

cap′ture (kap′chər) *v.t.* take prisoner;

seize; win. —*n.* **1,** act of capturing. **2,** who or what is captured.

cap′u·chin (kap′yû-shin) *n.* **1,** a long-tailed So. Amer. monkey. **2,** a hooded cloak. **3,** (*cap.*) a member of an order of Franciscan monks.

cap″y·ba′ra (kap″i-bä′rə) *n.* a So. Amer. rodent. Also, **cap″i·ba′ra.**

car (kär) *n.* **1,** automobile. **2,** any of a variety of vehicles. **3,** an elevator. **4,** a compartment for passengers or freight. —**car coat,** a medium-length overcoat. —**car hop,** a serving person in a drive-in restaurant. —**car jockey,** (*Slang*) a garage attendant.

ca″ra·ba′o (kär″ə-bä′ō) *n.* a large animal of the ox family; a water buffalo.

car″a·bin·eer′ (kar″ə-bə-nir′) *n.* a rifleman. Also, **car″bi·neer′.**

car′a·cole″ (kar′ə-kōl″) *n.* a half turn. —*v.i.* turn; go zigzag.

car′a·cul (kar′ə-kəl) *n.* the curly fleece of the newborn Astrakhan sheep, named for a lake in Pakistan.

ca·rafe′ (kə-raf′) *n.* a glass water bottle; decanter.

car′a·mel (kar′ə-məl) *n.* **1,** burnt sugar, as used for flavoring. **2,** a kind of candy. —**car′a·mel·ize″** (-īz) *v.t. & i.*

car′a·pace″ (kar′ə-pās″) *n.* the hard covering or shell of an animal.

car′at (kar′ət) *n.* **1,** a unit of weight for precious stones. **2,** a measure of purity of gold. Also, **kar′at.**

> **carat, caret, karat**
> ☛ Two of these words are related. *Carat* is a unit of weight for precious stones; *karat* is a unit for measuring the fineness of gold (it may also be spelled *carat*). A *caret* is a proofreading mark. ↔ *Carat* comes from Arabic *qira*, carob seed, which became a unit of measure.

car′a·van″ (kar′ə-van″) *n.* **1,** a group of travelers banded together for safety, esp. in desert regions of Asia and Africa. **2,** a large covered wagon; van. **3,** (*Brit.*) a house trailer.

car″a·van′sa·ry (kar″ə-van′sə-rē) *n.* an inn for caravan travelers.

car′a·vel″ (kar′ə-vel″) *n.* a small Portuguese sailing vessel.

car′a·way″ (kar′ə-wā″) *n.* a pungent seed used as a flavoring.

car′bide (kär′bīd) *n.* a chemical compound of carbon, esp. **calcium carbide,** used to make acetylene gas.

car′bine (kär′bīn) *n.* a short-barreled rifle. —**car″bi·neer′,** *n.*

car·bo- (kär-bō) *pref.* carbon.

car″bo·hy′drate (kär″bō-hī′drāt) *n.* a class of compounds of carbon, hydrogen, and oxygen, important in foods, as sugar and starch.

car′bo·lat″ed (kär′bə-lā″tid) *adj.* treated with carbolic acid.

car·bol′ic (kär-bol′ik) *adj.* pert. to **carbolic acid,** or phenol, a disinfectant.

car′bon (kär′bən) *n.* **1,** a chemical element, no. 6, symbol C, that occurs pure as diamond and graphite, impurely as coal, and in compounds to form organic substances. **2,** a rod of carbon used as an electrode. **3,** [**carbon paper**] a piece of paper backed with black preparation, for making duplicate copies. **4,** carbon copy. —**car·bon′ic** (-bon′ik) *adj.* —**car′bon·ize,** *v.t.* —**carbon black,** lampblack. —**carbon copy, 1,** a copy made using carbon paper. **2,** a replica; an almost exact copy. —**carbon dioxide** [also, **carbonic acid gas**] a heavy, colorless gas; dry ice. —**carbon 14,** a radioactive isotope of carbon used in dating archaeological and geological samples. —**carbon monoxide,** a colorless, odorless, poisonous gas. —**carbon te″tra·chlor′ide** (tet″rə-klôr′īd) a non-inflammable liquid used in fire extinguishers and as a solvent in cleaning fluids.

car′bon·ate″ (kär′bə-nāt″) *v.t.* charge (water) with carbon dioxide. —**carbonated water,** soda water.

car′bon·date″ *v.t.* determine the age of (an object) by measuring its content of carbon 14.

Car″bo·run′dum (kär″bə-run′dəm) *n.* (*T.N.*) an abrasive made of silicon and carbon.

car′boy (kär′boi) *n.* a large glass bottle protected with wickerwork or wood, for holding acids, etc.

> **carboy**
> ↔ Having nothing to do with either *car* or *boy*, the word comes from the Persian word *qaraba*, large flagon.

car′bun·cle (kär′bung-kəl) *n.* **1,** a garnet or its color. **2,** a circumscribed inflammation exuding pus.

car′bu·re″tor (kär′bə-rā″tər) *n.* a device for vaporizing a fuel to produce a combustible gas. —**car′bu·ret″** (-rāt″) *v.t.* —**car″bu·re′tion,** *n.*

car′cass (kär′kəs) *n.* the dead body of an animal.

car·cin′o·gen (kär-sin′ə-jən) *n.* (*Med.*) a

substance that causes cancer. —**car′cin·o·gen″ic**, *adj.*

car″ci·no′ma (kär′sə-nō′mə) *n.* (*Med.*) a malignant growth in body tissues; cancer.

card (kärd) *n.* **1,** a piece of thick paper or thin pasteboard, usually rectangular and printed, as *calling card, membership card, greeting card.* **2,** one of a set of such pieces printed for playing games: *playing card;* (*pl.*) any game played with such cards. **3,** a program of events; a bill of fare. **4,** (*Informal*) an amusing person. **5,** a brush or other implement for combing fibers. —*v.t.* **1,** comb (fibers). **2,** list; schedule. **3,** ask (a person) for identification or age verification.

car′da·mom (kär′də-məm) *n.* the aromatic seed of an E. Indian herb, used as a spice. Also, **car′da·mon** (-mən).

card′board″ *n.* thin stiff pasteboard.

card-′car″ry·ing *adj.* **1,** belonging to a certain organization or group. **2,** dedicated.

car′di·ac″ (kär′dė-ak″) *adj.* **1,** pert. to the heart. **2,** pert. to the upper part of the stomach.

car′di·gan (kär′də-gən) *n.* a close-fitting wool jacket or sweater, opening in the front.

---
cardigan
↔ Named for the 7th Earl of *Cardigan,* J. T. Brudenell, who liked to wear such clothing. He was well known as a participant in the Crimean War.

---

car′di·nal (kär′də-nəl) *adj.* **1,** of first importance; chief; fundamental. **2,** deep red. —*n.* **1,** a member of the Sacred College of the Rom. Cath. Church, ranking just below the pope. **2,** a No. Amer. finch. **3,** a deep red color. —**cardinal numbers,** one, two, etc., as distinguished from the ordinal numbers (first, second, etc.). —**cardinal points,** the compass directions.

car′di·nal·ate″ (kär′də-nə-lāt″) *n.* **1,** the rank of cardinal. **2,** the body of cardinals.

car′di·o- (kär-dė-ō) *pref.* heart.

car′di·o·gram″ *n.* a record made by a cardiograph.

car′di·o·graph″ *n.* an instrument for recording heart action. —**car″di·o·graph′ic,** *adj.*

car′di·o·pul′mo·nar·y resuscitation (-pûl′mə-ner-ė) CPR.

card′sharp″ *n.* a professional swindler at card games. Also, **card′sharp″er.**

care (kâr) *n.* **1,** attention; heed; solicitude; anxiety. **2,** a cause of worry, etc. **3,**

protection; charge. —*v.i.* **1,** be concerned, etc. **2,** provide (for). **3,** have an inclination (to) or affection (for).

ca·reen′ (kə-rēn′) *v.i.* **1,** sway or lean to one side, as a ship. **2,** (*Informal*) run or move at full speed; career.

---
careen, career
☛ Both words can mean to move at high speed, though *careen* emphasizes the instability of the vehicle. The other senses of the two words are independent.

---

ca·reer′ (kə-rir′) *n.* **1,** a general course of action, esp. progress in a lifework. **2,** a calling pursued as a lifework. **3,** speed. —*v.i.* run or move at full speed. ❏ *careen*

---
career, job, occupation, profession, trade, vocation
Words related to earning one's livelihood. A *job* is any task performed for pay. A *career* is the activity one pursues as one's life's work. An *occupation, trade,* or *vocation* is the activity that serves as the source of one's daily bread. A *profession* is a vocation requiring special knowledge or training.

---

care′free″ *adj.* free of anxiety or worry.

care′ful (kâr′fəl) *adj.* employing care; cautious. —**care′ful·ness,** *n.*

care′less (kâr′ləs) *adj.* **1,** inattentive; negligent; reckless. **2,** unworried. —**care′less·ness,** *n.*

ca·ress′ (kə-res′) *v.t.* touch with the hand to express affection. —*n.* an act of affection.

car′et (kar′ət) *n.* the mark (∧) used to show where to insert additional matter in a written or printed line. ❏ *carat*

care′tak″er *n.* a watchman or janitor.

care′worn″ *n.* showing fatigue, etc., from worry.

car′fare″ *n.* the charge for a ride on a streetcar, bus, etc.

car′go (kär′gō) *n.* the goods or merchandise carried by a ship.

car′hop″ *n.* a waiter or waitress in a drive-in restaurant. —*v.i.* work as a carhop.

car′i·bou″ (kar′ə-boo″) *n.* a No. Amer. reindeer.

car′i·ca·ture (kar′i-kə-chûr) *n.* a picture or verbal description that ludicrously exaggerates the characteristics of the thing depicted. —*v.t.* make a caricature of. —**car′i·ca·tur″ist,** *n.*

car′ies (kâr′ėz) *n.* decay, esp. of teeth. —**car′i·ous** (-ė-əs) *adj.*

car′il·lon″ (kar′ə-lon″) *n.* a set of bells

Carioca · 112 · **carrot**

tuned to play melodies. —**car″il·lon·neur′** (-lə-nēr′) *n.*

Car″i·o′ca (kär″ē-ō′kə) *n.* **1,** a native of Rio de Janeiro. **2,** (*l.c.*) a dance set to So. Amer. music; its music.

car′jack″ *v.t.* steal (a person's) car by force.

cark′ing (kär′king) *adj.* worrisome; anxious.

car′load″ *n.* capacity or contents of a railroad freight car.

car·min′a·tive (kär-min′ə-tiv) *adj.* tending to reduce flatulence.

car′mine (kär′min) *n. & adj.* a purplish-red color.

car′nage (kär′nij) *n.* the slaughter of many; a massacre.

car′nal (kär′nəl) *adj.* pert. to the body; not spiritual. —**car·nal′i·ty** (-nal′ə-tē) *n.*

car·na′tion (kär-nā′shən) *n.* **1,** a fragrant flower. **2,** a shade of pink.

car·nau′ba (kär-now′bə) *n.* the wax palm of Brazil; its wax.

car·nel′ian (kär-nēl′yən) *n.* a reddish, semiprecious stone.

car′ni·val (kär′nə-vəl) *n.* **1,** riotous revelry. **2,** the feasting season immediately preceding Lent. **3,** an amusement park set up temporarily.

carnival
↔ From Medieval Latin *carneleva-men*, removal of meat, as from one's diet during Lent.

car′ni·vore″ (kär′nə-vôr″) *n.* any animal living chiefly on flesh. —**car·niv′o·rous** (-niv′ə-rəs) *adj.*

car′ny (kär′nē) *n.* (*Slang*) a carnival worker.

car′ob (kar′əb) *n.* a Mediterranean tree; its seed pod, used as fodder and as a flavoring.

car′ol (kar′əl) *n.* a song of joy, esp. one sung at Christmas. —*v.i. & t.* sing joyously; celebrate in song.

car′om (kar′əm) *n.* **1,** (*Billiards*) a shot in which the cue ball is made to strike two other balls. **2,** any glancing blow or rebound. —*v.i.* rebound.

car′o·tene″ (kar′ə-tēn″) *n.* a hydrocarbon found in carrots and other plants, a source of vitamin A. Also, **car′o·tin** (-tin).

ca·rot′id (kə-rot′id) *adj.* pert. to an artery leading to the head.

ca·rouse′ (kə-rowz′) *v.i.* drink freely; revel noisily. —**ca·rous′al,** *n.*

car″ou·sel′ (kar′ə-sel′) *n.* **1,** a merry-go-round. **2,** a circular conveyor belt, as for luggage. ❑ *carousal*

carousal, carousel, carouse
☛ Do not confuse *carousal*, revelry, with *carousel*, a merry-go-round. ↔ *Carouse* comes from the German *gar aus trinken*, to drink full out.

carp (kärp) *v.i.* find fault. —*n.* any of several freshwater food fishes.

car′pal (kär′pəl) *adj.* pert. to the wrist. —**carpal tunnel syndrome,** a disorder of the hand and wrist.

car′pel (kär′pəl) *n.* (*Bot.*) a seed vessel in the pistil.

car′pen·ter (kär′pən-tər) *n.* a builder or repairer of wooden structures. —**car′pen·try,** *n.* —**carpenter ant,** an ant that nests in decaying wood.

carpenter
↔ From Latin *carpentum*, a type of carriage. A carpenter was originally a carriage-maker.

car′pet (kär′pit) *n.* a heavy cloth floor covering. —*v.t.* cover with or as with carpet. —**car′pet·ing,** *n.* such fabric.

car′pet·bag″ger (-bag″ər) *n.* one who carries all his or her possessions in one bag, esp. a Northerner in the South after the Civil War.

car pool an arrangement by which persons take turns driving each other (to work, shopping, etc.). —**car′pool″,** *v.i.*

car′port″ *n.* a roofed but otherwise open shelter for an automobile.

car″ra·geen″ (kar′ə-gēn″) *n.* an edible seaweed; Irish moss. —**car″ra·gee′nin** (-gē′nin) *n.* food additive made from carrageen.

car′rel (kar′əl) *n.* a cubicle in a library for study or reading.

car′riage (kar′ij) *n.* **1,** a wheeled vehicle for the conveyance of persons. **2,** any part of a machine or apparatus that carries another part. **3,** manner of carrying one's person; posture. **4,** the act of carrying, conveying, or transporting. —**carriage trade,** wealthy customers.

car′ri·er (kar′ē-ər) *n.* **1,** a company, as a railroad, engaged in public transportation. **2,** a naval vessel designed to carry airplanes. **3,** underwriter; insurer. **4,** one who delivers newspapers. —**carrier pigeon,** a pigeon trained to fly home, used to carry messages.

car′ri·on (kar′ē-ən) *n.* dead and putrefying flesh.

car′rot (kar′ət) *n.* a plant having an edible orange-yellow root.

fat, fāte, fär, fâre, fâll, ȧsk; met, hē, hėr, maybė; pin, pīne; not, nōte, ôr, tool

car″rou·sel′ (kar″ə-sel′) *n.* carousel.

car′ry (kar′ē) *v.t.* **1,** transport from place to place; convey. **2,** bear the weight of; support. **3,** adopt (a bill or motion); obtain election from (an electorate). **4,** be possessed of. **5,** transfer. **6,** keep (goods) in stock; have available for sale. —*v.i.* **1,** reach a distance, as a voice or missile. **2,** be adopted, as by a vote. **3,** (with *on*) display emotion. **4,** (with *on*) continue. —*n.* **1,** distance traversed. **2,** a portage. —**car′ry·ing charge,** interest. —**carry-on,** *adj.* designed to be carried in the passenger compartment of an airliner, not checked.

cart (kärt) *n.* a two-wheeled vehicle. —*v.t.* transport in a cart.

cart′age (kär′tij) *n.* **1,** conveyance in a cart. **2,** a fee therefore.

carte blanche (kärt′ blänsh′) (*Fr.*, blank document) unlimited authority.

car·tel′ (kär-tel′) *n.* a syndicate formed to seek a business monopoly.

cart′er (-ər) *n.* a truckman.

car′ti·lage (kär′tə-lij) *n.* a firm, elastic substance in the body; gristle. —**car″ti·lag′i·nous** (-laj′i-nəs) *adj.*

car·tog′ra·phy (kär-tog′rə-fē) *n.* the art and science of making maps. —**car·tog′ra·pher,** *n.* —**car″to·graph′ic,** *adj.* —**car″to·graph′i·cal·ly,** *adv.*

car′ton (kär′tən) *n.* a cardboard box, usually large.

car·toon′ (kär-toon′) *n.* **1,** a preparatory drawing (for a painting, sculpture, etc.). **2,** a drawing, often in caricature, made as a commentary on current events, or to illustrate a joke or narrative. —**car·toon′ist,** *n.*

car·touche′ (kär-toosh′) *n.* **1,** a carved convex architectural surface. **2,** a box for cartridges.

car′tridge (kär′trij) *n.* **1,** a cylindrical metal or cardboard case holding a charge of powder and shot. **2,** any similar sealed container.

cart′wheel″ *n.* **1,** a lateral handspring. **2,** (*Slang*) a large coin.

carve (kärv) *v.t. & i.* cut with an edged tool, esp. with skill.

car″y·at′id (kar″ē-at′id) *n.* a sculptured figure of a woman used as a supporting column.

car′wash″ *n.* an automatic machine for washing automobiles.

ca·sa′ba (kə-sä′bə) *n.* a variety of muskmelon. Also, **cas·sa′ba.**

Cas″a·no′va (kaz″zə-nō′və) *n.* a libertine; rake.

Casanova
↔ From the 18th-c. Italian adventurer Giovanni *Casanova*, who left memoirs of his innumerable affairs.

cas·cade′ (kas-kād′) *n.* **1,** a waterfall; a series of waterfalls. **2,** something likened to waterfalls. **3,** (*Computers*) to arrange several windows of information as though stacked in overlapping layers.

cas·ca′ra (kas-kar′ə) *n.* **1,** a kind of buckthorn. **2,** a laxative made from its bark.

case (kās) *n.* **1,** that which happens; actual circumstances. **2,** a particular instance among like instances. **3,** a question, problem, or state of things requiring discussion or decision; a cause of legal action. **4,** a statement of facts and reasons relevant to a decision. **5,** an instance of disease; a patient. **6,** (*Gram.*) one of the categories in the inflection of nouns, as *nominative case.* **7,** an outer covering or sheath; a box or receptacle. —*v.t.* **1,** put in a case; enclose. **2,** (*Slang*) survey, as for criminal intent.

case′ hard′en *v.t.* harden the surface of (metal), as by heat.

ca′se·in (kā′sē-in) *n.* a protein precipitated from milk.

case′ment (kās′mənt) *n.* a hinged frame for a glass window.

ca·serne′ (kə-zern′) *n.* a small barracks.

cash (kash) *n.* **1,** currency; specie. **2,** immediate payment. —*v.t.* exchange (a check, etc.) for cash. —**cash cow,** (*Informal*) a profitable business venture. —**cash flow, 1,** after-tax profit available for investment. **2,** relation of cash available for immediate use to funds tied up in investments. —**cash in,** (*Informal*) **1,** terminate a speculation, usually with profit. **2,** die. —**cash register,** a machine that holds and records money received.

cash′ew (kash′oo) *n.* a tropical American tree or its fruit, a small edible nut.

cash·ier′ (ka-shir′) *n.* an employee or officer who receives money, makes change, etc.; a treasurer. —*v.t.* dismiss in disgrace. —**cashier's check,** a check drawn by a bank for payment from its own treasury.

cashier
↔ The two senses of the word have totally different origins. The noun comes from *capsa,* the Latin word for case. The verb comes from French *casser,* to break (ultimately from Latin).

cash′mere (kash′mir) *n.* **1,** a fabric made from the hair of Kashmir goats. **2,** a twilled wool fabric.

cas'ing (kā'sing) *n.* a protective case or covering; a frame.

ca·si'no (kə-sē'nō) *n.* [*pl.* **-nos**] **1,** a building or room for indoor games. **2,** [also, **cas·si'no**] a card game.

cask (kȧsk) *n.* **1,** a barrel for holding liquids. **2,** its capacity.

cas'ket (kȧs'kit) *n.* **1,** a small box, esp. for jewels. **2,** a coffin.

cas·sa'va (kə-sä'və) *n.* a tropical plant cultivated for its starchy roots.

cas'se·role" (kas'ə-rōl") *n.* a baking dish with a cover; food cooked and served in such a dish.

cas·sette' (kə-set') *n.* **1,** a lightproof case for holding photographic or X-ray film. **2,** a compact container of recording tape.

cas'sia (kash'ə) *n.* **1,** a Chinese tree, or cinnamon obtained from it. **2,** a tropical tree or its pulpy pods, which yield senna.

cas'sock (kas'ək) *n.* a long, close-fitting clerical coat.

---

cassock, cossack

↔ Perhaps both derived from Turkish *quzzak*, nomad.

---

cas'so·war"y (kas'ə-wâr"ē) *n.* a large, flightless bird of Australia.

cast (kȧst) *v.t.* [*pret. & p.p.* **cast**] **1,** throw; hurl; fling. **2,** throw off; shed. **3,** plan; contrive; arrange; compute. **4,** select actors for (a play); assign (an actor) to a role. **5,** pour (molten metal, plaster, etc.) into a mold; make by this process. —*v.i.* **1,** throw. **2,** calculate; conjecture. —*n.* **1,** a throw. **2,** what is cast; something molded [also, **cast'ing**]. **3,** the list of actors in a play; the actors in a play collectively. **4,** tendency; expression; tinge. **5,** a computation.

---

cast, caste

☛ Do not confuse *caste*, a social class, and *cast*, with its wide range of meanings related to throwing.

---

cas"ta·net' (kas"tə-net') *n.* a shell of hard wood, used in pairs as clappers to provide a rhythmic beat.

---

castanets

↔ From the Spanish word for little chestnut, which they are thought to resemble.

---

cast'a·way" (kast'ə-wā") *n.* a person marooned, as by shipwreck.

caste (kȧst) *n.* **1,** one of the hereditary social classes among the Hindus. **2,** any group distinguished by its social position. ❑ *cast*

cas'tel·lat"ed (kas'tə-lā"tid) *adj.* built like a castle; having turrets and battlements. —**cas"tel·la'tion,** *n.*

cast'er (kȧs'tər) *n.* **1,** one who or that which casts. **2,** a small wheel attached to the leg of a piece of furniture. **3,** a small cruet or shaker.

---

caster, castor

☛ Though these two spellings can in some cases be used interchangeably, *castor* is the only correct spelling for the beaver or beaver oil.

---

cas'ti·gate" (kas'tə-gāt") *v.t.* **1,** criticize severely. **2,** punish; correct. —**cas"ti·ga'tion,** *n.*

cas'tile (kas'tēl) *n.* soap made with olive oil and soda.

cast-'i"ron *adj.* **1,** made of cast iron, an alloy of iron, carbon, etc. **2,** inflexible. **3,** hardy.

cas'tle (kȧs'əl) *n.* **1,** a fortified residence of feudal times. **2,** a fortress. **3,** an imposing building. **4,** a chess piece, the rook. —*v.t. & i.* (*Chess*) to move (the king) in castling. —**cas'tling,** *n.* (*Chess*) a special move involving both king and castle. —**castle in the air,** a daydream.

cas'tor (kas'tər) *n.* **1,** beaver; a glandular secretion of the beaver used in medicine and perfume. **2,** caster. —**cas'tor oil,** thick oil obtained from a bean (*castor bean*), used as a cathartic or lubricant. ❑ *caster*

cas'trate (kas'trāt) *v.t.* emasculate. —**cas·tra'tion,** *n.*

cas'u·al (kazh'ū-əl) *adj.* **1,** happening by chance; offhand. **2,** careless; negligent. **3,** occasional; irregular. —*n.* **1,** a worker employed only irregularly. **2,** a casualty. —**cas'u·al·ness,** *n.*

cas'u·al·ty (kazh'ū-əl-tē) *n.* **1,** an accident involving bodily injury or death. **2,** a person injured accidentally. **3,** (*Mil.*) a soldier lost through enemy action.

cas'u·ist·ry (kazh'oo-is-trē) *n.* specious reasoning. —**cas'u·ist,** *n.*

ca'sus bel'li (ka'səs bel'ī) (*Lat.*) a cause or justification for war.

cat (kat) *n.* **1,** a domesticated animal of the feline family. **2,** any feline animal, as lion, tiger, etc. **3,** (*Informal*) a spiteful woman. **4,** cat-o'-nine-tails. **5,** a caterpillar tractor. —**cat burglar,** an agile burglar who breaks into a building by climbing through upstairs windows. —**catnap,** a short sleep.

ca·tab'o·lism (kə-tab'ə-liz-əm) *n.* destructive metabolism. —**cat"a·bol'ic** (kat"ə-bol'ik) *adj.*

---

fat, fāte, fär, fâre, fâll, ȧsk; met, hē, hêr, maybė; pin, pīne; not, nōte, ôr, tool

cat·a·clysm (kat′ə-kliz-əm) *n.* a violent, usually destructive, upheaval. —**cat″a·clys′mic,** *adj.* —**cat″a·clys′mi·cal·ly,** *adv.*

cat·a·comb″ (kat′ə-kōm″) *n.* (usually *pl.*) an underground burial vault.

cat·a·falque″ (kat′ə-falk″) *n.* a dais for display of a coffin at a ceremonious public funeral.

cat·a·lep″sy (kat′ə-lep″sė) *n.* a morbid condition of muscular rigidity, loss of sensation, etc. —**cat″a·lep′tic,** *adj.*

cat·a·log″ (kat′ə-lâg″) *n.* a list of separate items; a register; a series of explanatory notes. —*v.t.* **1,** list. **2,** describe in explanatory notes. Also, **cat′a·logue″.**

ca·tal′pa (kə-tal′pə) *n.* a flowering tree of Asia and America.

ca·tal′y·sis (kə-tal′ə-sis) *n.* acceleration of a chemical reaction by a substance which itself remains unaffected. —**cat′a·lyst** (kat′ə-list) *n.* the substance used in catalysis. —**cat′a·lyt′ic,** *adj.* —**catalytic converter,** an antipollution device. —**cat′a·lyze″,** *v.t. & i.*

cat″a·ma·ran′ (kat″ə-mə-ran′) *n.* **1,** a raft. **2,** a boat with connected parallel hulls. **3,** a scold.

cat′a·mount″ (kat′ə-mownt″) *n.* a wild animal of the feline family; the cougar; the lynx.

cat′a·pult″ (kat′ə-pult″) *n.* a contrivance for hurling; a launching device for airplanes. —*v.t.* hurl by recoil. —*v.i.* leap suddenly.

cat′a·ract″ (kat′ə-rakt″) *n.* **1,** a large or spectacular waterfall; any furious downpour of water. **2,** an abnormality of the eye, characterized by opacity of the lens; the opacity itself.

ca·tarrh′ (kə-tär′) *n.* inflammation of the mucous membrane, esp. in the nose and throat. —**ca·tarrh′al,** *adj.*

ca·tas′tro·phe (kə-tas′trə-fè) *n.* a sudden or extreme disaster. —**cat″a·stroph′ic** (kat″ə-strof′ik) *adj.* —**cat″a·stroph′i·cal·ly,** *adv.* —**catastrophe theory,** (*Math.*) a theory for studying discontinuity.

cat″a·to′ni·a (kat″ə-tō′nė-ə) *n.* a muscular rigidity and insensitivity, symptom of certain mental disorders. —**cat″a·ton′ic** (kat″ə-ton′ik) *adj.*

cat′bird seat (*Informal*) a desirable or controlling position.

cat′boat″ *n.* a small sailboat.

cat′call″ *n.* a cry expressing disapproval, as in a theater.

catch (kach) *v.t.* **[caught] 1,** capture after pursuing; seize. **2,** overtake; intercept; reach. **3,** halt; check. **4,** entrap; deceive. **5,** get; receive; incur. **6,** understand; perceive. **7,** (*Informal*) see or hear (a performer or act). —*v.i.* take hold; become entangled. —*n.* **1,** the act of catching. **2,** a device for stopping or checking motion. **3,** what is caught. **4,** (*Informal*) something desirable to catch, as à matrimonial prospect. **5,** a trick; ruse. —**catch′ing,** *adj.* infectious.

catch′pen″ny *adj.* designed to be sold readily, though of little worth.

catch′phrase″ *n.* **1,** slogan. **2,** a phrase that attracts attention.

catch-22 a situation involving two mutually contradictory conditions.

> **catch-22**
> ↔ From the novel *Catch-22* (1961) by Joseph Heller.

catch′up (kech′əp) *n.* ketchup.

catch′word″ *n.* **1,** a slogan. **2,** a word at the top of a dictionary page to show the first or last main entry on it. **3,** a word at the bottom of a page to show the first word of the next page.

catch′y (kach′ė) *adj.* quick to win attention and favor.

cat″e·che′sis (kat″ə-kē′sis) *n.* [*pl.* **-ses** (-sēz)] oral religious instruction. —**cat″e·chet′ic** (-ket′ik) *adj.*

cat′e·chism (kat′ə-kiz-əm) *n.* a series of questions and the answers to them. —**cat′e·chize″** (-kīz″) *v.t.*

cat″e·chu′men (kat″ə-kū′mən) *n.* a student.

cat″e·gor′i·cal (kat″ə-gôr′i-kəl) *adj.* **1,** stated unconditionally; explicit. **2,** pert. to a category.

cat′e·go″ry (kat′ə-gôr″ė) *n.* a comprehensive division or class. —**cat′e·go·rize″,** *v.t.*

cat′e·nar·y (kat′ə-nār-ė) *n.* the curve assumed by a suspended cord.

ca′ter (kā′tər) *v.i.* make provision, as of food, service, etc. —**ca′ter·er,** *n.* a purveyor of food.

cat′er·cor″nered (kat′ər-kôr″nərd) *adj.* diagonal.

cat′er·pil″lar (kat′ə-pil″ər) *n.* the wormlike larva of a moth or butterfly. —*adj.* moving on treads, as some tractors.

> **caterpillar**
> ↔ From Old French *chatepelose,* hairy cat, of Latin origin.

cat′er·waul″ (kat′ər-wâl′) *v.i.* howl or screech like a cat. —*n.* such a sound.

cat′fish″ *n.* any of many smooth-skinned, blunt-headed fishes.

ca·thar′sis (kə-thär′sis) *n.* **1,** (*Med.*) purgation. **2,** any cleansing or release, as of pent-up emotions. —**ca·thar′tic** (-tik) *adj. & n.*

ca·the′dral (kə-thē′drəl) *n.* **1,** the principal church in a diocese. **2,** any imposing church edifice.

> **cathedral**
> ↔ From *cathedral church*, the church housing the *cathedra* (from the Greek), or bishop's throne.

cath′e·ter (kath′ə-tər) *n.* a tube used to drain the bladder. —**cath′e·ter·ize″**, *v.t.*

cath′ode (kath′ōd) *n.* the negative pole of an electric current; a negative electrode. —**cathode ray,** electrons issued from the cathode.

cath′o·lic (kath′ə-lik) *adj.* **1,** universal in extent, character, or application. **2,** (*cap.*) pert. to the Roman Catholic Church, or to any of certain other Christian churches. —*n.* (*cap.*) a member of a Catholic church. —**Ca·thol′i·cism** (kə-thol′ə-siz-əm) *n.* —**cath″o·lic′i·ty** (-lis′ə-tè) *n.* universality.

cat′house″ *n.* (*Slang*) a brothel.

cat′i·on (kat′ė-ən) *n.* a positively charged ion, molecule, or radical.

cat′kin (kat′kin) *n.* a scaly or downy spike of flowers.

cat′nip (kat′nip) *n.* a plant of the mint family, relished by cats.

> **catnip**
> ↔ A compound of *cat* and *nip*, from Medieval Latin *nepta*, catnip.

cat-″o'-nine-′tails (kat″ə-nīn′tālz) *n.* a whip formed of several thongs.

CAT scan (kat) a computerized X-ray photography used for diagnosis: *c(omputerized) a(xial) t(omography).*

cat's-′eye″ *n.* a chatoyant gem.

cat's-′paw″ *n.* a dupe.

cat′sup (kat′səp) *n.* ketchup.

cat′tail″ (kat′tāl″) *n.* a marsh plant with velvety spikes of brown flowers.

cat′tle (kat′əl) *n.* **1,** bovine animals. **2,** livestock generally. —**cattle call,** (*Slang*) an audition open to all.

> **cattle, chattel, capital**
> ↔ All three derive from Latin *capitale*, wealth. *Cattle* and *chattel* come by way of Old French *catel* and *chatel*, respectively. *Capital* probably came directly into English from Latin.

cat′ty (kat′è) *adj.* malicious. Also, **cat′-tish.** —**cat′ti·ness,** *n.*

cat′ty-cor″nered (kat′ė-kôr″nərd) *adj.* catercornered.

CATV *abbr.* a television distribution system that receives signals by antenna and distributes to subscribers by cable: *c(ommunity) a(ntenna) t(ele)v(ision).*

cat′walk″ (kat′wâk″) *n.* a narrow suspended path, as on a ship.

Cau·ca′sian (kâ-kā′zhən) *adj. & n.* "white" in race.

Cau′ca·soid (kâ′kə-zoid) *adj.* of the "white" race; Caucasian.

cau′cus (kâ′kəs) *n.* a meeting of the leaders of a political party. —*v.i.* meet to discuss party policy.

> **caucus**
> ↔ There are several theories about the origin of this word. The more picturesque—but not necessarily correct—is that it came from Algonquian *caucauasu,* counselor.

cau′dal (kâ′dəl) *adj.* **1,** like a tail. **2,** at or near the tail.

caught (kât) *v.* pret. & p.p. of *catch.*

caul (kâl) *n.* a sac sometimes covering the head of a child at birth, once thought to augur good luck.

caul′dron (kâl′drən) *n.* a large kettle. Also, **cal′dron.**

cau′li·flow″er (kâ′lə-flow″ər) *n.* **1,** a plant whose flower forms a compact head. **2,** the edible flower. —**cauliflower ear,** an ear mutilated, as in boxing.

caulk (kâk) *v.t.* make (a boat, boiler, tank, etc.) watertight. —*n.* **1,** [also, **caulk′ing**] a material used to caulk. **2,** a metal spike or spur on the bottom of a shoe. Also, **calk.**

cau·sal′i·ty (kâ-zal′ə-tė) *n.* the relation of cause and effect.

cau·sa′tion (kâ-zā′shən) *n.* **1,** act of causing. **2,** a cause. **3,** causality.

cause (kâz) *n.* **1,** that which produces an effect or a result. **2,** the reason or motive for an action. **3,** a subject of discussion or debate; a case for judicial decision. **4,** a doctrine, view, or side of a question. —*v.t.* make occur or be; bring about. —**caus′al,** *adj.*

cause cé·lè′bre (se-leb′rə) (*Fr.*) any much-discussed issue.

cau″se·rie′ (kō″zə-rė′) *n.* **1,** informal talk; a chat. **2,** a brief essay.

cause′way″ *n.* a raised road; a paved highway.

> **causeway**
> ↔ From Middle English *causey way,* limestone road.

caus′tic (kâs′tik) *adj.* **1,** capable of burning, corroding, or destroying animal tissue. **2,** severely critical or sarcastic. —*n.* a caustic substance. —**caus′ti·cal·ly,** *adv.*
❏ *holocaust*

cau′ter·ize″ (kâ′tər-īz″) *v.t.* burn with a hot iron or a caustic, esp. to prevent morbidity. —**cau″ter·i·za′tion,** *n.* —**cau′ter·y,** *n.* ❏ *holocaust*

cau′tion (kâ′shən) *n.* **1,** prudence in regard to danger; wariness. **2,** a warning of danger. —*v.t.* warn; admonish. —**cau′tion·ar·y** (-ner-ė) *adj.*

cau′tious (-shəs) *adj.* wary. —**cau′tious·ness,** *n.*

cav′al·cade″ (kav′əl-kād″) *n.* a procession of persons on horseback or in carriages.

cav″a·lier′ (kav″ə-lir′) *n.* **1,** a horseman; knight. **2,** a courtly or gallant person; a man who escorts a woman. —*adj.* haughty; disdainful; discourteously offhand.

cav′al·ry (kav′əl-rė) *n.* military troops that serve on horseback. —**mechanized cavalry,** troops serving in motor vehicles. ❏ *Calvary*

cav″a·ti′na (kav″ə-tė′nə) *n.* a simple song; in 18th-c. opera, a slow aria, usually followed by a cabaletta.

cave (kāv) *n.* a hollow place in a hillside, esp. a natural underground cavity of large size. —*v.i.* (with *in*) collapse.

ca′ve·at″ (ka′vė-at″) *n.* **1,** a warning. **2,** (*Law*) notice to suspend action until further hearing. —**caveat emp′tor** (emp′tôr) (*Lat.*) let the buyer beware.

cav′ern (kav′ərn) *n.* a cave.

cav′ern·ous (-əs) *adj.* **1,** containing caves. **2,** hollow; gaping.

cav′i·ar″ (kav′ė-är″) *n.* roe of fish, esp. sturgeon, prepared as a relish.

cav′il (kav′əl) *v.i.* find fault without good reason; carp. —*n.* a captious objection.

cav′i·ty (kav′ə-tė) *n.* any hollow place or space; esp., a hole in a tooth.

ca·vort′ (kə-vôrt′) *v.i.* prance about; caper.

caw (kâ) *n.* the call of a crow, or any similar sound.

cay (kā; kė) *n.* a small island.

cay·enne′ (kī-en′) *n.* a red pepper.

cayenne
↔ From *kyinha,* a So. Amer. Indian (Tupi) word for the pepper.

cay·use′ (kī-ūs′) *n.* an Indian pony.

CD compact disk. —**CD-ROM,** a com-

pact disk for storing digitized data that once written cannot be erased.

cease (sēs) *v.i.* **1,** stop doing an action; desist; come to rest. **2,** come to an end. —*v.t.* discontinue. —**cease′less,** *adj.* without stopping.

cease-′fire″ *n.* a suspension of military action.

ce′dar (sē′dər) *n.* any of several coniferous trees.

cede (sēd) *v.t.* yield and surrender to another; grant.

ce·dil′la (si-dil′ə) *n.* a sign ( ) attached to the bottom of a *c* to indicate that it is to be pronounced as *s.*

ceil′ing (sē′ling) *n.* **1,** the interior overhead surface, as of a room. **2,** the maximum altitude an aircraft can reach, or from which it has clear visibility of the earth; hence, any maximum. —**ceiling price,** a maximum price established by law.

Cel′a·nese″ (sel′ə-nēz″) *n.* (*T.N.*) a rayon fabric or yarn.

cel′e·brate″ (sel′ə-brāt″) *v.t.* **1,** commemorate (a day or event) with festivities, ceremonies, etc. **2,** perform (rites). **3,** make known with honor or praise; extol. —*v.i.* make merry. —**cel′e·brant,** *n.* —**cel′e·brat″ed,** *adj.* famous. —**cel″e·bra′tion,** *n.*

ce·leb′ri·ty (sə-leb′rə-tė) *n.* a famous person.

ce·ler′i·ty (sə-ler′ə-tė) *n.* rapidity of motion; swiftness.

cel′er·y (sel′ə-rė) *n.* a plant whose stalks are used as a food.

ce·les′ta (sə-les′tə) *n.* a keyboard glockenspiel. Also, **ce·leste′** (sə-lest′; cha-).

ce·les′tial (sə-les′chəl) *adj.* **1,** pert. to the sky. **2,** heavenly; divine.

cel′i·ba·cy (sel′ə-bə-sė) *n.* the state of being unmarried. —**cel′i·bate,** *adj. & n.*

celibate, chaste
☛ These words are often confused. *Celibate* means unmarried; *chaste* means abstaining from carnal love.

cell (sel) *n.* **1,** one of many like rooms, as in a prison. **2,** any small room. **3,** a group forming a unit in an organization, political party, etc. **4,** the structural unit of organic life. **5,** a device for producing an electric current chemically. **6,** (*Computers*) a rectangle for storing data in a spreadsheet at the intersection of a column and a row.

cel′lar (sel′ər) *n.* a room or rooms under a building, partly or wholly underground. —**cel′lar·age** (-ij) *n.* cellar space; storage space in a cellar; a charge for such space.

cel″lar·et′ (sel″ə-ret′) *n.* a cabinet for wine bottles.

cel′lo (chel′ō) *n.* [*pl.* **-los**] violoncello. —**cel′list,** *n.*

cel′lo·phane″ (sel′ə-fān″) *n.* a transparent plastic sheeting.

cel′lu·lar (sel′ū-lər) *adj.* pert. to, or consisting of, cells. —**cellular phone,** a portable telephone capable of transmitting to a series of regional transceivers connected to the conventional telephone system.

cell′u·lite″ (sel′yə-līt″) *n.* fatty deposits found in the thighs, etc.

cel′lu·loid″ (sel′yə-loid″) *n.* a nitrocellulose plastic compound.

cel′lu·lose″ (sel′yə-lōs″) *n.* the chief constituent of the cell walls of all plants, used in making plastic fibers, feed, fertilizers, etc.

Cel′si·us (sel′sē-əs) *adj.* centigrade.

Celsius, centigrade
↔ The *Celsius* temperature scale— identical with the *centigrade* scale— was named after the 18th-c. Swedish astronomer Anders *Celsius.*

Celt′ic (kel′tik; sel′-) *adj.* pert. to the Celts, a people including the Irish, Welsh, Gaels, and Bretons. —*n.* a Celtic language. Also, **Kelt′ic.**

cem′ba·lo (chem′bə-lō) *n.* **1,** a dulcimer. **2,** a harpsichord.

ce·ment′ (si-ment′) *n.* **1,** any of various adhesive plastic substances. **2,** pulverized limestone and clay, used in making concrete; Portland cement. —*v.t. & i.* join; bind.

---

cement, concrete
☛ Properly used, *cement* refers to the binding agent used in making *concrete*—not the *concrete* itself. However, the usage of *cement* for *concrete* is very common.

---

cem′e·ter″y (sem′ə-ter″ē) *n.* a burial ground.

ce′no·bite″ (sē′nə-bīt″) *n.* a member of a religious community. —**ce″no·bit′ic** (-bit′ik) *adj.* —**ce′no·bit″ism** (-bit″iz-əm) *n.*

cen′o·taph″ (sen′ə-taf″) *n.* an empty tomb as a memorial to someone buried elsewhere.

Cen″o·zo′ic (sen″ə-zō′ik) *adj.* pert. to a geological era, the age of man.

cen′ser (sen′sər) *n.* a vessel or pan in which incense is burned.

cen′sor (sen′sər) *n.* **1,** one empowered to judge the fitness of manuscripts, communications, etc. for publication. **2,** one who censures; a faultfinder. —*v.t.* judge criti-

cally; examine for fitness; delete as unsuitable. —**cen′sor·ship,** *n.* ❑ *censer*

cen·sor′i·ous (sen-sôr′ē-əs) *adj.* faultfinding; carping. —**cen·sor′i·ous·ness,** *n.*

cen′sure (sen′shər) *v.t.* reprove. —*n.* reproof. ❑ *censer*

---

censer, censor, censure
☛ Do not confuse these words. A *censer* is a container for incense, while a *censor* is a faultfinder. To *censor* is to examine something for fitness and often to delete parts deemed unsuitable. To *censure* is to criticize.

---

cen′sus (sen′səs) *n.* registration and enumeration of the population.

cent (sent) *n.* In U. S. coinage, a copper coin worth .01 dollar.

cen′tare (sen′tār) *n.* centiare.

cen′taur (sen′tôr) *n.* a mythological animal half horse and half man.

cen″te·nar′i·an (sen″tə-ner′ē-ən) *n.* a person aged 100 or more years.

cen′te·nar″y (sen′tə-ner″ē) *adj.* pert. to or consisting of 100. —*n.* a 100-year period. —**cen″te·nar′i·an,** *n.*

cen·ten′ni·al (sen-ten′ē-əl) *n. & adj.* the 100th anniversary.

cen′ter (sen′tər) *n.* **1,** the point equidistant from all extremities; the midpoint. **2,** the area near the middle. **3,** a pivot or axis. **4,** a principal object. **5,** position of a player in various games. **6,** a political party of moderate views. —*v.i. & t.* be or place at the center. Also, **cen′tre.** —**cen′trist,** *n.* a political moderate.

cen′ter·board″ *n.* a board lowered through the keel of a sailboat, to provide stability.

cen′ter·fold″ *n.* the central facing pages of a magazine, usu. with an additional foldout page or pages, showing a photograph, map, etc.

cen′ti- (sen′tə) *pref.* **1,** 100. **2,** 1/100th. —**cen′ti·gram,** *n.* 1/100th gram. —**cen′ti·me″ter,** *n.* 1/100th meter.

cen′ti·are″ (sen′tē-âr″) *n.* a square meter. Also, **cen′tare.**

cen′ti·grade″ (sen′tə-grād″) *adj.* **1,** divided into 100 degrees. **2,** pert. to the thermometer on which boiling and freezing points of water are 100° and 0° respectively. Also, **Cel′si·us.** ❑ *Celsius*

cen′ti·pede″ (sen′tə-pēd″) *n.* any of various insects having many legs.

cen′tral (sen′trəl) *adj.* in the center; conveniently located. —*n.* a telephone operator. —**cen·tral′i·ty,** *n.* —**central processing unit,** main processor of a computer.

---

cen′tral·ize″ (sen′trə-līz″) v.t. & i. **1,** put or come together at or near the center. **2,** bring or come under one control. —**cen″·tral·i·za′tion,** n.

cen′tri·fuge″ (sen′tri-fūj″) n. a machine that whirls a mixture to separate its ingredients.

cen·trif′u·gal (sen-trif′yə-gəl) adj. radiating or flying off or out, from a center.

cen·trip′e·tal (sen-trip′ə-təl) adj. progressing or stressed toward, or held to, the center.

cen·tu′ri·on (sen-tyûr′ē-ən) n. in ancient Rome, a military officer of medium rank, commanding 100 men.

cen′tu·ry (sen′chə-rē) n. **1,** a period of 100 years. **2,** 100 of anything.

ce·phal′ic (sə-fal′ik) adj. pert. to the head or skull.

ce·ram′ics (sə-ram′iks) n. **1,** (pl.) clay or porcelain objects. **2,** (sing.) the art or manufacture of such objects. —**ce·ram′ic,** adj.

ce′re·al (sir′ē-əl) adj. pert. to edible grain or seeds. —n. a food prepared from corn, wheat, etc.

---

cereal
↔ From Latin *Cerealis,* pert. to Ceres, goddess of agriculture.

---

cer″e·bel′lum (ser″ə-bel′əm) n. the rear lobe of the brain.

cer′e·bral (ser′ə-brəl) adj. pert. to the cerebrum or brain. —**cerebral palsy,** a crippling disease, characterized by paralysis or spasms, due to brain injury.

cer′e·brate″ (ser′ə-brāt″) v.i. think.

cer′e·brum (ser′ə-brəm) n. the front portion of the brain.

cere′ment (sir′mənt) n. **1,** the cloth in which a body is wrapped for embalming. **2,** (pl.) graveclothes.

cer″e·mo′ni·al (ser″ə-mō′nē-əl) adj. pert. to or being a ceremony or rite; formal. —n. rite.

cer″e·mo′ni·ous (ser″ə-mō′nē-əs) adj. **1,** elaborately polite. **2,** ceremonial. —**cer″e·mo′ni·ous·ness,** n.

cer′e·mo″ny (ser′ə-mō″nē) n. **1,** a formal occasion; rite. **2,** usages of politeness.

ce·rise′ (sə-rēs′) adj. cherry red.

ce′ri·um (sir′ē-əm) n. a metallic chemical element of the rare-earth group, no. 58, symbol Ce.

cer′tain (sēr′tən) adj. **1,** sure to occur; inevitable. **2,** established as true or sure. **3,** free from doubt; confident. **4,** definite; specified. **5,** definite but unspecified in amount, degree or identity; some. —**cer′·tain·ty,** n.

cer′tain·ly (-lē) adv. with certainty; without doubt. —interj. of course!

cer·tif′i·cate (sēr-tif′i-kət) n. **1,** a document of attestation. **2,** a written testimonial as to status, qualifications, etc. **3,** a banknote, bond, or similar financial document. —v.t. (-kāt″) certify by such a document. —**cer″ti·fi·ca′tion,** n.

cer′ti·fy″ (sēr′tə-fī″) v.t. **1,** attest to the truth or validity of. **2,** declare legally insane. —**cer′ti·fied″ check,** a check guaranteed by a bank.

cer′ti·tude″ (sēr′tə-tūd″) n. certainty; complete freedom from doubt.

ce·ru′le·an (sə-roo′lē-ən) adj. sky blue; light blue.

ce·ru′men (sə-roo′mən) n. earwax.

cer′vix (sēr′viks) n. **1,** the neck. **2,** a constricted necklike part, as of the uterus. —**cer′vi·cal,** adj.

Ce·sar′e·an (si-zãr′ē-ən) adj. pert. to Cesarean operation or section, delivery of a baby by cutting into the womb. Also, **Cae·sar′e·an.**

Cesarean
↔ So called from the unattested theory that Julius Caesar was born by this method.

---

ce′si·um (sē′zē-əm) n. a rare, monovalent metallic element, no. 55, symbol Cs.

ces·sa′tion (se-sā′shən) n. ceasing or discontinuance of action or motion.

ces′sion (sesh′ən) n. the act of ceding; transfer of rights or property; surrender.

cess′pool″ (ses′pool″) n. a pit for the reception of sewage.

ce·ta′cean (sə-tā′shən) adj. pert. to whales.

cha-′cha′ (chä′chä′) n. a Latin Amer. ballroom dance; its music.

chafe (chāf) v.t. **1,** abrade or roughen by friction. **2,** vex; annoy. —**chaf′ing dish,** a warming dish with its own heater.

chaff (chaf) n. **1,** the residue left from threshing grain. **2,** finely chopped straw for cattle food. **3,** gentle banter; raillery. —v.t. & i. tease; banter.

chaf′fer (chaf′ər) v.i. bargain; haggle. —n. haggling.

chaf′finch (chaf′inch) n. a common European finch.

cha·grin′ (shə-grin′) n. mental disquiet or grief; self-dissatisfaction. —v.t. render crestfallen.

chain (chān) n. **1,** a connected series of links of metal or other material. **2,** some-

---

thing that binds, restrains, or fetters. **3,** (*pl.*) bondage. **4,** a series of connected phenomena, events, objects, etc. **5,** a measuring instrument, 66 feet long (*surveyor's chain*) or 100 feet long (*engineer's chain*). —*v.t.* fasten with a chain; unite; restrain. —**chain gang,** a group of prisoners chained together. —**chain letter,** a letter sent from person to person according to a certain plan. —**chain reaction,** a series in which each effect causes the next one. —**chain store,** one of a group of retail stores owned and managed by the same company.

chain-'smoke″ *v.* to smoke (cigarettes, etc.) continuously.

chair (châr) *n.* **1,** a seat with a back, for one person. **2,** a chairperson; the office of chairperson. **3,** a position of authority; a professorship, as, the *chair* of physics. —*v.t.* act as chairperson of.

chair'per″**son** *n.* a presiding officer. Also, **chair'wo**″**man,** *n.fem.,* **chair'man** (-mən), *n.masc.*

chaise (shāz) *n.* **1,** an open horsedrawn vehicle; shay. **2,** [also, **chaise longue** (lâng)] an armchair whose seat extends to form a couch.

chal·ced'o·ny (kal-sed'ə-nē) *n.* a variety of quartz; a semiprecious stone.

chal·co- (chal-kō) *pref.* copper.

cha·let' (shä-lā') *n.* a style of country house, with a wide heavy roof.

chal'ice (chal'is) *n.* a cup-shaped vessel, esp. the cup from which the wine is administered at communion.

chalk (châk) *n.* **1,** a soft whitish variety of limestone. **2,** a crayon or cube of such substance. —*v.t.* **1,** treat with chalk. **2,** (with *up*) write; score; earn. —**chalk'board**″**,** *n.* blackboard. —**chalk'y,** *adj.* like chalk; very pale.

chal'lah (khä'lə) *n.* hallah.

chal'lenge (chal'inj) *n.* **1,** a call to battle or debate. **2,** a demand for explanation or identification. **3,** an objection. —*v.t.* **1,** invite to battle or debate. **2,** demand explanation of, etc. **3,** take exception to; object to.

chal'lis (shal'ē) *n.* a light cotton, wool, or rayon fabric, usu. printed.

cham'ber (chām'bər) *n.* **1,** a room, esp. an inner or secluded room; a bedroom. **2,** a legislative body or its meeting place. **3,** any enclosed space, hollow, or cavity. **4,** (*pl.*) a private office or apartment, esp. of a judge or lawyer. **5,** [also, **chamber pot**] a pot used in bedrooms, esp. as a urinal.

cham'ber·lain (chām'bər-lin) *n.* **1,** one responsible for the management of rooms. **2,** a supervisory official; treasurer; guardian.

cham'ber·maid″ *n.* a female servant who takes care of bedrooms.

cham'bray (sham'brā) *n.* a kind of gingham.

cha·me'le·on (kə-mē'lē-ən) *n.* **1,** a lizard-like reptile that can adapt its coloration to that of its surroundings. **2,** a fickle person.

> **chameleon**
> ↔ From Greek *khamaileōn*, ground lion.

cham'fer (cham'fər) *n.* a bevel on the edge of a board or other solid, usually of 45°. —*v.t.* bevel.

cham'ois (sham'ē) *n.* **1,** a Europ. antelope. **2,** its skin, or similar soft leather.

champ *v.t. & i.* bite into small pieces; munch; chew. —*n.* champion.

cham·pagne' (sham-pān') *n.* a sparkling white wine.

cham'pi·on (cham'pē-ən) *n.* **1,** the winner of a contest. **2,** one who defends a person or a cause. —*adj.* first among all competitors; preeminent. —*v.t.* defend; support. —**cham'pi·on·ship,** *n.* **1,** supremacy. **2,** support; defense.

> **champion**
> ↔ Germanic **kampion*, from Latin *campus*, arena; a champion was a gladiator.

chance (chàns) *n.* **1,** accident; fortuity. **2,** hazard; risk. **3,** a favorable contingency; an opportunity. **4,** an unexpected event. **5,** (often *pl.*) probability; likelihood. —*v.i. & t.* **1,** occur by accident. **2,** hazard. —*adj.* due to chance. —**chan'cy,** *adj.* hazardous; risky.

chan'cel (chàn'səl) *n.* an enclosed space about the altar of a church.

chan'cel·ler·y (chàn'sə-lə-rē) *n.* chancery.

chan'cel·lor (chàn'sə-lər) *n.* **1,** the judge in a court of equity or chancery. **2,** a high or the highest officer of certain universities, courts, etc.

chance-'med″**ley** *n.* **1,** killing by accident or in self-defense. **2,** haphazardness.

chan'cer·y (chàn'sə-rē) *n.* **1,** a court of equity. **2,** an office of public records. **3,** [also, **chan'cel·ler·y**] the court or office of a chancellor. —**in chancery,** in a helpless or embarrassing position.

chan'cre (shang'kər) *n.* a sore, esp. the initial lesion of syphilis.

chan'croid (shang'kroid) *n.* a venereal sore.

chan"de·lier' (shan"də-lir') *n.* a branched cluster of lights hung from a ceiling.

chan'dler (chắn'dlər) *n.* **1,** a dealer in specific supplies, provisions, etc. **2,** a maker of candles. —**chan'dler·y,** *n.*

change (chānj) *v.t.* **1,** make different; alter. **2,** replace by another; substitute. **3,** give and take reciprocally; exchange. —*v.i.* become different; pass from one condition or state to another. —*n.* **1,** alteration; modification; transformation. **2,** substitution; exchange. **3,** variety; novelty. **4,** money of small denomination; coins. —**change of life,** menopause.

change'a·ble (chān'jə-bəl) *adj.* variable; fickle; inconstant.

change'ful (-fəl) *adj.* variable; inconstant.

change'ling *n.* a child secretly substituted for another.

change-'up' *n.* in baseball, a slow pitch preceded by a fast windup.

chan'nel (chan'əl) *n.* **1,** the bed of a waterway; a navigable waterway. **2,** a means of access; a route. **3,** a furrow or groove. **4,** a frequency band, as in radio. **5,** (*pl.*) the prescribed routing of an application or order. —*v.t.* **1,** direct into a particular course. **2,** cut or form a channel in.

chan'son (shän'sən) *n.* (*Fr.*) a song.

chant (chȧnt) *n.* **1,** a song in which an indefinite number of syllables are intoned on each note, as in canticle-singing. **2,** any monotonous song or singing. —*v.t. & i.* sing; intone in a monotonous manner.

chan"te·relle' (shän"-tə-rel') *n.* **1,** a type of mushroom. **2,** the top string of the violin, lute, etc.

chan·teur' (shan-tûr') *n.masc.,* **chanteuse'** (shan-toos') *n.fem.* a singer, esp. of popular music.

chant'ey (chan'tē) *n.* a tune sung, esp. by sailors, to set the rhythm of united physical labor.

chan'ti·cleer" (chan'tə-klir") *n.* a cock; a male fowl.

> **chanticleer**
> ↔ A name derived from the Old French phrase *chante cler*, to sing clear. The name was used in many medieval fables.

chan'try (chȧn'trē) *n.* a chapel attached to a church, used for minor services.

Chan'u·kah (khän'ə-kə) *n.* Hanukkah.

cha'os (kā'os) *n.* the absence of form or order; utter confusion. —**cha·ot'ic** (-ot'ik) *adj.* —**cha·ot'i·cal·ly,** *adv.*

chap *v.t. & i.* [**chapped, chap'ping**] (of the skin) split in clefts; crack and roughen. —*n.* fellow; a familiar term for a man or boy.

chap"ar·ral' (chap"ə-ral') *n.* a dense thicket.

chap'book" *n.* a small book, esp. of poetry.

cha·peau' (sha-pō') *n.* [*pl.* **-peaux'** (-pō')] (*Fr.*) a hat.

chap'el (chap'əl) *n.* **1,** a small church; a subordinate place of worship in a church. **2,** a room for religious services in a school; the services held there.

> **chapel**
> ↔ From Latin *cappella,* diminutive of *cappa,* cloak. The name was first applied to the shrine built to hold the cloak of St. Martin of Tours.

chap'er·on" (shap'ə-rōn") *n.* an older person, usu. a married woman, accompanying younger unmarried persons, esp. women. —*v.t. & i.* attend as a chaperon. Also, **chap'er·one".**

chap'fal"len (chap'fâl"ən) *adj.* dejected.

chap'lain (chap'lin) *n.* a clergyman serving a special group, as a legislature, army, navy, etc.

chap'let (chap'lit) *n.* **1,** a wreath, as of flowers, worn on the head. **2,** a string of beads.

chaps *n.pl.* seatless riding breeches worn by Amer. cowboys.

chap'ter (chap'tər) *n.* **1,** a main division of a book or treatise. **2,** a council; assemblage. **3,** a branch of an association, fraternity, etc.

char (chär) *v.t.* [**charred, char'ring**] burn to charcoal; scorch. —*v.i.* **1,** become charcoal. **2,** do menial household tasks.

> **char, charwoman**
> ☞ *Char* in its sense of burning derives from *charcoal. Char* in the sense of do tasks is from Old English *cerr,* turn, related to English *chore.*

char'a·banc" (shär'ə-bank") *n.* a bus, esp. one for sightseeing or excursions.

> **charabanc**
> ↔ From the French phrase *char-à-bancs,* car with benches.

char'ac·ter (kar'ik-tər) *n.* **1,** the aggregate of properties and qualities that distinguishes one person or thing from another. **2,** a trait. **3,** good qualities. **4,** a person, esp. (*Informal*) an odd one; an actor or role in a play. **5,** a mark made in writing, printing, etc.

char″ac·ter·is′tic (-is′tik) *n.* a distinguishing quality or trait. —*adj.* typical. —**char″ac·ter·is′ti·cal·ly,** *adv.*

char′ac·ter·ize″ (-īz″) *v.t.* describe in terms of characteristics. —**char″ac·ter·iz·a′tion,** *n.*

cha·rade′ (shə-rād′) *n.* (often *pl.*) a game of pantomime acting to convey words and their syllables.

char′broil″ (chär′-) *v.t.* (*Informal*) to broil over charcoal embers.

char′coal″ (chär′kōl″) *n.* the residue of wood or other organic material reduced to carbon by imperfect combustion.

chard (chärd) *n.* a spinachlike vegetable: *Swiss chard.*

charge (chärj) *v.t.* **1,** put a load on or in; fill or occupy with something to be carried or retained. **2,** command; enjoin. **3,** accuse; blame. **4,** ask as a price; hold liable for payment. **5,** defer payment for. **6,** attack by rushing violently against. —*v.i.* make an onset. —*n.* **1,** a load; a burden; a filling. **2,** a command or instruction. **3,** a duty, responsibility, or encumbrance. **4,** an accusation. **5,** a price, cost, or fee. **6,** a violent onslaught. —**charge account,** an established line of credit with a retail store, bank, etc. —**charge card,** credit card.

char·gé′ d'af·faires′ (shär-zhā′ da-fār′) [*pl.* **char·gés′** (shär-zhā′)] **1,** a diplomatic officer who is temporarily in charge of an embassy or legation. **2,** a diplomatic envoy to a state to which a higher level diplomat is not assigned.

charg′er (chär′jər) *n.* **1,** a warhorse. **2,** a large platter or tray.

char′i·ot (char′ē-ət) *n.* **1,** an ancient two-wheeled horse-drawn vehicle. **2,** a carriage. —**char′i·ot·eer′** (-tir′) *n.* the driver of a chariot.

cha·ris′ma (kə-riz′mə) *n.* a power for eliciting enthusiastic popular support attributed to a person or a position.

char″is·mat′ic (kär″is-mat′ik) *adj.* **1,** having charisma. **2,** pert. to certain Christian denominations that seek an ecstatic religious experience. —*n.* the follower of such a religious denomination.

char′i·ty (char′ə-tē) *n.* **1,** the quality of sympathetic understanding; philanthropy; tolerance. **2,** alms. **3,** an organization devoted to the relief of the unfortunate. —**char′i·ta·ble,** *adj.*

char′la·tan (shär′lə-tən) *n.* a pretender; quack; mountebank.

charlatan
↔ From Italian *cialatore,* chatterer, + *cerretano,* native of Cerreto, a town in Italy known for its quacks.

char′ley horse (chär′lē) (*Informal*) a cramp in a muscle of arm or leg.

Charles′ton (chärlz′tən) *n.* a dance popular in the 1920s. —*v.i.* to dance the Charleston.

Char′lie (chär′lē) *n.* (*Communications*) the letter *c.*

char′lotte (shär′lət) *n.* a molded dessert. —**charlotte russe** (roos) Bavarian cream in a mold with ladyfingers.

charm (chärm) *n.* **1,** personal attractiveness; irresistible power to please or attract. **2,** a symbol of occult power, as an amulet. **3,** (*Physics*) a quantum number applied to different types of quarks. —*v.t. & i.* fascinate; enchant; captivate. —**charm′ing,** *adj.* highly attractive.

char′nel (chär′nəl) *n.* a place where dead bodies are deposited. —**charnel house,** a house or other building used as a charnel.

chart (chärt) *n.* **1,** a map; a drawn or written guide. **2,** a systematic record of development or change. —*v.t.* make a map of; record.

char′ter (chär′tər) *n.* **1,** a written instrument giving a right or privilege. **2,** a fundamental statement of purpose and scope; a constitution. —*v.t.* **1,** authorize; empower. **2,** lease or hire.

char·treuse′ (shär-trūz′) *n.* **1,** a liqueur. **2,** a greenish yellow color.

Chartreuse
↔ Named for the Carthusian monastery near Grenoble, France, where the liqueur is made.

char′wom″an *n.* a domestic servant hired by the day. ❑ *char*

char′y (chär′ē) *adj.* very cautious; suspicious. —**char′i·ness,** *n.*

chase (chās) *v.t.* **1,** [also, **give chase (to)**] follow after in order to overtake, capture, or kill; pursue; hunt. **2,** drive away. **3,** decorate (metal) by tooling. —*v.i.* move briskly. —*n.* **1,** the act of chasing. **2,** what is chased; quarry. **3,** the sport of hunting. **4,** a frame in which type is locked for printing.

chas′er (chā′sər) *n.* **1,** a milder drink taken after liquor. **2,** (*Informal*) a roué.

chasm (kaz′əm) *n.* **1,** a deep gulf or fissure. **2,** a wide divergency.

chas′sis (shas′ē) *n.* [*pl.* **-sis** (-ēz)] **1,** a supporting framework. **2,** the frame, wheels, and engine of an automobile, without the body; a radio receiving apparatus without a cabinet.

chaste (chāst) *adj.* **1,** abstaining from carnal love. **2,** pure; not ornate or fanciful in design. ❏ *celibate, incest*

chas·ten (chā′sən) *v.t.* **1,** punish; reprimand. **2,** make chaste.

chas·tise′ (chas-tīz′) *v.t.* punish, esp. corporally. —**chas·tise′ment,** *n.*

chas′ti·ty (chas′tə-tē) *n.* quality or state of being chaste.

chas′u·ble (chaz′yə-bəl) *n.* an ecclesiastical outer vestment.

chat *v.i.* [**chat′ted, -ting**] converse desultorily; make talk. —**chat′ty,** *adj.*

cha·teau′ (sha-tō′) *n.* [*pl.* **-teaux′** (-tōz′)] a French castle; an elaborate country house.

chat′e·laine″ (shat′lān″) *n.* **1,** the mistress of a castle, household, etc. **2,** a chain for holding trinkets worn around the waist.

cha·toy′ant (shə-toi′ənt) *adj.* changeable in color or luster.

> **chatoyant**
> ↔ From French *chatoyer*, to change luster like the eye of a cat.

chat′tel (chat′əl) *n.* a movable piece of personal property. ❏ *cattle*

chat′ter (chat′ər) *v.i.* **1,** make rapid clacking sounds having little or no meaning. **2,** talk rapidly but aimlessly. **3,** vibrate noisily. —*n.* **1,** chattering sounds as made by monkeys, birds, etc. **2,** idle or senseless talk; gossip.

chat′ter·box″ *n.* one who talks incessantly.

chauf′feur (shō′fər) *n.* one hired to drive an automobile.

> **chauffeur**
> ↔ French for stoker of a steam engine, from Old French *chauffer*, to heat.

chau·tau′qua (shə-tâ′kwə) *n.* a community assembly for educational or recreational purposes.

chau′vin·ism (shō′və-niz-əm) *n.* **1,** excessive and blindly prejudiced patriotism. **2,** excessive devotion to a cause. **3,** belief that one's sex should or does have predominance over the other sex. —**chau′vin·ist,** *n.* —**chau″vin·is′tic,** *adj.* —**chau″vin·is′ti·cal·ly,** *adv.*

> **chauvinism**
> ↔ From Nicolas *Chauvin*, a French soldier in Napoleon's army noted for his patriotic zeal.

cheap (chēp) *adj.* **1,** available at a low price. **2,** of little value. **3,** miserly; mean; petty. **4,** unfair, dishonorable. —**cheap′en,** *v.t. & i.* lessen in price, value, or reputation. —**cheap′ness,** *n.* —**cheap shot,** (*Slang*) an unfair comment.

> **cheap, inexpensive**
> ☛ Both words mean costing little, but *cheap* has a connotation of poor quality, a sense not shared by *inexpensive*.

cheap′skate″ *n.* a stingy person.

cheat (chēt) *v.t.* **1,** mislead; defraud; swindle. **2,** escape from; elude. —*v.i.* **1,** practice deception or trickery. **2,** be unfaithful. —*n.* **1,** a swindler, esp. a card sharper. **2,** an impostor. **3,** an act of fraud.

check (chek) *n.* **1,** an obstruction, hindrance, or stop; a device for stopping. **2,** a stoppage or rebuff. **3,** a test of operation; verification of accounts; investigation or examination (often **checkup**). **4,** a mark (√) indicating disposition or approval. **5,** a written order to a bank to pay money. **6,** a piece of paper used as a receipt, token, etc. **7,** one of a pattern of squares alternating in color. **8,** in chess, jeopardy of the king. **9,** a counter; a poker chip. —*v.t.* **1,** impede; stop. **2,** test; verify; investigate. **3,** make a check mark (√) upon. **4,** put or accept in temporary custody. **5,** send (baggage) under privilege of a passenger ticket. **6,** in chess, threaten to capture (the king). —*v.i.* **1,** make a test or investigation. **2,** prove to be right or accurate. **3,** pause; stop. **4,** in poker, stay in without betting. —*interj.* (*Informal*) correct! All right! —**check in,** register (at a hotel, etc.). —**check out, 1,** itemize. **2,** depart. **3,** (*Slang*) die. —**in check,** in chess, of the king, in jeopardy.

check′book″ *n.* a book containing blank checks.

check′er (chek′ər) *n.* **1,** one who checks; a record-keeper. **2,** one of the pieces for checkers. **3,** (*pl.*, *construed as sing.*) a game for two played on a board of 64 checkered squares (*checkerboard*). —**check′ered** (-ərd) *adj.* marked with a pattern of squares of alternating color.

check′mate″ *n.* **1,** (*Chess*) a position in which one's king is attacked and cannot escape capture. **2,** defeat; frustration. —*v.t.* put in checkmate; overthrow.

> **checkmate**
> ↔ From the Arabic *shah mat*, "the king is dead."

check′off″ (chek′âf″) *n.* the withholding of union dues from a payroll on behalf of the union.

Ched'dar (ched'ər) *n.* a smooth variety of cheese.

cheek (chēk) *n.* **1,** the side of the face below the eye-line. **2,** impudence; overweening self-assurance. **—cheek'y,** *adj.* impudent.

cheep (chēp) *n.* the high cry of a young bird; chirp. **—***v.t.* & *i.* chirp.

cheer (chir) *n.* **1,** state of mind. **2,** gaiety; animation. **3,** a shout of joy; applause. **—***v.t.* & *i.* **1,** encourage. **2,** applaud with shouts. **—cheers,** *interj.* a toast.

cheer'ful (-fəl) *adj.* full of cheer; blithe. **—cheer'ful·ness,** *n.*

cheer'i·o″ (chir'ē-ō″) *n.* & *interj.* hello or good-bye.

cheer'y (-ē) *adj.* in good spirits; gay. **—cheer'i·ness,** *n.*

cheese (chēz) *n.* a food made of aged milk solids. **—cheese off, (***Slang*) annoy; anger.

cheese'burg″er (chēz'bēr″gər) *n.* a hamburger grilled with cheese.

cheese'cake″ *n.* **1,** a kind of pie. **2,** (*Slang*) suggestive pictures of women.

cheese'cloth″ *n.* a coarse cotton cloth of open texture.

chees'y (chē'zē) *adj.* (*Informal*) unsubstantial; shoddy.

chee'tah (chē'tə) *n.* a leopardlike animal of Asia and Africa.

chef (shef) *n.* a head cook.

chef-d'oeu'vre (she-dövr') *n.* [*pl.* **chefs-** (she-)] a masterpiece.

chem'i·cal (kem'i-kəl) *adj.* pert. to chemistry. **—***n.* a substance produced by or used in a chemical process. **—chemical warfare,** use of chemical or bacterial agents against an enemy.

che·min' de fer' (shə-man' də fer') a gambling game, a variety of baccarat.

che·mise' (shə-mēz') *n.* a loose-fitting undergarment.

chem'is·try (kem'is-trē) *n.* the general science of the composition, properties, and phenomena of elementary substances. **—chem'ist,** *n.*

chem·o- (kē-mō; kem-ō) *pref.* chemical; chemically.

chem'ur·gy (kem'ər-jē) *n.* a branch of applied chemistry dealing with industrial uses of agricultural products.

che·nille' (shə-nēl') *n.* **1,** a fluffy yarn of cotton, silk, etc. **2,** a fabric woven with such yarn.

cheong'sam' (chong'säm') *n.* an Asian knee-length dress.

cheque (chek) *n.* (*Brit.*) check (def. 5).

cher'ish *v.t.* hold dear; treat with affection; nurse.

che·root' (shə-root') *n.* a cigar with square, open ends.

cher'ry (cher'ē) *n.* **1,** a tree bearing small, red, pitted fruit; its wood; its fruit. **2,** a bright red color.

cherry'stone″ *n.* **1,** the pit of a cherry. **2,** a small quahog clam.

cher'ub (cher'əb) *n.* **1,** [*pl.* **cher'u·bim**] an angel represented as a child with wings. **2,** a child with a round, plump face; a beautiful or innocent person. **—che·ru'bic** (che-roo'bik) *adj.* **—che·ru'bi·cal·ly,** *adv.*

cher'vil (chûr'vil) *n.* a plant used for seasoning.

chess (ches) *n.* a game for two played on a board of 64 checkered squares (*chessboard*).

chest *n.* **1,** a box, esp. a strong one for holding valuables. **2,** the human body between the neck and belly; the thorax. **3,** [also, **chest of drawers**] a bureau for clothes, etc. **4,** a public fund, as for charity.

ches'ter·field″ (ches'tər-fēld″) *n.* **1,** a single-breasted overcoat. **2,** a kind of sofa.

---

chesterfield
↔ The overcoat is named for the 19th-c. British statesman the 4th Earl of *Chesterfield*.

---

chest'nut (ches'nut) *n.* **1,** a tree of the beech family; its wood; its edible nut. **2,** a reddish brown color. **3,** (*Slang*) a hackneyed joke; anything repeated to the point of staleness. **—***adj.* reddish brown.

chest'y (ches'tē) *adj.* (*Informal*) **1,** conceited. **2,** having a well-developed bosom.

che·val' glass (shə-val') a long mirror pivoted in a frame.

chev″a·lier' (shev″ə-lir') *n.* **1,** knight; a gallant man. **2,** a rank of membership in an honorable order.

chev'i·ot (shev'ē-ət) *n.* a worsted fabric of twill weave.

chev'ron (shev'rən) *n.* a striped badge denoting military rank.

chew (choo) *v.t.* **1,** bite and grind with the teeth. **2,** meditate on; discuss. **—***n.* a portion chewed, as of tobacco. **—chew'y,** *adj.* **—chew the rag, (***Slang*) converse at length.

chi (kī) *n.* the 22nd letter of the Greek alphabet (X, x).

chi·a″ro·scu'ro (kē-är″ə-skûr'ō) *n.* **1,** the distribution of light and shade in a picture. **2,** a drawing in black and white. **3,** variety in a literary work.

chic (shēk) *adj.* stylish; fashionable.

chi·can′er·y (shi-kā′nə-rē) *n.* adroit but dishonest maneuvering or scheming.

Chi·ca′na (chė-kä′nä) *n.fem.*, **Chi·ca′no** (-nō) *n.masc.* an American of Mexican descent.

chi′chi″ (shē′shē″) *adj.* **1,** ornamental; showy. **2,** affected; pretentious. **3,** chic. —*n.* something chichi.

chick (chik) *n.* **1,** a young chicken or other bird. **2,** (*Slang, offensive*) a young girl.

chick′a·dee″ (chik′ə-dē″) *n.* a small No. Amer. bird of the titmouse family.

chick′en (chik′ən) *n.* **1,** a young domestic fowl. **2,** (*Slang, offensive*) a girl; a young woman. **3,** (*Slang*) coward. —*adj.* (*Slang*) cowardly; timid. —**chicken feed,** (*Slang*) a small sum of money. —**chick″-en·heart′ed,** *adj.* timid. —**chicken pox,** a mild, contagious, eruptive disease. —**chicken wire,** a lightweight wire fencing.

chick′pea″ *n.* a plant of the pea family; its hard, edible seed.

chic′le (chik′əl) *n.* a gum from certain trees, the basis of chewing gum.

chic′o·ry (chik′ə-rē) *n.* **1,** a plant whose root is used as a substitute or adulterant for coffee. **2,** a salad herb.

chide (chīd) *v.t. & i.* reprove mildly.

chief (chēf) *n.* **1,** the headman; commander; leader. **2,** the most important part or aspect. —*adj.* highest in rank or importance. —**Chief Executive,** the president.

chief′tain (-tən) *n.* the leader of a tribe, clan, or band.

chif·fon′ (shi-fon′) *n.* a thin, gauzelike fabric.

chif″fo·nier′ (shif″ə-nir′) *n.* a chest of drawers; a bureau.

chig′ger (chig′ər) *n.* **1,** the larva of certain mites whose bite causes severe itching. **2,** a flea: the *chigoe.*

chi′gnon (shēn′yon) *n.* a coil of hair, worn at the back of the neck by women.

chi·hua′hua (chė-wä′wä) *n.* a breed of tiny dog.

chil′blain″ (chil′blān″) *n.* a sore, esp. on the foot, resulting from exposure to cold.

child (chīld) *n.* [*pl.* **chil′dren** (chil′drən)] a young human offspring; an infant, boy or girl. —**child abuse,** mistreatment of a child by an adult, esp. a parent or guardian. —**with child,** pregnant. —**child′like″,**

adj. —**child′s play,** a very easy task. ❑ *childish*

child′birth″ *n.* the giving birth to a child; parturition.

child′hood″ *n.* the state or time of being a child.

child′ish *adj.* **1,** immature. **2,** silly. —**child′ish·ness,** *n.*

> **childish, childlike**
> ☛ *Childlike* means like a child; *childish* means the same thing, but the implication is derogatory, suggesting childlike behavior that is inappropriate.

child′proof″ *adj.* designed to be safe from tampering by children. —*v.t.* make a space childproof.

chil′dren (chil′drən) *n.* **1,** *pl.* of *child.* **2,** all the members of any group having a common experience, nationality, origin, etc.

chil′i (chil′ē) *n.* a hot seasoning made of dried pods of red pepper. —**chili con car′ne** (kon kär′nė) a Mexican dish of meat and chili, usu. with beans.

chill (chil) *n.* **1,** an acute sensation of cold, often with shivering. **2,** a degree of cold. —*v.t.* **1,** make cold. **2,** dispirit; discourage. —*v.i.* be fearful. —**chill′er,** *n.* a frightening experience, story, etc. —**chill′y,** *adj.* —**chill factor,** windchill.

chime (chīm) *n.* **1,** a bell or tube producing a bell-like tone; a set of such bells. **2,** harmonious sound or relation; concord. —*v.i.* **1,** produce harmonious sounds. **2,** harmonize; agree. **3,** (with *in*) add one's word; agree. —*v.t.* give forth (a sound).

chi·me′ra (ki-mir′ə) *n.* **1,** a mythical monster, part lion, goat, and serpent. **2,** a fantastic or vain hope. —**chi·mer′i·cal** (ki-mer′i-kəl) *adj.*

chim′ney (chim′nė) *n.* **1,** a tube, duct, or flue to carry off smoke. **2,** a volcanic vent. —**chimney pot,** a tubular cover put on top of a chimney to increase the draft. —**chimney sweep,** a person who cleans out chimneys.

> **chimney**
> ↔ From Greek *kaminos*, furnace; the word *chimney* for a long time meant fireplace.

chim″pan·zee′ (chim″pan-zē′) *n.* a large anthropoid ape of W. Africa. Also, *Informal,* **chimp.**

chin *n.* the point of the jaw. —*v.i.* [**chinned, chin′ning**] **1,** pull one's body upward toward an elevated horizontal bar, for exercise. **2,** (*Slang*) chat; talk.

chi′na (chī′nə) *n.* a porcelain ware; dishes; crockery. —**China syndrome,** the hypothetical results of a nuclear reactor meltdown.

chinch *n.* **1,** a bedbug. **2,** an insect that attacks grain plants.

chin·chil′la (chin-chil′ə) *n.* a small fur-bearing rodent of South America; its fur.

chine (chīn) *n.* **1,** the backbone of an animal. **2,** a cut of meat across the backbone. **3,** a ridge.

Chi·nese′ (chī-nēz′) *adj.* pert. to China. —*n.* [*pl.* **Chi·nese′**] **1,** the language of China. **2,** one descended from the people of China.

chink *n.* a small rift, fissure, or cleft. —*v.i.* **1,** crack. **2,** make a sharp metallic sound. —*v.t.* **1,** split. **2,** fill up cracks; caulk.

chi′no (chē′nō) *n.* **1,** a cotton fabric. **2,** (often *pl.*) an article of clothing made from this fabric.

Chi·nook′ (chi-nûk′) *n.* **1,** an Amer. Indian tribe. **2,** (*l.c.*) a warm, dry wind of the Rocky Mountains.

chintz (chints) *n.* a printed cotton fabric, usually glazed. —**chint′zy,** *adj.* (*Informal*) cheap.

chip *n.* **1,** a small fragment, as of wood or stone. **2,** a small disk used as a counter or token; poker chip. **3,** a small slice of semiconducting material imprinted with an electronic circuit for use in a computer, etc. —*v.t.* [**chipped, chip′ping**] cut or knock off fragments from. —*v.i.* **1,** break off in small pieces. **2,** (often with *in*) contribute a chip or money. —**a chip on one's shoulder,** a belligerent attitude. —**in the chips,** well off; wealthy.

chip′board″ *n.* a coarse paperboard.

chip′munk *n.* a small squirrel-like rodent.

chip′per (chip′ər) *v.i.* chirp; twitter. —*adj.* (*Informal*) lively; gay.

chi·ro- (kī-rō) *pref.* hand.

chi·rog′ra·phy (kī-rog′rə-fē) *n.* handwriting.

chi′ro·man″cy (kī′rə-man″sē) *n.* palmistry.

chi·rop′o·dy (kī-rop′ə-dē) *n.* the treatment of foot ailments. —**chi·rop′o·dist,** *n.*

chi″ro·prac′tic (kī″rō-prak′tik) *n.* the treatment of ailments by manipulating the bones. —**chi′ro·prac″tor,** *n.*

chirp (chẽrp) *n.* a short, shrill sound made by birds or insects. —*v.i.* utter with a chirp.

chir′rup (chir′əp) *n. & v.* chirp.

chis′el (chiz′əl) *n.* a bladed tool for cutting wood or metal. —*v.t. & i.* **1,** cut or trim with a chisel. **2,** (*Slang*) seek or ob-

tain an undue advantage; cheat. —**chis′-el·er,** *n.*

chit *n.* **1,** a pert young person (esp. a girl) or animal. **2,** a memorandum of indebtedness for a minor purchase.

---

chit
↔ The two senses have two quite different origins. In the sense of young person, from an Old English word for the young of an animal. In the sense of voucher, the word comes from Hindi *chitthi,* note.

---

chit′chat″ *n.* idle talk.

chit′ter·ling (chit′ər-ling) *n.* (usu. *pl.*) part of the small intestine, esp. of swine, cooked as food.

chiv′al·ry (shiv′əl-rē) *n.* **1,** the institution of medieval knighthood. **2,** gallantry; honor. —**chiv′al·ric, chiv′al·rous,** *adj.*

---

chivalry
↔ From Old French *chivalerie,* horsemanship; the word is related to *cavalry.*

---

chive (chīv) *n.* (usually *pl.*) an onionlike herb used for seasoning.

chlo′ral (klôr′əl) *n.* a hypnotic preparation from chlorine. —**chloral hydrate,** a solution of this substance.

chlor′dane (klôr′dān) *n.* an insecticide.

chlo′ride (klôr′īd) *n.* a compound of chlorine and one other element.

chlor′i·nate″ (klôr′ə-nāt″) *v.t.* combine or treat with chlorine. —**chlor″in·a′tion,** *n.*

chlo′rine (klôr′ēn) *n.* a gaseous chemical element, no. 17, symbol Cl.

---

chlorine
↔ From Greek *khlōros,* green-yellow, because of its color; the name was coined by 19th-c. British chemist Sir Humphry Davy.

---

chlo′ro·form″ (klôr′ə-fôrm″) *n.* a volatile, colorless liquid used as an anesthetic.

chlo′ro·phyll (klôr′ə-fil) *n.* the green coloring principle in plants.

chock (chok) *n.* a block of wood or stone used as a stop to prevent rolling. —**chock″-full′,** *adj.* full.

chock′a·block″ (chok′ə-blok″) *adj.* snugly fitted; crowded.

choc″o·hol′ic (chok″ə-hol′ik″) *n.* (*Informal*) a person having an abnormal craving for chocolate.

choc′o·late (chok′ə-lit) *n.* **1,** a food or flavoring made from the cacao bean. **2,** a beverage or candy flavored with it. **3,** a dark brown color.

choice (chois) *n.* **1,** the act of choosing. **2,** opportunity or right to choose; option. **3,** what is chosen; preference; alternative. **4,** the best part. —*adj.* superior; select; excellent. —**choice′ness,** *n.*

choir (kwīr) *n.* **1,** a chorus in a church; a group of angels singing. **2,** the choir's section in a church. —**choir′mas″ter,** *n.* a choir director.

choke (chōk) *v.t.* **1,** stop the breath of by stopping the windpipe; strangle. **2,** stop by filling; obstruct; stifle. —*v.i.* **1,** suffer constriction of the windpipe. **2,** be crammed full or overcrowded. **3,** (with *up*) be overcome by emotion or fear. —*n.* **1,** a constriction or blockage in a passage. **2,** an instrument for shutting off air from the carburetor of a gas engine. **3,** the central, inedible part of an artichoke.

chok′er (chō′kər) *n.* a high or tight collar or necklace.

chol′er (kol′ər) *n.* anger; ill-temper; irascibility. —**chol′er·ic,** *adj.*

chol′er·a (kol′ər-ə) *n.* **1,** an infectious disease, often fatal; the plague. **2,** a less serious disorder of the digestive organs.

cho·les′ter·ol (kə-les′tə-rol) *n.* a fatty alcohol found in bile, gallstones, etc., a possible cause of atherosclerosis.

> **cholesterol**
> ↔ A compound of the prefix *chole-*, bile, gall, and Greek *stereos*, solid.

chomp *v.* champ.

choose (chooz) *v.t.* [**chose** (chōz), **cho′sen**] select from two or more; give preference to; decide upon. —*v.i.* make a choice. —**choos′y,** *adj.* (*Informal*) hard to please.

chop *v.t.* [**chopped, chop′ping**] **1,** cut with a quick blow; hew. **2,** cut into pieces; mince. —*v.i.* **1,** make heavy strokes, as with an ax. **2,** turn or shift suddenly. —*n.* **1,** a cutting stroke; a hard blow. **2,** a slice of meat cut from the loin, containing the rib. **3,** a brisk, irregular motion of waves. **4,** (usu. *pl.*) the jaw. —**chop shop,** (*Informal*) a garage in which stolen cars are dismantled to get parts for resale. —**chop suey** (soo′ē) a Chinese-style stew developed in America. ❑ *chopstick*

chop′per *n.* **1,** a person or thing that chops. **2,** (*Informal*) a helicopter. **3,** (*Slang*) a customized motorcycle.

chop′py (-ē) *adj.* rough; jerky.

chop′stick″ *n.* **1,** a pencil-sized stick, two of which are used together by many Asian peoples as an eating utensil. **2,** (*pl.*) a

short waltz for piano, played with two outstretched forefingers.

> **chopstick, chop suey**
> ↔ *Chopstick* comes from Pidgin English *chop*, quick. The unrelated *chop suey* comes from Chinese *jaahp seui*, mixed bits.

cho′ral (kôr′əl) *adj.* pert. to a chorus or choir.

cho·rale′ (kə-rál′) *n.* **1,** a simple sacred tune. **2,** a chorus (def. 3).

chord (kôrd) *n.* **1,** a cord; a string of a musical instrument; an anatomical cord. **2,** a group of three or more tones sounding simultaneously. **3,** a straight line intersecting a curve at two points. **4,** a connecting member, as of a bridge truss. —**chord′al,** *adj.*

chore (chôr) *n.* a minor job; (*pl.*) routine household duties.

cho·re′a (kô-rē′ə) *n.* a spasmodic nervous disease; St. Vitus' dance.

cho″re·og′ra·phy (kôr″ē-og′rə-fē) *n.* the art of dancing; composition of exhibition dances. —**chor′e·o·graph″,** *v.t. & i.* —**cho″re·og′ra·pher,** *n.* a designer of dances.

cho′rine (kôr′ēn) *n.* (*Slang*) a cabaret or nightclub dancer.

chor′is·ter (kôr′is-tər) *n.* a member of a chorus.

chor′tle (chôr′təl) *n.* a gleeful chuckle. —*v.* chuckle and snort.

> **chortle**
> ↔ *Chuckle + snort.* One of many words coined by Lewis *Carroll*; this one first appeared in *Through the Looking Glass* (1871).

cho′rus (kôr′əs) *n.* **1,** a group of persons singing together. **2,** any group acting together in support of a soloist or principal. **3,** a composition for a chorus; a refrain; the principal melody of a popular song. **4,** a group of dancers or singers, or an interlocutor, who explain the action of a drama. —*v.t.* utter in concert.

chose (chōz) *v.* pret. of *choose.*

cho′sen (chō′zən) *v.* p.p. of *choose.*

chow *n.* **1,** [also, **chow-′chow′**] a Chinese breed of dog. **2,** (*Slang*) food; meals. —**chow mein** (mān) a Chinese dish of meat, vegetables, and fried noodles.

chow′chow″, *n.* **1,** a mixed, highly seasoned dish; a pickle preserve. **2,** (-chow′) chow (def. 1).

chow′der (-dər) *n.* a thick soup, usually of seafood, as clams.

---

tub, cūte, pûll; label; oil, owl, go, chip, she, thin, *th*en, sing, ink; *see p.* 6

chrism (kriz′əm) *n.* consecrated oil.

Christ (krīst) *n.* the Messiah; Jesus, as fulfilling his prophesied coming.

Christ
↔ From Greek *Christos*, the anointed one, a translation of Hebrew *mashiah*, Messiah.

---

chris′ten (kris′ən) *v.t.* **1,** baptize and receive into the Christian church. **2,** give a name to.

Chris′ten·dom (kris′ən-dəm) *n.* the Christian world; all Christians.

Chris′tian (kris′chən) *n.* one who professes the religious principles of Jesus Christ. —*adj.* pert. to these religious principles or any church based on them. —**Chris″ti·an′i·ty,** *n.* —**Christian name,** given name; first name. —**Christian Science,** the religious system of the Church of Christ, Scientist, that emphasizes the treatment of disease by mental and spiritual means.

Christ′mas (kris′məs) *n.* the festival celebrating the birth of Christ; Dec. 25.

chro·mat′ic (krō-mat′ik) *adj.* **1,** pert. to color. **2,** (*Music*) involving tones foreign to the diatonic scale. —**chro·mat′i·cal·ly,** *adv.*

chro·mat′o·graph″ (krō-mat′ə-graf″) *n.* a device for analyzing the constituent parts of a substance.

chrome (krōm) *n.* chromium, esp. in alloy or as a source of pigments. —**chro′-mic,** *adj.*

---

chrome
↔ From Greek *khrōma*, color, because of its brilliantly colored compounds.

---

chro′mi·um (krō′mē-əm) *n.* a metallic chemical element, no. 24, symbol Cr.

chro′mo (krō′mō) *n.* a lithograph in colors, esp. a copy of a painting.

chro·mo- (krō-mə) *pref.* **1,** color. **2,** chromium.

chro′mo·some″ (krō′mə-sōm″) *n.* a threadlike body in a germ cell, a carrier of hereditary characters.

chron- *pref.* of time. Also, **chron·o-.**

chron′ic (kron′ik) *adj.* of long standing; inveterate; continual. —**chron′i·cal·ly,** *adv.* ❏ *acute*

chron′i·cle (kron′i-kəl) *n.* an account of events in order of time; a history. —*v.t.* record or narrate in order of time. —**chron′i·cler,** *n.*

chron′o·graph″ (kron′ə-graf″) *n.* a stopwatch.

chron″o·log′i·cal (kron″ə-loj′i-kəl) *adj.* arranged in order of time.

chro·nol′o·gy (krə-nol′ə-jē) *n.* **1,** the science of determining the dates or historical order of past events. **2,** a statement of the order in time of particular events.

chro·nom′e·ter (krə-nom′ə-tər) *n.* a clock of great accuracy. —**chro·nom′e·try,** *n.*

chrys′a·lis (kris′ə-lis) *n.* the pupa of certain insects, as the moth.

chrys·an′the·mum (kri-san′thə-məm) *n.* a large flower.

chrys′o·lite″ (kris′ə-līt″) *n.* a semiprecious stone, green or yellow.

chub *n.* any of several freshwater or marine fishes.

chub′by (chub′ē) *adj.* plump.

chuck (chuk) *n.* **1,** a device to grip work in a turning machine. **2,** a cut of beef. —*v.t.* **1,** pat, usually on the chin. **2,** toss (often with *out*). —**chuck it,** (*Slang*) desist; quit. —**chuck wagon,** a wagon equipped with cooking facilities.

chuck′le (chuk′əl) *v.i.* laugh in a suppressed manner. —*n.* a subdued laugh.

chuck-′luck″ (chuk′luk″) *n.* a game of betting on casts of three dice.

chug *n.* a short explosive sound. —*v.i.* [**chugged, chug′ging**] make such sounds.

chug′a·lug″ (chug′ə-lug″) *v.t. & i.* drink the contents of a container without stopping.

chuk′ka (chuk′ə) *n.* an ankle-high boot.

---

chukka, chukker
☛ *Chukker* comes from Sanskrit *cakra*, wheel. The *chukka* is so called because it is supposed to resemble a polo boot.

---

chuk′ker (chuk′ər) *n.* one of the periods of play in polo. ❏ *chukka*

chum *n.* an intimate; a close companion. —**chum′my,** *adj.*

chump *n.* **1,** (*Informal*) a blockhead. **2,** a block of wood.

chunk *n.* **1,** an irregular solid piece, as of coal; a lump. **2,** a considerable amount. —**chunk′y,** *adj.* stocky; thickset.

Chun′nel (chun′əl) *n.* a railroad tunnel under the English Channel linking Great Britain and France.

church (chėrch) *n.* **1,** an edifice for religious worship; the chief services held there. **2,** a body or organization of Christian believers; a denomination. —**church′ly,** *adj.* devout. —**church′ key″** *n.* a can opener.

---

fat, fāte, fär, fāre, fâll, ȧsk; met, hē, hėr, maybè; pin, pīne; not, nōte, ôr, tool

> **church**
> ↔ From the Greek phrase *kyriakos domos*, the Lord's house.

church'go"er *n.* a person who goes to church regularly.

church'man (-mən) [*pl.* **-men**], **church'wo"man** *n.* 1, a member of the clergy. 2, an active member of a church.

churl (chĕrl) *n.* 1, a surly or coarse person. 2, peasant. **—churl'ish,** *adj.* rude; surly.

churn (chĕrn) *n.* 1, a device for agitating milk to make butter. 2, a similar agitating device. *—v.t.* agitate (milk) to make butter. *—v.i.* 1, operate a churn. 2, be nervously excited or agitated. 3, to engage in excessive trading (of stocks, etc.) to increase commissions.

chur'ro (chûr'ō) *n.* a type of deep-fried pastry.

chute (shoot) *n.* 1, an inclined trough, channel, or duct, esp. for the conveyance of fluid solids, as sand, by gravity. 2, any channel providing a steep descent. 3, a parachute.

chut'ney (chut'nė) *n.* an E. Indian condiment of mangoes, herbs and spices.

chutz'pa (khûts'pə) *n.* (*Informal*) effrontery; gall. Also, **chutz'pah.**

chyle (kīl) *n.* a fluid produced as part of digestion.

ciao (chow) *interj.* (*It., informal*) hello; good-bye.

ci·ca'da (si-kā'də) *n.* an insect that makes a shrill sound by vibrating certain membranes, as esp. the locust.

cic'a·trix (sik'ə-triks) *n.* [*pl.* **-tri'ces** (-trī'sėz)] the new tissue that forms a scar. Also, **cic'a·trice** (-tris).

cic'e·ly (sis'ə-lė) *n.* a plant of the parsley family.

cic"e·ro'ne (sis"ə-rō'nė) *n.* a guide.

-cide (sīd) *suf.* denoting a killer (of), or the act of killing. **— -cid'al,** *suf.* forming adjectives.

ci'der (sī'dər) *n.* expressed apple juice, fresh or slightly fermented.

> **cider**
> ↔ From Hebrew *shekhar*, strong drink (which correctly describes hard cider, if not its mild commercial cousin).

ci·gar' (si-gär') *n.* a cylindrical roll of tobacco leaves, for smoking.

cig"a·rette' (sig"ə-ret') *n.* shredded or granular tobacco contained within a paper tube, for smoking. Also, **cig"a·ret'.**

cig"a·ril'lo (sig"ə-ril'ō) *n.* a small, thin cigar.

ci·lan'tro (sə-län'trō) *n.* coriander.

cil'i·a (sil'ė-ə) *n.pl.* [*sing.* **-um** (-əm)] the eyelashes; similar short hairs or hairlike processes. **—cil'i·ar·y** (-er-ė) *adj.*

cinch (sinch) *n.* 1, a saddle girth. 2, (*Informal*) anything easy or sure of accomplishment. 3, a card game. *—v.t.* 1, tighten, as a surrounding band. 2, assure.

cin·cho'na (sin-kō'nə) *n.* a tropical tree; its bark, yielding quinine.

> **cinchona**
> ↔ From the 17th-c. Countess of *Cinchón*, who was (probably erroneously) considered important in the introduction of quinine to Europe.

cinc'ture (sink'chər) *n.* a girdle; a belt. *—v.t.* engirdle; encircle.

cin'der (sin'dər) *n.* a sandlike globular particle of burned matter; (*pl.*) ashes. **—cinder block,** a concrete building block containing coal cinders.

cin'e·ma (sin'ə-mə) *n.* a motion picture; a motion picture theater. **—cin"e·mat'ic,** *adj.*

> **cinema**
> ↔ From Greek *kinēma*, movement, through French *cinématographe*, coined by Auguste and Louis Jean Lumière at the turn of the 20th c.

Cin'e·ma·Scope" (sin'ə-mə-skōp") *n.* (*T.N.*) a wide-screen motion-picture system utilizing a special wide-angle lens.

cin'e·ma·theque" (-tek") *n.* (*Fr.*) a motion-picture theater, esp. one showing experimental films.

cin"e·ma·tog'ra·phy (-tog'rə-fė) *n.* the art or science of motion-picture photography. **—cin"e·ma·to·graph'ic,** *adj.* **—cin"e·ma·tog'ra·pher,** *n.*

ci'né·mä vé"ri·té' (sē'nä-mä vā"rē-tā') (*Fr.*) documentary filmmaking using real persons and events.

Cin'e·plex" (sin'ə-pleks") *n.* (*T.N.*) a theater complex containing multiple theaters.

Cin"e·ra'ma (sin"ə-rä'mə) *n.* (*T.N.*) a motion-picture system featuring a wide field of view, formed by projecting on a curved screen three films taken simultaneously from different angles.

cin"e·rar'i·um (sin"ə-rär'ė-əm) *n.* [*pl.* **-a** (-ə)] a place of deposit for the ashes of cremated dead.

cin'na·bar" (sin'ə-bär") *n.* a red mercuric sulfide: an ore of mercury.

---

tub, cūte, pŭll; labəl; oil, owl, go, chip, she, thin, *th*en, sing, ink; *see p.* 6

cin′na·mon (sin′ə-mən) *n.* the dried bark of a certain tree used as a spice. —*adj.* light brown.

ci′pher (sī′fər) *n.* **1,** the digit zero (0). **2,** any Arabic numeral. **3,** a secret code; the message written in it; the key to it. —*v.t.* calculate numerically. Also **cy′pher.**

cir′ca (sēr′kə) *prep.* (*Lat.*) about.

cir′cle (sēr′kəl) *n.* **1,** a closed curve, the locus of all points equidistant from a fixed point, or center, within. **2,** a ring. **3,** a cycle; a series culminating in a return to the starting point. —*v.t.* **1,** travel around the outside of. **2,** surround. —*v.i.* move in a circle.

cir′clet (sēr′klit) *n.* a ring.

cir′cuit (sēr′kit) *n.* **1,** a closed path providing continuous passage of fluids or electricity. **2,** a route regularly followed; an itinerary. —**cir′cuit·ry,** *n.* —**circuit breaker,** a thermal electric switch.

cir·cu′i·tous (sēr-kū′i-təs) *adj.* not direct; roundabout. —**cir·cu′i·tous·ness,** *n.*

cir′cu·lar (sēr′kyə-lər) *adj.* **1,** in the shape of a circle. **2,** roundabout; wandering. —*n.* a letter or brochure for general circulation.

cir′cu·late″ (sēr′kyə-lāt″) *v.i.* move through a circuit; (of persons) move about among other people. —*v.t.* disseminate; spread. —**cir′cu·la·to″ry,** *adj.*

cir′cu·la′tion (sēr″kyə-lā′shən) *n.* **1,** the act of diffusion or dissemination. **2,** continuous passage through a closed system, as the blood.

cir·cum- (sēr-kəm) *pref.* going around.

cir″cum·ci′sion (sēr″kəm-sizh′ən) *n.* removal of the foreskin of males, esp. as a religious rite. —**cir′cum·cise″** (-sīz″) *v.t.*

cir·cum′fer·ence (sər-kum′fər-əns) *n.* the distance around a circle, sphere, or other closed curved figure or object.

cir′cum·flex″ (sēr′kəm-fleks″) *n.* a diacritical mark (^), as ê.

cir″cum·lo·cu′tion (sēr″kəm-lō-kū′shən) *n.* studied indirectness of speech; evasion of a point.

cir″cum·scribe′ (sēr″kəm-skrīb′) *v.t.* limit; bound; restrain within fixed bounds. —**cir″cum·scrip′tion** (-skrip′shən) *n.*

cir″cum·spect″ (sēr″kəm-spekt″) *adj.* careful of one's behavior; discreet. —**cir″cum·spec′tion,** *n.*

cir′cum·stance″ (sēr′kəm-stans″) *n.* **1,** a concomitant condition or situation; one of the factors influencing a decision. **2,** (*pl.*) existing conditions; economic status. **3,** (*Archaic*) ceremonious display.

cir″cum·stan′tial (-stan′shəl) *adj.* **1,**

pert. to circumstances. **2,** based on incidental details; presumptive. **3,** carefully detailed. —**cir″cum·stan′tial′i·ty,** *n.*

cir″cum·stan′ti·ate″ (sēr″kəm-stan′shē-āt″) *v.t.* support with evidence; prove to be true; document. —**cir″cum·stan·ti·a′tion,** *n.*

cir″cum·vent′ (sēr″kəm-vent′) *v.t.* evade (an impediment) by going around it; outwit. —**cir″cum·ven′tion,** *n.*

cir′cus (sēr′kəs) *n.* **1,** a traveling show, including acrobats, clowns, wild animal displays, etc.; the company of performers in such show. **2,** any entertaining display likened to a circus; a good time. **3,** a circular area, as an arena or (*Brit.*) an open space where several streets converge.

cir·rho′sis (si-rō′sis) *n.* a disease, esp. of the liver, characterized by hardening of tissues.

cir′ro- (sir′ō) *pref.* cirrus.

cir′rus (sir′əs) *n.* [*pl.* **-ri** (-rī)] a cloud formation notably long, stratified, and of filamentous structure.

cis- (sis) *pref.* on this side of, as *cisalpine,* on this (the Roman) side of the Alps.

cis′tern (sis′tərn) *n.* an underground tank to hold a supply of fresh water.

cit′a·del (sit′ə-dəl) *n.* a fortress, usually at the edge of a town.

ci·ta′tion (sī-tā′shən) *n.* **1,** act or result of citing; a citing; quotation. **2,** a commendatory mention. **3,** an official summons.

cite (sīt) *v.t.* **1,** mention in specific connection; quote; refer to in support. **2,** summon officially, as to a court.

cith′a·ra (sith′ə-rə) *n.* an ancient musical instrument like a lyre.

cith′ern (sith′ərn) *n.* an ancient musical instrument like a guitar. Also, **cith′er, cit′-tern** (sit′ərn).

cit′i·fied″ (sit′i-fīd″) *adj.* **1,** having the habits of a city dweller. **2,** urbanized. —**cit′i·fy″,** *v.t.*

cit′i·zen (sit′ə-zən) *n.* **1,** an enfranchised member of a state or nation. **2,** civilian. —**cit′i·zen·ry** (-rē) *n.* citizens collectively. —**cit′i·zen·ship″,** *n.* —**citizens band,** one of several radio bands for private communications.

> **citizen, city**
> ↔ Both words come from Latin *civis.* *Citizen* derives more directly from Old French *citeain.*

cit′ric acid (sit′rik) an acid found in lemons and similar fruit.

cit′ron (sit′rən) *n.* a fruit resembling the

lemon; a candied preserve made of its rind.

cit″ron·el′la (sit″rə-nel′ə) *n.* an oil used in perfumes and soaps, and to repel insects.

cit′rus (sit′rəs) *n.* a species of tree, including the lime, lemon, etc. —*adj.* [also, **cit′rous**] containing citric acid.

cit′y (sit′ē) *n.* a large or important town. —**city hall,** the building in which the chief officials of a city government have their offices; (*fig.*) city government. ❏ *citizen*

cit′y-state′ *n.* a city having independent sovereignty.

civ′et (siv′it) *n.* **1,** (also, **civet cat**) a feline of Asia and Africa. **2,** a glandular secretion of the civet, used in perfumery.

civ′ic (siv′ik) *adj.* pert. to the affairs of a city or community, or to citizenship.

---

civic, civil
☛ *Civic* relates to a city or town or its inhabitants; *civil* relates to civilian, as distinguished from military or clerical, affairs.

---

civ′ics (siv′iks) *n.sing.* the study of the processes of government and duties of citizenship.

civ′il (siv′əl) *adj.* **1,** pert. to the state, its laws, administration, etc. **2,** pert. to a private citizen; not military, ecclesiastic, etc. **3,** courteous; polite. **4,** within a nation, as a *civil war.* —**civil defense,** defense of civilians against air raids, etc. —**civil disobedience,** noncooperation with government officers, as a method of protest. —**civil engineering,** the engineering of public-works construction, as bridges. —**civil law,** laws relating to private matters, rather than criminal, ecclesiastical, or military. —**civil liberty,** freedom of individual action and opinion. —**civil rights,** personal rights, as freedom of speech and freedom of assembly. —**civil service,** nonelected, permanent government employees collectively. ❏ *civic*

ci·vil′ian (si-vil′yən) *n.* one engaged in civil, not military, pursuits. —*adj.* not military.

ci·vil′i·ty (si-vil′ə-tē) *n.* politeness.

civ″i·li·za′tion (siv″i-lə-zā′shən) *n.* **1,** civilized peoples, states and facilities collectively. **2,** act of civilizing.

civ′i·lize″ (siv′ə-līz″) *v.t.* educate in the usages of organized society.

civ′vies (siv′ēz) *n.pl.* (*Informal*) civilian clothes (as opposed to military uniform). Also, **civ′ies.**

clab′ber (klab′ər) *n.* soured, coagulated

milk, not fully separated into curds and whey. —*v.i.* coagulate.

clack (klak) *n.* a quick, sharp, repeated sound. —*v.t. & i.* **1,** make a sharp, repeated sound; let the tongue vibrate. **2,** prattle.

clad (klad) *v.* clothed; dressed.

cla·dis′tics (klə-dis′tiks) *n.* (*constr. as pl.*) classification of organisms based on descent rather than anatomical similarity.

claim (klām) *v.t.* **1,** assert a right to; demand. **2,** (*Informal*) assert as fact; contend. —*n.* a demand for something due; the thing demanded. —**claim′ant,** *n.* —**claim′ing race,** a horse race among horses offered for sale at the same price.

clair·voy′ance (klār-voi′əns) *n.* extrasensory sight or perception. —**clair·voy′ant,** *n. & adj.*

clam (klam) *n.* **1,** any of several varieties of bivalve mollusks. **2,** an uncommunicative person. —*v.i.* **1,** gather clams. **2,** (with *up*) (*Informal*) stop talking. —**clam diggers,** knee-length pants.

---

clam, clammy
☛ These two words are unrelated. *Clam* (the mollusk) originally meant something that fastened, such as a clamp or fetter. *Clammy* comes from an ancient Germanic word for clay.

---

clam′bake″ *n.* **1,** a picnic at which clams are baked. **2,** any social gathering.

clam′ber (klam′bər) *v.i.* ascend by climbing, often with difficulty.

clam′my (klam′ē) *adj.* cold and damp. —**clam′mi·ness,** *n.* ❏ *clam*

clam′or (klam′ər) *n.* noise; noisy ado; a vociferous demand or complaint. —*v.i.* make an outcry; demand loudly. Also, **clam′our.** —**clam′or·ous,** *adj.*

clamp (klamp) *n.* a device for holding objects, or fastening them together temporarily. —*v.t.* fasten with or as with a clamp. —*v.i.* (with *down*) become strict.

clam′shell″ *n.* **1,** the shell of a clam. **2,** a dredging bucket having two hinged jaws.

clan (klan) *n.* **1,** a family or tribe, esp. Scottish. **2,** any social set; clique. —**clan′nish,** *adj.* —**clans′man** (klanz′mən) *n.masc.*, **clans′wo″man** *n.fem.* a kinsman.

clan·des′tine (klan-des′tin) *adj.* secret; covert; furtive.

clang (klang) *n.* the sound of a gong or hammer; the ring of metal when struck. —*v.i. & t.* make such a sound.

clan′gor (klang′ər) *n.* **1,** a clanging sound. **2,** clamor.

clank (klangk) *n.* a sharp, metallic sound.

—*v.t.* strike (an object) to produce such a sound. —*v.i.* give out such a sound.

clap (klap) *v.t.* **[clapped, clap′ping] 1,** strike together (as the hands) producing a sharp sound. **2,** place or dispose of hastily. —*v.i.* strike with the hands together, for applause, attention, etc. —*n.* **1,** the sound of clapping hands; applause. **2,** a blow with the flat of the hand. **3,** (*Vulgar*) gonorrhea.

clap′board (klab′ərd) *n.* **1,** a wooden board used for a type of siding for houses in which the boards overlap. **2,** (clap′-bôrd″) (*Motion Pictures*) a small board having a hinged stick used for synchronizing sound and image.

clap′per (klap′ər) *n.* the tongue of a bell.

clap′trap″ (klap′trap″) *n.* insincere and diversionary talk; nonsense.

claque (klak) *n.* a group of persons hired to applaud a performer.

---

claque, clique
☛ Do not confuse *claque*, a group of hired applauders, and *clique*, a social coterie.

---

clar′et (klar′ət) *n.* a red wine from Bordeaux; its color.

clar′i·fy″ (klar′ə-fī″) *v.t. & i.* **1,** make clear to the sight or understanding. **2,** free from turbidity; become clear. —**clar″i·fi·ca′tion,** *n.*

clar″i·net′ (klar″ə-net′) *n.* a single-reed woodwind instrument.

clar′i·on (klar′ē-ən) *adj.* obtrusively clear and high-pitched, as a trumpet's sound.

clar′i·ty (klar′ə-tē) *n.* clearness.

clash (klash) *v.i.* collide so as to make a loud, harsh noise; meet in conflict. —*v.t.* strike together violently and noisily. —*n.* a collision of physical objects, opinions, etc.; conflict.

clasp (klåsp) *n.* **1,** a small latch for holding two things together. **2,** a joining of the hands; an embrace. —*v.t.* fasten together; embrace; grasp.

class (klås) *n.* **1,** order or rank, esp. of persons; caste. **2,** a category. **3,** a group of persons with a common interest, esp. such a group in student session. **4,** (*Informal*) smartness; beauty; modishness. —*v.t.* arrange according to class; classify. —**class act,** (*Slang*) a person or thing of high quality, ability, etc. —**class action,** a legal suit brought on behalf of a group of people with a common complaint.

clas′sic (klas′ik) *n.* **1,** a creation of enduring value or esteem, as a musical or literary composition. **2,** a standard; a perfect specimen. **3,** (*pl.*) the literature of Greece and Rome. —*adj.* characterized by enduring value. —**clas′si·cal,** *adj.*

---

classic, classical
☛ Strictly speaking, *classical* refers to a period or style, e.g. the civilization of ancient Greece or Rome, or the latter half of the 18th c., when formality and balance were especially sought after. *Classic* assigns enduring value.

---

clas′si·cism (klas′i-siz-əm) *n.* **1,** purity and simplicity of style. **2,** advocacy of such a style.

clas′si·cist (-sist) *n.* **1,** an advocate of classicism. **2,** a classical scholar.

clas″si·fi·ca′tion (klas″i-fi-kā′shən) *n.* **1,** act of classifying. **2,** a class or category.

clas′si·fied″ (klas′i-fīd″) *adj.* **1,** arranged by topic, group, etc. **2,** (*Mil.*) secret, confidential, or restricted. —**classified ad,** a want ad, etc., arranged with others of the same nature.

clas′si·fy″ (klas′ə-fī″) *v.t.* **1,** sort into groups having common characteristics. **2,** assign a place in a group. **3,** (*Mil.*) place (a document) in a category of secrecy.

class′y (klas′ē) *adj.* (*Slang*) high-grade; modish.

clat′ter (klat′ər) *n.* a rattling or clashing sound, as of dishes roughly handled. —*v.i.* make such a sound.

clause (klâz) *n.* **1,** a sentence element containing at least a subject and verb. **2,** a stipulation, modification, or condition of a document; a paragraph. —**claus′al,** *adj.*

claus″tro·pho′bi·a (klâs″trə-fō′bē-ə) *n.* a morbid fear of being shut in or confined.

clav′i·chord″ (klav′ə-kôrd″) *n.* an ancient musical instrument, precursor of the piano.

---

clavichord, clavier
↔ Both words come from Latin *clavis*, key.

---

clav′i·cle (klav′ə-kəl) *n.* the collarbone.

clav′i·er (klav′ē-ər; klə-vir′) *n.* (*Music*) a keyboard instrument; a keyboard. ❏ *clavichord*

claw (klâ) *n.* **1,** a hook or talon on a limb, esp. the foot of a living creature. **2,** a tool or device for grasping. —*v.t. & i.* scratch; tear or rend.

clay (klā) *n.* **1,** plastic earth in the form of thick mud, used in making brick, for modeling, etc. **2,** the human body. **3,** one easily influenced.

clean (klēn) *adj.* **1,** free from dirt or irrelevant substances; pure; unadulterated. **2,** free from error or sin. **3,** fastidious. —*v.t.* remove foreign or superfluous material from; wash. —**clean′ness,** *n.* —**clean out, 1,** use up. **2,** empty of contents, occupants, etc. —**clean room,** a room that is kept free from contamination. —**clean up,** (*Informal*) make much money. —**come clean,** (*Informal*) confess.

---

clean, cleanse
☞ Both words mean the same thing, but *cleanse* is more formal and is used more often in religious or figurative contexts.

---

clean-′cut″ *adj.* **1,** shapely and clean-looking. **2,** sharply outlined; definite.

clean′er *n.* **1,** one who cleans. **2,** a washing agent.

clean′ly (klen′lē) *adj.* clean in habits; neat. —**clean′li·ness,** *n.*

cleanse (klenz) *v.t.* **1,** clean; dry-clean. **2,** absolve or free from guilt; purify. —**cleans′er** (klen′zər) *n.* ❑ *clean*

clear (klir) *adj.* **1,** easily understood or perceived; not turbid or cloudy; unobstructed; transparent. **2,** untroubled, innocent. —*v.t.* **1,** remove burdens or obstructions from; clarify; free from debt, encumbrance or accusation. **2,** make a net profit of. **3,** jump over. **4,** (with *up*) explain lucidly; solve. **5,** (often with *away* or *off*) remove; sweep away. —*v.i.* **1,** (often with *up*) become bright or unclouded. **2,** (of a check) be paid. **3,** (often with *out*) depart hastily; go. —**clear′ness,** *n.*

clear′ance (-əns) *n.* **1,** act of clearing. **2,** the space between two objects; room to pass. **3,** approval as free from objection; permission to proceed.

clear-′cut″ *adj.* distinct; obvious.

clear′ing (klir′ing) *n.* a tract of land cleared of trees. —**clearinghouse,** a cooperative institution through which banks settle their mutual accounts.

cleat (klēt) *n.* a crosspiece serving to join and strengthen a number of longitudinal strips; a similar crosspiece attached to increase traction.

cleav′age (klē′vij) *n.* **1,** act or result of cleaving, splitting, or division. **2,** the depression between a woman's breasts.

cleave (klēv) *v.i.* **1,** adhere; stick; cling. **2,** come apart; divide; split. —*v.t.* split; rend asunder; force apart.

---

cleave
↔ One of the rare words that have two contradictory meanings, which are derived from different Old English roots.

---

cleav′er (klē′vər) *n.* a heavy knife for chopping through bone.

clef (klef) *n.* (*Music*) a character placed at the beginning of a staff to indicate the location of the governing tonality.

cleft (kleft) *n.* a crack; crevice; split. —*v. p.p.* of *cleave.*

clem′a·tis (klem′ə-tis) *n.* a climbing vine bearing small white flowers.

clem′en·cy (klem′ən-sė) *n.* mildness; leniency; mercy.

clem′ent (klem′ənt) *adj.* **1,** merciful; lenient. **2,** mild; agreeable.

clench (klench) *v.t.* close tightly, as the fist or teeth.

clere′sto″ry (klir′stôr″ė) *n.* the upper part of a building, esp. a church, rising above the roofs and lighted with windows.

cler′gy (klėr′jė) *n.* **1,** priests, ministers, or ecclesiastical officials collectively. **2,** a member of the clergy. —**cler′gy·man** (-mən) [*pl.* **-men**], **cler′gy·wo″man,** *n.* any member of the clergy. ❑ *cleric*

cler′ic (kler′ik) *n.* **1,** a clerk. **2,** a member of the clergy.

---

cleric, clergy, clerk
↔ From Greek *klērikos,* pert. to inheritance, more specifically, Christian inheritance, i.e., the ministry. As clergy were virtually the only people at one time who could read and write, they filled posts that required those skills, i.e., clerical (secretarial) positions.

---

cler′i·cal (kler′ə-kəl) *adj.* **1,** pert. to the clergy or to affairs of the church. **2,** pert. to written records, copies, or office work.

clerk (klėrk) *n.* **1,** a salesperson in a shop. **2,** an assistant in an office. **3,** an official of a branch of government who keeps records. **4,** (*Archaic*) a lay officer of the church; any literate person. —*v.i.* serve as a clerk. —**clerk′ly,** *adj.* —**clerk′ship,** *n.* ❑ *cleric*

clev′er (klev′ər) *adj.* **1,** shrewd; quick to learn; skillful; quick-witted. **2,** ingenious. —**clev′er·ness,** *n.*

clev′is (klev′is) *n.* a U-shaped device for attaching a wagon, etc., to a drawbar for pulling.

---

clew (kloo) *n.* **1,** clue. **2,** part of a sail. **3,** a ball of yarn.

cli·ché′ (klē-shā′) *n.* (*Fr.*) **1,** a stereotype. **2,** an outworn expression; a stale or trite remark.

click (klik) *n.* a small, sharp snap. —*v.i.* **1,** make such a sound. **2,** (*Informal*) be successful.

cli·ent (klī′ənt) *n.* a customer, esp. the recipient of professional, esp. legal, services. —**client state,** a country dependent on another, larger country for its economic wellbeing and security.

cli″en·tele′ (klē″ən-tel′; klī″-) *n.* a body of clients of a lawyer, doctor, etc.; the customers of a business establishment.

cliff (klif) *n.* an abrupt wall of rock; precipice.

cliff′dwel″ler *n.* (*Informal*) a resident of a tall apartment building.

cliff′hang″er *n.* **1,** an event whose outcome is uncertain until the very end. **2,** an adventure serial.

cli·mac′ter·ic (klī-mak′tər-ik) *n.* a critical period, esp. the menopause. —*adj.* pert. to a critical time.

cli·mac′tic (klī-mak′tik) *adj.* pert. to a climax. —**cli·mac′ti·cal·ly,** *adv.* ❏ *climatic*

cli·mate (klī′mit) *n.* the customary pattern of the weather for any specific locality. —**cli·mat′ic,** *adj.* —**cli·mat′i·cal·ly,** *adv.*

> **climatic, climactic**
> ☛ Do not confuse *climatic*, pert. to the climate, with *climactic*, pert. to a climax.

cli′max (klī′maks) *n.* **1,** the culmination of one or more events. **2,** the highest point of action, stress, motion, etc. **3,** the most effective point of a narrative, drama, or argument. **4,** orgasm. —*v.t.* bring to the highest or most effective point.

> **climax**
> ↔ From Greek *klimax*, ladder; from steps leading to a goal, the word came to be applied to the goal itself.

climb (klīm) *v.t. & i.* **1,** ascend with effort; toil upward. **2,** rise slowly. **3,** (with *down*) descend. —*n.* an ascent.

clime (klīm) *n.* (*Poetic*) a place or region of the earth.

clinch (klinch) *v.t.* **1,** secure tightly; fasten by bending the point (of a nail, etc.) sideways after driving it through; clench. **2,** make certain of; consolidate. —*v.i.* (*Informal*) embrace; in boxing, grasp the opponent with the arms. —*n.* the result of

clinching. —**clinch′er,** *n.* that which clinches, esp. a decisive argument.

cling (kling) *v.i.* [**clung, cling′ing**] adhere; be fastened to; hold tenaciously to. —**cling′y,** *adj.*

cling′stone″ *n.* a peach whose stone clings to the flesh of the fruit.

clin′ic (klin′ik) *n.* **1,** a place for medical examination and treatment, often free, for experimental or instructive purposes. **2,** a class or meeting dealing with problems of a specific field of study. —**cli·ni′cian** (kli-ni′shən) *n.*

> **clinic**
> ↔ From Greek *klinē*, bed, perhaps through the phrase *klinike technē*, the art of treating bedridden patients, by way of French *clinique*.

clin′i·cal *adj.* **1,** pert. to or used in medical practice. **2,** analytical.

clink (klink) *n.* **1,** a high-pitched, fine sound, as of struck glass. **2,** (*Slang*) a jail.

> **clink**
> ↔ The jail is named for a prison in London, from Dutch *klink*, door latch.

clink′er (kling′kər) *n.* **1,** a vitreous residue of various fuels; a piece of slag. **2,** (*Informal*) error; boner.

clip (klip) *n.* **1,** a mechanical clasping device, as a *paper clip, cartridge clip.* **2,** a fast gait. —*v.t.* [**clipped** (klipt), **clip′ping**] **1,** fasten together by a spring-actuated device. **2,** cut, as with shears; truncate. **3,** cuff with a glancing blow. **4,** (*Slang*) cheat. —**clip art,** (*Computers*) pre-drawn computer graphics distributed for reuse. —**clip joint,** (*Slang*) an establishment that overcharges its customers.

clip′board″ *n.* **1,** a small portable writing surface having a clip at the top for holding papers. **2,** (*Computers*) a temporary storage area for text or graphics.

clip′per (klip′ər) *n.* **1,** any of various tools that cut by shearing. **2,** something that travels swiftly, esp. a square-rigged, speedy sailing ship, or an airliner.

clip′ping *n.* a piece clipped or cut out.

clique (klēk; klik) *n.* a small exclusive social coterie. —**cli′quish** (-kish) *adj.* ❏ *claque*

clit′o·ris (klit′ə-ris) *n.* a small erectile protuberance on the external genital parts of a female.

clo·a′ca (klō-ā′kə) *n.* [*pl.* **-cae** (-sē)] **1,**

a sewer. **2,** a privy. **3,** a cavity in certain animals. —**clo·a′cal,** *adj.*

cloak (klōk) *n.* **1,** a loose-fitting, sleeveless outer garment. **2,** a disguise; pretext; cover. —*v.t.* cover; conceal. —**cloak′-room″,** *n.* a room where coats, hats, etc., are left temporarily. —**cloak-and-dagger,** *adj.* pert. to espionage or secrecy.

clob′ber (klob′ər) *v.t.* (*Slang*) **1,** pummel; punish. **2,** frustrate; spoil. **3,** defeat soundly.

cloche (klōsh) *n.* **1,** a bell-shaped woman's hat. **2,** a bell-shaped or deep concave glass cover.

clock (klok) *n.* **1,** a stationary timepiece. **2,** a device that produces regular pulses, as in a computer. **3,** a vertical ornament on the ankle of a sock. —*v.t.* (*Informal*) measure the speed of; time.

clock′wise″ (klok′wīz″) *adj.* in the direction of travel of a clock's hands: from left to right around a circle.

clock′work″ *n.* the mechanism of a clock, or one similarly exact and inexorable.

clod (klod) *n.* **1,** a compacted chunk of earth. **2,** a stupid, stolid person. —**clod′-dish,** *adj.*

clod′hop″per *n.* **1,** a rustic; boor. **2,** (*pl.*) heavy work shoes.

clog (klog) *n.* **1,** a block or encumbrance; any impediment or hindrance. **2,** a type of thick-soled, often wooden, shoe. **3,** a dance in which heavy shoes tap the rhythm: *clog dance.* —*v.t.* [**clogged, clog′-ging**] encumber; hinder; impede. —*v.i.* **1,** become clogged. **2,** dance a clog dance.

cloi″son·né′ (kloi″zə-nā′) *n.* decorative work of enamel sections in a pattern of metal strips.

clois′ter (klois′tər) *n.* **1,** an arched walk surrounding a courtyard; an arcade or colonnade. **2,** a place of religious retirement. —**clois′tered** (-tərd) *adj.* **1,** secluded. **2,** having a cloister. —**clois′tral** (-trəl) *adj.*

clone (klōn) *v.t.* **1,** grow (an organism) from a single cell by asexual reproduction. **2,** copy or imitate so closely as to produce an almost identical twin. —*n.* an organism or copy so produced.

> **clone**
> ↔ The source reflects the original botanical sense; the word comes from Greek *klōn,* twig.

clop (klop) *n. & v.* make the sound of a hoof or wooden shoe against pavement.

close (klōz) *v.t.* **1,** stop up; shut. **2,** join; fill, as a gap. **3,** finish; conclude. —*v.i.* **1,** unite; come together. **2,** (with *in*) ap-

proach; draw near. **3,** come to an end; terminate. **4,** consummate a sale or agreement. **5,** fight in bodily contact; grapple. —*n.* **1,** conclusion; termination. **2,** (klōs) an enclosed yard; court. —*adj.* (klōs) **1,** near to; in contact with. **2,** restricted in space; wanting fresh air; stuffy. **3,** compact; dense. **4,** secretive; reticent. **5,** (*Informal*) penurious; miserly. —*adv.* (klōs) **1,** near. **2,** in a closed manner. —**close′ness** (klōs′-) *n.* —**close call** (klōs) (*Informal*) a narrow escape. —**closed car,** an automobile having windows and a hard top. —**closed circuit,** television transmission by wire to a limited number of receivers. —**closed shop,** a shop employing union members only.

closed-′cap″tioned (klōzd′kap′shənd) *adj.* (*TV*) of a television program, broadcast with captions for the hard-of-hearing requiring a decoder for viewing.

close-′fist″ed (klōs′-) *adj.* stingy.

close-′grained″ (klōs′-) *adj.* (of wood) having a fine texture.

close-′knit″ (klōs′-) *adj.* firmly bound together.

close′out (klōz′owt) *n.* a sale to liquidate stock.

clos′et (kloz′it) *n.* a small room for retirement or storage. —*adj.* secret. —**clos′-et·ed,** *adj.* shut up in a private room.

close-′up″ (klōs′-) *n.* a near view; a picture taken at close range.

clo′sure (klō′zhər) *n.* **1,** act of closing; state of being closed. **2,** that which closes, as a bottle cap.

> **closure, cloture**
> ☞ Do not confuse *closure,* the act of closing, with the very specific term *cloture,* the stopping of parliamentary debate.

clot (klot) *n.* soft or fluid matter, as blood or cream, coagulated into a mass. —*v.t. & i.* [**clot′ted, -ting**] form a clot. —**clot′ty,** *adj.*

cloth (klâth) *n.* **1,** fabric woven from filaments of wool, cotton, etc. **2,** (*pl.* klâthz) a specific piece of such material for a designated purpose. **3,** the professional dress of a clergyman. —*adj.* made of cloth.

clothe (klō*th*) *v.t.* [**clothed** or **clad, cloth′-ing**] attire; cover with, or as with, clothing.

clothes (klō*th*z) *n.pl.* **1,** wearing apparel. **2,** cloth coverings, esp. for beds. —**clothes′horse″,** *n.* (*Slang*) a person on whom clothes are unusually becoming. —**clothes′pin″,** *n.* a small clip for fastening clothes on a line. —**clothes′press″,** *n.* a chest or closet for storing clothes.

—**clothes'tree"**, *n.* an upright pole with arms for hanging hats and coats.

cloth'ier (klŏth'yər) *n.* a manufacturer or retailer of clothes.

cloth'ing (klō'thing) *n.* wearing apparel; cloth coverings in general.

clo'ture (klō'chər) *n.* the stopping of a debate by parliamentary rule. ❏ *closure*

cloud (klowd) *n.* **1,** white or gray masses of suspended water or ice particles at varying heights above the earth. **2,** anything resembling a cloud, as dust. **3,** anything that darkens, threatens, or obscures. —*v.t.* **1,** obscure; darken. **2,** place under suspicion; sully. —*v.i.* grow cloudy; become obscured. —**cloud'y,** *adj.* —**cloud chamber,** a vapor chamber for studying the movements of particles. —**cloud nine,** (*Informal*) a feeling of well-being.

> **cloud**
> ↔ From Old English *klud*, rocky hill, presumably from the resemblance to certain cloud formations.

cloud'ber"ry *n.* a variety of raspberry.

cloud'burst" *n.* a heavy rainfall.

clout (klowt) *v.t.* strike with the hand; cuff. —*n.* **1,** a blow. **2,** in baseball, a hard hit. **3,** (*Informal*) influence.

clove (klōv) *n.* **1,** one of the small bulbs from the mother bulb, as a clove of garlic. **2,** a spice, the dried flower buds of the clove tree.

> **clove**
> ↔ The garlic *clove* and the spice are not related. The spice comes from French *clou*, nail, so named because of its shape. The garlic *clove* is from an Old English word for bulb, and is related to *cleave* in its sense to split.

clo'ven (klō'vən) *adj.* parted; divided; split.

clo'ver (klō'vər) *n.* a common garden plant, useful as forage.

clo'ver·leaf" *n.* an arrangement of road intersections to avoid direct crossings; so-called from the resemblance to a four-leaf clover.

clown (klown) *n.* **1,** a comedian, esp. in a circus; a buffoon. **2,** (*Archaic*) a rustic; an uncouth person. —*v.i. & t.* act the buffoon; parody. —**clown'er·y,** *n.* —**clown'ish,** *adj.* rude or comical.

cloy (kloi) *v.t. & i.* surfeit; seem excessive. —**cloy'ing,** *adj.*

club (klub) *n.* **1,** a stick to be used as a weapon; a cudgel; a bat or stick as used in various games. **2,** any playing card designated by the trefoil (♣). **3,** a group of persons joined by a common interest; its quarters. —*v.t.* [**clubbed, club'bing**] **1,** strike or beat with a club. **2,** use as a weapon. **3,** pool; unite. —*v.i.* (with *together*) unite; act jointly. —**club car,** a railroad car equipped with a lounge, buffet, and other conveniences for passengers. —**club chair,** an easy chair. —**club sandwich,** a large multilayer sandwich with chicken, bacon, tomatoes, lettuce, and mayonnaise. —**club steak,** any of various cuts of beefsteak.

club'foot" *n.* a deformed foot.

cluck (kluk) *n.* **1,** the sound made by suddenly separating the tongue from the hard palate. **2,** the sound of a hen calling her chicks. —*v.i.* utter such sounds.

clue (kloo) *n.* a hint, indication or tangible guide to the solution of a mystery or problem. Also, **clew.** —**clue'less,** *adj.* (*Slang*) ignorant.

clump (klump) *n.* **1,** a shapeless mass of solid material. **2,** a cluster of trees or shrubs. —*v.i.* walk heavily and clumsily. —**clump'y,** *adj.*

clum'sy (klum'zē) *adj.* awkward; blundering; ill-adapted. —**clum'si·ness,** *n.*

clung (klung) *v.* pret. & p.p. of *cling.*

clunk (klunk) *n.* a dull, heavy, metallic sound. —*v.i.* make such a sound. —**clunk'er,** *n.* (*Slang*) something inferior; a lemon.

clus'ter (klus'tər) *n.* **1,** a closely grouped number of things, as fruits or persons; a bunch. **2,** (*Computers*) the smallest storage unit on a floppy or hard disk. —*v.i. & t.* bunch together. —**cluster college,** a small specialized residential college within a university.

clutch (kluch) *v.t.* **1,** grasp with the hands. **2,** (with *at*) try to grasp. —*v.i.* try to seize something. —*n.* **1,** (often *pl.*) a strong grip; powerful control. **2,** a device to engage a driven member with the driving force. **3,** (*pl.*) (*Slang*) a critical situation. **4,** a brood of eggs or chickens.

clut'ter (klut'ər) *n.* a disorderly state or litter. —*v.t.* (often with *up*) strew in confusion.

Clydes'dale" (klīdz'dāl") *n.* **1,** a breed of heavy draft horses. **2,** a breed of small Skye terriers.

clys'ter (klīs'tər) *n.* an enema.

co- (kō) *pref.* as one of two or more; jointly.

coach (kōch) *n.* **1,** carriage; passenger vehicle. **2,** a tutor or instructor. —*v.t.* instruct; train. —**coach'man** (-mən) [*pl.* **-men**], **coach'wom"an,** *n.* coach driver.

coach

↔ From Hungarian *kocsi szeker*, cart from Kocs (Hungary). The sense "instructor" apparently developed from the idea of a teacher as one who "transports" a person through an examination.

co·ad′ju·tor (kō-aj′ə-tər) *n.* an assistant, as of a bishop or prelate.

co·ag′u·late″ (kō-ag′yə-lāt″) *v.i.* become clotted or congealed. —*v.t.* curdle; congeal. —**co·ag′u·lant,** *n.* —**co·ag″u·la′tion,** *n.*

coal (kōl) *n.* **1,** a blackish carbonaceous mineral used as fuel. **2,** a lump of coal; (*pl.*) any burning lumps. —**coal oil,** kerosene.

co″a·lesce′ (kō″ə-les′) *v.i.* grow together; unite. —**co″a·les′cence,** *n.*

co″a·li′tion (kō″ə-lish′ən) *n.* **1,** a temporary alliance. **2,** fusion into one mass.

coarse (kôrs) *adj.* **1,** of rough finish or texture. **2,** crude; unrefined. —**coars′en** (kôr′sən) *v.t.* make coarse. —**coarse′-ness,** *n.*

coast (kōst) *n.* the shoreline; land by the sea. —*v.i.* proceed without power, by gravity or inertia. —**coast′al,** *adj.* —**Coast Guard,** a U.S. armed service.

coast′er (-ər) *n.* **1,** a vehicle that will coast, as a sled. **2,** a small table mat or dish, esp. for use under a glass. **3,** a serving tray on wheels. **4,** a roller coaster. —**coaster brake,** a bicycle brake operated by the pedals.

coat (kōt) *n.* **1,** an outer garment with sleeves. **2,** anything that covers the entire surface, as paint, an animal's fur, etc. —*v.t.* cover with a bonded or close-fitting layer of anything. —**coat′ing,** *n.* a layer of some substance, as paint. —**coat of arms,** a distinctive blazon on a shield.

co·au′thor *n.* one of two or more persons who write or compose something together. —*v.t.* write or compose together.

coax (kōks) *v.t. & i.* beg by fondling or flattery; wheedle; cajole.

co·ax″i·al (kō-ak′sè-əl) *adj.* having a common axis; (of a cable) capable of transmitting different and distinguishable impulses.

cob (kob) *n.* **1,** the spike upon which grains of corn grow: *corncob.* **2,** a small, strong horse. **3,** the male swan.

co′balt (kō′bâlt) *n.* a hard metallic element, no. 27, symbol Co. —*adj.* deep blue.

cob′ble (kob′əl) *v.t. & i.* make or repair shoes; mend or patch, esp. clumsily.

cob′bler (kob′lər) *n.* **1,** a shoemaker. **2,** a dessert or drink made with fruit.

cob′ble·stone″ *n.* a paving stone with convex upper surface.

CO′BOL (kō′bâl) *n.* (*Computers*) a standardized language for programming a computer: *Co(mmon) B(usiness) O(riented) L(anguage).*

co′bra (kō′brə) *n.* a poisonous snake of Asia and India.

cobra

↔ Short for Portuguese *cobra de capello,* hooded snake, of Latin origin.

cob′web″ (kob′web″) *n.* **1,** the net spun by the spider. **2,** any similar flimsy structure.

cobweb

↔ Originally, *cop web,* from Middle English *cop,* spider.

co′ca (kō′kə) *n.* the dried leaf of a So. Amer. shrub, used medicinally as a tonic, or mild stimulant.

co·caine′ (kō′kān′) *n.* an alkaloid of coca, used as an anesthetic and narcotic.

coc′cyx (kok′siks) *n.* [*pl.* **coc·cy′ges** (-sī′jēz)] a small bone at the base of the spinal column. —**coc·cyg′e·al** (-sij′è-əl) *adj.*

coch″i·neal′ (koch″ə-nēl′) *n.* a scarlet dye made from dried Central Amer. insects.

coch′le·a (kok′lè-ə) *n.* [*pl.* **-ae″** (-ē″)] a spiral canal in the internal ear. —**coch′-le·ar** (-ər) *adj.*

cock (kok) *n.* **1,** the male of various birds, esp. of domestic fowl; a rooster. **2,** a leader. **3,** a faucet or valve. **4,** a conical pile of hay. **5,** an upward tilt, as of a head, hat, etc. —*v.t.* **1,** turn up on one side. **2,** draw back the hammer of (a gun). —**cocked hat,** a hat with a wide brim turned up in flaps. —**knock into a cocked hat,** destroy; discredit.

cock·ade′ (-ād′) *n.* a rosette worn on the hat as a badge.

cock′a·ma″mie (kok′ə-mā″mè) *adj.* (*Slang*) absurd; ridiculous.

cock-′and-bull′ (kok′ən-bûl′) *adj.* of a story, absurd, but told as true.

cock″a·too′ (-ə-too′) *n.* a crested Australian parrot.

cockatoo

↔ From Malay *kakatua,* literally, old sibling.

cock′a·trice (kok′ə-tris) *n.* a fabulous deadly serpent.

cock′cha″fer (-chā″fər) *n.* a type of scarab beetle.

cock′crow″ *n.* dawn.

cock′er (-ər) *n.* a small long-haired hunting dog: *cocker spaniel.*

cock′er·el (-ər-əl) *n.* a young cock.

cock′eyed″ (-īd″) *adj.* **1,** cross-eyed. **2,** (*Slang*) twisted; absurd. **3,** (*Slang*) drunk.

cock′horse″ *n.* a child's rocking horse.

cock′le (kok′əl) *n.* **1,** a weed. **2,** an edible mollusk with two fluted shells. **3,** a shallow boat. **—cockles of the heart,** inmost depths of feeling.

cock′ney (kok′nė) *n.* a native of the East End of London; the dialect of this region.

> **cockney**
> ↔ From the Middle English *cokeney*, cock's egg, or, figuratively, foolish person.

cock′pit″ *n.* **1,** the space for pilots in an airplane or motorboat. **2,** a recess in the afterdeck of a yacht, etc. **3,** a place for cockfighting.

cock′roach″ *n.* an insect infesting houses.

> **cockroach**
> ↔ From the Spanish *cucaracha* (the famous song is about a cockroach!).

cocks′comb″ (koks′kōm″) *n.* a crimson-flowered plant: the *celosia.*

cock′sure″ *adj.* overconfident.

cock′tail″ *n.* a mixed drink, or dish of fruit, shellfish, etc. served before a meal. **—cocktail sauce,** a mixture of ketchup, horseradish, and spices.

cock′y (kok′ė) *adj.* conceited. **—cock′i·ness,** *n.*

co′co (kō′kō) *n.* the coconut palm.

co′coa (kō′kō) *n.* **1,** a powder made from cacao seed; a hot drink made from this powder and milk. **2,** a brown color. **—cocoa butter,** a waxy substance made from cacao seeds.

co·co·nut″ (kō′kə-nut″) *n.* the large, hard fruit of a tropical tree (*coconut palm*).

co·coon′ (kə-koon′) *n.* a silky case in which certain larvae develop.

co·cotte′ (kō-kot′) *n.* a harlot.

cod (kod) *n.* a No. Atlantic food fish. Also, **cod′fish″.**

co′da (kō′də) *n.* a concluding section of a musical composition.

cod′dle (kod′əl) *v.t.* **1,** humor; pamper. **2,** cook in hot but not boiling water.

code (kōd) *n.* **1,** a systematized collection of laws. **2,** any set of rules. **3,** a system of signals for telegraphic or secret communication. **—v.t. 1,** codify. **2,** encode. **—code word,** a euphemistic word or phrase used instead of a politically less acceptable one.

co′deine (kō′dēn) *n.* a narcotic derivative of opium.

co′dex (kō′deks) *n.* [*pl.* **-di·ces″** (-də-sēz″)] a manuscript, esp. of a classic book.

codg′er (koj′ər) *n.* (*Informal*) an old person.

cod′i·cil (kod′ə-səl) *n.* a supplement to a will.

cod′i·fy″ (kod′i-fī″) *v.t.* arrange systematically; reduce to a code. **—cod″i·fi·ca′tion,** *n.*

cod′piece″ *n.* in the 15th & 16th c., a flap hanging over the opening in the front of men's breeches.

co′ed″ (kō′ed″) (*Informal*) *n.* a female student in a coeducational college. **—adj.** coeducational.

> **coed**
> ☛ This word dates from a time when previously all-male colleges and universities were first admitting female students; its use now is at best out of date and is often considered sexist and offensive.

co″ed·u·ca′tion *n.* education of students of both sexes together. **—co″ed·u·ca′tion·al,** *adj.*

co″ef·fi′cient (kō″ə-fish′ənt) *n.* a multiplier.

co·e′qual *adj. & n.* equal in extent, rank, power, etc. **—co″e·qual′i·ty,** *n.*

co·erce′ (kō-ērs′) *v.t.* compel by force. **—co·er′cion** (-shən) *n.*

co·e′val (kō-ē′vəl) *adj.* of the same age; contemporary.

co″ex·ist′ *v.i.* exist together or at the same time. **—co″ex·ist′ence,** *n.* **—co″ex·ist′ent,** *adj.*

co″ex·tend′ *v.i.* extend equally in space or time. **—co″ex·ten′sive,** *adj.*

cof′fee (kâf′ė) *n.* **1,** a drink made from the seeds of a tropical shrub; the shrub or seeds (coffee beans). **2,** a brown color. **—coffeehouse, 1,** a public room where coffee and other refreshments are served. **2,** a café; nightclub. **—coffee klatsch** (kläch) an informal gathering at which coffee is served. **—coffee shop,** a restaurant serving simple meals. **—coffee table,** a low, usu. long, table set before a sofa.

> **coffee**
> ↔ From Arabic *qahwah*, perhaps from Kaffa, an area in Abyssinia.

cof·fer (kâf'ər) *n.* a chest, esp. one for valuables.

cof·fer·dam″ *n.* a watertight enclosure built in water, pumped dry to allow construction work.

cof′fin (kâf'in) *n.* a box in which a corpse is buried.

cog (kog) *n.* a tooth on a gearwheel. —**cog railway,** a railway on steep slopes that employs a gearwheel for traction.

co″gen·e·ra′tion (kō″jen-ə-rā′shən) *n.* the use of the heat produced by one process to fuel another.

co′gent (kō'jənt) *adj.* convincing; forcible. —**co′gen·cy,** *n.*

cog′i·tate″ (koj'ə-tāt″) *v.i.* & *t.* ponder; plan. —**cog″i·ta′tion,** *n.*

co′gnac (kon'yak) *n.* a Fr. brandy produced in the Cognac region.

cog′nate (kog'nāt) *adj.* related. —*n.* something related. —**cog·na′tion,** *n.* ❑ *native*

cog·ni′tion (kog-nish′ən) *n.* the process of acquiring a conscious awareness; perception; cognizance.

cog′ni·zance (kog'ni-zəns) *n.* **1,** awareness; notice. **2,** range of observation. —**cog′ni·zant,** *adj.*

cog·no′men (kog-nō′mən) *n.* **1,** a surname. **2,** among Romans, the third or family name. **3,** a nickname.

co″gno·scen′ti (kon″yə-shen′tē) *n.pl.* connoisseurs; those in the know.

cog′wheel″ *n.* a gearwheel.

co·hab′it (kō-hab'it) *v.i.* live together, esp. as husband and wife. —**co·hab″i·ta′-tion,** *n.*

co·here′ (kō-hir′) *v.i.* **1,** stick together. **2,** be logically consistent or connected. —**co·her′ence,** *n.* —**co·her′ent,** *adj.* ❑ *cohesive*

co·he′sion (kō-hē′zhən) *n.* a sticking together of like particles. —**co·he′sive** (-siv) *adj.*

---

cohesive, coherent
☞ Both words derive from *cohere,* to stick together, of Latin origin. *Cohesive* is most often used in the physical sense, *coherent* in the figurative, abstract sense.

---

co′hort (kō′hôrt) *n.* **1,** a band, esp. of warriors. **2,** (*Informal*) comrade.

co′host″ *n.* & *v.* host (as a program) jointly with another person.

coif (koif) *n.* **1,** a close-fitting peasant cap. **2,** a nun's hood-shaped cap. —*v.t.* provide with a headdress.

coif·feur′ (kwä-fēr′) *n.* a hairdresser.

coif·fure′ (kwä-fyûr′) *n.* a manner of arranging the hair; a headdress.

coign (koin) *n.* quoin.

coil (koil) *v.t.* & *i.* twist into spiral shape. —*n.* a length of coiled rope, wire, pipe, etc.

coin (koin) *n.* a piece of metal authorized for use as money. —*v.t.* **1,** make (metal) into money. **2,** make (money) by minting metal. **3,** invent, as a word. **4,** (*Informal*) gain (money) rapidly. —**coin′er,** *n.* a counterfeiter.

coin′age (koin'ij) *n.* **1,** the act or process of coining; money coined. **2,** currency. **3,** a thing invented.

co″in·cide′ (kō″in-sīd′) *v.i.* **1,** occupy the same space or time. **2,** correspond exactly. **3,** concur; agree.

co·in′ci·dence (kō-in′si-dəns) *n.* **1,** exact correspondence in space or time. **2,** a notable occurrence of events apparently accidental. —**co·in′ci·dent, co·in″ci·den′tal,** *adj.*

co·i′tus (kō′i-təs) *n.* sexual intercourse. Also, **co·i′tion** (kō-ish′ən).

coke (kōk) *n.* **1,** a fuel, the solid residue of coal baked but not burned. **2,** (*Slang*) cocaine. **3,** (*T.N.*) a brand of cola (def. 2): *Coca-Cola.*

co′la (kō′lə) *n.* **1,** kola. **2,** a carbonated soft drink flavored with an extract of the kola nut.

col′an·der (kol'ən-dər) *n.* a strainer used in cooking.

cold (kōld) *adj.* **1,** below the temperature comfortable to the body; chilling. **2,** lacking bodily heat. **3,** not heated. **4,** unresponsive; indifferent; lacking in enthusiasm. —*n.* **1,** a condition of low temperature. **2,** a sensation produced by lack of heat. **3,** an ailment affecting the mucous membranes of the nose and throat. —**cold′ness,** *n.* —**catch cold,** become sick with a cold. —**cold cream,** a cosmetic. —**cold duck,** a mixture of sparkling Burgundy and champagne. —**cold feet,** (*Informal*) lack or loss of courage. —**cold fusion,** nuclear fusion produced at low temperature. —**cold shoulder,** a rebuff; deliberate disregard. —**cold slaw,** (*Dial.*) coleslaw. —**cold sore,** a blister in the mouth. —**cold storage,** long-term storage. —**cold turkey,** (*Slang*) complete withdrawal from drugs, etc., as a cure for addiction. —**cold war,** a period of bitterly unfriendly diplomatic relations.

cold-′blood″**ed** (-blud″id) *adj.* **1,** deliberate; unsympathetic; cruel. **2,** pert. to fishes and reptiles. —**cold′blood″ed·ness,** *n.*

---

cole (kōl) *n.* a plant of the cabbage family; rape.

cole′slaw″ (kōl′slâ″) *n.* finely sliced cabbage.

col′ic (kol′ik) *n.* severe griping abdominal pains. —**col′ick·y,** *adj.*

col′i·se′um (kol″ə-sē′əm) *n.* a large public amphitheater.

co·li′tis (kō-lī′tis) *n.* inflammation of the colon.

col·lab′o·rate″ (kə-lab′ə-rāt″) *v.i.* **1,** work with another, esp. in writing. **2,** in wartime, cooperate with the enemy. —**col·lab″o·ra′tion,** *n.* —**col·lab″o·ra′tionist,** *n.* one who cooperates with the enemy. —**col·lab′o·ra″tor,** *n.* a joint author.

col·lage′ (kə-läzh′) *n.* (*Art*) a composition made of fragments of different materials stuck together.

col·lapse′ (kə-laps′) *v.i. & t.* **1,** break, fall in, or give way. **2,** fail. **3,** break down physically. **4,** fold up intentionally, as an umbrella. —*n.* a sudden failure or falling in. —**col·laps′i·ble,** *adj.*

col′lar (kol′ər) *n.* **1,** a band or harness worn around the neck. **2,** (*Slang*) an arrest. —*v.t.* **1,** put a collar on. **2,** grasp by the collar. **3,** (*Slang*) seize; apprehend; arrest.

col′lar·bone″ *n.* a bone connecting the breastbone with the shoulder blade; the clavicle.

col′lard (kol′ərd) *n.* a kind of kale.

col·late′ (kə-lāt′) *v.t.* **1,** compare in detail. **2,** put (pages, etc.) in proper order.

col·lat′er·al (kə-lat′ər-əl) *adj.* **1,** attendant on, but subordinate to, the main issue. **2,** side by side; parallel. **3,** descended from the same ancestor, but in a different line. —*n.* something given as additional security for a loan.

col·la′tion (ko-lā′shən) *n.* **1,** act of collating. **2,** a light meal.

col′league (kol′ēg) *n.* a professional associate.

---

colleague, college
↔ Both words derive from Latin *collega,* a chosen coworker, through *collegium,* fellowship.

---

col·lect′ (kə-lekt′) *v.t.* **1,** gather together. **2,** receive payment of. **3,** get (contributions, etc.) from others. **4,** acquire as a hobby. **5,** regain command of (oneself). —*v.i.* assemble; accumulate. —*n.* (kol′ekt) a short prayer. —**col·lect′i·ble** (-i-bəl) *n. & adj.* (pert. to) an item worth

collecting. —**col·lec′tion,** *n.* —**col·lec′tor,** *n.*

col·lec′tive (kə-lek′tiv) *adj.* **1,** combined. **2,** belonging to, or exercised by, an aggregate of persons. **3,** treating a number of objects as one unit, as *a collective noun.* —*n.* a collective enterprise. —**col·lec′tiv·ism,** *n.* the socialistic principle of state ownership. —**col·lec′tiv·ize,** *v.i. & t.* —**collective bargaining,** the process of fixing wages, hours, and other conditions for work for all employees by negotiation between their chosen representatives and the employer.

col·leen′ (ko-lēn′) *n.* girl.

col′lege (kol′ij) *n.* **1,** an institution of higher learning. **2,** one of the separate schools of a university. **3,** a body of persons having certain powers and rights.

col·le′gial (kə-lē′jəl) *adj.* **1,** collegiate. **2,** pert. to the relationship between colleagues.

col·le′gi·an (kə-lē′jė-ən) *n.* a college student.

col·le′gi·ate (kə-lē′jit) *adj.* **1,** pert. to a college or college customs. **2,** pert. to a church allied with others.

col·lide′ (kə-līd′) *v.i.* come into violent contact; conflict.

---

collision, crash
☛ The distinction is sometimes made between the *collision* between two *moving* objects and the *crash* of one object into another, which may be stationary.

---

col′lie (kol′ė) *n.* a Scot. sheep dog.

col′lier (kol′yər) *n.* **1,** a coal miner. **2,** a vessel for shipping coal. —**col′lier·y,** *n.* a coal mine.

col·lin′e·ar (kə-lin′ė-ər) *adj.* lying in the same straight line.

col′lins (kol′inz) *n.* a tall cocktail of liquor, lemon juice, sugar, and carbonated water.

col·li′sion (kə-lizh′ən) *n.* act or result of colliding; clash.

col′lo·cate″ (kol′ə-kāt″) *v.t.* place side by side; arrange in order. —**col″lo·ca′tion,** *n.*

col·lo′di·on (kə-lō′dė-ən) *n.* a cellulose solution used as a protective coating.

col′loid (kol′oid) *n.* (*Chem.*) a substance that, when dispersed in another medium, forms particles larger than molecules but smaller than particles of suspension.

col·lo′qui·al (kə-lō′kwė-əl) *adj.* belonging to ordinary, everyday speech. —**col·lo′qui·al·ism,** *n.* ❑ *argot*

---

fat, fāte, fär, fāre, fâll, åsk; met, hē, hėr, maybè; pin, pīne; not, nōte, ôr, tool

col·lo·qui·um (kə-lō′kwė-əm) *n.* a conference; discussion.

col′lo·quy (kol′ə-kwė) *n.* **1,** a conversation. **2,** a discussion; conference.

col·lude′ (kə-lood′) *v.i.* conspire. —**col·lu′sion** (-loo′zhən) *n.* —**col·lu′sive** (-siv) *adj.*

col·lyr′i·um (kə-lir′ė-əm) *n.* [*pl.* **-a** (-ə)] an eyewash.

co·logne′ (kə-lōn′) *n.* a fragrant toilet water.

co′lon (kō′lən) *n,* **1,** the large intestine. **2,** a mark (:) of punctuation, introducing an example or conclusion.

> **colon**
> (*Gram.*) This punctuation mark is often used incorrectly. Its principal use is to introduce a list or a phrase; the first word of the phrase so introduced is not capitalized unless it is a complete sentence. It should not be used between a preposition or a verb and its object.

colo′nel (kẽr′nəl) *n.* a military officer ranking between lieutenant colonel and brigadier general. —**colo′nel·cy** (-sė) *n.*

co·lo′ni·al (kə-lō′nė-əl) *adj.* being or pert. to a colony. —*n.* a native of a colony. —**co·lo′ni·al·ism,** *n.*

col′on·nade″ (kol′ə-nād″) *n.* a series of columns.

col′o·ny (kol′ə-nė) *n.* **1,** a body of people who settle in a new country but remain subject to the mother country; the place of settlement. **2,** people of one nationality or occupation living close together. —**col′o·nist,** *n.* —**col′o·nize″** (-nīz″) *v.t. & i.*

col′o·phon″ (kol′ə-fon″) *n.* a publisher's emblem.

col′or (kul′ər) *n.* **1,** any of the hues of the rainbow; also, any tint or shade made by mixing these hues. **2,** complexion. **3,** a pigment. **4,** outward appearance; general characteristics. **5,** (*pl.*) a flag. **6,** (*pl.*) a symbolic colored ribbon or ornament; the clothes of a jockey. **7,** (*Informal*) commentary in a sports broadcast. **8,** a skin complexion other than white: *a person of color.* **9,** (*Physics*) a property of quarks. —*v.t.* **1,** dye. **2,** misrepresent. —*v.i.* blush. Also, **col′our.** —**col″or·a′tion,** *n.* —**col′or·ant,** *n.* —**col′or·ize″,** *v.t.* add color to, esp. a black-and-white film. —**color line,** systematic segregation by races.

col″o·ra·tu·ra (kul″ə-rə-tûr′ə) *n.* **1,** florid passages in vocal music. **2,** a singer of coloratura, esp. a soprano of high range.

col′or-blind″ *adj.* unable to distinguish different colors normally.

col′or·cast″ *n.* a television broadcast in color. —*v.i. & t.* to broadcast in color.

col′or-code″ *v.t.* color (a wire, etc.) for purposes of identification.

col′ored (-ərd) *adj.* **1,** having color. **2,** belonging to a nonwhite race, esp. the Negro race. **3,** biased; deceptive. ❑ *African-American*

col′or·fast″ *adj.* having color that will not fade, wash out, etc.

col′or·ful (-fəl) *adj.* **1,** full of color. **2,** picturesque; dramatic.

col′or·ing *n.* **1,** complexion; hue. **2,** dye.

col′or·less *adj.* **1,** without color. **2,** lacking interest.

co·los′sal (kə-los′əl) *adj.* huge; gigantic.

co·los′sus (kə-los′əs) *n.* a gigantic statue; any great thing or person.

co·los′to·my (kə-los′tə-mė) *n.* a surgical operation to form an artificial opening to the colon.

co·los′trum (kə-los′trəm) *n.* milk secreted for several days before and after childbirth.

col′por″teur (kol′pôr″tər) *n.* a peddler of books, esp. religious books.

colt (kōlt) *n.* **1,** a young male horse. **2,** (*cap.*) (*T.N.*) a brand of revolver. —**colt′ish,** *adj.*

col′um·bine″ (kol′əm-bīn″) *n.* a plant having spurred flowers.

co·lum′bi·um (kə-lum′bė-əm) *n.* niobium.

col′umn (kol′əm) *n.* **1,** an upright pillar supporting some part of a building. **2,** anything resembling a pillar in use, position, or appearance. **3,** a vertical row of figures or type. **4,** a regular department in a newspaper. **5,** a formation or line of soldiers or ships. —**co·lum′nar** (kə-lum′nər) *adj.*

col′um·nist (kol′əm-nist) *n.* the writer of a regular newspaper feature.

com- (kom) *pref.* with; jointly; entirely.

co′ma (kō′mə) *n.* **1,** a state of prolonged stupor, caused by injury, disease, or poison. **2,** the head of a comet.

com′a·tose″ (kom′ə-tōs″) *adj.* **1,** in a coma. **2,** lethargic.

comb (kōm) *n.* **1,** a toothed instrument for arranging the hair, currying horses, carding wool or fibers, etc. **2,** a rooster's crest. **3,** reticulated cells, as a honeycomb. —*v.t.* **1,** dress (hair); card (wool, etc.). **2,** search thoroughly.

com′bat (kom′bat) *n.* a fight; a battle. —*v.t. & i* (kəm-bat′) fight against; oppose. —**com′bat·ant** (-bə-tənt) *n. & adj.* —**com·bat′ive** (-bat′iv) *adj.*

com″bi·na′tion (kom″bə-nā′shən) *n.* **1,**

a coming together so as to form a group, sum, product, etc.; the group, etc. so formed. **2,** a one-piece undergarment. **3,** the series of numbers which when dialed will open a keyless lock.

com·bine' (kəm-bīn') *v.t. & i.* join; unite. —*n.* (kom'bīn") **1,** a harvesting machine. **2,** (*Informal*) a union of important persons, parties, or corporations. —**com·bin"a·to'ri·al** (kəm-bī"nə-tôr'ē-əl) *adj.*

com'bo (kom'bō) *n.* (*Slang*) combination; esp. a small jazz or dance band.

com·bus'tion (kəm-bus'chən) *n.* the act or process of burning. —**com·bus'ti·ble,** *adj. & n.*

come (kum) *v.i.* [**came** (kām), **come, com'ing**] **1,** move toward; approach. **2,** arrive, in space, time, or sequence. **3,** appear as the result of something; be derived from. **4,** become. **5,** happen; occur. **6,** extend to a given point. **7,** be attained or acquired. —**come across, 1,** meet. **2,** deliver. —**come around, 1,** recover. **2,** submit. —**come off,** succeed; occur. —**come over,** happen to. —**come through, 1,** survive. **2,** produce as expected. —**come to,** regain consciousness.

come'back" *n.* (*Informal*) **1,** a recovery of lost position. **2,** a retort.

co·me'di·an (kə-mē'dē-ən) *n.* an actor or writer of comedy.

co·me"di·enne' (-en') *n.* a female comedian.

com'e·do" (kom'ə-dō") *n.* a blackhead.

come'down" *n.* a humiliating experience.

com'e·dy (kom'ə-dē) *n.* **1,** a light, amusing drama ending happily. **2,** the comic element in anything. **3,** any comic incident.

> **comedy**
> ↔ From a combination of Greek *kōmos,* merrymaking, and *aoidos,* singer.

come'ly (kum'lē) *adj.* good-looking. —**come'li·ness,** *n.*

come-'on" *n.* (*Slang*) a lure; gimmick.

com'er (kum'ər) *n.* (*Informal*) one likely to be successful.

co·mes'ti·ble (kə-mes'tə-bəl) *n. & adj.* edible.

com'et (kom'it) *n.* a moving celestial body with a luminous tail.

come-up'pance (-up'əns) *n.* (*Slang*) a humiliating or humbling experience.

com'fit (kum'fit) *n.* a bonbon.

com'fort (kum'fərt) *v.t.* console. —*n.* **1,** solace; consolation. **2,** one who brings solace. **3,** the feeling of consolation. **4,** a

state or feeling of well-being and content. **5,** (*pl.*) things that contribute to such a state. —**comforter,** a bed covering. —**comfort station,** rest room.

com'fort·a·ble (kum'fərt-ə-bəl) *adj.* **1,** affording ease. **2,** free from pain or distress. **3,** (*Informal*) sufficient.

com'fort·er *n.* **1,** a bed covering. **2,** a scarf. **3,** one who comforts. **4,** (*cap.*) the Holy Spirit.

com'fy (kum'fē) *adj.* (*Informal*) comfortable.

com'ic (kom'ik) *adj.* **1,** pert. to comedy. **2,** comical; funny. —*n.* **1,** a comedian. **2,** (*pl.*) comic pictures, esp. in a newspaper; funny papers. **3,** [also, **comic book**] a magazine presenting stories in cartoon style. —**com'i·cal,** *adj.* droll; funny; exciting mirth. —**comic strip,** a series of drawings in cartoon style, developing a narrative.

com'i·ty (kom'ə-tē) *n.* courtesy, esp. between nations.

com'ma (kom'ə) *n.* **1,** a punctuation mark (,) indicating a brief or minor pause. **2,** a caesura.

> **comma**
> (*Gram.*) Misuse of the comma can be best avoided if one remembers that the comma is the weakest of the separators—the period, semicolon, and colon are stronger. The comma should not be used to separate independent clauses; use a semicolon or period. It should not be used between a subject and its predicate. Do not use a comma after the last member of a series. And in general, do not use a comma unless it is needed for clarity.

com·mand' (kə-mánd') *v.t. & i.* **1,** order or require with authority. **2,** exercise supreme power (over). **3,** overlook, as from a height. —*n.* **1,** an order. **2,** authority to order. **3,** power to control; mastery; complete knowledge or skill. **4,** a naval or military force under the control of a certain officer. —**command performance,** a (theatrical, musical, etc.) performance before a king, etc.

com"man·dant' (kom"ən-dänt') *n.* the officer in command of a military installation, fortress, etc.

com"man·deer' (kom"ən-dir') *v.t.* **1,** seize for military purposes. **2,** seize arbitrarily.

com·mand'er (kə-man'dər) *n.* **1,** a leader; chief officer. **2,** in the U.S. Navy, the rank next below captain.

com·mand'ing (kə-man'ding) *adj.* **1,** in

command. **2,** imperative; imperious. **3,** affording a panoramic view. **4,** impressive.

com·mand′ment (kə-mand′mənt) *n.* **1,** a command; a charge. **2,** one of the Ten Commandments.

com·man′do (kə-mȧn′dō) *n.* [*pl.* **-dos**] a member of a body of picked troops for raiding enemy territory.

com·me′di·a dell′ar′te (kŏm·mä′dē-ä del-lär′tä) comedy of skill; a 16th-18th-c. improvisational theater.

com·mem′o·rate″ (kə-mem′ə-rāt″) *v.t.* **1,** honor the memory of in a formal manner. **2,** serve as a memento of. —**com·mem″o·ra′tion,** *n.* —**com·mem′o·ra″tive,** *adj.*

com·mence′ (kə-mens′) *v.t.* & *i.* begin.

com·mence′ment (-mənt) *n.* **1,** a beginning; **2,** the graduation exercises of a school or college.

com·mend′ (kə-mend′) *v.t.* **1,** praise. **2,** recommend. **3,** entrust or give in charge. —**com·mend′a·ble,** *adj.* —**com·mend′a·to·ry,** *adj.*

com″men·da′tion (kom″ən-dā′shən) *n.* a citation of praise.

com·men′su·ra·ble (kə-men′shə-rə-bəl) *adj.* comparable in measure; proportionate.

com·men′su·rate (kə-men′shə-rət) *adj.* **1,** of equal size. **2,** corresponding in amount, degree, or size; comparable. **3,** adequate.

com′ment (kom′ent) *n.* **1,** a remark or observation, esp. a note explaining or criticizing a book. **2,** talk; gossip. —*v.i.* make remarks.

com′men·tar″y (kom′ən-tār″ē) *n.* an explanatory discourse.

com′men·ta″tor (kom′ən-tā″tər) *n.* one who reports and comments on current events. —**com′men·tate″,** *v.i.*

com′merce (kom′ērs) *n.* **1,** trade on a large scale, esp. between countries; business. **2,** any intercourse.

com·mer′cial (kə-mēr′shəl) *adj.* **1,** pert. to, or engaged in, or accruing from, trade. **2,** suitable or designed for sale. —*n.* the advertising material on a radio or television program. —**com·mer′cial·ism** (-iz-əm) *n.* principles and practices of commerce; mercenary spirit. —**com·mer′cial·ize″** (-īz″) *v.t.* exploit; turn to account. —**com·mer″cial·ese′** (-ēz′) *n.* the jargon of business and commerce. —**commercial traveler,** a traveling salesman.

com·min′gle (kə-ming′gəl) *v.t.* & *i.* mingle together; blend.

com″mi·nute′ (kom″i-nūt′) *v.t.* pulverize. —**com″mi·nu′tion,** *n.*

com·mis′er·ate″ (kə-miz′ə-rāt″) *v.t.* pity; condole with. —**com·mis″er·a′tion,** *n.*

com″mis·sar′ (kom″ə-sär′) *n.* the head of a government department in the former U.S.S.R. —**com″mis·sar′i·at** (-sär′ē-ət) *n.* a department of a military or (in the former U.S.S.R.) government organization.

com″mis·sar″y (kom′ə-sär″ē) *n.* **1,** a store supplying food and supplies, as in a camp. **2,** a deputy.

com·mis′sion (kə-mish′ən) *n.* **1,** the act of doing or perpetrating. **2,** a warrant to inquire and report. **3,** a body of persons entrusted with special duties. **4,** a matter entrusted to another; assignment. **5,** authority to act as agent; also, the fee paid. **6,** a document conferring naval or military rank. **7,** an order to make or perform a work of art; the fee accompanying such an order. —*v.t.* **1,** delegate; appoint. **2,** confer rank or authority on. **3,** equip (a ship) for active service. **4,** order (as a work of art) to be made or performed.

com·mis′sion·er *n.* **1,** the head of a commission or of one of certain governmental departments. **2,** an agent.

com·mit′ (kə-mit′) *v.t.* [**com·mit′ted, -ting**] **1,** entrust to another's care. **2,** consign to custody. **3,** perpetrate (a sin, crime, etc.). **4,** refer to a committee, as a bill. **5,** involve in risk. **6,** bind (oneself); pledge. **7,** authorize the confinement of (a person) in a mental institution.

com·mit′ment (-mənt) *n.* **1,** act of committing. **2,** a pledge; something undertaken. Also, **com·mit′tal** (-əl) *n.*

com·mit′tee (kə-mit′ē) *n.* a body of persons appointed for specific duties. —**com·mit′tee·man** (-mən) · [*pl.* **-men**], **com·mit′tee·wom″an,** *n.* **1,** committee member. **2,** a ward or precinct leader.

com·mode′ (kə-mōd′) *n.* a small bedside cupboard.

com·mo′di·ous (kə-mō′dē-əs) *adj.* roomy and spacious. —**com·mo′dious·ness,** *n.*

com·mod′i·ty (kə-mod′ə-tē) *n.* **1,** an article of commerce. **2,** a useful thing.

com′mo·dore″ (kom′ə-dôr″) *n.* the senior or commanding officer of more than one ship or yacht; in the U.S. Navy, a rank next above captain.

com′mon (kom′ən) *adj.* **1,** shared by, or equally true of, two or more; joint; united. **2,** public; general. **3,** familiar; usual. **4,** not notable; ordinary. **5,** vulgar; coarse. —*n.* **1,** a tract of public land; a park. **2,** (*pl.*) a college dining hall; its food. **3,** (*pl.*) (*cap.*) the elective house of Parliament. **—common carrier,** a company that transports for hire. **—common law,** the system of law based on custom and court decisions, not statutes. **—Common Market,** European Economic Community. **—common noun,** a noun designating any of a class. **—common sense,** good judgment in simple matters. **—common stock,** shares of ownership of a company, having voting rights but no fixed dividend.

com″mon·al′i·ty (kom″ən-al′ə-tė) *n.* **1,** shared features. **2,** commonalty (def. 1).

com′mon·al·ty (kom′ən-əl-tė) *n.* **1,** the common people. **2,** the members of a corporation.

com′mon·er (kom′ən-ər) *n.* a person without noble rank.

com′mon·place″ *adj.* **1,** ordinary; not unusual or original. **2,** hackneyed; trite.

> **commonplace**
> ↔ Translation of Latin *locus communis*, translation in turn of Greek *koinos topos.*

com′mon·wealth″ *n.* a state or union of states.

com·mo′tion (kə-mō′shən) *n.* **1,** violent agitation. **2,** disorder; public unrest.

com·mu′nal (kə-myoo′nəl; kom′yoo-nəl) *adj.* pert. to, or owned by, a community; public.

com·mune′ (kə-mūn′) *v.i.* **1,** interchange thoughts and feelings; converse. **2,** take Communion. **—***n.* (kom′ūn) **1,** a small community having shared possessions, income, etc. **2,** an administrative unit in some countries.

com·mu′ni·cant (-kənt) *n.* one who communicates; one who takes communion.

com·mu″ni·cate″ (kə-mū′ni-kāt″) *v.t.* convey, impart. **—***v.i.* **1,** converse; get in touch by letter, etc. **2,** be connected, as rooms. **—com·mu′ni·ca·ble,** *adj.*

com·mu″ni·ca′tion (-kā′shən) *n.* **1,** act of communicating. **2,** a message. **3,** a means or way of communicating; passage.

com·mu′ni·ca·tive (-kə-tiv) *adj.* informative; talkative.

com·mun′ion (kə-mūn′yən) *n.* **1,** a sharing; fellowship. **2,** (*cap.*) celebration of the Lord's Supper.

com·mu″ni·qué′ (kə-mū″nə-kā′) *n.* an official communication or bulletin.

com′mu·nism (kom′yə-niz-əm) *n.* a so-

cial theory that the common people should own all property and means of production. **—com′mu·nize″** (-nīz″) *v.t.*

com′mu·nist (kom′yə-nist) *adj.* pert. to a political party or government advocating communism, esp. (*cap.*) in the former U.S.S.R. **—***n.* an advocate of such theory, or member of such government or such party.

com·mu′ni·ty (kə-mū′nə-tė) *n.* **1,** all persons living in a particular locality. **2,** a group having interests or religion in common. **3,** joint sharing. **—community antenna television,** CATV.

com′mu·tate″ (kom′yû-tāt″) *v.t.* change the direction of (an electric current). **—com′mu·ta″tor,** *n.*

com·mute′ (kə-mūt′) *v.t.* substitute another thing for, esp. to reduce the severity of a penalty, obligation, etc. **—***v.i.* travel daily between a city and suburb. **—com″mu·ta′tion,** *n.* **—com·mut′er,** *n.*

comp (komp) *n.* (*Informal*) a complimentary ticket, as for a concert.

com′pact (kom′pakt) *adj.* **1,** closely packed together; solid; dense. **2,** concise. **—***n.* **1,** a small case containing powder and rouge. **2,** an agreement; treaty. **3,** a small car: *compact car.* **—***v.t.* (kəm-pakt′) **1,** pack together closely; condense. **2,** form; compound. **—com·pact′or,** *n.* **—compact disc,** a small optical disc encoded (with data, music, etc.) to be read by means of a laser beam.

com·pa′dre (kəm-pä′drā) *n.* (*Sp.*) friend; companion.

com·pan′ion (kəm-pan′yən) *n.* **1,** an associate; comrade. **2,** a paid attendant. **3,** a mate; one of a pair of matched objects. **—com·pan′ion·a·ble,** *adj.* agreeable; friendly. **—com·pan′ion·ate** (-ət) *adj.* of or like a companion.

com·pan′ion·ship *n.* friendship.

com·pan′ion·way″ *n.* a stair from deck to cabins on a ship.

com′pa·ny (kum′pə-nė) *n.* **1,** a group of persons assembled, working, or associating together. **2,** someone to talk or commune with. **3,** guests. **4,** a business firm. **5,** a military unit; a ship's crew. **—part company,** separate. ❑ *firm*

com′pa·ra·ble (kom′pə-rə-bəl) *adj.* capable of being, or worthy to be, compared.

com·par′a·tive (kəm-par′ə-tiv) *adj.* **1,** relative; based on comparison. **2,** (*Gram.*) expressing a higher degree, as when modified by *more.* **—***n.* (*Gram.*) a comparative form.

com·pare′ (kəm-pār′) *v.t.* **1,** represent as

similar. **2,** note the resemblance and differences of. **3,** (*Gram.*) give the degrees of comparison of. —*v.i.* admit of comparison. —*n.* comparison.

---

compare, contrast
☞ Both words mean to observe two or more things to note how they relate. One *compares* to note similarities and differences; one *contrasts* only to note the differences.

---

com·par'i·son (kəm-par'i-sən) *n.* **1,** act of comparing. **2,** an illustration; simile. **3,** a comparable state or condition. **4,** (*Gram.*) the inflection of an adjective or adverb to show difference in degree.

com·part'ment (kəm-pärt'mənt) *n.* a chamber, cell, or space partitioned off. —*v.t.* divide into compartments. —**com·part"ment'al·ize** (-men'təl-īz) *v.t.*

com'pass (kum'pəs) *n.* **1,** extent within limits; boundary; range. **2,** an instrument showing the magnetic north. **3,** (often *pl.*) an instrument with two legs pivoted at one end, for describing circles, etc. —*v.t.* **1,** encompass; encircle. **2,** accomplish.

com·pas'sion (kəm-pash'ən) *n.* sympathy, esp. pity. —**com·pas'sion·ate,** *adj.* sympathetic; merciful.

com·pat'i·ble (kəm-pat'ə-bəl) *adj.* **1,** consistent. **2,** congenial; harmonious. —**com·pat"i·bil'i·ty,** *n.*

com·pa'tri·ot (kəm-pā'trē-ət) *n.* **1,** a fellow countryman. **2,** (*Informal*) colleague. —*adj.* of the same country.

com'peer (kom'pir) *n.* an associate, equal, or fellow.

com·pel' (kəm-pel') *v.t.* [**-pelled', -pel'-ling**] coerce; oblige.

com·pen'di·um (kəm-pen'dē-əm) *n.* a summary. —**com·pen'di·ous,** *adj.* concise.

com"pen·sate" (kom'pən-sāt") *v.t. & i.* **1,** make up (for); offset. **2,** pay (for); recompense. —**com·pen'sa·to·ry,** *adj.*

com"pen·sa'tion (kom"pən-sā'shən) *n.* **1,** act or result of compensating; offset; pay. **2,** regular payments, in lieu of wages, to a worker injured on the job: *workmen's compensation.*

com·pete' (kəm-pēt') *v.i.* contend with another; vie.

com'pe·tence (kom'pə-təns) *n.* **1,** fitness; adequacy. **2,** sufficient means for living comfortably.

com'pe·tent (-tənt) *adj.* **1,** capable; adequate. **2,** authorized.

com"pe·ti'tion (kom"pə-tish'ən) *n.* **1,** rivalry; the struggle for trade, preeminence,

etc. **2,** a match between contestants. —**com·pet'i·tive** (kəm-pet'ə-tiv) *adj.*

com·pet'i·tor (kəm-pet'i-tər) *n.* **1,** one who competes. **2,** opponent; rival.

com·pile' (kəm-pīl') *v.t.* collect from various sources, esp. literary material for a book. —**com"pi·la'tion** (kom"pə-lā'shən) *n.* —**com·pil'er,** *n.* a computer program that translates a high-level language into machine language.

com·pla'cen·cy (kəm-plā'sən-sē) *n.* self-satisfaction. Also, **com·pla'cence.**

com·pla'cent (kəm-plā'sənt) *adj.* **1,** self-satisfied. **2,** complaisant.

---

complacent, complaisant
☞ It is still best to retain the distinction between *complacent*, self-satisfied, and *complaisant*, agreeable.

---

com·plain' (kəm-plān') *v.i.* **1,** express pain, resentment, etc.; find fault. **2,** make a formal charge. —**com·plain'ant,** *n.* plaintiff.

com·plaint' (kəm-plānt') *n.* **1,** an expression of discontent, pain, etc. **2,** a bodily ailment. **3,** (*Law*) a statement of the cause of action in a civil suit.

com·plai'sant (kəm-plā'zənt) *adj.* agreeable; compliant. —**com·plai'sance,** *n.* ❑ *complacent*

com·pleat' (kəm-plēt') *adj.* (*Archaic*) complete.

com·plect'ed (kəm-plek'tid) *adj.* complexioned.

com'ple·ment (kom'plə-mənt) *n.* **1,** that which fills up or completes. **2,** one of two parts needed to form a whole. **3,** the officers and crew of a ship. **4,** (*Gram.*) a word that completes the predicate and is identified with the subject. —*v.t.* (-ment") fill out; complete.

com"ple·men'ta·ry (kom"plə-men'tə-rē) *adj.* **1,** completing. **2,** complementing each other. —**complementary colors,** pairs of colors that produce gray when mixed.

---

complementary, complimentary
☞ Do not confuse *complementary*, meaning serving to complete, and *complimentary*, meaning serving to convey a compliment. Originally, however, the words come from the same source, Latin *complementum.*

---

com·plete' (kəm-plēt') *adj.* **1,** having all its parts; whole. **2,** absolute; thorough. **3,** concluded. —*v.t.* supply what is lacking to. **2,** finish. —**com·ple'tion** (-plē'shən) *n.*

com·plex' (kəm-pleks') *adj.* **1,** composed

of many parts. **2,** involved; complicated; perplexing. —*n.* (kom'pleks) **1,** a complex condition or situation. **2,** an intricate assemblage of related buildings. **3,** (*Psych.*) a group of emotional experiences, often having an unsuspected effect. **4,** (*Informal*) an obsession. —**complex number,** a number expressed as the sum of a real number and an imaginary number.

com·plex′ion (kəm-plek′shən) *n.* **1,** the hue or texture of the skin, esp. of the face. **2,** general appearance; aspect. —**com·plex′-ioned** (-shənd) *adj.* having a specified complexion.

com·plex′i·ty (kom-plek′sə-tè) *n.* intricacy.

com·pli′ant (kəm-plī′ənt) *adj.* complying; yielding to the wishes of others. —**com·pli′ance,** *n.*

com′pli·cate″ (kom′plə-kāt″) *v.t.* **1,** render intricate or involved. **2,** aggravate. —**com″pli·ca′tion,** *n.*

com′pli·cat″ed *adj.* complex; (*Informal*) confusing.

com·plic′i·ty (kəm-plis′ə-tè) *n.* the state of being an accomplice.

com′pli·ment (kom′plə-mənt) *n.* **1,** an expression of praise or admiration. **2,** (*pl.*) formal greetings. —*v.t.* (-ment″) **1,** utter a compliment to. **2,** present with a gift or other favor. **3,** congratulate.

com″pli·men′ta·ry (kom″plə-men′tə-rè) *adj.* **1,** conveying or given as a compliment. **2,** given away free. ❑ *complementary*

com′plin (kom′plin) *n.* the last of the seven canonical hours; the service for it. Also, **com′pline.**

com·plot′ (kəm-plot′) *v.* plot together; conspire. —*n.* (kom′plot″) a conspiracy.

com·ply′ (kəm-plī′) *v.i.* acquiesce in another's wish, command, etc.

com·po′nent (kəm-pō′nənt) *adj.* forming a part of. —*n.* a constituent part.

com·port′ (kəm-pôrt′) *v.t.* behave (oneself). —*v.i.* (with *with*) accord; fit, suit. —**com·port′ment,** *n.* behavior.

---

comportment, deportment
☛ Both words refer to behavior and are generally interchangeable. However, *deportment* is more often used to refer to behavior in school.

---

com·pose′ (kəm-pōz′) *v.t.* **1,** form by putting parts together. **2,** be the parts of. **3,** construct in some creative way, esp. original music. **4,** calm; quiet. **5,** settle (differences); adjust. **6,** set (type). —*v.i.* write music. —**com·posed′,** *adj.* calm; serene.

—com·pos′er, *n.* one who composes music. ❑ *comprise*

com·pos′ite (kəm-pos′it) *adj. & n.* **1,** made up of distinct parts. **2,** (*Bot.*) having small flowers arranged compactly.

com″po·si′tion (kom″pə-zish′ən) *n.* act or result of composing; a piece of music, essay, etc.; a compound; structure.

com·pos′i·tor (kəm-poz′ə-tər) *n.* one who sets type.

com′post (kom′pōst) *n.* a mixture of decaying leaves, etc., used as fertilizer.

com·po′sure (kəm-pō′zhər) *n.* serenity; calmness.

com′pote (kom′pōt) *n.* **1,** stewed fruit. **2,** a small dish.

com·pound′ (kəm-pownd′) *v.t.* **1,** combine (two or more ingredients). **2,** form by mixing or joining. **3,** fail to prosecute (a criminal) for a consideration. —*adj.* (kom′pownd) composed of two or more elements. —*n.* (kom′pownd) **1,** something compound. **2,** an enclosure for houses; a reserved area, or area of confinement (as for prisoners, foreigners, etc.). —**compound fracture,** an open wound as well as a broken bone. —**compound interest,** interest paid on accrued interest, as well as on the capital.

com″pre·hend′ (kom″prè-hend′) *v.t.* **1,** include within a certain extent of time or space. **2,** understand. ❑ *comprise*

com″pre·hen′si·ble (kom″prè-hen′sə-bəl) *adj.* understandable; intelligible. —**com″pre·hen′si·bil′i·ty,** *n.*

com″pre·hen′sion (kom″prè-hen′shən) *n.* **1,** act or result of comprehending; power to comprehend. **2,** inclusion; perception.

com″pre·hen′sive (kom″prè-hen′siv) *adj.* of large scope; inclusive. —**com″pre·hen′sive·ness,** *n.*

com·press′ (kəm-pres′) *v.t.* reduce the bulk of by applied pressure; pack tightly together; condense. —*n.* (kom′pres) a soft pad used to apply moisture, pressure, etc. —**com·pres′sion** (-presh′ən) *n.* —**com·pres′sor** (-pres′ər) *n.* a device for compressing, esp. gas or air.

com·prise′ (kəm-prīz′) *v.t.* **1,** include. **2,** consist of.

com′pro·mise″ (kom′prə-mīz″) *n.* **1,** the settlement of differences by mutual concessions. **2,** a middle course; something intermediate. —*v.t.* **1,** adjust by compromise. **2,** expose to suspicion or scandal. —*v.i.* make a compromise.

comp·trol′ler (kən-trōl′ər) *n.* a chief accounting officer. Also, **con·trol′ler.** —**comp·trol′ler·ship,** *n.*

---

comprise, comprehend, include, compose, consist of
☛ These words share the concept of containment. One entity may *comprise, consist of,* or be *composed of* a number of other smaller entities. It may *include* those entities, among others, or it may *comprehend* a number of entities. One may *compose* a larger entity of smaller entities. The common expression *is comprised of* is incorrect; one should say *is composed of, consists of* or *comprises.*

---

com·pul'sion (kəm-pul'shən) *n.* **1,** the act of compelling; coercion. **2,** impulse.

com·pul'sive (-siv) *adj.* (*Psych.*) pert. to or compelled by a force of which the subject is not conscious.

com·pul'so·ry (-sə-rė) *adj.* **1,** compelling. **2,** obligatory.

com·punc'tion (kəm-punk'shən) *n.* a slight regret or prick of conscience.

com·pute' (kəm-pūt') *v.t. & i.* calculate; reckon. —**com"pu·ta'tion,** *n.*

com·put'er (kəm-pū'tər) *n.* **1,** that which computes. **2,** a computing machine, esp. an automatic electronic machine.

com·put'er·ize" *v.t. & i.* use or provide with computers. —**com·put"er·i·za'tion,** *n.*

com'rade (kom'rad) *n.* **1,** a close friend. **2,** a fellow member. **3,** a title of address in some 'Communist countries. —**com'rade·ship,** *n.*

Com'sat" (kom'sat") *n.* (often *l.c.*) a communications satellite.

con (kon) *v.t.* **[conned, con'ning] 1,** pore over; learn. **2,** (*Slang*) swindle. **3,** direct the course (of a ship). —*n.* (*Slang*) a convict. —*adv.* against. —**con game,** (*Slang*) a confidence game. —**con artist,** (*Slang*) a swindler. —**con man,** (*Slang*) confidence man. —**conning tower,** the pilot house of a submarine.

con- *pref.* a form of **com-.**

con·cat'e·nate" (kon-kat'ə-nāt") *v.t.* link together. —**con·cat"e·na'tion,** *n.*

con·cave' (kon-kāv') *adj.* with an outline or surface curved like the inside of a circle or ball; curved inward. —**con·cav'i·ty** (kən-kav'ə-tė) *n.*

---

concave, convex
☛ It is easy to confuse these concepts. A *concave* surface is curved like the inside of a circle or ball; a *convex* surface is like the outside.

---

con·ceal' (kən-sēl') *v.t.* keep secret or hidden; secrete; hide. —**con·ceal'ment,** *n.*

con·cede' (kən-sēd') *v.t.* **1,** grant, as a right or privilege. **2,** admit as true. **3,** give up as lost (as an election). —*v.i.* yield; admit defeat. ☐ *acknowledge*

con·ceit' (kən-sēt') *n.* **1,** an exaggerated opinion of one's own ability, etc. **2,** a quaint or humorous fancy. —**con·ceit'ed,** *adj.* vain.

con·ceive' (kən-sēv') *v.t. & i.* **1,** form in the mind; **2,** believe; have a feeling. **3,** become pregnant (with young). —**con·ceiv'a·ble,** *adj.* believable.

con'cen·trate" (kon'sən-trāt") *v.t.* **1,** bring together at one point; focus. **2,** increase the strength of by removing foreign elements. —*v.i.* **1,** meet at a common center. **2,** employ all one's power or attention.

con"cen·tra'tion (kon"sən-trā'shən) *n.* **1,** act or result of concentrating; assembly; intensification. **2,** close attention or application, as in study. —**concentration camp,** a camp in which prisoners or refugees are confined.

con·cen'tric (kən-sen'trik) *adj.* having a common center. —**con·cen'tri·cal·ly,** *adv.*

con'cept (kon'sept) *n.* a mentally conceived image; an idea or thought. —**con·cep'tu·al,** *adj.* —**con·cep'tu·al·ize",** *v.t.*

con·cep'tion (kən-sep'shən) *n.* **1,** act or effect of conceiving; an idea; notion. **2,** fertilization; pregnancy. **3,** beginning.

con·cern' (kən-sėrn') *v.t.* **1,** relate to. **2,** (with *in* or *with*) interest or occupy. **3,** disturb; trouble. —*n.* **1,** a matter of interest. **2,** solicitude; anxiety. **3,** a business firm. —**con·cern'ing,** *prep.* relating to; about.

con'cert (kon'sėrt) *n.* **1,** agreement in a plan or design. **2,** a musical performance. **3,** musical harmony; unison. —*v.t.* (kən-sėrt') contrive or plan by agreement. —**con·cert'ed,** *adj.* in unison; harmonious. —**con'cert·ize** (-īz) *v.i.* give a concert or concerts. —**in concert,** in unison; together.

---

concert, recital
☛ Although the distinction is not made consistently in daily speech, a *concert* is a musical performance by a group (playing *in concert*), while a *recital* is a musical performance by one or two performers.

---

con"cer·ti'na (kon"sər-tē'nə) *n.* a small accordion, hexagonal in shape.

---

concertina
↔ Coined by English instrument-maker Charles Wheatstone, perhaps on model of *concertino.*

---

con″cer·ti′no (kon″chər-tē′nō) *n.* **1,** a short concerto. **2,** a group of solo instruments.

con′cert·mas″ter *n.* the leader of an orchestra (after the conductor), usu. the leader of the first violins.

con·cer′to (kən-cher′tō) *n.* [*pl.* **-tos** (-tōz), **-ti** (-tè)] a musical composition, usually for a solo instrument with accompaniment.

con·ces′sion (kən-sesh′ən) *n.* **1,** the act or effect of conceding; the thing or point conceded. **2,** a grant or lease by an authority to a business. **—con·ces″sion·aire′** (-ə-nâr′) *n.* the recipient of such a grant or lease.

conch (konk; konch) *n.* a sea mollusk; its large, spiral shell.

con·cierge′ (kon-syerzh′) *n.* (*Fr.*) a doorkeeper or janitor.

con·cil′i·ate″ (kən-sil′ē-āt″) *v.t.* overcome the hostility of; pacify. **—con·cil′i·a′-tion,** *n.* **—con·cil′i·a·to·ry** (-ə-tôr-ē) *adj.*

con·cise′ (kən-sīs′) *adj.* brief and compact; terse. **—con·cise′ness,** *n.*

con·ci′sion (kən-sizh′ən) *n.* **1,** conciseness. **2,** a cutting off; schism.

con′clave (kon′klāv) *n.* **1,** a private assembly. **2,** the meeting of the cardinals for election of a Pope.

con·clude′ (kən-klood′) *v.t.* **1,** bring to an end; finish; decide finally; determine. **2,** deduce; infer. **—v.i. 1,** come to an end. **2,** decide.

con·clu′sion (kən-kloo′zhən) *n.* **1,** the end. **2,** the final part or stage. **3,** a result; outcome. **4,** a proposition inferred logically from premises. **—con·clu′sive** (-siv) *adj.* decisive.

con·coct′ (kən-kokt′) *v.t.* **1,** combine and prepare, as in cooking. **2,** devise; contrive, as a plot. **—con·coc′tion,** *n.*

con·com′i·tant (kon-kom′ə-tənt) *adj.* attending; going together. **—n.** an accompanying thing or circumstance. **—con·com′i·tance, con·com′i·tan·cy,** *n.*

con′cord (kon′kôrd) *n.* **1,** harmony; unanimity. **2,** peace. **3,** an agreement; a treaty.

con·cord′ance (kən-kôr′dəns) *n.* **1,** agreement. **2,** an index of words, as of those in the Bible. **—con·cord′ant,** *adj.*

con·cor′dat (kon-kôr′dat) *n.* a treaty.

Con′corde (kon′kôrd) *n.* (*T.N.*) a supersonic passenger aircraft.

con′course (kon′kôrs) *n.* **1,** a throng; crowd. **2,** an open place, as a public square. **3,** a wide street or arcade.

con′crete (kon′krēt) *adj.* **1,** existing in material form; real, not abstract. **2,** specific, not general. **3,** consisting of concrete. **—n.** a building material made of sand, cement, etc. **—v.i.** harden. **—con·crete′ness,** *n.* **—con·cre′tion,** *n.* **—con′cre·tize″** (kon′krə-tīz″) *v.t.* render concrete or tangible. □ *cement*

con′cu·bine″ (kon′kū-bīn″) *n.* a woman cohabiting with a man but not married to him. **—con·cu′bi·nage** (kon-kū′bə-nij) *n.*

con·cu′pis·cence (kon-kū′pə-səns) *n.* sensual appetite or desire. **—con·cu′pis·cent,** *adj.*

con·cur′ (kən-kẽr′) *v.i.* [**-curred′, -cur′-ring**] **1,** happen together; coincide; exist side by side. **2,** agree in opinion. **3,** (with *in*) act jointly. **—con·cur′rence,** *n.* **—con·cur′rent,** *adj.*

con·cus′sion (kən-kush′ən) *n.* the shock occasioned by a collision or blow.

con·demn′ (kən-dem′) *v.t.* **1,** express disapprobation of; censure. **2,** find guilty; sentence to punishment. **3,** pronounce unfit for use. **4,** claim for public use. **—con″dem·na′tion,** *n.*

---

condemn, contemn
☞ Do not confuse *condemn,* to censure, with *contemn,* a much rarer word meaning to scorn.

---

con·dense′ (kən-dens′) *v.t. & i.* **1,** make more compact. **2,** express in fewer words. **3,** compress; reduce (gas, vapor) to a liquid or solid. **—con′dens·ate″** (kon′dən-sāt″) *n.* **—con″den·sa′tion,** *n.* **—condensed milk,** evaporated milk with sugar added.

con·dens′er (-sər) *n.* a device for liquefying vapors, concentrating light rays or electric current, etc.

con″de·scend′ (kon″di-send′) *v.i.* **1,** deal as an equal with one of inferior rank. **2,** waive ceremony or dignity; deign (to do something). **3,** deal patronizingly, as though conscious of superior rank. **—con″de·scen′sion,** *n.*

con″de·scend′ing *adj.* **1,** complaisant; not haughty. **2,** patronizing.

con·dign′ (kən-dīn′) *adj.* fitting; deserved.

con′di·ment (kon′də-mənt) *n.* something to give relish to food, as pepper.

con·di′tion (kən-dish′ən) *n.* **1,** a mode or state of being of a person or thing. **2,** social rank. **3,** state of health. **4,** a stipulation or provision; a prerequisite. **—v.t. 1,** limit by, or subject to, a condition. **2,** put into a certain condition. **3,** modify the behavior, attitude, etc., of (a person or animal). **—con·di′tion·al,** *adj.* provisional.

con′do (kon′dō) *n.* (*Informal*) condominium.

con·dole′ (kən-dōl′) *v.i.* express sympathy for grief or misfortune.

con·do′lence (-əns) *n.* expression of sympathy.

con′dom (kon′dəm) *n.* a contraceptive or prophylactic device worn by the male.

con″do·min′i·um (kon″də-min′ē-əm) *n.* **1,** joint sovereignty over a territory by two or more nations. **2,** a cooperative apartment building or development jointly owned by its tenants who also own their own dwellings.

con·done′ (kən-dōn′) *v.t.* forgive, overlook, extenuate, or justify (another's offense, shortcomings, etc.). **—con·done′ment, con″do·na′tion** (kon″də-nā′shən) *n.*

con′dor (kon′dər) *n.* a large So. Amer. vulture.

con·duce′ (kən-doos′) *v.i.* (with *to*) contribute to a result. **—con·du′cive** (-siv) *adj.*

con·duct′ (kən-dukt′) *v.t.* **1,** act as leader of; guide; escort. **2,** manage; carry on. **3,** behave (oneself). **4,** transmit; convey. *—v.i.* act as a conductor. *—n.* (kon′dukt) **1,** management. **2,** deportment. **3,** escort. **—con·duc′tion,** *n.* **—con·duc′tive,** *adj.*

con·duct′ance (kən-duk′təns) *n.* the ability of a substance to conduct electricity.

con″duc·tiv′i·ty (kon″duk-tiv′ə-tē) *n.* power of transmitting heat, electricity, etc.

con·duc′tor (kən-duk′tər) *n.* **1,** one who leads, guides, or manages; esp. the director of an orchestra or chorus. **2,** the person in charge of a train, trolley car, etc. **3,** a substance that transmits heat, electricity, etc.

con′duit (kon′dwit) *n.* a channel or tube that conducts fluids, electric wires, etc.

cone (kōn) *n.* **1,** a solid generated by a line passing through a fixed point and a given plane curve. **2,** anything resembling this figure. **3,** the fruit of a conifer, as pine, fir, etc.; any similar fruit.

Con″e·sto′ga wagon (kon″ə-stō′gə) a heavy covered wagon.

Conestoga wagon, stogy
↔ Both words are derived from *Conestoga*, PA.
---

con·fab′u·late″ (kən-fab′yə-lāt″) *v.i.* converse. **—con′fab,** *n. & v.i.* (*Informal*) a conversation.

con·fect′ (kən-fekt′) *v.t.* **1,** make from ingredients; construct. **2,** make into a confection.

con·fec′tion (kən-fek′shən) *n.* **1,** a sweet preparation, esp. candy. **2,** a frilly dress.

---
confection, confetti
↔ Both words come from Latin *conficere*, to make, prepare. *Confetti* comes more directly from Italian *confetto*, a small sweet thrown during carnivals; later these sweets were replaced with colored paper.
---

con·fec′tion·a·ry (-er-ē) *n.* **1,** candy. **2,** a place where candy is made. *—adj.* pert. to confection.

con·fec′tion·er (-ər) *n.* one who sells or makes candy. **—con·fec′tion·er·y** (-er-ē) *n.* a confectioner's shop or place of manufacture.

con·fed′er·a·cy (kən-fed′ə-rə-sē) *n.* **1,** a league; alliance. **2,** (*cap.,* with *the*) the 11 southern states that seceded from the U.S. in 1860-61.

con·fed′er·ate (kən-fed′ər-ət) *adj.* **1,** united in a league; party to a confederation. **2,** (*cap.*) pert. to the Confederacy. *—n.* **1,** a member of a confederation. **2,** an accomplice. *—v.t. & i.* (-rāt′) unite in a league. **—con·fed′er·a′tion,** *n.* a league.

con·fer′ (kən-fēr′) *v.t.* **[-ferred′, -fer′-ring]** (with *on*) bestow. *—v.i.* consult together. **—con″fer·ee′** (kon″fə-rē′) *n.*

con′fer·ence (kon′fər-əns) *n.* **1,** a meeting for consultation or discussion. **2,** a league, as of churches, athletic teams, etc.

con·fess′ (kən-fes′) *v.t.* **1,** admit (having done something discreditable); acknowledge (guilt or belief). **2,** (of a priest) hear the confession of. *—v.i.* admit a crime, fault, etc. **—con·fes′sed·ly** (-id-lē) *adj.* by confession. ❑ *acknowledge*

con·fes′sion (kən-fesh′ən) *n.* the act or a statement of confessing. **—con·fes′sion·al** (-əl) *n.* a booth where a priest hears confessions.

con·fes′sor (kən-fes′ər) *n.* a priest who hears confessions.

con·fet′ti (kən-fet′ē) *n.* bits of colored paper thrown about in merrymaking. ❑ *confection*

con″fi·dant′ (kon″fi-dänt′) *n.* one trusted with secrets. Also, **con″fi·dante′,** *n.* (*usu. fem.*).

---
confidant, confident
☞ Do not confuse *confidant,* a noun meaning a trusted friend in whom one confides, and *confident,* an adjective meaning secure, optimistic.
---

con·fide′ (kən-fīd′) *v.t.* **1,** entrust. **2,** reveal privately. *—v.i.* (with *in*) **1,** have trust. **2,** entrust a secret.

con′fi·dence (kon′fi-dəns) *n.* **1,** firm trust; reliance. **2,** self-assurance; boldness.

3, an assured state of mind. **4,** a state of trust and intimacy. **5,** a secret confided. **—confidence game,** a scheme to obtain money fraudulently. **—confidence man,** a swindler.

con'fi·dent (kon'fi-dənt) *adj.* **1,** firmly trustful; sure. **2,** bold; self-assured. **3,** optimistic. ❏ *confidant*

con"fi·den'tial (kon"fi-den'shəl) *adj.* **1,** secret; private. **2,** entrusted with private affairs. **3,** intimate. **—con"fi·den"ti·al'i·ty,** *n.*

con·fig"u·ra'tion (kən-fig"yə-rā'shən) *n.* **1,** form. **2,** placement.

con·fine' (kən-fīn') *v.t.* **1,** restrict within bounds; imprison. **2,** keep indoors, as by sickness, esp. by childbirth. **—n.** (kon'fīn) (*usu. pl.*) a boundary or border. **—con·fine'ment,** *n.*

con·firm' (kən-fẽrm') *v.t.* **1,** establish more firmly; strengthen. **2,** put past doubt; verify. **3,** make valid. **4,** admit to church membership. **—con"fir·ma'tion,** *n.* **—con·firm'a·to"ry,** *adj.*

con·firmed' (kən-fẽrmd') *adj.* **1,** settled. **2,** inveterate; chronic.

con'fis·cate" (kon'fis-kāt") *v.t.* **1,** appropriate, by way of penalty, to public use. **2,** take away by, or as if by, authority. **—con"fis·ca'tion,** *n.*

con"fla·gra'tion (kon"flə-grā'shən) *n.* a large-scale fire.

con·flict' (kən-flikt') *v.i.* clash; be contrary. **—n.** (kon'flikt) **1,** a combat. **2,** discord; antagonism. **—conflict of interest,** a situation in which the demands of one job adversely or illegally affect the demands of another.

con·flu·ence (kon'flū-əns) *n.* **1,** a flowing together as of streams; their place of meeting. **2,** the coming together of people; a crowd. Also, **con'flux** (-fluks). **—con'flu·ent,** *adj.*

con·form' (kən-fôrm') *v.t.* bring into harmony; adapt. **—v.i.** be in accord; comply.

con"for·ma'tion (kon"fôr-mā'shən) *n.* **1,** structure. **2,** adaptation.

con·form'ist *n.* one who conforms, esp. to the usages of the Church of England.

con·form'i·ty (-ə-tė) *n.* accordance; agreement.

con·found' (kon-fownd') *v.t.* **1,** throw into confusion; perplex; astound. **2,** mistake for another. **—con·found'ed,** *adj.* (*Informal*) damnable.

con·frere (kon'frâr) *n.* a colleague.

con·front' (kən-frunt') *v.t.* **1,** stand facing; meet. **2,** meet in hostility. **3,** bring face to face (with). **—con"fron·ta'tion** (kon"frən-tā'shən) *n.*

con·fuse' (kən-fūz') *v.t.* **1,** throw into disorder. **2,** perplex; disconcert. **3,** mistake for another. **—con·fu'sion,** *n.*

con·fute' (kən-fūt') *v.t.* prove false; disprove. **—con"fu·ta'tion,** *n.*

con'ga (kong'gə) *n.* **1,** a Cuban dance. **2,** a tall bass drum beaten with the hands.

con·geal' (kən-jēl') *v.t. & i.* **1,** freeze; stiffen; harden, esp. as an effect of cold. **2,** coagulate; clot. **—con"ge·la'tion** (kon"jə-lā'shən) *n.*

con·gen'ial (kən-jēn'yəl) *adj.* **1,** kindred; like; sympathetic. **2,** agreeable; pleasing. **—con·ge"ni·al'i·ty,** *n.*

con·gen'i·tal (kən-jen'ə-təl) *adj.* existing at birth.

con'ger (kong'gər) *n.* a large marine eel.

con'ge·ries" (kon'jə-rēz") *n.sing. or pl.* collection into one heap; an aggregation.

con·gest' (kən-jest') *v.t.* **1,** overcrowd. **2,** overfill with blood. **—con·ges'tion,** *n.*

con·glom'er·ate (kən-glom'ər-ət) *adj.* collected or clustered together. **—n. 1,** a mass of varied and incongruous materials. **2,** a rock made of pieces of gravel. **3,** a company that operates businesses in a wide variety of unrelated fields. **—v.t. & i.** (-rāt") collect into a mass. **—con·glom"er·a'tion,** *n.*

con·grat'u·late" (kən-grach'ə-lāt") *v.t.* express (to a person) pleasure at his or her happiness or triumph; felicitate. **—con·grat"u·la'tion,** *n.*

con'gre·gate" (kon'gri-gāt") *v.t. & i.* gather together; assemble.

con"gre·ga'tion (kon"gri-gā'shən) *n.* **1,** act of congregating. **2,** a gathering, esp. of persons for religious worship.

con"gre·ga'tion·al *adj.* **1,** pert. to a congregation. **2,** (*cap.*) pert. to a certain Protestant denomination. **—Con"gre·ga'tion·al·ism** (-iz-əm) *n.* **—Con"gre·ga'tion·al·ist,** *adj. & n.*

con'gress (kon'gris) *n.* **1,** a formal meeting of delegates for discussion; a conference. **2,** (*cap.*) the legislative body of the U.S. **3,** intercourse. **—con·gres'sion·al** (kən-gresh'ən-əl) *adj.* **—con'gress·man** (-mən) [*pl.* **-men**], **con'gress·wom"an,** *n.* (often *cap.*) a member of the U.S. Congress.

con'gru·ent (kong'groo-ənt) *adj.* **1,** agreeing; harmonious. **2,** (*Geom.*) superposable. **—con'gru·ence,** *n.*

con·gru'i·ty (kong-groo'ə-tė) *n.* congruousness.

con'gru·ous (kong'groo-əs) *adj.* well

adapted; appropriate; consistent. —**con'-gru·ous·ness**, *n.*

con'ic (kon'ik) *adj.* [also, **con'i·cal**] having the shape of or like a cone. —*n.* [also, **conic section**] (*Geom.*) an ellipse, parabola, or hyperbola.

co·ni·fer (kon'i-fər) *n.* a cone-bearing plant. —**co·nif'er·ous** (kō-nif'ər-əs) *adj.*

con·jec'ture (kən-jek'chər) *n.* an opinion not founded on sufficient evidence; a guess; a surmise. —*v.t. & i.* guess. —**conjec'tur·al**, *adj.*

con·join' (kən-join') *v.t. & i.* join; associate. —**con·joint'**, *adj.*

con'ju·gal (kon'jə-gəl) *adj.* pert. to marriage; connubial. —**con"ju·gal'i·ty**, *n.*

con'ju·gate" (kon'jə-gāt") *v.t.* give in order the forms of (a verb). —*adj.* formed in a pair; coupled. —**con'ju·ga"tive**, *adj.*

con"ju·ga'tion (-gā'shən) *n.* **1,** inflection of verbs. **2,** conjunction.

con·junct' (kən-junkt') *adj.* joined together; united. —**con·junc'tive**, *adj.*

con·junc'tion (kən-junk'shən) *n.* **1,** act of joining. **2,** union; connection. **3,** a word that joins sentences, clauses, phrases, or words, as *and.*

con·junc"ti·vi'tis (kən-junk"tə-vī'tis) *n.* inflammation of the mucous membrane of the eyelids and eyeball (*conjunctiva*).

con·junc'ture (kən-junk'chər) *n.* **1,** a combination of circumstances. **2,** a crisis.

con'jure (kon'jər) *v.t. & i.* **1,** call up or bring about by, or as if by, magic; practice magic. **2,** (kon-jûr') entreat solemnly. —**con"ju·ra'tion**, *n.*

con'jur·er (kon'jər-ər) *n.* a magician. Also, **con'jur·or.**

conk (konk) (*Slang*) *v.t.* thump. —*v.i.* (with *out*) fail; stop running.

con·nect' (kə-nekt') *v.t. & i.* **1,** associate mentally. **2,** join; associate closely. **3,** (with *with*) establish communication or juncture. **4,** (*Slang*) attain one's goal or object. —**con·nec'tive**, *adj. & n.*

con·nec'tion (kə-nek'shən) *n.* **1,** the state of being connected; union; a connecting part. **2,** family relationship; a distant relative. **3,** (*pl.*) influential friends. **4,** continuity of words or ideas. **5,** a bond; tie. **6,** (often *pl.*) a meeting of trains, etc., for transfer of passengers. **7,** (*Slang*) a source of smuggled goods, esp. narcotics.

con·nip'tion (kə-nip'shən) *n.* (*Informal*) hysterical excitement.

con·nive' (kə-nīv') *v.i.* secretly abet or permit a wrong. —**con·niv'ance**, *n.*

con"nois·seur' (kon"ə-sēr') *n.* a discriminating critic.

con·note' (kə-nōt') *v.t.* imply; suggest; denote secondarily. —**con"no·ta'tion**, *n.*

con·nu'bi·al (kə-noo'bē-əl) *adj.* pert. to marriage; conjugal.

con'quer (kong'kər) *v.t.* **1,** subdue by force. **2,** overcome; surmount. **3,** resist, as temptation, a bad habit, etc. —**con'quer·or**, *n.*

con'quest (kon'kwest) *n.* **1,** subjugation by force; victory. **2,** that which is subdued or won.

con·quis'ta·dor" (kon-kwis'tə-dôr") *n.* a Spanish conqueror of the New World.

Con'rail" (kon'rāl") *n.* a government railway network in the U.S.: *Con(solidated) Rail (Corporation).*

con"san·guin'i·ty (kon"sang-gwin'ə-tē) *n.* relationship by blood. —**con"san·guin'e·ous** (-ē-əs) *adj.*

con'science (kon'shəns) *n.* one's moral sense of right and wrong.

con"sci·en'tious (kon"shē-en'shəs) *adj.* **1,** scrupulous. **2,** careful; meticulous. —**conscientious objector**, one who refuses to bear arms in a military conflict, for moral or religious scruple.

con'scion·a·ble (kon'shən-ə-bəl) *adj.* conforming to one's conscience; just.

con'scious (kon'shəs) *adj.* **1,** aware of one's existence, feelings, and thoughts. **2,** in a waking, not comatose, state. **3,** aware. **4,** intentional. —**con'scious·ness**, *n.* —**consciousness-raising**, *n.* a method of group therapy designed to heighten one's self-awareness.

con'script (kon'skript) *n.* one pressed into military or naval service. —*v.t.* (kən-skript') draft. —**con·scrip'tion**, *n.*

con'se·crate" (kon'si-krāt") *v.t.* dedicate to a sacred purpose or service. —**con"se·cra'tion**, *n.*

con·sec'u·tive (kən-sek'ū-tiv) *adj.* succeeding one another in regular order.

con·sen'sus (kən-sen'səs) *n.* **1,** agreement in opinion, feeling, etc. **2,** general agreement, as of opinion.

con·sent' (kən-sent') *v.i.* agree; yield; accede. —*n.* voluntary compliance; permission. —**con·sen'tient** (-shənt) *adj.* agreeing; unanimous.

con'se·quence (kon'sə-kwens) *n.* **1,** that which follows as the result of some preceding act, cause, etc. **2,** significance. **3,** distinction; importance in rank, etc.

con'se·quent (kon'sə-kwent) *adj.* **1,** resulting. **2,** following logically. —**con'se·quent·ly**, *adv.* in consequence of; therefore.

con″se·quen′tial (kon″si-kwen′shəl) *adj.* **1,** important. **2,** consequent.

con″ser·va′tion (kon″sər-vā′shən) *n.* preservation, esp. of natural resources. **—con″ser·va′tion·ist,** *n.*

con·serv′a·tive (kən-sẽr′və-tiv) *adj.* **1,** opposed to change. **2,** moderate; not extreme. **3,** protecting from loss, waste, or injury. **4,** preservative. **—***n.* **1,** a conservative person. **2,** (*cap.*) in some countries, a member of a conservative party. **—conserv′a·tism,** *n.*

con′ser·va″tor (kon′sər-vā″tər) *n.* **1,** one who conserves; protector. **2,** one who repairs and maintains a museum or library collection. **3,** (*Law*) guardian.

con·serv′a·to″ry (-tôr″ė) *n.* **1,** a greenhouse. **2,** a school, esp. of music.

con·serve′ (kən-sẽrv′) *v.t.* preserve from loss, waste, etc. **—***n.* (kon′sẽrv) a fruit preserve.

con·sid′er (kən-sid′ər) *v.t.* **1,** ponder; study. **2,** make allowance for. **3,** hold in esteem. **4,** believe; judge. **—***v.i.* reflect; meditate.

con·sid′er·a·ble *adj.* **1,** notable; important. **2,** not small. **—***n.* (*Informal*) a large amount or degree.

con·sid′er·ate (-ət) *adj.* thoughtful of others.

con·sid″er·a′tion *n.* **1,** careful reflection. **2,** thoughtfulness of others. **3,** something to be reckoned with. **4,** motive; reason. **5,** a fee; compensation. **6,** importance.

con·sid′ered (-ərd) *adj.* **1,** taken into account. **2,** deliberate; intentional.

con·sid′er·ing *prep.* taking into account; in view of.

con·sign′ (kən-sīn′) *v.t.* **1,** hand over; commit formally. **2,** assign. **3,** send or address (goods) to, for sale or custody. **—con″sign·ee′** (kon″sī-nē′) *n.* **—con·sign′or,** *n.*

con·sign′ment (-mənt) *n.* **1,** act of consigning; something consigned; a shipment. **2,** the condition that goods held for sale by an agent for a seller will not be paid for unless they are sold.

con·sist′ (kən-sist′) *v.i.* **1,** (with *of*) be composed. **2,** (with *in*) exist. ❏ *comprise*

con·sist′en·cy (-ən-sė) *n.* **1,** solidity; degree of density, esp. of liquids. **2,** harmony; correspondence. **3,** state of being consistent.

con·sist′ent (-ənt) *adj.* **1,** congruous; in accord. **2,** conforming regularly to the same pattern, habits, principles, etc.

con·sis′to·ry (kən-sis′tə-rė) *n.* an ecclesi-

astical council or meeting; its meeting place.

con″so·la′tion (kon″sə-lā′shən) *n.* act or effect of consoling; solace.

con′sole (kon′sōl) **1,** the cabinet containing the keyboard, etc. of an organ. **2,** a floor cabinet, as for a radio. **3,** the control unit, as of a computer. **4,** a supporting bracket. **—***v.t.* (kən-sōl′) comfort in time of sorrow; solace.

con·sol′i·date″ (kən-sol′ə-dāt″) *v.t.* **1,** make solid or firm; strengthen. **2,** unite firmly in one body; combine; merge. **—con·sol″i·da′tion,** *n.*

con″som·mé′ (kon″sə-mā′) *n.* a strong, clear meat soup.

con′so·nant (kon′sə-nənt) *adj.* **1,** agreeing in sound. **2,** consistent. **3,** relating to consonants. **—***n.* an alphabetical element other than a vowel. **—con′so·nance,** *n.*

con′sort (kon′sôrt) *n.* **1,** a husband or wife. **2,** the spouse of a more important person. **3,** a vessel sailing with another. **—***v.i.* (kən-sôrt′) (with *with*) associate; agree.

con·sor′ti·um (kən-sôr′tė-əm) *n.* **1,** international business agreement; cartel. **2,** society; association. **3,** a meeting; colloquium.

con·spec′tus (kən-spek′təs) *n.* an outline or summary of a subject.

con·spic′u·ous (kən-spik′ū-əs) *adj.* **1,** easily seen. **2,** attracting attention; notable; important. **—con·spic′u·ous·ness,** *n.*

con·spir′a·cy (kən-spir′ə-sė) *n.* a combination of persons for an evil purpose; a plot. **—con·spir′a·tor,** *n.* one who joins in a conspiracy.

con·spire′ (kən-spīr′) *v.i.* **1,** combine for an unlawful purpose; plot secretly. **2,** concur to one end.

con′sta·ble (kon′stə-bəl) *n.* an officer of the peace; a police officer.

con·stab′u·lar·y (kən-stab′yə-ler-ė) *n.* a body of constables; police. **—***adj.* [also, **con·stab′u·lar** (-lər)] pert. to police work.

con′stan·cy (kon′stən-sė) *n.* state of being constant; fidelity; stability.

con′stant (kon′stənt) *adj.* **1,** regularly recurring. **2,** ceaseless. **3,** steadfast; resolute. **4,** unvarying. **—***n.* **1,** something constant or unchanging. **2,** (*Math.*) a quantity which does not change value. ❏ *continual*

con″stel·la′tion (kon″stə-lā′shən) *n.* a group of fixed stars.

con″ster·na′tion (kon″stər-nā′shən) *n.* terrified amazement; dismay.

con′sti·pate″ (kon′sti-pāt″) *v.t.* **1,** cause

constipation in. **2**, clog; impede movement in.

con″sti·pa′tion (kon″sti-pā′shən) *n.* difficulty in moving the bowels. /

con·stit′u·en·cy (kən-stich′oo-ən-sė) *n.* a body of voters, customers, etc.

con·stit′u·ent (kən-stich′oo-ənt) *n.* **1**, a necessary part. **2**, a voter or resident in a legislative district. —*adj.* being one necessary part.

con′sti·tute″ (kon′sti-tūt″) *v.t.* **1**, make up; form as a necessary part. **2**, establish by lawful authority. **3**, appoint.

con″sti·tu′tion (kon″sti-too′shən) *n.* **1**, natural composition, qualities, structure, etc. **2**, a code of principles or laws forming the basis of a government or organization; the document of such a code.

con″sti·tu′tion·al (-əl) *adj.* **1**, inherent; basic; essential. **2**, beneficial to health. **3**, pert. to or in accordance with a written constitution. —*n.* an exercise, as a walk. —**con″sti·tu″tion·al′i·ty** (-al′ə-tė) *n.*

con·strain′ (kən-strān′) *v.t.* **1**, compel; oblige. **2**, bind; confine. **3**, repress; restrain. —**con·straint′**, *n.*

con·strict′ (kən-strikt′) *v.t.* cause to shrink; cramp; crush. —**con·stric′tion**, *n.* —**con·strict′ive**, *adj.* —**con·stric′tor**, *n.*

con·struct′ (kən-strukt′) *v.t.* **1**, build; make. **2**, frame in the mind. —*n.* (kon′-strukt) something constructed. —**con·struc′tor**, *n.* /

con·struc′tion (kən-struk′shən) *n.* **1**, the act or method of building or constructing; a structure; an interpretation. **2**, (*Gram.*) arrangement and connection of words in a sentence. **3**, act of construing. —**con·struc′tion·ist**, *n.* one who interprets (something written).

con·struc′tive (-tiv) *adj.* **1**, building; beneficial to progress. **2**, inferential.

con·strue′ (kən-stroo′) *v.t.* **1**, analyze grammatically. **2**, translate. **3**, interpret.

con″sub·stan″ti·a′tion (kon″səb-stan″-shė-ā′shən) *n.* the doctrine that the blood and body of Christ coexist in and with the bread and wine of the Eucharist.

con′sul (kon′səl) *n.* **1**, a diplomatic officer or agent of a government in a foreign country. **2**, (*Hist.*) a chief magistrate. —**con′su·lar**, *adj.* —**con′su·late** (-sə-lət) *n.*

con·sult′ (kən-sult′) *v.t.* **1**, ask the advice of; refer to. **2**, consider; have regard for. —*v.i.* confer. —**con·sult′ant**, *n.*

con″sul·ta′tion (kon″səl-tā′shən) *n.* act of consulting; conference. —**con·sul′ta·tive** (kən-sul′tə-tiv) *adj.* advisory.

con·sume′ (kən-soom′) *v.t.* **1**, devour;

eat; destroy. **2**, use up; spend, as time. —**con·sum′er**, *n.* the ultimate user of a commodity. —**con·sum′er·ism**, *n.* a movement to protect the rights of the consumer. —**consumer price index**, an index number reflecting changes in current prices of a selected list of products compared to a base period.

con′sum·mate″ (kon′sə-māt″) *v.t.* bring to completion or perfection. —*adj.* (kən-sum′it) complete; perfect. —**con″sum·ma′-tion**, *n.*

con·sump′tion (kən-sump′shən) *n.* **1**, the act or effect of consuming; the amount consumed. **2**, tuberculosis of the lungs.

con·sump′tive (-tiv) *adj.* wasteful. —*n. & adj.* (one) affected with tuberculosis.

con′tact (kon′takt) *n.* **1**, a meeting or touching of two things or (*Informal*) persons. **2**, a business or social acquaintance or introduction. —*v.t. & i.* (*Informal*) get in touch (with). —**contact lens**, a thin plastic shell fitted to the front of the eyeball under the eyelids to correct vision. —**contact man** *or* **woman**, a go-between.

con·ta′gion (kən-tā′jən) *n.* **1**, the communication of a disease by contact; the disease; plague. **2**, rapid spread of disease, feelings, etc.

con·ta′gious (kən-tā′jəs) *adj.* communicable; spreading. —**con·ta′gious·ness**, *n.*

---

contagious, infectious
☛ *Contagious* means communicable by contact; *infectious* means communicable by spread of germs, regardless of the medium.

---

con·tain′ (kən-tān′) *v.t.* **1**, keep within bounds; restrain; enclose. **2**, comprise; have a capacity of; hold. —**con·tain′er**, *n.* a vessel, can, box, bottle, etc.

con·tain″er·i·za′tion (kən-tān″ər-i-zā′-shən) *n.* the use in shipping of large containers that are transported as units in specially equipped transports. —**con·tain′-er·ize**, *v.t. & i.*

con·tam′i·nate″ (kən-tam′i-nāt″) *v.t.* make impure by mixture; taint; pollute. —**con·tam′i·nant**, *n.* —**con·tam″i·na′tion**, *n.*

con·temn′ (kən-tem′) *v.t.* scorn. ❑ *condemn*

con′tem·plate″ (kon′təm-plāt″) *v.t.* **1**, view or reflect upon attentively. **2**, intend; expect. —*v.i.* meditate. —**con″tem·pla′-tion**, *n.* —**con′tem·pla″tive**, *adj.*

con·tem″po·ra′ne·ous (kən-tem″pə-rā′nė-əs) *adj.* contemporary.

con·tem′po·rar″y (kən-tem′pə-rer″ė)

---

tub, cūte, pûll; labəl; oil, owl, go, chip, she, thin, *th*en, sing, ink; *see p. 6*

adj. **1,** living or occurring at the same time. **2,** of the same age. —*n.* a person contemporary with another.

> **contemporary, modern**
> ☞ *Modern* refers to something that has existed in recent, vaguely defined time. *Contemporary* refers to something happening at the same time as something else (or in the present time, if no comparative period is specified).

con·tempt′ (kən-tempt′) *n.* **1,** the act of despising. **2,** a feeling of disdain. **3,** (*Law*) defiance of a court, etc.

con·tempt′i·ble (kən-temp′tə-bəl) *adj.* meriting scorn; despicable. —**con·tempt″·i·bil′i·ty,** *n.*

con·temp′tu·ous (kən-temp′choo-əs) *adj.* expressing disdain; scornful. —**con·temp′tu·ous·ness,** *n.*

con·tend′ (kən-tend′) *v.i.* **1,** compete; struggle in opposition. **2,** assert in argument.

con′tent (kon′tent) *n.* **1,** (*pl.*) all that is contained in a receptacle. **2,** (*pl.*) subject matter, as of a book. **3,** the gist or substance, as of a sermon, etc. **4,** amount contained.

con·tent′ (kən-tent′) *adj.* satisfied; easy in mind. —*v.t.* satisfy. —**con·tent′ed,** *adj.* satisfied; placidly happy. —**con·tent′·ment,** *n.*

con·ten′tion (kən-ten′shən) *n.* **1,** act of contending; a struggle, debate, etc. **2,** rivalry; strife.

con·ten′tious (kən-ten′shəs) *adj.* argumentative. —**con·ten′tious·ness,** *n.*

con′test (kon′test) *n.* **1,** a struggle; fight; controversy. **2,** a competitive game. —*v.t.* (kən-test′) **1,** compete or vie for. **2,** challenge; dispute. —**con·test′ant,** *n.* one who competes.

> **contest**
> ↔ From Latin *contestari*, bear witness. The sense of adversarial relation in a lawsuit led to the present sense.

con′text (kon′tekst) *n.* **1,** related or adjoining passages of a book, etc. **2,** setting in which something occurs. —**con·tex′tual,** *adj.*

con·tig′u·ous (kən-tig′ū-əs) *adj.* touching at the border; adjoining. —**con″ti·gu′i·ty,** *n.*

con′ti·nence (kon′tə-nəns) *n.* **1,** self-restraint, esp. of sexual appetite. **2,** the ability to retain voluntarily a bodily discharge, as urine.

con′ti·nent (kon′ti-nənt) *n.* **1,** one of the six principal land masses of the globe. **2,** (*cap.,* with *the*) the mainland of Europe. —*adj.* exercising continence; chaste. —**con″ti·nen′tal,** *adj.* pert. to a continent, esp. (*cap.*) the mainland of Europe.

con·tin′gen·cy (kən-tin′jən-sē) *n.* **1,** a circumstance; what may happen. **2,** dependence.

con·tin′gent (kən-tin′jənt) *adj.* **1,** depending on something not certain; conditional. **2,** accidental. —*n.* **1,** a quota; a delegation. **2,** a fighting unit; detachment. —**contingent worker,** a temporary worker.

con·tin′u·al (kən-tin′ū-əl) *adj.* constant; often repeated. ❑ *continuous*

con·tin′u·ance (-əns) *n.* **1,** a keeping on; duration. **2,** uninterrupted succession. **3,** (*Law*) postponement.

con·tin″u·a′tion (-ā′shən) *n.* **1,** act of continuing; state of being continued. **2,** an extension or prolongation.

con·tin′ue (kən-tin′ū) *v.t.* **1,** prolong; extend. **2,** keep on with; not cease from. **3,** resume the course of. **4,** retain, as in office. —*v.i.* **1,** persist; keep on. **2,** resume after interruption. **3,** abide or stay. **4,** last; endure.

con″ti·nu′i·ty (kon″ti-nū′ə-tē) *n.* **1,** unbroken connection or sequence. **2,** a script for a motion picture, radio show, etc.

con·tin′u·ous (kən-tin′ū-əs) *adj.* without cessation or interruption.

> **continuous, continual, constant**
> ☞ These words mean continuing indefinitely, but *continuous* means continuing without interruptions, whereas *continual* implies repetition with intervals. *Constant* can mean either.

con·tin′u·um (kən-tin′ū-əm) *n.* [*pl.* **-a** (-ə)] **1,** a continuous whole. **2,** continuity. —**space-time continuum,** four-dimensional space, of which the dimensions are length, breadth, thickness, and time.

con·tort′ (kən-tôrt′) *v.t. & i.* twist out of shape.

con·tor′tion (kən-tôr′shən) *n.* a twisting out of shape. —**con·tor′tion·ist,** *n.* a performer who contorts his or her body.

con′tour (kon′tûr) *n. & adj.* the outline, as of a figure, coast, etc. —*v.t.* form the outline of; mark with contour lines. —**contour farming,** prevention of erosion by tilling land according to its shape. —**contour line,** a line connecting all points of equal elevation.

con′tra (kon′trə) *prep.* **1,** against. —*n.* a

member of a counterrevolutionary force in Nicaragua.

con·tra- (kon-tra) *pref.* against; opposite.

con'tra·band" (kon'trə-band") *adj.* prohibited by law from being imported or exported. —*n.* **1,** smuggling. **2,** smuggled goods.

con'tra·bass" (-bās") *adj.* denoting a musical instrument of deepest pitch or range in its family. —*n.* double bass.

con"tra·bas·soon' *n.* an instrument similar to the bassoon but pitched an octave lower.

con"tra·cep'tion (kon"trə-sep'shən) *n.* act or method of preventing conception; birth control. —**con"tra·cep'tive,** *n.* & *adj.*

con'tract (kon'trakt) *n.* **1,** a legal or business agreement. **2,** in certain games, the highest bid. **3,** (*Slang*) an agreement for murder. —*v.t.* (kən-trakt') **1,** make smaller; condense; abridge. **2,** acquire (a habit, disease, etc.); incur; enter into. —*v.i.* **1,** enter into an agreement. **2,** shrink.

con·trac'tile (kən-trak'til) *adj.* having the function or power of contracting, as a muscle.

con·trac'tion (-shən) *n.* **1,** a shrinking; shrinkage. **2,** a shortened form of a word or phrase. ❑ *abbreviation*

con·trac'tor (-tər) *n.* one who agrees to undertake a project, esp. in construction.

con·trac'tu·al (kən-trak'choo-əl) *adj.* pert. to a contract.

con"tra·dict' (kon"trə-dikt') *v.t.* **1,** assert the contrary of. **2,** deny the words of. **3,** be contrary to. —**con"tra·dic'tion,** *n.* —**con"tra·dic'to·ry,** *adj.*

con"tra·dis·tinc'tion *n.* direct contrast.

con'trail" (kon'trāl") *n.* a cloudlike trail caused by exhaust from a jet engine.

con"tra·in'di·cate *v.t.* discourage the use of (a treatment, etc.).

con·tral'to (kən-tral'tō) *n.* [*pl.* **-tos**] the lowest female voice.

con·trap'tion (kən-trap'shən) *n.* (*Informal*) a contrivance or gadget.

con"tra·pun'tal (kon"trə-punt'əl) *adj.* pert. to counterpoint.

con"tra·ri'e·ty (kon"trə-rī'ə-tè) *n.* **1,** contrariness. **2,** adversity.

con'tra·ri·wise" (kon'trer-ė-wīz") *adv.* **1,** in the opposite way or sense. **2,** perversely.

con'tra·ry (kon'trer-è) *adj.* **1,** diametrically opposed; opposite. **2,** conflicting. **3,** perverse. —*n.* the opposite in sense or meaning. —**con·tra'ri·ness,** *n.*

con·trast' (kən-tràst') *v.t.* & *i.* compare by showing differences. —*n.* (kon'trast) **1,** the act of contrasting. **2,** a striking difference. **3,** the ratio between light and dark in a scene. ❑ *compare*

con"tra·vene' (kon"trə-vēn') *v.t.* **1,** conflict with. **2,** violate. —**con"tra·ven'tion,** *n.*

con'tre·temps" (kon'trə-tän") *n.* [*pl.* **con'tre·temps"**] an embarrassing occurrence.

con·trib'ute (kən-trib'yət) *v.t.* **1,** give with others, as to a charity. **2,** write for a magazine, etc. —*v.i.* have a share; be of use. —**con"tri·bu'tion** (-bū'shən) *n.* —**con·trib'u·tive,** *adj.* —**con·trib'u·tor,** *n.* —**con·trib'u·to·ry,** *adj.* helping toward a result.

con·trite' (kən-trīt') *adj.* humbly penitent. —**con·tri'tion** (-trish'ən) *n.*

con·triv'ance (kən-trī'vəns) *n.* **1,** a mechanical device. **2,** a means of doing.

con·trive' (kən-trīv') *v.t.* devise or bring about by clever planning. —*v.i.* **1,** scheme. **2,** (with *to*) manage to.

con·trol' (kən-trōl') *v.t.* [**-trolled', -trol'-ling**] **1,** exercise power over; restrain; govern; dominate. **2,** regulate. **3,** verify by comparison. —*n.* **1,** restraint. **2,** authority to govern, regulate, or manage. **3,** (often *pl.*) the apparatus for operating a machine. —**con·trol'ler,** *n.* comptroller. —**controlled substance,** a substance whose production, sale, and use is restricted by law.

con"tro·ver'sial (kon"trə-vēr'shəl) *adj.* being or causing a controversy.

con'tro·ver"sy (kon'trə-vēr'sè) *n.* contention; an argument or debate.

con"tro·vert' (kon"trə-vėrt') *v.t.* **1,** argue against; dispute or deny. **2,** discuss; debate. —**con"tro·vert'i·ble,** *adj.*

con·tu'ma·cy (kon'tyû-mə-sè) *n.* contempt of authority. —**con"tu·ma'cious** (-mā'shəs) *adj.*

con·tu'me·ly (kon'tyû-mə-lè) *n.* contemptuous abuse. —**con"tu·me'li·ous** (-mē'lè-əs) *adj.*

con·tuse' (kən-tooz') *v.t.* bruise. —**con·tu'sion** (-zhən) *n.* a bruise.

co·nun'drum (kə-nun'drəm) *n.* a riddle; a hard question.

con"ur·ba'tion (kon"ər-bā'shən) *n.* a continuous network of cities and towns.

con"va·lesce' (kon"və-les') *v.i.* recover gradually after sickness. —**con"va·les'-cence,** *n.* —**con"va·les'cent,** *adj.* & *n.*

con·vec'tion (kən-vek'shən) *n.* **1,** transfer of heat, electricity, etc., in a fluid. **2,** (*Meteor.*) upward or downward movement of part of the atmosphere. —**con·vec'tive,** *adj.* —**con·vect',** *v.*

con·vene′ (kən-vēn′) *v.t. & i.* assemble for some public purpose.

con·ven′ience (kən-vēn′yəns) *n.* **1,** suitability; accessibility; opportuneness. **2,** (often *pl.*) that which adds to comfort; accommodation. **—con·ven′ient,** *adj.* **—convenience food,** packaged food designed for easy preparation. **—convenience store,** a retail store specializing in basic items and open long hours.

con′vent (kon′vent) *n.* **1,** a religious community. **2,** a monastery; esp., a home of nuns; nunnery.

con·ven′tion (kən-ven′shən) *n.* **1,** an assembly; a formal meeting. **2,** an agreement, esp. international. **3,** a fixed custom or usage. **—con·ven″tion·eer′,** *n.*

con·ven′tion·al (-əl) *adj.* **1,** conforming to custom; conservative. **2,** arbitrarily established. **3,** ordinary. **4,** of armament, not employing nuclear weapons. **—con·ven″tion·al′i·ty,** *n.* **—conventional memory,** (*Computers*) the first megabyte of computer memory, accessible by DOS.

con·verge′ (kən-vērj′) *v.i.* **1,** incline toward each other, as lines; tend to meet. **2,** intersect. **—con·ver′gence,** *n.* **—con·ver′gent,** *adj.*

con·ver′sant (kən-vēr′sənt) *adj.* acquainted; well-informed.

con″ver·sa′tion (kon″vər-sā′shən) *n.* informal, familiar talk. **—con″ver·sa′tion·al,** *adj.* **—con″ver·sa′tion·al·ist,** *n.*

con·verse′ (kən-vērs′) *v.i.* talk informally. **—n.** (kon′vērs) informal talk; conversation.

con′verse (kon′vērs) *adj.* transposed; reversed. **—n.** the reverse; opposite.

con·ver′sion (kən-vēr′zhən) *n.* act or effect of converting; change.

con·vert′ (kən-vērt′) *v.t.* **1,** change into another form; exchange. **2,** persuade to change in policy, religion, etc. **3,** (*Law*) appropriate illegally. **—n.** (kon′vērt) a converted person, esp. as to religion. **—con·vert′er, con·ver′tor,** *n.*

con·vert′i·ble *adj.* **1,** capable of being converted. **2,** of an automobile, having a folding top. **—n. 1,** a convertible automobile. **2,** a sofa, chair, etc. which changes into a bed. **—con·vert″i·bil′i·ty,** *n.*

con·vex′ (kon-veks′) *adj.* curved like the outside surface of a circle or sphere. **—con·vex′i·ty,** *n.* ❑ *concave*

con·vey′ (kən-vā′) *v.t.* **1,** carry from one place to another; transport. **2,** transmit. **3,** communicate; impart. **3,** (*Law*) transfer title of.

con·vey′ance *n.* **1,** act or result of con-

veying. **2,** a vehicle. **3,** (*Law*) a transfer of title; the document effecting such transfer.

con·vey′or *n.* a contrivance for conveying, as a moving belt.

con·vict′ (kən-vikt′) *v.t.* prove or find guilty. **—n.** (kon′vikt) a convicted prisoner.

con·vic′tion (kən-vik′shən) *n.* **1,** act or effect of convicting or convincing. **2,** a firm belief.

con·vince′ (kən-vins′) *v.t.* **1,** cause (a person) to believe. **2,** (*Informal*) persuade. **—con·vinc′ing,** *adj.* assuring by proof; persuasive.

> **convince, persuade**
> (*Gram.*) One can be *persuaded to do* something, but one is *convinced that* something is true or *convinced of* the truth of something.

con·viv′i·al (kən-viv′ē-əl) *adj.* **1,** fond of feasting; gay; jovial. **2,** festive. **—con·viv″i·al′i·ty,** *n.*

con″vo·ca′tion (kon″və-kā′shən) *n.* **1,** act or result of convoking. **2,** an assembly.

con·voke′ (kən-vōk′) *v.t.* summon to assemble.

con′vo·lute″ (kon′və-loot″) *adj.* rolled up; coiled. **—v.t.** form into a coil, spiral, or whorl. **—con″vo·lut′ed,** *adj.* complicated. **—con″vo·lu′tion,** *n.*

con·voy′ (kən-voi′) *v.t.* escort for protection. **—n.** (kon′voi) a protecting force or ship; a fleet or group under escort.

con·vulse′ (kən-vuls′) *v.t.* **1,** contract spasmodically. **2,** disturb violently. **3,** cause to laugh uncontrollably. **—con·vul′sion,** *n.* **—con·vul′sive** (-siv) *adj.*

co′ny (kō′nē) *n.* rabbit fur dyed to imitate sealskin.

coo (koo) *v.i.* murmur like a pigeon or dove; talk fondly.

cook (kûk) *v.t.* **1,** prepare (food) by heating; apply heat to. **2,** (with *up*) concoct. **3,** (*Informal*) ruin. **4,** (*Slang*) falsify. **—v.i. 1,** undergo cooking. **2,** work as a cook. **—n.** one who cooks food. **—cook′ery** (-ə-rē) *n.*

cook′book″ *n.* a book of recipes for cooking; any book of instructions. Also, **cook′er·y book** (-ə-rē).

cook′ie (kûk′ē) *n.* a small, flat cake. Also, **cook′y.**

cook′out″ *n.* an outing at which food is cooked and served.

Cook's tour 1, a brief, superficial tour. **2,** a complete, even overly thorough tour.

cook′top″ *n.* a cooking surface.

cool (kool) *adj.* **1,** neither warm nor very cold. **2,** calm; not excited. **3,** lacking cordiality. **4,** (of colors) green, blue, or violet. **5,** (*Informal*) not overstated. **6,** (*Slang*) excellent. **7,** (*Slang*) all right. —*v.t. & i.* **1,** make or become cool or cooler. **2,** (with *off*) become less angry, excited, etc. **3,** (with *it*) (*Slang*) relax. —**cool′ant** (-ənt) *n.* —**cool′ness,** *n.*

cool′er *n.* **1,** a cold room or space. **2,** a cold drink. **3,** (*Slang*) jail.

coo′lie (koo′lė) *n.* a Chinese unskilled laborer.

coon (koon) *n.* raccoon. —**coon's age,** (*Slang*) a long time.

coop (koop) *n.* **1,** a small crate or pen, as for poultry. **2,** any small place. **3,** (*Slang*) jail. —*v.t.* **1,** (with *up*) confine. **2,** (*Slang*) sleep during working hours; said of police officers.

co-′op (kō′op) *n.* a cooperative.

coop′er (koo′pər) *n.* one who makes barrels and casks. —**coop′er·age** (-ij) *n.*

co·op′er·ate″ (kō-op′ə-rāt″) *v.i.* work together toward a common goal. —**co·op″er·a′tion,** *n.*

co·op′er·a·tive (-tiv) *adj.* **1,** willing to cooperate. **2,** owned by those it serves, as a store by its customers. —*n.* [also, **co-′op**] a cooperative store, business, building, etc.

co-opt′ (kō-opt′) *v.t.* **1,** elect or appoint as a member; absorb. **2,** appropriate.

co·or′di·nate″ (kō-ôr′də-nāt″) *v.t.* bring into harmony or proper relation. —*adj.* (-nət) of the same rank or degree. —*n.* (-nət) (*Math.*) one of a set of numbers that determine the location of a point, line, etc. in a space. —**co·or′di·na″tor,** *n.*

co·or″di·na′tion (-nā′shən) *n.* **1,** act of coordinating. **2,** harmonious combination. **3,** ability to combine muscular functions effectively.

coot (koot) *n.* **1,** a swimming and diving bird. **2,** (*Informal*) a fool.

coot′ie (koo′tė) *n.* (*Slang*) a louse.

cop (kop) *n.* (*Slang*) a police officer. —*v.t.* [**copped, cop′ping**] **1,** steal. **2,** catch. —**cop a plea,** (*Slang*) turn state's evidence. —**cop out,** (*Slang*) give up; back out.

co·pa·cet′ic (kō-pə-set′ik) *adj.* (*Slang*) satisfactory; OK.

co′pal (kō′pəl) *n.* a resin used in varnishes.

copar′ent (kō-pâr′ənt) *n.* a divorced or separated parent who shares custody of the children equally with the other parent. —*v.t. & i.* act as a coparent.

co·part′ner *n.* a partner or associate. —**co·part′ner·ship″,** *n.*

cope (kōp) *n.* a mantle worn by priests. —*v.i.* contend or struggle successfully.

cope′stone″ *n.* **1,** a stone used in a coping. **2,** the top or crowning piece of a structure.

cop′ing (kō′ping) *n.* the uppermost stones or bricks in a wall. —**coping saw,** a narrow-bladed saw for cutting curves.

co′pi·ous (kō′pė-əs) *adj.* abundant; plentiful. —**co′pi·ous·ness,** *n.*

cop-′out″ (kop′out″) *n.* (*Slang*) the act or an instance of copping out; an excuse.

cop′per (kop′ər) *n.* **1,** a tough, ductile metallic element, no. 29, symbol Cu. **2,** its color, reddish brown. **3,** a penny. **4,** (*Slang*) a police officer. —**cop′per·y,** *adj.*

cop′per·head″ *n.* a venomous Amer. snake.

cop′pice (kop′is) *n.* a thicket of small trees; a copse.

cop′ra (kop′rə) *n.* the dried meat of the coconut, yielding oil.

co·pro′ces·sor *n.* a data-processing chip designed to handle certain specialized tasks in conjunction with the main processor.

copse (kops) *n.* a thicket.

cop′ter (kop′tər) *n.* (*Informal*) helicopter.

cop′u·la (kop′yə-lə) *n.* **1,** a link or coupling. **2,** (*Gram.*) [also, **linking verb**] a verb that connects the subject and predicate, as *to be, seem,* etc.

cop′u·late″ (-lāt″) *v.i.* unite. —**cop″u·la′tion,** *n.* —**cop′u·la″tive** (-lā″tiv) *adj.*

cop′y (kop′ė) *n.* **1,** an imitation; a reproduction. **2,** one of a number of duplicates, as a book, magazine, etc. **3,** matter to be set in type. —*v.t.* **1,** make a copy of. **2,** imitate. —**cop′y·ist,** *n.* ❏ *edition*

cop′y·cat″ *n.* (*Informal*) one who copies another's behavior, writings, etc.

cop′y·hold″er *n.* an assistant to a proofreader.

cop′y·read″er *n.* one who edits copy.

cop′y·right″ *n.* the sole right to reproduce a literary or artistic work. —*v.t.* secure such right on.

cop·y·writ″er *n.* one who writes text (*copy*), as for advertising.

co·quette′ (kō-ket′) *n.* a flirt.

cor′al (kôr′əl) *n.* **1,** a hard, horny skeleton of tiny marine animals; a hard, compact mass formed of these skeletons. **2,** the polyp that secretes such a skeleton. **3,** a yellowish-red color. —**coral snake,** a venomous snake of the so. U.S.

cor′bel (kôr′bəl) *n.* a bracket. —*v.t.* support or furnish with corbels.

cord (kôrd) *n.* **1,** string or small rope. **2,** any ropelike structure; a tendon. **3,** a cubic measure, 8 x 4 x 4 ft., used esp. for firewood. **4,** rib or ridge in a textile. —**cord′age** (-ij) *n.* cords, ropes, etc.

cor′dial (kôr′jəl) *adj.* friendly; hearty. —*n.* **1,** a sweet, aromatic liquor; liqueur. **2,** a stimulating beverage or medicine. —**cor·dial′i·ty** (-jal′ə-tē) *n.*

cor·dil·le′ra (kôr-dəl-yār′ə) *n.* an extensive chain of mountains.

cord′ite (kôr′dīt) *n.* a smokeless explosive powder.

cor′do·ba (kôr′də-bə) *n.* the monetary unit of Nicaragua.

cor′don (kôr′dən) *n.* **1,** a series or line, as of forts. **2,** an ornamental braid.

cor′do·van (kôr′də-vən) *n.* a goatskin or horsehide leather; its color, a dark grayish-brown.

cor′du·roy″ (kôr′də-roi″) *n.* a heavy, ribbed fabric; (*pl.*) trousers of this fabric.

---

corduroy

↔ Of uncertain origin, the word apparently has nothing to do with the French word for king, *roy.*

---

core (kôr) *n.* **1,** the innermost or essential part; pith. **2,** the center of an apple, pear, etc.

co″re·op′sis (kôr′ē-op′sis) *n.* a plant with a bright-yellow flower.

co″re·spond′ent (kō″rə-spon′dənt) *n.* a joint defendant in a divorce suit.

Cor′fam (kôr′fam) *n.* (*T.N.*) a synthetic leather substitute, used in making shoes, etc.

co″ri·an′der (kôr″ē-an′dər) *n.* an herb; its seeds, used in cookery.

cork (kôrk) *n.* **1,** the light, elastic outer bark of a species of oak. **2,** a piece of cork used as a stopper for a bottle. —*v.t.* seal; stop up.

cork′age (-ij) *n.* a restaurant's charge for serving a patron's liquor.

cork′er (-ər) *n.* (*Slang*) a good fellow, thing, joke, etc.

cork′ing *adj.* (*Slang*) very good.

cork′screw″ *n.* a metal spiral used for drawing out cork stoppers. —*adj.* twisted; tortuous. —*v.i.* follow a tortuous course.

corm (kôrm) *n.* a fleshy underground stem resembling a bulb.

cor′mo·rant (kôr′mə-rənt) *n.* a large fish-eating seabird. —*adj.* greedy.

corn (kôrn) *n.* **1,** a single seed of a cereal plant. **2,** grain: in the U.S., maize; in England, wheat; in Scotland, oats. **3,** a callus, esp. on a toe. **4,** (*Slang*) triteness; mawkishness. —*v.t.* preserve (beef) in brine. —**corn pone** (pōn) a hard cake made of cornmeal. —**corn sugar,** dextrose. —**corn syrup,** syrup made from cornstarch.

corn′ball″ *adj.* (*Slang*) corny.

corn′cob″ *n.* the hard core of an ear of corn.

cor′ne·a (kôr′nē-ə) *n.* the firm transparent covering of the eye.

cor′ne·ous (kôr′nē-əs) *adj.* horny.

cor′ner (kôr′nər) *n.* **1,** the intersection of, or the space between, two converging lines or surfaces; a point where streets meet; an angle. **2,** a nook. **3,** a region; a remote place. **4,** an awkward position. **5,** a monopoly. —*v.t.* **1,** force into a difficult position. **2,** monopolize. —**cut corners, 1,** take a shortcut. **2,** economize.

cor′ner·stone″ *n.* a stone, often inscribed, at a corner of a building; hence, a basis.

cor·net′ (kôr-net′) *n.* a brass musical instrument similar to the trumpet.

corn′flow″er *n.* any of several blue or white flowers.

cor′nice (kôr′nis) *n.* **1,** an ornamental molding at the top edge of a wall. **2,** an ornamented piece of wood or metal used to conceal drapery hardware.

corn′meal″ *n.* meal made from corn.

corn′row″ *n.* **1,** a type of tight braid. **2,** (*usu. pl.*) a hair style consisting of parallel rows of cornrow braids. —*v.t.* to arrange (hair) in cornrows.

corn′starch″ *n.* starch obtained from corn, used in puddings, etc.

cor′nu·co′pi·a (kôr″nū-kō′pē-ə) *n.* a horn overflowing with fruit, symbolizing abundance.

corn′y (kôr′nē) *adj.* (*Slang*) trite.

co·rol′la (kə-rol′ə) *n.* the petals of a flower collectively.

cor′ol·lar″y (kor′ə-ler′ē) *n.* **1,** (*Math.*) a proposition proved incidentally in proving another. **2,** a natural sequence or concomitant result.

co·ro′na (kə-rō′nə) *n.* **1,** the luminous circle on the rim of the sun; a similar luminous effect. **2,** a halo; crown. **3,** a kind of long cigar. —**co·ro′nal,** *adj.*

> **corona, coroner, coronet**
> ↔ These words all derive from Greek *korōnē,* something curved. The *coroner* was once an officer of the Crown (royalty), a superviser of the Crown's pleas.

cor′o·nach (kôr′ə-nəkh) *n.* a dirge.

cor′o·nar″y (kor′ə-ner″ē) *adj.* **1,** like a crown. **2,** pert. to arteries around the heart. —*n.* (*Informal*) a heart attack.

cor″o·na′tion (kor″ə-nā′shən) *n.* the crowning of a king or queen. —**cor′o·nate** (kôr′ə-nāt) *v.t.*

cor′o·ner (kor′ə-nər) *n.* the presiding officer at an inquest into a cause of death. ❑ *corona*

cor′o·net (kor′ə-net) *n.* **1,** a crown indicating noble rank. **2,** an ornamental headdress. ❑ *corona*

cor′po·ral (kôr′pə-rəl) *n.* the lowest noncommissioned army officer. —*adj.* pert. to the body. —**corporal punishment,** punishment inflicted on the body, as flogging.

> **corporal, corporeal**
> ☞ *Corporal* means pertaining to the body, *corporeal* means having a body.

cor′po·rate (kôr′pə-rət) *adj.* **1,** being or pert. to a corporation. **2,** pert. to a body.

cor″po·ra′tion (kôr′pə-rā′shən) *n.* **1;** a company or association chartered to act as an individual. **2,** a governing body. **3,** (*Slang*) a fat belly. ❑ *firm*

cor·po′re·al (kôr-pôr′ē-əl) *adj.* bodily; material; not spiritual. —**cor·po″re·al′i·ty,** *n.* ❑ *corporal*

corps (kôr) *n.* [*pl.* **corps** (kôrz)] **1,** persons associated in some way, considered as a group. **2,** (*Mil.*) a unit of two or more divisions; the officers of any unit; a special detail. —**corps′man** (kôrz′mən) *n.* a member of a corps, esp. the Medical Corps.

corpse (kôrps) *n.* a dead body.

cor′pu·lence (kôr′pyə-ləns) *n.* fatness; obesity. —**cor′pu·lent,** *adj.*

cor′pus (kôr′pəs) *n.* **1,** the body of a human or animal. **2,** a body of writings, as laws.

cor′pus·cle (kôr′pəs-əl) *n.* **1,** a minute body or cell in the blood. **2,** a minute particle.

cor·ral′ (kə-ral′) *n.* an enclosure for horses or cattle. —*v.t.* [**-ralled′, -ral′ling**] **1,** pen up. **2,** seize; collect.

cor·rect′ (kə-rekt′) *v.t.* **1,** note or mark errors in; edit. **2,** rectify. **3,** discipline. —*adj.* **1,** true; accurate. **2,** conforming to good taste, etc. —**cor·rec′tive,** *adj. & n.* —**cor·rect′ness,** *n.*

cor·rec′tion (kə-rek′shən) *n.* **1,** act of correcting. **2,** an emendation; rectification; adjustment; rebuke; discipline.

cor·rec′tion·al (-əl) *adj.* **1,** tending to or intended for correction or reformation. **2,** pert. to a penal institution. **3,** corrective.

cor′re·late″ (kor′ə-lāt″) *v.t.* show or find to be related or connected. —**cor″re·la′tion,** *n.*

cor·rel′a·tive (kə-rel′ə-tiv) *adj.* **1,** having a mutual relation. **2,** (*Gram.*) complementary, as *neither* and *nor.*

cor″re·spond′ (kor″ə-spond′) *v.i.* **1,** be similar or analogous. **2,** conform; match; fit. **3,** communicate by letter. —**cor″re·spond′ence,** *n.* —**correspondence school,** a school that instructs its students by mail.

cor″re·spond′ent (-ənt) *n.* **1,** a writer of letters. **2,** a reporter or agent in a distant place.

cor′ri·dor (kor′i-dər) *n.* **1,** a narrow passageway. **2,** a narrow tract giving access from a country to an outlying territory, city, etc., or the sea.

cor″ri·gen′dum (kôr″ə-jen′dəm) *n.* [*pl.* **-da** (-də)] something to be corrected, esp. in print.

cor″ri·gi·ble (kôr′ə-jə-bəl) *adj.* capable of being corrected or reformed. —**cor″ri·gi·bil′i·ty,** *n.*

cor·rob′o·rate″ (kə-rob′ə-rāt″) *v.t.* confirm (another's report). —**cor·rob″o·ra′tion,** *n.* —**cor·rob′o·ra·tive,** *adj.*

cor·rode′ (kə-rōd′) *v.t. & i.* wear or eat away gradually, esp. by chemical action.

cor·ro′sion (kə-rō′zhən) *n.* act or effect of corroding; a gradual eating or wearing away. —**cor·ro′sive** (-siv) *adj. & n.*

cor′ru·gate″ (kor′ə-gāt″) *v.t. & i.* make wrinkles or folds (in). —**cor″ru·ga′tion,** *n.* —**corrugated paper,** wrapping paper formed in ridges, for strength, then pasted between two flat sheets to form a board.

cor·rupt′ (kə-rupt′) *adj.* **1,** dishonest; open to bribery. **2,** debased; evil. **3,** tainted. —*v.t.* **1,** influence for evil; bribe; pervert. **2,** make impure; taint; injure. —**cor·rupt′i·ble,** *adj.* —**cor·rupt′ness,** *n.*

cor·rup′tion (kə-rup′shən) *n.* act or effect of corrupting; dishonesty; perversion.

cor·sage' (kôr-säzh') *n.* a small bouquet of flowers to be worn.

cor'sair (kôr'sär) *n.* a pirate.

cor"se·let' *n.* **1,** (kor"sə-let') a woman's undergarment. **2,** (kors'lit) armor for the upper body.

cor'set (kôr'sit) *n.* a stiffened girdle worn to shape the figure.

cor·tege' (kôr-tezh') *n.* **1,** a procession. **2,** a retinue.

cor'tex (kôr'teks) [*pl.* **-ti·ces"** (-ti-sēz')] *n.* **1,** bark, as of a tree. **2,** the layer of gray matter covering the brain. **—cor'ti·cal,** *adj.* **—cor'ti·cate** (-ti-kət) *adj.*

cor'ti·sone (kôr'ti-sōn) *n.* a hormone used in treating various diseases.

co·run'dum (kə-run'dəm) *n.* a very hard mineral used as an abrasive and, in some forms, a gem (ruby, sapphire, etc.).

cor'us·cate" (kôr'ə-skāt") *v.i.* emit vivid flashes of light; sparkle; gleam. **—cor"us·ca'tion,** *n.*

cor·vette' (kôr-vet') *n.* a small warship used as an escort.

cor'vine (kôr'vin) *adj.* pert. to the crow.

cor"y·phée' (kôr"ə-fā') *n.* a ballet dancer.

cos (kos) *n.* a kind of lettuce; romaine.

Co"sa No'stra (kō"sä nō'strä) (*It.*) the Mafia.

cosh (kosh) (*Brit.*) *n.* blackjack. **—v.t.** hit with a blackjack.

co·sig'na·to·ry *adj.* uniting with others in signing an agreement. **—n.** [also, **co·sign'-er**] a cosignatory person or power.

cos·met'ic (koz-met'ik) *n.* a preparation for beautifying the skin. **—adj. 1,** serving to beautify. **2,** serving to improve superficially the appearance of something. **—cos·met'i·cize", cos'me·tize",** *v.t.*

cos"me·tol'o·gy (koz"mi-tol'ə-gē) *n.* the art or profession of applying cosmetics. **—cos"me·tol'o·gist,** *n.*

cos'mic (kos'mik) *adj.* **1,** pert. to the universe; vast. **2,** orderly. **—cos'mi·cal·ly,** *adv.* **—cosmic rays,** certain rays or streams of particles which are present in space and of which the exact nature is not known.

cos·mo- (koz-mə) *pref.* of the cosmos.

cos'mo·drome" *n.* a Russian aerospace center.

cos·mog'o·ny (koz-mog'ə-nē) *n.* a theory or story of the origin of the universe.

cos·mol'o·gy (koz-mol'ə-jē) *n.* the branch of philosophy concerned with the origin and attributes of the universe, such as space, time, and causality. **—cos"mo·log'i·cal,** *adj.* **—cos·mol'o·gist,** *n.*

cos'mo·naut" (kos'mə-nât") *n.* a Russian astronaut.

cos·mop'o·lis (kos-mop'ə-lis) *n.* **1,** a city inhabited by persons of many nationalities. **2,** a city of international importance.

cos"mo·pol'i·tan (koz"mə-pol'ə-tən) *adj.* **1,** familiar with all the world; at home anywhere. **2,** peopled from all the world, as a city. **—n.** [also, **cos·mop'o·lite**] a cosmopolitan person.

cos'mos (koz'məs) *n.* **1,** the universe as an ordered whole. **2,** a tall annual plant with daisylike flowers.

Cos'sack (kos'ak) *n.* one of a Russian tribe famous as cavalrymen. ❏ *cassock*

cost (kâst) *n.* **1,** the price paid, or to be paid, for a thing or service; expense; outlay. **2,** loss of any kind; suffering. **—v.t.** [*pret. & p.p.* **cost**] **1,** have as a price. **2,** cause the loss of. **—v.i.** cause expenditure or loss.

co'star" (kō'stär") *n.* a performer who shares top billing with another.

cos'tard (kos'tərd) *n.* a large apple of England.

cos'tive (kos'tiv) *adj.* **1,** tending to cause constipation. **2,** constipated.

cost'ly (-lē) *adj.* expensive. **—cost'li·ness,** *n.*

cost-'plus" *n.* a fixed surcharge.

cost-'push inflation inflation caused by increases in production costs.

cos'tume (kos'tūm) *n.* **1,** dress in general; a particular style of dress. **2,** fancy dress; dress for stage wear. **—v.t.** furnish with a costume. **—cos'tum·er,** *n.* **—costume jewelry,** jewelry not containing precious stones.

> **costume, custom**
> ↔ Both words derive from Latin *consuetudo*, custom. *Costume* might be taken to mean the custom of a certain period in what concerns clothing.

co'sy (kō'zē) *adj.* cozy.

cot (kot) *n.* a small, light bed.

cote (kōt) *n.* a pen or coop.

co'te·rie (kō'tə-rē) *n.* a social group; set; clique.

co·til'lion (kō-til'yən) *n.* **1,** a fancy square dance. **2,** a ball.

cot'tage (kot'ij) *n.* a small house. **—cot'-tag·er,** *n.* **—cottage cheese,** a soft cheese made from sour milk curds. **—cottage industry,** a business in which products are produced by workers in their own homes.

cot'ter (kot'ər) *n.* **1,** a Scottish peasant. **2,** a split pin or bolt: *cotter pin.*

cot'ton (kot'ən) *n.* a soft white fibrous

mass from a plant (cotton plant); thread spun, cloth woven, etc. from cotton. —*v.i.* (with *to* or *up to*) (*Informal*) become friendly or attached (to). —**cot′ton·y,** *adj.*

---

cottage
↔ From Old English *cot(e)*, small house. Words ending in *-cote* (as *dovecote*) derive from the same source.

---

cot′ton·mouth″ *n.* a venomous snake of so. U.S.: *water moccasin.*

cot′ton·seed″ *n. & adj.* the seeds of cotton, which yield an oil.

cot′ton·tail″ *n.* a white-tailed rabbit.

cot′ton·wood″ (kot′ən-wûd″) *n.* an Amer. tree of the poplar family; the abele.

cot″y·le′don (kot″ə-lē′dən) *n.* (*Bot.*) the primary leaf of a plant.

couch (kowch) *n.* a lounge; a small bed. —*v.t.* **1,** express (meaning) in words. **2,** set; lay. —**couch potato,** (*Informal*) a person who spends much time watching television.

cou·chette′ (koo-shet′) *n.* **1,** a sleeping compartment on a train. **2,** a berth.

cou′gar (koo′gər) *n.* a large tawny Amer. wildcat; the puma.

cough (kâf) *v.i.* **1,** expel air from the lungs with effort and noise. **2,** (with *up*) expel by coughing, as phlegm; (*Slang*) surrender; pay out. —*n.* an act of coughing; a disease that causes coughing. —**cough drop,** a medicinal lozenge for soothing the throat.

---

cough
↔ The word is onomatopoetic—it comes from the sound of coughing, represented by Middle English *coghen.*

---

could (kûd) *v.* pret. of *can.*

cou′lee (koo′lē) *n.* a deep ravine.

cou′lomb (koo′lŏm) *n.* a unit of electric current, named for 18th-c. French physicist Charles Augustin de Coulomb.

coun′cil (kown′səl) *n.* a deliberative assembly. —**coun′cil·or,** *n.* —**coun′cil·man** (-mən) [*pl.* **-men**], **coun′cil·wom″an,** *n.*

---

council, counsel
☛ Do not confuse *council*, an assembly, and *counsel*, advice. Likewise, a *councillor* is an assembly member and a *counselor* is an adviser.

---

coun′sel (kown′səl) *n.* **1,** an interchange of opinions; consultation. **2,** advice. **3,** a lawyer; legal representative(s). —*v.t. & i.* advise; recommend. —**coun′se·lor,** *n.* □ *council*

count (kownt) *v.t.* **1,** enumerate one by one; reckon. **2,** consider; deem. —*v.i.* **1,** name numbers in order. **2,** be of value. **3,** (with *on*) depend; rely. **4,** (with *in*) include. —*n.* **1,** the act of reckoning. **2,** the result obtained. **3,** (*Law*) a charge in an indictment. **4,** a rank and title of nobility.

count′down″ *n.* a process of counting the seconds remaining before an event, esp. the launching of a spacecraft, is to occur.

coun′te·nance (kown′tə-nəns) *n.* **1,** the face. **2,** expression of the face. **3,** favor; approval. —*v.t.* **1,** aid; encourage. **2,** show approval of; tolerate.

count′er (kown′tər) *n.* **1,** a device for keeping count; a token. **2,** a bench or case over which goods are sold. **3,** the opposite or contrary. —*adj.* contrary; opposite. —*adv.* contrary. —*v.t. & i.* **1,** oppose; contradict. **2,** retaliate; strike back.

coun′ter- *pref.* denoting **1,** opposition. **2,** oppositeness. **3,** a complement.

coun″ter·act′ *v.t.* offset; neutralize. —**coun″ter·ac′tion,** *n.* —**coun″ter·act′ive,** *adj.*

coun′ter·at·tack″ *n.* an attack made to offset an enemy attack. —*v.i.* deliver a retaliatory attack (against).

coun′ter·bal″ance *n.* a weight or influence offsetting another. —*v.t.* offset with a counterbalance.

coun″ter·clock′wise *adj. & adv.* in reverse of clockwise.

coun″ter·cul″ture *n.* a subculture whose values and habits differ from those of society.

coun″ter·es′pi·o·nage *n.* the detection or frustration of enemy espionage.

coun′ter·feit (kown′tər-fit) *adj.* forged; spurious. —*n.* an imitation, esp. of a coin or banknote. —*v.t. & i.* imitate (money, etc.) fraudulently. —**coun′ter·feit·er,** *n.*

coun′ter·foil″ *n.* a part of a document, as the stub of a check, retained by the issuer.

coun″ter·in·sur′gen·cy *n.* the act of combating guerrilla warfare.

coun″ter·in·tel′li·gence *n.* measures taken to combat an enemy's information-gathering systems.

coun′ter·mand″ (kown′tər-månd″) *v.t.* revoke; overrule.

coun′ter·of·fen″sive *n.* counterattack.

coun′ter·pane″ *n.* a bedspread.

coun′ter·part″ *n.* **1,** a duplicate; facsimile. **2,** complement. **3,** a person or thing having the same function, etc. as another; equivalent.

coun'ter·point" (kown'tər-point") *n.* (*Music*) the combining of different melodies; hence, any element contrasted with another.

coun'ter·poise" *n.* a balancing weight; equilibrium.

coun"ter·pro·duc'tive *adj.* tending to produce results opposite those desired; self-defeating.

coun"ter·rev"o·lu'tion *n.* a revolution seeking to restore a former state of things. **—coun"ter·rev"o·lu'tion·ar·y,** *adj. & n.*

coun'ter·sign" *v.t.* add an authenticating signature to. **—***n.* a password.

coun'ter·sink" *v.t.* **1,** enlarge (a hole) to receive the head of a screw or nail. **2,** sink (the head of a screw) flush with the surface. **—***n.* a reamer for chamfering a hole.

coun'ter·spy" *n.* a spy who spies against other spies.

coun'ter·ten"or. *n.* **1,** a man's falsetto voice; a male alto. **2,** a high tenor.

coun"ter·vail' (-vāl') *v.t.* counteract; offset.

coun'ter·weight" *n.* a weight used to balance another.

count'ess (kown'tis) *n.* the wife of a count or earl.

count'less (-ləs) *adj.* so numerous as to be uncountable.

coun'tri·fied" (kun'trə-fīd") *adj.* (*Informal*) rustic in dress, manners, etc.

coun'try (kun'trē) *n.* **1,** land in general; a region; a particular kind of region. **2,** a nation, its territory or people. **3,** any rural region. **—***adj.* pert. to, or characteristic of, rural regions. **—country and western,** a kind of music. **—country club,** a suburban social club, usu. having facilities for golf, tennis, etc. **—the old country,** the foreign land from which a person or his or her ancestors emigrated, esp. Europe.

---

country
↔ From medieval Latin *contrata regio,* region lying on the opposite side (from the viewer, who is presumably in the city).

---

coun'try·man (-mən) *n.* [*pl.* **-men**] **1,** a native of one's own country. **2,** a rustic.

coun'try·side" *n.* the surrounding (rural) scene.

coun'ty (kown'tē) *n.* **1,** a political division of a state; its inhabitants. **2,** the domain of a count.

coup (koo) *n.* (*Fr.*) a sudden strategic

move; a blow; stroke. **—coup" de grâce'** (koo" də gräs') (*Fr.*) a merciful finishing blow. **—coup" d'é·tat'** (koo" dā-tä') (*Fr.*) a political stroke; a revolution. **—coup d'oeil** (koo döë') (*Fr.*) a glance.

coupe (koop) *n.* **1,** coupé. **2,** an ice cream sundae; the glass bowl or cup in which it is served.

cou·pé' (koo-pā') *n.* **1,** a two-doored closed automobile. **2,** a closed carriage for two.

cou'ple (kup'əl) *n.* **1,** two of a kind. **2,** two persons considered together, usu. because married, etc. **—***v.t.* connect; link; pair. **—coup'ler,** *n.*

---

couple
(*Gram.*) *Couple* is singular or plural depending on whether the two persons or things that compose it are considered as a unit (singular) or separately (plural).

---

coup'let (kup'lət) *n.* two successive rhyming lines.

coup'ling (kup'ling) *n.* a device for connecting things, as railroad cars, etc.

cou'pon (koo'pon) *n.* a slip to be detached from a bond, advertisement, etc. and exchanged for something.

cour'age (kēr'ij) *n.* lack of fear; bravery; valor.

cou·ra'geous (kə-rā'jəs) *adj.* intrepid; brave.

cour'i·er (kēr'ē-ər) *n.* **1,** a messenger. **2,** a paid escort of travelers.

course (kôrs) *n.* **1,** a moving forward; passage. **2,** the line of motion. **3,** the path or ground covered; a place for playing golf; a racetrack. **4,** progressive phases, as in a disease. **5,** a series, as of lectures, studies, etc. **6,** method of procedure. **7,** a succession of acts, practices, etc. **8,** any part of a meal served at one time. **—***v.t.* run, hunt, or chase after. **—***v.i.* move swiftly. **—of course,** obviously; certainly; yes, indeed.

cours'er (kôr'sər) *n.* **1,** a ploverlike bird. **2,** (*Poetic*) a swift horse.

court (kôrt) *n.* **1,** a space enclosed by buildings: *courtyard.* **2,** a level area for certain games, as tennis. **3,** a sovereign's household; a general reception hosted by a sovereign. **4,** a sovereign's authority. **5,** a hall of justice; a session there; the judge or judges presiding. **—***v.t.* **1,** seek the favor of. **2,** woo. **3,** aspire to; invite. **—***v.i.* woo. **—court'ly,** *adj.* elegant; refined; polite. **—court card,** in a deck of playing cards, the king, queen, or jack.

---

cour·te·ous (kẽr′tẻ-əs) *adj.* showing courtesy; polite.

cour′te·san (kôr′tə-zən) *n.* a harlot.

---

courtesan, courtier

↔ *Courtesan* was originally the feminine equivalent of the masculine *courtier,* i.e., a person of the court. This sense has been lost to the feminine form, leaving only the derived sense of paramour of a courtier, hence, prostitute.

---

cour′te·sy (kẽr′tə-sẻ) *n.* **1,** kind and thoughtful behavior toward another; politeness; gracious attention. **2,** a favor or indulgence.

court′house″ *n.* a building for law courts and governmental offices.

cour′ti·er (kôr′tẻ-ər) *n.* **1,** a person in attendance at a royal court. **2,** flatterer. ❑ *courtesan*

court-′mar″tial *n.* [*pl.* **courts-′mar″tial**] a military or naval court. —*v.t.* try by court-martial.

court′ship″ *n.* a wooing.

court′yard″ *n.* an enclosed yard in or near a building.

cous′cous (koos′koos) *n.* a No. Afr. dish made with semolina.

cous′in (kuz′ən) *n.* **1,** a child of one's uncle, aunt, or cousin. **2,** (*Slang*) a dupe. —*v.t.* (*Slang*) dupe. —**cous′in·ly,** *adj.*

---

cousin, cousin-german

☛ *Cousin* comes from Latin *consobrinus,* child of one's aunt; the meaning eventually broadened to cover any relative other than one's parents, sister, or brother. The *german* in *cousin-german* derives from Latin *germen,* sprout, the root word of English *germ.*

---

cous″in-ger′man (-jẽr′mən) *n.* [*pl.* **cous″-ins-ger′man**] first cousin. ❑ *cousin*

cou·ture′ (koo-tyûr′) *n.* dress design.

cou·tu·rier′ (koo-tûr-yā′) *n.* a dressmaker and designer.

cove (kōv) *n.* **1,** a sheltered inlet. **2,** (*Brit. Slang*) fellow; man.

cov′en (kuv′ən) *n.* band of witches, esp. 13.

cov′e·nant (kuv′ə-nənt) *n.* a solemn agreement. —*v.t. & i.* promise.

cov′er (kuv′ər) *v.t.* **1,** put something over or upon; lie upon; close the opening of; shield; protect; coat; clothe. **2,** extend over the entire surface of; hide; screen. **3,** travel or pass over. **4,** include; comprise. **5,** aim at directly, as with a gun. **6,** insure

for some specified risk. **7,** (*Informal*) report the news of (an event, place, etc.) —*v.i.* **1,** be spread or lie over an entire thing or surface. **2,** replace a hat. —*n.* **1,** something laid or lying over a thing to close, conceal, or protect it. **2,** a screen; disguise. **3,** shelter. **4,** table fittings for one person. —**cover charge,** a restaurant's extra charge for a floor show. —**cover girl,** (*Informal*) a young female cover model. —**cover model,** a person whose picture is used to decorate the cover of a magazine. —**cover story, 1,** a story which is advertised on the cover of a magazine. **2,** a story used to conceal the truth, provide an alibi, etc.

cov′er·age (-ij) *n.* **1,** protection by insurance or funds in reserve. **2,** the reporting of news; the extent or quality of the reports.

cov′er·alls (-âlz) *n.pl.* protective work garments.

cov′er·let (-lit) *n.* a bedspread.

cov′ert (kuv′ərt) *adj.* **1,** secret; hidden. **2,** sheltered. —*n.* a thicket; hiding place, esp. for game.

cov′er-up″ *n.* action taken to conceal information, as of an embarrassing or illegal event.

cov′et (kuv′it) *v.t.* long for; desire enviously. —**cov′et·ous,** *adj.*

cov′ey (kuv′ẻ) *n.* a small flock of birds, esp. quail.

co-″vi·vant′ (kō″vẻ-vänt′) *n.* roommate.

cow (kow) *n.* the female of various large animals, esp. of domestic cattle. —*v.t.* intimidate.

---

cow

↔ The name of the animal goes back through Germanic intermediaries to remote Indo-European roots. The verb comes from Old Norse *kuga,* oppress.

---

cow″a·bun′ga (kou″ə-bung′gə) *interj.* of exhilaration, often used by surfers.

cow′ard (kow′ərd) *n.* one who shrinks from pain or danger. —**cow′ard·ice** (-is) *n.* —**cow′ard·ly,** *adj.*

cow′bird″ *n.* a small No. Amer. blackbird.

cow′boy″ *n.* **1,** a male cowhand. **2,** a reckless person.

cow′catch″er *n.* the guarding front frame of a locomotive.

cow′er (kow′ər) *v.i.* bend down or crouch in fear, shame, etc.

cow′girl″ *n.* a female cowhand.

---

cow'hand" *n.* a worker on a cattle ranch. Also, **cow'punch"er.**

cow'hide" *n.* leather from the skin of cattle.

cowl (kowl) *n.* **1,** a monk's hooded garment; its hood. **2,** the front of an automobile's body. **3,** cowling.

cow'lick *n.* an unruly tuft of hair.

cowl'ing *n.* a metal cover or housing, esp. of an aircraft engine.

cow'man (kow'mən) *n.* [*pl.* **-men**] an owner of cattle; rancher.

co'work"er *n.* colleague.

cow'poke" (kow'pōk") *n.* cowboy.

cow'pox" (kow'poks") *n.* an eruptive disease of cows, caused by a virus used in smallpox vaccination.

cow'rie (kow'rē) *n.* a small marine shell, used for costume jewelry and by various peoples for money.

cow'slip (kow'slip) *n.* the marsh marigold.

cox'comb" (koks'kōm") *n.* **1,** a jester's cap. **2,** a vain, conceited fellow.

cox'swain (kok'sən) *n.* a helmsman of a rowed boat.

coy (koi) *adj.* exhibiting pretended shyness. —**coy'ness,** *n.*

> **coy, quiet**
> ↔ Both words derive from Latin *quietus,* but by differing routes: *coy* through Old French, *quiet* directly through Medieval Latin.

coy·o'te (kī-ō'tē) *n.* a small tawny wolf of western No. Amer.

coy'pu (koi'poo) *n.* a So. Amer. rodent.

coz'en (kuz'ən) *v.t. & i.* cheat; defraud. —**coz'en·age,** *n.*

co'zy (kō'zē) *adj.* warm and snug. —*n.* a padded cover, as for a teapot. —**co'ziness,** *n.*

CP/M *abbr.* (*Computers*) an early computer operating system: *C(ontrol) P(rogram for) M(icrocomputers).*

CPR cardiopulmonary resuscitation.

CPU central processing unit.

crab (krab) *n.* **1,** an edible crustacean. **2,** (*Informal*) a cross, surly person. **3,** a tree, the crab apple; its fruit. **4,** (*cap.*) a northern constellation; a sign of the zodiac: Cancer. —*v.i.* [**crabbed, crab'bing**] **1,** fish for crabs. **2,** (*Informal*) find fault. —**crab-grass,** a common lawn weed.

crab' ap"ple *n.* a variety of small, sour apple.

crab'bed (krab'id) *adj.* **1,** peevish; cross. **2,** cramped; illegible.

crab'by (-ē) *adj.* grouchy; surly.

crack (krak) *v.i. & t.* **1,** snap with a sudden sharp sound. **2,** split without separating. **3,** of a voice, break. **4,** (*Informal*) lose effectiveness or courage. **5,** (*Informal*) tell (a joke). **6,** distill (petroleum) under pressure. **7,** (with *down*) enforce regulations strictly; punish severely. —*n.* **1,** a sharp snapping sound or report. **2,** a narrow fissure; slight break. **3,** a resounding blow. **4,** (*Slang*) an attempt. **5,** (*Slang*) a gibe. **6,** (*Slang*) a variety of cocaine. —*adj.* (*Informal*) expert; excellent.

cracked (krakt) *adj.* **1,** broken. **2,** (*Informal*) crazy.

crack'er *n.* **1,** a thin, crisp biscuit. **2,** a poor white farmer of Ga. and Fla. —**crack'ers,** *adj.* (*Slang*) crazy.

Crack'er Jack" (*T.N.*) a popcorn confection.

crack'er·jack" *adj.* [also, **crack'ing**] (*Informal*) excellent; first-class.

crack'le (krak'əl) *v.i.* emit repeated, sharp, snapping noises. —*n.* pottery with fine cracks in the glaze. —**crack'ly,** *adj.*

crack'ling *n.* the crisp browned skin of roast pork.

crack'pot" (*Slang*) *n.* an eccentric person. —*adj.* eccentric; crazy.

cracks'man (-mən) *n.* [*pl.* **-men**] a burglar.

crack-'up *n.* **1,** a crash. **2,** collapse; defeat. **3,** (*Informal*) a physical or mental breakdown.

-cra·cy (krə-sē) *suf.* denoting government or governing body.

cra'dle (krā'dəl) *n.* a baby's crib, usually on rockers; hence, birthplace; origin; infancy. —*v.t.* place in, or hold as in, a cradle. —**cat's cradle,** a game played by forming designs with an endless loop of string; a design so formed.

craft (kráft) *n.* **1,** [*pl.* **craft**] a vessel; boat; ship, etc. **2,** a trade requiring skill; a guild. **3,** skill; dexterity. **4,** cunning; guile. —*v.t.* manufacture; make, esp. with skill. ❑ ability

crafts'per"son *n.* an artisan. Also, **crafts'man** (-mən) [*pl.* **-men**], **crafts'wom"an,** *n.* —**crafts'man·ship,** *n.*

craft'y (-ē) *adj.* guileful. —**craft'i·ness,** *n.*

crag (krag) *n.* a steep, rugged rock. —**crag'gy,** *adj.*

cram (kram) *v.t.* [**crammed, cram'ming**] **1,** fill overfull; pack or stuff in. **2,** eat greedily. —*v.i.* **1,** stuff oneself. **2,** study intensely for an examination.

cramp (kramp) *n.* **1,** a sudden, painful contraction of a muscle. **2,** (*pl.*) griping pain in the abdomen. —*v.t.* hinder from free action; hamper; confine narrowly. —**cramped,** *adj.* too small or close.

cran'ber"ry (kran'ber"ė) *n.* the tart red berry of a bog plant; the plant.

crane (krān) *n.* **1,** a large, long-legged wading bird. **2,** a machine for lifting and moving heavy weights; derrick. —*v.i. & t.* stretch out (the neck).

cra'ni·um (krā'nė-əm) *n.* the part of the skull containing the brain. —**cra'ni·al,** *adj.*

crank (krank) *n.* **1,** a device, as a bent axle, for imparting or converting rotary motion. **2,** an eccentric person. —*v.t. & i.* operate·by a crank.

crank'case" *n.* the housing for the crankshaft and its neighboring parts.

crank'shaft" *n.* the cranking shaft of an engine (esp. automobile).

crank'y (krang'kė) *adj.* irritable; hard to please. —**crank'i·ness,** *n.*

cran'ny (kran'ė) *n.* crevice; crack.

crape (krāp) *n.* crepe.

craps (kraps) *n.sing.* a gambling dice game. —**crap out,** lose. —**shoot craps,** play the game of craps. —**crap'shoot"er,** *n.*

crap'u·lent (krap'yə-lənt) *adj.* sick from excessive eating or drinking. —**crap'u·lence,** *n.*

crap'u·lous (-ləs) *adj.* **1,** characterized by excess in eating or drinking. **2,** crapulent.

crash (krash) *n.* **1,** a loud harsh sound of things breaking. **2,** a collision. **3,** financial failure or ruin. **4,** (*Computers*) a shutdown due to malfunction or software failure. **5,** a coarse, rough fabric of linen or cotton. —*v.t. & i.* **1,** smash; shatter. **2,** (*Slang*) intrude. **3,** (*Slang*) recover from a drug-induced experience. **4,** (*Slang*) spend the night; sleep. **5,** (*Computers*) freeze up or shutdown due to equipment or software failure. ❑ *collision*

crash-'dive" *v.i.* of a submarine, dive suddenly, to escape detection or attack.

crass (kras) *adj.* gross; obtuse. —**crass'ness,** *n.*

-crat (krat) *suf.* denoting a ruler; a member of a ruling body; or an advocate of a form of government.

crate (krāt) *n.* a box made of wooden slats. —*v.t.* put into a crate or protecting frame.

cra'ter (krā'tər) *n.* **1,** the mouth of a volcano. **2,** the pit made by an exploding bomb or shell.

cra·vat' (krə-vat') *n.* a necktie.

---

cravat
↔ From French *Cravate*, Croat, because Croatian mercenaries regularly wore linen scarves.

---

crave (krāv) *v.t.* **1,** long for. **2,** beg for.

cra'ven (krā'vən) *n.* a cowardly, abject person. —*adj.* cowardly.

crav'ing (krā'ving) *n.* extreme desire.

craw (krâ) *n.* the crop of a bird. —**stick in one's craw,** rankle.

craw'fish" (krâ'fish") *n.* a crustacean resembling a lobster. Also, **cray'fish** (krā'-). —*v.i.* (*Informal*) retreat from a position or opinion.

crawl (krâl) *v.i.* **1,** move on hands and knees or by drawing the body along the ground. **2,** advance slowly or feebly. **3,** be or feel overrun by creeping things. **4,** humiliate oneself to regain favor. —*n.* **1,** a creeping progress. **2,** a fast swimming stroke. —**crawl'y,** *adj.*

cray'on (krā'ən) *n.* a stick of chalk, wax, etc. for drawing or writing. —*v.t.* draw with crayons.

craze (krāz) *v.t. & i.* make or become insane. —*n.* **1,** a fad. **2,** a crack in the glaze of pottery.

cra'zy (krā'zė) *adj.* insane; wildly excited. —*n.* (*Slang*) a crazy or nonconforming person. —**cra'zi·ness,** *n.* —**crazy bone,** funny bone. —**crazy quilt,** a patchwork quilt.

creak (krēk) *v.i.* make a squeaking noise. —**creak'y,** *adj.*

cream (krēm) *n.* **1,** the rich, oily part of milk. **2,** something smooth like cream, as a sauce, paste, etc. **3,** the choice part of anything. **4,** a yellowish-white color. —*v.t.* **1,** beat to a smooth consistency. **2,** (*Slang*) whip soundly; thrash. —**cream'y,** *adj.* —**cold cream,** a cosmetic ointment. —**cream of tartar,** potassium bitartrate, an ingredient of baking powder. —**cream puff, 1,** a cream-filled pastry. **2,** (*Slang*) a weakling.

cream'er *n.* **1,** a cream pitcher. **2,** a non-dairy product used as a substitute for cream, in coffee, etc.

cream'er·y (-ə-rė) *n.* a factory where butter and cheese are made.

crease (krēs) *n.* a long thin mark made by folding; a wrinkle. —*v.t. & i.* make or become wrinkled.

cre·ate' (krė-āt') *v.t.* **1,** bring into being; cause to exist. **2,** invest with rank. **3,** give rise to; originate.

cre·a'tion (krė-ā'shən) *n.* **1,** act or result of creating; invention; an original product.

2, the world or universe. **3,** a woman's dress, hat, etc., of new and original design.

cre·a'tive (-tiv) *adj.* inventive; originating. **—cre·a'tive·ness,** *n.*

cre·a'tor (-tər) *n.* **1,** one who creates. **2,** (*cap.*) God.

crea'ture (krē'chər) *n.* **1,** a living animal or human. **2,** one created or controlled by another.

crèche (kresh) *n.* **1,** a tableau of the crib of Jesus in the stable of Bethlehem. **2,** a day-care center.

cre'dence (krē'dəns) *n.* belief.

cre·den'tials (kri-den'shəls) *n.pl.* attesting documents.

cre·den'za (kri-den'zə) *n.* a small sideboard, buffet, or table.

cred'i·ble (kred'ə-bəl) *adj.* worthy of belief; believable. **—cred"i·bil'i·ty,** *n.* **—credibility gap,** lack of confidence or trust between two entities (as between a government and its public).

---

credible, creditable, credulous

☛ Words from the same source, having to do with belief. *Credible* means believable; *creditable* means deserving of praise; *credulous* means gullible.

---

cred'it (kred'it) *n.* **1,** faith; belief. **2,** credibility. **3,** an acknowledgment of worth or accomplishment. **4,** good reputation, esp. in financial affairs; borrowing power. **5,** a sum in a person's favor in an account. **—v.t. 1,** believe; have faith in. **2,** acknowledge the worth of; record a payment received, etc. **—credit card,** a card used to purchase goods, etc., on credit.

cred'it·a·ble *adj.* deserving of esteem or praise. ❑ *credible*

cred'i·tor (kred'i-tər) *n.* one to whom money is owed.

cre'do (krē'dō) *n.* [*pl.* **-dos** (-dōz)] a statement of beliefs; a creed.

cre·du'li·ty (kre-dū'lə-tė) *n.* willingness to believe; gullibility.

cred'u·lous (krej'ə-ləs) *adj.* too willing to believe; gullible. ❑ *credible*

creed (krēd) *n.* **1,** a brief statement of belief, esp. religious. **2,** a sect; denomination; belief.

creek (krēk) *n.* a small river.

creel (krēl) *n.* **1,** a wickerwork basket for carrying fish. **2,** a framework for holding bobbins or spools in a spinning mill.

creep (krēp) *v.i.* [*pret. & p.p.* **crept** (krept)] **1,** move with the body close to the ground. **2,** move slowly, feebly, or stealthily. **3,** crawl. **4,** grow along the ground. **—n. 1,** a creeping movement. **2,**

(*Slang*) a disgusting person. **3,** (*pl.*) a sensation of unease, fear, etc.

creep'er *n.* **1,** a vine. **2,** (*pl.*) a garment worn by infants.

creep'y *adj.* **1,** creeping. **2,** causing the creeps. **—creep'i·ness,** *n.*

cre'mate (krē'māt) *v.t.* reduce to ashes, as a corpse. **—cre·ma'tion,** *n.*

cre'ma·to·ry (krē'mə-tôr-ė) *n.* a furnace for cremation. Also, **cre"ma·to'ri·um** (-tôr'ė-əm).

crème de ca·ca'o (krem' də kō'kō; kä-kä'ō) (*Fr.*) a liqueur flavored with chocolate.

crème' de la crème' (krem' də lä krem') (*Fr.*) cream of the cream; the very best.

crème de menthe (krem' də menth'; *Fr.* mänt') (*Fr.*) a mint-flavored liqueur.

cren'el (kren'əl) *n.* an opening in a battlement; embrasure. **—cren'el·ate"** (-āt") *adj.* **—cren"el·a'tion,** *n.*

Cre'ole (krē'ōl) *n.* **1,** an American of Fr. or Sp. ancestry. **2,** (*Informal*) erroneously, a person part black. **3,** a pidgin language, esp. the language of certain residents of Louisiana. **—adj.** in the style (as of cooking), dialect, etc. of Creoles.

cre'o·sote" (krē'ə-sōt") *n.* an oily liquid from wood tar, an antiseptic and preservative.

crepe (krāp) *n.* **1,** a crinkled fabric, usually of silk, often worn in black as a sign of mourning. Also, **crape. 2,** a pancake. **—crepe de Chine** (də shēn) a very thin silk crepe. **—crepes suzette** (krāp' soo-zet') Fr. pancakes cooked in burning liqueurs.

crep'i·tate" (krep'ə-tāt") *v.i.* crackle. **—crep'i·tant,** *adj.* **—crep"i·ta'tion,** *n.*

crept (krept) *v.* pret. & p.p. of *creep*.

cre·pus'cu·lar (kri-pus'kyə-lər) *adj.* pert. to twilight; dim.

cre·scen'do (krə-shen'dō) (*It., Music*) *adj. & adv.* gradually increasing in force or loudness. **—n.** a gradual increase in force or loudness.

cres'cent (kres'ənt) *adj.* **1,** growing; increasing. **2,** shaped like the new moon. **—n.** something in this shape.

cress (kres) *n.* a plant of the mustard family with crisp, pungent leaves.

crest (krest) *n.* **1,** a comb or tuft on a bird's head. **2,** the top of a helmet; the figure above an escutcheon. **3,** the top; peak, as of a hill, wave, etc. **—v.i.** form a crest; rise to a maximum.

crest'fall"en *adj.* dejected; abashed.

cre'tin (krē'tin) *n.* a person with a congenital thyroid deficiency, usu. resulting in idiocy. —**cre′tin·ism,** *n.*

> **cretin**
> ↔ From *crétin*, a Swiss-French word for a person having a physical or mental deformity. The source is Latin *christianus*, Christian.

cre·tonne′ (kri-ton′) *n.* an unglazed printed cotton fabric.

cre·vasse′ (krə-vas′) *n.* a crack, as in a glacier or levee.

crev′ice (krev′is) *n.* a crack; fissure.

crew (kroo) *n.* a working force, esp. of a ship or train. —*v.* pret. of *crow.* —**crew cut,** a very short haircut.

crew′el (kroo′əl) *n.* a worsted embroidery yarn.

crib (krib) *n.* **1,** a high-sided bed for a child. **2,** a slatted bin for storage of grain. **3,** (*Informal*) trot. —*v.t.* [**cribbed, crib′bing**] **1,** confine. **2,** (*Informal*) plagiarize; prepare (a language lesson) from a translation. —**crib′ber,** *n.* —**crib course,** an easy college course. —**crib death,** a sudden fatal affliction of unknown cause that strikes babies.

crib′bage (krib′ij) *n.* a card game.

crick (krik) *n.* **1,** a painful spasm, esp. of the neck or back. **2,** (*Dial.*) creek.

crick′et (krik′it) *n.* **1,** a jumping insect. **2,** a Brit. ball game similar to baseball. **3,** (*Informal*) fair play.

cri′er (krī′ər) *n.* one who cries, as a hawker or public announcer.

crime (krīm) *n.* **1,** an offense punishable by law. **2,** (*Informal*) a foolish or reprehensible act.

> **crime, crisis, critic**
> ↔ From Greek *krinein*, decide. *Crime* comes through Latin *crimen*, accusation. Greek *krisis* meant judgment (source of *critic*), then the turning point of a disease (source of *crisis*).

crim′i·nal (krim′i-nəl) *adj.* pert. to or constituting crime. —*n.* a person guilty of a crime. —**crim″i·nal′i·ty,** *n.*

crim′i·nal·ize″ (krim′ə-nəl-īz″) *v.t.* to make punishable as a crime. —**crim″i·nal·i·za′tion,** *n.*

crim″i·nol′o·gy (krim″i-nol′ə-jē) *n.* the study of crime or crime detection. —**crim″i·nol′o·gist,** *n.*

crimp (krimp) *v.t.* pinch into folds or flutings; give a wavy appearance to. —*n.* a fluting; a wave, as in hair. —**put a crimp in,** (*Slang*) hinder; obstruct.

crim′son (krim′zən) *n. & adj.* a deep-red color.

cringe (krinj) *v.i.* wince; shrink, esp. with fear or servility.

crin′kle (kring′kəl) *v.t. & i.* make wrinkles or ripples (in); twist. —**crink′ly,** *adj.*

crin′o·line (krin′ə-lin) *n.* **1,** a stiff cotton fabric. **2,** a hoop skirt.

crip′ple (krip′əl) *n.* a physically disabled person. —*v.t.* lame; disable.

cri′sis (krī′sis) *n.* [*pl.* **-ses** (-sēz)] a decisive point or condition; a turning point; climax. ❑ *crime*

crisp (krisp) *adj.* **1,** brittle; crumbly; short, as pastry; not limp. **2,** fresh. **3,** pithy; terse. **4,** crinkled; tightly curled. —*v.t.* curl; crimp. —*v.i.* become crisp. —**crisp′ness,** *n.*

criss′cross″ *adj.* formed in or marked by crossing lines. —*adv.* crosswise. —*n.* crisscross mark or pattern. —*v.i. & t.* form or mark (with) a crisscross.

> **crisscross**
> ↔ Variant of earlier *Christ cross*, the mark of the cross.

cri·te′ri·on (krī-tir′ē-ən) *n.* [*pl.* **-a** (-ə)] a standard for comparison or judgment.

crit′ic (krit′ik) *n.* **1,** one who appraises the merit of others' works, esp. artistic or literary. **2,** one who censures. ❑ *crime*

crit′i·cal (krit′i-kəl) *adj.* **1,** censorious. **2,** pert. to criticism. **3,** pert. to a crisis. **4,** indispensable; essential for success, proper functioning, etc. —**critical mass, 1,** the amount of fissionable material necessary to sustain a nuclear chain reaction. **2,** the amount necessary to achieve a desired result.

crit′i·cism (krit′i-siz-əm) *n.* the act or judgment of a critic.

> **criticism, critique**
> ☞ The two words mean the same thing, but *criticism* more commonly suggests a negative evaluation than *critique.*

crit′i·cize″ (krit′i-sīz″) *v.t. & i.* judge as a critic, esp. adversely.

cri·tique′ (kri-tēk′) *n.* a critical review. ❑ *criticism*

crit′ter (krit′ər) *n.* (*Dial.*) creature.

croak (krōk) *n.* a hoarse, guttural sound, as of a frog. —*v.i.* **1,** utter a croak. **2,** (*Slang*) die. —*v.t.* (*Slang*) kill.

croak′er (krō′kər) *n.* **1,** a frog or croaking fish. **2,** (*Slang*) a doctor.

cro·chet′ (krō-shā′) *n.* a kind of knitting

done with one hooked needle. —*v.t. & i.* make such work.

crock (krok) *n.* an earthenware vessel or jar. —**crocked** (krokt) *adj.* (*Slang*) drunk.

crock'er·y (-ə-rè) *n.* earthenware dishes.

Crock-'Pot'' *n.* (*T.N.*) an electric earthenware pot for slow cooking with low heat.

croc'o·dile'' (krok'ə-dīl'') *n.* a large horny-skinned aquatic reptile. —**crocodile tears,** insincere grief.

> **crocodile**
> ↔ From Greek *krokodilos*, crocodile. Some have proposed a derivation from the Greek roots *krokē*, pebbles, and *drilos*, worm—from the crocodile's penchant for lying in the sun.

cro'cus (krō-kəs) *n.* a dwarf bulb flowering in earliest spring.

crois·sant' (krwä-sän') *n.* a light crescent-shaped roll.

crom'lech (krom'lek) *n.* a prehistoric stone monument.

crone (krōn) *n.* an old woman.

cro'ny (krō'nè) *n.* a chum.

crook (krûk) *n.* **1,** a bend; curve; hook. **2,** a bent or curved staff, part, tool, etc. **3,** a dishonest person. —*v.t. & i.* bend; curve.

> **crook**
> ↔ All senses of the word—including the sense of criminal—come from the Old Norse *krokr*, hook.

crook'ed (krûk'id) *adj.* **1,** not straight; winding. **2,** dishonest. —**crook'ed·ness,** *n.*

croon (kroon) *v.t. & i.* sing softly and plaintively.

crop (krop) *n.* **1,** plants grown and harvested; the useful yield of a particular plant, field, or season. **2,** a riding whip. **3,** a pouch in a bird's gullet. **4,** hair cut close to the head. —*v.t.* [**cropped, crop'ping**] **1,** cut or bite off the tips of. **2,** cut short, as a tail, hair, etc. —*v.i.* (with *up*) appear unexpectedly.

crop'per (krop'ər) *n.* a fall from horseback; hence, a failure. —**come a cropper,** fail.

cro·quet' (krō-kā') *n.* a lawn game of driving balls through wickets.

cro·quette' (krō-ket') *n.* a fried portion of finely minced meat, rice, etc.

cro'sier (krō'zhər) *n.* crozier.

cross (krâs) *n.* **1,** two intersecting stakes, bars, or lines; (*cap.*) the cross on which Christ died; a replica of this as a religious symbol. **2,** hence, a burden; misfortune. **3,** an intermixture of breeds. —*adj.* **1,** trans-

verse; intersecting. **2,** contrary; opposed. **3,** peevish; fretful. **4,** hybrid. —*v.t.* **1,** draw (a line) or place (a thing) across another. **2,** (with *out*) cancel. **3,** go across. **4,** make the sign of the cross on or over. **5,** meet and pass. **6,** thwart; oppose. **7,** mix the breed of. —*v.i.* **1,** intersect. **2,** pass from one side to the other. **3,** meet and pass. **4,** interbreed. —**cross fire,** shooting from different positions so the lines cross. —**cross purposes,** conflicting purposes or tactics. —**cross section,** a cut through a solid; hence, a view of all parts or aspects.

cross- *pref.* **1,** across; transverse. **2,** opposing; antagonistic; counter.

cross'bar'' *n.* a transverse bar.

cross'bones'' *n.* crossed bones, a symbol of piracy.

cross'bow'' (-bō'') *n.* a bow mounted on a catapulting device.

cross'breed'' *v.t.* [*pret. & p.p.* **-bred''**] mix (breeds). —*n.* a hybrid produced by crossbreeding.

cross'cut'' *adj.* **1,** cut across the grain. **2,** adapted for cutting across.

cross-'dress'' *v.i.* dress in the clothes of the opposite sex. —**cross-''dress'er,** *n.*

cross-''ex·am'ine *v.t.* question a hostile witness or person. Also, **cross-''ques'tion.**

cross'eyed'' (-īd'') *adj.* having one or both eyes directed abnormally.

cross'hair'' *n.* (*often pl.*) two intersecting lines in the form of a cross, used in optical devices to center a target, as a pointer on a computer screen to locate a point, etc.

cross'hatch'' *v.t.* mark with crossed sets of parallel lines, as to shade a drawing. —*n.* an area so marked.

cross'ing *n.* **1,** an intersection of roads. **2,** a place suitable for crossing a road, river, etc. **3,** act of opposing.

cross'patch'' *n.* (*Informal*) a cross person.

cross-'pol''li·na'tion *n.* the transfer of pollen from one flower to another. —**cross-''pol'li·nate'',** *v.t.*

cross-ref'er·ence *n.* a note directing attention to another part of the same document. —**cross-''re·fer',** *v.i.*

cross'roads'' *n.* **1,** an intersection of roads. **2,** a critical point in time.

cross'town'' *adj.* **1,** across the width of a town. **2,** the other side of town.

cross'wise'' *adv.* across. Also, **cross'ways''.**

cross'word'' puzzle a game of fitting defined words to squares in a diagram.

crotch (kroch) *n.* the angle where two branches, legs, etc. divide.

crotch′et (kroch′it) *n.* **1,** an odd notion; a whim. **2,** (*Music*) a quarter note (see *note*).

crotch′et·y (kroch′it-ė) *adj.* given to odd or eccentric fancies; cranky.

cro′ton (krō′tən) *n.* any of various tropical herbs and shrubs yielding *croton oil*, a powerful purgative.

crouch (krowch) *v.i.* stoop low.

croup (kroop) *n.* a disease of young children marked by difficult breathing and hoarse coughing. —**croup′y,** *adj.*

crou′pi·er (kroo′pė-ər) *n.* an employee of a gambling casino.

crou′ton (kroo′ton) *n.* a small piece of toast put in soup, salad, etc.

crow (krō) *v.i.* **1,** [*pret.* also **crew**] utter the cry of a rooster. **2,** brag; gloat. —*n.* **1,** a rooster's cry. **2,** a large, glossy black bird; raven.

crow′bar″ (krō′bär″) *n.* a heavy iron bar used for prying.

crowd (krowd) *n.* **1,** a multitude; throng. **2,** the populace. **3,** (*Informal*) a clique; coterie. **4,** [also, **crwth** (krooth)] an ancient Celtic lyre. —*v.t.* **1,** squeeze; cram. **2,** fill to excess. —*v.i.* come in numbers; swarm.

crow′foot″ *n.* [*pl.* -**foots″**] a plant with leaves divided like a bird's foot.

crown (krown) *n.* **1,** a monarch's jeweled headdress; hence, the sovereign; royal authority. **2,** a wreath for the head. **3,** the highest part of anything. **4,** the exposed part of a tooth. **5,** any of various now obsolete coins, esp. an English silver coin worth 5 shillings. —*v.t.* **1,** put a crown on. **2,** confer honor or sovereignty upon. **3,** put the finishing touch to. **4,** (*Informal*) hit on the head. —**crown prince,** the heir apparent to a throne. —**crown saw,** a rotary saw formed of a hollow cylinder with teeth in its edge.

crow's-′foot″ *n.* [*pl.* -**feet**] a wrinkle shaped like a bird's foot.

crow's-′nest″ *n.* a lookout's perch.

cro′zier (krō′zhər) *n.* the pastoral staff of a bishop or abbot. Also, **cro′sier.**

cru′cial (kroo′shəl) *adj.* decisive; critical.

cru′ci·ble (kroo′sə-bəl) *n.* a cauldron for melting ores, metals, etc.

cru′ci·fer (kroo′sə-fər) *n.* a cross-bearer in a religious procession.

cru″ci·fix″ (kroo′si-fiks″) *n.* a representation of Christ on the cross.

cru″ci·fix′ion (kroo″sə-fik′shən) *n.* **1,** the act of crucifying. **2,** (*cap.*) the death of Christ on the cross.

cru′ci·form″ (kroo′sə-fôrm″) *adj.* cross-shaped.

cru′ci·fy″ (kroo′si-fī″) *v.t.* **1,** put to death by attaching to a cross. **2,** berate; scourge.

crud *n.* dirt; something inferior. —**crud′dy** (-ė) *adj.* (*Slang*) inferior; contemptible. ❏ *curd*

crude (krood) *adj.* **1,** in a raw or unprepared state. **2,** unrefined; unpolished. —**crude′ness, cru′di·ty,** *n.* —**crude oil,** unrefined petroleum.

cru″di·tés′ (kroo″di-tā′) *n.* (*Fr.*) an appetizer of raw vegetables.

cru′el (kroo′əl) *adj.* deliberately causing suffering to others; pitiless. —**cru′el·ty** (-tė) *n.*

cru′et (kroo′it) *n.* a glass vial, as for oil or vinegar.

cruise (krooz) *v.i.* **1,** drive or sail about with no definite destination. **2,** patrol a beat in a police car. **3,** operate a conveyance at the speed of maximum efficiency. **4,** (*Slang*) search for a sexual partner. —*n.* an ocean trip for pleasure. —**cruise control,** a device in a motor vehicle that automatically maintains a constant speed. —**cruise missile,** a guided missile designed to travel at low altitudes.

cruis′er (kroo′zər) *n.* **1,** a warship somewhat smaller than a battleship. **2,** a small yacht. **3,** a police car.

crul′ler (krul′ər) *n.* a ring or twist of deep-fried cake; a doughnut.

crumb (krum) *n.* **1,** a small fragment, esp. of bread. **2,** (*Slang*) an insignificant person. —**crumb′y,** *adj.*

crum′ble (krum′bəl) *v.t. & i.* break into small bits; disintegrate. —**crum′bly** (-blė) *adj.*

crum′my (krum′ė) *adj.* (*Slang*) of poor quality; inferior; shabby.

crum′pet (krum′pət) *n.* an unsweetened muffin, usually toasted before served.

crum′ple (krum′pəl) *v.t. & i.* rumple; wrinkle.

crunch (krunch) *v.t. & i.* chew, grind, or trample noisily. —*n.* a difficult situation caused by a shortage of something, as money.

crup′per (krup′ər) *n.* a strap holding a riding saddle steady.

cru·sade′ (kroo-sād′) *n.* a zealous campaign to defend a cause. —*v.i.* participate in a crusade. —**cru·sad′er,** *n.* one engaged in a crusade, esp. (*cap.*) in the "holy wars" of the Middle Ages.

cruse (krooz) *n.* an earthen bottle or jar.

crush (krush) *v.t.* **1,** squeeze out of shape; mash; rumple. **2,** grind into bits. **3,** con-

quer. —*v.i.* be pressed out of shape. —*n.*
1, sudden, violent pressure. **2,** a crowd. **3,**
(*Slang*) an infatuation; the object of it.

crust (krust) *n.* **1,** a hard outer layer or
coating; the outside of bread, a pie, etc.
2, an end (heel) of a loaf of bread. **3,** either of the two casings of a pie. **4,** (*Slang*)
nerve. —**crust′y,** *adj.* surly; curt.

crus·ta′cean (krus-tā′shən) *n.* a hard-
shelled, usually aquatic, animal, as a crab,
lobster, etc.

crutch (kruch) *n.* **1,** a support to fit under
the arm, used by the lame. **2,** any means
of support. **3,** a person, thing, fact, etc.,
that gives solace.

crux (kruks) *n.* a critical and puzzling
point or phase.

cru·zei′ro (kroo-zā′rō) *n.* the monetary
unit of Brazil.

cry (krī) *v.i.* **1,** call loudly. **2,** weep. **3,**
utter a characteristic sound, as an animal.
—*v.t.* **1,** proclaim. **2,** offer (wares) by
shouting. —*n.* **1,** any vehement outcry. **2,**
a shout to attract attention. **3,** a fit of
weeping. —**a far cry,** something almost
entirely different.

cry′ba″by *n.* (*Informal*) a chronic
complainer.

cry·o- (krī-ō) *pref.* cold; icy.

cry″o·gen′ics (krī″ə-jen′iks) *n.* (*Physics*)
the study of very low temperatures.

cry·on′ics (krī-on′iks) *n.sing.* the practice of freezing a dead diseased human
being for possible future thawing and
cure.

crypt (kript) *n.* **1,** an underground vault.
2, a secret code or cipher.

cryp′tic (krip′tik) *adj.* hidden; secret; occult. —**cryp′ti·cal·ly,** *adv.*

cryp′to·graph (krip′tə-gràf) *n.* **1,** a device for putting text into cipher. **2,** [also,
cryp′to·gram] a message in secret code or
cipher. —**cryp·tog′ra·pher** (-tog′rə-fər) *n.*
—**cryp·tog′ra·phy,** *n.*

crys′tal (kris′təl) *n.* **1,** transparent
quartz. **2,** a glass of unusual brilliance. **3,**
the transparent disk over a watch face. **4,**
a characteristically faceted body or particle. **5,** an electrical device for determining
frequency. —*adj.* clear. —**crys′tal·line**
(-lin) *adj.*

crys′tal-clear′ *adj.* (*Informal*) obvious;
evident.

crys′tal·lize″ (-līz″) *v.i. & t.* take, or
cause to take, definite form or shape, esp.
in crystals. —**crys″tal·li·za′tion,** *n.*

cub (kub) *n.* **1,** the young of the fox, bear,
wolf, lion, and tiger. **2,** a child. **3,** a junior
Boy Scout. **4,** a tyro. —*adj.* untrained.

cub′by·hole″ (kub′ē-) *n.* a small compartment or room. Also, **cub′by.**

cube (kūb) *n.* **1,** a solid with six square
faces, at right angles. **2,** the square of a
number again multiplied by the number.
—*v.t.* **1,** raise to the third power. **2,** cut
into cubes. —**cu′bic, cu′bi·cal,** *adj.*

---

cubical, cubicle
☞ Do not confuse *cubical*, cube-
shaped, with *cubicle*, a small room or
storage space.

---

cu′beb (kū′beb) *n.* the dried fruit of an
E. Indian shrub, used medicinally.

cu′bi·cle (kū′bə-kəl) *n.* a small room or
compartment. ❏ *cubical*

Cub′ism (kū′biz-əm) *n.* a form of modern art characterized by the use of geometrical forms. —**Cub′ist,** *n. & adj.*

cu′bit (kū′bit) *n.* an ancient measure of
length, about 18 inches.

cuck′old (kuk′əld) *n.* the husband of an
unfaithful wife. —*v.t.* seduce the wife of.

---

cuckold, cuckoo
☞ *Cuckold* was derived from *cuckoo*,
a reference to the bird's habit of laying its eggs in other birds' nests.
Cuckoo probably derived from the
French *cucu*, a word imitating the
sound of the bird's call.

---

cuck′oo (koo′koo) *n.* a Europ. bird uttering a sound like "cuckoo." —*adj.* (*Informal*) crazy. —**cuckoo clock,** a clock
from which a puppet cuckoo pops out to
call the hour. ❏ *cuckold*

cu′cum·ber (kū′kum-bər) *n.* a trailing
plant; its long, green, edible fruit.

cud (kud) *n.* **1,** swallowed food brought
up for rechewing by a ruminant. **2,** (*Slang*)
a wad for chewing. —**chew the cud,**
ruminate.

cud′dle (kud′əl) *v.t.* hug; embrace; fondle. —*v.i.* lie close and snug. —**cud′-
dle·some** (-səm) *adj.* affectionate.
—**cud′dly,** *adj.*

cudg′el (kuj′əl) *n.* a short thick club.
—*v.t.* beat with a club.

cue (kū) *n.* **1,** a guiding suggestion; hint.
2, in a play, the spoken words that signal
the next speech or action. **3,** a tapering
rod, used to strike a billiard ball: *cuestick.*
4, a pigtail. **5,** a queue; line. —*v.t.* remind
or signal to (an actor). —**cue ball,** in billiards, the ball struck by the cue.

cuff (kuf) *n.* **1,** an ornamental band or
fold, as on a sleeve. **2,** a slap. —*v.t.* slap.
—**cuff link,** a device for fastening a shirt
cuff. —**on the cuff,** (*Slang*) on credit.

---

cui·rass′ (kwi-ras′) *n.* a piece of body armor; a breastplate.

> **cue**
> ↔ The sense of hint or theatrical entrance may be a spelling of the letter *q*, perhaps an abbreviation for Latin *quando*, when. The cuestick in billiards is from French *queue*, tail, from Latin *coda*.

Cui″se·naire′ rod (kwē″zə-nãr′) (*T.N.*) any of a set of colored rods of varied lengths used for teaching arithmetic.

cui·sine′ (kwi-zēn′) *n.* kitchen; mode of cooking.

cul-′de-sac″ (kul′-də-sak″) *n.* **1,** a blind alley. **2,** any duct or cavity with only one opening.

-cule (kūl) *suf.* small; diminutive.

cu′li·nar″y (kū′lə-ner″ē; kul′ə-) *adj.* pert. to cooking or to the kitchen.

cull (kul) *v.t.* select and gather. —*n.* a rejected item.

cul′mi·nate″ (kul′mə-nāt″) *v.i.* reach the highest point. —**cul″mi·na′tion,** *n.*

cu·lottes′ (kū-lots′) *n.pl.* full trousers worn by women, having the appearance of an undivided skirt.

cul′pa·ble (kul′pə-bəl) *adj.* deserving censure; blameworthy. —**cul″pa·bil′i·ty,** *n.*

cul′prit (kul′prit) *n.* an offender; the guilty one.

> **culprit**
> ↔ Perhaps from a phrase in French law jargon, *culpable: prit d'averrer,* guilty: ready to prove. This could have been abbreviated *cul. prit* and at some point combined into one word.

cult (kult) *n.* the persons and rites associated with an object of worship or veneration.

cul′ti·vate″ (kul′tə-vāt″) *v.t.* **1,** prepare or condition (land) for crops. **2,** promote the growth of; foster; develop; refine. **3,** seek the society of. —**cul′ti·vat″ed,** *adj.* —**cul″·ti·va′tion,** *n.* —**cul′ti·va″tor,** *n.* a plowing machine.

cul′ture (kul′chər) *n.* **1,** a state of civilization; customs; esp., a high level of development. **2,** the growing of bacteria for scientific use; the product of such culture. **3,** tillage. **4,** improvement; refinement. —**cul′tur·al,** *adj.* —**cul′tured,** *adj.* —**culture shock,** the sense of disorientation caused by one of a certain cultural level encountering a society of a level markedly higher or lower.

cul′vert (kul′vərt) *n.* a conduit under a road, railroad, etc.

cum (kum) *prep.* (*Lat.*) **1,** along with; as well as. **2,** otherwise known as.

cum′ber (kum′bər) *v.t.* overload; hamper; impede. —**cum′ber·some, cum′brous,** *adj.* unwieldy; burdensome.

cum′in (kum′ən) *n.* a plant with aromatic seeds, used medicinally and for flavoring.

cum lau′de (kûm low′dē) (*Lat.*) with praise.

cum′mer·bund″ (kum′ər-bund″) *n.* a sash.

cu′mu·la″tive (kū′myə-lā″tiv) *adj.* increasing by accumulation.

cu′mu·lus (kū′myə-ləs) *n.* [*pl.* **-li** (-lī)] a cloud in the form of heaped-up white masses.

cu·ne′i·form″ (kū-nē′ə-fôrm″) *adj.* wedge-shaped, as the characters in ancient Persian, etc., inscriptions.

cun′ning (kun′ing) *adj.* ingenious; sly; (*Informal*) cute. —*n.* **1,** skill; expertise. **2,** craftiness; guile.

cup (kup) *n.* a bowl-shaped vessel, usually with a handle, to drink from; its contents or capacity; anything of similar concavity. —**cup′ful** (-fûl) *n.* —**cupped** (kupt) *adj.* held to form a hollow, as the hands. —**in one's cups,** tipsy; drunk.

cup′board (kub′ərd) *n.* a cabinet or closet fitted with shelves.

cup′cake″ *n.* a small cake.

cu·pid′i·ty (kū-pid′ə-tē) *n.* immoderate greed; avarice.

cu′po·la (kū′pə-lə) *n.* **1,** a dome rising above a roof. **2,** a furnace for melting iron.

cur (kėr) *n.* **1,** a snappish dog. **2,** a surly, ill-bred fellow.

> **cur**
> ↔ From Middle English *curredog,* growling dog.

cu′ra·çao″ (kyûr′ə-sow″) *n.* a liqueur flavored with orange peel.

cu·ra′re (kyû-rä′rē) *n.* a poisonous substance obtained from a So. Amer. plant.

cu′rate (kyûr′it) *n.* an assistant to a rector or vicar. —**cu′ra·cy** (-ə-sē) *n.*

cur′a·tive (kyûr′ə-tiv) *adj.* curing. —*n.* a remedy.

cu·ra′tor (kyû-rā′tər) *n.* the custodian of a museum, art gallery, etc. —**cu·ra′·tor·ship,** *n.*

curb (kėrb) *v.t.* **1,** hold in check; control. **2,** pull to the curb of the street. —*n.* **1,** a check; restraint. **2,** [also, **curb′stone″**] the raised edge of a street. **3,** a minor securities market.

curd (kĕrd) *n.* coagulated milk solids.

> **curd, crud**
> ↔ These two are ultimately the same word, and derive from Old English *crudan*, to press, which is also the source of *crowd*.

cur′dle (kĕr′dəl) *v.t. & i.* congeal, as into curd.

cure (kyūr) *n.* **1,** restoration to health. **2,** a method of treatment. **3,** a remedy. —*v.t.* **1,** heal; make well. **2,** remedy (an evil). **3,** preserve by drying or salting. —**cure-′all″,** *n.* a panacea.

cu·ré′ (kyū-rā′) *n.* (*Fr.*) a parish priest.

cu″ret·tage′ (kyūr″i-täzh′) *n.* the scraping of a bodily cavity.

cu·rette′ (kyə-ret′) *n.* a scoop-shaped surgical instrument.

cur′few (kĕr′fū) *n.* a time or signal (as a bell) after which all, or certain, persons must be indoors.

cu′ri·a (kyūr′ē-ə) *n.* [*pl.* **-ae″** (-ē″)] **1,** the administrative bodies through which the Pope governs the Roman Catholic Church (*Curia Romana*). **2,** the senate house of ancient Rome. **3,** the senate of other Italian cities.

cu′rie (kyūr′ē) *n.* a unit of radioactivity.

> **curie, curium**
> ↔ Both are named for the 20th-c. French physicists Pierre and Marie *Curie*, discoverers of radium.

cu′ri·o (kyūr′ē-ō) *n.* an object of art, esp. if rare or unusual.

cu″ri·os′i·ty (kyūr″ē-os′ə-tē) *n.* **1,** state of being curious. **2,** a rare or unusual thing.

cu′ri·ous (kyūr′ē-əs) *adj.* **1,** eager to learn; inquisitive; prying. **2,** (*Informal*) strange; odd; rare.

cu′ri·um (kyūr′ē-əm) *n.* an unstable, radioactive, metallic element, no. 96, symbol Cm. ☐ *curie*

curl (kĕrl) *n.* **1,** a ringlet of hair. **2,** something spiral-shaped. —*v.t. & i.* **1,** form into, or take the form of, a curl; coil. **2,** play at curling. —**curl′y,** *adj.* —**curling iron,** a heated rod for curling hair.

cur′lew (kĕr′loo) *n.* a wading bird with a long, slender bill.

curl′i·cue″ (kĕr′li-kū″) *n.* a fancy twist or curl. Also, **curl′y·cue″.**

curl′ing (kĕr′ling) *n.* a Scot. game, similar to bowls, played on ice.

cur·mudg′eon (kər-muj′ən) *n.* a churlish person.

cur′rant (kĕr′ənt) *n.* **1,** a shrub bearing red acid berries; the berry. **2,** a small seedless raisin.

> **currant**
> ↔ From Middle English *raisins of coraunce*, grapes from Corinth.

cur′ren·cy (kĕr′ən-sē) *n.* **1,** the state of being current; circulation. **2,** money in actual use.

cur′rent (kĕr′ənt) *adj.* **1,** widely circulated; prevalent. **2,** belonging to the immediate present. —*n.* **1,** a moving stream of water, air, electricity, etc. **2,** general course, as of events, opinions, etc.

cur·ric′u·lum (kə-rik′yə-ləm) *n.* **1,** a regular course of study. **2,** an accepted schedule; routine. —**cur·ric′u·lar,** *adj.* —**curriculum vi′tae,** vita. Also, *abbr.* **CV.**

cur′ry (kĕr′ē) *v.t.* **1,** rub down (a horse) with a comb. **2,** dress (leather). —*n.* a spice, sauce flavored with it, or food served with such a sauce, from India. —**cur′ry·comb″,** *n.* —**curry favor,** seek favor by flattery or cajolery.

curse (kĕrs) *n.* **1,** the invoking of evil on a person; the evil inflicted. **2,** an invocation of evil; oath; profanity. **3,** an affliction; bane. —*v.t.* **1,** call down evil upon; swear at profanely. **2,** blaspheme. **3,** harm; afflict. —*v.i.* swear profanely. —**curs′ed** (-sid) *adj.*

cur′sive (kĕr′siv) *adj.* in script.

cur′sor (kĕr′sər) *n.* on a computer video screen, a signal, usually blinking, showing the position of the next character to be displayed, etc.

cur′so·ry (kĕr′sə-rē) *adj.* hasty and superficial, as an examination, a glance, etc.

curt (kĕrt) *adj.* short; abrupt. —**curt′-ness,** *n.*

cur·tail′ (kər-tāl′) *v.t.* cut short; diminish in force, extent, quantity, or duration. —**cur·tail′ment,** *n.*

cur′tain (kĕr′tən) *n.* **1,** fabric hung to adorn or conceal, as at windows, before a stage, etc. **2,** a wall connecting two towers, etc. **3,** (*pl.*) (*Slang*) the end; ruin or death. —*v.t.* conceal. —**curtain call,** a reappearance of an actor, to receive applause. —**curtain raiser,** an act before the main show.

curt′sy (kĕrt′sē) *n.* a woman's deep bow with genuflection. Also, **curt′sey.**

cur·va′ceous (kĕr-vā′shəs) *adj.* (*Informal*) of a woman, having a well-rounded figure.

cur′va·ture (kĕr′və-chūr) *n.* a curving or degree of curve.

curve (kĕrv) *n.* a continuous bent line

---

fat, fāte, fär, fâre, fâll, ásk; met, hē, hĕr, maybē; pin, pīne; not, nōte, ôr, tool without angles. —*v.t. & i.* bend from a straight line.

cur′vet (kẽr′vit) *n.* a leap of a horse with all four legs in the air. —*v.t. & i.* (cause to) so leap.

cush′ion (kûsh′ən) *n.* **1,** a pillow or soft pad. **2,** something elastic to absorb shock. **3,** the padded rim of a billiard table. **4,** something to ease a hardship or absorb a blow. —*v.t.* **1,** hold or place in a soft base. **2,** absorb the impact or shock of.

cush′y (kûsh′ė) *adj.* (*Slang*) easy; soft; pleasant.

> **cushy**
> ↔ Not from cushion, but from Hindi *khush*, pleasant.

cusp (kusp) *n.* a point, as on the crown of a tooth or a crescent. —**cusp′ate** (-āt) *adj.*

cus′pid (kus′pid) *n.* a pointed tooth; canine.

cus′pi·dor″ (kus′pə-dôr″) *n.* a spittoon.

cuss (kus) (*Informal*) *v.i. & t.* swear (at); curse. —*n.* a fellow. —**cuss′ed** (-id) *adj.* (*Informal*) obstinate; perverse.

cus′tard (kus′tərd) *n.* a cooked dessert of eggs and milk.

> **custard**
> ↔ From Anglo-Norman *crustade*, crust, originally referring to an open meat or fruit pie.

cus·to′di·an (kus-tō′dė-ən) *n.* a caretaker; guardian; janitor.

cus′to·dy (kus′tə-dė) *n.* **1,** guardianship; care, esp. in trust. **2,** imprisonment; arrest. —**cus·to′di·al** (kəs-tō′dė-əl) *adj.*

cus′tom (kus′təm) *n.* **1,** usual practice or habit; convention. **2,** patronage. **3,** (*pl.*) duties levied on imported goods. —*adj.* made or making to order. —**cus′tom-built″,** *adj.* built to an individual's specifications. —**custom house,** a government office for collecting customs duties. —**cus′tom-made″,** *adj.* made to order for an individual customer. —**customs union,** an international agreement on tariff policies. ❑ *costume*

cus′tom·ar″y (kus′tə-mer″ė) *adj.* **1,** usual. **2,** established by custom.

cus′tom·er (kus′tə-mər) *n.* one who buys goods from another; a patron.

cus′tom·ize (-īz″) *v.t.* (*Informal*) make or alter to a customer's order.

cut (kut) *v.t.* [**cut, cut′ting**] **1,** penetrate or sever with a sharp edge; gash; reap; trim. **2,** intersect; divide into parts. **3,** cause pain to; injure; insult. **4,** hit; strike (at). **5,** shape, as a garment. **6,** abridge; reduce. **7,** absent one-self from. **8,** refuse to recognize; snub. —*v.i.* **1,** make a slit or gash. **2,** admit of being cut. **3,** go by a shorter route. **4,** (often with *out*) (*Slang*) leave. —*n.* **1,** the act or result of cutting. **2,** an engraved block for printing a picture; a picture so printed. **3,** style; manner. **4,** a glancing blow at a ball that causes it to spin. —**a cut above,** better than. —**cut′-and-dried″,** *adj.* by rote; invariable. —**cut in, 1,** move in sharply or suddenly. **2,** interrupt. **3,** add (an ingredient to a mixture). —**cut out,** (with *for* or *to be*) apt; suited. —**cut up,** act foolish or frivolous.

cu·ta′ne·ous (kū-tā′nė-əs) *adj.* pert. to the skin.

cut′a·way″ *n.* a long tailcoat.

cut′back″ *n.* **1,** a return to earlier events in a novel, movie, etc. **2,** a reduction; retrenchment.

cute (kūt) *adj.* **1,** winning; attractive. **2,** coy. —**cute′ness,** *n.* —**cute′sy** (-sė) *adj.* (*Informal*) very cute.

> **cute**
> ↔ Originally a shortened form of *acute*. The sense of attractive seems to have originated in American student slang.

cu′ti·cle (kū′tə-kəl) *n.* **1,** the outer layer of skin. **2,** the skin at the base of a fingernail.

cut′lass (kut′ləs) *n.* a short sword with a wide curved blade.

cut′ler (kut′lər) *n.* one who makes, repairs, or sells cutlery.

cut′ler·y (kut′lə-rė) *n.* edged or cutting tools collectively.

cut′let (kut′lit) *n.* **1,** a thin slice of meat. **2,** a croquette.

cut′off″ *n.* **1,** a shorter way. **2,** a valve. **3,** (*Music*) a signal (as by a conductor) to stop playing or singing. **4,** (*pl.*) short pants formed by cutting off the legs of long pants.

cut′purse″ *n.* a pickpocket.

cut-′rate″ *adj.* **1,** selling merchandise at a discount. **2,** cheap.

cut′ter *n.* **1,** one who or that which cuts. **2,** a swift ship; launch. **3,** a sleigh.

cut′throat″ *n.* a thug. —*adj.* relentless.

cut′ting (kut′ing) *n.* something cut off, as a shoot of a plant or a newspaper clipping. —*adj.* **1,** piercing; penetrating. **2,** sarcastic. —**cutting edge,** forefront; avant-garde.

cut′tle·fish″ (kut′əl-fish″) *n.* a marine mollusk.

cut′up″ *n.* a prankster; a boisterous fellow.

cut'worm" *n.* a caterpillar that cuts plants off near the ground.

-cy (sė) *suf.* of nouns [*pl.* **-cies**] denoting: **1,** qualities or abstract entities; **2,** arts or professions; **3,** offices.

cy'an (sī'an) *n.* greenish blue. —**cy·an'ic** (-ik) *adj.*

cy'a·nide" (sī'ə-nīd") *n.* potassium cyanide, a deadly poison.

cy·an'o·gen (sī-an'ə-jən) *n.* a colorless, poisonous gas.

cy"ber·na'tion (sī"bər-nā'shən) *n.* the automatic control of a process by use of computers.

cy"ber·net'ics (sī"bər-net'iks) *n.sing.* the comparative study of calculating machines and the human nervous system.

cy'borg (sī'bôrg) *n.* a human being modified by the provision of artificial organs.

cy'cla·mate" (sī'klə-māt") *n.* a sweetening agent.

cyc'la·men (sik'lə-mən) *n.* a plant of the primrose family.

cy'cle (sī'kəl) *n.* **1,** a period of years in which certain phenomena recur; any long period; an age. **2,** a series or round. **3,** one double alternation of alternating current. **4,** a bicycle, tricycle, etc. —*v.i.* **1,** return to the beginning or original condition; move in cycles. **2,** ride on a bicycle. —**cy'clic,** *adj.* —**cy'cli·cal·ly,** *adv.*

cy'clist (sī'klist) *n.* a bicycle rider.

cy'cloid (sī'kloid) *adj.* resembling or arranged in a circle. —*n.* a curve generated by a point on a circle that rolls on a straight line.

cy'clone (sī'klōn) *n.* **1,** a storm caused by rotating winds; tornado. **2,** hurricane. —**cy·clon'ic** (sī-klon'ik) *adj.*

cy"clo·pe'dic (sī"klə-pē'dik) *adj.* pert. to a cyclopedia (encyclopedia); hence, of great range. —**cy"clo·pe'di·cal·ly,** *adv.*

cy"clo·ra'ma (sī"klə-ra'mə) *n.* **1,** a pictorial representation of a scene in natural perspective in a cylindrical room. **2,** a curved backdrop used in a theater.

cy"clo·spo'rine (sī"klə-spôr'ēn) *n.* a drug used to suppress autoimmune reactions.

cy'clo·tron" (sī'klə-tron") *n.* an apparatus for bombarding the nuclei of atoms with other atomic particles.

cyg'net (sig'nit) *n.* a young swan.

cyl'in·der (sil'in-dər) *n.* **1,** a solid generated by the revolution of a rectangle on one of its sides. **2,** any body or space having this shape; the piston chamber of an engine, etc. —**cy·lin'dri·cal** (sə-lin'dri-kəl) *adj.*

cym'bal (sim'bəl) *n.* (*Music*) one of a pair of metal concave plates that ring when struck together. —**cym'bal·ist,** *n.*

cyn'ic (sin'ik) *n.* a sneering faultfinder. —**cyn'i·cism** (-siz-əm) *n.*

> **cynic**
> ↔ From their contempt for the weakness of their fellow humans, their name appears to be related to Greek *kuōn*, dog, perhaps a reference to their sneering.

cyn'i·cal (sin'i-kəl) *adj.* incredulous of the goodness of people; sarcastic.

> **cynical, skeptical**
> ☛ Two aspects of disbelief. The *cynical* person does not believe that humanity can be good, that goodness exists. The *skeptical* person doubts the truth of a certain assertion, but is not necessarily always doubting.

cy'no·sure" (sī'nə-shûr") *n.* a center of attention.

cy'press (sī'prəs) *n.* a cone-bearing evergreen tree.

cyst (sist) *n.* (*Pathol.*) a diseased sac in the body. —**cys'tic,** *adj.* —**cystic fibrosis,** a hereditary disease of infants and young children.

cys·ti'tis (sis-tī'tis) *n.* inflammation of the urinary bladder.

cy·tol'o·gy (sī-tol'ə-jē) *n.* the science treating of cells.

cy'to·plasm (sī'tə-plaz-əm) *n.* the protoplasm of a cell, exclusive of the nucleus. —**cy"to·plas'mic,** *adj.*

czar (zär) *n.* **1,** the title of the former emperors of Russia. **2,** a despot. **3,** a person of great wealth or power. Also, **tsar.** —**cza·ri'na** (zä-rē'nə) *n.fem.*

czar'das (chär'däsh) *n.* a Hungarian dance.

Czech (chek) *n. & adj.* of the Slavic people of Bohemia in Czechoslovakia, their language, etc.

D

D, d (dē) *n.* **1,** the fourth letter of the English alphabet. **2,** Roman numeral for 500.

dab *v.t. & i.* [**dabbed, dab'bing**] touch lightly; pat; moisten in spots. —*n.* **1,** a gentle blow. **2,** a small amount; bit. **3,** a flat fish.

dab'ble (dab'əl) *v.i.* **1,** splash or play in

water. **2,** do anything in a superficial manner. —**dab′bler** (-lər) *n.*

dab′chick″ *n.* a small grebe.

da ca′po (dä kä′pō) (*It.*, *Music*) from the beginning.

dace (dās) *n.* a small river fish.

da′cha (dä′chə) *n.* a Russian villa.

dachs′hund″ (däks′hûnd″) *n.* a small dog with a long body and very short legs.

> **dachshund**
> ↔ German for badger-dog; the dachshund was bred for badger-hunting.

Da′cron (dā′kron) *n.* (*T.N.*) a yarn or fabric made of a certain plastic.

dac′tyl (dak′təl) *n.* a metrical foot: one syllable stressed then two unstressed, as *ten′der-ly.* —**dac·tyl′ic,** *adj.*

dac″ty·lol′o·gy (dak″tə-lol′ə-jē) *n.* conversing by means of the fingers; language of the deaf and dumb.

dad *n.* (*often cap.*) (*Informal*) father. Also, **dad′dy** (-ē).

Da′da (dä′də) *n.* a style in art producing meaningless or apparently irrational expressions. —**da′da·ism,** *n.*

dad′dy-long′legs″ *n.* [*pl.* **-legs″**] an insect, the harvestman.

da′do (dā′dō) *n.* **1,** the part of a pedestal between the base and the cornice. **2,** a decorative covering for the lower part of a wall.

dae′dal (dē′dəl) *adj.* (*Poetic*) intricate.

daf′fo·dil (daf′ə-dil) *n.* an early spring flower, yellow in color, of the narcissus family.

daf′fy (daf′ē) *adj.* (*Informal*) crazy; silly. —**daf′fi·ness,** *n.*

daft (daft) *adj.* foolish; silly; insane.

dag′ger (dag′ər) *n.* **1,** a pointed short straight weapon for stabbing. **2,** a reference mark (†) in printing.

da·guerre′o·type″ (də-ger′ə-tīp″) *n.* **1,** an early process in photography. **2,** a picture produced by such process.

> **daguerreotype**
> ↔ Named for 19th-c. French painter and inventor Louis Jacques Mandé *Daguerre.*

Dag′wood (dag′wûd) *n.* a large sandwich with many ingredients.

> **Dagwood**
> ↔ A character who eats such sandwiches, in the comic strip *Blondie.*

dahl′ia (dàl′yə) *n.* a plant bearing large, brilliantly colored flowers.

> **dahlia, daisy**
> ☞ Two flowers with two very different origins. The *dahlia* was named after an 18th-c. Swedish botanist, Anders *Dahl,* who brought the plant back from Mexico. *Daisy* comes from Anglo-Saxon *daeges ēage,* day's eye, referring to the property of some species to remain open only in daylight.

dai′ly (dā′lē) *adj. & adv.* happening every day; diurnal. —*n.* a newspaper published every day. —**daily double,** a bet on two horses, one each in the first two races of a day's card, both of which must win to win the bet. —**daily dozen,** (*Informal*) a series of setting-up exercises.

dain′ty (dān′tē) *adj.* of delicate beauty or exquisite taste; neat; fastidious. —*n.* a delicacy; tidbit. —**dain′ti·ness,** *n.*

> **dainty, dignity**
> ↔ These two words have the same source: Latin *dignitas,* worthiness, dignity. They descend to us through different Old French and Middle English words.

dai′qui·ri (dī′kə-rē) *n.* a cocktail of rum, lemon or lime juice, and sugar.

dair′y (dār′ē) *n.* **1,** a milk farm. **2,** a building where milk is made into butter and cheese. **3,** a company or shop that makes or sells dairy products. —**dair′y·ing,** *n.* the business of running a dairy. —**dair′y·maid, dair′y·man** (-mən) [*pl.* **-men**] *n.*

da′is (dā′is) *n.* a raised platform.

> **dais, podium, rostrum, lectern**
> The first three are platforms for speakers (a *podium* is usually for one person, the others may be for any number). A *lectern* is a reading desk that is often found on one of those platforms.

dai′sy (dā′zē) *n.* **1,** a common spring wildflower. **2,** (*Slang*) something considered highly. —**daisy chain,** a string of daisies; hence, a series of related or interconnected things. —**daisy wheel,** a removable disk with printing characters used in some electronic printers and typewriters. ❑ *dahlia*

Da·lai′ La′ma (dä-lī′ lä′mə) title of the former sovereign and religious leader of Tibet.

dale (dāl) *n.* a small valley; a space between two hills.

dal′ly (dal′ē) *v.i.* **1,** play without seriousness; trifle, esp. with another's affections. **2,** idle; delay. —**dal′li·ance** (dal′yəns) *n.*

Dal·ma′tian (dal-mā′shən) *n.* a breed of dog having a white coat with dark spots, named for Dalmatia, a region in former Yugoslavia.

dal·mat′ic (dal-mat′ik) *n.* a loose-fitting ecclesiastical vestment.

dal′ton (dâl′tən) *n.* a unit of atomic mass.

> **dalton, daltonism**
> ↔ These two very different things were both named for 19th-c. English physicist John *Dalton.*

dal′ton·ism (dâl′tə-niz-əm) *n.* color-blindness, esp. as to red and green. ❑ *dalton*

dam *n.* **1,** a wall to confine a flow of water, as a river, and raise its level; a floodgate. **2,** any barrier or obstruction that stops a flow. **3,** the female parent of a quadruped. —*v.t.* [**dammed, dam′ming**] **1,** build a dam across (a stream, etc.). **2,** confine; shut up.

dam′age (dam′ij) *n.* **1,** hurt; harm; injury; loss. **2,** (*pl.*) (*Law*) money awarded for a loss sustained. —*v.t.* hurt; injure.

dam′a·scene″ (dam′ə-sēn″) *v.t.* decorate (metal) with a damask-like pattern. —*n.* damask.

> **damascene, damask, damson**
> ↔ These words all refer to objects connected with *Damascus,* Syria, a city famous for its products, esp. silk and steel.

dam′ask (dam′əsk) *n. & adj.* **1,** linen or silk woven into patterns, esp. for table linen. **2,** a rose color. ❑ *damascene*

dame (dām) *n.* **1,** (*cap.*) a British title of honor given to women, equivalent to Sir. **2,** (*Offensive*) a woman.

damn (dam) *v.t. & i.* **1,** condemn to hell. **2,** curse; swear. **3,** pronounce bad; censure. —*n.* an oath. —**damned,** *adj.* consigned to perdition; detestable.

dam′na·ble (dam′nə-bəl) *adj.* worthy of condemnation.

dam·na′tion (dam-nā′shən) *n.* **1,** condemnation. **2,** eternal punishment.

damp *adj.* moderately wet; moist. —*n.* **1,** a condition of extreme humidity; moisture. **2,** a poisonous vapor in coal mines. —*v.t.* **1,** moisten; wet. **2,** dispirit; deaden.

3, extinguish; smother. —**damp′en** (-ən) *v.t. & i.* make or become damp. —**damp′ness,** *n.*

damp-′dry″ *v.t.* dry partially.

damp′en (-ən) *v.t. & i.* **1,** make or become damp. **2,** deaden. **3,** depress.

damp′er (dam′pər) *n.* **1,** something that checks or discourages. **2,** a metal plate in a flue to regulate draft. **3,** (*Music*) a device in a piano to check vibration of the strings.

dam′sel (dam′zəl) *n.* a maiden; girl. —**damsel fly,** a slender-bodied, brilliantly colored insect.

dam′son (dam′zən) *n.* a black plum. ❑ *damascene*

dance (dåns) *v.i.* **1,** move the body and feet rhythmically to music. **2,** move quiveringly from emotion. **3,** bound up and down. —*v.t.* cause to move up and down. —*n.* **1,** a succession of ordered steps and movements to music; any similar ordered succession of movements. **2,** a tune to which people dance. **3,** a party for dancing; ball. —**danc′er,** *n.*

Danc′er·cise″ (-sīz″) *n.* (*T.N.*) a type of aerobic exercise employing jazz dancing.

dan′de·li″on (dan′də-lī″ən) *n.* a common herb with a large, bright yellow flower.

> **dandelion**
> ↔ From French *dent de lion,* lion's tooth, presumably because of the appearance of the plant's leaves.

dan′der (dan′dər) *n.* **1,** scurf from an animal's coat. **2,** (*Informal*) temper; anger.

dan′dle (dan′dəl) *v.t.* move (an infant) up and down in the arms or on the knee; fondle.

dan′druff (dan′drəf) *n.* a crust that forms on the scalp and comes off in small scales or dust.

dan′dy (dan′dē) *n.* **1,** a dude; fop. **2,** (*Slang*) something especially acceptable or excellent. —*adj.* very good; quite suitable. —**dan′di·fy,** *v.t.* make a dandy of. —**dan′dy·ism,** *n.* —**dandy fever,** dengue.

dan′ger (dān′jər) *n.* exposure to injury, loss, pain, or other evil.

> **danger**
> ↔ From Latin *domniarium,* dominion, with the idea that the danger comes from being in another's power.

dan′ger·ous (-əs) *adj.* **1,** not safe; hazardous. **2,** causing danger.

dan′gle (dang′gəl) *v.* hang or cause to hang loosely.

---

dangling modifier

(*Gram.*) A very common error in writing, in which a modifier does not clearly refer to another word in a sentence. *Coming in the door, the phone rang. Coming* does not refer to the subject, *phone*, or to any other word in the sentence. Differently stated: *Coming in the door, I heard the phone ring.* Now *coming* has a clear reference: *I*, the subject of the main clause.

Dan′ish pastry (dā′nish) a kind of sweet roll. Also, **Dan′ish.**

dank *adj.* unpleasantly damp; humid; moist. —**dank′ness,** *n.*

dan·seur′ (dän-sûr′) *n.masc.*, **dan·seuse′** (dän-sûz′) *n.fem.* a professional dancer.

daph′ne (daf′nė) *n.* a shrub bearing fragrant flowers.

dap′per (dap′ər) *adj.* 1, (of a man) carefully dressed and groomed; neat; trim. 2, small and lively.

dap′ple (dap′əl) *v.t.* mark with different-colored spots.

dare (dār) *v.t.* 1, challenge; defy. 2, face boldly. —*v.i.* [*pret.* **dared** or **durst** (dėrst)] have courage; venture. —*n.* a challenge. —**dar′ing,** *n.* boldness; recklessness; intrepidity.

dare′dev″il (dâr′dev″əl) *n.* a reckless person. —*adj.* rash; venturesome; reckless. —**dare′dev″il·try,** *n.*

dare′say″ *v.t. & i.* venture to say.

dark (därk) *adj.* 1, without illumination; unlighted. 2, not light in color, as skin or a shade. 3, shaded; obscure; concealed. 4, gloomy; dreary; morose; glowering. 5, wicked; sinister. —*n.* 1, absence of light; nightfall. 2, secrecy. 3, ignorance. 4, a color or shade not light. —**dark horse,** an unexpected contestant or winner; a long shot. —**dark′ness,** *n.* —**in the dark,** uninformed.

dark′en (där′kən) *v.t. & i.* 1, make or become dark or darker. 2, make or become sad, angry, etc.

dar′kle (där′kəl) *v.i.* 1, loom in the dark. 2, grow dark or gloomy. —**dark′ling,** *adj. & adv.* in the dark; obscure.

dark′room″ *n.* a darkened room, used for handling and developing photographic film.

dark′some (-səm) *adj.* (*Poetic*) dark; gloomy.

dark′y (där′kė) *n.* (*Offensive*) a Negro.

dar′ling (där′ling) *n. & adj.* favorite; dear; beloved.

darn (därn) *v.t.* 1, mend by interweaving stitches of yarn or thread. 2, (*Informal*) damn (*a mild form*). —*adj.* [also, **darned**] damned. —*n.* 1, a torn spot so mended. 2, a mild oath.

dar′nel (där′nəl) *n.* a common field weed.

darning needle 1, a large needle for darning clothes. 2, a dragonfly.

dart (därt) *n.* 1, a pointed missile, usually thrown by the hand as a weapon or in a game. 2, (*pl.*) a game of target shooting with darts. 3, a sudden, swift progressive movement; a dash. 4, a short seam. —*v.t. & i.* 1, throw or thrust suddenly. 2, suddenly spring or start forward.

dart′er (där′tər) *n.* a perchlike freshwater fish.

dar′tle (där′təl) *v.* dart repeatedly.

Dar′von (där′von) *n.* (*T.N.*) a painkilling drug.

dash *v.t.* 1, strike or thrust suddenly and violently, so as to shatter. 2, sprinkle; spatter. 3, (with *off*) sketch or write, in a hasty manner. 4, cast down; frustrate. —*v.i.* rush violently, esp. for a brief distance. —*n.* 1, a sudden and violent blow or thrust. 2, a splashing of a liquid; a small amount of a fluid added to a concoction, as for flavoring. 3, a vigorous, energetic manner; striking appearance or behavior. 4, a horizontal stroke (—) used in punctuation to signify a sudden change of thought. 5, a long signal in telegraphic code, transcribed as —. 6, a swift rush, esp. a short race. —**cut a dash,** show off.

dash

(*Gram.*) A punctuation mark, usually represented on a typewriter and some computer printers by two hyphens (—), that sometimes takes the function of a colon, semicolon, comma, or parenthesis. It is stronger than commas for setting off words or ideas you wish to emphasize. The dash is a powerful tool which is often overused—thereby losing its power.

dash′board″ (dash′bôrd″) *n.* a panel facing the driver of a vehicle.

dash′er (dash′ər) *n.* 1, that which dashes. 2, a plunging arm in a machine.

da·shi′ki (da-shē′kė) *n.* a brightly colored African robe or tunic.

dash′ing *adj.* high-spirited; gay; romantic.

dash′pot″ *n.* a device for dampening or cushioning movement, as in a meter.

das′tard (das′tərd) *n.* a coward. —**das′-tard·ly,** *adj.* cowardly; mean; reprehensible.

DAT *abbr.* magnetic tape containing material (music, speech, etc.) recorded with a digital rather than an analog signal: *d(igital) a(udio) t(ape).*

da′ta (dā′tə) *n.pl.* [*sing.* **da′tum** (-təm)] facts or truths given or admitted and used as a basis for conclusions. —**data bank, 1,** a collection of information on a subject or a group of related subjects. **2,** database. —**data processing,** the preparation of information for, or the processing of information by, a computer. —**data processor,** a computer.

---

data

(*Gram.*) *Data* is commonly used with either a singular or plural verb, though strictly speaking the plural is correct. In either case the word refers to a number of facts, each of which is a *datum.*

---

dat′a·base″ a computer file for data designed for easy access and organization.

da″ta·ma′tion (da″tə-mā′shən) *n.* automatic data processing.

date (dāt) *n.* **1,** the time or period of an event, usually stated by year and often month and day. **2,** a time of execution, as marked on a document, etc. **3,** (*Informal*) an appointment; engagement; the person with whom one has such a social appointment. **4,** a tree, the date palm, or its edible fruit. —*v.t.* **1,** mark with a time. **2,** note or set the time of. **3,** (*Informal*) make an appointment with, in courtship. —*v.i.* exist from a point in time. —**dating bar,** an establishment catering to singles. —**date rape,** sexual intercourse forced by one's date. —**to date,** until the present time.

dat′ed (dāt′id) *adj.* **1,** marked with a date; classified by date. **2,** old-fashioned.

date′line″ *n.* a line in a publication giving the date of an issue or of the report. —**date line,** [also, **international date line**] an imaginary line near 180° longitude, west of which it is one day later than to the east.

da′tive (dā′tiv) *n. & adj.* a grammatical case signifying the indirect object.

da·tu′ra (də-tyū′rə) *n.* a poisonous plant with a disagreeable odor and narcotic properties.

daub (dâb) *v.t. & i.* **1,** smear or cover roughly. **2,** spread or pat (a substance) on something. **3,** paint badly or coarsely. —*n.* **1,** a spot of paint, etc.; a smear. **2,** an inartistic painting. —**daub′er,** *n.* an inept painter.

---

daub

↔ This word—from Latin *dealbare,* whiten—comes from the process of applying whitewash (later, plaster or other substance) to a wall.

---

daugh′ter (dâ′tər) *n.* **1,** a girl or woman considered with reference to her parents. **2,** a female descendant of any degree. —**daughter cell,** a cell resulting from cell division. —**daugh′ter-in-law″,** *n.* a son's wife. —**daugh′ter·ly,** *adj.* like or befitting a daughter.

daugh′ter·board″ *n.* (*Computers*) an optional circuit board that plugs into a motherboard.

daunt (dânt) *v.t.* intimidate; discourage. —**daunt′less,** *adj.* fearless; intrepid.

dau′phin (dâ′fin) *n.* title of the heir apparent to the crown of France (1349-1830).

---

dauphin, dolphin

↔ These words are related; the region of France to which this word originally applied had three dolphins in its coat of arms. The region eventually became the inherited property of the eldest son of the French king, and the word came to be applied to the person as well as to the region.

---

dav′en·port″ (dav′ən-pôrt″) *n.* a sofa, often one convertible to a bed.

dav′it (dav′it) *n.* an apparatus for suspending, lowering, or hoisting a boat or anchor.

daw′dle (dâ′dəl) *v.i.* (*Informal*) idle; loiter; trifle; waste time. —*v.t.* (usu. with *away*) waste (time). —**daw′dler** (-dlər) *n.*

dawn (dân) *n.* **1,** the break of day. **2,** the beginning of anything. —*v.i.* **1,** begin to grow light. **2,** begin to open or expand. **3,** begin to be evident.

day (dā) *n.* **1,** the period between the rising and setting of the sun. **2,** the time of one rotation of the earth on its axis, 24 hours. **3,** (often *pl.*) an epoch; era. **4,** a definite period of glory, influence, activity, etc. —**call it a day,** cease effort or work. —**daybed,** a couch that may be used as a bed. —**day-′care″ center,** a supervised place where children can be left, usu. while parents work. —**day nursery,** a day-care center for preschool children.

day′book″ *n.* a journal; a diary.

day′break″ *n.* dawn; sunrise.

day′dream″ *n.* a train of fanciful thoughts while awake. —*v.i.* experience daydreams.

---

day letter a telegram sent by day but at a reduced rate for deferred delivery.

day′light″ *n.* light of the daytime hours. —**daylight saving time,** a reckoning of time, used in summer, that sets timepieces ahead by one hour in order to afford an extra period of daylight during early evening.

day′time″ *n.* the hours between sunrise and sunset.

daze (dāz) *n.* a sensation of confusion or bewilderment. —*v.t.* stun; bewilder; astound.

dazzle (daz′əl) *v.t.* overpower with an excess of light, brilliance, or magnificence.

de- (dè) *pref.* **1,** down, as in *degrade.* **2,** off; away; not; as in *detach, deformed.* **3,** same as *dis-.*

de″ac·ces′sion (dē″ak-se′shən) *v.t.* to sell (a work of art) from the collection of a museum, etc.

dea′con (dē′kən) *n.* a cleric or lay person who assists a minister. Also, **dea′con·ess,** *n.fem.* —**dea′con·ry,** *n.*

de·ac′ti·vate″ *v.t.* **1,** render inactive or safe. **2,** demobilize. —**de·ac″ti·va′tion,** *n.*

dead (ded) *adj.* **1,** not living; not existing; deceased. **2,** void; useless; forgotten. **3,** complete, as *a dead stop;* exact. **4,** lacking feeling; lacking the power to rebound; dull. **5,** lacking interest, appeal, or flavor. —*adv.* completely; exactly. —*n.* **1,** that or those which no longer exist. **2,** an extreme point: *the dead of night.* —**dead end,** a point at which a street or other passageway stops abruptly; (*fig.*) a procedure, etc., without likelihood of a successful outcome. —**dead heat,** a race in which two or more contestants finish exactly even. —**dead letter,** **1,** a letter that is unclaimed or cannot be delivered. **2,** an obsolete law that is still on the books. —**dead reckoning,** the calculation of a ship's place at sea from the log and compass. —**deadweight, 1,** a heavy, oppressive burden. **2,** the weight of a container or structure apart from its contents.

dead′beat″ *n.* (*Slang*) one who avoids paying.

dead′en (ded′ən) *v.t.* **1,** deprive of sensation; make less acute; dull; weaken; retard; lessen. **2,** make soundproof.

dead′eye″ *n.* **1,** a device used by seamen to extend the shrouds and stays. **2,** (*Slang*) an expert rifleman.

dead′head″ (*Informal*) *n.* **1,** one who obtains any privilege without paying for it. **2,** a commercial vehicle operating while empty. —*v.i.* of a commercial vehicle, to travel without cargo or passengers.

dead′line″ *n.* a time at or before which a task must be completed.

dead′lock″ *n.* an impasse.

dead′ly (ded′lè) *adj.* **1,** able to kill; lethal. **2,** relentless; malignant. **3,** suggestive of death or deadness. **4,** (*Informal*) exceedingly dull. —**dead′li·ness,** *n.* —**deadly sins,** the seven sins regarded in Christian religion as the source of all others: pride, covetousness, lust, anger, gluttony, envy, sloth.

---

deadly, deathly
☛ Both words are related to death. *Deadly* means able to kill, *deathly* means suggestive of death.

---

dead′pan″ (*Slang*) *adj.* of the face, lacking expression of any feeling. —*adv.* in a deadpan manner. —*n.* a face that has no expression.

dead′wood″ *n.* **1,** dead trees or branches. **2,** something or someone discarded or useless.

deaf (def) *adj.* **1,** unable to hear. **2,** refusing to listen; unpersuaded. —**deaf′ness,** *n.*

deaf′en (-ən) *v.t.* **1,** make deaf. **2,** seem too loud to (someone). —**deaf′en·ing,** *adj.* unpleasantly loud.

deaf-′mute″ *n.* one who is both deaf and dumb.

deal (dēl) *v.t.* [*pret. & p.p.* **dealt** (delt)] **1,** apportion; distribute. **2,** deliver, as a blow. —*v.i.* **1,** (with *out*) dispose (of); be concerned; negotiate. **2,** (with *in*) trade; do business. **3,** distribute playing cards in a game. —*n.* **1,** a transaction; a business arrangement; an agreement. **2,** a portion; a large quantity. **3,** the distribution of cards, the cards as distributed, and the play of them. —**a good** (or **great**) **deal, 1,** to a large degree; much. **2,** a favorable or profitable transaction.

deal′er (dē′lər) *n.* **1,** a merchant; one who buys and resells the product of another. **2,** one who deals (cards). —**deal′er·ship″,** *n.* the right to sell a manufacturer's product in a specific territory.

deal′ing (dē′ling) *n.* **1,** behavior; conduct. **2,** (usually *pl.*) business transactions.

dean (dēn) *n.* **1,** an ecclesiastical title, the head of a cathedral. **2,** the faculty head of a university or college. **3,** the senior member of any group. —**dean′er·y** (-ə-rè) *n.* the residence of a dean.

---

dean
↔ From Late Latin *decanus,* chief of ten (people).

---

dear (dir) *adj.* **1,** beloved. **2,** valuable. **3,** costly. **4,** a perfunctory salutation in letters, as *Dear Sirs.* —*n.* a term of endearment; darling. —**dear′ness,** *n.*

dearth (dērth) *n.* scarcity; lack.

death (deth) *n.* **1,** the act of dying; cessation, esp. of life. **2,** (*cap.*) the personification of the inevitability of death. **3,** lack of existence; the state of being dead. **4,** a plague; a fatal disease. —**death′bed″** *n.* the bed in which a person dies. —**death′less,** *adj.* immortal; of enduring value. —**death′ly,** *adv.* suggestive of death. —**death house,** a section of a prison reserved for persons condemned to death. —**death row,** a cell block for prisoners condemned to death. —**death squad,** a group of assassins, usu. operating for political reasons with the tacit approval of government. ❑ *deadly*

death′trap″ *n.* a structure or situation dangerous to life.

death′watch″ *n.* **1,** a vigil kept over a dying person. **2,** a guard set over a person condemned to death. **3,** a ticking beetle.

deb *n.* (*Informal*) debutante.

de·ba′cle (dā-bä′kəl) *n.* **1,** an utter failure; a sudden inglorious end. **2,** a stampede; panic; catastrophe. **3,** a sudden breaking of a jam of ice, logs, etc., in a river.

de·bar′ (di-bär′) *v.t.* [**de·barred′, -bar′ring**] shut out; exclude; preclude. —**de·bar′ment,** *n.*

de·bark′ (di-bärk′) *v.i. & t.* leave a ship to go ashore; disembark; land from a vessel. —**de″bar·ka′tion,** *n.*

de·base′ (di-bās′) *v.t.* degrade; adulterate. —**de·base′ment,** *n.*

de·bat′a·ble (di-bāt′ə-bəl) *adj.* subject to question or doubt; moot.

de·bate′ (di-bāt′) *v.i. & t.* **1,** discuss; engage in an argument for and against; dispute; contend. **2,** reflect; consider. —*n.* **1,** a controversy; a contest by argument. **2,** a quarrel.

de·bauch′ (di-bâch′) *v.t.* corrupt; ruin. —*v.i.* engage in wild and dissipated living. —*n.* an intemperate party; carousal. —**deb″au·chee′** (deb″ə-chē′) *n.*

de·bauch′er·y (-ə-rē) *n.* immoral and excessive indulgence.

de·ben′ture (di-ben′chər) *n.* **1,** a writ acknowledging a debt. **2,** an unsecured interest-bearing bond.

de·bil′i·tate″ (di-bil′ə-tāt″) *v.t.* weaken; enfeeble. —**de·bil″i·ta′tion,** *n.*

de·bil′i·ty (di-bil′ə-tē) *n.* feebleness.

deb′it *n.* **1,** a recorded item of money

owed; a charge. **2,** an entry on the left-hand side of the ledger, which carries all items charged to an account. —*v.t.* charge with or as a debt. —**debit card,** a card used in stores, machines, etc. to debit automatically the cost of goods or services from one's bank account.

deb″o·nair′ (deb″ə-nār′) *adj.* gay; light-hearted; affable; courteous.

---

debonair

↔ From the Old French phrase *de bon aire,* of good lineage.

---

de·bouch′ (di-boosh′; -bowch′) *v.i.* come out; emerge, as from a narrow passage into the open. —**de·bouch′ment,** *n.*

de″brief′ (dē″brēf′) *v.t.* interrogate about a mission just completed.

de·bris′ (de-brē′) *n.* fragments of a former whole; rubbish; ruins.

debt (det) *n.* **1,** that which is owed. **2,** an obligation to make payment in money or kind. —**debt′or,** *n.* one who owes something.

de·bug′ (dē-bug′) *v.t.* remove the errors from, as a computer program.

de·bunk′ (dē-bunk′) *v.t.* (*Informal*) strip of sham; show the falseness of.

de·but′ (di-bū′) *n.* a first public appearance. —*v.i.* make a debut.

deb′u·tant″ (deb′yû-tänt″) *n.* a beginner in a career, etc. —**deb′u·tante″** *n.* a young woman during her first season in society.

dec·a- (dek′ə) *pref.* ten; tenfold.

dec′ade (dek′ād) *n.* **1,** a period of ten consecutive years. **2,** a set of ten.

dec′a·dence (dek′ə-dəns) *n.* a process or state of decay or deterioration. —**dec′a·dent,** *adj.*

dec′a·gram *n.* a metric unit of weight, 10 grams.

de·caf′fein·ate″ (dē-kaf′ə-nāt″) *v.t.* remove the caffeine from.

dec″a·he′dron (dek″ə-hē′drən) *n.* a solid figure having 10 faces.

de·cal″co·ma′ni·a (di-kal″kə-mā′-ne-ə) *n.* **1,** a picture or design that can be transferred to wood, glass, china, or other smooth surfaces. Also (*Informal*) **de′cal** (dē′kal). **2,** the process of transferring such designs.

Dec′a·logue″ (dek′ə-lâg″) *n.* the Ten Commandments.

de·camp′ (di-kamp′) *v.i.* **1,** march off; break camp. **2,** depart unceremoniously; run away.

de·cant′ (di-kant′) *v.t.* **1,** pour gently, as wine from its sediment. **2,** transfer (a liquid) from one container to another. —**de-**

cant′er, *n.* a fancy bottle from which wine or liqueur is served.

de·cap′i·tate″ (di-kap′i-tāt″) *v.t.* cut off the head of; behead. **—de·cap″i·ta′tion,** *n.*

de·cath′lon (di-kath′lon) *n.* an athletic contest consisting of ten separate track or field events.

de·cay′ (di-kā′) *v.i. & t.* become dead matter; rot; decompose; deteriorate. *—n.* **1,** loss of soundness, health, substance, etc.; deterioration. **2,** dead or decomposed matter.

de·cease′ (di-sēs′) *n.* death; demise. *—v.i.* die. ❑ *predecessor*

de·ce′dent (di-sē′dent) *n.* (*Law*) one who is dead.

de·ceit′ (di-sēt′) *n.* **1,** the act of deceiving; fraud; cheating; artifice. **2,** something that tricks or deceives. **—de·ceit′ful,** *adj.* tending to deceive.

de·ceive′ (di-sēv′) *v.t.* give a false impression to; mislead; delude; cheat; trick. *—v.t.* be untruthful; lie; misrepresent.

de·cel′er·ate″ (dė-sel′ė-rāt″) *v.t. & i.* lessen the speed of; slow down. **—de·cel″er·a′tion,** *n.*

De·cem′ber (di-sem′bər) *n.* the 12th month of the year.

December
↔ *December* was the 10th month of the Roman calendar, which started with March; the name comes from Latin *decem,* 10.

---

de′cen·cy (dē′sən-sė) *n.* state or quality of being decent.

de·cen′ni·al (di-sen′ė-əl) *adj.* occurring once in 10 years; marking the end of a 10-year period. *—n.* observance of a tenth anniversary.

de′cent (dē′sənt) *adj.* **1,** respectable; ethical; moral. **2,** in good taste; becoming suitable; proper. **3,** virtuous; modest. **4,** fair; good enough.

de·cen′tral·ize″ *v.t. & i.* separate and distribute (offices, duties, etc.) of a government or agency.

de·cep′tion (di-sep′shən) *n.* **1,** the act of misleading. **2,** a misrepresentation; artifice; fraud. **—de·cep′tive,** *adj.* intended to or tending to deceive.

dec′i- (des′ə) *pref.* one-tenth; divided by 10.

dec′i·bel″ (des′ə-bel″) *n.* a unit for measuring the loudness of sounds. *Abbr.,* dB.

de·cide′ (di-sīd′) *v.i.* **1,** make up one's mind; settle or determine a question; render a decision. **2,** choose; exercise an option; *—v.t.* **1,** determine; settle. **2,**

arbitrate. **—de·cid′ed,** *adj.* **1,** unmistakable. **2,** determined.

de·cid′u·ous (di-sij′oo-əs) *adj.* **1,** shedding the leaves annually, as trees. **2,** falling off, as leaves; transitory.

dec′i·mal (des′ə-məl) *adj.* pert. to 10 or tenths. *—n.* a fraction with a power of 10 for its denominator. **—decimal point,** a dot to show that the number following is a decimal.

dec′i·mate″ (des′ə-māt″) *v.t.* destroy a great number of, literally one-tenth. **—dec″i·ma′tion,** *n.*

de·ci′pher (di-sī′fər) *v.t.* **1,** translate from cipher to clear language; decode. **2,** find the meaning of. **—de·ci′pher·ment,** *n.*

de·ci′sion (di-sizh′ən) *n.* **1,** the act of making up one's mind. **2,** determination; resolution. **3,** a judgment, as of a court of law.

de·ci′sive (di-sī′siv) *adj.* final; conclusive; resolute. **—de·ci′sive·ness,** *n.*

deck (dek) *n.* **1,** the floor of a ship. **2,** a package, as of playing cards. **3,** a tape deck. *—v.t.* (often with *out*) adorn; array. **—on deck,** (*Informal*) next in line; at hand.

deck′le (dek′əl) *n.* **1,** a device used in paper-making. **2,** the ragged edge characteristic of handmade paper. **—deck′le-edged″,** *adj.*

de·claim′ (di-klām′) *v.i. & t.* **1,** speak or write in an oratorical or pompous style. **2,** make a formal speech.

dec″la·ma′tion (dek″lə-mā′shən) *n.* act or result of declaiming. **—de·clam′a·to·ry** (di-klam′ə-tôr-ė) *adj.*

dec″la·ra′tion (dek″lə-rā′shən) *n.* **1,** act of declaring. **2,** statement; assertion. **3,** in card playing, the high bid.

de·clar′a·tive (di-klar′ə-tiv) *adj.* positive; constituting a statement. Also, **de·clar′a·to·ry** (-tôr-ė).

de·clare′ (di-klâr′) *v.t. & i.* **1,** assert explicitly; state; say. **2,** announce; proclaim formally. **3,** bid.

dé·clas·sé′ (dā-klä-sā′) (*Fr.*) *adj.* having lost social standing.

de·clas′si·fy″ *v.t.* remove (a document) from a classification of secrecy limiting its distribution.

de·clen′sion (di-klen′shən) *n.* **1,** descent. **2,** deterioration. **3,** (*Gram.*) inflection of nouns, etc.

de·cline′ (di-klīn′) *v.i.* **1,** bend or slant down; droop. **2,** approach termination; deteriorate. **3,** refuse. **4,** (*Gram.*) inflect, as a noun or adjective. *—v.t.* **1,** depress; bend down. **2,** refuse; reject. *—n.* **1,** a falling off; decay. **2,** a gradual diminishing. —**dec″li·na′tion** (dek″li-nā′shən) *n.*

de·cliv′i·ty (di-kliv′ə-tė) *n.* a downward slope.

de·coct′ (di-kokt′) *v.t.* extract by boiling. —**de·coc′tion,** *n.*

de·code′ (dė-kōd′) *v.t.* translate a message from code.

dé″col·le·tage′ (dā″kol-ə-täzh′) *n.* (*Fr.*) **1,** a low-cut neckline. **2,** a garment with such a neckline.

dé″col·le·té′ (dā″kol-tā′) *adj.* (*Fr.*) low-necked, as an evening gown.

de″com·pose′ *v.t. & i.* **1,** resolve into its original parts. **2,** decay. —**de″com·po·si′-tion,** *n.*

de″con·ges′tant *n.* a medication which relieves nasal or sinal congestion.

de″con·struc′tion *n.* a method of critical and philosophical analysis which questions the possiblity of coherent meaning in language.

de″con·trol′ *v.t.* make free of restrictions; deregulate.

dé·cor′ (dā-kôr′) *n.* (*Fr.*) a plan or theme of decorative arrangement, esp. of a room.

dec′o·rate″ (dek′ə-rāt″) *v.t.* **1,** embellish; ornament. **2,** reward or distinguish, as with a medal. **3,** paint; refinish. **4,** design and outfit (a room, show window, etc.). —**dec′o·ra″tor,** *n.*

dec″o·ra′tion (dek″ə-rā′shən) *n.* **1,** act of decorating. **2,** an ornament, medal, ribbon, etc. —**dec′o·ra·tive** (-rə-tiv) *adj.* adding beauty; ornamental.

dec′o·rous (dek′ə-rəs) *adj.* well-behavèd; proper; seemly.

de·co′rum (di-kôr′əm) *n.* propriety.

de″cou·page′ (dā″koo-päzh′) *n.* (*Fr.*) the act or result of decorating with paper cutouts.

de′coy (dē′koi) *n.* **1,** a live or imitation bird used as a lure to attract wildfowl. **2,** a stratagem. **3,** one who allures, as into a trap. —*v.t. & i.* lure; entice.

---

decoy
↔ Like many words brought into English, *decoy* is an example of importing the article with the noun. It comes from Dutch *de kooi,* the cage, from its earlier sense of a pond surrounded by nets.

---

de·crease′ (di-krēs′; dē′krēs) *v.i. & t.* become or make less; diminish; reduce. —*n.* a reduction; diminution; falling off.

de·cree′ (di-krē′) *n.* an edict; a law; a judgment, esp. of a court of equity. —*v.t. & i.* order; promulgate.

dec′re·ment (dek′rə-mənt) *n.* **1,** the act of becoming less; decrease. **2,** (*Math.*) negative increment.

de·crep′it (di-krep′it) *adj.* weakened, esp. by age; infirm. —**de·crep′i·tude″** (-tood″) *n.*

de·crep′i·tate″ (di-krep′ə-tāt″) *v.i. & t.* crackle, esp. in roasting. —**de·crep″i·ta′-tion,** *n.*

de″cre·scen′do (dé″-) (*It.*) *adv. & adj.* gradually decreasing in loudness. —*n.* a gradual decrease in loudness.

de·crim′i·nal·ize″ (de-krim′i-nəl-īz″) *v.t.* remove criminal penalties for use, possession, etc., of.

de·cry′ (di-krī′) *v.t.* blame; deplore; disparage; censure.

de·crypt′ (dė-kript′) *v.t.* to decode something that has been encrypted.

dec′u·ple (dek′yû-pəl) *adj.* tenfold. —*n.* a number repeated 10 times.

de·cus′sate (di-kus′āt) *v.t. & i.* intersect, like an X. —*adj.* intersecting. —**de″cus·sa′-tion,** *n.*

ded′i·cate″ (ded′i-kāt″) *v.t.* **1,** set aside or mark for a specific purpose, esp. testimonial; consecrate; devote. **2,** inscribe or address (a book, etc.) to someone. —**ded″i·ca′tion,** *n.* —**ded′i·ca·to·ry** (ded′i-kə-tôr-ė) *adj.*

de·duce′ (di-doos′) *v.t.* derive or conclude by reasoning. —**de·duc′i·ble,** *adj.*

de·duct′ (di-dukt′) *v.t.* take away; subtract. —**de·duct′i·ble,** *adj.* capable of being subtracted.

de·duc′tion (di-duk′shən) *n.* **1,** act or result of deducting or deducing. **2,** reasoning from the general to the particular. —**de·duc′tive,** *adj.*

---

deduction, induction
☞ Subtle distinctions differentiate these two logical terms. *Deduction* proceeds from a pair of propositions, deriving a conclusion from them (the *syllogism*). *Induction* examines an undetermined number of observations and draws a conclusion from them.

---

deed (dēd) *n.* **1,** a thing done; an act. **2,** an exploit. **3,** a legal document for conveying real estate. —*v.t.* transfer by deed; convey (def. 3).

dee′jay″ (dē′jā″) *n.* (*Slang*) a disc jockey.

deel′y bop″per (dē′lė) (*Slang*) a small hat with waving wire antennas.

deem (dēm) *v.t.* hold as an opinion; think; judge.

---

deep (dēp) *adj.* **1,** extending far downward, backward, or within. **2,** studiously engaged; absorbed. **3,** implicated; involved. **4,** profound; abstruse. **5,** wise; penetrating. **6,** low in pitch. **7,** dark and rich in color; intense. **8,** heartfelt. —*n.* **1,** the sea. **2,** the culminating point. —**deep′en,** *v.t. & i.* increase in depth. —**deep freeze,** period or state of suspended animation. —**deep′ness,** *n.* —**go off the deep end,** (*Informal*) be rash, extreme, or intemperate in behavior ·or expression.

deep-′freeze′ *v.t.* quick-freeze (food); store (food) in a frozen state.

deep-′fry′ *v.t.* fry in boiling oil or fat.

deep-′seat″ed *adj.* firmly imbedded.

deep-′set″ *adj.* placed far downward or inward, as *deep-set eyes.*

deep-′six′ *v.t.* (*Slang*) discard.

deer (dir) *n.* [*pl.* **deer**] a ruminant mammal, the male of which bears deciduous horns or antlers.

---

deer
↔ From Old English *deor,* animal (as opposed to human being); the Old English word for deer was *heorot,* source of *hart.*

---

de·es′ca·late (dė-es′kə-lāt) *v.t. & i.* to reduce the scope or intensity of. —**de·es″-ca·la′tion,** *n.*

de·face′ (di-fās′) *v.t.* mar the face or surface of; disfigure. —**de·face′ment,** *n.*

de fac′to (dē fak′tō) (*Lat.*) in fact; actual.

de·fal′cate (di-fal′kāt) *v.i.* misappropriate money, etc.; embezzle. —**de″fal·ca′-tion** (dē″fal-kā′shən) *n.* act of defalcating; the amount so taken.

de·fame′ (di-fām′) *v.t.* dishonor by injurious reports; slander. —**def″a·ma′tion** (def″ə-mā′shən) *n.* —**de·fam′a·to·ry** (di-fam′ə-tôr-ė) *adj.*

de·fault′ (di-fâlt′) *v.i. & t.* **1,** fail in fulfilling an obligation or duty, esp. legal or financial. **2,** (*Sports*) lose (a match) by failure to appear. —*n.* **1,** a deficiency; failure of duty. **2,** an initial setting which will be used unless altered by the user.

DEF′CON (def′kon) *n.* a military alert status for U.S. forces: *def(ense readiness) con(dition).*

de·feat′ (di-fēt′) *v.t.* **1,** conquer or overcome, in a battle or contest. **2,** thwart; baffle. —*n.* a setback; the act of defeating or being defeated; a loss. —**de·feat′ism,** *n.* the will to surrender without fighting. —**de·feat′ist,** *n.*

def′e·cate″ (def′ə-kāt″) *v.t.* clear of impurities. —*v.i.* have a bowel movement. —**def″e·ca′tion,** *n.*

de′fect (dē′fekt) *n.* **1,** a fault; an imperfection. **2,** a deficiency. —*v.i.* (di-fekt′) desert one country for another. —**de·fec′tion** (-fek′shən) *n.*

de·fec′tive (di-fek′tiv) *adj.* **1,** imperfect. **2,** subnormal (in intelligence). —*n.* a subnormal person. —**de·fec′tive·ness,** *n.*

---

defective, deficient
☞ *Defective* means having a defect, whereas *deficient* means lacking something, i.e., incomplete. Something may be *defective* because it is *deficient,* or vice versa.

---

de·fend′ (di-fend′) *v.t. & i.* **1,** guard against danger; shield. **2,** vindicate; uphold. **3,** contest (in court).

de·fend′ant (di-fen′dənt) *n.* (*Law*) one who is accused.

de·fend′er (di-fen′dər) *n.* **1,** one who guards. **2,** one who resists attack.

de·fense′ (di-fens′) *n.* **1,** resistance against assault. **2,** a fortification; a safeguard. **3,** a speech in vindication. **4,** (*Law*) the argument and evidence of the defendant; the defendant and his or her counsel. Also, **defence.** —**de·fense′less,** *adj.* helpless; vulnerable. —**de·fen′si·ble,** *adj.* capable of being ·defended.

de·fen′sive (di-fen′siv) *adj.* **1,** pert. to defense or to that which defends. **2,** [also, **on the defensive**] defending; fearing or expecting attack. —*n.* **1,** resistance to attack. **2,** a defending party or side. —**de·fen′sive·ness,** *n.*

de·fer′ (di-fēr′) *v.i. & t.* [**-ferred′, -fer′-ring**] **1,** yield to ·another's opinion. **2,** delay; postpone. —**de·fer′ment,** *n.* postponement.

def′er·ence (def′ə-rəns) *n.* submission to the judgment of another; respect. —**def″er·en′tial** (-ren′shəl) *adj.* respectful.

de·fi′ance (di-fī′əns) *n.* **1,** a challenge to fight. **2,** contempt of authority or an opposing force. —**de·fi′ant,** *adj.* full of antagonism; challenging.

de·fi′cient (di-fish′ənt) *adj.* inadequate; imperfect. —**de·fi′cien·cy,** *n.* ❑ *defective*

def′i·cit (def′ə-sit) *n.* a shortage, esp. in money; the excess of liabilities over assets. —**deficit spending,** the spending of money raised by borrowing rather than through taxation or earned revenue.

de·file′ (di-fīl′) *v.t.* soil; befoul; desecrate; sully. —*v.i.* march off in a line. —*n.* a narrow mountain passage. —**de·file′ment,** *n.* corruption; desecration.

de·fine' (di-fīn') *v.t.* **1,** set the limits of; prescribe. **2,** state the meaning of; describe; explain.

def'i·nite (def'ə-nit) *adj.* **1,** having fixed or clear limits; exact; certain. **2,** positive; unequivocal. —**definite article,** (*Gram.*) in English, *the.* —**def'i·nite·ness,** *n.*

> **definite, definitive**
> ☛ Do not confuse these two very similar words, which have distinct meanings. *Definite* means exact, certain; *definitive* means conclusive, final.

def"i·ni'tion (def"ə-nish'ən) *n.* **1,** act or effect of defining; a statement of the meaning of a word. **2,** degree of clarity; fineness of resolution.

de·fin'i·tive (di-fin'ə-tiv) *adj.* conclusive; fixed; final. —**de·fin'i·tive·ness,** *n.* ❑ *definite*

de·flate' (di-flāt') *v.t.* **1,** remove the air or gas from; reduce in size or importance. **2,** lower, as prices.

de·fla'tion (di-flā'shən) *n.* **1,** act of deflating. **2,** a decrease in volume and circulation of money. **3,** a condition in which the money in circulation is insufficient for the commodities on sale or being sold.

de·flect' (di-flekt') *v.i. & t.* turn aside; bend away. —**de·flec'tion,** *n.* —**de·flec'tive,** *adj.*

def"lo·ra'tion (def"lə-rā'shən) *n.* act or result of deflowering.

de·flow'er (di-flow'ər) *v.t.* **1,** strip of flowers. **2,** despoil of beauty. **3,** ravish.

de·fog' *v.t.* remove the fog or mist from.

de·fo'li·ate" (di-fō'lē-āt") *v.t. & i.* strip (a tree) of leaves. —**de·fo'li·ant** (-ənt) *n. & adj.* —**de·fo"li·a'tion,** *n.*

de·for'est *v.t.* clear of forests; remove trees from. —**de·for"est·a'tion,** *n.*

de·form' (di-fôrm') *v.t.* **1,** mar the natural shape of; disfigure. **2,** render ugly; spoil. —**de"for·ma'tion** (dē"fôr-mā'shən) *n.* —**de·formed',** *adj.* misshapen.

de·form'i·ty (di-fôr'mə-tė) *n.* physical malformation; defect in shape or structure.

de·fraud' (di-frâd') *v.t.* deprive of, by misrepresenting; cheat; dupe.

de·fray' (di-frā') *v.t.* pay for. —**de·fray'al,** *n.*

de·frost' (dė-frâst') *v.t.* thaw out (frozen foods). —**de·frost'er,** *n.* a device for melting frost on a windshield.

deft *adj.* dextrous; skillful. —**deft'ness,** *n.*

de·funct' (dė-funkt') *adj.* dead.

de·fuse' *v.t.* **1,** remove the fuse from; dis-

arm. **2,** render (a situation) less volatile by removal of dangerous elements.

de·fy' (di-fī') *v.t.* **1,** challenge; dare. **2,** brave; show contempt for.

de·gauss' (dė-gâs') *v.t.* to make nonmagnetic.

de·gen'er·a·cy (di-jen'ə-rə-sė) *n.* state of being degenerate; corruptness.

de·gen'er·ate" (di-jen'ə-rāt") *v.i.* pass from a better to an inferior state; deteriorate. —*adj.* (-ər-ət) degraded; worthless. —*n.* (-ər-ət) one of low morals. —**de·gen"er·a'tion,** *n.*

de·grade' (di-grād') *v.t.* **1,** reduce in rank or degree. **2,** demean; debase. **3,** decompose chemically. —**de·grad'a·ble,** *adj.* —**deg"ra·da'tion** (deg"rə-dā'shən) *n.*

de·gree' (di-grē') *n.* **1,** a step in a series. **2,** a stage of progress. **3,** grade; rank; station. **4,** (*Gram.*) a stage in the comparison of an adjective or adverb. **5,** a title indicating academic rank or achievement. **6,** a unit of temperature. **7,** intensive quantity; extent; measure. **8,** (*Geom.,* etc.) the 360th part of the circumference of a circle. **9,** the symbol (°) following a number. **10,** (*Law*) a distinction in culpability.

de·his'cence (di-his'əns) *n.* (*Bot.*) the opening of the capsules of plants to discharge seeds or pollen. —**de·his'cent,** *adj.*

de·hu'man·ize" (dė-hū'mə-nīz") *v.t.* make inhuman or impersonal.

de·hy'drate (dė-hī'drāt) *v.t. & i.* deprive of, or lose, water. —**de"hy·dra'tion,** *n.*

de"ice' (dē"īs') *v.t.* remove ice from. —**de"ic'er,** *n.* a device to remove ice or prevent it from forming, as on an airplane wing.

de'i·fy" (dē'ə-fī") *v.t.* make a god of; worship; exalt. —**de"i·fi·ca'tion** (-fi-kā'shən) *n.*

deign (dān) *v.i.* condescend; stoop (to an act). —*v.t.* grant.

de'ism (dē'iz-əm) *n.* belief in God. —**de'ist,** *n.*

de'i·ty (dē'ə-tė) *n.* **1,** divine nature. **2,** a god or goddess.

dé"jà vu' (dā"zhä voo') (*Fr.*) the illusion of having previously experienced something now actually experienced for the first time.

de·ject' (di-jekt') *v.t.* cast down; dishearten. —**de·ject'ed,** *adj.* sad; depressed. —**de·jec'tion,** *n.* sadness; gloom; discouragement.

dek·a- (dek-ə) *pref.* deca-.

de·late' (di-lāt') *v.t.* spread abroad; make public. —**de·la'tion,** *n.*

de·lay' (di-lā') *v.i. & t.* **1,** procrastinate;

wait; put off; defer; postpone. **2,** retard; detain. —*n.* a putting off; a postponement; a stay.

de·le (dē′lē) *v.t.* take out; delete.

de·lec′ta·ble (di-lek′tə-bəl) *adj.* delightful; very pleasing. —**de·lec″ta·bil′i·ty, de″lec·ta′tion** (dē″lek-tā′shən) *n.*

del′e·gate (del′i-gət) *n.* one who acts for or represents another or a group; an emissary. —*v.t.* (-gāt″) **1,** entrust; empower. **2,** send as a representative with power to transact business; depute.

del″e·ga′tion (del″i-gā′shən) *n.* **1,** act of delegating; what is delegated. **2,** a group of delegates.

de·lete′ (di-lēt′) *v.t.* take out; expunge; erase. —**de·le′tion,** *n.*

del″e·te′ri·ous (del″ə-tir′ē-əs) *adj.* injurious. —**del″e·te′ri·ous·ness,** *n.*

delft *n.* **1,** [also, **delf, delft′ware**] a kind of pottery decorated in colors. **2,** a shade of blue.

del′i (del′ē) *n.* (*Informal*) delicatessen.

de·lib′er·ate″ (di-lib′ər-āt″) *v.i. & t.* reflect carefully; consider. —*adj.* (-ət) **1,** careful; unhurried. **2,** intentional.

de·lib″er·a′tion (di-lib″ə-rā′shən) *n.* **1,** act of deliberating; careful thought. **2,** (*pl.*) conference or discussion among a deliberative body.

de·lib′er·a″tive (di-lib′ə-rā″tiv) *adj.* reflecting and weighing carefully. —**deliberative body,** a legislature, committee, etc.

del′i·ca·cy (del′i-kə-sē) *n.* the state or act of being delicate; a delicate thing, esp. a choice food.

del′i·cate (del′i-kət) *adj.* **1,** minutely perfect; exquisite. **2,** requiring tact or skill. **3,** fragile; of a weak constitution. **4,** considerate; tactful; sensitive. **5,** choice, as food.

del″i·ca·tes′sen (del″ə-kə-tes′ən) *n.pl.* prepared foods, as salads, cooked meats. —*n.sing.* a store where these are sold.

de·li′cious (di-lish′əs) *adj.* highly pleasing to the taste or smell; delightful. —**de·li′cious·ness,** *n.*

de·light′ (di-līt′) *n.* a high degree of pleasure or satisfaction, or that which affords it. —*v.t. & i.* thrill with pleasure. —**de·light′ful,** *adj.* very enjoyable; very attractive.

de·light′ed *adj.* greatly pleased. —*interj.* (I accept) with pleasure!

de·lim′it (dē-lim′it) *v.t.* place limits on; mark the limits of.

de·lin′e·ate″ (di-lin′ē-āt″) *v.t.* mark the outline of; describe; depict; sketch. —**de·lin″e·a′tion,** *n.*

de·lin′quent (di-ling′kwənt) *n.* one who fails to perform a duty or to fill an obligation; an offender; a culprit. —*adj.* **1,** neglectful of a duty or obligation. **2,** guilty of a crime or misdeed. —**de·lin′quen·cy,** *n.*

del″i·quesce′ (del″ə-kwes′) *v.i.* melt; become liquid from absorbing moisture. —**del″i·ques′cence,** *n.* —**del″i·ques′cent,** *adj.*

de·lir′i·um (di-lir′ē-əm) *n.* **1,** a temporary disordered mental state, marked by delusions. **2,** violent excitement; mad rapture. —**de·lir′i·ous,** *adj.* —**delirium tre′mens** (trē′mənz) delirium induced by excessive consumption of alcohol.

de·liv′er (di-liv′ər) *v.t.* **1,** set free; liberate; release. **2,** give or hand over; transport to a consignee. **3,** surrender; yield. **4,** give birth to. **5,** cast, as a blow; throw, as a ball. **6,** utter; enunciate. —*v.i.* **1,** to give birth. **2,** to fulfill a promise.

de·liv′er·ance (-əns) *n.* **1,** delivery, esp. from restraint; rescue. **2,** an expressed thought; a pronouncement.

de·liv′er·y (-ē) *n.* **1,** act of delivering; transport of goods, letters, etc. **2,** a handing over. **3,** release; rescue. **4,** the giving of birth. **5,** manner of delivering. **6,** something delivered.

dell (del) *n.* a small shady valley; a glen.

del·phin′i·um (del-fin′ē-əm) *n.* a handsome garden plant; the larkspur.

---

delphinium
↔ From Greek *delphis*, dolphin, probably so called from the shape of its nectar-producing organ.

---

del′ta (del′tə) *n.* **1,** the fourth letter of the Greek alphabet (Δ, δ). **2,** a triangular deposit at the mouth of a river split into branches. **3,** (*Communications*) the letter *d.* —**delta wing,** a triangular, swept-back airplane wing.

---

delta
↔ The triangular deposit is so called from the triangular shape of the capital Greek letter delta.

---

del′toid *adj.* triangular. —*n.* the shoulder muscle.

de·lude′ (di-lood′) *v.t.* convince that something false is true; deceive; cheat.

del′uge (del′ūj) *n.* a heavy downpour of rain; a flood. —*v.t.* **1,** overflow. **2,** overwhelm.

de·lu′sion (di-loo′zhən) *n.* **1,** a false belief. **2,** a persistent and false mental conception of facts as they relate to oneself. ❑ *allusion*

de·lu′sive (di-loo′siv) *adj.* **1,** being a de-

---

lusion. **2,** deluding. Also, **de·lu′so·ry** (-sə-rė) *adj.*

de·luxe′ (di-luks′) *adj.* of highest quality; luxurious.

delve (delv) *v.i.* **1,** dig. **2,** carry on laborious and continued research.

dem′a·gogue″ (dem′ə-gog″) *n.* **1,** an unprincipled popular orator or leader. **2,** a rabblerouser. —**dem′a·gog″uer·y** (-ə-rė) *n.* —**dem″a·gog′ic** (-goj′ik) *adj.* —**dem″a·gog′i·cal·ly,** *adv.*

> **demagogue**
> ↔ From a compound of Greek *demos,* common people, and *agōgos,* leader, applied in ancient Athens to leaders drawn from the people.

de·mand′ (di-månd′) *v.t.* **1,** claim by right. **2,** ask insistently. **3,** require; need; call for. —*n.* **1,** an authoritative claim. **2,** an urgent request. **3,** that which is demanded. **4,** the state of being sought after. **5,** (*Econ.*) the desire to purchase goods coupled with the power to do so. —**de·mand′ing,** *adj.* **1,** arduous, difficult. **2,** hard to please. —**demand-side,** *adj.* (*Econ.*) pert. to the theory that considers consumer demand as the determining factor of an economy.

de″mar·ca′tion (dė″mär-kā′shən) *n.* a marking of bounds. —**de·mar′cate** (dė-mär′kāt) *v.*

> **demarcation**
> ↔ From the Spanish phrase *linea de demarcación,* the boundary established in 1493 by Pope Alexander VI dividing the world between Spain and Portugal; of Germanic origin.

dé·marche′ (dā-märsh′) *n.* (*Fr.*) a way of procedure; a move or step, esp. one involving a change of policy.

de·mean′ (di-mēn′) *v.t.* **1,** debase; lower. **2,** (*Archaic*) comport or behave oneself.

de·mean′or (di-mēn′ər) *n.* behavior; bearing. Also, **de·mean′our.**

de·ment′ed (di-men′tid) *adj.* insane.

de·men′tia (di-men′shə) *n.* impairment of the mental powers; insanity. —**de·men′tia prae′cox** (prē′koks) schizophrenia.

de·mer′it (dė-mer′it) *n.* **1,** a fault. **2,** a mark given for bad conduct or deficiency.

dem·i- (dem-ė; -i) *pref.* **1,** half. **2,** inferior.

dem′i·god″ *n.* **1,** a lesser or minor deity. **2,** a being half god and half human.

dem′i·john″ (dem′i-jon″) *n.* a large jug, usually encased in wicker.

> **demijohn**
> ↔ This word results from a French habit of giving women's names to receptacles—in this case, *dame-jeanne,* Lady Jane.

de·mil′i·ta·rize″ (dė-mil′i-tə-rīz″) *v.t.* **1,** remove troops, fortifications, etc. from. **2,** transfer from military to civil control. **de·mil″i·ta·ri·za′tion,** *n.*

dem′i·monde″ (dem′i-mond″) *n.* women of poor reputation; the world in which they move. —**dem′i·mon·daine″** (-dān″) *n.* a member of the demimonde.

de·mise′ (di-mīz′) *n.* **1,** death. **2,** transfer of an estate by death. —*v.t. & i.* transfer, as an estate.

de·mit′ (di-mit′) *v.t.* [**-mit′ted, -ting**] resign.

dem′i·tasse″ (dem′i-tås″) *n.* a small cup of, or for, black coffee.

dem′o (dem′ō) *n.* (*Slang*) a demonstrator, used for selling.

de·mo′bi·lize″ (dė-mō′bə-līz″) *v.t.* disband, as troops. —**de·mo″bi·li·za′tion** (-li-zā′shən) *n.*

de·moc′ra·cy (di-mok′rə-sė) *n.* **1,** government by the people. **2,** political and social equality in general; belief in this. —**de·moc′ra·tize″** (-rə-tīz″) *v.t.*

dem′o·crat″ (dem′ə-krat″) *n.* **1,** a believer in democracy. **2,** one who treats all others as his or her equals. **3,** (*cap.*) a member of the Democratic political party in the U.S. —**dem″o·crat′ic,** *adj.* —**dem″o·crat′i·cal·ly,** *adv.*

> **democrat, Democrat**
> ☛ The lowercase *democrat* believes in the democratic process, i.e., government by the people. The uppercase *Democrat* is a member of the Democratic Party. Some use Democrat rather than Democratic as the uppercase adjective, probably to avoid the suggestion that the Democratic Party is democratic.

de·mod′ed (di-mō′did) *adj.* out of fashion. Also, (*Fr.*) **dé″mo·dé′** (dā″mō-dā′).

de·mod′u·late″ (dė-moj′ə-lāt″) *v.t.* detect (radio waves). —**de·mod″u·la′tion,** *n.*

de·mog′ra·phy (di-mog′rə-fė) *n.* the science of vital statistics relating to deaths, births, etc. —**de·mog′ra·pher,** *n.* —**dem″o·graph′ic** (dem′ə-graf′ik) *adj.* —**dem″o·graph′ics,** *n.pl.*

de·mol′ish (di-mol′ish) *v.t.* throw or pull down; destroy. —**dem″o·li′tion** (dem′ə-lish′ən) *n.* —**demolition derby,** an automobile contest in which contestants try to demolish their opponents' cars.

de'mon (dē'mən) *n.* **1,** an evil spirit; a devil. **2,** a wicked or cruel person. **3,** (*Informal*) an energetic person. —**de·mo'·ni·ac** (di-mō'nē-ak). **de″mo·ni'a·cal** (dē″mō-nī'ə-kəl) *adj.* —**de·mon'ic** (di-mon'ik) *adj.*

de·mon'e·tize″ (dē-mon'ə-tīz″) *v.t.* withdraw from use as money. —**de·mon″e·ti·za'tion** (-ti-zā'shən) *n.*

de″mon·ol'o·gy (dē″mən-ol'ə-jē) *n.* **1,** the study of demons or the belief in them. **2,** the doctrines of demon worshipers. —**de″mon·ol'o·gist,** *n.*

de·mon'stra·ble (di-mon'strə-bəl) *adj.* capable of proof by demonstration. —**de·mon″stra·bil'i·ty,** *n.*

dem'on·strate″ (dem'ən-strāt″) *v.t. & i.* **1,** describe or explain by use of examples. **2,** establish the truth of by reasoning; prove. **3,** exhibit and put to test publicly. **4,** point out; make evident. **5,** make a show of force; assemble to show approval or protest.

dem″on·stra'tion (-strā'shən) *n.* **1,** act of demonstrating; exhibition; display. **2,** manifestation of feelings; a show of force, protest, etc.

de·mon'stra·tive (di-mon'strə-tiv) *adj.* **1,** strongly exhibiting one's feelings. **2,** conclusive, as proof. **3,** (*Gram.*) pointing out an object, as *this, that.* —**de·mon'stra·tive·ness,** *n.*

dem'on·stra″tor (dem'ən-strā″tər) *n.* one who or that which demonstrates, esp. an automobile so used.

de·mor'al·ize″ (di-môr'ə-līz″) *v.t.* **1,** corrupt. **2,** deprive of spirit or energy; dishearten. **3,** throw into confusion or disorder. —**de·mor″al·i·za'tion** (-li-zā'shən) *n.*

de·mote' (di-mōt') *v.t.* reduce in rank or class. —**de·mo'tion,** *n.*

de·mot'ic (dē-mot'ik) *adj.* of the common people; popular.

de·mul'cent (di-mul'sənt) *adj.* softening; mollifying; soothing.

de·mur' (di-mėr') *v.i.* [**-murred', -mur'-ring**] take exception; object. —*n.* objection. —**de·mur'ral,** *n.*

de·mure' (di-myûr') *adj.* **1,** affectedly modest; prim. **2,** sedate. —**de·mure'ness,** *n.*

de·mur'rage (di-mėr'ij) *n.* detention of a vessel or freight car beyond the time stipulated; the charge for such delay.

de·mur'rer (di-mėr'ər) *n.* (*Law*) a plea that the case be dismissed though the facts alleged are conceded.

den *n.* **1,** a cave for a wild beast. **2,** a haunt; squalid resort. **3,** a small, snug private room. **4,** a unit of a Cub Scout pack.

de·na'ture (dē-nā'chər) *v.t.* change the nature of, esp. of alcohol to render it unfit to drink.

den'drite (den'drīt) *n.* **1,** the branching outer part of a neuron. **2,** a veining in certain impure minerals.

den·dro- (den-drō) *pref.* tree.

-den'dron (den'drən) *suf.* tree.

den'e·gate″ (den'i-gāt″) *v.t.* deny. —**den″e·ga'tion,** *n.*

den'gue (deng'gā) *n.* a tropical disease: *dandy-fever.*

de·ni'al (di-nī'əl) *n.* **1,** the act of contradiction; negation. **2,** refusal to grant a request. **3,** a refusal to accept or acknowledge. **4,** restraint of personal desires; poverty.

de·nier' (də-nir') *n.* the measure of weight or fineness of a yarn.

den'i·grate″ (den'i-grāt″) *v.t.* blacken in reputation; defame. —**den″i·gra'tion,** *n.*

den'im (den'əm) *n.* a coarse twilled cotton cloth.

> **denim**
> ↔ Originally French *serge de Nîmes*, serge fabric from the town of Nîmes, which was taken into English as *serge de Nim*. The last two words became over time *denim.*

den'i·zen (den'ə-zən) *n.* a dweller; an inhabitant.

de·nom'i·nate″ (di-nom'ə-nāt″) *v.t.* give a specific name to; designate.

de·nom″i·na'tion (di-nom″i-nā'shən) *n.* **1,** act of naming; a name. **2,** a religious sect. **3,** a unit in a series, as of quantity, value, etc.

de·nom'i·na″tor (di-nom'i-nā″tər) *n.* (*Math.*) the part of a fraction that represents the divisor: in ½, 2 is the denominator.

de·note' (di-nōt') *v.t.* **1,** point out and identify; designate. **2,** be a sign or symptom of; indicate. —**de″no·ta'tion** (dē″nō-tā'shən) *n.* —**de·no'ta·tive** (dē-nō'tə-tiv) *adj.*

dé″noue·ment' (dā″noo-män') *n.* the solution of a plot, as in a play.

> **dénouement**
> ↔ Literally, in French, the "unknotting" or "untying" of something, from Latin *nodus,* knot.

de·nounce' (di-nowns') *v.t.* **1,** blame or

brand publicly; stigmatize. **2,** inform against; condemn. **3,** announce the intention of abrogating a treaty. **—de·nounce′- ment,** *n.*

dense (dens) *adj.* **1,** having great closeness of parts; thick; compact. **2,** stupid. **—dense′ness, den′si·ty** (-sə-tė) *n.*

dent *n.* a small hollow or depression made by a blow. *—v.t. & i.* make a dent (in).

den′tal (den′təl) *adj.* pert. to the teeth. **—dental floss,** a waxed or unwaxed thread used for cleaning between teeth.

den′ti·frice (den′tə-fris) *n.* a preparation for cleaning the teeth.

den′tin *n.* the hard tissue of a tooth, under the enamel. Also, **den′tine.**

den′tist *n.* a doctor for the teeth. **— den′- tist·ry** (-rė) *n.* the science of treating the teeth; dental surgery.

den·ti′tion (den-tish′ən) *n.* **1,** the kind, number, and arrangement of the teeth in a human or animal. **2,** teething.

den′ture (den′chər) *n.* a set of false teeth.

de·nu′cle·ar·ize″ (dė-noo′klė-ə-rīz″) *v.t.* remove nuclear weapons or technology from.

de·nude′ (di-nūd′) *v.t.* strip or divest of all covering.

de·nun″ci·a′tion (di-nun″sė-ā′shən) *n.* act or result of denouncing. **—de·nun′ci- ate,** *v.t.* **—de·nun′ci·a·to·ry** (-ə-tôr-ė) *adj.*

Den′ver boot (den′vər) boot (def. 7).

de·ny′ (di-nī′) *v.t.* **1,** refuse to admit the truth of; contradict. **2,** refuse to give or grant. **3,** refuse to accept or admit. **4,** renounce; disown **—deny oneself,** do without. **—de·ni″a·bil′i·ty,** *n.* the ability to deny something.

de′o·dar″ (dē′ə-där″) *n.* an E. Indian evergreen tree.

de·o′dor·ant (dė-ō′dər-ənt) *n.* a preparation that destroys unpleasant odor. *—adj.* deodorizing.

de·o′dor·ize″ (dė-ō′də-rīz″) *v.t.* remove odor from. **—de·o″dor·i·za′tion,** *n.*

de·part′ (di-pärt′) *v.i.* **1,** go or move away; leave (often with *from*). **2,** deviate; abandon. **3,** die. **—de·par′ture** (di-pär′chər) *n.* **—the departed,** the deceased.

de·part′ment (di-pärt′ment) *n.* a separate part or division of a complex system; a branch of a business, government, etc. **—de·part″men′tal** (di-pärt″men′təl) *adj.* pert. to a department; organized into departments. **—de·part″men′tal·ize,** *v.t.*

—department store, a retail store dealing in many different kinds of merchandise.

de·pend′ (di-pend′) *v.i.* **1,** be contingent upon something; hang. **2,** (with *on* or *upon*) repose confidence; rely. **3,** (with *on*) rely upon for maintenance. **—de·pend′- a·ble,** *adj.* reliable; trustworthy. **—de- pen′dant,** *n.* ❑ *dependent*

de·pen′dence (-əns) *n.* **1,** reliance; trust. **2,** state of being physically or psychologically dependent; addiction.

de·pen′den·cy (di-pen′dən-sė) *n.* **1,** dependence. **2,** an appurtenance. **3,** a territory that is dependent upon, but not a part of, a nation.

de·pen′dent (di-pen′dənt) *adj.* **1,** depending (on) or subject (to). **2,** conditional. **3,** hanging down. *—n.* [also, **de·pen′dant**] one who is supported by another.

---

dependent, dependant
☛ Do not confuse *dependant,* a noun meaning someone who is supported by another, and *dependent,* which can mean the same thing, but also has other, adjectival senses.

---

de·per′son·a·lize″ *v.t.* render impersonal; remove the personality of.

de·pict′ (di-pikt′) *v.t.* portray by a picture or words. **—de·pic′tion,** *n.*

dep′i·late″ (dep′ə-lāt″) *v.t.* remove the hair from. **—dep″i·la′tion,** *n.*

de·pil′a·to·ry (di-pil′ə-tôr-ė) *n.* a preparation for removing unwanted hair. *—adj.* capable of removing hair.

de·plane′ *v.i.* disembark from an airplane.

de·plete′ (di-plēt′) *v.t.* exhaust by drawing away, as resources, strength, vital powers. **—de·ple′tion,** *n.*

de·plore′ (di-plôr′) *v.t.* regret; lament. **—de·plor′a·ble,** *adj.* lamentable; calamitous.

de·ploy′ (di-ploi′) *v.t. & i.* **1,** (*Mil.*) spread out on a more extended front. **2,** arrange or ready for use. **—de·ploy′- ment,** *n.*

de·pone′ (di-pōn′) *v.i.* (*Law*) give testimony under oath; depose. **—de·po′nent** (-ənt) *n.*

de·pop′u·late″ (dė-pop′yə-lāt″) *v.t.* deprive of inhabitants, as by killing or expelling them. **—de·pop″u·la′tion,** *n.*

de·port′ (di-pôrt′) *v.t.* **1,** transport forcibly; exile. **2,** behave (oneself). **—de″por- ta′tion** (dē″pôr-tā′shən) *n.* **—de″por·tee′,** *n.* one who is deported.

---

de·port′ment (-mənt) *n.* behavior; conduct. ❑ *comportment*

de·pose′ (di-pōz′) *v.t. & i.* **1,** remove from a high office. **2,** testify. —**de·pos′al** (-əl) *n.*

de·pos′it (di-poz′it) *v.t.* **1,** lay down; put; precipitate. **2,** place in safekeeping, esp. money in a bank. —*n.* **1,** anything entrusted, as money in a bank. **2,** a pledge; a part payment, **3,** that which is laid, thrown down, or settled, as sand from a body of water. **4,** a natural accumulation of a mineral in the earth.

dep″o·si′tion (dep″ə-zish′ən) *n.* **1,** act or effect of deposing. **2,** sworn testimony.

de·pos′i·tar″y (di-poz′ə-tār″ē) *n.* **1,** someone to whom something is given in trust. **2,** depository.

de·pos′i·to·ry (di-poz′ə-tôr-ē) *n.* a place where something is deposited; a bank.

de′pot (dē′pō) *n.* **1,** a warehouse; a railroad station. **2,** (*Mil.*) a redistribution point for supplies.

> **depot**
> ↔ From Latin *deponere*, put down; a *depot* is a place where something is deposited.

de·prave′ (di-prāv′) *v.t.* pervert; corrupt. —**de·prav′i·ty** (di-prav′ə-tē) *n.*

dep′re·cate″ (dep′rə-kāt″) *v.t.* plead against; express disapproval of. —**dep″re·ca′tion,** *n.* —**dep′re·ca·to·ry** (-kə-tôr-ē) *adj.*

> **deprecate, depreciate**
> ☛ Do not confuse these two very similar but unrelated words. *Deprecate* means to plead against; *depreciate* means to belittle.

de·pre′ci·ate″ (di-prē′shē-āt″) *v.i. & t.* **1,** become worth less; lessen the value of. **2,** belittle. —**de·pre″ci·a′tion,** *n.* a decrease in value; the amount of the decrease. ❑ *deprecate*

dep′re·date″ (dep′rə-dāt″) *v.t. & i.* lay waste; plunder. —**dep″re·da′tion,** *n.*

de·press′ (di-pres′) *v.t.* **1,** press or move downward. **2,** weaken. **3,** sadden. —**de·pres′sive** (-iv) *adj.* —**de·pres′sor,** *n.*

de·pres′sant (di-pres′ənt) *n. & adj.* a sedative.

de·pressed′ (di-prest′) *adj.* **1,** dejected. **2,** in a state of economic depression. **3,** lowered in position, amount, intensity, etc. **4,** indented; concave.

de·pres′sion (di-presh′ən) *n.* **1,** act of depressing, or state of being depressed. **2,** a hollow. **3,** an unwarranted and prolonged condition of emotional dejection. **4,** a period of decline in business activity. —**the (Great) Depression,** the depression in the U.S. during the 1930s.

dep″ri·va′tion (dep″ri-vā′shən) *n.* **1,** act of depriving; loss. **2,** poverty; want.

de·prive′ (di-prīv′) *v.t.* **1,** divest; strip. **2,** withhold; prevent from possessing.

de·pro′gram (dē-) *v.t.* rid or attempt to rid (a person) of beliefs acquired from a previous indoctrination.

depth *n.* **1,** deepness; distance measured downward, inward, or backward. **2,** intensity. **3,** profundity. **4,** (*pl.*) utmost depression of spirits. —**depth charge,** an explosive device set to explode at a certain depth, usu. used against submarines.

dep″u·ta′tion (dep″yə-tā′shən) *n.* **1,** appointment to act for another. **2,** a group of duties.

de·pute′ (di-pūt′) *v.t.* **1,** appoint as an agent. **2,** assign to an agent.

dep′u·tize″ (dep′yû-tīz″) *v.t.* appoint as agent.

dep′u·ty (dep′yə-tē) *n.* a representative assistant or agent (esp. of a public officer); one deputed.

de·rail′ (dē-rāl′) *v.i. & t.* run (a train) off the track. —**de·rail′ment,** *n.*

de·rail′leur (də-rā′lər) *n.* a device for shifting the chain on a bicycle from one sprocket wheel to another to change gears.

de·range′ (di-rānj′) *v.t.* **1,** disarrange. **2,** disorder the mind of. —**de·range′ment,** *n.*

der′by (dėr′bē) *n.* **1,** a man's hat with a stiff rounded crown and narrow brim. **2,** (*cap.*) any of several horse races.

> **derby**
> ↔ Named not for the town of Derby (which in England is pronounced där′bē), but for Edward Stanley, the twelfth Earl of Derby (same pronunciation as the town), who in 1780 instituted an annual race at Epsom Downs, England.

de·reg′u·late″ *v.t.* free from regulation (esp. governmental); decontrol. —**de″reg·u·la′tion,** *n.*

der′e·lict (der′ə-likt) *adj.* **1,** abandoned. **2,** unfaithful. —*n.* **1,** anything abandoned, esp. a ship. **2,** an outcast. **3,** one guilty of neglect. —**der″e·lic′tion,** *n.*

de·ride′ (di-rīd′) *v.t.* laugh at contemptuously; mock. —**de·ri′sive** (di-rī′siv) *adj.* showing contempt. —**de·ri′so·ry** (-sə-rē) *adj.* showing or deserving contempt.

de ri·gueur′ (də ri-gûr′) (*Fr.*) **1,** obligatory. **2,** suitable.

de·ri′sion (di-rizh′ən) *n.* **1,** act of deriding; ridicule. **2,** an object of ridicule or mockery.

der″i·va′tion (der″i-vā′shən) *n.* **1,** act of deriving. **2,** source.

de·riv′a·tive (di-riv′ə-tiv) *n. & adj.* what is derived.

de·rive′ (di-rīv′) *v.t. & i.* **1,** draw or receive from a source or origin. **2,** deduce; infer. **3,** trace the development of (a word).

derm-, -derm (dērm) *pref. & suf.* skin.

der′ma (dēr′mə) *n.* the true skin, below the epidermis. Also, **der′mis.**

der″ma·ti′tis (dēr″mə-tī′tis) *n.* inflammation of the skin.

der″ma·tol′o·gy (dēr″mə-tol′ə-jė) *n.* the science of the skin and its diseases. **—der″. ma·tol′o·gist,** *n.* a practitioner in this science.

der·nier′ cri (der-nyā′ krē′) (*Fr.*) the last word; the latest thing.

der′o·gate″ (der′ə-gāt″) *v.t. & i.* detract from; disparage; depreciate. **—der″o·ga′. tion,** *n.* **—de·rog′a·to·ry** (di-rog′ə-tôr-ė), **de·rog′a·tive,** *adj.*

der′rick (der′ik) *n.* **1,** an apparatus for hoisting; a crane. **2,** the framework over an oil well.

> **derrick**
> ↔ The word once meant gallows and came from the name of a famous 16th-c. hangman of Tyburn, England.

der·ri·ere′ (der-ė-er′) *n.* (*Informal*) buttocks; rump.

der′ring-do′ (der′ing-doo′) *n.* daring deeds; heroism.

der′rin·ger (der′in-jər) *n.* an antique short-barreled pistol.

> **derringer**
> ↔ Named for the 19th-c. American gunsmith Henry *Deringer*, who invented the weapon.

der′vish (dēr′vish) *n.* a member of a Mohammedan religious cult.

de·sal′i·nate″ (dė-sal′ə-nāt″) *v.t.* remove the salt from. Also, **de·sal′i·nize″** (-nīz″), **de·salt′.**

de″sa·pa·ra·ci′do (de″sä-pä″rä-sė′dō) *n.* (*Sp.*) esp. in Latin America, a person who has been secretly imprisoned or executed by a government.

des′cant (des′kant) *n.* **1,** a melody. **2,** a variation; varied discourse. **—v.t.** (des-kant′) **1,** sing. **2,** enlarge upon a topic.

de·scend′ (di-send′) *v.i.* **1,** move downward. **2,** slope downward. **3,** proceed from an original; be derived. **4,** lower oneself morally or socially. **5,** (with *upon*) come suddenly, violently, or in a hostile manner. **—v.t.** go down upon or along. **—de·scend′ent,** *adj.* descending.

de·scend′ant (di-sen′dənt) *n.* one descended from an ancestor. **—adj.** descendent.

de·scent′ (di-sent′) *n.* **1,** act or process of descending. **2,** a downward passage or slope. **3,** ancestral lineage.

de·scribe′ (di-skrīb′) *v.t.* **1,** portray in words. **2,** trace out; outline.

de·scrip′tion (di-skrip′shən) *n.* **1,** the act of representing a thing by words or pictures or signs; such a representation. **2,** a category. **—de·scrip′tive,** *adj.* serving to describe.

de·scry′ (di-skrī′) *v.t.* catch sight of; detect.

des′e·crate″ (des′ə-krāt″) *v.t.* treat with sacrilege; profane. **—des″e·cra′tion,** *n.*

de·seg′re·gate″ *v.t. & i.* rid of segregation. **—de·seg′re·ga′tion,** *n.*

de″se·lect′ *v.t.* discharge (a trainee) from a training program.

de·sen′si·tize″ *v.t.* make insensitive or less sensitive.

des′ert (dez′ərt) *n.* **1,** a dry sandy wasteland. **2,** a wilderness.

de·sert′ (di-zērt′) *v.t. & i.* **1,** abandon; forsake. **2,** leave (the army, etc.) without leave and not intending to return. **—n.** (often *pl.*) something deserved. **—desert′er,** *n.* one who deserts, esp. from military service. **—de·ser′tion** (di-zēr′shən) *n.*

> **desert, dessert**
> ☛ Do not confuse the two-*s dessert,* a sweet course, and the one-*s desert,* a noun and verb with several senses. ↔ The latter comes from Latin *deserere,* to abandon; the former comes from French *desservir,* to clear the table. The sense of *desert,* something deserved, comes from French *deservir,* to deserve.

de·serve′ (di-zērv′) *v.t. & i.* be entitled to receive, as reward or punishment; be worthy of. **—de·serv′ing,** *adj.* meritorious; worthy.

des′ic·cate″ (des′ə-kāt″) *v.i. & t.* **1,** dry up; wither. **2,** preserve (food) by drying. **—des′ic·cant** (-kənt) *n.* **—des″ic·ca′tion,** *n.*

de·sid′er·a′tum (di-sid″ə-rā′təm) *n.* [*pl.* **-ta** (-tə)] something desired or needed.

de·sign′ (di-zīn′) *v.t.* **1,** draw a plan or outline of; sketch. **2,** plan a detailed pattern. **3,** plan; contrive. **4,** intend; purpose. —*v.i.* do original artwork; make an original plan. —*n.* **1,** a preliminary drawing; a plan. **2,** the arrangement of details in a piece of art. **3,** a scheme, esp. a hostile scheme. —**de·sign′er,** *n. & adj.*

des′ig·nate″ (dez′ig-nāt″) *v.t.* **1,** mark; point out; specify. **2,** name. **3,** appoint. —**des″ig·na′tion,** *n.* —**designated driver,** a person who agrees to refrain from drinking to be able to drive home from a party, etc. —**designated hitter,** (*Baseball*) a player who is designated to bat for the pitcher.

de·sign′ing *adj.* craftily planning; artful. —*n.* the art of design.

de·sire′ (di-zīr′) *v.t.* **1,** wish or long for; crave. **2,** ask for; solicit. —*n.* **1,** a wish; craving; longing. **2,** sensual feeling. **3,** a request. **4,** an object wished for. —**de·sir′a·ble,** *adj.* worth desiring. —**de·sir′ous,** *adj.* feeling desire.

de·sist′ (di-zist′; -sist′) *v.i.* stop; forbear.

desk *n.* **1,** a table for writing, reading, or study. **2,** an official position or assignment, esp. in journalism. **3,** a small department, as of a foreign office. **4,** a hotel counter. —**desk′top″ publishing,** the design, preparation, and printing of business reports, newsletters, etc. by use of computers. *Abbr.,* **DTP.** —**desk′work″,** *n.* clerical work.

> **desk, dish, disk**
> ↔ All these words—and others— derive from Greek *diskos,* quoit, through Latin *discus,* which was also used figuratively for a circular shape.

desk′top″ *n.* **1,** the top surface of a desk. **2,** (*Computers*) a graphic representation of a desktop on a video screen.

des′o·late (des′ə-lət) *adj.* **1,** solitary; lonely; miserable. **2,** uninhabited; abandoned. **3,** barren; ravaged. —*v.t.* (-lāt″) make desolate. —**des″o·la′tion,** *n.*

de·spair′ (di-spâr′) *v.i.* give up all hope. —*n.* utter lack of hope.

des·patch′ (di-spach′) *v.t. & n.* dispatch.

des″per·a′do (des″pə-rä′dō) *n.* a reckless outlaw.

des′per·ate (des′pər-ət) *adj.* **1,** driven by despair; frantic; reckless. **2,** beyond hope. **3,** extremely dangerous. —**des″per·a′tion,** *n.*

des′pi·ca·ble (des′pi-kə-bəl) *adj.* to be despised; contemptible.

> **despicable, despise, despite**
> ↔ These words all derive from Latin *despicere,* to look down on from a height, i.e., scorn.

de·spise′ (di-spīz′) *v.t.* look down upon; scorn. ❑ *despicable*

de·spite′ (di-spīt′) *prep.* notwithstanding; in spite of. ❑ *despicable*

de·spoil′ (di-spoil′) *v.t.* pillage; plunder. —**de·spoil′ment,** *n.* —**de·spo″li·a′tion** (di-spō″lē-ā′shən) *n.* ❑ *spoil*

de·spond′ent (di-spon′dənt) *adj.* depressed; melancholy. —**de·spond′en·cy,** *n.*

des′pot (des′pət) *n.* an absolute ruler; a tyrant. —**des·pot′ic** (-pot′ik) *adj.* —**des·pot′i·cal·ly,** *adv.* —**des′pot·ism,** *n.*

des·sert′ (di-zèrt′) *n.* a sweet served as the last course of a meal. ❑ *desert*

de·sta′bil·ize″ (dē-stā′bə-līz″) *v.t.* render unstable.

des″ti·na′tion (des″tə-nā′shən) *n.* **1,** the predetermined end of a journey. **2,** the purpose for which anything is intended.

des′tine (des′tin) *v.t.* **1,** set apart; appoint for a special purpose. **2,** predetermine unalterably, as by divine decree.

des′ti·ny (des′tə-nē) *n.* **1,** fate; fortune. **2,** the inevitable. —**the Destinies,** the Fates.

des′ti·tute″ (des′tə-toot″) *adj.* **1,** (with *of*) wholly lacking (something needed). **2,** indigent; extremely poor. —**des″ti·tu′tion,** *n.*

de·stroy′ (di-stroi′) *v.t.* **1,** totally demolish; ruin; spoil. **2,** annihilate; slay. —**de·stroy′er,** *n.* **1,** one who destroys. **2,** a type of naval vessel.

des·truct′ (di-strukt′) *v.i.* be destroyed, esp. by a built-in device (also, **self-″destruct′**) —*v.t.* destroy.

des·truc′tion (di-struk′shən) *n.* **1,** the act of destroying; a scene of ruin. **2,** a force that destroys. —**de·struc′ti·ble,** *adj.*

des·truc′tive (-iv) *adj.* **1,** destroying. **2,** causing damage; hurtful.

des′ue·tude″ (des′wə-tūd″) *n.* disuse.

des′ul·to·ry (des′əl-tôr-ē) *adj.* aimless; disconnected; unmethodical.

> **desultory**
> ↔ From an unusual Latin word, *desultor,* a circus horseback rider who jumped from one horse to another while they were galloping. The idea of jumping from one thing to another led to the present sense of aimless.

de·tach′ (di-tach′) *v.t.* **1,** unfasten; disunite; separate. **2,** (*Mil.*) dispatch on a distinct mission.

de·tached' (-tacht') *adj.* **1,** separate; independent. **2,** impartial in judgment. **3,** preoccupied; aloof.

de·tach'ment (di-ţach'mənt) *n.* **1,** (*Mil.*) troops or ships detached for a special task. **2,** aloofness.

de·tail' (di-tāl'; dē'tāl) *v.t.* **1,** express by particulars; enumerate. **2,** (*Mil.*) appoint to a special duty. —*n.* **1,** an individual part; a particular. **2,** (*Mil.*) selection of an individual or a body of troops for a special service; those selected. —**de·tailed'**, *adj.* having many details; intricate.

de·tain' (di-tān') *v.t.* **1,** hold back; prevent from proceeding; delay. **2,** (*Law*) hold in custody. —**de·ten'tion**, *n.*

de·tect' (di-tekt') *v.t.* find out; discover (what is hidden or obscure). —**de·tec'tion**, *n.* —**de·tec'tor**, *n.*

de·tec'tive (di-tek'tiv) *n.* a person whose occupation is investigating crimes.

de·tent' (di-tent') *n.* a mechanical part that stops or checks motion, as a lock, catch, or pawl.

dé·tente' (dā-tänt') *n.* a relaxation, esp. of political relations between countries.

de·ter' (di-tẽr') *v.t.* **[-terred', -ter'ring]** discourage and stop, esp. by inciting fear or doubt. —**de·ter'ment**, *n.*

de·ter'gent (di-tẽr'jənt) *n.* a cleansing substance. —*adj.* cleansing.

de·te'ri·o·rate" (di-tir'ē-ə-rāt") *v.i. & t.* grow worse; reduce in worth; impair. —**de·te"ri·o·ra'tion**, *n.*

de·ter'mi·nate (di-tẽr'mi-nət) *adj.* definite; fixed.

de·ter"mi·na'tion (di-tẽr"mi-nā'shən) *n.* **1,** act of determining. **2,** a definite decision. **3,** firmness. **4,** exact measurement.

de·ter'mine (di-tẽr'min) *v.t.* **1,** resolve; decide. **2,** find out; ascertain. **3,** bring to a conclusion; end. **4,** give direction to. **5,** restrict. **6,** decree; ordain. —*v.i.* come to a decision. —**de·ter'mi·na·tive** (-nə-tiv) *adj.* —**de·ter'mined**, *adj.* resolute; firm.

de·ter'rent (di-tẽr'ənt) *adj.* deterring. —*n.* that which deters.

de·test' (di-test') *v.t.* dislike intensely; abhor. —**de·test'a·ble**, *adj.* hateful. —**de"tes·ta'tion** (dē"tes-tā'shən) *n.*

de·throne' (dē-thrōn') *v.t.* remove from a reigning or controlling position; depose. —**de·throne'ment**, *n.*

det'o·nate" (det'ə-nāt") *v.i. & t.* explode or cause to explode; explode loudly. —**det"o·na'tion**, *n.* —**det'o·na"tor**, *n.* a substance that causes explosion, as of a bomb.

de'tour' (dē'tûr') *n.* a roundabout way

used when the main route is temporarily closed; hence, an indirect procedure. —*v.i. & t.* go around.

de·tox'i·fy" (dē-tok'sə-fī") *v.t.* to remove poison or the effects of poison from. —**detox"i·fi·ca'tion**, *n.* Also, (*Slang*) **de'tox"**.

de·tract' (di-trakt') *v.t. & i.* (with *from*) disparage; reduce; take away a part, esp. from reputation. —**de·trac'tion**, *n.* —**de·trac'tive**, *adj.* —**de·trac'tor**, *n.*

de·train' *v.i. & t.* get off a railroad train. —**de·train'ment**, *n.*

det'ri·ment (det'rə-mənt) *n.* an injury or loss, or that which causes it. —**det"ri·men'tal** (-men'təl) *adj.*

de·tri'tus (di-trī'təs) *n.* (*Geol.*) loose particles eroded from solid rock by water or ice.

deuce (doos) *n.* **1,** (*Cards or Dice*) two. **2,** (*Tennis*) a tied score in a game. —**the deuce!** an exclamation of annoyance. —**deuc'ed** (doo'sid) *adj.* (*Informal*) confounded; annoying.

de'us ex ma'chi·na (dē'əs eks mä'ki-nə) a god from a machine; (*fig.*) a person, event, or object unexpectedly introduced into a story to resolve the plot.

deu·te'ri·um (doo-tir'ē-əm) *n.* a heavy isotope of hydrogen.

deu'ter·on (doo'tə-ron) *n.* the deuterium atom. Also, **deu'ton** (doo'ton).

de·val'u·ate" (dē-val'yû-āt") *v.t.* lower the value of, esp. of currency. Also, **de·val'ue**. —**de·val"u·a'tion**, *n.*

dev'as·tate" (dev'ə-stāt") *v.t.* **1,** lay waste; pillage. **2,** (*Informal*) overwhelm by disappointment, grief, etc.

de·vel'op (di-vel'əp) *v.i. & t.* **1,** advance or expand to a more complex or complete form; train; improve. **2,** unfold gradually; disclose; become apparent. **3,** process a photographic film, causing the image to become visible. **4,** elaborate; explain in full detail.

de·vel'op·ment (-mənt) *n.* **1,** act of developing or being developed. **2,** what is developed; a new or newly discovered event or fact. **3,** a group of buildings or land planned for buildings built or to be built by the same contractor. **4,** (*Music*) a section of a work in which themes previously announced are elaborated.

de'vi·ant (dē'vē-ənt) *adj.* departing from the norm. —*n.* a person or thing that departs from the norm.

de'vi·ate" (dē'vē-āt") *v.i. & t.* turn aside from a course; digress from a line of reasoning. —*n.* (-ət) a deviant; sexual pervert.

de·vice' (di-vīs') *n.* **1,** invention, esp. electrical or mechanical; contrivance; gadget. **2,** a scheme; trick. **3,** a heraldic design, as on a coat of arms. **4,** (*pl.*) will; inclination; pleasure.

dev'il (dev'əl) *n.* **1,** (*cap.*) the supreme evil spirit; Satan. **2,** any evil spirit; a demon. **3,** a cruel, fiendish person. **4,** a reckless person, as a *daredevil*. **5,** an expletive: *the devil!* **6,** a printer's errand boy. —*v.t.* **1,** (*Informal*) bother; torment. **2,** in cooking, season highly. —**dev'il·ish,** *adj.* **1,** fiendish. **2,** roguish. —**dev'il·ment, dev'-il·try** (-trē) *n.* mischief; roguishness. —**devil's advocate,** one who takes a position for the sake of argument, without necessarily accepting it. —**devil's food cake,** a rich chocolate cake.

> **devil**
> ↔ Not derived from *evil,* however appropriate, but from Greek *diabolos,* enemy.

dev'il·fish" *n.* a large marine animal, esp. a manta ray or an octopus.

dev'il·ish *adj.* **1,** like a devil. **2,** (*Informal*) excessive. —*adv.* (*Informal*) extremely.

devil-may-care *adj.* reckless; casual.

de·vi·ous (dē'vē-əs) *adj.* **1,** out of the direct or common way; circuitous. **2,** shifty; deceitful. —**de'vi·ous·ness,** *n.*

de·vise' (di-vīz') *v.t. & i.* **1,** think out; concoct; scheme. **2,** transmit (property) by will; bequeath. —*n.* a will; the act of transmitting by will. —**de·vis'er, de·vi'sor,** *n.* —**de·vi'see"** (-zē") *n.*

de·vi'tal·ize" (dē-vī'tə-līz") *v.t.* deprive of vitality; weaken in force or effect. —**de·vi"tal·i·za'tion,** *n.*

de·void' (di-void') *adj.* (with *of*) empty; destitute or lacking.

de·volve' (di-volv') *v.t. & i.* transmit or delegate to another; (with *upon*) pass to. —**dev"o·lu'tion** (dev"ə-loo'shən) *n.*

de·vote' (di-vōt') *v.t.* **1,** give or apply, as time to a hobby. **2,** consecrate or dedicate. —**de·vot'ed,** *adj.* ardently attached; dedicated.

dev"o·tee' (dev"ə-tē') *n.* one ardently devoted, as to religion; a zealot.

de·vo'tion (di-vō'shən) *n.* **1,** act of devoting; dedication; consecration. **2,** piety; godliness. **3,** affection; love; zeal. **4,** (*pl.*) prayers; religious worship.

de·vour' (di-vowr') *v.t.* **1,** swallow up; eat ravenously. **2,** consume; destroy. **3,** absorb; take in, as a book.

de·vout' (di-vowt') *adj.* devoted to religion or religious worship. —**de·vout'ness,** *n.*

dew (dū) *n.* small drops of moisture condensed from the atmosphere at night. —**dew'y,** *adj.* —**dew point,** the temperature at which dew forms.

dew'ber"ry (dū'ber"ē) *n.* a trailing plant or its fruit, similar to a blackberry.

dew'claw" *n.* a useless inner claw in the foot of some dogs.

dew'drop" *n.* a globule of dew.

dew'lap" (doo'lap") *n.* the pendulous skin under the throat of a number of animals.

dew'y (dū'ē) *adj.* **1,** moist with or like dew. **2,** fresh; young. —**dew'i·ness,** *n.*

Dex'e·drine" (dek'sə-drēn") *n.* (*T.N.*) an amphetamine used as a stimulant. Also, (*Slang*) **dex'ie** (dek'sē).

dex·ter'i·ty (deks-ter'ə-tē) *n.* manual or mental adroitness; skill. —**dex'ter·ous** (deks'tər-əs) *adj.*

dex'trin (dek'strin) *n.* a gummy product of starch, used as mucilage, etc.

dex'tro- (dek'strō) *pref.* right; turning to the right.

> **dextro-**
> ↔ From Latin *dexter,* on the right side, hence, by unfair extension, skillful.

dex'trose (deks'trōs) *n.* a form of sugar which is obtained commercially from starch.

dex'trous (deks'trəs) *adj.* dexterous.

dhole (dōl) *n.* a wild Asiatic dog.

dho'ti (dō'tē) *n.* loincloth.

dhow (dow) *n.* a light Arab sailing vessel.

di- (dī; di) *pref.* two; twofold; double.

di"a·be'tes (dī"ə-bē'tēz) *n.* a disease commonly due to the inability of the body to use sugar. —**di"a·bet'ic** (-bet'ik) *adj. & n.*

> **diabetes**
> ↔ From Greek *diabētēs,* passed through, from the excessive discharge of urine, a symptom of the disease.

di"a·bol'ic (dī"ə-bol'ik) *adj.* devilish; infernal. Also, **di"a·bol'i·cal.**

di·ac'o·nal (dī-ak'ə-nəl) *adj.* of or pert. to a deacon.

di·ac'o·nate (dī-ak'ə-nit) *n.* **1,** the office of a deacon. **2,** a body of deacons.

di"a·crit'i·cal (dī"ə-krit'ə-kəl) *adj.* serving to distinguish. —**diacritical mark,** [also, **di"a·crit'ic**] a mark that indicates the exact pronunciation of a letter; accent mark.

di'a·dem" (dī'ə-dem") *n.* **1,** a crown. **2,** a jeweled headband.

diadem
↔ From Greek *diadein*, to bind around; the term once referred to a regal headband worn by Alexander the Great and his successors.

di″aer′e·sis (dī-er″ə-sis) *n.* dieresis.

di″ag·nose′ (dī″əg-nōs′) *v.t.* ascertain; analyze; determine the nature of, esp. of a disease.

di″ag·no′sis (dī″ig-nō′sis) *n.* [*pl.* **-ses** (-sèz)] analysis of present condition, esp. of a disease. —**di″ag·nos′tic** (-nos′tik) *adj.* —**di″ag·nos′ti·cal·ly,** *adv.*

diagnosis, prognosis
☛ Two words of analysis of disease or other matters. *Diagnosis* refers to an examination of the nature of something, whereas *prognosis* attempts to forecast its future development.

di″ag·nos·ti′cian (dī″əg-nos-tish′ən) *n.* a doctor skilled in making diagnoses.

di·ag′o·nal (dī-ag′ə-nəl) *adj.* **1,** extending, as a line, from one angle to another not adjacent, within a polygon. **2,** oblique; slanting; marked by oblique lines. —*n.* a diagonal line or direction.

di′a·gram″ (dī′ə-gram″) *n.* a chart or plan, esp. a drawing made for demonstrating or graphic analysis. —*v.t.* chart; plan in detail. —**di″a·gram·mat′ic** (-grə-mat′ik) *adj.* —**di″a·gram·mat′i·cal·ly,** *adv.*

di′al (dī′əl) *n.* **1,** the face on which time is indicated, as on a clock or *sundial.* **2,** any face on which a pointer indicates something, as pressure. **3,** the rotary dial on a telephone, used to signal for connections. —*v.t.* **1,** measure or signal for, with a dial. **2,** select a number, as on a telephone dial or number pad. —**dial tone,** a buzzing signal indicating that a telephone number may be dialed.

di′a·lect″ (dī′ə-lekt″) *n.* **1,** the special idiom of a locality or class. **2,** jargon. —**di″a·lec′tal,** *adj.* ❏ *argot*

di″a·lec′tic (dī″ə-lek′tik) *adj.* **1,** relating to the art of reasoning or discussion. **2,** pert. to dialect. —*n.* **1,** the art of debating, or of logical discussion. **2,** (*pl.*) logic. —**di″a·lec′ti·cal·ly,** *adv.* —**di″a·lec·ti′cian,** *n.*

di′a·logue″ (dī′ə-lâg″) *n.* **1,** conversation between two or more persons. **2,** speeches spoken in a play. Also, **di′a·log″.**

di·al′y·sis (dī-al′ə-sis) *n.* [*pl.* **-ses″** (-sēz″)] the separation of substances by passing the solution containing them through a membrane. —**di″a·lyt′ic** (dī″ə-lit′ik) *adj.*

di·am′e·ter (dī-am′ə-tər) *n.* a line dividing a circle into halves; its length.

di″a·met′ri·cal (dī″ə-met′ri-kəl) *adj.* **1,** pert. to a diameter. **2,** absolute; complete. Also, **di″a·met′ric.**

dia′mond (dī″mənd) *n.* **1,** a form of pure carbon, extremely hard and brilliant; a precious stone. **2,** a quadrilateral, esp. a rhombus, viewed with an angle uppermost (◇). **3,** a playing card so marked. **4,** a baseball field, esp. the infield.

diamond
↔ The word comes from Latin *adamas*, diamond or other hard substance. The sense of quadrilateral shape comes from the shape of the diamond's facet.

dia′mond·back″ *n.* **1,** a kind of rattlesnake. **2,** a kind of terrapin.

Di″a·net′ics (dī″ə-net′iks) *n.sing.* (*T.N.*) a proposed therapy for mental disorders, esp. neuroses.

di″a·pa′son (dī″ə-pā′zən) *n.* **1,** the entire range of a voice or an instrument. **2,** correct tune or pitch.

di′a·per (dī′ə-pər) *n.* **1,** an infant's breechcloth. **2,** a white unbleached linen or cotton fabric with a woven pattern.

diaper
↔ From Greek *aspros*, white, through Greek *diaspros*, a white fabric.

di·aph′a·nous (dī-af′ə-nəs) *adj.* transparent or translucent.

di′a·phragm″ (dī′ə-fram″) *n.* **1,** the muscular partition that separates the thorax from the abdomen; the midriff. **2,** any thin piece of metal or other material that serves as a partition, as the vibrating disk of a telephone. **3,** a contraceptive device; pessary. —**di″a·phrag·mat′ic** (-frag-mat′ik) *adj.* —**di″a·phrag·mat′i·cal·ly,** *adv.*

di″ar·rhe′a (dī″ə-rē′ə) *n.* abnormally frequent evacuation of the bowels. —**di″ar·rhet′ic** (-ret′ik) *adj.*

di′a·ry (dī′ə-rē) *n.* a daily record; journal. —**di′a·rist,** *n.*

di·as′po·ra (dī-as′pə-rə) *n.* **1,** (often *cap.*) the Jews living among the Gentiles after the Babylonian captivity. **2,** the dispersion of a religious or political sect after conquest of its homeland.

di·as′to·le (dī-as′tə-lè) *n.* the rhythmical dilation of the heart.

di′a·ther″my (dī′ə-thēr″mē) *n.* (*Pathol.*)

treatment with radiant heat. —**di′·a·ther″-mic**, *adj.*

di′·a·tom (dī′ə-təm) *n.* any of a large family of microscopic, one-celled sea and freshwater plants.

di″·a·ton′·ic (dī″ə-ton′ik) *adj.* (*Music*) pert. to a normal scale—major or minor—of eight tones to the octave. —**di″-a·ton′i·cal·ly**, *adv.*

di′·a·tribe″ (dī′ə-trīb″) *n.* a bitter and abusive denunciation.

di·az′e·pam (dī-az′ə-pam) *n.* a tranquilizer and muscle-relaxing drug.

dib′ble (dib′əl) *n.* a gardening tool for making holes in the ground.

dibs (dibz) *n.* (*Slang*) a preemptive claim.

dice (dīs) *n.* **1,** (*pl.* of **die**) small cubes, esp. those having each face stamped with a different number of spots, used in games and in gambling. **2,** a dice game. —*v.t.* cut into small cubes, as food. —*v.i.* play at dice.

di′cey (dī′sė) *adj.* (*Slang*) dangerous; risky.

di·chot′o·my (dī-kot′ə-mė) *n.* a subdivision into two parts.

dick (dik) *n.* (*Slang*) a detective.

dic′kens (dik′ənz) *interj.* devil; deuce.

dick′er (dik′ər) *v.i.* (*Informal*) bargain; barter; haggle. —*n.* a haggling deal.

dick′ey (dik′ė) *n.* **1,** a child's bib. **2,** a separate or false shirt front. **3,** a woman's garment covering only the chest and worn under a suit coat or a bodice. **4,** a seat at the back of a vehicle. **5,** a small bird.

Dick test a test to determine susceptibility to scarlet fever, named for its inventor, U.S. internist G. F. Dick.

Dic′ta·phone″ (dik′tə-fōn″) *n.* (*T.N.*) a recording machine used for dictating.

dic′tate (dik′tāt) *v.t.* & *i.* **1,** express orally for another to write down. **2,** prescribe with authority; command. —*n.* **1,** an order; a command. **2,** a guiding principle; a maxim. —**dic·ta′tion,** *n.*

dic′ta·tor (dik′tā-tər) *n.* **1,** a person exercising unlimited powers of government; an absolute ruler. **2,** one who dictates. —**dic″ta·to′ri·al** (dik″tə-tôr′ė-əl) *adj.* —**dic·ta′tor·ship,** *n.*

dic′tion (dik′shən) *n.* **1,** manner of expression or choice of words in speaking or writing. **2,** enunciation.

dic′tion·ar·y (dik′shə-ner-ė) *n.* a book defining and listing in alphabetical order the principal words of a language, or a particular class of words.

dictionary, encyclopedia, thesaurus, glossary, lexicon
All of these books list words. A *dictionary* or *lexicon* defines a word and tells you how to use it. An *encyclopedia* discusses the subject represented by the word (and often related subjects) in detail. A *thesaurus* groups words that are related to one another in sense. A *glossary* lists words used in a particular specialized field and provides definitions. ↔ *Dictionary* comes from Latin *dictio*, word, from *dicere*, say.

Dic′to·graph″ (dik′tə-graf″) *n.* (*T.N.*) a recording instrument used chiefly for obtaining evidence secretly.

dic′tum (dik′təm) *n.* [*pl.* -**ta** (-tə)] a positive or authoritative statement.

did *v.* pret. of *do.*

di·dac′tic (dī-dak′tik) *adj.* instructive; expository. —**di·dac′ti·cal·ly,** *adv.*

did′dle (did′əl) *v.i.* & *t.* (*Slang*) **1,** waste time; dawdle. **2,** swindle.

di′do (dī′dō) *n.* (*Informal*) a prank; a caper.

di·dym′i·um (dī-dim′ė-əm) *n.* a mixture of neodymium and praesodymium, once thought to be a single element.

didymium
↔ Named by its discoverer, Swedish chemist Carl Mosander, from Greek *didymos*, twin.

die (dī) *v.i.* [**died, dy′ing**] **1,** cease to live; expire. **2,** come to an end. **3,** (with *away* or *out*) fade away. **4,** (with *for*) (*Informal*) desire keenly. —*n.* **1,** an engraved stamp used for impressing a design. **2,** any of various mechanical devices, as a tool for cutting the threads of screws. **3,** sing. of *dice.*

die′hard″ *n.* & *adj.* one who resists to the end; conservative.

diel′drin (dēl′drən) *n.* an insecticide.

di″e·lec′tric (dī″ə-lek′trik) *n.* a nonconducting substance. —*adj.* nonconducting.

di·er′e·sis (dī-er′ə-sis) *n.* [*pl.* -**ses** (-sēz)] **1,** the separate pronunciation of two adjacent vowels. **2,** a mark (¨) indicating such pronunciation.

die′sel (dē′zel) *n.* an internal-combustion engine employing the heat of compression to ignite fuel oil, named for its inventor, German engineer Rudolf Diesel.

di′et (dī′ət) *n.* **1,** food and drink regularly consumed. **2,** a prescribed course of food.

3, regimen. **4,** a formal public assembly. —*v.i.* eat according to a diet. —**di′e·tar·y** (-ter-ė) *adj.*

---

diet

↔ From Greek *diaita,* mode of living, or, more specifically, mode of eating, esp. a prescribed mode.

---

di″e·tet′ics (dī″ə-tet′iks) *n.* the science of regulating the diet.

di″e·ti′tian (dī″ə-tish′ən) *n.* one trained to plan meals. Also, **di″e·ti′cian.**

dif′fer (dif′ər) *v.i.* **1,** be unlike or distinct (with *from*). **2,** (with *with*) disagree, in opinion.

dif′fer·ence (dif′ər-əns) *n.* **1,** a dissimilarity; a distinction. **2,** a controversy; a dispute. **3,** discrimination. **4,** (*Math.*) the remainder after a number has been subtracted.

dif′fer·ent (dif′ər-ənt) *adj.* unlike; not the same. —**differently abled,** handicapped.

---

different

(*Gram.*) Though some grammarians dictate otherwise, *different* can be used with either *than* or *from*, and the two expressions are found about equally often in everyday speech and writing.

---

dif″fer·en′tial (dif′ə-ren′shəl) *n.* **1,** a difference between two comparable values. **2,** (*Math.*) a function that expresses the difference between two values of a variable quantity. **3,** in automobiles, a gear arrangement that allows the outer driving wheel to turn faster on a curve. —*adj.* making, showing, or having a difference.

dif″fer·en′ti·ate″ (dif″ə-ren′shė-āt″) *v.t.* & *i.* make, constitute, or observe a difference (between). —**dif″fer·en″ti·a′tion,** *n.*

dif′fi·cult″ (dif′ə-kult″) *adj.* **1,** presenting an obstacle or perplexing problem; not easy; hard to do or understand; arduous. **2,** hard to please or persuade; not compliant; troublesome.

dif′fi·cul·ty (dif′i-kul-tė) *n.* **1,** that which is hard to understand or to overcome. **2,** a troublesome or embarrassing situation; (*pl.*) want of money. **3,** an objection; reluctance.

dif′fi·dence (dif′ə-dəns) *n.* want of self-confidence; shyness. —**dif′fi·dent,** *adj.*

dif·frac′tion (di-frak′shən) *n.* **1,** in optics, the modification of light or deflection of its rays. **2,** a modification of sound waves passing by a large building, etc. —**dif·fract′,** *v.* —**dif·fract′ive,** *adj.*

dif·fuse′ (di-fūz′) *v.t.* & *i.* pour out and spread; send out in all directions; scatter. —*adj.* (di-fūs′) **1,** widely spread. **2,** verbose. —**dif·fu′sion** (-zhən) *n.* —**dif·fu′sive** (-siv) *adj.*

dig *v.t.* & *i.* (**dug, dig′ging**) **1,** turn up, or scoop out, as earth, with a trowel or spade; excavate. **2,** work hard; find out by effort or research. **3,** (with *in*) make a hole or trench for military protection. **4,** (with *up*) unearth; bring to light. **5,** (*Slang*) enjoy; appreciate. —*n.* **1,** a thrust; a poke. **2,** (*Informal*) a sarcastic remark.

di·gest′ (di-jest′) *v.t.* **1,** convert food in the body for assimilation. **2,** assimilate mentally; think over. —*n.* (dī′jest) a condensed collection or summary. —**di·gest′i·ble,** *adj.*

di·ges′tion (di-jes′chən) *n.* act or process of assimilating food. —**di·ges′tive,** *adj.*

dig′ger (dig′ər) *n.* **1,** that which digs. **2,** the stinger of an insect.

dig′gings (dig′ingz) *n.* **1,** an excavation or mine. **2,** (*Informal*) living quarters.

dig′it (dij′it) *n.* **1,** a finger or toe; **2,** any number under ten. —**dig′i·tal** (-i-təl) *adj.* —**digital audiotape,** DAT. —**digital computer,** a computer operating directly with digits.

---

digit

↔ From Latin *digitus,* finger, toe, pointer. The numerical sense clearly comes from the practice of counting on the fingers.

---

dig″i·tal′is (dij″ə-tal′is) *n.* **1,** a genus of plants, esp. the foxglove. **2,** a drug obtained from its leaves used as a heart stimulant.

dig′ni·fy″ (dig′nə-fī″) *v.t.* **1,** confer honor upon; ennoble. **2,** give an undeservedly important name to. —**dig′ni·fied,** *adj.* marked by dignity; noble; stately.

dig′ni·tar·y (dig′ni-ter-ė) *n.* one who holds an exalted rank or office.

dig′ni·ty (dig′nə-tė) *n.* **1,** worthiness; high rank. **2,** self-respecting or noble mien or deportment; importance. **3,** a high office or title. ❑ *dainty*

di′graph (dī′graf) *n.* two letters representing a single sound, as *th* in *the*.

di·gress′ (di-gres′) *v.i.* turn away from the main subject; deviate; wander. —**di·gres′sion** (-gresh′ən) *n.* —**di·gres′sive,** *adj.*

di·he′dral (dī-hē′drəl) *adj.* **1,** having two plane faces, as a crystal. **2,** forming an angle, as between the walls of a room.

---

fat, fāte, fär, fāre, fåll, åsk; met, hē, hėr, maybė; pin, pīne; not, nōte, ôr, tool

dike (dīk) *n.* **1,** an embankment built to prevent flooding by a river or the ocean. **2,** a channel for water.

dike, ditch
↔ These two words both derive from Old Norse *diki*, dike.

Di·lan′tin (dī-lan′tin) *n.* (*T.N.*) a drug used in treating epilepsy.

di·lap′i·date″ (di-lap′ə-dāt″) *v.t. & i.* ruin, or fall into partial or total ruin. —**di·lap′i·dat″ed,** *adj.* —**di·lap′i·da′tion,** *n.*

di·late′ (dī-lāt′) *v.t. & i.* **1,** expand; make larger; distend. **2,** expatiate (upon). —**di·la′tion, dil″a·ta′tion** (dil″ə-tā′shən) *n.* —**di·la′tor,** *n.*

dil′a·to·ry (dil′ə-tôr-ē) *adj.* given to delay; procrastinating.

dil′do (dil′dō) *n.* (*Slang*) an artificial substitute for an erect penis.

di·lem·ma (di-lem′ə) *n.* a choice between alternatives equally undesirable.

dil″et·tante′ (dil″ə-tänt′) *n.* one who pursues art or literature for amusement; a dabbler.

dil′i·gence (dil′ə-jəns) *n.* **1,** constant and persistent attention to one's work; industry. **2,** a public stagecoach. —**dil′i·gent,** *adj.*

diligence
↔ The sense of industry comes from Latin *diligentia*. The sense of stagecoach is from the French phrase *carosse de diligence*, express coach.

dill (dil) *n.* an aromatic herb.

dil′ly (dil′ē) *n.* (*Informal*) something unusually good or striking.

dil′ly·dal″ly (dil′ē-dal″ē) *v.i.* (*Informal*) loiter; waste time; vacillate.

dil′u·ent (dil′ū-ənt) *n.* a fluid used to dilute another.

di·lute′ (di-loot′) *v.t.* weaken by an admixture of water or other liquid; reduce in strength. —**di·lu′tion,** *n.*

di·lu′vi·al (di-loo′vē-əl) *adj.* **1,** pert. to a flood or deluge. **2,** pert. to any debris deposited by a flood.

dim *adj.* [**dim′mer, -mest**] **1,** not bright or clear; not well lighted. **2,** obscure; vague; not understood. **3,** not comprehending clearly. —*v.i. & t.* [**dimmed, dim′ming**] make dim or dimmer. —**dim′ness,** *n.*

dime (dīm) *n.* **1,** a U. S. silver coin worth ten cents. **2,** (*Slang*) a thousand dollars. —**dime novel,** a paperbound novel of adventure or romance. —**dime store,** a five-and-ten-cent store.

dime
↔ *Dime* originally meant the same as *tithe*, i.e., the tenth part. Its source is Latin *decima*, tenth part.

di·men′sion (di-men′shən) *n.* measure in one direction; length, breadth, or thickness. —**di·men′sion·al,** *adj.*

di·min′ish *v.t. & i.* make less or smaller by any means; lessen. —**dim″i·nu′tion** (dim″i-nū′shən) *n.*

di·min″u·en·do (di-min″yû-en′dō) *n.* (*Music*) a gradual lessening of the volume of sound.

di·min′u·tive (di-min′yə-tiv) *adj.* very small; tiny. —*n.* **1,** a small thing or person. **2,** a word form denoting smallness, affection, etc.

dim′i·ty (dim′ə-tē) *n.* a thin cotton fabric with woven corded stripes.

dim′mer (dim′ər) *n.* **1,** a device that reduces the intensity of a light. **2,** (*pl.*) dim lights. —*adj.* more dim.

dim′out″ *n.* a partial reduction in lighting in a city, to conserve electricity or escape attacking aircraft.

dim′ple (dim′pəl) *n.* **1,** a natural hollow in some soft part of the body, as in the cheek. **2,** a dent. —*v.i.* show a dimple, as by smiling.

dim′ sum″ *n.* (*Chin.*, a dot on the heart) small dumplings, usu. filled with meat, etc., and steamed or fried; snack.

dim′wit″ *n.* (*Slang*) a dull-witted or stupid person.

din *n.* a continued clattering or ringing noise; a clamor.

di·nar′ (dē-när′) *n.* the monetary unit of Yugoslavia, Iraq, Algeria, and other countries.

dine (dīn) *v.i.* eat the chief meal of the day. —*v.t.* give a dinner to or for.

din′er (dī′nər) *n.* **1,** one taking dinner. **2,** a railroad car, or similar structure, where meals are served.

di·ne′ro (dē-nā′rō) *n.* money.

di·nette′ (dī-net′) *n.* a small room or alcove in which to eat.

ding *n.* **1,** [also, **ding′dong″**] the sound of a bell. **2,** dent. —*v.t.* dent.

ding-′a-ling′ (ding′ə-ling′) *n.* (*Slang*) a stupid person.

ding′bat″ *n.* **1,** an eccentric or silly person. **2,** a character-sized decorative typographic symbol.

din′ghy (ding′ē) *n.* a small boat, usually for rowing.

din′gle (ding′gəl) *n.* a secluded valley.

din′go (ding′gō) *n.* a wild dog of Australia.

ding′us (ding′əs) *n.* (*Slang*) a gadget.

din′gy (din′jė) *adj.* dirty; not fresh; tarnished. —**din′gi·ness,** *n.*

dink *n.* (*Slang*) either of a couple, both of whom work and who have no children: *d(ouble) i(ncome) n(o) k(ids).*

dink′y (dink′ė) *adj.* small; tiny. —*n.* [also **dink′ey**] a little locomotive.

din′ner (din′ər) *n.* **1,** the principal meal. **2,** an entertainment; banquet. —**dinner jacket,** a man's semiformal jacket; tuxedo.

---

dinner, supper

☞ Although the distinction is not consistently observed, *dinner* properly refers to the main meal of the day, whenever it is served, while *supper* is always an evening meal, usually a light one. ↔ *Dinner* has a source word in Latin, *disjejunare,* which literally translates as "break fast." Nevertheless, the word in English has always referred to the main meal of the day.

---

di′no·saur″ (dī′nə-sôr″) *n.* **1,** an extinct gigantic reptile. **2,** anything outmoded or resistant to change. —**di″no·sau′ri·an** (-ė-ən) *adj.*

---

dinosaur

↔ A word coined in the 19th c. from Greek *deinos,* terrible, and *sauros,* lizard.

---

dint *n.* **1,** a dent. **2,** a power; force.

di′o·cese″ (dī′ə-sēs″) *n.* the district under the care of a bishop. —**di·oc′e·san** (dī-os′is-ən) *adj.*

di′ode (dī′ōd) *n.* in electronics, a vacuum tube or semiconductor device used as a rectifier.

di″o·ram′a (dī″ə-ram′ə) *n.* a continuous painting exhibited in a dark room with spectacular lighting effects. —**di″o·ram′ic,** *adj.*

di·ox′ide″ (dī-ok′sīd) *n.* (*Chem.*) an oxide having two oxygen atoms per molecule.

dip *v.t.* [**dipped, dip′ping**] **1,** immerse temporarily in a liquid. **2,** lower and raise, as a bird's wings. **3,** scoop up. —*v.i.* **1,** plunge into temporarily. **2,** (with *into*) investigate; be interested. **3,** incline downward. **4,** sink. —*n.* **1,** the act or result of dipping; a short swim. **2,** a sloping downward. **3,** a hollow; depression. **4,** a liquid to dip something in, as for eating, tinting or disinfection. **5,** a pickpocket. **6,** (*Slang*) an ineffectual person.

diph·the′ri·a (dif-thir′ė-ə) *n.* an infectious disease in which a membrane forms over the air passage.

diph′thong (dif′thâng) *n.* two adjacent vowels pronounced in one syllable. ,

di·plo′ma (di-plō′mə) *n.* a certificate given by a school or college showing graduation. —**dip′lo·mate″** (dip′lə-māt″) *n.* —**diploma mill,** (*Slang*) an educational institution granting diplomas fraudulently or without proper standards.

---

diploma, diplomat

↔ Originally, *diploma* was a Greek word meaning folded paper, hence, document.

---

di·plo′ma·cy (di-plō′mə-sė) *n.* **1,** the art of negotiation between nations. **2,** tact.

dip′lo·mat″ (dip′lə-mat″) *n.* **1,** an official representative of a country. **2,** one skilled in diplomacy. Also, **di·plo′ma·tist** (di-plō′mə-tist). ❏ *diploma*

dip″lo·mat′ic (-ik) *adj.* **1,** pert. to the work of a diplomat. **2,** tactful. —**dip″lo·mat′i·cal·ly,** *adv.*

di′pole″ (dī′pōl″) *n.* a pair of equal and opposite electric charges or magnetic poles. —**di·po′lar** (dī-pō′lər) *adj.*

dip′per (dip′ər) *n.* **1,** a utensil for ladling or scooping out something. **2,** (*cap.*) either of two constellations: *Big Dipper; Little Dipper.*

dip′py (dip′ė) *adj.* (*Slang*) **1,** crazy or eccentric. **2,** foolish.

dip″so·ma′ni·a (dip″sə-mā′nė-ə) *n.* an irresistible craving for intoxicants. —**dip″so·ma′ni·ac,** *n.*

dip′stick″ *n.* a measuring stick used for checking fluid levels.

DIP switch a type of electric switch, usu. small, used as control devices on electronic equipment: *d(ual) i(n-line) p(ackage) switch.*

dip′tych (dip′tik) *n.* **1,** an ancient two-leaved writing tablet. **2,** a pair of pictures or carvings hinged together.

dire (dīr) *adj.* dreadful; fearful; disastrous. —**dire′ful,** *adj.* —**dire′ness,** *n.*

di·rect′ (di-rekt′) *v.t.* **1,** aim or point toward an object. **2,** point out a course to. **3,** regulate; guide or lead. **4,** order; command. **5,** address (a letter); address (words) to a person. **6,** conduct an orchestra or choir. **7,** control the interpretation and dramatic performance of (a play, opera, etc.). —*adj.* **1,** straightforward; open; sincere. **2,** personal; firsthand. —**di·rect′ness,** .*n.* —**direct current,** electric current that flows always in the same direction.

di·rec′tion (di-rek′shən) *n.* **1,** relative

position, as along a line or to a place. **2,** act of directing; administration; management. **3,** the act of aiming or pointing out a course. **4,** an order; a regulation; instruction. **—di·rec′tion·al,** *adj.*

di·rec′tive (di-rek′tiv) *n.* an instruction; a statement of policy.

di·rect′ly (-lė) *adv.* **1,** in a direct line, course, or manner. **2,** immediately. **3,** expressly; clearly; precisely.

di·rec′tor (di-rek′tər) *n.* one who directs, esp. a company or theatrical production. **—di·rec′to·rate** (-ət) *n.* a body of directors. **—di·rec″tor′i·al** (-tôr′ė-əl) *adj.* **—di·rec′tor·ship,** *n.*

di·rec′to·ry (di-rek′tə-rė) *n.* **1,** a book listing names and addresses. **2,** (*cap.*) a French government, 1795-99, during the French Revolution.

dirge (dērj) *n.* music or poetry expressing grief; a funeral hymn.

> **dirge**
> ↔ From Latin *dirige*, direct, the first word of a line in the Latin office of the dead, Psalm 5, verse 8.

dir′i·gi·ble (dir′i-jə-bəl) *n.* a large cigar-shaped rigid airship, capable of being steered. **—adj.** capable of being directed or steered.

dirk (dērk) *n.* a dagger.

dirn′dl (dērn′dəl) *n.* a colorful peasant dress.

dirt (dērt) *n.* **1,** any filthy substance, as dust, mud, etc. **2,** earth or soil. **3,** anything mean or worthless; gossip. **—adj.** granular; unpaved, as a road. **—do one dirt,** (*Informal*) treat one abusively. **—eat dirt,** be humiliated. **—dirt bike,** trail bike.

> **dirt**
> ↔ By the process of sound reversal, *dirt* derives from Old Norse *drit*, excrement. Over time the sense was softened to its present one.

dirt-′cheap′ adj. & adv.(*Informal*) very cheap or cheaply.

dirt′y (dēr′tė) *adj.* **1,** soiling. **2,** unclean; sullied. **3,** base; low; contemptible. **4,** rainy (of the weather). **5,** obscene; pornographic. **—v.t.** sully. **—dirt′i·ness,** *n.* **—dirty pool,** (*Informal*) unethical conduct.

dis- *pref.* **1,** separate; not joined. **2,** not; negation in an active sense (thus: something *unproved* may never have been tried, something *disproved* has been tried and found false). [In addition to words defined in the text, the following words may be defined by assuming active lack or negation of the root word, which see in each case.

dis″ac·cord′
dis·af·firm′
dis″al·low′
dis″ap·pro·ba′tion
dis″ar·range′
dis″as·sem′ble
dis″as·so′ci·ate″
dis″be·lieve′
dis·bur′den
dis″con·nect′
dis·con″tin′u·ance
dis·coun′te·nance
dis″em·bark′
dis″em·bar′rass
dis″em·bod′y
dis″em·bow′el
dis″em·ploy′
dis″en·chant′
dis″en·cum′ber
dis″en·gage′
dis″en·tan′gle
dis″en·twine′
dis″es·tab′lish
dis″es·teem′
dis·fa′vor
dis·fran′chise

dis·har′mo·ny
dis·hon′est
dis″il·lu′sion
dis·in″cli·na′tion
dis″in·fec′tion
dis″in·gen′u·ous
dis·join′
dis·junc′tion
dis·loy′al
dis·o·blige′
dis·pir′it
dis″pro·por′tion
dis·rel′ish
dis″re·mem′ber
dis·re·spect′
dis·robe′
dis·rup′ture
dis·ser′vice
dis·sim′i·lar
dis″si·mil′i·tude
dis·sym′me·try
dis·trust′
dis·un′ion
dis″u·nite′
dis·use′

dis·a′ble (dis-ā′bəl) *v.t.* deprive of physical, mental, or legal power; incapacitate. **—dis″a·bil′i·ty,** *n.*

> **disability, inability**
> ☛ *Disability* is the incapacity to do something because of a handicap—physical, mental, etc. *Inability* is simply the lack of ability to do something, whatever the reason, but usually through incompetence, weakness, lack of training, etc.

dis·a·buse′ (dis″ə-būz′) *v.t.* set right; undeceive.

dis″ad·van′tage (dis″əd-vản′tij) *n.* **1,** that which prevents success or makes it difficult. **2,** a loss to profit, reputation, etc.; a drawback. **—dis″ad·van′taged,** *adj.* deprived of the basic requirements for normal development; underprivileged. **—dis·ad″van·ta′geous,** *adj.*

dis″af·fect′ *v.t.* make unfriendly or discontented. **—dis″af·fec′tion,** *n.* ill will.

> **disaffected, unaffected**
> ☛ *Disaffected* means discontented, esp. with an authority. *Unaffected* means not affected in its various senses, as uninfluenced or unaltered.

dis″a·gree′ *v.i.* **1,** (with *with*) differ. **2,** quarrel. **3,** be incompatible or unsuitable. **—dis″a·gree′a·ble,** *adj.* bad-tempered; distasteful.

dis″a·gree′ment *n.* **1,** act of disagreeing.

2, a quarrel; controversy. **3,** discrepancy; difference.

dis″ap·pear′ *v.i.* pass out of sight or existence; vanish. —**dis″ap·pear′ance,** *n.*

dis″ap·point′ (dis″ə-point′) *v.t. & i.* fail to fulfill the expectations of (someone). —**dis″ap·point′ment,** *n.*

dis″ap·prove′ *v.t. & i.* **1,** condemn. **2,** decline to sanction. —*v.i.* feel or express disfavor (with *of*). —**dis″ap·prov′al,** *n.*

dis·arm′ (dis-ärm′) *v.t.* **1,** deprive of weapons. **2,** deprive of resentment; make friendly. —*v.i.* reduce or curtail military power. —**dis·ar′ma·ment,** *n.* —**dis·arm′ing,** *adj.* inducing friendliness.

dis″ar·ray′ (dis″ə-rā′) *v.t.* **1.** divest; disrobe. **2,** throw into disorder; rout. —*n.* **1,** confusion. **2,** disorderly dress.

dis·as′ter (di-zas′tər) *n.* a great misfortune; a catastrophe. —**dis·as′trous,** *adj.*

---

disaster

↔ From Italian *disastro*, from *dis-*, away, + *astro*, star, from Greek *astron*, perhaps from the idea of an unfavorable star causing calamity on earth.

---

dis″a·vow′ *v.t.* disown; deny; repudiate. —**dis″a·vow′al,** *n.*

dis·band′ *v.i. & t.* dissolve, as a band or group; dismiss, as troops from an army. —**dis·band′ment,** *n.*

dis·bar′ (dis-bär′) *v.t.* **[-barred′, -bar′-ring]** withdraw the right (of a lawyer) to practice law. —**dis·bar′ment,** *n.*

dis·burse′ (dis-bērs′) *v.t.* pay out; expend. —**dis·burse′ment,** *n.*

disc (disk) *n.* disk.

dis·card′ (dis-kärd′) *v.t.* cast off; reject; throw away as useless. —*n.* (dis′kärd″) **1,** something cast off. **2,** a place of disposal.

dis·cern′ (di-zērn′) *v.t. & i.* distinguish by the eye or the intellect; perceive; discriminate. —**dis·cern′i·ble,** *adj.* —**dis·cern′ing,** *adj.* discriminating; keen. —**dis·cern′ment,** *n.*

dis·charge′ (dis-chärj′) *n.* **1,** the act of unloading. **2,** the act of firing a missile or a weapon. **3,** removal by taking away, settlement, or payment. **4,** a flowing out; emission. **5,** freeing, as of a prisoner; release, as of a soldier (also, a certificate of such release); dismissal, as of an employee. **6,** that which is emitted. **7,** performance; execution. —*v.t.* **1,** unload. **2,** emit (as water). **3,** set free; dismiss; absolve. **4,** fulfill (a duty); execute. **5,** fire, as a gun.

dis·ci·ple (di-sī′pəl) *n.* one who adheres to the doctrines of another; a follower, esp. (often *cap.*) an Apostle.

dis″ci·pli·nar′i·an (dis″ə-pli-nār′ē-ən) *n.* an exacting master.

dis′ci·pli·nar′y (dis′ə-pli-ner″ē) *adj.* pert. to or promoting discipline.

dis′ci·pline (dis′ə-plin) *n.* **1,** mental and moral training. **2,** obedience to rules. **3,** correction; chastisement. **4,** a set of regulations; regimen. **5,** a course of study; a science or art. —*v.t.* **1,** train. **2,** chastise.

dis·claim′ (dis-klām′) *v.t.* renounce; deny; disown. —**dis·claim′er,** *n.* a statement of disavowal.

dis·close′ (dis-klōz′) *v.t.* bring to light; uncover; make known. —**dis·clo′sure** (-klō′zhər) *n.*

dis′co (dis′kō) *n. & adj.* (*Informal*) (pert. to) a discotheque or its music.

dis·col′or (dis-kul′ər) *v.t. & i.* **1,** alter the natural hue of. **2,** stain. —**dis·col″or·a′-tion,** *n.*

dis″com·bob′u·late (dis″kəm-bob′ū-lāt) *v.t.* (*Slang*) confuse; disconcert.

dis·com′fit (dis-kum′fit) *v.t.* **1,** embarrass; frustrate. **2,** confuse. —**dis·com′fi-ture** (-fi-chər) *n.*

dis·com′fort *n.* uneasiness; pain.

dis″com·mode′ (dis″kə-mōd′) *v.t.* put to inconvenience; trouble.

dis″com·pose′ (dis″kum-pōz′) *v.t.* unsettle; agitate; disturb. —**dis″com·po′sure** (-pō′zhər) *n.* embarrassment.

dis″con·cert′ (dis″kən-sērt′) *v.t.* **1,** perturb; confuse. **2,** throw into disorder.

dis·con′so·late (dis-kon′sə-lət) *adj.* without consolation; sorrowful.

dis·con·tent′ *n.* want of satisfaction; uneasiness of mind. —*v.t.* make unhappy. —**dis″con·tent′ed,** *adj.* not contented; restive; unhappy. —**dis″con·tent′ment,** *n.*

dis″con·tin′u·ance *n.* lack of continued connection.

dis″con·tin′ue *v.t.* cease; break off; interrupt. —*v.i.* come to a stop or end. —**dis″-con·tin″u·a′tion,** *n.*

dis·con″ti·nu′i·ty *n.* a gap; lack of cohesion.

dis′cord (dis′kôrd) *n.* **1,** want of agreement; contention; strife. **2,** (*Music*) want of harmony; a dissonance. **3,** any confused noise. —**dis·cord′ance, dis·cord′-an·cy,** *n.* —**dis·cord′ant,** *adj.*

dis″co·theque″ (dis′kə-tek″) *n.* a nightclub where dance music is provided, usu. by recorded music. Also (*Informal*) **dis′co** (dis′kō).

dis′count (dis′kownt) *v.t.* **1,** deduct from the settlement of, as of a bill or charge

---

fat, fāte, fär, fāre, fâll, ásk; met, hē, hēr, maybè; pin, pīne; not, nōte, ôr, tool account. **2,** disregard; make allowance for exaggeration. **3,** lessen effectiveness of by anticipating the outcome. **4,** (*Com.*) buy or sell for less than face value, as a promissory note before maturity. —*n.* a deduction. —**discount rate,** rate of interest charged by the Federal Reserve Bank on borrowed money.

dis·cour′age (dis-kēr′ij) *v.t.* **1,** cause to lose spirit or hope. **2,** obstruct by opposition. **3,** dissuade (with *from*). —**dis·cour′-age·ment,** *n.*

dis′course (dis′kôrs) *n.* **1,** expression of ideas by words; a conversation. **2,** a formal discussion or written treatment of a subject. —*v.i.* (dis-kôrs′) converse; talk.

dis·cour′te·ous *adj.* uncivil; rude.

dis·cour′te·sy *n.* **1,** incivility; ill manners; rudeness. **2,** an impolite act.

dis·cov′er (dis-kuv′ər) *v.t.* gain first sight or knowledge of something hitherto unknown. —**dis·cov′er·er,** *n.*

dis·cov′er·y (-ē) *n.* **1,** act of discovering. **2,** something discovered.

dis·cred′it *v.t.* **1,** not to believe. **2,** injure the reputation of; destroy confidence in. —*n.* **1,** a loss of reputation or honor. **2,** doubt; disbelief. —**dis·cred′it·a·ble,** *adj.* blameworthy.

dis·creet′ (dis-krēt) *adj.* careful of appearances; tactful. —**dis·creet′ness,** *n.*

---

discreet, discrete

☛ Do not confuse *discreet*, meaning tactful, and *discrete*, separate. ↔ However, the two words come from the same source, Latin *discretus*, distinguished.

---

dis·crep′an·cy (dis-krep′ən-sē) *n.* an unexplained difference; inconsistency. —**dis·crep′ant,** *adj.*

dis·crete′ (dis-krēt′) *adj.* **1,** separate. **2,** discontinuous. —**dis·crete′ness,** *n.* ❑ *discreet*

dis·cre′tion (dis-kresh′ən) *n.* **1,** act or state of being discreet. **2,** judgment; power to decide. —**dis·cre′tion·a·ry** (-er-ē) *adj.*

dis·crim′i·nate (dis-krim′ə-nāt″) *v.i.* & *t.* **1,** judge (respective merits). **2,** treat differently on the basis of race, class, sex, etc. —**dis·crim′i·nat″ing,** *adj.* showing good taste. —**dis·crim″i·na′tion,** *n.* —**dis·crim′in·a·to″ry,** *adj.*

dis·cur′sive (dis-kēr′siv) *adj.* rambling from topic to topic; digressive. —**dis·cur′-sive·ness,** *n.*

dis′cus (dis′kəs) *n.* a heavy disk used in weight-throwing contests.

dis·cuss′ (dis-kus′) *v.t.* **1,** talk about; debate. **2,** speak or write about; explain. —**dis·cus′sant,** *n.* —**dis·cus′sion** (dis-kush′ən) *n.*

dis·dain′ (dis-dān′) *v.t.* & *i.* **1,** look down upon; scorn; despise. **2,** not deign or stoop. —*n.* scorn. —**dis·dain′ful,** *adj.*

dis·ease′ (di-zēz′) *n.* a condition of ill health; malady. —*v.t.* infect with disease.

dis″em·bow′el (dis″em-bow′əl) *v.t.* **1,** eviscerate. **2,** stab in the abdomen, as in harakiri. —**dis″em·bow′el·ment,** *n.*

dis″en·fran′chise *v.t.* disfranchise. —**dis″-en·fran′chise·ment,** *n.*

dis·fig′ure (dis-fig′yər) *v.t.* mar; deface. —**dis·fig′ure·ment,** *n.*

dis·fran′chise *v.t.* **1,** deprive of rights of citizenship, esp. the right to vote. **2,** deprive of a franchise. —**dis·fran′chise·ment,** *n.*

dis·gorge′ (dis-gôrj′) *v.t.* & *i.* throw out or emit, esp. violently; vomit. —**dis·gorge′-ment,** *n.*

dis·grace′ (dis-grās′) *n.* acute shame; ignominy; loss of reputation. —*v.t.* shame; discredit. —**dis·grace′ful,** *adj.* shameful.

dis·grun′tled (dis-grun′təld) *adj.* not contented; cross. —**dis·grun′tle,** *v.t.* —**dis·grun′tle·ment,** *n.*

dis·guise′ (dis-gīz′) *v.t.* conceal the identity or real nature of; give a misleading appearance to. —*n.* a covering that masks or misleads.

dis·gust′ *n.* extreme repugnance; loathing. —*v.t.* cause to feel loathing; offend. —**dis·gust′ing,** *adj.* loathsome.

dish *n.* **1,** a receptacle or vessel, esp. for food. **2,** a particular prepared food. **3,** (*Slang*) something very welcome, as (*Offensive*) a very attractive woman. **4,** fact or degree of concavity. —*v.t.* **1,** (often with *out* or *up*) serve, as food. **2,** make concave. ❑ *desk*

dis″ha·bille′ (dis″ə-bēl′) *n.* **1,** the state of being carelessly dressed; undress. **2,** a loose morning dress.

dish′cloth″ *n.* a cloth with which dishes are washed or dried.

dis·heart′en (dis-här′tən) *v.t.* cause to lose spirit or courage.

di·shev′el (di-shev′əl) *v.t.* muss, esp. the clothing or hair; tousle. —**di·shev′el·ment,** *n.*

dis·hon′or (dis-on′ər) *v.t.* **1,** bring shame upon. **2,** fail to meet (an obligation). —*n.* disgrace. —**dis·hon′or·a·ble,** *adj.*

dish′pan″ *n.* a pan in which dishes are washed.

dish′rag″ *n.* dishcloth.

---

dish'ware" *n.* china, etc., used in serving food.

dish'wash"er *n.* a machine for washing (and, usu., drying) dishes.

dish'wa"ter *n.* water in which dishes will be or have been washed.

dis·il·lu'sion *v.t.* deprive of illusions; disenchant. —*n.* freedom from illusions. —**dis"il·lu'sion·ment,** *n.*

dis"in·fect' *v.t.* remove infection or a source of infection from. —**dis"in·fect'ant,** *n.* a preparation for disinfecting.

dis·in"for·ma'tion *n.* false information, esp. false military information when deliberately supplied to an enemy. —**dis"in·form',** *v.t.* supply disinformation to.

> **disinformation**
> ↔ The English word is a translation of Russian *dezinformatsiya,* of French origin.

dis"in·her'it *v.t.* cut off (an heir) from an inheritance. —**dis"in·her'i·tance,** *n.*

dis·in'te·grate" *v.i. & t.* separate into parts; go to pieces. —**dis·in"te·gra'tion,** *n.*

dis"in·ter' *v.t.* [-terred', -ter'ring] dig up something buried; unearth. —**dis"in·ter'·ment,** *n.*

dis·in'ter·est·ed (dis-in'tə-res-tid) *adj.* **1,** unbiased; unselfish. **2,** not interested. —**dis·in'ter·est,** *n.*

> **disinterested, uninterested**
> ☛ It is useful to maintain a distinction between *disinterested,* in its sense of impartial, with *uninterested,* which means the opposite of *interested,* i.e., having no interest.

dis·joint'ed *adj.* not coherent; not properly connected.

dis·junct' (dis-junkt') *adj.* disconnected; distinct.

disk *n.* **1,** any flat circular plate or surface. **2,** (*Informal*) a phonograph record. Also, **disc. 3,** (*Computers*) a flexible or rigid magnetized disk used to store data: *floppy disk, hard disk.* —**disk brake,** a friction brake employing the pressure of brake pads against a disk. —**disc jockey,** an announcer (esp. on radio) who plays phonograph records, compact discs, etc. ❑ **desk**

disk·ette' (dis-ket') *n.* floppy disk.

dis·like' *n.* fixed aversion or distaste. —*v.t.* feel aversion toward. —**dis·lik'a·ble,** *adj.*

dis'lo·cate" *v.t.* **1,** displace; put out of joint or position. **2,** interrupt the continuity or order of. —**dis"lo·ca'tion,** *n.*

dis·lodge' *v.t.* remove or drive from a habitation or a position occupied. —**dis·lodg'ment,** *n.*

dis'mal (diz'məl) *adj.* gloomy; dreary; cheerless; doleful. —**dis'mal·ness,** *n.*

> **dismal**
> ↔ From Medieval Latin *dies mali,* evil days.

dis·man'tle (dis-man'təl) *v.t.* **1,** strip of equipment or defenses. **2,** take to pieces. —**dis·man'tle·ment,** *n.*

dis·may' (dis-mā') *v.t.* dishearten. —*n.* loss of courage; fright.

dis·mem'ber (dis-mem'bər) *v.t.* **1,** tear limb from limb. **2,** separate into parts. —**dis·mem'ber·ment,** *n.*

dis·miss' (dis-mis') *v.t.* **1,** send away; order or give permission to depart. **2,** discard; discharge from employment. **3,** put out of mind, as a subject. **4,** (*Law*) of a court, etc., refuse to continue to hear (an action, etc.). —**dis·miss'al,** *n.*

dis·mount' *v.i.* get off, as from a horse or bicycle. —*v.t.* **1,** unhorse. **2,** remove from a frame or setting, as a jewel. **3,** take apart, as a machine.

dis"o·be'di·ence *n.* refusal to obey. —**dis"o·be'di·ent,** *adj.*

dis"o·bey' *v.t. & i.* neglect or refuse to obey.

dis·or'der *n.* **1,** lack of order; confusion. **2,** tumult; disturbance of the peace. **3,** disturbance of the body or mind; a diseased state. —*v.t.* **1,** put in improper arrangement. **2,** unsettle the normal conditions of body or mind.

dis·or'dered *adj.* **1,** confused. **2,** mentally ill.

dis·or'der·ly *adj.* **1,** untidy. **2,** unruly; immoral. —**dis·or'der·li·ness,** *n.* —**disorderly house,** a house of prostitution.

dis·or'gan·ize" *v.t.* destroy the system or arrangement of. —**dis·or"gan·i·za'tion,** *n.* a breaking down or absence of system.

dis·or'i·ent *v.t.* confuse; cause to lose one's bearings. Also, (*Erroneous*) **dis·or'i·en·tate".**

dis·own' *v.t.* refuse to admit ownership or responsibility.

dis·par'age (dis-par'ij) *v.t.* speak slightingly of; discredit. —**dis·par'age·ment,** *n.*

dis'pa·rate (dis'pə-rət) *adj.* essentially different; unequal. —**dis·par'i·ty** (dis-par'ə-tē) *n.*

dis·pas'sion *n.* freedom from passion or emotion; impartiality. —**dis·pas'sion·ate,** *adj.*

dis·patch' (dis-pach') *v.t.* **1,** send off or away. **2,** transact speedily. **3,** kill. —*n.* **1,** a sending off or away. **2,** dismissal. **3,** speed; haste. **4,** a written message. Also, **des·patch′**.

dis·pel′ (dis-pel′) *v.t.* [**-pelled′, -pel′ling**] drive off or away.

dis·pen′sa·ry (dis-pen′sə-rè) *n.* **1,** a place where medicines are given out. **2,** a public medical clinic.

dis″pen·sa′tion (dis″pən-sā′shən) *n.* **1,** act of dispensing. **2,** that which is dispensed by God to man. **3,** a relaxation of a law, esp. ecclesiastical.

dis·pen′sa·to·ry (dis-pen′sə-tôr-è) *adj.* pert. to the dispensing of medicines. —*n.* **1,** a pharmacist's manual. **2,** a dispensary.

dis·pense′ (dis-pens′) *v.t.* **1,** deal out; distribute. **2,** administer, as laws. **3,** excuse; exempt. —*v.i.* **1,** (with *with*) permit the omission of; do without. **2,** compound (drugs, prescriptions). —**dis·pen′sa·ble,** *adj.*

dis·perse′ (dis-pērs′) *v.t.* **1,** scatter; diffuse. **2,** dissipate; cause to vanish. —*v.i.* separate. —**dis·per′sal** (-səl), **dis·per′sion** (-zhən) *n.*

dis·place′ *v.t.* **1,** put out of the usual or proper place; remove from office. **2,** replace. —**displaced homemaker,** a woman widowed, divorced, or separated after years of being a homemaker. —**displaced person,** one driven from his home by war.

dis·place′ment *n.* **1,** act of displacing. **2,** the weight or volume of water displaced by a submerged body. **3,** the volume swept out by a piston.

dis·play′ (dis-plā′) *v.t. & i.* show; exhibit; make manifest. —*n.* **1,** an exhibition. **2,** a device used to present the output of a computer, etc. in visual form. —*adj.* **1,** of type, large and designed to attract notice. **2,** used to display merchandise.

dis·please′ *v.t. & i.* offend; be disagreeable (to). —**dis·pleas′ure,** *n.* vexation.

dis·port′ (dis-pôrt′) *v.i.* make merry; play.

dis·pose′ (dis-pōz′) *v.t.* **1,** place in a particular order; arrange. **2,** regulate; adjust. **3,** incline the mind or heart of. —*v.i.* **1,** (with *of*) part with. **2,** control. —**dis·pos′a·ble,** *adj.* —**dis·pos′al,** *n.*

dis″po·si′tion (dis″pə-zish′ən) *n.* **1,** an arrangement of parts. **2,** definite settlement; ultimate destination. **3,** innate temper; natural tendency of the mind.

dis″pos·sess′ (dis″pə-zes′) *v.t.* deprive of actual occupancy; dislodge. —**dis″pos·ses′sion,** *n.*

dis·proof′ *n.* proof to the contrary; refutation.

dis·prove′ *v.t.* prove to be false or erroneous.

dis″pu·ta′tion (dis″pū-tā′shən) *n.* a controversy; debate. —**dis″pu·ta′tious,** *adj.*

dis·pute′ (dis-pūt′) *v.i.* argue; debate; wrangle. —*v.t.* argue about or against. —*n.* a controversy; a quarrel. —**dis·put′a·ble,** *adj.* —**dis·put′ant,** *n.*

dis·qual′i·fy″ *v.t.* make unfit or ineligible. —**dis·qual″i·fi·ca′tion,** *n.*

dis·qui′et (dis-kwī′ət) *v.t.* deprive of peace; make uneasy or restless. —*n.* an uneasy feeling or state; unrest. —**dis·qui′e·tude** (-ə-tood) *n.*

dis″qui·si′tion (dis″kwi-zish′ən) *n.* a dissertation; treatise.

dis″re·gard′ *v.t.* ignore. —*n.* failure to observe; neglect. —**dis″re·gard′ful,** *adj.*

dis″re·pair′ *n.* the state of being in bad condition.

dis″re·pute′ *n.* loss or want of good reputation. —**dis·rep′u·ta·ble** *adj.* of low character.

dis·rupt′ *v.t. & i.* break asunder; separate forcibly. —**dis·rup′tion,** *n.* —**dis·rup′tive,** *adj.*

diss (dis) *v.* (*Slang*) to show disrespect for. Also, **dis.**

dis·sat′is·fy″ *v.t.* fail to satisfy or please; render discontented. —**dis·sat″is·fac′tion,** *n.*

dis·sect′ (di-sekt′) *v.t.* **1,** cut in pieces; separate the parts of. **2,** examine point by point; analyze. —**dis·sec′tion,** *n.*

dis·sem′ble (di-sem′bəl) *v.t. & i.* **1,** give a false impression about; conceal one's real motives. **2,** pretend to disregard or ignore. —**dis·sem′blance** (-bləns) *n.*

---

dissemble, disassemble
☛ Do not confuse these two words, similar in sound but very different in meaning. *Dissemble* means to lie; *disassemble* means to take apart.

---

dis·sem′i·nate″ (di-sem′ə-nāt) *v.t.* scatter abroad; sow. —**dis·sem″i·na′tion,** *n.*

dis·sen′sion (di-sen′shən) *n.* violent disagreement; strife; discord.

dis·sent′ (di-sent′) *v.i.* feel or express a negative opinion. —*n.* difference of opinion. —**dis·sent′er,** *n.* one who disagrees, esp. with the doctrines of the Church of England.

dis·sen′tient (di-sen′shənt) *adj.* dissenting. —*n.* one who dissents. —**dis·sen′tious** (-shəs) *adj.*

dis″ser·ta′tion (dis″ər-tā′shən) *n.* a formal discourse or essay.

dis·sev′er (di-sev′ər) *v.t.* separate; divide. **—dis·sev′er·ance,** *n.*

dis′si·dence (dis′ə-dəns) *n.* difference in opinion; disagreement. **—dis′si·dent,** *adj. & n.*

dis·sim′u·late″ (di-sim′yə-lāt″) *v.t. & i.* disguise; make pretense; feign. **—dis·sim″·u·la′tion,** *n.*

dis′si·pate″ (dis′i-pāt″) *v.t.* **1,** scatter; dispel. **2,** expend wastefully. **—v.i. 1,** come to an end or vanish. **2,** act dissolutely. **—dis″si·pa′tion,** *n.*

dis′si·pat″ed (-id) *adj.* **1,** dissolute. **2,** dispersed.

dis·so′ci·ate″ (di-sō′shė-āt″) *v.t.* sever the connection of; separate. **—dis·so″ci·a′tion,** *n.*

dis′so·lute (dis′ə-loot) *adj.* loose in behavior and morals; wanton. **—dis′so·lute·ness,** *n.*

dis″so·lu′tion (dis″ə-loo′shən) *n.* act of dissolving or being dissolved.

dis·solve′ (di-zolv′) *v.t.* **1,** liquefy by means of heat or absorption. **2,** disunite; separate into parts; break up. **3,** solve; explain, as a mystery. **—v.i. 1,** become fluid. **2,** come to an end; crumble or waste away. **3,** disappear gradually; fade from sight. **—dis·sol′u·ble** (di-sol′yə-bəl) *adj.*

dis′so·nance (dis′ə-nəns) *n.* **1,** an inharmonious combination of sounds. **2,** disagreement; discord. **—dis′so·nant,** *adj.*

dis·suade′ (di-swād′) *v.t.* change from a purpose by advice, persuasion, or argument. **—dis·sua′sion** (-zhən) *n.*

dis′taff (dis′táf) *n.* **1,** a cleft stick for holding wool, flax, etc. in spinning. **2,** (*Hist.*) woman, her activities or work. **—distaff side,** the female line of descent in a family.

dis′tance (dis′təns) *n.* **1,** measure of interval in space or time. **2,** remoteness. **—v.t.** get far ahead of; surpass; outstrip.

dis′tant (dis′tənt) *adj.* **1,** situated at a different point in space or time. **2,** remote; far off. **3,** haughty; cool; reserved.

dis·taste′ (dis-tāst′) *n.* aversion; dislike. **—dis·taste′ful,** *adj.* displeasing; offensive.

dis·tem′per (dis-tem′pər) *n.* **1,** a serious disease of animals, esp. dogs. **2,** bad humor. **3,** mural paint or painting using eggs as sizing.

dis·tend′ *v.t.* dilate; expand. **—v.i.** swell. **—dis·ten′si·ble** (-ten′sə-bəl) *adj.* **—dis·ten′tion,** *n.*

dis′tich (dis′tik) *n.* (*Poetry*) a couplet.

dis·till′ (dis-til′) *v.i.* fall in drops. **—v.t. 1,** let fall in drops. **2,** purify. **3,** extract by process of distillation. **—dis′til·late,** *n.*

dis″til·la′tion (dis″tə-lā′shən) *n.* **1,** the vaporization and subsequent condensation of a liquid. **2,** a distilled liquid.

dis·till′er·y (dis-til′ə-rė) *n.* a place where alcoholic liquors are produced by distillation.

dis·tinct′ (dis-tinkt′) *adj.* **1,** separate; different. **2,** well-defined; not blurred; very plain; unmistakable; clear. **—dis·tinct′·ness,** *n.*

> **distinct, distinctive**
> ☞ *Distinct* means separate, different. *Distinctive* is more precise, emphasizing the special characteristics of the thing in question.

dis·tinc′tion (dis-tink′shən) *n.* **1,** act of distinguishing. **2,** a distinguishing quality or characteristic; difference in general. **3,** an honor; eminence; superiority.

dis·tinc′tive (dis-tink′tiv) *adj.* **1,** different; marking a difference. **2,** characteristic. **—dis·tinc′tive·ness,** *n.* ❏ *distinct*

dis·tin′guish (dis-ting′gwish) *v.t.* **1,** mark, recognize, or see as distinct or different. **2,** separate by classification. **3,** discern critically; judge. **4,** treat with honor. **—v.i.** make a distinction (between). **—dis·tin′guish·a·ble,** *adj.* capable of being perceived and recognized. **—dis·tin′guished,** *adj.* eminent; celebrated.

dis·tort′ (dis-tôrt′) *v.t.* twist out of shape; pervert; misrepresent. **—dis·tor′tion,** *n.*

dis·tract′ (dis-trakt′) *v.t.* **1,** divert the attention of. **2,** confuse; bewilder. **3,** derange.

dis·tract′ed (-id) *adj.* **1,** diverted. **2,** bewildered.

dis·trac′tion (dis-trak′shən) *n.* **1,** act of distracting or being distracted. **2,** what distracts; a diversion. **3,** frenzy; (*Informal*) madness.

dis·traint′ (dis-trānt′) *n.* (*Law*) a seizing of property, as for debt. **—dis·train′,** *v.t.*

dis·trait′ (dis-trāt′) *adj.* abstracted; absent-minded; inattentive.

dis·traught′ (dis-trât′) *adj.* bewildered; perplexed; deranged.

dis·tress′ (dis-tres′) *n.* **1,** pain or suffering of body or mind. **2,** calamity; adversity. **3,** the state of needing help; danger. **—v.t.** make miserable. **—dis·tress′ful,** *adj.* distressing.

dis·trib′ute (dis-trib′ūt) *v.t.* **1,** parcel out; apportion. **2,** classify. **3,** spread out. **—dis″tri·bu′tion** (dis″tri-bū′shən) *n.*

dis·trib′u·tor (dis-trib′yə-tər) *n.* **1,** one who distributes; esp., a wholesale dealer.

2, a device for distributing, esp. electricity to the spark plugs of an engine.

dis'trict (dis'trikt) *n.* a section of a city or state; a region in general. —**district attorney,** the public prosecutor for a city or county.

dis·turb' (dis-tẽrb') *v.t.* **1,** agitate; disquiet; molest. **2,** interfere with; interrupt. —**dis·turbed',** *adj.* mentally unsound; emotionally ill.

dis·turb'ance (-əns) *n.* **1,** something that disturbs; a feeling of disquiet; a disease. **2,** an illegally noisy commotion.

ditch (dich) *n.* a trench or channel dug in the earth. —*v.t.* **1,** drain by or surround with a ditch. **2,** throw or run into a ditch. **3,** (*Slang*) cast off; escape from. ❑ *dike*

dith'er (di*th*'ər) *n.* **1,** a nervous, excited state. **2,** commotion. —*v.t.* print or display an image using dithering. —**dith'er·ing,** *n.* a technique for approximating shades of gray by combining white and black dots, or hues by combining dots of the primary colors.

dith'y·ramb" (dith'ə-ram") *n.* a poem or discourse in impassioned mood.

dit'sy (dit'sė) *adj.* (*Informal*) frivolous; eccentric. —**ditz,** *n.* (*Slang*).

dit'to (dit'ō) *n.* [*pl.* **-tos**] **1,** the same thing; expressed by two small marks ("). **2,** (*cap., T.N.*) a duplicating process using ink transfer. —*v.t.* **1,** copy; repeat; echo. **2,** copy by the Ditto process.

> **ditto**
> ↔ From Latin *dictus*, said, through Italian dialectal *detto*.

dit'ty (dit'ė) *n.* a little song.

di"u·ret'ic (dī"yû-ret'ik) *adj.* promoting urination. —**di"u·re'sis** (-rē'sis) *n.*

di·ur'nal (dī-ẽr'nəl) *adj.* pert. to day; daily.

di'va (dē'vä) *n.* a prima donna.

div'a·gate" (div'ə-gāt") *v.i.* stray; digress. —**div"a·ga'tion,** *n.* digression.

di·van' *n.* **1,** a kind of sofa. **2,** a certain area of theater seating. **3,** a council of state in Turkey.

> **divan**
> ↔ From Persian *devan*, small book, which gradually acquired the sense of office, and hence, furniture within an office.

dive (dīv) *v.i.* [*p.t.* **dived** (dīvd) *or* **dove** (dōv)] **1,** plunge headfirst downward or forward, esp. into water. **2,** submerge. **3,** engage deeply in anything. —*n.* **1,** a headfirst plunge, esp. into water. **2,** (*Slang*) a

seamy place. **3,** (*Slang*) intentional loss of an athletic contest. —**dive bomber,** a bombing plane that aims its bombs by diving toward its target. —**div'er,** *n.* —**diving reflex,** a natural reflex that slows down the heartbeat and diverts blood to the brain to conserve oxygen in an emergency.

di·verge' (di-vẽrj') *v.i.* **1,** branch off in different directions. **2,** take different courses or ways (of thought; of life). **3,** differ from a typical form. —**di·ver'gence, di·ver'gen·cy,** *n.* —**di·ver'gent,** *adj.*

di·verse' (di-vẽrs') *adj.* essentially different; varied. Also, **di'vers** (dī'vərz). —**di·verse'ness,** *n.*

di·ver'si·fy" (di-vẽr'si-fī") *v.t.* give variety to. —**di·ver"si·fi·ca'tion** (-fi-kā'shən) *n.*

di·ver'sion (di-vẽr'zhən) *n.* **1,** act of diverting. **2,** a turning aside; a detour. **3,** recreation; amusement; a pastime. —**di·ver'sion·ar·y,** *adj.*

di·ver'si·ty (di-vẽr'sə-tė) *n.* **1,** essential difference. **2,** variety.

di·vert' (di-vẽrt') *v.t.* **1,** turn aside or away from a course or an aim. **2,** amuse; entertain.

di·vest' *v.t.* **1,** strip of clothes, arms, or equipment; despoil. **2,** deprive of rights, privileges, or authority. —**di·ves'ti·ture** (-ti-chər), **di·vest'ment,** *n.*

di·vide' (di-vīd') *v.t.* **1,** separate into parts or pieces. **2,** disjoin; sever the union of. **3,** make or keep distinct. **4,** distribute; share. **5,** (*Math.*) perform the process of division. —*v.i.* go apart. —*n.* a watershed. —**di·vid'ers,** *n.* compasses.

div'i·dend" (div'ə-dend") *n.* **1,** a sum to be divided and distributed, as to shareholders; the share of each. **2,** (*Math.*) a number or quantity to be divided by another.

div"i·na'tion (div'ə-nā'shən) *n.* the foretelling of the future or discovering of that which is hidden.

di·vine' (di-vīn') *adj.* **1,** of the nature of, proceeding from, or pert. to God; sacred. **2,** heavenly; excellent. —*n.* a clergyman. —*v.t.* learn by divination. —*v.i.* surmise. —**divine right,** the doctrine that kings derive the right to rule directly from God.

di·vin'er (di-vī'nər) *n.* **1,** one who divines. **2,** a rod supposed to locate subterranean water: *divining rod.*

di·vin'i·ty (di-vin'ə-tė) *n.* **1,** the character of being godly or divine. **2,** (*cap.*) God. **3,** a confection.

di·vis'i·ble (di-viz'ə-bəl) *adj.* capable of being divided, esp. (*Math.*) without a remainder. —**di·vis"i·bil'i·ty,** *n.*

di·vi'sion (di-vizh'ən) *n.* **1,** separation. **2,**

a partition. **3,** a definite part; a self-sufficient, large unit of an army. **4,** disunion; discord. **5,** (*Math.*) the process of finding how many times a number (divisor) or quantity is contained in another (dividend).

di·vi'sion·al (-əl) *adj.* pert. to a division. —*n.* (*pl.*) examinations of candidates for academic degrees.

di·vi'sive (di-vī'siv) *adj.* tending to create dissension.

di·vi'sor (di-vī'zər) *n.* (*Math.*) a number by which another is divided.

di·vorce' (di-vôrs') *n.* **1,** a legal dissolution of the marriage bond. **2,** complete separation. —*v.t.* obtain a divorce (from). —**di·vor"cé'** *n.masc.*, **di·vor·cée,** *n.fem.* (-sā') a divorced person. —**di·vorce'-ment,** *n.*

div'ot (div'ət) *n.* a piece of turf cut out by a golfer's club.

di·vulge' (di-vulj') *v.t.* tell or make known; reveal. —**di·vul'gence,** *n.*

> **divulge**
> ↔ From Latin *divulgare*, literally, make known to the common people, i.e., publish.

div'vy (div'ė) *v.t.* (*Slang*) divide into portions.

Dix'ie (dik'sė) *n.* the southern states of the U.S.

Dix'ie·crat" (-krat") *n.* a member of a faction of the southern wing of the Democratic Party.

Dix'ie·land" *n.* **1,** Dixie. **2,** a style of jazz music.

> **Dixieland**
> ↔ The popular name for the southern U.S. states, where this jazz style originated—*Dixie* or *Dixieland*—arose in the mid-19th c., perhaps from the *Mason-Dixon line* (see box under that entry).

diz'zy (diz'ė) *adj.* **1,** having a whirling sensation in the head; giddy. **2,** causing dizziness. **3,** (*Slang*) silly; foolish. —**diz'-zi·ness,** *n.*

djel·la'bah (jə-lä'bə) *n.* a loose-fitting Arab robe worn by men.

djinn (jin) *n.* a genie; spirit.

> **djinn**
> ↔ Although considered singular in English, in Arabic this word is the plural of *djinni*, demon; unlike English words, this word becomes plural by dropping a letter.

DNA (dē'en'ā') deoxyribonucleic acid, an essential constituent of chromosomes.

do (doo) *v.i.* [**did, done** (dun), **do'ing**] **1,** perform; carry out. **2,** perform the action or work required by the nature of the case, as *do one's hair.* **3,** cause; render. **4,** complete; finish. **5,** put forth; exert. **6,** (*Slang*) cheat; swindle. —*v.i.* **1,** work. **2,** act or behave. **3,** fare; prosper. **4,** serve the purpose. —*aux. v.* forming an emphatic pres. or past indicative with an infinitive, as *I did go.* —*n.* (*Informal*) **1,** bustle; ado. **2,** a party. **3,** (dō) (*Music*) the first tone of a scale. —**do'a·ble,** *adj.* —**do away with,** destroy. —**do for,** (*Slang*) **1,** destroy; kill. **2,** be sufficient for. **3,** take care of. —**do in, 1,** kill. **2,** swindle. —**do up, 1,** wrap. **2,** dress. —**make do,** use what is available.

> **do**
> ↔ The verb, and the noun meaning action, is from Old English *don*. The sense of a musical tone is from Italian *do*, an inversion of *ut*, another word for the first note of a scale (see *gamut*).

dob'bin (dob'in) *n.* a common name for a workhorse.

Do'ber·man pin'scher (dō'bər-mən pin'shər) a breed of slender, smooth-coated dog.

> **Doberman pinscher**
> ↔ German for Dobermann terrier, named for the 19th-c. German breeder Ludwig *Dobermann.*

doc (dok) *n.* (*Informal*) doctor.

do'cent (dō'sənt) *adj.* teaching. —*n.* instructor; lecturer.

doc'ile (dos'əl) *adj.* amenable; easily managed. —**do·cil'i·ty** (do-sil'ə-tė) *n.*

dock (dok) *n.* **1,** an enclosed water space in which a ship floats while being loaded or unloaded; a slip or pier; a wharf. **2,** the place where a prisoner stands in court. **3,** a coarse herb or weed. **4,** the stump of an animal's tail. —*v.t.* **1,** cut off; clip, as a dog's tail. **2,** deduct from, as wages. **3,** bring or draw (a vessel) into a dock. —*v.i.* **1,** arrive at a wharf or dock. **2,** join in space (as two spacecraft).

dock'age (-ij) *n.* **1,** act of docking. **2,** provision for docking a vessel; fee for use of a dock.

dock'et (dok'it) *n.* **1,** (*Law*) a list of cases for trial; any such agenda. **2,** (*Law*) a register of judgments. **3,** a package label. —*v.t.* **1,** summarize. **2,** enter in a court register. **3,** label; tag.

dock′yard″ *n.* a place where ships are built or repaired.

doc′tor (dok′tər) *n.* **1,** a physician. **2,** a person holding the highest degree a university can confer in his or her special field. —*v.t.* (*Informal*) **1,** treat medicinally. **2,** repair; patch up. **3,** adulterate; tamper with. —**doc′tor·ate** (-ət) *n.* the highest university degree.

> **doctor, physician**
> ☛ A *doctor* is one who received a doctoral degree from a university, whether in medicine, law, or another field. A *physician* is a doctor of medicine who is licensed by the state. ↔ *Doctor* comes from Latin *docere,* teach; it orig. meant teacher—the modern sense of medical practitioner arose in the 16th c.

doc″tri·naire′ (dok″trə-nâr′) *n.* one who acts by doctrine or theory without sufficient regard for practical considerations. —*adj.* obstinately impractical; theoretical.

doc′trine (dok′trin) *n.* a principle or body of principles; a tenet; a dogma. —**doc′tri·nal,** *adj.*

doc′u·dra″ma (dok′yə-drä″mə) *n.* a fictional drama based on real events.

doc′u·ment (dok′yə-mənt) *n.* a written or printed paper containing a record or statement. —*v.t.* (-ment″) cite or provide documents for authority. —**doc″u·men′tal,** *adj.* —**doc″u·men·ta′tion,** *n.*

doc″u·men·ta·ry (dok″yə-men′tə-rė) *adj.* **1,** of or pert. to documents. **2,** factual and educational, as a film. —*n.* an educational motion picture consisting of factual sequences.

dod′der (dod′ər) *v.i.* tremble; shake; totter.

do·dec·a- (dō-dek-ə) *pref.* twelve.

dodge (doj) *v.i.* & *t.* suddenly jump or step aside; evade. —*n.* an act of evasion; a trick, stratagem, or clever device.

do′do (dō′dō) *n.* **1,** an extinct flightless bird. **2,** (*Slang*) a stodgy, unimaginative person.

> **dodo**
> ↔ From Portuguese *doudo,* simpleton; the Portuguese explorers who discovered the bird on the island of Mauritius found it to be a clumsy bird and named it accordingly.

doe (dō) *n.* the female of the deer, most antelopes, the hare, and the rabbit.

do′er (doo′ər) *n.* **1,** one who does (something). **2,** one who accomplishes a great deal.

does (duz) *v.* 3rd pers. sing., pres. ind., of *do.*

doe′skin″ *n.* **1,** a fine leather. **2,** a finely twilled woolen cloth.

doff (dof) *v.t.* take off (any article of dress).

> **doff**
> ↔ A contraction of *do off.* In Middle English it was one of several similar forms of which only a few survive. Another common example is *don,* from *do on.*

dog (dâg; dog) *n.* **1,** a domesticated quadruped descended from different wild species of the genus *Canis,* as the wolf, fox, or jackal. **2,** a mechanical device for holding. **3,** (*Slang*) a fellow. **4,** (*Slang*) a mean, worthless fellow. —*v.t.* [dogged, dog′ging] hound; keep at the heels of; worry. —**dog days,** the hottest period of summer. —**dog it,** give up, through fear. —**dog tag,** a dog's license tag; (*Slang*) a soldier's identification tag. —**go to the dogs,** (*Informal*) go to ruin. —**put on the dog,** (*Informal*) behave or dress pretentiously.

dog′bane″ *n.* an herb with an intensely bitter root.

dog′cart″ *n.* **1,** a light horse-drawn vehicle. **2,** a cart drawn by dogs.

doge (dōj) *n.* title of the former rulers of Venice and Genoa.

dog′ear″ *n.* **1,** a dog's ear. **2,** a frayed corner. —*v.t.* turn down the corner of a page. —*v.i.* fray.

dog′fight″ *n.* combat between warplanes at close quarters.

dog′fish″ *n.* any of a variety of small sharks.

dog′ged (dog′id) *adj.* obstinate; persistent. —**dog′ged·ness,** *n.*

dog′ger·el (dâg′ər-əl) *n.* **1,** light, comic verse. **2,** poor verse.

dog′gy (dâg′ė) *n.* (*Informal*) a dog. —*adj.* **1,** like a dog. **2,** pretentious. —**doggy bag,** a bag to bring restaurant leftovers home.

dog′house″ *n.* a hut for a dog. —**in the doghouse,** (*Slang*) in disfavor.

do′gie (dō′gė) *n.* a stray calf.

dog′ma (dâg′mə) *n.* **1,** a rigidly held principle or doctrine, esp. in a religion; precept. **2,** a body of precepts. —**dog′-ma·tism,** *n.*

dog·mat′ic (dâg-mat′ik) *adj.* **1,** pert. to dogma. **2,** positive; adhering rigidly to a tenet. —**dog·mat′i·cal·ly,** *adv.*

---

tub, cūte, pûll; labəl; oil, owl, go, chip, she, thin, *th*en, sing, ink; *see p. 6*

dog-'tired' *adj.* extremely tired.

dog'tooth" *n.* [*pl.* **-teeth"**] **1,** eyetooth. **2,** an ornamental molding. —**dogtooth violet,** an early spring wildflower.

dog'trot" *n.* a slow running gait.

dog'wood" *n.* a shrub or tree bearing clusters of flowers.

doi'ly (doi'lè) *n.* a small ornamental mat for use on a table.

> **doily**
> ↔ *Doily* was originally a type of light fabric sold (and perhaps created) by a 17th-c. English draper named *Doily*. His name was also applied to a type of fringed napkin.

do-"it-your-self' *adj.* designed to be used or done by anyone. —**do-"it-your-self'er,** *n.*

Dol'by (dōl'bè) *n.* (*T.N.*) a device for reducing noise on recordings and in broadcasting. —**Dol'by-ize"** (-īz") *v.t.*

dol'ce (dōl'chä) (*It., Music*) *adj. & adv.* sweet and soft.

dol'drums (dōl'drəmz) *n. pl.* **1,** low spirits; the dumps. **2,** zones of calm air in the ocean near the Equator.

dole (dōl) *n.* **1,** alms. **2,** (*Brit.*) money granted to the unemployed. —*v.t.* hand out sparingly.

dole'ful (dōl'fəl) *adj.* showing sorrow; sad. —**dole'ful·ness,** *n.*

doll (dol) *n.* **1,** a toy, often a baby, for children; a puppet. **2,** (*Offensive*) a girl. —*v.i. & t.* (with *up*) (*Informal*) put on one's best clothes.

> **doll**
> ↔ *Doll* is one of a number of nicknames for Dorothy.

dol'lar (dol'ər) *n.* **1,** the basis of decimal coinage. **2,** a coin or treasury certificate of one dollar value, in the U.S. worth 100 cents. —**dollar diplomacy,** use (by the U.S.) of money to implement foreign policy.

> **dollar**
> ↔ From German *Joachimstaler*, a 16th-c. coin made from silver mined in Sankt *Joachimsthal*, Bohemia.

dol'lop (dol'əp) *n.* (*Informal*) a lump; mass.

dol'ly (dol'è) *n.* **1,** diminutive of *doll.* **2,** any of several mechanical devices, esp. a low platform on rollers for moving heavy loads.

dol'men (dol'mən) *n.* (*Archaeol.*) one of a number of ancient structures, believed to be tombs, formed by a horizontal slab

of rock set atop two or more upright stones.

dol'o·mite" (dōl'ə-mīt") *n.* a rock composed largely of calcium magnesium carbonate.

> **dolomite**
> ↔ Named from 18th-c. French mineralogist D. de *Dolomieu.*

do'lor (dō'lər) *n.* sorrow.

dol'or·ous (dol'ər-əs) *adj.* sad; mournful. —**dol'or·ous·ness,** *n.*

dol'phin (dol'fin) *n.* **1,** a sea mammal of the whale family. **2,** [*also,* **dol'phin·fish"**] either of two large game fishes. **3,** (*Naut.*) a cluster of piles used for mooring or as a fender. **4,** (*Astron.*) the constellation Delphinus. ❑ *dauphin*

dolt (dōlt) *n.* a dull, stupid person.

-dom (dəm) *suf.* the estate, condition or rank of, as *kingdom.*

do·main' (dō-mān') *n.* **1,** territory owned or governed. **2,** sphere of action or knowledge.

dome (dōm) *n.* **1,** a hemispherical roof; a large cupola. **2,** (*Slang*) head.

do·mes'tic (də-mes'tik) *adj.* **1,** relating to the household. **2,** pert. to one's own country; not foreign. **3,** tame, as an animal. —*n.* a household servant. —**do·mes'-ti·cal·ly,** *adv.* —**domestic partner,** spouse or lover, esp. in a homosexual relationship. —**domestic science,** the art or study of household management; home economics.

do·mes'ti·cate" (də-mes'ti-kāt") *v.t.* convert to home life; tame. —**do·mes"ti·ca'-tion,** *n.*

do"mes·tic'i·ty (dō"mes-tis'ə-tè) *n.* home life.

dom'i·cile (dom'ə-səl) *n.* a place of residence.

dom'i·nant (dom'ə-nənt) *adj.* **1,** exercising rule or authority. **2,** most conspicuous; overshadowing. —**dom'i·nance,** *n.*

dom'i·nate" (dom'ə-nāt") *v.t. & i.* govern; control; hold control; be most conspicuous. —**dom"i·na'tion,** *n.* ❑ *domineering*

dom"i·neer' (dom"ə-nir') *v.i. & t.* rule in an overbearing or arrogant manner; swagger; tyrannize. —**dom"i·neer'ing,** *adj.* overbearing.

> **domineering, dominating**
> ☛ Though these two words are similar in meaning, use *domineering* only if excess of arrogance is intended; *dominating* does not have this sense.
> ↔ Both words derive from Latin *dominari*, to control.

Do·min′i·can (də-min′ə-kən) *n. & adj.*
one of a Rom. Cath. religious order
founded by St. Dominic in the early
13th c.

dom′i·nie (dom′ə-nē) *n.* a clergyman;
priest.

do·min′ion (də-min′yən) *n.* **1,** supreme
authority; control. **2,** a territory under a
sovereign, now esp. one having strong
powers of self-government. **—Dominion
Day,** a legal holiday in Canada, July 1.

dom′i·no″ (dom′ə-nō″) *n.* **1,** a small tile
of wood or bone, marked with dots; (*pl.*)
a game played with such tiles. **2,** a masquerade costume, esp. a cloak; a half-
mask. **—domino theory,** the theory that if
one country is taken over by a colonizing
regime, esp. Communist, the neighboring
countries will soon be overrun in turn.

don *v.t.* **[donned, don′ning]** put on. ❏
doff

don *n.* **1,** (*cap.*) a Spanish noble; his title.
2, a fellow or tutor in an English university. **3,** the head of a Mafia family.

do·na′tion (dō-nā′shən) *n.* a gift; contribution. **—do′nate,** (dō′nāt) *v.t. & i.*

done (dun) *v.* p.p. of *do.* **—adj. 1,** executed; completed. **2,** worn out; used up. **3,**
cooked: *well done.* **4,** proper.

don′jon (dun′jən) *n.* the inner tower,
keep, or stronghold of a castle; dungeon.

don′key (dong′kè) *n.* **1,** an ass. **2,** a stupid or obstinate person.

don′ny·brook″ (don′ē-brûk″) *n.* free-
for-all; public altercation.

> **donnybrook**
> ↔ Named for the *Donnybrook* Fair,
> held annually in the early 19th c. in
> Ireland and famous for riotous
> behavior.

do′nor (dō′nər) *n.* one who gives.

do′nut (dō′nut) *n.* doughnut.

doo′dad *n.* (*Informal*) **1,** a trinket; gewgaw. **2,** a title for something whose name
is unknown or forgotten.

doo′dle (doo′dəl) *v.i.* **1,** (*Slang*) draw or
scribble aimlessly. **2,** play a bagpipe.

doo′dle·bug″ (doo′dəl-bug″) *n.* **1,** an insect larva. **2,** a contrivance for locating
water, minerals, etc., under the earth. **3,**
(*Informal*) a Geiger counter. **4,** (*Informal*)
a small vehicle.

doo′dle·sack″ *n.* bagpipe.

doo′hick″ey (doo′hik″ē) *n.* gadget;
doodad.

doom *n.* **1,** destiny, esp. when unhappy
or destructive; fate. **2,** a judgment; a sen-

tence. **3,** the Last Judgment: *doomsday.*
—v.t. condemn to ruin.

door (dôr) *n.* **1,** a barrier that swings on
hinges or slides for opening or closing a
passageway. **2,** any means of access, entrance, or exit.

door′keep″er *n.* **1,** one who guards an
entrance. **2,** [also, **door′man** (*pl.* **-men**)]
an attendant at the door of a hotel, club,
etc.

door′knob″ *n.* **1,** the handle of a door.
2, (*Slang*) a stupid person.

door′step″ *n.* threshold.

door′way″ *n.* the opening in which a
door is mounted.

doo′wop″ *n.* a style of jazz singing.

doo′zie (doo′zē) *n.* (*Informal*) something extraordinary. Also, **doo′zer.**

do′pa·mine″ (dō′pə-mēn″) *n.* a substance in the central nervous system, a deficiency of which is thought to cause
Parkinson's disease. Also, **L-dopa.**

dope (dōp) *n.* **1,** varnish, rubber cement,
etc., used in waterproofing, etc. **2,** (*Informal*) a narcotic drug; such drugs collectively. **3,** information; a private hint. **4,**
(*Slang*) a stupid person. **—v.t. 1,** (*Informal*) drug. **2,** (*Slang*) (with *out*) solve, as
a mystery. **—dop′ey,** *adj.*

Dopp′ler effect *or* **shift** (däp′lər) an
apparent change in the frequency of
sound, light, or radio waves reaching an
observer when the wave source and the
observer are in motion relative to one another, named for its discoverer, 19th-c.
Austrian physicist C. J. Doppler.

dork (dôrk) *n.* (*Slang*) a stupid or ineffectual person; nerd.

dorm (dôrm) *n.* (*Informal*) dormitory.

dor′mant (dôr′mənt) *adj.* in a state of
rest or inactivity. **—dor′man·cy,** *n.*

dor′mer (dôr′mər) *n.* a window in a projection under a gable.

dor′mi·to·ry (dôr′mə-tôr-ē) *n.* a building
or large room in which many persons
sleep. Also, (*Informal*) **dorm.**

dor′mouse″ (dôr′mows″) *n.* [*pl.* **-mice″**
(-mīs″)] a squirrel-like hibernating rodent.

dor′sal (dôr′səl) *adj.* pert. to, on, or situated near the back.

do′ry (dôr′ē) *n.* **1,** a small, flat-bottomed
boat. **2,** an edible sea fish. Also, **John
Dory.**

DOS (dâs) *n.* any of several microcom-
puter operating systems: *d(isk) o(p-
erating) s(ystem).*

dose (dōs) *n.* **1,** a prescribed quantity of
medicine to be taken at one time. **2,** anything disagreeable to take. **3,** (*Slang*) an

attack of venereal disease. —*v.t.* give a dose to. —**dos′age,** *n.*

do·sim′e·ter (dō-sim′ə-tər) *n.* a device for measuring doses, as of X rays.

doss (dôs) *n.* (*Brit.*) a place to sleep.

dos′si·er″ (dos′ė-ā″) *n.* a complete file of information on a person or affair.

dot *n.* **1,** a minute, round spot; a speck. **2,** a dowry. —*v.t. & i.* [**dot′ted, -ting**] mark with a dot or dots. —**on the dot,** exactly on time. —**dot matrix,** a system for forming characters and graphics in computer displays, printers, etc., using a matrix of small dots.

dot′age (dō′tij) *n.* **1,** senility. **2,** excessive fondness.

do′tard (dō′tərd) *n.* an old, foolish man.

dote (dōt) *v.i.* **1,** be weak-minded from age. **2,** (with *on*) lavish extravagant fondness.

dot′ty (dot′ė) *adj.* (*Informal*) crazy.

Dou′ay Bi′ble (doo′ā) an English translation of the Bible prepared by the Roman Catholic Church.

dou′ble (dub′əl) *adj.* **1,** being a pair; duplicated. **2,** twofold; twice as much, as large, as thick, etc. **3,** folded once. —*n.* **1,** a twofold quantity or size. **2,** a duplicate; a counterpart. **3,** a fold. **4,** an understudy. **5,** esp. in bridge, an increase in scoring values. **6,** (*Baseball*) a two-base hit. **7,** (*pl.*) esp. in tennis, a game with two on a side. —*v.t.* **1,** make double. **2,** contain twice as much or as many. **3,** fold once, as a blanket. **4,** repeat; duplicate. —*v.i.* **1,** increase or grow to twofold. **2,** turn in the opposite direction. —**doub′ly,** *adv.* —**double boiler,** a vessel for slow cooking over hot water or steam. —**double date,** (*Informal*) two unmarried couples joining in some social occasion. —**double dealing,** treachery. —**double jeopardy,** subjection to trial and possible punishment twice for the same offense. —**double meaning,** intentional ambiguity. —**double negative,** a grammatical error in which two negative words are used in the same clause to express a single negation. —**double standard,** a dual legal or moral code, as one stricter for women than for men. —**double take,** (*Slang*) sudden, delayed understanding. —**on the double,** at double rate; quickly.

dou′ble bass (bās) (*Music*) the largest and deepest-toned viol; bass viol.

dou′ble-bar′reled *adj.* **1,** having two barrels, as a gun. **2,** doubly effective.

dou′ble-blind′ *adj.* pert. to a test in which neither researchers nor subjects know which subjects will receive the active treatment and which will not.

dou′ble-breast′ed *adj.* (of a jacket, coat, etc.) having two rows of buttons.

dou″ble-cross′ *v.t.* (*Slang*) betray the confidence of; specif., promise (someone) to do something and then do something else. —*n.* betrayal.

dou′ble-deck′er *n.* **1,** a ship, bus, bunk, etc. having two decks or tiers. **2,** (*Informal*) a two-layered sandwich.

dou′ble-dip″ *v.i.* receive payment from two sources for the same time, as a salary and a pension. —**dou″ble-dip′per,** *n.*

double-″en·ten′dre (doo″blə-an-tän′-drə) *n.* (*Fr.*) an expression having two meanings, one usu. risqué.

dou′ble·head′er (dub′əl-hed′ər) *n.* **1,** two separate games played consecutively by the same teams on the same day. **2,** a train drawn by two engines.

dou′ble-joint′ed *adj.* having unusually flexible joints, esp. of the fingers.

dou″ble-knit″ *n.* a kind of knitted fabric.

dou″ble-park′ *v.t. & i.* park (an automobile) in the street, parallel with an automobile parked at the curb.

dou′ble·speak″ *n.* inflated, often deliberately obscure language.

dou′blet (dub′lət) *n.* **1,** a pair of like things. **2,** one of such a pair. **3,** a close-fitting jacket formerly worn by men.

dou′ble-talk″ *n.* rapid talk mingling real words with nonsense; gibberish.

dou·bloon′ (dub-loon′) *n.* a former Spanish gold coin.

doubt (dowt) *n.* **1,** an unsettled state of opinion; indecision. **2,** a matter of uncertainty. **3,** an objection. —*v.i.* feel doubt. —*v.t.* question the accuracy or honesty of. —**doubt′less,** *adj. & adv.* certainly. —**doubting Thomas,** a person disposed to doubt or question.

doubt′ful (-fəl) *adj.* **1,** feeling doubt; hesitant. **2,** unlikely.

douche (doosh) *n.* a liquid spray of water to clean or heal some organ of the body, or the instrument or syringe used. —*v.i. & t.* so spray.

dough (dō) *n.* **1,** the paste for bread or pastry ready to be baked. **2,** (*Slang*) money.

dough
↔ An Old English word derived from the Indo-European root for knead.

dough′boy″ a U.S. soldier, esp. in World War I.

dough'nut" *n.* a ring-shaped cake fried in deep fat. Also, **do'nut.**

dough'ty (dow'tē) *adj.* fearless; strong. —**dough'ti·ness,** *n.*

dour (dûr) *adj.* hard; inflexible; sour in mien. —**dour'ness,** *n.*

douse (dows) *v.t.* **1,** immerse in or splash with water. **2,** extinguish. —*v.i.* search for water or minerals with a divining rod.

dove (duv) *n.* **1,** a pigeon or related bird. **2,** an emblem of innocence and affection. **3,** an advocate of peace.

dove'cot" (-kot") *n.* a doves' house. Also, **dove'cote"** (-kōt").

dove'tail" (duv'tāl") *v.i. & t.* fit or adjust exactly, esp. for space saving; work together harmoniously. —*n.* a mortise and tenon in somewhat the shape of a dove's tail.

dow'a·ger (dow'ə-jər) *n.* **1,** a widow endowed with property from her husband. **2,** (*Informal*) a dignified-looking elderly woman.

dow'dy (dow'dē) *adj.* slovenly; illdressed. —**dow'di·ness,** *n.*

dow'el (dow'əl) *n.* a pin or tenon used for fastening together two pieces of wood, stone, etc.

dow'er (dow'ər) *n.* **1,** the property that a woman brings to her husband at marriage; dowry. **2,** real estate granted by law to a widow for her lifetime. **3,** one's portion of natural gifts. —*v.t.* supply with a dowry.

dow'itch·er (dow'ich-ər) *n.* a species of snipe.

---

down
↔ The sense of feathers comes from Old Norse *dunn.* The sense of downward comes from the Old English word *dun,* hill; the orig. sense of *down* was down from the hill (it is seen still in *downs,* a term for various low-lying regions in England).

---

down *adv.* **1,** [also, **down'ward** (-wərd)] in a descending direction; from higher to lower; from earlier to later times; from a greater to a less or lower rate. **2,** on the ground; at the bottom or lowest point; into disrepute. **3,** in writing; on paper. **4,** firmly; closely. —*adj.* **1,** downward. **2,** behind, in a score. **3,** dejected; ill-disposed. —*prep.* in a descending direction upon or along. —*n.* **1,** downward movement. **2,** (*Football*) a unit of play or progress. **3,** the soft feathers, as on a young bird; underplumage. **4,** any soft hairy growth. **5,** a hill; a dune. —*v.i. & t.* go or cause to go down. —**down payment,** an initial payment on an installment purchase. —**down-to-**

earth, *adj.* sensible; practical. —**down under,** in Australia or New Zealand.

down'cast" *adj.* dejected.

down'er (-ər) *n.* (*Slang*) **1,** a barbiturate depressant drug. **2,** a depressing event, report, etc.

down'fall" *n.* defeat; ruin.

down'grade" *n.* **1,** a downward slope or course. **2,** deterioration. —*v.t.* assign (a position or person) to lower status and salary.

down"heart'ed *adj.* discouraged.

down'hill" *adj. & adv.* in a descending direction down a slope.

down-'home' *adj.* informal; simple.

down'load" *v.t.* to transfer data from an external computer system to one's own system.

down'play" *v.t.* to play down.

down'pour" *n.* heavy rainfall.

down'right" *adj.* **1,** direct; plain; blunt. **2,** complete; utter; absolute. —*adv.* thoroughly; completely. —**down'right"ness,** *n.*

down'scale" *v.t. & i.* to reduce in expense, size, etc.

down'shift" *v.i. & t.* shift into a lower gear.

down'size" *v.t. & i.* reduce the size or scope of (an organization, etc.).

down'stage" *adj. & adv.* (*Theat.*) toward the front of the stage.

Down syndrome the abnormal condition of a mentally deficient child born with slanting eyes, large tongue, flattened skull, etc.; mongolism. Also, **Down's syndrome.**

Down syndrome
↔ Named for 19th-c. British physician L. H. *Down.*

---

down'stairs" *adv. & adj.* toward or on a lower floor.

down'town" *adv. & adj.* at, to, or of the business section of a city.

down'trod'den (-dən) *adv.* oppressed.

down'ward (-wərd) *adj.* [also, **down'- wards**] **1,** from a higher to a lower place, state, degree, etc. **2,** away from a source. —*adj.* descending.

down'y (dow'nē) *adj.* **1,** covered with down. **2,** like down; soft and fluffy. —**down'i·ness,** *n.*

dow'ry (dow'rē) *n.* the estate that a bride brings to her husband.

dowse (dows) *v.* **1,** douse. **2,** (dowz) search for underground water with a divining rod.

dox·ol'o·gy (doks-ol'ə-jē) *n.* a hymn or psalm of praise of God.

---

doy·en′, doy·enne′ (doi-yen′) *n.* a dean; senior member.

doze (dōz) *n.* a light sleep. —*v.i.* (often with *off*) nap.

doz′en (duz′ən) *n.* twelve units.

> **dozen**
> ↔ The word results from the gradual shortening over time of Latin *duodecim*, twelve.

drab *adj.* [**drab′ber, -best**] **1,** of a yellowish-gray tint. **2,** monotonous; dull. —*n.* **1,** a dull gray or brown color. **2,** cloth of this color. —**drab′ness,** *n.*

drach′ma (dräkh′mə) *n.* the monetary unit of Greece.

dra·co′ni·an (dra-kō′nė-ən) *adj.* (of laws) rigorous; harshly oppressive.

> **draconian**
> ↔ From the Athenian statesman Draco, who imposed a harsh code of laws in the 7th c. B.C.

draft (dråft) *n.* **1,** the act of drawing, dragging, or hauling. **2,** a drink. **3,** a heavy demand. **4,** conscription. **5,** the depth a loaded ship sinks in water. **6,** a written order for payment, as a check. **7,** a current of air; a device to produce or control the air flow. **8,** a first sketch; an outline. —*adj.* used for or capable of hauling. —*v.t.* make a draft of, upon, or from. Also, **draught.** —**draft′ee,** *n.* a conscript. —**on draft,** (of beer) drawn from a keg, not bottled.

> **draft, draught**
> ☞ These are variant spellings of the same word, but in American English *draft* is generally used for all senses except the plural *draughts,* checkers.

drafts′man (dråfts′mən) [*pl.* **-men**], **drafts′wom″an,** *n.* one who draws plans, sketches, or designs. Also, **draft′er.**

draft′y (dråf′tè) *adj.* causing or exposed to currents of air. —**draft′i·ness,** *n.*

drag *v.t. & i.* [**dragged, drag′ging**] **1,** pull; haul. **2,** (often with *along*) draw, move, or proceed slowly, heavily, or tiresomely. **3,** draw a grapnel through a body of water in search of something; dredge. **4,** harrow. **5,** (with *out*) prolong tediously. **6,** (*Slang*) race, esp. in automobiles. —*n.* **1,** something designed to be dragged or hauled; a brake; an impediment; hindrance. **2,** the act of dragging. **3,** (*Slang*) influence. **4,** (*Slang*) a street; district. **5,** a puff, as on a cigarette. **6,** (*Slang*) something boring or tiresome. **7,** (*Slang*) a woman's dress worn by a man. —**in drag,** (*Slang*) of a man,

dressed in women's clothing. —**drag strip,** a paved lane for automobile racing.

dra·gée′ (dra-zhā′) *n.* a sugar-coated candy, esp. a small, round candy used as decoration on cookies, etc.

drag′gle (drag′əl) *v.t.* soil by dragging through the mud. —*v.i.* trail on the ground.

drag′net″ *n.* **1,** a net for fishing. **2,** (*Informal*) a canvass, esp. by the police.

drag′o·man (drag′ō-mən) *n.* a professional interpreter or guide.

> **dragoman**
> ↔ From Akkadian (an extinct Semitic language of Babylonia) *targuman,* interpreter.

drag′on (drag′ən) *n.* a fabulous fire-breathing serpentine animal of great size and fierceness.

drag′on·fly″ (drag′ən-flī″) *n.* a large insect with two pairs of wings: *devil's darning needle.*

dra·goon′ (drə-goon′) *n.* an armed cavalry soldier. —*v.t.* persecute or oppress by armed force.

drain (drān) *v.t. & i.* **1,** draw off or flow off gradually. **2,** empty or exhaust gradually. —*n.* **1,** the act of draining. **2,** a passage or pipe used for draining.

drain′age (drā′nij) *n.* **1,** a gradual flowing off; that which flows off. **2,** a system of sewers for draining. **3,** area drained.

drake (drāk) *n.* the male duck.

dram *n.* **1,** a unit of weight, 1/16 ounce in avoirdupois weight. **2,** 1/8 fluid ounce. **3,** a small drink, esp. of spirits.

> **dram**
> ↔ Related to Greek *drakhmē,* drachma, a measure of weight and a silver coin.

dra′ma (drä′mə) *n.* **1,** a literary composition written for the stage; a play. **2,** that branch of literature dealing with the writing and production of plays; all plays, classic and modern. **3,** a human course of events.

Dram′a·mine (dram′ə-mēn) *n.* (*T.N.*) a drug used to prevent motion sickness.

dra·mat′ic (drə-mat′ik) *adj.* **1,** pert. to drama. **2,** intensely interesting; eventful. —**dra·mat′i·cal·ly.** *adv.*

dra·mat′ics (drə-mat′iks) *n.pl.* stage plays. —*n.sing.* **1,** the art or study of acting in, writing, and producing plays. **2,** histrionics.

dram′a·tist (dram′ə-tist) *n.* a playwright.

dram·a·tize" (-tīz") *v.t.* **1,** put in the form of a play. **2,** express dramatically. **—dram"·a·ti·za'tion** (-ti-zā'shən) *n.*

dram·a·tur"gy (drăm'ə-tēr"jē) *n.* the art or science of dramatic composition and representation. **dram'a·turge",** (-tērj) *n.* a specialist in dramaturgy. **—dram"a·tur'gi·cal,** *adj.*

drank *v.* p.t. of *drink.*

drape (drāp) *v.t.* **1,** cover with or adorn with cloth or hangings. **2,** arrange or adjust in folds. **—***n.* a heavy curtain. **—drap'er,** *n.* a dealer in cloths.

dra'per·y (drā'pə-rē) *n.* textile fabrics used for draping; (*pl.*) curtains.

dras'tic (dras'tik) *adj.* having extreme and immediate effect; radical; harsh. **—dras'ti·cal·ly,** *adv.*

draught (dráft) **1,** draft. **2,** (*pl.*) checkers. ❏ *draft*

draw (drâ) *v.t.* [**drew** (droo), **drawn, drawing**] **1,** pull; drag. **2,** take out, as money from a bank. **3,** derive; obtain from some source. **4,** induce; attract, as a crowd. **5,** deduce; infer. **6,** inhale; suck in. **7,** drain. **8,** tie (a game). **9,** (with *out*) extract the essence of; encourage to talk. **10,** (often with *out*) stretch; lengthen; prolong. **11,** obtain as due, as salary. **12,** sketch in lines of words; make a picture or draft of. **13,** disembowel; eviscerate (as poultry). **14,** of a vessel, have a draft of. **15,** play (a match) to a tie score. *—v.i.* **1,** move (toward or away). **2,** attract attendance. **3,** sketch. **4,** make a draft or a demand (upon). **5,** be susceptible to a draft, as a pipe. **6,** take a weapon out of its holder. **7,** tie (a score). **8,** draw lots. *—n.* **1,** the act of drawing; that which is drawn. **2,** a tie score. **3,** movable part of a drawbridge. **—draw a bead on,** aim at. **—draw a line,** fix a limit or barrier. **—draw back,** retreat; cower.

> **draw**
> ↔ The sense of pull, drag, is the more ancient, coming from Old English *dragan,* carry. The sense of sketch may refer to the dragging of the pencil across the page.

draw'back" *n.* a disadvantage; a hindrance.

draw'bridge" *n.* a bridge that can be raised or turned to permit vessels to pass through.

draw'er (drôr) *n.* **1,** a sliding box-shaped compartment in a piece of furniture. **2,** (drâ'ər) one who draws, esp. a check or draft. **3,** (*pl.*) (drôrz) an undergarment worn on the lower part of the body.

draw'ing (drâ'ing) *n.* **1,** the art of sketching, esp. pictures; a picture or illustration; a plan. **2,** the selection of the winners in a lottery. **—drawing card,** (*Informal*) a show or performer that attracts a large audience.

draw'ing room" *n.* **1,** a room used for the reception of company. **2,** a private compartment in a railroad car.

> **drawing room**
> ↔ This term has nothing to do with drawing, but rather with withdrawing, for it was the room to which the ladies withdrew after dinner.

drawl (drâl) *v.t. & i.* speak in a slow, dragged-out tone. *—n.* this manner of speech.

drawn (drân) *v.* p.p. of *draw.* *—adj.* **1,** disemboweled, as a fowl prepared for cooking. **2,** strained from weariness or grief. **3,** of a battle or contest, indecisive; tied.

dray (drā) *n.* a low horse-drawn cart for heavy loads. **—dray'age,** *n.* use of or charge for a dray. **—dray'horse",** *n.* **—dray'man** (-mən) *n.*

dread (dred) *v.t. & i.* fear greatly; be in great fear. *—n.* **1,** great fear. **2,** awe. *—adj.* fearsome.

dread'ful (-fəl) *adj.* **1,** causing great fear or awe. **2,** frightful; shocking; horrible. **—dread'ful·ness,** *n.*

dread'locks" *n.pl.* a braided hairstyle popular among Rastafarians.

dread'nought" (dred'nât") *n.* a powerful battleship.

dream (drēm) *n.* **1,** images or ideas occurring in the mind during sleep. **2,** a vision of the imagination. **3,** (*Informal*) something delightful. *—v.i. & t.* [*p.p.* **dreamed** *or* **dreamt** (dremt)] **1,** imagine during sleep. **2,** think idly; indulge in reverie. **3,** plan vaguely; be unduly hopeful (of). **4,** (with *up*) invent; devise. **—dream'er,** *n.* a visionary.

dream'land" *n.* sleep; the realm of fancy.

dream'y (drē'mē) *adj.* **1,** vague; fanciful. **2,** peaceful. **3,** delightful. **—dream'i·ness,** *n.*

drear'y (drir'ē) *adj.* dismal; gloomy; tedious. Also, **drear. —drear'i·ness,** *n.*

dreck (drek) *n.* (*Slang*) shoddy merchandise; trash; junk.

dredge (drej) *n.* a scooping machine or instrument for clearing a channel, as in a river. *—v.t. & i.* **1,** clear out by use of a dredge. **2,** sprinkle flour upon, as in roasting meat.

dregs (dregz) *n.pl.* worthless residue, as the sediment of wine.

drench *v.t.* wet thoroughly.

dress (dres) *v.t.* **1,** put clothes on; attire. **2,** bandage, as a wound. **3,** prepare; make ready. **4,** put in orderly arrangement, as the hair; adorn. —*v.i.* **1,** clothe oneself. **2,** come into proper alignment. —*n.* **1,** clothing; attire. **2,** a woman's frock. **3,** outward aspect; guise. **4,** formal, as *dress suit.* —**dress circle,** a section of a theater. —**dress down,** censure; discipline. —**dress rehearsal,** a final rehearsal of a play, concert, etc. —**dress up,** put on one's best clothes.

dres·sage′ (dre-säzh′) *n.* the training of a horse in precision movements; the execution of such movements.

dress′er (-ər) *n.* **1,** one who dresses another, esp. in the theater; one who adjusts, trims, etc. **2,** a bedroom chest of drawers with a mirror; a bureau.

dress′ing (-ing) *n.* **1,** the act of one who dresses. **2,** bandages applied to a wound. **3,** sauce or stuffing for food. **4,** a sizing, as starch, for fabrics. —**dressing gown,** a bathrobe; lounging robe.

dress″ing-down′ *n.* (*Informal*) a severe reprimand; a thrashing.

dress′mak″er *n.* a person who makes or alters women's clothing.

dress′y (-ē) *adj.* (of clothes) stylish or formal. —**dress′i·ness,** *n.*

drew (droo) *v.* pret. of *draw.*

drib *n.* a small quantity.

drib′ble (drib′əl) *v.i.* **1,** fall in drops. **2,** slaver. —*v.t.* **1,** let fall in drops. **2,** in some games, kick or bounce the ball forward. —*n.* a dripping of water.

drib′let (drib′lit) *n.* a tiny amount.

dri′er (drī′ər) *n.* **1,** a substance that accelerates drying. **2,** an apparatus for removing moisture. **3,** an ingredient added to promote quick drying.

drift *n.* **1,** the direction in which something is driven; the thing driven; the impelling force. **2,** a heap of any matter driven together, as by wind. **3,** a current, as of water; general current or intention; trend. —*v.i.* float or be carried at random by the force of wind or tide; hence, fig., be carried involuntarily into a course of action. —**drift′er,** *n.* a vagrant; hobo; one constantly on the move.

drift′wood″ *n.* wood and debris cast ashore by drift or tide.

drill (drill) *n.* **1,** a tool for boring holes. **2,** military training, esp. in parade exercises. **3,** teaching by repeated exercises; a test; quiz. **4,** an agricultural machine for planting seeds. **5,** a heavy cotton fabric. —*v.t. & i.* **1,** pierce with a drill. **2,** exercise; train; quiz. **3,** sow in rows, as wheat. —**drill′mas″ter,** *n.* a teacher, esp. of soldiers. —**drill press,** a machine for drilling.

drink *v.t.* [**drank, drunk, drink′ing**] **1,** swallow (a liquid). **2,** take in (a liquid) in any way; imbibe; absorb. **3,** (often with *in*) take in through the senses. —*v.i.* **1,** swallow water or other fluid; habitually imbibe alcoholic liquors. **2,** (with *to*) salute in drinking. —*n.* **1,** any liquid taken into the stomach. **2,** alcoholic liquor. **3,** a potion; a draft. **4,** (with *the*) the ocean, sea, etc. —**drink′er,** *n.* one who habitually drinks liquor.

drip *v.i. & t.* [**dripped, drip′ping**] fall or let fall in drops. —*n.* **1,** a falling in drops. **2,** a receptacle for catching the overflow. **3,** (*Slang*) an unattractive or boring person. —**drip′pings,** *n.pl.* fat that falls from meat in cooking.

drip-′dry′ *v.i. & t.* dry rapidly when hung up. —*adj.* designed for drip-drying.

drive (drīv) *v.t.* [**drove** (drōv), **driv′en** (driv′ən), **driv′ing**] **1,** force to move, esp. forward; impel; hammer in. **2,** set or direct in motion, as an automobile; carry forward. **3,** chase (game); hunt. **4,** incite to a course of action or a state of mind; urge; press. —*v.i.* **1,** be impelled. **2,** move forcibly. **3,** be conveyed, as in an automobile. **4,** aim; tend. **5,** in golf, hit the ball off the tee. **6,** work energetically. —*n.* **1,** a trip in an automobile. **2,** a private road; driveway. **3,** the urging together of animals, as for roundup. **4,** a campaign to collect something, as money, members, sales. **5,** extreme haste or strong action. **6,** the power to drive; energy; ambition. **7,** a driving mechanism, esp. a device used to read and write magnetic media. **8,** in golf, a hit off the tee. —**drive at,** (*Informal*) mean to say.

drive-′in″ *n.* a restaurant or theater serving people who remain in automobiles.

driv′el (driv′əl) *v.i.* **1,** drool; slaver. **2,** talk foolishly. —*n.* act or result of driveling.

driv′er (drī′vər) *n.* **1,** one who or that which drives; a chauffeur. **2,** a form of golf club (No. 1 wood).

drive′way″ *n.* a private lane.

driz′zle (driz′əl) *v.i.* rain in small drops. —*n.* a light rain.

drogue (drōg) *n.* a device used to slow

down a boat, airplane, etc., or, attached to a harpoon line, to tire a whale.

droid *n.* (*Informal*) android.

droll (drōl) *adj.* facetious; comical; amusing. —**droll′er·y,** *n.*

drom′e·dar·y (drom′ə-der-ė) *n.* the Arabian one-humped camel.

drone (drōn) *v.i. & t.* utter a dull, unvaried sound, as from a bee; hence, speak in a monotonous tone. —*n.* **1,** a monotonous, continued sound. **2,** the male honeybee. **3,** an idler. **4,** a robot airplane operated by remote control.

drool *v.i.* drivel; slaver, esp. with greed or anticipated pleasure.

droop *v.i.* **1,** sink or hang down, as from weakness or exhaustion. **2,** languish; decline. —*v.t.* let sink or hang down. —*n.* **1,** the act of drooping; a drooping state. **2,** (*Slang*) a killjoy. —**droop′y,** *adj.*

drop *n.* **1,** a small free-falling globule of liquid, as of rain; anything that resembles it; (*pl.*) a liquid medicine. **2,** a small quantity. **3,** a sudden fall or descent; the distance covered by such. **4,** a hanging; a curtain. **5,** a chute; a trapdoor. —*v.i. & t.* [**dropped, drop′ping**] **1,** fall or let fall in globules. **2,** drip. **3,** fall; descend. **4,** sink or let sink to a lower position, level, state, or condition. **5,** fall dead. **6,** let go; dismiss. **7,** utter or write in an offhand manner. **8,** (with *off*) diminish. **9,** (of cattle, etc.) give birth (to). —**drop′pings,** *n.pl.* animal dung. —**dropkick,** (*Football*) a kick given to a dropped ball on the rebound. —**drop out,** cease participation. —**drop shipment,** shipment by a manufacturer direct to his dealer's customer.

drop-″forge′ *v.t.* forge (metal) by dropping a heavy weight (*drop hammer*) on it.

drop′out″ *n.* one who has dropped out, esp. of school or society.

drop′per (drop′ər) *n.* a tube for dispensing liquid in drops.

drop′sy (drop′sė) *n.* an abnormal accumulation of serous fluid in the body. —**drop′si·cal** (-si-kəl) *adj.*

drosh′ky (drosh′kė) *n.* a Russian horse-drawn passenger vehicle, used as a cab.

dross (drâs) *n.* **1,** the waste matter thrown off from molten metal. **2,** any refuse.

drought (drowt) *n.* long-continued dry weather. Also, **drouth** (drowth).

drove (drōv) *v.* pret. of *drive.* —*n.* a number of cattle, sheep, etc. driven in a herd. —**drov′er,** *n.* a driver of or dealer in such animals.

drown *v.t. & i.* **1,** suffocate or be suffocated by immersion in water or other liq-

uid. **2,** flood; submerge; overwhelm. **3,** (with *out*) prevent from being heard, by creating a louder or more pervasive noise.

drowse (drowz) *v.i.* be half asleep; be heavy or dull. —*n.* a half-sleep.

drow′sy (drow′zė) *adj.* sleepy. —**drow′si·ness,** *n.*

drub *v.t.* [**drubbed, drub′bing**] beat; cudgel. —**drub′bing,** *n.* a bad beating or defeat.

drudge (druj) *v.i.* labor at hard, uninteresting tasks. —*n.* an overworked person; a spiritless toiler. —**drudg′er·y** (-ə-rė) *n.*

drug *n.* **1,** any substance used in the composition or preparation of medicines. **2,** a narcotic. **3,** a commodity unsalable because of overproduction. —*v.t.* [**drugged, drug′ging**] **1,** mix or dose with drugs. **2,** surfeit.

> **drug**
> ↔ This word is traced back to Old French *drogue*, but the path ends there in mystery.

drug′gist (-ist) *n.* a pharmacist.

drug′store″ *n.* a store that deals in drugs and, usually, other merchandise.

dru′id (droo′id) *n.* a priest of the ancient Celts.

drum *n.* **1,** a musical instrument consisting of a hollow frame covered on the top by a tightly stretched membrane which is beaten with sticks in playing. **2,** anything drum-shaped. **3,** a fish. **4,** a membrane in the ear: *eardrum.* —*v.i.* [**drummed, drum′ming**] **1,** play a drum. **2,** tap on something with the fingers. **3,** sound like a drum; resound. —*v.t.* **1,** (*Mil.*) expel formally. **2,** impress, as an idea into someone. **3,** (with *up*) attract or solicit, as trade. —**drum machine,** an electronic device for reproducing the sound of various drums and other percussion instruments. —**drum major** (*masc.*) or **majorette** (*fem.*), the leader of a marching corps of drummers or of a band.

> **drum**
> ↔ A shortening of *drumslade,* drumbeat. The word is related to *trumpet* and *trombone* and may have once referred to any loud instrument.

drum′lin *n.* (*Geol.*) a long narrow mound, formed by a glacier.

drum′mer (-ər) *n.* **1,** one who plays a drum. **2,** a traveling salesman.

drum′stick″ *n.* **1,** a stick with which a drum is beaten. **2,** the leg of a fowl.

drunk *v.* p.p. of *drink.* —*adj.* [also, **drunk′en** (-ən)] intoxicated by liquor. —*n.* **1,** a spree. **2,** an inebriated person. —**drunk′en·ness,** *n.*

drunk′ard (-ərd) *n.* a person given to excessive drinking of liquor.

drupe (droop) *n.* a stone fruit, as the plum, cherry, or peach. —**drupe′let,** *n.* a small drupe, as a section of a berry, containing a hard seed.

dry (drī) *adj.* **1,** without moisture; not wet. **2,** not giving milk, as a *dry cow;* empty, as a *dry well.* **3,** thirsty. **4,** barren; uninteresting. **5,** grave in manner but humorous or sarcastic. **6,** free from sweetness, as certain wines. **7,** (*Informal*) of or pert. to prohibition of alcoholic beverages. —*v.t. & i.* free from or lose moisture. —*n.* (*Informal*) prohibitionist. —**dry′ness,** *n.* —**dry cell,** a sealed storage battery. —**dry dock,** a structure for holding a ship out of water, for repairs, etc. —**dry goods,** textile fabrics, etc. —**dry ice,** frozen carbon dioxide. —**dry measure,** a system of units of volume or capacity used in measuring dry commodities, as grain. —**dry point,** a process of engraving on copper with a sharp-pointed tool; an engraving so made. —**dry rot,** a fungous disease of timber or other plants; fig., a concealed inward decay, as of public morals. —**dry run,** a rehearsal; demonstration. —**dry up, 1,** become arid or barren. **2,** (*Informal*) stop talking. —**drywall,** a prefabricated plaster wall panel.

dry′ad (drī′ad) *n.* a wood nymph.

dry-′clean″ *v.t.* wash (clothes, etc.) in benzene, gasoline, etc.

dry′er (drī′ər) *n.* drier.

dry′wall″ *v.t.* to install drywall.

du′al (doo′əl) *adj.* relating to or consisting of two parts; twofold.

du·al′i·ty (doo-al′ə-tē) *n.* the state of being twofold.

dub *v.t.* [**dubbed, dub′bing**] **1,** confer a new dignity or name upon. **2,** rub or dress so as to make smooth. **3,** record from or on a previous sound track.

dub′bin (dub′in) *n.* a mixture of oil and tallow for dressing leather.

du·bi·e·ty (doo-bī′ə-tē) *n.* doubtfulness.

du′bi·ous (doo′bē-əs) *adj.* **1,** of questionable value. **2,** doubtful; hesitating. —**du′bi·ous·ness,** *n.*

du′cal (doo′kəl) *adj.* of or pert. to a duke.

duc′at (duk′ət) *n.* **1,** a former Europ. gold coin. **2,** (*pl.*) (*Slang*) money.

du′ce (doo′chä) *n.* (*It.*) **1,** leader. **2,** (*cap.*)

Benito Mussolini, head of the Fascist Italian state from 1922 to 1943.

duch′ess (duch′əs) *n.* the wife of a duke.

duch′y (duch′ē) *n.* the territory of a duke or duchess; a dukedom.

duck (duk) *n.* **1,** any of many species of broad-, flat-billed water birds. **2,** (*Informal*) a likable person. **3,** a strong cotton or linen fabric; (*pl.*) clothes made of it. **4,** a diving inclination of the head. **5,** a brief dip or plunge in water. —*v.t. & i.* **1,** plunge briefly into water. **2,** bob or bow the head suddenly. **3,** dodge by bending down or aside suddenly. **4,** evade.

> **duck**
> ↔ The animal's name comes from the verb *duck,* which dates back to Middle English *duken.* The fabric comes from Dutch *doek,* a generic term for cloth.

duck′bill″ *n.* the platypus.

duck′ling *n.* a young duck.

duck′pin″ *n.* a small bowling pin; (*pl.*) a bowling game.

duck′y (duk′ē) (*Informal*) *adj.* excellent. —*n.* (as a term of address) darling; dear.

duct (dukt) *n.* **1,** any tube or canal by which a fluid is conducted or conveyed. **2,** a pipe for electric cables or wires. —**duct′less gland,** any of certain glands, as the thyroid, giving off their secretions directly into the bloodstream.

duc′tile (duk′təl) *adj.* **1,** capable of being drawn out into wire or threads. **2,** complying; easily led. —**duc·til′i·ty** (-til′ə-tē) *n.*

dud *n.* **1,** (*pl.*) (*Informal*) clothes. **2,** a bomb, shell, or firecracker that fails to explode. **3,** a failure.

dude (dood) *n.* **1,** an overdressed man; a fop. **2,** a city person; a tenderfoot. **3,** (*Slang*) a person. —**dud′ish,** *adj.* —**dude ranch,** a resort modeled on a cattle ranch. —**dude up,** (*Informal*) dress up stylishly.

dudg′eon (duj′ən) *n.* resentment; sullen anger.

due (doo) *adj.* **1,** owed; payable. **2,** suitable. **3,** expected or looked for. **4,** attributable. —*n.* **1,** that which is owed or required; a debt; an obligation. **2,** (*pl.*) a toll; a fee. —**due′bill″,** *n.* a written acknowledgment of a debt, made payable in goods or services. —**due to,** ascribable to; a result of. ❏ *because*

du′el (doo′əl) *n.* **1,** a premeditated combat between two persons with deadly weapons. **2,** any two-sided contest. —**du′el·ist,** *n.*

du·en′na (dū-en′ə) *n.* a chaperon.

du·et′ (doo-et′) *n.* (*Music*) a composition for two performers; the performance or performers.

duf′fel (duf′əl) *n.* **1,** a coarse woolen thick-napped cloth. **2,** a sportsman's or camper's outfit. **—duffel bag,** a large cloth carrying bag.

> **duffel**
> ↔ The fabric name comes from the name of the town where it originated, *Duffel*, Belgium.

duf′fer (duf′ər) *n.* **1,** a peddler. **2,** (*Slang*) a stupid or inefficient person; a poor player at a game.

dug *v.* pret. & p.p. of *dig.* —*n.* **1,** an udder or breast. **2,** a teat or nipple.

du′gong (doo′gong) *n.* a large sea mammal.

dug′out″ *n.* **1,** a boat hollowed out from a log. **2,** a shelter in the ground, esp. in trench warfare.

dui′ker (dī′kər) *n.* a small Afr. antelope.

duke (dook) *n.* **1,** a hereditary title of nobility equivalent to or next below a prince. **2,** the ruler of a duchy. **3,** (*pl.*) (*Slang*) fists. **—duke′dom** (-dəm) *n.* duchy.

> **duke**
> ↔ From Latin *dux*, leader (also source of Italian *duce*). Its French form *duc* was at one time the equivalent of English *earl.*

dul′cet (dul′sit) *adj.* sweet; harmonious; agreeable. ❏ *dulcimer*

dul′ci·mer (dul′sə-mər) *n.* **1,** a type of zither played with hammers, a precursor of the pianoforte. **2,** a similar folk instrument plucked with the fingers.

> **dulcimer**
> ↔ From the Latin phrase *dulce melos*, sweet melody. *Dulce* is also the source of English *dulcet*.

dull (dul) **1,** not understanding readily; stupid. **2,** tedious; boring; uninteresting. **3,** not quick or keen in perception. **4,** dismal; cheerless. **5,** not bright or clear; dim. **6,** not sharp; blunt. —*v.t. & i.* make or become dull. **—dull′ness,** *n.*

dull′ard (-ərd) *n.* a stupid person; a blockhead.

dulse (duls) *n.* an edible seaweed.

du′ly (doo′lē) *adv.* in a due manner; properly.

Du′ma (doo′mä) *n.* the former Russian lower house of parliament.

dumb (dum) *adj.* **1,** not having the power of speech. **2,** mute; silent. **3,** (*Informal*) stupid. **—dumb′ness,** *n.* **—dumb show,** pantomime.

> **dumb**
> ☛ Because *dumb* can mean mute or stupid, it is usually preferable to use *mute* when that sense is intended.

dumb′bell″ *n.* **1,** a weight for gymnastic exercise. **2,** (*Slang*) a dolt.

dumb·found′ (dum-fownd′) *v.t.* strike dumb; confuse; confound. Also, **dumb′-found″.**

dumb′wait″er *n.* an elevator to convey food or small articles.

dum′dum *n.* **1,** a soft-nosed bullet designed to spread on impact. **2,** (*Slang*) a stupid person.

> **dumdum**
> ↔ Named for the town in India, near Calcutta, where it was first produced.

dum′my (dum′ē) *n.* **1,** one who is dumb; a mute. **2,** a figurehead, model, effigy, etc. **3,** (*Card Games*) the high bidder's partner or his or her cards, exposed on the table. **4,** (*Informal*) a stupid person; a dolt. —*adj.* sham; set up for appearances only.

dump *v.t.* **1,** throw down or let slide down (a mass or body of something); unload. **2,** sell (quantities of stocks, merchandise, etc.) regardless of price. **3,** (*Computers*) display or print the contents of a data file or memory. —*n.* **1,** a place for dumping loads, esp. rubbish. **2,** (*Mil.*) a temporary storage place for supplies. **3,** (*pl.*) a state of depression; the doldrums. **4,** (*Informal*) a messy or dilapidated place.

dump′ish *adj.* morose; depressed in spirits. **—dump′ish·ness,** *n.*

dump′ling *n.* a lump of dough boiled in soup, stew, etc.

Dump′ster (dump′stər) *n.* (*T.N.*) a brand of large container used for disposal of trash, etc.

dump′y (-ē) *adj.* short and thick; squat. **—dump′i·ness,** *n.*

dun *v.t. & i.* [**dunned, dun′ning**] urge to pay a debt. —*n.* a demand for payment. —*adj.* of a dull grayish-brown color.

dunce (duns) *n.* a dull-witted stupid person; an ignoramus. **—dunce cap,** a cone of paper worn as a cap to mark a stupid student.

> **dunce**
> ↔ Named for a 13th-c. Scottish theologian, John *Duns*, whose followers were considered "enemies of learning."

dun′der·head″ (dun′dər-) *n.* a dunce.

dune (doon) *n.* a hill of sand heaped up by the wind. —**dune buggy,** a vehicle with large balloon tires for traveling on sand, etc.

dung *n.* animal excrement; manure.

dun″ga·ree′ (dung″gǝ-rē′) *n.* **1,** a coarse cotton material, generally blue. **2,** (*pl.*) work clothes made from this material.

dun′geon (dun′jǝn) *n.* **1,** a deep, dark place of confinement. **2,** the tower of a medieval castle.

dung′hill″ *n.* **1,** a heap of manure. **2,** anything mean, vile, or low.

dunk *v.t.* dip, esp. bread into coffee before eating it.

Dunk′ard (-ǝrd) *n.* one of a certain religious sect. Also, **Dunk′er.**

dun′nage (dun′ij) *n.* **1,** loose wood used to pack a ship's cargo. **2,** baggage.

du′o (doo′ō) *n.* a couple; pair.

du·o- *pref.* two.

du″o·dec′i·mal (doo″ǝ-des′ǝ-mǝl) *adj.* reckoning by twelves and the powers of twelve.

du″o·de′num (doo″ǝ-dē′nǝm) *n.* the first portion of the small intestine, immediately connected with the stomach. —**du″o·de′nal,** *adj.*

dupe (doop) *v.t.* deceive; trick; mislead. —*n.* a person easily deceived. —**dup′er·y,** *n.*

> **dupe**
> ↔ From the Middle French phrase *tête d'huppe,* head of hoopoo (a bird considered especially stupid).

du′ple (doo′pǝl) *adj.* double; twofold.

du′plex (doo′pleks) *adj.* **1,** double; twofold. —*n.* **1,** an apartment of two floors. **2,** a two-family house.

du′pli·cate (doo′plǝ-kit) *adj.* **1,** double; twofold. **2,** exactly like something done before. —*n.* an exact copy; a facsimile. —*v.t.* (-kāt″) make a copy or copies of. —**du″pli·ca′tion,** *n.* —**du′pli·ca″tor,** *n.*

du·plic′i·ty (doo-plis′ǝ-tē) *n.* bad faith; dissimulation; hypocrisy; double dealing.

du′ra·ble (dyûr′ǝ-bǝl) *adj.* lasting; longwearing; not perishable or changeable. —**du″ra·bil′i·ty,** *n.*

durable press permanent press.

du·ral′u·min (dyû-ral′yǝ-min) *n.* a strong and light alloy of aluminum.

dur′ance (dyûr′ǝns) *n.* imprisonment; involuntary confinement of any kind.

du·ra′tion (dyû-rā′shǝn) *n.* the length of time during which anything continues or lasts.

dur′bar (dēr′bär) *n.* in India, a prince's audience room, or an official audience or reception.

> **durbar**
> ↔ From the Urdu word for court, derived from Persian, entry door.

du·ress′ (dyû-res′) *n.* **1,** restraint of personal liberty; imprisonment. **2,** coercion.

dur′ing (dûr′ing) *prep.* in the time or course of; throughout the continuance of.

dur′mast (dēr′mast) *n.* a heavy, elastic variety of oak.

du′rum (dûr′ǝm) *n.* a hard wheat used in making macaroni.

dusk *n.* **1,** the state between light and darkness, esp. at twilight. **2,** partial darkness; shadow. **3,** swarthiness.

dusk′y (dus′kė) *adj.* dark, as at dusk. —**dusk′i·ness,** *n.*

dust *n.* **1,** fine, dry particles of earth or other matter. **2,** a dead body; remains. **3,** the ground; a low condition. **4,** a small quantity of any powdered substance sprinkled over something. —*v.t.* **1,** free from dust or sweep away dust from. **2,** sprinkle with a powder. —**dust bowl,** an area where the dry topsoil is blown about by the wind. —**dust cover,** a cover to keep out dust, as the jacket of a book.

dust′er (dus′tǝr) *n.* **1,** a cloth or implement for removing dust. **2,** a light overcoat. **3,** peignoir.

dust′man″ *n.* (*Brit.*) garbage or trash collector.

dust′y (dus′tė) *adj.* being covered with or charged with dust. —**dust′i·ness,** *n.*

Dutch (duch) *adj.* pert. to the Netherlands, its people or language. —**Dutch door,** a door with upper and lower sections that can be opened separately. —**Dutch oven,** a kettle for baking. —**Dutch treat,** a party in which each pays his or her share. —**Dutch uncle,** a severe but well-wishing critic. —**Dutch wife,** a bolster used as a sleeping companion.—**go Dutch,** each pay his or her own way. —**in Dutch,** in trouble.

> **Dutch**
> ↔ From Middle Dutch *duutsch,* which could mean either Dutch or Germanic. Note that the "Dutch" in Pennsylvania Dutch is in fact not "Dutch" but a misspelling of *Deutsch,* German.

du'te·ous (doo'tė-əs) *adj.* performing the duties required; obedient. —**du'te·ous·ness,** *n.*

du'ti·a·ble (doo'tė-ə-bəl) *adj.* subject to customs duty.

du'ti·ful (doo'ti-fəl) *adj.* **1,** duteous. **2,** loyal; diligent. —**du'ti·ful·ness,** *n.*

du'ty (doo'tė) *n.* **1,** good behavior owed to one's parents or superiors. **2,** service requisite to one's position. **3,** any moral obligation. **4,** a tax; excise or customs dues. —**du'ty-free",** *adj.* not dutiable.

du·vet' (doo-vā') *n.* a down-filled quilt; comforter.

du've·tyn" (doo'və-tēn") *n.* a soft woolen cloth with a long nap.

Dvo'rak keyboard (dvôr'ak) (*T.N.*) an arrangement of the keys of a typewriter or computer keyboard designed to allow faster typing speed.

dwarf (dwôrf) *n.* **1,** a person, animal, or plant much below ordinary size. —*adj.* below average size. —*v.t.* **1,** hinder from growing; stunt. **2,** cause to seem small by comparison. —*v.i.* become less. —**dwarf'-ish,** *adj.*

---

dwarf, midget
☛ Properly speaking, a *dwarf* is a person small and usually disproportioned because of the effects of dwarfism, a disease. A *midget* is a normally proportioned person who happens to be very small.

---

dweeb (dwēb) *n.* (*Slang*) a boring person; nerd.

dwell (dwel) *v.i.* [*pret. & p.p.* **dwelt** or **dwelled**] **1,** stay; remain. **2,** abide as a permanent resident; reside. **3,** (usually with *on*) dilate upon, as a topic. —**dwell'er,** *n.* a resident. —**dwell'ing,** *n.* a house for human occupation.

dwin'dle (dwin'dəl) *v.i.* diminish; become less; shrink; waste away.

dy'ad (dī'ad) *n.* **1,** two units treated as one. **2,** (*Chem.*) an element with a valence of two, as oxygen in H_2O. **3,** (*Biol.*) a secondary unit of organization; one of a pair of chromosomes.

dye (dī) *n.* **1,** a liquid or other matter used to change the color of something else. **2,** a particular color; tint. —*v.t.* [**dyed, dye'-ing**] change the color of, with a dye. —**dy'er,** *n.* —**dye'stuff"** *n.* a substance used for making dye. —**dyed'-in-the-wool",** *adj.* confirmed in character; thoroughgoing.

dyke (dīk) *n.* (*Slang*) a female homosexual; a lesbian.

dy·na- (dī'nə) *pref.* power.

dy·nam'ic (dī-nam'ik) *adj.* **1,** full of force and energy; active; potent. **2,** pert. to dynamics. —**dy·nam'i·cal·ly,** *adv.*

dy·nam'ics (dī-nam'iks) *n.* **1,** a branch of mechanics treating of motion. **2,** (construed as *pl.*) the principles of active operation in any field.

dy'na·mite" (dī'nə-mīt") *n.* **1,** an explosive, nitroglycerin mixed with sand. **2,** a precarious situation or plan. **3,** (*Informal*) something exciting. —*v.t.* blow up with dynamite.

---

dynamite
↔ The term was coined in Swedish, on Greek roots, by its inventor, Swedish manufacturer A. B. Nobel, who instituted the Nobel Prize.

---

dy'na·mo" (dī'nə-mō") *n.* [*pl.* **-mos"**] a machine that converts mechanical energy into electrical energy.

dy"na·mom'e·ter (dī"nə-mom'i-tər) *n.* an instrument for measuring force or power.

dy'nas·ty (dī'nəs-tė) *n.* **1,** a succession of rulers or monarchs of the same line or family. **2,** the period during which a dynasty rules. —**dy'nast,** *n.* a ruler. —**dy·nas'-tic,** *adj.*

dyne (dīn) *n.* (*Physics*) the unit of force in the centimeter-gram-second system.

Dy'nel (dī'nel) *n.* (*T.N.*) a synthetic, flame-resistant fiber; the yarn or fabric made from it.

dys- (dis) *pref.* with difficulty; difficulty.

dys'en·ter"y (dis'ən-ter"ė) *n.* a disease of the large intestine characterized by diarrhetic discharge of blood and mucus from the bowels.

dys·func'tion (dis-funk'shən) *n.* (*Med.*) impaired functioning, as of a bodily organ. —**dys·func'tion·al,** *adj.*

dys·lex'i·a (dis-leks'ė-ə) *n.* an impairment of the ability to read. —**dys·lex'ic,** *adj.*

dys·pep'sia (dis-pep'shə) *n.* impaired power of digestion.

dys·pep'tic (dis-pep'tik) *adj. & n.* (a person) afflicted with dyspepsia, hence gloomy or irritable. —**dys·pep'ti·cal·ly,** *adv.*

dys·pro'si·um (dis-prō'sė-əm) *n.* a metallic element, no. 66, symbol Dy, one of the rare earths.

dys·to'pi·a (dis-tō'pė-ə) *n.* a society characterized by human misery: opposed to *utopia.* —**dys·to'pi·an,** *adj.*

dys'tro·phy (dis'trə-fė) *n.* faulty nutrition.

E

E, e (ē) the fifth letter of the English alphabet.

each (ēch) *adj.* every (unit) (of a group or series considered one by one) —*pron.* every one individually. —*adv.* apiece. ❑ *both, either*

> **each, either**
> (*Gram.*) *Either,* a singular pronoun, refers to one or the other of two things or persons (but not both). *Each,* also singular, refers to both of two or more things or persons.

ea'ger (ē'gər) *adj.* having keen desire or longing; being impatient, intent, or earnest. —**ea'ger·ness,** *n.* —**eager beaver,** (*Slang*) an enthusiastic person.

ea'gle (ē'gəl) *n.* **1,** a large bird of prey. **2,** a conventional representation of an eagle. **3,** a U.S. $10 gold piece. **4,** in golf, two below par on a hole. —**ea'glet,** *n.* a young eagle.

ear (ir) *n.* **1,** the organ of hearing in mammals; the external part alone. **2,** the sense of hearing; ability to discriminate among sounds. **3,** attention; heed. **4,** something likened to an ear. **5,** the part of a cereal plant that contains the grains.

> **ear**
> ↔ The human ear and the ear of corn are unrelated, though both have ancient origins. The *ear* of corn comes from an Indo-European source word that also produced *acute.*

ear'drop" *n.* **1,** an earring with a pendant. **2,** (usu. *pl.*) medication for the ear.
ear'drum" *n.* the tympanum.
earl (ērl) *n.* a British nobleman ranking above a viscount and below a marquis. —**earl'dom,** *n.*
ear'ly (ēr'lē) *adv. & adj.* **1,** occurring near the beginning. **2,** of ancient date. **3,** before an appointed time. **4,** in the near future. —**ear'li·ness,** *n.* —**early bird,** early riser; first arrival. —**early on,** in the beginning stages of a process.
ear'mark" *n.* a mark of identification. —*v.t.* **1,** mark for identification. **2,** set aside for a specific purpose.
ear'muff" *n.* one of a pair of coverings for warming the ears.
earn (ērn) *v.t.* **1,** gain in return for labor or service, or as profit. **2,** deserve; merit. —**earn'ings,** *n.pl.* wages; profits.

ear'nest (ēr'nəst) *adj.* **1,** serious in purpose or effort; sincere. **2,** diligent; zealous. **3,** important; grave. **4,** showing sincerity. —*n.* a pledge. —**ear'nest·ness,** *n.* —**earnest money,** money given to bind a contract.

> **earnest**
> ↔ The adjective and noun senses are not related. The noun is of Germanic origin. The adjective comes from Hebrew '*eravon,* pledge.

ear'phone" *n.* a small speaker worn on the ear, for radio, telephone, etc.
ear'piece" *n.* a piece that covers or loops around the ear.
ear'plug" *n.* a stopper placed in the ear to reduce noise.
ear'ring" *n.* an ornament worn on the ear.
ear'shot" *n.* range of hearing.
ear'split"ting *adj.* extremely loud.
earth (ērth) *n.* **1,** (sometimes *cap.*) the globe or planet we inhabit. **2,** the solid matter of the globe. **3,** the loose material of the globe's surface; sand, soil, etc. **4,** the inhabitants of the globe; the world. —**earth science,** a science, such as geography, geology, etc., that deals with the earth.
earth'bound" *adj.* bound by earthly or mundane ties or interests.
earth'en (ēr'thən) *adj.* made of earth, clay, etc. —**earth'en·ware",** *n.* vessels of baked clay.
earth'ling *n.* **1,** an inhabitant of the earth; a mortal. **2,** a worldly person.
earth'ly (-lē) *adj.* **1,** worldly; material. **2,** (*Informal*) possible; conceivable. —**earth'li·ness,** *n.*
earth'nut" *n.* an edible nut or plant part that grows underground; a tuber.
earth'quake" *n.* a trembling or shaking of the earth's surface.
earth'shak"ing *adj.* (*Informal*) of great importance.
earth'work" *n.* a structure of earth, as a rampart.
earth'worm" *n.* any of various burrowing worms.
earth'y (ēr'thē) *adj.* **1,** of or like earth. **2,** worldly or coarse. —**earth'i·ness,** *n.*
ear'wax" *n.* a yellowish secretion of glands of the external ear.
ear'wig" *n.* a small harmless insect.

> **earwig**
> ↔ From Old English *ēarwicga,* ear insect, because it supposedly enters people's ears.

ease (ēz) *n.* **1,** physical comfort. **2,** mental tranquillity. **3,** freedom from difficulty; facility. **4,** unaffectedness. —*v.t.* **1,** put in a state of ease; rid of pain, anxiety, etc. **2,** lessen; mitigate. **3,** make less difficult. —*v.i.* (often with *off* or *up*) become less painful, severe, difficult, etc. —**at ease, 1,** in a state of ease. **2,** (*Mil.*) not at attention.

ea·sel (ē′zəl) *n.* a stand for supporting a picture, blackboard, etc.

> **easel**
> ↔ From Dutch *esel*, ass, because the device does an ass's work of holding up the canvas.

ease′ment (ēz′mənt) *n.* **1,** the act of easing. **2,** (*Law*) a right to use land owned by another person.

eas′i·ly (ē′zə-lē) *adv.* **1,** with ease. **2,** by far.

east (ēst) *n.* **1,** one of the four cardinal points of the compass, 90 degrees clockwise from north. **2,** (usu. *cap.*) a region lying in this direction, as Asia. —*adj.* in, toward, or from the east.

East′er (ēs′tər) *n.* the festival commemorating the resurrection of Jesus Christ, observed on the first Sunday after the first full moon that occurs on or after March 21.

> **Easter**
> ↔ From Old English *Eastre*, the name of a Germanic goddess, whose feast was celebrated at the time of the spring equinox.

east′er·ly (-lē) *adj. & adv.* toward or from the east.

east′ern (-tərn) *adj.* in or pert. to the east. —**east′ern·er,** *n.*

east′ward (-wərd) *adj. & adv.* toward the east.

eas′y (ē′zē) *adj.* **1,** not difficult. **2,** comfortable; tranquil. **3,** not oppressive. —*adv.* (*Informal*) easily. —**eas′i·ness,** *n.* —**easy chair,** a comfortable chair. —**go** or **be easy on,** treat with restraint. —**on easy street,** in comfortable circumstances.

eas′y·go″ing *adj.* calm and unhurried in manner or pace.

eat (ēt) *v.t.* **1,** take into the mouth and swallow for nourishment (esp. of nonliquid food). **2,** consume by corrosion, rust, etc. —*v.i.* dine; consume food. —*n.* (*pl.*) (*Informal*) food. —**eat′a·bles,** *n.pl.* articles of food. —**eat crow,** accept defeat or humiliation. —**eat dirt** or **humble pie,** apologize humbly. —**eat one's words,** retract what one has said. —**eat out,** eat a meal away from one's home, as in a restaurant.

eat′e·ry (ēt′ə-rē) *n.* (*Informal*) a lunchroom.

eau de Co·logne′ (ō″ də kə-lōn′) (*Fr.*) cologne.

eau″ de vie′ (ō″ də vē′) (*Fr.*) brandy.

eaves (ēvz) *n.pl.* the edge of a roof overhanging the walls.

eaves′drop″ *v.i.* listen secretly.

> **eavesdrop**
> ↔ From the idea that if one stood where water drops from the eaves, one could hear what went on in the house.

ebb (eb) *v.i.* flow back, as tidal water; recede; fall away. —*n.* **1,** a receding or ebbing. **2,** a decline.

eb′on·ite (eb′ə-nīt) *n.* hard rubber, esp. when black; vulcanite. —**eb′on·ize,** *v.t.*

eb′on·y (eb′ən-ē) *n.* a hard, durable wood from various trees. —*adj.* **1,** of ebony. **2,** black.

e·bul′li·ent (i-bul′yənt) *adj.* greatly excited or demonstrative; boiling. —**e·bul′li·ence,** *n.*

eb″ul·li′tion (eb″ə-lish′ən) *n.* **1,** a boiling up or overflow of liquid. **2,** an outburst of feeling, passion, etc.

ec′ce ho′mo (ek′ā hō′mō) (*Lat.*) behold the man.

ec·cen′tric (ek-sen′trik) *adj.* **1,** off center; not having the same center. **2,** elliptical, not circular. **3,** deviating from usual or recognized form; queer. —*n.* **1,** a queer or erratic person. **2,** a contrivance for transforming rotary to linear motion. —**ec·cen′tri·cal·ly,** *adv.* —**ec″cen·tric′i·ty** (ek″sən-tris′ə-tē) *n.*

ec·cle″si·as′tic (e-klē″zē-as′tik) *n.* a clergyman. —**ec·cle″si·as′ti·cal,** *adj.* pert. to the church or clergy.

ec·dy′si·ast (ek-diz′ē-ast) *n.* strip tease artist.

> **ecdysiast**
> ↔ Coined by H. L. Mencken, based on *ecdysis*, the process of shedding outer skin by snakes, shellfish, etc.

ech′e·lon″ (esh′ə-lon″) *n.* **1,** a level of command. **2,** a steplike deployment of military or naval units.

> **echelon**
> ↔ From French *échelon*, rung of a ladder, in turn derived from Latin *scala*, scale.

ech′o (ek′ō) *n.* **1,** repetition of a sound by reflection of the sound waves. **2,** sympathetic response; one who so responds.

3, (*Communications*) the letter *e*. —*v.i.* produce an echo. —*v.t.* repeat or imitate. —**ech·o'ic,** *adj.*

ech"o·lo·ca'tion *n.* the location of objects by use of radio waves, as in radar and sonar. Also, **ech"o·la'tion** (-lā'shən).

é·clair' (ā-klār') *n.* a frosted, filled cake.

é·clat' (ā-klä') *n.* brilliant effect; splendor.

ec·lec'tic (ek-lek'tik) *adj.* **1,** selective; not following any one school of thought. **2,** consisting of selections from various sources. —**ec·lec'ti·cal·ly,** *adv.* —**ec·lec'ti·cism,** *n.*

e·clipse' (i-klips') *n.* **1,** obscuration of the light of the sun by intervention of the moon (*solar eclipse*), or of the moon by intervention of the earth (*lunar eclipse*). **2,** any obscuration or diminution of light, brilliance, glory, etc. —*v.t.* **1,** cast a shadow upon. **2,** surpass.

e·clip'tic (i-klip'tik) *n. & adj.* the great circle which is the apparent annual path of the sun.

ec'logue (ek'log) *n.* a short pastoral poem.

ec·o- (ek-ə) *pref.* ecology.

ec'o·cide" (ek'ə-sīd") *n.* destruction of the natural environment.

e·col'o·gy (i-kol'ə-jė) *n.* **1,** (*Biol.*) the study of the relations between organisms and their environment. **2,** (*Sociol.*) the study of the causes and effects of the spatial distribution of population. —**e"co·log'i·cal** (ē"kə-loj'ə-kəl; ek'ə-) *adj.* —**e·col'·o·gist,** *n.*

> **ecology**
> ↔ Coined by the 19th-c. German zoologist Ernst Haeckel, based on Greek *oikos,* house, dwelling.

e"co·nom'ic (ē"kə-nom'ik; ek"ə-) *adj.* **1,** utilitarian. **2,** pert. to economics. —**e"co·nom'i·cal,** *adj.* thrifty.

e"co·nom'ics (ē"kə-nom'iks; ek"ə-) *n.* the science of the production and distribution of goods and services.

e·con'o·mist (i-kon'ə-mist) *n.* a scientist in the field of economics.

e·con'o·mize" (i-kon'ə-mīz") *v.i.* manage frugally.

e·con'o·my (i-kon'ə-mė) *n.* **1,** avoidance of or freedom from waste in expenditure or management; thrift. **2,** a system of management of resources, esp. pecuniary.

ec'o·sphere" (ek'ə-sfir") *n.* the part of the universe habitable by living organisms.

ec'o·sys"tem (ek'ō-sis"təm) *n.* an ecological community.

ec'ru (ek'roo) *adj. & n.* light tan.

ec'sta·sy (ek'stə-sė) *n.* overpowering emotion or exaltation; rapture. —**ec·stat'ic** (ek-stat'ik), *adj.* —**ec·stat'i·cal·ly,** *adv.*

ec·to- (ek'tō) *pref.* external; outer.

-ec'to·my (-ek'tə-mė) *suf.* surgical excision.

ec'to·plasm (ek'tə-plaz-əm) *n.* a visible exudation, in spiritualism.

é·cu' (ā-kū') *n.* [*pl.* **é·cus"** (ā-kū')] (*Fr.*) **1,** a triangular shield of the Middle Ages. **2,** a 14th-c. French coin.

ECU (ā-koo') *n.* the currency of account of the European Common Market: *E(uropean) C(urrency) U(nit).*

ec"u·men'i·cal (ek"yû-men'i-kəl) *adj.* **1,** general; universal. **2,** belonging to the whole Christian church.

ec'ze·ma (eg'zə-mə) *n.* an inflammation of the skin, often attended by exudation of lymph.

-ed *suf.* **1,** possessed of: forming adjectives from nouns, as *moneyed.* **2,** forming past tenses of verbs.

E'dam (ē'dəm) *n.* a yellow cheese.

ed'dy (ed'ė) *n.* a rotary motion in a stream of liquid or gas; a small whirl or vortex. —*v.i.* whirl; spin.

e'del·weiss" (ā'dəl-vīs") *n.* a flowering herb of alpine regions.

e·de'ma (ė-dē'mə) *n.* a disease in which body liquids collect in the tissues, causing swelling; dropsy. —**e·dem'ic** (ė-dem'ik) *adj.*

E'den (ē'dən) *n.* **1,** the garden that was the first home of Adam and Eve. **2,** any delightful region or residence; a paradise.

edge (ej) *n.* **1,** the extreme border or margin of anything; verge; brink; rim. **2,** the line of junction of two faces of a solid object; the sharpened edge of a blade. **3,** sharpness; keenness; acuteness. **4,** (*Informal*) advantage. —*v.t.* **1,** put an edge or border on. **2,** sharpen. **3,** (often with *out*) defeat by a slight margin. —*v.i.* move sidewise; advance gradually. —**edg'ing,** *n.* a border. —**edg'y** (ej'ė) *adj.* irritable; nervous. —**on edge,** edgy; impatient.

edge'wise" *adv.* **1,** in the direction of the edge. **2,** barely. Also, **edge'ways".**

ed'i·ble (ed'ə-bəl) *adj.* fit to be eaten as food. —*n.* something eatable. —**ed"i·bil'·i·ty,** *n.*

e'dict (ē'dikt) *n.* a decree or proclamation issued by an authority.

ed'i·fice (ed'ə-fis) *n.* a building, esp. one that is large and imposing.

ed'i·fy" (ed'i-fī") *v.t.* build up faith, belief, or knowledge in (a person); persuade; instruct. —**ed"i·fi·ca'tion** (-fi-kā'shən) *n.*

ed'it *v.t.* **1,** prepare (a manuscript) for publication by revising, correcting, etc. **2,** supervise (a publication) by collecting and preparing materials.

e·di'tion (i-dish'ən) *n.* the whole number of copies of a work printed at one time.

---

edition, issue, copy, printing
These words have varying meanings in reference to printed material, such as books and periodicals. A *copy* is one printed unit, such as a magazine or a book. An *issue*, when referring to a periodical, usually means all the copies printed on a certain day. *Edition*—often used interchangeably with *issue*—may refer to certain portions of an issue of a periodical; or it may mean all the copies of a certain book printed at the same time. There can be several *printings* (or more properly *impressions*) of the same *edition*, if no changes are made in the text.

---

ed'i·tor (ed'i-tər) *n.* **1,** one who edits; one who corrects, compiles, etc. **2,** one who selects the contents of a publication.

ed"i·to'ri·al (ed"i-tôr'ē-əl) *n.* an article presenting the opinion of an editor. —*adj.* pert. to editing or an editor. —**ed"i·to'ri·al·ize"** (-īz") *v.i.* express an opinion, esp. in reporting news.

ed'u·cate" (ed'yə-kāt") *v.t.* **1,** impart knowledge and training to; develop mentally and morally by instruction. **2,** send to school; provide schooling for. —**ed'u·ca·ble,** *adj.*

ed"u·ca'tion (ed"yə-kā'shən) *n.* **1,** act or process of educating; instruction. **2,** the science of teaching; pedagogy. —**ed"u·ca'tion·al,** *adj.*

ed"u·ca'tion·ist *n.* a person specializing in the theory and methods of education; sometimes used disparagingly.

ed'u·ca"tor (ed'yə-kā"tər) *n.* a teacher.

e·duce' (ē-dūs') *v.t.* draw out; elicit; develop. —**e·duc'tion** (-duk'shən) *n.*

-ee (ē) *suf.* **1,** the object or recipient of, as *draftee,* one who is drafted. **2,** a person in a specified condition. **3,** a person who performs a specified action.

eel (ēl) *n.* an elongated fish without ventral fins, resembling a snake.

e'en (ēn) (*Poetic*) *n.* evening. —*adv.* even.

e'er (ār) *adv.* (*Poetic*) ever.

-eer (ir) *suf.* one whose profession, occupation, activity or residence is. Also, **-ier.**

ee'rie (ir'ē) *adj.* inspiring fear; strange; weird. —**ee'ri·ness,** *n.*

ef·face' (e-fās') *v.t.* **1,** rub out; erase; obliterate. **2,** make inconspicuous. —**ef·face'ment,** *n.*

ef·fect' (e-fekt') *n.* **1,** what is produced by a cause; something that follows as a consequence; a result. **2,** power to produce results; force; validity. **3,** the state of being operative, in force, or active. **4,** (*pl.*) property, esp. personal. —*v.t.* produce as a result; be the cause or agent of; make happen; achieve. —**take effect,** begin to operate. ❏ *affect*

ef·fec'tive (e-fek'tiv) *adj.* **1,** productive; efficient. **2,** having a desired effect; successful. —**ef·fec'tive·ness,** *n.*

---

effective, effectual, efficacious
Three words having the same meaning, i.e., able to produce a desired effect. *Effective* is the most positive, highlighting the desired end itself. *Effectual* stresses the action of producing the effect. *Efficacious* stresses the efficiency of the means to the effect.

---

ef·fec'tu·al (e-fek'choo-əl) *adj.* producing a desired effect. —**ef·fec"tu·al'i·ty,** *n.* ❏ *effective*

ef·fec'tu·ate" (e-fek'choo-āt") *v.t.* make happen; cause. —**ef·fec"tu·a'tion,** *n.*

ef·fen'di (e-fen'dē) *n.* a Turkish title of respect.

ef·fem'i·nate (e-fem'ə-nət) *adj.* having the qualities of the female sex; womanish (applied to men). —**ef·fem'i·na·cy** (-nə-sē) *n.* ❏ *effete*

ef'fer·ent (ef'ə-rənt) *adj.* carrying away or outward, as nerve impulses.

ef"fer·vesce' (ef"ər-ves') *v.i.* **1,** bubble and hiss, like a boiling liquid. **2,** exhibit excitement or liveliness. —**ef"fer·ves'cence,** *n.* —**ef"fer·ves'cent,** *adj.*

ef·fete' (ə-fēt') *adj.* worn out by age; staled by usage; exhausted.

---

effete, effeminate
☞ These words, frequently confused, are actually very different. *Effete* means worn out, exhausted, and comes from Latin *fetus,* childbirth, in reference to the exhaustion which follows giving birth. *Effeminate* refers to a man having characteristics considered appropriate for women.

---

ef"fi·ca'cious (ef"i-kā'shəs) *adj.* having

power adequate to an intended purpose; effective; effectual. —**ef'fi·ca·cy** (-kə-sē) *n.* ❑ *effective*

ef·fi'cient (i-fish´ənt) *adj.* **1,** adequate in performance or operation; capable; competent. **2,** (of a machine) giving a relatively high output of work. **3,** acting as a cause; producing an effect; causative. —**ef·fi'cien·cy,** *n.*

ef'fi·gy (ef´ə-jē) *n.* a sculptured likeness or dummy of a person.

ef"flo·resce' (ef"lō-res´) *v.i.* **1,** burst into bloom; blossom. **2,** (*Chem.*) decompose into powdery substance. —**ef"flo·res'·cence,** *n.* —**ef"flo·res'cent,** *adj.*

ef'flu·ence (ef´loo-əns) *n.* **1,** act of flowing out. **2,** an emanation. Also, **ef'flux** (ef´luks).

ef'flu·ent (-ənt) *adj.* flowing out. *n.* **1,** effluence. **2,** sewage. ❑ *affluent*

ef·flu'vi·um (i-floo´vē-əm) *n.* [*pl.* **-a** (-ə)] an unpleasant vapor or emanation from something.

ef'fort (ef´ərt) *n.* **1,** voluntary exertion to perform an action. **2,** a strenuous attempt. **3,** a work; an achievement.

ef·fron'ter·y (i-frun´tə-rē) *n.* barefaced impropriety; shamelessness; impudence.

ef·ful'gent (i-ful´jənt) *adj.* radiantly bright. —**ef·fulge',** *v.t. & i.* —**ef·ful'·gence,** *n.*

ef·fuse' (e-fūz´) *v.t.* pour out; shed. —*v.i.* seep out; exude. —*adj.* (e-fūs´) loosely spread out. —**ef·fu'sion** (i-fū´zhən) *n.* —**ef·fu'sive** (-siv) *adj.* gushing.

eft *n.* **1,** a newt. **2,** a small lizard.

---

e.g., i.e.
☛ These two commonly used abbreviations are sometimes confused. *E.g.* stands for Latin *exempli gratia,* for example, and should be followed by one or more examples of whatever preceded the abbreviation. *I.e.* stands for Latin *id est,* that is, and should be followed by an explanation or amplification of what preceded it.

---

e·gad' (i-gad´) *interj.* a mild oath.

e·gal"i·tar'i·an (i-gal"ə-târ´ē-ən) *adj.* advocating equal rights for all. —*n.* one who advocates this. —**e·gal"i·tar'i·an·ism,** *n.*

egg (eg) *n.* **1,** the reproductive cell and its envelopes, as formed in a female animal. **2,** this cell and its nourishment enclosed in a hard rounded shell, such as produced by birds. **3,** anything resembling a hen's egg. —*v.t.* (usu. with *on*) incite; urge. —**egg cream,** a cold drink made of milk, syrup, and soda water.

---

egg
↔ The noun and verb senses are unrelated. The older, verb sense comes from Old Norse *eggja,* related to *edge.* The noun also comes from Old Norse, spelled the same way.

---

egg'head" *n.* (usu. contemptuous) intellectual; highbrow.

egg'nog" (eg´nog") *n.* a drink made of beaten eggs, sugar, and milk, often with an alcoholic beverage.

egg'plant" *n.* a plant having edible egg-shaped fruit, sometimes yellow.

e'gis (ē´jis) *n.* aegis.

eg'lan·tine (eg´lən-tīn") *n.* any of several brier plants.

e'go (ē´gō) *n.* [*pl.* **-gos**] the "I"; that which feels, acts, and thinks; the self. —**ego trip,** (*Slang*) something done to build one's self-esteem.

e"go·cen'tric (ē"gō-sen´trik) *adj.* self-centered; selfish; individualistic. —*n.* an egocentric person.

e'go·ism (ē´gō-iz-əm) *n.* **1,** the doctrine that self-interest is the basis of all behavior. **2,** conceit. —**e'go·ist,** *n.*

---

egoism, egotism
☛ *Egoism* means excessive interest in all aspects of oneself as opposed to others. *Egotism* has a narrower focus, excessive interest in one's own importance, characterized by the overuse of the pronoun "I" (which, in Latin, is *ego*).

---

e"go·ma'ni·a (ē"gō-mā´nē-ə) *n.* abnormally developed egotism. —**e"go·ma'ni·ac,** *adj. & n.*

e'go·tism (ē´gə-tiz-əm) *n.* the habit of talking too much about oneself; conceit. —**e'go·tist,** *n.* —**e"go·tis'tic** (-tis´tik) *adj.* —**e"go·tis'ti·cal·ly,** *adv.* ❑ *egoism*

e·gre'gious (i-grē´jəs) *adj.* **1,** (*Archaic*) remarkable; striking. **2,** extraordinarily flagrant. —**e·gre'gious·ness,** *n.*

e'gress (ē´grəs) *n.* **1,** the act of going out; departure. **2,** a way for going out; an exit. —**e·gres'sion** (i-gresh´ən) *n.*

e'gret (ē´grət) *n.* **1,** any of various herons. **2,** a plume from an egret.

E·gyp'tian (i-jip´shən) *adj.* pert. to Egypt, its people, customs, etc. —*n.* a native of Egypt.

eh (ā, e) *interj.* what?

ei'der (ī´dər) *n.* a large sea duck, whose breast feathers are prized for stuffing pillows, etc.

ei'der·down (n.) **1,** the down of the duck.

2, a quilt made of it. 3, a soft napped fabric of cotton or wool.

ei·det′ic (ī-det′ik) *adj.* based on intuition.

ei·do′lon (ī-dō′lən) *n.* [*pl.* **-la** (-lə)] **1,** an idealized image or likeness; idol. **2,** a specter or apparition.

eight (āt) *n. & adj.* the cardinal number between seven and nine, expressed by 8. —**eighth** (ātth) *adj. & n.*

eight′ ball″ in pool, a ball numbered 8 and colored black. —**behind the eight ball,** (*Slang*) in a predicament; helpless.

> **behind the eight ball**
> ↔ From certain forms of pool when the eight ball is between the cue ball and the target ball, causing the shooter to have an awkward shot.

eight″een′ (ā″tēn′) *n. & adj.* eight plus ten, 18. —**eight″eenth′** (-tēnth′) *adj. & n.*

eight′y (ā′tē) *n. & adj.* eight times ten, 80. —**eight′i·eth** (-əth) *adj. & n.*

ein′stein″i·um (īn′stīn″ē-əm) *n.* an unstable, radioactive chemical element, no. 99, symbol E, produced artificially, named for Ger.-Amer. physicist Albert Einstein.

eis·stedd′fod (ī-ste*th*′vod) *n.* an annual Welsh music festival and competition.

ei′ther (ē′*th*ər; ī′-) *adj.* **1,** one or the other of two. **2,** each of two. —*pron.* one or the other. —*adv.* also; further, esp. in emphatic denial. —*conj.* precedes the first of two coordinate alternatives, the second being preceded by *or.* ❑ *each*

> **either, each, neither, anyone, anybody, everyone, everybody, someone, somebody, noone, nobody**
> These indefinite pronouns all take singular verbs and singular pronouns: *Either* of the alternatives *is* acceptable.

e·jac′u·late″ (i-jak′yə-lāt″) *v.t.* **1,** utter suddenly and briefly; exclaim. **2,** emit forcibly; discharge. —**e·jac″u·la′tion,** *n.*

e·ject′ (i-jekt′) *v.t.* throw out; drive away; expel; evict. —**e·jec′tion,** *n.* —**e·jec′tor,** *n.*

eke (ēk) *v.t.* (with *out*) **1,** obtain with difficulty. **2,** supplement. —*adv.* (*Archaic*) also.

e·kis′tics (ē-kis′tiks) *n.* the science of urban planning and development.

> **ekistics**
> ↔ Coined by 20th-c. Greek urbanologist Constantine A. Doxiadus on the model of New Greek *oikistikos,* settlement.

e·lab′o·rate (i-lab′ə-rət) *adj.* **1,** worked out with great care or exactness. **2,** intricate; involved. —*v.t. & i.* (-rāt″) work out with precision, in full detail; add details. —**e·lab′o·rate·ness,** *n.* —**e·lab″o·ra′tion,** *n.*

é·lan′ (ā-län′) *n.* ardor; impetuous enthusiasm; dash.

e′land (ē′lənd) *n.* a large Afr. antelope.

> **eland**
> ↔ The Dutch (through Afrikaans) word for elk, applied to the animal by the Dutch in South Africa. Its source is Lithuanian *elnis.*

e·lapse′ (i-laps′) *v.i.* (of time) pass away.

e·las′tic (i-las′tik) *adj.* **1,** tending to revert to an original shape after distortion (of a solid); tending to expand (as a gas). **2,** highly flexible. **3,** recovering original form or condition readily; buoyant. —*n.* an elastic cord or band; rubber band. —**e·las′ti·cal·ly,** *adv.* —**e″las·tic′i·ty** (ē″las-tis′ə-tē) *n.*

> **elastic, elastomer**
> ↔ From the Greek verb *elaunein,* to forge. *Elastomer* was formed in English from *elastic* and Greek *meros,* a part.

e·las′to·mer (ē-las′tə-mər) *n.* an elastic substance. ❑ *elastic*

e·late′ (i-lāt′) *v.t.* make proud or exultant; gratify. —**e·la′tion,** *n.* great joy.

el′bow (el′bō) *n.* **1,** the joint connecting the long bones of the arm. **2,** an angle or bend. —*v.t. & i.* push with the elbows; jostle. —**elbow grease,** (*Informal*) energetic labor with the hands. —**el′bow·room″,** *n.* enough space for comfort.

eld′er (el′dər) *adj.* older; senior. —*n.* **1,** a senior in age. **2,** a leader or legislator in a tribe, community, or church. **3,** a shrub or small tree, bearing a reddish fruit.

eld′er·ber″ry *n.* the small dark berry of the elder plant, used in wine, medicine, etc.

eld′er·ly (-lē) *adj.* rather old. —**eld′er·li·ness,** *n.*

eld′est (el′dəst) *adj.* oldest.

El″ Do·ra′do (el″ də-rä′dō) *n.* a fabulously rich region; a golden opportunity.

> **El Dorado**
> ↔ A legendary city in Mexico sought by the Spanish explorers for the riches supposed to be there.

e′lect′ (i-lekt′) *v.t.* **1,** select for office by vote. **2,** choose; prefer; determine in favor of. —*adj.* **1,** voted into office but not yet inducted. **2,** chosen. **3,** superior; select; choice. —*n.* a person or persons chosen or worthy to be chosen.

-e·lect *suf.* indicating a position to which one has been elected but which one has not yet occupied.

e·lec′tion (i-lek′shən) *n.* act of electing; balloting. —**e·lec″tion·eer′** (-ir′) *v.i.* solicit votes.

e·lec′tive (i-lek′tiv) *adj.* **1,** chosen by election. **2,** having the duty or power to elect. **3,** optional. —*n.* an optional academic course.

e·lec′tor (i-lek′tər) *n.* **1,** one qualified to vote. **2,** in the U.S., a member of the electoral college. —**e·lec′to·rate** (-tər-ət) *n.* body of voters.

e·lec′tor·al (i-lek″tər-əl) *adj.* pert. to election or electors. —**Electoral College,** the body of persons chosen by popular vote to elect the president and vice-president of the U.S.

E·lec′tra complex (i-lek′trə) unconscious attachment of a daughter to her father.

> **Electra complex**
> ↔ From the story in Greek mythology about the daughter of Agamemnon who incited her brother Orestes to kill her mother and her mother's lover.

e·lec′tric (i-lek′trik) *adj.* **1,** of or pert. to electricity. **2,** operated by the power of electricity. **3,** startling; exciting. Also, **e·lec′tri·cal** (-tri-kəl). —**electrical storm,** a lightning storm. —**electric chair,** a chairlike device used for electrocution. —**electric eye,** a photoelectric cell.

e·lec″tri′cian (i-lek″trish′ən) *n.* a craftsman skilled in making, repairing or operating electric equipment.

e·lec″tric′i·ty (i-lek″tris′ə-tē) *n.* **1,** a force, manifest in magnetism, lightning, etc., utilized by man for power, light, etc. **2,** a flow of electric current.

e·lec′tri·fy″ (i-lek′tri-fī″) *v.t.* **1,** charge with electricity. **2,** equip for operation by electricity. **3,** startle greatly; thrill. —**e·lec″-tri·fi·ca′tion** (-fi-kā′shən) *n.*

e·lec·tro- (i-lek-trō) *pref.* pert. to or employing electricity.

e·lec′tro·cute″ (i-lek′trə-kūt″) *v.t.* kill by electric shock. —**e·lec″tro·cu′tion,** *n.* —**e·lec″tro·cu′tion·ist,** *n.*

e·lec′trode (i-lek′trōd) *n.* a conductor of electricity, esp. the terminal of such a conductor.

e·lec″tro·lier′ (i-lek″trə-lir′) *n.* a support

for electric lights, esp. one like a chandelier.

e·lec·trol′o·gist (i-lek-trol′ə-jist) *n.* one who removes warts, hair, etc. using electricity.

e·lec″trol′y·sis (i-lek″trol′ə-sis) *n.* the decomposition of a chemical compound by an electric current. —**e·lec″tro·lyt′ic** (-lit′ik) *adj.*

e·lec′tro·lyte″ (i-lek′trə-līt″) *n.* a liquid or solid that conducts electricity by flow of ions.

e·lec″tro·mag′net *n.* an iron core, magnetized by an electric current passing through a wire coiled around it. —**e·lec″-tro·mag·net′ic,** *adj.* —**e·lec″tro·mag·net′ic-al·ly,** *adv.* —**e·lec″tro·mag′net·ism,** *n.*

e·lec″tro·mo′tive (i-lek″trə-mō′tiv) *adj.* pert. to, or producing, electric current.

e·lec′tron (i-lek′tron) *n.* one of the fundamental particles of matter, believed to be the unit of negative electricity. —**electron gun,** a cathode-ray tube.

e·lec″tron′ic (-ik) *adj.* **1,** pert. to electronics. **2,** pert. to electrons. **3,** using electronics or electronic means (as to produce sound). —**e·lec″tron′i·cal·ly,** *adv.* —**electronic book,** a literary, reference, etc. work published in a computer-readable medium and read from the computer screen. —**electronic mail,** communication by message transmitted and stored electronically. —**electronic music,** music produced by a synthesizer, or by altering natural sounds electronically (*musique concrète*).

e·lec″tron′ics *n.* the science dealing with the action of electrons.

e·lec′tro·plate″ (i-lek′trə-plāt″) *v.t.* coat with metal by electrolysis.

e·lec′tro·shock″ *n.* a treatment for certain mental disorders using electric current. Also, **electroshock therapy, shock treatment.**

e·lec″tro·stat′ic (-stat′ik) *adj.* producing or containing static electricity. —**e·lec″-tro·stat′ics,** *n.sing.* the study of static electricity.

e·lec′tro·type″ (i-lek′trə-tīp″) *n.* a printing plate made by an electrolytic process; the print made from such a plate. —*v.t.* make an electrotype of.

el″ee·mos′y·nar·y (el″ə-mos′ə-ner-ē) *adj.* charitable.

el′e·gant (el′i-gənt) *adj.* having or exhibiting good taste; luxurious. —**el′e·gance,** *n.*

el″e·gi′ac (el″i-jī′-ək) *adj.* expressing sorrow.

el′e·gy (el′ə-jē) *n.* a mournful poem or

song, esp. in lament for the dead. —**el′e·gist,** *n.* —**el′e·gize″** (-jīz″) *v.t. & i.*

> **elegy, eulogy**
> ☛ Though both are generally associated with death, these two words are unrelated. *Elegy* comes from Greek *elegos*, song, lament. *Eulogy*, poem of praise, comes from Greek *eulogia*, blessing.

el′e·ment (el′i-mənt) *n.* **1,** that of which anything is in part composed; component; constituent. **2,** (*Chem.*) one of the substances of which all matter is composed, believed to be formed by particles or forces common to all. **3,** (*pl.*) rudimentary principles of an art or science. **4,** that in which something exists; proper or natural environment. **5,** (*pl.*) atmospheric forces. **6,** (*pl.*) the bread and wine used in the Eucharist. —**el″e·men′tal,** *adj.* basic; primal.

> **elemental, elementary**
> ☛ Do not confuse *elemental*, primal, pertaining to the elements, with *elementary*, simple, pertaining to basic facts.

el″e·men′ta·ry (-ə-rė) *adj.* simple; pert. to elements or first principles. —**elementary school,** kindergarten or first grade through seventh or eighth grades. ❑ *elemental*

el′e·phant (el′ə-fənt) *n.* a large mammal of Afr. and India having a long prehensile proboscis or trunk and long ivory tusks. —**el″e·phan′tine** (-fan′tin) *adj.* huge. —**white elephant,** a burdensome or embarrassing possession.

> **elephant**
> ↔ From Greek *elephas*, ivory; the term had already in ancient times also been applied to the animal itself.

el″e·phan·ti·a′sis (el″ə-fən-tī′ə-sis) *n.* a disease causing enlargement of bodily parts.

el′e·vate″ (el′i-vāt″) *v.t.* **1,** raise to a higher level or station; lift up. **2,** cheer.

el″e·va′tion (el″i-vā′shən) *n.* **1,** act of elevating. **2,** a high place; eminence. **3,** a drawing or plan of a vertical surface of a structure. **4,** altitude above the ground.

el′e·va″tor (el′i-vā″tər) *n.* **1,** a platform or small room capable of being raised or lowered to carry passengers or freight. **2,** a building for storage of grain, etc. **3,** a horizontal hinged flap on an airplane. —**elevator music,** (*Slang*) bland music; background music. —**elevator shoe** or **heel,** a very high heel, used to make one appear taller.

CHEMICAL ELEMENTS

actinium	mendelevium
aluminum	mercury
americium	molybdenum
antimony	neodymium
argon	neon
arsenic	neptunium
astatine	nickel
barium	niobium
berkelium	nitrogen
beryllium	nielsbohrium
bismuth	nobelium
boron	osmium
bromine	oxygen
cadmium	palladium
calcium	phosphorus
californium	platinum
carbon	plutonium
cerium	polonium
cesium	potassium
chlorine	praseodymium
chromium	promethium
cobalt	protactinium
copper	radium
curium	radon
dysprosium	rhenium
einsteinium	rhodium
erbium	rubidium
europium	ruthenium
fermium	rutherfordium
fluorine	samarium
francium	scandium
gadolinium	selenium
gallium	silicon
germanium	silver
gold	sodium
hafnium	strontium
hahnium	sulfur
hassium	tantalum
helium	technetium
holmium	tellurium
hydrogen	terbium
indium	thallium
iodine	thorium
iridium	thulium
iron	tin
krypton	titanium
lanthanum	tungsten
lawrencium	uranium
lead	vanadium
lithium	xenon
lutetium	ytterbium
magnesium	yttrium
manganese	zinc
meitnerium	zirconium

e·lev′en (i-lev′ən) *n. & adj.* the cardinal number between ten and twelve, expressed by 11. —**e·lev′enth** (-ənth) *adj. & n.* —**eleventh hour,** the last moment.

eleven
↔ Old English *ellefne*, from Indo-European roots meaning one left, i.e., after counting 10.

elf *n.* [*pl.* **elves** (elvz)] an imaginary tiny being of mischievous character; sprite; fairy. —**elf′in**, *adj.*

el′hi″ (el′hī″) *adj.* for use in grades 1 thru 12: el(ementary and) hi(gh school).

e·lic′it (i-lis′it) *v.t.* draw out; bring forth; evoke. —**e·lic″i·ta′tion**, *n.* ☐ *illicit*

e·lide′ (i-līd′) *v.t.* omit or slur over, as in speech.

el′i·gi′ble (el′i-jə-bəl) *adj.* **1,** fit to be chosen; worthy or deserving of choice. **2,** available and desirable as a husband. **3,** legally qualified. —**el″i·gi·bil′i·ty**, *n.*

e·lim′i·nate″ (i-lim′i-nāt″) *v.t.* **1,** get rid of; remove. **2,** omit; ignore. **3,** expel; secrete. **4,** kill. —**e·lim″i·na′tion**, *n.*

e·li′sion (i-lizh′ən) *n.* act or result of eliding; omission.

e·lite′ (ā-lēt′) *n.* a superior or choice part, esp. of a human society. —*adj.* select; elite. —**e·lit′ist**, *adj.* —**e·lit′ism**, *n.*

e·lix′ir (i-lik′sər) *n.* **1,** a supposed substance sought by alchemists to transmute baser metals into gold and to prolong life. **2,** a palatable medicine; any invigorating drink.

elixir
↔ From Greek *xēros*, dry, through Arabic *aliksīr* (the prefix *al* means the). It referred originally to a dry powder for treating wounds, and was later applied to a substance which would change base metal into gold and confer immortality.

elk *n.* **1,** a large deer. **2,** the wapiti.

ell (el) *n.* **1,** an addition to a building at right angles to the main part. **2,** a measure of length, 45 inches.

el·lipse′ (i-lips′) *n.* the curve traced by a moving point, the sum of whose distances from two fixed points (the *foci*) remains constant; a closed curve, somewhat oval-shaped. —**el·lip′ti·cal** (i-lip′ti-kəl) *adj.*

el·lip′sis (i-lip′sis) *n.* [*pl.* **-ses** (-sēz)] the omission of words in a text, sometimes indicated by (. . .).

el·lip′soid (i-lip′soid) *n.* (*Geom.*) a solid figure, all plane sections of which are ellipses or circles. —**el·lip·soi′dal** (-əl) *adj.*

elm *n.* a tree with wide-spreading branches; its wood.

el″o·cu′tion (el″ə-kū′shən) *n.* the study and practice of effective public speaking. —**el″o·cu′tion·ar·y**, *adj.* —**el″o·cu′tion·ist**, *n.*

e·lon′gate (i-lâng′gāt) *v.t.* make longer; extend. —*v.i.* become long or longer. —**e″lon·ga′tion** (ē″long-gā′shən) *n.*

e·lope′ (i-lōp′) *v.i.* **1,** run away with a lover. **2,** break loose from ties; escape. —**e·lope′ment**, *n.*

el′o·quent (el′ə-kwənt) *adj.* **1,** having the power to speak vividly and appropriately. **2,** stirring; persuasive. —**el′o·quence**, *n.*

else (els) *adv.* otherwise; differently; instead. —*adj.* besides; in addition.

else′where″ (els′hwâr″) *adv.* in or to another place.

e·lu′ci·date″ (i-loo′si-dāt″) *v.t.* make clear; explain. —**e·lu″ci·da′tion**, *n.*

e·lude′ (i-lood′) *v.t.* avoid or escape by stratagem or deceit; evade.

e·lu′sion (i-loo′zhən) *n.* act of eluding; evasion.

e·lu′sive (i-loo′siv) *adj.* hard to grasp or catch; slippery. Also, **e·lu′so·ry** (i-loo′sə-rē). —**e·lu′sive·ness**, *n.*

elves (elvz) *n.* pl. of *elf.*

E·ly′si·um (i-liz′ē-əm) *n.* **1,** in Gk. myth., the abode of the blessed after death. **2,** any place of exquisite happiness. —**E·ly′sian** (i-li′zhən) *adj.*

em *n.*(*Print.*) a square space in type: usually the pica, 12 points.

em- (em *or* im) *pref.* same as *en-.*

e·ma′ci·ate″ (i-mā′shē-āt″) *v.t.* make lean by gradual wasting away of flesh. —**e·ma″ci·a′tion**, *n.*

E-′mail″ (ē′-) *n.* electronic mail.

em′a·nate″ (em′ə-nāt″) *v.i.* flow out or issue; proceed from a source.

em″a·na′tion (em″ə-nā′shən) *n.* **1,** act or result of emanating. **2,** (*Chem.*) a gas given off by a radioactive substance.

e·man′ci·pate″ (i-man′si-pāt″) *v.t.* set free from a restraint; liberate. —**e·man″ci·pa′tion**, *n.* —**e·man′ci·pa″tor**, *n.*

e·mas′cu·late″ (i-mas′kyə-lāt″) *v.t.* **1,** castrate. **2,** deprive of manhood, strength, or vigor. —**e·mas″cu·la′tion**, *n.*

em·balm′ (em-bäm′) *v.t.* treat (a dead body) with balm, drugs, etc., to preserve it. —**em·balm′ment**, *n.*

em·bank′ *v.t.* enclose or confine with a ridge, as of earth. —**em·bank′ment**, *n.* a protecting bank or wall.

em·bar′go (em-bär′gō) *n.* a restraint, hindrance or prohibition, esp. of commerce or shipping by government order.

> **embargo, embarrass**
> ↔ Both words derive from a supposed Vulgar Latin verb *imbarricare*, place behind bars.

em·bark' (em-bärk') *v.i.* **1,** go aboard a ship. **2,** set out; make a start. —**em"bar·ka'tion,** *n.*

em·bar·ras' de ri·chesses' (äṅ-bä-rä' də rė-shes') (*Fr.*) an embarrassment of wealth; overabundance.

em·bar'rass (em-bar'əs) *v.t.* **1,** make self-conscious or ashamed; disconcert. **2,** perplex; hamper; impede. **3,** involve in financial difficulties. —**em·bar'rass·ment,** *n.* ❑ *embargo*

em'bas·sy (em'bə-sė) *v.t.* **1,** an ambassador and his or her staff. **2,** the headquarters of this body.

em·bat'tled (em-bat'əld) *adj.* prepared for or involved in battle.

em·bed' *v.t.* [**-bed'ded, -ding**] place in a bed; fix firmly in a surrounding substance. Also, **im·bed'.**

em·bel'lish (em-bel'ish) *v.i.* **1,** beautify with ornamentation; adorn. **2,** add fictitious detail to (a tale). —**em·bel'lish·ment,** *n.*

em'ber (em'bər) *n.* a smoldering coal; (*pl.*) dying remains. —**Ember Days,** an annual period of three days of fasting and prayer, observed in certain Catholic and Protestant churches.

em·bez'zle (em-bez'əl) *v.t.* take (property in trust) for one's own use. —**em·bez'zle·ment,** *n.*

em·bit'ter (em-bit'ər) *v.t.* make resentful. —**em·bit'ter·ment,** *n.*

em·bla'zon (em-blä'zən) *v.t.* **1,** depict on a heraldic shield. **2,** decorate; illuminate. **3,** celebrate; proclaim. —**em·bla'zon·ment,** *n.* —**em·bla'zon·ry** (-rė) *n.* heraldic decoration.

em'blem (em'bləm) *n.* an object or a design symbolizing an idea, quality, or the like; a flag; a badge. —**em"blem·at'ic** (-mat'ik) *adj.* —**em"blem·at'i·cal·ly,** *adv.*

em·bod'y (em-bod'ė) *v.t.* **1,** invest with a body; make concrete; express in concrete form. **2,** collect into a body; organize. **3,** comprise; include. —**em·bod'i·ment,** *n.*

em·bold'en em-bōl'dən) *v.t.* make bold; encourage.

em'bo·lism (em'bə-liz-əm) *n.* obstruction by a blood clot.

em·bon·point' (äṅ-boṅ-pwaṅ') *n.* (*Fr.*) plumpness; stoutness.

em·boss' (em-bâs') *v.t.* represent in raised designs or relief. —**em·boss'ment,** *n.*

em"bou·chure' (äm"bû-shûr') *n.* **1,** the mouth of a river or valley. **2,** the mouthpiece of a musical instrument; also, the adjustment of the lips in playing a wind instrument.

em·brace' (em-brās') *v.t.* **1,** clasp in the arms; hug. **2,** enclose; contain; include. **3,** take or receive willingly; adopt. —*n.* a hug; grasp.

em·bra'sure (em-brā'zhər) *n.* a flared opening for a window or door, having a larger aperture on one side of the wall than on the other.

em'bro·cate" (em'brō-kāt") *v.t.* moisten and rub (a bruised or injured part) with a liniment. —**em"bro·ca'tion,** *n.*

em·broi'der (em-broi'dər) *v.t.* **1,** decorate with ornamental needlework. **2,** embellish; elaborate. —**em·broi'der·y,** *n.*

em·broil' *v.t.* involve in contention or strife. —**em·broil'ment,** *n.*

em'bry·o" (em'brė-ō") *n.* **1,** an organism in its earliest stages of development after fertilization of the germ cell. **2,** the rudimentary or formative stage of anything. —*adj.* undeveloped. —**em"bry·on'ic** (-on'ik) *adj.* undeveloped; rudimentary. —**em"bry·on'i·cal·ly,** *adv.*

em"bry·ol'o·gy (em"brė-ol'ə-jė) *n.* the science of the origin and development of the embryo. —**em"bry·ol'o·gist** (-jist) *n.*

em'cee (em'sē) *n.* master of ceremonies. —*v.i. & t.* (*Informal*) act as master of ceremonies (for).

e·mend' (ė-mend') *v.t.* remove faults or errors from; revise; correct. Also, **e'men·date"** (ē'men-dāt"), **e"men·da'tion,** *n.* ❑ *amend*

em'er·ald (em'ər-əld) *n. & adj.* **1,** a variety of beryl, prized as a gem. **2,** of its color, green. —**Emerald Isle,** Ireland.

> **emerald**
> ↔ From Semitic *baraq*, to shine, through Greek *smaragdos*, green gem.

e·merge' (i-mėrj') *v.i.* rise out, as from water; come forth from something that conceals; become apparent. —**e·mer'gence** (-jəns) *n.* —**e·mer'gent,** *adj.*

e·mer'gen·cy (i-mėr'jən-sė) *n.* a sudden and urgent occasion for action; pressing necessity.

e·mer'i·tus (i-mer'i-təs) *adj. masc.,* **e·mer'i·ta** (-tə) *adj. fem.* (*Lat.*) retired from active duty but retaining honorary title.

e·mer′sion (i-mēr′shən) *n.* the act of emerging.

em′er·y (em′ə-rė) *n.* a mixture of pulverized minerals used as an abrasive.

e·met′ic (i-met′ik) *n.* a medicine to induce vomiting.

em′i·grant (em′i-grənt) *n.* one who emigrates. —*adj.* emigrating.

> **emigrant, immigrant**
> ☞ Both terms refer to people who move from one country to another and differ in point of view. An *emigrant* is one who *leaves* a country; an *immigrant* is one who *enters* a country.

em′i·grate″ (em′i-grāt″) *v.i.* leave a country or region to settle elsewhere. —**em″i·gra′tion,** *n.*

é′mi·gré″ (em′i-grā″) *n.* (*Fr.*) emigrant, esp. one leaving for political reasons.

em′i·nence (em′i-nəns) *n.* **1,** high repute. **2,** a hill. **3,** (*cap.*) title of honor of a cardinal.

em′i·nent (em′i-nənt) *adj.* **1,** high in rank, office, worth, etc. **2,** conspicuous; noteworthy. —**eminent domain,** the right of a government to buy property for public use.

> **eminent, imminent, immanent**
> ☞ These words are probably more often confused in pronunciation than in meaning. *Eminent* (em′-) means noteworthy, high-ranking. *Imminent* and *immanent* (im′-) mean, respectively, impending and intrinsic.

e·mir′ *n.* a Muslim prince.

> **emir, admiral**
> ↔ From Arabic *amir,* commander. This word is also the source of English *admiral.*

em′is·sar·y (em′i-ser-ė) *n.* a person sent out on a mission; an agent.

e·mis′sion (i-mish′ən) *n.* **1,** the act of emitting or issuing. **2,** something issued; emanation.

e·mit′ (i-mit′) *v.t.* [**-mit′ted, -ting**] **1,** send forth; give out; utter. **2,** issue.

e·mol′lient (i-mol′yənt) *n.* a substance that softens or soothes.

e·mol′u·ment (i-mol′ū-mənt) *n.* salary or fees for services; gain.

e·mote′ (ė-mōt′) *v.i.* (*Informal*) to express emotion. —**e·mot′ive,** *adj.*

e·mo′tion (i-mō′shən) *n.* **1,** a state of mind in which feeling, sentiment, or atti-tude is predominant (over cognition and volition). **2,** a specific feeling, as love, joy, etc.

e·mo′tion·al (-əl) *adj.* **1,** pert. to or affecting the emotions. **2,** easily stirred. —**e·mo′tion·al·ism,** *n.*

em·pa·na′da (em-pə-nä′də) *n.* (*Sp.*) a stuffed pastry turnover.

em′pa·thize″ (-thīz″) *v.i.* (with *with*) show empathy for.

em′pa·thy (em′pə-thė) *n.* **1,** sympathetic understanding of another person. **2,** projection of one's emotions on an object. —**em·path′ic** (em-path′ik), **em·pa·thet′ic** (-thet′ik) *adj.*

> **empathy, sympathy**
> ☞ Both words involve the sharing of another person's feelings. However, *empathy* is more restricted in its use, referring to the ability to imagine oneself in another's situation.

em″pen·nage′ (äṅ″pə-näzh′) *n.* (*Fr.*) the rear part of an airplane or airship.

em′per·or (em′pər-ər) *n.* the male ruler of an empire.

em′pha·sis (em′fə-sis) *n.* [*pl.* **-ses″** (-sēz″)] stress laid upon anything; vigor or force in expression. —**em·phat′ic** (em-fat′ik) *adj.* —**em·phat′i·cal·ly,** *adv.*

em′pha·size″ (em′fə-sīz″) *v.t.* place emphasis on; stress.

em″phy·se′ma (em″fi-sė′mə) *n.* abnormal distention produced by gas or air in any part of the body, esp. the lungs.

em′pire (em′pīr) *n.* **1,** a group of countries or peoples with a single government or emperor. **2,** supreme power. **3,** area of influence; domain.

em·pir′ic (em-pir′ik) *n.* **1,** one who follows an empirical method. **2,** a quack or charlatan. —**em·pir′i·cism** (-i-siz-əm) *n.*

em·pir′i·cal (em-pir′ə-kəl) *adj.* **1,** derived from experience. **2,** derived from observation without reliance on theory.

em·place′ment (im-plās′mənt) *n.* **1,** a gun or battery. **2,** a putting into place.

em·ploy′ (em-ploi′) *v.t.* **1,** use. **2,** give occupation to. —**em·ploy′ee′** (-ē″) *n.* —**em·ploy′er,** *n.* —**em·ploy′ment,** *n.*

em·po′ri·um (em-pôr′ė-əm) *n.* a shop that sells a variety of articles; department store.

em·pow′er (em-pow′ər) *v.t.* **1,** authorize; commission; license. **2,** to give greater rights to a certain group, esp. a minority group. —**em·pow′er·ment,** *n.*

em′press (em′pris) *n.* **1,** the woman ruler of an empire. **2,** the wife of an emperor.

emp′ty (emp′tė) *adj.* **1,** containing nothing. **2,** lacking in effect, value, etc.; meaningless. **3,** (*Informal*) hungry. —*v.t.* remove the contents of. —*v.i.* unload; discharge; become empty. —*n.* (*Informal*) an empty container or vehicle. —**emp′ti·ness,** *n.* —**empty nester,** (*Informal*) a person whose children have grown up and left home.

em″py·re′an (em″pǝ-rē′ǝn) *n.* the highest heaven, once supposed to be pure fire. —*adj.* celestial. —**em″py·re′al,** *adj.*

e′mu (ē′mū) *n.* a large flightless Australian bird.

em′u·late″ (em′yǝ-lāt″) *v.t.* strive to equal or excel; vie with. —**em″u·la′tion,** *n.* —**em′u·lous,** *adj.*

e·mul′si·fy″ (i-mul′si-fī″) *v.t.* make into an emulsion. —**e·mul″si·fi·ca′tion,** *n.*

e·mul′sion (i-mul′shǝn) *n.* a mixture of liquids, minute globules of one being suspended in a second that does not dissolve the first.

en *n.* (*Print.*) one-half em.

en- (en *or* in) *pref.* **1,** in; into. **2,** used to indicate a transitive verb.

-en (ǝn) *suf.* forming: **1,** verbs from nouns and adjectives, as *lengthen.* **2,** diminutive nouns, as *maiden.* **3,** adjectives meaning made of, as *golden.*

en·a′ble (en-ā′bǝl) *v.t.* make able; furnish with power, ability, or means; facilitate.

en·act′ (en-akt′) *v.t.* **1,** make into a law; decree; accomplish. **2,** act the part of (in a play). —**en·act′ment,** *n.*

e·nam′el (i-nam′ǝl) *n.* **1,** a glassy substance applied to pottery, metalware, etc. **2,** a paint that dries in a hard, glossy surface. **3,** the outermost and hardest part of a tooth. —*v.t.* apply enamel to; coat. —**e·nam′el·ware″,** *n.*

en·am′or (in-am′ǝr) *v.t.* (usu. used in passive with *of* or *with*) inflame with love; charm; captivate. Also, **en·am′our.**

en·camp′ (en-kamp′) *v.i.* form or lodge in a camp.

en·camp′ment (-mǝnt) *n.* **1,** the act of camping. **2,** a camp.

en·cap′su·late″ (in-kap′sǝ-lāt″) *v.t.* encase in a capsule. —**en·cap″su·la′tion,** *n.*

en·case′ (en-kās′) *v.t.* enclose in or as in a case. —**en·case′ment,** *n.*

-ence (ǝns) *suf.* forming nouns denoting act, state or quality. Also, **-en·cy** (ǝn-sė).

en·ceinte′ (än-sant′) *adj.* pregnant. —*n.* **1,** fortifications of a castle or town. **2,** the close of a cathedral.

en·ceph″a·li′tis (en-sef″ǝ-lī′tis) *n.* inflammation of the brain.

en·chant′ (en-chänt′) *v.t.* **1,** put a magical spell upon. **2,** delight to a high degree; charm; fascinate. —**en·chant′ment,** *n.* —**en·chant′er, en·chant′ress** (-rǝs) *n.*

en·chase′ (en-chās′) *v.t.* **1,** incrust with gems, etc.; inlay; ornament. **2,** chase, as metalwork; engrave; emboss.

en″chi·la′da (en″chi-lä′dä) *n.* (*Sp.*) a rolled-up tortilla, usu. filled with seasoned meat. —**whole enchilada,** (*Slang*) all of something, esp. something impressive.

en·ci′pher (in-sī′fǝr) *v.t.* convert (a message) into cipher; encode.

en·cir′cle (en-sēr′kǝl) *v.t.* **1,** form a circle around; enclose. **2,** move around; make a circle of. —**en·cir′cle·ment,** *n.*

en′clave (en′klāv) *n.* a country wholly surrounded by a foreign country.

en·close′ (en-klōz′) *v.t.* **1,** surround; shut in; confine. **2,** insert in the same envelope. Also, **in·close′.**

en·clo′sure (en-klō′zhǝr) *n.* **1,** act of enclosing. **2,** something enclosed. **3,** that which encloses, as a fence. Also, **in·clo′sure.**

en·code′ (in-cōd′) *v.t.* convert a message, etc., into code or some other language of communication.

en·co′mi·um (en-kō′mė-ǝm) *n.* extravagant praise. —**en·co′mi·ast″,** *n.* —**en·co″mi·as′tic,** *adj.*

en·com′pass (en-kum′pǝs) *v.t.* **1,** surround; encircle. **2,** contain. —**en·com′pass·ment,** *n.*

en′core (än′kôr) *n.* a repeated performance, or additional act. —*v.t.* call for an encore of or by.

> **encore**
> ↔ French for still, probably from the Latin phrase *hinc ad horam,* from then until this hour.

en·coun′ter (en-kown′tǝr) *v.t. & i.* **1,** meet, esp. by chance. **2,** meet in strife or contention. —*n.* a meeting or conflict. —**encounter group,** a group of persons meeting for various kinds of social interaction, usu. for purposes of therapy or self-analysis.

en·cour′age (en-kēr′ij) *v.t.* **1,** inspire with courage or confidence; lead on; incite. **2,** support. —**en·cour′ag·ing,** *adj.* promoting optimism. —**en·cour′age·ment,** *n.*

en·croach′ (en-krōch′) *v.i.* enter upon the domain of another; trespass; make inroads. —**en·croach′ment,** *n.*

en·cryp′tion (en-krip′shǝn) *n.* the process of encoding (a computer file, etc.) for security. —**en·crypt′**, *v.t.*

en·cum′ber (en-kum′bər) *v.t.* hinder, as with a load; burden with obligations or difficulties. —**en·cum′ber·ment,** *n.*

en·cum′brance (en-kum′brəns) *n.* **1,** a burden or hindrance. **2,** a legal obligation. **3,** a dependant, esp. a child.

en·cyc′li·cal (en-sik′li-kəl) *n.* a general letter from the Pope.

en·cy″clo·pe′di·a (en-sī″klə-pē′dė-ə) *n.* a work treating of various branches of knowledge, or various topics. —**en·cy″clo·pe′dic,** *adj.* wide in scope; comprehensive. —**en·cy″clo·pe″di·cal·ly,** *adv.* —**en·cy″clo·pe′dist,** *n.* a writer of encyclopedias. ❑ *dictionary*

> **encyclopedia**
> ↔ From the Greek phrase *enkuklios paideia,* general education. The application to reference works came in the 17th c.

end *n.* **1,** one of the terminal points or parts of something that is longer than it is wide. **2,** an outermost boundary. **3,** the terminal moment in time; finish; cessation; the concluding part. **4,** death; extinction. **5,** purpose; aim. **6,** outcome; result. **7,** the position of a player in football and other games. —*v.i.* **1,** come to an end; cease; finish. **2,** result. —**end run,** an evasion. —**end up,** reach a goal. —**end user,** the purchaser and user of a product, esp. computer software.

en·dan′ger (en-dān′jər) *v.t.* put into danger; expose to loss or injury. —**en·dan′ger·ment,** *n.* —**en·dan′gered species,** a species at risk of extinction, esp. as a result of the acts of man.

en·dear′ (en-dir′) *v.t.* make dear or beloved. —**en·dear′ment,** *n.*

en·deav′or (en-dev′ər) *v.i.* exert oneself to do something; strive. —*n.* effort. Also, **en·deav′our.**

en·dem′ic (en-dem′ik) *adj.* peculiar to a locality or a people (esp. of disease). —**en·dem′i·cal·ly,** *adv.*

> **endemic, epidemic, pandemic**
> ↔ These three words all contain the suffix *-demic,* from Greek *demos,* people. *Endemic* means indigenous to a region or people. *Pandemic* is broader, usually referring to an entire country or continent, or to the world. *Epidemic,* as an adjective, means affecting a large number of people.

end′game″ *n.* (*Chess*) the final stages of

a chess game; a similar stage of any competition.

end′ing *n.* **1,** act of coming or bringing to a close; termination. **2,** the final stage or part.

en·dive′ (en′dīv) *n.* a plant whose leaves are used in salad.

end′less (-ləs) *adj.* **1,** extending without end in space or time; infinite. **2,** having the ends joined to form a ring. **3,** innumerable. —**end′less·ness,** *n.*

end′most″ (end′mōst″) *adj.* at the very end; most remote.

en·do- (en-dō) *pref.* within.

en′do·crine″ (-krin″) *adj.* secreting internally. —**endocrine glands,** various ductless glands that directly affect certain organs of the body.

en·dog′e·nous (en-doj′ə-nəs) *adj.* derived from within.

en·dorse′ (en-dôrs′) *v.t.* **1,** approve; ratify; sustain. **2,** write one's name or initials upon, as a mark of approval, payment received, obligation, etc. Also, **in·dorse′.** —**en·dorse′ment,** *n.*

en·dow′ *v.t.* **1,** provide with a permanent source of income. **2,** bestow upon; give; furnish or equip. —**en·dow′ment,** *n.*

end′pa″per *n.* the heavy paper pasted inside the front and back covers of a book.

en·due′ (en-dū′) *v.t.* endow with some quality, ability, etc.

en·dure′ (en-dyûr′) *v.t.* **1,** undergo; sustain. **2,** sustain without impairment or yielding. **3,** bear with patience; put up with. —*v.i.* continue to exist. —**en·dur′ance,** *n.*

en·du′ro (en-dyû′rō) *n.* a long race, esp. for automobiles or motorcycles; a test of endurance.

end′ways″ (-wāz″) *adv.* **1,** with the end upward or forward. **2,** toward the ends; lengthwise. **3,** on end; end to end. Also, **end′wise″** (-wīz″).

en′e·ma (en′ə-mə) *n.* an injection of a liquid into the rectum.

en′e·my (en′ə-mė) *n.* **1,** one who opposes or seeks to inflict injury on another. **2,** an opposing military force; a hostile foreign country, or a national of such a country. **3,** anything injurious or antagonistic.

en″er·get′ic (en″ər-jet′ik) *adj.* manifesting energy; vigorous in action; powerful in force or effect. —**en″er·get′i·cal·ly,** *adv.*

en′er·gy (en′ər-jė) *n.* **1,** vigor in the exertion of power; strength in action; forcefulness of expression. **2,** action; activity; operation. **3,** (*Physics*) capacity to do work. —**en′er·gize″** (-jīz″) *v.t.* —**energy**

audit, an analysis of the energy consumption, as of a business or home.

en·er·vate″ (en′ər-vāt″) *v.t.* deprive of nerve or strength; weaken. —**en″er·va′-tion,** *n.*

> **enervate, invigorate, innervate**
> ☞ Be certain to use *enervate* to mean weaken rather than strengthen. The *e-* prefix means to remove. Some antonyms, meaning to infuse with energy, would be *innervate* or *invigorate.*

en″ fa·mille′ (än″ fä-mē′yə) (*Fr.*) at home; informally.

en·fant′ ter·ri′ble (än-fän′ te-rē′blə) *n.* (*Fr.*) **1,** prodigy. **2,** an unmanageable child; hence, an outspoken or unconventional person.

en″fi·lade′ (en″fə-lād′) *n.* a position allowing fire down the length of a line of enemy troops, trenches, etc. —*v.t.* attack in this manner.

en·force′ (en-fôrs′) *v.t.* **1,** put or keep in force; compel obedience to. **2,** impose by force. —**en·force′a·ble,** *adj.* —**en·force′-ment,** *n.*

en·fran′chise (en-frán′chīz) *v.t.* **1,** grant a franchise to. **2,** give the right to vote. —**en·fran′chise·ment,** *n.*

en·gage′ (en-gāj′) *v.t.* **1,** obtain the services or use of; employ; hire. **2,** betroth. **3,** bind by pledge or promise. **4,** gain the attention of; attract. **5,** meet in conflict with. **6,** interlock. —**en·gag′ing,** *adj.* attractive; pleasing.

en″ga·gé′ (än″gä-zhā′) *adj.* committed to a cause.

en·gage′ment (-mənt) *n.* **1,** act or effect of engaging; state of being engaged. **2,** betrothal.

en garde′ (än gärd′) on guard!; watch out!

en·gen′der (en-jen′dər) *v.t.* give rise to; bring forth; cause; excite.

en′gine (en′jən) *n.* **1,** any machine that converts energy into work. **2,** any mechanical contrivance. **3,** a railroad locomotive.

en″gi·neer′ (en″jə-nir′) *n.* **1,** one who operates an engine. **2,** one versed in the principles and practice of any department of engineering. —*v.t.* **1,** plan or direct, as an engineer. **2,** contrive.

en″gi·neer′ing *n.* **1,** the work or profession of an engineer. **2,** the science of making practical application of scientific knowledge. **3,** skillful management or contrivance.

en·gird′ (en-gērd′) *v.t.* surround; encircle; encompass. Also, **en·gir′dle.**

En′glish (ing′glish) *adj.* pert. to England, its people, customs, etc. —*n.* **1,** the English language. **2,** a spin given to a ball (in tennis, billiards, etc.) to cause it to curve. —**Basic English,** a select vocabulary of English words (orig. 750) intended as a teaching aid and an international language. —**English horn,** the alto instrument of the oboe family.

> **English**
> ↔ From Old English *Englisc,* from *Angle.* The English are named from the Angles, a people from the Jutland peninsula, who came to the British Isles in the 5th c.

en·grave′ (en-grāv′) *v.t.* **1,** cut in; produce by incision of a surface, as wood, metal, stone; carve in sunken patterns. **2,** produce by etching with acid, as in photoengraving. **3,** impress deeply.

en·grav′ing (en-grā′ving) *n.* **1,** the art of making designs by cutting or etching plates. **2,** an engraved plate. **3,** a print or impression from such a plate.

en·gross′ (en-grōs′) *v.t.* **1,** occupy wholly (as the attention of a person). **2,** write out in a document, in a special style of handwriting. **3,** monopolize the supply of. —**en·gross′ment,** *n.*

en·gulf′ *v.t.* swallow; submerge.

en·hance′ (en-háns′) *v.t.* raise to a higher degree; intensify; make more important or effective; improve the quality or clarity of. —**en·hance′ment,** *n.*

en″har·mon′ic (en″-) *adj.* (*Music*) of two notes, having the same pitch but written differently, as C sharp and D flat.

e·nig′ma (i-nig′mə) *n.* a riddle; anything puzzling. —**en″ig·mat′ic** (en″ig-mat′ik; ē″nig-) *adj.* —**en″ig·mat′i·cal·ly,** *adv.*

en·join′ *v.t.* **1,** command (a person) to do something; prescribe (a course of conduct). **2,** (*Law*) prohibit or restrain by injunction. —**en·join′der** (-dər) *n.* prohibition.

en·joy′ (en-joi′) *v.t.* **1,** feel joy in doing or perceiving; find pleasure in. **2,** have possession or use of. —**en·joy′ment,** *n.*

en·kin′dle (en-kin′dəl) *v.t.* **1,** excite; inflame. **2,** set on fire.

en·lace′ (en-lās′) *v.t.* **1,** encircle. **2,** entangle; intertwine. —**en·lace′ment,** *n.*

en·large′ (en-lärj′) *v.t.* **1,** make larger; extend; augment. **2,** increase in capacity or scope; expand. —*v.i.* **1,** become larger; expand. **2,** be diffuse in speaking or writing; expatiate. —**en·large′ment,** *n.* act or result of enlarging; esp., a photograph extended in size.

en·light′en (en-lī′tən) *v.t.* give intellectual or spiritual light to; impart knowledge to; instruct. **—en·light′en·ment,** *n.*

en·list′ *v.t. & i.* **1,** enter, as a name on a list; enroll. **2,** engage in a service or cause, as a military service. **—en·list′ment,** *n.* **—enlisted woman** or **man,** a member of the U.S. armed forces who is not a commissioned officer, warrant officer, or cadet. Also, **en·lis·tee′** (-tē′).

en·liv′en (en-lī′vən) *v.t.* give life or activity to; animate; make vigorous or gay. **—en·liv′en·ment,** *n.*

en masse′ (än mas′) (*Fr.*) all together; collectively.

en·mesh′ *v.t.* enclose in meshes; entangle.

en′mi·ty (en′mə-tē) *n.* hostility; hatred; ill will; antagonism.

en·no′ble (e-nō′bəl) *v.t.* elevate in rank, dignity, or worth. **—en·no′ble·ment,** *n.*

en′nui (än′wē) *n.* weariness or discontent arising from satiety or lack of interest; boredom.

e·nor′mi·ty (i-nôr′mə-tē) *n.* **1,** something outrageously offensive or heinous. **2,** atrociousness.

---

enormity, enormousness

☛ Although these two words can both mean very large size, *enormity* is almost always used in the figurative sense to indicate something offensive or atrocious; *enormousness* usually refers literally to size.

---

e·nor′mous (i-nôr′məs) *adj.* **1,** greatly exceeding the usual size; huge; immense. **2,** extremely wicked; atrocious. **—e·nor′-mous·ness,** *n.* ❏ *enormity*

e·nough′ (i-nuf′) *adj.* answering the purpose; adequate; sufficient; satisfactory. *—adv.* **1,** in sufficient quantity or degree. **2,** to a notable extent; fully.

en pas·sant′ (än pa·sänt′) (*Fr.*) **1,** in passing; by the way. **2,** (*Chess*) a method for capturing a pawn.

en·plane′ (en-plān′) *v.i.* board an airplane.

en·rage′ (en-rāj′) *v.t.* excite rage in; provoke anger or fury in.

en rap·port′ (än ra-pôr′) (*Fr.*) in harmony; in agreement.

en·rap′ture (en-rap′chər) *v.t.* put in rapture; delight extremely.

en·rich′ *v.t.* **1,** make rich; supply with abundant property. **2,** supply with anything (as knowledge) in abundance. **3,**

make better in quality. **4,** fertilize, as soil. **—en·rich′ment,** *n.*

en·roll′ (en-rōl′) *v.i. & t.* enlist. **—en·roll′-ment, en·rol′ment,** *n.*

en route (än root′) (*Fr.*) on the way.

en·sconce′ (en-skons′) *v.t.* **1,** settle firmly or snugly. **2,** cover; hide.

en·sem′ble (än-säm′bəl) *n.* **1,** the whole; all parts taken together. **2,** the costume of a person, esp. when all parts are in harmony.

en·shrine′ (en-shrīn′) *v.t.* **1,** enclose in or as in a shrine. **2,** preserve with care; cherish. **—en·shrine′ment,** *n.*

en·shroud′ (en-shrowd′) *v.t.* wrap in or as in a shroud; conceal.

en′sign (en′sīn) *n.* **1,** the identifying flag of a company of soldiers, army, nation, vessel, etc. **2,** a badge of rank or office; an emblem or token. **3,** (-sin) the lowest commissioned rank in the U.S. Navy. **—en′sign·ship,** (en′sin-ship) *n.*

en′si·lage (en′sə-lij) *n.* fodder preserved in a silo or pit.

en·sile′ (en-sīl′) *v.t.* preserve in a silo; prepare as ensilage.

en·slave′ (en-slāv′) *v.t.* make a slave of; put in bondage. **—en·slave′ment,** *n.*

en·snare′ (en-snār′) *v.t.* trap. **—en·snare′-ment,** *n.*

en·sue′ (en-soo′) *v.i.* **1,** follow in order; come after. **2,** follow as a consequence.

en·sure′ (en-shûr′) *v.t.* **1,** make sure or certain to occur, come, or be. **2,** make safe or secure. **3,** insure. ❏ *assure*

-ent (ənt) *suf.* forming adjectives or nouns denoting doing or doer.

en·tail′ (en-tāl′) *v.t.* **1,** limit the inheritance of (property) to a specified line of heirs. **2,** bring about; cause to ensue; involve as a consequence. **3,** impose as a burden. **—en·tail′ment,** *n.*

en·tan′gle (en-tang′gəl) *v.t.* **1,** involve in difficulties; perplex. **2,** make complicated. **—en·tan′gle·ment,** *n.*

en·tente′ (än-tänt′) *n.* an understanding, esp. among nations friendly to one another. Also, **en·tente′ cor·diale′** (kôr-dyal′).

en·ter (en′tər) *v.t.* **1,** come into; go into; penetrate. **2,** put in; insert. **3,** become a member of; join; admit to membership. **4,** take the first step in; begin upon; become involved in. **5,** make a record of; register. *—v.i.* **1,** come or go in. **2,** make a beginning. **3,** take an interest or part in an enterprise.

en·ter′ic (en-ter′ik) *adj.* intestinal. *—n.* typhoid fever.

en″ter·i′tis (en″tə-rī′tis) *n.* inflammation of the intestines.

en′ter·prise″ (en′tər-prīz″) *n.* **1,** something undertaken; a project, mission, business, etc., esp. one requiring boldness or perseverance. **2,** boldness in undertakings. —**en′ter·pris″ing,** *adj.* ready and energetic in carrying out projects. —**enterprise zone,** an area in which certain business incentives, such as reduced taxes, are provided to stimulate the economy.

en″ter·tain′ (en″tər-tān′) *v.t.* **1,** afford amusement or diversion. **2,** accommodate as a guest. **3,** admit into the mind; give heed to; harbor; take under consideration. —*v.i.* exercise hospitality; receive guests.

en″ter·tain′ment (-mənt) *n.* **1,** act or result of entertaining; state of being entertained. **2,** a show, party, etc.

en·thrall′ (en-thrâl′) *v.t.* **1,** captivate; charm. **2,** put or hold in bondage. —**en·thrall′ment,** *n.*

en·throne′ (en-thrōn′) *v.t.* place on a throne; invest with authority. —**en·throne′ment,** *n.*

en·thuse′ (en-thooz′; -thūz′) *v.* (*Informal*) —*v.t.* make enthusiastic. —*v.i.* become enthusiastic; show enthusiasm.

en·thu′si·asm (en-thoo′zė-az-əm) *n.* **1,** absorbing possession of the mind by an interest, study, or pursuit; ardent interest. **2,** (*Archaic*) extravagant religious fervor. —**en·thu′si·ast,** *n.* —**en·thu″si·as′tic,** *adj.* —**en·thu″si·as′ti·cal·ly,** *adv.*

---

enthusiasm
↔ From Greek *entheos*, inspired (by a god). During the Puritan era, it acquired a sense of excessive religious fervor, but this usage has become rare.

---

en·tice′ (en-tīs′) *v.t.* draw on by exciting hope or desire; allure; attract. —**en·tice′ment,** *n.*

en·tire′ (en-tīr′) *adj.* whole; complete; not broken or diminished; intact. —**en·tire′ness,** *n.*

en·tire′ty (-tė) *n.* **1,** the whole of something. **2,** completeness.

en·ti′tle (en-tī′təl) *v.t.* **1,** give a right to; furnish with grounds for a claim. **2,** give a title or name to.

en′ti·ty (en′tə-tė) *n.* **1,** something that has real existence; a thing. **2,** existence; being.

en·tomb′ (en-toom′) *v.t.* place in a tomb; bury. —**en·tomb′ment,** *n.*

en·to·mo- *pref.* meaning insect.

en″to·mol′o·gy (en″tə-mol′ə-jė) *n.* the study of insects. —**en″to·mo·log′i·cal,** *adj.* —**en″to·mol′o·gist,** *n.* ❑ *insect*

---

entomology, etymology
☞ Do not confuse *entomology*, the study of insects, with *etymology*, the study of word histories.

---

en″tou·rage′ (än″tû-räzh′) *n.* the attendants or followers of a person.

en·tr′acte′ (än-trakt′) *n.* **1,** an interval between acts of a play or opera. **2,** a musical piece, dance, etc., performed during this interval.

en′trails (en′trəlz) *n.pl.* **1,** the intestines or bowels. **2,** the internal parts or contents of anything.

en·train′ (en-trān′) *v.i.* board a train. —*v.t.* put on a train.

en′trance (en′trăns) *n.* **1,** the act of entering. **2,** a means or place of access; an opening or passage for entering.

en·trance′ (en-trăns′) *v.t.* **1,** fill with delight or wonder; enrapture. **2,** put in a trance.

en′trant (en′trənt) *n.* one who enters, as into a club, college, competition, etc.

en·trap′ *v.t.* [**-trapped′, -trap′ping**] catch in a trap; snare. —**en·trap′ment,** *n.*

en·treat′ (en-trēt′) *v.t.* ask earnestly; implore; beseech.

en·treat′y (en-trē′tė) *n.* **1,** act of entreating. **2,** a prayer; petition.

en′tre·côte″ (än′trə-kōt″) *n.* a rib or sirloin steak.

en′tree (än′trā) *n.* **1,** (U.S.) the main dish of a dinner. **2,** a dish served between chief courses of a dinner. **3,** the right or privilege of entering.

en·trench′ *v.t.* **1,** fortify by digging trenches around, or putting in a trench. **2,** establish in a position of security. —*v.i.* encroach; trespass. —**en·trench′ment,** *n.*

en·tre nous′ (än-trə noo′) (*Fr.*) between us.

en′tre·pôt″ (än′trə-pō″) *n.* **1,** a port or town to which goods are sent for distribution. **2,** a warehouse.

en″tre·pre·neur′ (än″trə-prə-nēr′) *n.* **1,** an employer of workmen. **2,** one who undertakes an enterprise.

en′tre·sol″ (än′trə-sōl″) *n.* mezzanine.

---

entropy
↔ Coined from Greek *tropē*, transformation, by the 19th-c. German physicist Rudolph Clausius, who formulated the second law of thermodynamics.

---

en′tro·py (en′trə-pė) *n.* (*Physics*) **1,** a measure of the unavailable energy in a thermodynamic system. **2,** the ultimate result of the degradation of matter and energy in the universe.

en·trust' *v.t.* **1,** (with *to*) transfer or commit, with confidence. **2,** (with *with*) charge with a trust or responsibility.

en'try (en'trė) *n.* **1,** the act of entering; entrance. **2,** an opening or passage for entering; a vestibule. **3,** an item entered in a register, account book, etc. —**entry-level,** *adj.* the level at which one begins with a company; relatively simple.

en·twine' (en-twīn') *v.t. & i.* curl about or together. —**en·twine'ment,** *n.*

e·nu'mer·ate" (i-nū'mə-rāt") *v.t.* **1,** name one by one; mention separately. **2,** count; ascertain the number of. —**e·nu"mer·a'-tion,** *n.*

e·nun'ci·ate" (i-nun'sė-āt") *v.t. & i.* utter or pronounce, as words or syllables, esp. with reference to manner. —*v.t.* proclaim; announce distinctly. —**e·nun"ci·a'tion,** *n.*

en·vel'op (en-vel'əp) *v.t.* surround entirely; form a covering about; wrap up. —**en·vel'op·ment,** *n.*

en've·lope (en'və-lōp) *n.* **1,** any covering or wrapping. **2,** a cover for a letter.

en·ven'om (en-ven'əm) *v.t.* **1,** make poisonous. **2,** imbue with malice.

en'vi·a·ble (en'vė-ə-bəl) *adj.* of an excellence to invite envy. —**en'vi·a·ble·ness,** *n.*

en'vi·ous (en'vė-əs) *adj.* feeling or showing envy. —**en'vi·ous·ness,** *n.*

en·vi'ron·ment (en-vī'rən-mənt) *n.* the aggregate of surrounding things or conditions; the totality of external influences on an organism. —**en·vi"ron·men'tal,** *adj.* —**en·vi"ron·men'tal·ism,** *n.* —**en·vi"ron·men'tal·ist,** *n.* one dedicated to the preservation of the natural environment.

en·vi'rons (en-vī'rənz) *n.pl.* the region surrounding a place; outskirts or suburbs.

en·vis'age (en-viz'əj) *v.t.* **1,** visualize. **2,** confront.

en·vi'sion (en-vizh'ən) *v.t.* contemplate in imagination, esp. future events.

en'voy (en'voi) *n.* **1,** an agent sent on a mission, esp. diplomatic. **2,** a postscript to a composition.

---

envoy, invoice
↔ *Envoy* in the sense of agent and the seemingly unrelated *invoice* both derive from Latin *inviare*, through French *envoyer*, send. *Envoy* in the sense of postscript comes from Old French *envoye*.

---

en'vy (en'vė) *n.* a feeling of mortification or discontent excited by seeing the superi-

ority or prosperity of another person; desire for the possessions or advantages of another; ill will combined with jealousy. —*v.t.* regard with envy.

en'zyme (en'zīm) *n.* a substance that acts as a catalyst in metabolism.

e·o- (ė-ō) *pref.* early; primeval.

e"o·lith'ic (ē"ə-lith'ik) *adj.* pert. to the earliest period of the Stone Age.

e'on (ē'ən) *n.* **1,** an indefinitely long period of time. **2,** the longest division of geologic time.

ep'au·let" (ep'ə-let") *n.* an ornamental badge on the shoulder.

é·pée' (ā-pā') *n.* a thin, pointed sword used in fencing.

e·pergne' (i-pērn') *n.* an ornamental table centerpiece.

e·phed'rine (i-fed'rin) *n.* a drug used to relieve nasal congestion.

---

ephedrine
↔ Named for Greek *Ephedra*, the genus of plants from which the drug was originally derived.

---

e·phem'er·al (i-fem'ər-əl) *adj.* lasting only one day or a very short time; transitory.

ep·i- *pref.* to; against; upon.

ep'ic (ep'ik) *adj.* **1,** pert. to a poem or poetry narrating in lofty style the achievements and adventures of a hero. **2,** of heroic character or style; imposing. —*n.* an epic poem or story. —**ep'i·cal·ly,** *adv.*

ep'i·cene" (ep'i-sēn") *adj.* **1,** both masculine and feminine. **2,** sexless; lacking vigor. **3,** effeminate.

ep'i·cen"ter (ep'ə-sen"tər) *n.* **1,** the parts of the earth immediately above the focus of an earthquake. **2,** focus; center.

ep'i·cure" (ep'ə-kyûr") *n.* **1,** one of refined taste in eating and drinking. **2,** one given to sensual pleasure. —**ep"i·cu·re'an** (-kyû-rē'ən) *adj.*

---

epicure
↔ So named because the epicure's lifestyle is best described in the writings of the Greek philosopher *Epicurus.*

---

ep"i·dem'ic (ep"ə-dem'ik) *adj.* (of a disease) appearing in a large number of cases at the same time in a locality. —*n.* a temporary prevalence of a disease in a community. —**ep"i·dem'i·cal·ly,** *adv.* □ *endemic*

ep"i·der'mis (ep"ə-dēr'mis) *n.* the outermost skin, membrane, integument, or layer of an organic body.

---

ep″i·glot′tis (ep″i-glot′is) *n.* the flap of cartilage that covers the glottis during swallowing.

ep′i·gram″ (ep′ə-gram″) *n.* a terse, witty saying, usually satirical. **—ep″i·gram·mat′ic** (-grə-mat′ik) *adj.* **—ep″i·gram·mat′i·cal·ly,** *adv.*

---

epigram, epigraph, epitaph, epithet

These four words share the Greek prefix *epi-*, which in this case means upon. *Epigram*, *epigraph*, and *epitaph* all refer to sayings. An *epigram* is a witty saying, irrespective of its use. *Epigraph* usually refers to an inscription on a monument or tombstone, for which *epitaph* is another word. An *epithet* is something else, namely, a word or phrase used to characterize a person or thing.

---

ep′i·graph″ (ep′ə-gráf″) *n.* **1,** an inscription. **2,** a quotation or motto at the beginning of a book or chapter. **—ep″i·graph′ic,** *adj.* ❏ *epigram*

e·pig′ra·phy (i-pig′rə-fė) *n.* **1,** the science of deciphering and explaining inscriptions. **2,** inscriptions collectively.

ep′i·lep″sy (ep′ə-lep″sė) *n.* a nervous disease characterized by muscular spasms and loss of consciousness.

ep″i·lep′tic (ep″ə-lep′tik) *adj.* pert. to epilepsy. **—n.** a person afflicted with epilepsy.

ep′i·logue″ (ep′ə-lâg″) *n.* the concluding part of a discourse; a section added at the end.

ep″i·neph′rine (ep″i-nef′rin) *n.* a drug used to stimulate the heart, etc.

E·piph′a·ny (i-pif′ə-nė) *n.* a Christian festival, Jan. 6.

e·pis′co·pa·cy (i-pis′kə-pə-sė) *n.* **1,** a form of church government in which the chief ministers are bishops. **2,** the office of a bishop. **—e·pis′co·pate** (-pət) *n.*

e·pis′co·pal (i-pis′kə-pəl) *adj.* **1,** pert. to a bishop. **2,** (*cap.*) designating a Protestant sect governed by bishops. **—E·pis″co·pa′lian** (-pāl′yən) *n.* a member of this sect.

ep′i·sode″ (ep′ə-sōd″) *n.* **1,** an incident in a series of events or a narrative; one happening. **2,** (*Music*) a digressive passage, as in a fugue. **—ep″i·sod′ic** (-sod′ik) *adj.* **—ep″i·sod′i·cal·ly,** *adv.*

e·pis″te·mol′o·gy (i-pis″tə-mol′ə-jė) *n.* the study of the nature, basis, limits, and validity of human knowledge.

e·pis′tle (i-pis′əl) *n.* a written communication; a letter, esp. a formal discourse, as (*cap.*) any of the apostolic letters in the New Testament. **—e·pis′to·lar·y** (-tə-ler-ė) *adj.*

ep′i·taph″ (ep′ə-tâf″) *n.* **1,** a memorial inscription on a monument. **2,** any similar commemorative writing. ❏ *epigram*

ep″i·tha·la′mi·um (ep″i-thə-lā′mė-əm) *n.* a song or poem in honor of a newly married person or pair.

ep′i·thet″ (ep′ə-thet″) *n.* a name or phrase used to characterize a person or thing. **—ep″i·thet′ic, ep″i·thet′i·cal,** *adj.* ❏ *epigram*

e·pit′o·me (i-pit′ə-mė) *n.* **1,** a brief summary of a subject or writing; an abridgment or abstract. **2,** the embodiment of the features of a group. **—e·pit′o·mize″** (-mīz″) *v.t.*

e plur′i·bus u′num (ē plûr′i-bəs oo′nəm) (*Lat.*) one out of many: motto of the U.S.

ep′och (ep′ək) *n.* **1,** a period of time marked by distinctive events; a division of a geologic period. **2,** a point of time distinguished by some remarkable event. **—ep′och·al** (-əl) *adj.*

ep′o·nym″ (ep′ə-nim) *n.* a person (real or imaginary) for whom something is named. **—ep·on′y·mous** (ə-pon′ə-məs) *adj.* **—ep·on′y·my** (ə-pon′ə-mė) *n.*

e·pox′y resin (ė-päks′ė) *n.* a thermosetting resin used as an adhesive or a protective coating. Also, **epoxy.**

ep′si·lon″ (ep′sə-lon″) *n.* the fifth letter of the Greek alphabet (E, ε).

Ep′som salts (ep′səm) hydrated magnesium sulfate, used as a cathartic.

eq′ua·ble (ek′wə-bəl) *adj.* uniform in action, intensity, or state; even; steady; tranquil. **—eq″ua·bil′i·ty,** *n.*

---

equable, equitable

☛ Both words have to do with uniformity. *Equable* means uniform in intensity, tranquil. *Equitable* means uniform in treatment, fair.

---

e′qual (ē′kwəl) *adj.* **1,** having one measure; the same in magnitude, quantity, degree, worth, etc. **2,** evenly balanced; level; uniform in operation. **—v.t.** be or become equal to; make or do something equal to. **—e·qual′i·ty** (i-kwol′ə-tė) *n.* **—Equal Rights Amendment,** a proposed amendment to the U.S. Constitution prohibiting discrimination based on sex. **—equal time,** the requirement of a radio or television station to provide equal airtime to all political candidates if time is provided to any.

e′qual·ize″ (ē′kwə-līz″) *v.t.* make equal or uniform. —**e″qual·i·za′tion,** *n.*

e′qual·iz″er (ē′kwə-līz″ər) *n.* **1,** a device for maintaining equal or uniform stress, potential, etc. among different parts of an apparatus. **2,** (*Slang*) a pistol.

e″qua·nim′i·ty (ē″kwə-nim′ə-tē) *n.* evenness of mind or temper; calmness under stress.

e·quate′ (i-kwāt′) *v.t.* state the equality of; put in an equation.

e·qua′tion (i-kwā′zhən) *n.* (*Math.*) a statement of relation between two quantities, indicated by an *equals sign* (=) or other symbol.

e·qua′tor (i-kwā′tər) *n.* **1,** a circle dividing the surface of a sphere into two equal parts. **2,** (*cap.*) such a circle on the earth equidistant between the North Pole and the South Pole. —**e″qua·tor′i·al** (ē″kwə-tôr′ē-əl) *adj.*

eq′uer·ry (ek′wə-rē) *n.* **1,** an attendant in a royal household. **2,** an officer in charge of horses.

e·ques′tri·an (i-kwes′trē-ən) *adj.* **1,** pert. to horsemen or horsemanship. **2,** mounted on horseback. —*n.* one who rides a horse. Also, **e·ques″tri·enne′** (-en′) *n.fem.*

e·qui- (ē-kwə; ek-wē) *pref.* equal.

e″qui·dis′tant (ē″kwə-dis′tənt) *adj.* equally distant.

e″qui·lat′er·al (ē″kwə-lat′ər-əl) *adj.* having all sides of equal length.

e·quil′i·brate″ (ē-kwil′ə-brāt″) *v.t. & i.* be or put in equal balance. —**e·quil″i·bra″-tion,** *n.*

e″qui·lib′ri·um (ē″kwə-lib′rē-əm) *n.* **1,** a state of rest or balance through equality of counteracting forces. **2,** mental stability.

e′quine (ē′kwīn) *adj.* pert. to or like a horse. —*n.* a horse.

e′qui·nox″ (ē′kwi-noks″) *n.* either of the two annual occasions, about Mar. 21 and Sept. 22, when night and day are of equal length. —**e″qui·noc′tial** (-nok′shəl) *adj.*

e·quip′ (i-kwip′) *v.t.* [**-quipped′, -quip′-ping**] fit out with what is needed to execute an undertaking; rig for service.

eq′ui·page (ek′wə-pij) *n.* a carriage.

e·quip′ment (i-kwip′mənt) *n.* **1,** act of equipping; state of being equipped. **2,** that which equips; supplies; gear.

e′qui·poise″ (ē′kwə-poiz″) *n.* **1,** equal distribution of weight. **2,** a counterbalance.

eq′ui·ta·ble (ek′wi-tə-bəl) *adj.* fair. —**eq′ui·ta·ble·ness,** *n.* ❑ *equable*

eq″ui·ta′tion (ek″wə-tā′shən) *n.* horsemanship.

eq′ui·ty (ek′wi-tē) *n.* **1,** impartial justice; fairness. **2,** (*Law*) the application of common principles of fair dealing, to supplement statute law. **3,** a net financial interest in a property.

e·quiv′a·lent (i-kwiv′ə-lənt) *adj.* **1,** the same in magnitude, meaning, effect, etc. **2,** corresponding in position or function. —*n.* substantially the same thing. —**e·quiv′a·lence,** *n.*

e·quiv′o·cal (i-kwiv′ə-kəl) *adj.* **1,** of uncertain meaning; ambiguous. **2,** of doubtful origin; dubious.

e·quiv′o·cate″ (i-kwiv′ə-kāt″) *v.i.* use ambiguous expressions; be evasive. —**e·quiv″o·ca′tion,** *n.*

-er (-ər) *suf.* **1,** added to verbs to denote a person or implement performing the act; added to nouns to denote a performer, follower, or resident of. **2,** forming the comparative degree of adjectives and adverbs.

e′ra (ir′ə) *n.* **1,** a period of time of distinctive historical character. **2,** (*Geol.*) a major period of geological time.

> **era**
> ↔ Descended from Greek *tropē*, transformation, by a circuitous route from Latin *aera*, a small Roman token used for counting.

e·rad′i·cate″ (i-rad′i-kāt″) *v.t.* pull up by the roots; destroy utterly. —**e·rad″i·ca′-tion,** *n.* —**e·rad′i·ca″tor,** *n.*

e·rase′ (i-rās′) *v.t.* rub or scratch out; clear (of writing, transcribed sound, recorded data, etc.). —**e·ras′er,** *n.* a utensil, device, or substance (as rubber) for erasing.

e·ras′ure (i-rā′shər) *n.* **1,** act of erasing. **2,** a place where something has been erased.

er′bi·um (ėr′bē-əm) *n.* a chemical element of the rare-earth group, no. 68, symbol Er.

ere (âr) *prep.* before (in time). —*conj.* before; sooner or rather than. —**ere″long′,** *adv.* before long.

e·rect′ (i-rekt′) *v.t.* **1,** build; construct. **2,** set up; establish; found. **3,** raise to an upright position. —*adj.* upright. —**e·rec′tile,** *adj.* capable of being erected. —**e·rec′-tion,** *n.*

er′e·mite″ (er′ə-mīt″) *n.* a hermit, esp. religious.

erg (ėrg) *n.* a unit of work. Also, **er′gon** (ėr′gon).

er'go (ēr'gō) *conj.* (*Lat.*) therefore.

er·go- (er-gə) *pref.* work.

er''go·nom'ics (er''gə-nom'iks) *n.* human engineering.

er·gos'ter·ol'' (ər-gos'tə-rōl'') *n.* a food supplement taken for its Vitamin D content.

er'got (ēr'gət) *n.* a fungus, in rye and other cereals, yielding a medicine used to check hemorrhage. —**er'go·tism,** *n.* a disease caused by ergot, marked by spasm and gangrene.

er'mine (ēr'min) *n.* **1,** a white-furred weasel; its fur. **2,** the office or dignity of a judge.

> **ermine**
> ↔ A shortening of Latin *Armenius mus,* Armenian rat.

e·rode' (i-rōd') *v.t. & i.* wear away slowly. —**e·ro'sive,** *adj.*

e·rog'e·nous (i-roj'ə-nəs) *adj.* producing sexual desire.

e·ro'sion (i-rō'zhən) *n.* a washing or wearing away of the earth's surface.

e·rot'ic (i-rot'ik) *adj.* pert. to sexual love. —**e·rot'i·cal·ly,** *adv.* —**e·rot'i·cism,** *n.*

> **erotic, erratic, esoteric, exoteric, exotic**
> ☛ Five similar-sounding words with fairly different meanings. *Erotic* means pertaining to sexual love, from Greek *Erōs,* the god of Love. *Exotic* means foreign or, by extension, strange, striking. *Esoteric* and *exoteric* are related. The more common of the two, *esoteric,* means understood by the select few; *exoteric* means readily understood by the general public. *Erratic* has nothing to do with the other words, meaning wandering or eccentric.

e·rot'i·ca (i-rot'i-kə) *n.pl.* erotic literature or art; pornography.

err (ēr; er) *v.i.* **1,** go astray; be mistaken; blunder. **2,** sin.

er'rand (er'ənd) *n.* **1,** a special business entrusted to a messenger; a commission. **2,** a short trip to execute a commission.

er'rant (er'ənt) *adj.* **1,** wandering; roving. **2,** deviating; erring. ❏ *arrant*

er·rat'ic (i-rat'ik) *adj.* **1,** wandering; off course. **2,** tending to err. **3,** eccentric. —**er·rat'i·cal·ly,** *adv.* ❏ *erotic*

er·ra'tum (i-rä'təm) *n.* [*pl.* **-ta** (-tə)] an error in a book; misprint. —**er·ra'ta,** *n.sing.* a list of errors or misprints.

er·ro'ne·ous (i-rō'nē-əs) *adj.* incorrect. —**er·ro'ne·ous·ness,** *n.*

er'ror (er'ər) *n.* **1,** a deviation from truth; a mistake; an inaccuracy. **2,** moral wrongdoing; an offense. **3,** difference from a true value or standard.

er'satz (er'zätz) *adj. & n.* substitute.

Erse (ērs) *n.* Gaelic.

erst'while'' (ērst'hwīl'') *adj.* former.

e·ruct' (i-rukt') *v.t. & i.* emit or issue violently, esp. wind from the stomach; belch. —**e·ruc'tate** (-tāt) *v.t. & i.* —**e·ruc''ta'-tion,** *n.*

er''u·di'tion (er''yû-dish'ən) *n.* knowledge gained by study; learning. —**er'u-dite''** (-dīt'') *adj.*

> **erudite**
> ↔ From Latin *erudire,* remove the roughness from.

e·rupt' (i-rupt') *v.i. & t.* burst forth suddenly and violently, like a volcano. —**e·rup'tive,** *adj.*

e·rup'tion (i-rup'shən) *n.* **1,** a bursting forth. **2,** a rash.

> **eruption, irruption**
> ☛ Do not confuse these two words, which both refer to bursting. An *eruption* is a bursting out, and an *irruption* is a bursting in.

er''y·sip'e·las (er''ə-sip'ə-ləs) *n.* an acute, infectious skin disease.

er''y·the'ma (er''i-thē'mə) *n.* [*pl.* **-ma·ta** (-mə-tə)] redness of the skin caused by local congestion of the blood.

es'bat *n.* a meeting of witches.

es·ca'late (es'kə-lāt'') *v.t. & i.* increase the scope or intensity of.

es'ca·la''tor (es'kə-lā''tər) *n.* a moving stairway for transporting passengers from one level to another. —**escalator clause,** a provision in labor contracts permitting periodic adjustment of wage scales.

es·cal'lop (es-kol'əp) *v.t.* **1,** bake (food) in a sauce, with crumbs on top. **2,** scallop. —*n.* scallop.

es'ca·pade'' (es'kə-pād'') *n.* a wild prank; a foolish adventure.

es·cape' (es-kāp') *v.i.* **1,** get away or flee, as from capture or confinement; evade or avoid threatened harm. **2,** leak out, as a liquid. —*v.t.* slip away from; elude. —*n.* act of escaping. —**escape clause,** a provision in a contract that permits a party to it to evade provisions of the contract under certain circumstances. —**escape velocity,** the velocity required for a spacecraft to escape the pull of gravity.

es·cape′ment (es-kāp′mənt) *n.* a contrivance for alternately releasing and stopping a moving part, as in a clock.

es·cap′ism (es-kāp′iz-əm) *n.* diversion of thought from unpleasant reality. **—es·cap′ist,** *n.*

es′ca·role″ (es′kə-rōl″) *n.* a broad-leaved variety of endive.

es·carp′ment (es-kärp′mənt) *n.* a precipitous slope; a cliff.

es″cha·tol′o·gy (es″kə-tol′ə-jē) *n.* the branch of theology that treats of last or final things, as death. **—es″cha·to·log′i·cal** (-tə-loj′i-kəl) *adj.*

es·chew′ (es-choo′) *v.t.* shun.

es·cort′ (es-kôrt′) *v.t.* accompany on a trip as a companion or protector; convoy. *—n.* (es′kôrt) one who escorts; a body of attendants.

es″cri·toire′ (es″kri-twär′) *n.* a writing desk or secretary.

es′crow (es′krō) *n.* a conditional contract of which the consideration is deposited in trust.

es·cu′do (es-koo′dō) *n.* [*pl.* **-dos**] a coin or monetary unit of various Spanish- and Portuguese-speaking countries.

es′cu·lent (es′kū-lənt) *adj.* fit to be used for food; edible.

es·cutch′eon (es-kuch′ən) *n.* the shield on which armorial bearings are emblazoned.

-ese (ēs *or* ēz) *suf.* denoting the language or inhabitants of a place or a situation; the jargon of an industry, etc.

Es′ki·mo″ (es′ki-mō″) *n.* [*pl.* **-mos**] **1,** one of the race indigenous to arctic North America. **2,** a malemute or husky.

e·soph′a·gus (ė-sof′ə-gəs) *n.* [*pl.* **-gi** (-jī)] the food canal of an animal, from mouth to stomach; the gullet.

es″o·ter′ic (es″ə-ter′ik) *adj.* understood by, or intended for, only a select few; secret; mysterious. **—es″o·ter′i·cal·ly,** *adv.* ❏ *erotic*

es′pa·drille″ (es′pə-dril″) *n.* a flat sandal.

es·pal′ier (es-pal′yər) *n.* **1,** a trellis for the branches of a fruit tree or bush. **2,** a tree or plant so grown.

es·par′to (i-spär′tō) *n.* [*pl.* **-tos**] a type of grass used for making paper, etc.

es·pe′cial (es-pesh′əl) *adj.* **1,** special; distinguished from others of the same kind. **2,** exceptional.

Es″pe·ran′to (es″pə-rán′tō) *n.* a proposed universal language based on European roots.

es′pi·o·nage″ (es′pė-ə-näj″) *n.* the practice of spying.

es′pla·nade″ (es′plə-näd″) *n.* a public ground for walking or riding; a level, open area.

es·pouse′ (es-powz′) *v.t.* **1,** take as a spouse; wed. **2,** adopt or advocate, as a cause. **—es·pous′al,** *n.*

es·pres′so (es-pres′sō) *n.* coffee brewed with forced steam.

espresso, express
↔ The Italian word for a type of coffee does not mean "express" but "expressed," i.e., "pressed out." Both come from Latin *expressus*, prominent, past participle of *exprimere*.

es·prit′ (es-prē′) *n.* (*Fr.*) liveliness; spirit; wit. **—esprit de corps** (də kôr) (*Fr.*) morale.

es·py′ (es-pī′) *v.t.* catch sight of.

-esque (esk) *suf.* like; having the style or manner of, as *picturesque, arabesque.*

es·quire′ (es-kwīr′) *n.* **1,** a title of politeness, added after a man's last name in addressing him by letter; usually *Esq.* When used for a lawyer, the title is used for both women and men. **2,** (*Hist.*) an attendant on a knight.

-ess (əs *or* is) *suf.* forming feminine nouns, as *seeress.*

es′say (es′ā) *n.* **1,** a literary composition on a particular subject. **2,** an effort or attempt. *—v.t.* (e-sā′) endeavor; try. **—es′say·ist,** *n.* ❏ *assay*

es′sence (es′əns) *n.* **1,** the distinctive characteristic of something. **2,** the inward nature or true substance of something. **3,** a liquid containing a substance in concentrated form, as a perfume.

essence
↔ From Latin *esse*, to be, through *essentia*, existence.

es·sen′tial (ə-sen′shəl) *adj.* **1,** absolutely necessary; indispensable. **2,** relating to inmost nature; basic; fundamental. **3,** pert. to or yielding a liquid essence. *—n.* a basic part or aspect; an element. **—essential oil,** a volatile oil in a plant giving it its characteristic odor or flavor.

es·tab′lish *v.t.* **1,** set up on a firm basis; found; fix. **2,** install, as in a position. **3,** show to be valid; prove.

es·tab′lish·ment (-mənt) *n.* **1,** act of establishing; state of being established. **2,** something established as a household, business, institution. **3,** (*cap.*) (*Informal*) the social institution and officials of a country or society.

---

fat, fāte, fär, fâre, fâll, ȧsk; met, hē, hẽr, maybė; pin, pīne; not, nōte, ôr, tool

es·tate' (es-tāt') *n.* **1,** a piece of landed property. **2,** a person's entire property and possessions. **3,** a person's worldly condition or circumstances; status; rank. **4,** a political or social class.

es·teem' (es-tēm') *v.t.* **1,** set a high value on; regard favorably. **2,** estimate; rate. —*n.* **1,** favorable opinion; respect. **2,** judgment of worth.

es'ter (es'tər) *n.* a chemical compound analogous to a salt and often fragrant.

es'thete (es'thēt) *n.* aesthete.

es·thet'ic (es-thet'ik) *adj. & n.* aesthetic.

es·thet'ics (-iks) *n.* aesthetics.

es'ti·ma·ble (es'ti-mə-bəl) *adj.* **1,** worthy of esteem. **2,** capable of being estimated or valued.

es'ti·mate" (es'tə-māt") *v.t.* form an opinion of, as to size, value, etc. —*n.* (es'tə-mət) **1,** an opinion, judgment, or approximate calculation; a tentative price or charge. **2,** esteem. —**es"ti·ma'tion** (-mā'shən) *n.*

es'ti·val (es'tə-vəl) *adj.* pert. to summer.

es'ti·vate" (es'tə-vāt") *v.i.* pass the summer; esp. (*Zool.*) be dormant in summer, as some mollusks. Also, **aes'ti·vate.** —**es·ti·va'tion,** *n.*

es·top' *v.t.* [**-topped', -top'ping**] prevent, bar, or stop. —**es·top'pel** (-əl) *n.*

es·trange' (es-trānj') *v.t.* cause to be hostile; alienate the affections of. —**es·trange'ment,** *n.*

es'tri·ol" (es'trē-ol") *n.* a female sex hormone.

es'tro·gen (es'trə-jən) *n.* a substance that stimulates production of certain sex hormones.

es'trous (es'trəs) *adj.* pert. to estrus. —**estrous cycle,** the physiological changes occurring during estrus.

es'trus (es'trəs) *n.* **1,** a passionate impulse or desire. **2,** (*Zool.*) heat; rut; the period of greatest female sexual receptivity. Also, **oes'trus.**

es'tu·ar·y (es'choo-er-ē) *n.* the mouth of a river, subject to tides.

-et *suf.* diminutive, as *owlet.*

e'ta (ā'tə) the seventh letter of the Greek alphabet (H, η).

é"ta·gère' (ā"tä-zher') *n.* (*Fr.*) a many-shelved cabinet; whatnot.

et cet'er·a (et set'ər-ə) (*Lat.*) and others; and so on: usually, **etc.,** *abbr.*

etch (ech) *v.t.* **1,** cut (the surface of a metal plate, etc.) with acid, in order to form a design. **2,** engrave with a stylus. —**etch'ing,** *n.* a printed impression from an etched plate.

e·ter'nal (i-tēr'nəl) *adj.* **1,** existing throughout all time; without beginning or end. **2,** incessant. **3,** (*cap.*) God.

e·ter'ni·ty (i-tēr'nə-tē) *n.* **1,** time without beginning or end; infinite duration. **2,** a seemingly endless period of time.

---

eternity, infinity
☞ *Eternity* refers to infinite time, time without end. *Infinity* means anything that is without end, whether in space or in time.

-eth *suf.* **1,** forming ordinal numbers, as *twentieth.* **2,** (*Archaic*) forming the third person singular of verbs, as *he readeth,* now *he reads.*

eth'ane (eth'ān) *n.* a colorless, combustible gas.

eth'a·nol (eth'ə-nâl) *n.* ethyl alcohol.

e'ther (ē'thər) *n.* **1,** a compound of sulfuric acid and alcohol, used as a solvent and anesthetic. **2,** the sky.

e·the're·al (i-thir'ē-əl) *adj.* **1,** airy; light; intangible. **2,** heavenly.

eth'ic (eth'ik) *adj.* ethical. —*n.* ethics.

eth'i·cal (eth'i-kəl) *adj.* in accordance with accepted principles of conduct.

eth'ics (eth'iks) *n.pl.* **1,** the principles of honor and morality. **2,** accepted rules of conduct. **3,** the moral principles of an individual.

E"thi·o'pi·an (ē"thē-ō'pē-ən) *adj.* pert. to Ethiopia. —*n.* **1,** a native of Ethiopia. **2,** (*Erroneous*) a Negro.

eth'nic (eth'nik) *adj.* **1,** pert. to a people distinguished by race, language, culture, etc. **2,** heathen; pagan. —**eth'ni·cal,** *adj.* —**eth·ni'ci·ty** (-ni'sə-tē) *n.*

eth·no- (eth-nō-) *pref.* race; people; nation.

eth"no·cen'tric (eth"nō-sen'trik) *adj.* believing in the superiority of one's own ethnic group.

eth·nol'o·gy (eth-nol'ə-jē) *n.* the science of the origin, history, customs, etc. of peoples. —**eth"no·log'i·cal,** *adj.* —**eth·nol'o·gist,** *n.*

e'thos (ē'thos) *n.* **1,** the character, ideals, etc. of a community or people. **2,** the quality of a work of art that produces a high moral impression, noble and universal.

eth'yl (eth'əl) *n.* (*Chem.*) a radical of alcohol. —**ethyl fluid,** tetraethyl lead, added to gasoline to reduce engine knock.

e'ti·o·late" (ē'tē-ə-lāt") *v.t. & i.* **1,** grow pale. **2,** weaken. —**e"ti·o·la'tion,** *n.*

e"ti·ol'o·gy (ē"tē-ol'ə-jē) *n.* the study of

---

causes. Also, **ae″ti·ol′o·gy.** —**e″ti·o·log′i·cal,** *adj.* —**e″ti·ol′o·gist,** *n.*

et′i·quette″ (et′i-ket″) *n.* the conventional requirements of polite behavior; proprieties of conduct; good manners.

E′ton jacket (ē′tən) a jacket with an open front, orig. worn by students at Eton College, England, now worn by both men and women. —**Eton collar,** a broad, exposed collar, such as is worn with an Eton jacket.

-ette (et) *suf.* **1,** little, small, as *kitchenette.* **2,** feminine, as *suffragette.* **3,** imitation, as *leatherette.*

é·tude′ (ā-tūd′) *n.* (*Fr.*) a musical composition intended as an exercise in technique, but often of aesthetic value; a study.

e·tui′ (ā-twē′) *n.* a small box, as for notions.

et″y·mol′o·gy (et″i-mol′ə-jė) *n.* **1,** the study of the structure and history of words. **2,** the derivation or history of a given word. —**et″y·mo·log′i·cal,** *adj.* —**et″y·mol′o·gist,** *n.* ❏ *entomology*

eu″ca·lyp′tus (ū″kə-lip′təs) *n.* a tree of the myrtle family; its wood or aromatic oil.

Eu′cha·rist (ū′kə-rist) *n.* the sacrament of the Lord's Supper; Holy Communion. —**Eu″cha·ris′tic,** *adj.*

> **eucharist**
> ↔ Etymologically, the word means "thanksgiving"; it is derived from Greek *eukharistos,* grateful.

eu′chre (ū′kər) *n.* a card game. —*v.t.* swindle; outsmart.

Eu·clid′e·an geometry (ū-klid′ē-ən) **1,** the system of geometry of Euclid (c. 300 B.C.). **2,** geometry.

eu·gen′ics (ū-jen′iks) *n.* the science of improving the human race through the regulation of parenthood, genetic engineering, etc. —**eu·gen′ic,** *adj.* —**eu·gen′i·cal·ly,** *adv.*

eu′lo·gy (ū′lə-jė) *n.* high praise; a speech or writing that lauds a person, esp. one deceased, or a thing. —**eu″lo·gis′tic** (-jis′tik) *adj.* —**eu″lo·gis′ti·cal·ly,** *adv.* —**eu′lo·gize″** (-jīz″) *v.t.* deliver a eulogy about. ❏ *elegy*

eu′nuch (ū′nək) *n.* a castrated man.

eu·pep′sia (ū-pep′shə) *n.* good digestion. —**eu·pep′tic** (-tik) *adj.*

eu′phe·mism (ū′fə-miz-əm) *n.* **1,** the use of a mild word in place of a plainer but possibly offensive one. **2,** a word or expression thus substituted. —**eu″phe·mis′tic** (-mis′tik) *adj.* —**eu″phe·mis′ti·cal·ly,** *adv.*

> **eunuch**
> ↔ From Greek *eunoukhos,* guard of the bed. The sense of castrated man comes from the practice of castrating these bed guards in Middle Eastern courts to make them safe for the harem.

eu·phen′ics (ū-fen′iks) *n.* the science of improving the human species by modifying biological development.

eu·pho′ni·ous (ū-fō′nė-əs) *adj.* pleasing in sound. —**eu·pho′ni·ous·ness,** *n.*

eu·pho′ni·um (ū-fō′nė-əm) *n.* a tenor tuba.

eu′pho·ny (ū′fə-nė) *n.* harmonious arrangement of sounds, esp. of words. —**eu·phon′ic,** *adj.* —**eu·phon′i·cal·ly,** *adv.*

eu·pho′ri·a (ū-fôr′ė-ə) *n.* a feeling or state of well-being.

eu′phu·ism (ū′fū-iz-əm) *n.* an excessively ornate style in writing. —**eu″phu·is′-tic,** *adj.* —**eu″phu·is′ti·cal·ly,** *adv.*

> **euphuism**
> ↔ For *Euphues,* a character in several works by 16th-c. English writer John Lyly.

Eur·a′sia (yû-rā′zhə) *n.* Europe and Asia considered as one continent.

Eur·a′sian (yû-rā′zhən) *n.* a person of mixed Europ. and Asiatic blood. —*adj.* **1,** pert. to Eurasia. **2,** of mixed European and Asiatic parentage.

eu·re′ka (yû-rē′kə) *interj.* (*Gk.*) I have found it!

> **eureka**
> ↔ Supposedly exclaimed by the Greek mathematician Archimedes when he discovered a method for distinguishing pure gold from alloy.

Eu′ro·dol″lar (yû′rō-dol″ər) *n.* (*usu.pl.*) U.S. dollars circulating among European banks.

Eu″ro·pe′an (yûr″ə-pē′ən) *adj.* pert. to Europe. —*n.* a native of Europe. —**European plan,** in hotel-keeping, rental of room only, with meals not included.

eu·ro′pi·um (yû-rō′pė-əm) *n.* a rare-earth chemical element, no. 63, symbol Eu.

eu·ryth′mics (ū-riᵗʰ′miks) *n.* **1,** the science of harmonious bodily movements. **2,** a system of musical education through bodily movements.

eu·ryth′my (ū-riᵗʰ′mė) *n.* harmony of movement or proportion. —**eu·ryth′mic,** *adj.*

Eu·sta′chian tube (ū-stā′shən) the canal between the eardrum and pharynx, named for 16th-c. Italian anatomist Bartolommeo Eustachio.

eu″tha·na′sia (ū″thə-nā′zhə) *n.* **1,** painless death. **2,** mercy killing.

eu·then′ics (ū-then′iks) *n.* **1,** the science of adjusting living conditions to improve the human race. **2,** the science of improving growth conditions of plants and animals.

eu″tro·phi·ca′tion (ū″trə-fi-kā′shən) *n.* the depletion of the oxygen in water by algae, caused by excess phosphates, nitrates, etc.

eu′tro·phy (ū′trə-fè) *n.* healthy nutrition. —**eu·troph′ic** (ū-trof′ik) *adj.*

e·vac′u·ate″ (i-vak′ū-āt″) *v.t.* **1,** make empty; free from something contained. **2,** vacate; withdraw from. **3,** excrete. —*v.i.* go elsewhere, esp. to avoid danger. —**e·vac″u·a′tion,** *n.*

e·vac′u·ee″ (-ē″) *n.* a person removed from a place of danger.

e·vade′ (i-vād′) *v.t.* **1,** escape from; avoid capture by; elude. **2,** circumvent by trickery. **3,** baffle.

e·val′u·ate″ (i-val′ū-āt″) *v.t.* **1,** ascertain the value or amount of. **2,** express numerically. —**e·val″u·a′tion,** *n.*

ev″a·nesce′ (ev″ə-nes′) *v.i.* fade away; disappear gradually; vanish. —**ev″a·nes′cence,** *n.* —**ev″a·nes′cent,** *adj.*

e·van′gel (i-van′jəl) *n.* the Christian gospel.

e″van·gel′i·cal (ē″van-jel′ə-kəl) *adj.* **1,** pert. to the Gospels or to evangelism. **2,** (of churches) adhering strictly to Protestant theology, esp. in interpretation of the Gospels.

e·van′ge·list (i-van′je-list) *n.* **1,** one of the apostles Matthew, Mark, Luke, John. **2,** a preacher of the gospel, esp. a revivalist. —**e·van′ge·lism,** *n.*

e·van′ge·lize″ (-līz″) *v.t. & i.* preach the gospel (to); convert to Christianity.

e·vap′o·rate″ (i-vap′ə-rāt″) *v.i.* **1,** pass off as vapor. **2,** disappear; be dissipated. —**e·vap″o·ra′tion,** *n.* —**evaporated milk,** milk concentrated by removal of some water by evaporation.

e·va′sion (i-vā′zhən) *n.* **1,** the act of evading. **2,** a trick or subterfuge; an equivocation.

e·va′sive (i-vā′siv) *adj.* **1,** using artifice to escape or avoid. **2,** escaping observation or understanding; elusive. —**e·va′siveness,** *n.*

eve (ēv) *n.* **1,** the night or the day before (a date, festival, etc.). **2,** the time just preceding an event. **3,** evening.

e′ven (ē′vən) *adj.* **1,** level; plane; smooth. **2,** uniform in action or character; unvarying. **3,** equal; on the same line or level. **4,** divisible by 2. **5,** whole; having no fractional part. **6,** not easily excited; placid. —*adv.* **1,** uniformly; equally; wholly; evenly. **2,** just; exactly; moreover; likewise; fully (used to emphasize or strengthen an assertion). —*v.t.* make even. —**e′ven·ness,** *n.* —**break even,** have neither a net profit nor a net loss. —**get even** (with), obtain revenge (upon). —**e′ven-ste′ven** (-stē′vən) *adj.* (*Informal*) not owing each other anything; tied.

e″ven-hand′ed (-han′did) *adj.* impartial; equitable; fair. —**e″ven-hand′ed·ness,** *n.*

eve′ning (ēv′ning) *n.* **1,** the latter part of the day; the time from sunset to darkness, or from first darkness to bedtime. **2,** the latter part or decline of any term of existence. —**evening star,** a bright planet, esp. Venus.

e′ven·song″ *n.* **1,** a song or hymn sung at evening. **2,** vespers.

e·vent′ (i-vent′) *n.* **1,** something that happens; an occurrence. **2,** an incident of special interest. **3,** an outcome, issue, or consequence. **4,** one item of a series.

e·vent′ful (-fəl) *adj.* **1,** full of striking events, as a period of time. **2,** having important results or outcome. —**e·vent′fulness,** *n.*

e′ven·tide″ (ē′vən-tīd″) *n.* evening.

e·ven′tu·al (i-ven′choo-əl) *adj.* **1,** happening or to happen finally; ultimate. **2,** contingent.

e·ven″tu·al′i·ty (i-ven″choo-al′ə-tè) *n.* an event that may come to pass.

e·ven′tu·ate″ (i-ven′choo-āt″) *v.i.* happen as an outcome; result. —**e·ven″tu·a′tion,** *n.*

ev′er (ev′ər) *adv.* **1,** at all times; always; continually. **2,** at any time. **3,** in any degree; at all.

ev′er·glade″ *n.* a tract of low, swampy ground.

ev′er·green″ *n.* a plant or tree that has green leaves throughout the entire year. —*adj.* always fresh.

ev″er·last′ing *adj.* **1,** perpetual; eternal. **2,** wearisome. —*n.* **1,** (*cap.*) God. **2,** a plant that does not wilt or fade when dried.

ev″er·more″ *adv.* forever after.

e·vert′ (i-vèrt′) *v.t.* turn outward or inside out. —**e·ver′sion,** *n.*

ev′er·y (ev′rè) *adj.* **1,** each without exception; all (of an aggregate taken one by one). **2,** the greatest possible, in extent or degree. **—every which way,** (*Informal*) in all directions. ❏ *either*

ev'er·y·bod"y *n.* every person. ❏ *anyone, either*

ev'er·y·day" *adj.* commonplace; usual.

ev'er·y·one" *n.* every person. ❏ *anyone, either*

ev'er·y·thing" *n.* all things.

ev'er·y·where" *adv.* **1,** in all places. **2,** wherever.

e·vict' (i-vikt') *v.t.* expel, esp. by judicial order; dispossess. **—e·vic'tion,** *n.*

ev'i·dence (ev'i-dəns) *n.* **1,** the means of proving or disproving an alleged fact; testimony, exhibits, etc., offered as proof; an indication of proof. **2,** the state of being clear or certain. **—v.t.** show clearly; prove. **—ev"i·den'tial** (-den'shəl) *adj.* **—in evidence,** plainly visible; conspicuous.

ev'i·dent (ev'i-dənt) *adj.* plainly seen or perceived; manifest; obvious. **—ev'i·dent·ly,** *adv.* apparently ❏ *apparently*

e'vil (ē'vəl) *adj.* **1,** immoral; wicked. **2,** harmful; disastrous. **3,** bad; ill-reputed. **—n. 1,** violation of moral principles; improper conduct. **2,** injury; misfortune. **3,** a cause of injury or mischief. **4,** a malady. **—e"vil·do'er,** *n.* one who sins. **—e'vil·ness,** *n.* **—evil eye,** a faculty of inflicting injury or bringing bad luck by a look; such a look. **—Evil One,** Satan.

e·vince' (i-vins') *v.t.* show clearly; **—e·vince'ment,** *n.*

e·vis'cer·ate" (i-vis'ə-rāt") *v.t.* **1,** remove the viscera from; disembowel. **2,** deprive of essential parts. **—e·vis"cer·a'tion,** *n.*

e·voke' (i-vōk') *v.t.* bring into the mind; cause to appear; call forth. **—ev'o·ca·ble** (ev'ə-kə-bəl) *adj.* **—ev"o·ca'tion,** *n.* **—e·voc'a·tive** (i-vok'ə-tiv) *adj.*

ev"o·lu'tion (ev"ə-loo'shən) *n.* **1,** the act of evolving; formation, growth, or development. **2,** (*Biol.*) the continuous modification of organic species; the steps in adaptation to environment. **3,** something evolved. **—ev"o·lu'tion·a·ry,** *adj.*

e·volve' (i-volv') *v.t.* **1,** form gradually, as though by unfolding; develop. **2,** emit. **—v.i.** come into being, or change, gradually.

ewe (ū) *n.* a female sheep.

ew'er (ū'ər) *n.* a water pitcher with a wide mouth.

ex (eks) *prep.* **1,** without; not including. **2,** from. **—n.** a former husband, boyfriend, etc.

ex- *pref.* **1,** out; out of. **2,** (hyphenated) former, as *ex-president.*

ex·ac'er·bate" (ig-zas'ər-bāt") *v.t.* embitter; make more bitter, angry or violent; irritate; aggravate. **—ex·ac"er·ba'tion,** *n.*

ex·act' (ig-zakt') *v.t.* compel to be paid or yielded; require. **—adj. 1,** strictly accurate or correct. **2,** admitting of no deviation; strict. **—ex·act'ing,** *adj.* holding to strict standards. **—ex·act'ness,** *n.*

ex·act'a (ig-zak'tə) *n.* perfecta.

> **exacta**
> ↔ Derived from the American Spanish *quiniela exacta,* exact quinella.

ex·ac'tion (ig-zak'shən) *n.* something exacted; extortion.

ex·ac'ti·tude (ig-zak'ti-tood) *n.* preciseness; strictness.

ex·ag'ger·ate" (ig-zaj'ə-rāt") *v.t.* **1,** represent as large, important, etc., beyond the truth; magnify falsely. **2,** enlarge or increase abnormally. **—v.i.** overstate. **—ex·ag'ger·at"ed,** *adj.* unduly enlarged. **—ex·ag"ger·a'tion,** *n.*

ex·alt' (ig-zâlt') *v.t.* **1,** elevate in rank, honor, power, etc. **2,** praise; extol. **3,** inspire; elate. **—ex"al·ta'tion,** *n.*

ex·am' (ig-zam') *n.* (*Informal*) a test, in school, usu. requiring a written answer; any examination.

ex·am"i·na'tion (ig-zam"i-nā'shən) *n.* **1,** act or process of examining or being examined. **2,** a series of questions asked as a test.

ex·am'ine (ig-zam'in) *v.t.* **1,** look at carefully; inspect; scrutinize. **2,** inquire into; investigate. **3,** test; interrogate.

ex·am'ple (ig-zam'pəl) *n.* **1,** one of a number of things that shows the character of all; a sample. **2,** a specimen or instance serving to illustrate or explain. **3,** a model.

ex·as'per·ate" (ig-zas'pə-rāt") *v.t.* irritate extremely; annoy; make angry. **—ex·as"per·a'tion,** *n.*

ex' ca·the'dra (eks' kə-thē'drə) (*Lat.*) from the chair (of office); with authority.

ex'ca·vate" (eks'kə-vāt") *v.t.* **1,** make a cavity or hollow in; dig into. **2,** form by scooping out material. **3,** unearth. **—ex"·ca·va'tion,** *n.* **—ex'ca·va"tor,** *n.*

ex·ceed' (ik-sēd') *v.t.* **1,** go beyond in quantity, degree, etc. **2,** be superior to; surpass. **—v.i.** be greater than others; excel. **—ex·ceed'ing·ly,** *adv.* extremely; (*Informal*) very.

ex·cel' (ik-sel') *v.t. & i.* **[-celled', -cel'ling]** be superior (to); surpass; outdo.

ex'cel·lence (ek'sə-ləns) *n.* great merit or efficiency.

ex·cel·len·cy (ek′sə-lən-sė) *n.* (usu. *cap.*) a title of address to certain high officials.

ex·cel·lent (ek′sə-lənt) *adj.* remarkably good; of superior merit.

ex·cel·si·or (ik-sel′sė-ər) *n.* wood shavings, used for packing.

ex·cept′ (ik-sept′) *prep.* leaving out; excluding; but for. —*conj.* **1,** with this exception; otherwise than. **2,** (*Archaic*) unless. —*v.t.* leave out; exclude. —*v.i.* make objection. ❑ *accept*

ex·cep′tion (ik-sep′shən) *n.* **1,** exclusion. **2,** something excepted; an instance not conforming to a general rule. **3,** an objection. **4,** slight anger or resentment. —**ex·cep′tion·a·ble,** *adj.* subject to objection. —**ex·cep′tion·al,** *adj.* unusual. —**take exception, 1,** make an objection. **2,** offense.

ex′cerpt (ek′sėrpt) *n.* an extract from something written or printed. —*v.t.* (ek-sėrpt′) cite or cull (such an extract).

| **excerpt, extract, abstract** |
| As nouns, *excerpt* and *extract* refer to a quoted passage from a larger work. An *abstract* is a summary of a document. |
---

ex·cess′ (ik-ses′; ek′ses) *n.* **1,** the state of being more or too much. **2,** a surplus or remainder. **3,** immoderate indulgence of the appetites. —*adj.* more than enough; extra.

ex·ces′sive (-siv) *adj.* **1,** superfluous. **2,** unduly great; extreme. —**ex·ces′sive·ness,** *n.*

ex·change′ (iks-chānj′) *v.t.* give in return for something else; give and receive reciprocally. —*v.i.* **1,** trade. **2,** be taken or received in exchanging. —*n.* **1,** the act of exchanging; mutual substitution. **2,** something given or received in exchanging; checks, drafts, etc. **3,** the rate at which one currency may be converted to another. **4,** a percentage or fee charged for exchanging. **5,** a place of exchange, as of stocks, drafts, etc.; a central telephone switchboard.

ex·cheq′uer (eks-chek′ər) *n.* **1,** a treasury, esp. a government treasury. **2,** (*Informal*) funds.

| **exchequer** |
| ↔ From Old French *eschequier,* chessboard, because of the design of the counting table on which accounts were once reckoned. |
---

ex′cise″ (ek′sīz″) *n.* a tax imposed on commodities, occupations, etc., within a country. —*v.t.* **1,** impose an excise tax upon. **2,** cut off or out; delete. —**ex·ci′sion** (ek-sizh′ən) *n.*

ex·cite′ (ik-sīt′) *v.t.* **1,** arouse the emotions of; stimulate. **2,** stir; agitate. **3,** produce a magnetic field in. —**ex·cit′a·ble,** *adj.* easy to excite. —**ex″ci·ta′tion** (ek″sī-tā′shən) *n.*

| **excite, incite** |
| ☛ Do not confuse *excite*, to arouse the emotions of, and *incite*, move to action. You *excite* someone, but you *incite* someone to perform an action. |
---

ex·cit′ed *adj.* **1,** emotionally aroused. **2,** enthusiastic.

ex·cite′ment (ik-sīt′mənt) *n.* **1,** the state of being excited. **2,** commotion; ado.

ex·cit′ing *adj.* **1,** tending to stir up. **2,** causing enthusiasm; appealing.

ex·claim′ (iks-klām′) *v.i.* cry out in astonishment, alarm, etc.; speak with vehemence. —*v.t.* say loudly and vehemently.

ex″cla·ma′tion (eks″klə-mā′shən) *n.* the act of exclaiming; what is exclaimed. —**exclamation point,** the symbol (!) used in punctuation for vehement expression.

| **exclamation point** |
| (*Gram.*) An important expressive tool that can easily lose its effect through overuse. The best rule is never to use one if another punctuation mark would be just as effective. |
---

ex·clam′a·to·ry (iks-klam′ə-tôr-ė) *adj.* **1,** spoken vehemently. **2,** marked with an exclamation point.

ex′clave″ (ek′sklāv″) *n.* a portion of a country physically separated from the main part.

ex·clude′ (ik-sklood′) *v.t.* **1,** shut out; omit. **2,** thrust out; eject; expel.

ex·clu′sion (ik-skloo′zhən) *n.* act of excluding; state of being excluded.

ex·clu′sive (ik-skloo′siv) *adj.* **1,** shutting out all others or all else from admission or consideration. **2,** incompatible with something else. **3,** (often with *of*) with the exception of. **4,** select; snobbish. **5,** (*Informal*) fashionable; stylish. —**ex·clu′sive·ness,** *n.*

ex·cog′i·tate″ (eks-koj′ə-tāt″) *v.t.* think out; contrive; devise. —**ex·cog″i·ta′tion,** *n.*

ex″com·mu′ni·cate″ (eks″kə-mū′ni-kāt″) *v.t.* cut off from communion or membership, esp. in respect to a church by ecclesiastical sentence. —**ex″com·mu″ni·ca′tion,** *n.*

ex·co′ri·ate″ (ik-skôr′ė-āt″) *v.t.* **1,** denounce or censure violently. **2,** remove the skin or outer covering from. —**ex·co″ri·a′tion,** *n.*

ex'cre·ment (eks'krə-mənt) *n.* waste matter eliminated from the living body, esp. the feces.

ex·cres'cence (ik-skres'əns) *n.* **1,** an abnormal outgrowth on a body, as a wart. **2,** a normal outgrowth, as hair. —**ex·cres'cent,** *adj.* superfluous.

ex·crete' (ik-skrēt') *v.t.* discharge from an organic body, as waste matter. —**ex·cre'ta** (-tə) *n.pl.* excreted matter. —**ex·cre'tion,** *n.* act of excreting; something excreted.

ex·cru'ci·at''ing (ek-skroo'shē-ā''ting) *adj.* extremely painful.

ex'cul·pate'' (eks'kul-pāt'') *v.t.* clear from a charge of fault or guilt; exonerate. —**ex''cul·pa'tion,** *n.* —**ex·cul'pa·to·ry** (iks-kulp'ə-tôr-ē) *adj.*

ex·cur'sion (ik-skėr'zhən) *n.* **1,** a journey, usually for a specific purpose, and return to the starting point; a jaunt. **2,** a train or boat ride at a reduced fare. **3,** a digression or deviation. —**ex·cur'sion·ist,** *n.* —**ex·cur'sive,** *adj.*

ex·cuse' (ik-skūz') *v.t.* **1,** pardon; forgive; overlook. **2,** apologize for; justify. **3,** release from an obligation or duty. **4,** refrain from exacting; remit. —*n.* (ik-skūs') **1,** a plea offered or reason given for excusing. **2,** a pretext or subterfuge. —**ex·cus'a·ble** (ik-skūz'ə-bəl) *adj.*

ex'e·cra·ble (ek'si-krə-bəl) *adj.* detestable. —**ex'e·cra·ble·ness,** *n.*

ex'e·crate'' (ek'sə-krāt'') *v.t.* **1,** detest utterly; abhor. **2,** denounce as abominable; curse.

ex''e·cra'tion *n.* **1,** the act of execrating. **2,** curse; denunciation.

ex''e·cute'' (ek'sə-kūt'') *v.t.* **1,** do; perform; carry out. **2,** enact. **3,** put to death according to law. —**ex·ec'u·tant** (ig-zek'yə-tənt) *n.*

ex''e·cu'tion (ek''si-kū'shən) *n.* **1,** act of executing. **2,** style or effectiveness of performance. **3,** capital punishment. —**ex''e·cu'tion·er,** *n.* the officer who inflicts capital punishment.

ex·ec'u·tive (ig-zek'yə-tiv) *adj.* **1,** concerned with doing, performing, or carrying into effect. **2,** pert. to management or administration. —*n.* a person or body having executive duties or abilities. —**Chief Executive,** the president of the U.S. —**executive privilege,** a right claimed by some presidents of the U.S. to withhold information from Congress.

ex·ec'u·tor (ig-zek'yə-tər) *n.* one designated to perform specified duties, esp. the provisions of a will. —**ex·ec'u·trix** (-triks) *n.fem.*

ex''e·ge'sis (ek''sə-jē'sis) *n.* interpretation, esp. of the Scriptures. —**ex'e·gete''** (-jēt'') *n.* an expert at exegesis. —**ex''e·get'ic** (-jet'ik) *adj.*

ex·em'plar (ig-zem'plər) *n.* an example, esp. an ideal one; a model.

ex·em'pla·ry (ig-zem'plə-rē) *adj.* **1,** worthy of imitation. **2,** serving as a model or example.

ex·em'pli·fy'' (ig-zem'pli-fī'') *v.t.* **1,** explain or illustrate by an example. **2,** be an example of. —**ex·em''pli·fi·ca'tion** (-fi-kā'shən) *n.*

ex·em'pli gra'ti·a (ek-sem'plē grä'tē-ä) (*Lat.*) for example. Abbr., **e.g.**

ex·empt' (ig-zempt') *v.t.* free from an obligation; except. —*adj.* excepted or released. —**ex·emp'tion,** *n.*

ex'e·quies (ek'si-kwēs) *n.pl.* obsequies.

ex'er·cise (ek'sər-sīz'') *n.* **1,** exertion of mind or body for development or training. **2,** active performance or use. **3,** a composition, drill, device, etc., designed for practice. **4,** (usually *pl.*) ceremonies; rites. —*v.t.* **1,** employ actively; perform; use. **2,** give practice or training to. **3,** make uneasy; disturb. —*v.i.* take bodily exercise.

> **exercise**
> ↔ From Latin *exercere*, remove restraint from, hence, train.

ex·ert' (ig-zėrt') *v.t.* **1,** put to use, as strength, ability, power, etc. **2,** bestir (oneself) vigorously.

ex·er'tion (ig-sėr'shən) *n.* **1,** act of exerting. **2,** a great effort.

ex''ha·la'tion (eks''ə-lā'shən) *n.* **1,** act of exhaling. **2,** what is exhaled.

ex·hale' (eks-hāl') *v.i.* breathe out. —*v.t.* give off as a vapor.

ex·haust' (ig-zâst') *v.t.* **1,** draw out the entire contents of; make empty or useless. **2,** tire out; fatigue. —*n.* the exhalation of waste gases, as from an engine. —**ex·haust'i·ble,** *adj.*

ex·haus'tion (ig-zâs'chən) *n.* **1,** act of exhausting; state of being exhausted. **2,** complete expenditure; utter fatigue. —**ex·haus'tive,** *adj.* thorough.

ex·hib'it (ig-zib'it) *v.t.* **1,** offer to view; place on show. **2,** manifest as a quality of character. —*v.i.* hold an exhibition. —*n.* **1,** exhibition. **2,** something exhibited; a concrete thing offered in evidence.

ex''hi·bi'tion (ek''sə-bish'ən) *n.* **1,** the act of exhibiting. **2,** a public display, as of works of art, goods, etc.

ex''hi·bi'tion·ist *n.* one who feels a compulsive urge to be noticed. —**ex″hi·bi′-tion·ism,** *n.*

ex·hib′i·tor (ig-zib′i-tər) *n.* one who displays, esp. the operator of a theater.

ex·hil′a·rate″ (ig-zil′ə-rāt″) *v.t.* make cheerful or joyous. —**ex·hil″a·ra′tion,** *n.*

ex·hort′ (ig-zôrt′) *v.t.* urge to a course of action; incite; admonish. —**ex″hor·ta′tion** (ek′sər-tā′shən) *n.*

ex·hume′ (ig-zūm′) *v.t.* dig up (something buried, esp. a body). —**ex″hu-ma′tion** (ek″sū-mā′shən) *n.*

ex·i·gen·cy (ek′si-jən-sė) *n.* **1,** a state of affairs requiring prompt action; an emergency. **2,** pressing necessity. —**ex′i·gent,** *adj.*

ex·ig′u·ous (ig-zig′ū-əs) *adj.* scanty; sparse. —**ex·ig′u·ous·ness,** *n.*

ex′ile (eg′zīl) *n.* **1,** expulsion from one's country; banishment. **2,** prolonged absence from home or country. **3,** one exiled. —*v.t.* banish.

ex·ist′ (ig-zist′) *v.i.* have actual being; be; live.

ex·ist′ence (-əns) *n.* **1,** state of existing; life. **2,** reality. —**ex·ist′ent,** *n.*

ex″is·ten′tial (eg″zis-ten′shəl) *adj.* **1,** pert. to existence. **2,** expressing the fact of existence.

ex″is·ten′tial·ism (eg″zis-ten′shəl-iz-əm) *n.* a humanistic philosophy stating that each person is responsible for forming his or her self and must with free will oppose an uncertain, purposeless, and seemingly hostile environment.

ex′it (eg′zit) *n.* **1,** a way of departure; a passage out. **2,** a departure. —*v.i.* go out or away. —**exit poll,** a poll taken of voters after they have cast their ballot.

ex″ li′bris (eks″ lē′bris) (*Lat.*) from the books (of).

ex·o- (ek-sō; ek-sə) *pref.* outside of.

ex″o·bi·ol′o·gy (ek″sō-bī-ol′ə-jė) *n.* the study of life in outer space, esp. on other planets.

ex′o·crine (ek′sə-krin) *adj.* secreting externally.

ex′o·dus (ek′sə-dəs) *n.* a mass departure.

ex″ of·fi′ci·o″ (eks″ ə-fish′ė-ō″) (*Lat.*) by right of office.

ex·og′e·nous (ek-soj′ə-nəs) *adj.* derived externally.

ex·on′er·ate″ (ig-zon′ə-rāt″) *v.t.* relieve of blame or accusation; exculpate; clear. —**ex·on″er·a′tion,** *n.*

ex·or′bi·tant (ig-zôr′bə-tənt) *adj.* going beyond usual or proper bounds; excessive

in cost or expense; inordinate. —**ex·or′bi-tance,** *n.*

ex′or·cise″ (ek′sôr-sīz″) *v.t.* **1,** expel (evil spirits) by magical or religious rites. **2,** rid of evil spirits, etc., by rites. —**ex′or·cism** (-siz-əm) *n.*

ex·or′di·um (ig-sôr′dė-əm) *n.* a beginning; esp., a preface or introduction. —**ex·or′di·al** (-əl) *adj.*

ex′o·sphere″ (ek′sō-sfir″) *n.* the outermost region of the atmosphere.

ex″o·ter′ic (ek″sə-ter′ik) *adj.* readily understood; commonplace. ❏ *erotic*

ex·ot′ic (ig-zot′ik) *adj.* **1,** of foreign origin or character; strange. **2,** (*Informal*) striking in appearance. **3,** (*Informal*) pert. to strip tease. —*n.* **1,** anything exotic. **2,** (*Informal*) a strip-tease dancer. —**ex·ot′i-cal·ly,** *adv.* ❏ *erotic*

ex·pand′ (ik-spand′) *v.t. & i.* **1,** increase in extent, bulk, amount, etc. **2,** spread or stretch out; unfold. —**expanded memory,** (*Computers*) additional memory accessed by swapping data in and out of a small section of conventional memory.

ex·panse′ (ik-spans′) *n.* an uninterrupted stretch or area.

ex·pan′sion (ik-span′shən) *n.* **1,** act of expanding; state of being expanded. **2,** an enlargement, increase, etc.

ex·pan′sion·ist *n.* an advocate of expansion, as of currency or territory. —**ex·pan′sion·ism** (-iz-əm) *n.*

ex·pan′sive (ik-span′siv) *adj.* **1,** wide; extensive; comprehensive. **2,** gregarious; sociable; friendly. —**ex·pan′sive·ness,** *n.*

ex par′te (eks pär′tė) (*Lat.*) from one side only; from a partisan point of view.

ex·pa′ti·ate″ (ik-spā′shė-āt″) *v.i.* deal with copiously, as in writing. —**ex·pa″ti·a′-tion,** *n.*

ex·pa′tri·ate (iks-pā′trė-ət) *n.* one living, as though permanently, away from his or her country. —*v.t.* (-āt″) banish. —**ex·pa″-tri·a′tion,** *n.*

ex·pect′ (ik-spekt′) *v.t.* **1,** look forward to; anticipate; await as likely to happen or appear. **2,** (*Informal*) suppose; conclude.

ex·pec′tan·cy (ik-spek′tən-sė) *n.* **1,** act of expecting; expectation. **2,** that which is expected. **3,** contingency.

ex·pec′tant (-tənt) *adj.* expecting; eagerly awaiting.

ex″pec·ta′tion (ek″spek-tā′shən) *n.* **1,** act of expecting; expectancy. **2,** something expected or awaited, as a legacy. **3,** (*pl.*) prospects of future good fortune.

ex·pec′to·rant (ik-spek′tə-rənt) *adj.* promoting expectoration. —*n.* an expectorant medicine.

ex·pec'to·rate" (ik-spek'tə-rāt") *v.i. & t.* spit out from the mouth. —**ex·pec"to·ra'·tion,** *n.*

> **expectorate**
> ↔ From Latin *expectorare,* to expel from the breast.

ex·pe'di·ent (ik-spē'dė-ənt) *adj.* **1,** serving to promote a desired object; advisable. **2,** conducive to present advantage or self-interest. —*n.* **1,** a means to an end. **2,** a makeshift. —**ex·pe'di·en·cy, ex·pe'·di·ence,** *n.*

ex'pe·dite" (eks'pə-dīt") *v.t.* **1,** quicken the progress of. **2,** dispatch. —**ex'pe·dit"er,** *n.* one who directs the course of a project through a series of government or business departments.

ex"pe·di'tion (eks"pə-dish'ən) *n.* **1,** an excursion made by a company of persons for a specific purpose. **2,** the state of being expedited; promptness or speed. —**ex"pe·di'tion·ar·y** (-er-ė) *adj.* making a journey.

ex"pe·di'tious (eks"pə-dish'əs) *adj.* quick. —**ex"pe·di'tious·ness,** *n.*

ex·pel' (ik-spel') *v.t.* **[-pelled', -pel'ling]** drive out or away; eject; emit. —**ex·pel'·lant,** *adj. & n.*

ex·pend' (ik-spend') *v.t.* **1,** use up. **2,** pay out; spend. —**ex·pend'a·ble,** *adj.* dispensable; not too valuable to spare.

ex·pend'i·ture (ik-spen'di-chər) *n.* **1,** consumption; disbursement. **2,** something expended; outlay.

ex·pense' (ik-spens') *n.* **1,** cost; charge; an expenditure. **2,** (*pl.*) charges, incurred for another, to be reimbursed. **3,** damage or loss.

ex·pen'sive (ik-spen'siv) *adj.* high in price or cost. —**ex·pen'sive·ness,** *n.*

ex·pe'ri·ence (ik-spir'ė-əns) *n.* **1,** the process or fact of learning by personally observing, encountering, testing, or undergoing something. **2,** knowledge or skill gained by this process. **3,** a particular instance of observing, encountering, etc.; an event in which one is involved. —*v.t.* meet, undergo, or feel. —**ex·pe'ri·enced,** *adj.* adept or knowing through experience; expert.

ex·per'i·ment (ik-sper'ə-mənt) *n.* **1,** a trial or test. **2,** the process of learning by observation. —*v.i.* make a trial or test. —**ex·per"i·men·ta'tion,** *n.*

ex·per"i·men'tal (-men'təl) *adj.* **1,** done as a trial. **2,** based on observation, not theory.

ex'pert (eks'pėrt) *adj.* having great knowledge or skill; learned; dexterous. —*n.* **1,** one especially skilled or learned; an authority. **2,** (*Mil.*) a rating in rifle marksmanship, above sharpshooter and marksman. —**ex·pert'ness,** *n.*

ex"per·tise' (eks"pėr-tēz') *n.* specialized skill; know-how.

ex'pi·a·ble (eks'pė-ə-bəl) *adj.* capable of being atoned for; pardonable.

ex'pi·ate" (eks'pė-āt") *v.t.* atone for; make amends for. —**ex"pi·a'tion,** *n.*

ex"pi·ra'tion (ek"spə-rā'shən) *n.* **1,** [also, **ex·pi'ry** (ik-spī'rė)] the end; termination. **2,** a breathing out.

ex·pir'a·to·ry (ik-spī'rə-tôr-ė) *adj.* pert. to emission of air from the lungs.

ex·pire' (ik-spīr') *v.i.* **1,** come to an end; die; close. **2,** breathe out; exhale. —*v.t.* breathe out; emit.

ex·plain' (ik-splān') *v.t.* **1,** make plain or clear to the mind. **2,** describe; interpret; analyze. **3,** show the cause or reason of; account for. **4,** (with *away*) nullify or remove the apparent import of. —*v.i.* give an explanation.

ex"pla·na'tion (ek"splə-nā'shən) *n.* **1,** the act of explaining; the facts or assertions that explain something. **2,** a clarification; solution; apology; excuse.

ex·plan'a·to·ry (ik-splan'ə-tôr-ė) *adj.* serving to explain.

ex'ple·tive (eks'plə-tiv) *adj.* added merely to fill out or to give emphasis (of a word or phrase). —*n.* an interjection; an oath or imprecation.

ex'pli·ca·ble (eks'pli-kə-bəl) *adj.* capable of being explained.

ex'pli·cate" (eks'pli-kāt") *v.t.* **1,** develop (an idea, etc.). **2,** analyze; explain. —**ex"·pli·ca'tion,** *n.*

ex·plic'it (eks-splis'it) *adj.* **1,** (of words, ideas) fully or clearly expressed, not merely implied; definite. **2,** (of persons) outspoken. —**ex·plic'it·ness,** *n.*

> **explicit, implicit**
> ☞ The distinction between these two words hinges upon the clarity and directness of a statement. If the meaning is clearly stated, it is *explicit;* if it is only implied or suggested, it is *implicit,* and interpretation is required to extract it.

ex·plode' (ik-splōd') *v.i.* **1,** burst suddenly; fly to pieces with noise and violence. **2,** break into action, speech, etc., suddenly and vehemently. —*v.t.* **1,** cause to explode. **2,** disprove; discredit. **3,** bring into discredit; expose. **—ex·plod′ed,** *adj.* showing the component parts of (a mechanism) separated but with indication of their relationship.

ex′ploit (eks′ploit) *n.* a notable achievement; conspicuous act or deed. *—v.t.* (iksploit′) **1,** make complete use of. **2,** turn to one's own advantage; utilize selfishly. **—ex″ploi·ta′tion,** *n.*

ex″plo·ra′tion (eks″splôr-ā′shən) *n.* **1,** the act of exploring. **2,** adventurous penetration of unknown territory. **—ex·plor′a·to·ry** (ik-splôr′ə-tôr-ė) *adj.*

ex·plore′ (ik-splôr′) *v.t.* **1,** travel over or through (a region) for purpose of observation and discovery. **2,** inquire into; examine; investigate. *—v.i.* engage in exploring.

ex·plor′er (ik-splôr′ər) *n.* one who explores unknown territories.

ex·plo′sion (iks-plō′zhən) *n.* the act of exploding; the loud noise attending such act.

ex·plo′sive (iks-plō′siv) *adj.* tending to explode. *—n.* that which explodes or causes explosion, as dynamite.

ex′po (ek′spō) *n.* (*Informal*) an exposition.

ex·po′nent (ik-spō′nənt) *n.* **1,** one who expounds or explains. **2,** representative, advocate, or symbol of something. **3,** (*Math.*) a superscript written after a quantity to indicate the power to which it is to be raised, as the ^{2} in 3^2 (=3 x 3). **—ex″po·nen′tial** (-nen′shəl) *adj.* ❑ *arithmetic*

ex·port′ (ik-spôrt′) *v.t.* send (a commodity) to another place or country for sale. *—n.* (eks′pôrt) **1,** something exported. **2,** the act or business of exporting. *—adj.* pert. to or suitable for exporting. **—ex″por·ta′tion,** *n.* **—ex·port′er,** *n.* one whose business is exporting merchandise.

ex·pose′ (ik-spōz′) *v.t.* **1,** lay open to view; uncover; reveal. **2,** show the secret intentions or motives of. **3,** leave unprotected. **4,** (*Photog.*) admit light to (a film or plate). **—ex·pos′al,** *n.* **—ex·pos′i·tor** (ikspos′ə-tər) *n.* one who or that which explains or expounds.

ex″po·sé′ (ek″spō-zā′) *n.* an exposure, esp. of something discreditable.

ex″po·si′tion (ek″spə-zish′ən) *n.* **1,** an exhibit or show, as of products of art or manufacture. **2,** the act of exposing or explaining. **3,** a detailed explanation.

ex·pos′i·to·ry (ik-spoz′ə-tôr-ė) *adj.* serving to explain.

ex″ post fac′to (eks″ pōst fak′tō) (*Lat.*) retroactively; subsequently.

ex·pos′tu·late″ (ik-spos′chə-lāt″) *v.i.* reason earnestly; remonstrate. **—ex·pos′tu·la′tion,** *n.*

ex·po′sure (ik-spō′zhər) *n.* **1,** the act of exposing; the state of being exposed. **2,** in photography, the admission of light to a sensitized plate or film; the duration of such action. **3,** the compass direction faced; aspect.

ex·pound′ (ik-spownd′) *v.t.* set forth the principles of; explain.

ex·press′ (ik-spres′) *v.t.* **1,** put (thoughts, ideas) into tangible or communicable form, as words, pictures, etc. **2,** manifest; reveal; make explicit. **3,** press or squeeze out. **4,** send as express. *—adj.* **1,** made known clearly or explicitly; directly stated or represented; precise. **2,** special; specially direct and fast. *—adv.* specially; by express. *—n.* **1,** a specially direct and fast train or other carrier. **2,** a system of rapid transportation of packages and money; goods transported by this system. **—express′i·ble,** *adj.* ❑ *espresso*

ex·pres′sion (ik-spresh′ən) *n.* **1,** the act of expressing. **2,** the word or phrase, picture, etc., that makes something known. **3,** the style in which something is expressed. **4,** outward manifestation; appearance of face; intonation of voice.

Ex·pres′sion·ism (iks-presh′ən-iz-əm) *n.* (*Art*) **1,** the effort to convey the artist's inner feelings rather than to represent external reality. **2,** free expression of one's individuality in writing, painting, etc.

ex·pres′sive (ik-spres′iv) *adj.* **1,** pert. to expression. **2,** revealing; readily understood. **—ex·pres′sive·ness,** *n.*

ex·pres′so (iks-pres′ō) *n.* (*Erroneous*) espresso.

ex·press′way″ (iks-pres′wā″) *n.* a highspeed, usually divided, limited-access highway.

ex·pro′pri·ate″ (iks-prō′prė-āt″) *v.t.* **1,** take for public use by right of eminent domain. **2,** dispossess. **—ex·pro″pri·a′tion,** *n.* **—ex·pro′pri·a″tor,** *n.*

ex·pul′sion (ik-spul′shən) *n.* the act of expelling or being expelled.

ex·punge′ (ik-spunj′) *v.t.* blot or wipe out; erase; destroy. **—ex·punc′tion** (ikspunk′shən) *n.*

ex′pur·gate″ (eks′pər-gāt″) *v.t.* purge or cleanse, esp. by deletion. **—ex″pur·ga′tion,** *n.* **—ex′pur·ga″tor,** *n.*

ex′qui·site (eks′kwi-zit; ik-skwiz′it) *adj.* **1,** exceedingly beautiful, fine, dainty, elegant, etc. **2,** giving pleasure or pain in the highest degree; intense; keen. **3,** very accurate; delicate in action or function. **—ex′qui·site·ness,** *n.*

ex′tant (eks′tənt) *adj.* in existence.

ex·tem″po·ra′ne·ous (ik-stem″pə-rā′-nēəs) *adj.* made, spoken, or performed without previous preparation; improvised at the moment. —**ex·tem″po·ra′ne·ous·ness,** *n.*

ex·tem′po·re (ik-stem′pə-rē) *adj. & adv.* impromptu.

ex·tem′po·rize″ (ik-stem′pə-rīz″) *v.t. & i.* speak extemporaneously; improvise.

ex·tend′ (ik-stend′) *v.t.* **1,** stretch out in space; carry forward; enlarge. **2,** continue in time; prolong; postpone. **3,** put forth; offer; bestow; impart. —*v.i.* **1,** be stretched or laid out. **2,** (with *to*) reach; include or cover. **3,** increase in length, duration, scope, etc.

ex·tend′ed (ik-sten′did) *adj.* stretched out; prolonged; extensive. —**extended memory,** (*Computers*) additional memory beyond conventional memory which can be directly accessed by a processor. —**extended play,** a 45-rpm recording of extended length. *Abbr.,* **EP.**

ex·ten′si·ble (ik-sten′sə-bəl) *adj.* capable of being extended.

ex·ten′sion (ik-sten′shən) *n.* **1,** the act of extending; state of being extended. **2,** an addition or prolongation. **3,** scope; range; extent.

ex·ten′sive (ik-sten′siv) *adj.* great in scope; thorough. —**ex·ten′sive·ness,** *n.*

ex·tent′ (ik-stent′) *n.* the space or degree to which something extends; length; bulk; size; limit.

ex·ten′u·ate″ (ik-sten′ū-āt″) *v.t.* make smaller in degree or appearance; make (a fault, crime, etc.) less blamable. —**ex·ten′-u·at″ed,** *adj.* shrunken; thin. —**ex·ten″u·a′-tion,** *n.*

ex·te′ri·or (ik-stir′ē-ər) *adj.* being outside; pert. to the outer surface, side, or part; outward; outlying. —*n.* the outer surface or part.

ex·ter′mi·nate″ (ik-stēr′mi-nāt″) *v.t.* destroy utterly; extirpate. —**ex·ter″mi·na′-tion,** *n.*

ex′tern″ (eks′tērn″) *n.* a person connected with an institution but not residing there.

ex·ter′nal (ik-stēr′nəl) *adj.* **1,** exterior. **2,** located outside and apart; separate. **3,** pert. to the outside of the body. **4,** outside the mind; having material existence. **5,** pert. to outward manifestation. —*n.* (*pl.*) outward appearances, manners, etc. —**ex·ter′nal·ism,** *n.* —**ex″ter′nal′i·ty,** *n.* —**ex·ter′nal·ize,** *v.t. & i.*

ex·tinct′ (ik-stinkt′) *adj.* **1,** extinguished,

as a fire. **2,** having ceased; out of existence; no longer living. —**ex·tinc′tion,** *n.*

ex·tin′guish (ik-sting′gwish) *v.t.* **1,** put out, as a fire; quench. **2,** put an end to; destroy; suppress. —**ex·tin′guish·er,** *n.* a device for putting out a fire. —**ex·tin′-guish·ment,** *n.*

ex·tir′pate″ (ek′stər-pāt″) *v.t.* pull up by the roots; eradicate; destroy totally. —**ex″-tir·pa′tion,** *n.*

ex·tol′ (ik-stōl′) *v.t.* [**-tolled′, -tol′ling**] speak in laudatory terms of; praise highly.

ex·tort′ (ik-stôrt′) *v.t.* obtain by force or compulsion; wrest from another by intimidation.

ex·tor′tion (ik-stôr′shən) *n.* exaction of payment by threat; blackmail. —**ex·tor′-tion·ate** (-ət) *adj.* exorbitant in price; demanding too much.

ex′tra (eks′trə) *adj.* more than what is usual, due, or expected; additional; supplementary. —*adv.* beyond the ordinary standard, amount, or degree; unusually. —*n.* **1,** something additional or superior. **2,** a special edition of a newspaper. **3,** an added worker, as an actor hired by the day.

ex′tra- *pref.* outside; beyond.

ex·tract′ (ik-strakt′) *v.t.* **1,** remove forcibly from a fixed position; pull out. **2,** separate, as a constituent part from the whole. **3,** derive from a particular source; deduce; select. —*n.* (eks′trakt) **1,** something extracted. **2,** a substance or preparation obtained by distillation or other chemical means. **3,** a passage from a book, etc.; excerpt; quotation. —**ex·trac′tor,** *n.* ❏ *excerpt*

ex·trac′tion (-shən) *n.* **1,** act of extracting. **2,** an extract or essence. **3,** descent; lineage; birth.

ex″tra·cur·ric′u·lar (ek″strə-kə-rik′yə-lər) *adj.* pert. to school activities outside the regular courses of study.

ex′tra·dite″ (eks′trə-dīt″) *v.t.* **1,** deliver up (a prisoner or fugitive) to another nation or jurisdiction. **2,** secure custody of a person by extradition. —**ex″tra·di′tion** (-dish′ən) *n.*

ex·tra′dos (eks-trā′dōs) *n.* the upper or convex surface of an arch or vault.

ex″tra·mu′ral (eks″trə-myûr′əl) *adj.* outside the walls, as of a college; not confined to one's own base or group.

ex·tra′ne·ous (ik-strā′nē-əs) *adj.* not belonging or proper to a thing; not intrinsic or essential; foreign. —**ex·tra′ne·ous·ness,** *n.*

ex·tra·or′di·nar″y (ik-strôr′də-ner″ē)

adj. **1,** not of the usual or regular kind. **2,** exceeding the common degree; remarkable; wonderful.

ex·trap′o·late″ (ik-strap′ə-lāt″) *v.t.* project on the basis of known data; surmise. —**ex·trap″o·la′tion,** *n.*

ex″tra·sen′so·ry *adj.* beyond the perception of the recognized senses.

ex″tra·ter·res′tri·al *adj.* beyond the limits of the earth.

ex″tra·ter″ri·to′ri·al *adj.* not subject to the jurisdiction of local authorities.

ex·trav′a·gant (ik-strav′ə-gənt) *adj.* **1,** wasteful of money; inclined to spend unnecessarily. **2,** high in price. **3,** profuse; irregular; fantastic. —**ex·trav′a·gance,** *n.*

ex·trav″a·gan′za (ik-strav″ə-gan′zə) *n.* a dramatic or musical show of elaborate or fantastic nature.

ex·treme′ (ik-strēm′) *adj.* **1,** utmost in degree, as largest, smallest, etc.; greatest in degree. **2,** farthest from the center. **3,** last; final. **4,** immoderate in action, opinion, etc. —*n.* **1,** the utmost or greatest degree. **2,** something immoderate or fantastic. **3,** the first or last. —**ex·treme′ly,** *adv.* exceedingly; very. —**ex·treme′ness,** *n.*

ex·trem′ist (ik-strē′mist) *n.* one who goes to extremes in opinions or actions. —**ex·trem′ism** (-iz-əm) *n.*

ex·trem′i·ty (ik-strem′ə-tē) *n.* **1,** the outer or terminal point; the limit or boundary. **2,** an end part; a hand, foot, etc. **3,** the utmost degree. **4,** (often *pl.*) a condition of great peril, distress, or want. **5,** (*pl.*) the last moments before death.

ex′tri·cate″ (eks′trə-kāt″) *v.t.* disentangle; set free; liberate. —**ex′tri·ca·ble,** *adj.* —**ex″tri·ca′tion,** *n.*

ex·trin′sic (iks-trin′sik) *adj.* **1,** being outside and separate; coming from without. **2,** not inherent or essential; extraneous. —**ex·trin′si·cal·ly,** *adv.*

ex′tro·vert″ (eks′trə-vērt″) *n. & adj.* **1,** (*Psychol.*) a person concerned chiefly with what is outside his or her own mind. **2,** an outgoing or boisterous person. —**ex″-tro·ver′sion** (-vēr′zhan) *n.*

ex·trude′ (ik-strood′) *v.t.* **1,** thrust out; expel. **2,** form (a plastic product) by ejection through a shaped opening. —*v.i.* project outward; protrude. —**ex·tru′sion** (-zhən) *n.* —**ex·tru′sive,** *adj.*

ex·u′ber·ant (ig-zoo′bər-ənt) *adj.* **1,** effusive in feeling or expression; lavish. **2,** copious to excess; overflowing. —**ex·u′-ber·ance,** *n.*

ex·ude′ (ig-zood′) *v.i.* ooze out, like sweat through the pores. —*v.t.* emit or discharge slowly. —**ex′u·date″** (eg′zə-

dāt″) *n.* something exuded. —**ex″u·da′tion** (eks″ū-dā′shən) *n.*

ex·ult′ (ig-zult′) *v.i.* show or feel congratulatory joy; rejoice in triumph. —**ex·ult′ant,** *adj.* rejoicing. —**ex″ul·ta′tion** (eks″əl-tā′shən) *n.*

ex′urb (eks′ērb) *n.* region beyond the city and suburbs, usually inhabited by the wealthy. —**ex·ur′ban·ite** (eks-ēr′bən-īt) *n.* one who lives in the exurbs.

ex·ur′bi·a (eks-ēr′bē-ə) *n.* the exurbs collectively.

ex·u′vi·ate″ (ig-zoo′vē-āt″) *v.t.* shed or cast off, as skin or shell; molt. —**ex·u″vi·a′-tion,** *n.*

eye (ī) *n.* **1,** the organ of vision in man and the higher animals. **2,** vision; the field of sight; observation; watchful attention. **3,** mental view; opinion; estimation. **4,** something resembling an eye; eyespot; a colored spot; a bud or shoot. **5,** a hole in an instrument or tool; a loop of rope or wire; a hook or catch. **6,** the center of a hurricane. —*v.t.* ogle; observe; watch. —**eye bank,** a storage facility for eye parts, esp. corneas, for transplant. —**eye-opener, 1,** a surprising occurrence. **2,** a drink of liquor early in the day. —**eye rhyme,** (*Poetry*) a type of rhyme employing paired words which appear to rhyme but whose true pronunciations do not: *love, prove.* —**eye shadow,** makeup used to color the eyelids.

eye′ball″ *n.* the ball-like mass of the eye. —*v.t.* (*Slang*) stare at; ogle.

eye′brow″ *n.* the hair on the ridge above the eye.

eye′ful (ī′fûl) *n.* **1,** (*Informal*) a full or satisfying look at something. **2,** (*Slang*) a beautiful or handsome person.

eye′glass″ *n.* **1,** (*pl.*) one of a pair of lenses worn before the eye to correct faulty vision. **2,** the eyepiece of an optical instrument.

eye′lash″ *n.* one of the hairs growing at the edge of the eyelid.

eye′let (ī′lət) *n.* a small round hole, as in paper, leather, fabric, etc. that is bound around the rim.

eye′lid″ *n.* the skin that moves over the eyeball.

eye′li″ner (ī′lī″nər) *n.* makeup used to outline the eye.

eye-opener 1, a surprising occurrence. **2,** a drink of liquor early in the day.

eye′piece″ *n.* the lens of an optical instrument to which the eye is applied.

eye′shade″ *n.* a visor.

eye′sight″ *n.* the faculty of seeing; vision.

eyes-′on″ly *adj.* confidential.

eye′sore″ *n.* an object of offensive appearance.

eye′spot″ *n.* **1,** a visual organ of lower animals. **2,** any eyelike spot of color.

eye′strain″ *n.* fatigue of the eye muscles caused by excessive or incorrect use of the eyes.

eye′tooth″ *n.* either of the two canine teeth of the upper jaw. **—cut one's eye-teeth,** gain understanding through age and experience.

eye′wash″ *n.* **1,** a lotion for the eyes. **2,** (*Slang*) specious talk; a lying excuse.

eye′wit″ness *n.* one who testifies concerning an occurrence which he has seen.

ey′rie (ār′ė; ī′rė) *n.* aerie.

F

F, f (ef) the sixth letter in the English alphabet.

fa (fä) *n.* (*Music*) the fourth tone of the diatonic scale.

Fa′bi·an (fā′bē-ən) *adj.* conservative; cautious in making change. —*n.* a member of the Fabian Society, a 19th-c. socialist organization in Great Britain.

> **Fabian**
> ↔ Named not for St. Fabian (3rd c. A.D.) but for *Fabius* Maximus, 3rd-c. Roman general and statesman, who defeated Carthaginian general Hannibal's forces by harassment without engaging in battle.

fa′ble (fā′bəl) *n.* **1,** a fictitious tale conveying a moral. **2,** a myth; legend. **3,** a lie. **—fa′bled,** *adj.* legendary; fictitious.

fab′ric (fab′rik) *n.* **1,** frame; structure; composition. **2,** a woven or knitted material; cloth.

fab′ri·cate″ (fab′rə-kāt″) *v.t.* **1,** build or manufacture. **2,** construct by assembling parts. **3,** concoct falsely. **—fab′ri·ca″tion,** *n.*

fab′u·list (fab′yə-list) *n.* **1,** an inventor of fables. **2,** liar.

fab′u·lous (fab′yə-ləs) *adj.* **1,** mythical; not actual. **2,** incredible; hence, immense or great. **—fab′u·lous·ness,** *n.*

fa·cade′ (fə-säd′) *n.* **1,** the chief exterior face of a building. **2,** the superficial aspect of something.

face (fās) *n.* **1,** the front of the head; countenance. **2,** expression; a look. **3,** out-ward aspect. **4,** prestige; reputation. **5,** effrontery. **6,** the principal surface of anything. —*v.t.* **1,** have the face or front toward. **2,** meet boldly; confront. **3,** cover the surface of, with anything. —*v.i.* front in any given direction. **—face card,** king, queen, or jack, in playing cards, **—face down,** abash; stare down. **—face up to,** confront boldly. **—face value, 1,** par or promised value. **2,** degree of validity claimed.

face-′lift″ing *n.* removal of wrinkles by plastic surgery. **—face-′lift″,** *n.* such an operation.

face-′off″ *n.* **1,** a method for putting the playing piece in play, as in hockey or lacrosse. **2,** a confrontation.

face-′sav″ing *adj.* serving to save one's prestige or pride.

fac′et (fas′it) *n.* **1,** one of the small surfaces of a cut gem. **2,** aspect; phase.

fa·ce′tious (fə-sē′shəs) *adj.* humorous; joking. **—fa·ce′tious·ness,** *n.*

fa′cia (fā′shə) *n.* (*Brit.*) dashboard.

fa′cial (fā′shəl) *adj.* of the face. —*n.* a facial massage.

-fa·cient (fā-shənt) *suf.* **1,** making; tending to make. **2,** that which makes.

fac′ile (fas′il) *adj.* **1,** ready; quick; skillful. **2,** affable. **3,** glib; flippant. **4,** easy to use.

fa·cil′i·tate″ (fə-sil′ə-tāt″) *v.t.* make easier. **—fa·cil″i·ta′tion,** *n.*

fa·cil′i·ty (fə-sil′ə-tė) *n.* **1,** ease. **2,** talent; dexterity. **3,** (*pl.*) conveniences; esp., a washroom. **4,** a building, etc., designed to serve a particular purpose.

fac′ing (fā′sing) *n.* **1,** an outer covering, as of different stone on a wall. **2,** a material on the edge of a garment.

fac·sim′i·le (fak-sim′ə-lė) *n.* an exact copy.

fact (fakt) *n.* **1,** something known to have occurred or to be true. **2,** the quality of being actual. **3,** the statement of something done or known to be true. **—in fact,** truly; actually. **—fact-′find″ing,** *adj.* investigatory.

fac′tion (fak′shən) *n.* **1,** a group or clique in a party, state, etc., seeking to promote partisan interests. **2,** strife; discord. **3,** in literature, films, etc., a blend of fact and fiction. **—fac′tion·al,** *adj.* **—fac′tion·al-ism,** *n.*

fac′tious (fak′shəs) *adj.* opposing; contentious. **—fac′tious·ness,** *n.*

> **factious, fractious**
> ☛ Do not confuse *factious*, contentious, with *fractious*, peevish, unruly.

fac·ti'tious (fak-tish'əs) *adj.* artificial; sham; made-up. —**fac·ti'tious·ness,** *n.*

---

factitious, fictitious, fictional
All three terms refer to information. *Factitious* means made-up, artificial (but existing nonetheless). *Fictitious* means false, imaginary (never having existed). *Fictional* means related to fiction, i.e., literature.

---

fac'toid (fak'toid) *n.* a questionable or unsubstantiated fact.

fac'tor (fak'tər) *n.* **1,** an agent, distributor, or private banker. **2,** any contributing cause or element. **3,** (*Math.*) one of the numbers which when multiplied together produce a given result. —*v.t.* **1,** handle as agent; lend money on accounts receivable. **2,** (*Math.*) produce from given factors; separate into factors. —**fac'tor·age** (-ij) *n.* business or commission of a factor.

fac·to'ri·al (fak-tôr'ē-əl) *adj.* **1,** pert. to a factor. **2,** (*Math.*) the product of consecutive integers from an integer to 1, written (!), as 3! (= $3 \times 2 \times 1$).

fac'to·ry (fak'tə-rē) *n.* **1,** a building for manufacturing. **2,** a place where goods, etc., are produced, esp. in quantity.

fac·to'tum (fak-tō'təm) *n.* a person hired to do all kinds of work.

---

factotum
↔ A *factotum* is literally someone who does everything, from Latin *facere*, to do, and *totum*, all.

---

fac'tu·al (fak'choo-əl) *adj.* **1,** pert. to facts. **2,** true; real; actual.

fac'u·la (fak'yə-lə) *n.* [*pl.* **-lae**″ (-lē″)] a spot or streak on the sun.

fac'ul·ta″**tive** (fak'əl-tā″tiv) *adj.* **1,** conferring or comprising a power. **2,** optional.

fac'ul·ty (fak'əl-tē) *n.* **1,** a physical or mental power. **2,** a special aptitude; ability; knack. **3,** the teaching body collectively of a school. ❑ *ability*

fad *n.* a passing style or interest. —**fad'dish,** *adj.* —**fad'dist,** *n.* one who follows fads.

fade (fād) *v.i.* **1,** lose color, freshness, or vigor. **2,** grow dim; die gradually. —*v.t.* **1,** cause to fade. **2,** (*Slang*) accept a bet, in craps. —**fade'less,** *adj.* permanent; eternal.

fag *v.t. & i.* [**fagged, fag'ging**] weary; exhaust. —*n.* (*Slang*) a cigarette.

fag'got (fag'ət) *n.* **1,** fagot. **2,** (*Slang, offensive*) a male homosexual.

fag'ot (fag'ət) *n.* a bundle of sticks used for fuel.

fag'ot·ing *n.* a kind of ornamentation in embroidery. Also, **fag'got·ing.**

Fahr'en·heit″ (far'ən-hīt″) *n.* a thermometric scale on which +32° is the freezing and +212° the boiling point of water.

Fahrenheit
↔ Named for its deviser, 18th-c. German physicist G. D. *Fahrenheit*, who also was the first to use mercury in thermometers.

---

fa·ience' (fī-äns') *n.* a kind of glazed pottery with highly colored decoration, named for the Italian city Faenza.

fail (fāl) *v.i.* **1,** fall short; be deficient. **2,** become weaker. **3,** prove to be lacking in what is expected or desired. **4,** go bankrupt. —*v.t.* **1,** not fulfill the expectations of; disappoint. **2,** assign a grade insufficient for passing.

fail'ing *n.* a fault. —*prep.* in the absence of; in default of.

faille (fāl; fīl) *n.* a ribbed silk or rayon fabric.

fail-'safe″ *adj.* **1,** automatically compensating for a mistake or failure. **2,** irreversibly reacting (as to launch a counterattack) on the occurrence of certain predetermined conditions.

fail'ure (fāl'yər) *n.* **1,** the act of failing; a falling short; nonperformance; deterioration; bankruptcy. **2,** an unsuccessful person or thing.

fain (fān) *adv.* (*Archaic*) willingly; gladly.

faint (fānt) *adj.* **1,** not easily seen or heard; weak in tone, color, sound, etc.; indistinct; pale. **2,** feeble; weak; about to swoon. —*n.* a swoon. —*v.i.* swoon. —**faint**″**heart'ed,** *adj.* diffident; timid. —**faint'ness,** *n.*

fair (fār) *adj.* **1,** good to look upon; beautiful. **2,** blond; light-colored. **3,** spotless; pure. **4,** legal; within bounds, as a hit ball in baseball. **5,** just; unbiased. **6,** passably good. **7,** clear; unclouded; bright; not stormy. **8,** womanly; feminine. —*adv.* **1,** according to rule. **2,** favorably; passably well. **3,** squarely. —*n.* **1,** a competitive exhibition of farm products, handwork, etc. **2,** a sale or bazaar, as for charity. **3,** a regular meeting, at a stated time and place, of buyers and sellers. —**fair'ness,** *n.* —**fair and square,** honest(ly). —**fair copy,** a final, corrected copy of a document. —**the fair sex,** (may be *offensive*) women. —**fair shake,** a fair chance.

fair, fairway

↔ The noun *fair* (meaning exhibition) comes from Latin *feriae*, holidays (when fairs are often held). The other parts of speech, of varying meanings, derive from Old English *faeger*, as does the word *fairway*, literally, a way that is clear.

fair′haired″ (-härd) *adj.* **1,** having blond hair. **2,** unduly favored.

fair′ly (-lè) *adv.* **1,** impartially; reasonably. **2,** tolerably; to a moderate degree. **3,** actually; positively.

fair′spo″ken *adj.* polite in speech.

fair-trade agreement an agreement under which a retailer must not undersell minimum price levels set by a manufacturer.

fair′way″ (fâr′wā″) *n.* **1,** (*Golf*) the mowed strip between tee and putting green. **2,** the navigable part of a river or harbor. ❏ *fair*

fair-′weath″er *adj.* (*Informal*) not dependable in time of trouble.

fair′y (fār′ē) *n.* a tiny spirit capable of assuming various forms and of interfering in human affairs. **—fair′y·land″,** *n.* the land where fairies live; any enchanting place. **—fairy tale, 1,** a story about fairies, for children. **2,** a preposterous tale; a lie.

fait ac·com·pli′ (fä tä-kom-plē′) (*Fr.*) an accomplished fact.

faith (fāth) *n.* **1,** belief without proof; confidence; reliance. **2,** belief in God. **3,** loyalty; fidelity to an agreement or promise. **4,** a religious creed. **—faith healing,** the curing of ills by prayer and religious faith alone.

faith′ful (-fəl) *adj.* **1,** loyal. **2,** conscientious. **3,** exact; true. **—faith′ful·ness,** *n.*

faith′less (-ləs) *adj.* false to a promise or obligation. **—faith′less·ness,** *n.*

fa·ji′ta (fä-hē′tä) *n.* a Mexican dish consisting of soft tortillas filled with sliced meat, vegetables, sauce, etc.

fake (fāk) *v.t. & i.* (*Informal*) **1,** imitate fraudulently; pretend; feign. **2,** improvise. **—adj.** not genuine. **—n. 1,** a counterfeit; a fraudulent imitation. **2,** a false pretender; an impostor. **—fake book,** a book of popular songs, giving only melody and chord symbols.

fak′er *n.* **1,** one who fakes. **2,** a swindler.

faker, fakir

☛ Unrelated words. A *faker* is one who fakes something. A *fakir* is a religious mendicant.

fa·kir′ (fə-kir′) *n.* a religious mendicant, esp. Muslim or Hindu. ❏ *faker*

fal′chion (fal′chən) *n.* a broad-bladed sword with a curved edge.

fal′con (fâl′kən) *n.* a small, swift hawk, esp. one trained to hunt.

fal′con·ry (-rē) *n.* the sport of hunting with falcons.

fal′de·ral″ (fal′də-ral″) *n.* nonsense. Also, **fol′de·rol″.**

fall (fâl) *v.i.* [**fell, fall′en, fall′ing**] **1,** drop or sink from a higher to a lower level; descend rapidly; decline. **2,** (sometimes with *down*) tumble to the ground, esp. after stumbling. **3,** die. **4,** come by chance. **5,** occur. **6,** pass from one condition to another. **7,** (with *away*) decline. **8,** (with *for*) be deceived by. **9,** (with *for*) become enamored of. **10,** (with *in*) take one's place in line; hence, agree. **11,** (with *out*) quarrel. **12,** (with *through*) not come to exist; miscarry. **—n. 1,** the act or result of falling. **2,** (often *cap.*) the season from Sept. 22 to Dec. 21; autumn. **—fall guy,** (*Slang*) victim; scapegoat; dupe. **—falling sickness,** epilepsy. **—falling star,** meteorite. **—fall off, 1,** decrease; diminish. **2,** separate; withdraw.

fal′la·cy (fal′ə-sē) *n.* **1,** an error or flaw, esp. in reasoning. **2,** a false idea. **—fal·la′·cious** (fə-lā′shəs) *adj.*

fall′-back″ *adj.* an alternative or reserve position, action, etc., usu. considered less desirable.

fal′li·ble (fal′ə-bəl) *adj.* apt to be mistaken; capable of committing error. **—fal″·li·bil′i·ty,** *n.*

Fal·lo′pi·an tubes (fə-lō′pē-ən) *n.* the two tubes that conduct the egg from the ovaries to the uterus.

Fallopian tubes

↔ Named for 16th-c. Italian anatomist Gabriello *Fallopio*, who first described them.

fall′out *n.* **1,** the falling of radioactive debris after a nuclear explosion. **2,** the debris itself. **3,** the reaction to or result of a statement or action.

fal′low (fal′ō) *adj.* **1,** plowed but not sowed. **2,** not in use; idle. **3,** a pale, yellowish color.

F.A.L.N. a military organization dedicated to achieving independence for Puerto Rico: *F(uerzas) A(rmadas de) L(iberación) N(acional)*, Armed Forces for National Liberation.

false (fâls) *adj.* **1,** not according to fact; untrue; erroneous; wrong. **2,** not truthful. **3,** treacherous; deceitful; disloyal. **4,** sham;

artificial. —**false′ness,** *n.* —**false alarm, 1,** an emergency alarm improperly or mistakenly sounded. **2,** any alarm or warning that turns out to be groundless.

false′hood″ (-hûd″) *n.* a lie.

fal·set′to (fâl-set′ō) *n.* [*pl.* **-tos**] a voice, esp. a man's voice, that is artificially high.

fal′sies (fâl′sēz) *n.pl.* forms worn by a woman to fill out her breasts.

fal′si·fy″ (fâl′si-fī″) *v.t.* **1,** misrepresent; deceive. **2,** alter fraudulently. —**fal″si·fi·ca′tion** (-fi-kā′shən) *n.*

fal′si·ty (fâl′sə-tē) *n.* **1,** the quality of being false. **2,** a lie.

falt′boat″ (fâlt′-) *n.* a small collapsible boat. Also, **fold′boat″.**

fal′ter (fâl′tər) *v.i.* **1,** be unsteady; stumble. **2,** be hesitant in speech; stammer. **3,** waver, in action or purpose.

fame (fām) *n.* renown; widespread reputation; rumor. —**famed,** *adj.*

fa·mil′iar (fə-mil′yər) *adj.* **1,** closely intimate. **2,** well versed or acquainted. **3,** well known and remembered; common. **4,** overfree; presuming. —*n.* **1,** an intimate associate. **2,** a spirit or demon supposed to attend on a person, esp. a witch or wizard. —**fa·mil′ial** (fə-mil′yəl) *adj.* —**fa·mil′i·ar′i·ty** (fə-mil″yar′ə-tē) *n.* —**fa·mil′i·ar·ize″** (-īz″) *v.t.* make well acquainted or well known.

> **familiar**
> ↔ From Latin *familiaris,* of a family; the sense has broadened over time.

fam′i·ly (fam′ə-lē) *n.* **1,** a household. **2,** kindred, esp. one's own spouse, parents, and children. **3,** descendants of a common ancestor; a tribe. **4,** lineage. **5,** a group of things with some common feature. **6,** (*Slang*) a unit of the Mafia. —**family leave,** a period of leave from employment for childbirth or postnatal child care. —**family planning,** a program for limiting the size of families; (*Informal*) birth control. —**family practice** *or* **medicine,** specialization in general medical practice. —**family tree,** a genealogical chart. —**in a family way,** (*Slang*) pregnant.

fam′ine (fam′in) *n.* extreme scarcity of food; starvation.

fam′ish *v.t. & i.* starve; suffer extreme hunger. —**fam′ish·ment,** *n.*

fa′mous (fā′məs) *adj.* **1,** widely known; renowned; noted or notorious. **2,** (*Informal*) excellent. —**fa′mous·ly,** *adv.* ❑ *notorious*

fam′u·lus (fam′yə-ləs) *n.* [*pl.* **-li″** (-lī″)] a servant or assistant.

fan *n.* **1,** a device for stirring the air, either mechanical or manual. **2,** (*Informal*) a devotee of a sport, hobby, etc. —*v.t. & i.* [**fanned, fan′ning**] **1,** drive air upon; wave a fan. **2,** rouse; excite. **3,** spread out like a fan. **4,** (*Baseball*) strike out.

> **fan, fanatic**
> ↔ *Fan* in the sense of circulating device comes from Latin *vannus,* a device for winnowing grain. *Fan* in the sense of devotee is a shortening of *fanatic,* from Latin *fanaticus,* pert. to a temple.

fa·nat′ic (fə-nat′ik) *n.* a zealot, esp. in religion. —*adj.* extreme; excessive. —**fa·nat′i·cal,** *adj.* —**fa·nat′i·cism,** *n.* ❑ *fan*

fan′ci·er (fan′sē-ər) *n.* one with a special interest, as in dogs or plants. —*adj.* comp. of *fancy.*

fan′ci·ful (fan′si-fəl) *adj.* **1,** whimsical; unreal, **2,** curiously designed.

fan′cy (fan′sē) *n.* **1,** the capacity for imaginative vision; an idea or notion of something unreal or fantastic but pleasing; a delusion. **2,** a whim. **3,** fondness; liking. —*adj.* **1,** chiefly imagined or imaginative; whimsical. **2,** not plain. **3,** of best quality; superfine. **4,** extravagant. **5,** done with skill. —*v.t.* **1,** imagine. **2,** suppose; assume. **3,** like; wish for; prefer. —**fan′cied,** *adj.* imaginary. —**fan′ci·ness,** *n.* —**fancy man** *or* **woman,** (*Slang*) a lover, esp. an adulterous lover of a married person.

fan′cy-free″ *adj.* carefree; not in love.

fan·dan′go (fan-dang′gō) *n.* [*pl.* **-gos**] a lively Spanish dance; the music for it.

fan′dom (fan′dəm) *n.* (*Informal*) fans collectively (as of a sport).

fan′fare″ (fan′fār″) *n.* a flourish of trumpets; ceremony; ostentation.

fan′fold″ *adj.* pert. to a continuous sheet of paper, folded like an accordion so that it can be stacked.

fang *n.* a sharp tooth, esp. of an animal or poisonous snake.

fan′jet″ *n.* a jet engine with a special air intake for increased thrust.

fan′light″ *n.* a fan-shaped window above a door.

Fan′nie Mae′ (fan′ē mā′) Federal National Mortgage Assoc.; the traded security representing mortgages guaranteed by it.

fan′ny (fan′ē) *n.* (*Slang*) buttocks.

fan′tail″ *n.* **1,** a fan-shaped end, part, or structure. **2,** a bird, fish, or plant having a fanlike tail or part. —*adj.* having such a part.

fan′tan″ *n.* **1,** a card game. **2,** a Chinese gambling game.

fan·ta′si·a (fan-tä′zhə) *n.* a fanciful or unconventional musical work.

fan·tas′tic (fan-tas′tik) *adj.* **1,** imagined or unreal and hardly possible. **2,** grotesque. —**fan·tas′ti·cal·ly,** *adv.*

fan′ta·sy (fan′tə-sė) *n.* **1,** unrestrained imagination. **2,** an illusory mental image; a visionary idea. Also, **phan′ta·sy.** —**fan′·ta·size,** *v.i.*

> **fantasy**
> ↔ From Greek *phantasia*, literally, a making visible, hence, idea, notion.

far (fär) *adj.* [**far′ther** (-*th*ər), **-thest**] **1,** remote in time or space. **2,** more distant of the two. —*adv.* **1,** widely. **2,** by a great deal. **3,** to a definite distance, point, or degree. —**a far cry, 1,** a great distance or length of time. **2,** disparate; incommensurate. —**as far as,** to the distance, extent, or degree that.

far′ad (far′əd) *n.* a unit of electrical capacitance.

> **farad**
> ↔ Named for 19th-c. English physicist Michael *Faraday*, who discovered electromagnetic induction.

farce (färs) *n.* **1,** a comedy of exaggerated humor. **2,** a mockery; a fiasco. **3,** forcemeat. —**far′ci·cal** (fär′si-kəl) *adj.*

> **farce, forcemeat**
> ↔ The theatrical sense of *farce* comes from Latin *farcire*, to stuff, with the idea that the play or other event was "forced" between the acts of another work. The same Latin verb is the source for *forcemeat*, which is not related to English *force*.

fare (fâr) *v.i.* **1,** proceed; go; travel. **2,** turn out; result. **3,** have good or bad health, fortune, or treatment. **4,** eat and drink. —*n.* **1,** the amount charged for passage; any charge or rate. **2,** a paying passenger. **3,** food served.

Far East a part of Asia including Japan, China, Vietnam, Korea, etc.

fare″well′ (fâr″wel′) *interj.* good-bye. —*n.* a leave-taking.

far″fetched′ (fär″fecht′) *adj.* too complex or unnatural to be readily grasped or believed.

far-″flung′ (fär″-flung′) *adj.* **1,** widely dispersed. **2,** extensive.

fa·ri′na (fə-rē′nə) *n.* meal or flour made

from cereal grains. —**fa″ri·na′ceous** (fa″rə-nā′shəs) *adj.*

farm (färm) *n.* a tract of land on which crops, animals, etc., are raised. —*v.t. & i.* **1,** use (land) as a farm. **2,** develop by cultivation. **3,** (with *out*) lease; assign. —**farm team,** (*Baseball*) a minor league team owned by a major league franchise.

farm′er (fär′mər) *n.* **1,** one who farms professionally. **2,** a rustic; yokel.

farm′ing *n.* agriculture.

farm′stead″ *n.* a farm and its buildings.

farm′yard″ *n.* an enclosed area around or adjoining buildings on a farm.

far′o (fâr′ō) *n.* a card game.

far-′out″ (*Slang*) *adj.* **1,** extreme. **2,** excellent; first-rate. —*interj.* excellent!

far·ra′go (fə-rä′gō) *n.* a confused mixture.

far′ri·er (far′ė-ər) *n.* one who shoes horses.

far′row (far′ō) *n.* a litter of pigs. —*v.t. & i.* give birth to (pigs). —*adj.* (of a cow) not pregnant.

> **farrow**
> ↔ The senses referring to pigs come from Old English *fearh*, pig. The sense referring to cows is from Old English *fearr*, ox.

far′see″ing *adj.* **1,** able to see distant objects. **2,** having foresight.

far′sight″ed (fär′sī″tid) *adj.* **1,** able to perceive distant sights. **2,** having foresight. —**far″sight′ed·ness,** *n.*

far′ther (fär′*th*ər) *adj. & adv.* more remote or extended, with reference to distance: comp. of *far.*

> **farther, further**
> (*Gram.*) *Further* can replace all senses of *farther*. However, *further* is generally used for expressions of time and degree; *farther* is used for physical distance.

far′ther·most″ *adj.* most remote.

far′thing (fär′*th*ing) *n.* a former Brit. coin worth ¼ penny.

far′thin·gale″ (fär′*th*ing-gāl″) *n.* a kind of hoop skirt.

fas′ces (fas′ėz) *n.* a bundle of rods bound and holding an ax blade, carried before Roman magistrates as a symbol of their power.

fas′ci·a (fash′ė-ə) *n.* [*pl.* **-ae** (-ė)] **1,** a flat surface beneath the eaves of a house. **2,** (*Anat.*) a connective tissue. ❑ *fasces*

fas′ci·cle (fas′i-kəl) *n.* **1,** a bundle; cluster. **2,** a number of sheets bound together; a part of a printed work.

---

fasces, fascism
↔ These words derive from Latin *fascis*, bundle. The political movement was so called from the idea that its members were "bundled" together (Italian *fascio*).

---

fas′ci·nate″ (fas′ə-nāt″) *v.t.* attract irresistibly; bewitch; enchant. —**fas″ci·na′tion,** *n.* —**fas′ci·na·tor,** *n.* a woman's lace scarf.

fas′cism (fash′iz-əm) *n.*(sometimes *cap.*) a governmental system characterized by nationalism, regimentation, rigid censorship, and suppression of opposition. ❑ *fasces*

fas′cist (fash′ist) (sometimes *cap.*) *n.* a supporter of fascism or a believer in its policies. —*adj.* reactionary; intolerant. —**fas·cis′tic** (fə-shis′tik) *adj.* —**fas·cis′ti·cal·ly,** *adv.*

fash′ion (fash′ən) *n.* **1,** prevailing mode, esp. of dress; present custom. **2,** people of polite society collectively. **3,** external shape; form. **4,** manner or way (of doing something). —*v.t.* make; fabricate; give a particular shape or form to. —**fashion plate,** a stylishly dressed person.

fash′ion·a·ble (-ə-bəl) *adj.* **1,** stylish. **2,** favored by polite society. —**fash′ion·a·ble·ness,** *n.*

fast (fàst) *adj.* **1,** moving at a rapid pace; swift; quick. **2,** without delay. **3,** conducive to rapidity, as a *fast track.* **4,** of a clock, showing too advanced time; of time (*Informal*) daylight saving. **5,** loose in morals; dissipated. **6,** firmly fixed; tight; steadfast. **7,** not subject to fading; lasting. —*adv.* **1,** rapidly. **2,** firmly; soundly. —*n.* voluntary abstinence from food. —*v.i.* abstain from eating. —**fast lane** or **track,** (*Slang*) a lifestyle characterized by rapid success and strong competition. —**fast time,** daylight saving time.

fast′back″ *n.* a sloping automobile roof; a car with such a roof.

fas′ten (fas′ən) *v.t. & i.* **1,** attach firmly; fix firmly in position; make secure. **2,** direct (the eyes, etc.) steadily. —**fas′ten·ing,** *n.* a clasp, lock, hook, etc.

fast-food *adj.* providing rapid preparation and service of food.

fas·tid′i·ous (fas-tid′ē-əs) *adj.* hard to please; overnice. —**fas·tid′i·ous·ness,** *n.*

fast′ness (fàst′nəs) *n.* **1,** state of being fast; speed. **2,** an impregnable place.

fast-′talk″ *v.t.* (*Slang*) persuade with glib or deceptive talk.

fat *adj.* **[fat′ter, -test] 1,** bulging with much, or too much, flesh; corpulent; plump. **2,** consisting of fat; greasy. **3,** rich in some desirable element. **4,** fertile; fruitful; profitable. —*n.* **1,** the oily solid substance in animal tissue, yellowish white in color; suet. **2,** the best part of anything. —**fat′ness,** *n.* —**chew the fat,** (*Slang*) chat; converse. —**fat cat,** (*Slang*) a wealthy person, esp. a contributor to a political campaign. —**fat chance,** (*Slang*) little or no chance. —**fat city,** (*Slang*) a state of material well-being. —**fat farm,** (*Slang*) a health spa, esp. for weight loss.

fa′tal (fā′təl) *adj.* **1,** causing death or ruin. **2,** fateful. —**fa′tal·ness,** *n.*

---

fatal, fateful
☛ Though *fatal* can mean *fateful,* usually a distinction is made. *Fatal* is taken to mean causing death; *fateful* means controlled by fate or momentous.

---

fa′tal·ism (fā′tə-liz-əm) *n.* the belief that all events are predetermined and hence inevitable. —**fa′tal·ist,** *n.* —**fa″tal·is′tic,** *adj.*

fa·tal′i·ty (fā-tal′ə-tē) *n.* a fatal disaster; a death in a disaster.

Fa′ta Mor·ga′na (fä′tə môr-gä′nə) a mirage seen on the coasts of Italy and Sicily.

Fata Morgana
↔ This is the Italian translation of *Morgan le Fay,* the fairy sister of King Arthur.

---

fat′back″ *n.* salt pork.

fate (fāt) *n.* **1,** a power that supposedly predetermines what is to happen. **2,** destiny; lot. **3,** ultimate outcome.

fat′ed (fā′tid) *adj.* **1,** predetermined by fate. **2,** doomed.

fate′ful (-fəl) *adj.* **1,** momentous. **2,** controlled by destiny. **3,** prophetic, **4,** disastrous. —**fate′ful·ness,** *n.* ❑ *fatal*

fat′head″ *n.* (*Informal*) a stupid person; dolt.

fa′ther (fä′thər) *n.* **1,** a male parent. **2,** (*cap.*) God. **3,** any ancestor. **4,** one who originates, makes possible, or inspires something. **5,** the title given to certain priests. **6,** one of the leading citizens. —*v.t.* beget; originate. —**fa′ther·hood″,** *n.* —**fa′ther-in-law″** *n.* the father of one's husband or wife.

fa′ther·land″ *n.* the land of one's birth or ancestry.

fa′ther·ly (-lē) *adj.* paternal; like a father. —**fa′ther·li·ness,** *n.*

fath'om (fath'əm) *n.* a nautical measure of length, 6 feet. —*v.t.* **1,** measure in fathoms; reach the bottom of. **2,** understand thoroughly. —**fath'om·less** (-ləs) *adj.* too deep to fathom.

fa·tigue' (fə-tēg') *n.* **1,** weariness from physical or mental exertion. **2,** (*pl.*) work clothes. —*v.t.* weary with labor. —**fat'i·ga·ble** (fat'i-gə-bəl) *adj.*

fat'so (fat'sō) *n.* (*Slang, offensive*) a fat person.

fat'ted (fat'id) *adj.* fattened.

fat'ten (fat'ən) *v.t.* **1,** feed so as to make fat. **2,** enrich; increase. —*v.i.* become fatter.

fat'ty (fat'ē) *adj.* of or like fat. —**fatty acid,** any of a class of acids present in animal and vegetable fats.

fa·tu'i·ty (fə-too'ə-tē) *n.* **1,** fatuousness. **2,** a foolish act or thing.

fat'u·ous (fach'oo-əs) *adj.* complacently silly; inane. —**fat'u·ous·ness,** *n.*

fau'cet (fâ'sit) *n.* a device for controlling the flow of a liquid from a pipe or container; a tap.

fault (fâlt) *n.* **1,** whatever is not perfect or not satisfactory; a defect; flaw; imperfection; failing; error; mistake. **2,** a cause for blame. **3,** a break in continuity, esp. in rock formation. **4,** in tennis, etc., an improper service. —*v.t.* blame —**fault'find'·ing,** *adj.* given to carping. —**fault'less,** *adj.* perfect; irreproachable. —**fault'y,** *adj.* having some defects; erroneous; erratic.

faun (fân) *n.* a Roman rural mythological being, part goat and part man.

fau'na (fâ'nə) *n.* the animals of a region or period.

> **fauna**
> ↔ From Latin *Fauna,* the Roman goddess of the countryside. Her name was used to refer to the animal life of a region by the Swedish naturalist Carolus Linnaeus.

Fauv'ism (fōv'iz-əm) *n.* a 20th-c. style of painting characterized by vivid colors and starkly contrasted contours. —**Fauv'ist,** *adj.*

faux (fō) *adj.* (*Fr.*) imitation; artificial. —**faux pas'** (pä') (*Fr.*) a false step; social error; mistake.

fa'vor (fā'vər) *n.* **1,** a spirit of approval, goodwill, or liking; partiality. **2,** an act of kindness or generosity. **3,** a small gift, esp. to a guest at a party; a token. **4,** in business idiom, a letter. **5,** (*pl.*) sexual intimacy. —*v.t.* **1,** prefer. **2,** advocate;

support. **3,** (*Informal*) resemble in facial aspect. Also, **fa'vour.**

fa'vor·a·ble (-ə-bəl) *adj.* **1,** inclined to approve; affirmative. **2,** advantageous. —**fa'vor·a·ble·ness,** *n.*

fa'vored (-vērd) *adj.* **1,** blessed. **2,** appealing. **3,** given special consideration.

fa'vor·ite (fā'vər-it) *adj.* preferred. —*n.* **1,** a person or thing preferred or popular. **2,** a contestant deemed most likely to win. —**fa'vor·it·ism,** *n.* partiality. —**favorite son,** at a U.S. presidential convention, a person favored as a nominee by the delegates from his state.

fawn (fân) *v.i.* show affection, as a dog, by hand-licking, etc.; hence, cringe and flatter. —*n.* **1,** a young deer. **2,** a very light tan color.

fax (faks) *n.* transmission of images by radio or wire; facsimile. —*v.t. & i.* send or communicate by fax.

fay (fā) *n.* an elf; fairy. —*adj.* **1,** elfin. **2,** (*Slang*) effeminate; homosexual.

faze (fāz) *v.t.* (*Informal*) ruffle; daunt.

> **faze, phase**
> ☛ Do not confuse *faze,* daunt, with *phase,* to schedule, synchronize.

fe'al·ty (fē'əl-tē) *n.* fidelity, esp. to a lord.

fear (fir) *n.* **1,** anticipation of misfortune or pain; the state of being afraid. **2,** something dreaded. **3,** anxiety. **4,** reverent awe, as of God. —*v.t. & i.* feel fear (of).

fear'ful (-fəl) *adj.* **1,** timid; apprehensive. **2,** fearsome. —**fear'ful·ness,** *n.*

fear'less (-ləs) *adj.* feeling no fear. —**fear'less·ness,** *n.*

fear'some (-səm) *adj.* causing fear; terrible. —**fear'some·ness,** *n.*

fea'si·ble (fē'zə-bəl) *adj.* **1,** possible of realization. **2,** suitable. —**fea"si·bil'i·ty,** *n.*

feast (fēst) *n.* **1,** a sumptuous meal. **2,** festival, esp. religious. —*v.t.* **1,** entertain with a feast. **2,** gratify; delight. —*v.i.* **1,** have a feast. **2,** dwell with delight.

feat (fēt) *n.* an act of remarkable skill or valor.

feath'er (feth'ər) *n.* **1,** one of the light outgrowths from a bird's skin. **2,** (*pl.*) plumage; hence, attire. **3,** something light. —*v.i. & t.* **1,** grow, or provide with, feathers. **2,** turn (an oar, a propeller blade, etc.) almost to a position parallel to the line of movement. —**feath'er·y,** *adj.*

feath'er·bed" *n.* **1,** a mattress or thick

quilt stuffed with feathers. **2,** (*Slang*) an easy task. —*v.i.* be paid for work not actually done.

feath′er·edge″ *n.* a very thin edge; the thinner edge, as of a board. —**feath′-er·edged″,** *adj.*

feath′er·weight″ *n.* a boxer of 118 to 126 pounds.

fea′ture (fē′chər) *n.* **1,** any part of the face; (*pl.*) facial appearance. **2,** a distinctive or prominent characteristic. **3,** an item of unusual interest or attraction; an article in a magazine, newspaper, etc. **4,** a motion picture of full length; the main motion picture shown in a theater. —*v.t.* give prominence to.

feb′ri·fuge″ (feb′ri-fūj″) *n.* a medicine to combat fever. —**feb″ri·fu′gal** (-fū′gəl) *adj.* acting against fever.

fe′brile (fē′brəl) *adj.* feverish.

Feb′ru·ar·y (feb′roo-er-ė) *n.* the second month of the year.

> **February**
> ↔ From Latin *februarius*, the source of which was *februa*, a word of the ancient Sabine people of Italy for a festival of purification.

fe′cal (fē′kəl) *adj.* pert. to feces.

fe′ces (fē′sėz) *n.pl.* excrement.

feck′less (fek′ləs) *adj.* feeble; ineffective.

fec′u·lent (fek′yə-lənt) *adj.* muddy; foul. —**fec′u·lence,** *n.*

fe′cund (fē′kund) *adj.* prolific; fertile. —**fe′cun·date″** (-dāt″) *v.* —**fe·cund′i·ty** (fi-kun′də-tė) *n.*

fed *v.* pret. & p.p. of *feed.* *n.* (*cap.*) (*Slang*) a federal investigative agent.

fed′er·al (fed′ər-əl) *adj.* pert. to a nation formed by the union of several sovereign states.

fed′er·al·ism (fed′ər-ə-liz-əm) *n.* the doctrine or practice of federal government; advocacy of a strong federal government. —**fed′er·al·ist,** *n.* —**fed′er·al·ize,** *v.t. & i.*

fed′er·ate″ (fed′ə-rāt″) *v.t. & i.* join (states, clubs, etc.) in a union.

fed″er·a′tion (fed″ə-rā′shən) *n.* **1,** act of uniting or being united. **2,** league; confederacy. —**fed′er·a″tive** *adj.*

fe·do′ra (fə-dôr′ə) *n.* a man's soft felt hat.

> **fedora**
> ↔ Probably named for the play *Fédora* (1882) by French playwright Victorien Sardou.

fee (fē) *n.* **1,** a charge for services, privileges, etc. **2,** a tip. **3,** land held under a feudal overlord. —*v.t.* give a fee to. —**fee simple,** absolute ownership.

> **fee**
> ↔ From Medieval Latin *feodum*, land given as a reward for service.

fee′ble (fē′bəl) *adj.* **1,** lacking energy or power; very weak; infirm. **2,** showing weakness; halfhearted; ineffective. —**fee′-ble·ness,** *n.*

fee″ble·mind′ed *adj.* **1,** having limited mental powers. **2,** (*Med.*) mentally retarded.

feed (fēd) *v.t. & i.* [*pret. & p.p.* **fed**] **1,** give food to. **2,** supply what is needed for the growth, operation, or maintenance of. **3,** satisfy; gratify. —*v.i.* take food; eat. —*n.* **1,** food, esp. for cattle, etc.; fodder. **2,** (*Informal*) a meal. **3,** a feeding mechanism. —**fed up,** (*Informal*) disgusted by too much of something.

feed′back″ *n.* a return of part of the output of a system to the input.

feed′bag″ *n.* a bag from which a horse feeds.

feed′lot″ *n.* a place where animals are fed, esp. to fatten for slaughter.

feel (fēl) *v.t.* [*pret. & p.p.* **felt**] **1,** perceive by the sense of touch; examine by touching. **2,** have a sensation of; be conscious of being, as warm, happy, etc. **3,** know intuitively; infer. **4,** suffer the consequences of. **5,** (often with *out*) explore by touch; find (one's way) cautiously by any means. —*v.i.* **1,** have a sensation of any kind; perceive oneself to be (in a certain condition, as ill). **2,** touch something to feel it; grope. **3,** be capable of, or experience, emotion. **4,** seem to the touch. —*n.* **1,** tactile quality of an object, material, etc. **2,** feeling. **3,** act of feeling. **4,** (*Informal*) aptitude; understanding.

feel′er (fē′lər) *n.* **1,** palpus. **2,** something said or done to find out the views of others.

feel′ing (fē′ling) *n.* **1,** the sense of touch. **2,** sensation of any kind. **3,** emotion; the capacity to feel emotion. **4,** an unreasoned conviction. —**feel′ing·ly,** *adv.* **1,** emotionally. **2,** sympathetically.

feet (fēt) *n.* pl. of *foot.*

feign (fān) *v.i. & t.* pretend.

feint (fānt) *n.* an apparent aiming at one point when another is the real object of attack. —*v.i.* make a feint.

feis′ty (fī′stė) *adj.* **1,** quarrelsome. **2,** frisky.

feisty
↔ A shortening of *fysting curre*, stinking cur, from Middle English *fysten*, to break wind.

feld'spar'' (feld'spär'') *n.* a mineral found in many common rocks, used in making porcelain.

fe·lic'i·tate'' (fi-lis'ə-tāt'') *v.t.* express happy sympathy with; congratulate. —**fe·lic''i·ta'tion,** *n.*

fe·lic'i·tous (fi-lis'ə-təs) *adj.* well chosen; apt. —**fe·lic'i·tous·ness,** *n.*

fe·lic'i·ty (fi-lis'ə-tė) *n.* **1,** happiness; a source of happiness. **2,** aptness; grace.

fe'line (fē'līn) *n.* an animal of the cat family. —*adj.* of the cat family; catlike; sly. —**fe·lin'i·ty** (fė-lin'ə-tė) *n.*

fell (fel) *v.t.* strike down by a blow or cut. —*adj.* ruthless; terrible. —*v.i.* pret. of *fall.* —*n.* pelt.

fell
↔ A word with many meanings of differing origins. The verb sense "to strike down" is related to *fall,* in the sense "to cause to fall." The adjective sense "ruthless" comes from Old French *fel,* fierce. The noun sense "pelt" is of Germanic origin, stemming from *fellam,* skin.

fel'lah (fel'ə) *n.* [*pl.* **-lahs**] a peasant or agricultural laborer.

fel'loe (fel'ō) *n.* the rim of a wheel when extended by spokes from a hub. Also, **fel'ly'** (-ė).

fel'low (fel'ō) *n.* **1,** a comrade. **2,** one of a pair; a mate; an equal. **3,** (*Informal*) a person, esp. male. **4,** a member of a learned society. **5,** a graduate student on a fellowship. —*adj.* in the same class, occupation, or condition. —**fellow feeling,** sympathy. —**fellow traveler,** one who supports an organization, esp. the Communist party, but is not a member. —**hail fellow,** a boisterously friendly acquaintance.

fellow
↔ From Old Norse *felagi,* to put down money, in the sense of someone putting money into a joint venture. From there to the sense of companion or fellow is not so long a voyage.

fel'low·ship (fel'ə-ship) *n.* **1,** a body of fellows or associates. **2,** companionship; community of interests. **3,** a grant of money for further study; scholarship.

fel'on (fel'ən) *n.* **1,** a person convicted of a felony; a criminal. **2,** an acute inflammation near the fingernail or toenail.

fel'o·ny (fel'ə-nė) *n.* a major crime. —**fe·lo'ni·ous** (fə-lō'nė-əs) *adj.*

felt *n.* a pressed fabric made of wool, hair, or fur. —*v.* pret. & p.p. of *feel.*

fe'male (fē'māl) *adj.* **1,** of the sex bearing young or yielding offspring. **2,** feminine. **3,** (*Mech.*) concave or having holes for the reception of a fitting part. —*n.* a female person, animal, or thing.

female, feminine
☛ *Female* indicates the sex of an organism. *Feminine* refers specifically to the qualities of woman. ↔ *Female* comes not from *male,* but from Latin *femella,* a diminutive form of *femina,* woman (which is also the source of *feminine*).

fem'i·nine (fem'ə-nin) *adj.* **1,** relating to, or like, woman. **2,** (*Gram.*) of the gender to which words applying to women belong. ❏ *female*

fem''i·nin'i·ty (-ə-tė) *n.* **1,** womanliness. **2,** females collectively.

fem'i·nism (fem'ə-niz-əm) *n.* advocacy of increased political activity or rights for women. —**fem'i·nist,** *n.*

femme'' fa·tale' (fäm'' fä-täl') [*pl.* **femmes fa·tales'** (fäm'' fä-tälz')] (*Fr.*) a dangerous, attractive woman; a seductress.

fe'mur (fē'mər) *n.* the thigh bone. —**fem'o·ral** (fem'ə-rəl) *adj.*

fen *n.* low, marshy ground.

fence (fens) *n.* **1,** an enclosing barrier. **2,** (*Slang*) a receiver of stolen goods. —*v.t.* (usually with *in*) surround with a fence. —*v.i.* **1,** use a sword or foil for sport or in self-defense. **2,** parry; evade. —**fenc'er,** *n.* one skilled in swordplay.

fenc'ing *n.* **1,** swordplay, esp. for sport. **2,** fences collectively.

fend *v.t.* ward off. —*v.i.* make shift: *fend for oneself.*

fend'er (fen'dər) *n.* a protective guard, as on an automobile or before a fireplace. —**fender bender,** (*Slang*) a minor automobile accident involving physical damage to a vehicle.

fe·nes'tra (fi-nes'trə) *n.* a windowlike opening.

fen''es·tra'tion (fen''ə-strā'shən) *n.* windows, their number and location.

Fe'ni·an (fē'nė-ən) *n.* a member of an Irish revolutionary organization.

Fenian
↔ From the legendary Irish Fenians, a group of warriors prepared to defend Ireland against its enemies.

fen'nel (fen'əl) *n.* an aromatic herb, used in cookery.

-fer (fər) *suf.* meaning that which carries.

fe'ral (fir'əl) *adj.* **1,** wild; untamed; hence, savage. **2,** having reverted to the wild state after escape or release from domesticity.

fer-"de-lance' (fer-"də-läns') *n.* a venomous snake.

fer·ma'ta (fer-mä'tə) *n.* (*Music*) the sustaining of a note, chord, or rest; the symbol (⌢) indicating such a sustaining.

fer'ment (fēr'ment) *n.* **1,** a substance that causes fermentation. **2,** commotion. —*v.t. & i.* (fər-ment') **1,** cause or undergo fermentation (in). **2,** excite; arouse; seethe.

ferment, foment
☛ Do not confuse *ferment*, excite, seethe, and *foment*, stir up, incite.

fer"men·ta'tion (fēr"mən-tā'shən) *n.* **1,** the chemical change produced in a substance by the action of organisms, as when milk sours. **2,** unrest; agitation.

fer'mi·um (fēr'mē-əm) *n.* an unstable, radioactive metallic element, no. 100, symbol Fm, produced artificially.

fermium
↔ Named in honor of Italian-American physicist Enrico *Fermi*, winner of the 1938 Nobel Prize.

fern (fērn) *n.* any of a large group of flowerless plants that propagate from spores. —**fern'er·y,** *n.* a collection of ferns; a place where ferns are grown.

fe·ro'cious (fə-rō'shəs) *adj.* very fierce; savage.

fe·roc'i·ty (fə-ros'ə-tē) *n.* cruel fierceness.

-fer·ous (fə-rəs) *suf.* containing; yielding; producing.

fer'ret (fer'it) *n.* a slim, lithe animal used to hunt rabbits and rats. —*v.t.* drive out of a hiding place; search out, as a criminal or a secret.

ferret
↔ From Latin *furittus*, little thief.

fer'ri-, fer'ro- (fer'ə) *pref.* iron.

Fer'ris wheel (fer'is) an amusement-park attraction, a large upright rotating wheel with seats for passengers, named for 19th-c. Amer. engineer G. W. G. Ferris.

fer"ro·mag·net'ic *adj.* behaving like iron in a magnetic field.

fer'rous (fer'əs) *adj.* containing or derived from iron.

fer'rule (fer'ool) *n.* a metal ring or cap for strengthening a tool handle, end of a cane, etc. Also, **fer'ule.**

fer'ry (fer'ē) *n.* **1,** provision for conveying passengers or goods across water. **2,** the boat or raft so used: *ferryboat.* —*v.t.* transport on a ferry.

fer'tile (fēr'təl) *adj.* **1,** producing crops, offspring, etc., abundantly; fruitful; prolific. **2,** capable of reproducing or developing. —**fer·til'i·ty** (fər-til'ə-tē) *n.*

fer'ti·lize" (fēr'tə-līz") *v.t.* make productive, as by impregnating (an egg, etc.) or enriching (the soil). —**fer"ti·li·za'tion** (-li-zā'shən) *n.* —**fer"ti·liz"er,** *n.* a substance that enriches the soil, as manure.

fer'ule (fer'əl) *n.* **1,** a ruler for punishing children. **2,** (-ool) ferrule.

fer'vent (fēr'vənt) *adj.* **1,** earnest; ardent. **2,** hot; glowing. —**fer'ven·cy,** *n.*

fer'vid (fēr'vid) *adj.* glowing with enthusiasm; vehement. —**fer'vid·ness,** *n.*

fer'vor (fēr'vər) *n.* **1,** ardent feeling; zeal. **2,** intense heat. Also, **fer'vour.**

fes'cue (fes'kū) *n.* a grass much used for pasture or lawns.

fes'tal (fes'təl) *adj.* pert. to a feast; gala.

festal, festive
☛ Both words may refer to feasts or festivals and the pleasures which accompany them. However, *festal* is more often used for solemn celebrations and rites.

fes'ter (fes'tər) *v.i.* **1,** become filled with pus; suppurate. **2,** rankle.

fes'ti·val (fes'ti-vəl) *n.* **1,** a feast or celebration, religious or anniversary. **2,** a gathering for entertainment or rejoicing. —*adj.* festive; joyous. —**festival seating,** unreserved seating, esp. at a rock concert.

fes'tive (fes'tiv) *adj.* pert. to a feast or festival; joyous; gay. —**fes'tive·ness,** *n.* ❑ *festal*

fes·tiv'i·ty (fes-tiv'ə-tē) *n.* **1,** gaiety; rejoicing. **2,** (*pl.*) festive observances or activities.

fes·toon' *n.* a rope of flowers, ribbons, etc., hung in a loop. —*v.t.* hang with festoons; decorate.

Fest'schrift" (fest'shrift") *n.* (*Ger.*) a collection of essays by various authors written in honor of a scholar, commemorating a special occasion, such as a birthday.

fe'tal (fē'təl) *adj.* pert. to a fetus. —**fetal**

alcohol syndrome, one of several birth defects caused by the mother's consumption of alcohol.

fetch (fech) *v.t. & i.* **1,** go after and bring back. **2,** sell for. **—fetch′ing,** *adj.* (*Informal*) alluring; attractive.

fete (fāt) *n.* a festival. *—v.t.* entertain in honor of. Also, **fête.**

fet′id *adj.* having an offensive stench. **—fet′id·ness,** *n.*

fet′ish *n.* **1,** an object supposed to embody a spirit; totem. **2,** an object of abnormal love or passion. **—fet′ish·ism,** *n.* **—fet′ish·ist,** *n.*

> **fetish**
> ↔ From Portuguese *feitiço*, charm, derived from Latin *factitius*, made by art.

fet′lock (fet′lok) *n.* a projection above and behind a horse's hoof; a tuft of hair at this point.

> **fetlock**
> ↔ The word comes not from *lock* but from Middle English *fitlok*, a variant of the word for foot.

fet′ter (fet′ər) *n.* **1,** a shackle. **2,** a check; restraint. *—v.t.* confine in fetters; restrain.

fet′ter·bush″ (fet′ər-bûsh″) *n.* an evergreen shrub.

fet′tle (fet′əl) *n.* state of health or spirits; condition.

fet″tuc·ci′ne (fet″ə-chē′nė) *n.pl.* (*It.*) a flat, narrow type of pasta.

fe′tus (fē′təs) *n.* the unborn young of an animal.

feud (fūd) *n.* a long-standing strife between clans or families; a quarrel. *—v.i.* quarrel. **—feud′ist,** *n.*

feu′dal (fū′dəl) *adj.* **1,** pert. to the system under which a vassal held land in fief from a lord to whom he owed allegiance and certain services. **2,** pert. to the period of the feudal system, the Middle Ages. **—feu′dal·ism,** *n.* practice or advocacy of the feudal system or a similar modern system.

fe′ver (fē′vər) *n.* **1,** a body temperature higher than normal; in humans, more than 98.6°F. (37°C.). **2,** a disease marked by weakness and high temperature. **3,** intense agitation.

> **fever, feverfew**
> ↔ *Fever* derives from Latin *febris*; spelling influenced by Old French *fievre*. The plant *feverfew* is so called because it was once used as a remedy for fever.

fe′ver·few″ (fē′vər-fū″) *n.* a perennial garden herb. ❑ *fever*

fe′ver·ish (fē′vər-ish) *adj.* **1,** having a fever. **2,** impatient; excited. **—fe′ver·ish·ness,** *n.*

few (fū) *adj.* not many. *—n.* **1,** a small group. **2,** (with *the*) the minority. **—quite a few,** (*Informal*) many.

> **fewer, less**
> (*Gram.*) *Fewer* refers to numbers of individual items, while *less* refers to bulk, quantity, or abstract nouns. As a result, *fewer* takes plural nouns, *less* takes singular nouns: *fewer people, less money, less love.* Although the distinction is not always observed, it is generally adhered to in formal writing.

Feyn′man diagram (fīn′mən) a graphic representation of the interaction of elementary particles.

fez *n.* a tasseled red cap formerly worn by Turks, named for a city in Morocco.

fi″an·cé′ *n.masc.,* **fi″an·cée′,** *n.fem.* (fē″än-sā′) person engaged to be married.

fi·as′co (fē-as′kō) *n.* [*pl.* **-cos**] an ignominious failure.

> **fiasco**
> ↔ From the Italian phrase *far fiasco*, literally, make a bottle, which is used in theater slang for "to botch a performance." The reason for the usage is unknown.

fi′at (fī′ət) *n.* a decree or sanction. **—fiat money,** paper currency made legal tender by fiat, not convertible into coin.

fib *n.* a trivial lie. *—v.i.* [**fibbed, fib′bing**] tell a fib.

fi′ber (fī′bər) *n.* **1,** one of the fine threadlike parts forming plant and animal tissue. **2,** a substance made of these parts, esp. when capable of being spun or woven. **3,** quality; character. Also, **fi′bre. —fi′brous,** *adj.* **—fiber optics,** transparent fibers of glass or plastic used to transmit light, often carrying coded information.

fi′ber·board″ *n.* a building material of compressed wood fiber.

fi′ber·fill″ *n.* a man-made material used as stuffing for quilts, etc.

fi′ber·glass″ *n.* glass drawn into a strong, pliable filament, used as a cord in automobile tires, in masses for insulation, or spun and woven into fabrics.

fi′ber·scope″ *n.* a flexible instrument for viewing inaccessible areas.

fi·bro′sis (fī-brō′sis) *n.* excess production of fibrous tissue in an organ, etc.

fib′u·la (fib′ū-lə) *n.* the thinner of the two bones of the lower leg.

-fic (fik) *suf.* causing; producing.

-fi·ca·tion (fi-kā′shən) *suf.* a making or being made.

fiche (fēsh) *n.* microfiche.

fich′u (fish′oo) *n.* a triangular scarf of lace, muslin, etc.

fick′le (fik′əl) *adj.* inconstant; changeable. —**fick′le·ness,** *n.*

fic′tion (fik′shən) *n.* **1,** literature in which the plot and the characters are imaginary. **2,** a statement contrary to fact. —**fic′-tion·al,** *adj.* —**fic′tion·al·ize″,** *v.t.* —**histori·cal fiction,** a type of prose literature utilizing historical personages and situations. ❑ *factitious*

fic·ti′tious (fik-tish′əs) *adj.* **1,** imaginary. **2,** feigned. **3,** false. —**fic·ti′tious·ness,** *n.* ❑ *factitious*

fic′tive (fik′tiv) *adj.* fictitious; imaginary; feigned.

fid′dle (fid′əl) *n.* a violin. —*v.i.* **1,** (*Informal*) play on the violin. **2,** move the hands and fingers idly; trifle. —**fid′dler,** *n.* —**fiddler crab,** a small crab, one of whose claws is disproportionately large.

> **fiddle**
> ↔ From the Latin verb *vitulari,* celebrate, from *Vitula,* the Roman goddess of victory. *Vitula* later referred to a stringed instrument played at a festival.

fid′dle-fad″dle (-fad″əl) *n.* (*Informal*) nonsense; trivialities.

fid′dle·sticks″ (fid′əl-stiks″) *interj.* nonsense!

fid′dling (fid′ling) *adj.* (*Informal*) trivial; ineffectual.

fi·del′i·ty (fi-del′ə-tè) *n.* **1,** faithfulness; loyalty. **2,** accuracy; exactness.

fidg′et (fij′it) *v.i.* **1,** make restless or uneasy movements; squirm. —*n.* (*pl.*) a restless mood. —**fidg′et·y,** *adj.*

fi·du′ci·ar·y (fi-doo′shè-er-ē) *adj.* pert. to a trust. —*n.* a trustee.

fie (fī) *interj.* for shame!

fief (fēf) *n.* an estate held under feudal law.

field (fēld) *n.* **1,** a tract of cleared land for cultivation, pasture, etc.; an area considered in relation to a specific use, as sports, hunting. **2,** a wide expanse; an unimpeded course. **3,** a sphere of activity; a class of enterprise, interest, study, etc.; a business. **4,** a battlefield; a battle; warfare.

5, a background, as of a photograph; a visible area; scope. **6,** a group considered as one for betting purposes; several unfavored horses in a race; several improbable numbers at dice; etc. —*v.t.* **1,** put a team into competition. **2,** catch and return (a ball). —**field day, 1,** an outing, esp. one devoted to athletic games. **2,** (*Informal*) an opportunity for unrestrained fun, etc. —**field glass,** binoculars. —**field goal, 1,** in football, a kick that sends the ball over the crossbar and between the goalposts. **2,** in basketball, a ball thrown through the basket. —**field hockey,** hockey played on a field with a ball. —**field house,** a building near an athletic field, housing dressing rooms, etc., and often a stadium. —**field marshal,** a high- or the highest-ranking military officer. —**field of honor,** the scene of a duel or battle. —**field rank,** (*Mil.*) the rank of major to colonel (*field officer*).

field′er (-ər) *n.* (*Baseball*) **1,** a player whose side is not at bat. **2,** an outfielder.

field′piece″ *n.* a cannon.

fiend (fēnd) *n.* **1,** a devil; a demon; a diabolically cruel person. **2,** (*Informal*) an addict of some practice, sport, etc. —**fiend′ish,** *adj.* cruel.

fierce (firs) *adj.* **1,** eager to kill or injure; savage; ferocious. **2,** violent; raging; intense. —**fierce′ness,** *n.*

fi′er·y (fīr′ē) *adj.* **1,** glowing, etc., like fire; burning; hot. **2,** passionate; spirited. —**fi′er·i·ness,** *n.*

fi·es′ta (fè-es′tə) *n.* a holiday or festival, esp. religious.

fife (fīf) *n.* a shrill musical instrument like a flute. —*v.t. & i.* to play the fife.

fif″teen′ (fif″tēn′) *n. & adj.* the cardinal number between fourteen and sixteen, expressed by 15. —**fif″teenth′** (-tēnth′) *n. & adj.*

fifth *n. & adj.* the ordinal of five, also written 5th. —*n.* **1,** one of 5 equal parts. **2,** a measure of liquor, one-fifth gallon. —**fifth column,** a body of citizens who serve enemy interests. —**fifth wheel,** (*Informal*) something superfluous. —**take the Fifth,** (*Informal*) refuse to testify or to answer a question, by invoking the Fifth Amendment to the U.S. Constitution, under which one cannot be required to testify against oneself.

> **fifth column**
> ↔ A translation of the Spanish phrase *quinta columna,* used during the Spanish Civil War to describe those in Madrid who were in sympathy with General Franco.

fif′ty (fif′tē) *n. & adj.* the cardinal number between forty-nine and fifty-one, expressed by 50. —**fif′ti·eth,** *n. & adj.* —**fifty-fifty,** *adv. & adj.* (*Informal*) in two equal shares.

fig *n.* a tropical tree; its pulpy, pear-shaped fruit.

fight (fīt) *v.i.* [*pret. & p.p.* **fought** (fât)] **1,** engage in combat. **2,** strive; contend. —*v.t.* **1,** war against. **2,** contend with. —*n.* **1,** a battle or contest. **2,** willingness to fight.

fight′er (-ər) *n.* **1,** one who fights. **2,** a warplane designed to fight enemy planes.

fig′ment (fig′mənt) *n.* something feigned or imagined; a pure invention.

fig″ur·a′tion (fig″yə-rā′shən) *n.* act or result of shaping, embellishing, or expressing by a figure.

fig′ur·a·tive (fig′yər-ə-tiv) *adj.* **1,** symbolical; not literal. **2,** full of figures of speech; flowery. —**fig′ur·a·tive·ness,** *n.*

fig′ure (fig′yər) *n.* **1,** form; shape; outline. **2,** a likeness of a form, as in art. **3,** the bodily form. **4,** an outline traced by a skater; a movement of a dance; the pattern of a fabric; a design, esp. an ornate one. **5,** a rhetorical symbol: *figure of speech.* **6,** a personage. **7,** a numerical symbol; (*pl.*) mathematics; computation. **8,** price. —*v.t.* **1,** (often with *out*) calculate; indicate by numbers. **2,** form; shape; portray, esp. in sculpture; see in imagination. **3,** ornament with a design. —*v.i.* **1,** take prominent part. **2,** (*Informal*) calculate; deduce. **3,** (with *on*) (*Informal*) count on; expect; anticipate. —**figure skating,** ice skating in which elaborate patterns are produced; a competitive sport involving such skating.

fig′ure·head″ (fig′yər-hed″) *n.* **1,** an ornamental figure on a ship's bow. **2,** a person of nominal but no real authority.

fig″ur·ine′ (fig″yû-rēn′) *n.* a small work of sculpture; a statuette.

fig′wort″ (fig′wûrt″) *n.* a type of flowering woodland plant.

---

figwort

↔ The *figwort* has nothing to do with fig in the modern sense, but derives from an obsolete sense of the word, hemorrhoids, which the plant was supposed to cure.

---

fil′a·ment (fil′ə-mənt) *n.* **1,** a fine thread-like fiber, as of a cobweb, wire, etc. **2,** the slender stalk bearing an anther in a flower.

fi′lar (fī′lər) *adj.* threadlike.

fil′bert (fil′bərt) *n.* the edible nut of the hazel; a hazelnut.

---

filbert

↔ Named after St. Philbert, because it is generally ripe by August 22, his saint day.

---

filch *v.t.* steal; pilfer. ❏ *rob*

file (fīl) *n.* **1,** a folder, case, or device for keeping papers in order; the papers so kept. **2,** a row of persons, esp. soldiers, one behind the other. **3,** a metal tool with a ridged surface for smoothing or cutting metal, wood, etc. **4,** (*Computers*) data, programs, or graphics stored on a storage medium, as floppy disk, magnetic disk, etc. —*v.t.* **1,** put (papers) in a file; record officially. **2,** smooth or cut with a file. —*v.i.* march in file. —**filing cabinet,** a set of drawers for holding filed papers. —**on file,** in a file and available for reference.

fi·let′ (fi-lā′) *n. & v.* fillet. —**filet mi·gnon′** (min-yon′) (*Fr.,* dainty fillet) a tenderloin of beefsteak.

fil′i·al (fil′ē-əl) *adj.* pert. to or appropriate to a son or daughter.

fil′i·bus″ter (fil′ə-bus″tər) *n.* **1,** the tactics, esp. in the U.S. Senate, of prolonged speaking to prevent or delay legislation. **2,** one who uses such tactics. **3,** a freebooter. —*v.i.* **1,** speak in a filibuster. **2,** act like or be a freebooter.

---

filibuster, freebooter

↔ These two words both derive from Dutch *vrijbuiter,* pirate, perhaps a critical reference to legislators who engage in such tactics.

---

fil′i·gree″ (fil′ə-grē″) *n. & adj.* ornamental openwork of fine wire. —*v.t.* make into or adorn with filigree.

---

filigree

↔ A compound of two Latin words, *filum,* thread, and *granum,* grain.

---

fil′ing (fī′ling) *n.* (usually *pl.*) a scrap filed off a larger piece.

fill (fil) *v.t.* **1,** occupy the entire capacity of. **2,** make full; be perceptible throughout; pervade. **3,** occupy (a position); perform the duties of. **4,** secure an occupant or incumbent for (a job, etc.) **5,** put an appropriate substance into (a cavity, hole, crack, etc.); stop up. **6,** feed to satiation. **7,** carry out (an order). —*v.i.* take in a filling quantity. —*n.* **1,** enough to satisfy. **2,** a filling. —**fill′er,** *n.* material used for filling, as the inside tobacco of a cigar, a base paint to fill cracks, etc. —**fill′ing,** *n.* that which is used to fill, as a material to fill a cavity in a tooth, or the crust of a pie. —**filling station,** a gas station. —**fill**

---

out, 1, complete (a document) by writing in the blank spaces. **2,** become rounded, inflated, or filled.

fil′let (fil′et) *n.* **1,** a narrow band for the hair. **2,** a thin, narrow strip, as a molding. **3,** [also, **fi·let′** (fi-lā′)] a boneless piece of meat or fish. —*v.t.* [**fil·let′ed** (fi-lād′)] to remove bones, etc., from (a piece of meat or fish).

fil′lip (fil′əp) *n.* **1,** a snap of the fingers. **2,** a stimulus; incentive.

fil′ly (fil′ė) *n.* a young mare.

film *n.***1,** a very thin layer, as of oil, coating the surface of something. **2,** a cellulose sheet, coated for photography; the developed negative of a picture. **3,** a mist; haze. **4,** a thin membrane. **5,** a motion picture. —*v.t.* photograph. —**film′dom** (-dəm) *n.* the motion picture industry. —**film′y,** *adj.*

film′ noir′ (nwär′) (*Fr.*) a type of motion picture characterized by grim, urban settings and an aura of mystery.

film′strip″ *n.* a strip of film intended for still projection.

fil′ter (fil′tər) *n.* **1,** any porous material for trapping solids from a fluid or the air. **2,** any similar device, as for separating light rays. —*v.t. & i.* pass through a filter.

filth *n.* **1,** foul matter; a dirty condition. **2,** corruption; obscene matter. **3,** (*Computers*) a program for converting text formatting from one system to another. —**filth′i·ness,** *n.* —**filth′y,** *adj.*

fil′trate (fil′trāt) *v.t. & i.* filter. —*n.* filtered liquid. —**fil·tra′tion,** *n.*

fin *n.* **1,** a membranous winglike projection from the body of a fish; anything resembling it. **2,** (*Slang*) a $5 bill. —**finned, fin′ny,** *adj.*

fi·na′gle (fi-nā′gəl) *v.t. & i.* obtain or contrive unscrupulously.

fi′nal (fī′nəl) *adj.* **1,** last; ultimate. **2,** decisive. —*n.* (*pl.*) **1,** a deciding contest. **2,** the last college examinations. —**fi′nal·ist,** *n.* one competing in the deciding match. —**fi·nal′i·ty** (fī-nal′ə-tė) *n.* —**fi′nal·ize,** *v.t.* (*Informal*) make final or definite. —**final solution,** genocide.

fi·na′le (fi-nä′lė) *n.* a closing scene, esp. of a musical performance.

fi·nance′ (fi-nans′; fī′nans) *n.* **1,** management of monetary affairs, esp. in banking and government. **2,** bankers, capitalists, and investors collectively. **3,** (*pl.*) monetary resources or revenue. —*v.t.* supply with money. —**fi·nan′cial** (-shəl) *adj.* —**finance company,** a company that lends money.

---

finance
↔ From Latin *finis*, end, in the sense of putting an end to a financial obligation. The same Latin word is the source of *final, finish,* and *fine,* among other words.

---

fin″an·cier′ (fin″ən-sir′) *n.* a capitalist or banker.

fin′back″ *n.* any of a genus of whales having large dorsal fins.

finch *n.* any of various small songbirds, as the sparrow.

find (fīnd) *v.t.* [*pret. & p.p.* **found**] **1,** locate by searching; come across by chance; discover. **2,** arrive at (a result, etc.); conclude; (*Law*) declare. —*n.* a valuable discovery. —**find′er,** *n.* one who or that which finds, esp. a device for locating a view for photographing.

fin de siè′cle (faṅ də sye′klə) (*Fr.*) end of the century, esp. the 19th c.

find′ing *n.* **1,** a decision or verdict. **2,** (*pl.*) small accessories or materials.

fine (fīn) *adj.* **1,** pure, as unalloyed gold; superior in quality, texture, etc. **2,** delicate, not coarse; of small diameter; ground into very small particles; very thin or keen, as a blade. **3,** discriminating. **4,** elegant; handsome. —*n.* **1,** a money penalty for a breach of law. **2,** (fē′ne) (*Music*) the end (of a piece or repeated section). —*v.t.* punish by a fine. —**fine′ness,** *n.* the degree of purity, thinness, etc. —**fine arts,** painting, engraving, architecture, and sculpture. —**fine print,** (*Informal*) small print in contracts, etc., often used for stipulations unfavorable to a party. —**in fine,** in short; finally.

fin′er·y (fī′nə-rė) *n.* showy clothes and jewelry.

fine-′spun″ *adj.* **1,** drawn out in a fine thread. **2,** highly or artificially subtle.

fi·nesse′ (fi-nes′) *n.* **1,** delicate skill. **2,** cunning; artful management. **3,** in card games, a play to trap an opponent's card. —*v.t. & i.* **1,** use or achieve by artifice. **2,** attempt a finesse (of) at cards.

fine-′tune′ *v.t.* **1,** tune (a radio, TV, etc.) for optimum reception. **2,** make delicate adjustments to something (as the economy) for best performance or results.

fin′ger (fing′gər) *n.* **1,** one of the five terminal members of the hand, esp. one other than the thumb. **2,** anything like or operating like a finger. —*v.t.* **1,** touch; handle. **2,** (*Slang*) inform against. **3,** perform with the fingers. —**fin′ger·ing,** *n.* (*Music*) the action or use of the fingers in playing; markings placed in music to

---

indicate such use. —**fin′ger·board″** *n.* the neck of a violin, guitar, or other stringed instrument. —**finger bowl,** a small dish of water for rinsing the fingers after a meal. —**finger wave,** a wave in the hair, done without a heated iron.

fin′ger·ling *n.* a finger-length fish.

fin′ger·nail″ *n.* the horny cap at the end of the finger.

fin′ger·print″ *n.* an impression of the lines on the tips of the fingers, used for identification.

fin′i·al (fin′ē-əl) *n.* the ornamental tip of a spire, cap on a shaft, etc.

fin′i·cal (fin′i-kəl) *adj.* unduly particular or fussy. Also, **fin′ick·ing, fin′ick·y.**

fi′nis (fin′is) *n.* the end.

fin′ish *v.t.* **1,** bring to an end; terminate. **2,** use up. **3,** complete; perfect. **4,** paint; polish. —*n.* **1,** the end. **2,** the final work done upon a thing. **3,** the way in which something is finished, as furniture. **4,** social polish; poise. —**finishing school,** a private secondary school for girls.

fin′ished *adj.* **1,** completed; perfected; polished. **2,** highly accomplished.

fi′nite (fī′nīt) *adj.* having limits; restricted. —**fi′nite·ness,** *n.*

fink (*Slang*) *n.* **1,** a strikebreaker. **2,** an informer. —*v.i.* **1,** (with *out*) quit; give up; let down. **2,** (with *on*) inform against.

fin′nan had′die (fin′ən had′ē) *n.* smoked haddock.

Finn′ish bath (fin′ish) a sauna followed by a plunge in cold water.

fiord (fyôrd) *n.* a narrow arm of the sea between high cliffs. Also, **fjord.**

fir (fėr) *n.* an evergreen, cone-bearing tree or its wood.

fire (fīr) *n.* **1,** the heat and light caused by burning. **2,** a burning of fuel; a conflagration, as of a building, forest, etc. **3,** a discharge of firearms. **4,** ardor; zeal; brilliancy. —*v.t.* **1,** set ablaze. **2,** subject to great heat. **3,** animate; inspire. **4,** discharge, as a gun. **5,** (*Informal*) dismiss from a job. —**fire engine,** a motor vehicle equipped to combat fires. —**fire escape,** an outdoor stairway or other structure designed to be used for escape from a burning building. —**fire off, 1,** discharge (as a firearm). **2,** write hastily and dispatch. —**fire tower,** a lookout tower used esp. to watch for forest fires. —**fir′ing line, 1,** the line from which weapons fire is directed against an enemy. **2,** a vulnerable frontline position.

fire′arm″ *n.* a weapon that propels a missile by an explosive.

fire′ball″ *n.* **1,** an early type of bomb. **2,** something like a ball of fire, as a luminous meteor. **3,** the cloud of hot, luminous gases produced by a nuclear explosion. **4,** (*Informal*) an extremely energetic person.

fire′bomb″ *n.* an incendiary bomb. —*v.t.* to attack with a firebomb.

fire′box″ *n.* the fuel chamber of a furnace or locomotive.

fire′brand″ *n.* **1,** a piece of burning wood. **2,** one who stirs up strife.

fire′break″ *n.* a strip of land cleared to check the spread of a forest fire.

fire′brick″ *n.* a brick capable of resisting high temperatures.

fire′bug″ *n.* (*Informal*) one who intentionally starts destructive fires.

fire′crack″er *n.* a small explosive-filled tube, set off to make a noise.

fire′damp″ *n.* a combustible gas occurring in coal mines.

fire′dog″ *n.* an andiron.

fire′fight″ *n.* an exchange of gunfire by opposing military forces.

fire′fight″er *n.* one employed to prevent or extinguish fires.

fire′fly″ *n.* a small beetle that emits light.

fire′man (-mən) *n.* [*pl.* **-men**] **1,** a firefighter. **2,** a stoker.

fire′place″ *n.* a recess lined with bricks or stones in which a fire is built for cooking or warmth.

fire′plug″ *n.* a street hydrant.

fire′proof″ *adj.* made of fire-resisting material. —*v.t.* render fireproof; treat or cover with fireproof material.

fire′side″ *n.* the hearth; home: —**fireside chat,** an informal speech by a political leader, esp. a U.S. president.

fire′storm″ *n.* **1,** an unusually intense fire. **2,** an atmospheric storm caused by the heat of a large fire.

fire′trap″ *n.* a building likely to be dangerous in case of fire.

fire′wa″ter *n.* (*Informal*) strong liquor.

fire′works″ *n.pl.* explosives set off to produce noise or display.

fir′kin (fėr′kin) *n.* a small cask or tub for butter, etc.

firm (fėrm) *adj.* **1,** not easy to shake, move, press in, puncture, etc.; steady; rigid; compact; solid; tough. **2,** stanch; loyal. **3,** positive; unalterable. —*n.* a business partnership; a company. —**firm′-ness,** *n.*

firm, company, corporation, partnership
A *firm* is a business partnership. The word should not be used to refer to a *company* or a *corporation*, which are incorporated business entities.

fir'ma·ment (fēr'mə-mənt) *n.* the visible sky; the heavens.

fir'man (fēr'mən) *n.* an edict issued by an Oriental sovereign.

firm'ware" *n.* (*Computers*) software that is permanently stored in read-only memory.

first (fērst) *adj.* **1,** foremost in time, place, importance, etc. **2,** the ordinal of one. —*adv.* before all others in place, time, rank, etc. —*n.* a person or thing that is first. —**first aid,** emergency treatment of the injured. —**First Lady,** the wife of the U.S. president or of a state governor. —**first lieutenant,** an army officer ranking below a captain and above a second lieutenant. —**first off,** (*Slang*) in the first place. —**first person,** (*Gram.*) the relation between a verb and its subject, so called when the subject is the speaker. —**first water,** the highest degree of fineness.

first'born' *adj.* eldest; first in order of birth.

first-'class" *adj.* of best quality.

first'hand" *adj.* direct, not by hearsay.

first-'rate" *adj.* of best quality; excellent. —*adv.* (*Informal*) very well.

firth (fērth) *n.* an arm of the sea.

fis'cal (fis'kəl) *adj.* pert. to financial matters, esp. governmental. —**fiscal year,** the 12-month period used for accounting purposes, which may or may not coincide with the calendar year.

fiscal
↔ From Latin *fiscus*, basket, hence, (public) purse.

fish *n.* [*pl.* **fishes** or **fish**] **1,** a completely aquatic vertebrate, usually with scales and fins. **2,** any of various other aquatic animals. **3,** fish flesh used as food. **4,** (*Slang*) a dupe. —*v.i.* & *t.* **1,** try to catch fish. **2,** search for anything hidden. **3,** seek to get indirectly; draw out. —**fish and chips,** deep-fried fish with French fried potatoes. —**fish story,** (*Informal*) an exaggerated or unbelievable narrative; tall tale.

fish'er (-ər) *n.* a person or vessel engaged in fishing. Also, **fish'er·man** (-mən), *n.masc.,* **fish'er·wom"an,** *n.fem.*

fish'er·y (-ə-rē) *n.* **1,** the business of fishing. **2,** a fishing ground.

fish'eye" lens a wide-angle lens giving a 180° view.

fish'hook" *n.* a hook used in catching fish.

fish'tail" *v.i.* (*Slang*) of the rear end of an automobile, swing uncontrollably from side to side.

fish'wife" *n.* **1,** a woman who sells fish. **2,** a scurrilous woman.

fish'y (-ē) *adj.* **1,** like fish in appearance, smell, etc. **2,** improbable; questionable. **3,** expressionless. —**fish'i·ness,** *n.*

fis'sile (fis'il; -əl) *adj.* fissionable.

fis'sion (fish'ən) *n.* a splitting into parts. —**fis'sion·a·ble,** *adj.* (of a chemical element) composed of atoms that will split.

fis'sure (fish'ər) *n.* a crack or cleft.

fist *n.* the hand clenched. —**fist'fight",** *n.* a fight with the fists. —**fist'ful,** *n.* handful. ❑ *five*

fist'ic (-ik) *adj.* pert. to boxing.

fist'i·cuffs" (-i-kufs") *n.pl.* a fistfight.

fis'tu·la (fis'chū-lə) *n.* an ulcerous passage from an abscess or an internal organ to the surface. —**fis'tu·lar,** *adj.*

fit *adj.* [**fit'ter, -test**] **1,** proper; suitable. **2,** ready; prepared; in top condition. —*v.t.* [**fit'ted, -ting**] **1,** adapt. **2,** (often with *out*) equip; supply. —*v.i.* **1,** be meet or proper. **2,** be of the right shape, size, etc. —*n.* **1,** something that is suitable. **2,** a convulsion; a sudden attack, as of epilepsy. **3,** an outburst, as of emotion, energy, etc. —**fit'ness,** *n.*

fit'ful (fit'fəl) *adj.* capricious; intermittent. —**fit'ful·ness,** *n.*

fit'ter (-ər) *n.* one who fits clothes on others.

fit'ting (-ing) *adj.* suitable; proper. —*n.* **1,** act of fitting. **2,** (*pl.*) furnishings.

five (fīv) *n.* & *adj.* the cardinal number between four and six, expressed by 5. —**five-and-ten,** *n.* (*Informal*) a department store specializing in low-priced items. —**five-o'clock shadow,** (*Slang*) a light beard.

five
↔ Traced back through Old English to the Indo-European root **pengke,* five, which also produced *fist, finger,* and *pentagon.*

fix (fiks) *v.t.* **1,** fasten firmly. **2,** settle definitely; establish (a time or place). **3,** make fast or permanent, as dye. **4,** arrange; repair. **5,** prepare. **6,** (*Slang*) bribe. **7,** (*Informal*) castrate or spay (an animal). —*n.* **1,** (*Informal*) a predicament. **2,** (*Slang*) a secret arrangement, usu. accomplished by means of a bribe. **3,** (*Slang*) a dose of a narcotic drug. **—fixed disk,** (*Computers*) hard disk. **—fix′ings,** *n.pl.* (*Informal*) trimmings.

fix·a′tion (fik-sā′shən) *n.* **1,** the state of being fixed. **2,** an obsession. **3,** a premature cessation of emotional development.

fix′a·tive (fik′sə-tiv) *adj.* serving to fix; making stable or permanent. **—n.** a preservative substance, as varnish to a drawing, etc.

fix′ture (fiks′chər) *n.* **1,** an article of furniture attached to the room. **2,** a person or thing that cannot be removed.

fizz (fiz) *v.i.* **1,** make a hissing sound; effervesce. **2,** a mixed drink. **—n.** such a sound.

fiz′zle (fiz′əl) **1,** make a hissing sound. **2,** (*Informal*) peter out; fail.—*n.* act or effect of fizzling.

fjord (fyôrd) *n.* fiord.

flab *n.* (*Informal*) excess body fat.

flab′ber·gast″ (flab′ər-gast″) *v.t.* (*Informal*) confound; astonish.

> **flabbergast**
> ↔ Possibly a fanciful formation from *flabby* and *aghast*. The relevance of *aghast* is clear, but how *flabby* fits in is less evident.

flab′by (flab′ē) *adj.* **1,** lacking firmness; jellylike. **2,** feeble. **—flab′bi·ness,** *n.*

flac′cid (flak′sid) *adj.* soft; flabby. **—flac-cid′i·ty** (-sid′ə-tė), **flac′cid·ness,** *n.*

flack (flak) *n.* **1,** a press agent. **2,** flak.

fla·con′ (flá-kän′) *n.* a small flask.

flag *n.* **1,** a piece of cloth bearing a design for display as a signal, standard, etc. **2,** an iris. **3,** a flagstone. **—v.t.** [**flagged, flag′-ging**] **1,** signal to with or as with a flag. **2,** pave with flagstones. **—v.i.** droop; grow languid. **—flag officer,** a naval officer of rank of commodore or higher.

> **flag, flagstone**
> ↔ *Flagstone* is derived from *flag,* in the sense of a paving stone, which in turn is derived from Middle English *flagge,* piece of sod, as is *flag* in the sense of iris. The other senses of the word may be a combination of *flap* and *fag* in an obsolete sense of flap.

flag′el·late″ (flaj′ə-lāt″) *v.t.* whip. **—flag′-el·lant,** (-lənt) *n.* one who flagellates herself or himself, esp. for religious purposes. **—flag″el·la′tion,** *n.*

flag′eo·let′ (flaj′ə-let′) *n.* a type of end-blown flute.

fla·gi′tious (flə-jish′əs) *adj.* grossly wicked. **—fla·gi′tious·ness,** *n.*

flag′on (flag′ən) *n.* a covered pitcher for liquors.

flag′pole″ *n.* a pole on which a flag is hung.

fla′grant (flā′grənt) *adj.* overtly outrageous. **—fla′gran·cy,** *n.* ❏ *blatant*

fla·gran′te de·lic′to (flə-gran′tė di-lik′tō) (*Lat., Law*) during the commission of the crime.

flag′ship″ *n.* the ship of the officer commanding a fleet.

flag′staff″ *n.* a staff by which a flag is hung or supported.

flag′stone″ *n.* a flat paving stone. Also, **flag.** ❏ *flag*

flail (flāl) *n.* a hand tool for threshing grain. **—v.t. & i. 1,** use a flail (on). **2,** whip; beat.

> **flail, flay**
> ☞ Two similar-sounding but unrelated words. To *flail* is to whip; *flay* means to strip the skin from (one could *flay* someone by *flailing* him).

flair (flâr) *n.* **1,** discriminating taste. **2,** a liking; bent.

> **flair, flare**
> ☞ Do not confuse these two homonyms. *Flair* means taste, *flare* means a light, signal.

flak *n.* **1,** antiaircraft fire. **2,** (*Slang*) criticism; complaints.

> **flak**
> ↔ An abbreviation of German *Fl(ieger)a(bwehr)k(anone),* air defense cannon.

flake (flāk) *n.* **1,** a small flat, scalelike particle. **2,** (*Slang*) an eccentric person. **—v.t. & i.** break or separate into flakes. **—flake out,** (*Slang*) sleep; lose consciousness.

flak′y (flā′kė) *adj.* **1,** like or consisting of flakes. **2,** of pastry, very short; crumbly. **3,** (*Slang*) odd or unusual in style or behavior. **—flak′i·ness,** *n.*

flam *v.t.* [**flammed, flam′ming**] delude; cheat. **—n. 1,** a trick; deception. **2,** a short roll on the drum.

flam·bé′ (fläm-bā′) *adj.* (*Fr.*) flaming.

flam′beau (flam′bō) *n.* **1,** a flaming torch. **2,** a large candlestick.

flam·boy′ant (flam-boi′ənt) *adj.* showy; ornate; gorgeous; florid. **—flam·boy′ance,** *n.*

flame (flām) *n.* **1,** burning gas or vapor; the luminous, quivering tongue it makes; (*pl.*) a state of combustion. **2,** burning zeal; ardor. **3,** (*Slang*) a sweetheart. —*v.i.* **1,** burn; shine. **2,** break out like flame, in anger or passion. —**flame thrower,** a weapon that throws a spray of burning oil.

fla·men′co (flə-meng′kō) *n.* an Andalusian gypsy dance.

---

flamenco, flamingo

↔ Despite its Spanish associations, *flamenco* comes from the Spanish word for *flamingo*, literally, Flemish. The bird was so named because of its reddish-pink coloring, supposedly resembling that of the Flemish. Likewise, the Andalusian dancers exhibited such coloring in complexion and dress.

---

flame′out″ *n.* the stalling of a jet engine due to malfunction or lack of fuel.

flam′ing *adj.* **1,** fiery. **2,** passionate; violent. **3,** flagrant.

fla·min′go (flə-ming′gō) *n.* [*pl.* **-gos**] a long-legged tropical bird with scarlet plumage. ❑ *flamenco*

flam′ma·ble (flam′ə-bəl) *adj.* inflammable. ❑ *inflammable*

flange (flanj) *n.* a projecting rim.

flank *n.* **1,** an animal's side between ribs and hip. **2,** the side of anything. **3,** (*Mil.*) the extreme right or left of an army or fleet. —*v.t.* **1,** stand at the flank. **2,** go around, or turn, the flank of.

flan′nel (flan′əl) *n.* **1,** a soft woolen fabric. **2,** (*pl.*) men's trousers made of flannel. **3,** (*pl.*) woolen undergarments. —**flannel cake,** a pancake.

---

flannel

↔ The word can be traced back to Welsh *gwlanen*, woolen cloth, from *gwlan*, wool.

---

flan″nel·et′ (flan″ə-let′) *n.* a cotton fabric, used for wearing apparel. Also, **flan″nel·ette′.**

flap *n.* **1,** anything broad, flat, and unusually flexible, hanging loose. **2,** the motion or noise of a swinging flap or wing. **3,** a slap. **4,** an argument; controversy. —*v.t.* [**flapped, flap′ping**] swing as a flap; beat (wings, etc.) up and down. —*v.i.* swing to and fro; flap wings.

flap′doo″dle (-dəl) *n.* nonsense.

flap′jack″ *n.* a large pancake.

flap′pa·ble (flap′ə-bəl) *adj.* (*Informal*) easily disturbed or upset; excitable.

flap′per (-ər) *n.* **1,** a flap. **2,** a young duck or bird. **3,** (*Informal*) a brash teenage girl. **4,** a young woman of the 1920s.

flare (flâr) *n.* **1,** a flaring, wavering light. **2,** a blazing light used as a signal. **3,** an outburst, as of temper. **4,** a spreading outward, as of a skirt. —*v.i.* **1,** be or form a flare. **2,** (often with *out* or *up*) burst into sudden flame, activity, or emotion. **3,** spread outward, as a skirt, etc. —**flare′-up″,** *n.* a burst of anger or flame. ❑ *flair*

flash *n.* **1,** a sudden transitory burst of light or flame; an instantaneous outburst or sensation, as of wit, understanding, etc. **2,** a glimpse. **3,** an instant; a moment. **4,** (*Informal*) ostentation. **5,** a brief bulletin. —*v.i.* **1,** blaze momentarily; be temporarily visible, brilliant, notable, etc. **2,** (*Slang*) to expose one's genitals momentarily. —*v.t.* send forth suddenly, esp. a signal or bulletin. —**flash′er,** *n.* —**flash gun,** a device that ignites a flashbulb. —**a flash in the pan,** a person, idea, etc. which is successful at first but which does not last. —**flash point,** the lowest temperature at which a vapor will ignite or explode.

flash′back″ *n.* a scene or event from the past, in a novel or motion picture.

Flash′bar″ *n.* (*T.N.*) (*Photog.*) a row of flashbulbs in a single housing, ignited successively.

flash′bulb″ *n.* (*Photog.*) a glass bulb containing magnesium foil and oxygen, giving a brief, brilliant flash of light when ignited.

flash′ card″ *n.* a card having words or pictures, used for drilling or for memorization.

flash′cube″ *n.* (*Photog.*) a plastic cube containing four small flashbulbs arranged to fire in sequence.

flash′ing *n.* pieces of metal for waterproofing roofing joints.

flash′light″ *n.* **1,** a small portable electric torch. **2,** a brilliant instantaneous light for taking pictures; a picture so taken.

flash′y (-ē) *adj.* showy; gaudy; momentarily brilliant. —**flash′i·ness,** *n.*

flask (flàsk) *n.* a narrow-necked glass or metal container.

flat *adj.* [**flat′ter, -test**] **1,** horizontally level and relatively smooth. **2,** spread out, lying, or fallen on a level surface; lying down; collapsed; (of feet) having fallen arches. **3,** without qualification; positive; exact. **4,** defeated; (*Slang*) penniless. **5,** dull; stale; insipid. **6,** (*Music*) below the true pitch. —*adv.* in a flat manner. —*n.* **1,** a plain; a shoal. **2,** the flat part of anything. **3,** (*Slang*) a deflated tire. **4,** (*Music*) a note, marked (ū), lowered a half tone in pitch. **5,** an apartment. —*v.t. & i.* [**flat'-ted, -ting**] lower (the pitch). —**flat'ness,** *n.*

flat'boat" *n.* a large flat-bottomed boat for transporting goods.

flat'car" *n.* a roofless, sideless freight car.

flat'fish" *n.* a broad, flat fish with both eyes on the upper side.

flat'foot" [*pl.* **-feet**"] **1,** a deformity of the foot due to fallen arches. **2,** (*Slang*) a police officer. —**flat'foot**"ed, *adj.*

flat'i"ron *n.* an iron for pressing clothes.

flat'line" *v.i.* (*Informal*) to die, as shown by a flat line on an EKG monitor. —**flat'-lin**"er, *n.* (*Informal*)

flat-'out" *adv.* at maximum speed.

flat'ten (-ən) *v.t.* **1,** make flat. **2,** knock down. —*v.i.* become flat or level.

flat'ter (flat'ər) *v.t.* **1,** seek to gratify by undue praise. **2,** portray too favorably. —**flat'ter·y,** *n.* adulation.

flat-'top" *n.* an aircraft carrier.

flat'u·lent (flach'ə-lənt) *adj.* **1,** producing or having gas in the stomach. **2,** pretentious. —**flat'u·lence,** *n.* ❏ *flavor*

fla'tus (flā'təs) *n.* intestinal gas. ❏ *flavor*

flat'ware" (flat'wār") *n.* **1,** table dishes that are flat, as plates. **2,** table utensils, usu. silver.

flaunt (flânt) *v.t. & i.* parade impudently; make a gaudy display (of).

---

flaunt, flout

☛ Do not confuse these two words which sound very similar but have very different meanings. *Flaunt* means to make a display of, whereas *flout* means to scoff at.

---

flau'tist (flâ'tist) *n.* a flutist.

fla'vor (flā'vər) *n.* **1,** that quality which affects the taste; usually the quality of appealing to the taste. **2,** a substance that imparts a distinctive taste. **3,** an interesting or distinctive quality in anything. —*v.t.* give flavor to. Also, **fla'vour.** —**fla'-vor·ing,** *n.* a substance that flavors.

---

flavor, flatus, flatulent

↔ All three words derive from Latin *flatus,* a blowing. *Flavor* comes via Middle French *flaur,* smell.

---

flaw (flâ) *n.* a defect; imperfection. —**flaw'less,** *adj.* without a flaw; perfect.

flax (flaks) *n.* a blue-flowered plant grown for its fiber, used for making linen, and its seeds, for linseed oil. —**flax'seed**", *n.*

flax'en (flak'sən) *adj.* **1,** made of flax. **2,** of a light yellow color, as hair.

flay (flā) *v.t.* **1,** strip the skin from. **2,** censure severely. ❏ *flail*

flea (flē) *n.* a small, leaping, blood-sucking insect. —**flea'bite**", *n.* an inconsequential injury. —**flea'bit**"ten, *adj.* (*Informal*) shabby; seedy. —**a flea in one's ear,** a warning hint; rebuke. —**flea collar,** an animal collar impregnated with insecticide or insect repellent. —**flea market,** a market for secondhand goods, usu. held outdoors.

flea'bag" *n.* (*Slang*) an old, run-down hotel, rooming house, etc.

flèche (flesh) *n.* **1,** a slender spire. **2,** any of the points of a backgammon board.

fleck (flek) *n.* a speck or small spot. —*v.t.* mark with spots.

fled *v.* pret. & p.p. of *flee.*

fledg'ling (flej'ling) *n.* **1,** a young bird just able to fly. **2,** a young, inexperienced person.

---

fledgling

↔ From the specialized verb *fledge,* furnish with feathers, or prepare (a young bird) for flight. From Middle Low German *vlugge,* ready to fly.

---

flee (flē) *v.i. & t.* [*pret. & p.p.* **fled**] take flight (from); escape.

fleece (flēs) *n.* the woolly coat of a sheep. —*v.t.* swindle. —**fleec'y,** *adj.* soft and woolly; resembling fleece, as clouds.

fleet (flēt) *adj.* able to run fast; rapid; swift. —*n.* an organized group of ships or vehicles. —**fleet'ing,** *adj.* swiftly passing; transitory. —**fleet'ness,** *n.* —**fleet admiral,** highest rank in the U.S. Navy.

flesh *n.* **1,** the mass of muscular tissue, containing some fat, that constitutes the soft substance of the animal body. **2,** a similar substance, as of fruit. **3,** meat. **4,** kindred. **5,** bodily appetites or sensibilities. —*adj.* [also, **flesh color**] of the color of a white person's skin; yellowish pink. —**flesh'ly,** *adj.* corporeal; worldly or sensual. —**flesh'y,** *adj.* plump. —**in the flesh,** in person.

flesh'pot" *n.* **1,** nightclub. **2,** (*pl.*) high living; luxury.

fletch'er (flech'ər) *n.* a maker of arrows.

fleur-'de-lis' (flêr"-də-lē') *n.* (*Fr.*) [*pl.* **fleurs-'de-lis'** (flêr"-də-lēz')] **1,** (*Hist.*) the royal emblem of France. **2,** the iris.

flew (floo) *v.* pret. of *fly.*

flex (fleks) *v.t.* **1,** bend, as a part of the body. **2,** contract (a muscle). —**flex'ion** (flek'shən) *n.*

flex'i·ble (flek'sə-bəl) *adj.* **1,** easily bent. **2,** adaptable. —**flex"i·bil'i·ty,** *n.*

---

flex′time″ *n.* a system which allows workers to choose their own schedule. Also, **flex′i·time″**.

flib′ber·ti·gib″bet (flib′ər-tė-jib″it) *n.* **1,** a frivolous or flighty person. **2,** an imp or fiend.

flick (flik) *n.* **1,** a light, sharp blow, as with the finger or a whip. **2,** (*Slang*) a motion picture. —*v.t.* to strike, as with the finger or a whip.

flick′er (flik′ər) *v.i.* **1,** vibrate; quiver. **2,** burn fitfully. —*n.* **1,** a wavering light. **2,** a briefly felt hope, feeling, etc. **3,** a large woodpecker.

fli′er (flī′ər) *n.* **1,** one who or that which flies; an aviator. **2,** a handbill. **3,** a risk; a speculative or incidental financial venture. Also, **fly′er.**

flight (flīt) *n.* **1,** the act, mode, or power of flying. **2,** swift motion caused by any propelling force. **3,** the distance or course a bird, missile, aircraft, etc. flies. **4,** a number of creatures or things flying together. **5,** (*fig.*) an imaginative or extravagant excursion or soaring. **6,** hasty departure. **7,** the stairs from one landing or story to the next. —**flight′less,** *adj.* incapable of flying. —**flight attendant,** an airline employee who serves passengers during flight.

flight′y (flī′tė) *adj.* given to whims, disordered fancies, etc.; capricious. —**flight′i·ness,** *n.*

flim′flam″ *n. & v.t.* humbug.

flim′sy (flim′zė) *adj.* **1,** loosely constructed or woven; unsubstantial. **2,** weak; ineffectual. —**flim′si·ness,** *n.*

flinch *v.i.* shrink from anything painful or unpleasant.

fling *v.t. & i.* [*pret. & p.p.* **flung**] throw with violence; cast; hurl. —*n.* **1,** the act of flinging. **2,** a brief time of unrestrained pleasure. **3,** a lively dance. **4,** (*Informal*) a try.

flint *n.* a very hard, dark gray quartz that will strike sparks from steel. —**flint′y,** *adj.* obdurate. —**flint glass,** a heavy, brilliant glass containing lead.

flint′lock″ *n.* an old type of musket.

flip *n.* **1,** a flick; snap. **2,** a sweet drink, usually containing wine or liquor. —*v.t.* [**flipped, flip′ping**] toss lightly. —*adj.* [**flip′per, -pest**] (*Informal*) pert. —**flip chart,** a series of charts, graphs, etc., hinged so that they can be flipped for sequential presentation. —**flip side,** (*Informal*) the other side (of a record).

flip′-flop″ (*Informal*) *v.i.* reverse direction. —*n.* **1,** reversal of direction. **2,** a bathing sandal.

flip′pant (flip′ənt) *adj.* disrespectful;

treating serious things lightly. —**flip′pan·cy,** *n.*

flip′per (flip′ər) *n.* **1,** a limb used for swimming, as of a seal. **2,** device in a pinball machine used to project the ball.

flirt (flėrt) *v.i.* **1,** play at being attracted; coquet. **2,** trifle (with an idea). —*n.* a flirtatious person.

flir·ta′tion (flėr-tā′shən) *n.* **1,** a transient, not serious, love affair. **2,** brief encounter.

flir·ta′tious (flėr-tā′shəs) *adj.* given to flirting. —**flir·ta′tious·ness,** *n.*

flit *v.i.* [**flit′ted, -ting**] move lightly and swiftly.

flit′ter (-ər) *v.i.* flutter.

fliv′ver (fliv′ər) *n.* (*Slang, obs.*) a small, cheap automobile.

float (flōt) *v.i.* **1,** be buoyed up by water or air. **2,** drift idly and gently. **3,** fluctuate freely in value, as currency. —*v.t.* **1,** cause to rest on, or rise to, the surface of a liquid. **2,** start; launch, as a company, rumor, etc. —*n.* **1,** something that floats, as an anchored raft, a buoy, etc. **2,** a decorated vehicle in a parade.

float′er *n.* **1,** (*Informal*) one who moves from place to place, esp. a laborer. **2,** an insurance policy that covers specified items no matter where they are.

float′ing *adj.* **1,** not attached. **2,** not fixed or settled. —**floating point,** a type of mathematical notation.

floc′cu·lent (flok′yə·lənt) *adj.* like tufts of wool; fleecy; flaky. —**floc′cu·lence,** *n.*

flock (flok) *n.* **1,** a number of animals or birds of one kind keeping together; a congregation, esp. of a church. **2,** a tuft of wool, cotton, etc. **3,** powdered fibers of wool, cotton, etc. —*v.i.* congregate; go in crowds.

floe (flō) *n.* a mass of floating ice.

flog *v.t.* [**flogged, flog′ging**] thrash.

flood (flud) *n.* **1,** a great volume of water overflowing land; a deluge. **2,** a great outpouring, as of work, light, etc.; a superfluity. **3,** inflow of the tide. —*v.t. & i.* **1,** overflow. **2,** issue or flow in great quantity. —**flood tide,** a rising tide.

flood′gate″ *n.* a gate regulating the flow of water in a channel; *fig.*, something that restrains an outburst.

flood′light″ *n.* a bright light illuminating a large area.

floor (flôr) *n.* **1,** the bottom surface of a room, cave, the ocean, etc. **2,** a story of a building. **3,** the right to address a meeting. —*v.t.* **1,** furnish with a floor. **2,** (*Informal*) knock down; confound. —**floor′ing,** *n.* material of which a floor is made. —**floor**

show, a show in a cabaret. —**floor′-walk″er,** *n.* a supervisor of sales in a store.

floo′zy (floo′zē) *n.* (*Slang*) **1,** a prostitute. **2,** a loose woman. Also, **floo′zie, floo′sy.**

flop *v.i.* [**flopped, flop′ping**] **1,** thrash about; flap. **2,** fall down clumsily. **3,** (*Slang*) fail. —*n.* (*Slang*) a failure. —**flop′py,** *adj.* lacking rigidity. —**floppy disk,** a small, flexible plastic disk used for storing data in a computer.

flop′house″ (flop′hows″) *n.* (*Slang*) a very cheap hotel.

flo′ra (flôr′ə) *n.* plant life peculiar to a region or era.

---

flora, floral, florin, flour, flower
↔ *Flora* was the Roman goddess of flowers, from Latin *flos,* flower. *Flora* was first applied in the 17th c. to plants in general. *Flower* and the *florin* ultimately trace back to the same root, as does *flour,* literally, the flower (finest part) of the grain.

---

flo′ral (flôr′əl) *adj.* of or pert. to flowers. ❏ *flora*

flor′id (flôr′id) *adj.* **1,** ruddy, as the complexion. **2,** highly ornate.

flor′in (flôr′in) *n.* **1,** the gulden. **2,** an Eng. two-shilling coin. ❏ *flora*

flo′rist (flôr′ist) *n.* one who raises or sells flowers as a business.

floss (flâs) *n.* **1,** the silky substance in certain plant pods. **2,** silk filaments used in embroidery, etc. **3,** dental floss. —*v.i. & t.* to clean teeth with dental floss.

floss′y *adj.* **1,** like floss. **2,** (*Slang*) fancy.

flo′tage (flō′tij) *n.* **1,** buoyancy. **2,** things afloat; flotsam. **3,** a fee for transporting railroad cars on floats.

flo·ta′tion (flō-tā′shən) *n.* **1,** act or state of floating. **2,** arrangement to receive a loan.

flo·til′la (flō-til′ə) *n.* a small fleet; a fleet of small vessels.

flot″ka′ti (flot″kä′tē) *n.* a type of rug made in Greece.

flot′sam (flot′səm) *n.* wreckage of a ship or its cargo, found floating.

flounce (flowns) *n.* **1,** a deep ruffle sewed at its upper edge, on a skirt. **2,** a petulant jerk of one's body. —*v.i.* move with a flounce.

floun′der (flown′dər) *v.i.* struggle awkwardly or helplessly. —*n.* a flatfish.

flour (flowr) *n.* the finely ground meal of grain, esp of wheat; hence, any fine, soft powder. —*v.t.* sprinkle with flour. —**flour′y,** *adj.* ❏ *flora*

---

flounder, founder
☞ Do not confuse *flounder,* to struggle, and *founder,* to sink (as a ship), fail, though the two words may be very closely related.

---

flour′ish (flēr′ish) *v.i.* thrive; prosper; be active. —*v.t.* **1,** wave about; hence, flaunt. **2,** embellish with a flourish. —*n.* anything done by way of display, as a decorative pen stroke, a fanfare, etc.

flout (flowt) *v.t. & i.* scoff (at). ❏ *flaunt*

flow (flō) *v.i.* **1,** both progress and move internally, as the stream of a liquid; circulate. **2,** issue from a source. **3,** proceed smoothly or evenly. **4,** rise, as the tide. —*n.* **1,** the act of flowing; the amount that flows. **2,** issuance; rise. —**flow chart,** a chart or diagram showing the successive steps in a procedure.

flow′er (flow′ər) *n.* **1,** the seed-producing part of a plant, esp. when colorful and fragrant; a blossom. **2,** a plant grown for its flowers. **3,** the state of efflorescence. **4,** the best part or finest example. **5,** youthful vigor. —*v.i.* blossom. —**flower child,** (*Slang*) a hippie. ❏ *flora*

flow′er·pot″ *n.* a pot to hold earth in which a flower grows.

flow′er·y (-ē) *adj.* **1,** of flowers. **2,** florid; full of ornate phrases. —**flow′er·i·ness,** *n.*

flown (flōn) *v. p.p.* of *fly.*

flu (floo) *n.* influenza.

flub *n., v.i. & t.* blunder; blooper.

fluc′tu·ate″ (fluk′chū-āt″) *v.i.* change continually; vary irregularly; rise and fall, like waves. —**fluc″tu·a′tion,** *n.*

flue (floo) *n.* a passageway for smoke, etc., as in a chimney.

flu′ent (floo′ənt) *adj.* facile in speech; voluble; smoothly flowing. —**flu′en·cy,** *n.*

fluff (fluf) *n.* **1,** a light puff of dust or nap; a downy mass, as hair. **2,** (*Slang*) a mistake. —*v.t.* puff up in a light mass. —**fluff′y,** *adj.* soft and light.

flu′gel·horn″ (floo′gəl-hôrn″) *n.* a type of bugle.

flu′id (floo′id) *adj.* **1,** capable of flowing; esp. liquid or gaseous. **2,** not rigid or fixed. —*n.* a liquid or a gas. —**flu·id′i·ty** (-ə-tē) *n.* —**fluid dram,** a measure of capacity, 1/8 of a fluid ounce. —**fluid drive,** a transmission using a hydraulic pump. —**fluid ounce,** a measure of capacity, 1/16 of a pint.

fluke (flook) *n.* **1,** that part of an anchor which catches and holds. **2,** the head of an arrow or harpoon; a lobe of a whale's tail. **3,** (*Slang*) an accidental stroke; a lucky chance. **4,** a type of flatfish, esp. the flounder. —**fluk′y,** *adj.* (*Informal*) unpredictable.

flume (floom) *n.* a natural or artificial channel for conveying water.

flum′mer·y (flum′ə-rē) *n.* **1,** agreeable nonsense. **2,** a porridge.

flum′mox (flum′əks) *v.t.* (*Slang*) confuse.

flung *v.* pret. & p.p. of *fling.*

flunk *v.t.* & *i.* (*Informal*) fail to award, or get, a passing grade. —**flunk out,** be dismissed, as from a school, for failure.

flunk′y (flung′kē) *n.* **1,** a liveried servant. **2,** a toady. Also, **flunk′ey.**

fluor- (flôr) *pref.* fluorine; fluoride.

fluo·res′cence (flô-res′əns) *n.* the property of becoming self-luminous, or emitting radiation, when exposed to the direct action of light rays; also, the emitted radiation. —**fluo·resce′,** *v.i.* —**fluo·res′cent,** *adj.* —**fluorescent light,** a mercury vapor lamp.

fluor′i·date″ (flôr′ə-dāt″) *v.t.* & *i.* add a fluoride (to a water supply) in order to prevent tooth decay. —**fluor″i·da′tion,** *n.*

fluor′ide (flô′rīd″) *n.* a chemical compound of fluorine with another element.

fluor′ine (flô′rēn″) *n.* a corrosive, pungent, gaseous element, no. 9, symbol F. —**fluor′i·nate″** (flôr′ə-nāt″) *v.t.*

fluor′o·scope″ (flôr′ə-skōp″) *n.* a device for exposing objects to radiation, as X rays, and viewing them on a screen.

flur′ry (flēr′ē) *n.* **1,** a sudden gust of wind. **2,** temporary ado or commotion. —*v.t.* fluster.

flush *v.i.* **1,** blush; glow. **2,** be startled from cover. —*v.t.* **1,** suffuse with color. **2,** elate; thrill. **3,** wash out with a copious flow of water. **4,** startle (a bird) from cover. —*n.* **1,** a blush; any warm coloring. **2,** a rush of water, as for cleansing. **3,** a rush of emotion; thrill. **4,** glow; vigor. **5,** a hand of cards all of the same suit. —*adj.* **1,** full; well filled. **2,** (*Informal*) prosperous; well supplied with money. **3,** in the same plane or line; level or even.

flus′ter (flus′tər) *v.t.* embarrass and confuse. —*n.* nervous confusion.

flute (floot) *n.* **1,** a tubular woodwind musical instrument. **2,** a groove or furrow, as in a pillar, or in a ruffle. —**flut′ed,** *adj.* grooved. —**flut′ist,** *n.*

flut′ter (flut′ər) *v.i.* & *t.* **1,** flap the wings rapidly, as a bird; hover. **2,** move or beat irregularly, as the heart. **3,** be agitated. **4,** wave, as a flag. —*n.* **1,** quick irregular motion; rapid vibration. **2,** agitation; stir. —**flut′ter·y,** *adj.* habitually fluttering.

flu′vi·al (floo′vē-əl) *adj.* pert. to rivers.

flux (fluks) *n.* **1,** a flowing, as of a liquid. **2,** continual change. **3,** a substance used to promote fusing of metals, prevent oxidation, etc. —**flux′ion** (fluk′shən) *n.*

fly (flī) *v.i.* [**flew** (floo), **flown** (flōn), **fly′-ing**] **1,** move more or less horizontally through the air, not touching ground; be airborne. **2,** pass swiftly. **3,** flee. **4,** wave in the air, as a flag. **5,** go by airplane. **6,** [*pret.* **flied** (flīd)] hit a baseball that is caught in the air. —*v.t.* **1,** cause to be airborne. **2,** operate, or travel over in, aircraft. **3,** flee from. —*n.* **1,** any of several two-winged insects, esp. the housefly. **2,** a fishhook disguised as a fly. **3,** a strip of cloth on a garment to hide a fastening. **4,** an extra roof for a tent. **5,** a baseball batted high in the air. —**flying boat,** a seaplane. —**flying buttress,** a supporting arch extending in the air from a wall to a pier. —**flying fish,** a fish with winglike fins, capable of brief flights out of the water. —**flying saucer,** a saucer-shaped illuminated object often reportedly seen in the skies. —**flying squirrel,** a squirrel having webs of skin, capable of long gliding leaps. —**on the fly,** in flight; hence, without stopping.

fly′blown″ *adj.* maggoty.

fly′boy″ *n.* (*Slang*) a member of the flight team of an aircraft; a member of the U.S. Air Force.

fly-′by-night″ *adj.* unreliable. —*n.* an unreliable person.

fly′catch″er *n.* a small insectivorous bird.

fly′leaf″ *n.* a blank leaf at the beginning or end of a book.

fly′pa″per *n.* sticky paper for catching flies.

fly′speck″ *n.* a fly's egg; a tiny spot.

fly′swat″ter (-swot″ter) *n.* a mat with a handle, for killing flies.

fly′way″ *n.* a migration route of birds.

fly′weight″ *n.* a boxer weighing 112 lbs. or less.

fly′wheel″ *n.* a heavy wheel that tends to stabilize the speed of a machine.

f-number (*Photog.*) the effective aperture of a lens divided by its focal length.

foal (fōl) *n.* a young horse, ass, etc. —*v.i.* & *t.* bring forth (a foal).

foam (fōm) *n.* & *v.i.* froth. —**foam′y,** *adj.* —**foam rubber,** latex in spongelike form.

fob *n.* **1,** a short watch chain. **2,** a small pocket for a watch. —*v.t.* **1,** (with *off*) palm off. **2,** cheat; trick.

fo'c's'le (fōk′səl) *n.* forecastle.

fo′cus (fō′kəs) *n.* [*pl.* **-cus·es** *or* **-ci** (-sī)] **1,** the point at which rays as of light, heat, etc., meet after reflection or refraction. **2,** focal length. **3,** an adjustment of eyes, camera, etc., for clear vision. **4,** a center, as of interest, activity, etc. —*v.t.* **1,** adjust the focus of. **2,** bring into focus —**fo′cal,** *adj.* —**focal length,** the distance from a lens to the plane of its focus. —**focal point, 1,** the point of focus of a lens. **2,** the center of attention.

fod′der (fod′ər) *n.* dried food, as hay, straw, etc., for livestock.

foe (fō) *n.* an enemy; an opponent. —**foe′-man** (-mən) *n.* [*pl.* **-men**] an enemy in war.

fog *n.* **1,** a heavy mist at or near the earth's surface. **2,** mental confusion. —*v.t. & i.* [**fogged, fog′ging**] make or become obscure or cloudy. —**fog′gy,** *adj.* thick with mist; obscure. —**Foggy Bottom,** the U.S. Dept. of State.

fog′bound″ *adj.* unable to navigate because of heavy fog.

fog′horn″ *n.* a horn for warning of an approach through fog.

fo′gy (fō′gē) *n.* one who is averse to change or to new ideas.

foi′ble (foi′bəl) *n.* a whimsy; a weakness.

foil *n.* **1,** a very thin sheet of metal. **2,** anything that sets off something by contrast. **3,** a blunted fencing sword. —*v.t.* baffle; frustrate.

foist *v.t.* palm off as genuine.

fold (fōld) *v.t.* **1,** bend double, as cloth, paper, etc.; restore to original shape by folding once or more. **2,** clasp together, as arms; bring toward the body; embrace. **3,** wrap (something) by folding paper over it. —*v.i.* **1,** double together. **2,** (*Slang*) close down, as a play. —*n.* **1,** a pleat. **2,** a pen for sheep. **3,** a flock of sheep; hence, any group under a leader, esp. a church congregation. —**folding money,** (*Informal*) paper money.

-fold *suf.* **1,** multiplied by. **2,** divided by.

fold′boat″ *n.* faltboat.

fold′er (fōl′dər) *n.* **1,** printed matter, as a map, circular, etc., folded into a booklet. **2,** a stiff folded holder for loose papers.

fo′li·age (fō′lē-ij) *n.* the leaves of plants.

fo′li·ate″ *v.t. & i.* (fō′lē-āt″) **1,** put forth or shape like leaves. **2,** number the leaves of (a book). —*adj.* (-ət) **1,** having leaves. **2,** leaflike. —**fo″li·a′tion,** *n.*

fo′lic acid (fō′lik) Vitamin M (a B vitamin), found in liver and leaves.

fo′li·o″ (fō′lē-ō″) *n.* **1,** a sheet of paper folded once. **2,** a book of sheets folded

once; a book of largest size. **3,** a page number.

folk (fōk) *n.* **1,** people in general. **2,** (*pl.*) one's relatives; people of a certain class. —*adj.* originating or widely used among the common people, as *folk song, folk music, folk dance.*

folk′lore″ *n.* the old traditions, beliefs, and superstitions of a people.

> **folklore**
> ↔ The word was coined by English scholar W. J. Thomas.

folk-′rock″ *n. & adj.* (*Music*) pert. to music combining a rock beat with folk-song lyrics.

folk′sy (-sē) *adj.* **1,** sociable; friendly and unpretentious. **2,** informal; rustic.

folk′ways″ *n.pl.* traditional customs.

fol′li·cle (fol′ə-kəl) *n.* **1,** a minute cavity or gland. **2,** a dry one-celled seed vessel. —**fol·lic′u·lar** (fə-lik′yə-lər) *adj.*

fol′low (fol′ō) *v.t.* **1,** come after in place or order of time; succeed. **2,** pursue. **3,** understand. **4,** emulate; accept as a guide or leader. **5,** result from. —*v.i.* **1,** go or come after another. **2,** arise as a natural consequence or inference; result. —**fol′-low·er,** *n.* an adherent; disciple. —**follow through,** continue or complete an action started. —**follow up,** continue to pursue or take advantage of (an opportunity, etc.).

fol′low·ing *n.* a body of supporters or patrons. —*adj.* coming next in order or time.

fol′low-through″ *n.* **1,** completion of a stroke, as in golf or tennis. **2,** exploitation of an advantage.

fol′low-up″ *n.* an act, letter, circular, call, etc., to sustain the effectiveness of a previous one.

fol′ly (fol′ē) *n.* **1,** lack of good sense; foolishness. **2,** a foolish act or undertaking. **3,** (*pl.*) a revue.

fo·ment′ (fō-ment′) *v.t.* stir up; incite. —**fo″men·ta′tion,** *n.* ❑ *ferment*

fond *adj.* **1,** loving. **2,** foolishly tender or trusting; doting. **3,** inclined toward. —**fond′ness,** *n.*

fon′dant (fon′dənt) *n.* a creamy sugar paste used in making candy.

fon′dle (fon′dəl) *v.t.* caress.

fon·due′ (fon-doo′) *n.* a baked pudding made of grated cheese or chocolate, butter, and eggs.

font *n.* **1,** a receptacle for baptismal water. **2,** a full assortment of one size and style of printing type.

food *n.* **1,** an edible substance, usually solid, for the nourishment of the body. **2,** anything that sustains or nourishes. —**food processor,** an electric kitchen appliance for chopping, pureeing, etc. —**food stamp,** a federal coupon redeemable for food.

food′stuff″ *n.* a grocery item.

fool *n.* **1,** a silly or stupid person. **2,** a court jester. —*v.t.* dupe; mislead. —*v.t.* **1,** play the fool. **2,** spend time idly. **3,** (with *with*) play or tamper (with). —**fool′er·y,** *n.* —**fool's gold,** a mineral which resembles gold.

fool′har″dy *adj.* foolishly rash. —**fool′har″di·ness,** *n.*

> **foolhardy**
> ↔ From Old French *fol hardi,* foolish-bold.

fool′ish *adj.* silly; unwise. —**fool′ish·ness,** *n.*

fool′proof″ *adj.* surely effective, even if mismanaged.

fools′cap″ (foolz′kap″) *n.* a size of paper, about 13 x 17 inches.

> **foolscap**
> ↔ So called not because it was used to make a dunce's cap but because the type of paper once had a watermark showing a fool's cap and bells.

foot (fût) *n.* [*pl.* **feet** (fēt)] **1,** the terminal part of the leg of a man or animal. **2,** anything that resembles a foot in shape, function, or position; the bottom or lowest point. **3,** a measure of length, 12 inches. **4,** tread; step. **5,** infantry. **6,** a group of syllables forming a metrical unit in a verse. —*v.t.* **1,** add up, as numbers in a column. **2,** (*Informal*) pay, as a bill.

foot′age (-ij) *n.* length in feet.

foot′ball″ *n.* a field game played with an inflated leather ball; the ball used.

foot-′can″dle *n.* a unit of illumination.

foot′er *n.* text appearing at the bottom of the page of a document, as for identification.

foot′fall″ *n.* the sound of a footstep.

foot′hill″ *n.* one of the lower hills at the base of a mountain range.

foot′hold″ *n.* a secure position.

foot′ing *n.* **1,** a foothold. **2,** an assured position. **3,** a foundation. **4,** basis; relative standing.

foot′less (-ləs) *adj.* **1,** having no feet. **2,** without foundation or basis. **3,** (*Informal*) awkward; inept.

foot′lights″ *n.pl.* **1,** the row of lights at

floor level in front of a stage. **2,** the theater; stage; theatrical life.

foot′lock″er *n.* a small trunk.

foot′loose″ *adj.* not tied down; free to travel.

foot′man (-mən) *n.* [*pl.* **-men**] a manservant for carriage, door, and table.

foot′note″ *n.* an explanatory note at the foot of a page.

foot′pad″ *n.* a robber.

foot-′pound″ *n.* the energy required to raise one pound one foot.

foot′print″ *n.* **1,** the mark made by a foot. **2,** the area occupied by the base of an object when placed on a surface.

foot′sore″ *adj.* **1,** having sore feet. **2,** tired of travel.

foot′step″ *n.* **1,** a tread of a foot or the sound it makes. **2,** (*pl.*) the example set by a predecessor.

foot′stool″ *n.* a low stool on which to rest one's feet while sitting.

foot′work″ *n.* **1,** agility on foot. **2,** laborious walking.

foo′zle (foo′zəl) *v.t.* & *i.* bungle. —*n.* blunder. —**foo′zler** (-zlər) *n.*

fop *n.* a man too concerned with dressing stylishly. —**fop′per·y** (-ə-rē) *n.* —**fop′pish,** *adj.*

for (fôr) *prep.* **1,** in order to obtain. **2,** to be used by, or given to; adapted to; appropriate to. **3,** in favor of. **4,** in place of; instead of; in consideration of. **5,** in honor of. **6,** because of; for want of. **7,** over the space of; during. **8,** toward. **9,** with regard to. —*conj.* because. —**for″asmuch′ as,** in view of the fact that; since.

for′age (for′ij) *n.* **1,** food for livestock, esp. pasturage. **2,** a search for food. —*v.i.* & *t.* raid for food.

fo·ra′men (fə-rā′mən) *n.* a hole or passage, esp. in a bone.

for′ay (fôr′ā) *n.* a raid for plunder. —*v.i.* make a raid; forage.

for·bear′ (fôr-bār′) *v.t.* [**-bore′, -borne′, -bearing**] refrain or abstain from. —*v.i.* hold back; be patient or lenient. —**forbear′ance,** *n.*

> **forbear, forebear**
> ☛ Do not confuse these two homonyms, differing by only one letter. *Forbear* (no *e*) is a verb meaning to refrain from. *Forebear* (with *e*) is a noun meaning ancestor.

for·bid′ (fôr-bid′) *v.t.* [**-bade′, -bid′den, -ding**] **1,** order (something) not to be done; refuse to permit; prohibit. **2,** order (someone) not to do something. **—for·bid′ding,** *adj.* repelling approach; disagreeable.

force (fôrs) *n.* **1,** the capacity for exerting strength; power; might. **2,** the power to coerce, persuade, convince, etc. **3,** meaning; import. **4,** military strength. **5,** a body of men prepared for action. **6,** (*pl.*) an army; physical resources. **7,** (*Physics*) the cause of motion, or a change in the motion, of a body. **—v.t. 1,** compel by physical, mental, or moral means. **2,** extort by violence. **3,** effect by effort. **4,** compel the acceptance of. **5,** hasten the growth of. **—force′ful,** *adj.* powerful; effective.

---

force, fort, effort
↔ From Latin *fortis*, strong, which also produced *fort* and *effort*.

---

forced *adj.* **1,** compulsory. **2,** strained; unnatural. **3,** caused by an emergency.

force″ ma·jeure′ (fôrs″ mä-zhûr′) (*Fr.*, superior force) (*Law*) an unavoidable and unanticipated event that may force the cancellation of a contract.

force′meat″ *n.* meat chipped fine and seasoned, used as stuffing. ❑ *farce*

for′ceps (fôr′səps) *n.* an instrument for grasping or extracting; pincers.

for′ci·ble (fôr′sə-bəl) *adj.* **1,** effective; convincing. **2,** resulting from the use of brute force.

ford (fôrd) *n.* a shallow place where a river can be crossed by wading. **—v.t.** pass across by a ford.

fore (fôr) *n.* the front. **—adv.** in or toward the bow of a ship. **—adj.** at or near the front; ahead, in time, rank, etc. **—interj.** (*Golf*) a warning to look out.

fore- (fôr) *pref.* **1,** front. **2,** previous; ahead of time. **3,** ahead in rank; superior.

fore-′and-aft′ *adj.* (*Naut.*) lying or running in the general direction of the length of a vessel.

fore′arm″ *n.* the arm between elbow and wrist.

fore′bear″ *n.* an ancestor. ❑ *forbear*

fore·bode′ *v.t. & i.* **1,** presage. **2,** have a premonition of. **—fore·bod′ing,** *n.* a feeling that evil is impending.

fore′cast″ *n.* a prediction. **—v.t.** (fôr-kåst′) **1,** foresee. **2,** predict.

fore′cas·tle (fōk′səl) *n.* **1,** the forward part of the upper deck of a vessel. **2,** in merchant ships, the seamen's quarters. Also, **fo′c′s′le.**

fore·close′ (fôr-klōz′) *v.t. & i.* (*Law*) take away the right to redeem (a mortgage). **—fore·clo′sure** (-klō′zhər) *n.*

fore′fa″ther *n.masc.* a male ancestor.

fore′fin″ger *n.* the finger next to the thumb.

fore′front″ *n.* the foremost place or part.

fore·go′ (fôr-gō′) *v.t.* precede. **—fore′go″-ing,** *adj.* that precedes, as a previous part of something written. **—fore′gone″,** *adj.* **1,** past. **2,** settled in advance.

---

forego, forgo
☛ Do not confuse these two homonyms, which are otherwise unrelated. *Forego* means to precede; *forgo* means to give up.

---

fore′ground″ *n.* the part of a picture, etc., represented as being nearest the observer.

fore′hand″ *adj.* **1,** made on the right side of the body (of a right-handed player), as a tennis stroke. **2,** done beforehand. **—fore′hand″ed,** *adj.* **1,** ahead of time. **2,** prudent; thrifty.

fore′head (fôr′id) *n.* the front of the head or face above the eyes and below the hairline.

for′eign (for′in) *adj.* **1,** situated outside one's own land. **2,** relating to, or dealing with, other countries. **3,** alien; not native. **4,** not pertinent. **—for′eign·er,** *n.* a resident or native of another country.

---

foreign
↔ From Latin *foras*, out of doors (*door* is related). Our current usage is a metaphorical sense which gained ascendancy over the earlier literal meaning.

---

fore″know′ *v.t.* [*pret. & p.p.* **-knew′**] know beforehand. **—fore·knowl′edge,** *n.*

fore′leg″ *n.* one of the front legs of an animal having four or more legs.

fore′lock″ *n.* a lock of hair at the forehead.

fore′man (-mən) [*pl.* **-men**], **fore′-wom″an,** *n.* **1,** a superintendent of workers. **2,** the spokesperson of a jury.

fore′mast″ *n.* the mast nearest the bow of a ship.

fore′most″ *adj. & adv.* first; chief.

fore′moth″er *n.fem.* a female ancestor.

fore′name″ *n.* first name. **—fore′named″,** *adj.* mentioned previously.

fore′noon″ *n.* morning.

fo·ren′sic (fə-ren′sik) *adj.* pert. to courts of law or to debate. **—fo·ren′si·cal·ly,** *adv.*

fore″or·di·na′tion (fôr″ôr-di-nā′shən) *n.* predestination.

fore′play″ *n.* sexual stimulation preceding intercourse.

---

fore′quar″ter *n.* one of the front quarters in cutting a carcass for meat.

fore′run″ner *n.* a predecessor; a precursor.

foresee′ *v.t.* [**-saw′, -seen′**] predict; anticipate.

fore·shad′ow *v.t.* give notice or indication of in advance.

fore″short′en *v.t.* **1,** gradually shorten the lines of (an object in a drawing) to give it the correct perspective. **2,** curtail.

fore′sight″ *n.* **1,** the power of foreseeing. **2,** prudent care for the future.

fore′skin″ *n.* the loose skin at the tip of the penis, removed during circumcision.

for′est (for′ist) *n.* a large area covered with a dense growth of trees. —**for′est·er,** *n.* one who works in a forest.

fore·stall′ *v.t.* thwart by action in advance.

for″est·a′tion (for″əs-tā′shən) *n.* the planting of forests.

for′es·try (-rē) *n.* the science of caring for forests.

fore′taste″ *n.* anticipation. —*v.t.* (fôr-tāst′) have previous experience of.

fore·tell′ *v.t. & i.* [*pret. & p.p.* **-told′**] prophesy.

fore′thought″ *n.* anticipatory care.

fore′to″ken *v.t.* foreshadow. —*n.* (fôr-tō′kən) an omen.

for·ev′er (fôr-ev′ər) *adv.* **1,** eternally. **2,** continually.

fore″warn′ *v.t.* warn of a coming event.

fore′word″ *n.* a preface in a book.

---

foreword, forward, froward
☛ These words are easily confused. A *foreword* is a preface; *forward* means near the front. Both are of Old English origin. *Froward* is unrelated, meaning willful; it is derived from Old Norse *fra*, from.

---

for′feit (fôr′fit) *n.* **1,** a deposit, hostage, or agreed penalty surrendered through neglect, default, a crime, error, etc. **2,** a fine; penalty. —*v.i. & t.* surrender (a forfeit). —**for′fei·ture** (-fi-chər) *n.*

for″fend′ (fôr″fend′) *v.t.* (*Archaic*) forbid; avert.

for·gath′er (fôr-gath′ər) *v.i.* assemble; associate.

forge (fôrj) *v.t.* **1,** hammer into shape while malleable through heat. **2,** shape out in any way; fashion. **3,** imitate fraudulently (a signature, document, etc.). —*v.i.* move ahead slowly but surely. —*n.* a smithy. —**forg′ing,** *n.* a piece of forged metal.

for′ger·y (fôr′jə-rē) *n.* fraudulent imita-

tion of a signature, document, etc.; the false signature or document.

for·get′ (fər-get′) *v.t.* [**for·got′, -got′ten** or **-got′, -get′ting**] **1,** be unable or fail to remember. **2,** omit or neglect (to act), unintentionally or willfully. **3,** (with *oneself*) act or speak improperly. —**for·get′ful,** *adj.* apt to forget; thoughtless. —**for·get′ful·ness,** *n.*

---

forget, forgive
☛ *Forget* is a compound of the prefix *for*, not, and *get*, in the figurative sense of losing one's hold on a memory. *Forgive*, on the other hand, results from the literal translation of the two elements of a Latin ancestor, *perdonare*: *per*, for, and *donare*, give.

---

for·get′-′me-not″ *n.* a tiny blue flower.

for·give′ (fər-giv′) *v.t.* [**for·gave′, -giv′en, -giv′ing**] **1,** grant pardon for (something) or to (someone). **2,** remit (a debt). **3,** cease to resent. —**for·give′ness,** *n.* willingness to forgive. —**for·giv′ing,** *adj.* ready to forgive. ❏ *forget*

for·go′ (fôr-gō′) *v.t.* [**for·went′, -gone′, -go′ing**] give up; let pass. ❏ *forego*

fo′rint (fô′rint) *n.* the monetary unit of Hungary.

fork (fôrk) *n.* **1,** a pronged tool for digging, lifting, etc., or for handling food at table. **2,** a division or branch, as of a road, stream, etc.; the place of such division. —*v.t.* use a fork on. **2,** (with *over*) (*Informal*) surrender. —*v.i.* separate into branches. —**forklift,** a vehicle with a pronged lifting platform.

for·lorn′ (fôr-lôrn′) *adj.* **1,** abandoned; forsaken. **2,** wretched. **3,** hopeless. —**for·lorn′ness,** *n.* —**forlorn hope, 1,** a desperate or hopeless enterprise. **2,** a group of soldiers picked for an expectedly perilous task.

---

forlorn hope
↔ Not from *hope*, but from Dutch *verloren hoop*, lost troop, referring to the advance attack party, sent into battle and expected not to return alive.

---

form (fôrm) *n.* **1,** external shape; structure; style. **2,** the human body. **3,** something that determines shape; a mold or pattern. **4,** a particular kind or condition. **5,** type in a frame ready for printing. **6,** a prescribed practice, as for conduct, ritual, etc.; a ceremony. **7,** manner of doing something. **8,** physical fitness. **9,** a document with blanks to be filled in. **10,** (*Gram.*) a change in a word, as by spelling, inflection, etc. —*v.t.* **1,** make; shape. **2,** train; mold, as character. **3,** be an element of; constitute. **4,** organize. **5,** develop. —*v.i.* take a definite shape or arrangement; develop. —**form letter, 1,** a letter duplicated for sending to a number of people. **2,** a standardized letter.

-form (fôrm) *suf.* in the form of; shaped.

for·mal (fôr′məl) *adj.* **1,** adhering to established form or mode; conventional; ceremonious; precise. **2,** not familiar or friendly in manner; stiff. **3,** perfunctory. —*n. (Informal)* **1,** a formal occasion. **2,** an evening dress. —**for′mal·ize,** *v.t.*

for·mal′de·hyde″ (fôr-mal′də-hīd″) *n.* a gas, used in solution, as a preservative and disinfectant: *form(ic) aldehyde.*

for′mal·ism (-liz-əm) *n.* strict adherence to prescribed or customary forms. —**for′mal·ist,** *n. & adj.* —**for″mal·is′tic,** *adj.*

for·mal′i·ty (fôr-mal′ə-tè) *n.* **1,** rigid conformity to conventions. **2,** ceremony; a rule of procedure; a perfunctory act.

for′mat (fôr′mat) *n.* the general style, appearance, or organization (of a book, program, etc.). —*v.t.* **1,** to design the style of. **2,** to prepare a computer disk for reading and writing.

---

format
↔ From the Latin phrase *liber formatus*, a book formed (in a certain way).

---

for·ma′tion (fôr-mā′shən) *n.* **1,** the process of shaping. **2,** that which is shaped. **3,** formal structure or arrangement, esp. of troops.

for′ma·tive (fôr′mə-tiv) *adj.* **1,** forming; shaping. **2,** pert. to development.

for′mer (fôr′mər) *adj.* **1,** preceding in time. **2,** the earlier or first-mentioned of two. —**for′mer·ly,** *adv.* in time past.

For·mi′ca (fôr-mī′kə) *n. (T.N.)* any of various laminated plastic products used in construction and in making furniture.

Formica, formication, mica
↔ These words look related, but in fact *formication* comes from Latin *formica,* ant. *Mica* is a Latin word for grain, and *Formica* was coined from it.

---

for″mi·ca′tion (fôr″mə-kā′-shən) *n.* a crawling sensation of the skin. ❏ *Formica*

for′mi·da·ble (fôr′mi-də-bəl) *adj.* **1,** exciting fear. **2,** hard to accomplish; alarmingly difficult. —**for″mi·da·bil′i·ty, for′mi·da·ble·ness,** *n.*

for′mu·la (fôr′mū-lə) *n.* **1,** a fixed rule

or form for saying or doing something. **2,** expression by symbols of the constituents of a chemical compound, or of a mathematical rule or principle. **3,** a recipe. —**for′mu·la·rize″,** *v.t.* —**for′mu·lism,** *n.*

for′mu·late″ (fôr′mū-lāt″) *v.t.* express as a formula; put into definite words. —**for′-mu·la′tion,** *n.*

for′ni·cate″ (fôr′ni-kāt″) *v.i.* consummate a love affair when not married. —**for″ni·ca′tion,** *n.*

for·sake′ (fôr-sāk′) *v.t.* [**for·sook′** (-sûk′), **-sak′en** (-sā′kən), **-sak′ing**] renounce; abandon.

for·sooth′ (fôr-sooth′) *adv. (Archaic)* in truth; indeed.

for·swear′ (fôr-swâr′) *v.t.* [**for·swore′, -sworn′, -swear′ing**] deny or renounce upon oath; abjure. —*v.i.* commit perjury. —**for·sworn′,** *adj.* perjured.

for·syth′i·a (fôr-sith′ē-ə) *n.* a shrub bearing yellow flowers, named for 18th-c. English horticulturist William Forsyth.

fort (fôrt) *n.* a strongly fortified place. ❏ *force*

forte (fôrt) *n.* a strong point; one's special talent. —*adj. & adv.* (fôr′tā) *(Music)* loud; loudly.

for″te·pi·a′no (fôr″tā-pē-ä′nō) *n.* a piano of the late 18th and early 19th c. ❏ *piano*

forth (fôrth) *adv.* **1,** onward or forward in time or place. **2,** into view; from under cover. **3,** away. —**and so forth,** et cetera.

FORTH *abbr. (Computers)* a programming language.

forth′com′ing *adj.* **1,** approaching in time. **2,** available when needed. **3,** candid; outgoing.

forth′right″ *adj.* outspoken; direct. —*adv.* **1,** directly. **2,** immediately. —**forth′-right″ness,** *n.*

forth″with′ *adv.* at once.

for′ti·eth (fôr′tē-əth) *adj. & n.* **1,** the ordinal of forty, also written 40th. **2,** one of 40 equal parts.

for″ti·fi·ca′tion (fôr″ti-fi-kā′shən) *n.* **1,** the act of strengthening. **2,** a fortified position.

for′ti·fy″ (fôr′ti-fī″) *v.t.* **1,** provide with military defenses. **2,** strengthen, against wear, etc. **3,** strengthen mentally, morally, or physically.

for·tis′si·mo″ (fôr-tis′i-mō″) *adj. & adv. (Lat., Music)* very loud.

for′ti·tude″ (fôr′tə-tūd″) *n.* the power to endure pain, hardship, etc.

fort′night″ (fôrt′nīt″) *n.* two weeks. —**fort′night″ly,** *adj. & adv.* (occurring) once each fortnight.

FOR'TRAN (fôr'tran) *n.* a computer language: *for(mula) tran(slation)*.

for'tress (fôr'tris) *n.* **1,** a fortified place; a group of forts. **2,** any stronghold.

for·tu'i·tous (fôr-tū'ə-təs) *adj.* coming by chance; accidental. **—for·tu'i·tous·ness, for·tu'i·ty,** *n.*

for'tu·nate (fôr'chə-nət) *adj.* **1,** having good fortune; lucky. **2,** resulting favorably.

for'tune (fôr'chən) *n.* **1,** success or failure as controlled or influenced by chance. **2,** wealth, esp. great wealth; good luck. **3,** chance; luck; destiny. **—fortune hunter,** one who seeks to marry for wealth.

for'tune-tel"ler *n.* a person who claims to be able to predict the future.

for'ty (fôr'tē) *n. & adj.* the cardinal number between thirty-nine and forty-one, expressed by 40. **—forty winks,** (*Informal*) a short nap.

fort'y-five" *n.* (*Informal*) **1,** a .45 caliber revolver or pistol. **2,** 45-rpm. disc.

for"ty-nin'er (fôr"tē-nī'nər) *n.* one who participated in the California gold rush of 1849.

fo'rum (fôr'əm) *n.* a public meeting; any medium for public discussion; a tribunal.

for'ward (fôr'wərd) *adj.* **1,** near or toward the front. **2,** well-advanced. **3,** eager; ready. **4,** presumptuous; bold. **—adv. 1,** onward; ahead; toward the front. **2,** forth; into view. **—v.t. 1,** further; encourage. **2,** send (freight, etc.). **3,** send (a letter, etc.) on to a new and different address. **—n.** in sports, a player stationed near the opponent's goal; (*Football*) a lineman. **—for'ward·ness,** *n.* ❑ *foreword*

fos'sil (fos'əl) *n.* **1,** remains or traces of a prehistoric plant or animal found in earth, rocks, etc. **2,** an outdated person or thing. **—fos'sil·ize"** (-īz") *v.t. & i.*

---

fossil
↔ From Latin *fodere*, to dig up.; the literal sense survives in the expression *fossil fuel*.

---

fos'ter (fâs'ter) *v.t.* **1,** nourish; bring up. **2,** cherish. **3,** promote the growth or development of. **—adj.** equivalent to parent or child though not so related by blood. **—fos'ter·ling,** *n.* foster child. **—foster home,** a home provided by foster parents. **—foster mother,** a woman who takes the place of a mother in caring for a child.

fought (fât) *v.* pret. & p.p. of *fight*.

foul (fowl) *adj.* **1,** disgusting to the senses by reason of decay, turpitude, filthiness, etc.; noisome; hateful. **2,** clogged, as a chimney; choked; entangled, as a rope. **3,** against the rules; out of legal bounds; unfair. **4,** base; vicious; scurrilous. **—n. 1,** a violation of the rules. **2,** a collision. **—v.t. 1,** defile. **2,** clog; entangle. **3,** collide with. **—v.i. 1,** become foul; commit a foul. **2,** (with *up*) (*Slang*) blunder. **—foul'ness,** *n.* **—fall foul of,** have trouble with; clash with.

fou·lard' (foo-lärd') *n.* a soft silk with a satin finish.

foul-'mouthed" (-mowthd") *adj.* given to filthy or abusive speech.

found (fownd) *v.t.* **1,** lay the basis or foundation of, as a building. **2,** establish, as a business or a dynasty. **3,** (with *on*) base. **4,** cast (metal) in a mold. **5,** pret. & p.p. of *find*. **—n.** food and lodging. **—found art,** a work of art composed of found objects. **—found object,** a natural or manufactured article considered as an esthetic object. **—found poem,** a poem composed of preexistent printed matter.

foun·da'tion (fown-dā'shən) *n.* **1,** the base on which a building rests; hence, basis; underlying principle. **2,** an endowment, as for research, a charity, etc. **3,** (also, **foundation garment**) a woman's undergarment.

foun'der (fown'dər) *v.i.* **1,** fill and sink, as a ship. **2,** go lame, as a horse. **3,** fail utterly. **—n. 1,** originator; charter member. **2,** one who casts metal. ❑ *flounder*

found'ling (fownd'ling) *n.* a deserted infant of unknown parentage.

found'ry (fown'drē) *n.* a place where metal is cast.

fount (fownt) *n.* a fountain; a source.

foun'tain (fown'tən) *n.* **1,** a natural spring; a source of water. **2,** an artificial jet of water; a basin to receive it. **—fountain pen,** a pen containing a reservoir for ink.

foun'tain·head" *n.* **1,** the head or source of a stream. **2,** a primary source, as of learning.

four (fôr) *n. & adj.* the cardinal number between three and five, expressed by 4. **—on all fours,** on four feet; on hands and knees (or feet).

four'flush"er (fôr'flush"ər) *n.* (*Slang*) a pretender.

four-'in-hand" *n.* **1,** a long necktie tied in a slip knot. **2,** a team of four horses driven by one person.

four-'o'clock" (fôr'ə-klok") *n.* a plant whose flowers open in the afternoon and close the next morning.

four'some *n.* four persons; a quartet.

four'square″ *adj.* steady; frank.

four'teen' (fôr″tēn′) *n. & adj.* the cardinal number between thirteen and fifteen, expressed by 14. —**four″teenth′**, *n. & adj.*

fourth (fôrth) *adj. & n.* the ordinal of four; 4th. —*n.* one of four equal parts. —**fourth dimension, 1,** a dimension in addition to length, width, and depth. **2,** time or duration, considered as a dimension in the space-time theory of relativity. **3,** something outside normal human experience not readily explainable scientifically. —**Fourth Estate,** the press; journalists collectively. —**the Fourth,** July 4, Independence Day.

fowl *n.* **1,** a domestic hen or cock; its flesh as food. **2,** birds in general, esp. those used for food. —**fowl′er,** *n.* one who hunts wild birds. —**fowl′ing,** *n.* the hunting of birds. —**fowling piece,** a shotgun.

fox (foks) *n.* **1,** a wild animal of the wolf family, noted for its cunning. **2,** a crafty person. —*v.t.* (*Slang*) outwit. —**foxed,** *adj.* discolored, stained, or spotted. —**fox terrier,** a small, usu. smooth-coated, terrier. —**fox-trot, 1,** a type of ballroom dance. **2,** in communications, the letter *f.*

> **fox, fox-trot**
> ↔ The animal is identified by its tail, and its name comes from an Indo-European root meaning tail. The dance name comes from a type of horse gait consisting of short steps, named in comparison to the pace of a fox.

fox'glove″ (foks′gluv″) *n.* a flowering plant, the source of digitalis.

fox'hole″ (foks′hōl″) *n.* a hastily dug pit for shelter from enemy fire.

fox'hound″ *n.* a breed of large, swift hounds trained for hunting.

fox'y (fok′sē) *adj.* **1,** clever; sly. **2,** foxed. —**fox′i·ness,** *n.*

foy'er (foi′ər) *n.* a lobby or entranceway, as of a hotel, theater, apartment, etc.

fra'cas (frā′kəs) *n.* a noisy fight.

frac'tal′ (frak′təl) *n.* a mathematically-generated geometric shape that contains an infinite amount of detail.

frac'tion (frak′shən) *n.* **1,** a part of a unit, or of a whole. **2,** a scrap; a fragment. —**frac′tion·al,** *adj.*

frac'tion·ate″ (-āt″) *v.t.* (*Chem.*) separate by distillation, crystallization, etc. —**frac″-tion·a′tion,** *n.*

frac'tious (frak′shəs) *adj.* **1,** cross; peevish. **2,** unruly. —**frac′tious·ness,** *n.* ❑ *factious*

frac'ture (frak′chər) *n.* a breaking, esp. of a bone. —*v.t. & i.* break.

frag'ile (fraj′əl) *adj.* easily broken; delicate; brittle. —**fra·gil′i·ty** (frə-jil′ə-tē) *n.*

frag'ment (frag′mənt) *n.* **1,** a part broken off. **2,** an unfinished part, as of a poem. —**frag′men·ta″ry,** *adj.* incomplete. —**frag″men·ta′tion,** *n.*

fra'grant (frā′grənt) *adj.* **1,** sweet-scented; pleasant. **2,** (*Informal*) having an unpleasant odor. —**fra′grance,** *n.*

frail (frāl) *adj.* **1,** fragile. **2,** morally or physically weak. —*n.* (*Slang, often offensive*) a woman. —**frail′ty** (-tē) *n.*

frame (frām) *v.t.* **1,** construct; fit together. **2,** compose or devise, as a law or a poem; utter or express. **3,** surround with a frame, as a picture. **4,** (*Slang*) incriminate (a person) on false evidence. —*n.* **1,** something made of parts fitted and joined. **2,** any kind of structure for enclosing, supporting, or holding something. **3,** bodily structure. **4,** a state of mind; mood. —**frame house,** a house built of wood.

frame'-up″ *n.* (*Slang*) something fraudulently prearranged.

frame'work″ *n.* the structure for supporting anything; an outline or basic plan.

franc (frank) *n.* the monetary unit of France, Belgium, and Switzerland.

> **franc**
> ↔ From Old French *franc,* in reference to the inscription on the earliest coins: *Francorum Rex,* king of the Franks.

fran'chise (fran′chīz) *n.* **1,** the right to vote. **2,** a special right granted, esp. by a government.

fran'ci·um (fran′sē·əm) *n.* an unstable radioactive chemical element, no. 87, symbol Fr.

franc'o·phone″ (frank′ə-fōn″) *n.* a person who speaks French, esp. as his or her principal language.

fran'gi·ble (fran′jə-bəl) *adj.* breakable. —**fran″gi·bil′i·ty,** *n.*

frank *adj.* unreserved in expressing one's sentiments; candid; undisguised. —*n.* **1,** the privilege of mailing letters free of postage. **2,** (*Informal*) frankfurter. —*v.t.* mark for free mailing. —**frank′ness,** *n.*

Frank'en·stein″ (frank′ən-stīn″) *n.* a fictional character (in a novel by Mary Shelley) who brought to life a creature (*Frankenstein's monster*) that destroyed him.

frank'furt'er (-fēr″tər) *n.* a reddish sausage of beef and pork. Also, *Informal*, **frank.**

> **frankfurter**
> ↔ German for Frankfort sausage, from *Frankfurt*, Germany.

frank′in·cense″ (frank′in-sens″) *n.* a gum resin burned as incense.

Frank′lin stove a heating stove, usually of cast iron, and often completely enclosed (named for Benjamin Franklin).

fran′tic (fran′tik) *adj.* frenzied; wild with excitement, pain, or fear. —**fran′ti·cal·ly,** *adv.*

frappe (frap) *n.* a milk shake with ice cream.

frap·pé′ (fra-pā′) *n.* (*Fr.*) a mixed cold drink.

fra·ter′nal (frə-tēr′nəl) *adj.* **1,** brotherly. **2,** pert. to a fraternity.

fra·ter′ni·ty (frə-tēr′nə-tē) *n.* **1,** brotherliness. **2,** a society, or group, of men with common interests or tastes. **3,** a college society or club.

frat′er·nize″ (frat′ər-nīz″) *v.t.* associate in a friendly manner. —**frat″er·ni·za′tion,** *n.*

frat′ri·cide″ (frat′rə-sīd″) *n.* the killer or killing of a brother.

Frau (frow) *n.* (*Ger.*) a wife; Mrs. —**Fräu′lein″** (froi′līn″) *n.* (*Ger.*) an unmarried woman; Miss.

fraud (frâd) *n.* **1,** deceit; a trick. **2,** (*Law*) dishonest practice; breach of confidence. **3,** (*Informal*) a cheat.

fraud′u·lent (frâ′dyə-lənt) *adj.* dishonest; based on or obtained by fraud. —**fraud′u·lence,** *n.*

fraught (frât) *adj.* filled (with).

> **fraught, freight**
> ↔ Both words derive from Middle Dutch *vrachten*, load.

fray (frā) *n.* a battle; skirmish. —*v.t. & i.* ravel; wear thin, as cloth.

fraz′zle (fraz′əl) *v.t. & i.* (*Informal*) **1,** fray. **2,** exhaust; weary. —*n.* a ragged end; an exhausted state.

freak (frēk) *n.* **1,** an abnormal person, plant, or thing. **2,** a whim; vagary. —**freak′ish,** *adj.* —**freak out,** (*Slang*) **1,** lose control of oneself under the influence of drugs; have a "bad trip." **2,** experience similar reaction without drugs.

freck′le (frek′əl) *n.* a light-brown spot on the skin, caused by sunlight. —*v.t. & i.* cause or acquire freckles. —**freck′ly** *adj.*

Fred′die Mac′ (fred′ē mak′) the Federal Home Loan Mortgage Corp.; the

traded security representing mortgages guaranteed by it.

free (frē) *adj.* **1,** enjoying personal liberty; not enslaved. **2,** enjoying civil or political liberty; self-governing. **3,** existing under civil liberty, as a country. **4,** unrestricted in opinion, choice, or action; independent. **5,** exempt, as from tax or restriction. **6,** obtained without cost; given without charge. **7,** lavish; profuse. **8,** not bound or restricted by force. **9,** unrestrained; unceremonious; not bound by fixed rules. **10,** not literal or exact. **11,** open to all. —*adv.* without charge. —*v.t.* unfetter; release; exempt; rid (with *of*). —**free agent,** a person not bound by contract, etc., and hence free to act. —**free lance,** a self-employed writer, artist, etc., who may sell to whom he or she pleases. —**free love,** sexual relations or cohabitation without marriage. —**free port,** an area allowing free passage of goods without import duties. —**free trade,** commercial trading between countries without government-imposed duties, etc. —**free university,** an informally organized forum offering classes in subject matter not usually available in regular university courses. —**free verse,** verse without rhyme or regular meter. —**free will,** free choice.

-free (frē) *suf.* free of; lacking.

free′base″ (*Slang*) *v.t.* **1,** purify (cocaine). **2,** use (cocaine) by heating it and inhaling the smoke. —*n.* purified cocaine.

free′bie (frē′bē) *n.* (*Slang*) something obtained or given free of cost.

free′boot″er (frē′boo″tər) *n.* a pirate. ❑ *filibuster*

freed′man (frēd′mən) [*pl.* -**men**], freed′wom″an, *n.* a person who has been freed from slavery.

free′dom (-dəm) *n.* the state of being free; personal liberty or national independence. —**freedom of the press,** the right to publish fact and opinion without censorship.

free-′for-all″ *n.* (*Informal*) a contest or fight open to all.

free-′form″ *adj.* **1,** not organized. **2,** spontaneous.

free′hand″ *adj.* roughly drawn by hand. —**free″hand′ed,** *adj.* generous.

free′hold″ *n.* land owned outright.

free′lance″ *adj.* pert. to or produced by a free lance. —*v.i.* operate as a freelance.

free-′load″er *n.* (*Slang*) **1,** a parasite; sponge. **2,** a crasher, as at a party. —**free′load″,** *v.i.*

free′man (-mən) *n.* a free person; a person entitled to citizenship.

Free′ma″son *n.* a member of the Free and Accepted Masons, a Christian secret order. —**free′ma″son·ry,** *n.* sympathetic fellowship.

free′si·a (frē′zhė-ə) *n.* a flowering plant, named for 19th-c. Swedish botanist E. M. Fries.

free′stone″ (frē′stōn″) *adj.* of a fruit, one whose pulp does not cling to the stone.

free′style″ *n.* **1,** a swimming competition allowing the swimmer choice of strokes. **2,** the crawl (def. 2).

free′think″er *n.* a person of independent religious opinions.

free′ware″ *n.* (*Computers*) software that can be distributed and used for free, but which cannot be sold for profit.

free′way *n.* a toll-free highway.

free′wheel″ing *adj.* (*Informal*) **1,** free of restraint. **2,** nonchalant; carefree.

free′will′ *adj.* voluntary.

freeze (frēz) *v.t.* [**froze** (frōz), **fro′zen, freez′ing**] **1,** cause to congeal; change from a liquid to a solid state by loss of heat. **2,** form ice on or in; injure or kill by cold. **3,** fix at the present place, condition, price, etc. —*v.i.* **1,** be turned into, or covered with, ice. **2,** be injured or killed by intense cold. **3,** suffer from, or as from, cold. —*n.* a freezing condition, as of weather. —**freeze out,** exclude.

freeze-′dry″ *v.t.* dehydrate by freezing and removing moisture by vacuum.

freez′er *n.* **1,** a machine for freezing ice cream, etc. **2,** a cold storage cabinet.

freight (frāt) *n.* **1,** transportation of goods by a common carrier. **2,** goods so transported; cargo; shipment. **3,** the charge for handling. **4,** a train carrying freight. —*v.t.* **1,** load with, or as with, cargo. **2,** ship (goods) by freight. —**freight′er,** *n.* a ship used to transport goods. ❏ *fraught*

French *adj.* pert. to France, its people, etc. —*n.* the language of France. —**French′man,** *n.* —**French cuff,** a double folding cuff, usually held together with a cuff link. —**French doors** or **windows,** a pair of doors opening in the middle. —**French dressing,** a salad dressing of oil, vinegar, salt, and spices. —**French fried potatoes,** also, **French fries,** strips of potato fried in deep fat. —**French horn,** a brass wind instrument having a coiled tube ending in a flaring mouth. —**French leave,** abrupt departure. —**French letter,** (*Slang*) a condom. —**French pancake,**

crêpe. —**French toast,** bread dipped in egg and milk and sautéed.

French′i·fy″ (fren′chi-fī″) *v.t.* (*Informal*) make French in taste, manners, or characteristics.

fre·net′ic (frə-net′ik) *adj.* frenzied. —**fre·net′i·cal·ly,** *adv.*

fren′zy (fren′zė) *n.* **1,** violent mental agitation. **2,** delirious excitement. —**fren′zied,** *adj.*

Fre′on (frē′on) *n.* (*T.N.*) a gas used as a refrigerant.

fre′quen·cy (frē′kwən-sė) *n.* **1,** repeated occurrence. **2,** the rate of recurrence of a given event in a given time. —**frequency modulation,** in radio, alteration of wavelength frequency to avoid distortion.

fre′quent (frē′kwənt) *adj.* **1,** happening often; occurring at short intervals. **2,** habitual; regular. —*v.t.* (*also,* frė-kwent′) go often or habitually to. —**fre″quen·ta′tion** (-tā′shən) *n.* —**fre″quen′ta·tive** (-tə-tiv) *adj.*

fres′co (fres′kō) *n.* a mural painting on damp plaster.

fresh *adj.* **1,** having its original qualities; not faded, worn, or stale. **2,** novel; new; recent. **3,** cool; refreshing; of wind, brisk. **4,** of water, not salt; of food, not canned, preserved, or salted; recently grown, picked, slaughtered, etc. **5,** rested; not tired; invigorated; healthy. **6,** of a cow, recently having calved. **7,** inexperienced. **8,** (*Slang*) impudent. —**fresh′ness,** *n.*

fresh′en (-ən) *v.t.* make fresh.

fresh′et (fresh′it) *n.* a sudden seasonal rise in the level of a stream.

fresh′man (-mən) *n.* [*pl.* **-men**] a male or female student in the first year in high school or college.

fresh′wa″ter *adj.* **1,** living in or accustomed to inland waters, not the sea. **2,** inexperienced, insignificant, or rustic.

fress (fres) *v.i.* (*Slang*) eat or snack voraciously.

fret *v.i.* [**fret′ted, -ting**] **1,** be continuously perturbed by worry, anxiety, annoyance, or resentment. **2,** become worn or corroded. —*v.t.* **1,** vex; irritate. **2,** chafe; rub. —*n.* **1,** irritation. **2,** a carved ornamental pattern: *fretwork.* **3,** a small ridge across the fingerboard of a stringed instrument. —**fret′ful,** *adj.* fretting; restless; peevish. —**fret saw,** a saw used for ornamental woodwork.

Freud′i·an (froi′dė-ən) *adj.* pert. to the theories of Sigmund Freud relating to neurotic and psychopathic conditions.

fri′a·ble (frī′ə-bəl) *adj.* easily crumbled. —**fri″a·bil′i·ty,** *n.*

fri′ar (frī′ər) *n.* a member of certain Rom. Cath. religious orders. —**fri′ar·y,** *n.* a monastery.

fric″as·see′ (frik″ə-sē′) *n.* a dish of meat or fowl cut in pieces and cooked in gravy. —*v.t.* so cook.

fric′tion (frik′shən) *n.* **1,** the rubbing of two surfaces together; opposition; conflict. **2,** the resistance to relative motion between two surfaces in contact. **3,** lack of harmony; conflict. —**fric′tion·al,** *adj.* —**friction tape,** a water-resistant insulating adhesive tape.

Fri′day (frī′dè) *n.* the sixth day of the week. —**man** or **girl Friday,** a loyal servant or person; a slavish follower.

> **Friday, man/girl Friday**
> ↔ From the name of the Scandinavian goddess of married bliss, *Frigg*; *Friday* is Frigg's day. The word is modeled after Latin *Veneris dies,* Venus's day. *Man Friday* (like the nonparallel derivative *girl Friday*) comes from the name of the loyal servant in Defoe's novel *Robinson Crusoe.*

fried (frīd) *v.* pret. & p.p. of *fry.* —*adj.* **1,** boiled in fat. **2,** (*Slang*) drunk.

friend (frend) *n.* **1,** a person on intimate and affectionate terms with another. **2,** a supporter; well-wisher. **3,** (*cap.*) a member of the Religious Society of Friends; a Quaker. —**friend′ly,** *adj.* amicable; not hostile; favorable. —**friend′li·ness,** *n.* —**friendly fire,** an attack on one's own allies, troops, etc., usually by accident. —**friend′ship,** *n.* the state of being friendly toward or intimate with another.

frieze (frēz) *n.* **1,** an ornamental or sculptured band around a wall. **2,** a heavy woolen cloth.

frig′ate (frig′it) *n.* **1,** (*Hist.*) a sailing warship, relatively equivalent to the modern cruiser. **2,** a modern light warship.

fright (frīt) *n.* **1,** sudden fear or terror. **2,** (*Informal*) a grotesque person or thing.

fright′en (-ən) *v.t.* terrify.

fright′ful (-fəl) *adj.* **1,** terrible. **2,** (*Informal*) unpleasant. —**fright′ful·ness,** *n.*

frig′id (frij′id) *adj.* **1,** icy; wintry. **2,** chilly in manner; formal. **3,** emotionally unresponsive. —**fri·gid′i·ty** (fri-jid′ə-tè) *n.*

frill (fril) *n.* **1,** a gathered or pleated ruffle; a trimming. **2,** (*Informal*) (*pl.*) affectations. **3,** a fancy detail or accessory. —**frill′y,** *adj.*

fringe (frinj) *n.* **1,** a raveled edge on a fabric; a fancy edging of tassels or twisted threads. **2,** border; outskirts. **3,** an extreme and unrepresentative part of a group, party, doctrine, etc. —*v.t.* furnish with a fringe; border. —**fringe benefit,** a benefit given in addition to salary or wages.

frip′per·y (frip′ə-rė) *n.* worthless finery; ostentation.

Fris′bee (friz′bè) *n.* (*T.N.*) a saucer-shaped object thrown from person to person.

> **Frisbee**
> ↔ The invention was supposedly inspired by the pie tins made by the *Frisbie* Pie Company, Bridgeport, CT (and others).

fri·sé′ (fri-zā′) *n.* (*Fr.*) an upholstery fabric, made of uncut loops.

frisk *v.i.* leap about; gambol. —*v.t.* (*Slang*) search (a person) for concealed weapons. —**frisk′y,** *adj.* playful.

frit′ter (frit′ər) *v.t.* waste on trifles, as time, energy, etc. —*n.* a small fried battercake.

> **fritter**
> ↔ The battercake name comes from French *friture,* from Latin *frictura,* a frying. The verb derives from Old English *fitt,* a part.

fritz (frits) —**on the fritz,** (*Informal*) not in working order.

fri·vol′i·ty (fri-vol′ə-tè) *n.* **1,** a frivolous act. **2,** merrymaking.

friv′o·lous (friv′ə-ləs) *adj.* **1,** not seriously intended; lacking in dignity; slight; trivial. **2,** silly; giddy. —**friv′o·lous·ness,** *n.*

friz *v.* form into crisp curls or tufts, as hair. —*n.* something frizzed. Also, **frizz.** —**friz′zy,** *adj.*

friz′zle (friz′əl) *v.t.* **1,** friz. **2,** cook with sizzling noise. —**friz′zly,** *adj.*

fro (frō) *adv.* back. —**to and fro,** back and forth.

frock (frok) *n.* **1,** a dress. **2,** a coarse outer garment worn by a monk, etc. —**frock coat,** a man's long-skirted coat.

frog (frâg) *n.* **1,** a small, tailless amphibian with great leaping and swimming ability. **2,** a lump of mucus in the throat. **3,** a flower holder. **4,** a fastening made of a button and a loop. **5,** a device that permits the intersection of two railway tracks.

frog′man; frog′wom″an *n.* a specially trained underwater swimmer.

frol′ic (frol′ik) *v.i.* [**-icked, -ick·ing**] play

merrily. —*n.* merrymaking; fun. —**frol'ic-some,** *adj.*

from *prep.* away; out of (a certain starting point); denoting removal, separation, distinction, etc.

frond *n.* a leaf of a fern, etc.

front (frunt) *n.* **1,** the foremost part or face of anything. **2,** manner of facing anything. **3,** position directly before a person or thing. **4,** land along the edge of a river, bay, etc. **5,** in war, the scene of actual fighting. **6,** bearing or demeanor. **7,** (*Informal*) an outward manifestation of wealth or importance. **8,** (*Informal*) a figurehead. **9,** (*Meteor.*) the surface of contact of two unlike air masses. **10,** a temporary coalition of political parties. —*adj.* pert. to, or situated at, the front. —*v.t.* confront; have the front toward; face. —*v.i.* **1,** face in a certain direction. **2,** (with *for*) (*Informal*) lend one's name or prestige (to). —**front foot,** a foot of frontage.

front'age (frun'tij) *n.* the distance a lot extends along a street, body of water, etc.

fron'tal (frun'təl) *adj.* **1,** at or of the front. **2,** pert. to the bone of the forehead.

fron·tier' (frun-tir') *n.* **1,** that part of a country that borders another country or an unsettled region. **2,** undeveloped spheres of knowledge, etc. —**fron·tiers'-man** (-tirz'mən) [*pl.* **-men**], **fron·tiers'-wom''an,** *n.*

fron'tis·piece'' (frun'tis-pēs'') *n.* an illustration facing the title page of a book.

---

frontispiece
↔ Not related to *piece,* the word derives from Latin *frontispicium,* examination of the face, which gradually was simplified to *face.*

---

front-'run''ner *n.* (*Informal*) the leader in a competition, contest, etc.

frost (frâst) *n.* **1,** frozen dew or vapor. **2,** freezing weather. **3,** a frozen state of the ground. **4,** (*Slang*) a failure. **5,** (*Informal*) a coolness between persons. —*v.t.* **1,** cover with frost. **2,** injure by freezing. **3,** ice (a cake). —**frost'ed,** *adj.* iced.

frost'bite'' *n.* injury to body tissues, caused by exposure to intense cold.

frost'ing *n.* **1,** a sugar coating for cake. **2,** a finish on metal or glass.

frost'y *adj.* **1,** cold. **2,** gray, as hair.

froth (frâth) *n.* **1,** mass of fine bubbles on the surface of a liquid, at the mouth of a hard-ridden horse, etc.; foam. **2,** anything light and trivial. —*v.t. & i.* foam.

froth'y *adj.* **1,** foaming. **2,** light; insubstantial.

frou'frou'' (froo'froo'') *n.* a rustling, esp. of a woman's silk dress.

fro'ward (frō'wərd) *adj.* willful; perverse. —**fro'ward·ness,** *n.* ❑ *foreword*

frown *n.* a wrinkling of the brows, as in anger, perplexity, etc. —*v.i.* **1,** so wrinkle the brow. **2,** (with *upon*) disapprove.

frowz'y (frow'zē) *adj.* slovenly; unkempt. —**frowz'i·ness,** *n.*

froze (frōz) *v.* pret. of *freeze.*

fro'zen (frō'zən) *adj.* **1,** congealed by cold. **2,** frigid. **3,** lacking emotion. **4,** refrigerated. **5,** fixed; not liquid, as assets. —*v.* p.p. of *freeze.*

fruc'ti·fy'' (fruk'tə-fī') *v.t.* make productive. —*v.i.* bear fruit. —**fruc''ti·fi·ca'tion** (-fi-kā'shən) *n.*

fruc'tose (fruk'tōs) *n.* an intensely sweet sugar that occurs in honey.

fru'gal (froo'gəl) *adj.* economical; not wasteful; not lavish; sparing. —**fru·gal'i·ty** (froo-gal'ə-tē), *n.*

fruit (froot) *n.* **1,** any natural, useful yield of a plant. **2,** the seed of a plant and its enveloping tissues. **3,** the sweet fruit of certain trees and vines, as peach, pear, grape, etc. **4,** a result; consequence. —**fruit'er·er,** *n.* a dealer in fruit. —**fruit'-ful,** *adj.* productive; profitable. —**fruit'less,** *adj.* unprofitable; barren.

fruit'cake'' *n.* **1,** a rich cake. **2,** (*Slang*) an eccentric; a crazy person.

fru·i'tion (froo-ish'ən) *n.* **1,** state of bearing fruit. **2,** realization; attainment, as of one's hopes.

fruit'y (-ē) *adj.* **1,** having the taste or flavor of fruit. **2,** spicy, as a story.

frump *n.* a dowdy person. —**frump'ish, frump'y,** *adj.*

frus'trate (frus'trāt) *v.t.* prevent from fulfilling plans, hopes, etc.; balk; thwart; nullify.

frus·tra'tion (frus-trā'shən) *n.* **1,** act of frustrating; state of being frustrated. **2,** extreme disappointment.

frus'tum (frus'təm) *n.* the remainder of a cone or pyramid after the top portion has been cut off.

fry (frī) *v.t. & i.* **1,** cook or be cooked in hot fat. **2,** (*Slang*) be electrocuted. **3,** be subjected to extreme heat. —*n.* **1,** a young fish. **2,** a swarm or brood of young; young children.

fuch'sia (fū'shə) *n.* a shrub or plant with drooping reddish tubular flowers; the color of the flower.

---

fat, fāte, fär, fāre, fâll, ȧsk; met, hē, hēr, maybė; pin, pīne; not, nōte, ôr, tool

fuchsia
↔ New Latin, named for 16th-c. German botanist Leonhard *Fuchs*.

fud′dle (fud′əl) *v.* [-**dled, -dling**] —*v.t.* muddle or intoxicate. —*v.i.* tipple.

fud′dy-dud′dy (fud′ē-dud′ē) *n.* **1,** a fogy. **2,** stuffed shirt.

fudge (fuj) *n.* **1,** nonsense. **2,** a creamy beaten chocolate candy. —*v.i.* cheat; hedge.

fu′el (fū′əl) *n.* **1,** combustible material burned to supply heat or power. **2,** a stimulant. —*v.t. & i.* furnish with, or take on, fuel. —**fuel injection,** a method of spraying fuel into the cylinders of an internal combustion engine.

fu′gi·tive (fū′jə-tiv) *adj.* **1,** fleeing; having run away. **2,** evanescent; fleeting. **3,** of literature, of passing interest; transitory. —*n.* one who flees from pursuit, duty, etc.

fugue (fūg) *n.* a musical composition in which the theme is reintroduced by various parts.

Füh′rer (fyū′rər) *n.* (*Ger.*) leader; applied esp. to Adolf Hitler.

-ful (fəl) *suf.* **1,** full of; filled. **2,** characterized by. **3,** tending to, as *harmful.*

ful′crum (fūl′krəm) *n.* the support on which a lever rests or turns.

ful·fill′ (fūl-fil′) *v.t.* **1,** carry into effect, as a promise. **2,** perform, as a duty. **3,** satisfy, as a desire. Also, **ful·fil′.** —**ful·fill′ment,** *n.*

ful′gent (ful′jənt) *adj.* shining brightly. —**ful′gent·ness,** *n.*

fu·lig′i·nous (fū-lij′ə-nəs) *adj.* sooty; smoky. —**fu·lig′i·nous·ness,** *n.*

full (fūl) *adj.* **1,** filled to capacity; holding all that can be held. **2,** complete according to standard; whole. **3,** rounded out; plump; ample. **4,** engrossed. **5,** abundantly supplied. **6,** at the peak of, as quality, force, volume, etc. —*adv.* **1,** entirely. **2,** exactly. —*n.* utmost extent. —**full′ness,** *n.* —**full blast, 1,** operating at capacity. **2,** thorough; unrestrained. **3,** at capacity; thoroughly. —**full stop,** a period (def. 3).

full′back″ *n.* in football, a player stationed behind the line.

full-blood′ed *adj.* **1,** of unmixed ancestry. **2,** virile.

full-blown′ *adj.* fully developed.

full-′bod″ied *adj.* having utmost flavor or strength, as a beverage.

full′er (fūl′ər) *n.* **1,** one who treats cloth to thicken it. **2,** a hammer with a cylindrical striking surface. —**fuller's earth,** a claylike substance used as a filter and blotting material.

fuller's earth
↔ Not named for someone called Fuller, but because it was used for cleaning (*fulling*) cloth.

full-′fledged″ *adj.* **1,** fully matured or developed. **2,** of first rank.

full-′time″ *adj. & adv.* working the customary number of hours, days, weeks, etc., for one's principal occupation.

ful′mar (fūl′mər) *n.* an Arctic seabird related to the petrel.

ful′mi·nate″ (ful′mə-nāt″) *v.t. & i.* **1,** explode; detonate. **2,** (with *against*) issue denunciations. —**ful″mi·na′tion,** *n.*

ful′some (fūl′səm) *adj.* cloying; offensively excessive; insincere. —**ful′some·ness,** *n.*

fulsome
☞ Beware this word. It means offensively excessive, not abundant or generous. If you mean to be complimentary, this is not the word to use.

fu′ma·role″ (fū′mə-rōl″) *n.* a hole from which volcanic gases issue.

fum′ble (fum′bəl) *v.i. & t.* **1,** grope about awkwardly; handle clumsily. **2,** in sports, fail to hold (the ball). —*n.* a slip; misplay.

fume (fūm) *n.* (usually *pl.*) smoke, gas, vapor, esp. if noxious. —*v.i.* **1,** emit fumes. **2,** be vexed; fret. —**fumed,** *adj.* colored by fumes, as woodwork.

fu′mi·gate″ (fū′mi-gāt″) *v.t.* treat with fumes to disinfect or to destroy pests. —**fu′mi·gant,** *n.* —**fu″mi·ga′tion,** *n.* —**fu″mi·ga″tor,** *n.*

fun *n.* anything that induces enjoyment, esp. mirthful; amusement; sport; joking.

fu·nam′bu·list (fū-nam′byə-list) *n.* a tightrope walker.

func′tion (funk′shən) *n.* **1,** proper action by which any person, organ, office, structure, etc. fulfills its purpose or duty. **2,** a public ceremony or occasion. **3,** (*Math.*) a quantity that depends on other quantities for its value. —*v.i.* perform a function; operate, in the natural or intended manner.

func′tion·al (-əl) *adj.* **1,** pert. to a function. **2,** designed to perform some function; useful. —**functional disease,** a disease characterized by a morbid change in the function, but not in the tissues, of an organ. —**func′tion·al·ism,** *n.* the doctrine that functional utility should determine design (of furniture, etc.).

func′tion·ar·y (-er-ē) *n.* an official.

fund *n.* **1,** a stock or supply, esp. of

money, set apart for a purpose. **2,** a store of anything, as knowledge. **3,** (*pl.*) available cash. —*v.t.* **1,** convert (a temporary debt) into a permanent debt bearing interest. **2,** provide funding for.

fun″da·men′tal (fun″də-men′-təl) *adj.* serving as, or being an essential part of, a foundation; basic; primary; elementary. —*n.* a basic principle. —**fun″da·men′tal·ist,** *n. & adj.* (one) who accepts the Bible as literally true. —**fun″da·men′tal·ism,** *n.*

fu·ne′bri·al (fū-nē′brė-əl) *adj.* funereal.

fu′ner·al (fū′nər-əl) *n.* the ceremony of burying a dead person. —**funeral director,** undertaker.

fu·ne′re·al (fū-nir′ė-əl) *adj.* **1,** dark; gloomy; sad. **2,** pert. to a funeral.

fun′gi·cide (fun′ji-sīd) *n.* an agent for destroying fungous growths, as athlete's foot.

fun′go (fung′gō) *n.* (*Baseball*) **1,** a long, slender bat used to hit practice balls. **2,** a ball hit for fielding practice.

fun′gus (fung′gəs) *n.* any of a group of non-green plants, including the molds, toadstools, rusts, etc. —**fun′gous,** *adj.*

fu·nic′u·lar (fū-nik′ū-lər) *adj.* pert. to, or worked by, a rope or cable. —*n.* a mountain cable railway.

funk *n.* (*Informal*) **1,** cowering fear. **2,** a state of depression. **3,** a style of blues music.

funk′y (funk′ė) *adj.* earthy; having a feeling of the blues.

fun′nel (fun′əl) *n.* **1,** a cone-shaped device for guiding something into a small opening. **2,** a smokestack. **3,** a shaft for ventilation.

fun′ny (fun′ė) *adj.* **1,** amusing; comical. **2,** (*Informal*) strange; odd. **3,** (*pl.*) (*Informal*) the comic strips; funny papers. —**fun′ni·ness,** *n.* —**funny bone** *n.* **1,** a nerve in the elbow. **2,** sense of humor. —**funny farm,** (*Slang*) an insane asylum. —**funny money,** (*Slang*) counterfeit or play money.

---

funny bone

⟨ ⟩ From the "funny" (i.e., strange) sensation when the nerve of the elbow is hit, and not, as some would have it, from a pun on *humerus,* the bone's Latin name, with *humerous,* funny.

---

fur (fėr) *n.* the soft, fine hair of certain animals; their dressed skins, used for clothing. —**furred,** *adj.*

fur′be·low″ (fėr′bə-lō″) *n.* **1,** a plaited

dress trimming; a flounce. **2,** any bit of finery.

fur′bish (fėr′bish) *v.t.* polish; burnish; renovate.

fu′ri·ous (fyûr′ė-əs) *adj.* **1,** raging; full of fury. **2,** violent, as a wind. **3,** energetic. —**fu′ri·ous·ness,** *n.*

furl (fėrl) *v.t.* roll up and fasten (a flag or sail).

fur′long (fėr′lâng) *n.* a measure of length, 220 yards.

---

furlong, furrow

↔ A compound of Old English *furh,* furrow, and *long:* a *furlong* was the length of a furrow, hence initially an imprecise measurement.

---

fur′lough (fėr′lō) *n.* **1,** leave of absence for a soldier, prisoner, etc. **2,** a temporary layoff from work.

fur′nace (fėr′nis) *n.* a structure in which fuel is burned to make heat.

fur′nish (fėr′nish) *v.t.* supply with what is needed, esp. furniture; provide. —**fur′nish·ings,** *n.pl.* fittings of any kind.

fur′ni·ture (fėr′nə-chər) *n.* **1,** movable articles, as chairs, desks, etc., for equipping a house, office, etc. **2,** any necessary apparatus.

fu′ror (fyûr′ôr) *n.* **1,** great excitement. **2,** a prevailing craze.

fur′ri·er (fėr′ė-ər) *n.* a maker of or dealer in fur garments.

fur′ring (fėr′ing) *n.* **1,** fur for a garment. **2,** in building, thin boards providing a basis for laths, plaster, etc.

fur′row (fėr′ō) *n.* **1,** a trench in the earth, esp. that made by a plow. **2,** a wrinkle. —*v.t.* make furrows in. ❑ *furlong*

fur′ry (fėr′ė) *adj.* **1,** covered with fur. **2,** made of or like fur. —**fur′ri·ness,** *n.*

fur′ther (fėr′thər) *adj.* [*superl.* **fur′thest**] **1,** more remote or extended, in figurative senses; comp. of *far.* **2,** additional. —*adv.* **1,** to a greater distance or extent. **2,** also. —*v.t.* promote or advance, as a cause. —**fur′ther·ance,** *n.* advancement. ❑ *farther*

fur′ther·more″ *adv.* besides; also.

fur′tive (fėr′tiv) *adj.* sly; stealthy; done by stealth. —**fur′tive·ness,** *n.*

fu′run·cle (fyûr′ung-kəl) *n.* a boil.

fu′ry (fyûr′ė) *n.* **1,** violent passion; great anger. **2,** fierceness; violence.

furze (fėrz) *n.* a shrub common in wastelands in Europe; gorse.

fuse (fūz) *n.* **1,** a casing filled with combustible material for exploding a shell, blast, etc. **2,** a protective strip of fusible

---

fat, fāte, fär, fâre, fâll, ȧsk; met, hē, hėr, maybė; pin, pīne; not, nōte, ôr, tool

metal inserted in an electric circuit. —*v.t. & i.* **1,** melt with extreme heat. **2,** blend, as if melted together; weld. Also, **fuze.** —**fus′i·ble,** *adj.* —**fus″i·bil′i·ty,** *n.*

fu·see′ (fū-zē′) *n.* **1,** a friction match that will burn in the wind. **2,** a warning flare.

fu′se·lage (fū′sə-lij) *n.* the body of an airplane.

fu′sel oil (fū′zəl) a poisonous liquid, a by-product of distilleries, used in solvents.

fu′si·form″ (fū′zə-form″) *adj.* spindle-shaped.

fu″sil·lade′ (fū″ze-lād′) *n.* simultaneous fire from many firearms.

fu′sion (fū′zhən) *n.* **1,** union by fusing. **2,** union of two or more political parties. **3,** in nuclear physics, union of parts of two atoms.

fuss (fus) *n.* **1,** much ado over trifles; bustle; confusion. **2,** (*Informal*) a petty quarrel. —*v.t.* worry, or be busy, over trifles. —*v.t.* confuse. —**fuss′y,** *adj.* unduly particular.

fuss′bud′get *n.* one who fusses about insignificant things.

fus′tian (fus′chən) *n.* **1,** a coarse cotton fabric. **2,** high-flown speech; bombast.

fus′ty (fus′tē) *adj.* **1,** musty; stuffy. **2,** old-fashioned. —**fus′ti·ness,** *n.*

fu′tile (fū′təl) *adj.* **1,** ineffectual. **2,** idle; trifling. —**fu·til′i·ty** (fū-til′ə-tē) *n.*

fu′ton (foo′ton) *n.* a thin Jap.-style mattress.

fu′ture (fū′chər) *adj.* **1,** yet to come or happen. **2,** relating to later time. —*n.* **1,** times to come. **2,** prospects. —**fu′tur·ism,** *n.* a style in the arts emphasizing the mechanisms and violence of modern life and rejecting the traditions of the past. —**future shock,** inability to deal with the rapidity of social and technological change.

fu″tur·is′tic (fū″chər-is′tik) *adj.* anticipating the supposed art forms of the future. —**fu″tur·is′ti·cal·ly,** *adv.*

fu·tu′ri·ty (fū-tyûr′ə-tē) *n.* **1,** the future; the state of being yet to come. **2,** a horse race in which the entries are named long in advance.

fuzz (fuz) *n.* **1,** fine, fluffy particles of wool, cotton, etc.; down. **2,** (*Slang*) police officer; the police. —**fuzz′y,** *adj.* —**fuzz′i·ness,** *n.* —**fuzz box,** an electronic device which gives a fuzzy quality to sound which is fed through it. —**fuzzy logic,** a branch of logic in which conclusions are not necessarily either true or false, but may be probably true or probably false.

Fuzz′bust″er, *n.* (*T.N.*) a device that detects and warns of radar speed-sensing devices.

-fy (-fī) *suf.* forming verbs meaning: **1,** make (as *simplify,* make simple). **2,** become (as *solidify,* become solid).

fyl′fot (fil′fot) *n.* swastika.

G

G, g (jē) the seventh letter of the English alphabet.

g (jē) *n.* **1,** gravity; acceleration of gravity. **2,** a unit of force equal to the force of gravity. **3,** (*Slang*) a grand; $1,000.

gab *v.i.* [**gabbed, gab′bing**] (*Informal*) talk idly; chatter. —*n.* idle talk. —**gab′by,** *adj.* very talkative.

gab′ar·dine″ (gab′ər-dēn″) *n.* cloth of wool or cotton, similar to serge.

gab′ble (gab′əl) *v.i.* **1,** cackle, as geese. **2,** talk volubly; jabber. —*n.* act or result of gabbling.

gab′fest″ *n.* (*Informal*) an informal get-together for conversation.

ga′ble (gā′bəl) *n.* the triangular expanse of wall between opposite edges of a sloping roof. —**ga′bled,** *adj.*

gad *n.* a pointed rod; a goad. —*v.i.* [**gad′ded, -ding**] ramble about idly. —*interj.* a euphemism for God. —**gad′der, gad′a·bout″,** *n.* one who travels about aimlessly.

gad′fly″ (gad′flī″) *n.* a stinging insect annoying to cattle.

gadg′et (gaj′it) *n.* any small device, esp. mechanical. —**gadg″e·teer′** (-ə-tir′) *n.* one who makes or collects many gadgets. —**gadg′et·ry** (-rē) *n.* gadgets.

gad″o·lin′i·um (gad″ə-lin′ē-əm) *n.* a metallic element of the rare-earth group, no. 64, symbol Gd.

> **gadolinium**
> ↔ From *gadolinite,* the name of the mineral from which it is extracted, from 19th-c. Finnish chemist J. *Gadolin,* who discovered the mineral.

Gael′ic (gā′lik) *adj.* pert. to the Celtic peoples, esp. Irish. —*n.* a language spoken by these peoples.

gaff (gaf) *n.* **1,** a stick with an iron hook, for landing fish. **2,** a spar to extend a sail. **3,** (*Slang*) persistent teasing; expense.

gaffe (gaf) *n.* a social blunder.

gaf′fer (-ər) *n.* **1,** (*Informal*) an old man. **2,** a gang boss, esp. in a carnival.

gag *n.* **1,** a thing thrust into the mouth

to prevent outcry; hence, restraint of free speech. **2,** (*Informal*) a joke. —*v.t.* **[gagged, gag′ging]** put a gag on; silence. —*v.i.* retch. —**gag order,** a court order prohibiting public disclosure of details of a trial in progress.

ga′ga (gä′gä) *adj.* (*Slang*) senseless.

ga·ga′ku (gä-gä′koo) *n.* the ancient court music of Japan.

gage (gāj) *n.* **1,** gauge. **2,** anything, as a glove, symbolizing a challenge. **3,** greengage.

gag′gle (gag′əl) *v.i.* **[-gled, -gling]** cackle. —*n.* a flock of geese.

gai′e·ty (gā′ə-tē) *n.* gayness; merrymaking; brightness.

gai′ly (gā′lē) *adv.* **1,** merrily. **2,** showily.

gain (gān) *v.t.* **1,** obtain (something valued or desired). **2,** acquire by accretion, as added weight. **3,** earn by effort. **4,** reach; arrive at. —*v.i.* **1,** benefit. **2,** make progress. **3,** put on weight. —*n.* **1,** profit. **2,** an increase. —**gain′ful,** *adj.* advantageous.

gain′er (gā′nər) *n.* a dive in which the diver faces forward and makes a backward somersault.

gain′say″ (gān′sā″) *v.t.* **[-said′, -say′ing]** contradict; dispute.

gait (gāt) *n.* manner of running or walking. —**gait′ed,** *adj.* (of a horse) trained to various gaits.

gai′ter (gā′tər) *n.* a cloth or leather covering for the leg or ankle; a spat.

gal *n.* (*Informal*) a woman or girl.

ga′la (gā′lə) *n.* a festival. —*adj.* festive. ❏ *gallant*

ga·lac·to- (gə-lak-tō) *pref.* milk.

gal′an·tine (gal′ən-tēn) *n.* a dish of chicken, veal, etc., served cold.

gal′ax·y (gal′ək-sē) *n.* **1,** a luminous band of stars. **2,** (*cap.*) the Milky Way. **3,** an assemblage of splendid persons or things. —**ga·lac′tic** (gə-lak′tik) *adj.*

> **galaxy**
> ↔ From Greek *galaxias kyklos*, milky way.

gale (gāl) *n.* **1,** a stiff wind. **2,** an outburst, as of laughter. **3,** a shrub.

ga·le′na (gə-lē′nə) *n.* a mineral, an important ore of lead and silver.

gal″i·ma·ti·as (gal″ə-mä′shē-əs) *n.* incoherent or nonsensical talk.

gall (gâl) *n.* **1,** a bitter secretion of the liver; bile. **2,** rancor. **3,** (*Slang*) impudence. **4,** a sore made by chafing. **5,** a lump made by insects on trees, esp. oaks. —*v.t. & i.* **1,** make sore by rubbing. **2,** vex;

annoy. —**gall bladder,** a sac in which the bile is stored.

gal′lant (gal′ənt) *adj.* **1,** brave; chivalrous. **2,** honorable; noble. **3,** (gə-länt′) courtly; attentive to women. —*n.* (gə-länt′) **1,** a dashing man of fashion. **2,** a ladies' man. —**gal′lant·ry** (-trē) *n.*

> **gallant, regale, gala**
> ↔ *Gallant* is from Old French *galer* (of Frankish origin), make merry, which also produced *regale* and perhaps *gala* as well.

gal′le·on (gal′ē-ən) *n.* a former Sp. sailing vessel.

gal·le·ri′a (gal-ə-rē′ə) *n.* a collection of small shops.

gal′ler·y (gal′ə-rē) *n.* **1,** a long narrow passage often open at one side; a veranda. **2,** a room or building for the exhibition of works of art. **3,** a balcony, as in a theater.

gal′ley (gal′ē) *n.* **1,** an ancient seagoing vessel propelled by oars and sails. **2,** a rowboat larger than a gig. **3,** the kitchen of a ship. **4,** an oblong, shallow tray to hold set-up type; a proof printed from this type.

gal′liard (gal′yərd) *n.* a lively dance.

Gal′lic (gal′ik) *adj.* pert. to the Gauls; French.

Gal′li·cism (gal′ə-siz-əm) *n.* **1,** a Fr. idiom. **2,** a Fr. word or phrase used in another language.

gal′li·um (gal′ē-əm) *n.* a rare metallic element, no. 31, symbol Ga.

> **gallium**
> ↔ Probably formed by a pun on the name of its discoverer, 19th-c. French chemist *Lecoq* de Boisbaudran: French *coq*, rooster, translated into Latin *gallus*.

gal′li·vant (gal′i-vant) *v.i.* seek pleasure frivolously; gad about.

gal′lon (gal′ən) *n.* a measure of capacity; four quarts.

gal′lop (gal′əp) *n.* a rapid, springing gait, esp. of a horse. —*v.t.* cause to gallop. —*v.i.* **1,** run or ride at a gallop. **2,** progress rapidly.

gal′lows (gal′ōz) *n.* a structure (*tree*) with two upright posts and a crossbar at the top, for hanging criminals.

> **gallows**
> ↔ From Germanic *galgon*, pole, presumably referring to the two upright poles which hold the crosspiece from which the victim is hung.

---

fat, fāte, fär, fâre, fâll, ȧsk; met, hē, hêr, maybè; pin, pīne; not, nōte, ôr, tool

gall'stone″ (gâl'stōn″) *n.* a stony mass formed in the gall bladder.

gal'lus·es (gal'ə-siz) *n.pl.* suspenders.

ga·loot′ (gə-loot′) *n.* (*Slang*) a clumsy or foolish fellow; yokel.

gal′op (gal'əp) *n.* a lively dance; the music for it.

ga·lore′ (gə-lôr′) *adj. & adv.* in plenty; in abundance.

> **galore**
> ↔ From Irish *go leor*, enough, of Gaelic origin.

ga·losh′ (gə-losh′) *n.* (usu. *pl.*) a high overshoe.

ga·lumph′ (gə-lumf′) *v.i.* to move ungracefully.

> **galumph**
> ↔ Coined by Lewis Carroll in *Through the Looking-Glass*, perhaps from *gal(lop)* + *(tri)umph*.

gal·van′ic (gal-van'ik) *adj.* **1,** pert. to a current of electricity. **2,** stimulating; electric; spasmodic. **—gal·van′i·cal·ly,** *adv.*

> **galvanic, galvanism, galvanize**
> ↔ From French *galvanique*, from the name of 18th-c. Italian physiologist Luigi *Galvani*.

gal′va·nism (gal'və-niz-əm) *n.* production of electricity by chemical action. ❑ *galvanic*

gal′va·nize″ (gal'və-nīz″) *v.t.* **1,** shock or stimulate, as by electricity. **2,** plate or coat with metal by means of electricity. **—galvanized iron,** iron sheeting plated with zinc. ❑ *galvanic*

gal″va·nom′e·ter (gal″və-nom'ə-tər) *n.* an instrument for detecting and measuring the strength and direction of an electric current.

gam *n.* **1,** a school of whales. **2,** (*Slang*) the human leg.

gam′bit *n.* **1,** in chess, an opening that loses a pawn or other piece but gains positional advantage. **2,** any apparent sacrifice in expectation of later gain.

> **gamble, game**
> ↔ *Game*, meaning pastime, and *gamble* both come from Old English *gaman*. *Game*, in the sense of lame, is a shortened form of *gammy*, from Middle French *gambi*, bent.

gam′ble (gam'bəl) *v.i.* **1,** risk money on a game of chance. **2,** hazard something of value on an uncertain event. **—v.t.** risk;

(with *away*) lose by gambling. **—n.** a risk. **—gam′bler,** *n.* **—gam′bling,** *n.*

gam·boge′ (gam-bōj′) *n.* a resin used as a yellow pigment or medicine.

gam′bol (gam'bəl) *v.i.* leap or skip about in frolic. **—n.** frolic.

gam′brel (gam'brəl) *n.* a joint in the hind leg of a horse. **—gambrel roof,** a roof in two sections of different slope, the outer being steeper.

game (gām) *n.* **1,** play; amusement. **2,** a contest played according to rules; a division of a contest; a winning score. **3,** a plan, scheme, or enterprise. **4,** wild animals, birds, or fish hunted for food or sport. **—adj.** (*Slang*) **1,** plucky. **2,** willing. **3,** lame. **—v.t. & i.** play games; gamble. **—game′ness,** *n.* **—game′ster** (-stər) *n.* a gambler. **—game plan,** a strategy for achieving a desired goal. **—game theory,** the application of mathematical laws of probability to finding the best strategy for winning at games, war, politics, etc. ❑ *gamble*

> **game, sport**
> ☞ Though these two words can be used interchangeably in some contexts, *sport* is generally used for games requiring physical strength.

game′cock″ *n.* a cock bred to fight in exhibitions.

game′keep″er *n.* a private game warden.

games′man·ship (gāmz'mən-ship) *n.* the art of winning games, esp. by deception or trickery.

gam′ete (gam'ēt) *n.* (*Biol.*) a cell that unites with another for reproduction.

gam′in *n.masc.,* **gam′ine** (-ēn) *n.fem.* a neglected child; street urchin.

gam′ing (gā'ming) *n.* the playing of a game for money.

gam′ma (gam'ə) *n.* the third letter of the Greek alphabet (H, γ). **—gamma glob′u·lin** (glob'yə-lin) a drug formerly used against infantile paralysis, often called **G.G. —gamma rays,** rays similar to X rays, emitted by radioactive elements.

gam′mon (gam'ən) *n.* **1,** a smoked ham. **2,** trickery; nonsense. **3,** backgammon; esp., in backgammon, a won game of double value. **—v.t.** deceive.

gam′ut (gam'ət) *n.* **1,** the whole range of accepted musical tones. **2,** range; scope. ❑ *gantlet*

> **gamut**
> ↔ From Latin *gamma ut*, the first note of a musical scale devised in the 11th c. by theorist Guido d'Arezzo.

gam′y (gā′mē) *adj.* **[-i·er, -i·est] 1,** having the flavor of game. **2,** spirited; plucky. **3,** racy; off-color.

gan′der (gan′dər) *n.* **1,** the male goose. **2,** (*Slang*) a careful look.

gang *n.* **1,** a group of persons acting or going about together. **2,** a set of tools, machines, etc. rigged to run simultaneously. —*v.i.* (with *up*) join forces against.

gang′bust″er *n.* **1,** a law enforcement officer specializing in gangs. —**like gangbusters,** (*Informal*) with great success, speed, etc.

gang′land″ *adj.* pert. to the criminal underworld, esp. organized crime.

gan′gling (gang′gling) *adj.* awkwardly tall and thin. Also, **gan′gly** (-glē). —**gan′gle** (-gəl) *v.i.*

gan′gli·on (gang′glē-ən) *n.* **1,** a knot on a nerve from which nerve fibers radiate. **2,** a mass of gray matter in the central nervous system.

gang′plank″ *n.* a movable ramp to a ship.

gan′grene (gang′grēn) *n.* the rotting away of body tissue resulting from stoppage of nourishment. —**gan′gre·nous,** *adj.*

gang′ster (gang′stər) *n.* a member of a lawless gang; a racketeer.

gang′way″ (gang′wā″) *n.* a passageway into or out of an enclosed space. —*interj.* stand aside! make way!

gan′net (gan′ət) *n.* a large seabird.

gant′let (gànt′lət) *n.* **1,** a form of punishment or hazing in which the victim runs between two lanes of people and is struck by them in passing. **2,** a series of unpleasant things or events. **3,** gauntlet.

> **gantlet, gauntlet, gamut**
> ☛ These words are frequently confused. *Gantlet* and *gamut* both are series of things: a *gantlet* is two rows of people meting out punishment and a *gamut* is the complete series of musical notes in the scale. Thus, you can *run the gantlet* or *run the gamut*, though the implications are different. A *gauntlet* is a medieval glove.

gan′try (gan′trē) *n.* a supporting structure, as a framework or bridge.

Gantt chart (gant) a diagram for scheduling tasks.

gaol (jāl) *n. & v.t.* (*Brit.*) jail. ❏ *jail*

gap *n.* **1,** an opening; a vacant space. **2,** a notch in a mountain ridge. **3,** a break in continuity.

gape (gāp) *v.i.* **1,** open the mouth wide;

yawn. **2,** be wide open. **3,** look amazed. —*n.* breach; gap.

gar (gär) *n.* a fish with a long, sharp snout.

ga·rage′ (gə-räzh′) *n.* a building where motor vehicles are stored or repaired. —*v.t.* put, keep, or service in a garage. —**garage sale,** a personal sale of used merchandise, clothing, etc.

> **garage**
> ↔ From Germanic *waron*, to watch over, through French *garer*, shelter.

Gar′and rifle (gar′ənd) a kind of semiautomatic repeating rifle.

garb (gärb) *n.* clothes, esp. of a distinctive calling or period; attire. —*v.t.* clothe.

gar′bage (gär′bij) *n.* **1,** waste matter from a kitchen; refuse. **2,** a worthless assortment; nonsense.

gar·ban′zo (gär-ban′zō) (*Sp.*) *n.* the chickpea.

gar′ble (gär′bəl) *v.t.* twist, in order to misrepresent; distort; misquote.

gar·çon′ (gär-sôn′) *n.* (*Fr.*) **1,** a boy. **2,** a waiter.

gar′den (gär′dən) *n.* **1,** a plot of ground where flowers, fruits, or vegetables are grown. **2,** a delightful spot. —*v.i.* lay out or work in a garden. —**gar′den·er,** *n.* one who tends a garden, esp. one employed to do so. —**garden variety,** common; regular.

> **garden, yard**
> ↔ Both words derive from Germanic **gardon*. *Yard* reached English through Germanic sources, *garden* through Romance sources.

gar·de′nia (gär-dē′nyə) *n.* the white or yellow flower of a tropical shrub.

> **gardenia**
> ↔ New Latin, coined by Linnaeus in honor of 18th-c. American naturalist Alexander *Garden*.

gar·gan′tu·an (gär-gan′tū-ən) *adj.* enormous; gigantic.

> **gargantuan**
> ↔ From *Gargantua*, the fictional character of enormous appetite in Rabelais' satirical novels *Gargantua* and *Pantagruel*.

gar′gle (gär′gəl) *v.i.* rinse the throat with medicinal liquid. —*n.* such a liquid.

gar′goyle (gär′goil) *n.* (*Archit.*) a grotesque stone image. ❏ *gargle*

gar′ish (gar′ish) *adj.* showy; overdecorated. —**gar′ish·ness,** *n.*

---

fat, fāte, fär, fâre, fâll, àsk; met, hē, hêr, maybè; pin, pīne; not, nōte, ôr, tool

gargle, gargoyle
↔ Both words derive from Latin *gargulio*, throat. *Gargoyles*, often used as rainspouts, were so named because of the idea that the rainwater was coming out of their throats.

gar'land (gär'lənd) *n.* **1,** a wreath of flowers or leaves. **2,** a literary anthology. —*v.t.* deck with garlands.

gar'lic (gär'lik) *n.* a bulb with a strong onionlike flavor. —**gar'lick·y, y,** *adj.*

gar'ment (gär'mənt) *n.* any article of clothing.

gar'ner (gär'nər) *v.t.* reap, gather, and store, as in a granary; collect.

gar'net (gär'nit) *n.* a clear deep-red stone, used as a gem.

gar'nish (gär'nish) *n.* a decoration, esp. for food. —*v.t.* **1,** adorn. **2,** garnishee. —**gar'nish·ment,** *n.*

gar"nish·ee' (gär"ni-shē') *v.t.* [**-eed'** (-ēd'), **-ee'ing**] (*Law*) attach a defendant's property which is in the possession of a third party, esp. wages. —*n.* a defendant whose property is attached.

gar'ni·ture (gär'ni-chər) *n.* decoration; trimming.

gar'ret (gar'ət) *n.* an attic.

gar'ri·son (gar'ə-sən) *n.* troops stationed in a fort or fortified town. —*v.t.* provide with or occupy as a garrison.

gar·rote' (gə-rōt') *v.t.* kill by strangulation. —*n.* a method of execution by strangulation.

gar·ru'li·ty (gə-roo'lə-tē) *n.* quality of being garrulous.

gar'ru·lous (gar'yə-ləs) *adj.* given to talking too much. —**gar'ru·lous·ness,** *n.*

gar'ter (gär'tər) *n.* a band or other device to keep up a stocking. —**garter snake,** a common and harmless striped snake.

gas *n.* **1,** any elastic, airlike fluid capable of indefinite expansion. **2,** such fluids used as anesthetic, fuel, etc. **3,** noxious fumes. **4,** (*Informal*) gasoline. —*v.i.* [**gassed, gas'sing**] (*Slang*) converse idly but at length. —*v.t.* poison with gas. —**gas'i·fy** (-i-fī) *v.t.* convert into gas. —**gas chamber,** a room in which a person is executed with gas. —**gas chromatograph,** a chromatograph for analyzing volatile substances. —**gas mask,** a mask worn for protection against poison gas. —**natural gas,** a mixture of gaseous hydrocarbons found in deposits in the earth often associated with petroleum, used as a fuel.

gas
↔ Coined by the 17th-c. Flemish chemist J. B. van Helmont, on the model of Greek *chaos*, atmosphere.

gas"con·ade' (gas"kə-nād') *n.* boastful talk.

gasconade
↔ From Latin *Vascones*, inhabitants of Basque country.

gas'e·ous (-ē-əs) *adj.* of or like gas.

gash *n.* a deep slash or cut. —*v.t.* cut deeply.

gas'ket (gas'kit) *n.* a strip of material used to seal a joint; a washer.

gas'o·hol" (gas'ə-hol") *n.* a mixture of gasoline and ethyl alcohol, used as a fuel.

gas'o·line" (gas'ə-lēn") *n.* an inflammable liquid distilled from petroleum, used esp. as a motor fuel. Also, **gas'o·lene".**

gasp (gàsp) *n.* a convulsive catching of the breath. —*v.i.* labor for breath painfully. —*v.t.* utter with quick, short breaths. —**last gasp,** dying breath; final effort.

gas'sy (gas'ē) *adj.* **1,** full of or like gas. **2,** (*Informal*) talkative; boastful.

gas'tric (gas'trik) *adj.* pert. to the stomach. —**gas·tri'tis** (-trī'tis) *n.* inflammation of the stomach.

gas·tro- (gas-trō) *pref.* of or pert. to the stomach.

gas·tron'o·my (gas-tron'ə-mē) *n.* the art of preparing good food. —**gas'tro·nome** (-trə-nōm) *n.* —**gas"tro·nom'ic** (-trə-nom'ik) *adj.* —**gas"tro·nom'i·cal·ly,** *adv.*

gat *n.* **1,** (*Hist.*) Gatling gun. **2,** (*Slang*) a pistol.

gate (gāt) *n.* **1,** an opening, esp. in a fence, hedge, or wall, for entrance and exit; a movable barrier at such an opening. **2,** an electronic device used in computers which emits a signal when certain input conditions are met. **3,** (*Slang*) the money received from sale of admission tickets. **4,** (*Slang*) dismissal.

gate'crash"er *n.* one who gains admission to a party, etc., without an invitation, or without paying.

gate'way" *n.* **1,** a means of access. **2,** (*Computers*) a link between computer networks.

gath'er (ga*th*'ər) *v.t.* **1,** bring together; assemble. **2,** cull; pick. **3,** acquire; gain; amass. **4,** recover; marshal. **5,** infer. **6,** draw (cloth) into folds; pleat. —*v.i.* **1,** congregate. **2,** increase. **3,** come to a head, as a boil. —*n.* a fold or pleat in cloth. —**gath'er·ing,** *n.* an assemblage.

Gat'ling gun an early type of machine gun having a cluster of barrels, named for 19th-c. U.S. inventor R. J. Gatling.

gauche (gōsh) *adj.* socially awkward. —**gau'che·rie** (gō'shə-rė) *n.*

gau'cho (gow'chō) *n.* a cowboy of South America.

gaud'y (gâ'dė) *adj.* **1,** gay; bright. **2,** showy without taste. —**gaud'i·ness,** *n.*

gauge (gāj) *n.* **1,** a standard of measurement. **2,** a graduated instrument for measuring. **3,** an instrument for measuring flow. —*v.t.* **1,** measure. **2,** estimate. Also, **gage.**

gaunt (gânt) *adj.* thin; haggard. —**gaunt'ness,** *n.*

gaunt'let (gânt'lət) *n.* **1,** a glove with a long, wide cuff. **2,** a challenge. **3,** a course beset by punishing or afflicting agencies. Also, **gant'let.** ❏ *gantlet*

gauss (gows) *n.* (*Physics*) a unit of magnetic induction, named for 19th-c. German mathematician Karl Friedrich Gauss.

gauze (gâz) *n.* a very thin, porous fabric of silk, cotton, etc.

---

gauze, gaze
↔ *Gauze* comes from French *gaze*, perhaps named after the city of Gaza, a city active in the production of gauze. *Gaze* is unrelated, tracing its roots to Frankish origins.

---

gave (gāv) *v.* pret. of *give.*

gav'el (gav'əl) *n.* a small mallet, used by a chairman or auctioneer.

ga'vi·al (gā'vė-əl) *n.* a crocodile of India and Pakistan.

ga·votte' (gə-vot') *n.* a dance similar to the minuet, but livelier.

gawk (gâk) *n.* an awkward fellow. —*v.i.* stare stupidly. —**gawk'y,** *adj.* clownish; clumsy.

gay (gā) *adj.* **1,** high-spirited; merry. **2,** bright; colorful; showy. **3,** dissipated; loose. **4,** homosexual. —*n.* a homosexual. *n.* —**gay'ness,** *n.*

gaze (gāz) *n.* a fixed, intent look. —*v.i.* look at intently. ❏ *gauze*

ga·ze'bo (gə-zē'bō) *n.* [*pl.* **-bos** or **-boes**] a summerhouse or garden pavilion.

ga·zelle' (gə-zel') *n.* a small, graceful antelope.

ga·zette' (gə-zet') *n.* **1,** a newspaper. **2,** an official government journal. —*v.t.* publish in such a journal.

gaz"et·teer' (gaz"ə-tir') *n.* a dictionary of geographical names.

gaz·pa'cho (gə-spä'chō) (*Sp.*) *n.* a cold soup of chopped vegetables, garlic, oil, and vinegar.

gear (gir) *n.* **1,** equipment; apparatus; tools. **2,** a harness, as for horses, and its appurtenances. **3,** a wheel or part that engages another part of a machine, as by meshing teeth; a working unit of a machine, as steering gear. **4,** the adjustment of parts of a machine, with respect to speed or efficiency, as in *high gear, in gear.* —*v.t.* **1,** equip; harness. **2,** adjust the operation or speed of, with gears.

gear'shift" *n.* a mechanism for changing gears in an automobile transmission.

gear'wheel" *n.* a wheel having cogs or teeth that engage with those of another wheel; cogwheel.

geck'o (gek'ō) *n.* a small nocturnal lizard.

gee (jē) *v.t., v.i. & interj.* turn or move to the right. —*v.i.* (*Informal*) suit; fit. —*interj.* an expletive of mild feeling.

geek (gēk) *n.* (*Slang*) a gullible or feeble-minded person.

geese (gēs) *n.* pl. of *goose.*

gee'zer (gē'zər) *n.* (*Slang*) an old man.

ge·fil'te fish (gə-fil'tə) (*Yiddish,* stuffed fish) chopped fish mixed with egg and seasonings, and cooked in broth.

Ge·hen'na (gi-hen'ə) *n.* a fiery place; hell.

Gehenna
↔ From the Hebrew phrase *ge ben Hinnom,* the valley of the son of Hinnom.

Gei'ger counter (gī'gər) a device for detecting radioactivity, named for 20th-c. German physicist Hans Geiger.

gei'sha (gā'shə) *n.* a Japanese woman skilled in the art of entertaining people, esp. men.

gel (jel) *n.* (*Chem.*) a jellylike or solid material formed by the coagulation of a colloidal solution. —*v.i.* [**gelled, gell'ing**] form or become a gel.

gel'a·tin (jel'ə-tin) *n.* a granular transparent substance that congeals when cold; jelly. —**ge·lat'i·nous** (jə-lat'i-nəs) *adj.*

ge·la'to (je-lä'tō) *n.* (*It.*) ice cream.

geld (geld) *v.t.* castrate. —**geld'ing,** *n.* a castrated animal, esp. a horse.

gel'id (jel'id) *adj.* very cold; icy. —**ge·lid'i·ty, gel'id·ness,** *n.*

gem (jem) *n.* **1,** a precious stone. **2,** an object of great beauty or worth.

gem'i·nate (jem'ə-nət) *adj.* in pairs, coupled. —*v.t. & i.* (-nāt") double. —**gem"i·na'tion,** *n.*

Gem′i·ni″ (jem′ə-nī″) *n.* a constellation, the Twins (see *zodiac*).

gems′bok (gemz′bok) *n.* a large straight-horned antelope of So. Afr.

ge·müt′lich (gə-müt′lik) *adj.* intimate; cheerful; warmhearted. —**Ge·müt′lich·keit″** (-kīt″) *n.* (*Ger.*) cheerfulness; cordiality.

gen′darme (zhän′därm) *n.* (*Fr.*) a police officer, esp. in France. —**gen·dar′me·rie** (-ə-rē) *n.* (*Fr.*) gendarmes collectively.

gen′der (jen′dər) *n.* in grammar, the classification as masculine, feminine, or neuter. —**gender gap,** the differences (economic, social, etc.) between women and men.

---

gender, sex
☞ Although *gender* is sometimes used as a synonym for *sex*, its specific meaning is a classification of nouns, affecting agreement of modifying adjectives, pronouns, etc., which may or may not actually correspond with the sex of the being represented. Thus *Mädchen* in German, which means young woman (female sex), is neuter in gender. Moreover, a masculine or feminine gender is assigned to many sexless things and in languages which do not have a neuter gender to all things: thus the French word for *ship* is *navire* (masculine) while the Italian word is *nave* (feminine).

---

gene (jēn) *n.* (*Biol.*) an element in the germ cell, concerned with the transmission of hereditary characteristics.

ge″ne·al′o·gy (jē″nē-al′ə-jē) *n.* record of descent from an ancestor; pedigree. —**ge″ne·a·log′i·cal,** *adj.* —**ge″ne·al′o·gist,** *n.* one whose vocation is tracing pedigrees.

gen′er·a (jen′ə-rə) *n.* pl. of *genus*.

gen′er·al (jen′ər-əl) *adj.* **1,** pert. or applicable to all or most of an entire class or category; universal; not limited in scope. **2,** widespread. **3,** not specific or detailed; vague; indefinite. **4,** usual; ordinary. **5,** chief; highest-ranking. —*n.* **1,** the highest-ranking army officer. **2,** [also, **general officer**] any officer ranking above a colonel. **3,** the masses; the populace. —**gen′er·al·ship,** *n.* —**General Assembly,** an organ of the United Nations composed of all member nations, each of which has one vote. —**general delivery,** a department of a post office that holds mail until picked up; mail sent to that department. —**general practitioner,** a medical doctor not limiting his or her practice to a specialty. Also, **GP.**

gen″er·al·is′si·mo″ (jen″ər-ə-lis′i-mō″) *n.* a supreme military commander.

gen″er·al′i·ty (jen″ər-al′ə-tē) *n.* **1,** the majority. **2,** a statement that is essentially true but not specific.

gen′er·al·ize″ (jen′ər-ə-līz″) *v.i.* draw conclusions from varied evidence. —*v.t.* consider as or arrange by classes. —**gen″·er·al·i·za′tion,** *n.*

gen′er·ate″ (jen′ə-rāt″) *v.t.* **1,** bring into life. **2,** produce; form. —**gen′er·a″tive,** *adj.*

gen″er·a′tion (jen″ə-rā′shən) *n.* **1,** production by natural or artificial means. **2,** the average difference in age between parent and child, usually counted as 30 years; each ancestor in a line of descent. **3,** all persons living at the same time. **4,** (*pl.*) descendants. —**generation gap,** (*Informal*) the difference in attitudes, mores, etc., between persons of different generations, esp. between parents and their children.

gen′er·a″tor (jen′ə-rā″tər) *n.* an apparatus for converting one type of energy into another, most often used to produce electricity.

ge·ner′ic (ji-ner′ik) *adj.* **1,** pert. to a genus or class. **2,** general, not specific. **3,** not marketed under a brand name. —**ge·ner′i·cal·ly,** *adv.*

gen″er·os′i·ty (jcn″ə-ros′ə-tē) *n.* quality of being generous; liberality.

gen′er·ous (jen′ər-əs) *adj.* **1,** free in giving; liberal. **2,** abundant. **3,** not mean or prejudiced.

gen′e·sis (jen′ə-sis) *n.* [*pl.* **-ses″** (-sēz″)] **1,** the origin of anything. **2,** (*cap.*) the first book of the Old Testament.

ge·net′ics (ji-net′iks) *n.pl.* the study of the evolution of species and of heredity. —**ge·net′ic,** *adj.* —**ge·net′i·cal·ly,** *adv.* —**genetic counseling,** the counseling of an individual with reference to the person's genetic history and its likely effects on the person's offspring. —**genetic engineering,** the modification of the DNA of an organism.

Ge·ne′va convention (jə-nē′və) one of several international agreements dealing with the treatment of sick, wounded, and prisoners, in time of war.

gen′ial (jēn′yəl) *adj.* **1,** friendly and kindly in manner; cordial; jovial. **2,** favorable to growth or comfort. —**ge″ni·al′i·ty** (jē″nē-al′ə-tē) *n.*

ge′nie (jē′nē) *n.* a mythical spirit having power to perform miraculous deeds.

---

genie, genius

↔ Both words derive from Latin *genius*, guardian spirit. *Genie* comes to English through French *génie*.

gen'i·tal (jen'ə-təl) *adj.* pert. to reproduction of animals. —*n.* (*pl.*) [also, **gen"i·ta'li·a** (jen"ə-tā'lē-ə)] the organs of reproduction.

gen'i·tive (jen'ə-tiv) *n.* the grammatical case expressing possession or source; the possessive.

gen'ius (jēn'yəs) *n.* **1,** the guiding spirit of a person or place. **2,** natural fitness; aptitude; talent; bent. **3,** exceptional mental and creative power. **4,** a person with such power. ❑ *ability, genie*

gen'o·cide" (jen'ə-sīd") *n.* deliberate extermination of an entire people.

gen'o·gram" (jen'ə-gram") *n.* a graphic family tree showing psychological connections between generations.

gen're (zhän'rə) (*Fr.*) *n.* **1,** variety; type. **2,** (*Painting*) portrayal of scenes from everyday life.

gent (jent) *n.* (*Informal*) gentleman.

gen·teel' (jen-tēl') *adj.* affectedly refined. —**gen·teel'ness,** *n.*

genteel, gentile, gentle

↔ All three words derive from Latin *gens*, race, and come to English through French *gentil*.

gen'tian (jen'shən) *n.* an herb bearing a blue flower.

gen'tile (jen'tīl) *n.* **1,** (*Bible*) a person not a Jew. **2,** in respect to any religious group, an outsider. ❑ *genteel*

gen·til'i·ty (jen-til'ə-tē) *n.* **1,** the state of being wellborn or wellbred; all persons of good or noble birth. **2,** gentleness; softness.

gen'tle (jen'təl) *adj.* **1,** mild in manner or disposition; tender; peaceful; tame. **2,** not rough or harsh; kind. **3,** of good birth; belonging to the gentry. —*v.t.* (*Informal*) soften; subdue. —**gen'tle·ness,** *n.* —**gentle sex** (often considered *Offensive*) women. ❑ *genteel*

gen'tle·folk" *n.pl.* persons of good breeding.

gen'tle·man (-mən) [*pl.* **-men**], **gen'·tle·wom"an,** *n.* **1,** a person of good birth. **2,** an honorable person of fine feelings. Also, **gen'tle·per"son,** *n.* —**gen'tle·man·ly, gen'tle·wo"man·ly,** *adj.* refined; well-behaved. —**gentleman farmer,** a person who farms for pleasure rather than for living income. —**gentlemen's agreement, 1,** an

agreement or promise binding as a matter of honor, but not of law. **2,** an unwritten agreement to discriminate against certain religious, social, or other groups.

gen'tri·fy (jen'trə-fī) *v.t. & i.* to upgrade (a neighborhood). —**gen"tri·fi·ca'tion,** *n.*

gen'try (jen'trē) *n.* **1,** people of good breeding and, usually, wealth. **2,** people of a particular class or group.

gen·u·flect' (jen'ū-flekt") *v.i.* bend the knee, esp. in worship. —**gen"u·flec'tion, gen"u·flex'ion,** *n.*

gen'u·ine (jen'yū-in) *adj.* **1,** not counterfeit; authentic. **2,** real; sincere. —**gen'u·ine·ness,** *n.*

ge'nus (jē'nəs) *n.* [*pl.* **gen'er·a** (jen'ə-rə)] (*Biol.*) a group of animals or plants having close relationship.

-gen·y (jə-nē) *suf.* denoting origin.

ge·o- (jē-ə-; -ō) *pref.* signifying earth.

ge'ode (jē'ōd) *n.* (*Geol.*) a hollow stone formed in concentric layers, often lined with crystals.

ge"o·des'ic (jē"ə-dē'sik) *adj.* pert. to the geometry of curved surfaces. —*n.* a line which is the shortest distance between its terminal points. —**geodesic dome,** a domed structure formed of interlocking polygons.

ge·od'e·sy (jē-od'ə-sē) *n.* the science of measuring the shape and area of the earth. —**ge"o·det'ic** (jē"ə-det'ik) *adj.*

ge·og'ra·phy (jē-og'rə-fē) *n.* the science that deals with the earth, its plants and animals, climate, population, industries, etc. —**ge·og'ra·pher,** *n.* —**ge"o·graph'i·cal** (jē"ə-graf'i-kəl) *adj.*

ge·ol'o·gy (jē-ol'ə-jē) *n.* the science that deals with the history of the earth and its changes, esp. as recorded in its rocks. —**ge"o·log'i·cal** (jē"ə-loj'i-kəl) *adj.* —**ge·ol'o·gist,** *n.*

ge·om'e·try (jē-om'ə-trē) *n.* that branch of mathematics dealing with the relations and measurements of lines, angles, surfaces, and solids. —**ge"o·met'ric** (jē"ə-met'rik), **ge"o·met'ri·cal,** *adj.* —**ge·om"e·tri'cian** (-trish'ən) *n.* —**geometric progression** or **series,** a series of numbers or terms, each of which is a constant multiple of the one preceding it, as 1, 2, 4, 8, etc. ❑ *arithmetic*

ge"o·phys'ics (jē"ō-fiz'iks) *n.* the study of the structure of the earth and the physical forces that affect it.

ge"o·pol'i·tics (jē"ō-pol'ə-tiks) *n.* the study or application of political science in the light of geographical influences and objectives.

fat, fāte, fär, fâre, fâll, ȧsk; met, hē, hėr, maybė; pin, pīne; not, nōte, ôr, tool

Geor'gian (jôr'jən) *adj.* **1,** pert. to the period (1714–1830) of the reigns of George I to George IV of England. **2,** a style of architecture, furniture, etc.

ge·ra'ni·um (jə-rā'nē-əm) *n.* **1,** a wild flower with pinkish-blue blossoms. **2,** a cultivated plant with large heads of white, pink, or red flowers.

> **geranium**
> ↔ From Greek *geranion*, from *geranos*, crane, from the supposed resemblance of the plant to a crane's bill.

ger'bil (jẽr'bəl) *n.* a small burrowing rodent of Asia and Africa.

ger"i·at'rics (jer"ē-at'riks) *n.* the study and treatment of diseases attendant on old age. **—ger"i·a·tri'cian** (-ə-trish'ən) *n.*

germ (jẽrm) *n.* **1,** a microbe. **2,** the earliest stage of an organism. **3,** source; origin. **—germ cell,** a cell having the function of reproduction.

> **germ, germane, German**
> ↔ The first two words (as well as the rare adjective *german*, related) derive from Latin *germen*, sprout. The nationality is apparently unrelated, of Latin origins perhaps going back to a Celtic ancestor.

Ger'man (jẽr'mən) *adj.***1,** pert. to Germany, its people, or language. **2,** (*l.c.*) born of the same father and mother. **3,** (*l.c.*) born of one's aunt or uncle. —*n.* a native, or the language, of Germany. **—German'ic** (-man'ik) *adj.* **—German measles,** a contagious disease resembling measles; rubella. **—German silver,** an alloy of copper, zinc, and nickel. ❑ *germ*

ger·mane' (jer-mān') *adj.* closely allied; relevant. ❑ *germ*

ger·ma'ni·um (jər-mā'nē-əm) *n.* a rare metallic element, no. 32, symbol Ge.

ger'mi·cide" (jẽr'mi-sīd") *n.* a substance to destroy germs. **—ger'mi·cid"al,** *adj.*

ger'mi·nal (jẽr'mə-nəl) *adj.* sprouting; budding.

ger'mi·nate" (jẽr'mə-nāt") *v.i.* begin to grow; sprout. **—ger"mi·na'tion,** *n.*

ger·ont- (jer-ənt) *pref.* old age.

ger"on·toc'ra·cy (jer"ən-tok'rə-sē) *n.* government by the aged.

ger"on·tol'o·gy (jer"ən-tol'ə-jē) *n.* the science that deals with the phenomena of old age.

ger'ry·man"der (ger'ē-man"dər; jer'-) *v.t.* change the boundaries of election districts to give one political party an unfair advantage.

> **gerrymander**
> ↔ A compound of Eldridge *Gerry*, a governor of Massachusetts, and *salamander*, inspired by the supposed resemblance of a newly redistricted Essex County, MA, to this animal.

ger'und (jer'ənd) *n.* a noun formed from a verb and ending in *-ing*.

ges'so (jes'ō) *n.* a preparation used as a base for painting.

gest (jest) *n.* **1,** a tale of adventure; a romance. **2,** deed; exploit. Also, **geste.**

ge·stalt' (gə-shtält') *n.* a structure (psychological, physical, or biological) having properties not derivable from the sum of its parts.

Ge·sta'po (gə-stä'pō) *n.* (*Ger.*) the state police of Nazi Germany.

> **Gestapo**
> ↔ An abbreviation of German *Ge(heime) Sta(ats)-Po(lizei)*, secret state police.

ges'tate (jes'tāt) *v.t.* carry in the womb during pregnancy. **—ges·ta'tion,** *n.* pregnancy.

ges·tic'u·late" (jes-tik'yə-lāt") *v.i.* make gestures to convey meaning. **—ges·tic"u·la'tion,** *n.*

ges'ture (jes'chər) *n.* **1,** a movement of head or limbs to convey feeling or to emphasize or illustrate. **2,** something said or done for effect only. —*v.i.* make gestures.

ge·sund'heit" (gə-zûnt'hīt") *interj.* (*Ger.*) used as a toast, or to a person who has sneezed.

get *v.t.* [**got** or **got'ten, get'ting**] **1,** acquire possession of, esp. by one's own efforts; obtain; receive. **2,** fetch. **3,** grasp; understand. **4,** cause to do or be done; cause to be; induce. **5,** produce; beget. —*v.i.* **1,** cause oneself to be or become; become. **2,** arrive. —*n.* offspring; a litter. **—get away (with),** *n.* escape (the consequences of). **—get back (at),** (*Slang*) obtain revenge (upon). **—get lost,** (*Slang*) go away! **—get off, 1,** depart. **2,** escape punishment. **—get on, 1,** progress; proceed; succeed. **2,** grow older. **—get through (to),** reach; establish communication with, esp. by telephone. **—get up, 1,** arise. **2,** assemble. **—get with (it),** (*Slang*) be or become up to date.

get'a·way" *n.* (*Slang*) escape.

get-'to·geth"er *n.* a social gathering, esp. a small one.

get′up *n.* (*Informal*) costume; manner of dress.

gew′gaw″ (gū′gâ″) *n.* a piece of minor jewelry; bauble; plaything.

gey′ser (gī′zər) *n.* a hot spring that periodically spouts hot water and steam.

ghast′ly (gåst′lē) *adj.* **1,** very pale; haggard. **2,** morally shocking. **—ghast′li·ness,** *n.*

> **ghastly, ghost**
> ↔ *Ghost* comes from Old English *gast,* ghost. Its spelling influenced the development of *ghastly,* which comes from the similar Middle English *gasten,* terrify.

gher′kin (gĕr′kin) *n.* a small cucumber used for pickles.

ghet′to (get′ō) *n.* [*pl.* **-tos**] **1,** the Jewish quarter in a city. **2,** any ethnic quarter. **3,** a slum. **—ghetto box** or **blaster,** (*Slang*) a large portable stereo.

> **ghetto**
> ↔ Venetian dialect for foundry, it was the name of an island near Venice where Jews were forced to live.

ghost (gōst) *n.* **1,** a disembodied human spirit, esp. such a spirit thought of as returning to haunt the living; a specter. **2,** a mere shadow; a glimmering. **—ghost′ly,** *adj.* like a ghost. **—ghost writer,** an author for whose work another receives credit. ❑ *ghastly*

ghoul (gool) *n.* **1,** an imaginary spirit who preys on the dead. **2,** a grave robber. **—ghoul′ish,** *adj.*

G.I. *abbr.* (*Slang*) a soldier in the U.S. Army: *g(overnment) i(ssue).*

gi′ant (jī′ənt) *n.* **1,** an imaginary being of superhuman size. **2,** a person, animal, plant, or thing of great size. **—adj.** huge.

gib′ber (jib′ər) *v.i.* talk nonsense; babble.

gib′ber·ish (jib′ər-ish) *n.* inarticulate talk; nonsense.

gib′bet (jib′ət) *n.* a gallows. **—v.t. 1,** execute by hanging. **2,** expose to ridicule, etc.

gib′bon (gib′ən) *n.* a small ape.

gib′bous (gib′əs) *adj.* convex, as the moon when more than half and less than full.

gibe (jīb) *v.t. & i.* mock; jeer; taunt. **—n.** a taunt.

gib′lets (jib′ləts) *n.pl.* the gizzard, liver, and heart of poultry.

Gib′son (gib′sən) *n.* a cocktail of gin and vermouth with pearl onions.

gid′dy (gid′ē) *adj.* **1,** dizzy. **2,** causing dizziness. **3,** frivolous. **—gid′di·ness,** *n.*

> **gibe, gybe, jibe**
> ☞ Three easily confusable words. *Gibe* means to jeer or taunt. *Gybe* means to shift from side to side, as the sail of a sailboat. *Jibe* is an alternate spelling for *gibe* and the more common spelling for *gybe*; it also has its own meaning, i.e., to be in harmony with.

gift *n.* **1,** something given; a donation; a present. **2,** the right or power to give. **3,** a natural talent. **—gift′ed,** *adj.* endowed with unusual talent. ❑ *ability*

gig *n.* **1,** a light, two-wheeled carriage. **2,** a ship's boat. **3,** any fancy, unusual hairdo. **4,** (*Slang, Music*) a playing engagement, as a concert.

gi·ga- (gig-ə) *pref.* billion.

gi·gan′tic (jī-gan′tik) *adj.* huge; enormous. **—gi·gan′ti·cal·ly,** *adv.*

gi·gan′tism (jī-gan′tiz-əm) *n.* abnormal increase in size of an organism or any of its parts.

gig′gle (gig′əl) *n.* a silly, half-suppressed laugh. **—v.i.** so laugh.

gig′o·lo″ (jig′ə-lō″) *n.* [*pl.* **-los″**] a man who, for pay, acts as an escort.

gig′ot (jig′ət) *n.* **1,** a puffed sleeve. **2,** a leg of mutton.

gigue (zhĕg) *n.* (*Fr.*) a jig.

Gi′la monster (hē′lə) a large poisonous lizard of the American Southwest, named for the Gila River, SW U.S.

gild *v.t.* **1,** overlay or coat with gold. **2,** give a bright but misleading appearance to.

gild′ing *n.* **1,** superficial or simulated gold. **2,** material for gilding, as gold leaf.

gill (gil) *n.* **1,** the breathing organ of fish. **2,** (jil) a liquid measure, one-fourth of a pint.

gil′ly·flow″er (jil′ē-flow″ər) *n.* **1,** a cultivated flower-bearing plant. **2,** a kind of apple.

gilt *n.* **1,** gilding, esp. with an imitation of gold. **2,** a young sow. **—adj.** gilded; imitative of gold.

gilt-′edged″ *adj.* **1,** having gilded edges. **2,** of highest quality.

gim′bals (jim′bəlz) *n.pl.* rings used for suspending anything, as a mariner's compass, so that it will remain level at all times.

gim′crack″ (jim′krak″) *n.* an intricate but useless device or ornament; a gewgaw.

gimp *n.* **1,** a braid used for trimming. **2,** one who limps; a cripple. **—v.i.** limp.

gin (jin) *n.* **1,** an uncolored alcoholic liquor, distilled from grain. **2,** a machine for separating the seeds from cotton. **3,** a snare; trap. **4,** [*also,* **gin rummy**] a card game for two. —*v.t.* put (cotton) through a gin.

> **gin**
> ↔ The drink is a shortened form of *geneva*, from Dutch *genever*, juniper, derived from Latin *juniperus*. The snare and the machine also come from a shortened form, but of another word, Old French *engin*, engine.

gin'ger (jin'jər) *n.* **1,** a tropical herb with a hot, spicy root, used in cooking and in medicine. **2,** a tawny, yellowish color. **3,** (*Informal*) vigor; vivacity.

gin'ger·bread" (jin'jər-bred") *n.* **1,** a cake flavored with ginger. **2,** excessively fancy decoration, in architecture.

> **gingerbread**
> ↔ From earlier *gingebras*, ginger paste, ultimately from Greek *zingiberis*, ginger.

gin'ger·ly (jin'jər-lè) *adv.* with extreme caution. —*adj.* slow and timid. —**gin'ger·li·ness,** *n.*

gin'ger·snap" (jin'jər-snap") *n.* a thin brittle cookie flavored with ginger.

ging'ham (ging'əm) *n.* a cotton dress fabric woven in checks, plaids, or stripes.

gin·gi·vi'tis (jin-jə-vī'tis) *n.* inflammation of the gums.

gink'go (ging'kō) *n.* a tree with fan-shaped leaves, native to Japan and China.

Gin'nie Mae' the Government National Mortgage Assoc.; the traded security representing mortgages guaranteed by it.

gin'seng (jin'seng) *n.* an herb or shrub whose aromatic root is used in medicine.

gip'sy (jip'sè) *n.* gypsy.

gi·raffe' (jə-raf') *n.* an Afr. ruminant animal with extremely long neck and legs.

gird (gėrd) *v.t.* [*pret. & p.p.* **girt** or **gird'ed**] **1,** confine with a belt; make fast by binding. **2,** encircle. **3,** prepare for action; equip.

gird'er (gėr'dər) *n.* a main supporting beam, esp. of steel.

gir'dle (gėr'dəl) *n.* **1,** a sash or belt for the waist. **2,** an elastic undergarment to support the abdomen and shape the body. **3,** a ring around a tree trunk. —*v.t.* bind; encircle.

girl (gėrl) *n.* **1,** female child or (often considered *Offensive*) a young woman. **2,** a maidservant. **3,** (*Informal*) sweetheart. —**girl'hood",** *n.* —**girl'ish,** *adj.* ❏ *lady*

> **girl**
> ↔ The Middle English ancestor of *girl* meant a child of either sex; the earlier roots of the word are unknown.

girl'friend" *n.* a female companion, sweetheart, or lover.

Girl Guide a member of the Girl Guides, a British association of girls.

Girl Scout a member of the Girl Scouts, an association of girls.

girth (gėrth) *n.* **1,** a band around an animal's body to secure a saddle or load. **2,** the distance around anything cylindrical; circumference.

gis'mo (giz'mō) *n.* gizmo.

gist (jist) *n.* the essence or substance of a matter; pith.

give (giv) *v.t.* [**gave** (gāv), **giv'en, giv'ing**] **1,** bestow; make a present of; donate. **2,** spend or pay, as money; exchange. **3,** supply; deliver; convey. **4,** (with *up*) yield; concede. **5,** utter; impart. —*v.i.* **1,** bestow alms. **2,** (usually with *in* or *up*) yield; surrender. **3,** afford an opening. —*n.* lack of resistance; elasticity. —**give off,** exude, emit, or produce. —**give way, 1,** fall back. **2,** surrender; give in.

give-'and-take' *n.* **1,** cooperative dealing by mutual concession and compromise. **2,** bantering conversation.

give'a·way" (giv'ə-wā") *n.* **1,** an unintentional betrayal; a revelation. **2,** something free; a premium; a bargain. —*adj.* being a giveaway.

give'back" *n.* **1,** wage or benefit concession made by employees in union negotiations. **2,** rebate.

giv'en (giv'ən) *adj.* **1,** addicted; inclined. **2,** granted; agreed. **3,** (of a name) first, not the surname.

giz'mo (giz'mō) *n.* gadget; contraption.

giz'zard (giz'ərd) *n.* the second stomach of a bird; a similar digestive organ in insects and earthworms.

gla'brous (glā'brəs) *adj.* (*Biol.*) devoid of hair or down; smooth.

gla·cé' (glà-sā') *adj.* (*Fr.*) **1,** glossy; smooth. **2,** covered with a hard, shiny sugar coating.

gla'cial (glā'shəl) *adj.* pert. to ice or glaciers.

gla'ci·ate (glā'shè-āt) *v.t.* **1,** cover with ice. **2,** (*Slang*) freeze (socially).

gla'cier (glā'shər) *n.* a slowly flowing mass or river of ice.

glad *adj.* [**glad′der, -dest**] **1,** joyful; bright; cheerful. **2,** joyous. —*n.* gladiolus. —**glad′den** (-ən) *v.t. & i.* cause to be, or become, glad. —**glad′ness,** *n.*

glade (glād) *n.* a clear space in a forest.

glad′i·a″tor (glad′ē-ā″tər) *n.* in ancient Rome, a man who fought in the arena with men or wild beasts.

glad″i·o′lus (glad″ē-ō′ləs) *n.* a bulbous plant with a tall spike of large flowers. Also, **glad″i·o′la** (-lə).

glad′some (glad′səm) *adj.* **1,** glad. **2,** causing gladness. —**glad′some·ness,** *n.*

Glad′stone″ bag a suitcase that opens into two equal compartments, named for 19th-c. British statesman W. E. Gladstone.

glair (glâr) *n.* the white of egg, used for sizing.

glam′our (glam′ər) *n.* alluring charm. Also, **glam′or.** —**glam′or·ize,** *v.t.* —**glam′or·ous,** *adj.*

glance (gláns) *n.* a brief, cursory look. —*v.i.* **1,** flash; gleam. **2,** take a hasty look. **3,** strike and be deflected.

gland *n.* an organ that secretes a substance to be used in the body. —**glan′du·lar** (glan′dyə-lər) *adj.*

glan′ders (glan′dərz) *n.* a contagious disease of horses.

glans (glanz) *n.* [*pl.* **glan′des** (glan′dēz)] the head of the penis or of the clitoris.

glare (glâr) *n.* **1,** a dazzling light. **2,** a fierce look. **3,** a slippery surface, as of ice. —*v.i.* **1,** shine dazzlingly. **2,** stare fiercely.

glar′ing *adj.* **1,** shining dazzlingly. **2,** obvious; notorious.

glas′nost (gläs′nōst) *n.* (*Russ.*) publicity; openness.

glas′phalt (glas′fâlt) *n.* a paving material composed of asphalt and glass.

glass (glás) *n.* **1,** a hard, brittle substance, usually transparent, made of silicates fused at high heat. **2,** an article, as a mirror, tumbler, etc., made of this substance; a telescope or binocular: *spyglass.* **3,** a tumblerful; the amount of liquid in a tumbler. **4,** (*pl.*) spectacles. —**glass′ful″,** *n.* —**glass harmonica,** a mechanical musical instrument composed of tuned glass bowls made to revolve and played with moistened fingers. —**glass wool,** massed glass fibers, used for insulation.

glass·ine′ (gla-sēn′) *n.* a thin transparent paper.

glass′y (glás′ē) *adj.* **1,** like glass, esp. in smoothness. **2,** staring; expressionless. —**glass′i·ness,** *n.*

glau·co′ma (glâ-kō′mə) *n.* a disease of the eye causing increased pressure within the eyeball.

glaze (glāz) *v.t.* **1,** furnish with glass, as a window sash. **2,** overlay (pottery, cloth, paper) with a glossy, hard surface. —*v.t.* become glassy. —*n.* a glassy appearance or sheen.

gla′zier (glā′zher) *n.* one who works with glass.

gleam (glēm) *n.* **1,** a brief flash of light. **2,** luster. —*v.i.* emit dim rays of light.

---

gleam, glimmer, glimpse
↔ These words come through Old English from an ancient Germanic root *glim-, brightness, glimpse.

---

glean (glēn) *v.t. & i.* **1,** gather (grain) after the reapers; pick up leavings. **2,** gather (as information) by slow, careful selection.

glee (glē) *n.* **1,** mirth; delight. **2,** a musical piece for three or more voices. —**glee′ful,** *adj.* exultantly happy. —**glee club,** a choral group.

glen *n.* a narrow valley; dale.

glen·gar′ry (glen-gar′ē) *n.* a Scottish cap.

glib *adj.* [**glib′ber, -best**] fluent but insincere. —**glib′ness,** *n.*

glide (glīd) *v.i.* move smoothly and easily. —*n.* **1,** a smooth, easy motion. **2,** the downward flight, without engine power, of an airplane. **3,** a metal button used on furniture legs to reduce friction when moving.

glid′er (glī′dər) *n.* **1,** a motorless aircraft resembling an airplane. **2,** a suspended swing.

glim′mer (glim′ər) *n.* a faint and wavering light. —*v.i.* shine faintly. —**glim′mer·ing,** *n.* a faint trace, of light or anything. ❑ *gleam*

glimpse (glimps) *n.* **1,** a momentary view. **2,** an inkling. —*v.t.* get a hasty view of. ❑ *gleam*

glint *n.* a streaked reflection of light; a flash. —*v.i.* flash; sparkle.

glis·sade′ (gli-säd′) *n.* **1,** a sliding down a snow slope in a standing position. **2,** a glide in dancing.

glis·san′do (gli-sän′dō) *n.* (*Music*) **1,** the effect of sliding the finger across the keys or strings of an instrument. **2,** a similar effect produced on a wind instrument.

glis′ten (glis′ən) *v.i.* shine with sparkling light; gleam.

glitch (glich) *n.* **1,** a sudden, brief surge of electrical power. **2,** a minor malfunction of an apparatus.

glit′ter (glit′ər) *v.i.* **1,** send off shoots of

---

fat, fāte, fär, fâre, fâll, ȧsk; met, hē, hěr, maybè; pin, pīne; not, nōte, ôr, tool light, as a gem; sparkle. **2,** be brilliant or showy. —*n.* **1,** sparkling light. **2,** splendor; allure.

glit″ter·a′ti (glit″ə-rä′tē) *n.pl.* glamorous and famous people.

glitz (glits) (*Slang*) *n.* flashy appearance or decoration. —**glitz′y,** *adj.*

gloam′ing (glō′ming) *n.* twilight.

gloat (glōt) *v.i.* **1,** gaze or ponder with spite, lust, or greed. **2,** show joy at another's misfortune.

glob *n.* a globule.

glob′al (glō′bəl) *adj.* worldwide. —**global warming,** the theory that the climate of planet earth is gradually becoming warmer as a result of the greenhouse effect.

globe (glōb) *n.* **1,** a sphere; a ball-shaped body. **2,** the earth. **3,** a sphere bearing a map of the earth. **4,** something of near-spherical shape, as an incandescent lamp, a bowl, etc.

globe′trot″ter *n.* one who travels all over the world.

glob′u·lar (glob′yə-lər) *adj.* spherical. —**glob″u·lar′i·ty** (-lar′ə-tē) *n.*

glob′ule (glob′ūl) *n.* a tiny, round particle.

glob′u·lin (glob′yû-lin) *n.* a protein soluble in pure water.

glock′en·spiel″ (glok′ən-spēl″) *n.* a musical instrument consisting of tuned bells or tubes played upon with hammers.

gloom *n.* **1,** dim shade; obscurity; cloudiness. **2,** melancholy; pessimism. —**gloom′y,** *adj.*

glop *n.* any thick semiliquid substance.

glo′ri·fy″ (glôr′i-fī″) *v.t.* **1,** worship. **2,** confer honor on. **3,** invest with beauty. —**glo″ri·fi·ca′tion,** *n.*

glo′ri·ous (glôr′ē-əs) *adj.* **1,** pert. to glory; blessed. **2,** illustrious; splendid. —**glo′ri·ous·ness,** *n.*

glo′ry (glôr′ē) *n.* **1,** exalted honor. **2,** splendor; radiance. **3,** celestial bliss. **4,** a source of pride. **5,** height of prosperity or renown. **6,** a halo. —*v.i.* exult; rejoice. —**glory hole, 1,** a storage locker. **2,** crew's quarters on a ship.

gloss (glâs) *n.* **1,** a smooth, mirrorlike finish; luster. **2,** a deceptive exterior. **3,** an explanation or annotation to clarify a word or phrase.

glos′sa·ry (glos′ə-rē) *n.* an explanatory list of terms used in a text. ❑ *dictionary*

gloss′y (-ē) *adj.* having a gloss or sheen; lustrous. —**gloss′i·ness,** *n.*

glot′tis (glot′is) *n.* the opening at the top of the windpipe and between the vocal cords. —**glot′tal** (-əl) *adj.*

glove (gluv) *n.* **1,** a covering for the hand, with compartments for the thumb and fingers. **2,** a padded covering for the hand, used in certain sports. —**glov′er,** *n.* a maker of gloves. —**glove compartment,** a small compartment in the dashboard of an automobile.

glow (glō) *v.i.* **1,** throw out heat and light without flame; display dull light. **2,** be flushed with heat or emotion; redden, as from exertion. **3,** shine brightly. —*n.* **1,** luminosity. **2,** brightness of color. **3,** ardor. **4,** bodily warmth.

glow′er (glow′ər) *v.i.* look menacing or angry; scowl; frown. —*n.* a frown; sullen stare.

glow′worm″ (glō′wĕrm″) *n.* an insect or its larva that glows in the dark.

glox·in′i·a (glok-sin′ē-ə) *n.* a plant having large bell-shaped flowers, named for 18th-c. Ger. botanist Benjamin Gloxin.

gloze (glōz) *v.t.* (with *over*) gloss over; explain away.

glu′cose (gloo′kōs) *n.* a light-colored syrup obtained from starch, cane sugar, etc., by the action of acids.

glue (gloo) *n.* a sticky, soluble substance that dries to a resinous hardness, used as an adhesive and sizing. —**glue′y,** *adj.*

glum *adj.* [**glum′mer, -mest**] disheartened; sullen. —**glum′ness,** *n.*

glu′on (gloo′on) *n.* a massless particle that binds quarks together.

glut *v.t.* [**glut′ted, -ting**] fill to overflowing; satiate; overstock. —*n.* **1,** a surfeit. **2,** supply exceeding demand.

glu′ten (gloo′tən) *n.* a sticky substance, highly nutritious, found in flour.

glu′ti·nous (gloo′tə-nəs) *adj.* sticky.

glut′ton (glut′ən) *n.* an excessive eater; a greedy person. —**glut′ton·ous,** *adj.* —**glut′ton·y,** *n.* greed. ❑ *gourmet*

glyc′er·in (glis′ər-in) *n.* a colorless syrupy liquid used in cosmetics, explosives, etc.

gly′co·gen (glī′kə-jən) *n.* the sugar formed in the body from carbohydrates.

glyph (glif) *n.* **1,** (*Archit.*) a groove or channel, usu. vertical, as in a sculptured decoration. **2,** a symbol used for nonverbal communication.

glyp′tic (glip′tik) *adj.* pert. to carving and engraving.

G-′man″ (jē′man″) *n.* (*Slang*) an agent of the FBI: *g(overnment) man.*

gnarl (närl) *n.* a knot on a tree. —*v.t.*

twist; knot. **—gnarled** (närld) *adj.* full of knots; twisted.

gnash (nash) *v.t.* grate or grind (the teeth) together.

gnat (nat) *n.* any of several small biting insects.

gnaw (nâ) *v.t. & i.* **1,** bite or wear away with the front teeth. **2,** consume; torture, as if by continual biting. **—gnaw′ing,** *n.* a continuous feeling of discomfort, as from hunger or remorse.

gneiss (nīs) *n.* rock composed of layers of quartz, mica, etc.

gnome (nōm) *n.* **1,** a dwarf, esp. an imaginary one living in the earth and guarding its treasures. **2,** an aphorism. **—gnom′ic,** *adj.*

---

gnome
↔ The word meaning dwarf was perhaps coined by the 16th-c. Swiss physician Paracelsus. The term for an aphorism derives from Greek *gnōmē*, intelligence.

---

gno′mon (nō′mon) *n.* the arm on a sundial which by its shadow shows the time of day.

gnos′tic (nos′tik) *adj.* **1,** possessing mystic knowledge. **2,** (*cap.*) a believer in Gnosticism, a mystic, quasi-religious philosophy.

gnu (noo) *n.* an Afr. antelope resembling an ox.

go (gō) *v.i.* **[went, gone, go′ing] 1,** move away (from where the speaker is); depart. **2,** be in motion; proceed; travel; be transported. **3,** succeed; fit; be suited. **4,** pass; elapse; cease to exist. **5,** extend; continue. **6,** operate; be in working order. **7,** be sold; be disposed of; be transferred. **8,** be a part of; belong. **—v.t. & i.** (*Informal*) say. **—n.** (*Informal*) **1,** ambition; energy. **2,** a success. **3,** an agreement. **4,** an attempt; a try. **5,** a Jap. board game of tactics. **—go back on,** (*Informal*) betray; fail to keep (one's word, etc.). **—go down,** (*Slang*) happen. **—go for,** (*Informal*) **1,** be attracted by; be infatuated with. **2,** attack. **—go in for, 1,** participate in. **2,** enjoy. **—go it,** (*Informal*) endure. **—go it alone,** (*Informal*) do something, esp. difficult or dangerous, by oneself. **—go one better,** (*Informal*) outdo; surpass. **—go over,** (*Informal*) succeed. **—go steady,** (*Informal*) have a constant boyfriend or girlfriend. **—go under,** (*Informal*) fail; be ruined.

go′a (gō′ə) *n.* an antelope of Tibet.

goad (gōd) *n.* **1,** a sharp stick for driving cattle. **2,** any incentive. **—v.t.** spur on, with or as with a goad; urge.

go-′a·head″ *n.* approval to proceed.

goal (gōl) *n.* **1,** the point that limits a race. **2,** the place, in some games, that players must reach to score; the score for reaching such a place. **3,** any object of ambition or desire. **—goal′ie, goal′keep″er, goal′tend″er,** *n.* in certain games, the player who guards the goal.

goat (gōt) *n.* **1,** an agile, horned ruminant animal about the size of a sheep, valued for its milk and hair. **2,** (*Informal*) the victim of a joke; an innocent sufferer. **—get one's goat,** (*Slang*) cause one to lose one's temper.

goat·ee′ (gō-tē′) *n.* a pointed beard.

goat′herd″ *n.* one who tends goats.

goat′skin″ *n.* leather made from the hide of a goat.

gob *n.* **1,** a mass or lump; a mouthful. **2,** (*Informal*) a sailor.

go′bang″ (gō′bang″) *n.* a Jap. board game similar to go (def. 5).

gob′bet (gob′it) *n.* a lump or fragment.

gob′ble (gob′əl) *v.t.* **1,** swallow hastily. **2,** (*Slang*) (often with *up*) seize greedily. **—v.i.** make a rattling noise in the throat, as a male turkey. **—n.** the cry of a male turkey. **—gob′bler,** *n.* a male turkey.

gob′ble·dy·gook″ (gob′əl-dė-gûk″) *n.* **1,** obscure, inflated language; officialese. **2,** meaningless confusion of words; nonsense. **3,** specialized, technical language; jargon.

go-′be·tween″ *n.* an intermediary.

gob′let (gob′lit) *n.* a drinking glass with a stem and base.

gob′lin *n.* a surly, malicious sprite.

go′by (gō′bė) *n.* a small spiny-finned fish.

go′cart″ (gō′kärt″) *n.* **1,** a child's walker. **2,** a small baby carriage or stroller. **3,** kart.

god *n.* **1,** (*cap.*) the Supreme Being, creator and master of all. **2,** any being considered as divine. **3,** an idol. **4,** a person or thing made the object of supreme devotion.

god′child″ *n.* a child one sponsors at baptism. **—god′daugh″ter, god′fa″ther, god′moth″er, god′par″ent, god′son″,** *n.*

god′dess (god′is) *n.* **1,** a female god. **2,** an extraordinary woman.

god′fa″ther *n.* **1,** a man who sponsors a child at baptism. **2,** the head of a criminal group, esp. a Mafia family.

god′head″ *n.* **1,** divinity. **2,** (*cap.*) God.

god′hood″ *n.* divinity.

god′less (-ləs) *adj.* impious; wicked. **—god′less·ness,** *n.*

---

god'ly (-lė) *adj.* pious. **—god'li·ness,** *n.*

god'send" *n.* an unlooked-for acquisition or piece of good fortune.

God'speed" *interj.* God speed you: a wish for success or prosperity.

god'wit *n.* a water bird akin to the snipe.

go'fer (gō'fər) *n.* (*Slang*) an employee hired primarily to run errands. Also, **go'pher.**

go-"get'ter *n.* (*Slang*) one who succeeds by vigorous pursuit of his or her object.

gog'gle (gog'əl) *v.i.* roll the eyes; blink. **—gog'gles,** *n.pl.* spectacles to protect against glare, dust, etc.

go-'go" (gō'-gō") *adj.* (*Slang*) modern; fashionable. Also, **à go-go. —go-go dancer,** a dancer who performs, often scantily clad, on a platform in a nightclub or bar.

go"ings-on' (gō"ingz-on') *n.* (*Informal*) events or actions; behavior.

goi'ter (goi'tər) *n.* morbid swelling of the thyroid gland.

go-'kart" *n.* kart.

gold (gōld) *n.* **1,** a precious metallic element, no. 79, symbol Au, used in coinage and jewelry. **2,** money; wealth. **3,** a bright yellow color. **—gold brick, 1,** anything sold as valuable that proves to be valueless. **2,** (*Slang*) in the U.S. Army, a soldier who cleverly evades onerous duty. **—gold digger,** (*Slang*) a person whose interest in others is mainly mercenary. **—gold leaf,** gold beaten into thin leaves. **—gold mine,** (*Slang*) anything productive of great wealth. **—gold standard,** a standard of value for a monetary system based on gold.

gold-'brick" (*Informal*) *v.t.* swindle; cheat. **—v.i.** shirk a duty; loaf.

gold'en (gōl'dən) *adj.* **1,** made of gold. **2,** yellow. **3,** most auspicious. **4,** very precious; excellent. **5,** most flourishing. **6,** glamorous. **7,** fiftieth: said of anniversaries. **—golden age,** an era of prosperity, progress, or development. **—golden-ager,** *n.* an elderly person, esp. one who has retired. **—golden parachute,** an agreement guaranteeing an executive of a company generous benefits if the company is sold or merged. **—golden rule,** a rule of conduct: Do unto others as you would have them do unto you. **—golden section, mean,** a ratio between two sections of a line such that the shorter is to the longer as the longer is to the whole.

gold'en·rod" *n.* a wildflower with yellow flower-heads.

gold-'filled" *adj.* heavily gold-plated.

gold'fish" *n.* a small orange-yellow fish of the carp family.

gold'smith" *n.* a worker in gold.

golf *n.* **1,** a game played on an extensive course, in which the object is to drive a ball into a series of holes in the smallest number of strokes. **2,** (*Communications*) the letter g.

Gol'go·tha (gol'gə-thə) *n.* **1,** Calvary. **2,** any place of suffering and slaughter.

gol'li·wog" (gol'ė-wog") *n.* a child's black doll.

golliwog
↔ From the name of a doll in a late 19th-c. series of children's books by Bertha and Florence Upton.

gol'ly (gol'ė) *interj.* an exclamation of delight or surprise.

go'mer (gō'mər) *n.* **1,** an altered bull. **2,** (*Slang*) an obnoxious person.

go·mo'ku (gô-mô'koo) *n.* (*Jap.*) gobang.

-gon *suf.* denoting geometrical figures.

go'nad (gō'nad) *n.* in biology, a sex gland.

gon'do·la (gon'də-lə) *n.* **1,** a narrow, one-oared boat used on the canals of Venice. **2,** an open railroad freight car. **3,** the control car of an airship. **4,** a cable car. **—gon"do·lier'** (-lir') *n.* the rower of a gondola.

gondola
↔ From Italian *gondolà*, roll, relating to the boat's motion on the water; origin uncertain.

Gond·wa'na (gond-wä'nə) *n.* a hypothetical land mass consisting of South America, Australia and Antartica before they separated.

gone (gân) *v.* p.p. of go. **—adj. 1,** ruined; failing. **2,** (*Informal*) (with *on*) in love; entranced. **—gon'er,** *n.* (*Slang*) a person or thing lost or past recovery.

gon'fa·lon (gon'fə-lən) *n.* a flag; standard.

gong (gâng) *n.* a metal disk giving a resonant tone when struck.

gon"or·rhe'a (gon"ə-rē'ə) *n.* a contagious disease of the genitals.

gon'zo (gon'zō) *adj.* (*Slang*) crazy; bizarre.

goo *n.* (*Slang*) a sticky substance. **—goo'ey** (-ė) *adj.*

goo'ber (goo'bər) *n.* the peanut.

good (gûd) *adj.* [**bet'ter, best**] **1,** worthy of respect or commendation, by being beneficial, honest, noble, etc. **2,** useful;

suited to the purpose; skillful or competent. **3**, virtuous; pure; well-behaved. **4**, thorough; complete; considerable. **5**, valid; genuine; worthy of being believed or trusted. **6**, pleasant; agreeable. —*n.* **1**, what is right, just, or desirable. **2**, virtuous persons. **3**, (*pl.*) merchandise, esp. textiles; possessions. **4**, (*pl.*) (*Slang*) evidence of guilt. —*interj.* expressing agreement, approval, or congratulation. —**Good Book**, the Bible. —**good Samaritan**, one who helps another in distress. —**goodwill**, **1**, kindly feeling; cheerful readiness. **2**, the value to a business of its established position and patronage.

good″-bye′ (gŭd″-bī′) *interj. & n.* **1**, a word spoken when parting from another; farewell. **2**, a parting, dismissal, or abandonment. Also, **good-″by′** [*pl.* **-bys′**], **good-″bye′**.

---

good-bye

↔ The *good* in *good-bye* comes from *God*, not *good*; the word is a contraction of "God be with you," its form being influenced by *good day* and *good night*.

Good Friday the Friday before Easter.

good′ies (gŭd′ēz) *n.pl.* candy.

good-″look′ing *adj.* handsome; comely.

good′ly (gŭd′lē) *adj.* adequate in quality, amount, etc.

good-′na″tured *adj.* having a pleasant disposition; friendly and cheerful.

good′ness (gŭd′nəs) *n.* **1**, the state, quality or degree of being good. **2**, heaven; providence. —*interj.* a mild exclamation.

good′y (gŭd′ē) *interj.* expressing delight. —*n.* (*Informal*) candy or delicacy. —**good′y-good′y**, *adj. & n.* priggish (person).

goof *n.* (*Slang*) a silly person. —*v.i.* make a mistake. —**goof′y**, *adj.* —**goof off**, (*Slang*) loaf.

goof′ball″ *n.* (*Slang*) **1**, a sleeping pill. **2**, a crazy person.

goo′gol (goo′gəl) *n.* a number equal to 1 followed by 100 zeros. —**goo′gol·plex″** (-pleks″) *n.* ten to the power of a googol.

---

googol, googolplex

↔ Both coined by mathematician Edward Kasner, supposedly suggested by his nine-year-old nephew.

---

gook (gŭk) *n.* **1**, sticky stuff. **2**, (*Slang, Offensive*) any dark-skinned foreigner.

goon *n.* **1**, (*Slang*) a hired thug. **2**, a stupid person.

goop *n.* **1**, (*Slang*) an uncouth person. **2**, a thick, viscid liquid; goo.

goose (goos) *n.* [*pl.* **geese** (gēs)] **1**, a large web-footed bird, esp. the female, similar to a duck; its flesh. **2**, a silly person. **3**, [*pl.* **goos′es**] a tailor's iron. —*v.t.* (*Slang*) jab (a person) in the backside. —**goose egg**, (*Slang*) zero. —**gooseflesh**, a roughened condition of the skin caused by cold or fear. Also, **goose pimples**. —**goose step**, a stiff-kneed marching step, as used by German soldiers.

goose′ber″ry (goos′ber″ē) *n.* a tart, greenish-brown berry, used in preserves.

goose′neck″ (goos′nek″) *n.* anything curved like a goose's neck, esp. an iron or rubber coupling.

go′pher (gō′fər) *n.* **1**, a ground squirrel of the prairies. **2**, a burrowing rodent with large cheek pouches. **3**, (*Slang*) a gofer.

Gor′di·an knot (gôr′dē-ən) an intricate problem. —**cut the Gordian knot**, solve a difficult problem.

Gordian knot

↔ The *Gordian knot* was tied by Gordius, the king of Phrygia, to be undone only by the person who was to rule Asia. The knot was cut by Alexander the Great.

---

gore (gôr) *n.* **1**, a wedge-shaped piece of cloth used to vary width, as of a garment or sail. **2**, blood. —*v.t.* pierce, as with a horn.

---

gore

↔ All three senses of the word come from Old English sources. *Gor*, dirt, produced the sense of blood. *Gar*, spear, produced the verb to pierce. *Gara*, corner, resulted in the wedge-shaped piece of cloth.

---

gorge (gôrj) *n.* **1**, a narrow ravine. **2**, the gluttonous eating of a big meal; a feast. **3**, food consumed; what has been swallowed. —*v.t. & i.* eat greedily; stuff.

gor′geous (gôr′jəs) *adj.* showy; magnificent. —**gor′geous·ness**, *n.*

Gor″gon·zo′la (gôr″gən-zō′lə) *n.* a strong Italian cheese, named for a town in Italy.

go·ril′la (gə-ril′ə) *n.* **1**, the largest known manlike ape. **2**, (*Slang*) a powerful, brutal man. ❑ *guerrilla*

---

gorilla

↔ From Greek *gorillas*, the name given by the explorer Hanno to a tribe of wild, hairy women.

---

fat, fāte, fär, fāre, fâll, àsk; met, hē, hêr, maybė; pin, pīne; not, nōte, ôr, tool

gork (gôrk) *n.* (*Slang*) a brain-dead person kept alive by artificial means.

gor'mand·ize" (gôr'mən-dīz") *v.i.* eat voraciously.

gorse (gôrs) *n.* a common Europ. weed; furze.

gor'y (gôr'ē) *adj.* **1,** like or covered with blood. **2,** involving bloodshed. —**gor'i·ness,** *n.*

gosh *interj.* a mild curse.

gos'hawk" (gos'hâk") *n.* a large hawk formerly used in falconry.

gos'ling (goz'ling) *n.* a young goose.

gos'pel (gos'pəl) *n.* **1,** the record of Christ's life and teachings. **2,** (*cap.*) any one of the first four books of the New Testament. **3,** any principle one believes in or preaches. **4,** absolute truth.

> **gospel**
> ↔ From Old English *godspel*, good news, a translation of Greek *evangelion*.

gos'sa·mer (gos'ə-mər) *n.* **1,** a cobweb. **2,** any thin, filmy material. —*adj.* cobweblike; unsubstantial.

gos'sip (gos'ip) *n.* **1,** trifling talk, esp. about other persons. **2,** [also, **gos'sip·er**] an idle talker. —*v.i.* discuss other persons' affairs.

got *v.* pret. & p.p. of *get.*

Goth'ic (goth'ik) *adj.* designating a type of architecture with pointed arches and high, steep roofs. —*n.* (*l.c.*) a style of printing type without serifs. —**gothic novel,** a terror story usually having a gloomy setting.

got'ten (got'ən) *v.* p.p. of *get.*

gouache (gwäsh) *n.* a way of painting with watercolors; a painting so made.

Gou'da (gow'də) *n.* a mild Dutch cheese.

gouge (gowj) *v.t.* **1,** scoop or tear out. **2,** (*Informal*) overcharge. **3,** (*Informal*) cheat. —*n.* a chisel.

gou'lash (goo'läsh) *n.* **1,** a highly seasoned stew. **2,** a jumble.

gourd (gôrd) *n.* **1,** the fleshy fruit of a vine related to the squash and cucumber. **2,** the dried shell of this fruit, used as a dipper or vessel.

> **gourmet, gourmand, glutton**
> ☛ The first two words are closely related, differing essentially in degree. A *gourmet* is a lover of fine food; so is a *gourmand*, but the latter overindulges in it, as does the *glutton*.

gour·mand' (goor-mänd') *n.* **1,** a glutton. **2,** a lover of good food. ❑ *gourmet*

gour·met' (goor-mā') *n.* a lover of good eating; an epicure.

gout (gowt) *n.* a painful inflammation of the joints, esp. of the big toe. —**gout'y,** *adj.* —**gout'i·ness,** *n.*

gov'ern (guv'ərn) *v.t. & i.* **1,** rule with authority. **2,** guide; control. **3,** determine.

> **govern, gubernatorial**
> ↔ Both words come from Greek *kyb-ernan*, to steer.

gov'er·ness (guv'ər-nəs) *n.fem.* a woman tutor for children.

gov'ern·ment (guv'ərn-mənt) *n.* **1,** regulation; management. **2,** a state's established form of political rule. **3,** the body of persons authorized to govern; the administration. —**gov"ern·men'tal** (-men'təl) *adj.*

> **government, junta, regime, administration**
> ☛ A *government* and a *junta* are ruling groups, with the distinction that a *junta* is in power after a coup and before a legal government has been established. A *regime* is a political system; however, the word is often used as a synonym for *government.* An *administration* is the officials who make up the executive branch of a government.

gov'er·nor (guv'ər-nər) *n.* **1,** one who governs; esp. the chief official of a state of the U.S. **2,** a device for regulating the speed of an engine.

gown *n.* **1,** a woman's dress. **2,** a loose robe worn officially by judges, clergymen, etc.; fig., the academic world. —*v.t.* put a gown on; dress.

goy (goi) *n.* [*pl.* **goy'im** (-im), **goys** (goiz)] (*often Offensive*) a non-Jewish person.

grab *v.t.* [**grabbed, grab'bing**] **1,** seize violently or suddenly; snatch. **2,** obtain by violent or illegal means. —*n.* seizure. —**grab'ber,** *n.*

grab-'bag" *n.* a miscellaneous collection.

grab'ble (grab'əl) *v.i.* **1,** grope about. **2,** sprawl; grovel.

grace (grās) *n.* **1,** ease and elegance of manner or movement; charm. **2,** (*often pl.*) liking; favor; good will. **3,** virtue; kindness; politeness. **4,** postponement, as of a penalty or obligation; clemency. **5,** a prayer for blessing at a meal. **6,** divine favor. —*v.t.* **1,** adorn. **2,** honor; favor. —**grace'ful,** *adj.* beautiful and elegant in

form, manner, and esp. movement.
—**grace note** (*Music*) a note not essential
but ornamental.

grac'ile (gras'il) *adj.* graceful; slender.

gra'cious (grā'shəs) *adj.* **1,** kindly; courteous. **2,** charming; attractive. **3,** generous;
magnanimous. —*interj.* a mild expression
of surprise. —**gra'cious·ness,** *n.*

grack'le (grak'əl) *n.* a blackbird.

grad *n.* (*Slang*) graduate.

gra'date (grā'dāt) *v.i.* pass gradually, as
from one color to another. —*v.t.* **1,** cause
to gradate. **2,** arrange by grades.

gra·da'tion (grā-dā'shən) *n.* **1,** the act or
process of classifying by grade, or becoming different in grade. **2,** a grade differing
only slightly from near grades.

grade (grād) *n.* **1,** a step in any series, as
of quality, etc.; degree. **2,** relative position
in any scale; rank; standing or a mark of
standing. **3,** one of the divisions of a
school course; also, the pupils in any of
these divisions. **4,** the rate of ascent and
descent of a highway or railroad; also, a
slope. —*v.t.* **1,** classify, as by relative quality; sort. **2,** make (a slope) level. —**grade
crossing,** two roads or tracks crossing at
the same level. —**grade point,** in education, a value assigned to each letter grade,
as A=4, B=3, etc. —**grade school,** a primary school, below high school.

gra'di·ent (grā'dē-ənt) *n.* the amount or
angle of slope.

grad'u·al (graj'oo-əl) *adj.* changing by
degrees; not sudden or abrupt.

grad'u·ate (graj'oo-ət) *n.* **1,** one who has
received an academic degree. **2,** a measuring glass. —*adj.* **1,** who has graduated. **2,**
pert. to academic graduates. —*v.t.* (-āt) **1,**
confer an academic degree upon. **2,** mark
with degrees; calibrate. —*v.i.* (-āt) **1,** receive a degree or diploma. **2,** pass gradually. —**grad"u·a'tion,** *n.*

graf·fi'to (grə-fē'tō) *n.* [*pl.* -**ti** (-tē)] an
inscription or design written or scratched
on a wall, stone, etc.

graft (gráft) *v.t.* **1,** unite or mix living tissue or plant shoots, for joint growth or
reproduction; crossbreed. **2,** dishonestly
accept (bribes, perquisites). —*n.* **1,** the act
of grafting; a part grafted. **2,** dishonest use
of office to get money or perquisites; anything so acquired.

gra'ham flour (grā'əm) a type of whole-
wheat flour, named for 19th-c. American
dietitian Sylvester Graham.

grail (grāl) *n.* a cup. —**Holy Grail,** in legend, the cup used by Jesus at the Last
Supper.

grain (grān) *n.* **1,** cereal grasses, or their

seeds. **2,** a tiny, hard particle. **3,** the smallest unit of weight; an infinitesimal
amount. **4,** the direction in which fibers
run; texture, as of wood, stone, etc. **5,** the
hair side of leather. —*v.t.* paint or emboss
in the pattern of the grain of wood,
leather, etc. —**grain'y,** *adj.* —**grain alcohol,** ethyl alcohol.

gram *n.* the unit of weight in the metric
system, .0353 avoirdupois ounce.

-**gram** *suf.* denoting a writing, as
telegram.

gram'mar (gram'ər) *n.* **1,** the study of
word endings and inflectional forms. **2,**
mode of speaking and writing according
to the principles of grammar. **3,** a book
on grammar. —**gram·mar'i·an** (grə-mãr'ē-
ən) *n.* a student of grammar. —**grammar
school** (*U.S.*) an elementary school,
grades 1 to 8.

gram·mat'i·cal (grə-mat'i-kəl) *adj.* **1,**
pert. to grammar. **2,** correct in grammar.

Gram'my (gram'ē) *n.* an award for excellence in sound recording.

gram'o·phone" (gram'ə-fōn") *n.* a
phonograph.

gram'pus (gram'pəs) *n.* a large sea mammal related to the dolphin.

gran'a·ry (gran'ə-rē) *n.* a storage place
for grain.

grand *adj.* **1,** imposing in size or effect;
majestic; splendid. **2,** dignified; lofty; eminent. **3,** belonging to high society; elegant.
4, main; comprehensive; all-embracing. **5,**
designating the second generation in ascent or descent, as *grandfather, grandson.*
6, (*Informal*) fine, very good. **7,** (*Slang*)
one thousand dollars. —**grand'ness,** *n.*
—**grand duke, 1,** a royal prince, esp. in
czarist Russia. **2,** the ruler of a grand
duchy, a principality ranking next below a
kingdom. —**grand jury,** a jury that indicts.
—**grand larceny,** the crime of stealing
something of great value. —**grand opera,**
opera (def. 1). —**grand piano,** a piano
with a horizontal, harp-shaped cabinet.
—**grand slam, 1,** (*Contract Bridge*) winning of all 13 tricks. **2,** (*Baseball*) a home
run with runners on all bases. **3,** in various
sports, the winning of several designated
major championships; hence, any substantial or total victory.. —**grand tour,** a tour
of Europe.

grande dame (gränd däm) (*Fr.*) **1,** a dignified elderly woman. **2,** the doyenne of a
field, as music or theater.

gran·dee' (gran-dē') *n.* a great nobleman; a man of comparable rank or
pretensions.

fat, fāte, fär, fâre, fâll, àsk; met, hē, hër, maybè; pin, pīne; not, nōte, ôr, tool

gran'deur (gran'jûr) *n.* **1,** grandness; illustriousness. **2,** conspicuous splendor.

grand'fa"ther *n.* the father of one's father or mother. **grandfather clause,** a legal provision protecting prior rights from the effects of a new law. —**grandfather clock,** a large pendulum clock. Also, **grandfather's clock.**

gran·dil'o·quent (gran-dil'ə-kwənt) *adj.* pompous, esp. in speech; bombastic. —**gran·dil'o·quence,** *n.*

gran'di·ose" (gran'dė-ōs") *adj.* **1,** ostentatiously imposing. **2,** bombastic; showy. —**gran"di·os'i·ty** (-os'ə-tė) *n.*

grand mal (gran' mäl') *n.* epilepsy.

Grand Prix' (grän prē') [*pl.* **Grand Prix**] (sometimes *l.c.*) any of several major races, as for automobiles, bicycles, etc.

grand'stand" *n.* the main structure for seating spectators at outdoor sporting events. —**grandstand play,** (*Slang*) a competitor's feat intended solely to impress an audience.

grange (grānj) *n.* **1,** (*Archaic*) a farm. **2,** (*cap.*) a national society of farmers; one of its branches.

gran'ite (gran'it) *n.* a hard, durable rock.

gran'ny (gran'ė) *n.* **1,** grandmother; an old woman. **2,** an incorrectly tied square knot. —**granny dress,** an old-fashioned dress, usu. ankle-length with ruffles or trimming.

gra·no'la (grə-nō'lə) *n.* an oat cereal flavored with raisins, nuts, etc.

grant (gránt) *v.t.* **1,** convey by deed. **2,** give; bestow. **3,** concede to be true. —*n.* the act of granting; also, the thing (land, money, etc.) given. —**gran·tee'** (-tē') *n.* the recipient of a grant. —**grant-'in-aid',** *n.* a type of financial grant. —**grant'or,** *n.*

grants'man·ship (grantz'mən-ship") *n.* the technique of applying for and obtaining financial grants. —**grants'man** (-mən) [*pl.* **-men**], **grants'wom"an,** *n.*

gran'u·late" (gran'yə-lāt") *v.t.* **1,** grind or form into granules. **2,** roughen the surface of. —**gran"u·la'tion,** *n.*

gran'ule (gran'ūl) *n.* a fine grain or particle. —**gran'u·lar,** *adj.* composed of or formed in grains.

grape (grāp) *n.* **1,** a juicy berry growing in clusters on a vine. **2,** wine. **3,** grape-sized cannon shot: *grapeshot.*

grape'fruit" *n.* a large citrus fruit.

grape'vine" *n.* **1,** the vine that bears grapes. **2,** (*Informal*) word-of-mouth transmission of information.

graph (gráf) *n.* a diagram showing the successive values of a changing quantity. —*v.t.* mark such values on cross-ruled paper (*graph paper*).

-graph (gráf) *suf.* a writing or picturing, as in *telegraph, photograph.*

graph'ic (graf'ik) *adj.* **1,** pert. to the arts of drawing, printing, engraving, etc. **2,** vivid; lifelike. —*n.* **1,** a product of the graphic arts. **2,** (*usu. pl.*) pictorial information displayed or printed by a computer. —**graph'i·cal·ly,** *adv.* —**graphic arts,** the pictorial arts: drawing, painting, engraving, etc.; sometimes also printing, process engraving, etc. —**graphical user interface,** (*Computers*) a type of computer interface designed to make use easier, through icons, menus, etc. *Abbr.,* **GUI.**

graph'ite (graf'īt) *n.* a soft, greasy natural carbon used in lead pencils and as a lubricant.

graph·ol'o·gy (gra-fol'ə-jė) *n.* the study of handwriting as an expression or indication of character. —**graph·ol'o·gist,** *n.*

-gra·phy (grə-fė) *suf.* writing or picturing, as in *photography, geography.*

grap'nel (grap'nəl) *n.* a hook with several prongs, for grappling.

grap'ple (grap'əl) *v.t.* **1,** lay fast hold of. **2,** (with *with*) deal with; try to overcome. —*v.i.* seize; come to close quarters with. —*n.* **1,** a grapnel. **2,** a clinch, as in wrestling. —**grap'pling iron,** grapnel.

grasp (grásp) *v.t.* **1,** seize and hold. **2,** understand. —*n.* **1,** a grip; clasp. **2,** possession. **3,** comprehension. —**grasp'ing,** *adj.* covetous; miserly.

grass (grás) *n.* **1,** green herbage sending up spikelike shoots or blades. **2,** any of a large family of plants with hollow stems and grainlike seed. **3,** a lawn; pasture. **4,** (*Slang*) marijuana. —**grass widow** or **widower,** (*Informal*) a person separated from her or his spouse.

grass'hop"per (grás'hop"ər) *n.* a large jumping insect destructive to crops.

grass'land (-lənd) *n.* permanent pasture.

grass"roots' *adj.* (*Informal*) emanating from the mass of people, as a cause, political movement, etc.

grass'y (-ė) *adj.* **1,** covered with grass. **2,** like grass.

grate (grāt) *v.t.* **1,** reduce to particles by rubbing on a rough surface. **2,** rub together with harsh sound. —*v.i.* **1,** make a rasping noise. **2,** cause irritation. —*n.* **1,** a frame of iron bars, as in a door or window. **2,** a box or frame of iron bars for holding burning fuel; a fireplace. —**grat'er,** *n.* a device for shredding or grating.

grate'ful (grāt'fəl) *adj.* **1,** thankful. **2,** soothing; pleasant.

grat'i·fy" (grat'i-fī") *v.t.* please; satisfy; indulge. —**grat"i·fi·ca'tion,** *n.*

gra·ti·né' (grat-ən-ā') *v.t.* (*Fr.*) bake or broil with topping of bread crumbs or grated cheese or both.

grat'ing (grā'ting) *n.* a latticework of wood or metal.

gra'tis *adv.* without charge.

grat'i·tude" (grat'i-tood") *n.* thankfulness.

gra·tu'i·tous (grə-tū'i-təs) *adj.* **1,** freely given. **2,** uncalled for. —**gra·tu'i·tous·ness,** *n.*

gra·tu'i·ty (grə-tū'i-tė) *n.* an extra payment, not owed; a tip.

grau'pel (grow'pəl) *n.* soft snow pellets.

gra·va'men (grə-vā'mən) *n.* (*Law*) the chief part of an accusation.

grave (grāv) *adj.* **1,** earnest; sedate; dignified. **2,** momentous; presenting a crisis. **3,** somber; not gay. **4,** (grä'vā) (*Music*) slow and solemn. —*n.* an excavation for the burial of a body; a tomb; hence, death. —*v.t.* engrave; impress (on the mind). —**grave'ness,** *n.* seriousness. —**grave accent** (grāv) the mark (`) placed over a letter. —**grave robber, 1,** a person who steals objects from graves. **2,** a person who steals corpses from graves, as for medical research.

grave'clothes" *n.pl.* wrappings in which a body is buried.

grav'el (grav'əl) *n.* fragments of rock larger than sand.

grav'en (grā'vən) *adj.* deeply carved or impressed; engraved.

grave'stone" *n.* a marker placed where a person is buried; a tombstone.

grave'yard" *n.* a cemetery. —**graveyard shift,** the latest work shift of the day, usu. beginning at midnight.

grav'i·tate" (grav'ə-tāt") *v.i.* **1,** yield to the force that draws bodies together. **2,** be attracted. —**grav"i·ta'tion,** *n.* —**grav"i·ta'tion·al,** *adj.* pert. to gravity or gravitation.

grav'i·ty (grav'ə-tė) *n.* **1,** the force that draws all objects toward the center of the earth. **2,** graveness.

gra·vure' (grə-vyûr') *n.* an intaglio printing process whereby liquid inks are deposited on paper from an engraved plate; such a plate; a print made by this process.

gra'vy (grā'vė) *n.* **1,** the juice that escapes from meat in cooking; also, a sauce made from this juice. **2,** (*Slang*) unearned profit. **3,** (*Slang*) graft. —**gravy boat,** a gravy dish. —**gravy train,** (*Slang*) a job, financial arrangement, etc. yielding high income with little effort.

---

gravy
↔ This word is a good demonstration of the effect of a simple misreading. *Gravy* probably resulted from a misreading of Old French *grané*, mistaking the *n* for a *v*. The ultimate source is Latin *granum*, seed.

---

gray (grā) *n.* a shade between, or mixture of, black and white. —*adj.* **1,** of this shade. **2,** cloudy; dismal. **3,** aged; (of hair) whitened by age. Also, **grey.** —**gray'ing,** *adj.* becoming gray. —**gray'ish,** *adj.* —**gray matter, 1,** neural tissue of the brain and spinal column. **2,** (*Informal*) brains; hence, intelligence. —**gray power,** political power of senior citizens collectively. —**gray scale,** a series of shades of gray from white to black.

gray'beard" *n.* an old man.

gray'ling *n.* a freshwater fish similar to trout.

graze (grāz) *v.t.* **1,** put (cattle) to pasture. **2,** brush lightly in passing. **3,** inflict a surface wound. —*v.i.* **1,** feed on grass, etc., as cattle. **2,** (often with *against*) barely touch. —*n.* a grazing touch; abrasion.

grease (grēs) *n.* **1,** animal fat; any oily matter. **2,** an oily lubricant much more viscous than liquid oil. —*v.t.* (*also,* grēz) **1,** lubricate, esp. with grease. **2,** (*Slang*) flatter; bribe. —**grease paint,** theatrical makeup.

greas'y (grē'sė) *adj.* **1,** oily in feel or appearance. **2,** slippery. —**greas'i·ness,** *n.* —**greasy spoon,** (*Slang*) a cheap, dirty restaurant or diner.

great (grāt) *adj.* **1,** conspicuously large or important; vast; numerous. **2,** extreme. **3,** long-continued. **4,** notable; renowned; magnificent. **5,** (*Informal*) most enjoyable. **6,** one step more remote in relationship, as *great-grandfather,* the father of a grandfather. —**great'ly,** *adv.* in or to a great degree. —**great'ness,** *n.* —**great-'aunt",** *n.* the aunt of a parent; grandaunt. —**great circle,** any circle on a sphere having the same diameter as the sphere. —**Great Dane,** a breed of very large dog. —**great-'un"cle,** *n.* the uncle of a parent: granduncle. ❑ *above*

great'coat" *n.* (*Brit.*) overcoat.

grebe (grēb) *n.* any of several diving birds allied to the loons.

Gre'cian (grē'shən) *adj.* pert. to Greece, esp. to the ancient Greeks and their culture; Greek.

---

greed (grēd) *n.* undue desire; avarice. —**greed′y**, *adj.* —**greed′i·ness**, *n.*

Greek (grēk) *adj.* pert. to Greece, its people and language. —*n.* **1,** a native or the language of Greece. **2,** (*Informal*) anything unintelligible. —*v.t.* to represent the overall appearance of a page without showing actual text. —**Greek fire,** an inflammable mixture.

green (grēn) *adj.* **1,** of the color of growing grass; a mixture of blue and yellow. **2,** unripe; immature; not dried, seasoned, etc. **3,** untrained; inexperienced. **4,** new; recent. **5,** pale; wan. **6,** pert. to environmental issues. —*n.* **1,** the color of growing grass. **2,** a common; a grassplot, esp. that around a hole on a golf course. **3,** (*pl.*) cut foliage, esp. evergreens, for decoration. **4,** (*pl.*) a cooked dish of leafy vegetables. **5,** (*Slang*) money, usu. paper money. —**green′ish,** *adj.* somewhat green. —**green′ness,** *n.* —**green belt, 1,** an area of parks, woods, etc. surrounding a residential area. **2,** an irrigated and cultivated strip of land adjoining a desert. —**Green Beret,** a member of the U.S. Army Special Forces specializing in guerrilla warfare. —**green card,** a card permitting foreign citizens to work in the U.S. —**green light,** (*Informal*) permission to proceed. —**green manure,** a crop plowed under as fertilizer. —**green onion,** scallion. —**green thumb,** the ability to make plants grow.

green′back″ *n.* a piece of U.S. paper money.

green′er·y (grē′nə-rė) *n.* **1,** green vegetation or foliage. **2,** a place for raising plants.

green-eyed″ (grēn-īd″) *adj.* (*Informal*) jealous.

green′gage″ (grēn′gāj″) *n.* a fine-flavored plum.

> **greengage**
> ↔ After 18th-c. English botanist Sir William *Gage*, who introduced it.

green′horn″ *n.* (*Informal*) an inexperienced person; ignoramus.

green′house″ *n.* a glass house in which plants are grown. —**greenhouse effect,** the trapping of the heat of the sun in the lower atmosphere.

green′mail″ *n.* one of several corporate stock maneuvers to avert a hostile takeover.

green′room″ *n.* a sitting room in a theater for the use of the performers when not on stage.

green′sward″ (-swôrd″) *n.* grassy land; a lawn.

greet (grēt) *v.t.* **1,** speak courteously to. **2,** welcome; receive.

greet′ing *n.* **1,** a spoken or written expression of salutation or good wishes. **2,** (*pl.*) a friendly message. —**greeting card,** a printed message of congratulation, goodwill, etc.

gre·gar′i·ous (gri-gār′ė-əs) *adj.* tending to live, associate, or congregate with others of the same kind; fond of company; sociable. —**gre·gar′i·ous·ness,** *n.*

Gre·gor′i·an calendar (gri-gôr′ė-ən) the calendar now in use, introduced by Pope Gregory XIII in 1582.

Gregorian chant a type of melody sometimes used in the ritual of the Roman Catholic Church.

grem′lin *n.* **1,** a mischievous imp. **2,** (*Informal*) the mysterious cause of a mechanical or other problem.

gre·nade′ (gri-nād′) *n.* a small bomb, usu. thrown by hand.

> **grenade, pomegranate**
> ↔ These two words are related by the resemblance of the former to the latter. From Old French *pome grenate*, pome having seeds.

gren″a·dier (gren″ə-dir′) *n.* **1,** a type of soldier. **2,** a No. Atlantic fish.

gren″a·dine′ (gren″ə-dēn′) *n.* **1,** a flavoring syrup made from pomegranate juice. **2,** a dress fabric.

grew (groo) *v.* pret. of *grow.*

grey (grā) *adj. & n.* gray.

grey′hound″ (grā′hownd″) *n.* a breed of tall, very slender, fleet dog.

> **greyhound**
> ↔ This word comes not from grey but from Old Norse *greyhundr*, bitch hound.

grid *n.* **1,** a grate or network of bars; gridiron. **2,** a rigid lead plate for conducting current in a storage battery. **3,** a grating between the electrodes of a vacuum tube.

grid′dle (grid′əl) *n.* a flat metal plate, heated from beneath, for cooking. —**grid′dle·cake″,** *n.* a pancake.

grid′i″ron (grid′ī″ərn) *n.* **1,** a metal cooking utensil of separated bars on which food is broiled. **2,** a football field. **3,** the beams and tackle above a theater stage by which scenery is hung and moved.

grid′lock″ *n.* **1,** a stoppage of the movement of traffic caused by an overly large number of vehicles. **2,** any situation in which progress is hampered.

---

t**u**b, c**ū**te, p**û**ll; lab**ə**l; **oi**l, **ow**l, g**o**, **ch**ip, **sh**e, **th**in, **th**en, si**ng**, i**nk**; *see p. 6*

grief (grēf) *n.* **1,** deep sorrow; also the cause of sorrow. **2,** disaster; failure.

griev'ance (grē'vəns) *n.* a real or fancied cause of complaint.

grieve (grēv) *v.t.* cause to suffer sorrow. —*v.i.* feel grief; mourn.

griev'ous (grē'vəs) *adj.* **1,** causing mental or physical pain, **2,** atrocious. —**griev'-ous·ness,** *n.*

grif'fin (grif'in) *n.* a fabulous creature with an eagle's head and wings and a lion's body.

grif'fon (grif'ən) *n.* **1,** a vulture. **2,** a Dutch breed of hunting dog.

grift *n.* (*Slang*) gambling pursuits generally. —**grift'er,** *n.* a confidence man or dishonest professional gambler.

grill (gril) *n.* **1,** a gridiron. **2,** a hotel bar or restaurant. **3,** a dish of various broiled meats. —*v.t.* **1,** broil (food) on a grill. **2,** subject to persistent questioning.

grille (gril) *n.* a metal grating.

grim *adj.* [**grim'mer, -mest**] **1,** forbidding. **2,** uncompromising; unyielding. **3,** frightful; cruel. —**Grim Reaper,** the personification of death as a human figure holding a scythe. —**grim'ness,** *n.*

grim'ace (grim'əs) *n.* a twisting of the face, expressive of pain, disgust, etc. —*v.i.* make a grimace.

gri·mal'kin *n.* **1,** a cat, esp. a female. **2,** a spiteful old woman.

grime (grīm) *n.* deeply ingrained dirt. —**grim'y,** *adj.* dirty.

grin *n.* a broad smile that shows the teeth. —*v.i.* [**grinned, grin'ning**] make a grin; smile broadly.

grind (grīnd) *v.t.* [**ground, grind'ing**] **1,** subject to friction between two abrasive surfaces, or against one surface, so as to reduce to particles, wear away, etc.; pulverize; grate; sharpen; smooth; machine; shape. **2,** operate (a grinding machine or wheel), as by pedaling or turning a handle. **3,** grit (the teeth); chew. **4,** oppress. —*v.i.* **1,** work at grinding. **2,** (*Slang*) work very hard.—*n.* **1,** a tedious routine. **2,** (*Slang*) a student who does nothing but study.

grind'er (grīn'dər) *n.* **1,** a device for grinding. **2,** (*Slang*) a large sandwich; a hero (def. 3).

grind'stone" *n.* a rotating abrasive wheel.

grin'go (gring'gō) *n.* (*Derog.*) in Latin Amer., a foreigner, esp. a person from the U.S.

grip *v.t. & i.* [**gripped, grip'ping**] **1,** grasp firmly. **2,** hold the interest of. —*n.* **1,** a

firm grasp; the power of firmness of a grasp or hold. **2,** a ritual manner of clasping hands. **3,** a handle or hilt; a device for grasping or attaching. **4,** power; control. **5,** (*Informal*) a valise. **6,** (*Slang*) a stagehand.

gripe (grīp) *v.t.* squeeze painfully; distress, esp. cause colic in. —*v.i.* **1,** have pain in the bowels. **2,** (*Slang*) complain. —*n.* **1,** a pang of colic. **2,** (*Informal*) a complaint. —**grip'er,** *n.* a chronic grumbler.

grippe (grip) *n.* influenza.

gri·sette' (gri-zet') *n.* (*Fr.*) a young Fr. working-class woman.

gris'ly (griz'lē) *adj.* gruesome; frightful. —**gris'li·ness,** *n.*

---

grisly, grizzly
☛ Do not confuse these two homonyms. *Grisly* means grim, frightful; *grizzly* means gray.

---

grist *n.* grain to be ground.

gris'tle (gris'əl) *n.* cartilage. —**gris'tly** (-lē) *adj.* composed of, or like, cartilage; tough.

grit *n.* **1,** tiny, rough particles; sand. **2,** a rough sandstone. **3,** pluck. **4,** (*pl.* used as *sing.*) coarsely ground hominy. —*v.t. & i.* [**grit'ted, -ting**] grate; grind.

grit'ty (-ē) *adj.* **1,** sandy; dirty. **2,** plucky.

griz'zled (griz'əld) *adj.* mixed with gray, as hair.

griz'zly (griz'lē) *adj.* streaked with gray. —**grizzly bear,** a large savage bear of western No. America. ❑ *grisly*

groan (grōn) *n.* a low, mournful sound uttered in pain or grief. —*v.t. & i.* utter such a sound.

groat (grōt) *n.* **1,** a former English silver coin worth fourpence. **2,** a very small sum. **3,** (*pl.*) crushed or coarsely ground grain.

gro'cer (grō'sər) *n.* a dealer in food supplies. —**gro'cer·ies** (-ēz) *n.pl.* food supplies. —**gro'cer·y,** *n.* a grocer's shop.

---

grocer, gross
↔ Despite their spelling, both words come from Latin *grossus*, large. The sense of *grocer* is a person who deals in wholesale goods in large quantities.

---

grog *n.* rum and water. —**grog'gy,** *adj.* confused and unsteady.

groin *n.* the depression between the abdomen and the thigh.

grom'met (grom'it) *n.* a ring or eyelet of metal.

groom *n.* **1,** a servant in charge of horses. **2,** a man at, or immediately before or after, his wedding. **3,** an attendant in a royal household. —*v.t.* **1,** tend (a horse). **2,** make neat and tidy. **3,** prepare (for a duty); coach; train. —**groom'ing,** *n.* personal appearance. —**grooms'man** (groomz'mən) *n.* male attendant.

> **grog**
> ↔ From *Old Grogram*, the nickname of the 18th-c. British admiral Edward Vernon, who introduced the drink. *Grogram* was a fabric of which the admiral's favorite overcoat was made.

groove (groov) *n.* **1,** a channel cut by a tool; rut; furrow. **2,** an unprogressive routine; habit. **3,** (*Slang*) a pleasurable experience. —*v.t.* **1,** cut a groove in. **2,** (*Slang*) enjoy oneself. —**groov'y,** *adj.* (*Slang*) wonderful.

grope (grōp) *v.i.* feel about with the hands, as in the dark; seek aimlessly.

gros'grain" (grō'grān") *n.* a heavy corded silk fabric.

gross (grōs) *adj.* **1,** whole, without deductions; total. **2,** thick; fat; coarse; hence, vulgar, indelicate. **3,** dull; dense. **4,** flagrant. —*n.* twelve dozen; 144. —*v.t.* make a profit of, before deductions for expenses or taxes. —**gross'ness,** *n.* vulgarity; indecency; obesity. —**gross national product,** the total value of the goods and services produced by a country during a specified period. —**gross out,** (*Slang*) to disgust; shock. ❏ *grocer*

gro·tesque' (grō-tesk') *adj.* contorted; fantastic. —*n.* something grotesque. —**gro·tesque'ness,** *n.*

> **grotesque, grotto**
> ↔ *Grotesque* means, literally, "like a grotto," from Italian *grotesco*. *Grotto* comes from Greek *kruptē*, vault, which also produced *crypt*.

grot'to (grot'ō) *n.* a cavern, esp. an artificial one; a bower. ❏ *grotesque*

grot'ty (grot'ē) *adj.* (*Slang*) filthy; seedy.

grouch (growch) *n.* (*Informal*) **1,** a fit of ill temper. **2,** a surly person. —*v.t.* complain. —**grouch'y,** *adj.*

ground (grownd) *n.* **1,** that part of the earth's surface that is not water; dry land; the composition of such surface; earth; soil. **2,** a specific region; area. **3,** a distance traversed. **4,** a foundation; subject matter; a basis; a reason. **5,** (*pl.*) a tract of land, esp. one attached to a dwelling. **6,** (*pl.*) waste matter in ground form, as *coffee grounds.* **7,** a conveyance of electrical current to the earth or a conductor of equivalent effect. —*adj.* **1,** prepared by grinding.

2, at the level of the ground. —*v.t.* **1,** set on the ground. **2,** (*Aviation*) forbid to fly. **3,** connect electrical current with the earth, etc. **4,** run (a ship) aground. **5,** teach fundamentals to. **6,** (*Informal*) forbid to participate in social activities. **7,** pret. & p.p. of *grind.* —*v.i.* come to rest on the ground. —**cover ground,** make progress. —**give ground,** yield; retreat. —**ground zero,** the point on the earth's surface on or above which a nuclear explosion takes place.

ground'er (grown'dər) *n.* (*Baseball*) a ball hit along the ground.

ground'hog" *n.* woodchuck. —**groundhog day,** Candlemas, Feb. 2.

ground'less (-ləs) *adj.* with no adequate reason.

ground'ling (grownd'ling) *n.* **1,** an animal or plant bound to or living close to the ground. **2,** a materialistic person.

ground'nut" *n.* (*Brit.*) the peanut.

grounds'keep"er *n.* a caretaker, as of an estate, arena, etc.

ground'swell" *n.* a surge of support, esp. for the general public.

ground'work" *n.* preparatory work; foundation; basis.

group (groop) *n.* a number of persons or things gathered or classified together, usually because of likeness or common purpose. —*v.t. & i.* combine in a unit.

group'er (groo'pər) *n.* an Atlantic food fish.

group'ie (groo'pē) *n.* (*Slang*) a person who follows a celebrity, rock group, etc.; fan.

grouse (grows) *n.* **1,** [*pl.* **grouse**] any of several game birds. **2,** (*Slang*) a complaint. —*v.i.* (*Slang*) grumble.

grout (growt) *n.* a thin mortar used to fill cavities between rocks, masonry, etc.

grove (grōv) *n.* a small wood; also, a group of cultivated fruit trees.

grov'el (gruv'əl) *v.i.* crawl or be prone upon the earth; hence, humble oneself.

grow (grō) *v.i.* [**grew** (groo), **grown** (grōn), **grow'ing**] **1,** increase in size, power, etc. **2,** arise naturally. **3,** become. —*v.t.* cause or permit to grow; plant and cultivate. —**grow up,** become adult; mature.

growl *n.* **1,** a deep snarling noise. **2,** a grumbling noise; complaint. —*v.t. & i.* make such a sound.

grown (grōn) *v.* p.p. of *grow.* —**grown'-up,** *n.* an adult.

growth (grōth) *n.* **1,** act, process, or result

of growing. **2,** a mass of morbid tissue, as a tumor.

grub *v.t.* **[grubbed, grub′bing] 1,** dig up by the roots. **2,** remove roots, etc., from (land). —*v.i.* dig in the ground; hence, toil. —*n.* **1,** the larva of an insect. **2,** (*Slang*) food. —**grub′by,** *adj.* dirty.

grub′stake″ *n.* the necessities for subsistence, supplied in anticipation of profits from prospecting.

grudge (gruj) *n.* a feeling of resentment; a cause of hostility.

gru′el (groo′əl) *n.* thin porridge.

gru′el·ing (groo′əl-ing) *adj.* arduous; exhausting.

grue′some (groo′səm) *adj.* horribly repulsive. —**grue′some·ness,** *n.*

gruff (gruf) *adj.* **1,** rough; hoarse. **2,** curt; surly. —**gruff′ness,** *n.*

grum′ble (grum′bəl) *n.* a growl; a discontented mutter. —*v.i.* complain in a mutter; growl.

grump′y (grum′pē) *adj.* surly; glum. —**grump′i·ness,** *n.*

grun′dy·ism (grun′dē-iz-əm) *n.* prudishness.

> **grundyism**
> ↔ After the character Mrs. *Grundy* in the play *Speed the Plough* by 18th-c. English playwright Thomas Morton.

grunge (grunj) *n.* filth; trash. —**grun′gy,** (grun′jē) *adj.* dirty; grubby. —**grun′gi·ness,** *n.*

grunt *n.* **1,** a deep guttural sound, as that made by a hog. **2,** (*Slang*) a foot soldier. —*v.t. & i.* utter a grunt.

Gru·yère′ (grə-yär′) *n.* a compact, pale-yellow cheese, often with small holes; Swiss cheese.

G-′string″ *n.* **1,** on a musical instrument, a string tuned to G. **2,** a breechcloth secured at the waist by a string.

gua″ca·mo′le (gwä″kə-mō′lē) *n.* a seasoned mixture of avocado, tomato, and onions.

gua·na′co (gwä-nä′kō) *n.* a large So. Amer. quadruped.

gua′no (gwä′nō) *n.* [*pl.* **-nos**] a fertilizer made from the droppings of seabirds.

gua·ra′ni (gwä-rä′nē) *n.* the monetary unit of Paraguay.

guar″an·tee′ (gar″ən-tē′) *n.* **1,** a statement that a thing is as represented; warranty. **2,** (*Law*) a promise to be responsible for another's debt or failure; property pledged as security for this promise. —*v.t.* **1,** insure; promise. **2,**

(*Law*) be responsible for. Also, **guar′an·ty″.** —**guar′an·tor″** (-tôr″) *n.*

guard (gärd) *v.t.* protect; keep safe. —*v.i.* be cautious. —*n.* **1,** a means of defense. **2,** a watchful state. **3,** a person or group of persons who guard; a sentry. **4,** a device to prevent injury. —**guard′ed,** *adj.* wary; reticent. —**guard′house″,** *n.* a military prison.

guard′i·an (gär′dē-ən) *n.* **1,** a warden. **2,** (*Law*) one entrusted with the person or property of another. —*adj.* guarding.

guards′man (gärdz′mən) [*pl.* **-men**], **guards′wom″an** *n.* **1,** a guard. **2,** a member of the U.S. National Guard. **3,** (*Brit.*) a member of a corps of troops designated to protect the sovereign.

gua′va (gwä′və) *n.* the pulpy fruit of a tropical tree.

gu″ber·na·to′ri·al (goo″bər-nə-tôr′ē-əl) *adj.* pert. to a governor. ❑ *govern*

gudg′eon (guj′ən) *n.* **1,** a small fish used as bait. **2,** one easily duped or cheated. **3,** a pivot. —*v.t.* dupe; swindle.

guer′don (gēr′dən) *n.* a reward.

Guern′sey (gērn′zē) *n.* one of a breed of dairy cattle.

guer·ril′la (gə-ril′ə) *n.* a person engaged in irregular warfare. —**guerrilla theater,** drama of social issue usu. performed outside on the street.

> **guerrilla, gorilla**
> ☛ Do not confuse *guerrilla,* a fighter, with *gorilla,* a manlike ape or an apelike man. ↔ *Guerrilla* is derived from Spanish *guerra,* war, of Germanic origin; a *guerrilla* (literally a little war) is a band of fighters.

guess (ges) *n.* an opinion reached at random or without reason; a conjecture. —*v.t.* **1,** form such an opinion; surmise. **2,** surmise correctly. —*v.i.* hazard an opinion. —**guess′work″,** *n.* the act of guessing; procedure based on guessing.

guess′ti·mate (ges′tə-mət) *n.* (*Informal*) an estimate, esp. one based on intuition.

guest (gest) *n.* **1,** a person entertained at the home of another. **2,** a patron of a hotel, etc. —*adj.* provided by or participating as a guest. —*v.t. & i.* (*Informal*) **1,** serve as guest host. **2,** appear as a guest.

guf·faw′ (gu-fâ′) *n.* a boisterous laugh. —*v.i.* laugh coarsely.

GUI (goo′ē) *abbr.* graphical user interface.

guid′ance (gī′dəns) *n.* the act of guiding; direction; management.

guide (gīd) *v.t.* **1,** show the way to; escort. **2,** direct; manage. —*n.* **1,** a person or thing that directs. **2,** a controlling device, as on a machine. **3,** a guidebook. —**guided missile,** a rocket-driven explosive missile carrying radio apparatus by which its course may be corrected from the ground.

guide'book" *n.* a book of directions and information for travelers.

guide'line" *n.* a recommendation or principle for determining a course of action.

guide'post" *n.* a post bearing a sign to direct travelers.

gui·don (gī'dən) *n.* a flag or pennant; a soldier who carries it.

guild (gild) *n.* an association of persons in a common trade, or having a common interest.

guil'der (gil'dər) *n.* **1,** gulden. **2,** the Austrian florin.

guile (gīl) *n.* craft; cunning. —**guile'ful,** *adj.* —**guile'less,** *adj.* naïve.

guil'lo·tine" (gil'ə-tēn") *n.* a machine for decapitating a person.

> **guillotine**
> ↔ Named for the 18th-c. French doctor Joseph Ignace *Guillotin,* who recommended the device to authorities during the French Revolution.

guilt (gilt) *n.* **1,** the fact of having violated law or right. **2,** a sense of having committed a wrong. —**guilt'y,** *adj.*

guimpe (gamp) *n.* a woman's outer garment for the neck and shoulders.

guin'ea (gin'ē) *n.* a former Brit. monetary unit, 21 shillings. —**guinea fowl,** an Afr. game bird, related to the pheasant. —**guinea hen,** a fowl domesticated for its meat and eggs. —**guinea pig,** a small, short-tailed rodent, much used in medical research; hence, a person used as a subject for experimentation.

gui·ro (gwē'rō) *n.* a So. Amer. musical instrument scraped with a stick.

guise (gīz) *n.* **1,** garb; dress; hence, semblance. **2,** cloak; cover.

gui·tar' (gi-tär') *n.* a 6- or 12-stringed musical instrument plucked with the fingers or a pick. —**gui·tar'ist,** *n.*

> **guitar, zither**
> ↔ Both words derive from Greek *kithara,* lyre. *Guitar* comes via Arabic *qitar; zither* comes via Latin *cithara.*

gu'lag (goo'läg) *n.* a forced-labor camp, esp. one in the former Soviet Union.

> **gulag**
> ↔ An acronym for Russian *G(lavnoe) u(pravlenie ispravitel'no-trudovykh) lag(erei),* Main Directorate of Corrective Labor Camps.

gulch *n.* a gorge; ravine.

gul'den (gŭl'den) *n.* the monetary unit of the Netherlands.

gulf *n.* **1,** an arm of the sea extending into the land. **2,** an abyss.

gull (gul) *n.* **1,** a web-footed seabird. **2,** a dupe. —*v.t.* trick; cheat.

gul'let (gul'it) *n.* the throat.

gul'li·ble (gul'ə-bəl) *adj.* easily deceived. —**gul"li·bil'i·ty,** *n.*

gul'ly (gul'ē) *n.* a narrow ravine.

gulp *v.t.* swallow hastily. —*v.i.* gasp; choke. —*n.* the act of gulping; a quantity gulped.

gum *n.* **1,** the firm flesh in which the teeth are set. **2,** a sticky substance. **3,** a tree yielding a viscid resin. **4,** chewing gum. —*v.t.* [**gummed, gum'ming**] **1,** stick together with gum. **2,** (*Slang*) clog; impede. —*v.i.* become sticky. —**gum'my,** *adj.* —**gum'mi·ness,** *n.* —**gum up,** spoil. —**gum arabic,** a gum derived from the acacia, used in medicines, etc.

gum'bo (gum'bō) *n.* [*pl.* **-bos** (-bōz)] **1,** a soup or dish made with okra. **2,** (*Informal*) sticky mud.

> **gumbo**
> ↔ Probably from a Bantu dialect word for okra, through Louisiana French.

gum'drop" *n.* a small candy made of gum arabic or gelatin.

gump'tion (gump'shən) *n.* (*Informal*) **1,** initiative; self-reliance. **2,** common sense.

gum'shoe" *n.* **1,** (*Informal*) an overshoe. **2,** (*Slang*) a detective.

gun *n.* **1,** any of various portable firearms. **2,** a cannon. **3,** in airplanes, the throttle. —*v.t.* [**gunned, gun'ning**] **1,** hurt with a gun. **2,** (with *for*) pursue. **3,** accelerate. —**at gunpoint,** with a gun pointing at one.

> **gun**
> ↔ From a Scandinavian female name, *Gunnhildr,* literally, war-war. Another example of naming weapons for women, of which the most celebrated case is *Big Bertha* of World War I.

gun'boat" *n.* a small warship carrying mounted guns. —**gunboat diplomacy,** diplomatic relations based on actual or implied threat of military action.

gun′cot″ton *n.* cotton treated with nitric acid, used in explosives; cellulose nitrate.

gung-′ho′ (gung′-hō′) *adj.* (*Informal*) enthusiastic.

gun′man (-mən) *n.* [*pl.* **-men**] a hired ruffian. Also, **gun′fight″er.**

gun′nel (gun′əl) *n.* **1,** a small blenny. **2,** gunwale.

gun′ner (gun′ər) *n.* the operator of a gun or cannon.

gun′ner·y (-ē) *n.* **1,** the making or operation of guns. **2,** artillery.

gun′ny (gun′ē) *n.* a coarse fabric made of jute or hemp fiber.

gun′play″ *n.* the firing of guns, esp. an exchange of shots.

gun′pow″der *n.* an explosive powder for use in guns, blasting, etc.

gun′run″ning *n.* the smuggling of firearms. —**gun′run″ner,** *n.*

gun′ship″ *n.* a heavily armed airplane or helicopter.

gun′sling″er *n.* a gunfighter.

gun′smith″ *n.* one who makes or repairs guns.

gun′wale (gun′əl) *n.* the upper edge of a ship's side. Also, **gun′nel.**

---

gunwale
↔ So called because it was the part of the boat (*wale*, side of boat) where the gun was mounted.

---

gup′py (gup′ē) *n.* a very small fish.

---

guppy
↔ Named for Trinidadan Rev. R.J.L. *Guppy*, who presented specimens of it to the British Museum.

---

gur′gle (gėr′gəl) *v.i.* make a bubbling sound, as water flowing from a bottle. —*n.* this sound.

gu′ru (goo′roo) *n.* a personal teacher and intellectual (and usu. spiritual or mystical) guide.

gush *v.i.* **1,** issue copiously and violently; flow out freely. **2,** (*Informal*) display sentiment effusively. —*v.t.* emit copiously. —*n.* a spouting forth.

gush′er (gush′ər) *n.* **1,** one given to sentimental display. **2,** an oil well with a copious natural flow.

gush′y (gush′ē) *adj.* (*Informal*) overdemonstrative. —**gush′i·ness,** *n.*

gus′set (gus′ət) *n.* a triangular piece of cloth inserted in a garment.

gus′sy (gus′ē) *v.i. & t.* (with *up*) (*Informal*) dress up; make pretty.

gust *n.* **1,** a sudden squall of wind. **2,** an outburst. —*v.i.* blow (of wind).

gus′ta·to·ry (gus′tə-tôr-ē) *adj.* pert. to the sense of taste.

gus′to (gus′tō) *n.* zest; enjoyment.

gust′y (gus′tē) *adj.* coming in gusts or squalls; windy. —**gust′i·ness,** *n.*

gut *n.* **1,** an intestine; (*pl.*) the bowels. **2,** animal intestines used as a string: *catgut.* **3,** a narrow defile; a channel. **4,** (*pl.*) (*Slang*) stamina; courage. —*v.t.* [**gut′ted, gut′ting**] **1,** disembowel. **2,** plunder of contents; destroy the insides of. —*adj.* (*Slang*) **1,** easy; simple. **2,** basic; fundamental. **3,** intuitive; nonintellectual. —**gut′sy,** *adj.* (*Slang*).

gut′ta-per′cha (gut′ə-pēr′chə) *n.* the dried juice of certain trees, which forms a whitish puttylike material.

gut′ter (gut′ər) *n.* **1,** a channel for carrying off water, as at the eaves of a roof or at a roadside. **2,** a debased state of living or thinking.

gut′ter·snipe″ (gut′ər-snīp″) *n.* a person, esp. a child, of lowly origin; a gamin.

gut′tur·al (gut′ər-əl) *adj.* pert. to or formed in the throat; hoarse.

guy (gī) *n.* **1,** a rope, chain, or wire used to steady something. **2,** (*Slang*) a person. —*v.t.* (*Informal*) tease.

---

guy
↔ The sense of a steadying wire or rope is of French origin. The other senses derive from 17th-c. English conspirator *Guy* Fawkes, who led the Gunpowder plot of 1605.

---

guz′zle (guz′əl) *v.t. & i.* drink too much or too rapidly.

gybe (jīb) *v.i.* jibe (def. 1). ❑ *gibe*

gym·kha′na (jim-kä′nə) *n.* **1,** place where athletic events are held; the events themselves. **2,** an equestrian competition. **3,** autocross.

---

gymkhana
↔ From Hindi *gedkhana*, ball house, racket court.

---

gym·na′si·um (jim-nā′zē-əm) *n.* **1,** building or room for athletic exercises. Also (*Informal*) **gym** (jim). **2,** (often *cap.*) in some countries, a secondary school preparing students for university.

gym′nast (jim′nast) *n.* one skilled in acrobatic and similar physical exercises. —**gym·nas′tifi** *n.pl.* such exercises. —**gymnas′tic,** *adj.* —**gym·nas′ti·cal·ly,** *adv.*

---

gymnasium
↔ From Greek *gymnos*, naked. As athletes tended to train naked, this word came to refer to the location where the training took place.

gy′′ne·col′o·gy (gī′′nə-kol′ə-jė) *n.* (*Med.*) the branch of medicine dealing with diseases of women. —**gy′′ne·col′o·gist,** *n.*

gy′no- (gī′nə) *pref.* female; woman.

gyp (jip) *n.* (*Slang*) a cheat; swindler. —*v.t.* [**gypped, gyp′ping**] cheat.

gyp′sum (jip′səm) *n.* a soft mineral, from which plaster of Paris is made.

gyp′sy (jip′sė) *n.* Romany. Also, **gip′sy.** —**gypsy cab,** (*Informal*) a taxicab licensed only to accept passengers by telephone, but that illegally accepts passengers on the street.

gypsy
↔ From earlier *gipcyan*, Egyptian; Egypt is where gypsies were at one time thought to have originated.

gy′rate (jī′rāt) *v.i.* move spirally; rotate. —**gy·ra′tion,** *n.*

gy·rene′ (jī-rēn′) *n.* (*Slang*) a U.S. Marine.

gy′ro- (jī′rō) denoting a ring or circle.

gy′ro·com′′pass (jī′rō-kum′′pəs) *n.* a motor-driven gyroscope placed with its axis parallel to that of the earth and thus indicating true north regardless of rotation of the earth and the movement of a ship.

gy′ro·scope′′ (jī′rə-skōp′′) *n.* an instrument employing a rotating wheel to stabilize ships, etc.

gyve (jīv) *n.* (usually *pl.*) a fetter for the leg; shackle. —*v.t.* fetter.

H

H, h (āch) **1,** the eighth letter of the English alphabet. **2,** (*cap.*) Roman numeral for 200. **3,** (*cap.*) (*Ger., Music*) the note B-natural.

habanera
↔ From Spanish *danza habanera,* dance of Havana. Note that although the word is frequently mispronounced (hä-bə-nye′rə), the "n" does not have a tilde (˜).

ha (hä) *interj.* expressing amusement, triumph or interrogation.

ha′′ba·ne′ra (hä′′bə-ne′rə) *n.* a Spanish dance.

ha′be·as cor′pus (hä′bė-əs kôr′pəs) (*Lat., Law*) a writ demanding that a prisoner be given an immediate hearing or else be released.

habeas corpus
↔ Latin for "you should have the body," the first words of a writ dating from the 13th c.

hab′er·dash′′er (hab′ər-dash′′ər) *n.* a dealer in accessory articles of men's wear. —**hab′er·dash′′er·y,** *n.* the shop of such a dealer.

haberdasher
↔ Probably from Anglo-Norman *hapertas,* a word of uncertain meaning (perhaps a type of cloth) and origin.

ha·bil′i·ment (hə-bil′ə-mənt) *n.* (usu. *pl.*) clothing; garments.

hab′it *n.* **1,** a tendency or disposition to act in a certain way, acquired by repetition of such acts. **2,** a usual mode of action; a custom or usage. **3,** a characteristic trait. **4,** (often *pl.*) a costume appropriate to a vocation or occasion. **5,** addiction. —*v.t.* clothe. —**hab′it·a·ble,** *adj.* capable of being lived in. —**hab′i·tant,** *n.*

hab′i·tat′′ (hab′ə-tat′′) *n.* the natural home of an animal or plant; the characteristics, as climate, etc., of such a region.

hab′′i·ta′tion (hab′′ə-tā′shən) *n.* **1,** a place of abode; a dwelling. **2,** the act of inhabiting.

ha·bit′u·al (ha-bich′oo-əl) *adj.* customary; by habit.

ha·bit′u·ate′′ (ha-bich′oo-āt′′) *v.t.* **1,** accustom. **2,** frequent. —**ha·bit′′u·a′tion,** *n.*

hab′i·tude′′ (hab′ə-tood′′) *n.* habitual attitude; usual condition or character; custom.

ha·bit′u·é′ (hə-bich′oo-ā′′) *n.* one who frequents a place.

ha·chure′ (ha-shûr′) *n.* shading of a drawing or map with lines; hatching.

ha′′ci·en′da (hä′′sė-en′də) *n.* a landed estate or the house on it.

hack (hak) *n.* **1,** a cut, gash, or notch. **2,** a tool for hacking, as an ax or hoe. **3,** a cough; an impediment in speech. **4,** a hackney; a taxicab. **5,** an overworked or jaded horse or person. **6,** a person hired to write according to demand. —*adj.* **1,** hired. **2,** hackneyed; trite. —*v.t.* **1,** notch or chop irregularly; strike. **2,** (with *out*) produce without enjoyment. **3,** hackney.

4, (*Slang*) do; perform. —*v.i.* **1,** make cuts or notches. **2,** cough repeatedly; stutter. **3,** drive a hackney or taxi-cab. **4,** write for hire. **5,** to gain unauthorized access to a computer system. —**hack around,** (*Slang*) loaf; idle.

---

hack, hackney, hackneyed
↔ These words come from the name of the borough of *Hackney*, England, a former center of horse breeding.

---

hack′er (-ər) *n.* **1,** one who hacks. **2,** one who works with computers, esp. one who attempts to gain unauthorized access to a computer system.

hack′ie (-ė) *n.* taxi driver.

hack′le (hak′əl) *n.* .**1,** the neck feathers of a fowl. **2,** a comb for dressing hemp, etc. **3,** erectile hair along the spine of certain animals. —*v.t.* **1,** comb. **2,** hack roughly.

hack′ney (hak′nė) *n.* a horse or carriage kept for hire. —*adj.* hired out. —*v.t.* make stale or trite by overuse. —**hack′-neyed,** *adj.* ❏ *hack*

hack′saw″ *n.* a saw for cutting metal.

had *v.* pret. & p.p. of *have.*

had′dock (had′ək) *n.* a No. Atlantic food fish similar to the cod.

Ha′des (hā′dēz) *n.* the abode of the dead; hell.

hadj (haj) *n.* the pilgrimage to Mecca. —**hadj′i** (haj′ė) *n.* a pilgrim.

had′ron (had′rən) *n.* a type of elementary particle.

haf′ni·um (haf′nė-əm) *n.* a metallic element, no. 72, symbol Hf.

haft (hȧft) *n.* the handle of a cutting or thrusting instrument.

hag *n.* **1,** a repulsive or malicious old woman. **2,** a witch or sorceress. **3,** a fish related to the lamprey.

hag′gard (hag′ərd) *adj.* wild-looking, as from terror, suffering, or fatigue. —**hag′-gard·ness,** *n.*

hag′gis (hag′is) *n.* a traditional Scottish pudding made of sheep or calf innards.

hag′gle (hag′əl) *v.i.* bargain in a petty manner; cavil. —*v.t.* cavil at. —*n.* dispute, esp. about price.

hag′i·o- (haj′ė-ō) *pref.* saint; sacred; holy.

ha-″ha′ (hä″-hä′) *n.* **1,** a laugh. **2,** (hä′-hä″) a sunken fence.

hai′ku (hī′koo) *n.* (*Jap.*) a Japanese lyric poem having 3 lines and 17 syllables.

hail (hāl) *v.t.* **1,** salute; welcome; cheer. **2,** cry out to. **3,** pour down like hail. —*v.i.* pour down hail. —*n.* **1,** a cry or call to attract attention. **2,** a salutation or greeting. **3,** pellets of ice falling in showers: *hailstones.* —**Hail Mary,** a prayer, the Ave Maria.

---

hail, hale
☛ Do not confuse *hail*, to greet, salute, and *hale*, to haul (or, as an adjective, healthy).

---

hail-′fel″low *n,* a pleasant or congenial companion.

hair (hār) *n.* **1,** one or the aggregate of the numerous fine filaments growing from the skin of most animals. **2,** any fine filament. **3,** a very small distance or degree. —**hair shirt,** a shirt made of rough cloth woven of horsehair, worn as a penance. —**hair trigger,** a trigger requiring very slight pressure to release.

hair′cloth″ *n.* an upholstery or lining fabric made of horsehair.

hair′cut″ *n.* a cutting or clipping of the hair.

hair′do″ (-doo″) *n.* any particular style of arranging hair; hairstyle.

hair′dress″er *n.* one who cuts and arranges hair.

hair′line″ *n.* a very thin line.

hair′piece″ *n.* a patch of human or artificial hair; toupee.

hair′pin″ *n.* a bent piece of wire, used to hold the hair in place. —*adj.* bent in form of a U.

hair-′rais″ing *adj.* frightening.

hair′split″ting *n.* & *adj.* the practice of making excessively fine distinctions.

hair′spray″ *n.* a substance sprayed on the hair to keep it in place.

hair′spring″ *n.* a fine spiral spring in a timepiece.

hair′y (-ė) *adj.* **1,** having much hair. **2,** (*Slang*) dangerous; difficult. —**hair′i-ness,** *n.*

hake (hāk) *n.* a sea fish.

hal′berd (hal′bərd) *n.* a medieval weapon, comprising a blade and spiked points on a long shaft.

hal′cy·on (hal′sė-ən) *n.* a marine bird, the kingfisher. —*adj.* calm; quiet; undisturbed.

---

halcyon
↔ From the phrase *halcyon days,* fourteen days of calm weather, from *halcyon,* a mythical bird bred in a floating nest that charmed the wind and waves into calm weather, from Greek *halkyōn.*

---

hale (hāl) *v.t.* drag forcibly; haul; pull.

—*adj.* (*Archaic*) in good health; robust. ❏ *hail*

half (hȧf) *n.* [*pl.* **halves** (hȧvz)] **1,** one of two equal parts into which something is divided. **2,** a tie score. **3,** 50 cents. —*adj.* **1,** being one half. **2,** partial; incomplete. —*adv.* **1,** to the extent or degree of a half. **2,** partly; somewhat. —**half brother** or **sister,** a brother or sister by one parent but not the other. —**half nelson** (nel′sən) a wrestling hold. —**half note,** (*Music*) a minim (see *note*). —**half′pen·ny** (hā′pə-nė) *n.* a British bronze coin. Also, **half′pence″.** —**half step,** (*Music*) a semitone.

---

half
(*Gram.*) *Half* may take a singular or plural verb, depending on whether the noun it modifies is singular or plural: "Half of the meat *was* eaten." "Half of the men *are* married."

---

half-′and-half″ *n.* a mixture of equal portions, esp. milk and cream, or ale or beer and stout.

half′back″ *n.* (*Football*) a player stationed behind the line.

half-′baked′ *adj.* not completely cooked; (*fig.*) uncompleted; immature.

half′breed″ *n.* an offspring of parents of different races.

half-′caste″ *n.* a person whose parents were of different castes.

half-″cocked′ *adj. & adv.* insufficiently prepared; superficial(ly).

half′heart″ed *adj.* showing little eagerness, enthusiasm, or generosity. —**half′- heart″ed·ness,** *n.*

half-′life″ *n.* **1,** the time required for half the atoms of a radioactive substance to undergo radioactive decay. **2,** (*Informal*) a period of success before something dies.

half-′mast″ *adv.* (of a flag) about halfway down its pole, as a mark of mourning or distress. Also, **half-′staff″.**

half′tone″ *n.* **1,** a process of photoengraving using a fine wire screen. **2,** a plate or print so made.

half′track″ *n.* a motor truck having treads instead of rear wheels.

half′way″ *adv. & adj.* **1,** to or at half the distance or middle point. **2,** partial. —**halfway house,** a rehabilitation center.

half′wit″ *n.* a feeble-minded person. —**half′wit″ted,** *adj.*

hal′i·but (hal′ə-bət) *n.* any of several large flatfishes.

halibut
↔ In Middle English the word meant holy flatfish, so called because it was eaten on holy days.

hal″i·to′sis (hal″ə-tō′sis) *n.* foul-odored breath.

hall (hâl) *n.* **1,** a building or a large room devoted to some public or common use. **2,** an antechamber or corridor giving entrance to other rooms. **3,** a main house. —**halls of ivy,** the academic world.

hal′lah (häl′ə) *n.* challah.

hal″le·lu′jah (hal″ə-loo′yə) *interj.* (*Hebrew*) Praise ye the Lord!

hall′mark″ (hâl′märk″) *n.* a mark, stamp, or attestation of quality.

---

hallmark
↔ The "hall" in *hallmark* refers specifically to Goldsmiths' Hall in London, home of the Goldsmiths' Company, which regulated the standards of purity in gold and silver.

---

hal·loo′ (ha-loo′) *interj.* to attract attention. —*v.i. & t.* shout; call.

hal′low (hal′ō) *v.t.* set apart as holy; regard as sacred; consecrate. —**hal′lowed** (hal′ōd, hal′ō-id) *adj.*

Hal″low·een′ (hal″ə-wēn′) *n.* the evening of October 31, the eve of All Saints' Day: (*all*) *Hallow(s) e(v)en.*

hal·lu″ci·na′tion (hə-loo″sə-nā′shən) *n.* **1,** an apparent perception of something not actually present. **2,** a false belief; illusion. —**hal·lu′ci·nate″,** *v.i.*

hal·lu′cin·o·gen″ (hə-loo′sə-nə-jən″) *n.* a drug that causes hallucinations. —**hal·lu″cin·o·gen′ic,** *adj.*

hall′way″ *n.* a vestibule; hall.

ha′lo (hā′lō) *n.* a circle of light around the head, as of a saint.

---

halo
↔ From Greek *halōs,* disk, orig. the threshing floor on which the oxen walked in a circle.

---

hal′o·gen (hal′ə-jən) *n.* any of the elements fluorine, chlorine, iodine, and bromine.

halt (hâlt) *v.i.* **1,** cease advancing; stop. **2,** waver; hesitate. —*v.t.* cause to halt. —*n.* a stop or pause. —*adj.* (*Archaic*) lame. —**halt′ing,** *adj.* hesitant.

hal′ter (hâl′tər) *n.* **1,** a rope or strap having a noose, for leading or confining an animal. **2,** a woman's waist held in place by bands tied around the back and neck.

hal′vah (häl′vä) *n.* a Turkish confection of sesame seeds and honey.

halve (hȧv) *v.t.* **1,** divide into two equal parts. **2,** reduce to a half. **3,** make equal scores in (a contest).

hal′yard (hal′yərd) *n.* a rope for raising and lowering a yard, sail, flag, etc.

ham *n.* **1,** the buttock of a hog; the meat from this quarter. **2,** the back of the knee; (*pl.*) the thighs. **3,** (*Slang*) an actor who overacts. **4,** (*Slang*) an amateur, esp. in radio. —*v.i.* [**hammed, ham′ming**] (*Slang*) overact.

> **ham**
> ↔ From Germanic *kham-, be crooked; *ham* originally referred to the back of the leg. *Ham* in the sense of bad actor (and that of an amateur radio enthusiast) is probably a shortening of *hamfatter*, from a minstrel song "The Ham-fat Man."

ham′burg″er (ham′bēr″gər) *n.* **1,** chopped beef: *hamburg steak.* **2,** a sandwich of such meat in a bun.

> **hamburger, burger**
> ↔ Short for *Hamburger steak,* i.e., steak as it is cooked in *Hamburg,* Germany. *Burger* results from a false division of *hamburger* into *ham* + *burger.*

ham′let (ham′lit) *n.* a small village.

ham′mer (ham′ər) *n.* **1,** an instrument for driving nails, beating metal, etc., comprising a heavy solid head set on a handle. **2,** any of various instruments for pounding or striking. **3,** a metal ball with a flexible handle used in throwing contests. —*v.t. & i.* **1,** beat, drive, etc., with or as with a hammer. **2,** (with *out*) execute laboriously.

ham′mer·head″ (-hed″) *n.* a kind of shark.

ham′mer·lock″ *n.* a wrestling hold.

ham′mock (ham′ək) *n.* a heavy cloth or mesh suspended by cords, used as a bed.

ham′per (ham′pər) *v.t.* impede in motion or progress; hinder. —*n.* a large covered basket.

ham′ster (ham′stər) *n.* a small burrowing rodent.

ham′string″ *n.* a tendon at the back of the knee. —*v.t.* [*pret. & p.p.* **ham′strung″**] cripple; disable.

hand *n.* **1,** the end of the human arm, from wrist outward, comprising the palm and fingers; a corresponding part of certain animals. **2,** something resembling a hand, as a pointer on a clock. **3,** style of handwriting; a person's signature. **4,** a unit of linear measure, 4 inches. **5,** a manual laborer; an employee. **6,** help; aid; agency; participation. **7,** (often *pl.*) custody; possession or control. **8,** the cards dealt to a player in a game; a player; the period from one deal to the next. —*adj.* **1,** of the hand; to be carried by or worn on the hand. **2,** operated or made by hand. —*v.t.* **1,** (often with *over*) deliver by hand. **2,** help; conduct. —**hand-in-glove,** very intimate; cooperating closely. —**hand organ,** a hurdy-gurdy. —**hand-to-mouth,** *adj.* barely supplying the minimum necessities of life; insecure. —**on hand,** available; present. —**hand truck,** truck (def. 2).

hand′bag″ *n.* a woman's purse.

hand′ball″ *n.* an athletic game.

hand′bill″ *n.* a printed notice.

hand′book″ *n.* **1,** a compact treatise; a guidebook. **2,** the business of a bookmaker.

hand′car″ *n.* a small hand-propelled railroad car.

hand′cuff″ *n.* (usually *pl.*) a shackle fitting on the wrist. —*v.t.* put handcuffs on.

-hand′ed (han′did) *suf.* supplied with or done by a specified number of hands.

hand′ful″ (-fûl″) *n.* **1,** what the hand can hold; a small quantity or number. **2,** (*Informal*) a difficult task.

hand′gun″ *n.* a firearm that can be held and fired in one hand.

hand′i·cap″ (han′di-kap″) *n.* **1,** an extra burden placed upon a superior competitor in a contest. **2,** any encumbrance or disadvantage. **3,** a contest in which some of the entrants are handicapped. —*v.t.* [**-capped″, -cap″ping**] **1,** place a handicap upon; rate. **2,** encumber; hinder. —**hand′-i·cap″per,** *n.*

> **handicap**
> ↔ From the 19th-c. *hand i' cap,* a betting game in which money was put into a cap before a horse race.

hand′i·craft″ (han′di-krȧft″) *n.* **1,** skilled labor with the hands. **2,** a manual art. *Also,* **hand′craft″.**

hand′i·ly (han′də-lē) *adv.* **1,** skillfully. **2,** easily; conveniently.

hand′i·work″ (han′di-wẽrk″) *n.* **1,** work done or something made by hand. **2,** the result of an action.

hand′ker·chief (hang′kər-chif) *n.* a small cloth carried for wiping the face or nose, etc.

han′dle (han′dəl) *v.t.* **1,** touch, manipulate, manage, or control with the hands. **2,** deal with; treat of. **3,** make use of; deal in; buy and sell. —*n.* **1,** the part of an implement, instrument, tool, or weapon made to be gripped by the hand. **2,** a title, as Mr. **3,** (*Slang*) name or nickname. —**han′dler,** *n.*

han′dle·bar″ *n.* (usually *pl.*) one of the two bars with which a bicycle or motorcycle is steered.

hand′made″ *adj.* not made by machinery.

hand′maid″ *n.* a female servant.

hand-′me-down″ *n.* a garment or other thing previously used by someone else. —*adj.* secondhand.

hand′out″ *n.* (*Slang*) something given to a beggar.

hand′sel (han′səl) *n.* a gift; token.

hand′set″ *n.* a telephone receiver and transmitter mounted on one handle.

hand′shak″ing *n.* (*Computers*) the exchange of signals between two devices.

hand′some (hand′səm) *adj.* **1,** agreeable to the eye. **2,** large; generous. —**hand′-some·ness,** *n.*

hands-′on′ *adj.* practical, as opposed to theoretical.

hand′spring″ *n.* a somersault.

hand′writ″ing *n.* **1,** writing done by hand. **2,** a style of such writing.

hand′y (han′dė) *adj.* **1,** ready at hand; accessible. **2,** well-suited to use; easy to handle; convenient. **3,** skillful in using the hands; dexterous. —**hand′i·ness,** *n.*

han′dy·man″, han′dy·wom″an *n.* a person employed to do odd jobs.

hang [*pret. & p.p.* **hung**] *v.t.* **1,** support from above and not from below; suspend. **2,** [*pret. & p.p.* **hanged**] suspend by the neck until dead. **3,** let dangle; let bend or droop downward. **4,** attach, as wallpaper. **5,** cause (a jury) to fail to reach a verdict. —*v.i.* **1,** be suspended; dangle; swing freely. **2,** [*pret. & p.p.* **hanged**] be executed by hanging. **3,** be contingent or dependent. **4,** hold fast; cling. **5,** (with *around* or *out*) linger; loiter. **6,** impend. **7,** come to a standstill. **8,** (*Computers*) crash. —*n.* **1,** the way something hangs. **2,** (*Informal*) the precise meaning, function, operation, etc. **3,** a trifle (in expletives). —**hang fire, 1,** be slow to explode. **2,** be slow in acting. —**hang gliding,** the individual sport of soaring with the aid of a kite-like glider. —**hang loose,** (*Slang*) stay relaxed. —**hang out,** (*Slang*) frequent a place; reside. —**hang tough,** (*Slang*) be inflexible. —**hang up,** end a telephone con-

nection by placing the receiver on the hook.

hang′ar (hang′ər) *n.* a shed for housing aircraft.

---
hangar, hanger
☞ Do not confuse *hangar,* a shelter for airplanes, and *hanger,* a device for hanging.

---

hang′dog″ *adj.* **1,** mean-looking. **2,** dejected.

hang′er *n.* a device for hanging something, as clothes. ❑ *hangar*

hang′er-on″ *n.* [*pl.* **hang′ers-on″**] a dependent; parasite.

hang′ing *n.* **1,** capital punishment on the gallows. **2,** a drapery, hung tapestry, etc.

hang′man (-mən) *n.* [*pl.* **-men**] an executioner.

hang′nail″ *n.* a tear in a fingernail or cuticle.

---
hangnail
↔ From Old English *angnaegl,* painful nail.

---

hang′out″ *n.* (*Slang*) a place one frequents.

hang′o″ver *n.* a belated effect of a previous act or condition; esp., illness induced by excessive drinking of liquor.

hang′up″ *n.* (*Slang*) **1,** a problem. **2,** an obsession; phobia.

hank *n.* a skein, as of thread or yarn; a coil or knot.

han′ker (hang′kər) *v.i.* have an uneasy craving; yearn keenly. —**han′ker·ing,** *n.*

han′ky (hang′kė) *n.* (*Informal*) handkerchief.

han′ky-pan′ky (hang′kė-pang′kė) *n.* trickery; legerdemain.

han′som (han′səm) *n.* a two-passenger carriage with an elevated rear seat for the driver.

---
hansom
↔ From the name of its 19th-c. patentee, James Aloysius *Hansom.*

Ha′nuk·kah″ (hä′nû-kä″) *n.* the Jewish Feast of the Dedication.

hap″haz′ard (hap″haz′ərd) *adj.* occurring by chance; accidental; random. —*adv.* at random.

---
haphazard, hapless, happen, happy
↔ These words attest to the existence of an earlier (but now archaic) word, *hap,* meaning luck, chance.

---

hap′less (hap′ləs) *adj.* unlucky; unfortunate. —**hap′less·ness,** *n.* ❑ *haphazard*

hap′pen (hap′ən) *v.i.* **1,** come to pass; take place; occur. **2,** occur by chance. ❑ *haphazard*

hap′pen·ing (hap′ən-ing) *n.* **1,** a theatrical event, usu. partially or wholly spontaneous, often involving audience participation. **2,** any spontaneous social occurrence.

hap′pen·stance″ (-stans″) *n.* a fortuitous happening.

hap′py (hap′ē) *adj.* **1,** glad; joyous; satisfied; pleased. **2,** giving pleasure; agreeable. **3,** lucky; fortunate. **4,** very fitting; apt; felicitous. —**hap′pi·ness,** *n.* —**hap′py-go-luck′y,** *adj.* unworried; irresponsible. —**happy hour,** the cocktail hour during which drinks are served with free snacks. ❑ *haphazard*

ha′ra-ki′ri (hä′rə-kir′ē) *n.* (*Jap.*) suicide by ripping open the abdomen with a knife.

ha·rangue′ (hə-rang′) *n.* a long vehement speech; a tirade. —*v.t. & i.* address in a harangue; declaim.

har′ass (har′əs) *v.t.* annoy by repeated attacks; disturb or torment persistently. —**har′ass·ment,** *n.*

har′bin·ger (här′bin-jər) *n.* a forerunner that gives notice of the coming of another.

har′bor (här′bər) *n.* **1,** a bay, cove, etc., that affords shelter or anchorage for ships. **2,** a refuge. —*v.t.* **1,** give shelter to; protect; conceal. **2,** have in the mind, as suspicious feelings. Also, **har′bour.** —**har′bor·age,** *n.* shelter.

hard (härd) *adj.* **1,** solid in substance or texture; resistant to penetration or cutting; unyielding. **2,** enduring; resistant; tough. **3,** firmly formed; tight. **4,** difficult; not easy to do, understand, etc. **5,** requiring or displaying great energy or exertion. **6,** harsh; severe; violent. **7,** shrewd; unsentimental; unfriendly. **8,** intoxicating; strong. —*adv.* **1,** vigorously; earnestly; intently. **2,** roughly; harshly. **3,** fully; closely. —**hard′ness,** *n.* —**hard and fast,** inflexible. —**hard liquor,** spiritous liquor of high alcoholic content. —**hard copy,** text which is printed or typewritten on paper, as opposed to displayed on a screen or stored in a computer. —**hard disk,** an electronic computer data storage system employing a magnetized metal disk in a sealed housing. —**hard lens,** a rigid plastic contact lens. —**hard money, 1,** coins. **2,** cash. —**hard of hearing,** somewhat deaf. —**hard put,** (with *to*) in great difficulty. —**hard rock,** aggressive, loud rock music. —**hard**

sell, high-pressure marketing. —**hard up,** short of funds. —**hard water,** water that contains mineral salts resistant to dissolving soap.

hard-′and-fast′ *adj.* binding; inflexible.

hard′ball″ *n.* **1,** baseball. **2,** aggressive or ruthless business practice: *play hardball.*

hard′bit″ten *adj.* obstinate; tough.

hard′board″ *n.* a building material made of compressed wood fibers.

hard″-boiled′ (-boild′) *adj.* **1,** boiled until hard, as eggs. **2,** (*Informal*) unpitying; without illusions; sophisticated.

hard-′core″ *adj.* **1,** uncompromising; committed. **2,** explicit; pornographic.

hard′en (här′dən) *v.t. & i.* make or become harder.

hard′fist″ed (-fis″tid) *adj.* **1,** stingy. **2,** tough; strict.

hard′ hat″ *n.* **1,** a protective head covering. **2,** (*Informal*) a construction worker.

hard′-head″ed *adj.* **1,** realistic; practical. **2,** obstinate.

hard′heart″ed *adj.* unfeeling; insensitive.

har′di·hood″ (här′dē-hûd″) *n.* boldness; venturesome spirit.

hard-′line″ *adj.* uncompromising; unyielding. —**hard-′lin″er,** *n.*

hard′ly (-lē) *adv.* **1,** barely; not quite. **2,** with little likelihood. **3,** harshly.

hard′nosed″ (-nōzd″) *adj.* (*Informal*) **1,** stubborn; persistent. **2,** determined.

hard′pan″ *n.* a layer of hard clay, etc., underlying soft soil.

hard′ship″ *n.* something that exacts endurance, as suffering, want, adversity.

hard′tack″ *n.* hard, dry biscuits.

hard′top″ *n.* an automobile with a fixed metal roof designed to resemble a convertible's.

hard′ware″ *n.* **1,** wares made of metal, as tools, cutlery, etc. **2,** in computers, the electronic and mechanical devices, as distinguished from the program and data software.

hard′wired″ (-wīrd″) *adj.* wired into a computer's circuitry, rather than stored in memory.

hard′wood″ *n.* **1,** deciduous timber. **2,** any heavy, compact, close-grained wood, as oak, maple, etc.

har′dy (här′dē) *adj.* capable of resisting hardship; strong; enduring. —**har′di·ness,** *n.*

hare (hār) *n.* a rodent similar to the rabbit.

hare′brained″ (hār′brānd″) *adj.* reckless; giddy. —**hare′brained″ness,** *n.*

Ha′re Krish′na (hä′rē krish′nə) (*Hindi*) a religious sect devoted to the Hindu god Krishna.

hare′lip″ (hār′lip″) *n.* a congenital deformation of the upper lip by a vertical cleft or fissure.

har′em (hâr′əm) *n.* **1,** the women in a Muslim residence; their quarters. **2,** (*Derog.*) a train of feminine admirers.

> **harem**
> ↔ From Arabic *harim*, women's quarters, forbidden place.

hark (härk) *v.i.* listen. —*interj.* Listen! Give attention! —**hark back,** retrace one's steps; revert.

hark′en (-ən) *v.i.* give heed. Also, **heark′en.**

Har′lem Renaissance (här′ləm) a flourishing of black American music and literature in Harlem, New York City, in the 1920s.

har′le·quin (här′lə-kwin) *n.* a clown; a jester. —**har″le·qui·nade′** (-kwə-nād′) *n.* a farce.

har′lot (här′lət) *n.* a prostitute.

> **harlot**
> ↔ This word used to mean beggar; its source is Old French *herlot*, of uncertain origin.

harm (härm) *n.* physical or moral injury; damage; detriment; wrong; mischief. —*v.t.* injure; hurt; be detrimental to. —**harm′-ful,** *adj.* injurious. —**harm′ful·ness,** *n.* —**harm′less,** *adj.* unable to harm. —**harm′-less·ness,** *n.*

har·mon′ic (här-mon′ik) *adj.* **1,** pert. to harmony. **2,** in harmony; concordant. —**har·mon′i·cal·ly,** *adv.*

har·mon′i·ca (här-mon′ə-kə) *n.* a small musical instrument played by blowing; a mouth organ. ❑ *harmony*

har·mon′ics (här-mon′iks) *n.* the science of musical sounds.

har·mo′ni·ous (här-mō′nē-əs) *adj.* **1,** pleasing to the ear or eye. **2,** agreeable; friendly. —**har·mo′ni·ous·ness,** *n.*

har·mo′ni·um (här-mō′nē-əm) *n.* a reed organ.

har′mo·nize″ (här′mə-nīz″) *v.t.* bring to accord or agreement. —*v.i.* sing in harmony. —**har″mo·ni·za′tion,** *n.*

har′mo·ny (här′mə-nē) *n.* **1,** (*Music*) the sound of two or more simultaneous tones; the structure and relationship of chords. **2,** a pleasing arrangement or combination

of parts; congruity. **3,** agreement, as in sentiments or interests; accord; peace and friendship.

> **harmony, harmonica**
> ↔ Both words derive ultimately from Greek *harmoniā*, joint, which in Greek musical terminology apparently meant scale. *Harmonica* is an alteration of *armonica*, a word coined by Benjamin Franklin (from Latin *harmonica*, harmonic) for a type of mechanical glass harmonica of his invention. The term was applied in the 19th c. to the mouth organ.

har′ness (här′nəs) *n.* **1,** the straps and other gear put on a horse or other draft animal; any similar arrangement of straps. **2,** (*Slang*) girdle. —*v.t.* **1,** put a harness on. **2,** link up for use; make useful application of. —**in harness,** employed; active; at work.

harp (härp) *n.* a musical instrument with strings played by plucking. —*v.i.* (*Informal*) (with *on*) speak or write of repetitiously. —**harp′ist,** *n.*

har·poon′ (här-poon′) *n.* a barbed spear attached to a rope, used in capturing large fish or whales. —*v.t.* strike with a harpoon.

harp′si·chord″ (härp′si-kôrd″) *n.* a keyboard musical instrument in which the strings are plucked by quills or quill-like plectrums.

har′py (här′pē) *n.* a repulsively greedy and unfeeling person.

> **harpy**
> ↔ From the legendary Greek monster having a woman's head and a bird's body, from Greek *arpyiai*, snatchers.

har′ri·dan (har′ə-dən) *n.* (*Offensive*) an odious old woman; a hag.

har′ri·er (har′ē-ər) *n.* **1,** a breed of hunting dog. **2,** a cross-country runner. **3,** a hawk.

har′row (har′ō) *n.* an agricultural implement, as a heavy frame set with iron teeth, used to break up clods. —*v.t.* **1,** draw a harrow over. **2,** affect the feelings of; distress. —**har′row·ing,** *adj.* distressing.

har′ry (har′ē) *v.t.* harass; ravage.

harsh (härsh) *adj.* **1,** rough to the senses; sharp, sour, discordant, irritating, etc. **2,** severe in character or effect; hard. —**harsh′ness,** *n.*

hart (härt) *n.* a male of the deer.

har′te·beest″ (här′tə-bēst″) *n.* a large So. Afr. antelope.

harts′horn″ *n.* **1,** antler of the hart. **2,** a solution of ammonia in water or alcohol.

har′um-scar′um (här′əm-skăr′əm) *adj.* giddy; rash.

har′vest (här′vəst) *n.* **1,** the gathering of crops. **2,** the season for gathering crops; autumn. **3,** a crop gathered, as grain. **4,** a supply of anything gathered and stored; the product of any labor. —*v.t. & i.* gather or reap, as grain.

> **harvest**
> ‹ › From Old English *haerfest*, which originally referred to the time of gathering crops, rather than the act.

har′vest·er (här′vəs-tər) *n.* a machine that harvests grain.

has (haz) *v.* 3rd person singular of *have.*

has-′been″ *n.* (*Informal*) a person formerly but no longer notable.

has′en·pfef′fer (hä′sən-fef″ər) *n.* (*Ger.*) rabbit stew.

hash *n.* **1,** a dish of chopped meat and potatoes. **2,** any mixture, or muddle. **3,** (*Slang*) hashish. —*v.t.* **1,** make hash of. **2,** botch; bungle. **3,** discuss. —**hash mark, 1,** military service stripe. **2,** a vertical stroke, as of a pencil. **3,** in football, the intersection of a sideline with a yard line.

hash′ish (hash′ēsh) *n.* a narcotic preparation made from Indian hemp.

hasp (håsp) *n.* a clasp for a door, etc.; a wire loop or hook.

has′si·um (has′ē-əm) *n.* a radioactive chemical element, no. 108; symbol Hs, produced artificially.

has′sle (has′əl) *n.* (*Informal*) an argument; quarrel.

has′sock (has′ək) *n.* **1,** a thick hard cushion used as a footstool. **2,** a clump or tuft of coarse grass.

has′ta la vis′ta (äs′tä lä vēs′tä) (*Span.*) until we meet again.

haste (hāst) *n.* **1,** swiftness; promptness. **2,** undue or rash quickness. —*v.i.* hasten.

has′ten (hā′sən) *v.i.* go, move, or act quickly; hurry. —*v.t.* cause to go fast or faster; accelerate.

hast′y (hās′tē) *adj.* **1,** unduly hurried or accelerated. **2,** thoughtless. —**hast′i·ness,** *n.* —**hasty pudding,** porridge.

hat *n.* a covering for the head, esp. one worn outdoors, having a crown and brim. —**pass the hat,** take a collection; ask for contributions. —**hat trick,** (*Sports*) the scoring of three goals in a single game by the same player.

hatch (hach) *v.t.* **1,** bring forth young from (an egg). **2,** contrive or produce (a plan, a result). **3,** mark lines for shading (a drawing). —*v.i.* **1,** emerge from a shell. **2,** be contrived or produced. —*n.* **1,** what is hatched; a brood. **2,** a fine line, as in engraving. **3,** an opening or door: *hatchway.* **4,** a cover for such an opening. —**hatch′er·y** (-ə-rē) *n.* a place for hatching eggs. —**hatch′ing,** *n.* fine lines, usu. parallel, used in shading or modeling.

hatch′back″ *n.* an automobile with a sloped roof which opens in the rear.

hatch′et (hach′it) *n.* **1,** a short-handled ax for use by one hand. **2,** a paid assassin. —**bury the hatchet,** make peace. —**hatchet job,** (*Informal*) a harsh verbal attack.

hatch′et·man″, hatch′et·wom″an *n.* hatchet (def. 2).

hatch′way″ *n.* **1,** a rectangular opening in a ship's deck. **2,** the opening of any trapdoor.

hate (hāt) *v.t.* **1,** regard with strong aversion or ill will; detest. **2,** find unpalatable or unappealing. —*v.i.* feel hatred. —*n.* **1,** passionate dislike or ill will. **2,** something hated.

hate′ful (hāt′fəl) *adj.* **1,** detestable; abhorrent. **2,** malicious; malevolent. —**hate′-ful·ness,** *n.*

hat′rack″ *n.* a rail or stand fitted with pegs to hold hats.

ha′tred (hā′trəd) *n.* passionate dislike; detestation.

hat′ter (hat′ər) *n.* one who makes or sells hats.

hau′berk (hâ′bərk) *n.* a coat of mail extending below the knees.

haugh′ty (hâ′tē) *adj.* disdainfully proud. —**haugh′ti·ness,** *n.*

haul (hâl) *v.t.* **1,** pull or draw with force; move by pulling; drag. **2,** (with *up*) call to account; arraign. —*v.i.* **1,** pull; tug. **2,** change direction; shift; veer. **3,** (with *off*) withdraw; pull back the arm preparatory to a blow. —*n.* **1,** a pulling with force. **2,** the distance through which something is hauled. **3,** a quantity gathered; (*Informal*) a valuable acquisition. —**haul′age,** *n.* the process of, or a fee for, hauling. —**haul′er,** *n.* one who hauls, esp. a trucker.

haunch (hânch) *n.* the fleshy part of the body above the thigh; hip.

haunt (hânt) *v.t.* **1,** reappear frequently after dying, as a ghost. **2,** visit frequently. —*v.i.* reappear, as a specter. —*n.* **1,** (often *pl.*) a place frequently visited. **2,** (hant) (*Dial.*) a ghost, or his visiting ground.

haus′frau″ (hows′frow″) *n.* a housewife.

haute′ cou·ture′ (ōt′ koo-tür′) (*Fr.*) high fashion.

haute′ cui·sine′ (ōt′ kwi-zēn′) (*Fr.*) gourmet cooking.

hau·teur′ (hō-tēr′) *n.* haughtiness.

haut″ monde′ (ō″ mōnd′) (*Fr.*) high society.

have (hav) *v.t.* [*present indicative:* I **have**; you **have** (*Archaic,* thou **hast**); he **has** (*Archaic,* **hath**); we, you, they **have**; *pret. & p.p.* **had; hav′ing**] **1,** possess; own; hold. **2,** acquire; obtain; receive. **3,** contain; comprise; be in part. **4,** hold in custody; control. **5,** hold in the mind; entertain; maintain. **6,** exhibit in action; exercise; show. **7,** possess knowledge of; be affected with; experience. **8,** procure to be done; permit; allow. **9,** (with *on*) wear. **10,** (*Slang*) outwit. —*aux. v.* used with a past participle to form a perfect tense, as I *have done* it, he *had gone.* —*n.* (*Informal*) a person or nation having material wealth: opposed to *have-not.* —**have at,** attack. —**have it in for,** hold a grudge against.

ha′ven (hā′vən) *n.* a harbor; a place of shelter or asylum.

have-′not″ *n.* (*Informal*) a person or nation lacking in material wealth.

hav′er·sack″ (hav′ər-sak″) *n.* a bag for provisions; knapsack.

> **haversack**
> ↔ Literally, oats bag, from German *Haber*, oats, and *Sack*, bag, from Old Norse.

hav′oc (hav′ək) *n.* general destruction; devastation.

haw (hâ) *interj.* **1,** a command to turn left. **2,** an expression marking indecision in speech. **3,** ha; a guffaw. —*v.i.* speak with hesitation.

hawk (hâk) *n.* **1,** any of numerous birds of prey. **2,** (*Informal*) an advocate of militaristic policies. **3,** a hard cough; a noisy effort to clear the throat. —*v.t.* offer for sale; peddle. —*v.i.* **1,** hunt with hawks. **2,** try to cough. **3,** peddle. —**hawk′er,** *n.* one who cries his wares; peddler.

hawk′eyed″ (hâk′īd″) *adj.* having keen vision.

haws (hâz) *n.pl.* a disease of the third eyelid of a horse.

haw′ser (hâ′zər) *n.* a rope or cable used on a ship for mooring, etc.

haw′thorn″ (hâ′thôrn″) *n.* a thorny shrub or small tree, much used in hedges.

hay (hā) *n.* grass cut and dried for use as fodder. —*v.i.* cut and dry grass for use as fodder. —**hay fever,** an allergic reaction to pollen with symptoms like those of a cold.

hay′cock″ *n.* a conical pile of hay in a field.

hay′mak″er *n.* (*Slang*) a decisive blow; knockout punch.

hay′seed″ *n.* (*Informal*) a rustic; a naïve person.

hay′stack″ *n.* a pile of hay.

hay′wire″ *adj.* (*Slang*) crazy; hopelessly confused.

haz′ard (haz′ərd) *n.* **1,** exposure to danger; risk; peril. **2,** a fortuitous event; chance; accident. **3,** something dangerous or obstructive; an obstacle. **4,** something risked. **5,** a dice game. —*v.t.* **1,** put up as a stake; expose to danger or loss. **2,** run the risk of incurring or bringing to pass. **3,** do or say tentatively. —**haz′ard·ous,** *adj.* dangerous.

haze (hāz) *n.* **1,** a thin mist or fog. **2,** obscurity; vagueness, as of thought. —*v.t.* play mischievous tricks on (a candidate for membership). —**haz′y,** *adj.* foggy; vague.

ha′zel (hā′zəl) *n.* **1,** any of several shrubs or small trees. **2,** a pale brown color. —**ha′-zel·nut″,** *n.*

H-′bomb″ *n.* hydrogen bomb.

he (hē) *pron.* [*poss.* **his;** *obj.* **him**] **1,** the third person sing. masc.; a male, other than the speaker and the person addressed. **2,** any male. —*adj.* (*Informal*) male.

> **he, she**
> Since English has no acceptable common-gender pronoun in the singular, *he* has generally been used for such situations. However, this is now often considered sexist. Avoid the problem by using *he or she,* or by restating the sentence in the plural and using *they.*

head (hed) *n.* **1,** the uppermost part of the human body, above the neck; the skull with its contents and integuments; the corresponding part of any animal. **2,** the head regarded as the seat of intelligence; understanding; will; inclination. **3,** the position or person of a leader or chief. **4,** the highest or foremost part; the top or summit; the obverse of a coin. **5,** the source, as of a stream. **6,** culmination; crisis; force; pressure. **7,** something like a head in position, form, or function; a rounded protuberance; the compact inflorescence of a plant, as cabbage; the membrane of a drum. **8,** an individual, taken as one of a number. **9,** a subject or topic; a title or subtitle; heading; headline. **10,** (*Slang*) a dope addict; one who takes drugs, esp. LSD. —*adj.* **1,** being at the head; foremost; principal. **2,** coming from in front. —*v.t.* **1,** be the chief of. **2,** go to the front of; lead; precede. **3,** turn or direct in advancing. **4,** oppose; check; restrain. —*v.i.* **1,** go in a direction. **2,** originate. **—lose one's head,** become excited or panicky.

head'ache" *n.* **1,** a pain in the head. **2,** (*Informal*) a troublesome person or circumstance.

head'cheese" *n.* a loaf made of the head and feet of hogs.

head'er (-ər) *n.* **1,** a brick or stone laid lengthwise across the thickness of a wall. **2,** (*Informal*) a plunge headfirst. **3,** text appearing at the top of each page of a document.

head'first' *adv.* **1,** with the head foremost. **2,** rashly; impetuously.

head'gear" *n.* a helmet; any covering for the head.

head'hunt"ing *n.* **1,** a primitive practice of hunting and decapitating a person, preserving the head as a trophy. **2,** the act of searching for new employees, esp. executives. **—head'hunt"er,** *n.*

head'ing (hed'ing) *n.* **1,** a title or caption. **2,** something that forms a head or front. **3,** the compass point toward which a craft is directed.

head'land (hed'lənd) *n.* a point of land projecting into the sea; a cape.

head'light" *n.* a lamp to illuminate the road ahead.

head'line" *n.* a title in large type, as in a newspaper. —*v.t.* give prominent billing to; advertise. **—head'lin"er,** *n.* lead performer.

head'lock" *n.* a wrestling hold.

head'long" *adv. & adj.* **1,** hastily; rashly. **2,** with head foremost.

head'man" *n.* chief; leader.

head'mas"ter, head'mis"tress, *n.* the principal of a school.

head-'on' *adj. & adv.* with the head or front first.

head'phone" *n.* a radio, telephone, or high-fidelity receiver held against the ear(s) by a clamp over the head. Also, **head'set".**

head'quar"ters *n.pl.* or *sing.* **1,** a principal office or residence. **2,** a seat of command. **—head'quar"ter,** *v.t. & i.*

head'ship *n.* the position of chief; leadership.

heads'man (hedz"mən) *n.* [*pl.*-**men**] an executioner.

head'stall" *n.* that part of a bridle which encompasses the head.

head'stone" *n.* a stone placed at the head of a grave.

head'strong" *adj.* obstinate; willful.

head'wait"er *n.* a person in charge of the waiters, busboys, etc. in a restaurant.

head'wat"ers *n.pl.* the source and earliest tributaries of a river.

head'way" *n.* **1,** motion or impetus forward. **2,** clear space in height, as under a bridge.

head'wind" *n.* a wind blowing opposite to the direction of one's travel.

head'y (hed'é) *adj.* exhilarating; intoxicating. **—head'i·ness,** *n.*

heal (hēl) *v.t.* **1,** make whole or sound; restore to health. **2,** cleanse; purify; remedy; repair. —*v.i.* grow whole or sound; get well. **—heal'er,** *n.*

health (helth) *n.* **1,** freedom from disease; good condition; normal and efficient functioning. **2,** bodily condition. **3,** a toast. **—health'ful,** *adj.* conducive to health. **—health'y,** *adj.* sound; in good condition. **—health club,** a club offering facilities for physical exercise. **—health maintenance organization,** a comprehensive health service plan. Also, **HMO.**

heap (hēp) *n.* **1,** a collection of things laid together, esp. in a raised pile. **2,** (*Informal*) a large number or quantity. **3,** (*Slang*) an automobile. —*v.t.* **1,** put together; pile; amass. **2,** bestow bountifully. **—heap'ing,** *adj.* above the level of the sides of a container.

hear (hir) *v.t.* [**heard, hear'ing**] **1,** perceive by ear. **2,** listen to; give attention to. **3,** be informed of. —*v.i.* **1,** possess the sense of hearing. **2,** be told; learn by report. **—hear'er,** *n.* one of an audience. **—hear! hear!,** an exclamation expressing approval.

hear'ing *n.* **1,** ability to perceive by ear. **2,** an opportunity to be heard. **3,** an examination in a court of law. **4,** earshot. **—hearing aid,** a device to amplify sounds for the hard-of-hearing. **—hearing-impaired,** hard of hearing.

hear'say" *n.* information communicated by another; gossip; rumor.

hearse (hėrs) *n.* a vehicle for bearing a corpse to a burial ground.

---

hearse, rehearse
↔ *Hearse* got its present meaning from the resemblance of an agricultural harrow to the triangular candle holder placed over the coffin at funeral services. *Rehearse* means to rake again, hence, to redo.

---

heart (härt) *n.* **1,** the principal organ that causes blood to circulate in the body. **2,** this organ regarded as the seat of vitality, intellect, emotion, etc. **3,** love; kindness; pity. **4,** courage; determination; enthusiasm. **5,** the inner, central, or essential part of anything. **6,** the symbol ♥; a playing card so marked. **—by heart,** by memory. **—take heart,** have courage. **—take to heart, 1,** think about earnestly. **2,** be queried about.

heart′ache″ *n.* mental anguish; sorrow or grief.

heart′break″ *n.* overwhelming sorrow or grief. **—heart′bro″ken,** *adj.*

heart′burn″ *n.* a burning sensation caused by stomach acidity.

heart′en (här′tən) *v.t.* incite with courage or good cheer; encourage.

heart′felt″ *adj.* felt deeply; sincere.

hearth (härth) *n.* **1,** a place where a fire is built; a section of floor in front of an open fire. **2,** the home or domestic circle; the fireside.

hearth′stone″ *n.* a stone or one of the stones forming a fireplace.

heart′land″ *n.* a region of special importance.

heart′less *adj.* unfeeling; cruel. **—heart′-less·ness,** *n.*

heart-′rend″ing *adj.* causing extreme grief or pity; harrowing.

heart′sick *adj.* unhappy; grieving. Also, **heart′sore″. —heart′sick″ness, heart′-sore″ness,** *n.*

heart′strings″ *n.pl.* the deepest feelings.

heart′throb″ *n.* **1,** a deep emotion or something that arouses it. **2,** sweetheart.

heart-′to-heart′ *adj.* confidential; unreservedly revealing, as a talk.

heart′y (här′tē) *adj.* **1,** friendly; cordial; affectionate. **2,** vigorous; enthusiastic; zealous. **3,** large; substantial. —*n.* a robust or brave person. **—heart′i·ness,** *n.*

heat (hēt) *n.* **1,** the condition, caused by friction, expenditure of energy, etc., that induces the sensation one feels when exposed to fire and causes substances to expand; the sensation, effect, etc., of being hot. **2,** high temperature; a hot condition, as of the atmosphere. **3,** passionate feeling; rage, vehemence, excitement, etc. **4,** the mating period of a female animal. **5,** one division of an athletic contest; one heating of metal in a furnace, etc. **6,** (*Slang*) the police or other authority. —*v.t.* **1,** make hot, hotter, or less cold. **2,** inflame with feeling. —*v.i.* **1,** become

warmer. **2,** become excited. **—heat′ed,** *adj.* excited; angry.

heat′er *n.* **1,** a device for heating. **2,** (*Slang*) a handgun.

heath (hēth) *n.* **1,** a tract of uncultivated wasteland. **2,** any of several evergreen shrubs.

hea′then (hē′thən) *n.* **1,** an irreligious person. **2,** a pagan.

---

heathen, pagan

↔ These two words both refer to people who are not Christian, Jewish, or Muslim. ↔ *Heathen* is derived from Old English *haethen,* perhaps with the idea of someone who lives on the heath, hence, someone from a wild, uncivilized area.

---

heath′er (he*th*′ər) *n.* a variety of heath common in Scotland.

heave (hēv) *v.t.* **1,** lift with marked effort; raise with exertion. **2,** throw upward and outward; toss; hurl. **3,** utter laboriously or painfully. —*v.i.* **1,** be raised, thrown, or forced up; swell up; bulge out. **2,** rise and fall, as the ocean. **3,** breathe laboriously; pant. **4,** vomit. —*n.* **1,** the act of heaving; an upward thrust or movement. **2,** the surface displacement of a geological fault. **3,** (*pl.*) a respiratory disease of horses. **—heave-′ho′,** *n.* (*Informal*) ejection; rejection.

heav′en (hev′ən) *n.* **1,** the abode of God; the place or state of existence of the blessed, after death. **2,** (*cap.*) God; Providence. **3,** a state of bliss; supreme happiness or exaltation. **4,** (usually *pl.*) the visible sky; the firmament.

heav′en·ly (-lē) *adj.* **1,** blissful; sublime. **2,** pert. to heaven; in the heavens.

heav′en·ward (-wərd) *adv. & adj.* toward heaven; upward; aloft.

heav′y (hev′ē) *adj.* **1,** having much weight; hard to lift or move. **2,** of high specific gravity; dense. **3,** great volume, force, intensity, etc.; thick, coarse, broad, deep, loud, etc. **4,** serious; intense; somber; dull; ponderous; sluggish. **5,** hard to bear; hard to do. **6,** pregnant. —*n.* a villainous character in a play. **—heav′i·ness,** *n.* **—heavy hydrogen,** deuterium. **—heavy metal,** a type of loud, rhythmic rock music. **—heavy water,** water in which hydrogen atoms have been replaced by deuterium.

heav′y-du′ty *adj.* capable of withstanding great wear, strain, etc.

heav′y-hand″ed *adj.* **1,** oppressive. **2,** clumsy.

heav′y·heart″ed *adj.* sad; mournful; dejected.

heav′y·set″ *adj.* stout; stocky.

heav′y·weight″ *n.* a boxer or wrestler weighing more than 175 lbs.

heb·dom′a·dal (heb-dom′ə-dəl) *adj.* weekly.

he·bet′ic (hi-bet′ik) *adj.* pert. to or occurring during puberty; immature.

He·bra′ic (hė-brā′ik) *adj.* **1,** of or like the Hebrews; Jewish. **2,** in or pert. to Hebrew.

He′brew (hē′broo) *n.* **1,** a Semitic language; the official language of Israel. **2,** a Jew.

hec′a·tomb″ (hek′ə-tōm″) *n.* a great slaughter; a mass sacrifice.

> **hecatomb**
> ↔ From Greek *hekatombē*, hundred cows, which indicates the original victims of the sacrifice.

heck′le (hek′əl) *v.t.* harass with questions, objections, jibes, etc.

hec′tare (hek′tār) *n.* a metric measure of land, 10,000 square meters or about 2 acres. *Abbr.,* **ha.**

hec′tic (hek′tik) *adj.* **1,** turbulent; excited; impassioned. **2,** feverish; consumptive.

hect·o- (hek-tə) *pref.* hundred.

hec′to·graph″ *n.* the process of copying writings by offset from a gelatin base.

hec′tor (hek′tər) *v.t.* bully; tease; harass. —*n.* a bully.

> **hector**
> ↔ From *Hektōr*, the Trojan hero of Homer's *Iliad*; orig. applied to London toughs.

hedge (hej) *n.* a barrier or fence formed by bushes or small trees growing close together. —*v.t.* **1,** enclose by a hedge. **2,** surround; hem in; obstruct. **3,** protect (a bet) by betting on both sides. —*v.i.* **1,** avoid a decisive course; veer aside; hesitate. **2,** provide a means of retreat or escape; protect a risk by some offsetting transaction.

hedge′hog″ *n.* **1,** a small insectivorous mammal. **2,** the porcupine.

hedge′hop″ *v.i.* **[hopped″, -hop″ping]** fly an airplane dangerously near the ground.

he′don·ism (hē′də-niz-əm) *n.* the doctrine that pleasure or happiness is the highest good. —**he′don·ist,** *n.* —**he″don·is′tic,** *adj.* —**he″don·is′ti·cal·ly,** *adv.*

-he′dron (hē′drən) *suf.* denoting a solid figure with several faces.

heed (hēd) *v.t. & i.* give attention; observe; consider. —*n.* careful notice or consideration. —**heed′ful,** *adj.* —**heed′less,** *adj.* neglectful; unwary.

hee′haw″ (hē′hâ″) *n.* the bray of an ass.

heel (hēl) *n.* **1,** the back part of the foot. **2,** the part of a stocking covering the heel; the rear support of a shoe. **3,** the rear, concluding, or final part of something. **4,** a tipping motion; a canted position. **5,** (*Slang*) a low character; a cad. —*v.t.* **1,** furnish with a heel. **2,** follow on the heels of; pursue. **3,** (*Informal*) arm; equip. **4,** cause to tilt. —*v.i.* **1,** tip to one side. **2,** run; dance.

heft *v.t.* heave; try the weight of by lifting. —*n.* weight.

heft′y (hef′tė) *adj.* **1,** heavy. **2,** muscular; strong. —**heft′i·ness,** *n.*

he·gem′o·ny (hi-jem′ə-nė) *n.* leadership or predominance, esp. by one member of a confederation of states.

He·gi′ra (he-jī′rə) *n.* the flight of Mohammed from Mecca, A.D. 622.

heif′er (hef′ər) *n.* a female cow that has not produced a calf.

heigh (hā) *interj.* a cry for attention.

height (hīt) *n.* **1,** vertical distance above the ground or base; altitude; elevation. **2,** distance upward; stature. **3,** elevation of degree or condition; eminence. **4,** the state of being high; loftiness. **5,** the highest part; top; apex. **6,** the highest degree; the culminating point.

height′en (hī′tən) *v.t.* **1,** increase the height of. **2,** intensify. —*v.i.* **1,** become higher. **2,** become more intense.

Heim′lich maneuver (hīm′lik) an emergency procedure for dislodging an object on which a person is choking, named after U.S. physician Henry J. Heimlich, who devised it.

hei′nous (hā′nəs) *adj.* wicked; reprehensible. —**hei′nous·ness,** *n.*

heir (ār) *n.* **1,** one who inherits property from another; one who will inherit. **2,** successor; beneficiary. —**heir apparent,** one who must inherit, if she or he survives. —**heir presumptive,** one who will inherit unless a more eligible candidate is born.

heir′loom″ (ār′loom″) *n.* a personal possession handed down from generation to generation in a family.

heist (hīst) (*Slang*) *n.* a burglary; the property stolen. —*v.t.* steal.

held *v.* pret. & p.p. of **hold.**

hel′den·ten″or (hel′dən-ten″ər) *n.* (*Ger.*) a tenor with a powerful voice, esp.

suited for singing in Wagnerian opera. Also, **heroic tenor.**

hel′i- *pref.* helicopter.

he″li·an′thus (hē″lė-an′thəs) *n.* a sunflower.

hel·i·co- (hel-i-kō) *pref.* spiral.

hel′i·cal (hel′i-kəl) *adj.* spiral.

hel′i·con (hel′i-kon) *n.* a bass tuba.

hel′i·cop″ter (hel′ə-kop″tər) *n.* an aircraft that is given vertical lift as well as propulsion by a horizontal propeller.

> **helicopter**
> ↔ From French *hélicoptère*, a coined compound of Greek *helix*, spiral, and *pteron*, wing.

he·li·o- (hē-lė-ə) *pref.* sun.

he′li·o·graph″ *n.* a device for signaling by reflecting the rays of the sun.

he′li·o·trope″ (hē′lė-ə-trōp″) *n.* **1,** a flower-bearing plant that turns toward the sun. **2,** a pale or pinkish purple color.

hel′i·pad *n.* a landing space for a helicopter.

hel′i·port″ (hel′i-pôrt″) *n.* an airport for helicopters.

he′li·um (hē′lė-əm) *n.* an inert gaseous chemical element, no. 2, symbol He.

he′lix (hē′liks) *n.* **1,** a spiral; a spiral part. **2,** a coil; the typical curve of a screw thread.

hell (hel) *n.* **1,** the abode or state of the wicked after death. **2,** any place or state of great suffering or misery. **3,** a place of low repute.

> **hell**
> ↔ From Old English *hell*, related to *helian*, conceal; *hell* originally denoted a covered or concealed place (and thus related to *hall*).

hell′bend″er (-ben″dər) *n.* **1,** a salamander. **2,** (*Slang*) a reckless debauch.

hell′bent″ *adj.* (*Slang*) recklessly determined to have or do at all costs.

hell′cat″ *n.* a violent woman.

Hel·len′ic (he-len′ik) *adj.* **1,** Greek. **2,** pert. to Amer. college fraternities and sororities.

hell′er (-ər) *n.* a wild or dissipated person.

hell′fire″ *n.* **1,** the fire of hell. **2,** punishment; retribution.

hell′hound″ *n.* a fiend.

hell′ion (hel′yən) *n.* a troublemaking, uncontrollable person.

hell′ish (-ish) *adj.* vile; unbearable. —**hell′ish·ness,** *n.*

hel·lo′ (he-lō′) *interj.* **1,** a greeting; a conventional salutation in telephoning. **2,** an exclamation of surprise.

helm *n.* **1,** the tiller or wheel controlling the rudder of a ship. **2,** the place or post of control.

hel′met (hel′mit) *n.* a protective covering for the head; any of various types of metal hats.

helms′man (helmz′mən) *n.* [*pl.* **-men**] a pilot.

hel′ot (hel′ət) *n.* a serf or slave.

help *v.t.* **1,** give aid to; assist in doing or attaining. **2,** bring relief to; succor; save. **3,** mitigate; relieve. **4,** repair; remedy. **5,** serve or distribute food (to). —*v.t.* give aid; be of service. —*n.* **1,** the act of helping; aid; relief; remedy. **2,** someone or something that helps; an assistant; servants, esp. domestic; a remedy. —**help′er,** *n.* an assistant. —**help′ful,** *adj.* useful. —**help′ing,** *n.* a portion of food served to a person at one time. —**help′less,** *adj.* entirely ineffective or dependent; unable to move or perform.

help′mate″ *n.* **1,** a spouse. **2,** a companion. Also, **help′meet″.**

> **helpmate, helpmeet**
> ↔ The original word is *helpmeet*, which resulted from a misreading of a Biblical passage from Genesis describing Eve as "an help meet for him," i.e., for Adam. This meant a help suitable for him, but came to be regarded as a single word; *helpmate* is a variant of the word under the influence of *mate*.

hel′ter-skel′ter (hel′tər-skel′tər) *adj.* & *adv.* with confused haste or commotion; in a disorderly hurry. —*n.* confused action; bustle.

helve (helv) *n.* the handle of an ax.

hem *n.* **1,** a fold on the edge of a cloth, sewed down to prevent raveling. **2,** an edge, rim, or border. —*v.t.* [**hemmed, hem′ming**] **1,** form a hem on. **2,** (often with *in*) enclose; limit. —*v.i.* clear the throat. —*interj.* a clearing of the throat; a mild exclamation to attract attention. —**hem and haw,** hesitate in speaking.

he-′man″ (hē′-man″) *n.* (*Informal*) a muscular, virile man.

he·ma·to- (hē-mə-tō) *pref.* hemo-.

he″ma·tol′o·gy (hē″mə-tol′ə-jė) *n.* a branch of biology dealing with the blood.

hem·i- (hem-ə) *pref.* half.

hem′i·sphere″ (hem′ə-sfir″) *n.* half of a sphere, esp. of the terrestrial globe or celestial sphere: the No. and So. hemispheres are regarded as divided by the equator, the W. and E. hemispheres by the Atlantic and Pacific oceans. **—hem″i·spher′i·cal** (-sfer′ə-kəl) *adj.*

hem′lock (hem′lok) *n.* **1,** an herb from which is obtained a powerful sedative. **2,** an evergreen tree of the spruce family.

he·mo- (hē-mə) *pref.* blood.

he′mo·glo″bin (hē′mə-glō″bin) *n.* the coloring matter of the red blood corpuscles.

he″mo·phil′i·a (hē″mə-fil′ē-ə) *n.* an affliction in which the blood does not coagulate readily. **—he″mo·phil′i·ac,** *n.* one so afflicted.

hem′or·rhage (hem′ə-rij) *n.* a discharge of blood from a ruptured blood vessel; hence, a substantial loss, as of assets, etc.

hem′or·rhoid″ (hem′ə-roid″) *n.* a swelling of a vein in the rectum; a pile.

he′mo·stat″ (hē′mə-stat″) *n.* an instrument for checking hemorrhage.

hemp *n.* any of various fibrous shrubs, used for cordage, fabrics, and narcotic drugs. **—hemp′en,** *adj.*

---

hemp, cannabis, canvas
↔ All three words probably come from a common source word for hemp (from which canvas was once made); the exact source is uncertain.

---

hem′stitch″ *n.* a hem joined where threads have been pulled to make a decorative pattern.

hen *n.* **1,** a female fowl, esp. a chicken. **2,** a censorious married woman.

hence (hens) *adv.* **1,** as a consequence; for this reason; therefore. **2,** from this time; in the future. **3,** from this place. **4,** from this source or origin.

hence″forth′ *adv.* from this time onward.

hench′man (hench′mən) *n.* [*pl.* **-men**] an attendant or follower; sidekick.

hen′na (hen′ə) *n.* an Asiatic shrub; a reddish-brown dye made from it. **—v.t.** dye (esp. hair) with henna.

hen′ner·y (-ə-rē) *n.* a henhouse.

hen′peck″ (hen′pek″) *v.t.* domineer over (said of a wife who thus rules her husband).

hen′ry (hen′rē) *n.* a unit of inductance, named for 19th-c. U.S. physicist Joseph Henry.

hep *adj.* (*Slang*) well-informed; being one of the elect. **—hep′cat″,** *n.* (*Slang, Archaic*) a jazz enthusiast. ❑ *hip*

he·pat′ic (hi-pat′ik) *adj.* pert. to the liver.

hep″a·ti′tis (hep″ə-tī′tis) *n.* inflammation of the liver.

hep·ta- (hep-tə) *pref.* seven.

hep·tath′lon *n.* a women's Olympic competition comprising seven track and field events.

her (hēr) *pron.* obj. and poss. case of *she.* ❑ *he*

her′ald (her′əld) *n.* **1,** an announcer; crier; publisher. **2,** one who proclaims in advance; forerunner; harbinger. **3,** a messenger. **4,** one who regulates the use of armorial bearings. **—v.t.** give tidings of; announce. **—he·ral′dic** (he-ral′dik) *adj.* **—her′ald·ry** (-rē) *n.* the art and science of armorial bearings.

herb (ērb, hērb) *n.* **1,** a plant whose stem does not become woody. **2,** such a plant used for medicine, flavoring, etc. **—her·ba′ceous** (hēr-bā′shəs) *adj.* **—herb′age,** *n.* herbs collectively or growing together. **—herb′al,** *adj.* **—herb′al·ist,** *n.* a collector or student of herbs.

her·bar′i·um (hēr-bār′ē-əm) *n.* **1,** a collection of dried plants, arranged systematically. **2,** a place where such a collection is kept.

her′bi·cide (hēr′bə-sīd) *n.* plant or weed killer.

her·biv′o·rous (hēr-biv′ə-rəs) *adj.* feeding on plants only. **—her′bi·vore″** (hēr′bi-vôr″) *n.*

her·cu′le·an (hēr-kū′lē-ən) *adj.* having or requiring prodigious strength, endurance, etc.

---

herculean
↔ After the Greek demigod *Hercules*, son of Zeus, who possessed superhuman strength.

---

herd (hērd) *n.* **1,** a number of animals together. **2,** a mob; rabble. **3,** [also, **herd′er**] one who tends a herd. **—v.t.** drive together; tend or lead. **—v.i.** go together; unite.

herds′man (hērds′mən) *n.* [*pl.* **-men**] one who tends a herd of animals.

here (hir) *adv.* **1,** in or toward this place. **2,** at this time or juncture. **—interj. 1,** I am present. **2,** come here! ❑ *there*

here′a·bout″ *adv.* about or near this place. Also, **here′a·bouts″**

here·af′ter *adv.* **1,** in the future. **2,** beyond this place or juncture. **—n.** future time, esp. after death.

here′by″ *adv.* by this means or agency; as a result of this.

---

he·red′i·tar·y (hi-red′ə-tār-ē) *adj.* **1,** passing naturally from parent to offspring; descending by inheritance. **2,** pert. to heredity.

he·red′i·ty (hə-red′ə-tē) *n.* the transmission of qualities or characteristics from parents to offspring.

here·in′ *adv.* **1,** in this place. **2,** in view of this.

here·of′ *adv.* of or concerning this.

her′e·sy (her′ə-sē) *n.* an unorthodox doctrine or opinion, esp. in religion.

her′e·tic (her′ə-tik) *n.* one who holds an unorthodox opinion. —*adj.* of such opinion. —**he·ret′i·cal** (hə-ret′i-kəl) *adj.*

here·to′ *adv.* to this.

here″to·fore′ *adv.* before this time.

here′up·on″ *adv.* at or immediately following this time or event.

her′it·a·ble (her′ə-tə-bəl) *adj.* capable of being inherited. —**her″it·a·bil′i·ty,** *n.*

her′it·age (her′ə-tij) *n.* **1,** something inherited. **2,** a condition, lot, or portion acquired by being born.

---

heritage, inheritance
☛ Both words refer to something handed down. *Heritage* is most often used in relation to tradition or birthright, which can be personal or national. *Inheritance* is more often used to refer to possessions to be passed on through the estate of a deceased person.

---

her·maph′ro·dite″ (hēr-maf′rə-dīt″) *n.* an animal or plant having both male and female organs of generation. —**her·maph″ro·dit′ic** (-dit′ik) *adj.*

---

hermaphrodite, hermetic
↔ *Hermaphrodite* is a compound of Greek *Hermes*, messenger of the gods, and *Aphrodite*, the goddess of love. Their son, *Hermaphroditos*, achieved his longed-for union with the nymph Salmacis, producing a demigod with dual sexual characteristics. *Hermetic* is derived from *Hermes Trismegistus*, supposed ancient author of various mystical writings.

---

her·met′ic (hēr-met′ik) *adj.* **1,** made airtight by sealing, as a container. **2,** mystic; isolated. —**her·met′i·cal·ly,** *adv.* ❏ *hermaphrodite*

her′mit (hēr′mit) *n.* one who lives alone and avoids the society of others; a recluse. —**her′mit·age,** *n.* the dwelling of a hermit.

her′ni·a (hēr′nē-ə) *n.* the protrusion of a bodily organ or tissue through its surrounding walls, esp. abdominal; a rupture. —**her′ni·ate** (-āt) *v.i.* rupture.

he′ro (hir′ō) *n.* **1,** a person, usually a man, admired for courage, fortitude, prowess, nobility, etc. **2,** the principal male character in a play, story, or poem. **3,** a submarine sandwich.

---

hero, heroin
↔ *Hero* comes from Greek *herōs*, person of superhuman ability. The name of the drug was coined in German from this same Greek word because of the feelings of courage and strength that the drug was supposed to inspire.

---

he·ro′ic (hi-rō′ik) *adj.* **1,** pert. to or like a hero. **2,** having recourse to extreme measures; daring; drastic. **3,** larger than lifesize (in art). —**he·ro′i·cal·ly,** *adv.*

he·ro′ics (hi-ro′iks) *n.* bombastic language; mawkish sentiment.

her′o·in (her′ō-in) *n.* a habit-forming drug, derivative of morphine. ❏ *hero*

her′o·ine (her′ō-in) *n.* **1,** a woman admired for courage, fortitude, prowess, nobility, etc. **2,** the principal female character in a play, story, or poem.

her′o·ism (her′ō-iz-əm) *n.* heroic qualities or conduct.

her′on (her′ən) *n.* a wading bird with long legs, neck, and bill.

her′pes (her′pēz) *n.* an inflammatory infection of the skin or mucous membrane. —**herpes zos′ter** (zos′tər) shingles.

her″pe·tol′o·gy (hēr″pə-tol′ə-jē) *n.* the branch of zoology dealing with reptiles and amphibians. —**her″pe·tol′o·gist,** *n.*

her′ring (her′ing) *n.* any of numerous small food fishes.

her′ring·bone″ (her′ing-bōn″) *n. & adj.* a pattern of oblique parallel lines in tiers alternating in direction.

hers (hērz) *pron.* poss. case of *she* used predicatively.

her·self′ (hēr-self′) *pron.* emphatic and reflexive form of *her.*

hertz (herts) *n.* [*pl.* **hertz**] a unit equaling one cycle (of a periodic process) per second, named for 20th-c. Nobel Prize-winning German physicist Heinrich Rudolf Hertz. *Abbr.,* **Hz.**

hes′i·tan·cy (hez′i-tən-sē) *n.* hesitation.

hes′i·tant (hez′i-tənt) *adj.* hesitating or prone to hesitate; irresolute.

hes′i·tate″ (hez′i-tāt″) *v.i.* **1,** hold back in doubt or indecision. **2,** falter in speech; stammer. **3,** pause. —**hes″i·ta′tion,** *n.*

Hes′sian (hesh′ən) *n.* a person of Hesse

(in Germany), esp. a soldier who fought against the colonial forces in the Revolutionary War.

het′er·o (het′ə-rō) *n.* (*Informal*) a heterosexual person.

het·er·o- (het-ər-ə) *pref.* different; other.

het′er·o·dox″ (het′ər-ə-doks″) *adj.* not orthodox; heretical. —**het′er·o·dox″y,** *n.*

het″er·o·ge′ne·ous (het″ər-ə-jē′nė-əs) *adj.* **1,** different in kind; widely dissimilar. **2,** composed of parts of different kinds; not homogeneous. —**het″er·o·ge′ne·ous·ness,** *n.*

het′er·o·sex′u·al (het″ər-ə-sek′shoo-əl) *adj.* **1,** pert. to different sexes. **2,** manifesting sexual desire toward a member of the opposite sex. —*n.* a heterosexual person. —**het″er·o·sex″u·al′i·ty,** *n.*

heu·ris′tic (hyû-ris′tik) *adj.* serving to demonstrate or reveal the truth. —**heu·ris′tic·al·ly,** *adv.*

hew (hū) *v.t. & i.* [*p.p.* **hewed** or **hewn**] **1,** cut with an ax, sword, etc.; chop. **2,** carve.

hex (heks) *v.t.* practice witchcraft on. —*n.* **1,** a spell. **2,** hexadecimal.

hex·a- (hek-sə) *pref.* six; sixfold.

hex″a·chlor′o·phene (heks″ə-klôr′ə-fēn) *n.* an antibacterial agent used esp. in soaps.

hex″a·dec′i·mal (hek″sə-des′ə-məl) *adj.* pert. to a numbering system of base 16, usu. employing the numerals 0 through 9 plus the letters A through F.

hex′a·gon″ (heks′ə-gon″) *n.* a plane figure having six sides. —**hex·ag′o·nal** (heks-ag′ə-nəl) *adj.*

hex′a·gram (heks′ə-gram) *n.* **1,** a six-pointed star; Mogen David. **2,** a six-sided figure.

hey (hā) *interj.* to draw attention.

hey′day″ (hā′dā″) *n.* highest vigor; full strength; acme.

> **heyday**
> ↔ From an exclamation of joy, *heyda,* on the model of *lackaday.*

hi·a′tus (hī-ā′təs) *n.* a space where something is missing; a gap; break.

hi·ba′chi (hi-bä′chė) *n.* a small charcoal-burning brazier.

hi·ber′nal (hī-bĕr′nəl) *adj.* pert. to winter.

hi′ber·nate″ (hī′bər-nāt″) *v.i.* pass the winter in seclusion and in a torpid condition, as do some animals. —**hi″ber·na′-tion,** *n.*

Hi·ber′ni·an (hī-bĕr′nė-ən) *adj.* Irish. —*n.* a native of Ireland.

hi·bis′cus (hī-bis′kəs) *n.* a shrub having large, showy flowers.

hic′cup (hik′up) *n.* **1,** a spasmodic, involuntary, audible cutting-off of indrawn breath. **2,** (*pl.*) such spasms. —*v.i.* have the hiccups. Also, **hic′cough** (hik′up).

hic′ ja′cet (hik yok′et) (*Lat.*) here lies (often the opening words on a tombstone).

hick (hik) *n.* (*Slang*) a person unfamiliar with city ways; a rustic. —*adj.* countrified.

hick′ey (hik′ė) *n.* **1,** an electronic fitting. **2,** (*Slang*) a mark on the skin caused by kissing.

hick′o·ry (hik′ə-rė) *n.* a No. Amer. tree or its tough, springy wood.

hi·dal′go (hi-dal′gō) *n.* a Spanish man of the lower nobility.

hide (hīd) *v.t.* [**hid** (hid), **hid′den** (hid′ən) or **hid, hid′ing** (hī′ding)] prevent from being discovered; secrete. —*v.i.* keep out of view. —*n.* **1,** the skin of an animal, raw or dressed. **2,** (*Slang*) the human skin.

Hide-′A-Bed″ (hīd′ə-bed″) *n.* (*T.N.*) a convertible sofa.

hide′a·way″ *n.* a hiding place; retreat.

hide′bound″ (hīd′bownd″) *adj.* narrow and stubborn in opinion.

hid′e·ous (hid′ė-əs) *adj.* frightful in appearance or character. —**hid′e·ous·ness,** *n.*

hide-′out″ *n.* a secret lodging; retreat.

hid′ing (hī′ding) *n.* **1,** the state of being hidden. **2,** (*Informal*) a thrashing.

hie (hī) *v.i.* go in haste.

hi·er-, hi·er·o- *pref.* sacred.

hi′er·arch″ (hī′ə-rärk″) *n.* one of authority in sacred matters. —**hi″er·ar′chal** (-əl) *adj.*

hi′er·ar″chy (hī′ə-rär″kė) *n.* **1,** a body of persons organized by rank, in church or government. **2,** a series of terms of different rank. —**hi″er·ar′chic, hi″er·ar′chi·cal,** *adj.*

> **hierarchy**
> ↔ From Greek *hieros,* holy, and *arkhēs,* ruling; the word originally referred to the power of the ruling high priest and gradually acquired its more generalized meaning.

hi″er·at′ic (hī″ə-rat′ik) *adj.* **1,** priestly. **2,** pert. to styles of art highly influenced by religion.

hi″er·o·glyph′ic (hī″ər-ə-glif′ik) *adj.* **1,** pert. to a system of writing by conventionalized pictures, esp. ancient Egyptian. **2,** hard to decipher. —*n.* a hieroglyphic symbol.

hi″er·o·phant′ (hī″ər-ə-fant′) *n.* interpreter of sacred mysteries or esoteric principles.

hig'gle·dy-pig'gle·dy (hig'əl-dĕ-pig'əl-dĕ) *adj. & adv.* in disorder or confusion; topsy-turvy. —*n.* a jumble; confusion.

high (hī) *adj.* **1,** rising far above, or situated above, the ground or a base. **2,** elevated in rank, etc. **3,** expensive. **4,** intensified; large in measure or amount. **5,** (of meat) slightly tainted. **6,** in the upper range of sounds; shrill. **7,** (*Informal*) under the influence of alcohol or drugs; tipsy. —*adv.* at a high place or level; to a high degree. —*n.* **1,** something that is high or highest. **2,** the automobile gear giving greatest forward speed. **3,** an area of high atmospheric pressure. **4,** (*Slang*) the effects of a stimulant or psychedelic drug; a trip. —**high fidelity,** the reproduction of audio signals through their full frequency range with a minimum of distortion. —**high five,** a mode of greeting by slapping of upraised hands signifying greeting, triumph, etc. —**high school,** the ninth or tenth to twelfth grades. —**high sea,** the open ocean. —**high time,** (*Informal*) almost too late.

> **high, highly (low, lowly)**
> *High* refers to physical location; *highly* is used figuratively to refer to relative rank, station, quality, etc. *Low* and *lowly* are used similarly.

high'ball" *n.* **1,** a drink of whiskey diluted with water, seltzer, etc. **2,** a railroad signal used to show a clear track. —*v.i.* (*Informal*) go ahead rapidly.

high'bind"er (-bīn"dər) *n.* **1,** a paid criminal, esp. Chinese. **2,** a swindler.

high'boy" *n.* a tall chest of drawers.

high'brow" *n.* (*Informal*) a person of intellectual tastes. —*adj.* intellectual; abstruse.

high"fa·lu'tin (hī"fə-loo'tən) *adj.* (*Informal*) pretentious.

high-'flown" *adj.* extravagant; bombastic; (esp. of language) fancy.

high'fly"er *n.* one extravagant in aims or pretensions.

high-'hand'ed *adj.* overbearing; arbitrary. —**high-'hand'ed·ness,** *n.*

high-'hat" *adj.* (*Slang*) snobbish. —*v.t.* treat condescendingly. —*n.* a percussion instrument formed of two cymbals operated by a pedal.

high' jinks" (hī' jinks") *n.pl.* (*Informal*) boisterous fun. Also, **hi'jinks".**

high'land" (-lənd) *n.* (often *pl.*) & *adj.* a mountainous region.

high'light" *n.* **1,** the point of most intense light. **2,** a conspicuous part or event. —*v.t.* **1,** emphasize. **2,** (*Art*) put highlight on. **3,** (*Computers*) to select a portion of a document, etc. —**high'light"er,** a marker containing a semitransparent color, used to mark text for emphasis.

high'ly (hī'lē) *adv.* **1,** in or to a great degree. **2,** favorably. **3,** in a high place or position. ❑ *high*

high-"mind'ed *adj.* **1,** having exalted principles or motives. **2,** arrogantly proud. —**high-"mind'ed·ness,** *n.*

high-'muck-'a-muck" (hī'muk'ə-muk") *n.* an important or high-ranking person, esp. when pompous.

high'ness (-nəs) *n.* **1,** the state of being high. **2,** (*cap.*) a title of address to royal persons.

high-'rise" *adj. & n.* (pert. to) a building with many stories.

high'road" *n.* **1,** a main road. **2,** any public route. **3,** an easy course.

high-'sound"ing *adj.* pretentious and imposing when read or spoken.

high'strung" *adj.* nervous; tense.

high'tail" *v.i.* (*Slang*) (often with *it*) escape in a great hurry.

high-'tech" (-tek") *adj.* technologically advanced or innovative.

high-'ten"sion *adj.* in electricity, involving high potential, usu. 1,000 volts or more.

high-'test" *adj.* of gasoline, etc., having a relatively low boiling point and a high octane rating.

high'toned" (-tōnd") *adj.* **1,** high in pitch. **2,** (*Informal*) stylish.

high'way" *n.* **1,** a main road. **2,** any public route, on land or water.

high'way·man (-mən) *n.* [*pl.* -men] a robber.

hi'jack" (hī'jak") *v.t.* (*Slang*) steal (contraband in transit).

hike (hīk) *v.i.* **1,** walk afield, for pleasure or training. **2,** (*Informal*) leave; walk away. **3,** raise with a jerk. **4,** increase. —*n.* **1,** a walking trip; a march. **2,** (*Informal*) an increase, as in prices.

hi·lar'i·ous (hi-lār'ē-əs) *adj.* **1,** merry; exhilarated. **2,** causing great mirth. —**hi·lar'-i·ty** (hi-lar'ə-tē) *n.*

hill (hil) *n.* **1,** a natural elevation of land. **2,** an artificial mound. —*v.t.* form into hills, as corn.

hill'bill"y (often *derog.*) *n.* a backwoods mountaineer. —*adj.* (esp. of music) in the style of mountain folk song.

hill'ock (hil'ək) *n.* a small hill.

hill'side" *n.* the side of a hill; sloping ground.

hill'y (-ė) *adj.* **1,** abounding in hills. **2,** steep. —**hill'i·ness,** *n.*

hilt *n.* the handle of a weapon, esp. of a sword or dagger.

him *pron.* objective case of *he.*

him·self' *pron.* emphatic form of *him*; reflexive form of *he.*

hind (hīnd) *adj.* [*superl.* **hind'most"** or **hind'er·most"** (hīn'dər-)] situated at the back; posterior. —*n.* a female deer.

hin'der (hin'dər) *v.t. & i.* prevent from acting or proceeding; impede.

hind'quar"ter *n.* **1,** the hind leg and loin of an animal, cut for meat. **2,** (*pl.*) the rump of an animal.

hin'drance (hin'drəns) *n.* **1,** act of hindering; a stopping or checking. **2,** an obstacle.

hind'sight" *n.* judgment of what should have been done, after the result is known.

Hin'du (hin'doo) *n. & adj.* East Indian, in language and religion (Brahman). —**Hin'du·ism,** *n.*

hinge (hinj) *n.* **1,** a joint that permits movement, as for a door. **2,** a similar anatomical joint, as the knee. **3,** that on which something turns or depends; a controlling principle. —*v.i. & t.* **1,** turn or depend (on). **2,** attach by a hinge.

hin'ny (hin'ė) *n.* **1,** a neigh. **2,** the offspring of a female donkey and a male horse.

hint *n.* a covert suggestion or implication; an indirect allusion. —*v.t. & i.* intimate; imply.

hin'ter·land" (hin'tər-land") *n.* **1,** territory lying back of a coastal region. **2,** a remote region.

hip *n.* **1,** the projecting, fleshy part of the body around the pelvis; the haunch. **2,** the hip joint. **3,** the fruit of a rose. —*adj.* (*Slang*) informed. —*interj.* a sound used in cheering.

---

hip, hep, hippie
↔ The noun *hippie* (and the adjective *hip*) come from the adjective *hep*, whose origin is uncertain. The rose fruit comes from Old English *heope.*

---

hip-'hop" *n.* a street culture combining rap music, break-dancing, graffiti, etc.

hip'hug"gers *n.* tight pants.

hipped (hipt) *adj.* (*Slang*) having an obsession.

hip'pie (hip'ė) *n.* a nonconformist person, usu. one who rejects conventional so-

cial behavior and dress, and often a user of drugs. Also, **hip'py.** ❑ *hip*

hip'po (hip'ō) *n.* (*Informal*) hippopotamus.

Hip"po·crat'ic oath (hip"ə-krat'ik) an oath embodying the obligations of a physician.

Hippocratic oath
↔ After its formulator, Greek physician *Hippocrates.*

---

hip'po·drome" (hip'ə-drōm") *n.* an arena for spectacular exhibitions, esp. involving horses.

hip"po·pot'a·mus (hip"ə-pot'ə-məs) *n.* a large Afr. herbivorous pachydermatous mammal that frequents rivers and lakes.

---

hippopotamus
↔ Literally, river horse, from Greek *hippos*, horse, and *potamos*, river.

---

hip'ster (hip'stər) *n.* (*Slang*) one who is up-to-date in attitudes and taste.

hir'cine (hėr'sīn) *adj.* goatlike, esp. in odor.

hire (hīr) *v.t.* **1,** engage the services or use of, for pay; employ; rent. **2,** (sometimes with *out*) grant the services or use of, for pay. —*v.i.* (with *out*) lend one's services for pay. —*n.* **1,** wages; rental. **2,** the act of hiring or being hired. **3,** a hired person, esp. a replacement worker; scab. —**hire'ling,** *n.* one serving only for pay.

hir·sute' (hėr-soot') *adj.* hairy. —**hir·sute'ness,** *n.*

his (hiz) *pron. poss.* form of *he.*

His·pan'ic (his-pan'ik) *adj.* **1,** Spanish. **2,** Latin American.

hiss (his) *v.t. & i.* **1,** make a sound like that of the letter *s* prolonged. **2,** express disapproval by making this sound. —*n.* such a sound.

hist *interj.* **1,** listen! **2,** silence!

his'ta·mine" (his'tə-mēn") *n.* an organic ammonia compound released by the body tissues in certain reactions, as of the common cold.

his·to- (his-tə) *pref.* tissue.

his'to·gram" (his'tə-gram") *n.* a graph in the form of rectangles of equal width and varying lengths.

his·tol'o·gy (his-tol'ə-jė) *n.* the science that treats of organic tissues. —**his"to·log'i·cal,** *adj.*

his·to'ri·an (his-tôr'ė-ən) *n.* a writer of, or an authority on, history.

his·tor'ic (his-tôr'ik) *adj.* **1,** in or pert. to history. **2,** important in history. Also, **his·tor'i·cal.**

---

historic, historical
☛ Although both words can mean the same thing, *historic* is more often used to mean significant in history.

his″to·ric′i·ty (his″tə-ris′ə-tē) *n.* historical authenticity.

his·to″ri·og′ra·phy (hi-stôr″ē-og′rə-fē) *n.* the method of historical study. **—his·to″ri·og′ra·pher,** *n.*

his′to·ry (his′tə-rē) *n.* **1,** the branch of knowledge concerned with ascertaining and recording past events. **2,** an oral or written narrative of past events. **3,** a systematic description of natural phenomena.

his″tri·on′ic (his″trē-on′ik) *adj.* **1,** pert. to actors or acting. **2,** pretended; artificial; affected. **—his″tri·on′i·cal·ly,** *adv.*

his″tri·on′ics (-iks) *n.pl.* **1,** theatricals. **2,** artificial speech or manner.

hit *v.t. & i.* **[hit, hit′ting] 1,** deal a blow to; strike; collide with. **2,** reach, as with a missile. **3,** move by a stroke. **4,** assail in speech. **5,** meet with; find; (with *on*) discover. **6,** agree with; suit. **7,** (*Slang*) kill. **8,** (*Slang*) burglarize. **—n. 1,** a blow, impact, or collision. **2,** (*Baseball*) a safely batted ball. **3,** (*Informal*) a successful performance or enterprise. **4,** a dose of a narcotic drug. **5,** (*Slang*) a killing, esp. one carried out by professional assassins. **6,** (*Computers*) a successful match in data retrieval. **—hit′ter,** *n.* **—hit-′and-run′,** *adj.* **1,** pert. to an automobile accident, usu. involving personal injury, in which the driver leaves the scene of the accident. **2,** (*Baseball*) a play in which the runner starts for the next base when the pitcher releases the ball and the batter must try to hit the ball. **—hit man,** a paid assassin.

hitch (hich) *v.t.* **1,** fasten as with a rope, esp. temporarily; tether. **2,** pull up; raise by jerks. **—v.i. 1,** be fastened, entangled. **2,** move jerkily. **3,** (*Informal*) work smoothly together; agree. **4,** (*Informal*) hitchhike. **—n. 1,** a joining or making fast. **2,** a device for attaching one thing to another, as a trailer to an automobile. **3,** a knot. **4,** a temporary stoppage or obstruction. **5,** a jerk; a limping gait. **6,** (*Informal*) a task; working period; prison sentence. **—hitch a ride,** hitchhike.

hitch′hike″ (hich′hīk″) *v.i.* travel by begging rides in strangers' automobiles.

hith′er (hith′ər) *adv.* to this place. **—adj.** on the nearer side. **—hith″er·to′,** *adv.* up to this time.

HIV *abbr.* human immunodeficiency virus, a frequent cause of AIDS.

hive (hīv) *n.* **1,** a swarm of bees; any shelter they inhabit. **2,** a roomful of busy people. **—v.i.** enter a hive.

hives (hīvz) *n.* an eruptive skin disease.

ho (hō) *interj.* to call attention, express surprise, amusement, etc.

hoa′gy (hō′gē) *n.* a submarine sandwich. Also, **hoa′gie.**

hoar (hôr) *adj.* **1,** white or gray, as frost. **2,** gray-haired with age. **—hoar′frost″,** *n.* frozen dew. **—hoar′y,** *adj.*

hoard (hôrd) *n.* a stock or store laid by for preservation or future use. **—v.t. & i.** **1,** amass; save. **2,** store up beyond one's own needs.

hoard, horde
☛ Do not confuse *hoard*, a stock of supplies, with *horde*, a flock.

hoarse (hôrs) *adj.* **1,** deep and harsh to the ear; raucous. **2,** having a husky voice. **—hoars′en,** *v.t. & i.* render or become hoarse. **—hoarse′ness,** *n.*

hoax (hōks) *n.* a mischievous deception; a practical joke. **—v.t.** deceive.

hob *n.* **1,** a shelf or projection in a fireplace. **2,** a stick used as a target. **3,** (*Informal*) mischief.

hob′ble (hob′əl) *v.i.* limp; proceed haltingly. **—v.t. 1,** fetter by tying the legs together. **2,** impede in any way. **—n. 1,** a limping gait. **2,** a rope used to tie the legs of an animal. **—hob′bling,** *adj.* limping. **—hobble skirt,** a skirt with a band near the ankles.

hob″ble·de·hoy′ (hob″əl-dē-hoi′) *n.* a clumsy or awkward youth.

hob′by (hob′ē) *n.* **1,** an occupation pursued for recreation. **2,** a stick or rocking vehicle with a horse's head, for children: *hobbyhorse.*

hobby
↔ A shortening of *hobbyhorse*, a figure of a horse used in the Morris dance. The *hobby* part probably comes from a pet form of *Robert* or *Robin*.

hob′gob″lin *n.* **1,** a mischievous imp. **2,** something that arouses fear.

hob′nail″ *n.* a large-headed nail protecting the sole of a heavy shoe.

hob′nob″ *v.i.* **[-nobbed″, -nob″bing]** associate constantly.

hobnob
↔ From the phrase *hab or nab*, to have or have not. How it achieved its present sense is uncertain.

ho′bo (hō′bō) *n.* [*pl.* **-boes**] **1,** a tramp;
vagrant. **2,** a migrant worker.

Hob′son's choice (hob′sən) a choice of
what is offered or nothing, i.e., a choice
offering no real alternative.

Hobson's choice

↔ In honor of a certain Englishman,
Thomas *Hobson*, who rented horses,
offering his clients only the horse
nearest the stable door.

---

hock (hok) *n.* **1,** a protruding joint in the
hind leg of a horse. **2,** a white Rhine wine.
—*v.t.* **1,** hamstring. **2,** (*Informal*) pawn.

hock′ey (hok′ē) *n.* a game played with a
puck and curved sticks, either on the
ground or on ice.

---

hockey

↔ Although its exact origin is uncertain, the word probably is related to
hook, in reference to the curved stick.

---

hock′shop″ *n.* (*Informal*) pawnshop.

ho′cus (hō′kəs) *v.t.* deceive by trickery.

ho′cus-po′cus (hō′kəs-pō′kəs) *n.* **1,** a
jocular incantation uttered by a conjurer.
2, a conjurer's trick; deception. —*v.t.* &
i. deceive.

hod *n.* **1,** a trough fixed on a long handle,
for carrying bricks or mortar. **2,** a coal
scuttle.

hodge′podge″ (hoj′poj″) *n.* an indiscriminate mixture; a jumble.

hoe (hō) *n.* a blade fixed on a long handle, for cultivating earth, cutting weeds,
etc. —*v.t. & i.* use a hoe (on).

hoe′cake″ *n.* a baked cornmeal cake.

hoe′down″ (hō′-) *n.* a square dance.

hog *n.* **1,** a pig, sow, or boar; a swine. **2,**
a domesticated swine fattened for market.
3, (*Informal*) a greedy or filthy person. **4,**
(*Slang*) a large motorcycle.—*v.t.* [**hogged,
hog′ging**] (*Slang*) take more than one's
share of. —**hog′gish,** *adj.*

ho′gan (hō′gan) *n.* a Navajo Indian hut.

hog′back″ *adj.* curved so as to be highest
at the middle.

hogs′head″ (hogz′hed″) *n.* **1,** a large barrel or cask. **2,** a unit of capacity.

hog′tie″ *v.t.* tie with all four feet together; hence, impede the movements or
actions of.

hog′wash″ *n.* **1,** swill given to hogs. **2,**
(*Informal*) trash; nonsense.

hog′wild′ *adj.* (*Slang*) berserk.

hoi pol·loi′ (hoi″ pə-loi′) (*Gr.*) the common people.

hoist *v.t.* raise or lift, esp. by machinery.

—*n.* **1,** a contrivance for lifting, as an elevator. **2,** a lift or boost.

hoi′ty-toi′ty (hoi′tē-toi′tē) *adj.* **1,** giddy.
2, haughty; pretentious.

ho′key (hō′kē) *adj.* **1,** excessively sentimental. **2,** phony.

ho′kum (hō′kəm) *n.* (*Slang*) **1,** nonsense;
buncombe. **2,** stereotyped humor.

hold (hōld) *v.t.* [*pret.* & *p.p.* **held**] **1,** keep
fast, as in grasp of the hand; retain; cling
to. **2,** keep back; withhold; restrain. **3,**
have in possession; own; occupy. **4,** engage in; pursue; sustain. **5,** contain; have
the capacity of. **6,** entertain in the mind;
maintain. **7,** rule legally. **8,** (with *up*) rob.
—*v.i.* **1,** maintain a grasp; adhere; cling.
2, (often with *out*) maintain a position or
condition. **3,** cease or pause; refrain. —*n.*
1, the act of holding fast; grasp; grip. **2,**
[also, **hold′er**] a part by which something
is held, as a handle. **3,** something that fixes
in place, supports, controls, or dominates.
4, a place of security or confinement. **5,**
the cargo space in a ship. **6,** (*Music*) a fer-
mata. —**hold′ing,** *n.* property owned, esp.
real estate or stocks. —**hold down, 1,**
curb; check. **2,** (*Slang*) retain (a job, etc.).
—**hold forth,** preach; harangue. —**holding
pattern,** a pattern of movement (usu. circular) in which aircraft are required to remain until given permission to land.
—**hold over, 1,** postpone. **2,** keep in force
or action. —**holding company, 1,** a company whose chief or sole business is to
acquire the securities of other companies.
2, an operating company that owns a controlling interest in the stock of another.
—**on hold, 1,** of a party in a telephone
conversation, temporarily disconnected.
2, in a state of abeyance or suspension.

hold′o″ver *n.* a thing or condition retained from a previous time.

hold′up″ (hōld′up) *n.* a robbery under
threat of bodily injury.

hole (hōl) *n.* **1,** an opening; aperture; per-
foration. **2,** a hollow place; cavity; excavation. **3,** any place that is dark, secluded,
or dingy; a hiding place; a dungeon. **4,**
(*Golf*) the course from one tee to the corresponding hole. **5,** (*Informal*) an embarrassing predicament. **6,** (*Informal*) a flaw.
—*v.t.* put into a hole. —*v.i.* (with *up*) go
into seclusion or hiding; hibernate.
—**hole′y,** *adj.* perforated. —**hole up,** go
into hiding.

hol′i·day″ (hol′ə-dā″) *n.* **1,** a commemorative day, fixed by law or custom, on
which business is suspended. **2,** a vacation.
—*adj.* festive; pert. to a holiday.

ho′lism (hō′liz-əm) *n.* **1,** (*Philos.*) the

---

fat, fāte, fär, fâre, fåll, åsk; met, hē, hêr, maybė; pin, pīne; not, nōte, ôr, tool theory that in nature organisms exist as whole entities which are more than the sum of their parts. **2,** (*Med.*) treatment of all the aspects of a patient's health. **—ho·lis′tic,** *adj.*

> **holism**
> ↔ Coined by South African politician Jan Christiaan *Smuts* from Greek *holos,* whole.

hol′land·aise″ sauce (hol′ən-dāz″) a sauce of egg yolks and butter seasoned with lemon or vinegar.

hol′ler (hol′ər) *v.t. & i. & n.* yell.

hol′low (hol′ō) *adj.* **1,** empty within; not solid. **2,** having a hole, cavity, or concavity; sunken, as cheeks. **3,** (of sound) low-pitched. **4,** of little worth; fruitless. **5,** insincere; false. **6,** hungry. **—n. 1,** an empty space, hole, or cavity. **2,** a valley. **—v.t.** (with *out*) make hollow. **—hol′low·ness,** *n.*

hol′low·ware″ *n.* silver serving dishes.

hol′ly (hol′ē) *n.* a shrub with glossy leaves and red berries much used for Christmas decoration.

hol′ly·hock″ (hol′ē-hok″) *n.* a tall plant bearing large flowers.

hol′mi·um (hōl′mē-əm) *n.* a rare-earth metallic element, no. 7, symbol Ho.

hol·o- (hol-ə) *pref.* whole, entire.

hol′o·caust″ (hol-′ə-kâst″) *n.* **1,** great destruction of life, esp. by fire. **2,** (usu. *cap.,* with *the*) the systematic killing of Jews in Nazi concentration camps during World War II.

> **holocaust**
> ↔ A compound of Greek *holos,* complete, and *kaustos,* burning (which produced such other words as *caustic* and *cauterize*).

hol′o·gram″ (hol′ə-gram″) *n.* an image produced on a sensitized surface by holography.

hol′o·graph″ (hol′ə-graf″) *n.* **1,** a document written in the hand of its author. **2,** a hologram. **—adj.** written in the hand of its author. **—v.** produce an image (of an object) using holography. **—hol″o·graph′ic,** *adj.*

ho·log′ra·phy (hō-log′rə-fē) *n.* a kind of three-dimensional lensless photography using lasers. **—hol″o·graph′ic,** *adj.*

hol′ster (hōl′stər) *n.* a leather case for carrying a pistol.

ho′ly (hō′lē) *adj.* **1,** sacred; declared sacred by church authority. **2,** devoted to the service of God or the church; reli-

gious. **3,** pious; devout; saintly. **—hol′i·ness,** *n.* **—holy of holies,** the innermost chamber of the Temple in Jerusalem in which the ark of the covenant was kept. **—Holy Week,** the week preceding Easter. **—Holy Communion,** Communion (def. 2). ❑ *hallow*

hom′age (hom′ij) *n.* respect or reverence; tribute.

hom′bre (om′brā) *n.* man.

hom′burg (hom′bėrg) *n.* a style of man's felt hat.

home (hōm) *n.* **1,** the house, etc., where one resides; one's native land. **2,** the burrow or retreat of an animal. **3,** the region in which something is common or native. **4,** an institution for sheltering orphans, the aged, etc. **5,** in games, the goal or principal base. **—v.i.** (with *in*) aim or be directed (toward). **—adj. 1,** domestic. **2,** to the point. **—adv. 1,** at, to, or toward home. **2,** to the point; effectively; all the way. **—hom′ey,** *adj.* (*Informal*) **—hom′ing,** *adj.* trained to return home from great distances. **—home′less,** *adj.* **—home economics,** the art or study of household management; domestic science. **—home stretch,** the final portion of a race, journey, effort, etc.

home′bod″y *n.* a person who would rather stay home than go out.

home′land″ *n.* one's native land.

home′ly (hōm′lē) *adj.* unattractive; plain. **—home′li·ness,** *n.*

home′made″ *adj.* made at home, not in a factory.

home′ma″ker *n.* one who manages a household.

ho′me·o- (hō-mē-ō) *pref.* similar.

ho″me·op′a·thy (hō″mē-op′ə-thē) *n.* treatment of disease with drugs that produce symptoms similar to those of the disease. **—ho′me·o·path″,** *n.* **—ho″me·o·path′ic,** *adj.* **—ho″me·o·path′i·cal·ly,** *adv.*

ho″me·o·sta′sis (hō″mē-ō-stā′sis) *n.* the tendency of a system to maintain internal stability.

hom′er (hō′mər) *n.* **1,** (*Baseball*) a home run. **2,** a homing pigeon.

home′sick″ *adj.* depressed by longing for home. **—home′sick″ness,** *n.*

home′spun″ *adj.* **1,** spun or woven at home, as cloth. **2,** plain; unpretentious.

home′stead″ *n.* land and dwelling occupied by their owner. **—home′stead″er,** *n.* one who establishes a homestead in unsettled territory. **—home′stead″ing,** *n.* a government program for revitalizing urban areas.

home′work″ *n.* any work, esp. school-work, assigned to be done at home.

hom′i·cide″ (hom′ə-sīd″) *n.* the killing of one human being by another. **—hom′i·cid′al,** *adj.*

hom″i·let′ic (hom″ə-let′ik) *adj.* being or like a sermon. **—hom″i·let′i·cal·ly,** *adv.*

hom″i·let′ics (-iks) *n.* the composition or preaching of sermons.

hom′i·ly (hom′ə-lė) *n.* a moralizing dis-course; a sermon.

hom′i·nid (hom′ə-nid) *n.* a member of the family Hominidae; man.

hom′i·ny (hom′ə-nė) *n.* corn, ground or in hulled kernels, boiled in water or milk.

hom·o- (hom-ə) *pref.* the same.

ho″mo·ge′ne·ous (hō″mə-jē′nė-əs) *adj.* **1,** composed of parts of the same kind; not heterogeneous. **2,** alike in kind. **—ho″-mo·ge·ne′i·ty** (-jə-nē′ə-tė) *n.*

ho·mog′e·nize″ (hə-moj′ə-nīz″) *v.t.* make homogeneous; mix thoroughly, as milk and cream. **—ho·mog″e·ni·za′tion,** *n.*

ho·mog′e·nous (hə-moj′ə-nəs) *adj.* **1,** having the same origin. **2,** homogeneous.

hom′o·graph″ (hom′ə-graf″) *n.* a word spelled the same as another but of differ-ent origin and meaning. **—hom″o-graph′ic,** *adj.*

---

homograph, homonym, homo-phone, synonym, antonym
Words describing the relationship be-tween two words. *Homographs* are words spelled the same but of differ-ent meaning (they may or may not be pronounced the same): *lead* (direct) and *lead* (metal). *Homonym* is some-times used for words that are both spelled and pronounced the same but have different meanings: *bear* (animal or to carry). *Homonym* may also refer to words that are pronounced the same but have different mean-ings, without regard to spelling: *peace* and *piece*; in this sense, it is the same as *homophone*. *Synonyms* are words that have the same or closely related meanings; *antonyms* have opposite meanings.

---

ho·mol′o·gous (hə-mol′ə-gəs) *adj.* hav-ing the same relative position, proportion, value, or structure. **—ho·mol′o·gy** (-jė) *n.*

hom′o·nym (hom′ə-nim) *n.* **1,** a word like another in sound and (often) spelling, but different in meaning, as *bear* (carry) and *bear* (mammal). **2,** homophone. ❑ *homograph*

hom′o·phile″ (hom′ə-fīl″) *adj.* **1,** pert. to

homosexuality; being homosexual. **2,** sup-portive of the rights of homosexuals. **—n.** a homosexual.

ho″mo·pho′bi·a (hō″-mə-) *n.* a fear or dislike of homosexuality. **—ho′mo-phobe″,** *n.*

hom′o·phone″ (hom′ə-fōn″) *n.* a word pronounced like another but different in meaning and spelling, as *too* and *two.* **—ho·moph′o·nous** (hə-mof′ə-nəs) *adj.* ❑ *homograph*

ho·moph′o·ny (hō-mof′ə-nė) *n.* **1,** same-ness of sound. **2,** music having a principal melody or leading voice: *monody.* **—hom″-o·phon′ic** (-fon′ik) *adj.*

ho″mo·sex′u·al (hō″mə-sek′shoo-əl) *adj.* feeling romantic love for persons of the same sex; gay. **—n.** a homosexual person, esp. male. **—ho″mo·sex″u·al′i·ty,** *n.*

---

homosexual
↔ Note that the first element of this word is Greek prefix *homo-,* same, not Latin *homo,* man. *Homosexual* can refer to either male or female partners.

---

ho·mun′cu·lus (hō-mung′kyə-ləs) *n.* **1,** a dwarf. **2,** a manikin.

hon′cho (hon′chō) *n.* (*Slang*) boss; leader.

hone (hōn) *n.* a stone for sharpening ra-zors, etc. **—v.t.** sharpen with a hone; whet. **—v.i.** (*Dial.*) yearn.

hon′est (on′ist) *adj.* **1,** having a sense of honor; upright and fair in dealing. **2,** sin-cere; truthful. **3,** genuine; unadulterated; virtuous. **—hon′es·ty,** *n.*

hon′ey (hun′ė) *n.* **1,** a sweet fluid pro-duced by bees from the nectar of flowers. **2,** something sweet or delightful. **3,** a term of endearment. **—hon′eyed,** *adj.* sweet; fawning.

hon′ey·bee″ *n.* a bee that gathers honey.

hon′ey·comb″ *n.* **1,** a wax structure formed by bees for storing honey. **2,** any structure having many cells. **—hon′ey-combed″,** *adj.*

hon′ey·dew″ *n.* a sweet plant substance. **—honeydew melon,** a white-fleshed vari-ety of muskmelon.

hon′ey·moon″ *n.* **1,** a trip taken alone by a newly married couple. **2,** a brief pe-riod of amity.

hon′ey·suck″le *n.* a sweet-scented shrub or vine.

ho·ni soit′ qui mal y pense′ (ō-nē swä′ kē mäl ē päns′) (*Fr.*) shamed be the per-son who thinks evil of it (motto of the Order of the Garter).

honk *n.* **1,** the cry of a wild goose. **2,** a similar sound, esp. of a warning horn. —*v.i.* utter such a sound.

honk′y (honk′ė) *n.* (*Slang, offensive*) a white man.

honk′y-tonk″ (-tonk″) *n.* (*Slang*) a cheap saloon or cabaret.

hon′or (on′ər) *n.* **1,** high esteem; deferential admiration. **2,** high reputation; credit for honesty, etc. **3,** fidelity to principles or obligations; fairness in dealing; conformance with high standards of behavior. **4,** high rank, achievement, or distinction. **5,** a title, decoration, diploma, etc. **6,** (preceded by *his, her* or *your*) a title of address to a mayor or judge. **7,** chastity in a woman. —*v.t.* **1,** hold in honor; respect. **2,** confer a mark of honor upon. **3,** treat with due respect; accept; credit; fulfill. Also, **hon′our.** —**do the honors,** act as host or hostess.

hon′or·a·ble (-ə-bəl) *adj.* **1,** worthy of respect. **2,** noble; upright. —**hon′or·a·ble·ness,** *n.*

hon″o·rar′i·um (on″ə-rãr′ė-əm) *n.* [*pl.* **-a** (-ə)] a fee, as for professional services.

hon′or·ar·y (on′ər-er-ė) *adj.* **1,** conferring honor, without usual requirements, duties, etc. **2,** done or given in token of honor. **3,** dependent on honor for fulfillment.

hon″o·rif′ic (on″ə-rif′ik) *adj.* conferring or expressing honor. —*n.* a term of respectful address.

hooch *n.* (*Slang*) alcoholic liquor.

> **hooch**
> ↔ From *hoochinoo*, the name of a Tlingit village in Alaska, reputedly a source for illicit liquor.

hood (hûd) *n.* **1,** a covering for the head, often attached to a cloak, etc. **2,** any hood-shaped covering, as over an automobile engine. **3,** (*Slang*) a hoodlum.

-hood (hûd) *suf.* the state or condition of being what is expressed by the foregoing word, as *likelihood,* the state of being likely.

hood′lum (hood′ləm) *n.* a rowdy; a ruffian.

hoo′doo *n.* **1,** voodoo. **2,** (*Informal*) bad luck; someone or something supposed to bring bad luck. —*v.t.* bring bad luck to.

hood′wink″ *v.t.* deceive; impose upon.

hoo′ey (hoo′ė) *n. & interj.* (*Slang*) nonsense.

hoof (hûf) *n.* [*pl.* **hoofs** *or* **hooves** (hûvz)] the horny casing that sheathes the foot of many quadrupeds; the entire foot. —*v.i.*

(*Informal*) walk; dance. —**hoof′er,** *n.* (*Slang*) a professional dancer.

hoo′ha″ (hoo′hä″) *n.* (*Informal*) commotion.

hook (hûk) *n.* **1,** a curved or angular piece of metal or the like, used to catch, hold, or sustain something. **2,** anything so bent or curved, as a spit of land. **3,** a curved course, as of a ball hit or thrown; a swinging blow in boxing; (*Golf*) an oblique stroke, veering to the left. —*v.t.* **1,** use or make a hook. **2,** catch by artifice; trap. **3,** (*Slang*) pilfer. **4,** (with *up*) connect. —*v.i.* **1,** become attached. **2,** bend or curve. —**by hook or crook,** by any means. —**hook and eye,** a fastening device used on clothes.

hoo′kah (hûk′ə) *n.* a pipe in which the smoke is cooled by being drawn through water. Also, **hoo′ka.**

hooked (hûkt) *adj.* **1,** bent in a loop. **2,** having a hook or hooks. **3,** caught on or as on a hook. **4,** addicted. —**hook′ed·ness,** *n.*

hook′er (hûk′ər) *n.* **1,** a boat. **2,** (*Slang*) prostitute. **3,** (*Slang*) a large alcoholic drink.

hook′up″ *n.* **1,** a system or network of devices, radio or TV stations, etc. **2,** a means for connecting to a supply, as of water, electricity, etc. **3,** (*Informal*) an alliance.

hook′worm″ *n.* a parasitic bloodsucking worm infesting the intestine.

hook′y (hûk′ė) *adj.* **1,** full of hooks or barbs. **2,** hook-shaped. —**play hooky,** be absent from school unjustifiably.

hoo′li·gan (hoo′lə-gən) *n.* (*Slang*) a hoodlum.

> **hooligan**
> ↔ Origin uncertain; perhaps derived from the Irish surname. Taken into Russian as *khuligan,* the word is widely used to refer to criminals, dissenters, etc.

hoop *n.* a circular band or ring, such as used on a barrel. —**hoop skirt,** a skirt stretched to bell shape over a framework.

hoop′la (hoop′lä) *n.* excitement; hullabaloo.

hoo·ray′ (hoo-rā′) *interj.* hurrah.

hoose′gow (hoos′gow) *n.* (*Slang*) a jail.

Hoo′sier (hoo′zhər) *n.* (*Slang*) a native of Indiana. —*adj.* of Indiana.

hoot *n.* **1,** the cry of an owl; any similar sound. **2,** a cry or noise of derision. **3,** (*Informal*) something very funny. —*v.i. & t.* utter this cry.

hootch (hooch) *n.* **1,** a thatched hut. **2,** (*Slang*) hooch.

hoot′e·nan″ny (hoo′tə-nan″ē) *n.* an assemblage of folk singers, usu. for public performance.

hop *v.i.* **1,** leap; move by short leaps. **2,** leap on one foot. **3,** (*Informal*) dance. **4,** (with *off*) begin a flight or journey. —*v.t.* [**hopped, hop′ping**] **1,** leap across. **2,** jump upon. —*n.* **1,** a short leap, esp. on one foot. **2,** a flight or journey. **3,** (*Informal*) a dance. **4,** (*Slang*) opium. **5,** a twining plant whose flowers (*hops*) are used in brewing.

hope (hōp) *v.t. & i.* expect or look forward to, with desire and confidence. —*n.* **1,** confidence in a future event; expectation of something desired. **2,** what is hoped for. **3,** something that arouses or justifies hope. —**hope′ful,** *adj.* —**hope′-ful·ly,** *adv.*

> **hopefully**
> ↔ This word means "with a feeling of hope"; it does not mean "it is hoped that." The common usage "Hopefully I will win the election" is incorrect.

hope′less *adj.* **1,** without hope. **2,** beyond repair, correction, or salvation.

hop′head″ *n.* (*Slang*) a user of drugs.

hopped-′up″ (hopt′-) *adj.* (*Slang*) **1,** under the influence of drugs; doped. **2,** very excited; enthusiastic.

hop′per (hop′ər) *n.* **1,** one who or that which hops, as certain insects. **2,** a trough or chute in a storage tank through which grain, coal, etc. is discharged.

hop′sack″ing *n.* **1,** a material of hemp and jute. **2,** a rough-surfaced cotton or wool clothing fabric. Also, **hop′sack″.**

hop′scotch″ *n.* a children's game, played by hopping from square to square.

> **hopscotch**
> ↔ A compound of *hop*, to jump, and *scotch*, a cut or score, referring to the lines scored in the ground over which the player hops.

hor′a (hôr′ə) *n.* a round dance of Israel.

ho′ral (hôr′əl) *adj.* hourly; relating to hours.

horde (hôrd) *n.* **1,** a large troop or flock; a multitude. **2,** a tribe, esp. of Asiatic nomads. ❏ *hoard*

hore′hound″ (hôr′hownd″) *n.* a perennial herb, used in making medicine and candy.

ho·ri′zon (hə-rī′zən) *n.* **1,** the apparent boundary between earth and sky. **2,** the limit of visual or intellectual perception.

> **horehound**
> ↔ This word has nothing to do with either *whores* or *hounds*. It comes from Old English *harhune*, from *har*, gray, + *hune*, horehound.

hor·i·zon′tal (hôr-ə-zon′təl) *adj. & n.* parallel to the earth's surface; at right angles to a vertical line.

hor′mone (hôr′mōn) *n.* any of various substances normally secreted by glands.

horn (hôrn) *n.* **1,** a hard, spikelike growth on the head, as of cattle; the substance of which it is composed. **2,** something shaped like, or made of, or suggesting a horn, as a cusp of the moon. **3,** any of a variety of musical wind instruments, usually made of brass; any of various noise-producing instruments. **4,** a megaphone. **5,** either of the alternatives of a dilemma. —*adj.* made of horn. —**horn in,** intrude, as in a conversation.

horn′bill″ (hôrn′bil″) *n.* a large bird.

horn′book″ *n.* formerly, a writing tablet bound with animal horn used for schoolwork.

hor′net (hôr′nit) *n.* a large insect of the wasp family.

horn′pipe″ (hôrn′pīp″) *n.* **1,** an old Welsh clarinet. **2,** a lively solo dance popular among sailors.

horn′swog″gle (hôrn′swog″əl) *v.t.* (*Slang*) swindle; hoax.

horn′y (hôr′nē) *adj.* **1,** consisting of or having a horn. **2,** (*Slang*) sexually excited.

ho·rol′o·gy (hô-rol′ə-jē) *n.* the art of making timepieces. —**hor′o·log′ic** (hôr′ə-loj′ik) *adj.* —**ho·rol′o·gist,** *n.*

hor′o·scope″ (hôr′ə-skōp″) *n.* a plan of the positions of the planets, used by astrologers. —**ho·ros′co·py** (hə-ros′kə-pē) *n.*

hor·ren′dous (hə-ren′dəs) *adj.* horrible; frightful.

> **horrendous, horrible, horrid, horrify, horror**
> ↔ All derive from Latin *horrere*, to stand on end (as hair), presumably from fear.

hor′ri·ble (hor′ə-bəl) *adj.* exciting horror; dreadful; deplorable. —**hor′ri·ble-ness,** *n.* ❏ *horrendous*

hor′rid (hor′id) *adj.* unpleasant; disagreeable. —**hor′rid·ness,** *n.*

hor′ri·fy″ (hor′ə-fī″) *v.t.* arouse horror. —**hor·rif′ic** (hə-rif′ik) *adj.* ❏ *horrendous*

hor′ror (hor′ər) *n.* **1,** a painful emotion

of fear or abhorrence; an intense aversion. **2,** that which excites such a feeling. ❏ *horrendous*

hors′ de com·bat′ (ôr də kōṁ-bä′) (*Fr.*) out of the fight; disabled.

hors d'oeuvre′ (ôr dövr′) *n.* [*pl.* **hors d'oeuvres′** (ôr dövr′)] (*Fr.*) a small bit of food, usu. served on a cracker or piece of bread; an appetizer.

horse (hôrs) *n.* **1,** a large, solid-hoofed domesticated quadruped, a draft or riding animal. **2,** a male horse; a stallion. **3,** a troop of horses; cavalry. **4,** a supporting frame on legs. **5,** a gymnastic apparatus. —*v.t.* provide with a horse; put on horseback. —*v.i.* (*Slang*) be playful or boisterous. —**horse chestnut,** a flowering tree, as the Ohio buckeye; its seed. —**horse latitude,** a zone of relative calm, near 30° north or south latitude. —**horse opera,** a western. —**horse sense,** (*Informal*) good sense.

horse′back″ *n.* the part of a horse's back on which a rider sits. —*adv.* on horseback.

horse′car″ *n.* a car drawn by a horse.

horse′feath″ers *interj.* (*Slang*) nonsense!

horse′fly″ *n.* gadfly.

horse′hair″ *n. & adj.* the mane and tail hair of a horse; a fabric woven from it.

horse′laugh″ *n.* a derisive laugh.

horse′less carriage an automobile.

horse′man (-mən) *n.* [*pl.* **-men**] the rider or trainer of a horse.

horse′man·ship *n.* **1,** the art of a horseman or horsewoman. **2,** equitation.

horse′play″ *n.* boisterous behavior.

horse′pow″er *n.* a unit for measuring rate of work.

horse′rad″ish *n.* a cultivated plant; its root, ground and used as a condiment.

horse′shoe″ *n.* **1,** the U-shaped iron plate nailed to a horse's hoof; anything so shaped. **2,** (*pl.*) a game of quoits played with horseshoes.

horse′whip″ *n.* a whip for urging a horse. —*v.t.* [**-whipped″, -whip″ping**] beat with a whip.

horse′wom″an *n.* a woman who rides or trains horses.

hors′y (hôr′sė) *adj.* **1,** like a horse; gross. **2,** interested in horses or horse racing. —**hors′i·ness,** *n.*

hor′ta·to·ry (hôr′tə-tôr-ė) *adj.* exhorting.

hor′ti·cul″ture (hôr′ti-kul″chər) *n.* the science and art of growing plants. —**hor″·ti·cul′tur·al,** *adj.*

ho·san′na (hō-zan′ə) *interj. & n.* (*He-*

brew, save, we pray) an exclamation in praise of God.

hose (hōz) *n.* **1,** a flexible tube for conveying water. **2,** [*pl.* **hose**] stockings or socks. —*v.t.* apply water through a hose.

ho′sier·y (hō′zhə-rė) *n.* stockings.

hos′pice (hos′pis) *n.* **1,** a shelter for travelers, or the destitute, maintained by a religious order. **2,** a nursing home, esp. for the terminally ill.

hos′pi·ta·ble (hos′pi-tə-bəl) *adj.* **1,** happy to welcome and entertain guests. **2,** receptive, as to ideas. —**hos′pi·ta·ble·ness,** *n.*

hos′pi·tal (hos′pi-təl) *n.* an institution for the care and treatment of the sick and injured; any similar establishment, as for repairs.

---

hospital, hotel, hostel
↔ These words have a common source, Latin *hospitale*, hospice.

---

hos″pi·tal′i·ty (hos″pə-tal′ə-tė) *n.* the reception of guests, esp. when friendly and warm.

hos″pi·tal·i·za′tion (hos″pi-təl-i-zā′shən) *n.* insurance covering expenses incurred in a hospital. —**hos′pi·tal·ize″,** *v.t.* put or treat in a hospital.

host (hōst) *n.* **1,** one who entertains another, esp. in his own house. **2,** the proprietor of an inn or restaurant. **3,** a great number of persons or things. **4,** (*cap.*) the bread consecrated in the Eucharist. **5,** an animal or plant that provides nutrition to a parasite. —*v.t.* (*Informal*) act as host of.

hos′tage (hos′tij) *n.* a person or thing held as a pledge or security for the performance of an action.

hos′tel (hos′təl) *n.* a lodging house or inn. Also, **hos′tel·ry** (-rė). ❏ *hospital*

host′ess (hōs′tis) *n.* **1,** a female host. **2,** a woman who greets patrons in a restaurant, etc. **3,** a female flight attendant.

hos′tile (hos′təl) *adj.* **1,** opposed in feeling or action; antagonistic. **2,** relating to an enemy.

hos·til′i·ty (hos-til′i-tė) *n.* **1,** antagonism. **2,** (*pl.*) warfare.

hos′tler (hos′lər) *n.* a servant who tends horses at an inn.

hot *adj.* [**hot′ter, -test**] **1,** having or giving the sensation of heat; of high temperature. **2,** pungent to the taste; biting. **3,** ardent in feeling; vehement; passionate. **4,** fresh; keen; brisk. **5,** (*Slang*) exciting; (of music) heightened by rhapsodic improvisation. **6,** (*Slang*) wanted by the police. **7,** (*Slang*) in good form, as an athlete; on a lucky streak, as a gambler. **8,** (*Slang*) sexually excited or exciting. **9,** (*pl.*) (*Slang*) sexual desire. —**hot air,** (*Slang*) empty talk. —**hot dog, 1,** a frankfurter on a roll. **2,** (*Informal*) a show-off, esp. in sports. —**hot flash,** a temporary sensation of heat experienced by some women during menopause. —**hot line,** an emergency telephone line. —**hot pants,** *n.pl.* pants with very short legs, usu. worn by women. —**hot plate,** a portable metal cooking or warming apparatus. —**hot rod,** (*Slang*) an automobile altered for greater speed. —**hot tub,** a large tub, usu. wooden, filled with hot water, often having a whirlpool and frequently placed outside.

hot′bed″ *n.* **1,** a glass-covered bed of soil. **2,** a place where growth is rapid.

hot′blood″ed *adj.* excitable; impetuous. —**hot′blood″ed·ness,** *n.*

hot′cake″ *n.* pancake.

hotch′potch″ *n.* hodgepodge.

ho·tel′ (hō-tel′) *n.* **1,** a public house that furnishes lodging, food, etc. to travelers or other guests. **2,** (*Communications*) the letter *h.* ◻ *hospital*

hot′foot″ *adv.* hastily; speedily. —*v.i.* go in haste.

hot′head″ed *adj.* of fiery temper; rash. —**hot′head″,** *n.* —**hot′head″ed·ness,** *n.*

hot′house″ *n.* a glass-covered area for raising plants.

hot′shot″ *n.* (*Slang*) a particularly energetic and skillful person.

hot-′wire″ *adj.* operated by the increased resistance of a wire through which electricity is made to pass. —*v.t.* (*Slang*) to start an automobile by bypassing the ignition switch.

hound (hownd) *n.* **1,** any of various hunting dogs. **2,** any dog. **3,** (*Slang*) a mean, contemptible fellow. **4,** (*Slang*) an addict. —*v.t.* harass.

hour (owr) *n.* **1,** measure of time equal to 60 minutes or one twenty-fourth of a solar day. **2,** a time of day. **3,** an indefinite period of time; a particular or appointed time.

hour′glass″ *n.* a device for measuring time by the flow of sand.

hou′ri (hû′rē) *n.* a beautiful maiden in the Mohammedan paradise.

hour′ly (-lē) *adj. & adv.* occurring each hour; continual or often.

house (hows) *n.* [*pl.* **hous′es** (how′ziz)] **1,** a building for human use or occupation, esp. a dwelling. **2,** any place of abode. **3,** something that contains or houses; a cell or compartment. **4,** a household. **5,** a fam-

ily including ancestors and descendants. **6,** a body of persons; a legislature; a commercial establishment; an audience in a theater. **7,** the management of a gaming house. —*v.t.* (howz) shelter. —**house music,** a style of popular dance music.

house′boy″ *n.* a young male servant.

house′break″er *n.* a burglar.

house′brok″en *adj.* trained to live in a house, as an animal.

house′hold″ *n.* all the permanent residents of a dwelling house. —**house′-hold″er,** *n.* one who owns a house; the head of a household.

house′keep″ing *n.* the maintenance and management of a house, including the serving of meals. —**house′keep″er,** *n.*

house′maid″ *n.* a female domestic servant. —**housemaid's knee,** inflammation of the bursa of the kneecap.

house′sit″ *v.t. & i.* to take care of a house while its occupants are away.

house′warm″ing *n.* a party to celebrate occupancy of a new house.

house′wife″ *n.* a married woman in charge of a household.

house′work″ *n.* cooking, cleaning, etc.

hous′ing (how′zing) *n.* **1,** houses collectively. **2,** the act of putting in a house; the business of providing houses. **3,** a cover, hood, or shield.

hove (hōv) *v.* pret. & p.p. of *heave.*

hov′el (huv′əl) *n.* a small, wretched house.

hov′er (huv′ər) *v.i.* **1,** remain over one place while fluttering in the air. **2,** linger about. **3,** continue in an undecided state.

hov′er·craft″ (huv′ər-kraft″) *n.* a motorized vehicle that travels over the surface of land or water supported on a cushion of air.

how *adv.* **1,** in what way or manner; by what means. **2,** to what extent; in what amount. **3,** in what state or condition. **4,** for what reason. —*interj.* a greeting.

how′dah (how′dä) *n.* a railed and canopied seat on the back of an elephant.

how′dy (how′dē) *interj.* hello; how do you do.

how·ev′er (how-ev′ər) *conj.* nevertheless; despite which. —*adv.* in whatever manner; to whatever extent or degree.

how′itz·er (how′it-sər) *n.* a rifled cannon for high-angle shots.

howl *v.i. & t.* **1,** utter a loud, prolonged, and mournful cry, as a wolf. **2,** cry out in pain, rage, etc. **3,** make a wailing sound, as the wind. **4,** laugh loudly. —*n.* such a cry. —**howl'ing**, *adj.* (*Slang*) great; wonderful.

howl'er (how'lər) *n.* **1,** one who or that which howls. **2,** a So. Amer. monkey. **3,** (*Informal*) an amusing blunder, joke, etc.

how"so·ev'er *adv.* **1,** in whatever manner. **2,** to whatever degree.

hoy'den (hoi'dən) *n.* a rowdy girl; a tomboy.

hua·ra'che (wə-rä'chė) *n.* a low-heeled sandal.

hub *n.* **1,** a block in the center of a wheel, esp. one to which spokes are joined. **2,** a center of intellectual, commercial, or other activity. —**the Hub**, Boston, Mass.

hub'bub (hub'ub) *n.* a noise as of many voices or sounds; uproar.

hu'bris (hū'bris) *n.* pride; arrogance.

hub'cap" *n.* a cover for the hub of a wheel.

huck'le·ber"ry (huk'əl-ber"ė) *n.* a low shrub or its dark-blue edible berry.

huck'ster (huk'stər) *n.* a street peddler, esp. of fruit and vegetables. —*v.t.* peddle.

hud'dle (hud'əl) *v.t.* draw closely together. —*v.t.* **1,** crowd together. **2,** (*Informal*) confer privately. —*n.* **1,** a confused mass; a crowd. **2,** (*Informal*) a secret conference.

hue (hū) *n.* **1,** a color; color in general. **2,** intensity of color. **3,** clamor, esp. in *hue and cry.*

huff (huf) *n.* a sudden swell of anger or resentment. —*v.i.* **1,** take offense. **2,** puff or blow; pant.

huff'ish *adj.* **1,** resentful; petulant. **2,** arrogant; swaggering. —**huff'ish·ness**, *n.*

huff'y *adj.* **1,** irascible; touchy. **2,** sulky. —**huff'i·ness**, *n.*

hug *v.t. & i.* [**hugged, hug'ging**] **1,** clasp tightly in the arms; embrace. **2,** cling to mentally. **3,** keep close to. —*n.* a close embrace.

huge (hūj) *adj.* very large. —**huge'ness**, *n.*

hug'ger-mug'ger (hug'ər-mug'ər) *n.* disorder; a muddle or jumble. —*adj.* **1,** confused. **2,** clandestine.

hu'la-hu'la (hoo'lə-hoo'lə) *n.* a Hawaiian dance. —**hula hoop**, a large hoop, usu. plastic, swung about the hips or waist.

hulk *n.* **1,** the hull of a ship, esp. one that is dismantled or wrecked. **2,** a bulky or unwieldy person or mass. —*v.i.* loom. —**hulk'ing**, *adj.*

hull (hul) *n.* **1,** the body of a ship, exclusive of masts and other superstructure. **2,** the fuselage of a seaplane. **3,** the shell, husk, etc., of a nut, fruit, or grain. —*v.t.* remove the hull of.

hul'la·ba·loo" (hul'ə-bə-loo") *n.* noisy confusion.

hum *v.t. & i.* [**hummed, hum'ming**] **1,** make a droning sound. **2,** vocalize with closed lips. **3,** make indistinct sounds; murmur. —*n.* a buzzing or droning sound. —*interj.* of hesitation, doubt, etc. —**hum'-ming**, *adj.* **1,** buzzing, etc. **2,** intensely active.

hu'man (hū'mən) *adj.* pert. to people or humankind; being a person; having the nature of a person. —*n.* a human being. —**human engineering**, the science of designing for the workplace; ergonomics.

hu·mane' (hū-mān') *adj.* **1,** inclined to treat others, and animals, with kindness; benevolent; compassionate. **2,** (of a branch of knowledge) tending to refine. —**hu·mane'ness**, *n.*

hu'man·ism (hū'mə-niz-əm) *n.* **1,** a system of thought predominantly centered on human interests. **2,** study of the humanities; literary culture. —**hu'man·ist**, *n.*

hu·man"i·tar'i·an (hū-man"ə-tār'ė-ən) *adj. & n.* concerned with the interests of all mankind; philanthropic.

hu·man'i·ty (hū-man'ə-tė) *n.* **1,** the human race; humankind. **2,** the quality of being human; human nature. **3,** humaneness. **4,** (usually *pl.*) any of the branches of learning embraced by philosophy, literature, languages, art, etc., excluding theology and natural and social sciences.

hu'man·ize" (hū'mə-nīz") *v.t.* make human or humane. —**hu"man·i·za'tion** (-i-zā'shən) *n.*

hu'man·kind" *n.* the human race.

hu'man·oid" (hū'mə-noid") *adj.* having human characteristics. —*n.* a humanoid being.

hum'ble (hum'bəl) *adj.* **1,** low in station; unimportant; lowly. **2,** meek or modest in manner. —*v.t.* abase; humiliate. —**hum'-ble·ness**, *n.* —**eat humble pie**, be humiliated.

---

humble, humble pie

↔ *Humble* comes from Latin *humilis*, lowly, which itself came from *humus*, earth. *Humble pie* is unrelated; it was originally a pie made from animal innards. Its source is the obsolete word *numbles*, fillet of venison, from Latin *lumulus*, loin.

---

hum'bug" *n.* **1,** a fraudulent trick; a hoax; sham. **2,** an impostor. —*v.t.* [**-bugged, -bug·ging**] delude.

hum″ding′er (hum″ding′ər) *n.* (*Slang*) a remarkable person or thing.

hum′drum″ *adj.* monotonous.

hu′mer·us (hū′mər-əs) *n.* [*pl.* **-i** (-ī)] the bone of the upper arm.

hu′mid (hū′mid) *adj.* moist; damp.

hu·mid′i·fy″ (hū-mid′ə-fī″) *v.t.* make damper. —**hu·mid″i·fi·ca′tion,** *n.*

hu·mid′i·stat″ (hū-mid′i-stat″) *n.* a device for measuring humidity.

hu·mid′i·ty (hū-mid′ə-tė) *n.* dampness; moisture in the air.

hu′mi·dor″ (hū′mə-dôr″) *n.* a container fitted to keep its contents moist, as for tobacco.

hu·mil′i·ate″ (hū-mil′ė-āt″) *v.t.* subject to shame or disgrace; abase in estimation; mortify. —**hu·mil″i·a′tion,** *n.*

hu·mil′i·ty (hū-mil′ə-tė) *n.* modesty in self-estimation; humbleness.

hum′ming·bird″ (hum′ing-bėrd″) *n.* a tiny bird whose wings hum from rapid vibration.

hum′mock (hum′ək) *n.* a knoll.

hu·mon′gous (hū-mung′gəs) *adj.* (*Slang*) very large; colossal.

hu′mor (hū′mər) *n.* **1,** the quality of inciting laughter, or of perceiving what is comical; drollery; facetiousness. **2,** mental state; mood. **3,** caprice; whim. **4,** droll literature. **5,** (*Biol.*) any body fluid. —*v.t.* indulge; cater to the whims of. Also, **hu′-mour.** —**hu′mor·ist,** *n.* a writer of humor. —**hu′mor·ous,** *adj.* funny; droll.

hu″mor·esque′ (hū″mə-resk′) *n.* a musical caprice.

hump *n.* a protuberance or swelling, esp. a natural or morbid curvature of the back. —*v.t. & i.* **1,** form or rise in a hump. **2,** (*Slang*) exert oneself.

hump′back″ *n.* **1,** a hump on the back. **2,** one who has a humpback. **3,** a kind of whale. —**hump′backed″,** *adj.*

humph (humf) *interj.* of contempt, doubt, dissatisfaction, etc.

hu′mus (hū′məs) *n.* decayed vegetable matter, important to the fertility of soil.

hunch *n.* **1,** hump. **2,** a premonition or suspicion. —*v.t.* thrust out or up in a hump. —*v.i.* sidle or lunge forward. —**hunch′back″,** *n.* humpback.

hun′dred (hun′drid) *n. & adj.* the cardinal number represented by 100, equal to ten times ten. —**hun′dredth,** *n. & adj.* the ordinal of this number, also written ten 100th.

hun′dred·fold″ *adv. & adj.* a hundred times.

hun′dred·weight″ *n.* 100 lbs in U.S., 112 lbs in England.

hung *v.* pret. & p.p. of *hang.*

hun′ger (hung′gər) *n.* **1,** craving for food. **2,** any strong desire. —*v.i.* feel hunger. —**hun′gry** (-grė) *adj.* —**hunger strike,** refusal to eat in an effort to force compliance with one's demands.

hung-up′ *adj.* (*Slang*) **1,** disturbed; depressed. **2,** obsessed; addicted.

hunk *n.* **1,** (*Informal*) a large piece, lump, or chunk. **2,** (*Slang*) a sexually attractive man. —**hunk′y,** *adj.* hunky-dory.

hun′ker (hung′kər) *v.i.* squat; crouch. —**hunker down,** (*Informal*) hold stubbornly to an opinion, policy, etc.

hun′ky-dor′y (hung′kė-dôr′ė) *adj.* (*Slang*) all right; satisfactory.

hunt *v.t. & i.* **1,** chase (animals) for the purpose of catching or killing. **2,** pursue; harry. **3,** look for; search. —*n.* **1,** the act or sport of chasing wild animals. **2,** a pack of hunting dogs; a group of hunters. **3,** any pursuit, search, or quest. —**hunt′er** *n.*

hur′dle (hėr′dəl) *n.* **1,** a barrier (as on a racetrack); a frame of crossed sticks, bars, etc., to be leaped over. **2,** an obstacle or difficulty. —*v.t.* **1,** leap over. **2,** circumvent or overcome by any means. —**hur′dler,** *n.*

---

hurdle, hurtle
☛ Do not confuse *hurdle*, to leap over, with *hurtle*, to rush.

---

hur′dy-gur′dy (hėr′dė-gėr″dė) *n.* a musical instrument played by turning a crank; a barrel órgan.

hurl (hėrl) *v.i. & t.* **1,** throw; fling. **2,** utter vehemently.

hurl′ing *n.* an Irish variant of hockey.

hur″ly-bur′ly (hėr″lė-bėr′lė) *n. & adj.* tumult; confusion.

hur·rah′ (hə-rä′) *interj.* of applause, approval, or elation.

hur′ri·cane″ (hėr′ə-kān″) *n.* a windstorm of intense severity; a tropical cyclone.

---

hurricane
↔ From a Caribbean native language, Taino, whose word for cyclone is *hurakan,* from *hura,* wind.

---

hur′ry (hėr′ė) *v.i.* move or act with haste. —*v.t.* urge onward; impel to greater rapidity; hasten. —*n.* haste.

hurt (hėrt) *v.t. & i.* **1,** cause bodily pain to. **2,** do harm or mischief to; injure; damage. **3,** grieve; distress. —*n.* **1,** an impairment; a wound, bruise, injury, etc. **2,** a cause of distress; an insult. **—hurt′ful,** *adj.* injurious.

hur′tle (hēr′təl) *v.i.* rush violently and noisily. ❑ *hurdle*

hus′band (huz′bənd) *n.* a married man, in relation to his wife. **—***v.t.* manage prudently; economize. **—hus′band·man** (-mən) *n.* a farmer.

> **husband**
> ↔ From Old Norse *husbondi*, master of the house.

hus′band·ry (-rė) *n.* **1,** farming; agriculture. **2,** thrifty management; frugality.

hush *interj.* to command silence. **—***v.i.* become quiet or silent. **—***v.t.* **1,** silence. **2,** calm; soothe; allay. **—***n.* silence or quiet, esp. after noise. **—hush-′hush′,** *adj.* highly confidential. **—hush money,** a bribe to buy silence.

hush′ pup″py (hush′pup″ė) *n.* **1,** a cornmeal fritter. **2,** (*pl.*) (*cap, T.N.*) lightweight rubber-soled shoes.

husk *n.* **1,** the outer covering of certain fruits and seeds, esp. corn. **2,** any similar dry covering. **—***v.t.* remove the husk from.

hus′ky (hus′kė) *adj.* **1,** strong; burly. **2,** dry in the throat; hoarse. **—***n.* a large Eskimo dog. **—hus′ki·ness,** *n.*

> **husky**
> ↔ The adjective and noun senses have totally different origins. The noun comes from the same Algonquin source as *Eskimo*. The adjective comes from *husk*, with reference to the dryness of the covering.

hus·sar′ (hû-zär′) *n.* a light-cavalryman.

hus′sy (huz′ė) *n.* (*Offensive*) a willful girl; a mean or worthless woman.

hust′ings (hus′tingz) *n.sing.* a platform or place where political candidates speak.

hus′tle (hus′əl) *v.i. & t.* **1,** move or act energetically; make haste. **2,** move by pushing or crowding. **3,** spirit away. **4,** (*Slang*) swindle. **5,** (*Slang*) ply the trade of a prostitute. **—***n.* a popular ballroom dance.

hus′tler (hus′lər) *n.* **1,** an energetic worker. **2,** (*Slang*) a minor swindler. **3,** (*Slang*) a prostitute.

hut *n.* a small, rude dwelling; a cabin.

hutch (huch) *n.* **1,** a box or coop for confining a small animal. **2,** a hut; a fisher's shanty.

hutz′pa (khûts′pə) *n.* chutzpah.

huz·za′ (hə-zä′) *interj.* hurrah.

hy′a·cinth (hī′ə-sinth) *n.* **1,** a bulbous

plant having spikes of bell-shaped flowers. **2,** a semiprecious stone.

hy′brid (hī′brid) *n.* **1,** the offspring of animals or plants of different varieties, species, or genera; a crossbreed or mongrel. **2,** any product or mixture of two heterogeneous things. **—***adj.* crossbred; diverse. **—hy′brid·ize″,** *v.t.*

hydr- *pref.* hydro.

hy·dran′gea (hī-drān′jə) *n.* a shrub having showy clusters of flowers.

hy′drant (hī′drənt) *n.* a pipe for drawing water from a main pipe.

hy′drate (hī′drāt) *n.* any compound containing water in chemical combination. **—hy·dra′tion,** *n.*

hy·drau′lic (hī-drâ′lik) *adj.* operated by water or other liquid. **—hy·drau′li·cal·ly,** *adv.*

hy·drau′lics (-liks) *n.* the science and engineering application of the motion of liquids.

hy·dro- (hī-drō) **1,** *pref.* water. **2,** hydrogen.

> **hydro-, hydrogen**
> ↔ The frequently encountered prefix *hydr(o)-* comes from Greek *hydōr*, water. *Hydrogen* was coined in French in the late 18th c. because of the property of the gas to form water when oxidized.

hy″dro·car′bon *n.* an organic compound of hydrogen and carbon.

hy″dro·e·lec′tric *adj.* pert. to the generation of electricity by water power.

hy′dro·foil″ *n.* a fin attached to a speedboat that lifts the hull above the water when a certain speed is reached.

hy′dro·gen (hī′drə-jən) *n.* a gas, the lightest of the chemical elements, no. 1, symbol H. **—hy·dro′gen·ate″** (hī-droj′ə-nāt″) *v.t.* combine with hydrogen. **—hydrogen bomb,** an atomic bomb based on fusion of an isotope of hydrogen. ❑ *hydro-*

hy·drom′e·ter (hī-drom′i-tər) *n.* an instrument for measuring the specific gravity of liquids.

hy″dro·pho′bi·a (hī″drə-fō′bė-ə) *n.* **1,** rabies. **2,** morbid fear of water.

hy′dro·plane″ *n.* **1,** a seaplane. **2,** a powerful motorboat designed to skim over the surface of the water. **3,** a horizontal rudder on a submersible boat. **—***v.i.* skim the surface of water in, or as in, a hydroplane.

hy″dro·pon′ics (-pon′iks) *n.* the cultivation of plants in a nutrient solution instead of soil.

hy′drous (hī′drəs) *adj.* containing water.

hy·e′na (hī-ē′nə) *n.* a carnivorous mammal of Afr. and Asia, whose cry resembles a laugh.

hy′giene (hī′jēn) *n.* the science that deals with the preservation of health.

hy″gi·en′ic (hī″jē-en′ik) *adj.* **1,** sanitary. **2,** pert. to hygiene. —**hy″gi·en′i·cal·ly,** *adv.*

hy·grom′e·ter (hī-grom′ə-tər) *n.* an instrument for measuring the humidity of the atmosphere.

hy′men (hī′mən) *n.* a membrane partly closing the vagina; maidenhead.

hy″me·ne′al (hī″mə-nē′əl) *adj.* pert. to marriage.

hymn (him) *n.* **1,** a song in worship of God. **2,** any song or ode of praise.

hym′nal (him′nəl) *n.* a book of hymns. —*adj.* pert. to hymns.

hymn′o·dy (him′nə-dē) *n.* the singing, composing, body, or study of hymns.

hype (hīp) *n.* (*Informal*) flattering publicity; puff.

hy·per- *pref.* over; in excess; exaggerated.

hy·per′bo·la (hī-pēr′bə-lə) *n.* a curve, one of the conic sections.

hy·per′bo·le (hī-pēr′bə-lē) *n.* obvious exaggeration; an extravagant statement.

hy″per·bol′ic (hī″pər-bol′ik) *adj.* **1,** pert. to or being a hyperbola. **2,** of or being hyperbole.

hy″per·gol′ic (hī″pər-gol′ik) *adj.* self-igniting: said of fuels.

hy′per·text″ *n.* (*Computers*) a method for linking related documents through key words.

hyphen

(*Gram.*) Most of the problems one encounters with hyphens concern the division of compound words. There are so many exceptions to the rules and disagreements among authorities about hyphenation that the best rule is to consult the dictionary. Compounds formed with prefixes such as *ante-, inter-, over-, post-, pre-* and *semi-* are usually closed, unless (a) the second element is capitalized or a numeral, as *post-1945, un-American*; (b) the word must be distinguished from a homonym, as *re-cover* from *re-cover*; (c) the second element consists of more than one word, as *non-English-speaking*. Newly invented compounds tend to be hyphenated at first and then to be closed when they become more familiar.

hy·per′tro·phy (hī-pēr′trə-fē) *n.* excessive development of an organ of the body.

hy′phen (hī′fən) *n.* the symbol (-) used to join the parts of compound words, indicate syllabication, etc. —*v.t.* hyphenate.

hy′phen·ate″ *v.t.* **1,** join with a hyphen. **2,** divide with a hyphen.

hyp·no′sis (hip-nō′sis) *n.* a condition similar to sleep, but usually induced artificially; a trance.

hypnosis

↔ From Greek *hypnos*, sleep. The term *hypnosis* was coined in the 19th c. by Dr. James Braid, and eventually replaced the earlier term *mesmerism*.

hyp·not′ic (hip-not′ik) *adj.* **1,** pert. to hypnosis; susceptible to hypnotism. **2,** inducing sleep. —**hyp·not′i·cal·ly,** *adv.*

hyp′no·tize″ (hip′nə-tīz″) *v.t.* put to sleep by persuasion or mental ascendancy. —**hyp′no·tism″,** *n.* —**hyp′no·tist″,** *n.*

hy′po (hī′pō) *n.* **1,** a photographic fixing agent. **2,** hypodermic.

hy·po- (hī-pō) *pref.* under.

hy″po·chon′dri·ac″ (hī″pə-kon′drē-ak″) *n. & adj.* one who is morbidly anxious about his or her health or suffers imagined ills. —**hy″po·chon′dri·a** (-ə) *n.*

hy·poc′ri·sy (hi-pok″rə-sē) *n.* false pretension to personal qualities or principles not actually possessed.

hyp′o·crite″ (hip′ə-krit″) *n.* one who pretends to beliefs, sentiments, etc., he or she does not actually feel. —**hyp″o·crit′i·cal,** *adj.*

hy″po·der′mic (hī″pə-dēr′mik) *adj.* under the skin. —*n.* **1,** a remedy applied under the skin. **2,** a syringe for hypodermic injection. —**hy″po·der′mi·cal·ly,** *adv.*

hy″po·gly·ce′mi·a (hī″pō-glī-sē′mē-ə) *n.* low level of sugar in the blood.

hy·pot′e·nuse″ (hī-pot′ə-noos″) *n.* the longest side of a right triangle.

hy·poth′e·cate″ (hī-poth′thə-kāt″) *v.t.* pledge to a creditor as security. —**hy·poth″e·ca′tion,** *n.*

hy·poth′e·sis (hī-poth′ə-sis) *n.* [*pl.* **-ses** (-sēz)] a tentative assertion about natural phenomena, assumed but not positively known; a postulate. —**hy·poth′e·size″** (-sīz″) *v.t. & i.*

hy″po·thet′i·cal (hī″pə-thet′i-kəl) *adj.* **1,** taken as a hypothesis. **2,** conjectural; supposed.

hys′sop (his′əp) *n.* an aromatic flowering herb.

hys·ter·ec'to·my (his-tə-rek'tə-mè) *n.* surgical removal of the uterus.

hys·te'ri·a (his-tir'è-ə) *n.* a disorder marked by violent emotional outbreaks.

hys·ter'ic (his-ter'ik) *n.* **1,** one subject to hysteria. **2,** (*pl.*) a fit of hysteria. —**hys·ter'- i·cal,** *adj.*

I

I, i (ī) **1,** the ninth letter of the English alphabet. **2,** (*cap.*) the personal pronoun, first person. **3,** the Roman numeral one.

i·am'bic (ī-am'bik) (*Prosody*) *n.* an iamb or iambus, a foot in poetry containing an unstressed then a stressed syllable, as *a- bout'.* —*adj.* (of verse) in iambics.

i·at''ro·gen'ic (ī-at''rə-jen'ik) *adj.* of an illness, caused by treatment.

I·ber'i·an (ī-bir'è-ən) *adj.* pert. to Iberia, the region of Spain and Portugal.

i'bex (ī'beks) *n.* a Europ. wild goat with long, curved horns.

i·bi'dem (ī-bē'dəm; ib'i-dəm) *adv.* (*Lat.*) in the same place. Abbr., **ibid.**

i'bis (ī'bis) *n.* a wading bird related to the heron and stork.

-i·ble (i-bəl) *suf.* same as **-able.**

i''bu·pro'fen (ī''bū-prō'fən) *n.* a drug used to treat inflammation and pain.

-ic (ik) *suf.* forming adjectives: **1,** like. **2,** pert. to. **3,** composed of. Also, **-i·cal** (i-kəl).

IC integrated circuit.

ice (īs) *n.* **1,** the solid form of water, pro- duced by freezing. **2,** any frozen liquid. **3,** a confection of frozen fruit juice. **4,** ice cream. **5,** icing. **6,** reserve; formality. **7,** (*Slang*) diamonds. **8,** (*Slang*) graft; bribes paid for freedom from arrest. —*v.t.* **1,** cool with ice. **2,** change into ice; freeze. **3,** cover with icing. —*v.i.* freeze. —*adj.* iced; icy. —**Ice Age,** the glacial epoch, from about 2 million to 10,000 B.C. —**icebox,** a refrigerator. —**ice cream,** a frozen confec- tion of cream, flavoring, and often eggs. —**ice hockey,** hockey played on ice. —**ice milk,** frozen custard. —**ice pack, 1,** a wa- terproof container for ice, used on the body to reduce swelling. Also, **ice bag. 2,** a large body of floating ice. —**ice water,** very cold water.

---

ice, icicle
↔ Though the source of *ice* is un- known, *icicle* is from Old English *is- gicel,* literally, "ice icicle."

---

ice'berg'' (īs'bėrg'') *n.* **1,** a mass of ice floating at sea. **2,** (*Informal*) a cold, un- emotional person.

ice'bound'' *adj.* frozen in or obstructed by ice.

ice'cap'' *n.* **1,** a large mass of ice. **2,** an ice pack designed for the head.

ice'man'' *n.* [*pl.* **-men**] a man who sells ice.

i'chor (ī'kôr) *n.* **1,** in Gk. mythology, the ethereal fluid flowing in the veins of the gods. **2,** an acrid watery discharge, as from an ulcer. —**i'chor·ous** (ī'kər-əs) *adj.*

ich'thy·o- (ik-thè-ō) *pref.* fish.

ich''thy·ol'o·gy (ik''thè-ol'o-jè) *n.* the study of fishes. —**ich'thy·o·log'i·cal,** *adj.* —**ich''thy·ol'o·gist,** *n.*

i'ci·cle (ī'si-kəl) *n.* a spike of ice formed when dripping water freezes. ❑ *ice*

ic'ing (ī'sing) *n.* a preparation of sugar used for covering cakes, etc; frosting.

ick'y (ik'è) *adj.* (*Informal*) **1,** sticky and unpleasant. **2,** disgusting.

i'con (ī'kon) *n.* **1,** a sacred image. **2,** on a computer screen, a symbol representing a file, option, function, etc.

i·con'o·clast (ī-kon'ə-klåst'') *n.* one who challenges cherished beliefs. —**i·con''o- clasm,** *n.* —**i·con''o·clas'tic,** *adj.* —**i·con''o- clas'ti·cal·ly,** *adv.*

i·con'o·scope'' (ī-kon'ə-skōp'') *n.* the large cathode-ray tube of a TV camera.

-ics (iks) *suf.* forming nouns, denoting fields of knowledge or activity.

-ics
(*Gram.*) Nouns ending in *-ics* may take a singular or plural verb, de- pending on use. Generally, words de- noting a science are singular; words referring to principles or practices are plural.

---

ic'tus (ik'təs) *n.* the moment of stress, as in a poetic line.

i'cy (ī'sè) *adj.* **1,** made of or abounding with ice. **2,** like ice; cold. —**i'ci·ly,** *adv.* —**i'ci·ness,** *n.*

id *n.* (*Psychoanal.*) a person's urge to pleasure and the exercise of the libido.

i·de'a (ī-dē'ə) *n.* **1,** something existing in the mind; conception; thought. **2,** an atti- tude of mind; opinion; belief; impression. **3,** a notion, vagary, or fantasy. **4,** a plan of action; purpose; intention.

i·de'al (ī-dē'əl) *n.* something imagined in a state of perfection; a goal; a model. —*adj.* **1,** perfect, highly desirable, worthy of emulation, etc. **2,** existing only in idea. **3,** not real; impractical; visionary.

---

i·de·al·ism (ī-dē'ə-liz-əm) *n.* **1,** a tendency to wish or believe things to be ideal, or better than they are. **2,** a constant effort to achieve perfection. —**i·de·al·ist,** *n.* —**i·de″al·is'tic,** *adj.* —**i·de″al·is'ti·cal·ly,** *adv.*

i·de·al·ize″ (ī-dē'ə-līz″) *v.t.* regard as ideal, usually in disregard of fact. —**i·de″al·i·za'tion,** *n.*

i·de·al·ly (ī-dē'ə-lè) *adv.* **1,** perfectly. **2,** if everything were as one wished.

i·dée fixe' (ē-dā fēks') [*pl.* **i·dées fixes** (ē-dā fēks')] (*Fr.*) a fixed idea; obsession.

i'dem (ī'dem) *adj. & pron.* the same (as before).

i·den'ti·cal (ī-den'ti-kəl) *adj.* **1,** being the same. **2,** exactly or much alike.

i·den″ti·fi·ca'tion (ī-den″tə-fi-kā'shən) *n.* **1,** act of identifying. **2,** a mark or means of identifying.

i·den'ti·fy″ (ī-den'ti-fī″) *v.t.* **1,** recognize or establish as being a particular kind, individual, etc. **2,** show to be identical. **3,** associate (oneself) in feeling, interest, etc.

i·den'ti·ty (ī-den'tə-tè) *n.* **1,** what a thing or person is; a name, classification, etc. **2,** recognizable individuality. **3,** sameness. **4,** exact or close likeness. —**identity crisis,** a psychological crisis caused by confusion about one's goals and role in society.

id·e·o- (id-ē-ō) *pref.* idea.

id'e·o·gram″ (id'ē-ə-gràm″) *n.* a written symbol that represents an idea directly. Also, **id'e·o·graph″** (-gràf″).

i″de·ol'o·gy (ī″dè-ol'ə-jè) *n.* **1,** the aggregate of ideas, beliefs, doctrines, etc., of a large group of persons; popularly, a system of government. **2,** the science of ideas. —**i″de·o·log'i·cal,** *adj.*

ides (īdz) *n.pl.* in ancient Rome, the 15th day of March, May, July, October; the 13th of other months.

id est' (*Lat.*) that is. Abbr., **i.e.** ❏ *e.g.*

id'i·o·cy (id'ē-ə-sè) *n.* the condition of an idiot.

id'i·om (id'ē-əm) *n.* **1,** a form of expression peculiar to a language. **2,** a dialect. **3,** the peculiar character of a language. **4,** a distinct style, as in music, art, etc.

id″i·o·mat'ic (id″ē-ə-mat'ik) *adj.* **1,** conforming to idiom. **2,** colloquial. —**id″i·o·mat'i·cal·ly,** *adv.*

id″i·o·syn'cra·sy (id″ē-ə-sin'krə-sè) *n.* a peculiarity, as of behavior.

id'i·ot (id'ē-ət) *n.* a person born mentally deficient, incapable of developing beyond a four-year mental level. —**id·i·ot'ic** (-ot'ik) *adj.* —**id·i·ot'i·cal·ly,** *adv.* —**idiot**

light, a warning light on an automobile instrument panel. —**idiot sa·vant'** (sä-vänt'; *Fr.* ē-dyō sä-vaǹ') a mentally deficient person with an exceptional talent in a certain field.

> **idiot**
> ↔ From Greek *idiōtēs*, private person. The sense was later extended to common person, and hence, ignorant person.

i'dle (ī'dəl) *adj.* **1,** doing nothing; inactive; unemployed. **2,** not in use or operation. **3,** lazy; slothful. **4,** useless; ineffective; futile. **5,** trivial; pointless; groundless. —*v.i.* **1,** pass the time in idleness. **2,** move slowly; saunter; loiter. **3,** (of a machine) run while not connected to do work. —*v.t.* cause to be idle. —**i'dle·ness,** *n.*

i'dler (ī'dlər) *n.* **1,** a gear or device that idles. **2,** a loafer.

i'dol (ī'dəl) *n.* **1,** an image of a deity, used as an object of worship. **2,** a person or thing adored or revered. **3,** a phantom; a false idea. —**i'dol·ize″,** *v.t.*

i″dol'a·ter (ī″dol'ə-tər) *n.* an idol worshiper. Also, **i″dol'a·tor.**

i·dol'a·try (ī-dol'ə-trè) *n.* the worship of idols. —**i·dol'a·trous,** *adj.*

i'dyll (ī'dəl) *n.* **1,** a descriptive or narrative poem, esp. pastoral. **2,** a simple, appealing episode or scene. Also, **i'dyl.** —**i·dyl'lic** (ī-dil'ik) *adj.* simple.

-ier (ir) *suf.* same as **-er** or **-eer.**

if *conj.* **1,** in case that; supposing that; on condition that. **2,** whether. **3,** even though. —*n.* a condition; a supposition. —**if'fy,** *adj.* (*Informal*) uncertain; contingent. ❏ *subjunctive*

> **if, whether**
> (*Gram.*) In formal usage, *if* and *whether* are not interchangeable. One frequently used test is to replace *whether* with *whether or not*; if the sentence still makes sense (i.e., if there are alternatives in question), do not use *if.*

ig'loo *n.* a domed Eskimo hut, made of blocks of snow and ice. Also, **ig'lu.**

ig'ne·ous (ig'nè-əs) *adj.* **1,** produced by intense heat, as rock of volcanic origin. **2,** pert. to fire.

ig'nis fat'u·us (ig'nəs fach'oo-əs) [*pl.* **ig'nes fat'u·i** (ig'nēz fach'oo-ī)] **1,** a flickering light sometimes seen at night over a marsh. **2,** something misleading; a delusion.

fat, fāte, fär, fåre, fåll, åsk; met, hē, hēr, maybè; pin, pīne; not, nōte, ôr, tool

ig·nite' (ig-nīt') *v.t. & i.* set on fire; begin to burn; kindle.

ig·ni'tion (ig-nish'ən) *n.* **1,** act of igniting; state of being ignited. **2,** a means, device, or process for igniting, esp. the electrical system of an internal combustion engine.

ig·no'ble (ig-nō'bəl) *adj.* **1,** low in character; base; dishonorable. **2,** low in birth or station. **—ig·no'ble·ness, ig″no·bil'i·ty,** *n.*

ig″no·min'i·ous (ig″nə-min'ē-əs) *adj.* causing or deserving humiliation, disgrace, or public contempt.

ig'no·min·y (ig'nə-min-ē) *n.* public disgrace.

ig″no·ra'mus (ig″nə-rā'məs) *n.* an ignorant person.

---

ignoramus
↔ From the name of an ignorant lawyer in a 17th-c. play by English playwright George Ruggle; based on Latin *ignoramus*, we ignore.

---

ig'no·rant (ig'nə-rənt) *adj.* **1,** having little or no knowledge; unlearned. **2,** unaware; uninformed. **—ig'no·rance,** *n.*

ig·nore' (ig-nôr') *v.t.* pass by without notice; pay no heed to.

i·gua'na (i-gwä'nə) *n.* a large lizard of tropical America.

ih·ram' (ē-räm') *n.* Muslim dress worn by men on pilgrimage to Mecca.

il- *pref.* same as **in-,** but used before an *l.*

il″e·i'tis (il″ē-ī'tis) *n.* inflammation of the ileum.

il'e·um (il'ē-əm) *n.* the part of the small intestine between the jejunum and the large intestine.

il'i·ac″ (il'ē-ak″) *adj.* pert. to the ilium, the large anterior bone of the pelvis.

ilk *n.* sort, kind, family, class, etc.

ill (il)' *adj.* **1,** impaired in health; unwell; sick. **2,** wicked; bad. **3,** causing evil; deleterious; malevolent. **4,** unfriendly; cross; crabbed. **5,** unfavorable; adverse. **6,** unskillful; bungling. **—adv.** [also, **ill'ly**] **1,** wickedly. **2,** unfortunately; unfavorably; in a hostile manner. **3,** with difficulty or hardship; faultily. **—n. 1,** a bodily ailment; disease. **2,** injury; harm; misfortune; trouble. **—ill'ness,** *n.* **—ill will,** hostility.

ill-″ad·vised' (-əd-vīzd') *adj.* showing poor judgment; unwise.

ill-'bred' *adj.* uncouth; impolite.

il·le'gal (i-lē'gəl) *adj.* contrary to law. **—il″le·gal'i·ty** (il″i-gal'ə-tē) *n.*

il·leg'i·ble (i-lej'ə-bəl) *adj.* impossible or hard to read. **—il·leg'i·bil'i·ty,** *n.*

il″le·git'i·mate (il″i-jit'ə-mət) *adj.* **1,** un-

lawful; invalid. **2,** born out of wedlock. **—il″le·git'i·ma·cy,** *n.*

ill-″fat'ed (-fā'təd) *adj.* **1,** doomed. **2,** unlucky.

ill-'fa″vored *adj.* ugly; unpleasant.

ill-″got'ten *adj.* obtained by illegal or dishonest means.

il·lic'it (i-lis'it) *adj.* **1,** unlawful; unlicensed. **2,** clandestine. **—il·lic'it·ness,** *n.*

---

illicit, elicit
☛ Do not confuse these words of similar sound and unrelated meanings. *Illicit* means unlawful; *elicit* means to evoke.

---

il·lim'it·a·ble (i-lim'i-tə-bəl) *adj.* infinite; too great to measure.

il·lin'i·um (i-lin'ē-əm) *n.* promethium.

il·lit'er·ate (i-lit'ər-ət) *adj.* unable to read and write. **—n.** an illiterate person. **—il·lit'er·a·cy,** *n.*

il·log'i·cal (i-loj'i-kəl) *adj.* contravening or disregarding the rules of logic. **—il·log'·i·cal'i·ty** (-kal'ə-tē) *n.*

ill-'starred″ *adj.* unfortunate.

il·lu'mi·nate″ (i-loo'mə-nāt″) *v.t.* **1,** furnish with a light; light up; enlighten. **2,** make clear; explain; elucidate. **3,** decorate in color by hand. **—il·lu″mi·na'tion,** *n.* **—il·lu'mi·na″tor,** *n.* Also, **il·lu'mine** (-min).

ill-″use' (-ūz') *v.t.* mistreat; abuse. **—n.** (-ūs') cruel or unjust treatment. Also, **ill-″us'age.**

il·lu'sion (i-loo'zhən) *n.* something that deceives the eye or mind; a mistaken perception or belief. **—il·lu'sive** (-siv), **il·lu'·so·ry** (-sə-rē) *adj.* ❑ *allusion*

il'lus·trate″ (il'ə-strāt″) *v.t.* **1,** furnish with pictures, diagrams, etc., to adorn or elucidate. **2,** make clear or intelligible, as with examples. **—il·lus'tra·tive** (i-lus'trə-tiv), *adj.*

il″lus·tra'tion (il″ə-strā'shən) *n.* **1,** something that illustrates, as a picture. **2,** act of illustrating.

il·lus'tra″tor (il'ə-strā″tər) *n.* an artist who makes illustrations for books or periodicals.

il·lus'tri·ous (i-lus'trē-əs) *adj.* very distinguished; conspicuous; eminent. **—il·lus'·tri·ous·ness,** *n.*

im- *pref.* same as **in-,** but used before *b, m,* or *p.* [In addition to words defined in the text, the following words formed by prefixing **im-** (=not) have merely the negative sense of the positive term. For pronunciation of such words, listed below or defined in the text, refer to the vocabulary

for the pronunciation of the positive
term.]

im·bal'ance
im·meas'ur·a·ble
im·mis'ci·ble
im·mit'i·ga·ble
im·mov'a·ble
im·mu'ta·ble
im·pal'pa·ble
im·par'i·ty
im·pas'sa·ble
im·pas'si·ble
im·pen'e·tra·ble
im·pen'i·tent
im″per·cep'ti·ble

im·per'ish·a·ble
im·per'ma·nent
im·per'me·a·ble
im·per'son·al
im″per·turb'a·ble
im″plau'si·ble
im·pol'i·tic
im·prac'ti·ca·ble
im·prac'ti·cal
im″pre·cise'
im·prob'a·ble
im·pro'bi·ty
im·prov'i·dent

im'age (im'ij) *n.* **1,** a representation of
the form and features of a person or thing,
in a picture, statue, etc. **2,** a reflection in
a mirror. **3,** a mental picture; a written
description; a figure of speech. **4,** any
counterpart or copy; a likeness or simili-
tude. **5,** symbol. —*v.t.* **1,** picture in the
mind; imagine. **2,** make an image of.

im'age·ry (-rė) *n.* **1,** imaginative thought
or expression. **2,** images collectively.

i·mag'i·nar·y (i-maj'ə-ner-ė) *adj.* existing only in the imagination or fancy; not
real. —**imaginary number** or **part,** (*Math.*)
the part of a complex number containing
the imaginary unit (as 3i in 5 + 3i). —
imaginary unit, the positive square root of
minus 1, symbol i.

i·mag″i·na'tion (i-maj″ə-nā'shən) *n.* **1,**
the act or faculty of forming mental images of objects. **2,** the faculty of forming
ideas and ideals. **3,** fancy, ideal, concept,
etc.

im·ag'i·na·tive (i-maj'ə-nə-tiv) *adj.* having lively imagination.

im·ag'ine (i-maj'in) *v.t.* **1,** form a mental
image of. **2,** think; believe; suppose; conjecture; guess, etc. —*v.i.* **1,** exercise the
imagination. **2,** think; fancy. —**im·ag'i·na-
ble,** *adj.*

i·ma'go (i-mā'gō) *n.* **1,** an insect in the
adult stage. **2,** (*Psychol.*) an idealized concept of a parent, formed in childhood and
retained in the adult unconscious mind.

i·mam' (i-mäm') *n.* a Muslim priest.

im'be·cile (im'bə-sil) *n.* a person of defective mentality, but above the level of
an idiot. —**im″be·cil'ic,** *adj.* —**im″be·cil'i-
ty,** *n.*

im·bed' *v.t.* [**-bed'ded, -ding**] embed.

im·bibe' (im-bīb') *v.t.* **1,** drink. **2,** absorb;
take in.

im'bri·cate (im'bri-kit) *adj.* **1,** overlapping like tiles, as fish scales, etc. **2,** decorated with designs like overlapping tiles.

Also, **im'bri·cat″ed** —*v.* (im'bri-kāt″)
overlap like tiles. —**im″bri·ca'tion,** *n.*

im·bro'glio (im-brōl'yō) *n.* an intricate,
confused, or perplexing state of affairs.

im·brue' (im-broo') *v.t.* wet; drench;
stain.

im·bue' (im-bū') *v.t.* saturate; dye; impregnate, as with sentiments, opinions,
etc. —**im·bue'ment,** *n.*

im'i·tate (im'ə-tāt″) *v.t.* **1,** copy in manner or action; follow as a model; mimic;
simulate. **2,** make a copy of. —**im'i·ta·ble**
(-tə-bəl) *adj.* —**im'i·ta″tive,** *adj.* —**im'i·ta″-
tor,** *n.*

im″i·ta'tion (im″ə-tā'shən) *n.* the act or
a product of imitating; a copy, likeness,
or counterfeit. —*adj.* made to imitate a
genuine, and usually superior, article.

im·mac'u·late (i-mak'yə-lit) *adj.* **1,** perfectly clean; spotless. **2,** free from moral
blemish; pure. —**im·mac'u·la·cy** (-lə-sė),
—**im·mac'u·late·ness,** *n.*

im'ma·nent (im'ə-nənt) *adj.* remaining
within; intrinsic. —**im'ma·nence,** *n.* ☐
eminent

im″ma·te'ri·al (im″ə-tir'ė-əl) *adj.* of little
or no significance; irrelevant. —**im″ma-
te'ri·al·ness,** *n.*

im″ma·ture' (im″ə-tyûr') *adj.* not ripe or
fully developed; youthful. —**im″ma·tur'i-
ty,** *n.*

im·me'di·a·cy (i-mē'dė-ə-sė) *n.* urgency,
because of lack of intervening time.

im·me'di·ate (i-mē'dė-ət) *adj.* **1,** without
any time intervening; instant. **2,** of the
present moment. **3,** not separated; next;
nearest. **4,** direct. —**im·me'di·ate·ness,** *n.*

im″me·mo'ri·al (im″ə-môr'ė-əl) *adj.* of a
time beyond memory, record, or
knowledge.

im·mense' (i-mens') *adj.* **1,** very large;
huge; vast. **2,** boundless. **3,** (*Slang*) excellent. —**im·men'si·ty** (i-men'sə-tė), **immense'ness,** *n.*

im·merse' (i-mėrs') *v.t.* **1,** plunge into,
esp. deeply. **2,** involve or interest deeply.

im·mer'sion (-zhən) *n.* act of immersing.
—*adj.* concentrated: *immersion course.*

im'mi·grant (im'i-grənt) *n.* one who im-
migrates. ☐ *emigrant*

im'mi·grate' (im'ə-grāt″) *v.t.* come to
settle in a new habitat or country. —**im″-
mi·gra'tion,** *n.*

im'mi·nent (im'ə-nənt) *adj.* **1,** likely to
occur soon; impending. **2,** jutting out;
overhanging. —**im'mi·nence,** *n.* ☐
eminent

im·mo'bile (i-mō'bəl) *adj.* not movable
or moving. —**im″mo·bil'i·ty** (-bil'ə-tė) *n.*

im·mo′bi·lize″ (i-mō′bə-līz″) *v.t.* render incapable of moving. —**im·mo″bi·li·za′-tion,** *n.*

im·mod′er·ate (i-mod′ər-ət) *adj.* not confined to just or reasonable limits; intemperate. —**im·mod″er·a′tion,** *n.*

im·mod′est (i-mod′ist) *adj.* **1,** not proper; indecent. **2,** boastful. —**im·mod′-es·ty,** *n.*

im′mo·late″ (im′ə-lāt″) *v.t.* kill as a sacrificial victim. —**im″mo·la′tion,** *n.*

im·mor′al (i-môr′əl) *adj.* not conforming to moral law. —**im″mo·ral′i·ty** (im″ə-ral′ə-tė) *n.* wickedness; vice. ❑ *amoral*

im·mor′tal (i-môr′təl) *adj.* not subject to death, cessation, or oblivion. —*n.* one who is immortal. —**im″mor·tal′i·ty** (im″ôr-tal′ə-tė) *n.*

im·mor′tal·ize″ (-īz″) *v.t.* make immortal or forever famous. —**im·mor″tal·i·za′tion,** *n.*

im″mor·telle′ (im″ôr-tel′) *n.* a plant or flower that retains form and color when it dies.

im·mune′ (i-mūn′) *adj.* not liable; exempt, as from a disease. —**im·mu′ni·ty** (i-mū′nə-tė) *n.*

im′mu·nize″ (im′yə-nīz″) *v.t.* protect, as from disease by inoculation. —**im″mu·ni·za′tion,** *n.*

im·mu·no- (i-myoo-nō) *pref.* immunity.

im·mure′ (i-myûr′) *v.t.* surround with walls; confine. —**im·mure′ment,** *n.*

imp *n.* a small prankish sprite or child. —**imp′ish,** *adj.* mischievous.

---
imp
↔ From Greek *emphytos*, engrafted, hence, new growth, child.

---

im′pact (im′pakt) *n.* **1,** the striking of one body against another; collision. **2,** the force of a collision. —*v.* (im-pakt′) **1,** press closely; pack in. **2,** (with *on*) have an impact or effect on. —**im·pact′ed,** *adj.* tightly packed; wedged in. —**im·pac′tion,** *n.*

im·pair′ (im-pâr′) *v.t. & i.* make or become worse; damage; weaken. —**im·pair′-ment,** *n.*

im·pa′la (im-pä′lə) *n.* a large Afr. antelope.

im·pale′ (im-pāl′) *v.t.* **1,** thrust a sharpened stake through; transfix. **2,** fence in. —**im·pale′ment,** *n.*

im·pan′el (im-pan′əl) *v.t.* enroll or summon (a jury). —**im·pan′el·ment,** *n.*

im·part′ (im-pärt′) *v.t.* **1,** make known; tell. **2,** give; bestow; share. —**im″par·ta′-tion,** *n.*

im·par′tial (im-pär′shəl) *adj.* not biased; equitable; just. —**im·par″ti·al′i·ty** (-shē-al′ə-tė) *n.*

im·pas′sa·ble (im-pas′ə-bəl) *adj.* **1,** that one cannot pass through. **2,** insurmountable.

---
impassable, impassible, impassive
☞ *Impassable* means that one cannot pass through. *Impassible* and *impassive* both mean lacking sensitivity, literally or figuratively.

---

im·passe′ (im-pas′) *n.* a condition in which progress or escape is blocked; a deadlock.

im·pas′si·ble (im-pas′i-bəl) *adj.* **1,** not suffering pain, harm, etc. **2,** impassive (def. 1). ❑ *impassable*

im·pas′sion (im-pash′ən) *v.t.* move or affect with passion. —**im·pas′sioned,** *adj.* filled with emotion; ardent.

im·pas′sive (im-pas′iv) *adj.* **1,** free of emotion; unmoved; apathetic. **2,** serene; calm. —**im·pas′sive·ness, im″pas·siv′i·ty** (im″pə-siv′ə-tė) *n.* ❑ *impassable*

im·pas′to (im-päs′tō) *n.* a thick covering of paint.

im·pa′tient (im-pā′shənt) *adj.* not tranquil; restive; eager. —**im·pa′tience,** *n.*

im·peach′ (im-pēch′) *v.t.* **1,** accuse (a public official) of misconduct. **2,** discredit; disparage. —**im·peach′ment,** *n.*

---
impeach
☞ Note that *impeach* means accuse, not to remove from office.

---

im·pec′ca·ble (im-pek′ə-bəl) *adj.* without fault or blemish; irreproachable. —**im·pec″ca·bil′i·ty,** *n.*

im″pe·cu′ni·ous (im″pə-kū′nė-əs) *adj.* without money; poor. —**im″pe·cu′ni·ous-ness,** *n.*

im·pe′dance (im-pē′dəns) *n.* (*Electricity*) the apparent resistance to the flow of an alternating current that corresponds to the actual resistance to the flow of a direct current.

im·pede′ (im-pēd′) *v.t.* check or retard the progress of; hinder; obstruct.

im·ped′i·ment (im-ped′ə-mənt) *n.* **1,** a load; hindrance. **2,** a physical defect that impairs speech. **3,** a bar to marriage. —**im·ped″i·men′ta** (-tə) *n.pl.* baggage.

im·pel′ *v.t.* [**-pelled′, pel′ling**] **1,** incite or constrain to an action; urge. **2,** drive onward.

im·pend′ *v.t.* be on the point of occurring; be imminent.

im·per′a·tive (im-per′ə-tiv) *adj.* **1,** expressing command; peremptory. **2,** not to be evaded; obligatory. **3,** (*Gram.*) of verbs, denoting the mood expressing command. —**im·per′a·tive·ness,** *n.*

im·per′fect (im-pēr′fikt) *adj.* **1,** faulty; defective; incomplete. **2,** (*Gram.*) of verbs, expressing past but not completed action; past progressive, as *he was singing.* —**im″per·fec′tion,** *n.*

im·per′fo·rate (im-pēr′fə-rit) *adj.* not pierced. —*n.* a postage stamp not perforated for separation.

im·pe′ri·al (im-pir′ė-əl) *adj.* **1,** pert. to an empire or emperor. **2,** august; commanding. **3,** grand; superior in size or quality. —*n.* **1,** a short narrow beard under the lower lip. **2,** a former Russian gold coin. —**imperial gallon,** a Brit. liquid measure, 1⅕ U.S. gallons.

> **imperial, imperious**
> ☛ Do not confuse *imperial*, pert. to an empire, and *imperious*, domineering.

im·pe′ri·al·ism (-iz-əm) *n.* the policy of expanding national territory. —**im·pe′ri·al·ist,** *n.* —**im·pe″ri·al·is′tic,** *adj.* —**im·pe″ri·al·is′ti·cal·ly,** *adv.*

im·per′il (im-per′əl) *v.t.* put in peril; endanger. —**im·per′il·ment,** *n.*

im·pe′ri·ous (im-pir′ė-əs) *adj.* **1,** domineering. **2,** imperative; urgent. —**im·pe′ri·ous·ness,** *n.* ❑ *imperial*

im·per′son·al (im-pēr′sə-nəl) *adj.* not personal; having no personality; hence, lacking human warmth, unfeeling. —**im·per″son·al′i·ty,** *n.*

im·per′son·ate″ (im-pēr′sə-nāt″) *v.t.* pretend or be; assume the character of; play the role of. —**im·per″son·a′tion,** *n.* —**im·per′son·a·tor,** *n.*

im·per′ti·nent (im-pēr′tə-nənt) *adj.* **1,** unmannerly in conduct; forward; insolent. **2,** not pertinent; irrelevant. —**im·per′ti·nence,** *n.*

im·per′vi·ous (im-pēr′vė-əs) *adj.* **1,** not permeable. **2,** resistant to persuasion. —**im·per′vi·ous·ness,** *n.*

im·pe′ti·go (im″pə-tī′gō) *n.* a contagious skin disease, esp. of children.

im·pet′u·ous (im-pech′oo-əs) *adj.* sudden and vehement in action. —**im·pet″u·os′i·ty** (-os′ə-tė), **im·pet′u·ous·ness,** *n.*

im′pe·tus (im′pə-təs) *n.* **1,** energy of motion; the power with which a moving body tends to maintain its velocity. **2,** impulse; incentive.

im·pi′e·ty (im-pī′ə-tė) *n.* lack of reverence; wickedness.

im·pinge′ (im-pinj′) *v.i.* (with *on, against,* etc.) **1,** collide. **2,** encroach. —**im·pinge′ment,** *n.*

im′pi·ous (im′pė-əs) *adj.* lacking reverence for God; profane. —**im′pi·ous·ness,** *n.*

im·pla′ca·ble (im-plā′kə-bəl) *adj.* not to be placated or appeased; inexorable. —**im·pla′ca·ble·ness, im·pla″ca·bil′i·ty,** *n.*

im·plant′ (im-plànt′) *v.t.* **1,** plant in the mind; inculcate; instill. **2,** set in a place; imbed. —*n.* (im′plant″) (*Med.*) something introduced into living tissue. —**im″plan·ta′tion.** *n.*

im′ple·ment (im′plə-mənt) *n.* **1,** an instrument, tool, or utensil. **2,** a means of doing or enacting; an agent. —*v.t.* (-ment″) **1,** enact; execute. **2,** provide with implements or means. —**im″ple·men·ta′tion,** *n.*

im′pli·cate″ (im′pli-kāt″) *v.t.* show to be involved or concerned with; entangle.

im″pli·ca′tion (im″pli-kā′shən) *n.* **1,** something implied; the act of implying. **2,** the condition of being implicated or involved.

im·plic′it (im-plis′it) *adj.* **1,** to be assumed, though not directly expressed; implied. **2,** unquestioning, as of faith. —**im·plic′it·ness,** *n.* ❑ *explicit*

im·plode′ (im-plōd′) *v.t. & i.* burst inward.

im·plore′ (im-plôr′) *v.t.* **1,** beseech; entreat. **2,** request urgently.

im·plo′sion (im-plō′zhən) *n.* a bursting inward. —**im·plo′sive,** *adj.*

im·ply′ (im-plī′) *v.t.* **1,** suggest or indicate without expressing directly. **2,** necessarily involve; entail.

> **imply, infer**
> ☛ Two words often confused. To *imply* is to suggest; to *infer* is to conclude by reasoning.

im″po·lite′ (im″pə-līt′) *adj.* discourteous. —**im″po·lite′ness,** *n.*

im·pon′der·a·ble (im-pon′dər-ə-bəl) *adj.* not to be weighed or evaluated; too vague to meditate upon. —**im·pon″der·a·bil′i·ty,** *n.*

im·port′ (im-pôrt′) *v.t.* **1,** bring in, as wares from a foreign country. **2,** denote; signify. **3,** have a bearing on. —*v.i.* be of importance. —*n.* (im′pôrt) **1,** something imported from abroad; the act or business of importing. **2,** meaning; implication. **3,** importance; consequence. —**im″por·ta′tion** (im″pôr-tā′shən) *n.*

im·por′tance (im-pôr′təns) *n.* state of being important.

im·por′tant (im-pôr′tənt) *adj.* **1,** of great weight in meaning, significance, or consequence. **2,** urgent. **3,** eminent; prominent; influential. **4,** pompous.

im″por·tune′ (im″pôr-tūn′) *v.t.* & *i.* **1,** beset with entreaties. **2,** ask for persistently; beg. —**im·por′tu·nate,** *adj.* —**im″·por·tu′ni·ty,** *n.*

im·pose′ (im-pōz′) *v.t.* **1,** lay as a burden; levy, inflict, or enforce. **2,** palm off. **3,** obtrude (oneself) upon others. **4,** lay on; put; lay out (printing type) in proper order. —**im·pos′ing,** *adj.* stately; impressive.

im″po·si′tion (im″pə-zish′ən) *n.* **1,** act or manner of imposing. **2,** a burden placed on another's goodwill.

im·pos′si·ble (im-pos′ə-bəl) *adj.* **1,** nonexistent or false; sure not to happen. **2,** not able to be done; utterly impracticable. **3,** (*Informal*) very unattractive. —**im·pos″si·bil′i·ty,** *n.*

im′post (im′pōst) *n.* a tax or tribute, esp. a customs duty.

im·pos′tor (im-pos′tər) *n.* one who deceitfully assumes a false name or character.

im·pos′ture (im-pos′chər) *n.* false assumption of another's name, etc.; any sham or hoax.

im′po·tent (im′pə-tənt) *adj.* lacking strength, power, or virility. —**im′po·tence, im′po·ten·cy,** *n.*

im·pound′ (im-pownd′) *v.t.* **1,** shut in a pen; restrain within bounds. **2,** seize and keep in custody. —**im·pound′age, im·pound′ment,** *n.*

im·pov′er·ish (im-pov′ər-ish) *v.t.* **1,** make indigent. **2,** cause to deteriorate. —**im·pov′er·ish·ment,** *n.*

im·prac′ti·cal (im-prak′ti-kəl) *adj.* not practical.

---

impractical, impracticable

☞ Do not confuse *impractical*, not practical, with *impracticable*, not feasible.

---

im·prac′ti·ca·ble (im-prak′ti-kə-bəl) *adj.* not feasible; which can not be done.

im′pre·cate″ (im′prə-kāt″) *v.t.* invoke a curse or evil upon. —**im″pre·ca′tion,** *n.*

im·preg′na·ble (im-preg′nə-bəl) *adj.* **1,** not to be taken or overcome by force; invincible. **2,** capable of being impregnated. —**im·preg″na·bil′i·ty,** *n.*

im·preg′nate (im-preg′nāt) *v.t.* **1,** make pregnant; fertilize. **2,** permeate or satu-

rate. —*adj.* impregnated. —**im″preg′na·tion,** *n.*

im″pre·sa′ri·o″ (im″prə-sär′é-ō″) *n.* a theatrical producer or manager, esp. of an opera company; any promoter.

---

impresario

↔ From Italian *impresa,* undertaking, from Latin *prendere,* take.

---

im·press′ (im-pres′) *v.t.* **1,** affect deeply as to mind or feelings. **2,** fix firmly in the mind. **3,** press; stamp; imprint. **4,** seize for public use; force into service. —*n.* (im′press) **1,** a product of stamping or printing. **2,** distinctive appearance or character. —**im·press′i·ble,** *adj.*

im·pres′sion (im-presh′ən) *n.* **1,** effect produced, as by perception or sensation; an idea, image, etc., esp. if vague. **2,** the act of impressing; a mark, mold, copy, etc., made by pressing, stamping, or printing. **3,** an edition. —**im·pres′sion·a·ble,** *adj.* easily impressed; susceptible.

Im·pres′sion·ism (-iz-əm) *n.* a style of nonobjective expression in art and music. —**Im·pres′sion·ist,** *adj.* & *n.*

im·pres′sive (-siv) *adj.* tending to excite admiration. —**im·pres′sive·ness,** *n.*

im·press′ment (-mənt) *n.* a forcing into service.

im″pri·ma′tur (im″pri-mä′tər) *n.* an official license to publish.

im·print′ *v.t.* produce or fix by, or as by, pressure; print; stamp. —*n.* (im′print) **1,** a distinctive mark; a maker's or seller's name, esp. a publisher's. **2,** effect produced; impression.

im·pris′on (im-priz′ən) *v.t.* put in prison; confine. —**im·pris′on·ment,** *n.*

im·promp′tu (im-promp′too) *adj.* **1,** done without previous preparation. **2,** hastily prepared; improvised. —*n.* an impromptu performance or composition. —*adv.* extemporaneously.

im·prop′er (im-prop′ər) *adj.* not proper; not moral; incorrect; indecorous. —**im·prop′er·ness,** *n.* —**improper fraction,** a fraction of which the numerator is equal to or greater than the denominator.

im″pro·pri′e·ty (im″prə-prī′ə-tè) *n.* improper action; an error; a breach of propriety.

im′prov (im′präv) *n.* (*Informal*) improvisation; improvised skit. Also, **im′pro** (-prō).

im·prove′ (im-proov′) *v.t.* **1,** make better. **2,** make (land) more valuable, esp. by erecting buildings. —*v.i.* become better; increase in value or utility.

---

im·prove′ment (-mənt) *n.* **1,** act or result of improving. **2,** construction, or a structure, that improves real property.

im′pro·vise″ (im′prə-vīz″) *v.t.* make or do hastily or without previous preparation; extemporize, esp. in music. —**im″·pro·vi·sa′tion,** *n.*

im·pru′dent (im-proo′dənt) *adj.* indiscreet; rash. —**im·pru′dence,** *n.*

im′pu·dent (im′pyə-dənt) *adj.* offensively forward in behavior; insolent; saucy. —**im′pu·dence,** *n.*

im·pugn′ (im-pūn′) *v.t.* challenge as false. —**im·pugn′ment,** *n.*

im′pulse (im′puls) *n.* **1,** force acting suddenly; a thrust or push. **2,** a stimulation of the mind to action; a sudden inclination. **3,** the intensity or momentum of a force; induced motion; impetus. —**im·pul′sion,** *n.* —**im·pul′sive,** *adj.* impetuous.

im·pu′ni·ty (im-pū′nə-tē) *n.* exemption from punishment.

im·pure′ (im-pyûr′) *adj.* **1,** not simple or homogeneous; mixed with extraneous matter; tainted. **2,** obscene. —**im·pure′ness,** *n.*

im·pur′i·ty (im-pyûr′ə-tē) *n.* **1,** something not pure; a flaw. **2,** impureness. **3,** that which makes impure, as a foreign ingredient, etc.

im·pute′ (im-pūt′) *v.t.* charge, ascribe, or attribute, esp. something discreditable. —**im″pu·ta′tion,** *n.*

in *prep.* denoting presence, existence, situation, inclusion, action, etc., within limits, as of place, time, condition, circumstances, etc. —*adv.* **1,** at, to, or toward (a place, condition, relation, etc.). **2,** inward; on the inside; at home; in occupancy. **3,** having the turn to play in a game. **4,** accepted; elected. —*adj.* (*Informal*) in vogue.

in- *pref.* **1,** in, as in *income.* **2,** used to form or intensify verbs, as *intrust*; often replaced by **en-**. **3,** not: used to impart a negative sense, as in *inactive.* (See also **un-**.) [In addition to words defined in the text, the following words formed by prefixing **in-** (=not) have merely the negative sense of the positive term. For pronunciation of such words, refer to the vocabulary for the pronunciation of the positive term.]

in″a·bil′i·ty
in″ac·ces′si·ble
in·ac′cu·rate
in·ac′tive
in·ad′e·quate
in″ad·mis′si·ble
in″ad·vis′a·ble
in·al′ien·a·ble

in″ef·fec′tu·al
in·ef′fi·ca·cy
in″ef·fi′cient
in″e·las′tic
in·el′e·gant
in·el′i·gi·ble
in·el′o·quent
in″e·qual′i·ty

in″ap′pli·ca·ble
in″ap·pre′ci·a·ble
in·apt′
in″ar·tis′tic
in·au′di·ble
in″aus·pi′cious
in·cal′cu·la·ble
in·ca′pa·ble
in·cer′ti·tude
in″ci·vil′i·ty
in·cog′ni·zant
in″com·bus′ti·ble
in″com·men′su·rate
in″com·mu′ni·ca·ble
in″com·plete′
in″com·pre·hen′·si·ble
in″com·press′ible
in″con·ceiv′a·ble
in″con·clu′sive
in″con·sid′er·ate
in″con·sist′ent
in″con·sol′a·ble
in″con·test′a·ble
in″con·tro·vert′i·ble
in″cor·po′re·al
in″cor·rect′
in″cor·rupt′i·ble
in·cur′a·ble
in·cu′ri·ous
in″de·ci′pher·a·ble
in·dec′o·rous
in″de·fen′si·ble
in″de·fin′a·ble
in″de·scrib′a·ble
in″de·struct′i·ble
in″di·rect′
in″dis·cern′i·ble
in″dis·pen′sa·ble
in″dis·put′a·ble
in″dis·sol′u·ble
in″dis·tinct′
in″di·vis′i·ble
in·ed′i·ble
in″ef·fec′tive

in″e·rad′i·ca·ble
in″es·cap′a·ble
in″ex·act′
in″ex·cus′a·ble
in″ex·haust′i·ble
in″ex·pe′di·ent
in″ex·pen′sive
in″ex′pert
in·ex′pi·a·ble
in″ex·plic′a·ble
in″ex·press′i·ble
in″ex·tin′guish·a·ble
in·ex′tri·ca·ble
in″fe·li′ci·tous
in·fer′tile
in·fre′quent
in″har·mo′ni·ous
in·hos′pi·ta·ble
in″hu·mane′
in·im′i·ta·ble
in″ju·di′cious
in·jus′tice
in·nu′mer·a·ble
in″ob·ser′vant
in·op′er·a·ble
in·op′er·a·tive
in·op″por·tune′
in″or·gan′ic
in·sa′ti·a·ble
in·sen′sate
in·sen′si·tive
in·sep′a·ra·ble
in″so·bri′e·ty
in·sol′u·ble
in″sub·stan′tial
in·suf′fer·a·ble
in″suf·fi′cient
in″sup·port′a·ble
in″sur·mount′a·ble
in·trac′ta·ble
in·var′i·a·ble
in·ver′te·brate
in·vis′i·ble
in·vul′ner·a·ble

in ab·sen′tia (in ab-sen′shə) (*Lat.*) in absence.

in″ad·vert′ent (in″əd-vēr′tənt) *adj.* **1,** unintentional; accidental. **2,** not attentive; negligent. —**in″ad·vert′ence,** *n.*

in·am″o·ra′ta (in-am″ə-rä′tə) *n.* a woman with whom one is in love; lover.

in·ane′ (in-ān′) *adj.* void of sense or intelligence; silly. —**in·an′i·ty** (in-an′ə-tē) *n.*

in·an′i·mate (in-an′i-mət) *adj.* not alive; quiescent.

in″a·ni′tion (in″ə-ni′shən) *n.* **1,** exhaustion from lack of nourishment; starvation. **2,** inanity.

in″ar·tic′u·late (in″är-tik′yə-lət) *adj.* **1,** not articulate. **2,** lacking facility in speech or expression. —**in″ar·tic′u·late·ness,** *n.*

in″as·much′ as (in″əz-much′) *adj.* **1,** in view of the fact; considering that. **2,** insofar as; to the degree of.

in″at·ten′tion (in″ə-ten′shən) *n.* failure to be attentive or thoughtful. —**in″at·ten′-tive** (-tiv) *adj.*

in·au′gu·ral (in-â′gyû-rəl) *adj.* inaugurating; pert. to an inauguration.

in·au′gu·rate″ (in-â′gyə-rāt″) *v.t.* **1,** make a formal beginning of; initiate. **2,** install in office. —**in·aug″u·ra′tion,** *n.*

in′board″ (in′bôrd″) *adj. & adv.* **1,** inside a ship's hull. **2,** toward the inside.

in′born″ (in′bôrn″) *adj.* implanted by nature; innate.

in′bred″ *adj.* **1,** produced by inbreeding. **2,** innate; ingrained in one's character.

in′breed″ing (in′brē″ding) *n.* the mating of closely related individuals. —**in′-breed″,** *v.i.*

In′ca (ing′kə) *n.* **1,** a member of an American Indian people of ancient Peru. **2,** a king of this people.

in″can·des′cent (in″kən-des′ənt) *adj.* **1,** rendered luminous by heat. **2,** white-hot; glowing; brilliant. —**in″can·des′cence,** *n.*

in″can·ta′tion (in″kan-tā′shən) *n.* the uttering of magical words.

in″ca·pac′i·tate″ (in″kə-pas′ə-tāt″) *v.t.* render unfit; disqualify. —**in″ca·pac″i·ta′-tion,** *n.*

in″ca·pac′i·ty (-ə-tė) *n.* inability to perform; incompetence.

in·car′cer·ate″ (in-kär′sə-rāt″) *v.t.* put or hold in prison. —**in·car″cer·a′tion,** *n.*

in·car′na·dine″ (in-kär′nə-dīn″) *adj.* **1,** flesh-colored. **2,** crimson.

in·car′nate (in-kär′nət) *adj.* embodied in flesh. —*v.t.* (-nāt) **1,** embody in flesh. **2,** typify. —**in″car·na′tion,** *n.* existence in bodily form.

in·cau′tious (in-kâ′shəs) *adj.* not cautious; done or uttered with insufficient thought or discretion. —**in·cau′tious·ness,** *n.*

in·cen′di·ar·y (in-sen′dė-er-ė) *adj.* **1,** pert. to arson. **2,** used in starting a fire. **3,** tending to excite violence; inflammatory. —*n.* **1,** one who or that which starts destructive fires. **2,** an agitator. —**in·cen′di·ar·ism** (-ə-riz-əm) *n.*

in′cense (in′sens) *n.* **1,** an aromatic material or the perfume it produces when burned. **2,** any agreeable odor.

in·cense′ (in-sens′) *v.t.* excite to anger or resentment; enrage. —**in·cense′ment,** *n.*

in·cen′tive (in-sen′tiv) *n.* something that incites to action; motive; spur. —*adj.* stimulating.

in·cep′tion (in-sep′shən) *n.* a beginning; initiation. —**in·cep′tive,** *adj.*

in·ces′sant (in-ses′ənt) *adj.* unceasing; continuing without interruption. —**in·ces′-san·cy,** *n.*

in′cest (in′sest) *n.* intercourse between closely related persons; such intercourse when considered a crime. —**in·ces′tuous** (in-ses′choo-əs) *adj.*

---

incest, chaste

↔ *Incest* comes from Latin *incestus,* impure, from *castus,* pure, the source of English *chaste.*

---

inch *n.* a unit of length, 1/12 of a foot. —*v.t. & i.* move by small degrees.

in·cho′ate (in-kō′it) *adj.* just begun; rudimentary. —**in·cho′ate·ness,** *n.*

inch′worm″ *n.* a measuring worm.

in′ci·dence (in′si-dəns) *n.* **1,** frequency or range of occurrence; extent of effects. **2,** manner or direction of a fall; course. **3,** partial coincidence.

in′ci·dent (in′si-dənt) *n.* **1,** an occurrence or event; a casual happening. **2,** an episode. **3,** a result or casual feature of something else. —*adj.* **1,** dependent; pertaining. **2,** falling or striking on something. **3,** likely to happen.

in″ci·den′tal (in″si-den′təl) *adj.* **1,** pert. to or constituting an incident. **2,** casual; minor.

in·cin′er·ate″ (in-sin′ə-rāt″) *v.t.* burn to ashes. —**in·cin″er·a′tion,** *n.* —**in·cin′er·a″-tor,** *n.* a furnace for burning waste.

in·cip′i·ent (in-sip′ė-ənt) *adj.* beginning to exist or appear. —**in·cip′i·ence, in·cip′-ien·cy,** *n.*

in·cise′ (in-sīz′) *v.t.* cut into; engrave.

in·ci′sion (in-sizh′ən) *n.* **1,** act of cutting into. **2,** a cut or gash.

in·ci′sive (in-sī′siv) *adj.* **1,** sharply expressive; penetrating; trenchant. **2,** adapted for cutting. —**in·ci′sive·ness,** *n.*

in·ci′sor (in-sī′zər) *n.* a tooth adapted for cutting.

in·cite′ (in-sīt′) *v.t.* **1,** move (a person) to action; urge or stimulate. **2,** stir up (an action); instigate. —**in·cite′ment,** *n.* ❑ *excite*

in·clem′ent (in-klem′ənt) *adj.* (of weather) harsh; tempestuous. —**in·clem′-en·cy,** *n.*

in″cli·na′tion (in′klə-nā′shən) *n.* **1,** a preference or liking; disposition; bent. **2,** the act of inclining; the state of being inclined. **3,** a slanted position; the angle of a slant.

in·cline′ (in-klīn′) *v.t.* **1,** have a tendency

or preference. **2,** be slanted or oblique. **3,** tend toward; approximate. —*v.t.* **1,** give a tendency to. **2,** bend; bow; slant. —*n.* (in′klīn) a slope.

in·close′ (in-klōz′) *v.t.* enclose.

in·clude′ (in-klood′) *v.t.* **1,** contain as a part; take in; embrace or cover. **2,** be composed of; comprise. —**in·clu′sion** (-zhən) *n.* ❏ *comprise*

in·clu′sive (in-kloo′siv) *adj.* **1,** including the stated limits. **2,** wide in extent; comprehensive. **3,** of language, not sexist; referring equally to both sexes. —**in·clu′sive·ness,** *n.* —**inclusive of,** including.

in″cog·ni′to (in″kog-nē′tō; in-kog′ni-tō″) *adj. & adv.* with real name or identity concealed.

in″co·her′ent (in″kō-hir′ənt) *adj.* **1,** without apparent unity or connection; incongruous. **2,** not logical or coordinated in expression; confused; chaotic. **3,** lacking physical cohesion. —**in″co·her′ence,** *n.*

in′come (in′kum) *n.* **1,** money received as wages, interest, etc. **2,** profit. —**income tax,** tax levied on annual income.

in′com″ing *adj.* **1,** entering; approaching. **2,** coming in as occupant or successor. **3,** accruing.

in″com·mode′ (in″kə-mōd′) *v.t.* subject to inconvenience. —**in″com·mo′di·ous,** *adj.*

in″com·mu″ni·ca′do (in″kə-mū″ni-kä′-dō) *adj.* shut off from any communication with others.

in·com′pa·ra·ble (in-kom′pə-rə-bəl) *adj.* **1,** without a rival; unequaled; matchless. **2,** not comparable. —**in·com″pa·ra·bil′i·ty,** *n.*

in″com·pat′i·ble (in″kəm-pat′ə-bəl) *adj.* not compatible; esp. of persons, unable to live together in harmony. —**in″com·pat·i·bil′i·ty,** *n.*

in·com′pe·tent (in-kom′pə-tənt) *adj.* not fit or capable. —*n.* one inadequate to a task, esp. mentally. —**in·com′pe·tence,** *n.*

in·con′gru·ous (in-kong′groo-əs) *adj.* **1,** out of place; unsuitable; inappropriate; inconsistent. **2,** composed of inharmonious parts; disjointed. —**in″con·gru·i′ty** (in″-kən-groo′ə-tē), **in·con′gru·ous·ness,** *n.*

in·con′se·quent (in-kon′sə-kwənt) *adj.* **1,** not consequent. **2,** fallacious. **3,** incongruous; irrelevant. —**in·con′se·quence,** *n.*

in″con·se·quen′tial (in″kon-sə-kwen′-shəl) *adj.* **1,** of no importance or effect; trivial. **2,** not consequent.

in″con·sid′er·a·ble (in″kən-sid′ər-ə-bəl)

adj. too few or small to matter; unimportant. —**in″con·sid′er·a·ble·ness,** *n.*

in″con·spic′u·ous (in″kən-spik′ū-əs) *adj.* too small or retiring to notice; not readily perceived. —**in″con·spic′u·ous·ness,** *n.*

in·con′stant (in-kon′stənt) *adj.* not loyal; not faithful. —**in·con′stan·cy,** *n.*

in·con′ti·nent (in-kon′tə-nənt) *adj.* not holding or held in; unrestrained; intemperate. —**in·con′ti·nence,** *n.*

in″con·ven′ience (in″kən-vēn′yəns) *n.* discomfort; trouble. —*v.t.* put to trouble. —**in″con·ven′ient,** *adj.* causing difficulty.

in·cor′po·rate″ (in-kôr′pə-rāt″) *v.t.* **1,** organize into a corporation; unite in a society, etc. **2,** combine; introduce as an integral part. —*v.i.* unite in a corporation, society, etc., or a body, mass, etc. —*adj.* (-rit) not corporeal; not having a material body. —**in·cor″po·ra′tion,** *n.*

in·cor′ri·gi·ble (in-kor′i-jə-bəl) *adj.* resistant to correction or reform; beyond reform. —**in·cor″ri·gi·bil′i·ty,** *n.*

in·cras′sate″ (in-kras′āt″) *v.t. & i.* thicken in consistency, as a liquid. —*adj.* thickened; swollen from fatness.

in·crease′ (in-krēs′) *v.t.* make greater; extend in bulk, size, number, degree, etc.; enlarge; augment; enhance. —*v.i.* **1,** become greater. **2,** multiply. —*n.* (in′krēs) **1,** the act of increasing. **2,** the amount, result, or product of increase. —**on the increase,** increasing.

in·cred′i·ble (in-kred′ə-bəl) *adj.* **1,** not believable. **2,** (*Informal*) extraordinary. —**in·cred″i·bil′i·ty,** *n.*

> **incredible, incredulous**
> ☛ Do not confuse *incredible,* unbelievable, with *incredulous,* skeptical.

in″cre·du′li·ty (in″krə-dū′lə-tē) *n.* disbelief; skepticism. —**in·cred′u·lous** (in-krej′ə-ləs) *adj.* ❏ *incredible*

in′cre·ment (in′krə-mənt) *n.* something added; augmentation; growth.

in·crim′i·nate″ (in-krim′ə-nāt″) *v.t.* show to be involved in a crime; charge; accuse. —**in·crim″i·na′tion,** *n.*

in·crust′ (in-krust′) *v.t.* form into a crust; cover or line with a hard coating. —**in″-crus·ta′tion,** *n.*

in′cu·bate″ (in′kyə-bāt″) *v.t.* **1,** hatch (eggs). **2,** maintain at a temperature favorable to growth. **3,** produce as though by hatching. —*v.i.* sit on eggs; brood. (def. 1). —**in″cu·ba′tion,** *n.* —**in′cu·ba″tor,** *n.* a heated apparatus for hatching eggs, nurturing babies, etc.

in′cu·bus (in′kyə-bəs) *n.* **1,** a male

demon imagined to disturb sleep; hence, a nightmare. **2,** a burden. ❑ *succubus*

in·cul′cate (in-kul′kāt) *v.t.* impress on the mind, as by admonition. —**in″cul·ca′-tion,** *n.*

in·cul′pa·ble (in-kul′pǝ-bǝl) *adj.* innocent; blameless.

in·cul′pate (in-kul′pāt) *v.t.* accuse, of wrongdoing. —**in″cul·pa′tion,** *n.*

in·cum′bent (in-kum′bǝnt) *adj.* **1,** resting on one as a duty or obligation. **2,** leaning on something. —*n.* an office-holder. —**in·cum′ben·cy,** *n.*

in″cu·nab′u·la (in″kū-nab′yǝ-lǝ) *n.pl.* [*sing.* **-lum** (-lǝm)] **1,** the place or period of beginning and earliest development, as of a race, art, etc. **2,** books printed before 1500 A.D. —**in″cu·nab′u·lar,** *adj.*

in·cur′ (in-kēr′) *v.t.* [**in·curred′, -cur′ring**] **1,** encounter as an experience. **2,** bring on oneself. —**in·cur′rence,** *n.*

in·cur′sion (in-kēr′zhǝn) *n.* a sudden running in; an inroad or invasion. —**in·cur′sive** (-siv) *adj.*

in·debt′ed (in-det′id) *adj.* owing; under obligation. —**in·debt′ed·ness,** *n.* fact of owing; amount owed.

in·de′cent (in-dē′sǝnt) *adj.* **1,** not fit to be done, seen, or heard in polite company; indelicate. **2,** immodest. —**in·de′-cen·cy,** *n.*

in″de·ci′sion (in″di-sizh′ǝn) *n.* vacillation; irresolution.

in″de·ci′sive (-sī′siv) *adj.* **1,** inconclusive. **2,** unable to decide. —**in″de·ci′sive·ness,** *n.*

in·deed′ (in-dēd′) *adv.* in fact; in reality; in truth. —*interj.* expressing doubt, surprise, or agreement.

in″de·fat′i·ga·ble (in″di-fat′ǝ-gǝ-bǝl) *adj.* not easily fatigued; not yielding to fatigue. —**in″de·fat′i·ga·bil′i·ty,** *n.*

in·def′i·nite (in-def′ǝ-nit) *adj.* **1,** having no fixed or specified limit; infinite. **2,** vague. **3,** indeterminate. —**indefinite arti-cle,** *a* or *an.* —**in·def′i·nite·ness,** *n.*

in·del′i·ble (in-del′ǝ-bǝl) *adj.* not capable of being deleted or obliterated. —**in·del″i·bil′i·ty,** *n.*

in·del′i·cate (in-del′i-kǝt) *adj.* coarse; gross; immodest; unrefined. —**in·del′i·ca·cy** (-kǝ-sè) *n.*

in·dem′ni·fy″ (in-dem′nǝ-fī″) *v.t.* compensate for or guarantee against damage, loss, or expenses incurred. —**in·dem″ni·fi·ca′tion,** *n.*

in·dem′ni·ty (in-dem′nǝ-tè) *n.* **1,** what is paid as compensation or reimbursement.

2, security given against damage or loss. **3,** exemption from liability.

in·dent′ *v.t.* make a dent, notch, or recess in; begin (a line of writing) to the right of the left margin. —**in″den·ta′tion** (in″den-tā′shǝn) *n.*

in·den′ture (in-den′chǝr) *n.* **1,** a contract binding a person to service, esp. an apprentice. **2,** a sealed deed, contract, etc. —*v.t.* so bind.

in″de·pen′dence (in″di-pen′dǝns) *n.* condition of being independent; freedom from control or influence. —**Independence Day,** July 4, on which date the Thirteen Colonies declared themselves sovereign.

in″de·pen′dent (in″di-pen′dǝnt) *adj.* **1,** not contingent on something else for existence, operation, etc. **2,** not influenced by others in opinion, conduct, etc. **3,** not affiliated; sovereign in authority. **4,** having ample income without working. —*n.* someone or something independent.

in-″depth′ *adj.* thorough; profound.

in″de·ter′min·a·ble (in″di-tēr′mǝ-nǝ-bǝl) *adj.* incapable of being determined, limited, established, etc.

in″de·ter′mi·nate (in″di-tēr′mǝ-nǝt) *adj.* **1,** not fixed or established; not precise or clear. **2,** not determinable. —**in″de·ter′mi·nate·ness,** *n.*

in′dex (in′deks) *n.* [*pl.* **in′dex·es, in′-di·ces″** (in′dǝ-sēz″)] **1,** an alphabetized list of items and their locations. **2,** a pointer; the symbol (☞). **3,** a quality, trait, etc. **4,** the forefinger. **5,** (*Math.*) an operative symbol, as an exponent. **6,** (*cap.*) a list of books forbidden to the Roman Catholic laity. **7,** price index. —*v.t.* **1,** furnish with or enter in an index. **2,** point out. **3,** to adjust wages, etc., in accordance with the fluctuations of an index, as a price index. —**index number,** a percent of something expressed as a number without a percent sign.

In′di·a (in′dè-ǝ) (*Communications*) the letter *i.* —**India ink,** a black drawing ink. —**India paper,** a very thin but tough paper, used chiefly for large reference works. —**India rubber,** natural rubber; caoutchouc.

In′di·an (in′dè-ǝn) *adj. & n.* **1,** pert. to the aboriginal inhabitants of North and South America; Native American. **2,** pert. to the inhabitants of India or the East Indies. —**Indian club,** a wooden club swung for exercise. —**Indian corn,** maize. —**Indian file,** single file. —**Indian giver,** a person who takes back a gift he or she made. —**Indian summer,** warm days late in the fall.

in'di·cate" (in'di-kāt") *v.t.* **1,** point out; direct attention to. **2,** imply. **—in"di·ca'-tion,** *n.*

in·dic'a·tive (in-dik'ə-tiv) *adj.* **1,** pointing out; betokening. **2,** (*Gram.*) of verbs, expressing a statement or question.

in'di·ca"tor (in'di-kā"tər) *n.* an instrument or part that indicates.

in·di'ci·a (in-dish'ē-ə) *n.pl.* [*sing.* **-di'ci·um** (-dish'ē-əm)] **1,** discriminating marks. **2,** printed marks to show payment of postage, as by postage meters.

in·dict' (in-dīt') *v.t.* charge with an offense, esp. a criminal one. **—in·dict'ment,** *n.*

> **indict, indite**
> ☞ Two homonyms related by origin. In current usage, *indict* means to charge with an offense; *indite* means to write. The Latin source word, *indicere*, meant to proclaim.

in·dif'fer·ent (in-dif'ər-ənt) *adj.* **1,** feeling no interest or anxiety; apathetic. **2,** unbiased; impartial. **3,** not making a difference. **4,** mediocre; moderate in amount or degree. **—in·dif'fer·ence,** *n.*

in·dig'e·nous (in-dij'ə-nəs) *adj.* originating in a particular region; native. **—in·dig'e·nous·ness,** *n.*

in'di·gent (in'di-jənt) *adj.* destitute; poor; needy. **—in'di·gence,** *n.*

in"di·gest'i·ble (in"di-jes'tə-bəl) *adj.* hard to digest or assimilate. **—in"di·gest'i·bil'i·ty,** *n.*

in"di·ges'tion (in"di-jes'chən) *n.* pain caused by inability to digest food properly.

in·dig'nant (in-dig'nənt) *adj.* feeling or showing anger, esp. righteous anger; resentful.

in"dig·na'tion (in"dig-nā'shən) *n.* righteous anger over injustice, etc.

in·dig'ni·ty (in-dig'nə-tē) *n.* an injury or affront to one's dignity; a slight; humiliation.

in'di·go" (in'di-gō") *n.* **1,** a dark blue dye. **2,** a violet-blue color.

> **indigo**
> ↔ From Greek *indikon*, Indian substance or dye.

in·dis·creet' (in-dis-krēt') *adj.* not prudent. **—in·dis·creet'ness,** *n.*

in"dis·crete' (in"dis-krēt') *adj.* not separated into parts. ❏ *indiscreet*

in·dis·cre'tion (-kresh'ən) *n.* act of being indiscreet; error of judgment.

in"dis·crim'i·nate (in"dis-krim'ə-nit) *adj.* not carefully selected; heterogeneous.

—in"dis·crim"i·na'tion, *n.* **—in"dis·crim'i-nate·ness,** *n.*

> **indiscreet, indiscrete**
> ☞ The second of these two words, the opposite of *discrete*, means not separated into parts. It is often confused in spelling for the more common *indiscreet*, meaning not prudent. Note that the noun form of *indiscreet* is *indiscretion*; the noun form of *indiscrete* is *indiscreteness*.

in"dis·posed' (in"dis-pōzd') *adj.* **1,** somewhat sick or ill. **2,** not inclined; unwilling. **—in"dis·po·si'tion** (-pə-zish'ən) *n.*

in·dite' (in-dīt') *v.t.* put into verbal form; write or compose. **—in·dite'ment,** *n.* ❏ *indict*

in'di·um (in'dē-əm) *n.* a rare, silver-white metallic element, no. 49, symbol In.

in"di·vid'u·al (in"di-vij'oo-əl) *adj.* **1,** relating to one person or thing. **2,** not divisible without loss of identity. **3,** single; particular. **4,** having peculiar characteristics. *—n.* a single person, animal, or thing.

in·di·vid'u·al·ism (-iz-əm) *n.* independence in personal behavior. **—in·di·vid'u·al·ist,** *n.* **—in·di·vid"u·al·is'tic,** *adj.* **—individual retirement account,** a plan which permits savings which are tax-free until retirement. *Abbr.,* **IRA**

in·di·vid"u·al'i·ty (-al'ə-tē) *n.* the state of being distinct and unlike others; peculiar character.

in"di·vid'u·al·ize" (in"di-vij'oo-ə-līz") *v.t.* **1,** differentiate; distinguish. **2,** mention or consider separately. **—in"di·vid"u·al·i·za'tion,** *n.*

in"di·vid'u·ate" (-āt") *v.t.* individualize.

in·doc'tri·nate" (in-dok'tri-nāt") *v.t.* imbue with a particular belief or principle. **—in·doc"tri·na'tion,** *n.*

In'do-Eu'ro·pe'an (in'dō-) *adj.* pert. to a family of languages spoken chiefly in Europe.

in'do·lent (in'də-lənt) *adj.* **1,** lazy; sluggish. **2,** giving little pain. **—in'do·lence,** *n.*

in·dom'i·ta·ble (in-dom'i-tə-bəl) *adj.* not able to be subdued or repressed. **—in·dom"i·ta·bil'i·ty,** *n.*

in'door" (in'dôr") *adj.* in a building; not in open air. **—in"doors',** *adv.*

in·dorse' (in-dôrs') *v.t.* endorse.

in·du'bi·ta·ble (in-doo'bi-tə-bəl) *adj.* not to be doubted; sure. **—in·du'bi·ta·ble·ness,** *n.*

in·duce' (in-dūs') *v.t.* **1,** lead by persuasion or influence; prevail upon; incite. **2,**

produce or cause. 3, produce by induction. **4,** infer.

in·duce′ment (-mənt) *n.* **1,** act or result of inducing. **2,** incentive.

in·duct′ (in-dukt′) *v.t.* **1,** install in office; initiate. **2,** enroll in military service.

in·duc′tance (in-duk′təns) *n.* the creation of an electromotive force by means of a varying current in an electric circuit.

in·duc′tion (in-duk′shən) *n.* **1,** installation of a person into office. **2,** the excitation of an electromagnetic field by a neighboring body, without direct contact. **3,** the process of drawing a general conclusion from particular facts. **4,** the act of inducing. —**in·duc′tive,** *adj.* ❑ *deduction*

in·due′ (in-dū′) *v.t.* endue.

in·dulge′ (in-dulj′) *v.t.* yield to or comply with (an inclination or person); humor. —*v.i.* yield to one's own inclination. —**in·dul′gent,** *adj.*

in·dul′gence (in-dul′jəns) *n.* **1,** gratification of desire. **2,** an extension of time. **3,** (*Rom. Cath.*) remission of punishment; relaxation of law.

in′du·rate (in′dyə-rət) *adj.* hardened.

in·dus′tri·al (in-dus′trē-əl) *adj.* pert. to large-scale manufacturing. —**in·dus′tri·al·ism,** *n.* —**in·dus′tri·al·ist,** *n.* —**industrial arts,** manual skills, and other skills related to industrial tools and techniques, taught as a course in school. —**industrial park,** a plot of land reserved for business and industrial buildings. —**Industrial Revolution,** the economic and social changes beginning in the late 18th c. as a result of the introduction of power-driven machines.

in·dus′tri·al·ize″ (in-dus′trē-əl-īz″) *v.t.* establish industries in (a country, city, etc.); organize the manufacturing activities of. —**in·dus″tri·al·i·za′tion,** *n.*

in·dus′tri·ous (in-dus′trē-əs) *adj.* hardworking; diligent; assiduous. —**in·dus′tri·ous·ness,** *n.*

in′dus·try (in′dəs-trē) *n.* **1,** a manufacturing trade. **2,** manufacturing and business generally. **3,** diligence; application to tasks.

in·e′bri·ate″ (in-ē′brē-āt″) *v.t.* make drunk; intoxicate. —*n.* **1,** a drunk person. **2,** a habitual drunkard. —**in·e″bri·a′tion,** *n.*

in″e·bri′e·ty (in″i-brī′ə-tē) *n.* drunkenness.

in·ef′fa·ble (in-ef′ə-bəl) *adj.* inexpressible; too sacred to speak of. —**in·ef′fa·bil′i·ty,** *n.*

in″e·luc′ta·ble (in″i-luk′tə-bəl) *adj.* not to be eluded or overcome.

in·ept′ *adj.* **1,** not apt, fit, or suited. **2,**

inefficient. —**in·ept′ness, in·ep′ti·tude** (in-ep′tə-tood) *n.*

in·eq′ui·ta·ble (in-ek′wi-tə-bəl) *adj.* unfair; unjust.

in·eq′ui·ty (in-ek′wə-tē) *n.* injustice; something that is unfair.

in·ert′ (in-ērt′) *adj.* **1,** having no inherent power to move or act. **2,** lacking active properties. **3,** sluggish. —**in·ert′ness,** *n.*

> **inert, inertia**
> ↔ From Latin *inertia*, lack of skill. The word was first applied in physics by the 17th-c. scientist Johannes Kepler.

in·er′tia (in-ēr′shə)) *n.* **1,** the property of matter whereby a body remains at rest or in uniform rectilinear motion unless acted upon by an external force. **2,** inertness; inactivity. ❑ *inert*

in es′se (in es′e) (*Lat.*) in being; in actuality.

in·es′ti·ma·ble (in-es′tə-mə-bəl) *adj.* not to be estimated; beyond measure. —**in·es″ti·ma·bil′i·ty,** *n.*

in·ev′i·ta·ble (in-ev′i-tə-bəl) *adj.* **1,** unavoidable. **2,** sure to come or happen. —**in·ev″i·ta·bil′i·ty,** *n.*

in·ex′o·ra·ble (in-ek′sə-rə-bəl) *adj.* not to be persuaded or moved; unrelenting. —**in·ex′o·ra·ble·ness,** *n.*

in″ex·pen′sive *adj.* not expensive; cheap. ❑ *cheap*

in″ex·pe′ri·ence (in″ik-spir′ē-əns) *n.* lack of the knowledge or skill usually gained from experience. —**in″ex·pe′ri·enced,** *adj.*

in ex·tre′mis (in eks-trē′mis) (*Lat.*) at the very end; near death.

in·fal′li·ble (in-fal′ə-bəl) *adj.* **1,** free from fallacy; not liable to error. **2,** unfailingly certain; trustworthy. —**in·fal″li·bil′i·ty,** *n.*

in′fa·mous (in′fə-məs) *adj.* notoriously evil; shamefully bad; wicked. —**in′fa·my** (in′fə-mē) *n.*

in′fan·cy (in′fən-sē) *n.* **1,** condition or period of being an infant. **2,** earliest and formative period of a movement, nation, art, etc.

in′fant (in′fənt) *n.* **1,** a baby or young child. **2,** (*Law*) anyone under legal age. —*adj.* **1,** being an infant, legally a minor. **2,** incipient.

in·fan′ta (in-fan′tə) *n.* a daughter of the king of Spain or Portugal. —**in·fan′te** (-tā) *n.* a son of the king of Spain or Portugal, but not heir to the throne.

in·fan′ti·cide (in-fan′ti-sīd) *n.* the killer or killing of an infant.

> **infant, infantry**
> ↔ *Infant* comes from Latin *infans*, which originally meant "unable to speak." The related *infantry* comes from Italian *infanteria*, youthful foot soldier.

in′fan·tile″ (in′fən-tīl″) *adj.* being or like a baby. —**infantile paralysis**, poliomyelitis.

in′fan·try (in′fən-trē) *n.* soldiers that serve on foot; a branch of military forces. —**in′fan·try·man** (-mən) [*pl.* -men], **in′fan·try·wom″an**, *n.* ❑ *infant*

in·fat′u·ate″ (in-fach′oo-āt″) *v.t.* inspire with foolish passion, esp. of love. —**in·fat″·u·a′tion**, *n.*

in·fect′ (in-fekt′) *v.t.* **1,** impregnate with germs; affect with disease. **2,** imbue; taint. —**in·fec′tion**, *n.*

in·fec′tious (-shəs) *adj.* **1,** communicable by transmission of germs. **2,** spreading rapidly; hard to resist. —**in·fec′tious·ness**, *n.* ❑ *contagious*

in·fer′ (in-fēr′) *v.t. & i.* [**in·ferred′, in·fer′·ring**] conclude by reasoning; derive from evidence. ❑ *imply*

in′fer·ence (in′fə-rəns) *n.* **1,** act of inferring. **2,** a conclusion or presumption. —**in″·fer·en′tial** (-ren′shəl) *adj.*

in·fe′ri·or (in-fir′ē-ər) *adj.* **1,** lower in rank, grade, etc. **2,** markedly poor in quality. **3,** lower in place or position. —*n.* someone or something inferior. —**in·fe″ri·or′i·ty** (-or′ə-tē) *n.*

in·fer′nal (in-fēr′nəl) *adj.* **1,** pert. to mythical lower regions. **2,** hellish; diabolical. **3,** (*Informal*) annoying; troublesome.

in·fer′no (in-fēr′nō) *n.* [*pl.* -nos] hell; the nether regions.

in·fest′ *v.t.* **1,** invade and swarm over, like vermin. **2,** pervade noxiously. —**in″fes·ta′·tion**, *n.*

in′fi·del (in′fə-dəl) *adj.* **1,** having no religious faith. **2,** not of a particular religion. —*n.* an unbeliever.

in″fi·del′i·ty (in″fə-del′ə-tē) *n.* **1,** unfaithfulness; disloyalty. **2,** lack of faith.

in′field″ (in′fēld″) *n.* (*Baseball*) the diamond; the four players (*infielders*) stationed there.

in′fight″ing (in′fīt″ing) *n.* rivalry within an organization or group.

in·fil′trate (in-fil′trāt) *v.t.* filter into or through; permeate. —**in″fil·tra′tion** (in″fəl-trā′shən) *n.*

in′fi·nite (in′fə-nit) *adj.* **1,** great beyond measurement or counting; without limit; interminable. **2,** absolute. —*n.* **1,** something limitless; boundless space. **2,** (*cap.*) God. —**in′fi·nite·ness**, *n.*

in″fin·i·tes′i·mal (in″fin-i-tes′ə-məl) *adj.* immeasurably small.

in·fin′i·tive (in-fin′ə-tiv) *n.* the form of a verb merely expressing its sense: used after *to*, as *to go*.

in·fin′i·ty (in-fin′ə-tē) *n.* **1,** boundless extension; unlimited quantity or number. **2,** the condition of being infinite. **3,** (*Math.*) increase to immeasurable magnitude; the symbol (∞) denoting this. ❑ *eternity*

in·firm′ (in-fērm′) *adj.* not in good health; weak; faltering.

in·fir′ma·ry (in-fēr′mə-rē) *n.* a place for the care of the sick or injured.

in·fir′mi·ty (in-fēr′mə-tē) *n.* illness; weakness.

in·flame′ (in-flām′) *v.t.* **1,** excite highly; make more violent; aggravate. **2,** affect with bodily inflammation. **3,** set on fire.

in·flam′ma·ble (in-flam′ə-bəl) *adj.* capable of burning; combustible. —**in·flam″·ma·bil′i·ty**, *n.*

> **inflammable, flammable**
> ☞ These two words—despite their appearance—are actually synonyms, meaning capable of burning. The opposite is expressed by *nonflammable*, *noninflammable*, or *incombustible*.

in″flam·ma′tion (in″flə-mā′shən) *n.* a morbid condition of the body characterized by heat, swelling, redness, etc.

in·flam′ma·to·ry (in-flam′ə-tôr-ē) *adj.* serving to inflame.

in·flate′ (in-flāt′) *v.t. & i.* **1,** fill with air or other gas; distend; swell. **2,** elate. **3,** (of currency, prices, etc.) raise or expand.

in·fla′tion *n.* **1,** act of inflating. **2,** an increase in volume and circulation of money. **3,** a condition in which the money in circulation is excessive for the commodities on sale or being sold. —**in·fla′·tion·ar·y**, *adj.*

in·flect′ (in-flekt′) *v.t.* **1,** turn from a direct course; bend. **2,** modulate (the voice); vary (a word) by inflection.

in·flec′tion (in-flek′shən) *n.* **1,** change of pitch or tone in speaking; modulation. **2,** variation of a word to show plurality, person, part of speech, etc. **3,** a bend or angle; a change of curvature. —**in·flec′tion·al** (-əl), **in·flec′tive**, *adj.*

in·flex′i·ble (in-flek′sə-bəl) *adj.* **1,** not to be bent; rigid. **2,** stubborn. —**in·flex″i·bil′·i·ty**, *n.*

in·flict' (in-flikt') *v.t.* impose (something undesired); cause to be suffered or borne. —**in·flic'tion,** *n.*

in-'flight" *adj.* occurring during an airplane flight.

in"flo·res'cence (in"flō-res'əns) *n.* **1,** the flowering part of a plant; flowers collectively; a flower. **2,** the fact or stage of blossoming. —**in"flo·res'cent,** *adj.*

in'flu·ence (in'floo-əns) *n.* **1,** power to control or affect others by authority, persuasion, example, etc. **2,** a person or thing that exerts such power. —*v.t.* exercise influence on.

in'flu·en'tial (-en'shəl) *adj.* **1,** able to exert much influence. **2,** influencing.

in'flu·en'za (in"floo-en'zə) *n.* a highly contagious disease characterized by nasal catarrh, bronchial inflammation, and prostration.

in'flux" (in'fluks") *n.* **1,** a flowing in. **2,** the place where something flows in. **3,** invasion.

in'fo (in'fō) *n.* (*Informal*) information.

in'fo·mer"cial (in'fō-mêr"shəl) *n.* (*Radio & TV*) a commercial designed to inform and instruct as well as sell.

in·form' (in-fôrm') *v.t.* **1,** communicate facts to; make known to; tell. **2,** instruct. —*v.i.* give information, esp. about a criminal. —**informed consent,** consent given by a patient for a medical procedure after being informed of the pertinent medical facts and risks.

in·for'mal (in-fôr'məl) *adj.* unconventional; familiar in manner; irregular. —*n.* a party at which formal dress is not required. —**in"for·mal'i·ty** (in"fôr-mal'ə-tè) *n.*

in·form'ant (in-fôr'mənt) *n.* one who communicates facts.

> **informant, informer**
> ☞ Both words refer to one who gives information. However, an *informer* is usually one who gives incriminating information about another.

in"for·ma'tion (in"fər-mā'shən) *n.* **1,** act or result of informing; news. **2,** an official criminal charge.

in·form'a·tive (in-fôr'mə-tiv) *adj.* imparting news or knowledge.

in·form'er (in-fôr'mər) *n.* **1,** one who exposes a wrongdoer to official punishment. **2,** informant. ❏ *informant*

in·fra- (in-frə) *pref.* below; beneath.

in·frac'tion (in-frak'shən) *n.* breach; violation.

in·fran'gi·ble (in-fran'jə-bəl) *adj.* **1,** unbreakable. **2,** inviolable.

in'fra·struc"ture *n.* **1,** the fundamental features of a system or organization. **2,** the basic facilities of a city, country, etc.

in"fra·red' *n. & adj.* radiation outside the visible spectrum, at the red (lower-frequency) end.

in·fringe' (in-frinj') *v.t.* violate; transgress. —*v.i.* encroach; trespass. —**in·fringe'ment,** *n.*

in·fu'ri·ate" (in-fyûr'ē-āt") *v.t.* make furious; enrage.

in·fuse' (in-fūz') *v.t.* **1,** cause to penetrate. **2,** permeate like a liquid; imbue. **3,** soak. —**in·fu'sion,** *n.*

in·gen'ious (in-jēn'yəs) *adj.* showing cleverness in contrivance or construction. —**in·gen'ious·ness,** *n.*

> **ingenious, ingenuous**
> ☞ Do not confuse *ingenious*, resourceful, with *ingenuous*, naïve.

in'gé·nue" (an'zhə-noo") *n.* an ingenuous young woman, in a play. Also, **in'ge·nue".**

in"ge·nu'i·ty (in"jə-nū'ə-tè) *n.* cleverness; inventiveness.

in·gen'u·ous (in-jen'ū-əs) *adj.* free from guile; candid; naïve. —**in·gen'u·ous·ness,** *n.* ❏ *ingenious*

in·gest' (in-jest') *v.t.* take into the body for digestion, as food. —**in·ges'tion,** *n.* —**in·ges'tive,** *adj.*

in'gle·nook" (ing'gəl-nûk") *n.* a corner near the fireplace of a dwelling.

in·glo'ri·ous (in-glôr'ē-əs) *adj.* dishonorable; shameful. —**in·glo'ri·ous·ness,** *n.*

in'got (ing'gət) *n.* a mass of metal roughly shaped by casting or rolling.

in·grain' (in-grān') *v.t.* fix firmly, as in the mind.

in'grate (in'grāt) *n.* one who is ungrateful.

in·gra'ti·ate" (in-grā'shē-āt") *v.t.* establish (oneself) in the favor of another. —**in·gra"ti·a'tion,** *n.*

in·grat'i·tude (in-grat'i-tood) *n.* ungratefulness.

in·gre'di·ent (in-grē'dè-ənt) *n.* an essential part of a compound or mixture; constituent; element.

in'gress (in'gres) *n.* entrance.

in'grown" *adj.* grown into the flesh, as an *ingrown* toenail.

in·gur'gi·tate" (in-gêr'jə-tāt") *v.t.* swallow; gulp. —**in·gur'gi·ta'tion,** *n.*

in·hab'it *v.t.* live or dwell in.

in·hab′i·tant (-tənt) *n.* a resident.

in·hal′ant (in-hā′lənt) *n.* medicinal vapor; an apparatus for dispensing it.

in·hale′ (in-hāl′) *v.t.* draw in by or as by breathing. —*v.i.* breathe in. —**in″ha·la′tion** (in″hə-lā′shən) *n.* —**in′ha·la″tor,** *n.* an apparatus for facilitating normal respiration or the inhalation of medical preparation.

in·here′ (in-hir′) *v.i.* be a basic and inseparable element; be innate or intrinsic. —**in·her′ence,** *n.*

in·her′ent (in-hir′ənt) *adj.* belonging intrinsically; innate. —**in·her′ence, in·her′en·cy,** *n.*

in·her′it *v.t. & i.* **1,** receive (property, etc.) as an heir; acquire by gift or succession. **2,** receive (qualities, etc.) from progenitors; possess intrinsically. —**in·her′it·ance,** *n.* —**in·her′i·tor,** *n.* —**in·her′i·trix,** *n.fem.* ❏ *heritage*

in·hib′it *v.t.* **1,** check or repress, as an impulse. **2,** forbid; prohibit. —**in·hib′i·tive,** *adj.*

in″hi·bi′tion (in″ə-bish′ən) *n.* the checking, restraining, or blocking of a mental process, physiological reaction, etc.

in-′house″ *adj.* produced within an organization.

in·hu′man *adj.* **1,** cruel; bestial. **2,** supernatural. —**in″hu·man′i·ty,** *n.*

in·hume′ (in-hūm′) *v.t.* inter. —**in″hu·ma′tion,** *n.*

in·im′i·cal (in-im′i-kəl) *adj.* **1,** harmful. **2,** like an enemy; hostile.

in·iq′ui·tous (i-nik′wə-təs) *adj.* **1,** lacking equity; grossly unjust. **2,** wicked; sinful. —**in·iq′ui·ty** (-tē) *n.*

in·i′tial (i-nish′əl) *adj.* **1,** placed at the beginning. **2,** pert. to the beginning or first stage. —*n.* the first letter of a word. —*v.t.* mark with the initials of one's name.

in·i′tial·ism *n.* an acronym whose letters are pronounced separately, not as a word. ❏ *abbreviation*

in·i′tial·ize″ (-īz) *v.t.* **1,** to set (a computer, etc.) to a starting value. **2,** (*Computers*) format a computer disk.

in·i′ti·ate″ (i-nish′ē-āt″) *v.t.* **1,** set going; begin; originate. **2,** give instruction to. **3,** induct into membership in a club, etc. —**in·i″ti·a′tion,** *n.*

in·i′ti·a·tive (i-nish′ē-ə-tiv) *n.* **1,** readiness and ability to initiate, take the lead, contrive, etc. **2,** the first step; leading movement.

in·ject′ (in-jekt′) *v.t.* **1,** put in by driving force, as a liquid into a cavity. **2,** insert; interject.

in·jec′tion (in-jek′shən) *n.* **1,** act or result of injecting; an enema, hypodermic, etc. **2,** a substance or thing injected. **3,** the process of boosting a spacecraft into orbit.

in·junc′tion (in-junk′shən) *n.* **1,** a command; order; admonition. **2,** the act of enjoining. —**in·junc′tive,** *adj.*

in′jure (in′jər) *v.t.* do harm to; hurt; damage; impair.

in·ju′ri·ous (in-jûr′ē-əs) *adj.* damaging; hurtful. —**in·ju′ri·ous·ness,** *n.*

in′ju·ry (in′jə-rē) *n.* act or result of injuring; hurt; damage.

ink *n.* **1,** a fluid used for writing or printing. **2,** an inky secretion ejected by certain animals for protection. —*v.t.* write or draw with ink; cover with ink. —**ink-′jet″ printer,** a printer that prints by spraying small ink dots onto paper.

---

ink
↔ From Greek *enkauton*, the purple ink used by Greek and Roman emperors for signing documents, from *enkaiein*, burn in.

---

ink′ling *n.* a vague idea or notion; a hint or intimation.

ink′well″ *n.* a cup for holding ink.

ink′y (-ē) *adj.* like ink; black.

in′laid″ (in′lād″) *adj.* **1,** set in a surface, as decorative material. **2,** formed or ornamented by this method.

in′land (in′lənd) *adj.* **1,** away from the coast or border. **2,** domestic to a country. —*adv.* toward the interior.

in-′law″ *n.* (*Informal*) a relative by marriage.

in′lay′ (in-lā′) *v.t.* [**in·laid′, in·lay′ing**] **1,** decorate with pieces set in the surface. **2,** apply to a surface, in a decorative pattern. **3,** graft (a shoot) upon a plant. —*n.* (in′lā″) **1,** something inlaid or for inlaying. **2,** a filling for a tooth.

in′let *n.* an arm of a sea or lake extending into the land.

in-′line″ *adj.* arranged in a line.

in lo′co pa·ren′tis (in lō′kō pə-ren′tis) (*Lat.*) in the place of a parent.

in′mate″ (in′māt″) *n.* an inhabitant or lodger, one confined in an institution.

in me′di·as res′ (in mā′dē-əs rās′) (*Lat.*) in the middle of things.

in me·mo′ri·am″ (in″ mə-môr′ē-äm″) (*Lat.*) in memory (of).

in′most″ (in′mōst″) *adj.* farthest within; deepest.

inn (in) *n.* **1,** a hotel, esp. a small one. **2,** a tavern. —**inn′keep″er,** *n.*

---

inn

↔ From an ancient Germanic word *innam*, place where one lives, lodging. The modern sense developed in the 14th c.

in'nards (in'ərdz) *n.pl.* the viscera.

in·nate' (i-nāt') *adj.* existing in one from birth; inborn. —**in·nate'ness,** *n.*

in'ner (in'ər) *adj.* [*superl.* **in'ner·most''**] **1,** situated in or farther within. **2,** mental or spiritual; not outward. **3,** private; concealed. —**inner city,** the central part of a city, esp. that part occupied by slums. —**inner sanctum,** a private retreat.

in'ner·vate'' (in'ər-vāt'') *v.t.* stimulate through the nerves; supply with nervous energy. —**in''ner·va'tion,** *n.* ❑ *enervate*

in'ning (in'ing) *n.* **1,** (*Baseball, Cricket*) a period in which each side has a turn at bat. **2,** (often *pl.*) a time of power.

in'no·cent (in'ə-sənt) *adj.* **1,** not guilty; upright; harmless. **2,** naïve; artless. **3,** devoid. —**in'no·cence,** *n.*

in·noc'u·ous (i-nok'ū-əs) *adj.* harmless. —**in·noc'u·ous·ness,** *n.*

in·nom'i·nate (i-nom'ə-nət) *adj.* anonymous; unnamed. —**innominate bone,** hipbone.

in'no·vate'' (in'ə-vāt'') *v.i. & t.* introduce something new. —**in''no·va'tion,** *n.* —**in'·no·va''tor,** *n.*

in''nu·en'do (in''ū-en·dō) *n.* an insinuation; unfriendly hint.

in·oc'u·late' (i-nok'yə-lāt'') *v.t.* **1,** inject an immunizing agent into. **2,** imbue. —**in·oc''u·la'tion,** *n.*

in''of·fen'sive (in''ə-fen'siv) *adj.* harmless; not annoying. —**in''of·fen'sive·ness,** *n.*

in·op'er·a·tive (in-op'ə-rə-tiv) *adj.* **1,** not operative or operating; destitute of activity or effect. **2,** (*Informal*) without meaning or effect.

in·or'di·nate (in-ôr'də-nət) *adj.* beyond proper limits; excessive.

in'pa''tient (in'pā''shənt) *n.* a hospital patient who is lodged there.

in'put (in'pût) *n.* **1,** the energy or power put in, as to operate a machine. **2,** the amount or share of a contribution. **3,** data entered into a computer. —*v.t.* enter (data) into a computer; hence, contribute (ideas, etc.) to a discussion.

in'quest (in'kwest) *n.* a legal inquiry, esp. as to the cause of death, before a jury.

in·qui'e·tude'' (in-kwī'ə-tūd'') *n.* unrest; uneasiness.

in·quire' (in-kwīr') *v.t. & i.* ask (about); seek knowledge (of). Also, **en·quire'.**

in·quir'y (in-kwīr'ė; in'kwə-rė) *n.* **1,** search for information or knowledge; interrogation; investigation. **2,** a question. Also, **en·quir'y.**

in''qui·si'tion (in''kwə-zish'ən) *n.* **1,** examination; a formal inquiry. **2,** (*cap., Hist.*) a court for the suppression of heresy.

in·quis'i·tive (in-kwiz'ə-tiv) *adj.* unduly curious; prying. —**in·quis'i·tive·ness,** *n.*

in·quis'i·tor (in-kwiz'i-tər) *n.* one who conducts an inquisition.

in re (in rā') (*Lat.*) re; concerning.

in'road'' (in'rōd'') *n.* a forcible or insidious encroachment; a raid. ❑ *raid*

in sae'cu·la sae·cu·lo'rum (in sek'yə-lə sek-yə-lôr'əm) (*Lat.*) for ever and ever.

in·sane' (in-sān') *adj.* crazy; not legally responsible for one's actions. —**insane asylum,** mental hospital. —**in·san'i·ty** (in-san'ə-tė) *n.*

in·sa'ti·ate (in-sā'shė-it) *adj.* **1,** insatiable. **2,** not satisfied.

in·scribe' (in-skrīb') *v.t.* **1,** write or engrave; mark with letters or signs. **2,** write or draw inside of.

in·scrip'tion (in-skrip'shən) *n.* something inscribed, as on a monument or coin. —**in·scrip'tive,** *adj.*

in·scru'ta·ble (in-skroo'tə-bəl) *adj.* not to be read by scrutiny or investigation; unfathomable; incomprehensible. —**in·scru''ta·bil'i·ty,** *n.*

in'seam' *n.* the seam from the crotch to the bottom of the trouser leg.

in'sect (in'sekt) *n.* **1,** any member of a class of tiny winged invertebrates. **2,** a contemptible person.

insect, entomology

↔ Both words derive from Greek *entomon*, literally, a segmented creature. *Insect* is from Latin *insectum*, a translation of the Greek word.

in·sec'ti·cide'' (in-sek'ti-sīd'') *n.* a substance to kill insects.

in''sec·tiv'o·rous (in''sek-tiv'ə-rəs) *adj.* feeding on insects.

in''se·cure' (in''si-kyûr') *adj.* **1,** feeling unsafe. **2,** not tightly fastened; not safe. —**in''se·cu'ri·ty,** *n.*

in·sem'i·nate'' (in-sem'ə-nāt'') *v.t.* sow seeds in; impregnate. —**in·sem''i·na'tion,** *n.*

in·sen'sate (in-sen'sāt) *adj.* **1,** inanimate. **2,** insensitive; unfeeling; cold. **3,** unaware.

insensate, insensible, insensitive
All three words mean lacking sensation, but with different nuances. *Insensate* is usually used in the figurative sense of unfeeling (synonymous with *insensitive*). *Insensible* is often used in the literal sense of deprived of sensation.

in·sen′si·ble (in-sen′sə-bəl) *adj.* **1,** deprived of sensation; unconscious; unfeeling. **2,** imperceptible. —**in·sen″si·bil′i·ty,** *n.* ❑ *insensate*

in·sen′si·tive (in-sen′si-tiv) *adj.* **1,** lacking sensibility; callous. **2,** lacking physical sensitivity. ❑ *insensate*

in·sert′ (in-sẽrt′) *v.t.* put in; place inside of or among. —*n.* (in′sẽrt) something inserted.

in·ser′tion (in-ser′shən) *n.* **1,** the act of inserting. **2,** an insert. **3,** the process of putting a spacecraft into orbit.

in′set″ *n.* something set in; an insert, esp. in a book, illustration, etc. —*v.t.* insert.

in·side′ (in-sīd′) *prep. & adv.* in or into; within a body or limit (of space or time). —*n.* **1,** the inner part; interior region; inner surface. **2,** the contents; (*pl.*) the alimentary tract; mental feelings. —*adj.* **1,** interior; internal. **2,** indoor. **3,** specially privileged.

in·sid′er (-ər) *n.* (*Informal*) one who has special access to secrets or privileges. —**insider trading,** illegal buying and selling of stocks based on privileged information.

in·sid′i·ous (in-sid′ē-əs) *adj.* **1,** operating stealthily with evil effect. **2,** deceitful; treacherous. —**in·sid′i·ous·ness,** *n.*

in′sight″ (in′sīt″) *n.* **1,** penetrating discernment; intuition. **2,** a sudden awareness.

in·sig′ni·a (in-sig′nē-ə) *n. sing. & pl.* [*sing.* also **in·sig′ne** (-nē)] a badge of office or honor; an emblem.

in″sig·nif′i·cant (in″sig-nif′ə-kənt) *adj.* without importance; trivial. —**in″sig·nif′i·cance,** *n.*

in″sin·cere′ (in″sin-sir′) *adj.* not sincere; hypocritical. —**in″sin·cer′i·ty** (-ser′ə-tē) *n.*

in·sin′u·ate″ (in-sin′ū-āt″) *v.t.* **1,** hint or suggest indirectly; imply slyly. **2,** introduce by devious means or by slow degrees. —**in·sin″u·a′tion,** *n.*

in·sip′id *adj.* **1,** lacking flavor or savor. **2,** uninteresting; dull. —**in″si·pid′i·ty** (in″si-pid′ə-tē) *n.*

in·sist′ *v.i.* **1,** (with *on*) enforce by command; assert or argue emphatically. **2,**

persevere in action. —**in·sist′ence,** *n.* —**in·sist′ent,** *adj.*

in″so·la′tion (in″sō-lā′shən) *n.* **1,** radiant energy from the sun. **2,** exposure to the sun's rays.

in′sole″ (in′sōl″) *n.* the inner sole of a shoe.

in′so·lent (in′sə-lənt) *adj.* contemptuously rude, disrespectful, or insulting. —**in′so·lence,** *n.*

in·sol′vent (in-sol′vənt) *adj.* having greater liabilities than assets; bankrupt. —**in·sol′ven·cy,** *n.*

in·som′ni·a (in-som′nē-ə) *n.* inability to sleep, esp. when chronic. —**in·som′ni·ac″** (-ak″) *n.*

in″so·much′ *adv.* inasmuch (as).

in·sou′ci·ant (in-soo′sē-ənt) *adj.* carefree; unconcerned. —**in·sou′ci·ance,** *n.*

in·spect′ (in-spekt′) *v.t.* look at closely; examine critically. —**in·spec′tion,** *n.* —**in·spec′tor,** *n.* one who inspects; a title of various executive or supervisory officers.

in″spi·ra′tion (in″spə-rā′shən) *n.* **1,** any influence, esp. supernatural or intuitive, that inspires thought or action; thought so suggested. **2,** the act of inspiring; the state of being inspired. —**in″spi·ra′tion·al,** *adj.*

in·spire′ (in-spīr′) *v.t.* **1,** stimulate to activity; animate; instigate; impel. **2,** breathe in; inhale. —**in·spir′a·to·ry** (-ə-tôr-ē) *adj.*

in·spir′it *v.t.* animate.

in·spis′sate (in-spis′āt) *v.t.* thicken (a liquid) by evaporation. —**in″spis·sa′tion,** *n.*

in″sta·bil′i·ty (in″stə-bil′ə-tē) *n.* unsteadiness; lack of firmness; changeability.

in·stall′ (in-stâl′) *v.t.* **1,** place in position for service or use. **2,** induct into office; seat. Also, **in·stal′.**

in″stal·la′tion (in″stə-lā′shən) *n.* **1,** act or result of installing. **2,** something installed, as a fixed machine. **3,** a tract of land and the buildings thereon devoted to military use.

in·stall′ment (in-stâl′mənt) *n.* one part of anything divided for periodical receipt or issuance, as a debt, a serial story, etc. Also, **in·stal′ment.** —**installment plan,** a method of payment by installments.

in′stance (in′stəns) *n.* **1,** an event that is one of many; a case; an example. **2,** instigation; suggestion.

in′stant (in′stənt) *n.* **1,** a small or infinitesimal interval of time; a moment. **2,** the present time or moment. *Abbr.,* **inst.** —*adj.* **1,** immediate. **2,** of present time, esp. of the present month. —**in″stan·ta′ne·ous** (-tā′nē-əs) *adj.* done in an instant. —**instant book,** a book produced quickly in response to a recent event. —**instant replay,** the recording and immediate re-broadcast of a portion of a live television broadcast.

> **instant**
> ↔ From Latin *instare*, be present, through the phrase *tempus instans*, present time.

in·stan'ter (in-stan'tər) *adv.* without delay; immediately.

in sta'tu quo' (in sta'too kwō') (*Lat.*) in the state in which (anything was or is); in the same condition.

in·stead' (in-sted') *adv.* in place (of another).

in'step" *n.* the arched upper surface of the human foot.

in'sti·gate" (in'sti-gāt") *v.t.* goad on, urge, or stimulate (a person); foment (an action). —**in"sti·ga'tion,** *n.* —**in'sti·ga"tor,** *n.*

in·still' (in-stil') *v.t.* **1,** infuse slowly into the mind or feelings. **2,** pour in by drops. —**in"stil·la'tion** (in"stə-lā'shən) *n.*

in'stinct (in'stinkt) *n.* **1,** an inborn tendency to act or respond in a particular way. **2,** aptitude. —**in·stinc'tive,** *adj.*

in'sti·tute" (in'sti-toot") *v.t.* set up; establish; appoint. —*n.* a corporate group, school, etc., devoted to scientific work, etc.

> **institute, institution**
> ☛ An *institution* can be an established custom, or an organization (and sometimes the building it occupies). An *institute* is an organization or foundation dedicated to public work or educational aims (or the building it occupies).

in"sti·tu'tion (in"sti-too'shən) *n.* **1,** an organization for the promotion of a particular object; the building it occupies. **2,** an established custom. **3,** act or result of instituting. **4,** a place for confinement of persons having special needs, as a mental hospital, old-age home, etc. —**in"sti·tu'-tion·al,** *adj.* ☐ *institute*

in"sti·tu'tion·al·ize" (-ə-līz") *v.t.* **1,** establish as an institution. **2,** to place (a person) in an institution.

in·struct' (in-strukt') *v.t.* **1,** give directions to; order; command. **2,** train. **3,** apprise.

> **instruct, instrument**
> ↔ Both words derive from Latin *in-struere,* teach, prepare.

in·struc'tion (in-struk'shən) *n.* **1,** act or result of instructing; teaching. **2,** an order; direction.

in·struc'tive (-tiv) *adj.* serving to teach or inform. —**in·struc'tive·ness,** *n.*

in·struc'tor (-tər) *n.* a teacher; in colleges, one below professorial rank.

in'stru·ment (in'strə-mənt) *n.* **1,** any mechanical device or contrivance; a tool, implement, or apparatus. **2,** a contrivance for producing musical sounds. **3,** a formal legal document. **4,** an agent, agency, or means. —**in"stru·men'tal,** *adj.* —**in"stru-men'tal·ist,** *n.* one who performs on a musical instrument. —**in"stru·men·tal'i·ty,** *n.* agency. —**in"stru·men·ta'tion,** *n.* orchestration. ☐ *instruct*

in"sub·or'di·nate (in"sə-bôr'də-nət) *adj.* disobedient; defiant. —**in"sub·or'di·na'-tion,** *n.*

in'su·lar (in'sū-lər) *adj.* **1,** pert. to an island; detached; hemmed in. **2,** provincial; narrow-minded. —**in"su·lar'i·ty** (-lar'ə-tē) *n.*

in'su·late" (in'sə-lāt") *v.t.* **1,** shield with material that isolates from heat, sound, electricity, etc. **2,** isolate. —**in"su·la'tion,** *n.* —**in'su·la"tor,** *n.* that which insulates, esp. a nonconductor of electricity.

in'su·lin (in'sə-lin) *n.* a preparation from the pancreas of animals, used in treating diabetes.

in·sult' *v.t.* cause to take offense; affront. —*n.* (in'sult) an affront to self-respect.

in·su'per·a·ble (in-soo'pər-ə-bəl) *adj.* incapable of being surmounted or overcome. —**in·su"per·a·bil'i·ty,** *n.*

in·sur'a·ble (in-shûr'ə-bəl) *adj.* acceptable to an underwriter. —**in·sur"a·bil'i·ty,** *n.*

in·sur'ance (in-shûr'əns) *n.* **1,** a contract whereby one party agrees to compensate another for loss through fire, death, etc. **2,** the business of insuring or underwriting. **3,** indemnity. **4,** assurance.

in·sure' (in-shûr') *v.t.* **1,** issue or obtain insurance on. **2,** assure. ☐ *assure*

in·sur'gent (in-sēr'jənt) *adj.* revolting against established government; engaged in insurrection. —*n.* one who revolts. —**in·sur'gence,** *n.*

in"sur·rec'tion (in"sə-rek'shən) *n.* armed resistance to authority; a limited rebellion. —**in"sur·rec'tion·ar·y,** *adj.* —**in"-sur·rec'tion·ist,** *n.*

in·tact' (in-takt') *adj.* remaining uninjured, unimpaired, whole, or complete. —**in·tact'ness,** *n.*

in·ta'glio (in-tà'lyō) *n.* **1,** incised engraving. **2,** the process of printing from engraved plates.

in'take" *n.* a taking or drawing in; consumption.

in·tan'gi·ble (in-tan'jə-bəl) *adj.* not able to be touched or grasped; vague. —**in·tan"-gi·bil'i·ty,** *n.*

in'te·ger (in'tə-jər) *n.* a whole number, not fractional.

in'te·gral (in'tə-grəl) *adj.* **1,** being an essential part of a whole; component; intrinsic. **2,** being an integer; involving integers. **3,** entire. **4,** (*Math.*) a measure of the area defined on top by the graph of a function, and on the bottom by the x-axis.

in'te·grate" (in'tə-grāt") *v.t.* form into a whole; bring together. —**in'te·gra·ble** (-grə-bəl) *adj.* —**integrated circuit,** a complete circuit, comprising transistors, resistors, and other components, inseparably associated in a single miniature unit.

in·te·gra'tion (-grā'shən) *n.* act or effect of integrating; mixing of persons of different races (esp. white and black), as in schools.

in·teg'ri·ty (in-teg'rə-tè) *n.* **1,** fidelity to moral principles; honesty. **2,** soundness; completeness.

in·teg'u·ment (in-teg'yə-mənt) *n.* a natural covering, as skin, shell, rind, etc.

in'tel·lect" (in'tə-lekt") *n.* **1,** the mind in its aspect of knowing and understanding (but not of feeling or willing). **2,** mental capacity.

in"tel·lec'tu·al (in"tə-lek'choo-əl) *adj.* pert. to, perceived by, or appealing to the intellect. —*n.* an intelligent and informed person.

in·tel'li·gence (in-tel'i-jəns) *n.* **1,** the power of knowing and understanding; mental capacity. **2,** news; information, esp. secret information. **3,** a staff of persons engaged in obtaining information. —**intelligence quotient,** a number representing a score made in an intelligence test; I.Q.

in·tel'li·gent (in-tel'i-jənt) *adj.* **1,** quick to understand. **2,** marked by or indicating intelligence.

in·tel"li·gent'si·a (in-tel"i-jen'sè-ə) *n.pl.* the highly educated classes; the intellectuals.

in·tel'li·gi·ble (in-tel'ə-jə-bəl) *adj.* capable of being understood; comprehensible. —**in·tel"li·gi·bil'i·ty,** *n.*

In·tel'sat" *n.* a communications satellite: *In(ternational) Tel(ecommunications) Sat-(ellite Organization).*

in·tem'per·ate (in-tem'pər-ət) *adj.* excessive; unrestrained; severe. —**in·tem'-per·ance, in·tem'per·ate·ness,** *n.*

in·tend' *v.t.* have in mind as a purpose; plan to do, use, give, etc. —**in·tend'ed,** *n.* (*Informal*) fiancé or fiancée.

in·tend'ant (in-ten'dənt) *n.* a manager or superintendent.

in·tense' (in-tens') *adj.* **1,** existing in high degree; strong; acute. **2,** vehement; earnest; ardent. —**in·tense'ness,** *n.*

in·ten'si·fy" (in-ten'si-fī") *v.t. & i.* make or become intense or more intense. —**in·ten"si·fi·ca'tion,** *n.*

in·ten'si·ty (-sə-tè) *n.* condition or degree of intenseness.

in·ten'sive (-siv) *adj.* **1,** extreme; very acute. **2,** requiring high consumption of energy. —*n.* (*Gram.*) a word or element that emphasizes another word, as *himself* in *he himself.* —**in·ten'sive·ness,** *n.* —**intensive care,** the use of specialized equipment to maintain the critically ill: *intensive care unit.*

in·tent' *n.* intention; aim; plan. —*adj.* **1,** firmly fixed or directed upon an object. **2,** earnest; sedulous.

in·ten'tion (-shən) *n.* **1,** the act of intending; something intended; purpose; aim. **2,** (*pl.*) (*Informal*) design with respect to proposing marriage. —**in·ten'-tion·al,** *adj.* done purposely.

in·ter' (in-tèr') *v.t.* [**in·terred', in·ter'ring**] place in a grave or tomb; bury. —**in·ter'-ment,** *n.*

in·ter- (in-tər) *pref.* between; among; together; mutually or reciprocally. [In addition to words defined in the text, the following words have the same sense as their root words, extended by the prefix to indicate interaction.]

in"ter·breed'	**in"ter·play'**
in"ter·col·le'gi·ate	**in"ter·plead'**
in"ter·co·lo'ni·al	**in"ter·ra'cial**
in"ter·com·mu'ni·cate"	**in"ter·scho·las'tic**
in"ter·de·nom'i·na'tion·al	**in"ter·stel'lar**
in"ter·de·pend'ent	**in"ter·trib'al**
in"ter·faith"	**in"ter·twine'**
in"ter·mix"	**in"ter·twist'**
in"ter·o"ce·an'ic	**in"ter·weave'**
in"ter·plan'e·tar·y	

in"ter·act' *v.i.* act on each other or one another. —**in"ter·ac'tion,** *n.* —**in"ter·ac'-tive,** *adj.*

in·ter'ca·lar·y (in-tər'kə-ler-è) *adj.* **1,** inserted in the calendar as an extra day, month, or year. **2,** interpolated.

in·ter'ca·late" (in-ter'kə-lāt") *v.t.* insert between others; interpolate. —**in·ter"ca·la'tion,** *n.*

in″ter·cede′ (in″tər-sēd′) v.i. mediate between two contending parties.

in″ter·cept′ (in″tər-sept′) v.t. **1,** interpose between. **2,** seize in passage; cut off. —n. (in′tər-sept″) **1,** a crossing. **2,** a message picked up off a radio, etc. **3,** an interception. —**in″ter·cep′tion,** n. —**in″ter·cep′tor,** n. a fighter airplane.

in″ter·ces′sion (in″tər-sesh′ən) n. **1,** act of interceding. **2,** a prayer for mercy. —**in′-ter·ces″sor** (-ses″ər) n.

in″ter·change′ v.t. **1,** put each (of two things) in the place of the other. **2,** transpose; exchange. **3,** alternate; vary. —v.i. change reciprocally. —n. **1,** mutual exchange; alternate succession. **2,** an intersection of two or more routes in a highway system. —**in″ter·change′a·ble** (-ə-bəl) adj.

in′ter·com″ (in′tər-kom″) n. a device for talking between rooms or offices of the same house or suite: intercom(munication).

in′ter·course″ (in′tər-kôrs″) n. **1,** communication between persons; exchange of ideas; conversation. **2,** sexual relations; coitus.

in′ter·dict″ (in′tər-dikt″) v.t. forbid peremptorily; restrain by injunction; debar. —n. **1,** a prohibitory order or decree. **2,** (Rom. Cath.) denial of certain sacraments. —**in″ter·dic′tion,** n.

in′ter·est (in′tər-ist) n. **1,** a feeling of concern, curiosity, etc.; the object that arouses such feeling. **2,** connection, esp. through investment, with a business. **3,** benefit; advantage; profit. **4,** (pl.) a group of persons or companies allied in business. **5,** selfish consideration. **6,** payment for the use of money; the rate or amount. —v.t. engage or excite the attention or curiosity of. —**in′ter·est·ing,** adj. attracting attention.

in′ter·face″ v.i. provide a link between two entities, regions, components, etc. —n. **1,** that which provides such a link. **2,** the connecting boundary between peoples, systems, etc.

in″ter·fere′ (in″tər-fir′) v.i. **1,** thrust oneself into the affairs of others; meddle. **2,** collide; be obstructive.

in″ter·fer′ence (in″tər-fir′əns) n. **1,** act of interfering. **2,** the interaction of waves of any kind, esp. the confusion of radio waves by extraneous waves.

in″ter·fer′on (in″tər-fēr′on) n. any of various proteins that inhibit the proliferation of an invading virus.

in′ter·im (in′tər-im) n. an intervening time; the meantime. —adj. provisional; temporary.

in·te′ri·or (in-tir′ē-ər) adj. **1,** being inside something; internal. **2,** inland; domestic; indoor; mental. —n. the internal part; the inside, as of a room, country, etc.

in″ter·ject′ (in″tər-jekt′) v.t. thrust between other things; insert; interpolate.

in″ter·jec′tion (-jek″shən) n. **1,** the act of interjecting. **2,** an interruption, esp. an exclamatory utterance.

in″ter·lace′ (in″tər-lās′) v.t. weave together; intersperse.

in″ter·lard′ (in″tər-lärd′) v.t. mix or insert among other things; diversify.

in″ter·leave′ (-lēv′) v.t. **1,** insert between leaves. **2,** provide (a book) with interleaved blank pages or illustrations.

in″ter·line′ v.t. **1,** insert between lines of writing. **2,** furnish (a garment) with an extra lining. —**in″ter·lin′e·ar** (-lin′ē-ər) adj. between lines. —**in″ter·lin′ing,** n. an extra, inside lining.

in″ter·lock′ v.t. & i. **1,** fasten or become fastened together. **2,** be connected so as to operate simultaneously or in desired sequence. —n. (in′tər-lok″) **1,** an interconnection. **2,** a mechanical interdependence whereby the operation of one part activates or prevents the operation of another part.

in″ter·lo·cu′tion (in″tər-lō-kū′shən) n. conversation; dialogue.

in″ter·loc′u·tor (in″tər-lok′yû-tər) n. **1,** one with whom one is conversing. **2,** the announcer in a minstrel troupe.

in″ter·loc′u·to·ry (in″tər-lok′yû-tôr-ē) **1,** of speech or conversation. **2,** interpolated. **3,** (of a legal ruling) not final.

in″ter·lope′ (in″tər-lōp′) v.i. intrude, as in a business, without right. —**in′-ter·lop″er,** n.

in′ter·lude″ (in′tər-lood″) n. **1,** an intervening time, period, or stage; an episode of such time. **2,** a short performance between acts.

in″ter·mar′ry v.i. marry within the limits of a family or group. —**in″ter·mar′riage,** n.

in″ter·me′di·a adj. relating to the combined use of several media.

in″ter·me′di·ar·y (in″tər-mē′dē-er-ē) adj. **1,** intermediate. **2,** serving as an intermediary. —n. a mediator; messenger; go-between.

in″ter·me′di·ate (in″tər-mē′dē-ət) adj. situated between two extremes; coming between, in position or degree; intervening. —v.i. (-āt″) mediate. —**intermediate school,** junior high school.

in″ter·mez′zo (in″tər-met′sō) n. [pl. **-zos**

or **-zi** (-sė)] a musical composition played between the acts of a play, etc.; an independent piece in similar style.

in·ter′mi·na·ble (in-tēr′mə-nə-bəl) *adj.* never-ending; long-drawn-out.

in″ter·min′gle (in″tər-ming′gəl) *v.t.* mix together; combine.

in″ter·mis′sion (in″tər-mish′ən) *n.* a period of temporary cessation; a pause or recess.

in″ter·mit′ (in″tər-mit′) *v.* [**-mit′ted, -mit′ting**] stop temporarily; suspend; delay.

in″ter·mit′tent (in″tər-mit′ənt) *adj.* ceasing and recurring at intervals. —**in″ter·mit′tence,** *n.*

in·tern′ (in-tĕrn′) *v.t.* confine within prescribed limits, esp. hold aliens, ships, etc., during a war. —*n.* [also, **in′terne″**] **1,** a doctor attached to a hospital's staff for training. **2,** an apprentice or trainee working in a profession to gain practical experience, esp. a college or graduate student. —**in″ter·nee′** (-nē′) *n.* one interned as a prisoner of war. —**in·tern′ment,** *n.* —**in·tern′ship,** *n.*

in·ter′nal (in-tēr′nəl) *adj.* **1,** situated within something; enclosed; inside. **2,** pert. to an inner part; domestic; subjective. **3,** (of a medicine, etc.) to be taken into the body. —**internal combustion,** power generated by an explosion inside a chamber, as in the cylinder of a gasoline engine. —**internal medicine,** a branch of medicine dealing with the diagnosis and nonsurgical treatment of the internal organs.

in″ter·na′tion·al *adj.* **1,** pert. to the relations between nations. **2,** involving more than one nation. —*n.* (*cap.*) any of several international federations of socialist or communistic groups.

in′terne″ (in′tĕrn″) *n.* intern.

in″ter·ne′cine (in″tər-nē′sin) *adj.* accompanied by mutual slaughter; extremely destructive.

---

internecine

↔ From Latin *internecare,* to slaughter utterly. The modern sense of mutual destruction comes from a misunderstanding by the eminent dictionary writer Dr. Samuel Johnson of the meaning of the prefix *inter-,* which in this case does not mean "between" but serves to intensify the meaning of the other part of the word, *necare,* to kill.

---

in·tern′ist (in-tĕrn′ist) *n.* a physician, internal medicine specialist.

in·ter′po·late″ (in-tēr′pə-lāt″) *v.t.* insert between other things; introduce (something new or extraneous). —**in″ter″po·la′tion,** *n.*

in″ter·pose′ (in″tər-pōz′) *v.t.* place between or among; interrupt with. —*v.i.* come between things or persons, as an obstacle or mediator. —**in″ter·po·si′tion** (-pə-zish′ən) *n.*

in·ter′pret (in-tēr′prit) *v.t.* **1,** show the meaning of; explain; elucidate; translate. **2,** construe in a particular way, as a part in a play. —**in·ter″pre·ta′tion,** *n.* —**in·ter′pre·ta″tive, in·ter′pre·tive,** *adj.*

in″ter·reg′num (in″tər-reg′nəm) *n.* an interval between one reign and the next; a breach of continuity.

in·ter′ro·bang″ (in-ter′ə-bang″) *n.* a punctuation mark (‽), not in general use, expressing both inquiry and exclamation. [*interro(gation point)* + *bang,* exclamation point]

in·ter′ro·gate″ (in-ter′ə-gāt″) *v.t. & i.* ask a question or questions (of). —**in·ter′ro·ga″tor,** *n.*

in·ter″ro·ga′tion (-gā′shən) *n.* **1,** a question or questioning. **2,** the symbol ?; question mark.

in″ter·rog′a·tive (in″tə-rog′ə-tiv) *adj.* asking a question. Also, **in″ter·rog′a·to·ry** (-tôr-ē).

in″ter·rupt′ (in″tə-rupt′) *v.t.* **1,** make a gap in; bring to a pause or stop. **2,** intrude upon the action or speech of. —**in″ter·rup′tion,** *n.*

in″ter·sect′ (in″tər-sekt′) *v.t. & i.* cut or divide; cross (one another).

in″ter·sec′tion (-sek′shən) *n.* **1,** the act of intersecting. **2,** a point where lines or roads meet.

in″ter·sperse′ (in″tər-spērs′) *v.t.* **1,** scatter among other things. **2,** diversify by placing various things here and there.

in″ter·state″ *adj.* between different states; in the U.S., concerning two or more states and therefore within federal jurisdiction. —*n.* a highway in the Interstate Highway System.

in·ter′stice (in-tēr′stis) *n.* [*pl.* **in·ter′sti·ces** (-siz)] an intervening space; a small narrow opening.

in″ter·ur′ban *adj.* between cities. —*n.* a transportation system running between cities.

in′ter·val (in′tər-vəl) *n.* **1,** the time between two events. **2,** an intermission. **3,** the distance between two objects; a difference in degree, etc. **4,** an empty space; a gap.

in″ter·vene′ (in″tər-vēn′) *v.i.* **1,** happen between things, persons, or events. **2,** intercede; interfere. **—in″ter·ven′tion** (-ven′shən) *n.*

in′ter·view″ (in′tər-vū″) *n.* **1,** a meeting of persons face to face. **2,** a questioning; examination. *—v.t.* meet to question.

in·tes′tate (in-tes′tāt) *adj.* **1,** having made no will. **2,** not bequeathed. *—n.* one who dies without having made a will. **—in·tes′ta·cy,** *n.*

in·tes′tine (in-tes′tin) *n.* the lower part of the alimentary tract; the bowel. **—in·tes′tin·al,** *adj.*

in·ti·fa′da (in-ti-fä′də) *n.* an Arab revolt, esp. against Israeli authority.

in′ti·ma·cy (in′ti-mə-sė) *n.* **1,** condition of being intimate. **2,** an act evidencing close familiarity with a person.

in′ti·mate (in′ti-mət) *adj.* **1,** close in personal relations; familiar; closely allied. **2,** personal; private. **3,** pert. to the inmost part or essential nature. *—n.* a close friend. *—v.t.* (-māt″) suggest; hint; imply. **—in″ti·ma′tion,** *n.* suggestion; a hint.

in·tim′i·date″ (in-tim′ə-dāt″) *v.t.* make timid or fearful; overawe. **—in·tim″i·da′-tion,** *n.*

in′to (in′too) *prep.* **1,** to and in, implying motion. **2,** (*Math.*) as a division of. **3,** (*Slang*) involved or interested in.

in·tol′er·a·ble (in-tol′ər-ə-bəl) *adj.* unbearable. **—in·tol″er·a·bil′i·ty, in·tol′er·a·ble·ness,** *n.*

in·tol′er·ant (in-tol′ər-ənt) *adj.* **1,** angered by contrary opinions or beliefs. **2,** unable to accept or bear. **—in·tol′er·ance,** *n.*

in″to·na′tion (in″tə-nā′shən) *n.* **1,** a particular modulation of the voice. **2,** the act of intoning. **3,** the relation of the pitch of a certain tone of a musical instrument or the voice to an accepted standard. **4,** the use of musical tones in speaking or chanting.

in·tone′ (in-tōn′) *v.t. & i.* **1,** utter in a singing voice; chant. **2,** utter in a particular tone, esp. a monotone.

in to′to (in tō′tō) (*Lat.*) in full; wholly.

in·tox′i·cant (in-tok′si-kənt) *n.* an intoxicating drink or drug.

in·tox′i·cate″ (in-tok′si-kāt″) *v.t.* **1,** make drunk with liquor. **2,** excite to elation, enthusiasm, etc. **3,** poison. *—v.i.* cause intoxication. **—in·tox′i·ca′tion,** *n.*

in·tra- (in-trə) *pref.* within.

in·trac′ta·ble (in-trak′tə-bəl) *adj.* **1,** stubborn; hard to control. **2,** (of a mate-

rial) hard to work with. **3,** hard to treat, as a pain.

in·tra′dos (in-trä′dōs) *n.* the interior curve or surface of an arch or vault.

in″tra·mu′ral (in″trə-myûr′əl) *adj.* confined to, or within the walls or limits of, a school, city, etc.

in·tran′si·gent (in-tran′sə-jənt) *adj.* refusing to agree or compromise. *—n.* one who is uncompromising. **—in·tran′si·gence,** *n.*

in·tran′si·tive (in-tran′sə-tiv) *adj.* (*Gram.*) of a verb, not acting directly on an object, as *I laugh, I go.*

in″tra·u′ter·ine (-ū′tər-in) *adj.* placed or found within the uterus. **—intrauterine device,** a contraceptive device placed within the uterus. Also, **IUD.**

in″tra·ve′nous (in″trə-vē′nəs) *adj.* within or into a vein.

in·trench′ *v.t.* entrench.

in·trep′id *adj.* undaunted; fearless. **—in″-tre·pid′i·ty** (in″trə-pid′ə-tė) *n.*

in′tri·cate (in′tri-kət) *adj.* perplexingly tangled; complex. **—in′tri·ca·cy** (-kə-sė) *n.*

in·trigue′ (in-trēg′) *v.t.* excite to interest or curiosity. *—v.i.* engage in underhand plotting. *—n.* a clandestine plot or love affair; plotting. **—in·tri′gant** (-trē′gənt) *n.*

in·trin′sic (in-trin′zik) *adj.* being an innate or essential part; inherent. **—in·trin′-si·cal·ly,** *adv.*

in·tro- (in-trō; in-trə) *pref.* within; into; inward.

in″tro·duce′ (in″trə-dūs′) *v.t.* **1,** bring into notice, use, or practice. **2,** begin; provide with a preface. **3,** present (a person) to another or to society. **4,** lead (a person) to a particular experience. **5,** put in; insert.

in″tro·duc′tion (in″trə-duk′shən) *n.* **1,** act or result of introducing. **2,** that which introduces, as a preface. **—in″tro·duc′to·ry** (-tə-rė) *adj.*

in′tro·it (in-trō′it) *n.* an antiphon sung at the beginning of mass or communion.

in″tro·spec′tion (in″trə-spek′shən) *n.* observation of one's own mental state.

in″tro·spec′tive (-tiv) *adj.* observing or tending to think about one's thoughts, feelings, etc.

in′tro·vert (in′trə-vėrt″) *n.* a person chiefly concerned with his or her own thoughts. *—v.t.* turn inward. **—in″tro·ver′-sion** (-vėr′zhən) *n.*

in·trude′ (in-trood′) *v.t.* thrust in forcibly. *—v.i.* thrust oneself in, esp. without warrant or welcome.

in·tru′sion (in-troo′zhən) *n.* **1,** act or result of intruding. **2,** an unwelcome visit or entrance.

in·tru′sive (in-troo′siv) *adj.* intruding; being an intrusion. **—in·tru′sive·ness,** *n.* ❑ *obtrusive*

in·trust′ *v.t.* entrust.

in″tu·i′tion (in″too-ish′ən) *n.* comprehension without effort of reasoning; instinctive knowledge. **—in·tu′it** (in-too′it) *v.i. & t.* **—in·tu′i·tive** (in-too′ə-tiv) *adj.*

in′un·date″ (in′un-dāte″) *v.t.* flood; deluge. **—in″un·da′tion,** *n.*

in·ure′ (in-yûr′) *v.t.* deaden the sensibility of; accustom; habituate. **—v.i.** (*Law*) pass (to); serve. **—in·ure′ment,** *n.*

in·vade′ (in-vād′) *v.t.* **1,** enter as an enemy; penetrate; raid. **2,** intrude upon; encroach upon.

in′va·lid (in′və-lid) *n.* a sick or disabled person. **—adj. 1,** infirm; sickly. **2,** (in-va′lid) not valid; without force.

in·val′i·date″ (in-val′i-dāt″) *v.t.* remove validity from; annul. **—in·val″i·da′tion,** *n.*

in·val′u·a·ble (in-val′ū-ə-bəl) *adj.* of immeasurably great value. **—in·val′u·a·ble·ness,** *n.*

> **invaluable, valuable, valueless**
> ☛ Despite appearances to the contrary, *invaluable* and *valuable* have the same general meaning, though *invaluable* is stronger; their antonym is *valueless*.

In·var′ (in-vär′) *n.* (*T.N.*) a nickel-steel alloy.

in·va′sion (in-vā′zhən) *n.* act or result of invading. **—in·va′sive** (-siv) *adj.*

in·vec′tive (in-vek′tiv) *n.* vehement denunciation or vituperation. **—adj.** censorious; abusive.

in·veigh′ (in-vā′) *v.i.* make a verbal attack.

> **inveigh**
> ↔ From Latin *vehere,* carry, which also produced *vehicle, invective,* and *vector,* among other words.

in·vei′gle (in-vā′gəl) *v.t.* lead astray artfully; entice. **—in·vei′gle·ment,** *n.*

in·vent′ *v.t.* **1,** be first to devise; originate. **2,** fabricate, as a story. **—v.i.** create something new. **—in·ven′tor,** *n.*

in·ven′tion (in-ven′shən) *n.* **1,** act of inventing. **2,** something invented; an original creation. **3,** a lie. **4,** imagination; skill or ingenuity in original contrivance.

in·ven′tive (in-ven′tiv) *adj.* apt at inventing; creative. **—in·ven′tive·ness,** *n.*

in′ven·to·ry (in′vən-tôr-ē) *n.* **1,** a descriptive list of articles; a catalog of contents, stock, etc. **2,** the value of a stock of goods. **—v.t.** list; catalog.

in″ver·ness′ (in″vər-ness′) *n.* a long, sleeveless cape.

in·verse′ (in-vērs′) *adj.* **1,** opposite or contrary in meaning, sense, application, etc. **2,** reversed in position or direction; inverted. **—n.** that which is inverse.

in·ver′sion (in-vēr′zhən) *n.* **1,** reversal; transposition. **2,** alteration of the natural order of words.

in·vert′ (in-vērt′) *v.t.* reverse in position or condition; turn over; transpose; reverse in meaning, application, tendency, etc. **—n.** (in′vert) the opposite or contrary thing.

in·vest′ *v.t.* **1,** put (money) to profitable use. **2,** install; endow. **3,** dress. **4,** hem in; besiege. **—v.i.** invest money.

in·ves′ti·gate″ (in-ves′ti·gāt″) *v.t. & i.* examine in detail; inquire into. **—in·ves″ti·ga′tion,** *n.* **—in·ves′ti·ga″tor,** *n.* **—in·ves′·ti·ga″tive,** *adj.*

in·ves′ti·ture (in-ves′ti-chər) *n.* **1,** act or effect of installing in office. **2,** a robe or token of office.

in·vest′ment (-mənt) *n.* act or result of investing; money invested.

in·vet′er·ate (in-vet′ər-ət) *adj.* firmly established or addicted by habit, custom, or usage. **—in·vet′er·a·cy,** *n.*

in·vid′i·ous (in-vid′ē-əs) *adj.* **1,** prompted by envy or ill will. **2,** unfair; odious. **—in·vid′i·ous·ness,** *n.*

in·vig′or·ate″ (in-vig′ə-rāt″) *v.t.* strengthen; animate. **—in·vig″or·a′tion,** *n.* ❑ *enervate*

in·vin′ci·ble (in-vin′sə-bəl) *adj.* unconquerable. **—in·vin″ci·bil′i·ty, in·vin′ci·ble·ness,** *n.*

in vi′no ve′ri·tas″ (in vē′nō ve′rē-täs″) (*Lat.*) in wine there is truth.

in·vi′o·la·ble (in-vī′ə-lə-bəl) *adj.* not to be violated; invulnerable. **—in·vi″o·la·bil′·i·ty,** *n.*

in·vi′o·late (in-vī′ə-lət) *adj.* **1,** not desecrated, infringed, or impaired. **2,** not to be violated.

in″vi·ta′tion (in″vi-tā′shən) *n.* **1,** act of inviting. **2,** a request to be present; an allurement. **—in″vi·ta′tion·al** (-əl) *adj.* open by invitation only.

in·vite′ (in-vīt′) *v.t.* **1,** ask (a person) to come; request the presence of. **2,** solicit, allure, tempt, etc. **3,** lay oneself open to. **—n.** (in′vīt) (*Slang*) an invitation. **—in·vit′·ing,** *adj.* alluring; tempting.

in vi′tro (ēn vē′trō) (*Lat.*) in a test tube.

in″vo·ca′tion (in″vō-kā′shən) *n.* **1,** act of invoking. **2,** a prayer.

in′voice (in′vois) *n.* a list of items shipped; a bill for them. —*v.t.* list and bill for. ❏ *envoy*

in·voke′ (in-vōk′) *v.t.* **1,** call on for aid or protection, esp. as addressing a deity. **2,** call for; utilize, as a law. —**in·voc′a·to·ry** (in-vok′ə-tôrė-) *adj.*

in·vol′un·tar″y (in-vol′ən-ter″ė) *adj.* **1,** not willed or intentional. **2,** done unwillingly. —**in·vol′un·tar″i·ness,** *n.*

in′vo·lute″ (in′və-loot″) *adj.* rolled inward; involved; intricate. —**in″vo·lu′tion,** *n.* something involute.

in·volve′ (in-volv′) *v.t.* **1,** contain or include; entail; imply. **2,** affect or be affected by. **3,** combine inextricably; implicate. **4,** make intricate or complex. —**in·volve′ment,** *n.*

in′ward (in′wərd) *adv.* [also, **in′wards**] toward the inside or center; in the mind or soul. —*adj.* **1,** being within; directed toward the inside or center. **2,** pert. to inner parts; in the mind. —**in′ward·ness,** *n.*

in′ward·ly (-lė) *adv.* **1,** toward the inside or center. **2,** privately; secretly. **3,** in a low tone; not aloud.

i′o·dine″ (ī′ə-dīn″) *n.* **1,** a nonmetallic chemical element, used medicinally, no. 53, symbol I. **2,** an antiseptic solution: *tincture of iodine.* —**i′o·dize″,** *v.t.* treat with iodine.

---

iodine

↔ From Greek *ion*, violet, because of the color of iodine vapor. The English term was coined by the British chemist Sir Humphry Davy, from the French term coined by Gay-Lussac.

---

i′on (ī′ən) *n.* an atom or molecule bearing an electric charge.

i·o′ni·um (ī-ō′nė-əm) *n.* a radioactive chemical element, no. 90, symbol Io.

i′on·ize″ (ī′ə-nīz″) *v.t.* form ions in; change to ions. —**i″on·i·za′tion,** *n.*

i·on′o·sphere″ (ī-on′ə-sfir″) *n.* the outer regions of the earth's atmosphere, from about 60 miles outward.

i·o′ta (ī-ō′tə) *n.* **1,** the ninth letter of the Greek alphabet (I, ι). **2,** a small quantity.

I O U *n.* a written acknowledgment of a debt: *I owe you.*

ip′e·cac″ (ip′ə-kak″) *n.* a So. Amer. shrub; an emetic drug made from it.

ip′se dix′it (ip′se dik′sit) (*Lat.*) **1,** he himself has said it. **2,** an unproved assertion.

ip′so fac′to (ip′sō fak′tō) (*Lat.*) by virtue of the same fact; by the nature of the deed.

I.Q. (ī′kū′) *n.* intelligence quotient.

ir- *pref.* not (the equivalent of **in-,** used before an initial r). [In addition to words defined in the text, the following words formed by prefixing **ir-** (= not) have merely the negative sense of the positive term.]

ir·ra′tion·al	ir″re·place′a·ble
ir″re·claim′a·ble	ir″re·press′i·ble
ir·rec′on·cil″a·ble	ir″re·proach′a·ble
ir″re·cov′er·a·ble	ir″re·sist′i·ble
ir·re·deem′a·ble	ir·res′o·lute″
ir″re·duc′i·ble	ir″re·spon′sive
ir·ref′u·ta·ble	ir″re·triev′a·ble
ir·rel′e·vant	ir·rev′er·ent
ir″re·me′di·a·ble	ir″re·vers′i·ble
ir″re·mov′a·ble	ir·rev′o·ca·ble
ir·rep′a·ra·ble	

i·ras′ci·ble (i-ras′ə-bəl) *adj.* easily provoked to anger; hot-tempered. —**i·ras″ci·bil′i·ty,** *n.*

i′rate (ī′rāt; ī-rāt′) *adj.* angry; incensed.

ire (īr) *n.* anger; resentment. —*v.t.* irritate; enrage.

i·ren′ic (ī-ren′ik) *adj.* tending to promote peace. —**i·ren′i·cal·ly,** *adv.*

ir″i·des′cent (ir″ə-des′ənt) *adj.* glittering with changeable colors, like a rainbow. —**ir″i·des′cence,** *n.*

i·rid′i·um (i-rid′ė-əm) *n.* a metallic chemical element, similar to platinum, no. 77, symbol Ir.

i′ris (ī′ris) *n.* **1,** the colored diaphragm of the eye surrounding the pupil. **2,** any of various flowering plants. **3,** the rainbow, or a similar iridescence.

I′rish (ī′rish) *adj.* pert. to Ireland, its people, customs, etc. —*n.* the Gaelic language; Erse. —**I′rish·man,** *n.*

irk (ērk) *v.t.* annoy; bore. —**irk′some,** *adj.* boring; annoying. —**irk′some·ness,** *n.*

i′ron (ī′ərn) *n.* **1,** a metallic chemical element, no. 26, symbol Fe; this metal, widely fabricated. **2,** a tool; implement, utensil, weapon, etc. of this metal; a harpoon; (*Slang*) a gun; (*pl.*) shackles; an implement for pressing clothes; a type of golf club. **3,** something hard, rigid, unyielding, etc. **4,** a tonic containing iron. —*adj.* **1,** made of iron. **2,** like iron; hard; enduring, steadfast, etc. —*v.t. & i.* press (clothes, etc.). —**Iron Age,** a period when iron implements were first used, about 1000 B.C. —**Iron Curtain,** a barrier to

---

travel and communication into and out of a country, by government restrictions and censorship. —**iron horse,** (*Informal*) **1,** a railroad locomotive. **2,** a bicycle or tricycle. —**iron lung,** a chamber in which a paralyzed person is placed to enable him or her to breathe. —**Iron maiden,** a medieval torture box containing metal spikes. —**pump iron,** lift weights.

i′ron·clad″ *adj.* **1,** armored, as a warship. **2,** unassailable; unbreakable, as an agreement.

i·ron′ic (ī-ron′ik) *adj.* **1,** being sarcastic. **2,** frustrating. Also, **i·ron′i·cal.**

i′ron·stone″ *n.* a kind of pottery.

i′ro·ny (ī′rə-nē) *n.* **1,** a figure of speech: emphasis by stating the opposite; covert sarcasm. **2,** the frustration of hopes.

> **irony**
> ↔ From Greek *eirōneiā*, feigned ignorance, a device used in debate.

ir·ra′di·ate″ (i-rā′dē-āt″) *v.t.* **1,** throw rays of light upon. **2,** make clear. **3,** treat with radiation, as food. —*v.i.* emit rays or radiant energy. —**ir·ra″di·a′tion,** *n.*

ir″re·den′tist (ir″i-den′tist) *n.* a member of a party advocating annexation of a region because of its ties.

ir″re·gard′less (ir″i-gärd′ləs) *adj.* (*Erroneous*) regardless.

ir·reg′u·lar (i-reg′yə-lər) *adj.* **1,** not regular. **2,** against the rules. **3,** (*Mil.*) not belonging to the established armed forces. —**ir·reg″u·lar′i·ty** (-lar′ə-tē) *n.*

ir″re·li′gious (ir″i-lij′əs) *adj.* **1,** not devout. **2,** profane. —**ir″re·li′gious·ness,** *n.*

ir″re·spec′tive (ir″i-spek′tiv) *adj.* regardless; independent (of).

ir″re·spon′si·ble (ir″i-spon′sə-bəl) *adj.* **1,** having no sense of responsibility; not trustworthy. **2,** not accountable, as for one's own actions. —**ir″re·spon″si·bil′i·ty,** *n.*

ir′ri·gate″ (ir′ə-gāt″) *v.t.* **1,** supply (land) with water through artificial channels. **2,** wash with a flow of liquid, as a wound. —**ir″ri·ga′tion,** *n.*

ir′ri·ta·ble (ir′ə-tə-bəl) *adj.* irascible. —**ir″ri·ta·bil′i·ty,** *n.*

ir′ri·tant (ir′ə-tənt) *n. & adj.* something that irritates.

ir′ri·tate″ (ir′ə-tāt″) *v.t.* **1,** excite to resentment or anger; vex; annoy. **2,** make sore or painful; chafe. —**ir″ri·ta′tion,** *n.* ❏ *aggravate*

ir·rup′tion (i-rup′shən) *n.* a bursting in; a sudden invasion. —**ir·rupt′,** *v.i.* —**ir·rup′-tive,** *adj.* ❏ *eruption*

is (iz) *v.* 3rd. pers. sing. pres. indicative of *be.*

-ise (īz) *suf.* same as **-ize.**

-ish *suf.* having some characteristics of.

i′sin·glass″ (ī′zing-glås″) *n.* **1,** a form of translucent gelatin. **2,** mica.

> **isinglass**
> ↔ Not from *glass*, but from Dutch *huisenblas*, sturgeon's bladder, the source of the material.

Is′lam (is′ləm) *n.* the Muslim religion; its followers and realm.

is′land (ī′lənd) *n.* **1,** a body of land entirely surrounded by water. **2,** something isolated or surrounded. —**is′land·er,** *n.* —**island universe,** a galaxy.

> **island, isle**
> ↔ The two words are only distantly related. *Island* comes from Old English *igland*, island land; the *s* probably was inserted by influence of French *isle*, island, which comes from Latin *insula*.

isle (īl) *n.* a small island. Also, **is′let** (ī′lət). ❏ *island*

ism (iz′əm) *n.* a distinctive doctrine, theory, or practice.

-ism (iz-əm) *suf.* of nouns, implying practice, system, doctrine, theory, or principle.

i′so- (ī-sə,-sō) *pref.* **1,** equal. **2,** (*Chem.*) isomeric.

i′so·bar″ (ī′sə-bär″) *n.* a line connecting, on a map, all places where the barometric pressure is the same.

i′so·late″ (ī′sə-lāt″) *v.t.* **1,** place apart; make separate. **2,** single out; rid of extraneous matter.

i″so·la′tion (ī″sə-lā′shən) *n.* **1,** the act of isolating; the state of being isolated. **2,** a national policy of nonparticipation in international affairs. —**i″so·la′tion·ism,** *n.* pursuit or support of this policy. —**i″so·la′tion·ist,** *n.*

i′so·mer (ī′sə-mər) *n.* a chemical compound of the same composition (as another) but in different arrangement. —**i″so·mer′ic** (-mer′ik) *adj.*

i″so·met′ric (ī″sə-met′rik) *adj.* **1,** of equal measure; regularly spaced. **2,** of muscular contraction, taking place against resistance, but without lengthening or shortening of the muscle fibers.

i·sos′ce·les″ (ī-sos′ə-lēz″) *adj.* (of a triangle) having two equal sides.

i′so·therm″ (ī′sə-thėrm″) *n.* a line connecting all places that have the same mean temperature. —**i″so·ther′mal,** *adj.*

i″so·ton′ic (ī″sō-tän′ik) *adj.* of muscle contraction, taking place without resistance but with lengthening or shortening of the muscle fibers.

i′so·tope″ (ī′sə-tōp″) *n.* a chemical element, nearly identical (with another or others) but differing in atomic weight.

Is·ra′el·i (iz-rā′ə-lē) *adj.* pert. to the modern country of Israel. —*n.* a citizen of Israel. —**Is′ra·el·ite″** (iz′rē-ə-līt″) *n.*

is′sue (ish′oo) *n.* **1,** the act of sending out; publication; emission. **2,** what is sent out, esp. a quantity issued at one time. **3,** an outflow; product, result, outcome, etc.; offspring or progeny. **4,** a point in question or dispute; a principal question. —*v.t.* **1,** send out; publish; promulgate; distribute. **2,** emit; discharge. —*v.i.* **1,** go or come out; flow out; emerge. **2,** arise as a result or yield. —**is′su·ance,** *n.* ❏ *edition*

-ist *suf.* of nouns denoting a supporter or adherent (of a doctrine, etc.), as *capitalist*; a practitioner or expert, as *strategist*; a performer on a named instrument, as *violinist*.

isth′mus (is′məs) *n.* a narrow strip of land connecting two larger bodies.

it *pron.* [*poss.* **its**] **1,** a personal pron., third person sing., neuter gender. **2,** a pron. of indefinite sense, as in *What is it?* **3,** a particle used for grammatical completeness in certain idiomatic constructions, as *It is ten o'clock. Let us call it a day.* —*n.* (*Informal*) **1,** a person who is the center of attention, or (esp. in children's games) solely given an onerous duty. **2,** (*Slang*) attractiveness to the opposite sex. —**it's** (its) *contraction* it is.

> **its, it's**
> (*Gram.*) These two forms are a common source of error. *It's* is a contraction of *it is; its* is the possessive form of *it.*

I·tal′ian (i-tal′yən) *adj. & n.* pert. to Italy or its inhabitants or language.

i·tal′ic (i-tal′ik) *n. & adj.* a style of type with sloped letters, thus: *italic.* —**i·tal′i·cize″** (-i-sīz″) *v.t.*

itch (ich) *v.i.* **1,** feel or produce an inclination to scratch an affected part. **2,** desire eagerly. —*n.* **1,** tingling sensation in the skin. **2,** an itching skin disease; scabies. **3,** a persistent desire. —**itch′y,** *adj.*

> **itch, scratch**
> (*Gram.*) An *itch* itches, but to relieve it you must *scratch* it (not *itch* it): as a verb, *itch* is only used intransitively.

-ite (-īt) *suf.* **1,** denoting a supporter, fol-

lower, associate, or inhabitant. **2,** denoting certain kinds of minerals, chemical compounds, etc.

i′tem (ī′təm) *n.* **1,** one article of a collection, list, etc. **2,** a separate article or piece, as in a newspaper.

i′tem·ize″ (ī′tə-mīz″) *v.t.* make a particularized list of. —**i″tem·i·za′tion** (-mi-zā′shən) *n.*

it′er·ate″ (it′ə-rāt″) *v.t.* utter or say again or repeatedly. —**it″er·a′tion,** *n.* —**it′er·a·tive,** *adj.*

i·tin′er·ant (ī-tin′ə-rənt) *adj.* traveling from place to place. —*n.* a traveler. —**i·tin′er·an·cy,** *n.*

i·tin′er·ar·y (ī-tin′ə-rer-ē) *n.* a plan of travel, esp. a proposed route.

-it′is (ī′təs) *suf.* (*Pathol.*) forming nouns, denoting an inflammation.

it·self′ *pron.* reflexive or emphatic form of *it.*

i′vo·ry (ī′və-rē) *n.* **1,** the bony substance of a tusk, esp. of an elephant. **2,** (*Slang*) a tooth; (*pl.*) piano keys; (*pl.*) dice. **3,** the color of ivory, creamy white. —**ivory tower, 1,** a dream world. **2,** an attitude of aloofness or isolation.

> **ivory**
> ↔ From Old French *ivurie* from Latin *eboreus*, probably derived from an African word.

i′vy (ī′vē) *n.* any of several climbing or trailing plants. —**Ivy League,** an association of colleges in the NE U.S.

-ize (īz) *suf.* forming verbs denoting application of the action denoted by the root, as *emphasize,* make emphatic.

iz′zard (iz′ərd) *n.* (*Informal*) z.

J

J, j (jā) the tenth letter of the English alphabet.

jab *v.t. & i.* [**jabbed, jab′bing**] strike suddenly and sharply; prod; poke. —*n.* a sharp thrust.

jab′ber (jab′ər) *v.i. & t.* talk rapidly in an incoherent way; chatter. —*n.* gibberish.

jab′ber·wock″y (jab′ər-wok″ē) *n.* gibberish; nonsensical speech.

> **jabberwocky**
> ↔ One of many words coined by Lewis Carroll, author of *Alice in Wonderland* and *Through the Looking-Glass,* in which the poem *Jabberwocky* appears.

ja·bot' (zha-bō') *n.* a frill or ruffle in a bosom of a shirt.

jac'a·mar (jak'ə-mär) *n.* a long-billed Amer. bird.

jac"a·ran'da (jak"ə-ran'də) *n.* a tall tropical tree valued for its wood.

jack (jak) *n.* **1,** a mechanical contrivance for lifting. **2,** an oscillating lever or fixed piece for transmitting motion. **3,** one of the face cards in a pack of playing cards; knave. **4,** a small flag. **5,** jackass; jackrabbit; jackdaw; any of several fishes, as the pike. **6,** (*Slang*) money. **8,** a small six-pronged metal object used in the game of jacks. **9,** (*pl., construed as sing.*) a children's game using a small ball and a set of small objects, such as jacks, stones, etc.. —*v.t.* (usually with *up*) hoist; raise.

jack'al (jak'əl) *n.* **1,** a wild dog of Asia and Africa. **2,** an accomplice, esp. one who performs dishonest tasks for another.

---

jackal, jackanapes
↔ Only one of these two words comes from *jack. Jackanapes* was, in Middle English, *Jakken-apes*, jack of the apes, a nickname for the 1st Duke of Suffolk, by reference to his coat of arms. *Jackal* derives from Persian *shagal.*

---

jack'a·napes" (jak'ə-nāps") *n.* an impertinent or obstreperous fellow. ❑ *jackal*

jack'ass" (-as") *n.* **1,** a male donkey. **2,** a stupid or foolish person.

jack'boot" *n.* a long boot reaching over the knee.

jack'daw" (-dâ") *n.* **1,** a Europ. crow. **2,** an Amer. grackle. **3,** a talkative person.

jack'et (jak'it) *n.* **1,** a tailless coat. **2,** any outer covering, as a protective wrapper on a book.

jack'fruit" *n.* a tropical tree of the mulberry family; its fruit.

jack'ham"mer *n.* a pneumatic hand drill.

jack-'in-the-box" *n.* a toy consisting of a box from which a compressed figure springs upward when the lid is released.

jack-'in-the-pul"pit *n.* [*pl.* **-pul"pits**] a No. Amer. flowering plant.

jack'knife" (jak'nīf") *n.* a large folding pocket knife.

jack'leg" *n.* an unskilled migrant worker.

jack-'of-all-trades' *n.* a handyman.

jack-'o'-lan"tern (jak'ə-lan"tərn) *n.* a carved hollowed pumpkin used for decorative illumination at Halloween.

jack pine a tree found in northern U.S. and Canada.

jack'pot" *n.* an unusually large prize, esp. the largest prize.

jack'rab"bit *n.* a large hare.

jack'screw" *n.* a jack for raising weights.

jack'straw" *n.* **1,** an effigy made of straw. **2,** a man without substance or means; a dependent. **3,** (*pl.*) a child's game using straws or strips.

---

jackstraw
↔ In English history, from *Jack Straw*, one of the leaders in the Wat Tyler revolution of 1381.

Jac"o·be'an (jak"ə-bē'ən) *adj.* pert. to or contemporary with James I of England (1603-1625).

Jacobean, Jacobite
↔ Both words are from New Latin *Jacobaeus*, from *Jacobus*, Latinized version of James.

Jac'o·bite (jak'ə-bīt) *n.* supporter of James II of England (1685-88) or the Stuart dynasty (1603-1714). ❑ *Jacobean*

jac'quard (jak'ärd) *n.* a fabric produced on a Jacquard loom. —**Jacquard loom,** a loom designed for producing intricate patterns.

---

jacquard
↔ Named for 19th-c. French inventor J. M. *Jacquard*.

Ja·cuz'zi (jə-koo'zė) *n.* (*T.N.*) a brand of whirlpool tub.

jade (jād) *n.* **1,** a green mineral prized for jewelry. **2,** a shade of green. **3,** (*Offensive*) a dissolute woman. **4,** an inferior or worn-out horse. —*v.t. & i.* make or become exhausted by overwork.

---

jade
↔ The name of the stone comes from Latin *ilia*, flanks, because the green stone was thought to cure certain body pains.

---

jae'ger (yā'gər) *n.* **1,** a predatory bird, the skua. **2,** a hunter. **3,** (*pl.*) (jā'gərz) long underwear.

jag *n.* **1,** a sharp notch or tooth. **2,** (*Slang*) a drinking spree.—**jag'gy,** *adj.*

jag'ged (jag'id) *adj.* having sharp projections; irregular.

jag'uar (jag'wär) *n.* a large, ferocious cat of Central and So. Amer.

ja"gua·ron'di (ja"gwə-ron'dė) *n.* a small tropical Amer. wildcat. Also, **ja"gua·run'di** (-run'dė).

jai′a·lai′ (hī ′ä-lī′) a game resembling squash but played with basketlike rackets.

jail (jāl) *n.* a place of detention for convicted criminals or persons awaiting trial. —*v.t.* put in a jail. —**jail′er,** *n.* an officer of a jail.

> **jail, gaol**
> ↔ These two very different-looking words have the same meaning and developed from the same Old French sources, in turn derived from Latin **caveola,* cage.

jail′bait″ *n.* (*Slang*) a girl under the legal age of consent.

jail′bird″ *n.* an ex-convict.

jake (jāk) (*Slang*) *adj.* all right. —*n.* bootleg liquor.

ja″la·pe′ño (hä″lə-pān′yō) *n.* a variety of hot red or green pepper.

ja·lop′y (jə-lop′ė) *n.* (*Informal*) a decrepit automobile.

jal′ou·sie (jal′oo-zė; -ə-sė) *n.* a blind or shutter made of slats set at an angle to admit air but exclude sun and rain.

jam *v.t.* [**jammed, jam′ming**] **1,** thrust or squeeze in so as to stick fast; crowd so as to hinder motion or extrication. **2,** interfere with (a radio broadcast) by another on the same frequency. —*v.i.* **1,** become wedged in place. **2,** (*Slang*) improvise together informally. **3,** (*Slang*) enliven. —*n.* **1,** an obstruction. **2,** a fruit preserve. **3,** (*Slang*) a predicament. —**jam session,** an impromptu jazz session.

jamb (jam) *n.* a vertical side member in the frame of a door or window.

jam″bo·ree′ (jam″bə-rē′) *n.* (*Slang*) a festive gathering.

> **jamboree**
> ↔ This word is possibly a combination of two words: *jabber* and *shivaree* have been mentioned. This is still conjectural, however.

jam-′packed″ *adj.* (*Informal*) full to capacity.

Jane Doe (*Law*) a female defendant or prisoner whose name is not known.

jan′gle (jang′gəl) *v.i. & t.* make a harsh or metallic sound. —*n.* **1,** a discordant sound. **2,** a quarrel or wrangle.

> **January**
> ↔ From the two-faced Roman god *Janus,* because the month looks back to the old year and forward to the new.

jan′i·tor (jan′ə-tər) *n.* the caretaker of a building; custodian.

Jan′u·ar″y (jan′yû-er″ė) *n.* the first month of the year.

ja·pan′ (jə-pan′) *n.* a varnish that gives a hard, glossy finish. —*v.t.* varnish with japan.

> **Japan**
> ↔ The name of the country is not Japanese but Chinese, from *jih pun,* sunrise. The word for lacquer comes from the name of the country.

Jap″a·nese′ (jap″ə-nēz′) *adj.* pert. to Japan. —*n.* **1,** the language of Japan. **2,** (-nēz′) one descended from the people of Japan.

jape (jāp) *n.* a joke or gibe.

ja·pon′i·ca (jə-pon′ə-kə) *n.* a shrub with scarlet flowers and yellow fruit; the Japanese quince.

jar (jär) *v.t. & i.* [**jarred, jar′ring**] **1,** jolt suddenly; rattle; make a harsh sound. **2,** affect unpleasantly; annoy or disconcert. **3,** clash; be inharmonious. —*n.* **1,** a harsh impact; a shock. **2,** a clash; conflict; discord. **3,** a wide-mouthed vessel.

jar″di·nière′ (jär″də-nir′) *n.* **1,** an ornamental flowerpot. **2,** diced vegetables used as a garnish.

jar′gon (jär′gən) *n.* **1,** confused or meaningless talk. **2,** language peculiar to a group or profession; cant. ❑ *argot*

jas′mine (jas′min) *n.* any of several shrubs bearing fragrant yellow or red flowers.

jas′per (jas′pər) *n.* a variety of quartz used for making ornaments.

jass (yäs) *n.* a card game for two persons.

ja′to (jā′tō) *abbr.* a system of propulsion using auxiliary rocket engines: *j(et-)a(ssisted) t(ake-)o(ff).*

jaun′dice (jân′dis) *n.* **1,** a disease that causes a yellowish tinge in the skin. **2,** a state of feeling that colors judgment, as jealousy, envy, etc. —*v.t.* affect with prejudice or envy. —**jaun′diced** (-dist) *adj.* adversely biased.

jaunt (jânt) *n.* a short trip, made for pleasure.

jaun′ty (jân′tė) *adj.* **1,** sprightly. **2,** smart in appearance. —**jaun′ti·ness,** *n.*

jave′lin (jav′lin) *n.* a spear made to be thrown by hand.

jaw (jâ) *n.* **1,** either of the two bony structures that form the mouth. **2,** anything likened to a jaw, for holding or seizing. —*v.i.* (*Slang*) talk; chatter; scold. —**Jaws of**

Life, (*T.N.*) a tool used to free people from wrecked vehicles.

jaw'bone'' *n.* **1,** a bone of the jaw. **2,** (*Slang*) credit. —*v.i.* **1,** chatter; scold. **2,** use government prestige to influence business and labor.

jaw'break''er (jâ'brā''kər) *n.* (*Informal*) **1,** any word hard to pronounce. **2,** a hard candy.

jay (jā) *n.* any of several common birds, as *blue jay.*

Jay'cee'' (jā'sē'') *n.* a member of a Junior Chamber of Commerce.

jay'walk'' (jā'wâk'') *v.i.* (*Informal*) cross a street against a traffic light, or between regular crossings.

jazz (jaz) *n.* **1,** dance music in a certain syncopated style. **2,** (*Slang*) foolishness; nonsense. —*v.t.* (*Slang*) (usu. with *up*) enliven. —*v.i.* (*Slang*) lie.

> **jazz**
> ↔ The origin of this word is not known, though it is generally assumed to be African. Before it was applied to syncopated music, the word was a slang term for sexual intercourse.

Jazz'er·cise'' (jaz'ər-sīz'') *n.* (*T.N.*) a style of physical exercise accompanied by jazz music.

jazz'y (jaz'ē) *adj.* (*Slang*) [-i·er, -i·est] **1,** containing or in the style of jazz. **2,** wildly exciting or energetic.

jeal'ous (jel'əs) *adj.* **1,** feeling or actuated by envy or resentment, as of a more successful rival. **2,** proceeding from distrust. **3,** intolerant of rivalry. —**jeal'ous·y,** *n.*

jean (jēn) *n.* **1,** a twilled cotton fabric. **2,** (*pl.*) trousers or overalls of jean.

> **jeans**
> ↔ From the Italian city Genoa, in the phrase *jean fustian,* fustian (a fabric), from Genoa.

jeep (jēp) *n.* a small multipurpose military automobile; (*cap., T.N.*) a similar civilian vehicle.

> **jeep**
> ↔ The origin of this name is variously ascribed to the abbreviation *G.P.* (general purpose) or the character "Eugene the Jeep" in the American cartoon "Popeye" by E. C. Segar.

jee'pers (jē'pərz) *interj.* of surprise, etc.

jeer (jir) *v.i. & t.* scoff at; deride; mock. —*n.* gibe; taunt.

Je·ho'vah (jė-hō'və) *n.* the name of God in the Old Testament.

> **Jehovah**
> ↔ New Latin. This word is an erroneous transliteration of Hebrew *adonai,* my lord.

je'hu (jē'hū) *n.* a reckless driver of a cart or car, named for a king of Israel noted for his chariot attacks.

je·june' (ji-joon') *adj.* deficient in sense, substance, or taste.

jell (jel) *v.i.* **1,** coagulate; become jelly. **2,** achieve a planned stage or form.

jel'ly (jel'ē) *n.* **1,** a semisolid food made by congealing fruit syrup or meat juice. **2,** any preparation of a soft, gelatinous consistency. —**jel'lied,** *adj.*

jel'ly bean'' *n.* a small oval candy with a soft chewy center.

jel'ly·fish'' (jel'ė-fish'') *n.* a marine invertebrate with a soft umbrella-shaped body, often with long tentacles.

je ne sais quoi' (zhə nə se kwä') (*Fr.,* I don't know what) an indefinable quality.

jen'net (jen'ət) *n.* **1,** a small Span. horse. **2,** (also, **gen'et**) a female donkey.

jen'ny (jen'ē) *n.* **1,** a type of spinning machine. **2,** the female of some species, as the ass. **3,** an airplane used for training fliers.

jeop'ard·y (jep'ər-dė) *n.* risk; danger. —**jeop'ard·ize'',** *v.t.* imperil.

> **jeopardy**
> ↔ From an Old French phrase, *jeu parti,* divided (hence uncertain) chance.

jer·bo'a (jėr-bō'ə) *n.* a small rodent of No. Afr. and Asia; jumping mouse.

jer''e·mi'ad (jer''ə-mī'ad) *n.* lamentation; a complaining tirade.

jerk (jėrk) *v.i. & t.* **1,** pull suddenly; tug or twist. **2,** cure (meat) in the sun. —*n.* **1,** a sudden start or thrust. **2,** (*Slang*) an inexpert or unsophisticated person.

jer'kin (jėr'kin) *n.* a sleeveless jacket.

jerk'wa''ter (jėrk'wâ''tər) *adj.* (*Informal*) located away from a main line; provincial.

> **jerkwater**
> ↔ So called from the jerking of water for steam locomotives in small towns along the line.

jerk'y (jėr'kė) *adj.* tending to jerk; spasmodic. —*n.* dried strips of meat. Also, **jerked meat.** —**jerk'i·ness,** *n.*

jer'ry (jer'ē) *n.* (*Brit.*) a nickname for a German or the Germans. —**jerry can,** a five-gallon can used for fuel or water. Also, **jer′ri·can.**

---

jerry, jerry-built
↔ The term *jerry* for "German" comes in fact from the latter word. *Jerry-built*, on the other hand, comes from a different word, English dialect *jerry*, meaning defective.

---

jer′ry-built″ (jer′ĕ-bilt″) *adj.* constructed hastily and with flimsy materials. —**jer′ry-build″** (-bild″) *v.t.* ❑ *jerry*

jer′sey (jēr′zĕ) *n.* **1,** a close-knitted fabric. **2,** a knitted shirt or jacket. **3,** (*cap.*) a breed of dairy cattle.

---

jersey
↔ After *Jersey*, one of the British Channel islands.

---

jest *v.i.* speak facetiously, playfully, or derisively. —*n.* a joke. —**jest′er,** *n.* a person retained to amuse a king; fool.

Jes′u·it (jezh′ū-it) *n.* a member of the Society of Jesus, a Roman Catholic religious order.

Je′sus freak (*Slang*) a member of a religious fundamentalist sect.

jet *n.* **1,** a gush of fluid from a spout. **2,** a spout. **3,** a black coal used in making ornaments. **4,** glossy black. **5,** an aircraft propelled by a jet engine. —*v.i. & t.* [**jet′-ted, -ting**] spurt; emit. —*adj.* black. —**jet engine,** an engine producing motion by jet propulsion. —**jet lag,** disorientation resulting from a rapid change of time zone without adequate time for adjustment of the body's biological clock. —**jet propulsion,** propelling force exerted (on aircraft or rockets) by exhaust of gases from burning. —**jet set,** (*Informal*) wealthy, usu. young, persons who travel long distances for parties and other social events. —**jet stream,** a high-speed air current.

---

jet, jettison, jetty
↔ The name of the black stone comes from Greek *gagatēs*, stone from Gagai, a town in Asia Minor that was a source for the stone. The other senses—as well as the words *jettison* and *jetty*— come from Latin *jacere*, throw.

---

jet′li·″ner (jet′lī″nər) *n.* a jet-propelled passenger airplane.

jet′port″ *n.* an airport suitable for jet airplanes.

jet′sam (jet′səm) *n.* goods thrown overboard to lighten a ship.

jet′ti·son (jet′ə-sən) *v.t.* throw goods overboard, to lighten a ship. ❑ *jet*

jet′ty (jet′ĕ) *n.* **1,** a pier built in water to deflect currents or shelter an anchorage. **2,** a landing wharf. ❑ *jet*

Jew (joo) *n.* a descendant of the Hebrew people or follower of their religion; an Israelite. —**Jew′ish,** *adj.*

jew′el (joo′əl) *n.* **1,** a gem; a precious stone, cut and polished, for adornment or for uses requiring great durability, as in the bearings of a watch. **2,** anything valuable. —**jew′el·er,** *n.* a seller of jewelry.

jew′el·ry (-rĕ) *n.* gems and precious metals made into ornaments.

Jew′ry (joo′rĕ) *n.* **1,** Jews collectively. **2,** a ghetto.

jew's-′harp″ (jooz′härp″) *n.* a metal reed in a round frame that is plucked and caused to sound different tones by movements of the mouth.

jez′e·bel (jez′ə-bel) *n.* an unscrupulous or vicious woman.

---

jezebel
↔ From *Jezebel*, wife of King Ahab (1 Kings 16:31), who influenced her husband and the people of Israel to turn from God.

---

jib *n.* **1,** a triangular sail set forward of a mast. **2,** a projecting arm, as in a gibbet or derrick.

jibe (jīb) *v.i.* **1,** shift abruptly from one side to the other, as the boom of a sail. **2,** (*Informal*) agree with; be in harmony with. —*n.* gibe. ❑ *gibe*

jif′fy (jif′ĕ) *n.* (*Informal*) a moment.

jig *n.* **1,** a tool for holding or guiding, as on a drill or lathe. **2,** a lively dance in triple time. —*v.i. & t.* [**jigged, jig′ging**] dance or play a jig; jump about.

jig′ger (jig′ər) *n.* **1,** a mast or sail near the stern, as on a yawl. **2,** a mechanical device that operates with a jerky motion, as a tripper. **3,** a 1½-oz. measure.

jig′gle (jig′əl) *v.i. & t.* move to and fro in quick, jerky motion. —*n.* act of jiggling; a jiggling motion.

jig′saw″ *n.* a saw designed to cut designs in wood. —**jigsaw puzzle,** a picture cut into many pieces to be fitted together.

ji·had′ (ji-had′) *n.* **1,** a Muslim religious war against unbelievers. **2,** any war or crusade in support of doctrine.

jilt *v.t.* dismiss (a sweetheart).

Jim Crow segregation of Negroes.

jim-′dan″dy *adj.* (*Informal*) excellent; first-rate.

jim′jams″ (jim′jamz″) *n.pl* **1,** jitters. **2,** delirium tremens.

---

tub, cūte, pûll; labəl; oil, owl, go, chip, she, thin, *th*en, sing, ink; *see p. 6*

jim′mie (jim′ė) *n.* a small chocolate sprinkle, usu. used on ice cream.

jim′my (jim′ė) *n.* a small prying tool used by burglars. —*v.t.* pry open.

jim′son weed (jim′sən) a noxious weed with white flowers; datura. Also, **James′-town weed.**

jin′gle (jing′gəl) *v.i. & t.* make tinkling sounds. —*n.* **1,** a metallic clinking sound. **2,** verse constructed more for sound than sense. **3,** verse set to music and used to advertise a product, service, etc.

jin′go (jing′gō) *n.* one who favors lavish armament or a bellicose foreign policy. —**jin′go·ism,** *n.*

> **jingo**
> ↔ From the refrain of a British music hall song ("We don't want to fight, but, by Jingo, if we do..."), a use of the exclamation *by jingo,* by God.

jinks *n.pl.* (*Informal*) pranks; lively merrymaking; usually *high jinks.*

jinn (jin) *n.pl.* [*sing.* **jin·ni′** (jin-ē′)] in Muslim mythology, a class of spirits lower than angels. ❏ *genie*

jin·rik′i·sha (jin-rik′shâ) *n.* (*Jap.*) a two-wheeled vehicle pulled by a man.

jinx (jinks) *n.* (*Informal*) a supposed influence for bad luck.

jit′ney (jit′nė) *n.* **1,** (*Informal*) a public cab. **2,** (*Slang*) a U.S. nickel.

jit′ter (jit′ər) *v.i.* show nervousness or apprehension. —*n.* nervousness. —**jit′-tery,** *adj.* very nervous.

jit′ter·bug″ *v.i.* [**-bugged″, -bug′ging**] dance to swing music with violent convulsive movements. —*n.* one who so dances.

jive (jīv) *n.* **1,** swing music. **2,** a patois used by jazz musicians. **3,** talk meant to deceive or confuse. —*v.t.* confuse, as by loud noise or rapid talk.

jo (jō) *n.* (*Scot.*) sweetheart.

job *n.* **1,** one's profession, trade, or employment. **2,** a specific task or stint of work. **3,** (*Informal*) matter; state of affairs. —*v.i.* [**jobbed, job′bing**] do work by the piece. —*v.t.* **1,** portion out work. **2,** buy or sell in large or odd quantities, for resale to retailers. —**job action,** an attempt by workers through work slowdown, etc., to achieve desired aims. —**job bank,** a service for matching persons seeking work with available positions. —**job′ber·y,** *n.* corruption in a position of trust. ❏ *career*

job′ber *n.* **1,** a wholesaler. **2,** one who does piecework.

jock (jok) *n.* (*Slang*) an athlete.

jock′ey (jok′ė) *v.t. & i.* **1,** bring about by skillful maneuvering. **2,** obtain advantage by trickery. —*n.* a professional rider of race horses. —**car jockey,** (*Slang*) a garage attendant. —**disc jockey,** a radio announcer on a program of recorded music.

jock′strap″ (jok′strap″) *n.* a supporter worn by male athletes.

jo·cose′ (jō-kōs′) *adj.* facetious; humorous. —**jo·cos′i·ty** (-kos′ə-tė) *n.*

joc′u·lar (jok′yə-lər) *adj.* playful; joking. —**joc″u·lar′i·ty** (-lar′ə-tė) *n.*

joc′und (jok′ənd) *adj.* cheerful; merry. —**jo·cun′di·ty** (jō-kun′də-tė) *n.*

jodh′purs (jod′pərz) *n.pl.* riding breeches, close-fitting below the knee, named for a former state in India.

Joe (jō) *n.* (*Informal*) a fellow.

jo′ey (jō′ė) *n.* **1,** (*Informal*) a fellow. **2,** the young of any animal, esp. a young child or kangaroo.

jog *v.t.* [**jogged, jog′ging**] **1,** push slightly; nudge. **2,** align the edges of (sheets of paper). —*v.i.* **1,** move with a jolting motion. **2,** (with *on* or *along*) proceed steadily or uneventfully. **3,** trot; amble; run at a leisurely pace, esp. as an exercise. —*n.* **1,** a poke; nudge. **2,** a projection; an irregularity of surface. **3,** a notch. —**jog′ger,** *n.*

jog′gle (jog′əl) *v.i. & t.* move joltingly; jiggle.

john (jon) *n.* **1,** (*Slang*) a prostitute's client. **2,** (*Informal*) a toilet.

John Bull **1,** an Englishman. **2,** the English people.

> **John Bull**
> ↔ From the principal character in the allegory *The History of John Bull,* by Scottish satirist John Arbuthnot.

John Doe (*Law*) a male defendant or prisoner whose name is not known.

John Han′cock (han′kok) (*Informal*) one's own signature.

> **John Hancock**
> ↔ From John *Hancock,* 18th-c. American statesman, whose signature on the Declaration of Independence is especially bold and legible.

john′ny (jon′ė) *n.* (*Informal*) a hospital gown. —**john′ny·cake″,** *n.* a cake or bread made with cornmeal. —**johnny-come-lately,** (*Informal*) newcomer.

joie de vi′vre (zhwä də vē′vrə) (*Fr.*) joy of living; pleasure in being alive.

join *v.t. & i.* **1,** put together; combine. **2,** unite with; become a member of. **3,** connect. —*n.* a joint.

join′er (-ər) *n.* **1,** one who joins. **2,** woodworker; carpenter. **3,** (*Informal*) one who joins many organizations. **—join′er·y,** *n.* woodworking; carpentry.

joint *n.* **1,** a place where two things come together and are united; a seam; a hinge. **2,** a large cut of meat. **3,** (*Slang*) a disreputable place. **4,** (*Slang*) a marijuana cigarette. **—adj. 1,** joined in relation or interest, as *joint* owners. **2,** shared by different individuals. **—v.t.** combine; unite closely; articulate.

join′ture (join′chər) *n.* (*Law*) an estate settled before marriage.

joist *n.* one of the horizontal timbers to which are fastened the boards of a floor or laths of a ceiling.

jo·jo′ba (hō-hō′bə) *n.* a desert shrub whose seeds are a source of an oil used in cosmetics and as a lubricant.

joke (jōk) *n.* something said or done to excite laughter; a jest. **—v.i.** say or do something playful; jest.

jok′er (jō′kər) *n.* **1,** one who jokes. **2,** an extra card in a pack of playing cards. **3,** a clause in a document that weakens its intended effect.

jol′li·fy″ (jol′ə-fī″) *v.* make or be jolly. **—jol″li·fi·ca′tion** (-fi-kā′shən) *n.*

jol′ly (jol′ē) *adj.* gaily cheerful; full of merriment. **—n.** (*pl.*) (*Slang*) excitement; pleasure. **—jol′li·ty** (-ə-tē) *n.* **—Jolly Rog′er** (rä′jər) a pirate flag.

jolt (jōlt) *v.t. & i.* shake with sudden jerks; move with a jerking motion. **—n.** a sudden jerk.

Jo′nah (jō′nə) *n.* one reputed to bring bad luck.

jon′gleur (jong′glər) *n.* a medieval wandering minstrel.

jon′quil (jong′kwil) *n.* a plant with pale yellow flowers.

jo′rum (jôr′əm) *n.* a large bowl for mixing liquors.

> **jorum**
> ↔ Probably from *Joram*, son of Toi, king of Hamath, who delivered gold, silver, and brass vessels to David (2 Sam. 8:10).

josh *v.t. & i.* (*Slang*) tease or chaff good-naturedly.

joss (jos) *n.* a Chinese god or idol.

jos′tle (jos′əl) *v.t.* **1,** push against; bump so as to render unsteady. **2,** (*Slang*) pick the pocket of. **—v.i. 1,** shove and be shoved about, as in a crowd. **2,** (*Slang*) pick pockets.

jot *n.* a very small quantity. **—v.t.** [**jot′-**

ted, -ting] (usually with *down*) make a written memorandum of.

joule (jowl) *n.* a unit of work, equal to 10,000,000 ergs, named for 19th-c. English physicist James P. Joule.

jounce (jowns) *v.i. & t.* shake up and down violently; bounce.

jour′nal (jēr′nəl) *n.* **1,** a record of daily transactions or events. **2,** a book for keeping such records. **3,** a newspaper or magazine.

jour″nal·ese′ (jēr″nə-lēz′) *n.* the style of writing characteristic of newspapers.

jour′nal·ism (jēr′nə-liz-əm) *n.* newspaper or magazine writing. **—jour′nal·ist,** *n.* **—jour″nal·is′tic,** *adj.* **—jour″nal·is′ti·cal·ly,** *adv.*

jour′ney (jēr′nē) *n.* a trip from one place to another. **—v.i.** travel.

jour′ney·man (-mən) [*pl.* **-men**], **jour′-ney·wom″an** *n.* a trained worker at a skilled trade.

> **journeyman, journeywoman**
> ↔ These words come not from *jour-ney*, trip, but from French *journée*, day, reflected in the basic sense of the word, a day worker.

joust (jowst) *n.* a combat between armored knights with lances.

Jove (jōv) *n.* Jupiter, supreme god of the Romans. **—Jo′vi·an,** *adj.*

jo′vi·al (jō′vē-əl) *adj.* cheerful; gay; jolly. **—jo″vi·al′i·ty** (-al′ə-tē) *n.*

jowl *n.* **1,** the cheek. **2,** a fold of flesh hanging from the jaw.

joy (joi) *n.* an emotion of sudden pleasure; exultant satisfaction; keen delight. **—joy′ful, joy′ous,** *adj.* **—joy ride,** (*Informal*) **1,** a ride for pleasure in an automobile, esp. when the car is used surreptitiously or driven recklessly. **2,** a trip (usu. on drugs). **—joystick,** the lever that controls the directions of an airplane's flight; any similar control, esp. one used for playing computer games.

ju′bi·lant (joo′bə-lənt) *adj.* triumphantly glad; exultant.

ju″bi·la′tion (joo″bə-lā′shən) *n.* rejoicing; glee.

ju′bi·lee″ (joo′bə-lē″) *n.* **1,** a special occasion or manifestation of joyousness. **2,** 50th anniversary.

> **jubilee**
> ↔ From Hebrew *yobhel*, ram's horn, the signal for the year of emancipation which occurs every 50 years.

Ju′da·ism (joo′də-iz-əm) *n.* the religion

of Jews, or adherence to it. **—Ju·da′ic** (joo-dā′ik) *adj.*

judge (juj) *v.t.* **1,** hear and determine authoritatively, as a controversy. **2,** hold as an opinion; deem; consider. **—v.i. 1,** pass judgment on a cause. **2,** make a critical determination; estimate the value or magnitude of anything. **—n. 1,** a public officer empowered to administer justice; a magistrate. **2,** an arbiter; one qualified to judge.

judg′ment (juj′mənt) *n.* **1,** the act of judging. **2,** the ability to make accurate determinations; discernment. **3,** a decision, award, or sentence, as of a court of law.

ju′di·ca″tive (joo′di-kā″tiv) *adj.* having ability to judge; judging.

ju′di·ca″tor (joo′di-kā″tər) *n.* one who acts as a judge; an arbiter.

ju′di·ca·to″ry (joo′di-kə-tôr″ė) *adj.* pert. to judgment or the courts. **—n. 1,** a court of justice. **2,** administration of justice.

ju′di·ca·ture (joo′də-kə-chər) *n.* **1,** the administration of justice. **2,** the whole body of judges and courts. **3,** the jurisdiction of a court.

ju·di′cial (joo-dish′əl) *adj.* pert. to a judge, to a court of law, or to the administration of justice.

---

judicial, judicious

☛ Do not confuse *judicial*, pertaining to the law, and *judicious*, prudent.

---

ju·di·ci·ar·y (joo-dish′ė-er-ė) *n.* **1,** the judicial branch of the government. **2,** judges collectively. **—adj.** pert. to court judges.

ju·di′cious (joo-dish′əs) *adj.* having or exercising sound judgment; prudent. **—ju·di′cious·ness,** *n.* ❏ *judicial*

ju′do (joo′dō) *n.* a system of exercise and personal defense.

jug *n.* **1,** a vessel for holding liquids; pitcher. **2,** (*Slang*) a jail.

ju′gal (joo′gəl) *adj.* pert. to the cheekbone.

jug′ger·naut″ (jug′ər-nât″) *n.* an irresistible force.

---

juggernaut

↔ An idol of the Indian god Vishnu, carried in a large cart from temple to temple. Pilgrims would sacrifice themselves by throwing themselves under its wheels.

---

jug′gle (jug′əl) *v.i.* **1,** perform feats of dexterity or legerdemain. **2,** practice artifice or imposture. **—v.t.** manipulate by trickery.

jug′gler (jug′lər) *n.* a performer of tricks

of dexterity, as tossing and keeping balls in the air. **—jug′gler·y,** *n.*

jug′u·lar (jug′yə-lər) *adj.* pert. to the neck, or to one of the large veins in the neck.

juice (joos) *n.* **1,** the watery part of vegetables, esp. of fruits. **2,** the fluid part of an animal body or substance. **3,** (*Slang*) motor fuel. **4,** (*Slang*) electric current. **5,** (*Slang*) power; influence.

juic′y (joo′sė) *adj.* **1,** full of juice. **2,** interesting; pithy. **—juic′i·ness,** *n.*

ju·jit′su (joo-jit′soo) *n.* a Japanese method of wrestling.

ju′jube (joo′joob) *n.* **1,** the fruit of several tropical Asian and Amer. trees. **2,** a jelly bean.

juke (jook) (*Football*) *v.i.* to make a deceptive move. **—v.t.** deceive someone by making such a move.

juke′box″ *n.* (*Slang*) a coin-activated phonograph.

---

jukebox

↔ From Gullah *juke house*, brothel. Gullah is a Creole language spoken by African-Americans along the Atlantic coast of the southern U.S.

---

ju′lep (joo′lip) *n.* a sweet drink. **—mint julep,** iced bourbon whiskey flavored with mint leaves.

ju′li·enne (joo′lė-en) *adj.* of vegetables, cut into thin strips. **—n.** a clear soup containing such vegetables.

ju′li·et (joo′lė-ət) *n.* (*Communications*) the letter *j.*

Ju·ly′ (jû-lī′) *n.* the seventh month of the year.

July

↔ *July* was the month during which Julius Caesar was born and got its name from him (not vice versa); earlier, the month was called *Quintilis*, fifth month.

---

jum′ble (jum′bəl) *v.t.* mix in a confused mass; put together without order. **—v.i.** become mixed. **—n. 1,** a confused mass or collection. **2,** a state of disorder. **3,** a thin, crisp, ginger-flavored cake.

jum′bo (jum′bō) *n.* [*pl.* **-bos**] a very large individual or thing of its kind. **—adj.** very large. **—jumbo jet,** a large, wide jet plane designed to hold over 400 persons.

---

jumbo

↔ From the name of the elephant displayed by American showman P. T. Barnum, origin uncertain.

---

jump *v.i.* **1,** spring from the ground or from any support; leap. **2,** move with a leap; jolt; throb. **3,** rise abruptly in amount, intensity, etc. —*v.t.* **1,** spring or leap over. **2,** cause to leap or jolt. **3,** give no heed to; disregard. —*n.* **1,** the act of jumping; a leap. **2,** a sudden rise; a jolt. **3,** an omission; an abrupt transition. **4,** (*Informal*) a position of advantage; a head start. —**jumping jack,** a type of physical exercise.

jump′er (-ər) *n.* **1,** one who jumps. **2,** any mechanical device that operates with a jumping motion. **3,** a loose outer garment; (*pl.*) overalls. **4,** a small, removable, rectangle-shaped plug used to connect two circuits on a circuit board.

jump-′start″ *v.t.* start an engine having a weak battery by using booster cables; hence, revitalize something weak, as an economy, business, etc.

jump′suit″ *n.* a one-piece suit worn by paratroopers; an article of clothing of a similar design for women or men.

jump′y (-ė) *adj.* nervous. —**jump′i·ness,** *n.*

jun′co (jung′kō) *n.* a snowbird.

junc′tion (junk′shən) *n.* **1,** act of joining or uniting; coalition. **2,** place of meeting or joining.

junc′ture (junk′chər) *n.* **1,** a point of time. **2,** a seam.

June (joon) *n.* the sixth month of the year.

> **June**
> ↔ From Latin *mensis Junius*, from *Juno*, Roman goddess of women, wife of Jupiter.

jun′gle (jung′gəl) *n.* **1,** a dense growth of rank and tangled vegetation; a wilderness. **2,** (*Slang*) a camping ground of tramps. —**asphalt jungle,** the city, esp. the inner city. —**jungle gym,** a playground structure for climbing.

jun′ior (joon′yər) *n.* **1,** one younger than another. **2,** one of less experience or inferior standing in his or her profession than another. **3,** a student in the next-to-last year of the high school or college course. —*adj.* **1,** younger. **2,** pert. to juniors. —**junior college,** a school teaching two years of a college course.—**junior high,** a school teaching grades 7, 8, and 9.

ju′ni·per (joo′nə-pər) *n.* a coniferous evergreen shrub, used in making gin and certain medicines.

junk *n.* **1,** worn-out or discarded material; trash. **2,** a Chinese sailing vessel. **3,** (*Slang*) narcotic drugs. —*v.t.* (*Informal*) throw away; discard. —**junk bond,** a high-

risk, high-yield corporate bond. —**junk food,** food with low nutritional value. —**junk mail,** third-class mail.

Jun′ker (yûng′kər) *n.* a member of the German aristocratic class.

jun′ket (jung′kit) *n.* **1,** a custard, milk sweetened and flavored, curdled with rennet. **2,** a picnic; an excursion. **3,** an excursion paid for at the taxpayers' expense. —*v.i. & t.* feast; regale; go on a pleasure trip.

jun′kie (jung′kė) *n.* (*Slang*) an addict or devotee, esp. someone addicted to a drug.

jun′ta (jun′tə, hûn-) *n.* **1,** a consultative or legislative assembly, esp. Spanish. **2,** a revolutionary caretaker government (usu. military). ❑ *government*

jun′to (jun′tō) *n.* [*pl.* **-tos**] a secret political combine.

Ju′pi·ter (joo′pi-tər) *n.* **1,** the chief god in Roman mythology. **2,** the largest planet in the solar system.

ju·rid′i·cal (jû-rid″ə-kəl) *adj.* relating to administrative law.

ju″ris·dic′tion (jûr″is-dik′shən) *n.* **1,** the right of making and enforcing laws. **2,** the domain over which a given authority extends.

ju″ris·pru′dence (jûr″is-proo′dəns) *n.* **1,** the science of law. **2,** the body of laws existing in a given state or nation.

ju′rist (jûr′ist) *n.* one who professes the science of law. —**ju·ris′tic,** *adj.*

> **jurist, juror**
> ☞ Do not confuse a *jurist*, an expert at law, and a *juror*, a member of a jury. Note that a jurist is not necessarily a judge.

ju′ror (jûr′ər) *n.* a member of a jury. Also, **ju′ry·man** (-mən) [*pl.* **-men**], **ju′ry·wom″an,** *n.* ❑ *jurist*

ju′ry (jûr′ė) *n.* a group of persons appointed to hear evidence and decide facts. —*adj.* (*Naut.*) rigged in an emergency; makeshift.

ju′ry-rig″ *v.t.* assemble quickly with materials at hand.

just *adj.* **1,** right in law or ethics: **2,** fairminded; good in intention; impartial. **3,** based on right; legitimate. **4,** in correct accordance with a standard. —*adv.* **1,** precisely. **2,** very nearly. **3,** barely; by a narrow margin. **4,** (*Informal*) wholly; positively. —**just′ness,** *n.* fairness.

jus′tice (jus′tis) *n.* **1,** conformity to moral principles or law; just conduct. **2,** merited reward or punishment. **3,** the administration of law; authority; jurisdiction. **4,** a judicial officer; a judge. **—justice of the peace**, a minor local judge.

jus'ti·fy" (jus'tə-fī") *v.t. & i.* **1**, prove or show to be just or conformable to justice, reason, law, etc. **2**, declare innocent or blameless. **3**, make precise; adjust; (*Printing*) make successive lines of type of equal length. **—jus"ti·fi'a·ble**, *adj.* defensible. **—jus"ti·fi·ca'tion**, *n.*

jut *v.i.* [**jut'ted, -ting**] (usually with *out*) extend beyond the main body or line. *—n.* a projection.

jute (joot) *n.* **1**, a plant that grows in warm, moist climate; its fiber. **2**, a coarse fabric made from jute.

ju've·nile (joo'və-nəl) *adj.* **1**, young; youthful. **2**, pert. to or suited for young persons. *—n.* a young person. **—juvenile delinquent**, a minor who commits criminal or antisocial acts. **—ju"ve·nil'i·ty**, *n.*

ju"ve·nil'i·a (joo"və-nil'ē-ə) *n.pl.* works produced in youth.

jux"ta·pose' (juks"tə-pōz') *v.t.* place side by side or close together. **—jux"ta·po·si'tion** (-pə-zish'ən) *n.*

K

K, k (kā) **1**, the eleventh letter of the English alphabet. **2**, thousand; kilo-.

ka·bob' (kə-bob') *n.* **1**, small cubes of meat or vegetables roasted on a skewer. **2**, roasted meat.

kad'dish (kad'ish) *n.* [*pl.* **kad'di·shim** (-im)] **1**, the doxology of the Jewish ritual. **2**, the prayer for the dead.

kaf'fee klatsch" (kä'fè kläch") an informal social gathering at which coffee is served.

Kai'ser (kī'zər) *n.* (*Ger.*) emperor; esp. Wilhelm II, German emperor during World War I.

ka"ka·po' (kä"kä-pō') *n.* [*pl.* **-pos**] a large nocturnal parrot of New Zealand.

kale (kāl) *n.* **1**, a variety of cabbage with curled or wrinkled leaves. **2**, (*Slang*) money.

ka·lei'do·scope" (kə-lī'də-skōp") *n.* an optical instrument for creating, by reflection, colorful symmetrical patterns. **—ka·lei"do·scop'ic** (-skop'ik) *adj.* **—ka·lei"do·scop'i·cal·ly**, *adv.*

kaleidoscope
↔ A compound of Greek *kalos*, beautiful *eidos*, shape, and *scopion*, look at.

kal'so·mine" (kal'sə-mīn") *v.t. & n.* calcimine.

ka"mi·ka'ze (kä"mi-kä'zè) (*Jap.*) *n.* aircraft pilot sworn to make suicidal attacks. *—adj.* pert. to a kamikaze.

Ka·nak'a (kə-nak'ə) *n.* a native Hawaiian.

kan"ga·roo' (kang"gə-roo') *n.* a marsupial of Australia having powerful hind legs developed for leaping. **—kangaroo court**, an unofficial group that acts as a court of law.

ka·o·lin (kā'ə-lin) *n.* a white clay used in making porcelain.

kaolin
↔ From *gao ling*, the name of a hill in Jiangxi province of China, source of the clay.

ka·on (kā'än) *n.* an unstable meson.

Ka·pell'meis"ter (kə-pel'mī"stər) *n.* (*Ger.*) a conductor (as of a choir or orchestra).

ka'pok (kā'pok) *n.* a tropical tree whose seeds yield a silky wool used for stuffing cushions, etc.

kap'pa (kap'ə) *n.* the tenth letter of the Greek alphabet (K, κ).

ka·put' (kä-pût') *adj.* (*Informal*) ruined; done for.

kaput
↔ From a French expression in cards, *être capot*, meaning to have made no tricks, i.e., to have zero score.

kar'a·kul (kar'ə-kəl) *n.* an Asiatic breed of sheep; its fur.

ka·ra·o'ke (kä-rä-ō'kā) *n.* (*Jap.*, empty orchestra) the practice of singing a song with a prerecorded accompaniment.

kar'at (kar'ət) *n.* carat.

ka·ra'te (kə-rä'tè) *n.* a Japanese system of self-defense. **—karate chop**, a slashing blow with the hand.

kar'ma (kär'mə) *n.* **1**, in Hinduism and Buddhism, the ethical consequences of the totality of one's actions that determine the destiny of one's subsequent existence or existences until one has achieved spiritual liberation. **2**, fate; destiny. **—kar'mic** (kär'mik) *adj.*

kart (kärt) *n.* a small-scale, often motorized, open racing car, usu. for children. Also, **go-'cart", go-'kart"**.

ka'ty·did (kā'tè-did) *n.* a large Amer. grasshopper.

ka'va (kä'vä) *n.* a Polynesian shrub of the pepper family; a beverage made from it.

Ka′wa·sa′ki disease (kä′wä-sä′kē) an acute illness affecting children.

kay′ak (kī′ak) *n.* a light Eskimo boat made of sealskins.

kay′o (kā′ō) *v.t.* (*Slang*) knock out, in pugilism.

ka·zoo′ (kə-zoo′) *n.* a musical instrument or toy consisting of a tube containing a membrane that vibrates sympathetically when the player hums into the tube.

kedge (kej) *v.t. & i.* pull or warp (a ship) by the rope of an anchor. —*n.* a small anchor.

keel (kēl) *n.* **1,** a central longitudinal member from which a frame is built upward, as on a ship. **2,** any central main stem, as on a leaf. —**keel over,** turn upside down.

keel′haul″ (kēl′hâl″) *v.t.* (*Naut.*) **1,** haul (a person) under the keel of a ship for punishment. **2,** reprimand severely.

keen (kēn) *adj.* **1,** having a sharp edge or point. **2,** acutely harsh or painful; biting. **3,** having sharp perception of senses or mind. **4,** intense in feeling; ardent. —*n.* lamentation for the dead. —*v.i.* wail; lament (esp. for the dead). —**keen′ness,** *n.*

keep (kēp) *v.t.* [*pret. & p.p.* **kept**] **1,** maintain possession or custody of; retain. **2,** continue or maintain in action or conduct. **3,** carry out; perform; observe; fulfill. **4,** preserve; protect; care for; support. **5,** hold; detain; restrain. —*v.i.* **1,** continue (action, state, etc.). **2,** endure; last. —*n.* **1,** board and lodging; subsistence; maintenance. **2,** the stronghold of a castle. —**keep′er,** *n.* a guardian, guard, or warden. —**keep′ing,** *n.* congruity; appropriateness. —**for keeps,** permanently.

keep′sake″ (kēp′sāk″) *n.* a souvenir or memento.

kees′hond″ (kās′händ″) *n.* [*pl.* **kees′hon″den** (-hän″dən)] a Dutch breed of companion dog.

ke·fir′ (kə-fēr′) *n.* a fermented drink made from cow's or goat's milk.

keg *n.* a small barrel.

keg′ler (keg′lər) *n.* bowler. —**keg′ling,** *n.*

kelp *n.* a large brown seaweed.

Kel′vin *adj.* pert. to a thermometer similar to the Celsius scale but with its 0° fixed at absolute zero (-273.13° C. or -459.6° F.).

> **Kelvin**
> ↔ Named for 19th-c. English physicist William Thompson, 1st Baron *Kelvin.*

ken *n.* range of sight or knowledge.

ken′nel (ken′əl) *n.* a house for a dog or (also *pl.*) dogs. —*v.t. & i.* lodge in a kennel.

> **kennel**
> ↔ From Old French *chenil*, from Latin *canis*, dog, the root word as well for *canine.*

ke′no (kē′nō) *n.* a lottery game, precursor of bingo.

> **keno**
> ↔ From French *quine*, five, with an ending borrowed from *lotto*; the game has five winning numbers.

Ke′ogh plan (kē′ō) a type of pension plan for self-employed persons.

kep′i (kep′ē) *n.* a French military cap.

kept *v.* pret. & p.p. of *keep.* —*adj.* financially supported by another.

ker′a·tin (ker′ə-tin) *n.* a protein which forms the basis of hair, horn, etc. —**ke·rat′i·nous** (kə-rat′i-nəs) *adj.*

kerb (kẽrb) *n.* (*Brit.*) street curb.

ker′chief (kẽr′chif) *n.* **1,** a cloth worn as a headdress, esp. by women. **2,** handkerchief.

kerf (kẽrf) *n.* a cut, as made by a saw.

kern (kẽrn) *v.t.* to tighten the space between characters to improve appearance.

ker′nel (kẽr′nəl) *n.* **1,** the substance, often edible, inside a nut or fruit stone. **2,** a grain or seed, as of corn. **3,** gist; nucleus. **4,** (*Computers*) a set of fundamental procedures.

ker′o·sene″ (ker′ə-sēn″) *n.* an oil, distilled from coal or petroleum, used for heat and illumination.

ker′sey (kẽr′zē) *n.* a coarse woolen cloth, usu. ribbed.

ketch (kech) *n.* a small sailing vessel.

ketch′up (kech′əp) *n.* a condiment consisting of tomatoes, onions, vinegar, and spices.

ket′tle (ket′əl) *n.* a covered vessel for the heating of liquids or for cooking.

ket′tle·drum″ *n.* **1,** a musical instrument consisting of a drumhead on a metal hemisphere, capable of being tuned. **2,** (*pl.*) tympani.

Kew′pie (kū′pē) *n.* (*T.N.*) a caricatural picture or doll of a cherub.

key (kē) *n.* **1,** an instrument for opening and closing a lock, valve, circuit, etc. **2,** a control lever operated by the fingers, as on a telegraph, typewriter, piano, horn. **3,** something explanatory; a translation of cipher, symbols, problems, perplexities, etc. **4,** (*Music*) the tonic note or name of a scale; a key signature; the tonality implied by a sequence of chords. **5,** pitch; degree of intensity; tone or mood. **6,** a reef or low island near the coast; cay. —*adj.* principal; fundamental. —*v.t.* provide with a key or reference system. —**keyed up,** tense.

key′board″ *n.* the row of keys for controlling a piano, typewriter, etc. —*v.t.* (*Informal*) type (something) into a computer. —**key′board″er,** *n.* one who types at a keyboard.

key′hole″ *n.* the opening through which a key is inserted in a lock.

key′note″ *n.* main theme or principle.

key′pad″ *n.* a small keyboard, esp. one composed largely of numbers for entering figures.

key′punch″ *n.* a machine, operated from a keyboard, that punches holes or notches in cards for use in data-processing machines.

key′stone″ *n.* the central stone bearing the pressure of other stones in an arch; hence, any essential member.

key′stroke″ *n.* a stroke of a key (of a keyboard).

khak′i (kak′ė) *n.* an olive-drab or yellowish-brown color or cloth.

khan (kån) *n.* **1,** an Asiatic title of respect. **2,** a caravansary.

khe·dive′ (kə-dēv′) *n.* formerly, title of the Turkish viceroy of Egypt.

kib′ble (kib′əl) *v.t.* grind coarsely. —*n.* coarsely ground grain, etc.

kib·butz′ (ki-bûts′) *n.* [*pl.* **kib″but·zim′** (ki″bût-sēm′)] in Israel, a communally owned, operated, and organized collective farm or settlement.

kib′itz·er (kib′it-sər) *n.* an onlooker who gives unwanted advice, esp. at a card game. —**kib′itz,** *v.i. & t.*

ki′bosh (kī′bosh) *n.* (*Slang*) **1,** nonsense. **2,** a ruinous curse or spell.

kick (kik) *v.t.* **1,** strike with the foot. **2,** strike in recoiling. —*v.i.* **1,** thrust the foot forward or outward. **2,** recoil, as a firearm. **3,** (with *off*) begin; initiate. **4,** (*Slang*) complain; resist. **5,** (with *in*) (*Slang*) contribute. —*n.* **1,** a blow with the foot. **2,** a recoil. **3,** (*Slang*) a complaint or objection. **4,** (*Informal*) vigor; excitement or thrill; the stimulating quality of liquor.

kick′back″ *n.* **1,** a violent reaction. **2,** the return of a portion of a worker's pay to an employer. **3,** (*Slang*) an amount returned, as graft money.

kick′box″ing *n.* a martial art combining karate and boxing. —**kick′box″er,** *n.*

kick′off″ *n.* **1,** in football, a place kick made to commence play. **2,** an event that begins something, as a fund drive.

kick′shaw″ (kik′shâ″) *n.* **1,** something fantastic and trifling. **2,** an unsubstantial dish or food.

---
kickshaw
↔ From the French phrase *quelque chose,* something.
---

kick′stand″ *n.* built-in stand for a bicycle, motorcycle, etc.

kick-′start″er *n.* a device for starting the engine of a motorcycle, etc., by foot. —**kick-′start″,** *v.t.* to start with a kickstarter; hence, begin (something) with an initial impetus.

kid *n.* **1,** a young goat. **2,** leather made from the skin of a young goat. **3,** (*Informal*) a child; youngster. —*v.t. & i.* [**kid′ded, -ding**] (*Slang*) tease.

kid′nap *v.t.* abduct, or carry off forcibly (a human being). —**kid′nap·ping,** *n.*

kid′ney (kid′nė) *n.* either of two bean-shaped organs that excrete urine. —*adj.* kidney-shaped.

kid′vid″ *n.* (*Slang*) a television show for children.

kiel′ba·sa (kil′bä-sə) *n.* an uncooked smoked Polish sausage.

kill (kil) *v.t.* **1,** put to death; slay. **2,** destroy; extinguish; nullify; cancel; veto; neutralize. —*n.* **1,** the act of killing. **2,** the culmination of a hunt or quest; an animal killed. **3,** a creek or river. —**kill′er bee,** an exceptionally aggressive African variety of honey bee.

kill′ing (kil′ing) *n.* **1,** the act of killing. **2,** (*Informal*) a highly successful stroke of business. —*adj.* **1,** deadly; exhausting. **2,** (*Informal*) funny.

kill′joy″ *n.* one who spoils the enjoyment of others.

kiln (kil) *n.* an oven for drying or baking, as bricks. —*v.t.* bake.

ki′lo (kē′lō) *n.* **1,** kilogram; kilometer. **2,** (*Communications*) the letter *k*.

kil·o- (kil-ə) *pref.* thousand; 1,000 times. *Abbr.,* **K.**

kil′o·cy″cle *n.* 1,000 cycles per second.

kil′o·gram″ *n.* 1,000 grams, equal to 2.2 pounds.

kil′o·me″ter (kil′ə-mē″tər; ki-lom′i-tər) *n.* 1,000 meters, about .62 mile.

kil′o·watt″ *n.* 1,000 watts. —**kilowatt-hour,** consumption of 1,000 watts throughout one hour.

kilt *n.* a short plaid skirt, esp. as worn by Scotsmen.

---

fat, fāte, fär, fâre, fâll, åsk; met, hē, hèr, maybè; pin, pīne; not, nōte, ôr, tool

kil′ter (kil′tər) *n.* (*Informal*) good working condition.

ki·mo′no (kə-mō′nō) *n.* [*pl.* **-nos**] **1,** a gownlike Japanese outer garment. **2,** a dressing gown; bathrobe.

kin *n.* **1,** one's relatives collectively. **2,** relationship of those having common descent. —*adj.* **1,** related by blood; of the same family or clan. **2,** of the same kind or nature. —**kin′ship,** *n.*

-kin *suf.* of diminutive nouns, as *lambkin.*

kind (kīnd) *n.* **1,** natural constitution or character. **2,** a class of persons or things of the same character; a category. **3,** an individual representative (of a class). —*adj.* of a sympathetic nature; benevolent. —**kind of,** (*Informal*) somewhat.

kin′der·gar″ten (kin′dər-gär″tən) *n.* a school or class for children of preschool age. —**kin′der·gart″ner** (-gärt″nər) *n.*

kin′dle (kin′dəl) *v.t.* **1,** set on fire. **2,** inspire; stir up. —*v.i.* **1,** catch fire. **2,** become animated.

kin′dling *n.* small pieces of material for starting fires.

kind′ly (kīnd′lē) *adj.* agreeable; considerate. —*adv.* **1,** in a kind way. **2,** if you please. —**kind′li·ness,** *n.*

kind′ness (-nəs) *n.* sympathetic nature; benevolence.

kin′dred (kin′drəd) *n.* **1,** consanguinity. **2,** kin; family or tribe. **3,** affinity. —*adj.* **1,** related by birth or descent. **2,** akin; allied. **3,** congenial.

kine (kīn) *n.pl.* (*Archaic*) cows.

kin″e·mat′ics (kin″ə-mat′iks) *n.sing.* a branch of dynamics dealing with motion considered apart from mass and force. Also, **cin″e·mat′ics** (sin″-).

kin′e·scope″ (kin′ə-skōp″) *n.* **1,** the tube and screen used in a television receiver. **2,** a film record of a television broadcast.

kin″es·the′sia (kin″əs-thē′zhə) *n.* the sensation of bodily tension or movement perceived through nerve ends in the muscles, tendons, and joints.

ki·net′ic (ki-net′ik) *adj.* caused by or pert. to motion. —**ki·net′i·cal·ly,** *adv.* —**kinetic art,** artwork that moves or appears to move.

kin′folk″ *n.pl.* relatives.

king *n.* **1,** a male sovereign; a monarch. **2,** a person or thing of preeminent rank in a class. **3,** a playing card bearing the picture of a king; the chief piece in chess; in checkers, a piece that has been crowned. —**king′ly,** *adj.* majestic. —**king′ship,** *n.*

king′craft″ *n.* the art of ruling as a king.

king′dom (-dəm) *n.* **1,** the realm of a king. **2,** any society or classification. **3,** one of the classes (animal, vegetable, mineral) of matter.

king′fish″er (-ər) *n.* a kind of diving bird.

king′mak″er *n.* a person with influence in the choosing of a king, political candidate, etc.

king′pin″ *n.* **1,** one of the bolts on which the steering axle of a vehicle pivots. **2,** (*Slang*) chief; boss.

king′post″ *n.* an important vertical structural beam of a roof.

king-′size″ *adj.* **1,** extra-large. **2,** pert. to a bed made of two twin-size beds joined together.

kink *n.* **1,** a knotlike curl, as in a wire. **2,** a muscular cramp. **3,** a mental twist; obstinate notion; crotchet. **4,** (*Slang*) eccentric sexual behavior. —*v.i. & t.* twist; curl. —**kink′y** (-ē) *adj.*

kin′ka·jou″ (king′kə-joo″) *n.* an animal with a long, prehensile tail.

kins′man (kinz′mən) [*pl.* **-men**], **kins′wom″an** *n.* a relative.

ki·osk′ (kē-osk′) *n.* a small building, as a newsstand or booth.

kip′per (kip′ər) *v.t.* prepare (fish) by salting and smoking. —*n.* a fish so prepared, esp. a herring.

Kir′li·an photography (kēr′lē-ən) a photographic process for recording electrical emanations from living objects.

kish′ke (kish′kə) *n.* (*Yiddish*) a type of baked sausage.

kis′met (kiz′met) *n.* fate; destiny.

kiss (kis) *v.t. & i.* **1,** touch (esp. the lips of another) with the lips, as a caress or salutation. **2,** touch gently in any way. —*n.* **1,** the act of kissing. **2,** a gentle touch or contact. **3,** a kind of candy. —**kiss′er,** *n.* (*Slang*) the face, mouth, or lips.

kit *n.* **1,** an assemblage of tools, materials, supplies, etc. **2,** a case for containing such an outfit. **3,** a small three-stringed violin. —**kit and caboodle,** everything; the whole lot.

kitch′en (kich′ən) *n.* a room in which food is cooked. —**kitch″en·ette′** (-ə-net′) *n.* a very small kitchen. —**kitchen police,** soldiers assigned to help in preparing and serving meals; assignment to this duty. Also, **KP.**

kite (kīt) *n.* **1,** a light contrivance, held captive by a long cord, designed to be supported in air by the wind. **2,** a variety of hawk. **3,** a fictitious commercial bill or check. —*v.t.* (*Slang*) cash (a check) against funds not yet deposited.

kith *n.* one's friends collectively (now used only in *kith and kin*).

kitsch (kitsh) *n.* something designed to appeal to popular taste.

kit′ten (kit′ən) *n.* a young cat. —**kit′-ten·ish,** *adj.* playful.

kit′ty (kit′ē) *n.* **1,** (*Cards*) a pool formed by players to defray expenses, etc. **2,** a collection or fund. **3,** pet name for a cat.

ki′wi (kē′wē) *n.* **1,** a flightless bird of New Zealand. **2,** (*Informal*) a nonflying aviation officer. —**kiwi fruit,** the edible fruit of the Chinese gooseberry, from New Zealand.

Klans′man (klanz′mən) *n.* [*pl.* **-men**] a member of the Ku Klux Klan.

Kleen′ex (klē′neks) *n.* (*T.N.*) a brand of soft paper handkerchief.

klep″to·ma′ni·a (klep″tə-mā′nē-ə) *n.* morbid addiction to stealing for psychological reasons rather than for economic need. —**klep″to·ma′ni·ac,** *n.*

klieg light (klēg) a very bright electric light for motion-picture photography, etc.

---
klieg light
↔ From German-American brothers *Kliegl,* both inventors.

---

kludge (klooj) *n.* (*Slang*) **1,** a poorly engineered and manufactured machine, esp. a computer. **2,** mismatched parts forming an imperfect whole.

klutz (kluts) *n.* (*Slang*) an inept or clumsy person.

knack (nak) *n.* aptitude; talent.

knap′sack″ (nap′sak″) *n.* a bag strapped to the shoulders.

knave (nāv) *n.* **1,** rascal. **2,** in playing cards, a jack. —**knav′e·ry** (nā′və-rē) *n.* dishonesty. —**knav′ish,** *adj.* dishonest.

knead (nēd) *v.t.* manipulate (dough, plastic material, the body in massaging, etc.) by squeezing, pressing, and thumping.

knee (nē) *n.* **1,** the joint between the two main parts of the leg. **2,** a hinge; a sharp bend or crook. —*v.t.* strike with the knee.

knee′cap″ *n.* the bone at the front of the knee joint.

knee-′jerk″ *adj.* thoughtless; in the manner of a reflex.

kneel (nēl) *v.i.* [*pret. & p.p.* **knelt**] rest on one or both bended knees. —**kneeling bus,** a bus that can lower its front corner containing the entrance door, to facilitate access for the elderly and the handicapped.

knell (nel) *n.* the sound of a bell, esp. when rung at a death or funeral.

knick′ers (nik′ərz) *n.pl.* short breeches gathered at the knee. Also, **knick′er·bock″-ers** (-bok″ərz).

---
knickers
↔ Short for *knickerbockers,* from Dietrich *Knickerbocker,* the fictitious author of Washington Irving's novel *History of New York* (1809).

---

knick′knack″ (nik′nak″) *n.* an unsubstantial article of food, furniture, or dress.

knife (nīf) *n.* [*pl.* **knives** (nīvz)] a cutting tool; a sharp-edged blade with attached handle. —*v.t.* cut or stab with or as with a knife. —**knife switch,** an electric switch having a pivoted blade that can be pressed between two metal clips to make contact and complete the circuit.

knight (nīt) *n.* **1,** medieval mounted soldier of noble birth. **2,** a title (marked in the Brit. Empire by the title Sir) conferred on men in recognition of merit. **3,** a chivalrous person. **4,** a chess piece. —**knight′hood,** *n.* —**knight′ly,** *adj.*

knight-″er′rant *n.* [*pl.* **knights-″er′rant**] a knight who wandered in quest of adventure. —**knight-″er′rant·ry,** *n.*

knish *n.* fried or baked dough stuffed with a filling.

knit (nit) *v.t. & i.* [**knit′ted** *or* **knit, -ting**] **1,** make (fabric) by interlooping a single strand of yarn on needles. **2,** join closely. **3,** contract (one's brows). **4,** grow together, as bones. —*n.* **1,** a style or stitch in knitting. **2,** knitted work.

knob (nob) *n.* **1,** a rounded projection. **2,** a hill. —**knob′by** (-ē) *adj.*

knob′ker″rie (nob′ker″ē) *n.* a heavy wooden club with a knob on one end.

knock (nok) *v.t.* **1,** hit; strike; rap. **2,** (*Slang*) criticize harshly. —*v.i.* **1,** strike a blow. **2,** collide. **3,** make a noise, as repeated blows or collisions; (of a motor) detonate. —*n.* **1,** the act of knocking. **2,** the sound of a knock. **3,** (*Slang*) a deprecating criticism or comment. —**knock down, 1,** sell finally, at auction. **2,** strike (an opponent) so that he falls, in pugilism. —**knocked down,** disassembled (as machinery) for shipment, storage, or repair. —**knock off, 1,** stop working. **2,** complete successfully. **3,** (*Slang*) kill. **4,** (*Slang*) copy. —**knock out,** eliminate or defeat finally; in pugilism, knock down (an opponent) so that he cannot rise and continue. —**knock up,** (*Slang*) to make pregnant.

---

fat, fāte, fär, fāre, fâll, ȧsk; met, hē, hėr, maybė; pin, pīne; not, nōte, ôr, tool

knock'er (-ər) *n.* **1,** one who knocks. **2,** a device for rapping at a door: *door-knocker.*

knock'kneed" (-nēd") *adj.* having legs that bend inward.

knock'off" *n.* (*Slang*) copy; reproduction, esp. of fashion design.

knock'out" *n.* **1,** victory won by knocking out an opponent. **2,** (*Slang*) a very prepossessing or beautiful thing or person. —**knockout drops,** chloral hydrate, when criminally used to drug someone.

knock'wurst" (näk'wẽrst") *n.* a kind of sausage.

knoll (nōl) *n.* a small rounded hill.

knot (not) *n.* **1,** an interlacement of loops in a cord, rope, or ribbon, drawn tight into a bunch, made for fastening or ornament. **2,** any bunch, cluster, lump, knob, or protuberance. **3,** a bond of association; a tie. **4,** a puzzle, problem, or perplexity. **5,** a unit of speed, one nautical mile per hour. **6,** the embedded end of a tree branch. —*v.t.* [**knot'ted, -ting**] **1,** fasten with a knot; form a knot in. **2,** form lumps. —*v.i.* become knotted, snarled, or lumpy. —**knot'ty** (-è) *adj.*

knot'hole" *n.* a hole left by the removal of a knot from wood.

knout (nowt) *n.* a whip or scourge. —*v.t.* flog with a knout.

know (nō) *v.t.* [**knew** (noo), **known** (nōn), **know'ing**] **1,** perceive as fact or truth. **2,** have information of; be acquainted with. **3,** recognize or distinguish in comparison. —*v.i.* **1,** have knowledge or information. **2,** have insight or perception.

know-'how" *n.* expertness. ❑ *ability*

know'ing *adj.* aware; shrewd.

knowl'edge (nol'ij) *n.* **1,** awareness of facts, truths, or principles; cognizance. **2,** erudition. **3,** what is known; a body of accumulated facts. —**knowl'edge·a·ble,** *adj.* wise.

known (nōn) *v.* p.p. of *know.*

knuck'le (nuk'əl) *n.* **1,** a joint of the finger. **2,** a cut of meat, esp. from the knee. **3,** a protuberance; a hinge. —*v.i.* **1,** (with *down*) apply oneself earnestly to a task. **2,** (with *under*) submit; yield.

knurl (nẽrl) *n.* one of a series of ridges, as on a thumbscrew, to afford a grip. —*v.t.* roughen.

KO (kā'yō) *n.* (*Slang*) knockout. Also, **K.O., k.o.**

ko·a'la (kō-ä'lə) *n.* a small Australian marsupial resembling a bear.

ko'an (kō'än) *n.* (*Jap.*) a paradoxical question.

Ko'be beef (kō'bē) meat from Japanese cattle, highly prized for its tenderness.

ko'bold (kō'bōld) *n.* a gnome.

Ko'dak (kō'dak) *n.* (*T.N.*) a small portable camera, esp. one with a universal lens.

kohl'ra"bi (kōl'rä"bè) *n.* a plant cultivated for its edible stem.

ko'la (kō'lə) *n.* a tree of the chocolate family; its seed (*kola nut*), used in drinks.

ko·lin'sky (kə-lin'skè) *n.* a Siberian mink, and its golden-brown fur.

kol·khoz' (kəl-kōz') *n.* (*Rus.*) in the former U.S.S.R., a collective farm.

> **kolkhoz**
> ↔ Abbreviation of Russian *kol(ektivnoe)   khoz(yaistvo),* collective economy.

Kom'on·dor" (kom'ən-dôr") *n.* a shaggy white Hungarian working dog.

kook *n.* (*Slang*) an eccentric or crazy person. —**kook'y** (-è) *adj.*

ko'peck (kō'pek) *n.* a former Russian coin.

> **kopek**
> ↔ From Russian *kopeika,* little spear, from the spear-carrying figure on the coin.

Ko·ran' (kō-rän') *n.* the sacred book of the Muslims.

ko'sher (kō'shər) *adj.* **1,** conformant to Jewish dietary law. **2,** (*Slang*) approved; genuine. **3,** (*Slang*) proper; conventional.

ko'to (kō'tō) *n.* (*Jap.*) a long-necked zither.

kow'tow' *v.i.* **1,** touch the forehead to the ground. **2,** fawn; cringe. —*n.* a low bow.

> **kowtow**
> ↔ From the Chinese *ke tou,* bump the head, from the approved sign of respect to the emperor of putting one's forehead to the ground.

kraal (kräl) *n.* **1,** a South African village. **2,** a cattle pen.

kraft (kråft) *n.* a heavy brown wrapping paper.

K ration *n.* a concentrated food product used as an emergency field ration by the U.S. Army.

> **K ration**
> ↔ The K is for Ancel *Keys,* 20th-c. American physiologist.

krem′lin *n.* **1,** a Russian castle. **2,** (*cap.*) former headquarters of the Soviet government, in Moscow.

kro′na (krō′nə) *n.* a Swedish coin.

kro′ne (krō′nə) *n.* any of various coins, Danish, Norwegian, or Austrian.

kryp′ton (krip′ton) *n.* an inert gaseous chemical element, no. 36, symbol Kr. —**kryp′ton·ite** (-īt) *n.* an imaginary element from the imaginary planet Krypton, in the comic strip "Superman."

ku′dos (kū′đos) *n.* glory; praise.

> **kudos**
> ↔ *Kudos* is a singular Greek word meaning praise or glory, and the final *s* is not a plural ending. However, the word is often used erroneously with a plural verb.

kud′zu (kûd′zoo) *n.* a fast-growing climbing vine from Asia.

Ku Klux Klan (koo′ kluks′ klan′) a secret terroristic society in the U.S., opposed to Negroes, Jews, and Roman Catholics.

> **Ku Klux Klan**
> ↔ A compound from Greek *kyklos*, circle, and *clan*, respelled to match the first two words.

ku·lak′ (koo-läk′) *n.* formerly, a free-holding peasant, in Russia.

ku′miss (koo′mis) *n.* a beverage made from fermented milk.

kum′quat (kum′kwot) *n.* a subtropical shrub with a pulpy citrus fruit, used chiefly for preserves.

kung′ fu′ (kung′ foo′) *n.* a Chinese martial art.

Kuo′min·tang′ (kwō′min′tang′) *n.* a former political party of China.

ku′ru (kû′roo) *n.* a fatal disease of the central nervous system.

ku′vasz (koo′väs) *n.* a large white Hungarian working dog.

kvetch (kvech) *v.i.* (*Slang*) gripe.

kwa′shi·or″kor (kwa′shē-ôr″kər) *n.* malnutrition in children caused by protein deficiency.

ky′an·iz·ing (kī′ən-īz-ing) *n.* a process for preserving wood, named after Irish inventor J. H. Kyan. —**ky′an·ize,** *v.t.*

Kyr′i·e″ e·le′i·son″ (kir′ē-ā″ ā-lā′ē-son″) a chant of prayer: *Lord, have mercy.*

L

L, l (el) the twelfth letter of the English alphabet. **2,** Roman numeral for 50.

la (lä) *n.* (*Music*) the sixth note of the diatonic scale. —*interj.* of surprise.

la′bel (lā′bəl) *n.* **1,** a slip of paper bearing a name, price, destination, or other particulars, to be fixed on an article or parcel. **2,** a mark or title of identification. **3,** any small strip or flap of paper, ribbon, etc. —*v.t.* attach or assign a label to.

la′bi·al (lā′bē-əl) *adj.* **1,** pert. to the lips or a liplike part. **2,** pert. to sounds produced by the lips, as *p.*

la′bile (lā′bil) *adj.* apt to lapse or err; unstable. —**la·bil′i·ty** (lə-bil′ə-tē) *n.*

la′bor (lā′bər) *n.* **1,** bodily toil for the earning of a livelihood. **2,** the class of persons engaged in such toil. **3,** hard work. **4,** a task. **5,** the pangs of childbirth; travail. —*v.i.* **1,** work; toil. **2,** be burdened or oppressed. **3,** be in travail. —*v.t.* work at persistently. Also, **la′bour.** —**Labor Day,** the first Monday in September, a federal legal holiday in the U.S. and Canada.

lab′o·ra·to·ry (lab′rə-tôr-ē) *n.* a room or building equipped for scientific research.

la′bored (lā′bərd) *adj.* done laboriously.

la·bo′ri·ous (lə-bôr′ē-əs) *adj.* **1,** not easy. **2,** diligent; assiduous. —**la·bo′ri·ous·ness,** *n.*

la·bur′num (lə-bėr′nəm) *n.* a small leguminous tree.

lab′y·rinth (lab′ə-rinth) *n.* **1,** an intricate combination of passages difficult to find a way through or out of; a maze. **2,** any thing or condition confusingly intricate. **3,** the canals in the human inner ear. —**lab″y·rin′thine** (-rin′thin) *adj.*

lac (lak) *n.* **1,** a resinous substance used in making varnishes. **2,** shellac. **3,** (*Pharm.*) milk.

lace (lās) *n.* **1,** an ornamental fabric or net of fine threads. **2,** a cord used for drawing together edges of cloth or leather. **3,** ornamental cord or braid. —*v.t.* **1,** bind with a lace. **2,** intertwine. **3,** add spirits to, as coffee. **4,** (*Informal*) beat; thrash.

lac′er·ate″ (las′ə-rāt″) *v.t.* **1,** tear roughly; mangle. **2,** afflict. —**lac″er·a′tion,** *n.*

lach′ry·mal (lak′rə-məl) *adj.* pert. to weeping or tears.

lach′ry·mose″ (-mōs″) *adj.* tending to shed or induce tears.

lac′ing (lā′sing) *n.* **1,** a cord fastening. **2,** a beating.

---

lack (lak) *n.* **1,** deficiency or absence of something needed, desired, or usual. **2,** what is lacking. —*v.t. & i.* be without; be deficient (in).

lack″a·dai′si·cal (lak″ə-dā′zi-kəl) *adj.* languid; listless.

lack′ey (lak′ē) *n.* **1,** a manservant; a liveried attendant. **2,** a servile follower.

> **lackey**
> ↔ This word came via French *laquais*, foot soldier, perhaps from Arabic *al-qadi*, judge.

lack′lus″ter *adj.* dull.

la·con′ic (lə-kon′ik) *adj.* expressing much in few words; pithy. —**la·con′i·cal·ly,** *adv.*

lac′quer (lak′ər) *n.* **1,** a varnish made with natural or synthetic resins. **2,** decorative work covered with lacquer and polished. —*v.t.* coat with lacquer.

la·crosse′ (lə-krâs′) *n.* an athletic field game played with a small ball and long-handled rackets (*crosses*).

> **lacrosse**
> ↔ Originally, in French, the *jeu de la crosse*, the game with the hooked stick.

lac·ta′tion (lak-tā′shən) *n.* **1,** the formation or secretion of milk. **2,** the period of suckling. —**lac′tate** (-tāt) *v.i.* secrete milk.

lac′te·al (lak′tē-əl) *adj.* pert. to milk; resembling milk.

lac′tic (lak′tik) *adj.* pert. to or derived from milk. —**lactic acid,** an acid found in sour milk, etc.

lac′tose″ (lak′tōs″) *n.* milk sugar.

la·cu′na (lə-kū′nə) *n.* a gap.

lac′y (lā′sē) *adj.* netlike. —**lac′i·ness,** *n.*

lad *n.* a boy or youth.

lad′der (lad′ər) *n.* **1,** an apparatus for ascending, comprising a series of horizontal bars fixed to one or two vertical posts. **2,** a blemish in a fabric, caused by the breaking of a warp thread. **3,** any means or way of ascent. —**fish ladder,** a series of pools so positioned as to allow fish to swim over a dam.

lad′der·man (-mən) *n.* a firefighter.

lad′die (làd′ē) *n.* lad.

lade (lād) *v.t.* [*p.p.* **lad′en**] **1,** load; burden. **2,** bail out with a ladle.

lad′ing (lā′ding) *n.* a cargo.

la′dle (lā′dəl) *n.* a spoon for dipping; a dipper. —*v.t.* dip out or convey with a ladle.

la·drone′ (la-drōn′) *n.* a robber; highwayman; thief; bandit.

la′dy (lā′dē) *n.* **1,** a woman of good breeding or social position. **2,** (*cap.*) a title in Brit. peerage. **3,** a wife; the mistress of a household. —*adj.* female. —**la′dies′ man,** a man who pays special attention to attracting women. —**lady-in-waiting,** a female attendant of a queen or princess.

> **lady, woman, girl**
> ↔ *Lady* comes from Old English *hlæfdige*, bread-kneader. In usage, *lady* is used as a formal term of address for a woman, in addition to its more specific sense of titled woman. However, it is much disparaged as a synonym for *woman*, which is the general term for a mature female person. *Girl* should be used only for a woman in her teens or younger.

la′dy·bug″ *n.* a small flying beetle. Also, **la′dy·bird″.**

la′dy·fin″ger *n.* a sponge cake shaped like a finger.

la′dy·kill″er *n.* (*Slang*) a man fascinating to women.

la′dy·like″ *adj.* befitting a lady, as in behavior.

la′dy·love″ *n.* sweetheart.

la′dy·ship″ *n.* term of address for a titled woman.

la′e·trile (lā′ə-tril″) *n.* a drug purported to be effective against some forms of cancer.

Laf′fer curve (laf′ər) (*Econ.*) a theoretical relationship between tax receipts and tax rates.

lag *v.i.* [**lagged, lag′ging**] **1,** move slowly; fall behind in progress; hang back. **2,** in games, drive a ball toward a line. —*n.* **1,** a falling behind; the amount of retardation. **2,** a hoop around a cylinder.

la′ger (lä′gər) *n.* aged beer.

> **lager**
> ↔ From German *lagerbier*, beer stored in a storeroom (*lager*).

lag′gard (lag′ərd) *n.* one who lags. —*adj.* lagging.

la·gniappe′ (lan-yap′) *n.* a tip; largess.

la·goon′ (lə-goon′) *n.* a shallow lake or channel.

la′ic (lā′ik) *adj.* pert. to the laity; secular.

laid (lād) *v.* pret. & p.p. of *lay.*

laid-′back′ *adj.* relaxed; calm.

lain (lān) *v.* p.p. of *lie.*

lair (lār) *n.* the den of a wild animal; a resting place.

laird (lārd) *n.* (*Scot.*) lord.

lais'sez-faire' (le'să-fār') let alone. —*n.* policy of noninterference. —**lais'sez-faire'**, *adj.* pert. to the principles of laissez-faire.

la'i·ty (lā'ə-tè) *n.* laymen; all those outside the clergy or a particular profession.

lake (lāk) *n.* **1,** a large body of water surrounded by land. **2,** a metallic pigment.

lal'ly·gag″ (lä'lè-gag″) *v.i.* (*Dial.*) loiter; dawdle. Also, **lol'ly·gag″**.

lam *v.t.* [**lammed, lam'ming**] (*Slang*) thrash; beat. —*v.i.* (*Slang*) run away.

la'ma (lä'mə) *n.* a priest or monk of the religion of Tibet.

---

lama, llama
☞ Do not confuse *lama*, a Tibetan priest, with *llama*, a South American mammal. They are usually pronounced alike but are unrelated in etymology. *Lama* is a Tibetan word, whereas *llama* is from the Quechua language of South America.

---

la'ma·ser″y (lä'mə-ser″è) *n.* a monastery of lamas.

La·maze' technique (lä-mäz') a method for childbirth without drugs, with the mother's active participation.

lamb (lam) *n.* **1,** a young sheep; its meat. **2,** one who is gentle, meek, or gullible.

lam·ba'da (läm-bä'də) *n.* a type of disco dance; its music.

lam·baste' (lam-bāst') *v.t.* whack; pound.

lamb'da (lam'də) *n.* the eleventh letter of the Greek alphabet (Λ, λ).

lam'bent (lam'bənt) *adj.* **1,** moving lightly; licking. **2,** softly bright; gleaming. —**lam'ben·cy** (-sè) *n.*

lamb'kin *n.* a little lamb.

lame (lām) *adj.* **1,** physically disabled; limping. **2,** ineffectual; halting. —*v.t.* make lame. —**lame duck,** (*Informal*) an officeholder soon to be succeeded. —**lame'ness,** *n.*

la·mé' (la-mā') *n.* a fabric made of metallic threads interwoven with silk, wool, or cotton.

lame'brain″ *n.* dunce.

la·mel'la (lə-mel'ə) *n.* a thin plate or scale. —**lam'el·lar** (lam'ə-lər), **lam'el·late,** *adj.*

la·ment' (lə-ment') *v.i. & t.* express sorrow (for); mourn; bewail. —*n.* an expression of grief; an elegy. —**lam'en·ta·ble** (lam'ən-tə-bəl) *adj.* regrettable. —**lam'en·ta'tion,** *n.*

lam'i·na (lam'ə-nə) *n.* **1,** a thin layer or scale. **2,** layers.

lam'i·nate″ (lam'ə-nāt″) *v.t.* press (layers) together. —*adj.* in layers. —**lam″i·na'tion,** *n.*

lamp *n.* **1,** a vessel for burning an illuminant; any device, chemical or electrical, for providing light. **2,** (*pl.*) (*Slang*) the eyes.

lamp'black″ *n.* soot used as a black pigment.

lam·poon' *n.* a satire aimed at a person. —*v.t.* assail in a lampoon.

---

lampoon
↔ First used in 1645, but of uncertain origin. Possibly from French *lampons*, let us drink.

---

lam'prey (lam'prè) *n.* a snakelike fish.

LAN (lan) a type of communications network: *l(ocal) a(rea) n(etwork).*

la·nai' (lə-nī') *n.* veranda; terrace.

lance (låns) *n.* a weapon comprising a sharp-pointed head on a long shaft. —*v.t.* prick or cut open.

lanc'er (lan'sər) *n.* **1,** a mounted soldier with a lance. **2,** (*pl.*) a kind of square dance.

lan'cet (lån'sit) *n.* a surgical knife. —**lancet arch,** an arch acutely pointed at the head.

land *n.* **1,** the surface of the earth, esp. the dry parts. **2,** a particular tract; a region or country. **3,** a tract as property; real estate. —*v.t.* **1,** discharge (passengers or freight); transfer to land. **2,** catch or capture. —*v.i.* **1,** disembark. **2,** arrive at a place or condition.

lan'dau (lan'dow) *n.* a carriage or automobile with a folding top.

land'ed (lan'did) *adj.* **1,** consisting of land, as landed property. **2,** owning land.

land'fall″ *n.* the land first sighted from the sea.

land'fill″ *n.* earth, gravel, etc., used to build up ground level or to fill in a swamp, etc.

land'hold″er *n.* an owner of land. Also, **land'own″er.**

land'ing *n.* **1,** a place where persons or goods are landed. **2,** a platform in a staircase. —**landing gear,** the wheels, pontoons, etc., on which an aircraft rests on land or water.

land'la″dy, land'lord *n.* **1,** an owner of rented land, buildings, etc. **2,** the proprietor of a hotel, etc.

land'locked″ (-lokt″) *adj.* (of water) sheltered or enclosed by land.

---

land'lub"ber (-lub"ər) *n.* one unaccustomed to being on a ship at sea.

land'mark" *n.* **1,** a conspicuous object serving to bound or identify a place. **2,** a memorable event.

land office a government office for registration of deeds. —**land-office business,** (*Informal*) a highly successful operation.

land-'poor" *adj.* owning much land but lacking capital because the land is unproductive or encumbered.

land'scape" *n.* a view or picture of rural scenery. —*v.t.* beautify (land). —*adj.* printed sideways on the page.

land'slide" *n.* **1,** the falling of a large mass of earth down a steep slope. **2,** an overwhelming victory.

lands'man 1, (lantz'mən) *n.* [*pl.* **-leit** (-līt)] a fellow Jew from one's own E. European district or town. **2,** (landz'mən) [*pl.* **-men**] a person who lives and works on land; landlubber.

lane (lān) *n.* **1,** a narrow passage; a rural road or path. **2,** a fixed route, as across an ocean.

lan'guage (lang'gwij) *n.* **1,** the aggregate of words composing a system of communication between persons in speech or writing. **2,** such a system peculiar to a country, race, etc. **3,** expression of thought in any way. **4,** linguistics. **5,** diction.

> **language**
> ↔ From French *langage* (from Latin *lingua*, tongue). The spelling was influenced by French *langue*, tongue.

lan'guid (lang'gwid) *adj.* **1,** sluggish from weakness, fatigue, or lack of energy. **2,** spiritless; listless. —**lan'-guid·ness,** *n.*

lan'guish (lang'gwish) *v.i.* be languid; droop, as from grief or longing. —**lan'-guish·ment,** *n.*

lan'guor (lang'gər) *n.* lack of spirit or vigor; dreaminess. —**lan'guor·ous,** *adj.*

lank *adj.* meagerly thin; gaunt. —**lank'y,** *adj.* slim and tall.

lan'o·lin (lan'ə-lin) *n.* a fat from sheep's wool, used in cosmetics, etc.

lan'tern (lan'tərn) *n.* **1,** a portable lamp. **2,** the lamp chamber of a lighthouse. —**lan'tern-jawed"** (-jâd") *adj.* thin-faced, with bulging jaws.

lan'tha·nide" (lan'thə-nīd") *n.* any of the rare-earth elements. Also, **lan'tha·non"** (-non").

lan'tha·num (lan'thə-nəm) *n.* a metallic element, usu. included with the rare-earth elements, no. 57, symbol La.

lan'yard (lan'yərd) *n.* a short length of cord used in rigging, etc.

lap *n.* **1,** the platform formed by the thighs when one sits. **2,** support or shelter, like the mother's lap to the child. **3,** the part of one body that lies on another; overlap. **4,** the distance or material required to go around something once. **5,** a rotating wheel for cutting or polishing gems. **6,** the act or sound of lapping liquid. —*v.t.* [**lapped, lap'ping**] **1,** fold; wrap. **2,** cover partly. **3,** get ahead of (a competitor) by one circuit of the racecourse. **4,** cut or polish with a lap wheel. **5,** lick up (a liquid) with the tongue. **6,** wash against; lick. —*v.i.* **1,** be folded. **2,** overlap. **3,** ripple, as waves. —**lap dog,** a small pet dog.

la·pel' (lə-pel') *n.* a fold in the front of a coat below the collar.

lap'i·dar·y (lap'ə-der-ė) *n.* **1,** a skilled worker on gems. **2,** an engraver of monuments.

lap'in *n.* a rabbit; rabbit fur.

lap'is laz'u·li" (lap'is laz'yû-lē") *n.* a semiprecious stone; its color, sky-blue.

Lapp (lap) *n.* one of a people of Mongolian descent, inhabiting Lapland. Also, **Lap'land"er** (-lan"dər).

lap'pet (lap'it) *n.* a loosely hanging part, as a flap; the wattle of a fowl.

lapse (laps) *n.* **1,** the passing by or away, as of time; termination or cessation, as of a privilege. **2,** a careless mistake; failure; error. —*v.i.* **1,** pass by or away gradually; end. **2,** deteriorate. **3,** err.

lap'sus ling'guae (lap'səs ling'gwė) (*Lat.*) a slip of the tongue.

lap'top" *n.* a small, lightweight portable computer.

lap'wing" *n.* a ploverlike Europ. bird; the pewit.

lar'board (lär'bərd) *adj.* (*Naut.*) left; port: opposite of *starboard.*

lar'ce·ny (lär'sə-nė) *n.* the wrongful taking of another's goods; theft. —**lar'ce·nous,** *adj.*

larch (lärch) *n.* a coniferous tree; its wood.

lard (lärd) *n.* a grease for cooking, prepared from hogs' fat. —*v.t.* **1,** grease. **2,** garnish or ornament.

lard'er (lär'dər) *n.* a pantry; a stock of food.

lar'don (lär'dən) *n.* a strip of salt pork, bacon, or suet, used for larding meat. Also, **lar·doon'** (lär-doon').

la′res et pe·na′tes (lār′ēz et pė-nä′tēz) (*Lat.*) household gods.

large (lärj) *adj.* great in size, amount, number, degree, range, scale, etc. —**at large, 1,** not caught or confined. **2,** at length; fully. **3,** (*Politics*) representing no specified district. —**large′ly,** *adv.* in great part. —**large′ness,** *n.*

large-′heart″ed (-här″tid) *adj.* sympathetic; generous. —**large-′heart″ed·ness,** *n.*

large-′scale″ *adj.* **1,** extensive. **2,** drawn to a larger scale, as a map.

lar·gess′ (lär-jės′) *n.* a liberal gift; generous bestowal of gifts.

lar′go (lär′gō) (*It., Music*) *adj.* slow. —*n.* a slow movement or work —**lar·ghet′to** (lär-get′tō) *adv. & adj.* (*It., Music*) somewhat slow.

lar′i·at (lar′ė-ət) *n.* **1,** a lasso. **2,** a rope used to picket a horse.

lark (lärk) *n.* **1,** any of numerous songbirds. **2,** a merry adventure; jovial frolic. —*v.i.* play pranks.

lark′spur″ (lärk′spēr″) *n.* a flowering plant; delphinium.

lar′rup (lar′əp) *v.t.* (*Informal*) flog; beat.

lar′va (lär′və) *n.* [*pl.* **-vae** (-vė)] the young of any animal that undergoes metamorphosis. —**lar′val,** *adj.*

lar″yn·gi′tis (lar″in-jī′tis) *n.* inflammation of the larynx.

lar′ynx (lar′inks) *n.* the part of the windpipe containing the vocal cords. —**la·ryn′ge·al** (lə-rin′jė-əl) *adj.*

la·sa′gna (lə-zä′nyə) *n.* (*It.*) broad flat noodles, usu. served with a sauce.

las′car (las′kər) *n.* an E. Indian sailor.

las·civ′i·ous (lə-siv′ė-əs) *adj.* **1,** inciting to lust. **2,** wanton; lewd. —**las·civ′i·ous·ness,** *n.*

la′ser (lā′zər) *n.* a device producing an intense, highly directional beam of light: *l(ight) a(mplification by) s(timulated) e(mission of electromagnetic) r(adiation).* —**laser bomb,** a bomb guided to its target by a laser beam. —**laser printer,** a type of dot matrix printer using a laser to form the pattern of dots.

la′ser·disc″ a digitally recorded disc used for music, images, etc. Also, **optical disc.**

lash *n.* **1,** the flexible part of a whip. **2,** a blow with a whip; a sweeping movement. **3,** a stroke of sarcasm or censure. **4,** eyelash. —*v.t.* **1,** flog. **2,** beat or dash against. **3,** assail violently with words. **4,** fasten with cord. —*v.i.* (with *out*) burst into violent action or speech.

lash′ing *n.* **1,** act or result of lashing or beating. **2,** tongue-lashing. **3,** a rope used for binding or fastening.

lass (las) *n.* girl. Also, **las′sie** (-ė).

las′si·tude″ (las′i-tūd″) *n.* weariness; languor.

las′so (las′ō) *n.* a rope with a noose used to catch animals. —*v.t.* catch in the noose of a lasso.

last (låst) *v.i.* **1,** continue to exist or progress; endure. **2,** continue unexhausted. —*n.* **1,** that which is after all others. **2,** end; conclusion. **3,** a model of the human foot, on which shoes are formed. —*adj.* **1,** being after all others in time, place, order, etc. **2,** being all that remains; final. **3,** most recent; latest. —*adv.* **1,** after all others. **2,** finally. **3,** on the most recent occasion. —**last′ly,** *adv.* in the last place; in conclusion. —**at last,** finally. —**last straw,** the final burden, indignity, etc., that goes beyond the limit of one's endurance. —**Last Supper,** the supper of Christ and his disciples on the night of Christ's betrayal.

last, latest
↔ *Last* meaning final is a shortening of *latest* (or, more precisely, an ancestor of *latest*). The verb meaning to endure and the noun from shoemaking are both derived from Old English *læstan*, to follow, continue. Both *last* and *latest* are superlatives of *late*; *last* is used to mean final, *latest* means happening later than all others, or most recent.

Las′tex (las′teks) *n.* (*T.N.*) elastic yarn consisting of silk, cotton, etc., wound around a latex rubber core.

last′ing (las′ting) *adj.* enduring; permanent.

latch (lach) *n.* a device for holding shut a door or gate. —*v.t.* lock.

latch′et (lach′ət) *n.* shoestring.

late (lāt) *adj.* **1,** coming after the usual or proper time. **2,** protracted in time. **3,** coming near the end. **4,** recent. **5,** recently changed, ended, or deceased. —*adv.* **1,** after the usual or proper time. **2,** not long since. —**lat′er,** *adv.* after some passage of time. —**late′ly,** *adv.* recently. —**late′ness,** *n.* —**of late,** recently.

la·teen′ (la-tēn′) *adj.* denoting a type of triangular sail.

la′tent (lā′tənt) *adj.* hidden; dormant; undeveloped. —**la′ten·cy,** *n.*

lat′er·al (lat′ər-əl) *adj.* pert. to the side.

la′tex (lā′teks) *n.* a milky liquid occurring in many plants, as rubber.

lath (låth) *n.* a narrow strip of wood; such strips collectively. —**lath′y,** *adj.* slender.

lath, lathe
☛ These two words are easily confused, though they are spelled and pronounced differently. A *lath* is a strip of wood, while a *lathe* is a woodworking machine. ↔ The two words are likewise unrelated in origin. *Lath* derives from Old English *lætt*; *lathe* goes back to Old Norse *hlath*, stack.

lathe (lā*th*) *n.* a machine that rotates wood or metal while it is shaped by a tool. —*v.t.* shape in a lathe. ❑ *lath*

lath′er (la*th*′ər) *n.* **1,** froth produced by soap and water. **2,** froth produced by profuse sweating. **3,** a state of excitement, fear, etc.

Lat′in *n.* **1,** the language spoken by the inhabitants of ancient Rome. **2,** a member of any Latin race. —*adj.* **1,** pert. to the Latin language. **2,** pert. to any people speaking a language derived from Latin. —**Latin alphabet,** the alphabet used for writing English and other W. European languages. —**Latin American,** pert. to the Spanish- and Portuguese-speaking American countries. —**Latin Quarter,** a community of artists or section where they live.

la·ti′na (lə-tē′na) *n.fem.*, **la·ti′no** (-nō) *n.masc.* (*Sp.*) a person of Spanish or Latin-Amer. descent.

lat′i·tude″ (lat′i-tūd″) *n.* **1,** freedom from narrow restriction. **2,** the distance of a point on the earth's surface from the equator. —**lat″i·tu′di·nal,** *adj.*

latitude, longitude
The potentially confusing question of which of these is which is rendered less confusing by remembering that *parallels* run parallel to the equator, *meridians* perpendicular to it: *latitude* is measured in degrees north or south of the equator, each change of 1 degree being marked by a *parallel*; *longitude* is measured in degrees east or west of the meridian passing through Greenwich, England (which is at 0° longitude), each change of 1 degree being marked by a *meridian.*

la·trine′ (lə-trēn′) *n.* a privy.

lat′ter (lat′ər) *adj.* **1,** being the second of two mentioned. **2,** more recent. —**Latter-Day Saints,** the Mormons. —**lat′ter·ly,** *adv.* **1,** recently. **2,** toward the end.

lat′tice (lat′is) *n.* an open network of laths, rods, etc.

laud (lâd) *v.t.* praise highly; extol. —**laud′-a·ble,** *adj.* worthy of praise.

lau′da·num (lâ′də-nəm) *n.* a medicinal tincture of opium.

laud′a·to·ry (lâd′ə-tôr-ė) *adj.* praising.

lauds (lâdz) *n.sing.* the second canonical hour, usu. beginning at dawn.

laugh (laf) *v.i.* **1,** make a convulsive or chuckling noise excited by merriment or pleasure. **2,** (with *at*) be amused by; deride. —*n.* an expression of mirth or joy by an explosive noise. —**laugh′a·ble,** *adj.* funny. —**laughing gas,** nitrous oxide, used as an anesthetic. —**laugh track,** (*Informal*) prerecorded laughter dubbed onto a TV show, etc.

laugh
↔ This word is traced back to Indo-European **klok-*, itself probably of imitative origin. The final *gh* was pronounced like German *ch* in medieval times.

laugh′ing·stock″ *n.* a person or thing ridiculed.

laugh′ter (-tər) *n.* the act or sound of laughing.

launch (lânch) *v.t.* **1,** set or slide (a boat) into the water. **2,** give initial impulse to; set going; esp. (*Computers*) run (a program). **3,** send forth; hurl. —*v.i.* begin action or speech. —*n.* a large open boat.

laun′der (lân′dər) *v.t. & i.* **1,** wash and iron (clothes). **2,** conceal the source or disposition of (money), as by passing it through foreign banks. —**laun′der·er,** *n.* Also, **laun′dress,** *n.fem.*

laun″der·ette′ (lân″dər-et′) *n.* an establishment offering coin-operated washing machines and dryers for public use.

Laun′dro·mat″ (lân′drə-mat″) *n.* (*T.N.*) a type of launderette.

laun′dry (lân′drė) *n.* **1,** an establishment for laundering. **2,** what is laundered. —**laundry list,** (*Informal*) a lengthy list, as of political promises, etc.

laundry, lavatory
↔ *Laundry* is a contraction of *lavendry*, which derives ultimately from Latin *lavare*, wash, as does *lavatory.*

Laur·a′sia (lô-rā′zhə) *n.* a hypothetical land mass consisting of North America and Eurasia before they separated.

lau′re·ate (lâ′rė-ət) *adj.* crowned with laurel, as a mark of honor. —*n.* one honored, esp. a poet.

lau′rel (lor′əl) *n.* **1,** a small evergreen tree; the bay tree. **2,** any of several trees and shrubs having similar leaves. **3,** a wreath of laurel leaves, as an emblem of honor. **4,** (*pl.*) honor for achievement.

la'va (lä'və) *n.* molten rock thrown out by a volcano.

la·va'bo (lə-vä'bō) *n.* **1,** a ritual act of hand-washing. **2,** a basin holding water for ablutions.

lav"a·liere' (làv"ə-lir') *n.* an ornament pendant from a chain, named for the Duchess de Lavallière, a mistress of Louis XIV.

lav'a·to·ry (lav'ə-tôr-ė) *n.* **1,** a small room for personal washing, esp. one also containing a toilet. **2,** a washbasin. ❑ *laundry, toilet*

lave (lāv) *v.i. & t.* wash; bathe. —**la·vage'** (lə-väzh') *n.*

lav'en·der (lav'ən-dər) *n.* **1,** an aromatic shrub used in perfumery. **2,** a pale blue-purple color.

lav'ish *adj.* extravagant; generous; abundant; profuse. —*v.t.* expend or bestow in generous amount. —**lav'ish·ness,** *n.*

law (lâ) *n.* **1,** a rule of action prescribed by an authority. **2,** a collection or system of such rules. **3,** jurisprudence; the profession dealing with legal procedure; the bar. **4,** a proposition asserting a natural truth. **5,** litigation. **6,** (*Informal*) a law-enforcement officer. **7,** (often *cap.*) the first five books of the Old Testament. —**law'a·bid"ing,** *adj.* obedient to the law. —**law'giv"er,** *n.* a legislator.

law'ful (-fəl) *adj.* allowed or sanctioned by law. —**law'ful·ness,** *n.*

> **lawful, legal, legitimate, licit**
> These four words are synonyms in the sense of "permitted by law," but each has its own nuance. *Lawful* and *licit* often refer to other than statutory laws, such as religious or moral laws. *Legal* is the term most often used for statutory law; it also means pertaining to law. *Legitimate* is more often used to mean valid.

law'less (-ləs) *adj.* **1,** contrary to or defiant of law. **2,** not regulated by laws. —**law'less·ness,** *n.*

law'mak"er *n.* a legislator.

law'man (lâ'mən) **lawwoman** *n.* an officer of the law.

> **lawn**
> ↔ The word for a grassy expanse is of Celtic origin; the fabric comes from the French town of *Laon*, where the cloth was first made.

lawn (lân) *n.* **1,** a tract of ground covered by mowed grass. **2,** a thin linen or cotton fabric.

law·ren'ci·um (lâ-ren'sė-əm) *n.* a radioactive chemical element, no. 103, symbol Lw, produced artificially, named for the Lawrence Radiation Laboratory in Berkeley, CA.

law'suit" *n.* an action to seek justice in a civil court.

law'yer (lâ'yər) *n.* a legal counselor. ❑ *attorney*

lax (laks) *adj.* **1,** lacking in strictness; careless; remiss. **2,** not tense or firm; relaxed. **3,** vague. —**lax'i·ty** (-ə-tė), **lax'-ness,** *n.*

lax'a·tive (lak'sə-tiv) *n. & adj.* a mild purgative.

lay (lā) *v.t.* [*pret. & p.p.* **laid** (lād)] **1,** cause to lie; put in a position, situation, or condition (with *up, down, by, away,* etc.); arrange. **2,** overthrow; allay. **3,** contrive. **4,** wager. **5,** bring forth (eggs). **6,** impute; ascribe. —*v.i.* bring forth eggs. —*v.* pret. of *lie.* —*n.* **1,** relative position or arrangement. **2,** a lyric poem or song. —*adj.* pert. to the laity. —**lay an egg,** (*Slang*) fail; flop. —**lay figure,** artist's dummy. —**lay for,** (*Informal*) prepare to attack. —**lay hold of,** seize; catch. —**lay off, 1,** measure off; mark the boundaries of. **2,** discharge an employee, usu. temporarily. **3,** (*Slang*) stop; cease. —**lay out, 1,** plan in detail. **2,** display. **3,** spend. —**lay person,** a member of the laity. ❑ *lie*

lay'a·way" plan a method of purchasing whereby the item to be purchased is reserved by a down payment until complete payment is given.

lay'er (lā'ər) *n.* **1,** a thickness of some material lying on another. **2,** that which lays.

lay·ette' (lā-et') *n.* an outfit of clothing, bedding, etc., for a newborn baby.

lay'man (-mən) *n.* [*pl.* **-men**] a lay person.

lay'off" (lā'âf') *n.* temporary suspension of employment.

lay'out" (lā'owt') *n.* **1,** a sketch, play, or design. **2,** an arrangement, as of furniture; a set of materials or tools; equipment.

lay'o"ver *n.* stopover.

lay'wom"an *n.* a female lay person.

laz'ar (laz'ər) *n.* a leper, esp. one who is a beggar.

laze (lāz) *v.i. & t.* lounge.

la'zy (lā'zė) *adj.* **1,** disinclined to exertion; indolent. **2,** slow; sluggish; languid. —**la'zi·ness,** *n.* —**lazy eye,** (*Informal*) dimness of sight apparently not caused by or-

---

fat, fāte, fär, fāre, fâll, åsk; met, hē, hėr, maybė; pin, pīne; not, nōte, ôr, tool

ganic defect. **—lazy Su′san** (soo′zən) a revolving tray for food.

la′zy·bones″ n. (*Informal*) a lazy person.

LCD *abbr.* liquid-crystal display.

lea (lē) n. a meadow.

leach (lēch) *v.t. & i.* wash or drain by percolation of liquid.

lead (led) n. **1,** a heavy, soft metal, chemical element, no. 82, symbol Pb. **2,** something made of lead; a weight, bullet, etc. **3,** graphite: *black lead.* —*v.t.* **1,** treat, weight, etc., with lead. **2,** (*Printing*) space between lines.

lead (lēd) *v.t.* [*pret. & p.p.* **led**] **1,** go before as a guide; conduct; influence; induce. **2,** direct; control. **3,** go or be first in. **4,** play as the first card. —*v.i.* **1,** act as a guide. **2,** provide passage or access; be conducive. **3,** go first; be in advance; be in command. **4,** make the first play. —*n.* **1,** guidance; direction. **2,** the condition of being first; precedence. **3,** a clue. **4,** the opening words of a story. **5,** the principal rôle. **6,** a wire for conducting electric current.

lead′en (led′ən) *adj.* **1,** made of lead. **2,** sluggish; gloomy. **3,** of a dull gray color.

lead′er (lē′dər) n. **1,** one who or that which leads; a chief director, etc. **2,** (*Brit.*) an editorial. **3,** (*Brit.*) a concertmaster. **—lead′er·ship,** n.

lead′er·board″ n. a sign showing the leading contenders in an athletic contest, etc.

lead′ing (lē′ding) *adj.* **1,** guiding. **2,** principal. —*n.* (led′ing) (*Printing*) space between lines of type. **—leading edge** (lē-), the latest (technology, etc.); state of the art. **—leading question** (lē′-) (*Law*) a question suggesting or inducing a desired reply.

leaf (lēf) n. [*pl.* **leaves** (lēvz)] **1,** a flat green blade growing from a stem of a plant. **2,** petal. **3,** a sheet of paper; a page. **4,** a sheet of wood, metal, etc. **—leaf′y,** *adj.*

leaf′age (lē′fij) n. foliage.

leaf′let (-lət) n. a pamphlet or circular.

league (lēg) n. **1,** a confederation of states, parties, etc.; alliance; association. **2,** a measure of distance, about 3 miles. —*v.t. & i.* combine.

leak (lēk) n. **1,** an unintended aperture allowing the escape of a fluid; any avenue of unintended entrance or escape, as of information. **2,** the act of leaking. —*v.t. & i.* **1,** enter, escape, or allow to escape through an unintended crack, etc. **2,** release information without authorization, usu. to the news media.

leak′age (lē′kij) n. act of leaking; the amount that leaks.

leak′y (lē′kė) *adj.* not perfectly sealed. **—leak′i·ness,** n.

lean (lēn) *v.i.* **1,** deviate from an upright position; tilt; bend. **2,** incline in feeling, opinion, etc. **3,** rest against or rely on something. —*v.t.* cause to rest against something. —*n.* **1,** a slant. **2,** meat without fat. —*adj.* **1,** not fat or plump; thin; spare. **2,** containing no fat. **3,** scanty; meager. **—lean′ness,** n.

lean′ing n. a tendency; desire.

lean-′to″ n. a rude shelter slanting from the ground to supporting posts.

leap (lēp) *v.i.* **1,** spring through the air; jump; bound. **2,** start eagerly. —*v.t.* jump over or across; vault. —*n.* **1,** a jump or bound. **2,** a sudden rise or start. **—leap year,** a year occurring once every four years containing an extra day (Feb. 29).

leap′frog″ n. a gymnastic game.

learn (lėrn) *v.t. & i.* **1,** acquire knowledge or skill (in). **2,** become informed of or acquainted (with). **3,** memorize. **—learn′ed** (lėr′nəd) *adj.* erudite. **—learn′er,** n. a student. **—learn′ing,** n. systematic knowledge. **—learning curve,** a graphic representation of the progress of learning (as to master a certain task) over time. **—learning disability,** a disorder that causes difficulty in learning.

> **learn, teach**
> (*Gram.*) Do not use *learn* for *teach.* To *learn* is to acquire knowledge, not to impart it.

learn′ing-dis·a″bled *adj.* having a learning disability.

lease (lēs) *v.t.* grant or obtain the use of (land, buildings, etc.) at a fixed rental. —*n.* a written instrument granting such use.

lease′hold″ n. property held under lease.

leash (lēsh) n. a cord or thong, esp. for restraining an animal. —*v.t.* hold in check.

least (lēst) *adj.* [*superl.* of **less**] little beyond all others. **—least′ways, least′wise,** *adv.* (*Informal*) at least. **—at least,** in any case. **—in the least,** at all.

leath′er (leth′ər) n. animal skin prepared for use by tanning, etc. —*v.t.* make, cover, or furnish with leather. **—leath′ern,** *adj.* made of leather. **—leath′er·y,** *adj.* tough, like leather.

leath″er·ette′ (-et′) n. imitation leather. Also, **leath″er·et′.**

leath′er·neck″ n. (*Slang*) a U.S. Marine.

leave (lēv) *v.t.* [*pret. & p.p.* **left**] **1,** go away from; quit. **2,** let remain. **3,** omit; postpone. **4,** (with *off*) stop doing; desist from. **5,** have remaining; bequeath. —*v.i.* go away; depart. —*n.* **1,** permission. **2,** a period of absence by permission. **3,** departure. **4,** (*pl.*) pl. of *leaf.* —**leaved** (lēvd) *adj.* having a leaf or leaves.

leav'en (lev'ən) *n.* **1,** a batch of fermenting dough. **2,** an influence that effects a gradual change. —*v.t.* add leavening to; change.

leav'en·ing *n.* that which causes a leaven; yeast.

leave-'tak″ing *n.* farewell.

leav'ings *n.pl.* residue.

Le·boy·er' birth (lə-bwä-yā') a method of natural childbirth.

lech'er (lech'ər) *n.* a lewd man.

> **lecher**
> ↔ Of Germanic origin, through Old French *lecheor,* one who licks.

lech'er·y *n.* **1,** excessive pursuit of sexual pleasure. **2,** suggestiveness. —**lech'er·ous,** *adj.*

lec'i·thin (les'ə-thin) *n.* a fatty substance found in various body fluids, in pus, and in egg yolks.

lec'tern (lek'tərn) *n.* a reading stand. ❑ *dais*

lec'tor (lek'tər) *n.* a reader.

lec'ture (lek'chər) *n.* **1,** a discourse to an audience; an address. **2,** a long, tedious reprimand. —*v.t.* address; rebuke. —**lec'-tur·er,** *n.* one who delivers addresses.

LED *abbr.* light-emitting diode.

led *v.* pret. & p.p. of *lead.*

ledge (lej) *n.* a flat projecting part; a rim; a shelf.

ledg'er (lej'ər) *n.* a book for recording debits and credits. —**ledger** or **leger line,** (*Music*) a short line above or below the staff extending its compass.

lee (lē) *n.* shelter; the side of a ship away from the wind. —**lee'ward** (-wərd) *adj.*

leech (lēch) *n.* **1,** a blood-sucking worm. **2,** an instrument for drawing out blood. **3,** a parasitic person.

leek (lēk) *n.* a bulbous plant allied to the onion.

leer (lir) *v.i.* cast a suggestive or malicious look. —*n.* an oblique glance. —**leer'y,** *adj.* (*Informal*) wary.

lees (lēz) *n.pl.* dregs.

lee'way″ *n.* room for movement, expansion, discretion, etc.

left *adj.* pert. to the side or direction that is westward as one faces north. —*n.* **1,** the left side. **2,** (often *cap.*) radical political parties. —*v.* pret. of *leave.* —**New Left,** a loosely organized political movement composed largely of young people seeking radical social and economic change.

> **left**
> ↔ This word comes from an Old English word meaning weak, a derivation which reflects the traditional prejudice against the left hand.

left-'hand″ed *adj.* [also, **left-'hand'**] **1,** preferring the use of the left hand. **2,** toward the left. **3,** (*Informal*) insincere. —*adv.* for or with the left hand.

left'ist *n. & adj.* (*Politics*) a radical. —**left'ism,** *n.*

left'o″ver *n.* a bit of food saved from a meal; hence, any remainder.

left-'wing″ *adj.* pert. to the parties or doctrines of the left.

left'y (-ē) *n.* (*Informal*) **1,** one who is left-handed. **2,** a leftist.

leg *n.* **1,** one of the limbs that support and move the human or animal body; any vertical supporting member. **2,** the part of a garment covering the leg. **3,** a straight segment. **4,** one contest of a series. —**leg'gy** (-ē) *adj.* having long legs. —**leg it,** walk; run fast. —**pull one's leg,** (*Slang*) fool one. —**shake a leg,** (*Slang*) hurry up.

leg'a·cy (leg'ə-sē) *n.* property left by will; a bequest.

le'gal (lē'gəl) *adj.* **1,** permitted or established by law; lawful. **2,** pert. to the practice or administration of law. —**le·gal'i·ty** (li-gal'ə-tē) *n.* lawfulness. —**le'gal·ize″** (-īz″) *v.t.* make legal. —**legal age,** the age at which a person acquires certain legal rights, as the right to sign contracts. —**legal tender,** currency that must be accepted by a creditor. ❑ *lawful*

> **legal, loyal**
> ↔ These two words share a common source, Latin *legalis,* legal, through Anglo-Norman *leal,* which was borrowed at two different times into English to produce our two, now quite distinct, forms.

leg'ate (leg'ət) *n.* an envoy.

leg'a·tee' (-ə-tē') *n.* one who receives a legacy.

le·ga'tion (li-gā'shən) *n.* the staff and headquarters of a diplomatic officer.

le·ga'to (li-gä'tō) *adj.* (*It., Music*) without breaks between the successive tones.

leg'end (lej'ənd) *n.* **1,** a widely accepted

but unverified story. **2,** an inscription; a caption; a written key. —**leg′end·ar″y,** *adj.*

leg″er·de·main′ (lej″ər-də-mān′) *n.* sleight of hand; conjuring.

-legged (legd *or* leg′gid) *suf.* having a specified leg or number of legs.

leg′gings (leg′ingz) *n.pl.* outer coverings for the legs.

leg′horn″ *n.* **1,** a small domestic fowl. **2,** a hat made of straw from Livorno (Leghorn), Italy.

leg′i·ble (lej′ə-bəl) *adj.* that may be read; written plainly. —**leg″i·bil′i·ty,** *n.*

le′gion (lē′jən) *n.* **1,** a large body of armed men. **2,** any multitude of persons or things. —**le′gion·ar·y,** *adj.*

le″gion·naire′ (lē″jə-nār′) *n.* a member of a legion. —**legionnaire's disease,** an acute respiratory infection, often fatal, apparently caused by airborne organisms transmitted by air conditioning.

leg′is·late″ (lej′is-lāt″) *v.i.* prepare and enact laws. —*v.t.* effect by legislation. —**leg′is·la″tor,** *n.*

leg″is·la′tion (lej″is-lā′shən) *n.* the enactment of laws; the laws. —**leg′is·la″tive,** *adj.*

leg′is·la″ture (lej′is-lā″chər) *n.* a body that prepares and enacts laws.

le·git′ (lə-jit′) *adj.* (*Slang*) legitimate; honest or respectable, as an occupation.

le·git′i·ma·cy (lə-jit′i-mə-sè) *n.* state of being legitimate; lawfulness.

le·git′i·mate (lə-jit′i-mət) *adj.* **1,** conforming to law; proper. **2,** born of parents legally married. **3,** logically correct; valid. **4,** regular; genuine. **5,** (*Theat.*) pert. to professionally produced stage plays. —*v.t.* (-māt″) make or declare to be legitimate. —**le·git′i·mize″** (-mīz″), **le·git′i·ma·tize″** (-mə-tīz″) *v.t.* —**le·git″i·mi·za′tion,** *n.* ❏ *lawful*

leg′man″ *n.* **1,** an agent working outside the office. **2,** a reporter covering news at the scene. **3,** gofer.

leg′ume (leg′ūm) *n.* a plant having pods that divide into halves, as peas and beans; the pods. —**le·gu′mi·nous** (lə-gū′mi-nəs) *adj.*

leg′work″ *n.* travel, esp. walking, as required by a job.

le′i (lā′ē) *n.* (*Hawaiian*) a wreath of flowers around the neck.

lei′sure (lē′zhər) *n.* **1,** freedom from necessary occupation; spare time. **2,** convenience. —*adj.* unoccupied; idle. —**lei′sure·ly** (-lè) *adj. & adv.* without

haste. —**lei′sured,** *adj.* having leisure. —**leisure wear,** casual clothing.

leit′mo·tif″ (līt′mō-tēf″) *n.* **1,** (*Music*) a recurring theme. **2,** a dominant motive or emotion. Also, **leit′mo·tiv″** (-tēf″).

lem′ma (lem′ə) *n.* **1,** a subsidiary theorem used to prove another. **2,** a word used in a heading, as of a dictionary.

lem′ming (lem′ing) *n.* a mouselike rodent of northern regions.

lem′on (lem′ən) *n.* **1,** a subtropical tree; its citrus fruit. **2,** a pale yellow color. **3,** (*Informal*) something inferior; a failure. —*adj.* light yellow. —**lemon law,** a law requiring manufacturers to repair or replace defective products.

lem″on·ade′ (-ād′) *n.* a beverage of sweetened lemon juice and water.

le′mur (lē′mər) *n.* a small arboreal mammal related to the monkey.

lend *v.t.* [*pret. & p.p.* **lent**] **1,** give temporary custody and use of. **2,** give use of (money), usually for a consideration. **3,** impart; furnish; accommodate (oneself) to. —*v.i.* make a loan (of or to). ❏ *loan*

length *n.* **1,** distance along a line; linear measure. **2,** the longest dimension of a body. **3,** duration in time. **4,** a piece, stretch, period, etc.

length′en (leng′thən) *v.t. & i.* make or become longer.

length′wise″ *adv.* in the direction of the longest axis. Also, **length′ways″.**

length′y (leng′thè) *adj.* very long. —**length′i·ness,** *n.*

le′ni·ent (lē′nè-ənt) *adj.* disposed to act without severity; merciful; gentle. —**le′-ni·en·cy** (-sè), **len′i·ty** (len′ə-tè) *n.*

len′i·tive (len′ə-tiv) *adj. & n.* **1,** soothing. **2,** mildly laxative.

lens (lenz) *n.* **1,** transparent glass, etc., having one or two curved surfaces, for altering the direction of light rays. **2,** a similar structure in the eye: *crystalline lens.*

Lent *n.* an annual period of fasting or penitence in Christian ritual. —*v.* (*l.c.*) *pret. & p.p.* of *lend.* —**Lent′en,** *adj.*

> **Lent**
> ↔ Derived from a much longer Germanic root *langgitinaz,* meaning long day, and originally referring to the lengthening of the day in the spring.

len′til *n.* a leguminous plant.

len′to (len′tō) *adj. & adv.* (*It., Music*) slow; slowly.

Le′o (lē′ō) *n.* a constellation, the Lion (see *zodiac*).

le·o·nine″ (lē′ə-nīn″) *adj.* like or pert. to a lion.

leop′ard (lep′ərd) *n.* a large ferocious animal of the cat family.

> **leopard**
> ↔ The name of this animal derives from the misconception that it was a crossbreed of the lion (Late Greek *leon*) and the leopard (*pardos*), though the animal to which the name was originally applied was what we now call a cheetah.

le′o·tard″ (lē′ə-tärd″) *n.* a close-fitting sleeveless garment worn by acrobats and dancers; (also *pl.*) tights.

> **leotard**
> ↔ Named for a 19th-c. French aerialist, Jules *Léotard*.

lep′er (lep′ər) *n.* one afflicted with leprosy.

lep′re·chaun″ (lep′ri-kân″) *n.* a helpful sprite, in Irish folklore, from Old Irish *luchorpán*, little body.

lep′ro·sy (lep′rə-sē) *n.* a chronic bacillic disease of the skin and nerves. —**lep′rous** (-rəs) *adj.*

Les′bi·an (lez′bē-ən) *n.* **1,** a resident of the island of Lesbos. **2,** (*l.c.*) a homosexual female.

lese maj′es·ty (lēz) (*Fr.*) an offense against, or indignity to, a sovereign or state's sovereignty.

le′sion (lē′zhən) *n.* an injury or wound.

less (les) *adv.* to a smaller extent or degree. —*adj.* [**less′er, least**] not so much, so large, or so important; smaller in extent. —*prep.* minus. ❑ *fewer*

-less (-ləs; -les) *suf.* without; lacking.

les·see′ (le-sē′) *n.* one to whom a lease is granted.

less′en (-ən) *v.t. & i.* make or become less.

les′son (les′ən) *n.* **1,** anything learned by study or experience. **2,** a session of instruction. **3,** a reproof or punishment. **4,** a reading from the Bible or other sacred text.

> **lesson**
> ↔ From Latin *lectio*, reading, in reference to a style of teaching that involves extensive reading and memorization.

les′sor (les′ôr) *n.* one who grants a lease.

lest *conj.* for fear that; to avoid.

let *v.t.* [**let, let′ting**] **1,** allow; permit. **2,** lease; rent out; assign. **3,** propose, cause, or do (as in *Let us go*). —*v.i.* be leased or rented. —*adj.* (*Tennis*) of a serve that hits the net and lands in the opponent's service court. —**let on, 1,** divulge. **2,** pretend.

-let *suf.* little.

let′down″ *n.* **1,** a decrease in force or tension. **2,** disappointment.

le′thal (lē′thəl) *adj.* causing death.

leth′ar·gy (leth′ər-jē) *n.* disinclination to move; sluggishness. —**le·thar′gic** (lə-thär′-jik) *adj.* —**le·thar′gi·cal·ly,** *adv.*

let′ter (let′ər) *n.* **1,** a sign representing a voiced sound; one of the characters in writing or printing. **2,** a written communication. **3,** (*pl.*) literature. **4,** literal wording. —*v.t.* mark with letters. —**letter bomb,** a bomb wrapped up and delivered with the mail. —**letter carrier,** one employed to deliver mail. —**letter of credit,** a draft on one bank by another, usually given to a traveler. —**letter of marque** (märk) (*Hist.*) a state's license to a shipowner to confiscate foreign shipping.

let′tered (-ərd) *adj.* **1,** in separate letters, not script. **2,** learned.

let′ter·head″ *n.* a printed heading on letter paper.

let′ter·ing *n.* the letters (usu. handdrawn) in an inscription, etc.

let′ter·man″ (-mən) [*pl.* **-men**], **let′-ter·wom**″**an** *n.* a person who has earned a letter, as for being on a certain team in sports.

let′ter-per′fect *adj.* exactly correct.

let′ter·press″ *n. & adj.* printing by direct impression of inked type on paper.

let′ter·set″ *n.* an offset printing method.

let′tuce (let′əs) *n.* a plant with large green leaves, used in salad.

> **lettuce**
> ↔ Originally, in Latin, *lactuca*, from Latin *lac*, milk, because of the milky substance contained in the stalk of the vegetable.

let′up″ *n.* a pause for rest.

le′u (le′ū) [*pl.* **le′i** (lā)] *n.* the monetary unit of Romania.

leu′co·cyte″ (loo′kə-sīt″) *n.* a white blood corpuscle.

leu·ke′mi·a (loo-kē′mē-ə) *n.* excessive production of white blood corpuscles.

lev *n.* the monetary unit of Bulgaria.

lev′ee (lev′ē) *n.* **1,** an embankment confining a river; a dike. **2,** a social reception, esp. for a large group.

lev′el (lev′əl) *adj.* **1,** being in a horizontal plane. **2,** having a smooth, even surface. **3,** (of two or more things) rising to the same elevation; equal in degree, etc. **4,** uniform; unbroken; even. —*n.* **1,** an imaginary line or plane parallel to the surface of water at rest. **2,** any instrument for determining such a line or plane. **3,** degree of elevation. **4,** a level surface. —*v.t.* **1,** make level. **2,** raze. **3,** aim. —*v.i.* **1,** seek or achieve a level condition. **2,** take aim; direct a purpose. **3,** (*Informal*) be honest or candid. —**lev′el·ness,** *n.*

lev′el·head″ed *adj.* calm and sound in judgment.

lev′er (lev′ər; lē′vər) *n.* **1,** a bar resting on and tending to rotate about a fixed point, the fulcrum, when force is applied at one end. **2,** a means or device used to achieve a desired end; tool.

lev′er·age (-ij) *n.* **1,** the action of a lever; the mechanical advantage it provides. **2,** force; coercion. **3,** speculation using borrowed funds. —*v.i.* to speculate using borrowed funds.

le·vi′a·than (li-vī′ə-thən) *n.* something of huge size, esp. a sea animal or ship.

Le′vi's (lē′vīz) *n.pl.* (*T.N.*) a brand of tight-fitting trousers of blue denim; blue jeans.

lev′i·tate″ (lev′ə-tāt″) *v.i. & t.* float or cause to float in air. —**lev″i·ta′tion,** *n.*

lev′i·ty (lev′ə-tē) *n.* **1,** lack of seriousness; frivolity. **2,** lightness in weight.

lev′y (lev′ē) *v.t.* **1,** assess or collect (taxes). **2,** raise or gather (troops). **3,** stir up; set in motion. —*n.* an assessing or assessment.

lewd (lood) *adj.* lascivious; indecent; obscene. —**lewd′ness,** *n.*

lew′is·ite″ (loo′ə-sīt″) *n.* a gas-producing agent used in chemical warfare, named for the chemist, Winford Lee Lewis, who developed it.

lex′i·cal (lek′si-kəl) *adj.* pert. to diction, vocabulary, or a lexicon.

lex″i·cog′ra·phy (lek″si-kog′rə-fē) *n.* the writing of dictionaries. —**lex″i·cog′ra·pher** (-kog′rə-fər) *n.* —**lex″i·co·graph′ic** (-kō-graf′ik) *adj.*

lex′i·con″ (lek′si-kon″) *n.* **1,** a dictionary. **2,** a special vocabulary. ❑ *dictionary*

Ley′den jar (lī′dən) an early form of electrical condenser or battery.

Lha″sa ap′so (lä″sä äp′sō) a Tibetan breed of terrier with a long, heavy coat.

li″a·bil′i·ty (lī″ə-bil′ə-tē) *n.* **1,** the state of being liable. **2,** a debt; a debit.

li′a·ble (lī′ə-bəl) *adj.* **1,** under legal obligation; responsible; answerable. **2,** affected by a present or future influence,

esp. injurious. **3,** (*Informal*) apt; likely; probable.

li′ai·son″ (lē′ə-zon″; lē-ā′zon) *n.* **1,** contact maintained between independent forces. **2,** (*Informal*) an illicit affair. —**li-aise′** (lē-āz′) *v.i.* act as or establish a liaison between.

li·a′na (lē-ä′nə) *n.* a tropical climbing or twining plant.

li′ar (lī′ər) *n.* one who tells a lie.

lib *n.* (*Informal*) liberation: *women's lib.* —**lib′ber,** *n.*

li·ba′tion (lī-bā′shən) *n.* **1,** a ceremonial pouring out of wine. **2,** (*Informal*) a drink; tippling.

li′bel (lī′bəl) *n.* defamation of a person in writing or printing. —**li′bel·ous,** *adj.*

> **libel, slander**
> ☞ *Libel* is defamation in writing or printing, *slander* is defamation in speech; in informal speech or writing, *libel* will serve for both circumstances.

lib′er·al (lib′ər-əl) *adj.* **1,** favoring progress and reform in social institutions, and the fullest practicable liberty of individual action. **2,** (*cap.*) (*Brit.*) of a certain political party. **3,** tolerant. **4,** not strict. **5,** bountiful; generous. —**lib′er·al·ism,** *n.* —**lib′er·al·ness,** *n.* —**liberal arts,** studies (as language, history, philosophy) providing general knowledge, rather than professional or vocational training.

> **liberal**
> ↔ From Latin *liber*, free; the word once meant generous, tolerant.

lib″er·al′i·ty (lib″ə-ral′ə-tē) *n.* tolerance; generosity.

lib′er·al·ize″ (-īz″) *v.t.* give broader range or greater tolerance to. —**lib″er·al·i·za′tion,** *n.*

lib′er·ate″ (lib′ə-rāt″) *v.t.* set free. —**lib″er·a′tion** (-ā′shən) *n.* —**lib″er·a′tion·ist,** *adj. & n.* —**liberation theology,** a theology stressing liberation from oppression.

lib″er·tar′i·an (lib″ər-tār′ē-ən) *n.* an advocate of the utmost personal freedom. —*adj.* pert. to or advocating such freedom. —**lib″er·tar′i·an·ism,** *n.*

lib′er·tine (lib′ər-tēn″) *n. & adj.* a dissolute or licentious person.

lib′er·ty (lib′ər-tē) *n.* **1,** freedom from bondage, captivity, restraint, etc. **2,** permission granted. **3,** a presumptuous act. —**at liberty,** not engaged; not employed.

li·bid′i·nous (li-bid′ə-nəs) *adj.* lewd; lustful.

li·bi′do (li-bē′dō) *n.* **1,** the will to live; all one's energies and desires. **2,** sexual drive.

Li′bra (lē′brə) *n.* a constellation, the Balance (see *zodiac*).

li′brar″y (lī′brer″ē) *n.* **1,** a collection of books, manuscripts, etc. **2,** a room or building where such a collection is available. —**li·brar′i·an,** *n.* a skilled worker in a library.

---
library
↔ From Medieval Latin *libraria,* from Latin *liber,* book, source word for many English derivatives, including *libretto* and *libel.*

---

li·bret′to (li-bret′ō) *n.* the text or words of a musical composition, esp. an opera. —**li·bret′tist,** *n.* the writer of a libretto.

Lib′ri·um (lib′rē-əm) *n.* (*T.N.*) a brand of chlordiazepoxide, used as a tranquilizer.

lice (līs) *n.* pl. of *louse.*

li′cense (lī′səns) *n.* **1,** permission to do something, esp. a formal authorization; an official permit. **2,** intentional unconventionality, in art. **3,** undue freedom of action or speech. —*v.t.* grant permission for; issue a license to; authorize. —**li″cen·see′** (-sē) *n.* one to whom a license is granted. —**li′cens·er, li′cen·sor,** *n.*

li·cen′ti·ate″ (lī-sen′shē-āt″) *n.* one licensed to practice a profession.

li·cen′tious (li-sen′shəs) *adj.* lewd; dissolute; immoral. —**li·cen′tious·ness,** *n.*

li′chee″ (lē′chē″) *n.* litchi.

li′chen (lī′kən) *n.* any of a variety of mosslike fungoid plants.

lic′it (lis′it) *adj.* lawful. ❏ *lawful*

lick (lik) *v.t.* **1,** pass the tongue over. **2,** stroke lightly. **3,** (*Informal*) thrash; whip; defeat. —*n.* **1,** a stroke with or as with the tongue. **2,** (*Informal*) a hard blow; a vigorous effort. **3,** a natural deposit of salt which animals lick. **4,** (*Informal*) gait.

lick″e·ty-split′ (lik″ə-tē-) *adv.* (*Informal*) extremely fast.

lic′o·rice (lik′ə-ris) *n.* a leguminous plant; its roots, used as flavoring.

---
licorice
↔ Not related to *liquor* (though its spelling was influenced by it), this word comes from Greek *glykurriza,* sweetroot, the plant originally used to flavor the candy.

---

lid *n.* **1,** a movable cover. **2,** eyelid. **3,** (*Slang*) a hat.

li′dar (lī′där) *n.* a device similar to radar using laser pulses instead of radio waves: *li(ght ra)dar.*

lie (lī) *v.i.* [**lay** (lā), **lain** (lān), **ly′ing**] **1,** rest in a recumbent or prostrate position; stretch out horizontally. **2,** be at rest; be buried; remain inactive. **3,** (with *down*) rest, press, weigh, or depend. **4,** be in a specified place, direction, or position; be found or occur. **5,** consist; comprise. **6,** [*pret. & p.p.* **lied**] speak falsely; have a deceitful appearance. —*n.* **1,** relative position, direction, etc. **2,** a falsehood; a false appearance. —**give the lie to,** accuse of lying. —**lie detector,** a polygraph used to determine whether the subject is telling the truth by analyzing his or her reaction to a series of questions. —**lie in,** be confined in childbirth. —**lie to,** (*Naut.*) head into the wind so as to be as stationary as possible.

---
lie, lay
(*Gram.*) Note the following inflected forms, frequently confused: *Lie* (rest), past tense *lay*, past participle *lain*. *Lie* (tell an untruth), past tense and past participle *lied*. *Lay*, past tense and past participle *laid*. The present participles of both words are formed normally by adding *-ing* to the verb.

---

lie′der·kranz″ (lē′dər-krants″) *n.* **1,** a German choral society. **2,** (*cap., T.N.*) a strong, creamy cheese.

lief (lēf) *adv.* willingly; gladly.

liege (lēj) *n.* in feudal custom, a lord or vassal. —*adj.* loyal.

lien (lēn) *n.* the right to hold another's property while pressing a claim against him or her.

lieu (loo) *n.* place; stead.

lieu·ten′ant (loo-ten′ənt; *Brit.* lef-) *n.* **1,** an officer next below the rank of captain (Army) or lieutenant commander (Navy). **2,** assistant; deputy. —**lieu·ten′an·cy** (-ən-sē) *n.* —**lieutenant colonel, commander, general,** officers of the grade next lower than colonel, commander, general, respectively. —**lieutenant governor,** the office in a U.S. state corresponding to vice-president in the U.S. government.

---
lieutenant
↔ Literally, one who holds the place of another, from French *lieu,* place, and *tenant,* holding.

---

life (līf) *n.* **1,** the aggregate of the powers of metabolism, reproduction, mobility, etc. **2,** animals and plants collectively. **3,** duration of existence. **4,** a condition or course of living; career; station. **5,** a biography. **6,** animation; vivacity; vigor. —**life**

belt, life buoy, life jacket, life net, life pre-server, life raft, articles designed to pro-tect one from drowning. —**life insurance,** insurance whose proceeds are payable when the insured person dies. —**life span,** the longest period of expectancy of life.

life′boat″ *n.* a boat in which to escape from a sinking ship.

life′guard″ *n.* one who patrols a beach to rescue bathers in peril.

life′less (-ləs) *adj.* **.1,** without life; dead. **2,** without spirit; dull; listless. —**life′-less·ness,** *n.*

life′line″ *n.* **1,** a cable by which a person can be hauled out of the water. **2,** a vital line of transportation or communication.

life′long″ *adj.* enduring throughout (one's) life.

---

lifelong, livelong

☛ *Lifelong* means specifically lasting the duration of one's life. *Livelong* is more general in use, meaning whole or entire. *Livelong* comes not from *life,* but from Middle English *lefe,* dear.

---

life′man·ship″ (līf′mən-ship″) *n.* the ability to deal successfully with life's problems.

lif′er (lī′fər) *n.* **1,** a person who has spent a lifetime in a certain occupation or the military. **2,** (*Slang*) one sentenced to prison until his death.

life′style″ *n.* a person's particular way of living.

life′time″ *n.* **1,** the duration of one's life. **2,** (*Informal*) a relatively long time. —*adj.* throughout one's life.

life′work″ *n.* the calling or occupation one adopts permanently.

lift *v.t.* **1,** move upward in space; raise; elevate. **2,** exalt. **3,** display; sing loudly with (the voice). **4,** (*Informal*) steal. —*v.i.* **1,** exert lifting force. **2,** rise. —*n.* **1,** the act of raising or rising; the distance, force applied, or weight lifted. **2,** a helping up-ward or onward; a ride. **3,** (*Brit.*) an eleva-tor. **4,** exaltation of feeling.

lift′off″ *n.* of an air- or spacecraft, the act or time of leaving the ground.

lig′a·ment (lig′ə-mənt) *n.* a band of tis-sue connecting bodily parts.

li′gate″ (lī′gāt) *v.t.* bind or join with a ligature.

lig′a·ture″ (lig′ə-chûr″) *n.* **1,** the act of tying up or binding; the band, bandage, etc., used. **2,** a stroke connecting letters, notes in music, etc.; the joint character, as æ.

li′ger (lī′gər) *n.* the offspring of a male lion and a female tiger.

light (līt) *n.* **1,** that which makes things visible; illumination. **2,** the state of being visible. **3,** electromagnetic radiation, esp. that to which the eye is sensitive. **4,** a source of illumination, as a lamp; a lumi-nous body. **5,** daytime. **6,** a window or windowpane. **7,** a means of igniting, as a match. **8,** clarification. **9,** (*pl.*) point of view; principles of conduct. **10,** that which is light. **11,** (*pl.*) lungs of an animal. **12,** an entry in a crossword puzzle. —*adj.* **1,** illuminated, not dark. **2,** pale or whitish in color. **3,** of little weight; not heavy; not heavy enough. **4,** of little density or spe-cific gravity. **5,** moderate. **6,** not burden-some or oppressive; easy. **7,** not serious or profound. **8,** reduced (as in calories, alcoholic content, etc.). —*v.t.* [*pret. & p.p.* **light′ed** or **lit**] **1,** illuminate. **2,** ignite. **3,** (with *up*) make bright. —*v.i.* **1,** catch fire; (often with *up*) become bright. **2,** dis-mount; alight. **3,** come to rest; land. **4,** (with *on*) come or meet by chance. **5,** (*In-formal*) (with *into*) attack. **6,** (with *out*) depart suddenly or quickly. **7,** (with *up*) ignite a cigarette. —**light′ness,** *n.* —**light-emitting diode,** a diode that produces light when a current passes through it. —**light meter,** a photometer. —**light opera,** operetta. —**light pen,** a hand-held light-sensitive pointing device for use with computers.

---

light

↔ The principal senses of this word are of Germanic origin. The word meaning illumination comes from *leukhtam.* Its homonym meaning not heavy comes from the adjective *ling-khtaz,* which also produced English *lung.*

---

light′en (-ən) *v.t. & i.* make or become light or lighter.

light′er (-ər) *n.* **1,** a device for igniting. **2,** a barge or boat for freight.

light′face″ *n.* (*Printing*) a type having thin light lines (opposed to **boldface**).

light-′fin″gered *adj.* addicted to stealing.

light-′foot″ed *adj.* nimble in footwork.

light′head″ed *adj.* **1,** dizzy. **2,** frivolous.

light′heart″ed *adj.* carefree.

light heavyweight a boxer weighing 160 to 175 pounds.

light′house″ *n.* a tower displaying a warning or guiding light.

light′ing *n.* a method or effect of il-lumination.

light′ning (līt′ning) *n.* a sudden flash of

---

tub, cūte, pûll; labəl; oil, owl, go, chip, she, thin, *th*en, sing, ink; *see p. 6*

light by the discharge of atmospheric electricity. —**lightning bug,** firefly. —**lightning rod,** a metal rod designed to ground the charge from a stroke of lightning.

light-'rail'' *adj.* pert. to a type of commuter rapid-transit rail system.

light'some (-səm) *adj.* **1,** cheerful; sportive. **2,** buoyant. —**light'some·ness,** *n.*

light'weight'' *n.* **1,** a boxer weighing 127 to 135 pounds. **2,** (*Informal*) one of small importance or intellect.

light-'year'' the distance a ray of light travels in a year, about 5,880 billion miles.

lig'ne·ous (lig'nē-əs) *adj.* of or like wood.

lig·ni- (lig-nē) *pref.* wood.

lig'ni·fy (lig'nə-fī) *v.t. & i.* make or become woody.

lig'nin *n.* a tissue found in wood.

lig'nite (lig'nīt) *n.* imperfectly formed coal, resembling wood.

like (līk) *v.t.* regard with favor; be pleased with; feel affection toward; enjoy. —*v.i.* feel inclined; wish; choose. —*adj.* **1,** having resemblance; similar; analogous; corresponding. **2,** characteristic of. —*n.* something equivalent or similar. —*adv.* (*Informal*) likely; probably. —*prep.* similar to; in the manner of. —*conj.* (*Informal*) as; as though. —**lik'a·ble,** *adj.* ❑ *as* **-like** *suf.* resembling.

> **-like**
> In compounds, the suffix is usually added without hyphen unless the preceding syllable ends in two *l*'s.

like'li·hood'' (-lē-hûd'') *n.* probability; expectancy.

like'ly (-lē) *adj.* **1,** probably destined to happen or be. **2,** credible. **3,** suitable; preferred. —**like'li·ness,** *n.*

like-'mind''ed *adj.* in agreement.

lik'en (lī'kən) *v.t.* represent as similar; compare.

like'ness (-nəs) *n.* **1,** a picture, etc., esp. a faithful one. **2,** resemblance.

like'wise'' *adv.* **1,** also; moreover. **2,** in like manner.

lik'ing (lī'king) *n.* a feeling of preference, favor, or enjoyment.

li'lac (lī'lək) *n.* **1,** a shrub having large clusters of fragrant flowers. **2,** a pale purple color.

Lil''li·pu'tian (lil''i-pū'shən) *adj. & n.* of minute size; tiny.

lilt *n.* gay, lively rhythm or tone.

lil'y (lil'ē) *n.* any of various bulbous plants with showy bell- or horn-shaped

flowers. —*adj.* **1,** pert. to the lily. **2,** white; pale; fair. **3,** pure; unsullied. —**lily-of-the-valley,** *n.* a type of lily. —**lily pad,** the floating leaf of the water lily.

> **Lilliputian**
> ↔ From *Lilliput,* the imaginary country inhabited by tiny people, in Jonathan Swift's *Gulliver's Travels.*

lil'y-liv''ered *adj.* cowardly.

li'ma (lē'mə) *n.* (*Communications*) the letter *l.* —**li'ma bean** (lī'mə) a bean with a flat, oval seed.

limb (lim) *n.* **1,** a member of an animal body apart from the head and trunk; a leg, arm, wing, etc. **2,** a large branch of a tree. **3,** a projecting part; an outgrowth, offshoot, etc. —**out on a limb,** (*Informal*) in a precarious situation.

lim'ber (lim'bər) *adj.* easily bent; flexible; supple. —*v.t. & i.* make limber; flex; exercise. —*n.* a wheeled carriage of a field gun.

lim'bo (lim'bō) *n.* **1,** a region where certain souls of the dead reside. **2,** fig., a place of oblivion or discord. **3,** a W. Indian dance.

Lim'burg''er (lim'bēr''gər) *n.* a kind of strong, soft cheese: named for a province in the Netherlands.

lime (līm) *n.* **1,** a tropical tree allied to the lemon; its greenish-yellow citrus fruit. **2,** oxide of calcium, prepared from limestone (*quicklime* or *unslaked lime*) used in cement and mortar. **3,** a sticky substance: *birdlime.* —**lim'y,** *adj.*

lime·ade' (līm-ād') *n.* a drink made of lime juice, sweetening, and water.

lime'light'' *n.* a strong light thrown on a stage; hence, publicity.

lim'er·ick (lim'ər-ik) *n.* a five-line stanza used in humorous verse.

> **limerick**
> ↔ The source of this word is the town of Limerick, Ireland, whose name was used in the refrain of a nonsense poem recited communally at social gatherings, in the standard limerick rhyme scheme of *aabba.*

lime'stone'' (līm'stōn'') *n.* rock composed chiefly of calcium carbonate.

lim'ey (lī'mē) *n.* (*Informal; often offensive*) a British sailor or ship.

lim'it *n.* **1,** an extreme point or line; boundary; terminal. **2,** a bound of any kind. —*v.t.* restrict; confine. —**lim''i·ta'-tion,** *n.*

lim'it·ed *n.* an express train. **—limited company,** a corporation.

> **limey**
> ↔ A shortening of *limejuicer*, a British slang term for sailors, based on the legal requirement for them to drink lime juice to avoid scurvy.

limn (lim) *v.t.* draw; portray.

lim'ou·sine" (lim'ə-zēn") *n.* **1,** an enclosed automobile. **2,** a large, luxury automobile driven by a chauffeur. *Slang,* **lim'o** (lim'ō).

> **limousine**
> ↔ From the town of *Limousin*, France, whose shepherds once wore a certain type of long cloak, possibly worn in such a car.

limp *v.i.* **1,** walk with a jerky or lame step. **2,** proceed in a halting, faulty manner. **—***n.* a lame walk or gait. **—***adj.* lacking rigidity or stiffness; flexible; flaccid. **—limp'ness,** *n.*

lim'pet (lim'pət) *n.* a sea mollusk.

lim'pid *adj.* transparent; clear; lucid. **—lim·pid'i·ty, lim'pid·ness,** *n.*

lin'age (līn'ij) *n.* **1,** the number of lines (of something in print). **2,** the amount paid per line (of a story, etc.).

linch'pin" *n.* a pin that holds a wheel on an axle.

lin'den (lin'dən) *n.* a tree with wide heart-shaped leaves.

line (līn) *n.* **1,** a straight mark of little breadth; a band, stripe, furrow, wrinkle, etc. **2,** a string, cord, or rope. **3,** a row or rank. **4,** a row of written or printed letters; a verse of poetry; a short written message. **5,** a connected series. **6,** a boundary or limit. **7,** a connecting wire, pipe, etc. **8,** a railroad, steamship, or other transport service. **9,** a direction; a bearing. **10,** business or occupation. **11,** (*Slang*) flirtatious banter. **12,** (*pl.*) plan of construction or action; words to be spoken in a play. **13,** (*Slang*) a dose of a powdered drug, as cocaine. **—***v.t.* **1,** bring into line; put in a row; mark with lines; delineate. **2,** provide with a lining. **—***v.i.* (often with *up*) form in a row; become aligned. **—line drive,** (*Baseball*), a low, hard-hit ball. **—line of credit,** the maximum amount of credit authorized to a borrower by a lender.

lin'e·age (lin'ē-ij) *n.* **1,** line of descent; family. **2,** linage.

lin'e·al (lin'ē-əl) *adj.* in direct line of descent.

lin'e·a·ment (lin'ē-ə-mənt) *n.* a feature, esp. facial.

lin'e·ar (lin'ē-ər) *adj.* **1,** involving measurement in only one dimension. **2,** composed of or involving lines.

line'back"er *n.* (*Football*) a player stationed behind the linemen.

line'man (-mən) [*pl.* **-men**], **line'wom"an** **1,** one who works on, or with, a line of wire, etc., as of long distance telephone. Also, **lines'man, -wom"an. 2,** (*Football*) a player in the forward line.

lin'en (lin'ən) *n. & adj.* **1,** thread, yarn, or cloth made from flax. **2,** (often *pl.*) articles usu. (or formerly) made of linen, esp. shirts, bedsheets, etc.

lin'er (lī'nər) *n.* **1,** a ship, airplane, etc., of a transport line. **2,** any instrument for drawing lines. **3,** a material for lining. **4,** (*Baseball*), a ball batted almost parallel to the ground; a line drive.

lines'man (līnz'mən) [*pl.* **-men**], **lines'-wom"an** *n.* **1,** (*Sports*) an official who watches boundaries or lines of a playing field. **2,** a lineman or linewoman.

line'up" *n.* an array or combination of persons or things.

ling *n.* a marine food fish.

-ling *suf.* **1,** denoting connection with, as *hireling.* **2,** diminutive, as *duckling.*

lin'ger (ling'gər) *v.i.* **1,** remain beyond a usual or appointed time. **2,** dawdle; delay.

lin"ge·rie' (län"zhə-rā') *n.* women's underclothing.

lin'go (ling'gō) *n.* (*Informal*) argot; lingua franca.

ling'on·ber"ry (ling'ən-ber'ē) *n.* a type of cranberry.

lin'gua fran'ca (ling'gwə frang'kə) **1,** a mixed language used in a number of Mediterranean ports. **2,** any international dialect.

lin'gual (ling'gwəl) *adj.* **1,** pert. to language. **2,** pert. to the tongue.

lin'guist (ling'gwist) *n.* one who knows languages; a polyglot.

lin·guis'tics (ling-gwis'tiks) *n.* the study of the structure and development of language. **—lin·guis'tic,** *adj.* **—lin·guis'ti·cal·ly,** *adv.*

lin'i·ment (lin'ə-mənt) *n.* a soothing liquid medicine for the skin.

lin'ing (lī'ning) *n.* an interior coating or layer.

link *n.* **1,** one of the pieces composing a chain. **2,** something that connects. **3,** a loop. **4,** a surveyor's unit of measure, 7.92 inches. **5,** (*pl.*) a golf course. **—link'age,** *n.*

lin′net (lin′it) *n.* a small Europ. songbird.

li·no′le·um (li-nō′lė-əm) *n.* a floor covering of heavily coated fabric.

Lin′o·type″ (lī′nə-tīp″) *n.* (*T.N.*) a typesetting machine which casts each line as a unit.

lin′sang″ *n.* a civet cat of Java.

lin′seed″ (lin′sēd″) *n.* seed of flax.

lin′sey-wool′sey (lin′zė-wûl′zė) *n.* a cloth of wool and linen or cotton.

lint *n.* small bits of fiber or thread.

lin′tel (lin′təl) *n.* a horizontal beam over a doorway, etc.

li′on (lī′ən) **1,** a large, ferocious cat of Afr. and Asia; esp., the male lion. **2,** a strong, courageous person. **3,** a sought-after person; a celebrity. —**lion′s share,** the largest part.

li′on·ess (-ə-nis) *n.* a female lion.

li′on·heart′ed *adj.* courageous.

li′on·ize″ (-īz″) *v.t.* treat as a celebrity.

lip *n.* **1,** either of the two fleshy parts forming the opening of the mouth. **2,** (*pl.*) speech; utterance. **3,** (*Slang*) impudent talk. **4,** a liplike organ or part; rim; edge. —**lip reading,** the reading of the movements of another's lips, as by a deaf person. —**lip service,** insincere praise or agreement.

li′pase (lī′pās) *n.* an enzyme that breaks down fats into acids and glycerin.

li′po·suc″tion (lī′-pō-) *n.* a procedure in cosmetic surgery for removing excess fat particles from bodily tissue.

lip′stick″ *n.* a stick of cosmetic used to color the lips.

lip-′sync″ (-sink″) *v.t. & i.* **1,** to synchronize recorded sound with lip movements, as of actors in a film. **2,** synchronize lip movements with recorded sound, as in a live performance.

liq′ue·fy″ (lik′wi-fī″) *v.t. & i.* make or become liquid. —**liq″ue·fac′tion,** *n.*

li·ques′cent (li-kwes′ənt) *adj.* **1,** melting; becoming liquid. **2,** tending to melt or liquefy. —**li·ques′cence,** *n.*

li·queur′ (li-kēr′) *n.* a sweet, flavored alcoholic liquor.

---

liqueur, liquor, spirits

☛ *Liquor* is the general term, applying to any distilled alcoholic beverage. *Liqueur* is a sweetish distilled alcoholic drink, usually served following a meal. *Spirits* refers to a strong distilled alcoholic drink.

---

liq′uid (lik′wid) *n.* any fluid substance neither solid nor gaseous. —*adj.* **1,** being

or pert. to a liquid. **2,** like a liquid: clear, transparent, flowing, etc. **3,** in cash or readily convertible to cash. —**li·quid′i·ty** (-ə-tė) *n.* —**liquid-crystal display,** a low-power display using rod-shaped molecules which change direction when a current passes through them. *Abbr.,* **LCD** —**liquid diet,** a diet consisting entirely of liquids.

liq′ui·date″ (lik′wi-dāt″) *v.t. & i.* **1,** pay or settle (debts, etc.); convert to cash. **2,** finally close (business affairs, etc.). **3,** (*Slang*) kill. —**liq″ui·da′tion,** *n.*

liq′uor (lik′ər) *n.* **1,** a distilled alcoholic beverage. **2,** any liquid. ❑ *liqueur*

li′ra (lē′rə) *n.* [*pl.* **li′re** (-rā)] the monetary unit of Italy.

lisle (līl) *adj.* knitted of fine, strong cotton or linen yarn.

lisp *n.* the pronouncing of *s* and *z* like *th.* —*v.t. & i.* so pronounce.

LISP *n.* a computer programming language: *lis(t) p(rocessing).*

lis′some (lis′əm) *adj.* supple.

list *n.* **1,** a record of a number of items; an enumeration. **2,** a leaning to one side, as of a ship. **3,** selvage. **4,** a ridge or furrow. **5,** (*pl.*) an arena for jousts. —*v.t.* make a record of; enter or arrange in a list. —*v.i.* **1,** tilt; careen. **2,** (*Archaic*) like; wish. **3,** (*Archaic*) listen. —**list price,** retail sales price.

lis′ten (lis′ən) *v.i.* **1,** try to hear. **2,** give heed; be compliant.

list′er (lis′tər) *n.* a plow for cutting furrows.

list′less (list′ləs) *adj.* indifferent; languid. —**list′less·ness,** *n.*

lit *v.* pret. & p.p. of *light.* —*adj.* (*Slang*) drunk.

lit′a·ny (lit′ə-nė) *n.* a ceremonial prayer with responses.

li′tchi (lē′chē) *n.* a Chinese tree; its sweet nut. Also, **li′chee.**

lite (līt) *adj.* (*Informal*) light (def. 8).

li′ter (lē′tər) *n.* a liquid measure, about 1.0567 U.S. quarts. Also, **li′tre.**

lit′er·a·cy (lit′ə-rə-sė) *n.* ability to read and write.

lit′er·al (lit′ər-əl) *adj.* **1,** in accordance with the strict meanings of words; not figurative or metaphorical. **2,** (of persons) strict in interpretation; unimaginative; prosaic. **3,** true to fact. **4,** pert. to letters of the alphabet. —**lit′er·al·ism,** *n.*

lit′er·ar·y (lit′ə-rer-ė) *adj.* **1,** pert. to literature. **2,** engaged in writing; learned in literature.

lit′er·ate (lit′ər-ət) *adj.* able to read and write. —*n.* one who is literate.

lit″e·ra′ti (lit″ə-rä′tē) *n.pl.* **1,** learned persons. **2,** the literary class.

lit″er·a′tim (lit″ər-ā′tim) *adj.* (*Lat.*) letter for letter.

lit′er·a·ture (lit′ər-ə-chûr) *n.* **1,** artistic writings. **2,** the aggregate of all writings of a people, period, topic, etc. **3,** literary work. **4,** (*Informal*) printed matter, esp. advertising pamphlets.

lith- *pref.* litho-.

-lith *suf.* stone.

lithe (līth) *adj.* easily bent; pliant; flexible; supple. Also, **lithe′some** (-səm). —**lithe′ness,** *n.*

lith′i·at″ed (lith′ē-ā″tid) *adj.* treated with lithium, which imparts a citrous flavor. —**lith′i·a water** (lith′ē-ə) lithiated water.

lith′i·um (lith′ē-əm) *n.* **1,** a metallic chemical element, no. 3, symbol Li. **2,** a form of lithium used in the treatment of certain mental disorders.

lith·o- (lith-ə) *pref.* stone.

lith′o·graph″ (lith′ə-gråf″) *n.* a print produced by lithography. —**lith″o·graph′ic,** *adj.* —**lith″o·graph′i·cal·ly,** *adv.*

li·thog′ra·phy (li-thog′rə-fē) *n.* printing, now usually by offset, from a stone or equivalent surface of which certain parts are chemically treated to reject ink. —**li·thog′ra·pher,** *n.*

lith′o·sphere″ (lith′ə-sfir″) *n.* the earth's crust.

lit′i·gant (lit′i-gənt) *n.* a disputant at law.

lit′i·gate″ (lit′i-gāt″) *v.i.* & *t.* contest in court. —**lit″i·ga′tion,** *n.*

li·ti′gious (li-tij′əs) *adj.* quick to litigate. —**li·ti′gious·ness,** *n.*

lit′mus (lit′məs) *n.* a substance that changes color in reaction to acid or alkaline presence. —**litmus paper,** a paper used to test for acids and bases. —**litmus test,** a revealing test based on one vital factor.

li′to·tes″ (lī′tə-tēz″) *n.* understatement; esp., a positive statement made by negating its opposite, as *He is not stupid* to mean *He is intelligent.*

lit′ter (lit′ər) *n.* **1,** a number of young brought forth at one birth. **2,** a portable bed. **3,** loose straw, etc., for bedding. **4,** rubbish; disorder. —*v.t.* scatter (things) about.

lit′ter·bug″ (lit′ər-bug″) *n.* (*Slang*) one who litters, esp. in public places.

lit′tle (lit′əl) *adj.* [**less** or **less′er, least** or **lit′tler, -tlest**] **1,** small in size, amount, number, degree, or duration; not large or much. **2,** unimportant; low in station. **3,**

petty; mean. —*adv.* **1,** in small degree; not much. **2,** not at all. —**lit′tle·ness,** *n.*

lit′tle·neck″ *n.* a small edible clam.

lit′to·ral (lit′ə-rəl) *adj.* & *n.* shore.

lit′ur·gy (lit′ər-jē) *n.* a ritual of public worship. —**li·tur′gi·cal** (li-têr′ji-kəl) *adj.*

liv′a·ble (liv′ə-bəl) *adj.* habitable; endurable.

live (liv) *v.i.* **1,** have life, as an animal or plant. **2,** remain alive; survive. **3,** continue in existence, operation, etc. **4,** dwell; reside. **5,** have experience. —*v.t.* pass (a kind of life); experience. —*adj.* (līv) **1,** having life; alive; energetic. **2,** burning; carrying electric current; unexploded (of a shell). **3,** performed at the time; not prerecorded. —**live wire** (līv) **1,** a wire carrying electric current. **2,** (*Slang*) a gogetter.

-lived (-līvd) *suf.* aged; having a specified life or existence.

live′li·hood″ (līv′lē-hûd″) *n.* an occupation that furnishes means of support.

live′long″ (liv′-) *adj.* entire. ❑ *lifelong*

live′ly (līv′lē) *adj.* **1,** full of life. **2,** vivid; bright. **3,** buoyant; elastic. —**live′li·ness,** *n.*

liv′en (lī′vən) *v.t.* & *i.* make or become lively.

liv′er (liv′ər) *n.* **1,** the vital organ that secretes bile, etc. **2,** an animal liver as meat.

liv′er·ied (liv′ər-ēd) *adj.* uniformed.

liv′er·ish (liv′ər-ish) *adj.* **1,** having a disorder of the liver. **2,** disagreeable in manner.

liv′er·wurst″ (liv′ər-wêrst″) *n.* liver sausage.

liv′er·y (liv′ə-rē) *n.* **1,** a uniform, esp. one worn by a domestic servant. **2,** the keeping and letting of horses for hire. —**liv′er·y·man″,** *n.*

live′stock″ (līv′-) *n.* useful domestic animals, esp. cattle.

liv′id *adj.* **1,** dull bluish in color, as a bruise. **2,** (*Informal*) furiously angry. **3,** pallid; ashen. —**liv′id·ness,** *n.*

liv′ing (liv′-) *n.* livelihood; (*Brit.*) a rector's post. —**living room,** a parlor. —**living will,** written directions to physicians whether or not to maintain life-support systems in the event of one's terminal illness.

liz′ard (liz′ərd) *n.* a small four-legged reptile with a long scaly body.

lla′ma (lä′mə) *n.* a large ruminant of So. Amer.; its fine, soft hair. ❑ *lama*

lla′no (lä′nō) *n.* [*pl.* **-nos**] a plain.

lo (lō) *interj.* look!; behold!

load (lōd) *n.* **1,** that which is carried in a conveyance; the amount that can be carried or contained at one time. **2,** a burden; demand of work. **3,** electrical power supplied or required by a machine, etc. **4,** (*Slang*) too much liquor imbibed. —*v.t.* **1,** put a load on or into; fill; charge. **2,** weigh down; burden; encumber; oppress. —*v.i.* take on a load. —**load′ed,** *adj.* (*Slang*) drunk.

load′stone″ *n.* lodestone.

loaf (lōf) *n.* [*pl.* **loaves** (lōvz)] a formed mass of bread, cake, or other food. —*v.i.* & *t.* lounge; idle away time.

> **loaf, loafer**
> ↔ *Loafer* does not derive from *loaf,* but the other way around. The source is German *Landläufer,* tramp. The other meaning of *loaf,* mass of bread, is derived from the Germanic noun **khlaibaz.*

loaf′er (-ər) *n.* **1,** an idler. **2,** a lounging shoe or slipper. ❑ *loaf*

loam (lōm) *n.* **1,** soil rich in organic matter. **2,** a mixture of sand, sawdust, etc., used to make molds.

loan (lōn) *n.* something lent; the act of lending. —*v.t.* & *i.* (*Informal*) lend. —**loan shark,** a usurer.

> **loan, lend**
> (*Gram.*) Generally accepted "good" usage prefers *lend* for the verb sense, although *loan* is widely used as well.

loath (lōth) *adj.* reluctant.

loathe (lōth) *v.t.* hate; detest. —**loath′ing,** *n.* aversion, disgust, or hatred. —**loath′some,** *adj.* hateful.

lob *v.t.* & *i.* [**lobbed, lob′bing**] strike or toss a ball so that it moves slowly in a high arc. —*n.* such a toss.

lob′by (lob′ė) *n.* **1,** a vestibule or anteroom. **2,** persons who seek to influence legislators. —*v.i.* solicit the support of legislators. —**lob′by·ist,** *n.*

lobe (lōb) *n.* a globular or rounded part, esp. of the ear or lung. —**lo′bar** (-ər) *adj.*

lob′lol·ly (lob′lol-ė) *n.* a bay or pine tree.

lo′bo (lō′bō) *n.* a large gray wolf of eastern U.S.

lo·bot′o·my (lō-bot′ə-mė) *n.* surgical cutting of brain tissue.

lob′ster (lob′stər) *n.* an edible marine crustacean having two large claws. —**lobster shift,** the working hours from midnight to 8 a.m.

lob′ule (lob′ūl) *n.* a small lobe, esp. of the brain. —**lob′u·late** (-yə-lət) *adj.*

lo′cal (lō′kəl) *adj.* **1,** pert. to situation in space; occurring in or particular to a specified place. **2,** (of a train, bus, etc.) stopping at many or all stations. —**local color,** the customs, speech, etc. of a region utilized in fiction.

lo-′cal″ (lō′kal″) *adj.* (*Informal*) low in calories.

lo·cale′ (lō-kal′) *n.* the scene of specified events.

lo·cal′i·ty (-kal′ə-tė) *n.* a place; community; section.

lo′cal·ize (-īz″) *v.t.* restrict to a particular place. —**lo″cal·i·za′tion,** *n.*

lo′cate (lō′kāt) *v.t.* **1,** discover or describe the place or locality of. **2,** establish in a particular place; settle. —**lo·ca′tion,** *n.* —**on location,** of a motion picture, advertisement, etc., photographed or recorded at the actual place depicted, not in a studio.

loc′a·tive (lok′ə-tiv) *adj.* & *n.* (*Gram.*) denoting a case that indicates place.

loch (lokh) *n.* (*Scot.*) a lake.

lock (lok) *n.* **1,** a device that fastens and prevents the opening, detachment, movement, etc. of a door, part, etc.; a catch or brake. **2,** a boxlike enclosure in a watercourse, with gates at each end, for moving boats from one level to another. **3,** any of various wrestling holds. **4,** a tress of hair; (*pl.*) hair of the head. —*v.t.* **1,** fasten, secure, or arrest. **2,** close (a lock). **3,** (with *up* or *in*) shut in; confine; isolate. **4,** (with *out*) exclude forcibly. **5,** fix or unite firmly. —*v.i.* **1,** become locked. **2,** to track a target, as with radar. —**lock′age** (-ij) *n.* a system of locks; the fee paid to use them. —**lock nut,** a nut designed not to come loose.

lock′box″ a strongbox or other locked container; esp., a locked box containing cable television decoding equipment.

lock′down″ *n.* confining prisoners to their cells, usu. as the result of a prison disturbance.

lock′er (-ər) *n.* a cabinet that can be locked.

lock′et (-it) *n.* a hinged case worn on a necklace.

lock′jaw″ *n.* tetanus.

lock′out″ *n.* the closing of a plant by an employer to force workers' compliance.

lock′smith″ *n.* a skilled worker on locks.

lock′step″ *n.* **1,** a style of military marching in which the steps are closely coordinated. **2,** an inflexible process.

lock′up″ *n.* (*Informal*) a jail.

---

fat, fāte, fär, fāre, fâll, ȧsk; met, hē, hėr, maybė; pin, pīne; not, nōte, ôr, tool

lo′co (lō′kō) *adj.* (*Slang*) crazy, as from eating locoweed, an intoxicating plant.

lo″co·mo′tion (lō″kə-mō′shən) *n.* **1,** the act or power of moving from place to place. **2,** a type of disco dance.

lo″co·mo′tive (-tiv) *adj.* pert. to or having the power of locomotion. —*n.* the self-propelled vehicle that pulls a railroad train.

lo″co·mo′tor (-tər) *adj.* pert. to locomotion. —**locomotor a·tax′i·a** (ə-tak′sē-ə) a form of paralysis.

lo′co·weed″ *n.* a plant of Central Amer. containing a poison that produces temporary mental imbalance.

lo′cum te′nens (lō′kəm ten′inz) (*Lat.*) a temporary substitute.

lo′cus (lō′kəs) *n.* [*pl.* **lo′ci** (lō′kē)] a place; locality.

lo′cust (lō′kəst) *n.* **1,** a variety of voracious grasshoppers or cicadas. **2,** a thorny, white-flowered tree.

lo·cu′tion (lō-kū′shən) *n.* style of speech; a phrase or expression.

lode (lōd) *n.* a mineral deposit or vein, esp. of metal ore.

lo′den (lō′dən) *n.* a woolen overcoat or outer jacket. Also, **loden coat.**

lode′star″ (lōd′stär″) *n.* a star that serves to guide, esp. Polaris.

lode′stone″ *n.* a mineral having magnetic attraction for iron. Also, **load′stone″.**

lodge (loj) *n.* **1,** a habitation. **2,** a fraternal society; its place. —*v.t.* **1,** provide lodging for; shelter; harbor. **2,** put in a place; deposit. **3,** file; deposit. —*v.i.* **1,** live in hired quarters. **2,** come to rest in a place. —**lodg′er,** *n.* one living in hired quarters. —**lodg′ing,** *n.* (often *pl.*) quarters hired for residence.

loess (les) *n.* a yellowish loam.

loft (lâft) *n.* **1,** the space directly under the roof of a building. **2,** a large room used for light manufacturing. **3,** a lifting stroke or impetus. —*v.t.* & *i.* send upward; rise.

loft′y (lâf′tē) *adj.* high; elevated; exalted. —**loft′i·ness,** *n.*

log (lâg) *n.* **1,** a bulky piece of timber; a section of the trunk or a large branch of a tree. **2,** a device for measuring the speed and progress of a ship; a record of this: *logbook.* **3,** a record or register. **4,** a stolid or stupid person. **5,** logarithm. —*v.t.* [**logged, log′ging**] **1,** cut into logs. **2,** record. —*v.i.* cut down trees; gather timber. —**log′ger,** *n.* one who cuts trees for lumber. —**log on,** sign on to a computer or computer system. —**log off,** sign off from a computer or computer system.

lo′gan·ber″ry (lō′gən-ber″ē) *n.* a berry similar to a blackberry.

> **loganberry**
> ↔ Named for the Amer. horticulturist James H. *Logan*, who developed the berry.

log′a·rithm (log′ə-ri*th*-əm) *n.* the exponent that must be applied to a fixed number (*base*) to produce a given number. —**log″a·rith′mic** (-mik) *adj.*

> **logarithm**
> ↔ From the Greek word *logos*, word, speech, and also, ratio, and *arithmos*, number. The word was coined by 17th-c. English mathematician John Napier.

loge (lōzh) *n.* a box or area of special seats in a theater.

log′ger·head″ (lâg′ər-hed″) *n.* a stupid person. —**at loggerheads,** engaged in dispute.

log′gia (loj′ə) *n.* a gallery or partly open room.

log′ic (loj′ik) *n.* the science of correct reasoning. —**lo·gi′cian** (lō-jish′ən) *n.*

log′i·cal (loj′i-kəl) *adj.* reasonable; persuasive; to be expected.

lo·gis′tics (lō-jis′tiks) *n.* (*Mil.*) the science of transport and supply. —**lo·gis′tic,** *adj.* —**lo·gis′ti·cal·ly,** *adv.*

log′jam″ *n.* **1,** a crowded mass of logs in a river. **2,** an impasse in work, negotiations, etc.

log′o·gram″ (lo′gə-gram″) *n.* a symbol standing for a frequently used word or phrase, such as & for *and.*

log′o·type″ (log′ə-tīp″) *n.* (*Printing*) a single piece of type containing two or more letters, a trademark, company symbol, etc. Also, **lo′go** (lō′gō).

log′roll″ing *n.* **1,** the rolling of floating logs with the feet. **2,** (*Informal*) the trading of favors among politicians.

-logue (lâg) *suf.* speech or writing. Also, **-log.**

lo′gy (lō′gē) *adj.* sluggish; dull.

loid *v.t.* (*Slang*) open a spring-locked door with a plastic card.

loin *n.* the part of a body between the lower ribs and hipbone; meat from this part of an animal. —**loin′cloth″,** *n.* a cloth worn around the hips.

loi′ter (loi′tər) *v.i.* **1,** linger idly. **2,** waste time; delay; lag.

loll (lol) *v.i.* lean or lie in a languid, indolent manner.

lol·la·pa·loo'za (lol'ə-pə-loo'zə) *n.* (*Slang*) something admirable or remarkable.

lol'li·pop" (lol'ė-pop") *n.* a kind of hard candy on the end of a stick.

lol'ly·gag" (lol'ė-gag") *v.i.* lallygag.

Lon'don broil (lun'dən) beefsteak served broiled and sliced.

lone (lōn) *adj.* **1,** being alone; solitary; isolated. **2,** unmarried.

lone'ly (-lė) *adj.* **1,** remote from other habitations. **2,** [also, **lone'some**] dejected from being alone. —**lone'li·ness, lone'-some·ness,** *n.*

lo'ner (lō'nər) *n.* (*Informal*) a person liking or living in solitude.

long (lâng) *adj.* **1,** having great extent in time or space. **2,** having a specified length or duration. **3,** far away; distant in time. **4,** tall; great in amount, number, or ratio. —*adv.* **1,** to a protracted extent, esp. in time. **2,** to a specified extent. —*n.* **1,** a long time. **2,** something long. —*v.i.* feel a strong desire; yearn; hanker. —**long distance,** telephone service between different cities. —**long face,** an expression of dejection or depression. —**long green,** (*Slang*) paper money. —**long jump,** an athletic contest; broad jump. —**long shot,** an entry, venture, etc., not very likely to win or to succeed. —**long ton,** 2,240 pounds.

long'boat" *n.* the principal boat carried aboard a merchant vessel.

long-'drawn" *adj.* prolonged. Also, **long-'drawn-'out'.**

lon·ge'vi·ty (lân-jev'ə-tė) *n.* duration of life; long life.

long'hair" *n. & adj.* (*Informal*) overly intellectual or refined.

long'hand" *n.* ordinary handwriting.

long'horn" *n.* a kind of cattle.

long'ing *n.* prolonged desire.

lon'gi·tude" (lon'jə-tūd") *n.* distance on the earth's surface east or west of a given meridian, esp. that of Greenwich. —**lon"-gi·tu'di·nal,** *adj.* ☐ *latitude*

long play (*T.N.*) a 12-inch 33-1/3 r.p.m. phonograph record. *Abbr.*, **LP.** —**long'-play"ing,** *adj.*

long-'range" *adj.* designed to travel long distances.

long'shore'man [*pl.* **-men**] (-mən), **long'shore'wom"an** *n.* one who loads or unloads ships.

long-stand"ing *adj.* existing or continuing for a long time.

long-'suf"fer·ing *adj.* bearing injuries or provocations with patience.

long-'term" *adj.* having a relatively long duration.

long'time" *adj.* long-standing.

long-'wind"ed *adj.* tediously long (of a speech, etc.). —**long'wind"ed·ness,** *n.*

loo *n.* **1,** a popular Eng. card game. **2,** (*Informal, Brit.*) toilet.

loo'ey (loo'ė) *n.* (*Slang*) lieutenant. Also, **loo'ie.**

loo'fah (loo'fə) *n.* **1,** a tropical vine of the gourd family; its fruit. **2,** dried material from the loofah gourd, used as a sponge.

look (lûk) *v.i.* **1,** use the eyes; exercise the power of vision. **2,** afford a view or outlook. **3,** keep watch; take heed. **4,** expect or hope (for). **5,** appear. —*v.t.* **1,** (usually with *up*) try to find. **2,** suggest by a look or appearance. —*n.* **1,** a visual examination or search. **2,** the act of looking. **3,** (often *pl.*) outward appearance or aspect. —**look'ing glass,** a mirror. —**look sharp,** be alert or careful.

look'er *n.* **1,** a watcher. **2,** a handsome person. —**look"er-on',** *n.* a spectator.

look'out" *n.* **1,** a watch kept; a watchman; his post. **2,** (*Informal*) an object of care or concern.

look-'see" *n.* (*Informal*) a look.

loom *n.* a machine for weaving cloth from yarn or thread. —*v.t.* weave on a loom. —*v.i.* **1,** come into view indistinctly. **2,** seem large or portentous.

loon *n.* **1,** a fish-eating diving bird. **2,** a stupid person.

loon'y *adj. & n.* (*Informal*) crazy. —**loony bin,** (*Slang*) an insane asylum.

loop *n.* **1,** a portion of rope, ribbon, etc., doubled back on itself to form an open eye. **2,** something of similar shape. **3,** (*Computers*) a series of commands which are repeated until a certain condition is met. —*v.t.* form a loop in; make into a loop; encircle with a loop. —*v.i.* move in a loop. —**looped** (loopt) *adj.* (*Informal*) drunk. —**loop'y,** *adj.* (*Slang*) eccentric or crazy. —**the Loop,** Chicago, IL.

loop'hole" *n.* **1,** an opening to fire an arrow or gun through or to admit light. **2,** any means of escape or evasion, esp. a means of evading a law.

loose (loos) *adj.* **1,** free from fetters or restraint; joined slackly or not at all; not tight or close; not bundled. **2,** open or porous. **3,** slack; diffuse; not concise. **4,** wanton; dissolute. —*v.t.* **1,** make loose; set free; release; untie. **2,** relax. —**loose'ness,**

n. —**at loose ends,** unoccupied; disorderly.

---

loose, loosen, lose
☞ Do not confuse these three words. *Loose* is an adjective meaning free or relaxed and a verb meaning to set free. *Lose* is a verb meaning to mislay or to be defeated. *Loosen* is also a verb, meaning to make or become loose.

---

loose-'leaf″ *adj.* having leaves or sheets which can be removed easily.

loos'en (loo′sən) *v.t. & i* make or become loose or looser. ❏ *loose*

loot *n.* booty seized in war; plunder; spoils; something stolen. —*v.t.* pillage; rob. —**loot′er,** *n.*

lop *v.t.* [**lopped, lop′ping**] **1,** cut off; trim by cutting off superfluous parts. **2,** let droop. —*v.i.* droop.

lope (lōp) *v.i.* move with a long, easy stride; canter. —*n.* this gait.

lop′sid″**ed** (lop′sī″did) *adj.* heavier on, or leaning to, one side. —**lop′sid**″**ed·ness,** *n.*

lo·qua′cious (lō-kwā′shəs) *adj.* talkative. —**lo·quac′i·ty** (-kwas′ə-tē) *n.*

lo′ran (lôr′an) *n.* an electronic device by which a navigator can determine his or her position from radio signals: *lo(ng) ra(nge) n(avigation).*

lord (lôrd) *n.* **1,** a master; a nobleman: a title of rank. **2,** (*cap.*) God; Jesus Christ. —**lord′ling,** *n.* a minor nobleman. —**lord′-ship,** *n.*

---

lord
↔ From Old English *hlafweard,* loaf-keeper, which was gradually shortened till it achieved its present form.

---

lord′ly (-lē) *adj.* **1,** imperious; insolent. **2,** befitting a lord; magnificent. —**lord′li-ness,** *n.*

lore (lôr) *n.* the store of knowledge about a particular subject.

lor′e·lei″ (lôr′ə-lī″) *n.* a siren (def. l).

lor·gnette′ (lôr-nyet′) *n.* eyeglasses mounted on a handle.

lor′i·keet″ (lôr′ə-kēt″) *n.* a small parrot, a kind of lory.

lorn (lôrn) *adj.* forsaken; desolate (*obs.* except in compounds, as *lovelorn*).

lor′ry (lor′ē) *n.* a truck, esp. (*Brit.*) a motor truck.

lo′ry (lôr′ē) *n.* a small Pacific parrot.

lose (looz) *v.t.* [*pret. & p.p.* **lost**] **1,** miss and not know where to find. **2,** be deprived of; be parted from. **3,** cease to have. **4,** cause or suffer defeat in (a game).

—*v.i.* suffer loss; be defeated. —**los′er,** *n.* ❏ *loose*

loss (lâs) *n.* **1,** failure to hold, keep, or preserve. **2,** that which is lost. **3,** wastage. **4,** defeat; ruin. —**at a loss,** bewildered; uncertain. —**loss leader,** an item sold at a loss to attract customers.

lost (lâst) *adj.* **1,** no longer possessed. **2,** wasted. **3,** unable to find one's way. —*v.* pret. & p.p. of *lose.* —**lost generation,** (*Hist.*) post-World War I expatriate Americans, esp. those living in Paris.

lot *n.* **1,** a station or condition determined by chance or destiny. **2,** a means of deciding something by chance. **3,** a distinct portion or parcel, esp. of land. **4,** (*Informal*) a great many; a great deal.

lo·thar′i·o (lō-thä′rē-ō) *n.* a seducer.

---

lothario
↔ A character in the play *The Fair Penitent* (1703) by Nicholas Rowe.

---

lo′tion (lō′shən) *n.* a liquid medicine for the skin.

lot′ter·y (lot′ə-rē) *n.* a method of selling numbered tickets and awarding prizes to the holders of certain numbers drawn by lot.

lot′to (lot′ō) *n.* a kind of lottery game; bingo.

lo′tus (lō′təs) *n.* **1,** a plant of Greek legend, possibly a jujube shrub or nettle tree. **2,** any of a variety of water lilies. **3,** a genus of leguminous plants. **4,** a sitting position in yoga, legs crossed over one another.

loud (lowd) *adj.* **1,** strongly audible. **2,** vehement; noisy. **3,** stormy; turbulent. **4,** urgent; emphatic. **5,** excessively showy; overdone. **6,** vulgar in manners or taste. —**loud′ness,** *n.*

loud′mouthed″ (-mowthd″) *adj.* arrogantly talkative. —**loud′mouth**″, *n.*

loud′speak″**er** *n.* a device for amplifying sound to make it widely audible.

Lou Gehr′ig's disease (loo ger′ig) an incurable disease affecting the brain and spinal cord: *amyotrophic lateral sclerosis.*

lounge (lownj) *v.i.* **1,** move or recline listlessly; loll. **2,** pass the time idly. —*n.* **1,** a public waiting room. **2,** a kind of long sofa. **3,** an indolent gait or stooping posture. —**lounge lizard,** (*Slang*) a fop who frequents bars in search of women.

loupe (loop) *n.* a magnifying glass held in the eye, used by jewelers, etc.

louse (lows) *n.* [*pl.* **lice** (līs)] **1,** a small blood-sucking insect; any of various other parasitic insects. **2,** (*Slang*) a contemptible

---

tub, cūte, pûll; labəl; oil, owl, go, chip, she, thin, *th*en, sing, ink; *see p. 6*

person. —*v.t.* (with *up*) (*Slang*) muddle or bungle; execute poorly.

lous'y (low'zė) *adj.* **1,** infested with lice. **2,** (*Slang*) mean or contemptible. **3,** (*Slang*) abundantly supplied. —**lous'i-ness,** *n.*

lout (lowt) *n.* an awkward, uncouth, or boorish fellow. —**lout'ish,** *adj.*

lou'ver (loo'vər) *n.* a slit, esp. one of a number serving as air vents.

love (luv) *n.* **1,** strong affection for another person, esp. of the opposite sex. **2,** an object of affection; a sweetheart. **3,** any strong liking or affection. **4,** (in games) a score of zero. —*v.t. & i.* have love, affection, or liking for. —**lov'a·ble,** *adj.* —**love seat,** a settee for two.

> **love**
> ↔ The sense of no score, as in tennis, derives from the principal meaning of the word, strong affection, as used in the phrase "play for love," i.e., for nothing. The source is Old English *lufu*, from the Indo-European root **leubh-*.

love'bird" *n.* **1,** a kind of parrot or parakeet, remarkable for the affection it shows its mate. **2,** (usu. *pl.*) lovers.

love'lorn" *adj.* forsaken by a loved one.

love'ly (-lė) *adj.* beautiful; delightful. —**love'li·ness,** *n.*

lov'er (luv'ər) *n.* **1,** one who loves, esp. a man who loves a woman. **2,** a sexual partner, esp. in an extramarital affair. **3,** one with a special liking for something.

love'sick" *adj.* disconsolate because of unrequited love.

lov'ing *adj.* very affectionate. —**loving cup,** a large cup from which many can drink; such a cup used as a trophy.

low (lō) *adj.* **1,** situated not far above the ground or base; not high; below a usual or standard level. **2,** deep. **3,** prostrate or dead. **4,** not high in scale, quality, or degree; moderate; simple. **5,** inferior. **6,** base; mean; coarse. **7,** not many in number. **8,** not loud; soft; feeble. **9,** dejected; depressed. —*adv.* **1,** in a low position, degree, etc. **2,** cheaply. **3,** in low tone or pitch; quietly. —*n.* **1,** that which is low. **2,** a low point; a time or feeling of depression. **3,** (*Meteorol.*) a low-pressure area. **4,** the lowest gear ratio for forward progress in an automobile transmission. **5,** the sound uttered by cattle. —*v.i.* sound or utter as cattle do; moo. ❏ *high*

low'ball" *n.* a variety of draw poker in which the lowest hand wins. —*v.t. & i.*

intentionally make a lower estimate for a service than one intends to charge.

low'boy" *n.* a chest of drawers on short legs.

low'brow" *adj.* (*Slang*) having low intellectual tastes. —*n.* a lowbrow person.

low'down" (*Slang*) *adj.* contemptible. —*n.* inside information.

low'er (lō'ər) *v.t.* **1,** cause to descend; take down. **2,** reduce; degrade; humble; humiliate. —*v.i.* **1,** decrease. **2,** descend; sink. —**low'er·case',** *adj.* in letters not capitals.

low'er (low'ər) *v.i.* **1,** scowl; frown. **2,** appear dark and threatening.

low-'key" *adj.* low in intensity; restrained.

low'land (lō'lənd) *n.* territory low in elevation.

low'ly (lō'lė) *adj.* humble. —**low'li·ness,** *n.* ❏ *high*

low-'mind"ed *adj.* having a vulgar mind. —**low-'mind"ed·ness,** *n.*

low-'rise" *adj.* having few stories and not equipped with elevators.

low-'spir"it·ed (-id) *adj.* dejected; depressed. —**low-"spir'it·ed·ness,** *n.*

lox (loks) *n.* smoked salmon.

loy'al (loi'əl) *adj.* **1,** faithful; constant in devotion or regard. **2,** manifesting fidelity. —**loy'al·ist,** *n.* one who remains loyal to a government during a rebellion. ❏ *legal*

loy'al·ty (-tė) *n.* state of being loyal; fidelity.

loz'enge (loz'ənj) *n.* **1,** a sweet pill. **2,** a diamond-shaped figure.

lu'au (loo'ow) *n.* a Hawaiian feast.

lub'ber (lub'ər) *n.* a clumsy or stupid fellow; an unskillful sailor. —**lub'ber·ly,** *adj.*

lube (loob) (*Slang*) *n.* lubrication. —*v.t.* lubricate.

lu'bri·cant (loo'bri-kənt) *n.* a material for lubricating, as grease.

lu'bri·cate" (loo'bri-kāt") *v.t.* **1,** apply oil or grease to. **2,** make slippery. —**lu"bri·ca'tion,** *n.*

lu'bri·cous (loo'bri-kəs) *adj.* **1,** smooth; slippery. **2,** unstable; shifty. **3,** lewd. —**lu·bric'i·ty** (loo-bris'ə-tė) *n.*

lu'cent (loo'sənt) *adj.* shining. —**lu'cence,** *n.*

lu·cerne' (loo-sėrn') *n.* alfalfa.

lu'cid (loo'sid) *adj.* **1,** clear; easily understood; distinct. **2,** sane; rational. **3,** shining. —**lu·cid'i·ty,** *n.*

Lu'cite (loo'sīt) *n.* (*T.N.*) an acrylic plastic having unusual transparency and properties of light transmission.

luck (luk) *n.* **1,** a trend of chance events. **2,** good fortune.

luck′y (-ė) *adj.* **1,** bringing good fortune; favorable. **2,** fortunate. **3,** chance; fortuitous. —**luck′i·ness,** *n.*

lu′cra·tive (loo′krə-tiv) *adj.* yielding gain; profitable.

lu′cre (loo′kər) *n.* money; profit (usually contemptuous).

lu′cu·brate″ (loo′kyû-brāt″) *v.i.* work or study laboriously, esp. at night. —**lu″cu·bra′tion,** *n.*

Lud′dite (lud′īt) *n.* one of a group of workers in early 19th-c. England militantly opposed to mechanization, named for their leader and originator, 18th-c. British worker Ned Ludd.

lu′di·crous (loo′di-krəs) *adj.* absurd; ridiculous. —**lu′di·crous·ness,** *n.*

luff (luf) *v.i.* turn the bow of a ship toward the wind. —*n.* the forward edge of a fore-and-aft sail.

lug *v.t. & i.* [**lugged, lug′ging**] carry or drag with effort. —*n.* **1,** a yank, tug, or haul. **2,** a projecting earlike part; a tab, flange, or cam. **3,** a sluggish fellow.

luge (loozh) *n.* **1,** a small sled. **2,** an Olympic sledding event.

lug′gage (lug′ij) *n.* trunks, valises, etc.; baggage.

lug′ger (lug′ər) *n.* a vessel rigged with lugsails. —**lug′sail″,** *n.* a quadrilateral sail.

lu·gu′bri·ous (loo-gū′brė-əs) *adj.* mournful; doleful; dejected. —**lu·gu′bri·ous·ness,** *n.*

lug′worm″ *n.* an annelid marine worm much used for bait.

luke′warm″ (look′wôrm″) *adj.* **1,** tepid; unenthusiastic. —**luke′warm″ness,** *n.*

lull (lul) *v.t.* soothe; assuage; calm. —*v.i.* become quiet; subside. —*n.* a period of temporary quiet or rest.

lull′a·by″ (lul′ə-bī″) *n.* a song to lull a child to sleep.

lu′lu″ (loo′loo″) *n.* (*Slang*) an exceptional person or incident.

lum·ba′go (lum-bā′gō) *n.* rheumatic pain in muscles of the back.

lum′bar (lum′bər) *adj.* pert. to the loins.

lum′ber (lum′bər) *n.* timber sawed or split for use. —*v.i.* walk clumsily.

lum′ber·jack″ *n.* one who cuts trees for lumber.

lum′ber·yard″ *n.* a place where building materials, esp. lumber, are sold.

lu′men (loo′mən) *n.* [*pl.* **lu′mi·na** (-mi-nə)] a unit of light flow.

lu′mi·nar·y (loo′mə-ner-ė) *n.* **1,** a celestial body, as the sun; a light. **2,** one who enlightens mankind. **3,** a celebrity; prominent person.

lu″mi·nes′cence (loo″mə-nes′əns) *n.* emission of light without heat. —**lu″mi·nesce′,** *v.i.* —**lu″mi·nes′cent,** *adj.*

lu′mi·nous (loo′mə-nəs) *adj.* **1,** giving out light. **2,** bright; resplendent. **3,** clear; lucid. **4,** intellectually brilliant. —**lu·mi·nos′i·ty** (-nos′ə-tė) *n.*

lum′mox (lum′əks) *n.* (*Informal*) a clumsy or stupid person.

lump *n.* **1,** a mass of solid matter with no particular shape. **2,** a protuberance, knob, or swelling. **3,** a dull, stolid person. —*adj.* in the form of a lump. —*v.t.* work into a mass; deal with as a whole. —*v.i.* **1,** form a lump. **2,** move heavily. —**lump′y, lump′ish,** *adj.* —**lump it,** endure something disagreeable.

lump·ec′to·my (lum-pek′tə-mė) *n.* surgical removal of a breast tumor.

lum′pen·pro″le·tar′i·at (lum′pən-prō″li-târ′ė-ət) *n.* (*Ger.*) the unskilled working class.

lu′na·cy (loo′nə-sė) *n.* insanity.

lu′nar (loo′nər) *adj.* pert. to the moon.

lu′na·tic (loo′nə-tik) *n.* a crazy person. —*adj.* crazy. —**lunatic fringe,** (*Informal*) those who espouse the most extreme causes, cults, and isms.

> **lunatic**
> ↔ From Latin *luna*, moon, from the idea that the phases of the moon affect a person's behavior.

lunch *n.* **1,** a midday meal. **2,** any light meal. —*v.i.* eat a lunch.

> **lunch, luncheon**
> ↔ It is unclear which word came first. *Lunch* originally meant a slice of food (perhaps from Spanish *lonja*, slice); a *luncheon* was a snack made of *lunches.* Our present word *lunch* may well have been derived later from *luncheon.*

lunch′eon (lun′chən) *n.* lunch.

lun″cheon·ette′ (-et′) *n.* a modest restaurant. Also, **lunch′room″.**

lune (loon) *n.* a figure bounded by two arcs of circles; a crescent. —**lu′nate** (-nāt) *adj.* —**lu·nette′** (-net′) *n.* something crescent-shaped.

lung *n.* one of the two large spongy organs of breathing in man and the higher vertebrates. —**iron lung,** a chamber to assist respiration by alternate pulsations of high and low air pressure.

lunge (lunj) *n.* a sudden forward movement. —*v.i.* so move.

lunk'head'' *n.* (*Informal*) a blockhead.

lu'pine (loo'pin) *adj.* pert. to a wolf.

lu'pus (loo'pəs) *n.* a bacterial skin disease.

lurch (lẽrch) *v.i.* sway suddenly to one side; list; stagger. —*n.* **1,** an act of lurching. **2,** an untenable situation; bad defeat in a game.

lure (lûr) *n.* something used to allure, entice, or trap; a bait or decoy. —*v.t.* entice.

lu'rid (lûr'id) *adj.* **1,** lighted up with a fiery glare. **2,** sensational; exaggerated. —**lur'id·ness,** *n.*

lurk (lẽrk) *v.i.* **1,** lie in concealment; exist unperceived or unsuspected. **2,** skulk; slink.

lus'cious (lush'əs) *adj.* very pleasing to taste or smell; delightful. —**lus'cious·ness,** *n.*

lush *adj.* **1,** fresh and juicy. **2,** luxuriant. —*n.* (*Slang*) a drunkard. —**lush'ness,** *n.*

lust *n.* intense longing for possession or enjoyment; passionate or lewd desire. —*v.i.* feel lust. —**lust'ful,** *adj.* feeling lust; lecherous.

lus'ter (lus'tər) *n.* **1,** the quality of shining with light emitted or reflected; radiance; glitter. **2,** a glossy finish. **3,** distinction; brilliancy. Also, **lus'tre.** —**lus'trous,** *adj.*

lust'y (lus'tè) *adj.* vigorous; robust; healthy; lively. —**lust'i·ness,** *n.*

lute (loot) *n.* a medieval musical instrument similar to a mandolin. —**lu'ta·nist** (loo'tə-nist) *n.*

lu·te'ti·um (loo-tē'shė-əm) *n.* a rare-earth metallic element, no. 71, symbol Lu.

Lu'ther·an (loo'*th*ə-rən) *adj. & n.* pert. to the Protestant Church founded by Martin Luther.

lux (luks) *n.* [*pl.* **lu'ces** (loo'sėz)] the international unit of illumination.

lux·u'ri·ant (lug-zhûr'ė-ənt) *adj.* **1,** growing or producing in abundance; plentiful; profuse. **2,** florid; superabundant. —**lux·u'ri·ance,** *n.*

lux·u'ri·ate'' (lug-zhûr'ė-āt'') *v.i.* enjoy luxury or abundance. —**lux·u''ri·a'tion,** *n.*

lux·u'ri·ous (lug-zhûr'ė-əs) *adj.* characterized by luxury.

lux'u·ry (luk'shə-rè) *n.* **1,** abundant means of self-indulgence. **2,** something enjoyable but not necessary; a delicacy.

-ly (-lė) *suf.* **1,** in a specified manner: forming adverbs, as *blindly.* **2,** like: forming adjectives, as *saintly.*

ly'can·thrope'' (lī'kən-thrōp'') *n.* a werewolf; an insane person who imagines himself to be a wolf. —**ly·can'thro·py** (līkan'thrə-pė) *n.*

ly·ce'um (lī-sè'əm) *n.* **1,** a literary association. **2,** a lecture hall.

---
lyceum
↔ From Greek *Lykeion*, a grove near Athens, from *Lykeios*, literally, wolf-slayer, an epithet for the god Apollo, whose temple stood near the grove.
---

lye (lī) *n.* a caustic solution of any alkaline salt, used in making soap.

ly''ing-in' *adj.* confinement in childbirth.

Lyme disease (līm) an acute inflammation caused by bacteria borne by ticks (named for Lyme, CT).

lymph (limf) *n.* a yellowish alkaline fluid in animal bodies. —**lym'phoid** (-foid) *adj.* —**lymph node,** lymph gland.

lym·phat'ic (lim-fat'ik) *adj.* **1,** pert. to lymph. **2,** sluggish.

lynch (linch) *v.t.* execute (a person) without authority or process of law. —**lynch law,** execution or punishment by an unauthorized mob.

---
lynch
↔ From the expression *lynch law,* from William *Lynch,* an American who established mob-rule tribunals.
---

lynx (links) *n.* a wildcat. —**lynx-'eyed'',** *adj.* having acute eyesight.

---
lynx
↔ The animal is so called because of its keen eyesight, from Greek *lyngx.*
---

ly''on·naise' (lī''ə-nāz') *adj.* esp. of potatoes, cooked with butter, parsley, and onions.

lyre (līr) *n.* a stringed musical instrument of ancient Greece.

lyre'bird'' *n.* an Australian bird.

lyr'ic (lir'ik) *adj.* **1,** pert. to singing; song-like. **2,** concerned with thoughts and feelings; romantic. **3,** (of a voice) delicate in quality and without great range. —*n.* **1,** a lyric poem or song. **2,** (*Informal*) the words of a song. —**lyr'i·cal,** *adj.* —**lyr'i·cist** (-sist) *n.*

-ly·sis (lə-sis) *suf.* disintegration; destruction.

M

M, m (em) **1,** the thirteenth letter of the English alphabet. **2,** Roman numeral for 1,000.

ma (mä) *n.* (*Informal*) mother.

ma'am (mâm; məm) *n.* (*Informal*) a term of address to women; madam.

ma·ca'bre (mə-kä'brə) *adj.* gruesome, as suggestive of the dance of death (*danse macabre*).

---

macabre

↔ From French *danse macabre*, a dance led by Death, a misreading of Middle French *danse macabé*, perhaps meaning dance of the Maccabees, a Jewish dynasty which was slaughtered.

---

mac·ad'am (mə-kad'əm) *n.* a road of crushed stone, usually with an asphalt surface. —*adj.* made of such materials. —**mac·ad'am·ize"** (-īz") *v.t.*

---

macadam

↔ Named for Scottish engineer John L. *McAdam*.

---

mac"a·da'mi·a (mak"ə-dā'mē-ə) *n.* an Australian tree; its hard-shelled, edible fruit (*macadamia nut*).

ma·caque' (mə-käk') *n.* a short-tailed monkey of Asia.

mac"a·ro'ni (mak"ə-rō'nē) *n.* **1,** thin tubes of dried wheat paste, as food. **2,** (*Slang*) a fop.

mac"a·ron'ic *adj.* of verse, mixing Latin with non-Latin words.

mac"a·roon' (mak"ə-roon') *n.* a small sweet cake.

ma·caw' (mə-kâ') *n.* a long-tailed parrot of tropical America.

mace (mās) *n.* **1,** a clublike weapon. **2,** a spice resembling nutmeg. **3,** (*cap., T.N.*) a chemical compound combining tear gas and chemical irritants, used to control riots, etc.

mac'er·ate" (mas'ə-rāt") *v.t.* **1,** separate or soften by digestion or soaking. **2,** make thin. —*v.i.* grow thin; waste away. —**mac"er·a'tion,** *n.*

Mach (mäk) *adv.* in relation to the speed of sound at a given altitude, as *Mach 2* = twice the speed of sound (2 being the Mach number), named for 19th-c. Austrian physicist Ernst Mach.

ma·che'te (mə-shet'ē) *n.* a heavy knife.

Mach"i·a·vel'li·an (mak"ē-ə-vel'ē-ən) *adj.* pert. to Niccolo di Bernardo Machia-velli, Italian statesman, or to his political philosophy of ruthlessness and unscrupulousness.

mach'i·nate" (mak'ə-nāt") *v.t. & i.* plan or plot, esp. with evil intent. —**mach"i·na'-tion,** *n.*

ma·chine' (mə-shēn') *n.* **1,** any device that transfers or converts energy from one form to another, esp. for manufacturing. **2,** an automobile. **3,** a sewing machine. **4,** persons acting together for a common purpose, as a *political machine.* —*v.t.* grind to a smooth finish with a machine. —**machine gun,** a mounted rifle that fires automatically and continuously. —**machine language,** a means of communicating directly with a computer, without the need for translation.

ma·chin'e·ry (mə-shē'nə-rē) *n.* **1,** machines or parts of machines, collectively. **2,** a system, not mechanical, designed to keep anything going.

ma·chin'ist (mə-shē'nist) *n.* a skilled operator of precision machinery; a toolmaker.

ma·chis'mo (mä-chēz'mō) *n.* (*Sp.*) masculinity; virility. ❑ *masochism*

ma'cho (mä'chō) *adj.* exhibiting machismo.

mack'er·el (mak'ər-əl) *n.* a food fish of the No. Atlantic.

mack'i·naw" (mak'ə-nâ") *n.* a short woolen outer coat.

---

mackinaw

↔ A variant spelling of *Mackinac*, a strait and an island in Michigan.

---

mack'in·tosh" (mak'in-tosh") *n.* a raincoat of rubber-coated cloth, named for its inventor, 19th-c. British chemist Charles Macintosh.

ma"cra·mé' (ma"krə-mā') *n.* lacework made of knotted heavy string or cord.

mac'ro (mak'rō) *n.* in computers, a small number of keystrokes which invoke a complex series of instructions.

macro- (mak-rə) *pref.* large; great.

ma"cro·bi·ot'ic (-bī-ot'ik) *adj.* pert. to the use of diet to prolong life. —**mac"ro-bi·ot'ics,** *n.pl,* construed as *sing.*

mac'ro·cosm (mak'rə-koz-əm) *n.* the great world; the universe.

ma'cron (mā'kron) *n.* the diacritical mark indicating a long vowel, as on ā.

mac"ro·scop'ic (mak"rə-skop'ik) *adj.* visible to the naked eye. —**mac"ro·scop'i·cal·ly,** *adv.*

mad *adj.* [**mad'der, -dest**] **1,** mentally deranged; irresponsible; irrational. **2,** of a dog, rabid. **3,** disorderly; ill-advised. **4,** infatuated; in love. **5,** (*Informal*) angry. —**mad′ness,** *n.*

mad′am (mad′əm) *n.* **1,** a polite term of address to a woman. **2,** a woman who operates a brothel. Also (*Fr.*) **ma·dame′** (mȧ-dȧm′) [*pl.* **mes·dames′** (mā-däm′)].

mad′cap″ *adj.* wild; flighty. —*n.* an unrestrained, adventurous person.

mad′den (mad′ən) *v.t.* **1,** make mad. **2,** infuriate.

mad′der (mad′ər) *n.* an herb; a dye, usually red, made from its root.

mad′ding (mad′ing) *adj.* (*Rare*) distracted; raging.

made (mād) *v.* pret. & p.p. of *make.* —*adj.* (*Informal*) **1,** artificially produced. **2,** assured of success.

ma·dei′ra (mə-dir′ə) *n.* a fine fortified wine resembling sherry.

> **madeira**
> ↔ From the *Madeira* Islands, a Portuguese possession off the coast of Africa.

mad′e·leine (mad′ə-lin) *n.* a small, shell-shaped cake.

mad″e·moi·selle′ (mad″mwə-zel′) *n.* [*pl.* **mes″de·moi·selles′** (mād″-)] an unmarried woman; miss.

made-′to-or′der *adj.* made specially for a customer: opposed to *ready-made.*

made-′up′ (mād′up′) *adj.* **1,** invented; fictional. **2,** adorned with cosmetics, as a face. **3,** put together; assembled.

mad′house″ *n.* **1,** a lunatic asylum. **2,** a place in a state of confusion.

mad′man″ [*pl.* **-men″**], **mad′wom″an** *n.* an insane person.

Ma·don′na (mə-don′ə) *n.* a picture or statue of the Virgin Mary.

mad′ras (mad′rəs) *n.* a cotton fabric, usually with a bright-colored design.

mad′ri·gal (mad′ri-gəl) *n.* **1,** a medieval poem or song. **2,** any part song, esp. one without accompaniment.

> **madrigal**
> ↔ From medieval Latin *matricalis*, simple, from Latin *matrix*, womb.

Mae·ce′nas (mī-sē′nəs) *n.* any generous patron of the arts.

> **Maecenas**
> ↔ From the Roman statesman Gaius Cilnius *Maecenas*, a friend of Virgil.

mael′strom (māl′strəm) *n.* a whirlpool; great and destructive agitation.

mae′nad (mē′nad) *n.* **1,** a priestess of Bacchus. **2,** a frenzied woman. —**mae·nad′ic,** *adj.*

maes′tro (mīs′trō) *n.* [*pl.* **-tros**] a master, esp. an eminent musical composer or conductor. Also, *n.fem.,* **maes′tra** (-trä).

Mae West (mā′ west′) an inflatable life jacket.

Ma′fi·a″ (mä′fē-ə) *n.* a Sicilian criminal organization, the Black Hand, active also in other countries. —**ma·fi·o′so** (mä-fē-ō′sō) *n.* a member of the Mafia.

mag′a·zine′ (mag′ə-zēn′) *n.* **1,** a periodical publication, issued not oftener than weekly. **2,** a depository for ammunition. **3,** a storehouse. **4,** a supply chamber, as in a weapon.

> **magazine**
> ↔ All senses ultimately derive from Arabic *makhazin*, storehouses; the journal is a "storehouse of information."

mag′da·lene″ (mag′də-len″) *n.* (*Heb.*, woman of Magdala, Palestine) a reformed prostitute.

ma·gen′ta (mə-jen′tə) *n.* & *adj.* a color or dye, reddish purple.

mag′got (mag′ət) *n.* the larva of an insect; a worm. —**mag′got·y,** *adj.*

Ma′gi (mā′jī) *n.pl.* [*sing.* **Ma′gus** (-gəs)] **1,** the "Three Wise Men," Matt. 2:1–12. **2,** (*l.c.*) priests, in ancient Persia.

mag′ic (maj′ik) *n.* **1,** the pretended art of controlling the supernatural; sorcery. **2,** legerdemain. **3,** charm; enchantment. —*adj.* [also **mag′i·cal**] **1,** as by supernatural agency. **2,** delightful. —**mag′i·cal·ly,** *adv.* —**magic bullet,** a remedy which causes no harmful side effects. —**magic lantern,** a projector. —**magic square,** an arrangement of integers in a square such that the sum of the numbers in each row, column, or diagonal is the same.

ma·gi′cian (mə-jish′ən) *n.* a conjurer.

mag′is·te′ri·al (maj″is-tir′ē-əl) *adj.* **1,** pert. to a magistrate. **2,** authoritative; imperious.

mag′is·trate″ (maj′is-trāt″) *n.* a minor judge or judicial officer. —**mag′is·tra·cy** (-trə-sē) *n.*

mag′ma (mag′mə) *n.* [*pl.* **mag′ma·ta** (-mə-tə)] *n.* (*Geol.*) the mass of molten material below the earth's crust.

mag·nan′i·mous (mag-nan′ə-məs) *adj.* generous; high-minded; noble. —**mag″na·nim′i·ty** (mag″nə-nim′ə-tē) *n.*

mag′nate (mag′nāt) *n.* a person of importance, esp. in industry.

magnate, magnet
☛ Do not confuse these two near-homonyms. A *magnate* is an important person, while a *magnet* is a body which attracts another. ↔*Magnate* comes from Latin *magnus*, large. *Magnet* comes from Greek *Magnēs*, the name for a region of Thessaly, Greece, also the source of *magnesium*, *magnesia* and *manganese*.

mag·ne'sia (mag-nē'zhə) *n.* an oxide of magnesium, used medicinally.

mag·ne'si·um (mag-nē'zhė-əm) *n.* a metallic chemical element, no. 12, symbol Mg.

mag'net (mag'nit) *n.* **1,** a body that attracts iron or steel; a lodestone. **2,** anything that draws persons toward it; an attraction. —**mag·net'ic** (-net'ik) *adj.* —**mag·net'i·cal·ly,** *adv.* —**magnetic field,** a space in which a magnetic force is present, as around a magnet or a conductor carrying an electric current. —**magnetic north,** north as indicated by a magnetic compass, as opposed to true north. —**magnet school,** a school having special programs to attract students throughout a school district. —**magnet train,** a train that runs on a cushion of air supported by magnetic repulsion. ❑ *magnate*

mag'net·ism (mag'nə-tiz-əm) *n.* **1,** the properties of attraction. **2,** charm. **3,** act or result of magnetizing.

mag'ne·tite" (mag'nə-tīt") *n.* an iron ore, often with magnetic properties; lodestone.

mag'net·ize" (mag'nə-tīz") *v.t.* **1,** make a magnet of. **2,** attract; influence.

mag·ne'to (mag-nē'tō) *n.* [*pl.* **-tos**] a generator of electricity by use of magnets.

mag'ne·tron" (mag'nə-tron") *n.* a vacuum tube for producing short radio waves.

mag·ni- (mag-nə) *pref.* large; great.

mag·nif'i·cent (mag-nif'ə-sənt) *adj.* **1,** great in size or extent. **2,** splendid; brilliant. **3,** noble; sublime. —**mag·nif'i·cence,** *n.*

mag·nif'i·co" (mag-nif'i-kō") *n.* a person of high rank or importance.

mag'ni·fy" (mag'nə-fī") *v.t.* **1,** make greater. **2,** make to appear greater. **3,** glorify; extol. —**mag"ni·fi·ca'tion,** *n.* —**mag'-ni·fi"er,** *n.*

mag·nil'o·quent (mag-nil'ə-kwənt) *adj.* affectedly lofty. —**mag·nil'o·quence,** *n.*

mag'ni·tude" (mag'nə-tūd") *n.* **1,** physical greatness; relative size. **2,** importance; moral greatness. **3,** the measure of brightness of a star.

mag·no'li·a (mag-nō'lē-ə) *n.* an evergreen tree with large, fragrant blossoms, named by Linnaeus for French botanist Pierre Magnol.

mag'num (mag'nəm) *n.* **1,** a two-quart wine bottle. **2,** [*pl.* **-na** (-nə)] a wrist bone.

mag'num o'pus (ō'pəs) (*Lat.*) major work; masterpiece.

mag'pie" (mag'pī") *n.* **1,** a noisy bird. **2,** a chattering person.

magpie
↔ The *mag* in *magpie* is the nickname for Margaret. The earlier name of the bird was *pie*, from Latin *pica*.

Mag'yar (mag'yär) *n.* a member of the predominant Hungarian race; the language of Hungary.

ma"ha·ra'jah (mä"hə-rä'jə) *n.* a ruling prince in India. Also, **ma"ha·ra'ja.**

ma"ha·ra'nee (-nė) *n.* a ruling princess in India.

ma·ha·ri'shi (mä-hə-rē'shė) *n.* a spiritual or mystical teacher.

ma·hat'ma (mə-hät'mə) *n.* a sage or saint in Brahmanism.

mah-'jongg" (mä'jâng") *n.* a Chinese game, played with domino-like tiles.

mahl'stick" (mäl'stik") *n.* a stick held by a painter as support for his brush.

ma·hog'a·ny (mə-hog'ə-nė) *n.* a tropical Amer. tree or its hard, reddish-brown wood.

Ma·hom'et·an (mə-hom'ə-tən) *n.* & *adj.* Mohammedan.

ma·hout' (mə-howt') *n.* the keeper and driver of an elephant.

maid (mād) *n.* **1,** a girl; an unmarried woman. **2,** a virgin. **3,** a female servant. —**maid in waiting,** a woman, often of noble birth, attendant on a queen or princess. —**maid of honor,** best woman.

maid'en (mā'dən) *n.* **1,** an unmarried girl or woman. **2,** a virgin. **3,** a new, untried animal or thing; a horse that has not won a race. —*adj.* unmarried; unused; first or earliest. —**maid'en·hood,** *n.* —**maid'en·ly,** *adj.* —**maiden name,** the surname of a woman before marriage. —**maiden voyage,** the first voyage of a ship.

maid'en·hair" (mā'dən-hâr") *n.* a delicate, feathery fern.

maid'en·head" *n.* the hymen.

mail (māl) *n.* **1,** letters or packages sent by post. **2,** the postal system. **3,** flexible armor of metal rings, interlinked. —*v.t.* send by mail. —**mailed,** *adj.* armored.

Mail'gram" *n.* (*T.N.*) a message transmitted electronically to a post office to be delivered as mail from there.

mail·lot' (mä-yō') *n.* (*Fr.*) **1,** tights. **2,** a woman's one-piece bathing suit.

mail'man'' *n.* [*pl.* **-men''**] a letter carrier.

mail-'or''der *adj.* pert. to the business of ordering and delivering goods by mail.

maim (mām) *v.t.* **1,** disable, by wounding or mutilation. **2,** impair.

> **maim, mayhem**
> ↔ Both words derive from Vulgar Latin **mahagnare*, to wound, through Old French.

main (mān) *adj.* **1,** chief; principal. **2,** sheer; utmost; as, by *main strength.* —*n.* **1,** a principal pipe or duct. **2,** the open ocean. **3,** strength; force. —**main'ly,** *adv.* chiefly. —**main drag,** (*Slang*) the principal street of a town. —**main line, 1,** a principal highway, railroad line, etc. **2,** (*Slang*) a principal vein.

main'frame'' *n.* a large computer.

main'land (-lənd) *n.* a principal mass of land; a continent.

main'line'' *v.i.* (*Slang*) inject a narcotic drug into a principal vein.

main'mast (-məst) *n.* the principal mast of a ship. —**main'sail** (-səl) *n.* the principal sail of a ship.

main'spring'' *n.* **1,** the principal spring in a watch. **2,** chief source or motive.

main'stay'' *n.* a chief support.

main'stream'' *n.* the predominant current or tendency of a movement, discipline, etc. —*v.t.* put (handicapped students) in regular classes. —**main'stream''ing,** *n.*

main·tain' (mān-tān') *v.t.* **1,** preserve; keep in condition. **2,** support; provide for. **3,** defend in argument. **4,** assert to be true. —**main'te·nance** (mān'tə-nəns) *n.*

mai' tai'' (mī' tī'') *n.* a cocktail made with rum, curaçao, and fruit juices.

maî''tre d'hô·tel' (me''tr dō-tel') *n.* (*Fr.*) **1,** a butler; headwaiter. **2,** the owner or manager of a hotel. Also, **maître d'** (mā''trə dē').

maize (māz) *n.* **1,** a cereal plant; Indian corn, in the U.S. called corn. **2,** a yellow color.

ma·jes'tic (mə-jes'tik) *adj.* possessing majesty; grand; sublime. —**ma·jes'ti·cal·ly,** *adv.*

maj'es·ty (maj'is-tē) *n.* **1,** stateliness; grandeur. **2,** sovereignty. **3,** a royal personage.

ma·jol'i·ca (mə-jol'ə-kə) *n.* decorative enameled Ital. pottery.

> **majolica**
> ↔ From Medieval Latin name for *Majorca,* the Spanish island where the pottery was made.

ma'jor (mā'jər) *adj.* **1,** greater in importance, quantity, or extent. **2,** senior. **3,** of legal age. **4,** (*Music*) pert. to a certain scale or larger interval. —*n.* **1,** an army officer ranking next above captain. **2,** a principal field of study. —*v.t.* (with *in*) adopt as a principal field of study. —**major general,** the fourth-highest-ranking army officer. —**major league,** one of the highest-ranking Amer. leagues of professional baseball teams.

> **major, mayor**
> ↔ Both words come from Latin *major,* larger, which in Medieval Latin was the title of various officials.

ma''jor·do'mo (-dō'mō) *n.* [*pl.* **-mos**] the manager of a large household or estate.

ma''jor·ette' (-et') *n.fem.* the leader of a marching band or formation. Also, **drum majorette.**

ma·jor'i·ty (mə-jor'ə-tē) *n.* **1,** the greater part or number; the excess of the greater over the smaller. **2,** full legal age. **3,** the military rank of a major. —**silent majority,** the presumed majority of the population which does not express its opinion in political action.

> **majority, plurality**
> The difference between these two terms can be crucial in an election. In a race between two candidates, the one receiving the *majority* of the votes has received more votes than his opponent, i.e., more than half the total. In a race among three or more candidates, the *plurality* is the excess of the leading candidate over the next-highest-scoring candidate.

make (māk) *v.t.* [*pret.* & *p.p.* **made** (mād)] **1,** bring into being. **2,** form; put in condition. **3,** compel. **4,** appoint. **5,** constitute; compose. **6,** judge; infer; estimate. **7,** arrive at; reach; achieve. **8,** earn; acquire. **9,** (with *out*) discern; understand; (*Informal*) assert. **10,** (with *up*) fabricate, as a story; adorn with cosmetics, as one's face; arrange, as type for printing. **11,** (with *up to*) ingratiate oneself with. **12,** (*Slang*) seduce. **13,** (*Slang*) identify. —*v.i.* **1,** cause to be as specified. **2,** be of effect; operate. **3,** go (toward or away from). **4,** (with *out*) fare. **5,** (with *up*) become reconciled; prepare one's face with cosmetics. —*n.* **1,** construction; nature; brand. **2,** the process of manufacture. —**make away with, 1,** steal. **2,** kill. **3,** eat all of. —**make one's way,** succeed. —**make out, 1,** write out (a form). **2,** see. **3,** get along; manage. **4,** (*Informal*) pet. —**make over, 1,** alter; remodel. **2,** transfer title to; hand over. —**make up, 1,** become reconciled. **2,** invent. **3,** prepare; apply cosmetics (to).

make-'be·lieve" *adj.* pretended. —*n.* pretense, as children's play.

make'o"ver *n.* a transformation.

make-'read"y *n.* adjustment to produce even printing.

make'shift" *n. & adj.* a temporary expedient.

make'up" *n.* **1,** composition: character or nature. **2,** the arrangement of type, etc. for printing. **3,** cosmetics; the use of cosmetics or costume.

mak'ings (mā'kingz) *n.pl.* ingredients necessary for making or producing something.

mal- *pref.* bad; imperfect.

mal'a·chite" (mal'ə-kīt") *n.* copper carbonate, an ore of copper, also used as a gem.

mal"ad·just'ed (mal"ə-jus'tid) *adj.* **1,** badly adjusted. **2,** (*Psych.*) not fully adapted to social living. —**mal"ad·just'ment,** *n.*

mal'a·droit' (mal"ə-droit') *adj.* inexpert; awkward.

mal'a·dy (mal'ə-dē) *n.* **1,** a disease. **2,** any disordered state or condition.

ma·laise' (ma-lez') *n.* (*Fr.*) an indefinite feeling of uneasiness or discomfort.

ma'la·mute" (mä'lə-mūt") *n.* a kind of Alaskan working dog having heavy fur.

mal'a·prop"ism (mal'ə-prop"iz-əm) *n.* a blunder in speech, through ignorance of a word or meaning.

> **malapropism**
> ↔ From Mrs. Malaprop, a character in the 18th-c. play *The Rivals* by Richard Sheridan. Her name was based on the adjective *malapropos*.

mal"ap·ro·pos' (mal"ap-rə-pō') *adj. & adv.* inappropriate.

ma'lar (mā'lər) *n.* the cheekbone.

ma·lar'i·a (mə-lãr'ē-ə) *n.* an intermittent or remittent fever. —**ma·lar'i·al, ma·lar'i·ous,** *adj.*

> **malaria**
> ↔ Italian *mal' aria,* bad air, the supposed cause of the disease.

ma·lar'key (mə-lär'kē) *n.* (*Slang*) empty talk; buncombe.

Ma·lay' (mə-lā') *n.* one of the indigenous peoples inhabiting the Malay Peninsula. —**Ma·lay'an,** *adj.*

mal'con·tent" (mal'kən-tent") *adj.* discontented. —*n.* a discontented person.

mal de mer' (mal də mer') (*Fr.*) seasickness.

male (māl) *adj.* **1,** pertaining to the sex that begets young. **2,** characteristic of this sex; masculine. **3,** (*Mech.*) shaped or having pins to be inserted into a socket. —*n.* **1,** a man. **2,** a male animal. —**male bonding,** close relationship between men. —**male chauvinism,** the attitude that men are superior to women.

> **male, masculine**
> ☞ *Male* indicates the sex of an organism. *Masculine* refers specifically to the qualities of a man, or to the masculine gender.

mal"e·dic'tion (mal"ə-dik'shən) *n.* **1,** evil speaking. **2,** a curse.

mal"e·fac'tor (mal'ə-fak"tər) *n.* **1,** a lawbreaker. **2,** one who does evil. —**mal"e·fac'tion,** *n.*

ma·lef'ic (mə-lef'ik) *adj.* harmful; doing mischief.

ma·lef'i·cent (mə-lef'ə-sənt) *adj.* having an evil effect or intent. —**ma·lef'i·cence,** *n.*

mal'e·mute" (mal'ə-mūt") *n.* a malamute.

ma·lev'o·lent (mə-lev'ə-lənt) *adj.* wishing evil to others; hostile. —**ma·lev'o·lence,** *n.*

mal·fea'sance (mal-fē'zəns) *n.* performance of a wrongful act. —**mal·fea'sant,** *adj.*

mal"for·ma'tion *n.* a faulty construction, as of a part of the body. —**mal·formed',** *adj.*

mal·func'tion *v.i.* operate imperfectly; fail to operate. —*n.* an act or instance of malfunctioning.

mal'ic (mal'ik) *adj.* pert. to apples.

mal'ice (mal'is) *n.* **1,** a disposition to inflict injury; ill will. **2,** a hostile act.

ma·li'cious (mə-lish'əs) *adj.* bearing malice; intending harm.

ma·lign' (mə-līn') *v.t.* speak ill of; defame. —*adj.* pernicious; malicious.

ma·lig'nant (mə-lig'nənt) *adj.* **1,** threatening danger. **2,** deadly or growing worse, as a cancerous tumor. —**ma·lig'nan·cy, ma·lig'ni·ty,** *n.*

ma·lin′ger (mə-ling′gər) *v.i.* feign illness. —**ma·ling′er·er**, *n.*

mall (mâl) *n.* **1,** a maul. **2,** a shaded public walk. **3,** a covered shopping center.

> **mall**
> ↔ A shortened form of *Pall Mall*, a street in London, England, having many clubs.

mal′lard (mal′ərd) *n.* the common wild duck.

mal′le·a·ble (mal′ē-ə-bəl) *adj.* **1,** capable of being extended by beating or rolling. **2,** adaptable. —**mal″le·a·bil′i·ty,** *n.*

mal′let (mal′it) *n.* **1,** a small wooden hammer. **2,** a long-handled club, as used in croquet or polo.

mal′low (mal′ō) *n.* a shrub or tree bearing pink or white flowers.

malm′sey (mäm′zė) *n.* a strong, sweet wine made mainly in Madeira.

> **malmsey**
> ↔ From *Monemvasia*, a town in Greece where the wine was originally produced.

mal″nu·tri′tion (mal″noo-trish′ən) *n.* imperfect, or lack of, nutrition.

mal·o′dor·ous (mal-ō′dər-əs) *adj.* having an offensive odor. —**mal·o′dor·ous·ness,** *n.*

mal·prac′tice (mal-prak′tis) *n.* improper conduct, esp. by a physician.

malt (mâlt) *n.* **1,** partially germinated grain, used in brewing. **2,** ale. —**malt′ed milk,** a preparation of dried milk and malted cereals; a drink of this mixed with milk and fruit flavoring. —**malt liquor,** a type of beer with a high alcoholic content.

Mal·tese′ (mâl-tēz′) *adj.* pert. to the island of Malta. —**Maltese cat,** a bluish-gray breed of cat. —**Maltese cross,** a cross of four equal arms, notched and wider at the end.

malt′ose (mâl′tōs) *n.* malt sugar, produced by conversion of starch.

mal·treat′ (mal-trēt′) *v.t.* treat badly; abuse. —**mal·treat′ment,** *n.*

ma′ma (mä′mə) *n.* mamma.

mam′ba (mäm′bə) *n.* a poisonous Afr. snake.

mam′bo″ (mäm′bō″) *n.* a lively ballroom dance.

mam′ma (mä′mə *or* mä-mä′) *n.* **1,** [also, **ma′ma**] mother. **2,** (mam′ə) [*pl.* **-mae** (-mė)] a gland secreting milk.

mam′mal (mam′əl) *n.* an animal whose young feed upon milk from the breast. —**mam·ma′li·an** (ma-mā′lė-ən) *adj.*

> **mammal**
> ↔ From *Mammalia*, the name for the class of animals that suckle their young coined by the Swedish scientist Linnaeus from Latin *mammalis*, of the breast.

mam′ma·ry (mam′ə-rē) *adj.* pert. to the mammae or breasts.

mam·mog′ra·phy (mam-og′rə-fė) *n.* X-ray photography of the breast (usu. used to detect cancer).

mam′mon (mam′ən) *n.* **1,** material wealth. **2,** (*cap.*) the apotheosis of riches and avarice.

mam′moth (mam′əth) *n.* an extinct species of very large elephant. —*adj.* gigantic; immense.

mam′my (mam′ė) *n.* **1,** mother. **2,** a female nurse.

·man *n.* [*pl.* **men**] **1,** a mammal of the genus *Homo.* **2,** a person; a human being. **3,** the human race; mankind. **4,** an adult human male. **5,** (*Informal*) a husband. **6,** a strong, virile, brave, or accomplished man. **7,** a piece in a game, as chess. **8,** (with *the*) (*Slang*) the police; authority, esp. white authority. —*v.t* [**manned, man′-ning**] supply with staff, as for service or defense. —**man about town,** a sophisticated, worldly man.

> **man, -man, woman**
> Because of its narrower meaning of male person, there has been an effort to avoid using *man* and its combining form *-man* in their long-established generic meaning of human being. It is this generic meaning which is found in *woman*, a compound of Old English *wif*, woman, and *man*, person. The generic *man* can usually be replaced by *human, human being,* or *person* (or its combining form *-person*). Such alternatives are sometimes suggested in this dictionary.

-man (mən) *suf.* [*pl.* **-men**] in compounds, denoting a man (or, often, person) who does, acts, has, etc., as indicated by the root word. ❏ *man*

man′a·cle (man′ə-kəl) *n.* (usually *pl.*) a shackle; handcuff. —*v.t.* fetter; restrain; make fast or secure.

man′age (man′ij) *v.t.* **1,** control physically, as a horse. **2,** control by direction or persuasion. **3,** contrive; bring about. —*v.i.* direct or control affairs. —**man′age·a·ble,** *adj.*

man'age·ment (-mənt) *n.* **1,** act of managing. **2,** owners and executives as distinguished from labor.

man'ag·er (man'ij-ər) *n.* one who directs any operations. —**man″a·ger′i·al** (-ə-jir′ē-əl) *adj.*

ma·ña'na (mä-nyä′nə) (*Sp.*) *adv. & n.* tomorrow; (*fig.*) (at) an indefinite time in the future.

man-'at-arms″ *n.* [*pl.* **men-'**] a soldier or armed attendant of medieval times.

man″a·tee' (man″ə-tē′) *n.* a seacow; a large sea mammal.

Man·chu' (man-choo′) *n.* a member of a tribe from Manchuria, long the rulers of China; their language. —**Man·chu'ri·an** (-chŭ′rē-ən) *adj.*

man'ci·ple (man′sə-pəl) *n.* a steward having authority to purchase goods.

man·da'mus (man-dä′məs) *n.* (*Lat.,* we command) (*Law*) a writ directing an inferior court, person, etc., to perform a specific act.

man'da·rin (man′də-rin) *n.* **1,** a Chinese official. **2,** a Chinese dialect. **3,** an Asiatic citrus fruit. **4,** a loose, wide sleeve; a woman's coat with such sleeves.

> **mandarin**
> ↔ The Chinese official comes from Sanskrit *mantrin,* counselor. The *mandarins* wore yellow robes, hence the connection with the orange.

man'date (man′dāt) *n.* **1,** a command. **2,** an order or injunction, as from a superior court to an inferior one. **3,** a commission, as to one nation to manage the affairs of another.

man'da·to·ry (man′də-tôr-ē) *adj.* compulsory; officially required.

man'di·ble (man′də-bəl) *n.* a bone of the lower jaw. —**man·dib'u·lar** (-dib′yə-lər) *adj.*

man'do·lin' (man′də-lin″) *n.* a musical instrument of the lute class, having metal strings in pairs.

man'drake (man′drāk) *n.* a poisonous herb of Europe. Also, **man·drag'o·ra** (man-drag′ə-rə).

man'drel (man′drəl) *n.* **1,** a cylindrical bar used to support work being turned on a lathe. **2,** a core for shaping metal or glass.

man'drill (man′dril) *n.* a large, ferocious Afr. baboon.

mane (mān) *n.* the long hair on the neck of some animals, as the horse or the lion. —**maned** (mānd) *adj.* having a mane.

ma·nege' (ma-nezh′) *n.* the art of training and riding horses; a riding school.

ma·neu'ver (mə-noo′vər) *n.* **1,** a planned and regulated strategic movement, particularly of troops or warships. **2,** an adroit move. —*v.t. & i.* manipulate; move skillfully. Also, **ma·noeu'vre.**

> **maneuver, manure**
> ↔ Both words are traced back to Latin *manu operari,* to work with the hand.

man'ful (-fəl) *adj.* brave. —**man'ful·ness,** *n.*

man'ga·nese″ (mang′gə-nēs″) *n.* a metallic chemical element, no. 25, symbol Mn. —**man·gan'ic** (man-gan′ik) *adj.*

mange (mānj) *n.* a skin disease of animals which causes loss of hair and eruptions.

man'gel-wur'zel (mang′gəl-wēr′zəl) *n.* a beetlike root used as fodder.

man'ger (mān′jər) *n.* a trough or box for feeding animals.

man'gle (mang′gəl) *v.t.* **1,** cut or slash; disfigure. **2,** mar. **3,** press in a mangle. —*n.* a machine for ironing cloth.

man'go (mang′gō) *n.* the luscious, slightly acid fruit of a tropical tree.

man'grove (man′grōv) *n.* a tropical tree, a source of tannic acid.

man'gy (mān′jē) *adj.* **1,** infected with mange. **2,** shabby; mean; petty. —**man'gi·ness,** *n.*

man'han'dle *v.t.* **1,** handle roughly. **2,** move by human energy.

Man·hat'tan (man-hat′ən) *n.* a cocktail of whiskey and sweet vermouth.

man'hole″ *n.* a hole for entering a sewer, steam boiler, etc.

man'hood″ (-hûd″) *n.* **1,** the state or condition of being a man; adulthood. **2,** courage; virility.

man-'hour″ *n.* a unit of work, that done by one person in one hour.

man'hunt″ *n.* a hunt for a person, as a lawbreaker.

ma·ni·a (mā′nē-ə) *n.* **1,** a form of insanity, marked by great excitement. **2,** a great desire or enthusiasm.

> **mania, phobia**
> ☛ Both these words suggest an abnormal degree: a *mania* is excess elation, *phobia* is excess fear.

-ma·ni·a (mā′nē-ə) *suf.* denoting love or enthusiasm for.

ma′ni·ac (mā′nė-ak) *n.* a madman. **—ma·ni′a·cal** (mə-nī′ə-kəl) *adj.*

man′ic (man′ik) *adj.* pert. to or affected with mania. **—manic depressive,** having a mental disorder marked by recurrent cycles of excitation and depression.

ma″ni·cot′ti (ma″nə-kot′ė) *n.* pasta filled with ricotta and ham.

man′i·cure″ (man′ə-kyûr″) *n.* care of the hands and fingernails. **—***v.t.* trim; polish. **—man′i·cur″ist,** *n.*

man′i·fest″ (man′ə-fest″) *adj.* readily perceived; obvious. **—***v.t.* demonstrate; give evidence of. **—***n.* a list of a shipment. **—man″i·fes·ta′tion,** *n.* a demonstration; display.

> **manifest, manifesto**
> ↔ Both words derive from Latin *manifestus,* literally, gripped by the hand, hence, palpable.

man″i·fes′to (man″ə-fes′tō) *n.* a public declaration; a proclamation. ❏ *manifest*

man′i·fold″ (man′ə-fōld″) *adj.* **1,** of many kinds; varied. **2,** having many parts, features, or activities. **3,** numerous. **—***n.* **1,** a carbon or duplicated copy; facsimile. **2,** thin paper for making many carbon copies. **3,** a pipe with several connections.

man′i·kin (man′ə-kin) *n.* **1,** a little man. **2,** a mannequin.

ma·nil′a (mə-nil′ə) *n.* **1,** a Philippine fiber used for cordage, heavy wrapping paper, etc. **2,** a cigar.

man′i·oc″ (man′ė-ok″) *n.* cassava; the starch derived from its roots.

man′i·ple (man′ə-pəl) *n.* a short narrow band worn over the left arm as a eucharistic vestment.

ma·nip′u·late″ (mə-nip′yə-lāt″) *v.t.* **1,** handle with skill. **2,** influence; manage. **3,** adapt or change. **—ma·nip′u·la·ble,** *adj.* **—ma·nip″u·la′tion,** *n.*

man′i·tou (man′i-too) *n.* an Indian spirit or god of nature.

man′kind″ *n.* humankind.

man′ly (-lė) *adj.* having the ideal qualities of a man. **—man′li·ness,** *n.*

man′na (man′ə) *n.* spiritual food.

man′ne·quin (man′ə-kin) *n.* **1,** a person who models clothes for sale. **2,** a dummy used by artists and tailors.

man′ner (man′ər) *n.* **1,** a mode of action; method. **2,** customary way of doing; habit; style. **3,** personal bearing and behavior. **4,** kind; sort. **5,** (*pl.*) polite, courteous deportment. **—man′ner·ly,** *adj.* **—man′ner·less,** *adj.* **—to the manner born,**

accustomed to a position or life-style from birth.

man′nered (man′ərd) *adj.* **1,** having manners of a specified sort. **2,** affected or artificial in style.

man′ner·ism (man′ə-riz-əm) *n.* a habitual peculiarity of deportment or speech; idiosyncrasy.

man′nish (-ish) *adj.* of a woman, unbecomingly masculine. **—man′nish·ness,** *n.*

ma·noeu′vre (mə-noo′vər) *v.* maneuver.

man-″of-war′ *n.* [*pl.* **men-″**] a warship.

ma·nom′e·ter (mə-nom′ə-tər) *n.* an instrument for measuring the pressure of gases or liquids. **—man″o·met′ric** (man″ə-met′rik) *adj.*

man′or (man′ər) *n.* in England, a landed estate, vested with certain rights. **—ma·no′ri·al** (mə-nôr′ė-əl) *adj.*

> **manor**
> ↔ From Latin *manere,* to remain or dwell, the source of many other English words, such as *remain* and *permanent.*

man′pow″er *n.* **1,** human muscle power. **2,** persons available for work, warfare, etc.

man·qué′ (mäng-kā′) *adj.* (*Fr.*) unsuccessful; unfulfilled.

man′sard (man′särd) *n.* a roof having two slopes, one steeper than the other.

manse (mans) *n.* a parsonage.

man′sion (man′shən) *n.* a large and stately residence.

man′slaugh″ter (man′slâ″tər) *n.* (*Law*) the unlawful killing of another without malice aforethought.

man′ta (man′tə) *n.* **1,** a coarse cotton cloth; a shawl or blanket made of this. **2,** a large ray; devilfish.

man′tel (man′təl) *n.* the facing above and around a fireplace. **—man′tel·piece″,** *n.* the shelf of a mantel.

> **mantel, mantle**
> ☞ These were originally variant spellings for the same word. Now, the distinction usually observed is between *mantel,* part of a fireplace, and *mantle,* a cloak or covering.

man′tel·et (mant′lit) *n.* **1,** a short cape. **2,** a shield or screen.

man·til′la (man-til′ə) *n.* **1,** a lace headcovering. **2,** a light cloak.

man′tis *n.* [*pl.* **-tes** (-tēz)] a carnivorous insect: *praying mantis.*

---

fat, fāte, fär, fāre, fâll, åsk; met, hē, hėr, maybė; pin, pīne; not, nōte, ôr, tool

man·tis′sa (man-tis′ə) *n.* the decimal part of a logarithm.

man′tle (man′təl) *n.* **1,** a loose cloak. **2,** any covering. **3,** an incandescent hood for a gas jet. —*v.t. & i.* cover or be covered. ❏ *mantel*

man′tra (man′trə) *n.* a sacred word or formula used in meditation.

man′u·al (man′ū-əl) *adj.* pert. to or done by the hands. —*n.* **1,** a book of instructions. **2,** a routine. **3,** an organ keyboard played by the hands.

man″u·fac′ture (man″yə-fak′chər) *n.* the making of goods, by hand or machinery. —*v.i.* engage in such a business. —*v.t.* **1,** make (goods); fabricate. **2,** produce artificially; invent. —**man″u·fac′tur·er,** *n.*

man″u·mis′sion (man″yə-mish′ən) *n.* liberation from slavery. —**man″u·mit′,** *v.t.* liberate.

ma·nure′ (mə-nyûr′) *n.* any substance, chiefly animal feces, used to fertilize land. ❏ *maneuver*

man′u·script″ (man′yə-skript″) *n.* **1,** a book or document written by hand. **2,** an original copy, not set in type. —*adj.* handwritten.

Manx (manks) pert. to the Isle of Man. —**Manx cat,** a tailless cat.

man′y (men′ē) *n.* a large number. —*adj.* **[more, most]** numerous.

Mao jacket (mow) a jacket with a high, broad collar, named for Chinese Communist leader Mao Zedong.

mao tai (mow′ tī′) *n.* **1,** a strong Chinese liquor. **2,** a type of rum cocktail.

map *n.* **1,** a drawing of all or a part of the earth's surface, or the heavens; a chart. **2,** (*Slang*) the face. —*v.t.* **[mapped, map′-ping] 1,** draw a map. **2,** (often with *out*) plan.

ma′ple (mā′pəl) *n.* a shade tree, valued for its hard wood and for the sugar-producing sap of some species.

Ma·quis′ (ma-kē′) *n.sing. & pl.* the French underground in World War II. —**ma·qui·sard′** (ma-kē-zär′) *n.* a member of the Maquis.

mar (mär) *v.t.* **[marred, mar′ring] 1,** disfigure; scratch. **2,** impair in quality.

mar′a·bou″ (mar′ə-boo″) *n.* **1,** a large stork. **2,** a marabou's plume or feathers, used for trimming.

ma·ra′ca (mə-rä′kə) *n.* a hollow gourd containing loose pebbles, used as a percussion instrument.

ma·ras′ca (mə-räs′kə) *n.* a small black variety of cherry.

mar″a·schi′no (mar″ə-skē′nō) *n.* a cordial distilled from the marasca. —**maraschino cherries,** cherries in a syrup flavored with maraschino.

mar′a·thon″ (mar′ə-thon″) *n.* **1,** a footrace of about 26 miles. **2,** any test of endurance.

> **marathon**
> ↔ From a famous battle between the Greeks and the Persians at Marathon. The race is a tribute to the messenger who brought the news of the Greek victory from Marathon to Athens, a distance of just over 26 miles.

ma·raud′ (mə-râd′) *v.i.* rove in search of plunder. —**ma·raud′er,** *n.*

mar′ble (mär′bəl) *n.* **1,** hard crystalline limestone, used in sculpture and architecture. **2,** a small ball of glass, agate, etc., used in a child's game. **3,** (*pl.*) the game played with such balls. —*adj.* made of, or like, marble. —**mar′ble·ize,** *v.t.* —**marble cake,** a cake streaked like marble from the mixture of light and dark (usu. chocolate) batters.

mar′bling (mär′bling) *n.* **1,** an imitation of, or appearance like, variegated marble. **2,** layers of fat and lean in meat. —**mar′-bled,** *adj.*

mar′ca·site″ (mär′kə-sīt″) *n.* a yellowish crystalline mineral, used in ornaments.

mar·cel′ (mär-sel′) *n.* a method of putting waves in hair, named for its originator, French hairdresser Marcel Grateau.

march (märch) *v.i.* **1,** proceed on foot. **2,** walk with regular, concerted steps, as soldiers. —*v.t.* cause to march. —*n.* **1,** the act of marching; progress from one place to another. **2,** the distance of a single marching. **3,** a musical composition, to whose rhythm persons march. **4,** border land; a frontier.

March *n.* the third month of the year.

mar·che′se (mär-kā′zā) *n.* an It. nobleman, equal in rank to a marquis.

mar′chion·ess″ (mär′shə-nes″) *n.* the wife or widow of a marquess. Also, (*It.*) **mar·che′sa** (mär-kā′zə).

march′pane″ (märch′pān″) *n.* marzipan.

march-′past″ *n.* procession.

Mar′di Gras′ (mär′dē grä′) (*Fr.*) the celebration of Shrove Tuesday.

mare (mär) *n.* **1,** a female horse. **2,** (mä′rā) [*pl.* **ma′ri·a** (mä′rē-ə)] a large flat area on the moon.

ma′re nos′trum (mä′rē nos′trəm) (*Lat.*) our sea, esp. the Mediterranean.

mare's-′nest″ (märz′nest″) *n.* a nonexistent discovery; a hoax.

mare's-ˈtail″ *n.* **1,** any of various plants. **2,** (*pl.*) long, narrow cirrus clouds.

marˈga·rine   (mär′jə-rin)   *n.*   oleomargarine.

> **margarine**
> ↔ The name comes from *margaric acid*, a term coined in France for an acid supposedly found in animal fats. The ultimate source of the word is Greek *margaritēs*, pearl.

mar″ga·riˈta (mär″gə-rē′tə) *n.* a cocktail made of tequila, lemon juice, and orange liqueur.

marˈgin (mär′jin) *n.* **1,** a bordering space, as along a river, or on a letter or page. **2,** allowance for error or security, as in a business transaction. **3,** the difference between selling price and cost.

marˈgi·nal (-əl) *adj.* **1,** on the edge. **2,** making little or no provision for error. **3,** barely acceptable.

mar″gi·naˈli·a (mär″jə-nā′lē-ə) *n.pl.* marginal notes.

marˈgrave (mar′grāv) *n.* a title of certain German nobles. **—mar′gra·vine′** (-grə-vēn″) *n.* the wife of a margrave.

mar″gueˈrite′ (mär″gə-rēt′) *n.* a daisy-like flower.

ma″ri·aˈchi (mä″rē-ä′chē) *adj.* pert. to a type of Mexican musical band or its music, used for dancing. **—n.** a member of such a band.

marˈi·gold″ (mar′i-gōld″) *n.* a flower, usually yellow or orange.

ma″ri·juaˈna (ma″rə-wä′nə) *n.* a hemplike plant whose leaves are smoked in cigarettes as a narcotic.

ma·rimˈba (mə-rim′bə) *n.* a musical instrument having strips of wood that produce bell-like tones when struck with hammers.

ma·riˈna (mə-rē′nə) *n.* a boat basin equipped to store and service small boats.

mar″i·nadeˈ′ (mar″ə-nād′) *n.* **1,** a sauce used in marinating. **2,** a pickle preserve.

> **marinade, marine**
> ↔ Ultimately *marinade* comes from Latin *marinus*, of the sea (also the source of *marine*), referring to preservation by soaking in brine.

mar″i·naˈra (mär″ə-när′ə) *adj.* made with tomatoes, onions, garlic, and seasonings.

marˈi·nate″ (mar′ə-nāt′) *v.t.* preserve by salting or pickling; steep in dressing. **—mar′i·naˈtion,** *n.*

ma·rineˈ (mə-rēn′) *adj.* pert. to the sea,

or navigation; nautical. **—n. 1,** shipping in general. **2,** a soldier serving on a ship; in U.S. (*cap.*) a member of the Marine Corps. ☐ *marinade*

marˈi·ner (mar′ə-nər) *n.* a sailor.

marˈi·o·nette′ (mar″ē-ə-net′) *n.* a puppet moved by strings.

marˈi·tal (mar′i-təl) *adj.* pert. to marriage or the married condition. **—marital rape,** sexual rape committed by a person against his or her spouse.

> **marital, martial**
> ☛ Two words sometimes confused. *Marital* means relating to marriage; *martial* means pertaining to war.

marˈi·time″ (mar′i-tīm″) *adj.* pert. to or bordering on the sea.

marˈjo·ram (mär′jə-rəm) *n.* an aromatic herb used as a flavoring.

mark (märk) *n.* **1,** a visible impression, as a line, stain, etc. **2,** a distinguishing symbol or peculiarity. **3,** a significant indication. **4,** a symbol denoting ownership or origin, as a *trademark*. **5,** a rating or grade, as in school. **6,** a target; a goal or aim. **7,** a Ger. monetary unit. **8,** a standard. **—v.t. 1,** make a mark on. **2,** notice. **—mark time, 1,** (*Mil.*) move the feet as in marching but without advancing. **2,** suspend progress; pause and wait. **—marked** (märkt) *adj.* branded; conspicuous; doomed.

markˈdown″ *n.* **1,** a marking for sale at a reduced price. **2,** the amount of such reduction.

markˈer (mär′kər) *n.* **1,** anything used as a mark; a counter, tombstone, etc. **2,** (*Slang*) a memorandum; an I.O.U.

marˈket (mär′kit) *n.* **1,** an assemblage of people, or a place, for buying and selling; a store. **2,** trade; rate of sale; demand. **—v.t.** offer for sale; sell. **—mar′ket·a·ble,** *adj.* **—market place,** an open space in a town where markets are held.

marksˈman (märks′mən) *n.* [*pl.* **-men**], **marks′wom″an** *n.* **1,** one skilled in shooting. **2,** (*Mil.*) a rating in rifle marksmanship, below expert and sharpshooter. **—marks′man·ship,** *n.*

markˈup″ *n.* the amount added to a cost price, for profit.

marˈlin (mär′lin) *n.* a large game fish.

marˈline·spike″ (mär′lin-spīk″) *n.* (*Naut.*) an iron spike used in twisting or splicing rope.

marˈma·lade″ (mär′mə-lād″) *n.* a preserve containing pieces of citrus fruit and rind.

marmalade
↔ From Greek *melimēlon*, a kind of apple; the early marmalades were made from quinces.

mar·mo′re·al (mar-môr′ė-əl) *adj.* of marble.

mar′mo·set″ (mär′mə-zet″) *n.* a small Central Amer. monkey.

mar′mot (mär′mət) *n.* any of various rodents, as the woodchuck.

ma·roon′ (mə-roon′) *v.t.* abandon on a desolate island; isolate. —*adj. & n.* dark red.

maroon
↔ The verb is derived from American Spanish *cimarrón*, wild, a term used for runaway slaves. The adjective comes from an old Italian word for the chestnut.

mar·quee′ (mär-kē′) *n.* **1,** a projecting roof above a door or sidewalk. **2,** such a projection over a theater entrance displaying information about current or future presentations.

mar′quess (mär′kwis) *n.* marquis.

mar′que·try (mär′kə-trė) *n.* inlaid work on furniture.

mar′quis (mär′kwis; mär-kē′) *n.* a nobleman, ranking above a count or earl and below a duke. Also (*Brit.*) **mar′quess.**

mar·quise′ (mär-kēz′) *n.* wife of a marquis.

mar″qui·sette′ (mär″kwi-zet′) *n.* a light, gauzelike fabric.

mar′riage (mar′ij) *n.* **1,** the legal union of a man and a woman; a wedding. **2,** the state of being married or united. —**mar′riage·a·ble,** *adj.* eligible to be married.

mar′ron (mä′rən) *n.* a chestnut, esp. candied. —**mar·rons′ gla·cés′** (mä-rōn′ gla-sā′) candied chestnuts.

mar′row (mar′ō) *n.* **1,** a soft tissue in the interior of the bones. **2,** the essence; the real meaning. **3,** vitality.

mar′ry (mar′ė) *v.t.* **1,** unite in wedlock. **2,** take for husband or wife. —*v.i.* wed.

Mars (märz) *n.* **1,** the planet fourth from the sun and nearest the earth. **2,** the Roman god of war.

Mar″seil·laise′ (mär″sā-yez′) *n.* the French national anthem.

marsh (märsh) *n.* low, wet land; a swamp. —**marsh′y,** *adj.* —**marsh gas,** a toxic inflammable gas.

mar′shal (mär′shəl) *n.* **1,** a high military officer. **2,** a judicial, or police, officer. **3,** a

person in charge of ceremonies, etc. —*v.t.* arrange in order; gather.

marsh′mal″low (märsh′mal″ō) *n.* a confection of gelatin and sugar.

mar·su′pi·al (mär-soo′pē-əl) *n.* a mammal having a *marsupium,* or external pouch, for its young, as the kangaroo.

mart (märt) *n.* a market.

mar′ten (mär′tən) *n.* an Amer. fur-bearing animal; its fur.

mar′tial (mär′shəl) *adj.* warlike; military; soldierly. —**martial arts,** one of the traditional Asian forms of self-defense, as karate, etc. —**martial law,** rule by military, not civil, authority. ❏ *marital*

Mar′tian (mär′shən) *adj.* pert. to the planet Mars. —*n.* a supposed inhabitant of this planet.

mar′tin (mär′tən) *n.* a swallowlike bird.

mar″ti·net′ (mär″tə-net′) *n.* a rigid disciplinarian.

martinet
↔ The source for this word is the French drillmaster General Jean *Martinet,* who invented a rigorous system of drill.

mar′tin·gale″ (mär′tən-gāl″) *n.* **1,** in a horse's harness, a strap between the girth and the bit. **2,** (*Naut.*) a short spar under the bowsprit.

mar·ti′ni (mär-tē′nė) *n.* a cocktail of gin or vodka and dry vermouth.

martini
↔ The name may come from *Martini* & Rossi, a manufacturer of vermouth.

mar′tyr (mär′tər) *n.* one who suffers in defense of a belief or cause. —**mar′tyr·dom,** *n.* —**mar′tyr·ize″** (-īz″) *v.t.*

martyr, victim
↔ *Martyr* comes from Greek *martyr,* witness, i.e., witness to the faith. A *martyr* suffers by conscious choice, usually in defense of a principle. A *victim* is the helpless or unwitting sufferer of a wrong.

mar′vel (mär′vəl) *n.* a wonderful or extraordinary thing. —*v.t. & i.* wonder at; be moved by wonder. —**mar′vel·ous,** *adj.* extraordinary.

Marx′ism (märk′siz-əm) *n.* the socialistic theory originated by the German economist Karl Marx. —**Marx′i·an,** *adj.* —**Marx′ist,** *n.*

Mary Jane (mâr′ė-jān′) (*Slang*) marijuana.

Mary Jane
↔ Erroneous translation of *marijuana*, supposing it to be a compound of *María* and *Juana*.

mar′zi·pan″ (mär′zə-pan″) *n.* an almond confection. Also, **march′pane″**.

marzipan
↔ The alternate spelling, *marchpane*, is closer to the original form of the word, Arabic *mawthapan*, seated king. The exact line of derivation from king to candy is conjectural.

mas·car′a (mas-kar′ə) *n.* a cosmetic used on the eyelashes.

mas″car·po′ne (mas″kär·pō′nė) *n.* (*It.*) a type of Italian soft cream cheese.

mas′cot (mas′kət) *n.* an animal or person supposed to bring good luck.

mas′cu·line (mas′kyə-lin) *adj.* male; manly; (of a woman) mannish. —**mas″culin′i·ty,** *n.* ❏ *male*

ma′ser (mā′sər) *n.* a device that amplifies or produces electromagnetic waves: *m(icrowave) a(mplification by) s(timulated) e(mission of) r(adiation)*.

mash *n.* a pulpy mixture, esp. of grain, etc., for feed, distilling, etc. —*v.t.* crush; make into a mash.

mash′er (-ər) *n.* **1,** a machine or implement for crushing. **2,** (*Slang*) a man who makes amorous advances to women with whom he is not acquainted.

mash′ie (mash′ė) *n.* a golf club used in making lofting shots, No. 5 iron.

mask (mȧsk) *n.* **1,** a covering for the face, worn for disguise, protection, etc. **2,** anything that conceals; a pretense. **3,** a masquerade. **4,** a likeness of a face, cast in plaster. —*v.t. & i.* disguise or conceal.

mas′o·chism (mas′ə-kiz-əm) *n.* pleasure derived from self-suffering or humiliation. —**mas′o·chist,** *n.* —**mas″o·chis′tic,** *adj.*

masochism, sadism
☛ Both these words refer to enjoyment derived from pain: *masochism* deals with experiencing pain, *sadism* deals with inflicting pain. Both words derive from personal names: *masochism* from L. von Sacher-*Masoch*, *sadism* from the Marquis de *Sade*.

ma′son (mā′sən) *n.* **1,** one who builds with brick, stone, etc. **2,** (*cap.*) a Freemason. —**Ma·son′ic** (mə-son′ik) *adj.* —**Mason jar,** a glass jar with an airtight closure.

Ma′son-Dix′on line (mā′sən-dik′sən) a surveyor's line, the boundary between Pennsylvania and Maryland, once considered as separating slave from free territory.

Mason-Dixon line
↔ From 18th-c. English surveyors Jeremiah *Dixon* and Charles *Mason*.

Ma′son·ite″ (mā′sə-nīt″) *n.* (*T.N.*) a brand of hardboard.

ma′son·ry (mā′sən-rė) *n.* **1,** stonework. **2,** (*cap.*) Freemasonry.

masque (mȧsk) *n.* **1,** a dramatic entertainment. **2,** a masquerade.

mas″quer·ade′ (mas″kə-rād′) *n.* **1,** a gathering where masks are worn. **2,** a disguise; concealment; false pretense. —*v.i.* go about under false pretenses.

mass (mas) *n.* **1,** a body of matter; a lump. **2,** a quantity of matter in a body. **3,** an assemblage of particles or things, as troops. **4,** (*pl.*) the proletariat. **5,** the bulk; the greater part. **6,** bulk; magnitude. **7,** (*cap.*) a church service. —*v.t.* collect into a mass. —*v.i.* assemble. —**mass media,** media which reach a large number of people, as radio, television, etc. —**mass meeting,** a large or general assembly. —**mass number,** the sum of the numbers of protons and neutrons in an atomic nucleus.

mass
↔ The sense of rite derives from the Latin word *missa*, sent, possibly from the final words of the Eucharist, *Ite, missa est*, "Go, it is dismissed." The sense of bulk comes from Greek *maza*, cake, lump.

mas′sa·cre (mas′ə-kər) *n.* the indiscriminate wholesale killing, esp. of humans. —*v.t.* kill; defeat decisively.

mas·sage′ (mə-säzh′) *n.* treatment of the muscles by rubbing, kneading, etc. —*v.t.* so treat.

mas·seur′ (ma-sėr′) *n.masc.,* **mas·seuse′** (-sûz′) *n.fem.* (*Fr.*) one who massages therapeutically.

mas′sif (mas′if) *n.* the dominant part of a mountain range.

mas′sive (mas′iv) *adj.* **1,** bulky; heavy. **2,** substantial; imposing. —**mas′sive·ness,** *n.*

mass-″pro·duce′ *v.t.* produce in large quantities, esp. by automatic machines. —**mass-″pro·duc′tion,** *n.*

mast (mȧst) *n.* **1,** a vertical support for yards, sails, etc., on a ship. **2,** any tall pole. **3,** the fruit of the oak and other trees used as food for hogs, etc.

mas·tec'to·my (mas-tek'tə-mė) *n.* the removal of a breast.

mas'ter (màs'tər) *n.* **1,** one who has chief authority or control. **2,** one eminently skilled in an occupation, art, or science. —*adj.* **1,** chief or principal; predominant. **2,** eminently skilled. —*v.t.* become master of; subdue. —**master bedroom,** the principal bedroom in a dwelling. —**master class,** a seminar or tutorial given by an expert in a certain field, esp. music. —**master hand,** an expert. —**master key,** a key opening many locks. —**master** or **mistress of ceremonies,** a person who introduces the speakers, performers, etc., as at a show. Also, **MC.** —**master sergeant,** a noncommissioned officer, ranking just below sergeant major (in the Air Force, just below senior master sergeant).

mas'ter·ful (-fəl) *adj.* **1,** authoritative; domineering. **2,** masterly. —**mas'ter·ful·ness,** *n.*

mas'ter·ly (-lè) *adj.* skilled. —**mas'ter·li·ness,** *n.*

mas'ter·mind" *n.* one who plans and directs an undertaking. —*v.t.* plan and control (an undertaking).

mas'ter·piece" *n.* a work of surpassing excellence. Also, **mas'ter·work".**

mas'ter·y (màs'tə-rè) *n.* power of control; command.

mast'head" *n.* **1,** the top of a ship's mast. **2,** a statement of ownership, etc., in a newspaper.

mas'tic (mas'tik) *n.* **1,** a resin. **2,** a cement used in masonry or plastering.

mas'ti·cate" (mas'tə-kāt") *v.t. & i.* **1,** chew. **2,** crush or knead into pulp. —**mas"ti·ca'tion,** *n.*

mas'tiff (màs'tif) *n.* a large dog.

---
mastiff
↔ The etymological meaning of the word is "tamed animal"; it derives from Latin *mansuetus*, tame.
---

mas·ti'tis (mas-tī'tis) *n.* inflammation of the breast.

mas'to·don" (mas'tə-don") *n.* an extinct, elephantlike mammal.

mas'toid *n.* a bony prominence below and behind the ear. —*adj.* **1,** pert. to the mastoid. **2,** shaped like a nipple. —**mas"toid·i'tis,** inflammation of the mastoid.

mas"tur·ba'tion (mas"tər-bā'shən) *n.* sexual self-gratification. —**mas'tur·bate",** *v.i.*

mat *n.* **1,** a piece of fabric, woven of straw, etc., used on the floor, on a table, etc. **2,** a thick mass, as of weeds or hair.

3, a lusterless surface. **4,** a matrix, in printing. **5,** a border placed around a picture, inside the frame (if any). —*v.t.* [**mat'ted, -ting**] **1,** cover with, or form into, a mat. **2,** finish with a dull surface. —*v.i.* become entangled. —*adj.* dull in surface.

---
mat
↔ The sense of woven or massed fibers—as well as the border in a frame—is Semitic in origin. The sense of dullness comes from Latin *mattus,* moist.
---

mat'a·dor" (mat'ə-dôr") *n.* in a bullfight, the one who kills the bull.

match (mach) *n.* **1,** an equal; a peer. **2,** a pair; a mating. **3,** a contest, as in golf. **4,** a chemical-tipped piece of wood, etc., that ignites on friction. —*v.t.* mate; bring into agreement; equal. —*v.i.* contend; correspond; suit; harmonize. —**match'less,** *adj.* having no equal.

match'lock" *n.* a musket in which the powder is ignited by a slow-burning cord.

match'mak"er *n.* one who arranges matrimonial matches, or athletic contests.

mate (māt) *n.* **1,** a husband or wife. **2,** one of a pair; a counterpart. **3,** a habitual associate. **4,** an officer on a merchant ship. **5,** checkmate. —*v.t.* join as a mate; marry; pair. —*v.i.* **1,** take a mate; marry. **2,** copulate.

ma·te'ri·al (mə-tir'ė-əl) *n.* **1,** a constituent principle or element; substance; raw matter to be developed. **2,** a textile fabric. —*adj.* **1,** physical; corporeal; not spiritual. **2,** important; essential.

ma·te'ri·al·ism (-iz-əm) *n.* devotion to material, rather than spiritual, needs or interests; self-interest. —**ma·te'ri·al·ist,** *n.* —**ma·te"ri·al·is'tic,** *adj.* —**ma·te"ri·al·is'ti·cal·ly,** *adv.*

ma·te'ri·al·ize" (-īz") *v.t. & i.* give or assume material form or perceptible existence (to) —**ma·te"ri·al·i·za'tion,** *n.*

ma·te'ri·al·ly (-ə-lè) *adv.* to an important extent.

ma·té·ri·el' (mə-tir-ė-el') *n.* (*Fr.*) equipment and supplies, esp. military.

ma·ter'nal (mə-tēr'nəl) *adj.* pert. to, befitting, or related to a mother.

ma·ter'ni·ty (mə-tēr'nə-tè) *n.* state of being a mother.

math *n.* (*Informal*) mathematics.

math"e·mat'i·cal (math"ə-mat'i-kəl) *adj.* **1,** pert. to mathematics. **2,** exact; precise.

math"e·mat'ics (math"ə-mat'iks) *n.sing.* the science of numbers in all their relations and applications. —**math″e·ma·ti′cian** (-mə-tish′ən) *n.*

> ### mathematics
> ↔ From Greek *manthanein*, to learn; *mathematics* originally covered a much wider area of the sciences than it does now.

mat′in·al (mat′ə-nəl) *adj.* pert. to matins or morning.

mat″i·nee′ (mat″ə-nā′) *n.* a daytime entertainment, as a concert, play, etc. —**matinee idol,** a highly popular male actor.

mat′ins (mat′inz) *n.pl.* **1,** one of the seven canonical hours, beginning properly at midnight. **2,** a morning service.

ma′tri- (mā-trė; mat-ri) *pref.* mother.

ma′tri·arch (mā′trė-ärk) *n.* a woman having chief authority in a household. —**ma″tri·ar′chal,** *adj.*

ma′tri·ar″chy (mā′trė-är″kė) *n.* a social system ruled by mothers or women.

mat′ri·cide″ (mat′ri-sīd″) *n.* the killer or killing of one's mother.

ma·tric′u·late″ (mə-trik′yə-lāt″) *v.t. & i.* enroll, or be enrolled, in a college. —**ma·tric′u·lant,** *n.* —**ma·tric″u·la′tion,** *n.*

mat′ri·mo″ny (mat′rə-mō″nė) *n.* the ceremony or sacrament of marriage. —**mat″ri·mo′ni·al,** *adj.*

ma′trix (mā′triks) *n.* [*pl.* **-tri·ces** (-tri-sėz)] **1,** that which forms or determines. **2,** a mold. **3,** (*Math.*) a rectangular array of quantities, such as a determinant.

ma′tron (mā′trən) *n.* **1,** a married woman. **2,** a woman in charge, as in an institution. —**ma′tron·ly,** *adj.* like a matron in manner or appearance; staid. —**matron of honor,** a married woman, attendant of the bride at a wedding; best woman.

matte (mat) *n.* **1,** an impure product of the smelting of certain ores. **2,** mat (def. 3).

mat′ted (mat′id) *adj.* covered with, or formed into, a mat or tangled mass.

mat′ter (mat′ər) *n.* **1,** the substance of which physical objects consist. **2,** any particular kind of substance, as *printed matter.* **3,** pus. **4,** the substance, as of a book. **5,** a thing of consequence; affair; business. —*v.i.* **1,** be of consequence. **2,** form or excrete pus.

mat′ter-of-course′ *adj.* occurring in the natural course of things.

mat′ter-of-fact′ *adj.* **1,** commonplace. **2,** unimaginative. **3,** unemotional.

mat′ting (mat′ing) *n.* matted fabric; material for making mats.

mat′tock (mat′ək) *n.* a tool like a pickax, but with one end broad.

mat′tress (mat′ris) *n.* a cloth case filled with padding and usu. having springs, used as or on a bed.

mat′u·rate″ (mach′û-rāt″) *v.i.* suppurate. —**mat″u·ra′tion,** *n.* —**ma·tur′a·tive** (mə-chû′rə-tiv) *adj.*

ma·ture′ (mə-tyûr′) *adj.* complete in natural growth; ripe; fully developed. —*v.t. & i.* age; become mature. —**ma·tu′ri·ty,** *n.*

ma·tu′ti·nal (mə-tū′tə-nəl) *adj.* in the morning.

mat′zoth (mät′sōth) *n.pl.* [*sing.* **mat′zo** (-zə)] unleavened bread.

maud′lin (mâd′lin) *adj.* tearfully, or drunkenly, sentimental.

> ### maudlin
> ↔ From *Magdalen*, the name of the woman Mary who was the first person to see Christ after he rose from the dead. She was generally represented in art as a weeping penitent.

maul (mâl) *n.* a heavy hammer. —*v.t.* handle roughly.

maun′der (mân′dər) *v.i.* talk or move about in a rambling way.

mau″so·le′um (mâ″sə-lė′əm) *n.* a grand and stately tomb.

> ### mausoleum
> ↔ From *Mausōleion*, the Greek name for the 4th-c.-B.C. tomb erected for Mausolus, king of Caria.

mauve (mōv) *n. & adj.* a color or dye, pale bluish purple.

ma′ven (mā′vən) *n.* an expert. Also, **ma′vin.**

mav′er·ick (mav′ər-ik) *n.* **1,** an unbranded cow or calf. **2,** a dissenter; nonconformist.

> ### maverick
> ↔ After Samuel *Maverick*, a Texas pioneer who refused to brand his calves.

ma′vis (mā′vis) *n.* the Europ. song thrush.

ma·vour′neen (mə-vûr′nēn) *n.* (*Irish*) my darling.

maw (mâ) *n.* the throat; gullet.

mawk′ish (mâ′kish) *adj.* nauseating; sickeningly sentimental. —**mawk′-ish·ness,** *n.*

---

max′i- (mak′sė) *pref.* especially large, long, etc.

max′i·dress″ *n.* a woman's ankle-length dress. —**max′i·skirt″,** *n.* a woman's ankle-length skirt. Also, *informal,* **max′i.**

max·il′la (mak-sil′ə) *n.* [*pl.* **-lae** (-ė)] the upper jawbone. —**max′il·lar·y** (mak′sə-ler-ė) *adj.*

max′im (mak′sim) *n.* a pithy expression of a general truth, or a rule of conduct.

max′i·mum (mak′si-məm) *n.* [*pl.* **-ma** (-mə) or **-mums**] *& adj.* the greatest quantity or amount possible. —**max′i·mal** (-məl) *adj.* —**max′i·mize** (-mīz) *v.t.* make as great as possible.

max·ixe′ (mak-sēks′) *n.* a type of syncopated Brazilian ballroom dance.

max′well (maks′wel) *n.* a unit of magnetic flux, named for Scottish physicist James C. Maxwell.

may (mā) *aux. v.* [*pret.* **might** (mīt)] expressing possibility, permission, wish, or contingency. ❏ *can*

May *n.* the fifth month of the year.

> **May**
> ↔ From Latin *Maius,* of Maia, the wife of the Roman god Vulcan.

Ma′ya (mä′yə) *n.* a member of a race formerly inhabiting Central Amer.; their language. —**Ma′yan,** *adj. & n.*

may′be (mā′bė) *adv.* perhaps.

May Day 1, May 1, often celebrated with a spring festival, and also by organized labor. **2,** a call of distress.

may′flow″er *n.* a spring-flowering plant, esp. the trailing arbutus.

may′fly *n.* an insect having a short adult life; an ephemerid.

may′hem (mā′hem) *n.* the infliction of serious bodily injury. ❏ *maim*

may″on·naise′ (mā″ə-nāz′) *n.* a thick salad dressing. Also, *informal,* **may′o** (mā′ō).

> **mayonnaise**
> ↔ Prob. from French *mahonnaise,* of Mahon, a town in Corsica, captured by the French in 1756.

may′or (mā′ər) *n.* the principal officer of a municipality. —**may′or·al** (mā′ər-əl) *adj.* —**may′or·al·ty,** *n.* ❏ *major*

May′pole″ *n.* a pole around which persons dance on May Day, holding streamers attached to its top.

May wine a white wine flavored with woodruff and orange slices.

maze (māz) *n.* **1,** a labyrinth; a deception. **2,** bewilderment. —**maz′y,** *adj.*

ma′zel tov″ (mä′zəl tov″) *interj.* (*Yiddish*) good luck; congratulations.

ma·zu′ma (mə-zoo′mə) *n.* (*Slang*) money.

ma·zur′ka (mə-zēr′kə) *n.* a lively Polish dance.

mbi′ra (em-bir′ə) *n.* an Afr. musical instrument, usu. played with the thumbs. Also, **thumb piano.**

McCoy, the (real) (mə-koi′) the real person or thing, not a substitute.

me (mē) *pron.* obj. of *I.*

me′a cul′pa (mā′ə kul′pə) (*Lat.,* I am to blame) an admission of fault.

mead (mēd) *n.* **1,** a fermented liquor of honey and yeast. **2,** (*Poetic*) meadow.

mead′ow (med′ō) *n.* a piece of land for raising hay or for pasture.

mead′ow·lark″ *n.* a yellow-breasted starling.

mea′ger (mē′gər) *adj.* lean; thin; without richness or fullness; scanty. —**mea′ger·ness,** *n.*

meal (mēl) *n.* **1,** a regular repast; sufficient food to satisfy the appetite. **2,** edible grain ground to a powder. **3,** any coarsely ground substance. —**meal ticket, 1,** a ticket for a meal at a restaurant. **2,** (*Slang*) a person or job depended upon for meals or financial support.

meal′y (mē′lė) *adj.* **1,** resembling, or covered with, meal. **2,** pale, as the complexion. —**meal′i·ness,** *n.*

meal′y·mouthed″ (mē′lė-mowthd″) *adj.* inclined to speak evasively; insincere.

mean (mēn) *v.t.* [*pret. & p.p.* **meant** (ment)] **1,** intend; purpose; have in mind for a particular use. **2,** signify; denote; express. —*v.i.* have intentions of some kind. —*adj.* **1,** inferior in quality; low in station; of small importance. **2,** miserly; stingy. **3,** (*Informal*) nasty; vicious; in poor health. **4,** (*Slang*) skillful. —*n.* **1,** something midway between two extremes. **2,** (*pl.*) what implements a plan; resources, esp. pecuniary. —**mean′y, mean′ie** (-ė) *n.* an unpleasant, often cruel, person. —**mean′ness,** *n.* ❏ *average*

me·an′der (mė-an′dər) *v.i.* wander aimlessly; pursue a winding course.

> **meander**
> ↔ From *Maeander,* a river in Turkey, known for its sinuosity.

mean′ing (mē′ning) *n.* that which is expressed; significance; import. —*adj.* significant. —**mean′ing·ful,** *adj.*

mean'time" *n.* the intervening time. —*adv.* in the interval. Also, **mean'while".**

mea'sles (mē'zəlz) *n.* an infectious, eruptive disease, chiefly in children.

mea'sly (mē'zlė) *adj.* **1,** infected with measles. **2,** (*Slang*) poor; inadequate. —**mea'sli·ness,** *n.*

meas'ure (mezh'ər) *n.* **1,** a unit or standard for determining extent, volume, quantity, etc., by comparison. **2,** any standard of comparison, estimation, or judgment. **3,** the instrument, act, or system of measurement. **4,** any definite quantity measured. **5,** a legislative bill. **6,** a rhythmical unit or movement, in poetry, music, or dance. —*v.t.* ascertain the extent of; estimate; appraise. —**meas'ure·less,** *adj.* unlimited. —**meas'ur·ing worm,** a type of caterpillar.

meas'ured *adj.* **1,** ascertained or regulated by measure. **2,** regular; deliberate.

meas'ure·ment (-mənt) *n.* **1,** act of measuring. **2,** the dimension, etc., ascertained.

meat (mēt) *n.* **1,** the flesh of animals, used for food. **2,** the edible part of anything; the material part; gist. —**meat'y,** *adj.* **1,** like meat. **2,** pithy.

Mec'ca (mek'ə) *n.* the holy city of Islam, goal of Muslim pilgrims; hence, a goal.

me·chan'ic (mə-kan'ik) *n.* **1,** [also, **mech"a·ni'cian** (mek"ə-nish'ən)] a skilled worker with tools. **2,** a sharper at cards, dice, etc.

me·chan'i·cal (mə-kan'ə-kəl) *adj.* **1,** pert. to, operated by, or produced by a mechanism or machine. **2,** artificial; not spontaneous; lacking in life or spirit. **3,** effected by physical forces; materialistic. —*n.* a layout for printing.

me·chan'ics (mə-kan'iks) *n.* **1,** the science of mechanical forces and motion. **2,** the science of machinery and mechanical appliances.

mech'an·ism (mek'ə-niz-əm) *n.* **1,** machinery. **2,** the agency by which an effect is produced or a purpose accomplished. **3,** mechanical execution. **4,** a belief that the processes of life are fully explainable by the laws of physics and chemistry. —**mech"a·nis'tic,** *adj.*

mech'a·nize" (mek'ə-nīz") *v.t.* **1,** make mechanical. **2,** (*Mil.*) equip with armored motor vehicles. —**mech"a·ni·za'tion,** *n.*

med'al (med'əl) *n.* a coinlike piece of metal inscribed to commemorate an event. —**med'al·ist,** *n.* one who has won a medal. —**Medal of Honor,** the highest U.S. military medal.

---

medal, metal
↔ Both words derive from Greek *metallon*; a *medal* was something made of metal.

---

me·dal'lion (mə-dal'yən) *n.* a large carved medal.

med'dle (med'əl) *v.i.* interfere unjustifiedly. —**med'dler** (-lər) *n.* —**med'dle·some,** *adj.* disposed to meddle.

me'di·a (mē'dė-ə) *n.* **1,** *pl.* of **medium. 2,** [*pl.* **-ae** (-ė)] the middle wall of an artery.

me'di·al (mē'dė-əl) *adj.* intermediate; average; ordinary.

me'di·an (mē'dė-ən) *adj.* being the dividing line or plane between two parts; middle. —**median strip,** a separating strip of pavement or landscaped earth in the center of a highway. ❏ *average*

me'di·ate" (mē'dė-āt") *v.t. & i.* reconcile (opposing forces); settle (a dispute); effect an agreement between others. —**me"di·a'tion,** *n.* —**me'di·a"tor,** *n.* ❏ *arbitrate*

med'ic (med'ik) *n.* (*Informal*) **1,** a doctor. **2,** a member of a medical corps.

Med'i·caid" (med'i-kād") *n.* a government program of medical aid for the poor.

med'i·cal (med'i-kəl) *adj.* **1,** pert. to the science or practice of medicine. **2,** curative.

me·dic'a·ment (mə-dik'ə-mənt) *n.* any substance for healing wounds or curing disease.

Med'i·care" (med'i-kār") *n.* a government program of medical aid for the aged.

med'i·cate" (med'i-kāt") *v.t.* treat with medicine.

med"i·ca'tion *n.* **1,** the use of medicine. **2,** a remedy.

med'i·cine (med'ə-sən) *n.* **1,** the science of treating disease or preserving health. **2,** a substance for treating disease; a remedy. —**me·dic'i·nal** (mə-dis'ə-nəl) *adj.* —**medicine ball,** a heavy ball, thrown for exercise. —**medicine man** *or* **woman,** among primitive peoples, a healer by magic.

med'i·co" (med'i-kō") *n.* [*pl.* **-cos**] (*Slang*) a doctor.

me"di·e'val (mē"dė-ē'vəl) *adj.* pert. to, or characteristic of, the Middle Ages. Also, **me"di·ae'val.**

me"di·o'cre (mē"dė-ō'kər) *adj.* of only moderate quality; ordinary. —**me"di·oc'ri·ty** (-ok'rə-tė) *n.*

med'i·tate" (med'i-tāt") *v.t.* intend; plan. —*v.i.* **1,** brood; reflect. **2,** engage in tran-

scendental meditation. —**med″i·ta′tion,** *n.*
—**med′i·ta″tive,** *adj.*

me′di·um (mē′dė-əm) *n.* **1,** something intermediate; a mean. **2,** an intervening substance, person, agency, or instrumentality, through which something exists or an effect is produced; in spiritualism, a person through whom the dead speak. **3,** [usually *pl.,* **me′di·a**] a publication, or other means of mass communication, esp. as used by an advertiser. **4,** (*Computers*) a material used for data storage. —*adj.* intermediate. —**me″di·um·is′tic,** *adj.* pert. to or having the abilities of a medium (def. 2).

med′lar (med′lər) *n.* a small tree, or its applelike fruit.

med′ley (med′lė) *n.* a mixture; a combination, as of songs.

me·dul′la (mə-dul′ə) *n.* (*Anat.*) the marrow or center of an organ, etc. —**medulla ob″lon·ga′ta** (ob″long-gä′tə) the part of the brain adjoining the spinal cord.

meed (mēd) *n.* (*Archaic*) recompense; reward.

meek (mēk) *adj.* submissive; humble. —**meek′ness,** *n.*

meer′schaum (mir′shəm) *n.* a silicate used for the bowls of tobacco pipes.

meet (mēt) *v.t.* [*pret. & p.p.* **met**] **1,** come together, or into contact, with. **2,** encounter; welcome. **3,** conform to; answer; refute. —*v.i.* **1,** (often with *with*) come together; combine; agree. **2,** come into contact. —*n.* a meeting, as of huntsmen. —*adj.* suitable.

meet′ing *n.* **1,** a coming together; a junction. **2,** an encounter, sometimes hostile, as a duel. **3,** an assembly or gathering. —**meetinghouse,** a church.

meg·a- (meg-ə) *pref.* **1,** great. **2,** a million times.

meg′a·cy″cle (meg′ə-sī″kəl) *n.* a million cycles: applied to wavelengths. Also, **meg′a·hertz″.**

meg′a·lith″ (meg′ə-lith″) *n.* a huge stone.

meg·al·o- (meg-ə-lə) *pref.* very large.

meg″a·lo·ma′ni·a *n.* a mania or delusion of greatness or wealth. —**meg″a·lo·ma′ni·ac,** *n.*

meg″a·lop′o·lis (meg″ə-lop′ə-lis) *n.* **1,** a very large city. **2,** the heavily populated region around a large city; urban area.

meg′a·phone″ (meg′ə-fōn″) *n.* an instrument for magnifying sound.

me·gil′lah (mə-gil′ə) *n.* a lengthy explanation.

me′grim (mē′grim) *n.* **1,** (*pl.*) lowness of spirit; "the blues." **2,** a headache.

mei·o′sis (mī-ō′sis) *n.* a process of cell division in which the number of chromosomes is halved.

mel′a·mine″ (mel′ə-mīn″) *n.* a type of thermoplastic.

meit′ner·i·um (mīt′nər-ė-əm) *n.* a radioactive chemical element, no. 109, symbol Mt, produced artificially.

mel″an·cho′li·a (mel″ən-kō′lė-ə) *n.* a mental disease marked by great depression of spirits. —**mel″an·cho′li·ac,** *n. & adj.*

mel′an·chol″y (mel′ən-kol″ė) *n.* a gloomy state of mind; depression. —*adj.* sad. —**mel″an·chol′ic,** *adj.* —**mel″an·chol′i·cal·ly,** *adv.*

> **melancholy**
> ↔ From Greek *melangkholia,* black bile, the one of the four humors which causes depression.

Mel″a·ne′sian (mel″ə-nē′zhən) *adj.* pert. to one of the principal regions of island groups in the So. Pacific.

mé·lange′ (mā-länzh′) *n.* (*Fr.*) a mixture; medley.

mel′a·nin (mel′ə-nin) *n.* the dark pigment in the hair, skin, etc. —**me·lan′ic** (mə-lan′ik) *adj.*

mel′a·nism (mel′ə-niz-əm) *n.* abnormal development of dark pigmentation in the skin.

mel·a·no- (mel-ə-nō) *pref.* black.

mel″a·no′ma (mel″ə-nō′mə) *n.* a dark-pigmented skin tumor.

Mel′ba toast (mel′bə) bread sliced very thin and well browned.

> **Melba toast**
> ↔ Named for the Australian operatic soprano Nellie *Melba,* whose name also graces the dessert *pêche Melba.*

meld *n.* a scoring combination of cards. —*v.t. & i.* **1,** announce or exhibit such cards. **2,** blend; merge.

me′lee (mā′lā) *n.* a general hand-to-hand fight.

mel′io·rate″ (mēl′yə-rāt″) *v.t. & i.* make or become better. —**mel″io·ra′tion,** *n.*

mel·lif′lu·ous (mə-lif′loo-əs) *adj.* smoothly and sweetly flowing; flowing with honey. Also, **mel·lif′lu·ent.** —**mel·lif′lu·ence, mel·lif′lu·ous·ness,** *n.*

mel′low (mel′ō) *adj.* **1,** soft, esp. from ripeness. **2,** softened; matured; good-humored. **3,** (*Slang*) relaxed; easygoing.

—*v.t.* & *i.* make or become mellow.
—**mel′low·ness,** *n.*

me·lo′de·on (mə-lō′dė-ən) *n.* a small
organ.

me·lod′ic (mə-lod′ik) *adj.* tuneful; pert.
to melody. —**me·lod′i·cal·ly,** *adv.*

me·lo′di·ous (mə-lō′dė-əs) *adj.* musical;
tuneful. —**me·lo′di·ous·ness,** *n.*

mel′o·dra″ma (mel′ə-drå″mə) *n.* a play
with a sensational plot and exaggerated
sentiment.

mel″o·dra·mat′ic (-drə-mat′ik) *adj.* affecting undue sentiment. —**mel″o·dra-
mat′i·cal·ly,** *adv.* —**mel″o·dra·mat′ics,**
n.sing. & pl.

mel′o·dy (mel′ə-dė) *n.* a tune; the air of
a musical composition; a succession of
musical tones.

mel′on (mel′ən) *n.* a large fruit with a
juicy flesh inside a rind.

> **melon**
> ↔ From Greek *mēlon,* which meant
> apple, through a complex route of
> expansion and then contraction back
> to the same spelling.

melt *v.t.* & *i.* **1,** make or become liquid
through heat. **2,** dissolve. **3,** dwindle;
blend. **4,** be softened to tenderness, sympathy, etc. —**melting pot,** a country or city
that assimilates and unites immigrants of
various national origins.

melt′down″ *n.* the melting of all or most
of the core of a nuclear reactor; hence, a
disastrous event. ❑ *China syndrome*

mem′ber (mem′bər) *n.* **1,** a part of any
aggregate or whole. **2,** a part of the body;
a vital organ; a limb. **3,** each of the persons composing a society, party, or legislative body. —**mem′ber·ship″,** *n.* the state of
being a member, as of a party; the total
number of such members.

mem′brane (mem′brān) *n.* a sheet of
thin tissue, lining an organ, connecting
parts, etc. —**mem′bra·nous** (-brə-nəs)
adj.

me·men′to (mə-men′tō) *n.* [*pl.* **-tos**] a
reminder; a souvenir.

mem′o (mem′ō) *n.* [*pl.* **-os**] a
memorandum.

mem′oir (mem′wär) *n.* **1,** a record of
facts. **2,** (*pl.*) a narrative of facts and
events, esp. of one's own life.

mem″o·ra·bil′i·a (mem″ər-ə-bil′ė-ə)
n.pl. [*sing.* **mem″o·rab′i·le** (-rab′ə-lė)]
memorable events.

mem′o·ra·ble (mem′ə-rə-bəl) *adj.* worthy to be remembered.

mem″o·ran′dum (mem″ə-ran′dəm) *n.*

[*pl.* **-dums** or **-da** (-də)] **1,** a record. **2,** a
note to help the memory.

me·mo′ri·al (mə-môr′ė-əl) *n.* **1,** a commemorative monument, etc. **2,** a petition.
—*adj.* commemorating. —**me·mo′ri·al·ize″**
(-īz″) *v.t.* —**Memorial Day,** a federal legal
holiday, the last Monday in May.

mem′o·rize″ (mem′ə-rīz″) *v.t.* commit to
memory. —**mem″o·ri·za′tion,** *n.*

mem′o·ry (mem′ə-rė) *n.* **1,** the mental
capacity of retaining and reviving impressions; remembrance; recollection. **2,** the
state of being remembered. **3,** that which
is remembered. **4,** the device or location,
as in a computer, where data are stored.

mem′sa″hib (mem′sä″ib) *n.* in India, a
term of respect for a European woman.

men *n.* pl. of *man.*

men′ace (men′is) *n.* a threat or threatening. —*v.t.* threaten.

mé·nage′ (mā-näzh′) *n.* (*Fr.*) a household. —**ménage′ à trois′** (ä trwä′) (*Fr.*)
three persons living together, usually of
mixed sexes.

me·nag′er·ie (mə-naj′ə-rė) *n.* a collection or exhibition of wild animals.

mend *v.t.* repair; make whole; correct;
improve. —*v.i.* improve in health; become
whole. —*n.* **1,** a mended place. **2,** recovery
from sickness.

men·da′cious (men-dā′shəs) *adj.* **1,** untrue. **2,** untruthful. —**men·dac′i·ty** (-das′ə-
tė) *n.*

> **mendacity, mendancy, mendicity**
> ☞ Do not confuse *mendacity,* un-
> truthfulness, and *mendicity* or *mendi-
> cancy,* both of which mean poverty.

men″de·le′vi·um (men″də-lē′vė-əm) *n.*
a radioactive chemical element, no. 101,
symbol Md.

> **mendelevium**
> ↔ Named for Russian chemist Dmitri
> I. *Mendeleev,* one of the developers
> of the periodic law.

men′di·cant (men′di-kənt) *n.* a beggar.
—*adj.* begging. —**men′di·can·cy, men·dic′-
i·ty** (men-dis′i-tė) *n.* ❑ *mendacity*

men·ha′den (men-hā′dən) *n.* [*pl.* **men·
ha′den**] a marine fish of the eastern U.S.,
used in making fertilizer.

men′hir *n.* an upright ornamental stone.

me′ni·al (mē′nė-əl) *n.* **1,** a domestic servant. **2,** a servile person. —*adj.* lowly;
servile.

men″in·gi′tis (men″in-jī′tis) *n.* inflammation of the membranes (*meninges*) of
the brain and spinal cord.

---

fat, fāte, fär, fâre, fâll, ȧsk; met, hē, hėr, maybė; pin, pīne; not, nōte, ôr, tool

Men′no·nite″ (men′ə-nīt″) *n.* a member of a certain fundamentalist Protestant sect, named for the Frisian religious leader *Menno* Simons.

men′o·pause″ (men′ə-pâz″) *n.* the final cessation of the menses; change of life. —**men″o·pau′sal** (-əl) *adj.*

me·no′rah (mə-nô′rə) *n.* the Judaic seven-branched candelabrum.

mensch (mensh) *n.* (*Yiddish, informal*) a human being, esp. one with compassion for one's fellow person.

men′ses (men′sēz) *n.pl.* the monthly discharge from the uterus.

Men′she·vik (men′shə-vik) *n.* a member of the minority Russian Social-Democratic Workers' party in Russia in opposition to the Bolsheviks. ❏ *Bolshevik*

men′stru·ate″ (men′stroo-āt″) *v.i.* discharge the menses. —**men″stru·al,** *adj.* —**men″stru·a′tion,** *n.*

men′sur·a·ble (men′shər-ə-bəl) *adj.* measurable. —**men″su·ra′tion,** *n.* the process of measuring.

men′sur·al (men′shər-əl) *adj.* pert. to measure.

-ment (mənt) *suf.* the act, fact, or result of doing (the root word).

men′tal (men′təl) *adj.* pert. to, or performed by, the mind or intellect. —**mental deficiency** *or* **retardation,** subnormal intellectual development, often caused by a defect in the central nervous system.

men′tal·ist (-ist) *n.* mind reader.

men·tal′i·ty (men-tal′ə-tē) *n.* **1,** mental capacity. **2,** the mind.

men′thol (men′thol) *n.* a crystalline substance derived from oil of peppermint, useful in treating nasal disorders. —**men′-tho·lat″ed,** *adj.* treated with or containing menthol.

men′tion (men′shən) *v.t.* refer to briefly or incidentally. —*n.* a brief reference.

men′tor (men′tôr) *n.* a wise adviser; a trusted teacher and counselor.

> **mentor**
> ↔ From Greek *Mentōr*, an adviser whom Odysseus put in charge of his son, Telemachus.

men′u (men′ū) *n.* **1,** a bill of fare. **2,** any listing of features, options, etc., as on a computer.

me·ow′ (mē-ow′) *n.* the whining sound made by a cat. —*v.i.* so cry.

me·per′i·dine″ (mə-per′ə-dēn″) *n.* a synthetic, morphine-like narcotic drug: *me(thyl pi)peridine.*

me·phi′tis (mi-fī′tis) *n.* a noxious or poi-sonous exhalation; a stench. —**me·phit′ic** (-fit′ik) *adj.*

mer′can·tile (mēr′kən-til) *adj.* pert. to merchants or trading; commercial. —**mer′-can·til·ism,** *n.*

Mer·ca′tor projection (mēr-kā′tər) a method of map-making in which the meridians and parallels of latitude are straight lines, intersecting at right angles, named for 16th-c. Flemish mapmaker Gerhardus Mercator.

mer′ce·nar″y (mēr′sə-ner″ē) *adj.* serving only for gain; avaricious. —*n.* a hired soldier; a hireling.

mer′cer (mēr′sər) *n.* a dealer in cloth. —**mer′cer·y,** *n.*

mer′cer·ize″ (mēr′sə-rīz″) *v.t.* treat cotton fabric with caustic alkali, to increase its luster and strength.

> **mercerize**
> ↔ Named for the 19th-c. English fabric maker John *Mercer,* who invented the process.

mer′chan·dise″ (mēr′chən-dīs″) *n.* commodities bought and sold. —*v.t. & i.* (-dīz″) market.

mer′chant (mēr′chənt) *n.* one who buys and sells commodities. —**merchant marine,** ships used in commerce; their crews.

mer′chant·man (mēr′chənt-mən) *n.* [*pl.* -men] a trading vessel.

mer′ci·ful (mēr′si-fəl) *adj.* compassionate; lenient.

mer′ci·less (-ləs) *adj.* pitiless. —**mer′ci-less·ness,** *n.*

mer·cu′ri·al (mər-kyûr′ē-əl) *adj.* **1,** [also, **mer·cur′ic**] pert. to mercury. **2,** sprightly; changeable.

Mer·cu′ro·chrome″ (mər-kyûr′ə-krōm″) *n.* (*T.N.*) an antiseptic or germicide.

mer′cu·ry (mēr′kyə-rē) *n.* **1,** a fluid metallic element, no. 80, symbol Hg. **2,** (*cap.*) the planet nearest the sun. —**mer′cur·ous,** *adj.*

> **mercury**
> ↔ From the name of a Roman god of commerce. The planet name came first, then the name of the element.

mer′cy (mēr′sē) *n.* **1,** compassionate leniency toward an enemy or wrongdoer. **2,** discretionary power to punish or spare. —**mercy killing,** the painless putting to death of persons suffering from incurable diseases; euthanasia. —**mercy seat,** the throne of God.

mere (mir) *adj.* simple; only. —*n.* a lake; pond. —**mere′ly** (-lē) *adv.* simply; solely.

---

tub, cūte, pûll; labəl; oil, owl, gō, chip, she, thin, *th*en, sing, ink; *see p. 6*

mer″e·tri′cious (mer″ə-trish′əs) *adj.* deceitfully alluring; tawdry. **—mer″e·tri′- cious·ness,** *n.*

mer·gan′ser (mər-gan′sər) *n.* a fish-eating duck.

merge (mĕrj) *v.i.* **1,** be absorbed; lose identity. **2,** unite. **—***v.t.* cause to be absorbed or united.

merg′er (mĕr′jər) *n.* a uniting of two or more businesses.

me·rid′i·an (mə-rid′ė-ən) *n.* **1,** a great circle, of the earth or the heavens, passing through the poles; half of this circle. **2,** the zenith; midday. **—me·rid′i·o·nal,** *adj.*

me·ringue′ (mə-rang′) *n.* a white-of-egg and sugar coating for pastry.

me·ri′no (mə-rē′nō) *n.* [*pl.* **-nos**] a sheep prized for its fine wool.

mer′it *n.* **1,** a commendable quality; worthiness. **2,** (*pl.*) the qualities by which something is evaluated. **—***v.t.* deserve.

mer″i·toc′ra·cy (mer″i-tok′rə-sė) *n.* government or leadership by the most talented.

mer″i·to′ri·ous (mer″i-tôr′ė-əs) *adj.* deserving of praise or reward.

merle (mĕrl) *n.* the Europ. blackbird.

mer′lin (mĕr′lin) *n.* a small hawk.

mer′maid″ (mĕr′-), **mer′man″** *n.* an imaginary marine being, with the tail of a fish.

---

mermaid, merman
↔ Compounds of Old English *mere*, lake, pond.

---

mer′ry (mer′ė) *adj.* **1,** festive. **2,** mirthful. **—mer′ri·ment,** *n.*

mer′ry-an′drew (-an′droo) *n.* a clown; buffoon.

mer′ry-go-round″ (mer′ė-gō-rownd″) *n.* a revolving platform fitted with hobbyhorses etc.

mer′ry·mak″er (-mā′kər) *n.* a reveler. **—mer′ry·mak″ing,** *n.*

Mer·thi′o·late″ (mər-thī′ə-lāt″) *n.* (*T.N.*) a red liquid compound of mercury used as an antiseptic and germicide.

me′sa (mā′sə) *n.* a tableland.

més·al′li·ance (mā-zal′ė-əns) *n.* (*Fr.*) a marriage with a social inferior.

mes·cal′ (mes-kal′) *n.* **1,** a cactus. **2,** an intoxicating beverage.

mes′ca·line″ (mes′kə-lēn″) *n.* a crystalline hallucinogenic compound. Also, **mez′ca·line″.**

mesh *n.* an open space of a net; a network. **—***v.t.* **1,** entangle; enmesh. **2,** engage, as gear teeth. **—***v.i.* become engaged; work efficiently (with another).

me·shug′ga (mə-shûg′ə) *adj.* (*Heb.*) crazy; nonsensical. **—me·shug′ga·na** (-gə-nə) *n.* (*Heb.*) crazy person.

mesh′work *n.* network.

mes′mer·ism (mes′mə-riz-əm) *n.* hypnotism. **—mes′mer·ic** (-mer′ik) *adj.* **—mes′mer·ist,** *n.* **—mes′mer·ize″,** *v.t.*

---

mesmerism
↔ From the inventor of "animal magnetism," Austrian doctor Franz Anton *Mesmer.*

---

mes·o- (me-zə) *pref.* middle.

Mes″o·lith′ic (me″zə-lith′ik) *adj. & n.* (pert. to) the middle period of the Stone Age.

me′son (mē′zon) *n.* an unstable nuclear particle of variable charge, first found in cosmic rays. Also, **mes′o·tron″** (mez′ə-tron″).

me′so·sphere″ *n.* an atmospheric layer above the ionosphere.

Mes″o·zo′ic (mez″ə-zō′ik) *adj.* pert. to a geological era, the age of reptiles.

mes·quite′ (mes-kēt′) *n.* a shrub of the S.W. U.S., on which grazing cattle feed.

mess (mes) *n.* **1,** an untidy condition or mass. **2,** a confused situation. **3,** a group taking meals together; such a meal. **—***v.t.* make untidy; muddle. **—***v.i.* **1,** eat in company. **2,** act or work haphazardly.

mes′sage (mes′ij) *n.* a verbal or written communication.

mes′sen·ger (mes′ən-jər) *n.* **1,** one who bears a message or goes on an errand. **2,** a chemical that carries genetic information: *messenger RNA.*

Mes·si′ah (mə-sī′ə) *n.* **1,** the prophesied deliverer of the Jews; a savior. **2,** to Christians, Jesus Christ. **—Mes″si·an′ic** (mes″ė-an′ik) *adj.*

mess′mate″ *n.* an associate in a ship's mess.

mess′y (-ė) *adj.* untidy. **—mess′i·ness,** *n.*

mes·ti′zo (mes-tē′zō) *n.masc.,* **mes·ti′za** (-ä) *n.fem.* (*Sp.*) a person of mixed blood, as Sp. and Amer. Indian.

met *v.* pret. & p.p. of *meet.*

met·a- (met-ə) *pref.* along with; after; over; also denoting change or transformation.

me·tab′o·lism (mə-tab′ə-liz-əm) *n.* the chemical process of absorbing food. **—met″a·bol′ic** (met″ə-bol′ik) *adj.* **—me·tab′o·lite** (-līt) *n.* a product of metabolism.

met″a·car′pus (met″ə-kär′pəs) *n.* [*pl.* **-pi**

(pī)] the part of the hand between the wrist and the fingers.

met′a·gal′ax·y *n.* the entire material universe, including all seen and unseen galaxies. —**met″a·ga·lac′tic,** *adj.*

met′al (met′əl) *n.* an elementary substance possessing opacity, conductivity, plasticity, and a peculiar luster, as gold, silver, etc.; an alloy of such substances. —**me·tal′lic** (mə-tal′ik) *adj.* —**me·tal′li·cal·ly,** *adv.* ❏ *medal*

> **metal, mettle**
> ↔ Their very different meanings belie the fact that these two words have the same origin, in Greek *metallon,* a mine.

met′al·loid″ (met′ə-loid″) *n.* an element having some but not all of the properties of a metal.

met′al·lur″gy (met′ə-lēr″jē) *n.* the science of separating metals from their ores, treating metals, and compounding alloys. —**met″al·lur′gic,** *adj.* —**met′al·lur″gist,** *n.*

met′a·mor′pho·sis (met″ə-môr′fə-sis) *n.* a complete change of form, structure, or appearance. —**met″a·mor′phic,** *adj.* —**met″a·mor′phose** (-fōz) *v.t. & i.*

met′a·phor″ (met′ə-fôr″) *n.* a figure of speech, based on some resemblance of a literal to an implied subject. —**met″a·phor′i·cal** (-fôr′i-kəl), **met″a·phor′ic,** *adj.*

met″a·phys′ics (met″ə-fiz′iks) *n.* philosophy in general; particularly the science of essential principles, or the more abstruse or abstract principles. —**met″a·phys′i·cal,** *adj.* concerned with the abstract. —**met″a·phy·si′cian,** *n.*

> **metaphysics**
> ↔ From the Greek phrase *ta meta ta physika,* the (works) after the *Physics,* referring to Aristotle's works.

met′a·plasm (met′ə-plaz-əm) *n.* the lifeless matter included with protoplasm in a cell.

me·tas′ta·sis (mə-tas′tə-sis) *n.* **1,** a change of substance. **2,** transference of a disease to another part of the body. **3,** a sudden rhetorical transition. —**met″a·stat′ic,** *adj.*

met″a·tar′sus (met″ə-tär′səs) *n.* [*pl.* **-si** (-sī)] the foot bone between the ankle and toes. —**met″a·tar′sal,** *adj.*

me·tath′e·sis (mə-tath′ə-sis) [*pl.* **-ses** (-sēz)] *n.* the transposition of letters or sounds, as in the pronunciation (aks) for *ask.* —**met″a·thet′ic** (met″ə-thet′ik) *adj.*

Met″a·zo′a (met″ə-zō′ə) *n.* all those ani-

mals which are above the Protozoa, and have two or more cells. —**met″a·zo′an,** *adj. & n.*

mete (mēt) *v.t.* apportion by measure.

me·temp″sy·cho′sis (mə-temp″sə-kō′sis) *n.* [*pl.* **-ses** (-sēz)] the passing of the soul after death into another body; reincarnation.

me′te·or (mē′tē-ər) *n.* matter from space (such as a meteoroid) that becomes luminous upon entering the earth's atmosphere.

me″te·or′ic (-or′ik) *adj.* **1,** pert. to a meteor. **2,** transiently brilliant. —**me″te·or′i·cal·ly,** *adv.*

me′te·or·ite″ (-īt″) *n.* a mass of stone or metal that reaches the earth from outer space.

me′te·or·oid″ (-oid″) *n.* a small celestial body traveling through space.

me″te·or·ol′o·gy (mē″tē-ə-rol′ə-jē) *n.* the scientific study of the atmosphere, the weather, etc. —**me″te·or·o·log′i·cal,** *adj.*

me′ter (mē′tər) *n.* **1,** the metric unit of length, 39.37 inches. **2,** poetic or musical rhythm or measure. **3,** an instrument that measures, as gas, water, etc. —*v.t.* measure or record by a meter. Also, **me′tre.**

me′ter·maid″ *n.* a policewoman assigned to check for parking violations.

meth′a·done″ (meth′ə-dōn″) *n.* a synthetic, morphinelike narcotic drug.

meth′ane (meth′ān) *n.* an inflammable natural gas.

meth′a·nol″ (meth′ə-nol″) *n.* wood alcohol.

Meth′e·drine″ (meth′ə-drēn″) *n.* (*T.N.*) a brand of amphetamine drug.

meth′od (meth′əd) *n.* systematic procedure; a plan or system of conduct or action. —**me·thod′i·cal,** *adj.* following a method; orderly. —**meth′od·ize″,** *v.t.*

Meth′od·ist (meth′ə-dist) *n.* a member of the United Methodist Church, a principal Protestant sect. —**Meth′od·ism,** *n.*

meth″od·ol′o·gy (meth″ə-dol′ə-jē) *n.* **1,** a system of methods. **2,** the branch of logic dealing with the principles of reasoning in scientific inquiry.

meth′yl (meth′il) *n.* a derivative of methane. —**methyl alcohol,** wood alcohol.

meth″yl·mer′cu·ry *n.* a highly toxic compound used as a pesticide.

me·tic′u·lous (mə-tik′yə-ləs) *adj.* finically careful. —**me·tic′u·lous·ness,** *n.*

mé·tier′ (mā-tyā′) *n.* (*Fr.*) **1,** profession; trade. **2,** appropriate field or surroundings.

mé·tis′ (mā-tēs′) *n.* (*Sp.*) **1,** a person of

mixed blood; halfbreed. **2,** a crossbred animal. Also, **mé·tif′** (-tēf′).

Met′ra·zol″ (met′rə-zōl″) *n.* (*T.N.*) a drug, a heart and lung stimulant.

met′ric (met′rik) *adj.* **1,** pert. to the meter (measure of length). **2,** pert. to measurement. —**metric system,** a decimal system of weights and measures.

met′ri·cal (met′ri-kəl) *adj.* **1,** composed in meter, as verse. **2,** metric.

met′ri·cize″ (met′ri-sīz″) *v.t.* convert to the metric system. —**met″ri·ca′tion,** *n.*

met′rics (met′riks) *n.* (*construed as sing.*) **1,** the science of meter. **2,** the art of composing metered verse.

met′ro (met′rō) *n.* **1,** the Paris subway; any subway. **2,** metropolitan region. —*adj.* metropolitan.

met′ro·nome″ (met′rə-nōm″) *n.* a mechanical contrivance for signaling intervals of time.

me·trop′o·lis (mə-trop′ə-lis) *n.* the chief city of a country or region.

> **metropolis**
> ↔ From Greek *mētropolis*, mother city.

met″ro·pol′i·tan (met″rə-pol′ə-tən) *adj.* characteristic of a metropolis. —*n.* **1,** an inhabitant of a metropolis. **2,** (*cap.*) a title in the Orthodox Church, equivalent to archbishop.

-me·try (mə-trē) *suf.* measurement.

met′tle (met′əl) *n.* natural temperament; courage. —**met′tle·some,** *adj.* spirited. ❏ *metal*

mew (mū) *n.* **1,** an enclosure. **2,** (*pl.*) a set of stables around a court. **3,** meow. —*v.i.* meow.

mewl (mūl) *v.i.* whine; whimper.

Mex′i·can (mek′si-kən) *adj. & n.* pert. to Mexico, its language or inhabitants.

mez′za·nine″ (mez′ə-nēn″) *n.* **1,** a low story between two principal stories. **2,** a theater balcony.

mez·zo- (met′sō-) *pref.* intermediate.

mez′zo-so·pran′o *n.* a voice intermediate between soprano and contralto. Also, **mez′zo.**

mez′zo·tint″ *n.* an engraving made by roughening a copper or other metallic surface.

mho (mō) *n.* a unit of electrical conductivity. ❏ *ohm*

mi (mē) *n.* (*Music*) the third tone in the diatonic scale.

mi·aou′ (mē-ow′) *n. & v.i.* meow.

mi·as′ma (mī-az′mə) *n.* noxious emanation.

mi′ca (mī′kə) *n.* a mineral readily separable into thin sheets. ❏ *Formica*

mice (mīs) *n. pl.* of *mouse.*

Mick′ey (mik′ē) *n.* (*Slang*) a drink containing knockout drops or a purgative. Also, **Mickey Finn.**

Mick′ey Mouse′ *adj.* (*often l.c., Slang*) petty; unimportant.

mi·cro- (mī-krə) *pref.* **1,** very small. **2,** one-millionth part. Also, before vowels, **mi′cr-.**

mi′crobe (mī′krōb) *n.* a germ; a bacterium. —**mi·cro′bic,** *adj.*

> **microbe**
> ↔ Coined from Greek *mikros*, small, and *bios*, life, by 19th-c. French surgeon Charles Sédillot.

mi′cro·bi·ol′o·gy *n.* the branch of biology dealing with microorganisms.

mi′cro·cas·sette″ *n.* a small tape cassette, used esp. for dictation.

mi′cro·cir″cuit *n.* integrated circuit.

mi″cro·com·pu′ter *n.* a small computer, esp. for personal or small-business use.

mi′cro·cosm (mī′krə-koz-əm) *n.* **1,** a little world; a world in miniature. **2,** fig., a human being.

mi′cro·dot″ *n.* **1,** printed matter reduced photographically to the size of a dot. **2,** a small pill of concentrated LSD.

mi′cro·fiche″ (-fēsh″) *n.* a card or sheet of microfilm containing information considerably reduced in size.

mi′cro·film″ *n.* the film used in microphotography.

mi′cro·graph″ *n.* **1,** a pantograph for drawing and engraving in microscopic size. **2,** a photograph or drawing of an object as seen through a microscope. —**mi·crog′raph·y** (mī-krog′rə-fē) *n.*

mi′cro·groove″ (mī′krə-groov″) *n.* **1,** an extremely narrow groove in a long-playing phonograph record. **2,** such a record.

mi·crom′e·ter (mī-krom′ə-tər) *n.* a precision instrument for measuring distances in thousandths of an inch or less.

mi′cron (mī′kron) *n.* [*pl.* **-cra** (-krə), **-crons**] one-millionth of a meter.

Mi″cro·ne′sian (mī″krə-nē′zhən) *adj.* pert. to a large group of islands in the So. Pacific, one of the three principal divisions of Oceania.

mi″cro·or′gan·ism (mī″krō-ôr′gə-niz-əm) *n.* an organism of microscopic size; a microbe, germ, etc.

mi′cro·phone″ *n.* an instrument that transforms sound waves into variations in an electric current; used esp. in telephonic and radio transmission and in recording.

mi″cro·pho′to·graph″ *n.* **1,** a minute film reproduction, esp. of printed or written matter, read by enlargement on a screen. **2,** photomicrograph. —**mi″cro·pho·tog′ra·phy,** *n.*

mi′cro·proc·es·sor *n.* an integrated circuit used as a CPU.

mi′cro·scope″ *n.* an instrument that magnifies objects not visible to the naked eye or too small to be seen distinctly.

mi″cro·scop′ic (-skop′ik) *adj.* **1,** pert. to a microscope. **2,** extremely small. —**mi″cro·scop′i·cal·ly,** *adv.*

mi′cro·sur″ger·y *n.* extremely delicate surgery performed under a microscope.

mi′cro·tome″ (-tōm″) *n.* an instrument for cutting tissue, etc., into thin sections for examination under the microscope.

mi′cro·wave″ *n.* (*Radio*) a very small electromagnetic wave having a wavelength less than one meter. —*v.t.* to cook using microwaves. —**microwave oven,** a cooking machine using microwaves to heat food.

mid *adj.* middle. —*prep.* amid; among.

mid- *pref.* middle.

mid′air″ *adj.* occurring in the air.

mid′day″ *n.* the middle of the day; noon.

mid′dle (mid′əl) *adj.* **1,** equally distant from the extremes or limits. **2,** intermediate; intervening. —*n.* **1,** the center; a middle point or area. **2,** the waist; the stomach. —**Middle Ages,** the period between classical antiquity and the Renaissance, roughly 500 to 1400 A.D. —**middle class,** an intermediate social or economic class. —**middle ear,** (*Anat.*) the tympanum. —**Middle East, 1,** a region including Iran, Iraq, and Afghanistan, and sometimes Burma, Tibet, and India. **2,** (*Brit.*) the Near East (def. 1). Also, **Mid′-east″.** —**middle-of-the-road,** *adj.* neutral; midway between extremes. —**middle school,** a division in some schools, often corresponding to junior high school. —**Middle West,** north central states of U.S.

mid′dle-aged′ (-ājd′) *adj.* intermediate in age; from about 45 to 60 years old.

mid′dle·man″ *n.* [*pl.* **-men**] an intermediary; esp. in business, a wholesaler or retailer.

mid′dle·weight″ (mid′əl-wāt″) *n.* a boxer weighing 148 to 160 lbs.

mid′dling (mid′ling) *adj.* **1,** of medium quality or size. **2,** (*Informal*) in moderate health.

mid′dy (mid′ē) *n.* **1,** a midshipman. **2,** a loose blouse with a sailor collar: *middy blouse.*

midge (mij) *n.* a small fly.

midg′et (mij′it) *n.* a very small person or thing. ❑ *dwarf*

mid′i (mid′ē) *n.* **1,** midiskirt. **2,** a standard protocol for encoding and transmitting musically related data between computers and/or musical devices: *M(usical) I(nstrument) D(igital) I(nterface).*

mid′i·dress″ (mid′ē-) *n.* a woman's dress of mid-calf length. —**mid′i·skirt″,** *n.* a woman's skirt of mid-calf length. Also, *informal,* **mid′i.**

mid′i″ron (mid′ī″ərn) *n.* a golf club used for long approach shots, No. 2 iron.

mid′land (mid′lənd) *adj.* in the interior of a country; inland.

mid′life″ *n.* middle age. —**midlife crisis,** psychological stress associated with middle age.

mid′night″ (mid′nīt″) *n.* 12 o'clock at night. —*adj.* **1,** at midnight. **2,** intensely black or dark. —**midnight sun,** the sun visible at midnight during the summer in Arctic or Antarctic regions.

mid′point″ *n.* **1,** a point at the middle of a line or curve. **2,** a moment midway between two points in time.

mid′riff″ (mid′rif) *n.* **1,** the diaphragm. **2,** a dress open at the midriff.

mid′ship″man (mid′ship″mən) *n.* [*pl.* **-men**] one in training to be a naval officer; her or his rank.

midst *n.* an interior or central position; middle.

mid′stream″ *n.* the middle of a stream, current of affairs, etc.

mid′sum″mer *n.* the middle of summer; the summer solstice.

mid′way″ (mid′wā″) *adj.* halfway. —*n.* a place for side shows at a fair.

> **midway**
> ↔ This comes from the *Midway* Plaisance, the main street at the 1893 Chicago Columbian Exposition.

Mid′west′ *n.* Middle West.

mid′wife″ *n.* a person who assists at childbirth. —*v.t.* assist in the birth or development of. —**mid′wife″ry,** *n.*

> **midwife**
> ↔ The *wife* in *midwife* meant woman in Old English and *mid* meant with; hence, the sense is woman with (another).

mid′win″ter *n.* the middle of winter; the winter solstice.

mien (mēn) *n.* a person's bearing, manner, appearance.

miff (mif) *v.t.* (*Informal*) offend.

might (mīt) *n.* effective power; ability. —*aux. v.* pret. of *may.*

might′y (mī′tė) *adj.* powerful; momentous. —*adv.* (*Informal*) very. —**might′i-ness,** *n.*

mi″gnon·ette′ (min″yə-net′) *n.* a fragrant garden plant.

mi′graine (mī′grān) *n.* a severe headache, sometimes accompanied by nausea.

> **migraine**
> ↔ From Greek *hēmikrania*, half-cranium, hence the sense, pain in one part of the head.

mi′grant (mī′grənt) *n.* one who or that which migrates. —*adj.* migrating.

mi′grate (mī′grāt) *v.i.* **1,** go from one country or place of residence to settle in another. **2,** move periodically from one region or latitude to another, esp. birds. —**mi·gra′tion,** *n.* —**mi′gra·to·ry,** *adj.*

mi·ka′do (mi-kä′dō) *n.* formerly, the emperor of Japan.

mike (mīk) (*Slang*) *n.* **1,** a microphone. **2,** (*Communications*) the letter *m.* —*v.t.* measure with a micrometer.

mil *n.* a unit of length, .001 inch.

milch *adj.* giving milk, as a cow.

mild (mīld) *adj.* even-tempered; gentle; temperate; moderate in intensity or degree; not severe, as weather; not sharp, as flavor. —**mild′ness,** *n.*

mil′dew (mil′doo) *n.* **1,** a fungus disease of plants. **2,** a white fungus coating on fabrics, leather, etc., from exposure to moisture. —*v.t. & i.* become covered with mildew.

mile (mīl) *n.* a Brit. and Amer. unit of distance, 5,280 ft. (*statute mile*) on land, 6,080 ft. (*nautical mile*) at sea.

> **mile**
> ↔ From Latin *mille*, thousand; the Roman mile was 1,000 paces (much shorter than our measure).

mile′age (mī′lij) *n.* **1,** the miles traveled in a given time. **2,** a fixed charge per mile. **3,** a traveling allowance.

mile′post″ *n.* **1,** a post marking the distance in miles along a highway. **2,** (*fig.*) an important point of time, as in a lifetime.

mil′er (mīl′ər) *n.* a runner trained to race a mile.

mile′stone″ (mīl′stōn″) *n.* **1,** a stone distance-marker along a highway. **2,** an important event in life; a birthday.

mil″i·ar′i·a (mil″ē-âr′ē-ə) *n.* an inflammatory skin disease. —**mil′i·ar·y,** *adj.*

mi·lieu′ (mē-lyû′) *n.* surroundings; environment.

mil′i·tant (mil′i-tənt) *adj.* **1,** aggressive. **2,** engaged in warfare. —*n.* one engaged in warfare. —**mil′i·tan·cy,** *n.*

mil′i·ta·rism (mil′ə-tə-riz-əm) *n.* extreme emphasis on military power in state policy. —**mil′i·ta·rist,** *n.* —**mil″i·ta·ris′tic,** *adj.*

mil′i·ta·rize″ (mil′i·tə-rīz″) *v.t.* equip or prepare for war. —**mil″i·tar·i·za′tion,** *n.*

mil′i·tar″y (mil′ə-ter″ė) *adj.* **1,** pert. to the army, a soldier, or affairs of war; soldierly. **2,** pert. to any arm or instrument of warfare. —*n.* the armed forces.

mil′i·tate″ (mil′ə-tāt″) *v.i.* have weight or force, against or for.

> **militate, mitigate**
> ☞ These two confusables have very different meanings. To *militate* is to have persuasive force; to *mitigate* is to moderate.

mi·li′tia (mi-lish′ə) *n.* a body of citizen soldiers, called out only in emergencies. —**mi·li′tia·man** (-mən) [*pl.* **-men**], **mi·li′tia·wom″an,** *n.*

milk *n.* **1,** a whitish liquid secreted by the mammary glands of female mammals for feeding their young. **2,** any liquid resembling this. —*v.t.* **1,** extract milk from a cow, etc. **2,** extract; draw out; exploit. —**milk fever,** a fever coincident with lactation. —**milk leg,** thrombosis and swelling of the large veins of the leg. —**milk of magnesia,** a mild laxative. —**milk shake,** an iced drink of milk, a flavoring syrup, and usu. ice cream, shaken together. —**milk tooth,** one of the temporary teeth of a young child or animal; baby tooth.

milk′maid″ *n.* a woman who milks cows; dairymaid.

milk′man″ *n.* [*pl.* **-men**] a man who delivers milk for a dairy.

milk′sop″ *n.* a soft, effeminate man.

milk′weed″ *n.* a plant having milky juice.

milk′wort″ (-wērt″) *n.* a flowering herb or shrub.

milk′y (mil′kė) *adj.* **1,** like milk. **2,** white. —**milk′i·ness,** *n.* —**Milky Way,** a luminous band in the heavens, composed of innumerable stars.

mill (mil) *n.* **1,** a manufacturing establishment; factory. **2,** a building equipped to grind grain into flour. **3,** any of various machines for grinding, or otherwise working materials into proper form. **4,** 1/10 of a cent in U.S. money. —*v.i.* move in a circle, as cattle. —*v.t.* **1,** grind, etc., in or with a mill. **2,** groove the edge of (a coin, etc.).

mil·len'ni·um (mi-len'ė-əm) *n.* **1,** 1,000 years; 1,000th anniversary. **2,** any period of universal happiness. —**mil·len'ni·al** (-əl) *adj.*

mill'er (mil'ər) *n.* **1,** one who operates a grain mill. **2,** a small moth.

mil'let (mil'it) *n.* a cereal grass, grown for grain or fodder.

mil·li- (mil-ə) *pref.* 1,000; in the metric system, 1/1,000th. —**mil'li·gram"**, 1/1000th gram. —**mil'li·me"ter,** *n.* 1/1000th meter.

mil'liard (mil'yərd) *n.* (*Brit.*) 1,000 million; billion.

mil'li·ner (mil'ə-nər) *n.* one who makes or sells women's hats. —**mil'li·ner"y,** *n.* women's hats.

> **milliner**
> ↔ From *Milaner,* an importer of goods from Milan, a center of fancy clothing and accessories.

mill'ing *n.* **1,** act or process of grinding, etc. **2,** the grooves or ridges on the edge of a coin. **3,** a slow circulating movement in a crowd of persons, cattle, etc. **4,** (*Slang*) a thrashing.

mil'lion (mil'yən) *n.* 1,000 times 1,000: 1,000,000.

mil"lion·aire' (mil"yə-nâr') *n.* a person worth 1,000,000 dollars, pounds, etc.; a very rich person.

mil'lionth (mil'yənth) *adj. & n.* the ordinal of 1,000,000, also written 1,000,000th; one of 1,000,000 equal parts.

mil'li·pede" (-pēd") *n.* any of several insects with a many-segmented body.

mill'race" *n.* the current of water that drives a mill, or the channel in which it flows.

mill'stone" *n.* **1,** one of two heavy circular stones between which grain is ground. **2,** a heavy burden.

mi'lo (mī'lō) *n.* a milletlike sorghum grown in the U.S. for forage.

milque'toast" (milk'-) *n.* (*Slang*) a timid person.

> **milquetoast**
> ↔ After a comic strip character, Caspar *Milquetoast,* created by cartoonist H. T. Webster.

mil'reis" (mil'rās") *n.* the former monetary unit of Brazil and Portugal.

milt *n.* **1,** the reproductive organs of male fish. **2,** fish sperm. —*adj.* breeding. —*v.t.* fertilize (roe) with milt.

mime (mīm) *n.* **1,** a mummer. **2,** in ancient drama, a farce.

mim'e·o·graph" (mim'ė-ə-gràf") *n.* a device for duplicating letters, etc., by means of stencils. —*v.t.* copy by mimeograph. Also, (*Informal*) **mim'e·o** (-ō).

mim'ic (mim'ik) *v.t.* [**mim'icked, mim'ick·ing**] imitate, esp. derisively. —*n.* an imitator; one apt at mimicking. —*adj.* **1,** imitative. **2,** simulated, esp. on a smaller scale.

mim'ic·ry (-rė) *n.* act or result of mimicking.

mi·mo'sa (mi-mō'sə) *n.* a tropical tree or shrub having globular flowers. —**mim"o·sa'ceous** (mim"ə-sā'shəs) *adj.*

Min"a·ma'ta disease (min"ə-mä'tə) a form of mercury poisoning.

min"a·ret' (min"ə-ret') *n.* a slender tower attached to a mosque.

min'a·to"ry (min'ə-tôr'ė) *adj.* menacing.

mince (mins) *v.t.* **1,** cut into small pieces. **2,** speak of euphemistically; minimize; moderate. —*v.i.* walk daintily; act or speak with affected delicacy. —**minc'ing,** *adj.* affectedly elegant.

mince'meat" *n.* **1,** a pie filling of minced suet, fruits, etc. **2,** anything chopped into small pieces.

mind (mīnd) *n.* **1,** that with which a living being feels, wills, and thinks; the ego. **2,** the intellect, as distinguished from feeling and volition; intellectual ability. **3,** reason; sanity. **4,** opinion; inclination; disposition. **5,** purpose; intention. **6,** memory. —*v.t. & i.* **1,** pay attention to; obey. **2,** take care of; attend to. **3,** care about; object to.

mind-'blow"ing (*Informal*) *adj.* **1,** shocking; surprising. **2,** hallucinogenic.

mind-'bog"gling *adj.* (*Informal*) overwhelming.

-mind'ed (mīn'dəd) *suf.* **1,** inclined. **2,** having such a mind, as *high-minded, weak-minded.*

mind-'ex·pand"ing *adj.* (of drugs) causing an apparent increase in one's sensitivity and understanding.

mind'ful (-fəl) *adj.* aware. —**mind'ful·ness,** *n.*

mind'less *adj.* thoughtless; heedless.

mind-'read"ing *n.* the art of reading or discerning another's thoughts. —**mind'read"er,** *n.*

mind′set″ *n.* (*Informal*) attitude; frame of mind.

mine (mīn) *pron.* poss. of *I;* belonging to me. —*n.* **1,** a deposit of mineral ores or coal, or the excavation made for removing them. **2,** an abounding source of anything. **3,** a charge of explosives submerged in the water or buried on land. **4,** an excavated passage for placing explosives under enemy fortifications. —*v.t. & i.* **1,** extract ores, etc. **2,** make subterranean passages. **3,** lay explosive mines. —**min′er,** *n.* —**min′ing,** *n.* —**mine field,** an area on land or water systematically covered with mines; hence an area of danger.

mine′lay″er *n.* a naval vessel specially equipped for placing mines.

min′er·al (min′ər-əl) *n.* **1,** an inorganic substance occurring in nature, of a definite chemical composition and definite structure. **2,** anything inorganic. —*adj.* **1,** of or pert. to minerals. **2,** containing minerals. —**mineral oil, 1,** petroleum. **2,** a laxative. —**mineral water,** water naturally or artificially impregnated with metallic salts. —**mineral wool,** an insulating material made from slag.

min′er·al·ize″ (-īz″) *v.t.* **1,** change (metal) to ore. **2,** change (organic matter) to a mineral; petrify. **3,** impregnate with minerals. —*v.i.* collect mineral specimens. —**min″er·al·i·za′tion,** *n.*

min″er·al′o·gy (min″ər-al′ə-jė) *n.* the science of minerals. —**min″er·al′o·gist,** *n.*

min″e·stro′ne (min″ə-strō′nė) *n.* an Ital. soup containing vegetables, herbs, etc.

mine′sweep″er *n.* a naval vessel that clears away mines.

min′gle (ming′gəl) *v.t. & i.* **1,** mix; blend; unite. **2,** associate.

mi·ni- (min-ė) *pref.* especially small, short, etc.

min′i·a·ture (min′ė-ə-chər) *n.* **1,** anything represented on a greatly reduced scale. **2,** anything small, esp. a portrait. —*adj.* small. —**min′i·a·tur·ize″,** *v.t.*

min′i·bike″ *n.* a small motorcycle.

min′i·bus″ *n.* a van or small bus.

min′i·cam″ (-kam″) *n.* a miniature camera, esp. for television.

min′i·com·pu′ter *n.* a medium-size computer, esp. for small-business use.

min′i·dress″ *n.* a very short dress for women. —**min′i·skirt″,** *n.* a very short skirt for women. Also, *informal,* **min′i.**

min′im (min′əm) *n.* **1,** the smallest unit of liquid measure, about one drop. **2,** something very small. **3,** (*Music*) an eighth note.

min′i·mal *adj.* representing or pert. to a minimum. —**minimal art,** a movement, esp. in painting and sculpture, rejecting complexity and tradition.

min′·i·mal·ism″ *n.* **1,** a musical style employing simple rhythms, harmonies, etc. **2,** a style of painting and sculpture characterized by simplicity of form and impersonality. —**min′i·mal·ist″,** *adj.*

min′i·mize″ (min′ə-mīz″) *v.t.* **1,** reduce to a minimum. **2,** belittle.

min′i·mum (min′ə-məm) *n.* the least possible, or lowest actual, degree, amount, etc. —**minimum wage,** the lowest wage payable to employees, as established by law.

min′ion (min′yən) *n.* **1,** an obsequious favorite, as of a prince. **2,** a subordinate.

min′i·ser′ies *n.* a short series of events; esp., a television program televised in several segments.

min′is·ter (min′is-tər) *n.* **1,** a member of the clergy; pastor. **2,** a diplomatic envoy. **3,** (esp. *Brit.*) a high state official, esp. head of a department. —*v.i.* (with *to*) attend; care for; contribute. —**min′is·trant** (-trənt) *n. & adj.*

---

minister
↔ From the Latin word for servant; a *minister* is a servant of the flock (or of God) or of the crown.

---

min″is·te′ri·al (-tir′ė-əl) *adj.* pert. to a minister or ministry.

min″is·tra′tion (-trā′shən) *n.* the act of serving or helping; an act of service or aid. —**min′is·tra″tive,** *adj.*

min′is·try (min′is-trė) *n.* **1,** the office or function of a clergyman or minister of state. **2,** the clergy, or the ministers of state, collectively. **3,** (*Brit.*) an administrative department of the government.

mink *n.* a fur-bearing aquatic animal; its fur.

min′ne·sing″er (min′ə-sing″ər) *n.* German lyric poet and singer of the 12th and 13th centuries.

min′now (min′ō) *n.* a small freshwater fish.

mi′nor (mī′nər) *adj.* **1,** lesser in importance, size, or extent. **2,** under legal age. **3,** (*Music*) pert. to a certain scale or smaller interval. —*n.* **1,** one not of legal age. **2,** a secondary field of study. —**minor league,** (*Baseball*) any of the leagues of Amer. baseball teams other than the two major leagues.

mi·nor′i·ty (mi-nor′ə-tė) *n.* **1,** the lesser part or number; less than half. **2,** a less numerous party or group, as political or racial, among a more numerous. **3,** the state of being below legal age.

min'ster (min'stər) *n.* a church or cathedral.

min'strel (min'strəl) *n.* **1,** originally, an itinerant musician or singer, esp. of ballads. **2,** a blackfaced singer or comedian. —**min'strel·sy,** *n.*

mint *n.* **1,** any of several aromatic herbs. **2,** a mint-flavored confection. **3,** a place where money is coined under governmental authority. **4,** a vast amount. —*adj.* unused (of a postage stamp). —*v.t.* coin (money). —**mint julep,** a drink made of whiskey, sugar, ice, and fresh mint.

mint'age (-ij) *n.* the process, result, or cost of minting.

min'u·end'' (min'ū-end'') *n.* a number from which another number is to be subtracted.

min''u·et' (min''ū-et') *n.* a slow and stately ballroom dance.

---

minuet

↔ From French *menu*, short, because the dancers' steps were very short.

---

mi'nus (mī'nəs) *prep.* **1,** less (by a certain amount). **2,** lacking. —*adj.* **1,** less than nothing; negative. **2,** (*Math.*) denoting subtraction, as the minus sign (–).

mi'nus·cule'' (min'ə''skyûl) *adj.* small, esp. of letters; not capital.

min'ute (min'it) *n.* **1,** the sixtieth part of an hour; sixty seconds. **2,** a short space of time. **3,** a moment; a point of time. **4,** a summary; a rough draft. **5,** (*pl.*) a record of the proceedings at a meeting. **6,** the sixtieth part of a degree. —*adj.* quickly prepared. —**minute steak,** a very thin cut of beefsteak that cooks very quickly.

mi·nute' (mī-nūt') *adj.* **1,** extremely small in size. **2,** very small in scope. —**mi·nute'ness,** *n.*

min'ute·man'' (min'it-man'') *n.* [*pl.* -**men**] **1,** a member of the Amer. militia of Revolutionary times. **2,** (*pl., cap.*) a reactionary political group.

mi·nu'ti·ae (mi-nū'shė-ė) *n.pl.* [*sing.* -**a** (-ə)] trivial details.

minx (minks) *n.* a pert girl.

mir (mēr) *n.* formerly, a community of Russian peasants, holding land in common.

mi·ra'bi·le dic'tu (mi-rab'ə-lė dik'too) (*Lat.*) marvelous to relate; strange to say.

mir'a·cle (mir'ə-kəl) *n.* **1,** an act or happening attributed to supernatural power. **2,** a wonderful thing.

mi·rac'u·lous (mi-rak'yə-ləs) *adj.* being, or like, a miracle; wonderful.

mi·rage' (mi-räzh') *n.* an optical illusion by which images of distant objects can be seen.

Mi·ran'da (mi-ran'də) *adj.* pert. to a 1966 court ruling requiring that a person taken into custody be informed of her or his constitutional right to remain silent or to be represented by a lawyer.

mire (mīr) *n.* **1,** wet, slimy ground; deep mud. **2,** filth. —*v.t.* **1,** sink or fix in mire. **2,** soil with filth. **3,** involve in difficulties. —*v.i.* sink in mire. —**mir'y,** *adj.* muddy; filthy.

mir'ror (mir'ər) *n.* **1,** a surface that reflects clear images; a looking glass. **2,** anything that gives a true picture or reflection. —*v.t.* reflect; imitate.

mirth (mērth) *n.* festive gaiety; amusement; laughter.

mirth'ful *adj.* **1,** full of mirth. **2,** causing mirth. —**mirth'less,** *adj.*

mis- *pref.* **1,** bad; wrong; erroneous. **2,** negative. **3,** hating.

mis''ad·ven'ture *n.* a mishap; ill fortune.

mis'an·thrope'' (mis'ən-thrōp'') *n.* a hater of humankind. Also, **mis·an'thro·pist** (mis-an'thrə-pist).

mis·an'thro·py (mis-an'thrə-pė) *n.* dislike of, or evil deeds toward, humankind. —**mis''an·throp'ic** (mis''ən-throp'ik) *adj.* —**mis''an·throp'i·cal·ly,** *adv.*

mis''ap·pre·hend' *v.t.* misunderstand. —**mis''ap·pre·hen'sion,** *n.*

mis''ap·pro'pri·ate'' *v.t.* put to a wrong or dishonest use, as funds. —**mis''ap·pro'pri·a'tion,** *n.*

mis''be·got'ten (mis''bė-got'ən) *adj.* illegitimate.

mis''be·have' *v.i.* behave badly. —**mis''be·hav'ior,** *n.*

mis''be·lieve' *v.t.* doubt.

mis''cal'cu·late'' *v.t. & i.* calculate incorrectly. —**mis''cal·cu·la'tion,** *n.*

mis·car'riage (mis-kar'ij) *n.* **1,** failure to arrive at a just result, as of justice. **2,** failure to arrive at destination, as a letter. **3,** untimely or premature delivery of young. —**mis·car'ry,** *v.i.*

mis''ce·ge·na'tion (mis''i-jə-nā'shən) *n.* interbreeding between races.

---

miscegenation

↔ Supposedly coined from Latin *miscere*, to mix, and *genus*, species, by 19th-c. U.S. journalist David G. Croly.

---

mis''cel·la'ne·ous (mis''ə-lā'nė-əs) *adj.*

---

consisting of a mixture; diversified; varied.

mis'cel·la"ny (mis'ə-lā"nè) *n.* a collection of unrelated or somewhat related items, as literary compositions on varied subjects. Also, **mis"cel·la'ne·a** (-ə) *n.pl.*

mis·chance' *n.* a mishap; ill luck.

mis'chief (mis'chif) *n.* **1,** an injury; a petty annoyance; trouble. **2,** a cause or source of trouble.

mis'chie·vous (mis'chə-vəs) *adj.* **1,** injurious; annoying. **2,** fond of mischief; teasing. —**mis'chie·vous·ness,** *n.*

mis'ci·ble (mis'ə-bəl) *adj.* capable of being mixed. —**mis"ci·bil'i·ty,** *n.*

mis"con·ceive' *v.t. & i.* misunderstand. —**mis"con·cep'tion,** *n.*

mis·con'duct (mis-kon'dukt) *n.* **1,** improper conduct. **2,** unlawful conduct, as by an official, lawyer, etc. —*v.t.* (mis"kən-dukt') mismanage.

mis"con·strue' *v.t.* misinterpret. —**mis"-con·struc'tion,** *n.*

mis·count' *v.t.* count incorrectly. —*n.* (mis'kownt) a wrong count.

mis'cre·ant (mis'krē-ənt) *n.* a villain; a scoundrel. —*adj.* villainous. —**mis'cre·ancy** (-ən-sè) *n.*

mis·cue' *n.* **1,** a slip of the cue (at billiards). **2,** a failure to take a hint, or to answer one's cue (in the theater). —*v.i.* make a miscue.

mis·deed' *n.* a wicked action.

mis"de·mean'or (mis"də-mē'nər) *n.* **1,** (*Law*) an offense less serious than a felony. **2,** misbehavior.

mis"di·rect' *v.t.* **1,** give erroneous information or instruction to. **2,** address incorrectly (a letter, etc.). —**mis"di·rec'tion,** *n.*

mise en scène (mē"zän-sen') (*Fr.*, put on stage) (*Theat.*) **1,** stage setting; production. **2,** staging; direction.

mi'ser (mī'zər) *n.* an avaricious, niggardly person; one who hoards money. —**mi'ser·ly,** *adj.* —**mi'ser·li·ness,** *n.*

mis'er·a·ble (miz'ər-ə-bəl) *adj.* **1,** wretched; unhappy; poor. **2,** manifesting, causing, or attended with, misery. **3,** mean; contemptible. **4,** (*Informal*) ailing.

mis'er·y (miz'ə-rè) *n.* **1,** physical or mental suffering; wretchedness; poverty. **2,** a cause of suffering. **3,** (*Informal*) a bodily ailment.

mis·fea'sance (mis-fē'zəns) *n.* the misuse of power; a wrongful exercise of lawful authority.

mis·fire' *v.i.* **1,** fail to explode or fire. **2,** go wrong; not produce the desired effect.

mis'fit *n.* **1,** something that does not fit,

as a garment of the wrong size; state of being unsuitable. **2,** a person poorly adapted to his or her job, society, etc.

mis·for'tune *n.* **1,** bad luck; adversity. **2,** a mishap; a calamity.

mis·giv'ing *n.* a feeling of doubt or apprehension.

mis·guide' *v.t.* advise badly; mislead.

mis·han'dle *v.t.* handle badly or roughly; maltreat.

mis'hap *n.* an unfortunate occurrence.

mish'mash" *n.* a jumble.

mis"in·form' *v.t.* give false information to. —**mis"in·for·ma'tion,** *n.*

mis"in·ter'pret *v.t.* understand, or explain, incorrectly.

mis·judge' *v.t. & i.* have an unjust or incorrect opinion (of). —**mis·judg'ment,** *n.*

mis·lay' *v.t.* [*pret. & p.p.* **mis·laid'**] **1,** lay away and forget. **2,** place incorrectly.

mis·lead' (mis-lēd') *v.t.* lead astray; lead into error; delude.

mis·man'age *v.t. & i.* manage badly. —**mis·man'age·ment,** *n.*

mis·match' *v.t.* match inaccurately or unsuitably. —*n.* a wrong or poor match, esp. a marriage between persons not suited for each other.

mis·no'mer (mis-nō'mər) *n.* a misapplied term, name, or designation; a misnaming.

mi·sog'a·my (mi-sog'ə-mē) *n.* hatred of marriage. —**mi·sog'a·mist,** *n.*

mi·sog'y·ny (mi-soj'ə-nē) *n.* hatred of women. —**mi·sog'y·nist,** *n.*

mis·place' *v.t.* **1,** put in a wrong place. **2,** bestow unwisely, as confidence.

mis'print" *n.* a typographical error. —*v.* (mis-print') print incorrectly.

mis·pri'sion (mis-prizh'ən) *n.* **1,** concealment of the crime of another, esp. of treason. **2,** any serious offense, esp. in a position of trust.

mis"pro·nounce' *v.t. & i.* pronounce incorrectly. —**mis"pro·nun"ci·a'tion,** *n.*

mis·quote' *v.t. & i.* quote incorrectly. —**mis"quo·ta'tion,** *n.*

mis·read' (mis-rēd') *v.t.* misinterpret.

mis"rep·re·sent' *v.t.* represent falsely or imperfectly. —**mis"rep·re·sen·ta'tion,** *n.*

mis·rule' *v.t.* govern badly. —*n.* **1,** bad or unwise rule. **2,** disorder.

miss (mis) *v.t.* **1,** fail to reach or attain what is aimed at, expected, or desired. **2,** feel the want of, or absence of. **3,** avoid. **4,** overlook. —*v.i.* fail to attain; be unsuccessful. —*n.* **1,** a failure to accomplish, etc.

2, a young woman; an unmarried woman. ❏ *Mrs.*

mis'sal (mis'əl) *n.* a prayer book.

mis·shap'en (mi-shā'pən) *adj.* deformed. —**mis·shap'en·ness,** *n.*

mis'sile (mis'əl) *n.* an object or weapon that can be hurled or shot.

miss'ing (mis'ing) *adj.* absent; lacking. —**missing link,** a hypothetical primate proposed as having linked ape and man, in evolution.

mis'sion (mish'ən) *n.* **1,** a sending; a charge to go and perform a specific service or duty. **2,** a delegation so sent. **3,** the service or duty for which one is sent. **4,** a self-imposed duty or function. **5,** an organized effort for the spread of religion in foreign lands.

mis''sion·ar''y (mish'ə-ner''ē) *n.* one sent to spread a religion or philosophy in a foreign land or to persons not of the same persuasion.

mis''si·sau'ga (mis''i-sâ'gə) *n.* a kind of snake.

mis'sive (mis'iv) *n.* a written message.

mis·speak' *v.* [**mis·spoke', mis·spo'ken**] speak or say incorrectly.

mis·spell' *v.t.* spell incorrectly.

mis·spent' *adj.* squandered. —**mis·spend',** *v.t.*

mis·state' *v.t.* state incorrectly or misleadingly. —**mis·state'ment,** *n.*

mis'step'' *n.* **1,** a stumble. **2,** a mistake in conduct.

mis'sus (mis'əz) *n.* **1,** wife. **2,** the mistress of a household. Also, **mis'sis.**

mist *n.* **1,** a cloud of minute globules of water, near the ground; a fog. **2,** a precipitation much finer than rain. **3,** a haze; something that veils or obscures. —*v.t. & i.* make or become misty.

mis·take' (mi-stāk') *v.t.* [**mis·took'** (-tûk'), **mis·tak'en, -tak'ing**] choose erroneously; regard (something) as other than it is; misunderstand. —*v.i.* be in error. —*n.* an error in action, opinion, or judgment. —**mis·tak'en,** *adj.* **1,** erroneous. **2,** being in error.

mis'ter (mis'tər) *n.* a conventional title for a man, usually written Mr.

mis·time' (mis-tīm') *v.t.* say or do inopportunely.

mis'tle·toe'' (mis'əl-tō'') *n.* a parasitic plant, with white berries, used in Christmas decorations.

---
mistletoe
↔ From Old English *mistel,* basil, and *tan,* twig.
---

mis'tral (mis'trəl) *n.* a cold, dry northwest wind from the Mediterranean.

mis·treat' *v.t.* treat badly; abuse. —**mis·treat'ment,** *n.*

mis'tress (mis'tris) *n.* **1,** a woman who has authority or control, as of a house or servants. **2,** the female owner, as of a dog. **3,** a woman having a continuing extramarital affair with a man who usu. provides financial support.

mis·tri'al (mis-trī'əl) *n.* (*Law*) a trial not concluded because of error, or because of disagreement of the jury.

mis·trust' *n.* lack of trust; suspicion. —*v.t. & i.* distrust. —**mis·trust'ful,** *adj.*

mist'y (mis'tē) *adj.* **1,** accompanied by, or resembling, mist. **2,** indistinct; obscure. **3,** (*Informal*) tearful. —**mist'i·ness,** *n.*

mis''un·der·stand' *v.t. & i.* [*pret. & p.p.* **mis''un·der·stood'**] misinterpret; understand wrongly.

mis''un·der·stand'ing *n.* **1,** disagreement. **2,** a misconception.

mis''un·der·stood' *adj.* **1,** incorrectly interpreted. **2,** unappreciated.

mis·us'age *n.* **1,** improper use, as of words. **2,** bad treatment.

mis·use' (mis-ūz') *v.t.* **1,** make a false or improper use of. **2,** maltreat. —*n.* (mis-ūs') improper use; abuse. ❏ *abuse*

mite (mīt) *n.* **1,** a very small sum of money, or contribution. **2,** a very small person or thing. **3,** an insect that infests plants and foods.

mi'ter (mī'tər) *n.* **1,** the official headdress of a bishop. **2,** a surface cut for a miter joint, a joining of two pieces beveled at equal angles. **3,** a jig or form for cutting such a surface. —*v.t.* cut so as to join in a miter joint. Also, **mi'tre.**

mit'i·gate'' (mit'ə-gāt'') *v.t. & i.* lessen or moderate in severity. —**mit'i·ga'tion,** *n.* ❏ *militate*

mi·to'sis (mī-tō'sis) *n.* a process of cell division in which the number of chromosomes is doubled.

mitt (mit) *n.* **1,** a long glove without fingers. **2,** (*Baseball*) a thickly padded glove. **3,** a mitten. **4,** (*Slang*) a hand.

mit'ten (mit'ən) *n.* a glove that encloses the four fingers together and the thumb separately.

mix (miks) *v.t.* **1,** unite or blend into one mass. **2,** mingle indiscriminately; crossbreed. **3,** (with *up*) confuse. —*v.i.* **1,** become mixed. **2,** associate. —*n.* **1,** a mixture. **2,** the final version of a recorded song.

mixed (mikst) *adj.* **1,** blended by mixing.

2, indiscriminate; assorted. **3,** (*Informal*) mentally confused. **—mixed metaphor,** the incongruous combination of two or more metaphors in the same sentence. **—mixed number,** a number consisting of an integer and a fraction.

mix′er (-ər) *n.* **1,** one who or that which mixes. **2,** a sociable person. **3,** a party.

mix′ture (miks′chər) *n.* the act, state, or result of mixing; a conglomeration; medley.

mix′up″ (miks′up″) *n.* a confused situation; a tangle.

miz′zen·mast″ (miz′ən-måst″) *n.* the after or third mast of a vessel. Also, **miz′zen.**

mne·mon′ic (ni-mon′ik) *adj.* pert. to or assisting the memory. **—***n.* an aid in remembering. **—mne·mon′i·cal·ly,** *adv.* **—mne·mon′ics,** *n.sing.* a technique for improving the memory.

mo′a (mō′ə) *n.* a large extinct bird of N.Z.

moan (mōn) *v.i.* **1,** utter a low inarticulate sound expressive of suffering. **2,** make a similar sound, as the wind. **—***n.* such a sound.

moat (mōt) *n.* a deep, water-filled trench around a fortified place.

mob *n.* **1,** an incoherent, disorderly crowd of people. **2,** any assemblage of persons or things (used disparagingly). **3,** the common mass of people. **—***v.t.* [**mobbed, mob′bing**] crowd around or attack.

---

mob, mobile

↔ From the Latin phrase *mobile vulgus,* fickle crowd, from *mobilis,* movable, fickle.

---

mo′bile (mō′bəl) *adj.* **1,** easily moving or movable. **2,** changing easily; facile; responsive. **—***n.* a sculpture whose parts may be moved by a breeze. **—mo·bil′i·ty** (mō-bil′ə-tē) *n.* **—mobile home,** a house trailer. ❑ *mob*

mo·bi·lize″ (mō′bə-līz″) *v.t. & i.* organize or put in readiness for service. **—mo″bi·li·za′tion,** *n.*

mob·oc′ra·cy (mob-ok′rə-sē) *n,* rule by the mob.

mob′ster (mob′stər) *n.* (*Slang*) one of a criminal mob; gangster.

moc′ca·sin (mok′ə-sən) *n.* **1,** a shoe of soft leather. **2,** a venomous water snake.

mo′cha (mō′kə) *n.* **1,** a choice coffee. **2,** a flavor of chocolate and coffee. **3,** a fine glove leather.

mock (mok) *v.t.* **1,** ridicule; deride;

mimic. **2,** defy; deceive. **—***v.i.* scoff; jeer. **—***adj.* being an imitation, as a *mock battle.* **—mock orange,** a shrub, the common syringa. **—mock turtle soup,** a soup made of veal or other meat and seasoned to imitate turtle soup.

mock′er·y (mok′ə-rē) *n.* **1,** ridicule; object of ridicule. **2,** an imitation; a travesty.

mock-″he·ro′ic *adj. & n.* (a work) burlesquing the heroic style.

mock′ing·bird″ (mok′ing-bėrd″) *n.* an imitative songbird of the So. U.S.

mock-′up″ (mok′up″) *n.* **1,** a model, built to scale, as of a machine. **2,** a layout of printed or other matter.

mod *adj.* (*Informal*) **1,** a style of dress fashionable in the 1960s. **2,** up-to-date.

mode (mōd) *n.* **1,** a manner of acting or doing; method. **2,** the manner of existence or action of anything. **3,** the customary usage; the prevailing fashion. **4,** (*Music*) a form of scale. **5,** (*Gram.*) mood. **—mod′al** (mō′dəl) *adj.*

mod′el (mod′əl) *n.* **1,** a standard for imitation or comparison. **2,** a copy, usually in miniature. **3,** an image for later reproduction. **4,** a subject for an artist. **5,** one employed to wear and display clothes, pose for pictures, etc. **—***adj.* **1,** serving as a model. **2,** exemplary. **—***v.t. & i.* **1,** form according to, or make, a model. **2,** act as a model.

mo′dem (mō′dem) *n.* a device for converting signals from one mode of transmission to another; esp. a device for transmitting data over telephone lines.

mod′er·ate (mod′ər-it) *adj.* **1,** restrained; temperate; kept or keeping within reasonable limits. **2,** medium; mediocre. **—***n.* one who avoids extreme opinions or actions. **—***v.t. & i.* (mod′ə-rāt″) **1,** make or become less severe or intense. **2,** preside over a meeting. **—mod″er·a′tion,** *n.* temperance. **—mod′er·a″tor,** *n.* a presiding officer.

mod″e·ra′to (mōd″ə-rä′tō) *adj. & adv.* (*It., Music*) moderate in tempo.

mod′ern (mod′ərn) *adj.* pert. to or characteristic of present or recent times. **—***n.* a person of the present era, or of modern tastes. ❑ *contemporary*

mod′ern·ism (-iz-əm) *n.* practice or advocacy of radically new customs, design, etc. **—mod′ern·ist,** *n. & adj.* **—mod″ern·is′tic,** *adj.*

mod′ern·ize″ (-īz″) *v.t. & i.* make or become modern; renovate. **—mod″ern·i·za′tion,** *n.*

mod′est (mod′ist) *adj.* **1,** manifesting humility, propriety, and restraint. **2,** moderate. **3,** decent; decorous. **—mod'es·ty,** *n.*

mod'i·cum (mod'ə-kəm) *n.* a small or moderate quantity.

mod'i·fy'' (mod'ə-fī'') *v.t.* **1,** change the properties, form, or function of. **2,** moderate. **3,** (*Gram.*) qualify or describe (another word). **—mod''i·fi·ca'tion,** *n.* **—mod'i·fi''er,** *n.*

mod'ish (mō'dish) *adj.* fashionable. **—mod'ish·ness,** *n.*

mo·diste' (mō-dēst') *n.* a maker or seller of women's hats, dresses, etc.

mod'u·lar (moj'oo-lər) *adj.* pert. to modulation; of a module.

mod'u·late'' (moj'ə-lāt'') *v.t.* **1,** make softer in tone; regulate. **2,** vary or inflect the sound or utterance of. **3,** (*Radio*) vary the frequency of the transmitted wave. **—mod''u·la'tion,** *n.* **—mod'u·la''tor,** *n.*

mod'ule (moj'ool) *n.* **1,** a unit of measure, esp. of building materials. **2,** a standardized unit. **3,** an independent unit of a space vehicle.

mo'dus op''e·ran'di (mō'dəs op''ə-ran'dī) (*Lat.*) method of working.

mo'dus vi·ven'di (mō'dəs vi-ven'dī) (*Lat.*) way of living or getting along.

mo'gul (mō'gəl) *n.* an important or powerful person; a member of the (orig. Mongolian) ruling class.

mo'hair'' (mō'hâr'') *n.* the fleece of an Angora goat; a fabric made of it.

---

mohair
↔ From Arabic *mukhayyar*, referring to a cloth made of goats' hair.

Mo·ham'med·an (mō-ham'ə-dən) *n.* a follower of Mohammed or his religion. **—adj.** Muslim.

Mohammedan, Muslim
☞ *Muslim* is generally the preferred word; *Mohammedan* is often considered offensive.

Mohs scale (mōz) a numerical scale for expressing the hardness of minerals, named for 19th-c. German mineralogist F. Mohs, who developed it.

moi'e·ty (moi'ə-tē) *n.* **1,** a half part. **2,** a share.

moil *v.i.* work hard. **—n.** drudgery. **—moil'er,** *n.*

moire (mwär) *n.* a watered silk or wool fabric.

moi·ré' (mwä-rā') *adj.* watered; wavelike.

moist *adj.* damp; slightly wet; tearful (of the eyes). **—moist'ness,** *n.*

mois'ten (mois'ən) *v.t. & i.* make or become damp.

mois'ture (mois'chər) *n.* diffused wetness. **—mois'tur·ize'',** *v.t.* **—mois'tur·iz·er,** *n.*

mo'lar (mō'lər) *n.* a grinding tooth.

mo·las'ses (mō-las'iz) *n.* a dark syrup produced in making sugar.

---

molasses
↔ From Late Latin *mellaceum*, new wine, from *mel*, honey.

---

mold (mōld) *n.* **1,** a shape or form, esp. for shaping molten or plastic material. **2,** something shaped in or on a mold, or the shape imparted to it. **3,** native character. **4,** a furry fungus growth, esp. on food or decaying matter. **5,** soft, rich earth. **—v.t.** shape, form, or fashion, esp. in or on a mold. **—v.t. & i.** make or become fungus mold. Also, **mould.** **—mold'y,** *adj.* covered with fungus mold.

mold'board'' (mōld'bôrd'') *n.* the curved surface of a plow·blade.

mold'er (mōl'dər) *v.i. & t.* turn to mold or dust by natural decay. **—n.** one who molds.

mold'ing (mōl'ding) *n.* **1,** (*Archit.*) a decorative border. **2,** something molded.

mole (mōl) *n.* **1,** a small dark permanent blemish on the human skin. **2,** a small mammal, living chiefly underground. **3,** a massive stone breakwater. **4,** an undercover agent, esp. one in place over a long period of time.

mol'e·cule'' (mol'ə-kūl'') *n.* **1,** the smallest possible physical unit of an element or compound, composed of atoms. **2,** a very small particle. **—mo·lec'u·lar** (mə-lek'yə-lər) *adj.*

mole'hill'' *n.* **1,** a small mound of earth raised by burrowing moles. **2,** an unimportant obstacle.

mole'skin'' (mōl'skin'') *n.* **1,** a stout cotton fabric. **2,** the soft gray fur of the mole.

mo·lest' (mə-lest') *v.t.* **1,** trouble; interfere with injuriously. **2,** to make improper sexual advances to. **—mo''les·ta'tion** (mō''les-tā'shən) *n.*

moll (mol) *n.* (*Slang*) the woman companion of a gangster.

mol'li·fy'' (mol'ə-fī'') *v.t.* **1,** soften. **2,** soothe; appease. **—mol''li·fi·ca'tion,** *n.* **—mol'li·fi''er,** *n.*

mol'lusk (mol'əsk) *n.* an invertebrate animal with a soft body and usually a hard shell, as a snail or oyster. Also, **mol'lusc.**

mol'ly·cod''dle (mol'ē-kod''əl) *n.* a pampered boy. **—v.t.** pamper.

Mol′o·tov″ cocktail (mol′ə-tof″) a bottle of gasoline ignited and hurled as an antitank weapon.

Molotov cocktail
↔ Named for Russian statesman and commissar of foreign affairs V. M. Molotov.

molt (mōlt) v.t. & i. shed feathers (as a bird) or skin (as a reptile). Also, **moult.** —n. the act or process of molting.

mol′ten (mōl′tən) adj. melted.

mo·lyb′de·num (mə-lib′də-nəm) n. an element used in alloys, no. 32, symbol Mo. —**mo·lyb′dic,** adj.

mom n. (Informal) mamma; mother.

mom-′and-pop′ (mom′ən-pop′) adj. (Informal) of a business, etc., operated by a family.

mo′ment (mō′mənt) n. **1,** an indefinitely small space of time; a minute. **2,** the present time; instant. **3,** importance; consequence.

mo′men·tar″y (mō′mən-ter″ē) adj. very brief. —**mo″men·tar′i·ly** (-tär′ə-lē) adv. for a moment; at any moment.

mo·men′tous (mō-men′təs) adj. of great consequence. —**mo·men′tous·ness,** n.

mo·men′tum (mō-men′təm) n. impetus; the quantity of motion of a body: the mass times the velocity.

mom′my (-ē) n. mom. —**mommy track,** (Informal) career path of women who choose time with their families over professional advancement.

mon′ad n. **1,** (Biol.) a single-celled organism. **2,** (Chem.) an element having a valence of one. **3,** a unit. —**mo·nad′ic,** adj.

mon′arch (mon′ərk) n. a hereditary sovereign; ruler. —**mo·nar′chal** (mə-när′kəl) adj.

mon′ar·chy (mon′ər-kē) n. a government headed by a monarch. —**mon′ar·chism** (-kiz-em) n. —**mon′ar·chist** (-kist) n. one who favors such form of government.

mon′as·ter·y (mon′ə-ster-ē) n. the premises occupied by monks.

mo·nas′tic (mə-nas′tik) adj. pert. to austere life in seclusion, as of monks. —**mo·nas′ti·cism,** n.

mon·aur′al (mon-ôr″əl) adj. **1,** pert. to or for use with one ear. **2,** monophonic.

Mon′day (mun′dē) n. the second day of the week.

Monday
↔ Monday is actually "moon's day," from Old English monandaeg, a translation of Latin lunae dies.

Mo·nel′ metal (mō-nel′) (T.N.) a nonrusting alloy of nickel.

mon′e·tar·ism″ (mon′ə-tə-riz″əm) an economic theory dealing with the effects of money in circulation.

mon′e·tar·y (mon′ə-ter-ē) adj. of or pert. to money.

mon′e·tize″ (mon′ə-tīz″) v.t. legalize as, or coin into, money.

mon′ey (mun′ē) n. **1,** coin; stamped metal or banknotes authorized as a medium of exchange. **2,** available assets; wealth; credit. —**mon′eyed,** adj. wealthy. —**money market,** a short-term trading in money. —**money of account,** a monetary unit used in computation but not issued as a coin or note. —**money order,** an order for payment of money, esp. one issued at a post office.

mon′ey·bags″ n.sing. (Slang) a rich person.

mon′ger (mung′gər) n. **1,** a dealer, as a fishmonger. **2,** one sordidly active, as a scandalmonger.

Mon·gol′i·an (mon-gō′lē-ən) adj. & n. **1,** pert. to Mongolia or to the yellow-skinned races of eastern Asia. **2,** [also, **mon′gol·oid** (-gə-loid)] afflicted with Down syndrome.

Mon′gol·ism (mong′gə-liz-əm) n. Down syndrome.

mon′goose (mong′goos) n. [pl. **-goos·es**] a slender ferretlike animal of India.

mongoose
↔ Not from goose, but from mangus, the word for the animal in the language of the state of Maharashtra, India.

mon′grel (mong′grəl) n. **1,** a dog of mixed breed. **2,** any plant, animal, or thing of mixed breed or elements. —adj. mixed; not pure.

mon′i·ker (mon′ə-kər) n. (Slang) a name or nickname.

mon′ism (mon′iz-əm) n. the metaphysical doctrine that mind and matter are not separate substances. —**mon′ist,** n.

mo·ni′tion (mə-nish′ən) n. a warning.

mon′i·tor (mon′i-tər) n. **1,** a pupil charged with overseeing other pupils. **2,** one who admonishes; a warning. **3,** a television receiver not having its own tuner; esp., the display unit for a computer. —v.t. & i. **1,** keep track of. **2,** listen to radio or television broadcasts for checking purposes. —**mon′i·tor·ship″,** n.

mon′i·to″ry (mon′i-tôr″ē) adj. admonishing. —n. an admonishing letter.

monk (munk) *n.* a man who is a member of a religious order. —**monk′ish,** *adj.*
—**monk's cloth,** a coarse, fabric used for draperies.

mon′key (mung′kė) *n.* **1,** any mammal of the order Primates except man, the lemur, and the apes. **2,** a mischievous child or person. **3,** any of various machines. —*v.t.* (*Informal*) trifle; fool. —**monkey business,** (*Slang*) playful, mischievous, or deceitful behavior. —**monkey jacket,** a sailor's jacket. —**mon′key·shine″,** *n.* (*Slang*) a mischievous prank. —**monkey suit,** (*Slang*) a tailcoat. —**monkey wrench,** an adjustable wrench.

monks′hood (munks′hûd) *n.* a plant having a hooded flower.

mon·o- (mon-ə) *pref.* single; alone.

mon′o·chord″ *n.* an instrument with one string and a movable bridge.

mon′o·chrome″ (mon′ə-krōm″) *n.* a painting in different shades of a single color. —**mon″o·chro·mat′ic,** *adj.* pert. to one color or one wavelength.

mon′o·cle (mon′ə-kəl) *n.* an eyeglass for one eye. —**mon·noc′u·lar** (mə-nok′yə-lər) *adj.* having, pert. to, or intended for one eye.

mon′o·dy (mon′ə-dė) *n.* **1,** a musical composition in which one voice part predominates. **2,** a mourner's lament, in a poem or ode. —**mo·nod′ic** (mə-nod′ik) *adj.*

mo·nog′a·my (mə-nog′ə-mė) *n.* the practice of marrying only once, or being married to only one person at a time. —**mo·nog′a·mist,** *n.* —**mo·nog′a·mous,** *adj.*

mon′o·gram″ (mon′ə-gram″) *n.* a design combining two or more letters, esp. initials.

mon′o·graph″ (mon′ə-grâf″) *n.* a treatise on a single subject. —**mon″o·graph′ic,** *adj.*

mon″o·ki′ni (-kē′nė) *n.* a topless bathing suit.

mon′o·lith (mon′ə-lith) *n.* a single stone; a structure of a single stone, as an obelisk.

mon″o·lith′ic (-ik) *adj.* **1,** formed from a single block of stone; massive; solid. **2,** formed from, or produced in or on, a single silicon chip.

mon′o·logue″ (mon′ə-lâg″) *n.* a discourse, poem, or dramatic part, by a single speaker. Also, **mon′o·log″.** —**mon′o·log″ist, mon′o·logu″ist,** *n.*

mon″o·ma′ni·a *n.* an exaggerated interest in one thing; a specific delusion. —**mon″o·ma′ni·ac,** *n.*

mon″o·met′al·lism (mon″ə-met′ə-liz″-əm) *n.* the use of one metal only as a monetary standard.

mo·no′mi·al (mo-nō′mė-əl) *adj. & n.* (an algebraic expression) consisting of only one term.

mon″o·nu·cle·o′sis (mon″ō-noo-clē-ō′sis) *n.* an infectious disease characterized by an abnormal increase in the number of white blood cells with one nucleus in the bloodstream.

mon″o·pho′bi·a *n.* morbid dread of being alone.

mon″o·phon′ic (mon″ə-fän′ik) *adj.* **1,** consisting of a solo voice with accompaniment. **2,** having only one part. **3,** pert. to sound transmission on a single channel. —**mo·noph′o·ny** (mə-nof′ə-nė) *n.*

mon′o·plane″ *n.* an airplane with one pair of wings.

mo·nop′o·list (mə-nop′ə-list) *n.* one who establishes or advocates a monopoly. —**mo·nop′o·lis″ti·cal·ly,** *adv.*

mo·nop′o·lize″ (-līz″) *v.t.* have exclusive control or possession of.

mo·nop′o·ly (mə-nop′ə-lė) *n.* **1,** exclusive control of a commodity. **2,** an exclusive privilege to carry on a traffic or service. **3,** the subject of, or a company having, a monopoly.

mon′o·rail″ 1, a single rail serving as the track for a train that either hangs from it or straddles it. **2,** a train that uses a monorail.

mo″no·so′dium glu′ta·mate (gloo′-tə-mət) *n.* a flavor enhancer. Abbr., **MSG.**

mon′o·syl″la·ble *n.* a word of one syllable. —**mon″o·syl·lab′ic,** *adj.*

mon′o·the″ism (mon′ə-thē″iz-əm) *n.* the doctrine or belief that there is but one God. —**mon′o·the″ist,** *n. & adj.* —**mon″o·the·is′tic,** *adj.*

mon′o·tone″ (mon′ə-tōn″) *n.* **1,** (*Music*) a single unvaried tone. **2,** speaking or singing without inflection or variation in pitch. **3,** sameness of style in writing.

mo·not′o·nous (mə-not′ə-nəs) *adj.* **1,** continued in the same tone. **2,** tiresome.

mo·not′o·ny (mə-not′ə-nė) *n.* boring lack of variety; sameness.

Mon′o·type″ (mon′ə-tīp″) *n.* **1,** (*T.N.*) a machine for setting type, which sets each character separately; type set by such a machine. **2,** (*l.c.*) a print from a picture painted on a metal or glass plate.

mon·sieur′ (mə-syû′) *n.* [*pl.* **messieurs′** (mā-syû′; mes′ərz)] (*Fr.*) **1,** mister. **2,** sir.

mon·si′gnor (mon-sēn′yər) *n.* a title given to certain male dignitaries of the Rom. Cath. Church.

mon·soon′ *n.* the seasonal wind, or the rainy season, of So. Asia.

mon′ster (mon′stər) *n.* **1,** a fabulous half-human animal. **2,** an abnormal or malformed animal or plant. **3,** a huge animal. **4,** a morally deformed person. —*adj.* huge.

mon′strance (mon′strəns) *n.* (*R.C.Ch.*) a receptacle in which the host is presented for adoration.

mon·stros′i·ty (mon-stros′ə-tē) *n.* state of being monstrous; anything monstrous.

mon′strous (mon′strəs) *adj.* **1,** abnormal. **2,** huge. **3,** frightful; shocking. —**mon′strous·ness,** *n.*

mon·tage′ (mon-täzh′) *n.* the combination of elements of different pictures, esp. photographic.

Mon′te Car′lo method (mon′tē kär′lō) a method of statistical analysis using a random variable.

Mon″tes·so′ri method (mon″tə-sôr′ē) a method of training young children emphasizing self-education through guidance rather than control, named for its creator, Italian educator Maria Montessori.

Mon″te·zu′ma′s revenge (mon″tə-zoo′məz) (*Slang*) diarrhea, esp. when contracted in Mexico.

Montezuma's revenge

↔ A humorous reference to the supposed revenge that *Montezuma II*, the last Aztec emperor of Mexico, would want to perpetrate on the Europeans who defeated him. *Montezuma* is Nahuatl for "angry nobleman."

---

month (munth) *n.* **1,** 1/12 solar year, about 30 days; 4 weeks. **2,** any of the 12 parts of the calendar year, as January, etc.

month′ly (-lē) *adj.* once a month; every month; continuing for a month. —*n.* **1,** a periodical published once a month. **2,** (*pl., slang*) menses.

mon′u·ment (mon′yə-mənt) *n.* **1,** a memorial structure or statue; a tomb or tombstone. **2,** any enduring memorial. —**mon″u·men′tal,** *adj.* imposing; notable.

moo *n.* the sound a cow makes.

mooch (*Slang*) *v.i.* **1,** skulk; hang about. **2,** make love by petting. —*v.t.* get without payment; cadge.

mood *n.* **1,** state of mind or feeling; disposition. **2,** (*pl.*) fits of uncertainty or gloominess. **3,** (*Gram.*) any of a series of verb inflections that denote whether a verb expresses fact, wish, or command.

mood′y (moo′dē) *adj.* gloomy; sullen; pensive. —**mood′i·ness,** *n.*

Moog′ syn′the·siz″er (mōg) (*T.N.*) a type of electronic synthesizer.

moon *n.* **1,** the heavenly body that revolves around the earth monthly and shines by the sun's reflected light. **2,** a lunar month. **3,** any planetary satellite. **4,** anything resembling an orb or a crescent. —*v.i.* behave listlessly or idly. —**moon′y,** *adj.* listless. —**moon blindness,** a disease of horses.

moon′beam″ *n.* a beam of light from the moon.

moon′calf″ *n.* an imbecile.

moon′flow″er *n.* a night-blooming plant.

Moon′ie (moo′nē) *n.* a member of Rev. Sun Myung Moon's Unification Church.

moon′light″ *n. & adj.* the light of the moon. —*v.i.* (*Informal*) work at a second job, usu. at night.—**moon′lit″,** *adj.*

moon′shine″ *n.* **1,** moonlight. **2,** nonsensical talk. **3,** (*Informal*) illicitly distilled liquor. —**moon′shin″er,** *n.* (*Informal*) an illicit distiller.

moon′stone″ *n.* a variety of feldspar used as a gem.

moon-′struck″ *adj.* crazed or bemused.

moor (mûr) *n.* a tract of open wasteland, often swampy; heath. —*v.t. & i.* secure (esp. a ship) in one place, by cables or anchors. —**moor′age,** *n.* a place for mooring.

Moor (mûr) *n.* any member of the dark-skinned No. African Muslim people who formerly occupied Spain.

moor′ing *n.* the cables for, or the place of, mooring.

Moor′ish (mûr′ish) *adj.* pert. to the Muslim Arabs of northwest Africa.

moose (moos) *n.sing. & pl.* a large antlered animal of the deer family.

moot *adj.* debatable.

---

moot

↔ From Old English *gemot*, meeting; hence, a subject raised at a meeting.

---

mop *n.* **1,** a bunch of yarn, etc., on a handle, for washing floors. **2,** a thick mass (as of hair). —*v.t.* [**mopped, mop′ping**] clean with or as with a mop; wipe clean.

mop′board″ *n.* a baseboard.

mope (mōp) *v.i.* be listless, gloomy, or melancholy. —**mop′ish,** *adj.*

mo·ped″ (mō′ped″) *n.* a motorbike (def. 1).

mop′pet (mop′it) *n.* a doll; a little girl; a child.

mo·quette′ (mō-ket′) *n.* a thick velvety carpet.

mo·raine′ (mə-rān′) *n.* the accumulation of boulders, gravel, etc. deposited by a glacier.

mor′al (mor′əl) *adj.* **1,** pert. to the distinction between right and wrong, and the rules of right conduct. **2,** conforming to these rules. **3,** based on ethical rather than legal rights. **4,** ethically or virtually, but not literally, true, as a *moral victory.* —*n.* **1,** the moral lesson in a fable, experience, etc. **2,** moral conduct or character. —**Moral Majority,** an association of fundamentalist Christians.

---

moral, morale
☛ Do not confuse *moral,* which deals with the question of right and wrong, and *morale,* with deals with one's confidence, faith, etc.

---

mo·rale′ (mə-ral′) *n.* moral or mental condition as regards courage, confidence, etc. ❏ *moral*

mor′al·ism (-iz-əm) *n.* **1,** belief in the practice of morality apart from religion. **2,** a maxim. —**mor′al·ist,** *n.* a moral person; a student or teacher of morality.

mor·al′i·ty (mə-ral′ə-tē) *n.* quality of being moral; virtue. —**morality play,** a type of medieval drama in which the characters personify moral qualities.

mor′al·ize″ (-īz″) *v.i. & t.* reflect on or explain in a moral sense.

mor′al·ly (-lē) *adv.* **1,** virtuously. **2,** practically.

mo·rass′ (mə-ras′) *n.* a marsh; bog.

mor″a·to′ri·um (môr″ə-tôr′ē-əm) *n.* an authorization to delay payment. —**mor′a·to·ry,** *adj.*

mo′ray (môr′ā) *n.* a savage eel.

mor′bid (môr′bid) *adj.* **1,** diseased. **2,** mentally unhealthy. —**mor·bid′i·ty, mor′-bid·ness,** *n.*

mor·da′cious (môr-dā′shəs) *adj.* violent in action; biting; acrid. —**mor·dac′i·ty** (-das′ə-tē) *n.*

mor′dant (môr′dənt) *adj.* **1,** biting; sarcastic. **2,** having the property to fix colors. —**mor′dan·cy,** *n.*

mor′dent (môr′dənt) *n.* (*Music*) a melodic embellishment.

more (môr) *adj.* **1,** [*superl.* **most**] in greater measure or number. **2,** additional. —*n.* a greater or additional quantity or number. —*adv.* to a greater extent. ❏ *above*

mo·reen′ (mə-rēn′) *n.* a heavy wool, or wool and cotton, fabric.

mo·rel′ (mə-rel′) *n.* an edible mushroom.

mo·rel′lo (mə-rel′ō) *n.* a dark-red variety of cherry.

more·o′ver *adv.* further; besides.

mo′res (môr′āz) *n.pl.* customs of behavior.

Mo·resque′ (mô-resk′) *adj. & n.* (pert. to) a Moorish style of decoration.

mor″ga·nat′ic (môr″gə-nat′ik) *adj.* denoting a marriage between a man of high rank and a woman who does not share his rank. —**mor″ga·nat′i·cal·ly,** *adv.*

---

morganatic
↪ From Germanic **morgangeba,* a gift from a husband to his wife which removed any further legal claim she or their offspring might have on his possessions.

---

morgue (môrg) *n.* **1,** a place where the bodies of unknown dead persons are kept until identified. **2,** the reference files of a newspaper.

---

morgue
↪ The word comes from the name of a building in Paris used to house unidentified dead bodies (and immortalized in the story by Edgar Allan Poe). The origin of the word is unknown.

---

mor′i·bund″ (môr′ə-bund″) *adj.* in a dying state.

Mor′mon (môr′mən) *n.* a member of the Church of Jesus Christ of Latter-Day Saints.

morn (môrn) *n.* morning.

morn′ing (môr′ning) *n.* **1,** the period between midnight and noon, or dawn and noon. **2,** the early part of anything. Also, **morn.** —**morning-after pill,** (*Informal*) a contraceptive pill taken after intercourse. —**morning sickness,** nausea in the morning, often accompanying early pregnancy. —**morning star,** the planet Venus.

morn′ing-glo″ry (môr′ning-glôr″ē) *n.* a climbing plant with cone-shaped flowers.

mo·roc′co (mə-rok′ō) *n.* a fine goatskin leather.

mo′ron (môr′on) *n.* **1,** a person whose mentality does not develop beyond the twelve-year-old level. **2,** (*Informal*) a fool; stupid person. —**mo·ron′ic,** *adj.*

---

mo·rose' (mə-rōs') *adj.* sullenly ill-humored. **—mo·rose'ness,** *n.*

morph-, mor·pho- (môrf; môr-fə) *pref.* form; as a *suf.,* **-morph, -mor·phic, -mor·phous.**

mor'phine (môr'fēn) *n.* a habit-forming narcotic, used medicinally to dull pain.

mor·phol'o·gy (môr-fol'ə-jē) *n.* the science of form and structure, as of animals and plants. **—mor″pho·log'ic, mor″pho·log'i·cal,** *adj.* **—mor·phol'o·gist,** *n.*

mor'ris (môr'is) *n.* an old English pastoral dance. Also, **morris dance.**

---

morris (dance), morris chair
↔ The dance comes not from a personal name but is a variant of *Moorish*, probably a reference to its origin. The chair is named after English furniture designer William *Morris*.

---

mor'ris chair a large armchair with an adjustable back and removable cushions. ❑ *morris*

mor'row (mor'ō) *n.* the next day after this.

Morse code (môrs) an alphabet of dots, dashes, and spaces, used in telegraphy and signaling, named for American inventor of the telegraph Samuel F. B. Morse.

INTERNATIONAL MORSE CODE

A	·-	N	-·	1	·----	;	-·-·-·
B	-···	O	---	2	··---	:	---···
C	-·-·	P	·--·	3	···--	'	·----·
D	-··	Q	--·-	4	····-	-	-····-
E	·	R	·-·	5	·····	/	-··-·
F	··-·	S	···	6	-····	()	-·--·-
G	--·	T	-	7	--···	_	··--·-
H	····	U	··-	8	---··	á	·--·-
I	··	V	···-	9	----·	ä	·-·-
J	·---	W	·--	0	-----	é	··-··
K	-·-	X	-··-	,	--··--	ñ	--·--
L	·-··	Y	-·--	.	·-·-·-	ö	---·
M	--	Z	--··	?	··--··	ü	··--

mor'sel (môr'səl) *n.* a small piece or quantity, esp. of food.

mor'tal (môr'təl) *adj.* **1,** subject to death; hence, human. **2,** deadly; fatal. **3,** implacable. **4,** grievous. **5,** (of a sin) causing the loss of divine grace. **—***n.* a human being.

mor·tal'i·ty (môr-tal'ə-tē) *n.* **1,** the condition of being mortal. **2,** deaths; death rate.

mor'tar (môr'tər) *n.* **1,** a bowl or device in which substances are pounded and ground. **2,** a cannon, firing at high angles; a similar device for hurling lifelines, etc. **3,** a mixture of cement used in building.

mor'tar·board″ *n.* **1,** a board for holding mortar. **2,** an academic cap with a flat, square top.

mort'gage (môr'gij) *n.* (*Law*) a conditional conveyance of property as security for a loan. **—***v.t.* put a mortgage on. **—mort″ga·gor'** (-jôr') *n.* one who so pledges property. **—mort″ga·gee'** (-jē') *n.* one who grants such a loan.

---

mortgage
↔ Literally, dead pledge, from an Old French word of Latin origin.

---

mor·ti'cian (môr-tish'ən) *n.* an undertaker.

mor'ti·fy″ (môr'tə-fī″) *v.t. & i.* **1,** humiliate. **2,** subject (the body) to ascetic discipline. **3,** affect with gangrene. **—mor″ti·fi·ca'tion,** *n.*

mor'tise (môr'tis) *n.* a cavity or recess to receive an inserted part, e.g., a tenon in joining wood. **—***v.t.* make, or fasten by, a mortise.

mor'tu·ar″y (môr'choo-er'ē) *n.* a place for temporary reception of the dead. **—***adj.* pert. to burial or death.

mo·sa'ic (mō-zā'ik) *n.* a picture or decoration composed of small pieces of material, separate photographs, etc. **—***adj.* **1,** pert. to a mosaic. **2,** composed of diverse elements. **3,** (*cap.*) pert. to Moses or his writings.

Mo·selle' (mō-zel') *n.* a German white wine.

mo'sey (mō'zē) *v.i.* (*Slang*) stroll.

Mos'lem (mos'ləm) *adj. & n.* Muslim.

mosque (mosk) *n.* a Muslim place of worship.

---

mosque
↔ From Arabic *masjid*, place of worship, from *sajada*, bow down.

---

mos·qui'to (mə-skē'tō) *n.* an insect that bites animals and draws blood. **—mosquito boat,** a fast motorboat equipped with torpedoes.

moss (mâs) *n.* a plant growing in tufts or mats, usually green, on moist ground, rocks, etc. **—moss'y,** *adj.*

moss'back″ *n.* a person of antiquated or conservative opinions.

most (mōst) *adj.* greatest in quantity or number. **—***n.* **1,** the greatest quantity or number. **2,** the majority. **—***adv.* **1,** to the greatest extent. **2,** (*Informal*) almost.

-most *suf.* a superlative: foremost.

most'ly (-lē) *adv.* chiefly; mainly.

mot (mō) *n.* a witticism.

mote (mōt) *n.* a speck, as of dust.

mo·tel' (mō-tel') *n.* motor court: *mo(tor ho)tel.*

---

fat, fāte, fär, fâre, fâll, ȧsk; met, hē, hêr, maybė; pin, pīne; not, nōte, ôr, tool

mo·tet′ (mō-tet′) *n.* a contrapuntal vocal composition, usu. sacred.

moth (mâth) *n.* **1,** a nocturnal insect resembling the butterfly. **2,** a larva that destroys woolen fabrics. —**moth′y,** *adj.* —**mothball,** a ball of naphthalene to repel clothes moths.

moth′eat″en *adj.* shabby.

moth′er (mu*th*′ər) *n.* **1,** a female parent. **2,** an elderly woman. **3,** the superior of a convent, etc. **4,** one who exercises the authority or protective care of a mother; a matron. **5,** a slimy substance formed by bacteria in vinegar, etc., during fermentation. —*adj.* **1,** maternal. **2,** native; giving origin. —*v.t.* **1,** give origin to. **2,** protect tenderly or solicitously. —**moth′er·hood,** *n.* —**mother hubbard** (hub′ərd) a full loose gown for women. —**mother supe·rior,** the woman superintendent of a convent. —**mother wit,** common sense.

moth′er·board″ *n.* the main circuit board of a computer.

moth′er-in-law″ *n.* the mother of one's wife or husband.

moth′er·land″ *n.* the land of one's birth or ancestry.

moth′er·ly (-lė) *adj. & adv.* like or befitting a mother. —**moth′er·li·ness,** *n.*

moth′er-of-pearl′ *n.* the iridescent lining of an oyster shell, etc.

mo·tif′ (mō-tēf′) *n.* a dominant theme; a short musical phrase.

mo′tile (mō′təl) *adj.* (*Biol.*) capable of moving spontaneously. —**mo·til′i·ty,** *n.*

mo′tion (mō′shən) *n.* **1,** the process, power, or manner of moving. **2,** a movement; gesture. **3,** a proposal; suggestion; application. —*v.t. & i.* direct by a motion or gesture. —**motion picture,** consecutive pictures shown so as to give an illusion of motion. —**motion sickness,** nausea induced by motion, as in a car, airplane, etc.

mo′ti·vate″ (mō′tə-vāt″) *v.t.* provide with a motive; induce. —**mo″ti·va′tion,** *n.*

mo′tive (mō′tiv) *n.* **1,** a mental force that induces an act; a determining impulse. **2,** intention; purpose; design. —*adj.* **1,** causing, or pert. to, motion. **2,** constituting a motive.

mot′ley (mot′lė) *adj.* **1,** composed of discordant elements; heterogeneous. **2,** consisting of, or wearing, a combination of different colors.

mo′to·cross″ (mō′tō-) *n.* a cross-country motorcycle race.

mo′tor (mō′tər) *n.* **1,** a source of mechanical power. **2,** a machine that trans-

forms the energy of water, steam, electricity, etc. into mechanical energy; engine. **3,** an automobile: *motor car.* —*adj.* **1,** causing or imparting motion. **2,** pert. to an automobile. —*v.i.* ride in an automobile. —**motor court,** a group of separate cabins or connected rooms serving as an inn for motorists. —**motor home,** a large van outfitted for occupancy. —**motor scooter,** a two-wheeled motorized vehicle less powerful than a motorcycle and having a seat that the driver does not straddle.

mo′tor·bike″ *n.* **1,** a bicycle propelled by a motor; a very light motorcycle. **2,** (*Informal*) a motorcycle.

mo′tor·boat″ *n.* a boat propelled by a gas or electric engine.

mo′tor·cade″ (-kād″) *n.* a procession of automobiles.

mo′tor·car″ *n.* automobile.

mo′tor·cy″cle *n.* a two-wheeled automotive vehicle for one or two passengers.

mo′tor·drome″ (-drōm″) *n.* a track for motorcycle or automobile racing.

mo′tor·ist *n.* one who travels in an automobile.

mo′tor·ize″ (-īz″) *v.t.* **1,** furnish with a motor. **2,** equip with motor-driven vehicles. —**mo″tor·i·za′tion,** *n.*

mo′tor·man (-mən) *n.* [*pl.* -**men**] the operator of a trolley car, etc.

mo′tor·mouth″ *n.* (*Slang*) a very talkative person.

Mo′town (mō′town) *n.* **1,** a nickname for Detroit, MI. **2,** a style of rhythm and blues music.

mot′tle (mot′əl) *v.t.* mark with different-colored spots. —*n.* a diversifying spot or blotch; variegated coloring. —**mot′tled,** *adj.*

mot′to (mot′ō) *n.* a phrase, or word, expressive of one's guiding principle.

moue (moo) *n.* (*Fr.*) a pout.

mou·lage′ (moo-läzh′) *n.* a plaster mold of a footprint, etc., to be used as evidence.

mould (mōld) *n.* mold.

moult (mōlt) *n.* molt.

mound (mownd) *n.* **1,** a natural or artificial elevation of earth. **2,** a raised mass of anything, as hay. —*v.t.* heap up.

mount (mownt) *v.t.* **1,** get up on; ascend. **2,** place at an elevation; set in proper position. **3,** equip with or place on a horse. **4,** preserve and stuff (as an animal skin). —*v.i.* **1,** ascend. **2,** rise in amount. —*n.* **1,** the act of mounting. **2,** a horse, etc., for riding. **3,** a support; setting. **4,** a mountain or hill.

moun′tain (mown′tən) *n.* **1,** a considerable and abrupt elevation of land. **2,** something resembling this in size. **3,** something relatively very large. **—mountain goat,** a long-haired antelope of the Rocky Mountains. **—mountain laurel,** an evergreen shrub with poisonous leaves. **—mountain lion,** a cougar.

moun″tain·eer′ (-ir′) *n.* **1,** one who lives in a mountainous region. **2,** a mountain climber.

moun′tain·ous *adj.* **1,** abounding in mountains. **2,** resembling a mountain; huge. **—moun′tain·ous·ness,** *n.*

moun′te·bank″ (mown′tə-bank″) *n.* a charlatan; an itinerant seller of quack medicines.

mount′ed (mown′tid) *adj.* **1,** riding, or serving while riding, as police on horseback. **2,** fixed on a support, etc.

moun′tie (mown′tė) *n.* (*Informal*) a mounted police officer, esp. (*cap.*) of Canada.

mount′ing *n.* a support; setting.

mourn (môrn) *v.i. & t.* **1,** feel or express sorrow, esp. for the dead. **2,** wear or display the customary tokens of sorrow. **3,** regret the loss of; deplore.

mourn′er *n.* one who mourns, esp. (at a funeral) a relative. **—mourners′ bench,** at a revival meeting, a seat for penitent sinners.

mourn′ful (-fəl) *adj.* **1,** sorrowful. **2,** gloomy; dreary. **—mourn′ful·ness,** *n.*

mourn′ing *n.* the conventional tokens of sorrow, as black dress, etc.

mouse (mows) *n.* [*pl.* **mice** (mīs)] **1,** a small rodent. **2,** (*Computers*) an input device with buttons controlling a cursor on a monitor. **—v.i. & t.** (mowz) hunt for mice; prowl about; search stealthily.

mous′er (mow′zər) *n.* an animal, esp. a cat, that catches mice.

mous·sa′ka (moo-sä′kə) *n.* (*Greek*) a dish of ground meat and eggplant.

mousse (moos) *n.* a frozen dessert of whipped cream, eggs, etc.

mousse″line′ (moos″lēn′) *n.* (*Fr.*) **1,** muslin. **2,** a very light fabric. **3,** a very thin blown glass used for goblets.

mous·tache′ (mus-tash′) *n.* mustache.

mous′y (mow′sė) *adj.* resembling a mouse; drab; colorless; quiet. **—mous′i·ness,** *n.*

mouth (mowth) *n.* [*pl.* **mouths** (mowthz)] **1,** the opening through or in which an animal takes food, masticates, and gives vocal utterance; the oral cavity. **2,** a similar opening, as of a cave, a vise, etc. **3,** the end of a river. **—v.t.** (mowth) **1,** utter pompously. **2,** put into, or rub with, the mouth. **3,** form (words) without uttering sound. **—v.i.** declaim pompously; make a grimace. **—mouth organ,** a harmonica.

mouth′ful (-fûl) *n.* **1,** enough to fill the mouth. **2,** (*Slang*) a sage remark.

mouth′piece″ (mowth′pēs″) *n.* **1,** a part of an instrument, etc., forming a mouth, or to which the mouth is applied. **2,** a person, newspaper, etc., acting as a spokesman for others. **3,** (*Slang*) a lawyer.

mouth′wash″ *n.* an antiseptic mouth-cleaning fluid used as a gargle.

mouth′wat″er·ing (-wât″ər-ing) *adj.* (*Informal*) appetizing; savorous.

mouth′y (mow′thė) *adj.* loudmouthed. **—mouth′i·ness,** *n.*

mou′ton (moo′ton) *n.* sheep's wool used as fur in garments.

mov′a·ble (moo′və-bəl) *adj.* which can be moved. **—n.** **1,** a piece of furniture not fixed in place. **2,** an article of personal property.

move (moov) *v.i. & t.* **1,** change from one place or residence to another; be or set in motion; advance. **2,** have a regular motion, esp. revolve. **3,** be sold (as stock); circulate (as in society); take action. **4,** make an application or proposal. **5,** arouse (the emotions of); touch the feelings of. **—n.** **1,** the act of moving; a change of residence; an action toward an end. **2,** in a game, the right or turn to play.

move′ment (moov′mənt) *n.* **1,** the act or manner of moving. **2,** a change of positions, as troops or ships. **3,** the progress of events; a tendency or trend. **4,** the suggestion of action, as in a painting. **5,** the works (of a watch, etc.). **6,** (*Music*) a principal division of a composition.

mov′er (moo′vər) *n.* **1,** a truckman who moves household things. **2,** (*Informal*) one who accomplishes things.

mov′ie (moo′vė) *n.* (*Informal*) a moving picture. **—mov′ie·go″er,** *n.*

mov′ing (moov′ing) *adj.* **1,** having or creating motion. **2,** actuating. **3,** exciting the emotions. **—moving picture,** motion picture. **—moving staircase** or **stairway,** an escalator.

mow (mō) *v.t. & i.* [*p.p.* **mowed** or **mown** (mōn)] **1,** cut down (grass, etc.) with a machine or scythe. **2,** cut down men in battle. **—n.** (mow) a place in a barn for storing hay.

mox′ie (mok′sė) *n.* (*Slang*) courage; pluck.

moz·ar′ab (mō-za′rəb) *n.* a Spanish Christian at the time of the Muslim domination of Spain. **—moz·ar′a·bic** (-ik) *adj.*

moz″za·rel′la (mot″sə-rel′ə) *n.* a soft white Ital. cheese.

Mr. (mis′tər) *abbr.* [*pl.* **Messrs.**; see *monsieur*] mister: a title before the surname or full name of a man without regard to his marital status.

Mrs. (miz′iz) *abbr.* [*pl.* **Mmes.**; see *madame*] mistress: a title before the surname or full name of a married or divorced woman.

Mrs., Miss, Ms.
☞ *Ms.* came into being as the woman's equivalent of Mr., i.e., a title which did not refer to marital status. It has gained increasingly in popularity since the 1950s, but some women still prefer the traditional Mrs. or Miss.

Ms. (miz) *abbr.* [*pl.* **Mses.**] a title before the surname or full name of a woman without regard to her marital status. ❑ *Mrs.*

mu (mū) the twelfth letter of the Greek alphabet (M, μ).

much *adj.* [**more, most**] in great quantity. —*n.* **1,** a great quantity. **2,** a great or important thing. —*adv.* **1,** to a great extent. **2,** approximately.

mu·cha′cha (moo-chä′chə) *n.fem.*, **mu·cha′cho** (-chō) *n.masc.* (*Sp.*) a young person; girl or boy.

mu′ci·lage (mū′sə-lij) *n.* **1,** an adhesive gum or glue. **2,** a gummy secretion in plants. **—mu″ci·lag′i·nous** (-laj′ə-nəs) *adj.*

muck (muk) *n.* **1,** filth; dirt. **2,** manure. **3,** highly organic soil. **4,** useless rock. **—muck′y,** *adj.*

muck′rake″ (muk′rāk″) *v.i.* (*Informal*) expose political corruption.

mu′cous (mū′kəs) *adj.* pert. to, or secreting, mucus. **—mucous membrane,** the membrane lining an internal organ.

---

mucous, mucus
☞ *Mucus* is the secretion of the *mucous* membrane.

---

mu′cus (mū′kəs) *n.* a viscid fluid secreted in the mucous membrane. ❑ *mucous*

mud *n.* wet, soft earth; mire. **—mud dauber,** a wasp.

mud′cat″ (mud′kat″) *n.* a large catfish.

mud′dle (mud′əl) *v.t. & i.* **1,** mix up; confuse. **2,** confuse mentally; intoxicate. **3,**

make muddy or turbid. —*n.* **1,** a mess. **2,** intellectual confusion.

mud′dle-head″ed *adj.* mentally confused or stupid; not thinking clearly.

mud′dler (mud′lər) *n.* **1,** a stick for mixing drinks. **2,** one who acts confusedly or haphazardly.

mud′dy (mud′ė) *adj.* **1,** covered or filled with mud. **2,** not clear; obscure. —*v.t.* make muddy. **—mud′di·ness,** *n.*

mud′guard″ *n.* a fender, as on an automobile.

mud hen a marsh bird, esp. a coot.

mud′sling″er *n.* one who makes unwarranted attacks on the character of an opponent, as in a political campaign. **—mud′sling″ing,** *n.*

mud′suck″er (mud′suk″ər) *n.* a Calif. fish.

muen′ster (mun′stər) *n.* (often *cap.*) a soft, mild Alsatian cheese.

mu·ez′zin (mū-ez′in) *n.* the crier who calls Muslims to prayer.

muff (muf) *n.* a cylindrical cover for warming both hands. —*v.t. & i.* (*Informal*) perform clumsily; bungle.

muf′fin (muf′in) *n.* a small round bread.

muf′fle (muf′əl) *v.t.* **1,** wrap up, esp. in a cloak or scarf. **2,** deaden (sound) by wrapping. —*v.i.* **1,** (with *up*) wrap oneself well. **2,** a heating chamber in a furnace.

muf′fler (muf′lər) *n.* **1,** a scarf. **2,** a device for deadening sound, as on an engine.

muf′ti (-tė) *n.* **1,** civilian dress. **2,** a Muslim religious officer.

mug *n.* **1,** a cup with a handle. **2,** (*Slang*) the mouth; the face; a wry expression. —*v.t. & i.* [**mugged, mug′ging**] (*Slang*) **1,** photograph. **2,** throttle from behind. **3,** grimace. **4,** overact. **—mug shot,** (*Slang*) a police photograph of a criminal or suspect. ❑ *rob*

mug′ger (mug′ər) *n.* **1,** a crocodile. **2,** one who mugs.

mug′gy (mug′ė) *adj.* (of weather, etc.) humid and hot. **—mug′gi·ness,** *n.*

mug′wump″ *n.* **1,** an independent in politics. **2,** an indecisive person.

---

mugwump
↔ From an American Indian word for war chief.

---

muk′luk *n.* an Eskimo sealskin or reindeer-skin boot or slipper.

mu·lat′to (mū-lat′ō) *n.* the offspring of a white person and a black. —*adj.* light-brown in color.

---

mul′ber″ry (mul′ber″ė) *n.* **1,** a tree or its berrylike, collective fruit. **2,** a dull reddish-purple color.

mulch *n.* a protective covering of straw, etc., around trees, etc.

mulct (mulkt) *v.t.* deprive of something by penalty or trickery. —*n.* a fine.

mule (mūl) *n.* **1,** the offspring of a mare and a male donkey. **2,** a stubborn person. **3,** a machine for spinning cotton. **4,** a slipper open at the heel. **5,** (*Slang*) a person who transports illegal drugs. —**mule skinner,** (*Informal*) muleteer.—**mul′ish,** *adj.* stubborn.

mu″le·teer′ (mū″lə-tir′) *n.* a driver of mules.

mu′ley (mū′lė) *n.* a cow. —*adj.* (of cattle) hornless.

mull (mul) *v.i.* ponder. —*v.t.* **1,** make a failure of. **2,** heat, sweeten, and spice, as wine or ale. **3,** think over. —*n.* a kind of muslin.

mul′lah (mul′ə) *n.* a religious teacher; judge.

mul′lein (mul′in) *n.* any of various flowering plants or weeds.

mul′let (mul′it) *n.* any of various marine or freshwater fishes.

mul′li·gan (mul′ə-gən) *n.* (*Slang*) a meat and vegetable stew.

mul″li·ga·taw′ny (mul″ė-gə-tâ′nė) *n.* a soup flavored with curry.

mul′lion (mul′yən) *n.* a vertical division between lights of a window or panels of wainscoting. —*v.t.* divide by mullions.

mul·ti- *pref.* many.

mul″ti·far′i·ous (mul″ti-fâr′ė-əs) *adj.* having many differing parts.

Mul′ti·graph″ (mul′ti-grȧf″) *n.* (*T.N.*) a small printing press.

mul″ti·lat′er·al *adj.* **1,** having many sides. **2,** including more than two nations, as a pact.

mul″ti·me′di·a *adj.* involving several different media, as of communication, entertainment, etc.

mul″ti·mil″lion·aire′ *n.* one who owns property worth several millions of dollars.

mul″ti·na′tion·al *adj.* including, involving or operating in several different countries.

mul″ti·par′tite (mul″tė-pär′tīt) *adj.* **1,** having many parts. **2,** of or between three or more nations.

mul′ti·ple (mul′ti-pəl) *adj.* manifold; having many parts, individuals, etc. —*n.* (*Math.*) the product of multiplying a number by a whole number. —**multiple sclerosis,** a hardening of the tissues in various

parts of the body, affecting the nervous system and causing defects in speech and sight, and weakness.

mul″ti·ple-choice′ *adj.* involving several choices, one of which must be chosen.

mul″ti·plex″ (-pleks″) *adj.* **1,** manifold. **2,** repeated many times. **3,** pert. to a system of transmitting several signals simultaneously on the same circuit or channel. —*v.t. & i.* encode or send (messages, etc.) by a multiplex system.

mul″ti·pli·cand′ (mul″tə-pli-kand′) *n.* a number to be multiplied by another.

mul″ti·pli·ca′tion (mul″tə-pli-kā′shən) *n.* act or process of multiplying; often indicated by the multiplication sign (× or ·).

mul″ti·plic′i·ty (mul″tə-plis′ə-tė) *n.* a great number.

mul′ti·ply″ (mul′ti-plī″) *v.t. & i.* **1,** increase the number or quantity. **2,** increase by propagation or procreation. **3,** (*Math.*) add as many units of one number as there are units in a second number. —**mul″ti·pli″er,** *n.*

mul′ti·task″ing *n.* in a computer, the nearly simultaneous execution of more than one program by a single CPU. —**mul′ti·task″,** *v.i.*

mul″ti·track″ing *n.* the technique of recording several separate sound tracks and later mixing them onto fewer tracks, usu. two. —**mul′ti·track″,** *v. & adj.*

mul′ti·tude″ (mul′ti-tood″) *n.* a great number; a crowd of persons. —**mul″ti·tu′di·nous,** *adj.*

mul″ti·ver′si·ty (-vēr′sə-tė) *n.* (*Informal*) a very large university.

mul″ti·vi′ta·min *n. & adj.* (a vitamin supplement) combining several different vitamins in one tablet, liquid, etc.

mum *adj.* [**mum′mer, -mest**] silent. —*n.* (*Informal*) **1,** a chrysanthemum. **2,** mother.

mum′ble (mum′bəl) *v.i. & t.* **1,** speak inarticulately or indistinctly. **2,** chew with the gums. —*n.* an inarticulate sound.

mum′ble·ty·peg″ (mum′bəl-ti-peg″) *n.* a game played with a knife.

mum′bo jum′bo (mum′bō jum′bō) **1,** an object of superstitious awe; a fetish. **2,** senseless incantation. **3,** a sorcerer.

mum′mer (mum′ər) *n.* one who wears a mask; a disguised reveler.

mum′mer·y (mum′ə-rė) *n.* **1,** a performance of mummers; burlesque. **2,** insincere ceremony.

mum′mi·fy″ (mum′ə-fī″) *v.t. & i.* make or become a mummy. —**mum″mi·fi·ca′tion,** *n.*

---

fat, fāte, fär, fāre, fâll, ȧsk; met, hē, hēr, maybė; pin, pīne; not, nōte, ôr, tool

mum′my (mum′ē) *n.* **1,** a human body embalmed by the ancient Egyptians; any desiccated corpse. **2,** a withered living being. **3,** (*Informal*) mother.

> **mummy**
> ↔ The word for embalmed body derives from Arabic *mumiya*, from *mum*, the wax used in embalming.

mumps *n.* an inflammation and swelling of the parotid glands.

> **mumps**
> ↔ From the earlier *mump*, grimace; presumably, from the facial expression caused by the disease.

munch *v.t. & i.* chew continuously and noisily.

mun′dane (mun′dān) *adj.* pert. to the world or universe; worldly. —**mun·dane′-ness,** *n.*

mung bean a leguminous plant having edible pods and sprouts.

mu·nic′i·pal (mū-nis′ə-pəl) *adj.* pert. to the government of a city.

mu·nic″i·pal′i·ty (mū-nis″i-pal′ə-tē) *n.* a city or town having corporate existence.

mu·nif′i·cent (mū-nif′i-sənt) *adj.* generous; spending liberally. —**mu·nif′i·cence,** *n.*

mu·ni′tion (mū-nish′ən) *n.* (usually *pl.*) materials for carrying on war, esp. ammunition.

mu′on (mū′on) *n.* a short-lived subatomic particle.

mu′ral (myûr′əl) *adj.* pert. to, or placed on, a wall. —*n.* a painting or photograph directly on or covering a wall.

mur′der (mēr′dər) *n.* homicide with malice aforethought. —*v.t.* **1,** kill with premeditated malice. **2,** kill barbarously. **3,** mar by poor execution. —**mur′-der·er,** *n.*

mur′der·ous *adj.* pert. to, or capable of, murder; deadly. —**mur′der·ous·ness,** *n.*

mu′ri·at′ic acid (myûr″ē-at′ik) hydrochloric acid.

murk (mērk) *n.* haze; gloom.

murk′y (mēr′kē) *adj.* **1,** dark. **2,** obscured; hazy. —**murk′i·ness,** *n.*

mur′mur (mēr′mər) *n.* **1,** a low, indistinct sound; a subdued hum, as of voices, a brook, the wind, etc. **2,** a muttered complaint. **3,** an abnormal sound in the body, esp. the heart. —*v.t. & i.* utter (such a sound). —**mur′mur·ous,** *adj.*

Mur′phy bed (mēr′fē) a bed that can be folded into a closet.

> **Murphy bed, Murphy's Law**
> ↔ The bed is named for Amer. inventor William *Murphy.* The law is named after a fictitious mechanic in U.S. Navy safety cartoons.

Mur′phy's Law (mēr′fēz) (*Slang*) the observation that anything that can go wrong will go wrong.

mur′rain (mur′ən) *n.* a disease of cattle, esp. anthrax.

mus′ca·dine (mus′kə-din) *n.* **1,** a variety of grape grown in the U.S. **2,** a variety of pear.

mus′cat (mus′kət) *n.* a variety of grape. —**mus″ca·tel′** (-tel′) *n.* a sweet wine made from the muscat.

mus′cle (mus′əl) *n.* **1,** a fixed bunch of fibers in an animal body which produces movement by contracting and dilating. **2,** muscular strength; brawn. —*v.i.* (with *in*) (*Informal*) force one's way in. —**mus′cle-bound″,** *adj.* having inelastic muscles.

> **muscle, mussel**
> ↔ From Latin *musculus*, little mouse, applied to the crustacean and the *muscle* because of their shape and movement.

Mus′co·vite″ (mus′kə-vīt″) *adj. & n.* of or pert. to Muscovy (Russia), its people or language.

mus′cu·lar (mus′kyə-lər) *adj.* of or pert. to muscle; very strong. —**mus″cu·lar′i·ty,** *n.* —**muscular dystrophy,** a hereditary disease characterized by progressive weakening of the muscles.

mus′cu·la·ture (mus′kyə-lə-chər) *n.* the number, kind, and arrangement of muscles in a part of or in the whole body.

muse (mūz) *v.i. & t.* **1,** ponder; reflect. **2,** gaze meditatively. —*n.* **1,** a poet's inspiration or genius. **2,** (*cap.*) a goddess presiding over one of the arts. —**mus′ing,** *adj. & n.*

mu·sette′ (mū-zet′) *n.* **1,** an early French bagpipe; a composition for this instrument. **2,** a small, high-pitched oboe. —**musette bag,** a bag for personal belongings.

mu·se′um (mū-zē′əm) *n.* a building for an exhibit of art, science, etc.

> **museum, music**
> ↔ Both words derive from Greek *mousa*, muse.

mush *n.* **1,** anything soft and pulpy. **2,** a food, made of meal and water. **3,** (*Informal*) maudlin sentiment. **4,** a journey over snow with a dog team. —*v.i.* drive a dog team.

mush′room″ *n.* any of various large fungi, esp. the edible varieties. —*v.i.* grow or spread rapidly.

mush′y (-ė) *adj.* **1,** pulpy. **2,** sentimental. —**mush′i·ness,** *n.*

mu′sic (mū′zik) *n.* **1,** the combining of sounds and tones as a form of artistic expression. **2,** a composition rendered by instruments or singing voices; a copy or copies of such a composition. **3,** any pleasing combination of sounds, as of the wind. —**music box,** a mechanical musical instrument. ❑ *museum*

mu′si·cal (-əl) *adj.* **1,** pert. to, producing, or skilled in, music. **2,** melodious; harmonious. —*n.* [also, **musical comedy**] a light drama composed chiefly of music. —**mu″si·cal′i·ty,** *n.*

mu″si·cale′ (mū″zi-kal′) *n.* a program of music.

> **musicale**
> ↔ From French *soirée musicale,* musical evening.

mu·si′cian (mū-zish′ən) *n.* one who composes or performs music.

mu″si·col′o·gy (mū″zi-kol′ə-jė) *n.* the study of the history, forms, and methods of music. —**mu″si·col′o·gist,** *n.*

musk *n.* an odoriferous animal secretion used in perfumery. —**musk′y,** *adj.*

mus′keg *n.* a bog.

mus′kel·lunge″ (mus′kə-lunj″) *n.* a large freshwater game fish.

mus′ket (mus′kit) *n.* a large caliber gun for soldiers.

mus″ket·eer′ (mus″kə-tir′) *n.* a soldier, orig. one who carried a musket.

mus′ket·ry (-rė) *n.* **1,** troops armed with muskets. **2,** firing practice.

musk′mel″on (musk′mel″ən) *n.* a small sweet variety of melon.

musk ox a ruminant mammal intermediate between the sheep and the ox.

musk′rat″ *n.* a No. Amer. aquatic rodent; its fur.

Mus′lim (muz′ləm) *adj.* pert. to the religion or civilization of Islam. —*n.* a follower of Islam. ❑ *Mohammedan*

mus′lin (muz′lin) *n.* a cotton fabric, esp. used for sheets.

> **muslin**
> ↔ From Arabic *muslin,* cloth from Mosul, Iraq.

mu′so (mū′zō) *n.* (*Slang*) a musician, esp. of rock and roll.

muss (mus) *n.* an untidy or confused state. —*v.t.* disarrange. —**muss′y,** *adj.*

mus′sel (mus′əl) *n.* any bivalve mollusk, esp. the freshwater clam or a mollusk of the family Mytelidae. ❑ *muscle*

must *v.i.* be obliged or compelled to. —*n.* **1,** (*Informal*) a necessary thing. **2,** new wine. —*adj.* (*Informal*) required.

mus′tache (mus′tash) *n.* the hair on a man's upper lip. Also, **mous·tache′, mus·ta′chio** (mus-tä′-shó) *n.*

mus′tang *n.* an Amer. wild horse.

> **mustang**
> ↔ From Mexican Spanish *mestengo,* stray animal (that got mixed into the herd).

mus′tard (mus′tərd) *n.* a plant; its seed made into a paste, used as a condiment or medicinally. —**mustard gas,** a chemical liquid used in warfare. —**mustard plaster,** a poultice containing mustard, used as a counterirritant, as for chest colds.

mus′te·line″ (mus′tə-līn″) *adj.* designating a large family of fur-bearing mammals.

mus′ter (mus′tər) *v.t.* **1,** assemble, esp. troops. **2,** (with *in*) enlist; (with *out*) discharge. **3,** (with *up*) gather; summon (up). —*v.i.* assemble. —*n.* assembly; enrollment list.

mus′ty (mus′tė) *adj.* **1,** having a stale odor or taste. **2,** antiquated. —**mus′ti·ness,** *n.*

mu′tate (mū′tāt) *v.t. & i.* change; alter. —**mu′ta·ble,** *adj.* —**mu′tant,** *adj. & n.*

mu·ta′tion *n.* (*Biol.*) a sudden change in characteristics.

mu·ta′tis mu·tan′dis (mū-tā′tis mū-tan′dis) (*Lat.*) the necessary changes having been made.

mute (mūt) *adj.* **1,** silent; not speaking. **2,** incapable of speech. —*n.* **1,** one incapable of speech. **2,** a device to deaden the resonance of a musical instrument. —*v.t.* deaden the resonance of. —**mute′ness,** *n.*

mu′ti·late″ (mū′tə-lāt″) *v.t.* maim or disfigure, esp. by depriving of a limb. —**mu″ti·la′tion,** *n.*

mu″ti·neer′ (mū″tə-nir′) *n.* one who commits mutiny.

mu′ti·nous (-nəs) *adj.* **1,** being or pert. to mutiny. **2,** rebellious.

mu′ti·ny (mū′tə-nė) *n.* a revolt, esp. by soldiers or seamen, against lawful authority. —*v.i.* revolt.

mutt (mut) *n.* (*Slang*) **1,** a stupid person. **2,** a mongrel dog.

mut′ter (mut′ər) *v.t. & i.* utter indistinctly in a low tone; grumble.

mut′ton (mut′ən) *n.* the flesh of a grown sheep, used as food.

mut′ton·chops″ *n.pl.* a style of side whiskers.

mu′tu·al (mū′choo-əl) *adj.* **1,** preferred, exerted, or performed by each of two with respect to the other; reciprocal. **2,** pert. alike to both or all sides; shared alike. **3,** denoting a company whose members share the expenses and the profits. —**mu″-tu·al′i·ty,** *n,* reciprocity. —**mutual fund,** an investment company whose resources are pooled and invested.

muu′muu″ (moo′moo″) *n.* a loose Hawaiian dress.

Mu′zak (mū′zak) *n.* (*T.N.*) a system of transmitting recorded music to hotels, offices, etc.; hence, the music transmitted.

mu·zhik′ (moo-zhik′) *n.* (*Russ.*) a Russian peasant.

muz′zle (muz′əl) *n.* **1,** the mouth of a gun barrel. **2,** the jaws and nose of an animal. **3,** a device to prevent an animal from biting. —*v.t.* **1,** equip with a muzzle to prevent biting. **2,** restrain from speech.

muz′zy (muz′ē) *adj.* dazed.

my (mī) *pron.* poss. form of *I.* —*interj.* expressing surprise.

my″as·the′ni·a (mī″əs-thē′nē-ə) *n.* abnormal muscle weakness.

my·col′o·gy (mī-kol′ə-jē) *n.* **1,** the study of fungi. **2,** the fungi of a region. —**my″-co·log′i·cal,** *adj.*

my″e·li′tis (mī″ə-lī′tis) *n.* inflammation of the spinal cord. —**my″e·lit′ic** (-lit′ik) *adj.*

My′lar (mī′lär) *n.* (*T.N.*) a polyester film.

my′na (mī′nə) *n.* an Asiatic bird, sometimes taught to talk. Also, **mi′na; my′nah.**

my·o- (mī-ō) *pref.* muscle.

my·o′pi·a (mī-ō′pē-ə) *n.* nearsightedness. —**my·op′ic** (-op′ik) *adj.* —**my·ope′,** *n.*

my·o′sis (mī-ō′sis) *n.* abnormal contraction of the pupil of the eye. —**my·ot′ic** (-ot′ik) *adj.*

my″o·so′tis (mī″ə-sō′tis) *n.* the forget-me-not.

my′o·ther″a·py (mī′ō-) *n.* a type of muscular therapy using pressure points.

myr′i·ad (mir′ē-əd) *n. & adj.* **1,** 10,000. **2,** many.

myr′mi·don″ (mēr′mə-don″) *n.* a follower who obeys without question or scruple.

myrrh (mēr) *n.* an aromatic resin of certain plants, used for incense.

myr′tle (mēr′təl) *n.* any of various evergreen plants.

my·self′ (mī-self′) *pron.* [*pl.* **our·selves′**]

1, an emphatic form of *I.* **2,** the reflexive form of *me.*

mys·te′ri·ous (mis-tir′ē-əs) *adj.* pert. to a mystery; obscure; puzzling. —**mys·te′-ri·ous·ness,** *n.*

mys′ter·y (mis′tə-rē) *n.* **1,** a fact or phenomenon whose meaning or cause is unknown; an enigma or puzzle. **2,** a story or novel about crime, esp. murder. **3,** a religious sacrament; (*pl.*) ancient religious rites. —**mystery play,** a medieval religious drama based on the Scriptures.

> **mystery**
> ↔ From Greek *muein*, keep secret, source of *mystēs*, initiated person.

mys′tic (mis′tik) *adj.* **1,** known only to those of special comprehension or especially initiated; obscure. **2,** occult. **3,** pert. to mystery or mysticism. —*n.* one who believes in, or practices, mysticism. —**mys′-ti·cal,** *adj.*

mys′ti·cism (mis′tə-siz-əm) *n.* a mode of thought founded on spiritual illumination or intuition.

mys′ti·fy″ (mis′tə-fī″) *v.t.* perplex; bewilder. —**mys″ti·fi·ca′tion,** *n.*

mys·tique′ (mis-tēk′) *n.* semimystical beliefs and attitudes surrounding a person, institution, etc., and endowing him or her or it with a special aura and significance.

myth (mith) *n.* **1,** a legendary story; fable. **2,** a fictitious person, thing, or happening. —**myth′i·cal,** *adj.*

my·thol′o·gy (mi-thol′ə-jē) *n.* a body or system of myths concerning a particular person or race. —**myth″o·log′i·cal** (mith″ə-loj′i-kəl) *adj.*

N

N, n (en) the fourteenth letter of the English alphabet.

nab *v.t.* [**nabbed, nab′bing**] (*Informal*) **1,** seize suddenly. **2,** arrest.

na′bob (nā′bob) *n.* a very rich person, esp. one whose riches were acquired in the Far East.

na·celle′ (nə-sel′) *n.* a cabin or enclosed shelter on an aircraft.

na′cho (nä′chō) *n.* (*Sp.*) a tortilla chip, usu. served with a sauce and topped with melted cheese.

na′cre (nā′kər) *n.* mother-of-pearl.

na′dir (nā′dər) *n.* **1,** that point of the heavens directly below the observer. **2,** the lowest point.

---

nadir, zenith
In astronomy and in figurative uses these terms describe, respectively, the lowest and highest points.

---

nag *v.t. & i.* [**nagged, nag′ging**] annoy by constant scolding or urging. —*n.* **1,** (*Informal*) a horse, esp. an inferior horse. **2,** a nagging person.

nai′ad (nī′ad) *n.* a water nymph of springs and streams.

na·if′ (nä-ēf′) *n.* a naïve person.

nail (nāl) *n.* **1,** the horny covering at the end of a finger or toe. **2,** a slender pointed piece of metal, used to hold things together, esp. wood. —*v.t.* **1,** fasten with nails. **2,** (*Informal*) catch; secure. **3,** detect and expose.

nail′set″ *n.* a metal punch for sinking the head of a nail.

nain′sook (nān′sûk) *n.* (*Hindi*, pleasurable to the eye) a fine, soft cotton fabric.

na·ïve′ (nä-ēv′) *adj.* unsophisticated; artless. —**na·ïve″té′** (-tā′) *n.*

na′ked (nā′kid) *adj.* **1,** unclothed; nude. **2,** without the usual covering; bare; exposed. **3,** plain; undisguised. **4,** (*Law*) lacking in some essential detail required for confirmation, authentication, etc.

nam′by-pam′by (nam′bē-pam′bē) *adj.* insipid; inanely sentimental.

---

namby-pamby
↔ A derisive nickname for 18th-c. poet *Ambrose* Philips, based on his first name, first used in a poem by Henry Carey.

---

name (nām) *n.* **1,** a word by which a person, place, or thing is known. **2,** a descriptive word or title. **3,** reputation, good or bad. **4,** fame; great reputation. **5,** a family; clan. **6,** a famous person. —*v.t.* **1,** give a name to. **2,** mention; specify. **3,** appoint. **4,** identify.

name′less (-ləs) *adj.* **1,** obscure. **2,** anonymous. **3,** illegitimate. **4,** indescribable or unmentionable. —**name′less·ness,** *n.*

name′ly (-lē) *adv.* that is to say.

name′sake″ *n.* one who is named for another.

nan·keen′ (nan-kēn′) *n.* **1,** a yellow cotton cloth. **2,** (*pl.*) trousers made of it. **3,** (*cap.*) a type of porcelain. Also, **nan′kin.**

nan′ny (nan′ē) *n.* **1,** a child's word for nurse. **2,** a female goat. **3,** trained child care specialist.

na′no- (na′nō) *pref.* one-billionth.

nap *n.* **1,** the soft, fuzzy surface of some fabrics. **2,** a short sleep. —*v.t.* [**napped,**

nap′ping] **1,** take a short sleep. **2,** be off guard.

na′palm (nā′päm) *n.* jellied gasoline, used in incendiary weapons: *na(phthene) palm(itate).*

nape (nāp) *n.* the back of the neck.

na′per·y (nā′pə-rē) *n.* table linens.

naph′tha (naf′thə) *n.* a volatile liquid distilled from petroleum, used for dry cleaning, etc.

naph′tha·lene″ (naf′thə-lēn″) *n.* a coal tar derivative, used for dyes or as a moth repellent.

naph′thene (naf′thēn) *n.* a hydrocarbon found in petroleum.

nap′kin *n.* a small square of cloth or paper, esp. one used at table.

na·po′le·on (nə-pō′lē-ən) *n.* **1,** a former Fr. gold coin. **2,** a rich layered pastry. **3,** a high boot.

narc (närk) *n.* (*Slang*) a federal narcotics inspector.

nar′cis·sism (när′-sə-siz-əm) *n.* an abnormal tendency to admire one's own perfections. Also, **nar′cism** (-siz-əm).

nar·cis′sus (när-sis′əs) *n.* a spring-flowering bulbous plant.

nar·co′sis (när-kō′sis) *n.* stupor induced by drugs. Also, **nar′co·tism** (när′kə-tiz-əm). —**nar′co·tize″,** *v.t.* stupefy; affect with a narcosis.

nar·cot′ic (när-kot′ik) *n. & adj.* a drug that dulls the senses, relieves pain, and produces sleep.

nard (närd) *n.* an aromatic ointment made from an E. Indian herb; the herb.

nar′es (när′ēz) *n.pl.* [*sing.* **nar′is**] the nostrils. —**nar′i·al,** *adj.*

nar′ghi·le (när′gi-le) *n.* an Oriental tobacco pipe; hookah.

---

narghile
↔ From Persian *nargil,* coconut, from which the bowl of the pipe was first made.

---

nark (närk) *n.* (*Slang*) an informer.

nar′rate″ (na′rāt″) *v.t. & i.* give an account (of); relate. —**nar·ra′tion,** *n.*

nar′ra·tive (när′ə-tiv) *n.* a story. —*adj.* of or being a story. —**nar′ra″tor,** *n.*

nar′row (när′ō) *adj.* **1,** of small width; not broad. **2,** limited in extent, resources, point of view, etc. **3,** with little margin; close. —*v.t. & i.* lessen; contract. —*n.* (*pl.*) the shallow part of a river; a strait. —**nar′row-gauge″,** *adj.* having (railroad) tracks less than the usual 56 inches apart. —**nar′row-mind″ed,** *adj.*

---

fat, fāte, fär, fåre, fåll, åsk; met, hē, hèr, maybē; pin, pīne; not, nōte, ôr, tool shallow; intolerant; bigoted. —**nar'-row·ness**, *n.*

nar'thex (när'theks) *n.* vestibule.

nar'whal (när'wəl) *n.* an arctic sea mammal, related to the whale, with a long, straight tusk.

nar'y (när'ē) *adj.* (*Dial.*) not; no.

na'sal (nā'zəl) *adj.* pert. to the nose; pronounced through the nose. —**na'sal·ize"**, *v.t.* pronounce through the nose.

nas'cent (nā'sənt) *adj.* beginning to exist or to grow. —**nas'cen·cy**, *n.*

nas·tur'tium (na-stēr'shəm) *n.* a plant bearing fragrant flowers.

nas'ty (nas'tē) *adj.* **1,** physically filthy; offensive. **2,** indecent; objectionable. **3,** stormy, as weather. **4,** troublesome. **5,** vicious. —**nas·ti·ness**, *n.*

na'tal (nā'təl) *adj.* pert. to one's birth. —**na·tal'i·ty** (nə-tal'ə-tē) *n.* birthrate.

na'tant (nā'tənt) *adj.* swimming; floating.

na·ta'tion (na-tā'shən) *n.* the art or act of swimming. —**na"ta·to'ri·um,** (na"tə-tôr'ē-əm) *n.* a swimming pool. —**na'ta·to"ry,** *adj.*

na'tion (nā'shən) *n.* **1,** a race of people having a common descent, language, and culture. **2,** a body of people constituting a political unit under one government.

na'tion·al (nash'ən-əl) *adj.* common to the whole nation; public; governmental. —*n.* a citizen. —**national debt,** money owed by the federal government to private individuals or organizations. —**National Guard,** the militia of the U.S. states, each commanded by the governor except in wartime. —**National Socialism,** the principles of the German government under Hitler.

na'tion·al·ism (nash'ə-nə-liz-əm) *n.* advocacy of the utmost political advancement of one's nation or people. —**na'tion·al·ist,** *n.* —**na"tion·al·is'tic,** *adj.*

na"tion·al'i·ty (nash"ə-nal'ə-tē) *n.* **1,** membership in a particular nation. **2,** a race of people; a nation.

na'tion·al·ize" (-īz") *v.t.* place under government control or ownership. —**na"tion·al·i·za'tion,** *n.*

na'tive (nā'tiv) *adj.* **1,** pert. to one by birth or by the place of one's birth. **2,** not of foreign origin or production. **3,** natural; innate. —*n.* **1,** one born in a certain place or country. **2,** one of the original inhabitants. —**na'tive-born",** *adj.* —**Native American,** an American Indian.

---

native, nature
↔ Both words derive from Latin *nasci,* be born, which produced many English words, including *pregnant* and *cognate.*

---

na·tiv'i·ty (nā-tiv'ə-tē) *n.* **1,** birth; also, time, place, and manner of birth. **2,** (*cap.*) the birth of Christ.

NATO (nā'tō) *n. & adj.* a group of nations cooperating to oppose aggression: *N(orth) A(tlantic) T(reaty) O(rganization).*

nat'ty (nat'ē) *adj.* (*Informal*) smartly spruce; trim. —**nat'ti·ness,** *n.*

nat'u·ral (nach'ə-rəl) *adj.* **1,** not artificial; formed by nature. **2,** pert. to, or in a state of, nature. **3,** proper; reasonable; not unusual. **4,** innate. **5,** easy; unaffected; kindly. **6,** (*Music*) neither sharp nor flat. **7,** (of children) illegitimate. —*n.* **1,** something that is natural. **2,** (*Informal*) a person or thing sure to succeed. **3,** an idiot. —**nat'u·ral·ness,** *n.* —**natural history,** the study of plant and animal life, behavior, etc. —**natural selection,** survival of the fittest.

nat'u·ral·ism (-iz-əm) *n.* **1,** close adherence to nature or reality in painting, poetry, etc. **2,** a view of the world which takes account only of natural elements and forces.

nat'u·ral·ist (-ist) *n.* a scholar of plant and animal life.

nat'u·ral·ize" (-īz") *v.t.* admit (an alien) to citizenship. —**nat"u·ral·i·za'tion,** *n.*

na'ture (nā'chər) *n.* **1,** the material universe; the forces at work in the universe, independently of mankind or its acts. **2,** the essential character of a person or thing. **3,** kind; sort. —**na'tur·ist,** *n.* a nudist. ❑ *native*

Nau'ga·hyde" (nô'gə-hīd") *n.* (*T.N.*) a brand of simulated leather.

naught (nât) *n.* **1,** nothing. **2,** a zero; a cipher (0).

naugh'ty (nâ'tē) *adj.* **1,** disobedient. **2,** improper. —**naugh'ti·ness,** *n.*

nau'sea (nâ'shə) *n.* **1,** an inclination to vomit. **2,** a feeling of disgust. ❑ *noisome*

nau'se·ate" (nâ'zē-āt") *v.t.* sicken.

nau'seous (nâ'shəs) *adj.* **1,** causing nausea; nauseating. **2,** experiencing nausea; nauseated. —**nau'seous·ness,** *n.*

nautch (nâch) *n.* an Indian ballet.

nau'ti·cal (nâ'ti-kəl) *adj.* pert. to ships, seamen, or navigation.

nau'ti·lus (nâ'tə-ləs) *n.* a mollusk with a spiral chambered shell.

---

na'val (nā'vəl) *adj.* pert. to a navy.

---

naval, navel

☛ Do not confuse *naval*, pertaining to a navy, and *navel*, an anatomical term for the bellybutton.

---

nave (nāv) *n.* **1,** the main body of a church from chancel to entrance. **2,** the hub of a wheel.

na'vel (nā'vəl) *n.* the depression in the center of the abdomen. —**navel orange,** a type of small, seedless orange. ❑ *naval*

nav'i·ga·ble (nav'i-gə-bəl) *adj.* **1,** affording passage to ships. **2,** capable of being steered, as a dirigible.

nav'i·gate'' (nav'i-gāt'') *v.t. & i.* **1,** travel by water; sail over or on. **2,** sail or steer a ship. —**nav''i·ga'tion,** *n.* —**nav'i·ga''tor,** *n.* one who plots the course of ships or aircraft.

nav'vy (nav'ė) *n.* (*Brit.*) an unskilled laborer.

na'vy (nā'vė) *n.* **1,** all the war vessels of a nation. **2,** (usually *cap.*) a nation's naval organization. —**navy bean,** a variety of small white bean. —**navy blue,** a deep, dark blue.

nay (nā) *n.* **1,** no; a refusal. **2,** a negative vote. —*adv.* not only so, but; indeed.

Naz''a·rene' (naz''ə-rēn') *n. & adj.* of or pert. to Nazareth. —**the Nazarene,** Jesus Christ.

Na'zi (nät'sė) *n.* a member of the former National Socialist party, which controlled Germany from 1933 to 1945: *Nazi(onal-sozialist).* —**Na'zism** (nät'siz-əm) *n.* the principles of this party, quasi-fascistic and racist.

N-'bomb'' *n.* neutron bomb.

né (nā) *adj.* (*Fr.,* born) of a man, originally known as.

Ne·an'der·thal'' (nė-an'dər-täl'') *adj.* pert. to a species of man existing in the Paleolithic period.

Neanderthal

↔ From the *Neanderthal,* a valley in Germany, where specimens were first found pointing to the existence of the species.

---

neap (nēp) *adj.* designating the lowest high tide in the lunar month.

near (nir) *adj.* **1,** not remote; close to; close. **2,** closely akin. **3,** intimate, as friends. **4,** on the left (opposed to *off*). **5,** (*Informal*) stingy. —*adv.* **1,** not far off. **2,** closely. **3,** nearly. —*prep.* close by or to. —*v.i. & t.* come close (to). —**near''by',** *adj., adv. & prep.* close at hand. —**near'-**ness, *n.* —**near beer,** a malt liquor with a very low alcoholic content.

---

near, neighbor

↔ The Old English ancestor of these words meant nearer; it was the comparative form of *neah,* which produced the first syllable of *neighbor.* The second syllable came from Old English *gebur,* dweller.

Near East 1, a region including S.W. Asia (Syria, Turkey, Jordan, etc.) and sometimes the Balkans and Egypt. **2,** (*Brit.*) the Balkans.

near'ly *adv.* **1,** closely. **2,** almost.

near'sight''ed *adj.* able to see clearly only at short distances; myopic. —**near'-**sight''ed·ness, *n.*

neat (nēt) *adj.* **1,** tidy; orderly. **2,** adroit; effective. **3,** pure; undiluted. —**neat'ness,** *n.*

neb'bish (neb'ish) *n.* a meek or uninteresting person.

neb'u·la (neb'yə-lə) *n.* [*pl.* **-lae** (-lė), **-las**] a luminous patch in the sky made by distant star clusters or masses of gas. —**neb'u·lar,** *adj.*

neb'u·lous (neb'yə-ləs) *adj.* **1,** cloudy; hazy. **2,** indistinct; vague; confused. —**neb''u·los'i·ty, neb'u·lous·ness,** *n.*

nec'es·sar''y (nes'ə-ser'ė) *adj.* **1,** inevitably resulting from the nature of things. **2,** required; essential; indispensable. —*n.* an essential thing. —**nec''es·sar'i·ly** (-ə-lė) *adv.* inevitably.

ne·ces'si·tate'' (nə-ses'ə-tāt'') *v.t.* render unavoidable; compel.

ne·ces'si·tous (nə-ses'ə-təs) *adj.* very poor; needy.

ne·ces'si·ty (nə-ses'ə-tė) *n.* **1,** the state or fact of being inevitable or necessary. **2,** something essential, esp. to existence. **3,** poverty; great need. **4,** compulsion.

neck (nek) *n.* **1,** the slender part of the body between the head and shoulders. **2,** in a garment, the part closest to the neck. **3,** something resembling a neck; an isthmus. —*v.i.* (*Slang*) kiss and pet.

neck'er·chief (nek'ər-chif) *n.* a scarf worn around the neck. Also, **neck'cloth''.**

neck'lace (nek'ləs) *n.* any flexible ornament worn around the neck.

neck'tie'' (nek'tī'') *n.* a decorative band worn around the neck. —**neck'tie party,** (*Slang*) a public hanging, esp. without trial.

neck'wear'' *n.* neckties, etc.

nec·ro- (nek-rō) *pref.* dead; death; corpse.

---

ne·crol'o·gy (nek-rol'ə-jė) *n.* **1,** an obituary. **2,** a list of persons who have died. —**ne·crol'o·gist,** *n.*

nec'ro·man"cy (nek'rə-man"sė) *n.* **1,** divination by conversing with the dead. **2,** magic in general.

ne·crop'o·lis (nek-rop'ə-lis) *n.* a cemetery, esp. of ancient times.

ne·cro'sis (ne-krō'sis) *n.* death of bodily tissue; gangrene. —**ne·crot'ic** (-krot'ik) *adj.*

nec'tar (nek'tər) *n.* **1,** in mythology, the wine of the gods. **2,** any delicious drink. **3,** a sweet secretion. —**nec'tar·ous,** *adj.*

nec"ta·rine' (nek"tə-rēn') *n.* a form of peach with a smooth skin.

née (nā) *adj.* (*Fr.,* born) of a woman, whose maiden name was.

need (nēd) *n.* **1,** necessity or lack; urgent want. **2,** time of difficulty; emergency. **3,** poverty. —*v.t.* be in want of. —*v.i.* **1,** be obliged. **2,** be necessary. —**need'ful,** *adj.* necessary; requisite.

nee'dle (nē'dəl) *n.* **1,** a slender pointed instrument with a hole for thread, used in sewing. **2,** any of various similar instruments, as for knitting, in a phonograph, on a hypodermic syringe, etc. **3,** a leaf of a pine tree. **4,** the pointer on the dial of an instrument, esp. the magnetized pointer in a compass. **5,** something resembling a needle, as an obelisk. —*v.t.* (*Informal*) vex or goad by repeated gibes.

nee'dle·point" *n.* **1,** lace made on a paper pattern. **2,** a kind of embroidery.

need'less (-ləs) *adj.* unnecessary. —**need'less·ness,** *n.*

nee'dle·work" *n.* sewing or embroidery.

need'y (nē'dė) *adj.* very poor. —**need'i·ness,** *n.*

ne'er (nār) *contr.* never.

ne'er-'do-well" (nār'doo-wel") *n.* an idle, worthless person.

ne·far'i·ous (ni-fâr'ė-əs) *adj.* unspeakably wicked. —**ne·far'i·ous·ness,** *n.*

ne·gate' (ne-gāt') *v.t.* deny; nullify. —**ne·ga'tion,** *n.*

neg'a·tive (neg'ə-tiv) *adj.* **1,** expressing denial or refusal; not affirmative; not positive. **2,** lacking positive or distinguishing qualities. **3,** (*Math.*) denoting subtraction; minus. **4,** having an excess of electrons. —*n.* **1,** a negative statement, reply, or word. **2,** in a debate, the side that denies or refutes. **3,** (*Photog.*) a plate or film from which a print is made; the image in reverse. —*v.t.* refuse assent. —**negative income tax,** a method of public relief; guaranteed annual income. —**neg'a·tiv-**

ism, *n.* a tendency to view the world with a skeptical attitude.

neg·lect' (ni-glekt') *v.t.* **1,** disregard. **2,** be remiss about; leave uncared for. **3,** fail in duty or performance through carelessness. —*n.* **1,** lack of attention or care. **2,** negligence. —**neg·lect'ful,** *adj.* careless.

neg"li·gee' (neg"lə-zhā') *n.* a woman's loose, informal house gown.

neg'li·gent (neg'lə-jənt) *adj.* **1,** guilty of or characterized by neglect, esp. of duty. **2,** (*Law*) failing to exercise due care. —**neg'li·gence,** *n.*

neg'li·gi·ble (neg'li-jə-bəl) *adj.* of little importance. —**neg"li·gi·bil'i·ty,** *n.*

né·go·ci·ant' (nā-gō-sē-änt') *n.* (*Fr.*) wine merchant.

ne·go'ti·a·ble (ni-gō'shė-ə-bəl) *adj.* capable of being negotiated; transferable. —**ne·go"ti·a·bil'i·ty,** *n.*

ne·go'ti·ate' (ni-gō'shė-āt") *v.i.* discuss with others the terms of a diplomatic, political, or business matter. —*v.t.* **1,** bring about by mutual discussions. **2,** sell (notes, securities, etc.). **3,** (*Informal*) handle. —**ne·go'ti·ant,** *n.* —**ne·go"ti·a'tion,** *n.*

Ne·gri'to (ni-grē'tō) *n.* a member of one of the dwarfish Negroid peoples of Asia or Africa.

Ne'gro (nē'grō) *n.* a member of the darkest-skinned, or black, race. —*adj.* of, or pert. to, this race. —**Ne'gress,** *n.fem.* —**Ne'groid** (-groid) *adj.* ❑ *African-American*

ne'gus (neg'əs) *n.* a beverage of hot water and wine, sweetened and spiced, named for English Colonel Francis Negus, its inventor.

Neh'ru jacket (nā'roo) a long jacket with a high collar, similar to a Mao jacket, named for Jawaharlal Nehru, Indian political leader.

neigh (nā) *n.* the prolonged cry of a horse; a whinny. —*v.i.* whinny.

neigh'bor (nā'bər) *n.* **1,** one who lives near another. **2,** a person or thing next or near another. **3,** a fellow being. —*v.t.* adjoin; be near to. Also, **neighbour.** —**neigh'bor·ing,** *adj.* nearby. ❑ *near*

neigh'bor·hood" *n.* **1,** the vicinity; a district of a particular kind. **2,** the persons in a locality.

neigh'bor·ly (-lė) *adj.* appropriate to a neighbor; accommodating. —**neigh'-bor·li·ness,** *n.*

nei'ther (nē'thər; nī'-) *adj., adv., conj. & pron.* not either. ❑ *either*

nel'son (nel'sən) *n.* a hold in wrestling.

Nem'bu·tal" (nem'byə-tâl") *n.* (*T.N.*) a

barbiturate used as a sedative and analgesic.

nem'e·sis (nem'ə-sis) *n.* [*pl.* **-ses''** (-sēz'')] an agent of vengeance.

> ### neither, neuter
> ↔ Etymologically *neither* is not the negative of *either*, but is derived from Old English *nāhwaether*, not one of two. *Neuter*, from Latin *ne uter*, has the same base meaning.

ne·o- (nē-ō) *pref.* new; recent.

ne''o·clas'si·cism *n.* any revival of classic style in the arts. **—ne''o·clas'sic,** *adj.*

ne''o·con·serv'a·tism *n.* conservatism in politics combining elements of capitalism and the welfare state. **—ne''o·con·serv'a·tive,** *n.*

ne''o·dym'i·um (nē''ō-dim'ē-əm) *n.* a rare-earth metallic element, no. 60, symbol Nd.

Ne''o·lith'ic (nē''ō-lith'ik) *adj. & n.* (pert. to) the later Stone Age.

ne·ol'o·gism (nē-ol'ə-jiz-əm) *n.* a new word, usage, or expression. Also, **ne·ol'o·gy.**

ne''o·my'cin (-mī'sin) *n.* an antibiotic drug.

ne'on (nē'on) *n.* an inert gaseous element, no. 10, symbol Ne, used in electric signs.

ne'o·nate'' (nē'ə-nāt'') *n.* a newborn child.

ne'o·phyte'' (nē'ə-fīt'') *n.* **1,** a beginner; a novice. **2,** a convert.

ne'o·plasm'' (nē'ə-plaz''-əm) *n.* any morbid growth, as a tumor. **—ne''o·plas'tic,** *adj.*

ne'o·prene'' (nē'ə-prēn'') *n.* a kind of synthetic rubber.

ne''o·ter'ic (nē''ə-ter'ik) *adj.* recent; modern. **—n.** a modern writer, etc.

ne·pen'the (ni-pen'thē) *n.* anything that induces forgetfulness of pain or care.

neph'ew (nef'ū) *n.* a son of one's sister or brother.

neph'rite (nef'rīt) *n.* a variety of jade.

ne·phri'tis (ni-frī'tis) *n.* inflammation of the kidneys.

ne plus ul'tra (nā plus ul'trə) (*Lat.*) no more beyond; the ultimate.

nep'o·tism (nep'ə-tiz-əm) *n.* undue favoritism to relatives. **—ne·pot'ic** (nə-pot'ik) *adj.* **—ne·pot'i·cal·ly,** *adv.*

nep·tu'ni·um (nep-tū'nē-əm) *n.* an artificially produced radioactive element, no. 93, symbol Np.

nerd (nērd) *n.* (*Slang*) an uninteresting person.

ne're·id (nir'ē-id) *n.* a sea nymph.

nerve (nērv) *n.* **1,** a bundle of fibers, one of many conveying impulses of motion and sensation from the brain to all parts of the body. **2,** force; energy. **3,** courage. **4,** (*pl.*) acute nervousness. **5,** (*Slang*) audacity. **—v.t.** give strength or courage to. **—nerve cell, 1,** any cell of the nervous system. **2,** a ganglion. **—nerve gas,** a chemical weapon which attacks the nervous system.

nerve'less (-ləs) *adj.* **1,** lacking courage. **2,** listless; weak. **—nerve'less·ness,** *n.*

nerv'ous (nēr'vəs) *adj.* **1,** made up of, or affecting, the nerves. **2,** high-strung; easily agitated. **3,** timid; uneasy. **—nerv'ous·ness,** *n.* **—nervous breakdown,** a condition characterized by fatigue, lethargy, worry, and lack of energy. **—nervous system,** the bodily system that receives stimuli and transmits impulses.

ner'vure (nēr'vyûr) *n.* a vein in a leaf or insect's wing.

nerv'y (nēr'vē) *adj.* brash; bold.

nes'cience (nesh'əns) *n.* ignorance. **—nes'cient,** *adj.*

ness (nes) *n.* a promontory or cape.

-ness (nəs) *suf.* quality or state of being (the root word): added to adjectives to form nouns. (A terminal *-y* regularly changes to *-i* before *-ness.*)

nest *n.* **1,** a place used by or made by birds, insects, turtles, etc., for laying eggs and hatching young. **2,** any snug retreat. **3,** a graduated set of articles, as bowls, tables, etc., fitted one within the other. **—v.i.** sit on or build a nest. **—nest egg,** a fund of money saved for an emergency.

nes·tle (nes'əl) *v.i. & t.* **1,** lie close and snug. **2,** settle comfortably; snuggle.

nest'ling (nest'ling; nes'-) *n.* a young bird in the nest.

net *n.* **1,** a contrivance made of coarse string tied in meshes, for catching fish, birds, etc. **2,** a snare; a trap. **3,** a fine fabric of open mesh for dresses, veils, etc. **4,** anything woven or tied in meshes. **5,** clear profit. **—adj. 1,** remaining as profit after all necessary deductions (taxes, expenses, etc.). **2,** without discount. **—v.t.** [**net'ted, -ting**] **1,** capture, as with a net. **2,** spread a net over. **3,** earn as clear profit. **—net worth,** the total assets of an entity minus its total liabilities.

neth'er (ne*th*'ər) *adj.* under; lower. **—neth'er·most'',** *adj.* lowest, deepest, etc. **—neth'er·ward** (-wərd) *adv.* toward the depths. **—nether world,** hell.

net'ting (net'ing) *n.* any meshed fabric of thread, rope, wire, etc.

---

fat, fāte, fär, fāre, fâll, àsk; met, hē, hėr, maybé; pin, pīne; not, nōte, ôr, tool

net′tle (net′əl) *n.* a coarse herb with stinging hairs. —*v.t.* vex. —**net′tle·some** (-səm) *adj.*

net′work″ *n.* **1,** anything of intersecting lines resembling a net. **2,** a chain of radio or television stations. **3,** an interconnected system of computers: *local area network.* —*v.i.* to pool information, resources, etc., with others in the same field. —**net′work″ing,** *n.*

neu′ral (nyûr′əl) *adj.* pert. to the nerves or the nervous system.

neu·ral′gia (nyû-ral′jə) *n.* an acute intermittent pain along the course of a nerve. —**neu·ral′gic,** *adj.* —**neu·ral′gi·cal·ly,** *adv.*

---

neuralgia, neuritis
☛ *Neuralgia* is a pain originating within a nerve. *Neuritis* is the inflammation of a nerve (which might cause *neuralgia*).

---

neu″ras·the′ni·a (nyûr″əs-thē′nė-ə) *n.* nervous exhaustion. —**neu″ras·then′ic** (-then′ik) *adj. & n.*

neu·ri′tis (nyû-rī′tis) *n.* inflammation or continued pain in a nerve. ❑ *neuralgia*

neu·ro- (nyû-rō) *pref.* nerve.

neu·rol′o·gy (nyû-rol′ə-jė) *n.* the branch of science dealing with the nervous system and its diseases. —**neu″ro·log′i·cal,** *adj.* —**neu·rol′o·gist,** *n.*

neu′ron (nyûr′on) *n.* a nerve cell. Also, **neu′rone** (-ōn)

neu″ro·pa·thol′o·gy *n.* (*Med.*) the study of the diseases of the nervous system. —**neu″ro·pa·thol′o·gist,** *n.*

neu·ro′sis (nyû-rō′sis) *n.* [*pl.* **-ses** (sēz)] a functional nervous disease or emotional disorder. —**neu·rot′ic** (-rot′ik) *adj. & n.* —**neu·rot′i·cal·ly,** *adv.*

neu′ter (noo′tər) *adj.* **1,** (*Gram.*) neither masculine nor feminine. **2,** (*Zool.*) sexless; (*Bot.*) asexual. —*v.t.* render neuter. ❑ *neither*

neu′ter·cane″ (noo′tər-kān″) *n.* a subtropical cyclone.

neu′tral (noo′trəl) *adj.* **1,** taking neither side in a war, quarrel, or dispute. **2,** with no decided qualities or characteristics; indifferent. **3,** of a color, gray; subdued in tone. —*n.* a neutral power, one of its subjects or its vessels. —**neutral spirits,** ethyl alcohol of higher than 190 proof.

neu·tral′i·ty (noo-tral′ə-tė) *n.* state of being neutral.

neu′tral·ize″ (noo′trə-līz″) *v.t.* **1,** render neutral or inactive. **2,** counteract. —**neu″tral·i·za′tion,** *n.*

neu·tri′no (noo-trē′nō) *n.* a neutral particle.

neu′tron (noo′tron) *n.* a minute uncharged particle of matter. —**neutron bomb,** a high-energy bomb which kills living things but inflicts little physical damage on buildings, etc. —**neutron star,** (*Astron.*) a dense star composed primarily of neutrons.

né·vé′ (nā-vā′) *n.* granular snow. Also, **firn.**

nev′er (nev′ər) *adv.* **1,** not ever. **2,** not at all. —**never-never land, 1,** wilderness. **2,** an imaginary place. **3,** an imagined existence.

nev″er·more′ *adj.* never again.

nev″er·the·less′ (nev″ər-*th*ə-les′) *adv. & conj.* in spite of that; yet.

ne′vus (ne′vəs) *n.* [*pl.* **-vi** (-vī)] a mole or birthmark.

new (noo) *adj.* **1,** recently made, discovered, invented, etc. **2,** unfamiliar. **3,** not the same as before; different. **4,** not used before. **5,** starting afresh; unaccustomed. **6,** not previously well known. —*adv.* recently; freshly. —**new′ish,** *adj.* —**new′ness,** *n.* —**New Age,** a cultural movement emphasizing mysticism and Oriental themes. —**new journalism,** a style of journalism characterized by a more personal, less objective manner of reporting. —**New Left,** a political movement that advocates radical change. —**new math,** a system of teaching mathematics based on set theory. —**new moon,** the phase of the moon when it is in conjunction with the sun, its dark side turned toward the earth. —**new wave, 1,** a type of film-making. **2,** a type of rock music related to punk rock.

new′born″ *adj.* **1,** born recently. **2,** reborn.

new′com″er *n.* one recently arrived.

new′el (noo′əl) *n.* **1,** the center pillar of a flight of winding stairs. **2,** a post on a stairway.

new″fan′gled (-fang′gəld) *adj.* **1,** novel. **2,** fond of novelty. —**new·fan′gled·ness,** *n.*

---

newfangled
↔ From Old English *newe,* new, + *fangol,* inclined to take.

---

new-′fash″ioned *adj.* **1,** made in a new form or style. **2,** lately come into fashion.

New′found·land (noo′fənd-lənd) *n.* a very large, shaggy dog.

new′ly (noo′lė) *adv.* **1,** recently; lately. **2,** anew; afresh.

new′ly·wed″ *n.* a person recently married.

---

news (nooz) *n.sing.* **1,** tidings, esp. of recent public events. **2,** the reports published in a newspaper. **3,** (*Informal*) a matter not previously known. —**news'boy", news'girl",** *n.* a boy or girl who sells or delivers newspapers. —**news'cast",** *n.* a radio or TV broadcast of current news. —**news'deal"er,** *n.* a person who sells newspapers. —**news'man", news'wom"an,** *n.* a person who writes, edits, reports, etc., the news. —**news'pa"per,** *n.* a printed publication giving chiefly news. —**news'print",** *n.* a cheap paper used in newspapers. —**news'reel",** *n.* motion pictures of current events. —**news'stand",** *n.* a stand where newspapers are sold.

news'let"ter *n.* a periodical news bulletin, usu. for a particular special interest group.

news'mon"ger *n.* a gossip.

new'speak" *n.* the intentional use of ambiguous and misleading language.

> **newspeak**
> ↔ Coined by novelist George Orwell in his novel *1984*.

news'wor"thy *adj.* worthy of being reported as news; of general interest.

news'y (noo'zē) *adj.* full of news; informative. —**news'i·ness,** *n.*

newt (noot) *n.* a small, semiaquatic salamander.

> **newt**
> ↔ A misdivision of the Middle English phrase *an ewte,* an eft.

New Testament the books of the Holy Bible relating to Jesus Christ or Christianity.

New Year a year just beginning. —**New Year's Day,** Jan. 1. —**New Year's Eve,** Dec. 31.

next (nekst) *adj. & adv.* **1,** nearest. **2,** immediately following in time, place, order, etc. —*prep.* nearest to.

nex'us (nek'səs) *n.* [*pl.* **nex'us**] **1,** a tie; link. **2,** a connected series.

ni'a·cin (nī'ə-sin) *n.* nicotinic acid.

nib *n.* **1,** the point of anything, esp. of a pen. **2,** a bird's beak.

nib'ble (nib'əl) *v.i. & t.* bite off small pieces (of). —*n.* **1,** a small bite. **2,** in computers, half a byte.

nib'lick (nib'lik) *n.* a golf club for high lofting shots; no. 9 iron.

nibs (nibż) *n.* (*Informal*) an important person, as *his nibs* or *her nibs.*

nice (nīs) *adj.* **1,** requiring precision or tact. **2,** subtle, as a distinction. **3,** delicately sensitive; minutely accurate. **4,** fastidious; refined; discriminating. **5,** (*Informal*) pleasing or pleasant; attractive; kind. —**nice'ness,** *n.*

> **nice**
> ↔ The source of this word is Latin *nescius,* ignorant; only by a very tortuous path did it reach its present sense of pleasant.

nice-"nel'ly·ism (-nel'ē-iz-əm) *n.* a euphemism.

ni'ce·ty (nī'sə-tē) *n.* **1,** precision; accuracy. **2,** a minute distinction or detail. **3,** something choice. **4,** (usu. *pl.*) refinement.

niche (nich) *n.* **1,** a recess in a wall, as for a vase, statue, etc. **2,** a suitable place or position.

Ni'chrome (nik'rōm) *n.* (*T.N.*) an alloy of nickel, chromium, and iron.

nick (nik) *n.* **1,** a notch. **2,** a slightly chipped place, as on a dish. **3,** the exact moment (of time). —*v.t.* **1,** make a notch in; chip. **2,** (*Slang*) steal; shoplift.

nick'el (nik'əl) *n.* **1,** a hard silvery-white metallic element much used in alloys, no. 28, symbol Ni. **2,** a U.S. five-cent coin. —**nickel** or **German silver,** an alloy of nickel, copper, and zinc, used for tableware, etc.

> **nickel**
> ↔ Coined by a Swedish mineralogist from German *Kupfernickel,* lit., copper-demon, used by miners as a term for nickel-bearing ore.

nick"el·o'de·on (nik"ə-lō'dē-ən) *n.* **1,** a movie theater with an admission price of five cents. **2,** a jukebox.

nick'er (nik'ər) *v.i.* **1,** neigh. **2,** laugh; snicker. —*n.* a neigh; a vulgar laugh.

nick'name" (nik'nām") *n.* an additional or substitute name.

> **nickname**
> ↔ The result of the improper division of Middle English *an ekename,* an added name.

nic'o·tine" (nik'ə-tēn") *n.* a poisonous, colorless, oily liquid extracted from tobacco. —**nic'o·tin"ic acid,** a B vitamin derived from nicotine; niacin.

> **nicotine**
> ↔ From Jacques *Nicot,* the French ambassador to Lisbon, Portugal, who supposedly introduced tobacco to France.

ni'dus (nī'dəs) *n.* [*pl.* **-di** (-dī)] **1,** a nest, esp. for insects' eggs. **2,** a place where disease germs may develop.

niece (nēs) *n.* a daughter of one's brother or sister.

niels·bohr′i·um (nēlz-bō′rē-əm) *n.* a radioactive chemical element, no. 107, symbol Ns, produced artificially.

Niel′sen rating (nēl′sən) a system of ranking (television programs) on the basis of the estimated number of viewers.

nif′ty (nif′tē) (*Slang*) *adj.* smart; stylish. —*n.* a smart remark.

nig′gard (nig′ərd) *n.* a stingy person; a miser. —*adj.* **1,** niggardly. **2,** scanty; inadequate.

nig′gard·ly (nig′ərd-lē) *adj.* stingy; miserly. —**nig′gard·li·ness,** *n.*

nig′gle (nig′əl) *v.t. & i.* **1,** trifle (with); perform too meticulously. **2,** cheat.

nigh (nī) *adj., adv. & prep.* near.

night (nīt) *n.* **1,** the time from sunset to sunrise. **2,** nightfall. **3,** darkness; also, a time of affliction or ignorance. —**night blindness,** poor vision at night; nyctalopia. —**night crawler,** a large earthworm. —**night letter,** a telegram transmitted at a reduced rate, during the night. —**night owl,** a person accustomed to late hours.

night′cap″ (nīt′kap″) *n.* **1,** a cap worn at night in bed. **2,** a drink taken just before retiring. **3,** the last event in an evening program.

night′clothes″ *n.pl.* bedclothes.

night′club″ *n.* a cabaret.

night′dress″ *n.* a garment worn in bed.

night′fall″ *n.* the coming of night.

night′gown″ *n.* **1,** a dressing gown. **2,** a loose shift worn in bed.

night′hawk″ *n.* **1,** any of various nocturnal hawks. **2,** (*Informal*) night owl.

night′ie (-ē) *n.* (*Informal*) a nightgown.

night′in·gale″ (nīt′ən-gāl″) *n.* a European thrush famous for its song.

---
nightingale
↔ From Old Eng. *nihtegale,* night singer (from Old Eng. *galan,* to sing).

---

night′ly (-lē) *adj.* **1,** happening at night. **2,** happening every night. **3,** pert. to night. —*adv.* every night.

night′mare″ *n.* **1,** any oppressive terrifying dream. **2,** any threatening, haunting thought or experience. —**night′mar″ish,** *adj.*

---
nightmare
↔ A Middle English word from Old English *maere,* an evil spirit.

---

night′rid″er *n.* a member of a lawless band that commits crimes of violence at night.

night′shade″ *n.* any of several poisonous plants, as belladonna or henbane.

night′shirt″ *n.* a loose knee-length garment formerly worn in bed by men.

night′spot″ *n.* (*Informal*) a nightclub.

night′stick *n.* a billy.

night′time″ *n.* night.

night′y (-ē) *n.* (*Informal*) nightie.

ni′hil·ism (nī′ə-liz-əm) *n.* **1,** a doctrine that denies moral principles and social obligations. **2,** an extreme anarchistic movement. —**ni′hil·ist,** *n.* —**ni″hil·is′tic,** *adj.*

ni′hil ob′stat (nī′hil ob′stat) (*Lat., R.C.Ch.*) permission to publish a book.

-nik *suf.* designating one who advocates or is associated with.

nil *n.* nothing.

nil des″pe·ran′dum (nil des″pə-ran′dəm) (*Lat.*) despair of nothing.

nim′ble (nim′bəl) *adj.* **1,** lively; quick; agile. **2,** alert; acute. —**nim′ble·ness,** *n.*

nim′bus (nim′bəs) *n.* in art, a bright cloud or a halo around the head of a divine or saintly person.

NIM′BY (nim′bē) an expression of opposition to the location of civic projects in one's own neighborhood: *n(ot) i(n) m(y) b(ack) y(ard).*

nin′com·poop″ (nin′kəm-poop″) *n.* a simpleton.

nine (nīn) *n. & adj.* the cardinal number between eight and ten, expressed by 9. —**ninth,** *adj. & n.* —**nine days' wonder,** an event or person arousing short-lived excitement.

nine′pins″ *n.sing.* a bowling game using nine pins.

nine′teen″ (nīn′tēn″) *n. & adj.* nine plus ten: 19. —**nine′teenth,** *adj. & n.* —**nineteenth hole,** (*Informal*) a clubhouse, bar, or other place where golfers gather after playing a round.

nine′ty (nīn′tē) *n. & adj.* ten times nine: 90. —**nine′ti·eth,** *adj. & n.* —**ninety-day wonder,** in World War II, an officer commissioned after a ninety-day training course; hence, an inexperienced person.

nin′ja (nin′jə) *n.* a Jap. warrior having special training in martial arts.

nin′ny (nin′ē) *n.* a simpleton.

ni′non (nē′non) *n.* a sheer chiffon fabric.

ni·o′bi·um (nī-ō′bē-əm) *n.* a steel-gray metallic element, no. 41, symbol Nb.

nip *v.t.* [**nipped, nip′ping**] **1,** pinch; bite. **2,** pinch off. **3,** benumb; blast, as by cold. **4,** check in growth, as a plot. **5,** drink in sips. —*n.* **1,** a pinch; bite. **2,** chill or sting in the air. **3,** a small drink. —**nip and tuck,** (in a contest) almost exactly even; unpredictable in outcome. —**nip in the bud,** arrest at the start of development.

---

nip, nipper

↔ *Nip* comes from Old Norse *hnippa*, thrust, steal: a *little nipper* is, etymologically, a little thief.

---

nip′per (nip′ər) *n.* **1,** the large claw of a crab or lobster. **2,** (*pl.*) pincers. **3,** (*Informal*) a small boy. ❏ *nip*

nip′ple (nip′əl) *n.* **1,** the milk duct of the female breast. **2,** the mouthpiece of a nursing bottle. **3,** a short piece of pipe threaded at both ends.

Nip″pon·ese′ (nip″ə-nēz′) *n.* & *adj.* Japanese.

nip′py (nip′ē) *adj.* sharp; biting.

nir·va′na (nir-vä′nə) *n.* a state of detachment and dispassion.

Ni′sei′ (nē′sā′) *n.* a native U.S. citizen of Japanese ancestry.

Nis′sen hut (nis′ən) a shelter in the form of a metal half-cylinder, named for its inventor, Canadian engineer Lt. Col. Peter Nissen.

nit *n.* the egg or young of a parasitic insect, as the louse.

ni′ter (nī′tər) *n.* nitrate of potassium, a white salt used in gunpowder; saltpeter. Also, **ni′tre.**

ni′ton (nī′ton) *n.* radon.

nit′pick″ *v.i.* concentrate on petty details.

ni′trate (nī′trāt) *n.* a chemical compound of nitric acid, used as a fertilizer.

ni′tric (nī′trik) *adj.* **1,** containing nitrogen. **2,** pert. to niter. —**nitric acid,** a corrosive compound of nitrogen, used in making dyes, explosives, plastics, etc.

ni′tri·fy (nī′trə-fī) *v.t.* **1,** combine with nitrogen. **2,** impregnate with nitrates, as soil. —**ni″tri·fi·ca′tion,** *n.*

ni″tro·cel′lu·lose (nī″trə-sel′yə-lōs) *n.* a plastic compound of nitrogen and cellulose.

ni′tro·gen (nī′trə-jən) *n.* a colorless, odorless gaseous element, no. 7, symbol N, forming four-fifths of the volume of the earth's atmosphere.

ni″tro·glyc′er·in (nī″trə-glis′ər-in) *n.* a highly explosive oil.

ni′trous (nī′trəs) *adj.* containing nitrogen. —**nitrous oxide,** an anesthetic: *laughing gas.*

nit″ty-grit′ty (nit″ē-grit′ē) *n.* (*Slang*) the essential facts, issues, elements, etc.

nit′wit *n.* (*Slang*) a stupid person.

nix (niks) *n., adv. & interj.* (*Slang*) nothing; no. —*v.t.* (*Slang*) veto. —*n.* a male water sprite.

nix′ie (-ē) *n.* **1,** a female water sprite. **2,** an improperly addressed and undeliverable piece of mail.

no (nō) *adv.* a word of denial, refusal, or dissent; a negative. —*adj.* not any; not at all. —*n.* **1,** a denial or refusal. **2,** a negative vote. ❏ *either*

nob *n.* (*Slang*) **1,** a socially prominent person. **2,** the head.

No·bel′ Prize (nō-bel′) a prize in money given for an achievement in science, literature, or the advancement of peace, endowed by Alfred Nobel, Swed. inventor.

no·bel′i·um (nō-bel′ē-əm) *n.* a radioactive chemical element, no. 102, symbol No, produced artificially.

no·bil′i·ty (nō-bil′ə-tē) *n.* state of being noble.

no′ble (nō′bəl) *adj.* **1,** of high birth, rank, or title. **2,** of lofty character. **3,** stately; imposing. **4,** admirably conceived or executed. **5,** choice; excellent. —*n.* a peer: *nobleman, noblewoman.*

no·blesse′ o·blige′ (nō-bles′ ō-blēzh′) (*Fr.,* nobility obliges) the supposed moral and social obligations of the nobility.

no′bod″y (nō′bod″ē) *n.* **1,** no one. **2,** a person of no social standing.

nock (nok) *n.* a notch in a bow or arrow.

noct- (nokt) *pref.* night.

noc·tur′nal (nok-tûr′nəl) *adj.* **1,** pert. to, or occurring in, the night. **2,** active at night, as certain animals.

noc′turne (nok′tûrn) *n.* a meditative, pensive musical piece.

nod *n.* an inclination of the head, as in a greeting; approval, command, etc. —*v.t. & i.* [**nod′ded, -ding**] **1,** incline the head in assent, etc. **2,** drowse; become inattentive.

nod′dy (nod′ē) *n.* **1,** a simpleton; fool. **2,** a shorebird.

node (nōd) *n.* **1,** a knot; knob. **2,** a hard swelling. **3,** a point of intersection, as of two great circles. **4,** a point in a vibrating body that remains relatively at rest. **5,** (*Computers*) the point of connection between a network and a workstation. —**nod′al** (nō′dəl) *adj.*

nod′ule (nod′ūl) *n.* a little knot or lump. —**nod′u·lous,** *adj.*

no′dus (nō′dəs) *n.* **1,** a knot. **2,** a complication, as in a drama.

No·el′ (nō-el′) *n.* Christmas.

no-′fault″ *adj.* of a type of insurance

---

under which claims are paid without regard to fault.

no-'frills'' *adj.* **1,** simple, unadorned. **2,** of a type of reduced-fare service, as on an airplane, offering few or no extra benefits.

nog'gin (nog'in) *n.* **1,** a small mug. **2,** a small amount of liquor; a gill. **3,** (*Informal*) the head.

Noh (nō) *n.* a type of Japanese dance-drama. Also, **No.**

noil *n.* a short fiber, esp. of wool.

noise (noiz) *n.* **1,** a sound of any kind, esp. when loud or disagreeable. **2,** outcry; clamor. **3,** interference; static. —*v.t.* spread the report of; make public. —**nois'y,** *adj.* full of, or making, loud sounds. ❑ *noisome*

noi'some (noi'səm) *adj.* **1,** ill-smelling; disgusting. **2,** injurious.

> **noisome, noisy**
> ☛ These similar-sounding words mean quite different things. *Noisome* means ill-smelling; it is related to *annoying,* not *noise. Noisy* means loud. *Noise,* oddly enough, comes from Latin *nausea,* which also produced English *nausea.*

no'lens vo'lens (nō'ləns vō'ləns) (*Lat.*) willy-nilly.

nol'le pros'e·qui'' (nol'ē pros'i-kwī) (*Lat.*) to be unwilling to prosecute.

no-'load'' *adj.* of an investment fund, not charging a commission.

no'lo con·ten'de·re (nō'lō kən-ten'də-rē) (*Lat.*) I am unwilling to contest: a plea in court accepting punishment but not admitting guilt.

no'mad (nō'mad) *n.* a member of a roving tribe; a wanderer. —**no·mad'ic,** *adj.* —**no·mad'i·cal·ly,** *adv.*

no man's land 1, territory between entrenched enemy forces. **2,** wasteland.

nom de guerre (nom'' də gār') (*Fr.*) a pseudonym assumed for a certain activity.

nom de plume (nom' də ploom'') (*Fr.*) a pen name.

no'men·cla''ture (nō'mən-klā''chər) *n.* a system of names.

nom'i·nal (nom'i-nəl) *adj.* **1,** existing in name only; so-called. **2,** so small as to be virtually nothing. **3,** pert. to a name. —**nominal value,** the named or face value; par value.

nom'i·nate'' (nom'ə-nāt'') *v.t.* **1,** propose for an elective office. **2,** appoint to an office. —**nom'i·na'tion,** *n.*

nom'i·na·tive (nom'i-nā-tiv) *adj.* **1,** requiring nomination. **2,** (*Gram.*) designating the case of the subject of a verb. —*n.* this case.

nom'i·nee'' (nom'i-nē'') *n.* a person nominated for office.

non- *pref.* used freely before nouns, adjectives, and adverbs with the general meaning of *not,* being less emphatic than *un-* or *in-.*

non'age (non'ij) *n.* legal minority; immaturity.

non''a·ge·nar'i·an (non''ə-jə-nār'ē-ən) *n.* a person 90 years of age or older, but less than 100.

non''ag·gres'sion *n.* a refraining from aggression, esp. in international relations.

non'a·gon'' (non'ə-gon'') *n.* a polygon having nine sides and nine angles.

non''a·ligned' (-ə-līnd') *adj.* neutral, as of a nation.

non'bel·lig'er·ent *n. & adj.* (being) a nation that is not at war but is openly assisting a nation at war.

nonce (nons) *n.* the time being; this one time. —**nonce word,** a word coined and used on a single occasion.

non'cha·lance (non'shə-ləns) *n.* coolness; disinterested self-possession. —**non'-cha·lant** (-lənt) *adj.*

> **nonchalant**
> ↔ From Latin *calere,* to be hot or, figuratively, worried.

non'com'' (non'kom'') *n.* (*Informal*) a noncommissioned officer.

non·com'bat·ant *n.* **1,** a person in the armed forces whose duties do not include fighting. **2,** a civilian in wartime.

non''com·mis'sioned *adj.* not having a commission, as an officer of the rank of corporal or sergeant.

non''com·mit'tal (-kə-mit'əl) *adj.* not committing oneself or itself to a positive view or course.

non''com·pli'ance *n.* failure or refusal to comply; disobedience.

non com'pos men'tis (non kom'pos men'tis) (*Lat.*) not of sound mind.

non''con·duc'tor *n.* a substance that does not readily conduct electricity, heat, etc.

non''con·form'i·ty *n.* refusal or failure to conform, esp. to some established church. —**non''con·form'ist,** *n.*

non''co·op·er·a'tion *n.* **1,** failure to work together harmoniously. **2,** refusal to perform civic duties in protest against an unpopular administration.

---

non″dair′y *adj.* not containing any milk products.

non′de·script″ (non′də-skript″) *adj.* not easily classified; of no particular kind or sort.

none (nun) *pron.* **1,** no one. **2,** not any. —*adv.* in no degree. —*adj.* not any. —**none″the·less′,** *adv.* no less; nevertheless.

> **none**
> (*Gram.*) *None* takes a singular verb when it means not any or not one. In other cases, it takes a plural verb.

non″ef·fec′tive *n.* a soldier or sailor not fit for duty.

non·en′ti·ty (non-en′tə-tė) *n.* **1,** a person or thing of no importance. **2,** something not exciting.

nones (nōnz) *n.* **1,** in ancient Rome, the 7th of March, May, July, and October, and the 5th of other months. **2,** the 5th canonical hour, beginning about 3:00 p.m.; a service at this hour.

non″es·sen′tial *adj. & n.* (something) not essential or necessary.

none′such″ (nun′such″) *n.* a person or thing that has no equal.

none′the·less′ *adv.* nevertheless.

non″ex·ist′ence *n.* condition of not existing; something that does not exist. —**non″ex·ist′ent,** *adj.*

non·fea′sance (non-fē′zəns) *n.* (*Law*) omission to do something that should have been done.

non″fic′tion *n.* literature dealing with real persons and events, as history or biography.

non″he′ro *n.* a person or character lacking the usual attributes of a hero.

non″in·ter·ven′tion *n.* refusal to intervene, esp. in the affairs of other nations.

non″in·va′sive (non″in-vā′siv) *adj.* **1,** of a malignancy, not invading healthy cells. **2,** not penetrating body tissue.

no-′no″ (nō′nō) *n.* something forbidden.

non″pa·reil′ (non″pə-rel′) *adj.* having no equal; peerless. —*n.* **1,** some one or thing having no equal. **2,** a size of type. **3,** a kind of chocolate candy coated with small sugar pellets. **4,** a brightly colored finch of the So. U.S.

non″per″son *n.* **1,** a person treated or ignored as though nonexistent. **2,** a person with no standing in society.

non·plus′ *v.t.* perplex; confound.

non″prof″it *adj.* not intended to earn a profit, as an incorporated charity.

non·res′i·dent *adj.* exercising rights or performing duties (as of franchise, membership, position, etc.) while residing relatively far away. —*n.* one who lives elsewhere.

non″sec·tar′i·an (non″sek-tār′ė-ən) *adj.* favoring no particular religious sect, as a school, association, etc.

non′sense *n.* senseless or absurd words, ideas, or conduct. —**non·sen′si·cal,** *adj.*

non se′qui·tur (non sek′wi-tər) (*Lat.*) a conclusion which does not logically follow from its premises.

non′stop′ *adj. & adv.* without a single stop, as a journey.

non″sup·port′ *n.* (*Law*) failure to provide maintenance by one who is obligated to do so.

non″un′ion *adj.* **1,** not conforming to trade-union requirements. **2,** not having membership in, or a contract with, a trade union.

non″vi′o·lence *n.* **1,** abstention on principle from all forms of violence. **2,** the doctrine of such abstention in the effort to achieve one's objectives.

noo′dle (noo′dəl) *n.* **1,** dough rolled into thin, flat strips; a form of macaroni. **2,** (*Slang*) the head.

nook (nûk) *n.* a recess; an out-of-the-way corner or retreat.

noon *n.* twelve o'clock midday; 12 M. —**noon′day″,** *adj.* at noon. —**noon′time″, noon′tide″,** *n.* noon.

> **noon**
> ↔ *Noon* comes from Latin *nona hora,* the ninth hour (*noon* was originally the ninth hour after sunrise).

noose (noos) *n.* **1,** a loop with a sliding knot, as in a lasso. **2,** (with *the*) death by hanging.

no′pal (nō′pəl) *n.* a cactus, the prickly pear.

nor (nôr) *conj.* and not; neither.

Nor′dic (nôr′dik) *adj.* **1,** pert. to or designating a Caucasian race characterized by blond hair, blue eyes, and tall stature, as the Scandinavians and Anglo-Saxons. **2,** pert. to certain types of skiing events. —*n.* a person of Nordic ancestry.

norm (nôrm) *n.* **1,** a standard; pattern. **2,** a type.

nor′mal (nôr′məl) *adj.* **1,** conforming to a certain type or standard; regular; average. **2,** free from mental defect. —*n.* the standard; the average. —**nor′mal·cy, nor′mal·i·ty,** *n.* state of being normal; a normal condition. —**nor′mal·ize″,** *v.t. & i.* make or become normal; standardize.

—**nor′ma·tive,** *adj.* —**normal school,** a college where teachers are trained.

Nor′man (nôr′mən) *n.* [*pl.* **-mans**] **1,** one of the French who conquered England in 1066. **2,** a native of Normandy. —*adj.* of the Normans or Normandy.

Norse (nôrs) *adj.* **1,** pert. to ancient Scandinavia. **2,** Norwegian.

north (nôrth) *n.* **1,** the point of the compass on the right hand of a person facing the setting sun; the direction toward that point. **2,** a region or country lying north of another; (*cap.*, with *the*) the northern part of the U.S., esp. the region lying north of Maryland, the Ohio River, and Missouri. —*adj. & adv.* in, toward, or from the direction of north. —**north′er·ly** (nôr′thər-lė) *adj.* in or toward the north. —**north′ward,** *adv.*

north″east′ *n. & adj.* midway between north and east. —**north·east′er** (nôr-ēs′tər) *n.* a gale from the northeast. —**north″east′ern,** *adj.*

north′er (nôr′thər) *n.* a strong, cold wind from the north.

north′ern (nôr′thərn) *adj.* pert. to, living in, coming from, or going toward the north. —**north′ern·er,** *n.* a resident or native of the north. —**northern lights,** the aurora borealis. —**north′ern·most″,** *adj.* farthest north.

north′land (-lənd) *n.* **1,** a northern region, or the northern part of any country. **2,** (*cap.*) the Scandinavian Peninsula.

North Pole 1, the north end of the earth's axis of rotation. **2,** the zenith of this point.

North Star Polaris, a bright star near the North Pole of the heavens.

north″west′ *n. & adj.* midway between north and west. —**north″west′er** (nôr-wes′tər) *n.* a gale from the northwest. —**north″west′ern,** *adj.*

Nor·we′gian (nôr-wē′jən) *adj. & n.* pert. to Norway or its language or inhabitants.

nor′·west′er (nôr-wes′tər) *n.* a seaman's oilskin raincoat.

nose (nōz) *n.* **1,** that feature of the face above the mouth, containing the nostrils or respiratory passage; the organ of smell. **2,** sense of smell, as of a dog. **3,** something likened to a nose in shape; the forward or projecting part of anything. —*v.t. & i.* **1,** detect by smell. **2,** rub with the nose. **3,** push slowly forward, as a ship. **4,** (with *out*) (*Informal*) defeat by a narrow margin. **5,** pry curiously. —**nose′bleed″,** a bleeding from the nose. —**nose cone,** the part of a space vehicle that contains the instrumentation and that returns to earth at the end of a mission; the forward end of a rocket or missile. —**nose′dive,** *n.* a headlong plunge of an airplane. —**nos′ey, nos′y,** *adj.* prying. —**nose job,** a cosmetic operation altering the shape of the nose.

nose′gay″, *n.* a bouquet.

nosh *n. & v.i.* (*Slang*) snack. —*v.i.* snack.

no-′show″ *n.* (*Informal*) a person who does not show up, as for a reserved space.

nos·tal′gia (nos-tal′jə) *n.* homesickness; sentimental recollection of the past. —**nos·tal′gic** (-jik) *adj.* —**nos·tal′gi·cal·ly,** *adv.*

nos·tol′o·gy (nos-tol′ə-jė) *n.* the study of senility.

nos′tril (nos′trəl) *n.* an external opening of the nose.

no-′strings″ *adj.* free of conditions or obligations.

nos′trum (nos′trəm) *n.* **1,** a medicine, esp. a quack remedy. **2,** any cure-all scheme or device.

not *adv.* a word expressing denial, refusal, or negation.

no′ta be′ne (nō′tə bē′nė) (*Lat.*) note well; mark carefully. *Abbr.,* **N.B.**

no′ta·ble (nō′tə-bəl) *adj.* worthy of note; remarkable; eminent. —*n.* a prominent or important person. —**not″a·bil′i·ty,** *n.* ❑ *notorious*

no′ta·rize″ (nō′tə-rīz″) *v.t.* attest to (a sworn·statement).

no′ta·ry (nō′tə-rė) *n.* a person licensed to attest deeds, take affidavits, etc.: *notary public.* —**no·tar′i·al** (nō-tär′ė-əl) *adj.*

no·ta′tion (nō-tā′shən) *n.* **1,** the act of taking notes; a note. **2,** a system, or set of symbols, for representing numbers and quantities by symbols, in mathematics and music. —**no′tate** (-tāt) *v.t.*

notch (noch) *n.* **1,** a nick or slot in the edge of something. **2,** a narrow defile between mountains.

notch′back″ *n.* an automobile roof having a deck at the rear.

note (nōt) *n.* **1,** a mark or record to assist the memory. **2,** fame or distinction; importance or consequence. **3,** notice; heed. **4,** an annotation, as in a book. **5,** a memorandum. **6,** a short letter; also, a formal diplomatic communication. **7,** (*pl.*) a brief record of facts, impressions, a speech, etc. **8,** a written promise to pay. **9,** a sound; cry; a musical tone or a symbol of it in musical notation. —*v.t.* **1,** observe carefully. **2,** make a record of. **3,** make mention of. —**note′wor·thy,** *adj.* notable.

note′book″ *n.* **1,** a book of blank pages

NOTES: **1,** double whole note (breve). **2,** whole note (semibreve). **3,** half note (minim). **4,** quarter note (crochet). **5,** eighth note (quaver). **6,** sixteenth note (semiquaver). **7,** thirty-second note (demisemiquaver). **8,** sixty-fourth note (hemidemisemiquaver).

for making notes. **2,** a small portable computer.

not'ed *adj.* **1,** famous; well known. **2,** noticed.

noth'ing (nuth'ing) *n.* **1,** that which does not exist; absence of everything; not anything. **2,** a trifle. **3,** a zero. —*adv.* in no way. —**noth'ing·ness,** *n.* nonexistence.

no'tice (nō'tis) *n.* **1,** observation; attention; cognizance. **2,** any written statement giving an order, information, or warning. **3,** a brief review, as of a book, play, etc. **4,** public attention. —*v.t.* **1,** perceive; observe. **2,** remark upon; acknowledge. **3,** heed. —**no'tice·a·ble,** *adj.*

no'ti·fy" (nō'ti-fī") *v.t.* give attention to; inform. —**no"ti·fi·ca'tion,** *n.*

no'tion (nō'shən) *n.* **1,** a general idea; a somewhat vague belief. **2,** a view; an opinion. **3,** a whim; a fancy. **4,** (*pl.*) various small wares. —**no'tion·al,** *adj.*

no"to·ri'e·ty (nō"tə-rī'ə-tē) *n.* state or fact of being notorious.

no·to'ri·ous (nō-tôr'ē-əs) *adj.* widely but not favorably known.

> **notorious, notable**
> ☞ This word is generally agreed not to be synonymous with *notable* or *famous,* because it has a pejorative connotation.

not"with·stand'ing *adv.* nevertheless. —*prep.* in spite of. —*conj.* although.

nou'gat (noo'gət) *n.* a glazed candy. —**nou'ga·tine** (-tēn) *n.* a chocolate-covered nougat.

nought (nât) *adv., adj. & n.* naught.

noun (nown) *n.* (*Gram.*) a word denoting a person, place, thing, or concept.

nour'ish (nûr'ish) *v.t.* **1,** supply with substances that are assimilated and maintain life and growth; feed. **2,** foster; maintain.

nour'ish·ment (-mənt) *n.* **1,** feeding. **2,** food.

nou"veau riche' (noo"vō rēsh') [*pl.* **nou"veaux riches'** (noo"vō rēsh')] (*Fr.,* new rich) (pert. to) the newly rich.

nou·velle' cui·sine' (noo-vel' kwē-zēn') (*Fr.,* new cooking) a modified form of Fr. cooking.

no'va (nō'və) *n.* a star that increases greatly in brightness and then gradually wanes.

nov'el (nov'əl) *adj.* previously unknown; unusual; new and striking. —*n.* a long narrative portraying fictitious characters and events in a realistic manner. —**nov"el·ette',** *n.* a short novel. —**nov'el·ist,** *n.* a writer of novels. —**nov'el·ize",** *v.t.*

no·vel'la (nō-vel'lə) *n.* a short story.

nov'el·ty (nov'əl-tē) *n.* **1,** the quality of being new and fresh. **2,** a new experience or thing. **3,** a new or unusual article of trade.

No·vem'ber (nō-vem'bər) *n.* **1,** the eleventh month of the year. **2,** (*Communications*) the letter *n.*

> **November**
> ↔ Literally, the ninth month (the year used to begin with March), from Latin *novem,* nine.

no·ve'na (no-vē'nə) *n.* a devotion consisting of nine days of prayer.

nov'ice (nov'is) *n.* **1,** a beginner. **2,** a monk or nun who has not yet taken vows.

no·vit'i·ate (nō-vish'ē-ət) *n.* a probationary period.

no'vo·caine" (nō'və-kān") *n.* a local anesthetic. Also, **pro'caine** (prō'-).

NOW account a type of savings account upon which checks can be drawn: *n(egotiable) o(rder of) w(ithdrawal).*

now *adv.* **1,** at the present time; at once. **2,** but lately. **3,** nowadays; under existing circumstances. —*conj.* since. —*n.* this very time. —*adj.* current; up-to-date. —**now'a·days",** *adv.* at present; in this age.

no'way" *adv.* in no way, manner, or degree. Also, **no'ways".**

no'where" (nō'hwār") *adv.* in, at, or to no place; not anywhere.

no'wise" (nō'wīz") *adv.* in no way.

nox'ious (nok'shəs) *adj.* injurious. —**nox'ious·ness,** *n.*

noz'zle (noz'əl) *n.* a terminal spout, as on a hose or pipe.

nth (enth) *adj.* **1,** (*Math.*) being the last term, or any at random, of a series. **2,** superlative.

---

noxious, obnoxious
☛ These terms are related. The more general, *obnoxious*, means objectionable, and can be applied to persons or things. *Noxious* means injurious and is not applied to persons.

---

nu (noo) *n.* the thirteenth letter of the Greek alphabet (N, ν).

nu·ance′ (noo-äns′) *n.* a delicate degree or shade of difference.

nub *n.* **1,** a knob. **2,** (*Informal*) the gist of a story.

nub′bin (nub′in) *n.* **1,** a small piece. **2,** an underdeveloped corn ear.

nub′ble (nub′əl) *n.* **1,** a small piece or lump. **2,** a protuberance. —**nub′bly,** *adj.* lumpy.

nu′bi·a (noo′bē-ə) *n.* a wrap of soft fleecy material worn by women.

nu′bile (noo′bil) *adj.* **1,** (of a young woman) marriageable. **2,** (*Informal*) (of a young woman) sexually attractive. —**nu·bil′i·ty,** *n.*

nu′cle·ar (noo′klē-ər) *adj.* **1,** being or pert. to a nucleus. **2,** pert. to the study of atomic nuclei. —**nu′cle·ate** (-ət) *adj.* —**nuclear energy,** energy released by the fusion or fission of atomic nuclei. —**nuclear fission,** the breakdown of the atomic nucleus of an element into two or more nuclei of lower atomic number, part of the mass being converted into energy. —**nuclear fusion,** the fusion of atomic nuclei to transform elements, with release of large quantities of energy. —**nuclear physics,** the branch of physics that deals with the structure and transformations of nuclei. —**nuclear winter,** a prolonged period of extreme cold which might result from nuclear war.

nu·cle′ic acid (noo-klā′ik) any of several complex acids found in all living cells.

nu′cle·on (noo′klē-än) *n.* a proton or neutron, esp. in a nucleus.

nu″cle·on′ics (noo″klē-on′iks) *n.sing.* nuclear physics.

nu′cle·us (noo′klē-əs) *n.* [*pl.* **-i** (-ī)] **1,** a central mass about which other matter collects; a starting point for growth or development. **2,** (*Biol.*) the kernel of a cell. **3,** (*Physics*) the center of an atom.

nude (nood) *adj.* naked; bare. —*n.* in art, an undraped figure. —**nude′ness,** *n.* —**nud′ism,** *n.* the practice of going naked. —**nud′ist,** *n.*

nudge (nuj) *v.t.* **1,** prod gently, as a hint or signal. **2,** (*nooj*) (*Slang*) bore; pester.

—*n.* **1,** a gentle prod. **2,** (nooj) (*Slang*) a bore; pest.

nu′di·ty (noo′də-tē) *n.* nudeness.

nu′ga·to″ry (noo′gə-tôr″ē) *adj.* **1,** worthless. **2,** ineffectual.

nug′get (nug′ət) *n.* a lump, esp. of native gold.

nui′sance (noo′səns) *n.* an annoying or obnoxious person or thing.

nuke (nook) *v.t.* (*Slang*) **1,** to destroy with nuclear weapons. **2,** to cook in a microwave oven.

null (nul) *adj.* **1,** of no effect. **2,** nonexistent. —**null and void,** utterly without validity. —**null modem,** (*Computers*) a connection between two devices made without a modem, as with a cable.

nul′li·fy″ (nul′i-fī″) *v.t.* **1,** render invalid. **2,** make ineffective. —**nul″li·fi·ca′tion,** *n.*

nul′li·ty (nul′ə-tē) *n.* something invalid, null, without legal force, etc.

numb (num) *adj.* without sensation; powerless to feel or act. —*v.t.* make numb. —**numb′ness,** *n.*

num′ber (num′bər) *n.* **1,** the sum of an aggregation of persons or things. **2,** the symbol that stands for this sum. **3,** a particular numeral assigned to one of a series. **4,** (*Gram.*) inflection of nouns depending on quantity, as singular or plural. **5,** a large, but not precisely counted, aggregation. **6,** (*pl.*) a considerable aggregation; superiority. **7,** (*pl.*) a type of lottery. **8,** one issue of a periodical. **9,** a musical composition; a verse; a recitation; an act, as in vaudeville; (*Informal*) a routine; bit. —*v.t.* **1,** count. **2,** include in a class. **3,** assign a number to. **4,** limit in number. —**num′ber·less,** *adj.* too many to number; countless. —**do a number on,** (*Slang*) humiliate; undermine the confidence of. —**numbered account,** a bank account whose owner is identified only by a number. —**number-cruncher,** (*Slang*) **1,** a computer; calculator. **2,** a person who deals with numbers; accountant. —**numbers game** or **pool** or **racket,** an illegal lottery. —**by the numbers,** (*Informal*) according to standard procedures. ❑ *amount*

nu′mer·al (noo′mər-əl) *n. & adj.* a symbol or word denoting a number, as *9* or *nine.*

nu′mer·ate″ (noo′mə-rāt″) *v.t.* enumerate; count. —**nu′mer·a·ble,** *adj.* —**nu″mer·a′tion,** *n.*

nu′mer·a″tor (noo′mə-rā″tər) *n.* in a fraction, the number above the line showing how many parts of a unit are taken.

---

tub, cūte, pŭll; labəl; oil, owl, go, chip, she, thin, *th*en, sing, ink; *see p.* 6

numerals
Although there is difference of opinion about when to use figures and when to use words (some say use words up to ten, others say up to one hundred), a useful rule for general writing is to spell out numbers that can be expressed in one or two words. Moreover, words should be used at the beginning of a sentence and when large round numbers are involved.

nu·mer′i·cal (noo-mer′i-kəl) *adj.* pert. to, or expressed in, numbers.

nu″mer·ol′o·gy (noo″mə-rol′ə-jē) *n.* the study of the occult meaning of numbers. —**nu″mer·ol′o·gist,** *n.*

nu′mer·ous (noo′mər-əs) *adj.* a great many. —**nu′mer·ous·ness,** *n.*

nu″mis·mat′ics (noo″miz-mat′iks) *n.* the study or collecting of coins and medals. —**nu″mis·mat′ic,** *adj.* —**nu·mis′ma·tist** (-mə-tist) *n.*

num′skull″ (num′skul″) *n.* a dolt.

nun *n.* a woman living under religious vows in a convent. —**nun′ner·y** (-ə-rē) *n.* a convent.

nun
↔ From Medieval Latin *nunna,* old woman (*nunnus* means old man); later applied to monks and nuns.

nun′ci·o (nun′shē-ō″) *n.* a diplomatic agent of the Pope. —**nun′ci·a·ture** (-ə-chər) *n.* the office or term of a nuncio.

nup′tial (nup′shəl) *adj.* pert. to marriage or a wedding ceremony. —*n.* (*pl.*) a wedding.

nurse (nērs) *n.* **1,** a person in charge of young children. **2,** one who cares for the sick. —*v.t.* **1,** take care of, as children or invalids. **2,** suckle; feed from the breast. **3,** foster; encourage. —**nurs′ing home,** a private home for elderly persons and invalids.

nurse′maid″ *n.* a person who takes care of children. —*v.t.* act as nursemaid to.

nurs′er·y (nēr′sə-rē) *n.* **1,** a room set apart for children. **2,** day nursery. **3,** a place where young trees, shrubs, and plants are grown for sale. —**nurs′er·y·man** (-mən) *n.* one whose business is the growing of young trees, plants, etc. —**nursery rhyme,** a story for children written in rhymed verse.

nurs′ling (nērs′ling) *n.* **1,** an infant. **2,** any person or thing receiving tender care.

nur′ture (nēr′chər) *v.t.* **1,** give nourishment to; feed. **2,** rear; train.

nut *n.* **1,** the fruit of certain trees, consisting of a kernel in a hard shell; the kernel itself. **2,** a small perforated metal block internally threaded to fit a bolt. **3,** a difficult problem. **4,** (*Slang*) the head. **5,** (*Slang*) fixed expenses; overhead. **6,** (*Slang*) a crazy person.

nu·ta′tion (noo-tā′shən) *n.* **1,** a wedding. **2,** (*Pathol.*) an involuntary shaking of the head. —**nu′tant** (noo′tənt) *adj.*

nut′crack″er *n.* **1,** an instrument for cracking nuts. **2,** a Europ. bird that feeds on nuts.

nut′hatch″ (nut′hach″) *n.* a small bird that creeps on tree trunks.

nut′meg *n.* the seed of an East Indian tree, used as a spice.

nu′tri·a (noo′trē-ə) *n.* the coypu or its fur, resembling beaver.

nu′tri·ent (noo′trē-ənt) *n. & adj.* (something) affording nutrition.

nu′tri·ment (noo′trə-mənt) *n.* nourishment.

nu·tri′tion (noo-trish′ən) *n.* **1,** the process by which food is converted into living tissue. **2,** the act of nourishing; food. —**nu·tri′tion·al,** *adj.* —**nu·tri′tion·ist,** *n.* —**nu·tri′tious,** *adj.* nourishing. —**nu′tri·tive** (-trə-tiv) *adj.*

nuts (nutz) (*Slang*) *interj.* of disgust or defiance. —*adj.* crazy.

nut′shell″ *n.* **1,** the shell of a nut. **2,** a pithy condensation; summary. —**in a nutshell,** in few words.

nut′ty (-ē) *adj.* **1,** like a nut, esp. in flavor. **2,** (*Slang*) crazy. —**nut′ti·ness,** *n.*

nuz′zle (nuz′əl) *v.t. & i.* **1,** dig, push, or rub with the nose. **2,** nestle; snuggle.

nyc″ta·lo′pi·a (nik″tə-lō′pē-ə) *n.* night blindness.

ny′lon (nī′lon) *n.* a synthetic thermoplastic product that can be spun into fibers of great toughness and elasticity, used in hosiery, clothing, bristles, cordage, etc.

nylon
↔ A nonsense term coined by the du Pont Chemical Co., using the suffix *-on,* already appearing in *rayon* and *cotton.*

nymph (nimf) *n.* **1,** (*Myth.*) a semidivine maiden inhabiting streams, forests, hills, etc. **2,** a beautiful young woman. **3,** the young of certain insects.

nym″pho·ma′ni·a (nim″fə-mā′nē-ə) *n.* uncontrollable amorous passion in a woman. —**nym″pho·ma′ni·ac,** *n.*

O

O, o (ō) **1,** the fifteenth letter of the English alphabet. **2,** (*cap.*) as a numeral, zero. —*interj.* an intensifier used in direct address: *O Lord!*

O, oh

(*Gram.*) *O* is always capitalized and is generally used as a form of direct address; it is not followed by any punctuation. The interjection *oh* can be capitalized or not and is usually followed by a comma or an exclamation point.

---

oaf (ōf) *n.* a simpleton; a lout. —**oaf′ish**, *adj.*

oak (ōk) *n.* a valuable hardwood tree, whose fruit is the acorn. —**oak′en**, *adj.* —**Oak Leaf Cluster,** an insignia, traditionally in the shape of oak leaves, signifying that a medal previously awarded has been earned again.

oa′kum (ō′kəm) *n.* loose rope fibers, used for calking ships.

---

oakum

↔ This word has nothing to do with oak, but comes from Old English *acumba*, offcombings.

---

oar (ôr) *n.* **1,** a shaft of wood, broad at one end, for rowing a boat. **2,** an oarsman. —**oar′lock″,** *n.* a U-shaped oar rest on the side of a boat. —**oars′man** (ôrz′mən) *n.* a rower.

o·a′sis (o-ā′sis) *n.* [*pl.* **-ses** (-sēz)] a fertile spot in a desert; a watering place.

oat (ōt) *n.* a cereal plant or its seeds, used for food, esp. for horses. —**oat′en,** *adj.* —**oat′er,** (*Slang*) horse opera. *n.* —**feel one's oats,** feel lively. —**sow (one's) wild oats,** indulge in youthful excesses.

oath (ōth) *n.* **1,** a solemn statement, with God as witness. **2,** a curse.

oat′meal″ *n.* **1,** crushed and hulled oats. **2,** oat porridge.

ob- *pref.* **1,** toward; facing. **2,** against. **3,** upon or over.

ob″bli·ga′to (ob″lə-gä′tō) *n.* [*pl.* **-tos, -ti** (-tē)] (*Music*) an accompaniment of independent importance.

ob′du·rate (ob′dyə-rət) *adj.* resisting entreaty; hard-hearted. —**ob′du·ra·cy,** *n.*

o′be·ah (ō′bē-ə) *n.* a religion of the W. Indies employing witchcraft; a fetish used in that religion.

o·be′di·ent (ō-bē′dē-ənt) *adj.* submissive to authority; willing to obey. —**o·be′di·ence,** *n.*

o·bei′sance (ō-bā′səns) *n.* **1,** a bow, as a mark of deference. **2,** deference. —**o·bei′sant,** *adj.*

ob′e·lisk (ob′ə-lisk) *n.* **1,** a four-sided shaft of stone tapering to a pyramidal apex. **2,** (*Printing*) the dagger (†).

o·bese′ (ō-bēs′) *adj.* very fat. —**o·bes′i·ty,** *n.*

o·bey′ (ō-bā′) *v.t.* comply with the command of. —*v.i.* do as bidden.

ob·fus′cate (ob-fus′kāt) *v.t.* darken; obscure; bewilder. —**ob″fus·ca′tion,** *n.*

o′bi (ō′bē) *n.* **1,** a broad sash worn by Japanese women. **2,** obeah.

O′bie (ō′bē) *n.* one of several awards given annually for excellence in off-Broadway theaters.

ob′i·ter dic′tum (ob′i-tər dik′təm) (*Lat.*) a passing remark; an incidental opinion.

o·bit′u·ar″y (ō-bich′oo-er″ē) *n.* a notice, esp. in a newspaper, of a person's death, with a brief biography. Also, *Informal,* **o′bit** (ō′bit). —*adj.* pert. to the death of a person or persons.

ob′ject (ob′jikt) *n.* **1,** a material thing. **2,** a person or thing to which action or feeling is directed. **3,** purpose; goal; aim. **4,** (*Gram.*) a word, phrase, or clause toward which the action of the verb is directed. —**object lesson,** a practical illustration or example. —**ob′ject-or″i·ent·ed** (*Computers*) **1,** pert. to graphics programs that treat objects as a series of mathematical instructions rather than as dots. **2,** pert. to a programming technique that treats a set of instructions as an object.

ob·ject′ (əb-jekt′) *v.i.* offer opposition; disapprove.

ob·jec′ti·fy (ob-jek′tə-fī) *v.t.* give form and shape to. —**ob″jec′ti·fi·ca′tion,** *n.*

ob·jec′tion (ob-jek′shən) *n.* **1,** an expression of opposition or disapproval. **2,** an adverse reason.

ob·jec′tion·a·ble (-ə-bəl) *adj.* undesirable; unpleasant.

ob·jec′tive (-tiv) *n.* **1,** a goal; aim. **2,** the lens nearest the object observed, as in a microscope. —*adj.* **1,** dealing with external facts and not with thoughts and feelings. **2,** free from personal prejudices; unbiased. —**objective case,** (*Gram.*) the case of the object of a verb or preposition. —**ob″jec·tiv′i·ty** (ob″jek-tiv′ə-tē) *n.*

ob·jet′ d'art′ (ob-zhe″ där′) [*pl.* **objets d'art** (ob-zhe″-)] (*Fr.*) a small work of art.

---

ob′jur·gate″ (ob′jər-gāt″) *v.t.* berate; rebuke. **—ob″jur·ga′tion,** *n.* **—ob·jur′ga·to·ry** (əb-jûr′gə-tôr-ė) *adj.*

ob′late (ob′lāt) *adj.* flattened at the poles. **—n.** (*Rom. Cath.*) a secular person devoted to monastic work.

ob·la′tion (ob-lā′shən) *n.* a religious offering; sacrifice.

ob′li·gate″ (ob′lə-gāt″) *v.t.* bind by some legal or moral tie, sense of duty, etc. ❑ *oblige*

ob″li·ga′tion (-gā′shən) *n.* **1,** the binding power of a promise, contract, sense of duty, etc. **2,** a debt. **3,** the state of being bound to something.

ob·lig′a·to″ry (ob-lig′ə-tôr″ė) *adj.* compulsory; necessary.

o·blige′ (ə-blīj′) *v.t.* **1,** bind, constrain, or compel by any physical, moral, or legal force or influence. **2,** lay under obligation by some favor; render a favor to. **—o·blig′ing,** *adj.* accommodating; courteous.

---
oblige, obligate
☞ These two words can be used synonymously. However, *oblige* is often used with reference to a favor rather than a binding duty. ↔ Both words come from Latin *ligāre*, to tie.

---

ob·lique′ (ə-blēk′) *adj.* **1,** slanting. **2,** indirectly aimed or expressed. **—oblique angle,** an angle other than a right or straight angle.

ob·liq′ui·ty (ō-blik′wə-tė) *n.* **1,** the state of being oblique. **2,** immorality; an immoral act.

ob·lit′er·ate″ (ə-blit′ə-rāt″) *v.t.* blot out; efface entirely. **—ob·lit″er·a′tion,** *n.*

ob·liv′i·on (ə-bliv′ė-ən) *n.* **1,** the state of being forgotten. **2,** forgetfulness. **—ob·liv′i·ous,** *adj.* forgetful; unmindful.

ob′long (ob′lâng) *adj.* **1,** longer than broad and with sides parallel. **2,** elongated. **—n.** a rectangle.

ob′lo·quy (ob′lə-kwė) *n.* **1,** abusive language; slander. **2,** disgrace.

ob·nox′ious (əb-nok′shəs) *adj.* odious; objectionable. **—ob·nox′ious·ness,** *n.* ❑ *noxious*

o′boe (ō′bō) *n.* a double-reed woodwind instrument with a penetrating tone. **—o′bo·ist,** *n.*

---
oboe
↔ From French *hautbois*, oboe, literally, high wood. There was an earlier English version *hautboy*, but a spelling influenced by the Italian form of the word eventually prevailed.

---

ob·scene′ (əb-sēn′) *adj.* offensive to modest sensibilities (said of words, pictures, etc.); indecent; lewd. **—ob·scen′i·ty** (-sen′ə-tė) *n.*

---
obscene, pornographic
☞ *Obscene* means highly offensive, and may refer to standards other than sexual; *pornographic* refers specifically to material that is intended to stimulate sexual thoughts.

---

ob·scur′ant (əb-skyûr′ənt) *n.* one who strives to prevent inquiry, enlightenment, or reform. **—ob·scur′ant·ism,** *n.* **—ob·scur′ant·ist,** *n.*

ob·scure′ (əb-skyûr′) *adj.* **1,** vague; not clearly expressed. **2,** murky; dim. **3,** remote; hidden. **4,** humble; lowly.

ob·scu′ri·ty (əb-skûr′ə-tė) *n.* **1,** state of being obscure. **2,** lack of fame or recognition.

ob′se·quies (ob′sə-kwėz) *n.pl.* funeral rites.

ob·se′qui·ous (əb-sē′kwė-əs) *adj.* fawning; servile; deferential. **—ob·se′qui·ous·ness,** *n.*

ob·serv′ance (əb-zėr′vəns) *n.* **1,** the act of complying with some law, custom, rule, etc. **2,** a customary rite or ceremony.

---
observance, observation
☞ Do not confuse *observance*, the act of complying with a law, and *observation*, the act of noticing.

---

ob·serv′ant (əb-zėr′vənt) *adj.* **1,** taking keen notice. **2,** apt at noticing details; attentive; mindful.

ob″ser·va′tion (ob″zər-vā′shən) *n.* **1,** the act of seeing and noting; notice. **2,** the observing of scientific phenomena; the record so obtained. **3,** a remark or comment. **4,** the faculty of observing. ❑ *observance*

ob·serv′a·to″ry (ob-zėr′və-tôr″ė) *n.* **1,** (*Astron.*) a building equipped with instruments for studying natural phenomena. **2,** a high tower for affording an extensive view.

ob·serve′ (əb-zėrv′) *v.t.* **1,** take note of; watch. **2,** remark; comment. **3,** comply with; obey. **4,** celebrate with due ceremony. **—ob·serv′er,** *n.* a spectator.

ob·sess′ (əb-ses′) *v.t.* dominate the mind. **—v.i.** think obsessively about something.

ob·ses′sion (-sesh′ən) *n.* **1,** excessive preoccupation with an idea or delusion. **2,** the idea or delusion.

ob·sid′i·an (ob-sid′ē-ən) *n.* a dark volcanic rock resembling glass.

ob″so·les′cent (ob″sə-les′ənt) *adj.* becoming obsolete. **—ob″so·les′cence,** *n.*

ob′so·lete″ (ob′sə-lēt″) *adj.* gone out of use; out of date. **—ob′so·lete″ness,** *n.*

ob′sta·cle (ob′stə-kəl) *n.* an obstruction; hindrance.

ob·stet′rics (əb-stet′riks) *n.* the medical specialty of care during pregnancy and childbirth. **—ob·stet′ric, ob·stet′ri·cal,** *adj.* **—ob″ste·tri′cian** (ob″stə-trish′ən) *n.*

ob′sti·nate (ob′sti-nət) *adj.* stubbornly persistent. **—ob′sti·na·cy,** *n.*

ob·strep′er·ous (əb-strep′ər-əs) *adj.* noisy; unruly. **—ob·strep′er·ous·ness,** *n.*

ob·struct′ (əb-strukt′) *v.t.* **1,** block so as to prevent passing; interfere with. **2,** retard; delay. **3,** shut out from sight, as a view.

ob·struc′tion (-struk′shən) *n.* **1,** a barrier or hindrance. **2,** systematic and persistent efforts to delay legislation. **—ob·struc′tion·ist,** *n.* one who willfully impedes progress, esp. in a legislative body. **—ob·struc′tive,** *adj.*

ob·tain′ (əb-tān′) *v.t.* get possession of, esp. by some effort; acquire. **—v.i.** be established or in vogue.

ob·trude′ (əb-trood′) *v.t.* **1,** thrust forward unasked. **2,** push out; form by forcing through an opening of proper shape. **—v.i.** intrude. **—ob·tru′sion** (-zhən) *n.* **—ob·tru′sive** (-siv) *adj.* given to intruding; showy, distracting, etc.

---

obtrusive, intrusive

☞ Literally, *obtrusive* means sticking out and *intrusive* means thrusting in. The former word is more often used of objects, the latter of persons.

---

ob·tund′ *v.t.* reduce the force or intensity of; dull; blunt; deaden.

ob·tuse′ (əb-toos′) *adj.* **1,** not sensitive; stupid. **2,** blunt in form. **3,** of angles, larger than a right angle. **—ob·tuse′ness,** *n.*

ob·verse′ (ob-vērs′) *adj.* **1,** facing the observer; on the top or front side. **2,** (*Bot.*) narrower at the base than at the top. **—n.** (ob′vērs) **1,** the side of a coin bearing the head or main design. **2,** a counterpart. **—ob·vert′** (əb-vērt′) *v.t.*

ob′vi·ate″ (ob′vē-āt″) *v.t.* meet and clear away, as difficulties; make unnecessary. **—ob″vi·a′tion** (-ā′shən) *n.*

ob′vi·ous (ob′vē-əs) *adj.* plainly seen or understood; evident. **—ob′vi·ous·ness,** *n.*

oc″a·ri′na (ok″ə-rē′nə) *n.* an egg-shaped musical wind instrument.

---

ocarina

↔ From Italian *ocarina*, little goose (from Latin *auca*), because of a supposed resemblance to the goose egg.

---

oc·ca′sion (ə-kā′zhən) *n.* **1,** a special event, ceremony, etc. **2,** reason; motive; need. **3,** opportunity; a favorable moment. **4,** a cause; that which brings about an unexpected result. **5,** a particular time; the time of a special happening. **—v.t.** cause; bring about.

oc·ca′sion·al (-əl) *adj.* **1,** occurring now and then. **2,** incidental.

oc′ci·dent (ok′si-dənt) *n.* **1,** the west. **2,** (*cap.*) Europe and the Western Hemisphere. **—oc″ci·dent′al,** *adj.* ❑ *Asian, oriental*

oc′ci·put″ (ok′sə-put″) *n.* the back part of the skull. **—oc·cip′i·tal** (ok-sip′ə-təl) *adj.*

oc·clude′ (ə-klood′) *v.t.* **1,** shut in or out; also, close, as pores. **2,** absorb. **—oc·clu′sion** (-zhən) *n.*

oc·cult′ (o-kult′) *adj.* **1,** beyond ordinary understanding. **2,** secret; known only to the initiated. **3,** dealing with the supernatural or magical: the occult sciences. **—n.** something occult or supernatural. **—oc·cult′ism,** *n.* **—oc·cult′ist,** *adj.*

oc″cul·ta′tion (ok″ul-tā′shən) *n.* the disappearance from view, esp. of a star or planet.

oc′cu·pan·cy (ok′yə-pən-sē) *n.* act of occupying; state of being an occupant.

oc′cu·pant (ok′yə-pənt) *n.* one who resides in a place; a tenant.

oc″cu·pa′tion (ok″yə-pā′shən) *n.* **1,** possession; occupancy. **2,** the stationing of controlling forces in enemy territory. **3,** means of filling one's time; regular employment; a job. **—oc″cu·pa′tion·al,** *adj.* pert. to an occupation, esp. a trade. **—occupational therapy,** the treatment of mental and physical disorders by suitable work. ❑ *career*

oc′cu·py″ (ok′yə-pī″) *v.t.* **1,** become established in, as a building, enemy territory, etc. **2,** hold, as an office. **3,** take up or fill, as space, time, attention, etc. **4,** engage the attention of; employ.

oc·cur′ (ə-kėr′) *v.i.* [**oc·curred′, -cur′-ring**] **1,** take place; happen. **2,** come to mind. **3,** be found; exist. **—oc·cur′rence,** *n.* a happening. **—oc·cur′rent,** *adj.*

o′cean (ō′shən) *n.* **1,** the body of salt water covering three-fourths of the earth's surface; any of the five great divisions of this body. **2,** a vast amount. **—o"ce·an'ic** (ō"shē-an'ik) *adj.*

---

ocean
↔ From Greek *Ōkeanós*, in mythology, a Titan, guardian of the great sea encircling the globe.

---

o'cean·aut" (-nât) *n.* aquanaut.

o"ce·an'ics (ō"shē-an'iks) *n.sing.* the study of the ocean.

o"cean·og'ra·phy (ō"shən-äg'rə-fē) *n.* a branch of geography dealing with the ocean and its phenomena.

o·cel'lus (ō-sel'əs) *n.* **1,** an eyelike spot of color, as in a peacock's tail. **2,** one of the minute single eyes of insects and various other animals. **—o·cel'lar** (-ər), *adj.* **—o·cel'late** (-ət) *adj.*

oc'e·lot" (os'ə-lot") *n.* an Amer. leopardlike cat.

o'cher (ō'kər) *n.* an earth containing iron, used as a yellow or orange pigment. Also, **o'chre.**

o'clock' (ə-klok') *adv.* on the clock; hours, etc., since noon or midnight.

oct- (okt) *pref.* eight.

oc'ta·gon" (ok'tə-gon") *n.* a polygon with eight sides and eight angles. **—oc·tag'o·nal** (ok-tag'ə-nəl) *adj.*

oc'tal (ok'təl) *adj.* pert. to a number system on the base 8.

oc'tane (ok'tān) *n.* **1,** an isomeric hydrocarbon found in petroleum. **2,** the measure of the power-producing quality of gasoline. **—octane number** or **rating,** a number representing the antiknock property of gasoline.

oc'tant (ok'tant) *n.* **1,** the eighth part of a circle, 45°. **2,** a navigational instrument resembling a sextant.

oc'tave (ok'tiv) *n.* **1,** (*Music*) a note eight diatonic degrees above or below another note; an interval of eight degrees; the whole series of notes within this interval. **2,** (*Poetry*) a group of eight lines. **3,** a period of eight days.

oc·ta'vo (ok-tā'vō) *adj.* of a book, having pages about 6 x 9 inches, or somewhat less; written 8vo.

oc·tet' (ok-tet') *n.* a group of, or a composition for, eight voices or instruments.

Oc·to'ber (ok-tō'bər) *n.* the tenth month of the year.

October
↔ From Latin *octo*, eight, as October was the eighth month, counting from March, which once was the first month of the year.

---

oc"to·ge·nar'i·an (ok"tə-jə-nār'ē-ən) *n.* a person at least 80 but less than 90 years of age.

oc'to·pus (ok'tə-pəs) *n.* a sea mollusk having eight arms with sucking disks.

oc"to·roon' (ok"tə-roon') *n.* a person having one-eighth black ancestry.

oc'u·lar (ok'yə-lər) *adj.* **1,** pert. to the eye. **2,** perceived by the eye; visual. **—n.** the eyepiece of an optical instrument.

oc'u·list (ok'yə-list) *n.* a doctor who examines and treats the eye; ophthalmologist.

---

oculist, optician, optometrist
☞ These terms are often confused. An *oculist* is an eye doctor, an ophthalmologist. An *optician* sells eyeglasses, lenses, etc. An *optometrist* tests eyesight and prescribes corrective lenses, etc.

OD (ō'dē') *v.i.* (*Slang*) take an overdose of a drug, often with fatal results.

o'da·lisque (ō'də-lisk) *n.* a female slave in a harem. Also, **o'da·lisk.**

odd (od) *adj.* **1,** eccentric; queer; strange. **2,** casual; occasional; differing from the ordinary. **3,** not paired; lacking a mate. **4,** extra; left over after an even division; not exactly divisible by two. **5,** a small surplus; a little more. **—adv.** more or less. **—odd'ness,** *n.*

odd'ball" *n.* an eccentric person.

odd'i·ty (-ə-tē) *n.* a strange person or thing.

odd'ment (od'mənt) *n.* an odd article; a remnant.

odds (odz) *n.pl.* **1,** excess in favor of one as compared with another; advantage; superiority. **2,** balance of probability. **3,** in sports, a handicap. **4,** variance; disagreement. **—odds-'on',** *adj.* likely to win. **—at odds,** in disagreement. **—odds and ends,** miscellaneous articles.

ode (ōd) *n.* a lyric poem of exalted and dignified style. **—od'ic,** *adj.*

o'di·ous (ō'dē-əs) *adj.* deserving of hate; repugnant. **—o'di·ous·ness,** *n.*

---

odious, odorous
☞ These two similar-sounding words are unrelated. *Odious* means hateful, *odorous* means having an odor.

---

o'di·um (ō'dē-əm) *n.* **1,** hatred. **2,** disgrace. **3,** censure; reproach.

o·dom'e·ter (ō-dom'ə-tər) *n.* an instrument for measuring the distance traveled by a wheeled vehicle.

---

o·don·tol·o·gy (ō″don-tol′ə-jė) *n.* the study of the teeth.

o′dor (ō′dər) *n.* **1,** effect on the sense of smell, pleasant or unpleasant. **2,** repute. Also, **o′dour.** —**in bad odor,** in ill repute.

o·dor·if′er·ous (ō″də-rif′ər-əs) *adj.* giving forth an odor. —**o·dor·if′er·ous·ness,** *n.*

o′dor·ous (ō′dər-əs) *adj.* having an odor, esp. a fragrant one. ❏ *odious*

od′ys·sey (äd′ə-sė) *n.* a long wandering; an intellectual or spiritual quest.

Oed′i·pus complex (ed′ə-pəs) unconscious attachment of a son to his mother. —**oed′i·pal** (-pəl) *adj.*

> **Oedipus complex**
> ↔ In Greek mythology, *Oedipus* was a king of Thebes who unknowingly killed his father and wed his mother.

o′er (ôr) *adv. & prep.* (*Poetic*) over.

oer′sted (ēr′sted) *n.* a unit of magnetic intensity, named for 19th-c. Danish physicist H. C. Oersted.

of (uv) *prep.* **1,** indicating separation, derivation, source, or origin: from. **2,** concerning; about. **3,** indicating composition or substance. **4,** indicating possession: belonging to. **5,** containing.

o′fay (ō′fā) *n.* (*Slang, offensive*) a white person. Also, **fay.**

off (âf) *adv.* **1,** away; at, or to, a distance. **2,** not on, touching, or attached. **3,** so as to stop or end entirely. **4,** away from work. —*prep.* **1,** away from. **2,** deviating from standard. **3,** to seaward of. **4,** less than. **5,** temporarily relieved of. **6,** (*Slang*) refraining from. —*adj.* **1,** on the right side of a vehicle or animal (opposed to *near*). **2,** disengaged, as an *off day*. **3,** below normal. **4,** disconnected; discontinued. **5,** provided for. **6,** (*Informal*) in error. —*v.t.* (*Slang*) to kill. —**off and on,** intermittently. —**off limits,** not allowed. —**off the cuff,** (*Slang*) extemporaneous(ly). —**off the hook,** (*Slang*) free of responsibility, blame, etc. —**off-′the-wall′,** *adj.* (*Slang*) eccentric; outrageous. —**take off,** leave.

of′fal (âf′əl) *n.* refuse; garbage.

off-″base′ *adj.* **1,** (*Baseball*) not touching a base. **2,** mistaken; in error.

off′beat″ *n.* (*Music*) an unaccented part of a measure. —*adj.* **1,** stressing the offbeat. **2,** unusual; eccentric.

off-″Broad″way (-brâd′wā) *adj.* pert. to professional theater in New York not in the traditional commercial theaters or district. —**off-″off-′Broad″way,** *adj.* pert. to

the more experimental or avant-garde New York theater.

off-′chance″ *n. & adj.* a remote possibility.

off-col′or *adj.* **1,** of poor color; inferior, as a gem. **2,** (*Informal*) improper; risqué.

of·fend′ (ə-fend′) *v.t.* cause resentment in; displease. —*v.i.* **1,** sin. **2,** cause indignation, dislike, or resentment.

> **offend**
> ↔ Originally, the opposite of *defend*, i.e., strike against. Its source was Latin *offendere*.

of·fend′er *n.* **1,** one who offends; a culprit. **2,** an aggressor.

of·fense′ (ə-fense′) *n.* **1,** an attack; assault. **2,** a cause of displeasure; an affront. **3,** anger; annoyance. **4,** a sin. **5,** [also, (of′ens)] the attacking side. Also, **of·fence′.**

of·fen′sive (ə-fen′siv) *adj.* **1,** offending. **2,** attacking. —*n.* **1,** the state of being the attacker. **2,** an aggressive campaign; an attack. —**of·fen′sive·ness,** *n.*

of′fer (of′ər) *v.t. & i.* **1,** present or put forward for acceptance. **2,** put forward, as a suggestion; propose; suggest. **3,** volunteer (to do something). **4,** present as an act of devotion to God. **5,** present for sale. **6,** tender as a bid. —*n.* the act of offering; condition of being offered; a proposal; a bid. —**of′fer·ing,** *n.* something offered; a gift, esp. in an offertory.

of′fer·to″ry (of′ər-tôr′ė) *n.* the offering and collection of gifts at a religious service; the rites at that time.

off′hand″ *adj. & adv.* **1,** impromptu. **2,** free and easy. —**off′hand″ed,** *adj.* casual.

of′fice (of′is) *n.* **1,** a position of trust, esp. in public service. **2,** the duties of such a position. **3,** official employment. **4,** a service or task. **5,** a prescribed form of worship. **6,** a room for transacting business. **7,** the quarters and staff of a governmental department. —**office boy** *or* **girl, 1,** a young employee who does errands and menial tasks. **2,** a person treated like an office boy or girl.

of′fi·cer (of′ə-sər) *n.* **1,** a holder of public or civil office. **2,** a person of (usually, commissioned) rank in an army, navy, etc. **3,** a policeman or policewoman. **4,** an executive in a society, corporation, etc.

of·fi′cial (ə-fish′əl) *n.* a person holding office. —*adj.* **1,** pert. to an office or to the discharge of the duties of an office. **2,** properly authorized. **3,** formal. —**of·fi′cial·dom** (-dəm) *n.* the official class. —**of·fi′cial·ism,** *n.* red tape.

official, officious

☛ *Official* refers to an office or an office-holder; *officious* means annoyingly intrusive (an *official* may often be *officious*).

of·fi'ci·ate" (-shė-āt") *v.i.* **1,** act in an official capacity, esp. on some special occasion. **2,** conduct a religious service. **—of·fi'ci·ant,** *n.* **—of·fi"ci·a'tion,** *n.*

of·fi'cious (ə-fish'əs) *adj.* acting unduly important; meddling; intrusive. **—of·fi'cious·ness,** *n.* ❏ *official*

off'ing *n.* a place or result to be reached in the future but at present remote. **—in the offing,** in the near future.

off'ish *adj.* (*Informal*) reserved or distant in manner. **—off'ish·ness,** *n.*

off-'key" *adj.* **1,** out of tune. **2,** unusual; abnormal.

off-'load" *v.t.* unload (from a truck, etc.).

off'print" *n.* a separate reprint of a magazine, etc., article. **—v.t.** make an offprint of.

off-'road" *adj.* designed for use or taking place on unpaved roads or other rough terrain.

off-'sea"son *adj. & n.* (pert. to) a less busy period of the year for a business, sport, etc.

off'set" *v.t.* [**-set"**, **-set"ting**] **1,** place (one thing) over against another; balance. **2,** (of printing) blot. **—n. 1,** something that balances or compensates. **2,** the start. **3,** a type of lithography.

off'shoot" *n.* **1,** a branch from a main stem. **2,** a lateral branch, as of a family.

off"shore' *adv. & adj.* **1,** a short distance out to sea. **2,** away from the shore.

off'side" *adj.* (*Sports*) away from the proper side; ahead of the ball or puck.

off'spring" (âf'spring") *n.* a child or children; a descendant.

off-'the-rack' *adj.* ready-made.

off-"the-rec'ord *adj.* unofficial; informal.

off'track" *adj.* handled away from the track, as of parimutuel betting.

off-'white" *adj.* of a grayish white.

oft (âft) *adv.* (*Poetic*) often.

of'ten (âf'ən) *adv.* many times; in many cases. Also, **oft, of'ten·times".**

often

↔ Originally, *often* was the declined form of *oft* used before vowels and *h*.

o·gee' (ō-jē') *n.* an S-shaped curve.

o'give (ō'jiv) *n.* **1,** a pointed arch. **2,** a

diagonal rib in a Gothic vault. **—o·giv'al** (ō-jī'vəl) *adj.*

o'gle (ō'gəl) *v.i. & t.* stare (at) covetously; leer.

OG'PU (og'poo) *n.* the security police of the former U.S.S.R. from 1923 to 1934.

o'gre (ō'gər) *n.* **1,** in fairy tales, a man-eating giant. **2,** a terrifying person.

ogre

↔ From Latin *Orcus*, the Roman god of the underworld.

oh (ō) *interj.* expressing surprise, pain, etc. ❏ *O*

ohm (ōm) *n.* the unit of electrical resistance. **—ohm'age,** *n.* **—ohm'ic,** *adj.* **—ohm'me"ter,** *n.* a device to measure resistance, named after the 19th-c. German physicist Georg Ohm.

-oid *suf.* like; resembling.

oil *n.* **1,** any of various vegetable, animal, or mineral substances that tend to reduce the friction of surfaces rubbing against each other, are inflammable, and are used for heat, lubrication, medicines, perfumes, etc. **2,** in art, a paint made of oil mixed with pigment; a picture painted in oils. **—v.t. 1,** lubricate or treat with oil. **2,** (*Informal*) placate; flatter. **—oil'er,** *n.* a tankship for transporting oil. **—oil color,** a pigment ground in oil. **—oil spill,** the accidental leaking of oil into a body of water. **—strike oil,** (*Informal*) make a profitable discovery.

oil'cloth" *n.* cloth coated with a glossy, water-resistant substance.

oil'pa"per *n.* paper waterproofed by being steeped in oil.

oil'skin" *n.* **1,** a cloth made waterproof with oil. **2,** (*pl.*) garments made of this cloth.

oil'stone" *n.* a fine-grained variety of quartz, used for whetstones.

oil'y (oi'lė) *adj.* **1,** like oil. **2,** smooth in manner; unctuous; fawning. **—oil'i·ness,** *n.*

oink *n.* the cry of a pig. **—v.i.** make this sound.

oint'ment (oint'mənt) *n.* a salve for healing or beautifying the skin.

O.K. (ō-kā') (*Informal*) *adj. & adv.* satisfactory; all right. **—v.t.** approve. Also, **o·kay'.**

O.K.

↔ Dating from the mid-19th c., this abbreviation supposedly comes from *orl korrect,* a phonetic spelling of "all correct."

o·ka′pi (ō-kä′pē) *n.* an Afr. mammal related to the giraffe.

o′kie (ō′kē) *n.* (*Offensive*) a migrant worker.

o′kra (ō′krə) *n.* a vegetable grown for its edible green mucilaginous pods.

-ol·a·try (ol-ə-trē) *suf.* excessive, or idolatrous, worship of.

old (ōld) *adj.* **1,** advanced in years; having existed or lived long, or for most of its life span. **2,** of a (specified) age. **3,** of long standing. **4,** experienced. **5,** not new, fresh, or recent. **6,** not modern; antique. **7,** belonging to an earlier time, stage, etc. **—old′ness,** *n.* **—old boy network,** a mutually supportive group of men, usu. who were comrades in school or college. **—Old Glory,** the flag of the U.S.; the Stars and Stripes. **—old guard,** a conservative faction. **—old hand,** a person of much experience or skill. **—old hat,** old-fashioned; out of date. **—old lady,** (*Informal*) **1,** one's mother or wife. **2,** one in command. **—old maid, 1,** an elderly woman who has never married. **2,** (*Informal*) a prim, fastidious person. **3,** a children's card game. **—old man,** (*Informal*) **1,** one's father or husband. **2,** one in command. **—Old Testament,** all the books of the Holy Bible written before the Christian era. **—old wives' tale,** a traditional, often superstitious, belief. **—Old World,** Europe and Asia.

old′en (ōl′dən) *adj.* ancient.

old-fash′ioned *adj.* **1,** holding to old ideas or customs. **2,** out of style. **—***n.* a cocktail of sweetened whiskey, soda, bitters, and fruit.

old′ie (ōld′ē) *n.* (*Informal*) something old.

old-′school′ *adj.* having customs, education, etc., of a bygone age.

old′ster (-stər) *n.* an elderly person.

Old-′Style″ *adj.* according to the Julian calendar, several days earlier than the modern calendar.

old-′time″ *adj.* of, or characteristic of, old times. **—old-′tim′er,** *n.* (*Informal*) one who has grown old in a place, profession, etc.

o·lé′ (ō-lā′) *interj.* (*Sp.*) of approval or encouragement.

o″le·ag′i·nous (ō″lē-aj′ə-nəs) *adj.* oily; unctuous. **—o″le·ag′i·nous·ness,** *n.*

o″le·an′der (ō″lē-an′dər) *n.* a poisonous evergreen shrub with showy red or white blossoms.

o′le·in (ō′lē-in) *n.* an oily substance found in most animal and vegetable fats and oils.

o″le·o·mar′ga·rine (ō″lē-ō-mär′jə-rin) *n.* an animal and vegetable fat used like butter; margarine. Also, **o′le·o″.**

ol·fac′to·ry (ol-fak′tə-rē) *adj.* pert. to the sense of smell.

ol′i·gar″chy (ol′ə-gär″kē) *n.* government in which power is in the hands of a few. **—ol″i·gar′chic,** *adj.*

o′li·o″ (ō′lē-ō″) *n.* **1,** a stew. **2,** a medley; miscellany.

ol′ive (ol′iv) *n.* **1,** an evergreen tree of warm climates grown for its fruit, wood, or oil; its small, oval fruit, ripe or green. **2,** a yellowish-green color. **—olive branch,** a symbol of peace. **—olive drab, 1,** a dull greenish brown. **2,** a woolen cloth of this color, used for military uniforms. **—olive oil,** oil pressed from olives, used in food and medicines.

ol″la (ol′ə) (*Sp.*) *n.* a wide-mouthed jar. **—ol″la po·dri′da,** (ol′ə pə-drē′də) (*Sp.*) **1,** a type of stew. **2,** hodgepodge.

O·lym′pi·ad (o-lim′pē-ad) *n.* **1,** in ancient Greece, the four-year period between Olympic games. **2,** a modern tournament of Olympic games.

O·lym′pic games (ō-lim′pik) **1,** athletic contests in ancient Greece. **2,** international athletic contests, held every four years in a different country.

om *n.* a word used as a mantra.

o′mah″ (ō′mä″) *n.* the sasquatch.

om′buds·man (äm′buds-mən) [*pl.* **-men**], **om′buds·wom″an** *n.* a government official who investigates complaints from the public; a similar position in a corporation or other organization. Also, **om′buds·per″son,** *n.*

> **ombudsman**
> ↔ A Swedish word meaning legal representative, from Old Norse *umbothsmathr.*

o·me′ga (ō-mē′gə) *n.* the 24th and last letter of the Greek alphabet (Ω, ϖ).

om′e·let (om′lit) *n.* beaten eggs cooked as a pancake. Also, **om′e·lette.**

> **omelet**
> ↔ Metathetic form of Old French *alemette*, thin plate, from Latin *lamella.*

o′men (ō′mən) *n.* a sign or event prophetic of the future; an augury.

o″mer·tà′ (ō″mer-tä′) *n.* (*It.*) a code of secrecy or silence.

om′i·cron″ (om′i-kron″) *n.* the fifteenth letter of the Greek alphabet (O, o).

om'i·nous (om'i-nəs) *adj.* foretelling disaster; threatening. **—om'i·nous·ness,** *n.*

o·mis'sion (ō-mish'ən) *n.* **1,** neglect or failure to do something. **2,** the act of leaving out; the thing left out.

o·mit' (ō-mit') *v.t.* [**o·mit'ted, -ting**] **1,** leave out. **2,** leave undone; neglect.

om·ni- (om-nə) *pref.* all.

om'ni·bus" (om'nə-bus") *n.* **1,** a large passenger motor vehicle. **2,** a volume of related literary works. **—adj.** comprising or providing for many objects or items.

om"ni·far'i·ous (-fär'ė-əs) *adj.* of all varieties, forms, or kinds.

om·nif'er·ous (om-nif'ə-rəs) *adj.* producing all kinds.

om·nip'o·tent (om-nip'ə-tənt) *adj.* having infinite power. **—om·nip'o·tence,** *n.*

om"ni·pres'ent *adj.* present everywhere at the same time. **—om"ni·pres'ence,** *n.*

om·nis'cient (om-nish'ənt) *adj.* all-knowing. **—om·nis'cience,** *n.*

om"ni·um-ga'ther·um (om"nė-əm-ga'thə-rəm) *n.* a hodgepodge.

om·niv'o·rous (om-niv'ə-rəs) *adj.* eating both animal and vegetable foods; devouring everything. **—om·niv'o·rous·ness,** *n.*

on *prep.* **1,** above and in contact with. **2,** dependent on; supported by. **3,** near or adjacent to. **4,** in regard to. **5,** at the time of. **6,** (*Informal*) at the expense of. **—adv.** **1,** in or into place or position. **2,** in progress. **3,** into action or use. **4,** forward. **—on ice,** (*Informal*) **1,** a sure thing. **2,** in reserve. **—on line, 1,** ready for use. **2,** computerized. **—on the nose,** (*Informal*) precisely. **—on to,** (*Slang*) aware of.

on'a·ger (on'ə-jər) *n.* **1,** a wild ass of Central Asia. **2,** a medieval war-engine for throwing large boulders.

on-'air' *adj.* broadcasting.

o'nan·ism (ō'nə-niz-əm) *n.* **1,** uncompleted sexual intercourse. **2,** masturbation. **—o'nan·ist,** *n.* **—o"nan·is'tic,** *adj.*

---
onanism
↔ From the Biblical *Onan,* son of Judah, who "spilt his seed upon the ground" to avoid impregnating his brother's wife (Gen. 38:9).
---

once (wuns) *adv.* **1,** at one time; formerly. **2,** one time only. **3,** even for one time; ever. **—conj.** whenever; as soon as. **—n.** one time. **—at once, 1,** simultaneously. **2,** immediately.

once-'o"ver *n.* (*Slang*) a single, comprehensive inspection.

one (wun) *n.* **1,** the lowest whole number, expressed by 1 (ordinal, *first*). **2,** a single person or thing; a unit. **—adj.** **1,** a single. **2,** any. **3,** some. **4,** the same. **5,** united. **—pron.** someone; anyone. **—all one,** all the same. **—one by one,** singly. **—one-night stand, 1,** a theatrical performance scheduled for one night only. **2,** (*Informal*) casual sex.

---
one
(*Gram.*) There has always been a question of which possessive pronoun should follow the impersonal *one*: *One is the master of one's* (or *his* or *her*) *destiny.* Repeating *one* often sounds stilted, but using a gender-specific pronoun is objected to by many writers. In speech, the problem is often avoided by the grammatically incorrect solution of using a plural possessive pronoun: *One is the master of their destiny.* This approach is not yet considered acceptable in most formal writing, however.
---

one-'horse" *adj.* (*Informal*) small and unimportant.

one'ness (-nəs) *n.* **1,** unity. **2,** uniformity. **3,** constancy in feeling or purpose.

one-"li'ner (-lī'nər) *n.* (*Informal*) a short joke.

on'er·ous (on'ər-əs) *adj.* burdensome. **—on'er·ous·ness,** *n.*

one·self' *pron.* reflexive form of *one.* **—be oneself,** behave as usual.

one'sid"ed *adj.* **1,** unequal. **2,** unfair; partial. **—one'sid"ed·ness,** *n.*

one'time" *adj.* former.

one-'to-one' *adj.* involving interaction between two persons.

one-'track" *adj.* **1,** having one track. **2,** (*Informal*) narrow; restricted.

one-'way" *adj.* permitting traffic in one direction only.

on'go"ing *adj.* continuing without interruption.

on'ion (un'yən) *n.* a plant with a pungent edible bulb.

on'ion·skin" (un'yən-skin") *n.* a very thin translucent paper.

on'look"er (-ər) *n.* spectator.

on'ly (ōn'lė) *adj.* **1,** single; sole. **2,** best. **—adv.** **1,** alone; solely. **2,** merely; no more than. **—conj.** but; excepting that.

on"o·mat"o·poe'ia (on"ə-mat"ə-pē'ə) *n.* imitation of natural sounds in word formation or rhetoric. **—on"o·mat"o·po·et'ic** (-pō-et'ik) *adj.*

on'rush" *n.* a rush forward.

---

on'set" *n.* **1,** an attack. **2,** a beginning; start.

on'side" *adj. & adv.* (*Sports*) at or toward the proper position.

on'slaught" (on'slât") *n.* a violent attack.

on'to (on'too) *prep.* to a place on; upon.

on·to- (on-tə) *pref.* existence; being.

on·tog'e·ny (on-toj'ə-nē) *n.* the entire development and history of an individual organism. **—on"to·ge·net'ic,** *adj.*

on·tol'o·gy (on-tol'ə-jē) *n.* the branch of metaphysics dealing with the nature of being. **—on"to·log'i·cal** (on"tə-loj'i-kəl), *adj.* **—on·tol'o·gist,** *n.*

o'nus (ō'nəs) *n.* a burden; a charge.

on'ward (on'wərd) *adv. & adj.* toward the front; forward. **—on'wards,** *adv.*

on'yx (on'iks) *n.* a quartz with parallel colored bands.

o·o- (ō-ə) *pref.* egg.

oo'dles (oo'dəlz) *n.pl.* (*Informal*) a large quantity.

oo'long (oo'lâng) *n.* a variety of tea.

oomph (oomf) *n.* (*Slang*) **1,** sex appeal. **2,** energy; pep.

oops *interj.* expressing surprise, dismay, etc. at a blunder.

ooze (ooz) *n.* soft mud or slime, esp. on the bed of the ocean. **—v.i.** seep or leak slowly. **—oo'zy,** *adj.*

o·pac'i·ty (ō-pas'ə-tē) *n.* state of being opaque.

o'pah (ō'pä) *n.* a brilliantly colored oceanic food fish.

o'pal (ō'pəl) *n.* an iridescent mineral valued as a gem. **—o'pal·ine** (-in) *adj.*

o·pal·esce' (ō-pə-les') *v.i.* give forth a play of colors like an opal. **—o"pal·es'-cence,** *n.* **—o"pal·es'cent,** *adj.*

o·paque' (ō-pāk') *adj.* **1,** not letting light through. **2,** dull. **3,** obscure. **4,** stupid. **—o·paque'ness,** *n.*

op art optical art.

op-'ed" *adj.* pert. to the page opposite the editorial page in a newspaper when composed of commentary, editorial essays, etc.

o'pen (ō'pən) *adj.* **1,** permitting passage through; not shut or closed. **2,** without a cover; not protected. **3,** unfilled, as a position; unengaged, as time. **4,** free to use; public. **5,** unrestrained; unrestricted. **6,** undecided. **7,** without concealment; frank. **8,** spread out; unfolded. **9,** ready. **10,** immune from attack. **—v.t. 1,** unfasten; raise the covering of; move aside. **2,** remove obstructions from. **3,** unfold; spread out. **4,** reveal; disclose. **5,** make accessible, esp. for trade, settlement, etc. **6,** start; initiate. **7,** make an opening in. **—v.i. 1,** afford a view, entrance, or egress, etc. **2,** unfold; come apart; become open. **3,** become more visible. **4,** commence. **—n. 1,** the outdoors. **2,** public view. **—o'pen·er,** *n.* **—o'pen·ness,** *n.* **—open admissions,** a policy of admitting students regardless of previous academic record. **—open architecture,** (*Computers*) hardware design which is made public to allow third-party design of peripherals and clones. **—open classroom,** a style of education departing from traditional fixed desks and curriculum. **—open door,** in diplomacy, free and equal trade opportunities for all. **—open enrollment, 1,** open admissions. **2,** a policy in public schools allowing parents to choose the school of their choice within a system regardless of location. **—open housing,** the sale or rental of housing without discrimination. **—open marriage,** a marriage in which each spouse is free to engage in sexual relationships with other partners. **—open shop,** a shop open to nonunion labor.

o"pen-air' *adj.* happening out of doors.

o"pen-and-shut" *adj.* perfectly obvious.

o"pen-end' *adj.* having no predetermined duration or amount. Also, **o"pen-end'ed.**

o'pen·hand"ed *adj.* generous.

o'pen-hearth" *adj.* pert. to a process of making steel.

o'pen·ing *n.* **1,** a beginning. **2,** an open space; a gap, breach, clearing, etc. **3,** a business opportunity; vacancy. **4,** a formal beginning, as of a sale, a theatrical production, etc.

o'pen-mind"ed *adj.* unprejudiced. **—o'pen-mind"ed·ness,** *n.*

o'pen-mouthed" (-mowthd") *adj.* gaping with astonishment.

o'pen·work" *n.* ornamental work, such as lace, embroidery, etc., made with openings in the material.

op'er·a (op'ər-ə) *n.* **1,** a drama wholly sung. **2,** pl. of *opus.* **—op"er·at'ic,** *adj.* **—op"er·at'i·cal·ly,** *adv.* **—opera glass,** a small binocular. Also, **opera glasses.**

op'er·a·ble (op'ər-ə-bəl) *adj.* **1,** permitting surgical treatment. **2,** that can be put into operation; practicable.

op'er·and (op'ər-and) *n.* (*Math.*) a value operated on by an operator.

op'er·ate" (op'ə-rāt") *v.i.* **1,** perform or be at work; act. **2,** be effective. **3,** perform a surgical operation. **4,** deal heavily in securities, etc. —*v.t.* direct the working of. —**op′er·ant** (-ənt) *adj. & n.*

op″er·a′tion (op″ər-ā′shən) *n.* **1,** act or method of working; action; agency. **2,** (*Mil.*) a strategic project, movement, or campaign. **3,** surgical treatment. **4,** a business transaction. —**op″er·a′tion·al,** *adj.*

op′er·a·tive (op′ə-rə-tiv) *adj.* **1,** acting; effective. **2,** practical. **3,** pert. to surgical operations. **4,** significant. —*n.* **1,** a workman. **2,** a private detective; secret agent.

op′er·a″tor (-tər) *n.* **1,** one who runs something. **2,** one who makes connections in a telephone exchange. **3,** a speculator. **4,** (*Math.*) a letter or other character signifying an operation to be performed. **5,** (*Informal*) someone adept at accomplishing something, esp. through dishonest or evasive means.

op″er·et′ta (op″ə-ret′ə) *n.* a drama set to light, diverting music.

oph′i·cleide″ (of′ə-klīd″) *n.* an obsolete form of bass bugle.

o·phid′i·an (ō-fid′ē-ən) *adj.* pert. to snakes.

oph·thal′mic (of-thal′mik) *adj.* pert. to the eye.

oph″thal·mol′o·gy (of″thəl-mol′ə-jē) *n.* the medical specialty of the eye and its diseases.

oph″thal·mol′o·gist (-jist) *n.* a doctor of medicine with a specialty in ophthalmology.

oph·thal′mo·scope″ (of-thal′mə-skōp″) *n.* an instrument for examining the interior of the eye, esp. the retina. —**oph·thal″mo·scop′ic,** *adj.*

o′pi·ate (ō′pē-ət) *n. & adj.* **1,** a narcotic drug, esp. one containing opium. **2,** anything that dulls sensation.

o·pine′ (ō-pīn′) *v.i. & t.* give an opinion; think.

o·pin′ion (ə-pin′yən) *n.* **1,** a conclusion; view. **2,** a view held by many at once: public opinion. **3,** estimation; judgment.

o·pin′ion·at″ed (ə-pin′yə-nā″tid) *adj.* obstinate in one's opinion.

o′pi·um (ō′pē-əm) *n.* a narcotic drug derived from the poppy.

o·pos′sum (ō-pos′əm) *n.* a marsupial of the eastern U.S.

op·po′nent (ə-pō′nənt) *n.* an antagonist; adversary.

op″por·tune′ (op″ər-tūn′) *adj.* timely; appropriate. —**op″por·tune′ness,** *n.*

op″por·tun′ism (op″ər-tū′niz-əm) *n.* quickness to grasp opportunities, often unscrupulously. —**op″por·tun′ist,** *n.*

op″por·tu′ni·ty (op″ər-tū′ni-tē) *n.* a favorable occasion or time.

op·pose′ (ə-pōz′) *v.t.* **1,** set against or opposite to (something else). **2,** be hostile to; object to; resist. **3,** contrast; offset. —**op·pos′a·ble,** *adj.*

op′po·site (op′ə-zit) *adj.* **1,** situated on the other side; facing. **2,** going the other way. **3,** radically different. —*n.* something opposite. —**opposite number,** a person having the same rank or duties as one, but in a different country, company, etc.

---

opposite, apposite
☞ These two words are unrelated. *Opposite* means facing, on the other side; *apposite* means appropriate.

---

op″po·si′tion (op″ə-zish′ən) *n.* **1,** act of opposing; state of being opposite. **2,** resistance; antagonism. **3,** the political party opposed to the party in power.

op·press′ (ə-pres′) *v.t.* **1,** lie heavily on (the mind); weigh down. **2,** treat tyrannically. —**op·pres′sion** (-presh′ən) *n.* —**op·pres′sive** (-pres′iv) *adj.* —**op·pres′sor,** *n.* a tyrant.

op·pro′bri·ous (ə-prō′brē-əs) *adj.* abusive; insulting; vile. —**op·pro′bri·um,** *n.* infamy; reproach.

op·pugn′ (ə-pūn′) *v.t.* oppose, as by argument; attack or resist. —**op·pug′nant** (ə-pug′nənt) *adj.* —**op·pug′nan·cy** (-nən-sē) *n.*

opt *v.i.* make a choice.

op′tic (op′tik) *adj.* pert. to vision or to the eye. —*n.* (*Slang*) the eye. —**op′ti·cal,** *adj.* —**optical art,** a movement, esp. in painting and sculpture, specializing in geometric construction, optical illusion, and mechanical devices. Also, **op art.** —**optical disk, 1,** compact disk. **2,** a type of computer data storage device similar to a compact disk. —**optical fiber,** a glass thread used to transmit light waves transporting data.

op·ti′cian (op-tish′ən) *n.* one who makes and sells eyeglasses, etc. ❏ *oculist*

op′tics *n.* the science that deals with vision and light.

op′ti·mism (op′tə-miz-əm) *n.* **1,** the belief that good will prevail. **2,** cheerful hopefulness. —**op′ti·mist,** *n.* —**op″ti·mis′-tic,** *adj.* —**op″ti·mis′ti·cal·ly,** *adv.*

---

optimism
↔ An 18th-c. French coinage based on Latin *optimum*, best, to describe the doctrine of the German philosopher Leibniz.

---

op'ti·mum (op'ti-məm) *n. & adj.* the best; the most favorable. **—op'ti·mal** (-məl) *adj.* **—op'ti·mize** (-mīz) *v.t.* make best use of.

op'tion (op'shən) *n.* **1,** the right or power of choice. **2,** the thing that is or may be chosen. **3,** a purchased right to buy later. **—op'tion·al,** *adj.*

op·tom'e·try (op-tom'ə-trē) *n.* the measurement of vision and fitting of glasses. **—op·tom'e·trist,** *n.* ❏ *oculist*

op'u·lent (op'yə-lənt) *adj.* wealthy; abundantly supplied. **—op'u·lence,** *n.*

o'pus (ō'pəs) *n.* [*pl.* **op'e·ra**] a work, esp. of music. **—o'pus·cule"** (-kūl") *n.* a minor work; a small book.

or (ôr) *conj.* a connective between words, clauses, terms, etc., indicating an alternative or explanation.

-or (ôr, ər) *suf.* denoting **1,** nouns of agency, as *operator.* **2,** adjectives of comparison, as *major.*

or'a·cle (or'ə-kəl) *n.* **1,** a deity that utters answers to questions; hence, an authoritative voice. **2,** the answers given. **—o·rac'u·lar** (â-rak'yə-lər) *adj.*

o'ral (ôr'əl) *adj.* **1,** spoken; not written. **2,** pert. to the mouth. **—oral history,** history based on verbal (often tape-recorded) information from witnesses.

---

oral, verbal

☛ *Oral* means of the mouth; *verbal* simply means utilizing words, which can be written or spoken. Do not use *verbal* if you wish to be specific about the means of communication.

---

or'ange (or'inj) *n.* **1,** the round, juicy, deep yellow citrus fruit of a tropical evergreen tree; the tree. **2,** a reddish-yellow color. **—orange pe'koe** (pē'kō) a black tea from Ceylon or India. **—orange stick,** a rod of orangewood used in manicuring.

or"ange·ade' (-ād') *n.* a drink of orange juice mixed with water and sugar.

Or'ange·man (-mən) *n.* [*pl.* **-men**] an Irish Protestant.

or'ange·wood" *n.* the wood of the orange tree.

o·rang'u·tan" (ō-rang'ū-tan") *n.* an ape of Borneo and Sumatra.

o·rate' (ō-rāt') *v.i.* deliver an oration.

o·ra'tion (ō-rā'shən) *n.* a formal and dignified public speech.

or'a·tor (or'ə-tər) *n.* an eloquent public speaker.

or"a·to'ri·o (ôr"ə-tôr'ē-ō) *n.* a composition for choral singing, usually on a sacred theme.

or'a·to·ry (or'ə-tôr-ē) *n.* **1,** eloquent public speaking. **2,** a place for prayer. **—or"a·tor'i·cal,** *adj.*

orb (ôrb) *n.* **1,** a sphere; globe; esp. a heavenly body. **2,** (*Poetic*) the eye. **—or·bic'u·lar** (ôr-bik'yə-lər) *adj.*

or'bit (ôr'bit) *n.* **1,** a regular circuit or path, esp. of a planet around a star or a satellite around a planet. **2,** the eye socket. **—***v.i. & t.* travel or cause to travel in an orbit (around). **—or'bit·al,** *adj.*

or'chard (ôr'chərd) *n.* a grove of fruit trees.

or'ches·tra (ôr'kə-strə) *n.* **1,** a group of players on various musical instruments. **2,** the main floor of a theater. **—or·ches'tral,** *adj.*

---

orchestra

↔ From Greek *orkhēstra*, the space in front of a theater stage where the chorus danced.

---

or"ches·tra'tion (ôrk"əs-trā'shən) *n.* **1,** music arranged in separate parts for an orchestra. **2,** the planning of a stratagem. **—or'ches·trate",** *v.t. & i.*

or·ches'tri·on (ôr-kes'trē-ən) *n.* a mechanical musical instrument that imitates the sound of an orchestra.

or'chid (ôr'kid) *n.* **1,** any of a large order of tropical plants with brilliant flowers. **2,** a bluish purple. **—or"chi·da'ceous** (-dā'shəs) *adj.*

---

orchid

↔ From Greek *orkhis*, testicle, from the shape of the plant's tuberous roots.

---

or·dain' (ôr-dān') *v.t.* **1,** decree; enact. **2,** appoint. **3,** confer holy orders upon.

or·deal' (ôr-dēl') *n.* a severe test; a trying experience.

or'der (ôr'dər) *n.* **1,** an authoritative direction; a command. **2,** a direction to buy, sell, or furnish something. **3,** a sequence; systematic arrangement. **4,** class; kind; rank. **5,** a classification of plants and animals. **6,** a prescribed mode of procedure. **7,** (*pl.*) religious ordination; clerical rank. **8,** a society of persons, esp. monastic. **9,** an honorary society or institution. **10,** conformity to law or authority. **—***v.t.* **1,** command; bid. **2,** direct; manage. **3,** give an order for. **—***v.i.* give a command. **—in order to,** for the purpose of. **—out of order, 1,** not in accordance with parliamentary rules. **2,** not in working condition.

or'der·ly (ôr'dər-lē) *adj.* **1,** arranged in order; neat; tidy. **2,** well managed. **3,**

peaceable. —*n.* **1,** an officer's aide. **2,** a hospital attendant. **—or'der·li·ness,** *n.*

or'di·nal (ôr'də-nəl) *adj.* defining a thing's position in a series, as first, second, etc. —*n.* an ordinal number.

or'di·nance (ôr'də-nəns) *n.* a law or decree; a regulation.

> **ordinance, ordnance**
> ☞ Do not confuse *ordinance*, a decree, with *ordnance*, weapons.

or'di·nar"y (ôr'də-ner"ē) *adj.* **1,** usual; customary. **2,** mediocre. —*n.* **1,** the usual condition, etc. **2,** a regular meal at a fixed price; an inn serving such a meal.

or"di·na'tion (ôr"də-nā'shən) *n.* act or effect of ordaining.

ord'nance (ôrd'nəns) *n.* **1,** heavy artillery. **2,** weapons of all kinds, ammunition, etc. ❑ *ordinance*

or'dure (ôr'dyûr) *n.* excrement; dung.

ore (ôr) *n.* a mineral or rock from which metal is extracted.

o·reg'a·no (ō-reg'ə-nō) *n.* an aromatic herb.

O're·o (ôr'ē-ō) *n.* (*Slang, derogatory*) a black person perceived to have attitudes and values typical of white society.

or'gan (ôr'gən) *n.* **1,** a part of a plant or animal body which does some vital work. **2,** a medium of communication, esp. a sectarian or political newspaper. **3,** a large musical instrument played by releasing compressed air through pipes (*pipe organ*); an instrument providing similar sound electronically (*electronic organ*). **4,** any of various other wind instruments, as a barrel organ, mouth organ, etc. **—or'gan·ist,** *n.* **—organ grinder,** one who operates a hand organ in the streets and solicits money. **—organ loft,** the place where the pipes of an organ are placed.

or'gan·dy (ôr'gən-dē) *n.* a sheer, stiffened muslin.

or·gan'ic (ôr-gan'ik) *adj.* **1,** pert. to an organ of the body. **2,** pert. to or derived from plant and animal matter; containing carbon. **3,** systematized. **4,** structural. **5,** of foods, produced without use of fertilizers, pesticides, etc. **—organ'i·cal·ly,** *adv.*

or'gan·ism (ôr'gə-niz-əm) *n.* any living thing; any whole with interdependent parts.

or'gan·i·za'tion (ôr"gə-nə-zā'shən) *n.* **1,** the process of organizing. **2,** that which is organized, as a business, a club, etc.

or'gan·ize" (ôr'gə-nīz") *v.t.* **1,** unite the separate elements of into a smoothly working unit. **2,** set going; start. —*v.i.*

combine. **—organized labor,** workers belonging to labor unions.

or·gan'za (ôr-gan'zə) *n.* a light, stiff fabric of silk, rayon, etc.

or'gasm (ôr'gaz-əm) *n.* a paroxysm resulting from intense sexual excitement. **—or·gas'tic,** *adj.*

or'gy (ôr'jē) *n.* **1,** a drunken carousal. **2,** excessive indulgence. **—or"gi·as'tic,** *adj.* **—or"gi·as'ti·cal·ly,** *adv.*

or'i·bi (ôr'ə-bē) *n.* a small So. Amer. antelope.

o'ri·el (ôr'ē-əl) *n.* a large bay window projecting from an upper story.

o'ri·ent (ôr'ē-ənt) *n.* **1,** the east. **2,** (*cap.*) the Asiatic countries. —*v.t.* [also, (*Erroneous*) **o'ri·en·tate"**] **1,** place so as to face the east. **2,** adjust with relation to circumstances, facts, etc. **—o"ri·en·ta'tion,** *n.*

o"ri·en'tal (ôr"ē-en'təl) *adj.* **1,** eastern. **2,** (often *cap.*) of the Far East. —*n.* a native or inhabitant of the Orient.

> **oriental, occidental**
> ☞ These words, which divide the world into halves based on our position in it, are perceived as ethnocentric and should be avoided when applied to persons. *Asian,* or a more precise indication of origin (*Chinese, Japanese,* etc.), is to be preferred. ↔ *Oriental* comes from Latin *oriens,* rising (sun); *occidental* comes from Latin *occidentalis,* western.

or'i·fice (or'ə-fis) *n.* a mouthlike aperture.

o"ri·ga'mi (or"ə-gä'mē) *n.* the Jap. art of paper folding.

or'i·gin (or'ə-jin) *n.* **1,** a source; a beginning. **2,** (often *pl.*) ancestry.

o·rig'i·nal (ə-rij'i-nəl) *adj.* **1,** occurring first. **2,** not copied or imitated. **3,** novel; fresh. **4,** creative; inventive. —*n.* a model, pattern, or first and authentic example. **—o·rig"i·nal'i·ty** (-nal'ə-tē) *n.*

o·rig'i·nate" (ə-rij'i-nāt") *v.t. & i.* begin; initiate. **—o·rig"i·na'tion,** *n.* **—o·rig'i·na"tor,** *n.*

o'ri·ole" (ôr'ē-ōl") *n.* an Amer. bird with black and orange plumage.

O·ri'on (ō-rī'ən) *n.* **1,** in Gk. myth., a giant hunter slain by Artemis. **2,** a constellation near the Equator.

or'i·son (or'i-zən) *n.* a prayer.

Or'lon (ôr'lon) *n.* (*T.N.*) a weather-resistant synthetic fabric used for outer clothing.

or'mo·lu" (ôr'mə-loo") *n.* **1,** gold prepared for gilding. **2,** imitation gold.

or′na·ment (ôr′nə-mənt) *n.* **1,** anything that beautifies or adorns. **2,** a person who confers grace or honor to his or her position, society, etc. —*v.t.* adorn. —**or″na·men′tal** (-men′təl) *adj.* —**or″na·men·ta′tion,** *n.*

or·nate′ (ôr-nāt′) *adj.* elaborately adorned. —**or·nate′ness,** *n.*

or′ner·y (ôr′nə-rė) *adj.* (*Dial.*) of ugly disposition; hard to manage.

or″ni·thol′o·gy (ôr″ni-thol′ə-jė) *n.* the study of birds. —**or″ni·tho·log′i·cal** (-thə-loj′i-kəl) *adj.* —**or″ni·thol′o·gist,** *n.*

o·rog′e·ny (ô-roj′ə-nė) *n.* the process of mountain formation. Also, **or″o·gen′e·sis** (ôr″ə-jen′ə-sis) *n.*

o′ro·tund″ (ôr′ə-tund″) *adj.* **1,** rich and full (of the voice). **2,** pompous (of rhetoric or delivery).

> **orotund**
> ↔ A contraction of the Latin phrase *ore rotundo*, with round mouth.

or′phan (ôr′fən) *n.* **1,** a child bereft by death of its parents. **2,** the last line of a paragraph that is stranded at the top of the following page. —*adj.* **1,** bereft of parents. **2,** unprotected. **3,** of or to orphans. —*v.t.* bereave of parents. —**or′phan·age** (-ij) *n.* a home for orphans. —**or′-phan·hood″,** *n.*

or′rer·y (ôr′ə-rė) *n.* a machine representing the motions and phases of the planets; a planetarium.

> **orrery**
> ↔ From Charles Boyce, Earl of *Orrery*, who commissioned the construction of such a device.

or′ris (or′is) *n.* a kind of iris; its root, used for perfume.

or′thi·con (ôr′thi-kon) *n.* a television camera tube.

or·tho- *pref.* straight; upright; correct.

or″tho·don′tia (ôr″thə-don′shə) *n.* a branch of dentistry dealing with irregularities of the teeth and the correction of them, esp. by mechanical means. —**or″tho·don′tist,** *n.*

or″tho·don′tics (or″thə-dän′tiks) *n.sing.* orthodontia.

or′tho·dox″ (ôr″thə-doks′) *adj.* **1,** holding sound, generally accepted views, esp. on religion. **2,** approved; conventional. —**Orthodox Church,** a Christian church in eastern Europe. —**or′tho·dox″y** (-ė) *n.*

or·thog′o·nal (ôr-thog′ə-nəl) *adj.* of right angles; rectangular.

or·thog′ra·phy (ôr-thog′rə-fė) *n.* correct spelling. —**or″tho·graph′ic,** *adj.*

or″tho·pe′dic (ôr″thə-pē′dik) *adj.* (*Med.*) pert. to or employed in orthopedics. —**or″tho·pe′di·cal·ly,** *adv.*

or″tho·pe′dics (-diks) *n.sing.* prevention or correction of physical deformities, esp. in children.

or″tho·pe′dist (-dist) *n.* a doctor of medicine with a specialty in orthopedics.

or′to·lan (ôr′tə-lən) *n.* a Europ. bunting; the bobolink.

-o·ry (ôr-ė; ə-rė) *suf.* **1,** pert. to; characterized by; effecting; expressing. **2,** a place for; an instrument for.

o′ryx (ō′riks) *n.* a large straight-horned Afr. antelope.

or′zo (ôr′zō) *n.* rice-shaped pasta.

Os′car (os′kər) *n.* **1,** (*Informal*) the statuette signifying an Academy Award, given annually for various achievements in motion pictures; the award itself. **2,** (*Communications*) the letter *o.*

> **Oscar**
> ↔ Supposedly named after her uncle by an employee of the Academy of Motion Picture Arts and Sciences, which presents the award.

os′cil·late″ (os′ə-lāt″) *v.i.* **1,** move to and fro, as a pendulum. **2,** vacillate; fluctuate. —**os″cil·la′tion,** *n.* —**os′cil·la″tor,** *n.*

os·cil′lo·scope″ (ə-sil′ə-skōp″) *n.* an instrument for tracing a graphic picture of an electric wave on a fluorescent screen.

os′cu·late″ (os′kyə-lāt″) *v.t. & i.* kiss. —**os″cu·lant** (-lənt) *adj.* —**os″cu·la′tion,** *n.*

-ose (ōs) *suf.* **1,** full of. **2,** like. **3,** used to name various carbohydrates.

o′sier (ō′zhər) *n.* a willow whose twigs are used for baskets, etc.

-o·sis (ō-sis) *suf.* [*pl.* **-o·ses** (-sėz)] abnormal condition of.

os′mi·um (oz′mė-əm) *n.* a hard, heavy metallic element, no. 76, symbol Os, similar to platinum.

os·mo′sis (oz-mō′sis) *n.* the tendency of liquids to pass through porous partitions and become diffused.

os′prey (os′prė) *n.* a large fish-eating bird.

os′se·ous (os′ė-əs) *adj.* made of or like bone.

os′si·fy″ (os′i-fī″) *v.t. & i.* change into bone. —**os″si·fi·ca′tion,** *n.*

os′su·ar·y (os′ū-er-ė) *n.* a vessel or place for the bones of the dead.

tub, cūte, pûll; labəl; oil, owl, go, chip, she, thin, *th*en, si**ng**, i**ng**k; *see p. 6*

os·ten′si·ble (os-ten′sə-bəl) *adj.* appearing outwardly; professed.

os″ten·ta′tion (os″ten-tā′shən) *n.* a pretentious display. —**os″ten·ta′tious,** *adj.*

os·te·o- (os-tė-ə) *pref.* bone.

os″te·ol′o·gy (os″tė-ol′ə-jė) *n.* the science dealing with the bones.

os″te·op′a·thy (ȯs″tė-op′ə-thė) *n.* a system of medicine which holds that disease is chiefly due to derangement of the bones. —**os′te·o·path″** (os′tė-ə-path″) *n.*

os″ti·na′to (os″ti-nä′tō) *n.* (*It., Music*) a short melodic phrase repeated over and over at the same pitch.

os′tra·cize″ (os′trə-sīz″) *v.t.* banish from society, etc. —**os′tra·cism,** *n.*

---

ostracism
↔ From Greek *ostrakon*, a piece of pottery such as the ones used to vote on the banishment of a Greek citizen in ancient times.

---

os′trich *n.* a very large flightless bird of Africa, valued for its plumes.

o·tal′gi·a (ō-tal′jė-ə) *n.* earache.

oth′er (u*th*′ər) *adj.* **1,** different from the one just mentioned. **2,** the remaining one or ones. **3,** additional. **4,** different; not the same. —*adv.* otherwise. —*pron.* **1,** the second of two. **2,** a different person or thing.

oth′er·wise″ *adv.* in a different way. —*conj.* else.

oth″er·world′ly *adj.* **1,** concerned with another world, as the world to come or the world of the imagination. —**oth″er·world′li·ness,** *n.*

o′tic (ō′tik) *adj.* of the ear.

o′ti·ose″ (ō′shė-ōs″) *adj.* **1,** inactive; idle. **2,** careless; ineffective; futile. —**o″ti·os′i·ty** (-os′ə-tė) *n.*

o·ti′tis (ō-tī′tis) *n.* inflammation of the ear.

o·tol′o·gy (ō-tol′ə-je) *n.* the medical specialty of the ear and its diseases. —**o·tol′o·gist,** *n.*

ot′ter (ot′ər) *n.* an aquatic animal; its dark-brown fur.

ot′to·man (ot′ə-mən) *n.* **1,** a cushioned footstool or bench. **2,** a corded fabric. **3,** (*cap.*) a Turk.

ou″bli·ette′ (oo″blė-et′) *n.* a dungeon or pit with an opening only at the top.

ouch (owch) *interj.* an exclamation of pain.

ought (ât) *aux.v.* be bound, or obliged, or sure (to): followed by an infinitive.

Oui′ja (wē′jə) *n.* (*T.N.*) a board and pointer supposed mystically to spell out words.

ounce (owns) *n.* **1,** a measure of weight, one-twelfth of a pound troy, one-sixteenth of a pound avoirdupois. **2,** one-sixteenth of a pint: *fluid ounce.* **3,** the snow leopard of Asia.

---

ounce
↔ The measure derives from Latin *uncia,* twelfth part. The leopard's name comes from Old French *lonce,* misperceived as *once* preceded by the definite article.

---

our (owr) *pron. & adj.* poss. form of *we.* —**ours,** *pron.* form of *our* used predicatively. —**our·selves′,** *pron.*

-ous (əs) *suf.* **1,** full of; having; like. **2,** (*Chem.*) in a compound, denoting a lower valence than that denoted by -ic.

oust (owst) *v.t.* drive out. —**oust′er,** *n.* ejection.

out (owt) *adv.* **1,** away from or not in a place, position, state, etc. **2,** into sight or existence; forth. **3,** to exhaustion, extinction, or conclusion. **4,** at variance; in error; minus. **5,** not in vogue. **6,** by reason of. **7,** (*Baseball*) temporarily retired from action. —*n.* (*Informal*) **1,** a means of escape or excuse. **2,** (*pl.*) bad terms. **3,** one who is out. —*v.i.* **1,** become known. **2,** reveal one's homosexuality. —**out to lunch,** (*Informal*) **1,** crazy. **2,** oblivious.

out- *pref.* away; beyond; outside; outer: used in many compounds.

out′age (-ij) *n.* a period of suspension of operation or service.

out-′and-out′ *adj.* absolute; complete.

out-″bal′ance *v.t.* outweigh.

out·bid′ *v.t.* bid more than.

out′board″ *adj. & adv.* (located) on or to the outside of a boat, aircraft, etc.; (located) away from the center.

out′bound″ *adj.* going away.

out·brave′ *v.t.* **1,** surpass in daring or courage. **2,** overcome; defy successfully.

out′break″ *n.* **1,** a sudden eruption; an outburst. **2,** a riot or insurrection.

out′build″ing *n.* a small, detached building, subordinate to another.

out′burst″ *n.* a sudden pouring forth; an outbreak of emotion.

out′cast″ *n.* **1,** a person cast out, as from home. **2,** discarded matter.

out·class′ *v.t.* be ahead of; surpass.

out′come″ *n.* the result, consequence, or issue.

out′crop″ *n.* rock projecting upward through the ground.

---

fat, fāte, fär, fåre, fåll, åsk; met, hē, hèr, maybė; pin, pīne; not, nōte, ôr, tool

out'cry" *n.* a loud cry, as of distress; clamor. —*v.t.* (owt-krī') cry louder than.

out·dat'ed *adj.* obsolete; out-of-date; antiquated. —**out·date'**, *v.t.*

out·dis'tance *v.t.* go farther than.

out·do' *v.t.* do better than; surpass; excel.

out'door" *adj.* in open air, not in a building. —**out·doors'**, *adv. & n.*

out'er (ow'tər) *adj.* **1,** exterior. **2,** farther out.. —**out'er·most"**, *adj.* farthest out. —**outer space, 1,** space beyond the earth's atmosphere. **2,** interstellar space.

out·face' *v.t.* **1,** face or stare down. **2,** confront boldly; defy.

out'field" *n.* (*Baseball*) the part of a baseball field outside the diamond; the three players (*outfielders*) stationed there.

out'fit" *n.* **1,** equipment for a special purpose, trade, etc.; fittings. **2,** a special group of persons, as a company, a military unit. —*v.t.* [**-fit'ted, -ting**] equip.

out·flank' *v.t.* go beyond the extent of (an opposing military force's) flank.

out·fox' *v.t.* outwit.

out'go" *n.* **1,** expenditure. **2,** outflow.

out'go"ing *adj.* **1,** going out; vacating; retiring. **2,** extrovert.

out·grow' *v.t.* **1,** grow too large or able for. **2,** surpass in growing.

out'growth" *n.* a natural development or result; an offshoot.

out·guess' *v.t.* penetrate the designs of; outwit.

out'house" *n.* **1,** an outbuilding. **2,** a privy.

out'ing *n.* a pleasure trip.

out'land" *n.* outlying land. —*adj.* foreign. —**out'land"er,** *n.* a foreigner; stranger.

out·land'ish (owt-lan'dish) *adj.* unfamiliar; bizarre; odd.

out·last' *v.t.* last longer than; outlive.

out'law" *n.* a habitual criminal. —*v.t.* **1,** make illegal or legally unenforceable. **2,** deprive of the protection of the law. —**out'law"ry,** *n.*

out'lay" *n.* expenditure, as of money, effort, etc.

out'let" *n.* **1,** a means of exit or escape. **2,** a market for goods. **3,** a letting out; discharge.

out'line" *n.* **1,** the line tracing the exterior shape of an object. **2,** a drawing showing only this shape. **3,** a rough draft, as of a speech, plan, etc. **4,** a summary; (*pl.*) the gist. —*v.t.* make an outline of; describe briefly.

out·live' *v.t.* live longer than.

out'look" *n.* **1,** a view or scene from a place. **2,** the prospect for the future. **3,** mental attitude.

out'ly"ing (owt'lī"ing) *adj.* remote from the center; outside a boundary.

out'mod'ed (-mō'did) *adj.* out of fashion.

out'most" *adj.* outermost.

out·num'ber *v.t.* be more numerous than.

out-'of-bod'y *adj.* pert. to the sensation of perceiving or observing oneself from outside one's own body.

out-'of-date' *adj.* no longer in style; antiquated; obsolete.

out-"of-door' *adj.* outside; outdoor. —**out-"of-doors'**, *adv. & n.*

out-"of-the-way' *adj.* secluded.

out'pa"tient *n.* a person treated at, but not staying in, a hospital.

out'place"ment *n.* to assist an employee about to be dismissed in finding a new position.

out'post" *n.* a station distant from an army; troops stationed there as a guard.

out'pour" *n.* a pouring out; effusion. Also, **out'pour"ing.**

out'put" *n.* **1,** production of goods, crops, work, etc. **2,** the amount produced; yield. **3,** computerized data transmitted to an outside medium, storage device, etc. —*v.t.* transmit data from a computer.

out'rage" *n.* **1,** a shameful wrong. **2,** cruel or wanton violence. —*v.t.* **1,** assault. **2,** transgress shamefully. **3,** offend grossly.

> **outrage**
> ↔ Not connected with *rage*, this word comes from Latin *ultra*, beyond, through Old French *outrage*.

out·ra'geous (-rāj'əs) *adj.* **1,** flagrantly contrary to law, order, or decency. **2,** remarkable. —**out·ra'geous·ness,** *n.*

out·rank' *v.t.* rank higher than.

ou·tré' (oo-trā') (*Fr.*) *adj.* **1,** extravagantly odd or exaggerated. **2,** improper.

out·reach' *v.t. & i.* **1,** extend beyond; surpass. **2,** outwit. —*n.* (out'rēch") **1,** the extent of effectiveness or influence. **2,** extension of services to nontraditional recipients.

out'rid"er *n.* a horseback rider attending a carriage.

out'rig"ger *n.* a projection from the side of a ship or boat, to give stability, support oars, etc.

out'right" *adv.* **1,** all at once; entirely. **2,**

openly. —*adj.* **1,** complete; total. **2,** unqualified.

out·run′ *v.t.* run faster than.

out′set″ *n.* the beginning.

out·shine′ *v.t.* shine more brightly than; surpass in fame.

out″side′ *n.* **1,** the region beyond an enclosure or boundary. **2,** the outer surface; external aspect. **3,** the utmost limit. —*adj.* **1,** external. **2,** coming from beyond a given place or group. **3,** apart from one's regular occupation. —*adv.* **1,** on or to the outer side. **2,** outdoors. —*prep.* **1,** outward from. **2,** beyond. **3,** (*Informal*) except for. —**out″sid′er,** *n.* one not belonging to a particular set, etc.

out′size″ *n.* a size not standard; esp., an unusually large size. —**out′sized″,** *adj.*

out′skirts (owt′skĕrtz) *n.pl.* an outer part; a bordering district.

out′smart′ *v.t.* (*Informal*) outwit.

out′sourc″ing (-sôr″sing) *n.* the acquisition of manufacturing parts from abroad or from nonunion suppliers to cut costs.

out′spo″ken (owt′spō″kən) *adj.* frank; said without reserve.

out·stand′ing *adj.* **1,** prominent; notable. **2,** not paid or settled. **3,** standing apart; detached; opposing.

out′sta″tion *n.* an outpost.

out·stay′ *v.t.* stay longer than.

out·strip′ *v.t.* get ahead of; surpass; outdo.

out′take″ *n.* material prepared (for a film, etc.) and subsequently eliminated.

out·talk′ *v.t.* **1,** talk longer or more effectively than. **2,** overpower by talking.

out·vote′ *v.t.* defeat in an election or a vote.

out′ward (-wərd) *adj.* **1,** going away. **2,** external; seen from the outside. **3,** visible. —*adv.* [also, **out′wards**] toward the outside; out.

out·wear′ *v.t.* **1,** last longer than. **2,** wear out; exhaust.

out·weigh′ *v.t.* exceed in weight, importance, or influence.

out·wit′ *v.t.* get the better of by superior cleverness.

out′work″ *n.* one of the minor defenses constructed in advance of the main fortification.

out·worn′ *adj.* **1,** obsolete; outgrown. **2,** worn out, as clothes; exhausted.

ou′zel (oo′zəl) *n.* the Europ. blackbird.

ou′zo (oo′zō) *n.* an anise-flavored Gk. liqueur.

o′val (ō′vəl) *adj.* elliptical. —**Oval Of-**

fice, the office of the President of the U.S., where official business is conducted.

o′va·ry (ō′və-rė) *n.* the organ in a female in which the egg cells are formed. —**o·var′i·an** (ō-vār′ė-ən) *adj.*

o·vate′ (ō-vāt′) *adj.* egg-shaped.

o·va′tion (ō-vā′shən) *n.* enthusiastic public acclaim.

ov′en (uv′ən) *n.* a chamber, as in a stove, for baking or drying.

o′ver (ō′vər) *prep.* **1,** higher than; above; covering. **2,** above and across; to or on the other side of. **3,** more than. **4,** during. **5,** about; concerning. **6,** in preference to. —*adv.* **1,** on the top. **2,** across. **3,** yonder; on the other side. **4,** from one to another. **5,** so as to show the other side. **6,** above the rim or top. **7,** from beginning to end. **8,** in excess. **9,** once more. **10,** at one end. **11,** (*Informal*) successfully. —*adj.* **1,** higher up. **2,** in excess; surplus. **3,** finished; past. —**over and above,** in addition to; besides. ❑ *above*

o′ver- *pref.* over; beyond; extra.

o″ver·a·chieve′ *v.i.* perform beyond expectations, as academically. —**o″ver·a·chiev′er,** *n.*

o″ver·act′ *v.i. & t.* be excessively dramatic; overplay.

o″ver·age′ *adj.* beyond the proper age; too old.

o′ver·age (-ij) *n.* excess of goods, money, etc.

o′ver·all *adj.* extending to both or all extremes; covering all parts. —*n.* (*pl.*) a one-piece outer garment worn to protect the clothes.

o″ver·awe′ *v.t.* restrain or subdue by awe, fear, or superior influence.

o″ver·bal′ance *v.t.* **1,** outweigh. **2,** tip over.

o″ver·bear′ing (-bār′ing) *adj.* haughty; arrogant; dictatorial.

o″ver·bid′ *v.t.* bid higher than. —*v.i.* bid too much. —*n.* a higher bid.

o″ver·blown′ *adj.* **1,** past the time of blossoming. **2,** pretentious.

o″ver·board′ *adv.* **1,** off a ship into the water. **2,** (*Informal*) to a rash or extravagant extent.

o″ver·book′ *v.t.* accept more reservations for (an airplane, concert, etc.) than there are seats available.

o′ver·call″ *v.t. & n.* bid higher than (another bid), in a card game.

o″ver·cast′ *adj.* **1,** darkened, esp. by clouds. **2,** sewn by long stitches over an edge, as to prevent raveling.

o′ver·clothes″ *n.pl.* outer garments, as for outdoor wear.

o″ver·cloud′ *v.t. & i.* overspread with clouds; make or become gloomy.

o′ver·coat″ *n.* a long outer coat, esp. for cold weather.

o″ver·come′ *v.t.* **1,** defeat; conquer. **2,** successfully resist (an impulse, etc.). —*adj.* feeling great emotion.

o′ver·dose″ *n.* an excessive dose, as of medicine. —*v.t.* (ō″vər-dōs′) give too large a dose to.

o′ver·draft″ *n.* **1,** a draft exceeding one's credit balance, esp. at a bank. **2,** any excess draft or demand. **3,** an air draft above a fire, or passing downward.

o″ver·draw′ *v.t. & i.* **1,** draw out or back too much or too far. **2,** exaggerate in depicting.

o″ver·dress′ *v.i. & t.* dress too ostentatiously.

o″ver·drive′ *v.t.* drive or work too hard; push to excess. —*n.* (ō′vər-drīv″) a gear arrangement whereby a wheel or propeller rotates faster than the driving shaft.

o′ver·due′ *adj.* due at a previous time; past due.

o″ver·es′ti·mate″ (-māt″) *v.t. & i.* **1,** rate too highly. **2,** estimate to be more than the reality. —*n.* (-mət) an excessive estimate. —**o″ver·es″ti·ma′tion,** *n.*

o″ver·flow′ *v.t. & i.* **1,** flood. **2,** run over the edge or boundary (of). —*n.* (ō′vər-flō″) **1,** a flowing over; that which flows over. **2,** an outlet for excess fluid.

o″ver·grown′ *adj.* **1,** covered with a growth of vegetation, hair, etc. **2,** grown too large.

o′ver·hand″ *adj. & adv.* with the hand above or raised.

o″ver·hang′ *v.t. & i.* [-hung, -hang′ing] **1,** extend or project over. **2,** impend; threaten. —*n.* (ō′vər-hang″), a projecting part; the extent of this projection.

o′ver·haul″ *v.t.* **1,** examine or repair thoroughly. **2,** overtake. —*n.* inspection.

o′ver·head″ *adj.* **1,** above one's head; in the sky. **2,** applicable to all; average. —*n.* the fixed expenses of a business, as for rent, etc. —*adv.* (ō″vər-hed′) **1,** aloft; on high. **2,** so as to be completely submerged.

o″ver·hear′ *v.t. & i.* hear without the speaker's knowledge or intention.

o″ver·joy′ *v.t.* make exceedingly glad; overcome with joy. —**o″ver·joyed′,** *adj.*

[The following words may be defined by assuming the prefix *over-* to mean "excessive" in the case of nouns; "too much, too far, too long," etc. in the case of verbs; "too" or "excessively" in the case of adjectives and adverbs.]

o″ver·a·bun′dance, *n.*
o″ver·ac′tive, *adj.*
o″ver·am·bi′tious, *adj.*
o″ver·anx′ious, *adj.*
o″ver·bold′, *adj.*
o″ver·bur′den, *v.t.*
o″ver·bus′y, *adj.*
o″ver·buy′, *v.i. & t.*
o″ver·cap′i·tal·ize″, *v.t.*
o″ver·care′ful, *adj.*
o″ver·cau′tious, *adj.*
o″ver·charge′, *v.i. & t.*
o″ver·con·fi′dent, *adj.*
o″ver·con·serv′a·tive, *adj.*
o″ver·cook′, *v.t.*
o″ver·crit′i·cal, *adj.*
o″ver·crowd, *v.t.*
o″ver·cu′ri·ous, *adj.*
o″ver·do′, *v.i. & t.*
o″ver·done′, *v.t.*
o″ver·ea′ger, *adj.*
o″ver·eat′, *v.i.*
o″ver·e·mo′tion·al, *adj.*
o″ver·em′pha·size″, *v.t.*
o″ver·en·thu′si·as″tic, *adj.*
o″ver·ex·cite′, *v.t.*

o″ver·ex′er·cise″, *v.i. & t.*
o″ver·ex·ert′, *v.i.*
o″ver·ex·pan′sion, *n.*
o″ver·ex·pose′, *v.t.*
o″ver·fa·mil′iar, *adj.*
o″ver·fa·tigue′, *v.t.*
o″ver·feed′, *v.t.*
o″ver·fill′, *v.t.*
o″ver·fond′, *adj.*
o″ver·has′ty, *adj.*
o″ver·heat′, *v.t. & i.*
o″ver·in·dulge′, *v.i.*
o″ver·load′, *v.t.*
o″ver·long′, *adv. & adj.*
o″ver·mod′est, *adj.*
o″ver·pay′, *v.t. & i.*
o″ver·pay′ment, *n.*
o″ver·plump′, *adj.*
o″ver·pop′u·la′tion, *n.*
o″ver·praise′, *v.t.*
o″ver·pro·duce′, *v.i. & t.*
o″ver·pro·duc′tion, *n.*
o″ver·qual′i·fied, *adj.*
o″ver·re·li′gious, *adj.*
o″ver·ripe′, *adj.*
o″ver·rule′, *v.t.*

o″ver·scru′pu·lous, *adj.*
o″ver·sell′, *v.t. & i.*
o″ver·sen′si·tive, *adj.*
o″ver·set′, *v.i.*
o″ver·sim″pli·fi·ca′tion, *n.*
o″ver·sim′pli·fy″, *v.t. & i.*
o″ver·spread′, *adj. & v.t.*
o″ver·stay′, *v.i.*
o″ver·stim′u·late″, *v.t.*
o″ver·stock′, *v.t.*
o″ver·stock″, *n.*
o″ver·strict″′, *adj.*
o″ver·stu′di·ous, *adj.*
o″ver·sub·scribe′, *v.t.*
o″ver·sus·pi′cious, *adj.*
o″ver·sweet′, *adj.*
o″ver·talk′a·tive, *adj.*
o″ver·task′, *v.t.*
o″ver·tax′, *v.t.*
o″ver·tire′, *v.t. & i.*
o″ver·trained′, *adj.*
o″ver·val″u·a′tion, *n.*
o″ver·val′u,e *v.t.*
o″ver·ve′he·ment, *adj.*
o″ver·write′, *v.i. & t.*
o″ver·zeal′ous, *adj.*

o′ver·kill″ *n.* the nuclear capacity to de-stroy many times the total population of an enemy nation or of the world; hence, excess capability, capacity, or action.

o′ver·land″ (-lənd″) *adj. & adv.* across dry land; by land.

o″ver·lap′ *v.t. & i.* cover partly and ex-tend beyond. —*n.* (ō′vər-lap″) the part lapping over.

o″ver·lay′ *v.t.* **1,** place on something else. **2,** cover, esp. with a decorative layer. —*n.* (ō′vər-lā″) something laid on something else.

---

overlay, overlie
☛ *Overlay* describes the action of placing something over something else. *Overlie* describes the fact of something lying on top of something else. One can *overlay* linoleum on a wood floor; as a result, the linoleum then *overlies* the wood floor.

---

o″ver·leap′ *v.t.* **1,** leap over; pass beyond. **2,** omit; disregard.

o″ver·lie′ *v.t.* **1,** lie over or upon. **2,** smother (as an infant) by lying upon.

o″ver·look′ *v.t.* **1,** fail to notice. **2,** ignore; condone. **3,** afford a view of, from a higher position. **4,** supervise.

---

overlook, oversee
☛ In common usage, these similar words have different (though related) meanings. *Overlook* means to ignore; have a view of. It can also—but sel-dom does—mean the same as *over-see*, to supervise.

---

o′ver·lord″ *n.* **1,** a master; a chief lord. **2,** boss; overseer.

o′ver·ly (-lė) *adv.* excessively.

o″ver·match′ *v.t.* **1,** surpass. **2,** put in competition against another greatly superior.

o″ver·much′ *adj. & adv.* too much. —*n.* an excessive amount.

o′ver·night″ *adj.* **1,** done during the night. **2,** intended for one night's use. —*adv.* (ō″vər-nīt′) during the night. —*n.* **1,** the previous evening or night. **2,** (*Infor-mal*) an overnight pass or trip.

o′ver·pass″ *n.* a bridge over a road. —*v.t.* (ō″vər-pàs′) *v.t.* go over or beyond; surmount.

o″ver·play′ *v.t. & i.* act or make a play with more force than is proper; exaggerate.

o″ver·pleased′ (-plēzd′) *adj.* too pleased (used chiefly in the negative, to express dissatisfaction).

o″ver·pow′er *v.t.* **1,** conquer or subdue by superior force. **2,** overwhelm, as with emotion. **3,** equip with too much power.

o″ver·rate′ *v.t.* value too highly; overestimate.

o″ver·reach′ *v.t. & i.* **1,** stretch beyond. **2,** reach too far; miss. **3,** outwit.

o″ver·ride′ *v.t.* **1,** prevail over; outweigh; overrule. **2,** trample down. **3,** extend over; overlap.

o″ver·run′ *v.t.* **1,** swarm over in great numbers. **2,** roam over; spread through-out. **3,** run beyond; exceed. **4,** take posses-sion of (a country) by invasion. —*n.* (o′ver-run″) the act or result of exceeding (a budget, limit, etc.).

o′ver·seas″ (-sēz″) *adj.* **1,** situated be-yond a sea; foreign. **2,** pert. to sea travel. —*adv.* (ō″vər-sēz′) beyond a sea; abroad.

o″ver·see′ *v.t.* **1,** supervise; direct. **2,** ob-serve; watch. —**o″ver·se″er,** *n.* ❏ *overlook*

o″ver·shad′ow *v.t.* **1,** darken, as by cast-ing a shadow on. **2,** cause to seem less important.

o′ver·shoe″ *n.* a shoe worn over another; a waterproof shoe, as a rubber or galosh.

o″ver·shoot′ *v.t. & i.* shoot or go beyond (a proper mark or limit).

o′ver·shot″ *adj.* **1,** driven from above, as a water wheel. **2,** with the upper jaw over-hanging the lower, as on a dog.

o′ver·sight″ *n.* **1,** an omission or error due to failure to notice. **2,** supervision; care.

o′ver·size″ *adj.* larger than is usual or proper. —*n.* an oversize article. Also, **o′ver·sized″.**

o′ver·skirt″ *n.* an outer skirt, esp. one worn over another.

o″ver·sleep′ *v.i.* sleep too late.

o″ver·state′ *v.t.* state too strongly; exag-gerate. —**o″ver·state′ment,** *n.*

o″ver·step′ *v.t.* go beyond; transgress.

o″ver·strung′ *adj.* **1,** too tightly strung. **2,** highly nervous.

o″ver·stuffed′ (-stuft″) *adj.* (of furni-ture) covered with thick stuffing and upholstery.

o·vert′ (ō-vėrt′) *adj.* plain to the view; open.

o″ver·take′ *v.t.* catch up with, as in pursuing.

o′ver-the-count′er *adj.* **1,** sold direct to buyers, as in a retail store. **2,** aboveboard.

o″ver·throw′ *v.t.* **1,** defeat; force out of power; put an end to. **2,** knock down; upset. —*n.* defeat; demolition.

o′ver·time″ *n.* **1,** time spent working after regular hours; pay for such work. **2,**

---

fat, fāte, fär, fâre, fâll, àsk; met, hē, hėr, maybė; pin, pīne; not, nōte, ôr, tool an extra period beyond the usual, as in sports. —*adj. & adv.* requiring extra time. —*v.t.* (ō"vər-tīm') give too much time to, as in photographic processes.

o'ver·tone" *n.* **1,** a higher, secondary tone of a basic musical tone. **2,** (*pl.*) additional meaning; connotation.

o"ver·top' *v.t.* **1,** rise above. **2,** exceed. **3,** surpass; outdo.

o'ver·trick" *n.* in bridge, a trick won in excess of the contract.

o'ver·trump" *v.t.* play a higher trump than.

o'ver·ture' (ō'vər-chûr") *n.* **1,** an orchestral prelude to an opera, play, etc. **2,** a proposal; a suggestion that negotiations begin.

o"ver·turn' *v.t. & i.* **1,** overthrow. **2,** upset; capsize.

o'ver·view" *n.* a comprehensive survey or view.

o"ver·ween'ing (ō"vər-wē'ning) *adj.* arrogant; presumptuous.

o"ver·weigh' *v.t.* **1,** exceed in weight. **2,** weigh down; oppress. —**o'ver·weight**" (-wāt") *adj.*

o"ver·whelm' *v.t.* **1,** cover, bury, load, or weigh upon overpoweringly; crush; oppress. **2,** overcome with emotion.

o"ver·work' *v.i.* work too hard. —*v.t.* **1,** weary with too much work. **2,** excite excessively. **3,** elaborate too much. —*n.* (ō'vər-wērk") extra work.

o"ver·wrought' *adj.* **1,** weary or nervous, esp. from overwork or excitement. **2,** too elaborate.

o'vi·duct" (ō'vi-dukt") *n.* the duct or passage through which the ovum or egg of an animal passes from the ovary.

o'vine (ō'vīn) *adj.* pert. to sheep.

o·vip'a·rous (ō-vip'ə-rəs) *adj.* producing eggs.

o'void (ō'void) *adj.* egg-shaped.

ov'u·late" (ov'vyə-lāt") *v.i.* produce or lay an egg or eggs. —**o"vu·la'tion,** *n.*

ov'ule (ov'ūl) *n.* a rudimentary egg or seed.

o'vum (ō'vəm) *n.* [*pl.* **o'va** (-və)] the female reproductive cell.

owe (ō) *v.t.* **1,** be under obligation to pay, render, etc. **2,** be indebted to or for. —**ow'ing,** *adj.* owed; due. —**owing to,** because of. ❏ *because*

owl *n.* **1,** a nocturnal bird of prey, with hooked beak and strong claws. **2,** a solemn person. **3,** a person of nocturnal habits. —**owl'et,** *n.* a young, or small, owl. —**owl'ish,** *adj.* affecting a solemn or wise manner.

own (ōn) *v.t.* **1,** possess by right. **2,** (often with *up*) admit; concede. —*adj.* belonging to or concerning only oneself or itself. —**own'er,** *n.* —**own'er·ship**", *n.* ❏ *acknowledge*

ox (oks) *n.* [*pl.* **ox'en** (-ən)] **1,** the emasculated adult male of the domestic cattle family. **2,** any member of the bovine family.

ox·al'ic acid (oks-al'ik) a poisonous acid used in bleaching, dyeing, etc.

ox'a·lis (ok'sə-lis) *n.* a plant with white or pink flowers.

ox'blood" *n.* **1,** the blood of an ox. **2,** a deep red color.

ox'bow" (oks'bō") *n.* **1,** in a yoke, the U-shaped piece that fits over the neck of the animal. **2,** a U-shaped bend in a river.

ox'eye" (oks'ī") *n.* **1,** a daisylike plant. **2,** a small U.S. shorebird, as the sandpiper.

ox'ford (oks'fərd) *n.* **1,** a low shoe. **2,** a cotton or rayon fabric used as shirting. —**oxford gray,** a dark gray.

ox'ide (ok'sīd) *n.* a compound of oxygen with another element.

ox'i·dize" (ok'sə-dīz") *v.t. & i.* combine with oxygen. —**ox'i·dant** (-dənt) *n.* —**ox"·i·da'tion,** *n.*

ox"y·a·cet'y·lene (ok"sė-ə-set'ə-lēn) *adj.* pert. to a gas that burns with a very hot flame, used for welding and cutting metal.

ox'y·gen (ok'sə-jən) *n.* a gaseous element, no. 8, symbol O, colorless, odorless, and essential to all life. —**ox'y·gen·ate**" (-āt") *v.t.* —**oxygen mask,** a mask worn over the nose and kept supplied with oxygen. —**oxygen tent,** an enclosure supplied with oxygen in which a patient is kept for aid in breathing.

> **oxygen**
> ↔ An 18th-c. French coinage based on Greek *oxys*, acid, + *-genes*, formation.

ox"y·mo'ron (oks"ē-môr'on) *n.* a statement which is seemingly self-contradictory.

o'yez (ō'yes; -yez) *interj.* hear! attention!

oys'ter (ois'tər) *n.* an edible saltwater bivalve mollusk. —**oyster plant,** a vegetable, the salsify.

Oz'a·lid (oz'ə-lid) *n.* (*T.N.*) a copying process producing a copy resembling a blueprint.

o'zone (ō'zōn) *n.* **1,** an ionized form of

oxygen. **2,** (*Informal*) pure air. **—ozone layer,** a layer of ozone in the earth's upper atmosphere which absorbs ultraviolet radiation. Also, **o′zone shield.**

P

P, p (pē) **1,** the sixteenth letter of the English alphabet. **2,** (*Brit.*) penny.

pa (pä) *n.* (*Informal*) papa.

Pab′lum (pab′ləm) *n.* **1,** (*T.N.*) a brand of cereal for infants. **2,** (*l.c.*) bland writing or thinking.

pab′u·lum (pab′yə-ləm) *n.* **1,** food. **2,** insipid ideas.

PAC (pak) *n.* political action committee.

pa′ca (pä′kə) *n.* a large spotted rodent of So. Amer.

pace (pās) *n.* **1,** a single step or its distance. **2,** mode or rate of walking or progressing; gait; speed. **3,** a gait of horses. **4,** (*pl.*) gaits; accomplishments. **—v.t. 1,** set the rate for. **2,** (usu. with *off*) measure by counting steps. **3,** walk back and forth across. **—v.i.** walk in even steps; go at a pace. **—pac′er,** *n.* a pacing horse.

pa′ce (pä′chā) *prep.* (*Lat.*) with due respect to.

pace′mak″er *n.* **1,** one who sets the pace, as in a race; a leader. **2,** a machine for regulating the heartbeat.

pace′set″ter *n.* pacemaker (def. 1).

pa·chi′si (pa-chē′zè) *n.* a game resembling backgammon, played with counters and dice.

pach′y·derm″ (pak′i-dėrm″) *n.* a thick-skinned quadruped, esp. an elephant or rhinoceros. **—pach″y·der′ma·tous,** *adj.*

pach″y·san′dra (pak″i-san′drə) *n.* an evergreen plant used as a ground cover.

pa·cif′ic (pə-sif′ik) *adj.* peaceable; conciliatory; calm. **—n.** (*cap.*) the Pacific Ocean. **—pa·cif′i·cal·ly,** *adv.* **—Pacific Rim,** countries on the edge of the Pacific Ocean, esp. Japan and the U.S. west coast.

pac′i·fi″er (pas′i-fī″ər) *n.* a simulated nipple for a baby.

pac′i·fism (-fiz-əm) *n.* total opposition to war. **—pac′i·fist,** *n.*

pac′i·fy″ (-fī″) *v.t.* appease; calm. **—pac″i·fi·ca′tion,** *n.*

pack (pak) *n.* **1,** a bundle tied up; a packing; a package, esp. of cards or cigarettes. **2,** a group of persons or animals; a gang. **—v.t. 1,** put in a bundle or a piece of bag-

gage. **2,** compress; cram; fill (a space). **3,** carry, esp. on the back. **4,** (with *off*) send away. **—v.i.** stow personal things for traveling. **—adj.** used to carry things. **—pack animal,** a beast of burden. **—pack rat, 1,** a desert rodent. **2,** a hoarder.

pack′age (-ij) *n.* **1,** a small wrapped bundle. **2,** (*Informal*) a comprehensive plan or proposition. **—v.t.** put into a package, esp. for marketing. **—pack′ag·ing,** *n.* **—package store,** a liquor store.

pack′er (-ər) *n.* one who packs; esp. a wholesale supplier of meat.

pack′et (-it) *n.* **1,** a small, compact bundle or portion. **2,** a small merchant ship.

pack′ing *n.* material for a protective wad.

pack′sack″ *n.* a large knapsack.

pack′sad″dle *n.* a pair of sacks or bags joined by straps and hung over the back of a pack animal.

pack′thread″ *n.* a heavy twine.

Pac-′Man defense (pak′man) a response to a corporate takeover attempt in which the company facing takeover threatens to take over the original predator company.

pact (pakt) *n.* an agreement.

pad *n.* **1,** a small wad of something soft; a cushion. **2,** the soft sole of an animal's paw. **3,** a leaf of a water lily. **4,** a writing tablet. **5,** (*Slang*) quarters where a person lives or sleeps. **6,** (*Slang*) graft. **—v.t.** [**pad′ded, -ding**] **1,** fill out or cushion with pads. **2,** add needless or fraudulent items to. **—v.i.** walk or trot steadily. **—pad′-ding,** *n.*

pad′dle (pad′əl) *n.* a short oar; a similar broad-bladed implement. **—v.i. & t. 1,** propel (a canoe). **2,** dabble (as the feet) in shallow water. **3,** spank. **—paddle wheel,** a large wheel with boards around the rim for propelling a boat (*paddleboat*).

pad′dock (pad′ək) *n.* a small enclosed field near a stable.

pad′dy (pad′ê) *n.* **1,** rice in the husk, either in the field or gathered. **2,** a field where rice is grown.

pad′dy wagon (pad′ê) *n.* an enclosed police truck used to carry prisoners. Also, **Black Maria.**

pa′di·shah″ (pa′di-shä″) *n.* great king; emperor.

pad′lock″ (pad′lok″) *n.* a portable lock with a hinged arm. **—v.t.** fasten with a padlock; close officially.

pad′nag″ *n.* an easygoing saddle horse.

pa′dre (pä′drā) *n.* **1,** a priest. **2,** a chaplain.

pae′an (pē′ən) *n.* a song of joy.

pa·el′la (pä-ā′lə) *n.* (*Sp.*) a type of Sp. stew.

pa′gan (pā′gən) *n.* an idolater. —*adj.* heathenish; irreligious. —**pa′gan·dom,** *n.* —**pa′gan·ism,** *n.* —**pa′gan·ize,** *v.t.* ☐ *heathen*

page (pāj) *n.* **1,** one side of a printed leaf of a book, etc. **2,** a messenger boy, esp. one in an honorary position. —*v.t.* **1,** number the pages of. **2,** summon (a person) from a crowd by calling his or her name. —**pag′er,** *n.* a radio device for paging someone. —**page description language,** (*Computers*) a progamming language used to tell a printer how to print a formatted page.

pag′eant (paj′ənt) *n.* a showy spectacle. —**pag′eant·ry** (-rė) *n.*

page′boy″ *n.* **1,** a page (def. 2). **2,** a hairstyle in which the hair is curled under at the shoulder.

pag′i·nate″ (pag′i-nāt″) *v.t.* number the pages of. —**pag″i·na′tion,** *n.*

pa·go′da (pə-gō′də) *n.* in the Far East, a many-storied tower.

paid (pād) *v.* pret. & p.p. of *pay.*

pail (pāl) *n.* an open vessel for carrying liquids; a bucket.

pain (pān) *n.* **1,** suffering of body or mind. **2,** (*pl.*) great care. —*v.t.* cause suffering to. —**pain′ful,** *adj.*

pain′kill″er *n.* an anesthetic.

pains′tak″ing (pānz′tāk″ing) *adj.* very careful.

paint (pānt) *n.* **1,** a pigmented oil or liquid that forms a coloring or protective coating when dry. **2,** rouge. **3,** a pinto horse. —*v.t.* & *i.* **1,** apply paint (to). **2,** portray, esp. with oil paints on canvas; make paintings. —**paint′er,** *n.* one who paints (houses, etc., or paintings) professionally. —**paint′ing,** *n.* a painted picture.

paint′ball *n.* a type of war-game using paint-pellet airguns.

pair (pār) *n.* **1,** a matched set of two things. **2,** a married couple. **3,** two cards of the same rank. —*v.t.* & *i.* **1,** match (two things). **2,** (often with *off* or *up*) join or go off in couples.

pais′ley (pāz′lė) *n.* & *adj.* a thin, soft woolen fabric.

pa·jam′as (pə-jàm′əz) *n.pl.* loose coat and trousers for sleeping or lounging. Also, *Brit.,* **py·jam′as.**

pal *n.* (*Slang*) friend; chum.

pal′ace (pal′is) *n.* **1,** the residence of a sovereign. **2,** a magnificent building.

---

palace, palatine
↔ From Latin *Palatium*, the Palatine hill in Rome where the emperor Caesar Augustus built a "palatial" house.

---

pal′a·din (pal′ə-din) *n.* a heroic champion.

pal′an·quin′ (pal″ən-kēn′) *n.* a litter borne by several persons.

pal′at·a·ble (pal′ə-tə-bəl) *adj.* tasty; acceptable. —**pal″at·a·bil′i·ty,** *n.*

pal′ate (pal′it) *n.* **1,** the roof of the mouth. **2,** the sense of taste; liking. —**pal′-a·tal,** *adj.*

---

palate, palette, pallet
☛ Three easily confused homonyms. The *palate* is the roof of the mouth. A *palette* is the paint board used by artists. *Pallet* is most often used to mean a platform or bed.

---

pa·la′tial (pə-lā′shəl) *adj.* grand, like (or as in) a palace.

pa·lat′i·nate″ (pə-lat′i-nāt″) *n.* a palatine's state or domain.

pal′a·tine″ (pal′ə-tīn″) *adj.* having royal privileges. —*n.* a palatine nobleman. ☐ *palace*

pa·lav′er (pə-lav′ər) *n.* idle talk; cajolery. —*v.i.* chat.

pale (pāl) *adj.* **1,** wan; lacking color; in a light shade. **2,** faint; lacking brilliance. —*n.* **1,** a pointed stake; picket. **2,** a strictly bounded area. —*v.t.* & *i.* make wan; dim. —**pale′ness,** *n.* —**beyond the pale,** out of bounds.

pale′face″ *n.* (*Slang*) a white person (supposedly so called by Amer. Indians).

pa·le·o- *pref.* **1,** remote in the past. **2,** early; primitive.

pa″le·og′ra·phy (pā″lė-og′rə-fė) *n.* the study of ancient written documents and methods of writing; those methods collectively. —**pa″le·og′ra·pher,** *n.* —**pa″le·o·graph′ic,** *adj.*

Pa″le·o·lith′ic (pā″lė-ə-lith′ik) *adj.* & *n.* (pert. to) the Old Stone Age.

pa″le·on·tol′o·gy (pā″lė-ən-tol′ə-jė) *n.* the scientific study of life in past geologic periods. —**pa″le·on·to·log′i·cal,** *adj.* —**pa″le·on·tol′o·gist,** *n.*

Pa″le·o·zo′ic (pā″lė-ə-zō′ik) *adj.* & *n.* (pert. to) a geological era, the age of invertebrates.

Pal′es·tine″ Liberation Organization (pal′əs-tīn″) an organization of Arab groups dedicated to the recovery of Palestine from Israel.

---

pal′ette (pal′it) *n.* the thin board on which an artist mixes his colors. ❑ *palate*

pal′frey (pâl′frè) *n.* a saddle horse.

pal′i·mo″ny (pal′ə-mō-nè) *n.* money paid by one member of an unmarried partnership to the other after the relationship ends.

pal′imp·sest″ *n.* a parchment from which one writing has been erased to make space for another.

pal′in·drome″ (pal′in-drōm″) *n.* a word or sentence whose letters read the same backward as forward, as *level.*

pal′ing (pāl′ing) *n.* a row of pales; fencing.

pal′i·node″ (pal′ə-nōd″) *n.* a retraction. —*v.* recant. —**pal″in·o′di·al** (-dè-əl) *adj.*

pal″i·sade′ (pal″ə-sād′) *n.* **1,** a fence of pointed stakes. **2,** (*pl.*) a line of sheer cliffs.

pall (pâl) *n.* **1,** a cloth thrown over a coffin. **2,** the coffin. **3,** a gloomy, blanketing effect. —*v.i.* become boring. —*v.t.* satiate; depress.

pal·la′dium (pə-lā′dè-əm) *n.* **1,** a rare metallic element of the platinum group, no. 46, symbol Pd. **2,** any safeguard, esp. of liberty or rights. —**pal·la′dous** (-dəs) *adj.* containing palladium.

> **palladium**
> ↔ The element is named after the meteorite *Pallas*, which in turn is named for the Greek goddess *Pallas* Athena. The sense of safeguard comes from the statue of Athena, the Palladium, which was considered to safeguard the citizens of Troy.

pall′bear″er *n.* a coffin-bearer at a funeral.

pal′let (pal′it) *n.* **1,** a board for drying ceramics, bricks, etc. **2,** palette. **3,** a bed of straw or rags. ❑ *palate*

pal′li·ate″ (pal′è-āt″) *n.* **1,** make excuses for, as a crime. **2,** relieve without curing, as a disease. —**pal″li·a′tion,** *n.* —**pal′li·a″tive,** *n. & adj.*

pal′lid (pal′id) *adj.* pale; wan.

pall-″mall′ (pel″mel′) *n.* an old game in which a wooden ball was driven through a raised ring at the end of an alley; the alley.

pal′lor (pal′ər) *n.* paleness.

palm (päm) *n.* **1,** that surface of the hand toward which the fingers bend; a similar part, as of a glove. **2,** any of various tropical trees. **3,** a leaf of this tree as a symbol of victory. —*v.t.* **1,** conceal in the hand. **2,** (with *off*) get rid of unfairly.

—**Palm Sunday,** the Sunday before Easter, commemorating Christ's entry into Jerusalem.

pal′mate (päl′māte) *adj.* **1,** like a hand with the fingers extended. **2,** web-footed. —**pal·ma′tion,** *n.*

palm′er (-ər) *n.* a pilgrim returning from the Holy Land.

pal·met′to (pal-met′ō) *n.* [*pl.* -tos] a palm tree with fan-shaped leaves.

palm′is·try (pä′mis-trè) *n.* fortune-telling from the markings of the palm. —**palm′ist,** *n.*

palm′y (pä′mè) *adj.* flourishing.

pal″o·mi′no (pal″ə-mē′nō) *n.* [*pl.* -nos] a gray or golden horse, usually with near-white mane and tail, bred in the S.W. U.S.

pa·loo′ka (pə-loo′kə) *n.* (*Slang*) **1,** an inept or clumsy person. **2,** (*Boxing*) an inexperienced or inept boxer.

pal′pa·ble (pal′pə-bəl) *adj.* readily perceived; obvious. —**pal′pa·ble·ness,** *n.*

pal′pate (pal′pāt) *v.t.* examine by touch; manipulate. —**pal·pa′tion,** *n.*

pal′pi·tate″ (pal′pə-tāt″) *v.i.* pulsate; throb. —**pal″pi·ta′tion,** *n.*

pal′pus (pal′pəs) *n.* [*pl.* **-pi** (-pī)] a sense organ of an insect, crustacean, etc. Also, **palp.**

pal′sy (pâl′zè) *n.* paralysis; commonly, uncontrolled shaking. —*v.t.* paralyze. —**pal′sied,** *adj.*

pal′ter (pâl′tər) *v.i.* play false; trifle.

pal′try (pâl′trè) *adj.* worthless; trifling. —**pal′tri·ness,** *n.*

pal′u·dal (pal′yə-dəl) *adj.* marshy.

pam′pas (pam′pəz) *n.pl.* in So. Amer., vast treeless plains. —**pam·pe′an** (pam-pē′ən) *adj.*

pam′per (pam′pər) *v.t.* overindulge; humor.

pam·pe′ro (päm-per′ō) *n.* [*pl.* -ros] a cold, dry wind of Argentina and Brazil.

pam′phlet (pam′flit) *n.* a small printed tract; a booklet. —**pam″phlet·eer′** (-flə-tir′) *n.* a writer of polemical essays.

> **pamphlet**
> ↔ This odd word appears to have originated in a 12th-c. satiric Latin poem, *Pamphilus, seu de Amore,* "Pamphilus, or On Love."

pan *n.* **1,** a hollow vessel for cooking. **2,** any similar shallow vessel. **3,** a depression. —*v.t. & i.* [**panned, pan′ning**] **1,** cook or wash in a pan. **2,** (*Slang*) criticize harshly. **3,** yield gold. **4,** (with *out*) succeed. **5,**

move (a camera) toward or away from its object, or so as to follow a moving object.

pan- *pref.* all; every; united.

pan″a·ce′a (pan″ə-sē′ə) *n.* a remedy for all ills.

pa·nache′ (pə-nash′) *n.* flair; flamboyance.

pa·na′da (pə-nä′də) *n.* (*Sp.*) a bread pudding.

pan′a·ma″ (pan′ə-mä″) *n.* a hat woven of fine-leaf shoots or straws.

Pan-″A·mer′i·can *adj.* embracing all the sovereign countries of the Western Hemisphere; lit., all-American.

pan″a·tel′a (pan″ə-tel′ə) *n.* a cigar that is relatively long and slender. Also, **pan″e·tel′a.**

pan′cake″ (pan′kāk″) *n.* **1,** a thin, fried battercake. **2,** (*Aviation*) an abrupt, almost vertical landing. **3,** a flat facial powder.

pan″chro·mat′ic (pan″krō-mat′ik) *adj.* sensitive to light of all colors.

pan′cre·as (pan′krē-əs) *n.* a large gland secreting a digestive fluid (*pancreatin*); when used as meat, the gland is called *sweetbread.* —**pan″cre·at′ic,** *adj.*

pan′da (pan′də) *n.* **1,** a raccoonlike animal of India. **2,** [*also,* **giant panda**] a bearlike animal of Tibet.

pan·dem′ic (pan-dem′ik) *adj.* **1,** common to or characteristic of a whole people. **2,** affecting a very high proportion of the population (of a country or an area), as a disease. ❏ *endemic*

pan″de·mo′ni·um (pan″də-mō′nē-əm) *n.* a wild, lawless uproar.

---

pandemonium
↔ Coined by English poet John Milton from Greek *pan,* all, and *daimōn,* demon.

---

pan′der (pan′dər) *n.* **1,** one who assists others to gratify their baser passions. **2,** a pimp. —*v.i.* act as a pander.

---

pander
↔ From the character *Pandaro* in Boccaccio's *Filostrato,* who acted as go-between in the affair between Troilus and Cressida.

---

pan′dit *n.* in India, a wise person; scholar.

pan-dow′dy (pan-dow′dē) *n.* a pudding of bread and apples baked together.

pane (pān) *n.* a sheet of glass in a door or window; a rectangular section, as in a ceiling.

pan″e·gyr′ic (pan″ə-jir′ik) *n.* an oration or writing of high praise.

pan′el (pan′əl) *n.* **1,** a flat section, raised or sunken, in a wall, door, etc. **2,** a strip inserted in a skirt. **3,** a list of eligible jurors; a group of speakers. —*v.t.* form with, divide into, or decorate with panels. —**pan′eled,** *adj.* —**pan′el·ing,** *n.* —**panel truck,** a small, fully enclosed truck, usu. used for deliveries.

pan′el·ist (-ist) *n.* a member of a panel; one of several persons who discuss events, play games, etc. on a radio or television show.

pan″e·tel′a (pan″ə-tel′ə) *n.* panatela.

pan-′fry″ *v.t.* fry (food) in a pan, usu. with little or no liquid.

pang *n.* a sudden sharp pain or feeling of emotion.

Pan·gae′a (pan-jē′ə) *n.* a hypothetical land mass consisting of all the continents before they separated.

pan·go′lin (pan-gō′lin) *n.* a scaly anteater of Afr. and Asia.

pan·guin′gue (päng-gēng′gē) *n.* a card game related to rummy.

pan′han″dle *n.* **1,** the handle of a pan. **2,** (often *cap.*) a narrow strip of land extending from a territory. —*v.i. & t.* (*Slang*) beg. —**pan′han″dler** (-dlər) *n.* (*Slang*) a street beggar.

Pan″hel·len′ic (pan″hə-len′ik) *adj.* **1,** embracing all the states of ancient Greece. **2,** representing all fraternities and sororities in a college.

pan′ic (pan′ik) *n.* **1,** a sudden, extreme fright. **2,** rapidly spreading alarm, esp. in financial circles. **3,** (*Informal*) something extremely funny. **4,** any of several species of grass. —*v.t. & i.* affect or be affected with panic. —**pan′ick·y** (-ik-ē) *adj.* —**pan′ic-strick″en, pan′ic-struck″,** *adj.*

pan·jan′drum (pan-jan′drəm) *n.* a pretentious public official.

---

panjandrum
↔ Coined as a pseudo-Latin word by 18th-c. English dramatist Samuel Foote.

---

pan′nier (pan′yər) *n.* a basket, usually of wicker, esp. one of a pair.

pan′o·ply (pan′ə-plē) *n.* **1,** a full set of armor. **2,** splendid array.

pan″o·ram′a (pan″ə-ram′ə) *n.* an unbroken or widely extended view. —**pan″o·ram′ic,** *adj.* —**pan″o·ram′i·cal·ly,** *adv.*

pan′pipe″ *n.* a simple wind instrument consisting of reeds or tubes of graduated length. Also, **Pan's pipes.**

pan′sy (pan′zē) *n.* **1,** a plant of the violet

---

family, with velvety, variously colored flowers. **2,** (*Slang*) a pantywaist.

---

pansy, pantry
↔ Pansies are evidently supposed to convey good thoughts. The word derives from Latin *pensare*, think, through Middle French *pensée*. *Pantry* comes to English by a similar route, from Latin *panis*, bread, through Old French *paneterie*, bread room.

---

pant *v.i.* **1,** breathe deeply and rapidly; throb. **2,** yearn.

pan″ta·lets′ (pan″tə-letz′) *n.pl.* a woman's long drawers.

pan″ta·loons′ (pan″tə-loonz′) *n.pl.* trousers. ❏ *pants*

pant′dress″ *n.* a dress with a divided skirt.

pan′the·ism (pan′thė-iz-əm) *n.* **1,** the doctrine that the existing universe is God. **2,** the worship of all gods. —**pan′the·ist,** *n.* —**pan″the·is′tic,** *adj.* —**pan″the·is′ti·cal·ly,** *adv.*

pan′the·on″ (pan′thė-on″) *n.* **1,** a dedicated building, as a temple or mausoleum. **2,** (*cap.*) a temple of ancient Rome, dedicated to all the gods.

pan′ther (pan′thər) *n.* **1,** a leopard. **2,** the American puma or cougar.

pan′ties (pan′tėz) *n.pl.* (*Informal*) a woman's short drawers.

pan′tile (pan′tīl) *n.* a roofing tile in the shape of a horizontal S.

pan′to·graph″ (pan′tə-gráf″) *n.* **1,** an instrument for copying a drawing to a given scale. **2,** the extensible wire contact on an electric locomotive. —**pan″to·graph′ic,** *adj.* —**pan″to·graph′i·cal·ly,** *adv.*

pan′to·mime″ (pan′tə-mīm″) *n.* acting, or a play, done solely by gestures and facial expressions. —*v.t. & i.* express by pantomime. —**pan″to·mim′ic** (-mim′ik) *adj.*

pan′try (pan′trė) *n.* a small room for storing food and dishes. ❏ *pansy*

pants *n.pl.* (*Informal*) **1,** trousers. **2,** drawers. —**pants role,** a role of a young boy in an opera sung by a woman dressed as a boy.

---

pants, pantaloons
↔ *Pants* is short for *pantaloons*, which comes from the Italian commedia dell'arte character *Pantalone* (or more properly, from his trousers).

---

pant′suit″ *n.* a woman's ensemble of jacket and pants.

pan′ty-hose″ *n.* stockings and panties combined in one garment worn by women.

pan′ty-waist″ *n.* **1,** a child's undergarment. **2,** (*Slang*) a childish or timorous person; an effeminate man.

pan′zer (pan′zər) *adj.* (*Ger.*) armored, as a division of troops.

pap *n.* a soft food for babies or invalids.

pa′pa (pä′pə) *n.* **1,** father. **2,** (*Communications*) the letter *p*.

pa′pa·cy (pä′pə-sė) *n.* the office, term, jurisdiction, or institution of the Pope. —**pa′pal,** *adj.*

pa·pa·raz′zo (pä-pä-rät′sō) *n.* a freelance photographer specializing in photographing celebrities for publication.

---

paparazzo
↔ From a character in Federico Fellini's film *La Dolce Vita.*

---

pa·paw′ (pâ-pâ′) *n.* pawpaw.

pa·pa′ya (pə-pä′yə) *n.* a tropical tree or its sweet, juicy fruit.

pa′per (pä′pər) *n.* **1,** a thin, flexible material made in sheets of pressed wood pulp, rag fiber, etc. **2,** a newspaper. **3,** an essay; article. **4,** a document; (*pl.*) credentials. **5,** bank notes; bills of exchange. —*adj.* of or on paper. —*v.t.* **1,** cover with wallpaper. **2,** fill (a theater) with an unpaying audience. —**pa′per·y,** *adj.* —**paper clip,** a metal clip for holding sheets of paper together. —**paper nautilus,** a variety of thin-shelled sea mollusk. —**paper tiger,** an individual or organization apparently powerful but in reality weak or ineffectual. —**paper trail,** a sequence of documents providing written evidence of an action, etc.

pap′er·back″ *adj.* bound with paper, instead of cardboard, etc. —*n.* a paperback book.

pa′per·board″ *n.* cardboard.

pa′per·hang″er *n.* **1,** one who hangs wallpaper as a trade. **2,** (*Slang*) a passer of bad checks.

pa′per·weight″ *n.* a weight to hold down loose papers.

pa′per·work″ *n.* the writing or processing of records, reports, etc.

pa″pier-mâ·ché′ (pä″pər-mə-shā′) *n.* a plastic material of ground or compressed paper.

---

papier-mâché
↔ The term was probably coined from French elements, not by the French, but by the English. It means, literally, mashed paper.

---

pa·pil′la (pə-pil′ə) *n.* [*pl.* **-lae** (-ė)] a small nipplelike projection. —**pap′il·lar·y** (pap′ə-ler-ė) *adj.*

---

fat, fāte, fär, fāre, fâll, ȧsk; met, hē, hėr, maybė; pin, pīne; not, nōte, ôr, tool

pa·pil·lon′ (pä-pē-yôń′) (*Fr.*) *n.* a breed of toy dog related to the spaniel.

pap′il·lote″ (pap′ə-lōt″) *n.* **1,** a curl-paper used by women to hold their hair in place. **2,** (pä-pē-yōt′) a frilled ring of paper used to decorate a lamb chop. **3,** (pä-pē-yōt′) a piece of greased paper or foil in which food is cooked.

pa′pist (pā′pist) *n.* one who favors Roman Catholicism or papal supremacy.

pa·poose′ (pa-poos′) *n.* a No. Amer. Indian baby.

pa′pri·ka (pä′pri-kä) *n.* a mild red pepper.

Pap test a test to detect cancer in smears of various bodily secretions, esp. from the cervix and the vagina, named for U.S. scientist George Papanicolaou, who developed the test. Also, **Pap smear.**

pap′u·la (pap′yə-lə) *n.* [*pl.* **-lae** (-lė)] a pimple. Also, **pap′ule** (-ūl). —**pap′u·lar,** *adj.*

pa·py′rus (pə-pī′rəs) *n.* a paper made by the ancient Egyptians from the papyrus plant; a manuscript written on it.

par (pär) *n.* **1,** full or nominal value of money, stocks, etc. **2,** equal footing. **3,** an accepted standard; (*Golf*) a score for each hole based on length and two putts for the green.

para- *pref.* **1,** beside; beyond. **2,** (*Med.*) faulty; abnormal. **3,** guarding against.

par′a·ble (par′ə-bəl) *n.* a fictitious story pointing a moral.

pa·rab′o·la (pə-rab′ə-lə) *n.* a curve formed by the intersection of a cone by a plane parallel to its side. —**par″ə·bol′ic** (par″ə-bol′ik) *adj.*

par′a·chute″ (par′ə-shoot″) *n.* an apparatus to retard the speed of a falling body. —*v.i.* descend by parachute. —**par′a·chut″ist,** *n.*

Par′a·clete″ (par′ə-klēt″) *n.* the Holy Ghost or Holy Spirit.

pa·rade′ (pə-rād′) *n.* **1,** a formal procession; troops assembled for review. **2,** a display; a passing in review. —*v.t. & i.* pass in review.

par′a·digm″ (par′ə-dīm″) *n.* **1,** (*Gram.*) a list of the inflected forms of a word. **2,** pattern; model.

par′a·dise″ (par′ə-dīs″) *n.* **1,** heaven. **2,** a place of extreme beauty or of supreme happiness. **3,** (*cap.*) the garden of Eden. —**par″a·dis′i·ac** (-dis′ē-ak) *adj.*

par′a·dox″ (par′ə-doks″) *n.* **1,** a seemingly absurd but possibly true statement. **2,** something self-contradictory. —**par″a·dox′i·cal,** *adj.*

par′af·fin (par′ə-fin) *n.* **1,** an odorless, waxy substance used for candles, sealing, etc. **2,** (*Brit.*) kerosene. Also, **par′af·fine.**

par′a·foil″ (par′ə-foil″) *n.* an inflatable wing-shaped structure used as a kite or parachute.

par′a·glid″er *n.* a parachute used for re-entering spacecraft, etc.

par′a·gon″ (par′ə-gon″) *n.* a model of perfection.

par′a·graph″ (par′ə-gråf″) *n.* **1,** a separate section of a writing, usually having an indented first line, or marked by the sign ¶. **2,** a brief item, as in a newspaper.

par′a·keet″ (par′ə-kēt″) *n.* a small, long-tailed parrot.

par·al′de·hyde″ (pə-ral′də-hīd″) *n.* a liquid used as a sedative and hypnotic.

par′al·lax″ (par′ə-laks″) *n.* the apparent shifting of an object when the observer's position changes.

par″a·le′gal *adj. & n.* (someone) trained but not fully licensed in law.

par′al·lel″ (par′ə-lel″) *adj.* **1,** of lines or planes, never intersecting; equidistant at all points. **2,** similar; analogous. **3,** (*Computers*) pert. to the transmission of data one word at a time. —*n.* **1,** something parallel or similar to another. **2,** comparison. **3,** one of the imaginary lines indicating degrees of latitude. —*v.t.* **1,** compare. **2,** run parallel to. **3,** correspond to. —**par′al·lel′ism,** *n.* —**parallel circuit,** a circuit in which each device receives its current independently of others on the same circuit. —**parallel processing,** the simultaneous use in a computer of multiple processors to achieve the solution of a problem.

par″al·lel′e·pi′ped (-ə-pī′pid) *n.* a solid figure with six sides, all parallelograms.

par″al·lel′o·gram″ (-ə-gram″) *n.* a quadrilateral whose opposite sides are parallel.

pa·ral′y·sis (pə-ral′ə-sis) *n.* complete or partial loss of power to feel or move. —**par″a·lyt′ic** (par″ə-lit′ik) *adj. & n.*

par′a·lyze″ (par′ə-līz″) *v.t.* **1,** affect with paralysis. **2,** render helpless or ineffective.

par″a·me′ci·um (pa″rə-mē′shė-əm) *n.* [*pl.* **-ci·a** (-shė-ə)] a slipper-shaped protozoan.

par″a·med′i·cal *adj. & n.* (pert. to) a person who assists a physician. Also, **par″a·med′ic.**

pa·ram′e·ter (pə-ram′ə-tər) *n.* **1,** (*Math.*) a variable quantity whose values depend on the special case. **2,** a basic factor in determining the nature of a system.

par″a·mil′i·tar″y *adj.* being supplementary to regular military forces.

par′a·mount″ (par′ə-mownt″) *adj.* superior to all others.

par′a·mour″ (par′ə-mûr″) *n.* a lover, esp. an illicit one.

par′ang *n.* a large knife used by Malays.

par″a·noi′a (par″ə-noi′ə) *n.* insanity marked by delusions of grandeur or persecution. **—par′a·noid,** *n. & adj.* **—par″a·noi′ac,** *n.*

par′a·pet (par′ə-pət) *n.* **1,** (*Mil.*) a rampart; breastwork. **2,** a low wall at the edge of a balcony, bridge, etc.

par″a·pher·nal′ia (par″ə-fər-nāl′yə) *n.pl.* **1,** personal belongings. **2,** equipment; trappings.

> **paraphernalia**
> ↔ From Greek *parapherna*, a married woman's property excluding her marriage dowry.

par′a·phrase″ (par′ə-frāz″) *n.* an expression of the same meaning in other words. **—***v.t. & i.* restate.

par′a·ple′gi·a (par″ə-plē′jē-ə) *n.* paralysis from the waist down. **—par″a·pleg′ic** (-plē′jik) *n. & adj.*

par′a·pro·fes′sion·al *adj. & n.* (pert. to) one who assists a professional.

par″a·psy·chol′o·gy *n.* the study of phenomena not explainable by accepted laws of nature.

par′a·sail″ *n.* a type of parachute.

par′a·sail″ing *n.* the sport of soaring using a parasail towed by a land- or water-based vehicle.

par′a·sang″ (par′ə-sang″) *n.* an ancient Persian measure, about 3½ miles.

par′a·site″ (par′ə-sīt″) *n.* **1,** an organism that lives in or on another (called the *host*) from which it receives its nutrition. **2,** a person who lives at the expense of another. **—par″a·sit′ic** (-sit′ik), **par″a·sit′i·cal,** *adj.*

par′a·sol″ (par′ə-sâl″) *n.* a light umbrella used as a dainty sunshade.

par″a·thy′roid *adj.* designating any of four small hormone-producing glands beside the thyroid gland. **—***n.* an extract of these glands, or their secretions, used in treating tetany.

par′a·troop″er (par′ə-troo″pər) *n.* a soldier dropped by parachute, esp. in enemy territory. **—par′a·troops″,** *n.pl.*

par′a·vane″ (par′ə-vān″) *n.* a device to protect vessels against mines.

par′boil″ (pär′boil″) *v.t.* **1,** cook partially in boiling water. **2,** overheat.

par′cel (pär′səl) *n.* **1,** a package. **2,** a small piece, as of land. **3,** an integral part: *part and parcel.* **—***v.t.* separate and dole out. **—parcel post,** postal transmission of packages.

parch (pärch) *v.t. & i.* **1,** dry out by heat. **2,** shrivel; dry up.

Par·chee′si (pär-chē′zē) *n.* (*T.N.*) an adaptation of the game of pachisi.

parch′ment (-mənt) *n.* sheep- or goatskin prepared to take writing; paper resembling it; a document written on it.

> **parchment**
> ↔ From Greek *Pergamenos*, of Pergamum, a city in ancient Turkey, where the material was supposedly first used.

pard (pärd) *n.* **1,** leopard. **2,** (*Slang*) partner.

par′don (pär′dən) *v.t.* excuse; forgive, as a person or offense; free (a person) from penalty. **—***n.* a release from punishment. **—par′don·a·ble,** *adj.*

pare (pâr) *v.t.* **1,** cut or shave off the skin or edge of. **2,** reduce.

par″e·gor′ic (par″ə-gor′ik) *n.* a medicine for relieving pain or diarrhea. **—***adj.* relieving pain.

par′ent (pār′ənt) *n.* **1,** a father or mother; a progenitor. **2,** a cause; source. **—***v.t.* (*Informal*) to act as parent of. **—par′ent″ing,** *n.* **—par′ent·age** (-tij) *n.* **—pa·ren′tal** (pə-ren′təl) *adj.* **—par′ent·hood″,** *n.*

pa·ren′the·sis (pə-ren′thə-sis) *n.* [*pl.* **-ses** (-sēz)] **1,** an inserted explanatory word, phrase, clause, etc. **2,** either of the curves ( ) enclosing insertions. **—par″en·thet′i·cal,** *adj.*

> **parentheses**
> (*Gram.*) Parentheses are for setting off inserted (parenthetical) material. In some cases they are similar in function to commas and dashes, but parentheses are more formal and the material they enclose is usually more distantly related to the rest of the sentence. They are also used for specialized purposes, such as enclosing corrections or errors in quoted matter, enclosing letters or numbers indicating divisions, and enclosing question marks or exclamation points used to express an editorial opinion.

pa·re′sis (pə-rē′sis) *n.* partial paralysis. **—pa·ret′ic** (-ret′ik) *adj. & n.*

par ex″cel′lence′ (pär ek″sə-läns′) (*Fr.*) above all others; preeminent.

par·fait' (pär-fā') *n.* **1,** a frozen dessert of whipped cream, egg, etc. **2,** ice cream in a glass with a flavored syrup and whipped cream.

pa·ri·ah (pə-rī'ə) *n.* an outcast.

pa·ri·e·tal (pə-rī'ə-təl) *adj.* **1,** pert. to a wall-like structure, esp. the sides of the skull. **2,** resident within, or having charge over, the walls or buildings of a college. —*n.* (*pl.*) the rules of conduct for a dormitory, etc.

par'i·mu'tu·el (par'ė-mū'choo-əl) *n.* (usu. *pl.*) method of dividing money bet on horse races, etc., among winning bettors.

par'ing (pãr'ing) *n.* something pared off; slice; peel.

pa'ri pas'su (pä'rė pä'soo) (*Lat.*) at an equal rate.

Par'is green a poisonous green powder used as a pigment and as an insecticide.

par'ish *n.* **1,** the district under a clergy's care. **2,** a county.

pa·rish'ion·er (pə-rish'ən-ər) *n.* a member of a church parish.

par'i·ty (par'ə-tė) *n.* equality; equality with or equivalence to a fixed value or standard.

park (pärk) *n.* **1,** ground set apart for public use, esp. for recreation or sports. **2,** the grounds adjoining a country house. —*v.t. & i.* **1,** leave (an automobile) temporarily on a street or in a lot. **2,** temporary investment in securities considered unlikely to lose value. —**industrial park,** an area zoned for industrial and business use and characterized by coordinated building or plant design.

par'ka (pär'kə) *n.* a shirtlike coat made of fur or fleece-lined wool, usually hooded.

Par'kin·son's disease (pär'kin-sunz) a progressive nervous disorder, named for the 19th-c. English physician James Parkinson, who first described it.

Par'kin·son's law the opinion, expressed facetiously as if a natural law, that work expands to fill the amount of time available for it, formulated by English author C.N. Parkinson.

park'way" *n.* a wide, landscaped thoroughfare.

par'lance (pär'ləns) *n.* way of speaking; language.

par·lay' (pär-lā') *v.t.&i.* bet a previously won bet and its winnings. —*n.* (pär'lā) such a bet.

par'ley (pär'lė) *n.* a conference, esp. between hostile parties. —*v.i.* confer; hold a parley.

par'lia·ment (pär'lə-mənt) *n.* a legislative assembly, esp. (*cap.*) of Great Britain.

---

parliament
↔ From French *parler*, talk, through *parlement*, legislative body.

---

par"lia·men'ta·ry (-men'tə-rė) *adj.* pert. to the rules of procedure of legislative bodies. —**par"lia·men·tar'i·an** (-tär'ė-ən) *n.* one versed in such procedure.

par'lor (pär'lər) *n.* **1,** a reception or lounging room. **2,** a private meeting or dining room in a hotel, etc.; a shop. Also, **par'lour.** —**parlor car,** an extra-fare railroad car.

par'lor·maid" *n.* housemaid.

par'lous (pär'ləs) *adj.* dangerous.

Par"me·san' cheese (pär"mə-zän') a dry Ital. cheese made from skim milk.

Parmesan cheese
↔ From Italian *parmigiano*, pertaining to Parma, Italy.

Par·nas'sus (pär-nas'əs) *n.* a center of, or inspiration for, poetic or artistic works.

pa·ro'chi·al (pə-rō'kė-əl) *adj.* **1,** pert. to a parish. **2,** local; provincial. —**parochial school,** one maintained by a church parish, esp. Rom. Cath.

par'o·dy (par'ə-dė) *n.* a humorous imitation of an author's or artist's style; a burlesque. —*v.t.* imitate (an author, etc.) in a derisive manner. —**par'o·dist,** *n.*

pa·role' (pə-rōl') *n.* **1,** a prisoner's promise not to escape. **2,** a conditional release from prison. —*v.t.* release on parole.

pa·rot'id (pə-rot'id) *adj.* **1,** designating either of two salivary glands adjacent to the ears. **2,** near the ears.

par'ox·ysm (par'ək-siz-əm) *n.* a spasm; violent outburst.

par·quet' (pär-kā') *n.* **1,** [also, **par'quet·ry** (-ki-trė)] inlaid flooring of different woods. **2,** the main floor of a theater.

par'ri·cide" (par'ə-sīd") *n.* the killer or killing of one's parent.

par'rot (par'ət) *n.* **1,** a tropical bird of brilliant plumage, capable of imitating speech. **2,** one who echoes the words of another. —*v.t.* imitate.

par'ry (par'ė) *v.t.* turn aside; ward off. —*n.* a warding off.

parse (pärs) *v.t.* resolve (a sentence) into its grammatical parts.

---

par'sec'' (pär'sek'') *n.* a unit of distance, about 3.26 light-years.

Par'see (pär'sē) *n.* a member of a Zoroastrian sect in India.

par'si·mo'ny (pär'sə-mō'nē) *n.* excessive frugality. —**par''si·mo'ni·ous,** *adj.* stingy.

pars'ley (pärs'lē) *n.* an herb with aromatic leaves used as a garnish and seasoning.

pars'nip (pärs'nip) *n.* a plant with a white, edible root.

par'son (pär'sən) *n.* a member of the clergy; preacher.

> **parson, person**
> ↔ These two words were once the same word, deriving from Latin *persona,* character, human being. The reason for the split into two words is unknown.

par'son·age (-ij) *n.* the residence of a member of the clergy, provided by the church.

part (pärt) *n.* **1,** a piece of a whole; a section; an essential element, as of a machine. **2,** a person's share or duty. **3,** a role, as in a play. **4,** in music, the melody assigned to any voice or instrument. **5,** a side in a dispute. **6,** (*pl.*) abilities. **7,** a division in the hair. —*v.t.* **1,** divide into sections. **2,** separate; hold apart. —*v.i.* **1,** become separated or sundered. **2,** (with *with*) let go. —**part'i·ble,** *adj.* —**part'ing,** *n.* —**part and parcel,** an integral part. —**part of speech,** a classification of the form or function of a word, as noun, adjective, etc. —**part song,** a choral composition, usu. in four parts and unaccompanied.

par·take' (pär-tāk') *v.i.* [-**took'**, -**tak'en**] have or take a share.

par·terre' (pär-tār') *n.* **1,** the rear of a theater's main floor. **2,** an ornamental pattern of flower beds.

par''the·no·gen'e·sis (pär''thə-nō-jen'ə-sis) *n.* reproduction from an unfertilized egg.

par'tial (pär'shəl) *adj.* **1,** affecting a part only; not total. **2,** (with *to*) having a liking for. **3,** biased. —*n.* an overtone. —**par''ti·al'i·ty** (-shē-al'ə-tē) *n.*

par'ti·ceps cri'mi·nis (pär'tə-seps krim'ə-nis) (*Law*) accomplice in crime.

par·tic'i·pant (pär-tis'ə-pənt) *n.* one who participates.

par·tic'i·pate'' (pär-tis'ə-pāt') *v.i.* have a share; take part in something. —**par·tic''i·pa'tion,** *n.*

par'ti·ci''ple (pär'tə-sip''əl) *n.* a part of a verb which functions as an adjective. —**par''ti·cip'i·al,** (-ē-əl) *adj.*

par'ti·cle (pär'tə-kəl) *n.* **1,** a minute piece or amount. **2,** (*Gram.*) a small word other than a noun or verb, as an article (*the*), conjunction, etc.

par'ti·col''ored (pär'tē-kul''ərd) *adj.* variegated.

par·tic'u·lar (pər-tik'yə-lər) *adj.* **1,** belonging or relating to a single person, place, or thing; not general. **2,** apart from others; separate. **3,** unusual; notable. **4,** detailed; careful. **5,** nice; fastidious. —*n.* an item; detail. —**par·tic''u·lar'i·ty** (-lar'ə-tē) *n.* —**par·tic'u·lar·ize'',** *v.t.* specify in detail. —**par·tic'u·lar·ly,** *adv.* especially; specifically.

par·tic'u·late (pär-tik'yə-lət) *adj.* consisting of separate particles.

par'ti·san (pär'tə-zən) *n.* **1,** an adherent, often biased, of a party or cause. **2,** a guerrilla. —*adj.* **1,** pert. or belonging to a political party. **2,** biased. —**par''ti·san·ship'',** *n.*

par·ti'tion (pär-tish'ən) *n.* **1,** division; separation. **2,** that which separates, esp. a dividing wall. —*v.t.* **1,** divide by a partition. **2,** divide into shares.

par'ti·tive (pär'ti-tiv) *adj.* **1,** serving to divide into parts. **2,** indicating a part, as *some.* —*n.* a partitive word.

part'ly (pärt'lē) *adv.* in part; in some degree; not wholly.

part'ner (pärt'nər) *n.* one who is associated with another, as in business, dancing, marriage, etc.

part'ner·ship'' *n.* **1,** the state of being partners. **2,** a business firm of partners, not incorporated. ❑ *firm*

par'tridge (pär'trij) *n.* a game bird; the quail; ruffed grouse.

part-'time'' *adj.* requiring less than the usual working time.

par''tu·ri'tion (pär''tyû-rish'ən) *n.* childbirth. —**par·tur'i·ent** (-rē-ənt) *adj.*

par'ty (pär'tē) *n.* **1,** a body of persons; a detachment of troops; an organization of persons acting together politically. **2,** a person concerned in some action, as a contract; (*Informal*) a person. **3,** a social gathering. —**party line, 1,** a telephone line shared by different houses. **2,** the dogma of a political party. —**party wall,** a wall common to two houses.

par've·nu'' (pär'və-nū'') *n.* (*Fr.*) an upstart; one newly rich.

par'vis (pär'vis) *n.* an outer court, front yard, porch, or portico of a church, palace, etc.; a room over such a porch.

pas (pä) *n.* (*Fr.*) a step in dancing; a dance.

pas·cal' (pas·kal') *n.* **1,** a unit of pressure. **2,** (*cap.*) a computer language.

> **pascal, paschal**
> ↔ *Pascal* refers to the 17th-c. French philosopher and mathematician Blaise *Pascal.* The adjective *paschal* comes from the Aramaic word for Passover.

pas'chal (pas'kəl) *adj.* pert. to Easter, or to the Passover. ❏ *pascal*

pa'sha (pä'shə) *n.* a Turkish title of authority. Also, **pa'cha.** —**pa·sha'lik** (pə-shä'lik) *n.* territory governed by a pasha.

pas'quin (pas'kwin) *n.* a lampoon; satire. Also, **pas"quin·ade'** (-kwə-nād').

pass (pås) *v.i.* **1,** move from one place or condition to another. **2,** vanish; (often with *away* or *on*) die. **3,** be enacted, as a law. **4,** undergo a test or pursue a course of study successfully. **5,** occur; happen. **6,** (with *on*) pronounce an opinion. **7,** go by unnoticed. **8,** be accepted at face value. **9,** take no action; decline to bid. —*v.t.* **1,** go by or over. **2,** spend, as time. **3,** undergo successfully. **4,** gain the approval of; give legal effect to. **5,** utter; pronounce. **6,** hand over; transfer. —*n.* **1,** an act of passing. **2,** a defile in the mountains. **3,** state of affairs, as a *sorry pass.* **4,** a free ticket; (*Mil.*) a written leave of absence. **5,** (*Slang*) a feinted blow. **6,** (*Slang*) an amorous advance. —**bring to pass,** cause to happen. —**come to pass,** happen. —**pass muster,** be found up to standard. —**pass out,** (*Informal*) faint. —**pass the buck,** shift responsibility.

> **passed, past**
> (*Gram.*) The past tense and past participle of *pass* is *passed. Past* was originally a variant of *passed.*

pass'a·ble *adj.* **1,** navigable; traversable. **2,** only fairly good.

pas"sa·cag'li·a (pä"sə-kä'lyə) *n.* a musical composition on a ground bass.

pas'sage (pas'ij) *n.* **1,** a passing or moving. **2,** a means of passing, as a channel, alley, etc. **3,** a voyage, usu. by sea; accommodations for it. **4,** an excerpt from a book, speech, etc. **5,** enactment, as of a law. **6,** an interchange, as of vows, blows, etc. **7,** lapse, as of time.

pas'sage·way" *n.* passage (def. 2).

pass'book" *n.* a bank book.

pas·sé' (p̄.-sā') *adj.* outmoded.

pas'sel (pas'əl) *n.* (*Dial.*) a large number.

pas'sen·ger (pas'ən-jər) *n.* a traveler on some form of conveyance. —**passenger-mile,** *n.* one passenger transported one mile.

passe" par·tout' (pas pär-too') (*Fr.*) **1,** a means by which one can pass anywhere, as a master key. **2,** a picture mounting.

pass"er·by' *n.* [*pl.* **pass"ers·by'**] one who happens to go by.

pas'ser·ine (pas'ər-in) *adj. & n.* pert. to or belonging to the order of perching birds, embracing more than half of all birds.

pass-'fail' *adj.* of a grading system employing only two levels of achievement, pass or fail.

pas'sim (pas'im) *adv.* (*Lat.*) at different places; here and there.

pass'ing *n.* death. —*adj.* **1,** now happening; current. **2,** cursory. **3,** fleeting. —**passing note,** (*Music*) a transitional, unaccented note, not a part of the harmony.

pas'sion (pash'ən) *n.* **1,** intense emotion: anger; rage; ardent love; zeal; enthusiasm. **2,** the object of admiration. **3,** (*cap.*) the sufferings of Christ in his last days, in preparation for the Crucifixion. —**pas'sion·ate** (-ət) *adj.* —**Passion play, 1,** a dramatic representation of scenes from the Passion of Jesus. **2,** similar dramatic treatment of the suffering and death of a famous religious or spiritual leader.

pas'sive (pas'iv) *adj.* **1,** unresisting; not opposing. **2,** not acting, but acted upon; (*Gram.*) naming that form of a transitive verb in which the subject is acted upon. —**pas'sive·ness,** *n.* —**passive restraint,** a safety device activated automatically to protect a passenger in a vehicle in case of collision.

pas·siv'i·ty (pə-siv'ə-tē) *n.* unresisting acceptance.

pass'key" *n.* a master key.

Pass'o"ver *n.* the feast of unleavened bread (Ex. 12).

pass'port" *n.* **1,** official permission to travel. **2,** a means to an end. **3,** a document of identification.

pass'word" *n.* a secret word to distinguish friend from foe or to prove authorization to enter.

past (påst) *adj.* **1,** gone by in time. **2,** just gone by. **3,** no longer in office. **4,** (*Gram.*) indicating a time gone by. —*n.* **1,** bygone time; events of that time. **2,** a person's past history, esp. a discreditable one. —*prep.* beyond in time, position, or condition. —*adv.* by. —**past master, 1,** a Freemason. **2,** an expert. ❏ *passed*

pas'ta (päs'tə) *n.* a dough of flour and water, shaped, and dried, usu. cooked by boiling.

paste (pāst) *n.* **1,** an adhesive substance, usually one containing starch. **2,** dough for pastry or macaroni, etc. **3,** a material ground to a creamy consistency. **4,** a compound used for making artificial gems. —*v.t.* **1,** cause to adhere with paste. **2,** (*Slang*) wallop.

paste'board" *n.* **1,** a board made from paper pasted or pressed together. **2,** (*Slang*) a ticket or playing card. —*adj.* flimsy; unsubstantial.

pas·tel' *n.* a pale and light shade of color; a drawing with pastel crayons.

pas'tern (pas'tərn) *n.* the part of a horse's foot between the fetlock and the hoof.

pas'teur·ize" (pas'tə-rīz") *v.t.* partially sterilize a liquid, as milk, by heating it. —**pas"teur·i·za'tion,** *n.*

> **pasteurize**
> ↔ From the 19th-c. French chemist Louis *Pasteur*, who invented a method for sterilization of milk.

pas·tiche' (pas-tēsh') *n.* a medley, combining various works or styles; potpourri. Also, **pas·tic'cio** (-tē'chō).

pas·tille' (pas-tēl') *n.* **1,** a cone of incense. **2,** a medicated lozenge.

pas'time" (pås'tīm") *n.* an agreeable occupation; amusement.

pas'tor (pås'tər) *n.* a minister in charge of a parish; a member of the clergy. —**pas'tor·ate** (-ət) *n.*

pas'tor·al (-əl) *adj.* **1,** pert. to the duties of a pastor. **2,** pert. to shepherds or country life. —*n.* a work, esp. a poem, dealing with country life.

pas"to·rale' (pas"tə-räl') *n.* a musical composition suggestive of rustic life.

pas·tra'mi (pəs-trä'mē) *n.* smoked, highly seasoned beef.

pas'try (pās'trē) *n.* food with a shortened crust, as pies, patties, etc.

pas'ture (pås'chər) *n.* grassland for grazing cattle. —*v.t.* put to graze. —**pas'tur·age** (-ij) *n.*

past'y (pās'tē) *adj.* **1,** of or like paste. **2,** pale. —*n.* **1,** a meat pie. **2,** a patch used by exotic dancers to cover the nipple. —**past'i·ness,** *n.*

pat *v.t.* [**pat'ted, -ting**] tap or stroke gently with the hand. —*n.* **1,** a light blow. **2,** a small molded mass. —*adj.* [**pat'ter, -test**] apt. —*adv.* exactly.

pat-'a-cake" (pat'ə-kāk") *n.* a children's game played to a nursery rhyme. Also, **pat'ty-cake".**

patch (pach) *n.* **1,** a piece of cloth, metal, etc., used to cover a hole or worn place. **2,** a small piece, as a plot of ground. —*v.t.* **1,** mend with a patch. **2,** (with *up*) repair; reconcile. —**patch test,** a skin test for tuberculosis. —**patch'y,** *adj.*

patch'board" *n.* a board allowing interconnection of various electrical or electronic devices in different combinations.

patch'cord" *n.* an electrical wire used for connections on a patchboard.

patch'work" *n.* something made up of fragments of different kinds, colors, or shapes.

pate (pāt) *n.* the top of the head.

pâ·té' (pä-tā') *n.* **1,** an appetizer made of chopped liver. **2,** a pasty (def. 1). —**pâté de foie gras** (-də fwä grä') a paste made of fat goose livers.

pa·tel'la (pə-tel'ə) *n.* the kneecap.

pat'en (pat'ən) *n.* the plate holding consecrated bread.

pat'ent (pat'ənt; pā'-) *n.* an official document (*letters patent*) granting a privilege, esp. a temporary monopoly to an inventor. —*adj.* **1,** open for all to read; plain; obvious. **2,** patented. —*v.t.* obtain a patent for. —**pat"ent·ee'** (pat"ən-tē') *n.* one to whom a patent is issued. —**patent leather,** a leather or coated fabric with a hard, glossy surface. —**patent medicine,** a packaged medicine with patented name.

pa'ter (pā'tər) *n.* **1,** paternoster. **2,** father. —**pa"ter·fa·mil'i·as** (-fə-mil'ē-əs) *n.* head of a household.

pa·ter'nal (pə-tēr'nəl) *adj.* **1,** fatherly. **2,** inherited from, or related through, a father.

pa·ter'nal·ism (-iz-əm) *n.* excessive governmental regulation. —**pa·ter'nal·is"tic,** *adj.* —**pa·ter"nal·is'ti·cal·ly,** *adv.*

pa·ter'ni·ty (pə-tēr'nə-tē) *n.* male parentage; fatherhood.

pa'ter·nos"ter (pā'tər-nos"tər) *n.* a prayer, esp. the Lord's Prayer.

path (påth) *n.* **1,** a footway; any road. **2,** course; track. —**path'way",** *n.*

pa·thet'ic (pə-thet'ik) *adj.* exciting pity. —**pa·thet'i·cal·ly,** *adv.* —**pathetic fallacy,** ascription of human attributes to inanimate objects.

path'find"er *n.* a pioneer.

-path·ic *suf.* disease.

path·o- (path-ə) *pref.* disease.

path'o·gen' (path'ə-jən) *n.* a cause of disease. —**path"o·gen'ic** (path"ə-jen'ik) *adj.* causing disease.

pa·thol′o·gy (pə-thol′ə-jē) *n.* the science of the nature and origin of disease. —**path″o·log′i·cal,** *adj.* —**pa·thol′o·gist,** *n.*

pa′thos (pā′thos) *n.* a quality that evokes pity or sadness. ❑ *bathos*

-path·y (pə-thē) *suf.* **1,** feeling. **2,** disease.

pa′tience (pā′shəns) *n.* **1,** endurance of pain or provocation without complaint. **2,** the power to wait calmly. **3,** perseverance. **4,** (*Cards*) solitaire.

pa′tient (pā′shənt) *adj.* having patience. —*n.* a person under medical care.

pat′i·na (pat′ə-nə; pə-tē′nə) *n.* a film that forms on a surface, esp. of bronze; a mellowing due to age.

pa′ti·o″ (pȧ′tē-ō″) *n.* a courtyard.

pat′ois (pat′wä) *n.* a dialect. ❑ *argot*

pat·ri- (pat-rə) *pref.* father.

pa′tri·arch″ (pā′trē-ärk″) *n.* **1,** a father or ruler of a tribe. **2,** a high church dignitary. **3,** a venerable old man. —**pa′tri·ar′chal,** *adj.* —**pa′tri·ar″chate** (-kit) *n.* —**pa′tri·ar″chy,** *n.* government by the father or fathers.

pa·tri′cian (pə-trish′ən) *n.* an aristocrat. —*adj.* of noble birth.

pat′ri·cide″ (pat′rə-sīd″) *n.* one who kills his or her father; such a killing. —**pat″ri·cid′al** (-əl) *adj.*

pat′ri·mon″y (pat′rə-mō″nē) *n.* **1,** an inheritance from any ancestor. **2,** the endowment of a church. —**pat″ri·mo′ni·al,** *adj.*

pa′tri·ot (pā′trē-ət) *n.* one who loves and defends his or her country. —**pa″tri·ot′ic** (-ot′ik) *adj.* —**pa″tri·ot′i·cal·ly,** *adv.* —**pa′tri·ot·ism,** *n.*

pa·trol′ (pə-trōl′) *v.t. & i.* [**pa·trolled′, -trol′ling**] traverse as a guard. —*n.* **1,** the act of patrolling; a person or troop that patrols. **2,** a unit of Boy Scouts, etc. —**pa·trol′man** (-mən) [*pl.* **-men**], **pa·trol′wom″an,** *n.* a police officer. —**patrol wagon,** a police vehicle for transporting prisoners; Black Maria.

pa′tron (pā′trən) *n.* **1,** an influential supporter or donor. **2,** a guardian saint. **3,** a regular customer of a shop. —**patron saint,** a saint considered to have a special interest in a person, organization, etc.

> **patron, pattern**
> ↔ These seemingly unrelated words both come from Latin *pater*, father, and did not develop their separate senses and spellings until the 17th c.

pa′tron·age (-ij) *n.* **1,** support; favor. **2,**

customers. **3,** the power to appoint jobholders.

pa′tron·ize″ (-īz″) *v.t.* **1,** give one's support or custom to. **2,** treat with condescension.

pat″ro·nym′ic (pat″rə-nim′ik) *n.* a surname. —*adj.* being or pert. to a surname.

pat′sy (pat′sē) *n.* (*Slang*) the unwitting victim of a scheme, plot, or practical joke; a dupe; gull.

pat′ten (pat′ən) *n.* a shoe with a wooden sole.

pat′ter (pat′ər) *v.i.* **1,** make quick, short taps; run with short steps. **2,** talk glibly. —*v.t.* repeat mechanically. —*n.* **1,** a succession of light taps. **2,** rapid, glib speech.

> **patter**
> ↔ The sense of quick talk comes from the rapid recitation of the Lord's Prayer in Latin, which begins "*Pater* noster," Our Father.

pat′tern (pat′ərn) *n.* **1,** an example; ideal. **2,** a model to be copied. **3,** a decorative design. —*v.t.* (with *after*) make conform (to some pattern). ❑ *patron*

pat′ty (pat′ē) *n.* **1,** a cup-shaped shell of pastry. **2,** a shaped mound of chopped meat.

pat′ty-cake″ (pat′ē-kāk″) *n.* pat-a-cake.

pau′ci·ty (pâ′sə-tē) *n.* smallness of quantity or number.

Paul′ Pry′ an inquisitive person.

> **Paul Pry**
> ↔ From the name of a character in a play by 19th-c. English playwright John Poole.

paunch (pânch) *n.* the belly.

pau′per (pâ′pər) *n.* a destitute person; a recipient of charity. —**pau′per·ism,** *n.* —**pau′per·ize″** (-īz″) *v.t.* impoverish.

pause (pâz) *n.* an interval of silence or inaction. —*v.i.* stop, hesitate, or linger for a time.

pav′an (pav′ən) *n.* a slow, stately dance. Also, **pav′ane.**

pave (pāv) *v.t.* **1,** cover with bricks, cement, etc. **2,** facilitate. —**pave′ment, pav′ing,** *n.* a paved surface, as a sidewalk.

pa·vé′ (pə-vā′) *n.* (*Fr.*) a type of jewelry setting in which the gems are set very close together.

pa·vil′ion (pə-vil′yən) *n.* a light building or tent for recreation, etc.

paw (pâ) *n.* an animal's foot with nails or claws. —*v.t. & i.* **1,** strike or scrape with the foot. **2,** touch, stroke, or handle rudely.

---

pawl (pâl) *n.* a short pivoted bar acting as a brake in a machine.

pawn (pân) *n.* **1,** the chess piece of least value; hence, a person used as a tool. **2,** a pledge; something pawned. —*v.t.* deposit as security for a loan. —**pawn′bro″ker,** *n.* a person licensed to lend money on pledged property. —**pawn′shop″,** *n.*

paw′paw″ (pâ′pâ″) *n.* a tree of the So. U.S. or its edible fruit.

pax (päks) *n.* (*Lat.*) peace.

pay (pā) *v.t.* [**paid** (pād), **pay′ing**] **1,** compensate (a person) for services rendered or goods supplied. **2,** discharge, as a debt; hand over, as money. **3,** render, as a compliment. **4,** be profitable to. —*v.i.* **1,** discharge a debt. **2,** be advantageous. —*n.* **1,** wages; salary. **2,** employment for gain. —**pay′a·ble,** *adj.* & *n.* (amount) due. —**pay dirt, 1,** earth containing a remunerative quantity of gold. **2,** (*Informal*) something profitable. —**pay out, 1,** expend. **2,** let out. —**pay station** or **telephone,** a public coin-operated telephone.

pay′day″ *n.* the day on which employees receive their pay.

pay·ee′ (pā-ē′) *n.* one who receives payment.

pay′load″ *n.* the weight a vehicle carries in freight or paying passengers.

pay′mas″ter *n.* the official who pays laborers, troops, etc.

pay′ment (-mənt) *n.* **1,** act of paying. **2,** that which is paid.

pay′off″ *n.* a final reckoning.

pay·o′la (pā-ō′lə) *n.* a bribe paid to receive a certain service.

pay′roll″ *n.* a list of persons to be paid (wages), or the wages paid.

pa·zazz′ (pə-zaz′) *n.* pizazz.

PCB polychlorinated biphenyl: a toxic chemical.

PDL *abbr.* page description language.

pea (pē) *n.* the round, edible green seed of a leguminous vine; the vine. —**pea jacket,** a heavy woolen coat worn by sailors.

peace (pēs) *n.* **1,** freedom from war or civil disorder. **2,** a contract to end war. **3,** harmony in human relations. **4,** tranquillity; quietness. —**peace′a·ble,** *adj.* not quarrelsome; loving peace. —**Peace Corps,** a volunteer organization of the U.S. government that sends skilled persons abroad to help underdeveloped countries. —**peace dividend,** the amount to be saved from reduction of military budget which could be used for domestic economy. —**peace officer,** a police officer,

constable, sheriff, etc. —**peace pipe,** the calumet.

peace′ful (-fəl) *adj.* **1,** quiet; tranquil. **2,** peaceable. —**peace′ful·ness,** *n.*

peace′nik *n.* (*Informal*) an advocate of the cause of peace.

peace′time″ *n.* a period of not being at war.

peach (pēch) *n.* **1,** a round juicy fruit with a fuzzy, red-tinged skin; the tree bearing it. **2,** a yellowish-red color. **3,** (*Slang*) a person highly approved of. —*v.i.* (*Slang*) inform.

> **peach**
> ↔ From Latin *persica*, short for *malum Pericum*, Persian apple.

peach′y (-ē) *adj.* **1,** peachlike. **2,** (*Slang*) excellent. —**peach′i·ness,** *n.*

pea′cock″ (pē′kok″) *n.* a male peafowl with long brilliant tail feathers.

pea′fowl″ *n.* a type of bird found in Asia and Africa; a peacock or peahen.

pea′hen″, *n.* a female peafowl.

peak (pēk) *n.* **1,** the pointed end of anything. **2,** a steep mountain. **3,** a visor. **4,** the highest point. —*v.i.* look sickly; become emaciated. —**peak′ed** (-id) *adj.* thin; sickly.

peal (pēl) *n.* the loud ringing of a bell, or of thunder, laughter, etc. —*v.t.* & *i.* ring.

pea′nut″ (pē′nut″) *n.* **1,** a plant of the pea family whose pods ripen underground; its edible nutlike seed. **2,** a small person. —**peanut butter,** a paste made of ground peanuts.

pear (pâr) *n.* the juicy fruit of a tree related to the apple; the tree.

pearl (pērl) *n.* **1,** a hard lustrous body found in the shells of certain mollusks and valued as a gem. **2,** a pale, bluish-gray color. **3,** a size of type. —**pearl′y,** *adj.* like pearl; lustrous.

pear′main″ (-mān″) *n.* a variety of apple.

peas′ant (pez′ənt) *n.* a countryman; rustic. —**peas′ant·ry** (-rē) *n.*

peat (pēt) *n.* partly decomposed vegetable matter found in bogs, used, when dried, for fuel.

peb′ble (peb′əl) *n.* a small stone worn smooth by water. —*v.t.* grain, as leather. —**peb′bly,** *adj.*

pe·can′ (pi-kän′) *n.* a species of hickory tree or its thin-shelled nut.

pec″ca·dil′lo (pek″ə-dil′ō) *n.* a trifling offense.

pec′cant (pek′ənt) *adj.* sinning; guilty; causing offense. —**pec′can·cy** (-kən-sē) *n.*

pec'ca·ry (pek'ə-rė) *n.* a hoglike animal of tropical America.

pec·ca'vi (pe-kä've) *n.* [*pl.* -vis] (*Lat.*) I have sinned: a confession of guilt.

peck (pek) *n.* **1,** a unit of capacity: in dry measure, eight quarts or one-fourth of a bushel. **2,** a quick, sharp stroke, as with a bird's beak or a pointed tool. **3,** (*Informal*) a kiss. —*v.t.* & *i.* **1,** strike or pick up with, or as with, the beak. **2,** nag. **3,** eat in bits. **4,** (*Informal*) kiss. —**peck'ing order,** (*Informal*) a hierarchy.

pecs (peks) *n.* (*Informal*) pectoral muscles.

pec'tin (pek'tin) *n.* a substance that causes jelling. —**pec'tic,** *adj.*

pec'to·ral (pek'tə-rəl) *adj.* pert. to the chest.

pec'u·late'' (pek'yə-lāt'') *v.t.* & *i.* embezzle. —**pec''u·la'tion,** *n.*

pe·cul'iar (pi-kūl'yər) *adj.* **1,** characteristic of or belonging exclusively to. **2,** special. **3,** odd; queer. —**pe·cu''li·ar'i·ty,** *n.*

pe·cu'ni·ar''y (pi-kū'nė-er''ė) *adj.* pert. to, or consisting of, money.

ped'a·gogue'' (ped'ə-gog'') *n.* a schoolteacher. Also, **ped'a·gog''.** —**ped'a·go''gy** (-gō''jė) *n.* —**ped''a·gog'i·cal** (-goj'i-kəl) *adj.*

ped'al (ped'əl) *adj.* pert. to the foot. —*n.* a lever worked by the foot, as of a bicycle, organ, etc. —*v.t.* & *i.* work the pedals (of).

---

pedal, peddle
☞ Don't confuse *pedal,* a device operated by the foot, and *peddle,* to sell.

Pe·da'lo (pə-dä'lō) *n.* (*T.N.*) a pedal-operated recreational pontoon boat. Also, **pedal boat.**

ped'ant (ped'ənt) *n.* one who parades or overvalues his or her learning. —**pe·dan'tic** (pə-dan'tik) *adj.* —**pe·dan'ti·cal·ly,** *adv.* —**ped'ant·ry** (-rė) *n.*

ped'dle (ped'əl) *v.i.* & *t.* sell from house to house. —**ped'dler,** *n.* ❏ *pedal*

ped'er·as''ty (ped'ə-ras''tė) *n.* anal intercourse, esp. between man and boy. —**ped'er·ast'',** *n.*

ped'es·tal (ped'is-təl) *n.* a supporting base, as of a column.

pe·des'tri·an (pə-des'trė-ən) *n.* one who walks. —*adj.* **1,** walking. **2,** prosaic; unimaginative.

pe''di·at'rics (pē''dė-at'riks) *n.* (*Med.*) the medical care and treatment of children. —**pe''di·a·tri'cian** (pē''dė-ə-trish'ən) *n.*

ped'i·cab'' (ped'i-kab'') *n.* a foot-propelled vehicle for hire.

ped'i·cure'' (ped'ə-kyûr'') *n.* the care of the feet.

ped'i·gree'' (ped'ə-grē'') *n.* **1,** lineage; descent. **2,** a genealogical record. —**ped'·i·greed'',** *adj.* of known and pure breeding.

---

pedigree
↔ From Old French *pie' de grue,* crane's foot, a reference to the shapes of the lines in a genealogical chart.

---

ped'i·ment (ped'ə-ment) *n.* a triangular gable over the front of a building.

ped'lar (ped'lər) *n.* (*Brit.*) peddler.

pe''do·don'tia (pe''dō-don'shə) *n.* dentistry as applied to children.

pe·dom'e·ter (pi-dom'ə-tər) *n.* an instrument for recording steps taken in walking.

ped'o·phile'' (ped'ə-fīl'') *n.* an adult who is sexually attracted to children; a child molester.

peek (pēk) *v.i.* peep slyly. —*n.* a sly peep.

peek'a·boo'' (-ə-boo'') *n.* a child's peeking game. —*adj.* revealing; ephemeral.

peel (pēl) *v.t.* strip the covering from, as the rind, skin, or bark. —*v.i.* become stripped. —*n.* [also, **peel'ing**] the rind.

peen (pēn) *n.* the shaped top of a hammer's head.

peep (pēp) *v.i.* **1,** begin to appear. **2,** peer slyly or furtively. **3,** chirp; cheep. —*n.* **1,** a sly or furtive look. **2,** a glimpse. **3,** the cry of a small bird. —**peep'er,** *n.* a young frog. —**peep'hole'',** *n.* —**peeping Tom,** a person who likes to watch others in secret.

---

peeping Tom
↔ From the legend of Lady Godiva, who rode naked through the streets of Coventry to protest taxes. All the townspeople stayed inside out of respect, except for Tom the tailor: peeping Tom.

---

peer (pir) *n.* **1,** an equal; match. **2,** a nobleman. —*v.i.* look sharply or curiously. —**peer'age,** *n.* the nobility. —**peer'less,** *adj.* matchless. —**peer pressure,** influence exerted upon one by others of the same age, social group, etc. —**peer review,** judging of one's work by others in the same field.

peer'ess (pir'əs) *n.* **1,** the wife of a peer. **2,** a woman having the rank of a peer.

peeve (pēv) (*Informal*) *v.t.* & *i.* make or become ill-tempered. —*n.* an annoyance.

pee'vish (pē'vish) *adj.* fretful; irritable. —**pee'vish·ness,** *n.*

pee'wee" (pē'wē") *n.* (*Dial.*) **1,** a small child, person, or animal; a runt. **2,** a small marble.

peg *n.* **1,** a tapering pin of wood or metal. **2,** (*Brit.*) a drink of liquor. —*v.t.* [**pegged, peg'ging**] **1,** fasten or mark with pegs. **2,** set at a certain price. —**peg leg,** a wooden leg. —**take down a peg,** humble.

peg'board" *n.* a perforated board used for hanging things with pegs.

peign·oir' (pān-wär') *n.* a woman's dressing gown; duster.

pe"jo·ra'tion (pej"ə-rā'shən) *n.* **1,** deterioration. **2,** a change for the worse in the meaning of a word.

pe·jo'ra·tive (pi-jôr'ə-tiv) *adj.* disparaging; depreciating. —*n.* a disparaging term.

Pe'king·ese" (pē'kə-nēz") *n.* a small Chinese dog.

pe'koe (pē'kō) *n.* a black India tea.

pel'age (pel'ij) *n.* the hair, fur, or other soft covering of a mammal.

pe·lag'ic (pə-laj'ik) *adj.* marine; oceanic.

pel"er·ine' (pel"ə-rēn') *n.* a woman's cape with pointed ends.

pelf *n.* booty; money.

pel'i·can (pel'ə-kən) *n.* a large water bird with a pouch under its bill.

pel·la'gra (pə-lā'grə) *n.* a disease, characterized by dermatitis, affecting the nervous system, caused by deficient diet.

pel'let (pel'ət) *n.* a little ball of dough, lead, etc.; a pill.

pell-'mell' (pel'mel') *adv.* in confusion; headlong.

pel·lu'cid (pə-loo'sid) *adj.* **1,** clear; limpid. **2,** easily understood; perfectly clear.

pe·lo'ta (pə-lō'tə) *n.* jai alai.

pel"o·ton' (pel"ə-ton') *n.* a type of ornamental glass.

pelt *n.* **1,** a hide, esp. with fur. **2,** a blow; a beating down, as of rain. —*v.t.* assail with missiles. —*v.i.* **1,** beat violently. **2,** move rapidly.

pel'vis *n.* [*pl.* **-ves** (-vēz)] the basin-shaped group of bones that support the spine. —**pel'vic** (-vik) *adj.*

pem'mi·can (pem'ə-kən) *n.* a dried meat paste, made into cakes.

pen *n.* **1,** a small enclosure for animals. **2,** an instrument for writing with ink. —*v.t.* [**penned, pen'ning**] **1,** shut in; enclose. **2,** write. —**pen name,** a pseudonym.

pe'nal (pē'nəl) *adj.* pert. to or inflicting punishment. —**pe'nal·ize"** (-īz") *v.t.* inflict a penalty upon.

pen'al·ty (pen'əl-tē) *n.* a punitive forfeit; punishment.

---

pen, pencil

↔ Despite their similarity, these two writing implements have different origins. *Pen* comes from Latin *penna*, feather (early pens were in fact feathers or quills). *Pencil* comes from Latin *penicillus*, painter's brush, from *peniculus*, little tail (which is also the source of *penis*). The other senses of *pen* are of unknown origin.

---

pen'ance (pen'əns) *n.* self-inflicted punishment for sin.

pe·na'tes (pə-nä'tēz) *n.pl.* the household gods of the ancient Romans.

pence (pens) *n.pl.* (*Brit.*) pennies.

pen'chant (pen'chənt) *n.* a strong inclination or predilection.

pen'cil (pen'səl) *n.* **1,** a cylinder, as of wood, enclosing a soft, solid substance for writing, marking, etc. **2,** rays of light diverging from or converging to a given point. —*v.t.* write, draw, or mark with, or as with, a pencil. ❑ *pen*

pend *v.i.* hang, as if balanced; await settlement.

pend'ant (pen'dənt) *n.* a hanging ornament.

pend'ent (pen'dənt) *adj.* **1,** hanging. **2,** pending. —**pen'den·cy,** *n.*

pen'du·lous (pen'jə-ləs) *adj.* hanging loosely. —**pen'du·lous·ness,** *n.*

pen'du·lum (pen'jə-ləm) *n.* a weight suspended on a swinging arm.

pen'e·trate" (pen'i-trāt") *v.t.* **1,** pierce into or through. **2,** enter and become part of; permeate. **3,** see into; understand. —*v.i.* enter and make way. —**pen'e·tra·ble,** *adj.* —**pen'e·tra"tive,** *adj.* keen. —**pen"e·tra'tion,** *n.*

pen'guin (peng'gwin) *n.* a flightless aquatic bird.

pen"i·cil'lin (pen"ə-sil'ən) *n.* a powerful, bacteria-killing substance obtained from a green mold (*penicillium*).

pen·in'su·la (pə-nin'sə-lə) *n.* a body of land almost surrounded by water. —**pen·in'su·lar,** *adj.*

pe'nis (pē'nis) *n.* the male organ through which urine and sperm are discharged.

pen'i·tent (pen'ə-tənt) *adj.* repentant; contrite. —*n.* a penitent person. —**pen'i·tence,** *n.* —**pen"i·ten'tial** (-ten'shəl) *adj.*

pen"i·ten'tia·ry (pen"ə-ten'shə-rē) *n.* a prison for criminals.

pen'knife" *n.* a pocket knife.

pen'light" *n.* a small flashlight.

---

pen'man (-mən) *n.* [*pl.* **-men**] one skilled in handwriting. —**pen'man·ship**, *n.* handwriting.

pen'nant (pen'ənt) *n.* a long, narrow flag, often one awarded to a victor.

pen'nate (pen'āt) *adj.* winged.

pen'non (pen'ən) *n.* a small triangular flag.

pen'ny (pen'è) *n.* **1,** a copper coin worth one U.S. cent. **2,** (*Brit.*) formerly, one-twelfth of a shilling, now one-hundredth of a pound. —**pen'ni·less**, *adj.* destitute. —**pen'ny-an'te,** *adj.* insignificant. —**penny arcade,** an amusement center. —**penny-wise and pound-foolish,** niggardly in unimportant matters. —**pretty penny,** a fairly large sum of money.

pen'ny-pinch"er *n.* a niggardly person.

pen'ny·roy"al *n.* **1,** a plant of the mint family. **2,** any of various herbs.

pen'ny·weight" *n.* a measure of weight, one-twentieth of a troy ounce.

pe·nol'o·gy (pè-nol'ə-jè) *n.* the science of prison management. —**pe"no·log'i·cal** (pē"nə-loj'i-kəl) *adj.* —**pe·nol'o·gist,** *n.*

pen'sion (pen'shən) *n.* **1,** a regular payment for past services. **2,** (pän-syôn") (*Fr.*) a boarding house. —*v.t.* retire and pay a pension to. —**pen'sion·er,** *n.* one who is pensioned.

pen'sive (pen'siv) *adj.* reflective; thoughtful. —**pen'sive·ness,** *n.*

pen'stock" *n.* a trough or pipe for conveying water, as to a water wheel.

pent *adj.* (often with *up*) confined; shut up.

pen·ta- (pen-tə) *pref.* five.

pen'ta·cle (pen'tə-kəl) *n.* **1,** a five-pointed star. **2,** hexagram.

pen'ta·gon (pen'tə-gon) *n.* a five-sided figure. —**pen·tag'o·nal** (-tag'ə-nəl) *adj.*

pen·tam'e·ter (pen-tam'ə-tər) *n. & adj.* (a line of verse) having five metrical feet.

Pen'ta·teuch" (pen'tə-tūk") *n.* the first five books of the Bible.

pen·tath'lon *n.* an athletic contest consisting of five events.

Pen'te·cost" (pen'tə-kâst") *n.* a Christian festival, Whitsunday.

> **Pentecost**
> ↔ From the Greek phrase *pentēkostē hēmera,* fiftieth day.

pent'house" (pent'hows") *n.* an apartment or house on the roof of a building.

pe·nu'che (pə-noo'chè) *n.* a kind of fudge.

pe'nult (pē'nult) *n.* the next-to-last syllable.

> **penthouse**
> ↔ The "house" in *penthouse* is actually a mispronunciation (influenced surely by *house*) of the ending of Middle English *pentis,* which derives from Old French *apentiz,* hang against.

pe·nul'ti·mate (pi-nul'ti-mət) *adj.* next to last.

pe·num'bra (pi-num'brə) *n.* **1,** partial shadow. **2,** a fringe. **3,** the gray border around a sunspot. —**pe·num'bral,** *adj.*

pe·nur'i·ous (pə-nyûr'è-əs) *adj.* stingy; miserly. —**pe·nur'i·ous·ness,** *n.*

pen'u·ry (pen'yə-rè) *n.* extreme poverty.

pe'on (pē'on) *n.* in Lat. Amer., a day laborer. —**pe'on·age,** *n.* virtual slavery; serfdom.

pe'o·ny (pē'ə-nè) *n.* a plant bearing large, globular flowers.

peo'ple (pē'pəl) *n.* **1,** a whole of a particular body or group of persons. **2,** (*n.pl.*) the populace; the masses. **3,** (*n.pl.*) (*Informal*) persons; relatives. —*v.t.* populate.

pep (*Slang*) *n.* energy; vigor. —*v.t.* [**pepped, pep'ping**] (with *up*) stimulate. —**pep'py,** *adj.* —**pep talk,** a brief speech designed to excite or encourage the listener.

pep'lum (pep'ləm) *n.* a short fitted overskirt.

pep'per (pep'ər) *n.* **1,** a pungent spice. **2,** a garden plant or its edible fruit. —*v.t.* **1,** season with pepper. **2,** sprinkle (on); pelt. —**pepper pot,** any of various highly seasoned stews.

pep'per-and-salt' *adj.* mixed black and white.

pep'per·corn" *n.* **1,** the berry of the pepper plant. **2,** a small particle.

pep'per·mint" (pep'ər-mint") *n.* a pungent herb, its oil, or candy flavored with it.

pep'per·y (-è) *adj.* **1,** hot; biting. **2,** hot-tempered. —**pep'per·i·ness,** *n.*

pep'sin *n.* a digestive substance in the gastric juice. —**pep'tic,** *adj.* pert. to digestion.

per (pēr) *prep.* **1,** by means of; through. **2,** for or to each.

per- (per) *pref.* **1,** through. **2,** thoroughly; utterly; very. **3,** (*Chem.*) the maximum or an unusual amount.

per"ad·ven'ture (pēr"-) *adv.* perhaps.

per·am'bu·late" (pər-am'byə-lāt") *v.i.* walk about. —**per·am'bu·la'tion,** *n.* —**per·am'bu·la·to"ry** (-lə-tôr"è) *adj.*

per·am′bu·la″tor (-lā″tər) *n.* a baby carriage. Also, **pram.**

per an′num (an′əm) (*Lat.*) each year.

per·cale′ (pər-kāl′) *n.* a closely woven cotton fabric.

per cap′i·ta (kap′ə-tə) (*Lat.*) per person.

per·ceive′ (pər-sēv′) *v.t.* become aware of through the senses or the understanding. **—per·ceiv′a·ble,** *adj.*

per·cent′ (pər-sent′) *n.* parts per hundred, symbol %.

per·cent′age (-ij) *n.* **1,** rate or proportion per hundred; proportion; commission. **2,** (*Informal*) profit; advantage.

per·cen′tile (pər-sen′tīl; -til) *n.* one of 100 equal consecutive groups arranged in order of magnitude, or the points dividing them. **—adj.** pert. to a percentile or to a division by percentiles.

per′cept (pĕr′sept) *n.* a perception. **—per·cep′tu·al** (pər-sep′shoo-əl) *adj.*

---

percept, precept
☞ Do not confuse *percept*, a perception, with *precept*, a maxim.

---

per·cep′ti·ble (pər-sep′tə-bəl) *adj.* perceivable. **—per·cep″ti·bil′i·ty,** *n.*

per·cep′tion (pər-sep′shən) *n.* the act or faculty of perceiving; something perceived.

per·cep′tive (-tive) *adj.* quick to perceive. **—per·cep′tive·ness,** *n.*

perch (pĕrch) *n.* **1,** any of various edible fishes. **2,** any of several units of measure, as a rod, a sq. rod, etc. **3,** a support, esp. a roost for birds. **—v.t.** place on a perch. **—v.i.** roost.

per·chance′ (pər-cháns′) *adv.* perhaps.

Per′che·ron″ (pĕr′chə-ron″) *n.* one of a breed of draft horses.

per·cip′i·ent (pər-sip′ē-ənt) *adj.* perceiving. **—per·cip′i·ence,** *n.*

per′co·late″ (pĕr′kə-lāt″) *v.t.* pass (a liquid) through a porous substance. **—v.i.** seep; filter. **—per′co·la′tion,** *n.* **—per′co·la″tor,** *n.* a pot for cooking coffee.

per·cus′sion (pər-kush′ən) *n.* the forcible striking of one body against another. **—per·cuss′,** *v.t.* **—per·cus′sion·ist,** *n.* a musician who plays percussion instruments. **—percussion cap,** a cap filled with powder on the end of a cartridge. **—percussion instrument,** a drum, cymbals, etc.

per di′em (pər dē′əm) (*Lat.*) **1,** by the day. **2,** a fixed allowance for each day's expenses; daily expense account.

per·di′tion (pər-dish′ən) *n.* **1,** utter ruin. **2,** eternal damnation.

per·dur′a·ble (pər-) *adj.* everlasting; imperishable.

per″e·gri·na′tion (per″ə-grə-nā′shən) *n.* a wandering about from place to place.

per′e·grine (per′ə-grin) *adj.* foreign; migratory; wandering. **—n.** a swift, courageous kind of falcon. Also, **per′e·grin.**

per·emp′to·ry (pə-remp′tə-rē) *adj.* **1,** admitting no refusal. **2,** dogmatic; dictatorial.

per·en′ni·al (pə-ren′ē-əl) *adj.* **1,** lasting several years, as a plant. **2,** long-lasting; continuing. **—n.** a perennial plant. ❑ *annual*

pe″res·troi′ka (per″ə-stroi′kə) *n.* (*Russ.*) reform; reconstruction.

per′fect (pĕr′fikt) *adj.* **1,** complete in every detail. **2,** without defect; flawless. **3,** of the highest type. **4,** exact; precise. **5,** thoroughly learned or skilled. **6,** (*Informal*) utter; complete. **7,** (*Gram.*) denoting the tense of a verb that expresses completed action. **—n.** the perfect tense. **—v.t.** (pər-fekt′) **1,** complete; finish. **2,** make perfect. **—per·fec′tion** (pər-fek′shən), **per′fect·ness,** *n.* **—per·fec′tion·ist,** *n. & adj.* **—per·fec′tion·ism,** *n.*

per·fec′ta (pər-fek′tə) *n.* a wager in horseracing requiring correct choice of first and second place in exact order to win; exacta.

per·fec′to (pĕr-fek′tō) *n.* a shape of cigar.

per′fi·dy (pĕr′fə-dē) *n.* breach of faith; treachery. **—per·fid′i·ous,** *adj.*

per′fo·rate″ (pĕr′fə-rāt″) *v.t.* bore through; make a series of holes in. **—adj.** perforated.

per″fo·ra′tion (pĕr″fə-rā′shən) *n.* **1,** act of perforating. **2,** a hole or row of holes, as in paper.

per·force′ (pər-fôrs′) *adv.* of necessity.

per·form′ (pər-fôrm′) *v.t.* **1,** carry out; do. **2,** discharge, as a duty, etc. **3,** act (a play or part); render (music). **—v.i.** **1,** work; operate. **2,** act, sing, or play in public. **—performing arts,** those arts, as drama, music, etc., which involve public performance.

per·form′ance (-əns) *n.* **1,** the act of performing; execution. **2,** a thing performed. **3,** a musical, dramatic, or other entertainment. **4,** efficiency. **—performance art,** a form of live performance combining several media, such as music, dancing, and drama.

per·fume′ (pər-fūm′) *v.t.* make fragrant. **—n.** **1,** a pleasant scent; aroma. **2,** a volatile sweet-smelling liquid.

---

per·fum′e·ry (pər-fūm′ə-rē) n. **1,** perfumes in general. **2,** a place where perfumes are made or sold.

per·func′to·ry (pər-funk′tə-rē) adj. done merely from a sense of duty; casual; superficial.

per′go·la (pēr′gə-lə) n. a latticework over a walk; an arbor.

per·haps′ (pər-haps′) adv. maybe.

pe′ri (pir′ē) n. an elf; fairy.

per″i·cyn′thi·on (per″ə-sin′thē-on) n. the point nearest the moon in the lunar orbit of a satellite.

per′i·dot (per′ə-dot) n. green chrysolite, used as a gem.

per′i·gee (per′ə-jē) n. the point of the orbit of a satellite of the earth which is nearest the earth. **—per″i·ge′al, per″i·ge′an,** adj.

per″i·he′li·on (-hē′lē-ən) n. [pl. -li·a (-lē-ə)] the point of the orbit of a planet or comet which is nearest the sun.

per′il (per′əl) n. danger; risk. —v.t. imperil. **—per′il·ous,** adj.

per·im′e·ter (pə-rim′i-tər) n. the outer boundary; circumference.

pe′ri·od (pir′ē-əd) n. **1,** an era; epoch. **2,** a specified division of time; a recurring event or its duration. **3,** the sign (.) marking the end of a declarative sentence; the sentence itself. **4,** termination. **5,** an occurrence of menstruation.

pe″ri·od′ic (pir″ē-od′ik) adj. recurring at regular intervals. **—pe″ri·o·dic′i·ty** (-ə-dis′ə-tē) n. **—periodic table** or **chart,** a grouping of the atomic elements by atomic numbers or weights.

pe″ri·od′i·cal (pir″ē-od′ə-kəl) adj. **1,** periodic. **2,** published at regular intervals. —n. a periodical magazine.

per″i·pa·tet′ic (per″ə-pə-tet′ik) adj. walking about; itinerant.

pe·riph′e·ry (pə-rif′ə-rē) n. the outer boundary line.

pe·riph′er·al (pə-rif′ə-rəl) adj. on the periphery. —n. equipment linked to a computer to enhance or extend its functions. Also, **peripheral unit.**

pe·rique′ (pə-rēk′) n. a strong-flavored tobacco from Louisiana.

> **perique**
> ↔ Perhaps from the nickname of the Louisiana farmer who first grew it, *Pierre* Chenet.

per′i·scope″ (per′ə-skōp″) n. an instrument for seeing above or around an obstacle. **—per″i·scop′ic** (-skop′ik) adj.

per′ish v.i. waste away; disappear; die.

—per′ish·a·ble, adj. & n. mortal; easily spoiled, as goods.

per″i·stal′sis (per″ə-stal′sis) n. involuntary muscular movements of some organs, esp. the alimentary canal.

per′i·style″ n. a row of columns surrounding a building, an open court, etc.; the enclosed space.

per″i·to·ne′um (per″ə-tə-nē′əm) n. the membrane lining the abdominal cavity.

per″i·to·ni′tis (per″ə-tə-nī′tis) n. inflammation of the peritoneum.

per′i·wig (per′i-wig) n. peruke.

per′i·win″kle (per′ə-wing″kəl) n. a trailing evergreen plant with blue flowers; myrtle.

per′jure (pēr′jər) v.t. make (oneself) guilty of perjury. **—per′jured,** adj. constituting, or guilty of, perjury. **—per′jur·er,** n.

per′ju·ry (pēr′jə-rē) n. the willful giving of false testimony under oath.

perk (pērk) v.t. & i. **1,** (with *up*) lift (one's head, ears) eagerly; be cheered. **2,** percolate. —n. (*Slang*) perquisite. **—perk′y,** adj. jaunty; pert.

per′ma·frost″ (pēr′mə-) n. permanently or perennially frozen subsoil, usu. in arctic regions.

Perm·al·loy″ (pērm′ə-loi″) n. (*T.N.*) an iron-nickel alloy easily magnetized and demagnetized.

per′ma·nent (pēr′mə-nənt) adj. lasting; fixed, not temporary. **—per′ma·nence,** n. **—permanent press,** a treatment for fabrics so that they hold their shape after washing. **—permanent wave** [also, *informal,* **permanent** or **perm**] a long-lasting artificial wave for the hair. ❏ *manor*

per′me·a·ble (pēr′mē-ə-bəl) adj. porous. **—per″me·a·bil′i·ty,** n.

per′me·ate″ (pēr′mē-āt″) v.t. & i. seep through the pores (of); penetrate; spread through. **—per″me·a′tion,** n.

per·mis′si·ble (pər-mis′ə-bəl) adj. allowable. **—per·mis″si·bil′i·ty,** n.

per·mis′sion (pēr-mish′ən) n. act of permitting; consent; license.

per·mis′sive (pər-mis′iv) adj. **1,** permitted. **2,** permitting; tolerant.

per′mit (pēr′mit) n. a written license to do something. —v.t. (pər-mit′) [**per·mit′-ted, -ting**] **1,** allow. **2,** give formal consent to. —v.i. make possible.

per″mu·ta′tion (pēr″mū-tā′shən) n. any possible arrangement of any units in a group.

per·mute′ (pər-mūt′) v.t. **1,** alter. **2,** make permutations of.

per·ni'cious (pər-nish'əs) *adj.* highly destructive; ruinous. —**per·ni'cious·ness,** *n.*

per·nick'et·y (pər-nik'ə-tè) *adj.* (*Informal*) persnickety.

per"o·ra'tion (per"ə-rā'shən) *n.* an emphatic or summarizing conclusion of a speech. —**per"o·rate"** (-rāt") *v.i.*

per·ox'ide (pə-rok'sīd) *n.* **1,** a chemical compound with a high oxygen content. **2,** hydrogen peroxide, an antiseptic liquid.

per"pen·dic'u·lar (per"pən-dik'yə-lər) *adj.* **1,** perfectly vertical. **2,** (*Geom.*) meeting a line or surface at right angles. —*n.* a vertical line. —**per"pen·dic"u·lar'i·ty,** *n.*

per'pe·trate" (per'pə-trāt") *v.t.* commit (a crime); be guilty of. —**per"pe·tra'tion,** *n.* —**per'pe·tra"tor,** *n.*

per·pet'u·al (pər-pech'oo-əl) *adj.* **1,** everlasting. **2,** continuous.

per·pet'u·ate" (-āt") *v.t.* cause to continue indefinitely; preserve from oblivion. —**per·pet"u·a'tion,** *n.*

perp (perp) *n.* (*Slang*) perpetrator.

per"pe·tu'i·ty (per"pə-tū'ə-tè) *n.* endless existence or duration.

per·plex (pər-pleks') *v.t.* make confused or bewildered; puzzle. —**per·plex'i·ty,** *n.*

per'qui·site (per'kwi-zit) *n.* extra payment received because of one's regular work, as a tip.

per se' (per sā') (*Lat.*) by itself.

per'se·cute" (per'si-kūt") *v.t.* **1,** harass persistently, esp. make suffer for divergent principles. —**per"se·cu'tion,** *n.* —**per'se·cu"tor,** *n.*

---

persecute, prosecute
☛ Do not confuse *persecute*, to harass, with *prosecute*, to bring legal proceedings against.

---

per"se·vere' (per"sə-vir') *v.i.* persist in something undertaken. —**per"se·ver'-ance,** *n.*

Per'sian (per'zhən) *adj. & n.* pert. to ancient Persia, or Iran, or its people or language. —**Persian blinds,** adjustable shutters for the outside of a window. Also, **per·siennes'** (per-zyen'). —**Persian lamb,** the fur of the older Karakul lamb.

per'si·flage" (per'si-fläzh") *n.* flippant, bantering talk.

per·sim'mon (pər-sim'ən) *n.* a tree or its pulpy, acid fruit.

per·sist' (pər-zist') *v.i.* **1,** continue despite opposition. **2,** endure; recur. —**per·sis'tence, per·sist'en·cy,** *n.* —**per·sist'ent,** *adj.*

per·snick'e·ty (pər-snik'ə-tè) *adj.* (*In-*

formal) excessively meticulous. Also, **per·nick'e·ty.**

per'son (per'sən) *n.* **1,** a human being. **2,** the human body. **3,** (*Gram.*) the distinction between the speaker (*first person*), person spoken to (*second person*), and person spoken of (*third person*). ☐ *parson*

-per·son *suf.* designating an agent of unspecified sex.

-person
(*Gram.*) The *-person* form replaces paired sex-specific forms *-man* and *-woman* or *-er* and *-ess*, in words such as *chairperson*. While these forms have by no means achieved universal acceptance, they are widely found.

---

per·so'na (pər-sō'nə) *n.* [*pl.* **-nae** (-nè)] (*Lat.*) **1,** person; personality. **2,** facade; mask. **3,** (*pl.*) the characters in a play.

per'son·a·ble (-ə-bəl) *adj.* attractive in manner and appearance.

per'son·age (-ij) *n.* **1,** an important person. **2,** a part or character in a play.

per'son·al (-əl) *adj.* **1,** one's own; private. **2,** done by oneself, not a representative or representation. **3,** (of a remark) invidious. **4,** (*Gram.*) denoting person. **5,** of property, movable. —**personal computer,** a computer designed for personal use. —**personal information manager,** (*Computers*) a program designed to keep track of addresses, dates, etc. *Abbr.,* **PIM.**

---

personal, personnel
☛ Do not confuse *personal*, private, pert. to a person, with *personnel*, staff, work force. Note the difference in the number of n's.

---

per·son·al'i·ty (per"sən-al'ə-tè) *n.* **1,** distinctive character; individuality. **2,** (*pl.*) gossip. **3,** (*Informal*) celebrity.

per'son·al·ize" (-īz") *v.t.* **1,** typify; make personal. **2,** mark or identify, as by initialing. —**per"son·al"i·za'tion,** *n.*

per'son·al·ty (-tè) *n.* (*Law*) personal property; movable possessions.

per·so'na non gra'ta (pər-sō'nə nōn grä'tə) (*Lat.*) an unacceptable or unwanted person.

per·son'i·fy" (pər-son'ə-fī") *v.t.* **1,** attribute human qualities to (an object, quality, etc.). **2,** exemplify; typify. —**per·son"i·fi·ca'tion,** *n.*

per"son·nel' (per"sə-nel') *n.* employees (of a particular employer). ☐ *personal, personage*

per·spec'tive (pər-spek'tiv) *n.* **1,** point

---

of view. **2,** the proper relative position of objects or phenomena one perceives.

per"spi·ca'cious (pēr"spə-kā'shəs) *adj.* mentally acute. —**per"spi·cac'i·ty** (-kas'-ə-tė) *n.*

per·spic'u·ous (pər-spik'ū-əs) *adj.* easily understood; lucid. —**per"spi·cu'i·ty** (-spi-kū'ə-tė) *n.*

per·spire' (pər-spīr') *v.i. & t.* excrete waste fluids through the pores; sweat. —**per"spi·ra'tion,** *n.*

per·suade' (pər-swād') *v.t.* prevail upon by argument or entreaty; convince. ☐ *convince*

per·sua'sion (pər-swā'zhən) *n.* **1,** act or effect of persuading. **2,** a conviction; way of thinking. —**per·sua'si·ble,** *adj.* —**per·sua'sive** (-siv) *adj.* serving to persuade.

pert (pērt) *adj.* saucy; impudent. —**pert'-ness,** *n.*

per·tain' (pər-tān') *v.i.* (with *to*) **1,** belong as a part. **2,** have reference or relation; relate; bear upon; be connected with.

per"ti·na'cious (pēr"ti-nā'shəs) *adj.* stubbornly holding to an opinion, purpose, etc. —**per"ti·nac'i·ty** (-nas'ə-tė) *n.*

per'ti·nent (pēr'tə-nənt) *adj.* to the point; appropriate; relevant; pertaining. —**per'ti·nence,** *n.*

per·turb' (pər-tērb') *v.t.* agitate; disturb greatly. —**per"tur·ba'tion,** *n.*

per·tus'sis (pər-tus'əs) *n.* whooping cough.

pe·ruke' (pə-rook') *n.* a wig.

pe·ruse' (pə-rooz') *v.t.* read attentively. —**pe·rus'al,** *n.*

Pe·ru'vi·an (pə-roo'vė-ən) *adj.* of or pert. to Peru. —*n.* a native or citizen of Peru.

per·vade' (pər-vād') *v.t.* spread through every part of; permeate. —**per·va'sive,** *adj.*

per·verse' (pər-vērs') *adj.* self-willed; contrary. —**per·verse'ness,** *n.* —**per·ver'-si·ty,** *n.*

per·vert' (pər-vērt') *v.t.* **1,** divert from its intended meaning, use, etc. **2,** lead astray; corrupt. —*n.* (pēr'vērt) a perverted person, esp. one who engages in sexual perversion. —**per·ver'sion** (-zhən) *n.*

Pe'sach (pe'säk) *n.* the Passover.

pe·se'ta (pə-sā'tə) *n.* the monetary unit of Spain.

pes'ky (pes'kė) *adj.* (*Informal*) troublesome. —**pes'ki·ness,** *n.*

pe'so (pā'sō) *n.* [*pl.* **-sos**] a coin of varying value used in Latin Amer.

pes'sa·ry (pes'ə-rė) *n.* **1,** any of various

appliances placed in the vagina for support or medication. **2,** a diaphragm (def. 3).

pes'si·mism (pes'ə-miz-əm) *n.* a tendency to expect the worst. —**pes'si·mist,** *n.* —**pes"si·mis'tic,** *adj.* —**pes"si·mis'ti·cal·ly,** *adv.*

pest *n.* **1,** a pestilence. **2,** a person or thing that annoys; nuisance. **3,** an insect or small animal that destroys plants, etc.

---

pest, pester

↔ These two words, surprisingly enough, are not related. *Pest* comes from Latin *pestis*, plague; *pester* is from Vulgar Latin *impastoriare*, to hobble, through Middle French *empestrer*.

---

pes'ter (pes'tər) *v.t.* annoy; harass. ☐ *pest*

pest'house" *n.* a hospital ward isolated because of infectious disease.

pest'i·cide" (pest'ə-sīd") *n.* an agent (as a chemical) used to kill pests.

pes·tif'er·ous (pes-tif'ər-əs) *adj.* **1,** bearing infection; noxious. **2,** (*Informal*) annoying. —**pes·tif'er·ous·ness,** *n.*

pes'ti·lence (pes'tə-ləns) *n.* a devastating epidemic disease. —**pes"ti·len'tial** (-len'shəl) *adj.*

pes'ti·lent (pes'tə-lənt) *adj.* **1,** poisonous. **2,** injurious to morals. **3,** troublesome.

pes'tle (pes'əl) *n.* a tool for pounding substances in a mortar.

pes'to (pes'tō) *n.* a sauce of basil, pine nuts, olive oil, and cheese.

pet *n.* **1,** an animal or bird that is cherished. **2,** a favorite. **3,** a sulking mood. —*adj.* **1,** loved and fondled. **2,** favorite. **3,** expressing fondness. —*v.t. & i.* [**pet'ted, -ting**] **1,** fondle; engage in amorous caresses. **2,** sulk.

---

pet

↔ The sense of cherished person or animal comes perhaps from the phrase *petty lamb*, little lamb. The sense of sulking mood is of uncertain origin.

---

pet'al (pet'əl) *n.* a leaf of a flower.

pe·tard' (pi-tärd') *n.* an ancient cannon or bomb attached to a gate or wall, to blow a hole in it.

pet'cock" *n.* a small faucet.

pe'ter (pē'tər) *v.i.* (*Informal*) (with *out*) become exhausted.

Pe'ter Prin"ci·ple the opinion, stated as

a law, that employees are promoted to the level of their own incompetence.

pe'ter·sham (pē'tər-shəm) *n.* a heavy overcoat; the woolen cloth of which it was made, named for 19th-c. British Viscount Petersham.

pet'i·ole'' (pet'ė-ōl'') *n.* a leafstalk.

pe·tite' (pə-tēt') *adj.* (*Fr.*) little. **—petite'ness,** *n.*

pe·tit four' (pet'ė fôr') [*pl.* **pe'tits fours'** (pet'ė-fôrz')] a small frosted cake covered completely with icing.

pe·ti'tion (pə-tish'ən) *n.* **1,** an earnest entreaty; prayer. **2,** a formal written request. —*v.t.* address a petition to. **—pe·ti'tion·er,** *n.*

pe'tit jury (pet'ė) a jury that decides the facts of a case in a court trial.

pet'nap''ping *n.* (*Informal*) stealing of a pet, esp. for ransom.

pet'rel (pet'rəl) *n.* a seabird.

> **petrel**
> ↔ Perhaps from *St. Peter*, because of his reported act of walking on water (Matthew 14:29).

pet'ri·fy'' (pet'rə-fī'') *v.t. & i.* **1,** turn into stone. **2,** paralyze or stupefy, as with fear. **—pet''ri·fac'tion,** *n.*

pet·ro- (pet-rō) *pref.* **1,** stone. **2,** oil.

pet'ro·dol'lar *n.* a dollar earned, esp. by a foreign country, from the sale of crude oil.

pe·trog'ra·phy (pi-trog'rə-fė) *n.* the scientific study and classification of rocks. **—pet''ro·graph'ic** (pet''rə-graf'ik) *adj.*

pet'rol (pet'rəl) *n.* (*Brit.*) gasoline.

pet''ro·la'tum (pet''rə-lā'təm) *n.* an oil obtained from petroleum.

pe·tro'le·um (pə-trō'lė-əm) *n.* unrefined oil obtained from the earth.

pe·trol'o·gy (pi-trol'ə-jė) *n.* the study of rocks.

pet'ti·coat'' (pet'ė-kōt'') *n.* a woman's underskirt.

pet'ti·fog''ger (pet'ė-fog''ər) *n.* a scheming lawyer. **—pet'ti·fog',** *v.i.*

pet'tish (pet'ish) *adj.* peevish. **—pet'tish·ness,** *n.*

pet'ty (pet'ė) *adj.* on a small scale; trivial; mean. **—pet'ti·ness,** *n.* **—petty cash,** cash on hand for minor expenditures. **—petty officer,** a noncommissioned naval officer.

pet'u·lant (pech'ə-lənt) *adj.* peevish; capricious. **—pet'u·lance,** *n.*

pe·tu'ni·a (pə-tū'nė-ə) *n.* a plant or its funnel-shaped flower.

pew (pū) *n.* a bench for worshipers in a church.

pe'wee' (pē'wē) *n.* a small Amer. fly-catcher; the phoebe.

pew'ter (pū'tər) *n.* an alloy of tin and lead, antimony, or bismuth.

pe·yo'te (pā-yō'tē) *n.* a stimulant drug derived from mescal.

pH a measure of the acidity or alkalinity of a solution.

pha'e·ton (fā'ə-tən) *n.* **1,** a light four-wheeled carriage. **2,** a convertible sedan.

> **phaeton**
> ↔ From the Latin name for Greek *Phaethōn*, a son of Helios who drove his chariot too close to the sun and was struck down by Zeus.

-phage (fāj) *suf.* an eater of. **— -pha·gous** (fā-gəs) *suf.* forming adjectives.

phag'o·cyte'' (fag'ə-sīt'') *n.* a white corpuscle in the blood, capable of destroying bacteria.

pha·lan'ger (fə-lan'jər) *n.* a long-tailed arboreal marsupial of Australia.

pha'lanx (fā'lanks) *n.* **1,** a body of troops in close formation; a solid group. **2,** [*pl.* **pha·lan'ges** (fə-lan'jēz)] any of the bones of the fingers or toes.

phal'a·rope'' (fal'ə-rōp'') *n.* a small coastal wading bird.

phal'lus (fal'əs) *n.* a symbol or image of the male reproductive organ; the organ itself. **—phal'lic,** *adj.*

phan'tasm (fan'taz-əm) *n.* **1,** a specter. **2,** fantasy; an illusion.

phan·tas''ma·go'ri·a (fan-taz''mə-gôr'ė-ə) *n.* **1,** a succession of illusive images, as in a dream. **2,** a similar fantastic exhibition.

phan'ta·sy (fan'tə-sė) *n.* fantasy.

phan'tom (fan'təm) *n.* an apparition; specter; something unreal. **—adj.** illusive; ghostly.

Phar'aoh (fār'ō) *n.* **1,** a title of ancient Egyptian kings. **2,** (*l.c.*) a tyrant. **—phar''a·on'ic** (fār''ā-on'ik) *adj.*

> **Pharaoh**
> ↔ From Egyptian phrase for great house, orig. referring to the palace.

Phar'i·see'' (far'ə-sē'') *n.* **1,** a member of a Jewish sect of 1st c. A.D. **2,** (*l.c.*) one who follows the letter, not the spirit, of the (religious) law. **—phar''i·sa'ic** (-sā'ik) *adj.* **—phar''i·sa'i·cal·ly,** *adv.*

phar''ma·ceu'tics (fär''mə-soo'tiks) *n.* pharmacy (def. 1). **—phar''ma·ceu'tic, phar''ma·ceu'ti·cal,** *adj.*

phar″ma·col′o·gy (-kol′ə-gė) *n.* the science of drugs. —**phar″ma·co·log′i·cal,** (-kə-loj′ə-kəl) *adj.* —**phar″ma·col′o·gist,** *n.*

phar″ma·co·poe′ia (-kō-pē′yə) *n.* an official list of drugs and medicines.

phar′ma·cy (fär′mə-sė) *n.* **1,** the art of compounding drugs according to prescription. **2,** a drugstore. —**phar′ma·cist** (-sist) *n.*

phar′ynx (far′inks) *n.* [*pl.* **pha·ryn′ges** (fə-rin′jėz), **phar′ynx·es**] the passage connecting the mouth with the esophagus. —**pha·ryn′ge·al** (fə-rin′jė-əl) *adj.* —**phar″yn·gi′tis** (-jī′təs) *n.*

phase (fāz) *n.* the aspect in which a thing appears; a stage. —*v.t.* **1,** put in phase; synchronize. **2,** (with *out*) gradually remove from service. **3,** (with *in*) gradually come into service. **4,** (with *down*) gradually reduce. ❑ *faze*

pheas′ant (fez′ənt) *n.* a long-tailed game bird.

> **pheasant**
> ↔ From Greek *phasianos*, bird from the Phasis River, in the Caucasus.

phe″no·bar′bi·tal″ (fē″nō-bär′bi-tâl″) *n.* a drug used as a hypnotic.

phe′nol (fē′nol) *n.* carbolic acid.

phe·nom′e·non″ (fi-nom′ə-non″) *n.* [*pl.* **-na** (-nə)] **1,** any observable fact in nature. **2,** an odd or notable thing. —**phe·nom′e·nal,** *adj.*

> **phenomenon**
> ☞ Despite the error commonly made in speech, *phenomena* is plural; *phenomenon* is the singular form.

phew (fū) *interj.* of disgust, weariness, relief, or surprise.

phi (fī) *n.* the 21st letter of the Greek alphabet (Φ, φ).

phi′al (fī′əl) *n.* vial.

phil- (fil) *pref.* loving; fond of.

phi·lan′der (fi-lan′dər) *v.i.* make trifling love to a woman; flirt.

phi·lan′thro·py (fi-lan′thrə-pė) *n.* **1,** love of mankind; altruism. **2,** a benevolent act, gift, etc. —**phil″an·throp′ic** (fil″ən-throp′ik) *adj.* —**phil″an·throp′i·cal·ly,** *adv.* —**phi·lan′thro·pist** (-thrə-pist) *n.*

phi·lat′e·ly (fi-lat′ə-lė) *n.* the collecting and study of stamps and related postal materials. —**phi·lat′e·list,** *n.*

-phile *suf.* one who loves.

phil″har·mon′ic (fil″här-mon′ik) *adj.* **1,** fond of or devoted to music. **2,** a type of orchestra.

phi·lip′pic (fi-lip′ik) *n.* an oration full of bitter invective.

> **philippic**
> ↔ From the speeches delivered by Greek orator Demosthenes against *Philip*, king of Macedonia.

Phil′ip·pine (fil′ə-pēn) *adj.* pert. to the Philippine Islands or Republic.

Phi·lis′tine (fi-lis′tin) *n.* an uncultured, materialistic person.

phil″o·den′dron (fil″ə-den′drən) *n.* a tropical Amer. climbing plant.

phi·lol′o·gy (fi-lol′ə-jė) *n.* the science of the origins, laws, etc. of languages. —**phil″o·log′i·cal,** *adj.* —**phi·lol′o·gist,** *n.*

phi·los′o·pher (fi-los′ə-fer) *n.* **1,** a student of philosophy. **2,** a philosophical person. —**philosopher's stone,** a magical substance believed by alchemists to have the power, among others, to change base metal into gold.

phil″o·soph′i·cal (fil″o-sof′ə-kəl) *adj.* **1,** pert. to philosophy. **2,** serene in adversity. Also, **phil″o·soph′ic.**

phi·los′o·phy (fi-los′ə-fė) *n.* **1,** the science dealing with the general causes and principles of things. **2,** personal attitude. —**phi·los′o·phize″** (-fīz″) *v.i.*

phil′ter (fil′tər) *n.* a love potion. Also, **phil′tre.**

phle·bi′tis (fli-bī′tis) *n.* inflammation of a vein.

phle·bot′o·my (fle-bot′ə-mė) *n.* bloodletting as a therapeutic measure; bleeding.

phlegm (flem) *n.* **1,** thick mucus secreted in throat and bronchi. **2,** sluggishness; apathy.

phleg·mat′ic (fleg-mat′ik) *adj.* **1,** apathetic; unexcitable. **2,** pert. to phlegm. —**phleg·mat′ic·al·ly,** *adv.*

phlo·gis′ton (flō-jis′tən) *n.* fire considered as an element present but latent in all combustible substances and released when burning occurs.

phlox (floks) *n.* a tall summer perennial bearing large flower heads.

-phobe (fōb) *suf.* one who fears or hates.

-pho·bi·a *suf.* fear.

pho·bi·a (fō′bė-ə) *n.* an irrational fear or dread. ❑ *mania*

phoe′be (fē′bē) *n.* a bird, a small Amer. flycatcher; pewee; pewit.

phoe′nix (fē′niks) *n.* a fabled bird that burned itself and rose from its own ashes.

phon- (fōn) *pref.* sound; voice; speech.

phone (fōn) *n. & v.* (*Informal*) telephone. —**phone phreak, (***Slang*) a person who makes free telephone calls illegally.

-phone (fōn) *suf.* **1,** sound. **2,** speaking.

pho′neme (fō′nēm) *n.* a basic, distinctive unit of speech.

pho·net′ic (fō-net′ik) *adj.* pert. to speech sounds; in spelling, using always the same symbol for each sound. —**pho·net′i·cal·ly,** *adv.* —**pho·net′ics,** *n.sing.*

phon′ic (fon′ik) *adj.* pert. to sound, esp. speech sounds. —**phon′ics,** *n.sing.* the use of phonetics in teaching reading.

pho′no·graph″ (fō′nə-gráf″) *n.* a record player. —**pho″no·graph′ic,** *adj.*

pho′ny (fō′nē) (*Informal*) *adj.* fake; spurious. —*n.* a fake or faker.

phoo′ey (foo′ē) *interj.* of disgust.

phos′gene (fos′jēn) *n.* a poisonous gas used in chemical warfare.

phos′phate (fos′fāt) *n.* **1,** a compound of phosphorus used as a fertilizer. **2,** an effervescent drink.

phos′phor (fos′fər) *n.* a chemical that gives off visible light when struck by ultraviolet radiation. ❏ *phosphorus*

phos″pho·res′cence (fos″fə-res′əns) *n.* the property of giving out luminous light without sensible heat. —**phos″pho·res′-cent,** *adj.*

phos′pho·rus (fos′fə-rəs) *n.* a waxy, luminous nonmetallic element, no. 15, symbol P. —**phos′phor·ous,** *adj.*

---

phosphorus, phosphor
↔ From Greek *Phōsphoros* (lit., light-bearing), the morning star, i.e., Venus.

---

phot (fot) *n.* a unit of illumination.

pho′to (fō′tō) *n.* photograph. —**photo finish,** a race so close that the winner must be determined from a photograph. —**photo opportunity,** time set aside for photographers to photograph government officials after a news conference. Also, **photo op.**

pho·to- (fō′tō) *pref.* **1,** light. **2,** photographic.

pho″to·con″duc·tiv′i·ty *n.* (*Physics*) the increase of electrical conductivity caused by the absorption of radiation. —**pho″to·con·duc′tive,** *adj.*

pho′to·cop″y *n.* a photographic reproduction of printing, drawing, etc. —*v.t. & i.* make a photocopy (of). Also, **pho″to·dup′li·cate,** *n. & v.t.*

pho″to·e·lec′tric cell a device for controlling an electric circuit by light falling on it: *electric eye.* Also, **pho′to·cell″.**

pho″to·en·grav′ing *n.* a reproduction of pictures on letterpress printing plates by a photographic process. —**pho″to·en-grave′,** *v.t.*

pho″to·gen′ic (-jen′ik) *adj.* which looks good when photographed.

pho′to·graph″ (fō′tə-gráf″) *n.* a picture made by exposing a chemically treated surface to light. —*v.t.* make a photograph of. —*v.i.* **1,** take photographs. **2,** be a (good, bad, etc.) subject for photography. —**pho″to·graph′ic,** *adj.* —**pho″to·graph′i-cal·ly,** *adv.*

pho·tog′ra·phy (fə-tog′rə-fē) *n.* the taking of photographs. —**pho·tog′ra·pher,** *n.*

pho·tom′e·ter (fō-tom′ə-tər) *n.* an instrument for measuring the intensity of light; light meter.

pho″to·mi′cro·graph″ (-mī′krə-gráf″) *n.* a photograph taken through a microscope. —**pho″to·mi·crog′ra·phy** (-mī-krog′rə-fē) *n.*

pho′ton (fō′ton) *n.* a particle of radiant energy moving with the velocity of light.

pho″to-off′set *n.* lithography from plates made photographically.

pho′to·play″ *n.* a motion picture.

pho′to·sphere″ *n.* the gaseous, luminous envelope of the sun.

Pho′to·stat″ *n.* **1,** (*T.N.*) a device for producing a facsimile or negative copy, photographed directly onto paper. **2,** (*l.c.*) such a copy. —*v.t.* (*l.c.*) copy using the Photostat. Also, **stat.** —**pho″to·stat′ic,** *adj.*

pho″to·syn′the·sis *n.* the process by which plants make carbohydrates from light and air.

phrase (frāz) *n.* **1,** a group of words used as though one. **2,** a short, pithy expression. **3,** (*Music*) a group of notes played or sung connectedly in a particular way. —*v.t.* express in words.

phra″se·ol′o·gy (frā″zē-ol′ə-jē) *n.* choice of words.

phre·net′ic (fri-net′ik) *adj.* **1,** insane; violent. **2,** fanatic; zealous. —**phre·net′i-cal·ly,** *adv.*

phren′ic (fren′ik) *adj.* **1,** pert. to the diaphragm. **2,** mental.

phre·nol′o·gy (fre-nol′ə-jē) *n.* character-reading from the form of the skull. —**phre·nol′o·gist,** *n.*

phthi′sis (thī′sis) *n.* **1,** tuberculosis of the lungs. **2,** bodily decay.

phy·col′o·gy (fī-kol′ə-jē) *n.* the branch of botany dealing with algae.

phy·lac′ter·y (fə-lak′tə-rē) *n.* **1,** a small leather box containing scriptures, worn by pious Jews. **2,** an amulet; talisman.

---

fat, fāte, fär, fāre, fåll, åsk; met, hē, hėr, maybė; pin, pīne; not, nōte, ôr, tool

phyl′lo (fē′lō) *n.* a flaky, layered pastry used in Greek and Middle Eastern cooking.

phy·lo- (fī-lō) *pref.* tribe or race.

phy·log′e·ny (fī-loj′ə-nē) *n.* racial history; the evolution of a type or species of animal or plant. Also, **phy″lo·gen′e·sis** (fī″lə-). —**phy″lo·gen′ic, phy″lo·ge·net′ic,** *adj.*

phy′lum (fī′-ləm) *n.* [*pl.* **-la** (-lə)] a primary division of the animal or vegetable kingdom.

phys″i·at′rics (fiz″ē-at′riks) *n.* a system of medicine founded on the healing powers of nature.

phys′ic (fiz′ik) *n.* a medicine; specif., a cathartic.

phys′i·cal (fiz′i-kəl) *adj.* **1,** pert. to the body. **2,** pert. to nature or to the material. **3,** pert. to physics. —*n.* (*Informal*) a medical examination. —**physical education,** instruction in hygiene, exercises for the body, etc.

phy·si′cian (fə-zish′ən) *n.* a healer; esp. a doctor of medicine. ❑ *doctor*

phys′ics (fiz′iks) *n.* the science dealing with the properties of matter and energy. —**phys′i·cist** (-i-sist) *n.*

phy·si·o- (fiz-ē-ō) *pref.* **1,** nature; natural. **2,** physical.

phys″i·og′no·my (fiz″ē-og′nə-mē) *n.* the face; external aspect.

phys·si·og′ra·phy (fiz-ē-og′rə-fē) *n.* physical geography or geophysics.

phys″i·ol′o·gy (fiz″ē-ol′ə-jē) *n.* the science dealing with the processes of living. —**phys″i·o·log′i·cal,** *adj.* —**phys″i·ol′o·gist,** *n.*

phys″i·o·ther′a·py *n.* treatment of disease by the use of heat, massage, etc. —**phys″i·o·ther′a·pist,** *n.*

phy·sique′ (fi-zēk′) *n.* the structure and development of the body.

phy·to- (fī-tō) *pref.* plant; plant life; vegetable.

pi (pī) *n.* **1,** the sixteenth letter of the Greek alphabet (Π, π), also (π) denoting the ratio of the circumference of a circle to its diameter, about 3.1416. **2,** a jumbled mass of printing type. —*v.t.* [**pied, pie′ing**] jumble (type).

pi″a·nis′si·mo″ (pē″ə-nis′i-mō″) *adj.* & *adv.* (*It., music*) very soft.

pi·an′ist (pē-an′ist; pē′ə-nist) *n.* one who plays on the piano.

pi·an′o (pē-an′ō) *n.* [*pl.* **-os**] a large stringed musical instrument with a keyboard. —*adj.* & *adv.* soft. —**pi·an′o·forte″** (-fôrt″) *n.* a piano. —**piano roll,** a roll of

heavy paper on which is recorded mechanically, by means of holes, the notes of a work as performed by a pianist, to be reproduced on a player piano.

---

piano
↔ From the Italian phrase *gravicembalo col piano e forte,* harpsichord with soft and loud, i.e., that can play soft and loud, which the harpsichord itself can only do to a very limited extent. The 18th-c. piano is commonly called the *fortepiano,* to distinguish it from the modern form.

---

pi·as′ter (pē-as′tər) *n.* a coin, of varying value, of various countries, as Turkey and Egypt.

pi·az′za (pē-az′ə) *n.* **1,** a porch. **2,** (pē-ät′sə) a public square or walk.

pi′broch (pē′brokh) *n.* a wild, irregular kind of bagpipe music.

pi′ca (pī′kə) *n.* (*Printing*) twelve points; a type of this depth.

pic′a·dor″ (pik′ə-dôr″) *n.* a mounted bullfighter.

pic″a·resque′ (pik″ə-resk′) *adj.* (of fiction) episodic and dealing with rogues.

pic″a·yune′ (pik″ə-ūn′) *adj.* trifling; of little value.

pic′ca·lil″li (pik′ə-lil″ē) *n.* a pickle of chopped vegetables.

pic′co·lo″ (pik′ə-lō″) *n.* [*pl.* **-los″**] a small, high-pitched flute. —**pic′co·lo″ist,** *n.*

pick (pik) *n.* **1,** any of various pointed tools, large or small, as for loosening rock, chopping ice, etc.; a pickax. **2,** a hand-gathered crop. **3,** first choice; hence, the choicest. —*v.t.* **1,** prick, pierce, clean, open, etc., with a pointed tool. **2,** (often with *up*) acquire; gain; gather, as crops; take up; lift; pluck. **3,** (often with *out*) choose; select. **4,** rob; open (a lock) without a key. **5,** pull apart; shred. **6,** provoke (a quarrel); (with *on*) nag unfairly; tease. —*v.i.* **1,** use a pointed instrument. **2,** nibble at food. **3,** select. **4,** (with *up*) improve; recover. —**pick′er,** *n.* one who chooses wisely. —**pick′y,** *adj.* choosy; finicky.

pick′a·back″ *adv.* (riding) on a person's back and shoulders.

pick′a·nin″ny (pik′ə-nin″ē) *n.* (*Offensive*) a black child.

pick′ax″ *n.* a heavy, wooden-handled digging tool.

---

pickax
↔ Not an ax at all, this implement gets its name from Old French *picois,* a pick.

---

pick'er·el (pik'ər-əl) *n.* an edible fish of the pike family.

pick'et (pik'it) *n.* **1,** a pointed stake. **2,** a small body of troops sent out to scout, guard, etc. **3,** a person, as a striking workman, stationed outside a place to protest its operations. —*v.i. & t.* **1,** be or post a picket outside a place. **2,** tether.

pick'ings (-ingz) *n.pl.* (*Informal*) things gleaned or pilfered.

pick'le (pik'əl) *n.* **1,** a food preserved in brine or a vinegar solution. **2,** (*Informal*) a difficult or dangerous situation. —*v.t.* preserve as a pickle. —**pick'led,** *adj.* (*Slang*) drunk.

pick-'me-up'' *n.* a stimulating drink.

pick'pock''et *n.* one who steals from others' pockets.

pick'up *n.* **1,** an acquaintance met without an introduction. **2,** power of acceleration. **3,** a small open-body motor truck. **4,** (*Slang*) improvement, as in business. **5,** a device that receives audio or video signals, as a microphone. **6,** reception of sounds or images for broadcasting. —*adj.* made of odds and ends.

pic'nic (pik'nik) *n.* an outdoor meal. —*v.i.* [**pic'nicked, -nick'ing**] go on a picnic. —**pic'nick·er,** *n.*

pi·co- (pē-kō) *pref.* one trillionth.

pi'cot (pē'kō) *n.* a small projecting loop on the edge of lace, fabric, etc.

pic'to·graph'' (pik'tə-gràf'') *n.* a pictorial symbol used in writing. —**pic''to·graph'ic,** *adj.* —**pic·tog'ra·phy,** (-tog'rə-fē) *n.*

pic·tor'i·al (pik-tôr'ē-əl) *adj.* expressed in, consisting of, or illustrated by pictures.

pic'ture (pik'chər) *n.* **1,** a painting, photograph, etc., depicting a person, object, or scene; an image; likeness. **2,** a description in words. **3,** (often *pl.*) (*Informal*) a motion picture. —*v.t.* **1,** portray, depict. **2,** imagine. —**picture tube,** a kinescope. —**picture window,** a large window offering a panoramic view.

Pic'ture·phone'' *n.* (*T.N.*) a type of telephone providing both audio and visual communication.

pic·tur·esque' (pik-chər-esk') *adj.* colorful; vivid. —**pic·tur·esque'ness,** *n.*

pid'dle (pid'əl) (*Informal*) *v.i.* **1,** dawdle; putter. **2,** urinate. —*v.t.* waste (time). —**pid'dling,** *adj.* trifling; petty.

pidg'in (pij'ən) *n.* a dialect formed of limited vocabulary and simplified grammar; esp., *pidgin English,* used between Asian and English-speaking traders.

pie (pī) *n.* **1,** food baked in a pastry crust.

2, pi (def. 2). —**pie chart,** a chart in the shape of a round pie divided into sectors.

pie'bald'' (pī'bâld'') *adj.* having patches of color. —*n.* a piebald animal, esp. a horse.

piece (pēs) *n.* **1,** a fragment; a part or portion; a tract. **2,** a separate article, as of furniture, etc. **3,** an amount of work to be done. **4,** a definite quantity, as of cloth. **5,** one of the figures used in a game, as chess. **6,** a short literary or musical composition. **7,** a coin. **8,** a rifle or cannon. —*v.t.* (often with *out*) extend or enlarge by adding material. —**piece goods,** dry goods. —**piece of eight,** an old Span. coin.

pièce de ré·sis·tance' (pyes də rā-zēs-täns') (*Fr.*) the main dish, event, etc.

piece'meal'' *adv.* bit by bit; gradually.

piece'work'' *n.* work paid for by the piece or job.

pied (pīd) *adj.* of several colors. —**pied piper,** a person who convinces others to follow him or her.

pied-'à-terre' (pyād'a-tār') *n.* [*pl.* **-terres'** (-tār')] (*Fr.*) a place (as an apartment) where one can stay when necessary.

pied'mont'' (pēd'mont) *n.* located at the base of a mountain or mountain range.

pie-'eyed'' (-īd'') *adj.* drunk.

pie'plant'' *n.* rhubarb.

pier (pir) *n.* **1,** a breakwater; a wharf projecting into the water. **2,** a support of a bridge span. **3,** solid masonry between windows, etc. —**pier glass,** a large high mirror.

pierce (pirs) *v.t.* **1,** make a hole in. **2,** stab; enter painfully. **3,** force a way into or through. **4,** wound or affect keenly. —**pierc'ing,** *adj.* (of sound) shrill.

pi'e·ty (pī'ə-tē) *n.* reverence for God; devoutness.

pi·e''zo·e·lec'tric (pē-ā''zō-ē-lek'trik) *adj.* having the capacity to transform vibrations into electric current.

pif'fle (pif'əl) *n.* (*Slang*) nonsense.

pig *n.* **1,** a hog, esp. a young one. **2,** a greedy or dirty person. **3,** a mass of cast molten metal. **4,** (*Vulgar*) a policeman. —*v.i.* (with *out*) (*Slang*) to overeat. —**pig'let** (-lit) *n.* a small or young pig. —**pig iron,** crude iron cast into molds for further processing. —**pig Latin,** dog Latin.

pi'geon (pij'ən) *n.* **1,** a dove or related bird. **2,** (*Slang*) a dupe. —**clay pigeon,** a disk of baked clay used as a target in trap shooting.

pi′geon-heart″ed *adj.* easily frightened; meek.

pi′geon·hole″ *n.* a small open compartment in a desk. —*v.t.* **1,** file in a pigeonhole; lay aside and ignore. **2,** classify.

pi′geon-toed″ (-tōd″) *adj.* having the toes turned in.

pig′gish (pig′ish) *adj.* like a pig; gluttonous or dirty. —**pig′gish·ness,** *n.*

pig′gy (-gė) *n.* a small pig. —*adj.* piggish. —**piggy bank,** a hollow statuette of a pig, used as a savings bank; any similar savings receptacle.

pig′gy·back″ *adv.* **1,** pickaback. **2,** on a railroad flatcar. —*n.* a system of freight transport utilizing special railroad flatcars to carry truck trailers.

pig′head″ed *adj.* stubborn.

pig′ment (pig′mənt) *n.* **1,** coloring matter. **2,** the natural coloring matter in the tissues of an animal or plant. —**pig′men·tar·y,** *adj.* —**pig″men·ta′tion,** *n.*

pig′skin″ *n.* **1,** leather from pigs' skin. **2,** (*Informal*) a football.

pig′sty″ *n.* sty. Also **pig′pen″.**

pig′tail″ *n.* a long hanging braid of hair.

pike (pīk) *n.* **1,** a steel-pointed weapon; a lance. **2,** an edible freshwater fish. **3,** a main road; turnpike.

pik′er (pī′kər) *n.* (*Slang*) one who bets or spends in a small way.

pike′staff″ *n.* a staff with a metal point on the end.

pi·laf′ (pi-läf′) *n.* a dish of boiled rice and meat. Also, **pi·lau′** (-low′).

pi·las′ter (pi-las′tər) *n.* a rectangular column built partly in a wall.

pil′chard (pil′chərd) *n.* **1,** a small marine fish, like a herring. **2,** a sardine.

pile (pīl) *n.* **1,** soft hair; nap on cloth. **2,** a large supporting timber, etc., set in the ground. **3,** a massive edifice. **4,** a heap or mass. **5,** a pyre. **6,** (*Informal*) a large quantity; a fortune. **7,** a series of metal plates for producing electric current. **8,** an atomic pile. **9,** (*pl.*) hemorrhoids. —*v.t.* **1,** heap up. **2,** load: —*v.i.* (with *up*) form a heap; accumulate. —**pile driver,** a machine which drives piles by dropping a heavy weight (*drop hammer*) upon them.

pile-′up″ *n.* **1,** a collision involving several automobiles, people, etc. **2,** congestion, as in the air.

pil′fer (pil′fər) *v.t. & i.* steal surreptitiously in small amounts. —**pil′fer·er,** *n.*

pil′grim *n.* **1,** one who travels, esp. to a holy place as an act of devotion. **2,** (*cap.*) one of the earliest English settlers in Massachusetts. —**pil′grim·age,** *n.* a journey.

pill (pil) *n.* **1,** a small tablet of medicine. **2,** (*Slang*) a ball, as in baseball. **3,** (*Slang*) a disagreeable person. **4,** (with *the*) an oral contraceptive pill.

pil′lage (pil′ij) *v.t. & i.* plunder, esp. in war; sack. —*n.* plunder.

pil′lar (pil′ər) *n.* a supporting or ornamental column; any mainstay.

pill′box″ *n.* **1,** a small box for pills. **2,** (*Mil.*) a low, fortified machine-gun position.

pil′lion (pil′yən) *n.* an extra rear saddle or motorcycle seat.

pil′lo·ry (pil′ə-rė) *n.* a frame to hold an offender for exposure to public ridicule. —*v.t.* **1,** punish in the pillory. **2,** invoke scorn upon.

pil′low (pil′ō) *n.* a soft cushion to rest the head upon. —*v.t.* lay on a pillow. —**pil′low·case″, pil′low·slip″,** *n.* a cover for a pillow.

pi′lot (pī′lət) *n.* **1,** one who steers or controls a ship or aircraft. **2,** a leader; guide. **3,** a prototype. —*v.t.* direct the course of. —**pilot lamp,** an indicator lamp on a motor, etc. —**pilot light,** a small flame from which to ignite a larger.

pils′ner (pilz′nər) *n.* **1,** a light Bohemian beer. Also, **pils. 2,** a tall tapering glass.

PIM *abbr.* personal information manager.

pi·men′to (pi-men′tō) *n.* [*pl.* **-tos**] *n.* **1,** the berry of a W. Indies tree; allspice; also, the tree. **2,** pimiento.

pi·mien′to (pi-myen′tō) *n.* [*pl.* **-tos**] a sweet red pepper.

pimp *n.* an agent or exploiter of prostitutes. —*v.i.* pander.

pim′per·nel″ (pim′pər·nel″) *n.* a plant with flowers which close in bad weather.

pim′ple (pim′pəl) *n.* a small eruption on the skin. —**pim′ply,** *adj.*

PIN *abbr.* a number assigned to an individual to gain access to a banking account, etc.: *p(ersonal) i(dentification) n(umber).*

pin *n.* **1,** a pointed piece, esp. of thin wire, to join or attach things; a peg or bolt; a fastening device employing a pin. **2,** a piece of jewelry attached by a pin; a brooch. **3,** any of various pieces cut from a cylinder, as used in machines, bowling, etc. —*v.t.* [**pinned, pin′ning**] **1,** hold fast, esp. with a pin. **2,** (*Informal*) give a fraternity pin to (a girl) as a token of intention to become engaged. —**pin money,** a small amount of money, usu. for personal expenses. —**pins and needles,** a tingly sensation. —**on pins and needles,** nervous or tense; insecure.

pi′ña co·la′da (pē′nyə kə-lä′də) a drink of rum, pineapple juice, and coconut.

pin′a·fore″ (pin′ə-fôr″) *n.* a child's apron or sleeveless dress.

pi·ña′ta (pēn-yä′tə) *n.* (*Sp.*) a papier-mâché figure (as of an animal) stuffed with candy, toys, etc. for parties.

pin′ball″ *n.* a game in which a small metal ball bumps against various targets causing scores to be electrically recorded.

pince-′nez′ (pans′-nā′) *n.* (*Fr.*, pinches the nose) eyeglasses held on the nose by a spring.

pin′cers (pin′sərz) *n.pl. or sing.* **1,** a gripping tool, two arms hinged off-center. **2,** the gripping claws of lobsters, crabs, etc. **3,** (*Mil.*) simultaneous attacks from different directions. Also, **pinch′ers** (pin′chərz).

pinch *v.t. & i.* **1,** nip or squeeze between two surfaces. **2,** cramp; afflict, as with cold, poverty, etc.; be frugal. **3,** (*Slang*) capture; arrest. **4,** (*Slang*) steal. —*n.* **1,** a squeeze; nip. **2,** a tiny amount. **3,** painful stress. **4,** a critical juncture; emergency. **5,** (*Slang*) a raid; arrest.

pinch-′hit″ *v.i.* **1,** (*Baseball*) go to bat for another. **2,** act as substitute, esp. in an emergency.

pin′cush″ion *n.* a small cushion in which to keep pins.

pine (pīn) *n.* a cone-bearing evergreen tree with needle-shaped leaves; its timber. —*v.i.* **1,** grieve; languish. **2,** long (for). —**pinecone,** the cone-shaped fruit of the pine.

pin′e·al (pin′ē-əl) *adj.* shaped like a pine cone. —**pineal body** or **gland,** a small vestigial organ of unknown function attached to the brain.

pine′ap″ple (pīn′ap″əl) *n.* **1,** a tropical plant or its sweet, juicy fruit. **2,** a small bomb in this shape.

> **pineapple**
> ↔ The Middle English ancestor of this word, *pinappel*, meant pinecone (fruit of the pine), and later became attached to the larger fruit because of its resemblance to a pinecone.

pin′feath″ers *n.* feather stems just emerging.

ping *n.* **1,** the whistling sound of a projectile. **2,** motor knock. —*v.i.* make a pinging sound.

Ping-′Pong″ *n.* (*T.N.*) table tennis.

pin′head″ *n.* (*Informal*) **1,** a person with a very small head. **2,** a dolt.

pin′hole″ *n.* a tiny hole or dent.

pin′ion (pin′yən) *n.* **1,** a small gear wheel. **2,** the end segment of a bird's wing; a feather; a wing. —*v.t.* restrain, as by cutting the wings or pinning the arms.

pink *n.* **1,** a garden plant or its spicy, fringed flower. **2,** a light-red color. **3,** a person mildly inclined to communism. **4,** the best degree. —*v.t.* **1,** pierce; prick. **2,** finish with a serrated edge.

> **pink, pinkeye, pinkie**
> ↔ The origin of *pink* is a Dutch word for small (also the source of *pinkie*); *pinkeye* refers not to the color of the affected eye, but to its appearance. Dutch *pinck oogen,* of which *pinkeye* is a translation, meant small-eyed.

pink-′col″lar *adj.* pert. to an occupation in which women predominate.

pink′eye″ *n.* a contagious disease of the eye; conjunctivitis. ❑ *pink*

pink′ie (-ē) *n.* the little finger. ❑ *pink*

pink′ster (-stər) *n.* Whitsuntide. Also, **pinx′ter.** —**pinkster flower,** a variety of azalea.

pin′nace (pin′is) *n.* a light, two-masted vessel; a small boat.

pin′na·cle (pin′ə-kəl) *n.* **1,** a sharp point or peak; a spire. **2,** the highest point; acme.

pin′nate (pin′āt) *adj.* shaped like a feather.

pi′noch″le (pē′nuck″əl) *n.* a card game.

pi′ñon (pin′yən) *n.* a variety of pine tree; its fruit.

pin′point″ *n.* extreme exactitude; a pin's point or similar fineness. —*v.t.* locate exactly, as for precision bombing.

pin′set″ter *n.* an automatic device in a bowling alley that sets up the pins and returns the ball. Also, **pin′spot″ter.**

pin′stripe″ *adj.* (of a fabric) having thin lines of a different color. —*n.* **1,** a fabric so woven. **2,** any such line or stripe.

pint (pīnt) *n.* a measure of capacity, sixteen liquid oz., one-half quart.

pin′tail″ *n.* a wild duck with a pointed tail.

pin′to (pin′tō) *adj.* mottled. —*n.* a piebald horse or pony.

pin-′up *n.* an attractive person or a picture of such a person suitable for hanging.

pin′wheel″ *n.* **1,** a wheel that spins on a pin when blown upon. **2,** revolving fireworks.

pinx′ter (pink′stər) *n.* pinkster.

pin′y (pī′nē) *adj.* of the pine.

Pin'yin' *n.* a system for transliterating Chinese.

pi″o·neer' (pī″ə-nir') *n.* one who goes ahead; an early settler. —*v.t. & i.* do or be first.

pi'ous (pī'əs) *adj.* **1,** godly; devout. **2,** pretending piety. —**pi'ous·ness,** *n.*

pip *n.* **1,** a disease of fowls. **2,** a spot on a radar screen. **3,** a small seed, as of an apple; something like it, as a spot on dice, a suit symbol on playing cards, etc. **4,** (*Slang*) something remarkable.

pipe (pīp) *n.* **1,** a long tube for conveying a fluid. **2,** a tube and its attached bowl, for smoking. **3,** one of the tubes of an organ. **4,** (*Archaic*) a musical wind instrument. **5,** a shrill voice; a bird's note. **6,** a wine measure, usu. 126 gallons. —*v.t.* **1,** supply with, or convey by or as by, pipe. **2,** (*Naut.*) summon or salute with the sound of a whistle or pipe. **3,** utter in a shrill voice; whistle. —*v.i.* **1,** chirp; whistle. **2,** play on a pipe. —**pipe down,** (*Slang*) be quiet. —**pipe dream,** a vain hope. —**pipe up,** (*Informal*) speak up.

pipe'line″ *n.* **1,** a pipe for conveying oil or gas over long distances. **2,** a means of obtaining secret information.

pip'er *n.* a flutist or bagpiper. —**pay the piper, 1,** bear the costs (of something). **2,** suffer the consequences (of an action).

pipe'stem″ *n.* the stem of a pipe. —*adj.* (*Informal*) very thin, as a person's legs.

pi·pette' (pī-pet') *n.* a small tube. Also, **pi·pet'.**

pip'ing (pī'ping) *n.* **1,** a system of pipes. **2,** a trim of covered cord. —**piping hot,** very hot.

pip'it *n.* a small bird resembling the lark that sings in flight.

pip'pin (pip'in) *n.* **1,** a variety of apple. **2,** (*Slang*) something lovely.

pip'squeak″ *n.* (*Slang*) an unimportant, usu. small person, esp. one who is obtrusive or presumptuous.

pi'quant (pē'kənt) *adj.* agreeably pungent; attractive though racy. —**pi'quan·cy,** *n.*

pique (pēk) *v.t.* **1,** wound the pride of; nettle. **2,** arouse the interest of. —*n.* wounded pride; umbrage.

pi·qué' (pē-kā') *n.* a ribbed fabric.

pi·quet' (pi-kā') *n.* a card game for two.

pi·ran'ha (pi-ron'yə) *n.* a small tropical fish, voracious and typically vicious.

pi'rate (pī'rət) *n.* **1,** a sea-robber; a pirate's ship. **2,** hijacker. **3,** one who steals a literary or artistic idea. —*v.t.* **1,** rob at sea. **2,** publish without legal right. —**pi'-**

ra·cy (pī'rə-sė) *n.* —**pi·rat'i·cal** (pī-rat'i-kəl) *adj.*

pi·rogue' (pi-rōg') *n.* a canoe hollowed out from the trunk of a tree.

pir″ou·ette' (pir″ə-wet') *n.* in ballet dancing, a spinning on the toes.

pis″ca·to'ri·al (pis″kə-tôr'ė-əl) *adj.* pert. to fishing or those who fish.

Pis'ces (pis'ēz) *n.* a constellation, the Fish (see *zodiac*).

pis·ci- (pis-i) *pref.* fish.

pish *interj.* nonsense!

pis'mire (pis'mīr) *n.* an ant.

pis·ta'chi·o″ (pis-tä'shė-ō″) *n.* [*pl.* **-os″** (-ōz″)] a tree bearing a greenish edible nut; the nut.

pis'til *n.* (*Bot.*) the seed-bearing organ of a flower.

pis'tol (pis'təl) *n.* a small firearm held and fired by one hand. —**pis'tol-whip″,** *v.t.* beat with a pistol.

pis·tole' (pis-tōl') *n.* a former gold coin of various countries, esp. Spain.

pis'ton (pis'tən) *n.* a cylinder moving within a fitting bore to impart motion.

pit *n.* **1,** a hole in the ground; an abyss; a mine, or shaft in a mine. **2,** a depression; a small scar. **3,** a small arena; (*Brit.*) the cheaper seats in a theater. **4,** an area for trading in a stock or grain exchange, etc. **5,** the stone of a fruit. **6,** (*pl.*) (*Slang*) the worst. —*v.t.* [**pit'ted, -ting**] **1,** make scars in. **2,** match (one person or force) against another. **3,** remove the pits from, as fruit. —**pit viper,** a snake having a deep pit in the skin between the eye and the nostril.

pi'ta (pē'tə) *n.* a round, flat bread often filled with meat, etc.

pit'a·pat″ (pit'ə-pat″) *n.* a succession of taps; a light quick step.

pitch (pich) *v.t.* **1,** hurl; toss; throw. **2,** set up, as a tent. **3,** (*Music*) start (a tune) by sounding the keynote. —*v.i.* **1,** toss something; specif., throw a ball to a batter. **2,** encamp. **3,** plunge headlong; also, incline; slope. **4,** (with *on* or *upon*) decide. **5,** rise and fall, as a ship at sea. —*n.* **1,** a throw; toss. **2,** a headlong fall. **3,** the fore-and-aft plunging of a ship. **4,** the extreme point or degree or height or depth. **5,** slope; a declivity. **6,** (*Music*) highness or lowness of tone. **7,** a thick black substance; tar. **8,** the number of characters per inch of a certain size of type. **9,** (*Computers*) the number of spaces between pixels on a video screen. **10,** (*Cricket*) the area of the playing field between the wickets. —**pitch dark,** complete dark. —**pitch in,** (*Informal*) set to work with energy. —**pitch into,**

(*Informal*) attack. —**pitch pipe,** a harmonica-like device for giving the pitch (as to singers, etc.).

pitch-'black' *adj.* as black as pitch.

pitch'blende'' (pich'blend'') a lustrous black mineral, a source of radium and uranium.

pitch'er (-ər) *n.* **1,** a vessel with a handle for holding liquids. **2,** (*Baseball*) the player who pitches. **3,** a golf club for lofting shots, No. 7 iron.

pitch'fork'' *n.* a tool for lifting hay.

pitch'man'' *n.* [*pl.* **-men''**] a hawker.

pit'e·ous (pit'ė-əs) *adj.* sad; arousing pity. —**pit'e·ous·ness,** *n.* ❏ *pitiable*

pit'fall'' *n.* a trap; a hidden danger.

pith *n.* **1,** the spongy tissue in the stems of certain plants. **2,** the essential part; gist. **3,** vigor. —**pith'y,** *adj.*

pit'i·a·ble (pit'ė-ə-bəl) *adj.* deserving pity. —**pit'i·a·ble·ness,** *n.*

> **pitiable, piteous, pitiful**
> Similar words with slightly different meanings. *Pitiable* and *pitiful* mean deserving pity; *piteous* means arousing pity. *Pitiful* also means paltry, and once meant compassionate.

pit'i·ful (-fəl) *adj.* **1,** deserving pity. **2,** paltry. —**pit'i·ful·ness,** *n.* ❏ *pitiable*

pit'i·less (-ləs) *adj.* unmerciful. —**pit'i·less·ness,** *n.*

pi'ton (pē'ton) *n.* (*Mountain Climbing*) a metal spike driven into rock or ice, used to secure a rope.

pit'tance (pit'əns) *n.* a very small and inadequate quantity, esp. of money.

pit'ter-pat''ter (pit'ər-pat''ər) *n.* pit-a-pat.

pi·tu'i·tar''y (pi-tū'ə-ter''ė) *adj. & n.* (pert. to) a small endocrine gland.

pit'y (pit'ė) *n.* **1,** a feeling of compassion for another's grief or suffering. **2,** a cause of regret. —*v.t.* feel compassion for.

più (pyoo) *adv.* (*It.*) more.

piv'ot (piv'ət) *n.* a pin on which an object turns; hence, a cardinal or critical point. —*v.i.* turn; hinge. —**piv'ot·al,** *adj.*

pix'el (pik'səl) *n.* one of the small dots that make up the picture on a television screen.

pix'ie (pik'sė) *n.* a mischievous elf. Also, **pix'y.**

pix'i·lat''ed (pik'sə-lā''tid) *adj.* (*Informal*) mentally eccentric.

piz'za (pēt'tsə) *n.* an Italian baked dish resembling a pie, made of leavened bread dough rolled out into a thin sheet (usu. round) and topped with a tomato sauce and cheese and other seasonings. —**piz''ze·ri'a** (pēt''tsə-rē'ə) *n.* a restaurant specializing in pizza.

piz''zi·ca'to (pit''sə-kä'tō) *adj.* (*It.*) played by plucking the strings with the fingers.

plac'ard (plak'ərd) *n.* a notice posted in a public place; poster. —*v.t.* place a poster on.

pla'cate (plā'kāt) *v.t.* pacify; conciliate. —**pla'ca·to·ry** (-kə-tôr-ė) *adj.*

place (plās) *n.* **1,** region; locality; spot; a particular spot or building. **2,** room to stand or sit in. **3,** the proper or allocated position for anything. **4,** a job; situation. **5,** social status; duty. **6,** second in a horse race. —*v.t.* **1,** put or set in a particular position; set in order; arrange. **2,** find a home or job for. **3,** put; repose. **4,** locate; identify, as by association. —*v.i.* finish second. —**place kick,** (*Football*) a kick of the ball held upright on the ground. —**place setting,** the necessary eating utensils for one person. —**take place,** occur.

> **place**
> ↔ From Greek *plateia*, broad, flat, which also is the source of *piazza* and *plate*.

pla·ce'bo (plə-sē'bō) *n.* **1,** (*Med.*) an inert medicine prescribed to humor or pacify a patient. **2,** (*Rom. Cath. Ch.*) the vespers for the dead. **3,** a control dose given to one of two groups in a medical experiment.

> **placebo**
> ↔ From Latin *placere*, to please; the *placebo* was supposed to please the patient (if not provide a cure).

place'ment (-mənt) *n.* **1,** act or result of placing. **2,** employment. **3,** a place kick.

pla·cen'ta (plə-sen'tə) *n.* the organ in the womb to which the fetus is attached.

plac'er (plà'sər) *n.* in mining, a place where sand, gravel, etc. is washed for gold.

plac'id (plas'id) *adj.* serene; unruffled. —**pla·cid'i·ty,** *n.*

plack'et (plak'it) *n.* a slit in a skirt, coat tail, etc.

pla'gia·rism (plā'jə-riz-əm) *n.* the offering of another's artistic or literary work, ideas, research, etc. as one's own. —**pla'gia·rist,** *n.* —**pla'gia·rize'',** *v.t. & i.*

plague (plāg) *n.* **1,** a pestilential epidemic disease. **2,** severe trouble; scourge. **3,** (*Informal*) a nuisance. —*v.t.* **1,** harass; annoy. **2,** afflict with the plague. —**pla'guy,** *adj.*

plaice (plās) *n.* a kind of flatfish or flounder.

plaid (plad) *n.* a wool fabric with a tartan or similar pattern; the pattern itself. —*adj.* having a crossbarred pattern.

plain (plān) *adj.* **1,** flat; level; unobstructed; open. **2,** easily understood. **3,** sheer; downright. **4,** without a figured pattern. **5,** not handsome or fancy; homely. **6,** simple; sincere; frank. —*n.* an extent of level country. —**plain′ness,** *n.*

plain′clothes″ *adj.* not in uniform, as a detective.

plains′man (plānz′mən) *n.* [*pl.* **-men**] a dweller on an undeveloped plain.

plain′song″ *n.* a liturgical chant.

plain-′spo″ken *adj.* frank. —**plain-″spo′ken·ness,** *n.*

plaint (plānt) *n.* **1,** a sad song; lamentation. **2,** a complaint.

plain′tiff (plān′tif) *n.* (*Law*) the person who brings suit.

---

plaintiff, plaintive
☞ Do not confuse the legal term *plaintiff*, a person who brings a suit, and *plaintive*, an adjective meaning mournful.

---

plain′tive (plān′tiv) *adj.* mournful. —**plain′tive·ness,** *n.* ❏ *plaintiff*

plait (plāt) *n.* **1,** a braid, as of hair. **2,** an overlapping fold; pleat. —*v.t.* braid (hair).

plan *n.* **1,** a diagram or drawing, esp. of an uncompleted structure. **2,** arrangement of parts in a certain design. **3,** a formulated scheme for getting something done. —*v.t.* [**planned, plan′ning**] **1,** make a design or diagram of. **2,** devise ways and means for. —*v.i.* decide on future acts. —**plan′ner,** *n.* —**planned parenthood,** the advance planning of family size by parents; (*cap.*) an organization dedicated to promoting this.

plane (plān) *adj.* level; flat. —*n.* **1,** a flat or level surface. **2,** a grade or level, as of thought, etc. **3,** an airplane. **4,** a tool for smoothing wood. **5,** a type of tree, as the sycamore. —*v.t.* smooth with a plane. —*v.i.* to glide, as in a hydroplane.

plan′et (plan′it) *n.* a celestial body revolving around the sun. —**plan′e·tar·y,** *adj.*

---

planet
↔ From Greek *planētēs,* a wanderer, referring to the motion of the planets across the skies.

---

plan″e·tar′i·um (plan″i-tār′ē-əm) *n.* [*pl.* **-a** (-ə)] a device to represent the heavenly bodies and their movement; the auditorium or building housing it.

plan′e·tar″y (plan′ə-ter″ē) *adj.* **1,** pert. to a planet or the planets. **2,** pert. to system of gears, esp. an automobile transmission.

plan″e·tes′i·mal (plan″ə-tes′ə-məl) *n.* one of numerous small solid heavenly bodies which may have united to form the planets and moons of our solar system.

plan′et·oid″ *n.* a minor planet; asteroid.

plank *n.* **1,** a long, thick board. **2,** an item of a political party's platform. —*v.t.* **1,** cover with planks. **2,** (with *down*) pay; deliver. **3,** cook and serve on a board.

plank′ton (plank′tən) *n.* the microscopic animals and plants that drift freely in natural bodies of water and on which most marine life feeds.

plant (plant) *n.* **1,** a living organism, lacking voluntary motion, usually rooted in and growing from the soil. **2,** a seedling or cutting; anything planted. **3,** a factory; a business building and its equipment. —*v.t.* **1,** put in the ground to grow. **2,** set firmly in position. **3,** implant or engender, as ideas, etc. **4,** (*Slang*) secrete (something) to trick or incriminate someone —**plant louse,** aphid.

plan′tain (plan′tin) *n.* **1,** a common weed with broad leaves. **2,** a tropical tree; its bananalike fruit.

plan·ta′tion (plan-tā′shən) *n.* a large estate on which cotton, sugar, or some other crop is cultivated.

plant′er *n.* **1,** a rich farmer; a plantation owner. **2,** a small plant-holder. —**planter's punch,** a sweetened drink of rum and lemon or lime juice.

plaque (plak) *n.* **1,** an ornamental or commemorative tablet. **2,** a patch of skin disease. **3,** mucus containing bacteria on a tooth.

plash *n.* **1,** a splash. **2,** a puddle. —*v.t.* & *i.* **1,** splash. **2,** bend down and interweave the branches of, as a hedge.

plas′ma (plaz′mə) *n.* **1,** the liquid part of blood, lymph, or milk. **2,** charged particles. **3,** a green quartz.

plas′ter (plàs′tər) *n.* **1,** a wet paste of lime, sand, water, etc., that dries to a hard smooth finish. **2,** a remedy spread on cloth and applied to the body. —*v.t.* **1,** apply plaster to. **2,** spread on. —**plas′tered,** *adj.* (*Slang*) drunk. —**plas′ter·ing,** *n.* —**plaster of Paris,** a white paste used in molding.

plas′ter·board″ *n.* a layered building material for walls, etc.

plas′tic (plas′tik) *adj.* **1,** capable of being molded, esp. by pressure; pliant. **2,**

(*Slang*) phony; not trustworthy. —*n*. **1,** a plastic substance, esp. one of a group of synthetic materials used as substitutes for wood, metal, etc. **2,** [also, **plastic money**] credit card(s). —**plas′ti·cal·ly,** *adv.* —**plastic arts,** the arts of modeling or molding plastic materials, as plaster, clay, etc. —**plastic surgery,** surgery to correct deformities or repair mutilations. —**plastic wood,** a plastic that dries to the consistency of wood.

plas·tic′i·ty (plas-tis′ə-tē) *n.* state of being plastic.

plate (plāt) *n.* **1,** a thin flat sheet of metal, glass, etc.; such a sheet used or prepared for any purpose, as printing, photography, etc. **2,** a shallow dish for food; its contents. **3,** gold and silver table dishes and utensils. **4,** a denture; a setting for false teeth. **5,** in an electron tube, the electrode to which the electrons flow. **6,** (*Baseball*) home base. —*v.t.* apply a coating of metal to. —**plate glass,** a superior kind of thick glass, rolled and polished, used for mirrors, shop windows, etc.

pla·teau′ (pla-tō′) *n.* **1,** an extent of elevated land; a tableland. **2,** a period or area of little change.

plat′en (plat′ən) *n.* **1,** the plate that presses paper against printing type. **2,** the roller of a typewriter.

plat′form (plat′fôrm) *n.* **1,** a raised flooring. **2,** a statement of political policies.

plat′i·num (plat′ə-nəm) *n.* **1,** a precious silver-white metallic element, no. 78, symbol Pt. **2,** of a recording, having sold a million copies. —**platinum blonde,** a woman with hair of extremely pale yellow.

plat′i·tude″ (plat′i-tood″) *n.* a trite, obvious remark. —**plat″i·tu′di·nous,** *adj.*

pla·ton′ic (plə-ton′ik) *adj.* solely spiritual; not sensual. —**pla·ton′i·cal·ly,** *adv.*

pla·toon′ (plə-toon′) *n.* a body of troops, comprising several squads; (*Sports*) a specialized group of players. —*v.t. & i.* (*Sports*) to alternate players at the same position.

---

platoon
↔ From French *peloton*, little ball, extended over time to refer to a small group of people.

---

plat′ter (plat′ər) *n.* **1,** a broad shallow dish for serving food. **2,** a phonograph record.

plat′y·pus (plat′ə-pəs) *n.* a small, egg-laying, aquatic mammal with a bill like a duck's.

plau′dit (plâ′dit) *n.* (usually *pl.*) applause.

plau′si·ble (plâ′zə-bəl) *adj.* seemingly true or trustworthy. —**plau″si·bil′i·ty,** *n.*

play (plā) *v.i.* **1,** move lightly and quickly; flicker; dart. **2,** engage in a game; take recreation. **3,** act; behave. **4,** act on the stage; perform music. —*v.t.* **1,** engage in (a game); compete against; bet on. **2,** perform upon (a musical instrument). **3,** perform (a play, musical composition, trick, etc.); assume the role of. **4,** put in operation or motion. —*n.* **1,** brisk or free motion; freedom; scope. **2,** amusement; diversion; fun; jest. **3,** a dramatic work. **4,** in a game, one's turn to act; the move made or action taken. —**make a play for,** try to obtain; solicit; woo. —**play around,** (*Informal*) flirt; dally. —**play at,** do inexpertly or halfheartedly. —**play back,** replay, as a record. —**play down,** depreciate. —**play down to,** (*Informal*) treat in a condescending manner. —**playing card,** one of the pasteboard or plastic cards, 2¼ or 2½ by 3½ inches, used in many games. —**play on words,** a pun. —**play up,** emphasize.

play′act″ *v.i.* **1,** pretend; make believe. **2,** behave artificially. —**play′act″ing,** *n.*

play′bill″ *n.* a theater program.

play′boy″ *n.* (*Slang*) a rich, frivolous man.

play′er *n.* **1,** a performer in a game, play, etc. **2,** (*Informal*) a participant, as in a conference. —**player piano,** a piano which automatically plays music recorded mechanically on piano rolls.

play′ful *adj.* frolicsome; jocular. —**play′ful·ness,** *n.*

play′girl″ *n.* (*Slang*) a beautiful, pleasure-seeking woman; the companion of a playboy.

play′go″er *n.* one who regularly attends plays.

play′ground″ *n.* a field for games, etc.

play′house″ *n.* **1,** theater. **2,** a small house for children's play.

play′let (plā′lit) *n.* a short dramatic play.

play′mate″ *n.* a companion at play. Also, **play′fel″low.**

play-′off″ *n.* a contest to decide a previous tie.

play′thing″ *n.* a toy.

play′wright″ *n.* a dramatist.

pla′za (plä′zə) *n.* an open square.

plea (plē) *n.* **1,** an entreaty. **2,** pretext; excuse. **3,** (*Law*) a defendant's answer to the charge against him. —**plea bargaining,** agreement in advance of trial between

---

prosecution and defense for a certain plea and sentence.

plead (plēd) *v.i.* **1,** (with *with*) try to persuade; beg; implore. **2,** (*Law*) present a plea. —*v.t.* urge or allege as an excuse or defense. —**plead′ings,** *n.pl.* statements made in court.

pleas′ance (plez′ əns) *n.* a secluded formal garden attached to a mansion.

pleas′ant (plez′ ənt) *adj.* agreeable. —**pleas′ant·ness,** *n.*

pleas′ant·ry (plez′ ən-trē) *n.* **1,** banter. **2,** a jest.

please (plēz) *v.t.* give satisfaction or delight to. —*v.i.* **1,** give satisfaction. **2,** choose; wish; think fit. —*adv.* if you so wish: a polite form in imperative construction, short for if you please, as in *please do this.* —**pleas′ing,** *adj.* attractive; agreeable.

pleas′ure (plezh′ ər) *n.* **1,** a feeling of enjoyment or delight. **2,** a cause or source of this feeling. **3,** desire; preference. —**pleas′ur·a·ble,** *adj.*

pleat (plēt) *n.* a fold, as of cloth. —*v.t.* lay in folds.

plebe (plēb) *n.* at the U.S. military and naval academies, a fourth-classman (freshman).

ple·be′ian (pli-bē′ ən) *adj.* pert. to the common people; vulgar. —*n.* one of the common people.

pleb′i·scite″ (pleb′ ə-sīt″) *n.* a vote by the whole people.

plebs (plebz) *n.sing.* [*pl.* **ple′bes** (plē′bēz)] in ancient Rome, the populace.

plec′trum (plek′ trəm) *n.* a small flat implement for plucking the strings of a musical instrument.

pledge (plej) *n.* **1,** a thing given as security. **2,** a promise. **3,** a candidate for admission to a fraternity or sorority who has not yet been initiated. —*v.t.* **1,** pawn. **2,** promise, esp. a donation.

ple·na·ry (plen′ ə-rē) *adj.* **1,** full; unqualified. **2,** fully attended or constituted.

plen″i·po·ten′ti·ar″y (plen″i-pō-ten′shē-er″ē) *n.* an emissary, as an ambassador, with full powers. —*adj.* having full powers.

plen′i·tude″ (plen′ i-tood″) *n.* abundance; fullness.

plen′te·ous (plen′ tē-əs) *adj.* abundant. —**plen′te·ous·ness,** *n.*

plen′ti·ful (plen′ ti-fəl) *adj.* **1,** ample. **2,** fruitful. —**plen′ti·ful·ness,** *n.*

plen′ty (plen′ tē) *n.* an adequate supply; abundance.

ple′num (plē′ nəm) *n.* **1,** fullness; the op-

posite of vacuum. **2,** a quantity of air, etc., under greater than atmospheric pressure. **3,** a full meeting or assembly.

ple′o·nasm″ (plē′ ə-naz″əm) *n.* redundancy, or an instance of it.

pleth′o·ra (pleth′ ə-rə) *n.* overfullness; superabundance.

pleu′ra (plŭr′ ə) *n.* the membrane lining of the chest. —**pleu′ral,** *adj.* —**pleu·ris′tic,** *adj.*

pleu′ri·sy (plŭr′ ə-sē) *n.* inflammation of the pleura.

Plex′i·glas″ (plek′ sə-glàs″) *n.* a clear thermoplastic compound.

plex′us (plek′ səs) *n.* a network, as of blood vessels and nerve fibers. —**plex′i·form,** *adj.*

pli′a·ble (plī′ ə-bəl) *adj.* **1,** flexible. **2,** compliant. —**pli″a·bil′i·ty,** *n.*

pli′ant (plī′ ənt) *adj.* supple; pliable. —**pli′an·cy,** *n.*

pli′ers (plī′ ərz) *n.pl.* pincers with long, blunt jaws.

plight (plīt) *n.* **1,** condition; predicament. **2,** a pledge. —*v.t.* **1,** pledge, as one's word, honor, etc. **2,** betroth.

Plim′soll mark (plim′səl) a line showing a ship's safe load capacity.

> **Plimsoll mark**
> ↔ From the 19th-c. British politician Samuel *Plimsoll*, who thought of the need for the marking.

plinth *n.* the slab at the base of a column, pedestal, statue, etc.

Pli′o·film″ (plī′ ə-) *n.* (*T.N.*) a plastic that forms flexible, transparent sheets, used for raincoats, etc.

PLO *Abbr.* Palestine Liberation Organization.

plod *v.i.* [**plod′ded, -ding**] **1,** trudge. **2,** toil; drudge. —**plod′der,** *n.*

plop *n.* the sound of something falling into liquid with little splashing. —*v.i. & t.* [**plopped, plop′ping**] fall, drop, or set with a plop.

plot *n.* **1,** a small piece of ground. **2,** a plan or map. **3,** an intrigue; conspiracy. **4,** the plan of a novel, play, etc. —*v.t.* [**plot′ted, -ting**] **1,** chart; map; plan. **2,** contrive. —*v.i.* conspire.

plot′ter *n.* **1,** one who or that which plots. **2,** (*Computers*) a printer that draws images using computer-directed pens.

plov′er (pluv′ ər) *n.* a shorebird akin to the sandpiper.

plow *n.* an implement that furrows and turns over the soil; a similar instrument, as a snowplow. —*v.t. & i.* **1,** till with a

plow. 2, move, cleave, or push through. Also, (*Brit.*) **plough. —plow′man** (-mən) *n.*

plow′share″ *n.* the cutting blade of a plow.

ploy (ploi) *n.* **1,** a game; an escapade or trick. **2,** a stratagem or remark that subtly puts an antagonist at a disadvantage in a game or in argument or conversation.

pluck (pluk) *v.t.* **1,** pull off or up; pick. **2,** strip (a fowl) of feathers. **3,** jerk; twitch. **4,** twang, as a banjo. **5,** (*Slang*) rob; fleece. **—***n.* **1,** a twitch; tug; twang. **2,** courage; spirit. **—pluck′y,** *adj.* spirited; courageous.

plug *n.* **1,** a stopper. **2,** a connection, as for a hose, an electrical wire, etc. **3,** a cake of tobacco. **4,** (*Informal*) a favorable remark. **5,** (*Slang*) something unfit or worthless, esp. a horse. **6,** an artificial lure in fishing. **—***v.t.* **[plugged, plug′ging] 1,** stop up with a plug. **2,** (*Informal*) shoot. **3,** (*Informal*) publicize. **—***v.i.* work steadily. **—plug′ger,** *n.* a dogged worker. **—plug′-ug″ly,** *n.* (*Slang*) a rowdy; tough; gangster's henchman.

plug·o′la (plug-ō′lə) *n.* (*Slang*) payola paid to receive a plug on radio or TV.

plum *n.* **1,** the juicy, smooth-skinned fruit of a tree similar to the peach; the tree. **2,** a raisin. **3,** a prize or reward; a good thing. **4,** a bluish-red color.

> **plum, prune**
> ↔ Both words derive from Greek *proumnon,* plum; *prune* comes from the Latin descendant and *plum* from a Germanic derivative of the Latin word.

plum′age (ploo′mij) *n.* **1,** feathers. **2,** (*Humorous*) bright or fancy clothing.

plumb (plum) *n.* **1,** a ball of lead dropped on a line (*plumb line*) for testing perpendicularity, depth, etc. **2,** the vertical. **—***v.t.* test by a plumb line. **—***adj.* vertical. **—***adv.* **1,** vertically. **2,** exactly. **3,** (*Informal*) utterly.

plum·ba′go (plum-bā′gō) *n.* graphite, used in lead pencils, etc.

plumb′er (plum′ər) *n.* **1,** a worker on water pipes, bathroom fixtures, steam fittings, etc. **2,** (*Slang*) an undercover agent, esp. one assigned to stop leakage of information. **—plumber's helper,** a plunger.

plumb′ing *n.* **1,** the trade of a plumber. **2,** piping and attached fixtures.

plume (ploom) *n.* a feather or bunch of feathers. **—***v.t.* preen or adorn (oneself).

plum′met (plum′it) *n.* a plumb. **—***v.i.* plunge straight down.

plump *v.i. & t.* **1,** drop suddenly and heavily. **2,** (with *for*) support (as a candidate) vigorously. **—***n.* a heavy fall. **—***adj.* fat; well-rounded. **—***adv.* heavily; flatly. **—plump′ness,** *n.*

plun′der (plun′dər) *v.t.* rob; take by force. **—***n.* **1,** robbery. **2,** booty.

plunge (plunj) *v.t.* **1,** thrust suddenly (into a liquid, flesh, etc.). **2,** cast or throw (into a state or condition, as war, debt, etc.). **—***v.i.* **1,** dive or leap. **2,** rush headlong. **3,** bet recklessly. **—***n.* a sudden dive or leap.

plung′er *n.* **1,** a mechanical part that moves up and down, as a piston. **2,** an implement for unclogging a toilet. **3,** (*Slang*) a reckless gambler.

plunk *v.i.* make a quick, hollow, heavy, often metallic sound. **—***v.t.* **1,** twang. **2,** drop or slap down. **—***n.* the sound of plunking.

plu″per′fect (ploo″pēr′fikt) *adj. & n.* (*Gram.*) past perfect, as *I had done it.*

plu′ral (plûr′əl) *adj.* designating more than one. **—***n.* (*Gram.*) a plural form.

plu·ral′i·ty (plû-ral′ə-tē) *n.* the receipt of more votes than any other candidate; the amount of excess. ❑ *majority*

plus *adj.* **1,** indicating addition. **2,** additional. **3,** positive; greater than zero. **—***prep.* with the addition of. **—***n.* **1,** the plus sign (+). **2,** something additional. **—plus fours,** long baggy knickerbockers.

plush *n.* a fabric like velvet, but with a longer pile. **—***adj.* (*Informal*) luxurious; showy.

plu·toc′ra·cy (ploo-tok′rə-sē) *n.* **1,** government by the rich. **2,** the influential rich.

plu′to·crat″ (ploo′tə-krat″) *n.* **1,** a very rich person. **2,** an adherent of plutocracy. **—plu″to·crat′ic,** *adj.* **—plu″to·crat′i·cal·ly,** *adv.*

plu·to′ni·um (ploo-tō′nē-əm) *n.* a radioactive chemical element, no. 94, symbol Pu.

plu′vi·ous (ploo′vē-əs) *adj.* pert. to rain; rainy. **—plu′vi·al,** *adj.*

ply (plī) *n.* a layer or strand. **—***v.t.* **1,** wield diligently. **2,** work at steadily. **3,** address persistently, as with questions. **4,** offer (to someone) frequently and persistently, as drink. **—***v.i.* travel a course regularly.

ply′wood″ *n.* several layers of wood laminated together.

PMS premenstrual syndrome.

pneu·mat′ic (nū-mat′ik) *adj.* **1,** pert. to

air. **2,** inflated with air. **3,** worked by compressed air. **—pneu·mat′i·cal·ly,** *adv.*

pneu·mo- (noo-mō) *pref.* the lungs.

pneu·mo′ni·a (noo-mō′nyə) *n.* inflammation of the tissues of the lungs. **—pneumon′ic** (-mon′ik) *adj.*

poach (pōch) *v.t. & i.* **1,** cook (food) in simmering water. **2,** trespass, esp. to hunt or fish. **—poach′er,** *n.* a trespasser.

pock (pok) *n.* a pus-filled eruption, as in smallpox. **—pock′mark″,** *n.*

pock′et (pok′it) *n.* **1,** a pouch inserted in a garment; its contents, esp. money. **2,** a cavity or hollow. **3,** an isolated area, group, etc. **—***adj.* of small size. **—***v.t.* **1,** put in a pocket. **2,** appropriate; accept. **3,** suppress. **—in one's pocket,** under one's domination or control. **—line one's pockets,** get much money. **—pocket battleship,** a heavily armed vessel, smaller than usual because of treaty limitations. **—pocket billiards,** a game of sinking balls in pockets on a billiard table. **—pocket park,** a small city park. **—pocket veto,** the holding of a bill by a chief executive until it expires by law, in effect, a veto.

pock′et·book″ *n.* a purse.

pock′et·knife″ *n.* a folding knife to be carried in the pocket.

po′co (pō′kō) *adv.* (*It.*) somewhat. **—poco a poco,** *adv.* (*It.*) little by little; gradually.

pod *n.* **1,** the seed case of certain plants, as the pea or bean. **2,** a podlike container, as a spacecraft compartment, etc. **3,** a herd of seals or whales.

po·di′a·try (pō-dī′ə-trē) *n.* (*Med.*) the treatment of disorders of the feet. **—po·di′a·trist,** *n.*

po′di·um (pō′dē-əm) *n.* [*pl.* **-a** (-ə)] a speaker's or conductor's platform; dais. ❑ *dais*

po′em (pō′im) *n.* a composition in verse; lofty or imaginative writing or artistic expression.

po′e·sy (pō′ə-sē) *n.* **1,** poetry. **2,** the art of writing poetry.

po′et (pō′it) *n.* **1,** one who writes poems or is capable of lofty artistic expression. **—poet laureate,** the official poet of a state or nation.

po′et·as″ter (pō′it-as″tər) *n.* a writer of poor verse.

po·et′ic (pō-et′ik) *adj.* **1,** of or pert. to poetry. **2,** befitting poetry. Also, **po·et′i·cal.** **—poetic justice,** an ideal distribution of rewards and punishments. **—poetic license,** deviation from form to achieve a poetic effect.

po′et·ry (-rē) *n.* **1,** expression in poems. **2,** poems collectively. **3,** poetic qualities, spirit, or feeling. Also, **po′e·sy** (-zē).

po·go′ni·a (pə-gō′nē-ə) *n.* a type of orchid usu. having a single pale rose flower.

po′go stick (pō′gō) a pole with a spring, for making small hops.

po′grom (pō′grəm) *n.* an organized massacre, esp. of Jews.

poi *n.* (*Hawaiian*) a Hawaiian dish made from the root of the taro.

poign′ant (poin′yənt) *adj.* biting; painfully acute; affecting. **—poign′an·cy,** *n.*

poi′lu (pwä′loo) *n.* (*Fr.*, hairy) a Fr. soldier.

poin·ci·a′na (poin-sē-a′nə) *n.* a tropical tree bearing showy orange or scarlet flowers.

---

poinciana, poinsettia

↔ The *poinciana* was named for a 17th-c. governor of the French Antilles, M. de *Poinci.* The *poinsettia* was named for a 19th-c. American minister to Mexico, J. R. *Poinsett.*

---

poin·set′ti·a (poin-set′ē-ə) *n.* a plant with large scarlet leaves. ❑ *poinciana*

point *n.* **1,** a sharp or tapering end. **2,** a telling or essential feature. **3,** precise degree. **4,** aim; purpose. **5,** an exact spot or time. **6,** a unit of counting, measuring, or scoring. **7,** a unit of measurement for type; about 1/72 inch. **8,** one of the divisions of a compass. **9,** the period, esp. as a decimal mark. **10,** a percentage point. **—***v.t.* **1,** aim. **2,** (with *out*) indicate the direction or position of. **3,** (with *up*) emphasize. **—***v.i.* **1,** indicate direction with, or as with, the finger. **2,** tend; lead. **3,** face. **—point′y,** *adj.* pointed. **—point man, 1,** the soldier in charge of an infantry patrol. **2,** the principal contact person for a project, work team, etc. **—point of no return,** the place or moment in a journey or proceedings when one can no longer return or retreat. **—point of order,** a question as to whether proceedings are according to parliamentary law. **—point of view,** one's aspect of a subject or thing.

point-′blank″ *adj.* direct; straightforward.

point′ed (-id) *adj.* sharp; pertinent; intended to affect a person. **—point′ed·ness,** *n.*

point′er (-ər) *n.* **1,** a hand on a clock, etc. **2,** a tapering rod for pointing. **3,** a hunting dog. **4,** a bit of advice; a tip.

poin′til·lism (pwan′tə-liz-əm) *n.* a method of Fr. impressionist painters in which color is applied in small dots on a white field.

point'less (-ləs) *adj.* meaningless; purposeless. **—point'less·ness,** *n.*

point'y-head'ed *adj.* (*Slang, disparaging*) intellectual.

poise (poiz) *n.* **1,** equilibrium. **2,** carriage; bearing; self-possession. **—v.t. & i.** balance.

poi'son (poi'zən) *n.* **1,** a substance that causes injury or death upon ingestion, contact, or injection. **2,** any baneful influence or doctrine. **—v.t.** give poison to; corrupt or spoil with poison. **—poi'son·ous,** *adj.* **—poison ivy, oak, sumac,** plants that cause irritation of the skin. **—poison pill,** a strategy taken by a company to avoid a hostile takeover, esp. by making the takeover prohibitively expensive.

> **poison**
> ↔ From Latin *potio*, drink, also the source of English *potion*.

poke (pōk) *v.t.* **1,** thrust away, down, or through. **2,** jab; prod, as with a stick. **—v.i.** **1,** search; pry; grope. **2,** make a thrust. **3,** dawdle. **—n.** **1,** a thrust; nudge. **2,** a projecting brim on a bonnet. **3,** a bag; sack. **4,** a dawdler.

pok'er (pō'kər) *n.* **1,** a steel bar for stirring a fire. **2,** a card game. **—poker face,** (*Informal*) an expressionless face.

pok'y (pō'kė) *adj.* **1,** slow; boring. **2,** of a room, small and shabby. **—n.** (*Informal*) a jail. Also, **pok'ey. —pok'i·ness,** *n.*

po'lar (pō'lər) *adj.* pert. to, or at, the poles of a sphere, esp. of the earth. **—polar bear,** a large, creamy-white bear of the Arctic.

Po·la'ris (pō-lär'is) *n.* the North Star; the polestar.

po·lar'i·ty (pō-lär'ə-tė) *n.* the property whereby like magnetic poles repel and unlike poles attract each other.

po''lar·i·za'tion (pō''lər-ə-zā'shən) *n.* a state in which light rays exhibit different qualities in different directions. **—po'lar·ize''** (-īz'') *v.t.*

Po'lar·oid'' *n.* (*T.N.*) **1,** an optical glass used to polarize light to reduce glare, create the illusion of three-dimensional pictures, etc. **2,** a camera which takes pictures with a film that develops rapidly by itself.

pol'der (pōl'dər) *n.* reclaimed marshland that has been brought under cultivation.

pole (pōl) *n.* **1,** either end of the axis of a sphere; specif. either end (North Pole or South Pole) of the earth's axis. **2,** either

end of a magnet or terminal of an electric cell. **3,** a long, slender, tapering piece of wood. **4,** a measure of length, a rod, 5½ yds. **5,** (*cap.*) a native of Poland. **—v.t.** **1,** propel by a pole. **2,** support by poles. **—pole vault,** an athletic contest of leaping, aided by a long pole.

pole'ax'' *n.* **1,** a battle-ax with a hook or spike opposite the blade. **2,** an ax with a hammer face opposite the blade, for slaughtering cattle. **—v.t.** fell with or as with a poleax.

pole'cat'' (pōl'kat'') *n.* **1,** a small Europ. animal of the weasel family. **2,** in the U.S., a skunk.

> **polecat**
> ↔ From Old French *pol*, chicken; the polecat preyed on poultry.

po·lem'ic (pō-lem'ik) *n.* argument about doctrines. **—po·lem'i·cal,** *adj.* **—po·lem'ics,** *n.sing.* the art or practice of disputation.

pole'star'' *n.* **1,** the North Star. **2,** a guide; lodestar.

po·lice' (pə-lēs') *n.sing. & pl.* **1,** the civil department that maintains order and enforces the law. **2,** (*Mil.*) the work of keeping a camp clean. **—v.t.** **1,** guard and maintain order in. **2,** clean up, as a camp. **—police dog,** a German shepherd dog. **—police lock,** a lockable brace attached to a door to prevent it from being forced open. **—police officer,** a member of a police force. **—police state,** a territory, country, etc., governed by a repressive government.

po·lice'man (-mən) [*pl.* **-men**], **po·lice'wom''an** *n.* police officer.

pol'i·cy (pol'ə-sė) *n.* **1,** a course of conduct based on principle or advisability. **2,** a contract of insurance. **3,** a form of lottery.

pol''i·o·my''e·li'tis (pō''lė-ō-mī''ə-lī'tis) *n.* a spinal paralysis; infantile paralysis. Also, **pol'i·o.**

-po·lis *suf.* city.

pol'ish *v.t.* **1,** make smooth and glossy, as by rubbing. **2,** give elegance or refinement to. **—n.** **1,** a smooth, glossy finish. **2,** a mixture for polishing. **3,** refinement; elegance. **—polish off,** dispose of quickly.

Pol'ish (pō'lish) *adj. & n.* of or pert. to Poland or its people, language, etc.

Po·lit'bu''ro (pə-lit'byûr''ō) *n.* a policy-forming committee in a communist party.

po·lite' (pə-līt') *adj.* **1,** courteous; well-bred. **2,** refined. **—po·lite'ness,** *n.*

pol'i·tic (pol'ə-tik) *adj.* **1,** consisting of

citizens. **2,** wise; expedient. **3,** shrewd; crafty.

po·lit′i·cal (pə-lit′i-kəl) *adj.* pert. to governmental affairs or to politics. —**political action committee,** a political organization which lobbies and makes campaign donations in support of a cause. *Abbr.,* **PAC.** —**political science,** the science of the principles and conduct of government. —**politically correct,** (*Informal*) not offensive to any special interests.

pol″i·ti′cian (pol″ə-tish′ən) *n.* **1,** one skilled or active in politics. **2,** a statesman.

po·lit′i·cize″ (pə-lit′ə-sīz″) *v.i.* engage in political discussion or action. —*v.t.* make the subject of political discussion or dispute.

pol′i·tick″ (-tik″) *v.i.* engage in politics.

po·lit′i·co (pə-lit′i-kō) *n.* (*Slang*) a politician.

pol′i·tics (pol′ə-tiks) *n.sing.* **1,** the science of government. **2,** the activities of a political party. **3,** (construed as *pl.*) political opinions.

pol′i·ty (pol′ə-tē) *n.* a system of government.

pol′ka (pōl′kə) *n.* a lively dance; the music for it. —*v.i.* dance the polka. —**polka dots,** a pattern of round spots on a fabric.

poll (pōl) *n.* **1,** the voting at an election; the number of votes cast. **2,** (*pl.*) a place of voting. **3,** a survey of opinion. **4,** the head. —*v.t.* **1,** register the votes of; ask the opinions of. **2,** receive as votes. **3,** clip; shear; cut off. —**poll tax,** a tax on individuals who vote.

> **poll**
> ↔ From a Middle Low German word for the head; a voting *poll* is a counting of heads, a *poll tax* a *per capita* (per head) tax.

pol′lack (pol′ək) *n.* a marine food fish of the cod family.

pol′lard (pol′ərd) *n.* **1,** a tree cut back nearly to the trunk, to produce a dense head of branches. **2,** a stag, ox, etc. without horns.

pol′len (pol′ən) *n.* the fertilizing element of a plant, a fine yellow powder. —**pollen count,** a measure of the pollen in the air.

pol′li·nate″ (pol′ə-nāt″) *v.t.* fertilize (a flower). —**pol″li·na′tion,** *n.*

pol′li·wog″ (pol′ē-wog″) *n.* a tadpole.

poll′ster (pōl′stər) *n.* one who takes a poll, as of individual opinions.

pol·lute′ (pə-loot′) *v.t.* make impure; soil; defile. —**pol·lu′tion,** *n.*

Pol″ly·an′na (pol″ē-an′ə) *n.* an overoptimistic person.

> **Pollyanna**
> ↔ From a character in a novel by 19th-c. American writer Eleanor Porter.

po′lo (pō′lō) *n.* a game similar to hockey but played on horseback. —**polo shirt,** a short-sleeved knitted shirt.

pol″o·naise′ (pol″ə-nāz′) *n.* **1,** a stately Polish dance; the music for it. **2,** an outer dress for women.

po·lo′ni·um (pə-lō′nē-əm) *n.* a radioactive element, no. 84, symbol Po.

pol′ter·geist″ (pōl′tər-gīst″) *n.* a noisy and mischievous ghost.

pol·troon′ *n.* a coward. —**pol·troon′er·y,** *n.*

pol·y- (päl-ē) *pref.* many.

pol′y·an″dry (-an″drē) *n.* the state or practice of having more than one male mate or husband at the same time. —**pol″y·an′drous,** *adj.*

pol′y·chrome″ *adj.* having various colors. —*n.* a work of art done in several colors. Also, **pol″y·chro·mat′ic,** *adj.*

pol″y·clin′ic *adj.* treating various diseases. —*n.* a hospital or clinic that treats various diseases.

pol″y·dac′tyl *adj.* having too many fingers or toes. —**pol″y·dac′tyl·ism,** *n.*

pol″y·es′ter (päl′ē-es′tər) *n.* **1,** an ester used in making fibers, resins, and plastics. **2,** a polyester fiber, often blended with other fibers (as cotton or wool). **3,** a polyester resin used for making packaging or backing films or for molding and laminating.

pol″y·eth′yl·ene *adj.* a type of plastic.

po·lyg′a·my (pə-lig′ə-mē) *n.* the state or practice of having more than one mate (husband or wife) at the same time. —**po·lyg′a·mist,** *n.* —**po·lyg′a·mous,** *adj.*

pol′y·glot″ *adj.* knowing or comprising several languages.

pol′y·gon″ *n.* a closed plane figure with many sides and angles.

pol′y·graph″ (päl′ē-graf″) *n.* **1,** a device that records tracings of several different signals at once (as of blood pressure, respiration, etc.). **2,** lie detector. —*v.t.* to test (someone) with a polygraph.

po·lyg′y·ny (pə-lig′ə-nē) *n.* the state or practice of having more than one female mate or wife at the same time. —**po·lyg′y·nous** (-nəs) *adj.*

pol″y·he′dron (-hē′drən) *n.* [*pl.* **-dra** (-drə)] a many-sided solid.

pol'y·math″ (-math″) *n.* a person having extensive knowledge.

pol'y·mer (-mər) *n.* a chemical compound with very complex and heavy molecules.

Pol″y·ne′sian (pol″i-nē′zhən) *adj.* & *n.* of or pert. to the peoples of the So. Pacific islands called Oceania.

pol″y·no′mi·al (-nō′mė-əl) *adj.* containing many names or terms. —*n.* an algebraic expression consisting of two or more terms.

pol'yp (pol′ip) *n.* **1,** an invertebrate marine animal. **2,** a small tumor.

po·lyph′o·ny (pə-lif′ə-nė) *n.* **1,** (*Music*) a combining of two or more individual but harmonizing melodies. **2,** a multiplicity of sounds (as in an echo). —**pol″y·phon′ic** (pol″ə-fän′ik) *adj.*

pol″y·sty′rene *n.* a clear, hard plastic.

pol'y·syl′la·ble *n.* a word having many (usually four or more) syllables. —**pol″y·syl·lab′ic** (-si-lab′ik) *adj.*

pol″y·tech′nic *adj.* teaching many sciences. —*n.* a technical school.

pol'y·the·ism″ *n.* belief in more than one god. —**pol″y·the″ist,** *n.* —**pol″y·the·is′tic,** —**pol″y·the·is′ti·cal,** *adj.*

pol'y·to″nal *adj.* (*Music*) having more than one tonal center or key. —**pol″y·to·nal′i·ty,** *n.*

pol″y·un·sat′u·rat·ed *adj.* of animal or vegetable fats, having molecules with many double or triple bonds (associated with lower concentration of cholesterol in the blood). —**pol″y·un·sat′u·rate** (-rit) *n.*

pol'y·ur′e·thane″ (päl′ė-yûr′ə-thān″) *n.* any of various polymers used in making resins, flexible and rigid foams, and elastic, rubberlike substances.

pol″y·vi′nyl *n.* one of several thermoplastic vinyls. —**polyvinyl chloride,** a resin used in coatings, piping, etc.

pom'ace (pum′is) *n.* a crushed pulpy residue.

po·made′ (pō-mād′) *n.* a scented ointment.

po′man·der (pō′man-dər) *n.* a mixture of aromatic substances; the container for this mixture.

pome (pōm) *n.* the typical fruit of the apple family. —**po·ma′ceous** (-mā′shəs) *adj.*

pome′gran″ate (pom′gran″it) *n.* a tropical tree; its pulpy fruit. ❏ *grenade*

Pom″er·a′ni·an (pom″ə-rā′nė-ən) *n.* a small, long-haired dog.

pom'fret (pom′frit) *n.* a food fish of the North Atlantic and Pacific.

pom'mel (pum′əl) *n.* a rounded knob on a saddle, etc. —*v.t.* pummel.

pomp *n.* splendor; showy display.

pom'pa·dour″ (pom′pə-dôr″) *n.* a hairdress, the hair straight back from the forehead.

pom'pa·no″ (pom′pə-nō″) *n.* a food fish of tropical seas.

pom-′pom″ *n.* **1,** a many-barreled antiaircraft gun. **2,** pompon. —**pom-pom girl,** a cheerleader.

pom'pon *n.* **1,** a fluffy ball of feathers, wool, etc. **2,** a globelike flower, as a chrysanthemum.

pomp′ous (pom′pəs) *adj.* ostentatiously dignified or lofty. —**pom·pos′i·ty** (-pos′ə-tė), **pom′pous·ness,** *n.*

pon'cho (pon′chō) *n.* [*pl.* **-chos**] **1,** a blanket used as a cloak, with a hole in it for the head. **2,** a similar rainproof cloak.

pond *n.* a body of standing water, usu. smaller than a lake.

pon'der (pon′dər) *v.t.* & *i.* reflect (upon or over); consider deeply.

pon'der·ous (pon′der-əs) *adj.* very heavy; hence, unwieldy; tedious. —**pon′der·ous·ness,** *n.*

pone (pōn) *n.* a cornmeal bread.

pon·gee′ (pon-jē′) *n.* a soft silk fabric.

pon'iard (pon′yərd) *n.* a dagger.

pon'tiff (pon′tif) *n.* a bishop; specif. the Pope. —**pon·tif′i·cal,** *adj.*

pon·tif′i·cate (pon-tif′i-kət) *n.* the office of a bishop. —*v.i.* (-kāt″) assume an air of infallibility; speak pompously. —**pon·tif′i·ca′tion,** *n.*

pon·toon′ *n.* **1,** a flat-bottomed boat. **2,** a floating support for a temporary bridge; a buoy. **3,** a float for a seaplane.

po'ny (pō′nė) *n.* **1,** a horse of a small, stocky breed. **2,** (*Slang*) a trot; crib. **3,** a small liqueur glass. **4,** a medium-sized car. —**pony express,** a former system of mail delivery by relays of horses and riders.

po'ny·tail″ *n.* a woman's hairstyle.

Pon'zi (pon′zė) *n.* a type of business fraud in which old investors are paid off with money obtained from new ones. Also, **Pon'zi game, Pon'zi scheme.**

pooch *n.* (*Slang*) dog.

poo'dle (poo′dəl) *n.* a breed of dog with wiry curled hair.

pooh (poo) *interj.* of contempt. —**pooh″-pooh′,** *v.t.* treat with contempt; make light of.

Pooh′-Bah″ (poo′ bä′) a pompous person, esp. a public official.

---

fat, fāte, fär, fâre, fâll, àsk; met, hē, hếr, maybė; pin, pīne; not, nōte, ôr, tool

Pooh-Bah
↔ The name of a pompous public official in Gilbert & Sullivan's operetta *The Mikado*.

pool *n.* **1,** a still, deep place in a river; a pond; puddle. **2,** an open tank of water for swimming. **3,** pocket billiards. **4,** the totality of bets made on a contingency; pot. **5,** a combination of business interests or investors. —*v.t.* put into a common fund.

poop *n.* **1,** a raised deck in a ship's stern. **2,** (*Slang*) information. —*v.t.* (of a wave or a gust of wind) strike. —**pooped,** *adj.* (*Slang*) fatigued.

poop′er-scoop″er (poo′pər-skoo″pər) *n.* a device for picking up dog or cat excrement.

poor (pûr) *adj.* **1,** needy; not rich. **2,** lacking desirable qualities; inferior. **3,** spiritless. **4,** unfortunate; to be pitied. **5,** humble. —**poor boy,** (*Informal*) a submarine sandwich. —**poor farm,** a farm for paupers.

poor′house″ *n.* a home for paupers.

poor′ly (-lė) *adv. & adj.* not well.

poor-′mouth″ (*Slang*) *v.i.* use one's alleged poverty as an excuse. —*v.t.* disparage.

pop *n.* **1,** a short explosive sound. **2,** a soft drink. **3,** (*Informal*) papa. —*v.i.* [**popped, pop′ping**] **1,** make such a sound; burst. **2,** appear or disappear suddenly. —*v.t.* **1,** cause to burst or explode. **2,** put (in) quickly. —*adj.*(*Informal*) popular. —**pop art,** a movement, esp. in painting and sculpture, dealing with objects from everyday life and borrowing the techniques of commercial art. —**pop the question,** (*Informal*) propose marriage.

pop′corn″ *n.* a maize whose kernels burst when heated.

Pope (pōp) *n.* the bishop of Rome, leader of the Rom. Cath. Church. —**pop′-ish,** *adj.* (*Derog.*) pert. to this church.

pope
↔ From Greek *pappas*, father (the pope may be considered the father of the Rom. Cath. Church).

pop′eyed″ (-īd″) *adj.* having bulging eyes.

popinjay
↔ Not a jay, but a parrot is the source of this word, which comes from Arabic *babagha*, parrot.

pop′gun″ *n.* a toy gun.

pop′in·jay″ (pop′in-jā″) *n.* **1,** a woodpecker. **2,** a vain person.

pop′lar (pop′lər) *n.* a tree with light soft wood; the wood.

pop′lin *n.* a ribbed fabric.

poplin
↔ From Italian *papalina*, papal; so called because it was made at Avignon, a papal capital.

pop′o″ver *n.* a light muffin.

pop′pet (pop′it) *n.* a valve that opens by lifting from its seat.

pop′py (pop′ė) *n.* a flowering plant with a milky narcotic juice.

pop′py·cock″ (pop′ė-kok″) *n.* (*Informal*) nonsense; vain talk.

pop-′top′ *adj.* of a can, having a removable tab for opening. —*n.* such a can.

pop′u·lace (pop′yə-lis) *n.* the common people; the multitude.

pop′u·lar (pop′yə-lər) *adj.* **1,** pert. to, or intended for, the common people. **2,** generally liked. —**pop″u·lar′i·ty** (-lar′ə-tė) *n.* —**pop′u·lar·ize″** (-īz″) *v.t.* —**popular front,** a temporary coalition of political parties.

pop′u·late″ (pop′yə-lāt″) *v.t.* supply with inhabitants.

pop″u·la′tion (pop″yə-lā′shən) *n.* **1,** total number of inhabitants of a place. **2,** the process of populating. —**population explosion,** an unusually large increase in annual population growth.

pop′u·lism (pop′yə-liz-əm) *n.* a political philosophy in support of the common people. —**pop′u·list,** *adj. & n.*

pop′u·lous (pop′yə-ləs) *adj.* thickly inhabited. —**pop′u·lous·ness,** *n.*

por′ce·lain (pôr′sə-lin) *n.* a fine, white, translucent china.

porcelain
↔ The unusual derivation of this word is from Italian *porcellana*, a type of shell which apparently looked like the vulva of a sow (*porcella*).

porch (pôrch) *n.* **1,** a covered approach to a doorway. **2,** a veranda.

por′cine (pôr′sīn) *adj.* pert. to swine.

por′cu·pine″ (pôr′kyə-pīn″) *n.* a small animal with sharp spines on its body and tail.

pore (pôr) *n.* a tiny opening, esp. in the skin. —*v.i.* (with *over*) meditate; ponder.

por′gy (pôr′jė) *n.* a small, edible sea fish.

pork (pôrk) *n.* the flesh of swine as food. —**pork′er,** *n.* a swine, esp. a young hog fattened for market. —**pork′y,** *adj.* pork-like; fat. —**pork barrel,** a government grant used for political patronage.

pork′pie″ *n.* a flat, low-crowned hat.

por′no (pôr′nō) (*Slang*) *adj.* pornographic. —*n.* pornography. Also, **porn.**

por·nog′ra·phy (pôr-nog′rə-fė) *n.* obscene art, writings, etc. —**por″no·graph′ic** (pôr″nə-graf′ik) *adj.* —**por″no·graph′i·cal·ly,** *adv.* ❏ *obscene*

> **pornography**
> ↔ From Greek *pornē*, prostitute; the word literally means the depiction of prostitutes, at first applied to classical drawings, such as the paintings at Pompeii.

por′ous (pôr′əs) *adj.* permeable by fluids. —**po·ros′i·ty** (pə-ros′ə-tė), **por′ous·ness,** *n.*

por′phy·ry (pôr′fə-rė) *n.* a hard, purplish-red rock embedded with crystals. —**por″phy·rit′ic** (-rit′ik) *adj.*

por′poise (pôr′pəs) *n.* a whalelike sea mammal, about six ft. long.

por′ridge (pôr′ij) *n.* a thin boiled cereal.

por′rin·ger (pôr′in-jər) *n.* a dish for cereal.

port (pôrt) *n.* **1,** a coast city where ships load and unload; a harbor; a haven. **2,** a porthole; an outlet. **3,** the left side of a ship. **4,** a sweet, dark-red wine. **5,** a socket on a computer for connecting peripherals. —*v.t.* **1,** turn (the helm) to the left. **2,** (*Mil.*) hold (a rifle) diagonally across the body. **3,** to transfer data from one medium or system to another. —**port of call,** an intermediate stop in an itinerary, shipping route, etc. —**port of entry,** a port where imports can enter.

> **port, porter**
> ↔ The name of the wine comes from the Portuguese town of *Oporto. Porter,* on the other hand, is short for *porter's ale,* perhaps because it was popular with porters. The other senses of *port* are all of Latin origin.

port′a·ble (pôrt′ə-bəl) *adj.* capable of being carried; easily conveyed. Also, **port′a·tive,** *adj.*—**port″a·bil′i·ty,** *n.*

por′tage (pôr′tij) *n.* **1,** the act or place of carrying boats overland from one stream to another. **2,** a fee for conveyance.

por′tal (pôr′təl) *n.* a doorway. —**portal-to-portal,** *adj.* of salary, including time spent traveling to and from one's working place.

por″ta·men′to (pôr″tə-men′tō) *n.* (*It.,*

Music) a gliding from one tone to another.

port·cul′lis (pôrt-kul′is) *n.* a gate that slides up and down, esp. as used in medieval castles.

porte-″co·chere′ (pôrt″-kō-shār′) *n.* a covered carriage entrance.

por·tend′ (pôr-tend′) *v.t.* give a warning of; presage.

por′tent (pôr′tent) *n.* a dire or evil omen.

por·ten′tous (pôr-ten′təs) *adj.* **1,** foreshadowing evil. **2,** solemn. —**por·ten′-tous·ness,** *n.*

por′ter (pôr′tər) *n.* **1,** one who carries baggage; a sleeping-car attendant. **2,** a doorkeeper or janitor. **3,** a heavy, dark beer. —**por′ter·age,** *n.* transport or fees for it. ❏ *port*

por′ter·house″ *n.* a choice cut of beef; a T-bone steak.

port·fo′li·o (pôrt-fō′lė-ō) *n.* **1,** a flat case for carrying documents; a briefcase. **2,** the office of a cabinet minister. **3,** an itemized account of securities, etc., held by an investor.

port′hole″ *n.* a round window in a ship's side; an aperture in a wall.

por′ti·co″ (pôr′ti-kō″) *n.* a roof supported by columns, used as a porch or a detached shed.

por·tiere′ (pôr-tyār′) *n.* a curtain hung in a doorway.

por′tion (pôr′shən) *n.* **1,** a part of a whole. **2,** a share. **3,** lot; destiny. **4,** a dowry. —*v.t.* **1,** allot in shares. **2,** dower.

port′ly (pôrt′lė) *adj.* **1,** fat; stout. **2,** stately; dignified. —**port′li·ness,** *n.*

port·man′teau (pôrt-man′tō) *n.* a traveling bag or suitcase. —**portmanteau word,** a word made by combining parts of other words, as brunch: br(*eakfast and l*)unch.

> **portmanteau**
> ↔ In French the word refers to a court official assigned to carry the king's cloak (*manteau*), and to the bag in which he carried it.

por′trait (pôr′trit) *n.* a picture of a person, esp. one done in oils. —*adj.* printed vertically on the page. —**por′trai·ture** (-trə-chər), **por′trait·ist,** *n.*

por·tray′ (pôr-trā′) *v.t.* **1,** picture; describe vividly. **2,** enact. —**por·tray′al,** *n.*

Por′tu·guese (pôr′tyə-gėz) *adj. & n.* of or pert. to the people of Portugal, their language, etc. —**Portuguese man-of-war,** a tropical, brilliantly colored marine invertebrate, with tentacles over ten feet long.

por″tu·la′ca (pôr″chə-lä′kə) *n.* a low-growing annual plant.

pose (pōz) *v.t.* **1,** place (a model) suitably. **2,** propound, as a question. —*v.i.* **1,** act as a model. **2,** make a pretense. —*n.* **1,** attitude; position. **2,** an affectation.

pos′er (pō′zər) *n.* **1,** [also, **po·seur′** (-zėr′)] an affected person; pretender. **2,** a puzzling question.

posh *adj.* (*Informal*) luxurious; exclusive.

pos′it (poz′it) *v.t.* **1,** put in place or relation; dispose. **2,** present as a fact or datum; stipulate.

po·si′tion (pə-zish′ən) *n.* **1,** the place occupied by a person or thing; situation. **2,** bodily attitude or posture. **3,** point of view; opinion. **4,** rank; station, esp. high standing. **5,** a job; occupation. —*v.t.* put in proper position; locate. —**po·si′tion·al,** *adj.*

pos′i·tive (poz′ə-tiv) *adj.* **1,** stated explicitly; definite. **2,** confident; dogmatic. **3,** affirmative. **4,** real; actual; of numbers, greater than zero; plus. **5,** proving the presence of something in question. **6,** in photography, showing light and shade as in the original. **7,** (*Gram.*) noting the simple form of an adjective or adverb. **8,** (*Electricity*) having a deficiency of electrons. —*n.* something positive. —**pos′i·tive·ness,** *n.*

pos′i·tron″ (poz′ə-tron″) *n.* a particle of positive electricity having the same mass as an electron.

pos′se (pos′ė) *n.* a body of persons helping a law officer.

posse
↔ A shortening of *posse comitatus,* force of the county empowered by the sheriff. From Latin *posse,* to be able.

pos·sess′ (pə-zes′) *v.t.* **1,** have as one's property; own; have as a quality. **2,** obtain power over; dominate. —**pos·ses′sor,** *n.*

pos·sessed′ (pə-zest′) *adj.* **1,** in possession (of). **2,** afflicted by evil spirits.

pos·ses′sion (pə-zesh′ən) *n.* **1,** the state of having or controlling. **2,** something owned. **3,** state of being possessed.

pos·ses′sive (-zes′iv) *adj.* **1,** pert. to ownership; jealous in ownership. **2,** (*Gram.*) denoting a possessor. —**pos·ses′sive·ness,** *n.*

pos′si·ble (pos′ə-bəl) *adj.* **1,** capable of existing, occurring, or being done. **2,** that

may do; worth consideration. **3,** conceivable. —**pos″si·bil′i·ty,** *n.*

possible, probable
☞ Do not confuse *possible,* capable of occurring, and *probable,* likely to occur.

pos′si·bly (pos′ə-blė) *adv.* by any possibility; perhaps.

pos′sum (pos′əm) *n.* (*Informal*) an opossum. —**play possum,** feign death.

post (pōst) *n.* **1,** an upright timber or stake. **2,** a station; assignment; job. **3,** a military station or its garrison; a trading station. **4,** a system or means of conveying letters, packages, etc.; the mail. —*v.t.* **1,** fasten (a notice) in a public place. **2,** mail (a letter). **3,** station at a post, as a sentry. **4,** transfer to, or enter in, a ledger. **5,** (*Informal*) supply with information. —*v.i.* **1,** travel in haste. **2,** move up and down in the saddle, when riding. —**post chaise,** a horsedrawn coach. —**post exchange,** (also *cap.*) a store or canteen for soldiers at an army post. *Abbr.* **PX.** —**post office, 1,** formerly, the government department for the transmission of mail; now, the Postal Service. **2,** a branch office of the Postal Service.

post- (pōst) *pref.* after.

post′age (pōs′tij) *n.* the fee for conveying letters or packages; mailing charges. —**postage meter,** a machine which prints postage on mail and records accumulated postage expenditures. —**postage stamp,** an official stamp showing prepayment of postage.

post′al (pōs′təl) *adj.* pert. to the mail service. —**postal card,** postcard. —**postal note,** a check issued by the post office for transmission of money; a postal money order. —**Postal Service,** a U.S. government corporation that handles the mail.

post′card″ *n.* a card prepared for correspondence on one section or side and address on the other.

post′date′ *v.t.* **1,** date (a contract, check, etc.) with a date later than the current one. **2,** be subsequent to in time.

post′er *n.* a posted notice; a placard.

poste″ res·tante′ (pōst′ res-tänt′) (*Fr.*) a place where mail is held until called for.

pos·te′ri·or (pos-tir′ė-ər) *adj.* **1,** located in the back or rear. **2,** later. —*n.* the rump.

pos·ter′i·ty (pos-ter′ə-tė) *n.* **1,** descendants collectively. **2,** all future generations.

pos′tern (pos′tərn) *n.* a rear or secondary entrance.

post'fix'' *v.t.* add at the end; suffix.

post·grad'u·ate *adj.* pert. to study after graduation from a school or college. —*n.* a postgraduate student.

post'haste'' *adv.* by fastest means; speedily.

post'hu·mous (pos'tū-məs) *adj.* **1,** done by or awarded to a person now dead. **2,** born after the father's death.

pos·til'lion (pōs-til'yən) *n.* a rider on one of a team of two or four horses.

post'lude'' (pōst'lood'') *n.* (*Music*) an added or concluding piece.

post'man (-mən) *n.* [*pl.* **-men**] a letter carrier.

post'mark'' *n.* an official mark canceling a postage stamp and giving the date and place of mailing.

post'mas''ter, post'mis''tress, *n.* a person in charge of a post office. —**Postmaster General,** the official in charge of the Postal Service.

post''me·rid'i·an *adj.* occurring after noon.

post me·rid'i·em (-əm) (*Lat.*) after noon, usu. *abbr.* P.M.

post·mod'ern·ism *n.* a reaction in the arts beginning in the late 1960s to the modernism of the preceding decades.

post''mor'tem (pōst''môr'təm) *adj.* after death. —*n.* **1,** an autopsy. **2,** (*Slang*) discussion of card play after a game.

post'na'sal *adj.* behind the nose.

post'paid'' *adj.* with postage prepaid.

post·par'tum (-pär'təm) *adj.* of or occurring after birth.

post·pone' (pōst-pōn') *v.t.* defer until later; delay. —**post·pone'ment,** *n.*

post'script'' (pōst'skript') *n.* **1,** a paragraph added to a letter finished and signed; any added part. **2,** (*cap.*) (*T.N.*) a page description language for use in computers and printers.

pos'tu·lant (pos'chə-lənt) *n.* a candidate for membership, esp. in a religious order.

pos'tu·late (pos'chə-lāt') *v.t. & i.* assert or assume as a basis for reasoning. —*n.* (-lət) **1,** an assumption; hypothesis. **2,** a prerequisite.

pos'ture (pos'chər) *n.* **1,** bodily position; carriage. **2,** attitude. —*v.i.* pose.

post''war'' *adj.* after any given war, esp. World War II.

po'sy (pō'zè) *n.* a flower.

pot *n.* **1,** a round deep vessel, as for cooking. **2,** an aggregate of stakes to be won; a prize. **3,** a basket for catching fish, lobsters, etc. **4,** (*Informal*) potbelly. **5,**

(*Slang*) marijuana. —*v.t.* [**pot'ted, -ting**] **1,** preserve in pots; plant in a pot. **2,** shoot (game) for food. —**go to pot** (*Informal*) go to pieces; be ruined. —**pot cheese,** cottage cheese. —**pot roast,** braised beef.

po'ta·ble (pō'tə-bəl) *adj.* drinkable. —*n.* (*pl.*) beverages.

pot'ash'' *n.* a white chemical obtained by leaching wood ashes.

po·tas'si·um (pə-tas'ė-əm) *n.* a soft, silvery-white metallic element, no. 19, symbol K, used in drugs, fertilizers, etc. —**po·tas'sic,** *adj.*

> **potassium**
> ↔ Coined by English chemist Sir Humphry Davy from Dutch *potasch,* potash.

po·ta'to (pə-tā'tō) *n.* a plant or its important edible tuber. —**potato chip,** a fried thin slice of potato. —**small potatoes,** (*Slang*) something or someone insignificant.

pot'bel''ly *n.* (*Informal*) a fat or protruding belly.

pot'boil''er *n.* a work of art or literature produced solely for making a living.

po·teen' (pō-tēn') *n.* in Ireland, illicitly distilled liquor. Also, **po·theen'** (-thēn').

po'ten·cy (pō'ten-sè) *n.* state or quality of being potent; power; ability.

po'tent (pō'tənt) *adj.* **1,** wielding power; strong; effective. **2,** capable of procreation.

po'ten·tate'' (pō'tən-tāt'') *n.* a ruler; monarch.

po·ten'tial (pə-ten'shəl) *adj.* **1,** possible. **2,** latent. —*n.* something that has the possibility of becoming actual. —**po·ten''ti·al'i·ty** (-shė-al'ə-tè) *n.*

pot'head'' *n.* (*Slang*) one who uses marijuana, esp. to excess.

poth'er (poth'ər) *n.* confusion; bustle. —*v.t.* bother; perplex. —*v.i.* make a commotion.

pot'herb'' *n.* a plant boiled for food or used for seasoning.

pot'hold''er *n.* a thick cloth used as protection for the hand when picking up a hot utensil.

pot'hole'' *n.* a round depression (in a rock, road, etc.) caused by erosion, traffic, etc.

pot'hook'' (pot'hûk'') *n.* **1,** a hook used to lift or suspend pots. **2,** any S-shaped figure, as in writing; (*Humorous*) any stenographic symbol.

po'tion (pō'shən) *n.* a drink, as of medicine or poison.

pot′latch (pot′lach) *n.* a ceremonious distribution of gifts.

pot′luck″ (pot′luk″) *n.* **1,** whatever food is on hand, without special buying. **2,** a meal for which the participants bring the food to be shared.

pot′pie″ *n.* **1,** a meat pie. **2,** a stew of meat and dumplings.

pot·pour′ri (pot-pûr′ē; pō-poo-rē′) *n.* a mixture or medley of spices, foods, musical or literary compositions, etc.

pot′sherd″ (-shērd″) *n.* a broken piece of earthenware.

pot′shot″ *n.* **1,** a random shot, or one at close range. **2,** a random critical remark.

pot′tage (pot′ij) *n.* a stew.

pot′ted (pot′id) *adj.* **1,** put into, cooked, or preserved in a pot. **2,** (*Slang*) tipsy; drunk.

pot′ter (pot′ər) *n.* one who makes pottery. —*v.i.* busy oneself over trifles; loiter; dawdle. —**potter's field,** a place for the burial of paupers or criminals. —**potter's wheel,** a rotating disk on which a potter shapes clay.

pot′ter·y (-ē) *n.* dishes, vases, etc., molded from clay and baked.

pot′ty (-ē) *n.* (*Informal*) toilet, esp. a child's toilet. —*adj.* (*Slang*) slightly crazy.

pouch (powch) *n.* **1,** a small bag or sack. **2,** a marsupium.

poult (pōlt) *n.* the young of the domestic fowl, pheasant, etc.

poul′tice (pōl′tis) *n.* a soft, warm mass applied to a sore spot.

poul′try (pōl′trē) *n.* domestic fowls collectively. —**poul′ter·er,** *n.* a dealer in poultry.

pounce (powns) *v.i.* (often with *on* or *upon*) swoop and seize suddenly. —*n.* a sudden spring.

pound (pownd) *n.* **1,** a measure of weight, sixteen avoirdupois or twelve troy ounces. **2,** the Brit. monetary unit; its symbol (£). **3,** an enclosure for stray animals. **4,** the symbol #, as on a telephone or computer keyboard. —*v.t.* **1,** beat; pummel. **2,** crush. —*v.i.* **1,** hammer away steadily. **2,** plod heavily. —**pound′age,** *n.* —**pound cake,** a rich, sweet cake.

pound′al (pown′dəl) *n.* the force which, acting for one second upon a mass of one pound, gives it a velocity of one foot per second.

pour (pôr) *v.t.* **1,** cause to flow downward in a stream. **2,** send forth copiously. —*v.i.* **1,** flow. **2,** rain hard. **3,** issue in great numbers.

pour·boire′ (pûr-bwär′) *n.* (*Fr.*) a tip to a servant.

pout (powt) *v.i.* protrude the lips, as in sullenness. —*n.* a sulky mood.

pout′er pigeon a pigeon with a puffed-out crop.

pov·er·ty (pov′ər-tē) *n.* **1,** lack of money; need. **2,** lack; scarcity. —**poverty level** *or* **line,** the level of income below which one is considered legally impoverished. —**pov′er·ty-strick′en,** *adj.* impoverished.

pow′der (pow′dər) *n.* **1,** a mixture of fine, dry particles, as pulverized talc used as a cosmetic; gunpowder; a dose of medicinal powder. **2,** (*Slang*) sudden departure. —*v.t.* **1,** sprinkle with or as with powder. **2,** reduce to powder. —**pow′der·y,** *adj.* —**powder blue,** a pale blue. —**powder keg,** a situation liable to explode, as in war. —**powder puff, 1,** a pad for applying powder. **2,** an effeminate man. —**powder room,** a lavatory for women. —**take a powder,** (*Slang*) depart quickly or suddenly.

pow′er (pow′ər) *n.* **1,** ability to do or act. **2,** physical or mental strength or energy; influence; control. **3,** an influential person; a nation considered as a military force. **4,** the magnifying capacity of a lens. **5,** any of the products obtained by multiplying a number by itself repeatedly; as, 2 x 2 = 4 (2nd power) x 2 = 8 (3rd power), etc. —**power of attorney,** legal authority to act for another. —**power politics,** diplomacy based on the threat of force. —**power user,** (*Computers*) a person who uses the more advanced capabilities of computers. ❑ *ability*

pow·er- *pref.* impelled by an engine.

pow′er·boat″ *n.* motorboat.

pow′er·bro″ker *n.* a person wielding great power, esp. political or financial.

pow′er·ful *adj.* strong; influential; mighty. —**pow′er·ful·ness,** *n.*

pow′er·house″ *n.* **1,** a plant for generating electricity. **2,** (*Informal*) something very strong.

pow′er·less *adj.* helpless; without authority. —**pow′er·less·ness,** *n.*

pow′wow″ *n.* **1,** among N. Amer. Indians, a ceremony or conference. **2,** (*Informal*) any conference. —*v.i.* confer.

pox (poks) *n.* a disease marked by eruptive pocks.

prac′ti·ca·ble (prak′ti-kə-bəl) *adj.* capable of being done or used. —**prac″ti·ca·bil′i·ty,** *n.*

prac′ti·cal (prak′ti-kəl) *adj.* **1,** usable; useful. **2,** taught by or derived from experience; advisable. **3,** inclined to action rather than theory. **4,** pert. to actual practice or action; not theoretical. —**prac″ti·cal′i·ty,** *n.* —**practical joke,** one that causes discomfort or embarrassment to someone. —**practical nurse,** an experienced nurse who is not registered and not a graduate of a nursing school. ❑ *practicable*

---

practicable, practical
☞ These two words have similar, though distinct, meanings. *Practicable* means capable of being done; *practical* means useful.

---

prac′ti·cal·ly (-ė) *adv.* **1,** in practice; actually. **2,** (*Informal*) nearly; in effect.

prac′tice (prak′tis) *n.* **1,** actual performance. **2,** frequent performance; custom; usage. **3,** the exercise of a profession, esp. medical. **4,** repeated exercise, to gain skill —*v.t.* **1,** carry out in action. **2,** do repeatedly, esp. to gain skill. **3,** follow as a profession. —*v.i.* **1,** perform certain acts often. **2,** engage in a profession. Also (*Brit.*) **prac′tise.** —**prac′ticed,** *adj.* skilled; proficient.

prac′ti·cum (prak′ti-kəm) *n.* the part of a college or university course consisting of practical work.

prac·ti′tion·er (prak-tish′ən-ər) *n.* **1,** one engaged in a profession. **2,** in Christian Science, an authorized healer.

prag·mat′ic (prag-mat′ik) *adj.* **1,** based on utility or effect; practical. **2,** matter-of-fact. **3,** dogmatic. —**prag·mat′i·cal·ly,** *adv.* —**prag′ma·tism,** *n.*

prai′rie (prār′ė) *n.* a broad, level, treeless grassland. —**prairie chicken,** a kind of grouse. —**prairie dog,** a rodent of Amer. prairies. —**prairie oyster, 1,** a raw egg, often with seasonings. **2,** calf testes used as food. —**prairie schooner,** a covered wagon. —**prairie wolf,** a coyote.

praise (prāz) *v.t.* **1,** commend warmly. **2,** glorify the attributes of (God). —*n.* compliments; applause.

praise′wor″thy *adj.* commendable. —**praise′wor″thi·ness,** *n.*

pra′line (prä′lēn) *n.* a confection of browned sugar and nuts.

---

praline
↔ Named for its creator, 17th-c. French chef Marshall du Plessis-*Praslin.*

---

pram *n.* perambulator.

prance (prȧns) *v.i.* **1,** step proudly (of a horse's gait). **2,** strut. —*n.* a prancing gait or stride.

pran′di·al (pran′dė-əl) *adj.* pert. to a meal, esp. dinner.

prank *n.* a playful or mischievous act. —**prank′ish,** *adj.* —**prank′ster,** *n.*

pra″se·o·dym′i·um (prā″zė-ō-dim′ė-əm) *n.* a rare-earth metallic element, no. 59, symbol Pr.

---

praseodymium
↔ The element is named for the color of its salts, from Greek *prasios,* green, + *didymium.*

---

prate (prāt) *v.t. & i.* chatter; babble; talk too much.

prat′fall″ (prat′fâl″) *n.* a fall on the buttocks.

prat′tle (prat′əl) *v.i.* talk idly, like a child. —*n.* such talk.

prawn (prân) *n.* an edible shrimplike crustacean.

prax′is (prak′sis) *n.* **1,** art learned by experience. **2,** established practices; customs. **3,** a manual or textbook of such practices.

pray (prā) *v.i.* ask God's grace. —*v.t.* **1,** beg; entreat. **2,** petition for. —*adv.* (*Archaic*) please.

prayer (prâr) *n.* **1,** a supplication to God; (*pl.*) a religious service. **2,** entreaty; petition. —**prayer book,** a book of forms for prayers. —**prayer shawl,** a tallith.

prayer′ful (-fəl) *adj.* **1,** devout. **2,** entreating. —**prayer′ful·ness,** *n.*

praying mantis an insect with long forelegs; mantis.

pre- (prē) *pref.* before, in time, place, rank, sequence, etc.

preach (prēch) *v.t. & i.* **1,** deliver (a sermon). **2,** advocate earnestly; exhort. **3,** give advice importunately. —**preach′ment,** *n.* —**preach′y,** *adj.* moralizing; didactic.

preach′er *n.* **1,** a member of the clergy. **2,** anyone who preaches.

preach′i·fy″ (-ə-fī″) *v.i.* (*Informal*) give prolonged, tiresome moral advice.

pre′am·ble (prē′am″bəl) *n.* introductory remarks; a preface.

pre·am′pli·fi″er *n.* an electronic device used to modify a signal for an amplifier. Also, *informal,* **pre′amp.**

pre″ar·range′ *v.t.* arrange beforehand. —**pre″ar·range′ment,** *n.*

pre·car′i·ous (pri-kār′ė-əs) *adj.* uncertain; insecure. —**pre·car′i·ous·ness,** *n.*

pre·cau′tion (pri-kâ′shən) *n.* **1,** an act done in advance to assure safety or benefit. **2,** prudent foresight. —**pre·cau′tion·ar·y,** *adj.*

---

pre·cede' (prè-sēd') *v.t. & i.* go before in place, time, rank, or importance. **—pre·ced'ing,** *adj.*

> **precede, proceed**
> ☞ Do not confuse *precede*, to go before, with *proceed*, go forward.

prec'e·dence (pres'i-dəns) *n.* **1,** the act of going before. **2,** the right of taking a more honored position.

prec'e·dent (pres'i-dənt) *n.* an identical or analogous previous example. *—adj.* (prè-sē'dənt) preceding.

pre·cen'tor (prè-sen'tər) *n.* one who leads singing in church; a soloist. **—pre·cen'tor·ship",** *n.*

pre'cept (prē'sept) *n.* a rule for moral conduct; maxim. **—pre·cep'tor,** *n.* a teacher. ❑ *percept*

pre'cinct (prē'sinkt) *n.* **1,** district. **2,** (*pl.*) environs.

pre"ci·os'i·ty (presh"ē-os'ə-tē) *n.* over-niceness; affectation.

pre'cious (presh'əs) *adj.* **1,** of great value. **2,** held in great esteem; dear. **3,** overrefined; affectedly clever or delicate. *—adv.* (*Informal*) very. **—pre'cious·ness,** *n.*

prec'i·pice (pres'ə-pis) *n.* a very steep or overhanging cliff. **—pre·cip'i·tous** (pri-sip'i-təs) *adj.*

pre·cip'i·tant (pri-sip'ə-tənt) *adj.* rushing headlong; abrupt; hasty. *—n.* an agent that causes precipitation. **—pre·cip'i·tan·cy,** *n.*

pre·cip'i·tate" (pri-sip'ə-tāt") *v.t.* **1,** cast headlong. **2,** cause to happen suddenly or too soon. **3,** (*Chem.*) change from a state of solution to solid form. *—v.i.* (*Chem.*) separate from a solution, as a solid. *—adj.* (-tət) **1,** headlong. **2,** acting hastily and unwisely. **3,** extremely sudden or abrupt.

pre·cip"i·ta'tion (pri-sip"i-tā'shən) *n.* **1,** act of hurling down or falling headlong. **2,** impetuous action. **3,** (*Chem.*) the process or effect of precipitating. **4,** rain, sleet, or snow; the quantity that falls.

pre·cip'i·tous (pri-sip'ə-təs) *adj.* **1,** overhasty; rash. **2,** steep.

pré·cis' (prā-sē') *n.* a concise summary.

pre·cise' (pri-sīs') *adj.* **1,** exactly defined; definite; accurate. **2,** punctilious; formal. **3,** exact; identical. **—pre·cise'ness,** *n.*

pre·ci'sian (pri-sizh'ən) *n.* a stickler for the rules.

pre·cis'ion (pri-sizh'ən) *n.* preciseness; accuracy.

pre·clude' (pri-klood') *v.t.* impede; prevent. **—pre·clu'sion,** *n.* **—pre·clu'sive,** *adj.*

pre·co'cious (pri-kō'shəs) *adj.* prematurely developed, esp. mentally. **—pre·co'cious·ness, pre·coc'i·ty** (pri-kos'ə-tē) *n.*

pre"con·ceive' *v.t.* form an idea or opinion of in advance. **—pre"con·cep'tion,** *n.*

pre"con·di'tion (prē'-) *n.* a requirement for beginning something, as negotiations.

pre·cur'sor (pri-kèr'sər) *n.* a predecessor; a premonitory forerunner. **—pre·cur'so·ry** (-sə-rē) *adj.*

pre·da'cious (pri-dā'shəs) *adj.* predatory. Also, **pre·da'ceous.** **—pre·dac'i·ty** (-das'ə-tē) *n.*

pred'a·tor (pred'ə-tər) *n.* an organism or person that lives by preying on other organisms.

pred'a·to"ry (pred'ə-tôr"ē) *adj.* **1,** plundering. **2,** preying upon others.

pred'e·ces"sor (pred'i-ses"ər) *n.* one who preceded another in the same position, etc.

> **predecessor, decease**
> ↔ Both words derive from Latin *decedere*, to go away. A *predecessor* is one who goes away first.

pre"des"ti·na'tion *n.* **1,** the belief that God has ordained all events to come. **2,** fate; destiny.

pre·des'tine *v.t.* decide the course or fate of beforehand.

pre"de·ter'mine *v.t.* **1,** decide or ascertain beforehand. **2,** predestine.

pre·dic'a·ment (pri-dik'ə-mənt) *n.* a trying or dangerous situation; a dilemma.

pred'i·cate (pred'ə-kət) *n.* **1,** (*Gram.*) the part of a sentence that tells something about the subject. **2,** what is predicated. *—v.t.* (-kāt") **1,** assert; declare. **2,** base.

pred'i·ca"tive (pred'i-kā"tiv) *adj.* (*Gram.*) of an adjective, being in the predicate and modifying the subject, as *clear* in *The sky is clear.*

pre·dict' (pri-dikt') *v.t. & i.* foretell; prophesy. **—pre·dic'tion,** *n.*

pre"di·lec'tion (prē"də-lek'shən) *n.* partiality; liking.

pre"dis·pose' *v.t.* **1,** give a tendency or inclination to. **2,** dispose in advance. **—pre"dis·po·si'tion,** *n.* innate tendency.

pre·dom'i·nate" (pri-dom'i-nāt") *v.i. & t.* prevail (over); control; be the chief element. **—pre·dom'i·nance,** *n.* **—pre·dom'i·nant,** *adj.*

pree'mie (prē'mē) *n.* (*Informal*) a premature baby.

pre·em'i·nent (prè-em'i-nənt) *adj.* eminent above others. **—pre·em'i·nence,** *n.*

pre·empt' (prè-empt') *v.t. & i.* **1,** occupy; seize; buy or do before another can. **2,** supplant. —**pre·emp'tion,** *n.* —**pre·emp'tive,** *adj.* —**pre·emp'tor,** *n.*

preen (prēn) *v.t.* **1,** smooth (feathers) with the beak. **2,** trim or adorn (oneself).

pre·fab'ri·cate" *v.t.* manufacture parts of, for later assembly, as houses. Also, *informal,* **pre'fab.** —**pre·fab"ri·ca'tion,** *n.*

pref'ace (pref'is) *n.* an introduction, as to a book or speech. —*v.t.* **1,** give a preface to. **2,** introduce; precede. —**pref'a·to·ry,** *adj.*

pre'fect (prē'fekt) *n.* **1,** a chief magistrate; an administrative head. **2,** a monitor in school. —**pre'fec·ture** (-fek-shər) *n.*

pre·fer' (pri-fēr') *v.t.* [**pre·ferred', -fer'ring**] **1,** choose, rather than another; like more. **2,** advance; bring forward. —**pref'er·a·ble** (pref'ər-ə-bəl) *adj.* —**preferred stock,** stock that receives a dividend before common stock.

pref'er·ence (pref'ə-rəns) *n.* **1,** act of preferring; choice; favor. **2,** preferred or superior position.

pref"er·en'tial (pref"ər-en'shəl) *adj.* favored; based on preference.

pre·fer'ment (pri-fēr'mənt) *n.* promotion.

pre·fig'ure *v.t.* **1,** presage. **2,** imagine in advance. —**pre·fig"u·ra'tion,** *n.* —**pre·fig'u·ra·tive,** *adj.* —**pre·fig'ure·ment,** *n.*

pre'fix (prē'fiks) *v.t.* fix or place before. —*n.* in compound words, one or more letters or syllables that go before and qualify another word.

preg'na·ble (preg'nə-bəl) *adj.* capable of being taken by force.

preg'nant (preg'nənt) *adj.* **1,** carrying unborn young. **2,** fertile; inventive. **3,** full of significance. —**preg'nan·cy,** *n.* ❏ *native*

pre·hen'sile (pri-hen'sil) *adj.* fitted for grasping or holding, as claws.

pre"his·tor'ic *adj.* preceding recorded history. —**pre"his·tor'i·cal·ly,** *adv.*

pre·judge' *v.t.* judge or condemn before proper inquiry.

prej'u·dice (prej'ə-dis) *n.* **1,** an opinion, often unfavorable, formed without adequate reasons; bias. **2,** disadvantageous effect. —*v.t.* **1,** cause prejudice in. **2,** damage. —**prej"u·di'cial** (-dish'əl) *adj.*

prel'ate (prel'it) *n.* a high ecclesiastical dignitary. —**prel'a·cy,** *n.*

pre·lim'in·ar'y (pri-lim'i-ner'ē) *adj.* leading up to something more important. —*n.* (usu. *pl.*) a preparatory act, feature, test, etc..

prel'ude (prel'ūd) *n.* **1,** something pre-liminary or introductory. **2,** (*Music*) an introductory movement. —*v.t.* introduce.

pre"ma·ture' *adj.* happening before maturity or too soon; overhasty.

pre"med'i·cal *adj.* preparing for the study of medicine. Also, *informal,* **pre·med'.**

pre·med'i·tate" *v.t. & i.* consider or plan beforehand. —**pre·med"i·ta'tion,** *n.*

pre·men'strual syndrome the physical and emotional changes preceding the onset of menstruation. *Abbr.,* **PMS.**

pre'mi·er (prē'mē-ər) *adj.* chief; foremost. —*n.* the chief minister of state; prime minister.

pre·miere' (pri-myār'; *Informal* pri-mir') *n.* a first performance; opening. —*v.t. & i.* (*Informal*) have or present a premiere (of).

prem'ise (prem'is) *n.* **1,** a previous statement from which something is inferred or concluded. **2,** (*pl.*) real estate; a building and grounds.

pre'mi·um (prē'mē-əm) *n.* **1,** a prize; reward; anything given as an inducement. **2,** an amount to be paid for insurance. **3,** an excess of value over cost.

pre·mo'lar (prē-mō'lər) *adj.* situated in front of the molar teeth. —*n.* a premolar tooth.

pre"mo·ni'tion (prē"mə-nish'ən) *n.* a foreboding, as of impending danger.

pre·mon'i·to·ry (pri-mon'ə-tôr-ē) *adj.* forewarning.

pre"na'tal *adj.* occurring or existing before birth.

pre·oc'cu·py" (prē-ok'yə-pī") *v.t.* take the attention of, to the exclusion of other matters; engross; absorb. —**pre·oc'cu·pied",** *adj.* —**pre·oc"cu·pa'tion,** *n.*

pre"or·dain' *v.t.* decree beforehand. —**pre"or·di·na'tion,** *n.*

prep *adj.* (*Informal*) preparatory; as, a *prep* school. —*v.t.* (*Slang*) prepare, as for an operation.

prep"a·ra'tion (prep"ə-rā'shən) *n.* the act, means, or result of preparing.

pre·par'a·to·ry (pri-par'ə-tôr-ē) *adj.* serving to make ready. —**preparatory school,** a school preparing students to enter college. Also, **prep school.**

pre·pare' (pri-pār') *v.t.* **1,** make ready for a particular purpose. **2,** instruct. **3,** provide; fit out. **4,** make; manufacture; compound. **5,** cook; concoct. —*v.i.* **1,** put things in readiness. **2,** make oneself ready.

pre·par'ed·ness *n.* the state of being prepared, esp. for war.

pre·pay' (prė-pā') *v.t.* pay or pay for in advance. **—pre'paid"**, *adj.*

pre·pon'der·ate" (pri-pon'də-rāt") *v.i.* exceed in weight, influence, number, etc.; prevail. **—pre·pon'der·ance**, *n.* **—pre·pon'der·ant,** *adj.*

prep"o·si'tion (prep"ə-zish'ən) *n.* (*Gram.*) a part of speech serving to show the relation between a noun or pronoun and some other word. **—prep"o·si'tion·al,** *adj.*

pre"pos·sess' (prē"pə-zes') *v.t.* **1,** impress favorably at the outset, **2,** dominate, as a prejudice. **—pre"pos·sess'ing,** *adj.* arousing favorable bias.

pre·pos'ter·ous (pri-pos'tər-əs) *adj.* contrary to common sense; utterly absurd. **—pre·pos'ter·ous·ness,** *n.*

---
preposterous
↔ This word itself is self-contradictory, meaning roughly "before/afterish," and meant originally backwards, out of order.

---

prep'pie (prep'ė) *n.* one who attends or has attended a prep school. **—***adj.* having the characteristics of a preppie. Also, **prep'py.**

pre'puce (prē'pūs) *n.* **1,** the foreskin. **2,** a similar covering for the clitoris.

pre'quel (prē'kwəl) *n.* a sequel dealing with events prior to those dealt with in the previous work.

pre·req'ui·site *adj.* necessary as an antecedent condition. **—***n.* something needed in advance or at the outset.

pre·rog'a·tive (pri-rog'ə-tiv) *n.* a right or privilege inherent in one's office or position.

pres'age (pres'ij) *n.* an omen; foreboding. **—***v.t.* (pri-sāj') give a warning of; foretell.

pres'by·ter (prez'bi-tər) *n.* **1,** a Presbyterian elder or minister. **2,** a title of some members of the clergy.

Pres"by·te'ri·an (prez"bi-tir'ė-ən) *adj. & n.* pert. to a Prot. church governed by its ministers and elders.

pres'by·ter"y (-ter"ė) *n.* **1,** a ruling council of a church; its jurisdiction. **2,** a priest's residence.

pre'school *adj.* of the time in a child's life before it enters school (usu. six years of age).

pre'sci·ence (presh'ė-əns) *n.* foreknowledge; foresight. **—pre'sci·ent** (-ənt) *adj.*

pre·scribe' (prė-skrīb') *v.t.* **1,** lay down beforehand as a rule. **2,** advise the use of

(a medicine). **—***v.i.* **1,** lay down rules. **2,** advise remedies.

---
prescribe, proscribe
☛ Do not confuse *prescribe*, lay down a rule, with *proscribe*, to prohibit.

---

pre'script (prē'skript) *n.* a rule.

pre·scrip'tion (pri-skrip'shən) *n.* **1,** authoritative directions, esp. for a medicine. **2,** the medicine. **—pre·scrip'tive,** *adj.*

pres'ence (prez'əns) *n.* **1,** the fact of being present. **2,** immediate vicinity. **3,** a person's bearing, demeanor, etc. **4,** a spirit. **—presence of mind,** alertness in emergencies.

pres'ent (prez'ənt) *adj.* **1,** being at the place in question; here. **2,** being or occurring at this time; not past or future. **—***n.* **1,** time now passing. **2,** the present tense. **3,** a gift.

pre·sent' (pri-zent') *v.t.* **1,** make a gift to; offer as a gift. **2,** introduce; exhibit; display. **—pre·sent'a·ble,** *adj.* in fit shape to be offered or seen.

pres"en·ta'tion (prez"ən-tā'shən) *n.* **1,** act of presenting. **2,** something presented; an exhibition, show, etc.

pre·sen'ti·ment (pri-zen'tə-mənt) *n.* a foreboding; premonition.

pres'ent·ly (-lė) *adv.* **1,** soon. **2,** at this time.

pre·sent'ment (-mənt) *n.* **1,** presentation. **2,** (*Law*) a statement or charge of an offense by a grand jury, based on its own knowledge.

pres"er·va'tion (prez"ər-vā'shən) *n.* act or effect of preserving.

pre·serv'a·tive (pri-zerv'ə-tiv) *adj.* serving to keep alive or sound. **—***n.* a substance used to preserve something, esp. food.

pre·serve' (pri-zėrv') *v.t.* **1,** keep safe or free from harm. **2,** keep alive or permanent. **3,** retain (a quality, condition). **4,** keep (food) from decay by canning, etc. **—***n.* **1,** (usu. *pl.*) fruit, jam, or jellies. **2,** ground set aside for the protection of game.

pre·set' (prē-set') *adj. & v.t.* set in advance. **—***n.* (prē'set) a switch, such as a button, that activates a preset appliance.

pre·side' (pri-zīd') *v.i.* act as chairperson of a meeting; act as head.

pres'i·den·cy (prez'i-dən-sė) *n.* **1,** office, function, etc., of a president. **2,** a territory governed by a president.

pres'i·dent (prez'i-dənt) *n.* **1,** (often *cap.*) the highest executive officer of a republic, company, club, college, etc. **2,** a chairperson. —**pres″i·den′tial** (-den′shəl) *adj.*

pre·sid′i·o (pri-sid′ė-ō) *n.* (*Sp.*) a fort.

pre·sid′i·um (pri-sid′i-əm) *n.* **1,** an administrative or executive committee. **2,** (*cap.*) the permanent committee within the Supreme Soviet of the former U.S.S.R.

press (pres) *v.t.* **1,** bear down upon; weigh heavily upon. **2,** compress; squeeze out. **3,** clasp in the arms. **4,** smooth or flatten by pressure. **5,** thrust upon others; push; thrust aside. **6,** urge on; hurry. **7,** conscript; draft. —*v.i.* **1,** bear heavily. **2,** crowd. **3,** hurry. —*n.* **1,** a crowding pressure. **2,** urgency. **3,** a chest, as for clothes. **4,** a machine that exerts pressure, as for printing. **5,** the practice and industry of printing or publishing. **6,** periodicals, newspapers, and their representatives, collectively. —**press′ing,** *adj.* urgent; persistent. —**press agent,** one employed to solicit favorable publicity. —**press conference,** an interview given to the collected press at an appointed time. —**press kit,** a packet containing various items of publicity to be given to the press, usu. at a press conference.

press′man (-mən) *n.* [*pl.* **-men**] operator of a printing press

press′mark″ *n.* the catalog number of a library book.

pres′sure (presh′ər) *n.* **1,** a bearing down; squeezing. **2,** the exertion of influence or authority. **3,** trouble; burden. **4,** demand, on one's time or energy. —**pressure cooker,** an airtight vessel for cooking food under high steam pressure. —**pressure group,** a group using lobbying, propaganda, etc., to influence decisions, such as legislation. —**pressure point, 1,** a region of the body where it is possible to obstruct blood circulation and produce fainting or necrosis. **2,** an area sensitive to pressure applied to produce a certain effect.

pres′sur·ize″ (presh′ər-īz″) *v.t.* supply with compressed air to increase the air pressure.

pres″ti·dig″i·ta′tion (pres″tə-dij″ə-tā′shən) *n.* sleight of hand. —**pres″ti·dig′i·ta′tor,** *n.*

pres·tige′ (pres-tēzh′) *n.* influence arising from reputation or esteem. —**pres·tig′ious** (-tij′əs) *adj.*

pres′to (pres′tō) *adv.* quickly.

pre·sume′ (pri-zoom′) *v.t.* **1,** take for granted; assume. **2,** take upon oneself; dare. —*v.i.* behave with undue familiarity. —**pre·sum′a·ble,** *adj.*

pre·sump′tion (pri-zump′shən) *n.* **1,** the act of presuming. **2,** something believed on inconclusive evidence. **3,** arrogance; boldness.

pre·sump′tive (pri-zump′tiv) *adj.* justifying or based on presumption.

pre·sump′tu·ous (pri-zump′tyû-əs) *adj.* arrogant; overbold. —**pre·sump′tu·ous·ness,** *n.*

pre″sup·pose′ (prē″sə-pōz′) *v.i.* **1,** assume in advance. **2,** imply as an antecedent fact. —**pre″sup·po·si′tion,** *n.*

pre·teen′ (prē-tēn′) *adj. & n.* of a boy or girl younger than 13, usu. between the ages of 9 and 12. Also, **pre·teen′ag·er,** *n.*

pre·tend′ (pri-tend′) *v.t.* **1,** make believe; feign. **2,** profess falsely. —*v.i.* **1,** make pretense. **2,** assert a claim, as to a throne, etc. **3,** (with *to*) venture; aspire.

pre·tend′er (-ər) *n.* **1,** one who makes a false show, as of learning. **2,** a claimant, esp. to a throne.

pre·tense′ (pri-tens′; prē′tens) *n.* **1,** a sham; false profession; pretext. **2,** a claim. Also, **pre·tence′.**

pre·ten′sion (pri-ten′shən) *n.* **1,** a claim; allegation. **2,** (often *pl.*) ostentation.

pre·ten′tious (pri-ten′shəs) *adj.* ostentatious; showy. —**pre·ten′tious·ness,** *n.*

pre·ter- *pref.* beyond; more than.

pret′er·it (pret′ər-it) *adj.* (*Gram.*) expressing action or existence in the past. —*n.* the past tense.

pre″ter·nat′u·ral *adj.* extraordinary.

pre′text (prē′tekst) *n.* an ostensible reason; excuse.

pret′ti·fy″ (prit′i-fī″) *v.t.* make pretty, esp. by gaudy embellishment.

pret′ty (prit′ė) *adj.* pleasing, esp. to the eye; attractive. —*adv.* (*Informal*) fairly; tolerably. —**pret′ti·ness,** *n.*

pret′zel (pret′səl) *n.* a hard dry biscuit crusted with salt, in form of a stick or knot.

pre·vail′ (pri-vāl′) *v.i.* **1,** be victorious. **2,** (with *on* or *upon*) persuade. **3,** be prevalent.

prev′a·lent (prev′ə-lənt) *adj.* of wide use or occurrence; widespread. —**prev′a·lence,** *n.*

pre·var′i·cate″ (pri-var′ə-kāt″) *v.i.* be evasive; lie. —**pre·var″i·ca′tion,** *n.* —**pre·var′i·ca″tor,** *n.*

pre·vent′ (pri-vent′) *v.t.* hinder or keep from doing or happening; impede.

pre·ven′ta·tive (pri-ven′tə-tive) *n.* that which prevents. —*adj.* preventing; precautionary. Also, **pre·ven′tive.**

pre·ven′tion (pri-ven′shən) *n.* act or effect of preventing.

pre′view″ (prē′vū″) *n.* **1,** an advance showing, as of a motion picture before general release. **2,** [also, **pre′vue″**] an excerpt from a motion picture shown to advertise it. —*v.t.* show or see in advance.

pre′vi·ous (prē′vē-əs) *adj.* earlier; prior; foregoing. —**pre′vi·ous·ness,** *n.*

pre·vi′sion (prē-vizh′ən) *n.* foreknowledge; premonition.

pre·war′ *adj.* before any given war, esp. World War II.

prex′y (prek′sē) *n.* (*Slang*) president.

prey (prā) *n.* **1,** an animal killed by another for food. **2,** any victim. **3,** predatory habits, as *a bird of prey.* —*v.i.* (with *on* or *upon*) **1,** seize and devour an animal. **2,** plunder. **3,** victimize.

price (prīs) *n.* **1,** a consideration, esp. money, demanded in exchange for something. **2,** cost or sacrifice. **3,** the offer of a reward. **4,** an acceptable bribe. —*v.t.* set or ask the price of. —**price′less,** *adj.* invaluable. —**price control,** legislative control of pricing. —**price support,** government intervention in the market to maintain a predetermined price level. —**price war,** a competition between businessmen through use of unusually low prices.

prick (prik) *n.* **1,** a tiny hole or wound made by a pointed instrument. **2,** a stinging sensation. —*v.t.* **1,** make a tiny hole in. **2,** cause sharp pain to. **3,** (with *up*) raise (ears) as does a dog or horse.

prick′le (prik′əl) *n.* a small thornlike projection. —*v.i.* tingle; sting. —**prick′ly,** *adj.* —**prickly heat,** an inflammation of the sweat glands. —**prickly pear,** a variety of cactus; its fruit.

pride (prīd) *n.* **1,** a sense of one's own worth; self-respect. **2,** undue self-esteem; haughtiness. **3,** a feeling or object of delight. —*v.t.* be proud of (oneself). —**pride′ful,** *adj.*

prie-″dieu′ (prē″-dyö′) *n.* (*Fr.*) a kneeling desk for prayer.

priest (prēst) *n.* a person authorized to perform religious rites. —**priest′craft″,** *n.* —**priest′ess,** *n.* a female priest. —**priest′hood,** *n.* —**priest′ly,** *adj.*

prig *n.* **1,** one who makes a show of virtue. **2,** (*Slang*) a thief. —*v.t.* [**prigged, prig′ging**] (*Slang*) steal. —**prig′gish,** *adj.*

prim *adj.* [**prim′mer, -mest**] stiffly formal; demure. —**prim′ness,** *n.*

pri′ma·cy (prī′mə-sē) *n.* state of being first in rank, importance, etc.

pri′ma don′na (prē′mə don′ə) **1,** the principal female singer in an opera. **2,** a temperamental person.

pri′ma fa′cie (prī′mə fā′shə) (*Lat.*) apparent; at first sight.

pri′mal (prī′məl) *adj.* **1,** original; primeval. **2,** primary. —**primal therapy,** [also, **primal scream therapy**] psychotherapy involving the reliving of past traumatic events.

pri·ma′ri·ly (prī-mer′ə-lē) *adv.* **1,** principally. **2,** at first; originally.

pri′ma·ry (prī′mer-ē) *adj.* coming first; chief; principal; original; earliest; preliminary; elementary. —*n.* **1,** the first. **2,** an election to nominate candidates. —**primary colors,** in the spectrum, red, green, and blue; in pigments, red, yellow, and blue. —**primary school,** a school offering the first three grades of elementary school and sometimes kindergarten.

pri′mate (prī′mit) *n.* **1,** an archbishop. **2,** (-māt″) one of an order of animals that includes man, the apes, etc.

prime (prīm) *adj.* **1,** first in order of time, rank, degree. **2,** of highest quality. **3,** of a number, divisible only by itself and unity. —*n.* **1,** the first part; earliest stage. **2,** the part of highest quality. **3,** the period of greatest vigor. **4,** [also, **prime rate**] the lowest interest rate charged by a lender to its best-rated customers. —*v.t.* prepare; make ready; supply with priming. —**prime meridian,** the meridian which passes through Greenwich, England; 0°. —**prime minister,** in some countries, the chief executive or cabinet officer. —**prime rib,** a cut of beef, the first two ribs of the forequarter. —**prime time,** in broadcasting, the evening hours during which the largest audience is tuned in.

prim′er *n.* **1,** (prī′mər) that which primes; an instrument or charge to promote ignition. **2,** (prim′ər) an elementary textbook, esp. a reader.

pri·me′val (prī-mē′vəl) *adj.* pert. to earliest times; primitive.

prim′ing (prī′ming) *n.* **1,** powder, fuel, etc. used to ignite a charge, as in a firearm. **2,** the adding of liquids to a pump, to start it. **3,** a first coat of paint.

prim′i·tive (prim′ə-tiv) *adj.* **1,** early in the history of the world or man; original. **2,** simple; crude. **3,** basic. —*n.* **1,** an untrained artist. **2,** a basic form of a word or equation.

pri″mo·gen′i·ture (prī″mə-jen′ə-chər) *n.* **1,** the fact of being the firstborn. **2,** the eldest son's right of inheritance or succession. —**pri″mo·gen′i·tor,** *n.*

pri·mor′di·al (prī-môr′dē-əl) *adj.* original; earliest.

---

tub, cūte, pûll; labəl; oil, owl, go, chip, she, thin, *th*en, sing, ink; *see p.* 6

primp *v.i. & t.* dress (oneself) with elaborate care; prink.

prim′rose″ (prim′rōz″) *n.* a spring-flowering plant; its yellow flower. —**primrose path,** devotion to pleasure.

prince (prins) *n.* **1,** a ruler of a principality or small state. **2,** a monarch. **3,** the title of a son of a sovereign. **4,** a title of high nobility. **5,** a preeminent person. —**prince′dom,** *n.* —**prince consort,** the husband of a reigning female sovereign. **prince′ly** *adj.* **1,** royal. **2,** lavish; magnificent. —**prince′li·ness,** *n.*

prin′cess (prin′ses) *n.* **1,** a nonreigning female member of a ruling family. **2,** the consort of a prince. **3,** the daughter of a sovereign. **4,** a preeminent person.

prin′ci·pal (prin′sə-pəl) *adj.* first in rank or importance; chief. —*n.* **1,** one who takes a leading part. **2,** the head of a school. **3,** capital bearing interest. **4,** the employer of an agent. **5,** the chief perpetrator of a crime. —**principal parts,** the principal inflected forms of a verb.

---

principal, principle
☛ Two often-confused words. *Principal* as an adjective means chief; as a noun it means someone or something important. *Principle* is only a noun, meaning a doctrine.

---

prin″ci·pal′i·ty (prin″sə-pal′ə-tē) *n.* the domain of a prince.

prin′ci·ple (prin′sə-pəl) *n.* **1,** a fundamental truth or doctrine on which others are based. **2,** (*pl.*) rules of conduct or ethical behavior. —**prin′ci·pled,** *adj.* ❏ *principal*

prink *v.t. & i.* dress up; adorn.

print *n.* **1,** a mark made by impression. **2,** a seal or die.· **3,** anything printed; (of a book) publication. **4,** cloth stamped with a design. —*v.t.* **1,** impress; stamp. **2,** produce (reading matter from type, a photograph from a film, etc.). **3,** form (letters) in imitation of type. —**printed circuit,** a circuit made by depositing conducting material on a surface between two terminals.

print′er (-ər) *n.* **1,** one whose business or trade is printing. **2,** a device for copying (not applied to printing machinery). **3,** a high-speed typewriter. —**printer's devil,** an errand boy in a print shop.

print′ing *n.* **1,** the process of producing the printed portion of books, etc. **2,** the use of capital letters only, in handwriting. **3,** something printed. ❏ *edition*

print-out″ *n.* the typed or printed output of a computer, etc.

pri′or (prī′ər) *adj.* preceding in time, order, or importance. —*adv.* (with *to*) previous. —*n.* a male superior in a religious order or house (*priory*). —**prior restraint,** (*Law*) censorship in advance of publication.

pri′or·ess (-is) *n.* a female superior in a religious order or house (*priory*).

pri·or′i·ty (prī-or′ə-tē) *n.* **1,** the state of being prior. **2,** a right of precedence. —**pri·or′i·tize″** (-tīz) *v.t.* arrange in order of priority.

prise (prīz) *v.t.* pry (def. 1).

prism (priz′əm) *n.* **1,** a solid figure whose sides are parallelograms and whose ends are similar equal polygons and parallel. **2,** a transparent body that separates light into its component colors. —**pris·mat′ic,** *adj.*

pris′on (priz′ən) *n.* a jail; any place of confinement. —**pris′on·er,** *n.* one confined in or as in prison or forcibly restrained.

---

prison
↔ From Latin *praehendere*, to seize, also the source of *apprehend*, *comprehensive*, etc.

---

pris′sy (pris′ē) *adj.* (*Informal*) prim. —**pris′si·ness,** *n.*

pris′tine (pris′tēn) *adj.* original; primitive; unspoiled.

pri′va·cy (prī′və-sē) *n.* state of being private or alone.

pri′vate (prī′vit) *adj.* **1,** personal; not public. **2,** secret, confidential; being alone. **3,** retired; secluded. —*n.* a soldier of lowest rank. —**private detective,** a detective not working for an official police force. —**private eye,** a private detective.

pri″va·teer′ (prī″və-tir′) *n.* a ship operating under a letter of marque; its commander.

pri·va′tion (prī-vā′shən) *n.* want; destitution.

priv′et (priv′it) *n.* an evergreen shrub, much used for hedges.

priv′i·lege (priv′ə-lij) *n.* a special advantage enjoyed by a person. —*v.t.* **1,** grant a privilege to. **2,** (with *from*) exempt. **3,** authorize.

priv′i·leged (-lijd) *adj.* **1,** favored. **2,** exempt. **3,** confidential.

priv′y (priv′ē) *adj.* **1,** (with *to*) admitted to a secret. **2,** private. —*n.* a small building used as a toilet. —**privy council,** a small advisory body.

prix′ fixe′ (prē′ fēks′) [*pl.* **prix fixes** (prē′ fēks′] (*Fr.*) (at a) fixed price; table d'hôte.

---

prize (prīz) *n.* **1,** a reward given as a symbol of superiority. **2,** anything highly valued. **3,** a ship seized from an enemy. —*v.t.* **1,** value highly. **2,** [also, **prise**] pry. —*adj.* **1,** worthy of or given as a prize. **2,** outstanding; superior. —**prize ring,** a boxing ring; hence, prizefighting as a profession. **prize′fight″** *n.* a professional boxing match. —**prize′fight″er,** *n.* —**prize′- fight″ing,** *n.*

pro (prō) *n.* [*pl.* **pros**] **1,** a proponent. **2,** (*Informal*) a professional, esp. in sports. —*adv.* for the affirmative. —*prep.* for.

pro- *pref.* **1,** in favor of. **2,** on behalf of.

pro′a (prō′ə) *n.* a Malay canoe with an outrigger and a lateen sail.

pro·ac′tive *adj.* anticipatory.

pro-′am″ (prō′am″) *adj.* of a competition including both professionals and amateurs.

prob″a·bil′i·ty (prob″ə-bil′ə-tē) *n.* **1,** likelihood. **2,** that which appears true or likely. **3,** (*pl.*) relative chances of occurrence; expectancy.

prob′a·ble (prob′ə-bəl) *adj.* to be expected; likely. —**prob′a·bly,** *adv.* ❑ *possible*

pro′bate (prō′bāt) *n.* (*Law*) official proof of a will. —*adj.* **1,** related to the proof of wills. **2,** having jurisdiction over wills, as a probate court. —*v.t.* submit for probate.

pro·ba′tion (prō-bā′shən) *n.* **1,** a method or period of test or trial. **2,** conditional release of a prisoner. —**pro·ba′tion·a·ry,** *adj.* —**pro·ba′tion·er,** *n.* one who is being tested.

pro′ba·tive (prō′bə-tiv) *adj.* **1,** serving to test or prove. **2,** pert. to proof. Also, **pro′- ba·to″ry** (-tôr″e).

probe (prōb) *n.* **1,** a surgical instrument for exploring cavities, etc. **2,** a searching investigation. —*v.t. & i.* search (into); explore.

pro′bi·ty (prō′bə-tē) *n.* integrity.

prob′lem (prob′ləm) *n.* **1,** a difficult or perplexing matter; a troublesome person. **2,** a proposition to be worked out. —**prob″lem·at′ic** (-lə-mat′ik), **prob″- lem·at′i·cal,** *adj.* questionable; doubtful.

pro bo′no (prō bō′nō) (*Lat.*) for the (public) good.

pro·bos′cis (prō-bos′is) *n.* a long flexible nose or snout.

pro·caine′ (prō-kān′) *n.* a local anesthetic.

pro·ce′dure (prə-sē′jər) *n.* **1,** a course or mode of action; a step taken. **2,** customary process. —**pro·ce′dur·al,** *adj.*

pro·ceed′ (prə-sēd′) *v.i.* **1,** go forward; continue or renew progress. **2,** issue; come forth. **3,** begin and carry on legal action. ❑ *precede*

pro·ceed′ing *n.* **1,** a measure or step taken; a legal action. **2,** (*pl.*) business done; a record of it.

pro′ceeds (prō′sēdz) *n.pl.* money taken in.

proc′ess (pros′es) *n.* **1,** course; progress; lapse (of time). **2,** a series of changes leading to some result. **3,** a series of operations, as in manufacturing. **4,** (*Anatomy*) an outgrowth; protuberance. **5,** (*Law*) a summons. —*v.t.* subject to a special treatment.

pro·ces′sion (prə-sesh′ən) *n.* an array, formal march, or orderly series; those constituting it.

pro·ces′sion·al (-əl) *adj.* pert. to a procession. —*n.* **1,** a hymn to which clergy and choir enter. **2,** a procession.

proc′es·sor (pros′es-ər) *n.* **1,** a person or machine that processes. **2,** a computer or the principal microchip in a computer.

pro-choice′ *adj.* advocating legalized abortion.

pro·claim′ (prō-klām′) *v.t.* declare publicly; announce officially.

proc″la·ma′tion (prok″lə-mā′shən) *n.* act or result of proclaiming; announcement.

pro·cliv′i·ty (prō-kliv′ə-tē) *n.* inclination; tendency; predisposition. ❑ *acclivity*

pro·con′sul *n.* in ancient Rome, the governor of a province. —**pro·con′su·lar,** *adj.* —**pro·con′sul·ate, pro·con′sul·ship,** *n.*

pro·cras′ti·nate″ (prō-kras′tə-nāt″) *v.i.* delay action. —**pro·cras″ti·na′tion,** *n.* —**pro·cras′ti·na″tor,** *n.*

pro′cre·ate″ (prō′krē-āt″) *v.t.* engender; —**pro″cre·a′tion,** *n.*

proc·tol′o·gy (prok-tol′ə-jē) *n.* (*Med.*) the study and treatment of rectal and anal diseases.

proc′tor (prok′tər) *n.* **1,** a supervising official, esp. in a college. **2,** a representative in a church court. —**proc·to′ri·al** (-tôr′ē-əl) *adj.*

proc′u·ra″tor (prok′yû-rā″tər) *n.* a manager, spec. a colonial financial officer for ancient Rome.

pro·cure′ (prō-kyûr′) *v.t.* **1,** contrive (an effect). **2,** obtain. —**pro·cure′ment,** *n.*

pro·cur′er (prō-kyûr′ər) *n.* a pimp.

prod *n.* a goad. —*v.t.* [**prod′ded, -ding**] goad; poke.

prod′i·gal (prod′i-gəl) *adj.* **1,** lavish;

wasteful. **2,** bountiful. —*n.* a spendthrift. —**prod″i·gal′i·ty,** *n.*

pro·di′gious (prə-dij′əs) *adj.* vast; huge; immense. —**pro·di′gious·ness,** *n.*

prod′i·gy (prod′ə-jē) *n.* **1,** something remarkable; a marvel. **2,** a portent. **3,** an exceptionally talented person, esp. a child.

---

prodigy, progeny, protégé
☛ The first two words are frequently confused. A *prodigy* is an exceptionally talented person, esp. a child. *Progeny* are descendants. A *protégé* is a person, esp. someone having special talents, protected or sponsored by another person.

---

pro·duce′ (prə-dūs′) *v.t.* **1,** bring out; exhibit. **2,** bear, yield. **3,** bring about; effect. **4,** make; manufacture. —*v.i.* yield. —*n.* (prod′ūs) yield; products, esp. agricultural.

prod′uct (prod′ukt) *n.* **1,** that which is produced; an effect; result. **2,** the number resulting from multiplication.

pro·duc′tion (prə-duk′shən) *n.* **1,** act of bringing forward. **2,** a product of physical or mental labor; esp., a theatrical presentation.

pro·duc′tive (prə-duk′tiv) *adj.* **1,** creative; fertile. **2,** profitable. —**pro·duc′tive-ness,** *n.*

pro′em (prō′em) *n.* an introduction; preface. —**pro·e′mi·al** (prō-ē′mē-əl) *adj.*

pro·fane′ (prə-fān′) *adj.* **1,** not sacred; irreverent; blasphemous. **2,** vulgar. —*v.t.* **1,** desecrate. **2,** pollute; debase. —**prof″a·na′tion** (prof″ə-nā′shən) *n.*

---

profane
↔ Literally, "outside the temple," from Latin *profanus.*

---

pro·fan′i·ty (prə-fan′ə-tē) *n.* **1,** blasphemy; swearing. **2,** irreverence.

pro·fess′ (prə-fes′) *v.t.* **1,** declare openly. **2,** affirm faith in. **3,** make a pretense of. —**pro·fessed′,** *adj.* avowed.

pro·fes′sion (prə-fesh′ən) *n.* **1,** an avowal. **2,** a vocation, esp. in a branch of science or learning; the body of persons engaged in such a vocation. ❏ *career*

pro·fes′sion·al *adj.* pert. to or engaged in a profession, or in a sport for pay. —*n.* one working for pay, not an amateur. —**pro·fes′sion·al·ism,** *n.*

pro·fes′sor (prə-fes′ər) *n.* a teacher of high rank. Also, (*Slang*) **prof.** —**pro″fes·sor′i·al** (prō″fə-sôr′ē-əl) *adj.*

prof′fer (prof′ər) *v.t.* tender, as an offer. —*n.* an offer.

pro·fi′cient (prə-fish′ənt) *adj.* skilled. —*n.* an expert. —**pro·fi′cien·cy,** *n.*

pro′file (prō′fīl) *n.* **1,** a side view of a face. **2,** a contour. **3,** a colorful biographical sketch. —*v.t.* draw or make a profile of.

prof′it *n.* **1,** advantage; benefit. **2,** monetary gain; excess of returns over costs; benefit. —*v.t.* benefit. —*v.i.* **1,** improve; make progress. **2,** gain; become richer. —**prof′it·a·ble,** *adj.* yielding a profit.

prof″it·eer′ (prof″i-tir′) *n.* one who profits unduly from the sale of necessities. —*v.i.* profit unduly.

prof′li·gate (prof′li-gət) *adj.* dissolute; recklessly extravagant. —*n.* a spendthrift. —**prof′li·ga·cy,** *n.*

pro for′ma (prō fôr′mə) (*Lat.*) for form's sake.

pro·found′ (prə-fownd′) *adj.* **1,** deep; thorough. **2,** intense; deeply felt. —**pro·found′ness,** *n.*

pro·fun′di·ty (prə-fun′də-tē) *n.* **1,** profoundness; intellectual deepness. **2,** that which is profound.

pro·fuse′ (prə-fūs′) *adj.* liberal to excess; copious; abundant. —**pro·fu′sion** (-zhən) *n.*

pro·gen′i·tor (prō-jen′ə-tər) *n.* an ancestor in the direct line.

prog′e·ny (proj′ə-nē) *n.* offspring; descendants. ❏ *prodigy*

pro·ges′ter·one″ (prō-jes′tə-rōn″) *n.* a sex hormone.

prog·no′sis (prog-nō′sis) *n.* a forecast. *adj.* —**prog·nos′ti·cal·ly,** *adv.* ❏ *diagnosis*

prog·nos′tic (prog-nos′tik) *adj.* **1,** pert. to, or serving as a ground for, prognosis. **2,** foretelling. —*n.* **1,** an omen. **2,** a prediction. **3,** a prognostic symptom.

prog·nos′ti·cate″ (prog-nos′tə-kāt′) *v.t.* foretell; predict. —**prog·nos″ti·ca′tion,** *n.*

pro′gram″ (prō′gram″) *n.* **1,** a printed list of events, performers, etc., in any public entertainment. **2,** a plan of procedure. **3,** a sequence of coded instructions for a digital computer. —*v.t.* schedule. Also, **pro′-gramme.** —**pro′gram·mer,** *n.* —**program trading,** market trading in groups of securities governed by complex formulas requiring computerized computations.

prog′ress (prog′res) *n.* **1,** a moving forward. **2,** advance; development. —*v.i.* (prə-gres′) **1,** proceed; advance. **2,** grow; develop.

pro·gres′sion (prə-gresh′ən) *n.* **1,** a moving forward. **2,** a sequence, as of events. **3,** a series in which there is a constant

---

relation between each item and the one preceding it.

pro·gres'sive (prə-gres'iv) *adj.* **1**, moving forward. **2**, advocating new ideas, methods, etc. **3**, (*Gram.*) indicating action going on at the time, as *is going; was going.* —*n.* one who is not conservative. —**pro·gres'sive·ness**, *n.*

pro·hib'it (prō-hib'it) *v.t.* **1**, forbid. **2**, prevent; hinder. —**pro·hib'i·to·ry**, *adj.*

pro"hi·bi'tion (prō"ə-bish'ən) *n.* act or effect of forbidding; esp. (*U.S.*) the period 1920–33 when the 18th Amendment was in effect. —**pro"hi·bi'tion·ist**, *n.* one favoring prohibition of alcoholic liquors.

pro·hib'i·tive (prə-hib'ə-tiv) *adj.* tending to preclude or discourage, as a high price. —**pro·hib'i·tive·ness**, *n.*

proj'ect (proj'ekt) *n.* **1**, a plan; scheme. **2**, a piece of research; a problem undertaken in school. **3**, a public works development, esp. in housing. —*v.t.* (prə-jekt') **1**, cast forward; impose. **2**, devise. **3**, cause (light, shadow) to fall on a surface, as a screen. —*v.i.* jut out; protrude.

pro·jec'tile (pro-jek'til) *n.* a missile, as a bullet. —*adj.* impelling, or impelled, forward.

pro·jec'tion (prə-jek'shən) *n.* **1**, act or effect of projecting. **2**, a part that juts out. **3**, the act or result of projecting a figure on another surface, esp. an image on a screen or the surface of the earth on a plane surface. —**pro·jec'tion·ist**, *n.*

pro·jec'tor (prə-jek'tər) *n.* an optical instrument that projects an image, as a motion picture.

pro·lac'tin (prō-lak'tin) *n.* a pituitary hormone that stimulates the secretion of milk.

pro·lapse (prō'laps) *n.* a falling or slipping out of normal position, as of the uterus.

pro·late (prō'lāt) *adj.* extended; elongated, as a spheroid.

pro"le·tar'i·at (prō"lə-tār'ē-ət) *n.* the laboring class. —**pro"le·tar'i·an**, *adj. & n.*

> **proletariat**
> ↔ From Latin *proles*, offspring: a *proletarius* was a citizen only good for producing children.

pro-life' *adj.* opposed to legalized abortion.

pro·lif'er·ate" (prō-lif'ə-rāt") *v.i.* **1**, grow by multiplication of elementary parts, as in budding. **2**, spread or multiply rapidly. —**pro·lif"er·a'tion**, *n.* —**pro·lif"er·ous**, *adj.*

pro·lif'ic (prō-lif'ik) *adj.* **1**, producing young, fruit, etc., abundantly. **2**, producing much work, etc. —**pro·lif'i·cal·ly**, *adv.*

pro·lix' (prō-liks') *adj.* long and wordy; tedious. —**pro·lix'i·ty**, *n.*

PRO'LOG (prō'lâg) *n.* (*Computers*) a programming language used in artificial intelligence: *pro(gramming in) log(ic).*

pro'logue (prō'lâg) *n.* the introduction to a poem, play, etc.

pro·long' (prə-lâng') *v.t.* extend in time or length. —**pro"lon·ga'tion**, (prō"long-gā'shən) *n.*

prom"e·nade' (prom"ə-nād') *n.* **1**, a stroll for pleasure; a place for strolling. **2**, [also (*informal*) **prom**] a dance; ball. —*v.i. & t.* take a stroll.

pro·me'thi·um (prə-mē'thē-əm) *n.* a rare-earth metallic element, no. 61, symbol Pm.

> **promethium**
> ↔ Named after the Titan *Prometheus*, who brought fire to humankind,

prom'i·nent (prom'ə-nənt) *adj.* **1**, standing out; jutting. **2**, conspicuous; distinguished. —**prom'i·nence**, *n.*

pro·mis'cu·ous (prə-mis'kū-əs) *adj.* **1**, of all sorts and kinds; indiscriminate. **2**, not discriminating in choice of companions, esp. in sexual relations. —**prom"is·cu'i·ty** (prom"is-kū'ə-tē) *n.*

prom'ise (prom'is) *n.* **1**, one's pledge to another that one will or will not do something. **2**, ground for hope. **3**, indication of future excellence. —*v.t.* **1**, engage to do or give; give one's word to. **2**, afford hope or expectation (of). —**prom'is·ing**, *adj.* encouraging; apparently due to succeed.

prom'is·so·ry (-sôr-ē) *adj.* stating an obligation to pay, as *a promissory note.*

pro'mo (prō'mō) *n.* (*Informal*) **1**, promotion. **2**, an item of promotional advertising.

prom'on·to"ry (prom'ən-tôr"ē) *n.* high land jutting into the sea; a headland.

pro·mote' (prə-mōt') *v.t.* **1**, encourage the growth or improvement of. **2**, raise to a higher rank, class, or position. —**pro·mot'er**, *n.* one who helps to start an enterprise.

pro·mo'tion (prə-mō'shən) *n.* **1**, act or effect of promoting. **2**, advancement in rank. **3**, an enterprise being promoted.

prompt *adj.* **1**, quick to act. **2**, given without delay. **3**, on time. —*v.t.* **1**, move or incite to action. **2**, remind (an actor, speaker) of his or her lines. —*n.* (*Computers*) a message to an operator from an operating system, usu. requesting or awaiting a response. —**promp'ti·tude** (-ti-tood) *n.* —**prompt'ness**, *n.*

prom'ul·gate" (prom'əl-gāt") *v.t.* make known publicly; proclaim. —**prom"ul·ga'-tion**, *n.*

prone (prōn) *adj.* **1,** lying face downward. **2,** having a natural tendency; inclined. —**prone'ness**, *n.*

prong *n.* a sharp point, as a tine.

prong'horn" *n.* a No. Amer. ruminant resembling an antelope.

pro'noun (prō'nown) *n.* a word (as *he, it*) used to represent a noun previously stated or understood. —**pro·nom'in·al**, (-nom'i-nəl) *adj.*

pro·nounce' (prə-nowns') *v.t.* **1,** declare; utter. **2,** utter the recognized sound of (a word, etc.). —*v.i.* **1,** give as one's opinion. **2,** articulate words. —**pro·nounced'**, *adj.* clearly so; decided. —**pro·nounce'ment**, *n.* a formal announcement.

pron'to (pron'tō) *adv.* (*Informal*) at once; immediately.

pro·nun"ci·a'tion (prə-nun"sē-ā'shən) *n.* the uttering of words, esp. with correct sounds and stresses.

proof *n.* **1,** evidence that establishes a fact. **2,** a test; trial. **3,** an impression from composed type, taken for correction. —*adj.* **1,** (often as a *suf.*) able to withstand. **2,** of liquors, times ½ of 1% absolute alcohol, as, 90 proof is 45% alcohol. —**proof'ing**, *n.* a treatment to make something waterproof, fireproof, etc.; the chemical used.

proof'read" *v.t. & i.* [*pret. & p.p.* -**read** (-red)] read and correct.

prop *v.t.* [**propped, prop'ping**] support or keep from falling, as by placing something under or against. —*n.* **1,** a support. **2,** an airplane or boat propeller. **3,** a property (def. 4).

prop"a·gan'da (prop"ə-gan'də) *n.* ideas disseminated to support a doctrine. —**prop"a·gan'dist**, *n.* —**prop"a·gan'dize"** (-dīz") *v.t. & i.*

---

propaganda

↔ A shortened form of the Latin phrase *congregatio de propaganda fide*, congregation for propagating the faith.

---

prop'a·gate" (prop'ə-gāt") *v.t.* **1,** cause to multiply by natural processes. **2,** spread; disseminate. —*v.i.* have offspring. —**prop"a·ga'tion**, *n.*

pro'pane (prō'pān) *n.* (*Chem.*) a hydrocarbon, found in petroleum.

pro·pel' (prə-pel') *v.t.* [**pro·pelled', -pel'-ling**] drive forward by force. —**pro·pel'-lant** (-ənt) *n.* a propelling agent, as a fuel or an explosive.

pro·pel'ler (prə-pel'ər) *n.* a device with blades which revolves to drive forward a ship or airplane.

pro·pen'si·ty (prə-pen'sə-tė) *n.* a natural tendency; bent.

prop'er (prop'ər) *adj.* **1,** particularly suited; natural. **2,** fit; appropriate. **3,** taken in a strict sense. **4,** accurate. **5,** decent; respectable. **6,** of a noun, naming one particular person, place, etc. —**prop'er·ness**, *n.*

prop'er·ty (prop'ər-tė) *n.* **1,** an essential attribute or quality. **2,** ownership. **3,** a thing owned, esp. real estate; a possession. **4,** (usu. *pl.*) items in a stage setting. —**prop'er·tied** (-tēd) *adj.* owning real estate.

---

property, propriety

↔ These two words both spring from the same Latin source, *proprietas*, ownership, through two slightly different Middle English words.

---

proph'e·cy (prof'ə-sė) *n.* a prediction of the future.

proph'e·sy" (prof'ə-sī") *v.t. & i.* predict; foretell.

proph'et (prof'it) *n.* **1,** one who predicts. **2,** a spokesman, esp. one inspired by God.

proph'et·ess (-i-tis) *n.* a female prophet.

pro·phet'ic (prə-fet'ik) *adj.* **1,** pert. to prophecy or a prophet. **2,** presaging. —**pro·phet'i·cal·ly**, *adv.*

pro"phy·lax'is (prō"fə-lak'sis) *n.* (*Med.*) preventive treatment. —**pro"phy·lac'tic**, *n. & adj.*

pro·pin'qui·ty (prō-ping'kwi-tė) *n.* nearness, in time, place, or blood.

pro·pi'ti·ate" (prō-pish'ė-āt") *v.t.* appease; conciliate. —**pro·pi'ti·a'tion**, *n.* —**pro·pi'ti·a·to·ry** (-ė-ə-tôr-ė) *adj.*

pro·pi'tious (prə-pish'əs) *adj.* **1,** kindly disposed. **2,** favorable. —**pro·pi'tious·ness**, *n.* ❏ *auspicious*

prop'jet engine a turbo-propeller engine.

pro·po'nent (prə-pō'nənt) *n.* one who proposes or supports something.

pro·por'tion (prə-pôr'shən) *n.* **1,** the relation of one thing or part to another in respect to size, degree, or quantity. **2,** symmetrical arrangement; harmony. **3,** just or proper share. **4,** (*pl.*) dimensions. —**pro·por'tion·al**, *adj.* —**pro·por'tion·ate** (-ət) *adj.*

pro·pose' (prə-pōz') *v.t.* **1,** offer for con-

---

siideration, acceptance, admission, or adoption. **2,** put forward as a plan; suggest. —*v.i.* **1,** intend. **2,** make an offer of marriage. —**pro·pos'al,** *n.*

prop"o·si'tion (prop"ə-zish'ən) *n.* **1,** a subject for study, discussion, etc.; a problem. **2,** (*Informal*) a project, undertaking, situation, etc. **3,** a proposal. —*v.t.* (*Slang*) make a proposal to, esp. of sexual relations.

pro·pound' (prə-pownd') *v.t.* offer for consideration, as a question; set forth (a theory, etc.).

pro·pri'e·tar"y (prə-prī'ə-ter"ē) *adj.* **1,** pert. to an owner; holding property. **2,** privately owned; patented.

pro·pri'e·tor *n.* an owner. —**pro·pri'e·tor·ship",** *n.*

pro·pri'e·ty (prə-prī'ə-tē) *n.* **1,** fitness; rightness. **2,** correct behavior; decorum. **3,** (*pl.*) the standards of conduct approved by society. ❏ *property*

pro·pul'sion (prə-pul'shən) *n.* **1,** a propelling forward. **2,** driving force.

pro ra'ta (prō" rā'tə) (*Lat.*) in proportion.

pro·rate' (prō-rāt') *v.t.* divide proportionally. —**pro·ra'tion,** *n.*

pro·rogue' (prō-rōg') *v.t.* temporarily discontinue meetings of, esp. the British Parliament. —**pro"ro·ga'tion** (prō"rə-gā'shən) *n.*

pro·sa'ic (prō-zā'ik) *adj.* unromantic; commonplace. —**pro·sa'i·cal·ly,** *adv.*

pro·sce'ni·um (prō-sē'nē-əm) *n.* **1,** a stage. **2,** the front of the stage, before the curtain.

pro·scribe' (prō-skrīb') *v.t.* **1,** prohibit. **2,** banish. —**pro·scrip'tion** (-skrip'shən) *n.* —**pro·scrip'tive** (-tiv) *adj.* ❏ *prescribe*

prose (prōz) *n.* ordinary language; not poetry. —**pros'y,** *adj.* dull.

pros'e·cute" (pros'ə-kūt") *v.t.* **1,** institute legal proceedings against. **2,** pursue (an object). —*v.i.* **1,** sue. **2,** act as prosecutor. —**prosecuting attorney,** the state's attorney. ❏ *persecute*

pros"e·cu'tion (-kū'shən) *n.* **1,** act or result of prosecuting. **2,** the side that prosecutes. **3,** the prosecutor and his staff.

pros'e·cu"tor (pros'ə-kū"tər) *n.* one who prosecutes, esp. the public prosecutor or state's attorney.

pros'e·lyte" (pros'ə-līt") *n.* a convert from one creed, sect, or party to another. —**pros'e·ly·tize"** (-lə-tīz") *v.t. & i.* attempt to convert.

pro'sit (prō'sit) *interj.* (*Ger.*) (as a toast) may it do good!

pros'o·dy (pros'ə-dē) *n.* the study of metrical versification.

pros'pect (pros'pekt) *n.* **1,** a view; scene. **2,** what one hopes for; expectation. **3,** a possible buyer, client, etc. —*v.t. & i.* explore (a district) for ores, oil, etc. —**pros·pec'tive,** *adj.* expected. —**pros'pec·tor,** *n.* one who seeks ores.

pros·pec'tus (prə-spek'təs) *n.* a descriptive pamphlet; catalog.

pros'per (pros'pər) *v.i.* succeed; thrive.

pros·per'i·ty (pros-per'ə-tē) *n.* **1,** success. **2,** a period of economic well-being.

pros'per·ous (-pər-əs) *adj.* **1,** thriving; successful. **2,** favorable.

pros'tate (pros'tāt) *n. & adj.* a gland in males which surrounds the base of the urethra and discharges into it. —**pro·stat'ic** (prō-stat'ik), *adj.*

> **prostate, prostrate**
> ☛The *prostate* is a gland; *prostrate* is a verb and adjective having to do with lying down.

pros'the·sis (pros'thə-sis) *n.* the supplying of an artificial part of the body; such a part.

pros'ti·tute" (pros'tə-tūt") *v.t.* devote (one's honor, talents, person) to base purposes. —*n.* a person who engages in sexual acts for money. —**pros"ti·tu'tion,** *n.*

pros'trate (pros'trāt) *adj.* **1,** lying flat; laid low. **2,** bowing low. —*v.t.* **1,** throw (oneself) down; lay or lie flat. **2,** overthrow. **3,** cause to succumb. —**pros·tra'tion,** *n.* ❏ *prostate*

pro"tac·tin'i·um (prō"tak-tin'ē-əm) *n.* a short-lived radioactive chemical element formed from uranium 235, no. 91, symbol Pa. Also, **pro"to·ac·tin'i·um** (prō"tō-).

pro·tag'o·nist (prō-tag'ə-nist) *n.* the leading figure, as in a play.

pro'te·an (prō'tē-ən) *adj.* readily assuming many shapes.

> **protean**
> ↔ Named for the constantly changing sea god *Proteus*.

pro·tect' (prə-tekt') *v.t.* shield from harm, damage, etc. —**pro·tec'tor,** *n.*

pro·tec'tion *n.* **1,** act or effect of protecting; that which keeps safe. **2,** support of domestic prices by a tariff. **3,** immunity from arrest, purchased by bribery. —**pro·tec'tion·ist,** *n. & adj.* —**pro·tec'tion·ism,** *n.*

pro·tec'tive *adj.* **1,** serving to protect or supply protection. **2,** wishing to protect. —**pro·tec'tive·ness,** *n.*

---

pro·tec′tor·ate (-ət) *n.* a state controlled and protected by a stronger state.

pro·té·gé″ (prō′tə-zhā″) *n.* a person protected or aided by another. ❑ *prodigy*

pro·te·in (prō′tēn) *n.* an organic substance, an essential element of diet.

> **protein**
> ↔ Coined by 19th-c. Dutch chemist Gerardus Mulder, based on Greek *prōteios*, primary.

pro tem′po·re (prō tem′pə-rē) (*Lat.*) for the time being.

pro′test (prō′test) *v.i. & t.* **1,** declare solemnly. **2,** remonstrate; formally object to. **3,** declare to be dishonored by nonpayment, as a check, etc. —*n.* a formal declaration of disapproval. —**prot″es·ta′tion** (prot″is-tā′shən) *n.*

Prot′es·tant (prot″is-tənt) *adj.* pert. to a Christian church not Roman or Orthodox Catholic. —*n.* a member of such a church. —**Prot′es·tant·ism,** *n.*

pro″tha·la′mi·um (prō″thə-lā′mē-əm) *n.* a pre-wedding ode.

> **prothalamium**
> ↔ Coined (as *prothalamion*) by 16th-c. English poet Edmund Spenser.

pro·to- (prō-tō) *pref.* first in time; principal; chief.

pro′to·col″ (prō′tə-kol″) *n.* **1,** a draft of a treaty or agreement. **2,** the formal procedure in official or diplomatic society. **3,** (*Computers*) a standard for communication between devices.

pro′ton (prō′ton) *n.* a particle of the atom, carrying a positive charge of electricity.

pro′to·plasm″ (prō′tə-plaz″əm) *n.* the substance of which all animal and plant cells are composed. —**pro″to·plas′mic,** *adj.*

pro′to·type″ (prō′tə-tīp″) *n.* the original form; pattern; model.

Pro″to·zo′a (prō″tə-zō′ə) *n.pl.* all animals that consist of a single cell. —**pro″to·zo′an,** *adj. & n.*

pro·tract′ (prō-trakt′) *v.t.* **1,** prolong. **2,** draw to scale; chart. —**pro·trac′tion,** *n.*

pro·trac′tor (-ər) *n.* **1,** a muscle that extends a part of the body. **2,** a device for measuring or drawing angles.

pro·trude′ (prō-trood′) *v.i. & t.* stick out; project. —**pro·tru′sion** (-troo′zhən) *n.*

pro·tu′ber·ant (prō-tū′bər-ənt) *adj.* bulging out; prominent. —**pro·tu′ber·ance,** *n.*

proud (prowd) *adj.* **1,** haughty; arrogant.

2, self-respectful. **3,** being gratified or elated. **4,** imposing; splendid. **5,** spirited. —**proud′ness,** *n.* —**proud flesh,** excessive granulation of a healing wound or sore.

prove (proov) *v.t.* **1,** test the qualities of. **2,** make certain, by adducing evidence. **3,** probate. **4,** make a proof of (type). —*v.i.* turn out (to be). —**prov′en,** *adj.* proved. —**proving ground,** a place or occasion for testing.

prov′e·nance (prov′ə-nəns) *n.* source; derivation.

prov′en·der (prov′ən-dər) *n.* dry food for animals; fodder.

prov′erb (prov′ĕrb) *n.* **1,** a well-known truth expressed as a maxim. **2,** a byword. —**pro·ver′bi·al** (prə-vĕr′bē-əl) *adj.*

pro·vide′ (prə-vīd′) *v.t.* **1,** procure beforehand. **2,** (with *with*) furnish —*v.i.* **1,** furnish supplies; take precautions. **2,** supply what is needed. **3,** stipulate. —**pro·vid′ed, pro·vid′ing,** *conj.* on the condition that.

prov′i·dence (prov′i-dəns) *n.* **2,** thrift; economy. **2,** (*cap.*) God; divine care.

prov′i·dent (prov′i-dənt) *adj.* thrifty; foresighted.

prov″i·den′tial (prov″i-den′shəl) *adj.* **1,** of or by divine guidance. **2,** opportune.

prov′ince (prov′ins) *n.* **1,** an administrative division of a country. **2,** (*pl.*) rural regions. **3,** a proper sphere of action. **4,** a division or department of knowledge.

pro·vin′cial (prə-vin′shəl) *adj.* **1,** of a province. **2,** rustic. **3,** narrow; not cosmopolitan. —**pro·vin′cial·ism,** *n.*

pro·vi′sion (prə-vizh′ən) *n.* **1,** preparation. **2,** (*pl.*) stores; supplies, as of food. **3,** a proviso; condition, as in a contract. —*v.t.* supply with a store of food.

pro·vi′sion·al *adj.* **1,** conditional. **2,** temporary.

pro·vi′so (prə-vī′zō) *n.* [*pl.* **-sos** (-zōz)] a condition, esp. in a contract. —**pro·vi′so·ry** (-zə-rē) *adj.*

prov″o·ca′tion (prov″ə-kā′shən) *n.* **1,** act or effect of provoking. **2,** a cause of anger or resentment. **3,** stimulus; incitement.

pro·voc′a·tive (prə-vok′ə-tiv) *adj.* serving to provoke, arouse, or stimulate. —**pro·voc′a·tive·ness,** *n.*

pro·voke′ (prə-vōk′) *v.t.* **1,** incense; irritate. **2,** arouse; goad. **3,** incite; stir up.

pro·vo·lo′ne (prō-və-lō′nē) *n.* a mild Ital. cheese.

prov′ost (prov′əst) *n.* a supervisor or head. —**provost marshal,** a chief of military police.

prow *n.* the foremost surface of a ship; bow.

prow'ess (prow'is) *n.* **1,** valor. **2,** great skill or ability.

prowl *v.i. & t.* roam about stealthily. —*n.* act of prowling. —**prowl car,** a radio-equipped police automobile.

prox'i·mate (prok'si-mət) *adj.* next; immediate.

prox·im'i·ty (prok-sim'ə-tė) *n.* nearness. —**proximity fuse,** a device to explode a bomb when it approaches its object.

> **proximity, proxy**
> ↔ These two words are unrelated. *Proximity* comes from Latin *proximus,* next. *Proxy,* also of Latin origin, comes from *procuratio,* caring for.

prox'y (prok'sė) *n.* **1,** authority to act for another. **2,** the person so authorized. ❏ *proximity*

prude (prood) *n.* an affectedly modest person. —**prud'er·y,** *n.* —**prud'ish,** *adj.* —**prud'ish·ness,** *n.*

> **prude, prudent**
> ↔ These words are unrelated. *Prude* comes, by devious route, from French *prudefemme,* respectable woman. *Prudent* derives from Latin *providens,* prudent.

pru'dence (proo'dəns) *n.* discretion; foresight; careful judgment. —**pru·den'tial** (-den'shəl) *adj.*

pru'dent (proo'dənt) *adj.* **1,** judicious; wise. **2,** discreet; circumspect. —**pru·den'tial** (-den'shəl) *adj.* ❏ *prude*

prune (proon) *n.* a dried plum. —*v.t. & i.* trim off something superfluous, esp. branches. ❏ *plum*

pru'ri·ent (prûr'ė-ənt) *adj.* lewd in thought. —**pru'ri·ence,** *n.*

Prus'sian (prush'ən) *adj.* pert. to Prussia or its people. —**Prussian blue,** a dark blue dye or pigment.

pry (prī) *n.* a lever. —*v.t.* **1,** raise or move by a lever. **2,** extract or move with difficulty. —*v.i.* peer curiously or impertinently.

psalm (säm) *n.* a sacred song or poem. —**psalm'ist,** *n.* —**psal'mo·dy** (sä'mə-dė; sal'-) *n.*

> **psalm**
> ↔ From Greek *psallein,* to pluck, as the strings of a harp to accompany singing of songs.

Psal'ter (sâl'tər) *n.* the Book of Psalms.

psal'ter·y (sâl'tə-rė) *n.* an ancient musical instrument like the zither.

pseu'do (soo'dō) *adj.* feigned; sham.

pseu·do- *pref.* false; sham.

pseu'do·nym'' (soo'də-nim'') *n.* a false name; pen name. —**pseu·don'y·mous,** (soo-don'ə-məs) *adj.*

pshaw (shâ) *interj.* of disdain.

psi (sī) *n.* the 23rd letter of the Greek alphabet (Ψ, ψ).

psit''ta·co'sis (sit''ə-kō'sis) *n.* a contagious disease of birds, transferable to man: *parrot fever.*

pso·ri'a·sis (sô-rī'ə-sis) *n.* a chronic skin disease characterized by scaly, reddish patches.

psych (sīk) *v.i.* (*Slang*) **1,** (with *out*) figure out the motives or behavior of); outwit. **2,** talk oneself out of or into; lose one's nerve. **3,** (with *up*) prepare mentally and emotionally.

psy'che (sī'kė) *n.* the human soul.

psy''che·del'ic (sī''kə-del'ik) *adj.* pert. to or causing a state of extreme calm, heightened senses, aesthetic perception, and frequently hallucination and distortion of perception.

psy·chi'a·try (sī-kī'ə-trė) *n.* (*Med.*) the medical specialty dealing with mental diseases. —**psy''chi·at'ric** (sī'kė-at'rik) *adj.* —**psy·chi'a·trist,** *n.*

> **psychiatrist, psychologist**
> A *psychiatrist* is a medical doctor specializing in mental disorders. A *psychologist* is not necessarily a medical doctor and may deal with normal psychology.

psy'chic (sī'kik) *adj.* **1,** pert. to the mental or spiritual life. **2,** pert. to mysterious mental forces. **3,** sensitive to such forces. —*n.* a person esp. susceptible to psychic forces. —**psy'chi·cal·ly,** *adv.*

psy'cho (sī'kō) *n.* (*Slang*) a deranged person.

psy·cho- *pref.* of the mind; by mental processes.

psy''cho·a·nal'y·sis *n.* a method of relieving mental disorders by a study of the unconscious emotional life of the patient. —**psy''cho·an'a·lyze,** *v.t.* —**psy''cho·an'a·lyst,** *n.*

psy'cho·dra''ma *n.* the use of improvisational theater in treating mental patients; such theater.

psy''cho·ki·ne'sis (-kə-nē'səs) *n.* the displacement of an object by strength of will.

psy·chol'o·gy (sī-kol'ə-jė) *n.* **1,** the study

of the mind and mental activities. **2,** (*Informal*) attitude. **3,** (*Informal*) the use of stratagems. **—psy″cho·log′i·cal,** *adj.* **—psy″chol′o·gist,** *n.* ❑ *psychiatrist*

psy″cho·pa·thol′o·gy *n.* the medical specialty dealing with mental illness and abnormality.

psy·chop′a·thy (sī-kop′ə-thė) *n.* mental disease, esp. one characterized by antisocial behavior.

psy″cho·path′ic (-ik) *adj.* pert. to psychopathy. **—psy′cho·path″,** *n.* **—psy″cho·path′i·cal·ly,** *adv.*

psy·cho′sis (sī-kō′sis) *n.* [*pl.* **-ses** (sėz)] a mental disease characterized by a loss of touch with reality. **—psy·chot′ic** (-kot′ik) *adj.*

psy″cho·so·mat′ic (sī″kō-sō-mat′ik) *adj.* pert. to the relation between mental and physical disorders, as a physical disease induced by emotional factors.

psy″cho·ther′a·py *n.* treatment of mental disease, esp. by psychoanalysis, psychodrama, etc. **—psy″cho·ther′a·pist,** *n.*

ptar′mi·gan (tär′mə-gən) *n.* a kind of grouse.

> **ptarmigan**
> ↔ From Gaelic *tarmachan,* spelled in pseudo-Greek style.

PT boat a small, lightly armored motor torpedo boat: *p(atrol) t(orpedo) boat.*

pter″o·dac′tyl (ter″ə-dak′til) *n.* an extinct large flying reptile.

ptis′an (tiz′ən) *n.* **1,** a mild herbal drink; barley water. **2,** tisane.

pto′maine (tō′mān) *n.* a chemical compound, often poisonous, found in decaying organic matter. **—ptomaine poisoning,** an acute intestinal disorder caused by toxic bacilli; formerly attributed to ptomaines.

pub *n.* (*Brit.*) public house; tavern.

pu′ber·ty (pū′bər-tė) *n.* **1,** the age or period at which a person first can procreate. **2,** the developmental process resulting in puberty; sexual maturation.

pu′bes (pū′bēz) *n.* the front bone of the pelvis, or its region, where hair grows at puberty; the hair itself. **—pu′bic,** *adj.*

pu·bes′cent (pū-bes′ənt) *adj.* arrived, or arriving, at puberty. **—pu·bes′cence,** *n.*

pub′lic (pub′lik) *adj.* **1,** pert. to the people at large. **2,** open to, or shared by, the people. **3,** known to all; not secret. **4,** engaged in service to the people. **—***n.* the entire community or a specified group. **—public access television,** television channel(s) made available to community

groups or individuals for noncommercial broadcasting. **—public address system,** the apparatus necessary to provide amplified sound for public assemblies. **—public domain, 1,** public land. **2,** works whose copyrights have expired. **—public defender,** a lawyer available for people without the means to hire an attorney. **—public enemy,** a criminal at large. **—public house,** (*Brit.*) a bar; pub. **—public relations,** organized publicity. **—public school, 1,** a school paid for by public funds. **2,** (*Brit.*) a private boarding school. **—public servant,** an elected or appointed employee of the government. **—pub″lic-spir′it·ed,** seeking the best interests of the community. **—public television,** public service and educational television not accepting commercial advertising.

pub′li·can (pub′lə-kən) *n.* **1,** (*Brit.*) an innkeeper. **2,** in ancient Rome, a tax collector.

pub″li·ca′tion (pub″li-kā′shən) *n.* **1,** the act or business of publishing. **2,** a book, periodical, etc.

pub′li·cist (pub′li-sist) *n.* **1,** a writer on current affairs, esp. international. **2,** one who is retained to manage publicity for another.

pub·lic′i·ty (pub-lis′ə-tė) *n.* **1,** a bringing to public attention. **2,** common knowledge; notoriety.

pub′li·cize″ (pub′li-sīz″) *v.t.* make known by publicity.

pub′lish *v.t.* **1,** make generally known; proclaim. **2,** print and offer for sale, as a book, etc.

puce (pūs) *adj.* of a purple-brown color.

puck (puk) *n.* **1,** the sliding disk used in hockey. **2,** (*cap.*) a mischievous sprite.

puck′er (puk′ər) *v.i. & t.* draw up into small bulges or wrinkles. **—***n.* **1,** a furrow. **2,** a state of agitation.

puck′ish (puk′ish) *adj.* mischievous. **—puck′ish·ness,** *n.*

pud′ding (pûd′ing) *n.* a soft, bulky dessert.

> **pudding**
> ↔ Perhaps from Latin *botellus,* sausage. *Pudding* once meant sausage, then later referred to food cooked in a casing.

pud′dle (pud′əl) *n.* **1,** a small pool of muddy water. **2,** a watertight covering of clay mixed with water. **—***v.t.* convert (pig iron) into wrought iron. **—pud′dling,** *n.*

pu·den′dum (poo-den′dəm) *n.* [*pl.* **-da** (-də)] **1,** (usu. *pl.*) the external genital parts of the female; vulva. **2**, (*pl.*) all the female genital parts.

pudg′y (puj′ė) *adj.* short and fat.

pueb′lo (pweb′lō) *n.* [*pl.* **-los** (lōz)] a Lat. Amer. or Indian village of adobe houses.

pu′er·ile (pū′ər-il) *adj.* childish; trivial. —**pu″er·il′i·ty**, *n.*

pu·er′per·al (pū-ēr′pər-əl) *adj.* pert. to childbirth.

puff (puf) *n.* **1**, a short blast, as of wind, smoke, etc. **2**, a light, fluffy pad. **3**, a light, porous pastry. **4**, (*Informal*) undue praise; a plug. —*v.i.* **1**, emit a puff. **2**, breathe hard. —*v.t.* **1**, expel with puffs; smoke with puffs. **2**, (usually with *up* or *out*) distend; inflate. **3**, praise. —**puff′y**, *adj.* —**puff adder, 1,** a large, extremely venomous Afr. snake. **2**, a small, harmless snake of No. Amer.

puff′ball″ *n.* a ball-shaped mushroom.

puff′er·y (puf′ər-ė) *n.* extravagant praise, as in advertising.

puf′fin (puf′in) *n.* a bird of the auk family.

pug *n.* **1**, a small dog with a squat, wrinkled face. **2**, a short, tip-tilted nose: *pug-nose.* **3**, (*Slang*) pugilist.

pu′gil·ist (pū′jə-list) *n.* a professional boxer. —**pu′gil·ism**, *n.* —**pu″gi·lis′tic**, *adj.*

pug·na′cious (pug-nā′shəs) *adj.* given to fighting; quarrelsome. —**pug·nac′i·ty** (-nas′ə-tė) *n.*

puke (pūk) *v.t. & i.* (*Vulgar*) vomit.

puk′ka (puk′ə) *adj.* **1**, genuine. **2**, first-rate.

pul′chri·tude″ (pul′kri-tood″) *n.* beauty. —**pul″chri·tu′di·nous**, *adj.*

pule (pūl) *v.i.* whine; whimper.

pu′li (poo′lė) *n.* a Hungarian breed of farm dog.

pull (pul) *v.i.* **1**, draw with force toward one; tug. **2**, extract, as a tooth. **3**, pluck; gather. **4**, rip; rend. **5**, (*Baseball*) hit (a ball) so as to cause it to go toward the left (for a right-handed batter). —*v.i.* **1**, draw, drag, tug, etc. **2**, move; be under way. —*n.* **1**, the effort exerted in hauling, drawing, etc. **2**, a device for pulling. **3**, a hard climb. **4**, (*Slang*) influence. —**pull one's leg**, perpetrate a hoax; trick; fool. —**pull through**, help or come through a danger, illness, etc., successfully.

pul′let (pul′it) *n.* a young hen.

pul′ley (pul′ė) *n.* a wheel, or series of wheels, used with a rope or belt to transmit power.

Pull′man (pul′mən) *n.* (*T.N.*) an extra-fare railroad car for sleeping or lounging.

Pullman
↔ From the inventor of the Pullman railway carriage, the American designer George M. *Pullman.*

pull′o″ver *n.* a sweater pulled on over the head.

pull-′out″ *n.* **1**, the maneuver of bringing an airplane to level flight from a dive. **2**, a retreat; evacuation.

pull-′up″ *n.* **1**, the maneuver of putting an airplane into a sharp climb from level flight. **2**, chin-up.

pul′mo·nar″y (pul′mə-ner″ė) *adj.* pert. to the lungs.

Pul′mo″tor (pul′mo″tər) *n.* (*T.N.*) an apparatus for pumping air into the lungs.

pulp *n.* **1**, the fleshy part of a fruit. **2**, a moist mixture of wood fibers, etc., from which paper is made. **3**, a cheap paper; a magazine printed on it. —*v.t.* reduce to a pulp. —**pulp′y**, *adj.*

pul′pit (pul′pit) *n.* **1**, the stand from which a sermon is preached. **2**, preachers collectively.

pulp′wood″ *n.* soft wood mashed to a pulp for making paper.

pul′que (pul′kė) *n.* a Mexican fermented drink made from agave juice.

pul′sar (pul′sär) *n.* a rapidly pulsating radio source from space of very short but gradually lengthening period: *puls(ating st)ar.*

pul′sate (pul′sāt) *v.i.* beat; throb. —**pul·sa′tion**, *n.*

pulse (puls) *n.* the throbbing of arteries as blood is pumped along them by the heart. —*v.i.* pulsate.

pul′ver·ize″ (pul′və-rīz″) *v.t.* grind or crush into a fine powder.

pu′ma (pū′mə) *n.* the cougar.

pum′ice (pum′is) *n.* a light spongy volcanic rock used in polishing, etc.

pum′mel (pum′əl) *v.t.* **1**, beat with the fists. **2**, pommel.

pump *n.* **1**, a machine for moving, or compressing, liquids or gases. **2**, a shoe without straps or lacings. —*v.t.* **1**, move (a fluid) by means of a pump. **2**, (*Informal*) draw information from. **3**, (often with *up*) inflate.

pumpernickel, pumpkin
↔ In all likelihood, neither word is related to *pump. Pumpernickel* is probably from a German word meaning, euphemistically, "smelly Nicholas." Why it was applied to the bread is pure speculation. *Pumpkin* comes from Greek *pepōn*, ripe melon.

pum′per·nick″el (pum′pər-nik″əl) *n.* a coarse, dark brown rye bread.

pump′kin *n.* a vine or its large, deep yellow, gourdlike fruit. ❑ *pumpernickel*

pun *n.* a humorous play on words of similar sound. —**pun′ster,** *n.*

punch *n.* **1,** a blow, as with the fist. **2,** a tool for stamping holes. **3,** a mixed beverage. **4,** energy; force. —*v.t.* **1,** strike, as with the fist. **2,** poke; prod; hence, herd, as cattle. **3,** perforate or impress with a punch. **4,** select a number on a telephone number pad. —**punch line,** the final line of a joke, story, etc. that makes the principal point. —**punch out, 1,** record one's time of departure from work by punching a time clock. **2,** knock out; beat up.

> **punch**
> ↔ The sense of a thrusting blow is from Middle English. The *punch* that perforates, and related senses, is short for *puncheon* (def. 3). The beverage is of uncertain origin.

punch′card″ *n.* a card having holes or notches punched in particular positions with assigned meaning for use in automatic data-processing machines.

punch-′drunk″ *adj.* having confused or dazed actions, due to head injuries.

pun′cheon (pun′chən) *n.* **1,** a large cask. **2,** an upright timber. **3,** a punching tool.

punch′y (-ē) *adj.* (*Informal*) confused; dazed; punch-drunk.

punc·til′i·o (punk-til′ē-ō) *n.* correct formal behavior.

punc·til′i·ous (punk-til′ē-əs) *adj.* scrupulously careful. —**punc·til′i·ous·ness,** *n.*

punc′tu·al (punk′choo-əl) *adj.* seldom late; prompt. —**punc″tu·al′i·ty,** *n.*

punc′tu·ate″ (punk′choo-āt″) *v.t.* separate into sentences, clauses, and the like, by means of certain marks, as period, comma, dash, etc. —**punc″tu·a′tion,** *n.* —**punctuated equilibrium,** a theory of evolution stating that evolutionary change comes in bursts rather than evenly.

punc′ture (punk′chər) *v.t.* prick; make a small hole in. —*n.* act or effect of puncturing.

pun′dit *n.* a learned man.

pung *n.* a low horse-drawn sleigh.

pun′gent (pun′jənt) *adj.* **1,** stinging to the taste or smell. **2,** caustic; biting. —**pun′gen·cy,** *n.*

pun′ish *v.t.* inflict a penalty on (a person) or for (an offense). —**pun′ish·a·ble,** *adj.*

pun′ish·ment (-mənt) *n.* act or effect of punishing; penalty.

pu′ni·tive (pū′nə-tiv) *adj.* pert. to, or inflicting, punishment. Also, **pu′ni·to·ry,** *adj.*

punk *n.* **1,** dry, crumbly wood, or a fungus, used as a tinder. **2,** (*Slang*) a worthless youth. **3,** (*Slang*) a style of clothing and makeup associated with punk rock. —*adj.* (*Slang*) of low quality. —**punk rock,** a variety of rock music characterized by violence and obscenity.

punt *n.* **1,** a flat-bottomed boat. **2,** (*Football*) a kick of a football dropped from the hands, before it touches the ground. —*v.t. & i.* **1,** propel a punt. **2,** kick (a football).

pu′ny (pū′nē) *adj.* feeble; petty. —**pu′ni·ness,** *n.*

> **puny**
> ↔ From Old French *puisne*, born afterward or later.

pup *n.* **1,** [also, **pup′py**] a young dog. **2,** the young of various mammals. —**pup tent,** a small tent.

pu′pa (pū′pə) *n.* [*pl.* **-pae** (pē)] the stage in an insect's life between the larval and adult stages.

pu′pil (pū′pəl) *n.* **1,** a person receiving instruction. **2,** the dark center of the eye.

> **pupil, puppet, puppy**
> ↔ All three words come from Latin *pupus* and *pupa,* boy and girl. *Puppet* and *puppy* derive from later French forms of the word.

pup′pet (pup′it) *n.* a doll moved by wires; hence, a person or state controlled by another. —**pup″pet·eer′** (-ir′) *n.* —**pup′pet·ry** (-rē) *n.* ❑ *pupil*

pup′py (pup′ē) *n.* **1,** a pup. **2,** a conceited, impertinent young man. —**puppy love,** immature love. ❑ *pupil*

pur′blind″ (pēr′blīnd″) *adj.* partly blind; hence, obtuse; dull. —**pur′blind″ness,** *n.*

pur′chase (pēr′chəs) *v.t.* buy. —*n.* **1,** the act of buying; something bought. **2,** a hold or leverage for moving heavy bodies.

pur′dah (pēr′də) *n.* **1,** a curtain. **2,** seclusion of women, in India.

pure (pyûr) *adj.* **1,** free from pollution. **2,** chaste. **3,** genuine; sincere. **4,** abstract, as sciences. **5,** sheer; simple. —**pure′ness,** *n.*

pure′bred″ *adj. & n.* of a breed that has maintained certain desirable characteristics through generations of descent.

pu·rée′ (pyû-rā′) *n.* a thick soup or sauce of sieved vegetables, fruit, etc. —*v.t.* rub or pass through a sieve to make a smooth sauce; make into a similar sauce by means of a blender, etc.

pur·ga·tive (pērg'ə-tiv) *n.* that which purges. —*adj.* purging.

pur·ga·to··ry (pēr'gə-tôr"ė) *n.* ·(*Rom. Cath.*) a place where penitent souls are purified.

purge (pērj) *v.t.* **1,** cleanse from impurities, bodily or spiritual. **2,** flush (the bowels) by a physic. **3,** remove disloyal members from (a state or party). —*n.* **1,** the act of purging. **2,** a physic; purgative. —**pur·ga'tion** (pēr·gā'shən) *n.*

pu·ri·fy (pyûr'i-fī") *v.t.* make pure. —**pu"ri·fi·ca'tion,** *n.*

Pu·rim' (poo-rēm') *n.sing.* a Jewish holiday, the Feast of Lots.

pur'ist (pyûr'ist) *n.* & *adj.* (a person) insistent on exactness. —**pur'ism,** *n.*

Pu'ri·tan (pyûr'ə-tən) *n.* **1,** a member of a Protestant group of the 16th and 17th c. **2,** (*l.c.*) a religious zealot who frowns on frivolity. —**pu"ri·tan'i·cal** (-tan'i-kəl) *adj.*

pu'ri·ty (pyûr'i-tė) *n.* pureness.

purl (pērl) *n.* **1,** a knitting stitch. **2,** a ripple; eddy. —*v.i.* make purls.

pur'lieus (pēr'looz) *n.pl.* outskirts, environs.

pur·loin' (pər-loin') *v.t.* steal.

pur'ple (pēr'pəl) *n.* **1,** a bluish-red color. **2,** an emperor's robe of this color; regal power. —*adj.* of a purple color; hence, regal. —**pur'plish,** *adj.* —**Purple Heart,** a medal awarded to one wounded in action.

> **purple**
> ↔ From Greek *porphyra*, a type of shellfish from which a purple dye was obtained.

pur·port' (pər-pôrt') *v.t.* profess; seem to mean. —*n.* (pēr'pôrt) meaning; import.

pur'pose (pēr'pəs) *v.t.* intend; mean. —*n.* **1,** intention; aim. **2,** intended effect; use. —**pur'pos·ive,** *adj.* —**on purpose,** intentionally.

pur'pose·ful *adj.* **1,** determined; resolved. **2,** serving a purpose. —**pur'pose·ful·ness,** *n.*

pur'pose·ly *adj.* deliberately; intentionally.

purr (pēr) *v.t.* make a low vibrating sound, as a contented cat. —*n.* this sound.

purse (pērs) *n.* **1,** any small receptacle for carrying money; hence, means; finances. **2,** a sum of money collected as a gift or offered as a prize. —*v.t.* pucker (the lips). —**purse strings,** power or control over money or spending.

purs'er (pēr'sər) *n.* an officer on a ship or airplane in charge of accounts and passenger welfare.

purs'lane (pērs'lān) *n.* a low, spreading plant used as a potherb and in salads.

pur·su'ant (pər-soo'ənt) *adj.* **1,** following. **2,** (with *to*) according. —**pur·su'ance,** *n.*

pur·sue' (pər-soo') *v.t.* **1,** follow with intent to catch. **2,** proceed along; continue. **3,** seek after. **4,** be engaged in.

pur·suit' (pər-soot') *n.* **1,** act of following. **2,** carrying out. **3,** an occupation.

pur'sy (pēr'sė) *adj.* fat and short-winded.

pu'ru·lent (pyûr'ə-lənt) *adj.* full of, or discharging, pus. —**pur'u·lence,** *n.*

pur·vey' (pər-vā') *v.t.* & *i.* provide (food supplies). —**pur·vey'or,** *n.*

pur'view (pēr'vū) *n.* **1,** scope; extent of anything. **2,** range of physical or mental vision.

pus *n.* the yellowish-white matter in an inflamed sore. —**pus'sy** (pus'ė) *adj.*

push (pûsh) *v.t.* **1,** thrust forcibly against, in order to move. **2,** advance or extend by effort. —*v.i.* **1,** exert impelling pressure. **2,** force one's way. —*n.* **1,** a shove. **2,** a crowd of people. **3,** (*Informal*) energy; enterprise. —**push'er,** *n.* (*Slang*) a dealer in illegal drugs.

push-'but"ton *adj.* automatic; done by, or as though by, merely sending an electrical signal by pushing a button.

push'cart" *n.* a cart pushed by hand, used by a vendor, etc.

push'o"ver *n.* (*Slang*) a weak-willed person; an easy task.

push'pin" *n.* a thumbtack.

push-'up" *n.* a physical exercise of raising the body with the arms.

push'y *adj.* aggressive.

pu"sil·lan'i·mous (pū"sə-lan'ə-məs) *adj.* mean-spirited; cowardly. —**pu"sil·la·nim'i·ty** (-lə-nim'ə-tė) *n.*

puss (pûs) *n.* **1,** [also, **pus'sy, pus'sy·cat"**] a cat. **2,** (*Slang*) the face or mouth.

puss'y·foot" *v.t.* move warily or fearfully; hedge.

pussy willow a small willow tree.

pus'tule (pus'chûl) *n.* a small, pus-filled pimple. —**pus'tu·lar,** *adj.*

put (pût) *v.t.* [**put, put'ting**] **1,** set, lay, or cause to be in any place, position, or condition. **2,** assign; attribute. **3,** propound; propose for attention. **4,** (with *across* or *over*) accomplish; effect the acceptance of. **5,** (with *by*) save, as money. **6,** (with *up*) give lodging to. **7,** (with *up* *with*) tolerate. —*v.i.* **1,** (with *about*) turn. **2,** (with *on*) pretend. **3,** (with *out*) set forth. —**put down,** (*Slang*) **1,** suppress; smash. **2,** snub. **3,** attribute. **4,** inscribe; write down. —**put forward,** propose. —**put in, 1,** interpose; insert. **2,** spend, as time. —**put off, 1,** postpone. **2,** get rid of (a person) by evasion. **3,** take off. —**put on,** (*Slang*) kid; mock. —**put out, 1,** vex; offend. **2,** inconvenience. **3,** extinguish; blind. **4,** expel. **5,** expend. —**put** (something) **over on,** deceive. —**put upon,** impose on.

pu·ta·tive (pū'tə-tiv) *adj.* supposed; reputed.

put'down" *n.* (*Slang*) insult; slight; rejection.

put-'on" *n.* (*Informal*) a deception; hoax.

pu'tre·fy" (pū'trə-fī") *v.i. & t.* decay or cause to decay. —**pu"tre·fac'tion,** *n.*

pu·tres'cence (pū-tres'əns) *n.* process of becoming rotten. —**pu·tres'cent,** *adj.*

pu'trid (pū'trid) *adj.* rotten; foul.

putsch (pûch) *n.* (*Ger.*) a minor rebellion or uprising; a coup.

putt (put) *n.* (*Golf*) a stroke made to send a ball along the ground. —*v.t. & i.* make (the ball) so roll. —**putt'er,** *n.* a golf club for this purpose.

put'tee (put'ė) *n.* a legging.

put'ter (put'ər) *v.i.* busy oneself in an ineffective manner.

put'ty (put'ė) *n.* a soft, doughy cement for filling cracks, etc.

put-'up" *adj.* fraudulently prearranged.

puz'zle (puz'əl) *n.* a perplexing problem; a device or toy to test one's ingenuity. —*v.t.* perplex. —*v.i.* ponder. —**puz'-zle·ment,** *n.*

PVC polyvinyl chloride.

Pyg'my (pig'mė) *n.* one of a dwarf race of central Africa; hence (*l.c.*) a dwarf.

pygmy
↔ From Greek *pugmē*, a measure of length, later, dwarfish. It was applied to an Afr. people in the 19th c.

py·jam'as (pə-jàm'əs) *n.pl.* pajamas.

py'lon (pī'lon) *n.* **1,** a gateway formed of one or two truncated pyramids. **2,** a high tower.

py·lo'rus (pī-lôr'əs) *n.* the opening from the stomach to the intestines. —**py·lor'ic,** *adj.*

py"or·rhe'a (pī"ə-rē'ə) *n.* inflammation of the gums, with discharge of pus.

pyr'a·mid (pir'ə-mid) *n.* (*Geom.*) a solid whose base is a polygon and whose sides are all triangles meeting in a common point; anything so shaped. —*v.i. & t.* reinvest (profits or winnings) for greater profit. —**py·ram'i·dal** (pi-ram'ə-dəl) *adj.*

pyre (pīr) *n.* a heap of wood for burning a corpse.

Py'rex (pī'reks) *n.* (*T.N.*) a heat-resistant glassware used for cooking utensils.

py·rex'i·a (pī-rek'sė-ə) *n.* (*Med.*) fever. —**py·ret'ic,** *adj.*

pyr'i·dine" (pir'ə-dēn") *n.* a colorless liquid, of pungent odor, used as a solvent and germicide and in medicine.

py'rite (pī'rīt) *n.* fool's gold. —**py·rit'ic** (-rit'ik) *adj.*

py'ro- (pī-rə) *pref.* heat; fire.

py"ro·ma'ni·a *n.* a mania for starting fires. —**py"ro·ma'ni·ac,** *n.*

py"ro·tech'nics *n.* a display of fireworks.

py·rox'y·lin (pī-rok'sə-lin) *n.* guncotton; nitrocellulose, esp. in solution.

Pyr'rhic victory (pir'ik) a victory gained at too great cost.

Pyrrhic victory
↔ From a remark by the king of Epirus, *Pyrrhus*, who said that another costly victory over the Romans would ruin him.

py'thon (pī'thon) *n.* a large snake that crushes its prey.

python
↔ From the name of the large dragon guarding the chasm at Delphi, killed by Apollo, who then established his temple there.

py'tho·ness (pī'thə-nis) *n.* a woman with the gift of prophecy; a witch.

pyx (piks) *n.* **1,** a small box or vase in which the consecrated wafer of the Eucharist is kept. **2,** a chest in which specimen coins are deposited.

Q

Q, q (kū) *n.* seventeenth letter of the English alphabet.

Qi·a'na (kė-ä'nə) *n.* (*T.N.*) a silklike nylon fabric.

qua (kwā; kwä) *adv.* as being; in the manner or capacity of.

Quaa'lude (kwā'lood) *n.* (*T.N.*) a brand of methaqualone, a barbituate sedative. Also, *slang,* **lude.**

quack (kwak) *n.* **1,** the cry of a duck; a similar harsh, flat sound. **2,** a false pretender to medical skill. —*v.i.* make a noise as a duck. —*adj.* fraudulent. —**quack′er·y,** *n.* deceptive practice.

> **quack**
> ↔ The word for the cry of the duck is imitative of the actual sound. The word for a fake doctor comes from Dutch *quacksalver,* which loosely means someone who chatters about his or her medicines.

quad (kwod) *n.* **1,** quadrangle (def. 2). **2,** blank metal used to space type. **3,** (*Informal*) a quadruplet.

quadr- *pref.* four; fourth.

Quad″ra·ges′i·ma (kwod″rə-jes′ə-mə) *n.* the first Sunday in Lent.

quad′ran″gle (kwod′rang″gəl) *n.* **1,** a plane figure with four sides and four angles. **2,** the square-shaped court of a college or like group of buildings. —**quad·ran′gu·lar** (kwə-drang′gyə-lər) *adj.*

quad′rant (kwod′rənt) *n.* **1,** the fourth part. **2,** a quarter of a circle. **3,** an instrument for measuring altitudes.

quad′ra·phon″ic (kwod′rə-fon″ik) *adj.* recorded or reproduced on four separate channels.

quad·rat′ic (kwod-rat′ik) *adj.* **1,** belonging to a square. **2,** (*Math.*) concerning the square as the highest power of an unknown quantity. —**quad·rat′ics,** *n.sing.* (*Math.*) the study of quadratic equations.

quad·ren′ni·al (kwod-ren′ē-əl) *adj.* **1,** every four years. **2,** for four years' duration. —*n.* a fourth anniversary.

quad″ri·lat′er·al (kwod″rə-lat′ər-əl) *n.* a plane figure with four straight sides. —*adj.* four-sided.

qua·drille′ (kwə-dril′) *n.* a dance for four or more couples.

quad·riv′i·um (kwod-riv′ē-əm) *n.* geometry, astronomy, arithmetic, and music.

quad·roon′ (kwod-roon′) *n.* a person of one-quarter Negro blood.

quad′ru·ped″ (kwod′rû-ped″) *n.* a four-footed animal. —*adj.* four-footed.

quad·ru′ple (kwo-droo′pəl) *adj.* four times. —*v.t.* (kwod-rû′pəl) multiply by four. —**quad·ru′plet** (kwo-drup′lit) *n.* one of four offspring born of one birth.

quad·ru′pli·cate (kwod-rûp′li-kət) *n. & adj.* four identical copies; the fourth such copy. —*v.t.* (-kāt″) make four copies of.

quaff (kwåf) *v.t. & i.* drink deeply.

quag′ga (kwag′ə) *n.* a zebralike animal of So. Afr., now extinct.

quag′ma (kwag′mə) *n.* a theoretical type of plasma.

quag′mire″ (kwag′mīr″) *n.* **1,** an area of muddy ground; a marsh. **2,** a difficult position or situation. —**quag′gy,** *adj.*

qua′hog (kwâ′hog) *n.* a large, edible clam of the Atlantic coast.

quail (kwāl) *v.i.* cower; shrink away; flinch; lose courage. —*n.* **1,** a game bird related to the partridge, esp. the bobwhite. **2,** the partridge.

quaint (kwānt) *adj.* pleasingly odd or unusual. —**quaint′ness,** *n.*

quake (kwāk) *v.i.* tremble; shake; shudder. —*n.* a shaking or tremulous agitation, esp. an earthquake.

Quak′er (kwā′ker) *n.* a member of the Society of Friends, a Christian religious sect. —**Quak′er·ism,** *n.*

qual″i·fi·ca′tion (kwol″i-fi-kā′shən) *n.* **1,** act or result of qualifying. **2,** a quality that meets some requirement. **3,** modification; restriction.

qual′i·fied″ (kwol′i-fīd″) *adj.* **1,** fit; competent. **2,** limited; restricted.

qual′i·fy″ (kwol′i-fī″) *v.t.* **1,** modify; limit; restrict. **2,** establish the authority of; empower; instruct; fit. **3,** soften; assuage. —*v.t.* fill requirements for a place or occupation.

qual′i·ta″tive (kwol′i-tā″tiv) *adj.* relating to quality, not quantity.

qual′i·ty (kwol′i-tē) *n.* **1,** essential nature. **2,** a trait; characteristic. **3,** high birth or rank. **4,** superiority, relatively considered.

qualm (kwäm) *n.* **1,** a twinge of conscience; compunction. **2,** a sudden sensation of nausea.

quan′da·ry (kwon′də-rē) *n.* state of bewilderment or perplexity; a dilemma.

quan′ti·ta″tive (kwon′ti-tā″tiv) *adj.* relating to quantity of measurement.

quan′ti·ty (kwon′ti-tē) *n.* **1,** amount; weight; bulk. **2,** a portion, esp. a large amount. **3,** a number. **4,** duration (of a sound). ❑ *amount*

quan′tize (kwän′tīz) *v.t.* to express in multiples of a discrete value.

quan′tum (kwon′təm) *n.* [*pl.* **-ta** (tə)] **1,** amount. **2,** the smallest unit of radiant energy. —**quantum jump** or **leap,** a rapid, significant change; breakthrough. —**quantum theory,** a hypothesis in physics that the emission of radiant energy is not continuous.

quar′an·tine″ (kwor′ən-tēn″) *n.* **1,** time

during which an incoming ship is held for inspection for contagious disease or plant and animal pests. **2,** the place where such a ship is held. **3,** a period of enforced seclusion, usually to prevent contagion. —*v.t.* isolate.

> **quarantine**
> ↔ From Latin *quadraginta*, forty, through Italian *quarantina*, a period of forty days.

quark (kwärk) *n.* a hypothetical particle.

> **quark**
> ↔ Coined by American physicist Murray Gell-Mann after a word in James Joyce's *Finnegans Wake.*

quar′rel (kwor′əl) *n.* a squabble; disagreement; dispute; petty fight. —*v.i.* find fault; dispute. —**quar′rel·some,** *adj.* disposed to quarrel.

quar′ry (kwor′ē) *n.* **1,** an open excavation from which building materials, as stone, are taken. **2,** prey; any object of eager pursuit. —**quar′ri·er,** *n.*

quart (kwôrt) *n.* a unit of capacity; in liquid measure equal to two pints or 1/4 gallon, in dry measure, 1/8 peck.

quar′ter (kwôr′tər) *n.* **1,** one-fourth of the whole. **2,** a U.S. silver coin; one-fourth dollar or 25 cents. **3,** three consecutive months. **4,** section; region; locality. **5,** one leg of an animal with bordering parts for use as meat. **6,** mercy. **7,** (*pl.*) a specific dwelling place; station; lodgings. —*v.t.* **1,** divide into four equal parts. **2,** furnish with lodgings. —**quarter horse,** a breed of horse noted for its endurance. —**quarter note,** (*Music*) a crotchet (see *note*). —**quarter tone,** (*Music*) an interval one-half as long as a semitone.

quar′ter·back″ *n.* (*Football*) the back who directs the play of a team.

quar′ter·deck″ *n.* (*Naut.*) an upper deck used by officers.

quar′ter·ly (-lē) *n.* a periodical published each three months.

quar′ter·mas″ter *n.* (*Mil.*) a supply officer.

quar′ter·staff″ *n.* an old Eng. weapon consisting of a stout pole about 6 ft. long.

quar·tet′ (kwôr-tet′) *n.* **1,** a group of four. **2,** (*Music*) a composition in four parts. Also, **quar·tette′.**

quar′to (kwôr′tō) *n.* [*pl.* **-tos**] a book whose pages are about 9 by 12 inches.

quartz (kwôrts) *n.* a common hard mineral occurring in many varieties, some prized as semiprecious stones.

qua′sar (kwā′zär) *n.* **1,** a quasi-stellar radio source, one of the brightest and most distant bodies in the universe, emitter of very intense radio and visible radiation. **2,** [also, **quasi-stellar object** or **QSO**] a quasar not emitting any radio signals but producing very intense visible radiation.

quash (kwosh) *v.t.* **1,** crush; subdue. **2,** annul.

qua′si (kwā′zī; kwä′sē) *adj.* seeming; as though. —*adv.* seemingly; almost.

qua′si- *pref.* almost; purportedly but not wholly genuine.

quas′sia (kwosh′ə) *n.* a medicinal bitter extracted from the bark and wood of an Amer. tree.

> **quassia**
> ↔ Named for a Dutch slave, *Quassi,* who discovered the special properties of the plant.

qua·ter′na·ry (kwə-tēr′nə-rē) *adj.* consisting of or arranged in fours. —*n.* **1,** the number four. **2,** a group of four.

quat′rain (kwot′rān) *n.* a stanza of four lines, usually rhyming alternately.

qua′ver (kwā′vər) *v.i.* **1,** shake; tremble; vibrate. **2,** sing or speak in a tremulous tone. **3,** (*Music*) trill. **4,** (*Music*) an eighth note (see *note*). —*n.* a shaking or trembling, esp. of the voice.

quay (kē, kwā) *n.* a dock for landing and loading a ship's cargo.

quea′sy (kwē′zē) *adj.* **1,** sick at the stomach. **2,** easily nauseated; squeamish. —**quea′si·ness,** *n.*

Que·bec′ (kwi-bek′) *n.* (*Communications*) the letter *q.*

queen (kwēn) *n.* **1,** a female sovereign. **2,** the wife of a king. **3,** the most notable woman in a particular sphere. **4,** the perfect female bee, ant, or termite. **5,** a playing card depicting a queen. **6,** the most valuable piece in chess. **7,** (*Offensive*) a homosexual. —**queen′dom** (-dəm) *n.* —**queen′ly** (-lē) *adj.* —**queen mother,** the widow of a king and mother of a present sovereign.

> **queen**
> ↔ From the prehistoric Indo-European word for woman. A *queen* was, at one time, the wife of any important personage.

queen-′size″ *adj.* pert. to a bed size, usu. 60 by 72 inches.

queer (kwir) *adj.* **1,** odd; strange; eccentric. **2,** (*Offensive*) homosexual. —*v.t.* (*In-*

formal) spoil; upset. —*n.* (*Slang*) counterfeit money. —**queer′ness**, *n.*

quell (kwel) *v.t.* **1,** subdue; crush. **2,** allay; quiet.

quench (kwench) *v.t.* **1,** satisfy, as thirst. **2,** extinguish or put out, as a fire. **3,** repress or still, as anger. **4,** cool (hot metal) suddenly.

quer′cine (kwẽr′sin) *adj.* of or pert. to the oak tree.

quer′u·lous (kwer′ə-ləs) *adj.* habitually complaining; fretful.

que′ry (kwir′ė) *n.* a question; an inquiry. —*v.t. & i.* question; doubt.

quest (kwest) *n.* a search; pursuit. —*v.i.* go in search.

ques′tion (kwes′chən) *n.* **1,** an interrogation; inquiry. **2,** doubt; dispute; controversy. **3,** a subject under discussion; a motion to be voted upon. —*v.i.* ask; examine. —*v.t.* **1,** inquire of. **2,** doubt; challenge; take exception to. —**ques′tion·a·ble,** *adj.* subject to doubt. —**ques′tion·ing·ly,** *adv.* —**question mark,** the mark of punctuation (?) denoting inquiry or doubt; the interrogation point.

> **question mark**
> (*Gram.*) The most frequent use of the question mark is to end a sentence which poses a question. However, when enclosed in parentheses, it can signify doubt, uncertainty, or even an ironical or humorous intention. These special uses should be employed sparingly.

ques″tion·naire′ (-nãr′) *n.* a series of questions to be answered.

quet·zal′ (ket-säl′) *n.* **1,** a Central Amer. bird. **2,** the monetary unit of Guatemala.

queue (kū) *n.* **1,** a waiting line. **2,** hair braided and worn as a pigtail. —*v.i.* (with *up*) get in line.

quib′ble (kwib′əl) *v.i.* equivocate; bring up trifling objections. —*n.* an evasive argument.

quiche (kēsh) *n.* a custard pie, often made with cheese and bacon.

quick (kwik) *adj.* **1,** fast; speedy; rapid. **2,** perceptive; alert. **3,** hasty; easily aroused. **4,** (*Archaic*) living. —*n.* **1,** living beings. **2,** sensitive flesh. **3,** the most sensitive part. —*adv.* quickly. —**quick′ness,** *n.* —**quick fix,** a superficial or hasty solution or repair.

quick′en (kwik′ən) *v.t. & i.* make or become faster and more active.

quick-′fro″zen *adj.* (of food) frozen rap-

idly to zero or below, for preservation. —**quick-′freeze′,** *v.t.*

quick′ie (-ė) *n.* (*Slang*) something done, produced, etc., in haste.

quick′lime″ *n.* a caustic substance made from limestone.

quick′sand″ *n.* a bog.

quick′sil″ver *n.* metallic mercury.

quick′step″ *n.* a fast marching pace, as of soldiers.

quick-′tem″pered *adj.* irascible.

quick-′wit″ted *adj.* mentally alert; quick to think and act. —**quick-′wit″ted·ness,** *n.*

quid (kwid) *n.* **1,** a cud; a lump for chewing, as gum or tobacco. **2,** (*Brit. slang*) a pound sterling.

quid′di·ty (kwid′i-tė) *n.* **1,** essence. **2,** a trifling nicety.

quid′nunc″ (kwid′nungk″) *n.* a gossip.

quid pro quo (kwid′ prō kwō′) (*Lat.*) something in return; an exchange.

qui·es′cent (kwī-es′ənt) *adj.* still; resting; tranquil. —**qui·es′cence,** *n.*

> **quiescent, quiet**
> ☞ Though these two words both have the sense of tranquil, *quiescent* is used to indicate a lack of motion or activity, whereas *quiet* usually indicates the absence of noise.

qui′et (kwī′ət) *adj.* **1,** still; smooth; tranquil. **2,** silent; noiseless. **3,** composed; subdued. **4,** modest; not glaring. —*v.t.* calm; pacify; hush; allay. —*v.i.* become calm; abate. —*n.* **1,** repose; rest; stillness. **2,** peace. **3,** composure; calmness. **4,** silence. —**qui′et·ness,** *n.* ◻ *coy, quiescent*

qui′e·tude (kwī′ə-tood) *n.* repose; rest; tranquillity.

qui·e′tus (kwī-ē′təs) *n.* **1,** release, as from debts. **2,** death.

quill (kwil) *n.* **1,** a stiff feather from a bird; its stem. **2,** a pen made from a feather. **3,** a sharp spine, as of a porcupine. **4,** a pick used for playing certain string instruments.

quilt (kwilt) *n.* a warm, padded bed cover. —*v.t. & i.* make a quilt.

quince (kwins) *n.* a fruit tree or its yellow applelike fruit.

> **quince**
> ↔ From Greek *mēlon Kudōnion,* apple from Khaniá, Crete.

quin′cunx (kwing′kunks) *n.* an arrangement of five objects.

qui′nine (kwī′nīn) *n.* a bitter alkaloid

obtained from cinchona bark, used medicinally, esp. for malaria.

Quin″qua·ges′i·ma (kwing″kwə-jes′ə-mə) *n.* the Sunday before Lent; Shrove Sunday.

quin·que- (kwin′kwe) *pref.* five.

quin′sy (kwin′zė) *n.* severe inflammation of the throat and tonsils accompanied by swelling and pus.

quint (kwint) *n.* **1,** a set or sequence of five. **2,** (*Music*) a fifth. **3,** (*Informal*) a quintuplet.

quin′tal (kwin′təl) *n.* a weight, orig. 100 pounds, now varying in different countries.

quin·tes′sence (kwin-tes′əns) *n.* the concentrated and purest essence of anything; the perfect form. **—quin″tes·sen′-tial,** *adj.*

quin·tet′ (kwin-tet′) *n.* a group of five. Also, **quin·tette′.**

quin·tu′ple (kwin-too′pəl) *adj.* five times. **—***v.t.* multiply by five. **—quintu′-plet** (kwin-tup′lit) *n.* one of five offspring born of one birth.

quin·tup′li·cate (kwin-tup′li·kit) *n.* five identical copies; the fifth such copy. **—***v.t.* (-kāt″) make five copies of.

quip (kwip) *n.* a witty remark. **—***v.i.* [**quipped, quip′ping**] make quips. **—quip′ster,** *n.*

quire (kwīr) *n.* 1/20th ream; 24 (sometimes 25) uniform sheets of paper.

quirk (kwėrk) *n.* **1,** idiosyncrasy; deviation. **2,** a quick turn. **—quirk′y,** *adj.*

quirt (kwėrt) *n.* a riding whip.

quis′ling (kwiz′ling) *n.* a traitor who helps an enemy occupy his country.

> **quisling**
> ↔ From Vidkun *Quisling*, a Norwegian politician, leader of the Norwegian fascist party.

quit (kwit) *v.t. & i.* [**quit′ted, -ting**] **1,** leave; abandon; resign. **2,** satisfy; clear. **—***adj.* (with *of*) discharged or released from (a debt, obligation, etc.).

quit′claim″ *n.* (*Law*) **1,** a document by which a claim, right, or title to an estate is relinquished to another. **2,** a transfer without warranty. **—***v.t.* give up a claim to; relinquish.

quite (kwīt) *adv.* **1,** wholly; completely. **2,** considerably; very.

quits (kwitz) *adj.* (*Informal*) on even terms; released from obligation.

quit′tance (kwit′əns) *n.* **1,** a discharge from obligation; receipt. **2,** recompense.

quit′ter (kwit′ər) *n.* (*Informal*) one who

abandons a task through discouragement or fear.

quiv′er (kwiv′ər) *v.i.* quake; shiver; flutter. **—***n.* **1,** a tremor; shiver. **2,** a case for holding arrows.

qui vive″ (kē vēv′) (*Fr.*) who goes there? **—on the qui vive,** alert.

quix·ot′ic (kwiks-ot′ik) *adj.* absurdly or extravagantly romantic or chivalrous; impractical; visionary.

> **quixotic**
> ↔ After the title character of Miguel Cervantes's episodic novel *Don Quixote de la Mancha*.

quiz (kwiz) *n.* **1,** a puzzling question or series of questions; bantering. **2,** an examination in school; a question-and-answer program on radio or television. **—***v.t.* [**quizzed, quiz′zing**] **1,** chaff; make sport of. **2,** question. **3,** peer at.

quiz′zi·cal (kwiz′i-kəl) *adj.* **1,** bantering; teasing. **2,** odd; comical.

quod′li·bet″ (kwod′lə-bet″) *n.* **1,** a subject of academic debate. **2,** (*Music*) a composition combining known tunes, usu. to humorous effect.

quod e′rat de″mon·stran′dum (kwod er′at dem″ən-strän′dəm) (*Lat.*) which was to be proved.

quoin (koin) *n.* **1,** an external angle of a building; a stone forming such an angle. **2,** a wedgelike device used in printing for locking up type.

quoits (kwoits) *n.sing.* a game of pitching rings, as of iron or rubber, at a peg. **—quoit,** *n.* such a ring.

quon′dam (kwon′dam) *adj.* former; in time past.

Quon′set hut (kwon′sət) a prefabricated metal shelter.

> **quotation marks**
> (*Gram.*) Double quotation marks (", ") are generally used to enclose cited material. If quotation marks within quotation marks are needed, then single quotes (', ') are used. The placement of ending punctuation marks depends on the mark: commas and periods are placed within the marks, while semicolons and colons are placed outside. When citing titles of works, as a general rule, complete works (printed books, magazines, plays, etc.) are underlined or set in italics, while articles and short stories (as well as university theses) are enclosed in quotation marks.

quo′rum (kwôr′əm) *n.* the number of members who must be present to validate a meeting.

quo′ta (kwō′tə) *n.* the share or proportion assigned to one of a group.

quo·ta′tion (kwō-tā′shən) *n.* **1,** repetition of words previously uttered or written. **2,** a citation of a price. **—quotation mark,** a mark of punctuation: " or ' (*quote*), " or ' (*unquote*).

quote (kwōt) *v.t. & i.* **1,** repeat, copy or cite words previously uttered. **2,** give the current market price of. **3,** enclose within quotation marks. **—n.** (*Informal*) quotation.

quoth (kwōth) *v.* (*Archaic*) says.

quo·tid′i·an (kwō-tid′ē-ən) *adj.* daily.

quo′tient (kwō′shənt) *n.* the number produced by dividing a given number by another.

qwer′ty (kwĕr′tē) *adj.* having a certain layout for the keys of a typewriter or computer keyboard in which the first six letters of the top row are "qwerty."

R

R, r (är) the eighteenth letter of the English alphabet.

rab′bet (rab′it) *n.* a slot or groove made in a board to receive the edge of another board; a joint so made. **—v.t. & i. 1,** cut a rabbet in. **2,** join or be joined by a rabbet.

rab′bi (rab′ī) *n.* master; a Jewish doctor of scriptural law. **—rab′bin·ate** (-ə-nət) *n.* **—rab·bin′i·cal** (rə-bin′i-kəl) *adj.*

rab′bit (rab′it) *n.* **1,** a small rodent related to the hare. **2,** Welsh rabbit. **—rabbit ears,** a type of indoor television antenna having two aerials. **—rabbit punch,** a blow on the back of the neck.

rab′ble (rab′əl) *n.* crowd; mob; the masses.

rab′ble·rou″ser (-row″zər) *n.* one who stirs up the masses; demagogue.

rab′id *adj.* **1,** furious; raging. **2,** zealous; fanatical. **3,** affected with or pert. to rabies. **—ra·bid′i·ty** (rə-bid′ə-tē) *n.*

ra′bies (rā′bēz) *n.* an infectious disease: *hydrophobia.*

> **rabies, rage**
> ↔ These two words both have their origin in Latin *rabies,* fury, frenzy.

rac·coon′ (ra-koon′) *n.* a small carnivorous No. Amer. mammal.

race (rās) *n.* **1,** a contest or effort to reach a goal first; a rush. **2,** a rapid current of water. **3,** an ethical, tribal, or national stock. **4,** any class or group, esp. of persons, considered as a class apart. **—v.i. & t.** engage in a contest of speed; run swiftly; cause to run. **—rac′er,** *n.* a racing car or its driver.

race′horse″ *n.* a horse bred and trained for racing.

race′track″ *n.* a track for racing, esp. for horse racing.

race′way″ *n.* **1,** a channel for water. **2,** a racetrack.

ra·chi′tis (rə-kī′tis) *n.* rickets. **—ra·chit′ic** (rə-kit′ik) *adj.*

ra′cial (rā′shəl) *adj.* pert. to a race (of people).

rac′ism (rā′siz-əm) *n.* prejudice against certain peoples. **—rac′ist,** *n.*

rack (rak) *n.* **1,** an open framework or stand for holding articles. **2,** a toothed bar engaging a gear. **3,** an ancient instrument of torture; hence, pain or distress. **4,** a gait of a horse between a trot and a gallop. **5,** the neck of mutton, pork, or veal. **—v.t. 1,** strain; worry. **2,** place on a rack. **3,** (of a horse) go at a rack. **4,** (with *up*) score; chalk up. **—rack rent,** excessive rent.

> **rack, wrack**
> ↔ The various senses of the versatile word *rack* have varying origins. The senses of framework and torture go back to Middle Dutch *rac.* The pace of a horse is perhaps related to *rock.* The cut of meat is of uncertain origin.
> ☞ *Rack* should not be confused with *wrack,,* which means wreck or ruin and is used nowadays only in the phrase *wrack and ruin.*

rack′et (rak′it) *n.* **1,** a disorderly, confused noise; din; hurly-burly. **2,** a dishonest enterprise. **3,** [also, **rac′quet**] the bat used in tennis, squash, etc. **4,** (*pl.*) an indoor ball game. **—v.i.** engage in an illegal activity.

rack″et·eer′ (-ə-tir′) *n.* one engaged in a dishonest enterprise; a gangster.

ra·clette′ (rä-klet′) *n.* a Swiss dish of melted cheese and boiled potatoes.

rac″on·teur′ (rak″on-tēr′) *n.* a skillful narrator of anecdotes.

rac′quet·ball″ *n.* a game combining elements of tennis and squash played on an indoor court.

rac′y (rās′ē) *adj.* **1,** piquant; spicy. **2,** (*Informal*) suggestive; off-color. **—rac′i·ness,** *n.*

ra′dar (rā′där) *n.* a device timing the

echo of radio waves to detect objects they strike: *ra(dio) d(etecting) a(nd) r(anging)*.

ra′dar·scope″ *n.* an oscilloscope used to display radar signals.

ra′di·al (rā′dē-əl) *n.* **1,** pert. to a radius; of or being radii. **2,** pert. to a type of tire construction in which the belts are placed directly across the direction of travel.

ra′di·an (rā′dē-ən) *n.* (*Math.*) in a circle, the angle opposing an arc equal in length to the radius, approx. 57°.

ra′di·ant (rā′dē-ənt) *adj.* **1,** emitting rays; shining; sparkling. **2,** beaming, as with kindness or joy. —**ra′di·ance,** *n.*

ra′di·ate″ (rā′dē-āt″) *v.i. & t.* **1,** issue and proceed in rays from a point, as heat or light. **2,** spread in all directions from a central source. —**ra″di·a′tion,** *n.* —**radiation sickness** or **syndrome,** sickness caused by exposure to radiation (as from nuclear explosion or from x-rays), characterized by loss of hair, nausea, bleeding, etc.

ra′di·a″tor (rā′dē-ā″tər) *n.* an apparatus, as a grill, that radiates heat waves, as to warm a room, dispel the heat from an automobile engine, etc.

rad′i·cal (rad′i-kəl) *adj.* **1,** (*Math.*) pert. to a root. **2,** drastic. **3,** advocating drastic reform of existing institutions. —*n.* **1,** an extreme liberal in politics. **2,** (*Math.*) a root; the sign (√) expressing it. **3,** (*Gram.*) a root. **4,** (*Chem.*) a group of atoms remaining unchanged in many reactions. —**rad′i·cal·ism,** *n.*—**rad′i·cal·ize″,** *v.t.* —**radical chic,** the patronage of radical extremists by celebrities.

ra·dic′chi·o (ra-dēk′ē-ō) *n.* a type of chicory with reddish leaves.

ra′di·o″ (rā′dē-ō″) *n.* **1,** wireless telephone and telegraph transmission and reception. **2,** a receiving set for sounds so transmitted. —*v.t. & i.* send (a message) by radio. —**radio astronomy,** a branch of astronomy dealing with radio signals received from outer space or with the use of radar for celestial observation. —**radio button,** (*Computers*) a small, button-like graphic which can be clicked with a mouse to select an option. —**radio galaxy,** a galaxy which emits unusually large amounts of radiation. —**radio station,** a place from which radio broadcasts are made. —**radio telescope,** a combination of radio receiver and antenna used for celestial observations.

ra″di·o·ac′tive *adj.* spontaneously radiating energy in atoms or particles of atoms. —**ra″di·o·ac·tiv′i·ty,** *n.*

ra′di·o·car′bon *n.* radioactive carbon, used in dating organic remains.

ra′di·o·gram″ *n.* a message sent by radio.

ra′di·o·graph″ *n.* an image produced on a sensitized surface by radiation other than light, as x-rays or gamma rays. —**ra″di·og′ra·phy** (-og′rə-fē) *n.*

ra″di·ol′o·gy (rā″dē-ol′ə-jē) *n.* the study or use of x-rays and radioactive substances —**ra″di·ol′o·gist,** *n.*

ra″di·om′e·ter (rā″dē-om′ə-tər) *n.* an instrument for detecting and measuring small amounts of radiant energy.

ra′di·o·phone″ *n.* **1,** a device for communication by radio waves rather than by wires. **2,** an apparatus for the production of sound by means of radiant energy. Also, **ra″di·o·te′le·phone.** —**ra′di·o·te·leph′o·ny,** *n.*

ra″di·os′co·py (rā″dē-os′kə-pē) *n.* the examination of the interior of opaque objects by x-rays or gamma rays.

ra′di·o·sonde″ (-sōnd″) *n.* (*Meteor.*) a radio transmitter held aloft by a balloon for broadcasting atmospheric temperature, pressure, etc.

ra″di·o·tel′e·graph″ *n.* a wireless telegraph. —*v.t.* telegraph by radio. —**ra″di·o·te·leg′ra·phy,** *n.*

ra″di·o·ther′a·py *n.* treatment by x-rays or radioactive rays.

ra′di·o·thon″ (-thon″) *n.* a lengthy radio program in support of a cause.

rad′ish *n.* the crisp, pungent root of a garden plant; the plant.

ra′di·um (rā′dē-əm) *n.* a metallic chemical element, no. 88, symbol Ra, found in pitchblende.

ra′di·us (rā′dē-əs) *n.* [*pl.* **-i** (-ī)] **1,** a line drawn from the center of a circle or sphere to the circumference or surface. **2,** the measure of this line; any limited area.

ra′dix (rā′diks) *n.* [*pl.* **rad′i·ces** (rad′ə-sēz)] **1,** the root of a plant. **2,** (*Math.*) the base number of a system, as ten in the decimal system. **3,** a root word.

ra′dome″ (rā′dōm″) *n.* on an airplane, the exterior dome-shaped housing for the radar antenna.

ra′don (rā′don) *n.* a radioactive gaseous element formed in the disintegration of radium, no. 86, symbol Rn.

raf′fi·a (raf′ē-ə) *n.* a species of palm, used for weaving.

raff′ish (raf′ish) *adj.* rowdy. —**raff′-ish·ness,** *n.*

raf′fle (raf′əl) *n.* a lottery to dispose of one prize, usually merchandise. —*v.t.* (often with *off*) dispose of by raffle.

raft (ráft) *n.* **1,** a wooden platform to float in water. **2,** (*Informal*) an accumulation; a collection.

raft'er (ráf'tər) *n.* a sloping beam of a roof.

rag *n.* **1,** a worn or worthless piece of cloth. **2,** (*pl.*) shabby clothes. **3,** (*pl.*) (*Slang*) any clothes, as *glad rags.* **4,** (*Informal*) jazz music: *ragtime.* —*adj.* made of or with rags, as paper. —*v.t.* [**ragged, rag'ging**] (*Slang*) badger; tease.

ra'ga (rä'gä) *n.* (*Music*) any of the traditional modal patterns of Hindu music.

rag'a·muf''fin (rag'ə-muf''in) *n.* a ragged person.

> **ragamuffin**
> ↔ After Middle English *Ragamoffyn*, a demonic character in the poem *Piers Plowman.*

rage (rāj) *n.* **1,** violent anger; fury. **2,** extreme violence; intensity. **3,** enthusiasm; vogue; a fad. —*v.i.* **1,** be furious with anger. **2,** storm. **3,** have furious course or effect. ❏ *rabies*

rag'ged (rag'id) *adj.* **1,** tattered; frayed; shaggy; dressed in worn-out clothes. **2,** slipshod. —**rag'ged·ness,** *n.*

rag'lan (rag'lən) *n.* a topcoat with the sleeves extending down from the collar without shoulder seams, named after Brit. Field Marshal Lord Raglan.

ra·gout' (ra-goo') *n.* (*Fr.*) a highly seasoned stew of meat and vegetables.

rag'tag'' *n.* (*Contemptuous*) ragged people; the rabble. Also, **ragtag and bobtail** (bob'tāl'').

rag'time'' *n.* an early form of jazz music.

rag'weed'' (rag'wēd'') *n.* an herb whose pollen aggravates some asthmatic symptoms.

raid (rād) *n.* a hostile or predatory incursion; a sudden onset. —*v.t. & i.* attack; rob.

> **raid, road, inroad**
> ↔ These words derive from Old English *rād*, whose original sense was closer to *raid* (this sense is also preserved in *inroad*).

rail (rāl) *n.* **1,** a bar passing from one support to another, as for a barrier. **2,** a metal bar used to form a track for a wheeled vehicle. **3,** transportation by railroad. **4,** a small wading bird. —*v.i.* speak bitterly; scoff; inveigh. —*v.t.* (with *in* or *off*) enclose with rails. —**rail'ing,** *n.* a barrier made of rails; a fence.

rail'head'' *n.* **1,** a railroad supply center.

2, the farthest point to which rails have been laid.

rail'ler·y (rā'lə-rė) *n.* banter.

rail'road'' *n.* [also, **rail'way''**] a common carrier operating trains over permanent tracks of rails; the tracks. —*v.t.* (*Slang*) **1,** force and speed to a conclusion. **2,** devise false evidence against; frame. —**rail'road''ing,** *n.* work pert. to the operation of a railroad.

rail'way'' *n.* railroad.

rai'ment (rā'mənt) *n.* clothing.

rain (rān) *n.* **1,** water falling in drops from the clouds. **2,** a shower or outpouring of anything. —*v.i.* produce water falling in drops. —*v.t.* shower down; give abundantly. —**rain check,** a ticket for future use, given to ticketholders of an event stopped by rain or other natural phenomenon; hence, a standing invitation. —**rain'mak''er,** *n.* (*Slang*) a person who attracts much new business to a company.

rain'bow'' *n.* an arc of prismatic colors. —*adj.* comprising different racial, ethnic, etc. groups.

rain'coat'' *n.* a light waterproof outer coat.

rain'drop'' *n.* a drop of rain.

rain'fall'' *n.* rain.

rain'storm'' *n.* a heavy rain.

rain'y *adj.* constantly or often raining. —**rain'i·ness,** *n.*

raise (rāz) *v.t.* **1,** move to a higher place; hoist; elevate. **2,** increase the height or amount of; build up. **3,** cause to rise. **4,** grow or breed, as crops, cattle; bring up. **5,** muster; collect; procure, as an army or money. —*n.* (*Informal*) an increase in pay.

> **raise, raze**
> ☛ Do not confuse these two homonyms. To *raise* is to elevate; to *raze* is to demolish.

raised (rāzd) *adj.* **1,** leavened. **2,** in relief, as carving.

rai'sin (rā'zən) *n.* a dried grape.

rai''son d'ê'tre (rā''zōn de'trə) (*Fr.*) reason for being; justification for existence.

ra'jah (rä'jə) *n.* an E. Indian prince.

rake (rāk) *n.* **1,** a long-handled toothed implement for scraping loose materials together; a similar implement. **2,** an idle, dissolute man; a libertine. **3,** a slope. —*v.t.* **1,** gather or smooth with or as with a rake; (with *up*) glean. **2,** ransack. **3,** scratch. **4,** (*Mil.*) fire upon, lengthwise. **5,** cause to incline.

rake
↔ There are several unrelated senses. The scraping *rake* is of Old Norse origin. The dissolute *rake* is a shortening of *rakehell*, from Middle English *rakel*, rough, hasty. The sloping *rake* is of unknown origin.

rake-'off" *n.* (*Slang*) a rebate or commission, usually illegal.

rak'ish (rāk'ish) *adj.* **1**, (*Naut.*) inclined, as a mast. **2**, jaunty. **3**, dissolute. —**rak'-ish·ness,** *n.*

ral"len·tan'do (räl"ən-tän'dō) *adv., adj. & n.* (*It., Music*) slowing gradually.

ral'ly (ral'ė) *v.t.* **1**, draw or call together for a common purpose. **2**, assemble and reconstitute as a disorganized army. **3**, banter; tease. —*v.i.,* **1**, reunite. **2**, recover energy or effectiveness. —*n.* **1**, a renewal of energy in joint action. **2**, in tennis, a sustained exchange. **3**, a quick recovery. **4**, a mass meeting. **5**, a race or test among sport cars.

RAM random access memory.

ram *n.* **1**, a male sheep. **2**, (*cap.*) Aries, a sign of the zodiac. **3**, an instrument of war for battering; the armored prow of a warship. —*v.t.* [**rammed, ram'ming**] **1**, batter. **2**, force or drive down. **3**, stuff; cram.

ram'ble (ram'bəl) *v.i.* **1**, roam or wander about; rove. **2**, digress. —*n.* a sauntering walk. —**ram'bler,** *n.* **1**, a wanderer. **2**, a climbing rose. —**ram'bling,** *adj.* wandering; roundabout; digressive.

ram'bler *n.* **1**, a wanderer. **2**, a climbing rose.

ram·bunc'tious (ram-bunk'shəs) *adj.* boisterous. —**ram·bunc'tious·ness,** *n.*

ram'e·kin (ram'ə-kin) *n.* an individual baking dish. Also, **ram'e·quin.**

ram'ie (ram'ė) *n.* an Asiatic perennial shrub; its fiber.

ram"i·fi·ca'tion (ram"i-fi-kā'shən) *n.* **1**, a branch; subdivision. **2**, the consequence or extended effect of an action.

ram'i·fy" (ram'ə-fī") *v.i. & t.* form or divide into branches.

ram'jet engine the simplest type of jet engine.

ramp *n.* **1**, a sloping passageway. **2**, a vegetable. —*v.i.* rear or spring up; act violently.

ram'page (ram'pāj) *n.* violent, furious, or excited behavior. —*v.i.* (ram-pāj') act or move more violently. —**ram·pa'geous,** *adj.*

ramp'ant (ram'pənt) *adj.* raging and unchecked.

ram'part (ram'pärt) *n.* **1**, a mound, usu-

ally with a parapet, surrounding a fortified place. **2**, a bulwark; a protective barrier.

ram'rod" *n.* **1**, a rod for tamping the charge of a muzzle-loading gun. **2**, someone very strict.

ram'shack"le (ram'shak"əl) *adj.* tumbledown; rickety. ❑ *ransack*

ran *v.* pret. of *run*.

ranch *n.* a large farm for raising livestock. —*v.i.* conduct, or work on, a ranch. —**ranch'er,** *n.* owner of a ranch. —**ranch'-style,** *adj.* of a house, having one story.

ran·che'ro (ran-chā'rō) *n.* (*Sp.*) a rancher.

ran'cho (ran'chō) *n.* [*pl.* **-chos**] (*Sp.*) **1**, a rude hut. **2**, a ranch.

ran'cid (ran'sid) *adj.* having a rank, tainted smell or taste. —**ran·cid'i·ty,** *n.*

ran'cor (rang'kər) *n.* bitter animosity; spitefulness. Also, **ran'cour.** —**ran'cor·ous,** *adj.*

rand *n.* the monetary unit of the Union of So. Africa.

ran'dom (ran'dəm) *adj.* haphazard; casual. —**at random,** haphazardly. —**random access memory,** (*Computers*) computer memory which is available for running programs and for temporary storage.

ran'dom·ize" (-īz") *v.t.* make random. —**ran"dom·i·za'tion,** *n.*

rand'y (ran'dė) *adj.* **1**, vulgar; bawdy. **2**, (*Slang*) lascivious.

ra'nee (rä'nė) *n.* rani.

rang *v.* pret. of *ring*.

range (rānj) *v.t.* **1**, dispose in a row or rows of; set in definite order. **2**, oppose. **3**, rove over or along. —*v.i.* **1**, be in or form a parallel line or direction. **2**, roam; wander. **3**, travel a certain distance or direction. **4**, vary, within specified limits. —*n.* **1**, a series in a lane or row. **2**, scope; extent. **3**, distance from one point to another. **4**, a large tract of land for grazing. **5**, a course for shooting or target practice. **6**, a cooking stove. **7**, a chain of mountains. —**range finder,** an instrument for determining the distance of a target from a gun, etc.

rang'er (rān'jər) *n.* **1**, a trooper patrolling a wide area. **2**, (*cap.*) an Amer. soldier trained for raiding.

rang'y (rān'jė) *adj.* **1**, tall and slender. **2**, spacious; roomy.

ra'ni (rä'nė) *n.* in India, the wife of a rajah, or a reigning princess. Also, **ra'nee.**

rank *n.* **1**, a row, esp. one conceived as horizontal; a line; formation. **2**, a class, order. **3**, relative position; standing, as social, ordinal, etc. **4,** (*pl.*) (*Mil.*) enlisted men. —*v.t.* **1,** arrange in lines or formations. **2,** assign to a particular class. **3,** take precedence of or over; rate above. —*v.i.* occupy a relative position. —*adj.* **1,** strong in growth, as weeds; rich and fertile. **2,** offensive; unmitigated. **3,** obscene; indecent. —**rank′ing,** *adj.* —**rank and file,** the common people; people indiscriminately.

ran′kle (rang′kəl) *v.i.* fester; be irritating.

> **rankle**
> ↔ From Medieval Latin *dracunculus*, snake, or, by extension, a wound caused by the bite of a snake.

ran′sack (ran′sak) *v.t.* **1,** search thoroughly. **2,** plunder.

> **ransack, ramshackle**
> ↔ These two words share their origin in Old Norse *rannsaka*, literally, house search.

ran′som (ran′səm) *n.* the price or cost of redeeming a hostage. —*v.t.* redeem by paying.

rant *v.i.* declaim violently and with little sense; rave.

rap *v.i. & t.* **[rapped, rap′ping] 1,** strike (with) a quick sharp blow, **2,** (with *out*) utter sharply; communicate by raps. **3,** criticize adversely. **4,** (*Informal*) converse. —*n.* (*Informal*) **1,** a cutting remark. **2,** a bit. **3,** (*Slang*) penalty. **4,** a blow. **5,** a style of vocal popular music consisting of rhythmic chanting against a rock background. —**rap session,** (*Informal*) a freewheeling conversation. —**rap sheet,** a police record of arrests and convictions.

ra·pa′cious (rə-pā′shəs) *adj.* greedy; grasping; predatory. —**ra·pa′cious·ness,** *n.*

ra·pac′i·ty (rə-pas′ə-tē) *n.* rapaciousness.

rape (rāp) *n.* **1,** forcible seizing and violation; ravishing. **2,** carrying off by force. **3,** a plant grown for fodder and oil. —*v.t.* **1,** force to have sexual intercourse. **2,** carry off violently.

rap′id *adj.* **1,** moving swiftly. **2,** requiring little time. —*n.* (usu. *pl.*) a swift current in a river. —**rap′id·ness,** *n.* —**rapid transit,** subway or trolley lines. —**rapid eye movement,** rapid movement of the eyes during dreaming sleep. *Abbr.,* **REM.**

rap′id-fire″ *adj.* **1,** capable of firing shots in rapid succession. **2,** characterized by rapidity, sharpness, etc., as questioning.

ra·pid′i·ty (rə-pid′ə-tē) *n.* rapidness; swiftness; speed.

ra′pi·er (rā′pē-ər) *n.* a long, narrow, pointed two-edged sword.

rap′ine (rap′in) *n.* plundering.

> **rapine, ravine**
> ↔ Originally the same word, derived from Latin *rapina*, plunder. A *ravine* was a gorge carved out by plundering, impetuous water.

rap·pel′ (ra-pel′) *v.i.* to descend a mountain using a rope.

rap·port′ (ra-pôr′) *n.* harmonious relation; accord.

rap″proche″ment′ (rä″prōsh″män′) *n.* (*Fr.*) an establishment of harmonious relations.

rap·scal′lion (rap-skal′yən) *n.* (*Informal*) a scamp; a rascal.

rapt *adj.* ecstatically engrossed or bemused. —**rapt′ness,** *n.*

rap·tor′i·al (rap-tôr′ē-əl) *adj.* **1,** predatory. **2,** fitted for seizing and holding prey, as claws of birds.

rap′ture (rap′chər) *n.* ecstatic joy. —**rap′tur·ous,** *adj.*

ra′ra a′vis (rār′ə ā′vis) (*Lat.,* rare bird) a rare or unusual thing.

rare (rār) *adj.* **1,** thin, not dense; sparse. **2,** very uncommon; remarkable; excellent; choice. **3,** (of meat) not thoroughly cooked. —**rare′ness,** *n.*

rare′bit (rār′bit) *n.* Welsh rabbit.

rare-earth element or **metal** any of a series of metallic elements, nos. 58-71, whose oxides are found in relatively scarce minerals and are very difficult to separate.

rar′e·fy″ (rār′ə-fī″) *v.t. & i.* make or become thin or less dense. —**rar″e·fac′tion,** *n.*

rare′ly (rār′lē) *adv.* seldom; uncommonly.

rare′ripe″ *adj.* ripening early. —*n.* a rareripe fruit, esp. a variety of peach.

rar′ing *adj.* eager.

rar′i·ty (rār′ə-tē) *n.* **1,** state of being uncommon. **2,** something unusual.

ras′cal (ras′kəl) *n.* **1,** a scoundrel. **2,** a scamp. —**ras·cal′i·ty,** *n.*

rash *adj.* too hasty in judgment, speech, or action; reckless; precipitate. —*n.* an eruption on the skin. —**rash′ness,** *n.*

> **rash, rather**
> ↔ These two words are distantly related in an unrecorded Germanic source. *Rather* originally meant more quickly, hence, sooner.

rash′er (rash′ər) *n.* a slice, or small serving, of bacon or ham.

rasp *v.t.* grate with a coarse, rough instrument. —*v.i.* irritate (one's nerves). —*n.* a coarse file. —**rasp′ing,** *adj.* (of a voice, etc.) harsh.

rasp′ber″ry (ràz′ber″ė) *n.* **1,** a sweet, red or black, edible berry from a plant of the rose family. **2,** (*Slang*) an expression of derision.

Ras″ta·far′i·an·ism (ras″tə-fär′ė-ə-niz-əm) *n.* a religious cult originating in Jamaica. —**Ras″ta·far′i·an,** *adj. & n.*

ras′ter (ras′tər) *n.* **1,** (*TV*) the parallel lines produced on the screen by the scanner. **2,** (*Computers*) the lines of dots printed by a dot-matrix printer. —**ras′ter·ize,** *v.t.* to translate an image or text into raster lines.

rat *n.* **1,** a rodent similar to the mouse but larger. **2,** (*Slang*) a betrayer or informer; a contemptible person. **3,** a bulging roll of hair. —*v.i.* [**rat′ted, -ting**] **1,** catch or kill rats. **2,** (*Slang*) be a betrayer; inform. —**rat pack,** (*Informal*) a gang of young people, esp. a group of young actors and actresses. —**rat race,** the competitive, pointless daily routine of life.

ratch′et (rach′it) *n.* **1,** a pivoted piece or part that checks backward motion of a toothed bar or wheel. **2,** the wheel or bar itself.

rate (rāt) *n.* **1,** amount, quantity, range, or degree, measured according to some standard. **2,** a price; a fixed charge. —*v.t.* **1,** appraise; fix the relative scale, rank, or position of. **2,** (*Informal*) deserve. **3,** scold; censure. —*v.i.* (*Informal*) have (a certain) standing. —**at any rate,** in any case; at least.

rat′fink″ (*Slang*) *n.* **1,** fink. **2,** an obnoxious person.

rath′er (ràth′ər) *adv.* **1,** sooner; preferably. **2,** more correctly. **3,** on the contrary. **4,** somewhat considerably. ❑ *rash*

raths′kel″ler (rots′kel″ər) *n.* (*Ger.*) a barroom in a cellar.

rat′i·fy″ (rat′ə-fī″) *v.t.* **1,** accept and sanction formally. **2,** confirm; establish. —**rat″-i·fi·ca′tion,** *n.*

rat′i·né′ (rat″ə-nā′) *n.* a heavy woolen cloth used for linings.

rat′ing (rā′ting) *n.* **1,** relative standing; appraisal. **2,** rank of a noncommissioned sailor or seaman. **3,** a scolding.

ra′tio (rā′shō) *n.* the relation between two quantities; proportion.

ra″ti·oc′i·nate″ (rash″ė-os′ə-nāt″) *v.i.* reason. —**ra″ti·oc″i·na′tion,** *n.*

ra′tion (rā′shən) *n.* **1,** an allowance, esp. of a necessity. **2,** (*pl.*) meals. —*v.t.* apportion.

ra′tion·al (rash′ən-əl) *adj.* **1,** of, pert. to, or attributable to reason or the power of reasoning; sane. **2,** acting in accordance with reason. **3,** (*Math.*) designating a number that can be represented as the quotient of two integers or polynomials. —**ra″tion·al′i·ty,** *n.*

ra″tion·ale′ (rash″ə-nal′) *n.* the rational basis for something; justification.

ra′tion·al·ism (-iz-əm) *n.* a doctrine that places reason above faith. —**rà′tion·al·ist,** *n.*

ra′tion·al·ize″ (-īz″) *v.t. & i.* explain or interpret according to supposed reason. —**ra″tion·al·i·za′tion,** *n.*

rat′line (rat′lĭn) *n.* (*Naut.*) a rope hung horizontally, used as a step in climbing. Also, **rat′lin.**

rats′bane″ (rats′bān″) *n.* rat poison, esp. white arsenic.

rat·tan′ (ra-tan′) *n.* **1,** a climbing palm whose stems are used for wickerwork, canes, etc. **2,** a cane.

rat′ter (rat′ər) *n.* a dog or cat that kills rats.

rat′tle (rat′əl) *v.i. & t.* **1,** make or cause to make a rapid succession of clicking sounds. **2,** talk rapidly. **3,** move with a clatter. **4,** (*Informal*) confuse. —*n.* **1,** the act or effect of rattling. **2,** a toy that produces a clattering sound. **3,** one of the horny cells at the end of a rattlesnake's tail.

rat′tle·brain″ *n.* a giddy, chattering person.

rat′tle·snake″ *n.* a venomous Amer. snake whose tail rattles when shaken. Also (*Informal*) **rat′tler** (rat′lər).

rat′tle·trap″ *n.* a shaky, rickety object, esp. a vehicle. —*adj.* shaky.

rat′trap″ *n.* (*Slang*) **1,** a hopeless situation. **2,** a shabby, disreputable place.

rat′ty (rat′ė) *adj.* seedy. —**rat′ti·ness,** *n.*

rau′cous (râ′kəs) *adj.* harsh of voice; hoarse. —**rau′ci·ty** (râ′sə-tė) *n.*

raunch′y (rân′chė) *adj.* (*Slang*) **1,** obscene; indecent. **2,** lustful.

rav′age (rav′ij) *v.t. & i.* lay waste; devastate; pillage. —*n.* devastation.

---

ravage, ravish, ravished, ravenous
☛ Similar-sounding words with very different meanings. To *ravage* is to devastate; to *ravish* is to enrapture or rape. Note that *ravished* is not a synonym for *ravenous*, which means very hungry.

rave (rāv) *v.i. & t.* talk insanely, extravagantly, or overenthusiastically. —*n.* (*Informal*) unrestrained praise; the object of it. —*adj.* (*Informal*) extremely enthusiastic.

rav'el (rav'əl) *v.t. & i.* **1,** draw apart thread by thread; fray. **2,** disentangle or become disentangled.

ra'ven (rā'vən) *n.* a large, glossy, black crow. —*adj.* deep, lustrous black.

rav'en (rav'ən) *v.t. & i.* **1,** obtain by violence. **2,** swallow greedily. —**rav'en·ing**, *adj.* eager for prey. —**rav'en·ous** (-əs) *adj.* furiously hungry or greedy. ❏ *ravage*

ra·vine' (rə-vēn') *n.* a deep valley. ❏ *rapine*

rav'ing (rā'ving) *adj.* **1,** talking wildly; mad. **2,** (*Informal*) superlative. —*n.* (often *pl.*) irrational, incoherent talk.

ra″vi·o·li (ra″vē-ō'lē) *n.pl.* an Ital. dish of chopped meat, cheese, etc., wrapped in dough.

rav'ish *v.t.* **1,** seize and carry off. **2,** enrapture. **3,** rape sexually. —**rav'ish·ing**, *adj.* entrancing. —**rav'ish·ment**, *n.* ❏ *ravage*

raw (râ) *adj.* **1,** uncooked. **2,** in a natural state or condition; not processed by manufacture, etc. **3,** harsh, sharp, or chilly; bleak, as of weather. **4,** without covering, as of skin; naked. **5,** untried; untrained; inexperienced. **6,** crude; rough. —*n.* **1,** a raw article or condition. **2,** a sore place. —**raw material,** a substance of which manufactured goods are made. —**raw'ness,** *n.*

raw'boned″ (-bōnd″) *adj.* gaunt.

raw'hide″ *n.* **1,** untanned leather. **2,** a leather whip.

ray (rā) *n.* **1,** a line of light; a similar emanation from a central source. **2,** a beam of intellectual light. **3,** a stripe. **4,** one of several lines emanating from a point. **5,** a sea fish, as the skate, etc. —*v.i.* radiate.

ray'on (rā'on) *n.* a silklike cellulose yarn or fabric.

raze (rāz) *v.t.* level to the ground; tear down; demolish. ❏ *raise*

ra'zor (rā'zər) *n.* a sharp-edged instrument used for shaving. —*adj.* extremely sharp. —**razor cut,** a type of haircut using a straight razor.

ra'zor·back″ *n.* **1,** a hog with a back like a sharp ridge. **2,** a whale with a similar back.

razz (raz) *v.t. & i.* (*Informal*) tease; heckle.

razz'le-daz'zle (raz'əl-daz'əl) *n.* (*Slang*) **1,** bewildering or noisy confusion. **2,** ostentatious display; deceptive maneuverings.

razz'ma·tazz″ (raz'mə-taz″) *n.* (*Informal*) razzle-dazzle.

re (rā) *n.* (*Music*) the second tone in the diatonic scale.

re (rē) *n.* (*Lat., Law*) (preceded by *in*) in the case of.

re- (rē) *pref.* **1,** back; denoting reverse action. **2,** (with hyphen when necessary to avoid ambiguity), again; anew. [In addition to words defined in the text, the following words may be defined by adding *again* to the root word.]

re″ad·just'	re″en·force'
re″ap·pear'	re″en'ter
re″ap·point'	re″es·tab'lish
re″arm'	re·fit'
re″ar·range'	re·heat'
re″as·sem'ble	re·kin'dle
re″as·sert'	re·load'
re·born'	re·mar'ry
re·build'	re·name'
re″com·mence'	re·o'pen
re·con'quer	re·paid'
re·con'sti·tute	re″pub·li·ca'tion
re-″cre·ate'	re·pub'lish
re″dis·cov'er	re·read'
re·ech'o	re·set'
re″e·lect'	re″u·nite'
re″em·bark'	re·vis'it

reach (rēch) *v.t. & i.* **1,** stretch out; extend outward. **2,** attain; arrive at; extend as far as. **3,** obtain access to; establish communication with. **4,** influence. **5,** hand over; deliver. **6,** strive. —*n.* **1,** the act or capacity of stretching out for something. **2,** a continuous stretch or course. **3,** the distance one can reach. **4,** range of capacity or ability.

re·act' *v.i.* **1,** act in a reverse or opposite direction. **2,** act mutually or reciprocally upon each other. **3,** respond. **4,** return to a former condition.

re·act'ance (-əns) *n.* impedance due to capacitance or inductance or both.

re·act'ant (rē-ak'tənt) *n.* an initial factor in a chemical reaction.

re·ac'tion (rē-ak'shən) *n.* **1,** an opposed or return action. **2,** a response. **3,** a tendency to revert, as to former customs or ideology. **4,** mutual or reciprocal action. **5,** a chemical change.

re·ac'tion·ar·y *adj. & n.* (one) favoring a return to old, esp. conservative, ways and methods.

re·act'i·vate *v.t.* make active or functional again.

re·ac'tor (rē-ak'tər) *n.* **1,** a chemical reagent. **2,** a device in which a nuclear chain reaction may be initiated and controlled to produce heat or for production of other fissionable materials. Also, **atomic reactor** or **pile, nuclear reactor.**

read (rēd) *v.t. & i.* [*pret. & p.p.* **read** (red)] **1,** understand (something written or printed) by interpretation of the signs used. **2,** understand by observation or scrutiny. **3,** utter aloud (written words); recite. **4,** peruse (a book, etc.); study. **5,** infer. **6,** solve (a riddle); tell fortunes. **7,** perform music at sight. **8,** interpret in a certain way, as music, etc. **—read-only memory,** ROM.

read′a·ble *adj.* **1,** legible. **2,** interesting.

read′er *n.* **1,** a person who reads or likes to read. **2,** in some churches, a minor clerical order. **3,** a book for the teaching of reading. **4,** an interpreter. **5,** an anthology. **—read′er·ship″,** *n.*

read′i·ly (red′ə-lė) *adv.* **1,** willingly. **2,** easily.

read′ing (rē′ding) *n.* **1,** act of reading. **2,** a recital; rendition. **3,** interpretation; inference. **4,** the study of reading. **5,** printed matter. **6,** the indication on a graduated instrument.

read′out″ *n.* **1,** presentation of computer data, usu. on a screen in digital form. **2,** printout.

read′y (red′ė) *adj.* **1,** prepared for immediate use or action. **2,** willing. **3,** about (to). **4,** immediately available; handy. **5,** prompt; facile; quick. **—read′i·ness,** *n.*

read′y-made″ *adj.* **1,** manufactured before being offered for sale, as clothes. **2,** unoriginal.

---

ready-made

↔ This term was introduced in French by 20th-c. French artist Marcel Duchamp.

---

re·a′gent (rė-ā′jənt) *n.* a substance that causes chemical reaction.

re′al (rē′əl) *adj.* **1,** existing, not imaginary; actual. **2,** genuine; true; authentic. **3,** of property, immovable, as lands. **—real estate,** land, together with any buildings on it. **—real number,** a number without an imaginary part. **—real time,** the actual time it takes to do something, as for a computer to process information.

re′al·ism (rē′ə-liz-əm) *n.* **1,** interest only in the actual or real, not in the ideal or abstract. **2,** fidelity to actual appearance or fact, as in art.

re′al·ist (rē′əl-ist) *n.* one who tries to see or portray things as they are, not idealized. **—re″al·is′tic,** *adj.* **—re″al·is′ti·cal·ly,** *adv.*

re·al′i·ty (rė-al′ə-tė) *n.* **1,** state of actual existence. **2,** fact; truth.

re′al·ize″ (rē′ə-līz″) *v.t.* **1,** recognize the nature or existence of. **2,** comprehend; understand, or feel distinctly. **3,** achieve. **4,** make a profit of or on. **5,** exchange for cash. **—v.i.** convert property into cash; profit. **—re″al·i·za′tion,** *n.*

re′al·ly (rē′ə-lė) *adv.* **1,** as a fact; truly; actually. **2,** indeed.

realm (relm) *n.* a domain; sphere.

Re·al″po·li·tik′ (rē-al″po-li-tēk′) *n.* a policy of national development and expansion based on practicality rather than theory or ethics.

Re′al·tor′ (rē′əl-tôr″) *n.* (*T.N.*) a member of a certain real-estate brokers' organization; a real-estate agent.

re′al·ty (rē′əl-tė) *n.* real estate.

ream (rēm) *n.* **1,** a quantity of paper, usually 500 sheets. **2,** (*pl.*) (*Informal*) a large quantity. **—v.t.** enlarge and smooth (a hole).

ream′er (rē′mər) *n.* **1,** a tool for enlarging holes. **2,** a device for extracting juice from an orange, etc.

reap (rēp) *v.t.* **1,** cut with a sickle or other implement and gather; harvest. **2,** garner as the fruit of one's labors. **—reap′er,** *n.* a machine for reaping.

rear (rir) *n.* **1,** the back; a position lying backward; the background. **2,** (*Mil.*) the body of an army or fleet that comes last. **—adj.** hindmost. **—v.t.** **1,** set or hold up; elevate. **2,** build; construct; erect. **3,** foster; nurture; train, as children. **4,** raise, as plants or animals. **—v.i.** **1,** rise on the hind legs, as a horse. **2,** (with *up*) express resentment. **—rear admiral,** a naval officer ranking above captain and commodore. **—rear guard,** a detachment to follow and protect a marching army.

rear′end″ *v.t.* to strike the back (of a vehicle) with one's own vehicle.

rear′most *adj.* last of all.

rear′ward (-wərd) *adj. & adv.* at or toward the rear. Also, **rear′wards.**

rea′son (rē′zən) *n.* **1,** a statement given to create, confirm, or justify a belief, conclusion, or action; a promise; ground; excuse. **2,** intellect; the faculty of understanding, inferring, and deducing, esp. as man does. **3,** sanity. **4,** moderation; right. **—v.i.** exercise the mind; reflect; think. **—rea′son·ing,** *n.*

---

reason is because

(*Gram.*) *The reason is because...* is not considered good style. You should write instead *The reason is that...*

---

rea′son·a·ble *adj.* **1,** rational. **2,** amenable to sound sense. **3,** not exceeding the bounds of common sense; sensible. **4,** moderate in amount or price.

re″as·sur′ance *n.* **1,** restored confidence. **2,** something that reassures.

re″as·sure′ *v.t.* instill confidence in.

Ré′au·mur scale (rā′ə-myûr) a temperature calibration scale on which the freezing and boiling points of water are 0°R and 80°R, respectively, named for 18th-c. French physicist René Réaumur.

re′bate (rē′bāt) *n.* a return of part of a payment. —*v.t.* (rė-bāt′) return (part of a payment received).

re′bec (rē′bek) *n.* (*Music*) a medieval string instrument, played with a bow.

re·bel′ (ri-bel′) *v.i.* **1,** make war against one's government; revolt against any authority or order. **2,** refuse or dislike to do something expected. —*n.* (reb′əl) **1,** one who rebels. **2,** an unconventional person.

re·bel′lion (ri-bel′yən) *n.* **1,** an armed revolt. **2,** a spirit of resistance to authority.

re·bel′lious (ri-bel′yəs) *adj.* rebelling; defiant; resisting control. —**re·bel′liousness,** *n.*

re′birth″ *n.* **1,** a new or second birth; reincarnation. **2,** a revival; renaissance.

re·bound′ *v.i.* spring back; bounce. —*n.* (rē′bownd) **1,** the act of flying back; recoil. **2,** (*Informal*) recovery from an unhappy love affair.

re·buff′ (ri-buf′) *v.t.* & *n.* snub.

re·buke′ (ri-būk′) *v.t.* chide; reprimand. —*n.* reproof.

re′bus (rē′bəs) *n.* a representation of words or phrases by means of figures or pictures.

---

rebus
↔ From the Latin phrase *non verbis sed rebus,* not by words but by things.

---

re·but′ (ri-but′) *v.t.* disprove by argument or evidence; refute, esp. in a debate. —**re·but′tal,** *n.*

re·cal′ci·trant (ri-kal′si-trənt) *adj.* refusing to submit; refractory. —*n.* a recalcitrant person. —**re·cal′ci·trance,** *n.*

---

recalcitrant
↔ From the Latin verb *recalcitrare,* to kick back, from Latin *calx,* heel.

---

re·call′ (ri-kâl′) *v.t.* **1,** remember; recollect. **2,** call back; summon anew. **3,** revoke; countermand. —*n.* **1,** the act of recalling; revocation. **2,** the right to vote

an elected official out of office. **3,** a signal (by flag, bugle, etc.).

re·cant′ (ri-kant′) *v.t.* & *i.* contradict formally one's previous assertion; retract. —**re″can·ta′tion** (rē″kan-tā′shən) *n.*

re·cap′ (rė-kap′) *v.t.* put a new tread on (a worn tire). **2,** recapitulate. —*n.* **1,** (rē′kap) a recapped tire. **2,** (*Informal*) recapitulation.

re″ca·pit′u·late″ *v.t.* **1,** summarize; review. **2,** repeat (past stages of evolution) in development. —**re″ca·pit″u·la′tion,** *n.*

re·cap′ture *v.t.* seize, remember, or enjoy again. —*n.* **1,** a taking again; recovery. **2,** lawful seizure of property or earnings by a government.

re·cede′ (ri-sēd′) *v.i.* **1,** withdraw; fall away. **2,** turn back or aside. **3,** incline or slope backward.

re·ceipt′ (ri-sēt′) *n.* **1,** the act or state of receiving. **2,** something received, esp. (*pl.*) money taken in. **3,** a written acknowledgment of having received something, esp. money. **4,** a recipe. —*v.t.* give a receipt for; acknowledge payment of.

---

receipt, receive, recipe
↔ These words all come from Latin *recipere,* to receive. *Receipt* came through Old French, while *recipe* came directly from the Latin.

---

re·ceiv′a·ble *adj.* owing to oneself. —*n.* (usu. *pl.*) an account due from another.

re·ceive′ (ri-sēv′) *v.t.* **1,** get by transfer as from a primary source, as money, a wound, an impression, etc. **2,** give admission, recognition, or welcome to. **3,** hold; contain. —*v.i.* **1,** come into custody of something by transfer. **2,** greet and entertain visitors. **3,** deal in stolen goods. ❏ *receipt*

re·ceiv′er *n.* **1,** one who or that which receives (taxes, etc.). **2,** a dealer in stolen goods. **3,** one appointed to handle the affairs of a bankrupt. **4,** an instrument for receiving signals, sounds, etc. **5,** a receptacle.

re·ceiv′er·ship″ *n.* (*Law*) **1,** the office or function of a receiver (def. 3). **2,** state of being in the hands of a receiver.

re·cen′sion (ri-sen′shən) *n.* a critical revision, as of a book; the revised text.

re′cent (rē′sənt) *adj.* **1,** of or pert. to time not long past. **2,** of relatively modern date; fresh. —**re′cent·ly,** *adv.* not long ago.

re·cep′ta·cle (ri-sep′tə-kəl) *n.* **1,** a container, as a wastebasket. **2,** an electrical outlet.

re·cep′tion (ri-sep′shən) *n.* **1,** the act or

manner of receiving; a letting in. **2,** a greeting or welcome. **3,** a formal entertainment of guests. —**re·cep′tion·ist,** *n.* one employed to greet visitors.

re·cep′tive (ri-sep′tiv) *adj.* **1,** willing or ready to receive or accept. **2,** able to hold and contain. —**re·cep′tive·ness, re·cep·tiv′·i·ty,** *n.*

re·cep′tor (ri-sep′tər) *n,* a sensory nerve ending; a sense organ.

re′cess (rē′ses) *n.* **1,** an interval of relief; a rest period. **2,** an alcove; a niche; a nook. **3,** *(pl.)* a place of retirement or seclusion. —*v.t.* (rė-ses′) **1,** put in, make, or order a recess. **2,** set back. —*v.i.* adjourn for a short time.

re·ces′sion (rė-sesh′ən) *n.* **1,** act of receding. **2,** a recessed place. **3,** a brief decline in business prosperity.

re·ces′sion·al (rė-sesh′ən-əl) *n.* a hymn sung while clergy and choir retire at the end of a church service.

re·ces′sive (rė-ses′iv) *adj.* **1,** tending to recede. **2,** tending to yield.

re·cher·ché′ (rə-sher-shā′) *adj.* (*Fr.*) **1,** studied or refined; careful. **2,** rare.

re·cid′i·vism (ri-sid′ə-viz-əm) *n.* relapse into crime by a convicted criminal. —**re·cid′i·vist,** *n.* —**re·cid′i·vous,** *adj.*

rec′i·pe (res′ə-pė) *n.* **1,** directions, as for preparing a specific dish. **2,** a medical prescription. **3,** any formula for producing a desired effect. ❏ *receipt*

re·cip′i·ent (ri-sip′ė-ənt) *n.* one who receives or accepts something. —*adj.* receiving; receptive.

re·cip′ro·cal (ri-sip′rə-kəl) *adj.* in mutual relation; concerning, given, or owed by each with regard to the other. —*n.* (*Math.*) **1,** the quotient resulting from the division of unity by a quantity, as the reciprocal of 4 is ¼. **2,** a complement.

re·cip′ro·cate″ (ri-sip′rə-kāt″) *v.t. & i.* **1,** give and return mutually; act in return or response. **2,** (*Mech.*) move backward and forward. —**re·cip′ro·ca′tion,** *n.* —**reciprocating engine,** one in which the pistons move back and forth.

rec″i·proc′i·ty (res″i-pros′ə-tė) *n.* mutual exchange or aid; cooperation.

re·ci′sion (ri-sizh′ən) *n.* a cutting off; resection or annulment.

re·cit′al (ri-sīt′əl) *n.* act of reciting; esp. a musical performance. ❏ *concert*

rec″i·ta′tion (res″i-tā′shən) *n.* **1,** a reciting or recital. **2,** a piece recited; a declamation.

rec″i·ta·tive′ (res″i-tə-tēv′) *n.* a passage in an opera or oratorio intermediate between speaking and singing.

re·cite′ (ri-sīt′) *v.t.* **1,** deliver orally (something memorized); rehearse. **2,** give an account or statement of; tell. **3,** enumerate. —*v.i.* state or perform a lesson, etc.

reck (rek) *v.t. & i.* heed.

reck′less (rek′ləs) *adj.* daring; imprudent; foolhardy. —**reck′less·ness,** *n.*

reck′on (rek′ən) *v.t.* **1,** count; compute. **2,** hold in estimation as; regard. —*v.i.* **1,** figure up. **2,** rely; depend. **3,** (*Informal*) think; suppose; guess.

reck′on·ing *n.* **1,** an accounting. **2,** a final settlement.

re·claim′ *v.t.* **1,** recover or assert right to (something lost or surrendered). **2,** redeem; save (something abandoned or neglected). **3,** fit for cultivation or other use. **4,** reform; tame. —**rec″la·ma′tion** (rek″lə-mā′shən) *n.*

re·cline′ (ri-klīn′) *v.i.* lie down.

re·cluse′ (ri-kloos′) *n.* a person who lives in seclusion; a hermit. —**re·clu′sion,** *n.* —**re·clu′sive,** *adj.*

rec″og·ni′tion (rek″əg-nish′ən) *n.* the act of recognizing; acceptance; notice.

re·cog′ni·zance (ri-kog′nə-zəns) *n.* **1,** (*Law*) a surety bond. **2,** recognition.

rec′og·nize″ (rek′əg-nīz″) *v.t.* **1,** identify or acknowledge something or someone as previously known. **2,** acknowledge or accept formally. **3,** appreciate. —**rec′og·niz″a·ble,** *adj.*

re·coil′ (ri-koil′) *v.i.* spring back; react. —*n.* (rē′koil″) the act or extent of recoiling.

> **recoil**
> ↔ Not related to *coil,* but derived from Latin *culus,* rump, through French *reculer.*

rec″ol·lect′ (rek″ə-lekt′) *v.t.* bring back to the mind; remember. —**rec″ol·lec′tion,** *n.* the act of recalling; something remembered.

re·com′bi·nant (ri-kom′bə-nənt) *adj.* pert. to the combination of genetic materials in new ways.

rec″om·mend′ (rek″ə-mend′) *v.t.* **1,** put in a favorable light before another; state to be worthy. **2,** advise. —**rec″om·men·da′·tion,** *n.*

rec′om·pense″ (rek′əm-pens″) *v.t.* pay, in return for something. —*n.* remuneration; repayment.

rec″on·cile″ (rek′ən-sīl″) *v.t.* **1,** restore to union and friendship after estrangement.

2, adjust; settle. **3,** bring to agreement. **4,** make consistent. —**rec″on·cil″i·a′tion** (-sil″ė-ā′shən) *n.*

rec′on·dite″ (rek′ən-dīt″) *adj.* hard to understand; deep in meaning.

re″con·di′tion (rē″-) *v.t.* restore to original condition; repair; renovate.

re·con′nais·sance (ri-kon′ə-səns) *n.* act of reconnoitering.

re″con·noi′ter (rē″kə-noi′tər) *v.t. & i.* make a preliminary inspection of (a region, enemy's position, etc.).

re″con·sid′er *v.t.* think about again, esp. to change a decision. —**re″con·sid·er·a′-tion,** *n.*

re″con·struct′ *v.t.* construct again; rebuild.

re″con·struc′tion *n.* **1,** act of rebuilding. **2,** (*cap.*) the return of the Confederate States to the Union after the Civil War.

re·cord′ (ri-kôrd′) *v.t.* **1,** write down, so as to keep as evidence. **2,** register; enroll, as voters or pupils. **3,** transcribe for reproduction by phonograph, etc. —*n.* (rek′ərd) **1,** the act of recording; an account or report. **2,** all the known facts; previous experience. **3,** a disk to reproduce sound on. **4,** the highest achievement in a competition. —*adj.* exceeding all others; best of its kind to date. —**record player,** a machine for reproducing sounds recorded on grooved disks.

---

record, recorder
↔ From Latin *recordari*, to remember. The instrument *recorder* comes from an obsolete sense of *record*, to practice.

---

re·cord′er *n.* **1,** an official who keeps records. **2,** a registering instrument. **3,** a type of flute. ❑ *record*

re·cord′ing *n.* a phonograph record, recorded tape, etc.

re·count′ (ri-kownt′) *v.t.* **1,** tell; relate; narrate in order or detail. **2,** (rē″kownt′) count again. —*n.* (rē′kownt″) a second enumeration.

re·coup′ (ri-koop′) *v.t. & i.* recover (one's losses).

re′course (rē′kôrs) *n.* a source of or appeal for help.

re·cov′er (ri-kuv′ər) *v.t.* get or obtain (something lost) again; regain; save. —*v.i.* **1,** grow well again after illness; come back to a former, better state. **2,** (*Law*) obtain a judgment, as for damages.

re·cov′er·y (-ə-rė) *n.* act or fact of recovering; what is recovered.

rec′re·ant (rek′rė-ənt) *adj.* **1,** craven;

cowardly. **2,** unfaithful to duty. —*n.* a coward or traitor. —**rec′re·an·cy** (-ən-sė) *n.*

rec′re·ate″ (rek′rė-āt″) *v.t.* refresh after toil or exertion; divert. —*v.i.* take recreation.

rec″re·a′tion (rek″rė-ā′shən) *n.* diversion from toil; play. —**rec″re·a′tion·al,** *adj.* —**rec″re·a′tive,** *adj.* —**recreational vehicle,** a vehicle, usu. a van, outfitted for recreational purposes. Also, **RV.**

re·crim′i·nate″ (ri-krim′ə-nāt″) *v.i.* answer an accusation with another. —**re·crim″i·na′tion,** *n.*

re″cru·desce′ (rē″kroo-des′) *v.i.* **1,** become raw or sore again. **2,** break out afresh. —**re″cru·des′cence,** *n.* —**re″cru·des′cent,** *adj.*

re·cruit′ (ri-kroot′) *v.t. & i.* **1,** enlist (new men), esp. for an army, **2,** gather or recover (strength, provisions, etc.). —*n.* a newly enlisted member, esp. a soldier or sailor. —**re·cruit′ment,** *n.*

rec′tal (rek′təl) *adj.* of or pert. to the rectum.

rec′tan′gle (rek′tang″gəl) *n.* a parallelogram having all right angles. —**rec·tan′-gu·lar** (-gyə-lər) *adj.*

rec·ti- (rek-tə) *pref.* straight.

rec′ti·fy″ (rek′ti-fī″) *v.t.* make right or straight; correct; amend. —**rec″ti·fi·ca′-tion,** *n.* —**rec′ti·fi″er,** *n.*

rec′ti·lin′e·ar *adj.* composed of straight lines.

rec′ti·tude″ (rek′ti-tūd″) *n.* **1,** rightness of principle or practice. **2,** correctness; freedom from error.

rec′to (rek′tō) *n.* [pl. **-tos**] the right-hand, odd-numbered page of an open book.

rec′tor (rek′tər) *n.* **1,** a priest or clergyman in charge of a parish. **2,** the head of a school or college. —**rec′tor·ate** (-ət) *n.*

rec′to·ry (rek′tə-rė) *n.* a parsonage.

rec′tum (rek′təm) *n.* the terminal section of the intestine.

---

rectum
↔ From the same root as *right*. The anatomical sense is from the Latin phrase *rectum intestinum*, straight intestine, as contrasted with the convolutions of the small intestine.

---

re·cum′bent (ri-kum′bənt) *adj.* leaning, reclining. —**re·cum′ben·cy,** *n.*

re·cu′per·ate″ (ri-kū′pə-rāt″) *v.i.* **1,** recover health. **2,** recover from pecuniary loss. —*v.t.* regain. —**re·cu″per·a′tion,** *n.* —**re·cu′per·a·tive,** *adj.*

re·cur′ (ri-kẽr′) *v.i.* [**-curred′, -cur′ring**]

---

appear again; return. —**re·cur'rence,** *n.*
—**re·cur'rent,** *adj.*

re·cu'sal (ri-kyoo'zəl) *n.* the disqualification of a judge from a lawsuit, usu. because of conflict of interest.

rec'u·sant (rek'yə-zənt) *n. & adj.* (one who is) obstinate in refusal to comply. —**rec'u·san·cy** (-zən-sè) *n.*

re·cy'cle *v.t.* reuse, esp. by reducing to component parts or materials. —**re·cy'cla·ble** (-sī'klə-bəl) *adj.*

red *n.* **1,** a bright color, the color of fresh blood; any dark shade of this color, as crimson, scarlet, etc. **2,** a radical; specif., a communist. —*adj.* **[red'der, -dest]** of this color. —**red'dish,** *adj.* —**red'ness,** *n.* —**Red Cross,** an organization that helps victims of war and disaster. —**red flag,** a signal of danger. —**red hat,** (*Informal*) a Rom. Cath. cardinal. —**red herring,** a false, diversionary clue. —**red light,** a signal to stop. —**red light district,** one where brothels are located. —**red man,** (*sometimes offensive*) a No. Amer. Indian. —**red pepper, 1,** cayenne pepper. **2,** the sweet pepper. —**red shift,** a shift in the spectrum toward longer wavelengths, sometimes caused by the Doppler effect. —**red tape,** excessive and tedious adherence to form and routine. —**red tide,** seawater colored red by presence of large quantities of an organism fatal to certain marine life.

re·dact' (ri-dakt') *v.t.* edit. —**re·dac'-tion,** *n.*

red-'blood"ed *adj.* vigorous.

red'breast" *n.* a robin.

red'cap" *n.* a porter in a railroad station.

red'coat" *n.* (*Hist.*) a Brit. soldier.

red'den (red'ən) *v.t. & i.* make or become red; blush.

re·deem' (ri-dēm') *v.t.* **1,** buy back; pay off (a loan or debt). **2,** liberate from captivity or obligation by paying ransom. **3,** perform or fulfill a promise. **4,** atone for; compensate for. —**re·deem'a·ble,** *adj.*

re·deem'er *n.* one who ransoms or atones for another; (*cap.*) Jesus Christ.

re·demp'tion (ri-dem'shən) *n.* act or result of redeeming; salvation. —**re·demp'-tive,** *adj.*

red-'eye" *n.* (*Informal*) an overnight commercial airline flight leaving late at night and arriving early the next morning.

red'hand"ed *adj.* overtly guilty.

red'head" *n.* a person with red hair. —**red'head"ed,** *adj.*

red-'hot" *adj.* **1,** very hot; intense. **2,** very new; affording unusual opportunity.

red'in·gote" (red'ing-gōt") *n.* a long, double-breasted overcoat, now worn only by women.

re"di·rect' *adj.* (*Law*) designating the examination of a witness by the party calling him or her, after cross-examination. —*v.t.* direct again.

re·dis'trict *v.t.* divide again into districts.

red-'let"ter *adj.* memorable; auspicious.

red'lin"ing *n.* **1,** the practice of banks and insurance companies of designating certain areas, esp. ghetto areas, as bad risks. **2,** the printing of added or revised text in a special manner to distinguish it from unchanged text. —**red'line",** *v.t.*

red'neck" *n.* (*Derog.*) a reactionary, often bigoted, person, esp. from the rural working class.

red'o·lent (red'ə-lənt) *adj.* having or diffusing a sweet (or, sometimes, offensive) scent; fragrant. —**red'o·lence,** *n.*

re·dou'ble *v.t. & i.* **1,** double again. **2,** increase greatly. **3,** echo.

re·doubt' (ri-dowt') *n.* a small fort.

re·doubt'a·ble (ri-dow'tə-bəl) *adj.* causing dread or respect; formidable.

re·dound' (ri-downd') *v.t.* **1,** roll or flow back. **2,** accrue.

re·dress' (ri-dress') *v.t.* set right; remedy. —*n.* (rē'dres") relief; atonement; compensation.

red'shirt" *v.t.* to delay the acceptance of (a player) to a college sports team to extend the player's period of eligibility. —**red'shirt"ing,** *n.*

red'skin" *n.* (*sometimes offensive*) an Amer. Indian. Also, **red man.**

re·duce' (ri-doos') *v.t.* **1,** bring down; diminish in size, quantity, or value. **2,** weaken; degrade. **3,** bring to any specified state, condition, or form. **4,** subdue; raze. —*v.i.* (*Informal*) make oneself less fat, esp. by diet. —**re·duc'tion** (ri-duk'shən) *n.*

re·duc'ti·o ad ab·sur'dum (ri-duk'shè-ō ad ab-sēr'dəm) (*Lat.*) reduction to absurdity.

re·dun'dant (ri-dun'dənt) *adj.* **1,** superfluous; esp., using more words than are needed. **2,** serving as a backup for a system. —**re·dun'dan·cy,** *n.*

red'wood" *n.* a sequoia.

reed (rēd) *n.* **1,** any tall, broad-leaved grass growing near water, or its hollow or pulp-filled stem. **2,** a musical pipe; reed instrument. **3,** (*Music*) a thin, vibratory reed tongue used in a mouthpiece. —**reed'y,** *adj.*

reef (rēf) *n.* **1,** a low rocky or sandy ridge

near the water line; a shoal; a sand bar. **2,** (*Naut.*) a part of a sail that can be rolled up. —*v.t.* roll up. —**reef knot,** a square knot.

reef′er *n.* **1,** a short outer coat. **2,** (*Slang*) a marijuana cigarette.

reek (rēk) *v.t.* **1,** give off an offensive odor. **2,** be full of something offensive. —*n.* an offensive odor.

reel (rēl) *n.* **1,** any of various revolving devices for winding yarn, fishing lines, etc. **2,** a spool of motion-picture film. **3,** a lively dance. **4,** a staggering motion; a sensation of dizziness. —*v.t.* **1,** wind upon a reel. **2,** (with *off*) utter fluently and rapidly. **3,** (with *in*) draw in with a reel. —*v.i.* **1,** whirl. **2,** stagger. —**reel-to-reel,** *adj.* of a tape recorder that passes tape from one reel to another; opposed to cassette.

re·en′try *n.* a return, as of a spacecraft into the earth's atmosphere.

reeve (rēv) *v.t.* (*Naut.*) pass the end of a rope through a hole, as in a block. —*n.* **1,** a bird, the female of the ruff. **2,** a sheriff, bailiff, or similar officer.

re·fec′tion (ri-fek′shən) *n.* refreshment; a repast.

re·fec′to·ry (ri-fek′tə-rē) *n.* a dining room.

re·fer′ (ri-fēr′) *v.t.* [**re·ferred′, -fer′ring**] **1,** submit (to another person of authority) for consideration and decision. **2,** direct (someone to another person or source). **3,** assign. —*v.i.* (with *to*) **1,** relate. **2,** have recourse; appeal. **3,** allude; direct the attention. —**re·fer′ral,** *n.* ❑ *allude*

ref·er·ee′ (ref″ə-rē′) *n.* a person deputed to settle a matter in dispute; an umpire. —*v.t. & i.* arbitrate. Also, *Informal,* **ref.**

ref′er·ence (ref′ə-rəns) *n.* **1,** act of referring; consultation. **2,** a casual mention. **3,** a written recommendation. **4,** a citation. —**reference book,** a book of systematically arranged information. —**re·fer′ent** (rə-fēr′ənt) *adj.*

ref″er·en′dum (ref″ə-ren′dəm) *n.* a popular vote; plebiscite.

re·fill′ (rē-fil′) *v.t.* fill again. —*n.* (rē′fil″) a supply to replace one used or worn out.

re·fine′ (ri-fīn′) *v.t.* **1,** bring or reduce to a pure state. **2,** give culture to; polish. —**re·fined′,** *adj.* cultivated; pure.

re·fine′ment (-mənt) *n.* **1,** act of refining; cultivation. **2,** elegance.

re·fin′er (ri-fīn′ər) *n.* a person or establishment that makes gasoline from petroleum, sugar from cane, etc. —**re·fin′er·y,** *n.* a refiner's factory.

re·flect′ (ri-flekt′) *v.t.* **1,** throw back, as

rays of light or heat after they strike a surface. **2,** present an image of; mirror. **3,** bring about. **4,** ponder. —*v.i.* **1,** throw back rays, etc. **2,** meditate. **3,** (with *on*) bring reproach or blame.

re·flec′tion (ri-flek′shən) *n.* **1,** act or result of reflecting. **2,** an image, as in a mirror. **3,** meditation. **4,** comment. **5,** an unfavorable remark; slur. Also, **re·flex′ion.**

re·flec′tive (ri-flek′tiv) *adj.* **1,** reflecting. **2,** being, or pert. to, reflection.

re·flec′tor (ri-flek′tər) *n.* **1,** a part for reflecting light. **2,** a reflecting telescope.

re′flex (rē′fleks) *n.* an involuntary action of the nervous system in response to some stimulus. —*adj.* **1,** pert. to such an action. **2,** cast, bent, or turned back. —*v.t.* (ri-fleks′) bend or turn back. —**reflex camera,** a camera in which viewing is accomplished by means of a ground glass screen upon which the image focused by the lens is reflected by a mirror.

re·flex′ive (ri-flek′siv) *adj.* (*Gram.*) denoting action upon the subject, as in *he wrongs himself.*

re″flex·ol′o·gy (rē″fleks-ol′ə-jē) *n.* a type of massage concentrating on the feet to reduce tension.

re′flux″ (rē′fluks″) *n.* a flowing back, as of a tide; ebb.

re·for′est (rē-fôr′əst) *v.t.* replant with trees. —**re″for·es·ta′tion,** *n.*

re·form′ (ri-fôrm′) *v.t.* **1,** make over; change, esp. to a better state; improve. **2,** cause (a person) to abandon evil ways. —*v.i.* abandon evil ways. —*n.* **1,** change or improvement, esp. in social institutions. **2,** betterment of conduct. —**re·form′er,** *n.* one who urges betterment of conditions or morals. —**reform school,** a reformatory.

re-″form′ (rē-″fôrm′) *v.t. & i.* **1,** form again; reconstruct. **2,** make different in shape or form.

ref″or·ma′tion (ref″ər-mā′shən) *n.* **1,** a change for the better. **2,** (*cap.*) the 16th-c. movement that led to the formation of Protestant churches.

re·form′a·to·ry (ri-fôr′mə-tôr-ē) *n.* a place of detention for juvenile criminals.

re·fract′ (ri-frakt′) *v.t.* bend abruptly; esp., deflect a ray of light. —**re·frac′tive,** *adj.*

re·frac′tion (ri-frak′shən) *n.* an oblique direction given a ray of heat, light, or sound, passing into a different medium or through a medium of varying density.

re·frac′to·ry (ri-frak′tə-rē) *adj.* **1,** unmanageable; unyielding. **2,** resistant.

re·frain′ (ri-frān′) *v.i.* hold oneself back;

abstain; forbear. —*n.* something repeated, esp. a phrase or verse in a poem or song; a chorus.

> **refrain**
> ↔ The noun and verb senses are un-related. The noun comes from Provençal *refranh*, from Latin *re-fringere*, break off. The verb is also of Latin origin, from *refrenare*, hold back.

re·fran'gi·ble (ri-fran'jə-bəl) *adj.* capa-ble of being refracted. —**re·fran"gi·bil'i·ty,** *n.*

re·fresh' (ri-fresh') *v.t.* make fresh again; invigorate; stimulate. —*v.i.* become fresh.

re·fresh'er (-ər)' *adj.* serving as a review of a subject already studied. —*n.* some-thing that refreshes.

re·fresh'ment (-mənt) *n.* **1,** act or result of refreshing. **2,** (*pl.*) a light meal served at a party.

re·frig'er·ant (ri-frij'ər-ənt) *n. & adj.* a substance that causes cooling.

re·frig'er·ate" (ri-frij'ə-rāt") *v.t.* make cold; freeze (food or liquids). —**re·frig"er·a'tion,** *n.*

re·frig'er·a"tor (ri-frij'ə-rā"tər) *n.* a cabi-net for cold storage.

re"fu'el *v.t. & i.* supply or take in fresh fuel.

ref'uge (ref'ūj) *n.* a shelter or protection from danger or distress; an asylum.

ref"u·gee' (ref"ū-jē') *n.* one who flees for safety.

re·ful'gence (rė-ful'jəns) *n.* brilliant light; splendor. —**re·ful'gent,** *adj.*

re·fund' (rė-fund') *v.t.* **1,** pay back. **2,** (rē"-) refinance, as by a new bond issue. —*n.* (rē'fund") a repayment.

re·fur'bish *v.t.* clean and polish; renovate.

re·fus'al (ri-fūz'əl) *n.* **1,** act or result of refusing. **2,** first option (to buy, sell, etc.).

re·fuse' (ri-fūz') *v.t. & i.* **1,** decline to do or grant; deny. **2,** decline to accept; reject.

ref'use (ref'ūs) *n.* garbage; rubbish.

ref"u·ta'tion (ref"ū-tā'shən) *n.* act or re-sult of refuting; that which refutes.

re·fute' (ri-fūt') *v.t.* defeat by argument or proof; disprove.

re·gain' (ri-gān') *v.t.* **1,** get again; re-cover. **2,** get back to; reach again.

re·gal (rē'gəl) *adj.* royal; majestic. —**re·gal'i·ty** (ri-gal'ə-tē) *n.*

re·gale' (ri-gāl') *v.t. & i.* entertain sump-tuously; divert; feast. —**re·gale'ment,** *n.* ❏ *gallant*

re·ga'li·a (ri-gā'lē-ə) *n.pl.* **1,** emblems; in-signia. **2,** personal finery. ❏ *regale*

> **regale, regalia**
> ↔ These two very similar words have different origins. *Regale* comes from Old French *rigale*, making merry. *Re-galia* is from Medieval Latin *regalia*, kingly trappings.

re·gard' (ri-gärd') *v.t.* **1,** look upon; ob-serve; consider. **2,** have a particular atti-tude toward; esteem. **3,** have relation to; concern. —*n.* **1,** reference; respect. **2,** a particular feeling, esp. of respect. **3,** scru-tiny. **4,** concern; interest. —**re·gard'ful,** *adj.* thoughtful; attentive. —**re·gard'ing,** *prep.* in reference to; concerning.

re·gard'less *adj.* indifferent; not caring. —*adv.* notwithstanding.

re·gat'ta (ri-gä'tə) *n.* a boat race, esp. of yachts.

re'gen·cy (rē'jən-sē) *n.* **1,** a board of re-gents. **2,** state of being a regent. **3,** govern-ment by a regent. **4,** a style of furniture and interior decoration.

re·gen'er·ate" (rė-jen'ər-āt") *v.t.* **1,** make over completely; reform thoroughly. **2,** bring into existence again. **3,** (*Electricity*) amplify the input by part of the output. —*v.i.* be formed again or improved. —*adj.* (-ət) reformed. —**re"gen·er·a'tion,** *n.* —**re·gen'er·a·tive,** *adj.*

re'gent (rē'jənt) *n.* **1,** one who governs when the legitimate ruler cannot. **2,** one of a board governing education, a col-lege, etc.

reg'gae (reg'ā) *n.* a style of Jamaican popular music.

reg'i·cide" (rej'ə-sīd") *n.* the killing or killer of a king. —**reg"i·ci'dal,** *adj.*

re·gime' (rā-zhēm') *n.* **1,** the mode, sys-tem, style, or rule of management or gov-ernment. **2,** regimen. ❏ *government*

reg'i·men (rej'ə-mən) *n.* a system of reg-ulation or remedy.

reg'i·ment (rej'ə-mənt) *n.* a body of sol-diers, usu. two or three battalions com-manded by a colonel. —*v.t.* systematize; bring under strict and uniform control. —**reg"i·men'tal,** *adj.* pert. to a regiment. —**reg"i·men'tals,** *n.pl.* military dress. —**reg"i·men·ta'tion,** *n.* act or effect of regimenting.

re'gion (rē'jən) *n.* **1,** a large area of in-definite extent; a country. **2,** a district; sec-tion. **3,** a sphere or realm. —**re'gion·al,** *adj.* —**re'gion·al·ism,** *n.*

reg'is·ter (rej'is-tər) *n.* **1,** an official writ-ten record; a record book; a recording de-vice. **2,** (*Music*) a part or all of the compass or range of a voice or instrument. **3,** a device for regulating the passage of heat or air. **4,** in printing, exact adjustment of position. **5,** a recording office. —*v.t.* **1,** enter in a register; record. **2,** mark or indicate on a scale. **3,** demonstrate (some kind of emotion). **4,** insure delivery of (a letter). —*v.i.* **1,** cause one's name to be recorded. **2,** place printing type or plates in proper position. **3,** (*Informal*) create an impression. —**registered nurse,** a graduate trained nurse licensed by a state authority.

reg′is·trar″ (rej′is-trär″) *n.* a recording officer.

reg″is·tra′tion (rej″is-trā′shən) *n.* **1,** act of registering or being registered. **2,** the number of persons registered. **3,** in organ and harpsichord playing, the stops used for a particular work or passage.

reg′is·try (rej′is-trė) *n.* act or place of recording.

reg′nal (reg′nəl) *adj.* of or pert. to a reign or reigning.

reg′nant (reg′nənt) *adj.* reigning.

re′gress (rē′gres) *n.* passage back; return. —*v.i.* (ri-gres′) go back; retrogress. —**re·gres′sion** (ri-gresh′ən) *n.* —**re·gres′sive** (ri-gres′iv) *adj.*

re·gret′ (ri-gret′) *v.t.* **1,** look back at with sorrow; lament. **2,** be distressed on account of; rue. —*n.* **1,** grief; a painful sense of loss. **2,** (*pl.*) an oral or written message note declining an invitation. —**re·gret′ful,** *adj.*

re·group′ *v.i. & t.* form again into groups.

reg′u·lar (reg′yə-lər) *adj.* **1,** conforming to a rule, law, type, prescribed mode, customary form, or design; normal; customary. **2,** steady; rhythmical. **3,** (*Mil.*) professional. **4,** (*Informal*) thorough; sportsmanlike. —**reg″u·lar′i·ty** (-lar′ə-tė) *n.*

reg′u·late″ (reg′yə-lāt″) *v.t.* **1,** direct or govern by rule. **2,** put or keep in good order. **3,** adjust (an instrument, as a clock). —**reg″u·la′tion,** *n.* —**reg′u·la″tor,** *n.*

re·gur′gi·tate″ (rė-gêr′ji-tāt″) *v.t. & i.* **1,** bring back (specif., food from the stomach). **2,** (*Slang*) recite from memory. —**re·gur″gi·ta′tion,** *n.*

re″ha·bil′i·tate″ (rē″hə-bil′ə-tāt″) *v.t.* restore to good condition or respectable position. —**re″ha·bil″i·ta′tion,** *n.* Also, (*Informal*) **re′hab″.**

re′hash (rē′hash) *n.* something made over but with nothing new in substance.

—*v.t.* (rė-hash′) **1,** make into a different form. **2,** go over again, as an argument.

re·hearse′ (ri-hērs′) *v.t.* **1,** practice (as a play) for a public performance. **2,** repeat. **3,** enumerate. —*v.i.* perform for practice. —**re·hears′al,** *n.* ❑ *hearse*

rehearse
↔ From Old French *herce*, harrow. To *rehearse* was to rake over, hence, repeat.

Reich (rīkh) *n.* (Ger., kingdom) Germany; the German state.

reign (rān) *n.* **1,** sovereignty; royal or supreme power. **2,** the time during which a sovereign rules. —*v.i.* rule.

reign, rein, reindeer
☞ Do not confuse *reign*, rule, with *rein*, restraint. ↔ Both words are of Latin origin and have nothing to do with *reindeer*, which is a compound of two Old Norse words, *hreinn* and *dyr*, meaning "reindeer animal."

re″im·burse′ (rē″im-bērs′) *v.t.* pay back; restore; refund. —**re″im·burse′ment,** *n.*

rein (rān) *n.* **1,** a long strap attached to a bridle, by which the rider or driver controls a horse. **2,** (usually *pl.*) any means of restraint or control. —*v.t.* restrain. ❑ *reign*

re″in·car′nate *v.t.* endow a spirit with a new or different body.

re″in·car·na′tion *n.* **1,** a rebirth in a new embodiment. **2,** the belief that souls are reborn.

rein′deer″ (rān′dir″) *n.* a deer used as a draft animal in Arctic regions. ❑ *reign*

re″in·force′ (rē″in-fôrs′) *v.t.* strengthen by supplying additional men, materials, support, etc. Also, **re″en·force′.**

re″in·force′ment (-mənt) *n.* **1,** act or effect of reinforcing. **2,** that which reinforces; (*Mil.*, often *pl.*) new troops, ships, etc.

re″in·state′ (rē″in-stāt′) *v.t.* restore to a former position. —**re″in·state′ment,** *n.*

re·it′er·ate″ *v.t.* repeat; iterate. —**re·it″er·a′tion,** *n.*

re·ject′ (ri-jekt′) *v.t.* **1,** throw away as useless; discard. **2,** refuse to accept; decline. **3,** refuse to grant; deny. —*n.* (rē′jekt) **1,** an imperfect article; a second. **2,** something rejected. —**re·jec′tion,** *n.*

re·joice′ (ri-jois′) *v.i. & t.* feel joy and gladness; exult; gladden.

re·join′ (ri-join′) *v.t. & i.* **1,** answer. **2,** (rē″join′) unite or join again.

re·join′der (-dər) *n.* a reply.

re·ju've·nate" (ri-joo'və-nāt") *v.t.* make youthful; renew; refresh. **—re·ju've·na'-tion,** *n.*

re·ju've·nes'cence (ri-joo"və-nes'əns) *n.* a renewal of the appearance, powers, or feeling of youth. **—re·ju've·nes'cent,** *adj.*

re·lapse' (ri-laps') *v.i.* slip back into a former state, as illness or evil ways. *—n.* (rē'laps") a recurrence of illness; a backsliding.

re·late' (ri-lāt')· *v.t.* **1,** connect with (something else). **2,** tell; narrate. **3,** ally by kinship. *—v.i.* have reference, kinship, or connection with something. **—re·lat'ed,** *adj.* associated; connected; akin.

re·la'tion (ri-lā'shən) *n:* **1,** narration; a narrative. **2,** kinship; a kinsman. **3,** (*pl.*) affairs; dealings. **4,** bearing; close connection. **5,** reference. **6,** proportion; ratio. **—re·la'tion·ship,** *n.*

rel'a·tive (rel'ə-tiv) *adj.* **1,** having bearing on something; close in connection. **2,** belonging to or respecting something else. **3,** comparative, not absolute. **4,** (*Gram.*) referring to an antecedent. *—n.* a person connected by blood or affinity. **—rel'a·ti·vis'tic,** *adj.* **—relative humidity,** the ratio of the water vapor in the atmosphere to the amount required to saturate it.

rel"a·tiv'i·ty (rel"ə-tiv'ə-tē) *n.* **1,** quality or state of being connected with; interdependence. **2,** a theory in physics (the Einstein theory) that motion, time, space, etc., are not absolute; that time is a dimension; etc.

re·lax' (ri-laks') *v.t. & i.* make or become less tense, severe, assiduous, or the like; slacken; ease; unbend. **—re·lax'ant** (-ənt) *n. & adj.* **—re"lax·a'tion** (rē"-) *n.*

> **relax, relish**
> ↔ Oddly enough, these two words both come from Latin *relaxare*, to loosen. *Relish* came via Old French *relais*, remainder.

re'lay (rē'lā) *n.* **1,** a fresh supply of men or animals held in readiness; a shift. **2,** a race among teams of successive runners. *—v.t.* send by a series of messengers or media.

re·lease' (ri-lēs') *v.t.* **1,** set free; unfasten. **2,** free from pain, obligation, penalty, etc. **3,** let be shown or sold, as a motion picture or book. *—n.* **1,** liberation, as from prison. **2,** discharge or freedom from any burden. **3,** a news item, motion picture, etc., made available for publication. **4,** a surrender of a claim.

rel'e·gate" (rel'ə-gāt") *v.t.* send away or out of the way; consign. **—rel"e·ga'tion,** *n.*

re·lent' (ri-lent') *v.i.* become less obdurate; feel compassion; soften; yield. **—re·lent'less,** *adj.* ever harsh or pressing.

rel'e·vant (rel'ə-vənt) *adj.* concerning the case in question; pertinent; applicable. **—rel'e·vance,** *n.*

re·li'a·ble (ri-lī'ə-bəl) *adj.* dependable; trustworthy. **—re·li"a·bil'i·ty,** *n.*

re·li'ance (ri-lī'əns) *n.* confidence; trust. **—re·li'ant,** *adj.*

rel'ic (rel'ik) *n.* **1,** that which remains after decay of the rest. **2,** a memento held in religious veneration. **3,** (*pl.*) remains.

rel'ict (rel'ikt) *n.* a widower or, esp., a widow.

re·lief' (ri-lēf') *n.* **1,** the act of relieving; alleviation; comfort. **2,** that ·which removes or lessens pain, want, etc. **3,** assistance given to the poor. **4,** release from a post of duty by a substitute; the substitute. **5,** the projection of a figure from a plane surface.

re·lieve' (ri-lēv') *v.t.* **1,** remove or lessen anything that weighs down or pains; alleviate. **2,** free from pain, want, anxiety, etc.; comfort. **3,** substitute for. **4,** heighten the effect or interest of, by contrast or variety. **5,** remove (an officer, etc.) from a post of duty.

re·li'gion (ri-lij'ən) *n.* **1,** a system of faith in and worship of a deity. **2,** devoutness; dedication to a holy life. **3,** a doctrine or custom accepted on faith.

re·lig"i·os'i·ty (ri-lij"ē-os'ə-tē) *n.* excessive or affected religiousness; religious sentimentality.

re·li'gious (ri-lij'əs) *adj.* **1,** pert. to a religion. **2,** devout. **3,** conscientious; diligent. *—n.* a monk or nun.

re·lin'quish (ri-ling'kwish) *v.t.* give up; desist from; quit; surrender. **—re·lin'-quish·ment,** *n.*

rel'i·quar"y (rel'ə-kwär"ē) *n.* a repository for relics.

rel'ish *v.t.* be pleased with; enjoy; esp., eat with pleasure. *—n.* **1,** a pleasing taste; flavor. **2,** appreciation; gusto. **3,** an appetizer. ❑ *relax*

re·live' (rē-liv') *v.t.* live or experience again.

re·lle'no (rə-yā'nō) *adj.* (*Sp.*) stuffed: *chili relleno.*

re·lo'cate *v.t. & i.* move. **—re"lo·ca'tion,** *n.*

> **reluctant, reticent**
> ☛ Both words indicate unwillingness. *Reluctant* means unwilling to act; *reticent* means unwilling to speak.

re·luc′tant (ri-luk′tənt) *adj.* acting or doing with positive disinclination; unwilling. —**re·luc′tance,** *n.*

re·ly′ (ri-lī′) *v.i.* (with *on*) have confidence; trust; depend.

REM *abbr.* rapid eye movement.

rem *n.* a measure of radiation.

re·main′ (ri-mān′) *v.i.* **1,** continue in a place; stay. **2,** continue in a specified state without change. **3,** endure; last. **4,** be left after something has been taken away. **5,** be held in reserve. —*n.* (*pl.*) that which is left; a dead body; relics. ❑ *manor*

re·main′der (-dər) *n.* **1,** anything left after the removal of a part. **2,** a surplus. **3,** (*Math.*) the sum left after subtraction, or left over after division. —*v.t.* sell leftover stock at a loss.

re·mand′ (ri-mand′) *v.t.* send, call, or order back.

re·mark′ (ri-märk′) *v.t. & i.* **1,** note in the mind; observe. **2,** express by way of comment. —*n.* a casual statement.

re·mark′a·ble *adj.* worthy of notice; extraordinary.

re·me′di·al (ri-mē′dē-əl) *adj.* serving to cure or correct.

rem′e·dy (rem′ə-dē) *n.* **1,** any treatment that cures a disease. **2,** anything that corrects or counteracts an evil. **3,** (*Law*) redress. —*v.t.* **1,** cure; heal. **2,** remove something evil from; counteract; redress. —**re·me′di·a·ble** (rə-mē′dē-ə-bəl) *adj.*

re·mem′ber (ri-mem′bər) *v.t.* **1,** retain in the mind; recall; recollect. **2,** observe, as an anniversary. **3,** acknowledge (some service) with money; tip. **4,** (with *to*) convey regards from someone (to someone). —*v.i.* utilize the memory.

re·mem′brance (ri-mem′brəns) *n.* **1,** act of remembering; something remembered. **2,** memory. **3,** a souvenir; a greeting card, gift, etc. —**Remembrance Day,** a legal holiday in Canada, Nov. 11.

re·mem′bran·cer (ri-mem′brən-sər) *n.* one who or that which reminds; a reminder.

re·mind′ (ri-mīnd′) *v.t.* put in mind; recall to the memory or notice of. —**re·mind′ful,** *adj.* reminiscent.

rem″i·nisce′ (rem″ə-nis′) *v.t.* recall the past to mind.

rem″i·nis′cence (rem″ə-nis′əns) *n.* **1,** recollection. **2,** something remembered, esp. nostalgically. —**rem″i·nis′cent,** *adj.*

re·mise′ (ri-mīz′) *n.* (*Law*) a surrender or release, as of a claim. —*v.t.* release.

re·miss′ (ri-mis′) *adj.* negligent; dilatory. —**re·miss′ness,** *n.*

re·mis′sion (ri-mish′ən) *n.* **1,** a giving up or discharge, as of a debt. **2,** the act of forgiving; pardon. **3,** abatement.

re·mit′ (ri-mit′) *v.t.* [**re·mit′ted, -ting**] **1,** pardon; forgive. **2,** refrain from enacting. **3,** make less intense or violent; slacken. **4,** restore; replace. **5,** send in payment for goods received. **6,** (*Law*) transfer (a case) to a lower court. —*v.i.* **1,** abate. **2,** send payment. —**re·mit′tal,** *n.*

re·mit′tance (ri-mit′əns) *n.* money sent. —**remittance man,** an exile living on remittances from home.

re·mit′tent (ri-mit′ənt) *adj.* temporarily abating; esp. of a disease the symptoms of which diminish considerably but never disappear entirely. —*n.* a remittent fever.

rem′nant (rem′nənt) *n.* **1,** a small remainder; a remainder of a bolt of cloth, ribbon, etc. **2,** a last trace; vestige.

re·mod′el *v.t.* make over; reform; recondition.

re·mon′strance (ri-mon′strəns) *n.* an objection; protest.

re·mon′strate (ri-mon′strāt) *v.i.* present strong reasons against something; object; protest. —**re″mon·stra′tion** (rī″mən-strā′-shən) *n.* —**re·mon′stra·tive″,** *adj.*

rem′o·ra (rem′ə-rə) *n.* a parasitical marine fish.

re·morse′ (ri-môrs′) *n.* self-accusatory regret. —**re·morse′ful,** *adj.* regretful and conscious of guilt. —**re·morse′less,** *adj.* relentless.

re·mote′ (ri-mōt′) *adj.* **1,** far away; distant; not closely connected. **2,** alien; foreign. **3,** slight; inconsiderable. —**re·mote′ness,** *n.* —**remote control,** a device for controlling something (as a television set) from a distance.

re·mount′ *v.t. & i.* mount again, as a horse, picture, etc. —*n.* a fresh horse.

re·mov′a·ble (ri-moov′ə-bəl) *adj.* not fixed. —*n.* (usu. *pl.*) furniture and loose possessions.

re·move′ (ri-moov′) *v.t.* **1,** change from one place to another; transfer; move. **2,** displace, as from an office. **3,** destroy. —*v.i.* transfer from one residence, place, etc., to another. —*n.* **1,** change of place. **2,** interval; distance. —**re·mov′al,** *n.*

re·mu′ner·ate (ri-mū′nə-rāt″) *v.t.* pay (a person) for any service, loss, or expense; recompense. —**re·mu″ner·a′tion,** *n.* —**re·mu′ner·a·tive,** *adj.* profitable.

ren″ais·sance′ (ren″ə-säns′) *n. & adj.* a new emergence or revival, specif. (*cap.*) of art and literature after the Dark Ages.

re′nal (rē′nəl) *adj.* pert. to the kidneys.

re·nas'cence (ri-nas'əns) *n.* a rebirth; renaissance. —**re·nas'cent,** *adj.*

ren·coun'ter (ren-kown'tər) *n.* **1,** a combat or engagement. **2,** a contest; debate. **3,** a casual meeting. Also, **ren·con'tre** (-kän'tər). —*v.* meet; encounter.

rend *v.t. & i.* [*pret. & p.p.* **rent**] tear apart violently; split.

ren'der (ren'dər) *v.t.* **1,** cause to be or become. **2,** afford for use or benefit; present. **3,** give or pay back; return. **4,** translate. **5,** reproduce; represent, as a part in a play. **6,** reduce; melt; clarify by frying.

ren'dez·vous" (rän'dā-voo") *n.* [*pl.* **-vous"** (-vooz")] **1,** a place of meeting. **2,** an appointment. —*v. t. & i.* assemble.

ren·di'tion (ren-dish'ən) *n.* the act of rendering; a translation; interpretation; performance.

ren'e·gade" (ren'ə-gād") *n.* one who deserts his or her faith, cause, party, etc.; a turncoat; a traitor.

re·nege' (ri-nig') *v.i.* **1,** in card-playing, deviate from rule, esp. by revoking. **2,** (*Informal*) back down. —*n.* a reneging.

re·new' (ri-nū') *v.t.* **1,** make fresh or vigorous again. **2,** make again; reaffirm, as a promise. **3,** replenish. **4,** grant again; extend the term of. —**re·new'al,** *n.* act or effect of renewing; extension of a contract.

ren·i- (ren-i; rē-ni) *pref.* kidney.

ren'net (ren'it) *n.* **1,** the fourth stomach of a calf. **2,** a substance derived from this stomach, used to curdle milk; rennin.

ren'nin (ren'in) *n.* a substance that coagulates milk; rennet.

re·nounce' (ri-nowns') *v.t. & i.* refuse to acknowledge; abandon. —**re·nounce'ment,** *n.*

ren'o·vate" (ren'ə-vāt") *v.t.* restore to freshness or new condition. —**ren"o·va'-tion,** *n.* —**ren'o·va"tor,** *n.*

re·nown' (ri-nown') *n.* a great reputation for achievements; fame. —**re·nowned'** (-nownd') *adj.* famous.

rent *n.* **1,** payment for the use of property. **2,** an opening made by tearing; a separation. —*adj.* torn. —*v.t.* **1,** let; grant the use of, for payment. **2,** hire. —*v.i.* be leased or let out. —*v.* pret. & p.p. of *rend.* —**rent strike,** refusal by tenants to pay rent.

rent'al (ren'təl) *n.* **1,** the rate paid as rent. **2,** income from rented property. —*adj.* pert. to rent.

re·nun"ci·a'tion (ri-nun"sē-ā'shən) *n.* act of renouncing, esp. as a voluntary sacrifice. —**re·nun'ci·a·to"ry** (-sē-ə-tôr'ē) *adj.*

re·or'gan·ize" *v.t. & i.* organize again or in a new way, esp. of a business or corporation, —**re·or"gan·i·za'tion,** *n.*

rep *n.* **1,** a corded fabric. **2,** (*Slang*) reputation. **3,** (*Informal*) representative.

re·pair' (ri-pār') *v.i.* go to a specified place. —*v.t.* **1,** restore to good condition. **2,** make amends for; make good. —*n.* **1,** act of restoring to good condition. **2,** good condition. —**re·pair'man"** [*pl.* **-men**] *n..*

rep'a·ra·ble (rep'ə-rə-bəl) *adj.* capable of being repaired.

rep"a·ra'tion (rep"ə-rā'shən) *n.* the act of making amends; (*pl.*) compensation for damage.

rep"ar·tee' (rep"ər-tē') *n.* a ready, pertinent, and witty reply; an exchange of such replies.

re·past' (ri-pàst') *n.* a meal.

re·pa'tri·ate" (rē-pā'trē-āt") *v.t. & i.* **1,** restore to one's own country. **2,** restore to citizenship. —**re·pa"tri·a'tion,** *n.*

re·pay' (rē-pā') *v.t.* **1,** pay back; refund. **2,** requite; return, as a visit. —**re·pay'-ment,** *n.*

re·peal' (rē-pēl') *v.t.* recall or annul (a law); revoke; abrogate. —*n.* act of repealing; esp. (U.S., often *cap.*) the 21st Amendment, repealing the 18th (Prohibition) Amendment.

re·peat' (rē-pēt') *v.t.* **1,** do, make, or perform again. **2,** say again; reiterate. **3,** say over from memory; recite. —*v.i.* **1,** say or do as before. **2,** vote more than once for one candidate at one election. —*n.* (*Music*) a sign (:) that a passage is to be repeated. —**re·peat'ed,** *adj.* frequent.

re·peat'er *n.* **1,** one who repeats. **2,** a watch that strikes. **3,** an automatic firearm.

re·pel' (ri-pel') *v.t.* [**re·pelled', -pel'ling**] **1,** drive back; force to return; check the advance of. **2,** resist; oppose; reject. **3,** arouse repulsion in; disgust. —*v.i.* be disgusting. —**re·pel'lence,** *n.* —**re·pel'lent,** *adj.*

re·pent' (ri-pent') *v.i. & t.* regret, grieve for, or do penance for (a sin or crime). —**re·pent'ance,** *n.* —**re·pent'ant,** *adj.*

re"per·cus'sion (rē"pər-kush'ən) *n.* **1,** the reaction to, or result of, an action. **2,** a rebounding; echo. —**re"per·cus'sive,** *adj.*

rep'er·toire" (rep'ər-twär") *n.* a list of the works a performer or company can perform.

rep'er·to·ry (rep'ər-tôr-ē) *n.* **1,** repertoire. **2,** an inventory; a stock. **3,** a storage location. —*adj.* designating a theatrical company performing various plays or operas.

rep″e·ti′tion (rep″ə-tish′ən) *n.* the act or result of repeating. —**re·pet′i·tive** (ri-pet′ə-tiv) *adj.* —**repetitive strain injury,** muscular strain resulting from activities such as typing or playing certain musical instruments. Also, **RSI.**

rep″e·ti′tious (rep″ə-tish′əs) *adj.* characterized by undue or tiresome repetition. —**rep″e·ti′tious·ness,** *n.*

re·pine′ (ri-pīn′) *v.i.* complain; mourn.

re·place′ (ri-plās′) *v.t.* **1,** put back; restore; return. **2,** take the place of. **3,** substitute for.

re·place′ment (-mənt) *n.* **1,** act or effect of replacing. **2,** a substitute.

re·play (rē-plā′) *v.t.* play again. —*n.* (rē′plā″) a playing again.

re·plen′ish (ri-plen′ish) *v.i.* fill again. —**re·plen′ish·ment,** *n.*

re·plete′ (ri-plēt′) *adj.* completely filled; stuffed. —**re·ple′tion,** *n.*

re·plev′in (ri-plev′ən) *n.* (*Law*) the recovery of one's property held by another, subject to later court judgment. —*v.t.* seize by replevin. Also, **re·plev′y** (-ē).

rep′li·ca (rep′li-kə) *n.* an exact copy; a duplicate; esp., an exact copy (of a work of art) made by the original artist.

rep′li·cate (rep′li-kāt) *v.t.* **1,** fold back. **2,** reproduce, esp. by genetic processes. —*n.* (-kit) something replicated.

re·ply′ (ri-plī′) *v.t. & i.* say in answer; respond. —*n.* an answer.

re·port′ (ri-pôrt′) *n.* **1,** a statement of facts or figures ascertained by investigation; an account or accounting. **2,** a rumor. **3,** (*pl.*) a record of court judgments and opinions. **4,** the sound of an explosion. —*v.i.* **1,** serve as a reporter. **2,** present oneself for duty. —*v.t.* **1,** give an account of; relate. **2,** say. —**re·port′ed·ly,** *adv.* —**report card, 1,** a school report giving a student's grades, teachers' comments, etc. **2,** an evaluation of work done, etc. (as of a politician).

re·port′age (rə-pôr′tij) *n.* the act or result of reporting, as of news.

re·port′er *n.* one who reports: a newspaper writer; a court stenographer.

rep″or·tor′i·al (rep″ər-tôr′ē-əl) *adj.* pert. to reporters or their work.

re·pose′ (ri-pōz′) *n.* **1,** a state of rest; sleep. **2,** tranquillity; composure. —*v.i.* **1,** lie at rest; be tranquil. **2,** be situated. **3,** rely. —*v.t.* **1,** lay; place. **2,** set at rest. —**re·pos′al,** *n.* —**re·pose′ful,** *adj.*

re″pos·sess′ (rē″pə-zes′) *v.t.* reclaim, esp. for nonpayment of money due. Also, (*Informal*) **re′po** (rē′pō).

re·pos′i·to·ry (ri-poz′i-tôr-ē) *n.* a place where things are situated or stored.

re″pos·sess′ *v.t.* regain possession of, esp. something leased or sold conditionally. —**re″pos·ses′sion,** *n.*

re·pous·sé (rə-poo-sā′) *adj.* (*Fr.*) of a design, hammered in relief.

rep″re·hend′ (rep″ri-hend′) *v.t.* chide sharply; reprove; censure. —**rep″re·hen′-sion** (-hen′shən) *n.* —**rep″re·hen′sive,** *adj.* censorious.

rep″re·hen′si·ble (rep″ri-hens′ə-bəl) *adj.* highly blameworthy.

rep″re·sent′ (rep″ri-zent′) *v.t.* **1,** portray; depict; describe. **2,** play the role of; impersonate. **3,** denote; symbolize; stand for. **4,** speak and act for; be a substitute for. **5,** set forth; assert. **6,** be composed of; consist in. **7,** be a representative for, as in a legislature.

rep″re·sen·ta′tion (-zen-tā′shən) *n.* **1,** act or result of representing; a portrayal; description. **2,** a statement; a claim; a complaint. **3,** the right to be represented in a governing body. **4,** a delegation.

rep″re·sen′ta·tive (-zen′tə-tiv) *adj.* **1,** serving to represent. **2,** composed of delegates of the people. **3,** typical; characteristic. —*n.* one who or that which represents; an agent, delegate, or substitute; a U.S. congressman, member of the House of Representatives.

re·press′ (ri-pres′) *v.t.* **1,** put down; subdue; crush. **2,** keep under due restraint. —**re·pres′sion** (-presh′ən) *n.* —**re·pres′-sive** (-pres′iv) *adj.*

re·prieve′ (ri-prēv′) *v.t.* **1,** grant a respite to; spare for a time. **2,** suspend or delay the execution of (a criminal). —*n.* a respite.

rep′ri·mand″ (rep′rə-mand″) *v.t.* reprove severely; censure, esp. publicly. —*n.* a severe reproof.

re·print′ *v.t.* print again. —*n.* (rē′print″) a reproduction or new edition of something printed.

re·pris′al (ri-prī′zəl) *n.* any act done in retaliation.

re·prise′ (ri-prēz′) *n.* (*Music*) a repetition of a main theme.

re·proach′ (ri-prōch′) *v.t.* charge with a fault; upbraid. —*n.* **1,** a severe expression of censure. **2,** shame; disgrace. **3,** a cause or object of disgrace. —**re·proach′ful,** *adj.* accusing; expressing blame.

rep′ro·bate″ (rep′rə-bāt″) *n.* one who is

profligate or unprincipled. —*adj.* unprincipled; wicked. —*v.t.* **1,** condemn; censure. **2,** reject. —**rep″ro·ba′tion,** *n.*

re″pro·duce′ *v.t.* **1,** make a copy of; duplicate. **2,** procreate. **3,** produce again. —*v.i.* **1,** beget; generate offspring. **2,** be capable of being copied, as by printing.

re″pro·duc′tion *n.* **1,** act, process, or result of reproducing. **2,** a copy, picture, etc. —**re″pro·duc′tive,** *adj.*

re·prog′ra·phy (rė-prog′rə-fė) *n.* the photocopying of graphic material.

re·proof′ (ri-proof′) *n.* an expression of blame; rebuke.

re·prove′ (ri-proov′) *v.t.* censure; chide. —**re·prov′al,** *n.*

rep′tile (rep′til; -tīl) *n.* **1,** a creeping animal, as the snake, lizard, crocodile, etc. **2,** a low, mean person. —**rep·til′i·an,** *adj.*

re·pub′lic (ri-pub′lik) *n.* a nation whose government is wholly elected, having no king.

> **republic**
> ↔ From the Latin phrase *res publica,* public matter, i.e., the state.

re·pub′li·can (ri-pub′li-kən) *adj.* **1,** being, pert. to, or favoring a republic. **2,** (*cap.*) designating one of the two chief political parties in the U.S. —*n.* **1,** one who favors republican government. **2,** (*cap.*) a member or adherent of the Republican party. —**re·pub′li·can·ism,** *n.*

re·pu′di·ate″ (ri-pū′dė-āt″) *v.t.* **1,** refuse to acknowledge or to pay. **2,** cast away; reject; renounce. —**re·pu″di·a′tion,** *n.*

re·pug′nance (re-pug′nəns) *n.* **1,** a feeling of distaste or aversion. **2,** state of being repugnant.

re·pug′nant (re-pug′nənt) *adj.* **1,** highly distasteful; offensive. **2,** contrary in nature.

re·pulse′ (ri-puls′) *v.t.* **1,** beat or drive back; repel. **2,** refuse; reject. —*n.* **1,** a driving back. **2,** refusal; denial.

re·pul′sion (ri-pul′shən) *n.* **1,** act or effect of repulsing. **2,** repugnance.

re·pul′sive (ri-pul′siv) *adj.* **1,** repelling. **2,** offensive; causing intense aversion. —**re·pul′sive·ness,** *n.*

rep′u·ta·ble (rep′yə-tə-bəl) *adj.* held in esteem; respectable. —**rep″u·ta·bil′i·ty,** *n.*

rep″u·ta′tion (rep″yə-tā′shən) *n.* **1,** the estimation of a person or thing by the community. **2,** fame.

re·pute′ (ri-pūt′) *n.* reputation; esp., good reputation. —*v.t.* hold in thought; regard; deem; estimate. —**re·put′ed,** *adj.*

supposed to be. —**re·put′ed·ly,** *adv.* supposedly.

re·quest′ (ri-kwest′) *n.* **1,** an asking for something; a petition; demand. **2,** that which is asked for. —*v.t.* express desire for; ask. —*adj.* at someone's request.

re′qui·em (rek′wė-əm) *n.* a Mass for the dead; music for such a Mass.

re·quire′ (ri-kwīr′) *v.t.* **1,** ask or claim, as by right; demand; exact. **2,** order to do something; call on. **3,** need; want. —**re·quire′ment,** *n.*

re″qui·es′cat in pa′ce (rek″wė-es′kat in pä′che) (*Lat.*) may he (she) rest in peace.

req′ui·site (rek′wə-zit) *adj.* required; indispensable. —*n.* something essential or indispensable.

req″ui·si′tion (rek″wi-zish′ən) *n.* **1,** act of demanding. **2,** a written order, as for supplies. —*v.t.* order; seize officially.

re·quite′ (ri-kwīt′) *v.t.* repay (either good or evil); recompense; retaliate. —**re·quit′al,** *n.*

rere′dos (rir′i-dos) *n.* a screen or background, esp. behind an altar.

re′run″ (rē′run″) *v.t. & n.* replay.

re·scind′ (ri-sind′) *v.t.* abrogate; repeal; take back.

re·scis′sion (ri-sizh′ən) *n.* act of rescinding.

re′script (rē′skript) *n.* an edict.

res′cue (res′kū) *v.t.* deliver from danger or evil; liberate. —*n.* an act of rescuing.

re·search′ (ri-sėrch′; rē′sėrch) *n.* study or investigation of facts, esp. scientific, not readily available. —*v.t.* conduct researches into or concerning. —**re′search″er,** *n.* one who does research, esp. in assembling facts for a writer.

re·sec′tion (ri-sek′shən) *n.* a cutting or paring off, esp. of a bone.

re·sem′blance (ri-zem′bləns) *n.* similarity, esp. in appearance.

re·sem′ble (ri-zem′bəl) *v.t.* have similarity to; look alike.

re·sent′ (ri-zent′) *v.t.* consider to be an injury or an affront. —**re·sent′ful,** *adj.* angry at having been injured. —**re·sent′ment,** *n.*

re·ser′pine (ri-sûr′pin) *n.* a tranquilizer and sedative.

res″er·va′tion (rez″ər-vā′shən) *n.* **1,** the act of keeping back or withholding. **2,** anything withheld, as a qualification on a statement or contract. **3,** something reserved for future use or occupation. **4,** a misgiving. **5,** a qualification of approval. **6,** a tract of public land set aside for some special use.

---

re·serve' (ri-zērv') *v.t.* **1,** retain or set apart for future or special use. **2,** keep as one's own. —*n.* **1,** that which is kept for future or special use, esp. capital retained for future or contingent liabilities. **2,** a reservation. **3,** self-restraint; a distant manner. **4,** fighting men subject to call but not on active duty. —**re·served'**, *adj.* reticent; self-restrained.

re·serv'ist (ri-zērv'ist) *n.* a member of a military reserve force.

res'er·voir" (rez'ər-vwär") *n.* a supply stored for future use; a place of such storage, esp. of water.

res' ges'tae (räs' jes'tė) (*Lat.*) **1,** things done; exploits. **2,** (*Law*) admissible evidence in a trial.

re·side' (ri-zīd') *v.i.* **1,** dwell permanently or for a considerable time. **2,** be inherent in, as a quality.

res'i·dence (rez'i-dəns) *n.* **1,** act or period of residing. **2,** a dwelling.

res'i·den·cy (rez'i-dən-sė) *n.* **1,** residence. **2,** an official residence. **3,** living where one's official duties lie.

res'i·dent (rez'i-dənt) *n.* one who dwells (in a certain place). —**res"i·den'tial** (-den'shəl) *adj.* pert. to or consisting of dwellings.

re·sid'u·al (rə-zij'oo-əl) *adj.* remaining; left over. —*n.* **1,** a residual quantity or substance. **2,** (usu. *pl.*) payment given to a performer in a recorded advertisement, concert, etc., each time it is replayed.

re·sid'u·ar·y (rə-zij'oo-er-ė) *adj.* **1,** remaining in an estate after deducting specific bequests. **2,** inheriting a residuary estate.

res'i·due" (rez'i-dū") *n.* that which is left over; the remainder; the rest.

re·sid'u·um (ri-zij'oo-əm) *n.* [*pl.* **-a** (-ə)] **1,** a residue. **2,** any residual product.

re·sign' (ri-zīn') *v.i.* **1,** submit oneself; be reconciled; endure with patience. **2,** give up an office, position, or post. —*v.t.* **1,** relinquish. **2,** submit. —**re·signed'**, *adj.* reconciled (to some ill).

res"ig·na'tion (rez"ig-nā'shən) *n.* **1,** act or result of resigning. **2,** uncomplaining acceptance of misfortune.

re·sil'i·ent (ri-zil'yənt) *adj.* **1,** springing back; rebounding. **2,** buoyant; not readily discouraged. —**re·sil'ience, re·sil'ien·cy,** *n.*

res'in (rez'in) *n.* **1,** a hardened secretion of many plants, esp. trees, used in varnish, medicines, etc. **2,** rosin. —**res'in·ous,** *adj.*

re·sist' (ri-zist') *v.t.* **1,** oppose; exert physical or moral force against. **2,** withstand.

—*v.i.* make opposition to. —**re·sist'i·ble,** *adj.* —**re·sis'tive,** *adj.*

re·sist'ance (-əns) *n.* **1,** the act or power of resisting; the degree of an opposing force. **2,** the extent to which an electrical conductor impedes a flow of current. —*adj.* utilizing electrical resistance.

re·sist'ant (-ənt) *adj.* resisting.

re·sist'or (ri-zis'tər) *n.* a resistant device used in an electric circuit for protection or control.

res'o·lute (rez'ə-loot) *adj.* having a fixed purpose; unwavering.

res"o·lu'tion (rez"ə-loo'shən) *n.* **1,** the quality of having a fixed purpose; determination; firmness. **2,** something determined upon; a decision of a legislative body. **3,** the act of resolving; an analysis; a solution or answer.

re·solve' (ri-zolv') *v.t.* **1,** determine; decide; express as a resolution. **2,** separate into constituent parts; reduce by mental analysis; solve. —*v.i.* **1,** establish a purpose; determine in the mind. **2,** become by analysis. —*n.* **1,** a resolution. **2,** firmness or fixedness of purpose; determination. —**re·solved'**, *adj.* determined; firm.

res'o·nant (rez'ə-nənt) *adj.* **1,** resounding; capable of decided sympathetic vibrations. **2,** having a rich, vibrant tone. —**res'o·nance,** *n.*

res'o·nate" (rez'ə-nāt") *v.i.* have or produce resonance; vibrate sympathetically.

res'o·na"tor (-ər) *n.* **1,** a device for increasing the vibrancy of tone. **2,** an instrument used in the analysis of sound. **3,** the high-frequency circuits of a radio receiving set. **4,** a small auxiliary muffler.

res·or'cin·ol (rez-ôr'si-nol) *n.* a derivative of benzene, used in medicines.

re·sort' (ri-zôrt') *v.i.* **1,** (with *to*) have recourse; apply. **2,** go customarily or frequently. —*n.* **1,** a place frequently visited. **2,** the act of having recourse to; a source of aid.

re·sound' (ri-zownd') *v.i.* **1,** ring with echoing sounds; reverberate; be filled with sound. **2,** give forth a loud sound.

re·sound'ing *adj.* **1,** ringing. **2,** thorough.

re·source' (ri-sôrs') *n.* **1,** any source of aid or support; an expedient to which one may resort. **2,** (*pl.*) available means; funds or supplies; assets. **3,** (*pl.*) the natural or collective wealth of a country. —**re·source'-ful,** *adj.* clever in finding and utilizing resources. —**re·source'ful·ness,** *n.*

re·spect' (ri-spekt') *v.t.* **1,** treat with special consideration or high regard; heed. **2,** have reference to; relate to. —*n.* **1,** high esteem; courteous or considerate treatment. **2,** a point; a particular; a feature. **3,** (*pl.*) compliments.

re·spect′a·ble *adj.* **1,** worthy of esteem; highly regarded. **2,** decent. **3,** fairly good or large. —**re·spect″a·bil′i·ty,** *n.*

re·spect′ful *adj.* deferent.

re·spect′ing *prep.* regarding; concerning.

re·spec′tive (-spek′tiv) *adj.* pertaining individually to each. —**re·spec′tive·ly,** *adv.* with each in proper order.

res″pi·ra′tion (res″pə-rā′shən) *n.* breathing. —**res′pi·ra·to″ry** (res′pə-rə-tôr″ē) *adj.*

res′pi·ra″tor (res′pə-rā″tər) *n.* **1,** a device to produce involuntary breathing. **2,** a mask to exclude noxious gases or substances.

re·spire′ (ri-spīr′) *v.i. & t.* breathe.

res′pite (res′pit) *n.* **1,** an interval of rest or relief. **2,** a postponement. —*v.t.* relieve temporarily; delay; postpone.

re·splend′ent (ri-splen′dənt) *adj.* shining with brilliant luster; splendid. —**re·splend′ence,** *n.*

re·spond′ (ri-spond′) *v.i.* **1,** give an answer; make a reply. **2,** show reaction to a force or stimulus.

re·spond′ent (ri-spon′dənt) *adj.* answering; responsive. —*n.* (*Law*) defendant.

re·sponse′ (ri-spons′) *n.* **1,** an answer or reply. **2,** a reaction. **3,** a verse said or sung by choir or congregation in reply to one read by the pastor. —**re″spon·sor′i·al** (ri″-spon-sôr′ē-əl) *adj.*

re·spon″si·bil′i·ty (ri-spon″sə-bil′ə-tē) *n.* **1,** the state of being responsible. **2,** a duty; charge.

re·spon′si·ble (ri-spon′sə-bəl) *adj.* **1,** answerable; accountable. **2,** able to satisfy any reasonable claim. **3,** involving important work or trust.

re·spon′sive (ri-spon′siv) *adj.* **1,** readily answering or reacting. **2,** constituting an answer or reaction. **3,** pert. to the use of responses. —**re·spon′sive·ness,** *n.*

rest *n.* **1,** a state of quiet or repose. **2,** freedom from care; peace; quiet. **3,** sleep. **4,** a place of quiet; a shelter. **5,** that upon which something leans for support. **6,** (*Music*) a silence or pause between tones; the symbol for this silence. **7,** that which is left; remainder. —*v.i.* **1,** cease action or performance; be without motion; pause. **2,** take repose; be tranquil. **3,** have a foundation; be supported. **4,** remain. **5,** lean; trust; rely. —*v.t.* **1,** place at rest; give repose to. **2,** lay or place, as on a foundation. **3,** leave; allow to stand. —**rest room,** lavatory (def. 1).

res′tau·rant (res′tə-rənt) *n.* a place

where meals are sold; a public eating house.

> **restaurant**
> ↔ Literally, a place where one is restored, from Latin *restaurare*, restore.

res″tau·ra·teur′ (res″tə-rə-tēr′) *n.* (*Fr.*) the proprietor or manager of a restaurant.

rest′ful *adj.* promoting comfort or tranquillity. —**rest′ful·ness,** *n.*

res″ti·tu′tion (res″tə-tū′shən) *n.* **1,** the act of returning or restoring to someone what is his or hers. **2,** the act of making amends. **3,** restoration.

res′tive (res′tiv) *adj.* **1,** uneasy; impatient. **2,** refractory.

> **restive, restless**
> ☞ These two words share similar senses. Both can mean impatient, but *restive* more often is used in the sense of intractable.

rest′less (-ləs) *adj.* **1,** unable to rest or sleep; uneasy. **2,** unsettled; continually moving. —**rest′less·ness,** *n.* ❏ *restive*

res″to·ra′tion (res″tə-rā′shən) *n.* **1,** the act of restoring or being restored. **2,** that which is restored. **3,** (*cap.*) the reestablishment of the British monarchy in 1660.

re·stor′a·tive (ri-stôr′ə-tiv) *adj.* healing; stimulating. —*n.* a food, drink, or medicine that heals or stimulates.

re·store′ (ri-stôr′) *v.t.* **1,** bring back to a former state; return to a former position. **2,** heal; cure. **3,** renew or reestablish after interruption. **4,** return (something lost or taken) to the owner.

re·strain′ (ri-strān′) *v.t.* hold back; check; repress; restrict; confine.

re·straint′ (ri-strānt′) *n.* **1,** the act of holding back; hindrance; confinement. **2,** reserve; self-control. **3,** a limitation.

re·strict′ (ri-strikt′) *v.t.* attach limitations to; limit; restrain. —**re·stric′tion,** *n.* —**re·stric′tive,** *adj.*

re·sult′ (ri-zult′) *v.i.* **1,** proceed or arise as a consequence or effect; be the outcome. **2,** (with *in*) terminate. —*n.* **1,** a consequence; effect; outcome. **2,** (*Math.*) a quantity or value obtained by calculation.

re·sult′ant (ri-zul′tənt) *adj.* following as a result or consequence. —*n.* that which follows as a consequence.

re·sume′ (ri-zoom′) *v.t.* take up again after interruption; begin again. —*v.i.* proceed after interruption.

ré′su·mé′ (rez′oo-mā′) *n.* (*Fr.*) a summary, esp. of a person's achievements.

re·sump′tion (ri-zum′shən) *n.* act or effect of resuming.

re·surge′ (rē-sērj′) *v.i.* rise again; revive; reappear. —**re·sur′gent,** *adj.* —**re·sur′gence,** *n.*

res″ur·rect′ (rez″ə-rekt′) *v.t.* **1,** restore to life; reanimate; renew; reconstruct. **2,** bring back from the dead. **3,** disinter.

res″ur·rec′tion (rez″ə-rek′shən) *n.* **1,** act or result of resurrecting. **2,** (*cap.*) the rebirth of souls on the judgment day. **3,** (*cap.,* with *the*) the rising of Christ from the dead.

re·sus′ci·tate″ (ri-sus′ə-tāt′) *v.t. & i.* revive; bring to life again. —**re·sus″ci·ta′tion,** *n.*

re·ta′ble (ri-tā′bəl) *n.* a shelf above an altar for candles, flowers, etc.

re′tail (rē′tāl) *n.* the sale of commodities in small quantities to the ultimate consumer. —*adj.* pert. to such sales. —*v.t.* **1,** sell to the ultimate consumer. **2,** (ri-tāl′) tell in detail. —**re′tail″er,** *n.* the keeper of a store.

re·tain′ (ri-tān′) *v.t.* **1,** hold or keep in possession, use, or practice. **2,** keep in mind; remember. **3,** engage the services of. —**retaining wall,** a wall to prevent a mass of earth from slipping.

re·tain′er *n.* **1,** that which holds in, as a retaining wall. **2,** a servant long employed. **3,** a fee paid to secure services, esp. of a lawyer.

re·take′ (rē-tāk′) *v.t.* **1,** take again; recapture. **2,** photograph again. —*n.* (rē′tāk″) a second photographing, as of a motion picture scene.

re·tal′i·ate″ (ri-tal′ē-āt′) *v.t. & i.* return like for like, esp. evil for evil. —**re·tal″i·a′tion,** *n.* —**re·tal′i·a·to·ry,** *adj.*

re·tard′ (ri-tärd′) *v.t.* **1,** make slow or slower; obstruct. **2,** defer; postpone. —**re·tar′dant,** *adj.* —**re″tar·da′tion,** *n.* —**re·tar′ded,** *adj.*

re·tard′ate (rē-tär′dāt) *n.* a mentally retarded person.

retch (rech) *v.i.* strain, as in vomiting; try to vomit.

re·ten′tion (ri-ten′shən) *n.* **1,** act or result of retaining. **2,** memory. —**re·ten′tive,** *adj.* serving or tending to retain.

ret′i·cent (ret′ə-sənt) *adj.* disposed to be silent; reserved. —**ret′i·cence,** *n.* ❑ *reluctant*

ret′i·cle (ret′i-kəl) *n.* a glass plate divided into small squares by fine lines, as used in a telescope to locate stars, etc.

re·tic′u·late (ri-tik′yə-lāt″) *adj.* being or resembling a network. Also, **re·tic′u·lar**

(-lər). —*v.t. & i.* form or form into a network.

ret′i·cule″ (ret′ə-kūl″) *n.* a woman's handbag, orig. of network.

ret′i·na (ret′i-nə) *n.* the innermost coating of the back of the eye, extending in to the optic nerve and receiving the images of vision. —**ret′i·nal,** *adj.*

ret′i·nue″ (ret′ə-nū″) *n.* a body of followers or attendants.

re·tire′ (ri-tīr′) *v.i.* **1,** draw back; retreat. **2,** go into a private place. **3,** withdraw from business or public life. **4,** go to bed. —*v.t.* **1,** take or lead back; withdraw. **2,** make inactive; relieve of duty. **3,** withdraw from circulation, as bonds. —**re·tire′ment,** *n.*

re·tired′ *adj.* **1,** having discontinued work after long service. **2,** sequestered; secluded.

re·tir′ing *adj.* diffident; shy.

re·tort′ (ri-tôrt′) *v.t.* **1,** return or turn back, as an argument upon the originator; retaliate. **2,** reply sharply. —*v.i.* make a sharp reply. —*n.* **1,** a retaliatory remark. **2,** a glass vessel with a long neck, used in chemistry.

re·touch′ (rē-tuch′) *v.t.* alter details of (a painting, photograph, film, or engraving) for improvement.

re·trace′ (rē-trās′) *v.t.* **1,** go back over; trace backward. **2,** trace again, as a drawing.

re·tract′ (ri-trakt′) *v.t.* **1,** draw back or in, as a cat's claws. **2,** take back; undo; recant. —*v.i.* **1,** shrink back; recede. **2,** undo or unsay what has been previously done or said.

re·trac′tile (ri-trak′til) *adj.* capable of being drawn back in.

re·trac′tion (ri-trak′shən) *n.* a disclaimer of, or apology for, an incorrect statement.

re·trac′tive (-tiv) *adj.* drawing back in.

re·trac′tor *n.* **1,** a muscle that draws back a part of the body. **2,** anything that serves to retract.

re·tread′ (rē-tred′) *v.t.* **1,** tread again. **2,** recap or cut grooves in (a tire). —*n.* (rē′-tred″) a retreaded tire.

re·treat′ (ri-trēt′) *n.* **1,** the act of withdrawing; a backward movement under enemy pressure. **2,** a state of seclusion; retirement. **3,** a place of retirement, privacy, or security. **4,** an asylum. **5,** (*Mil.*) the bugle call that signals retirement from action. —*v.i.* go back; run from an enemy.

re·trench′ (ri-trench′) *v.t. & i.* cut down; curtail, esp. expenses; economize. —**re·trench′ment,** *n.*

ret″ri·bu′tion (ret″rə-bū′shən) *n.* reward or punishment for past good or evil, esp. punishment for evil. —**re·trib′u·tive** (ri-trib′yû-tiv) *adj.*

re·trieve′ (ri-trēv′) *v.t. & i.* **1,** find again; recover; regain. **2,** search for and bring in killed or wounded game.

re·triev′er (ri-trē′vər) *n.* a dog bred or trained to bring in game.

ret·ro- (ret-rō) *pref.* back; backward; behind.

ret″ro·ac′tive (ret″rō-) *adj.* applicable to past events, as a law. —**ret″ro·ac·tiv′i·ty,** *n.*

ret′ro·fit (ret′rō-) *v.t.* **1,** modify equipment to incorporate improvements. **2,** install new equipment in an older facility.

ret′ro·grade″ (ret′rə-grād″) *adj.* **1,** moving or directed backward; retreating. **2,** deteriorating. —*v.i.* go or move backward; lose ground; deteriorate. —**ret″ro·gra·da′tion,** *n.*

ret′ro·gress″ (ret′rə-gres″) *v.i.* revert to a worse condition; decline. —**ret″ro·gres′sion** (-gresh′ən) backward movement; deterioration. —**ret″ro·gres′sive,** *adj.*

ret′ro·rock″et *n.* an auxiliary rocket or jet engine on a spacecraft or satellite used to slow down its speed, as for landing on a celestial body.

ret′ro·spect″ (ret′rə-spekt″) *n.* the act of looking backward; contemplation of the past.

ret″ro·spec′tion (-spek′shən) *n.* the act of looking backward (in time).

ret″ro·spec′tive (-iv) *adj.* **1,** looking back on or occurring in the past. **2,** retroactive. —*n.* an exhibition of the works of an artist, composer, etc., covering a wide period of his or her career.

re″trous·sé′ (ret″roo-sā′) *adj.* (*Fr.*) (of a nose) turned up.

ret′si·na (ret′sə-nə; ret-sē′nə) *n.* a Greek resinated wine.

re·turn′ (ri-tērn′) *v.i.* **1,** come or go back to a former place, position, or state. **2,** recur. **3,** make a reply; retort. —*v.t.* **1,** send or give back; restore. **2,** cast back; reflect. **3,** repay; requite. **4,** report. **5,** elect or reelect to office. **6,** yield (a profit). —*n.* **1,** the act or an act of returning; a recurrence; repayment. **2,** (*pl.*) a result, esp. of an election. **3,** a profit or yield. **4,** a reply. **5,** a report on one's earnings, for income tax purposes. —**re·turn′ee″,** *n.*

Reuben
↔ After the Amer. restaurateur Arnold *Reuben*, who created the sandwich.

Reu′ben (roo′bən) *adj.* denoting a toasted sandwich of corned beef, sauerkraut, and Swiss cheese.

re·un′ion (rē-ūn′yən) *n.* **1,** the act of uniting again. **2,** a gathering of friends, relatives, etc.

re·up′ *v.i.* (*Slang*) reenlist.

rev (*Slang*) *v.t.* [**revved, rev′ving**] increase the number of revolutions per minute of (a motor). —*n.* a revolution.

re·vamp′ (rē-vamp′) *v.t.* remodel; renovate.

re·veal′ (ri-vēl′) *v.t.* make known; disclose; divulge.

rev′eil·le (rev′ə-lē) *n.* (*Mil.*) a bugle call sounded at daybreak.

rev′el (rev′əl) *v.i.* **1,** join in merrymaking; carouse. **2,** take great pleasure (in); delight (in). —*n.* a boisterous merrymaking. —**rev′el·ry,** *n.*

rev″e·la′tion (rev″ə-lā′shən) *n.* **1,** the act of revealing; a disclosure, esp. by supernatural means. **2,** a striking accession of information.

re·venge′ (ri-venj′) *v.t.* inflict punishment because of; avenge. —*n.* retaliation of wrongs. —**re·venge′ful,** *adj.* seeking vengeance. ❑ *avenge*

rev′e·nue″ (rev′ə-nū″) *n.* **1,** income from real or personal property. **2,** the income of a state from taxation. **3,** the department that collects such taxes, etc. —**revenue sharing,** the return of part of federal tax revenues to the states, state to city, etc.

re·ver′ber·ate″ (ri-vēr′bə-rāt″) *v.t.* return as sound; reecho. —**re·ver″ber·a′tion,** *n.* a series of echoes. Also, *Informal,* **re′-verb″** (rē′vērb″) *n.*

reverberate
↔ From Latin *verberare,* to whip; the sounds that reverberate "whip" back and forth, or echo.

re·vere′ (ri-vir′) *v.t.* regard with deepest respect and awe; venerate. —*n.* revers.

rev′er·ence (rev′ər-əns) *n.* **1,** act of revering; veneration. **2,** title of certain clergymen. **3,** a bow or curtsy.

rev′er·end (rev′ər-ənd) *adj.* deserving of respect: applied to a clergyman. —*n.* (*Informal*) a clergyman.

rev′er·ent (rev′ər-ənt) *adj.* **1,** respectful. **2,** devout. —**rev″er·en′tial** (-en′shəl) *adj.* characterized by awe or respect.

rev′er·ie (rev′ə-rē) *n.* a state of fanciful meditation; a daydream.

re·vers′ (rə-vir′) *n. sing. & pl.* a part of a garment turned back, as a lapel. Also, **re·vere′.**

re·verse' (ri-vērs') *adj.* turned backward; opposite; contrary. —*n.* **1,** a change to an opposite form, state, condition, or direction. **2,** a change of fortune, specif. for the worse. **3,** the opposite; the contrary, esp., the back of a coin or medal. —*v.t.* **1,** turn about, around, upside down, or in an opposite direction. **2,** set aside; annul, as a legal decree. —*v.i.* change to an opposite position, direction, motion, etc. —**re·ver'sal,** *n.* —**re·vers'i·ble,** *adj.* —**reverse annuity mortgage,** a type of mortgage esp. for elderly persons which provides an annuity until the security is sold.

re·ver'sion (ri-vēr'zhən) *n.* **1,** act or result of reverting. **2,** the right of future possession of a property. —**re·ver'sion·ar·y,** *adj.*

re·vert' (ri-vērt') *v.i.* go back to a former place, position, or state.

re·vet' (ri-vet') *v.t.* put a facing of masonry on an embankment, etc. —**re·vet'ment,** *n.*

re·view' (ri-vū') *n.* **1,** a going over anything again; an examination. **2,** a survey of the past. **3,** a critical report, as of a book or play; a periodical devoted to critical articles. **4,** (*Mil.*) a formal inspection; parade. **5,** (*Law*) a judicial reconsideration by a higher court. —*v.t.* **1,** look back upon. **2,** repeat; examine again. **3,** write about critically. **4,** (*Mil.*) make a formal inspection of. —**re·view'er,** *n.* one who reviews; a critic.

> **review, revue**
> ☛ A *revue* is a musical entertainment; the word has no other senses. *Review* is seldom used in this sense.

re·vile' (ri-vīl') *v.t.* abuse in speech or writing. —**re·vile'ment,** *n.*

re·vise' (ri-vīz') *v.t.* make changes or corrections in; amend. —*n.* **1,** a review and correction. **2,** a proof sheet taken after corrections have been made.

re·vi'sion (ri-vizh'ən) *n.* act or result of revising.

re·viv'al (ri-vīv'əl) *n.* **1,** act or effect of reviving; restoration. **2,** a meeting to promote religious awakening. **3,** the presentation of a play, film, etc., formerly presented. —**re·viv'al·ism,** *n.* —**re·viv'al·ist,** *n.*

re·vive' (ri-vīv') *v.i.* come back to life after apparent death; be renewed or refreshed. —*v.t.* **1,** bring back to life or use. **2,** refresh; recall; reawaken. **3,** produce again (a play, etc., formerly presented).

rev'o·ca·ble (rev'ə-kə-bəl) *adj.* subject to being revoked.

rev"o·ca'tion (rev"ə-kā'shən) *n.* annulment; recall.

re·voke' (ri-vōk') *v.t.* annul by taking back; repeal; cancel. —*v.i.* in card playing, fail to follow suit when able and obliged to do so. —*n.* in card playing, act or instance of revoking.

re·volt' (ri-vōlt') *n.* an uprising against government or authority; rebellion; insurrection. —*v.i.* break away from established authority; rebel. —*v.t.* repel; shock. —**re·volt'ing,** *adj.* repulsive.

rev"o·lu'tion (rev"ə-loo'shən) *n.* **1,** the act of revolting. **2,** a complete rotation. **3,** the act of traveling completely around a circuit. **4,** a cycle. **5,** a total change of conditions, specif. a radical social or political change; a major revolt.

rev"o·lu'tion·ar·y (-er-ė) *adj.* **1,** pert. to a revolution. **2,** revolving. **3,** drastic; radical. —*n.* a revolutionist.

rev"o·lu'tion·ist *n.* one who participates in a revolution.

rev"o·lu'tion·ize" (-īz") *v.t.* effect an extreme change in.

re·volve' (ri-volv') *v.i.* **1,** turn or roll around on an axis; rotate. **2,** move about a center. **3,** pass through periodic changes; recur. —*v.t.* turn or cause to roll around, as on an axis. —**revolving charge account,** a charge account that charges a fixed rate of interest each month on the balance remaining due at the beginning or end of that month or on the average balance due during that month. —**revolving fund,** one maintained by balanced borrowings and repayments.

re·volv'er *n.* a repeating pistol having a revolving cylinder to hold cartridges.

re·vue' (ri-vū') *n.* a musical variety show, usually of parodies. ❏ *review*

re·vul'sion (ri-vul'shən) *n.* a sudden, violent change of feeling.

re·ward' (ri-wôrd') *v.t.* **1,** repay, as for good conduct or merit; recompense. **2,** make a return for. —*n.* **1,** a repayment or prize for merit or accomplishment. **2,** profit. **3,** a sum of money offered for the finding of a criminal or of a lost article. —**re·ward'ing,** *adj.* ❏ *award*

re·write' (rē-rīt') *v.t.* write again in different words or form. —*n.* (rē'rīt") something rewritten, esp. a newspaper story from oral report.

rex (reks) *n.* [*pl.* **re'ges** (re'ges)] (*Lat.*) a king.

Reye's syndrome (rīz) a rare but often fatal children's disease, associated with the use of aspirin.

rhap'so·dize'' (rap'sə-dīz'') *v.t. & i.* speak or write rhapsodically.

rhap'so·dy (rap'sə-dė) *n.* **1,** an expression of extravagant enthusiasm. **2,** a musical composition in irregular form with striking changes of tempo and rhythm. —**rhap·sod'ic** (-sod'ik) *adj.* —**rhap·sod'i·cal·ly,** *adv.*

rhe'a (rē'ə) *n.* the three-toed ostrich.

-rhe·a (rē-ə) *suf.* flow; discharge.

rhe'ni·um (rē'nė-əm) *n.* a rare heavy metallic element, symbol Re, no. 75.

rhe·o- (rē-ō, rē-ə) *pref.* flow; current.

rhe'o·stat'' (rē'ə-stat'') *n.* a resistance coil for regulating or adjusting electric current. Also, **resistance box.**

rhe'sus (rē'səs) *n.* a macaque.

rhet'o·ric (ret'ə-rik) *n.* **1,** the study of effective use of language. **2,** (*Informal*) inflammatory language. **3,** pompous or insincere language. —**rhet''o·ri'cian** (-rish'ən) *n.*

rhe·tor'i·cal (rə-tôr'i-kəl) *adj.* **1,** pert. to rhetoric. **2,** for effect only; not intended to be taken literally.

rheum (room) *n.* a cold.

rheu·mat'ic (roo-mat'ik) *adj.* pert. to rheumatism. —*n.* one subject to rheumatism. —**rheumatic fever,** a disease, usually of children, affecting the joints and heart. —**rheu·mat'i·cal·ly,** *adv.*

> **rheumatic**
> ↔ From Greek *rheuma*, flow, from the idea that rheumatic joints were caused by watery secretions.

rheu'ma·tism (roo'mə-tiz-əm) *n.* a disease characterized by inflammation of the joints. —**rheu'ma·toid,** *adj.*

Rh factor a property of the blood which when present (Rh positive) may cause agglutination of the red cells.

> **Rh factor**
> ↔ For *Rhesus factor*, because it was first found in the blood of rhesus monkeys.

rhi'nal (rī'nəl) *adj.* pert. to the nose; nasal.

rhine'stone'' (rīn'stōn'') *n.* **1,** imitation diamond. **2,** rock crystal.

rhi·ni'tis (rī-nī'tis) *n.* an inflammation of the nasal mucous membrane.

rhi·no- (rī'nō) *pref.* nose.

> **rhinoceros**
> ↔ The name refers to the animal's most prominent feature, from Greek *rhinokerōs*, horned nose.

rhi·noc'er·os (rī-nos'ər-əs) *n.* a large pachyderm with one or two upright horns on the snout. Also, **rhi'no** (rī'nō).

rhi''no·vi'rus (rī''nō-vī'rəs) *n.* a virus causing various respiratory infections, including the common cold.

rho (rō) *n.* the seventeenth letter of the Greek alphabet (P, ρ).

rho'di·um (rō'dė-əm) *n.* a metallic chemical element, no. 45, symbol Rh.

rho''do·den'dron (rō''də-den'drən) *n.* any of various hardy shrubs bearing flowers in clusters.

rhom'boid (rom'boid) *n.* a parallelogram with opposite sides equal and no right angle.

rhom'bus (rom'bəs) *n.* an equilateral parallelogram with no right angle.

rhu'barb (roo'bärb) *n.* **1,** a garden plant with tender, pink, acid leafstalks, used for sauce, pies, etc. **2,** the root of an Oriental rhubarb, used in medicines. **3,** (*Slang*) noisy objection to an arbiter's decision.

rhyme (rīm) *n.* **1,** agreement in the terminal sounds of words or verses. **2,** a couplet or short poem containing rhymes. **3,** a word that rhymes with another. —*v.i. & t.* make a rhyme or rhymes. Also, **rime.** —**rhyme'ster,** *n.* a writer of light or mediocre verse.

> **rhyme, rime**
> ☛ It is best to maintain the spelling distinction between *rhyme*, an agreement of sounds between words, and *rime*, hoarfrost, though the latter spelling was once used for both senses.

rhythm (rith'əm) *n.* **1,** movement characterized by equal or regularly alternating beats. **2,** that quality in music or poetry which is produced by a regular succession of accents; cadence. **3,** recurrence at regular or uniform intervals. —**rhyth'mic, rhyth'mi·cal,** *adj.* —**rhythm and blues,** a style of popular music characterized by strong, driving rhythm. —**rhythm method,** a method of birth control based on abstention from sexual intercourse during ovulation.

ri·al' (rė-äl') *n.* a monetary unit of Iran.

ri·al'to (rė-al'tō) *n.* **1,** a theatrical district, esp. in New York City. **2,** a market place, esp. (*cap.*) in Venice.

ri·a'ta (rė-ä'tə) *n.* a lariat.

rib *n.* **1,** one of the series of curved bones enclosing the chest of man and animals. **2,** something likened to such a bone; a slender elongated member, timber, or ridge. —*v.t.* [ribbed, rib'bing] 1, strengthen or support by ribs. 2, (*Informal*) tease.

rib'ald (rib'əld) *adj.* coarsely humorous. —rib'ald·ry, *n.*

rib'bon (rib'ən) *n.* 1, a narrow strip of fabric, as silk; a similar strip of paper, metal, etc., or of color. 2, a tape for trimming. 3, (*pl.*) shreds. 4, an inked tape for a typewriter. Also, rib'and (-ənd). —*v.t.* 1, adorn with ribbons. 2, streak; stripe. 3, shred.

ri''bo·fla'vin (rī''bō-flā'vin) *n.* a vitamin, esp. vitamin B$_2$.

ri'bo·nu·cle''ic acid (rī'bō-noo-klā''ik) a molecule important in transmitting genetic information. Also, RNA.

ri'bo·some'' (rī'bə-sōm'') *n.* particles in a cell that synthesize proteins and enzymes.

rice (rīs) *n.* the grain from a plant grown in warm climates. —*v.t.* press into shreds. —ric'er, *n.* a utensil for ricing potatoes, etc. —rice paper, a thin paper made from rice, straw, or the pith of a shrub.

rich *adj.* 1, having much money or great possessions; wealthy. 2, abundantly supplied; abounding. 3, productive; fertile. 4, elegant; luxurious; costly. 5, full in tone; strong in color; vivid. 6, containing desirable, nutritious, or fattening ingredients. 7, (*Informal*) preposterous. —rich'es, *n.pl.* wealth. —rich'ness, *n.*

Rich'ter scale (rikh'tər) a logarithmic scale from 1 to 10, used to indicate the force of an earthquake.

rick (rik) *n.* a heap or pile, as of hay.

rick'ets (rik'its) *n.* a disease characterized by softness of the bones and distortions, usu. caused by malnutrition.

rick·ett'si·a (ri-ket'sė-ə) *n.* the microorganisms which cause typhus and other diseases.

rick'et·y (rik'ə-tė) *adj.* 1, tottering; shaky. 2, affected with rickets.

rick'ey (rik'ė) *n.* a cold drink made of lime juice, carbonated water, and gin: *gin rickey.*

rick'rack'' (rik'rak'') *n.* a narrow zigzag openwork braid used for trimming.

rick'shaw (rik'shâ) *n.* (*Informal*) jinrikisha.

ric''o·chet' (rik''ə-shā') *n.* a rebounding or a skipping of an object passing over a flat surface. —*v.i.* rebound and glance off.

ri·cot'ta (rė-kot'ə) *n.* Ital. cottage cheese.

rid *v.t.* [rid, rid'ding] free from anything superfluous or objectionable. —*adj.* clear or relieved (of). —get rid of, 1, get free of. 2, do away with.

rid'dance (rid'əns) *n.* the act of ridding; deliverance. —good riddance, a welcome relief.

rid'den (rid'ən) *v.* p.p. of *ride.*

-rid·den *suf.* obsessed with; oppressed by; full of.

rid'dle (rid'əl) *n.* 1, a puzzling question; an enigma; a perplexing person or thing. 2, a coarse sieve. —*v.t.* 1, fill with holes, by or as by shot. 2, sift through a coarse sieve.

ride (rīd) *v.i.* [rode (rōd), rid'den (rid'ən), rid'ing] 1, be carried on an animal's back or in a vehicle, ship, or plane. 2, (of a ship) float. 3, move on or about something. 4, carry passengers. 5, climb up, as an ill-fitting coat. —*v.t.* 1, sit on and manage (a horse) in motion. 2, travel on, through, or over. 3, treat harshly; tease; harass. —*n.* a journey on which one is borne.

rid'er (rīd'ər) *n.* 1, one who or that which rides. 2, a clause added to a document.

rid'er·ship'' *n.* the people who ride (as the subway, etc.).

ridge (rij) *n.* 1, the crest of two sloping surfaces rising to meet at an angle. 2, a mountain or hill in this form. —*v.t. & i.* form into, provide with, or mark with ridges.

ridge'pole'' *n.* the horizontal timber at the top of a roof.

rid'i·cule'' (rid'ə-kūl'') *n.* incitement of contemptuous laughter; derision. —*v.t.* make to appear absurd.

ri·dic'u·lous (ri-dik'yə-ləs) *adj.* laughable; absurd; preposterous. —ri·dic'u·lous·ness, *n.*

rid'ing (rīd'ing) *n.* (*Brit.*) a district.

> **riding**
> ↔ This general term for a district used to refer specifically to any of the three districts in Yorkshire, England. The word derives, not from *ride*, but from Old Norse *thridjung*, a third part.

rife (rīf) *adj.* prevalent; current.

riff (rif) *n.* a note or phrase serving to punctuate swing music.

rif'fle (rif'əl) *n.* 1, a ripple, as on water. 2, a method of shuffling cards. 3, grooves on the bottom of a sluice for catching particles of mineral. —*v.* [-fled (-əld), -fling] 1, form or become a riffle. 2, flutter, as pages. 3, shuffle (cards).

riff'raff'' (rif'raf'') *n.* 1, scraps; rubbish; trash. 2, the rabble.

ri'fle (rī'fəl) *v.t.* 1, search, esp. to rob; ransack; plunder. 2, cut spiral grooves in (the bore of a gun barrel). —*n.* a portable firearm or a cannon having a rifled bore. —**ri′fle·man** (-mən) *n.* —**ri′fling,** *n.* spiral grooves cut in the bore of a gun causing the bullet to spin.

rift *n.* an opening made by splitting; a cleft or crevice; a fissure.

rig *v.t.* [rigged, rig′ging] **1,** fit with necessary equipment, as a ship with sails. **2,** (with *out*) dress, oddly or gaudily. **3,** raise or lower (prices) artificially. —*n.* **1,** (*Naut.*) arrangement of masts, sails, etc. **2,** dress; equipment. **3,** a light horse-drawn vehicle.

rig″a·doon′ (rig″ə-doon′) *n.* a former lively dance for one couple; the music for this dance.

rig′a·ma·role″ (rig′ə-mə-rōl″) *n.* rigmarole.

rig′ger (rig′ər) *n.* a mover of heavy objects.

rig′ging (rig′ing) *n.* (*Naut.*) rig, especially sails, masts, etc.

right (rīt) *adj.* **1,** in conformity with the moral law or standards; just; good. **2,** in conformity with truth, fact, or reason; correct; also orderly. **3,** proper; fitting; convenient. **4,** in good condition. **5,** pert. to the side or direction that is eastward when one faces north. **6,** conservative, in politics. **7,** straight; direct. —*adv.* **1,** directly. **2,** justly. **3,** properly. **4,** correctly; exactly. **5,** very. **6,** toward the right side. —*n.* **1,** conformity to an authoritative standard. **2,** that which conforms to a rule. **3,** a just claim or title. **4,** the right side or direction. **5,** (*cap., Brit.*) the Conservative party. —*v.t.* **1** set straight; adjust or correct. **2,** vindicate. —*v.i.* resume a vertical position. —**right angle,** an angle of 90° —**right of way, 1,** the right to proceed before another. **2,** land over which a railroad, etc., may pass. **3,** a right of passage. —**right on,** (*Slang*) exactly right! —**right triangle,** a triangle with one right angle. —**right wing,** members of an ultraconservative political party.

right′a·bout″ *n.* the opposite direction. —*adv.* in a half circle.

right′eous (rī′chəs) *adj.* virtuous; devout. —**right′eous·ness,** *n.*

right′ful *adj.* having or being based on a just claim. —**right′ful·ness,** *n.*

right-′hand″ *adj.* to the right; for the right hand. —**right-hand man,** a chief assistant. —**right-′hand″ed,** *adj.* more adept with the right hand than with the left.

right′ist *n.* a conservative in politics. —**right′ism,** *n.*

right-′to-die′ *adj.* favoring euthanasia or the withdrawal of artificial means of life support for the terminally ill or incurably comatose.

right-′to-life′ *adj.* seeking to protect the rights of an unborn child.

right-′wing′ *adj.* ultraconservative.

rig′id (rij′id) *adj.* **1,** stiff, not pliant or easily bent; inflexible; unyielding. **2,** strict; exacting. —**ri·gid′i·ty,** *n.*

rig″ma·role″ (rig″mə-rōl″) *n.* long, incoherent discourse; nonsense; unnecessary formalities.

> **rigmarole**
> ↔ This unusual word comes from *ragman role,* a catalog, also perhaps a list of characters in a game.

rig′or (rig′ər) *n.* **1,** stiffness; inflexibility. **2,** strictness; austerity; sternness. Also, **rig′our.** —**rig′or·ous,** *adj.* —**ri″gor mor′tis** (rīg″ər môr′tis) (*Lat.*) the stiffening of the body after death.

rile (rīl) *v.t.* (*Informal*) annoy; vex.

rill (ril) *n.* a small brook.

rim *n.* **1,** the border, edge, or margin of anything. **2,** of a wheel, the outer part. —*v.t.* [rimmed, rim′ming] surround with a rim or border.

rime (rīm) *n.* **1,** rhyme. **2,** white frost; hoarfrost. —*v.t. & i.* rhyme. —**rim′y,** *adj.* ❑ *rhyme*

rind (rīnd) *n.* an outer covering; a thick skin.

ring *v.i.* [rang, rung, ring′ing] **1,** resound, as a bell when struck. **2,** give a signal with a bell. **3,** sound loudly and clearly. **4,** have the sensation of a humming or buzzing sound. **5,** reverberate; reecho. —*v.t.* **1,** cause (a bell, etc.) to sound. **2,** announce; celebrate. **3,** (with *up*) (*Brit.*) telephone to. **4,** (with *in*) introduce unfairly. **5,** [*pret. & p.p.* **ringed**] encircle; surround with, or as with, a ring. —*n.* **1,** the sound of a bell; a peal or clang; resonance. **2,** a telephone call. **3,** a circular band or hoop; an ornamental band for the finger, etc. **4,** anything circular; arrangement or array in a circle. **5,** a group. **6,** an area for sports, exhibitions, etc.; arena. **7,** prizefighting.

ringed (ringd) *adj.* **1,** encircled. **2,** formed into or like a ring. **3,** wearing a ring or rings. **4,** marked with rings.

ring′er *n.* **1,** in quoits, a cast that encircles the pin. **2,** (*Slang*) a person who greatly resembles another: *dead ringer.* **3,** (*Slang*) a superior athlete, racehorse, performer, etc., usu. entered at the last minute, often under an assumed name. **4,** (*Slang*) one who votes fraudulently.

ring′lead″er *n.* a leader in mischief or objectionable acts.

ring′let *n.* a curl of hair.

ring′mas″ter *n.* one in charge of the performances in a circus ring, or, often, of the entire circus.

ring′side″ *n.* the seating space next to a boxing ring.

ring′worm″ *n.* a contagious skin disease.

rink *n.* a section of ice, or a floor, for skating; the building containing it.

rink′y-dink″ (ring′kė-dink″) *adj.* (*Slang*) cheap; shabby.

rinse (rins) *v.t.* wash lightly, esp. wash out (soap) with fresh water. —*n.* a light wash, as for removing soap, dyeing hair, etc.

ri′ot (rī′ət) *n.* **1,** a disturbance arising from disorderly conduct; a brawl. **2,** revelry. **3,** confusion; a haphazard mixture. **4,** (*Slang*) a cause of hearty laughter. —*v.i.* act without restraint. —**ri′ot·ous,** *adj.*

rip *v.t. & i.* [ripped, rip′ping] **1,** tear or cut open or off; slit; undo a seam. **2,** saw (wood) with the grain. **3,** (*Informal*) utter with violence. **4,** (with *off*) (*Slang*) cheat; steal. —*v.i.* **1,** be torn or split open. **2,** (*Informal*) rush headlong. —*n.* **1,** a rent or tear made by ripping. **2,** a rapid. **3,** (*Informal*) a dissolute person. —**rip′per,** *n.* —**rip cord,** a cord for opening a parachute during descent.

ri·par′i·an (ri-pār′ė-ən) *adj.* pert. to, or situated on, the bank of a river, lake, etc.

ripe (rīp) *adj.* **1,** ready for harvest; mature. **2,** in the best condition for use. **3,** ready for action or effect. —**ripe′ness,** *n.*

rip′en (rī′pən) *v.t. & i.* make or become ripe; mature.

rip′off″ *n.* (*Slang*) a deception; swindle.

ri·poste′ (ri-pōst′) *n.* a return thrust in fencing; a clever retort.

rip′ping (rip′ing) *adj.* splendid.

rip′ple (rip′əl) *n.* **1,** the light ruffling of the surface of the water; a little wave. **2,** a sound of a like that of water running over a stony bottom. —*v.t. & i.* **1,** form ripples (in). **2,** make a sound like rippling water. —*v.t.* agitate; mark with ripples. —**rip′plet,** *n.* a small ripple. —**ripple effect,** the gradually spreading effect of a single event.

rip′roar″ing *adj.* boisterously exhilarating; hilarious; jolly.

rip′saw″ *n.* a saw with coarse teeth, for sawing with the grain.

rip′snort″er (rip′snôr″tər) *n.* (*Slang*) **1,** a violent storm, person, etc. **2,** a person of striking energy or ability.

rip′tide″ *n.* a strong undertow.

RISC (risk) *Abbr.* a microprocessor designed with a limited set of instructions

for accomplishing certain specified tasks: r(educed) i(nstruction) s(et) c(omputer).

rise (rīz) *v.i.* [**rose** (rōz), **ris′en** (riz′ən), **ris′ing**] **1,** move from a lower to a higher position; move upward. **2,** stand up. **3,** slope or extend upward; stand in height. **4,** swell, as dough. **5,** emerge; come into sight or existence. **6,** increase in force, value, position, etc. **7,** elevation in rank, wealth, or importance. **8,** take up arms; rebel. **9,** (*Slang*) an irritated reaction or retort. —*n.* **1,** ascent; emergence; appearance. **2,** degree of ascent. **3,** an elevated place. **4,** spring; source; origin. **5,** increase.

ris′er (rī′zər) *n.* **1,** one who rises, esp. from sleep. **2,** the vertical piece which separates two stairs. **3,** (*pl.*) sets of stairs used as a multileveled platform, as for singers.

ris′i·ble (riz′ə-bəl) *adj.* **1,** having the faculty of laughing. **2,** exciting laughter. —**ris″i·bil′i·ty,** *n.*

risk *n.* **1,** exposure to loss or harm; danger; peril. **2,** chance; hazard. **3,** a contingency covered by insurance. —*v.t.* **1,** expose to injury or loss. **2,** take the chance of. —**risk′y,** *adj.*

ri·sot′to (rė-zot′tō) *n.* (*It.*) rice cooked with meat stock and flavorings.

ris·qué′ (ris-kā′) *adj.* somewhat indelicate, as a story; daring.

ris·sole′ (rė-sōl′) *n.* a small fried roll of chopped meat or fish.

ri″tar·dan′do (rē″tär-dän′dō) *adj., adv. & n.* (*It., Music*) becoming slower gradually.

rite (rīt) *n.* a ceremonial, religious, or other solemn service; ritual.

ri″te·nu′to (rē″tə-noo′tō) *adj.* (*It., Music*) slower; held back.

rit′u·al (rich′oo-əl) *adj.* pert. to or consisting of ceremonials. —*n.* a prescribed form or manner.

rit′u·al·ism (rich′oo-ə-liz-əm) *n.* **1,** insistence upon or fondness for ritual. **2,** the study of rituals. —**rit′u·al·ist,** *n.* —**rit″u·al·is′tic,** *adj.* —**rit″u·al·is′ti·cal·ly,** *adv.*

ritz (rits) *n.* ostentatious display. —**ritz′y** (rit′sė) *adj.* (*Slang*) luxurious; showy and costly.

ri′val (rī′vəl) *n.* one who is in pursuit of the same object or thing; an opponent. —*adj.* competing. —*v.t.* **1,** stand in competition with. **2,** emulate. **3,** be equal to. —**ri′val·ry,** *n.*

---

rival

↔ A *rival* is literally one who uses the same stream as another, from Latin *rivalis*, stream.

---

rive (rīv) *v.t. & i.* [*p.p.* **riv'en** (riv'ən)] rend asunder by force.

riv'er (riv'ər) *n.* **1,** a large stream of water flowing throughout the year. **2,** a copious flow.

riv'et (riv'it) *n.* a malleable metal pin or bolt used to fasten pieces together. —*v.t.* fasten with such a pin; fasten firmly.

Ri·vie'ra (ri-vye'rä) *n.* the Mediterranean coast of France and Italy.

riv'u·let (riv'yə-lət) *n.* a small stream or brook.

RNA ribonucleic acid.

roach (rōch) *n.* **1,** a common freshwater fish. **2,** a cockroach.

road (rōd) *n.* **1,** a public way for passage or travel; a highway. **2,** any means or way of approach. **3,** an anchorage. —**on the road,** traveling; on tour. —**road company,** the touring cast of a play, musical, etc. ❑ *raid*

road"a·bil'i·ty *n.* the ease of handling of a vehicle on a road.

road'bed" *n.* the foundation of a railroad track or highway.

road'house" *n.* a restaurant and dance hall by a road.

road'kill" *n.* an animal killed on the road by a passing motor vehicle.

road'run"ner *n.* a fast-running crested cuckoo of S.W. No. Amer.

road'stead" (-sted") *n.* an anchorage.

road'ster (-stər) *n.* **1,** a small open automobile. **2,** a driving horse.

road'way" *n.* a road.

roam (rōm) *v.i. & t.* travel aimlessly; rove; wander over.

roan (rōn) *adj.* of a horse, having a bay, sorrel, or chestnut color interspersed with gray or white. —*n.* **1,** a roan animal. **2,** a sheepskin leather in imitation of morocco, used in bookbinding.

roar (rôr) *v.i.* **1,** bellow; cry aloud. **2,** make a full, deep sound, as of wind, waves, or a crowd. **3,** guffaw. —*v.t.* shout. —*n.* a roaring sound, as of a lion.

roar'ing *adj.* **1,** that roars. **2,** extremely active; outstanding.

roast (rōst) *v.t.* **1,** cook (as meat) before an open fire, or in an oven. **2,** heat to excess. **3,** (*Slang*) ridicule or castigate. —*v.i.* be heated; be cooked by roasting. —*n.* a cut of meat suitable for roasting. —**roast'er,** *n.* a pan or chamber for roasting; a pig, chicken, etc., suitable for roasting.

rob *v.t.* [**robbed, rob'bing**] strip or deprive (someone) of something by force. —**rob'ber,** *n.* —**rob'ber·y,** *n.*

rob, mug, burglarize, steal, filch
These words all refer to the taking of something that belongs to someone else. *Rob, mug,* and *burglarize* refer to the person, place, or business stolen from. *Rob* is the most general term and can be used of a person or place. *Burglarize* is used mostly of places. *Mug* is used only of persons. *Steal* and *filch* refer to the items stolen.

robe (rōb) *n.* **1,** a gown or a long, loose outer garment, sometimes symbolizing honor or authority. **2,** (*pl.*) dress; attire. **3,** a dressed pelt, blanket, etc., used as a wrap. —*v.t.* clothe.

rob'in *n.* a red-breasted migratory thrush of No. Amer. Also, **robin red'breast.**

ro'bot (rō'bət) *n.* an automaton resembling a human being. —**robot bomb, robot plane,** one that guides itself or is controlled by radio.

robot
↔ From the 1920 play *R.U.R.* by Czech playwright Karel Capek, based on the Czech word *robota,* drudgery.

ro·bot'ics (rō-bot'iks) *n.sing.* the technology of robots.

ro·bust' (rō-bust') *adj.* **1,** strong; vigorous. **2,** rough; boisterous; rude. **3,** requiring vigor. —**ro·bust'ness,** *n.*

roc (rok) *n.* a fabulous large bird.

roc'am·bole" (rōk'əm-bōl") *n.* a European plant of the onion family used in seasoning.

rock (rok) *n.* **1,** a mass of stony material; a fragment or piece of it. **2,** a foundation; strength. **3,** (*pl.*) (*Slang*) money; jewels. **4,** a backward and forward movement. **5,** rock-'n'-roll. —*v.t. & i.* move backward and forward; sway. —**on the rocks, 1,** in or into a state of disaster or bankruptcy. **2,** poured straight over ice (as whiskey). —**rock and rye,** rye whiskey flavored with sugar crystals (rock candy). —**rock crystal,** a transparent variety of quartz. —**rock garden,** one grown among rocks. —**rocking horse,** a child's riding toy. —**rock salt,** a mineral salt. —**rock wool,** an insulating material.

rock
↔ The sense of a swaying motion comes from Old English *roccian.* The sense of a mass of stone is from Old French *roque.*

rock'a·bil"ly (rok'ə-bil"ē) *n.* a combination of country and western and rock-'n'-roll music.

rock″bot′tom *adj.* **1,** lowest possible. **2,** basic; fundamental.

rock′bound″ *adj.* **1,** surrounded by rocks. **2,** impenetrable.

rock′er *n.* **1,** a curved piece on which a cradle or chair moves backward and forward. **2,** a chair so mounted: *rocking chair.* **3,** an oscillating part in a machine.

rock′et (rok′it) *n.* a tube propelled into the air by self-contained explosives, used in fireworks, warfare, etc. —*v.i.* rise with great rapidity.

rock′et·ry (-rē) *n.* the science and technology of rockets.

rock′-'n'-roll′ (rok′ən-rōl′) *n.* a style of popular music characterized by a heavily accented beat.

rock′ribbed″ (rok′ribd″) *adj.* **1,** marked by rocky ridges. **2,** inflexible; unyielding.

rock′y (-ē) *adj.* **1,** of or like stone; rough with, or as with, crushed stone. **2,** shaky. —**rock′i·ness,** *n.*

Rocky Mountain spotted fever an infectious disease transmitted by ticks.

ro·co′co (rə-kō′kō) *n.* an extremely ornate style of ornamentation. —*adj.* in this style.

rod *n.* **1,** a slender, straight stick. **2,** a scepter; fig., authority. **3,** a switch used for chastisement. **4,** a measure of length, 16 feet. **5,** a fishing pole. **6,** a nerve ending in the retina. **7,** (*Slang*) a pistol.

rode (rōd) *v.* pret. of *ride.*

ro′dent (rō′dənt) *n.* a member of an order of gnawing mammals with sharp, strong teeth.

ro·de′o (rō-dā′ō) *n.* **1,** a roundup of cattle. **2,** a public performance of horsemanship, lassoing, etc.

rod″o·mon·tade′ (rod″ə-mon-tād′) *n.* vainglorious boasting; bravado.

> **rodomontade**
> ↔ From the character *Rodomante*, a boastful king of Algiers in two poems of 16th-c. Italian poet Ludovico Ariosto.

roe (rō) *n.* **1,** a small, agile, very graceful deer of Europe and Asia. **2,** the doe of the stag or red deer. **3,** the eggs of a fish or of various crustaceans.

roe′buck″ *n.* the male of a species of deer, the roe deer.

roent′gen (rent′gən) *n.* a unit of x-radiation. —**Roent′gen ray,** x-ray.

ro·ga′tion (rō-gā′shən) *n.* a litany or supplication.

> **roentgen**
> ↔ Named after 19th-c. German physicist Wilhelm *Roentgen.*

rog′er (roj′ər) *interj.* (*Slang*) very well; order received.

rogue (rōg) *n.* **1,** a dishonest person; a knave. **2,** a mischievous or playful person. —**ro′guish** (-gish) *adj.* —**rogue's gallery,** a collection of photographs of known criminals.

ro′guer·y (rō′gə-rē) *n.* **1,** knavishness. **2,** a knavish act.

roil *v.t.* **1,** make turbid by stirring up (water, etc.). **2,** annoy; vex.

roist′er (rois′tər) *v.i.* bluster; swagger; bully; be noisy. —**roist′er·er,** *n.*

role (rōl) *n.* **1,** an actor's part. **2,** function. —**role model,** a person whose behavior is emulated by others, esp. by those younger.

Rolf′ing (rolf′ing) *n.* (*T.N.*) a type of deep massage therapy.

roll (rōl) *v.i.* **1,** move along a surface by turning over and over. **2,** travel on wheels. **3,** revolve. **4,** sway. **5,** move in ripples, as waves. **6,** make a deep prolonged sound. **7,** be wound or curled in cylindrical form. **8,** turn over and over while lying down; wallow. —*v.t.* **1,** cause to roll or rotate; whirl. **2,** give expression to a prolonged deep sound. **3,** (often with *up*) wrap around an axis. **4,** press or level with rollers. **5,** trill, esp. the letter *r.* —*n.* **1,** something wound into a cylinder. **2,** a small bread; a biscuit. **3,** a list of names. **4,** the act of rolling. **5,** a deep, prolonged, or sustained sound. **6,** a swell or undulation of the surface. **7,** a swagger. **8,** a streak of good luck. —**roll call,** a calling of names to which those present must answer. —**rolling mill,** an establishment that makes steel sheets, bars, etc. —**rolling pin,** a wooden cylinder for rolling dough. —**rolling stock,** railroad cars.

roll′back″ *n.* a reduction to a previous, lower level, as of prices.

roll′bar″ *n.* a rigid curved bar covering the passenger area of an automobile to protect occupants if the car should overturn.

roll′er *n.* **1,** a cylinder used as a wheel, bearing, core, pressing surface, etc. **2,** a heavy wave. —**roller bearing,** a bearing in which revolving cylinders bear the shaft. —**roller coaster,** a miniature railway used at amusement parks. —**roller derby,** a contest played between two teams on roller skates. —**roller skate,** a shoe or attachment with small wheels.

Rol′ler·blade″ *n.* (*T.N.*) a type of roller skate having only one set of in-line rollers.

rol′lick (rol′ik) *v.i.* frolic; be gay. —**rol′-lick·ing,** *adj.*

roll′o″ver *n.* **1,** a rolling over. **2,** the extension of the term of an obligation.

roll′top″ desk a desk with a cover that slides upward.

ro′ly·po″ly (rō′lē-pō″lē) *adj.* round; pudgy. —*n.* a kind of dessert.

> **roly-poly**
> ↔ From earlier *rowly-powly,* a type of game with balls, lit., worthless fellow.

ROM computer memory whose contents can be read but not changed or overwritten, usu. used to hold operating system instructions: *r(ead-)o(nly) m(emory).*

Ro′man (rō′mən) *adj.* **1,** pert. to Rome. **2,** (*l.c.*) denoting any printing type not italic. **3,** denoting the numerals (as I = 1, V = 5, X = 10, etc.) used in ancient Rome. **4,** pert. to the Rom. Cath. Church.—*n.* a citizen or inhabitant of Rome. —**Roman alphabet,** Latin alphabet. —**Roman candle,** a kind of colorful firework. —**Roman nose,** a nose with a prominent bridge.

ro·man à clef′ (rō-mä na klä′) (*Fr.*) a work of historical fiction.

Roman Catholic a member of the Christian church of which the Pope, or Bishop of Rome, is the pontiff.

ro·mance′ (rō-mans′) *n.* **1,** a tale or novel of extraordinary, not real or familiar, life. **2,** a fiction; a falsehood. **3,** a love affair. —*adj.* (*cap.*) denoting a language almost wholly derived from Latin, as Italian, Spanish, French. —*v.i.* **1,** make up fanciful tales. **2,** (*Informal*) make love.

Ro″man·esque′ (rō″mən-esk′) *n.* the early medieval style of architecture in W. Europe. —*adj.* pert. to or designating this style.

Ro·ma′ni·an (rō-mā′nē-ən) *adj.* of or pert. to Romania, its people, or their language. —*n.* a native or citizen of Romania. Also, **Ru·ma′ni·an, Rou·ma′ni·an.**

ro·man′tic (rō-man′tik) *adj.* **1,** fanciful; fabulous; pert. to romance. **2,** given to sentimental or amorous feelings. **3,** in art and literature, imaginative and free from classical rule. —*n.* a romantic person; romanticist. —**ro·man′ti·cal·ly,** *adv.* —**ro·man′ti·cism,** *n.*

Rom′a·ny (rom′ə-nē) *n.* a gypsy; the gypsy language. —*adj.* belonging to or relating to the gypsies. —**Romany rye** (rī) a

person, not a gypsy, who associates with gypsies.

Ro′me·o (rō′mē-ō) *n.* **1,** (*Informal*) a lover. **2,** (*l.c.*) (*Communications*) the letter *r.*

> **Romeo**
> ↔ After the hero of the tragedy *Romeo and Juliet* by William Shakespeare.

romp *v.i.* **1,** leap and frisk about in play. **2,** win easily. —*n.* **1,** boisterous play. **2,** an easy win. —**romp′ers,** *n.pl.* a small child's costume.

ron′deau (ron′dō) *n.* [*pl.* **-deaux** (-dōz)] (*Fr.*) a Fr. lyric poem.

ron′do (ron′dō) *n.* [*pl.* **-dos**] (*Music*) a work in which the principal theme is often repeated.

rood *n.* **1,** a crucifix. **2,** a varying unit of measurement.

roof *n.* **1,** the external upper covering of a building, car, etc. **2,** any house. **3,** an upper limit. —*v.t.* cover with a roof; shelter. —**roof′er,** *n.* —**roof′ing,** *n.* a material for making a roof. —**roof garden,** a restaurant on top of a building.

roof′tree″ *n.* **1,** the ridgepole of a roof. **2,** a roof. **3,** home.

rook (rûk) *n.* **1,** a Europ. crow. **2,** a piece used in chess; a castle. —*v.i. & t.* cheat. —**rook′er·y,** *n.* a roost for rooks.

rook′ie (rûk′ē) *n.* (*Slang*) an inexperienced recruit; a beginner, as a policeman in training, etc.

room *n.* **1,** extent of space, great or small. **2,** space or place unoccupied or unobstructed. **3,** freedom; opportunity. **4,** an apartment; chamber. —*v.i.* (*Informal*) lodge. —**room′er,** *n.* a lodger. —**room′ful,** *n.* —**rooming house,** a house where rooms are let.

room·ette′ (rû-met′) *n.* a small private compartment in a railroad sleeping car.

room′mate″ *n.* one with whom one shares living quarters.

room′y (rûm′ē) *adj.* spacious. —**room′i·ness,** *n.*

roor′back (rûr′bak) *n.* a false story defaming a political candidate.

> **roorback**
> ↔ From Baron von *Roorback,* imaginary author of an imaginary 19th-c. travel book.

roost *n.* **1,** a pole, a perch, or a place for fowls to rest at night. **2,** (*Informal*) a temporary abiding place. —*v.i.* **1,** perch, as a bird. **2,** (*Informal*) lodge.

---

fat, fāte, fär, fâre, fâll, ȧsk; met, hē, hėr, maybē; pin, pīne; not, nōte, ôr, tool

roost'er (roos'tər) *n.* the male of the domestic chicken; a cock.

root *n.* **1,** the part of a plant that grows downward into the soil. **2,** the foundation of anything. **3,** a source, origin, or cause. **4,** (*Math.*) a quantity that when multiplied by itself a certain number of times will produce a given quantity. **5,** (*Math.*) a quantity that, when substituted for the unknown quantity in an equation, satisfies the equation. **6,** the part of a word that conveys its essential meaning. **7,** (*pl.*) a person's ethnic and cultural origins. —*v.t.* **1,** plant firmly; fix. **2,** tear up or out, as by the roots. —*v.i.* **1,** take root; be firmly fixed; be established. **2,** turn up the earth with the snout. **3,** (*Informal*) cheer; (with *for*) wish well. —**root'er,** *n.* (*Informal*) a supporter; one who applauds. —**root beer,** a beverage flavored with aromatic roots.

root'stock" *n.* **1,** a plant stem resembling a root. **2,** the primary ground or cause of anything.

rope (rōp) *n.* **1,** a thick, strong cord made of several strands twisted together. **2,** a row or string of things. **3,** a stringy, glutinous formation. **4,** death by hanging. —*v.t.* **1,** fasten or enclose with a strong cord; catch; lasso. **2,** (*Slang*) (with *in*) fool; trick.

Roque'fort (rōk'fərt) *n.* a strong French cheese, veined with mold.

ror'qual (rôr'kwəl) *n.* a finback whale.

Ror'schach test (rôr'shäk) a personality and intelligence test consisting of 10 inkblot designs to be described by the subject in his or her own terms, named for 20th-c. Swiss psychiatrist Hermann Rorschach.

ro'sa·ry (rō'zə-rē) *n.* **1,** (*Rom. Cath.*) a string of beads used in counting prayers. **2,** a garland or bed of roses. **3,** an anthology.

rosary
↔ From Latin *rosarium*, rose garden. The English term was used as the title for a collection of prayers, and was later extended to the string of beads used to count off prayers.

rose (rōz) *n.* **1,** a thorny shrub bearing flowers in various colors. **2,** a light crimson color. —*adj.* light crimson. —*v.* pret. of *rise.* —**rose diamond,** one with a faceted top and flat bottom. —**rose fever,** a form of hay fever caused by grass pollen, occurring in the spring. —**rose window,** a circular window with elaborate radiating tracery.

ros'e·ate (rō'zē-ət) *adj.* **1,** rose-colored; blushing. **2,** optimistic.

rose'bud" *n.* the bud of a rose.

rose'bush" *n.* the bush on which roses grow.

rose'mar"y (rōz'mār"ē) *n.* a fragrant evergreen shrub.

rosemary
↔ From Latin *ros,* dew + *marinus,* marine, i.e., dew of the sea.

ro·sette' (rō-zet') *n.* a design or ornament in circular, roselike form.

rose'wa"ter *n.* a water scented with oil of roses.

rose'wood" *n.* a tree, or its reddish, fragrant wood.

Rosh" Ha·sha'na (rosh" hä-shä'nə) the Jewish New Year.

Ro"si·cru'cian (rō"zi-kroo'shən) *n.* a member of a supposed secret society claiming knowledge of the occult sciences. —*adj.* pert. to this society.

ros'in (roz'in) *n.* the solid substance (*resin*) left after the distillation of the oil of turpentine. —*v.t.* rub with rosin.

ros'ter (ros'tər) *n.* **1,** a list of names. **2,** a schedule; a program.

ros'trum (ros'trəm) *n.* a pulpit or platform for a speaker. ◻ *dais*

ros'y (rō'zē) *adj.* **1,** rose-colored. **2,** favorable; promising. **3,** blushing; blooming. —**ros'i·ness,** *n.*

rot *v.i.* [**rot'ted, -ting**] **1,** undergo natural decomposition; decay. **2,** become corrupt; deteriorate. —*n.* **1,** the process or result of decaying. **2,** a parasitic disease. **3,** (*Slang*) nonsense; humbug.

ro'ta·ry (rō'tə-rē) *adj.* turning, as a wheel on its axis. —*n.* a traffic circle.

ro'tate (rō'tāt) *v.i. & t.* **1,** revolve or move around a center or axis. **2,** alternate serially. —**ro·ta'tion,** *n.* —**ro'ta·tor cuff** (-tər) a group of muscles supporting the shoulder, often injured in sports.

rote (rōt) *n.* **1,** mechanical routine in learning; repetition without attention to meaning. **2,** a medieval string musical instrument.

ro·tis'se·rie (rō-tis'ə-rē) *n.* a broiler with a rotating spit for roasting meat.

ro"to·gra·vure' (rō"tə-grə-vyûr') *n.* a process for gravure printing from cylindrical plates.

ro'tor (rō'tər) *n.* a rotating part of a machine.

rot'ten (rot'ən) *adj.* **1,** having rotted; decayed. **2,** (*Informal*) very bad. **3,** (*Slang*) contemptible. —**rot'ten·ness,** *n.*

rot'ter (rot'ər) *n.* a scoundrel; cad.

Rott'wei"ler (rot'wī"lər) *n.* a German breed of cattle dog.

ro·tund' (rō-tund') *adj.* round or rounded out; bulbous; obese. **—ro·tun'·di·ty,** *n.*

ro·tun'da (rō-tun'də) *n.* a round building or room, esp. one with a dome.

rou'ble (roo'bəl) *n.* ruble.

rou·é' (roo-ā') *n.* a dissolute man; a rake.

rouge (roozh) *n.* **1,** a red cosmetic or coloring for the skin. **2,** a red powder or paste used for polishing. **—***v.t.* & *i.* apply rouge (to).

rough (ruf) *adj.* **1,** not smooth to the touch or to the sight; uneven. **2,** left in a natural or incomplete state; crude; approximate. **3,** severe; harsh. **4,** lacking refinement; uncouth. **5,** boisterously violent. **—***n.* **1,** (with *the*) crudeness; rawness. **2,** in golf, the untrimmed grass bordering the fairway. **—***adv.* in a crude, coarse, or harsh manner. **—rough it,** endure hardships. **—rough'ness,** *n.* **—Rough Rider,** in the Span. Amer. war, a member of a volunteer cavalry regiment organized and commanded by Theodore Roosevelt.

rough'age (ruf'ij) *n.* coarse, bulky food.

rough-'and-read'y *adj.* crude but effective.

rough-'and-tum'ble *adj.* & *n.* (characterized by) rough action or fighting.

rough'en (-ən) *v.t.* make rough.

rough-'hew" *v.t.* **1,** hew without smoothing, as timber. **2,** give a crude form to.

rough'house" *n.* boisterous play. **—***v.t.* treat violently but in fun.

rough'neck" *n.* a boor; a rowdy.

rough'rid"er *n.* one who breaks in wild horses.

rough'shod" *adj.* **1,** shod with spiked horseshoes. **2,** ruthless.

rou·lade' (roo-läd') *n.* (*Fr.*) **1,** meat rolled around a filling and cooked. **2,** (*Music*) a rapid succession of notes in a melody.

rou·lette' (roo-let') *n.* **1,** a game of betting on the number at which a revolving wheel will stop. **2,** a cutting tool using a rowel.

round (rownd) *adj.* **1,** having the shape, or approximately the shape, of a circle, cylinder, or sphere. **2,** having curved sections, lines, or surfaces; convex. **3,** easy, smooth and brisk in motion. **4,** full; liberal. **5,** approximate. **—***n.* **1,** a round object. **2,** series; circuit; course or tour of duty. **3,** a period of action between inter-

missions. **4,** a rung of a ladder or chair. **5,** a cut of beef: *round steak.* **6,** ammunition for a single shot or volley. **—***v.t.* **1,** give rotundity to. **2,** (with *out*) complete or perfect. **3,** encircle; encompass. **4,** make a course along or around. **5,** (with *up*) drive or gather (cattle, etc.) together. **—***v.i.* **1,** grow or become rotund. **2,** mature; develop. **—***adv.* **1,** on all sides, so as to surround. **2,** with a rotating movement. **3,** in, within, or through a circuit. **4,** in circumference. **5,** from beginning to end. **—***prep.* around; about. **—round'ness,** *n.* **—round robin,** an act in which all members of a group participate. **—round table,** a group assembled for discussion. **—round trip,** one to a place and back again.

round'a·bout" *adj.* circuitous; indirect. **—***n.* **1,** a circuitous course, statement, etc. **2,** a merry-go-round. **3,** (*Brit.*) a rotary.

round'el (rown'dəl) *n.* **1,** a rondeau. **2,** something round, esp. a window.

roun'de·lay" (rown'də-lā") *n.* **1,** any song in which an idea, line, or refrain is continually repeated. **2,** a dance in a circle.

> **roundelay**
> ↔ Not a *lay* at all, *roundelay* comes from Middle French *rondelet*, little circle.

round'er 1, one who travels a circuit. **2,** a dissolute person; an idler.

round'house" *n.* a circular building where locomotives are repaired.

round'ly (-lè) *adv.* vigorously; earnestly; frankly.

round-'the-clock' *adj.* lasting more than 24 hours; continual.

round'up *n.* **1,** a gathering or driving together. **2,** a summation.

round'worm" *n.* a parasitic worm, esp. one infesting the human intestine.

rouse (rowz) *v.t.* cause to start up from sleep, inactivity, indifference, etc.; stir up; provoke. **—***v.i.* start or rise up; be stirred to action.

roust'a·bout" (rowst'ə-bowt") *n.* **1,** a laborer on a wharf or river boat. **2,** a laborer at odd jobs.

> **rout, route**
> ☞ Do not confuse these two similar-looking words, which have totally different meanings. *Rout* means (among other things) a retreat; *route* means a road.

rout (rowt) *n.* **1,** a confused retreat after a defeat. **2,** a disorderly crowd; the rabble.

—*v.t.* **1,** disperse by defeating; drive away in disorder. **2,** (with *out*) turn out. **3,** cut away. —**rout′er,** *n.* a tool for cutting grooves, recesses, etc.

route (root) *n.* **1,** a way; road. **2,** a course; line of travel. —*v.t.* send by a certain route. ❏ **rout**

rou·tine′ (roo-tēn′) *n.* a customary procedure or course of action. —*adj.* entirely customary; not deviating from routine.

roux (roo) *n.* (*Fr.*) a mixture of flour and melted butter for thickening gravy or soup.

rove (rōv) *v.i. & t.* wander at pleasure; roam; ramble.

rov′er (-ər) *n.* **1,** a pirate or a pirate ship. **2,** a wanderer. **3,** a fickle person.

row (rō) *n.* **1,** a series of persons or things in a straight line. **2,** a ride in a rowboat. —*v.t. & i.* propel (a boat) by means of oars.

row (row) *n.* a noisy disturbance; a quarrel. —*v.i.* quarrel.

row′boat″ (rō′bōt″) *n.* a small boat propelled by oars.

row′dy (row′dė) *n.* a rough, quarrelsome person. —*adj.* rough; disreputable. —**row′dy·ish,** *adj.* —**row′dy·ism,** *n.*

row′el (row′əl) *n.* **1,** the wheel of a horseman's spur. **2,** a similar wheel for cutting, perforating, etc.

row′lock (rō′-) *n.* an oarlock.

roy′al (roi′əl) *adj.* **1,** pert. or related to a king or queen. **2,** majestic. **3,** large or superior of its kind.

roy′al·ist *n.* an adherent of a king or monarchy. —*adj.* pert. to royalists. —**roy′al·ism,** *n.*

roy′al·ty (-tė) *n.* **1,** the state or condition of being royal; royal persons collectively. **2,** a fee paid for the use of prerogatives such as a patent, copyright, etc.

RSVP(*Fr., répondez s'il vous plaît,* please respond) *v.i.* to respond to an invitation. —*n.* **1,** a response to an invitation. **2,** on an invitation, a request for a response.

rub *v.t.* [**rubbed, rub′bing**] **1,** apply pressure and friction by motion over the surface of. **2,** smooth, polish, clean, etc., by rubbing. **3,** affect as if by friction; annoy; disturb. —*v.i.* move or act with friction; rub something. —*n.* **1,** the act of rubbing. **2,** (*Informal*) a disturbing factor. —**rub it in,** emphasize or reiterate something disagreeable. —**rub out,** (*Slang*) murder.

rub-′a-dub″ (rub′ə-dub″) *n.* the sound of a drum when beaten.

ru·ba′to (roo-bä′tō) *adj. & adv.* (*It.*) per-

formed with a certain freedom of rhythm, to heighten the effect. —*n.* **1,** a rubato style of performance. **2,** a passage so played.

rub′ber (rub′ər) *n.* **1,** one who or that which rubs. **2,** something made of rubber, esp. a pencil eraser. **3,** an elastic, tough, waterproof substance obtained from the sap of various tropical trees. **4,** a series of games, usually three. —*adj.* made of rubber. —**rubber cement,** an adhesive containing rubber and naphtha. —**rubber check,** (*Slang*) a check that is worthless.

rub′ber·ize (-īz″) *v.t.* waterproof (as cloth) with rubber.

rub′ber·neck″ *n.* (*Slang*) **1,** an inquisitive person. **2,** a sightseeing bus. —*v.i.* stretch the neck to look.

rub″ber·stamp′ *v.t.* **1,** imprint with inked rubber type. **2,** (*Informal*) approve without scrutiny.

rub′ber·y *adj.* tough and elastic. —**rub′ber·i·ness,** *n.*

rub′bish (rub′ish) *n.* waste material; trash; litter.

rub′ble (rub′əl) *n.* **1,** rough broken stones. **2,** trash.

rub′down″ *n.* a massage of the body, esp. after exercise.

rube (roob) *n.* (*Slang*) a crude or clownish countryman.

ru·bel′la (roo-bel′ə) *n.* a mild contagious disease: *German measles.*

ru·bi·cund″ (roo′bə-kund″) *adj.* inclining to redness; ruddy.

ru·bid′i·um (roo-bid′ė-əm) *n.* a metallic element, no. 37, symbol Rb.

ru′ble (roo′bəl) *n.* the monetary unit of Russia. Also, **rou′ble.**

ru′bric (roo′brik) *n.* **1,** a heading or caption in a book or other writing. **2,** a rule for the conduct of religious worship.

ru′by (roo′bė) *n.* **1,** a clear, red precious stone, a variety of corundum. **2,** a pure crimson red color.

ruche (roosh) *n.* a frill or strip of dress trimming. Also, **ruch′ing** (roo′shing).

ruck (ruk) *n.* **1,** a fold or crease. **2,** the common run of persons or things.

ruck′sack″ *n.* a knapsack.

ruck′us (ruk′əs) *n.* (*Slang*) a noisy disturbance.

ruc′tion (ruk′shən) *n.* a disturbance; a row; rumpus.

rud′der (rud′ər) *n.* a flat piece hinged vertically, used for directing a ship or airplane.

rud′dy (rud′ė) *adj.* of a red color, esp. healthily red. —**rud′di·ness,** *n.*

---

tub, cūte, pŭll; labəl; oil, owl, go, chip, she, thin, *th*en, sing, ink; *see p.* 6

rude (rood) *adj.* **1,** rough; crude; primitive. **2,** ill-bred; discourteous; impolite. **3,** sturdy; rugged. **4,** tempestuous, as weather. —**rude′ness,** *n.*

ru′di·ment (roo′di-mənt) *n.* **1,** an undeveloped state. **2,** (usu. *pl.*) an element or first principle, as of an art or science. —**ru″di·men′ta·ry** (-men′tə-rė) *adj.*

rue (roo) *v.t.* repent of; regret; feel sorrow or suffering on account of. —*n.* a garden plant used in medicine. —**rue′ful,** *adj.* sorrowful.

ruff (ruf) *n.* **1,** a large, projecting, frilled collar of fine material. **2,** a breed of domestic pigeons. **3,** in card playing, an act of trumping. —*v.* in cards, play a trump. —**ruffed grouse,** partridge.

ruf′fi·an (ruf′ė-ən) *n.* a brutal man; a thug; rowdy. —**ruf″fi·an·ly,** *adj.*

ruf″fle (ruf′əl) *v.t.* **1,** draw up into gathers, folds, or pleats. **2,** disturb the arrangement, orderliness, or composure of; rumple; ripple; agitate. —*n.* **1,** a gathered border or trimming. **2,** a low beat of a drum.

rug *n.* **1,** a thick, heavy floor covering. **2,** a lap robe.

rug′by (rug′bė) *n.* a Brit. form of football.

> **rugby**
> ↔ From the *Rugby* School in England, where the game was first played.

rug′ged (rug′id) *adj.* **1,** having a rough surface; shaggy; hilly; uneven. **2,** unpolished; uncultivated. **3,** harsh; austere. **4,** fierce; tempestuous. **5,** (*Informal*) robust; strong. —**rug′ged·ness,** *n.*

ru′in (roo′in) *n.* **1,** collapse, moral or physical; downfall; overthrow. **2,** that which promotes decay or destruction. **3,** (often *pl.*) anything, as a building, in a state of destruction, decay, or wreck. —*v.t.* damage essentially and irreparably. —**ru″in·a′tion,** *n.* —**ru′in·ous,** *adj.*

rule (rool) *n.* **1,** a regulation for standard procedure; a law. **2,** an established method or way of doing anything. **3,** government; supreme authority. **4,** a scaled strip; ruler. **5,** a printed or drawn straight line. —*v.t.* **1,** determine; settle. **2,** govern; control. **3,** mark with lines. —*v.i.* **1,** have power or command. **2,** prevail; decide. —**rule of thumb,** a practical method; a rough guide.

rul′er (roo′lər) *n.* **1,** one who governs. **2,** a scaled strip of wood, metal, etc. with a straight edge, used for measuring and drawing lines.

rul′ing *n.* an authoritative decision. —*adj.* governing; chief; prevalent.

rum *n.* **1,** an alcoholic liquor distilled from sugar cane. **2,** any strong alcoholic drink. **3,** a card game; rummy. —*adj.* (*Slang*) queer; odd; droll. —**rum runner,** *n.* a smuggler of, or vehicle or ship carrying, contraband liquor.

Ru·ma′ni·an (roo-mā′nė-ən) *n. & adj.* Romanian.

rum′ba (rum′bə) *n.* a fast dance, originally Cuban, or the music for it.

rum′ble (rum′bəl) *v.i.* **1,** make a deep, heavy, continuous sound. **2,** move with such a sound; roll heavily or noisily. **3,** (*Slang*) fight. —*v.t.* utter, or cause to make, such a sound. —*n.* **1,** a rumbling sound. **2,** an open seat at the back of a roadster or coupé. **3,** (*Slang*) a street fighter.

rum′dum″ (*Slang*) *n.* **1,** a lush. **2,** a stupid or inept person. —*adj.* **1,** having a tendency to drunkenness. **2,** ordinary; lacking skill.

ru′men (roo′min) *n.* **1,** the first stomach of a cow or other ruminant. **2,** the cud.

ru′mi·nant (roo′mi-nənt) *n.* a cud-chewing animal. —*adj.* **1,** cud-chewing. **2,** contemplative.

ru′mi·nate″ (roo′mə-nāt″) *v.i.* **1,** chew the cud. **2,** meditate; ponder. —*v.t.* **1,** chew again. **2,** turn over in the mind. —**ru″mi·na′tion,** *n.*

rum′mage (rum′ij) *v.t. & i.* hunt through; ransack. —*n.* **1,** a search. **2,** odds and ends. —**rummage sale,** a sale of miscellaneous articles.

rum′my (rum′ė) *n.* **1,** a card game. **2,** (*Slang*) an alcoholic. —*adj.* rum.

ru′mor (roo′mər) *n.* **1,** popular report. **2,** an unconfirmed but widely circulated story; a piece of gossip. Also, **ru′mour.**

rump *n.* **1,** the back parts of an animal; the buttocks. **2,** a remnant.

rum′ple (rum′pəl) *v.t. & i.* make uneven; wrinkle; become mussed. —*n.* a wrinkle.

rum′pus (rum′pəs) *n.* (*Informal*) a noisy or disorderly commotion; a brawl. —**rumpus room,** a room for games and play.

run *v.i.* [**ran, run, run′ning**] **1,** move swiftly on foot. **2,** make haste; rush; flee; steal away; abscond. **3,** pursue a course; travel. **4,** perform a regular passage from place to place. **5,** flow. **6,** discharge a fluid, as tears; become fluid. **7,** extend from point to point; spread. **8,** operate; work. **9,** be a candidate for office; compete in a race. **10,** go or pass by; elapse, as time. **11,** (with *to*) have a proclivity or general tendency. **12,** have a certain direction, course, tenor, or form. **13,** keep going; continue. **14,** ravel. **15,** average. —*v.t.* **1,** cause (anything) to go or to function; direct; operate. **2,** accomplish; undertake. **3,** travel past or through successfully. **4,** smuggle. **5,** sew several stitches at the same time. —*n.* **1,** the act of moving at a rapid pace. **2,** a passage; journey; trip; distance covered. **3,** a current; a flow. **4,** course; progress; a continued course. **5,** a tendency; general character. **6,** a general and extraordinary demand, as on a bank. **7,** in baseball, the act of making a score. **8,** in certain card games, a sequence. **9,** free access to a place. **10,** a place where animals may range. **11,** a herd or school moving together. **12,** a small stream of water; a brook. **13,** a ravel, as in hose. **14,** a series of successes. **15,** (*Music*) a roulade. —**run′ny,** *adj.* —**run down, 1,** disparage. **2,** enumerate; list. **3,** unwind, as a clock. —**run in,** arrest and confine. —**run-of-the-mill,** *adj.* average.

run′a·bout″ *n.* a light, open automobile or motorboat.

run′a·round″ *n.* **1,** (*Informal*) an abscess near a fingernail or toenail. **2,** (*Slang*) an evasion. **3,** type set around an illustration.

run′a·way″ *adj.* **1,** escaped; out of control. **2,** eloping. —*n.* **1,** a horse, etc. that has escaped. **2,** an easy victory, as in a race.

run′ci·ble spoon (run′si-bəl) a fork with three broad tines, one edged, curved like a spoon.

> **runcible**
> ↔ This odd word was coined by 19th-c. Amer. poet Edward Lear in his poem "The Owl and the Pussycat."

run-″down′ *adj.* **1,** in poor health or condition. **2,** of a clock, etc., not wound.

run′down″ *n.* (*Informal*) narrative.

rune (roon) *n.* **1,** a character of an ancient Europ. alphabet. **2,** an obscure saying. —**ru′nic,** *adj.*

rung *n.* a rounded bar forming the crosspiece of a ladder, a brace on a chair, a spoke, etc. —*v.* p.p. of *ring.*

run′nel (run′əl) *n.* a small stream.

run′ner (run′ər) *n.* **1,** one who runs; a messenger; a racer. **2,** the base on which a sled, etc., slides. **3,** a shoot from a plant. **4,** a narrow rug or table scarf.

run″ner-up′ *n.* the contestant finishing in second place.

run′ning (-ing) *n.* **1,** act of one who or that which runs. **2,** competition. —*adj.* **1,** that runs. **2,** cursory; hasty. **3,** continuous; persistent. —**running board,** a ledge at the side of a vehicle. —**running head,** the heading at the top of each page of a book. —**running light,** a light (for visibility, navigation, etc.) on a boat, ship, or aircraft. —**running mate,** a competitor or candidate allied with another.

run′off″ *n.* **1,** water flowing off the land. **2,** a deciding contest.

runt *n.* **1,** any undersized animal, esp. the smallest of a litter. **2,** a small or contemptible person.

run-′through″ *n.* a rehearsal at which a work is performed complete, with few stops.

run′way″ *n.* a channel; course; a level strip for airplanes landing and taking off.

ru·pee′ (roo-pē′) *n.* a monetary unit of India.

rup′ture (rup′chər) *n.* **1,** the act or result of breaking; a breach of peace. **2,** hernia, esp. abdominal hernia. —*v.t.* **1,** break; burst. **2,** cause to suffer from hernia. —*v.i.* suffer a break.

ru′ral (rûr′əl) *adj.* pert. to the country or to country life. —**rural free delivery,** free delivery of mail in rural districts. *Abbr.,* **RFD.**

ruse (rooz) *n.* artifice; trickery; a stratagem.

rush *v.i.* **1,** move or drive forward with violent haste. **2,** move or act with undue eagerness; hurry. —*v.t.* **1,** cause to go swiftly or violently. **2,** (*Football*) carry (the ball) forward. **3,** cause to hasten; push. **4,** (*Slang*) entertain, to induce to join a fraternity or sorority. **5,** (*Informal*) court. —*n.* **1,** a driving forward with eagerness and haste. **2,** an eager demand; a run. **3,** (*Informal*) urgent pressure. **4,** a scrimmage. **5,** (*pl.*) the first prints of a motion picture film, for inspection. **6,** any of various hollow-stemmed water plants. **7,** (*Slang*) a sudden feeling of excitement or pleasure, as from a drug. —**rush hour,** a time of heaviest traffic.

rusk *n.* a sweet, toasted bread or biscuit; zwieback.

rus′set (rus′it) *n.* **1,** a reddish-brown color. **2,** a kind of winter apple with a brownish skin. —*adj.* reddish-brown.

Rus′sian (rush′ən) *adj.* pert. to Russia, its people, or its language. —**Russian roulette,** a type of duel or act of bravado performed with a gun loaded with one bullet.

rust *n.* **1,** the reddish coating that forms on iron exposed to air and moisture. **2,** any corrosive formation. **3,** an orange-red color. —*v.i.* become rusty. —**rust belt,** the older industrial area of the northeastern and midwestern U.S.

rus'tic (rus'tik) *adj.* **1,** pert. to the country; rural. **2,** unsophisticated; simple. **3,** rude; simply constructed. —*n.* a country person. —**rus'ti·cal·ly,** *adv.* —**rus·tic'i·ty** (-tis'ə-tė) *n.*

rus'ti·cate'' (rus'ti-kāt'') *v.t. & i.* send or go to live in the country. —**rus''ti·ca'tion,** *n.*

rus'tle (rus'əl) *v.i. & t.* **1,** make a murmuring sound by the rubbing of parts against each other. **2,** (*Informal*) stir about. **3,** (*Slang*) steal (cattle). —*n.* the sound of rustling. —**rus'tler,** *n.* a cattle thief.

rust'y (rus'tė) *adj.* **1,** covered with rust. **2,** out of practice. **3,** reddish. **4,** hoarse. —**rust'i·ness,** *n.*

rut *n.* **1,** a narrow track worn or cut in the ground. **2,** an established habit or mode of procedure. **3,** the period of heat in various animals. —*v.t.* [**rut'ted, rut'ting**] trace furrows in. —**rut'ted,** *adj.* furrowed.

ru''ta·ba'ga (roo''tə-bā'gə) *n.* a variety of nutritious turnip.

ru·the'ni·um (roo-thē'nė-əm) *n.* a rare metallic element, no. 44, symbol Ru.

ruth'less (rooth'lis) *adj.* having no pity; merciless. —**ruth'less·ness,** *n.*

rye (rī) *n.* **1,** a hardy cereal plant or its seeds. **2,** whiskey made of rye.

S

S, s (es) the nineteenth letter of the English alphabet.

's (s or z; see p. 8) *suf.* marking the possessive form of nouns. —*contr.* is: as, *he's* (he is). ❑ *possessives*

Sab'bath (sab'əth) *n.* a day of rest and religious dedication.

sab·bat'i·cal (sə-bat'i-kəl) *adj.* pert. to a rest period or (*cap.*) to the Sabbath. —**sabbatical year,** a year's leave of absence (every seventh year).

sa'ber (sā'bər) *n.* a one-edged, curved sword. —**saber-rattling,** *n.* actions or policies that threaten war. —**saber saw,** a portable electric jigsaw.

Sa'bin vaccine (sā'bin) a live attenuated virus taken orally to combat infantile paralysis, named for U.S. physician A. B. Sabin.

sa'ble (sā'bəl) *n.* **1,** an animal of the marten family; its fur. **2,** the color black. **3,** (*pl.*) mourning garments. —*adj.* **1,** made of sable fur. **2,** black.

sa·bot' (sa-bō') *n.* a wooden shoe.

sab'o·tage'' (sab'ə-täzh'') *n.* malicious destruction. —*v.t.* wilfully and maliciously destroy or impede.

> **sabotage**
> ↔ From French *sabot*, clog (a type of wooden shoe). The word means, literally, walking in wooden shoes, i.e., walking noisily or clumsily.

sab''o·teur' (sab''ə-tēr') *n.* one who commits sabotage.

sa'bra (sä'brə) *n.* a native-born Israeli.

sab'u·lous (sab'yə-ləs) *adj.* sandy; gritty. —**sab''u·los'i·ty** (-los'ə-tė) *n.*

sac (sak) *n.* a pouch or cavity in an animal or plant.

sac'cha·rin (sak'ə-rin) *n.* a chemical sweetening compound.

sac'cha·rine (sak'ə-rin) *adj.* **1,** sweet; sugary. **2,** insincerely polite, sympathetic, or flattering; fulsome.

sac''er·do'tal (sas''ər-dō'təl) *adj.* pert. to a priest or to priestly functions.

sa'chem (sā'chəm) *n.* **1,** a No. Amer. Indian chief. **2,** a high official of a political party.

sa·chet' (sa-shā') *n.* a small bag of perfuming herbs, etc.

sack (sak) *n.* **1,** pillage. **2,** a bag, esp. a large one. **3,** (*Slang*) discharge from employment. **4,** a strong white wine. —*v.t.* **1,** plunder. **2,** put into a sack. **3,** (*Informal*) discharge. **4,** (*Football*) tackle the quarterback behind the line of scrimmage.

sack'but (sak'but) *n.* an early form of trombone.

sack'cloth'' *n.* a coarse cloth, symbol of mourning.

sac'ral (sak'rəl) *adj.* **1,** sacred. **2,** of the sacrum.

sac'ra·ment (sak'rə-mənt) *n.* a devotional rite or symbol. —**sac''ra·men'tal,** *adj.*

sa'cred (sā'krid) *adj.* dedicated to a deity; holy; inviolable. —**sac'red·ness,** *n.* —**sacred cow,** something beyond question; a taboo.

sac'ri·fice'' (sak'rə-fīs'') *n.* **1,** an offering, as to God or a deity. **2,** a voluntary loss. **3,** (*Baseball*) a hit made to advance a runner, although the batter is put out. —*v.t.* make a sacrifice of. —*v.i.* make a sacrifice hit.

sac'ri·lege (sak'rə-lij) *n.* profanation of something sacred. —**sac''ri·le'gious** (-lij'əs) *adj.*

---

fat, fāte, fär, fãre, fâll, àsk; met, hē, hėr, maybė; pin, pīne; not, nōte, ôr, tool

sacrilegious

↔ This word is frequently misspelled because of its supposed derivation from *religious*. In fact, it derives from the Latin words *sacra*, sacred things, and *legere*, to steal.

sac'ris·ty (sak'ris-tė) *n.* the place where sacred vessels and vestments are kept. —**sac'ris·tan** (-tən) *n.* the church official in charge of them.

sacristan, sexton

↔ These words both derive from Latin *sacristanus*, a religious official. *Sexton* came by way of Anglo-French.

sac"ro·il'i·ac (sak"rō-il'ė-ak) *n. & adj.* (pert. to) the region between the sacrum and the small intestine.

sac'ro·sanct" (sak'rə-sankt") *adj.* exceedingly sacred.

sac'rum (sak'rum) *n.* the posterior wall of the pelvis.

SAD seasonal affective disorder.

sad, sate, satiate, satisfy

↔ These words all derive from the same Germanic source meaning enough. *Sad* came through Old English. The other words came via Latin *satis*, enough.

sad *adj.* sorrowful; causing sorrow. —**sad'ness,** *n.* —**sad sack,** (*Slang*) an ineffectual or hopeless person.

sad'den (sad'ən) *v.t. & i.* make or become sad.

sad'dle (sad'əl) *n.* 1, a seat for a rider. 2, a cut of meat. —*v.t.* 1, put a saddle on. 2, burden. —**saddle horse,** a horse trained to carry a saddle and rider.

sad'i"ron *n.* a flatiron.

sad'ism (sād'iz-əm) *n.* gratification derived from causing pain. —**sad'ist,** *n.* —**sa·dis'tic** (sə-dis'tik) *adj.* —**sa·dis'ti·cal·ly,** *adv.* ❑ *masochism*

sa"do·mas'o·ch·ism (sā"dō-mas'ə-kiz-əm) *n.* combined sadism and masochism.

sa·fa'ri (sə-fär'ė) *n.* an expedition, esp. for hunting.

safe (sāf) *adj.* 1, free from danger or injury; secure. 2, unharmed. 3, trustworthy. —*n.* 1, a repository for valuables. 2, (*Slang*) a condom. —**safe'ness,** *n.* —**safe house,** a building considered safe for clandestine activities. —**safe sex,** sexual activities employing precautions, such as condoms, to avoid sexually transmitted disease.

safe-"con'duct *n.* the right to go unmo-

lested from one place to another, as during a war; a document granting such a right.

safe'crack"er *n.* a burglar who opens and robs safes.

safe-"de·pos'it box a steel box kept in a bank's vault.

safe'guard" *n.* a means of security or protection. —*v.t.* protect.

safe'keep"ing *n.* care.

safe'ty (-tė) *n.* 1, safeness. 2, protection; safekeeping. 3, a device to prevent injury or accident. 4, (*Football*) a down behind one's own goal line, scoring 2 points for the opponents. —**safety belt,** a belt fastened across the body for protection, in an airplane, automobile, etc. —**safety glass,** unshatterable glass. —**safety match,** a match requiring a prepared surface for striking. —**safety pin,** a pin with a sheathed point. —**safety net,** a net used to prevent injury from falling; hence, any protective measure. —**safety razor,** one with a guarded blade. —**safety valve, 1,** an automatic escape valve. **2,** an outlet for the emotions.

saf'flow"er (saf'low"ər) *n.* a plant whose florets are used in some drugs and dyes and whose oil is used for cooking, etc.

saf'fron (saf'rən) *n.* 1, a crocus. 2, a condiment made from the crocus. 3, a deep orange color.

sag *v.i.* [**sagged, sag'ging**] 1, droop; hang unevenly. 2, decline in price. —*n.* a sinking; a dip.

sa'ga (sä'gə) *n.* a narrative of heroic exploits.

sa·ga'cious (sə-gā'shəs) *adj.* wise. —**sa·gac'i·ty** (sə-gas'ə-tė) *n.*

sag'a·more (sag'ə-môr) *n.* a No. Amer. Indian chief.

sage (sāj) *adj.* profoundly wise. —*n.* 1, a wise person. 2, an herb for seasoning. 3, a bush: *sagebrush.*

Sag"it·ta'ri·us (saj"i-tär'ė-əs) *n.* a constellation, the Archer (see *zodiac*).

sa'go (sā'gō) *n.* [*pl.* **-gos**] a starch obtained from certain palms.

sa·gua'ro (sə-gwä'rō) *n.* [*pl.* **-ros**] a giant cactus.

sa'hib (sä'ib) *n.* (*Indian*) master.

said (sed) *v.* pret. & p.p. of *say.* —*adj.* aforementioned.

sail (sāl) *n.* 1, a piece of canvas, etc., spread to the wind to propel a ship. 2, a voyage. —*v.i.* move along in or as in a vessel. —*v.t.* 1, manage (a vessel). 2, travel over. —**set sail,** begin a voyage.

sail'board" *n.* a small flat sailboat.

sail'boat" *n.* a boat equipped with sails.

sail'cloth" *n.* heavy canvas or duck suitable for making ship's sails.

sail'fish" *n.* **1,** a large seafish with a high dorsal fin. **2,** a small sailboat.

sail'or (-ər) *n.* **1,** a mariner; an enlisted seaman. **2,** a flat-brimmed hat, usually of straw.

sail'plane" *n.* a type of glider.

sain'foin (sān'foin) *n.* a wild grass used as a ground cover and for forage.

saint (sānt) **1,** a person who has been canonized. Abbr., **St. 2,** a person who has died and is in heaven. **3,** a person of great purity. **—saint'hood,** *n.*

Saint Ber·nard' (bər-närd') one of a breed of large, shaggy working dogs.

saint'ed *adj.* **1,** canonized. **2,** sacred. **3,** saintly.

Saint El'mo's fire (el'mōz) St. Elmo's fire.

saint'ly *adj.* being or befitting a saint. **—saint'li·ness,** *n.*

saith (seth) *v.* (*Archaic*) says.

sake (sāk) *n.* **1,** interest; account. **2,** purpose.

sa'ke (sä'kė) *n.* a Jap. rice liquor.

sa·laam' (sə-läm') *n.* an obeisance.

sal'a·ble (sāl'ə-bəl) *adj.* sellable.

sa·la'cious (sə-lā'shəs) *adj.* impure; obscene. **—sa·la'cious·ness,** *n.*

sal'ad (sal'əd) *n.* a dish of uncooked green herbs, fruit, cold vegetables; etc. **—salad days,** a period of youth, inexperience, and usu. poverty.

sal'a·man"der (sal'ə-man"dər) *n.* **1,** a lizardlike amphibian. **2,** a mythical animal able to live in fire.

sa·la'mi (sə-lä'mė) *n.* a spicy Italian sausage.

sal'a·ry (sal'ə-rė) *n.* compensation for work. **—sal'a·ried,** *adj.*

> **salary**
> ↔ From Latin *salarium*, an allowance given to Roman soldiers for buying salt, from *sal,* salt, a word which produced a large number of descendants, including *salary, salami, sauce,* and *sausage.*

Sal'chow (sal'kow) *n.* (*Skating*) a type of jump.

sale (sāl) *n.* **1,** an act of selling. **2,** a selling at a reduced price. **—sales tax,** a tax on retail sales.

sales'man (-mən) [*pl.* **-men**], **sales'wom"an** *n.* one whose profession or specialty is selling. **—sales'clerk",** *n.*

—sales'man·ship, *n.* ability to sell. **—sales'per"son,** *n.*

sa'li·ent (sā'lė-ənt) *adj.* conspicuous; projecting. **—n.** a projecting angle. **—sa'li·ence,** *n.*

sa'line (sā'lēn) *adj.* pert. to salt.

sa·li'va (sə-lī'və) *n.* a fluid secreted in the mouth. **—sal'i·va·ry** (sal'ə-ver-ė) *adj.* **—sal'i·vate"** (sal'ə-vāt") *v.i.* secrete saliva.

Salk vaccine (sâk) a vaccine used to combat infantile paralysis, named for U.S. bacteriologist Dr. Jonas Salk.

sal'low (sal'ō) *adj.* of an unhealthy, yellowish complexion. **—sal'low·ness,** *n.*

sal'ly (sal'ė) *n.* **1,** a rushing forth; a sortie. **2,** a witty remark. **—v.i.** set out briskly.

Sal'ly Mae (mā) Student Loan Marketing Assoc.; the traded security representing loans guaranteed by it.

sal"ma·gun'di (sal"mə-gun'dė) *n.* **1,** a hash or stew. **2,** any mixture.

sal'mi (sal'mė) *n.* a ragout of the meat of game birds, stewed in wine. Also, **sal'mis.**

salm'on (sam'ən) *n.* a marine and freshwater food fish.

> **salmon, salmonella**
> ↔ *Salmon* is, literally, the leaping fish, from Latin *salmo,* probably from *salire,* jump. *Salmonella* has nothing to do with *salmon* the fish; it is named after the 19th-c. American surgeon Daniel E. Salmon.

sal"mon·el'la (sal"mə-nel'ə) *n.* a rod-shaped pathogenic bacterium. ❑ *salmon*

sa·lon' (sə-lon') *n.* **1,** a drawing room. **2,** a fashionable gathering. **3,** a beauty parlor.

> **salon, saloon**
> ☛ Do not confuse the one-*o* salon, meaning a drawing room or a parlor, and *saloon,* a tavern. ↔ Etymologically, the two words are the same, deriving from a Germanic root through French *salon.* English *salon* retains the French spelling, while *saloon* is an Anglicized version.

sa·loon' (sə-loon') *n.* **1,** a barroom. **2,** a public hall. **3,** a sedan. ❑ *salon*

sal·sa (säl'sə) *n.* (*Sp.*) **1,** a Latin Amer. dance. **2,** a sauce.

sal'si·fy (sal'sə-fė) *n.* a vegetable, the oyster plant.

salt (sâlt) *n.* **1,** a mineral, sodium chloride, found in deposits or in seawater, used as a seasoning. **2,** (*pl.*) a medicinal compound. **3,** piquancy; spice; wit. **4,** (*Informal*) a sailor. **—v.t.** season or preserve

with salt. —**salt′ed,** *adj.* —**salt′y,** *adj.*
—**salt away,** (*Informal*) store up; save.
—**salt lick,** a natural deposit of salt, which
animals come to lick. —**salt water, 1,** seawater; the sea. **2,** a solution of salt in
water.

sal″ta·rel′lo (sal″tə-rel′ō) *n.* a lively Italian dance.

sal·ta′tion (sal-tā′shən) *n.* **1,** leaping;
dancing. **2,** an abrupt change or
transition.

salt′cel″lar *n.* a dish or shaker for salt.

> **saltcellar**
> ↔ Not from *cellar*, but from French
> *saliere*, salt container. A *saltcellar* is,
> literally, a "salt salt container."

sal·tine′ (sâl-tēn′) *n.* a crisp, square
cracker topped with coarse salt.

salt′pe′ter (-pē′tər) *n.* niter.

salt′wa″ter *adj.* **1,** inhabiting ocean waters. **2,** pert. to or consisting of salt water.
—**saltwater taffy,** a flavored sugar candy.

salt′y (sâl′tē) *adj.* **1,** containing or tasting
of salt. **2,** piquant; witty; racy. —**salt′i-
ness,** *n.*

sa·lu′bri·ous (sə-loo′brē-əs) *adj.* favorable to health. —**sa·lu′bri·ous·ness, sa·lu′-
bri·ty,** *n.*

sa·lu′ki (sə-loo′kē) *n.* an Asiatic breed
of hunting dog.

> **saluki**
> ↔ Arabic, from *Saluq,* a city in
> Arabia.

sal′u·tar″y (sal′yə-ter″-ē) *adj.* **1,** healthful. **2,** beneficial.

sal″u·ta′tion (sal″yû-tā′shən) *n.* **1,** act of
greeting or saluting. **2,** the formal opening
of a letter.

sa·lu′ta·to·ry (sə-loo′tə-tôr-ē) *adj.* pert.
to a salutation. —*n.* an address of welcome. —**sa·lu″ta·to′ri·an,** *n.* the second-
highest-ranking student in a graduating
class.

sa·lute′ (sə-loot′) *v.t. & i.* **1,** greet; kiss.
2, honor formally. —*n.* an act of greeting
or tribute.

sal′vage (sal′vij) *n.* the saving of property from danger of loss; the property
saved. —*v.t.* save.

sal·va′tion (sal-vā′shən) *n.* **1,** deliverance; that which saves. **2,** redemption.
—**Salvation Army,** a religious and charitable body, organized on military lines.

salve (sàv) *n.* **1,** a healing ointment. **2,**
anything that soothes. —*v.t.* heal; soothe.

sal′ver (sal′vər) *n.* a tray.

> **salver**
> ↔ From Spanish *salva* (Latin *salvare,*
> save), a tray on which food was given
> to a king after it had been tested for
> safety.

sal′vo (sal′vō) *n.* **1,** a discharge of artillery. **2,** a round of applause.

sa·mar′i·um (sə-mar′ē-əm) *n.* a rare-
earth metallic element, no. 62, symbol Sm.

sa·mar′skite (sə-mär′skit) *n.* a black
mineral, source of uranium and rare-earth
metals, named for 19th-c. Russian engineer V. E. Samarskii-Bykhovets.

sam′ba (sàm′bə) *n.* **1,** a So. Amer. dance.
2, a card game, three-pack canasta.

same (sām) *adj.* **1,** identical; agreeing in
kind, degree, or amount. **2,** just mentioned. **3,** unchanged. —*pron.* the same
person or thing.

same′ness (-nis) *n.* **1,** identity. **2,**
monotony.

sam′i·sen (sam′ə-sen″) *n.* a Jap. three-
stringed musical instrument.

sa′miz·dat″ (sa′mèz-dat″) *n.* an underground system in the former U.S.S.R. for
printing and distributing government-
banned literature.

sam′o·var″ (sam′ə-vär″) *n.* a copper urn
for making tea.

Sam″o·yed′ (sam″ə-yed′) *n.* a white-
haired Siberian dog.

sam′pan″ *n.* a small skifflike boat of
China, Indochina, etc.

sam′ple (sam′pəl) *n.* **1,** a representative
specimen. **2,** a digitized recording of a
sound, song, etc., combined with other
samples for various purposes. —*v.t.* **1,**
test; taste. **2,** to make a sample of a sound,
song, etc.

sam′pler *n.* **1,** a piece of embroidery. **2,**
one who samples. **3,** a machine that records electronic samples.

sam′u·rai″ (sam′û-rī″) *n. sing. & pl.* a
member of the Jap. military class.

san″a·to′ri·um (san″ə-tôr′ē-əm) [*pl.* **-a**
(-ə)] *n.* a sanitarium.

> **sanatorium, sanitarium**
> ☞ Many usage experts to the con-
> trary, these two words are now used
> as synonyms. The distinction once
> made between *sanatorium* for institu-
> tions treating tuberculosis and *sani-
> tarium* for those treating mental
> illness is rarely observed today.

sanc′ti·fy″ (sank′tə-fī″) *v.t.* **1,** make holy;
purify. **2,** consecrate. —**sanc″ti·fi·ca′tion,**
n.

sanc'ti·mo"ny (sank'tə-mō"nė) *n.* hypocritical devoutness. —**sanc"ti·mo'ni·ous,** *adj.*

sanc'tion (sank'shən) *n.* **1,** authorization. **2,** ratification. **3,** a nonmilitary punitive act by one nation against another. —*v.t.* **1,** countenance; approve. **2,** ratify.

> **sanction**
> ☞ *Sanction* is one of a small number of words having contradictory meanings. It can mean to approve something, or to punish it, depending on context. Be certain that the context is clear.

sanc'ti·ty (sank'tə-tė) *n.* holiness; sacredness.

sanc'tu·ar"y (sank'chû-er"ė) *n.* **1,** a sacred place. **2,** a place of refuge. **3,** a wildlife preserve.

sanc'tum (sank'təm) *n.* **1,** a sacred place. **2,** a private retreat.

sanc'tum sanc·to'rum (sank'təm sanktôr'əm) (*Lat.*) **1,** holy of holies. **2,** a sacred and inviolable place.

sand *n.* **1,** the fine debris of rocks, in soil-like particles. **2,** (*pl.*) a desert or beach. **3,** (*Informal*) grit; pluck. —*v.t.* **1,** sprinkle with sand. **2,** sandpaper. —**sand'er,** *n.* —**sand bar,** a ridge of sand. —**sand dollar,** any of several varieties of flat, diskshaped sea urchins.

san'dal (san'dəl) *n.* a low shoe.

> **sandal, sandalwood**
> ↔ The two words are unrelated. The foot covering is from Greek *sandalon,* wooden shoe, of uncertain origin. The wood comes ultimately from Sanskrit *candanah.*

san'dal·wood" *n.* a fragrant Asiatic tree or its wood. ❏ *sandal*

san'da·rac (san'də-rak) *n.* a No. Afr. tree; a resin obtained from it, used in varnish, incense, etc.

sand'bag" *n.* a sand-filled bag. —*v.t.* (*Slang*) hit or betray unexpectedly.

sand'blast" *v.t.* clean (stone, etc.) with sand driven by air.

sand'hog" *n.* a worker in tunnel construction.

sand-'lot" *adj.* pert. to amateur sports, esp. baseball, played in a city on undeveloped lots.

S and M sadomasochism.

sand'man" *n.* [*pl.* **-men"**] a fabled spirit that makes children sleepy.

sand'pa"per *n.* paper coated with an abrasive, esp. sand. —*v.t.* rub sandpaper on, to smooth.

sand'pi"per (sand'pī"pər) *n.* a small wading bird.

sand'stone" *n.* soft, crumbly rock.

sand'wich *n.* **1,** meat, cheese, etc., between two slices of bread. **2,** something similarly compacted. —*v.t.* insert between two other things. —**sandwich man,** (*Informal*) a person who carries advertising placards (*sandwich boards*) held in front and in back by two straps over the shoulders.

> **sandwich**
> ↔ Named for John Montagu, the fourth Earl of *Sandwich,* who, rather than leave the gambling table, had a snack brought to him. That snack tended to be something similar to our present-day *sandwich.*

sand'y (san'dė) *adj.* **1,** of or like sand. **2,** yellowish, as *sandy hair.* **3,** gritty. —**sand'i·ness,** *n.*

sane (sān) *adj.* **1,** mentally sound. **2,** reasonable. —**sane'ness,** *n.*

San'for·ized" (san'fə-rīzd") *adj.* (*T.N.*) designating a process to prevent shrinking.

sang *v.* pret. of *sing.*

sang-froid' (saṅ-frwä') *n.* (*Fr.,* cold blood) calmness; indifference.

san·gri'a (san-grē'ə) *n.* a punch made of wine and fruit juice.

san'gui·nar"y (sang'gwi-ner"ė) *adj.* **1,** bloody. **2,** bloodthirsty. ❏ *sanguine*

san'guine (sang'gwin) *adj.* **1,** hopeful; confident; cheerful. **2,** ruddy.

> **sanguine, sanguinary**
> ☞ In current usage, these two words, once synonyms, have distinct meanings. *Sanguine* means optimistic; *sanguinary* means bloody.

san"i·tar'i·um (san"ə-tār'ė-əm) *n.* an establishment for invalids. ❏ *sanatorium*

san'i·tar"y (san'ə-ter"ė) *adj.* **1,** pert. to conditions affecting health. **2,** hygienic. —**sanitary napkin,** an absorbent pad worn by women during menstruation.

san"i·ta'tion (san"ə-tā'shən) *n.* the process of garbage disposal, sewage, etc.

san'i·tize" *v.t.* **1,** clean; sterilize. **2,** make less objectionable or offensive by removing the offending element.

san'i·ty (san'ə-tė) *n.* saneness.

sank *v.* pret. of *sink.*

sans (sanz) *prep.* (*Archaic*) without.

sans-"cu·lotte' (sanz"-kyû-lot') *n.* a radical revolutionary.

San'skrit *n.* the ancient literary language of India.

sap *n.* **1,** the fluid that circulates in a plant. **2,** (*Slang*) a fool. **3,** (*Mil.*) a ditch dug to approach an enemy position. —*v.t.* [**sapped, sap'ping**] undermine. —**sap'per,** *n.* a soldier who digs or fights in saps.

sap'id *adj.* tasty; agreeable. —**sa·pid'i·ty** (sə-pid'ə-tē) *n.* —**sap'or** (sā'pər) *n.*

sa'pi·ent (sā'pē-ənt) *adj.* wise. —**sa'pi·ence,** *n.*

sap'ling *n.* a young tree.

sap'phire (saf'īr) *n.* **1,** a precious stone, a transparent blue variety of corundum. **2,** deep blue.

sap'py (sap'ē) *adj.* **1,** full of sap or vitality. **2,** (*Slang*) foolish. —**sap'pi·ness,** *n.*

sap'suck"er *n.* a small spotted woodpecker of the U.S.

sar'a·band" (sar'ə-band") *n.* **1,** a lively Span. castanet dance. **2,** a slow, stately Span. dance.

Sar'a·cen (sar'ə-sən) *n.* (formerly) a Muslim.

sa·ran' (sə-ran') *n.* a thermoplastic vinyl used for packaging, etc.

sar'casm (sär'kaz-əm) *n.* bitter irony; taunting comment.

sar·cas'tic (sär-kas'tik) *adj.* being or using sarcasm. —**sar·cas'ti·cal·ly,** *adv.*

---

sarcastic, sardonic
☛ These words have similar though distinct meanings. *Sarcastic* means cruelly ironic, taunting. *Sardonic* means scornful, but with a sense of humor rather than cruelty. ↔ *Sardonic* owes its origin to the plant known in Latin as *herba Sardonia,* plant from Sardinia, because it caused facial contortions when eaten.

---

sar·co'ma (sär-kō'mə) *n.* a malignant tumor of the connective tissue.

sar·coph'a·gus (sär-kof'ə-gəs) *n.* an ornamental stone coffin.

---

sarcophagus
↔ From Greek *sarkophagos,* literally, flesh-eating. The word originally referred to a type of limestone used for coffins because it accelerated decomposition.

---

sard (särd) *n.* a reddish chalcedony.

sar·dine' (sär-dēn') *n.* a small fish allied to the herring, often canned in oil.

sar·don'ic (sär-don'ik) *adj.* sneering; sarcastic. —**sar·don'i·cal·ly,** *adv.* ❏ *sarcastic*

sar'do·nyx (sär'də-niks) *n.* a semiprecious stone.

sar·gas'so (sär-gas'ō) *n.* a seaweed. Also, **sar·gas'sum** (-əm).

sarge (särj) *n.* (*Informal*) sergeant.

sa'ri (sä'rē) *n.* a single long piece of silk or cotton, wrapped around the body and over the head, the principal garment of a Hindu woman.

sa·rong' (sä-râng') *n.* a Malay woman's one-piece garment, wrapped around the lower body like a skirt.

sar"sa·pa·ril'la (sas"pə-ril'ə) *n.* a tropical Amer. plant; a soft drink made from its root.

sar·to'ri·al (sär-tôr'ē-əl) *adj.* **1,** pert. to a tailor or his or her work. **2,** pert. to clothing., esp. tailored.

SASE (es-ā-es-ee) *abbr.* self-addressed, stamped envelope.

sash *n.* **1,** the framed part of a window. **2,** a band worn around the waist.

sa·shay' (sa-shā') *v.i.* (*Informal*) move glidingly.

sa·shi'mi (sä-shē'mē) *n.* raw fish served in thin slices.

sas'quatch" (sas'kwach") *n.* a large manlike animal believed to exist in the N.W. U.S.; Bigfoot.

sass (sas) (*Slang*) *n.* saucy or insolent talk; sauce. —*v.t.* speak insolently to (a person). —**sass'y,** *adj.* —**sas'si·ness,** *n.*

sas'sa·by (sas'ə-bē) *n.* a large So. Afr. antelope.

sas'sa·fras" (sas'ə-fras") *n.* a No. Amer. tree; the aromatic bark of the root.

sat *v.* pret. & p.p. of *sit.*

Sa'tan (sā'tən) *n.* the chief evil spirit; the devil. —**sa·tan'ic** (sə-tan'ik) *adj.* —**sa·tan'i·cal·ly,** *adv.*

satch'el (sach'əl) *n.* a small bag, used as luggage.

sate (sāt) *v.t.* satisfy; fill. ❏ *sad*

sa·teen' (sa-tēn') *n.* a cotton fabric resembling satin.

sat'el·lite" (sat'ə-līt") *n.* **1,** a moon. **2,** an attendant; follower. **3,** a country supposedly independent but actually controlled by another. **4,** [also, **artificial satellite**] a device designed to be placed in orbit around the earth or other celestial body. —**satellite dish,** a round, concave antenna for receiving radio, TV, etc., signals from orbiting satellites.

sa'ti·ate" (sā'shē-āt") *v.t.* surfeit; oversatisfy; glut. —**sa"ti·a·ble,** *adj.* —**sa"ti·a'tion,** *n.* ❏ *sad*

sa·ti'e·ty (sə-tī'ə-tē) *n.* state of being satiated; surfeit.

sat′in (sat′ən) *n. & adj.* a lustrous fabric. —**sat′in·y,** *adj.*

> **satin**
> ↔ From Arabic *zaituni*, from Zaitun, the Arabic name for the port of Tsinkiang, China.

sat′in·wood″ *n.* an E. Indian tree or its fine, hard wood.

sat′ire (sat′īr) *n.* the use of irony, ridicule, etc., in writing. —**sa·tir′i·cal** (sə-tir′ə-kəl) *adj.* —**sat′i·rist,** *n.* —**sat′i·rize″** (sat′ə-rīz″) *v.t.*

sat″is·fac′tion (sat″is-fak′shən) *n.* act, means, or result of satisfying. —**sat″is·fac′-to·ry** (-tə-rė) *adj.*

sat′is·fy″ (sat′is-fī″) *v.t.* **1,** gratify completely; supply the needs of. **2,** pay fully. **3,** convince. **4,** fulfill the conditions of. **5,** atone for. ❏ *sad*

sa·to′ri (sə-tō′rė) *n.* in Zen Buddhism, a state of enlightenment.

sat′rap (sat′rap) *n.* a subordinate ruler. —**sat′rap·y** (-rə-pė) *n.*

sat′u·rate″ (sach′ə-rāt″) *v.t.* soak; impregnate fully. —**sat″u·ra′tion,** *n.* —**sat′u·rat″ed,** *adj.* (*Chem.*) a state of animal or vegetable fats, associated with higher concentrations of cholesterol in the blood. —**saturation diving,** a diving method which reduces the decompression time of divers.

Sat′ur·day (sat′ər-dė) *n.* the seventh day of the week, observed by some Christians and Judaism as the Sabbath. —**Saturday-night special,** a cheap handgun.

> **Saturday, saturnalia, saturnine**
> ↔ *Saturday* is, literally, Saturn's day, from Latin *Saturni dies*, from *Saturnus*. Also related to Saturn are *saturnalia*, referring to the revels of the festival of Saturn, and *saturnine*, referring to the astrological characterization of those born under the sign of Saturn as gloomy of temperament.

sat″ur·na′li·a (sat″ər-nā′lė-ə) *n.* an occasion of unrestrained revelry; orgy. ❏ *Saturday*

sat′ur·nine″ (sat′ər-nīn″) *adj.* morose; phlegmatic. ❏ *Saturday*

sat′yr (sat′ər) *n.* **1,** a sylvan deity, half human and half goat. **2,** a man subject to uncontrollable amorous passion.

sat″y·ri·a·sis (sat″ə-rī′ə-sis) *n.* uncontrollable amorous passion in a man.

sauce (sâs) *n.* **1,** a relish or appetizer. **2,** a compote of fruit. **3,** (*Informal*) pertness; insolence. **4,** (*Slang*) liquor. —*v.t.* **1,** sea-

son; give zest to. **2,** (*Informal*) address impertinently.

sauce′pan″ *n.* a small cooking pan with a handle.

sau′cer (sâ′sər) *n.* a small, round dish.

sau′cy (sâ′sė) *adj.* pert; insolent. —**sau′ci·ness,** *n.*

sau″er·brat″en (sow′ər-brä″tən) *n.* (*Ger.*) a pot roast of meat marinated in vinegar.

sau″er·kraut″ (sow′ər-krowt″) *n.* (*Ger.*) fermented, sour cabbage.

sau′na (sâ′nə) *n.* **1,** a Finnish steam bath using water thrown on heated rocks. **2,** a similar bath using dry heat from heated rocks.

saun′ter (sân′tər) *v.i.* walk in a leisurely way; stroll.

sau′sage (sâ′sij) *n.* minced meat, seasoned, often stuffed into a membranous tube.

sau·té′ (sō-tā′) *v.t.* pan-fry.

Sau·terne′ (sō-tĕrn′) *n.* a sweet, white California wine.

Sau·ternes′ (sō-tĕrn′) *n.* (*Fr.*) a sweet, white French wine or the region in France where it is produced.

sav′age (sav′ij) *adj.* **1,** uncivilized; uncultivated. **2,** ferocious; barbarous. —*n.* a savage person. —**sav′age·ry** (-rė) *n.*

> **savage**
> ↔ From Latin *silva*, woods. A *savage* was a person of the woods.

sa·van′na (sə-van′ə) *n.* a grassy plain with scattered trees. Also, **sa·van′nah.**

sa·vant′ (sa-vänt′) *n.* a person of learning.

save (sāv) *v.t.* **1,** preserve from danger, injury, or loss; deliver from sin. **2,** conserve; set apart; hoard. **3,** (*Theol.*) deliver from the power or penalty of sin. —*v.i.* **1,** put aside money for the future. **2,** be frugal. **3,** last without spoiling, as food. —*prep. & conj.* except. —*n.* **1,** (*Hockey*) the prevention by the goalie of a scoring attempt. **2,** (*Baseball*) a credit given to a relief pitcher for preserving a team's lead.

sav′ing *n.* **1,** economy. **2,** a reduction in expenditure. **3,** (*pl.*) money put aside. —*adj.* redeeming. —*prep. & conj.* save.

sav′ior (sāv′yər) *n.* **1,** a rescuer. **2,** (*cap.*) [usu. Sav′iour] Jesus Christ.

sa′voir-faire′ (sav′wär-fâr′) *n.* (*Fr.*) knowledge of what to do; poise.

sa′vor (sā′vər) *n.* taste; flavor. —*v.i.* taste; season. Also, **sa′vour.**

sa′vor·y (sā′və-rė) *adj.* tasty; agreeable. —*n.* **1,** (*Brit.*) a highly flavored dish served as an appetizer or dessert. **2,** either of two herbs used for seasoning.

sa·voy' (sə-voi') *n.* [*pl.* **-voys**] a variety of cabbage.

sav'vy (sav'ē) (*Slang*) *v.t. & i.* understand. —*adj.* knowledgeable. —*n.* understanding.

saw (sâ) *n.* **1,** a metal blade with teeth, used for cutting. **2,** a proverb. —*v.t. & i.* **1,** cut with or use a saw. **2,** cut or move as a saw does. **3,** pret. of *see.*

saw'bones" *n.sing.* (*Slang*) a surgeon.

saw'buck" *n.* **1,** a sawhorse. **2,** (*Slang*) a $10 bill.

---
sawbuck
↔ A compound of *saw* and earlier *buck,* sawbuck, perhaps from Dutch *zaagbok,* sawhorse. The sense of $10 bill comes from the resemblance of "X" (ten) to the shape of the sawhorse.

---

saw'dust" *n.* tiny fragments of wood resulting from cutting wood with a saw.

saw'horse" *n.* a support for holding wood while it is sawed.

saw'mill" *n.* a mill where logs are sawed into planks.

saw-'toothed" *adj.* having teeth resembling those of a saw; serrate.

saw'yer (sâ'yər) *n.* **1,** one who saws wood. **2,** a kind of beetle.

sax (saks) *n.* saxophone.

sax'horn" *n.* any of a family of brass wind instruments used chiefly in military bands.

---
saxhorn, saxophone
↔ These instruments—and many others—were the invention of and named after 19th-c. Belgian inventor Adolphe *Sax.*

---

sax'i·frage (sak'si-frij) *n.* any of a genus of perennial herbs.

---
saxifrage
↔ From Late Latin *saxifraga,* from Latin *saxum,* stone, and *frangere,* break. The plant was so called because it grew in the crevices of rocks, thus giving the impression it had split them.

Sax'on (sak'sən) *adj.* **1,** pert. to an ancient Teutonic people. **2,** pert. to Saxony. —*n.* a Saxon person.

sax'o·phone" (sak'sə-fōn") *n.* a brass wind instrument. Also, *informal,* **sax.** ❏ *saxhorn*

say (sā) *v.t.* [*pret. & p.p.* **said** (sed)] **1,** utter, express, or declare in words; tell. **2,** suppose. **3,** decide. —*n.* **1,** what one has to

say. **2,** the opportunity to speak or decide. —*adv.* for example.

say'ing *n.* a proverbial expression.

say-'so" *n.* (*Informal*) **1,** a personal assertion. **2,** a decision.

scab (skab) *n.* **1,** an incrustation formed over a healing sore. **2,** a strikebreaker. —*v.i.* act as a scab. —**scab'by,** *adj.*

scab'bard (skab'ərd) *n.* a sheath for a sword, etc.

sca'bies" (skā'bēz") *n.* an infectious parasitic skin disease.

sca'brous (skā'brəs; ska'-) *adj.* **1,** scabby or scaly. **2,** full of difficulties. **3,** risqué or salacious.

scads (skadz) *n.pl.* (*Slang*) a large amount.

scaf'fold (skaf'əld) *n.* **1,** a temporary supporting platform. **2,** a platform for a gallows. —**scaf'fold·ing,** *n.* a scaffold for workmen.

scag (skag) *n.* (*Slang*) heroin.

sca'lar (skā'lər) *adj.* one-dimensional; having magnitude without direction. —*n.* a scalar quantity.

scal'a·wag" (skal'ə-wag") *n.* (*Informal*) a worthless person; a scamp.

scald (skâld) *v.t.* **1,** burn with a boiling liquid or steam. **2,** cook slightly. **3,** cleanse with boiling water. —*n.* **1,** a sore caused by scalding. **2,** a disease of fruit.

scale (skāl) *n.* **1,** a thin, horny piece of cuticle, as on a fish. **2,** a flake; a scab. **3,** (*sing.* or *pl.*) a balance for weighing. **4,** (*Music*) a series of tones at fixed intervals. **5,** a series of marks for measurement or computation. **6,** a gradation. **7,** a system of proportion. **8,** a table of prices, wages, etc. —*v.t.* **1,** deprive of scales; clean. **2,** skip, as a stone over water. **3,** weigh. **4,** climb up or over. **5,** project or adjust according to scale.

sca'lene (skā'lēn) *adj.* (*Geom.*) **1,** denoting a triangle with no two sides equal. **2,** having the axis oblique, as a cone.

scal'lion (skal'yən) *n.* a variety of onion with a small bulb.

scal'lop (skal'əp) *n.* **1,** a bivalve mollusk; its wavy-edged shell. **2,** one of a series of small curves cut in the edge of a garment, etc. —*v.t.* **1,** cut (an edge) in a wavy line. **2,** escallop.

scalp (skalp) *n.* the integument of the upper part of the head. —*v.t.* **1,** remove the scalp of. **2,** (*Informal*) buy and sell (tickets) for quick profit. —**scalp'er,** *n.* a ticket broker who charges exorbitant prices.

scal'pel (skal'pəl) *n.* a light, straight surgical knife.

---

scam (skam) *n.* (*Slang*) a swindle.

scamp (skamp) *n.* a rascal.

scam′per (skam′pər) *v.i.* run quickly.

scam′pi (skam′pē) *n.pl.* shrimp cooked in garlic sauce.

scan (skan) *v.t.* [**scanned, scan′ning**] **1,** examine minutely; scrutinize. **2,** glance over hastily. **3,** read for metrical structure. **4,** traverse (a text, picture, etc.) with a laser beam or other source in order to transmit it to a computer or other device. —*v.i.* conform to a meter.

scan′dal (skan′dəl) *n.* **1,** public disgrace; a cause of disgrace. **2,** gossip. —**scan′-dal·ize″** (-īz″) *v.t.* shock.

scan′dal·mon″ger (skan′dəl-mung″gər) *n.* one who gossips.

scan′dal·ous (-əs) *adj.* **1,** disgraceful. **2,** defamatory.

Scan″di·na′vi·an (skan″di-nā′vē-ən) *adj.* pert. to Scandinavia, its people or languages. —*n.* an inhabitant of Scandinavia.

scan′di·um (skan′dē-əm) *n.* a white metallic element, sometimes included with the rare-earth elements, no. 21, symbol Sc.

scan′ner *n.* **1,** something or someone that scans. **2,** a device that translates images into electronic data for use in a computer.

scan′sion (skan′shən) *n.* analysis of metrical verse.

scant (skant) *adj.* scarcely sufficient. —**scant′y,** *adj.* small; scant.

scant′ling (-ling) *n.* **1,** timber of small cross section relative to length, as a joist; such timbers collectively. **2,** an upright piece in a house frame.

scape′goat″ (skāp′gōt″) *n.* one made to bear the blame for others' misdeeds.

scape′grace″ (skāp′grās″) *n.* a graceless fellow; a scamp.

scap′u·la (skap′yə-lə) *n.* the shoulder blade.

scap′u·lar (-lər) *adj.* pert. to the scapula. —*n.* a sleeveless monastic robe hung from the shoulders.

scar (skär) *n.* a mark remaining after a wound has healed. —*v.t. & i.* [**scarred, scar′ring**] mark with a scar; form a scar in healing.

scar′ab (skar′əb) *n.* **1,** a beetle. **2,** an amulet in the form of a beetle.

scarce (skārs) *adj.* **1,** insufficient; not abundant. **2,** uncommon; rare. —**scarce′ness,** *n.*

scarce′ly *adv.* hardly; barely; probably not.

scar′ci·ty (skär′sə-tē) *n.* scarceness; shortage; dearth.

scare (skār) *v.t.* **1,** frighten. **2,** (with *up*) get. —*v.i.* become frightened.

scare′crow″ *n.* **1,** a semblance of a man, set up to frighten crows. **2,** a poorly dressed person. **3,** a thin person.

scare′head″ *n.* a headline in very large type.

scarf (skärf) *n.* **1,** a decorative strip of material; a muffler; a cravat. **2,** a joint for uniting two timbers. —*v.t.* (*Slang*) (often with *down*) eat quickly.

scar′i·fy″ (skar′ə-fī″) *v.t.* **1,** scratch. **2,** harass. —**scar″i·fi·ca′tion,** *n.*

scar′la·ti′na (skär″lə-tē′nə) *n.* scarlet fever, esp. a mild form of it.

scar′let (skär′lit) *n. & adj.* a brilliant red color. —**scarlet fever,** a contagious febrile disease.

scarp (skärp) *n.* **1,** a steep slope. **2,** an escarpment.

scar′y (skār′ē) *adj.* **1,** causing fright. **2,** timid. —**scar′i·ness,** *n.*

scat (skat) *v.t.* [**scat′ted, -ting**] (*Informal*) drive off. —*interj.* Go away! —**scat singing,** a style of jazz singing using nonsense syllables.

scathe (skāth) *v.t.* **1,** criticize severely. **2,** injure. —**scath′ing,** *adj.*

sca·tol′o·gy (ska-tol′ə-jē) *n.* **1,** the study of animal excretions. **2,** any writing about what is considered morally or physically filthy. —**scat″o·log′i·cal** (skat″ə-loj′i-kəl) *adj.*

scat′ter (skat′ər) *v.t.* **1,** throw loosely about. **2,** dispose. **3,** put to flight. —*v.i.* disperse. —**scatter rug,** a small rug used with others.

scat′ter·brain″ *n.* a giddy person.

scaup (skâp) *n.* any of several common species of duck.

scav′en·ger (skav′in-jər) *n.* **1,** an animal or organism that devours refuse. **2,** a street cleaner. —**scav′enge,** *v.i. & t.*

> **scavenger**
> ↔ From Flemish *scauwen*, look at, through Anglo-French *scawager*, a tax inspector.

sce·nar′i·o″ (si-när′ē-ō″) *n.* the outline of a drama or motion picture; hence, a likely course of action.

scene (sēn) *n.* **1,** the place where anything is done or takes place. **2,** a stage setting; a division of a play. **3,** a particular incident. **4,** a view; a picture. **5,** an exhibition of strong feeling. **6,** (*Slang*) situation.

scen′er·y (sē′nə-rē) *n.* **1,** the aggregate of features in a view. **2,** stage settings.

scen′ic (sē′nik) *adj.* pert. to scenery; abounding in fine scenery. —**scen′i·cal·ly,** *adv.* —**scenic railway,** a miniature railroad providing a brief sightseeing tour of a resort, amusement park, etc.

scent (sent) *n.* **1,** an odor. **2,** the course of an animal. **3,** a perfume. **4,** the sense of smell. —*v.t.* **1,** smell. **2,** suspect. **3,** perfume.

scep'ter (sep'tər) *n.* a staff emblematic of royalty. Also, **scep'tre.**

scep'tic (skep'tik) *n.* skeptic.

sched'ule (skej'ūl) *n.* **1,** a statement of contents, details, etc. **2,** agenda. **3,** a timetable. —*v.t.* place on a schedule; plan.

sche'ma (skē'mə) *n.* [*pl.* **-ma·ta** (-mə-tə)] scheme; diagram; plan.

sche·mat'ic (skē-mat'ik) *adj.* pert. to a scheme or diagram. —*n.* a schematic drawing. —**sche·mat'i·cal·ly,** *adv.* —**sche'-ma·tize,** *v.t.*

scheme (skēm) *n.* **1,** a regular or formal plan; a system. **2,** a plot; an intrigue. —*v.t. & i.* plan; plot. —**schem'er,** *n.* —**schem'ing,** *adj.* plotting; crafty.

scher·zan'do (sker-tsän'dō) *adj. & adv.* (*It., Music*) playful; sportive.

scher'zo (sker'tzō) *n.* (*Music*) a movement of a light or playful nature.

Schick test (shik) a diphtheria immunity test, named for U.S. pediatrician Béla Schick.

schip'per·ke (ship'ər-kē) *n.* a Belgian breed of terrier used as watchdogs.

schism (siz'əm; skiz-) *n.* a division or separation. —**schis·mat'ic,** *adj.*

schist (shist) *n.* a crystalline rock formed in parallel layers.

schiz·o- (skiz-ō; skit-sō) *pref.* split.

schiz''o·phre'ni·a (skit''sə-frē'nē-ə) *n.* a mental disorder, splitting of the personality. —**schiz'oid, schiz''o·phren'ic** (-fren'ik) *adj.*

---

schizophrenia, split personality
☛ Be careful not to confuse these two types of mental disability. *Schizophrenia* does refer to a split (↔ from Greek *schizein*, split), but it is the split between reality and fantasy. The *schizophrenic* suffers from hallucinations. A person with a *split personality* has two or more distinct personalities, each with its own character traits and behavior, within the same mind.

---

schle·miel' (shlə-mēl') *n.* (*Slang*) an ineffective and somewhat stupid or unpractical person.

schlep (shlep) *v.t.* [**schlepped, schlep'ping**] (*Slang*) lug awkwardly or with difficulty; transport.

schli·ma'zel (shli-mä'zəl) *n.* (*Slang*) a bungler; unlucky person.

schlock (shlok) *n.* (*Slang*) cheap or tawdry merchandise.

schmaltz (shmalts) *n.* (*Slang*) **1,** flattery. **2,** trite or sentimental writing, music, etc.; corn. —**schmaltz'y,** *adj.*

schmat'te (shmä'tə) *n.* **1,** a ragged garment. **2,** anything worthless.

schmear (shmir) *n.* (*Slang*) the totality of something.

schmo (shmō) *n.* (*Slang*) a stupid person.

schmooze (shmooz) *v.i. & n.* (*Slang*) chat.

schmuck (shmuk) *n.* (*Slang*) a stupid, gullible, or clumsy person.

schnapps (shnäps) *n.* liquor.

schnau'zer (shnow'zər) *n.* a Ger. breed of terrier.

schnit'zel (shnit'zəl) *n.* a veal cutlet.

schnook (shnûk) *n.* (*Slang*) a dupe.

schnor'rer (shnôr'ər) *n.* a parasite.

schnoz'zle (shnoz'əl) *n.* (*Slang*) the nose.

schol'ar (skol'ər) *n.* **1,** a student. **2,** a learned person. —**schol'ar·ly,** *adj.*

schol'ar·ship'' *n.* **1,** learning; erudition. **2,** monetary assistance granted to a scholar.

scho·las'tic (skə-las'tik) *adj.* **1,** pert. to schools, scholars, or education. **2,** pedantic. —*n.* a pedantic person.

scho·las'ti·cism (skə-las'tə-siz-əm) *n.* **1,** a philosophicical and theological system based on the authority of the church and the writings of Aristotle, prevalent in the Middle Ages. **2,** narrow adherence to traditional doctrines or methods.

school (skool) *n.* **1,** an educational establishment. **2,** a united group or sect. **3,** a specific method, etc. **4,** a large body of fish, whales, etc. —*v.t.* educate; train. —**school board,** a body governing local schools. —**school'book'',** *n.* textbook. —**school'ing,** *n.* education; learning. — **school'marm''** (-märm'') *n.* (often considered *offensive*) a woman schoolteacher, or any prim woman (formerly thought to be typical of schoolteachers).

---

school
↔ A *school* of fish and a *school* of children are not the same word. The latter derives from Latin *scola*, of Germanic origin. The former also comes from a Germanic source, but through Middle Dutch *schole*, group.

---

schoon'er (skoo'nər) *n.* **1,** a sailing vessel. **2,** a tall glass for beer.

schot'tische (shot'ish) *n.* a Scottish dance, similar to the polka.

schtick (shtik) *n.* (*Slang*) act; bit; routine.

schuss (shûs) *n.* (*Skiing*) a steep, straight run. —*v.i.* make such a run.

schwa (shwä) *n.* the indeterminate vowel sound of most unaccented syllables in English; the symbol ə for it.

sci·at·ic (sī-at'ik) *adj.* pert. to or affecting the hip.

sci·at'i·ca (sī-at'i-kə) *n.* pain and tenderness in a sciatic nerve.

sci'ence (sī'əns) *n.* **1,** a branch of knowledge; what is known concerning a subject. **2,** (*Informal*) natural science, as physics or chemistry. **3,** special skill. —**natural science, 1,** any of the sciences dealing directly with the physical world, as biology, chemistry, physics, etc. **2,** these sciences collectively. —**science fiction,** fiction based on scientific fact or imagining.

sci″en·tif'ic (sī″ən-tif'ik) *adj.* **1,** pert. to science. **2,** systematic and accurate. —**sci″en·tif'i·cal·ly,** *adv.* —**scientific creationism,** the belief that science supports the biblical account of creation. Also, **creation science.**

sci'en·tist (sī'ən-tist) *n.* one versed in a science.

scim'i·tar (sim'ə-tər) *n.* a curved, single-edged sword.

scin·til'la (sin-til'ə) *n.* the least particle; a trace.

scin'til·late″ (sin'tə-lāt″) *v.i.* emit sparks; twinkle; shine. —**scin″til·la'tion,** *n.*

sci'on (sī'ən) *n.* **1,** a descendant. **2,** a shoot or twig used for grafting.

scis'sors (siz'ərz) *n.pl.* or *sing.* a cutting instrument consisting of two pivoted blades.

scle·ro'sis (skli-rō'sis) *n.* [*pl.* **-ses** (-sēz)] a hardening of a tissue or part. —**scle·rot'ic,** *adj.*

scoff (skof) *v.i.* (with *at*) jeer. —*v.t.* (*Slang*) eat quickly.

scoff'law″ *n.* one who scoffs at or disobeys the law.

scold (skōld) *v.t. & i.* chide; find fault. —*n.* a railing woman.

sconce (skons) *n.* **1,** a wall bracket for candles, etc. **2,** a defensive bulwark. **3,** (*Archaic*) the head.

scone (skōn) *n.* a soft cake or biscuit.

> **scone**
> ↔ A Scottish word from Dutch, *schoonbrood*, beautiful bread.

scoop (skoop) *n.* **1,** an instrument for hollowing out anything. **2,** a hollow. **3,** the act of scooping. **4,** (*Informal*) a journalistic beat. —*v.t.* **1,** (with *out*) remove or hollow with a scoop. **2,** publish news earlier than.

scoot (skoot) *v.i.* go hastily; dart. —*v.t.* eject.

scoot'er *n.* **1,** a child's foot-propelled vehicle. **2,** an iceboat. **3,** a motor scooter.

scope (skōp) *n.* **1,** outlook; intellectual range. **2,** room for free observation or action. **3,** extent; length; sweep.

-scope (skōp) *suf.* a means or instrument for viewing.

sco·pol'a·mine″ (skō-pol'ə-mēn″) *n.* an alkaloid used as a depressant and as an anesthetic in obstetrics; truth serum.

scor·bu'tic (skôr-bū'tik) *adj.* pert. to or affected with scurvy.

scorch (skôrch) *v.t. & i.* **1,** burn superficially; singe. **2,** parch. **3,** criticize caustically. —*n.* a superficial burn. —**scorched-earth policy,** total destruction of one's own territory, to impede an invader.

scorch'er *n.* anything that scorches; (*Informal*) very hot day; caustic statement.

score (skôr) *n.* **1,** the points made in a game or match. **2,** a reckoning; account. **3,** a notch; a scratch. **4,** reason; ground. **5,** twenty; (*pl.*) many. **6,** a copy of a musical composition. —*v.i. & t.* **1,** make, record, or write a score. **2,** berate. **3,** orchestrate. **4,** (often with *with*) (*Informal*) seduce. **5,** win success or advantage.

> **score**
> ↔ All senses of the word derive from the basic sense of cutting: the *score* in a game is recorded by cutting notches in wood; the musical *score* is a system of staves connected by a score mark. The word is of Old Norse origin.

sco'ri·a (skôr'ė-ə) *n.* [*pl.* **-ae** (-ė)] slag.

scorn (skôrn) *n.* contempt; disdain. —*v.t.* **1,** disdain. **2,** reject.

scorn'ful (-fəl) *adj.* full of or expressing contempt.

Scor'pi·o (skôr'pė-ō) *n.* a constellation, the Scorpion (see *zodiac*).

scor'pi·on (skôr'pė-ən) *n.* a venomous arachnid.

Scot (skot) *n.* a native or inhabitant of Scotland. —**Scots,** *adj.* —**Scots'man** (-mən), **Scots'wom″an,** *n.*

> **Scot, Scots, Scotch, Scottish**
> A person from Scotland is either a Scot or a Scotswoman or Scotsman; avoid using *Scotch* in this sense. Likewise, *Scottish* or *Scots* are preferred to *Scotch* as an adjective. *Scotch* should be used for the whiskey, and in certain widely used expressions, such as *Scotch terrier*. ↔ *Scot* comes from Late Latin *Scotti*, the Irish.

Scotch (skoch) *adj.* Scottish. —*n.* **1,** a

whiskey distilled in Scotland. **2,** (*l.c.*) a cut. **3,** (*l.c.*) a block or wedge. —*v.t.* (*l.c.*) **1,** cut; crush. **2,** block (a wheel). **3,** thwart; obstruct; hinder. **—Scotch broth,** a soup made of lamb stock and barley. **—Scotch Tape,** (*T.N.*) an adhesive cellulose tape. **—Scotch terrier** [also, **Scot′tie** (skot′ė)] a short-legged, small terrier. ❏ *Scot*

scot-′free″ (skot′frē″) *adj.* safe; clear; without charge or tax.

> **scot-free**
> ↔ This word is not related to Scotland, but to an old Scandinavian word, *scot,* money paid as tax.

Scotland Yard the police headquarters in London, England.

Scot′tish (skot′ish) *adj.* of or pert. to Scotland. ❏ *Scot*

scoun′drel (skown′drəl) *n.* an unprincipled person; a villain. **—scoun′drel·ly,** *adj.*

scour (skowr) *v.t. & i.* **1,** clean by friction; brighten. **2,** cleanse dirt from. **3,** search through; range.

scourge (skėrj) *n.* **1,** a whip. **2,** an affliction; a cause of affliction. —*v.t.* **1,** whip. **2,** afflict.

scout (skowt) *n.* **1,** a soldier, airplane, etc., sent to reconnoiter. **2,** an observer. **3,** (*cap.*) a Boy Scout or Girl Scout. **4,** (*Informal*) fellow. —*v.t. & i.* **1,** reconnoiter. **2,** ridicule.

> **scout**
> ↔ From Latin *auscultare,* listen, through Old French.

scout′mas″ter, scout′mis″tress *n.* adult leader of a troop of Scouts.

scow (skow) *n.* a large, flat-bottomed boat for freight.

scowl (skowl) *v.i.* lower the brows; look gloomy, severe, or angry. —*n.* an angry frown.

scrab′ble (skrab′əl) *v.i.* **1,** scratch. **2,** scrawl. **3,** scramble. —*n.* (*cap.; T.N.*) a board game based on crossword puzzles and anagrams.

scrag′gly (skrag′lė) *adj.* irregular; ragged. **—scrag′gy,** *adj.* thin; scrawny.

scram (skram) *v.i.* **[scrammed, scram′-ming]** (*Slang*) go away.

scram′ble (skram′bəl) *v.i.* **1,** struggle along as if on all fours. **2,** strive eagerly and rudely. **3,** (*Football*) to run from pursuers without blocking. **4,** (of aircraft) to take off to intercept enemy aircraft.—*v.t.* mix together. —*n.* act of scrambling. **—scrambled eggs, 1,** eggs mixed and fried.

2, (*Slang*) yellow braid worn by a naval officer.

scram′jet″ *n.* a ramjet engine with special thrust at supersonic speeds: *s(upersonic) c(ombustion) ramjet.*

scrap (skrap) *n.* **1,** a detached portion; a fragment. **2,** (*pl.*) fragments of food. **3,** discarded iron or steel. **4,** (*Slang*) a fight or quarrel. —*v.t.* **[scrapped, scrap′ping] 1,** break up. **2,** discard as useless. —*v.i.* (often with *with*) (*Slang*) fight.

scrap′book″ *n.* a blank book for pictures, clippings, etc.

scrape (skrāp) *v.t.* **1,** shave or abrade the surface of. **2,** (with *out* or *off*) remove; erase. **3,** (with *together* or *up*) collect. —*v.i.* **1,** rub lightly. **2,** get by with difficulty. **3,** save. —*n.* **1,** the act or sound of scraping. **2,** an embarrassing predicament. **—scrap′er,** *n.* **—scrap′ing,** *n.*

scrap′ple (skrap′əl) *n.* a highly spiced sausagelike food served at breakfast.

scrap′py (skrap′ė) *adj.* (*Slang*) pugnacious. **—scrap′pi·ness,** *n.*

scratch (skrach) *v.t. & i.* **1,** mark or wound slightly. **2,** rub, as with the fingernails, to relieve itching. **3,** scribble. **4,** dig with the claws. **5,** rub roughly; grate against. **6,** erase. **7,** withdraw from a race. —*n.* **1,** an act or result of scratching. **2,** a position without allowance or penalty. **—scratch′y,** *adj.* **—scratch hit,** (*Baseball*) a lightly hit ground ball that makes a hit. **—scratch pad,** a memorandum pad. ❏ *itch*

scrawl (skrâl) *v.t.* write or draw carelessly. —*n.* a careless script.

scraw′ny (skrâ′nė) *adj.* meager; lean. **—scraw′ni·ness,** *n.*

scream (skrēm) *v.i. & t.* **1,** utter a sharp, piercing outcry. **2,** emit a shrill sound. **3,** (*Informal*) laugh immoderately. —*n.* **1,** a screaming sound. **2,** (*Informal*) a joker; something funny. **—scream′er,** *n.* a banner headline in a newspaper.

screech (skrēch) *v.i. & t.* scream harshly. —*n.* a shriek. **—screech′y,** *adj.*

screed (skrēd) *n.* **1,** a harangue. **2,** a section of plastering.

screen (skrēn) *n.* **1,** any partition or curtain that conceals or protects. **2,** a protective formation, as of troops. **3,** a pretext. **4,** a sieve. **5,** a surface on which motion pictures are projected; motion pictures collectively. —*v.t. & i.* **1,** conceal; protect. **2,** sift. **3,** film; exhibit. **—screen saver,** a computer program that blanks or writes special material to a video screen to prevent burnin.

screen′play″ *n.* a play or script followed in making a motion picture.

screw (skroo) *n.* **1,** a nail-like device having an external thread that turns in a nut or is driven into wood. **2,** a propeller. **3,** coercion. **4,** (*Slang*) a prison guard. —*v.t. & i.* **1,** turn (a screw); attach by a screw. **2,** twist; contort. **3,** (with *up*) (*Slang*) bungle; botch.

screw′ball″ *n. & adj.* (*Slang*) an eccentric person.

screw′driv″er *n.* a tool for turning screws. **2,** (*Informal*) a cocktail made with vodka and orange juice.

screw′up″ *n.* a blunder.

screw′y (-ē) *adj.* **1,** twisted; tortuous; spiral. **2,** (*Slang*) crazy; eccentric; inexplicable. —**screw′i·ness,** *n.*

scrib′ble (skrib′əl) *v.t. & i.* write carelessly. —*n.* a scrawl.

scribe (skrīb) *n.* **1,** a penman; a public writer. **2,** (*Informal*) an author. —*v.t.* mark or score with a pointed tool.

scrim (skrim) *n.* coarse cotton or linen fabric.

scrim′mage (skrim′ij) *n.* **1,** a skirmish; a tussle. **2,** (*Football*) the clash of opposing lines; a practice game. —*v.i.* engage in a scrimmage.

scrimp (skrimp) *v.t. & i.* be sparing in or of; pinch. —**scrimp′y,** *adj.* meager.

scrim′shaw″ *n.* a carved decoration on ivory, bone, etc. —*v.t. & i.* carve such decorations.

scrip (skrip) *n.* a certificate promising future payment.

script (skript) *n.* **1,** handwriting; printing type like handwriting. **2,** the manuscript of a play or motion picture.

scrip′ture (skrip′chər) *n.* **1,** (often *cap.*) the Bible. **2,** any sacred writing. —**scrip′tur·al,** *adj.*

scrive′ner (skriv′nər) *n.* scribe.

scrod (skrod) *n.* a young codfish or haddock.

scrof′u·la (skrof′yə-lə) *n.* a disorder characterized by glandular swelling. —**scrof′u·lous,** *adj.*

scroll (skrōl) *n.* **1,** a roll of paper or parchment, esp. a writing. **2,** a spiral or coiled ornament. —*v.t. & i.* to move text up or down on a computer screen. —**scroll′work″,** *n.* spiral decoration. —**scroll saw,** a thin saw for cutting irregular shapes.

Scrooge (skrooj) *n.* a disagreeable, stingy person.

Scrooge
↔ From the character in Charles Dickens's *A Christmas Carol.*

---

scro′tum (skrō′təm) *n.* the pouch of skin containing the testicles.

scrouge (skrowj) *v.t.* (*Informal*) squeeze; crowd.

scrounge (skrownj) *v.t. & i.* obtain by sponging on or pilfering from another person. —*n.* one who does so.

scrub (skrub) *v.t. & i.* [**scrubbed, scrub′bing**] **1,** cleanse by rubbing hard. **2,** to clean a gas or smoke, as in a smokestack. **3,** (*Informal*) cancel. —*n.* **1,** underbrush. **2,** a worn-out or inferior animal. **3,** anything inferior. **4,** (*Sports*) a substitute player. **5,** a form of baseball. —*adj.* makeshift. —**scrub′by,** *adj.*

scruff (skruf) *n.* the nape of the neck. —**scruff′fy,** *adj.* unkempt; shabby.

scrump′tious (skrump′shəs) *adj.* (*Slang*) very fine; first-rate; delicious.

scrunch (skrunch) *v.t. & i.* crunch or crush. —*n.* a crumbling sound.

scru′ple (skroo′pəl) *n.* **1,** a conscientious reluctance. **2,** a small amount. —*v.i.* hesitate.

scru′pu·lous (skroop′yə-ləs) *adj.* **1,** upright; moral. **2,** exact; punctilious. —**scru′pu·lous·ness,** *n.*

scru′ti·nize″ (skroo′tə-nīz″) *v.t.* observe or investigate closely.

scru′ti·ny (skroo′tə-nē) *n.* close observation; examination.

SCSI (skuz′ē) a protocol for interfacing peripheral devices with a computer: *S(mall) C(omputer) S(ystem) I(nterface).*

scu′ba (skoo′bə) *n.* a breathing device used for extended periods of underwater swimming: *S(elf-)C(ontained) U(nderwater) B(reathing) A(pparatus).* Also, **SCUBA.**

scud (skud) *v.i.* [**scud′ded, -ding**] **1,** move quickly. **2,** run before a gale.

scuff (skuf) *v.t.* **1,** spoil the finish by scraping. **2,** scrape with the feet. —*v.i.* shuffle. —*n.* **1,** a blemish; scuffmark. **2,** a type of slipper.

scuf′fle (skuf′əl) *v.i.* **1,** fight or struggle confusedly. **2,** shuffle. —*n.* **1,** a brief, rough fight. **2,** a shuffle.

scull (skul) *n.* **1,** an oar. **2,** a light racing boat for one rower. —*v.t. & i.* propel (a boat) with a scull.

scul′ler·y (skul′ə-rē) *n.* a back kitchen.

scul′lion (skul′yən) *n.* a menial kitchen servant.

sculp′ture (skulp′chər) *n.* **1,** the art of carving or shaping figures. **2,** a piece of such work. —*v.* [also, **sculpt**] carve, chisel, or engrave. —**sculp′tur·al,** *adj.* —**sculp′tor,** *n.*

---

fat, fāte, fär, fāre, fâll, ásk; met, hē, hēr, maybē; pin, pīne; not, nōte, ôr, tool

scum (skum) *n.* **1,** a film of extraneous matter on a liquid. **2,** refuse. **3,** worthless person or persons. —**scum′my,** *adj.*

scum′ble (skum′bəl) *v.t.* rub (a painting or drawing) to spread and soften the colors or tones.

scup (skup) *n.* the porgy.

scup′per (skup′ər) *n.* an opening to let water run off the deck of a ship.

scup′per·nong″ (skup′ər-nong″) *n.* a muscadine grape of the U.S.

scurf (skẽrf) *n.* flakes of skin that are shed, as dandruff. —**scurf′y,** *adj.*

scur′ril·ous (skẽr′ə-ləs) *adj.* indecently or grossly abusive; offensive. —**scur·ril′i·ty,** *n.*

scur′ry (skẽr′ė) *v.i.* hurry along; scamper. —*n.* a scampering rush.

scur′vy (skẽr′vė) *n.* a disease characterized by swelling, hemorrhages, etc., caused by improper diet. —*adj.* low; contemptible.

scutch′eon (skuch′ən) *n.* **1,** escutcheon. **2,** a metal plate or shield, as that which covers a keyhole, etc.

scut′tle (skut′əl) *n.* **1,** a container for coal. **2,** a hurried run. **3,** a small opening. —*v.i.* hurry. —*v.t.* sink (a ship) by cutting holes in the bottom.

scut′tle·butt″ *n.* **1,** a cask. **2,** (*Slang*) gossip.

scythe (sīth) *n.* an instrument with a long blade for cutting grass.

sea (sē) *n.* **1,** the salt waters on the earth's surface; the ocean. **2,** a region of the ocean; a large lake. **3,** a swell; a large wave. **4,** an overwhelming quantity. —**at sea,** perplexed. —**sea biscuit, 1,** a large, crisp unleavened cracker. **2,** hardtack. —**sea cucumber,** a small invertebrate sea animal. —**sea dog, 1,** an experienced sailor. **2,** the harbor seal. —**sea elephant,** a large seal. —**sea foam,** meerschaum. —**sea gull,** a marine bird; gull. —**sea horse,** a fish with a head suggesting a horse's. —**sea legs,** ability to walk (as on a ship) without losing balance. —**sea level,** the mean level of the sea. —**sea lion,** a variety of seal. —**sea shell,** the shell of any sea mollusk. —**sea urchin,** a spiny sea animal.

sea′bed″ *n.* bed (def. 3).

Sea′bee″ *n.* a member of a U.S. Navy construction battalion.

sea′board″ *n.* coast.

sea′coast″ *n.* seashore.

sea′far″er (-fär″ər) *n.* a traveler by sea. —**sea′far″ing,** *adj.*

sea′food″ *n.* edible marine fish or shellfish.

sea′go″ing *adj.* used for, or suitable for, ocean travel.

seal (sēl) *n.* **1,** an impressed device used to authenticate a document; a stamp for impressing the device. **2,** a tight closure; a substance used to effect it. **3,** a marine carnivorous mammal; its fur; its skin used for leather. —*v.t.* **1,** authenticate, close, or secure with a seal. **2,** determine irrevocably. **3,** close; confine. **4,** hunt seals. —**seal′ant,** *n.* a substance used for sealing.

Sea′lab″ *n.* a special U.S. Navy ship for underwater exploration.

Sea′ly·ham″ (sē′lė-ham″) *n.* a shaggy terrier of Welsh origin.

seam (sēm) *n.* **1,** the line formed by joining two edges, esp. in sewing. **2,** a fissure or gap; a ridge. **3,** a stratum. —*v.t. & i.* sew a seam.

sea′man (-mən) *n.* [*pl.* **-men**] **1,** a sailor. **2,** a naval rank below petty officer. —**sea′man·ship,** *n.* skill in the operation of a ship.

seam′ster (-stər), **seam′stress** (-stris) *n.* a person who sews; tailor.

seam′y (sē′mė) *adj.* sordid.

---

seamy, steamy
☞ These similar-sounding words have slightly different meanings. *Seamy* means sordid, while *steamy,* in its figurative sense, means sensual.

---

sé′ance (sā′äns) *n.* a session or meeting of spiritualists.

sea′plane″ *n.* an airplane, often with pontoons, designed for taking off and landing on water.

sea′port″ *n.* a city having a harbor on the sea.

sear (sir) *v.t.* **1,** burn or brown the surface of. **2,** make callous. **3,** dry up.

search (sẽrch) *v.t.* **1,** go through and examine carefully; explore. **2,** probe. **3,** penetrate. **4,** (with *out*) look for; seek. —*v.i.* seek; investigate. —*n.* process of searching; investigation. —**search warrant,** a legal order authorizing a search.

search′ing *adj.* keen; penetrating.

search′light″ *n.* an electric light that sends a concentrated beam.

sea′scape″ (-skāp″) *n.* a view or picture of the sea.

sea′shore″ *n.* land by the sea; a beach.

sea′sick″ *adj.* nauseated by the rolling of a vessel. —**sea′sick″ness,** *n.*

sea′side″ *n.* seashore.

sea′son (sē′zən) *n.* **1,** a quarter of the year: spring, summer, autumn, or winter. **2,** a particular period as to weather, business activity, fashion, etc. **3,** a suitable time. —*v.t.* **1,** mature; ripen. **2,** render palatable with spices, herbs, etc. **3,** give zest to; qualify; imbue. **4,** inure; accustom. —*v.i.* mature. —**seasonal affective disorder,** a period of mental depression caused by the lack of sunlight in winter.

> **season**
> ↔ Literally, a time for sowing, from Latin *satio*, act of sowing, through Old French *seson*.

sea′son·a·ble *adj.* suitable; opportune; timely.

sea′son·al *adj.* pert. to, or depending upon, the season.

sea′son·ing *n.* spices, etc.

seat (sēt) *n.* **1,** a place or thing to sit on. **2,** that part of a chair, garment, etc., on which one sits. **3,** a site; location. **4,** a right to sit or attend. —*v.t.* **1,** place on a seat; locate; fix. **2,** furnish with seats or room for sitting. —**seat belt,** a protective belt worn in automobiles and aircraft.

sea′wa″ter *n.* the salt water of the ocean.

sea′way″ *n.* **1,** headway, for a ship. **2,** a channel provided for seagoing ships.

sea′weed″ *n.* a plant growing in the sea.

sea′wor″thy *adj.* in condition for sea travel.

se·ba′ceous (si-bā′shəs) *adj.* being, containing, or secreting fat.

se′cant (sē′kənt) *n.* **1,** (*Geom.*) a line across an arc. **2,** a trigonometric ratio.

se·cede′ (si-sēd′) *v.i.* withdraw, esp. from a political or religious organization.

se·ces′sion (si-sesh′ən) *n.* act of seceding, as (*cap.*) that of the Confederate States in 1861. —**se·ces′sion·ist,** *n.* one who favors secession.

se·clude′ (si-klood′) *v.t.* shut away; keep in solitude.

se·clu′sion (si-kloo′zhən) *n.* **1,** act or effect of secluding. **2,** a secluded condition or place; solitude. —**se·clu′sive** (-siv) *adj.*

sec′ond (sek′ənd) *adj.* **1,** next after the first in order, time, value, etc.; the ordinal of two. **2,** subordinate. **3,** another. —*n.* **1,** the one next after the first. **2,** a supporter; an attendant in a prize fight or duel. **3,** an imperfect product. **4,** the sixtieth part of a minute. —*v.t.* support; assist. —**second fiddle,** a minor role. —**second hand,** the pointer on a timepiece that indicates the seconds. —**second nature,** habit. —**second sight,** clairvoyance. —**second thought,** reconsideration. —**second wind,** renewed breath control or energy, after an initial exhaustion.

sec′on·dar·y (sek′ən-der-ē) *adj.* **1,** of a second class or group. **2,** subordinate; de-

rived, not primary. —*n.* (*Electricity*) an induction coil or circuit. —**secondary school,** a high school.

sec′ond·class″ *adj.* **1,** in the next-to-highest class. **2,** inferior.

sec′ond-guess″ *v.t.* **1,** anticipate the actions or decisions of. **2,** criticize or analyze (actions or decisions) with the benefit of hindsight, after the fact.

sec″ond·hand′ *adj.* **1,** not original. **2,** previously used.

sec′ond-rate″ *adj.* inferior.

sec′ond-sto′ry man *adj.* a burglar.

sec′ond-string″ *adj.* of a secondary level of ability, achievement, etc.

se′cre·cy (sē′krə-sē) *n.* **1,** the state of being secret. **2,** secretive manner; strict silence.

se′cret (sē′krit) *adj.* **1,** kept private or concealed. **2,** not apparent; mysterious. —*n.* something not revealed. —**secret service,** a governmental branch that investigates secretly: (*cap.*) in the U.S., a bureau of the Treasury Dept.

> **secret, secrete, secretary**
> ☛ The easiest way to distinguish *secret* and *secrete* is to remember that *secret* is a noun or an adjective, never a verb, and *secrete* is only a verb. ↔ All three words derive from Latin *secretus*, secret; a *secretary* is a confidential aide.

sec″re·tar′i·at (sek″rə-ter′ē-ət) *n.* an administrative bureau.

sec′re·tar′y (sek′re-ter″ē) *n.* **1,** a recording or corresponding officer. **2,** a stenographer. **3,** a cabinet minister. **4,** a confidential aide. **5,** a writing desk. —**sec″re·tar′i·al,** *adj.* ❏ *secret*

sec′re·tar′y-gen′er·al *n.* the head of a secretariat.

se·crete′ (si-krēt′) *v.t.* **1,** hide. **2,** produce by secretion. —**se·cre′to·ry** (-tə-rē) *adj.* ❏ *secret*

se·cre′tion (si-krē′shən) *n.* **1,** the process of preparing substances by glandular activity. **2,** the product secreted.

se′cre·tive (sē′kri-tiv) *adj.* maintaining secrecy; reticent.

sect (sekt) *n.* a religious denomination. —**sec·tar′i·an** (sek-tār′ē-ən) *adj. & n.*

> **sect, section**
> ↔ Despite their apparent similarity, these two words are not related. *Sect* comes ultimately from Latin *sequi*, follow; *section* comes from Latin *secare*, to cut.

sec'ta·ry (sek'tə-rē) *n.* a religious dissenter.

sec'tion (sek'shən) *n.* **1,** a part cut or separated; a distinct portion. **2,** a region. **3,** the act of cutting; a surgical operation. **4,** a tract of U.S. public land, a mile square. **5,** a train scheduled jointly with another. ❑ *sect*

sec'tion·al *adj.* **1,** composed of several sections. **2,** local. —*n.* a piece of furniture made up of several parts. —**sec'tion·al·ism,** *n.* undue regard for local interests.

sec'tor (sek'tər) *n.* **1,** a plane figure enclosed between the arc of a circle and two radii. **2,** a mathematical scale. **3,** a combat area. **4,** (*Computers*) on a computer disk, an area comprising a number of clusters.

sec'u·lar (sek'yə-lər) *adj.* temporal; worldly; not of the church. —**sec'u·lar·ism,** *n.* —**sec'u·lar·ize",** *v.t.*

se·cure' (si-kyūr') *adj.* **1,** free from danger; safe. **2,** firm; stable. **3,** certain. —*v.t.* **1,** make safe; make certain. **2,** obtain. **3,** fasten.

se·cur'i·ty (si-kyūr'ə-tē) *n.* **1,** safety. **2,** a guaranty or pledge. **3,** a bond or stock certificate. —**security blanket,** anything that makes one feel secure, esp. an object.

se·dan' (si-dan') *n.* a two-seated closed automobile. —**sedan chair,** a vehicle for one person, borne by two porters.

se·date' (si-dāt') *adj.* quiet; composed; serious. —**se·date'ness,** *n.*

sed'a·tive (sed'ə-tiv) *adj.* tending to soothe or calm. —*n.* a calming medicine.

sed'en·tar"y (sed'ən-ter"ē) *adj.* **1,** characterized by a sitting position. **2,** taking little physical exercise.

Se'der (sā'dər) *n.* the Jewish feast of the Exodus.

sedge (sej) *n.* a grasslike plant.

sed'i·ment (sed'ə-mənt) *n.* the matter that settles to the bottom of a liquid; dregs. —**sed"i·men'ta·ry,** *adj.* —**sed"i·men·ta'tion,** *n.*

se·di'tion (si-dish'ən) *n.* incitement of rebellion. —**se·di'tious,** *adj.*

se·duce' (si-doos') *v.t.* lead astray; entice away from duty, rectitude, or chastity. —**se·duc'er,** *n.*

se·duc'tion (si-duk'shən) *n.* act or effect of seducing.

se·duc'tive (-tiv) *adj.* tending to seduce; enticing.

sed'u·lous (sej'ə-ləs) *adj.* diligent; persevering. —**se·du'li·ty** (sə-dū'lə-tē) *n.* —**sed'u·lous·ness,** *n.*

see (sē) *v.t.* [**saw** (sâ), **seen** (sēn), **see'ing**]

1, perceive by the eye; observe; view. **2,** comprehend. **3,** make sure. **4,** escort; attend. **5,** visit. **6,** in poker, etc., meet or call (a bet). —*v.i.* **1,** have the power of sight. **2,** understand. **3,** consider. —*n.* the seat or jurisdiction of a bishop. —**see'ing,** *conj.* inasmuch as. —**See'ing Eye,** an organization that trains dogs to guide blind persons. —**seeing-eye dog,** a dog trained to guide the blind.

seed (sēd) *n.* [*pl.* **seeds** or **seed**] **1,** the fertilized and natural ovule of a plant. **2,** semen, sperm, etc. **3,** offspring; descendants. **4,** origin. —*v.t.* **1,** plant. **2,** distribute (players) evenly in a tournament. —*v.i.* produce seed. —**go to seed,** decline in vigor, freshness, prosperity, etc. —**seed money,** funds given to support the initiation of a project. —**seed pearl,** a very small pearl.

seed'ling *n.* a young plant.

seed'y (sē'dē) *adj.* **1,** gone to seed; shabby. **2,** (*Informal*) not well. —**seed'i·ness,** *n.*

seek (sēk) *v.t.* [*pret. & p.p.* **sought** (sât)] **1,** go in search or quest of. **2,** resort to. **3,** attempt; endeavor.

seem (sēm) *v.i.* **1,** appear; appear to be. **2,** appear to oneself.

seem'ing *adj.* ostensible; apparent. —*n.* an appearance.

seem'ly (-lē) *adj.* becoming; proper; decent. —**seem'li·ness,** *n.*

seen (sēn) *v.* p.p. of *see.*

seep (sēp) *v.i.* ooze gently through pores. —*n.* a pool of water, oil, etc., seeping from the ground. —**seep'age** (-ij) *n.*

seer (sir) a prophet; clairvoyant.

seer'suck"er (sir'suk"ər) *n.* a crinkled cotton fabric.

---

seersucker
↔ This unusual word comes from a Persian word, *shir-o-shakar*, meaning milk and sugar, in reference to the stripes of the fabric.

---

see'saw" (sē'sâ") *n.* **1,** a board balanced on a support, on which two children move alternately up and down. **2,** any up-and-down movement. —*v.i.* move like a seesaw.

seethe (sēth) *v.i.* **1,** boil. **2,** be agitated.

seg'ment (seg'mənt) *n.* a part cut off; a section. —*v.t. & i.* divide into segments. —**seg"men·ta'tion,** *n.*

se'go (sē'gō) *n.* a perennial herb. Also, **sego lily.**

seg're·gate" (seg'rə-gāt") *v.t. & i.* separate or detach from others.

segregate
↔ From Latin *segregare*, place apart from the flock (*grex*).

seg″re·ga′tion (-gā′shən) *n.* act or effect of segregating; esp., separation of black and white persons. —**seg″re·ga′tion·ist,** *n. & adj.*

seg′ue (seg′wā) *n.* (*Radio & TV*) a brief musical passage between episodes.

seiche (sāsh) *n.* a sudden large wave in a lake, etc.

seine (sān) *n.* a large fishing net.

seism (sī′zəm) *n.* an earthquake. —**seis′mal** (-məl), **seis′mic** (-mik), *adj.*

seis′mo·graph″ (sīz′mə-gråf″) *n.* a device that records earthquakes.

seis·mol′o·gy (sīz-mŏl′ə-jē) *n.* the science of earthquakes. —**seis″mo·log′i·cal,** *adj.* —**seis·mol′o·gist,** *n.*

seize (sēz) *v.t.* **1,** grasp suddenly. **2,** comprehend. **3,** take legal or forcible possession of. **4,** afflict.

sei′zure (sē′zhər) *n.* **1,** the act of seizing. **2,** a sudden attack; a fit.

sel′dom (sel′dəm) *adv.* rarely; infrequently.

se·lect′ (si-lekt′) *v.t.* choose. —*adj.* **1,** choice. **2,** fastidious; exclusive. —**se·lec″tee′,** *n.* one selected for anything, esp. one drafted for military service.

se·lec′tion (si-lek′shən) *n.* act of choosing; a thing or things chosen.

se·lec′tive (-tiv) *adj.* **1,** pert. to or determined by selection. **2,** careful in choosing. —**selective service,** conscription of selected persons; draft.

se·lec′tiv′i·ty (-tiv′ə-tē) *n.* **1,** the quality of being selective. **2,** (*Radio & TV*) precision in tuning qualities.

se·lect′man (-mən) [*pl.* **-men**], **se·lect′·wom″an** *n.* a member of a town governing board.

sel′e·nite″ (sel′ə-nīt″) *n.* a variety of gypsum.

se·le′ni·um (sə-lē′nē-əm) *n.* a nonmetallic toxic chemical element, no. 34, symbol Se.

sel″e·nol′o·gy (sel″ə-nŏl′ə-jē) *n.* the study of the moon.

self *n.* [*pl.* **selves** (selvz)] **1,** a person in his relations to his own person. **2,** nature; individuality. **3,** personal interest and benefit. —*pron.* (*Informal*) myself, himself, herself, etc. —*adj.* single; uniform; unmixed.

self- *pref.* **1,** expressing reflexive action: on or to oneself or itself. **2,** in or by oneself or itself. [In addition to words defined in the text, the following words formed by prefixing *self-* may be defined by reference to the root word.]

self-″ad·dressed′
self-″as·sur′ance
self-″com·mand′
self-″com·pla′cent
self-″con·tained′
self-″con·trol′
self-″de·cep′tion
self-″de·ni′al
self-″de·struc′tion
self-″dis′ci·pline
self-″ed′u·cat″ed
self-″es·teem′
self-″ex·plan′a·to·ry
self-″gov′erned
self-″help′
self-″im·posed′
self-″in·duced′
self-″in·dul′gent

self-″in·flict′ed
self-″load′ing
self-″love′
self-″pit′y
self-″pol·li·na′tion
self-″pres″er·va′tion
self-″pro·pelled′
self-″pro·tec′tion
self-″re·li′ance
self-″re·proach′
self-″re·straint′
self-″sac′ri·fice″
self-″ser′vice
self-″styled′
self-″sup·port′
self-″sus·tain′ing
self-″taught′
self-″wind′ing

self-″cen′tered *adj.* absorbed in oneself.

self-″con′fi·dence *n.* the state of not feeling the need of assistance. —**self-″con′·fi·dent,** *adj.*

self-″con′scious *adj.* ill at ease when with others. —**self-″con′scious·ness,** *n.*

self-″de·feat′ing *adj.* having a result opposed to its purpose.

self-″de·fense′ *n.* protection of oneself when attacked.

self-″des·truct′ *v.i.* be destroyed by means of a self-contained mechanism.

self-″de·ter″mi·na′tion *n.* determination of one's own course; autonomy.

self-″ef·fac′ing *adj.* diffident; very modest. —**self-″ef·face′ment,** *n.*

self-″ev′i·dent *adj.* obvious; requiring no proof.

self-″ex·pres′sion *n.* utilization or pursuit of an outlet for one's personality.

self-″im·por′tant *adj.* pompous. —**self-″·im·por′tance,** *n.*

self-″in′ter·est *n.* personal advantage.

self′ish *adj.* devoted only to oneself. —**self′ish·ness,** *n.*

self′less *adj.* entirely unselfish. —**self′·less·ness,** *n.*

self-″made′ *adj.* successful wholly by one's own efforts.

self-″pos·sessed′ *adj.* composed.

self-″re·al·i·za′tion *n.* the development of one's potential abilities, personality, etc.

self-″re·li′ance *n.* self-confidence. —**self-″re·li′ant,** *adj.*

self-″re·spect′ *n.* becoming pride.

self-″right′eous *adj.* righteous in one's own esteem. —**self-″right′eous·ness,** *n.*

self′same″ *adj.* identical.

self-"sat'is·fied" *adj.* complacent. **—self'-sat"is·fac'tion,** *n.*

self-"seek'ing *adj.* selfish.

self-"start'er *n.* **1,** an electric motor that cranks an automobile engine. **2,** a person that starts something on his or her own initiative.

self-"suf·fi'cient *adj.* **1,** requiring no help, companionship, etc. **2,** unduly self-confident.

self-"willed' *adj.* obstinate.

sell (sel) *v.t.* [*pret. & p.p.* **sold** (sōld)] **1,** transfer to another for money. **2,** keep for sale. **3,** betray. **4,** cause acceptance. *—v.i.* **1,** engage in selling. **2,** be in demand; be sold. **3,** (with *out*) yield. *—n.* (*Slang*) a swindle or hoax. **—sell'er's market,** a market in which goods are relatively scarce and prices are relatively high.

sell'out" *n.* **1,** a complete disposal by selling, as of theater seats. **2,** a betrayal.

sel'tzer (sel'tsər) *n.* an effervescent mineral water, or carbonated water resembling it.

sel'vage (sel'vij) *n.* the finished edge of a fabric. Also, **sel'vedge.**

se·man'tic (si-man'tik) *adj.* pert. to meaning in language. **—se·man'tics,** *n.sing.* the study of meaning.

sem'a·phore" (sem'ə-fôr") *n.* a signaling device or method.

sem'blance (sem'bləns) *n.* **1,** a likeness; an image. **2,** outward appearance.

se'men (sē'mən) *n.* the male reproductive fluid.

se·mes'ter (si-mes'tər) *n.* a major division of the academic year, usu. one half.

sem·i- (sem-ē) *pref.* **1,** half. **2,** partly. **3,** once every half, as *semiannual.* ❑ *bi-*

sem"i·an'nu·al *adj.* once every six months.

sem'i·breve" (-brēv") *n.* (*Music*) a whole note (see *note*).

sem'i·cir"cle *n.* half a circle. **—sem"i·cir'cu·lar,** *adj.*

sem'i·co"lon *n.* a mark of punctuation (;) used to separate major sentence elements more distinctly than the comma.

---

semicolon
(*Gram.*) The *semicolon* is one of the more powerful and, at the same time, least difficult punctuation marks to use properly. It is used solely as a separator, dividing two or more complete statements or dividing halves of statements which employ a conjunctive adverb (such as *however, therefore,* etc.). It is also used to separate items of a sequence when those items may include commas.

---

sem"i·con·duc'tor *n.* a solid (such as silicon or germanium) having more conductivity than an insulator but less than good conductors; used in transistors, etc.

sem"i·fi'nal *adj.* a round or match in a contest, next to the final one. *—n.* [*also,* **sem"i·fi'nals**] this round, match, or matches. **—sem"i·fi'nal·ist,** *n.*

sem"i·month'ly *adj.* **1,** once every two weeks. **2,** once every two months. ❑ *bi-*

sem'i·nal (sem'ə-nəl) *adj.* **1,** pert. to seed or semen. **2,** being the inspiration for future developments.

sem'i·nar" (sem'ə-när") *n.* a small group, or course, for advanced study.

sem'i·nar"y (sem'ə-ner"ē) *n.* **1,** a school of religious study, as for the ministry. **2,** a school for young women.

sem"i·pre'cious *adj.* of less than the highest (gem) value.

sem"i·pri'vate *adj.* used or shared by two (or three) persons.

sem"i·pro·fes'sion·al *adj. & n.* (of or for) one who is professional part of the time. Also, **sem"i·pro'.**

sem'i·qua"ver (-kwā"vər) *n.* (*Music*) a sixteenth note (see *note*).

Sem'ite (sem'īt) *n.* a member of any Semitic people.

Se·mit'ic (sə-mit'ik) *adj.* relating to the Semites or their languages, such as Hebrew, Aramaic, Assyrian, and Arabic.

sem'i·tone" *n.* (*Music*) the interval between adjacent tones of the chromatic scale, as A to A-sharp.

sem"i·trail'er *n.* a trailer with no wheels in the front, that part being supported by the tractor.

sem"o·li'na (sem"ə-lē'nə) *n.* the hard, coarse part of the wheat, used for pasta.

sem'per fi·de'lis (sem'pər fi-del'is) (*Lat.*) ever faithful.

sem'per pa·ra'tus (sem'pər pə-rä'təs) (*Lat.*) ever ready.

sen *n.* a Jap. coin, 1/100 yen.

sen'ate (sen'it) *n.* a legislative assembly; (*cap.*) the upper legislative house of the U.S. and (*l.c.*) of some U.S. states.

---

senate, senior
↔ Etymologically, an assembly of elders, from Latin *senex*, old, of which *senior* was the comparative.

---

sen'a·tor (sen'ə-tər) *n.* a member of a senate, as (*cap.*) of the U.S. Senate. **—sen"-a·to'ri·al** (-tôr'ē-əl) *adj.*

send *v.t. & i.* [*pret. & p.p.* **sent**] **1,** cause to go; dispatch. **2,** impel. **3,** (with *out*, etc.) produce or give off. **4,** (*Slang*) stimulate or excite. —**send′er,** *n.* **1,** one who sends. **2,** a transmitter.

send-′off″ *n.* **1,** a start. **2,** a farewell demonstration.

send-′up″ *n.* (*Slang*) parody.

se·nes′cent (sə-nes′ənt) *adj.* growing old. —**se·nes′cence,** *n.*

sen′es·chal (sen′ə-shəl) *n.* the manager of a nobleman's estate.

se′nile (sē′nīl) *adj.* pert. to or characterizing old age. —**se·nil′i·ty** (sə-nil′ə-tē) *n.*

sen′ior (sēn′yər) *adj.* **1,** older; elder. **2,** older in office or service. **3,** pert. to the last year of a high school or college course, —*n.* **1,** a person who is older or of higher rank. **2,** a member of the senior class. —**senior citizen,** an elderly person, esp. one 65 years old or older. ❏ *senate*

sen·ior′i·ty (sē-nyor′ə-tē) *n.* state of being older in years, service, etc.

sen′na (sen′ə) *n.* a cathartic drug derived from cassia.

se·ñor′ (sā-nyôr′) *n.* (*Sp.*) **1,** mister. **2,** sir.

se·ño′ra (-nyō′rə) *n.* (*Sp.*) a married woman; Mrs. —**se″ño·ri′ta** (sā″nyə-rē′tə) *n.* (*Sp.*) a young or unmarried woman.

sen′sate (sen′sāt) *adj.* perceived by the senses.

sen·sa′tion (sen-sā′shən) *n.* **1,** a mental impression caused by an affection of a bodily organism; sensitive apprehension. **2,** a state of, or the cause of, excited interest or feeling.

sen·sa′tion·al (-əl) *adj.* intended to thrill. —**sen·sa′tion·al·ism,** *n.*

sense (sens) *n.* **1,** a special faculty of sensation: sight, smell, taste, touch, or hearing. **2,** consciousness; understanding; discriminative perception. **3,** practical intelligence. **4,** meaning. **5,** intention. **6,** consensus. **7,** algebraic sign (+ or -). —*v.t.* perceive by or as by the senses.

sense′less (-ləs) *adj.* **1,** unconscious. **2,** stupid. **3,** nonsensical. —**sense′less·ness,** *n.*

sen″si·bil′i·ty (sen″sə-bil′ə-tē) *n.* **1,** mental receptivity. **2,** capacity for the more refined feelings.

sen′si·ble (sen′sə-bəl) *adj.* **1,** reasonable. **2,** aware; cognizant. **3,** perceptible through the senses. **4,** capable of sensation.

---

sensible, sensitive
☛ Both words refer to the senses, literal or figurative. A *sensible* person has good sense; a *sensible* sensation can be perceived through the senses. A *sensitive* person has keen senses or is especially responsive (and hence easily offended).

---

sen′si·tive (sen′sə-tiv) *adj.* **1,** pert. to the senses; capable of receiving sensations. **2,** of keen sensibility; easily hurt. **3,** quickly responsive; readily affected. —*n.* one with heightened sensory perceptions. —**sen′si·tive·ness, sen″si·tiv′i·ty,** *n.* ❏ *sensible*

sen′si·tize″ (-tīz″) *v.t.* treat so as to make sensitive.

sen′sor (sen′sər) *n.* a device that responds to a physical stimulus (as heat or light) by emitting a signal for measurement, operating a control, etc.

sen′so·ry (sen′sə-rē) *adj.* pert. to sensation or the senses.

sen′su·al (sen′shû-əl) *adj.* pert. to the senses; not intellectual; carnal; voluptuous. —**sen′su·al·ism,** *n.* —**sen′su·al·ist,** *n.*

---

sensual, sensuous
☛ The textbook distinction between these two words is that *sensual* means pertaining to the senses and, by extension, voluptuous; *sensuous* means affecting the senses, especially in a delicate, refined manner. In common usage, the two words are often used interchangeably.

---

sen″su·al′i·ty (sen″shoo-al′ə-tē) *n.* unrestrained self-gratification.

sen′su·ous (sen′shû-əs) *adj.* affecting, or affected through, the senses. ❏ *sensual*

sent *v.* pret. & p.p. of *send.*

sen′tence (sen′təns) *n.* **1,** a number of words constituting a complete statement, inquiry, etc. **2,** the punishment determined for a convicted criminal. **3,** an opinion. —*v.t.* pronounce sentence upon.

sen·ten′tious (sen-ten′shəs) *adj.* given to the use of maxims; didactic.

sen′tient (sen′shənt) *adj.* having the power of feeling or perception. —**sen′tience,** *n.*

sen′ti·ment (sen′tə-mənt) *n.* **1,** higher feeling; emotion. **2,** tender susceptibility. **3,** an opinion; mental attitude. **4,** an expression of feeling.

sen″ti·men′tal (sen″tə-men′təl) *adj.* **1,** of a tender nature. **2,** mawkish. **3,** appealing to the feelings. —**sen″ti·men′tal·ist,** *n.* a sentimental person. —**sen″ti·men·tal′i·ty** (-tal′ə-tē) *n.* state of being sentimental; emotionalism.

sen′ti·nel (sen′tə-nəl) *n.* a soldier stationed as a guard.

sen′try (sen′trē) *n.* a guard; a sentinel.

se′pal (sē′pəl) *n.* a small leaf forming part of a flower.

sep′a·rate″ (sep′ə-rāt″) *v.t.* **1,** disunite;

---

disconnect. **2,** divide, place, or keep apart. —*v.i.* **1,** part. **2,** come apart; open. —*adj.* (-rət) **1,** divided; apart. **2,** distinct; individual. —**sep′a·ra·ble,** *adj.* —**sep′a·rat·ist** (-rə-tist) *adj. & n.*

sep″a·ra′tion (sep″ə-rā′shən) *n.* **1,** act or effect of separating. **2,** that which separates; a partition, etc. **3,** a limited divorce.

sep′a·ra″tor *n.* an apparatus for separating cream from milk.

se′pi·a (sē′pė-ə) *n. & adj.* a dark brown color.

sep′pu·ku (sep′oo-koo) *n.* harakiri.

sep′sis *n.* bacterial infection accompanied by formation of pus.

sept *n.* a group believing itself descended from a common ancestor.

sept- *pref.* seven.

Sep·tem′ber (sep-tem′bər) *n.* the ninth month of the year.

September
↔ From Latin *septem*, seven. The month was the seventh of the year (which then began with March).

---

sep·tet′ *n.* **1,** a group of seven. **2,** a composition in seven parts. Also, **sep·tette′.**

sep′tic (sep′tik) *adj.* pertaining to decay. —**septic tank,** a tank for sewage disposal.

sep″ti·ce′mi·a (sep″tə-sē′mė-ə) *n.* blood poisoning.

sep″tu·a·ge·nar′i·an (sep″choo-ə-ji-nãr′- ėən) *n. & adj.* (a person) aged 70 or more years.

Sep″tu·a·ges′i·ma (sep″choo-ə-jes′ə- mə) *n.* the third Sunday before Lent.

sep′tum (sep′təm) *n.* [*pl.* **-ta** (-tə)] a dividing wall or membrane.

sep′tu·ple (sep′tə-pəl) *adj.* seven times. —*v.t.* multiply by seven. —**sep·tup′let** (-tup′lit) *n.* one of seven offspring born of one birth.

sep′ul·cher (sep′əl-kər) *n.* a tomb; a burial vault. Also, **sep′ul·chre.**

se·pul′chral (sə-pul′krəl) *adj.* **1,** pert. to burial. **2,** deep; hollow in tone. **3,** gloomy.

sep′ul·ture (sep′əl-chər) *n.* **1,** burial. **2,** sepulcher. —*v.t.* bury.

se′quel (sē′kwəl) *n.* **1,** a continuation. **2,** a consequence.

se′quence (sē′kwəns) *n.* **1,** a succession. **2,** order of succession. **3,** a series; (*Music*) three or more repetitions of a phrase at different pitch levels. —**se′quenc·er,** *n.* an electronic instrument for storing musical notes, etc. —**se′quent,** *adj. & n.* —**se·quen′tial** (si-kwen′shəl) *adj.*

se·ques′ter (si-kwes′tər) *v.t.* put aside; seclude. —**se″ques·tra′tion** (sē″-) *n.*

se′quin (sē′kwin) *n.* **1,** a spangle. **2,** a former gold coin.

se·quoi′a (si-kwoi′ə) *n.* either of two very large coniferous trees of California.

---

sequoia
↔ The tree was named for a Cherokee scholar who developed a system for writing the Cherokee language.

---

se·ragl′io (si-ral′yō) *n.* **1,** a harem. **2,** a Turkish palace.

se·ra′pe (se-rä′pė) *n.* a bright-colored shawl or wrap.

ser′aph (ser′əf) *n.* [*pl.* **ser′a·phim** (-ə- fim) or **ser′aphs**] an angel. —**se·raph′ic** (sə-raf′ik) *adj.*

Serb (sẽrb) *adj. & n.* pert. to Serbia, its people, language, etc. Also, **Ser′bi·an** (sẽr′bė-ən).

sere (sir) *adj.* withered; dry.

ser″e·nade′ (ser″ə-nād′) *n.* an evening song of love. —*v.t.* entertain with a serenade.

---

serenade
↔ Literally, serene music, from Latin *serenus* through Italian *sereno*. The idea of night music comes from a mistaken association with Italian *sera*, evening.

---

ser″e·na′ta (ser″ə-nä′tə) *n.* (*Music*) **1,** a secular cantata. **2,** an instrumental composition in several movements.

ser″en·dip′i·ty (ser″ən-dip′ə-tė) *n.* an assumed talent for making discoveries by accident.

---

serendipity
↔ An odd word coined by Horace Walpole from *Serendip,* an old name for Sri Lanka and part of the title of a fairy tale "The Three Princes of Serendip."

---

se·rene′ (sə-rēn′) *adj.* **1,** tranquil; calm. **2,** clear. —**se·rene′ness,** *n.*

se·ren′i·ty (sə-ren′ə-tė) *n.* tranquillity; sereneness.

serf (sẽrf) *n.* a peasant attached to a feudal estate. —**serf′dom,** *n.*

serge (sẽrj) *n.* a twilled worsted fabric.

---

serge
↔ From Latin phrase *lana serica,* wool of the Seres, a Chinese people.

---

ser′geant (sär′jənt) *n.* **1,** a noncommissioned officer, ranking above a corporal.

2, a police or court officer. **—sergeant-at-arms,** an official appointed to maintain order, as in a court.

se'ri·al (sir'ė-əl) *adj.* **1,** published in installments. **2,** successive. **3,** (*Music*) composed on the basis of predetermined series of pitches, numbers, etc. **4,** (*Computers*) pert. to the transmission of data one bit at a time. —*n.* a serial story. **—serial killer,** a murderer using a consistent method on a series of victims over a period of time. **—serial number,** an identifying number for something produced as part of a series, as a manufactured article, etc.

se'ri·al·ism (-iz-əm) *n.* (*Music*) a method of composition utilizing serial techniques.

se'ri·al·ize" (-īz") *v.t.* **1,** publish in installments. **2,** (*Music*) compose music using serial techniques.

se"ri·a'tim (sē"rė-ā'tim) *adv.* one after another.

se'ries (sir'ėz) *n.* a continued succession of similar things. **—in series,** in sequence.

ser'if *n.* a short cross-line on a letter of type.

se'ri·ous (sir'ė-əs) *adj.* **1,** grave; solemn. **2,** in earnest. **3,** weighty; critical. **—se'ri·ous·ness,** *n.*

ser'mon (sėr'mən) *n.* **1,** a religious discourse. **2,** any admonitory speech. **—ser'mon·ize"** (-īz") *v.t.* preach; moralize.

ser'pent (sėr'pənt) *n.* **1,** a snake. **2,** (*cap.*) Satan. **3,** an obsolete wooden bass trumpet.

ser'pen·tine" (sėr'pən-tēn") *adj.* **1,** winding about; tortuous. **2,** wily; treacherous. —*n.* a greenish silicate mineral.

ser'rate (ser'āt) *adj.* having sharp teeth. **—ser·ra'tion,** *n.*

ser'ried (ser'ēd) *adj.* pressed closely together.

se'rum (sir'əm) *n.* **1,** the clear liquid in the blood. **2,** immunized blood serum. **—se'rous,** *adj.*

ser'vant (sėr'vənt) *n.* one who serves, esp. a domestic employee.

serve (sėrv) *v.t.* **1,** attend or wait upon; work for. **2,** aid. **3,** (with *for*) be a substitute for. **4,** avail. **5,** (*Law*) give (a summons, etc.) to. **6,** (*Tennis*) put (the ball) in play. **7,** (of animals) mate with. **8,** supply. —*v.i.* **1,** act as a servant or waiter. **2,** suffice; be convenient. **3,** serve something. —*n.* (*Tennis*) the act or manner of serving. **—serv'ing,** *n.* a portion of something served, as food.

ser'ver *n.* **1,** a waiter. **2,** (*Computers*) the

central processing unit of a computer network.

ser'vice (sėr'vis) *n.* **1,** act or result of serving; duty performed or needs supplied. **2,** (often *pl.*) religious worship. **3,** a set of dishes, etc. **—ser'vice·a·ble,** *adj.* useful. **—service mark,** trademark. **—service module,** the part of a spacecraft containing fuel cells, the engines, and propellant tanks. **—service station, 1,** a filling station. **2,** a place where a service is offered.

ser'vice·man", ser'vice·wom"an *n.* **1,** a member of an armed force. **2,** a repairer.

ser'vi·ette' (sėr"vė-et') *n.* a napkin.

ser'vile (sėr'vil) *adj.* menial; obsequious. **—ser·vil'i·ty,** *n.*

ser'vi·tor (sėr'vi-tər) *n.* an attendant; a waiter.

ser'vi·tude" (sėr'vi-tood") *n.* slavery.

ser·vo- (sėr-vō) *pref.* indicating devices using a servomotor.

ser"vo·mech'a·nism (sėr"vō-mek'ə-niz-əm) *n.* an automatic control device, triggered by mechanical or electrical impulses, that operates a machine or maintains performance of a machine at a desired standard. Also, **ser'vo** (*Informal*).

ser'vo·mo"tor *n.* a motor that supplements a control device (such as a servomechanism).

ses'a·me (ses'ə-mė) *n.* a tropical herbaceous plant; its edible seed.

ses·qui- (ses'kwė) *pref.* one and a half.

ses'sile (ses'əl) *adj.* attached by the base; permanently attached.

ses'sion (sesh'ən) *n.* **1,** the sitting or meeting of a court, council, class, etc. **2,** one period in a series.

set *v.t.* **[set, set'ting] 1,** put in a certain place or position; fix; establish. **2,** adjust. **3,** start; employ; assign. **4,** mount, as a gem. **5,** adapt to music. **6,** (with *down*) write. **7,** arrange (type) for printing. **8,** (with *forth*) express. —*v.i.* **1,** sink; settle. **2,** become fixed. **3,** (with *out* or *forth*) begin. **4,** sit on eggs, as a hen. —*n.* **1,** a related group; a collection. **2,** a number of persons customarily associated. **3,** a hardening. **4,** a tendency. **5,** build; carriage. **6,** a stage setting; scenery. **7,** a scoring unit, as in tennis. **8,** of a saw, the bending of adjacent teeth in opposite directions. —*adj.* **1,** placed; fixed. **2,** obstinate. **3,** prescribed. **—set back,** hinder; delay. **—set theory,** a branch of mathematics dealing with the manipulation of sets. **—set up,** establish. **—set upon,** attack.

set'back" *n.* **1,** a reverse; a recession. **2,**

a setting of part of a building behind a lower part.

set′screw″ *n.* a screw for clamping an adjustable part on another.

set·tee′ (se-tē′) *n.* a small sofa; a bench with a back.

set′ter (set′ər) *n.* a kind of long-haired hunting dog.

set′ting *n.* **1,** environment; scene; scenery. **2,** a mounting, as for a jewel. **3,** music composed for a text; libretto, etc.

set′tle (set′əl) *v.t.* **1,** fix in position or condition; establish; decide. **2,** adjust, as a dispute. **3,** calm. **4,** colonize. **5,** clear of dregs. **6,** pay (a bill). —*v.i.* **1,** become fixed; come to rest. **2,** establish a permanent residence. **3,** become clear. **4,** sink. **5,** decide; arrange; agree. —*n.* a bench.

set′tle·ment *n.* **1,** act or result of settling; an adjustment; payment. **2,** a small colony. **3,** a welfare establishment.

set′tler (-lər) *n.* a colonizer.

set-′to″ *n.* (*Informal*) a fight.

set′up″ *n.* **1,** a system. **2,** (*Slang*) a contest easy to win. **3,** a glass with ice, etc., for mixing a drink.

sev′en (sev′ən) *n. & adj.* the cardinal number between six and eight, expressed by 7. —**sev′enth,** *adj. & n.* —**seventh heaven,** bliss.

sev′en·teen″ (-tēn″) *n. & adj.* seven plus ten; also expressed by 17. —**sev″en·teenth′** (-tēnth′) *n. & adj.*

sev′en·ty (-tē) *n. & adj.* ten times seven; also expressed by 70. —**sev′en·ti·eth** (-tē-əth) *n. & adj.*

sev′er (sev′ər) *v.t. & i.* separate; divide into parts; cut apart.

sev′er·al (sev′ər-əl) *adj.* **1,** three or more, but not many. **2,** various. **3,** individual; separate. **4,** distinct. —*n.* a few.

sev′er·ance (sev′ər-əns) *n.* **1,** the act of severing or the state of being severed. **2,** break off, as a relationship, employment, etc. **3,** [also, **severance pay**] money paid to a tenured worker who is dismissed.

se·vere′ (si-vir′) *adj.* **1,** serious or earnest; austere. **2,** rigorous; trying. **3,** harsh. **4,** sharp; distressing; extreme. —**se·ver′i·ty** (-ver′ə-tē) *n.*

sew (sō) *v.t. & i.* join or attach by means of a thread, wire, etc.

sew′age (soo′ij) *n.* waste matter.

sew′er (soo′ər) *n.* a conduit for carrying off waste water and refuse. —**sew′er·age,** *n.* a system of sewers.

sex (seks) *n.* **1,** the anatomical and physiological distinction between male and female. **2,** either males or females, con-sidered collectively. **3,** sexual intercourse. —**sex appeal,** the quality of attracting amatory interest. —**sex object,** (*Informal*) someone appreciated or exploited for sexual reasons alone. —**sex surrogate,** a sexual partner employed in sex therapy. —**sex symbol,** a person considered especially sexually appealing. —**sex′less,** *adj.* ❏ gender

sex- *pref.* six.

sex″a·ge·nar′i·an (seks″ə-jə-nār′ē-ən) *adj. & n.* (a person) aged 60 or more years.

sex′ism (sekz′iz-əm) *n.* bias or discrimination by one sex against the other. —**sex′ist,** *n. & adj.*

sex′pot″ *n.* (*Informal*) a sexy woman.

sex′tant (seks′tənt) *n.* **1,** one-sixth of a circle. **2,** an instrument used in navigation.

sex·tet′ (seks-tet′) *n.* **1,** a group of six, esp. musicians. **2,** a composition for six instruments. Also, **sex·tette′.**

sex′ton (seks′tən) *n.* a minor official of a church. ❏ sacristan

sex′tu·ple (seks′tə-pəl) *adj.* of six parts; six times as great; sixfold. —*v.* make or become six times as great. —**sex·tup′let** (-tup′lit) *n.* a set of six.

sex′u·al (sek′shoo-əl) *adj.* **1,** pert. to sex. **2,** (*Informal*) pert. to carnal love. —**sex″u·al′i·ty** (-al′ə-tē) *n.* —**sexual harassment,** unwelcome sexual innuendo or advances made by one person to another, esp. an employer to an employee.—**sexual intercourse** or **relations,** coitus.

sex′y *adj.* (*Slang*) concerned with or suggesting carnal love. —**sex′i·ness,** *n.*

sfor·zan′do (sfôr-tsän′dō) (*It., Music*) *adj.* strongly accented. —*n.* a strong accent.

shab′by (shab′ē) *adj.* **1,** seedy; (of clothes) much worn. **2,** mean; contemptible. —**shab′bi·ness,** *n.*

shack (shak) *n.* a rough cabin. —**shack up,** (*Slang*) live with.

shack′le (shak′əl) *n.* **1,** a fetter; hobble. **2,** a coupling device. **3,** the bar of a padlock. —*v.t.* **1,** chain with shackles. **2,** hamper.

shad *n.* an Amer. food fish.

shad′dock (shad′ək) *n.* an E. Indian tree; its pear-shaped citrus fruit. Also, **pom′·e·lo″** (pom′ə-lō″).

> **shaddock**
> ↔ Named for 17th-c. English seaman Captain *Shaddock*.

shade (shād) *n.* **1,** darkness caused by interception of rays of light. **2,** a shaded place. **3,** a dark area. **4,** a trace. **5,** a ghost. **6,** a screen against light. **7,** a gradation of color; a hue to which black has been added. **8,** (*pl., Informal*) sunglasses. —*v.t.* **1,** screen from light. **2,** obscure; darken.

shad′ing (shā′ding) *n.* **1,** a slight difference. **2,** application of shade.

shad′ow (shad′ō) *n.* **1,** the dark image of a body intercepting the light. **2,** shade. **3,** an inseparable companion. **4,** a spy. **5,** a phantom. —*v.t.* **1,** shade; cloud. **2,** trail; stay near. —**shad′ow·y,** *adj.*

shad′ow·box″ing *n.* exercise by boxing with an imaginary opponent. —**shad′-ow·box″,** *v.i.*

shad′ow·graph″ *n.* a picture produced by casting a shadow, as of the hands, on a screen.

shad′y (shā′dè) *adj.* **1,** affording shade. **2,** (*Informal*) of doubtful character. —**shad′i·ness,** *n.*

shaft (shàft) *n.* **1,** a long, slender, cylindrical body, as an arrow, spear handle, etc. **2,** a bar transmitting motion. **3,** passage, as in a mine, or for an elevator. **4,** harsh criticism. —*v.t.* criticize harshly.

shag *v.t.* [**shagged, shag′ging**] **1,** roughen. **2,** fetch. —*n.* **1,** a rough surface; a coarse material. **2,** a fabric with a nap. **3,** a hopping dance step.

shag′gy (shag′è) *adj.* having rough hair or nap; unkempt. —**shag′gi·ness,** *n.*

shah (shä) *n.* king; esp., the former monarch of Iran.

shake (shāk) *v.t.* [**shook** (shûk), **shak′en, shak′ing**] **1,** cause to vibrate or tremble; agitate. **2,** loosen. **3,** weaken; cause to doubt. **4,** (with *up*) disturb; upset; jar. **5,** (with *down*) (*Slang*) extort money from. —*v.i.* be agitated; tremble; totter. —*n.* **1,** an act of shaking. **2,** (*pl.*) the ague. **3,** (*Informal*) an instant. **4,** a shaken drink, often with ice cream. **5,** (*Music*) a trill. —**shake a leg,** (*Slang*) bestir oneself. —**fair shake,** just treatment.

shake′down″ *n.* **1,** preparation or conditioning, as of a new ship. **2,** (*Slang*) extortion. **3,** a makeshift bed, as of straw.

shak′er *n.* **1,** a perforated container for dispensing salt, etc. **2,** (*cap.*) a member of a celibate religious sect.

shake′up″ *n.* a reorganization.

shak′o (shā′kō) *n.* [*pl.* **-os**] a high, plumed military hat.

shak′y *adj.* **1,** trembling. **2,** insecure; wavering. —**shak′i·ness,** *n.*

shale (shāl) *n.* a rock that splits readily into thin leaves.

shall (shal) *aux. v.* [*pret.* **should** (shûd)]

1, (first person) expressing the future: am or are going to or sure to. **2,** (second and third persons) must.

---

shall, will

(*Gram.*) Everyone has learned in school how these words are *supposed* to be used, but very few actually employ those rules consistently. The distinction is between what one *wants* to do or *must* do (volition) and what one *intends* to do (prediction): *shall* expresses volition, *will* expresses prediction. *Should* and *would* are to be used in the same way.

---

shal′lop (shal′əp) *n.* a light open boat.

shal·lot′ (shə-lot′) *n.* an onionlike vegetable.

---

shallot

↔ From Latin *Ascalonia caepa*, onion from Ascalon, an ancient port in Palestine. The word reached English by way of Old French *eschalotte*.

---

shal′low (shal′ō) *adj.* **1,** not deep. **2,** superficial. —*n.* a shoal.

sha·lom′ (shä-lōm′) *interj.* (*Hebrew*) peace. —**sha·lom′ a·lai′chem** (ə-lā′kəm) (*Hebrew*) peace be with you.

sham *adj.* counterfeit; pretended. —*n.* an imposture; make-believe; an imitation. —*v.i. & t.* [**shammed, sham′ming**] pretend; feign.

sha′man (shā′mən) *n.* a religious person.

sham′ble (sham′bəl) *v.i.* walk awkwardly. —*n.* **1,** a shambling walk. **2,** (*pl.*) a slaughterhouse. **3,** (*pl.*) a scene of devastation.

shame (shām) *n.* **1,** a remorseful consciousness of guilt. **2,** disgrace or dishonor; a cause of it. —*v.t.* **1,** make ashamed. **2,** disgrace. **3,** influence by reproach. —**shame′ful,** *adj.* disgraceful. —**shame′less,** *adj.* overbold; conscienceless.

shame′faced″ *adj.* ashamed; showing shame.

---

shamefaced

↔ The *faced* in this word is not from *face*, but from *fast*, firm; the original form of the word was *shamefast*.

---

sham′my (sham′è) *n.* chamois.

sham·poo′ *v.t.* wash (the hair). —*n.* a washing of the hair; a preparation for it.

sham′rock″ (sham′rok″) *n.* a three-leaved plant, emblem of Ireland.

sham·us (shām′əs) *n.* (*Slang*) a private detective.

---

fat, fāte, fär, fāre, fâll, àsk; met, hē, hèr, maybè; pin, pīne; not, nōte, ôr, tool

shan′dy (shan′de) *n.* a beverage of lemonade and beer.

shang′hai (shang′hī) *v.t.* abduct and force to serve as a seaman; hence, abduct (a person.)

Shan″gri-la′ (shang″gri-lä′) *n.* a hidden or remote paradise.

> **Shangri-la**
> ↔ From the imaginary paradise in the novel *Lost Horizon* (1933) by James Hilton.

shank *n.* **1,** the leg between the knee and the ankle. **2,** the part of a tool, etc., that connects the acting part with the handle. **3,** (*Informal*) the latter part, as, *shank of the evening.* —**by shank's-′mare″,** on foot.

shan′tung *n.* a silk fabric.

shan′ty (shan′tè) *n.* **1,** a rough or flimsy hut or house. **2,** chantey.

shape (shāp) *n.* **1,** form; outward contour; appearance. **2,** proper form. **3,** condition. —*v.t.* **1,** give form to; create. **2,** adapt. **3,** express. —*v.i.* **1,** take form. **2,** (with *up*) come out; reach proper form. —**shape′ly,** *adj.* pleasingly formed.

shard (shärd) *n.* a fragment of a brittle substance, as glass.

share (shâr) *n.* **1,** a portion; an allotted part. **2,** a unit of stock in a corporation. **3,** a plow blade. —*v.t.* **1,** divide; apportion. **2,** have jointly. —*v.i.* **1,** partake. **2,** give a portion to others.

share′crop″per *n.* a farmer who divides the crop with his or her landlord.

share′hold″er *n.* stockholder.

share′ware″ *n.* computer software distributed free for a trial period, with subsequent payment if the program is used.

shark (shärk) *n.* **1,** a large and ferocious marine fish. **2,** a predatory person. **3,** (*Slang*) an expert.

shark′skin″ *n.* a heavy suiting fabric.

sharp (shärp) *adj.* **1,** having a fine cutting edge or point. **2,** well-defined; distinct. **3,** abrupt; angular. **4,** keenly affecting a sense: pungent, shrill, keenly cold, etc. **5,** acute; keen. **6,** barely honest. **7,** (*Music*) of a note, marked #, raised a half tone. **8,** (*Music*) above the intended pitch. —*adv.* sharply; quickly; exactly. —*n.* **1,** a needle. **2,** (*Music*) a tone raised half a step; the sign (#) indicating this. **3,** a sharper. **4,** (*Informal*) an expert. —**sharp′ness,** *n.*

sharp′en (shär′pən) *v.t. & i.* make or become sharp. —**sharp′en·er,** *n.* a tool or machine for sharpening an edge or point.

sharp′er *n.* a swindler.

sharp′ie (shär′pè) *n.* **1,** a type of small

sailboat. **2,** (*Slang*) a stylish person. **3,** (*Slang*) a sly person.

sharp′shoot″er *n.* **1,** a person skilled in shooting. **2,** (*Mil.*) a rating in rifle marksmanship, below expert and above marksman. **3,** a sharper.

shat′ter (shat′ər) *v.i. & t.* **1,** break in pieces. **2,** disorder; impair.

shave (shāv) *v.t.* **1,** slice with a keen instrument. **2,** make bare. **3,** cut down gradually. **4,** come very close to. —*v.i.* remove hair with a razor. —*n.* **1,** an act of shaving. **2,** [also, **close shave**] (*Informal*) a narrow escape.

shav′er *n.* **1,** one who or that which shaves. **2,** (*Informal*) a youngster.

shave′tail″ *n.* (*Slang*) a newly appointed second lieutenant.

> **shavetail**
> ↔ The term originally referred to a newly broken mule, because in the army their tails were shaved for identification.

shav′ing *n.* a thin slice, esp. of wood.

shawl (shâl) *n.* a loose covering for the shoulders.

shay (shā) *n.* a light carriage.

she (shē) *pron.* [*poss.* **her** (hēr), **hers;** *obj.* **her**] **1,** the third person, sing., fem., nominative; a female person other than the speaker and the person addressed. **2,** any female. ❏ *he*

s/he *pron.* she or he: sometimes used to avoid using *he* when the sex of the person referred to is unknown.

sheaf (shēf) *n.* [*pl.* **sheaves** (shēvz)] a bundle, as of grain, papers, etc.

shear (shir) *v.t.* **1,** clip or cut. **2,** remove by clipping, as fleece. —**shears,** *n.sing. & pl.* large scissors.

> **shear, sheer**
> ☛ Do not confuse these homonyms. *Shear*, a verb, means to cut. *Sheer*, an adjective, has several meanings, among them diaphanous and precipitous.

sheath (shēth) *n.* a case or covering; a scabbard.

sheathe (shē*th*) *v.t.* put into a sheath; enclose; cover.

sheath′ing (shē′*th*ing) *n.* **1,** a covering or outer layer. **2,** the boards first put on the framework of a house.

she·bang′ (shə-bang′) *n.* (*Slang*) establishment; outfit.

shed *v.t.* [**shed, shed′ding**] **1,** throw off, molt, or cause to flow off. **2,** disperse, as

light. —*v.i.* cast or let fall a covering, etc.
—*n.* a rude structure for shelter or
storage.

sheen (shēn) *n.* luster.

sheep (shēp) *n.sing. & pl.* **1,** a ruminant
mammal, valued for its flesh, skin, fleece,
etc. **2,** a timid person. **3,** ignorant imita-
tors. —**sheep′ish,** *adj.* embarrassed,
timid.

sheep′dog″ *n.* any of several dogs
trained to herd and guard sheep.

sheep′fold″ *n.* a pen or shelter for
sheep.

sheep′shank″ *n.* a kind of knot made in
a rope to shorten it temporarily.

sheep′skin″ *n.* **1,** sheep's fur; a garment
made of it. **2,** parchment; (*Informal*) a
diploma.

sheer (shir) *adj.* **1,** very thin; diaphanous.
2, unmixed; absolute. **3,** precipitous.
—*adv.* **1,** absolutely; quite. **2,** steeply.
—*v.i.* (with *off*) swerve. ❏ *shear*

sheet (shēt) *n.* **1,** a rectangular piece of
cloth bedding. **2,** a broad, flat, very thin
piece of anything. **3,** a newspaper. **4,** an
expanse or surface. **5,** a rope fastened to
a sail. —**sheet′ing,** *n.*

sheik (shēk) *n.* **1,** an Arab chief. **2,**
(*Slang*) a bold lover.

shek′el (shek′əl) *n.* **1,** the monetary unit
of Israel. **2,** a silver coin of the ancient
Jews. **3,** (*pl., Slang*) money.

shel′drake″ (shel′drāk″) *n.* any of several varieties of duck.

> **sheldrake**
> ↔ The *shel-* in *sheldrake* comes from
> a dialect word *sheld*, meaning
> multicolored.

---

shelf *n.* [*pl.* **shelves**] **1,** a horizontal plank
for supporting objects. **2,** a ledge. **3,** a reef.
—**on the shelf,** discarded or retired.

shell (shel) *n.* **1,** a hard outer case or covering. **2,** something flimsy, hollow, or concave. **3,** a light racing boat. **4,** a projectile;
a cartridge, esp. a shotgun cartridge. **5,**
(*Computers*) a program simplifying the
interface between the user and the operating system of a computer. —*v.t.* **1,** remove, or take out of, the shell. **2,**
bombard. —**shell game,** a swindling game.
—**shell out,** (*Informal*) hand over; pay.
—**shell shock,** a psychoneurosis caused by
battle strain.

shel·lac′ (shə-lak′) *n.* a purified plastic
resin; a varnish made from it. —*v.t.* paint
with shellac.

shell′fish″ *n.* an aquatic animal having a
shell, as an oyster, lobster, etc.

shel′ter (shel′tər) *n.* whatever shields or
protects; a refuge; a roofed place. —*v.t. &
i.* house; protect.

shelve (shelv) *v.t.* **1,** put on a shelf. **2,** put
aside; put off. **3,** furnish with shelves.

she·nan′i·gan (shə-nan′ə-gən) *n.* (*Informal*) foolery; a prank.

shep′herd (shep′ərd), **shep′herd·ess** (-is)
n. **1,** a sheep-herder. **2,** a pastor; (*cap.*)
Jesus Christ. **3,** a breed of dog.

sher′bet (shēr′bət) *n.* an ice containing
milk.

> **sherbet, syrup**
> ↔ Both words derive from Arabic
> *shariba*, drink, by way of Turkish.
> *Sherbet* once referred to a drink made
> with melted snow.

---

sher′iff (sher′if) *n.* the chief law-enforcement officer of a county.

> **sheriff**
> ↔ From an Old English compound of
> *scir*, shire, county, and *gerefa*, reeve,
> local official.

Sher′pa (shēr′pə) *n.* a member of a Tibetan people, often used as Himalayan
guides; hence, (*l.c.*) an expert assigned to
help prepare a summit meeting.

sher′ry (sher′ē) *n.* a strong wine of
southern Spain.

Shet′land (shet′lənd) *n.* **1,** a small,
rough-coated pony. **2,** a soft, loosely
twisted wool.

shew (shō) *v.* (*Brit.*) show.

shi·at′su (shē-ät′soo) *n.* a Jap. massage
technique.

shib′bo·leth″ (shib′ə-leth″) *n.* a password; a slogan.

> **shibboleth**
> ↔ A Hebrew word for stream, used
> as a password because the *sh* sound
> was difficult for enemy tribes to
> pronounce.

---

shield (shēld) *n.* **1,** a broad plate of defensive armor. **2,** anything that protects.
3, an escutcheon. —*v.t.* protect; screen.
—**shield law,** a law protecting journalists
from having to disclose their sources.

shift *v.t.* transfer to another place or person; change; exchange. —*v.i.* **1,** change
place, position, direction, etc. **2,** alter. **3,**
get along. —*n.* **1,** a change; a turning. **2,** a
group of workmen; the time they work.
3, an expedient; a resource. **4,** a woman's
chemise. —**shift′less,** *adj.* lazy. —**shift′y,**
adj. tricky; evasive. —**shift key,** a key on
a typewriter or computer keyboard that

---

determines whether a character will be uppercase or lowercase.

Shih Tzu (shē′ tzoo′) *n.* a Chinese breed of dog.

Shi′ite (shē′īt) *n.* an Islamic sect that regards Ali, the son-in-law of Mohammed, to be Mohammed's legitimate successor.

shik′sa (shik′sə) *n.* (*Yiddish, disparaging*) a non-Jewish female.

shill (shil) *n.* (*Slang*) an accomplice to a peddler, gambler, etc.

shil·le′lagh (shə-lā′lė) *n.* a cudgel.

shil′ling (shil′ing) *n.* **1,** a former Brit. monetary unit. **2,** the monetary unit of Kenya and other Afr. states.

shil′ly-shal′ly (shil′ė-shal′ė) *v.i.* act in an irresolute manner.

shim *n.* a wedge or strip of wood, metal, etc., used to fill in or bring one part level with another. —*v.t.* adjust with a shim.

shim′mer (shim′ər) *v.i.* shine with a tremulous light. —**shim′mer·y,** *adj.*

shim′my (shim′ė) *n.* **1,** abnormal vibration; jiggling. **2,** a jazz dance. **3,** (*Informal*) a chemise. —*v.i.* dance the shimmy.

shin *n.* **1,** the front of the leg from knee to ankle. **2,** the tibia. —*v.t. & i.* [shinned, shin′ning] [also, shin′ny] climb by hugging with arms and legs.

shin′bone″ *n.* the tibia.

shin′dig″ *n.* (*Slang*) a dance or party.

shin′dy (shin′dė) *n.* (*Slang*) **1,** shindig. **2,** an uproar or fracas.

shine (shīn) *v.t.* **1,** cause to gleam. **2,** polish. —*v.i.* [*pret. & p.p.* **shone** (shōn)] **1,** glow; appear bright; gleam. **2,** excel. —*n.* **1,** light; luster. **2,** fair weather. —**shin′y,** *adj.* —**take a shine to,** (*Informal*) take a liking to.

shin′er *n.* **1,** a minnow. **2,** (*Slang*) a black eye. **3,** (*Informal*) a liking. **4,** (*Informal*) a prank.

shin′gle (shing′gəl) *n.* **1,** a thin piece of wood, etc., used as roofing. **2,** closely bobbed hair. **3,** a small signboard. **4,** a gravelly beach. —*v.t.* **1,** roof with shingles. **2,** cut (hair) short.

shin′gles (shing′gəlz) *n.* an inflammatory skin disease.

shin′ny (shin′ė) *n.* a game similar to hockey. —*v.i.* (with *up*) climb; shin.

Shin′to (shin′tō) *n.* a Jap. religion; ancestor worship.

ship *n.* **1,** a large vessel, usually seagoing. **2,** an aircraft. —*v.t.* [shipped, ship′ping] **1,** put or take on board a ship or boat. **2,** send or transport. —*v.i.* embark. —**ship′-per,** *n.* one who ships goods; consignor.

-ship *suf.* denoting office, occupation, condition, character, etc.

ship′board″ *n.* any deck or interior part of a ship.

ship′build″ing *n.* construction of ships.

ship′load″ *n.* a full load for a (particular) ship.

ship′mate″ *n.* a fellow sailor.

ship′ment *n.* **1,** act or result of shipping. **2,** a quantity of goods shipped.

ship′ping *n.* **1,** the business of transporting goods. **2,** ships collectively.

ship′shape″ *adj.* in good order.

ship′wreck″ *n.* **1,** the sinking or destruction of a ship. **2,** ruin. —*v.t.* ruin.

ship′wright″ *n.* a shipbuilder.

ship′yard″ *n.* a place where ships are built.

shire (shīr) *n.* a county.

shirk (shėrk) *v.t. & i.* evade work, responsibility, etc. —**shirk′er,** *n.*

shirr (shėr) *v.t.* **1,** draw up (a fabric). **2,** bake (eggs).

shirt (shėrt) *n.* a garment for the upper body. —**shirt′ing,** *n.* material for shirts.

---

shirt, skirt
↔ Both words are Germanic in origin, from a source meaning short garment.

---

shirt′waist″ *n.* an outer shirt.

shish′ ke·bab″ (shish′ kə-bob″) *n.* meat cubes and vegetables roasted and served on skewers.

shiv *n.* (*Slang*) a knife used as a weapon.

shiv′a·ree″ (shiv′ə-rē″) *n.* a mock serenade of newlyweds.

shiv′er (shiv′ər) *v.i.* tremble or quiver with cold or fear. —*n.* shake. —**shiv′er·y,** *adj.*

shlep *v.t.* (*Slang*) schlep.

shoal (shōl) *n.* **1,** a sandbank in the water. **2,** a group of fish. **3,** a crowd. —*adj.* shallow. —*v.i.* **1,** become shallow. **2,** throng together.

shoat (shōt) *n.* a young weaned pig.

shock (shok) *n.* **1,** a violent collision. **2,** any sudden, violent impact. **3,** a condition of prostration; a stroke. **4,** the sensory impression caused by an electric current. **5,** a group of sheaves of grain in a field. **6,** a thick mass, as of hair. —*v.t.* **1,** affect with a shock; surprise; outrage; horrify. **2,** stack (grain). —**shock′er,** *n.* a sensational novel, film, etc. —**shock absorber,** a device for retarding rebound. —**shock therapy,** treatment of certain diseases by inducing electric or other shock. —**shock troops,**

---

experienced assault troops. **—shock wave, 1,** the blast caused by an explosion. **2,** the blast caused when the speed of an object in a medium exceeds the speed at which the medium can transmit sound (as when an aircraft exceeds the speed of sound).

shock′ing *adj.* causing surprise, consternation, or indignation.

shod *v.* pret. & p.p. of *shoe.*

shod′dy (shod′ė) *n.* **1,** a low-quality fabric; anything inferior. **2,** sham. —*adj.* **1,** inferior. **2,** sham; ungenerous. **—shod′diness,** *n.*

shoe (shoo) *n.* **1,** a covering for the human foot. **2,** a horseshoe. **3,** an outer covering or housing, as a tire. **4,** part of a brake. **5,** a block in sliding contact with a third rail to transmit current to an electric motor. —*v.t.* [*pret.* & *p.p.* **shod**] put shoes on.

shoe′bill″ *n.* an African wading bird.

shoe′horn″ *n.* a device used to slip one's feet into shoes.

shoe′lace″ *n.* shoestring.

shoe′mak″er *n.* cobbler.

shoe′string″ *n.* **1,** a lace for tying a shoe. **2,** very limited capital, in business.

shoe′tree″ *n.* a form for keeping shoes in shape.

sho′far (shō′fər) *n.* a ram's horn used as a wind instrument, esp. in Jewish services.

sho′gun (shō′gən) *n.* a member of the former ruling aristocracy of Japan.

sho′ji (shō′zhė) *n.* a framework covered with paper or other translucent material, used in Jap. houses as a door, wall, etc.

shone (shōn) *v.* pret. & p.p. of *shine.*

shoo *interj.* begone! **—shoo-′in″,** *n.* an easy victory, esp. in an election.

shook (shûk) *v.* p.t. of *shake.*

shoot *v.t.* [*pret.* & *p.p.* **shot**] **1,** hit, wound, or kill with a missile from a weapon. **2,** discharge (a weapon). **3,** send out or forth. **4,** traverse rapidly. **5,** take a picture of. —*v.i.* **1,** discharge a missile; fire. **2,** hunt. **3,** dart forth or along. **4,** be emitted; sprout. **5,** (with *up*) grow rapidly. **6,** (with *up*) (*Slang*) inject oneself with a drug, esp. heroin. —*n.* **1,** a shooting party. **2,** a sprout. **—shooting gallery,** an establishment where one can shoot at targets. **—shooting iron,** (*Slang*) a firearm. **—shooting star,** a meteor. **—shoot the bull,** (*Slang*) converse informally.

shoot′out″ *n.* **1,** a gunfight. **2,** (*Informal*) a military skirmish; a fiercely contested sports match. **3,** (*Soccer*) a tie-breaker.

shop *n.* **1,** a store. **2,** a workroom; a fac-

tory; (*Informal*) an office. **3,** one's own business. —*v.i.* & *t.* [**shopped, shop′ping**] visit stores as a customer. **—talk shop,** talk about one's business or profession.

shop′keep″er *n.* a tradesman.

shop′lift″er *n.* one who steals from shop counters. **—shop′lift″,** *v.i.* & *t.*

shoppe (shop) *n.* shop.

shop′per (shop′ər) *n.* **1,** one who shops. **2,** one sent to buy from a competitor, for comparison of goods.

shop′worn″ *adj.* deteriorated by display.

shore (shôr) *n.* **1,** land adjacent to water. **2,** a prop. —*v.t.* (with *up*) prop. **—shor′ing,** *n.* props.

shore′bird″ *n.* a bird found most often by the seashore.

shore′line″ *n.* the line where water and shore meet.

shorn (shôrn) *v.* p.p. of *shear.*

short (shôrt) *adj.* **1,** not long; not tall. **2,** brief; concise. **3,** deficient; (with *of*) insufficiently supplied with. **4,** of vowels, not prolonged in utterance. **5,** of stocks, not possessed at time of sale. **6,** crumbling readily, as pastry. **7,** curt. **8,** of odds, almost even. —*adv.* **1,** briefly. **2,** abruptly. **3,** insufficiently. —*n.* **1,** whatever is short. **2,** (*pl.*) short trousers or drawers. **—in short order,** quickly and efficiently. **—short circuit,** a low-resistance electrical connection, usually accidental. **—short cut,** a shorter route or method. **—short order,** an order for food cooked quickly on request. **—short-order cook,** a cook specializing in short orders, as in a diner. **—short shrift,** little delay or mercy. **—short story,** a relatively brief prose narrative.

short′age (-ij) *n.* deficiency.

short′bread″ *n.* a rich cake made short with butter.

short′cake″ *n.* a cake or biscuit covered with fruit.

short-″change′ *v.t.* (*Informal*) give inadequate change to; cheat.

short′com″ing *n.* a failing.

short′en *v.t.* make shorter.

short′en·ing *n.* fat used in baking.

short′fall″ *n.* the amount by which the actual number falls short of the expected or desired amount.

short′haired″ *adj.* having short hair. Also, **short′hair″.**

short′hand″ *n.* a system of taking notes.

short′hand″ed *adj.* having too few workers.

Shorthand Outlines

Gregg 〳〵⌒⌐⌐〵⌒⌐

Pitman 〇 • ⌐⌐ ⌐ ⌐〵

---

short'horn" *n.* one of a breed of cattle.

short'lived" (-līvd") *adj.* of brief life or duration.

short'ly (-lè) *adv.* **1,** in a short time; soon. **2,** briefly; concisely. **3,** curtly.

short"sight'ed *adj.* **1,** nearsighted. **2,** lacking foresight; not provident. **—short"-sight'ed·ness,** *n.*

short'stop" *n.* (*Baseball*) an infield position between second and third base.

short-"tem'pered *adj.* easily roused to anger.

short-'term" *adj.* lasting for a relatively short time.

short'wave' *n.* a radio wave 60 meters or less in length. **—adj.** pert. to or using shortwaves.

short-'wind"ed (-win"did) *adj.* tending to be out of breath after little exertion. **—short-'wind"ed·ness,** *n.*

shot *n.* **1,** an act of shooting. **2,** the distance traveled by a bullet or missile in flight. **3,** small pellets. **4,** one who shoots. **5,** a move or stroke in a game. **6,** (*Slang*) a guess. **7,** (*Slang*) a drink; one injection of a drug. **8,** a photograph. **9,** the ball used in the shot put. **—adj.** woven with threads of different colors. **—v.** pret. & p.p. of *shoot.* **—shot put,** a contest at hurling a heavy metal ball.

shot'gun" *n.* **1,** a gun firing charges of small shot. **2,** (*Football*) an offensive formation. **—shotgun wedding,** (*Jocular*) a wedding forced upon the bridegroom.

should (shud) *aux.v.* **1,** pret. or subjunctive of *shall.* **2,** ought to. ❏ *shall*

shoul'der (shōl'dər) *n.* **1,** a part of the body from the side of the neck to the upper joint of the arm (or foreleg). **2,** a ledge. **3,** the unpaved side of a road. **—v.t. & i. 1,** carry on, or as on, the shoulder. **2,** push with the shoulder. **—shoulder blade,** a flat bone in the shoulder; scapula.

shout (showt) *v.i. & t.* **1,** cry out. **2,** laugh noisily. **—n.** a loud cry.

shove (shuv) *v.t.* **1,** push along a surface. **2,** jostle. **—v.i. 1,** push. **2,** (with *off*) depart. **—n.** a push.

shov'el (shuv'əl) *n.* **1,** a long-handled implement with a broad scoop. **2,** a machine for excavating. **—v.t. & i.** transfer with a shovel.

show (shō) *v.t.* [*p.p.* **shown** (shōn) or **showed**] **1,** allow to be seen; exhibit; indicate. **2,** instruct; guide. **3,** (with *up*) expose the faults of. **—v.i. 1,** be seen; appear. **2,** finish third in a horse race. **3,** (with *off*) perform ostentatiously. **4,** (with *up*) appear; stand out. **—n. 1,** a theatrical performance. **2,** an exhibition. **3,** ostentatious display. **4,** (*Informal*) a chance.

show'boat" *n.* **1,** a river boat used as a traveling theater. **2,** a show-off. **—v.i.** show off; parade.

show'case" *n.* **1,** a glass case for the display of articles, as in a store or museum. **2,** any situation or location that displays talent, beauty, etc.

show'down" *n.* a final disclosure or test.

show'er (show'ər) *n.* **1,** a light rain; a spray. **2,** a large number. **3,** a bestowal of gifts. **4,** a shower bath. **—v.t. 1,** wet copiously. **2,** bestow or scatter abundantly. **—v.i. 1,** rain. **2,** take a shower bath. **—show'er·y,** *adj.* raining intermittently. **—shower bath,** a bath in water poured down from above.

show'ing *n.* **1,** act of displaying. **2,** performance.

show'man (-mən) *n.* [*pl.* **-men**] one who puts on a show. **—show'man·ship,** *n.*

shown (shōn) *v.* pret. & p.p. of *show.*

show-'off" *n.* one given to ostentation.

show'piece" *n.* something on display, esp. a particularly good example of a style, etc.

show'place" *n.* a place that is noted for its beauty, interest, etc.

show'room" *n.* a room for exhibition of goods for sale.

show'y *adj.* **1,** imposing. **2,** gaudy. **—show'i·ness,** *n.*

shrank *v.* pret. of *shrink.*

shrap'nel (shrap'nəl) *n.* a bursting projectile that showers missiles; the missiles collectively.

---

shrapnel
↔ After British General Henry *Shrapnel,* who invented the bomb.

---

shred *v.t.* [**shred'ded, -ding**] tear or cut into small pieces or strips. **—n. 1,** a small strip. **2,** a particle.

shrew (shroo) *n.* **1,** a scolding woman. **2,** a small mouselike animal. **—shrew'ish,** *adj.*

shrewd (shrood) *adj.* astute; quick-witted. **—shrewd'ness,** *n.* ❏ *shrew*

shriek (shrēk) *n.* a shrill outcry or utterance. **—v.t. & i.** utter such a cry.

shrift *n.* a shriving. **—short shrift, 1,** disposition without delay. **2,** little or insufficient attention.

---

shrew, shrewd

↔ The original sense of *shrew* was wicked man. and *shrewd* meant dangerous, wicked. These senses may have come from the notion that the *shrew* (the animal) had a poisonous bite. It is unclear why the senses of both words have been modified over time.

---

shrike (shrīk) *n.* the butcherbird.

shrill (shril) *adj.* sharp, high, and piercing in sound. —*v.t. & i.* utter (such a sound). —**shrill′ness,** *n.*

shrimp *n.* **1,** an edible, long-tailed crustacean. **2,** a small person.

shrine (shrīn) *n.* a consecrated or hallowed place.

shrink *v.i.* [shrank, shrunk, shrink′ing] **1,** contract spontaneously; diminish; shrivel. **2,** draw back; recoil. —*n.* (*Slang*) a psychiatrist or psychoanalyst. —*v.t.* cause to contract; lessen. —**shrink′age,** *n.* —**shrinking violet,** (*Informal*) a shy person.

shrink-′wrap″ *v.t.* wrap an item in a clinging plastic film.

shrive (shrīv) *v.t. & i.* [shrived or shrove, shriv′en (shriv′ən)] grant absolution to; impose penance on; confess.

---

shrive, Shrove Tuesday

↔ *Shrive* comes from Latin *scribere*, write, prescribe penances. *Shrove Tuesday* is so called because of the traditional practice of going to confession before the beginning of Lent.

---

shriv′el (shriv′əl) *v.t. & i.* contract; wrinkle; wither.

shroud (shrowd) *n.* **1,** a burial cloth. **2,** something that envelops or conceals. **3,** (*pl.*) (*Naut.*) strong guy ropes. —*v.t.* cover; obscure.

Shrove Tuesday (shrōv) the day before Lent. ❑ *shrive*

shrub *n.* a woody plant smaller than a tree. —**shrub′ber·y,** *n.*

shrug *v.t. & i.* [shrugged, shrug′ging] raise and contract the shoulders, expressing doubt, indifference, etc. —*n.* such a gesture.

shrunk *v.* p.p. of *shrink.*

shrunk′en *adj.* having shrunk.

shtetl (shtet′əl) *n.* (*Yiddish*) a Jewish community in eastern Europe.

shtick (shtik) *n.* (*Slang*) schtick.

shuck (shuk) *n.* **1,** a husk or pod, as of

corn. **2,** a shell. **3,** (*Slang*) a put-on; deception. —*v.t.* **1,** remove the husk or shell from. **2,** deceive. —**shucks,** *interj.* expressing deprecation, frustration, etc.

shud′der (shud′ər) *n.* a convulsive tremor of the body, as from horror, etc. —*v.i.* tremble violently.

shuf′fle (shuf′əl) *v.t. & i.* **1,** move with scraping feet. **2,** mix. **3,** shift evasively. —*n.* an act of shuffling.

shuf′fle·board″ *n.* a game played by pushing disks toward marked squares on a board or court.

shun *v.t.* [shunned, shun′ning] keep away from; avoid; refrain from.

shun′pike″ *n.* a road taken to avoid the tollgates of a toll road.

shunt *v.t.* **1,** turn aside. **2,** shift (as a train). **3,** (with *off*) relegate; foist. —*n.* **1,** a shift or shifting. **2,** a conductor carrying off a small part of the current in a circuit.

shush *v.t. & interj.* silence.

shut *v.t.* [shut, shut′ting] **1,** close; bring together. **2,** (with *in* or *up*) confine; prevent access to. **3,** (with *out*) exclude; prevent from scoring. —*v.i.* **1,** become closed; close. **2,** (with *down*) discontinue. **3,** (with *up*) (*Informal*) stop talking. —*adj.* closed.

shut′down″ *n.* a temporary closing or discontinuance.

shut-′eye″ *n.* (*Informal*) sleep.

shut-′in″ *adj.* confined to a house, hospital, etc. —*n.* one so confined.

shut-′off″ *n.* a device for shutting off, as a valve.

shut′out″ *n.* **1,** exclusion. **2,** a game in which one team does not score.

shut′ter (-ər) *n.* one who or that which shuts, esp. a hinged panel for a window, a device for a camera, a movable slide, etc.

shut′ter·bug″ *n.* (*Informal*) an avid amateur photographer.

shut′tle (shut′əl) *n.* **1,** a device for passing thread in a loom or sewing machine. **2,** a train or airline traveling back and forth for a short distance. **3,** space shuttle. —*v.t. & i.* move to and fro.

shut′tle·cock″ *n.* a ball, usu. of cork, with a tail of feathers, used in *badminton* and *battledore and shuttlecock*.

shy (shī) *adj.* **1,** timid; bashful. **2,** cautious; wary. **3,** scant; short. —*v.i.* start back in fear. —*v.t.* throw. —*n.* a start, as in fear. —**shy′ness,** *n.*

Shy′lock (shī′lok) *n.* (often *l.c.*) a usurious moneylender.

shy′ster (shī′stər) *n.* a professional person, esp. a lawyer, who uses underhand or unethical methods.

> ### shyster
> ↔ Possibly from a mid-19th-c. New York lawyer named *Scheuster*, known for his suspect practices.

si (sē) *n.* (*Music*) the seventh tone of the diatonic scale. Also, **ti** (tē).

si′a·mang (sē′ə-mang) *n.* a large black gibbon of Sumatra.

Si″a·mese′ (sī″ə-mēz′) *adj. & n.* pert. to Siam (Thailand), its people, language, etc.; Thai. **—Siamese twins,** twins born with joined bodies.

sib *n.* a kinsman.

sib′i·lant (sib′ə-lənt) *adj.* having a hissing sound. **—***n.* *s* or *z.* **—sib′i·lance,** *n.* **—sib′i·late,** *v.t. & i.* pronounce with a hiss. **—sib″i·la′tion,** *n.*

sib′ling *n.* a full brother or sister.

sib′yl (sib′il) *n.* a female prophet or fortune-teller.

> ### sibyl
> ↔ From Greek *Sibylla*, a maiden given the gift of prophecy by Apollo.

sic (sik) *adv.* (*Lat.*) (quoted) exactly as written, even though incorrect. **—sic tran′sit glo′ri·a mun′di** (tran′sit glôr′ē·ə mun′dē) (*Lat.*) so passes away the glory of the world.

sick (sik) *adj.* **1,** ill. **2,** nauseated. **3,** depressed. **4,** disgusted. **5,** (with *of*) satiated. **—***n.* sick people. **—***v.t.* set upon, esp. of a dog. **—sick bay,** a ship's hospital. **—sick′ness,** *n.*

sick′bed″ *n.* **1,** a sick person's bed. **2,** a bedridden person's state.

sick′en (-ən) *v.t. & i.* make or become sick. **—sick′en·ing,** *adj.* causing nausea or disgust.

sick′le (sik′əl) *n.* a short-handled scythe with a curved blade. **—sickle cell anemia,** a disease of the blood occurring most frequently in black people.

sick′ly *adj.* **1,** unhealthy in fact or appearance. **2,** mawkish. **3,** feeble. **—sick′li·ness,** *n.*

sick′out″ *n.* an organized work protest in which employees feign illness to stay away from the job.

side (sīd) *n.* **1,** a terminal surface or line. **2,** either half, as of the body, right or left. **3,** an aspect; a point of view. **4,** a position in a lawsuit, game, etc. **—***adj.* being on, coming from, or aimed toward one side. **—***v.i.* (with *with*) ally oneself. **—side arm,** a small weapon carried at the side, as a pistol. **—side effect,** a reaction or result produced (as by a drug) in addition to the desired effect. **—side whiskers,** whiskers worn long when the chin is clean-shaven.

side′arm″ *adj. & adv.* thrown with the arm held between the shoulder and the hip.

side′board″ *n.* a piece of dining-room furniture.

side′burns″ *n.pl.* short side whiskers.

> ### sideburns
> ↔ Derived from name of the U.S. Civil War general who wore his whiskers in this fashion, Ambrose E. *Burnside*. They were formerly called *burnsides* in his honor.

side′car″ *n.* **1,** a small car attached to a motorcycle. **2,** a cocktail made with brandy and Cointreau.

side′kick″ *n.* (*Informal*) buddy.

side′light″ *n.* **1,** an incidental aspect of anything. **2,** a narrow window beside a door.

side′line″ *n.* a secondary occupation or line of merchandise. **2,** a hobby. **3,** (*Sports*) a side boundary.

side′long″ *adj.* to the side; sideways. **—***adv.* sideways.

side′man″ *n.* an instrumental musician in a jazz or rock band.

side′piece″ *n.* a handgun.

si·de′re·al (sī-dir′ē-əl) *adj.* pert. to the stars; based on fixed stars.

side′sad″dle *n.* a saddle allowing a person to sit with both legs on the same side of the horse. **—***adv.* sitting on or as if on a sidesaddle.

side′show″ *n.* an incidental attraction, as at a circus.

side′slip″ *n.* of a banked airplane, a sliding sideways and down.

side′split″ting *adj.* uproariously funny.

side′step″ *v.t. & i.* evade.

side′stroke″ *n.* a stroke in swimming.

side′swipe″ *v.t.* strike glancingly. **—***n.* a glancing collision.

side′track″ *v.t.* **1,** move to a siding. **2,** divert.

side′walk″ *n.* the paved path for foot traffic beside a street.

side′wall″ *n.* the lateral surface of a vehicle tire.

side′ward″ *adj.* directed or moving to one side. **—***adv.* [also, **side′wards″**] toward the side.

side′ways″ *adj. & adv.* to the side; from one side. Also, **side′wise″.**

side′wind″er (-wīn″dər) *n.* **1,** a small rattlesnake. **2,** (*Slang*) a blow from the side. **3,** (*cap.*) a kind of air-to-air missile fired from an aircraft.

sid′ing (sī′ding) *n.* **1,** a track for idle railroad cars. **2,** boards or other material for the sides of a frame house.

si′dle (sī′dəl) *v.i.* move obliquely; edge along. —*n.* this movement.

SIDS sudden infant death syndrome.

siege (sēj) *n.* **1,** a prolonged surrounding of a place by an enemy. **2,** a long illness. —**siege guns,** artillery used to bombard a fortress.

si·en′na (sė-en′ə) *n.* a brown pigment or color.

> **sienna**
> ↔ From Italian *terra de Siena*, soil from Siena, Italy.

si·er′ra (sė-er′ə) *n.* **1,** mountains in a succession of peaks. **2,** (*Communications*) the letter *s*.

si·es′ta (sė-es′tə) *n.* a midday nap.

> **siesta**
> ↔ A Spanish word from Latin *sexta hora*, sixth hour, the time of the nap.

sieve (siv) *n.* **1,** a straining pan. **2,** a leakage of information. —*v.t.* sift.

sift *v.t.* **1,** separate the large from the small. **2,** scrutinize.

sigh (sī) *v.i. & t.* breathe out audibly, expressing disappointment. —*n.* an act or sound of sighing.

sight (sīt) *n.* **1,** the faculty of vision; visual perception. **2,** point of view. **3,** a coming into view. **4,** something seen; something unusual (interesting, distressing) to see. **5,** (*Informal*) a surprising number. **6,** an aid to aiming. **7,** aim. —*v.t.* get sight of; aim at. —**sight′ed,** *adj.* able to see. —**sight′-less,** *adj.* blind. —**sight′ly,** *adj.* pleasing to the eye. —**at sight, 1,** as soon as seen. **2,** on demand.

> **sight, site**
> ☞ These homophones are unrelated. *Sight* is the faculty of vision; a *site* is a location.

sight-′read″ (-rēd″) *v.t. & i.* read (music, a language, etc.) at sight.

sight′see″ing *n.* brief visiting of places of interest. —**sight′see″** *v.i.* —**sight′se″er,** *n.*

sig′ma (sig′mə) *n.* the 18th letter of the Greek alphabet (Σ, σ, ς).

sign (sīn) *n.* **1,** a mark or symbol. **2,** a display board. **3,** a gesture. **4,** a symptom. **5,** a trace. —*v.t.* **1,** affix a signature to;

write (one's name). **2,** indicate by sign. **3,** (with *on*) engage to do service. **4,** communicate in sign language. —*v.i.* **1,** write one's signature. **2,** (with *off*) end. **3,** communicate in sign language. —**sign language,** a system of communication among deaf people, using gestures.

sig′nal (sig′nəl) *n.* **1,** a sign carrying a message, often in code. **2,** a radio wave. —*adj.* **1,** serving as a signal. **2,** eminent; conspicuous. —*v.t. & i.* make a signal (to). —**sig′nal·ize″** (-īz″) *v.t.* indicate distinctly. —**sig′nal·ly,** *adv.* notably.

sig′na·to·ry (sig′nə-tôr-ė) *n.* one who signs. —*adj.* signing.

sig′na·ture (sig′nə-tyûr) *n.* **1,** a person's name in his or her own handwriting. **2,** any distinguishing sign. **3,** (*Printing*) a batch of pages resulting from a single sheet folded and cut; the sheet; a sign printed on the first page of each batch for identification.

sign′board″ *n.* a large mounting for advertising signs.

sig′net (sig′nət) *n.* a small seal, as on a ring.

sig·nif′i·cance (sig-nif′i-kəns) *n.* **1,** the real or implied meaning. **2,** consequence. **3,** expressiveness. —**sig·nif′i·cant,** *adj.* —**significant other,** (*Informal*) spouse; lover.

sig′ni·fy″ (sig′ni-fī″) *v.t.* mean; suggest. —*v.i.* to engage in a game of verbal insults, esp. popular among African-Americans. Also, **the dozens.** —**sig″ni·fi·ca′tion,** *n.*

si·gnor′ (sē-nyôr′) *n.* (*It.*) a gentleman; Mr.; sir. Also, **si·gno′re** (-e) [*pl.* **-ri** (-ė)].

si·gno′ra (-ä) *n.* a married woman. —**si″gno·ri′na** (-rē′nä) *n.* a young girl or an unmarried woman.

sign′post″ *n.* a post bearing a sign or signs.

Sikh (sēk) *n.* a member of a certain Hindu religious sect.

si′lage (sī′lij) *n.* fodder stored in a silo.

si′lence (sī′ləns) *n.* **1,** the absence of sound. **2,** abstention from speech or noise. **3,** absence of mention. **4,** secrecy. —*v.t.* restrain from making sound or speech. —**si′lenc·er,** *n.* a device to silence a firearm.

si′lent (sī′lənt) *adj.* **1,** making no sound. **2,** tacit. —**silent majority,** the supposed politically inactive (usually conservative) majority of a country's voters. —**silent partner,** an inactive partner.

si′lex (sī′leks) *n.* **1,** flint; silica. **2,** (*cap., T.N.*) a heat-resistant glass of fused quartz.

sil″hou·ette′ (sil″û-et′) *n.* **1,** an outline drawing. **2,** a two-dimensional outline, as of a ship. —*v.t.* represent in silhouette.

> **silhouette**
> ↔ Named for 18th-c. French politician Étienne de *Silhouette*, for reasons that are obscure.

sil′i·ca (sil′ə-kə) *n.* **1,** silicon dioxide. **2,** sandlike particles of hard stone. —**si·li′ceous** (si-lish′əs) *adj.*

> **silica, silicon, silicone**
> ↔ All three words are based on Latin *silex*, flint. *Silicon* was coined in the early 19th c. by British chemist Thomas Thomson.

sil′i·cate (sil′i-kət) *n.* a salt derived from silica.

sil′i·con (sil′i-kən) *n.* a crystalline chemical element, no. 14, symbol Si. ❏ *silica*

sil′i·cone″ (sil′ə-kōn″) *n.* any of various silicon compounds having high resistance to heat and water. ❏ *silica*

sil″i·co′sis (sil″i-kō′sis) *n.* a disease caused by inhaling stone dust.

silk *n.* **1,** a fine soft fiber, produced by the silkworm; a thread or fabrics made from it. **2,** similar filament produced by some spiders or other organisms. **3,** the filaments on an ear of corn. —**silk′en, silk′y,** *adj.*

silk-′screen″ *adj.* designating a method of reproducing by means of a stencil of silk cloth. —*v.t. & i.* print by this method.

silk-′stock″ing *adj.* luxurious. —*n.* a rich or aristocratic person.

silk′worm″ *n.* a moth larva from whose cocoon silk is spun.

sill (sil) *n.* a horizontal foundation, as of a door.

sil′ly (sil′ė) *adj.* **1,** foolish; witless. **2,** ridiculous. **3,** stunned. —**sil′li·ness,** *n.*

> **silly**
> ↔ The Old English ancestor of *silly*, *gesaelig*, meant blessed, as does the German cognate *selig*. The shift in meaning happened during the Middle English period.

si·lo (sī′lō) *n.* an airtight storehouse for grain, etc.

silt *n.* earthy sediment.

sil′ver (sil′vər) *n. & adj.* **1,** a precious metallic chemical element, no. 47, symbol Ag. **2,** silver coin; money. **3,** silver tableware. **4,** a lustrous, grayish-white color. **5,** the 25th anniversary. —**sil′ver·y,** *adj.* —**silver certificate,** a former U.S. piece of

paper money redeemable in silver. —**silver fox,** a fox with black, silver-gray-tipped fur; the fur. —**silver lining,** a fortunate or hopeful circumstance in an otherwise gloomy situation. —**silver screen, 1,** a projection screen. **2,** (*cap.*) motion pictures.

sil′ver·fish″ *n.* **1,** any of various fish. **2,** a wingless insect common as a household pest.

sil′ver·plate″ *n.* tableware or other item plated with silver.

sil′ver·smith″ *n.* a craftsman who makes articles of silver.

sil′ver·ware″ *n.* tableware and dishes of silver.

s′il vous plaît (sēl voo ple′) (*Fr.*) if you please; please.

sim′i·an (sim′ė-ən) *adj.* pert. to an ape or monkey. —*n.* monkey or ape.

sim′i·lar (sim′ə-lər) *adj.* resembling. —**sim″i·lar′i·ty** (-lar′ə-tė) *n.*

sim′i·le″ (sim′ə-lė″) *n.* a comparison, as a figure of speech.

si·mil′i·tude″ (si-mil′i-tood″) *n.* **1,** resemblance. **2,** a comparison.

sim′mer (sim′ər) *v.i. & t.* continue in a state just below the boiling point. —*n.* this state of heat.

si·mol′e·on (si-mō′lė-ən) *n.* (*Slang*) a dollar.

si′mon·ize″ (sī′mən-īz″) *v.t.* clean and polish (an enameled surface, as of an automobile).

si′mon-pure′ (sī′mən-pyûr′) *adj.* genuine.

> **simon-pure**
> ↔ From a character in the play *A Bold Stroke for a Wife* (1718) by Susanna Centlivre.

si′mo·ny (sī′mə-nė) *n.* the selling of ecclesiastical offices, indulgences, etc. —**si′mon·ist,** *n.*

> **simony**
> ↔ From the Biblical *Simon* Magus (Acts 8:18-20), who attempted to buy from Simon Peter the power of conferring the Holy Ghost.

si·moom′ *n.* a hot wind.

simp *n.* (*Slang*) a fool.

sim·pa′ti·co (sim-pä′tė-kō) *adj.* (*It.*) of similar or compatible temperament; congenial.

sim′per (sim′pər) *v.i. & t.* smile or say in a silly manner.

sim′ple (sim′pəl) *adj.* **1,** elementary; not

complicated. **2,** plain; not elaborate. **3,** pure; absolute. **4,** unaffected; unassuming. **5,** insignificant. **6,** humble. **7,** easily deceived; silly. **8,** (*Archaic*) a medicinal herb.

sim′ple-mind″ed *adj.* foolish.

sim′ple·ton (-tən) *n.* a fool.

sim·plic′i·ty (sim-plis′ə-tē) *n.* condition of being simple.

sim′pli·fy (sim′pli-fī″) *v.t.* make easier or less complex. —**sim″pli·fi·ca′tion,** *n.*

sim·plis′tic (sim-plis′tik) *adj.* tending to oversimplify; naïve.

sim″u·la′crum (sim″yə-lā′krəm) *n.* [*pl.* **-cra** (-krə)] an unreal semblance; a shadowy image.

sim′u·late″ (sim′yə-lāt″) *v.t.* **1,** pretend. **2,** imitate; resemble. **3,** create a model or likeness of.

sim″u·la′tion (-lā′shən) *n.* **1,** the act or result of imitating or pretending. **2,** the representation of or prediction of the results of a process or series of processes by means of computers.

si′mul·cast″ (sī′məl-) *v.t.* **1,** broadcast simultaneously by radio and television. **2,** broadcast at the same moment that it happens. —*n.* such a broadcast.

si″mul·ta′ne·ous (sī″məl-tā′nē-əs) *adj.* existing, occurring, or operating at the same time. —**si″mul·ta·ne′i·ty** (-tə-nā′ə-tē), **si″mul·ta′ne·ous·ness,** *n.*

sin *n.* **1,** a transgression of the law of God. **2,** a serious fault; an error. —*v.i.* [**sinned, sin′ning**] commit a sin. —**sin′ful,** *adj.* —**sin′ner,** *n.* —**sin tax,** a tax on something considered by some to be a vice, such as gambling or liquor.

since (sins) *adv.* **1,** from then till now. **2,** subsequently. **3,** before now; ago. —*prep.* throughout all the time, or at some time, following. —*conj.* **1,** from the time when; during the time after. **2,** because. ❑ *because*

---

sin·cere′ (sin-sir′) *adj.* free from falsehood, pretense, or deceit. —**sin·cer′i·ty** (-ser′ə-tē) *n.*

sine (sīn) *n.* a trigonometric ratio.

si′ne·cure″ (sī′nə-kyûr″) *n.* an easy job. ❑ *sine*

si′ne di′e (sī′ne dē′ā) (*Lat.*) without (setting) a day (to meet again).

si′ne qua non′ (sē′ne kwä nōn′) (*Lat.*, without which nothing) an absolute necessity.

sin′ew (sin′ū) *n,* **1,** a tendon. **2,** strength; vigor. **3,** a mainstay.

sin′ew·y (-ē) *adj.* **1,** strong. **2,** vigorous. **3,** stringy.

sing *v.i.* [**sang, sung, sing′ing**] **1,** utter words or sounds musically. **2,** murmur, whistle, etc. —*v.t.* utter musically; chant. —*n.* a gathering of persons for singing.

singe (sinj) *v.t.* burn superficially.

Sing″gha·lese′ (sing″gə-lēz′) *adj.* of Ceylon. —*n.* a native of Ceylon; its language.

sin′gle (sing′gəl) *adj.* **1,** pert. to one person or thing; individual. **2,** alone; detached. **3,** unmarried. —*v.t.* (with *out*) select individually. —*n.* **1,** that which is single. **2,** (*Baseball*) a one-base hit. **3,** (*pl.*) (*Tennis*) a contest between two players. —*v.i.* (*Baseball*) hit a single. —**sin′gle·ness,** *n.* —**single file,** a line of people or things, one behind the other.

---

single out, signal out
☞ *Single out* is the correct expression for choose. *Signal out* does not exist (except as a confusion for the former).

---

sin″gle-breast′ed (-bres′tid) *adj.* (of a coat or vest) overlapping only enough to allow fastening.

sin″gle-hand′ed *adj. & adv.* **1,** unaided. **2,** done with one hand.

single-lens reflex a camera which allows viewing through the same lens which exposes the film. *Abbr.* **SLR.**

sin″gle-mind′ed *adj.* undeviating. —**sin″gle-mind′ed·ness,** *n.*

sin′gle·ton (-tən) *n.* (*Card Games*) a holding of one card in a suit.

sin′gle·tree″ *n.* a pivoted bar on a carriage, etc., to which a horse's harness is attached. Also, **whif′fle·tree″.**

sin′gly (sing′glē) *adv.* **1,** separately; individually. **2,** one at a time.

sing′song″ *adj.* monotonously rhythmical.

sin′gu·lar (sing′gyə-lər) *adj.* **1,** unusual. **2,** eccentric. **3,** (*Gram.*) denoting or relating to one person or thing. —**sin″gu·lar′i·ty** (-lar′ə-tē) *n.*

---

sin·is·ter (sin'is-tər) *adj.* **1,** malicious; harmful; ominous. **2,** bad; corrupt. **3,** on the left side.

sink *v.i.* [**sank, sunk, sink'ing**] **1,** fall or decline; settle. **2,** become submerged. **3,** incline downward. **4,** decrease. —*v.t.* **1,** force downward. **2,** place by excavation. **3,** diminish. **4,** suppress; overwhelm. —*n.* **1,** a basin, esp. in a kitchen; a drain. **2,** a low area. —**sink'a·ble,** *adj.* —**sinking fund,** a fund held in reserve to pay off the principal of a debt.

sink'er *n.* **1,** a weight on a fishing line. **2,** (*Slang*) a doughnut.

sink'hole" *n.* a hole caused by the action of water on soluble rock.

Sinn Fein (shin fān) a revolutionary Irish society.

Si·no- (sī-nō-) *pref.* Chinese.

sin·u·ous (sin'ū-əs) *adj.* **1,** full of curves; winding. **2,** devious. —**sin"u·os'i·ty, sin'u·ous·ness,** *n.*

si'nus (sī'nəs) *n.* a cavity or recess, esp. in the skull. —**si"nus·i'tis** (-ī'təs) *n.* inflammation of the sinuses.

Sioux (soo) *adj. & n.sing. & pl.* (pert. to) a tribe of No. Amer. Indians.

sip *v.t. & i.* [**sipped, sip'ping**] drink little by little. —*n.* a small quantity sipped.

si'phon (sī'fən) *n.* **1,** a bent tube used to draw a liquid over an elevation. **2,** a bottle for aerated water. —*v.t.* draw off with a siphon.

sip'per (sip'ər) *n.* a tube for sipping.

sir (sẽr) *n.* **1,** a respectful term of address to a man. **2,** (*cap.*) the title of a knight or baronet.

sire (sīr) *n.* **1,** a father; a male parent. **2,** a term of address to a sovereign. —*v.t.* beget.

si'ren (sī'rən) *n.* **1,** a mythical alluring sea nymph. **2,** an alluring and dangerous woman. **3,** a device for producing a whistle; its sound.

sir'loin (sẽr'loin) *n.* a cut of beef.

si·roc'co (sə-rok'ō) *n.* a hot southeast wind from N. Afr.

sir'up *n.* syrup.

si'sal (sī'səl) *n.* a hemplike fiber taken from the agave.

sis'sy (sis'ė) *n.* (*Informal*) **1,** an effeminate boy. **2,** a timid or cowardly person.

sis'ter (sis'tər) *n.* **1,** [also, *informal,* **sis**] a female relative having the same parents as another. **2,** a fellow person, female. **3,** one of a sisterhood; a nun. **4,** (*Informal*) a feminist.

sis'ter·hood" *n.* **1,** state of being a sister or sisters. **2,** an association of women.

sis'ter-in-law" *n.* [*pl.* **sis'ters-**] **1,** the sister of one's spouse. **2,** the wife of one's brother.

sis'ter·ly *adj.* befitting a sister. —**sis'ter·li·ness,** *n.*

sit *v.i.* [**sat, sit'ting**] **1,** take a posture with back erect, body bent at the hips; be seated. **2,** perch. **3,** remain. **4,** be located; be in office; convene. —**sit'ter,** *n.* a part-time nurse for children. —**sit'ting,** *n.* the act or period of sitting; session. —**sit-down strike,** occupation of an employer's premises by strikers. —**sitting duck,** an easy target. —**sitting room,** a parlor.

si·tar' (sē-tär') *n.* an Indian plucked-string instrument with a long neck and sympathetic strings.

sit'com" (sit'kom") *n.* a situation comedy.

site (sīt) *n.* location.

sit-'in" *n.* a nonviolent demonstration, usu. involving the obstruction of a public place by sitting there and refusing to move unless carried away.

sit'u·ate" (sich'oo-āt") *v.t.* place in a particular place. —*adj.* located.

sit"u·a'tion (sich"oo-ā'shən) *n.* **1,** location. **2,** condition. **3,** a job. —**situation comedy,** a dramatic comedy, esp. on television, in which characters in a certain situation find themselves in different comic, often grotesque, circumstances. —**situation ethics,** a system of morality based on specific situations rather than general principles. —**situation room,** a room in a office or military center in which current operations information is assembled.

sit'up" *n.* an exercise.

si'tus (sī'təs) *n.* location; situation.

sitz bath (sits; zits) a tub bath taken with water covering only the legs and hips.

six (siks) *n. & adj.* the cardinal number between five and seven, expressed by 6. —**sixth,** *n. & adj.* —**sixth sense,** intuition.

six'pence (-pəns) *n.* an obsolete Brit. coin worth six pennies. —**six'pen"ny,** *adj.*

six-'shoot"er *n.* (*Informal*) a revolver, esp. of .45 caliber.

six·teen' (-tēn') *n. & adj.* ten plus six, also expressed by 16. —**six·teenth'** (-tēnth') *adj. & n.*

six'ty (-tė) *n. & adj.* ten times six, also expressed by 60. —**six'ti·eth** (-tė-əth) *adj. & n.*

size (sīz) *n.* **1,** bulk; volume; extent. **2,** a standard measure for clothes, etc. **3,** a gluey substance for bonding or glazing, as starch. —*v.t.* **1,** (with *up*) estimate. **2,** starch, glaze, etc. —**siz'a·ble,** *adj.* fairly large. **—siz′ing,** *n.* material for glazing, etc.

siz′zle (siz′əl) [**siz′zled, siz′zling**] *v.i.* **1,** sputter. **2,** (*Informal*) be very hot. **—n.** a sputtering sound.

skag *n.* (*Slang*) heroin.

skate (skāt) *n.* **1,** a steel runner for gliding. **2,** a roller skate. **3,** a fish of the ray family. **—v.i.** glide or roll on skates.

skate′board″ *n.* a short board mounted on roller-skate wheels.

ske·dad′dle (ski-dad′əl) *v.i.* (*Slang*) run away.

skeet (skēt) *n.* a form of trapshooting.

> **skeet**
> ↔ This unusual word was coined by an entrant in a contest seeking a name for the sport.

skein (skān) *n.* a coiled length of yarn or thread.

skel′e·ton (skel′ə-tən) *n.* **1,** the assemblage of bones of the body. **2,** an inner framework. **3,** an outline. **4,** [also, **skeleton in the closet**] a scandal; embarrassing secret. **—adj. 1,** skeletal. **2,** condensed or synoptic in form. **—skel′e·tal,** *adj.* pert. to or like a skeleton. **—skeleton key,** a key for opening many different locks.

skep′tic (skep′tik) *n.* one inclined to doubt. Also, **scep′tic. —skep′ti·cal,** *adj.* doubting; incredulous. ❑ *cynical*

skep′ti·cism (skep′ti-siz-əm) *n.* inclination to doubt; questioning nature. Also, **scep′ti·cism.**

sketch (skech) *n.* **1,** a rough drawing. **2,** an outline; synopsis. **3,** a short humorous act; skit. **—v.t.** delineate or describe roughly. **—sketch′y,** *adj.* not detailed.

skew (skū) *v.i.* swerve. **—adj.** oblique or distorted.

skew′er (skū′ər) *n.* a long pin; a spit used in roasting meat. **—v.t.** fasten or pierce with or as with a skewer.

ski (skē) *n.* a long wooden runner for gliding on snow. **—v.i.** [**skied, ski′ing**] travel on skis. **—ski′er,** *n.*

ski′bob″ *n.* a small, steerable vehicle on skis.

skid *n.* **1,** a timber or metal band forming a track. **2,** a supporting runner. **3,** a friction brake. **4,** a framework. **5,** an act of skidding. **—v.t. & i.** [**skid′ded, -ding**] **1,** slide without rotating. **2,** swerve. **—skid row** or **road,** a street or section where vagrants and alcoholics live.

skid·doo′ (ski-doo′) *interj.* (*Slang*) go away!

skiff (skif) *n.* a small boat.

skif′fle (skif′əl) *n.* music played on unusual instruments.

ski·jor′ing (skē-jôr′ing) *n.* a sport in which a skier is pulled by a horse.

skill (skil) *n.* technical ability or knowledge; expertness. **—skill′ful, skil′ful, skilled,** *adj.* ❑ *ability*

skil′let (skil′it) *n.* **1,** a frying pan. **2,** a long-handled saucepan.

skim *v.t. & i.* [**skimmed, skim′ming**] **1,** lift or scrape off the top of (a liquid). **2,** read superficially. **3,** glide lightly (over). **4,** take (the best parts) of something. **5,** take for illegal purposes. **—skim milk,** milk without its natural cream.

ski′mo·bile″ *n.* snowmobile.

skimp *v.t. & i.* provide meagerly; scrimp. **—skimp′y,** *adj.* meager.

skin *n.* **1,** the outer covering of a body. **2,** a pelt. **3,** a rind or peel. **—v.t.** [**skinned, skin′ning**] **1,** remove the skin from; peel. **2,** (*Slang*) swindle. **—v.i.** (*Slang*) abscond. **—skin flick,** (*Slang*) a pornographic movie. **—skin game,** (*Informal*) **1,** a fraud; swindle. **2,** (*Golf*) a type of game having a prize for each hole. Also, **skins.**

skin-′deep′ *adj. & adv.* superficial; slight.

skin′div″er *n.* a diver who penetrates deep water carrying a supply of oxygen but not wearing a diver's suit. **—skin′div″-ing,** *n.*

skin′flint″ *n.* a stingy, grasping person; tightwad.

skin′head″ *n.* a working-class person with a shaved head.

skink *n.* a small, smooth-scaled lizard.

skin′ner *n.* **1,** one who skins. **2,** a driver of teams of mules.

skin′ny (skin′ē) *adj.* lean; underweight; thin. **—n.** (*Slang*) gossip; information. **—skin′ni·ness,** *n.*

skin′ny·dip″ *v.i.* swim in the nude.

skin′tight″ *adj.* fitting closely to or like the skin.

skip *v.i.* [**skipped, skip′ping**] **1,** jump lightly. **2,** bounce; ricochet. **3,** pass over something. **4,** (*Informal*) flee. **—v.t. 1,** jump over. **2,** cause to ricochet. **3,** (*Informal*) evade. **—n.** act of skipping.

skip′per (skip′ər) *n.* captain of a ship; chief; master. **—v.t.** act as skipper of.

skirl (skėrl) *n.* the sound of the bagpipe. **—v.t.** sound loudly and shrilly.

skir′mish (skėr′mish) *n.* a minor battle. **—v.i.** engage in a skirmish.

skirt (skėrt) *n.* **1,** a garment, or part of it, hanging down from the waist. **2,** an apron.

3, (*Slang, offensive*) a woman. —*v.t.* lie or pass along the border of. ❏ *shirt*

skit *n.* a short, comic play.

skit′ter (skit′ər) *v.i. & t.* glide lightly or swiftly; skim along the surface.

skit′tish (skit′ish) *adj.* **1,** apt to shy. **2,** restless. **3,** coy.

skit′tles (skit′əlz) *n.pl.* ninepins.

skive (skīv) *v.t.* slice (leather) thinly.

skiv′er (ski′vər) *n.* **1,** a thin slice of leather. **2,** a knife for skiving.

skiv′vy (skiv′ē) *n.* **1,** a man's undershirt. **2,** (*pl.*) a man's undershirt and briefs.

skoal (skōl) *interj.* of salutation in toasting.

skul·dug′ger·y (skul-dug′ə-rē) *n.* dishonest trickery.

skulk *v.i.* **1,** sneak away. **2,** slink. **3,** malinger.

---
skulk, sulk
☞ Two words frequently confused. *Skulk* means to sneak or slink; *sulk* means to be resentful.

---

skull (skul) *n.* the bony framework of the head. —**skull and crossbones,** a human skull above two crossed bones, used to label poisons (formerly an emblem on pirates' flags).

skull′cap″ *n.* a brimless, close-fitting cap.

skunk *n.* **1,** a small fur-bearing animal of the weasel family that ejects a fetid fluid. **2,** (*Informal*) a contemptible person. —*v.t.* (*Slang*) keep scoreless. —**skunk cabbage,** a foul-smelling plant.

sky (skī) *n.* the surrounding space as seen from the earth. —**sky marshal,** a law enforcement officer assigned to an aircraft to deter skyjackers. —**sky pilot,** (*Slang*) a clergyman.

sky′cap″ *n.* a porter at an airport.

sky′div″ing *n.* the sport of jumping from an airplane and performing various gymnastic maneuvers before opening the parachute. —**sky′dive″,** *v.i.*

Skye terrier a small, short-legged, usually white terrier.

sky-′high′ *adj. & adv.* very high.

sky′jack″ (-jak″) *v.t.* to hijack an airplane, esp. when in the air.

Sky′lab″ *n.* an orbiting space station.

sky′lark″ *n.* a lark that sings as it flies.

sky′light″ *n.* a window in a ceiling.

sky′line″ *n.* **1,** tall buildings seen outlined against the sky. **2,** the visible horizon.

sky′rock″et *n.* a small rocket used in fireworks. —*v.i.* achieve wealth, fame etc., rapidly.

sky′scrap″er *n.* a tall building.

sky′ward (-wərd) *adj.* toward the sky. —*adv.* [also, **sky′wards**] at or toward the sky.

sky′writ″ing *n.* writing trailed in smoke from an airplane.

slab *n.* a flat, thick piece.

slack (slak) *adj.* **1,** loose, not taut. **2,** slow; sluggish. **3,** negligent. —*n.* **1,** a slack condition or part. **2,** a decrease in activity. **3,** (*pl.*) loose trousers. —**slack′en,** *v.t. & i.* make or become more slack. —**slack′er,** *n.* a shirker, esp. of military service.

slag *n.* **1,** the waste matter from smelting. **2,** lava. —**slag′gy,** *adj.*

slain (slān) *v.* p.p. of *slay.*

slake (slāk) *v.t.* **1,** appease, as thirst, wrath, etc. **2,** abate. **3,** treat (lime) with water.

sla′lom (slä′ləm) *n.* a skiing race.

slam *v.t. & i.* [**slammed, slam′ming**] **1,** shut or strike with violence or noise. **2,** (*Slang*) criticize adversely. —*n.* **1,** a bang. **2,** (*Slang*) criticism. **3,** (*Card Games*) the winning of all the tricks. —**slam dancing,** a form of violent dancing. —**slam dunk,** (*Basketball*) an especially forceful dunk shot.

slam-′bang″ *adv.* (*Informal*) suddenly, noisily, or violently. —*adj.* **1,** noisy. **2,** violent. **3,** carelessly fast.

slam′mer (slam′ər) *n.* (*Slang*) prison.

slan′der (slan′dər) *n.* **1,** aspersion. **2,** (*Law*) defamation by oral utterance. —*v.t.* defame. —**slan′der·ous,** *adj.* ❏ *libel*

slang *n.* **1,** language of coarse, familiar, or jocular character, regarded as below the level of written or colloquial speech. **2,** jargon; cant. ❏ *argot*

slant (slant) *v.i. & t.* **1,** lie obliquely. **2,** have a bias; incline. —*n.* **1,** an oblique direction or position. **2,** bias. **3,** point of view.

slap *v.t.* [**slapped, slap′ping**] **1,** strike with the open hand or with something flat. **2,** strike with. **3,** rebuke. —*n.* act of slapping; a slapping blow.

slap′dash″ *adv.* hastily and carelessly. —*adj.* carelessly hasty.

slap-′hap″py *adj.* (*Slang*) **1,** dazed or mentally impaired from blows on the head. **2,** silly; foolish.

slap′jack″ *n.* a children's card game.

slap′stick″ *n.* **1,** a device used to make a slapping sound. **2,** rough comedy. —*adj.* like or characteristic of slapstick.

slash *v.t.* **1,** hack violently. **2,** make slits in. —*v.i.* make a wide cutting stroke. —*n.* **1,** a slashing stroke; a wound. **2,** an ornamental slit. **3,** debris of felled trees. **4,** (usu. *pl.*) a swampy tract. **—slash′er,** *n.* (*Slang*) a horror film.

slat *n.* a strip of wood, etc.; a lath.

slate (slāt) *n.* **1,** a fine-grained rock, easily split. **2,** a thin piece of this rock, as for writing upon. **3,** a written record. **4,** a dull bluish-gray color. **5,** a list of candidates. **—v.t. 1,** cover with slate. **2,** destine.

slath′er (slath′ər) *v.t.* **1,** spread thickly with or on. **2,** apply liberally; lavish.

slat′tern (slat′ərn) *n.* **1,** prostitute. **2,** a slovenly or untidy woman. **—slat′tern·ly,** *adj.*

slaugh′ter (slâ′tər) *n.* **1,** the killing of domestic animals for food. **2,** massacre; carnage. **—v.t.** kill; massacre. **—slaugh′-ter·house″,** *n.*

Slav (släv) *n. & adj.* a member of one of the peoples dominant in E. Europe.

slave (slāv) *n.* **1,** a person who is the property of another. **2,** an addict. **3,** a drudge. **—v.i.** drudge. **—slav′ish,** *adj.* **—slave driver,** a hard taskmaster. **—slave trade,** the buying and selling of human beings as slaves.

---

slave
↔ The resemblance of this word to Slav is an indication of their common origin, from an ancient Slavic word, *Sloveninu,* through Greek and Latin descendants.

---

slave′hold″ing *n.* the ownership of slaves. **—adj.** owning slaves. **—slave′-hol″der,** *n.* one who owns slaves.

slav′er (slā′vər) *n.* **1,** a trader in slaves. **2,** a ship carrying slaves.

slav′er (slav′ər) *v.i.* **1,** let saliva dribble from the mouth. **2,** show inordinate desire. **—n. 1,** saliva. **2,** drivel.

slav′er·y (slā′və-rė) *n.* **1,** the condition of a slave; bondage. **2,** the practice of enslaving humans. **3,** drudgery.

slav′ey (slā′vė) *n.* (*Informal*) a maid of all work.

Slav′ic (släv′ik) *adj.* pert. to the Slavs, as Russians, Poles, etc., and their languages.

slaw (slâ) *n.* chopped cabbage served as a salad; coleslaw.

slay (slā) *v.t.* [**slew, slain, slay′ing**] **1,** kill by violence. **2,** (*Slang*) affect powerfully.

slea′zy (slē′zė; slā′-) *adj.* **1,** flimsy, unsubstantial. **2,** sordid; squalid. **3,** mean; contemptible. **—sleaze,** *n.* **—slea′zi·ness,** *n.*

sled *n.* a vehicle mounted on runners for moving on snow or ice. **—sled′ding,** *n.* (*Informal*) going.

sledge (slej) *n.* **1,** a large sled. **2,** a large, heavy hammer: *sledgehammer.*

sleek (slēk) *adj.* **1,** smooth and glossy. **2,** well-groomed. **3,** suave. **—v.t.** preen. **—sleek′ness,** *n.*

sleep (slēp) *n.* **1,** the natural state of bodily rest, marked by suspension of consciousness. **2,** inactivity; repose. **—v.i.** [*pret. & p.p.* **slept**] **1,** get to sleep. **2,** lie in death. **3,** (with *away, off,* etc.) pass, as time, a condition, etc. **—v.t.** furnish sleeping accommodations for. **—sleeping bag,** a lined bag in which to sleep on the ground. **—sleeping car,** a railroad car having berths, and sometimes compartments, for sleeping. **—sleeping pill,** a barbiturate. **—sleeping policeman,** an artificial bump in a road designed to slow down a car. **—sleeping sickness,** a disease that causes extreme lethargy.

sleep′er *n.* **1,** one who sleeps. **2,** a railroad car with berths. **3,** a railroad tie. **4,** (*Informal*) an unexpected success.

sleep′less *adj.* **1,** without sleep. **2,** never resting; vigilant.

sleep′walk″ *v.i.* somnambulate.

sleep′y (-ė) *adj.* **1,** anxious to sleep; drowsy. **2,** tranquil; quiet. **—sleep′i·ness,** *n.*

sleet (slēt) *n.* partly frozen rain. **—v.i.** produce sleet.

sleeve (slēv) *n.* **1,** the part of a garment that covers the arm. **2,** a tubular covering or jacket.

sleigh (slā) *n.* a horse-drawn sled.

sleight (slīt) *n.* an artful feat, esp. of conjuring: *sleight-of-hand.*

slen′der (slen′dər) *adj.* **1,** small in width or diameter. **2,** scanty. **3,** weak. **—slen′-der·ness,** *n.*

slen′der·ize″ (-īz″) *v.i. & t.* (*Informal*) make, or become, or make to seem, more slender.

slept *v.,* p.t. & p.p. of *sleep.*

sleuth (slooth) *n.* **1,** (*Informal*) a detective. **2,** a bloodhound.

slew (sloo) *v.* pret. of *slay.* **—v.i.** veer; twist. **—n.** [also, **slue**] **1,** a twist. **2,** (*Informal*) a great number.

slice (slīs) *n.* **1,** a thin, broad piece. **2,** an act of cutting. **3,** a slicer. **4,** (*Golf*) an oblique stroke, veering to the right. **—v.t. & i.** cut into slices. **—slic′er,** *n.*

slick (slik) *adj.* **1,** sleek. **2,** ingenious; sly. **—n. 1,** a smooth patch. **2,** a magazine printed on coated paper. **—v.t.** (often with *up*) make smooth, sleek, or elegant.

slick′er *n.* **1,** an oilskin coat. **2,** (*Informal*) a sly fellow; a swindler.

---

slide (slīd) *v.i.* [*pret.* & *p.p.* **slid**] **1,** slip over a smooth surface. **2,** go smoothly. **3,** deteriorate. —*v.t.* cause to glide. —*n.* **1,** an act of sliding; a place for sliding. **2,** an avalanche. **3,** a sliding part. **4,** a picture on glass, for projection on a screen. —**slide fastener,** a zipper. —**slide rule,** a device for calculating, by the relative position of two graduated rulers. —**sliding scale,** a basis for varying prices, wages, etc., according to conditions.

slight (slīt) *adj.* **1,** small. **2,** of little importance. **3,** slender; frail. —*v.t.* **1,** disdain; ignore. **2,** do negligently. —*n.* discourteous neglect.

slim *adj.* [**slim′mer, -mest**] **1,** slender; thin. **2,** meager. —**slim′ness,** *n.*

slime (slīm) *n.* an offensive viscous liquid. —**slim′y,** *adj.*

sling *n.* **1,** a device for hurling a missile by hand; *slingshot.* **2,** a loop for suspending a load. **3,** a cocktail of gin, water, and lemon juice. —*v.t.* [*pret.* & *p.p.* **slung**] **1,** fling. **2,** suspend, etc., by a sling.

sling′shot″ *n.* a forked stick with an elastic band for shooting small missiles.

slink *v.i.* [*pret.* & *p.p.* **slunk**] go in a furtive manner.

slip *v.i.* [**slipped, slip′ping**] **1,** lose hold; slide back. **2,** (often with *up*) err. **3,** slide; decline; deteriorate. **4,** move quietly. —*v.t.* **1,** put or move quietly. **2,** cast off. **3,** of animals, bring forth (young). —*n.* **1,** an act of slipping. **2,** a woman's undergarment. **3,** a pillowcase. **4,** the space between two wharves. **5,** a strip, as of paper. **6,** a slender person. —**slip cover,** a removable cloth cover for a piece of furniture.

slip′knot″ *n.* **1,** a knot used to form a noose of variable size. **2,** a knot easily untied.

slip-′on″ *adj.* designed to be slipped on easily. —*n.* a slip-on garment.

slip′o″ver *n.* a sweater, etc., to be pulled over the head.

slip′page (-ij) *n.* act, result, or extent of slipping.

slip′per (-ər) *n.* a low shoe.

slip′per·y *adj.* **1,** offering little friction, as though greasy. **2,** sly; insecure. —**slip′-per·i·ness,** *n.*

slip′shod′ *adj.* negligent; careless; slovenly.

slip′stream″ *n.* the air forced back by an aircraft propeller.

slip-′up″ *n.* a careless error.

slit *v.t.* [**slit′ted** or **slit, slit′ting**] **1,** make a long narrow cut in. **2,** cut into strips. —*n.* a long, narrow, straight cut or aperture.

slith′er (sli*th*′ər) *v.i.* slide; go unsteadily; slip. —**slith′er·y,** *adj.*

sliv′er (sliv′ər) *n.* a fragment broken off; a splinter.

slob *n.* (*Slang*) a slovenly or uncultivated person.

slob′ber (slob′ər) *v.i.* & *t.,* & *n.* slaver; drool. —**slob′ber·y,** *adj.*

sloe (slō) *n.* a small, black plum. —**sloe′-eyed″,** *adj.* dark-eyed. —**sloe gin,** an alcoholic beverage flavored with sloes.

slog *v.i.* [**slogged, slog′ging**] plod.

slo′gan (slō′gən) *n.* a distinctive phrase or cry, used as a rallying cry, motto, catch-phrase in advertising, etc.

sloop *n.* a one-masted sailboat.

slop *n.* **1,** a puddle. **2,** an unappetizing mess. **3,** (*pl.*) waste liquid; sewage. —*v.t.* & *i.* [**slopped, slop′ping**] **1,** spill; splash. **2,** (*Informal*) be effusive.

slope (slōp) *n.* a slanting surface; slant. —*v.i.* be slanting or oblique. —*v.t.* cause to slant.

slop′py (-ė) *adj.* **1,** untidy. **2,** splashing. —**slop′pi·ness,** *n.* —**sloppy Joe, 1,** a dish of ground meat and a sauce, served on a bun. **2,** a baggy sweater worn by girls.

slosh *n.* **1,** slush. **2,** nonsense. —*v.t.* & *i.* muddle; mix; splash.

slot *n.* a long narrow aperture or recess. —**slot′ted,** *adj.* —**slot car,** a small, electric toy car raced on a special track. —**slot machine,** a device for vending, gambling, etc., activated by dropping a coin in a slot.

sloth (slâth) *n.* **1,** laziness; indolence. **2,** a small arboreal mammal of So. America. —**sloth′ful,** *adj.*

slouch (slowch) *v.i.* bend downward; droop. —*n.* **1,** a drooping posture. **2,** an inept person.

slough (slow) *n.* **1,** a mudhole; bog. **2,** condition of helplessness or degradation. **3,** (sloo) a swamp.

slough (sluf) *n.* a molted part, as the skin of a snake. —*v.t.* **1,** molt; cast off; shed. **2,** discard. Also, **sluff.**

slov′en (sluv′ən) *n.* one who is habitually untidy. —**slov′en·ly,** *adj.*

slow (slō) *adj.* **1,** taking a relatively long time. **2,** dull-witted. **3,** tardy; sluggish. **4,** slack. **5,** tedious. —*v.t.* & *i.* make or become slow. —*adv.* (*Informal*) slowly. —**slow′ness,** *n.*

slow′down″ *n.* a slowing down, esp. of the rate of production, as by workers to enforce demands upon the management.

slow-′mo″tion *adj.* denoting a technique

that depicts motion at less than its actual speed.

slow′poke″ *n.* (*Slang*) one who thinks or acts slowly.

slow-′wit″ted *adj.* dull in mind.

sludge (sluj) *n.* slush; ooze.

slue (sloo) *n. & v.* slew.

sluff (sluf) *v.t. & n.* (*Card Games*) discard a card (so as to avoid losing a trick).

slug *n.* **1,** a billet or ingot; a lead weight or bullet; a counterfeit coin; a bar of metal. **2,** a snaillike terrestrial mollusk. **3,** a heavy blow. **4,** a drink of liquor or other beverage. —*v.t.* [**slugged, slug′ging**] strike heavily. —**slug′ger,** *n.*

slug′gard (slug′ərd) *n.* one habitually lazy or slow,

slug′gish (slug′ish) *adj.* lazy; torpid.

sluice (sloos) *n.* a channel for carrying off surplus water; the stream of water. —*v.t.* drench.

slum *n.* (often *pl.*) a squalid residential section. —*v.i.* [**slummed, slum′ming**] visit the slums, esp. as a sightseer.

slum′ber (slum′bər) *v.i. & t., & n.* sleep. —**slum′ber·ous,** *adj.*

slum′lord″ *n.* landlord of a slum building.

slump *v.i.* sink heavily. —*n.* a sudden sinking or decline.

slung *v.* pret. & p.p. of *sling.*

slunk *v.* pret. & p.p. of *slink.*

slur (slėr) [**slurred, slur′ring**] *v.t.* **1,** run together (as separate words or notes). **2,** (usually with *over*) treat slightingly; ignore. **3,** disparage. —*n.* **1,** a slurred utterance; (*Music*) a curved line indicating a slurring of notes. **2,** a disparaging remark. **3,** a blot or stain. —**slur′ry,** *adj.*

slurp (slėrp) *v.t. & i.* sip or eat noisily.

slush *n.* **1,** watery snow. **2,** a watery mixture of mud, etc. **3,** drivel. **4,** bribery. —*v.t.* splash; flush. —**slush fund,** a fund, usu. secret, of money used for bribery.

slut *n.* **1,** a slovenly woman. **2,** a female dog. —**slut′tish,** *adj.*

sly (slī) *adj.* [**sly′er, sly′est**] **1,** meanly artful; cunning; shrewd. **2,** stealthy; insidious. **3,** roguish. —**sly′ness,** *n.*

sly′boots″ *n.* (*Informal*) a sly person.

smack (smak) *v.t.* **1,** separate (the lips) with a sharp sound. **2,** slap. **3,** kiss noisily. —*v.i.* **1,** make a sharp sound; slap. **2,** (with *of*) suggest. —*n.* **1,** a smacking noise. **2,** a resounding blow. **3,** a trace; suggestion; taste. **4,** a small fishing vessel. **5,** (*Slang*) heroin. —*adv.* squarely and abruptly. —**smack-dab,** *adv.* (*Informal*) squarely. —**smack′er,** *n.* (*Slang*) a dollar.

small (smâl) *adj.* **1,** little; of limited scope; restricted. **2,** humble. **3,** mean; petty. —*n.* a thin or narrow part. —**small arms,** hand guns. —**small fry,** youngsters. —**small hours,** late hours. —**small potatoes,** (*Informal*) of little consequence. —**small talk,** chatter.

small-′mind″ed *adj.* narrow in outlook, sympathy, etc.

small′pox″ *n.* an acute contagious disease often leaving pockmarks on its survivors.

small-′time″ *adj.* (*Slang*) of minor importance.

smart (smärt) *v.i.* **1,** sting. **2,** feel physical or mental distress. —*v.t.* cause to smart. —*n.* **1,** a sting. **2,** mental distress. —*adj.* **1,** keen; acute; severe. **2,** brisk. **3,** clever; shrewd. **4,** vivacious; witty. **5,** neat; fashionably groomed. —**smart′en,** *v.t.* make neat, spruce, etc. —**smart′ness,** *n.* —**smart a′leck** (a′lək) a cocky person. —**smart bomb,** a bomb with its own internal guidance system. —**smart money,** (*Informal*) money bet or invested by one supposed to have superior judgment. —**smart set,** (*Informal*) those who are up-to-date, esp. in clothing styles, etc.; fashionable society.

smash *v.t.* **1,** break to pieces. **2,** defeat utterly. **3,** strike against something. —*v.i.* **1,** break to pieces; be ruined, bankrupt, etc. **2,** dash against something. —*n.* **1,** a violent blow. **2,** destruction. **3,** a sweet drink. —**smash-′up″,** *n.* a collision.

smat′ter·ing (smat′ər-ing) *n.* a slight or superficial knowledge or assortment.

smear (smir) *v.t.* **1,** overspread with grease, dirt, paint, etc.; daub. **2,** soil; sully. —*n.* a smudge.

smear′case″ *n.* cottage cheese.

smell (smel) *v.t.* **1,** perceive through the nose. **2,** inhale the odor of. **3,** detect or discover as though by smell. —*v.i.* inhale or give out an odor, esp. an offensive odor. —*n.* **1,** the sense of smell. **2,** odor; scent; aroma. **3,** the act of smelling. **4,** a trace. —**smell′y,** *adj.* having a strong or offensive odor. —**smelling salts,** a pungent restorative.

smelt *v.t.* melt (ore). —*n.* a small food fish.

smelt′er (smel′tər) *n.* a place where ore is melted, to yield metal.

smid′gen (smid′jən) *n.* a very small amount.

smi′lax (smī′laks) *n.* any of various woody vines.

smile (smīl) *n.* **1,** a widening of the mouth, with parted lips, indicating pleasure, amusement, or favor. **2,** a favoring aspect. —*v.i.* & *t.* **1,** assume, or express by, a smile. **2,** favor.

smirch (smẽrch) *v.t.* soil; discolor; sully. —*n.* a stain; smear.

smirk (smẽrk) *n.* an affected or knowing smile. —*v.i.* so smile.

smite (smīt) *v.t.* [**smote** (smōt), **smit′ten** (smit′ən)] **1,** strike with a hard blow; afflict. **2,** affect; captivate.

smith *n.* a worker in metal; a blacksmith. —**smith′y,** *n.* his workshop.

smith′er·eens″ (smith′ə-rēnz″) *n.pl.* (*Informal*) fragments.

smith′son·ite″ (smith′sən-īt″) *n.* zinc carbonate, an ore of zinc, named for 18th-c. English chemist James Smithson.

smock (smok) *n.* a thin, loose outer robe. —*v.t.* apply smocking to.

smock′ing (-ing) *n.* embroidery stitches that gather material into folds.

smog *n.* (*Informal*) an irritating mixture of smoke and fog.

smoke (smōk) *n.* **1,** the visible vapor given off by a burning substance. **2,** something unsubstantial. **3,** a cigar or cigarette. —*v.i.* **1,** emit smoke. **2,** draw and emit the fumes of burning tobacco. —*v.t.* **1,** puff the smoke of (tobacco, opium, etc.). **2,** treat with smoke. **3,** (with *out*) drive into view. —**smoke and mirrors,** (*Informal*) exaggerated claims or simulated demonstrations made in promoting a product. —**smokeless powder,** white gunpowder, which burns with little smoke. —**smoke screen,** an obscuring cloud of, or as of, smoke. —**smoking gun,** conclusive evidence of a crime. —**smoking jacket,** a jacket worn for indoor lounging.

smoke′house″ *n.* a shed for smoking meat.

smok′er *n.* **1,** one who smokes. **2,** a train car in which smoking is permitted. **3,** a social meeting, esp. for men.

smoke′stack″ *n.* an upright pipe carrying off smoke.

smok′y (smō′kė) *adj.* **1,** smoking; visibly vaporous. **2,** dark; cloudy; grayish-blue. —**smok′i·ness,** *n.*

smol′der (smōl′dər) *v.i.* **1,** burn and smoke without flame. **2,** exist in a suppressed state.

smooch *v.i.* (*Slang*) kiss amorously; pet.

smooth (smooth) *adj.* **1,** having an even surface; not obstructed. **2,** without sudden jolts or breaks; uniform. **3,** not lumpy. **4,** bland. **5,** harmonious. **6,** tranquil. **7,** mild. **8,** flowing, as speech. —*v.t.* **1,** make

smoother. **2,** calm; allay; mollify; palliate. —**smooth′ness,** *n.*

smor′gas·bord″ (smôr′gəs-bôrd″) *n.* (*Swedish*, sandwich table) a buffet composed of hors d'oeuvres, casseroles, etc.

smote (smōt) *v.* p.t. of *smite.*

smoth′er (smuth′ər) *v.t.* **1,** suffocate; cover so as to deprive of air. **2,** stifle; repress or suppress. —*v.i.* be smothered. —**smoth′er·y,** *adj.*

smoul′der (smōl′dər) *v.i.* smolder.

smudge (smuj) *n.* **1,** a dirty mark; a blot or smear. **2,** a smoky fire. —*v.t.* & *i.* stain; blacken. —**smudg′y,** *adj.*

smug *adj.* [**smug′ger, -gest**] self-satisfied. —**smug′ness,** *n.*

smug′gle (smug′əl) *v.t.* & *i.* transport (goods) secretly, esp. to avoid payment of duties. —**smug′gler,** *n.*

smut *n.* **1,** sooty matter. **2,** obscenity. —**smut′ty,** *adj.*

smutch (smuch) *v.* & *n.* smudge.

snack (snak) *n.* a small portion, esp. of food.

sna″fu′ (sna″foo′) (*Slang*) *n.* a badly confused or bungled situation: *s(ituation) n(ormal): a(ll) f(ouled) u(p).* —*adj.* in disorder.

snag *n.* an obstruction; an obstacle. —*v.t.* [**snagged, snag′ging**] **1,** impede; entangle. **2,** trap, as with a snag. —**snag-′toothed″, snag′gle-toothed″,** *adj.* with teeth projecting awry.

snail (snāl) *n.* **1,** a mollusk with a spiral shell. **2,** a slow mover.

snail′paced″ *adj.* sluggish.

snake (snāk) *n.* **1,** any of an order of reptiles with elongated, tubular, limbless bodies: serpent. **2,** a treacherous person. —*v.t.* drag by jerks; haul at the end of a chain or rope. —**snake check,** examine in advance, looking for unintended consequences.

snak′y *adj.* **1,** pert. to snakes. **2,** flexible; sinuous. **3,** treacherous.

snap *v.i.* [**snapped, snap′ping**] **1,** make a sudden sharp sound; click. **2,** break suddenly. **3,** move suddenly. **4,** (with *at*) bite suddenly. **5,** speak sharply. —*v.t.* **1,** make a clicking sound. **2,** break. **3,** retort. **4,** (with *up*) grab. **5,** take an instantaneous photograph of. —*n.* **1,** a sharp sound; a click. **2,** a quick motion. **3,** something that snaps. **4,** a thin, brittle cake. **5,** briskness; vigor. **6,** a brief spell. **7,** (*Slang*) an easy task. —*adj.* **1,** offhand. **2,** easy. **3,** operated by a device that snaps.

snap′drag″on (snap′drag″ən) *n.* a flowering plant.

snap'per (-ər) *n.* **1,** a large marine fish. **2,** a snapping turtle.

snap'pish (-ish) *adj.* apt to bite or snap. —**snap'pish·ness,** *n.*

snap'py (-ė) *adj.* **1,** snapping; crackling. **2,** brisk; cold and stimulating, as weather. **3,** (*Informal*) smart, as dress; lively and clever, as repartee; quick. **4,** snappish. —**snap'pi·ness,** *n.*

snap'shot″ *n.* a photograph.

snare (snãr) *n.* **1,** a trap. **2,** a cord, as one stretched across a head of a drum (*snare drum*). —*v.t.* catch, entangle.

snarl (snärl) *v.t. & i.* **1,** utter an angry cry, as a dog; speak angrily. **2,** entangle; become entangled. —*n.* **1,** act of snarling; a surly tone. **2,** a tangled mass.

snatch (snach) *v.t.* seize abruptly or violently. —*v.i.* grab hastily. —*n.* **1,** the act of snatching; (*Slang*) a kidnapping. **2,** a fragment or bit.

snaz'zy (snaz'ė) *adj.* fancy; flashy.

sneak (snēk) *v.i.* go or act in a stealthy, furtive manner; slink; skulk. —*v.t.* **1,** do furtively. **2,** (*Informal*) steal. —*n.* **1,** one who sneaks. **2,** (*pl.*) [also, **sneak'ers**] soft-soled low shoes. —**sneak'y,** *adj.* —**sneak thief,** a thief who does not break his or her way in.

sneer (snir) *v.i.* express scorn, as by a grimace. —*v.t.* utter with a sneer. —*n.* a contemptuous expression or utterance.

sneeze (snēz) *n.* a sudden, involuntary, spasmodic expulsion of air through the nose and mouth. —*v.i.* make a sneeze. —**sneeze at,** (*Informal*) treat with scorn.

snick'er (snik'ər) *v.i. & t.* laugh in a suppressed manner. —*n.* giggle.

snick'er·snee″ *n.* (usu. *jocular*) a cutting weapon.

snide (snīd) *adj.* mean; invidious.

sniff (snif) *v.i. & t.* **1,** draw in air audibly. **2,** (with *at*) show scorn or disdain (of). —*n.* a sniffling. —**snif'fy,** *adj.*

snif'fle (-əl) *v.i.* sniff repeatedly.

snif'ter (snif'tər) *n.* **1,** a pear-shaped brandy glass. **2,** (*Slang*) a small drink.

snip *v.t. & i.* cut off with one light stroke. —*n.* **1,** the act or result of snipping. **2,** (*Informal*) an insignificant person. **3,** (*pl.*) shears.

snipe (snīp) *n.* a long-billed wading bird. —*v.i.* **1,** hunt snipe. **2,** shoot, esp. from a concealed position. —**snip'er,** *n.* a sharpshooter.

snip'pet (snip'ət) *n.* **1,** a small piece snipped off. **2,** (*Informal*) a small or insignificant person.

snip'py (-ė) *adj.* snappish; curt. —**snip'-pi·ness,** *n.*

snitch (snich) (*Slang*) *v.t.* steal. —*v.i.* turn informer.

sniv'el (sniv'əl) *v.i.* **1,** weep and sniffle. **2,** pretend contrition; whine.

snob *n.* one who unduly esteems social position. —**snob'bish,** *adj.* —**snob'bish·ness, snob'ber·y,** *n.*

---

snob
↔ This word originally meant shoemaker. It was borrowed by Cambridge University students to refer to townspeople, hence (from the students' standpoint) persons of a lower order.

---

snood *n.* a band or fillet to confine the hair.

snook'er (snûk'ər) *n.* a form of pocket billiards.

snoop (*Informal*) *v.i.* prowl and spy. —*n.* one who snoops. —**snoop'y,** *adj.*

snoot (*Informal*) *n.* the nose or face. —**snoot'y,** *adj.* snobbish. —**snoot'i·ness,** *n.*

snooze (snooz) *n. & v.i.* (*Informal*) sleep; doze; nap.

snore (snôr) *v.i.* breathe with a hoarse noise during sleep. —*n.* a snoring sound.

snor'kel (snôr'kəl) *n.* a device to supply air to the engine of a submarine or to an underwater swimmer.

snort (snôrt) *v.i.* **1,** force air audibly through the nose. **2,** scoff. —*n.* a snorting sound or act —*v.t.* (*Slang*) inhale cocaine.

snot *n.* (*Vulgar*) mucus from the nose.

snot'ty *adj.* (*Informal*) snobbish; impudent. —**snot'ti·ness,** *n.*

snout (snowt) *n.* the forepart of an animal's head, esp. the nose.

snow (snō) *n.* **1,** water vapor frozen into crystals, falling to earth in flakes; a fall of snow; fallen snow. **2,** something very white. **3,** (*Slang*) cocaine or heroin. —*v.i. & t.* send down or fall as snow. —*v.t.* (*Slang*) flatter. —**snow job,** (*Slang*) flattery to attain a desired favor. —**snow under,** bury.

snow'ball″ *n.* **1,** snow, pressed into a ball. **2,** crushed ice flavored with fruit syrup. —*v.i.* (*Informal*) increase rapidly.

snow'bank″ *n.* a heap of snow.

snow'belt″ *n.* a region of unusually heavy snowfall.

snow'bird″ *n.* **1,** (*Informal*) a seasonal resident in a warm climate, on vacation from a colder region. **2,** (*Slang*) a drug addict.

snow-'blind" *adj.* having the eyesight impaired by the glare of snow.

snow'bound" *adj.* confined by impassable snow.

snow'clad" *adj.* topped with snow, as a mountain.

snow'drift" *n.* drifted snow.

snow'drop" *n.* a white flower blooming in the spring.

snow'fall" *n.* a fall of snow.

snow'flake" *n.* **1,** a snow crystal. **2,** a bulbous plant with white flowers.

snow'man" *n.* **1,** a crude statue of a human figure, made of snow. **2,** yeti.

snow'mo·bile" *n.* a small motor vehicle on skis, driven by a belt, for traveling on snow.

snow'plow" *n.* a blade for pushing aside snow.

snow'shoe" *n.* a network in a frame, worn for walking on snow.

snow'storm" *n.* a heavy snowfall; blizzard.

snow'y *adj.* **1,** pert. to snow. **2,** clear white; spotless; immaculate. **—snow'i-ness,** *n.*

snub *v.t.* **[snubbed, snub'bing] 1,** check or stop suddenly. **2,** slight; ignore. **—adj.** (of the nose) turned up at the tip. **—snub'by,** *adj.*

snuff (snuf) *v.t. & i.* sniff. **—v.t.** extinguish, as a candle. **—n. 1,** sniff. **2,** powdered tobacco.

snuff'box" *n.* a pocket container for snuff.

snuf'fle (snuf'əl) *v.i. & t., & n.* sniff or sniffle.

snug *adj.* **[snug'ger, -gest] 1,** comfortable; cozy. **2,** fitting closely. **3,** compact; neat. **—snug'ness,** *n.*

snug'gle (snug'əl) *v.i. & t.* cuddle; nestle.

so (sō) *adv.* **1,** in the degree, amount, manner, etc., expressed or implied. **2,** very; extremely. **3,** such being the case. **4,** consequently. **—interj.** expressing mild surprise.

soak (sōk) *v.i.* be permeated by a liquid; become thoroughly wet; permeate. **—v.t. 1,** drench; saturate. **2,** absorb. **3,** (*Slang*) charge exorbitantly. **—n.** (*Slang*) an immoderate drinker.

so-'and-so" *pron.* **1,** someone whose name is not known or specified. **2,** (*Slang*) a contemptible person.

soap (sōp) *n.* **1,** a substance used for cleansing. **2,** (*Slang*) flattery: *soft soap.* **3,** (*Slang*) money used for building. **—v.t.** cover or treat with soap. **—no soap,**

(*Slang*) definitely not. **—soap opera,** a sentimental radio or television drama.

soap'box" *n.* the podium of an unauthorized orator.

soap'er (-ər) *n.* (*Slang*) soap opera.

soap'stone" *n.* a soft stone, a variety of talc.

soap'suds" *n.* suds.

soap'y (-ē) *adj.* **1,** containing soap. **2,** flattering. **—soap'i·ness,** *n.*

soar (sôr) *v.i.* **1,** fly upward; glide in air. **2,** rise higher, or to great height.

sob *v.i. & t.* **[sobbed, sob'bing]** weep convulsively. **—n.** a convulsive catching of the breath in weeping. **—sob sister,** (*Slang*) a writer of sentimental human-interest stories. **—sob story,** a story told to arouse pity or generosity.

so'ber (sō'bər) *adj.* **1,** not intoxicated. **2,** sedate; serious; solemn. **3,** subdued, as in color. **—v.t. & i.** make or become sober. **—so'ber·ly,** *adv.* seriously. **—so'ber·ness,** *n.*

so·bri'e·ty (sō-brī'ə-tē) *n.* soberness, not drunkenness.

so'bri·quet" (sō'bri-kā") *n.* (*Fr.*) a nickname. Also, **sou'bri·quet.**

so-"called" *adj.* thus (perhaps unjustifiably) designated.

soc'cer (sok'ər) *n.* a form of football.

---

soccer
↔ From (*As*)*soc*(*ciation Football*) + *-cer*, referring to the rules of the Football Association as opposed to the rules of rugby football.

---

so'cia·ble (sō'shə-bəl) *adj.* gregarious; friendly; amiable. **—n.** a social gathering. **—so"cia·bil'i·ty,** *n.*

so'cial (sō'shəl) *adj.* **1,** pert. to communal activities; gregarious; friendly. **2,** pert. to or tending to advance human society. **3,** fashionable. **4,** of disease, venereal. **—n.** a social gathering. **—social climber,** one who seeks social advancement. **—Social Register,** a book listing members of fashionable society. **—social science,** a science dealing with society and its institutions. **—social security,** a general insurance and old-age-pension plan. **—social work,** a profession dealing with the problems of the underprivileged persons of society.

so'cial·ism (-iz-əm) *n.* ownership of exploitable capital and means of production by the government, not by individuals or by private enterprise. **—so'cial·ist,** *n.* **—so"cial·ist'ic** (-is'tik) *adj.*

so'cial·ite" (sō'shə-līt") *n.* a member of fashionable society.

---

so″**ci·al**′**i·ty** (sō″shē-al′ə-tė) *n.* the state, tendency, or practice of being social.

so′**cial·ize**″ (-īz″) *v.t.* make social or socialistic. —**socialized medicine,** medical care provided by the state. —**so**″**cial·i·za**′**tion,** *n.*

so·ci′**e·ty** (sō-sī′ə-tė) *n.* **1,** human beings collectively. **2,** the fashionable world. **3,** a community. **4,** an association. **5,** companionship. —**so·ci**′**e·tal,** *adj.*

so·ci·o- *pref.* society; social; sociological.

so″**ci·ol**′**o·gy** (sō″shē-ol′ə-jė) *n.* the science of human society. —**so**″**ci·o·log**′**i·cal** (-ə-loj′i-kəl) *adj.* —**so**″**ci·ol**′**o·gist,** *n.*

so″**ci·o·path**′**ic** (-path′ik) *adj.* antisocial.

sock (sok) *n.* **1,** a short stocking. **2,** (*Slang*) a hard blow. —*v.t.* (*Slang*) hit hard. —**socked in,** (*Slang*) closed because of bad weather.

sock″**dol**′**a·ger** (sok″dol′ə-jər) *n.* (*Slang*) something that brings decisive defeat; knockout punch.

sock′**et** (sok′it) *n.* a hollow into which something is fitted.

sock′**eye** *n.* a species of red salmon.

sod *n.* **1,** the upper layer of grassy land. **2,** a piece of turf. —*v.t.* cover with sods.

so′**da** (sō′də) *n.* **1,** sodium or one of its oxides. **2,** water charged with carbon dioxide; any drink prepared with it: *soda water.* —**soda fountain,** a counter at which ice cream and drinks are served. —**soda jerk,** (*Slang*) a clerk at a soda fountain. —**soda pop,** a carbonated soft drink.

so·dal′**i·ty** (sō-dal′ə-tė) *n.* an association.

sod′**den** (sod′ən) *adj.* soaked; bloated.

so′**di·um** (sō′dė-əm) *n.* a metallic chemical element, no. 11, symbol Na. —**sodium chloride,** salt. —**sodium silicate,** water-glass.

sod′**om·y** (sod′əm-ė) *n.* unnatural sexual intercourse. —**sod**′**om·ite**″, *n.* —**sod**′**om·ize**″, *v.t.*

> **sodomy**
> ↔ From Old French *sodomie*, for the Biblical city *Sodom* (Gen. 18-19).

so′**fa** (sō′fə) *n.* a long, upholstered seat with a back and arms.

so′**far**″ *n.* a system for locating very distant underwater objects: *so(und) f(ixing) a(nd) r(anging).*

soft (sâft) *adj.* **1,** yielding readily to pressure; not hard or stiff. **2,** agreeable to the touch; mild, bland, delicate, melodious, etc. **3,** kind, lenient, etc. **4,** not robust. **5,** easy. **6,** (of water) relatively free of mineral salts. **7,** not sharp, as outlines. —*adv.*

in a soft manner. —*interj.* (*Archaic*) be quiet! not so fast! —**soft**′**ness,** *n.* —**soft coal,** bituminous coal. —**soft drink,** a sweet beverage containing no alcohol. —**soft soap,** (*Informal*) flattery.

soft′**ball**″ *n.* baseball played with a larger, softer ball; the ball used.

soft-′**bound**″ *adj.* paperback.

soft-′**core**″ *adj.* less explicit than hard-core.

sof′**ten** (sâf′ən) *v.t.* & *i.* make or become softer. —**sof**′**ten·er,** *n.*

soft′**heart**″**ed** *adj.* very sympathetic.

soft-′**ped**″**al** *v.t.* tone down; suppress.

soft-′**shoe**″ *adj.* of a type of exhibition dancing without metal taps on the shoes.

soft-′**spo**″**ken** *adj.* beguiling; persuasive.

soft′**ware**″ *n.* written or printed information or data for use with computers; program(s).

soft′**y** (sâf′tė) *n.* (*Informal*) **1,** a weak-willed or softhearted person. **2,** a person of scant endurance.

sog′**gy** (sog′ė) *adj.* sodden. —**sog**′**gi·ness,** *n.*

soi-di·sant′ (swä dē-zän′) *adj.* (*Fr.*) so-called.

soi·gné′ (swä-nyā′) *adj.* (*Fr.*) well-groomed; neat in personal appearance.

soil *n.* **1,** the portion of the earth's surface in which plants grow. **2,** land. **3,** filth. —*v.t.* stain; defile; make dirty or foul. —*v.i.* become soiled.

soi·rée′ (swä-rā′) *n.* (*Fr.*) a social gathering in the evening.

so′**journ** (sō′jėrn) *v.i.* dwell temporarily. —*n.* a temporary stay.

sol *n.* (sōl) **1,** (*Music*) the fifth tone of the diatonic scale. **2,** the monetary unit of Peru. **3,** (sol) (*cap.*) the sun.

sol′**ace** (sol′is) *n.* comfort in sorrow. —*v.t.* comfort.

so′**lar** (sō′lər) *adj.* pert. to the sun. —**solar energy,** the energy which can be produced from the sun's rays or the effects of the sun's rays or gravity. —**solar panel,** a bank of light-sensitive solar cells, used to generate electricity, as for a spacecraft. —**solar plex**′**us** (plek′səs) the system of nerves behind the stomach. —**solar sail,** a flat sail attached to a spacecraft to receive propulsive force from the sun's radiation. —**solar system,** a sun and the planets revolving around it. —**solar wind,** charged particles emitted from the sun's surface.

so·lar′**i·um** (sō-lâr′ė-əm) *n.* [*pl.* **-a** (-ə)] a glass-enclosed room; sunroom.

sold (sōld) *v.* pret. & p.p. of *sell.*

sol′der (sod′ər) *n.* a fusible metal. —*v.t.* join with solder. —**soldering iron,** a tool for melting solder.

sol′dier (sōl′jər) *n.* a person engaged in military service; one of an army. —*v.i.* **1,** serve as a soldier. **2,** (*Informal*) malinger. —**sol′dier·ly,** *adj.* —**sol′dier·y,** *n.* soldiers collectively. —**soldier of fortune,** a mercenary or adventurer.

> **soldier**
> ↔ From Latin *solidus,* a gold coin. A *soldier* was a mercenary, working for pay.

sole (sōl) *n.* **1,** the undersurface of the foot, or of a shoe. **2,** any of several flatfishes. —*adj.* unique; only; alone.

sol′e·cism (sol′ə-siz-əm) *n.* an error, as in grammar.

sol′emn (sol′əm) *adj.* **1,** sober in manner or aspect. **2,** gravely impressive. —**so·lem′ni·fy** (sə-lem′ni-fī) *v.t.* —**so·lem′ni·ty** (sə-lem′nə-tè) *n.*

sol′em·nize″ (-nīz″) *v.t.* **1,** perform (a ceremony); celebrate with ceremonies. **2,** render solemn. —**sol″em·ni·za′tion,** *n.*

so′le·noid″ (sol′ə-noid″) *n.* a tubular wire coil for producing a magnetic field, used in switches.

sol-′fa″ (sōl′fä″) *n.* (*Music*) a set of syllables naming the notes of the diatonic scale.

sol·feg′gio (sol-fej′ō) *n.* **1,** a vocal exercise. **2,** a system for teaching music using sol-fa syllables.

so·lic′it (sə-lis′it) *v.t.* **1,** seek to obtain; request. **2,** address entreaties to; petition. —*v.i.* seek to obtain something. —**so·lic″i·ta′tion,** *n.*

so·lic′i·tor (sə-lis′ə-tər) *n.* **1,** one who solicits. **2,** (*Brit.*) a lawyer who prepares cases for barristers. —**solicitor general, 1,** a high officer of the U.S. Dept. of Justice, ranking next below the Attorney General. **2,** the chief law officer in some U.S. states. ❑ *attorney*

so·lic′i·tous (sə-lis′ə-təs) *adj.* anxious.

so·lic′i·tude (sə-lis′ə-tood) *n.* anxiety or concern for the welfare of others.

> **solid, stolid**
> ☛ Two easily confused words. *Solid* means dense, sound. *Stolid* means impassive.

sol′id *adj.* **1,** existing in three-dimensional space. **2,** compact; undivided; dense. **3,** firm; hard; strong. **4,** united; unanimous. **5,** reliable; financially sound. —*n.* **1,** a three-dimensional body. **2,** a

solid substance. —**so·lid′i·ty,** *n.* —**solid-state,** *adj.* using only semiconductors, such as transistors and diodes.

sol″i·dar′i·ty (sol″i-dar′ə-tè) *n.* union; community of interests.

so·lid′i·fy″ (sə-lid′ə-fī″) *v.t. & i.* make or become solid. —**so·lid″i·fi·ca′tion,** *n.*

sol′i·dus (sol′ə-dəs) *n.* **1,** a gold coin of ancient Rome. **2,** the slant line (/).

so·lil′o·quy (sə-lil′ə-kwè) *n.* the act of talking to oneself. —**so·lil′o·quize″** (-kwīz″) *v.i. & t.*

sol′ip·sism″ (sol′ip-siz″əm) *n.* the doctrine that since all knowledge is subjective, the self is the only entity directly known.

sol′i·taire″ (sol′ə-tār″) *n.* **1,** a puzzle or game played by one person alone. **2,** a precious stone, esp. a diamond, set alone.

sol′i·tar″y (sol′ə-ter″è) *adj.* **1,** alone. **2,** single; sole. **3,** characterized by solitude; not social.

sol′i·tude″ (sol′ə-tood″) *n.* the state of being alone or remote.

so′lo (sō′lō) *n.* [*pl.* **-los**] **1,** a performance by one person alone. **2,** a composition performed by one performer. —*adj.* alone; performed alone. —**so′lo·ist,** *n.*

sol′o·mon (sol′ə-mən) *n.* a wise man.

> **solomon, solon**
> ↔ Two words derived from ancient men of great wisdom. *Solomon* was the 10th-c.-B.C. king of Israel and son of David. *Solon* was a 6th-c.-B.C. Athenian statesman.

so′lon (sō′lon) *n.* a lawmaker. ❑ *solomon*

so long (*Informal*) good-bye.

sol′stice (sol′stis) *n.* either of the two times when the sun is at its greatest distance from the celestial equator, about June 21 and Dec. 21.

sol′u·ble (sol′yə-bəl) *adj.* **1,** capable of being dissolved. **2,** capable of being solved. —**sol″u·bil′i·ty,** *n.*

sol′ute (sol′oot) *n.* a dissolved substance. —*adj.* dissolved.

so·lu′tion (sə-loo′shən) *n.* **1,** an explanation or answer. **2,** a fluid containing something dissolved.

solve (solv) *v.t.* find the answer to (a problem, puzzle, etc.); clear up.

sol′ven·cy (sol′vən-sè) *n.* ability to pay all just debts.

sol′vent (sol′vənt) *adj.* **1,** able to pay all just debts. **2,** having the power of dissolving. —*n.* a fluid that dissolves a specified substance.

so'ma (sō'mə) *n.* [*pl.* **-ma·ta** (-mə-tə)] the whole body of an organism, excluding its germ cells. —**so·mat'ic** (-mat'ik) *adj.*

som'ber (som'bər) *adj.* **1,** dark in color; dull. **2,** gloomy; dismal. Also, **som'bre.** —**som'ber·ness,** *n.*

som·bre'ro (som-brār'ō) *n.* [*pl.* **-ros**] (*Sp.*) a broad-brimmed Mexican hat.

some (sum) *adj.* **1,** of an unspecified but considerable number or quantity. **2,** certain (one or ones) not specified. **3,** (*Slang*) considerable; notable. —*pron.* an unspecified number or portion. —*adv.* (*Slang*) somewhat or considerably. ☐ *either*

-some (səm) *suf.* **1,** showing a tendency (to), as *meddlesome.* **2,** a group, as *threesome.*

some'bod"y *pron.* a person unspecified. —*n.* a person of consequence.

some'day" *adv.* on some indefinite day.

some'how" *adv.* in an unspecified way.

some'one" *pron.* somebody.

some'place" *adv.* & *n.* somewhere.

som'er·sault" (sum'ər-sâlt") *n.* an acrobatic turning over of the body.

---

somersault
↔ Not related to *summer,* but derived from Provençal *sobresaut,* a jumping over.

---

some'thing" *n.* an unspecified thing.

some'time" *adv.* at some indefinite time. —*adj.* **1,** former. **2,** occasional.

some'times" *adv.* occasionally.

some'way" *adv.* in some way or manner not specified or known. Also, **some'ways".**

some'what" *adv.* to some extent. —*n.* some part.

some'where" *adv.* in, at, or to some unspecified place. —*n.* an unspecified place.

som"me·lier' (sum"əl-yā') *n.* (*Fr.*) a wine steward.

som·nam'bu·lism" (som-nam'byə-liz"əm) *n.* sleepwalking. —**som·nam'bu·late"** (-lāt") *v.i.* & *t.* walk, etc., in one's sleep. —**som·nam'bu·list,** *n.*

som'no·lent (som'nə-lənt) *adj.* **1,** sleepy. **2,** causing sleep. —**som'no·lence,** *n.*

son (sun) *n.* **1,** a male in relation to his parents. **2,** (*cap.*) Jesus Christ. —**son'**-**ship,** *n.*

so'nar (sō'när) *n.* a device to time the echo of sound waves in water, used in detecting submarines or obstructions and measuring depths: *so*(*und*) *na*(*vigation*) *r*(*anging*).

so·na'ta (sə-nä'tə) *n.* a musical composition in contrasted movements. —**so"na-**

ti'na (sä"nə-tē'nə) *n.* a simplified or short sonata.

son et lu·mière (sôn-nā lü-myer') (*Fr.* sound and light) a nighttime spectacle usu. demonstrating with sound and lights the history of a building, monument, etc.

song (sâng) *n.* **1,** a short poem set to music. **2,** poetry. **3,** the act or sound of singing.

song'bird" *n.* a bird that sings; hence, a singer, esp. of popular music.

song'fest" *n.* a gathering for communal singing.

song'ster (-stər), **song'stress** (-stris) *n.* a singer, poet, or songbird.

son'ic (son'ik) *adj.* **1,** of or pert. to sound. **2,** of the speed of sound. —**sonic boom,** a sound like the blast of an explosion produced by a shock wave when it reaches the ground.

son-'in-law" *n.* [*pl.* **sons-'**] the husband of one's daughter.

son'net (son'it) *n.* a fourteen-line poem. —**son"ne·teer',** *n.*

son'ny (sun'ē) *n.* (often *Disparaging*) a term of address to a boy.

son'o·gram" (son'ə-gram") *n.* the graphic representation of reflected sound waves in an ultrasound examination, as of a fetus.

so·no'rous (sə-nôr'əs) *adj.* richly resonant in sound; deep; full. —**so·nor'i·ty** (sə-nôr'ə-tē) *n.*

soon *adv.* **1,** in a short time; before long. **2,** promptly; quickly.

soot (sût) *n.* a black substance, chiefly carbon, produced by faulty combustion. —**soot'y,** *adj.*

sooth *n.* (*Archaic*) truth. —**sooth'say"er,** *n.* a fortune-teller.

soothe (sooth) *v.t.* **1,** calm; mollify. **2,** allay (pain, etc.).

sop *n.* **1,** something dipped in a liquid, as bread. **2,** something that pacifies; a bribe. —*v.t.* & *i.* [**sopped, sop'ping**] **1,** dip; soak. **2,** (with *up*) absorb. —**sop'ping,** *adj.* drenched.

soph'ism (sof'iz-əm) *n.* an adroit but fallacious argument. —**soph'ist,** *n.* —**so·phis'tic** (sə-fis'tik) *adj.* —**so·phis'ti·cal·ly,** *adv.*

so·phis'ti·cate" (sə-fis'ti-kāt") *v.t.* make less natural, more worldly. —*n.* a sophisticated person. —**so·phis"ti·ca'tion,** *n.*

so·phis'ti·cat"ed *adj.* **1,** experienced and worldly-wise; artificial. **2,** complex; advanced.

soph'ist·ry *n.* use of a sophism.

soph'o·more" (sof'ə-môr") *n.* a second-year student. —**soph″o·mor′ic,** *adj.* immature; superficial.

so′por (sō′pər) *n.* an unnaturally deep sleep; lethargy; stupor.

so″po·rif′ic (sop″ə-rif′ik) *adj.* **1,** causing sleep. **2,** sleepy. —*n.* something that causes sleep.

sop′py (-ė) *adj.* **1,** soaked. **2,** rainy. **3,** (*Slang*) mawkish. —**sop′pi·ness,** *n.*

so·pran′o (sə-prän′ō) *n.* [*pl.* **-os**] the highest singing voice in women; the singer; the voice part.

sor′cer·y (sôr′sə-rė) *n.* witchcraft; magic. —**sor′cer·er, sor′cer·ess,** *n.*

sor′did (sôr′did) *adj.* **1,** mercenary. **2,** ignoble; base. **3,** squalid. —**sor′did·ness,** *n.*

sore (sôr) *adj.* **1,** sensitive; painful. **2,** suffering pain. **3,** (*Informal*) offended; angry. —*n.* an inflamed or infected spot. —**sore′head″,** *n.* (*Slang*) a disgruntled person. —**sore′ly,** *adv.* very. —**sore′ness,** *n.*

sor′ghum (sôr′gəm) *n.* a cereal grass; a syrup made from it.

so·ror′i·ty (sə-rôr′ə-tė) *n.* a women's society, esp. in college. —**so·ror′al,** *adj.* sisterly.

sor′rel (sor′əl) *n.* **1,** any of various plants. **2,** a light reddish-brown color; a horse of this color.

sor′row (sor′ō) *n.* **1,** distress of mind; sadness; grief. **2,** a cause of grief. —*v.i.* grieve. —**sor′row·ful,** *adj.*

---

sorrow, sorry
↔ Oddly enough, these two words are not related, though both are of Germanic origin. *Sorrow* comes from a source meaning care. *Sorry* comes from a different Germanic root meaning pain, both physical and mental.

---

sor′ry (sor′ė) *adj.* **1,** feeling sorrow, regret, or pity. **2,** deplorable. **3,** worthless; mean; poor. ❏ *sorrow*

sort (sôrt) *n.* **1,** a class, kind, variety, species, etc. **2,** nature; character. **3,** way; fashion. —*v.t.* **1,** classify. **2,** separate from others that differ.

sor′tie (sôr′tē) *n.* **1,** a sally of troops. **2,** a combat mission of aircraft.

S O S (es′ō″es′) a call for help.

so-′so″ *adj. & adv.* fair; mediocre; indifferently.

sot *n.* a habitual drunkard. —**sot′tish,** *adj.*

sot′to vo′ce (sot′tō vō′che) (*It.*) under the breath; softly.

sou (soo) *n.* a Fr. coin of low value, equal to five centimes.

sou·brette′ (soo-bret′) *n.* (*Fr.*) an actress who plays a pert young woman, usu. a servant.

souf·flé′ (soo-flā′) *n.* a fluffy baked dish.

sought (sât) *v.* pret. & p.p. of *seek.*

soul (sōl) *n.* **1,** the spiritual part of man. **2,** emotional feeling. **3,** nobility; courage. **4,** the essential part of anything; a leader. **5,** the personification of a quality. **6,** a human being. **7,** (*Slang*) a unique quality attributed to U.S. blacks, resulting from a combination of racial pride, tradition, and social customs. **8,** [*also*, **soul music**] a popular form of African-American gospel music. —*adj.* (*Slang*) pert. to the usages, customs, and traditions of African-Americans: applied to food, music, etc. —**soul′ful,** *adj.* expressing deep feeling. —**soul brother** or **sister,** (*Slang*) a black; occasionally applied to a person who is not a black who is known to be sympathetic to the black cause. —**soul food,** traditional African-American food.

sound (sownd) *n.* **1,** the sensation produced in the organs of hearing by certain vibrations in the air. **2,** these vibrations; any auditory effect. **3,** the general effect or tone. **4,** a narrow passage of water; an inlet. —*v.i.* **1,** make a sound. **2,** make a particular sound or impression. **3,** measure depth at sea. **4,** seek information. —*v.t.* **1,** cause to make a sound. **2,** utter. **3,** measure the depth of water. **4,** investigate. —*adj.* **1,** in good condition; healthy. **2,** reliable; substantial. **3,** honorable. —**sound′ness,** *n.* —**sound bite,** a short audio segment inserted into a filmed or prerecorded program. —**sounding board, 1,** a thin plate of wood adding resonance. **2,** a sound-reflecting canopy, as over a pulpit. **3,** an agency, device, etc., that serves to spread information, etc. —**sound off, 1,** call out one's name. **2,** (*Slang*) utter complaint, reproof, etc. —**sound track,** that part of a movie film carrying the sound record.

sound′ly (-lė) *adv.* **1,** in a sound state or manner. **2,** completely; thoroughly.

sound′proof″ *adj.* insulating against or resisting the passage of sound.

soup (soop) *n.* **1,** a cooked liquid food. **2,** something thick, as fog. **3,** (*Slang*) any potent liquid, as nitroglycerin. —**soup up,** (*Slang*) make more powerful, as an automobile engine.

---

soup
↔ The French source for this word, *soupe*, originally referred to bread that was soaked in liquid (like English *sop*). The term eventually was transferred to the liquid itself.

---

soup′y (soo′pė) *adj.* like soup; (of fog) thick. **—soup′i·ness,** *n.*

sour (sowr) *adj.* **1,** having an acid or tart taste. **2,** fermented. **3,** unpleasant. **4,** morose in disposition. **5,** excessively acid, as soil. *—v.t. & i.* make or become sour; spoil. **—sour′ness,** *n.***—sour grapes,** a pretense of not wanting something unobtainable.

> **sour grapes**
> ↔ An allusion to the Aesopian fable "The Fox and the Grapes," in which the fox disparaged as sour the grapes that were too high to reach.

source (sôrs) *n.* a place from which something comes; origin. *—v.t.* **1,** to find a source for. **2,** to reveal the source of.

sour·dine′ (sûr-dēn′) *n.* mute.

sour′dough″ *n.* **1,** fermented dough, used in breadmaking. **2,** a seasoned prospector.

sour′puss″ (sowr′pus″) *n.* (*Slang*) a person with a peevish look or disposition.

sou′sa·phone″ (soo′sə-fōn″) *n.* a form of tuba.

> **sousaphone**
> ↔ Named for the conductor who inspired its invention, U.S. bandleader John Philip *Sousa.*

souse (sows) *v.t. & i.* **1,** drench; soak. **2,** pickle. **3,** (*Slang*) intoxicate. *—n.* (*Slang*) a drunkard; a drinking spree.

south (sowth) *n.* **1,** the point of the compass opposite north. **2,** (often *cap.*) [also, **south′land″**] a region in this direction, esp. the former Confederate States. *—adj. & adv.* toward, in, or from the south.

south″east′ *n., adj., & adv.* midway between south and east. **—south″east′er·ly,** *adj. & adv.* **—south″east′ern,** *adj.*

south″east′er *n.* a wind or storm from the southeast.

south′er·ly (su*th*′ər-lē) *adj. & adv.* toward or from the south.

south′ern (su*th*′ərn) *adj.* in or pert. to the south. **—south′ern·er,** *n.* **—southern lights,** aurora australis.

south′paw″ *n. & adj.* (*Slang*) a left-handed person.

south″west′ *n., adj., & adv.* midway between south and west. **—south″west′er·ly,** *adj.* **—south″west′ern,** *adj.*

south″west′er (sowth″-; sow″-) *n.* **1,** a storm from the southwest. **2,** a waterproof hat. **3,** a waterproof oilskin slicker.

sou″ve·nir′ (soo″və-nir′) *n.* **1,** a memento or keepsake. **2,** a memory.

sou·vla′ki (soo-vlä′kė) *n.* shish kebab.

sou′·west′er (sow-wes′ter) *n.* southwester.

sov′er·eign (sov′rin) *n.* **1,** one having supreme power; a monarch. **2,** a Brit. gold coin worth one pound. *—adj.* **1,** having supreme power. **2,** supreme; greatest. **—sov′er·eign·ty,** *n.*

so′vi·et″ (sō′vė-et″) *n.* **1,** in Russia, a council, esp. a town meeting. **2,** (*cap.*) an inhabitant of the former U.S.S.R. *—adj.* pert. to a soviet or (*cap.*) the former U.S.S.R.

sow (sō) *v.t. & i.* **1,** scatter or plant (seed). **2,** scatter seed over (land). **3,** disseminate.

sow (sow) *n.* a female hog.

soy (soi) *n.* a plant or its edible seed (*soybean*). Also, **soy′a** (-ə).

sox (soks) *n.pl.* (*Informal*) socks.

spa (spä) *n.* **1,** a mineral spring. **2,** a health resort.

space (spās) *n.* **1,** the unlimited expanse in all directions in which material objects exist. **2,** a particular portion of this expanse. **3,** enough room. **4,** a blank area. *—v.t.* place a certain distance apart. **—spac′ey,** *adj.* spaced-out. **—space cadet,** (*Slang*) a person out of touch with reality; a flighty person. **—space heater,** a small heater used to heat a relatively small space. **—space shuttle,** a spacecraft designed to enter space and return to earth to be used again. **—space station,** a structure with living spaces, laboratories, etc., placed in permanent orbit in space. **—space suit,** a protective garment worn in space that provides pressurized air for breathing and other life-supporting necessities.

space′craft″ *n.* a vehicle built for travel in space.

spaced-′out′ *adj.* (*Slang*) confused or dazed by or as if by use of drugs; spacey.

space′ship″ *n.* an aircraft that can travel beyond the atmosphere of the earth.

space-′time′ *n.* the four-dimensional continuum in which all things exist.

space′walk″ *n.* activity outside a spacecraft in space.

spa′cious (spā′shəs) *adj.* roomy; broad. **—spa′cious·ness,** *n.*

spade (spād) *n.* **1,** a long-handled tool for digging. **2,** the symbol ♠; a playing card so marked. *—v.t.* dig with a spade.

spa′dix (spā′diks) *n.* a spikelike flower head.

spa·ghet′ti (spə-get′ė) *n.* a cordlike, solid food pasta of Ital. origin. **—spaghetti western,** a western movie made in Italy.

span *n.* **1,** the full extent or stretch of anything; a space of time. **2,** the distance between two supports of a bridge; a bridge. **3**, the distance between thumb and little finger when extended: about 9 inches. **4**, a pair (of horses or other draft animals). —*v.t.* [**spanned, span′ning**] **1**, measure. **2**, extend or reach over.

span′gle (spang′gəl) *n.* a small glittering piece. —*v.t.* decorate with spangles.

span′iel (span′yəl) *n.* any of various hunting or pet dogs.

Span′ish *adj.* of or pert. to Spain, its people, or their language. —*n.* **1**, the language of Spain. **2**, the Spanish people. —**Spanish fly,** a diuretic and aphrodisiac.

spank *v.t.* strike on the buttocks with the open hand; punish. —*n.* a slap. —**spank′- ing,** *adj.* **1**, exceptional. **2**, brisk.

span′ner (span′ər) *n.* (*Brit.*) a wrench.

spar (spär) *n.* **1**, a pole on a mast; a mast. **2**, a part of the frame of an airplane. **3**, any of various lustrous minerals. **4**, (*all caps.*) a member of the women's reserve of the U.S. Coast Guard. —*v.i.* [**sparred, spar′ring**] **1**, box cautiously or for practice. **2**, wrangle; dispute. **3**, fight with spurs, as cocks do.

spare (spār) *v.t. & i.* **1**, show mercy to. **2**, refrain from injuring, using, saying, etc. **3**, dispense with. —*adj.* **1**, in excess; in reserve. **2**, meager. **3**, lean. **4**, frugal. —*n.* an extra or reserve thing, as a tire.

spare′rib″ *n.* an upper pork rib.

spar′ing (spār′ing) *adj.* economical; scanty; restricted.

spark (spärk) *n.* **1**, a fiery particle. **2**, an electrical discharge or arc. **3**, (*Informal*) a suitor. —*v.i. & t.* **1**, produce or issue as sparks. **2**, (*Informal*) court; woo. —**spark plug, 1**, the sparking device in an engine. **2**, (*Slang*) one who encourages or inspires others.

spar′kle (spär′kəl) *v.i.* **1**, emit little sparks. **2**, glitter. **3**, effervesce. **4**, be vivacious. —*n.* scintillation.

spar′kler (spär′klər) *n.* something that sparkles; a gem; a kind of firework.

spar′row (spar′ō) *n.* any of various small birds.

sparse (spärs) *adj.* **1**, thinly distributed. **2**, thin; scanty. —**sparse′ness, spar′si·ty,** *n.*

Spar′tan (spär′tən) *adj.* **1**, simple; unadorned. **2**, strictly disciplined and courageous. —*n.* a person of enduring courage, self-denial, or discipline.

Spartan
↔ From Latin *Spartanus*, Sparta, a city in ancient Greece famous for its discipline.
---

spasm (spaz′əm) *n.* **1**, a sudden, involuntary contraction of the muscles. **2**, a brief burst of activity or feeling.

spas·mod′ic (spaz-mod′ik) *adj.* **1**, pert. to or like a spasm. **2**, violent but intermittent. —**spas·mod′i·cal·ly,** *adv.*

spas′tic (spas′tik) *adj.* characterized by spasms. —*n.* one afflicted with a spastic disease. —**spas′ti·cal·ly,** *adv.*

spat *n.* **1**, a petty dispute. **2**, a light blow. **3**, a splash, as of rain. **4**, (*pl.*) short cloth gaiters. **5**, a young oyster. —*v.i. & t.* [**spat′ted, -ting**] quarrel; strike lightly.

spate (spāt) *n.* a freshet; storm.

spa′tial (spā′shəl) *adj.* pert. to, being, or existing in space.

spat′ter (spat′ər) *v.t. & i.* **1**, scatter or sprinkle in small drops. **2**, a splash. —*n.* a sprinkling.

spat′u·la (spach′ə-lə) *n.* a flat-bladed implement for mixing or spreading. —**spat′u·late** (-lət) *adj.* shaped like a spatula.

spav′in *n.* a diseased condition of the hock of a horse. —**spav′ined,** *adj.*

spawn (spân) *n.* **1**, the eggs of fishes, etc. **2**, offspring. —*v.t. & i.* (esp. of fishes) produce offspring.

spay (spā) *v.t.* remove the ovaries of (a female animal).

speak (spēk) *v.i. & t.* [**spoke, spo′ken, speak′ing**] **1**, utter words; express. **2**, talk; converse. **3**, deliver a public address.

speak′eas″y *n.* (*Slang*) an illegal barroom.

speak′er (-ər) *n.* **1**, one who speaks. **2**, an orator. **3**, a presiding officer, as (*cap.*) of the U.S. House of Representatives. **4**, loudspeaker. —**speak′er·ship″,** *n.*

speak′er·phone″ *n.* a combination microphone and loudspeaker for telephone communication.

speak′ing *adj.* **1**, talking. **2**, lifelike.

spear (spir) *n.* **1**, a long-handled, sharp-headed weapon; any similar instrument. **2**, a blade of grass; a shoot. —*v.t.* **1**, pierce with a spear. **2**, capture. —**spear carrier,** a supernumerary, esp. in an opera production.

spear′head″ *n.* **1**, the sharp point of a spear. **2**, a leader or leading force.

spear′mint″ *n.* the common mint used for flavoring.

spec (spek) *n.* **1**, specification. —**on spec,** made or built in the hope of future sale.

spe′cial (spesh′əl) *adj.* **1**, of a particular kind; being a particular one. **2**, peculiar to a particular person, thing, or purpose. **3**, unusual; exceptional. —*n.* **1**, a special person or thing. **2,** a radio or TV program not appearing regularly. —**Special Olympics,** an athletic competition for children and adults with mental or physical handicaps, modeled on the Olympics.

spe′cial·ist *n.* one who specializes, esp. in a medical field.

spe″ci·al′i·ty (spesh″ė-al′ə-tė) *n.* **1,** a special characteristic; a distinctive feature or quality. **2,** (*pl.*) details; particulars.

spe′cial·ize″ (-īz″) *v.i.* pursue a particular course of study or work. —**spe″cial·i·za′-tion,** *n.*

spe′cial·ty (-tė) *n.* **1,** a particular or preferred item, subject, skill, etc. **2,** a novelty.

spe′cie (spē′shė) *n.* money in the form of coin.

> **specie, species**
> ☞ The second is not the plural of the first, though the two words are both derived from Latin *species,* appearance. *Specie* means coined money; *species* means a kind (or kinds, it being both singular and plural).

spe′cies (spē′shėz) *n.sing. & pl.* **1,** a category of biological classification, lower than a genus. **2,** any class of persons or things. ❑ *specie*

spe′cies·ism (-iz-əm) *n.* discrimination against, or exploitation of, animals by humans.

spe·cif′ic (spə-sif′ik) *adj.* **1,** explicit; definite. **2,** of a particular kind. —*n.* **1,** something specific. **2,** a medicinal remedy. —**spe·cif′i·cal·ly,** *adv.* —**specific gravity,** the density of a substance relative to that of water.

spec″i·fi·ca′tion (spes″ə-fi-kā′shən) *n.* **1,** a statement of particulars, as of dimensions, materials, etc.; a single item in such a statement. **2,** act or result of specifying.

spec′i·fy″ (spes′ə-fī″) *v.t.* **1,** name expressly. **2,** state as a condition.

spec′i·men (spes′ə-mən) *n.* an individual or part used as a typical example of the whole.

spe′cious (spē′shəs) *adj.* apparently, but not actually, sound; deceptive. —**spe″cios′-i·ty** (-os′i-tė) *n.*

speck (spek) *n.* a tiny particle; a spot. —*v.t.* spot.

speck′le (spek′əl) *v.t.* mark with small spots.

spec′ta·cle (spek′tə-kəl) *n.* **1,** a striking sight or view. **2,** a large public display. **3,** (*pl.*) [also, *Informal,* **specs**] eyeglasses.

spec·tac′u·lar (spek-tak′yə-lər) *adj.* impressive; thrilling.

spec′ta·tor (spek′tā-tər) *n.* an onlooker; a witness.

spec′ter (spek′tər) *n.* **1,** a ghost. **2,** a source of terror. Also, **spec′tre.** —**spec′-tral** (-trəl) *adj.*

spec·tro- (spek-trə) *pref.* spectrum.

spec′tro·gram″ *n.* a graph of a spectrum.

spec′tro·graph″ *n.* **1,** a spectroscope designed to graph spectra. **2,** a spectrogram.

spec·trol′o·gy (spek-trol′ə-jė) *n.* the study of spectrums, esp. to determine the constituent elements of bodies. —**spec·trol′o·gist,** *n.*

spec·trom′e·ter (spek-trom′ə-tər) *n.* any of various optical instruments, for measuring wavelength, index of refraction, etc.

spec′tro·scope″ (spek′trə-skōp″) *n.* an instrument for producing the spectrum of any light. —**spec″tro·scop′ic** (-skop′ik) *adj.* —**spec″tro·scop′i·cal·ly,** *adv.*

spec′trum (spek′trəm) *n.* the band of colors formed by dispersed light.

spec′u·late″ (spek′yə-lāt″) *v.i.* **1,** meditate or ponder; reflect. **2,** theorize; conjecture. **3,** make a risky investment. —**spec″u·la′tion,** *n.* —**spec′u·la·tive″** (spek′yə-lə-tiv″) *adj.* —**spec′u·la″tor,** *n.*

speech (spēch) *n.* **1,** the power of speaking. **2,** a particular utterance; an address. **3,** a language. **4,** a manner of speaking. —**speech′less,** *adj.* deprived of speech by emotion, as surprise.

speech′i·fy″ (-ə-fī″) *v.i.* (*Derogatory*) make speeches.

speed (spēd) *n.* **1,** rapidity of motion or performance. **2,** rate of progress or motion. **3,** (*Slang*) any amphetamine, esp. Methedrine. —*v.t.* [*pret. & p.p.* **speed′ed** or **sped**], expedite. **2,** (with *up*) increase the speed of. —*v.i.* **1,** move, etc., with rapidity. **2,** (with *up*) increase speed. —**speed bump,** a low ridge placed crosswise in a road to force drivers to proceed slowly. —**speed′er,** *n.* one who drives at an illegally high speed.

> **speed, velocity**
> Two terms with differing technical senses. *Speed* is the rate of motion of a body; *velocity* is speed in a certain direction. The distinction is not observed in everyday, non-technical use.
> ↔ *Speed* had two senses—the current one, quickness, and a primary sense, now obsolete, success. In *Godspeed* it is the primary sense that is intended.

fat, fāte, fär, fâre, fâll, àsk; met, hē, hėr, maybè; pin, pīne; not, nōte, ôr, tool

speed'boat" *n.* a motorboat built and powered for speed.

speed·om'e·ter (spĕ-dom'i-tər) *n.* a device that indicates the rate of speed of an automobile, etc.

speed'ster (-stər) *n.* **1,** a speeder. **2,** a low two-seated automobile.

speed'way" *n.* a road designed for fast automobile travel or for races.

speed'y *adj.* **1,** rapid. **2,** prompt; not delayed. —**speed'i·ness,** *n.*

spe"le·ol'o·gy (spē"lē-ol'ə-jē) *n.* the scientific study of caves. —**spe·le'an** (spə-lē'ən) *adj.* pert. to caves.

spell (spel) *v.t.* **1,** form or express by or in letters. **2,** (of letters) form or constitute (a word). **3,** (with *out*) make plain. **4,** replace temporarily; relieve. **5,** —*v.i.* form words with the proper letters. —*n.* **1,** a charm; an enchantment. **2,** a turn of work. **3,** a short period. —**spell'er,** *n.* **1,** one who spells. **2,** an elementary spelling textbook.

spell'bind" *v.t.* entrance; fascinate. —**spell'bound",** *adj.*

spell'down" *n.* a spelling bee in which a contestant is eliminated after a certain number of mistakes.

spell'ing *n.* **1,** orthography. **2,** the letters forming a word. —**spelling bee,** a contest in spelling words.

spe·lunk'er (spĕ-lung'kər) *n.* one who explores caves.

spend *v.t.* [*pret. & p.p.* **spent**] **1,** pay or give out (money, etc.). **2,** consume; use up. **3,** employ or while away (time). —*v.i.* pay out money, etc.

spend'thrift" *n. & adj.* an extravagant person; a prodigal.

---

spendthrift
↔ The second half of this word comes from an earlier sense of *thrift,* wealth.

---

spent *adj.* exhausted. —*v.* pret. & p.p. of *spend.*

sperm (spĕrm) *n.* the male reproductive cell: *spermatozoon.* —**sperm oil,** oil from the head of the *sperm whale.*

sper"ma·ce'ti (spĕr"mə-sē'tĕ) *n.* a waxy residue of sperm oil, used in making ointments, cosmetics, etc.

spew (spū) *v.t. & i., & n.* vomit.

sphere (sfir) *n.* **1,** a round solid body; a globe. **2,** a field of knowledge, influence, or activity. —**spher'i·cal** (sfer'i-kəl) *adj.*

sphe'roid (sfir'oid) *n.* the solid generated by rotation of an ellipse. —**sphe·roid'al,** *adj.*

sphinc'ter (sfink'tər) *n.* a ringlike muscle.

sphinx (sfinks) *n.* **1,** a mythical creature, usually half human and half lion. **2,** an enigmatic or inscrutable person.

spice (spīs) *n.* **1,** an aromatic or pungent vegetable substance used for seasoning food. **2,** anything that gives zest or piquancy. —*v.t.* add spice to. —**spic'y,** *adj.*

spick-'and-span' (spik'ən-span') *adj.* **1,** neat. **2,** new and fresh.

spic'ule (spik'ūl) *n.* a small piece of hard material, as bone or rock, esp. one needle-shaped. —**spic'u·late** (-lāt) *adj.*

spi'der (spī'dər) *n.* **1,** an eight-legged arachnid, esp. one that spins a web. **2,** something resembling a spider. **3,** a frying pan, esp. one having short feet. —**spi'der·y,** *adj.*

spiel (spēl) *n.* (*Slang*) a persuasive talk. —**spiel'er,** *n.* a barker.

spiff'y (spif'ē) *adj.* (*Slang*) spruce; smart.

spig'ot (spig'ət) *n.* a faucet.

spike (spīk) *n.* **1,** a large metal nail. **2,** a sharp-pointed projection. **3,** an ear, as of wheat. **4,** (*Volleyball*) a hard smash from close to the net. **5,** a surge of electric power through a circuit. —*v.t.* **1,** pierce with a spike; furnish with spikes. **2,** make useless; frustrate. **3,** (*Slang*) add alcohol or liquor to (a drink). **4,** (*Football*) to slam (the ball) to the ground in the endzone after scoring a touchdown. **5,** (*Volleyball*) smash the ball hard from close to the net. **6,** (*Slang*) to refuse to run a story in a newspaper.

spill (spil) *v.t.* **1,** cause or allow to run or fall out. **2,** shed (blood). **3,** let the wind out (of a sail). **4,** divulge. —*v.i.* run or fall out; overflow. —*n.* **1,** a running out. **2,** (*Informal*) a fall.

spill'way" *n.* an outlet for surplus water.

spilt *adj.* spilled.

spin *v.t.* [**spun, spin'ning**] **1,** draw out and twist into threads, as wool, etc. **2,** make with threads; fabricate. **3,** cause to revolve rapidly. **4,** (with *out*) prolong. —*v.i.* **1,** revolve rapidly. **2,** move, ride, etc., rapidly. —*n.* **1,** a spinning motion; a spiral course. **2,** a rapid ride. **3,** an interpretation put on something. —**spin doctor,** (*Slang*) one who applies his or her own interpretation to the news. —**spinning reel,** a type of fishing reel in which the line is wound on a stationary spool by a metal arm. —**spinning rod,** a rod designed for use with a spinning reel. —**spinning wheel,** a machine once used in the home to spin thread or yarn.

spin'ach (spin'ich) *n.* a vegetable having edible green leaves.

---

spi′nal (spī′nəl) *adj.* of, in, or pert. to the spine. —**spinal column,** the series of vertebrae. —**spinal cord,** the nervous tissue inside the spinal column.

spin′dle (spin′dəl) *n.* a slender pointed rod or pin, esp. one used in spinning. —**spin′dling, spin′dly,** *adj.* tall and slender.

spin′drift″ *n.* a windswept spray.

spine (spīn) *n.* **1,** the backbone. **2,** any bony part, as a quill. **3,** a thorn. —**spine′less,** *adj.* feeble; irresolute.

spin′et (spin′it) *n.* a small piano or harpsichord.

spin′na·ker (spin′ə-kər) *n.* a triangular sail.

spin′ner *n.* **1,** one who or that which spins. **2,** an artificial fly or revolving lure used in angling.

spin-′off″ *n.* **1,** the transfer of a branch of a corporation's activities to a smaller corporation controlled by it. **2,** any product derived from a larger, usu. unrelated, enterprise. **3,** (*Radio & TV*) a program whose characters or other features derive from another program.

spin′ster (spin′stər) *n.* an unmarried woman.

> **spinster**
> ↔ From Middle English *spinnestere,* woman who spins.

spin′y (spī′nē) *adj.* **1,** having or covered with spines. **2,** spinelike. —**spin′i·ness,** *n.*

spi′ra·cle (spī′rə-kəl) *n.* a small aperture; a vent or air hole.

spi·rae′a (spī-rē′ə) *n.* any of various flower-bearing shrubs.

spi′ral (spī′rəl) *n.* **1,** a curve winding around a fixed point and continually receding from it. **2,** a coil; a helix. —*adj.* coiled. —*v.i. & t.* go or cause to go in a spiral or winding course.

spire (spīr) *n.* **1,** an upright structure tapering to a point, as a steeple. **2,** the top. **3,** the shoot of a plant.

spir′it *n.* **1,** the inspiring principle or dominant influence. **2,** soul. **3,** the nature of a person; disposition; attitude. **4,** (often *pl.*) vivacity; optimism. **5,** (*cap.*) in the Trinity, the Holy Spirit. **6,** the essence or real meaning. **7,** a supernatural being; an angel; a fairy; a ghost. **8,** a chemical distillation; (*pl.*) strong distilled alcoholic liquor. —*v.t.* (with *away*) carry off secretly. —**spir′it·ed,** *adj.* full of courage, vigor, etc. —**spir′it·u·ous,** *adj.* alcoholic. —**spirit level,** a level (def. 2) using an air bubble in a glass tube full of liquid.

spir′it·u·al (spir′i-choo-əl) *adj.* **1,** pert. to the soul or spirit. **2,** relating to sacred things. —*n.* a religious song, esp. of African-American origin. —**spir″it·u·al′i·ty,** *n.*

spir′it·u·al·ism *n.* belief in communication with the spirits of the dead. —**spir′it·u·al·ist,** *n.*

spi′ro·graph″ (spī′rə-graf″) *n.* **1,** an instrument for recording movements in breathing. **2,** (*cap., T.N.*) a device for drawing various geometric figures.

spit *v.i. & t.* [**spat** or **spit, spit′ting**] **1,** eject saliva from the mouth. **2,** spew out. **3,** [*pret. & p.p.* **spit′ted**] impale on a sharp stick, etc. —*n.* **1,** saliva. **2,** the image of a person. **3,** a sharp stick or bar. **4,** a narrow point of land. —**spitting image,** (*Informal*) perfect likeness.

spit′ball″ *n.* **1,** a wad of paper chewed and rolled into a ball for use as a missile. **2,** (*Baseball*) a curve pitched by moistening the ball with saliva (now against the rules).

spite (spīt) *n.* ill will; malevolence. —*v.t.* thwart. —**spite′ful,** *adj.* malicious. —**in spite of,** notwithstanding.

spit′fire″ *n.* **1,** a hot-tempered person. **2,** (*cap.*) a Brit. fighter plane.

spit′tle (-əl) *n.* **1,** saliva. **2,** a frothy insect secretion.

spit·toon′ (spi-toon′) *n.* a cuspidor.

spitz (spits) *n.* any of several types of dog having pointed ears and a stocky body, as the Pomeranian.

splash *v.t.* **1,** spatter, as with water or mud. **2,** dash or throw about (water, etc.). —*v.i.* spatter water, or in water. —*n.* **1,** the act or sound of splashing. **2,** a quantity splashed. **3,** an ostentatious display. —**splash′y,** *adj.*

splash-′down″ *n.* the return landing of a spacecraft or missile on the water; hence, any landing on water.

splat *n.* the center upright member of the back of a chair.

splat′ter (splat′ər) *v.t. & i.* splash.

splay (splā) *v.i. & t.* spread out. —*adj.* spread out; turned outward; awkward. —**splay′foot″,** *n.*

spleen (splēn) *n.* **1,** an organ in the abdomen in which the blood is modified. **2,** ill humor; melancholy. **3,** anger; malice. —**splen′ic** (-ik), **sple·net′ic** (spli-net′ik) *adj.*

splen′did *adj.* excellent; admirable; grand.

splen·dif′er·ous (splen-dif′ə-rəs) *adj.* (*Informal*) extremely gorgeous or sumptuous.

splen′dor (splen′dər) *n.* brilliant luster;

magnificence; grandeur. Also, **splen′dour.**
—**splen′dor·ous,** *adj.*

splice (splīs) *v.t.* join together, as two ropes, genes, etc. —*n.* a joint of ropes.

spline (splīn) *n.* a thin strip of wood.

splint *n.* **1,** a thin piece of wood, etc., used to immobilize a fractured bone. **2,** a thin strip for weaving a basket, etc.

splin′ter (splin′tər) *n.* a sharp, thin, split-off piece of wood, bone, etc. —*v.t. & i.* break into splinters.

split *v.t. & i.* [**split, split′ting**] **1,** rend or cleave lengthwise. **2,** burst asunder. **3,** divide; disunite. **4,** (*Slang*) leave; depart. —*n.* **1,** a crack or rent. **2,** a division; a schism. **3,** a split willow twig. **4,** (*Informal*) a bottle of half the usual size. —*adj.* divided; cleft. —**split′ting,** *adj.* extreme; severe, as a headache. —**split infinitive,** (*Gram.*) an expression in which a word is placed between the *to* of an infinitive and the verb: *to fully understand.* ❑ *schizophrenia*

split-′lev″el *adj.* having two levels, one higher than, and adjacent to, the other.

splotch (sploch) *n.* a large, ill-defined spot. —*v.t.* blot.

splurge (splėrj) *n.* an extravagant display or expenditure. —*v.i.* spend extravagantly or ostentatiously.

splut′ter (splut′ər) *v.i. & t.* talk or utter incoherently; sputter.

spoil *v.t.* **1,** seriously impair. **2,** overindulge, as a child. **3,** plunder; despoil. —*v.i.* decay; become tainted. —*n.* (*pl.*) plunder. —**spoil′age,** *n.*

> **spoil, despoil**
> ↔ These two words have a common origin in Latin *spoliare,* strip of possessions. The sense of *spoil* modified during the 16th c. to its present usage.

spoil′er *n.* a hinged flap on an airplane wing used to regulate lift.

spoil′sport″ *n.* one who spoils the pleasure or enjoyment of others.

spoke (spōk) *n.* one of the bars joining the hub and rim of a wheel. —*v.* pret. of *speak.*

spo′ken (spō′kən) *v.* p.p. of *speak.* —*adj.* oral, not written.

spokes′man (spōks′mən) [*pl.* **-men**], **spokes′wom″an, spokes′per″son** *n.* one who speaks for others.

spo″li·ate″ (spō′lė-āt″) *v.t.* despoil; plunder. —**spo″li·a′tion,** *n.*

spon′dee (spon′dė) *n.* a poetic foot comprising two long syllables. —**spon·da′ic** (-dā′ik) *adj.*

sponge (spunj) *n.* **1,** a marine invertebrate; its dried, absorbent framework. **2,** any similar absorbent substance. **3,** (*Informal*) a parasitical person. —*v.t. & i.* **1,** wipe with a sponge. **2,** (*Informal*) live at the expense of another. —**spon′gy,** *adj.* —**sponge cake,** a light cake made without shortening.

spon′sor (spon′sər) *n.* **1,** one who vouches for another; a godparent. **2,** a buyer of radio or television time. —*v.t.* vouch for; be a patron of. —**spon′sor·ship,** *n.*

> **sponsor, spouse**
> ↔ Both words derive from Latin *spondere,* to promise solemnly, and both refer to persons who have made solemn promises to others.

spon″ta·ne′i·ty (spon″tə-nē′ə-tė) *n.* natural, impulsive action; spontaneousness.

spon·ta′ne·ous (spon-tā′nė-əs) *adj.* **1,** proceeding from internal impulse. **2,** arising naturally; instinctive. —**spon·ta′ne·ous·ness,** *n.* —**spontaneous combustion,** a burning ignited by the heat of internal chemical action.

spoof *v.t. & i., & n.* (*Slang*) hoax; tease.

> **spoof**
> ↔ From *Spoof,* a hoaxing game invented by British comedian Arthur Roberts.

spook *n.* **1,** (*Informal*) a ghost. **2,** (*Slang*) a spy. —*v.t. & i.* frighten. —**spook′y,** *adj.* —**spook′iness,** *n.*

spool *n.* a small cylinder on which thread, wire, etc. are wound.

spoon *n.* **1,** a utensil consisting of a concave bowl and a handle. **2,** any implement or object resembling this. **3,** a wooden-faced golf club (No. 3 wood). —*v.t. & i.* **1,** convey in a spoon. **2,** (*Informal*) pet; make love. —**spoon′ful** (-fûl) *n.* [*pl.* **-fuls**].

spoon′bill″ *n.* any of various wading birds, as the shovelbill.

spoo′ner·ism″ (spoo′nər-iz″əm) *n.* a slip of the tongue in which sounds are transposed.

> **spoonerism**
> ↔ After 19th-c. English clergyman William *Spooner,* who apparently had the habit of reversing the initial letters of words.

spoon-′fed″ *adj.* **1,** given food with a spoon, as a child. **2,** pampered. —**spoon′-feed″,** *v.t.*

spoor (spûr) *n.* the track or trail of a wild animal.

spo·rad'ic (spô-rad'ik) *adj.* appearing at irregular intervals; occasional. **—spo·rad'-i·cal·ly,** *adv.*

spore (spôr) *n.* a germ; a seed; a source of being.

spor'ran (spor'ən) *n.* a large purse worn suspended from the belt by Scottish highlanders.

sport (spôrt) *n.* **1,** an outdoor or athletic pastime. **2,** fun; diversion. **3,** jesting; a subject of diversion. **4,** (*Informal*) a sportsmanlike person; a sporting man. *—v.t.* (*Informal*) display ostentatiously. *—v.i.* play; frolic. ❑ *game*

sport'ing *adj.* **1,** relating to outdoor pastimes. **2,** sportsmanlike. **3,** pert. to gambling. **—sporting house,** house of prostitution.

spor'tive (spôr'tiv) *adj.* frolicsome; jesting. **—spor'tive·ness,** *n.*

sports'cast" *n.* a broadcast of a sporting event. **—sports'cast"er,** *n.*

sports'man (-mən) [*pl.* **-men**], **sports'-wom"an** *n.* **1,** one who engages in field sports. **2,** a fair contestant. **—sports'-man·like",** *adj.* having the qualities of a sportsman, as courteous, fair, etc. **—sports'-man·ship",** *n.* fair play.

sports'wear" *n.* clothes for engaging in or attending sporting events.

sport'y (spôr'tē) *adj.* **1,** sporting. **2,** flashy. **—sport'i·ness,** *n.*

spot *n.* **1,** a stain; a blemish. **2,** a small mark; a speck. **3,** a place; a site. *—v.t.* [**spot'ted, -ting**] **1,** stain; mark with spots. **2,** note; recognize. **3,** place. **4,** (*Informal*) give a handicap of or to. *—v.i.* become spotted. **—on the spot, 1,** handy. **2,** in an embarrassing position.

spot'less *adj.* unsullied; clean.

spot'light" *n.* **1,** a device, often movable, that focuses brilliant light on a small area. **2,** the center of attraction.

spot'ter (-ər) *n.* one who watches and locates.

spot'ty (-ē) *adj.* occurring in spots; irregular. **—spot'ti·ness,** *n.*

spouse (spows) *n.* one's husband or wife. ❑ *sponsor*

spout (spowt) *v.t. & i.* **1,** discharge or issue forth, in a stream. **2,** utter or declaim volubly. *—n.* a tube or opening that guides a flow.

sprain (sprān) *n.* a violent straining of muscles and ligaments.

sprang *v.* pret. of *spring.*

sprat *n.* a small European herring.

sprawl (sprâl) *v.i. & t.* **1,** be stretched out carelessly; be spread out aimlessly. **2,** scramble. *—n.* a sprawling posture.

---

sprain, strain
☞ Both words have to do with injury caused by exertion, but *sprain* is more specific; it refers to an injury to the ligaments of a joint. *Strain* can be a synonym for *sprain*, but has many other senses.

---

spray (sprā) *n.* **1,** finely divided water or other liquid blown by air. **2,** an atomizer. **3,** a branch of a tree or of a flowering plant; a similar ornament or design. *—v.t. & i.* scatter or apply as a spray. **—spray gun,** a pistol-shaped device for spraying paint.

spread (spred) *v.t. & i.* [*pret. & p.p.* **spread**] **1,** stretch out; unfold. **2,** flatten out in a sheet; distribute evenly. **3,** set out; display. **4,** disperse; scatter; disseminate. **5,** extend. **6,** push apart. *—n.* **1,** extension or expansion. **2,** an expanse. **3,** a feast; a spread food, as jam. **4,** a coverlet. **5,** [*also,* **point spread**] a method for gambling on sporting events based on the expected difference in scores between competitors. **—spread'er,** *n.*

spread-'ea"gle *adj.* **1,** sprawling. **2,** (*Informal*) boastful or bombastic. *—v.t.* stretch out; send sprawling.

spread'sheet" a mathematical worksheet arranged in columns and rows; a computer program emulating such a worksheet.

spree (sprē) *n.* a lively frolic.

sprig *n.* a small branch; a shoot.

spright'ly (sprīt'lē) *adj. & adv.* lively; animated. **—spright'li·ness,** *n.*

spring *v.i.* [**sprang, sprung, spring'ing**] **1,** leap. **2,** rise up or issue forth suddenly. **3,** recoil; warp. *—v.t.* **1,** cause to leap or rise. **2,** disclose or produce suddenly. **3,** release the spring of, as a trap; (*Slang*) provide bail for. *—n.* **1,** a leap. **2,** (often *cap.*) the vernal season, in No. Amer. approx. March 21 to June 21. **3,** the beginning or freshest time of anything. **4,** water rising to the surface of the earth. **5,** any source of supply. **6,** an elastic strip of steel or spiral wire. **7,** elasticity; motive power. **8,** a split; a warp. **—spring chicken,** a young, naïve person, esp. a woman. **—spring fever,** a lazy feeling that comes with spring weather.

spring'board" *n.* a diving board.

spring'bok *n.* a So. Afr. gazelle.

spring'er *n.* a spaniel used in hunting.

spring'time" *n.* the spring.

---

spring'y *adj.* resilient; elastic; agile. —**spring'i·ness,** *n.*

sprin'kle (spring'kəl) *v.t.* **1,** scatter in drops or particles. **2,** bespatter. **3,** distribute; diversify. —*v.i.* rain slightly. —*n.* a light rain; a spray. —**sprin'kler,** *n.* a device for sprinkling water. —**sprin'kling,** *n.* a small scattered amount.

sprint *n.* a short run at full speed. —*v.i.* run at full speed.

sprit *n.* a small spar that crosses a sail diagonally.

sprite (sprīt) *n.* **1,** an elf; a fairy. **2,** (*Computers*) a moving element in a graphic display.

spritz'er (sprit'sər) *n.* a drink of wine and soda water.

sprock'et (sprok'it) *n.* a projection on a wheel that engages a chain or a hole.

sprout (sprowt) *v.i. & t.* **1,** begin to grow. **2,** put forth shoots. —*n.* a shoot or bud.

spruce (sproos) *adj.* trim and neat in appearance. —*v.t. & i.* (with *up*) make neat. —*n.* a coniferous evergreen tree; its wood.

> **spruce**
> ↔ *Spruce* was the Old English word for Prussia, from Medieval Latin *Prussia*. The wood came originally from that country. The sense of dapper refers to the obsolete phrase *spruce leather*, leather from Prussia.

sprung *v.* p.p. of *spring.*

spry (sprī) *adj.* nimble; lively. —**spry'ness,** *n.*

spud *n.* **1,** a small-bladed spade or chisel. **2,** (*Informal*) a potato.

spume (spūm) *v.t. & i., & n.* foam; froth.

spu·mo'ne (spoo-mō'nè) *n.* (*It.*) ice cream containing chopped fruit or nuts.

spun *v.* pret. & p.p. of *spin.*

spunk *n.* **1,** (*Informal*) mettle; pluck. **2,** tinder. —**spunk'y,** *adj.* bold; courageous.

spur (spėr) *n.* **1,** a pointed instrument worn on the heel, to goad a horse; any similar projection. **2,** an incentive. **3,** a short ridge, a railroad track, etc., branching from a main line. —*v.t.* [**spurred, spur'ring**] goad; incite. —*v.i.* press forward; hasten.

spu'ri·ous (spyûr'ē-əs) *adj.* not genuine or authentic; counterfeit. —**spu'ri·ous·ness,** *n.*

spurn (spėrn) *v.t.* **1,** reject with disdain. **2,** kick.

spurt (spėrt) *n.* **1,** a forcible gush of liquid. **2,** a short, sudden effort. —*v.i. & t.* gush or advance suddenly.

sput'nik *n.* (*Russ.*) artificial satellite, esp. one launched by the former U.S.S.R.

sput'ter (sput'ər) *v.i. & t.* **1,** spit out or emit small particles explosively. **2,** speak or utter explosively and incoherently. —*n.* an act or result of sputtering.

spu'tum (spū'təm) *n.* [*pl.* **-ta** (-tə)] spittle, esp. when mixed with mucus.

spy (spī) *n.* **1,** a secret watcher. **2,** a secret agent in enemy territory. —*v.i.* observe secretly. —*v.t.* **1,** (with *on*) observe secretly. **2,** (with *out*) discover by observation. **3,** catch sight of; see.

spy'glass *n.* a hand telescope.

squab (skwob) *n.* a young, unfledged pigeon. —**squab'by,** *adj.* short and stout.

squab'ble (skwob'əl) *n.* a petty quarrel. —*v.i.* bicker.

squad (skwod) *n.* a small party or group, esp. of soldiers. —**squad car,** a cruising police car.

squad'ron (skwod'rən) *n.* an operating unit of warships, cavalry, aircraft, etc.

squal'id (skwol'id) *adj.* dirty; filthy; degraded. —**squal'id·ness,** *n.*

squall (skwâl) *n.* **1,** a sudden, violent gust of wind. **2,** (*Informal*) a commotion. **3,** a scream or cry. —*v.i.* cry violently. —**squall'y,** *n.*

squal'or (skwol'ər; skwā'lər) *n.* filthy and depressed condition.

squan'der (skwon'dər) *v.t.* spend wastefully; dissipate.

square (skwār) *n.* **1,** a plane figure having four equal sides and four right angles. **2,** an open area in a city. **3,** a city block. **4,** an instrument for determining right angles. **5,** the result obtained by multiplying a number by itself. —*adj.* **1,** like a square; at right angles. **2,** straight, level, or even. **3,** equitable; honest. **4,** unequivocal. **5,** satisfying, as a meal. —*v.t.* **1,** make square. **2,** adjust; true. **3,** settle (a debt). —*v.i.* **1,** agree (with). **2,** (with *off*) prepare to box. —**square dance,** one for four or more couples. —**square deal,** (*Informal*) a mutually honest transaction. —**square knot,** a secure but easily untied knot formed of two interlocking half loops. —**square root,** the number of which a given number is the square. —**square shooter,** (*Informal*) an honest person.

square-'rigged *adj.* designating a vessel having square principal sails.

squash (skwosh) *v.t.* **1,** press into pulp; crush. **2,** (*Informal*) suppress; silence. —*v.i.* **1,** be crushed. **2,** make a splashing sound. —*n.* **1,** the act or sound of squashing. **2,** a game played with rackets in a walled court: *squash rackets.* **3,** a trailing plant of the melon family; its green or yellow fruit, used as a vegetable. —**squash′y,** *adj.* soft and wet; easily crushed.

squat (skwot) *v.i.* [**squat′ted, -ting**] **1,** sit close to the ground; crouch. **2,** settle on public land. —*adj.* [**squat′ter, -test**] short and thick. —*n.* a squatting posture. —**squat′ter,** *n.*

squaw (skwâ) *n.* (often *Offensive*) a Native American woman, esp. a wife.

squawk (skwâk) *v.i.* **1,** make a loud, harsh outcry. **2,** (*Informal*) complain loudly. —*n.* act of squawking.

squeak (skwēk) *n.* **1,** a short, sharp, shrill sound. **2,** (*Informal*) a narrow escape; a close thing. —*v.t. & i.* make a squeaking sound.

squeal (skwēl) *n.* **1,** a prolonged shrill cry. **2,** (*Slang*) the act of an informer. —*v.t. & i.* utter a squeal. —*v.i.* (often with *on*) (*Slang*) inform (on someone). —**squeal rule,** (*Informal*) a proposed law requiring clinics to inform parents of contraceptive devices sought by their children.

squeam′ish (skwē′mish) *adj.* easily nauseated; fastidious; prudish.

squee′gee (skwē′jē) *n.* a rubber blade for wiping water from panes.

squeeze (skwēz) *v.t.* **1,** exert pressure upon; compress; force; cram. **2,** express; extract. —*v.i.* press; push. —*n.* **1,** the act of squeezing. **2,** a handshake; a hug; an embrace. **3,** (*Informal*) a predicament.

squelch (skwelch) *v.t.* suppress. —*n.* (*Informal*) a crushing remark.

squib (skwib) *n.* **1,** a short, satirical writing. **2,** a firecracker. —*v.t. & i.* write or assail with a squib.

squid (skwid) *n.* a sea mollusk having ten arms with sucking disks.

squig′gle (skwig′əl) *n.* a wriggly line or scrawl. —*v.i.* wriggle and squirm.

squint (skwint) *v.i.* look askance, obliquely, or with narrowed eyes.

squire (skwīr) *n.* **1,** a landed proprietor. **2,** a lady's escort. **3,** an attendant. **4,** a justice of the peace. —*v.t.* attend; escort.

squirm (skwērm) *v.i.* **1,** wriggle. **2,** writhe mentally. —*n.* a wriggle.

squir′rel (skwėr′əl) *n.* a bushy-tailed, arboreal rodent.

squirt (skwėrt) *v.t. & i.* eject or issue suddenly in a thin stream. —*n.* **1,** a thin stream of water, etc. **2,** (*Informal*) a small, insignificant fellow.

SST supersonic transport.

stab *v.t. & i.* [**stabbed, stab′bing**] **1,** pierce with, or thrust with, a pointed weapon. **2,** betray. —*n.* act of stabbing; a thrust or wound.

sta′bile (stā′bəl) *adj.* fixed in position; stationary.

sta·bil′i·ty (stə-bil′ə-tē) *n.* firmness; permanence.

sta′bi·lize″ (stā′bə-līz″) *v.t.* make stable; steady. —**sta″bi·li·za′tion,** *n.*

sta′ble (stā′bəl) *n.* **1,** a building for horses, cattle, etc. **2,** a collection of racing horses. —*adj.* **1,** firmly fixed; steady. **2,** not changing or wavering. —*v.t.* lodge in a stable.

stac·ca′to (stə-kä′tō) *adj.* (*It., Music*) **1,** abrupt. **2,** separated by slight pauses.

stack (stak) *n.* **1,** an orderly pile or heap. **2,** a chimney or funnel. **3,** (*pl.*) bookshelves. —*v.t.* **1,** pile in a stack. **2,** prearrange, esp. (of cards) dishonestly.

sta′di·um (stā′dē-əm) *n.* a structure of tiers of seats enclosing an athletic field.

> **stadium**
> ↔ From Greek *stadion*, the racetrack at Olympia or its length. The English derivative (through Latin) was originally a unit of measurement.

staff (staf) *n.* **1,** a stick or pole; a cane. **2,** a body of workers or assistants. **3,** the lines and spaces on which musical notes are written. —*v.t.* provide with a staff. —**staff′er,** *n.* (*Informal*) a member of a staff.

stag *n.* **1,** an adult male deer. **2,** (*Informal*) a man not accompanied by a woman. —*adj.* (*Informal*) for men only.

stage (stāj) *n.* **1,** a single time, period, or step of a gradual process. **2,** a raised platform, esp. in a theater. **3,** the theatrical profession; drama. **4,** a station for changing horses. —*v.t.* exhibit on a stage. —**stage fright,** nervousness caused by public appearance. —**stage whisper,** a whisper intended to be overheard.

stage′coach″ *n.* a horse-drawn public passenger coach.

stage′hand″ *n.* a worker who handles the sets, etc., in a theater.

stage-′struck″ *adj.* obsessed with a desire to perform before an audience.

stag′fla′tion (-flā′shən) *n.* (*Informal*) combined recession and inflation.

stag′ger (stag′ər) *v.i.* move unsteadily; falter. —*v.t.* **1,** cause to falter; shock. **2,** arrange in a zigzag order. —*n.* **1,** an unsteady movement. **2,** (*pl.*) a cerebral and spinal disease of horses, etc.

stag′ing (stā′jing) *n.* **1,** the act of putting a play, etc., on a stage. **2,** scaffolding.

stag′nant (stag′nənt) *adj.* not moving; stagnating. —**stag′nan·cy,** *n.*

stag′nate (stag′nāt) *v.i.* **1,** cease to run or flow; lose freshness. **2,** be or become inactive. —**stag·na′tion,** *n.*

stag′y (stā′jė) *adj.* theatrical. —**stag′i·ness,** *n.*

staid (stād) *adj.* sober and sedate; not flighty. —**staid′ness,** *n.*

stain (stān) *n.* **1,** a discoloration. **2,** a blot; a taint. **3,** a liquid for coloring wood. —*v.t. & i.* discolor. —**stainless steel,** an alloy of steel with chrome, nickel, etc., to inhibit rusting.

stair (stâr) *n.* **1,** a step, or series of steps, rising to a higher level. **2,** (*pl.*) such steps collectively.

stair′case″ *n.* a flight of stairs. Also, **stair′way″.**

stair′well″ *n.* a vertical opening containing a staircase.

stake (stāk) *n.* **1,** a pointed stick or post. **2,** money wagered; (*Informal*) capital. **3,** that which is risked or to be gained. —*v.t.* **1,** mark, support, etc., with stakes. **2,** hazard or wager. —**stake out,** keep under surveillance.

stake′out″ *n.* a concealed location for surveillance, usu. used by police.

sta·lac′tite (stə-lak′tīt) *n.* a calcium deposit hanging from the roof of a cave.

> **stalactite, stalagmite**
> ↔ The *stalactite* starts at the top and grows downward (etymologically, it means "something that drips"); the *stalagmite* starts at the bottom and grows up (its source meaning is "something dropped").

stal′ag *n.* (*Ger.*) a German prisoner-of-war camp.

sta·lag′mite (stə-lag′mīt) *n.* a formation similar to a stalactite, but rising from the floor. ❏ *stalactite*

stale (stāl) *adj.* **1,** not fresh. **2,** trite. **3,** physically overtrained. —*v.t. & i.* make or become stale. —**stale′ness,** *n.*

stale′mate″ *n.* a deadlocked situation. —*v.t.* deadlock; thwart.

stalk (stâk) *v.i.* **1,** walk with slow, dignified strides. **2,** approach game stealthily. —*v.t.* approach stealthily. —*n.* **1,** an act of stalking. **2,** the principal stem or support, esp. of a plant. —**stalk′y,** *adj.* tall and thin.

stall (stâl) *n.* **1,** a compartment, esp. one for an animal in a stable; a booth; a seat or pew. **2,** a state of arrested operation or motion. **3,** (*Informal*) a delaying pretext.

—*v.t. & i.* **1,** cause to stick or stop. **2,** (*Informal*) evade; delay.

stal′lion (stal′yən) *n.* a male horse kept for breeding.

stal′wart (stâl′wərt) *adj.* strong and brave. —*n.* a stalwart person.

sta′men (stā′mən) *n.* the pollen-bearing organ of a plant.

stam′i·na (stam′ə-nə) *n.* lasting strength; endurance.

> **stamina**
> ↔ *Stamina* is the plural of Latin *stamen*, the male reproductive organ of a flower, thus the metaphorical sense of life-giving force or vigor.

stam′mer (stam′ər) *v.i. & t.* speak or utter with involuntary breaks and repetitions. —*n.* a stammering.

> **stammer, stutter**
> ☞ These two speech defects are slightly different. A *stammer* is characterized by hesitations and stops; a *stutter* by repetition of consonants.

stamp *v.t.* **1,** crush or pound; strike the foot down on. **2,** impress; seal. **3,** characterize. **4,** affix a stamp on. —*v.i.* strike the foot down; walk heavily. —*n.* **1,** a downward thrust of the foot. **2,** a device for stamping; a die. **3,** a mark; a seal; a piece of adhesive paper, as postage. —**stamp′ing ground,** a place one frequents.

stam·pede′ (stam-pēd′) *n.* a concerted, panic-stricken rush. —*v.i. & t.* move in a stampede.

stance (stans) *n.* posture; (*Golf*) the position of the feet.

stanch (stänch) *v.t.* stop the flow of a liquid, esp. blood. —*adj.* **1,** firm. **2,** trustworthy; loyal. **3,** watertight, as a ship. Also, **staunch.** —**stanch′ness,** *n.*

stan′chion (stan′shən) *n.* a post or pillar.

stand *v.i.* [*pret. & p.p.* **stood** (stůd)] **1,** be in or assume an upright position. **2,** be stagnant; stop. **3,** be situated. **4,** continue. **5,** (with *for*) be representative. **6,** move (back, aside, etc.). —*v.t.* **1,** set upright. **2,** (with *for*) tolerate. **3,** endure. **4,** (with *by*) support; abide by. —*n.* **1,** an act of standing. **2,** a determined position. **3,** a structure, platform, or piece of furniture; a grandstand, etc. **4,** a growth, as of grain. —**stand down,** withdraw. —**stand pat,** decline to change.

stan′dard (stan′dərd) *n.* **1,** a basis of comparison; a criterion; measure. **2,** a flag or emblem. **3,** something upright or standing. —*adj.* serving as a basis of comparison.

stan'dard·ize" (-īz") *v.t.* make uniform. **—stan"dard·i·za'tion,** *n.*

stand'by" *n.* a reliable supporter or resource.

stand'ee *n.* (*Informal*) one who stands, as at a theatrical performance.

stand-'in" *n.* a temporary substitute for a motion-picture actor, etc.

stand'ing *n.* **1,** rank; reputation. **2,** length of experience, etc. —*adj.* **1,** upright. **2,** continuing; permanent.

stand'off" *n.* **1,** a state of being evenly matched. **2,** a tie. **—stand·off'ish,** *adj.* aloof.

stand'out" *n.* something conspicuous, esp. for excellence.

stand'pipe" *n.* a large vertical pipe or water tower.

stand'point" *n.* point of view.

stand'still" *n.* a halt.

stan'za (stan'zə) *n.* a unit, several lines, of a poem or song.

staph'y·lo·coc"cus (staf'ə-lə-kok"əs) *n.* [*pl.* **-coc"ci** (-kok"sī)] a parasitic bacterium. Also, *Informal,* **staph.**

sta'ple (stā'pəl) *n.* **1,** a loop of wire, driven as a nail or fastener. **2,** a principal commodity. **3,** a raw material. —*adj.* chief or principal, as commodities; basic. —*v.t.* fasten with staples. **—sta'pler,** *n.* a device for driving staples.

star (stär) *n.* **1,** a body in space, esp. one outside the solar system; a sun. **2,** a figure (★) representing this. **3,** an asterisk (*). **4,** a distinguished or leading performer. —*v.t. & i.* [**starred, star'ring**] **1,** mark with a star. **2,** feature. —*adj.* brilliant; leading. **—star'dom,** *n.* **—star chamber,** a severe and arbitrary court.

star'board (stär'bərd) *n., adj. & adv.* (*Naut.*) the right side, as one faces the bow of a vessel.

starch (stärch) *n.* **1,** a carbohydrate occurring in cereals, potatoes, etc.; this substance prepared for stiffening, etc. **2,** formality. —*v.t.* stiffen with starch.

starch'y (stär'chė) *adj.* **1,** full of starch. **2,** (*Informal*) formal in manner. **—starch'i·ness,** *n.*

stare (stär) *v.i. & t.* gaze steadily and fixedly. —*n.* a steady gaze.

star'fish" *n.* a star-shaped sea animal.

star'gaz"er *n.* an idle dreamer. **—star'-gaze",** *v.i.*

stark (stärk) *adj.* **1,** sheer; downright. **2,** rigid. **3,** desolate; naked. —*adv.* entirely; absolutely. **—stark'ness,** *n.*

star'let (stär'lət) *n.* a young motion picture actress.

star'light" *n.* light from the stars, or a time when stars can be seen.

star'ling (stär'ling) *n.* any of various birds.

star'ry (-ė) *adj.* sparkling with, or as with, stars. **—star'ri·ness,** *n.*

Stars and Stripes the flag of the U.S.A.

star-'span'gled *adj.* dotted with stars. **—the Star-Spangled Banner,** the U.S. flag or the U.S. national anthem.

start (stärt) *v.i.* **1,** begin or enter upon an action, etc.; set out. **2,** make a sudden involuntary move; jerk. —*v.t.* originate; set in motion; establish; begin. —*n.* **1,** a beginning; the outset. **2,** a lead. **3,** a twitch; a jerk.

star'tle (stär'təl) *v.t.* surprise; alarm; shock. **—star'tling,** *adj.*

star·va'tion (stär-vā'shən) *n.* act or process of starving; famishment.

starve (stärv) *v.i.* **1,** die of hunger. **2,** suffer from hunger or want. —*v.t.* cause to starve.

starve'ling *adj.* **1,** starving. **2,** emaciated. **3,** meager, as in supply. —*n.* someone or something that is starved.

stash *v.t.* (*Slang*) put away; hide. —*n.* a place where something is hidden; something hidden.

stat *n.* (*Informal*) **1,** photostat. **2,** statistic.

-stat *suf.* **1,** stationary. **2,** a device for various purposes. **3,** an agent that inhibits growth.

state (stāt) *n.* **1,** mode or form of existence; position; situation; condition; structure. **2,** dignity; ceremony; great style. **3,** the whole people; a nation; a civil community, esp. (often *cap.*) one of the states of the U.S. —*adj.* **1,** pert. to civil government. **2,** pert. to a state of the U.S. **3,** ceremonious. —*v.t.* declare. **—state'hood,** *n.* **—state of the art,** as advanced as permitted by current technology.

stat'ed (stā'tid) *adj.* **1,** settled. **2,** explicit.

state'house" *n.* a state capitol.

state'ly (-lė) *adj.* majestic; dignified. **—state'li·ness,** *n.*

state'ment (-mənt) *n.* **1,** a spoken or written declaration. **2,** an accounting.

state'room" *n.* a private room on a train or ship.

state'side" *adj. & adv.* in or toward the United States.

states'man (-mən) [*pl.* **-men**], **states'wom"an** *n.* a leader in government. **—states'man·ship,** *n.*

stat'ic (stat'ik) *adj.* **1,** fixed; stationary; stagnant. **2,** pert. to a stationary charge of electricity. **3,** (*Radio & TV*) pert. to atmospheric electrical interference. —*n.* (*Radio & TV*) static interference. —**stat′i·cal·ly,** *adv.*

sta′tion (stā′shən) *n.* **1,** an assigned place or position. **2,** a headquarters. **3,** standing. —*v.t.* assign; place. —**station break,** a break in programming during which a radio or TV station identifies itself, and often commercials are presented. —**station house,** a police station. —**station wagon,** a large automobile designed to carry both passengers and baggage.

sta′tion·ar″y (stā′shə-ner″ē) *adj.* not moving; fixed; not changing.

---

stationary, stationery

☛ Do not confuse the *a* version, *stationary*, meaning not moving, and the *e* version, *stationery*, meaning writing materials. ↔ The *e* version derives from Medieval Latin *stationarius*, a trader who maintained a permanent stall, and frequently these traders were booksellers.

---

sta′tion·er (stā′shə-nər) *n.* a dealer in stationery.

sta′tion·er·y (stā′shə-ner″ē) *n.* writing materials, esp. paper. ❏ *stationary*

sta′tion·mas″ter *n.* a person in charge of a railroad station.

sta·tis′tics (stə-tis′tiks) *n.sing.* **1,** the science of collecting and interpreting numerical data. **2,** (constr. as *pl.*) the data. —**sta·tis′ti·cal,** *adj.* —**stat″is·ti′cian** (stat″is-tish′ən) *n.*

stat′u·ar·y (stach′oo-er-ē) *n.* statues collectively.

. **stat′ue** (stach′oo) *n.* a carved or molded figure, esp. of a person.

stat″u·esque′ (stach″oo-esk′) *adj.* of dignified bodily form and posture.

stat′u·ette″ (stach′oo-et″) *n.* a small statue.

stat′ure (stach′ər) *n.* **1,** a person's natural height. **2,** elevation; standing.

sta′tus (stā′təs; stat′əs) *n.* **1,** relative standing. **2,** position; condition.

sta′tus quo (kwō) (*Lat.*, state in which [things were]) the existing state or condition.

stat′ute (stach′ût) *n.* an ordinance or law. —**stat′u·to·ry,** *adj.*

staunch (stânch) *adj.* stanch.

stave (stāv) *n.* **1,** a pale or piece of wood, esp. for the side of a barrel. **2,** a stanza. **3,** (*Music*) a staff. —*v.t.* **1,** (with *in*) crush in; break. **2,** (with *off*) avert; keep off.

stay (stā) *v.i.* **1,** remain. **2,** hold out; per-

severe. **3,** stop; pause; linger. —*v.t.* **1,** halt; restrain. **2,** suspend; delay. **3,** prop up; support. —*n.* **1,** a pause or halt; indefinite sojourn. **2,** a stoppage or suspension. **3,** a prop. **4,** (*pl.*) a corset. **5,** (*Naut.*) a guy rope or wire.

stead (sted) *n.* place.

stead′fast″ *adj.* firm; resolute. —**stead′fast·ness,** *n.*

stead′y (sted′ē) *adj.* **1,** firmly fixed. **2,** regular; uniform. **3,** resolute. **4,** industrious. —*v.t. & i.* make or become steady. —*n.* (*Informal*) a regular sweetheart. —**stead′i·ness,** *n.*

steak (stāk) *n.* a thick slice of meat, esp. beef.

steal (stēl) *v.t.* [**stole** (stōl) **sto′len, steal′ing**] **1,** take dishonestly and secretly. **2,** obtain surreptitiously or by surprise. —*v.i.* **1,** practice theft. **2,** move stealthily. —*n.* (*Informal*) a great bargain. ❏ *rob*

stealth (stelth) *n.* a secret or furtive procedure. —**stealth′y,** *adj.*

steam (stēm) *n.* **1,** water in a gaseous state, esp. when produced by boiling. **2,** (*Informal*) energy; enthusiasm. —*v.i.* give out, or move by, steam. —*v.t.* **1,** treat with steam. **2,** (*Informal*) (with *up*) arouse enthusiasm in. —**steam engine,** an engine in which steam supplies the power.

steam′boat″ *n.* steamship.

steam′er *n.* **1,** a device for steaming. **2,** a steamship.

steam′fit″ter *n.* a skilled worker who installs pipes, etc., that carry steam at high pressure.

steam′roll″er *n.* **1,** a steam-driven engine for leveling roads. **2,** (*Informal*) any agency that ruthlessly overrides and crushes. —*v.t.* [also, **steam′roll″**] (*Informal*) crush. —**steam shovel,** a steam-powered machine for excavating.

steam′ship″ *n.* a ship propelled by a steam engine.

steam′y *adj.* **1,** vaporous; misty. **2,** (*Informal*) excited or energetic; sensual. —**steam′i·ness,** *n.* ❏ *seamy*

steed (stēd) *n.* a horse.

steel (stēl) *n.* **1,** iron modified to increase its hardness, toughness, etc. **2,** something made of steel. —*v.t.* instill with courage or resolution. —**steel wool,** long steel shavings compressed into a pad for use as an abrasive.

steel′y (stē′lē) *adj.* hard; unflinching. —**steel′i·ness,** *n.*

steel′yard″ *n.* a balance scale.

steen′bok (stēn′bok) *n.* a small So. Afr. antelope.

---

tub, cūte, pŭll; labəl; oil, owl, go, chip, she, thin, *th*en, sing, ink; *see p. 6*

steep (stēp) *adj.* **1,** almost perpendicular; precipitous. **2,** (*Informal*) excessive, as a price. —*v.i. & t.* soak; saturate. —**steep′en,** *v.i. & t.* —**steep′ness,** *n.*

stee′ple (stē′pəl) *n.* a lofty tower, esp. on a church; a spire.

stee′ple·chase″ *n.* a horse race over obstacles.

stee′ple·jack″ *n.* a person who repairs steeples, etc.

steer (stir) *v.t. & i.* **1,** direct and govern; guide; pilot. **2,** follow (a course). —*n.* a castrated male bovine, raised for beef. —**steering wheel,** a wheel used to guide a ship, automobile, etc.

steer′age (-ij) *n.* lowest class in a passenger ship.

steers′man (stirz′mən) *n.* [*pl.* **-men**] a pilot.

stein (stīn) *n.* a mug for beer.

stele (stēl) *n.* **1,** an upright slab of stone, usu. bearing an inscription or sculptured design. **2,** the central cylinder in the stem of a plant.

stel′lar (stel′ər) *adj.* starlike; pert. to stars.

St. El′mo's fire (el′mōz) a glow due to atmospheric electricity, named for the 4th-c. patron saint of sailors.

stem *n.* **1,** the main body of a plant, the supporting stalk. **2,** a stemlike part, as of a goblet. **3,** ancestry. **4,** (*Gram.*) the unchanged part in a series of inflectional forms. **5,** (*Slang*) a street. —*v.t.* [**stemmed, stem′ming**] stop; check; stanch.

stem′ware″ *n.* glassware having a stem.

stench *n.* an offensive odor.

sten′cil (sten′səl) *n.* a form cut so that a design or letters can be rubbed through it; such a design or letters.

ste·nog′ra·phy (stə-nog′rə-fē) *n.* the art of writing in shorthand. —**ste·nog′ra·pher,** *n.* —**sten″o·graph′ic** (sten″ə-graf′ik) *adj.* —**sten″o·graph′i·cal·ly,** *adv.*

sten′o·type″ (sten′ə-tīp″) *n.* a keyboard instrument for writing phonetic shorthand.

sten·to′ri·an (sten-tôr′ē-ən) *adj.* loud and powerful in sound.

> **stentorian**
> ↔ After *Stentor,* a Greek warrior and herald in the Trojan War with a particularly loud voice.

step *n.* **1,** one completed movement in walking, running, or dancing. **2,** the distance of a step; a short distance. **3,** gait; pace. **4,** a support for the foot. **5,** gradation; degree; interval. **6,** an expedient; a measure. —*v.i.* [**stepped, step′ping**] **1,**

walk; go. **2,** dance. **3,** press with the foot. —*v.t.* **1,** (with *off*) measure by steps. **2,** perform, as a dance. **3,** grade; vary.

step- *pref.* indicating relationship through the marriage of a parent, as *stepfather, stepson,* etc.

step-′down″ *adj.* (*Electricity*) converting from a higher to a lower voltage. —*n.* a decrease.

step′fam″i·ly *n.* a family composed of a parent, a stepparent, and a child or children by a previous marriage.

step-′ins″ *n.pl.* a woman's undergarment.

step′lad″der *n.* a short ladder held erect by a frame.

steppe (step) *n.* an extensive, treeless plain.

step′ping-stone″ *n.* **1,** something to step and pause on briefly. **2,** a means for advancement.

step-′up″ *adj.* (*Electricity*) converting from a lower to a higher voltage. —*n.* an increase.

-ster (stər) *suf.* occupation.

stere (stir) *n.* a cubic meter.

ster′e·o (ster′ē-ō) *n.* (*Informal*) **1,** a stereoscopic photograph. **2,** stereophonic reproduction. **3,** a stereophonic sound system. —*adj.* (*Informal*) **1,** stereoscopic. **2,** stereophonic.

ster′e·o- *pref.* solid; three-dimensional.

ster″e·o·phon′ic (ster″ē-ə-fän′ik) *adj.* pert. to or rendering the illusion of true auditory perspective, usu. through the use of two or more microphones for recording and speakers for playback.

ster′e·o·scope″ (ster′ē-ə-skōp″) *n.* an optical instrument that makes photographs appear three-dimensional. —**ster″e·o·scop′ic** (-skop′ik) *adj.*

ster′e·o·type″ (ster′ē-ə-tīp″) *n.* **1,** a type plate cast from a mold. **2,** a convention. **3,** something conforming to a standard pattern. —*v.t.* make a stereotype of. —*adj.* hackneyed; unoriginal. —**ster″e·o·typ′i·cal,** *adj.*

ster′ile (ster′il) *adj.* **1,** free from living germs. **2,** barren; unproductive. —**ste·ril′i·ty,** *n.* —**ster′i·lize″** (-līz″) *v.t.*

ster′ling (stēr′ling) *adj.* **1,** (of silver) of standard pureness, 92½%. **2,** (of money) in Brit. money, measured by the pound sterling. **3,** of great excellence.

> **sterling**
> ↔ The *sterling* was once an English silver penny; the pound sterling once designated a literal pound of sterlings (240 coins).

stern (stẽrn) *adj.* harsh; austere; severe. —*n.* the hinder part, esp. of a ship. —**stern′ness,** *n.*

ster′num (stẽr′nəm) *n.* [*pl.* **-nums; -na** (-nə)] the breastbone.

ster′to·rous (stẽr′tə-rəs) *adj.* characterized by noisy breathing.

stet *n.* (*Lat.*) a proofreader's mark: *let it stand.*

steth′o·scope″ (steth′ə-skōp″) *n.* (*Med.*) an instrument for listening to sounds in the chest.

ste′ve·dore″ (stē′və-dôr″) *n.* one who loads or unloads vessels.

stew (stoo) *v.t. & i.* **1,** cook by simmering or slowly boiling. **2,** (*Informal*) fret; worry. —*n.* **1,** a dish of stewed meat, etc. **2,** (*Informal*) a state of agitation; a predicament. —**stewed,** *adj.* (*Informal*) drunk.

stew′ard (stoo′ərd) *n.* **1,** a manager or trustee; a chief servant. **2,** flight attendant. —*v.t. & i.* guard; conserve. —**stew′ard·ship,** *n.*

stick (stik) *n.* **1,** a piece of wood, generally small and slender. **2,** a club; a rod; a cane. **3,** any slender piece. **4,** (*pl.*) (*Informal*) rural regions. **5,** a stab. —*v.t.* [*pret. & p.p.* **stuck** (stuk)] **1,** stab; pierce; prod. **2,** thrust (a pin, etc.). **3,** put. **4,** attach; fasten. **5,** (*Informal*) nonplus; puzzle. **6,** (*Slang*) impose upon. —*v.i.* **1,** remain; adhere; cling; abide. **2,** extend or protrude. **3,** (with *at*) scruple. **4,** be held fast; stall. —**stick-in-the mud,** an old-fashioned, ultraconservative person. —**stick shift,** a manual transmission.

stick′er *n.* **1,** a persistent person. **2,** an adhesive label. **3,** (*Informal*) a puzzling problem. —**sticker price,** the retail price before any discounts.

stick′ler (stik′lər) *n.* one who is insistently precise. —**stick′le,** *v.i.*

stick-′to-it-ive·ness″ *n.* determination; tenacity.

stick′up″ *n.* (*Slang*) a holdup robbery.

stick′y (-ē) *adj.* **1,** adhesive; humid. —**stick′i·ness,** *n.*

stiff (stif) *adj.* **1,** rigid; not easily bent. **2,** moving with difficulty. **3,** formal; unbending. **4,** awkward. **5,** strong; hard; severe. **6,** expensive. —*n.* (*Slang*) a corpse. —**stiff′ness,** *n.*

stiff′en (stif′ən) *v.t. & i.* make or become stiff. —**stiff′en·ing,** *n.*

stiff-′necked″ (-nekt″) *adj.* **1,** suffering from stiffness of the neck. **2,** (*Informal*) obstinate. **3,** (*Informal*) haughty.

sti′fle (stī′fəl) *v.t.* **1,** smother; suffocate. **2,** extinguish. **3,** suppress. —*v.i.* suffocate.

stig′ma (stig′mə) *n.* **1,** a brand or mark of infamy; a disgrace. **2,** [*pl.* **stig·ma·ta** (stig-mä′tə)] wounds corresponding to those of Christ crucified. **3,** (*Bot.*) the part of the pistil that receives the pollen. —**stig·mat′ic** (-mat′ik) *adj.* —**stig·mat′i·cal·ly,** *adv.* —**stig′ma·tize″** (-mə-tīz″) *v.t.*

stile (stīl) *n.* a series of steps over a fence or wall.

sti·let′to (sti-let′ō) *n.* [*pl.* **-tos**] a slender, triangular-bladed dagger.

still (stil) *adj.* **1,** motionless; tranquil; silent. **2,** not sparkling, as wine. —*v.t.* silence. —*n.* **1,** silence. **2,** a distilling apparatus. **3,** a single photograph of a scene in a motion picture. —*adv.* **1,** now as previously. **2,** nevertheless. —*conj.* nevertheless. —**still′ness,** *n.* —**still′ly,** *adj.* quiet. —**still life,** a painting of inanimate objects.

still′born″ *adj.* dead when born.

Still′son wrench (stil′sən) (*T.N.*) a monkey wrench used esp. for round objects.

stilt *n.* **1,** a high post. **2,** (*pl.*) two poles to extend the length of the legs, for walking above ground level. —**stilt′ed,** *adj.* stiffly formal.

Stil′ton cheese a rich waxy English mold cheese.

stim′u·lant (stim′yə-lənt) *n.* that which stimulates.

stim′u·late″ (stim′yə-lāt″) *v.t.* **1,** excite to action; invigorate. **2,** quicken. —**stim″u·la′tion,** *n.*

stim′u·lus (stim′yə-ləs) *n.* [*pl.* **-li″** (-lī″)] **1,** an excitation of a sense organ; what excites it. **2,** an incentive; any prod to action.

sting *v.t. & i.* [*pret. & p.p.* **stung**] **1,** pain by pricking. **2,** distress. **3,** goad into action. —*n.* **1,** the venomous organ of a bee, etc. **2,** a sharp pain. **3,** (*Slang*) confidence game. **4,** (*Slang*) an apparently illegal operation run by undercover agents to trap criminals.

sting′er *n.* **1,** that which stings or astounds. **2,** a sting of a bee, etc. **3,** a cocktail of brandy and liqueur.

sting′ray″ *n.* a flat sea animal with a barbed tail. Also, **sting′a·ree** (-ə-rē).

stin′gy (stin′jē) *adj.* **1,** niggardly. **2,** scanty. —**stin′gi·ness,** *n.*

stink *v.i.* [**stank, stunk, stink′ing**] **1,** emit a strong offensive smell. **2,** have a bad reputation. **3,** (*Slang*) be incompetent, mediocre, or very bad. —*n.* **1,** a bad smell. **2,** (*Slang*) a protest. —**stink′er,** *n.* (*Slang*) a mean or dishonorable person.

stink′o (-ō) *adj.* (*Slang*) drunk.

stint *v.t. & i.* be stingy toward; restrict. —*n.* **1,** limitation. **2,** an allotted task.

sti′pend (stī′pend) *n.* fixed pay.

stip′ple (stip′əl) *v.t.* mark with dots or a grained pattern.

stip′u·late″ (stip′yə-lāt″) *v.t. & i.* **1,** settle by agreement. **2,** make a condition of; require. —**stip″u·la′tion,** *n.* a condition; requirement.

stir (stēr) *v.t. & i.* [**stirred, stir′ring**] **1,** set in motion; arouse; awake. **2,** circulate; agitate. **3,** move; move briskly. —*n.* **1,** activity; bustle; commotion. **2,** emotion. **3,** (*Slang*) a prison.

stir-′fry″ *v.t. & i.* cook by stirring in a wok with a small amount of hot oil. —*n.* food so cooked.

stir′ring (stēr′ing) *adj.* **1,** moving; affecting. **2,** rousing; thrilling.

stir′rup (stēr′əp) *n.* a loop to support a rider's foot. —**stirrup cup,** a farewell drink.

stitch (stich) *n.* **1,** in sewing, knitting, etc., one whole movement of the needle; its result. **2,** (*Informal*) a bit of clothing. **3,** a sudden muscular pain. **4,** (*pl.*) (*Informal*) unrestrained laughter. —*v.t. & i.* **1,** make stitches; sew. **2,** staple.

stoat (stōt) *n.* an ermine.

stock (stok) *n.* **1,** a stem; a race or line of descent; a breed. **2,** a family of languages. **3,** livestock. **4,** a principal supporting part. **5,** a supply of merchandise for sale. **6,** a reserve supply. **7,** the shares of a corporation: *capital stock.* **8,** the broth from boiling meat. **9,** a flowering garden plant. **10,** a wide necktie reaching to the chin. **11,** (*pl.*) a framework for confining petty offenders. **12,** the shoulder support of a gun; butt. —*adj.* **1,** kept on hand; staple; commonplace. **2,** pert. to a repertory theatrical company. —*v.t.* **1,** furnish with stock. **2,** keep on hand. —*v.i.* (with *up*) lay in a supply. —**stock exchange,** an association of stockbrokers. —**stock-in-trade,** *n.* the equipment necessary to ply one's trade; hence, the abilities, tricks, etc. of one's profession. —**stock market,** stock exchange. —**take stock in,** attach importance to.

stock·ade′ (stok-ād′) *n.* an enclosure of upright posts.

stock′brok″er *n.* a broker in corporate stocks.

stock′hold″er *n.* an owner of corporate stock.

Stock′holm syndrome (stok′hōlm) the tendency for hostages to identify with their captors.

stock′i·net″ an elastic machine-knitted fabric.

stock′ing (stok′ing) *n.* a knitted covering for the foot and lower leg.

stock′pile″ *n.* a reserve supply.

stock-″still′ *adj.* motionless.

stock′y (-ē) *adj.* short and thick. —**stock′-i·ness,** *n.*

stock′yard″ *n.* **1,** an enclosure for livestock. **2,** a slaughterhouse.

stodg′y (stoj′ē) *adj.* heavy and dull. —**stodg′i·ness,** *n.*

sto′gy (stō′gē) *n.* **1,** a long, coarse cigar. **2,** a heavy shoe. ❑ *Conestoga wagon*

sto′ic (stō′ik) *n.* one indifferent to pain or pleasure. —**sto′i·cal,** *adj.* —**sto′i·cal·ly,** *adv.* —**sto′i·cism** (-siz-əm) *n.*

> **stoic**
> ↔ From the supposed lecturing place (the *stoa,* porch) of the Greek philosopher Zeno, whose teachings form the basis for the sense of *stoic.*

stoke (stōk) *v.t. & i.* supply with fuel; tend. —**stok′er,** *n.* one who tends fire, as in a boiler.

STOL a type of aircraft requiring very little runway length: *s(hort) t(ake)o(ff and) l(anding).*

stole (stōl) *n.* **1,** an ecclesiastical vestment. **2,** a woman's long neckpiece of fur, etc. —*v.* pret. of *steal.*

sto′len (stō′lən) *v.* p.p. of *steal.*

stol′id *adj.* impassive. —**sto·lid′i·ty** (stə-lid′i-tē) *n.* ❑ *solid*

sto′ma (stō′mə) *n.* [*pl.* **sto′ma·ta** (stō′mə-tə)] an opening, as in the skin.

stom′ach (stum′ək) *n.* **1,** the digestive organ. **2,** the abdomen or belly. **3,** appetite for food. **4,** inclination; liking. —*v.t.* put up with; endure.

stom′ach·ache″ *n.* indigestion.

stom′ach·er (-ər) *n.* a garment covering the stomach.

sto·mach′ic (stō-mak′ik) *adj.* aiding digestion. —*n.* a tonic.

stomp *v.* (*Dial.*) stamp. —*n.* **1,** (*Dial.*) stamp. **2,** a heavy dance.

stone (stōn) *n.* **1,** the substance of rock; a piece of rock; something made of rocks. **2,** a gem. **3,** a hard, rounded object, as a *hailstone.* **4,** a unit of weight, 14 lbs. **5,** a playing piece in various games (as go, bowls, etc.). —*adj.* of stone. —*adv.* (in compounds) completely, as *stone-deaf.* —*v.t.* throw stones at. —**stoned,** *adj.* (*Slang*) intoxicated with alcohol or drugs. —**Stone Age,** the era when stone implements were first used. **—a stone's throw,** a short distance.

stone'wall" *v.i.* (*Slang*) refuse to give information so as to obstruct an investigation.

stone'ware" *n.* a coarse pottery.

ston'y (stō'nė) *adj.* **1,** pert. to, or abounding in, stone. **2,** unfeeling; merciless. **—ston'i·ness,** *n.*

stood (stûd) *v.* pret. & p.p. of *stand.*

stooge (stooj) *n.* (*Informal*) the foil for a comedian; a compliant dupe.

stool *n.* **1,** a single seat or rest without arms or back. **2,** an evacuation of the bowels. **3,** a decoy. **—stool pigeon,** (*Slang*) a spy; an informer.

stoop *v.i.* **1,** bend the body forward and downward. **2,** descend; condescend; lower oneself (to). **—n. 1,** a stooping movement or position. **2,** a small porch and the steps to it.

stop *v.t.* [**stopped, stop'ping**] **1,** close up or block up, as a hole. **2,** check; impede; restrain. **3,** cease from; discontinue. **—v.i. 1,** halt. **2,** cease; desist. **3,** tarry; make a stay. **4,** (with *by*) (*Informal*) drop in. **—n. 1,** the act or result of stopping. **2,** a place where trains, etc., stop. **3,** an obstacle. **4,** (*Music*) a hole, fret, organ control, etc. **—stop'page** (-ij) *n.*

stop'cock" *n.* a valve.

stop'gap" *n.* & *adj.* a temporary expedient.

stop'light" *n.* **1,** a red light displayed as a signal to traffic to stop. **2,** a warning light at the rear of an automobile.

stop'o"ver *n.* a brief stay, esp. one imposed by carrier schedules.

stop'per (stop'ər) *n.* one who or that which stops, esp. a closure for a bottle.

stop'ple *n.* a stopper in an organ pipe, flute, etc., to regulate pitch. **—v.t.** close or fit with a stopple.

stop'watch" *n.* a watch whose movement can be stopped, as for timing races; chronograph.

stor'age (stôr'ij) *n.* act or fact of storing; safekeeping.

store (stôr) *n.* **1,** a place where goods are stored or kept for sale. **2,** a supply for future use. **—v.t. 1,** stock. **2,** put away. **—store'room", store'house",** *n.* a repository. **—set store by,** esteem highly.

store'keep"er *n.* **1,** the proprietor of a store or ship. **2,** one in charge of stores, as in a military depot.

sto'ried (stôr'ēd) *adj.* **1,** celebrated in story. **2,** having stories.

stork (stôrk) *n.* a wading bird.

storm (stôrm) *n.* **1,** an atmospheric disturbance, with high wind, rain, or snow, etc. **2,** a vehement outbreak; a tumult. **3,** a violent assault. **—v.i. 1,** blow, rain, etc. **2,** fume; rage. **3,** move with violence. **—v.t.** attack. **—storm'y,** *adj.* **—storm cellar,** an underground room for refuge from storms. **—storm window,** an insulating window outside a window.

sto'ry (stôr'ė) *n.* **1,** a literary narrative; an account. **2,** the plot of a novel, drama, etc. **3,** (*Informal*) a lie. **4,** [also, **sto'rey**] a floor of a building.

---

story

↔ All senses derive ultimately from Latin *historia,* history. The sense of floor of a building comes from the practice of painting a building with historical scenes.

---

sto'ry·tell"er *n.* **1,** one who tells stories. **2,** a liar.

stoup (stoop) *n.* a basin for holy water.

stout (stowt) *adj.* **1,** bulky in figure; corpulent. **2,** bold and brave; firm. **—n.** strong ale, beer, or porter. **—stout'ness,** *n.*

stout'heart"ed *adj.* courageous; resolute.

stove (stōv) *n.* an apparatus for furnishing heat or for cooking. **—v.** pret. of *stave* (*in*). **—stove'pipe",** *n.* a pipe for carrying off smoke from a stove. **—stovepipe hat,** (*Informal*) a tall silk hat.

stow (stō) *v.t.* **1,** pack (cargo, etc.); put away. **2,** (*Slang*) desist from. **—stow'age,** *n.*

stow'a·way" *n.* one who hides aboard a ship or other vehicle.

stra·bis'mus (strə-biz'məs) *n.* an ailment of the eye; cross-eyes. **—stra·bis'mal** (-məl) *adj.*

strad'dle (strad'əl) *v.i. & t.* **1,** sit or stand astride. **2,** (*Informal*) favor both sides. **—n.** a straddling.

Strad"i·var'i·us (strad"ə-vãr'ē-əs) *n.* a fine violin made by one of the Stradivari family.

strafe (strāf) *v.t.* fire at (ground troops) from an airplane.

strag'gle (strag'əl) *v.i.* **1,** wander away; stray. **2,** spread irregularly or untidily. **—strag'gly,** *adj.*

straight (strāt) *adj.* **1,** without bend or deviation. **2,** upright; honorable. **3,** regular; unmodified; undiluted. **4,** consecutive. **5,** proper; correct. **6,** (*Informal*) heterosexual. **—n.** (*Card Games*) five cards in sequence. **—adv.** directly; at once. **—straight'ness,** *n.* **—straight arrow,** (*Infor-*

mal) a morally upright person. **—straight man,** the foil for a comedian.

straight-′arm″ *v.t.* ward off (an opponent) by holding the arm out straight.

straight′a·way″ *adj. & n.* (a road) without a curve, as a race course. *—adv.* (*Informal*) straightway.

straight′edge″ *n.* a ruler.

straight′en *v.t. & i.* make or become straight.

straight″for′ward *adj.* **1,** direct. **2,** honest; open.

straight′way″ *adv.* at once.

strain (strān) *v.t.* **1,** stretch to the utmost or beyond the proper limit. **2,** sprain. **3,** press through a filter. *—v.i.* exert oneself. *—n.* **1,** a stretching or deforming force or effect. **2,** great effort. **3,** a passage of music. **4,** streak; trace. **—strained,** *adj.* affected; forced. **—strain′er,** *n.* a filter or sieve. ❏ *sprain*

strait (strāt) *n.* [also, **straits**] **1,** a narrow connecting passage of water. **2,** a position of difficulty or need. *—adj.* narrow; confined; strict.

strait′en (strā′tən) *v.t.* impoverish; confine.

strait′jack″et *n.* a restraining coat. *—v.t.* put in or as in a straitjacket.

strait′laced″ *adj.* strict; puritanical.

strand *v.t. & i.* **1,** drive or run aground. **2,** leave in a helpless position. *—n.* **1,** a piece of twisted yarn; a filament; a tress of hair; a string, as of pearls. **2,** a beach.

strange (strānj) *adj.* **1,** unfamiliar; new; unusual; surprising. **2,** alien; foreign. **3,** reserved; distant. **—strange′ness,** *n.*

stran′ger (strān′jər) *n.* **1,** a person not known. **2,** a newcomer.

stran′gle (strang′gəl) *v.t. & i.* kill by choking.

stran′gu·late″ (strang′gyə-lāt″) *v.t.* obstruct; compress. **—stran″gu·la′tion,** *n.*

strap *n.* a narrow strip of leather, etc. *—v.t.* **[strapped, strap′ping]** fasten, sharpen, or chastise with a ′strap. **—strapped,** *adj.* (*Informal*) without funds. **—strap′ping,** *adj.* (*Informal*) tall and robust.

strap′hang″er *n.* (*Informal*) a standing passenger on a bus or subway.

stra′ta (strā′tə; strat′ə) *n.* pl. of *stratum.*

strat′a·gem (strat′ə-jəm) *n.* a means of deception; a trick.

stra·te′gic (strə-tē′jik) *adj.* **1,** pert. to strategy. **2,** of vital importance. Also, **stra·te′gi·cal. —Strategic Defense Initiative,** a military defense strategy using high-technology equipment in space. Also (*informal*) **Star Wars.**

---

stratagem, strategy

☛ Although these two words are often used as synonyms, they have distinct meanings. A *stratagem* is a trick intended to deceive, whereas a *strategy* is the science of tactical planning. ↔ Both words derive from Greek *stratēgós*, general of an army.

---

strat′e·gy (strat′ə-jē) *n.* **1,** the skillful employment and coordination of tactics. **2,** artful planning and management. **—strat′e·gist,** *n.* ❏ *stratagem*

strat′i·fy″ (strat′ə-fī″) *v.t.* form in layers. **—strat″i·fi·ca′tion,** *n.*

strat′o·sphere″ (strat′ə-sfir″) *n.* the region of the earth's atmosphere six to sixty miles above sea level.

stra′tum (strā′təm) *n.* [*pl.* **stra′ta, stra′tums**] a layer, as of the earth's crust, of the atmosphere, etc.

straw (strâ) *n.* **1,** a single stalk of grain; such stalks when dried. **2,** a paper tube. **3,** a trifle. *—adj.* **1,** of straw. **2,** ineffective. **3,** pale yellow. **—straw boss,** (*Informal*) a subforeman. **—straw man,** *n.* **1,** a fabricated person; front. **2,** an imaginary opponent, easily defeated. **—straw vote,** an unofficial test vote.

straw′ber″ry *n.* a low herb, its red fruit, or the color of the fruit.

stray (strā) *v.i.* wander; deviate. *—n.* **1,** a lost domestic animal. **2,** a homeless person. *—adj.* **1,** wandering. **2,** isolated; casual.

streak (strēk) *n.* **1,** a line, stripe, or mark. **2,** a stratum or vein. **3,** a disposition; a trait. **4,** (*Informal*) a run of good or bad luck. *—v.t.* mark with streaks. *—v.i.* **1,** move rapidly. **2,** become streaked. **3,** (*Slang*) run naked in public. **—streak′y,** *adj.*

stream (strēm) *n.* **1,** a course of running water. **2,** any continuous flow. *—v.t. & i.* flow in a stream. **—stream of consciousness,** a literary technique attempting to represent the natural flow of human thought.

stream′er *n.* **1,** a pennant. **2,** a headline across five or more newspaper columns.

stream′let *n.* a small stream, as of droplets.

stream′line″ *v.t.* **1,** shape so as to offer little wind resistance, like a drop of water. **2,** modernize by eliminating superfluities.

stream′lin″er *n.* a streamlined train.

street (strēt) *n.* **1,** a passageway for vehicles and pedestrians in a town or city. **2,**

---

the part of such a passageway used by vehicles. **3,** such passageway and its abutting properties. **4,** a stock exchange. —**street person,** (*Informal*) **1,** a homeless person or a vagrant living in the streets. **2,** a criminal working in the streets. —**street price,** the actual price for which an item is available, as opposed to the manufacturer's suggested retail price.

street′car″ *n.* a trolley car.

street′walk″er *n.* a prostitute.

street′wise″ *adj.* (*Informal*) having experience with and understanding of conditions in urban areas, esp. those characterized by poverty and a high crime rate.

strength (strength) *n.* **1,** the power of exerting muscular force; power; vigor. **2,** potency; efficacy. —**strength′en,** *v.t. & i.* make or grow stronger.

stren′u·ous (stren′ū-əs) *adj.* energetic; vigorous. —**stren′u·ous·ness,** *n.*

strep″to·coc′cus (strep″tə-kok′əs) *n.* [*pl.* **-coc′ci″** (-kok′sī″)] a microorganism that forms chains, causing certain diseases. Also, **strep.** —**strep throat,** sore throat with fever caused by streptococcus infection.

strep″to·my′cin (strep″tə-mī′sin) *n.* an antibiotic effective against certain diseases.

stress (stres) *n.* **1,** importance; emphasis; accent on a word or syllable. **2,** a strain. **3,** chronic pressure; tension. —*v.t.* **1,** emphasize; accent. **2,** subject to strain. —**stress test,** a test of how something reacts under stress; esp., a test of a person's cardiovascular system during physical exertion.

stretch (strech) *v.t.* **1,** draw out or extend to full length or extent. **2,** extend too far. **3,** (*Informal*) exaggerate. —*v.i.* **1,** extend over a distance, period of time, etc. **2,** be elastic. **3,** reach. **4,** (with *out*) recline; be prolonged. **5,** extend one's limbs. —*n.* **1,** an extent of distance, area, or time. **2,** the act of stretching. **3,** a straightaway. **4,** (*Slang*) a term of imprisonment.

stretch′er (-ər) *n.* **1,** a litter. **2,** a device for stretching.

strew (stroo) *v.t.* [*p.p.* **strewed** or **strewn** (stroon)] **1,** scatter. **2,** overspread by scattering.

stri′a (strī′ə) *n.* [*pl.* **-ae** (ē)] a groove or ridge. —**stri′ate** (-āt) *adj.*

strick′en (strik′ən) *v.* a p.p. of *strike.* —*adj.* strongly affected or afflicted; struck; wounded.

strict (strikt) *adj.* **1,** precise. **2,** exacting; severe. —**strict′ness,** *n.*

stric′ture (strik′chər) *n.* **1,** a sharp criti-

cism; censure. **2,** a morbid contraction of a canal in the body.

stride (strīd) *v.i.* [**strode** (strōd), **strid′den** (strid′ən), **strid′ing**] walk with long steps. —*n.* **1,** a long step or its distance; a striding gait. **2,** (usu. *pl.*) progress.

stri′dent (strī′dənt) *adj.* creaking; harsh; grating. —**stri′den·cy,** *n.*

strife (strīf) *n.* conflict; discord; a quarrel.

strike (strīk) *v.t.* [**struck** (struk), **strik′ing**] **1,** give a blow to; hit; attack. **2,** inflict (a blow, etc.). **3,** cause to ignite. **4,** stamp out; print. **5,** effect. **6,** come upon suddenly. **7,** appear to. **8,** lower; pull down. **9,** cancel. **10,** assume (a posture, pose, etc.). **11,** form (an acquaintance, etc.). —*v.i.* **1,** inflict a blow. **2,** run aground. **3,** grab at bait. **4,** (*Naut.*) yield. **5,** (with *out*) go; proceed. **6,** (with *upon*) discover. **7,** (with *out*) (*Baseball*) have three strikes; (*Informal*) fail. **8,** engage in a strike. —*n.* **1,** a refusal by employees to work. **2,** (*Baseball*) a suitable pitch not hit. **3,** (*Bowling*) a knocking down of all pins with the first bowl. **4,** a discovery; an accession. —**strik′er,** *n.*

> **strike, stroke**
> ↔ Both words derive from a Germanic source meaning to touch lightly. While *stroke* has retained this sense, *strike* has developed more violent connotations.

strike′break″er *n.* a worker who replaces striking employees.

strike′out″ *n.* (*Baseball*) the act or instance of striking out.

strik′ing *adj.* impressive.

string *n.* **1,** a line, thread, cord, or thong; a tendril. **2,** (*pl.*) stringed musical instruments. **3,** a series; a chain. **4,** (*Informal*) a limitation or condition. **5,** (*Computers*) a group of letters or other characters treated as a unit. —*v.t.* [*pret. & p.p.* **strung**] **1,** make a string of. **2,** (with *up*) hang. **3,** (*Slang*) hoax. —**string′y,** *adj.* —**stringed** (stringd) *adj.* having strings. —**string bean, 1,** a leguminous garden vegetable. **2,** (*Slang*) a tall, thin person. —**string theory,** (*Physics*) a theory which deals with elementary particles as stringlike objects rather than as points.

strin′gent (strin′jənt) *adj.* **1,** vigorous; exacting; urgent. **2,** straitened. —**strin′gen·cy,** *n.*

string′er (-ər) *n.* **1,** a long horizontal timber. **2,** one of the sloping sides of a stairway. **3,** a part-time newspaper reporter.

strip *v.t.* [**stripped, strip′ping**] **1,** (with *of*) take away; deprive; divest. **2,** deprive of clothing. **3,** tear off (the thread of a screw, the teeth of a gear, etc.). —*v.i.* **1,** remove one's clothes. **2,** (with *off*) separate. —*n.* **1,** a narrow piece, as of cloth or territory. **2,** a continuous series. **3,** a runway. —**strip′per,** *n.* —**strip tease,** a dance in which the dancer gradually disrobes.

stripe (strīp) *n.* **1,** a streak or band of a different color or nature. **2,** a kind; character. **3,** (*pl.*) insignia. **4,** a whip stroke given in punishment.

strip′ling *n.* a youth.

strive (strīv) *v.i.* [**strove,** (strōv), **striv′en** (striv′ən), **striv′ing**] **1,** make strenuous effort; endeavor. **2,** struggle; fight.

strob′o·scope″ (strob′ə-skōp″) *n.* an instrument for studying rapid revolution or motion. Also, **strobe.**

strode (strōd) *v.* pret. of *stride.*

stroke (strōk) *n.* **1,** a sweeping movement. **2,** a mark, as of a pen. **3,** an act of striking; a blow; a sudden affliction. **4,** a coup. **5,** a caress. —*v.t.* rub gently. ❑ *strike*

stroll (strōl) *v.i.* walk leisurely; saunter. —*v.t.* saunter through. —*n.* a walk for pleasure. —**stroll′er,** *n.* a baby carriage.

strong (strâng) *adj.* **1,** possessing or exerting great physical or moral power. **2,** powerful. **3,** extreme in kind; intense. **4,** rancid. —**strong′ness,** *n.* —**strong force,** (*Physics*) the force which holds together the nucleus of the atom.

strong-′arm″ *adj.* violent. —*v.t.* coerce by violence.

strong′box″ *n.* chest; coffer; safe.

strong′hold″ *n.* a fortress.

strong′man″ *n.* **1,** a man having exceptional muscular strength. **2,** a dictator.

stron′ti·um (strän′tė-əm; -chəm) *n.* a metallic element, no. 38, symbol Sr. —**strontium 90,** a heavy radioactive isotope of strontium found in nuclear fallout.

> **strontium**
> ↔ From the *Strontian* region of Scotland, a source for the element.

strop *n.* a strap to sharpen razors.

stro′phe (strō′fė) *n.* a stanza or longer section of a poem.

strove (strōv) *v.* pret. of *strive.*

struck *v.* pret. & p.p. of *strike.*

struc′ture (struk′chər) *n.* **1,** that which is built. **2,** form; the mode of construction or organization. —**struc′tur·al,** *adj.*

stru′del (stroo′dəl) *n.* a filled pastry made of very thin dough.

strug′gle (strug′əl) *v.i.* & *t.* labor or contend urgently or strenuously.

strum *v.i.* & *t.* [**strummed, strum′ming**] play carelessly on a stringed instrument.

strum′pet (strum′pət) *n.* a prostitute.

strung *v.* pret. & p.p. of *string.* —**strung out,** (*Slang*) **1,** exhausted. **2,** weakened by alcohol, drugs, etc.

strut *v.i.* [**strut′ted, -ting**] walk pompously. —*n.* **1,** a strutting walk. **2,** a brace or support.

strych′nine (strik′nin) *n.* a colorless, odorless crystalline poison.

stub *n.* **1,** a projection; a short remaining piece. **2,** a space for memoranda, as in a checkbook. —*v.t.* [**stubbed, stub′bing**] strike (the toe).

stub′ble (-əl) *n.* **1,** stubs of grain. **2,** rough growth, as of beard.

stub′born (stub′ərn) *adj.* **1,** obstinately determined or perverse. **2,** tough. —**stub′-born·ness,** *n.*

stub′by (-ė) *adj.* thickset; bristly. —**stub′-bi·ness,** *n.*

stuc′co (stuk′ō) *n.* daubed plaster or cement on walls.

stuck (stuk) *v.* pret. & p.p. of *stick.* —**stuck-′up′,** *adj.* haughty.

stud *n.* **1,** a protuberance, as a knob. **2,** an upright support. **3,** a buttonlike fastener. **4,** an establishment for breeding, as horses or dogs. **5,** a male animal used for breeding. **6,** (*Slang*) an especially virile or handsome man. **7,** a form of poker. —*v.i.* [**stud′ded, -ding**] **1,** set with studs. **2,** scatter over at intervals. —**stud farm,** stud (def. 4).

stu′dent (stoo′dənt) *n.* one who studies; a pupil; a scholar.

stud′ied (stud′ėd) *adj.* **1,** deliberate. **2,** carefully considered.

stu′di·o″ (stoo′dė-ō″) *n.* an artist's workroom; a place for painting, broadcasting, etc.

stu′di·ous (stoo′dė-əs) *adj.* **1,** diligent in study. **2,** thoughtfully attentive. —**stu′di-ous·ness,** *n.*

stud′y (stud′ė) *n.* **1,** the mental effort of understanding. **2,** an exercise. **3,** a branch of learning. **4,** deep meditation. **5,** deliberate contrivance. **6,** a portrait or sketch. **7,** a room for study. —*v.i.* try to learn; ponder; plan. —*v.t.* examine thoughtfully.

stuff (stuf) *n.* **1,** material. **2,** rubbish. —*v.t.* **1,** cram full. **2,** pack tightly. —*v.i.* eat greedily. —**stuffed shirt,** (*Slang*) a pompous person. —**stuff′ing,** *n.* filling.

stuff′y (-ė) *adj.* **1,** poorly ventilated. **2,** dull; prudish. —**stuff′i·ness,** *n.*

stul′ti·fy″ (stul′tə-fī″) *v.t.* make absurd or ineffectual. —**stul″ti·fi·ca′tion,** *n.*

stum'ble (stum'bəl) *v.i.* **1,** strike the foot; trip. **2,** stagger. **3,** blunder. **4,** (with *on* or *across*) discover accidentally. —*n.* a false step; a blunder. —**stumbling block,** an obstacle; a cause of downfall.

stump *n.* **1,** the truncated lower part of a tree. **2,** any remaining part or stub. **3,** (*pl.*) (*Informal*) legs. **4,** a political rostrum. —*v.t.* **1,** nonplus. **2,** (*Informal*) make political speeches in. —*v.i.* **1,** walk heavily. **2,** make political speeches.

stump'y *adj.* **1,** stocky. **2,** abounding in stumps.

stun *v.t.* [**stunned, stun'ning**] **1,** deprive of consciousness by a blow, etc. **2,** astound; bewilder; stupefy. —**stun'ning,** *adj.* (*Informal*) strikingly beautiful. —**stun gun,** a battery-powered electrical device that delivers a shock, used to immobilize an attacker temporarily.

stung *v.* pret. & p.p. of *sting.*

stunk *v.* p.p. of *stink.*

stunt *v.t.* check or hinder the growth or development of. —*v.i.* (*Informal*) perform a stunt. —*n.* an athletic or other feat done to impress an audience. —**stunt man** or **woman,** a person who substitutes for an actor in performing a hazardous or difficult physical feat.

stu'pe·fy" (stū'pə-fī") *v.t.* deprive of sensibility; shock. —**stu"pe·fac'tion** (-fak'-shən) *n.* ❏ *stupid*

stu·pen'dous (stū-pen'dəs) *adj.* astounding; prodigious.

stu'pid (stū'pid) *adj.* **1,** lacking ordinary activity of mind. **2,** inane. —**stu·pid'i·ty** (stū-pid'ə-tē) *n.*

> **stupid, stupor, stupefy**
> ↔ All three words derive from Latin *stupēre*, to be numb, and all three used to denote mental numbness. The sense of *stupid* as lacking intelligence is a later development.

stu'por (stoo'pər) *n.* insensibility. ❏ *stupid*

stur'dy (stēr'dė) *adj.* strong; robust; unyielding. —**stur'di·ness,** *n.*

> **sturdy**
> ↔ Oddly, this word derives from Vulgar Latin *exturdīre*, dazed like a drunken thrush, from Latin *turdus*, thrush. The modern sense of robust developed after the word was borrowed from Old French.

stur'geon (stēr'jən) *n.* any of various large fishes.

Sturm" und Drang' (shtoorm" ûnt dräng') (*Ger.*, storm and stress) a development in German Romantic literature.

stut'ter (stut'ər) *v.t.* & *i.* utter or speak with breaks and repetitions; stammer. —*n.* a stuttering. ❏ *stammer*

sty (stī) *n.* **1,** a pen for swine. **2,** any filthy place. **3,** an inflammation of the eyelid.

styg'i·an (stij'ė-ən) *adj.* dark; infernal.

style (stīl) *n.* **1,** a characteristic mode of expression or action. **2,** the prevalent fashion. **3,** a stylus; the pointer on a sundial; any pen, pin, or peg. **4,** a trade name. **5,** (*Computers*) the formatting and character attributes of a section of text. —*v.t.* **1,** design. **2,** name. **3,** shape the hair. —**styl'ish,** *adj.* fashionably elegant. —**styl'ist,** *n.* one whose style is distinctive. —**style sheet,** (*Computers*) a collection of styles.

styl'ize *v.t.* conform to a particular style, esp. in an artificial manner; conventionalize. —**sty"li·za'tion,** *n.*

sty'lo·graph" *n.* a fountain pen having a fine tube instead of a nib.

sty'lus (stī'ləs) *n.* **1,** a pointed instrument, as for writing on wax. **2,** a phonograph needle.

sty'mie (stī'mė) *n.* (*Golf*) obstruction by the opponent's ball; hence, any minor but insurmountable obstacle. —**sty'mied,** *adj.*

styp'tic (stip'tik) *adj.* checking bleeding.

sty'rene (stī'rēn) *n.* a thermoplastic substance.

Sty'ro·foam" (stī'rə-fōm") *n.* (*T.N.*) a rigid plastic foam made from polystyrene.

sua'sion (swā'zhən) *n.* a persuasive effort.

suave (swäv) *adj.* urbane; bland. —**suav'i·ty,** *n.*

sub *n.* (*Informal*) substitute, submarine, etc. —*v.i.* as substitute (for).

sub- *pref.* **1,** under. **2,** inferior.

sub·al'tern (sub-âl'tərn) *n.* a junior officer.

sub"a·tom'ic *adj.* pert. to the particles or phenomena inside the atom.

sub'com·mit"tee *n.* a committee acting for a larger committee.

sub'com"pact *n.* & *adj.* (of) an automobile smaller than a compact.

sub·con'scious (sub-kon'shəs) *adj.* present in the mind but beyond consciousness.

sub·con'ti·nent *n.* a large area of land smaller than a continent.

sub·con'tract *n.* a contract to provide services or materials necessary for another contract. —*v.t.* & *i.* make a subcontract for.

sub'cul"ture *n.* a unified group or movement within a culture from which it is in some way distinguished.

sub″cu·ta′ne·ous (sub″kū-tā′nė-əs) *adj.* beneath the skin.

sub′deb″ *n.* (*Informal*) a teenage girl, usually under eighteen, not yet a debutante. Also, **sub″deb·u·tante′.**

sub″di·vide′ *v.t.* divide (esp. real estate) into smaller parts. —**sub″di·vi″sion,** *n.*

sub·due′ (səb-doo′) *v.t.* **1,** overcome by force; conquer. **2,** prevail over. **3,** repress. **4,** soften; allay.

sub′head″ *n.* **1,** the title of a section under a main title; a subordinate heading. **2,** an official ranking next below the head.

sub·in′dex *n.* a symbol written to the right of and slightly below another symbol, as x_0 (read "x sub-zero").

sub·ja′cent (sub-jā′sənt) *adj.* underlying.

sub′ject (sub′jikt) *n.* **1,** a topic; a theme; a person or idea being discussed. **2,** one under the authority of another, esp. a king. **3,** a recipient of treatment. **4,** (*Gram.*) the word representing the person or thing acting. —*adj.* **1,** under the power of another. **2,** (with *to*) exposed or liable to; conditioned upon. —*v.t.* (sub-jekt′) **1,** treat. **2,** expose. —**sub″jec′tion** (-jek′shən) *n.* —**subject matter,** substance (of a book, etc.).

sub·jec′tive (sub-jek′tiv) *adj.* **1,** pert. to the thinking subject; not objective. **2,** introspective. —**sub″jec·tiv′i·ty,** *n.*

sub′join′ *v.t.* add below.

sub ju′di·ce (sub joo′di-sè) (*Lat.*) before the court; under consideration.

sub′ju·gate″ (sub′jə-gāt″) *v.t.* **1,** vanquish. **2,** make subservient. —**sub″ju·ga′-tion,** *n.*

sub·junc′tive (səb-junk′tiv) *adj.* (*Gram.*) expressing contingency, doubt, or supposition, not reality.

sub′lease″ *n.* a lease granted by a lessee. —*v.t.* [*also,* **sub′let″**] grant or receive a sublease.

sub′li·mate″ (sub′lə-māt″) *v.t.* **1,** elevate; purify. **2,** turn into, or replace with, more wholesome interests or activities. **3,** vaporize by heat and allow to solidify again. —**sub″li·ma′tion,** *n.*

sub·lime′ (sə-blīm′) *adj.* exalted; lofty. —**sub·lim′i·ty** (-lim′ə-tè) *n.*

sub·lim′i·nal (sub-lim′ə-nəl) *adj.* subconscious.

sub″ma·chine′ gun a portable machine gun.

sub″ma·rine′ *adj.* under water. —*n.* **1,** a boat able to submerge. **2,** (*Informal*) a large sandwich; a hero.

sub·merge′ (səb-mėrj′) *v.t. & i.* sink below the surface, as of water. Also, **submerse′.** —**sub·mer′gence,** **sub·mer′sion,** *n.*

sub·mers′i·ble (sub-mėr′sə-bəl) *adj.* capable of being submerged. —*n.* a submarine.

sub″mi·cro·scop′ic *adj.* too small to be seen with an optical microscope.

sub·min′i·a·ture *adj.* smaller than miniature.

sub·mis′sion (səb-mish′ən) *n.* act or effect of submitting.

sub·mis′sive (-mis′iv) *adj.* yielding; obedient.

sub·mit′ (səb-mit′) *v.t. & i.* [**sub·mit′-ted, -ting**] **1,** yield. **2,** refer to another. **3,** propose.

sub·nor′mal *adj.* below average, esp. in intélligence.

sub·or′bi·tal *adj.* following a path too low for an orbit.

sub·or′di·nate (sə-bôr′di-nət) *adj. & n.* secondary; inferior. —**sub·or′di·na′tion,** *n.*

sub·orn′ (sə-bôrn′) *v.t.* bribe to perform an unlawful act. —**sub″or·na′tion** (sub″ər-nā′shən) *n.*

sub·poe′na (səb-pē′nə) *n.* a writ summoning a witness. —*v.t.* serve a subpoena on. Also, **sub·pe′na.**

sub′ro·gate″ (sub′rə-gāt″) *v.t.* transfer (a claim, etc.). —**sub″ro·ga′tion,** *n.*

sub ro′sa (sub rō′zə) (*Lat.*, under the rose, an ancient symbol of secrecy) secretly.

sub·scribe′ (səb-skrīb′) *v.t. & i.* **1,** give consent to. **2,** endorse. **3,** engage to receive a magazine, etc., periodically.

sub′script″ *n.* something written low, as a subindex.

sub·scrip′tion (-skrip′shən) *n.* **1,** a signature; assent. **2,** agreement to pay, contribute, etc. **3,** an order for a periodical, season tickets, etc.

sub′se·quent (sub′sə-kwənt) *adj.* following in time; later; succeeding. —**sub′se-quence,** *n.*

sub·serve′ *v.t.* serve to promote (a purpose, plan, etc.); be useful to.

sub·ser′vi·ent (səb-sėr′vė-ənt) *adj.* **1,** subordinate. **2,** servile. —**sub·ser′vi·ence,** *n.*

sub′set″ *n.* (*Math.*) a set, each of whose elements belongs to a given set.

sub·side′ (səb-sīd′) *v.i.* **1,** abate. **2,** sink lower. —**sub·sid′ence,** *n.*

sub·sid′i·ar″y (səb-sid′ė-er″ė) *adj.* lending assistance; supplementary; secondary. —*n.* **1,** a subsidiary thing or person. **2,** a company owned or controlled by a larger company.

sub′si·dize″ (sub′sə-dīz″) *v.t.* support financially.

sub′si·dy (sub′sə-dē) *n.* pecuniary aid.

sub·sist′ (səb-sist′) *v.i.* **1,** exist; have the means to live. **2,** continue. —**sub·sist′ence,** *n.*

sub′soil″ *n.* the soil next below the topsoil.

sub·son′ic *adj.* **1,** pert. to speed less than that of sound in air. **2,** moving or capable of moving at subsonic speed.

sub′stance (sub′stəns) *n.* **1,** any particular kind of corporeal matter; material. **2,** subject matter. **3,** wealth. —**substance abuse,** drug or alcohol addiction.

sub″stan′dard *adj.* of a level of quality, size, etc., below an established standard.

sub·stan′tial (-stan′shəl) *adj.* **1,** real; actual. **2,** genuine.

sub·stan′ti·ate″ (-stan″shē-āt″) *v.t.* establish by evidence. —**sub·stan″ti·a′tion,** *n.*

sub′stan·tive (-stən-tiv) *n.* **1,** (*Gram.*) a noun or pronoun, or a phrase or clause functioning like a noun. **2,** something that exists. —*adj.* **1,** pert. to a noun, etc. **2,** real; existing independently; essential.

sub′sti·tute″ (sub′stə-tūt″) *n.* a person or thing serving in place of another. —*v.t. & i.* supply or serve as a substitute. —**sub″sti·tu′tion,** *n.*

sub·sume′ (-soom′) *v.t.* bring (a class, case, etc.) under a larger class. —**sub·sump′tion** (-sump′shən) *n.*

sub·teen′ *n. & adj.* younger than thirteen.

sub·tend′ *v.t.* **1,** lie under or opposite to. **2,** enclose.

sub′ter·fuge″ (sub′tər-fūj″) *n.* an artifice; an evasion.

sub″ter·ra′ne·an (sub″tə-rā′nē-ən) *adj.* underground; hidden.

sub′text″ *n.* an implied meaning.

sub′ti″tle *n.* **1,** a secondary title. **2,** printed words shown in the course of a motion picture, usu. translating the dialogue into a different language.

sub′tle (sut′əl) *adj.* **1,** delicate; refined. **2,** artful; crafty. **3,** discerning; discriminating; shrewd. Also, **sub′tile.** —**sub′tle·ness, sub′tle·ty,** *n.*

sub·tract′ (sub-trakt′) *v.t. & i.* take away; deduct. —**sub·trac′tion,** *n.*

sub′tra·hend″ (sub′trə-hend″) *n.* a quantity to be subtracted.

sub·trop′i·cal *adj.* near the tropics; almost tropical.

sub′urb (sub′ẽrb) *n.* a district outside of, but adjoining, a city. —**sub·ur′ban** (sə-bẽr′bən) *adj.* —**sub·ur′ban·ite,** *n.*

sub·urb′i·a (sə-bẽr′bē-ə) *n.* the suburbs collectively.

sub·ven′tion *n.* a financial grant, esp. from governments.

sub·ver′sive (-vẽr′siv) *adj.* tending or intended to overthrow (a government, etc.).

sub·vert′ (səb-vẽrt′) *v.t.* overthrow; destroy. —**sub·ver′sion,** *n.*

sub′way″ *n.* **1,** an underground railway. **2,** an underground pedestrian passage.

suc·ceed′ (sək-sēd′) *v.i.* **1,** accomplish what is attempted; terminate, usually well. **2,** follow; come next. —*v.t.* come after; be heir to.

suc·cess′ (sək-ses′) *n.* **1,** a favorable termination. **2,** a person or thing that prospers. —**suc·cess′ful,** *adj.*

suc·ces′sion (-sesh′ən) *n.* **1,** a following in order; descent. **2,** the act or right of succeeding.

suc·ces′sive (-ses′iv) *adj.* following in order.

suc·ces′sor (-ses′ər) *n.* one who follows or replaces another.

suc·cinct′ (sək-sinkt′) *adj.* concise; brief. —**suc·cinct′ness,** *n.*

suc′cor (suk′ər) *n.* help. Also, **suc′cour.**

suc′co·tash″ (suk′ə-tash″) *n.* a dish of lima beans and corn.

suc′cu·bus (suk′yə-bəs) [*pl.* **-bi** (-bī)] *n.* a female demon imagined to disturb sleep.

> **succubus, incubus**
> ↔ These two demonic spirits, which have sexual intercourse with sleeping persons, get their names from their position, the *succubus* below, the *incubus* above. Both are of Latin origin.

suc′cu·lent (suk′yə-lənt) *adj.* **1,** juicy. **2,** interesting. —**suc′cu·lence, suc′cu·len·cy,** *n.*

suc·cumb′ (sə-kum′) *v.i.* **1,** give way under pressure; yield. **2,** die.

such *adj.* **1,** of that kind, character, or extent; like; similar. **2,** the same as previously specified or mentioned. **3,** of that class or character. —*pron.* **1,** such a person or thing; such persons or things. **2,** the same.

such′like″ *adj.* of this same kind; similar. —*pron.* persons or things of an indicated kind.

suck (suk) *v.t. & i.* **1,** draw into the mouth by creating a partial vacuum with the lips and tongue. **2,** absorb; inhale. **3,** (*Slang*) be inferior, disgusting, etc. —**suck up,** (*Slang*) toady; be obsequious.

suck′er *n.* **1,** one who or that which sucks. **2,** any of various fishes. **3,** (*Infor-*

mal) a lollipop. **4,** (*Informal*) a dupe; a gull. **5,** (*Slang*) any person or object.

suck′le (suk′əl) *v.i. & t.* nurse at the breast. **—suck′ling,** *n.* a baby at the breast.

su′cre (soo′kre) *n.* the monetary unit of Ecuador.

su′crose (soo′krōs) *n.* cane sugar.

suc′tion (suk′shən) *n.* the process or condition of sucking; sucking force.

sud′den (sud′ən) *adj.* happening or done unexpectedly; abrupt. **—sud′den·ness,** *n.* **—sudden death,** in sports, games, etc., a method of breaking a tie in which the first contestant to score a point wins. **—sudden infant death syndrome,** death from sudden stoppage of breathing in an otherwise healthy child. Also, **crib death.**

su′dor (soo′dər) *n.* sweat; perspiration. **—su″dor·if′ic** (-if′ik) *adj.*

suds (sudz) *n.pl.* **1,** water foaming with soap. **2,** (*Slang*) beer.

sue (soo) *v.t. & i.* **1,** institute process in law against. **2,** make a petition; woo.

suede (swād) *n.* undressed leather, esp. kid.

su′et (soo′it) *n.* fatty tissue.

suf′fer (suf′ər) *v.i. & t.* **1,** feel or undergo pain; sustain damage or loss. **2,** allow; permit; tolerate.

suf′fer·ance (suf′ər-əns) *n.* **1,** tacit consent. **2,** endurance.

suf·fice′ (sə-fīs′) *v.i.* be enough or adequate. **—***v.t.* satisfy.

suf·fi′cien·cy (sə-fish′ən-sē) *n.* **1,** adequacy. **2,** a sufficient income.

suf·fi′cient (sə-fish′ənt) *adj.* adequate; enough.

suf′fix (suf′iks) *n.* a terminal formative element added to a word or root to make a derivative word. **—***v.t.* (sə-fiks′) attach at the end.

suf·fo·cate″ (suf′ə-kāt″) *v.t. & i.* **1,** kill by impeding respiration. **2,** stifle; smother. **—suf′fo·ca′tion,** *n.*

suf·fra·gan (suf′rə-gən) *adj. & n.* assistant (bishop).

suf′frage (suf′rij) *n.* the political right or act of voting.

suf·fra·gist (suf′rə-jist) *n.* a person advocating suffrage, esp. for women. Also, (*Informal*) **suf″fra·gette′** (-jet′) *n.fem.*

suf·fuse′ (sə-fūz′) *v.t.* overspread, as with a liquid or tincture. **—suf·fu′sion,** *n.*

sug′ar (shûg′ar) *n.* a sweet crystalline substance. **—***v.t.* **1,** sweeten. **2,** make agreeable. **—***v.i.* form sugar. **—sug′ar·y,** *adj.* **—sugar beet,** a white beet yielding sugar. **—sugar cane,** a tall grass yielding

sugar. **—sugar daddy,** (*Informal*) a wealthy man who spends money on a young woman in return for intimacy.

sug′ar-coat″ *v.t.* **1,** cover with sugar. **2,** make more palatable.

sug′ar·plum″ *n.* a candy.

sug·gest′ (səg-jest′) *v.t.* **1,** propose for consideration. **2,** intimate. **3,** call to mind by association.

sug·gest′i·ble *adj.* **1,** easily influenced. **2,** that may be suggested.

sug·ges′tion (-jes′chən) *n.* **1,** act or result of suggesting; a proposal; hint. **2,** a small amount; a trace.

sug·ges′tive (-jes′tiv) *adj.* **1,** tending to suggest. **2,** suggesting something improper.

su′i·cide″ (soo′ə-sīd″) *n.* **1,** intentional self-destruction. **2,** one who takes his own life. **—su″i·ci′dal** (-sī′dəl) *adj.*

su′i gen′e·ris (soo′ē jen′ə-ris) (*Lat.*) of its own kind; unique.

suit (soot) *n.* **1,** a set of garments. **2,** a suing in a court of law. **3,** a petition or appeal. **4,** a courtship. **5,** a division of the pack of playing cards: spades, hearts, diamonds, or clubs. **6,** (*Slang, disparaging*) a male executive. **—***v.t. & i.* **1,** adapt. **2,** be appropriate. **3,** satisfy.

suit′a·ble *adj.* appropriate; becoming. **—suit″a·bil′i·ty,** *n.*

suit′case″ *n.* a rectangular traveling bag.

suite (swēt) *n.* **1,** a series or set. **2,** a retinue.

suit′ing *n.* cloth for making a suit.

suit′or *n.* a man who courts a woman.

su′ki·ya′ki (soo′kē-yä′kē) *n.* a Jap. dish of sliced meat and vegetables fried together.

Suk′koth″ (sū′koth″) *n.* the Jewish feast of thanksgiving.

sul′fa (sul′fə) *n. & adj.* designating certain antibacterial compounds.

sul′fur (sul′fər) *n.* a nonmetallic chemical element, no. 16, symbol S, used in medicine, gunpowder, etc. Also, **sul′phur.** **—sul·fur′ic** (-fyûr′ik) *adj.* **—sul′fur·ous,** *adj.*

sulk *v.i.* be silently resentful. **—***n.* a sullen mood. ❑ *skulk*

sulk′y (sul′kē) *adj.* morose. **—***n.* a light two-wheeled carriage used in trotting races. **—sulk′i·ness,** *n.*

sul′len (sul′ən) *adj.* morose; gloomy. **—sul′len·ness,** *n.*

sul′ly (sul′ē) *v.t.* stain; defile.

sul′phur (sul′fər) *n.* sulfur.

sul′tan (sul′tən) *n.* the sovereign of a

Muslim country. —**sul·tan′a** (-tä′nə) *n.* the wife or concubine of a sultan. —**sul′-tan·ate″** (-tə-nāt″) *n.*

sul′try (sul′trē) *adj.* **1,** very hot and moist. **2,** passionate. **3,** (*Slang*) salacious —**sul′tri·ness,** *n.*

sum *n.* **1,** the aggregate; total. **2,** a quantity of money. —*v.t.* [**summed, sum′ming**] **1,** add together. **2,** (with *up*) condense; recapitulate.

su′mac (soo′mak; shoo′-) *n.* a shrub; its leaves, used in tanning.

sum′ma cum lau′de (sûm′ə kûm low′dā) (*Lat.*) with the highest praise: used on diplomas to award the highest grades.

sum′ma·ry (sum′ə-rē) *n.* a condensed statement. —*adj.* **1,** brief; concise. **2,** (*Law*) immediately judged. —**sum·mar′-i·ly** (səmar′ə-lē) *adv.* —**sum′ma·rize″** (-rīz″) *v.t.*

sum·ma′tion (sə-mā′shən) *n.* a summing up; total.

sum′mer (sum′ər) *n. & adj.* (often *cap.*) the warm season; in the No. Hemisphere, approx. June 21 to Sept. 21. —**sum′-mer·y,** *adj.*

sum′mer·house″ *n.* a small shelter in a garden.

sum′mer·time *n.* summer.

sum′mit (sum′it) *n.* the top; the highest point or degree. —**summit meeting,** a meeting among heads of state.

sum′mit·ry (-rē) *n.* the political strategy of using conferences between heads of state to discuss and deal with international problems.

sum′mon (sum′ən) *v.t.* **1,** call or send for, with authority; call together. **2,** (with *up*) rouse. —**sum′mons,** *n.* an order to appear.

su′mo (soo′mō) *n.* (*Jap.*) a type of Jap. wrestling.

sump *n.* **1,** a pit in which water collects. **2,** an open drain. **3,** a reservoir. **4,** a cesspool.

sump′tu·ous (sump′choo-əs) *adj.* lavish; luxurious; grand. —**sump′tu·ous·ness,** *n.*

sun *n.* **1,** the central body of a solar system. **2,** the sunshine. **3,** anything splendid or luminous. —*v.t. & i.* [**sunned, sun′ning**] expose to the sun. —**sun bath,** exposure of the body to direct rays of the sun. —**Sun Belt,** the south and southwest of the U.S.

sun′bathe″ *v.i.* take a sun bath, esp. in the nude.

sun′beam″ *n.* a beam of sunlight.

sun′bon″net *n.* a bonnet shading the face.

sun′burn″ *n.* a burning of the skin from exposure to the sun. —*v.t. & i.* affect or be affected by sunburn.

sun′dae (sun′dē) *n.* ice cream with syrup, fruit, etc.

Sun′day (sun′dē) *n.* the first day of the week, observed by most Christians as the Sabbath.

> **Sunday**
> ↔ From a translation of Latin *diēs sōlis,* day of the sun.

sun′der (sun′dər) *v.t. & i.* part; sever.

sun′di″al *n.* a device on which a shadow indicates the time.

sun′down″ *n.* dusk; nightfall.

sun′dry (sun′drē) *adj.* several; various. —**sun′dries,** *n.pl.* miscellaneous articles.

sun′fish″ *n.* **1,** a large seafish. **2,** any of numerous varieties of small freshwater fish. **3,** (*cap.,* *T.N.*) a type of small sailboat.

sun′flow″er *n.* a tall plant bearing showy yellow flowers.

sung *v.* p.p. of *sing.*

sun′glass″ *n.* **1,** a lens for producing heat by focusing the rays of the sun. **2,** (*pl.*) spectacles of tinted glass.

sunk *v.* p.p. of *sink.*

sunk′en (sunk′ən) *adj.* **1,** submerged. **2,** on a lower level. **3,** concave; hollow.

sun′lamp″ *n.* an ultraviolet lamp used for therapeutic purposes or to produce artificial sunburn.

sun′light″ *n.* light from the sun. —**sun′-lit,** *adj.*

Sun′ni (sûn′ē) *n.* a member of an Islamic sect that regards the first four caliphs to be Mohammed's legitimate successors.

sun′ny (-ē) *adj.* **1,** bright with sunshine. **2,** cheerful. —**sun′ni·ness,** *n.*

sun′rise″ *n.* appearance of the sun above the horizon.

sun′roof″ *n.* a section in an automobile roof which can be opened to let in the sun.

sun′set″ *n.* disappearance of the sun below the horizon. —**sunset law,** a law providing for the automatic termination of a government program unless reauthorized by the legislature.

sun′shade″ *n.* a shield from the sun, as a parasol.

sun′shine″ *n.* **1,** bright sunlight. **2,** cheer. —**sunshine law,** a law requiring a government agency to open its meetings to the public.

sun'spot" *n.* a dark patch appearing on the sun.

sun'stroke" *n.* prostration from the sun's rays or heat.

sun'tan" *n. & v.t. & i.* tan.

sun'up" *n.* sunrise.

sup *v.i.* [**supped, sup'ping**] eat the evening meal.

su'per (soo'pər) *n.* (*Informal*) superintendent, supernumerary, etc. —*adj.* (*Informal*) excellent. —*adv.* very.

su·per- (soo-pər) *pref.* over, above, or beyond; superior; superlative; transcending.

su'per·an'nu·at"ed (-an'ū-ā"tid) *adj.* too old; past retirement age.

su·perb' (sû-pêrb') *adj.* magnificent; elegant; excellent.

su'per·car'go *n.* a person in charge of a cargo in transit.

su'per·charg"er *n.* a mechanism to force air into an engine.

su'per·cil'i·ous (soo"pər-sil'ė-əs) *adj.* haughtily contemptuous. —**su"per·cil'i·ous·ness,** *n.*

> **supercilious**
> ↔ Literally, of the eyebrows, from the notion of haughtiness as being symbolized by a raising of the eyebrows. The word is a compound of Latin *super*, above, and *cilium*, eyelash.

su'per·con"duc·tiv'i·ty *n.* unusually high conductivity, esp. in metals at very low temperatures.

su'per·cool" *v.t. & i.* cool (a liquid) below its freezing point without solidifying it.

su"per·e'go *n.* (*Psychoanal.*) a moral conscience that regulates the ego.

su"per·er'o·gate" (soo"pər-er'ə-gāt") *v.i.* do more than duty requires. —**su"per·er·og'a·to"ry** (-e-rog'ə-tôr-ė) *adj.*

su"per·fec'ta (soo"pər-fek'tə) *n.* a perfecta requiring the correct choice of the first four finishers of a race in order to win.

su"per·fi'cial (soo"pər-fish'əl) *adj.* **1,** lying on the surface; external. **2,** not deep or thorough. —**su"per·fi"ci·al'i·ty** (-fish"ė-al'ə-tė) *n.*

su·per·flu·ous (soo-pêr'floo-əs) *adj.* more than is needed. —**su"per·flu'i·ty** (-ə-tė) *n.*

su'per·fund" *n.* a large fund established for an especially costly project.

su"per·heat' *v.t. & i.* heat (a liquid) above its boiling point without vaporizing it.

su"per·he'ro *n.* an imaginary being having superhuman abilities, as *Superman.*

su"per·het'er·o·dyne" (soo"pər-het'ə-rə-dīn") *adj.* pert. to a radio receiver that changes the frequency of the incoming wave.

su"per·high'way *n.* a multilane divided highway.

su"per·hu'man *adj.* surpassing ordinary human power.

su"per·im·pose' *v.t.* lay (something) over something else.

su"per·in·tend' (soo"pər-in-tend') *v.t.* have charge of; manage. —**su"per·in·tend'ent,** *n.*

su·pe'ri·or (sə-pir'ė-ər) *adj.* **1,** higher in rank or office. **2,** more excellent; greater; higher. **3,** proud. —*n.* **1,** one superior to another. **2,** the head of a convent, etc. —**su·pe"ri·or'i·ty** (-or'ə-tė) *n.*

su·per'la·tive (sə-pėr'lə-tiv) *adj.* **1,** surpassing all others; supreme. **2,** excessive. **3,** (*Gram.*) expressing the highest degree by being, or as though, modified by *most.*

su'per·man", su'per·wom"an *n.* a person of extraordinary powers.

> **superman**
> ↔ A translation (popularized by its use by George Bernard Shaw in his play *Man and Superman*) of German *Übermensch,* coined by 19th-c. German philosopher Friedrich Wilhelm Nietzsche to mean an outstanding human being.

su'per·mar"ket *n.* a self-service retail market, usu. one of a chain, that sells food and other convenience items.

su·per'nal (soo-pėr'nəl) *adj.* **1,** lofty. **2,** celestial.

su"per·nat'ur·al *adj.* beyond the normal; not to be explained rationally.

su"per·no'va *n.* an explosion of a star and the resulting release of energy and light.

su"per·nu'mer·ar"y (soo"pər-nū'mər-er"ė) *n.* an extra person or thing; a theatrical extra.

su'per·pose' *v.t.* superimpose. —**su"per·po·si'tion,** *n.*

su'per·pow"er *n.* a leading country of the world.

su'per·scribe" *v.t.* write on or over. —**su"per·scrip'tion,** *n.*

su'per·script" *n.* a symbol written to the

right of and slightly above another symbol, as x′ (read "x-prime").

su″per·sede′ (soo″pər-sēd′) *v.t.* **1**, replace; supplant. **2**, set aside.

su″per·son′ic (soo″pər-son′ik) *adj.* **1**, above the audible limit. **2**, exceeding the speed of sound.

su′per·sta″tion *n.* an independent radio or TV station whose signal is broadcast by satellite to cable systems.

su″per·sti′tion (soo″pər-stish′ən) *n.* an unreasoning belief in an omen, supernatural agency, etc. —**su″per·sti′tious,** *adj.*

su′per·struc″ture *n.* something erected on a foundation.

su′per·ti″tle *n.* a translation of the words being sung projected above the stage in a theatrical production. Also, (*T.N.*) **Sur′-ti″tle** (sēr′-).

su″per·vene′ (soo″pər-vēn′) *v.i.* be added; occur unexpectedly. —**su″per·ven′tion,** *n.*

su′per·vise″ (soo′pər-vīz″) *v.t.* oversee; have charge of. —**su″per·vi′sion** (-vizh′ən) *n.* —**su′per·vi′sor,** *n.* —**su″per·vi′so·ry,** *adj.*

su·pine′ (soo-pīn′) *adj.* lying on the back. —**su·pine′ness,** *n.*

sup′per (sup′ər) *n.* a light evening meal. —**supper club,** a restaurant offering entertainment; nightclub. ❑ *dinner*

sup·plant′ (sə-plänt′) *v.t.* displace and take the place of.

sup′ple (sup′əl) *adj.* pliant; flexible; limber. —**sup′ple·ness,** *n.*

sup′ple·ment (sup′lə-mənt) *n.* an addition to something substantially completed. —*v.t.* (-ment″) add to. —**sup″ple·men′tal** (-əl), **sup″ple·men′ta·ry** (-ə-rē) *adj.*

sup′pli·ant (sup′lē-ənt) *n.* a petitioner. —*adj.* supplicating. Also, **sup′pli·cant** (-li-kənt).

sup′pli·cate″ (sup′li-kāt″) *v.i. & t.* entreat; petition. —**sup″pli·ca′tion,** *n.*

sup·ply′ (sə-plī′) *v.t.* furnish; provide. —*n.* **1**, the act of providing. **2**, a store or stock. **3**, the quantity available. **4**, one who fills a vacant position. —**sup·pli′er,** *n.* —**supply-side,** *adj.* (*Econ.*) pert. to the theory that considers the availability of capital to be the determining factor of an economy.

sup·port′ (sə-pôrt′) *v.t.* **1**, bear; hold up. **2**, uphold; back; speak for; encourage; aid. **3**, provide for; maintain. **4**, act with or accompany (a performer). **5**, put up with; endure. —*n.* **1**, maintenance. **2**, a base; something that supports. —**sup·port′a·ble,** *adj.* endurable; tenable.

sup·pose′ (sə-pōz′) *v.t.* make a hypothesis; assume. —**sup·pos′ed·ly,** *adv.*

sup″po·si′tion (sup″ə-zish′ən) *n.* act or result of supposing.

sup·pos″i·ti′tious (sə-poz″i-tish′əs) *adj.* **1**, pretended; spurious. **2**, supposed. Also, **sup″po·si′tious** (sup″ə-zish′əs).

sup·pos′i·tor″y (sə-päz′ə-tôr″ē) *n.* a small capsule of medication, usu. cylindrical or oval, introduced into the rectum, vagina, etc., where it is melted by body temperature.

sup·press′ (sə-pres′) *v.t.* **1**, restrain; abolish. **2**, repress. **3**, withhold from publication. —**sup·press′ant,** *adj. & n.* —**sup·pres′sion** (-presh′ən) *n.* ❑ *repress*

sup′pu·rate″ (sup′yə-rāt″) *v.i.* produce pus. —**sup″pu·ra′tion,** *n.*

su·pra- (soo-prə) *pref.* above.

su·prem′a·cy (soo-prem′ə-sē) *n.* state of being supreme; highest power. —**su·prem′a·cist,** *n.* one who believes in the suprem′acy of (a specified thing).

su·preme′ (sə-prēm′) *adj.* highest; utmost. —**Supreme Being,** God.

sur·cease′ (sēr-sēs′) *n.* cessation; end.

sur′charge″ (sēr′chärj″) *n.* an extra charge.

sur·cin″gle (sēr′sing″gəl) *n.* **1**, a girth for a horse. **2**, a girdle.

sur′coat (sēr′-) *n.* an outer coat or garment.

surd (sērd) *n.* (*Math.*) an irrational number.

sure (shûr) *adj.* **1**, confident; undoubting. **2**, certain. **3**, stable; unfailing; infallible. —*adv.* (*Informal*) surely. —**sure′ly,** *adv.* securely; certainly; doubtless. —**sure′-ness,** *n.*

sure′fire″ *adj.* (*Informal*) certain; assured of success.

sur·e′ty (shûr′ə-tē) *n.* **1**, security against loss or damage; a pledge. **2**, a guarantor; a sponsor.

surf (sērf) *n.* the swell of the sea that breaks on the shore. —*v.i.* ride waves on a surfboard. —**surf′ing,** *n.* —**surf and turf,** (*Informal*) a dish combining steak and seafood.

sur′face (sēr′fis) *n.* **1**, the outside; an outer face. **2**, external appearance. —*adj.* pert. to the surface; superficial.

surf′board″ *n.* a board on which one stands in the sport of riding crests of waves.

sur′feit (sēr′fit) *n.* excess, esp. in eating or drinking; satiety. —*v.t.* satiate.

surge (sērj) *n.* **1**, a large wave or billow; swell. **2**, (*Elect.*) a sudden increase in power in a circuit. —*v.i. & t.* swell.

sur'geon (sẽr'jən) *n.* a physician who practices surgery.

> **surgeon**
> ↔ From Greek *kheirurgía*, work of the hands, distinguishing the *surgeon* from the general medical practitioner who administers drugs.

sur'ger·y (sẽr'jə-rė) *n.* **1,** the treatment of disease, injury, etc. by manual or instrumental operations. **2,** an operating room.

sur'gi·cal (sẽr'ji-kəl) *adj.* pert. to surgery.

sur'ly (sẽr'lė) *adj.* ill-humored; ill-tempered. —**sur'li·ness,** *n.*

> **surly**
> ↔ A variant of *sirly*, lordly, by a shift of meaning through *haughty*.

sur·mise' (sẽr-mīz') *n.* a conjecture; a guess. —*v.t. & i.* guess.

sur·mount' (sẽr-mownt') *v.t.* **1,** pass over. **2,** overcome; prevail over. —**sur·mount'a·ble,** *adj.*

sur'name" (sẽr'nām") *n.* a family name.

sur·pass' (sẽr-pás') *v.t.* be greater than; exceed; transcend. —**sur·pass'ing,** *adj.* greatly excelling; extraordinary.

sur'plice (sẽr'plis) *n.* a white, loose-fitting clerical vestment.

sur'plus (sẽr'pləs) *n.* **1,** what is left over. **2,** the excess of assets over liabilities. —*adj.* left over; excess. —**sur'plus·age** (-ij) *n.*

sur·prise' (sər-prīz') *v.t.* **1,** come upon unexpectedly. **2,** strike with astonishment. —*n.* **1,** a surprising act or event. **2,** astonishment.

sur·re'al·ism (sə-rē'ə-liz-əm) *n.* art interpreting the workings of the unconscious mind. —**sur·re'al·ist,** *n. & adj.* —**sur·re'al,** *adj.*

sur·ren'der (sə-ren'dər) *v.t.* give up; relinquish. —*v.i.* give oneself up; yield. —*n.* a yielding.

sur·rep·ti'tious (sẽr"əp-tish'əs) *adj.* **1,** done by stealth; clandestine. **2,** acting in a stealthy way. —**sur"rep·ti'tious·ness,** *n.*

sur'rey (sẽr'ė) *n.* a light, four-wheeled carriage.

sur'ro·gate" (sẽr'ə-gāt") *n.* **1,** a deputy; a substitute. **2,** a judge having jurisdiction over the probate of wills, estates, etc. —**surrogate mother, 1,** a woman who acts in place of a child's biological mother. **2,** a woman who carries to term a child for another woman, either through implanta-

tion of the woman's embryo or by impregnation by the woman's husband.

sur·round' (sə-rownd') *v.t.* enclose on all sides; encompass; encircle. —**sur·round'ings,** *n.pl.* environment.

sur'tax" (sẽr'taks") *n.* an additional tax, esp. on income.

sur·veil'lance (sẽr-vā'ləns) *n.* **1,** a careful watch. **2,** supervision. —**sur·veil'lant,** *adj.*

sur·vey' (sẽr-vā') *v.t.* **1,** view; scrutinize. **2,** determine the boundaries, extent, position, etc., of a piece of land. —*n.* (sẽr'vā) **1,** a general view. **2,** a statistical study. **3,** a surveying. —**sur·vey'or,** *n.*

sur·viv'al (sẽr-vī'vəl) *n.* **1,** fact of surviving. **2,** something that has survived.

sur·vive' (sẽr-vīv') *v.i.* continue to live. —*v.t.* outlive; outlast. —**sur·vi'vor,** *n.*

sus·cep'ti·ble (sə-sep'tə-bəl) *adj.* **1,** (with *of* or *to*) capable of being affected. **2,** (with *to*) liable. **3,** impressionable. —**sus·cep"ti·bil'i·ty,** *n.*

su'shi (soo'shė) *n.* a Jap. dish consisting of a piece of raw fish or seafood served with a small cake of rice.

sus'lik *n.* a ground squirrel of Asia and Europe; its fur.

sus·pect' (sə-spekt') *v.t.* **1,** imagine to be guilty, without proof. **2,** distrust; doubt; mistrust. **3,** surmise. —*n.* (sus'pekt) a suspected person. —*adj.* (sus'pekt) open to suspicion; doubtful.

sus·pend' (sə-spend') *v.t.* **1,** hold from above and keep from falling; cause to hang. **2,** interrupt; delay. **3,** defer; postpone. **4,** debar temporarily. —*v.i.* cease; stay.

sus·pend'er *n.* **1,** (*pl.*) straps to hold up the trousers. **2,** a garter.

sus·pense' (sə-spens') *n.* anxious expectancy or indecision.

sus·pen'sion (sə-spen'shən) *n.* **1,** act or result of suspending. **2,** a temporary stoppage; stay. —**suspension bridge,** a bridge held up by cables hung between towers.

sus·pen'so·ry (sə-spen'sə-rė) *adj.* suspending. —*n.* a bandage or appliance that holds something up.

sus·pi'cion (sə-spish'ən) *n.* **1,** the act of suspecting. **2,** a slight trace.

sus·pi'cious (sə-spish'əs) *adj.* exciting or feeling suspicion. —**sus·pi'cious·ness,** *n.*

sus·pire' (sə-spir') *v.i.* sigh; breathe.

sus·tain' (sə-stān') *v.t.* **1,** maintain; support; keep alive. **2,** assist. **3,** endure; undergo. **4,** corroborate; affirm. **5,** of a tone, prolong. —**sustaining program,** a radio or television program that is not sponsored.

sus'te·nance (sus'tə-nəns) *n.* **1,** act of sustaining. **2,** nourishment; means of living.

sut'ler (sut'lər) *n.* a peddler who follows an army.

su'tra (soo'trə) *n.* a Hindu or Buddhist religious text.

sut·tee' (sut-ē') *n.* the self-cremation of a widow in her husband's funeral pyre, formerly practiced by Hindus.

su'ture (soo'chər) *n.* **1,** a sewing together of a wound, etc. **2,** the thread used. —*v.t.* sew (a wound).

su'ze·rain (soo'zə-rən) *n.* a sovereign or state that exercises political control over a dependent state. —**su'ze·rain·ty,** *n.*

svelte (svelt) *adj.* slender, graceful, sleek, etc.

swab (swob) *n.* **1,** a mop. **2,** a bit of cotton for cleansing or medicating. —*v.t.* [**swabbed, swab'bing**] mop; wipe with a swab.

swad'dle (swod'əl) *v.t.* wrap (a newborn child).

swag *n.* (*Slang*) loot.

swag'ger (swag'ər) *v.i.* **1,** strut. **2,** bluster. —*n.* a gait suggesting arrogance.

swain (swān) *n.* a male escort; a lover.

swal'low (swol'ō) *v.t.* **1,** take into the stomach through the throat. **2,** accept credulously; take patiently. **3,** suppress; retract. —*v.i.* perform the motions of swallowing. —*n.* **1,** the act of swallowing. **2,** a mouthful. **3,** any of various long-winged, graceful birds. —**swal''low·tail',** *n.* a cutaway dress coat.

swam *v.* pret. of *swim.*

swa'mi (swä'mē) *n.* **1,** lord; master: used of a Hindu religious teacher or monk. **2,** seer; prophet.

swamp (swomp) *n.* **1,** a marsh; a bog. —*v.t. & i.* **1,** flood; fill (a boat) with water. **2,** overwhelm.

swan (swon) *n.* a large, white swimming bird with a gracefully curved neck. —**swan song,** the last work or performance.

swank *n.* (*Slang*) pretentious smartness. —*adj.* [also, **swank'y**] stylish.

swans-'down'' *n.* **1,** very soft down from a swan. **2,** a fabric of similar softness.

swap (swop) *v.t. & i.* [**swapped, swap'-ping**] barter; exchange.

sward (swôrd) *n.* turf.

swarm (swôrm) *n.* **1,** a colony of honeybees. **2,** a mob. —*v.i.* throng.

swarth'y (swôr'thē) *adj.* dark in complexion. Also, **swart.** —**swarth'i·ness,** *n.*

> **swap**
> ↔ The modern sense of exchanging things comes from the act of striking hands together to seal a bargain. The word derives from a Germanic source meaning hit.

swash (swosh) *v.t. & i.* splash.

swash'buck''ler (-buk''lər) *n.* a swaggering bully; adventurer; daredevil. —**swash'buck''le,** *v.i.*

swas'ti·ka (swos'ti-kə) *n.* a form of cross adopted as the emblem of the Nazi party. Also **swas'ti·ca.**

swat (swot) *v.t.* [**swat'ted, -ting**] (*Informal*) hit sharply. —*n.* a blow.

SWAT (swot) *n.* a special division of a law enforcement agency trained to deal with unusually dangerous situations: *s(pecial) w(eapons) a(nd) t(actics).*

swatch (swoch) *n.* a sample strip of cloth.

swath (swoth) *n.* **1,** a mowed path. **2,** the sweep of a scythe.

swathe (swāth) *v.t.* bind with a bandage; wrap.

sway (swā) *v.t. & i.* **1,** bend back and forth. **2,** rule. **3,** prejudice; influence. **4,** vacillate. —*n.* rule.

sway'back'' *n.* abnormal sagging of the back, esp. in horses. —**sway'backed** (-bakt) *adj.*

swear (swār) *v.i. & t.* [**swore** (swôr), **sworn, swear'ing**] **1,** affirm something on oath. **2,** promise on oath; vow. **3,** curse. **4,** (*Informal*) (with *off*) give up (a habit, etc.).

sweat (swet) *v.i.* **1,** perspire heavily. **2,** exude or condense moisture. **3,** (*Informal*) drudge; suffer; wait impatiently. —*v.t.* **1,** excrete or exude. **2,** cause to sweat. —*n.* the process or product of sweating. —**sweat'y,** *adj.* perspiring.

sweat'er (swet'ər) *n.* a knitted garment for the upper body.

sweat'shirt'' *n.* a warm pullover shirt, worn by athletes.

sweat'shop'' *n.* a factory where workers are oppressed.

Swed'ish (swē'dish) *adj. & n.* of or pert. to Sweden, its people, language, etc.

sweep (swēp) *v.t.* [*pret. & p.p.* **swept**] **1,** move by, or as by, a long brushing stroke. **2,** brush over with a broom; clear. **3,** pass over. **4,** drag over; trail. —*v.i.* **1,** clear with a broom. **2,** move steadily. **3,** move ceremoniously. —*n.* **1,** an act of sweeping. **2,** reach; range; an extent; a curve. **3,** one who sweeps, esp. chimneys.

---

tub, cūte, pûll; labəl; oil, owl, go, chip, she, thin, *th*en, sing, ink; *see p. 6*

—**sweep′ing,** *adj.* of wide range; overwhelming.

sweep′stakes″ *n.* a gambling transaction; a lottery.

sweet (swēt) *adj.* **1,** having the taste of sugar or honey. **2,** pleasing. **3,** amiable. **4,** dear; precious. **5,** nonacid; fresh. **6,** fragrant. —*n.* a candy, dessert, etc. —**sweet′ness,** *n.* —**sweet pea,** a climbing plant or its fragrant flower. —**sweet potato,** a climbing plant or its edible yellow root. —**sweet spot,** the area of a tennis, squash, etc., racquet designed to produce optimûm rebound. —**sweet tooth,** (*Informal*) a liking for candy, etc.

sweet′bread″ *n.* the pancreas of an animal, used as meat.

sweet′bri″er *n.* a long-stemmed rose; the eglantine.

sweet′en (-ən) *v.t. & i.* **1,** make or become sweet or sweeter. **2,** (*Informal*) render more pleasant or palatable. —**sweet′en·ing,** *n.*

sweet′heart *n.* a person beloved.

sweet′ie (-ē) *n.* (*Informal*) sweetheart.

sweet′meat″ *n.* a candy.

sweet-′talk″ *v.t.* cajole; flatter.

sweet Wil′liam (wil′yəm) a small flower of the pink family.

swell (swel) *v.i. & t.* [*p.p.* **swelled** or **swol′len** (swō′lən)] **1,** grow in bulk; bulge; expand. **2,** rise, as a wave. **3,** show elation. —*n.* **1,** an increase; a bulge. **2,** a wave. **3,** (*Music*) an increase in loudness followed by a decrease; the sign (< >) indicating this. **4,** (*Slang*) a socially prominent person. —*adj.* (*Slang*) **1,** elegant. **2,** excellent.

swell′ing *n.* a swollen part; a protuberance.

swel′ter (swel′tər) *v.i. & t.* suffer from heat. —**swel′ter·ing,** *adj.* sultry.

swept *v.* pret. & p.p. of *sweep.*

swerve (swērv) *v.i. & t.* turn aside suddenly. —*n.* a sudden veering.

swift *adj.* **1,** moving with great speed; rapid. **2,** prompt. —*n.* a long-winged bird. —**swift′ness,** *n.*

swig *v.t. & i.* [**swigged, swig′ging**] drink by large drafts. —*n.* a drink; a deep draft.

swill (swil) *n.* garbage; hogwash. —*v.t. & i.* drink greedily.

swim *v.i.* [**swam, swum, swim′ming**] **1,** propel oneself through the water. **2,** be immersed. **3,** be dizzy. —*v.t.* swim across. —*n.* **1,** act or period of swimming. **2,** a smooth, easy movement. **3,** (*Informal*) the trend of fashion, etc. —**swim′mer,** *n.* —**swim′ming·ly,** *adv.* easily; prosperously.

swin′dle (swin′dəl) *v.t. & i.* cheat; defraud. —*n.* an act or instance of swindling. —**swin′dler,** *n.*

swine (swīn) *n.sing. & pl.* **1,** the domestic hog. **2,** any animal of the hog family. **3,** a contemptible person. —**swin′ish,** *adj.*

swing *v.i. & t.* [*pret. & p.p.* **swung**] **1,** move to and fro, while suspended; sway. **2,** (*Informal*) be hanged. **3,** (*Informal*) manage. **4,** (*Slang*) be promiscuous. —*n.* **1,** a seat suspended by ropes. **2,** steady rhythm. **3,** the natural rhythm or movement (of something). **4,** (*Informal*) a style of dance music. —**swing shift,** (*Informal*) a shift of work from 4 p.m. to midnight.

swing′er *n.* (*Slang*) one who adopts in his or her life-style the permissive moral and intellectual attitudes of present-day youth.

swipe (swīp) *v.t. & i.* **1,** strike with a long, sweeping blow. **2,** (*Informal*) steal. —*n.* a sweeping blow.

swirl (swērl) *v.i. & t.* whirl; eddy. —*n.* a twist; a curl. —**swirl′y,** *adj.*

swish *v.i. & t.* **1,** whisk; flourish. **2,** rustle. —*n.* a swishing sound or act. —*adj.* swishy. —**swish′y,** *adj.* (*Slang*) effeminate.

Swiss (swis) *adj.* pert. to Switzerland, its people, etc. —*n.* a Swiss citizen. —**Swiss cheese,** a pale yellow cheese having many holes.

switch (swich) *n.* **1,** a flexible twig or rod. **2,** a device for making or breaking an electric current. **3,** a change; a device for changing, as a *railroad switch.* **4,** a tress of hair. —*v.t.* **1,** whip. **2,** shift; divert. —*v.i.* change course.

switch′back″ *n.* **1,** a zigzag road or railroad. **2,** a roller coaster.

switch′blade″ *n.* a pocket knife with an automatic mechanism for opening.

switch′board″ *n.* a device for making telephone connections.

switched-′on″ *adj.* (*Informal*) **1,** in an elated mood; high (as on drugs). **2,** sophisticated; up-to-date.

switch-′hit″ter *n.* (*Baseball*) a batter who can bat right- or left-handed.

switch′man (-mən) *n.* [*pl.* **-men**] a tender of a railroad switch.

swiv′el (swiv′əl) *n.* a pivoted support. —*v.t. & i.* pivot.

swiz′zle stick (swiz′əl) a stick for stirring drinks.

swol′len (swō′lən) *adj.* swelled.

swoon *v.i. & n.* faint.

swoop *v.i.* sweep down. —*n.* a sudden sweeping down.

sword (sôrd) *n.* **1,** a weapon with a long

---

edged blade. **2,** (*Fig.*) warfare; military power.

sword'bill" *n.* a hummingbird of So. Amer.

sword'fish" *n.* a large fish with a hard, pointed beak.

sword'play" *n.* the art or practice of fighting with swords; fencing.

swords'man (sôrdz'mən) *n.* [*pl.* **-men**] a skilled fencer. —**swords'man·ship"**, *n.* skill at fencing.

swore (swôr) *v.* pret. of *swear.*

sworn (swôrn) *v.* p.p. of *swear.*

swum *v.* p.p. of *swim.*

swung *v.* pret. & p.p. of *swing.*

syb'a·rite" (sib'ə-rīt") *n.* a self-indulgent, luxury-loving person. —**syb"a·rit'ic** (-rit'ik) *adj.* —**syb"a·rit'i·cal·ly,** *adv.*

> **sybarite**
> ↔ From Greek *Sybarítēs*, inhabitant of Sybaris, an ancient Greek colony in S. Italy known for its taste for self-indulgence.

syc'a·more" (sik'ə-môr") *n.* **1,** (*U.S.*) the buttonwood or any plane tree. **2,** (*Eng.*) the maple.

syc'o·phant (sīk'ə-fənt) *n.* a servile flatterer. —**syc'o·phan·cy** (-fən-sè) *n.*

syl·lab'i·cate" (sil-lab'i-kāt") *v.t.* form or divide into syllables. Also, **syl·lab'i·fy"** (-fī"). —**syl·lab"i·ca'tion, syl·lab"i·fi·ca'-tion,** *n.*

syl'la·ble (sil'ə-bəl) *n.* the smallest separately articulated element in human utterance; one of the parts into which a word is divided. —**syl·lab'ic** (si-lab'ik) *adj.* —**syl·lab'i·cal·ly,** *adv.*

syl'la·bus (sil'ə-bəs) *n.* a compendium; an abstract.

> **syllabus**
> ↔ This word resulted from a misprint for *sittybas*, from Greek *sittyba*, table of contents.

syl'lo·gism (sil'ə-jiz-əm) *n.* a logical statement consisting of two premises and a conclusion, as "All men are human. John is a man. Therefore, John is human." —**syl"lo·gis'tic,** *adj.*

sylph (silf) *n.* **1,** an imaginary being. **2,** a slender woman.

syl'van (sil'vən) *adj.* **1,** pert. to the woods. **2,** wooded; woody.

sym"bi·o'sis (sim"bī-ō'sis) *n.* the living together of different species of organisms.

sym'bol (sim'bəl) *n.* **1,** an object standing for or representing something else; an emblem. **2,** a letter, figure, or character. —**sym·bol'ic** (-bol'ik) *adj.* —**sym·bol'i·cal·ly,** *adv.* —**sym'bol·ize"** (-līz") *v.t.*

sym'bol·ism (-iz-əm) *n.* **1,** the art or practice of representing things by symbols. **2,** a set of symbols. **3,** symbolic meaning.

sym'me·try (sim'ə-trè) *n.* **1,** regularity of accordance or form. **2,** excellence of proportion. —**sym·met'ri·cal** (si-met'ri-kəl) *adj.*

sym"pa·thet'ic (sim"pə-thet'ik) *adj.* **1,** feeling sympathy; compassionate. **2,** sharing a feeling. —**sym"pa·thet'i·cal·ly,** *adv.* —**sympathetic string,** a string in a stringed instrument designed to vibrate in sympathy with the bowed or struck strings.

sym'pa·thize" (-thīz") *v.i.* feel or express sympathy.

sym'pa·thy (sim'pə-thè) *n.* **1,** fellow feeling; compassion. **2,** condolence. **3,** agreement; approval; accord. ❑ *empathy*

sym'pho·ny (sim'fə-nè) *n.* **1,** an elaborate musical composition for an orchestra. **2,** any harmony of sounds, words, or colors. —**sym·phon'ic** (-fon'ik) *adj.* —**sym·phon'i·cal·ly,** *adv.*

sym·po'si·um (sim-pō'zè-əm) *n.* **1,** a meeting for discussion. **2,** a collection of writings on one subject.

> **symposium**
> ↔ From Greek *sumposion*, a meeting with drinking.

symp'tom (simp'təm) *n.* a sign or indication, esp. of a particular disease. —**symp"-to·mat'ic,** *adj.* —**symp"to·mat'i·cal·ly,** *adv.*

syn- (sin) *pref.* with; together.

syn'a·gogue" (sin'ə-gog") *n.* an organization or assembly of Jews for religious instruction and worship; the building where this is held.

syn'apse (sin'aps) *n.* the place where impulses pass between cells.

sync (sink) *n.* (*Informal*) synchronization.

syn'chro·mesh" (sin'krə-mesh") *adj.* designed to produce synchronized, smooth shifting of gears: a *synchromesh transmission.*

syn'chro·nize" (sing'krə-nīz") *v.i.* agree in time; occur at the same time. —*v.t.* cause to agree in time. —**syn"chro·ni·za'-tion,** *n.*

syn'chro·nous (sing'krə-nəs) *adj.* **1,** simultaneous. **2,** recurring together. **3,** (*Computers*) controlled by a clock.

syn'co·pate" (sing'kə-pāt") *v.t.* (*Music*)

accent beats normally unaccented. —**syn″-co·pa′tion,** *n.*

syn′co·pe (sing′kə-pē) *n.* **1,** a contraction. **2,** brief loss of consciousness.

syn′dic (sin′dik) *n.* **1,** a person appointed to transact business for a corporation, estate, etc. **2,** a civil magistrate of various countries.

syn′di·cate (sin′di-kət) *n.* **1,** an association of persons or corporations in a particular enterprise. **2,** an agency that supplies features for simultaneous publication in different newspapers. —*v.t.* (-kāt″) **1,** combine. **2,** distribute (newspaper features). —**syn″di·ca′tion,** *n.*

syn′drome (sin′drōm) *n.* a set of symptoms that characterize a certain disease or condition.

syn′er·gism (sin′ər-jiz-əm) *n.* the combined effect of two or more agents (as drugs) that is greater than the effect of either of the agents used alone.

syn′er·gy (sin′ər-jē) *n.* combined action or operation, as of muscles, drugs, etc. —**syn·er·get′ic, syn·er′gic,** *adj.*

syn′od (sin′əd) *n.* an ecclesiastical council. —**syn′od·al,** *adj.*

syn′o·nym (sin′ə-nim) *n.* a word having the same, or nearly the same, meaning as another. —**syn·on′y·mous** (si-non′ə-məs) *adj.* ❏ *homograph*

syn·op′sis (si-nop′sis) *n.* [*pl.* **-ses** (-sēz)] a summary; outline. —**syn·op′tic,** *adj.* —**syn·op′ti·cal·ly,** *adv.*

syn′tax (sin′taks) *n.* the due arrangement of words and phrases in a sentence. —**syn·tac′ti·cal** (sin-tak′ti-kəl) *adj.*

syn′the·sis (sin′thə-sis) *n.* [*pl.* **-ses″** (-sēz″)] the combination of separate elements into a complex whole; the product. —**syn′the·size″** (-sīz″) *v.t.*

syn′the·si″zer (sin′thə-sī″zər) *n.* someone or something that synthesizes; esp., a machine that reconstructs a given sound by recreating and combining its component frequencies.

syn·thet′ic (sin-thet′ik) *adj.* **1,** pert. to or based on synthesis. **2,** artificial. —**syn·thet′i·cal·ly,** *adv.*

syph′i·lis (sif′ə-lis) *n.* a chronic, infectious venereal disease. —**syph″i·lit′ic,** *adj. & n.*

> **syphilis**
> ↔ From *Syphilus,* the name of a shepherd who, according to a 16th-c. Veronese doctor, was the first recorded sufferer from the disease.

sy·rin′ga (sə-ring′gə) *n.* a flowering shrub, esp. the mock orange.

sy·ringe′ (sə-rinj′) *n.* a device used to draw in and eject a liquid.

syr′inx (sir′ingks) *n.* panpipe.

syr′up (sir′əp) *n.* any concentrated solution of sugar, flavored or medicated. Also, **sirup.** —**syr′up·y,** *adj.* ❏ *sherbet*

SYS′OP″ (sis′op″) *n.* the manager of an electronic bulletin board system: *sys(tem) op(erat*ȯr*).*

sys′tem (sis′təm) *n.* **1,** a number of things adjusted as a connected whole; a scheme, plan, or method. **2,** regular method or order. **3,** a concurrence of bodily parts. **4,** the entire body.

sys″te·mat′ic (-at′ik) *adj.* following a system; methodical. —**sys″te·mat′i·cal·ly,** *adv.*

sys′tem·a·tize″ (-ə-tīz″) *v.t.* make systematic.

sys·tem′ic (sis-tem′ik) *adj.* pert. to a system, esp. the body. —**sys·tem′i·cal·ly,** *adv.*

sys′to·le (sis′tə-lē) *n.* the normal contraction of the heart.

syz′y·gy (siz′i-jē) *n.* **1,** (*Astron.*) the alignment of three celestial bodies, esp. the sun, the earth, and a planet or the moon. **2,** any two related things.

T

T, t (tē) the twentieth letter of the English alphabet. —**to a T,** exactly.

tab *n.* **1,** a flap or strap. **2,** a tag; label. **3,** a bill; accounting. **4,** tablet. **5,** a group of blank spaces treated as a unit. —*v.t.* to put a tab (on). —*v.i.* to insert or move the distance of a tab.

Ta·bas′co (tə-bas′kō) *n.* (*T.N.*) a very spicy seasoning made from pepper.

tab′by (tab′ē) *n.* **1,** a female cat. **2,** an old maid. **3,** any watered silk fabric. —*adj.* striped or brindled.

> **tabby**
> ↔ The name of the cat comes from the fabric, which in turn was named after the suburb of Baghdad *Al-'at-tabiya,* which in turn got its name from Prince Attab, a noble resident of the suburb.

tab′er·nac″le (tab′ər-nak″əl) *n.* **1,** a place or house of worship. **2,** a receptacle for the Eucharist.

tab′la (täb′lä) *n.* a small tuned hand drum of India.

---

fat, fāte, fär, fâre, fåll, åsk; met, hē, hêr, maybè; pin, pīne; not, nōte, ôr, tool

tab′la·ture (tab′lə-chər) *n.* a system of musical notation using letters, numbers, or symbols other than notes.

ta′ble (tā′bəl) *n.* **1,** an article of furniture having a flat top supported on legs. **2,** a plane surface; a level tract of ground; a plateau. **3,** food served; fare. **4,** persons gathered at a table. **5,** an arrangement of written or printed information for classification in small space. **6,** a list. —*v.t.* **1,** place on a table. **2,** postpone discussion of. —**table tennis,** a game like tennis, usually played indoors on a large table; Ping-Pong. —**turn the tables,** bring about a reversal of circumstances or relations.

tab′leau (tab′lō) *n.* **1,** a picture. **2,** a striking scene. **3,** an arrangement or array.

ta·bleau′ vi·vant′ (tä-blō′ vē-vän′) [*pl.* **ta·bleaux′ vi·vants′** (tä-blō′ vē-vän′)] (*Fr.*) living tableau; a representation of a scene by posed costumed persons.

ta′ble·cloth″ *n.* a cloth cover for a table.

ta′ble d'hôte′ (tä′bəl dōt′) [*pl.* **ta′bles d'hôte′** (tä′bəls-)] (*Fr.*) a fixed meal of several courses served at a fixed price.

ta′ble·hop″ *v.i.* (*Informal*) go from table to table, visiting friends, as in a restaurant.

ta′ble·land″ *n.* a plateau.

ta′ble·spoon″ *n.* a spoon holding ½ fluid ounce. —**ta′ble·spoon″ful** *n.* [*pl.* **-fuls**].

tab′let (tab′lit) *n.* **1,** a small flat slab or piece, esp. one intended to receive an inscription. **2,** a number of sheets of paper bound together. **3,** a flattish cake, as of soap; a pill.

tab′loid *n.* a newspaper printed on sheets about 15″ x 11″ in size. —*adj.* smaller than the usual size.

---

tabloid
↔ Orig. a trade name for a brand of medicine tablet (from Old French *tablete*). Because a tablet also meant a flat slab or table, the diminutive term *tabloid* came to be used for the relatively small newspaper which featured "condensed" news.

---

ta·boo′ *n.* a ban or prohibition. —*adj.* prohibited; ostracized. Also, **ta·bu′.**

ta′bor (tā′bər) *n.* a small drum.

tab″o·ret′ (tab″ə-ret′) *n.* **1,** a low stand. **2,** a frame for embroidery. **3,** a stool.

tab′u·la ra′sa (täb′yə-lə rä′sə) (*Lat.*) a blank slate or tablet; hence, the mind before it has received any sensory information.

tab′u·lar (tab′yə-lər) *adj.* pert. to, or in the form of, a table.

tab′u·late″ (tab′yə-lāt″) *v.t.* enter in a table or list; put in the form of a table. —**tab″u·la′tion,** *n.* —**tab′u·la″tor,** *n.*

ta·chom′e·ter (tə-kom′ə-tər) *n.* an instrument for measuring velocity.

tach″y·car′di·a (tak″ē-kär′dē-ə) *n.* relatively rapid heart beat.

tach′y·on″ (tak′ē-on″) *n.* (*Physics*) a particle that moves faster than the speed of light.

tac′it (tas′it) *adj.* **1,** implied or understood, not expressed. **2,** silent. —**tac′-it·ness,** *n.*

tac′i·turn″ (tas′ə-tėrn″) *adj.* saying little; reserved in speech. —**tac″i·turn′i·ty,** *n.*

tack (tak) *n.* **1,** a small, short nail with a large head. **2,** any temporary fastening; a basting stitch. **3,** a course in sailing, esp. one obliquely toward the wind; a leg of a zigzag course. **4,** a course in general; a line of procedure. **5,** food; fare. —*v.t.* **1,** nail with tacks; attach, esp. temporarily. **2,** steer (a sailing vessel) on a tack. **3,** baste. —*v.i.* change course.

tack′le (tak′əl) *n.* **1,** an apparatus for moving heavy loads. **2,** equipment or gear, as for fishing. **3,** the act of seizing or tackling. **4,** a position on a football team. —*v.t.* **1,** grasp. **2,** undertake to deal with.

tack′y (tak′ē) *adj.* **1,** sticky; adhesive. **2,** (*Informal*) dowdy. —**tack′i·ness,** *n.*

ta′co (tä′kō) *n.* a Mexican dish of a tortilla filled with meat, cheese, etc.

tact (takt) *n.* good judgment in dealing with persons; diplomacy. —**tact′ful,** *adj.* —**tact′less,** *adj.*

tac′tic (tak′tik) *n.* a particular expedient. —**tac′ti·cal,** *adj.* —**tac·ti′cian** (-tish′ən) *n.*

tac′tics (tak′tiks) *n.sing.* the art of maneuvering forces in battle.

tac′tile (tak′til) *adj.* pert. to the sense of touch. —**tac·til′i·ty,** *n.*

tac′tu·al (tak′choo-əl) *adj.* **1,** pert. to or arising from touch. **2,** communicating the feeling of contact.

tad *n.* (*Informal*) **1,** a small child. **2,** a small amount.

tad′pole″ (tad′pōl″) *n.* a frog or toad in the larval stage.

tae kwon do (tī′ kwon′ dō′) (*Korean,* way of the fist) a Korean martial art.

tael (tāl) *n.* a Chinese unit of weight; a money based on this weight.

taf′fe·ta (taf′i-tə) *n. & adj.* a lustrous silk or rayon fabric.

taf′fy (taf′ē) *n.* a candy made of molasses and sugar.

tag *n.* **1,** a label tied or attached to something. **2,** a tatter. **3,** a binding on the end of a cord, ribbon, etc. **4,** something added, or at the end; a refrain, a moral, etc. **5,** a children's game in which one must pursue and touch another. —*v.t.* **[tagged, tag'-ging] 1,** furnish with a tag. **2,** (*Informal*) follow closely. —*v.i.* (with *along*) go as a follower. —**tag day,** a day on which contributions are solicited in exchange for tags. —**tag sale,** a sale of used and unwanted items.

tai chi (tī'jē') (*Chinese,* fist of the Great One) a Chinese system of exercise, characterized by slow, stylized movement. Also, **t'ai chi ch'uan** (chwän').

tai'ga (tī'gə) *n.* a subarctic forest, as in Siberia.

tail (tāl) *n.* **1,** the posterior extremity of an animal, esp. a projecting appendage. **2,** any flexible appendage. **3,** the rear, bottom, concluding, or inferior part of anything. **4,** (*pl.*) the reverse of a coin. —*v.t. & i.* follow after. —**tail spin,** a spiral, nearly vertical descent by an airplane. —**tail wind,** a wind blowing in the direction of travel of an airplane.

tail'board" *n.* the hinged platform at the rear of a truck. Also, **tail'gate".**

tail'coat" *n.* a man's coat with a long tail, for formal dress.

tail'gate" *n.* tailboard. —*v.t. & i.* **1,** (*Informal*) to follow a vehicle very closely, in another vehicle. **2,** (*Informal*) to picnic, esp. outside a football stadium.

tail'light" *n.* a warning light at the rear of a vehicle.

tai'lor (tā'lər) *n.* one whose business is to make and mend outer garments. —*v.t.* **1,** shape (a garment) to fit the body. **2,** outfit with clothing. —**tai'lor-made",** *adj.* made to exact order.

tail'pipe" *n.* (*Automobiles*) the pipe discharging exhaust gases from the muffler.

taint (tānt) *n.* **1,** a stain or blemish. **2,** contamination. —*v.t.* tinge with something deleterious; corrupt.

taj (täzh) *n.* (*Arabic*) an Arab conical cap.

take (tāk) *v.t.* **[took** (tûk), **tak'en] 1,** get by one's own action. **2,** seize; capture. **3,** accept willingly; receive; swallow, absorb, etc. **4,** understand; construe. **5,** be affected by or infected with. **6,** attack and surmount. **7,** (often with *in*) deceive; trick. **8,** carry; carry off; remove. **9,** conduct; escort. **10,** choose; select. **11,** be the subject of; experience. **12,** need; require. **13,** subtract. **14,** (with *up*) enter into or upon. **15,** attract; please. **16,** (with *on*) undertake to do; employ; consume; acquire. **17,** ascertain, as by measurement. **18,** (often with *down*) write down; record. **19,** do; make;

perform; execute, etc. **20,** (with *after*) resemble. —*v.i.* **1,** have effect; operate; develop. **2,** be successful; win favor. **3,** apply oneself. **4,** make one's way; proceed. **5,** admit of being taken. —*n.* **1,** the act of taking; what is taken. **2,** (*Slang*) gross income or net profit. **3,** (*Informal*) point of view; opinion. —**take-'home" pay** net wages received after deduction of taxes, etc. —**take the cake,** (*Informal*) win first prize. —**take a powder,** (*Slang*) leave. —**take out, 1,** date. **2,** (*Slang*) kill. ❑ *bring*

take'off" *n.* **1,** a beginning, as of an airplane flight. **2,** (*Informal*) a burlesque; an imitation.

take'out" *n.* (*Informal*) food prepared at a restaurant to be taken out by the purchaser.

take'o"ver *n.* the act or an instance of taking over, as of a company.

tak'ing *adj.* captivating.

talc (talk) *n.* a soft mineral, magnesium silicate.

tal'cum (tal'kəm) *n.* pulverized talc used as a powder.

tale (tāl) *n.* **1,** a narrative of events, real or imaginary. **2,** rumor. —**tale'bear'er,** *n.* informer.

tal'ent (tal'ənt) *n.* **1,** an inborn ability or aptitude. **2,** a person of ability. **3,** performer. **4,** an ancient widely variable unit of weight. —**tal'ent·ed,** *adj.* ❑ *ability*

ta'les (tā'lēz) *n.* a number of persons summoned to serve on a jury panel. —**tales'man** (tālz'mən) *n.* a person so summoned; substitute juror.

tal'is·man (tal'is-mən) *n.* [*pl.* **-mans**] an inscribed amulet or charm.

---

talisman
↔ This word is not a compound of *-man*, but is derived from Medieval Greek *telesma*, ritual object, which came to English via Arabic and French.

---

talk (tâk) *v.i.* **1,** utter words by the voice; speak. **2,** interchange thoughts; converse. **3,** chatter; prate; gossip. —*v.t.* **1,** say; speak. **2,** discuss. —*n.* **1,** the act of talking; speech; conversation. **2,** a conference or discussion. **3,** report; rumor. **4,** a subject of talk. **5,** manner of talking; language; dialect. —**talking machine,** a phonograph. —**talking picture** [also, (*Informal*) **talkie**], a motion picture with vocal sound. —**talk show,** (*Informal*) a radio or TV program consisting of interviews, sometimes with viewers or listeners participating by telephone.

talk′a·tive (-ə-tiv) *adj.* inclined to talk much. —**talk′a·tive·ness,** *n.*

talk′ing-to″ *n.* (*Informal*) a scolding.

tall (tâl) *adj.* **1,** having relatively great stature; high. **2,** having a specified height. **3,** (*Informal*) difficult to believe; extraordinary. —**tall′ness,** *n.*

tall′boy″ *n.* highboy.

tal′low (tal′ō) *n.* an oily substance used for making candles, soap, etc. .

tal′ly (tal′ē) *n.* **1,** an account kept of items; a reckoning or score. **2,** a tag or label. **3,** agreement. —*v.t.* **1,** record; register; score. **2,** count; enumerate. **3,** furnish with a tally; tag. 4, cause to correspond. —*v.i.* be in correspondence; accord.

tal′ly·ho″ (tal′ē-hō″) *n.* a coach drawn by four horses. —*interj.* used by hunters on sighting a fox.

Tal′mud *n.* a collection of authoritative dicta on Jewish religious law and life.

tal′on (tal′ən) *n.* **1,** a claw, esp. of a bird of prey. **2,** playing cards remaining after the deal.

ta′lus (tā′ləs) *n.* **1,** [*pl.* **-li** (-lī)] the anklebone. **2,** a slope.

tam *n.* tam-o′-shanter.

ta·ma′le (tə-mä′lē) *n.* a Mexican dish of corn and minced meat.

tam′a·rack″ (tam′ə-rak″) *n.* an American larch tree.

tam′a·rind (tam′ə-rind) *n.* a tropical tree or its sweet fruit.

tam″bou·rine′ (tam″bə-rēn′) *n.* a small single-headed drum with jingling metal disks set in its frame.

tame (tām) *adj.* **1,** changed from the wild state; domesticated. **2,** gentle; tractable; docile. **3,** dull; insipid. —*v.t.* make tame. —**tam′a·ble,** *adj.* —**tame′ness,** *n.*

tam-″o′-shan′ter (tam″ə-shan′tər) *n.* [also, **tam**] a Scottish flat cap or hat (from the name of the hero of a poem by Robert Burns).

tamp *v.t.* press down by repeated strokes; pound lightly. —**tamp′er,** *n.*

tam′per (tam′pər) *v.i.* meddle; touch improperly or harmfully.

> **tamper, tinker**
> ☞ Both words mean to fuss with something, but there is a difference in the result. To *tamper* is to meddle harmfully; to *tinker* is to fuss clumsily, perhaps, but not harmfully.

tam′pon *n.* **1,** an absorbent plug to stop or absorb hemorrhage. **2,** a type of sanitary napkin.

tan *v.t.* [**tanned, tan′ning**] **1,** convert (a hide) into leather. **2,** make brown by exposure to the sun. **3,** (*Informal*) thrash. —*v.i.* become tanned. —*n.* & *adj.* a yellowish-brown color, as from exposure to the sun.

tan′a·ger (tan′ə-jər) *n.* a small songbird.

tan′bark″ *n.* crushed bark used for tanning.

tan′dem (tan′dəm) *adv.* one behind another.

tang *n.* **1,** a strong or distinctive taste or flavor. **2,** a sharp sound; a twang. **3,** a slender projecting part of an object. —*v.i.* clang; twang. —**tang′y,** *adj.*

tan′ge·lo (tan′jə-lō) *n.* a cross between a tangerine and a grapefruit.

tan′gent (tan′jənt) *n.* **1,** a straight line marking the direction of motion of a point at any instant in generating a plane curve. **2,** a sudden divergence from one course to another. **3,** a trigonometric ratio. —*adj.* **1,** touching. **2,** being a tangent. —**off on a tangent,** digressing.

tan·gen′tial (-jen′shəl) *adj.* **1,** pert. to a tangent. **2,** touching. **3,** digressive.

tan″ge·rine′ (tan″jə-rēn′) *n.* **1,** a small, loose-skinned variety of orange. **2,** a reddish-orange color.

> **tangerine**
> ↔ The word originally meant "from Tangiers," the city from which the fruit was originally exported.

tan′gi·ble (tan′jə-bəl) *adj.* **1,** capable of being touched; having corporeal existence. **2,** definite or concrete; capable of being realized. —**tan″gi·bil′i·ty,** *n.*

tan′gle (tang′gəl) *v.t.* **1,** unite confusedly; snarl. **2,** catch, as in a trap; perplex. —*v.i.* be or become tangled. —*n.* a mass of tangled fibers; a confused jumble.

tan′go (tang′gō) *n.* **1,** a So. Amer. round dance for couples. **2,** (*Communications*) the letter *t.*

tan′gram (tang′grəm) *n.* a Chinese puzzle consisting of a square cut into seven pieces.

tank *n.* **1,** a large receptacle for storing fluids. **2,** a pool of water. **3,** an armored self-propelled combat vehicle. —**tank′age** *n.* —**tanked,** *adj.* (*Slang*) drunk. —**tank suit,** a one-piece bathing suit. —**tank top,** a type of sleeveless shirt. —**tank up,** (*Informal*) **1,** fill a gas tank. **2,** drink.

> **tank**
> ↔ *Tank* was the codeword for the armored vehicle while under development. The source is Sanskrit *tadaga,* pond.

tank′ard (tank′ərd) *n.* a large drinking cup with a hinged lid.

tank′er *n.* a ship for transporting oil.

tan′ner (tan′ər) *n.* **1,** one who tans hides. **2,** (*Brit.*) a sixpence. **—tan′ner·y,** *n.* a tanner's place of business.

tan′nin *n.* a substance used in tanning hides: *tannic acid.*

tan′sy (tan′zė) *n.* a flowering weed.

tan′ta·lize″ (tan′tə-līz″) *v.t.* tease by arousing and disappointing expectation.

> **tantalize**
> ↔ From the story of Tantalus, mythical king of ancient Phrygia, who was punished for his disrespect of the gods by being made to stand for eternity in water up to his chin, with delicious fruit overhead. If he stooped to drink, the water disappeared; if he reached for the fruit, the wind blew it away.

tan′ta·lum (tan′tə-ləm) *n.* a corrosion-resistant metallic element with high melting point, no. 73, symbol Ta.

tan′ta·mount″ (tan′tə-mownt″) *adj.* equivalent, as in value, force, or effect.

tan′trum (tan′trəm) *n.* (*often used in pl.*) a fit of temper.

Tao′ism (dow′iz-əm) *n.* a Chinese religious system. **—Tao′ist,** *adj. & n.*

tap *v.t.* **[tapped, tap′ping] 1,** strike lightly; pat. **2,** pierce or unplug (a container) to draw off liquid. **3,** provide outlets for (an electric wire, etc.). **4,** cut an internal screw thread in, **5,** connect into so as to listen, as a telephone line. *—v.i.* strike light blows; rap audibly. *—n.* **1,** a gentle blow; an audible rap. **2,** (*pl., construed as sing.*) a military signal on a bugle or drum: *lights out.* **3,** a piece of leather or metal fastened to the bottom of a shoe. **4,** a plug, faucet, or spigot in a hole. **5,** an outlet. **6,** an instrument for cutting internal screw threads. **—on tap, 1,** ready to be drawn, as liquor from a cask. **2,** ready for use. **—tap dance,** one in which the rhythm is tapped with the feet.

tape (tāp) *n.* a long, narrow band of flexible material. *—v.t.* bind or fasten with tape. **—tape deck,** a tape recorder without an amplifier included. **—tape measure,** a tape marked for measuring distance. **—tape recorder,** a device for recording sound on magnetized plastic tape. **—tape recording,** a recording made using a tape recorder.

ta′per (tā′pər) *v.i.* **1,** become gradually slenderer at one end. **2,** become gradually less; diminish. *—v.t.* make in tapered

form; cause to diminish. *—v.i.* (with *off*) gradually reduce consumption of something. *—n.* **1,** gradual diminution of width. **2,** a slender candle.

tap′es·try (tap′is-trė) *n.* a woven fabric reproducing elaborate designs, often pictorial.

tape′worm″ *n.* a parasitic worm that lives in the intestines of humans and animals.

tap″i·o′ca (tap″ė-ō′kə) *n.* a starchy food substance used in pudding for thickening, etc.

ta′pir (tā′pər) *n.* a tropical hoofed mammal resembling swine.

tap′pet (tap′it) *n.* a cam.

tap′room″ *n.* a barroom.

tap′root″ *n.* a main root.

taps *n.sing.* see *tap, n.,* def. 2.

tap′ster *n.* a bartender.

tar (tär) *n.* **1,** any of various dark, viscid products obtained from organic substances, as wood, coal, etc.; pitch. **2,** a sailor. *—v.t.* **[tarred, tar′ring]** smear with, or as with, tar. **—tar′ry** (tär′ė) *adj.*

tar″an·tel′la (tär″ən-tel′ə) *n.* a whirling Ital. dance; its music.

> **tarantella**
> ↔ The dance is named from the spider *tarantula*, which was named for the Italian seaport *Taranto*. The bite of the spider evidently caused a nervous disorder, one of whose symptoms was an uncontrollable whirling.

ta·ran′tu·la (tə-ran′chə-lə) *n.* any of various large spiders.

tar′dy (tär′dė) *adj.* **1,** not punctual; late. **2,** moving slowly; sluggish. **—tar′di·ness,** *n.*

tar′dy·on″ (tär′dė-on″) *n.* a particle that moves at less than the speed of light.

tare (tār) *n.* **1,** a weed; vetch. **2,** the weight of a container or vehicle without contents.

tar′get (tär′git) *n.* **1,** a design of concentric circles, aimed at in a shooting contest. **2,** anything aimed or shot at. **3,** a goal or objective.

tar′iff (tar′if) *n.* **1,** the duties levied on imports; customs. **2,** any table or system of charges; a price list.

Tar′mac (tär′mak) *n.* **1,** (*T.N.*) a paving substance used for roads, airport runways, etc. **2,** (*l.c.*) a road paved with Tarmac, esp. an airport runway.

tarn (tärn) *n.* a small mountain lake or pool.

tar′nish (tär′nish) *v.t.* **1,** dull the luster

---

fat, fāte, fär, fāre, fâll, åsk; met, hė, hėr, maybė; pin, pīne; not, nōte, ôr, tool of; discolor. **2,** cast a stain upon; sully. —*v.i.* become tarnished. —*n.* discoloration or impurity.

ta'ro (tä'rō) *n.* a starchy, tuberous plant of tropical regions.

ta'rot (ta'rō) *n.* **1,** any of a set of 22 pictorial playing cards used for fortune-telling. **2,** a card game played with the 22 tarots added to 52 cards of the usual suits.

tar·pau'lin (tär-pâ'lin) *n.* a cloth cover of waterproofed canvas.

tar'pon (tär'pon) *n.* a large game fish of warm Atlantic regions.

tar'ra·gon" (tar'ə-gon") *n.* a plant whose leaves are used in seasoning.

tar'ry (tar'ē) *v.i.* **1,** remain in a place; stay; sojourn. **2,** delay or be tardy; linger.

tar'sus (tär'səs) *n.* [*pl.* **-si** (-sī)] a bone structure joining ankle and foot. —**tar'sal,** *adj.*

tart (tärt) *adj.* **1,** acid or sour to the taste. **2,** sharp in character or expression; biting; sarcastic, etc. —*n.* **1,** a small fruit pie. **2,** (*Slang, offensive*) a woman of low character. —**tart'ness,** *n.*

tar'tan (tär'tən) *n.* a woolen or worsted cloth with a pattern of crossing varicolored stripes; a plaid.

Tar'tar (tär'tər) *n.* Tatar.

tar'tar (tär'tər) *n.* **1,** an earthy substance deposited on the teeth by the saliva. **2,** potassium tartrate as used in various drugs. **3,** an adversary hard to overcome. —**tar·tar'ic** (-tar'ik) *adj.* —**cream of tartar,** purified tartar, used in baking. —**tartar sauce,** mayonnaise dressing with chopped pickles, herbs, olives, and capers. —**tartar steak,** chopped beef, eaten raw.

Ta'sa·dy" (tä'sə-dī) *n.* a Stone Age people of the Philippines.

task (tàsk) *n.* **1,** a definite amount of work to be done; a job or stint. **2,** a burdensome piece of work. —*v.t.* put a strain upon. —**task force,** a naval force acting as a unit.

task'mas"ter, task'mis"tress, *n.* one who assigns tasks (esp., hard tasks) to others.

Tas·ma'ni·an devil (taz-mā'nē-ən) a burrowing carnivorous marsupial of Tasmania.

Tass (tas) *n.* the official news agency of the former U.S.S.R. (from the Russian acronym for Telegraph Agency of the Soviet Union).

tas'sel (tas'əl) *n.* a pendent fringe of threads.

taste (tāst) *v.t. & i.* **1,** try or perceive the flavor of by taking into the mouth. **2,** eat or drink a little of. —*v.i.* have a specified flavor. —*n.* **1,** the sense by which flavor or savor is perceived, operating through organs in the mouth. **2,** flavor or quality as perceived by these organs. **3,** the act of tasting. **4,** a portion tasted; a morsel. **5,** a liking; predilection; relish. **6,** particular preference. **7,** good judgment in aesthetic matters. —**taste'ful,** *adj.* showing good taste. —**tast'y,** *adj.* palatable. —**taste bud,** one of special organs of taste, a group of cells on the tongue.

tat *v.t. & i.* [**tat'ted, -ting**] knot thread with a shuttle, to make lace.

ta·ta'mi (tə-tä'mē) *n.* (*Jap.*) a floor covering.

Ta'tar (tä'tər) *n.* one of an Asiatic people related to the Turks.

tat'ter (tat'ər) *n.* **1,** a torn piece of cloth hanging from a garment. **2,** (*pl.*) ragged or torn clothing.

tat"ter·de·mal'i·on (tat"ər-də-māl'yən) *n.* a ragged fellow.

tat'ter·sall" (tat'ər-sâl") *n. & adj.* (of cloth) consisting of dark squares on a light background.

tat'ting (tat'ing) *n.* a kind of knotted lace made of thread.

tat'tle (tat'əl) *v.i.* **1,** gossip; divulge secrets. **2,** talk idly; chatter. —*v.t.* disclose by tattling. —*n.* idle talk; gossip. —**tat'tler, tat'tle·tale",** *n.* a gossip; an informer.

tat·too' (ta-too') *n.* **1,** a picture, etc., inscribed on the skin by the insertion of pigments. **2,** a bugle or drumming signal calling soldiers to their quarters. —*v.t.* mark with tattoos.

tattoo
↔ The two senses of this word are unrelated. The military sense comes from Dutch *taptoe*, turn off the (beer) taps. The body decoration sense is of Polynesian origin.

tau (tow) *n.* the 19th letter of the Greek alphabet (T, τ).

taught (tât) *v.* pret. & p.p. of *teach.* ❏ *taut*

taunt (tânt) *v.t.* **1,** reproach scornfully; ridicule. **2,** twit; provoke. —*n.* a gibe; taunting statement. ❏ *taut*

taupe (tōp) *n. & adj.* mole-colored; gray-brown.

tau'rine (tâ'rīn) *adj.* pert. to, or resembling, a bull.

Tau'rus (tôr'əs) *n.* a constellation, the Bull (see *zodiac*).

taut (tât) *adj.* **1,** stretched or drawn tight; tense, not slack. **2,** tidy; neat. —**taut'en,**

v.t. & i. make or become taut. —**taut'-ness,** *n.*

---

taut, taught, taunt
☛ Do not confuse these similar-looking words, which are unrelated. *Taut,* an adjective, means tight; *taught* is the past tense of *teach*; *taunt,* a verb and noun, means ridicule.

---

tau·tog' (tâ-tog') *n.* a food fish of the U.S. Atlantic coast.

tau·tol'o·gy (tâ-tol'ə-jē) *n.* needless repetition of the same idea in other words. —**tau"to·log'i·cal** (tâ"tə-loj'ə-kəl) *adj.*

tav'ern (tav'ərn) *n.* **1,** a house in which liquor is sold to be drunk on the premises. **2,** an inn.

taw (tâ) *n.* a game played with marbles; a marble; a line from which the players shoot.

taw'dry (tâ'drē) *adj.* showy but tasteless; gaudy; cheap. —**taw'dri·ness,** *n.*

---

tawdry
↔ From *St. Audrey,* referring to Etheldrida, 7th-c. queen of Northumbria, who attributed a tumor of the neck to her fondness for neckerchiefs. Her canonized name was later used for lace neckties made of cheap material.

---

taw'ny (tâ'nē) *adj. & n.* of a yellowish-brown color; tan. —**taw'ni·ness,** *n.*

tax (taks) *n.* **1,** an enforced contribution to the public funds, levied on persons, property, or income by governmental authority. **2,** a burdensome charge, obligation, or task. **3,** (*Informal*) any charge. —*v.t. & i.* **1,** levy a tax (on). **2,** lay a burden on. **3,** accuse; blame. —**tax shelter,** an investment designed to minimize income tax liability.

tax·a'tion (tak-sā'shən) *n.* act or effect of levying a tax.

tax'i (tak'sē) *n.* [also, **tax'i·cab"**] an automobile for public hire for short trips. —*v.i.* **1,** go by taxicab. **2,** (of an airplane) move on land or water. —**taxi dancer,** a girl who acts as dancing partner for pay. —**taxi squad,** (*Football*) a group of players hired to practice with a team.

tax'i·der"my (tak'sə-dėr"mē) *n.* the art of preserving and stuffing the skins of animals. —**tax'i·der"mist,** *n.*

tax'i·me"ter *n.* a device installed in a taxi for computing the fare.

tax·on'o·my (taks-on'ə-mē) *n.* the science of classification of plants and animals. —**tax"o·nom'i·cal** (-ə-nom'ə-kəl) *adj.* —**tax·on'o·mist,** *n.*

tax'pay"er *n.* one who pays taxes.

Tay-'Sachs' disease (tā-saks') a rare hereditary disease of children, usu. fatal.

tea (tē) *n.* **1,** an oriental plant whose dried leaves, infused with hot water, make a beverage; the beverage; a similar beverage made of other plants. **2,** a light evening meal. **3,** an afternoon reception. —**tea ball,** a small, porous bag or container of tea leaves. —**tea rose,** a yellowish-pink rose having a scent similar to that of tea. —**tea wagon,** a small serving table on wheels.

teach (tēch) *v.t.* [*pret. & p.p.* **taught** (tât)] **1,** impart knowledge or practical skill to; educate; instruct. **2,** impart knowledge of. —*v.i.* give lessons. ❑ *learn*

teach'er (-ər) *n.* one who teaches, esp. in a school.

teach-'in" *n.* an extended series of classes, lectures, and seminars on a certain subject, usu. as a means of social protest.

tea'cup" *n.* a cup in which tea or another hot beverage is served. —**tea'cup·ful,** *n.*

teak (tēk) *n.* a large Indian tree; its hard, durable wood.

tea'ket"tle *n.* a kettle with a spout, in which water is boiled.

teal (tēl) *n.* a wild duck.

team (tēm) *n.* **1,** a group of persons joined together in an action, esp. in a game. **2,** two or more horses, oxen, etc., harnessed together. —*v.t. & i.* join together in a team.

team'mate" *n.* a member of the same team.

team'ster (-stər) *n.* a driver of a team or truck.

team'work" *n.* coordination of effort.

tea'pot" *n.* a pot with a spout, in which tea is steeped.

tear (tir) *n.* **1,** [also, **tear'drop"**] a drop of the liquid flowing from the eye. **2,** (*pl.*) sorrow; grief. **3,** a drop of any liquid. —**tear gas** (tir) a gas that temporarily blinds, used as a weapon.

tear (târ) *v.t.* [**tore** (tôr), **torn** (tôrn), **tear'-ing**] **1,** pull apart or into pieces. **2,** make (holes, etc.) by rending forcibly. **3,** lacerate. **4,** (with *off, out, down,* etc.) drag violently; remove; raze; wrench. **5,** affect with grief or pity. —*v.i.* **1,** become torn. **2,** move or act with haste or violence. —*n.* **1,** a rip, rent, or fissure. **2,** turbulent motion; violent haste; an outburst of emotion. **3,** (*Slang*) a spree.

tear'drop" (tir'-) *n.* a tear.

---

tear'ful (tir'fəl) *adj.* weeping; sorrowful. —**tear'ful·ness,** *n.*

tear'jerk"er (tir'jẽr"kər) *n.* an overly sentimental play, movie, etc.

tea'room" *n.* a small restaurant.

tear'y (tir'ė) *adj.* nearly weeping. —**tear'i·ness,** *n.*

tease (tēz) *v.t.* **1,** worry or plague with persistent requests, insinuations, etc.; chaff with good-humored jests. **2,** separate the fibers of (wool, etc.). —*n.* one who teases. —**teas'er,** *n.* (*Informal*) an intriguing problem.

tea'sel (tē'zəl) *n.* **1,** a plant with thorny leaves or blooms. **2,** a device for raising the nap of cloth.

tea'spoon" *n.* a small spoon for table use, 1/3 tablespoon in capacity. —**tea'spoon·ful** (-fûl) *n.* [*pl.* **-fuls**].

teat (tēt) *n.* a nipple of the mammary gland.

tech'ie (tek'ė) *n.* (*Informal*) an enthusiast for technology, esp. computers.

tech·ne'ti·um (tek-nē'shė-əm) *n.* a radioactive metallic element, no. 43, symbol Tc, produced artificially.

tech'nic (tek'nik) *n.* **1,** technique. **2,** (*pl.*) technical rules, terms, etc. —*adj.* technical.

tech'ni·cal (tek'ni-kəl) *adj.* **1,** pert. to the methods or technique of an art, science, etc. **2,** peculiar to a particular art, etc.; esoteric. **3,** insistent on exact details or construction.

tech"ni·cal'i·ty (tek"ni-kal'ə-tė) *n.* **1,** technical character. **2,** detail of technique; a technical term or point. **3,** an insignificant point.

tech·ni'cian (tek-nish'ən) *n.* **1,** a skilled worker in a technical field. **2,** one skilled in technique.

Tech'ni·col"or (tek'ni-kul"ər) *n.* (*T.N.*) a method of making motion pictures in color.

tech·nique' (tek-nēk') *n.* **1,** method of performance. **2,** technical skill.

tech·no- (tek-nō) *pref.* using or pert. to technology.

tech·noc'ra·cy (tek-nok'rə-sė) *n.* a plan of social reform based on greater control and utilization of industrial power. —**tech'no·crat",** *n.*

tech·nol'o·gy (tek-nol'ə-jė) *n.* industrial arts collectively; the systematic knowledge of a particular art. —**tech"no·log'i·cal,** *adj.*

tec·ton'ics (tek-ton'iks) *n.* **1,** constructive arts. **2,** structural geology. —**tec·ton'ic,** *adj.* —**tectonic plate,** (*Geol.*) slablike sections of earth that support continents.

ted'dy bear (ted'ė bãr") a child's toy stuffed bear.

teddy bear
↔ Named for President *Theodore* Roosevelt, because he reportedly saved a bear cub's life.

te'di·ous (tē'dė-əs) *adj.* long, slow, and tiresome. —**te'di·ous·ness,** *n.*

te'di·um (tē'dė-əm) *n.* tediousness.

tee (tē) *n.* **1,** the letter *t*; something shaped like a capital T. **2,** the starting place in the play of a hole of golf. **3,** a small peg used to elevate a golf ball. —**tee off,** drive a golf ball. —**teed off,** (*Slang*) annoyed. —**tee shirt,** T-shirt.

teem (tēm) *v.i.* be full, prolific, or abundant.

-teen (tēn) *suf.* plus ten, as in *fourteen.*

teen'age" *adj.* 13 to 19 years old. —**teen'a"ger,** *n.*

teens (tēnz) *n.pl.* the ages 13 to 19 inclusive.

tee'ny (tē'nė) *adj.* (*Informal*) tiny.

tee'ny-bop"per (tē'nė-bäp"ər) *n.* (*Slang*) a young teenage girl who follows the latest fads; used esp. in the 1960s.

tee'pee (tē'pē) *n.* a tent of No. Amer. Indians. Also, **te'pee.**

tee'ter (tē'tər) *v.i. & t.* move back and forth; seesaw; move unsteadily. —*n.* a seesaw; a seesaw motion.

tee'ter-tot"ter *n.* a seesaw.

teeth (tēth) *n.* pl. of *tooth.*

teethe (tēth) *v.i.* grow teeth.

tee·to'tal (tė-tō'təl) *adj.* **1,** pert. to total abstinence from intoxicating liquor. **2,** absolute; entire. —**tee·to'tal·er,** *n.*

teetotal
↔ Coined by 19th-c. Englishman R. Turner, based on *total.* It apparently has nothing to do with *tea,* however.

tee·to'tum (tē-tō'təm) *n.* a top spun with the fingers.

Tef'lon *n.* (*T.N.*) a substance used as a coating on cooking utensils, razor blades, etc., to prevent sticking or catching.

teg'men (teg'mən) *n.* [*pl.* **-mi·na** (-mə-nə)] a covering.

teg'u·ment (teg'yə-mənt) *n.* a natural covering; integument.

tek'tite (tek'tīt) *n.* glass objects of uncertain (prob. extraterrestrial) origin found in various parts of the world.

tel·e- (tel-ə) *pref.* **1,** distant; far off. **2,** television.

tel′e·cast″ (-kåst″) *n. & v.* broadcast by television.

tel″e·com·mu″ni·ca′tion *n.* the science of communication at a distance (by radio, cable, etc.).

Tel″e·cop′i·er *n.* (*T.N.*) a facsimile machine.

tel′e·gen′ic (tel″ə-jen′ik) *adj.* that which looks good when shown on television.

tel′e·gram″ *n.* a message sent by telegraph.

tel′e·graph″ *n.* an apparatus and system for transmitting code messages by electric currents in wires. —*v.t. & i.* 1, send a telegram (to or about). 2, (*Informal*) give advance notice (of). —**te·leg′ra·pher** (tə-leg′rə-fər) *n.* —**te·leg′ra·phy,** *n.*

tel′e·ki·ne′sis (tel″ə-kə-nē′sis) *n.* the movement of objects by methods not explainable by natural laws.

tel′e·mark″ (tel′ə-märk″) *n.* a skiing maneuver.

tel″e·mar′ket·ing *n.* advertising or selling by telephone.

te·lem′e·try (tə-lem′ə-trē) *n.* transmission of radio signals and coded data from a space vehicle or satellite to a station on the earth, or vice versa. —**te·lem′e·ter,** *n.* a device used in telemetry.

te″le·ol′o·gy (tē″lē-ol′ə-jē) *n.* 1, the study of purpose in nature. 2, the doctrine that natural phenomena tend to a final purpose. —**te″le·o·log′i·cal,** *adj.*

te·lep′a·thy (tə-lep′ə-thē) *n.* communication between minds by means other than the ordinary and normal. —**tel″e·path′ic,** (tel″ə-path′ik) *adj.* —**tel″e·path′i·cal·ly,** *adv.*

tel′e·phone″ (-fōn″) *n.* an apparatus and system for transmitting speech and sounds by electric currents in wires. —*v.t. & i.* speak to or call by telephone. —**tel″e·phon′ic** (-fon′ik) *adj.* —**tel″e·phon′i·cal·ly,** *adv.* —**te·leph′o·ny** (tə-lef′ə-nē) *n.*

tel″e·pho′to *adj.* (of a lens) permitting photography at a distance. —*n.* (*cap., T.N.*) a picture transmitted by electric wire: *telephotograph.* —**tel″e·pho″to·graph′ic,** *adj.* —**tel″e·pho·tog′ra·phy** (-tog′rə-fē) *n.*

tel′e·play″ *n.* a play written for television.

tel′e·port″ (-pôrt″) *v.t.* move (a person or object) without physical contact either by mystical means or by conversion of matter to energy for transmission. —**tel″e·por·ta′tion,** *n.*

tel′e·print″er *n.* a teletypewriter.

Tel′e·Promp″Ter *n.* (*T.N.*) a device used in television for cueing a performer's lines.

tel′e·ran″ *n.* a system of aircraft navigation: *tele(vision) r(adar) a(ir) n(avigation).*

tel′e·scope″ *n.* an optical instrument by means of which distant objects are made to appear nearer and larger. —*v.t. & i.* slide, fit, or come together like a collapsing telescope; shorten.

tel″e·scop′ic (-skop′ik) *adj.* 1, pert. to a telescope; visible only through a telescope. 2, farseeing. —**tel″e·scop′i·cal·ly,** *adv.*

tel′e·thon″ *n.* a lengthy, continuous television program, usu. for raising money for charity.

Tel′e·type″ *n.* (*T.N.*) an apparatus and system for transmitting typewritten messages electrically.

tel″e·van′ge·list (tel″-) *n.* an evangelical preacher using television to promulgate doctrine.

tel′e·vise″ (-vīz″) *v.t.* send (a picture, show, etc.) by television.

tel′e·vi″sion (-vizh″ən) *n.* an apparatus and system for transmitting visual images by wireless electrical or electronic means.

tel′ex (tel′eks) *n.* a system of communication using interconnected teletypewriters; a message transmitted by telex: *tel(eprinter) ex(change).*

tell (tel) *v.t.* [*pret. & p.p.* **told** (tōld)] 1, make known; disclose; communicate. 2, give an account of; narrate; relate. 3, express in words; say. 4, explain. 5, inform. 6, discern; recognize. 7, command; bid. 8, assert positively. 9, count; enumerate. —*v.i.* 1, give an account; make a report. 2, be an indication or evidence of something. 3, have force or effect; produce a severe effect. —**tell off,** rebuke. —**tell on,** inform against.

tell′er *n.* one who tells or counts; esp., a bank clerk.

tell′ing *adj.* effective; striking.

tell′tale″ *n.* 1, a tattler. 2, an indicator or gauge. —*adj.* that reveals or betrays; significant.

tel·lur′i·an (te-lûr′ē-ən) *adj.* of the earth. —*n.* an inhabitant of the planet earth.

tel·lu′ri·um (te-lûr′ē-əm) *n.* a chemical element, symbol Te, no. 52.

tel′ly (tel′ē) *n.* (*Brit.*) television.

tem′blor″ (tem′blôr″) *n.* an earthquake; one tremor of an earthquake.

te·mer′i·ty (tə-mer′ə-tē) *n.* boldness;

rashness. **—tem″er·ar′i·ous** (tem″ə-rãr′ē-əs) *adj.*

---

temerity, timidity, timorousness
☛ These similar-looking words are antonyms. *Temerity* means boldness, the opposite of *timidity* and *timorousness.*

---

temp *n.* a temporary worker.

tem′per (tem′pər) *n.* **1,** state of mind or feelings; mood; disposition. **2,** irritability. **3,** calmness of mind; self-restraint. **4,** the state of a metal as to hardness and elasticity. **5,** a modifying substance. **—v.t. 1,** moderate; mitigate. **2,** bring to a desired condition. **3,** modify by admixture. **4,** (*Music*) adjust the pitch of.

tem′per·a (tem′pər-ə) *n.* in painting, distemper.

tem′per·a·ment (tem′pər-ə-mənt) *n.* **1,** the tendencies peculiar to an individual; natural disposition. **2,** tendency to act without self-restraint. **3,** the plan of tuning for a musical instrument.

tem″per·a·men′tal (-men′təl) *adj.* **1,** having a strongly marked temperament; irritable or sensitive. **2,** constitutional; innate.

tem′per·ance (tem′pər-əns) *n.* moderation, esp. in the use of intoxicating liquors.

tem′per·ate (tem′pər-ət) *adj.* moderate. **—tem′per·ate·ness,** *n.* **—Temperate Zone,** either of two parts of the earth's surface lying between the tropics and the polar circles.

tem′per·a·ture″ (tem′pər-ə-chûr″) *n.* **1,** condition with respect to hotness or coldness. **2,** (*Informal*) fever. **—temperature-humidity index,** a number estimating the level of comfort for a human being of a certain combination of temperature and humidity.

tem′pered (tem′pərd) *adj.* **1,** moderated; made less violent. **2,** having a specified disposition, as *good-tempered.* **3,** of metals, modified by heat treatment. **4,** (*Music*) tuned to a certain temperament.

tem′pest (tem′pist) *n.* a violent windstorm; any great commotion or tumult.

tem·pes′tu·ous (tem-pes′choo-əs) *adj.* stormy; tumultuous. **—tem·pes′tu·ous·ness,** *n.*

tem′plate (tem′plāt) *n.* a pattern or guide used in shaping a piece of work. Also, **tem′plet.**

tem′ple (tem′pəl) *n.* **1,** an edifice dedicated to the service of a deity; a church. **2,** a revered headquarters. **3,** the flattened area at the side of the head above the cheek.

tem′plet (tem′plit) *n.* template.

tem′po (tem′pō) *n.* **1,** rate of movement, as in music. **2,** a favorable movement for action.

tem′po·ral (tem′pə-rəl) *adj.* **1,** pert. to time. **2,** of the present life or this world; worldly; secular.

tem′po·rar″y (tem′pə-rer″ē) *adj.* lasting for a time only.

tem′po·rize″ (tem′pə-rīz″) *v.i.* **1,** defer action or decision to gain time; delay. **2,** yield temporarily.

tempt *v.t.* **1,** induce or incite; entice; dispose to evil. **2,** be attractive to; allure; invite. **3,** risk provoking; defy. **—tempt′er,** *n.*

temp·ta′tion (temp-tā′shən) *n.* act or effect of tempting; an inducement; enticement.

tem·pu′ra (tem-pû′rə) *n.* a Jap. dish of meat, fish, etc., cooked with butter and fried.

tem′pus fu′git (tem′pəs fū′jit) (*Lat.*) time flies.

ten *n. & adj.* the cardinal number between nine and eleven, expressed by 10.

ten′a·ble (ten′ə-bəl) *adj.* capable of being held or maintained. **—ten·a·bil′i·ty, ten′a·ble·ness,** *n.*

ten′ace (ten′is) *n.* (*Card Games*) a holding of two cards near but not adjacent in rank.

te·na′cious (tə-nā′shəs) *adj.* **1,** holding fast; retentive. **2,** persistent in an opinion or view; stubborn. **3,** sticky or viscous. **4,** highly cohesive; tough.

te·nac′i·ty (tə-nas′ə-tē) *n.* quality of being tenacious.

ten′ant (ten′ənt) *n.* one who holds property by lease or rent. **—v.t. & i.** inhabit. **—ten′an·cy,** *n.* **—ten′an·try,** *n.* tenants collectively.

Ten Commandments a series of rules for moral behavior, given by God to Moses (Ex. 20).

tend *v.i.* **1,** be inclined or disposed. **2,** lead in a particular direction. **3,** attend. **—v.t.** take care of; wait upon; attend.

ten′den·cy (ten′dən-sē) *n.* **1,** disposition to act in a particular way. **2,** a particular inclination; a mode, direction, or outcome.

ten·den′tious (ten-den′shəs) *adj.* **1,** opinionated; biased. **2,** serving or written as propaganda. **—ten·den′tious·ness,** *n.*

ten′der (ten′dər) *adj.* **1,** soft in substance, not hard or tough. **2,** delicate in constitution, health, etc.; gentle; sensitive. **3,** affectionate; sentimental; considerate. **4,** immature. **5,** requiring careful handling; critical. —*n.* **1,** one who tends; an attendant. **2,** an auxiliary boat or railroad car. **3,** an offer; the act of tendering. **4,** something offered; money that must be accepted in payment of a debt: *legal tender.* —*v.t.* offer; present for acceptance. —**ten′der·ness,** *n.*

ten′der·foot″ *n.* a soft or inexperienced person; a novice.

ten″der·heart′ed *adj.* kind; sympathetic. —**ten″der·heart′ed·ness,** *n.*

ten′der·ize″ (-īz″) *v.t.* make tender.

ten′der·loin″ *n.* **1,** a cut of tender meat. **2,** the underworld section of a city.

ten′don (ten′dən) *n.* a band of tough, fibrous tissue; a sinew.

ten″don·i′tis (-ī′tis) *n.* inflammation of a tendon. Also, **ten″di·ni′tis.**

ten′dril *n.* a threadlike growth from the stem of a vine.

ten′e·brous (ten′ə-brəs) *adj.* dark; gloomy.

ten′e·ment (ten′ə-mənt) *n.* **1,** a multiple dwelling, esp. of inferior class. **2,** any dwelling occupied by a tenant. **3,** an apartment in a multiple dwelling. **4,** any place of abode.

ten′et (ten′ət) *n.* any opinion, principle, or doctrine held to be true.

ten-′four′ *interj.* (*Slang*) CB radio term for message received, affirmative.

ten′nis (ten′is) *n.* a game of propelling a ball, struck by a racket, across a net.

ten′on (ten′ən) *n.* a projecting end for insertion into a mortise. —*v.t.* make or join by a tenon.

ten′or (ten′ər) *n.* **1,** the general course of a thought, saying, discourse, etc.; purport; drift. **2,** a male singing voice of high range.

ten′pen·ny (-pə-nė) *adj.* **1,** (*Obsolete*) [also, **ten′pence** (-pəns)] 10 Brit. pennies in value. **2,** of a nail; 3 in. long.

ten′pins″ *n.sing.* a bowling game.

ten′rec (ten′rik) *n.* a mammal of Madagascar.

tense (tens) *adj.* **1,** stretched tight; strained to stiffness; taut. **2,** in a state of mental strain or nervous tension. —*v.t. & i.* make or become tense. —*n.* (*Gram.*) time of the action of a verb. —**tense′-ness,** *n.*

---

tense, terse
☞ Do not confuse *tense*, tight, taut, with *terse*, brief, concise.

---

ten′sile (ten′sil) *adj.* **1,** pert. to tension. **2,** ductile.

ten′sion (ten′shən) *n.* **1,** the act of stretching; the state of being strained or tense. **2,** mental strain; excitement. **3,** an opposition of physical or electrical forces; pressure. —**ten′sion·al,** *adj.*

ten′si·ty (ten′sə-tė) *n.* a state of tension.

ten′sor (ten′sər) *n.* **1,** a muscle that tightens or stretches a part. **2,** a set of equations describing the properties of space. —**Ten′sor light** (*T.N.*) a high-intensity light with hinged shaft.

tent *n.* a portable shelter of cloth, skins, etc., supported by one or more poles. —*v.i.* live in a tent.

ten′ta·cle (ten′tə-kəl) *n.* **1,** a slender appendage of an animal; a feeler. **2,** any sensitive filament.

ten′ta·tive (ten′tə-tiv) *adj.* based on or done as a trial; experimental. —**ten′ta·tive·ness,** *n.*

ten′ter·hook″ (ten′tər-hûk″) *n.* a hook used to hold cloth stretched on a drying frame. —**on tenterhooks,** in a state of suspense; apprehensive.

tenth *adj.* the ordinal of ten, also written 10th. —*n.* one of ten equal parts.

ten′u·ous (ten′ū-əs) *adj.* **1,** thin in consistency; rarefied. **2,** slender or small. **3,** of slight significance. —**ten′u·ous·ness,** *n.*

ten′ure (ten′yər) *n.* **1,** the holding of something, as property, office, etc. **2,** the period of such holding. **3,** permanent status in a job, usu. awarded after a period of probation. —**tenure-track,** *adj.* of a job, leading to consideration for tenure.

te·nu′to (te-noo′tō) *adj.* (*It., Music*) held; sustained.

te′pee (tē′pē) *n.* teepee.

tep′id *adj.* moderately warm; lukewarm. —**te·pid′i·ty,** *n.*

te·qui′la (te-kē′lə) *n.* an alcoholic liquor of Mexico and Central Amer.

ter′bi·um (tėr′bē-əm) *n.* a metallic rare-earth chemical element, symbol Tb, no. 65.

ter″cen·ten′ar·y (tėr″sən-ten′ə-rė) *adj.* pert. to or comprising 300 years. —*n.* the 300th anniversary.

ter′gi·ver·sate″ (tėr″ji-vər-sāt″) *v.i.* change one's opinions or principles; be fickle. —**ter″gi·ver·sa′tion,** *n.*

ter″i·ya′ki (ter″i-yä′kė) *n.* a Jap. dish of marinated meat or fish broiled on a skewer.

term (tėrm) *n.* **1,** a word or phrase, esp. one particular to some branch of knowledge. **2,** the period of time through which

---

fat, fāte, fär, fāre, fâll, ȧsk; met, hē, hēr, maybė; pin, pīne; not, nōte, ôr, tool

something lasts, as a course of instruction in a school or college. **3,** (*pl.*) conditions offered for acceptance; rates. **4,** (*pl.*) relative position; circumstances. **5,** a mathematical expression treated as a unit. —*v.t.* apply a term to; name; call; designate. —**term insurance,** life insurance effective for a limited number of years.

ter′ma·gant (tēr′mə-gənt) *n.* a quarrelsome or shrewish woman.

> **termagant**
> ↔ From Old French *Tergavan,* an imaginary deity found in medieval morality plays.

ter′mi·na·ble (tēr′mə-nə-bəl) *adj.* that may be terminated.

ter′mi·nal (tēr′mə-nəl) *adj.* **1,** situated at or forming the extremity, boundary, or limit of something. **2,** final. **3,** pert. to a terminus. —*n.* **1,** a terminal part or structure. **2,** a principal railroad, bus, etc., station. **3,** an electrical connection. **4,** (*Computers*) a device for inputting or outputting data. —**terminal leave,** leave with pay (accumulated unused leave) given to a member of the armed forces before discharge.

ter′mi·nate″ (tēr′mə-nāt″) *v.t.* **1,** bring to an end; finish; conclude. **2,** form the end, boundary, or limit of. —*v.i.* **1,** come to an end; cease. **2,** result. —**ter″mi·na′tion,** *n.*

ter′mi·na″tor (tēr′mə-nā″tər) *n.* the line between the light and dark portions of the moon's or a planet's disk.

ter″mi·nol′o·gy (tēr″mə-nol′ə-jē) *n.* the vocabulary of terms peculiar to a particular subject.

ter′mi·nus (tēr′mə-nəs) *n.* [*pl.* **-ni″** (-nī″)] **1,** an end, extremity, boundary, or limit. **2,** terminal (def. 2).

ter′mite (tēr′mīt) *n.* a social insect that burrows into and undermines wooden structures; white ant.

tern (tērn) *n.* an aquatic bird of the gull family.

ter′na·ry (ter′nə-rē) *adj.* **1,** based on the number three. **2,** having three parts. **3,** third in order or rank.

terp″si·cho·re′an (tērp″si-kə-rē′ən) *adj.* pert. to dancing. —*n.* a dancer.

> **terpsichorean**
> ↔ After Greek *Terpsikhor,* the muse of dancing.

ter′race (ter′əs) *n.* **1,** an elevated tract of flat ground; one of a series of tracts at different levels. **2,** an outdoor promenade; a balcony. **3,** a street cut in a slope. —*v.t.* cut in a series of terraces.

ter′ra cot′ta (ter′ə kot′ə) *n.* **1,** a hard earthenware; something made of it. **2,** an orange-brown color. —**ter′ra-cot′ta,** *adj.*

ter′ra fir′ma (ter′ə fēr′mə) (*Lat.*) solid ground.

ter·rain′ (tə-rān′) *n.* a tract of land with regard to its suitability to a particular purpose.

ter′ra in·cog′ni·ta (ter′ə in-kog′ni-tə) (*Lat.*) unknown or uncharted land; the unknown.

Ter″ra·my′cin (ter″ə-mī′sin) *n.* (*T.N.*) an antibiotic drug.

ter′ra·pin (ter′ə-pin) *n.* any of several freshwater and tidewater turtles.

ter·rar′i·um (tə-rār′ē-əm) *n.* **1,** a place where land animals are kept. **2,** a small indoor glass-enclosed garden.

ter·raz′zo (te-rät′tsō) *n.* a flooring of cemented stone or marble chips.

ter·res′tri·al (tə-res′trē-əl) *adj.* **1,** pert. to the earth or dry land. **2,** worldly; mundane. **3,** living on land.

ter′ri·ble (ter′ə-bəl) *adj.* **1,** such as to excite terror; dreadful; fearsome. **2,** excessive; severe. **3,** (*Informal*) unpleasant; unskillful. —**ter′ri·ble·ness,** *n.* —**ter′ri·bly,** *adv.* (*Informal*) very.

ter′ri·er (ter′ē-ər) *n.* any of several breeds of small dog.

ter·rif′ic (tə-rif′ik) *adj.* **1,** causing terror. **2,** (*Informal*) extraordinary; extreme; extraordinarily good. —**ter·rif′i·cal·ly,** *adv.* —**ter·rif′ic·ness,** *n.*

ter′ri·fy″ (ter′i-fī″) *v.t.* fill with terror; frighten.

ter′ri·to″ry (ter′i-tôr″ē) *n.* **1,** a tract of land; a region or district. **2,** a domain; realm. **3,** (*cap.*) a region belonging to the U.S., not a state. —**ter″ri·to′ri·al,** *adj.*

ter′ror (ter′ər) *n.* **1,** intense fear, fright, or dread; a cause of fear. **2,** the use of violence as a political instrument; a period of such violence.

ter′ror·ism (ter′ər-iz-əm) *n.* the use of terror and intimidation to gain one's political objectives. —**ter′ror·ist,** *n. & adj.*

ter′ror·ize″ (-īz″) *v.i. & t.* dominate by intimidation; fill with dread.

ter′ry (ter′ē) *n.* [also, **terry cloth**] a fabric with a pile of loops.

terse (tērs) *adj.* saying much in few words; brief and pithy; concise. —**terse′ness,** *n.* ❑ *tense*

ter′ti·ar″y (tēr′shē-er″ē) *adj.* third in order or rank.

tes′la (tes′lə) *n.* a unit of magnetic induction, named for U.S. physicist Nikola Tesla.

tes′sel·late″ (tes′ə-lāt″) *v.t.* form into a variegated pattern of small squares. —**tes″sel·lat″ed,** *adj.* —**tes″sel·la′tion,** *n.*

tes′ser·a (tes′ər-ə) *n.* [*pl.* **-ae** (-ē)] a small square of marble, glass, etc., used in mosaic work.

test *n.* a critical trial or examination; a trial. —*v.t.* subject to a test; try; assay. —**test tube,** a hollow glass cylinder, closed at one end, used in chemical experiments.

> **test**
> ↔ From Latin *testum*, pot, because pots were used to test how metals reacted to heat.

tes′ta·ment (tes′tə-mənt) *n.* **1,** a document directing disposition of property after death of the owner; a will. **2,** an agreement; a covenant between God and man. **3,** (*cap.*) either of the two major parts of the Bible; the Mosaic dispensation (*Old Testament*) or Christian dispensation (*New Testament*). —**tes″ta·men′ta·ry,** *adj.*

tes′tate″ (tes′tāt″) *adj.* having made a valid will.

tes′ta″tor (tes′tā″tər) *n.* (*Law*) one who makes a will. —**tes·ta′trix** (tes-tā′triks) *n.* (*Law*) a female testator.

test-′drive″ *v.t.* drive before buying, to test for roadworthiness.

tes′ter (tes′tər) *n.* a canopy.

tes′ti·cle (tes′tə-kəl) *n.* the male sex gland. Also, **tes′tis** [*pl.* **-tes** (-tēz)].

tes′ti·fy″ (tes′tə-fī″) *v.i.* give testimony, esp. under oath; attest to facts. —*v.t.* give evidence of.

tes″ti·mo′ni·al (tes″tə-mō″nē-əl) *n.* **1,** a written recommendation or certificate. **2,** an expression of esteem or appreciation. —*adj.* pert. to testimony or a testimonial.

tes′ti·mo″ny (tes′tə-mō″nē) *n.* **1,** a statement made under oath by a witness. **2,** evidence; proof. **3,** open declaration, as of faith.

tes·tos′ter·one″ (tes-tos′tə-rōn″) *n.* the hormone secreted by the testicles, used medicinally.

tes′ty (tes′tē) *adj.* ill-tempered; irascible; petulant. —**tes′ti·ness,** *n.*

tet′a·nus (tet′ə-nəs) *n.* an infectious, often fatal, bacillic disease, marked by rigid spasm of voluntary muscles, as lockjaw.

tetch′y (tech′ē) *adj.* (*Dial.*) touchy; peevish. —**tetch′i·ness,** *n.*

tête-′à-tête′ (tāt′ə-tāt′) *n.* a private conversation, esp. between two persons. —*adj.* & *adv.* (in) private.

teth′er (teth′ər) *n.* a rope to restrain a grazing animal; a halter or leash. —*v.t.* restrain with a tether. —**teth′er·ball″** *n.* a game involving a ball attached to a pole.

tet·ra- (tet-rə) *pref.* four.

tet′ra·chord″ *n.* (*Music*) a diatonic series of four tones.

tet″ra·eth′yl *adj.* pert. to tetraethyl lead: see *ethyl.*

Tet″ra·gram′ma·ton″ (-gram′ə-ton″) *n.* (*Greek,* having four letters) the letters JHVH (or YHWH, etc.), representing the name of God, rendered in English as Jehovah (or Yahweh, etc.).

te·tral′o·gy (te-träl′ə-jē) *n.* a series of four related dramas, operas, etc.

te′trarch (te′trärk) *n.* one of four joint rulers. —**te′trar·chy** (-kē) *n.*

tet″raz·zi′ni (tet″rə-zē′nē) *adj.* of food, served over pasta with a cream sauce.

> **tetrazzini**
> ↔ After the famous Italian operatic soprano Luisa *Tetrazzini,* for whom it was first made.

Teu·ton′ic (tū-ton′ik) *adj.* pert. to the Teutons, or Germanic peoples.

Tex′as lea′guer (tek′səs lē′gər) (*Baseball*) a batted ball that falls safely between infielders and outfielders.

Tex-′Mex′ (teks′-meks′) *adj.* pert. to the culture of the S.W. U.S., combining Texan and Mexican features.

text (tekst) *n.* **1,** the main body of a book; the actual wording of anything written or printed; the author's words. **2,** the subject of a discourse; a theme or topic. **3,** a passage of Scripture taken as a theme. **4,** the words of a song, oratorio, etc. **5,** a style of printing type (𝕬); Old English. —**text file,** (*Computers*) a data file containing only alphanumeric characters and no formatting information.

text′book″ *n.* a book used for instruction.

tex′tile (teks′til) *adj.* pert. to weaving or fabrics. —*n.* cloth.

tex′tu·al (teks′chû-əl) *adj.* being or pert. to a text.

tex′ture (teks′chər) *n.* **1,** the particular arrangement of the constituent parts of any body; structure. **2,** surface characteristics.

-th *suf.* **1,** condition of being, as *warmth.* **2,** denoting ordinal numbers, as *fourth.* **3,** denoting an equal part of a division.

tha·las′sic (thə-las′ik) *adj.* pert. to the sea; marine.

tha·las·so- (thə-las-ō) *pref.* sea.

tha·lid′o·mide (thə-lid′ə-mīd) *n.* a sedative drug found to cause birth defects.

thal′li·um (thal′ē-əm) *n.* a metallic chemical element; no. 81, symbol Tl.

than (*th*an) *conj.* a particle used to introduce the second member of a comparison.

---

than, then

☞ These two words are frequently confused, esp. in pronunciation. *Than* (*th*an) is a conjunction connecting two things that are to be compared. *Then* (*th*en) is an adverb of time describing sequence of events. ↔ Etymologically, the two words are the same and at one time both referred to time.

---

than″a·tol′o·gy (than″ə-tol′ə-jē) *n.* the study and treatment of conditions surrounding death.

than″a·top′sis (than″ə-top′sis) *n.* a view or contemplation of death.

thane (thān) *n.* **1,** a knight or baron. **2,** a Scottish chief.

thank *v.t.* express gratitude to. —*n.* (*pl.*) an expression of gratitude. —**thanks to,** as a result of; due to. —**thank you,** *interj.* expressing gratitude. Also, **thanks.**

thank′ful (-fəl) *adj.* grateful. —**thank′-ful·ness,** *n.*

thank′less (-ləs) *adj.* **1,** unappreciated. **2,** ungrateful. —**thank′less·ness,** *n.*

thanks″giv′ing *n.* **1,** the act or occasion of giving thanks, esp. to God. **2,** (*cap.*) a U.S. holiday, the last Thursday in November.

that (*th*at) *adj. & pron.* [*pl.* **those**] **1,** (*demonstrative*) indicating or emphasizing a person or thing. **2,** (*relative*) as a subject or object in a relative clause, usually one defining or restricting its antecedent. —*adv.* to such an extent or degree. —*conj.* **1,** the following; namely. **2,** for this purpose.

thatch (thach) *n.* **1,** a covering, as for a roof, of straw, rushes, leaves, etc. **2,** the hair covering the head. —*v.t.* cover with a thatch.

thaw (thâ) *v.i.* **1,** of ice, melt. **2,** become so warm as to melt ice. **3,** become less formal or reserved. —*v.t.* cause to thaw. —*n.* the act or process of thawing.

the (*th*ə; emphatic or isolated, *th*ē) *def. art.* used before a noun or pronoun to particularize it, indicate an individual, mark a generic term, emphasize preeminence, etc.

the′a·ter (thē′ə-tər) *n.* **1,** a building or room fitted with a stage or screen and tiers of seats for spectators. **2,** dramatic works or performances collectively. **3,** a field of operations. Also, **the′a·tre.**

the·at′ri·cal (thē-at′ri-kəl) *adj.* **1,** pert. to the theater. **2,** affected; histrionic. —*n.* (*pl.*) dramatic productions.

the·at′rics (thē-at′riks) *n.* **1,** the art of staging dramatic performances. **2,** histrionics.

thé dan·sant′ (tā dän-sän′) [*pl.* **thés dan·sants′** (tā dän-sän′)] (*Fr.*) a tea dance.

thee (thē) *pron.* **1,** (*Archaic or poetic*) obj. sing of *thou.* **2,** (*Dial.*) you (*sing.*).

theft *n.* the act or an instance of stealing; larceny.

their (*th*ār) *pron.* poss. of *they;* in the predicate, **theirs** (*th*ārz). ❑ *he*

---

their, there, they're

☞ Three frequently confused homonyms. *Their* is a possessive form of *they, there* is an adverb of place, and *they're* is the contraction of *they are.*

---

the′ism (thē′iz-əm) *n.* the belief in the existence of a God. —**the′ist,** *n.* —**the·is′-tic,** *adj.* —**the·is′ti·cal·ly,** *adv.*

them (*th*em) *pron.* obj. of *they.*

theme (thēm) *n.* **1,** a subject of discourse or discussion; a topic. **2,** a brief essay. **3,** a principal subject in a musical composition. **4,** an identifying melody. —**the·mat′ic** (thē-mat′ik) *adj.* —**theme park,** an amusement park organized around a central idea.

them·selves′ (-selvz′) *pron.* emphatic form of *them;* reflexive form of *they.*

then (*th*en) *adv.* **1,** at that time. **2,** afterward; next in order. **3,** at another time. **4,** in that case; for this reason; therefore. **5,** on the other hand. —*adj.* being at that time. ❑ *than*

thence (*th*ens) *adv.* **1,** from that place. **2,** from that time; afterward. **3,** from that source; for that reason. —**thence′forth″,** *adv.* from that time or place onward.

the·o- (thē-ə) *pref.* of God or gods.

the·oc′ra·cy (thē-ok′rə-sē) *n.* government by priests.

the·ol′o·gy (thē-ol′ə-jē) *n.* the systematic study of God and His divinity. —**the″o·log′-i·cal** (-ə-loj′ə-kəl) *adj.* —**the″o·lo′gi·an** (-lō′jē-ən) *n.*

the·or′bo (thē-ôr′bō) *n.* a lutelike musical instrument of the 17th c.

the′o·rem (thē′ə-rəm) *n.* **1,** a statement of something to be proved; a theoretical proposition that has been deduced from other statements. **2,** a formula or equation expressing a natural law.

---

the″o·ret′i·cal (thē″ə-ret′i-kəl) *adj.* **1,** in accordance with a theory. **2,** impractical.

the′o·rist (thē′ə-rist) *n.* one who studies or draws conclusions from theory.

the′o·ry (thē′ə-rė) *n.* **1,** a set of propositions describing the operation and causes of natural phenomena. **2,** a proposed but unverified explanation. **3,** the principles of an art, as distinguished from its practice. —**the′o·rize″** (-rīz″) *v.i.*

the·os′o·phy (thē-os′ə-fė) *n.* any philosophical or religious system based on a claim of special insight into the divine nature; specif. Brahmanism or metempsychosis. —**the″o·soph′i·cal** (-sof′i-kəl) *adj.* —**the·os′o·phist,** *n.*

ther″a·peu′tic (ther″ə-pū′tik) *adj.* pert. to the curing of disease; having remedial effect. —**ther″a·peu′ti·cal·ly,** *adv.* —**ther″a·peu′tics,** *n.* the branch of medicine concerned with this.

ther′a·py (ther′ə-pė) *n.* the treatment of a disease; a remedial process. —**ther′a·pist,** *n.*

there (*th*ār) *adv.* **1,** in, at, or to that place. **2,** at that point in time, action, etc. **3,** in that respect; in those circumstances. **4,** an introductory word before the verb *be* when the subject is placed after it, as in *there is hope.* —*interj.* see! ❏ *their*

---

there is, there are, here is, here are

(*Gram.*) In sentences beginning with *there,* be certain that the connecting verb agrees with the true subject which follows it. Thus, "*There is* a tavern in the town," but "*There are* taverns in the town."

---

there- *pref.* adding a sense of time, place, direction, or agency, as in:

there′a·bout″	there″in·af′ter
there′a·bouts″	there·in′to
there·af′ter	there·of′
there·at′	there·on′
there·by′	there·to′
there·from′	there·un′der
there·in′	there·with′

there′for″ *adv.* for that person or thing.

---

therefor, therefore
☛ Once variant spellings, these two words now have distinct meanings. Be careful not to confuse them.

---

there′fore″ *adv.* for that reason; as a result; consequently. ❏ *therefor*

ther′e·min (ther′ə-min) *n.* an electronic musical instrument played by moving the hands between two antennas, named for the 19th-c. Russian inventor Leo Theremin.

there″to·fore′ (*th*ār″tə-fôr′) *adv.* before that time.

there″up·on′ *adv.* then; after that.

there″with·al′ *adv.* in addition to that; following that.

therm- (therm) *pref.* heat. Also, **ther·mo-** (thėr-mə; -mō).

ther′mal (thėr′məl) *adj.* pert. to heat or temperature. —**thermal pollution,** the pollution of a body of water by the addition of heated water, as from the cooling system of a nuclear reactor, thereby changing the mean temperature and affecting wildlife.

therm·is′tor (ther-mis′tər) *n.* an electrical resistor sensitive to heat.

ther′mo·cou′ple (thėr′mō-kup″əl) *n.* a device for measuring temperature.

ther″mo·dy·nam′ics *n.* the science concerned with the conversion of heat to energy, the control of temperature, etc. —**ther″mo·dy·nam′ic,** *adj.*

ther·mom′e·ter (thėr-mom′i-tər) *n.* an instrument for measuring temperature. —**ther″mo·met′ric,** *adj.*

ther″mo·nu′cle·ar *adj.* pert. to the extremely high temperatures required to initiate nuclear fusion, as in a hydrogen bomb, or released as a result of nuclear fission, as in the bombardment of uranium.

ther″mo·plas′tic *n. & adj.* (pert. to) a plastic that may be heated and molded more than once.

ther′mos (thėr′məs) *n.* a container insulated so as to maintain the temperature of its contents; a vacuum bottle. Also, **thermos bottle.**

ther″mo·set′ting *adj.* pert. to a plastic that can be molded only once.

ther′mo·sphere″ *n.* the outermost layer of atmosphere, in which temperatures increase with altitude.

ther′mo·stat″ (thėr′mə-stat″) *n.* an instrument for maintaining a desired temperature.

-ther·my (thėr-mė) *suf.* heat.

the·sau′rus (thė-sôr′əs) *n.* [*pl.* **-ri** (rī)] **1,** a collection of words classified by meaning. **2,** any repository; treasury. ❏ *dictionary*

these (thēz) *pron. & adj.* pl. of *this.*

the′sis (thē′sis) *n.* [*pl.* **-ses** (sės)] **1,** a proposition advanced for discussion, proof, etc. **2,** the subject of a composition. **3,** an essay or dissertation, esp. by a candidate for a degree.

thes'pi·an (thes'pē-ən) *adj.* of the drama. —*n.* an actor.

thespian
↔ From the reputed founder of Greek drama, *Thespis*, a poet who flourished in the 6th c. B.C.

the'ta (thā'tə) *n.* the eighth letter of the Greek alphabet (Θ, θ).

thew (thū) *n.* muscle; sinew.

they (*th*ā) *pl. pron.* [*poss.* **their** or **theirs**; *obj.* **them**] nominative plural of *he, she,* and *it.* ❏ *their*

thi'a·mine (thī'ə-min) *n.* vitamin B₁.

thick (thik) *adj.* **1,** having relatively great extent between opposite sides. **2,** having a specified measure between opposite sides. **3,** compactly arranged; dense. **4,** abundant; abounding with something. **5,** heavy; profound; obscure; intense, etc. **6,** mentally dull. **7,** (*Informal*) close in friendship; intimate. **8,** (*Informal*) disagreeable; unacceptable. —*n.* the thickest part. —**thick'en,** *v.t. & i.* make or become thick. —**thick'ness,** *n.*

thick'et (thik'it) *n.* a concentration of shrubs, trees, etc.

thick'set" *adj.* **1,** growing or occurring close together. **2,** heavily built; stout.

thick-'skinned" *adj.* not sensitive.

thief (thēf) *n.* [*pl.* **thieves** (thēvz)] **1,** one who steals; one who commits larceny or robbery. **2,** any lawless wrongdoer.

thieve (thēv) *v.i.* be a thief; steal. —**thiev'er·y,** *n.* —**thiev'ing, thiev'ish,** *adj.*

thigh (thī) *n.* the part of the leg between the hip and the knee in humans; a corresponding part.

thim'ble (thim'bəl) *n.* **1,** a metal cap worn on the finger to push a needle in sewing. **2,** a sleeve; bushing. —**thim'-ble·ful,** *n.* a very small amount.

thim'ble·rig" *v.t.* [-**rigged", -rig"ging**] swindle.

thin *adj.* [**thin'ner, -nest**] **1,** having relatively little extent between opposite sides; very narrow. **2,** having the constituent parts loose or sparse; not dense. **3,** lacking richness or strength; flimsy; transparent; weak, etc. —*v.t. & i.* make to become thin or thinner. —**thin'ness,** *n.*

thine (*th*īn) *pron.* poss. of *thou.*

thing *n.* **1,** a material object without life. **2,** a matter, affair, fact, circumstance, action, deed, etc. **3,** (*pl.*) personal possessions. **4,** a living being. **5,** (*Informal*) what one is most comfortable or most adept at doing. —**the thing,** (*Informal*) that which is proper or fashionable.

thing
↔ The original meaning of *thing* was assembly, from a Germanic root word meaning time. The sense development was through "something discussed by an assembly" to "a subject" to "an object."

thing'um·a·bob" (thing'əm-ə-bob") *n.* (*Informal*) thing. Also, **thing'um·bob", thing'um·a·jig".**

think *v.t.* [*pret. & p.p.* **thought** (thât)] **1,** hold as a belief or opinion; judge; consider. **2,** form a mental concept of; imagine. **3,** hold or bear in mind; recollect. **4,** reflect upon; meditate; ponder. **5,** expect. **6,** (with *up*) invent. —*v.i.* **1,** exercise the mind; cogitate; reflect. **2,** have an opinion or belief. **3,** (with *of*) bring something to mind; remember; make a discovery or invention; have expectation; show consideration. —**think tank,** (*Informal*) a group of experts engaged in research and problem-solving.

thin'ner (-ər) *n.* a solvent.

thin-'skinned" *adj.* very sensitive; touchy.

third (thẽrd) *n. & adj.* the member of a series next after the second. —*n.* one of three equal parts. —**third class, 1,** a class of mail, comprising printed matter such as advertising circulars, books, etc. **2,** next below second class. —**third degree,** an examination accompanied by torture or intimidation. —**third estate,** the commons. —**third person,** (*Gram.*) one other than the speaker and person spoken to. —**third rail,** a live rail supplying power to an electric locomotive. —**third world,** (often *cap.*) the developing countries of the world, esp. in Asia and Africa.

third-'rate' *adj.* inferior.

thirst (thẽrst) *n.* **1,** bodily need of drink. **2,** an ardent desire or craving for anything. —*v.i.* feel thirst. —**thirst'y,** *adj.* feeling thirst.

thir·teen' (thẽr-tēn') *n. & adj.* the cardinal number between twelve and fourteen, expressed by 13. —**thir·teenth',** *adj. & n.*

thir'ty (thẽr'tē) *n. & adj.* the cardinal number between twenty-nine and thirty-one, expressed by 30. —**thir'ti·eth,** *adj. & n.*

this (*th*is) *pron.* [*pl.* **these** (*th*ēz)] *& adj.* a demonstrative term indicating a person or thing immediately present, nearby, nearer than another, or previously referred to. —*adv.* to the specified extent or degree.

this'tle (this'əl) *n.* any of several plants having prickly stems and leaves.

this'tle·down" *n.* the silky fibers attached to the dried flower head of the thistle.

thith'er (thi*th*'ər) *adv.* to or toward that place.

tho (thō) *adv.* (*Informal*) though.

thole (thōl) *n.* a pin that acts as the fulcrum for an oar.

Thomp'son submachine gun (tom'sən) a portable automatic weapon. Also, **Tom'my** (tom'ė) **gun**.

thong (thâng) *n.* **1,** a narrow strip of leather. **2,** an open sandal. **3,** a type of very skimpy two-piece bathing suit.

tho'rax (thôr'aks) *n.* the part of the body between the neck and abdomen. **—tho·rac'ic** (thə-ras'ik) *adj.*

tho'ri·um (thôr'ė-əm) *n.* a radioactive chemical element, symbol Th, no. 90.

thorn (thôrn) *n.* **1,** a sharp excrescence on a plant; a spine or prickle. **2,** any of various thorny shrubs. **3,** something that wounds or annoys. **—thorn'y,** *adj.*

thor'ough (thėr'ə) *adj.* **1,** done completely or perfectly; fully executed. **2,** leaving nothing undone; exhaustive in action or operation. **3,** being completely such. **—thor'ough·ness,** *n.*

> **thorough, through**
> ↔ These are ultimately the same word, from Old English *thurh*, through, of Germanic origin.

thor'ough·bred" *adj.* **1,** bred from the best stock. **2,** superior. **—***n.* a thoroughbred person or animal, esp. a racehorse.

thor'ough·fare" *n.* a main road.

thor'ough·go"ing *adj.* complete; consummate.

thorp (thôrp) *n.* a hamlet; village.

those (thōz) *pron.* pl. of *that.*

thou (thow) *pron.* [*poss.* **thy** (*th*ī), **thine** (*th*īn)] (*Archaic*) sing. pron. of the second person.

though (thō) *conj.* **1,** in spite of the fact that; although. **2,** even if. **3,** nevertheless; yet. **4,** if. **—***adv.* however.

thought (thât) *n.* **1,** the act or product of thinking; mental activity; an idea, opinion, etc. **2,** attention; regard or care. **—***v.* pret. & p.p. of *think.*

thought'ful (-fəl) *adj.* **1,** pensive. **2,** considerate. **—thought'ful·ness,** *n.*

thought'less (-ləs) *adj.* inconsiderate; careless. **—thought'less·ness,** *n.*

thou'sand (thow'zənd) *n. & adj.* the cardinal number for ten times one hundred, expressed by 1,000. **—thou'sandth,** *adj. & n.*

thrall (thrâl) *n.* **1,** one in bondage; a serf or slave. **2,** slavery. **—thral'dom, thrall'-dom,** *n.*

thrash *v.t.* **1,** beat or whip, as for punishment. **2,** defeat thoroughly. **3,** thresh. **—***v.i.* toss about violently.

thrash'er (thrash'ər) *n.* a thrushlike songbird.

thread (thred) *n.* **1,** a fine cord made of twisted fibers, used in weaving or sewing. **2,** any fine filament. **3,** something thin and long. **4,** the spiral groove or ridge of a screw or a nut. **5,** a theme; sequence. **—***v.t.* **1,** pass a thread through the eye of (a needle). **2,** string, as beads. **3,** form a screw thread on or in. **4,** pervade; steer through (something narrow or intricate). **—***v.i.* move in a winding course.

thread'bare" *adj.* **1,** shabby; scanty. **2,** trite; hackneyed.

thread'y *adj.* **1,** like thread; filamentous. **2,** very thin, slight, or feeble. **—thread'i·ness,** *n.*

threat (thret) *n.* **1,** a declaration of intention or determination to harm another. **2,** an indication of impending danger or evil.

threat'en (thret'ən) *v.t. & i.* utter or be a threat (against). **—threat'ened species** (-ənd) a species likely to become endangered.

three (thrē) *n. & adj.* the cardinal number between two and four, expressed by 3 (ordinal, *third*).

three-'deck'er *n.* something with three layers, esp. a sandwich made with three slices of bread.

three-"di·men'sion·al *adj.* **1,** having three dimensions, i.e., height, width, and depth. **2,** lifelike; realistic. **3,** having an illusion of depth, often achieved through stereoscopic means. Also, **3-D.**

three'fold" *adj.* times three; in three parts.

three'pence (thrip'əns) *n.* (*Obsolete*) a Brit. coin worth three pennies. **—three'-pen"ny** (thrip'ə-nė) *adj.*

thren'o·dy (thren'ə-dė) *n.* a song of lamentation; a dirge.

thresh *v.t.* **1,** beat (a cereal plant) with a flail, to separate the grain or seeds. **2,** discuss (a matter) exhaustively.

thresh'old (thresh'ōld) *n.* **1,** a doorsill. **2,** a point of beginning.

threw (throo) *v.* pret. of *throw.*

thrice (thrīs) *adj.* three times.

thrift *n.* economical management; the saving of money. **—thrift'y,** *adj.* **—thrift**

shop, a store selling used or donated items, usu. to raise money for charity.

thrill (thril) *v.t.* **1,** affect with a sudden wave of emotion or sensation, esp. of pleasure. **2,** cause to vibrate or quiver. —*v.i.* **1,** be thrilled. **2,** produce a thrill. —*n.* **1,** a sudden keen emotion. **2,** a tremor, or tingling; vibration. —**thrill′er,** *n.* an exciting story, play, etc., esp. when of small artistic value.

thrive (thrīv) *v.i.* be fortunate or successful; prosper; flourish.

throat (thrōt) *n.* **1,** the passage from the mouth to the stomach or lungs. **2,** the front of the neck. **3,** any narrowed part or passage.

throat′y (-ė) *adj.* (of sounds) produced or modified in the throat. —**throat′i·ness,** *n.*

throb *v.i.* [**throbbed, throb′bing**] **1,** beat, as the heart, with increased force or rapidity. **2,** pulsate; vibrate. **3,** feel emotion. —*n.* a strong pulsation.

throe (thrō) *n.* **1,** a violent pang; a spasm or paroxysm. **2,** (*pl.*) convulsive pain.

throm·bo′sis (throm-bō′sis) *n.* clotting of the blood in any part of the circulatory system.

throm′bus (throm′bəs) *n.* [*pl.* **-bi** (-bī)] a clot in a blood vessel.

throne (thrōn) *n.* **1,** the ceremonial chair of a sovereign, bishop, etc. **2,** sovereign power.

throng (thrâng) *n.* a large crowd or multitude. —*v.i.* assemble in large numbers. —*v.t.* fill with a crowd.

thros′tle (thros′əl) *n.* a Europ. thrush.

throt′tle (throt′əl) *n.* a valve regulating the admission of fuel to an engine. —*v.t.* **1,** strangle; suffocate. **2,** silence. **3,** check.

through (throo) *prep.* **1,** from one side or end of the other; completely across or over. **2,** between or among the parts of. **3,** within the limits of; during the period of. **4,** to the end of. **5,** by agency of. **6,** by reason or in consequence of. —*adv.* **1,** from one side or end to the other. **2,** from beginning to end; all the way. **3,** thoroughly. **4,** to the end or completion. —*adj.* passing or extending to a destination with little or no interruption. ❏ *thorough*

through·out′ *pret. & adv.* in every part (of).

through′put″ *n.* the output of a machine.

through′way″ *n.* thruway.

throw (thrō) *v.t.* [**threw** (throo), **thrown** (thrōn), **throw′ing**] **1,** toss or fling through the air with a jerk of the arm; propel in any way; cast; hurl. **2,** put carelessly. **3,** bring to the ground. **4,** shape, as on a lathe. **5,** lose (a contest) intentionally. —*v.i.* make a cast, etc. —*n.* **1,** the act or a result of throwing. **2,** the distance traveled or displacement of a moving part. **3,** a scarf or blanket. —**throw up,** vomit.

throw′a·way″ *n.* an advertising circular. —*adj.* intended to be discarded; hence, of a comment, off-hand, casual.

throw′back″ *n.* an instance of atavism.

thrown (thrōn) *v.* p.p. of *throw.* —**thrown in,** added without extra charge.

thru (throo) *prep.* (*Informal*) through.

thrum *v.t. & i.* [**thrummed, thrum′ming**] play (a stringed instrument) by plucking; drum or tap idly (on).

thrush *n.* **1,** any of numerous songbirds. **2,** a disease caused by a fungus.

thrust *v.t.* [*pret. & p.p.* **thrust**] **1,** push forcibly; shove. **2,** compel; drive; force. **3,** stab. —*v.i.* make a thrust; lunge. —*n.* **1,** a push, lunge, or stab. **2,** force exerted linearly. **3,** meaning; import.

thru′way (throo′wā) *n.* a high-speed divided highway, sometimes having a toll.

thud *n.* a dull, blunt, or hollow sound. —*v.i. & t.* [**thud′ded, -ding**] make a thud.

thug *n.* a professional cutthroat.

> **thug**
> ↔ From Hindi *thag,* thief, orig. members of an organization of assassins and robbers in India.

thu′li·um (thoo′lė-əm) *n.* a rare-earth metallic element, no. 69, symbol Tm.

thumb (thum) *n.* the shortest and thickest finger of the hand. —*v.t.* **1,** run through with the thumb; handle. **2,** solicit (a ride) by pointing with the thumb. —**all thumbs,** awkward. —**under one's thumb, 1,** readily available. **2,** controlled by.

thumb′nail″ *n.* the nail on the thumb. —*adj.* very small or brief.

thumb′screw″ *n.* **1,** a screw that may be turned by hand. **2,** an instrument of torture.

thumb′tack″ *n.* a tack that may be driven by the thumb.

thump *n.* **1,** a heavy blow. **2,** the dull sound of a blow. —*v.t. & i.* pound.

thump′ing *adj.* (*Informal*) heavy; big; excellent.

thun′der (thun′dər) *n.* **1,** the loud atmospheric noise that often follows lightning. **2,** any loud noise. **3,** vehement and threatening utterance. —*v.i.* **1,** give forth a resounding noise. **2,** utter denunciation.

—*v.t.* utter or move with great noise. —**thun′der·ous,** *adj.*

thun′der·bird″ *n.* in Amer. Ind. folklore, the spirit or god of thunder, lightning, and rain.

thun′der·bolt″ *n.* **1,** a flash of lightning. **2,** a sudden, violent, or astonishing event.

thun′der·clap″ *n.* a crash of thunder.

thun′der·cloud″ *n.* an electrically charged cloud producing thunder and lightning.

thun′der·head″ *n.* one of the round swelling cumulus clouds which frequently develop into thunderclouds.

thun′der·show″er (-show″ər) *n.* a brief rain and electrical storm.

thun′der·storm″ *n.* a storm of lightning and thunder and, usually, heavy but brief rain.

thun′der·struck″ *adj.* very astonished; thrown into consternation.

thur′i·ble (thûr′ə-bəl) *n.* a censer.

Thurs′day (thẽrz′dè) *n.* the fifth day of the week.

> **Thursday**
> ↔ A translation of Latin *dies Iovis*, Jupiter's day, which became in Germanic languages Thor's day.

thus (*th*us) *adv.* **1,** in this way. **2,** in consequence; accordingly. **3,** so.

thwack (thwak) *v.t.* strike with something flat. —*n.* a whack.

thwart (thwôrt) *v.t.* prevent from accomplishing a purpose; frustrate; baffle. —*n.* a transverse part.

thy (*th*ī) *pron. poss.* of *thou.* —**thy·self′,** *pron.* reflexive and emphatic form of *thou.*

thyme (tīm) *n.* a plant of the mint family; a seasoning.

thy′mus (thī′məs) *n.* a ductless gland near the neck.

thy′roid (thī′roid) *n.* a ductless gland near the neck which regulates metabolism.

ti (tē) *n.* (*Music*) si.

ti·ar′a (tē-är′ə) *n.* **1,** an ornament worn on the head by women. **2,** a diadem worn by the Pope.

tib′i·a (tib′ê-ə) *n.* [*pl.* **-ae** (-ē)] the shinbone.

tic (tik) *n.* a twitching of the face.

tick (tik) *n.* **1,** a slight, sharp sound, as of a clock. **2,** a small mark; a dot. **3,** a small quantity; an instant of time. **4,** any of various parasitic insects or arachnids. **5,** the cloth case of a mattress, pillow, etc., made of ticking. **6,** (*Informal*) score or account;

credit. —*v.i.* make a slight, esp. a recurrent, sound. —*v.t.* mark with a tick.

tick′er *n.* **1,** something that ticks; (*Slang*) a watch; the heart. **2,** a telegraph instrument that prints on a tape.

tick′et (tik′it) *n.* **1,** a slip of paper entitling one to admission, service, etc. **2,** a label or tag. **3,** a party's list of candidates. **4,** a license. **5,** (*Informal*) proper procedure. **6,** a police summons. —*v.t.* **1,** furnish with a ticket; label. **2,** schedule.

tick′ing *n.* a strong material of linen or cotton, usu. striped.

tick′le (tik′əl) *v.t.* **1,** touch so as to produce a tingling sensation. **2,** amuse; gratify. —*v.i.* produce or feel a tingling sensation. —**tick′ler,** *n.* a reminder.

tick′lish *adj.* **1,** sensitive to tickling. **2,** requiring careful handling; risky. —**tick′lish·ness,** *n.*

tick″tack·toe′ (tik″tak-tō′) *n.* a game of placing three naughts or crosses in a row. Also, **tic″tac·toe′, tit″tat·toe′.**

tick′tock″ (-tok″) *n.* the sound of a clock ticking.

tick′y-tack″y (tik′ē-tak′ē) *adj.* **1,** cheap; inferior. **2,** insubstantial.

tid′al (tī′dəl) *adj.* pert. to or being a tide. —**tidal wave,** a very large ocean wave.

tid′bit″ *n.* a savory bit, esp. of food.

tid′dly·winks″ (tid′lē-winks″) *n.* a table game of snapping small disks into a cup.

tide (tīd) *n.* **1,** the periodic rise and fall of terrestrial water. **2,** a movement; a flow, current, or stream. —*v.t.* bear; carry.

> **tide, tidings, tidy**
> ↔ All three words derive from a prehistoric Germanic root meaning time, season (as in "Christmastide").

tide′land″ *n.* land which is alternately covered and left dry by the ebb and flow of the tide.

tide′wa″ter *n.* water that rises and falls with the tides.

tid′ings (tī′dingz) *n.pl.* news. ❑ *tide*

ti′dy (tī′dè) *adj.* **1,** kept in good order; neat. **2,** (*Informal*) fairly large; apt. —*v.t. & i.* make neat. —**tid′i·ness,** *n.* ❑ *tide*

tie (tī) *v.t.* [**tied, ty′ing**] **1,** attach or make fast by a knotted cord, etc.; bind; fasten or join in any way. **2,** restrict; constrain. **3,** make the same score, as in a contest. —*v.i.* **1,** make equal scores. **2,** join. —*n.* **1,** anything that binds or unites. **2,** a cravat; necktie. **3,** a connecting beam; a transverse timber. **4,** equality of scores. —**tie down, 1,** confine; restrict. **2,** keep occupied. **—tie up, 1,** keep busy. **2,** hinder; prevent. **3,** fasten securely.

tie-'dye" *v.t.* dye a fabric by a process in which certain parts are tied in knots to reduce or eliminate penetration of the dye.

tie-'in" *n.* **1,** connection; relationship. **2,** a newspaper article mentioning merchandise advertised nearby. **3,** a retailer's advertisement placed near that of the manufacturer.

tier (tir) *n.* a row or rank, esp. one of several at different levels.

tie-'up" *n.* a stoppage.

tiff (tif) *n.* **1,** a petty quarrel. **2,** a peevish mood. —*v.i.* quarrel.

tif'fa·ny (tif'ə-nē) *n.* a kind of gauze muslin; silk. **—Tiffany glass,** a stained glass used in lamps, windows, and other objects.

ti'ger (tī'gər) *n.* **1,** a large, carnivorous feline of Asia. **2,** a person of great fierceness. **—tiger lily,** a variety of lily bearing showy yellow flowers with black spots.

ti'ger's-eye" *n.* an ornamental quartz stone.

tight (tīt) *adj.* **1,** firmly fixed in place. **2,** fitting closely, esp. too closely. **3,** stretched taut; tense. **4,** compact in texture; dense. **5,** hard to obtain. **6,** (*Informal*) stingy. **7,** (*Slang*) drunk; tipsy. —*adv.* securely; tensely. **—tight'en,** *v.t. & i.* **—tight'ness,** *n.*

tight-'fist"ed *adj.* parsimonious.

tight-'lipped" *adj.* secretive.

tight'rope" *n.* a stretched rope on which acrobats walk.

tights *n.pl.* close-fitting trousers worn by acrobats, dancers, etc., and as an undergarment.

tight'wad" *n.* (*Slang*) a stingy person.

ti'glon (tī'glon) *n.* the offspring of a male tiger and a female lion.

ti'gress (tī'gris) *n.* **1,** a female tiger. **2,** a fierce or courageous woman.

til'de (til'də) *n.* a diacritical mark (~) as on ñ to indicate a nasal sound resembling *nyuh* (nyə).

tile (tīl) *n.* **1,** a thin slab or plate of baked clay, etc., used as building material. **2,** a block used in masonry construction. **3,** a pottery tube or pipe. **4,** tiles collectively. —*v.t.* **1,** construct, cover, or drain with tiles. **2,** (*Computers*) to arrange several windows of information in separate, not overlapping frames on a video screen.

till (til) *n.* a drawer, tray, or box for keeping money or valuables. —*v.t. & i.* cultivate (land); plow. —*prep. & conj.* until.

till'age (-ij) *n.* cultivation of land; tilled land.

till'er (-ər) *n.* **1,** a farmer. **2,** a lever that controls a rudder.

tilt *v.i. & t.* **1,** lean or incline away from a vertical or normal position; slant. **2,** engage in a joust or combat; make thrusts (at); charge. **3,** forge (steel). —*n.* **1,** a sloping position. **2,** a joust, contest, or dispute; a thrust. **3,** an awning. **—full tilt,** full speed.

tilth *n.* **1,** act or result of tilling. **2,** depth of cultivation. **3,** crop.

tim'bale (tim'bəl) *n.* a small pastry cup filled with cooked food.

tim'ber (tim'bər) *n.* **1,** growing trees. **2,** wood; a wooden member or beam. **3,** personal character; quality. —*v.t.* furnish with timber. **—timber line,** the height or line, on mountains or in polar regions, beyond which trees do not grow.

tim'bre (tim'bər) *n.* the quality or tone color of a sound.

tim'brel (tim'brəl) *n.* a tambourine.

time (tīm) *n.* **1,** the relationship of any event to any other, as being before, simultaneous, or after; continuous duration. **2,** the measurement of duration, as by a clock. **3,** an epoch, era, period, season, etc. **4,** an extent of duration, as an hour, day, etc.; hours worked, or the pay therefor; a prison term. **5,** a point of time; a particular occasion. **6,** (often *pl.*) a historical period; a state of affairs. **7,** leisure; opportunity. **8,** one of several recurrent instances. **9,** (*pl.*) a term denoting multiplication, as in *two times six.* **10,** rhythm; tempo; meter; rate. —*adj.* **1,** pert. to time. **2,** equipped with a timing device. **3,** pert. to installment buying. —*v.t.* **1,** determine the moment, duration, or rate of. **2,** choose the time or occasion for. **3,** regulate as to time. **—at times,** occasionally. **—on time, 1,** punctual. **2,** by installment payments. **—serve time,** be imprisoned. **—time clock,** one that records hours worked. **—time exposure,** exposure of film for more than one-half second; a picture so taken. **—time frame,** period of time. **—time out,** a rest period. **—time signature,** (*Music*) a sign indicating meter. **—time warp,** a hypothetical aberration in the progress of time. **—time zone,** an area throughout which standard time is the same.

time-'hon"ored *adj.* respected by reason of age.

time'keep"er *n.* **1,** one who records a worker's hours worked and wages due. **2,** one who watches the time, as in a contest.

---

time'less (-ləs) *adj.* unending. —**time'-less·ness,** *n.*

time'line" *n.* a schedule detailing the sequence of events in time.

time'ly *adj.* opportune. —**time'li·ness,** *n.*

time'piece" *n.* a clock, watch, etc.

tim'er (tī'mər) *n.* **1,** one who or that which measures or records time. **2,** a device for supplying the spark in an internal combustion engine.

time-'shar"ing *n.* **1,** a system of joint ownership of a property among owners who take turns using it. **2,** the simultaneous use of a central computing unit by users at a number of remote locations.

time'ta"ble *n.* a schedule of the times of planned occurrences, esp. a railroad schedule.

time'worn" *adj.* **1,** worn or impaired by time or use. **2,** out-of-date.

tim'id *adj.* **1,** easily alarmed; fearful; shy. **2,** characterized by fear. —**ti·mid'i·ty, tim'id·ness,** *n.* ❑ *temerity*

tim'ing (tī'ming) *n.* synchronization; effective choice of a time.

tim'or·ous (tim'ə-rəs) *adj.* timid. —**tim'or·ous·ness,** *n.*

tim'o·thy (tim'ə-thē) *n.* a grass grown for hay, named for 18th-c. American farmer Timothy Hanson.

tim'pa·ni (tim'pə-nē) *n.* tympani.

tin *n.* **1,** a metallic chemical element, no. 50, symbol Sn. **2,** sheet iron or steel coated with tin: *tin plate.* **3,** a container made of tin plate: *tin can.* —*adj.* **1,** made of tin, or tin plate. **2,** worthless; counterfeit. —*v.t.* **[tinned, tin'ning] 1,** coat with tin. **2,** preserve in tin cans. —**tin liz'zie** (liz'ē) a Model T Ford; hence, an antiquated car.

tin'a·mou (tin'ə-moo) *n.* a So. Amer. bird resembling a partridge.

tinc'ture (tink'chər) *n.* **1,** a solution of a medicinal substance in alcohol. **2,** a tinge. —*v.t.* tinge.

tin'der (tin'dər) *n.* any easily ignited material. —**tin'der·box,** *n.* (*Informal*) something easily inflammable.

tine (tīn) *n.* a slender projection; a prong, as of a fork.

tin'foil" *n.* a thin sheet of tin, used to wrap various merchandise.

ting *n.* a high-pitched metallic sound. —*v.t. & t.* make this sound.

tinge (tinj) *v.t.* **1,** color slightly; tint. **2,** imbue slightly with something, as flavor. —*n.* **1,** a moderate degree of coloration. **2,** a slight admixture of anything.

tin'gle (ting'gəl) *v.i.* have a prickling or stinging sensation. —*n.* this sensation.

tin'horn" *n.* a professional gambler who bets small amounts; a piker. —*adj.* a gambler or gambling game despised for cheapness.

tink'er (tink'ər) *n.* **1,** a mender of metal household utensils. **2,** a bungler. **3,** a repairer; jack-of-all-trades. —*v.i. & t.* **1,** work as a tinker; meddle (with). **2,** work unskillfully or without effect. —**tinker's dam,** something worthless. ❑ *tamper*

tin'kle (ting'kəl) *v.i.* give forth a short, light, metallic sound. —*n.* such a sound.

tin'ny (tin'ē) *adj.* like tin; flimsy; metallic in sound; sour in taste. —**tin'ni·ness,** *n.*

Tin' Pan" Alley a street or district largely occupied by publishers and composers of popular music; also, the composers, etc., collectively.

tin'sel (tin'səl) *n.* **1,** a glittering material of metal in sheets or strips. **2,** false show. —*v.t.* decorate. —**Tin'sel·town",** *n.* (*Informal*) Hollywood, CA.

tint *n.* **1,** a variety of a color; a hue to which white has been added. **2,** a pale color. —*v.t.* color slightly.

tin"tin·nab"u·la'tion (tin"ti-nab"yə-lā'shən) *n.* the sound of bells ringing.

tin'type" *n.* a photograph on a metal plate.

ti'ny (tī'nē) *adj.* very small.

-tion (shən) *suf.* see *-ation.*

tip *n.* **1,** the extremity of something long and slender; an outermost point; the top or apex. **2,** a small piece attached to an extremity. **3,** a light blow; a tap. **4,** the state of being tilted. **5,** a small present of money. **6,** a bit of information or advice. —*v.t.* **[tipped, tip'ping] 1,** form the tip of. **2,** strike lightly or obliquely. **3,** tilt; overturn. **4,** give a tip to. —*v.i.* **1,** tilt; incline; be overturned; topple. **2,** give tips.

tip'off" *n.* a warning or hint.

tip'pet (tip'it) *n.* a covering for the neck and shoulders, esp. a scarf or muffler wound around the neck.

tip'ple (tip'əl) *v.i. & t.* drink (intoxicating liquor) habitually. —**tip'pler,** *n.* a habitual drinker.

tip'staff" *n.* a minor police or court officer.

tip'ster (-stər) *n.* (*Informal*) one who furnishes private information.

tip'sy (-sē) *adj.* slightly intoxicated. —**tip'-si·ness,** *n.*

tip'toe" *n.* a movement or posture on the toes. —*adj.* standing or moving on tiptoe, to reach high or walk quietly. —*v.i.* move on tiptoe.

tip'top" *n. & adj.* (pert. to) the highest point or quality.

ti'rade (tī'rād) *n.* a long speech or writing of censure or denunciation.

tire (tīr) *v.i.* become weary or jaded. —*v.t.* make weary; fatigue. —*n.* [also, *Brit.*, **tyre**] a rubber or iron hoop around a wheel. —**tired,** *adj.* weary; impatient; dissatisfied. —**tire'less,** *adj.* diligent; untiring. —**tire'some,** *adj.* tedious.

ti·sane' (ti-zän') *n.* an infusion of dried leaves or flowers used medicinally or as a beverage.

tis'sue (tish'oo) *n.* **1,** the cellular substance of which living bodies are composed. **2,** a woven fabric, esp. one very light and thin. **3,** thin, translucent paper: *tissue paper.*

tit *n.* **1,** a small bird, esp. the titmouse. **2,** teat. —**tit for tat,** equivalent given in return or as retribution; an eye for an eye.

ti'tan (tī'tən) *n.* a person or thing of enormous size and strength. —**ti·tan'ic,** *adj.* —**ti·tan'i·cal·ly,** *adv.*

ti·ta'ni·um (tī-tā'nē-əm) *n.* a metallic chemical element, no. 22, symbol Ti.

tit'bit" *n.* tidbit.

tithe (tīth) *n.* a tenth part; a tax; a contribution to a church, etc. —*v.t. & i.* pay a tithe.

ti'tian (tish'ən) *n. & adj.* a yellow-red color.

---

titian
↔ From the professional name of 16th-c. It. painter *Tiziano* Vecellio.

---

tit'il·late" (tit'ə-lāt") *v.t.* excite agreeably; tickle. —**tit"il·la'tion,** *n.*

tit'i·vate" (tit'i-vāt") *v.t.* (*Informal*) dress smartly; spruce up. —**tit"i·va'tion,** *n.*

ti'tle (tī'təl) *n.* **1,** a name assigned to distinguish an individual thing. **2,** a descriptive heading or caption. **3,** a word or phrase denoting rank, honors, etc. **4,** the rank of champion. **5,** right to the possession of property. **6,** a division of a statute or law. —*v.t.* give a name or appellation to. —**title role,** the role from which the name of a play, etc., is derived.

ti'tled (tī'təld) *adj.* bearing a title, esp. of nobility.

tit'mouse" (tit'mows") *n.* [*pl.* **-mice"**] a small bird.

---

titmouse
↔ This word comes not from *mouse*, but from *mose*, an earlier word for the bird. *Tit* meant small creature.

---

tit'ter (tit'ər) *v.i. & n.* laugh in a restrained manner; giggle; snicker.

tit'tle (tit'əl) *n.* a very small mark, dot, thing, etc.; a particle.

tit'tle-tat"tle *n. & v.i.* chatter; gossip.

tit'u·lar (tit'yə-lər) *adj.* of, being, or pert. to a title; by virtue of one's title. —**tit"u·lar'i·ty,** *n.*

tiz'zy (tiz'ē) *n.* dither.

TM *abbr.* transcendental meditation.

T-'man" *n.* (*Informal*) a law enforcement agent employed by the U.S. Treasury.

TNT (tē'en-tē') *n.* trinitrotoluene, a powerful explosive.

to (too) *prep.* **1,** indicating motion or purpose toward something. **2,** indicating a destination, result, outcome, limit, or point of space, time, or degree. **3,** indicating relations, as comparison, opposition, agreement, accompaniment, contiguity. **4,** a particle used before the infinitive of a verb. —*adv.* toward someone or something, usually implied; in an inward direction. —**to and fro,** alternately toward and away from a point.

toad (tōd) *n.* a terrestrial member of the frog family.

toad'stool" (tōd'stool") *n.* a fungus having an umbrellalike cap on a stalk.

toad'y (tō'dē) *n.* a servile, fawning person; a sycophant. —*v.i.* fawn.

toast (tōst) *n.* **1,** sliced bread browned by heat. **2,** a complimentary sentiment endorsed by drinking; the person complimented. —*v.t.* **1,** expose to heat. **2,** compliment by a toast. —**toast'er,** *n.* a device for making toast.

toast'mas"ter, toast'mis"tress *n.* a master of ceremonies at a dinner.

to·bac'co (tə-bak'ō) *n.* a plant whose large leaves, containing nicotine, are prepared for smoking and chewing, and snuff. —**to·bac'co·nist** (-ə-nist) *n.* a dealer in tobacco.

to·bog'gan (tə-bog'ən) *n.* a boardlike sled with low or no runners. —*v.i.* **1,** coast on snow. **2,** fall rapidly or abruptly. **3,** move without effort.

to'by (tō'bē) *n.* **1,** a small jug or mug. **2,** (*Slang*) a long, cheap cigar.

toc·ca'ta (tə-kä'tə) *n.* (*Music*) a virtuosic keyboard composition.

toc'sin (tok'sin) *n.* a warning bell or signal.

to·day' (tə-dā') *n. & adj.* **1,** the present day. **2,** the present period.

tod'dle (tod'əl) *v.i.* walk with short, unsteady steps. —*n.* a toddling walk.

---

tub, cūte, pûll; labəl; oil, owl, go, chip, she, thin, *th*en, sing, ink; *see p. 6*

tod'dy (tod'ė) *n.* a hot drink of whiskey diluted and sweetened.

to-do' (tǝ-doo') *n.* commotion; fuss.

toe (tō) *n.* **1,** a digit of the foot. **2,** the forepart of a hoof. **3,** the part of a stocking or shoe that covers the toes. **4,** a part resembling a toe; a projection, stud, etc. —*v.t. & i.* touch, reach, strike, etc., with the toes. —**toe the mark,** behave as instructed.

toe'hold *n.* **1,** a slight or precarious grip, with or as with the toes. **2,** a wrestling grip upon an opponent's foot.

toe'nail" *n.* a nail of a toe.

toff (tof) *n.* (*Brit., Informal*) a fashionable person; a member of the upper class.

tof'fee (tof'ė) *n.* taffy. Also, **tof'fy.**

to'fu" (tō'foo") *n.* a soft, white food, high in protein, made from curdled soybean milk.

tog *n.* (*Informal*) (usually *pl.*) a garment. —**tog'ge·ry** (tog'ǝ-rė) *n.* (*Informal*) clothes; togs. —**togged out,** dressed.

to'ga (tō'gǝ) *n.* a loose outer garment, as that of the ancient Romans; a robe.

to·geth'er (tǝ-geth'ǝr) *adv.* **1,** in conjunction; in one gathering, mass, or body. **2,** simultaneously; contemporaneously. **3,** with each other; in common; mutually. **4,** in or into junction or union. **5,** without intermission or interruption.

tog'gle (tog'ǝl) *n.* **1,** a transverse pin or bar. **2,** a linkage of levers to produce motion at right angles to a thrust. —**toggle switch,** an electric switch actuated by a toggle lever.

toil *v.i.* **1,** work hard; labor. **2,** move or travel with difficulty or weariness. —*n.* **1,** fatiguing labor. **2,** a laborious task. **3,** (*pl.*) a net for trapping game.

toile (twäl) *n.* a thin linen fabric.

---

toilet, bathroom, lavatory, washroom, water closet
    Although these terms are all used to refer to a room containing a toilet bowl, strictly speaking they are not synonymous. The *toilet* is the actual fixture. A *lavatory* or *washroom* is a room for washing up, which may or may not have a toilet. Similarly, a *bathroom* is a room with a bathtub in it and may or may not have a toilet. A *water closet* is a small closet-like room containing only a toilet fixture.

---

toi'let (toi'lit) *n.* **1,** a water closet, bathroom, or dressing room. **2,** the process of dressing, including bathing, makeup, etc.; personal appearance as a result of this. **3,**

a dressing table. —**toilet set,** articles as comb, brush, etc. —**toilet water,** a light perfume.

toi'let·ry (-rė) *n.* an article or preparation used in dressing, as a cosmetic.

toi·lette' (twä-let') *n.* **1,** toilet (def. 2). **2,** one's style of dress.

toil'worn" *adj.* affected by much toil or use.

to'ka·mak" (tō'kǝ-mak") *n.* (*Physics*) a type of nuclear fusion reactor.

To·kay' (tō-kā') *n.* **1,** a rich, heavy Hungarian wine. **2,** a similar California wine. **3,** a sweet variety of grape.

toke (tōk) *n.* (*Slang*) a puff on a cigarette, esp. of marijuana. —*v.t.* puff (on a cigarette).

to'ken (tō'kǝn) *n.* **1,** something regarded as representing something else; a sign or symbol; a keepsake or memento. **2,** an indication, symptom, or evidence. **3,** a special coin issued as a ticket. **4,** a representative of a minority group, esp. one who is included for reasons other than merit. —*adj.* serving only as an expression of good faith. —**to'ken·ism,** *n.* making a minimal effort for the sake of appearance.

tol·bu'ta·mide" (tol-byoo'tǝ-mīd") *n.* a drug used in the treatment of diabetes.

told (tōld) *v.* pret. & p.p. of *tell.*

tole (tōl) *n.* lacquered or enameled metalware, usu. decorated.

tol'er·a·ble (tol'ǝr-ǝ-bǝl) *adj.* **1,** endurable. **2,** somewhat good; not bad. —**tol'er·a·ble·ness,** *n.*

tol'er·ance (tol'ǝr-ǝns) *n.* **1,** disposition to be patient and fair; freedom from bigotry. **2,** power of enduring or resisting the action of a drug. **3,** allowed variation from standard dimensions. —**tol'er·ant,** *adj.*

tol'er·ate" (tol'ǝ-rāt") *v.t.* **1,** allow to be, be done, or be practiced; permit. **2,** bear with patience; endure without complaint or ill effect. —**tol"er·a'tion,** *n.*

toll (tōl) *n.* **1,** a fee or tax collected for a particular service. **2,** a succession of slow single strokes of a bell; one such stroke. —*v.t.* **1,** cause (a bell) to toll. **2,** announce, signal, etc., by a bell. —*v.i.* give forth slow repeated sounds. —**toll call,** a long-distance telephone call.

toll'gate" *n.* a point at which tolls are collected.

toll'house" *n.* a booth, cabin, etc., at which tolls are paid. Also, **toll'booth".** —**Toll House cookies,** chocolate chip cookies.

tol'u·ene" (tol'yû-ēn") *n.* a liquid deriva-

---

tive of coal tar, used as a solvent, detonator, etc. Also, **tol′u·ol** (-ol).

tom *n.* the male of various animals, as the cat.

tom′a·hawk″ (tom′ə-hâk″) *n.* a Native Amer. stone-headed hatchet.

to·ma′to (tə-mā′tō) *n.* a plant bearing a pulpy fruit, usu. red.

tomb (toom) *n.* **1,** an excavation made to receive a dead body; a grave. **2,** a monument to one dead: *tombstone.* **3,** death.

tom′boy″ *n.* an athletic, boylike girl.

tomb′stone″ *n.* a stone marker for a grave.

tom′cat″ *n.* a male cat.

Tom Col′lins (kol′inz) a tall iced drink of gin, lemon or lime juice, sugar, and carbonated water.

tome (tōm) *n.* a large book.

tom″fool′er·y *n.* silly or prankish behavior.

Tom′my (tom′é) *n.* a British soldier.

Tom′my gun″ *n.* (*Slang*) a Thompson submachine gun.

tom′my·hawk″ *n.* tomahawk.

tom′my·rot″ (tom′é-rot″) *n.* (*Slang*) nonsense.

to·mor′row (tə-mor′ō) *n. & adj.* **1,** the day after this day. **2,** the future; a future day.

tom′tit″ *n.* a small bird.

tom-′tom″ *n.* **1,** a primitive drum. **2,** a drum used in bands.

-to·my (tə-mé) *suf.* cutting, denoting a surgical operation.

ton (tun) *n.* **1,** a unit of weight: 2,000 lbs. avoirdupois (*short ton*) or 2,240 lbs. (*long ton*), or 1,000 kilograms (*metric ton*). **2,** a variable unit of volume or capacity, as 40 cubic feet (*shipping ton*) or 35 cubic feet of salt water (*displacement ton*). **3,** (*Informal*) any large amount.

ton′al (tōn′əl) *adj.* pert. to a tone or to tonality.

to·nal′i·ty (tō-nal′ə-té) *n.* **1,** (*Music*) a system of tones; key. **2,** a color scheme.

tone (tōn) *n.* **1,** any resonant sound. **2,** a sound of definite pitch; a musical note. **3,** a sound with respect to its pitch, volume, and timbre. **4,** accent, inflection, or modulation, esp. of the voice. **5,** a color; a shade or tint. **6,** the state of tension or firmness proper to bodily tissues. **7,** prevailing character; style; temper; spirit; tenor. **8,** elegance; stylishness. —*v.t.* give a proper or desired tone to. —**tone arm,** a phonograph pick-up. —**tone color,** timbre. —**tone deaf,** unable to perceive differences in musical tones by hearing. —**tone down,** reduce, in intensity of sound, color, etc.; subdue. —**tone poem,** a musical composition suggestive of poetic images or sentiments.

ton′er (tō′nər) *n.* **1,** a powder used in xerographic copying machines. **2,** a chemical solution used in developing film.

tong (tong) *n.* a Chinese political party or private society.

tongs (tongz) *n.pl.* an implement for grasping and lifting something.

tongue (tung) *n.* **1,** a fleshy, freely movable organ in the mouth, the principal organ of taste (in humans, also of speech). **2,** an animal's tongue as meat. **3,** speech or talk; a language or dialect. **4,** a tonguelike part, as the clapper of a bell, a strip of leather in a shoe, a small strip of land projecting into water, etc. —*v.t.* **1,** sound with the tongue. **2,** put a tongue on. —**tongue and groove,** a joint formed by a projecting strip on one piece of wood which fits into a groove in another. —**tongue in cheek,** facetiously.

tongue-′lash″ing *n.* a scolding.

tongue-′tied″ *adj.* **1,** having an impediment of the speech. **2,** speechless from shyness or astonishment.

tongue′twist″er *n.* a word or phrase difficult to pronounce because of an unusual combination of sounds.

ton′ic (ton′ik) *n.* **1,** a medicine that improves the bodily tone. **2,** anything that imparts strength or vigor. **3,** the first degree of a musical scale; the keynote. **4,** quinine water. **5,** pop. —*adj.* **1,** invigorating. **2,** pert. to a musical tone or tones. **3,** pert. to muscular tension. —**ton·ic′i·ty** (-is′ə-té) *n.*

to·night′ (tə-nīt′) *n. & adj.* (pert. to) the present or coming night. Also, (*Informal*) **to·nite′.**

ton′nage (tun′ij) *n.* **1,** capacity or displacement in tons. **2,** ships collectively.

ton·neau′ (tə-nō′) *n.* the interior of a closed automobile body.

ton′sil (ton′səl) *n.* either of two masses of lymphoid tissue at the back of the mouth.

ton″sil·lec′to·my (-lek′tə-mé) *n.* removal of the tonsils.

ton″sil·li′tis (-lī′tis) *n.* inflammation of the tonsils.

ton·sor′i·al (ton-sôr′é-əl) *adj.* pert. to a barber.

ton′sure (ton′shər) *n.* **1,** the cutting or shaving of hair from the head. **2,** a shaved spot on the head of a priest or monk.

ton′y (tōn′ē) *adj.* (*Informal*) stylish. —**ton′i·ness,** *n.*

too *adv.* **1,** in addition; also; furthermore. **2,** more than enough; beyond what is normal or proper. **3,** exceedingly; extremely.

took (tûk) *v.* pret. of *take.*

tool *n.* **1,** any implement for working, cutting, shaping, etc. **2,** an unwitting or compliant agent of another. —*v.t. & i.* shape, etc., with a tool; ornament (the cover of a book, etc.).

toot *n.* **1,** the sound of a horn. **2,** (*Slang*) drunken revelry. —*v.t. & i.* blow or make the sound of a horn.

tooth *n.* [*pl.* **teeth** (tēth)] **1,** one of the hard bodies set in a row in the jaw. **2,** any toothlike projection, as on a comb; a cog on a wheel. **3,** something sharp, distressing, or destructive. **4,** taste; relish. —**tooth′y,** *adj.* —**in the teeth of,** in defiance of; straight against. —**tooth and nail,** with all one's strength and means. —**tooth powder,** a powder used for cleaning the teeth.

tooth′ache″ *n.* pain in a tooth.

tooth′brush″ *n.* a small, long-handled brush for cleaning the teeth.

tooth′paste″ *n.* a paste used for cleaning the teeth.

tooth′pick″ *n.* a small pointed piece of wood or plastic for cleaning the teeth.

tooth′some (-səm) *adj.* **1,** palatable. **2,** (*Informal*) attractive; voluptuous. —**tooth′some·ness,** *n.*

too′tle (too′təl) *v.i.* toot gently or repeatedly. —*n.* a tootling sound.

toot′sy (tût′sē) *n.* (*Slang*) a woman's foot, esp. a small foot. Also, **toot′sie.**

top *n.* **1,** the highest point or part of anything; the summit or apex. **2,** the highest position in rank, etc. **3,** the most perfect example or type; the best. **4,** a lid or cover; a roof. **5,** a toy, made to spin on its point. —*adj.* highest; uppermost; foremost; chief; principal. —*v.t.* [**topped, top′ping**] **1,** be the top of. **2,** furnish with a top. **3,** reach the top of. **4,** rise above; surpass. **5,** get over; vault; cross. **6,** complete; perfect. **7,** remove the top of; prune. **8,** hit (a ball) above the center. —**top gun,** (*Informal*) an ace pilot; a leader in a certain field. —**top hat,** a high silk hat. —**top kick,** (*Informal*) a first sergeant; a boss. —**top secret,** the highest classification of secrecy in the U.S. government.

to′paz (tō′paz) *n.* **1,** a gem, silicate of aluminum. **2,** a yellow variety of sapphire or quartz. —*adj.* yellow.

top′coat″ *n.* a light overcoat.

top-′drawer″ *adj.* first-rate.

tope (tōp) *v.i.* drink intoxicating liquor habitually. —**top′er,** *n.*

top′flight″ *adj.* of highest class.

top′gal″lant *n.* (*Naut.*) the mast, sail, or rigging above the topmast and below the royal.

top-′heav″y *adj.* likely to topple; structurally unsound. —**top-′heav″i·ness,** *n.*

top-′hole″ *adj.* (*Brit.*) excellent.

top′ic (top′ik) *n.* a subject or theme of a discourse, etc.

top′i·cal (top′i-kəl) *adj.* **1,** pert. to matters of current interest. **2,** pert. to the topic. **3,** local. —**top″i·cal′i·ty,** *n.*

top′knot″ *n.* a tuft of hair on top of the head; a crest.

top′less (top′ləs) *adj.* wearing nothing above the waist.

top′mast″ *n.* (*Naut.*) a mast on top of a lower mast.

top′most″ *adj.* highest.

top′notch″ *adj.* (*Informal*) excellent.

to·pog′ra·phy (tə-pog′rə-fē) *n.* the relief features of a land area; the surface configuration of anything. —**top″o·graph′i·cal,** *adj.*

top′per *n.* **1,** top hat. **2,** a woman's topcoat.

top′ping *n.* a top layer or covering. —*adj.* (*Informal*) excellent.

top′ple (top′əl) *v.i.* fall down with the top or head foremost; tumble as from being too heavy at the top.

tops *adj.* (*Slang*) the very best.

top′sail (top′səl) *n.* a sail above a lower sail.

top′side″ *n.* the upper part of a ship's side.

top′soil″ *n.* surface soil, essential to agriculture.

top′sy-tur′vy (top′sē-tēr′vē) *adj. & adv.* upside down; in reverse of normal position or order; disorderly. —**top′sy-tur′vi·ness,** *n.*

toque (tōk) *n.* **1,** a woman's hat with little or no brim. **2,** a knitted winter cap.

To′rah (tō′rə) *n.* **1,** the Pentateuch. **2,** the Scriptures of Judaism.

torch (tôrch) *n.* **1,** something burning carried in the hand to give light; (*Brit.*) a flashlight. **2,** a portable instrument producing a jet of flame. **3,** any source of illumination or enlightenment. —**torch song,** a song of unrequited love.

torch′bear″er *n.* a leader; (*Informal*) a zealous adherent.

torch′light″ *n.* light given by a torch.

tore (tôr) *v.* pret. of *tear*.

tor′e·a·dor″ (tôr′ĕ-ə-dôr″) *n.* (*Bull-fighting*) an assistant of the matador.

tor·ment′ (tôr-ment′) *v.t.* **1,** afflict with pain or misery; distress, worry, or annoy. **2,** stir up; disturb. —*n.* (tôr′ment) suffering; something that torments. —**tor·men′-tor,** *n.*

torn (tôrn) *v.* p.p. of *tear*.

tor·na′do (tôr-nā′dō) *n.* a destructive whirling.

> **tornado**
> ↔ This word does not derive from *turn*, despite the storm's violent whirling, but from Spanish *tronada*, thunderstorm, from Latin *tonare*, thunder. Its present form is from confusion with Spanish *tornado*, turned.

tor·pe′do (tôr-pē′dō) *n.* **1,** a self-propelled missile containing an explosive charge, launched in water. **2,** a submarine mine. **3,** a charge of explosive. **4,** (*Slang*) a hired ruffian.

tor′pid (tôr′pid) *adj.* sluggish; slow; inactive. —**tor·pid′i·ty,** *n.*

tor′por (tôr′pər) *n.* **1,** sluggishness in bodily functioning; stupor. **2,** stupidity. **3,** inactivity; lethargy.

torque (tôrk) *n.* a force that tends to cause torsion or rotation.

tor′re·fy (tôr′ə-fī) *v.t.* dry or parch with heat. —**tor″re·fac′tion,** *n.*

tor′rent (tôr′ənt) *n.* **1,** an abundant and violent flow of water; a heavy rain. **2,** an overwhelming flow of anything. —**tor·ren′tial** (-shəl) *adj.*

tor′rid (tor′id) *adj.* **1,** hot, dry, and arid in climate. **2,** ardent; passionate. —**Torrid Zone,** the zone centered on the Equator.

tor′sion (tôr′shən) *n.* the act or result of twisting. —**tor′sion·al,** *adj.*

tor′so (tôr′sō) *n.* [*pl.* **-sos**] the trunk of the human body.

tort (tôrt) *n.* (*Law*) a civil wrong calling for compensation in damages.

tor″tel·li′ni (tôr″tə-lē′nē) *n.pl.* small pasta rings filled with meat or vegetables.

tor″ti·col′lis (tôr″ti-kol′is) *n.* a twisted neck; wryneck.

tor·ti′lla (tôr-tē′yə) *n.* a Mexican cake of unleavened cornmeal.

tor′toise (tôr′təs) *n.* a turtle of a terrestrial variety.

> **tortoise**
> ↔ This word derives from Late Latin *tartarucha*, of the underworld.

tor′toise·shell″ *adj.* of tortoise shell, or its yellow-and-brown coloring.

tor·to′ni (tôr-tō′nē) *n.* a rich It. ice cream with fruit and nuts.

tor′tu·ous (tôr′choo-əs) *adj.* full of twists and turns; winding; crooked. —**tor′tu·ous·ness,** *n.*

> **tortuous, torturous**
> ☞ *Tortuous* means winding, crooked; *torturous* means causing torture.

tor′ture (tôr′chər) *n.* **1,** the act of willfully inflicting severe pain. **2,** excruciating pain or anguish. **3,** a cause of anguish. —*v.t.* **1,** subject to torture. **2,** distort. —**tor′tur·er,** *n.* —**tor′tur·ous,** *adj.* ❑ *tortuous*

To′ry (tôr′ē) *n. & adj.* one who is conservative in political views, esp. a supporter of an established monarchy or aristocracy.

> **Tory**
> ↔ Orig. a term for Irish guerrilla, then applied to Irish Catholic royalists, and finally to the British political party.

toss (tâs) *v.t.* **1,** throw or fling, esp. with little effort. **2,** tumble about; agitate. **3,** jerk. —*v.i.* **1,** be pitched or rocked about; sway. **2,** move restlessly. —*n.* a throw, fling, jerk, or pitch. —**toss for it,** decide something by the way a tossed coin falls.

toss′pot″ (tâs′pot″) *n.* (*Informal*) a heavy drinker; toper; tippler.

toss-′up″ *n.* **1,** the tossing of a coin. **2,** (*Informal*) an even chance.

tos·ta′da (tō-stä′dä) *n.* (*Sp.*) a fried tortilla filled with shredded meat, etc.

tot *n.* **1,** a small child. **2,** a small quantity. —*v.t.* [**tot′ted, -ting**] (usu. with *up*) add.

to′tal (tō′təl) *adj.* **1,** pert. to the whole; taking all together. **2,** being or comprising the whole. **3,** complete; absolute. —*n.* **1,** the sum; the whole or aggregate. —*v.t. & i.* **1,** ascertain the sum of; add up. **2,** amount to. **3,** (*Slang*) destroy completely. —**total war,** war waged with greatest possible effort.

to·tal″i·tar′i·an (tō-tal″i-tār′ē-ən) *adj.* pert. to a government that suppresses opposition. —*n.* an adherent of such government. —**to·tal″i·tar′i·an·ism,** *n.*

to·tal′i·ty (tō-tal′ə-tē) *n.* an entirety; a whole.

to′tal·i·za′tor (tō′təl-i-zā″tər) *n.* a device for registering parimutuel ticket sales. Also, **to′tal·iz″er.**

tote (tōt) *v.t.* (*Informal*) carry. —**tote bag,** a large handbag. —**tote board,** (*In-*

formal) an electrical display board for racetrack calculations.

to'tem (tō'təm) *n.* an emblem of a clan or family. **—to'tem·ism,** *n.* **—totem pole,** a post carved or painted with totems, erected by certain Native Americans.

tot'ter (tot'ər) *v.i.* **1,** walk unsteadily. **2,** sway or shake as if about to fall. **—n.** an act of tottering.

tou·can' (too-kän') *n.* a tropical Amer. bird with an enormous beak and brilliant plumage.

touch (tuch) *v.t.* **1,** perceive by physical contact; feel by tactile sense. **2,** be or come in contact with. **3,** reach; stop at; equal; attain. **4,** put the hand on; handle. **5,** refer or allude to; deal with. **6,** pertain or relate to. **7,** (with *up*) modify; improve. **8,** affect, as with pity. **9,** tinge; imbue. **10,** (*Slang*) borrow or beg money from. **—v.i. 1,** come or be in contact. **2,** (with *on* or *upon*) allude to something briefly. **—n. 1,** the sense of feeling. **2,** the act of touching; adjacency. **3,** communication. **4,** a quality perceptible to the touch. **5,** a small quantity or degree. **6,** a detail of handiwork. **7,** skill or style in execution. **—touch and go,** a precarious state of affairs.

touch'back" *n.* (*Football*) the grounding of the ball by a player behind his or her own goal line.

touch'down" *n.* (*Football*) a scoring play.

tou·ché' (too-shā') *interj.* (*Fr.*) acknowledgment of a point scored, in fencing, conversation, etc.

touched (tucht) *adj.* **1,** affected with emotion. **2,** mentally feeble; eccentric.

touch'ing *prep.* in reference to. **—adj.** emotionally affecting.

touch'stone" *n.* a test or criterion.

Touch'Tone" *adj.* (*T.N.*) designating a telephone operated by push buttons.

touch-'type" *v.i.* type using a system assigning one or more keys to each finger.

touch'y *adj.* **1,** irritable. **2,** risky; delicate. **—touch'i·ness,** *n.*

tough (tuf) *adj.* **1,** not easily broken or cut. **2,** flexible without brittleness; hardy. **3,** stiff in consistency; difficult to chew. **4,** unyielding; hardened; incorrigible. **5,** troublesome; hard to do or bear. **6,** violent; severe. **7,** rowdy; vicious. **—n.** a ruffian or bully. **—tough'en,** *v.t.* make tougher. **—tough'ness,** *n.*

tou·pee' (too-pā') *n.* a hairpiece.

tour (tûr) *n.* **1,** a journey to several places in succession. **2,** a period of work or duty. **—v.i. & t.** travel about. **—touring car,** an

open automobile for five or more passengers. **—tour'ist,** *n.* a traveler for pleasure. **—tourist class,** service below first class; second class.

tour de force (toor' də fôrs') (*Fr.*) a feat of skill or strength.

Tou·rette's' syndrome (too-rets') a nervous disorder that features spasms and, often, uncontrollable swearing.

tour'ism (tûr'iz-əm) *n.* **1,** travel for pleasure. **2,** the economic activities related to and dependent on tourism.

tour'ma·line (tûr'mə-lēn) *n.* a mineral, a gem when transparent.

tour'na·ment (tûr'nə-mənt) *n.* a meeting for contests.

tour'ney (tûr'nè) *n.* tournament.

tour'ni·quet (tûr'ni-ket) *n.* a tight bandage to stop bleeding.

tou'sle (tow'zəl) *v.t.* rumple.

tout (towt) *v.i.* **1,** sell horse-race betting information. **2,** solicit business, votes, etc. **3,** spy. **—v.t. 1,** praise highly. **2,** sell a betting tip to. **—n.** one who touts.

to·var'isch (tō-vä'rish) *n.* (*Russian*) comrade; citizen.

tow (tō) *v.t.* drag by a rope, chain, etc. **—n. 1,** the act or means of towing. **2,** the fiber of flax, hemp, or jute. **—tow'age,** *n.* **—tow truck** a truck equipped for towing vehicles.

TOW missile a type of wire-guided anti-tank missile: *t(ube-launched) o(ptically-guided) w(ire-tracked) missile.*

to·ward' (tôrd, twôrd) *prep.* **1,** in the direction of. **2,** in furtherance of. **3,** with respect to; concerning. **4,** near. Also, **towards'.**

tow'el (tow'əl) *n.* a cloth or paper for wiping. **—tow'el·ing,** *n.* material used for towels.

tow'er (tow'ər) *n.* a high, slender building or structure. **—v.i.** rise aloft; stand high. **—tow'er·ing,** *adj.*

tow'head"ed (tō) *adj.* having flax-colored hair.

tow'hee (tō'hē) *n.* any of several Amer. finches, esp. the chewink.

town *n.* **1,** an inhabited place, larger than a village. **2,** [also, **town'ship**] a division of a county. **3,** a city or borough. **—town hall,** headquarters of a town's government. **—town meeting,** a meeting of the citizens of a town.

town'house", *n.* a house in the city, esp. one of a row of such houses sharing common side walls.

town'ship" *n.* **1,** a unit of territory, varying in size and function in different states and countries, in the U.S. usually six miles square. **2,** a town.

towns'man (townz'mən) *n.* [*pl.* **-men**] an inhabitant of a town or of the same town. **—towns'peo"ple, towns'folk"**, *n.pl.*

tow'path" *n.* the path on the bank of a canal or river traveled by animal or man towing a boat.

tox·e'mi·a (tok-sē'mē-ə) *n.* the presence of toxins in the blood. **—tox·e'mic,** *adj.*

tox'ic (tok'sik) *adj.* **1,** poisonous. **2,** pert. to a toxin. **—tox·ic'i·ty** (toks-is'ə-tē) *n.* **—toxic shock syndrome,** an often fatal bacterial infection, sometimes caused by tampons.

tox"i·col'o·gy (tok"si-kol'ə-jē) *n.* the science of poisons. **—tox"i·co·log'i·cal,** *adj.* **—tox"i·col'o·gist,** *n.*

tox'in (tok'sin) *n.* a poisonous product of microorganisms.

toy (toi) *n.* **1,** any article played with by a child; a plaything. **2,** a trinket; a trifle. **3,** a dog of small size. **—adj. 1,** made as a plaything. **2,** diminutive. **—v.i. 1,** play. **2,** act idly; trifle.

toy'on (toi'ən) *n.* an evergreen shrub with white flowers and red berries.

trace (trās) *n.* **1,** a mark, track, or any evidence of someone or something formerly present or existent. **2,** a very small quantity of something. **3,** a line or sketch. **4,** a strap, rope, or chain for hitching a draft animal. **5,** a bar or lever for transferring motion. **—v.i. 1,** follow the footprints or track of. **2,** determine the course, development, or history of. **3,** find evidence of; investigate. **4,** copy (a drawing, etc.) by marking the lines on superimposed transparent paper. **5,** make a plan of.

trac'er (trās'ər) *n.* one who or that which traces. **—adj.** that which traces. **—skip tracer,** detective who seeks debt-evaders. **—tracer bullet,** one that blazes in flight, to indicate its course.

trac'er·y (trā'sə-rē) *n.* **1,** ornamental openwork built in a window. **2,** any delicate interlacing.

tra'che·a (trā'kē-ə) *n.* [*pl.* **-ae** (-ē")] the tube that conveys air from the larynx to the lungs; the windpipe. **—tra'che·al,** *adj.*

tra"che·ot'o·my (trā"kē-ot'ə-mē) *n.* the cutting of an opening into the trachea.

trac'ing (trās'ing) *n.* a traced copy.

track (trak) *n.* **1,** marks left in the ground, as footprints, a rut, etc. **2,** a system of rails to support and guide a moving vehicle, esp. a railroad. **3,** a path laid out for a race; running and field sports. **4,** a path or trail. **5,** a course of motion, travel, action, etc. **6,** (*Slang*) scar from a hypodermic

needle. **—v.t. 1,** pursue; trace. **2,** make a track on; make footprints with (mud, etc.). **3,** traverse; explore. **—keep track of,** keep within sight or knowledge. **—make tracks,** (*Slang*) go away. **—track (and field) meet,** a series of track and field contests. **—track lighting,** movable lights attached to a permanent mounted current-conducting track. **—track record,** (*Informal*) performance record in a certain job, duty, etc. **—track suit,** a sweat suit worn by athletes," esp. runners. **—track system,** a system in education for separating students into groups based on ability, disability, interests, etc.

track'ball" *n.* a small ball rotating in a fixed housing, used to move the cursor on a computer screen.

tract (trakt) *n.* **1,** an expanse of land or water; a region. **2,** a particular system in the body. **3,** a brief printed treatise.

trac'ta·ble (trak'tə-bəl) *adj.* **1,** easily led; docile; compliant. **2,** easily managed, worked, or wrought. **—trac"ta·bil'i·ty,** *n.*

trac'tate (trak'tāt) *n.* a tract (def. 3).

trac'tion (trak'shən) *n.* **1,** the act of dragging or hauling; the state of being drawn. **2,** power of pulling or attracting. **3,** adhesive friction. **—trac'tive,** *adj.*

trac'tor (trak'tər) *n.* a self-propelled vehicle that pulls heavy loads.

trade (trād) *n.* **1,** the business of buying and selling; commerce. **2,** a sale or exchange. **3,** an occupation, esp. skilled mechanical work. **4,** the persons engaged in the same occupation. **5,** customers. **—v.t.** buy, sell, barter, or exchange. **—v.i.** engage in commerce. **—trad'er,** *n.* **—trade name,** a name coined to identify a product; trademark. **—trade union,** an organization of workers in a skilled trade. **—trade wind,** a prevailing wind relied upon by ships. **—trading card,** a small card depicting an athlete, etc., traded, esp. by children. **—trading post,** a station of a trader in a sparsely settled region. **—trading stamp,** a stamp given as a premium by a merchant, good for merchandise. ❑ *career*

trade-'in" *n.* property given in part payment of a purchase.

trade-'last" *n.* a compliment reported to another on condition of receiving one in return.

trade'mark" *n.* a patented name or visual mark attached to a product.

trade-'off" *n.* **1,** a stalemate. **2,** an exchange.

trades'man (trādz'mən) [*pl.* **-men**] **trades'wom"an** *n.* a shopkeeper; merchant.

tra·di′tion (trə-dish′ən) *n.* the handing down of customs, practices, doctrines, etc.; something so handed down. **—tra·di′tion·al**, *adj.* **—tra·di′tion·al·ism**, *n.* **—tra·di′tion·al·ist**, *n.*

tra·duce′ (trə-dūs′) *v.t.* defame; slander.

traf′fic (traf′ik) *n.* **1,** the coming and going of persons, vehicles, etc. **2,** commercial dealings; the transportation of goods. **—traf′fick·er**, *n.—v.i.* [**-ficked, -fick·ing**] carry on traffic; deal. **—traffic circle,** a road intersection designed to avoid cross traffic. **—traffic light,** a stoplight (def. 1).

tra·ge′di·an (trə-jē′dē-ən), **tra·ge″di·enne′** (-en′) *n.* an actor in a tragedy.

trag′e·dy (traj′ə-dē) *n.* **1,** a lamentable event or state of affairs; a disaster or calamity. **2,** a drama with an unhappy ending.

---

tragedy

↔ Etymologically, a *tragedy* is a goat-song, from Greek *tragos*, goat, and *ōidē*, song. The reason for the derivation is unclear.

---

trag′ic (traj′ik) *adj.* being or suggesting a tragedy; very unhappy. Also, **trag′i·cal.**

trag″i·com′e·dy (traj″i-) *n.* a drama or incident of mixed tragic and comic character. **—trag″i·com′ic,** *adj.*

trail (trāl) *v.t.* **1,** drag loosely, as along the ground; draw along behind. **2,** follow the trail of; track. **3,** (*Informal*) follow behind, as in a race. **4,** make a path through; mark out. **—v.i.** **1,** hang down or be dragged loosely behind something. **2,** proceed idly or lazily; loiter or straggle. **3,** be dispersed. **—n.** **1,** a rough path. **2,** a track or scent. **3,** something that trails behind. **—trail bike,** a motorcycle designed for use on trails and other rough terrain. **—trail mix,** (*Informal*) a snack food consisting of fruit, nuts, and raisins.

trail′blaz″er *n.* one who goes first, a pioneer or originator.

trail′er (trā′lər) n. **1,** a vehicle drawn by another. **2,** a kind of mobile house drawn by an automobile. **3,** a trailing plant. **4,** brief excerpts from a motion picture to advertise it.

train (trān) *n.* **1,** a railroad locomotive and the cars connected to it. **2,** a procession of persons, vehicles, etc., traveling together. **3,** a body of attendants; a retinue. **4,** something that trails along behind; a trailing skirt. **5,** a series of events, ideas, etc. **—v.t.** **1,** subject to discipline and instruction; make proficient or fit. **2,** aim or direct, as a gun. **—v.i.** undergo or impart training.

train·ee′ (trā-nē′) *n.* one who receives training, esp. military.

train′er *n.* **1,** one who trains others. **2,** in some sports, one who gives rubdowns, applies bandages, etc.

train′man (-mən) *n.* [*pl.* **-men**] a member of a railroad conductor's crew.

traipse (trāps) *v.i.* **1,** walk carelessly or idly. **2,** trail untidily.

trait (trāt) *n.* a distinguishing feature or quality.

trai′tor (trā′tər) *n.* one who betrays; one guilty of treason. **—trai′tor·ous,** *adj.*

tra·jec′to·ry (trə-jek′tə-rē) *n.* the curve described by a projectile in flight.

tram *n.* a wheeled car; (*Brit.*) a streetcar. **—tram′way″,** *n.*

tram′mel (tram′əl) *n.* **1,** an impediment. **2,** an instrument for drawing ellipses. **3,** a shackle. **—v.t.** shackle; hamper.

tramp *v.i.* **1,** walk with a heavy step. **2,** walk steadily or resolutely; trudge. **3,** travel about as a vagabond. **—v.t.** **1,** traverse on foot. **2,** trample underfoot. **—n.** **1,** a heavy tread. **2,** the sound of a heavy footstep. **3,** a long walk. **4,** a vagabond who lives by begging or stealing. **5,** a freight ship without fixed ports of call. **6,** (*Slang*) a prostitute.

tram′ple (tram′pəl) *v.t.* **1,** step heavily upon; crush with the feet. **2,** suppress by force.

tram″po·line′ (tram″pə-lēn′) *n.* a sheet of canvas attached by springs to a frame, used for tumbling.

trance (tráns) *n.* **1,** a state of partial unconsciousness. **2,** a daze.

tran′quil (trang′kwil) *adj.* calm; serene; undisturbed. **—tran·quil′li·ty,** *n.* **—tran′quil·ize″** (-īz″) *v.t.* **—tran′quil·iz″er,** *n.* a drug used to reduce tension.

trans- *pref.* across; beyond.

trans·act′ *v.t. & i.* carry through (dealings, etc.) to a conclusion; perform; do. **—trans·ac′tion,** *n.* performance; a deal. **—transactional analysis,** a type of psychotherapy dealing esp. with social interaction.

trans″at·lan′tic *adj.* **1,** crossing the Atlantic Ocean. **2,** situated across the Atlantic.

trans″ceiv′er (tran-sē′vər) *n.* a combined radio transmitter and receiver.

tran·scend′ (tran-send′) *v.t.* go or be beyond (a limit, etc.); surpass; excel. **—tran·scend′ence,** *n.* **—tran·scend′ent,** *adj.*

tran″scen·den′tal (tran″sən-den′təl) *adj.*

---

beyond ordinary experience. —**Transcendental Meditation,** (*T.N.*) a method of meditation for increasing mental effectiveness and reducing anxiety and tension. Also, **TM.**

tran″scen·den′tal·ism (-iz-əm) *n.* a philosophy based on reasoning or intuition, not empiricism.

trans″con·ti·nen′tal *adj.* crossing, or situated across, a continent; (*U.S.*) coast-to-coast.

tran·scribe′ (tran-skrīb′) *v.t.* **1,** make a written copy of. **2,** put into writing; write in other characters; transliterate. **3,** make a phonograph recording of. **4,** arrange (a musical composition) for other instruments.

tran′script (tran′skript) *n.* a written copy.

tran·scrip′tion (-skrip′shən) *n.* **1,** act or result of transcribing. **2,** a transcript. **3,** a record for broadcasting.

trans·du′cer (-doo′sər) *n.* a device that converts energy from one form to another.

tran′sept *n.* that part of a cross-shaped church at right angles to the nave.

trans·fer′ (trans-fēr′) *v.t.* [**trans·ferred′, -fer′ring**] **1,** move or convey from one place to another. **2,** make over custody or ownership of. **3,** copy or impress (a design, etc.) from one surface to another. —*n.* (trans′fēr) **1,** the act or means of transferring. **2,** a ticket valid as fare on another car of a transit system. **3,** something to be transferred, as a design. —**trans″fer·ee′,** *n.* —**trans·fer′ence,** *n.* —**trans·fer′or,** *n.*

trans·fig″u·ra′tion (trans-fig″yə-rā′-shən) *n.* **1,** transfigurement. **2,** (*cap.*) the change in appearance of Christ on the Mount.

trans·fig′ure *v.t.* **1,** change the outward form or appearance of; transform. **2,** give a glorified appearance to; exalt. —**trans·fig′ure·ment,** *n.*

trans·fix′ *v.t.* **1,** pierce through; fasten by pinning down. **2,** make motionless with amazement, etc. —**trans·fix′ion,** *n.*

trans·form′ *v.t.* change in form, appearance, or condition.

trans″for·ma′tion *n.* **1,** act or effect of transforming. **2,** a wig.

trans·form′er *n.* an apparatus for changing electric current.

trans·fuse′ (trans-fūz′) *v.t.* transfer (liquid) by or as by pouring; inject; infuse. —**trans·fu′sion,** *n.* a transfer of blood from one person to another.

trans·gress′ (trans-gres′) *v.t. & i.* **1,** go beyond (a limit, etc.). **2,** break or violate (a law or rule.). —**trans·gres′sion** (-gresh′ən) *n.* —**trans·gres′sor** (-gres′ər) *n.*

tran′sient (tran′shənt) *adj.* passing with time; not enduring; temporary; momentary. —*n.* **1,** one who stays briefly, as a guest. **2,** (*Physics*) a decaying signal. —**tran′sience,** *n.*

tran·sis′tor (tran-sis′tər) *n.* a small electronic device used instead of a tube, to modify the signal.

tran′sit *n.* **1,** passage or conveyance from one place to another. **2,** a surveying instrument for measuring angles.

tran·si′tion (-zish′ən) *n.* a change from one place or state to another. —**tran·si′-tion·al,** *adj.*

tran′si·tive (tran′sə-tiv) *adj.* **1,** (*Gram.*) (of a verb) taking a direct object. **2,** making, or having power to make, a transition.

tran′si·to″ry (tran′sə-tôr″ē) *adj.* lasting only for a time; fleeting.

trans·late′ (trans-lāt′) *v.t.* **1,** express the sense in words of another language. **2,** explain by using other words. **3,** transfer. —**trans·la′tion,** *n.* —**trans·la′tor,** *n.*

trans·lit′er·ate″ (trans-lit′ər-āt″) *v.t.* spell in another alphabet. —**trans″lit·er·a′tion,** *n.*

trans·lu′cent (trans-loo′sənt) *adj.* transmitting light without being transparent. —**trans·lu′cence,** *n.*

> **translucent, transparent**
> ☛ Something that is *translucent* lets light come through, but diffuses it. A *transparent* object allows light to come through essentially unaffected.

trans″mi·gra′tion *n.* passage, esp. of a soul reborn in another body. —**trans·mi′-grate,** *v.i.*

trans·mis′si·ble *adj.* capable of being transmitted. —**trans·mis′si·bil′i·ty,** *n.*

trans·mis′sion (trans-mish′ən) *n.* **1,** the act or result of transmitting. **2,** a system of gears for transmitting power in an automobile.

trans·mit′ *v.t.* [**trans·mit′ted, -ting**] **1,** send onward or along; hand over, or down to, a recipient or destination. **2,** communicate; emit. —**trans·mit′tal,** *n.*

trans·mit′ter (-ər) *n.* the sending part of a radio or telephone apparatus.

trans·mog′ri·fy″ (-mog′rə-fī″) *v.t.* transform, as by magic. —**trans·mog″ri·fi·ca′-tion,** *n.*

trans·mute' (trans-mūt') *v.t. & i.* change from one nature, form, or substance to another. —**trans″mu·ta'tion,** *n.*

tran'som (tran'səm) *n.* **1,** a beam above a door separating it from a window. **2,** a hinged window or panel above a door. **3,** any crossbeam.

trans·par'ent (trans-par'ənt) *adj.* **1,** permitting distinct vision through a solid substance. **2,** easily understood; manifest. —**trans·par'ence, trans·par'en·cy,** *n.* ❑ *translucent*

tran·spire' (tran-spīr') *v.i.* **1,** emit a vapor; exhale or perspire. **2,** escape through pores. **3,** become known. **4,** happen; occur. —**tran″spi·ra'tion,** *n.*

trans·plant' *v.t.* remove from one place and plant, fix, or establish in another.

tran·spon'der (tran-spon'dər) *n.* a transceiver activated by a predetermined signal.

trans·port' (trans-pôrt') *v.t.* **1,** carry from one place to another; convey. **2,** imbue with strong emotion. **3,** carry into banishment. —*n.* (trans'pôrt) **1,** the act or business of transporting. **2,** a means of transport, esp. a ship for carrying troops. **3,** rapture.

trans″por·ta'tion (trans″pôr-tā'shən) *n.* **1,** act or result, or a means, of conveying. **2,** traveling expenses.

trans·pose' (trans-pōz') *v.t.* **1,** alter the position or order of. **2,** exchange the places of. **3,** [also *v.i.*] arrange or perform (music) in a different key. —**trans″po·si'tion,** *n.*

trans·sex'u·al *n. & adj.* (pert. to) a person who has undergone, or desires to undergo, a change of sex.

trans·ship' *v.t. & i.* ship by more than one carrier.

tran″sub·stan'ti·ate″ (tran″səb-stan'shē-āt″) *v.t.* **1,** change from one substance into another. **2,** (*Theol.*) change (the bread and wine of the Eucharist) into the body and blood of Christ. —**tran″sub·stan″ti·a'tion,** *n.*

trans·ver'sal (trans-vẽrs'əl) *n.* a line intersecting two or more other lines.

trans·verse' (trans-vẽrs') *adj.* lying across something; extending from side to side.

trans·vest'ism (tranz-vest'iz-əm) *n.* desire to wear or the practice of wearing the clothes of the opposite sex. Also, **transves'ti·tism.** —**trans·vest'ite** (-īt) *n.*

trap *n.* **1,** any contrivance for catching something, esp. animals; a pitfall or snare; a stratagem. **2,** a U-bend in a pipe. **3,** (*pl.*) baggage; equipment; the percussion instruments of a band. **4,** a door in a floor,

ceiling, or roof; trapdoor. **5,** a light two-wheeled carriage. **6,** a device for throwing clay pigeons. —*v.t.* [**trapped, trap'ping**] catch in a trap; ensnare in any way. —*v.i.* trap animals.

trap'door″ *n.* a door in a floor, ceiling, or roof.

tra·peze' (tra-pēz') *n.* a horizontal bar suspended by two ropes, used for gymnastic exercises.

---

trapeze, trapezium, trapezoid
↔ All three words derive from Greek *trapezion,* small four-footed table (from *tetra,* four, and *peza,* foot). Euclid applied the term to the table-shaped geometric figure, the quadrilateral.

---

tra·pe'zi·um (tra-pē'zē-əm) *n.* a quadrilateral plane figure having no two sides parallel. ❑ *trapeze*

trap'e·zoid″ (trap'i-zoid″) *n.* a quadrilateral figure with two sides parallel. ❑ *trapeze*

trap'per (-ər) *n.* one who traps animals, esp. fur-bearing animals.

trap'pings (-ingz) *n.pl.* equipment.

Trap'pist (trap'ist) *adj.* pert. to a Rom. Cath. order of monks.

trap'rock″ *n.* an igneous rock, as basalt.

trap'shoot″ing *n.* the sport of shooting at flying targets.

trash *n.* anything worthless or useless; waste material; rubbish. —*v.t.* (*Slang*) **1,** vandalize. **2,** run down; disparage. **3,** discard. —**trash'y,** *adj.*

trau'ma (trou'mə) *n.* **1,** a bodily injury. **2,** a mental shock. —**trau·mat'ic,** *adj.* —**trau·mat'i·cal·ly,** *adv.*

trav'ail (trav'āl; trə-vāl') *n.* hard labor. —*v.i.* **1,** toil hard. **2,** suffer the pangs of childbirth.

trav'el (trav'əl) *v.i.* **1,** go from place to place; make a journey. **2,** move on a fixed track, as a mechanical part. **3,** advance; proceed. **4,** (*Informal*) move speedily. —*v.t.* pass over or through. —*n.* the act of traveling. —**tra'vel·er,** *n.* —**traveler's check,** a check signed by the purchaser when bought and again when cashed.

trav'eled (trav'əld) *adj.* **1,** having traveled widely. **2,** experienced. **3,** used by travelers, as a road.

trav'e·logue″ (trav'ə-lâg″) *n.* a lecture or motion picture describing a journey. Also, **trav'e·log″.**

trav'erse (trav'ərs) *v.t.* [also, (trə-vers')] **1,** pass across, over, or through. **2,** contradict; obstruct. **3,** turn and aim (a gun).

---

fat, fāte, fär, fãre, fâll, ásk; met, hē, hẽr, maybė; pin, pīne; not, nōte, ôr, tool

—*n.* something that lies or moves crosswise; a crosswise barrier. —*adj.* transverse. —**traverse rod,** a mechanical curtain rod.

trav'er·tine" (trav'ər-tīn") *n.* a soft, straw-colored form of limestone.

trav'es·ty (trav'is-tè) *n.* a burlesque of a literary or dramatic composition; any debased likeness. —*v.t.* imitate grotesquely.

trawl (trâl) *n.* a fishing net or line dragged by a boat. —*v.i.* fish with a trawl. —**trawl'er,** *n.* a fishing boat.

tray (trā) *n.* a flat vessel or shallow box for holding something.

treach'er·ous (trech'ə-rəs) *adj.* **1,** committing treachery. **2,** deceptive; unreliable. —**treach'er·ous·ness,** *n.*

treach'er·y (trech'ə-rè) *n.* violation of allegiance or faith; betrayal of trust; treason or perfidy.

trea'cle (trē'kəl) *n.* molasses.

---
treacle
↔ The ultimate origin of this word is Greek *thērion,* wild beast, through Latin *theriaca,* antidote for a poisonous bite. The reference is probably to the earlier use of treacle as a general-purpose remedy.
---

tread (tred) *v.i.* [**trod, trod'den** (-dən), **tread'ing**] set the foot down; step; walk. —*v.t.* **1,** walk on, in, or along. **2,** trample. **3,** execute by walking or dancing. —*n.* **1,** a stepping; the sound of a step; a single step. **2,** the undermost surface, as of a shoe, tire, etc., that touches the ground or road. **3,** a bearing surface, as of a rail or stair. —**tread water, 1,** swim so as to remain upright with the head above water. **2,** barely survive without improving one's lot. **3,** not make progress.

trea'dle (tred'əl) *n.* a lever operated by the foot.

tread'mill" *n.* **1,** a mill powered by animals walking on a wheel, etc. **2,** any monotonous and wearisome routine.

trea'son (trē'zən) *n.* violation of the allegiance due a state. —**trea'son·a·ble,** *adj.* constituting treason. —**trea'son·ous,** *adj.*

treas'ure (trezh'ər) *n.* **1,** an accumulation of money or jewels. **2,** anything prized highly. —*v.t.* **1,** collect and save; retain carefully. **2,** regard as precious; prize. —**treasure trove** (trōv) money or valuables (of an unknown owner) found in the earth.

treas'ur·er (trezh'ər-ər) *n.* the officer in charge of funds.

treas'ur·y (trezh'ə-rè) *n.* **1,** the funds of a government, corporation, etc.; the department administering them. **2,** a place where money or valuables are kept.

treat (trēt) *v.t.* **1,** regard, behave toward, or deal with; discuss. **2,** apply methods of relief or cure to (a patient or disease). **3,** subject to a process. **4,** entertain by paying for food, drink, amusement, etc. —*v.i.* **1,** discuss something. **2,** carry on negotiations. **3,** bear the expense of regalement. —*n.* **1,** entertainment paid for; one's turn to pay. **2,** (*Informal*) anything enjoyable.

trea'tise (trē'tis) *n.* a book treating of a particular subject.

treat'ment (-mənt) *n.* **1,** act or manner of dealing with something. **2,** therapy.

trea'ty (trē'tè) *n.* a written agreement between nations.

tre'ble (treb'əl) *adj.* **1,** threefold. **2,** high in pitch; soprano. —*n.* a high-pitched part, tone, etc. —*v.t. & i.* triple. —**treble clef,** a G clef on the second line of a staff.

tree (trē) *n.* **1,** a large perennial plant with a single permanent woody trunk. **2,** any of various devices or parts in the form of a pole, bar, etc. **3,** the representation of a hierarchical structure as the branches of a tree, as a genealogical diagram: *family tree.* —*v.t.* drive into a tree.

tre'foil" (trē'foil") *n.* a three-leaved plant, esp. the clover.

trek *v.i.* [**trekked, trek'king**] travel; migrate. —*n.* a journey.

trel'lis (trel'is) *n.* a framework of crossbars; a lattice.

trem'a·tode" (trem'ə-tōd") *n.* any of a class of parasitic flatworms.

trem'ble (trem'bəl) *v.i.* **1,** shake or vibrate with continued movement; shiver; quake. **2,** be agitated by fear. **3,** vacillate. —*n.* a shivering or vibratory motion. —**trem'bly,** *adj.*

tre·men'dous (tri-men'dəs) *adj.* **1,** very great in size, amount, degree, etc.; huge; gigantic. **2,** (*Informal*) excellent. —**tre·men'dous·ness,** *n.*

trem'o·lo" (trem'ə-lō") *n.* [*pl.* **-los"**] rapid reiteration of a musical tone or tones.

trem'or (trem'ər) *n.* a shake, quiver, or vibration; a trembling or vibratory movement.

trem'u·lous (trem'yə-ləs) *adj.* **1,** trembling; unsteady. **2,** fearful; timid; irresolute. **3,** wavy, as a line. —**trem'u·lous·ness,** *n.*

trench *n.* a long, narrow excavation in the ground, esp. as a shelter in warfare; a ditch or furrow. —*v.t. & i.* dig a trench (in); fortify. —**trench coat,** a heavy raincoat. —**trench mouth,** an infectious disease of the mucous membranes of the throat and mouth.

trench′ant (tren′chənt) *adj.* **1,** keenly effective; incisive. **2,** thoroughgoing. —**trench′an·cy,** *n.*

trench′er *n.* a wooden platter for serving meat.

trench′er·man (tren′chər-mən) *n.* [*pl.* -men] a heavy eater.

trend *n.* tendency to go in a particular direction or course; drift, bent, or inclination. —**trend′y,** *adj.* (*Informal*). chic; up-to-date.

tre·pan′ (trə-pan′) *n.* a cylindrical saw; a boring instrument. —*v.t.* [-panned′, -pan′-ning] cut with a trepan.

tre·pang′ (trė-pang′) *n.* a sea cucumber, often dried, smoked, and used as food. Also, **bêche-de-mer.**

tre·phine′ (tri-fīn′) *n.* a cylindrical saw used in brain surgery.

trep″i·da′tion (trep″ə-dā′shən) *n.* tremulous agitation, as from alarm.

tres′pass (tres′pəs) *v.i.* **1,** enter without right upon another's land; encroach. **2,** commit a wrong; transgress; sin. —*n.* an offense; sin.

tress (tres) *n.* **1,** a lock or braid of hair. **2,** (*pl.*) the hair of the head.

tres′tle (tres′əl) *n.* **1,** a short horizontal bar supported by legs; a sawhorse. **2,** a bridge supported by framework.

trey (trā) *n.* a playing card, die, domino, etc., with three spots.

tri- (trī) *pref.* three.

tri′ad (trī′ad) *n.* **1,** a group of three closely related things. **2,** (*Music*) a chord of three tones.

tri·age′ (trė-äzh′) *n.* the act of sorting, esp. of combat casualties for treatment.

tri′al (trī′əl) *n.* **1,** an action in a judicial court to determine a cause. **2,** a test; an examination. **3,** a try or attempt. **4,** the state of being tried or tested; probation. **5,** a hardship. —*adj.* **1,** pert. to a trial. **2,** done as a test or experiment. —**trial and error,** a method of solving a problem by a series of guesses. —**trial balance,** a statement of the current totals in a ledger. —**trial balloon,** an act or statement to test public reaction.

tri′an″gle (trī′ang″gəl) *n.* **1,** a plane figure formed by three straight lines. **2,** a drawing instrument in this shape. **3,** a steel bar bent into a triangle used as a musical percussion instrument. **4,** three persons involved in emotional conflict. —**tri·an′gu·lar** (trī-ang′gyû-lər) *adj.*

tri·an″gu·la′tion (trī-ang″gyû-lā′shən) *n.*

a measuring by inferring unknown sides or angles of a triangle. —**tri·ang′u·late″** (-lāt″) *v.t.*

tri·ath′lon (trī-ath′lon) *n.* an athletic contest involving swimming, bicycling, and running.

tribe (trīb) *n.* **1,** an aggregate of people united by common ancestry, intermarriage, or allegiance. **2,** any class or body of individuals. —**trib′al,** *adj.* —**tribes′-man, tribes′wom″an** *n.*

trib″u·la′tion (trib″yə-lā′shən) *n.* a state, cause, or instance of affliction or suffering.

tri·bu′nal (trī-bū′nəl) *n.* a court of justice.

trib′une (trib′ūn) *n.* **1,** a person who upholds or defends popular rights. **2,** a dais or pulpit.

trib′u·tar″y (trib′yə-ter″ė) *n.* **1,** a river, brook, etc. that flows into another body of water. **2,** one who pays tribute. —*adj.* contributory.

trib′ute (trib′ūt) *n.* **1,** a gift or compliment as a mark of gratitude or respect. **2,** any forced payment.

trice (trīs) *n.* an instant; moment.

tri″cen·ten′ni·al *adj. & n.* tercentenary.

tri′ceps (trī′seps) *n.sing.* a three-headed muscle, esp. the extensor muscle along the back of the upper arm.

trich″i·no′sis (trik″ə-nō′sis) *n.* a disease caused by a parasitic worm.

trick (trik) *n.* **1,** any method of deceiving; a stratagem, ruse, or wile. **2,** a practical joke, prank, or hoax. **3,** a peculiar habit or mannerism. **4,** a batch of playing cards, one played from each hand. **5,** (*Informal*) a woman. **6,** a turn of work or duty. **7,** (*Slang*) an act of prostitution; a prostitute's client. —*adj.* fraudulent; crafty; unreliable; unusual. —*v.t. & i.* **1,** dupe; swindle. **2,** (with *out*) dress; array.

trick′er·y (-ə-rė) *n.* deception.

trick′le (trik′əl) *v.i.* flow slowly, irregularly, or by drops. —*v.t.* cause to trickle. —*n.* a trickling flow. —**trickle-down,** *adj.* pert. to a theory of economics that financial help from government to big business will eventually benefit the general public.

trick′ster (-stər) *n.* a deceiver; a joker.

trick′track″ *n.* a variety of backgammon. Also, **tric′trac′.**

trick′y *adj.* **1,** crafty. **2,** unreliable; ticklish. —**trick′i·ness,** *n.*

tri′col′or (trī′kul′ər) *n.* a flag of three colors.

tri′corne (trī′kôrn) *n.* a three-cornered cocked hat.

tri′cot (trē′kō) *n.* a knitted fabric.

tri′cy·cle (trī′sik-əl) *n.* a three-wheeled vehicle for a child; a velocipede.

tri′dent (trī′dənt) *n. & adj.* a spear or fork having three prongs.

tried (trīd) *v.* pret. & p.p. of *try.*

tri·fec′ta (trī-fek′tə) *n.* a wager in horseracing requiring correct choice of first, second, and third place in exact order to win.

tri′fle (trī′fəl) *n.* something trivial or insignificant. —*v.i.* **1,** deal with something lightly or idly. **2,** waste time; dally. —**tri′fler** (-flər) *n.* —**tri′fling,** *adj.* insignificant.

> ### trifle, trivial
> ↔ These two words are unrelated, though they have similar sounds and senses. *Trifle* comes from Old French *trufle,* mockery. *Trivial* is from Latin *trivialis,* pert. to the crossroads, hence, commonplace.

tri·fo′cal (trī-fō′kəl) *adj.* having three focal points. —*n.* (*pl.*) eyeglasses having lenses of three different strengths.

trig *adj.* [**trig′ger, -gest**] **1,** neat; spruce. **2,** in good condition. —*n.* a block used to check the motion of a wheel, cask, etc.

trig′ger (trig′ər) *n.* a lever for releasing a spring, esp. on a firearm. —*v.t. & i.* initiate; cause.

trig″o·nom′e·try (trig″ə-nom′ə-trē) *n.* the branch of mathematics that deals with measurement of and by means of triangles. —**trig″o·no·met′ric** (-nə-met′rik) *adj.*

trill (tril) *n.* **1,** a rapid alternation of two adjacent musical tones. **2,** any quavering, tremulous sound. **3,** a warbling, as of a bird. —*v.i. & t.* sound vibrantly.

tril′lion (tril′yən) *n. & adj.* the cardinal number represented by 1 followed by twelve zeros (U.S. & Fr.) or eighteen zeros (Brit. & Ger.).

tril′li·um (tril′ē-əm) *n.* a plant of the lily family.

tril′o·gy (tril′ə-jē) *n.* a group of three related things, as plays.

trim *v.t.* [**trimmed, trim′ming**] **1,** make neat or orderly. **2,** remove by clipping or pruning. **3,** deck with ornaments. **4,** (*Informal*) defeat. —*v.i.* come to a desired adjustment or position. —*n.* **1,** position, condition, or order. **2,** dress, equipment, or decoration; ornamental borders or furnishings. —*adj.* [**trim′mer, -mest**] **1,** neat; spruce; smart. **2,** in good order or condition. —**trim′mer,** *n.* —**trim′ming,** *n.* —**trim′ness,** *n.*

tri·mes′ter (trī-mes′tər) *n.* a period of three months.

trin′i·ty (trin′ə-tē) *n.* a group of three, esp. (*cap.*) Father, Son, and Holy Ghost or Spirit.

trin′ket (tring′kit) *n.* a trifling ornament or keepsake.

tri′o (trē′ō) *n.* a group of three.

tri′ode (trī′ōd) *n.* an electron tube containing three elements.

trip *n.* **1,** a journey or voyage. **2,** a catching of the foot against an obstacle; a stumble. **3,** a slip or error. **4,** a light, short step. **5,** a catch or trigger; a sudden release, as by a trigger. **6,** (*Slang*) the hallucinations, heightened perceptions, etc., experienced under the influence of a hallucinogenic drug. —*v.i.* [**tripped, trip′ping**] **1,** stumble. **2,** make a mistake. **3,** run or step lightly; skip. **4,** have a psychedelic experience. —*v.t.* **1,** cause to stumble, fall, or err. **2,** perform with a tripping step. **3,** release suddenly. —**trip′per,** *n.*

tri·par′tite (trī-pär′tīt) *adj.* embracing three parties, as a treaty.

tripe (trīp) *n.* **1,** the stomach of a cow or ox, prepared as food. **2,** (*Slang*) anything worthless.

trip′ham″mer *n.* a heavy hammer allowed to fall by a tripping device.

triph′thong″ (trif′thâng″) *n.* three adjacent vowels pronounced in one syllable.

tri′ple (trip′əl) *adj.* consisting of three parts; threefold; of three kinds. —*n.* a threefold object or amount; (*Baseball*) a three-base hit. —*v.t. & i.* multiply by three.

trip′let *n.* one of three offspring born at one birth; one of a group of three; (*pl.*) the three collectively.

tri′plex (trip′leks) *adj.* threefold. —*n.* something triple; an apartment having three stories.

trip′li·cate″ (trip′li-kāt″) *v.t.* make in three copies. —*adj.* (-kət) made in three copies. —*n.* (-kət) the third copy. —**trip″li·ca′tion,** *n.*

tri′pod (trī′pod) *n.* a stand having three legs. —**trip′o·dal** (trip′ə-dəl) *adj.*

trip′ping *adj.* light and lively.

trip′tych (trip′tik) *n.* three pictures, etc., esp. in hinged frames.

tri′reme (trī′rēm) *n.* a galley with three tiers of oars.

tri·sect′ (trī-sekt′) *v.t.* divide in three parts. —**tri·sec′tion,** *n.*

trite (trīt) *adj.* stale; hackneyed. —**trite′ness,** *n.*

tri′tium (trish′əm) *n.* an isotope of hydrogen.

trit′u·rate″ (trich′ə-rāt″) *v.t.* grind to powder. —**trit″u·ra′tion,** *n.*

tri′umph (trī′umf) *n.* **1,** the winning of a war or contest; success. **2,** exultation over victory or success. —*v.i.* win; succeed.

tri·um′phal (trī-um′fəl) *adj.* pert. to or commemorating a victory.

tri·um′phant (trī-um′fənt) *adj.* victorious; exulting in victory.

tri·um′vir (trī-um′vər) *n.* a member of a triumvirate.

tri·um′vi·rate (trī-um′və-rit) *n.* three joint rulers; their government.

triv′et (triv′it) *n.* **1,** a three-legged stool or stand. **2,** a short-legged plate to put under a hot platter.

triv′i·a (triv′ē-ə) *n.pl.* trivial matters or things.

triv′i·al (triv′ē-əl) *adj.* of little importance or significance. —**triv″i·al′i·ty,** *n.* ❏ *trifle*

triv′i·um (triv′ē-əm) *n.* grammar, logic, and rhetoric, three of the seven liberal arts.

-trix *suf.* denoting a feminine agent, as *executrix.*

tro′che (trō′kē) *n.* a medicinal tablet or pill.

tro′chee (trō′kē) *n.* (*Prosody*) a metrical foot of two syllables, long then short. —**tro·cha′ic** (-kā′ik) *adj. & n.*

trod *v.* pret. of *tread.*

trod′den (trod′ən) *v.* p.p. of *tread.*

trog′lo·dyte″ (trog′lə-dīt″) *n.* **1,** a dweller in a cave. **2,** one who lives in seclusion. —**trog″lo·dyt′ic** (-dit′ik) *adj.*

troi′ka (troi′kə) *n.* **1,** a team of three horses; the carriage they draw. **2,** a group of three; triumvirate.

Tro′jan horse (trō′jən) an ostensible gift intended as a trap.

troll (trōl) *v.i. & t.* **1,** sing in a full, jovial tone; sing a round. **2,** fish with a moving line. **3,** turn around; roll. —*n.* **1,** a round song. **2,** equipment for trolling. **3,** a fairy dwarf.

trol′ley (trol′ē) *n.* **1,** a pulley or block moving on an overhead wire, to convey loads or feed electric current. **2,** a streetcar.

trol′lop (trol′əp) *n.* **1,** a slovenly woman. **2,** a prostitute.

trom′bone (trom′bōn) *n.* a musical wind instrument having a sliding U-shaped section. —**trom′bon·ist,** *n.*

tromp *v.i.* (*Slang*) **1,** defeat soundly. **2,** trample upon. —*v.i.* walk noisily or heavily.

trompe l'oeil (trômp′ loi′) (*Fr.,* trick the eye) a method of painting for reproducing through fine detail the illusion of three-dimensional depth and photographic realism.

troop *n.* **1,** an assemblage of people; a herd or flock; a multitude. **2,** a unit of armed forces; (*pl.*) a body of soldiers. —*v.i. & t.* flock together; march or maneuver. —**troop′er,** *n.* a policeman or soldier.

---

troop, troupe, trooper, trouper
Troop and *troupe* are, in fact, the same word, orig. meaning flock, but *troupe,* the French form, is now used as a specialized word for a group of performers. A similar distinction is observed for *trooper* (a police officer or member of a troop) and *trouper* (a member of a troupe).

---

trope (trōp) *n.* a figure of speech; metaphor.

tro′phy (trō′fē) *n.* **1,** something captured in war, hunting, etc. **2,** a prize or medal, etc.

-tro·phy (trə-fē) *suf.* denoting nourishment.

trop′ic (trop′ik) *n.* **1,** either of the two parallels of latitude 23½° distant from the equator, north (tropic of Cancer) and south (tropic of Capricorn). **2,** (*pl.*) the region lying between these two parallels; the Torrid Zone. —**trop′i·cal,** *adj.* pert. to Torrid Zone.

tro′pism (trō′piz-əm) *n.* (*Biol.*) the tendency of an organism to face an external energy source, such as light.

trop′o·sphere″ (trop′ə-sfir″) *n.* the layer of atmosphere about 6 to 12 miles above the earth's surface.

-tro·py (trə-pē) *suf.* growth. Also, **-trop·ism.**

trot *v.i.* [**trot′ted, -ting**] go at a pace between a walk and a run. —*v.t.* **1,** cause (a horse) to trot. **2,** (with *out*) produce for inspection. —*n.* **1,** a trotting gait. **2,** (*Informal*) an illicit translation used by students; a crib.

troth (trâth) *n.* **1,** a promise to marry. **2,** (*Archaic*) truth.

trot′line″ *n.* a long fishing line with numerous hooks.

trot′ter (trot′ər) *n.* **1,** a trotting horse. **2,** pig's foot, as food.

trou′ba·dour″ (troo′bə-dôr″) *n.* an itin-

---

erant lyric poet or singer, esp. of So. France.

trou'ble (trub'əl) *v.t.* **1,** disturb in the mind; annoy; worry. **2,** put to inconvenience. —*n.* **1,** discomfort; distress; inconvenience. **2,** a cause or source of trouble. —**trou'ble·some,** *adj.* causing trouble. —**trou'blous,** *adj.*

trou'ble·shoot"er *n.* one who locates and eliminates sources of trouble.

trough (trâf) *n.* **1,** a long narrow container for water, food for animals, etc. **2,** a shallow open ditch; a deep groove.

trounce (trowns) *v.t.* defeat decisively; thrash.

troupe (troop) *n.* a traveling theatrical company. —*v.i.* travel as member of a troupe. —**troup'er,** *n.* ❑ *troop*

trou'sers (trow'zərz) *n.pl.* a garment extending downward from the waist, covering each leg separately. —**trou'ser,** *adj.*

trous·seau' (troo-sō') *n.* a bride's clothes and other outfits.

trout (trowt) *n.* [*pl.* **trout**] a freshwater game fish.

trou·vère (troo-vār') *n.* (*Fr.*) a medieval narrative or epic poet of No. France.

trow (trō) *v.i.* (*Archaic*) believe.

trow'el (trow'əl) *n.* a short-handled tool with a flat or concave blade, for digging, spreading, etc.

troy (troi) *adj.* pert. to a system of weights used for gold, silver, etc., named for Troyes, France.

tru'ant (troo'ənt) *n. & adj.* one who is absent without leave, esp. a student. —**tru'an·cy,** *n.*

truce (troos) *n.* **1,** a negotiated suspension of hostilities. **2,** a respite.

truck (truk) *n.* **1,** an automotive vehicle for carrying heavy loads. **2,** a frame on wheels for carrying loads; such a frame supporting a railway car or locomotive. **3,** the top of a mast. **4,** vegetables grown for marketing. **5,** miscellaneous articles. **6,** dealings; barter. —*v.t.* **1,** transport by truck. **2,** barter; peddle. —*v.i.* **1,** use or drive a truck. **2,** deal; bargain. **3,** (*Slang*) move ahead; stroll. —**truck'age,** *n.* the act or cost of transporting goods. —**truck'er,** *n.* truck driver. —**truck farm,** a farm growing garden vegetables for sale.

truck'le (truk'əl) *n.* a small wheel, pulley, or caster. —*v.i.* be tamely submissive or obsequious. —**truckle bed,** a bed that can be pushed under another bed when not in use.

truck'man (-mən) *n.* [*pl.* **-men**] the

owner or operator of a motor truck used as a common carrier; truck driver.

truc'u·lent (truk'yə-lənt) *adj.* **1,** overbearing; cruel. **2,** bad-tempered. **3,** self-assertive. —**truc'u·lence,** *n.*

trudge (truj) *v.i.* walk, esp. laboriously or wearily.

trud'gen (truj'ən) *n.* a swimming stroke combining the crawl and the scissors kick, named for its inventor, 19th-c. English swimmer John Trudgen.

true (troo) *adj.* **1,** being in accordance with fact; not false. **2,** correct; accurate. **3,** genuine. **4,** firm in adherence to principles; faithful; loyal; truthful. **5,** sure; reliable. **6,** rightful; legitimate. —*n.* that which is true. —*v.t.* make true; shape or adjust exactly. —*adv.* in a true or truthful manner. —**true'ness,** *n.* —**tru'ly,** *adv.* —**true bill,** an indictment by a grand jury. —**true blue,** loyal.

truf'fle (truf'əl) *n.* a subterranean edible fungus.

tru'ism (troo'iz-əm) *n.* an obvious truth.

trump *n.* **1,** a playing card or suit given temporary rank higher than all cards of other suits. **2,** (*Informal*) a delightful person. —*v.t.* **1,** take with a trump card. **2,** (with *up*) fabricate deceitfully. —*v.i.* play a trump card.

trump'er·y (-ə-rè) *n. & adj.* something showy but of little value.

trum'pet (trum'pit) *n.* **1,** a musical wind instrument of the brass family. **2,** a noise-making toy. **3,** a loud cry, as of an elephant. **4,** a hearing aid: *ear trumpet.* —*v.i. & t.* **1,** make a trumpet's sound. **2,** proclaim. —**trum'pet·er,** *n.*

trun'cate (trung'kāt) *v.t.* reduce in size by cutting off a part. —**trun·ca'tion,** *n.*

trun'cheon (trun'chən) *n.* a baton or staff of office; a police officer's club.

trun'dle (trun'dəl) *n.* a small wheel, roller, or caster. —*v.t. & i.* **1,** move on trundles. **2,** roll along; whirl; rotate. —**trundle bed,** truckle bed.

trunk *n.* **1,** the main stem of a tree. **2,** the human or animal body without the head and limbs. **3,** the proboscis of an elephant. **4,** a large box or chest for carrying clothes in traveling. **5,** the main part or line of something having branches. **6,** (*pl.*) short trousers or breeches. —*adj.* pert. to a main line. —**trunk'ful,** *n.* —**trunk line, 1,** a transportation or supply route for long distance through traffic; main line. **2,** a direct link between two telephone offices or switchboards.

truss (trus) *v.t.* fasten; bind securely; confine closely. —*n.* **1,** a rigid framework, as to support a bridge. **2,** a belt worn for support, as of a hernia. **3,** a bundle or pack.

trust *n.* **1,** reliance on the integrity, veracity, etc. of a person; confidence. **2,** confident expectation. **3,** expectation of future payment; credit. **4,** management of property by one party (trustee) for the benefit of another (beneficiary); property given or held in trust. **5,** a group or company controlling a number of other companies. **6,** any monopolistic organization. —*adj.* pert. to a trust. —*v.t.* rely on; believe; give credit to. —*v.i.* have confidence; be trustful. —**trust company,** a bank that administers trusts.

trus·tee′ (trus-tē′) *n.* one to whom property is entrusted for management. —**trus·tee′ship,** *n.*

> **trustee, trusty**
> ☛ Do not confuse these two nouns, the latter of which, *trusty,* refers only to a prison inmate granted special privileges.

trust′ful *adj.* confiding. —**trust′ful·ness,** *n.*

trust′wor″thy *adj.* reliable. —**trust′wor″thi·ness,** *n.*

trust′y *adj.* reliable. —*n.* a convict trusted not to escape. —**trust′i·ness,** *n.* ☐ *trustee*

truth (trooth) *n.* **1,** conformity of assertion to fact or reality; the state of being true. **2,** that which is true; a fact; reality. —**truth serum,** a drug used to induce a person to talk freely, esp. sodium pentathol.

truth′ful *adj.* **1,** speaking the truth, esp. habitually. **2,** correct; true. —**truth′ful·ness,** *n.*

try (trī) *v.t.* [*pret. & p.p.* **tried** (trīd)] **1,** attempt to do or accomplish; essay; undertake. **2,** test. **3,** examine judicially; subject to trial. **4,** subject to strain, trouble, or affliction. **5,** (with *out*) refine; render. —*v.i.* make an attempt to trial. —*n.* an attempt or effort. —**try′ing,** *adj.* annoying; tiring.

try′out″ *n.* a trial to determine fitness.

tryst (trist) *n.* an appointed meeting, esp. between lovers.

tsar (tsär) *n.* czar. —**tsar·ev′na,** *n.* czarevna. —**tsar′e·vitch,** *n.* czarevitch. —**tsa·ri′na** *n.* czarina.

tset′se (tset′sē) *n.* an Afr. blood-sucking fly that transmits diseases.

T-′shirt″ *n.* a shirt with short sleeves and no collar, used both as an undershirt for men and as an outer shirt by both sexes.

tsim′mis (tsim′is) *n.* (*Informal*) a complicated affair.

T square a T-shaped ruler for drawing parallel lines.

tsu·na′mi (tsoo-nä′mē) *n.* a sea wave caused by a submarine earthquake.

tub *n.* **1,** a tanklike vessel for bathing: *bathtub.* **2,** a shallow cylindrical vessel. **3,** (*Informal*) a slow or clumsy boat. **4,** (*Informal*) a bath.

tu′ba (too′bə) *n.* (*Music*) a bass wind instrument of the brass family.

tub′by (tub′ē) *adj.* **1,** short and fat. **2,** having a dull sound. —**tub′bi·ness,** *n.*

tube (toob) *n.* **1,** a long, hollow cylinder of metal, glass, etc. **2,** a duct, canal, pipe, etc., for containing or conveying fluid. **3,** a bulb of glass fitted with electrodes. **4,** a tunnel; a subway. **5,** (*Slang*) a television receiver. —**tubing,** *n.* a piece of tube; material for tubes; tubes collectively. —**tube sock,** a long sock without a shaped heel.

tu′ber (too′bər) *n.* a plant having an enlarged fleshy rootlike part, as the potato. —**tu′ber·ous,** *adj.*

tu′ber·cle (too′bər-kəl) *n.* a small, rounded protuberance or excrescence, as on a bone. —**tubercle bacillus,** the organism causing tuberculosis.

tu·ber′cu·lin (too-bēr′kyə-lin) *n.* a preparation used in treating and testing for tuberculosis.

tu·ber″cu·lo′sis (too-bēr″kyû-lō′sis) *n.* **1,** an infectious disease marked by the formation of tubercles. **2,** this disease affecting the lungs; consumption. —**tu·ber′cu·lar, tu·ber′cu·lous,** *adj.*

tube′rose″ *n.* a bulbous plant bearing white flowers.

> **tuberose**
> ↔ This word has nothing to do with *rose.* It is derived from Latin *tuberosus,* tuberous, referring to its root structure.

tu′bu·lar (too′byû-lər) *adj.* being or pert. to a tube or tubes.

tuck (tuk) *v.t.* **1,** press into a narrow space; cram. **2,** cover snugly with wrappings. **3,** make tucks in. —*v.i.* draw together; contract. —*n.* a flat fold in cloth. —**tuck pointing,** brickwork that has mortar projecting from the mortar joint. —**tuck shop,** (*Brit.*) a variety store.

tuck′er (-ər) *n.* **1,** one who tucks. **2,** a neckcloth. —**tuckered out,** (*Informal*) fatigued.

-tude (tūd) *suf.* quality, state, etc.

Tu′dor (too′dər) *adj.* pert. to an Eng. dynasty or its period, 1485–1603.

Tues′day (tūz′dė) *n.* the third day of the week.

> **Tuesday**
> ↔ Translation of Latin *dies Martis*, Mars' day, replacing the god's name with the Germanic equivalent, *Tiu*.

tuft *n.* a small bunch of fibrous material, as hair, feathers, grass, etc., bound at one end. **—tuft′ed,** *adj.*

tug *v.t.* [**tugged, tug′ging**] pull with force or effort; drag; haul; tow. **—***v.i.* exert effort in pulling ·or otherwise. **—***n.* **1,** a strong pull; a sudden jerk. **2,** a boat for towing: *tugboat.* **3,** a strenuous contest or struggle. **4,** a strap; trace. **—tug of war,** a pulling contest.

tu·i′tion (too-ish′ən) *n.* **1,** a fee for instruction. **2,** the act or business of teaching. **—tu·i′tion·al,** *adj.*

tu′lip (too′lip) *n.* a bulbous plant bearing cup-shaped flowers.

> **tulip, turban**
> ↔ Both words derive from Persian *dulband*, turban; the flower was so called because of its supposed resemblance to the headwear.

tulle (tool) *n.* a fine fabric; silk or rayon net.

tum′ble (tum′bəl) *v.i.* **1,** lose footing or support; fall down. **2,** descend rapidly, as prices. **3,** roll about; toss; pitch. **4,** perform gymnastic exercises. **5,** (*Slang*) (often with *to*) become suddenly aware of something. **—***v.t.* **1,** cast down; upset. **2,** throw or move about; put in disorder. **3,** rotate in a box of abrasive material, for cleaning. **—***n.* **1,** an act of tumbling; a fall or turn. **2,** a state of confusion. **3,** (*Slang*) a sign of recognition.

tum′ble-down″ *adj.* dilapidated; ruinous; ready to fall.

tum′bler (tum′blər) *n.* **1,** a drinking glass. **2,** a gymnast; an acrobat. **3,** a lever, pin, etc., that holds the bolt of a lock. **4,** a cog or rotating part.

tum′ble·weed″ *n.* a U.S. weed that breaks off at the roots in the fall and blows around.

tum′brel (tum′brəl) *n.* a dump cart. Also, **tum′bril.**

tu·mes′cent (tū-mes′ənt) *adj.* swelling; forming into a tumor. **—tu·mes′cence,** *n.*

tu′mid (too′mid) *adj.* **1,** swollen; protuberant. **2,** pompous. **—tu·mid′i·ty,** *n.*

tum′my (tum′ė) *n.* (*Informal*) stomach; belly.

tu′mor (too′mər) *n.* an abnormal swelling in the body. Also, **tu′mour.**

tu′mult (too′mult) *n.* **1,** the commotion and uproar of a multitude. **2,** violent disturbance; high excitement. **—tu·mul′tu·ous,** *adj.*

tun *n.* a large cask.

tu′na (too′nə) *n.* a large, oceanic food and game fish.

tun′dra (tun′drə) *n.* a level, treeless plain of Arctic regions.

tune (toon) *n.* **1,** a succession of tones having musical coherence; an air or melody. **2,** adjustment to proper pitch or frequency. **3,** harmony; accord. **4,** good condition. **—***v.t. & i.* adjust to a proper pitch or frequency; bring or come into harmony. **—tune′ful,** *adj.* melodious. **—tune′less,** *adj.* **—tuning fork,** a pronged instrument that vibrates at an exact pitch.

tun′er *n.* **1,** one who or that which tunes. **2,** a radio receiver without amplifier or speakers.

tune-′up″ *n.* (*Informal*) an adjustment of an engine to return it to optimal functional efficiency.

tung′sten (tung′stən) *n.* a metallic chemical element, no. 74, symbol W.

tu′nic (too′nik) *n.* a short coat or shirt; a blouse.

tun′nel (tun′əl) *n.* **1,** an underground roadway or passage. **2,** the burrow of an animal. **—***v.t. & i.* penetrate by digging. **—tunnel vision,** a lack of peripheral vision.

tun′ny (tun′ė) *n.* a large food fish of the mackerel family.

tu′pe·lo (too′pə-lō) *n.* any of several No. Amer. trees; their wood.

tur′ban (tėr′bən) *n.* **1,** a headdress formed by winding a long scarf around the head. **2,** a brimless hat. ❑ *tulip*

tur′bid (tėr′bid) *adj.* **1,** clouded, opaque, or muddy, as a liquid. **2,** confused, muddled. **—tur·bid′i·ty,** *n.*

> **turbid, turgid**
> ☛ These two words sound related but are not. *Turbid* means clouded, confused. *Turgid* means tumid, swollen.

tur′bine (tėr′bin) *n.* a motor in which a vaned wheel is made to revolve by a flow of liquid or gas.

tur·bo- (tėr-bō) *pref.* turbine-driven.

tur′bo·fan″ *n.* a type of turbojet engine with added thrust.

tur′bo·jet″ *n.* a jet-propulsion engine supercharged by a turbine.

tur′bo·pro·pel″ler engine an engine combining the thrust of a turbine-powered propeller with the additional thrust of hot exhaust gases. Also, **tur′bo·prop″.**

tur′bot (tẽr′bət) *n.* a variety of flatfish.

tur′bo·train″ *n.* a train pulled by a gas-turbine locomotive.

tur′bu·lent (tẽr′byû-lənt) *adj.* disturbed; tumultuous; riotous. —**tur′bu·lence,** *n.*

tu·reen′ (tû-rēn′) *n.* a deep dish with a cover, for holding soup.

turf (tẽrf) *n.* **1,** the matted grass, roots, earth, mold, etc., covering grassland. **2,** a section of this cut out; a sod. **3,** a racetrack for horses; horse-racing. **4,** peat. **5,** (*Slang*) territory; neighborhood. —*v.t.* cover with turf. —**turf′y,** *adj.*

tur′gid (tẽr′jid) *adj.* tumid. ❏ *turbid*

tur′key (tẽr′kè) *n.* **1,** a large American fowl. **2,** (*Slang*) a failure, esp. a play; a flop. **3,** (*Slang*) an ineffective person; loser. —**turkey buzzard,** a vulture. —**turkey trot,** a ragtime dance.

> **turkey**
> ↔ The *turkey* is not from Turkey, nor was the name originally intended for this bird. The name was first applied to the African guinea-fowl and was later transferred to our turkey because of a supposed resemblance between the two birds.

Turk′ish (tẽr′kish) *adj.* pert. to Turkey, its people, language, etc. —**Turkish bath,** a steam bath. —**Turkish towel,** a thick towel with a long nap.

tur′mer·ic (tẽr′mər-ik) *n.* an E. Indian plant, used for making a condiment, a yellow dye, etc.

tur′moil (tẽr′moil) *n.* commotion; tumult; agitation.

turn (tẽrn) *v.t.* **1,** move to or from a position; shift or twist. **2,** move to a new direction, course, or purpose. **3,** reverse; fold back. **4,** revolve or rotate; shape or perform by rotating. **5,** alter or change in a specified way. **6,** make sour or fermented. **7,** meditate on. **8,** go around; pass beyond. —*v.i.* **1,** rotate or revolve. **2,** assume a new direction, course, position, etc. **3,** change; become different. **4,** (with *on*) attack. **5,** become sour; ferment. **6,** be or become curved; bend. —*n.* **1,** movement about a center; a rotation or revolution; a twist. **2,** a change of direction, course, or position. **3,** a bend, curve, angle, fold, etc. **4,** one's occasion to act; a spell of work, duty, etc. **5,** a change in appearance, condition, or

character. **6,** trend; tendency; bent. **7,** (*Informal*) a nervous shock. —**to a turn,** perfectly. —**turn in,** go to bed. —**turn off, 1,** extinguish, shut off, etc. **2,** turn away (from); esp., exit (from), as a road. **3,** (*Slang*) lose or cause to lose interest, enthusiasm, etc. —**turn on,** (*Slang*) **1,** use or cause to use a hallucinogenic drug. **2,** experience or cause to experience without drugs the sense stimulation usu. associated with their use. **3,** make or become elated, excited, etc.

turn′a·bout″ *n.* **1,** a turning to the opposite direction. **2,** alternation of privileges.

turn′coat″ *n.* a renegade.

turn′er *n.* **1,** a woodworker. **2,** a gymnast.

turn′ing *n.* **1,** act or result of turning. **2,** place of turning; a bend; curve. —**turning point, 1,** a critical point. **2,** a change for the better.

tur′nip (tẽr′nip) *n.* a plant whose root and leaves are used as vegetables.

turn′key″ *n.* a jailer. —*adj.* ready to use, occupy, etc.

turn′off″ *n.* **1,** a branch of a road; an exit, esp. from a main thoroughfare. **2,** (*Slang*) something that causes one to lose interest, enthusiasm, etc.

turn′out″ *n.* **1,** those who attend a meeting, etc. **2,** output. **3,** costume; outfit.

turn′o″ver *n.* **1,** rate or volume of business. **2,** rate of change in personnel employed. **3,** a small semicircular pie.

turn′pike″ *n.* a toll highway.

turn′stile″ *n.* a device of revolving arms to bar passage or count those passing through.

turn′ta″ble *n.* **1,** a revolving platform to change the direction of a locomotive. **2,** the rotating disk of a record player; the record player itself.

tur′pen·tine″ (tẽr′pən-tīn″) *n.* an oily substance extracted from several trees, used in making paint.

tur′pi·tude″ (tẽr′pi-tood″) *n.* wickedness; depravity. —**tur″pi·tud′i·nous,** *adj.*

tur′quoise (tẽr′kwoiz) *n.* an opaque semiprecious stone; its blue-green color.

tur′ret (tẽr′it) *n.* **1,** a small tower rising from a larger building. **2,** an attachment on a lathe for holding and applying several tools. **3,** a gun tower on a fort or battleship.

tur′tle (tẽr′təl) *n.* any of an order of reptiles having two surfaces of strong shell, from between which the head and limbs protrude. —**turn turtle,** capsize; upset.

tur′tle·dove″ (-duv″) *n.* a variety of dove.

> **turtledove**
> ↔ The *turtledove* is not related to the *turtle*, either biologically or etymologically (though *turtle* once also meant *turtledove*). The first part of its name comes from Latin *turtur*, a word of imitative origin based on the bird's cooing.

tur′tle·neck″ *n.* a shirt or sweater with a high, tight-fitting collar.

tush *interj.* of disapproval. —*n.* (*Slang*) buttocks.

tusk *n.* **1,** a long pointed tooth. **2,** a toothlike part, as a prong. —**tusk′er,** *n.* a tusked animal.

tus′sle (tus′əl) *n.* scuffle.

tus′sock (tus′ək) *n.* a clump or tuft of growing grass.

tut *interj.* of mild reproach.

tu′te·lage (too′tə-lij) *n.* guardianship; instruction. —**tu′te·lar·y,** *adj.*

tu′tor (too′tər) *n.* a teacher, esp. one engaged for private instruction. —*v.t. & i.* **1,** instruct, esp. privately. **2,** study under a tutor. —**tu′tor·age,** *n.* —**tu·tor′i·al** (-tôr′ē-əl) *adj.*

tut′ti-frut′ti (too′tē-froo′tē) *n.* a preserve of mixed fruits.

tu′tu (too′too) *n.* a short ballet skirt of several layers.

tu·whit′ tu·whoo′ (tû-hwit′tû-hwoo′) the cry of the owl.

tux (tuks) *n.* (*Informal*) tuxedo.

tux·e′do (tuk-sē′dō) *n.* **1,** a man's tailless evening coat; dinner jacket. **2,** a dinner jacket and accompanying pants.

> **tuxedo**
> ↔ From the *Tuxedo* Park Country Club near Tuxedo Lake in New York State where the jacket was apparently first worn in the U.S. The word is of Native American origin.

TV (tee′vee′) *n.* (*Informal*) television. —**TV dinner,** (*Informal*) a precooked, packaged dinner which requires only to be heated for use.

twad′dle (twod′əl) *v.i. & t.* talk in a trivial and tedious manner. —*n.* idle, senseless talk or writing.

twain (twān) *n.* (*Archaic*) two.

twang *n.* **1,** the sharp sound of a tense string when plucked. **2,** a nasal tone of voice. —*v.i. & t.* make such a sound.

tweak (twēk) *v.t.* **1,** pinch and pull or

twist. **2,** make a small modification, as to a mechanism. —*n.* a jerk or twist.

tweed (twēd) *n.* a coarse wool cloth; (*pl.*) garments of this fabric.

tweet (twēt) *n. & v.* chirp.

tweet′er (twē′tər) *n.* a loudspeaker responsive only to the higher frequencies and used only for reproducing high-pitched sounds.

tweez′ers (twē′zərz) *n.pl.* a small two-pronged gripping tool. —**tweeze,** *v.t.*

Twelfth Night the evening preceding the twelfth day after Christmas.

twelve (twelv) *n.* the cardinal number between eleven and thirteen, expressed by 12. —**twelfth,** *adj. & n.*

twelve′month″ *n.* a year.

twen′ty (twen′tē) *n.* a cardinal number between nineteen and twenty-one, expressed by 20. —**twen′ti·eth,** *adj. & n.*

twen″ty-one′ *n.* **1,** twenty plus one. **2,** a card game, blackjack.

twerp (twĕrp) *n.* (*Informal*) an insignificant, ineffective person.

twice (twīs) *adv.* **1,** two times. **2,** doubly.

twice-′told″ *adj.* hackneyed.

twid′dle (twid′əl) *v.t.* twirl, esp. with the fingers. —*v.i.* play idly.

twig *n.* a small shoot of a tree or other plant.

twi′light″ (twī′līt″) *n.* **1,** light from the sky when the sun is below the horizon. **2,** early evening. —**twilight sleep,** a state of semiconsciousness, usu. given by scopolamine, produced to reduce pain, esp. of childbirth. —**twilight zone,** (*Informal*) an indefinite boundary between two areas, conditions, etc.

twill (twil) *n.* a fabric woven so as to show parallel diagonal lines.

twin *n.* **1,** one of two offspring brought forth at a birth. **2,** one of two persons or things closely alike. —*adj.* **1,** being one of twins. **2,** occurring in pairs.

twine (twīn) *n.* **1,** a strong cord or string. **2,** something twisted. —*v.t. & i.* **1,** twist together; interweave. **2,** meander.

twinge (twinj) *n.* a sudden sharp pain.

twi′night″ (twī′-) *adj.* (*Baseball*) of a game beginning during twilight and continuing into the evening. Also, **twi′nite″.**

twin′kle (twing′kəl) *v.i.* **1,** shine with quick, irregular gleams. **2,** (of the eyes) sparkle with amusement or kindliness. —*n.* a gleam; gleams of light.

twin′kling *n.* **1,** intermittent shining. **2,** an instant.

twirl (twĕrl) *v.t.* cause to revolve rapidly;

spin; whirl. —*v.i.* **1,** rotate; be whirled about. **2,** wind; coil. —*n.* **1,** a rapid spin; a gyration. **2,** a curl or convolution. —**twirl′er,** *n.* (*Baseball*) a pitcher.

twist *v.t.* **1,** wrap (something flexible) around and around; combine by winding. **2,** wring out of shape; distort; warp. **3,** cause to rotate; turn. **4,** form by bending, curving, etc. **5,** pervert in meaning; misinterpret; misapply. —*v.i.* **1,** be bent or coiled; wind; twine. **2,** rotate or revolve; move in a spiral course. **3,** change direction. **4,** be or become distorted in shape. —*n.* **1,** a bend, curve, knot, etc. **2,** a tangle, kink, crook, etc. **3,** a twisting motion or course. **4,** spin imparted to a ball. **5,** something formed by twisting. **6,** a dance in which one contorts the torso. —**twist′er,** *n.* a tornado.

twit *v.t.* taunt; reproach. —*n.* a gibe or reproach.

twitch (twich) *v.t.* **1,** pull or move with a quick jerk. **2,** pinch; squeeze. —*v.i.* jerk suddenly, as from muscular spasm. —*n.* **1,** a sudden muscular contraction; a twinge. **2,** a slight, sudden movement. **3,** a tug or jerk.

twit′ter (twit′ər) *v.i.* **1,** chirp rapidly or excitedly. **2,** giggle.

two (too) *n.* the cardinal number, one plus one, expressed by 2 (ordinal, *second*).

two-′bit″ *adj.* (*Slang*) cheap; worthless. —**two bits,** twenty-five cents.

two-′by-four″ *n.* a timber approx. two inches thick and four inches wide.

two-′edged″ *adj.* **1,** having two sharp edges. **2,** doubly effective.

two-′faced″ *adj.* deceitful; hypocritical.

two′fer (too′fər) *n.* (*Slang*) two tickets for the price of one.

two-′fist″ed *adj.* vigorous, as in a fight.

two′fold″ *adj.* times two; double.

two′pence (tup′əns) *n.* (*Brit., obs.*) two pennies. —**two′pen″ny** (tup′nė) *adj.*

two′some *n.* two persons; a duo.

two-′step″ *n.* a dance.

two-′time″ *v.t.* (*Informal*) deceive; esp., be unfaithful to.

two-′way″ *adj.* operating, or permitting operation, in either of two directions.

-ty (tė) *suf.* **1,** of numerals, times ten, as *sixty*. **2,** quality, state, etc.

ty·coon′ (tī-koon′) *n.* (*Informal*) a wealthy and powerful business leader.

tyke (tīk) *n.* **1,** a dog. **2,** a child.

tym′pa·ni (tim′pə-nė) *n.pl.* [*sing.* **-no** (-nō)] orchestral kettledrums. —**tym′pa-nist,** *n.* Also, **tim′pa·ni.**

tym′pa·num (tim′pə-nəm) *n.* **1,** a stretched membrane; a drum or tambourine. **2,** the eardrum or middle ear. **3,** a vibrating device, as the diaphragm of a telephone. —**tym·pan′ic,** *adj.*

type (tīp) *n.* **1,** a kind or class. **2,** a typical person or thing. **3,** a model or pattern. **4,** a rectangular block bearing a letter or character in relief, used in printing; such printing blocks collectively. **5,** a printed character. —*v.t. & i.* **1,** ascertain the type of. **2,** symbolize. **3,** typewrite. —**Type A,** (*Psychol.*) pert. to a tense, competitive behavioral pattern. —**Type B,** (*Psychol.*) pert. to a relaxed, noncompetitive behavioral pattern.

type′cast″ *v.t.* **1,** cast (an actor, etc.) in a role especially appropriate for him. **2,** cast repeatedly in the same type of role.

type′face″ *n.* a particular style of printing type.

type′script″ *n.* typewritten copy.

type′set″ter *n.* compositor.

type′writ″er (tīp′rī″tər) *n.* a machine for writing letters and characters like those produced by printing type. —**type′write″,** *v.t. & i.* —**type′writ″ing,** *n.*

ty′phoid fever (tī′foid) *n.* an infectious bacillic disease marked by inflammation and ulceration of the intestines.

---

typhoid fever, typhus

☛ While the words naming these two diseases have in fact the same derivation (from Greek *typhos*, vapor), the diseases are not the same. *Typhoid fever* is an infectious disease transmitted through food; *typhus* is transmitted by lice.

---

ty·phoon′ (tī-foon′) *n.* a cyclone of the W. Pacific Ocean.

ty′phus (tī′fəs) *n.* an acute infectious disease carried by lice. ❏ *typhoid fever*

typ′i·cal (tip′i-kəl) *adj.* **1,** pert. to a type. **2,** conforming to a type; being a representative specimen.

typ′i·fy″ (tip′i-fī″) *v.t.* **1,** exemplify. **2,** represent by a type of symbol.

typ′ist (tīp′ist) *n.* one who operates a typewriter.

ty′po (tī′pō) *n.* (*Informal*) a typographical error.

ty·pog′ra·phy (tī-pog′rə-fė) *n.* **1,** the art or work of setting type. **2,** the style of printed matter. —**ty·pog′ra·pher,** *n.* —**ty″-po·graph′i·cal,** *adj.* —**typographical error,** an error made in the setting of type or in typing [also, *informal,* **ty′po** (tī′pō)].

tyr′an·nize″ (tir′ə-nīz″) *v.i. & t.* dominate tyrannically. .

tyr·an′no·saur″ (tir-an′ə-sôr″) *n.* a great carnivorous dinosaur.

tyr′an·ny (tir′ə-nē) *n.* unrestrained exercise of power; unmerciful rule. —**ty·ran′ni·cal** (tī-ran′i-kəl), **tyr′an·nous** (tir′ə-nəs) *adj.*

ty′rant (tī′rənt) *n.* a despot; an absolute ruler. .

ty′ro (tī′ro) *n.* a beginner in learning something; a novice.

tzar (tsär) *n.* czar. —**tzar·ev′na,** *n.* czarevna. —**tzar′e·vitch,** *n.* czarevitch. —**tza·ri′na** *n.* czarina.

tzet′ze (tset′sē) *n.* tsetse.

U

U, u (ū) the 21st letter of the English alphabet.

u·biq′ui·tous (ū-bik′wə-təs) *adj.* existing everywhere; inescapable. —**u·biq′ui·tous·ness,** *n.* —**u·biq′ui·ty,** *n.*

U-′boat″ (ū′bōt″) *n.* a submarine, esp. German.

> ### U-boat
> ↔ An abbreviation of German *Unterseeboot,* underwater boat.

ud′der (ud′ər) *n.* the baggy mammary gland of a cow.

ugh (u; ug; ukh) *interj.* expressing aversion, disgust, or horror.

ug′ly (ug′lē) *adj.* **1,** unpleasing or repulsive in appearance. **2,** disagreeable; inclement; threatening. —**ug′li·ness,** *n.* —**ugly duckling,** an unpromising child who becomes handsome or beautiful as an adult.

u′kase (ū′kās) *n.* an edict; decree.

U·krain′i·an (ū-krā′nē-ən) *n. & adj.* of or pert. to the Ukraine, a large region and republic in the former Soviet Union, its people, language, etc.

u″ku·le′le (ū″kə-lā′lē) *n.* a Hawaiian four-stringed musical instrument resembling a small guitar.

> ### ukulele
> .↔ From Hawaiian, leaping flea.

ul′cer (ul′sər) *n.* **1,** an infected sore. **2,** a moral blemish. —**ul′cer·ous,** *adj.*

ul′cer·ate″ (-āt″) *v.t. & i.* (cause to) become ulcerous. —**ul″cer·a′tion,** *n.*

ul′na (ul′nə) *n.* [*pl.* **-nae** (-nē)] the large bone of the forearm. —**ul′nar,** *adj.*

ul′ster (ul′stər) *n.* an overcoat, named for the province in Ireland.

ul·te′ri·or (ul-tir′ē-ər) *adj.* **1,** kept concealed. **2,** in the future. .

ul′ti·mate (ul′tə-mət) *adj.* **1,** being the last, as of a series; most remote. **2,** eventual; final; decisive. —*n.* the final stage or degree. .

ul″ti·ma′tum (ul″tə-mā′təm) *n.* a final statement of conditions.

ul′ti·mo (ul′tə-mō) (*Lat.*) *adv.* in the month which preceded the present.

ul′tra (ul′trə) *adj.* beyond the ordinary; extreme; superlative; excessive.

ul·tra- *pref.* beyond; excessive; superlative. [In the following compounds, the prefix adds merely the sense of "overmuch" to the adjective.] **ul″tra·con·serv′a·tive,** *adj.* —**ul″tra·fash′ion·a·ble,** *adj.* —**ul″tra·mod′ern,** *adj.* —**ul″tra·re·li′gious,** *adj.*

ul′tra·fiche″ (-fēsh″) *n.* a very small size of microfiche.

ul′tra·high″ frequency designating frequencies from 300 to 3,000 megacycles. Also, **UHF.**

ul″tra·ma·rine″ *n.* a deep blue color.

ul″tra·mon′tane (-mon′tān) *adj.* **1,** south of the Alps; in Italy. **2,** recognizing the Pope as head of all Christianity.

ul′tra·son′ic *adj.* supersonic.

ul′tra·sound″ *n.* ultrasonic sound, esp. when used for cleaning, diagnosis, etc.

ul″tra·vi′o·let *adj.* pert. to invisible rays lying beyond violet in the spectrum.

ul′u·late″ (ūl′yə-lāt″) *v.i.* howl like a wolf; wail. —**ul″u·la′tion,** *n.*

um′ber (um′bər) *n.* a reddish-brown pigment.

um·bil′i·cal (um-bil′i-kəl) *adj.* pert. to the umbilicus. —**umbilical cord,** the tube through which a mother nourishes a fetus.

um·bil′i·cus (um-bil′i-kəs) *n.* [*pl.* **-i·ci** (-sī)] the depression in the middle of the abdomen.

um′bra (um′brə) *n.* [*pl.* **-brae** (-brē)] shadow; a dark spot.

um′brage (um′brij) *n.* **1,** resentment. **2,** foliage. —**um·bra′geous** (-brā′jəs) *adj.*

um·brel′la (um-brel′ə) *n.* **1,** a portable screen from rain or the sun. **2,** aerial protection given by fighter planes to troops or ships below. **3,** a name, organization, etc. which includes a variety of small entities, often unrelated, under its control.

u′mi·ak (oo′mē-ak) *n.* an open boat used by Eskimos.

um′laut (ûm′lowt) *n.* (*Ger.*) modification

of a vowel sound, or the diacritical mark (¨) as in ä, ö, ü, in transliteration indicated by *e* following the vowel.

um·pire (um'pīr) *n.* an arbiter; referee. Also, *Informal,* **ump.**

ump'teen (ump'tēn) *adj.* (*Informal*) a fairly large, but indefinite, number.

un- *pref.* not; signifying the converse, reversal, or absence of some quality, action, or condition.

un″a·bridged' (un″ə-brijd') *adj.* **1,** not shortened; not restricted. **2,** (of a dictionary) not a condensation or shorter version of a larger dictionary; omitting no applicable material.

un·ad·vised' (un-əd-vīzd') *adj.* ill-advised.

un-″A·mer'i·can *adj.* **1,** not befitting a loyal U.S. citizen. **2,** not consistent with American beliefs, customs, etc.

u·nan'i·mous (ū-nan'ə-məs) *adj.* being of one mind; all agreeing, without exception. **—u″na·nim'i·ty** (ū″nə-nim'ə-tē) *n.*

un·as·sum'ing *adj.* modest; retiring.

un·at·tached' *adj.* **1,** free; loose. **2,** (*Mil.*) not assigned to any unit or duty. **3,** not betrothed, romantically committed, escorted, etc.

un″a·ware' *adj.* not conscious (of something); not knowing or realizing. **—un″-a·wares',** *adv.*

un·bal'anced *adj.* mentally deranged.

un″be·known' (un″bė-nōn') *adj.* (*Informal*) unknown. Also, **un″be·knownst'** (-nōnst').

un″be·lief' *n.* lack of belief, esp. in religious dogma. **—un″be·liev'er,** *n.*

un·bend' *v.t.* [**-bent', -bend'ing**] **1,** release from strain or tension. **2,** straighten; untie. **—v.i. 1,** relax; become less formal, etc. **2,** become unbent. **—un·bend'ing,** *adj.*

un·blessed' *adj.* **1,** denied a blessing. **2,** wretched; unhappy. Also, **un·blest'.**

un·blush'ing *adj.* shameless.

un·bos'om (un-bûz'əm) *v.t. & i.* disclose (thoughts, feelings).

un·bound'ed *adj.* without boundaries or limits; vast.

un·break'a·ble *adj.* **1,** incapable of being broken. **2,** resistant to breaking.

un·bri'dled (un-brī'dəld) *adj.* unrestrained; uncontrolled.

un·called-'for″ (un-kâld'-fôr″) *adj.* **1,** unwarranted; impertinent; improper. **2,** not claimed, as merchandise.

un·can'ny *adj.* eerie; weird; mysterious. **—un·can'ni·ness,** *n.*

un·cap' *v.t.* [**-capped', -cap'ping**] remove the cap or cover from.

un·cer'tain *adj.* **1,** not certain; doubtful. **2,** unsteady or hesitant; not firm. **—un·cer'tain·ty,** *n.*

un·chal'lenged (un-chal'ənjd) *adj.* unquestioned; acknowledged; agreed.

un'ci·al (un'shė-əl) *adj.* designating a style of majuscule writing used from the 4th to 10th c. **—n.** an uncial letter or manuscript.

[In the following words, formed of words defined elsewhere in the dictionary, the prefixed *un-* forms an antonym of the root word.]

un″a·bashed'
un″a·bat'ed
un·a'ble
un·ac'cent·ed
un″ac·cept'a·ble
un″ac·com'pa·nied
un″ac·count'a·ble
un″ac·cus'tomed
un″ac·quaint'ed
un″a·dorned'
un″a·dul'ter·at″ed
un″af·fect'ed
un″a·fraid'
un'aid'ed
un″al'ien·a·ble
un″al·loyed'
un″al'ter·a·ble
un″am·big'u·ous
un″am·bi'tious
un″an·nounced'
un″an'swer·a·ble
un″an·tic'i·pat·ed

un″ap'pe·tiz″ing
un″ap·pre'ci·a″tive
un″ap·proach'a·ble
un·apt'
un·arm'
un″a·shamed'
un·asked'
un″as·sail'a·ble
un″as·sist'ed
un″at·tain'a·ble
un″at·trac'tive
un″at·tend'ed
un·au·thor'ized
un″a·vail'a·ble
un″a·vail'ing
un″a·void'a·ble
un·bal'ance
un·bar'
un·bear'a·ble
un·beat'en
un″be·com'ing
un″be·liev'a·ble

un″be·liev'ing
un·bi'ased
un·bid'den
un·bind'
un·bleached'
un·blink'ing
un·bolt'
un·born'
un·bound'
un·bowed'
un·brace'
un·braid'
un·bro'ken
un·buck'le
un·bur'den
un·busi'ness·like″
un·but'ton
un·caused'
un·ceas'ing
un″cer·e·mo'ni·ous
un·chain'
un·change'a·ble

---

fat, fāte, fär, fāre, fâll, ask; met, hē, hėr, maybė; pin, pīne; not, nōte, ôr, tool

un'cle (ung'kəl) *n.* **1,** a brother of one's father or mother. **2,** the husband of one's aunt. **3,** any elderly man, regarded familiarly. **4,** (*Slang*) a pawnbroker. —**Uncle Sam,** the U.S., its government or people. —**Uncle Tom,** a black having a submissive attitude toward whites.

un·com'mon *adj.* not common or usual; out of the ordinary; exceptional. —**un·com'mon·ness,** *n.*

un"con·cern' *n.* lack of anxiety; indifference. —**un"con·cerned',** *adj.*

un·con'scion·a·ble *adj.* **1,** not in accord with conscience; unscrupulous. **2,** unduly excessive.

un·con'scious *adj.* **1,** not aware (of something). **2,** having lost consciousness; being in a stupor, faint, etc. **3,** not endowed with awareness of one's own existence. **4,** pert. to mental processes not consciously perceived. —**un·con'scious·ness,** *n.*

un·couth' *adj.* **1,** ill-mannered; clumsy. **2,** strange; unusual. —**un·couth'ness,** *n.*

un·cov'er *v.t.* remove a cover from; lay bare; reveal. —*v.i.* take off one's hat.

unc'tion (unk'shən) *n.* **1,** the act of anointing with oil. **2,** anything soothing; a divine or spiritual influence. —**extreme unction,** a sacrament administered to one in imminent danger of death.

unc'tu·ous (unk'choo-əs) *adj.* oily; suave. —**unc'tu·ous·ness,** *n.*

un·cut' *adj.* **1,** (of a stone) not cut or polished. **2,** unabridged; complete.

un"de·ceive' *v.t.* free from a mistaken idea or belief.

un'der (un'dər) *prep.* **1,** beneath and covered by; below the surface of. **2,** in a lower place or position. **3,** receiving; bearing; undergoing. **4,** less than. **5,** inferior to. **6,** subject to. **7,** in accordance with. **8,** in. **9,** during the existence of. —*adv.* lower. —*adj.* **1,** beneath. **2,** lower; subordinate. —**under secretary,** a deputy to a secretary in a U.S. government department, ranking next under the head. —**under way** *or* **weigh,** (*Naut.*) no longer in port, station, etc. ❏ *below*

---

under way, under weigh

☛ The first form, with *way*, is the original form, but both versions are acceptable. The second, formed with a strictly nautical term, should probably be reserved for use in nautical situations.

---

un·der- *pref.* **1,** below; lower in place or rank. **2,** lesser in degree, esp. less than a proper or usual degree.
[In the following words, the prefix *under-* implies sense 1.]

un'der·arm'	un"der·cov'er
un'der·bel"ly	un'der·cur'rent
un'der·bod"ice	un'der·gar"ment
un'der·car"riage	un'der·grad'u·ate
un'der·class'man	un'der·growth"
un"der·clothes"	un'der·hung'

---

un·changed'	un"com·plain'ing	un·daunt'ed
un·chang'ing	un"com·pli·men'ta·ry	un"de·cid'ed
un·char'i·ta·ble	un·com'pro·mis"ing	un"de·feat'ed
un·chart'ed	un"con·di'tion·al	un"de·fend'ed
un·chaste'	un"con·di'tioned	un"de·filed'
un·checked'	un"con·form'i·ty	un"de·fined'
un·Chris'tian	un"con·nect'ed	un"dem·o·crat'ic
un·cir'cum·cised	un"con'quer·a·ble	un"de·mon'stra·tive
un·civ'il	un"con·sti·tu'tion·al	un"de·ni'a·ble
un·civ'i·lized"	un"con·trol'la·ble	un"de·nom"i·na'tion·al
un·clad'	un"con·ven'tion·al	un"de·served'
un·claimed'	un·cooked'	un"de·sign'ing
un·clasp'	un·cork'	un"de·sir'a·ble
un·clean'	un"cor·rupt'ed	un"de·vel'oped
un·clench'	un·count'ed	un"dig'ni·fied"
un·cloak'	un·cou'ple	un"di·min'ished
un·clog'	un·cov'er	un"dip·lo·mat'ic
un·close'	un·crit'i·cal	un"di·rect'ed
un·clothe'	un·crossed'	un"dis·cov'ered
un·cloud'ed	un·crowned'	un"dis·mayed'
un·coil'	un·cul'ti·vat"ed	un"dis·patched'
un·com'fort·a·ble	un·cul'tured	un"dis·put'ed
un"com·mit'ted	un·cured'	un"dis·tin'guished
un"com·mu'ni·ca"tive	un·curl'	un"dis·turbed'
un"com·par'a·ble	un·dam'aged	un"di·vid'ed

---

un″der·laid′
un″der·prop′
un′der·sea″
un′der·shirt″
un′der·shorts″
un′der·side″
un′der·sign′
un′der·skirt″
un′der·slung″
un′der·soil″
un′der·waist″
un′der·wa′ter

[In the following words, the prefix *under*- implies sense 2.]

un″der·act′
un″der·armed′
un″der·bid′
un″der·bred′
un″der·charge′
un″der·de·vel′op
un′der·do′
un″der·ex·pose′
un″der·feed′
un″der·nour′ish
un″der·pay′
un″der·play′
un″der·priv′i·leged
un″der·sized′
un″der·staffed′
un″der·stock′
un″der·trump′
un″der·val′ue
un″der·weight″

un″der·a·chieve′ *v.i.* not produce results (as in school) commensurate with one's assumed potential. —**un″der·a·chiev′er,** *n.*

un″der·age′ *adj.* of less than legal or suitable age.

un′der·boss″ *n.* (*Slang*) the second in command in a Mafia family.

un′der·brush″ *n.* shrubs, etc., growing under trees.

un′der·class″ *n.* the lowest social stratum, characterized by poverty and social instability.

un′der·clothes″ *n.pl.* **1,** underwear. **2,** any clothes worn under outer clothes.

un′der·coat″ *n.* **1,** a protective coating to the underside of a vehicle. **2,** a preparatory coating, as of paint.

un″der·cut′ *v.t.* **1,** cut so as to leave an overhanging edge. **2,** undersell. **3,** strike (a ball) on the underside.

un′der·dog″ *n.* one who gets the worst of it, or is at a disadvantage, in a struggle.

un′der·drawers″ *n.pl.* drawers.

un″der·es′ti·mate″ (-es′ti-māt″) *v.t.* estimate at too low a value, amount, rate, etc. —*n.* (-mət) too low an estimate. —**un″der·es″ti·ma′tion,** *n.*

un″der·fed′ *adj.* very thin, from malnutrition.

un″der·foot′ *adj. & adv.* **1,** under the foot; lying on the ground. **2,** in the way.

un″der·go′ *v.t.* [**-went′, -gone′, -go′ing**] be subjected to; experience; sustain.

un″der·ground″ *adj.* **1,** sunken, buried. **2,** done or acting in secrecy. **3,** pert. to anything (as movies, publications, etc.) that is experimental, radical, unconventional, etc. —*n.* **1,** (*Brit.*) subway. **2,** a secret organization opposing government or occupation forces. —**underground railway,** (*Hist.*) a system for helping escaped slaves to reach safety, esp. in Canada.

un′der·hand″ *adj. & adv.* **1,** secret and mean; sly; deceitful. **2,** with the hand below the shoulder or under the object.

un′der·hand″ed *adj.* underhand.

un″der·lie′ *v.t.* [**-lay′, -ly′ing**] **1,** be situated under. **2,** be the basis or foundation of.

un′der·line″ *v.t. & n.* underscore.

un′der·ling (-ling) *n.* one in a subordi-

[In the following words, formed of words defined elsewhere in the dictionary, the prefixed *un*- forms an antonym of the root word.]

un·dou′ble
un·drape′
un·dress′
un·dy′ing
un·earned′
un·eat′a·ble
un·ed′u·cat″ed
un″em·bar′rassed
un″e·mo′tion·al
un″en·dur′a·ble
un″en·force′a·ble
un″en·light′ened
un·en′vied
un·e′qual
un·e′qualed
un″e·quiv′o·cal
un·err′ing
un″es·sen′tial
un·eth′i·cal
un·e′ven
un″e·vent′ful
un″ex·cep′tion·a·ble
un″ex·cep′tion·al
un″ex·pect′ed
un″ex·pired′
un″ex·plained′
un″ex·plored′
un″ex·pressed′
un″ex·pres′sive
un·ex′pur·gat″ed
un·fail′ing
un·fair′
un·faith′ful
un·fal′ter·ing
un″fa·mil′iar
un·fash′ion·a·ble
un·fas′ten
un·fath′om·a·ble
un·fa′vor·a·ble
un·feigned′
un·fenced′
un·fet′ter
un·fet′tered
un·fil′ial
un·fin′ished
un·fit′
un·flinch′ing
un″fore·seen′
un″for·get′ta·ble
un″for·giv′a·ble
un″for·got′ten
un·formed′
un″fre·quen′ted
un·friend′ly
un·fruit′ful
un″ful·filled′
un·gen′er·ous
un·gird′
un·gov′ern·a·ble
un·grace′ful
un·gra′cious
un·grate′ful
un·grudg′ing
un·guard′ed
un·hal′lowed
un·ham′pered

fat, fāte, fär, fâre, fâll, ȧsk; met, hē, hêr, maybē; pin, pīne; not, nōte, ôr, tool nate or inferior position (usually in disparagement).

un″der·mine′ *v.t.* **1,** dig a hole or passage under. **2,** weaken or injure by secret or underhand means.

un′der·most″ *adj.* lowest.

un″der·neath′ (-nēth′) *prep. & adv.* beneath; under; below. ❏ *below*

un′der·pants″ *n.pl.* drawers.

un′der·pass″ *n.* a passage or road under a railroad, road, etc.

un″der·pin′ *v.t.* [-pinned′, -pin′ning] support; stay. —**un′der·pin″ning,** *n.*

un″der·rate′ *v.t.* rate too low; underestimate.

un′der·score′ *v.t.* print or draw a line under; emphasize. —*n.* such a line.

un″der·sell′ *v.t.* [-sold′, -sell′ing] **1,** sell for a lower price than. **2,** understate the virtues of.

un′der·shot″ *adj.* **1,** driven by water underneath. **2,** (of the lower jaw) protruding.

un″der·stand′ *v.t. & i.* **1,** grasp the meaning (of); comprehend. **2,** have full knowledge (of). **3,** be told (of); realize; believe. **4,** sympathize (with).

un″der·stand′ing *n.* **1,** intelligence; mental apprehension and appreciation. **2,** good relations. **3,** a private or unexpressed agreement. **4,** sympathy. —*adj.* intelligent; sympathetic.

un″der·state′ *v.t.* state with less than due emphasis; represent in lesser degree than the reality. —**un″der·state′ment,** *n.*

un′der·steer″ *n.* the tendency of an automobile to turn less than normal as the wheel is turned.

un′der·stood′ (un″dər-stûd′) *adj.* **1,** inferred. **2,** agreed.

un′der·stud″y *n.* one trained to substitute for an actor or actress. —*v.t.* act as an understudy to.

un″der·take′ *v.t.* **1,** try to do; attempt. **2,** engage to perform or execute. —**un′-der·tak″er,** *n.* a funeral director.

un″der·tak′ing *n.* **1,** a project, esp. a business venture. **2,** the business of preparing the dead for burial and arranging funerals.

un″der-the-coun′ter *adj.* illegal; illicit; unlawful.

un′der·things″ *n.pl.* underclothes.

un′der·tone″ *n.* **1,** a tone of less than normal loudness in speaking. **2,** a tone, hue, etc., lying under another.

un′der·tow″ *n.* a strong current below the surface of water, as the backflow from a beach.

un′der·way′ *adj.* **1,** (*Naut.*) under way. **2,** moving; in motion.

un′der·wear″ *n.* garments worn beneath the outer clothing; underclothes.

un″der·whelm′ *v.t.* (*Informal*) fail to impress.

un′der·world″ *n.* **1,** the community of criminal or degraded persons. **2,** Hades or hell.

un″der·write′ *v.t.* **1,** subscribe to; en-

un·harmed′	un″in·spired′	un·love′ly
un·harm′ful	un″in·tel′li·gent	un·luck′y
un·har′ness	un″in·tel′li·gi·ble	un·make′
un·hatched′	un″in·ten′tion·al	un·man′age·a·ble
un·health′ful	un·in·ter·est·ed	un·manned′
un·heard′	un·in·ter·est·ing	un·man′ner·ly
un·heed′ed	un″in·ter·rupt′ed	un·marked′
un·hes′i·tat″ing	un″in·vit′ed	un·mar′ried
un·hitch′	un·is′sued	un·mask′
un·hook′	un·just′	un·matched′
un·hur′ried	un·kind′	un·meas′ured
un·hurt′	un·knot′	un·mer′ci·ful
un″i·den′ti·fied	un·lace′	un·mer′it·ed
un″im·ag′i·na·ble	un″la·ment′ed	un·mind′ful
un″im·ag′i·na″tive	un·lash′	un″mis·tak′a·ble
un″im·paired′	un·latch′	un·mit′i·gat·ed
un″im·peach′a·ble	un·leash′	un·mixed′
un″im·proved′	un·li′censed	un″mo·lest′ed
un″in·flect′ed	un·lim′ber	un·moved′
un″in·formed′	un·lim′it·ed	un·mov′ing
un″in·hab′it·a·ble	un·link′	un·mus′i·cal
un″in·hab′it·ed	un·list′ed	un·muz′zle
un″in·hib′it·ed	un·lit′	un·named′
un″in·i′ti·at″ed	un·load′	un·nat′u·ral
un·in′jured	un·lock′	un·nec′es·sar″y

dorse; guarantee; indemnify. **2,** insure
against loss.

un'der·writ"er *n.* **1,** one in the insurance
business. **2,** one who subscribes to bonds,
etc., for resale.

un·dis'ci·plined (un-dis'ə-plind) *adj.* unruly; not controllable.

un"dis·guised' (un"dis-gīzd') *adj.* lacking
disguise or pretense; candid; open.

un·do' *v.t.* **[-done' -do'ing] 1,** annul; reverse (the effect of). **2,** spoil; ruin. **3,** unfasten. **—un·do'ing,** *n.* ruin; destruction.

un·doubt'ed (un-dow'tid) *adj.* not questioned: obviously true. **—un·doubt'ed·ly,**
adv. surely.

un·due' *adj.* **1,** unwarranted; disproportionate; excessive. **2,** not yet payable.

un'du·lant (un'dyə-lənt) *adj.* waving; wavy.
—undulant fever, a recurrent disease usually contracted from bacteria in raw milk.

un'du·late" (un'dyə-lāt") *v.i. & t.* move
or be formed in waves; rise and fall. *—adj.*
(-lət) wavy. **—un"du·la'tion,** *n.*

un·du'ly *adv.* **1,** without warrant or right.
2, excessively.

un·earth' *v.t.* **1,** discover; bring to light.
2, dig up; disinter.

un·earth'ly *adj.* **1,** supernatural; weird. **2,**
(*Informal*) extraordinary.

un·eas'y *adj.* **1,** not comfortable in mind
or body; disturbed; restless. **2,** not easy
in manner; constrained. **—un·eas'i·ly,**
adv. **—un·eas'i·ness,** *n.*

un"em·ployed' (un"əm-ploid') *adj.* **1,**

without a job; out of work. **2,** not in use.
—un"em·ploy'ment, *n.*

un·end'ing *adj.* without end, or seemingly so.

un·e'ven *adj.* not even. **—uneven bars,**
an apparatus in gymnastics consisting of
two parallel bars at different heights.

un"ex·am'pled (un"eg-zam'pəld) *adj.*
without precedent.

un"ex·cep'tion·a·ble *adj.* beyond
criticism.

---

unexceptionable, unexceptional
☞ These words have distinctly different meanings. *Unexceptionable* means
beyond criticism; *unexceptional*
means common, ordinary, in no way
exceptional.

---

un·feel'ing *adj.* **1,** hardhearted; unsympathetic. **2,** insensitive; devoid of feeling.
—un·feel'ing·ness, *n.*

un·flap'pa·ble *adj.* (*Slang*) not easily
confused or excited.

un·fledged' (-flejd') *adj.* **1,** too young to
fly. **2,** undeveloped; immature.

un·fold' *v.t. & i.* **1,** open or spread out.
2, reveal or become revealed.

un·for'tu·nate *adj.* **1,** not lucky. **2,** regrettable. *—n.* a pitiable person.

un·found'ed (un-fown'did) *adj.* without
foundation; not based on fact; unwarranted.

un·frock' *v.t.* deprive of ecclesiastical
rank or status.

[In the following words, formed of words defined elsewhere in the dictionary, the prefixed *un-* forms an antonym of the root word.]

un·neigh'bor·ly
un·no'ticed
un"ob·served'
un"ob·struct'ed
un"ob·tru'sive
un·oc'cu·pied"
un"of·fend'ing
un·o'pened
un·or'gan·ized"
un·or'tho·dox
un·pack'
un·paid'
un·pal'at·a·ble
un·par'don·a·ble
un"par·lia·men'ta·ry
un·pen'
un·peo'pled
un"per·turbed'
un·pin'
un·planned'
un·pleas'ing
un·plowed'

un·plug'
un·pol'ished
un"pol·lut'ed
un·prec'e·dent·ed
un"pre·dict'a·ble
un·prej'u·diced
un"pre·med'i·tat"ed
un"pre·pared'
un"pre·tend'ing
un"pre·ten'tious
un·print'a·ble
un"pro·duc'tive
un"pro·fes'sion·al
un"prof'it·a·ble
un·prom'is·ing
un"pro·nounce'a·ble
un"pro·tect'ed
un"pro·voked'
un·pub'lished
un·pun'ished
un·qual'i·fied
un·quench'a·ble

un·ques'tion·a·ble
un·ques'tioned
un·qui'et
un·read'
un·read'a·ble
un·read'y
un·real'
un·rea'son·a·ble
un·rea'son·ing
un"rec·og·niz'a·ble
un"rec'og·nized"
un"re·cord'ed
un·reel'
un"re·fined'
un"re·flect'ing
un"re·gen'er·ate
un"re·lat'ed
un"re·lent'ing
un"re·li'a·ble
un"re·lieved'
un"re·li'gious
un"re·mem'bered

un·furl' *v.t.* spread out, as a flag; display.

un·fur'nished (un-fēr'nisht) *adj.* without furniture.

un·gain'ly (un-gān'lē) *adj.* clumsy; awkward; uncouth. —*adv.* awkwardly.

un·god'ly *adj.* **1,** wicked; sinful. **2,** (*Informal*) outrageous; atrocious. —**un·god'li·ness,** *n.*

un″gram·mat'i·cal *adj.* not in conformity to rules of grammar.

un'guent (ung'gwənt; un'jənt) *n.* an ointment; salve.

un'gu·late (ung'gyə-lət) *adj.* **1,** having hoofs. **2,** hooflike. —*n.* a hoofed mammal.

un·hand' *v.t.* take the hand from; let go; release.

un·hand'y *adj.* **1,** not easy to manage; inconvenient. **2,** not skillful.

un·hap'py *adj.* **1,** sad. **2,** unfortunate. —**un·hap'pi·ness,** *n.*

un·health'y *adj.* **1,** in poor health. **2,** unwholesome; likely to turn out badly. —**un·health'i·ness,** *n.*

un·heard-'of″ (un-hērd'uv″) *adj.* not hitherto known or existent; unprecedented.

un·hinge' *v.t.* **1,** remove the hinges of; take off of hinges. **2,** detach; derange. **3,** unbalance mentally; discompose; craze. —**un·hinged',** *adj.*

un·hol'y *adj.* **1,** sinful; impious. **2,** (*Informal*) extreme; unseemly. —**un·ho'li·ness,** *n.*

un·horse' *v.t.* **1,** throw down from a horse. **2,** dislodge.

u·ni- (ū-nə) *pref.* one; having only one; single.

u″ni·cam'er·al (ū'nə-kam'ə-rəl) *adj.* (of a legislature) having only one chamber.

u″ni·cel'lu·lar *adj.* consisting of a single cell.

u'ni·corn″ (ū'nə-kôrn″) *n.* a fabulous animal with a single long horn and usually the body of a horse.

u'ni·cy″cle *n.* a one-wheeled vehicle with footpedals.

u'ni·form″ (ū'nə-fôrm″) *adj.* **1,** unchanging; even; regular. **2,** the same as others. —*n.* **1,** a distinctive dress worn by all the members of a military force, a society, etc. **2,** (*Communications*) the letter *u.* —**u″ni·form'i·ty,** *n.*

u'ni·fy″ (ū'nə-fī″) *v.t.* collect, class, or form into a single whole; make uniform. —**u″ni·fi·ca'tion,** *n.* —**Unification Church,** a religious sect founded by Rev. Sun Myung Moon.

u″ni·lat'er·al (ū″nə-lat'ər-əl) *adj.* **1,** affecting or done by only one party (of two or more). **2,** having or pert. to only one side.

un″im·por'tant *adj.* not important; insignificant. —**un″im·por'tance,** *n.*

un'ion (ūn'yən) *n.* **1,** the act of joining two or more things into one. **2,** something made by uniting; a league, combination, compound, etc. **3,** marriage. **4,** an organi-

un″re·mit'ting	un·seal'	un·so'cia·ble
un″re·quit'ed	un·sea'son·a·ble	un·sold'
un″re·served'	un·sea'soned	un·sol'dier·ly
un″re·sist'ing	un·seat'	un″so·phis'ti·cat″ed
un″re·strained'	un″se·cured'	un·sought'
un″re·strict'ed	un·see'ing	un·spar'ing
un·rig'	un·seem'ly	un·spoiled'
un·right'eous	un·seen'	un·spo'ken
un·ripe'	un·set'	un·sports'man·like″
un·ri'valed	un·set'tle	un·spot'ted
un·robe'	un·set'tled	un·sta'ble
un·roll'	un·shack'le	un·stained'
un·ruf'fled	un·shad'ed	un·states'man·like″
un·sad'dle	un·shaped'	un·strained'
un·safe'	un·shape'ly	un·strap'
un·said'	un·shav'en	un·string'
un·sal'a·ble	un·sheathe'	un″sub·dued'
un·san'i·tar·y	un·shod'	un″sub·stan'tial
un″sat·is·fac'to·ry	un·sight'ly	un″suc·cess'ful
un·sat'is·fied	un·skilled'	un·suit'a·ble
un·sat'u·rat·ed	un·skill'ful	un·suit'ed
un·sa'vo·ry	un·sling'	un·sul'lied
un·schooled'	un·snap'	un″sup·port'ed
un″sci·en·tif'ic	un·snarl'	un″sur·passed'
un·screw'	un·so'ber	un″sus·pect'ed

zation of workers: a labor or trade union. **5,** a flag symbolizing union; a jack: *union jack.* **6,** a coupling device. **—un′ion·ism,** *n.* **—un′ion·ize″** (-īz″) *v.t. & i.* organize in a labor union. **—union shop, 1,** a shop where labor relations are controlled by fixed contract between employer and labor union. **2,** closed shop. **—union suit,** a one-piece undergarment.

u·nique′ (ū-nēk′) *adj.* **1,** being the only one of its kind. **2,** unusual; rare. **—u-nique′ness,** *n.*

u′ni·sex″ *adj.* designed for both sexes alike, as clothing.

u′ni·son (ū′nə-sən) *n.* **1,** coincidence in pitch of two or more tones. **2,** accord in sentiment or action.

u′nit (ū′nit) *n.* **1,** a single thing or person. **2,** a group of things or persons regarded as a single entity. **3,** a component part. **4,** any standard quantity used as a measure. **5,** the quantity and integer 1. **—u′ni·tar″y** (ū′ni-ter″ē) *adj.* **—u′ni·tize″,** *v.t.* **—unit pricing,** a system of commodity pricing based on a standard measure.

---

unit
↔ The word was coined by 16th-c. English mathematician John Dee.

U″ni·ta′ri·an (ū″ni-tār′ē-ən) *adj. & n.* of a sect that believes God exists in one person, not the Trinity.

u·nite′ (ū-nīt′) *v.t. & i.* **1,** combine so as to form one; make a union (of); connect. **2,** join in feeling or sympathy; agree. **—u-nit′ed,** *adj.* **—United Nations,** an organi-

zation comprising representatives of most of the countries of the world.

u′ni·ty (ū′nə-tē) *n.* **1,** the state of being united or uniform. **2,** the quantity and integer 1. **3,** harmony among elements.

u′ni·valve″ (ū′ni-valv″) *n.* a mollusk having only one shell.

u″ni·ver′sal (ū″nə-vēr′səl) *adj.* **1,** pert. to the, or a, universe; generally applicable. **2,** comprehensive; wide in scope. **3,** widely adaptable or effective in different directions, as of a mechanical contrivance. **—u″ni·ver·sal′i·ty,** *n.* **—universal joint** or **coupling,** a coupling of two rotating shafts, so designed that the shafts can be moved in any direction. **—Universal Product Code,** a ten-digit bar code used to identify products. Abbr., **UPC.**

U″ni·ver′sal·ist *adj. & n.* pert. to a Christian denomination or its doctrine of universal salvation.

u′ni·verse″ (ū′nə-vērs″) *n.* **1,** the totality of all existing things. **2,** the whole world; all mankind. **3,** an individual's own sphere or ken. **—island universe,** any of the collections of stars in space; a galaxy.

u″ni·ver′si·ty (ū″nə-vēr′sə-tē) *n.* an institution of higher learning, embracing both colleges and postgraduate schools.

U′nix (ū′niks) *n.* (*T.N.*) a computer operating system and file manager.

un·kempt′ *adj.* not combed, as hair; untidy. **—un·kempt′ness,** *n.*

un·known′ *adj.* **1,** not known, discovered, determined, or identified. **2,** unfamiliar. **—***n.* something unknown; (*Math.*)

[In the following words, formed of words defined elsewhere in the dictionary, the prefixed *un-* forms an antonym of the root word.]

un″sus·pect′ing	un·ti′dy	un·wa′ver·ing
un″sus·pi′cious	un·touched′	un·wea′ried
un″sus·tained′	un·trained′	un·weave′
un·sweet′ened	un·tram′meled	un·wed′
un·swept′	un·tried′	un·wel′come
un·swerv′ing	un·trimmed′	un·well′
un″sym·pa·thet′ic	un·trou′bled	un·wept′
un·tack′	un·true′	un·wil′ling
un·taint′ed	un·tu′tored	un·wind′
un·tak′en	un·twist′	un·wise′
un·tamed′	un·used′	un·wom′an·ly
un·tan′gle	un·ut′ter·a·ble	un·work′a·ble
un·tar′nished	un·var′y·ing	un·world′ly
un·tast′ed	un·veil′	un·wor′thy
un·taught′	un·ver′i·fied	un·wound′ed
un·ten′a·ble	un·vexed′	un·wrap′
un·ten′ant·ed	un·vis′it·ed	un·yoke′
un·teth′er	un·voiced′	un·youth′ful
un·thank′ful	un·want′ed	un·zip′
un·thread′	un·warped′	
un·throne′	un·war′y	

---

fat, fāte, fär, fâre, fâll, ȧsk; met, hē, hër, maybė; pin, pīne; not, nōte, ôr, tool a symbol for an unknown quantity. —**un·know'a·ble,** *adj.* beyond the range of human knowledge. —**un·know'ing,** *adj.* ignorant; unsophisticated. —**Unknown Soldier,** an unidentified soldier killed in battle who is buried with full military honors as a representative of all the unidentified soldiers killed in a war.

un·law'ful *adj.* against the law. —**un·law'ful·ness,** *n.*

un·lead'ed (un-led'id) *adj.* of motor fuel, containing no lead.

un·learn' *v.t.* put out of the mind or memory; forget.

un·leash' *v.t.* release from, or as from, a leash; let loose.

un·leav'ened (un-lev'ənd) *adj.* (of bread) not raised with yeast, etc.

un·less' (un-les') *conj.* if it be not that; if not; except in case that.—*prep.* except.

un·let'tered (un-let'ərd) *adj.* lacking book knowledge; uneducated.

un·lib'e·rat"ed *adj.* **1,** not liberated; captive. **2,** following traditional sex roles.

un·like' *adj.* not like; different; dissimilar. —*prep.* differently from. —**un·like'-ness,** *n.*

un·like'ly *adj. & adv.* **1,** not probable. **2,** having little prospect of success; unpromising. —**un·like'li·ness,** *n.*

un·looked-'for" (un-lûkt'for") *adj.* unexpected.

un·loose' (un-loos') *v.t.* loosen; untie; release.

un·luck'y *adj.* **1,** having bad luck. **2,** regrettable. —**un·luck'i·ness,** *n.*

un·make' *v.t.* **1,** take apart; reduce to original components. **2,** ruin; destroy; depose.

un·man' *v.t.* **1,** deprive of manly spirit; dishearten. **2,** emasculate. **3,** deprive of men, as a ship. —**un·man'ly,** *adj.* not befitting a man; weak. —**un·manned',** *adj.* unstaffed.

un·mean'ing (un-mē'ning) *adj.* **1,** without meaning or significance. **2,** expressionless, as a face.

un·men'tion·a·ble *adj.* not fit to be mentioned. —*n.* (usu. *pl.*) any undergarment.

un·mor'al *adj.* **1,** having no moral aspect. **2,** neither moral nor immoral.

un·nerve' *v.t.* cause to lose courage or resolution.

un·num'bered (un-num'bərd) *adj.* **1,** innumerable; very many. **2,** not numbered.

un"of·fi'cial *adj.* **1,** lacking official sanction. **2,** tentative.

un·pack' *v.t. & i.* remove a packing or something that has been packed (from).

un·par'al·leled" (un-par'ə-leld") *adj.* having no parallel or equal; unmatched.

un"per'son *n.* a person treated as, or as if, nonexistent.

unperson
↔ The word was coined by 20th-c. British novelist George Orwell in his novel *1984*.

un·pleas'ant *adj.* **1,** displeasing. **2,** disagreeable in manner, disposition, etc. —**un·pleas'ant·ness,** *n.*

un"plumbed' (-plumd') *adj.* unfathomed; unexplored.

un·pop'u·lar *adj.* disliked by many people. —**un·pop"u·lar'i·ty,** *n.*

un·prac'ticed (un-prak'tist) *adj.* **1,** not done usually or at all. **2,** not trained; unskillful.

un·prec'e·dent"ed (un-pres'ə-den"tid) *adj.* having no precedent; unexampled.

un·prin'ci·pled (un-prin'sə-pəld) *adj.* lacking moral principles; unscrupulous; wicked.

un·quote' *v.t.* close a quotation. —*n.* a mark (as ") so signifying.

un·rav'el *v.t.* **1,** separate the threads or fibers of; disentangle. **2,** free from perplexity; solve.

un·re'al (un-rē'əl) *adj.* **1,** not real. **2,** unpractical; visionary. **3,** (*Slang*) unbelievable.

un·re"con·struct'ed *adj.* not ready for social change.

un·rest' *n.* lack of rest or quiet; a state of agitation.

un·rid'dle *v.t.* solve, as a riddle; interpret; fathom.

un·rip' *v.t.* [-ripped', -rip'ping] rip; tear apart.

un·rul'y (un-roo'lē) *adj.* not submissive; balky; ungovernable. —**un·ru'li·ness,** *n.*

un·say' *v.t.* retract or recant (something said).

un·scathed' (un-skāth d') *adj.* not injured; unharmed.

un·scram'ble *v.t.* make orderly; disentangle.

un·scru'pu·lous *adj.* not honest, ethical, etc. —**un·scru'pu·lous·ness,** *n.*

un·self'ish *adj.* not putting one's own interests first. —**un·self'ish·ness,** *n.*

un·sex' (un-seks') *v.t.* deprive (a person) of the qualities of his or her sex.

un·shak'a·ble (un-shāk'ə-bəl) *adj.* determined; not open to persuasion.

un·shak'en *adj.* having lost no faith, resolution, force, etc.

un·smil'ing (un-smī'ling) *adj.* serious in demeanor; dour.

un·sound' *adj.* **1,** not sound; diseased, decayed, or defective. **2,** not well founded; invalid. **3,** financially insecure; unreliable.

un·speak'a·ble (un-spē'kə-bəl) *adj.* inexpressible; very bad.

un·stead'y *adj.* **1,** not steady; shaky. **2,** not reliable or resolute. **—un·stead'i·ness,** *n.*

un·stop' *v.t.* open; release.

un·strung' *adj.* **1,** removed from a string; with strings relaxed. **2,** nervously upset; distraught.

un·stud'ied (un-stud'ēd) *adj.* not affected in manner; artless; natural.

un·sung' *adj.* not duly honored.

un·sure' *adj.* **1,** not sure. **2,** not confident; hesitant.

un·think'a·ble (un-think'ə-bəl) *adj.* **1,** unworthy of consideration. **2,** inconceivable. **—un·think'ing,** *adj.* showing lack of thought; heedless.

un·tie' *v.t.* undo (a knot); release the fastenings of; set free.

un·til' *conj. & prep.* up to the time that; when or before.

un·time'ly *adj.* **1,** premature. **2,** inopportune; inconvenient. **—un·time'li·ness,** *n.*

un·tir'ing (un-tīr'ing) *adj.* unceasing in effort; not yielding to fatigue. **—un·tir'ing·ness,** *n.*

un'to *prep.* (*Archaic*) to; until.

un·told' *adj.* **1,** not told or revealed. **2,** not counted; too vast to be measured.

un·touch'a·ble (un-tuch'ə-bəl) *adj.* **1,** loathsome to the touch. **2,** that which cannot be reached. **3,** impalpable; intangible. *—n.* a member of the lowest caste in India, whose touch is thought to pollute.

un·to·ward' (un-tôrd') *adj.* unfavorable; troublesome.

un·truth' *n.* a falsehood; lie. **—un·truth'ful,** *adj.*

un·u'su·al *adj.* strange; uncommon. **—un·u'su·al·ness,** *n.*

un·var'nished (un-vär'nisht) *adj.* **1,** not varnished. **2,** not embellished or disguised; stark.

un·want'ed *adj.* not wanted; not desired.

---

unwanted, unwonted
☞ These two homophones have very different meanings. *Unwanted* means not wanted, not desired. *Unwonted* means not customary, out of the ordinary.

---

un·war'rant·a·ble (-ə-bəl) *adj.* lacking justification; without authority; unjust. Also, **un·war'rant·ed.**

un·washed' (un-wosht') *adj.* not washed; (of persons) unclean and vulgar.

un·whole'some *adj.* not healthful; unhealthy. **—un·whole'some·ness,** *n.*

un·wield'y (un-wēl'dē) *adj.* too large or bulky to be easily handled. **—un·wield'i·ness,** *n.*

un·wit'ting (un-wit'ing) *adj.* not knowing or realizing; unaware.

un·wont'ed *adj.* not usual or customary. ☐ *unwanted*

un·writ'ten *adj.* not written. **—unwritten law,** a custom that is observed as though it were formal law; esp., that crimes in defense of honor should not be punished.

up *adv.* **1,** in, toward, or to a more elevated position; to an erect position; higher. **2,** at or to a source or point of importance. **3,** to an equally advanced point or extent. **4,** well prepared or equipped. **5,** into activity. **6,** in process of happening. **7,** ended. **8,** together or close. *—prep.* **1,** to a higher position on or in; near the top of. **2,** toward the source, center, interior, etc., of. *—adj.* **1,** going or tending to higher position. **2,** cheerful; optimistic. *—n.* an upward movement; improvement. *—v.t.* [**upped, up'ping**] (*Informal*) make larger; bid or bet higher than. **—up-and-coming,** *adj.* promising. **—up to snuff,** sharp; alert.

up'beat" *n.* (*Music*) a beat preceding a downbeat. *—adj.* (*Informal*) lively; brisk.

up·braid' *v.t.* blame; rebuke.

up'bring"ing *n.* childhood training; rearing.

UPC *abbr.* Universal Product Code.

up'chuck" *v.i.* (*Slang*) vomit.

up'com"ing *adj.* coming soon.

up'coun"try *n.* a region away from the seacoast or lowlands. *—adj. & adv.* in or toward such a region.

up'date" *n.* a revision incorporating latest news, documents, etc. *—v.t.* to revise.

up'draft" *n.* a rising air current.

up·end' *v.t.* set on end; turn the top upward. *—v.i.* stand on end.

up'front' *adj.* **1,** in view; in cash. **2,** honest; candid.

up'grade" *n.* **1,** an upward slope; rising grade. **2,** improvement. *—adj. & adv.* upward. *—v.t.* **1,** put in a higher grade or classification than previously. **2,** improve.

up·heav'al (up-hē'vəl) *n.* **1,** a bursting upward, as in an earthquake. **2,** a violent disturbance, as a revolution.

---

up'hill" *adj. & adv.* on or toward the top of a hill.

up·hold' *v.t.* [**-held'**, **-hold'ing**] support; advocate; confirm.

up·hol'ster (up-hōl'stər) *v.t.* provide (the framework of furniture) with cushions, covering, etc. **—up·hol'ster·er,** *n.* **—up·hol'ster·y,** *n.* the process or result of upholstering.

up'keep" *n.* maintenance.

up'land (-lənd) *n. & adj.* **1,** upcountry. **2,** high land.

up'lift' *v.t.* elevate. **—n.** (up'lift) **1,** raising; elevation. **2,** moral advancement; inspiration.

up'load" *v.t.* (*Computers*) transfer data from one's own computer to an external system.

up'most *adj.* uppermost.

up·on' (ə-pon') *prep.* **1,** up and on. **2,** on.

up'per (up'ər) *adj.* **1,** higher in place or position. **2,** superior in rank, station, etc. **—n. 1,** an upper part or section; the part of a shoe above the sole. **2,** (*Slang*) a stimulant drug. **—on one's uppers,** poverty-stricken. **—upper house,** the senior or smaller of two legislative bodies, as the U.S. Senate. **—the upper hand,** mastery.

up"per·case' *adj. & n.* capital (of a letter).

up"per·class' *adj.* pert. to or characteristic of a high-ranking social or scholastic class.

up"per·class'man (-mən) *n.* [*pl.* **-men**] a junior or senior in school or college.

up'per·cut" *n.* an upward blow.

up'per·most" *adj. & adv.* highest in place, position, rank, power, etc.

up'pish (up'ish) *adj.* insolent; haughty. Also, **up'pi·ty** (up'ə-tē). **—up'pish·ness,** *n.*

up·raise' *v.t.* raise; lift up.

up'right" *adj.* **1,** vertical or erect. **2,** honest; righteous. **—n.** something standing erect or vertical, as a supporting post. **—adv.** vertically. **—up'right"ness,** *n.* **—upright piano,** one in which the strings and sounding board are placed vertically.

up"ris'ing (up"rīz'ing) *n.* rebellion; insurrection.

up'roar" *n.* violent disturbance and noise; bustle and clamor.

---

uproar
↔ No relation to *roar*, this word derives from Dutch *oproer*, a motion upward, tumult.

---

up·roar'i·ous (up-rôr'ē-əs) *adj.* **1,** clamorous. **2,** hilarious. **—up·roar'i·ous·ness,** *n.*

up·root' *v.t.* tear out by the roots; remove forcibly.

up'scale" *adj.* luxurious; expensive.

up·set' *v.t.* **1,** knock down from an erect or normal posture; overturn; throw into confusion. **2,** overthrow; spoil. **3,** perturb. **—n.** (up'set) **1,** a fall; an overturning. **2,** an unexpected result. **—adj.** overturned; disordered; disturbed.

up'shift" *n.* **1,** an improvement. **2,** a shift from a lower gear to a higher gear. **—v.i.** so shift.

up'shot" *n.* result.

up'side-"down' *adj. & adv.* **1,** having on top the side that should be on the bottom. **2,** in total disorder.

up'si·lon" (ūp'sə-lon") *n.* the twentieth letter of the Greek alphabet (Y, υ).

up·stage' *adj. & adv.* (*Theat.*) at or to the back of the stage; (*Informal*) haughty. **—v.t. 1,** cause (an actor, singer, etc.) to face away from the audience. **2,** draw attention from (a person, subject, etc.).

up'stairs' *adj., adv. & n.* (in, to, etc.) the second or a higher story.

up·stand'ing *adj.* highly respectable; upright.

up'start" *n.* a presumptuous person.

up'state" *adj., adv. & n.* (*Informal*) (of or from) the interior or northern part of a state.

up'stream" *adj. & adv.* to or toward the source of a river, etc.; against the current.

up'surge" *n.* an increasing wave or movement, as of emotion.

up'swing" *n.* a marked improvement.

up'take" *n.* **1,** a ventilating pipe or shaft. **2,** comprehension; awareness.

up'tick" *n.* (*Econ.*) an improvement in the national economy.

up-"tight' *adj.* (*Slang*) **1,** tense; nervous. **2,** conventional in attitude.

up-'to-date" *adj.* **1,** in accordance with, or conforming to, the latest ideas or fashions; modern. **2,** extending to the present time.

up'town" *adj., adv. & n.* (in or to) a section away from the main business district.

up'turn" *n.* **1,** a turning over or up. **2,** a change for the better.

up'ward (up'wərd) *adv.* [*also,* **up'-wards"**] **1,** toward a higher position, degree, etc. **2,** toward the source, interior, etc. **3,** in the upper part. **4,** more. **—adj.** moving or directed upward. **—upward mobility,** the possibility or ability to improve one's financial, social, or professional position. **—upwards of,** (*Informal*) somewhat more than.

---

ur- (ûr) *pref.* original; earliest; most authentic.

u·ra′ni·um (yû-rā′nê-əm) *n.* a radioactive chemical element, no. 92, symbol U.

urb (ērb) *n.* an urban area.

ur′ban (ēr′bən) *adj.* pert. to, comprising, living in, or characteristic of a city. **—ur′-ban·ite,** *n.* **—urban renewal,** reconstruction or rehabilitation of blighted urban areas. **—urban sprawl,** the tendency of the city to expand.

---

urban, urbane

☞ These two words have the same root, but divergent meanings. *Urban* means relating to a city; *urbane* means sophisticated (presumably from having lived in a city). ↔ Both words derive from Latin *urbanus,* of the city.

---

ur·bane′ (ēr-bān′) *adj.* affable; suave. **—ur·ban′i·ty** (-ban′ə-tė) *n.* ❑ *urban*

ur″ban·ol′o·gy *n.* the study of urban problems.

ur′chin (ēr′chin) *n.* a mischievous child; any small child.

-ure (-yər) *suf.* forming abstract nouns of action, agency, state, or result.

u·re′a (yû-rē′ə) *n.* a substance found in urine, used in plastics.

u·re′mi·a (yû-rē′mê-ə) *n.* a morbid bodily condition caused by retention of waste products. **—u·re′mic,** *adj.*

u·re′ter (yû-rē′tər) *n.* the tube carrying urine from kidney to bladder.

u·re′thra (yû-rē′thrə) *n.* the tube through which urine is discharged from the bladder.

urge (ērj) *v.t.* **1,** push onward; drive vigorously. **2,** exhort. **3,** advocate earnestly. **—n.** an impelling force; an impulse.

ur′gen·cy (ēr′jən-sė) *n.* **1,** insistence. **2,** imperative necessity.

ur′gent (ēr′jənt) *adj.* **1,** imperative; needed at once. **2,** insistent.

-ur·gy (ēr-jė) *suf.* technology.

u′ric (yûr′ik) *adj.* of or pert. to urine or urea.

u′rin·al (yûr′i-nəl) *n.* a receptacle to receive urine.

u″ri·nal′y·sis (yûr″i-nal′ə-sis) *n.* an analysis of a specimen of urine, made for medical purposes.

u′ri·na·ry (-ner-ė) *adj.* pert. to the organs that excrete urine.

u′ri·nate″ (-nāt″) *v.t.* discharge urine. **—u″ri·na′tion,** *n.*

u′rine (yûr′in) *n.* a fluid secretion of the kidneys, excreting waste products.

urn (ērn) *n.* **1,** a vase with a base. **2,** a vessel for making tea, coffee, etc.

u·rol′o·gy (yûr-ol′ə-jė) *n.* the study and treatment of organs that excrete urine. **—u″ro·log′i·cal,** *adj.* **—u·rol′o·gist,** *n.*

ur′sine (ēr′sīn) *adj.* pert. to a bear; bearlike.

ur″ti·car′i·a (ēr″ti-kār′ė-ə) *n.* an eruptive skin disease; hives. **—ur″ti·car′i·al,** *adj.*

us *pron.* obj. of *we.*

us′age (ū′sij) *n.* **1,** customary practice or way of acting or doing; an established way of using words or phrases. **2,** the use or enjoyment of something.

us′ance (ū′zəns) *n.* **1,** the time allowed by custom for payment of foreign bills of exchange. **2,** income derived from ownership of wealth.

use (ūz) *v.t.* **1,** employ for a purpose; put to service. **2,** consume or expend. **3,** treat. **—n.** (ūs) **1,** the act of using, employing, or putting to service; the state of being used. **2,** utility; service. **3,** an instance or way of using something. **—us′a·ble** (ū′zə-bəl) *adj.* **—us′er** (ū′zər) *n.* **—used to** (ūs′tū) accustomed to (with a noun); in past time did. **—user-friendly,** *adj.* designed with the needs of users in mind; easy to use.

use′ful (ūs′fəl) *adj.* having a practical function, purpose, or effect; worthwhile. **—use′ful·ness,** *n.*

use′less (ūs′ləs) *adj.* without function or effect; not useful. **—use′less·ness,** *n.*

ush′er (ush′ər) *n.* **1,** one who escorts persons to seats in a church, theater, etc. **2,** one in charge of a door. **—v.t.* **1,** escort. **2,** (with *in*) introduce; contribute to the beginning of.

u′su·al (ū′zhû-əl) *adj.* **1,** ordinary; normal. **2,** customary; habitual. **—u′su·al·ly,** *adv.* on most occasions.

u′su·fruct″ (ū′zū-frukt″) *n.* the right to use; the yield from use.

u·surp′ (ū-sērp′) *v.t.* seize and hold (office, power, etc.) by force and without right. **—u″sur·pa′tion,** *n.*

u′su·ry (ū′zhə-rė) *n.* exorbitant interest paid or charged. **—u′su·rer,** *n.* **—u·sur′i·ous** (ū-zhûr′ė-əs) *adj.*

ut (ût) *n.* (*Music*) do.

u·ten′sil (ū-ten′səl) *n.* an implement, instrument, or vessel, esp. one used in preparing food.

u′ter·us (ū′tər-əs) *n.* [*pl.* **-i** (-ī)] the organ in which the fetus rests and grows; the womb. **—u′ter·ine** (-in) *adj.*

u′tile (ū′təl) *adj.* useful.

u·til″i·tar′i·an (ū-til″ə-târ′ē-ən) *adj.* useful rather than ornamental.

u·til′i·ty (ū-til′ə-tė) *n.* **1,** the state of being useful; something useful. **2,** a public service, as an agency supplying electricity, water, etc. —**utility man,** one who does any odd jobs.

u′ti·lize″ (ū′tə-līz″) *v.t.* make use of; put to service. —**u″ti·li·za′tion,** *n.*

ut′most″ (ut′mōst″) *adj.* **1,** of the greatest degree, quantity, etc. **2,** at the farthest or outermost point. —*n.* the limit. Also, **ut′ter·most.**

U·to′pi·an (ū-tō′pė-ən) *adj.* relating to an imaginary ideal state (Utopia) or condition; hence, idealistic but not practical.

> **Utopian**
> ↔ From *Utopia,* coined by English scholar Sir Thomas More as a name for an imaginary and ideal island community. The word is based on Greek *ou,* not, + *topos,* place.

ut′ter (ut′ər) *v.t.* **1,** give audible expression to; say. **2,** issue; emit. —*adj.* complete; absolute; unconditional.

ut′ter·ance *n.* **1,** act of uttering; issuance; something said. **2,** manner of speaking.

ut′ter·most″ *adj. & n.* utmost.

U-′turn″ *n.* **1,** a U-shaped turn. **2,** a reversal, as of policy, politics, etc.

u′vu·la (ū′vyə-lə) *n.* the fleshy conical body hanging down from the soft palate in the back of the mouth. —**u′vu·lar** (-lər) *adj.*

ux·o′ri·ous (uk-sôr′ē-əs) *adj.* excessively fond of one's wife. —**ux·o′ri·ous·ness,** *n.*

U′zi (oo′zė) *n.* a type of submachine gun, named for Israeli officer Uziel Gal.

V

V, v (vē) **1,** the 22nd letter of the English alphabet. **2,** Roman numeral for 5.

va′can·cy (vā′kən-sė) *n.* **1,** state of being vacant; a vacant space. **2,** an available job, space, etc.

va′cant (vā′kənt) *adj.* **1,** having no contents; empty; devoid of something. **2,** having no occupant; untenanted. **3,** idle; disengaged. **4,** vacuous; stupid.

va′cate″ (vā′kāt″) *v.t.* **1,** make vacant; quit; empty. **2,** make void; annul.

va·ca′tion (vā-kā′shən) *n.* **1,** a period of release from work; holiday. **2,** act of vacating. —**va·ca′tion·ist,** *n.*

vac′ci·nate″ (vak′sə-nāt″) *v.t.* inoculate

with a vaccine, esp. to immunize against smallpox. —**vac″ci·na′tion,** *n.*

vac·cine′ (vak-sēn′) *n.* a weakened virus introduced into a healthy body to induce immunity against the disease.

> **vaccine**
> ↔ From New Latin *variolae vaccinae,* cowpox, from Latin *vacca,* cow. The cowpox virus was proposed by British physician Edward Jenner to be used to produce antibodies against smallpox.

vac·cin′i·a (vak-sin′ė-ə) *n.* cowpox.

vac′il·late″ (vas′ə-lāt″) *v.i.* **1,** waver in opinion, sentiment, determination, etc.; be irresolute. **2,** sway; stagger. —**vac″il·la′tion,** *n.*

vac′u·ole″ (vak′ū-ōl″) *n.* **1,** a cavity in the protoplasm of a cell. **2,** a tiny cell or cavity in the tissue of organisms.

vac′u·ous (vak′ū-əs) *adj.* **1,** showing no intelligence; blank. **2,** empty; unfilled. —**va·cu′i·ty** (-kū′ə-tė) *n.*

vac′u·um (vak′ū-əm) *n.* **1,** space void of matter. **2,** a space largely exhausted of air or gas. —*v.t. & i.* (*Informal*) clean with a vacuum cleaner. —**vacuum aspiration,** a form of abortion. —**vacuum bottle,** thermos. —**vacuum cleaner,** a device that sucks in dust, etc., for housecleaning. —**vacuum-packed,** *adj.* packed in a container from which the air is removed. —**vacuum tube,** a sealed tube of glass or metal, used in electronic devices, as radio.

va′de me′cum (vä′dė mā′kəm) (*Lat.,* go with me) a guide, esp. a guidebook.

vag′a·bond″ (vag′ə-bond″) *adj.* having no settled habitation; wandering; nomadic. —*n.* **1,** a wanderer; esp. a worthless vagrant; a tramp.

va·gar′y (və-gâr′ė) *n.* a capricious or extravagant thought or action.

va·gi′na (və-jī′nə) *n.* the passage from vulva to uterus in a female animal. —**vag′i·nal** (vaj′i-nəl) *adj.*

va′grant (vā′grənt) *adj.* **1,** vagabond. **2,** uncertain; erratic (as ideas). —*n.* **1,** a vagabond. **2,** one without visible or reputable means of support. —**va′gran·cy,** *n.*

vague (vāg) *adj.* **1,** not definite, precise, or clear. **2,** mentally confused. **3,** indistinct to sight or other sense. —**vague′ness,** *n.*

vain (vān) *adj.* **1,** ineffective; futile. **2,** of no real value; trivial. **3,** excessively proud of oneself; conceited. —**vain′ness,** *n.*

vain·glo′ri·ous *adj.* inordinately proud,

boasting, or pretentious. —**vain·glo'ri·ous·ness**, *n.* —**vain"glo'ry**, *n.*

val'ance (val'əns) *n.* a short drape or curtain used as an ornamental border.

vale (vāl) *n.* (*Poetic*) valley. —*interj.* (vä'le) farewell.

val"e·dic'tion (val"ə-dik'shən) *n.* a farewell; a bidding farewell.

val"e·dic'to·ry (val"ə-dik'tə-rė) *adj.* bidding farewell; farewell. —*n.* an oration of farewell, esp. by a member of a graduating class. —**val"e·dic·to'ri·an**, (-tôr'ė-ən) *n.* one who delivers a valedictory, usu. the top academic student in the graduating class.

va'lence (vā'ləns) *n.* (*Chem.*) the relative combining capacity of an atom compared with the hydrogen atom. Also, **va'len·cy**.

Va·len"ci·ennes' (və-len"sė-enz') *n.* a kind of fine lace, named for a city in France.

-va·lent (vā-lənt) *suf.* having a valency of, as *univalent*.

val'en·tine" (val'ən-tīn") *n.* 1, a sentimental missive sent on St. Valentine's Day, Feb. 14. 2, a sweetheart chosen on this day.

---

valentine

↔ The word honors the 3rd-c. Saint *Valentine*, a Christian martyr who died in Rome.

---

va·le'ri·an (və-lir'ė-ən) *n.* 1, a perennial herb. 2, a drug made from it, used to quiet the nerves.

---

valerian

↔ Named for *Valeria*, a province of ancient Rome.

---

val'et (val'ət, va-lā') *n.* 1, a personal servant. 2, one whose business is pressing and cleaning clothes. —**valet parking**, a parking system in which an employee parks the car for the client.

---

valet, varlet

↔ These words are both derived from Celtic *wasso*, squire, through Vulgar Latin and Old French.

---

val"e·tu"di·nar'i·an (val"ə-tū"də-nār'ė-ən) *n. & adj.* (one) in poor health; invalid.

Val·hal'la (val-hal'ə) *n.* in Norse mythology, the final resting place for the souls of heroes slain in battle.

val'iant (val'yənt) *adj.* 1, brave; courageous. 2, showing valor. —**val'ian·cy**, *n.*

val'id *adj.* 1, well supported by fact;

sound; just. 2, legally effective or binding. —**va·lid'i·ty** (və-lid'ə-tė) *n.*

val'i·date" (val'i-dāt") *v.t.* make valid. —**val"i·da'tion**, *n.*

va·lise' (və-lēs') *n.* a small leather traveling bag.

Val'i·um (val'ė-əm) *n.* (*T.N.*) a tranquilizing drug.

val'ley (val'ė) *n.* 1, a relatively low tract of land between hills. 2, the lowlands along the course of a river. 3, any hollow, depression, or dip.

val'or (val'ər) *n.* strength of mind in braving danger. Also, **val'our.** —**val'or·ous**, *adj.*

val'or·ize" (val'ə-rīz") *v.t.* fix and maintain an arbitrary price of (a commodity) by governmental action. —**val"or·i·za'tion**, *n.*

val'u·a·ble (val'ū-ə-bəl) *adj.* of great value or price. —*n.* (usually *pl.*) an expensive personal possession, as a jewel. —**val'u·a·ble·ness**, *n.* ❏ *invaluable*

val"u·a'tion (val"ū-ā'shən) *n.* 1, act of appraising or estimating value. 2, estimated worth.

val'ue (val'ū) *n.* 1, that for which something is regarded as useful or desirable; utility, merit, or worth. 2, price. 3, import. 4, degree; number; amount; duration, etc. —*v.t.* 1, regard as desirable or useful. 2, estimate the value of. —**val'ued**, *adj.* highly regarded. —**val'ue·less**, *adj.* worthless. —**value-added tax**, a tax based on the amount added to the value of a product at each stage of production. ❏ *invaluable*

valve (valv) *n.* 1, any device used to control the flow of a fluid through a pipe, vent, etc. 2, a hinged lid or flap, as of the shell of a clam, etc. 3, an electron tube. —**val'vu·lar** (val'vyə-lər) *adj.*

va·moose' (va-moos') *v.i.* depart rapidly; run away.

vamp *n.* 1, the front part of the upper of a shoe or boot. 2, a patch added to something old. 3, an improvised musical accompaniment. 4, (*Slang*) a flirtatious woman. —*v.t.* 1, repair; patch; renovate. 2, (*Slang*) use feminine wiles on.

vam'pire (vam'pīr) *n.* 1, a supposed bloodsucking monster. 2, any of various bloodsucking or similar bats. 3, an extortionist, esp. a flirtatious or predatory woman.

---

vampire, werewolf

☛ These words are frequently used as synonyms. However, a *vampire* is a bloodsucking person; a *werewolf* is a person transformed into a wolf.

---

van *n.* **1,** a large covered wagon or truck. **2,** (*Brit.*) a light delivery truck; a baggage or freight car. **3,** vanguard.

va·na'di·um (və-nā'dė-əm) *n.* a rare element, no. 23, symbol V, used to harden steel.

> **vanadium**
> ↔ From Icelandic *Vanadis*, a name for the goddess Freya.

Van Al'len radiation belt (van al'ən) a belt of ionizing radiation surrounding the earth and extending from approx. 500 miles to approx. 30,000 miles into space, named for U.S. physicist J. A. Van Allen.

van'dal *n.* one who willfully destroys things of beauty. **—van'dal·ism,** *n.* wanton destruction. **—van'dal·ize",** *v.t.*

> **vandal**
> ↔ From the name of the Germanic tribe who sacked Rome in 455 A.D.

van·dyke' (-dīke') *n.* (often *cap.*) a short pointed beard, named for 17th-c. Flemish painter Sir Anthony Van Dyck.

vane (vān) *n.* **1,** a device that turns with the wind and shows its direction: *weathervane.* **2,** blade, plate, fin, etc., moved by a fluid stream.

van'guard" (van'gärd") *n.* the foremost units, as of an advancing army; the leaders, as of a social movement.

va·nil'la (və-nil'ə) *n.* a tropical orchid; a flavoring extract made from its bean. **—adj.** (*Informal*) simple; plain.

va·nil'lin (və-nil'ən) *n.* an artificial compound giving a vanilla flavor.

van'ish *v.i.* **1,** fade from sight; disappear. **2,** pass away; cease to exist. **3,** (*Math.*) become zero. **—vanishing point,** the point toward which receding parallel lines seem to converge.

van'i·ty (van'ə-tė) *n.* **1,** excessive pride; excessive attention to one's appearance. **2,** futility; worthlessness. **3,** a thing or trait regarded as vain. **4,** a small cosmetic case carried by a woman. **5,** a woman's dressing table. **—vanity plate,** an automobile license plate having a word or message chosen, usu. at additional cost, by the licensee rather than by the issuing authority.

van'quish (vang'kwish) *v.t.* defeat in battle or contest.

van'tage (van'tij) *n.* a position affording superior power or opportunity.

vap'id *adj.* lacking animation or flavor. **—va·pid'i·ty** (və-pid'ə-tė), **vap'id·ness,** *n.*

va'por (vā'pər) *n.* **1,** a gas made visible by particles of liquid or dust, as steam, fog, smoke. **2,** any matter in gaseous state. **3,** something unsubstantial or transitory. **4,** (*pl.*) (*Archaic*) harmful exhalations formerly supposed to reside within the body and cause psychological problems. **5,** (*pl.*) depression; hypochondria. *—v.t. & i.* change to vapor. Also, **va'pour.** **—vapor trail,** contrail.

va'por·ize" (-īz") *v.t. & i.* make or become vapor. **—va"por·i·za'tion,** *n.*

va'por·ous (-əs) *adj.* **1,** pert. to or of vapor. **2,** unsubstantial; vague. **—va'por·ous·ness,** *n.*

va'por·ware" *n.* (*Computers*) software repeatedly announced as about to be released but never actually appearing on the market.

va·que'ro (va-kā'rō) *n.* (*Sp.*) a herdsman or cowboy.

var·ac'tor (var-ak'tər) *n.* a type of semiconductor capacitor: *var(iable re)actor.*

var'i·a·ble (vār'ė-ə-bəl) *adj.* **1,** tending to change; not constant. **2,** capable of being varied. *—n.* that which varies. **—var"i·a·bil'i·ty,** *n.* **—variable rate mortgage,** a type of mortgage in which interest rates are keyed to money market rates.

var'i·ance (vār'ė-əns) *n.* act or effect of varying; difference. **—at variance,** in disagreement.

var'i·ant (vār'ė-ənt) *adj.* tending to change; different; diverse. *—n.* an altered form of something.

var"i·a'tion (vār'ė-ā'shən) *n.* **1,** the act or process of varying; change; modification. **2,** a point or aspect of difference. **3,** the amount of change; variance. **4,** a different form. **5,** (*Music*) a theme repeated with changes or elaborations.

var"i·cel'la (var"i-sel'lə) *n.* chicken pox.

var'i·col'ored (vār'ė-kul"ərd) *adj.* variegated; motley.

var'i·cose" (vār'i-kōs") *adj.* dilated; abnormally swollen, esp. of veins. **—var"i·cos'i·ty** (-kos'ə-tė) *n.*

var'ied (vār'ėd) *adj.* **1,** assorted; differing. **2,** altered.

var'i·e·gat"ed (vār'ė-ə-gā"təd) *adj.* marked with different colors. **—var'i·e·gate",** *v.t.* **—var"i·e·ga'tion,** *n.*

va·ri'e·ty (və-rī'ə-tė) *n.* **1,** a mixture of different things. **2,** difference or discrepancy. **3,** a variant; a subdivision. **4,** vaudeville. **—variety store,** a store offering a wide variety of merchandise.

var'i·fo"cal lens (var'ə-fō"kəl) zoom lens.

var″i·form″ (var′ə-fôrm″) *adj.* varied in form; having different shapes.

va·ri′o·la (və-rī′ə-lə) *n.* smallpox. **—va·ri′o·lous,** *adj.*

var″i·om′e·ter (vār″ē-om′ə-tər) *n.* an instrument for regulating or measuring electrical variations.

var″i·o′rum (vār″ē-ôr′əm) *adj.* presenting several versions (of a text).

var′i·ous (vār′ē-əs) *adj.* **1,** differing; having diverse features; not uniform. **2,** some; several; many. **—var′i·ous·ness,** *n.*

var′let (vär′lit) *n.* (*Archaic*) a rascal. **—var′let·ry,** *n.* (*Archaic*) the rabble. ❑ *valet*

var′mint (vär′mənt) *n.* (*Dial.*) **1,** an insect; bug; any undesirable creature. **2,** a low or rascally person.

var′nish (vär′nish) *n.* **1,** a resinous coating material that produces a glossy surface. **2,** superficial social polish. **—v.t.** finish with, or as with, varnish.

var′si·ty (vär′sə-tē) *n.* the principal team of a school or college in a given sport.

var′y (vār′ē) *v.t.* **1,** make different; alter. **2,** make of different kinds; diversify. **3,** (*Music*) embellish with variations. **—v.i.** **1,** be different or diverse. **2,** undergo change. **3,** be variable.

vas *n.* [*pl.* **va′sa** (vā′-sə)] (*Anatomy*) duct; vessel. **—vas de′fe·rens** (def′ə-renz) the duct that carries sperm to the penis.

vas′cu·lar (vas′kyə-lər) *adj.* pert. to bodily ducts that convey fluid, as blood and lymph. **—vas″cu·lar′i·ty** (-lar′ə-tē) *n.*

vase (vās) *n.* a hollow vessel, as for holding cut flowers, etc.

va·sec′to·my (va-sek′tə-mē) *n.* a surgical method of sterilization of a male.

Vas′e·line″ (vas′ə-lēn″) *n.* (*T.N.*) a greasy petroleum product used as an ointment and lubricant.

vas″o·mo′tor (vas″ō-mō′tər) *adj.* regulating the blood vessels.

vas′sal (vas′əl) *n.* **1,** a feudal tenant. **2,** a subject, follower, or retainer. **—vas′sal·age,** *n.*

vast (våst) *adj.* very great in extent, quantity, etc. **—vast′ness,** *n.*

VAT *abbr.* value-added tax.

vat *n.* a large container for liquids.

vat′ic (vat′ik) *adj.* prophetic.

Vat′i·can (vat′i-kən) *n.* the palace of the Pope, at Rome.

vaude′ville (vod′vil) *n.* a theatrical show comprising separate acts of different kinds. **—vaude·vil′lian** (-yən) *n. & adj.*

> **vaudeville**
> ↔ From the *vau de Vire,* a region of France noted for satirical folksongs.

vault (vâlt) *n.* **1,** a chamber with an arched or concave roof, esp. one underground; any underground room. **2,** a chamber used as a safe. **3,** a jump; the act of vaulting. **—v.i. & t.** jump or leap, esp. with aid of the hands resting on something.

vaunt (vânt) *v.t.* speak of boastfully.

VCR *abbr.* videocassette recorder.

V-′Day′ day of victory (in World War II): in Europe (*V-E Day*), May 8, 1945, and over Japan (*V-J Day*), Sept. 2, 1945.

VDT *abbr.* video display terminal.

veal (vēl) *n.* the meat of a calf.

vec′tor (vek′tər) *n. & adj.* a line graphically representing both magnitude and direction; a quantity which may be represented by such a line. **—vector graphics,** object-oriented graphics.

Ve′da (vā′də) *n.* one of the Hindu scriptures. **—Ve′dic,** *adj.*

Ve·dan′ta (vā-dän′tə) *n.* a Hindu philosophy, a derivation of the Vedas.

ve·dette′ (və-det′) *n.* (*Naval*) a small scouting boat.

vee′jay″ (vē′jā″) *n.* video jockey.

veep (vēp) *n.* (*Slang*) vice-president.

veer (vir) *v.i.* change direction, as wind. **—n.** a change of direction.

veer′y (vir′ē) *n.* a thrush of E. U.S. noted for its song.

veg′e·ta·ble (vej′tə-bəl) *n.* **1,** any herbaceous plant used wholly or in part for food. **2,** any plant. **3,** an uninteresting or ineffectual person. **4,** a brain-damaged or brain-dead person. **—adj.** **1,** being an edible plant. **2,** belonging to the plant kingdom. **—veg′e·tal** (vej′ə-təl) *adj.* **—vegetable marrow,** a kind of oblong squash.

veg″e·tar′i·an (vej′ə-tār′ē-ən) *n. & adj.* one who eats no meat.

veg′e·tate″ (vej′ə-tāt″) *v.i.* **1,** grow or live like a plant. **2,** be mentally inactive. **—veg′e·ta·tive,** *adj.*

veg″e·ta′tion (vej″ə-tā′shən) *n.* **1,** plants collectively. **2,** the act of vegetating.

ve′he·ment (vē′ə-mənt) *adj.* showing strength or impetuosity in feeling; eager, fervent, or passionate. **—ve′he·mence,** *n.*

ve′hi·cle (vē′ə-kəl) *n.* **1,** any carriage or conveyance on wheels or runners. **2,** any medium for producing effects. **3,** (*Painting*) a liquid, as linseed oil, with which a

---

pigment is mixed. —**ve·hic′u·lar** (vĕ-hik′yû-lər) *adj.*

veil (vāl) *n.* **1,** a piece of light fabric worn over the face or head. **2,** anything that screens or conceals. —*v.t.* **1,** cover with a veil. **2,** hide; disguise. —**take the veil,** become a nun.

vein (vān) *n.* **1,** one of the tubes that convey blood to the heart. **2,** a riblike part supporting a membrane, as a leaf. **3,** a stratum or deposit; a lode. **4,** a fissure or cavity; a small natural watercourse. **5,** a streak or stripe. —*v.t.* furnish or mark with veins. —**vein′y,** *adj.*

Vel′cro (vel′krō) *n.* (*T.N.*) a plastic fastener consisting of tiny interlocking hooks.

veldt (velt) *n.* the open, scrubby country of So. Afr. Also, **veld.**

vel′lum (vel′əm) *n.* **1,** parchment made from calfskin. **2,** a paper of similar texture.

ve·loc′i·pede″ (və-los′ə-pēd″) *n.* a light vehicle with three wheels propelled by foot power; a tricycle.

ve·loc′i·ty (və-los′ə-tē) *n.* quickness or rate of motion; speed. ❑ *speed*

ve·lours′ (və-loor′) *n.* velvet.

ve·lure′ (və-lūr′) *n.* a velvet.

vel′vet (vel′vit) *n.* **1,** a fabric with a thick, soft pile. **2,** something of similar texture. **3,** (*Slang*) net profit. —**vel′vet·y,** *adj.*

vel″ve·teen′ (vel″və-tēn′) *n.* a cotton fabric woven like velvet.

ve′nal (vē′nəl) *adj.* open to bribery; corrupt. —**ve·nal′i·ty** (vē-nal′ə-tē) *n.*

---
venal, venial

☛ *Venal* (without an *i*) means corrupt; *venial* (with an *i*) means not depriving the soul of divine grace. A sin is *venial*, not *venal*. (The opposite is a *mortal sin*, which causes the death of the soul.)

---

vend *v.t. & i.* sell; purvey. —**ven·dee′,** *n.* buyer. —**vend′i·ble,** *adj.* —**vending machine,** a coin-slot machine for selling merchandise.

ven·det′ta (ven-det′ə) *n.* a feud.

ven′dor (ven′dər) *n.* **1,** a seller; a peddler. **2,** a vending machine. Also, **vend′er.**

ven·due′ (ven-dū′) *n.* a public auction.

ve·neer′ (və-nir′) *n.* **1,** a thin layer of fine wood or other material applied as an outer coating. **2,** one of the layers in plywood. **3,** outward show to give a fair appearance; superficial ornamentation. —*v.t.* **1,** cover with veneer. **2,** make into plywood.

ven′er·a·ble (ven′ər-ə-bəl) *adj.* **1,** worthy of veneration. **2,** old and dignified; ancient. —**ven″er·a·bil′i·ty, ven′er·a·ble·ness,** *n.*

ven′er·ate″ (ven′ə-rāt″) *v.t.* regard with reverence. —**ven″er·a′tion,** *n.*

ve·ne′re·al (və-nir′ē-əl) *adj.* pert. to diseases arising from copulation.

ven′er·y (ven′ə-rē) *n.* hunting; the chase.

Ve·ne′tian (və-nē′shən) *adj. & n.* of or pert. to Venice. —**Venetian blind,** a screen for a window, having adjustable horizontal slats.

venge′ance (ven′jəns) *n.* retributive punishment; revenge.

venge′ful (venj′fəl) *adj.* seeking revenge. —**venge′ful·ness,** *n.*

ve′ni·al (vē′nē-əl) *adj.* **1,** pardonable; excusable. **2,** (of a sin) not causing the loss of divine grace. —**ve″ni·al′i·ty,** *n.* ❑ *venal*

ve·ni′re (və-nī′rē) *n.* (*Law*) a writ requiring a sheriff to summon qualified citizens to act as jurors. —**ve·ni′re·man** (vi-nī′rē-mən) *n.* [*pl.* **-men**] one summoned to be a juror.

ven′i·son (ven′ə-zən) *n.* the flesh of a deer or like animal.

ven′om (ven′əm) *n.* **1,** poison secreted by snakes, spiders, etc. **2,** spite; malice; virulence. —**ven′om·ous,** *adj.*

ve′nous (vē′nəs) *adj.* of or pert. to the veins.

vent *n.* **1,** a small aperture or passage; an outlet. **2,** an emission or discharge. **3,** utterance. —*v.t.* **1,** let out; discharge. **2,** utter.

ven′ti·late″ (ven′tə-lāt″) *v.t.* let fresh air into; expose to the action of air. —**ven″ti·la′tion,** *n.* —**ven′ti·la″tor,** *n.* a device, as an opening, shaft, fan, etc., for ventilating.

ven′tral (ven′trəl) *adj.* pert. to the abdominal side of the body.

ven′tri·cle (ven′tri-kəl) *n.* a small cavity or hollow organ of the body; esp., a chamber of the heart. —**ven·tric′u·lar** (-yû-lər) *adj.*

ven·tril′o·quism (ven-tril′ə-kwiz-əm) *n.* the art of uttering sounds so that they seem to come from a source other than the speaker. —**ven·tril′o·quist,** *n.*

ven′ture (ven′chər) *n.* a hazardous enterprise. —*v.t.* **1,** expose to risk; stake. **2,** expose oneself to the risk of; utter daringly. —*v.i.* risk. —**ven′tur·ous,** *adj.* venturesome. —**at a venture,** at random.

ven′ture·some (-səm) *adj.* **1,** daring. **2,** hazardous; dangerous. —**ven′ture·some·ness,** *n.*

ven'ue (ven'ū) *n.* the scene of a crime or the jurisdiction of a court.

ve·ra'cious (və-rā'shəs) *adj.* **1,** disposed to tell the truth. **2,** true. —**ve·ra'cious·ness,** *n.*

ve·rac'i·ty (və-ras'ə-tē) *n.* truthfulness; accuracy.

ve·ran'da (və-ran'də) *n.* an open porch or gallery, usually roofed.

verb (vērb) *n.* a word that expresses action or existence; a part of speech that predicates and combines with a subject to form a sentence.

verb'al (vēr'bəl) *adj.* **1,** expressed in words. **2,** oral, not written. **3,** pert. to a verb.

ver'bal·ism *n.* **1,** something expressed orally. **2,** wordiness. **3,** a wordy expression. —**ver'bal·ist,** *n.* ☐ *oral*

ver'bal·ize'' (-īz'') *v.i.* be verbose. —*v.t.* express in words. —**ver''bal·i·za'tion,** *n.*

ver·ba'tim (vər-bā'təm) *adj.* in exactly the same words.

ver·be'na (vər-bē'nə) *n.* a plant with showy flowers.

ver'bi·age (vēr'bē-ij) *n.* wordiness; verbosity.

ver·bose' (vər-bōs') *adj.* using more words than are necessary; wordy. —**verbos'i·ty** (-bos'ə-tē) *n.*

ver'dant (vēr'dənt) *adj.* **1,** green with vegetation. **2,** inexperienced. —**ver'dan·cy,** *n.*

ver'dict (vēr'dikt) *n.* **1,** the finding of a jury. **2,** any judgment or decision.

ver'di·gris'' (vēr'də-grēs'') *n.* a greenish patina that forms on copper, brass, or bronze.

---

verdigris
↔ This word comes from Old French *vertegrez*, green of Greece, though no one knows why the term came to be applied to the patina on copper.

---

ver'dure (vēr'jər) *n.* **1,** green vegetation. **2,** greenness, esp. of growing plants. **3,** fresh or healthy condition.

verge (vērj) *n.* **1,** brink; edge; rim. **2,** a point or limit beyond which something begins. **3,** a staff of authority. —*v.i.* be at a border; approach.

ver'ger (vēr'jər) *n.* a minor church officer, as an usher or sexton.

ver'i·fy'' (ver'ə-fī'') *v.t.* ascertain or prove to be true. —**ver''i·fi·ca'tion,** *n.*

ver'i·ly (ver'ə-lē) *adv.* (*Archaic*) truly; really.

ver''i·si·mil'i·tude'' (ver''i-si-mil'ə-tūd'') *n.* an appearance of truth.

ver'ism (ver'iz-əm) *n.* the attempt to depict reality in art and literature.

ver'i·ta·ble (ver'i-tə-bəl) *adj.* true; genuine. —**ver''i·ta·bil'i·ty,** *n.*

ver'i·ty (ver'ə-tē) *n.* **1,** the quality of being true or real. **2,** a truth; a reality.

ver'juice'' (vēr'joos'') *n.* **1,** the juice of a sour fruit. **2,** tartness.

ver·mi- (vēr-mə) *pref.* wormlike.

ver''mi·cel'li (vēr''mə-sel'ē) *n.* a thin spaghetti.

ver·mic'u·late (vēr-mik'yû-lət) *adj.* **1,** marked with wavy lines. **2,** infested with worms.

ver'mi·form'' (vēr'mə-fôrm'') *adj.* long and slender, resembling a worm.

ver·mil'ion (vər-mil'yən) *n. & adj.* a bright yellow-red color.

ver'min (vēr'min) *n.pl.* or *sing.* **1,** small noxious animals collectively, esp. insects that infest the body, houses, etc. **2,** an obnoxious person or persons. —**ver'min·ous,** *adj.*

ver·mouth' (vər-mooth') *n.* a spiced wine. Also, **ver·muth'.**

ver·nac'u·lar (vər-nak'yə-lər) *adj. & n.* pert. to the native or common language of a place or group.

ver'nal (vēr'nəl) *adj.* **1,** pert. to spring. **2,** pert. to early age; youthful.

ver'ni·er (vēr'nē-ər) *n.* **1,** an auxiliary device to measure fractional parts of subdivisions of a graduated scale. **2,** a device designed to give greater accuracy of adjustment to a piece of machinery, named for 17th-c. French inventor Pierre Vernier.

ve·ron'i·ca (və-ron'i-kə) *n.* **1,** any of various plants or shrubs. **2,** a napkin or piece of cloth impressed with the face of Christ.

---

veronica
↔ Medieval Latin, perhaps from *vera iconica*, true image, referring to the image of Christ said to have been transferred to the handkerchief given to him by St. Veronica on the way to Calvary.

---

ver'sa·tile (vēr'sə-til) *adj.* **1,** having ability in many different fields. **2,** pivoted so as to swing or turn freely. —**ver''sa·til'i·ty,** *n.*

verse (vērs) *n.* **1,** metrical composition; poetry. **2,** a line of poetry or prose. **3,** a poem. **4,** a stanza.

versed (vērsd) *adj.* experienced; practiced; skilled.

ver'si·cle (vēr'sə-kəl) *n.* one of a succession of short verses said or sung alternately.

ver·si·fy" (vĕr'sə-fī") *v.t. & i.* write in poetry. —**ver"si·fi·ca'tion,** *n.*

ver'sion (vĕr'zhən) *n.* **1,** a particular form or variant of something; a particular translation. **2,** a narration from a particular point of view.

ver'so (vĕr'sō) *n.* **1,** a left-hand page of a book. **2,** the reverse side.

verst (vĕrst) *n.* a Russian measure of distance, equaling 3,500 ft.

ver'sus (vĕr'səs) *prep.* against, as opposing parties in a lawsuit or contest.

ver'te·bra (vĕr'tə-brə) *n.* [*pl.* **-brae** (-brē) or **-bras**] any of the bone segments forming the spinal column. —**ver'te·bral,** *adj.*

ver'te·brate" (vĕr'tə-brāt") *adj.* having a spine or backbone. —*n.* a vertebrate animal.

ver'tex (vĕr'teks) *n.* [*pl.* **-es** or **ver'ti·ces"** (-tə-sēz")] the highest point; a point where two lines intersect.

ver'ti·cal (vĕr'tə-kəl) *adj.* being perpendicular to the horizon; upright. —*n.* **1,** something vertical, as a line, supporting post, etc. **2,** an upright position. —**ver'ti·cal·ness,** *n.*

ver·tig'i·nous (vĕr-tij'ə-nəs) *adj.* **1,** turning around; whirling; **2,** unstable.

ver'ti·go" (vĕr'tə-gō") *n.* a disordered condition marked by dizziness.

ver'vain (vĕr'vān) *n.* a weedy plant with small flowers.

verve (vĕrv) *n.* enthusiasm; dash.

ver'y (ver'ē) *adv.* to a high degree; greatly; extremely. —*adj.* **1,** [*superl.* **ver'i·est**] true; actual; genuine. **2,** exact; innermost.

very high frequency designating radio frequencies from 30 to 300 megacycles. Also, **VHF.**

ve·si'ca (və-sē'kə) *n.* [*pl.* **-cae** (-sè)] a bladder or sac. —**ves'i·cal** (ves'ə-kəl) *adj.*

ves'i·cle (ves'ə-kəl) *n.* a bladderlike structure, cavity, sac, or cyst.

ve·sic'u·lar (ve-sik'yû-lər) *adj.* pert. to or like a vesicle. —**ve·sic'u·late** (-lət) *adj.* having vesicles.

ves'per (ves'pər) *n.* **1,** evening; the evening star. **2,** (*pl.*) a religious service held in late afternoon; evensong.

ves'per·tine" (ves'pər-tīn") *adj.* pert. to, or happening in, the evening.

ves'sel (ves'əl) *n.* **1,** a ship or other craft for traveling on water. **2,** a hollow container. **3,** a tube or duct.

vest *n.* a short sleeveless garment worn by men under the coat; any similar gar-

ment. —*v.t.* **1,** clothe; cover or adorn with fabric. **2,** endow with something, as authority. **3,** put (rights, property, etc.) in possession of someone.

ves'tal (ves'təl) *adj.* virginal; chaste. —*n.* **1,** a virgin. **2,** a nun.

vest'ed (ves'tid) *adj.* **1,** owned securely. **2,** clothed; robed.

vest·ee' (ves-tē') *n.* a vestlike front piece in a woman's dress.

ves'ti·bule" (ves'tə-būl") *n.* a hall or antechamber between an outer door and inner room.

ves'tige (ves'tij) *n.* a remainder or evidence of something no longer present; a trace. —**ves·tig'i·al** (-tij'əl) *adj.*

vest'ment (-mənt) *n.* a garment, esp. an official or ceremonial dress.

vest-'pock"et *adj.* small enough to fit in a vest pocket; miniature.

ves'try (ves'trē) *n.* **1,** a room in a church where vestments are kept. **2,** a chapel. **3,** a church committee.

ves'try·man (-mən) [*pl.* **-men**], **ves·try·wom"an** *n.* a member of a church committee.

ves'ture (ves'chər) *n.* **1,** garments. **2,** any covering. —*v.t.* clothe.

vet *n.* **1,** veteran (of a war). **2,** veterinarian. —*v.t.* **1,** (*Informal*) work as a veterinarian. **2,** examine thoroughly.

vetch (vech) *n.* any of several leguminous plants used for forage.

vet'er·an (vet'ər-ən) *n.* **1,** one who has had long experience. **2,** a former soldier or other member of the armed services. —*adj.* having long experience. —**Veterans Day,** a federal legal holiday, Nov. 11.

vet'er·in·ar"y (vet'ər-ə-ner"ē) *adj.* pert. to medical and surgical care of domestic animals. —*n.* [also, **vet"er·i·nar'i·an**] one who practices veterinary medicine.

ve'to (vē'tō) *n.* **1,** rejection by one branch of government of measures proposed by another. **2,** the right to reject. **3,** any ban or prohibition. —*v.t.* reject; prohibit; refuse to endorse.

vex (veks) *v.t.* **1,** make angry or displeased. **2,** annoy; worry; harass.

vex·a'tion (veks-ā'shən) *n.* annoyance; irritation. —**vex·a'tious,** *adj.*

vi'a (vī'ə) *prep.* by way of; by a route through.

vi'a·ble (vī'ə-bəl) *adj.* **1,** capable of living, esp., able to live outside the womb. **2,** (*Informal*) workable; practical. —**vi"a·bil'i·ty,** *n.*

vi'a·duct" (vī'ə-dukt") *n.* a bridge for carrying a road, railroad, waterway, etc. over a depression.

vi′al (vī′əl) *n.* a small bottle or flask.

vi′and (vī′ənd) *n.* an article of food.

vi·at′i·cum (vī-at′ə-kəm) *n.* **1,** communion given to a dying person. **2,** an allowance for traveling expenses.

vibes (vībz) *n.pl.* (*Slang*) **1,** vibrations; intuitive feelings. **2,** vibraphone.

vi′bra·phone″ (vī′brə-) *n.* a musical percussion instrument similar to a marimba but having metal chimes and an electric mechanism for producing vibrato. Also, **vi′bra·harp″**.

vi′brant (vī′brənt) *adj.* **1,** vibrating; resonant. **2,** full of vigorous enthusiasm. **—vi′-bran·cy,** *n.*

vi′brate (vī′brāt) *v.i.* **1,** swing to and fro, as a pendulum; oscillate. **2,** move rapidly to and fro, as a plucked string; quiver; resound; thrill. **—vi·bra′tion,** *n.* **—vi′bra·tor,** *n.* **—vi′bra·to·ry** (-brə-tôr-ė) *adj.*

vi·bra′to (vi-brä′tō) *n.* a tremulous effect or tremolo produced in singing and on various instruments.

vi·bur′num (vi-bēr′nəm) *n.* any of various shrubs or small trees, usu. bearing white flowers.

vic′ar (vik′ər) *n.* **1,** an assistant clergy. **2,** one in charge of a dependent parish or chapel. **3,** a deputy. **—Vicar of Christ,** the Pope.

vic′ar·age (-ij) *n.* the residence or office of a vicar.

vi·car′i·ous (vī-kār′ė-əs) *adj.* substituting for, or feeling in place of, another. **—vi·car′i·ous·ness,** *n.*

vice (vīs) *n.* **1,** any immoral or evil practice. **2,** prostitution. **3,** a defect; a bad habit. **—prep.** instead of; in place of.

---

vice, vise
☞ These two words are usually pronounced the same, but they are unrelated. A *vice* is an evil practice; a *vise* is a clamp.

---

vice- (vīs) *pref.* denoting a deputy or subordinate.

vice″ge′rent (-jir′ənt) *n.* a deputy.

vi·cen′ni·al (vī-sen′ė-əl) *n. & adj.* **1,** 20 years. **2,** the 20th anniversary.

vice-″pres′i·dent *n.* an officer of a government, corporation, etc., ranking next below the president. **—vice-″pres′i·den·cy,** *n.*

vice′roy (-roi) *n.* a deputy king. **—vice″-re′gal,** *adj.* **—vice′roy·ship,** *n.*

vice′ ver′sa (vīs′ vēr′sə) conversely; denoting reciprocal relationship or reversal of order.

vi′chy (vish′ė) *n.* **1,** a carbonated, naturally effervescent water; soda. **2,** (*cap.*) an alkaline, still water from Vichy, France (*eau de Vichy*).

vi′chys·soise″ (vish′ė-swäz″) *n.* a soup made with potatoes, leeks, and heavy cream, and served chilled.

vi·cin′i·ty (vi-sin′ə-tė) *n.* the region surrounding or near a place; the neighborhood.

vi′cious (vish′əs) *adj.* **1,** addicted to vice; wicked; depraved. **2,** evil; pernicious. **3,** faulty; defective. **4,** malicious; spiteful. **—vi′cious·ness,** *n.* **—vicious circle,** a series of successively consequent effects in which the last affects the first.

---

vicious, viscous
☞ Two words frequently confused. *Vicious* means wicked (the word is related to *vice*); *viscous* means having high viscosity.

---

vi·cis′si·tude″ (vi-sis′i-tūd″) *n.* **1,** change of condition; succession of one set of circumstances by another. **2,** (*pl.*) good or bad fortune.

vic′tim (vik′tim) *n.* **1,** one who suffers from a harmful agency. **2,** one who is cheated or duped. **—vic′tim·ize″** (-mīz″) *v.t.* ❏ *martyr*

vic′tor (vik′tər) *n.* **1,** one who wins. **2,** (*Communications*) the letter *v*.

vic·to′ri·a (vik-tôr′ė-ə) *n.* a kind of horse-drawn carriage. **—Victoria Day,** a legal holiday in Canada, the Monday before May 25.

---

victoria
↔ Named for Queen *Victoria* of England.

Vic·to′ri·an (vik-tôr′ė-ən) *adj.* **1,** pert. to the time of Queen Victoria of England, 1837–1901. **2,** prudish; smug.

vic′to·ry (vik′tə-rė) *n.* **1,** the winning of a contest or battle. **2,** any successful performance. **—vic·to′ri·ous** (-tôr′ė-əs) *adj.*

Vic·tro′la (vik-trō′lə) *n.* (*T.N.*) an early phonograph.

vict′ual (vit′əl) *n.* (*pl.*) food or provisions, esp. for human beings. **—v.t. & i.** supply with or obtain provisions. **—vict′ual·er,** *n.* a supplier of food; a restaurateur.

---

victuals
↔ The pronunciation of this unusual word reflects French *vitaille*, the immediate source of the word, but the spelling is from its more distant source, Latin *victualia*, provisions.

---

vi·cu′ña (vī-kū′nyə) *n.* **1,** a wild ruminant of the Andes, related to the llama. **2,** a fabric made from the wool of this animal.

vi·de′ (vē′de) *v.* (*Lat.*) see.

vi·de′li·cet″ (vi-dā′li-ket″) *adv.* (*Lat.*) namely; that is to say.

vid′e·o (vid′ē-ō) *adj.* pert. to television. —*n.* **1,** television. **2,** a videotape, esp. containing a prerecorded program. **3,** a promotional film designed to accompany a recording. —**video jockey,** a person who plays videotapes, as at a discotheque.

vid′e·o·disk″ *n.* a disk on which video images and sound are recorded, to be played back later.

vid″e·og′ra·phy (vid″ē-og′rə-fē) *n.* picture-taking with a television camera recording on videotape. —**vid″e·og′ra·pher,** *n.* —**vid″e·o·graph′ic,** *adj.*

vid′e·o·phone″ *n.* a Picturephone.

vid′e·o·tape″ *n.* a tape for recording video images for playback; the process by which this is done. —*v.t. & i.* record on videotape.

vid′e·o·text″ *n.* information transmitted over wires for display on a television set or monitor; esp. a two-way interactive data system.

vie (vī) *v.i.* [**vied, vy′ing**] strive for superiority; compete.

Vi″en·nese′ (vē″ə-nēz′) *adj. & n.* of or pert. to Vienna.

Viet″cong′ (vyet″kong′) *n.* [*pl.* **Viet″cong′**] a member of the former National Liberation Front of So. Vietnam; the Front itself.

view (vū) *n.* **1,** examination by eye; inspection; survey. **2,** range of vision. **3,** what is seen; scene, prospect, etc. **4,** mental contemplation; visualization. **5,** a particular aspect or mental attitude; an opinion, judgment, theory, etc. **6,** purpose; aim. —*v.t.* **1,** look at. **2,** consider; regard in a particular way. —**in view of,** in consideration of.

view′er *n.* **1,** one who or that which views. **2,** a device used for viewing, as of photographic slides, etc.

view′find″er *n.* a finder.

view′point″ *n.* **1,** a place from which something may be seen. **2,** attitude of mind: *point of view.*

vi·ges′i·mal (vi-jes′i-məl) *adj.* twentieth; by twenties.

vig′il (vij′əl) *n.* **1,** a keeping awake; a watch kept at night. **2,** watchful attention at any time.

vig′i·lant (vij′ə-lənt) *adj.* alert to detect danger. —**vig′i·lance,** *n.*

vig″i·lan′te (vij″ə-lan′tē) *n.* one of a group of self-appointed citizens acting to maintain order.

vi·gnette′ (vin-yet′) *n.* **1,** a photograph shaded at the edges so as to have no clear border. **2,** a descriptive literary sketch. **3,** a decorative illustration in a book. —*v.t.* **1,** outline; describe. **2,** make a (photographic) vignette of.

vig′or (vig′ər) *n.* **1,** active strength of body; good physical condition. **2,** mental energy. **3,** strength or force in general; powerful action; potency. Also, **vig′our.** —**vig′or·ous,** *adj.*

vi′king (vī′king) *n.* a Scandinavian mariner of the Middle Ages.

vile (vīl) *adj.* **1,** morally base; depraved; villainous. **2,** repulsive; obnoxious; disgusting. **3,** low in station; mean. **4,** of small value; paltry. —**vile′ness,** *n.*

vil′i·fy″ (vil′ə-fī″) *v.t.* defame. —**vil″i·fi·ca′tion,** *n.*

vil′i·pend″ *v.t.* **1,** treat contemptuously. **2,** vilify.

vil′la (vil′ə) *n.* a rural or suburban mansion; a large country residence.

vil′lage (vil′ij) *n.* a small assemblage of houses, less than a town. —**vil′lag·er,** *n.*

vil′lain (vil′ən) *n.* **1,** the chief antagonist of the hero in a play or novel. **2,** a wicked person; rascal; scoundrel. —**vil′lain·ous,** *adj.* —**vil′lain·y,** *n.*

vil″la·nelle′ (vil″ə-nel′) *n.* a French verse form.

vil′lein (vil′ən) *n.* under the feudal system, a member of the class who were serfs with respect to their lords, but freemen with respect to others. —**vil′lein·age,** *n.*

vim *n.* energy; impetuosity.

vin″ai·grette′ (vin″ə-gret′) *n.* a small ornamental bottle or box for holding smelling salts, etc. —**vinaigrette sauce,** a sauce of vinegar, oil, and seasonings.

vin′ci·ble (vin′sə-bəl) *adj.* conquerable. —**vin″ci·bil′i·ty,** *n.*

vin′cu·lum (ving′kyə-ləm) *n.* [*pl.* **-la** (-lə)] **1,** a bond of union; a tie. **2,** (*Math.*) a line drawn over two or more algebraic quantities to show that they are to be treated as one term.

vin′di·cate″ (vin′də-kāt″) *v.t.* **1,** clear, as from an accusation or imputation. **2,** maintain as true or correct. **3,** regain possession of (property) by legal procedure. —**vin″di·ca′tion,** *n.*

vin·dic′tive (vin-dik′tiv) *adj.* disposed to seek revenge; bitter. —**vin·dic′tive·ness,** *n.*

vine (vīn) *n.* **1,** any plant with a long slender stem that trails on the ground or climbs upright objects. **2,** the grape plant. **3,** wine.

vin′e·gar (vin′ə-gər) *n.* **1,** a sour liquid obtained by fermentation of fruit juices. **2,** sourness of speech, temper, etc. —**vin′e·gar·y,** *adj.*

> **vinegar**
> ↔ From Old French *vyn egre,* sour wine, of Latin origin.

vine′yard″ (vin′yərd) *n.* a plantation for grapes, esp., for wine-making.

vin′i·cul″ture (vin′ə-) *n.* the cultivation of grapes for wine.

vi′nous (vī′nəs) *adj.* pert. to wine or vines.

vin′tage (vin′tij) *n.* **1,** the wine from a particular crop of grapes; the crop or output of anything. **2,** the gathering of grapes; the harvest season. **3,** wine-making. —*adj.* exceptionally fine.

vint′ner (vint′nər) *n.* a dealer in wines.

vi′nyl (vī′nil) *adj. & n.* **1,** (pert. to) certain compounds used in plastics (*vinyl resins,* as styrene, Vinylite, Koroseal, etc.). **2,** (pert. to) a type of plastic fabric.

vi′ol (vī′əl) *n.* a stringed musical instrument similar in shape to a violin but with more than four strings. —**vi′ol·ist,** *n.*

vi·o′la (vē-ō′lə) *n.* the alto instrument of the violin family. —**vi·o′list,** *n.*

vi′o·late″ (vī′ə-lāt″) *v.t.* **1,** break or infringe, as a law or a contract. **2,** break in upon; do violence to. **3,** treat with irreverence; desecrate; profane. **4,** molest (a woman) sexually. —**vi′o·la·ble,** *adj.* —**vi″o·la′tion,** *n.* —**vi′o·la·tor,** *n.*

vi′o·lent (vī′ə-lənt) *adj.* **1,** acting with, or characterized by, strong physical force. **2,** vehement; passionate; furious. —**vi′o·lence,** *n.*

vi′o·let (vī′ə-lit) *n.* **1,** any of numerous herbs bearing small short-stemmed flowers; the flower. **2,** a blue or reddish-blue color; the spectrum color of highest frequency visible to the eye.

vi″o·lin′ (vī″ə-lin′) *n.* a stringed musical instrument played with a bow; the treble member of the modern family of such instruments. —**vi″o·lin′ist,** *n.*

> **violoncello**
> ↔ Note the spelling of this word: it is not *violincello,* despite the fact that the instrument is a member of the violin family. The name comes from the *violone.*

vi″o·lon·cel′lo (vē″ə-lon-chel′ō) *n.* the

tenor instrument of the violin family. Also, **cel′lo.** —**vi″o·lon·cel′list,** *n.*

vi″o·lo′ne (vē″ə-lō′nā) *n.* a contrabass viol.

vi·os′ter·ol″ (vī-os′tər-ol″) *n.* a prepared oil that supplies vitamin D.

V.I.P. (vē′ī′pē′) *n.* (*Slang*) very important personage.

vi′per (vī′pər) *n.* **1,** a venomous snake. **2,** a malignant or treacherous person. —**vi′per·ous, vi′per·ish,** *adj.*

> **viper**
> ↔ This word is a contraction of Latin *vivipera,* giving birth to live young, from a mistaken belief common in earlier time.

vi·ra′go (vi-rä′gō) *n.* **1,** an ill-tempered or violent woman. **2,** (*Archaic*) a woman of great stature, strength, and courage.

vi′ral (vī′rəl) *adj.* pert. to, or resulting from, a virus.

vir′e·lay (vir′ə-lā) *n.* an old French poetic form.

vir′e·o (vir′ē-ō) *n.* [*pl.* **-e·os**] any of several small Amer. songbirds.

vir′gin (vėr′jin) *n.* **1,** a person who has not had sexual intercourse. **2,** (*cap.*) Mary, mother of Jesus. —*adj.* **1,** being a virgin; pure. **2,** fresh; new; unused. —**vir·gin′i·ty,** *n.* —**virgin birth,** the doctrine that Jesus was miraculously born of a virgin mother.

vir′gin·al (-əl) *adj.* **1,** virgin. **2,** pure; fresh. —*n.* a small harpsichord.

Vir·gin′ia creeper (vər-jin′yə) a No. Amer. vine; woodbine.

Virginia reel a type of square dance.

vir·gin′i·um (vər-jin′ē-əm) *n.* francium.

Vir′go (vėr′gō) *n.* a constellation, the Virgin (see *zodiac*).

vir″i·des′cent (vir″i-des′ənt) *adj.* greenish. —**vir″i·des′cence,** *n.*

vir′ile (vir′əl) *adj.* **1,** of or like a man; masculine; manly. **2,** capable of procreating. **3,** forceful. —**vi·ril′i·ty** (və-ril′ə-tē) *n.*

vir·tu′ (vər-too′) *n.* the quality of being artistic, rare, etc.; objects having this quality.

vir′tu·al (vėr′choo-əl) *adj.* **1,** existing in power or effect, but not actually. **2,** equivalent to, though somewhat different or deficient. —**vir·tu·al′i·ty,** *n.* —**virtual reality,** a hypothetical three-dimensional space created by means of computer graphics.

vir′tue (vėr′choo) *n.* **1,** conformity to moral law; uprightness; rectitude. **2,** a commendable quality. **3,** chastity. **4,** inherent power; effect. **—by virtue of,** by authority of; because of.

vir″tu·os′i·ty (vēr″choo-os′ə-tē) *n.* great individual skill.

vir″tu·o′so (vēr″choo-ō′sō) *n.* [*pl.* **-sos, -si** (-sē)] **1,** one who has great skill in a fine art, as music. **2,** a connoisseur.

vir′tu·ous (vēr′choo-əs) *adj.* moral; upright; chaste. **—vir′tu·ous·ness,** *n.*

vir′u·lent (vir′yə-lənt) *adj.* **1,** like a poison; deadly; malignant. **2,** bitterly hostile; acrimonious. **—vir′u·lence,** *n.*

vi′rus (vī′rəs) *n.* **1,** an agent of infection, esp. one smaller than common bacteria. **2,** a pernicious influence. **3,** (*Computers*) a program inserted into a computer system as a prank or to cause damage.

vi′sa (vē′zə) *n.* an endorsement making a passport valid for entry into a particular country. Also, **vi·sé′** (-zā′).

vis′age (viz′ij) *n.* **1,** the face, esp. of a human being. **2,** countenance; appearance; aspect.

vis″-à-vis′ (vē″zä-vē′) *prep.* face to face.

vis′cer·a (vis′ər-ə) *n.pl.* [*sing.* **vis′cus** (-kəs)] **1,** the soft interior parts of the body. **2,** the bowels. **—vis′cer·al,** *adj.*

vis′cid (vis′id) *adj.* having a glutinous consistency; sticky. **—vis·cid′i·ty, vis′cid·ness,** *n.*

vis′cose (vis′kōs) *n. & adj.* a solution of cellulose used in making rayon.

vis·cos′i·ty (vis-kos′ə-tē) *n.* thickness of consistency of a liquid; resistance to flow.

vis′count (vī′kownt) *n.* a nobleman ranking next below a count (or earl). **—vis′count″ess,** *n.* wife of a viscount.

vis′cous (vis′kəs) *adj.* **1,** viscid. **2,** having high viscosity. ❑ *vicious*

vise (vīs) *n.* an apparatus for gripping and holding an object while work is performed on it. Also, **vice.** ❑ *vice*

vis′i·ble (viz′ə-bəl) *adj.* **1,** capable of being seen. **2,** open to view; conspicuous. **3,** perceptible to the mind. **—vis″i·bil′i·ty,** *n.*

vi′sion (vizh′ən) *n.* **1,** the sense of sight; ability to see. **2,** the ability to visualize; foresight. **3,** a pleasing or vivid scene. **4,** a supernatural or prophetic presentiment, as in a dream or trance. **5,** a fanciful or unpractical view. **—vision quest,** an attempt to communicate with the spirit world through fasting, prayer, etc.

vi′sion·ar·y (-er-ē) *adj.* **1,** unpractical. **2,** given to idealistic theorizing. *—n.* a dreamer; theorizer.

vis′it (viz′it) *v.t.* **1,** go to see (a person, place, etc.); call upon. **2,** stay with, as a guest. **3,** afflict, as with suffering; assail. *—v.i.* make calls. *—n.* a friendly or official call; a stay as a guest. **—vis′i·tor,** *n.*

vis′it·ant (viz′i-tənt) *n.* one visiting for a short period.

vis″i·ta′tion (viz″i-tā′shən) *n.* **1,** an official visit. **2,** a boon or affliction regarded as an act of God. **3,** (*cap.*) the visit of the Virgin Mary to her cousin Elizabeth (Luke 1:39).

vi′sor (vī′zər) *n.* a part projecting above the eyes, as on a cap, to shade or protect them. Also, **vi′zor.**

vis′ta (vis′tə) *n.* a view or prospect, esp. one of great depth.

vis′u·al (vizh′ū-əl) *adj.* **1,** pert. to vision; used in seeing; optical. **2,** visible to the eye or mind. *—n.* pictoral elements (as opposed to aural) in a presentation. **—visual arts,** the arts whose objects are appreciated by viewing, as painting, sculpture, photography, etc.

vis′u·al·ize″ (vizh′ū-ə-līz″) *v.t.* **1,** form a mental image of. **2,** make perceptible. *—v.i.* form mental images. **—vis″u·al·i·za′tion,** *n.*

vi′ta (vī′tə) *n.* [*pl.* **vi′tae** (vī′tē)] biographical résumé. Also, **curriculum vitae.**

vi′tal (vī′təl) *adj.* **1,** pert. to life; alive. **2,** essential to existence or well-being. **3,** critically important. **4,** invigorating. **5,** fatal. **—vi′tal·ness,** *n.* **—vital signs,** bodily symptoms indicative of basic bodily functions, as heartbeat, pulse rate, etc. **—vital statistics,** birth and death records. **—vi′tals,** *n.pl.* vital organs of the body.

vi·tal′i·ty (vī-tal′ə-tē) *n.* **1,** the power to live; the principle of life. **2,** vigor; energy.

vi′tal·ize″ (vī′təl-īz″) *v.t.* give life, vigor, or vitality to. **—vi″tal·i·za′tion,** *n.*

vi′ta·min (vī′tə-min) *n.* a food constituent essential to the proper functioning of the body. Also, **vi′ta·mine.**

---

vitamin

↔ Originally coined in German by biochemist Casimir Funk, on the mistaken belief that vitamins contained amino acids.

---

vi′ti·ate″ (vish′ē-āt″) *v.t.* make faulty or imperfect; contaminate; spoil; invalidate. **—vi″ti·a′tion,** *n.*

vit′i·cul″ture (vit′ə-) *n.* the cultivation of grapes. **—vit″i·cul′tur·al,** *adj.*

vit′re·ous (vit′rē-əs) *adj.* **1,** pert. to or consisting of glass. **2,** resembling glass, as in hardness, finish, etc. **—vit″re·ous·ness,** *n.* **—vitreous humor,** the jellylike fluid in the eye.

vit′ri·fy″ (vit′ri-fī″) *v.t. & i.* change to a glassy state by heat. —**vit″ri·fi·ca′tion, vit″ri·fac′tion,** *n.*

vit′ri·ol (vit′ré-əl) *n.* **1,** sulfuric acid. **2,** any metallic sulfate of glassy appearance. **3,** something extremely caustic, as criticism. —**vit″ri·ol′ic,** *adj.* —**vit″ri·ol′i·cal·ly,** *adv.*

vi·tu′per·ate″ (vī-tū′pə-rāt″) *v.t.* address or find fault with abusively. —**vi·tu″per·a′-tion,** *n.* —**vi·tu′per·a·tive** (-ə-tiv), **vi·tu′per·ous** (-əs) *adj.*

vi′va (vē′və) *interj.* long live (the person or thing named). —*n.* a shout of "viva."

vi·va′cious (vī-vā′shəs) *adj.* animated; lively; sprightly. —**vi·va′cious·ness,** *n.*

vi·vac′i·ty (vi-vas′ə-tè) *n.* high spirits; vivaciousness.

vi·var′i·um (vi-vâr′ē-əm) *n.* a place where animals are kept in a natural setting.

vi′va vo′ce (vī′vä vō′che) (*Lat.*) orally.

vive le roi′ (la reine′) (vēv lə rwä′; lä ren′) (*Fr.*) long live the king (the queen).

viv′id *adj.* **1,** lifelike; animated; bright. **2,** clearly perceptible. **3,** vigorous or lively in action. —**viv′id·ness,** *n.*

viv′i·fy″ (viv′ə-fī″) *v.t.* enliven; give life to.

vi·vip′a·rous (vī-vip′ə-rəs) *adj.* bearing young alive, not in eggs. —**vi·vip′a·rous·ness,** *n.*

viv′i·sect″ (viv′ə-sekt″) *v.t.* dissect the living body of (an animal), for experimental purposes. —**viv″i·sec′tion,** *n.*

vix′en (vik′sən) *n.* **1,** a female fox. **2,** an ill-tempered woman. —**vix′en·ish,** *adj.*

vi·zier′ (vi-zir′) *n.* a chief minister of a Muslim sovereign.

vi′zor (vī′zər) *n.* visor.

vizs′la (vish′lə) *n.* a Hungarian breed of hunting dog.

vo′ca·ble (vō′kə-bəl) *n.* any word, regarded as a group of letters or sounds, without reference to meaning. —*adj.* that which may be spoken.

vo·cab′u·lar″y (vō-kab′yû-ler″é) *n.* **1,** the words of a language collectively. **2,** the stock of words used by a particular person, group, etc. **3,** a written list of words, as a dictionary.

vo′cal (vō′kəl) *adj.* **1,** pert. to the voice, speech, or singing. **2,** pert. to expression in speech; able or insistent in speaking. —*n.* **1,** a vocal sound, esp. a vowel. **2,** (*Informal*) the singing part of a musical performance. —**vo′cal·ist,** *n.* a singer. —**vo′cal·ize″** (-īz″) *v.t. & i.* utter; sing.

—**vocal cords,** membranes in the larynx that vibrate to produce sound.

vo·ca′tion (vō-kā′shən) *n.* **1,** a particular profession, business, or occupation; calling. **2,** a summons or feeling of being called to a particular activity, esp. religious. —**vo·ca′tion·al,** *adj.* pert. to an occupation; giving training for a trade. ❑ *career*

voc′a·tive (vok′ə-tiv) *adj. & n.* calling by name; (*Gram.*) designating the case of one directly addressed.

vo·cif′er·ate″ (vō-sif′ə-rāt″) *v.i. & t.* cry out noisily; shout. —**vo·cif″er·a′tion,** *n.*

vo·cif′er·ous (vō-sif′ə-rəs) *adj.* exclaiming; clamorous; noisy. —**vo·cif′er·ous·ness,** *n.*

vod′ka (vod′kə) *n.* a Russian alcoholic liquor distilled from cereals or potatoes.

vogue (vōg) *n.* prevalent fashion; popularity.

voice (vois) *n.* **1,** sound uttered by the mouth of a living creature, esp. human. **2,** the vocal sounds characteristic of a particular person. **3,** expression by, or as though by, speaking, singing, etc. **4,** the right to speak, vote, etc. **5,** a person or agency by which something is revealed. **6,** a singer; his role or part. **7,** (*Gram.*) a relative verb inflection, active (as, *I do it*) or passive (as, *it is done by me*). —*v.t.* give utterance to. —**voiced,** *adj.* —**voice′less,** *n.* —**voice box,** larynx. —**voice mail,** a spoken message that is stored digitally in a computer for later replay. —**voice-stress analysis,** the analysis of stress in a human voice, to determine truthfulness, etc.

-voiced *suf.* having a specified kind of voice, as soft-voiced.

voice-′o″ver *n.* (*Informal*) in motion pictures and television, a voice of a narrator, etc., not actually appearing on camera.

voice′print″ *n.* the distinctive pattern of wavy lines made by an individual's voice on a sound spectrograph: used for identification.

void *adj.* **1,** not legally binding; invalid; null. **2,** having no contents; vacant. **3,** ineffectual. —*v.t.* **1,** nullify. **2,** empty; evacuate. —*n.* a vacuum; empty place. —**void′ness,** *n.*

voile (voil) *n.* a thinly woven dress fabric.

vol′a·tile (vol′ə-təl) *adj.* **1,** changing to vapor readily or rapidly. **2,** fickle; frivolous. **3,** transient; unstable. —**vol″a·til′i·ty,** *n.*

vol·can′ic (vol-kan′ik) *adj.* **1,** pert. to a volcano. **2,** violently eruptive. —**vol·can′i-**

cal·ly, *adv.* —**vol′can·ism** (vol′kən-iz-əm) *n.*

vol·ca′no (vol-kā′nō) *n.* a vent in the earth's surface, commonly at the top of a mountain, from which molten rock and heated gases issue or have issued.

> **volcano, vulcanize**
> ↔ Both words derive from Latin *Volcanus,* Vulcan, the Roman god of fire.

vole (vōl) *n.* a small rodent of the rat family.

vo·li′tion (vō-lish′ən) *n.* the act or power of willing; voluntary action. —**vo·li′tion·al,** *adj.*

vol′i·tive (vol′ə-tiv) *adj.* expressing a wish.

vol′ley (vol′ē) *n.* **1,** a flight or discharge of a number of missiles at one time. **2,** the sound of concerted explosions. **3,** (*Games*) the striking of a ball before it touches the ground. —*v.t. & i.* send or fly in a volley.

vol′ley·ball″ *n.* a game played by volleying a large ball back and forth over a high net.

vol′plane (vol′plān) *v.i.* glide in an airplane without motor power. —*n.* a glide without motor power.

volt (vōlt) *n.* **1,** a unit of electrical force. **2,** a sideward step.

> **volt**
> ↔ The electrical unit is named for It. physicist Alessandro *Volta.*

volt′age (vōl′tij) *n.* the force of an electric current, expressed in volts.

vol·ta′ic (vol-tā′ik) *adj.* pert. to electric current. —**voltaic cell,** a device for generating electricity.

volte-″face′ (vōlt″-fäs′) *n.* (*Fr.*) a reversal.

volt′me″ter *n.* a device for measuring voltage.

vol′u·ble (vol′yə-bəl) *adj.* speaking fluently; glib. —**vol″u·bil′i·ty,** *n.*

vol′ume (vol′ūm) *n.* **1,** a book, esp. one of a set. **2,** amount or capacity measured in three dimensions; cubic magnitude. **3,** mass or quantity, esp. a large amount. **4,** loudness or softness; roundness of tone.

vol″u·met′ric (vol″yə-met′rik) *adj.* pert. to measurement or analysis by volume.

vo·lu′mi·nous (və-loo′mi-nəs) *adj.* **1,** having many volumes; copious; prolix. **2,** large in bulk. —**vo·lu′mi·nous·ness,** *n.*

vol′un·tar″y (vol′ən-ter″ē) *adj.* **1,** done of one's own accord or free choice. **2,** controlled by the will. **3,** having the power of making free choice. —*n.* a piece of music

interpolated in a church service. —**vol′un·tar″i·ness,** *n.*

vol″un·teer′ (vol″ən-tir′) *n. & adj.* one who enters into any service of his own free will. —*v.i.* offer or undertake to do something. —*v.t.* offer or state voluntarily.

vo·lup′tu·ar·y (və-lup′choo-er-ē) *n.* a sensualist.

vo·lup′tu·ous (və-lup′choo-əs) *adj.* seeking, affording, or suggestive of pleasure. —**vo·lup′tu·ous·ness,** *n.*

vo·lute′ (və-loot′) *n. & adj.* a spiral or whorled formation.

vom′it *v.i.* **1,** eject the contents of the stomach through the mouth; throw up. **2,** be emitted; come out with force or violence. —*v.t.* throw up; emit. —*n.* the act of vomiting; what is thrown up.

vom′i·to″ry (vom′i-tôr″-ē) *n.* **1,** an emetic. **2,** a doorway for entrance and exit.

voo′doo *n. & adj.* **1,** a form of witchcraft or conjuration. **2,** a fetish of voodoo worship. —**voo′doo·ism,** *n.*

vo·ra′cious (vō-rā′shəs) *adj.* greedily devouring; ravenous. —**vo·ra′cious·ness, vo·rac′i·ty** (vō-ras′ə-tē) *n.*

vor′tex (vôr′teks) *n.* **1,** a whirling motion or mass; a whirlpool or eddy. **2,** destructive force that draws one in. —**vor′ti·cal** (-tə-kəl) *adj.*

vo′ta·ry (vō′tə-rē) *n. & adj.* **1,** one bound by a vow, as a monk or nun. **2,** a devotee.

vote (vōt) *n.* **1,** a formal expression of choice. **2,** the right to choose or elect; franchise; suffrage. **3,** votes collectively; a decision made by voting. **4,** a ballot. —*v.i.* indicate a choice. —*v.t.* (often with *in*) enact, establish, grant, declare, etc., by voting. —**vot′er,** *n.*

vo′tive (vō′tiv) *adj.* **1,** in accordance with a vow. **2,** optional, not prescribed. —**vo′tive·ness,** *n.*

vouch (vowch) *v.t.* assert; attest. —*v.i.* (with *for*) attest or warrant to be true, reliable, etc.

vouch′er (-ər) *n.* a receipt or authorization for an expenditure.

vouch″safe′ *v.t.* bestow or grant condescendingly.

vow *n.* a solemn promise or pledge. —*v.t.* promise solemnly; swear. —**take vows,** enter a religious order.

vow′el (vow′əl) *n. & adj.* **1,** a speech sound uttered without friction and with more or less open mouth. **2,** a letter standing for such a sound: in English, *a, e, i, o, u,* sometimes *y.*

vox′ po′pu·li (voks′ pop′yə-lī) (*Lat.*) the voice of the people; public opinion.

voy′age (voi′ij) *n.* a journey to a distant place, esp. by water. —*v.i. & t.* travel (to). —**voy′ag·er,** *n.*

vo·ya·geur′ (vwä-yä-zhĕr′) *n.* [*pl.* -**geurs′** (-zhĕr′)] (*Fr.*) **1,** in Canada, one of those employed by fur companies to maintain communication and transportation with distant stations. **2,** traveler.

voy·eur′ (vwä-yẽr′) *n.* (*Fr.*) a person who enjoys observing sexual acts or objects.

vul′can·ite″ (vul′kən-īt″) *n.* hard rubber, used for making combs, etc. ❑ *volcano*

vul′can·ize″ (vul′kə-nīz″) *v.t.* **1,** treat (rubber) with sulfur and heat. **2,** patch (as a tire) with rubber fused by heat. —**vul″-can·i·za′tion,** *n.* ❑ *volcano*

vul′gar (vul′gər) *adj.* **1,** ignorant of or deficient in good taste; coarse; unrefined. **2,** plebeian. **3,** ordinary; common. —**vul′-gar·ness,** *n.*

vul·gar′i·an (vul-gãr′ē-ən) *n.* a vulgar person.

vul′gar·ism (vul′gə-riz-əm) *n.* a word or expression not in good usage.

vul·gar′i·ty (vul-gãr′ə-tė) *n.* **1,** the state of being vulgar. **2,** something vulgar.

Vul′gate (vul′gāt) *n.* a Latin version of the Bible, the authorized version of the Rom. Cath. Church. —*adj.* (*l.c.*) common; in popular use.

vul′ner·a·ble (vul′nər-ə-bəl) *adj.* **1,** susceptible of being wounded, assaulted, or conquered. **2,** open to reproof. **3,** not resistant to evil influence. —**vul″ner·a·bil′i·ty,** *n.*

vul′pine (vul′pīn) *adj.* pert. to a fox; foxlike.

vul′ture (vul′chər) *n.* **1,** a large carrion-eating bird. **2,** a rapacious or ruthless person. —**vul′tur·ine** (-rīn), **vul′tur·ous,** *adj.*

vul′va (vul′və) *n.* the external parts of the female genital organs.

W

W, w (dub′əl-yû) the 23rd letter of the English alphabet.

wab′ble (wob′əl) *v.i.* wobble.

WAC (wak) *n.* a member of the U.S. Women's Army Corps.

wack′o (wak′ō) *adj. & n.* (*Slang*) crazy.

wack′y (wak′ė) *adj.* (*Slang*) **1,** slightly demented. **2,** odd. —**wack,** *n.* an eccentric person. —**wack′i·ness,** *n.*

wad (wod) *n.* **1,** a small mass of soft mate-rial; a packing or filling. **2,** (*Slang*) a roll of money. —*v.t.* [**wad′ded, -ding**] form into or pack with a wad.

wad′ding (wod′ing) *n.* material for stuffing; wads collectively.

wad′dle (wod′əl) *v.i.* rock from side to side in walking. —*n.* a rocking gait. —**wad′dler** (-dlər) *n.*

wad′dy (wäd′ė) *n.* **1,** a native war club. **2,** a walking stick.

wade (wād) *v.i.* **1,** walk through a substance that impedes, as water, sand, etc. **2,** make progress against obstacles. **3,** (with *in*) begin vigorously. —*v.t.* pass or cross by wading.

wad′er (wād′ər) *n.* **1,** one who wades. **2,** a long-legged bird. **3,** (*pl.*) high boots.

wa′di (wä′dė) *n.* in No. Afr., a river channel, usually dry.

WAF *n.* a member of Women in the Air Force.

wa′fer (wā′fər) *n.* **1,** a thin, usu. sweetened, delicate cake. **2,** any similar disk, as a communion wafer. —**wa′fer·y,** *adj.*

waf′fle (wof′əl) *n.* a flat pancake baked in a mold. —*v.i.* (*Informal*) speak or write in a weighty style, but communicate little; equivocate. —**waffle iron,** a griddle with a hinged cover, both having indented surfaces, for baking waffles.

waft (wȧft) *v.t.* bear or convey through, or as through, a buoyant medium, as water or air. —*n.* something wafted; a gust.

wag *v.i. & t.* [**wagged, wag′ging**] move or cause to move from side to side. —*n.* **1,** a shake; an oscillation. **2,** one who jokes; a wit. —**wag the tongue,** (*Informal*) talk.

wage (wāj) *v.t.* engage in; carry on, as a war. —*n.* rate of payment for work; (*pl.*) recompense; pay.

wa′ger (wā′jər) *n.* a bet. —*v.t. & i.* bet.

wag′ger·y (wag′ə-rė) *n.* **1,** jocularity; waggishness. **2,** a joke.

wag′gish (wag′ish) *adj.* jocular. —**wag′-gish·ness,** *n.*

wag′gle (wag′əl) *v.t. & i.* wag.

wag′on (wag′ən) *n.* **1,** a wheeled vehicle, esp. a four-wheeled freight vehicle. **2,** a railroad freight car. Also, (*Brit.*) **wag′gon.** —**wag′on·er,** *n.* —**on the wagon,** abstaining from liquor.

wag″on·ette′ (wag″ə-net′) *n.* a four-wheeled pleasure vehicle with two lengthwise seats facing each other, and a cross seat in front.

wag′tail″ *n.* any of several small birds with a wagging tail.

wa'hoo (wa'hoo) *n.* **1,** any of several trees or shrubs. **2,** a food fish.

waif (wāf) *n.* **1,** a homeless person, esp. a child. **2,** a stray animal or thing.

wail (wāl) *v.i. & t.* express sorrow by a mournful sound; lament. —*n.* a plaintive cry or sound. —**wail'ful,** *adj.*

wain'scot (wān'skət) *n.* a wooden lining, usually paneled, of the walls of a room. —**wain'scot"ing,** *n.*

wain'wright" (wān'rīt") *n.* a wagon maker.

waist (wāst) *n.* **1,** the part of the human body between the ribs and the hips. **2,** a middle part. **3,** an undergarment. **4,** a bodice; a blouse.

waist'coat" (wāst'kōt; (*Brit.*) wes'kət) *n.* a man's vest.

waist'line" *n.* the body between ribs and hips.

wait (wāt) *v.i.* **1,** remain, expecting something. **2,** (with *on*) attend as a servant. **3,** (*Archaic*) call (upon); visit. —*n.* a stay; a delay.

wait'er (-ər), **wait'ress** *n.* **1,** a server at the table. **2,** a tray. Also, **wait'per"son, wait'ron,** *n.*

waive (wāv) *v.t.* relinquish; forgo; defer for the present.

> **waive, wave**
> ☞ These homonyms are unrelated. To *waive* is to relinquish; to *wave* is to flutter.

waiv'er (wā'vər) *n.* (*Law*) the intentional relinquishment of a right or claim.

wake (wāk) *v.i.* [*pret.* **waked** or **woke** (wōk)] **1,** stop sleeping; be unable to sleep. **2,** become active. —*v.t.* **1,** rouse from sleep. **2,** arouse; reanimate. —*n.* **1,** an all-night watch over a corpse; a vigil. **2,** the track left by a boat in the water. —**wake-'up'** call, a call to wake a person up; hence, a warning; reminder to stay alert.

wake'ful (-fəl) *adj.* unable to sleep. —**wake'ful·ness,** *n.*

wak'en (wā'kən) *v.t.* wake.

wake-'rob"in *n.* **1,** (*U.S.*) any of several trilliums. **2,** (*Brit.*) a plant of the arum family.

Wal'dorf salad (wâl'dôrf) a salad of diced apples, walnuts, and vegetables mixed with mayonnaise, named for the Waldorf Hotel, New York City.

wale (wāl) *n.* **1,** a streak or stripe produced by a blow; a welt. **2,** a ridge or plank along the edge of a ship. **3,** a ridge in cloth.

walk (wâk) *v.i.* **1,** move by steps with a moderate gait; go or travel on foot. **2,** wander about. **3,** behave in any particular manner. **4,** (*Baseball*) achieve first base on balls. —*v.t.* **1,** move over on foot at a moderate gait. **2,** lead or drive at a moderate speed; carry. **3,** take for a stroll. —*n.* **1,** a stroll; a distance covered by walking. **2,** way of living. **3,** range or sphere of action. **4,** gait; carriage. **5,** a path. **6,** a slow pace or gait. **7,** (*Baseball*) a base on balls. —**walking papers,** (*Slang*) notice of dismissal. —**walking stick,** a cane.

walk'a·bout" *n.* an informal outing in a public place by a celebrity.

walk'a·way" *n.* an easy victory. Also, **walk'o"ver.**

walk'ie-talk'ie (-ē) *n.* (*Slang*) a portable radio receiving and transmitting set.

walk-'in" *adj. & n.* **1,** large enough to walk into, as a closet. **2,** having a direct entrance from the street. **3,** a person who arrives without an appointment. **4,** walkover.

walk-'on" *n.* **1,** a minor, nonspeaking role in a theatrical production. **2,** (*Sports*) a player who has not been scouted or recruited.

walk'out" *n.* (*Informal*) a labor strike.

walk'o"ver *n.* (*Informal*) an easy victory.

walk'up" *n.* (*Informal*) an apartment not served by an elevator.

walk'way" *n.* a pedestrian passage.

wall (wâl) *n.* **1,** a structure of stone, brick, or other materials, serving to enclose, divide, support, or defend. **2,** a solid fence. **3,** any enclosing part or shell. —*v.t.* enclose or seal with, or as with, a wall; fortify.

wal'la·by (wol'ə-bē) *n.* any of the smaller kangaroos of Australia.

wal"la·roo' (wol"ə-roo') *n.* any of several large kangaroos.

wall'board" *n.* fibers, minerals, etc., pressed into thick sheets.

wal'let (wol'it) *n.* **1,** a pocketbook, esp. one in which bank notes, papers, etc. lie flat. **2,** a bag or kit.

wall'eye" *n.* **1,** an eye in which the iris is light-colored. **2,** strabismus. **3,** a large staring eye. **4,** any of various fishes with large staring eyes. —**wall'eyed",** *adj.*

wall'flow"er *n.* **1,** a Europ. perennial plant. **2,** (*Informal*) a person unable to attract a partner at a dance.

wal'lop (wol'əp) *v.t.* **1,** beat soundly. **2,** defeat conclusively. —*n.* a heavy blow.

wal'low (wol'ō) *v.i.* **1,** roll the body in sand, mire, etc. **2,** dwell with satisfaction in. —*n.* **1,** the act of wallowing. **2,** a place where animals, as hogs, wallow.

wall′pa″per *n.* paper for covering the walls of a room. —*v.t.* cover with wallpaper.

Wall Street 1, a street in New York City, the financial center of the U.S. **2,** the financial interests of the U.S. collectively.

wal′nut (wâl′nut) *n.* **1,** any of various trees bearing edible, hard-shelled nuts; the wood or nut of such a tree. **2,** a shade of brown.

wal′rus (wol′rəs) *n.* a large, carnivorous Arctic sea mammal related to the seal. —**walrus mustache,** a mustache with the ends hanging down.

waltz (wâlts) *n.* **1,** a dance for couples, in 3/4 time; music for such a dance. **2,** (*Slang*) easy or effortless progress. —*v.t. & i.* dance (a waltz).

wam′pum (wom′pəm) *n.* **1,** small shell beads used for money by No. Amer. Indians. **2,** (*Slang*) money.

wan (won) *adj.* [**wan′ner, -nest**] of a sickly hue; pale; colorless. —**wan′ness,** *n.*

wand (wond) *n.* a slender stick; a rod, esp. one used by a conjurer.

wan′der (won′dər) *v.i.* **1,** roam; ramble; stroll. **2,** go astray; err. **3,** be delirious. —*v.t.* travel aimlessly about. —**wan′-der·er,** *n.* —**Wandering Jew, 1,** a legendary character who insulted Christ and was condemned to wander on the earth until Christ's return. **2,** (*l.c.*) any of several trailing plants.

wan′der·lust″ *n.* restless desire to roam.

wane (wān) *v.i.* decrease, as in size; decline. —*n.* decreasing.

wan′gle (wang′gəl) *v.i. & t.* (*Informal*) contrive; accomplish or obtain by shrewdness.

Wan′kel engine (wäng′kəl) an internal combustion engine in which pistons are replaced by a single rotor, named for German engineer Felix Wankel.

wan′na·be″ (won′ə-bē″) *n.* (*Slang*) a dreamer; wishful-thinker.

want (wont) *v.t.* **1,** feel a desire for. **2,** be without; lack. **3,** require; need. —*v.i.* be lacking or deficient; be in need. —*n.* **1,** lack or scarcity of what is needed or desired; poverty. **2,** a desire. —**want′ing,** *adj.* lacking; needed. —**want ad,** (*Informal*) a short advertisement for something desired.

wan′ton (won′tən) *adj.* **1,** unrestrained; wild; reckless. **2,** heartless; malicious. **3,** dissolute. —*n.* an unrestrained or disso-lute person. —*v.i.* revel. —*v.t.* squander. —**wan′ton·ness,** *n.*

wap′i·ti (wop′ə-tē) *n.* the No. Amer. stag or elk.

war (wôr) *n.* **1,** armed conflict among nations; such conflict between parties in the same state (*civil war*). **2,** any strife or conflict. **3,** the profession of arms. —*v.i.* [**warred, war′ring**] carry on a war. —**at war,** engaged in warfare; warring. —**war dance, war paint, war whoop,** respectively, a dance, a facial paint worn, or a cry, used by primitive peoples to arouse warlike emotions or frighten an enemy. —**war game,** a military training exercise. —**war horse, 1,** a horse trained for battle; hence, an experienced campaigner of any sort. **2,** (*Informal*) a work of art which has become hackneyed through constant repetition.

war′ble (wôr′bəl) *v.i. & t.* **1,** carol or sing. **2,** sound vibratingly; quaver. —*n.* a song, esp. of a bird. —**war′bler,** *n.* any of various songbirds.

ward (wôrd) *v.t.* (with *off*) fend off; turn aside; repel. —*n.* **1,** the act of keeping guard. **2,** one under guardianship, esp. a minor. **3,** a political division of a city. **4,** one of the sections of a hospital. **5,** a curved ridge of metal inside a lock; a notch on a key that fits it. —**ward heeler,** (*Informal*) a minor political worker.

-ward (wərd) *suf.* forming adjectives and adverbs: in the direction of. Also, **-wards** (wərdz) *suf.* forming adverbs.

ward′en (wôr′dən) *n.* **1,** a guard or guardian. **2,** the chief officer of a prison. **3,** the title of various chief officers. **4,** a kind of pear.

ward′er (wôr′dər) *n.* a keeper; a guard.

ward′robe″ *n.* **1,** a cabinet for clothes. **2,** one's supply of clothing.

ward′room″ *n.* the quarters of officers, except the captain, on a war vessel.

ward′ship″ *n.* custody.

ware (wâr) *n.* **1,** (usually *pl.*) articles of merchandise. **2,** a term used in compounds, denoting articles, as *chinaware*.

ware′house″ *n.* a place for storage. —**warehouse club,** a club for buying goods at low prices.

war′fare″ *n.* the waging of war.

war′head″ *n.* a compartment containing an explosive charge, at the forward part of a torpedo or other missile.

war′like″ *adj.* disposed to make war.

war′lock″ *n.* (*Archaic*) one in league with the devil; a sorcerer or wizard.

---

war′lord″ *n.* a military commander exercising civil authority.

warm (wôrm) *adj.* **1,** having a moderate degree of heat; communicating or causing heat. **2,** having the sensation of heat. **3,** hearty; earnest; affectionate; intimate. **4,** new; fresh. **5,** close, in a guessing game. —*v.t. & i.* make or become warm. —**warm′ness,** *n.* —**warm up, 1,** practice before a contest, performance, etc. **2,** reheat.

warm′blood″ed (-blûd″id) *adj.* **1,** denoting animals, esp. mammals, with warm blood. **2,** ardent; impulsive. —**warm′blood″ed·ness,** *n.*

warm′heart″ed *adj.* kindly; generous; sympathetic. —**warm′heart″ed·ness,** *n.*

war′mong″er (-mong″gər) *n.* one who incites to warfare.

warmth (wôrmth) *n.* warmness; ardor.

warn (wôrn) *v.t.* **1,** put on guard; caution. **2,** advise; notify.

warn′ing *n.* **1,** a caution; admonition. **2,** (*Brit.*) notice of dismissal or resignation from a job. —*adj.* that which warns.

warp (wôrp) *v.t.* **1,** turn or twist out of shape; distort; pervert. **2,** pull (a ship) with a rope. **3,** twist (the wings of an airplane) to maintain balance. **4,** time warp. —*v.i.* **1,** be twisted out of proper shape. **2,** swerve. —*v.t.* haul a ship. —*n.* **1,** a twist; distortion. **2,** the lengthwise threads on a loom. —**warp′age,** *n.*

war′path″ *n.* among Native Americans, a warring campaign. —**on the warpath,** bellicose; wrathful.

war′plane″ *n.* a plane designed for fighting.

war′rant (wor′ənt) *n.* **1,** that which attests or proves; a guarantee. **2,** sanction; justification. **3,** (*Law*) a writ authorizing an arrest, search, or seizure. —*v.t.* **1,** guarantee; indemnify. **2,** authorize; justify. **3,** affirm. —**war′ran·tor,** *n.* —**warrant officer,** an Army or Navy officer below commissioned but above noncommissioned rank.

war′ran·ty (wor′ən-tē) *n.* a guarantee; assurance.

war′ren (wor′ən) *n.* **1,** a shelter or pen for rabbits or game. **2,** any crowded section.

war′rior (wôr′yər) *n.* a fighting man.

war′ship″ *n.* a ship designed for fighting.

wart (wôrt) *n.* a small, hard growth on the skin. —**wart′y,** *adj.*

wart′hog″ *n.* a large, ugly Afr. wild swine.

war′y (wār′ē) *adj.* cautious of danger; alert. —**war′i·ness,** *n.*

was (wuz) *v.* pret. of *be.* —**was′n′t** (wuz′ənt) contraction of *was not.*

wash (wosh) *v.t.* **1,** cleanse in or with a liquid, esp. water. **2,** flow over or against; wet. **3,** (with *away*) remove; absolve. **4,** sweep. **5,** process by immersing in a liquid. —*v.i.* **1,** cleanse oneself, etc., in or with water. **2,** stand cleansing by water without injury. **3,** flow. **4,** (*Informal*) hold up under scrutiny, as a theory. —*n.* **1,** a cleansing by water; articles to be cleansed. **2,** the flow, sweep, or sound of a body of water. **3,** the wake of a vessel. **4,** waste articles or liquid; alluvia. **5,** a liquid for washing. **6,** a body of water. —**wash′a·ble,** *adj.* that can safely be washed in water. —**washed out, 1,** faded. **2,** fatigued. **3,** expelled after failure. —**washed up,** (*Informal*) spent; finished. —**wash out,** (*Slang*) fail.

wash′ba″sin *n.* a basin used for washing clothes, dishes, etc.

wash′board″ *n.* a corrugated board for scrubbing clothes.

wash′bowl″ *n.* a basin.

wash′cloth″ *n.* a cloth for use in washing oneself. Also, **wash′rag″.**

wash′er (-ər) *n.* **1,** one who or that which washes; a washing machine. **2,** a small metal gasket.

wash′er·man (-mən) [*pl.* **-men**], **wash′er·wom″an** *n.* a launderer.

wash′ing *n.* clothes to be washed. —**washing machine,** a machine for washing clothes. —**washing soda,** sodium bicarbonate.

wash′out″ *n.* **1,** a place where soil or a foundation has been eroded. **2,** (*Slang*) a failure.

wash′rag″ *n.* washcloth.

wash′room″ *n.* a lavatory (def. 1). ❑ *toilet*

wash′stand″ *n.* a cabinet or fixture for holding a washbowl.

wash′tub″ *n.* a tub for washing clothes.

wash′wom″an *n.* [*pl.* **-wom″en**] a washerwoman.

wash′y (wosh′ē) *adj.* **1,** watery; moist. **2,** weak; diluted. **3,** insubstantial; feeble. —**wash′i·ness,** *n.*

WASP (wosp) *abbr.* white Anglo-Saxon Protestant.

wasp (wosp) *n.* an insect related to the bee.

wasp′ish *adj.* **1,** peevish. **2,** slenderwaisted. —**wasp′ish·ness,** *n.*

was′sail (wos′əl) *n.* **1,** a toast. **2,** a drink of spiced ale. **3,** a drinking party. —*v.i.* carouse.

Was'ser·mann test (wäs'ər-mən) a test for syphilis, named for German physician August von Wassermann.

waste (wāst) *adj.* **1,** desolate; uninhabited; untilled; unproductive. **2,** rejected as unfit for use; unused. —*v.t.* **1,** devastate; ruin. **2,** consume or wear away the strength and substance of. **3,** squander; throw away. **4,** (*Slang*) kill. —*v.i.* decay or diminish in strength, substance, or value; wear or pine away. —*n.* **1,** a desolate place or region. **2,** gradual loss or decay. **3,** broken, spoiled, useless, or superfluous material; refuse. **4,** useless expenditure. **5,** a drain pipe. —**wast'age,** *n.*

waste'bas"ket *n.* a receptacle for unwanted papers.

waste'ful (-fəl) *adj.* needlessly spending or spent. —**waste'ful·ness,** *n.*

waste'land" *n.* **1,** a barren uncultivated region. **2,** a place without artistic, intellectual, etc. resources.

wast'rel (wās'trəl) *n.* a spendthrift; a profligate.

watch (woch) *v.i.* **1,** be attentive, circumspect, or closely observant. **2,** keep vigil. **3,** keep guard. **4,** wait. —*v.t.* **1,** look at attentively. **2,** take care of; tend; guard. —*n.* **1,** a keeping awake for the purpose of attending, guarding, or preserving; vigil. **2,** close, constant observation; supervision. **3,** a force on duty, esp. for guarding; a sentinel. **4,** a period of duty; on a ship, four hours. **5,** a timepiece carried in the pocket or worn on the wrist.

watch'band" *n.* a strap or bracelet of leather, metal, etc., used to hold a wristwatch.

watch'dog" *n.* **1,** a dog trained to bark a warning. **2,** a guardian.

watch'ful (-fəl) *adj.* alert. —**watch'-ful·ness,** *n.*

watch'man (-mən) *n.* [*pl.* **-men**] a guard.

watch'night" *n.* a prayer service held on New Year's Eve.

watch'tow"er *n.* a tower in which to post a lookout.

watch'word" *n.* **1,** a secret password. **2,** a slogan; a rallying cry.

wa'ter (wot'ər, wâ'-) *n.* **1,** the transparent, odorless, tasteless fluid, H_2O, that falls in rain. **2,** a body of water; (*pl.*) a flood. **3,** any liquid secretion of an animal body. **4,** transparency denoting the fine properties of a precious stone. —*v.t.* **1,** moisten; irrigate. **2,** supply with water. **3,** dilute; assign unjustified value to (a stock). **4,** produce a gleaming, wavy pattern upon (a fabric). —*v.i.* **1,** give off or fill up with liquid. **2,** get or take in water. —**of**

the first water, of the finest quality. —**water ballet,** choreographed movements performed in the water. —**water biscuit,** a kind of cracker. —**water buffalo,** a carabao. —**water cannon,** a hose used to shoot water at high pressure, as for dispersing demonstrators. —**water chestnut,** a plant or its edible nutlike fruit. —**water closet, 1,** a device, with a seat, for disposing of excrement. **2,** a toilet room. ❑ *toilet* —**water cooler,** a device for cooling and dispensing drinking water. —**water gap,** a cleft in a mountain ridge through which a stream flows. —**water ice,** a frozen dessert like ice cream, made without milk. —**watering hole, 1,** a place where animals drink. **2,** (*Informal*) a place, as a bar, where one can get something to drink. —**watering place,** a spa. —**watering pot,** a can with a perforated spout, for spraying on flowers. —**water lily,** a plant with floating leaves and showy flowers, that grows in water. —**water moccasin, 1,** a venomous snake of the So. U.S. **2,** any of several harmless snakes. —**water nymph,** a naiad. —**water pipe,** a hookah. —**water polo,** a ball game played by swimmers. —**water power,** power derived from a flow or fall of water. —**water rat,** an aquatic rodent, as the muskrat. —**water table,** the level below which the soil is saturated with water. —**water tower, 1,** a tower used as a reservoir for water. **2,** a fire-fighting apparatus. —**water wheel,** a wheel turned by water power. —**water wings,** inflated bags used to support a person in water.

wa'ter·bed" *n.* a watertight sac filled with heated water, used as a mattress.

wa'ter·col"or, *n.* **1,** a paint soluble in water. **2,** a picture painted with such paint.

wa'ter·course" *n.* a stream or river, or its bed.

wa'ter·craft" *n.* **1,** any boat or ship. **2,** skill in sailing or in aquatic sports.

wa'ter·cress" *n.* a salad herb.

wa'ter·fall" *n.* a cascade; a cataract.

wa'ter·front" *n.* docks, etc., at the water's edge.

Wa'ter·gate" *n.* a scandal in government, usu. involving misuse of power and subsequent coverup.

Watergate
↔ From the Watergate apartment-office complex in Washington, DC, in which the Democratic Party national headquarters, scene of a politically-motivated break-in in 1972, was located.

wa'ter·glass" *n.* a substance that forms a protective coating.

wa′ter·line″ *n.* the line at which a floating body is out of the water.

wa′ter·logged″ (-lâgd″) *adj.* saturated so as to sink in water.

Wa′ter·loo *n.* a final defeat, from the village in Belgium where Napoleon I was defeated.

wa′ter·mark″ *n.* a design impressed in paper during its manufacture.

wa′ter·mel″on *n.* a large edible melon.

wa′ter·pick″ *n.* a device for cleaning teeth with a stream of water under pressure.

wa′ter·proof″ *adj.* impervious or resistant to water.

wa′ter·re·pel′lent *adj.* treated to repel water, as cloth, but not entirely waterproof.

wa′ter·re·sis′tant *adj.* resistant to penetration by water, but not entirely waterproof.

wa′ter·shed″ *n.* **1,** a ridge off which water flows or drains. **2,** the area drained by a river. **3,** a dividing or transitional point.

wa′ter·side″ *n.* a shore or bank.

wa′ter·ski″ *v.i.* ski on water while being pulled by a motorboat.

wa′ter·spout″ *n.* a gyrating column of rising moisture, caused by a whirlwind at sea.

wa′ter·tight″ *adj.* **1,** impenetrable by water. **2,** that which cannot be evaded or controverted.

wa′ter·way″ *n.* a course navigable by water.

wa′ter·works″ *n.* a system for supplying water to a city.

wa′ter·y (-ē) *adj.* **1,** pert. to or consisting of water; wet; dripping. **2,** thin, as a liquid. **—wa′ter·i·ness,** *n.*

watt (wot) *n.* a unit of electrical activity or power, named for 19th-c. Scottish inventor James Watt. **—watt′age,** *n.*

wat′tle (wot′əl) *n.* **1,** a framework of poles. **2,** a rod; a twig. **3,** a fleshy lobe hanging from the throat of a bird or the mouth of a fish. **—***v.t.* interweave.

wave (wāv) *v.i.* **1,** move up and down or to and fro; undulate; flutter. **2,** have a curved form or direction. **3,** give a signal by waving the hands. **—***v.t.* **1,** move to and fro; brandish. **2,** shape in undulations or curves. **—***n.* **1,** a ridge in the surface of a liquid. **2,** (*pl.*) the sea. **3,** an influx of anything. **4,** a gesture or signal made by moving the hand. **5,** a curl in the hair. **6,** (*cap.*) a woman serving in the U.S. Navy. **—wave band,** a range of frequencies assigned to a particular form of broadcasting, as television, AM radio, etc. ❑ *waive*

wave′length″ **1,** the distance between two particles in the same phase of a wave: now applied chiefly to the band assigned to a radio or television transmitting station. **—on the same wavelength,** in rapport.

wave′let *n.* a ripple.

wa′ver (wā′vər) *v.i.* **1,** sway; falter. **2,** be irresolute; vacillate. **—***n.* a wavering motion.

wav′y (wāv′ē) *adj.* **1,** abounding in waves. **2,** curly. **—wav′i·ness,** *n.*

wax (waks) *v.i.* increase in size; grow, specif. of the moon. **—***v.t.* put wax on. **—***n.* a thick, sticky substance secreted by bees; any similar oily substance. **—wax bean,** a yellow string bean. **—wax paper,** paper coated with paraffin.

wax′en (wak′sən) *adj.* **1,** yellowish, as wax. **2,** of the consistency of wax.

wax′wing″ *n.* a passerine bird.

wax′work″ *n.* **1,** a figure, or figures, modeled in wax. **2,** (*pl.*) an exhibit of such figures.

wax′y (-ē) *adj.* like wax. **—wax′i·ness,** *n.*

way (wā) *n.* **1,** a course leading from one place to another; a road, passage, route, etc. **2,** room for passage. **3,** a journey. **4,** distance. **5,** direction. **6,** a respect; a particular. **7,** condition or state. **8,** a plan; mode; method. **9,** progress; headway. **10,** (*pl.*) the timbers on which a ship is built and launched. **—give way, 1,** make way. **2,** break down. **—out of the way,** unusual; extraordinary. **—way station,** a minor railroad station, or similar station for other mode of travel.

way′bill″ *n.* a descriptive list of goods sent by a common carrier.

way′far″er *n.* a traveler, esp. on foot.

way′lay″ *v.t.* ambush.

way-′out″ *adj.* (*Slang*) **1,** unusual; strange. **2,** excellent.

-ways (wāz) *suf.* indicating manner, direction, or position.

way′side″ *n.* the side of a road; a secluded place.

way′ward″ (-wərd) *adj.* **1,** rebellious; perverse. **2,** irregular; accidental. **—way′-ward·ness,** *n.*

we (wē) *pron. pl.* of *I* (*poss.* **our, ours;** *obj.* **us**) the first person, nominative, *pl.*; used as sing. by monarchs and editors (the editorial *we*).

weak (wēk) *adj.* **1,** lacking physical strength or endurance. **2,** lacking moral or mental strength or firmness. **3,** inadequate or unsatisfactory; faulty. **4,** (*Com.*) tending downward in price. —**weak'ly,** *adj. & adv.* —**weak force,** (*Physics*) a type of force between elementary particles. —**weak sister,** (*Derog.*) coward.

weak'en (-ən) *v.t. & i.* make or become weaker.

weak'fish" *n.* an edible sea fish.

weak-'kneed" *adj.* irresolute; easily controlled.

weak'ling *n.* a weak person.

weak'ness *n.* **1,** state of being weak. **2,** a weak point; fault or defect. **3,** (*Informal*) a fondness; an uncontrollable desire.

wealth (welth) *n.* **1,** valuable and large material possessions; riches. **2,** profusion; abundance. **3,** all property. —**wealth'i-ness,** *n.* —**wealth'y,** *adj.*

wean (wēn) *v.t.* **1,** accustom (a child or young animal) to food other than mother's milk. **2,** alienate.

weap'on (wep'ən) *n.* any instrument used in fighting. —**weap'on-ry,** *n.*

wear (wâr) *v.t.* [**wore** (wôr), **worn** (wôrn), **wear'ing**] **1,** carry or bear on the body, as clothing. **2,** consume or deteriorate by friction or frequent use. **3,** make weary. **4,** bear; show. —*v.i.* **1,** last or hold out. **2,** waste; diminish. —*n.* **1,** use; deterioration. **2,** garments. —**wear'a-ble,** *adj.* —**wear'-ing,** *adj.* tiring. —**wear and tear,** loss by waste, deterioration, etc., sustained in ordinary use.

wea'ry (wir'ē) *adj.* **1,** exhausted either physically or mentally; tired. **2,** discontented. **3,** causing fatigue. —*v.t. & i.* tire. —**wea'ri-ness,** *n.* —**wea'ri-some,** *adj.* tiresome.

wea'sel (wē'zəl) *n.* a small carnivorous mammal. —**weasel words,** evasive language.

weath'er (we*th*'ər) *n.* **1,** the state of the atmosphere in regard to heat, cold, wetness, dryness, humidity, storm, etc. **2,** bad or stormy weather. —*v.t.* **1,** bear up against and survive. **2,** condition by exposure. **3,** (*Naut.*) sail to windward of. —*adj.* (*Naut.*) windward. —**under the weather,** (*Informal*) **1,** ill. **2,** drunk. —**weather strip,** a strip to seal a crack around a window, etc. —**weather vane,** a device that turns with the wind, to show its direction.

weath'er-beat"en *adj.* marked or hardened by exposure.

weath'er-board" *n.* clapboard.

weath'er-bound" *adj.* delayed by bad weather.

weath'er-cock" *n.* a figure of a bird, on top of a weather vane.

weath'er-glass" *n.* an instrument for indicating the state of the atmosphere, as a barometer.

weath'er-ing *n.* the action of the elements on rock, wood, etc.

weath'er-ize" (-īz) *v.t.* to prepare a building for cold weather by adding insulation, etc.

weath'er-man", weath'er-wom"an *n* a person whose job is to forecast the weather. —**Weath'er-men",** *n.pl.* the members of a radical political organization.

weath'er-proof" *adj.* resistant to rain, wind, etc.

weave (wēv) *v.t.* [**wove** (wōv), **wo'ven, weav'ing**] **1,** form by interlacing flexible parts, as threads; produce (a fabric) on a loom. **2,** contrive or construct. —*v.i.* **1,** become interlaced. **2,** wind in and out. —*n.* a pattern produced by weaving.

web *n.* **1,** that which is woven. **2,** a trap, plot, or scheme. **3,** the membrane of skin connecting the toes of a bird or animal, as a duck. —**webbed,** *adj.* —**web'bing,** *n.* —**web'foot"ed,** *adj.*

wed *v.t. & i.* [**wed'ded** or **wed, wed'ding**] take for husband or wife; marry; unite closely.

wed'ding (wed'ing) *n.* an occasion or anniversary of marriage.

wedge (wej) *n.* **1,** a triangular-shaped solid, used to separate, split, or raise objects. **2,** an act that serves to introduce or divide. —*v.t.* **1,** use a wedge on. **2,** compress closely. —*v.i.* force one's way.

wedg'ie (wej'ē) *n.* a woman's shoe giving elevation as with a high heel but with the sole almost flat.

wed'lock" *n.* matrimony.

---

wedlock

↔ From Old English *wedlac*, a pledging of troth. The suffix *-lāc* has nothing to do with *lock*, but is a verbal suffix reinforcing *wed*.

Wednes'day (wenz'dē) *n.* the fourth day of the week.

Wednesday

↔ From *Woden's day*, a Germanic translation of Latin *Mercurii dies*, Mercury's day.

---

wee (wē) *adj.* [**we'er, we'est**] tiny.

weed (wēd) *n.* **1,** a useless or characteristically unwanted plant. **2,** (*Informal*) tobacco. **3,** (*pl.*) a widow's mourning attire. **4,** (*Slang*) marijuana. —*v.t.* free from obnoxious plants. —*v.i.* root up weeds.

---

fat, fāte, fär, fãre, fâll, àsk; met, hē, hêr, maybè; pin, pīne; not, nōte, ôr, tool

—**weed out,** remove weeds or other undesirable elements (from).

weed′y (-ē) *adj.* **1,** like a weed; lanky. **2,** being or like widow's weeds. **3,** abounding in weeds. —**weed′i·ness,** *n.*

week (wĕk) *n.* **1,** a period of seven consecutive days. **2,** the working days of the week. —**week′day″,** *n.* any day but Sunday or sometimes Saturday. —**week′ly,** *adj.* & *adv.* occurring once each week.

week′end″ *n.* the period from the end of the working week through Sunday. —*adj.* of or on a weekend. —*v.i.* spend the weekend. —**week′end″er,** *n.*

ween′ie (wē′nē) *n.* (*Informal*) a frankfurter.

weep (wēp) *v.i.* [*pret.* & *p.p.* **wept**] **1,** shed tears; lament. **2,** drip; give out moisture. **3,** droop. —*v.t.* shed, as tears. —**weep′ing,** *adj.* drooping, as the branches of a tree: as, *weeping willow.* —**weep′y,** *adj.*

wee′vil (wē′vəl) *n.* any of various beetles.

weft *n.* the woof.

weigh (wā) *v.t.* **1,** determine the heaviness of. **2,** consider; ponder. **3,** (*Naut.*) raise or lift up. **4,** (with *down*) burden; oppress. —*v.i.* have weight or influence.

weight (wāt) *n.* **1,** the downward force of a body; heaviness. **2,** mass. **3,** something used on account of its heaviness. **4,** a system of units for expressing the heaviness of bodies. **5,** pressure; care; burden. **6,** importance; influence. —*v.t.* **1,** add to the heaviness of. **2,** adjust the proportions of.

weight′less *adj.* having no weight, esp. as a result of a lack of gravitational pull, as in space. —**weight′less·ness,** *n.*

weight′lift″ing *n.* the act or sport of lifting weights. —**weight′lift″er,** *n.*

weight′y (-ē) *adj.* **1,** momentous; influential. **2,** burdensome. —**weight′i·ness,** *n.*

Wei′ma·ran″er (wī′mə-rän″ər) *n.* German breed of sporting dog, named for the city of Weimar, Germany.

weir (wir) *n.* **1,** a dam. **2,** a fence set in a stream for catching fish.

weird (wird) *adj.* unearthly; uncanny. —**weird′ness,** *n.* —**Weird Sisters,** the Fates.

weird′o (-ō) *n.* (*Slang*) an eccentric person.

welch *v.i.* welsh.

wel′come (wel′kəm) *adj.* gladly received or permitted. —*n.* a kindly, warm greeting; hospitable reception. —*v.t.* receive gladly.

weld *v.t.* unite (pieces of metal); join.

—*n.* a solid union; a welt where union was made.

wel′fare″ (wel′fār″) *n.* **1,** prosperous or healthy condition. **2,** charity. —**welfare mother,** a woman with children who receives government assistance. —**welfare state, 1,** a social system under which the state assumes primary responsibility for the physical, mental, and social well-being of its citizens. **2,** a nation, state, etc. in which the system of the welfare state is adopted.

wel′kin *n.* (*Archaic*) the sky; the firmament.

well (wel) *n.* **1,** an excavation in the ground as a source of water, oil, gas, etc. **2,** a spring. **3,** any source of origin or supply; a fount. **4,** a dangerous depression; a whirlpool. —*v.i.* issue; pour forth. —*adv.* [**bet′ter, best**] **1,** in a good, right, or worthy manner; abundantly. **2,** favorably. **3,** conveniently. —*adj.* in good health. —**as well (as),** also.

well-″ap·point′ed *adj.* furnished with all requisites.

well-″bal′anced *adj.* **1,** properly adjusted or proportioned. **2,** sensible.

well-″be′ing *n.* good health; welfare.

well″born′ *adj.* of gentle or noble birth.

well″bred′ *adj.* having good manners.

well-″de·fined′ *adj.* leaving no room for doubt; clear.

well-″dis·posed′ *adj.* favorable.

well-′done″ *adj.* cooked thoroughly.

well-′fed′ *adj.* prosperous-looking.

well-′fixed″ *adj.* (*Informal*) well-to-do.

well-″found′ed *adj.* based on good reasons or grounds.

well′head″ *n.* a source.

well-″heeled′ *adj.* (*Slang*) wealthy.

well-″in·formed′ *adj.* abreast of current events.

well-″in·ten′tioned *adj.* having laudable motives.

well-′known″ *adj.* **1,** famous. **2,** fully known. **3,** generally acknowledged.

well-′man″nered *adj.* polite; courteous.

well-″mean′ing *adj.* having good intentions. —**well-″meant′,** *adj.*

well-′nigh″ *adv.* very nearly.

well-″off″ *adj.* wealthy or fortunate.

well-″read′ (-red′) *adj.* having read many books; educated.

well-″round′ed *adj.* complete.

well′spring″ *n.* a constant source.

well-′to-do″ *adj.* prosperous; wealthy.

welsh *v.i.* fail to pay a gambling loss. Also, **welch.**

Welsh *adj. & n.* of or pert. to Wales, its people, language, etc. —**Welsh′man,** *n.* —**Welsh corgi** (kôr′gė) a Welsh breed of short-legged dog. —**Welsh rabbit** [or, **rare′bit**] melted cheese served on toast.

welt *n.* **1,** a strip of material, esp. leather, standing out. **2,** a wale.

wel′ter (wel′tər) *v.i.* **1,** wallow (in something). **2,** roll or toss; be tossed. —*n.* **1,** rolling or wallowing motion. **2,** turmoil; ferment.

wel′ter·weight″ (wel′tər-wāt″) *n.* a boxer weighing 136 to 147 lbs.

Welt′schmerz″ (velt′shmerts″) *n.* (*Ger.*) dejection at the state of the world; pessimism.

wen *n.* a small, benign tumor.

wench *n.* **1,** a girl or young woman. **2,** a prostitute. —*v.i.* consort with prostitutes.

wend *v.i.* proceed; go. —*v.t.* direct (one's way or course).

went *v.* pret. of *go.*

wept *v.* pret. & p.p. of *weep.*

were (wėr) *v.* pret. & subjunctive of *be.*

were′wolf″ (wėr′wûlf″) *n.* [*pl.* **-wolves**] in folklore, a human being turned into a wolf. ❏ *vampire*

Wes′ley·an (wez′lė-ən) *n.* a Methodist.

> **Wesleyan**
> ↔ From 18th-c. English theologian John *Wesley.*

west *n.* **1,** the direction lying on the left hand when one faces the north; the point where the sun sets at the equinox. **2,** any place to the west; (*cap.*) Europe and the Americas. —*adj. & adv.* toward the sunset. —**west′er·ly,** *adj.* toward the west. —**west′ward,** *adj.* —**West Point,** the site of the U.S. Military Academy.

west′ern (wes′tərn) *adj.* pert. to the west. —*n.* (*Informal*) a story or motion picture depicting life in the western U.S. or the 19th c. —**west′ern·er,** *n.* —**west′-ern·most″,** *adj.*

wes′tern·ize″ *v.t. & i.* adopt the social, economic, etc. customs of Europe or, esp., America.

wet *adj.* [**wet′ter, -test**] **1,** covered with or permeated by a moist or fluid substance. **2,** rainy. **3,** (*Informal*) opposed to Prohibition. —*n.* **1,** moisture, specif. rain. **2,** (*Informal*) a person, state, etc., opposed to Prohibition. —*v.t. & i.* [**wet′ted, -ting**] drench with water or other fluid; urinate. —**wet′ness,** *n.* —**wet blanket,** (*Slang*) a depressing person. —**wet nurse,** a woman employed to suckle the infant of another.

—**wet suit,** a close-fitting heat-retaining suit worn in cold water.

wet′back″ *n.* a person who enters the U.S. illegally, usually from Mexico, to take a temporary job.

weth′er (weth′ər) *n.* a castrated ram.

whack (hwak) *v.t. & i.* strike a smart, resounding blow. —*n.* **1,** a heavy blow. **2,** (*Informal*) an attempt. —**whacked out,** (*Slang*) crazy; intoxicated. —**whack′ing,** *adj.* (*Slang*) enormous.

whale (hwāl) *n.* **1,** any of an order of marine mammals; the largest known animals. **2,** (*Informal*) anything huge. —*v.i.* pursue the business of whale fishing. —*v.t.* (*Informal*) thrash; castigate. —**whal′er,** *n.* a whaling ship.

whale′back″ *n.* a type of freight steamer.

whale′boat″ *n.* a large rowboat originally used by whale fishermen.

whale′bone″ *n.* baleen; a flexible strip of it, used to stiffen a corset.

whal′ing **1,** the work or business of whale fishing. **2,** a thrashing. —*adj.* (*Informal*) whopping.

wham (hwam) *n.* a powerful blow; its sound. —*v.t. & i.* [**whammed, wham′-ming**] smash (into) with great force and noise.

wham′my (hwam′ė) *n.* (*Slang*) a hex; a magic spell.

whang (hwang) (*Informal*) *n.* a resounding blow; a bang. —*v.t.* strike with a blow or bang.

whang′ee (hwang′ė) *n.* **1,** a Chinese species of bamboo. **2,** walking stick made of the stalk of the plant.

wharf (wôrf) *n.* [*pl.* **wharves** (wôrvz)] a mooring platform for ships; a dock; a pier. —**wharf′age,** *n.*

wharf′in·ger (hwôr′fin-jər) *n.* one who owns or has charge of a wharf.

what (hwot) *pron. sing. & pl.* **1,** which thing or things. **2,** that which. —*adj.* **1,** (*interrogative*) which. **2,** any; whatever. **3,** (*exclamatory*) how extraordinary!; how large! **4,** in part; partly. —*conj.* but that.

what·ev′er *pron.* **1,** anything which; all that. **2,** no matter what. —*adj.* **1,** any or all that. **2,** of any kind.

what′not″ *n.* **1,** a stand to display small ornaments. **2,** anything indiscriminately.

what·so·ev″er *adj. & pron.* of whatever nature or kind.

wheal (hwēl) *n.* **1,** a pimple or small itching swelling on the skin. **2,** a wale.

wheat (hwēt) *n.* any of various cereal plants whose grain is ground into flour and makes bread. —**wheat'en,** *adj.* of wheat. —**wheat germ,** the embryo of the wheat kernel, used as a source of vitamins.

whee'dle (hwē'dəl) *v.t. & i.* cajole; gain by flattery; coax.

wheel (hwēl) *n.* **1,** a circular frame or disk capable of turning on an axis. **2,** a bicycle. **3,** a firework that revolves while burning. **4,** the office of pilot or driver. **5,** a turning maneuver; a circular course. **6,** (*pl.*) machinery. **7,** (*Slang*) an important person. **8,** an instrument of torture. **9,** (*pl.*) (*Slang*) an automobile or other vehicle. —*v.t.* cause to turn; cause to move on or as on wheels. —*v.i.* **1,** turn; rotate. **2,** move on wheels or on a bicycle. —**wheel and deal,** (*Informal*) operate to gain a political or commercial advantage. —**fifth wheel,** something superfluous or useless. —**wheel horse, 1,** the horse at the pivot of a team. **2,** an essential worker. —**wheel housing,** the space reserved from an automobile seat or body to give play to the wheels.

wheel'bar"row *n.* a vehicle for pushing light loads.

wheel'base" *n.* the distance between centers of axles on a vehicle.

wheel'chair" *n.* a conveyance for an invalid.

wheeled *adj.* having (such, or so many) wheels.

wheel'er-deal'er *n.* (*Slang*) a clever operator.

wheel'ie (wē'lē) *n.* a maneuver performed on a two-wheeled vehicle in which the front wheel leaves the ground.

wheel'wright" *n.* a maker of wheels.

wheeze (hwēz) *v.i.* breathe with difficulty and audibly. —*n.* **1,** the sound of such a breath. **2,** a joke. —**wheez'y,** *adj.*

whelk (hwelk) *n.* **1,** an edible, spiral-shelled mollusk. **2,** a wheal.

whelm (hwelm) *v.t.* **1,** engulf; submerge. **2,** overcome; overwhelm. —*v.i.* roll so as to engulf.

whelp (hwelp) *n.* the young of certain animals, as the dog. —*v.i. & t.* bring forth young.

when (hwen) *adv.* **1,** at what or which time. —*conj.* **1,** as soon as. **2,** at which time. —*n.* a time specified.

whence (hwens) *adv.* from that or which place.

when"ev'er *adv. & conj.* at whatever time.

where (hwâr) *adv.* **1,** at or in what place. **2,** to which place? whither? —*conj.* **1,** at,

in, or to the place in which. **2,** whereas. **3,** when. —*n.* place; situation.

where'a·bouts" *n.* location.

where·as' *conj.* this being the case.

where·at' *adv.* at which. —*conj.* whereupon.

where'by" *adv.* for which reason; how.

where'fore" *adv. & conj.* **1,** why? **2,** consequently. —*n.* a reason.

where·from' *conj.* from which; whence.

where·in' *adv.* in which.

where·of' *conj.* of what, which, or whom.

where·to' *adv.* to what place, point, or end. —*conj.* to which or whom.

where·up·on" *adj.* at which juncture.

wher·ev'er *conj.* in, at, or to whatever place. Also, **where"so·ev'er.**

where·with' *adv.* with which.

where'with·al' *n.* the means; money.

wher'ry (hwer'ē) *n.* a light boat.

whet (hwet) *v.t.* [**whet'ted, -ting**] **1,** sharpen. **2,** excite.

wheth'er (hweth'ər) *conj.* **1,** introducing the first of two or more alternatives, the second being introduced by *or.* **2,** introducing a single alternative, the other being implied. ❏ *if*

whet'stone" *n.* a stone for sharpening knives, etc.

whey (hwā) *n.* the watery part of milk. —**whey'ey** (hwā'ē) *adj.*

which (hwich) *pron.* **1,** (*interrogative*) what one? (of several). **2,** (*relative*) the one that. **3,** (*relative*) that (with additional information). —*adj.* indicating one of a number of known or specified things.

which·ev'er *pron. & adj.* any one. Also, **which"so·ev'er.**

whid'ah bird (hwi'də) an Afr. weaver bird.

whiff (hwif) *n.* a puff; a slight current or gust of air, smoke, etc. —*v.i. & t.* blow; puff.

whif'fet (whif'ət) *n.* **1,** (*Informal*) an insignificant person. **2,** a snappish little dog.

whif'fle (hwif'əl) *v.i.* **1,** blow in gusts; veer, as the wind. **2,** be fickle or unsteady. —*v.t.* disperse; scatter.

Wif'fle Ball" (*T.N.*) **1,** a lightweight, perforated ball shaped like a baseball, golfball, etc., used for practice. **2,** a game played with a Wiffle Ball.

whif'fle·tree" *n.* whippletree.

Whig (hwig) *n.* (*Hist.*) a member of: **1,** an English political party, later known as Liberals. **2,** a 19th-c. U.S. political party.

Whig
↔ From the *Whiggamores*, 17th-c. Scottish political rebels, perhaps from Scots *whig*, egg on, + *more*, horse.

while (hwīl) *n.* a space of time, esp. a short time. —*conj.* [also, **whilst**] **1,** during or in the time that; as long as. **2,** though; whereas. —*v.t.* (with *away*) cause (time) to pass. ☐ *although*

whi'lom (hwī'ləm) *adj.* former. —*adv.* (*Archaic*) formerly; at times.

whim (hwim) *n.* a fancy; a capricious desire.

whim'per (hwim'pər) *v.i.* & *t.* cry with a low, whining voice; utter plaintively. —*n.* a low, peevish cry.

whim'si·cal (hwim'zi-kəl) *adj.* quaintly humorous; odd. —**whim"si·cal'i·ty, whim'si·cal·ness,** *n.*

whim'sy (hwim'zē) *n.* a fanciful notion.

whine (hwīn) *v.i.* & *t.* **1,** utter a plaintive, prolonged nasal sound. **2,** complain in a feeble way. —*n.* a whining utterance or tone.

whin'ny (hwin'ē) *n.* the cry of a horse; a low or gentle neigh. —*v.i.* utter this sound.

whip (hwip) *v.t.* [**whipped, whip'ping**] **1,** punish with a scourge, rod, etc.; flog; beat. **2,** move or pull with a sudden quick motion; jerk; snatch. **3,** overlay or wrap with cord. **4,** bring or keep together. **5,** sew with an over-and-over stitch. **6,** beat into a froth. **7,** defeat thoroughly. —*v.i.* **1,** move suddenly and nimbly; thrash around. **2,** in fishing, cast. —*n.* **1,** an instrument for lashing; a scourge. **2,** a driver. **3,** a swishing or whipping motion. **4,** a conveyance for hoisting. **5,** a preparation of beaten eggs, cream, etc. **6,** a party disciplinarian in a legislature. —**whip hand,** control. —**whipping boy,** a scapegoat.

whip'cord" *n.* a ribbed fabric.

whip'lash" *n.* **1,** the flexible striking end of a whip. **2,** a twisting of the spine, as from an accident.

whip'per·snap"per (hwip'ər-snap"ər) *n.* an insignificant, but presumptuous, person, esp. male.

whip'pet (hwip'it) *n.* **1,** a kind of dog, a cross between a greyhound and a terrier. **2,** something slight and speedy; a small, fast tank.

whip'ple·tree" (hwip'əl-trē") *n.* a crossbar at the front of a horse-drawn vehicle to which the harness is attached.

whip'poor·will" (hwip'ər-wil") *n.* an Amer. nocturnal bird; its cry.

whip'saw" *n.* a narrow saw in a frame. —*v.t.* (*Slang*) defeat doubly.

whir (hwēr) *v.i.* [**whirred, whir'ring**] fly, dart, revolve, or move quickly with a buzzing sound. —*n.* a buzzing sound.

whirl (hwērl) *v.t.* **1,** cause to revolve rapidly; rotate. **2,** carry swiftly away. —*v.i.* **1,** revolve swiftly. **2,** reel. —*n.* **1,** a spinning movement or sensation. **2,** a round of parties, events, etc. —**whirl'ing der'vish,** a member of a sect of Turkish dervishes whose ritual involves a stylized whirling dance.

whirl'i·gig (hwērl'ə-gig) *n.* something that revolves.

whirl'pool" *n.* a circular eddy in a body of water.

whirl'wind" *n.* **1,** a destructive wind moving in a vortex. **2,** a rushing force.

whir'ly·bird" (hwer'lē-) *n.* (*Informal*) a helicopter.

whish (hwish) *v.i.* move with, or make, a swishing or whistling sound. —*n.* such a sound.

whisk (hwisk) *v.t.* **1,** sweep or brush with a light, rapid motion. **2,** move quickly. **3,** (with *away, off,* etc.) carry suddenly and rapidly. —*v.i.* move nimbly and swiftly. —*n.* **1,** a small brush: *whiskbroom.* **2,** a rapid, light, sweeping motion.

whisk'er (hwisk'ər) *n.* a hair on the face, esp. (*pl.*) those on a man's face. —**whisk'ered,** *adj.*

whis'key (hwis'kē) *n.* **1,** a strong alcoholic liquor, made chiefly from grain. **2,** (*Communications*) the letter *w.* Also, **whis'ky.**

whis'per (hwis'pər) *v.i.* **1,** speak softly with the breath, without vibration of the vocal cords. **2,** gossip; plot. **3,** make a low rustling sound. —*v.t.* say under the breath; say secretly. —*n.* **1,** a whispering voice or utterance. **2,** a hint or insinuation. **3,** a low, rustling sound.

whist (hwist) *n.* a game of cards, the forerunner of bridge. —*interj.* hush!

whis'tle (hwis'əl) *v.i.* **1,** make a shrill or musical sound by forcing the breath through pursed lips or air through a pipe. **2,** move with a whizzing sound. **3,** (*Informal*) desire in vain. —*v.t.* **1,** sound by whistling. **2,** signal to, by whistling. —*n.* **1,** a whistling sound; a device for producing it. **2,** (*Informal*) the throat. —**whis'tler,** *n.* —**whistle stop,** a short stop, as for a political speech.

whis'tle-blow"er *n.* a person who exposes corporate or government corruption or improper actions.

whit (hwit) *n.* a little; a jot.

white (hwīt) *adj.* **1,** of the color of pure snow. **2,** of a light color; gray. **3,** fair-skinned. **4,** pale. **5,** pure. **6,** blank; unprinted. **7,** (*Informal, sometimes offensive*) sportsmanlike; honorable. —*n.* a white color; something of this color, as: the albumen of an egg; a member of the Caucasian race; a part of the eyeball. —*v.t.* make white. —**white′ness,** *n.* —**whit′ish,** *adj.* —**white ant,** a termite. —**white elephant,** a burdensome or useless possession. —**white feather,** a symbol of cowardice. —**white flag,** a symbol of surrender or peaceful intent. —**white gold,** a white alloy of gold, used for jewelry. —**white hat,** (*Informal*) a good guy. —**white heat,** intense heat, excitement, etc. —**white hole,** *n.* (*Astron.*) a hypothetical astronomical body once proposed as the counterpart of a black hole. —**white knight, 1,** hero; champion. **2,** (*Informal*) a company that intervenes to prevent the takeover of another company. —**white lead,** lead carbonate, used in paints; a paint containing it. —**white lie,** a harmless falsehood. —**white noise,** a mixture of sound waves spreading over a wide frequency range. —**white paper,** a government report; hence, any authoritative report. —**white plague,** tuberculosis. —**white sale,** a sale of household articles, esp. linens. —**white slave,** a woman forced into prostitution. —**white whale,** the beluga.

white-′bread′ *adj.* possessing the bland values of middle-class white society.

white′cap″ *n.* a wave with a foaming crest.

white-′col″lar *adj.* pert. to clerical or professional workers.

white′fish″ *n.* any of various white or silvery food fish.

White′hall″ *n.* **1,** a former palace in London. **2,** a street in London bordered by government offices, hence the British government.

white-″hot′ *adj.* intensely hot.

White House 1, the residence of the President of the U.S. in Washington, D.C. **2,** the presidential office, authority, etc.

white-′liv″ered *adj.* cowardly.

whit′en (hwīt′ən) *v.t. & i.* make or become whiter.

white′out″ *n.* a situation of zero visibility caused by a heavy snowstorm.

white-′shoe′ *adj.* (*Informal*) being a member of or pert. to elite society.

white′wall″ *n.* a tire having a band of white around the visible outer side.

white′wash″ *v.t.* **1,** paint with whitewash. **2,** cover up the faults or defects of. **3,** (*In-*formal) defeat, when the loser fails to score. —*n.* **1,** a white paint, usu. of quicklime and water. **2,** the covering up of wrongdoing or defects. **3,** (*Informal*) a victory over a scoreless opponent.

whith′er (hwi*th*′ər) *adv.* wherever; to which place.

whit′ing (hwīt′ing) *n.* **1,** any of various edible fish. **2,** a powdered chalk.

Whit′sun·tide″ (hwit′sən-tīd″) *n.* the eighth week after Easter, beginning with Whitsunday. —**Whit′sun,** *adj.*

whit′tle (hwit′əl) *v.t. & i.* cut or form with a knife; pare. —**whit′tler** (-lər) *n.*

whiz *v.i.* [**whizzed, whiz′zing**] **1,** make a humming or hissing sound. **2,** move rapidly; rush. —*n.* **1,** a sound made by rapid motion through the air. **2,** (*Slang*) someone very capable. —**whiz′zer,** *n.*

who (hoo) *pron. sing. & pl.* [*poss.* **whose** (hooz), *obj.* **whom** (hoom)] **1,** what or which person or persons? **2,** that person; those persons.

---

who's, whose

☞ Do not confuse these two words. *Whose* is the possessive of *who.* *Who's* is a contraction of *who is* (or sometimes *who has*).

---

whoa (hwō) *interj.* stop!

who·dun′it (hoo-dun′it) *n.* (*Slang*) a detective story or drama.

who·ev′er *pron.* no matter who. Also, **who″so·ev′er.**

whole (hōl) *adj.* **1,** not broken or injured; intact; unimpaired. **2,** entire; complete. **3,** having full blood relationship. —*n.* **1,** the complete thing; the total. **2,** an organic unity. —**whole′ness,** *n.* —**whol′ly,** *adv.* —**out of whole cloth,** fabricated. —**whole hog,** (*Slang*) all the way. —**whole note,** a semibreve (see *note*). —**whole number,** an integer.

whole′heart″ed *adj.* sincere; enthusiastic. —**whole′heart″ed·ness,** *n.*

whole′sale″ (hōl′sāl″) *n.* sale of goods in quantity to retailers. —*adj.* **1,** pert. to trade with dealers. **2,** in great quantities; extensive; indiscriminate. —*v.t.* sell by wholesale. —**whole′sal″er,** *n.*

whole′some (hōl′səm) *adj.* **1,** contributing to health of body, mind, or character. **2,** healthy or sound-looking. —**whole′some·ness,** *n.*

whole′wheat″ *adj.* made of the complete wheat kernel.

whom (hoom) *pron.* objective of *who.*

whoop (hwoop) *v.i.* **1,** shout; halloo; hoot. **2,** gasp after coughing, as in the disease *whooping cough.* —*n.* **1,** a loud call or shout. **2,** a gasp.

whoo′pee (hwoo′pē) (*Slang*) *interj.* expressing hilarity.

whoops (hwoops) *interj.* expressing enthusiasm, or surprise at an error.

whoosh (hwoosh) *v.i.* move rapidly with a rushing sound. —*n.* a rushing sound.

whop′per (hwop′ər) *n.* (*Informal*) anything unusually large, esp. a lie. —**whop′ping,** *adj.* (*Informal*) very large.

whore (hôr) *n.* an unchaste woman; a prostitute. —*v.i.* **1,** act as a whore. **2,** consort with whores. —**whore′dom** (-dəm) *n.* —**whor′ish,** *adj.*

whorl (hwêrl) *n.* a spiral or coil-shaped part or pattern.

whose (hooz) *pron. poss.* of *who* or *which.* ❑ *who's*

why (hwī) *adv.* **1,** used interrogatively, for what cause, reason, or purpose? **2,** on account of which. —*n.* the reason or cause. —*interj.* used as an expletive.

wi′ca (wik′ə) *n.* **1,** witchcraft. **2,** a witch. —**wi″ca·pho′bi·a,** *n.* fear of witches.

wick (wik) *n.* a strip or cord that draws up the fuel that burns in a lamp or candle.

wick′ed (wik′id) *adj.* **1,** evil; sinful. **2,** harmful; pernicious. **3,** difficult; disagreeable. **4,** (*Informal*) mischievous. —**wick′ed·ness,** *n.*

wick′er (wik′ər) *n. & adj.* a small pliant twig. —**wick′er·work″,** *n.* anything made of wicker.

wick′et (wik′it) *n.* **1,** a small gate or window. **2,** in croquet, an arch. **3,** in cricket, one of the goals.

wick′i·up″ (wik′ē-up″) *n.* the rude hut of certain Native Americans.

wide (wīd) *adj.* **1,** having considerable extension from side to side; broad. **2,** having a specified width. **3,** vast; spacious. **4,** embracing many subjects. **5,** spread apart; open. **6,** deviating or far from a point. —*adv.* **1,** a long way; afar. **2,** extensively; far apart. **3,** astray. —**wide′ness,** *n.*

wide-′an″gle *adj.* of a lens, having greater than a 50° angle of coverage.

wide-′a·wake″ *adj.* fully awake.

wide-′eyed″ (-īd″) *adj. & adv.* having the eyes widely open, as with astonishment.

wid′en (wīd′ən) *v.t. & i.* make or become wider.

wide-′o″pen *adj.* (*Informal*) **1,** of a town, lax in enforcement of laws. **2,** of liquor sales, gambling, etc., unrestrained.

wide′spread″ *adj.* covering a great area, or known to many persons.

widg′eon (wij′ən) *n.* a duck, the baldpate. Also, **wi′geon.**

wid′ow (wid′ō) *n.* **1,** a woman who has not remarried since the death of her husband. **2,** (*Card Games*) additional cards dealt to the table. **3,** the first line of a paragraph, stranded at the bottom of a page. **4,** a very short last line of a paragraph. —*v.t.* bereave of a spouse. —**wid′ow·hood″,** *n.*

wid′ow·er *n.* a man who has not remarried since the death of his wife.

width *n.* linear extent from side to side.

wield (wēld) *v.t.* **1,** use or exert (power, etc.). **2,** handle; brandish.

wie′ner (wē′nər) *n.* a kind of small sausage. Also, **wie′ner·wurst″** (-wûrst″).

wife (wīf) *n.* [*pl.* **wives** (wīvz)] a woman wedded to a man; a man's spouse. —**wife′hood,** *n.* —**wife′ly,** *adj.* befitting a wife.

---

wife

↔ Originally this word meant "woman"; the specific application to "married woman" dates from the Old English period. Its source is a prehistoric Germanic root.

---

wig *n.* an artificial covering of hair for the head. —**wigged,** *adj.*

wig′gle (wig′əl) *v.t. & i., & n.* wobble; wriggle. —**wig′gly,** *adj.*

wight (wīt) *n.* (*Archaic*) a person.

wig′wag″ *v.i. & t.* [**wig′wagged″, -wag″ging**] **1,** move or cause to move to and fro. **2,** signal by waving flags. —*n.* a system of signaling with two flags.

wig′wam″ (wig′wom) *n.* the tent or hut of a Native American; teepee.

wild (wīld) *adj.* **1,** living or growing in a natural state; not domesticated; not cultivated. **2,** stormy; violent. **3,** savage; ferocious. **4,** extravagant; fantastic. **5,** reckless; rash. **6,** wide of the mark. **7,** disorderly; boisterous. **8,** (*Informal*) ardent; enthusiastic. —*n.* (often *pl.*) an uninhabited or uncultivated region. —**wild′ness,** *n.* —**wild card, 1,** a playing card of arbitrary denomination. **2,** (*Sports*) an unranked player entered into a tournament at the discretion of the tournament committee. —**wild oats,** youthful indiscretions.

wild-′card″ *adj.* (*Informal*) **1,** unpredictable. **2,** (*Sports*) designating a player or team that is entered into a tournament or playoff without qualifying in the regular manner.

wild′cat″ (wīld′kat″) *n.* **1,** any of various small, untamed cats, as the lynx. **2,** a quick-tempered person. —*adj.* **1,** specula-

tive; unsound. **2,** of a strike, unsanctioned.
—*v.t.* **[-cat″ted, -ting]** drill wells experimentally for oil or gas.

wil′de·beest″ (wil′də-bēst″) *n.* a gnu.

wil′der·ness (wil′dər-nəs) *n.* an uninhabited tract of land; a desert.

wild-′eyed″ *adj.* staring wildly; wildly excited or angry.

wild′fire″ *n.* a spreading, uncontrollable fire.

wild′fowl″ *n.* **1,** a game bird, esp. a duck or goose. **2,** game birds collectively.

wild-goose′ chase the pursuit of something unattainable; a futile chase or search.

wild′ing (wīl′ding) *n.* **1,** something wild, as a plant, animal, etc. **2,** a rampage, as of youths.

wild′life″ *n.* wild, undomesticated animals living in their natural habitat.

wild′wood″ *n.* a wild or unfrequented wood; a forest.

wile (wīl) *n.* a sly trick; a stratagem. —*v.t.* **1,** lure; entice. **2,** (with *away*) pass (time) pleasantly. —**wil′y,** *adj.*

will (wil) *n.* **1,** the faculty of conscious and deliberate action; volition. **2,** desire; choice; pleasure. **3,** purpose; determination. **4,** a legal document to dispose of property after the owner's death. —*aux. v.* [*pret.* **would**] **1,** expressing the future: am, is, are, etc., about to, sure to, determined to, etc. **2,** expressing desire: wish, want. **3,** is able to; can. —*v.t.* [*pret. & p.p.* **willed**] **1,** determine; decide. **2,** bequeath. **3,** compel by force of will. ❏ *shall*

will′ful (-fəl) *adj.* **1,** deliberate; intentional. **2,** obstinate; headstrong. Also, **wil′ful.** —**will′ful·ness,** *n.*

wil′lies (wil′ēs) *n.pl.* (*Informal*) nervousness; the jitters.

will′ing *adj.* **1,** favorably disposed; amenable. **2,** voluntary. **3,** eager to serve or comply. —**will′ing·ness,** *n.*

wil′li·waw″ *n.* a cold wind blowing from the coastal mountains toward the sea; any gust or squall.

will-′o′-the-wisp′ (wil′ə-thə-wisp′) *n.* **1,** a light (from burning gas) that flits over marshes. **2,** an elusive or misleading hope.

wil′low (wil′ō) *n.* **1,** any of a genus of trees or shrubs with slender flexible twigs, valuable for wickerwork; its wood. **2,** (*Baseball, Cricket*) the bat. —**wil′low·y,** *adj.* supple.

will′pow″er *n.* strength of will; self-discipline.

wil′ly-nil′ly (wil′ē-nil′ē) *adv.* regardless of one's wishes: *will ye, nill ye.*

wilt *v.i. & t.* **1,** become or make limp or drooping. **2,** weaken.

Wil′ton (wil′tən) *n.* a heavy carpet, orig. made at Wilton, Eng.

wim′ble (wim′bəl) *n.* a tool for boring.

wimp *n.* an ineffectual person. —**wimp′i·ness, wimp′ish·ness,** *n.* —**wimp′y,** *adj.*

wim′ple (wim′pəl) *n.* a woman's head covering, as worn by nuns.

win *v.t.* [**won,** (wun), **win′ning**] **1,** acquire by effort; gain. **2,** be victorious in. **3,** gain the favor of. **4,** prevail on; induce. **5,** reach; attain. —*v.i.* gain one's end; be successful or victorious. —*n.* (*Informal*) a victory. —**win′ner,** *n.*

wince (wins) *v.i.* shrink, as in pain or from a blow; start back. —*n.* a flinch.

winch *n.* hoisting machine.

wind *n.* **1,** a natural current of air. **2,** air artificially put in motion. **3,** breath; the power of respiration. **4,** idle talk; bombast. **5,** scent. **6,** flatulence. **7,** (*pl.*) wind instruments. —*v.t.* put out of breath. —**wind′ed,** *adj.* out of breath. —**wind instrument,** any musical instrument sounded by air. —**wind sleeve,** a windsock. —**wind tunnel,** a tunnellike structure for testing wind resistance.

wind (wīnd) *v.i.* [**wound** (wownd), **wind′ing**] **1,** go in a devious course; twist. **2,** entwine itself round something. **3,** (*Informal*) (with *up*) come to a conclusion; end. —*v.t.* **1,** turn; coil; twist. **2,** entwine; enfold. **3,** insinuate; worm. **4,** (*Informal*) (with *up*) bring to a conclusion. —*n.* [also, **wind′ing**] a turn; a bend. —**winding sheet,** a cloth in which a corpse is wrapped for burial.

wind′bag″ *n.* (*Slang*) a chatterer; a braggart.

wind′blown″ (wind′-) *adj.* made disorderly by the wind, as hair.

wind′break″ (wind′-) *n.* something to break the force of the wind, as a fence or a growth of trees.

wind′break″er (wind′-) *n.* a lightweight outer jacket.

wind′bro″ken (wind′-) *adj.* of a horse, having the heaves.

wind′burn″ (wind′-) *n.* skin burn caused by the wind.

wind′cane″ (wind′-) *n.* a windsock.

wind′chill″ (wind′-) *n.* the cooling effect of wind, expressed as a combination of wind speed and temperature.

wind′fall″ (wind′-) *n.* **1,** an unexpected

and fortunate acquisition. **2,** something blown down by the wind, as fruit.

wind′flow″er (wind′-) *n.* the anemone.

wind′jam″mer (wind′jam″ər) *n.* a sailing ship.

wind′lass (wind′ləs) *n.* a machine for hoisting.

wind′mill″ (wind′-) *n.* a mill driven by blades turned by the wind.

win′dow (win′dō) *n.* **1,** an opening in the wall of a building to let in light and air. **2,** any similar opening. **3,** a moment period· of time especially favorable for a certain occurrence: *window of opportunity, launch window.* **4,** (*Computers*) a rectangular area on a computer screen inside which information is displayed. —**window box,** a box of soil in which to grow plants, placed below a window. —**window dressing,** a display in a store's window; any display designed to impress. —**window envelope,** an envelope with a transparent panel.

win′dow·pane″ *n.* a glass pane in a window.

win′dow·shop″ *v.i.* [**-shopped″, -shop″-ping**] look at display windows without intending to buy.

wind′pipe″ (wind′-) *n.* the trachea.

wind′row″ (wind′rō″) *n.* a ridge of hay, etc., arranged for drying.

wind′shield″ (wind′-) *n.* a glass shield before a driver of an automobile.

wind′sock″ (wind′-) *n.* a device used to show the direction of the wind. Also, **wind sleeve, wind′cone″.**

wind′storm″ (wind′-) *n.* a violent wind with little or no rain.

wind′surf″ing (wind′-) *n.* a type of sailing on a surfboard equipped with a sail.

wind′up″ (wīnd′-) *n.* (*Informal*) **1,** a conclusion. **2,** (*Baseball*) a pitcher's preparatory movements.

wind′ward (wind′wərd) *adv. & adj.* toward the wind.

wind′y (win′dē) *adj.* **1,** marked by much blowing of wind. **2,** voluble; wordy. —**wind′i·ness,** *n.*

wine (wīn) *n.* the fermented juice of fruit or plants, specif. of the grape. —*v.t.* regale with alcoholic liquors. —*v.i.* drink wine. —*adj.* a dark red color. —**wine′bib″ber,** *n.* a heavy drinker. —**win′er·y,** *n.* a place where wine is made.

wine′sap″ *n.* a red apple.

wine′skin″ *n.* a goatskin container for wine.

wing *n.* **1,** a limb, usually occurring in pairs, by which certain animals fly; any similar appendage. **2,** flight. **3,** one of the chief supporting planes of an airplane. **4,** a part of a building projecting from the main part. **5,** one of the sides of a stage of a theater. **6,** anything projecting to the side. **7,** (*pl.*) an emblem worn by a military flier. **8,** protection. —*v.t.* **1,** equip with wings. **2,** traverse in flight. **3,** accomplish by means of flight. **4,** shoot; wound; disable. —*v.i.* **1,** fly; soar. **2,** (with *it*) (*Informal*) improvise; do without forethought. —**wing chair,** an upholstered chair with winglike projections of the back. —**wing collar,** a high, stiff man's collar with pointed winglike corners.

wing′ding″ *adj.* (*Slang*) a wild, lavish party.

winged (wingd) *adj.* **1,** having wings. **2,** swift; rapid. **3,** lofty; elevated; sublime.

wing′spread″ *n.* the distance, tip to tip, of outstretched wings. Also, **wing′span″.**

wink *v.i.* **1,** close and open the eye quickly, as a signal. **2,** (with *at*) condone. —*n.* an act of winking. —**forty winks,** a short nap. —**wink at,** overlook; condone.

win′kle (wing′kəl) *n.* **1,** a large sea snail with a spiral shell. **2,** a periwinkle.

win′ning (win′ing) *adj.* **1,** that wins. **2,** attractive. —*n.pl.* gains.

win′now (win′ō) *v.t.* **1,** drive off chaff from (grain) by a current of air. **2,** sift; weed out; test. —*v.i.* **1,** winnow grain. **2,** flutter.

wi′no (wī′nō) *n.* (*Slang*) a person habitually drunk on wine.

win′some (-səm) *adj.* charming. —**win′-some·ness,** *n.*

win′ter (win′tər) *n. & adj.* **1,** (often *cap.*) the cold season; in the No. Hemisphere, approximately Dec. 22 to March 21. **2,** a period of dreariness or adversity. **3,** old age. —*v.i.* spend or pass the winter. —*v.t.* keep or shelter during the winter. —**win′-ter·ize″** (-īz″) *v.t.* prepare for winter. —**winter wheat,** wheat planted in the fall.

win′ter·green″ *n.* an evergreen plant bearing aromatic leaves and berries.

win′ter·kill″ *v.t.* kill (a plant) by exposure to winter cold. —*v.i.* die from exposure to the cold.

win′ter·time″ *n.* winter.

win′try (win′trē) *adj.* of or like winter; cold; forbidding. —**win′tri·ness,** *n.*

wipe (wīp) *v.t.* **1,** clean or dry by gently rubbing, as with a soft cloth. **2,** remove, as dirt. **3,** cleanse. —*n.* **1,** an act of wiping. **2,** (*Slang*) a handkerchief. —**wipe out, 1,** destroy. **2,** (*Informal*) murder. **3,** in skiing, etc., lose balance and fall.

wire (wīr) *n.* **1,** a pliable thread or slender rod of metal; a piece of this material. **2,** a telegram. —*v.t.* **1,** provide with wire. **2,** snare. **3,** send a telegram; telegraph to. —*v.i.* telegraph. —**wire recording,** recording of sound on magnetized wire.

wired (wīrd) *adj.* (*Slang*) high on drugs.

wire′hair″ *n.* a type of fox terrier: *wire-haired terrier.*

wire′less (-ləs) *n.* a telegraph or telephone not requiring connection by wires; radio.

Wire′pho″to *n.* (*T.N.*) [*pl.* -tos] a method or apparatus for transmitting photographs by wire; a photograph so transmitted.

wire′pull″ing *n.* the use of influence to gain unfair advantage.

wire′tap″per (wīr′tap″ər) *n.* one who taps telephone wires to get information, messages, etc., by listening to someone's telephone conversations. —**wire′tap″,** *n. & v.t. & i.*

wir′ing *n.* a system of connected wires.

wir′y (wīr′ē) *adj.* lean but muscular. —**wir′i·ness,** *n.*

wis′dom (wiz′dəm) *n.* **1,** the power or faculty of forming a sound judgment in any matter; sagacity; experience. **2,** erudition. —**wisdom tooth,** the third molar, in the back of the jaw.

wise (wīz) *adj.* **1,** having the power of discerning and judging rightly. **2,** having knowledge; learned. **3,** experienced; cunning. **4,** judicious. **5,** (*Slang*) too smart; aware. **6,** (*Informal*) impudent; rude. —*n.* **1,** wise persons collectively. **2,** manner; way; mode.

-wise *suf.* forming adverbs: in the manner of, as *likewise;* in the direction of, as *sidewise;* (*Informal*) with respect to, as *performance-wise.*

wise′a″cre *n.* one who affects wit or cleverness.

> **wiseacre**
> ↔ Unrelated to *acre,* this word comes from Middle Dutch *wijssager,* soothsayer, prophet.

wise′crack″ *n. & v.i.* (*Slang*) quip. —**wise′crack″er,** *n.*

wish *v.t.* **1,** long for; desire; crave. —*v.i.* form or express a desire. —*n.* **1,** eager desire or longing. **2,** a request. **3,** the thing desired.

wish′bone″ *n.* **1,** the forked bone in front of the breast of a fowl. **2,** (*Football*) an offensive formation.

wish′ful (-fəl) *adj.* based on desire; desirous. —**wish′ful·ness,** *n.*

wish′y-wash″y (wish′ē-wosh′ē) *adj.* (*Informal*) **1,** feeble. **2,** vacillating.

wisp *n.* **1,** a tuft of hay or straw, hair, etc. **2,** a fragment. —**wisp′y,** *adj.*

wist *v.* (*Archaic*) knew.

wis·ta′ri·a (wis-tār′ē-ə) *n.* a climbing shrub bearing clusters of purplish or white flowers. Also, **wis·te′ri·a** (-tir′ē-ə).

> **wistaria**
> ↔ Named for 18th-c. U.S. anatomist Caspar *Wistar.*

wist′ful (wist′fəl) *adj.* longing, but with little hope. —**wist′ful·ness,** *n.*

wit *n.* **1,** cleverness; intelligence; sense; (often *pl.*) power to reason. **2,** clever, amusing sayings and writings; one apt at making them. —**to wit,** namely.

witch (wich) *n.* **1,** a person with magic powers derived from evil spirits; a sorcerer or sorceress. **2,** a hag; a crone. —*v.t.* **1,** work witchcraft on. **2,** effect by witchcraft. **3,** charm; fascinate. —**witch′er·y,** *n.* —**witch′ing,** *adj.* bewitching; fascinating. —**witch doctor,** a medicine man. —**witch hazel,** a shrub bearing yellow flowers; a soothing lotion prepared from its bark. —**witch hunt,** a search for and prosecution of political dissidents on the pretext of the public good.

witch′craft″ *n.* magic.

with *prep.* **1,** accompanying; beside; carrying. **2,** possessing; holding. **3,** opposed to; against; compared to. **4,** using. **5,** having in association or connection, or as a reason. **6,** away from. —**with it,** (*Slang*) hip; up-to-date; aware.

with·al′ (with-âl′) *adv.* considering everything; besides.

with·draw′ (with-drâ′) *v.t.* take back; recall; retract. —*v.i.* retire; retreat. —**withdraw′al,** *n.*

withe (wīth) *n.* a tough, flexible twig, esp. of willow.

with′er (with′ər) *v.i. & t.* **1,** shrivel up; dry out; decay. **2,** languish. **3,** abash.

with′ers (with′ərz) *n.pl.* the highest part of the back of a horse.

with·hold′ (with-hōld′) *v.t.* [-held′, -hold′ing] **1,** restrain. **2,** refuse to grant or release. —**withholding tax,** a deduction from wages for payment of tax.

with·in′ (with-in′) *adv.* **1,** pert. to the inside; indoors; internally; inwardly. —*prep.* in; inside of; not exceeding.

with·out′ (with-owt′) *adv.* on or as to the outside; outdoors; externally. —*prep.* **1,** outside of; beyond. **2,** lacking; independent of.

with·stand' *v.t.* [*pret. & p.p.* **with·stood'**] resist successfully; oppose.

wit'less (-ləs) *adj.* stupid; foolish. —**wit'less·ness,** *n.*

wit'ness (wit'nəs) *v.t.* **1,** see or know by personal presence. **2,** attest to (a document) by one's signature. **3,** testify. —*n.* **1,** one who sees personally. **2,** one who gives evidence or witnesses a document. **3,** testimony.

wit'ti·cism (wit'i-siz-əm) *n.* a witty remark.

wit'ting·ly (wit'ing-lē) *adv.* knowingly.

wit'ty (wit'ē) *adj.* characterized by or apt at making original and clever remarks. —**wit'ti·ness,** *n.*

wive (wīv) *v.t. & i.* marry.

wives (wīvz) *n.* pl. of *wife.*

wiz'ard (wiz'ərd) *n.* **1,** one supposed to have magic powers; a sorcerer. **2,** an unusually skilled person. —*adj.* **1,** enchanting. **2,** (*Brit. Slang*) superb. —**wiz'ard·ry,** *n.* **1,** sorcery. **2,** admirable skill.

wiz'ened (wiz'ənd) *adj.* dried up; shriveled.

woad (wōd) *n.* a European plant formerly cultivated for the blue dye obtained from its leaves; the dye.

wob'ble (wob'əl) *v.i.* **1,** move from side to side; rock. **2,** tremble. —*n.* a rocking motion. —**wob'bly** (-lē) *adj.*

woe (wō) *n.* **1,** intense unhappiness; grief; sorrow. **2,** an affliction.

woe'be·gone'' *adj.* sorrowful.

woe'ful (-fəl) *adj.* **1,** sorrowful. **2,** causing or expressing woe. —**woe'ful·ness,** *n.*

wok (wok) *n.* a Chinese bowl-shaped cooking utensil.

woke (wōk) *v.* pret. of *wake.*

wold (wōld) *n.* in England, a tract of treeless, rolling country; a down or moor.

wolf (wûlf) *n.* [*pl.* **wolves** (wûlvz)] **1,** a wild, carnivorous animal of the dog family. **2,** a cruel, cunning, greedy person. **3,** (*Slang*) a man who makes advances to many women. —*v.t.* devour ravenously. —**wolf'ish,** *adj.* —**cry wolf,** raise a false alarm. —**wolf pack,** a group of submarines hunting together for enemy shipping.

wolf'hound'' *n.* a large hound used to hunt wolves.

wolf'ram (wûl'frəm) *n.* a mineral, a source of tungsten. Also, **wolf'ram·ite''** (-īt'').

wolfs'bane'' *n.* aconite or monkshood.

wol''ver·ine' (wûl''və-rēn') *n.* **1,** a small, ferocious, carnivorous animal, related to

the marten. **2,** (*cap.*) (*Informal*) an inhabitant of Michigan.

wom'an (wûm'ən) *n.* [*pl.* **wom'en** (wim'ən)] **1,** an adult human female; a wife; a female attendant. **2,** the female sex. **3,** feminine nature. —**wom'an·kind'',** *n.* —**wom'an·like'',** *adj.* —**wom'an·ly,** *adj.* befitting a woman. □ *lady, man*

wom'an·hood'' *n.* the state of being a woman; women collectively.

wom'an·ish *adj.* **1,** feminine. **2,** effeminate.

wom'an·ize'' *v.t.* make more feminine. —*v.i.* (*Slang*) chase after women.

womb (woom) *n.* the uterus.

wom'bat *n.* an Australian marsupial resembling a small bear.

wom'en (wim'ən) *n.* pl. of *woman.* —**wom'en·folk'',** *n.* —**women's liberation,** a movement advocating the liberation of women from traditional, subservient roles in society. Also, (*informal, often derog.*) **women's lib.**

won (wun) *v.* pret. & p.p. of *win.*

won'der (wun'dər) *n.* **1,** a strange thing; a cause of surprise or admiration; a marvel; a prodigy. **2,** astonishment. —*v.i.* **1,** entertain doubt or curiosity; speculate. **2,** marvel. —**won'der·ment,** *n.* —**won'drous,** *adj.*

won'der·ful (-fəl) *adj.* **1,** extraordinary; marvelous. **2,** delightful. —**won'der·ful·ness,** *n.*

won'der·land'' *n.* a wonderful place.

wonk *n.* (*Slang*) **1,** an obsessive student; grind. **2,** (*Offensive*) an unattractive person.

wont *adj.* accustomed; in the habit. —*n.* custom; habit; practice. —**wont'ed,** *adj.*

woo *v.t. & i.* seek the favor or love of; court. —**woo'er,** *n.*

wood (wûd) *n.* **1,** the hard, fibrous substance of the body of a tree. **2,** (often *pl.*) a forest. **3,** timber. —**wood alcohol,** methyl alcohol. —**wood pulp,** wood fibers, prepared for use in manufacturing paper.

wood'bine'' (wûd'bīn'') *n.* **1,** honeysuckle. **2,** the Virginia creeper.

wood'block'' *n.* **1,** a woodcut. **2,** a musical percussion instrument.

wood'chuck'' (wûd'chuk'') *n.* a burrowing hibernating marmot; the ground hog.

wood'cock'' *n.* a game bird. —**Scotch woodcock,** a dish of scrambled eggs on toast or crackers spread with anchovy paste.

wood'craft'' *n.* the art of living on nature.

---

wood'cut" n. a printing block of wood; a print made from one.

wood'ed adj. thick with trees.

wood'en (-ən) adj. **1,** made of wood. **2,** inflexible; unimaginative. **3,** not sensitive; expressionless. **—wood'en·head"ed,** adj. stupid; obstinate.

wood'land (-lənd) n. a forest.

wood'man (-mən) n. [pl. **-men**] **1,** a woodcutter; lumberman. **2,** one who dwells in the woods. **3,** a forester.

wood'note" n. a wild or natural song, as of a forest bird.

wood'peck"er n. a bird that bores into trees with its bill.

wood'ruff" (-ruf") n. a small sweet-scented European herb.

wood'shed" n. a shed for storing cut firewood. **—v.i.** (Informal) do extra study.

woods'man (wûdz'mən) n. [pl. **-men**] a forester.

woods'y adj. belonging to, associated with, or suggestive of the woods.

wood'wind" n. a musical wind instrument, as the flute, clarinet, etc.

wood'work n. interior trim and fixtures made of wood.

wood'y (-ė) adj. **1,** wooded. **2,** of or resembling wood. **—wood'i·ness,** n.

woof n. **1,** the crosswise threads in weaving. **2,** a suppressed bark or growl of a dog. **—v.i.** make such a sound.

woof'er (wûf'ər) n. a loudspeaker responsive only to the lower frequencies and used for reproducing low-pitched sounds.

wool (wûl) n. **1,** the fleece of the sheep; any fabric or yarn made of it. **2,** kinky hair.

wool'en (-ən) adj. & n. made of wool. Also, **wool'len.**

wool'gath"er·ing n. desultory thought causing inattention.

wool'ly (-ė) adj. **1,** of or like wool. **2,** (Informal) confused; blurred. **3,** (Informal) exciting. **—wool'lies,** n.pl. woolen clothes. **—wool'li·ness,** n. **—woolly bear,** a hairy caterpillar.

wool'sack" n. the wool-stuffed seat of the Lord Chancellor, in the Eng. House of Lords; hence, the office of the Lord Chancellor.

wooz'y (woo'zė) adj. (Slang) **1,** confused; befuddled. **2,** shaky. **—wooz'i·ness,** n.

Worces'ter·shire sauce (wûs'tər-shër) a piquant sauce of soy, vinegar, and many other ingredients, named for a former county in England.

word (wėrd) n. **1,** a sound or combination of sounds, or its graphic representation, expressing an idea; a term. **2,** (pl.) speech; written words; a song lyric; a quarrel. **3,** information; a report; a command; a signal or password; a motto. **4,** a promise. **5,** (cap.) Holy Scripture. **6,** (Computers) the string of bytes which is treated as a unit by a computer. **—v.t.** express in words; phrase. **—word'age,** n. **—word'ing,** n. phrasing. **—word'less,** adj. silent; tacit. **—the last word,** the ultimate authority; (Slang) the latest thing. **—word for word,** verbatim; literally. **—word processing,** using a computer for writing, as letters, contracts, etc.

word'book" n. **1,** a dictionary; vocabulary. **2,** an opera libretto.

word'play" n. repartee; pun.

word'y (-ė) adj. verbose. **—word'i·ness,** n.

wore (wôr) v. pret. of wear.

work (wėrk) v.i. **1,** put forth effort; labor; toil; strive. **2,** act; operate, esp. effectively. **3,** ferment; seethe. **4,** make way slowly. **5,** be employed; perform labor. **—v.t. 1,** prepare or fashion by labor; operate; employ. **2,** sew; embroider. **3,** do; accomplish. **4,** (often with on, etc.) affect; influence; persuade; provoke. **5,** exact labor or service from. **6,** solve. **—n. 1,** effort or exertion; toil; labor. **2,** employment; a job; an undertaking; a project. **3,** a product of effort; deed; performance. **4,** (pl.) a factory. **5,** (pl.) a mechanism, as of a watch. **6,** (pl.) the entire output of an artist, writer, etc. **7,** (pl.) engineering structures, esp. public ones. **8,** (pl., Informal) everything; the whole thing. **—work ethic,** the belief that hard work is beneficial in developing a person's character. **—work force,** all the workers of an employer, country, etc. **—work out, 1,** develop; study. **2,** solve. **3,** exhaust, as a mine. **4,** exercise.

-work suf. product of (what is specified).

work'a·ble (-ə-bəl) adj. **1,** feasible; practicable. **2,** tractable. **—work"a·bil'i·ty,** n.

work"a·hol'ic (-ə-hol'ik) n. (Slang) one who works excessively, as though addicted to work.

work'a·day" adj. commonplace; matter-of-fact.

work'bench" n. a table on which to do work.

work'book" n. an instructive manual or drill book.

work'day" n. hours worked in a day. Also, **working day.**

work′er (-ər) *n.* one who works; esp., a laborer. —**worker's compensation,** insurance provided by employers for their employees while on the job..

work′horse″ *n.* **1,** a horse used for labor. **2,** (*Informal*) a hard-working person.

work′house″ *n.* a poorhouse or small prison.

work′ing *adj.* **1,** that works. **2,** effective; in operation. —*n.* **1,** operation; fermentation. **2,** (*pl.*) the parts of a mine. —**work′-ing·man″, work′ing·wom″an,** *n.* a laborer.

work′man (-mən) *n.* [*pl.* -**men**] a skilled worker; artisan. —**work′man·like″,** *adj.* competently executed. —**work′man-ship″,** *n.*

work′out″ *n.* **1,** a performance for practice or exercise. **2,** (*Informal*) a trying experience.

work′shop″ *n.* a building or room in which work is done.

work′sta″tion *n.* a computer terminal connected with a remote central computer.

work′wom″an *n.* a skilled female worker; artisan.

world (wērld) *n.* **1,** the whole creation; the universe; the earth. **2,** the human race; mankind. **3,** a class or society of persons; a sphere; realm. **4,** material concerns. **5,** public or social life. **6,** a particular part of the earth. **7,** a great number or quantity. —**world music,** the music of non-western nations.

world′beat″er *n.* one who is unusually good at what he or she does.

world-′class′ *adj.* outstanding; of international quality competitiveness.

world′ling *n.* one devoted to the pleasures and interests of this life.

world′ly (-lė) *adj.* **1,** mundane; material; not spiritual. **2,** sophisticated. —**world′li-ness,** *n.* —**world′ly-wise″,** *adj.* experienced; knowing; shrewd.

world′wide″ *adj.* throughout the earth.

worm (wērm) *n.* **1,** any small, creeping tube-shaped animal. **2,** a contemptible person; an unfortunate person. **3,** something that silently harasses. **4,** any device resembling a worm, as a spiral part. **5,** (*pl.*) any disease caused by parasitic worms. —*v.i.* work or act slowly, stealthily, or secretly. —*v.t.* free from worms. —**worm′y,** *adj.* —**worm gear,** a wheel driven by a screw.

worm-′eat″en *adj.* **1,** eaten or bored into by worms. **2,** old; worn-out; worthless.

worm′hole″ *n.* **1,** a hole made by a worm. **2,** (*Astron.*) a hypothetical passage-way in space connecting a black hole and a white hole.

worm′wood″ (wērm′wûd″) *n.* **1,** a bitter herb used in tonics and in absinthe. **2,** bitterness.

worn (wôrn) *v.* pret. & p.p. of *wear.* —*adj.* weary. —**worn′ness,** *n.*

worn-″out′ *adj.* **1,** unfit for use. **2,** exhausted.

wor′ry (wēr′ė) *v.t.* **1,** cause to feel anxious; harass; bother. **2,** grasp with the teeth and shake. —*v.i.* **1,** be anxious; fret. **2,** (*Informal*) manage somehow. —*n.* anxiety; trouble. —**wor′ri·er,** *n.* —**wor′ri·ment** (-mənt) *n.* (*Informal*) worry. —**wor′ri-some** (-səm) *adj.* causing worry. —**worry beads,** a string of beads toyed with for relaxation or distraction.

wor′ry·wart″ (-wôrt) *n.* (*Informal*) someone who worries excessively.

worse (wērs) *adj.* & *adv.* comp. of *bad, ill, badly.* —**wors′en,** *v.t. & i.*

wor′ship (wēr′ship) *n.* **1,** reverence and homage, esp. to God. **2,** religious services. **3,** a title of honor. —*v.t.* **1,** pay divine honors to; adore (God). **2,** love or admire inordinately. —*v.i.* perform or attend religious services. —**wor′ship·er,** *n.* —**wor′ship·ful,** *adj.*

worst (wērst) *adj.* & *adv.* superl. of *bad, ill, badly.* —*v.t.* defeat. —*n.* that which is worst.

wor′sted (wûs′tid) *n.* **1,** a tight-twisted woolen yarn; fabric made of it. **2,** a woolen yarn for knitting, named for Worstead, a parish in England.

wort (wērt) *n.* **1,** a plant, herb, or vegetable: used in old plant names, as *colewort.* **2,** the infusion of malt which, after fermentation, becomes beer.

worth (wērth) *adj.* **1,** meriting; deserving. **2,** having a specified value. **3,** equivalent in value to. **4,** possessing. —*n.* **1,** value, esp. in money. **2,** excellence; merit.

worth′less (-ləs) *adj.* useless; worth nothing; undeserving. —**worth′less·ness,** *n.*

worth″while′ *adj.* serving a useful purpose. —**worth″while′ness,** *n.*

wor′thy (wēr′*th*ė) *adj.* deserving respect. —**wor′thi·ness,** *n.*

would (wûd) *v.* pret. of *will.*

would-′be″ *adj.* hoping or pretending to be.

wound (woond) *n.* **1,** an injury to flesh or tissue, esp. one caused by violence. **2,** any injury; something that hurts. —*v.t. & i.* **1,** hurt by violence. **2,** hurt the feelings (of).

wound (wownd) *v.* pret. & p.p. of *wind* (wīnd).

wove (wōv) *v.* pret. of *weave*.

wo'ven (wō'vən) *v.* p.p. of *weave*.

wow *interj.* expressing admiration or wonder. —*v.t.* (*Slang*) captivate. —*n.* **1,** a distortion of fidelity in sound reproduction. **2,** (*Slang*) a wonderful person, thing, or performance.

wrack (rak) *n.* wreck. ❏ *rack*

wraith (rāth) *n.* an apparition; a specter; a ghost. —**wraith'y,** *adj.*

wran'gle (rang'gəl) *v.i.* argue noisily; dispute. —*v.t.* round up (livestock). —*n.* a noisy quarrel. —**wran'gler,** *n.*

wrap (rap) *v.t.* [**wrapped, wrap'ping**] **1,** cover with (paper, etc.); envelop; make into a bundle. **2,** roll or fold (paper, etc.) around. —*n.* a cloak or shawl; (*Informal*) an overcoat. —**wrap up, 1,** conclude; work out the details of. **2,** summarize. —**wrapped up in,** engrossed.

wrap'a·round'' *adj.* designating a garment that wraps around the body before being fastened.

wrap'per (-ər) *n.* **1,** any covering. **2,** a dressing gown.

wrap'ping (rap'ing) *n.* that which wraps; material for wrapping.

wrap'up'' *n.* summary; précis.

wrasse (ras) *n.* any of various marine fishes.

wrath (ràth) *n.* **1,** fierce anger; rage. **2,** vengeance. —**wrath'ful,** *adj.*

wreak (rēk) *v.t.* inflict.

> **wreak, wreck**
> ☛ Do not confuse these two words. To *wreck* is to cause the ruin of; to *wreak* is to inflict, as to *wreak havoc*.

wreath (rēth) *n.* something twisted or formed into a circular band; a garland.

wreathe (rēth) *v.t.* form by twisting; intertwine; encircle.

wreck (rek) *n.* **1,** destruction, disruption, or ruin. **2,** one who or that which is in a state of ruin; remains; a shipwrecked vessel. —*v.t.* cause the ruin or demolition of. —**wreck'age,** *n.* ❏ *wreak*

wreck'er (-ər) *n.* **1,** one who wrecks. **2,** a vehicle for removing or towing wrecked cars.

wren (ren) *n.* any of a family of small, migratory songbirds.

wrench (rench) *n.* **1,** a violent, sudden twist or jerk; a sprain. **2,** a grasping tool. —*v.t.* **1,** give a sudden twist to; distort. **2,** sprain. **3,** wrest forcibly.

wrest (rest) *v.t.* remove or seize by, or as if by, violent twisting; wring; wrench.

wres'tle (res'əl) *v.i.* **1,** struggle, as two persons each trying to throw the other to the mat in a contest. **2,** contend; grapple; strive. —*v.t.* contest with in wrestling. —*n.* a wrestling match. —**wres'tler,** *n.* —**wres'-tling,** *n.*

wretch (rech) *n.* **1,** one who is very unhappy or unfortunate. **2,** a contemptible person.

wretch'ed *adj.* **1,** miserable. **2,** mean; lowly. —**wretch'ed·ness,** *n.*

wrig'gle (rig'əl) *v.i.* **1,** move along sinuously; writhe; squirm. **2,** make way by opportunism and shrewdness. —*n.* a squirming motion. —**wrig'gler,** *n.* —**wrig'-gly,** *adj.*

wright (rīt) *n.* a worker.

wring (ring) *v.t.* [**wrung** (rung), **wring'-ing**] **1,** twist or flex forcibly. **2,** distress. **3,** squeeze out; extort. —*v.i.* writhe. —*n.* a twist. —**wring'er,** *n.* a device for pressing water from washed clothes. —**wring'ing wet,** drenched.

wrin'kle (ring'kəl) *n.* **1,** a slight ridge or furrow in a surface; a crease in the skin, esp. one caused by old age. **2,** (*Informal*) a good or new idea. —*v.t.* & *i.* crease; pucker.

wrist (rist) *n.* **1,** the joint between the hand and the forearm. **2,** a connecting stud or pin: *wrist pin.* —**wrist watch,** a watch strapped to the wrist.

wrist'let *n.* a band around the wrist.

writ (rit) *n.* **1,** (*Law*) a written order or document. **2,** Scripture.

write (rīt) *v.t.* [**wrote** (rōt), **writ'ten** (rit'ən), **writ'ing**] **1,** form (letters or characters) on a surface by hand. **2,** set down for reading, as with a pen or typewriter; cause to be written, as by dictation. **3,** cover with writing. **4,** (with *off*) treat as a loss; forget about. —*v.i.* **1,** write words or characters. **2,** work as an author. **3,** conduct a correspondence. —**writer's cramp,** a muscular spasm in the hand caused by holding a writing implement for a long period of time.

write-'in'' *adj.* pert. to votes, written or sent in, or to a candidate voted for or elected by such votes.

write-'off'' *n.* an amount, person, etc., considered lost and hence canceled.

write-'up'' *n.* a written account, esp. a laudatory description.

writhe (rīth) *v.i.* twist one's body, as from pain.

writ′ing (rīt′ing) *n.* **1,** written matter; a literary work. **2,** handwriting.

writ′ten (rit′ən) *v.* p.p. of *write.*

wrong (râng) *adj.* **1,** deviating from right, truth, or morals. **2,** not correct in fact; mistaken. **3,** unsuitable; improper. —*adv.* not rightly; incorrectly; amiss. —*n.* evil; harm; injury. —*v.t.* **1,** do harm to; treat unfairly. **2,** unjustly blame or disapprove of.

wrong′do″er (-doo″ər) *n.* a sinner. —**wrong′do″ing,** *n.*

wrong′ful (-fəl) *adj.* injurious; unlawful. —**wrong′ful·ness,** *n.*

wrong″head′ed *adj.* obstinately opinionated; misguided and stubborn. —**wrong″head′ed·ness,** *n.*

wrote (rōt) *v.* pret. of *write.*

wroth (roth) *adj.* very angry.

wrought (rât) *v. & adj.* worked; formed, fashioned, or hammered. —**wrought iron,** iron purified of carbon. —**wrought-″up′,** *adj.* disturbed; excited.

wrung (rung) *v.* pret. & p.p. of *wring.*

wry (rī) *adj.* **1,** twisted to one side; askew; distorted. **2,** ironic. —**wry′ness,** *n.*

wry′neck″ *n.* **1,** spasmodic contraction of the neck muscles; torticollis. **2,** a bird resembling a woodpecker.

Wun′der·kind″ (vûn′dər-kint″ *n.* (*Ger.*) child prodigy.

wy′an·dotte″ (wī′ən-dot″) *n.* a breed of domestic fowl.

WYSIWYG (wiz′ė-wig″) a type of computer representation that accurately displays actual typefaces, etc.: *W(hat) Y(ou) S(ee) I(s) W(hat) Y(ou) G(et).*

X

X, x (eks) **1,** the 24th letter of the English alphabet. **2,** the legal signature of an illiterate person. **3,** Roman numeral for 10.

xan·tho- (zan-thə) *pref.* yellow.

xan′thous (zan′thəs) *adj.* yellow; yellow-skinned.

X′-chro″mo·some *n.* a female sex chromosome.

xe′bec (zē′bek) *n.* a small Mediterranean three-masted vessel. Also, **ze′bec.**

xe′ni·a (zē′nė-ə) *n.* (*Bot.*) the effect of pollen on a seed or fruit, other than on the embryo.

xen·o- (zen-ə) *pref.* alien.

xe′non (zē′non) *n.* an inert gaseous chemical element, no. 54, symbol Xe.

xen″o·pho′bi·a (zen″ə-fō′bė-ə) *n.* fear or hatred of foreigners.

xe·ro- (zir-ə) *pref.* dry.

xe·rog′ra·phy (zi-räg′rə-fė) *n.* copying by use of light action on an electrically charged photoconductive insulating surface that transfers a special printing powder only from those areas that remain electrically charged, thereby reproducing the image to be copied.

xe′ro·phyte″ (zir′ə-fīt″) *n.* a plant that grows in arid regions, as the cactus. —**xe″·rophyt′ic** (-fit′ik) *adj.* —**xe″ro·phyt′i·cal·ly,** *adv.*

Xe′rox (zi′-räks) *n.* (*T.N.*) **1,** a machine that copies by xerography. **2,** a copy made by xerography. —*v.t.* (*l.c.*) to copy by xerography.

xi (zī or sī) *n.* the fourteenth letter of the Greek alphabet (Ξ, ξ).

X′mas (eks′məs) *abbr.* Christmas.

X-′rat″ed *adj.* racy; pornographic; hence, of movies, literature, etc., for adults only; not suitable for children.

x-′ray″ (eks′-rā″) *n.* **1,** (*pl.*) electromagnetic radiations of extremely short wavelength and high penetrating power, commonly used to photograph the interior of solids and for the treatment of skin or cancerous diseases. **2,** a photograph made by x-rays. **3,** (*Communications*) the letter *x.* —*v.t.* examine, photograph, or treat by x-rays. —**x-′ra·di·a′tion,** *n.*

xy′lem (zī′lem) *n.* the woody tissue of plants.

xy·lo- (zī-lə) *pref.* wood; wooden.

xy·log′ra·phy (zī-log′rə-fė) *n.* wood engraving. —**xy′lo·graph″,** *n.* —**xy″lo·graph′ic,** *adj.* —**xy″lograph′i·cal·ly,** *adv.*

xy′loid (zī′loid) *adj.* resembling wood.

xy′lo·phone″ (zī′lə-fōn″) *n.* a musical instrument comprising a series of wooden bars processed to sound musical tones when struck with wooden hammers. —**xy′lo·phon″ist,** *n.*

Y

Y, y (wī) the 25th letter of the English alphabet.

-y (ė; i) *suf.* forming adjectives: **1,** of the nature of, as *misty.* **2,** being, as *guilty.*

yacht (yot) *n.* a pleasure ship used solely for its owner's personal purposes. —*v.i.* travel in a yacht. —**yacht′ing,** *n.* —**yachts′-man** (-mən) [*pl.* -**men**], **yachts′wom″an,** *n.* the owner of a yacht.

ya'hoo (yä'hoo) *n.* a coarse, uncouth person.

> **yahoo**
> ↔ From the novel *Gulliver's Travels* by 18th-c. English satirist Jonathan Swift.

Yah'weh (yä'we) *n.* variant transliteration of Jehovah.

yak *n.* a long-haired Asiatic ox.

yam *n.* **1,** a tuberous root cultivated as food. **2,** the sweet potato.

yam'mer (yam'ər) (*Informal*) *v.i.* **1,** whimper; whine. **2,** shout; yell. **3,** talk persistently. **4,** lament. —*n.* an act of yammering.

yang *n.* the masculine force in Chinese philosophy, opposed to yin.

yank *v.t. & i.* pull suddenly; jerk. —*n.* **1,** a jerk. **2,** (*cap.*) (*Slang*) Yankee.

Yan'kee (yang'kė) *n.* **1,** a citizen of the U.S. **2,** a native of the NE states. **3,** in the So. U.S., any native of the No. states. **4,** (*Communications*) the letter *y.* —*adj.* pert. to Yankees.

> **yankee**
> ↔ Originally a nickname for Dutchmen, perhaps from Dutch *Janke*, a diminutive for the name *Jan.* It first referred to New Englanders, but gradually spread to include all inhabitants of the U.S.

yap *v.i.* [**yapped, yap'ping**] **1,** yelp. **2,** talk foolishly, or in a barking manner. —*n.* a yelp.

ya·pok' *n.* a small, aquatic opossum of Central and So. Amer, named for the Oyapok River in So. Amer.

yard (yärd) *n.* **1,** the ground adjoining a building. **2,** an enclosure or area in which any work is carried on. **3,** a unit of linear measure, equal to 3 ft. **4,** a rod or spar, esp. a crosswise piece on a mast. —**yard goods,** goods sold by length, as fabrics, etc. —**yard sale,** garage sale. —**the whole nine yards,** (*Informal*) the whole thing. ❑ *garden*

yard'age (-ij) *n.* distance or area in yards.

yard'arm" *n.* (*Naut.*) an end of a yard.

yard'mas"ter *n.* one who superintends a railway yard.

yard'stick" (yärd'stik") *n.* **1,** a calibrated stick one yard long. **2,** any standard of measurement.

yare (yär) *adj.* (*Naut.*) of a ship, easily handled.

yar'mul·ke (yar'məl-kə) *n.* a skullcap worn by Jewish males.

yarn (yärn) *n.* **1,** fibers of cotton, wool, etc., twisted together. **2,** a tale, esp., a fabricated one. —*v.i.* tell or exchange stories.

yar'row (yar'ō) *n.* a plant related to the aster; milfoil.

yash·mak' (yäsh-mäk') *n.* a veil worn in public by Muslim women to cover the face.

yaw (yâ) *v.i.* turn to one side, heading off course. —*n.* a deviation.

yawl (yâl) *n.* a small two-masted sailing vessel.

yawn (yân) *v.i.* **1,** open the mouth involuntarily in reaction from fatigue or sleepiness. **2,** open wide; extend far. —*n.* a yawning.

yawp (yâp) (*Informal*) *v.i.* **1,** yelp. **2,** make a loud, uncouth sound, as an audible yawn. **3,** talk noisily. —*n.* **1,** a yelp. **2,** a loud sound or cry. **3,** noisy talk.

yaws (yâz) *n.pl.* a skin disease.

Y'-chro"mo·some *n.* a male sex chromosome.

y·clept' (i-klept') *v.* (*Archaic*) named.

ye (yē) *pron. pl.* **1,** (*Obs.*) you. **2,** (*Erroneous*) the.

> **ye**
> ↔ The use of *ye* for *the* resulted from a misreading of the runic thorn (þ), pronounced (th), which was represented by *y.*

yea (yā) *adv.* **1,** yes. **2,** truly; indeed. —*n.* an affirmative vote.

year (yir) *n.* **1,** the period of one revolution of the earth about the sun, about 365 days. **2,** the period from Jan. 1 to the next Dec. 31 inclusive (calendar year); any period of 365 or 366 consecutive calendar days. **3,** the period of an annually recurring activity, as a school year. **4,** (*pl.*) age; old age; time. —**year'ly,** *adj. & adv.*

year'book" *n.* an annual publication, usually dealing with events of the past year.

year'ling (yir'ling) *n.* an animal one year old, or in its second year.

yearn (yērn) *v.i.* desire strongly; long for something. —**yearn'ing,** *n.*

yeast (yēst) *n.* **1,** a yellowish substance, an aggregate of minute fungi, used to leaven bread and ferment liquors. **2,** any froth or spume. —*v.i.* ferment.

yeast'y (-ė) *adj.* frothy; light. —**yeast'i·ness,** *n.*

yecch (yekh) *interj.* yuck. Also, **yech.**

yegg (yeg) *n.* (*Slang*) a robber, esp. one who cracks safes.

yell (yel) *v.i.* cry out; shout. —*v.t.* utter in a loud, piercing tone. —*n.* **1,** a shout or scream. **2,** a cry or slogan uttered in concert by a crowd.

yel′low (yel′ō) *n.* the color of lemons, the yolk of an egg, etc.; a hue between orange and green in the spectrum. —*adj.* **1,** of this color. **2,** yellow-skinned; belonging to the Mongolian race. **3,** (*Informal*) cowardly; contemptible. **4,** offensively sensational (of newspapers). —**yellow-dog contract,** (*Slang*) a contract in which workers agree not to join a union. —**yellow fever,** an infectious febrile disease, also called *yellow jack.* —**yellow jacket,** a variety of wasp. —**yellow pages,** a telephone directory of businesses and services. —**yellow peril,** (*Offensive*) Asian peoples, when viewed as dangerous because so numerous.

yel′low·bel′ly *n.* (*Slang*) a coward.

yelp *v.i.* give a quick, shrill cry, like a dog. —*n.* a sharp cry; a bark.

yen *n.* **1,** the monetary unit of Japan. **2,** (*Informal*) yearning.

yen′ta (yen′tə) *n.* (*Slang*) a nosy, gossiping person.

yeo′man (yō′mən) *n.* [*pl.* **-men**] **1,** a petty officer of the U.S. Navy whose duties are clerical. **2,** (*Brit.*) an independent farmer; (*Archaic*) an attendant or servant. —**yeo′man·ry,** *n.* yeomen collectively. —**yeoman service,** vigorous and effective work.

yes *adv.* a word expressing affirmation, agreement, consent. —**yes′man″,** *n.* one who always agrees with a superior.

ye·shi′va (ye-shē′və) *n.* an Orthodox Jewish school.

yes′ter- (yes′tər) *adj.* past. —**yes″ter-eve′, yes″ter·night′, yes″ter·year′,** *n.*

yes′ter·day (yes′tər-dā) *n.* **1,** the day preceding the present day. **2,** time of the immediate past. —*adv.* on yesterday.

yet *adv.* **1,** at or up to the present or some future time; hitherto; already. **2,** as formerly; still; in continuation. **3,** in addition; besides; moreover. —*conj.* nevertheless; notwithstanding.

ye′ti (ye′tè) *n.* a humanoid beast, by some supposed to exist in Tibet, also called *abominable snowman.*

yew (ū) *n.* an evergreen coniferous tree; its wood.

Yid′dish (yid′ish) *n.* a language of the Jews, incorporating Hebrew, German, and other words.

yield (yēld) *v.t. & i.* **1,** produce in payment. **2,** bring forth by natural process; bear (as fruit); produce. **3,** surrender; relinquish. —*v.i.* give way; assent; comply. —*n.* what is produced. —**yield′ing,** *adj.* compliant; tractable.

yin *n.* the female force in Chinese philosophy, opposed to yang.

yip *v.i.* [**yipped, yip′ping**] (*Informal*) bark sharply; yelp. —*n.* a yelp.

yip′pie (yip′ė) *n.* a radical hippie activist

> **yippie**
> ↔ An abbreviation of *Youth International Party.*

yo′del (yō′dəl) *v.i. & t.* sing with alternation between ordinary voice and falsetto.

yo′ga (yō′gə) *n.* a Hindu ascetic philosophy.

yo′gi (yō′gė) *n.* one who practices or teaches yoga.

yo′gurt (yō′gûrt) *n.* a curdled milk food.

yoicks (yoiks) *interj.* a cry of fox hunters.

yoke (yōk) *n.* **1,** a contrivance for fastening together the necks of two draft animals, as oxen. **2,** anything resembling a yoke in form or use, as the collarpiece of a garment. **3,** something that binds or holds parts together. **4,** servitude; slavery. —*v.t.* put a yoke on; couple; link.

yo′kel (yō′kəl) *n.* a rustic; an awkward person.

yolk (yōk) *n.* **1,** the yellow substance of an egg. **2,** the vital or essential part of anything.

Yom Kip·pur′ (yom kə-poor′) a fast day, the Day of Atonement, in Judaism.

yon *adj.* (*Poetic*) yonder.

yon′der (yon′dər) *adv. & adj.* in that (distant or more distant) place.

yore (yôr) *adv.* (*Archaic*) long ago.

York′shire pudding (yôrk′shər) a batter pudding baked in roast-meat drippings, named for a former county of England.

you (ū) *pron. sing. & pl.* [*poss.* **your** (yûr), **yours**] the personal pronoun of the second person; in nominative it always takes a plural verb. ❑ *your*

young (yung) *adj.* **1,** being in an early stage of life or growth; not yet mature. **2,** recent; not fully developed. **3,** having the appearance and vigor of youth. **4,** inexperienced. —*n.* offspring. —**young′ish,** *adj.* —**young′ness,** *n.* —**young blood, 1,** youthful vigor, ideas, etc. **2,** a relatively young person or persons. —**young Turk,** an aggressive reformer; revolutionary.

fat, fāte, fär, fåre, fåll, åsk; met, hē, hĕr, maybė; pin, pīne; not, nōte, ôr, tool

young′ling *n.* **1,** any young person or thing. **2,** a beginner. —*adj.* youthful; young.

young′ster (-stər) *n.* a young person.

your (yûr) *pron.* poss. of *you*. —**yours,** poss. of *you,* used predicatively. —**yourself′,** emphatic and reflexive form of *you.*

> **your, you're**
> ☛ Do not confuse these two forms. *Your* is the possessive form of *you. You're* is a contraction for *you are.*

youth (ūth) *n.* **1,** the period of life from puberty to maturity; adolescence. **2,** the earliest stage. **3,** the condition of being young. **4,** the qualities of early age, as vigor. **5,** a young person, esp. male; young persons collectively. —**youth′ful,** *adj.* —**youth′ful·ness,** *n.*

yowl *v.i.* utter a long wailing cry; howl. —*n.* such a cry.

yo′yo (yō′yō) *n.* **1,** toy consisting of two thick disks designed to be spun out and reeled in by a string. **2,** (*Slang*) an eccentric or crazy person.

yt·ter′bi·um (i-tēr′bē-əm) *n.* a metallic chemical element, no. 70, symbol Yb.

> **ytterbium, yttrium**
> ↔ The names of both elements are derived from *Ytterby,* a quarry near Stockholm, Sweden.

yt′tri·um (it′rē-əm) *n.* a metallic chemical element, no. 39, symbol Yt.

yu·an′ (ū-än′) *n. sing. & pl.* the monetary unit of China.

yuc′ca (yuk′ə) *n.* a plant of the lily family.

yuck (yuk) *interj.* an expression of disgust. —*n.* something disgusting. —**yuck′y,** *adj.*

Yu′go·slav″ (ū′gō-släv″) *adj. & n.* of or pert. to the former Yugoslavia, its people, its language, etc.

yule (ūl) *n.* Christmas or the Christmas season. Also, **yule′tide″.**

yum′my (yum′ē) *adj.* (*Informal*) delicious.

yup′pie (yup′ē) *n.* a prosperous middle-class professional person.

> **yuppie**
> ↔ An abbreviation of *Young Upwardly Mobile Professional.*

Z

Z, z (zē) the 26th letter of the English alphabet.

za·ba·glio′ne (zä-bəl-yō′nė) *n.* (*It.*) a foamy dessert custard with Marsala wine.

za′ny (zā′nė) *n.* **1,** a clownish person; an amusing fool, a simpleton.

zap *v.t.* (*Slang*) **1,** kill or wipe out with a sudden burst, as of electricity, firepower, etc. **2,** cook in a microwave oven.

zeal (zēl) *n.* fervent ardor; eagerness; enthusiasm; diligence.

zeal′ot (zel′ət) *n.* one who is fanatically earnest.

zeal′ous (zel′əs) *adj.* diligent; earnest. —**zeal′ous·ness,** *n.*

ze′bec (zē′bek) *n.* xebec.

ze′bra (zē′brə) *n.* an Afr. mammal related to the horse, marked with alternate light and dark stripes.

ze′bu (zē′bū) *n.* a bovine animal having a hump over the shoulders, domesticated in the Asia.

zed *n.* (*Brit.*) the letter z.

Zeit′geist″ (tsīt′gīst″) *n.* (*Ger.*) the spirit of the time; the moral and intellectual thought or feeling characteristic of an age or period.

Zen *n.* a school of Buddhism which stresses meditation.

ze·na′na (ze-nä′nə) *n.* in India, the living quarters of the women; the harem.

ze′nith (zē′nith) *n.* **1,** the point in the sky directly above an observer or place on the earth. **2,** the highest point of anything; culmination. ❑ *nadir*

zeph′yr (zef′ər) *n.* a mild, gentle breeze.

Zep′pe·lin (zep′ə-lin) *n.* a type of dirigible balloon with a cigar-shaped bag, named for German general Count Ferdinand von Zeppelin.

ze′ro (zir′ō) [*pl.* **-ros**] *n.* **1,** the symbol 0, meaning the absence of quantity; the cipher. **2,** the first or lowest point on a scale of measurement, as a thermometer. **3,** naught; nothing. —*v.t.* **1,** adjust to a zero point. **2,** (with *in*) aim at the center (on). —**zero-coupon bond,** a bond bearing no interest but sold below face value. —**zero hour,** a time set for the commencement of action. —**zerobase budgeting,** a process in which the entire budget is reviewed every year. —**zero population growth,** the principle that births and deaths in a given year should be equal. —**zero-sum game,** a game in which losses are considered as negative and the sum of winnings and losses are always zero; hence, a game in which there is always a loser.

ze′ro-ze′ro *adj.* of an atmospheric condition characterized by zero ceiling and zero visibility.

zest *n.* **1,** keen relish; hearty enjoyment; gusto. **2,** piquant or appealing flavor; an enjoyable quality. **—zest′ful,** *adj.* **—zest′y,** *adj.*

ze′ta (zā′tə) *n.* the sixth letter of the Greek alphabet (Z, ζ).

zig′zag″ *n.* a sharp angle or series of such angles; a line or course that turns abruptly from side to side. **—adj.** having sharp turnings or angles. **—v.i. & t. [-zagged″, -zag″ging]** advance or form in zigzags.

zilch *n.* (*Slang*) zero.

> **zilch**
>
> ↔ From the character *Mr. Zilch,* from the humor magazine *Ballyhoo.*

zil′lion (zil′yən) *adj.* an indefinite, very large number.

zinc (zink) *n.* a metallic chemical element, no. 30, symbol Zn. **—zinc ointment,** a salve containing zinc oxide. **—zinc oxide,** an oxide of zinc, an antiseptic.

zing *n.* **1,** a high-pitched humming sound. **2,** (*Informal*) vitality; energy. **—interj.** an exclamation of enthusiasm. **—v.i.** make a high-pitched humming sound. **—zing′er** *n.* (*Informal*) a sharp or witty retort.

zin′ni·a (zin′ē-ə) *n.* a plant having showy yellow or red flowers, named for 18th-c. German botanist J. G. Zinn.

Zi′on (zī′ən) *n.* **1,** a hill in Jerusalem, designated as holy. **2,** heaven.

Zi′on·ism (zī′ə-niz-əm) *n.* advocacy of the establishment and support of a Jewish nation (now Israel) in Palestine. **—Zi′on·ist,** *n.*

zip *n.* **1,** the sound of a bullet in flight. **2,** energy; vim. **3,** (*Informal*) zero. **—v.i. [zipped, zip′ping]** sound or move with a zip. **—v.t.** fasten with a zipper. **—zip gun,** a homemade .22-caliber pistol.

ZIP code 1, [also, **ZIP code number**] a special 5- or 9-digit number assigned by the U.S. Postal Service to each of the many postal districts throughout the U.S. to speed the distribution of mail. **2,** the entire system of ZIP code numbers: *Z*(one) *I*(mprovement) *P*(rogram).

zip′per (zip′ər) *n.* a fastening device that causes two strips of metal or plastic studs to interlock.

zip′py (-ē) *adj.* pert; lively. **—zip′pi·ness,** *n.*

zir′con (zėr′kon) *n.* a common silicate mineral used as a gem.

zir·co′ni·um (zėr-kō′nē-əm) *n.* a metallic element, no. 40, symbol Zr.

zit *n.* (*Informal*) a pimple.

zith′er (zith′ər) *n.* a musical instrument comprising a number of strings stretched over a flat sounding board, played with the fingers or a plectrum. ❏ *guitar*

zi′ti (zē′tē) *n.* a type of tubular pasta.

zlo′ty (zlâ′tē) *n.* [*pl.* **-tys**] the monetary unit of Poland.

zo′di·ac″ (zō′dē-ak″) *n.* the imaginary belt in the sky in which lie the apparent paths of the sun, moon, and principal planets. There are twelve signs of the zodiac:

Aquarius (*Water Bearer*)	**Virgo** (*Virgin*)
Pisces (*Fish*)	**Libra** (*Balance*)
Aries (*Ram*)	**Scorpio** (*Scorpion*)
Taurus (*Bull*)	**Sagittarius** (*Archer*)
Gemini (*Twins*)	
Cancer (*Crab*)	**Capricorn** (*Goat*)
Leo (*Lion*)	

zo·di′a·cal (zō-dī′ə-kəl) *adj.* pert. to the zodiac.

zo′ic (zō′ik) *adj.* pert. to animal life.

zom′bi (zom′bē) *n.* **1,** a snake deity worshiped by certain tribes of Afr. and the W.I. **2,** a dead body brought to life. Also, **zom′bie.**

zone (zōn) *n.* **1,** a part of the surface of a sphere lying between two parallel planes. **2,** any of the five arbitrary divisions of the surface of the earth: North Frigid, North Temperate, Torrid, South Temperate, South Frigid. **3,** region; district; any distinct, defined, or delimited area. **—v.t. 1,** encircle like a belt. **2,** divide into or mark with zones. **—zon′al,** *adj.*

zonked (zänkt) *adj.* (*Slang*) under or as if under the influence of a hallucinogenic drug. **—zonk,** *v.t.*

zoo *n.* **1,** an enclosure where live animals are kept for public exhibition. **2,** (*Informal*) a place characterized by disorder. **—zoo event,** (*Astron.*) an occurrence of unknown origin.

zo·o- (zō-ə) *pref.* pert. to living animals.

zo″o·log′i·cal (zō″ə-loj′i-kəl) *adj.* pert. to zoology. **—zoological garden**

zo·ol′o·gy (zō-ol′ə-jē) *n.* the general science of animal life. **—zo·ol′o·gist,** *n.*

zoom *v.i. & t.* fly (an aircraft) on a sudden upward course. **—zoom lens** [also, **var′i·fo″cal lens**], a motion-picture or television camera lens permitting change in the image size without loss of focus.

zo′o·phyte″ (zō′ə-fīt″) *n.* an animal that looks like a plant, as a coral. **—zo″o·phyt′ic** (-fit′ik) *adj.*

zoot suit (*Slang*) an extreme costume

popular during the 1940s among young male jitterbugs.

zor'il (zôr'il) *n.* a South African animal resembling the skunk.

Zo"ro·as'tri·an (zō"rə-as'tre-ən) *adj.* pert. to Zoroaster, Persian prophet of 1000 B.C., his religion or philosophy.

Zou·ave' (zoo-äv') *n.* formerly, a brightly dressed French infantryman.

zounds (zowndz) *interj.* of surprise, a shortening of *(God')s wounds.*

zoy'si·a (zoi'sė-ə) *n.* a type of grass, named for 18th-c. German botanist Karl von Zois.

ZPG *abbr.* zero population growth.

zuc·chet'to (zû-ket'tō) *n.* [*pl.* **-tos**] (*It.*) a small round skullcap worn by Rom. Cath. clergymen.

zuc·chi'ni (zû-kē'nė) *n.* [*pl.* **-nis**] a variety of summer squash, used as a vegetable.

Zu'lu (zoo'loo) *adj. & n.* **1,** of or pert. to a So. African people, their language, etc. **2,** (*l.c.*) (*Communications*) the letter *z.*

zwie'back" (tswē'bäk") *n.* a kind of toasted bread prepared in small pieces.

Zwing'li·an (zwing'lė-ən) *adj.* pert. to Ulrich Zwingli, 1484–1531, Swiss Protestant reformer.

zy'de·co" (zī'di-kō") *n.* a type of Cajun blues music.

zyme (zīm) *n.* the specific principle regarded as the cause of a zymotic disease.

zy·mo- (zī-mō) *pref.* pert. to leaven.

zy·mo'sis (zī-mō'sis) *n.* **1,** an infectious or contagious disease. **2,** fermentation as a supposed cause of disease. —**zy·mot'ic** (-mot'ik) *adj.*

zy'mur·gy (zī'mər-jė) *n.* (*Chem.*) the science and study of fermentation, as in brewing.

ABBREVIATIONS
Including all abbreviations used in this Dictionary.

A.A., Alcoholics Anonymous.
AAA, American Automobile Association.
A. & M., Agricultural and Mechanical.
A.A.U., Amateur Athletic Union.
A.B., Bachelor of Arts.
A.B.A., American Bar Association; American Basketball Association.
abbr., abbreviation.
ABC, American Broadcasting Company; Argentina, Brazil, and Chile.
ABM, antiballistic missile.
AC, alternating current.
A.C., before Christ; athletic club.
A/C, account; air conditioning.
acct., account; accountant.
A.D., Anno Domini; active duty.
A.D.A., Americans for Democratic Action.
adj., adjective; (*cap.*) Adjutant.
Adm., Admiral.
ADT, Atlantic Daylight Time.
adv., adverb.
advt., advertisement.
ae., aet., aetat., aetatis, (*Lat.*) aged.
AEC, Atomic Energy Commission.
AEF, American Expeditionary Force.
aero., aeronautical; aeronautics.
A.F. & A.M., Ancient Free and Accepted Masons.
AFB, Air Force Base.
AFC, automatic frequency control.
A.F.L., A.F. of L., American Federation of Labor.
Afr., Africa, African.
A.F.T., American Federation of Teachers.
AFTRA, American Federation of Television and Radio Artists.
A.I.D., Agency for International Development.
AIDS, acquired immunodeficiency syndrome.
A.H., anno Hegirae.
AK, Ak., Alaska.
a.k.a., also known as; alias.
AL, American League.
AL, Al., Ala., Alabama.
Alas., Alaska.
A.L.P., American Labor Party.
Alta., Alberta.
AM, amplitude modulation.
A.M., Master of Arts.
A.M., a.m., ante meridiem.
A.M.A., American Medical Association.
Amer., America; American.
AMG, Allied Military Government.
amp., ampere; amperage.
AMVETS, American Veterans of World War II, Korea, and Vietnam.
anat., anatomical; anatomy.
anon., anonymous.

ANTA, American National Theater and Academy.
AP, Associated Press.
APB, all points bulletin.
APO, Army Post Office.
APR, annual percentage rate.
Apr., April.
apt(s)., apartment(s).
AR, Ar., Arkansas.
A.R.C., American (National) Red Cross.
Arch., Archbishop; (*l.c.*) architect.
archit., architect; architecture.
arith., arithmetic; arithmetical.
Ariz., Arizona.
Ark., Arkansas.
ARM, adjustable rate mortgage.
art., article.
AS, American Samoa.
A-S., A.S., Anglo-Saxon.
ASAP, as soon as possible.
A.S.C., American Society of Cinematographers.
ASCAP, American Society of Composers, Authors, and Publishers.
ASCII, American Standard Code for Information Interchange.
ASEAN, Association of Southeast Asian Nations.
assn., association.
assoc., associate; association.
asst., assistant.
Assyr., Assyrian.
AST, Atlantic Standard Time.
astron., astronomy.
Atl., Atlantic.
ATM, automated teller machine.
att., atty., attorney.
ATV, all-terrain vehicle.
Aug., August.
Aus., Austl., Australia.
Aust., Austria; Austrian.
aux., auxiliary.
A.V., Authorized Version (of the Bible); audiovisual.
av., average.
avdp., avoirdupois.
Ave., Av., Avenue.
AWOL, absent without official leave.
AZ, Az., Arizona.

B.A., Bachelor of Arts; Buenos Aires.
Bart., Bt., Baronet.
B.B.A., Bachelor of Business Administration.
BBB, Better Business Bureau.
BBC, British Broadcasting Corporation.
bbl., barrel; barrels.
B.C., British Columbia; before Christ.

B.C.E., before the Christian (or Common) era.

B.D., Bachelor of Divinity.

bd., board.

BEF, British Expeditionary Force or Forces.

Belg., Belgian; Belgium.

Benj., Benjamin.

b.f., boldface (type).

B.F.A., Bachelor of Fine Arts.

bhp, brake horsepower.

Bib., Bible; Biblical.

b.i.d., twice a day (in prescription).

biol., biology.

B/L, bill of lading.

bldg., blg., building.

Blvd., boulevard.

BLT, bacon, lettuce, and tomato (sandwich).

BMI, Broadcast Music, Inc.

bn., battalion.

bot., botany.

B.P.O.E., Benevolent and Protective Order of Elks.

Braz., Brazil; Brazilian.

Brig., Brigadier.

Brit., British.

bro., bros., brother(s).

B.S., B.Sc., Bachelor of Science.

B/S, bill of sale.

B.S.A., Boy Scouts of America.

bsh., bushel; bushels.

B.T.U., British thermal unit(s).

Bulg., Bulgaria; Bulgarian.

B.V., B.V.M., Blessed Virgin (Mary).

BX, base exchange.

b/w, black and white.

B.W.I., British West Indies.

BYO, bring your own.

C., Celsius; centigrade.

C.A., Central America; Coast Artillery; chartered accountant.

CA, Ca., California.

ca., circ., (*Lat.* circa) about.

CAA, Civil Aeronautics Authority.

CAB, Civil Aeronautics Board.

CAD/CAM, computer-aided design/computer-aided manufacturing.

Cal., Calif. California.

Can., Canada; Canadian.

cap., capital(ized).

Capt., Captain.

car., carat.

CARE, Cooperative for American Relief Everywhere.

CAT, computerized axial tomography.

CATV, Community Antenna Television.

CB, citizens band.

C.B., Companion of the Bath.

CBC, Canadian Broadcasting Corporation.

C.B.I., China, Burma, India

CBS, Columbia Broadcasting System.

CBX, computerized branch exchange.

cc, carbon copy; cubic centimeters.

CCC, Civilian Conservation Corps; Commodity Credit Corporation.

CCTV, closed-circuit television.

CD, compact disk; certificate of deposit.

cd., cord.

Cdr., commander.

CD-ROM, compact disk read-only memory.

CDT, central daylight time.

C.E., Civil Engineer; Common Era.

cent., centigrade; centimeter; century.

CENTO, Central Treaty Organization.

CEO, chief executive officer.

cert., certificate, certify.

CETA, Comprehensive Employment and Training Act.

cf., (*Lat.* confer) compare; (*Baseball*) center fielder.

cg, centigram.

C.G., Coast Guard.

Ch., China; Chinese; church; (*l.c.*) chapter.

Chas., Charles.

Ch.E., Chemical Engineer.

chem., chemistry; chemical; chemist.

chm., chairman.

Chr., Christian.

Chron., Chronicles.

CIA, Central Intelligence Agency.

CID, Criminal Investigation Department.

Cie., (*Fr.* compagnie) company.

C. in C., Commander-in-Chief.

CIO, Congress of Industrial Organizations.

cit., cited; citation.

ck., check.

cl., centiliter(s).

CLU, Civil Liberties Union.

cm., centimeter(s).

Cmdr., commander.

CO, conscientious objector; Colorado.

C.O., Commanding Officer.

Co., company; county; Colorado.

c/o, care of.

COD, cash on delivery; collect on delivery.

C. of N., Commonwealth of Nations.

Col., Colonel; Columbia; Colorado.

COLA, cost-of-living adjustment.

colloq., colloquial.

Colo., Colorado.

Com., Commander; Commodore; commerce.

comp., comparative.

Comr., Commissioner.

Cong., Congregational; Congress; Congressional.

conj. conjunction.

Conn., Connecticut.

cont., continued.

contr., contract; contralto.

Cor., Corinthians.

CORE, Congress of Racial Equality.

Corp., Corporal; Corporation.

CP, Communist Party.

C.P.A., Certified Public Accountant.

CPI, consumer price index.
Cpl., Corporal.
C.P.O., Chief Petty Officer.
CPR, cardiopulmonary resuscitation.
CPU, central processing unit.
C.R., Costa Rica.
cr., credit; creditor.
CRT, cathode-ray tube.
C.S.A., Confederate States of America.
CST, Central Standard Time.
CT, Ct., Connecticut.
ct., cent(s); carat.
cu., cubic.
CV, curriculum vitae.
cwt., hundredweight.
CYO, Catholic Youth Organization
CZ, C.Z., Canal Zone (Panama).
Czech., Czechoslovakia.

D.A., District Attorney.
D.A.R., Daughters of the American Revolution.
DAV, Disabled American Veterans.
dB, decibel.
d/b/a, doing business as.
DC, direct current.
d&c, dilation and curettage.
D.C., District of Columbia.
D.C.M., Distinguished Conduct Medal.
D.D., Doctor of Divinity.
D.D.S., Doctor of Dental Surgery.
DDT, dichloro-diphenyl-trichloroethane (an insecticide).
DE, De., Delaware.
Dec., December.
Del., Delaware.
Dem., Democratic; Democrat.
Den., Denmark.
dept., department.
derog., derogatory.
Deut., Deuteronomy.
DEW, distant early warning.
DFC, Distinguished Flying Cross.
DFM, Distinguished Flying Medal.
dial., dialect(ical).
dir., director.
dl, deciliter; deciliters.
D.Litt., Doctor of Letters.
D.M.D., Doctor of Dental Medicine.
dm, decimeter; decimeters.
DMZ, demilitarized zone.
DNA, deoxyribonucleic acid.
do., ditto.
DOA, dead on arrival.
DOS, disk operating system.
doz., dozen; dozens.
DP, displaced person.
dpi, dots per inch.
dpt., department.
Dr., Doctor; (*l.c.*) debit; debtor; dram.
D.Sc., Doctor of Science.
D.S.C., Distinguished Service Cross.
D.S.M., Distinguished Service Medal.
D.S.O., Distinguished Service Order.

DST, Daylight Saving Time.
DTP, desktop publishing.
DTs, delirium tremens.
DUI, driving under the influence (of alcohol, drugs, etc.).
D.V.M., Doctor of Veterinary Medicine.
DWI, driving while intoxicated.
dwt., pennyweight.
dz., dozen; dozens.

E., east.
ECA, Economic Cooperation Administration.
Eccl., Ecclesiastes.
econ., economics.
Ecua., Ecuador.
ed., editor(ial).
E.D.T., Eastern daylight time.
Edw., Edward.
E.E., Electrical Engineer.
E.E.C., European Economic Community.
EEG, electroencephalogram.
EEO, Equal Employment Opportunity.
EFTA, European Free Trade Association.
Eg., Egypt; Egyptian.
e.g., (*Lat.* exempli gratia) for example.
EKG, electrocardiogram.
Eliz., Elizabeth; Elizabethan.
EMT, Emergency Medical Technician.
ENE, east-northeast.
Eng., England; English.
engr., engineer.
Ens., Ensign.
E.P.A., Environmental Protection Agency.
ERA, earned-run average; Equal Rights Amendment.
ESE, east-southeast.
ESL, English as a second language.
ESP, extrasensory perception.
esp., especially.
Esq., Esqr., Esquire.
EST, Eastern Standard Time.
Est., Estonia; established.
Esth., Esther.
ETA, estimated time of arrival.
et al., (*Lat.* et alia) and others.
etc., (*Lat.* et cetera) and so forth.
Eth., Ethiopia.
ETO, European Theater of Operations.
et seq., (*Lat.* et sequentia) and the following.
Eu., Europ., European.
EVA, extravehicular activity.
Ex., Exodus.
expr., expressive.
Ez., Ezr., Ezra.
Ezek., Ezekiel.

F., Fahrenheit; Fellow; French.
FAA, Federal Aviation Administration.
F. & A. M., Free and Accepted Masons.
F.A.O., Food and Agriculture Organization.
FBI, Federal Bureau of Investigation.
FCA, Farm Credit Administration.

FCC, Federal Communications Commission.

FDA, Food and Drug Administration.

FDIC, Federal Deposit Insurance Corporation.

FEA, Federal Energy Administration.

Feb., February.

Fed., Federal.

fem., feminine.

FET, Federal Excise Tax.

ff., and following (pages).

F.F.V., First Families of Virginia.

FHA, Federal Housing Administration.

F.I.C.A., Federal Insurance Contributions Act.

FIFO, (*Computers*) first in, first out.

fig., figuratively.

Fin., Finland; Finnish.

fl., flourished.

FL, Fl., Fla., Florida.

Flem., Flemish.

FM, frequency modulation.

fn., footnote.

f.o.b., free on board.

F.O.E., Fraternal Order of Eagles *or* Elks.

FOI, Freedom of Information Act.

F.P.C., Federal Power Commission.

F.P.O., Fleet Post Office.

Fr., Father; French.

Fri., Friday.

ft., feet; foot; fort.

FTC, Federal Trade Commission.

fwd., forward.

f/x, special effects.

FY, fiscal year.

FYI, for your information.

G, general audiences (a motion picture rating); German.

GA, Ga., Georgia.

Gal., Galatians.

gal., gallon; gallons.

GAO, General Accounting Office.

G.A.R., Grand Army of the Republic.

GATT, General Agreement on Tariffs and Trade.

G.B., Great Britain.

gent., gentleman.

Geo., George.

geom., geometrical; geometry.

Ger., German; Germany.

GHQ, General Headquarters.

G.I., general (or Government) Issue; a private soldier.

GIGO, (*Computers*) garbage in, garbage out.

Gk., Greek.

gm., gram; grams.

GMT, Greenwich mean time.

GNP, gross national product.

GOP, Grand Old Party (Republican party).

Gov., governor.

Govt., government.

G.P., general practitioner.

GPO, Government Printing Office.

GPU, (formerly) Soviet Secret Police.

gr., grain, gross.

gram., grammar.

Gr. Br., Gr. Brit., Great Britain.

G.S.A., Girl Scouts of America.

GU, Guam.

ha, hectare.

Hag., Haggai.

hdqrs., headquarters.

hdw., hardware.

Heb., Hebrew(s).

H.E.W., Department of Health, Education, and Welfare.

HI, H.I., Hawaiian Islands.

hist., historical.

HIV, human immunodeficiency virus.

H. J., here lies.

H. M., His (Her) Majesty.

HMO, health maintenance organization.

H.M.S., His (Her) Majesty's Ship.

Hon., Honorable.

hp, horsepower.

HQ, headquarters.

H.R., House of Representatives.

hr., hour; hours.

H.R.H., His (Her) Royal Highness.

H.S., high school.

ht., height.

HUD, Department of Housing and Urban Development.

Hz, hertz.

I., Island(s); Isle(s).

IA, Ia., Iowa.

ibid., (*Lat.* ibidem) in the same place.

IC, integrated circuit.

ICBM, Intercontinental Ballistic Missile.

ICC, Interstate Commerce Commission.

ID, identification.

ID, Ida., Idaho.

i.e., (*Lat.* id est) that is.

IHS, Jesus.

IL, Il., Ill., Illinois.

ILGWU, International Ladies' Garment Workers' Union.

I.L.O., International Labor Organization.

I.M.F., International Monetary Fund.

imit., imitative.

in., inch; inches.

IN, In., Ind., Indiana.

inc., inclosure; (*cap.*) incorporated.

incl., inclusive.

inf., infinitive.

I.N.R.I., (*Lat.* Iesus Nazarenus Rex Iudeorum) Jesus of Nazareth, King of the Jews.

INS, International News Service.

inst., the present month.

interj., interjection.

intl., international.

I/O, input/output.

I.O.O.F., Independent Order of Odd Fellows.
I.O.U., I owe you.
I.Q., intelligence quotient.
Ire., Ireland.
I.R.A., Irish Republican Army; individual retirement account.
IRBM, intermediate-range ballistic missile.
IRO, International Refugee Organization.
IRS, Internal Revenue Service.
Is., is., island; islands; (*cap.*) Isaiah.
I.S., intermediate school.
ISBN, International Standard Book Number.
ISO, International Standardization Organization.
It., Ital., Italian; (*l.c.*) italic (type).
ITO, International Trade Organization.
IUD, intrauterine device.
IV, intravenous.
IWW, Industrial Workers of the World.

Jan,, January.
Jap., Japan; Japanese.
Jas., James.
jct., junction.
J.D., (*Lat.* Juris Doctor) Doctor of Laws.
JDL, Jewish Defense League.
j.g., junior grade.
J.H.S., junior high school.
Jno., John.
Jos., Joseph; Josiah.
Josh., Joshua.
J.P., Justice of the Peace.
jr., junior.
Judg., Judges.
JV, junior varsity.

K, king (*Chess*); thousand.
k., karat.
Kan., Kans., Kas., Kansas.
K.C., King's Counsel; Knights of Columbus.
kc., kilocycle(s).
K.G., Knight (of the Order) of the Garter.
kg., keg(s); kilogram(s).
K.G.B., the intelligence agency of the former Soviet Union.
kilo., kilogram(s); kilometer(s).
K.K.K., Ku Klux Klan.
km., kilometer; kilometers.
K.O., knockout.
K. of P., Knights of Pythias.
KP, kitchen police.
K.T., Knight Templar.
Kt., knight.
kw., kilowatt(s).
KY, Ky., Kentucky.

L, large; liter.
L., Latin.
LA, La., Louisiana.
Lab., Labrador.
Lam., Lamentations.
LAN, local area network.

Lat., Latin; latitude.
lb., lbs. (*Lat.* libra) pound(s).
LBO, leveraged buyout.
LC, landing craft; **LS,** landing ship; **LCI,** landing craft, infantry; **LCP,** landing craft, personnel; **LST,** landing ship, tank; etc.
l.c., lowercase (type).
LCD, liquid crystal display.
LED, light-emitting diode.
L.I., Long Island.
LIFO, (*Computers*) last in, first out.
Lieut., Lt., Lieutenant.
Litt.D., Doctor of Literature.
LL.B., Bachelor of Laws.
LL.D., Doctor of Laws.
LM, LEM, lunar (excursion) module.
LNG, liquefied natural gas.
loc. cit., (*Lat.* loco citato) in the place cited.
long., longitude.
L.O.O.M., Loyal Order of Moose.
LP, long play.
LPG, liquefied petroleum gas.
L.P.G.A., Ladies' Professional Golf Association.
LSD, lysergic acid diethylamide (a halucinogenic drug).
LSI, landing ship infantry.
LST, landing ship tank.
Ltd., Limited.

M, medium; meter.
M., Monsieur; meridies, midday.
m., meter(s); noon; married.
MA, Ma., Mass., Massachusetts.
M.A., Master of Arts.
Macc., Maccabees.
Maj., Major.
Man., Manitoba.
Mar., March.
masc., masculine.
MASH, mobile army surgical hospital.
math., mathematics.
M.B.A., Master of Business Administration.
MC, Master of Ceremonies; Member of Congress.
M.D., Doctor of Medicine.
MD, Md., Maryland.
mdse., merchandise.
M.D.T., mountain daylight time.
ME, Me., Maine.
M.E., Methodist Episcopal; Mechanical Engineer.
mech., mechanics.
med., medicine.
Medit., Mediterranean.
memo., memorandum.
Messrs., Messieurs.
meteorol., meteorology.
Mex., Mexican.
mfg., manufacturing.
mfr., manufacturer.

Mgr., Manager; Monsignor.
MHz, megahertz.
MI, Mi., Mich., Michigan.
mi., mile.
MIA, missing in action.
Mic., Micah.
mil., military.
min., mineral; mineralogy.
Minn., Minnesota.
MIRV, multiple independently targetable re-entry vehicle.
misc., miscellaneous.
Miss., Mississippi.
ml, milliliter.
Mlle., Mademoiselle.
MM., Messieurs.
mm, millimeter(s).
Mme., Madame.
MN, Mn., Minnesota.
MO, Mo., Missouri.
M.O., money order; (*Lat.* modus operandi) mode of operation.
mo., month(s).
Mon., Monday.
Mont., Montana.
M.P., military police; Member of Parliament.
mph, miles per hour.
Mr., Mister.
Mrs., Mistress.
MRV, multiple re-entry vehicle.
M.S., Master of Science.
MS, Ms., Mississippi.
Ms., a title for an unmarried woman, or for one whose marital status is unknown.
ms., manuscript.
MSG, monosodium glutamate.
Msgr., Monsignor.
M/Sgt., Master Sergeant.
M.S.T., Mountain Standard Time.
MT, Montana.
Mt., mountain; Montana.
MVD, the former Soviet Ministry of Internal Affairs.
MVP, most valuable player.
myth., mythology.

n., noun.
N., north.
N.A., North America.
NA, N/A, not applicable; not available.
NAACP, National Association for the Advancement of Colored People.
NAB, National Association of Broadcasters.
NAM, National Association of Manufacturers.
NASA, National Aeronautics and Space Administration.
NASCAR, National Association for Stock Car Auto Racing.
NASDAQ, National Association of Securities Dealers.
natl., national.

NATO, North Atlantic Treaty Organization.
naut., nautical.
NB, Nb., Nebraska.
N. B., New Brunswick; note well.
NBA, National Basketball Association.
NBC, National Broadcasting Company.
NC, N.C., North Carolina; no charge.
N.C.A.A., National Collegiate Athletic Association.
NCO, noncommissioned officer.
ND, N.D., North Dakota.
NE, northeast.
N. E., New England.
Nebr., Neb., Nebraska.
Neh., Nehemiah.
NET, National Educational Television.
Neth., Netherlands.
Nev., Nevada.
NFL, National Football League.
N. F., Newf., Newfoundland.
NG, no good.
NH, N.H., New Hampshire.
NHL, National Hockey League.
NJ, N.J., New Jersey.
NKVD, the former Soviet Secret Police.
NL, National League; New Latin.
N.L.R.B., National Labor Relations Board.
NM, N.M., New Mexico.
NNE, north-northeast.
NNW, north-northwest.
No., north; northern; number.
nom., nominative.
Nor., Norwegian; Norway.
Nov., November.
NOW, negotiable order of withdrawal; National Organization for Women.
NP, no protest; notary public..
NRA, National Recovery Administration; National Rifle Association.
N.S., New Style; Nova Scotia.
NSA, National Student Association; National Security Agency.
NSC, National Security Council.
NSF, National Science Foundation.
N. T., New Testament.
NTA, sodiumnitrilotriacetate, used in some detergents as a substitute for phosphates.
Num., Numbers.
NV, Nevada.
NW, northwest.
NY, N.Y., New York.
N.Y.C., New York City.
N.Z., New Zealand.

O, old.
O., Ohio.
O.A.S., Organization of American States.
OAU, Organization of African Unity.
ob., (*Lat.* obiit) he (she) died.
Obad., Obadiah.

O.B.E., Officer (of the Order) of the British Empire.

obj., objective; object.

OCR, optical character recognition.

OCS, Officer Candidate School.

Oct., October.

OD, overdose.

O.D., Officer of the Day; overdraft; olive drab (uniforms).

O/D, overdraft.

O.E.D., Oxford English Dictionary.

OEM, original equipment manufacturer.

OEO, Office of Economic Opportunity.

O.E.S., Order of the Eastern Star.

OH, Oh., Ohio.

OK, Ok., Okla., Oklahoma.

O.M.B., Office of Management and Budget.

Ont., Ontario.

OPA, Office of Price Administration.

OPEC, Organization of Petroleum Exporting Countries.

op., (*Lat.* opus) work.

op. cit., (*Lat.* opere citato) in the work cited.

OR, operating room.

OR, Or., Ore., Oreg., Oregon.

orch., orchestra.

orig., original(ly).

O.S., Old Style; ordinary seaman.

OSS, Office of Strategic Services.

O.T., Old Testament.

OTB, off-track betting.

OTC, one-stop inclusive tour charter.

OTS, Officers' Training School.

OWI, Office of War Information.

Ox., Oxford.

Oxon., (*Lat.* Oxoniensis) of Oxford.

oz., ounce(s).

p., page.

PA, Pa., Pennsylvania.

PA, public address.

P.A., Purchasing Agent; Press Agent.

PAC, political action committee.

Pac., Pacif., Pacific.

p. adj., participial adjective.

Pan., Panama.

par., paragraph; parallel.

Para., Paraguay.

paren., parentheses.

part., participle.

PATH, Port Authority Trans-Hudson.

pathol., pathology.

pat. pend., patent pending.

payt., payment.

PBS, Public Broadcasting Service.

PBX, private branch (telephone) exchange.

PC, personal computer; politically correct.

pc., piece.

p.c., percent; postcard.

PCB, polychlorinated biphenyl (a poisonous industrial chemical).

PCP, phencyclidine (a hallucinogenic drug).

pct., percent.

P.D., Police Department.

pd., paid.

P.D.Q., (*Slang*) pretty damn quick.

P.D.T., Pacific daylight time.

P.E.N., (International Association of) Poets, Playwrights, Editors, Essayists and Novelists.

Penn., Penna., Pennsylvania.

Pers., Persia; Persian.

pert., pertaining.

Peruv., Peruvian.

Pfc., Private First Class.

PG, parental guidance recommended (a motion picture rating).

P.G.A., Professional Golfers' Association.

pH, a measure of acidity or alkalinity.

phar., pharm., pharmaceutical; pharmacopoeia; pharmacy.

Ph.B., Bachelor of Philosophy.

Ph.D., Doctor of Philosophy.

Phil., Philemon; Philip; Philippians; Philippine.

Phila., Philadelphia.

photog., photography.

P.I., Philippine Islands; private investigator.

PIN, personal identification number.

pk., peck.

pkg., package(s).

pkwy., parkway.

pl., plural.

P.L.O., Palestine Liberation Organization.

plupf., pluperfect.

P.M., p.m., post meridiem; post-mortem; (*cap.*) Prime Minister; Postmaster.

P.O., post office; purchase order.

POE, port of entry.

Pol., Poland; Polish.

Port., Portugal; Portuguese.

pos., possessive.

POSSLQ, person of the opposite sex sharing living quarters.

POW, prisoner of war.

p.p., parcel post; past participle; postpaid.

P.P.S., post postcriptum.

P.Q., Province of Quebec.

PR, P.R., Puerto Rico; public relations.

pr., pair.

pref., prefix.

prep., preposition; preparatory.

pret., preterit.

Prof., professor.

pron., pronoun.

Prot., Protestant.

pro tem., for the time being.

Prov., Proverbs; (*l.c.*) province.

prox., (*Lat.* proximo) next (month).

P.S., postscript.

Ps., Psalm(s).

P.S.T., Pacific Standard Time.

psychoanal., psychoanalysis.

pt., point; pint.

p/t, part time.
PTA, Parent-Teacher Association.
PT boat, patrol torpedo boat.
p.t.o., please turn over (the page).
PVC, polyvinyl chloride.
Pvt., Private.
PWA, Public Works Administration.
PX, Post Exchange.

Q., Quebec.
Q.E.D., (*Lat.* quod erat demonstrandum) which was to be demonstrated.
QMC, Quartermaster Corps.
qt., quart.
qty., quantity.
Que., Quebec.
q.v., (*Lat.* quod vide) which see.

R, restricted (a motion picture rating).
R.A.F., Royal Air Force.
RAM, random access memory.
R & B, rhythm and blues.
R & D, research and development.
R & R, rest and rehabilitation (relaxation).
RBI, run(s) batted in.
R. C., Red Cross; Reserve Corps; Roman Catholic.
RCAF, Royal Canadian Air Force.
RCMP, Royal Canadian Mounted Police.
R.D., Rural Delivery.
REM, rapid eye movement.
Rep., Republican; Representative.
Rev., Revelation; Reverend.
RF, radio frequency.
RFD, Rural Free Delivery.
RI, R.I., Rhode Island.
RIP, (*Lat.* requiescat in pace) rest in peace.
rm., ream (paper); room.
RN, Registered Nurse.
RNA, ribonucleic acid.
Robt., Robert.
ROM, read-only memory.
Rom., Roman; Romans; Romania; Romanian.
Rom. Cath., Roman Catholic.
ROTC, Reserve Officers' Training Corps.
rpm, revolutions per minute.
RR, railroad; Right Reverend; Rural Route.
RRSP, Registered Retirement Savings Plan.
R.S.V., Revised Standard Version (of the Bible).
R.S.V.P., (*Fr.* répondez, s'il vous plaît) please reply.
rt., right.
Rus., Russ., Russia; Russian.
RV, recreational vehicle.
Rx, (*Med.*) prescription.
Ry., Railway.

S., small.
S., south.

S.A., South Africa; South America; corporation; (*Slang*) sex appeal.
SAC, Strategic Air Command.
SALT, strategic arms limitation treaty.
Salv., Salvador; Salvator.
SAM, surface-to-air missile.
Sam., Sam'l, Samuel.
S.A.R., Sons of the American Revolution.
S.A.S.E., self-addressed stamped envelope.
Sask., Saskatchewan.
SAT, Scholastic Aptitude Test.
Sat., Saturday; Saturn.
sc., science.
s.c., small capitals.
SC, S.C., South Carolina.
Scand, Scandinavian.
Scot., Scottish; Scotland.
SD, S.D., South Dakota.
SDA, Students for Democratic Action; Seventh-Day Adventist.
SDI, Strategic Defense Initiative.
SDS, Students for a Democratic Society.
SE, southeast.
SEATO, Southeast Asia Treaty Organization.
SEC, Securities and Exchange Commission.
Sen., Senate.
Sept., September.
seq., (*Lat.* sequens) the following.
SF, sf, science fiction.
sgd., signed.
Sgt., Sergeant.
SHAEF, Supreme Headquarters Allied Expeditionary Forces.
Shak., Shakespeare.
S. I., Staten Island.
Sib., Siberia; Siberian.
Sic., Sicily; Sicilian.
Sig., sig., signor.
sing., singular.
S.J., Society of Jesus (Jesuits).
Slav., Slavic; Slavonian.
SLR, single-lens reflex (camera).
So., south; southern.
sop., soprano.
S.O.S., a radio distress signal.
SP, shore patrol.
Sp., Span., Spain; Spaniard; Spanish.
SPAR, Coast Guard Women's Reserve.
SPCA, Society for Prevention of Cruelty to Animals.
S.P.C.C., Society for Prevention of Cruelty to Children.
spec., specifically.
SPQR, (*Lat.* Senatus Populusque Romanus) the Senate and the Roman people.
sq., square.
sqq., and the following ones.
Sr., Senior; Señor; Sister.
Sra., Señora.
SRO, standing room only.
SS., Saints.
SS, steamship; Social Security.

SSE, south-southeast
S/Sgt., Staff Sergeant.
S.S.R., the former Soviet Socialist Republic.
SSS, Selective Service System.
SST, supersonic transport.
SSW, south-southwest.
St., Saint (Fr. *fem.* **Ste.**); Strait; Street.
STOL, short takeoff and landing (aircraft).
suf., suff., suffix.
Sun., Sund., Sunday.
superl., superlative.
supt., superintendent.
S.W., southwest.
SWAT, special weapons and tactics.
Swed., Sweden; Swedish.
Swtz., Swit., Switz., Switzerland.
Syr., Syria.

t., ton.
TA, teaching assistant.
TB, t.b., tuberculosis.
TBA, to be announced.
tbsp., tablespoon.
TD, touchdown.
Tenn., Tennessee.
Tex., Texas.
TGIF, thank God it's Friday.
THC, tetra-hydrocannabinol (the principal chemical in marijuana).
Th.D., Doctor of Theology.
Theat., theatrical.
Theo., Theodore; Theodosia.
THI, temperature-humidity index.
Thos., Thomas.
Thurs., Thursday.
Tim., Timothy.
TKO, technical knockout.
TLC, tender loving care.
TM, transcendental meditation.
TN, Tn., Tennessee.
T.N.T., trinitrotoluene (explosive).
T.N., trade name.
tp., twp., township.
Tr., Troop.
treas., treasurer; treasury.
tsp., teaspoon.
TT, Trust Territories.
Tues., Tuesday.
TV, television.
TVA, Tennessee Valley Authority.
TX, Tx., Texas.

U.A.W., United Auto, Aircraft, or Agricultural Implements Workers.
u.c., upper case (type).
U.D.C., United Daughters of the Confederacy.
UFO, unidentified flying object.
UHF, ultrahigh frequency.
U.K., United Kingdom.
Ukr., Ukraine.
UL, Underwriters Laboratories.

ult., last month.
U.M.W., United Mine Workers.
U.N., United Nations.
UNESCO, United Nations Educational, Scientific and Cultural Organization.
UNICEF, United Nations Children's Fund.
UNRRA, United Nations Relief and Rehabilitation Administration.
UP, United Press.
UPC, universal product code.
UPS, United Parcel Service.
Uru., Uruguay.
U.S., United States (of America).
U.S.A., Union of South Africa; United States Army; United States of America.
U.S.A.F., United States Air Force.
U.S.C.G., United States Coast Guard.
USDA, United States Department of Agriculture.
USES, United States Employment Service.
U.S.I.A., United States Information Agency.
U.S.M.A. United States Military Academy.
U.S.M.C., United States Marine Corps.
U.S.N., United States Navy.
U.S.N.A., United States Naval Academy.
U.S.N.R., United States Naval Reserve.
U.S.O., United Service Organizations.
U.S.P., United States Pharmacopoeia.
USPS, United States Postal Service.
U.S.S., United States Ship, or Steamer.
U.S.S.R., formerly, Union of Soviet Socialist Republics.
usu., usually.
UT, Ut., Utah.

v., verb; versus.
VA, Veterans Administration.
VA, Va., Virginia.
VAT, value-added tax.
V.C., Victoria Cross; Vietcong.
VCR, videocassette recorder.
V.D., venereal disease.
Venez., Venezuela.
vet., veteran; veterinarian.
V.F.W., Veterans of Foreign Wars.
VHF, very high frequency.
VHS, video home system.
VI, V. I., Virgin Islands.
v.i., verb intransitive.
V.I.P., very important person.
VISTA, Volunteers in Service to America.
viz., namely.
V.M.D., Doctor of Veterinary Medicine.
VOA, Voice of America.
vol., volume.
V.P., Vice-President.
V.S., Veterinary Surgeon.
vs., versus.
VT, Vt., Vermont.
v.t., verb transitive.
VTOL, vertical takeoff and landing (aircraft).

W., west.
w., watt.
w/, with.
WA, Wa., Washington.
WAAC, Women's Auxiliary Army Corps.
WAAF, Women's Auxiliary Air Force.
WAC, Women's Army Corps.
WAF, Women in the Air Force.
Wash., Washington.
WASP, Women's Air Force Service Pilots; white Anglo-Saxon Protestant.
WATS, wide-area telecommunications service.
WAVES, Women Accepted for Volunteer Emergency Service (U. S. Navy).
W.C., WC, water closet.
W.C.T.U., Women's Christian Temperance Union.
Wed., Wednesday.
W.H.O., World Health Organization.
W. I., West Indies.
WI, Wi., Wis., Wisc., Wisconsin.
wk., week; work.
Wm., William.
WNW, west-northwest.
W.O., Warrant Officer.
w/o, without.
WPA, Works Progress Administration.
WPB, War Production Board.
w.p.m., words per minute.

WRENS, Women's Royal Naval Service.
WSW, west-southwest.
WV, Wv., W.Va., West Virginia.
WW, World War.
WY, Wy., Wyo., Wyoming.

X, restricted to adults only (a motion picture rating).
X-C, cross-country.
XL, extra large.
Xmas, Christmas.

Y., Young Men's Christian Association.
yd., yard(s).
Y.M.C.A., Young Men's Christian Association.
Y.M.H.A., Young Men's Hebrew Association.
yr., year(s).
Y.T., Yukon Territory.
Yuc., Yucatan.
Y.W.C.A., Young Women's Christian Association.
Y.W.H.A., Young Women's Hebrew Association.

Zech., Zechariah.
Zeph., Zephaniah.
ZIP, Zone Improvement Plan.
ZPG, zero population growth.

GAZETTEER

An otherwise unidentified entry in the Gazetteer denotes an independent or self-governing country. A dependency is indicated by the name of the mother country, in parentheses. The following special abbreviations are used: *Fr. C.*, French Community; *Br. C. of N.*, (British) Commonwealth of Nations; and *Trust.*, Trusteeship. For the United States, the 1990 census has been used. United States Government and United Nations reports or estimates have been followed for most other countries, and for the majority of countries the estimates are as of July 1992. For some cities, population figures are also given for the urbanized area (urb.), which includes the city proper and its suburban fringe.

Abidjan (ä″bi-jän′) City (cap. of Ivory Coast) pop. 1,423,323.

Abu Dhabi (ä′boo *th*ä′bē) City (cap. of United Arab Emirates) pop. 722,000.

Abyssinia, see *Ethiopia.*

Accra (ə-krä′) City (cap. of Ghana) pop. 867,459.

Addis Ababa (ad′is ab′ə-bə) City (cap. of Ethiopia) pop. 1,739,130.

Adelaide (ad′ə-lād) City (Australia) pop. 1,013,000.

Aden (ä′dən) City (cap. of Yemen) pop. 271,590.

Admiralty Islands part of Papua New Guinea, 820 sq. mi., pop. 27,600.

Adriatic Sea (a″drė-at′ik) between Italy & Yugoslavia 50,000 sq. mi.

Aegean Sea (ė-jē′ən) between Greece & Turkey, 40,000 sq. mi.

Afghanistan (af-gan′is-tan″) 251,773 sq. mi., pop. 16,494,000, cap. Kabul.

Africa (af′ri-kə) Continent, 11,700,000 sq. mi., pop. 661,951,000.

Ahmedabad (ä′məd-ä-bäd) City (India) pop. 2,872,865.

Akron (ak′rən) City (OH) pop. 223,019.

Alabama (al″-ə-ba′mə) State (U.S.) 52,423 sq. mi., pop. 4,089,232, cap. Montgomery.

Alaska (ə-las′kə) State (U.S.) 570,833 sq. mi., pop. 570,345, cap. Juneau.

Albania (al-bān′yə) 11,096 sq. mi., pop. 3,322,000, cap. Tiranë (Tirana).

Albany (âl′bə-nė) City (cap. of NY) pop. 101,082, urb. 861,424.

Alberta (al-bėr′tə) Prov. (Canada) 248,800 sq. mi., pop. 2,472,500, cap. Edmonton (ed′mən-tən) (pop. 823,000).

Albuquerque (al″bə-kėr′kė) City (NM) pop. 384,736, urb. 589,131.

Aleutian Islands (ə-loo′shən) (U.S.) 6,800 sq. mi., pop. 7,768.

Alexandria (al″ig-zan′drē-ə) City (Egypt) pop. 3,170,000.

Algeria (al-jir′ė-ə) 851,284 sq. mi., pop. 27,321,000, cap. Algiers.

Algiers (al-jērs′) City (cap. of Algeria) pop. 1,523,000, urb. 1,740,461.

Alma-Ata (al′mə-ə-tä′) City (cap. of Kazakhstan) pop. 1,108,000.

Amazon River (am′ə-zon) (Brazil) 4,000 miles.

Amman (äm′män) City (cap. of Jordan) pop. 936,000.

Amsterdam (am′stər-dam″) City (cap. of Netherlands) pop. 693,209, urb. 1,034,562.

Anaheim (an′ə-hīm) City (CA) pop. 266,408.

Anchorage (ank′ə-rij) City (AK) pop. 226,338.

Andaman Islands (an′də-man) (India) 2,508 sq. mi., pop. 279,111, cap. Port Blair (blãr).

Andaman Sea (an′də-man) part of Bay of Bengal, 218,100 sq. mi.

Andorra (an-dôr′ə) 191 sq. mi., pop. 55,615, cap. Andorra la Vella (Andorra la Vieja) (lä vä′yä, lä vē-ä′hä), pop. 16,151.

Angola (ang-gō′lə) 481,351 sq. mi., pop. 9,143,000, cap. Luanda.

Anguilla Island (ang-gwē′la) (B.W.I.) 34 sq. mi., pop. 7,006.

Ankara (ang′kə-rə) City (cap. of Turkey) pop. 2,541,899, urb. 3,022,236.

Annapolis (ə-nap′ə-lis) City (cap. of MD) pop. 33,187.

Antananarivo (än-tä-nä-nä-rē′vō) City (cap. of Madagascar) pop. 802,000.

Antarctica (ant-ärk′ti-kə) Continent, 5,000,000 sq. mi.

Antigua and Barbuda (an-tē′gwə, bär-boo′də) (Br.) 171 sq. mi., pop. 64,406, cap. St. Johns.

Antilles (an-til′lėz) a chain of Caribbean islands, divided into the **Greater Antilles** and **Lesser Antilles.**

Antilles, Netherlands (an-til′lėz) (Neth.) 310 sq. mi., pop. 184,990, cap. Willemstad.

Antwerp (ant′wərp) City (Belgium) pop. 483,199.

Apia (ä-pē′ä) City (cap. of W. Samoa) pop. 35,000.

Arabia (ə-rā′bė-ə) Peninsula, SW Asia; includes Saudi Arabia, Yemen, Oman, Kuwait, Qatar, and Bahrain.

Aral Sea (ar′əl) (Kazakhstan and Uzbekistan) 24,904 sq. mi. Also, **Lake Aral.**

---

fat, fāte, fär, fãre, fâll, åsk; met, hē, hėr, maybė; pin, pīne; not, nōte, ôr, tool

Arctic Ocean (ärk'tik) 5,540,000 sq. mi.

Argentina (är-jən-tē'nə) 1,078,266 sq. mi., pop. 33,275,000, cap. Buenos Aires.

Arizona (ar-i-zō'nə) State (U.S.) 113,508 sq. mi., pop. 3,749,693, cap. Phoenix.

Arkansas (är'kən-sâ) State (U.S.) 52,078 sq. mi., pop. 2,371,950, cap. Little Rock.

Arlington (är'ling-tən) City (TX) pop. 261,721.

Armenia, Republic of (är-mē'nē-ə) 11,544 sq. mi., pop. 3,300,000, cap. Yerevan.

Aruba (ä-roo'bä) Island (part of Neth. Antilles) 75 sq. mi., pop. 65,117.

Ascension Island (ə-sen'shən) (Br.) 34 sq. mi., pop. 1,486, cap. Georgetown.

Asia (ā'zhə) Continent, 17,400,000 sq. mi., pop. (without former U.S.S.R.) 3,046,000,000.

Asunción (ä-soon-syân') City (cap. of Paraguay) pop. 607,000.

Athens (ath'ənz) City (cap. of Greece) pop. 885,737, urb. 3,027,331.

Atlanta (at-lan'tə) City (cap. of GA) pop. 394,017, urb. 2,959,950.

Atlantic Ocean (at-lan'tik) 41,000,000 sq. mi., inc. Arctic Ocean.

Augusta (ə-gus'tə) City (cap. of ME) pop. 21,325.

Aurora (ə-rôr'ə) City (CO) pop. 222,103.

Austin (âs'tin) City (cap. of TX) pop. 465,622, urb. 846,227.

Australia (âs-trāl'yə) **1, Commonwealth of** (C. of N.) 2,974,581 sq. mi., pop. 16,849,496, cap. Canberra. **2,** Continent, 2,948,366 sq. mi.

Austria, Republic of (âs'trē-ə) 82,369 sq. mi., pop. 7,915,000, cap. Vienna.

Azerbaijan, Republic of (ä"zər-bī-jän') 33,011 sq. mi., pop. 7,000,000, cap. Baku.

Azores Islands (ə-zôrz') (Port.) 890 sq. mi., pop. 252,000, cap. Ponta Delgada (pon'tə del-gä'də).

Azov, Sea of (ā'zof) No. of the Black Sea, 14,000 sq. mi.

Baffin Bay (baf'in) between Greenland & Baffin Island, approx. 180,000 sq. mi.

Baghdad (bag'dad) City (cap. of Iraq) pop. 2,200,000, urb. 3,400,000.

Bahamas, Commonwealth of the (bə-hä'məs; -hä'-) (C. of N.) 4,375 sq. mi., pop. 259,386, cap. Nassau.

Bahrain, State of (bä'rān) 268 sq. mi., pop. 568,471, cap. Manama.

Baikal, Lake (bī-kal') (Russia) 11,780 sq. mi.

Bakersfield (bā'kərs-fēld) City (CA) pop. 174,820, urb. 543,477.

Baku (bä-koo') City (cap. of Azerbaijan) pop. 1,741,000.

Balearic Islands (bal"ē-a'rik) (Sp.) 1,936

sq. mi., pop. 558,287, cap. Palma (päl'mä).

Balkan States (bâl'kən) Albania, Bulgaria, Greece, Romania, Turkey & Yugoslavia.

Baltic Sea (bâl'tik) between Germany & Scandinavia, 163,000 sq. mi.

Baltimore (bâl'ti-môr) City (MD) pop. 736,014, urb. 2,382,172.

Bamako (bä-mä-kō') City (cap. of Mali) pop. 646,163.

Bandar Seri Begawan (bän-där' se'rē be-gä'wän) City (cap. of Brunei) pop. 51,000.

Bangkok (bang'kok) City (cap. of Thailand) pop. 4,697,071, urb. 6,000,000.

Bangladesh, People's Republic of [formerly **East Pakistan**] (bang'glə-desh") 54,501 sq. mi., pop. 122,255,000, cap. Dhaka.

Bangui (bäng'gē) City (cap. of C. Afr. Republic) pop. 473,817, urb. 596,000.

Banjul (ban-jool') City [formerly **Bathurst**] (cap. of Gambia) pop. 49,181, urb. 109,986.

Barbados (bär-bā'dōz) (C. of N.) 166 sq. mi., pop. 255,338, cap. Bridgetown.

Barcelona (bär-sə-lō'nə) City (Spain) pop. 1,707,000.

Barents Sea (bar'ənts) No. of Scandinavia & Russia, 529,096 sq. mi.

Basse-Terre (bäs-tār') **1,** City (cap. of St. Kitts and Nevis) pop. 15,726. **2,** City (cap. of Guadeloupe) pop. 14,000. .

Basutoland (bə-soo'tō-land) see *Lesotho.*

Bathurst (bath'ērst) see *Banjul.*

Baton Rouge (bat'ən roozh) City (cap. of LA) pop. 219,531, urb. 470,050.

Bechuanaland (bech"û-ä'nə-land) see *Botswana.*

Beijing (bā'jing') City (cap. of People's Republic of China) pop. 15,000,000.

Beirut [*Fr.* **Beyrouth**] (bā-root') City (cap. of Lebanon) pop. 900,000.

Belarus, Republic of (be-lä'rəs) (formerly Byelorussia) 80,134 sq. mi., pop. 10,200,000, cap. Minsk.

Belfast (bel'fâst) City (cap. of No. Ireland) pop. 390,700.

Belgium, Kingdom of (bel'jəm) 11,775 sq. mi., pop. 10,041,000, cap. Brussels.

Belgrade [*Serb.* **Beograd**] (bel'grād, be'ə-gräd) City (cap. of Serbia) pop. 1,553,000.

Belize (be-lēz') 8,766 sq. mi., pop. 235,998, cap. Belmopan (pop. 60,000).

Belo Horizonte (be"lō-rē-zon'te) City (Brazil) pop. 2,122,073.

Bengal, Bay of (ben-gäl') between India and Indo-China, approx. 650,000 sq. mi.

Benghazi (ben-gä'zē) City (cap. of Libya) pop. 282,192.

Benin, Republic of (be-nēn′) [formerly **Dahomey**] 42,471 sq. mi., pop. 5,167,000, cap. Porto-Novo.

Bering Sea (bir′ing) between Alaska & Siberia, 878,000 sq. mi.

Berlin (bər-lin′) City (cap. of Germany) pop. 3,000,000.

Bermuda (bər-mū′də) Island (Br.) 21 sq. mi., pop. 60,686, cap. Hamilton.

Bern (bērn) City (cap. of Switzerland) pop. 135,718, urb. 298,820.

Bhutan, Kingdom of (boo″tän′) 18,000 sq. mi., pop. 1,699,000, cap. Thimphu.

Birmingham 1, (bēr′ming-əm) City (England) pop. 1,074,900. **2,** (bēr′mingham″) City (AL) pop. 265,968, urb. 840,140.

Biscay, Bay of (bis′kā) bay off coasts of France & Spain, 160,000 sq. mi.

Bismarck (biz′märk) City (cap. of ND) pop. 49,256, urb. 83,831.

Bismarck Archipelago (biz′märk) part of Papua New Guinea; includes New Britain, New Ireland, New Hanover, and the Admiralty Islands.

Bissau (bi-sow′) City (cap. of Guinea-Bissau) pop. 109,214.

Black Sea, between Europe & Asia, 170,000 sq. mi.

Bloemfontein (bloom′fon-tān″) City (jud. cap. of So. Africa) pop. 104,381, urb. 232,984.

Bogotá (bo″go-tä′) City (cap. of Colombia) pop. 4,176,769.

Boise (boi′zė) City (cap. of ID) pop. 295,851.

Bolivia (bə-liv′ė-ə) 412,777 sq. mi., pop. 7,493,000, cap. La Paz, also Sucre (legal).

Bombay (bom-bā′) City (India) pop. 8,243,405.

Bonn (bon) City (Germany) pop. 279,718.

Bordeaux (bôr-dō′) City (France) pop. 266,662, urb. 628,000.

Borneo (bôr′nė-ō) Island (Indonesia & Malaysia) 289,000 sq. mi., pop. 6,800,000.

Bosnia and Herzegovina (bäz′nė-ə, her″tsə-gō-vē′nə) 19,741 sq. mi., pop. 4,365,000, cap. Sarajevo.

Boston (bäs′tən) City (cap. of MA) pop. 574,283, urb. 5,050,761.

Bothnia, Gulf of (both′nė-ə) between Sweden & Finland, 43,000 sq. mi.

Botswana, Republic of (bot-swä′nə) [formerly **Bechuanaland**] (C. of N.) 238,605 sq. mi., pop. 1,326,000, cap. Gaborone.

Bratislava (brat″ə-slä′və) City (cap. of Slovak Republic) pop. 444,482.

Brazil, Federative Republic of (brə-zil′) 3,286,170 sq. mi., pop. 161,038,000, cap. Brasilia (pop. 1,576,657).

Brazzaville (brä″zä-vēl′) City (cap. of Republic of Congo) pop. 596,200.

Bridgetown (brij′town) City (cap. of Barbados) pop. 7,466.

Brisbane (briz′bān) City (Australia) pop. 1,215,300.

British Columbia (kə-lum′bė-ə) Prov. (Canada) 359,279 sq. mi., pop. 3,138,900, cap. Victoria (pop. 64,379).

Brunei Darussalam, State of (brû-nī′) (Borneo) 2,226 sq. mi., pop. 276,984, cap. Bandar Seri Begawan.

Brussels [*Fr.* **Bruxelles**] (brus′əlz, brooksel′) City (cap. of Belgium) pop. 139,678, urb. 976,536.

Bucharest [*Rom.* **Bucuresti**] (boo′kə-rest″, boo″koo-resht′) City (cap. of Romania) pop. 1,975,508.

Budapest (boo′du-pest″) City (cap. of Hungary) pop. 2,109,137.

Buenos Aires (bwā′nes ī′res) City (cap. of Argentina) pop. 2,983,000, urb. 11,125,554.

Buffalo (buf′ə-lō) City (NY) pop. 328,123, urb. 1,189,288.

Bujumbura (boo″jam-bûr′ə) City (cap. of Burundi) pop. 215,243.

Bulgaria, Republic of (bul-ger′ė-ə) 42,796 sq. mi., pop. 8,831,000, cap. Sofia.

Burkina Faso (bər-kē′nə fä′sō) (formerly Upper Volta) 105,869 sq. mi., pop. 9,960,000, cap. Ouagadougou.

Burma (bēr′mə), see *Myanmar.*

Burundi, Republic of (bû-rûn′dė) 10,744, sq. mi., pop. 6,218,000, cap. Bujumbura.

Byelorussian S.S.R. (bye″lə-rush′ən), see *Belarus.*

Cairo (kī′rō) City (cap. of Egypt) pop, 6,052,836, urb. 10,099,000.

Calcutta (kal-kut′ə) City (India) pop. 3,305,006, urb. 9,194,018.

Calgary (kal′gə-rė) City (Canada) pop. 592,743, urb. 706,000.

California (kal-i-fôr′nė-ə) State (U.S.) 156,299 sq. mi., pop. 30,379,872, cap. Sacramento.

Cambodia, State of (kam-bō′dė-ə) 70,238 sq. mi., pop. 7,450,000, cap. Phnom Penh.

Cameroon, Republic of (käm-ə-roon′) 161,787 sq. mi., pop. 13,083,000, cap. Yaoundé.

Canada (kan′ə-də) (C. of N.) 3,621,616 sq. mi., pop. 27,693,000, cap. Ottawa.

Canal Zone, see *Panama.*

Canary Islands (kə-ner′ė) (Sp.) 2,894 sq. mi., pop. 944,448, cap. Las Palmas, Santa Cruz (läs päl′mäs, san′tə krooz).

Canberra (kan′ber-ə) City (cap. of Australia, pop. 289,000.

Canton [*Chinese* **Kwangchou**] (kan-ton′, gwäng-jō′) City (China) pop. 3,400,000.

Cape Town City (legis. cap. of So. Africa) pop. 776,617, urb. 1,911,521.

Cape Verde, Republic of (kāp vērd) 1,557 sq. mi., pop. 410,535, cap. Praia.

Caracas (kə-rä′kəs) City (cap. of Venezuela) pop. 1,246,677, urb. 3,247,498.

Caribbean Sea (kar″ə-bē′ən; kə-rib′ė-ən) between So. America & West Indies, 750,000 sq. mi.

Caroline Islands (kar′ə-līn) U.S. Trust., 525 sq. mi., pop. 66,900, cap. Truk (trûk).

Carson City (kär′sən) City (cap. of NV) pop. 40,443.

Casablanca (kas″ə-blang′kə) City (Morocco) pop. 1,495,000, urb. 2,408,600.

Caspian Sea (kas′pė-ən) between Europe & Asia, 169,383 sq. mi.

Castries (kä′strēz) City (cap. of St. Lucia) pop. 56,147.

Cayenne (kī-en′) City (cap. of Fr. Guiana) pop. 38,093.

Cayman Islands (kī-män′) (Br.) 104 sq. mi., pop. 30,440, cap. Georgetown.

Celebes (sel′ə-bėz), see *Sulawesi*.

Central African Republic (af′ri-kən) (Fr. C.) 238,000 sq. mi., pop. 3,107,000, cap. Bangui.

Central America (ə-mer′i-kə) region comprising Guatemala, Belize Honduras, El Salvador, Nicaragua, Costa Rica, and Panama.

Ceylon (sė-lon′) see *Sri Lanka*.

Chad, Republic of (chäd) (Fr. C.) 455,598 sq. mi., pop. 5,351,000, cap. N'Djamena.

Changsha (chäng′shä) City (cap. of Hunan China) pop. 1,066,030, urb. 2,459,920.

Channel Islands (chan′əl) (Br.) 75 sq. mi., pop. 135,694, cap. St. Helier.

Charleston (chärls′tən) 1, City (cap. of WV) pop. 57,287, urb. 250,454. 2, City (SC) pop. 80,414, urb. 506,875.

Charlotte (shär′lət) City (NC) pop. 395,934, urb. 1,162,093.

Charlotte Amalie (shär′lət ə-mä′lė-ə) City (cap. of U.S. Virgin Islands) pop. 12,372.

Chengdu (chung′du′) City (China) pop. 2,499,000, urb. 4,025,180.

Cheyenne (shī-en′) City (cap. of WY) pop. 50,008.

Chicago (shi-kä′go) City (IL) pop. 2,783,726, urb. 8,239,820.

Chile (chil′ė) 286,396 sq. mi., pop. 13,740,000, cap. Santiago.

China, Republic of (chī′nə) 1, [People's Republic of China] 3,768,727 sq. mi., pop. 1,187,998,000, cap. Beijing (Peking). 2, [The Republic of China] see *Taiwan*.

Chosen (chō′sen′) see *Korea*.

Christmas (kris′məs) 1, Island [Kiritimati] (Australia) 64 sq. mi., pop. 3,524. 2, Islands (Kiribati) 184 sq. mi.

Chongqing [*Chinese* **Pahsien**] (chung′-ching′, bä-shyen′) City (China) pop. 2,121,000, urb. 2,395,000.

Cincinnati (sin-si-na′tė) City (OH) pop. 364,040, urb. 1,817,571.

Ciudad Trujillo (syoo′däd troo-hē′yō) former name of Santo Domingo.

Cleveland (klēv′lənd) City (OH) pop. 505,616, urb. 2,859,644.

Cocos Islands (ko′kəs) (Australia) 5 sq. mi., pop. 569.

Cologne [*Ger.* **Köln**] (kə-lōn, köln) City (Germany) pop. 934,375.

Colombia, Republic of (kə-lum′bė-ə) 439,828 sq. mi., pop. 34,943,000, cap. Bogotá.

Colombo (kə-lum′bō) City (cap. of Sri Lanka) pop. 604,000.

Colorado (kol-ə-rad′ō) State (U.S.) 103,595 sq. mi., pop. 3,376,669, cap. Denver.

Colorado Springs City (CO) pop. 281,140, urb. 397,014.

Columbia (kə-lum′bė-ə) City (cap. of SC) pop. 98,052, urb. 453,331.

Columbus (kə-lum′bəs) 1, City (cap. of Ohio) pop. 632,910, urb. 1,345,450. 2, City (GA) pop. 179,278.

Comoros, Federal Islamic Republic of the (ko-mō′rō) 863 sq. mi., pop. 511,651, cap. Moroni.

Conakry (kon′ə-krē″) City (cap. of Guinea) pop. 705,000.

Concord (kon′kôrd) City (cap. of NH) pop. 36,006.

Congo (kon′gō) region in C. Africa, 1, **Democratic Republic of Congo** [formerly Belgian Congo], see *Zaire*. 2, **Republic of the Congo** [formerly Moyen Congo] (Fr. C.) 175,676 sq. mi., pop. 2,447,000, cap. Brazzaville.

Connecticut (kə-net′i-kət) State (U.S.) 4,872 sq. mi., pop. 3,291,094, cap. Hartford.

Constantinople, see *Istanbul*.

Cook Islands (kûk) (New Zeal.) 90 sq. mi., pop. 18,072, cap. Rarotonga (pop. 9,281).

Copenhagen (kō″pən-hā′gən) City (cap. of Denmark) pop. 619,000, urb. 876,960.

Coral Sea, part of Pacific Ocean NE of Australia.

Corpus Christi (kôr′pəs kris′tė) City (TX) pop. 257,453, urb. 349,894.

Corsica (kôr′si-kə) Island (Fr.) 3,367 sq. mi., pop. 248,000, cap. Ajaccio (ä-yät′chō).

Costa Rica, Republic of (kos′tə-rē′kə) 19,239 sq. mi., pop. 3,265,000, cap. San José.

Côte d'Ivoire (kōt dė-vwär′) 124,503 sq. mi., pop. 14,027,000, cap. Abidjan.

Cotonou (kō-tō-noo′) City (de facto cap. of Benin) pop. 383,250.

Crete (krēt) Island (Greece) 3,232 sq. mi., pop. 483,075, cap. Canea (kə-nē′ə).

Croatia (krō-ā′shə) (formerly part of Yugoslavia) 21,829 sq. mi., pop. 4,763,000, cap. Zagreb.

Cuba, Republic of (kū′bə) 42,857 sq. mi., pop. 10,957,000, cap. Havana.

Curaçao (kûr′ə-sow) Island (part of Neth. Antilles) 173 sq. mi., pop. 159,072.

Cyprus, Republic of (si′prəs) (C. of N.) 3,572 sq. mi., pop. 723,371, cap. Nicosia.

Czech Republic (chek) 30,448 sq. mi., pop. 10,298,731, cap. Prague.

Czechoslovakia (chek″ō-slō-väk″yə) see *Czech Republic* and *Slovak Republic.*

Dacca (dak′a) City (cap. of Bangladesh) pop. 1,679,572, urb. 3,458,602.

Dahomey (da-hō′mè) see *Benin.*

Dakar (dä-kär′) City (cap. of Senegal) pop. 798,792.

Dalian (dä′lyän′) [formerly **Dairen**] City (China) pop. 595,000.

Dallas (dal′əs) City (TX) pop. 1,006,877, urb. (Dallas-Fort Worth) 4,037,282.

Damascus [*Arabic* **Esh Shâm**] (də-mas′kəs, ash-sham′) City (cap. of Syria) pop. 1,343,000.

Danzig (dan′tsig) see *Gdansk.*

Dar es Salaam (där′es sə-läm′) City (de facto cap. of Tanzania) pop. 1,096,000.

Davis Strait (dā′vis) between Greenland & Baffin Island.

Dayton (dā′tən) City (OH) pop. 182,044, urb. (Dayton-Springfield) 951,270.

Dead Sea, between Palestine & Jordan, 340 sq. mi.

Delaware (del′ə-wâr) State (U.S.) 1,932 sq. mi., pop. 679,942, cap. Dover.

Delhi (del′ė) City (India) pop. 4,884,234, urb. 5,729,283.

Denmark, Kingdom of (den′märk) 16,556 sq. mi., pop. 5,176,000, cap. Copenhagen.

Denver (den′vər) City (cap. of CO) pop. 467,610, urb. 1,622,980.

Des Moines (di moin′) City (cap. of IA) pop. 193,187, urb. 392,928..

Detroit (dė-troit′) City (MI) pop. 1,027,974, urb. 5,187,171.

Dili (dil′ė) City (cap. of Port. Timor) pop. 52,158.

District of Columbia (kə-lum′-bė-ə) (U.S.) 63 sq. mi., pop. 606,900.

Djakarta (jə-kär′tə) see *Jakarta.*

Djibouti, Republic of (ji-boo′tė) [formerly **French Territory of the Afars and Issas**] 9,000 sq. mi., pop. 401,579, cap. Djibouti, pop. 100,000, urb. 290,000.

Dodecanese Islands (dō-dek′ə-nēz) (Greece) 1,030 sq. mi., pop. 123,021.

Dodoma (dō′dō-mä) City (cap. of Tanzania) pop. 45,703.

Doha (dō′hə) City (cap. of Qatar) pop. 217,294.

Dominica, Commonwealth of (dō-min′i-kə) (C. of N.) 290 sq. mi., pop. 88,406, cap. Roseau.

Dominican Republic (də-min′ə-kən) 19,129 sq. mi., pop. 7,657,000, cap. Santo Domingo.

Douglas (dug′ləs) City (cap. of Isle of Man) pop. 20,368.

Dover (dō′vər) City (cap. of DE) pop. 27,630, urb. 110,993.

Dresden (drez′dən) City (Germany) pop. 515,892.

Dublin [*Gaelic* **Baile Atha Cliath**] (dub′-lin, blâ-klē′ə) City (cap. of Republic of Ireland) pop. 502,749, urb. 920,956.

Durban (dēr′bən) City (So. Africa) pop. 634,301, urb. 982,075.

Dushanbe (doo-shän′bə) City (cap. of Tajikistan) pop. 582,000.

Ecuador, Republic of (ek′wə-dôr) 115,000 sq. mi., pop. 11,179,000, cap. Quito.

Edinburgh (ed′ən-bēr″ə) City (cap. of Scotland) pop. 433,480.

Edmonton (ed′mən-tən) City (Alta.) pop. 532,250, urb. 803,500.

Egypt, Arab Republic of (ē′jipt) 386,659 sq. mi., pop. 57,669,000, cap. Cairo.

Eire (er′ə) former name for the *Republic of Ireland.*

El Aiiún (el″ ä-yoon′) City (cap. of W. Sahara) pop. 28,010.

Ellesmere Island (elz′mèr) (Canada) 82,119 sq. mi., pop. 150.

Ellice Islands (el′is) see *Tuvalu.*

El Paso (el pas′o) City (TX) pop. 515,342, urb. 591,610.

El Salvador, Republic of (el säl-vä-dôr′) 13,176 sq. mi., pop. 5,699,000, cap. San Salvador.

England and Wales (ing′glənd, wälz) 58,340 sq. mi., pop. 48,827,000, cap. London.

Equatorial Guinea, Republic of (gi′nè) 10,832 sq. mi., pop. 399,055, cap. Malabo.

Erie, Lake (ir′ė) (Great Lakes) 9,940, sq. mi.

Eritrea (er-i-trē′ə) (Ethiopia) 15,754 sq. mi., pop. 1,589,400, cap. Asmara (äs-mä′rä).

Erivan, see *Yerevan.*

Estonia, Republic of (es-tō′nyə) 17,838 sq. mi., pop. 1,581,000, cap. Tallinn.

Ethiopia, People's Democratic Republic of (ē″thė-ō′pė-ə) 350,000 sq. mi., pop. 56,082,000, cap. Addis Ababa.

Europe (ū′rəp) Continent, 1,920,000 sq. mi., pop. 640,000,000. (without former U.S.S.R.).

Faroe Islands (fer′ō) (Den.) 540 sq. mi., pop. 49,025, cap. Thorshavn.

Falkland Islands or **Islas Malvinas** (fâk′lənd, ēz′läs mäl-vē′näs)) (Br.) incl. S. Georgia, 5,618 sq. mi., pop. 2,721, cap. Stanley.

Fiji, Republic of (fē′jė) (C. of N.) 7,055 sq. mi., pop. 756,762, cap. Suva.

Finland, Republic of (fin′lənd) 130,500 sq. mi., pop. 5,016,000, cap. Helsinki.

Florence (*It.* **Firenze**) (flôr′əns, fē-ren′zä) City (Italy) pop. 438,304.

Florida (flor′i-də) State (U.S.) 54,153 sq. mi., pop. 13,276,771, cap. Tallahassee.

Formosa, see *Taiwan.*

Fort-de-France (fôr′-dē-fräns″) City (cap. of Martinique) pop. 97,814.

Fort Lauderdale (lâ′dər-dāl″) City (Florida) pop. 149,377, urb. 1,255,488.

Fort Wayne (wān) City (IN) pop. 173,072, urb. 456,281.

Fort Worth (wėrth) City (TX) pop. 447,619.

France (frans) 212,736 sq. mi., pop. 57,566,000, cap. Paris.

Frankfort (frank′fərt) City (cap. of KY) pop. 25,968.

Franz Josef Land (fränts′ yō′zef länt″) Arctic archipelago (Russia) 8,000 sq. mi.

Freetown (frē′town) City (cap. of Sierra Leone) pop. 469,776.

Fremont (frē′mänt) City (CA) pop. 173,339.

French Indo-China (in′dō-chī′nə) former Fr. terr., now: Cambodia, Laos, Vietnam.

French Sudan (soo-dan′) see *Mali.*

Fresno (frez′nō) City (CA) pop. 354,202.

Friendly Islands, see *Tonga.*

Funafuti (foo-nä-foo′ti) City (cap. of Tuvalu) pop. 2,000.

Fundy, Bay of (fun′dė) between Nova Scotia & New Brunswick, 6,300 sq. mi.

Gabon (gä-bôn′) (Fr. C.) 103,088 sq. mi., pop. 1,123,000, cap. Libreville.

Gaborone (gä-bə-rō′nē) City (cap. of Botswana) pop. 138,000.

Galapagos Islands (gä-lä′pä-gos) (Ecuador) 3,042 sq. mi., pop. 2,391, cap. San Cristobal (san krəs-tō′bəl).

Galilee, Sea of (gal′ə-lē″) (Israel) 64 sq. mi.

Gambia, Republic of The (gam′bė-ə) (C. of N.) 3,999 sq. mi., pop. 930,249, cap. Banjul.

Gangtok City (cap. of Sikkim) pop. 36,768.

Garland (gär′lənd) City (TX) pop. 180,650.

Gdansk (gə-dänsk′) City (Poland) pop. 469,726.

Geneva (jə-nē′və) City (Switzerland) pop. 162,735, urb. 385,653.

Genoa [*It.* **Genova**] (jen′ō-ə, je-nō′və) City (Italy) pop. 843,632.

Georgetown (jôrj′town) **1,** City (cap. of Cayman Islands) pop. 13,700. **2,** City (cap. of Guyana) pop. 182,000.

Georgia (jôr′jə) State (U.S.) 58,056 sq. mi., pop. 5,463,105, cap. Atlanta.

Georgia, Republic of (jôr′jyə) 28,687 sq. mi., pop. 5,500,000, cap. Tiflis (Tbilisi) (tif′lis, tbi′lė-se) (pop. 1,095,000).

Germany, Federal Republic of (jėr′mə-nė), comprising former German Democratic Republic (East Germany) and Federal Republic of Germany (West Germany), 137,838 sq. mi., pop. 80,768,000, cap. Berlin.

Ghana, Republic of (gä′nə) (C. of N.) 88,802 sq. mi., pop. 16,699,000, cap. Accra.

Gibraltar (ji-brâl′tər) (Br.) 2 sq. mi., pop. 30,689.

Gibraltar, Strait of, between Spain & Africa.

Gilbert Islands (gil′bərt) see *Kiribati.*

Glasgow (glas′kō) City (Scotland) pop. 703,186.

Glendale (glen′dāl) City (CA) pop. 180,038.

Gôa, Daman, and Diu (gō′ə, da-man′, dė′oo) (India) 1,426 sq. mi., pop. 857,180, cap. Panjim (bän-zhen′).

Godthaab (native *Nuuk*) (gât′hâp; nûk) City (cap. of Greenland) pop. 9,561.

Gold Coast, former name of *Ghana.*

Gorky (gôr′kė) City (Russia) pop. 1,425,000.

Grand Rapids City (MI) pop. 189,126, urb. 937,891.

Grand Turk City (cap. of Turks and Caicos Islands) pop. 3,098.

Great Bear Lake (Canada) 12,275 sq. mi.

Great Britain, see *United Kingdom.*

Great Lakes, chain of 5 lakes between U.S. & Canada: Erie, Huron, Michigan, Ontario, Superior.

Great Salt Lake (UT) 2,560 sq. mi.

Great Slave Lake (Canada) 10,980 sq. mi.

Greece (grēs) 51,182 sq. mi., pop. 10,079,000 cap. Athens.

Greenland (native *Kalaalit Nunaat*) (grēn′lənd; kə-lät lit nû′nat) (Den.) 839,999 sq. mi., pop. 56,752, cap. Godthaab.

Greensboro (grēnz′bə-rə) City (NC) pop. 183,521, urb. 1,050,304.

Grenada (grə-nä′də) 133 sq. mi., pop. 83,325, cap. St. George's.

Guadalajara (gwä″thä-lä-hä′rä) City (Mexico) pop. 1,352,109.

Guadeloupe (gwä″də-loop′) (Fr.) 688 sq. mi., pop. 417,540, cap. Basse-Terre.

Guam (gwäm) U.S. Terr., 206 sq. mi., pop. 145,935, cap. Agana (ə-gä′nyə) (pop. 881).

Guatemala, Republic of (gwät′ə-mä-lə) 45,452 sq. mi., pop. 9,832,000, cap. Guatemala City (pop. 754,243).

Guiana (gė-ä′nə) see *Guyana*.

Guiana, Dutch (gė-ä′nə) see *Suriname*.

Guiana, French (gė-ä′nə) (Fr.) 35,135 sq. mi., pop. 133,376, cap. Cayenne (kī-en′).

Guinea, Republic of (gin′ė) 96,525 sq. mi., pop. 7,820,000, cap. Conakry.

Guinea-Bissau, Republic of (gin′ė-bi-sow′) [formerly *Portuguese Guinea*] 13,948 sq. mi., pop. 1,072,000, cap. Bissau.

Guinea, Equatorial (gin′ė), see *Equatorial Guinea*.

Guyana, Co-operative Republic of (gė-ä′nə) (C. of N.) 89,480 sq. mi., pop. 736,640, cap. Georgetown.

Hague, The [*Dutch* 's **Gravenhage**] (hāg, skrä″vən-hä′kə) City (Netherlands) pop. 570,765.

Haiti, Republic of (hā′tė) 10,714 sq. mi., pop. 6,579,000, cap. Port-au-Prince.

Halifax (hal′ə-faks) City (cap. of Nova Scotia) pop. 114,590, urb. 306,300.

Hamburg (ham′bėrg) City (Germany) pop. 1,595,255.

Hamilton (ham′il-tən) **1,** City (cap. of Bermuda) pop. 3,000. **2,** City (Canada) pop. 306,434, urb. 583,000.

Hanoi (ha-noi′) City (cap. of Vietnam) pop. 897,500, urb. 2,570,905.

Harare (hə-rä′rä) City (cap. of Zimbabwe) pop. 730,000.

Harbin (här′bin) City (Manchuria) pop. 2,800,000.

Harrisburg (har′is-bėrg) City (cap. of PA) pop. 52,376, urb. 587,986.

Hartford (härt′fərd) City (cap. of CT) pop. 139,739, urb. 1,157,585.

Havana [*Sp.* **La Habana**] (hə-van′ə, lä ä-vä′nä) City (cap. of Cuba) pop. 2,077,938.

Hawaii (hä-wä′ė) State (U.S.) 6,425 sq. mi., pop. 1,134,750, cap. Honolulu.

Helena (hel′ə-nə) City (cap. of MT) pop. 24,569.

Helsinki (hel′sing-kė) City (cap. of Finland) pop. 488,777, urb. 971,733.

Hialeah (hī″ə-lē′ə) City (FL) pop. 188,004.

Hiroshima (hi″rō-shē′mə, *Jap.* hė-râsh′mä) City (Japan) pop. 542,000.

Hispaniola (his-pan″ė-ō′lə) Island; includes Haiti and Dominican Republic.

Ho Chi Minh City (formerly, **Saigon**) (hō chē min) City (Vietnam) pop. 2,700,849, urb. 3,419,978.

Holland, see *Netherlands*.

Holy See, see *Vatican City*.

Honduras, Republic of (hon-door′əs) 43,277 sq. mi., pop. 5,236,000, cap. Tegucigalpa.

Hong Kong (hong′ kong′) (Br. until 1997, then China) 391 sq. mi., pop. 5,922,000, cap. Victoria.

Honiara (hō′nē-är″ə) City (cap. of Solomon Islands) pop. 30,413.

Honolulu (ho″nə-loo′loo) City (cap. of HI) pop. 365,272, urb. 836,231.

Honshu (hon′shoo) Island (Jap.) 88,000 sq. mi., pop. 81,560,000, cap. Tokyo.

Houston (hūs′tən) City (TX) pop. 1,630,553, urb. 3,731,131.

Huang or **Yellow River** (hwäng) (China) 3,000 miles.

Hudson Bay, bay of No. Canada, 281,900 sq. mi.

Hungary (hung′gə-rė) 35,875 sq. mi., pop. 10,324,000, cap. Budapest.

Huntington Beach (hun′ting-tən) City (CA) pop. 181,519.

Huron, Lake (hyû′rən) (Great Lakes) 23,010 sq. mi.

Hyderabad (hi′dēr-ə-bȧd″) City (India) pop. 2,093,488, urb. 3,673,000.

Iceland (īs′lənd) 39,709 sq. mi., pop. 261,270, cap. Reykjavik.

Idaho (i′də-hō) State (U.S.) 82,413 sq. mi., pop. 1,039,295, cap. Boise.

Ifni (ēf′nė) (Morocco) 579 sq. mi., pop. 52,000.

Illinois (il-ə-noi′) State (U.S.) 55,645 sq. mi., pop. 11,542,841, cap. Springfield.

India, Republic of (in′dė-ə) (C. of N.) 1,059,342 sq. mi., pop. 903,178,000, cap. New Delhi.

Indiana (in″dė-an′ə) State (U.S.) 35,932 sq. mi., pop. 5,609,616, cap. Indianapolis (in″dė-ən-ap′ə-lis) (pop. 741,952, urb. 1,380,491).

Indian Ocean, between Africa & Australia, 28,350,000 sq. mi.

Indo-China (in′dō-chī′nə) Peninsula comprising Myanmar, Thailand, Cambodia, Laos, Vietnam, and Malaya.

Indonesia, Republic of (in″dō-nē′zhə) 575,892 sq. mi., pop. 198,919,000, cap. Jakarta.

Iowa (i′ə-wə) State (U.S.) 55,965 sq. mi., pop. 2,795,220, cap. Des Moines.

Iran, Islamic Republic of [formerly **Persia**] (ī-ran′, pēr′zhə) 628,000 sq. mi., pop. 63,370,000, cap. Tehran.

Iraq, Republic of [formerly **Mesopotamia**] (i-rak′, mes″ō-pō-tā′mė-ə) 116,600 sq. mi., pop. 19,162,000, cap. Baghdad.

---

fat, fāte, fär, fāre, fâll, ȧsk; met, hē, hėr, maybė; pin, pīne; not, nōte, ôr, tool

Ireland, Northern (īr'lənd) (U.K.) 5,238 sq. mi., pop. 1,570,000, cap. Belfast.

Ireland, Republic of (īr'lənd) 26,601 sq. mi., pop. 3,530,000, cap. Dublin.

Irish Sea, between Ireland & Great Britain, 75,000 sq. mi.

Islamabad (is-läm'ə-bàd″) City (cap. of Pakistan), pop. 204,364.

Isle of Man (Br.) 221 sq. mi., pop. 64,068, cap. Douglas.

Israel, State of (iz-rė-əl) 7,992 sq. mi., pop. 4,919,000, cap. Jerusalem.

Istanbul [formerly **Constantinople**] (is″tan-bool', kon″stan-ti-nō'pəl) City (Turkey) pop. 6,293,397, urb. 6,678,000.

Italy, Republic of (it'ə-lė) 116,000 sq. mi., pop. 58,019,000, cap. Rome.

Ivory Coast, see *Côte d'Ivoire.*

Jackson (jak'sən) City (cap. of Miss.) pop. 196,637, urb. 395,396.

Jacksonville (jak'sən-vil) City (FL) pop. 672,971, urb. 906,727.

Jakarta (jə-kär'tə) City (cap. of Indonesia) pop. 7,885,519.

Jamaica (jə-mā'kə) Island (C. of N.) 4,450 sq. mi., pop. 2,530,000, cap. Kingston.

Jamestown City (cap. of Saint Denis) pop. 1,576.

Japan (jə-pan') 144,550 sq. mi., pop. 124,907,000, cap. Tokyo.

Japan, Sea of (jə-pan') between Japan and Korea, 391,100 sq. mi.

Java and Madura (jä'və, mä-doo'rä) (Indonesia) 51,032 sq. mi., pop. 78,000,000.

Jefferson City (jef'ər-sən) City (cap. of MO) pop. 35,481.

Jersey City (jėr'zė) City (NJ) pop. 223,532.

Jerusalem (jə-roo'sə-lem) City (cap. of Israel) pop. 493,500.

Johannesburg (jō-han'is-bėrg″) City (Union of So. Africa) pop. 632,369, urb. 1,609,408.

Jordan, Hashemite Kingdom of [formerly **Transjordan**] (jōr'dən) 37,300 sq. mi., pop. 3,707,000, cap. Amman.

Juneau (joo'nō) City (cap. of AK) pop. 26,751.

Kabul (kä'bûl) City (cap. of Afghanistan) pop. 1,424,400.

Kampala (käm-pä'lä) City (cap. of Uganda) pop. 330,700.

Kampuchea (käm-pū-chē'ə) see *Cambodia.*

Kanpur (kän'pûr) City (India) pop. 1,481,789, urb. 1,639,064.

Kansas (kan'zəs) State (U.S.) 81,781 sq. mi., pop. 2,494,560, cap. Topeka.

Kansas City (kan'zəs) **1,** City (MO) pop. 435,146. **2,** City (KS) pop. 161,087. **3,** urban area (KS-MO) pop. 1,582,875.

Karachi (ke-rä'chė) City (former cap. of Pakistan) pop. 5,180,562, urb. 8,014,000.

Katmandu (kät-män-doo') City (cap. of Nepal) pop. 235,160.

Kazakhstan, Republic of (kä″zäk-stän') 1,064,092 sq. mi., pop. 16,500,000, cap. Alma-Ata.

Keeling Islands (kē'ling) see *Cocos Islands*

Kentucky (kən-tuk'ė) State (U.S.) 39,669 sq. mi., pop. 3,713,475, cap. Frankfort.

Kenya, Republic of (kěn'yə) (C. of N.) 224,960 sq. mi., pop. 27,109,000, cap. Nairobi.

Kharkov (kär'kof) City (Russia) pop. 1,587,000.

Khartoum (kär-toom') City (cap. of Sudan) pop. 561,000.

Kiev (kē'yef) City (Ukraine) pop. 2,544,000.

Kigali (kē-gä'lē) City (cap. of Rwanda) pop. 116,227.

Kingston (kings'tən) City (cap. of Jamaica) pop. 104,041, urb. 524,638.

Kingstown City (cap. of St. Vincent and the Grenadines) pop. 22,500.

Kinshasa [formerly **Leopoldville**] (kinshä'sä) City (cap. of Zaire) pop. 3,741,000.

Kiribati, Republic of (ki-ri-bäss') 264 sq. mi., pop. 76,320, cap. Tarawa.

Kishinev (kish'ə-nef) City (cap. of Moldova) pop. 663,000.

Kitakyushu (kē″tä-kū'shoo) City (Japan) pop. 1,039,482.

Kobe (kō'be) City (Japan) pop. 1,447,547.

Korea (kō-rē'ə) **1,** Democratic People's Republic of Korea (North Korea) 47,862 sq. mi., pop. 22,646,000, cap. Pyongyang. **2,** Republic of Korea (South Korea) 37,424 sq. mi., pop. 44,614,000, cap. Seoul.

Kota Kinabalu (kō'tə kin'-ə-bə-lū″) City (cap. of Sabah) pop. 108,725.

Kuala Lumpur (kwä'lä lûm'pûr) City (cap. of Malaysia) pop. 919,610.

Kuching (koo'ching) City (cap. of Sarawak) pop. 63,491.

Kuril Islands or **Chishima** (koo-rēl', chė-shē'mä) (Russia) 6,020 sq. mi., pop. 15,000.

Kuwait, State of (kû-wät') 5,991 sq. mi., pop. 1,698,000, cap. Kuwait City (pop. 99,609).

Kuybyshev (kyu'bi-shef″) City (Russia) pop. 1,280,000.

Kwangchou, see *Canton.*

Kyoto (kyō'tō) City (Japan) pop. 1,474,507.

Kyrgyzstan, Republic of (kir-gēz'stän) 77,838 sq. mi., pop. 4,300,000, cap. Bishkek (pop. 552,000).

---

tub, cūte, pûll; labəl; oil, owl, go, chip, she, thin, *th*en, sing, ink; *see p. 6*

Labrador (lab'rə-dôr") (Newfoundland) 112,000 sq. mi., pop. 21,300, cap. Battle Harbour.

Lagos (lä'gâs) City (cap. of Nigeria) pop. 1,060,848.

Lahore (lə'hôr) City (Pakistan) pop. 2,952,689.

Lansing (lan'sing) City (cap. of Mich.) pop. 127,321, urb. 432,674.

Laos, People's Democratic Republic of (lä'ōs) 89,343 sq. mi., pop. 4,569,000, cap. Vientiane.

La Paz (lä päz') City (cap. of Bolivia) pop. 976,800.

Las Vegas (läs vā'gəs) City (NV) pop. 258,295, urb. 825,737.

Latvia, Republic of (lat'vė-ə) 24,954 sq. mi., pop. 2,680,000, cap. Riga (rē'gä) (pop. 910,000).

Lebanon, Republic of (leb'ə-nən) 3,475 sq. mi., pop. 3,499,000, cap. Beirut.

Leeds (lēdz) City (England) pop. 506,100.

Leeward Islands (lē'wərd) (Br.) 423 sq. mi., pop. 32,000, cap. St. John's.

Leipzig (līp'sig) City (Germany) pop. 590,291.

Leningrad (len'in-grad") City (Russia) pop. 4,948,000.

Leopoldville (lē'ə-pōld-vil) see *Kinshasa*.

Lesotho, Kingdom of [formerly **Basutoland**] (lə-sō'tō) (C. of N.) 11,716 sq. mi., pop. 1,896,000, cap. Maseru.

Lexington (lek'sing-tən) City (KY) pop. (Lexington-Fayette City) 225,366, urb. 405,936.

Liberia, Republic of (lī-bir'ė-ə) 43,000 sq. mi., pop. 2,875,000, cap. Monrovia.

Libreville (lē'brə-vėl") City (cap. of Gabon) pop. 57,000.

Libya, Socialist People's Arab Jamahiriya (lib'ė-ə) 679,358 sq. mi., pop. 4,618,000, cap. Tripoli, Benghazi.

Liechtenstein, Principality of (lik'tənstīn) 65 sq. mi., pop. 28,806, cap. Vaduz.

Lilongwe (li-lâng'wä) City (cap. of Malawi) pop. 253,973.

Lima (lē'mə) City (cap. of Peru) pop. 5,826,000, urb. 6,233,800.

Lincoln (link'ən) City (cap. of NE) pop. 191,972, urb. 213,641.

Lisbon [*Port.* **Lisboa**] (liz'bən, lēzh-bō'ə) City (cap. of Portugal) pop. 828,000, urb. 1,611,887.

Lithuania, Republic of (lith"ū-ā'nyə) 24,151 sq. mi., pop. 3,754,000, cap. Vilnyus (Vilna) (vil'nė-ûs, vil'nə) (pop. 592,000).

Little Rock (lit'əl rok") City (cap. of AR) pop. 175,795, urb. 513,117.

Liverpool (liv'ər-pool) City (England) pop. 688,000.

Ljubljana (loo"blē-ä'nə) City (cap. of Slovenia) pop. 224,817.

Lodz City (Poland) pop. 857,485.

Lomé (lō-mā') City (cap. of Togo) pop. 220,000.

London (lun'dən) City (cap. of England) pop. 6,735,353.

Long Beach (lâng' bēch') City (CA) pop. 429,433.

Los Angeles (los an'jə-ləs) City (CA) pop. 3,485,398, urb. 14,531,529.

Louisiana (lū-ēz"ė-an'ə) State (U.S.) 44,521 sq. mi., pop. 4,251,569, cap. Baton Rouge.

Louisville (loo'i-vil) City (KY) pop. 269,063, urb. 948,829.

Loyalty Islands (lâ'yəl-tė) (Fr.) 800 sq. mi., pop. 11,500, cap. Lifou (lė-foo').

Luanda (lû-än'də) City (cap. of Angola) pop. 475,328.

Lubbock (lub'ək) City (TX) pop. 186,206, urb. 222,636.

Lusaka (loo-sä'kə) City (cap. of Zambia) pop. 982,000.

Lüshun [formerly **Port Arthur**] (lyoo'-shûn') City (China) pop. 1,650,000.

Luxembourg, Grand Duchy of (luk'səmbėrg) 999 sq. mi., pop. 396,003, cap. Luxembourg (pop. 86,000).

Lyon (lė-ōn') City (France) pop. 527,800, urb. 1,170,000.

Macao (mə-kow') (Port.) 6 sq. mi., pop. 481,199, cap. Macao.

Macedonia, Republic of (mä-sə-dō'nė-ə) (formerly part of Yugoslavia) 9,928 sq. mi., pop. 2,033,964, cap. Skopje.

Madagascar, Democratic Republic of [formerly **Malagasy Republic**] (mad-ə-gas'kər, mä-lä-gä'sė) 241,094 sq. mi., pop. 13,006,000, cap. Antananarivo.

Madeira Islands (mə-dir'ə) (Port.) 308 sq. mi., pop. 268,600, cap. Funchal (fûn-shäl').

Madison (mad'i-sən) City (cap. of Wis.) pop. 191,262, urb. 367,085.

Madras (ma-dräs') City (India) pop. 3,276,622, urb. 4,289,347.

Madrid (mə-drid') City (cap. of Spain) pop. 2,991,223, urb. 4,513,000.

Madura (mä-doo'rə) Island (Indonesia) 1,725 sq. mi., pop. 2,400,000, cap. Pamekasan (pä"mä-kə-sän').

Magellan, Strait of (mə-jel'ən) at so. tip of So. America.

Maine (mān) State (U.S.) 30,995 sq. mi., pop. 1,234,602, cap. Augusta.

Malabo [formerly **Santa Isabel**] (mal'ə-bō, sän'tä ē-sä-bel') City (cap. of Equatorial Guinea) pop. 34,980.

Malacca, Strait of (mə-lak'ə) between Sumatra & Malaya.

Malawi, Republic of [formerly **Nyasaland**] (mä-lä'wē) (C. of N.) 48,443 sq. mi., pop. 9,777,000, cap. Lilongwe.

Malaysia [formerly **Federation of Malaya**] (mə-lā′zhə) (C. of N.) 128,430 sq. mi., pop. 18,845,000, cap. Kuala Lumpur.

Maldives, Republic of (mal′dīv) 115 sq. mi., pop. 243,094, cap. Male (mä-lā′) (pop. 46,334).

Mali, Republic of [formerly **French Sudan**] (mä′lē) 584,942 sq. mi., pop. 8,869,000, cap. Bamako.

Malta, Republic of (mâl′tə) (C. of N.) 122 sq. mi., pop. 361,894, cap. Valletta.

Managua (mä-nä′gwä) City (cap. of Nicaragua) pop. 608,020.

Manama (mä-nä′mə) City (cap. of Bahrain) pop. 151,000.

Manchester (man′ches-tər) City (England) pop. 445,927.

Manchuria (man-chûr′ē-ə) (China) 412,801 sq. mi., pop. 53,000,000, cap. Shenyang.

Manila (mə-nil′ə) City (cap. of Philippines) pop. 1,856,375, urb. 6,720,050.

Manitoba (man-i-tō′bə) Prov. (Canada) 219,723 sq. mi., pop. 1,026,241, cap. Winnipeg.

Maputo (mə-pū′tō) City (cap. of Mozambique) pop. 882,601.

Marianas Islands (mar″ē-an′əs) U.S. Trust., 247 sq. mi., pop. 16,600, cap. Saipan (sī-pan′).

Marquesas Islands (mär-kā′səs) (Fr.) 480 sq. mi., pop. 4,838, cap. Atuana (ä″tû-ä′nä).

Marseille (mär-sā′) City (France) pop. 867,260, urb. 1,080,000.

Marshall Islands, Republic of the (mär′shəl) 74 sq. mi., pop. 51,982, cap. Majuro.

Martinique (mär-ti-nēk′) (Fr.) 425 sq. mi., pop. 376,980, cap. Fort-de-France.

Maryland (mer′i-lənd) State (U.S.) 9,837 sq. mi., pop. 4,859,790, urb. Annapolis.

Maseru (maz′ə-roo″) City (cap. of Lesotho) pop. 29,049.

Masqat, see *Muscat.*

Massachusetts (mas-ə-choo′səts) State (U.S.) 7,824 sq. mi., pop. 5,995,959, cap. Boston.

Mata Utu (ma′ta oo′too) City (cap. of Wallis and Futuna Islands) pop. 3,000.

Mauritania, Islamic Republic of (mâ-rə-tā′nē-ə) 328,185 sq. mi., pop. 2,125,000, cap. Nouakchott.

Mauritius (mâ-rish′əs) **Island** (C. of N.) 720 sq. mi., pop. 1,101,000, cap. Port Louis.

Mbabane (m-bä-bä′nə) City (cap. of Swaziland) pop. 38,290.

Medellín (mā″thä-yēn′) City (Colombia) pop. 1,452,392.

Mediterranean Sea (med″i-tə-rā′nē-ən) between Europe & Africa, 1,145,000 sq. mi.

Melbourne (mel′bərn) City (Australia) pop. 2,965,600.

Memphis (mem′fis) City (TN) pop. 610,337, urb. 1,007,306.

Mesa (mā′sə) City (AZ) pop. 288,091.

Mesopotamia, see *Iraq.*

Mexico (United Mexican States) (mek′si-kō) 760,373 sq. mi., pop. 94,450,000, cap. Mexico City (pop. 8,831,079, urb. 20,899,000).

Mexico, Gulf of, off so. U.S. and east Mexico, 700,000 sq. mi.

Miami (mī-am′ē) City (FL) pop. 358,548, urb. 1,937,094.

Michigan (mish′i-gən) State (U.S.) 56,954 sq. mi., pop. 9,367,627, cap. Lansing.

Michigan, Lake (Great Lakes) 22,400 sq. mi.

Micronesia, Federated States of (mī″krə-nē′zhə) 270 sq. mi., pop. 117,588.

Midway Island (U.S.) 2 sq. mi., pop. 2,000.

Milan [*It.* **Milano**] (mi-lan′, mē-lä′nō) City (Italy) pop. 1,548,580.

Milwaukee (mil-wâ′kē) City (WI) pop. 628,088, urb. 1,607,183.

Minneapolis (min-ē-ap′ə-lis) City (MN) pop. 368,383, urb. 1,538,834.

Minnesota (min-i-sō′tə) State (U.S.) 79,548 sq. mi., pop. 4,432,361, cap. St. Paul.

Minsk City (cap. of Belarus) pop. 1,543,000.

Mississippi (mis″i-sip′ē) State (U.S.) 47,233 sq. mi., pop. 2,592,003, cap. Jackson.

Mississippi-Missouri River (U.S.) 3,710 miles.

Missouri (mə-zûr′ē) State (U.S.) 68,945 sq. mi., pop. 5,157,751, cap. Jefferson City.

Mobile (mō′bēl) City (AL) pop. 196,278, urb. 476,923.

Mogadishu (mog″ə-dish′oo) City (cap. of Somalia) pop. 700,000.

Moldova, Republic of (mōl-dō′və) (former Moldavian S.S.R.) 13,012 sq. mi., pop. 4,300,000, cap. Kishinev.

Monaco, Principality of (mon′ə-kō) 370 acres, pop. 30,212, cap. Monaco, pop. same.

Mongolia, People's Republic of (mon-gō′lē-ə) 625,946 sq. mi., pop. 2,367,000, cap. Ulan Bator.

Monrovia (mən-rō′vē-ə) City (cap. of Liberia) pop. 421,058.

Montana (mon-tan′ə) State (U.S.) 145,392 sq. mi., pop. 808,487, cap. Helena.

Montenegro (mon-te-nā′grō) Republic, formerly part of Yugoslavia, 5,333 sq. mi., pop. 616,327, cap. Podgorica (pop. 54,500).

Monterrey (mon″tə-rä′) City (Mexico) pop. 1,084,696.

Montevideo (mon″ti-vi-dā′ō) City (cap. of Uruguay) pop. 1,310,000.

Montgomery (mont-gum′ə-rė) City (cap. of AL) pop. 187,106, urb. 292,517.

Montpelier (mont-pēl′yər) City (cap. of VT) pop. 8,247.

Montreal (mon″trė-âl′) City (Que.) pop. 980,354, urb. 3,021,300.

Montserrat Islands (mont-sə-rat′) (Br.) 32 sq. mi., pop. 12,661, cap. Plymouth (plim′əth).

Morocco, Kingdom of (mə-rok′ō) 171,031 sq. mi., pop. 27,264,000, cap. Rabat-Salé.

Moroni (mô-rō′nė) City (cap. of Comoros) pop. 17,800, urb. 28,000.

Moscow [*Russ.* **Moskva**] (mos′kō, mus-kvä′) City (cap. of Russia) pop. 8,818,000.

Mozambique, Republic of (mō″zəm-bēk′) 297,731 sq. mi., pop. 16,104,000, cap. Maputo.

Mukden, see *Shenyang.*

Munich [*Ger.* **München**] (mū′nik, myün′chən) City (Germany) pop. 1,206,394.

Muscat (mus′kat) City (cap. of Oman) pop. 85,000.

Myanmar, Union of (myän′mär) (formerly Burma) 261,789 sq. mi., pop. 43,456,000, cap. Yangon.

Nagoya (nə-goi′ə) City (Japan) pop. 2,147,667.

Naha (nä-hä) City (cap. of Ryukyu) pop. 284,000.

Nairobi (nī-rō′bė) City (cap. of Kenya) pop. 1,162,189.

Namibia, Republic of (nä-mē′bė-ə) 318,261 sq. mi., pop. 1,632,000, cap. Windhoek.

Nanjing (nan′jing′) City (China) pop. 2,091,400, urb. 3,682,070.

Naples [*It.* **Napoli**] (nā′pəlz, nä′pō-lė) City (Italy) pop. 1,267,073.

Nashville (nash′vil) City (cap. of TN) pop. (Nashville-Davidson City) 510,784, urb. 985,026.

Nassau (nas′â) City (cap. of Bahamas) pop. 153,620.

Nauru, Republic of [formerly **Pleasant Island**] (nä-oo′roo) 8.22 sq. mi., pop. 9,581, cap. Yaren.

N'Djamena (en-jä′mä-nä) City (cap. of Chad) pop. 180,000.

Nebraska (nə-bras′kə) State (U.S.) 76,644 sq. mi., pop. 1,592,717, cap. Lincoln.

Nepal, Kingdom of (ni-pâl′) 54,000 sq. mi., pop. 20,574,000, cap. Katmandu.

Netherlands, Kingdom of the or **Holland** (ne*th*′ər-lənds, hol′ənd) 12,883 sq. mi.,

pop. 15,194,000, cap. Amsterdam (seat of government, The Hague).

Nevada (ni-vä′də) State (U.S.) 109,893 sq. mi., pop. 1,283,832, cap. Carson City.

Newark (noo′ərk) City (NJ) pop. 275,221.

New Britain Islands (brit′ən) (part of Papua New Guinea) 14,600 sq. mi., pop. 154,000, cap. Rabaul.

New Brunswick (brunz′wik) Prov. (Canada) 27,895 sq. mi., pop. 724,300, cap. Fredericton (fred′rik-tən) (pop. 43,723).

New Caledonia (kal″ə-dō′nė-ə) (Fr.) 7,201 sq. mi., pop. 178,056, cap. Nouméa.

New Delhi (del′ė) a section of Delhi (cap. of India) pop. 273,036.

Newfoundland (noo′fənd-lənd) Prov. (Canada) 152,734 sq. mi., pop. 573,000, cap. St. John's.

New Guinea (gin′ė) see *Indonesia* and *Papua New Guinea.*

New Guinea, Netherlands (gin′ė) see *Indonesia.*

New Hampshire (hamp′shər) State (U.S.) 8,993 sq. mi., pop. 1,104,695, cap. Concord.

New Hebrides Islands (heb′ri-dēz) see *Vanuatu.*

New Ireland (īr′lənd) Island (part of Papua New Guinea) 3,800 sq. mi., pop. 59,543.

New Jersey (jēr′zė) State (U.S.) 7,468 sq. mi., pop. 7,760,487, cap. Trenton.

New Mexico (mek′si-kō) State (U.S.) 121,335 sq. mi., pop. 1,547,721, cap. Santa Fe.

New Orleans (ôr′lė-ənz) City (LA) pop. 496,938, urb. 1,285,270

Newport News (noo′pôrt) City (VA) pop. 170,045.

New York (yôrk) **1,** State (U.S.) 47,377 sq. mi., pop. 18,057,602, cap. Albany. **2,** City (NY) pop. 7,322,564, urb. 19,342,013.

New Zealand (zē′lənd) (C. of N.) 103,934 sq. mi., pop. 3,308,000, cap. Wellington.

Niamey (nė-ə-mā′) City (cap. of Niger) pop. 350,000.

Nicaragua, Republic of (nik″ə-rä′gwə) 57,143 sq. mi., pop. 3,987,000, cap. Managua.

Nicobar Islands (nik-ō-bär′) see *Andaman Islands*

Nicosia (nik″ō-sē′ə) City (cap. of Cyprus) pop. 166,900.

Niger, Republic of (nī′jər) 501,930 sq. mi., pop. 8,337,000, cap. Niamey.

Nigeria, Federal Republic of (nī-jir′ė-ə) (C. of N.) 372,674 sq. mi., pop. 130,167,000, cap. Lagos.

Nile River (nīl) (Arab Republic of Egypt) 4,145 miles.

Norfolk (nôr′fək) **1,** City (VA) pop.

261,229, urb. 2,082,914. **2,** Island (Austl.) 13 sq. mi., pop. 1,000.

North America (ə-mer′i-kə) Continent, 8,500,000 sq. mi., pop. 279,000,000.

North Carolina (kar-ə-lī′nə) State (U.S.) 48,843 sq. mi., pop. 6,736,827, cap. Raleigh.

North Dakota (də-kō′tə) State (U.S.) 69,300 sq. mi., pop. 634,604, cap. Bismarck.

Northern Mariana Islands, Commonwealth of (mä-rē-ä′nə) U.S. Commonwealth, 183.5 sq. mi., pop. 48,363, cap. Saipan.

Northern Rhodesia (rō-dē′zhə) see *Zambia.*

North Sea, off NW Europe, 222,000 sq. mi.

Northwest Territories (Canada) 1,258,217 sq. mi., pop. 45,741, cap. Yellowknife.

Norway, Kingdom of (nôr′wä) 124,560 sq. mi., pop. 4,314,000, cap. Oslo.

Nouakchott (nwäk′shôt) City (cap. of Mauritania) pop. 400,000.

Nouméa (noo-mā′ə) City (cap. of New Caledonia) pop. 65,110, urb. 97,581.

Nova Scotia (nō-və skō′shə) Prov. (Canada) 20,743 sq. mi., pop. 892,000, cap. Halifax (hal′i-faks) (pop. 114,594).

Novosibirsk (nō-vō-si-birsk′) City (Russia) pop. 1,423,000.

Nuku'alofa (noo-koo″ə-lō′fə) City (cap. of Tonga) pop. 29,000.

Nyasa Lake (nī-as′ə) (Africa) 11,430 sq. mi.

Nyasaland (nī-as′ə-land) see *Malawi.*

Oakland (ōk′lənd) City (Calif.) pop. 372,242.

Ob-Irtysh River (ôb′ir-tish′) (Russia) 3,460 miles.

Odessa (ō-des′ə) City (Ukraine) pop. 1,141,000.

Ohio (ō-hī′ō) State (U.S.) 41,004 sq. mi., pop. 10,938,800, cap. Columbus.

Okhotsk, Sea of (ō-kotsk′) (Russia) 537,500 sq. mi.

Oklahoma (ōk-lə-hō′mə) State (U.S.) 68,655 sq. mi., pop. 3,174,775, cap. Oklahoma City (pop. 444,719, urb. 958,839).

Olympia (ō-lim′pyə) City (cap. of WA) pop. 33,840, urb. 161,238.

Omaha (ō′mə-hâ) City (NE) pop. 335,795, urb. 639,580.

Oman, Sultanate of (ō′man) 82,000 sq. mi., pop. 1,644,000, cap. Muscat.

Ontario (on-tãr′ē-o) Prov. (Canada) 363,282 sq. mi., pop. 9,747,600, cap. Toronto.

Ontario, Lake (Great Lakes) 7,540 sq. mi.

Oregon (or′ə-gon) State (U.S.) 96,184 sq. mi., pop. 2,921,921, cap. Salem.

Orkney Islands (ôrk′nė) (Scotland) 376 sq. mi., pop. 17,300, cap. Kirkwall (kėrk′wâl).

Orlando (ôr-lan′dō) City (FL) pop. 164,293, urb. 1,224,852.

Osaka (ō-sä′kə) City (Japan) pop. 2,644,691.

Oslo (oz′lō) City (cap. of Norway) pop. 454,927, urb. 726,440.

Ottawa (ot′ə-wə) City (cap. of Canada) pop. 295,163, urb. 853,200.

Ouagadougou (wä″gà-doo′goo) City (cap. of Burkina Faso) pop. 307,937.

Pacific Islands (pə-sif′ik) consisting of the Caroline, Marshall, and Marianas Islands, 687 sq. mi., pop. 136,810.

Pacific Ocean, 70,000,000 sq. mi.

Pakistan, Islamic Republic of [formerly **West Pakistan**] (pak′i-stan) (C. of N.) 310,236 sq. mi., pop. 125,214,000, cap. Islamabad.

Palau Islands (pä-low′) U.S. Trust. (part of Caroline Islands) 175 sq. mi., pop. 15,122, cap. Koror (kâ-rôr′).

Palestine (pal′əs-tīn″) see *Israel.*

Panama, Republic of (pan′ə-mä) 28,576 sq. mi., pop. 2,582,000, cap. Panama (pop. 431,937).

Panama Canal, between Pacific Ocean & Gulf of Mexico, 50 mi.

Papeete (pä-pė-ä′te) City (cap. of Fr. Polynesia) pop. 22,278.

Papua New Guinea (pap′ū-ə) (C. of N.) 90,540 sq. mi., pop. 4,101,000, cap. Port Moresby.

Paraguay, Republic of (par′ə-gwä) 150,518 sq. mi., pop. 5,071,000, cap. Asunción.

Paramaribo (par″ə-mar′i-bō) City (cap. of Suriname) pop. 192,000.

Paris (par′is) City (cap. of France) pop. 2,590,771, urb. 8,612,531.

Peking, see *Beijing.*

Pennsylvania (pen″sil-vä′ni-ə) State (U.S.) 44,888 sq. mi., pop. 11,961,074, cap. Harrisburg.

Pernambuco, see *Recife.*

Persia, see *Iran.*

Persian Gulf, between Iran & Arabia, 88,800 sq. mi.

Perth (pėrth) City (Australia) pop. 1,083,400.

Peru, Republic of (pə-roo′) 513,000 sq. mi., pop. 23,210,000, cap. Lima.

Philadelphia (fil-ə-del′fė-ə) City (PA) pop. 1,585,577, urb. 5,892,937.

Philippines, Republic of the (fil′e-pēnz″) 115,600 sq. mi., pop. 68,464,000, cap. Quezon City (de facto cap., Manila.)

Phnom Penh (nom-pen′) City (cap. of Cambodia) pop. 400,000.

---

tub, cūte, pûll; labəl; oil, owl, go, chip, she, thin, *th*en, sing, ink; *see p. 6*

Phoenix (fē′niks) City (cap. of AZ) pop. 983,403, urb. 2,238,480.

Phoenix Islands (fē′niks) (Kiribati) 16 sq. mi., pop. 850.

Pierre (pir) City (cap. of SD) pop. 11,973.

Pitcairn Island (pit′kärn) (Br.) 1.7 sq. mi., pop. 61, cap. Adamstown.

Pittsburgh (pits′bėrg) City (PA) pop. 369,879, urb. 2,394,811.

Poland, Republic of (pō′lənd) 119,734 sq. mi., pop. 38,519,000, cap. Warsaw.

Polynesia, French (pol″i-nē′zhə) Fr. Terr., 1,544 sq. mi., pop. 210,333, cap. Papeete.

Port Arthur and Dairen (dī′ren) see *Lüshun, Talien.*

Port-au-Prince (por″tō-prins′) City (cap. of Haiti) pop. 470,000, urb. 738,342.

Portland (pôrt′lənd) City (OR) pop. 437,319, urb. 1,793,476.

Port-Louis (pôr″lwē′) City (cap. of Mauritius) pop. 139,000.

Port Moresby (môrz′bė) City (cap. of Papua New Guinea) pop. 152,000.

Port-of-Spain City (cap. of Trinidad and Tobago) pop. 56,649.

Porto-Novo (pôr″tō-nō′vō) City (cap. of Benin) pop. 144,000.

Portugal, Republic of (pôr′chə-gəl) 35,413 sq. mi., pop. 10,486,000, cap. Lisbon.

Prague [*Czech* **Praha**] (präg, prä′hä) City (cap. of Czech Republic) pop. 1,209,149.

Praia (prī′ə) City (cap. of Cape Verde) pop. 57,748.

Pretoria (pri-tôr′ė-ə) City (admin. cap. of So. Africa) pop. 443,059, urb. 822,925.

Prince Edward Island, Prov. (Canada) 2,184 sq. mi., pop. 130,400, cap. Charlottetown.

Providence (prov′i-dəns) City (cap. of RI) pop. 160,728, urb. 1,134,350.

Puerto Rico (pwer″tō rē′kō) (U.S.) 3,423 sq. mi., pop. 3,797,000, cap. San Juan.

Pusan (pû-sän) City (So. Korea) pop. 3,514,798.

Pyong Yang (pyûng′yäng′) City (cap. of No. Korea) pop. 1,350,000.

Qatar, State of (kä′tär) 4,000 sq. mi., pop. 499,115, cap. Doha.

Québec (kwi-bek′; *Fr.* kā-) Prov. (Canada) 523,860 sq. mi., pop. 6,770,800, cap. Québec (pop. 166,474, urb. 615,400).

Queen Elizabeth Islands (i-liz′ə-bəth) (Canada) 134,920 sq. mi., pop. 310.

Quezon City (kā′sōn) City (cap. of Philippines) pop. 1,546,019.

Quito (kē′tō) City (cap. of Ecuador) pop. 1,500,000

Rabat-Salé (rə-bät′-sä-lā′) City (cap. of Morocco) pop. 556,000, urb. 841,800.

Raleigh (râ′lė) City (cap. of NC) pop. 207,951, urb. 855,545.

Rangoon (rang-goon′) see *Yangon.*

Rarotonga (rä-rō-tông′gä) City (cap. of Cook Islands) pop. 11,000.

Recife or **Pernambuco** (re-sē′fə, pēr′nəmboo′kō) City (Brazil) pop. 1,298,627.

Red Sea, between Asia & Africa, 178,000 sq. mi.

Regina (rə-jī′nə) City (cap. of Sask.) pop. 162,610.

Réunion (rā-û-nyôṅ′) Island (Fr.) 970 sq. mi., pop. 639,622, cap. Saint-Denis.

Reykjavik (rā′kyə-vēk″) City (cap. of Iceland) pop. 97,000, urb. 140,273.

Rhode Island (rōd ī′lənd) State (U.S.) 1,055 sq. mi., pop. 1,004,328, cap. Providence.

Rhodesia, see *Zimbabwe.*

Richmond (rich′mənd) City (cap. of VA) pop. 203,056, urb. 865,640.

Rio de Janeiro (rē′ō dā jə-nā′rō) City (Brazil) pop. 5,615,149.

Rio de Oro (rē′o dā ō′rō) see *Spanish Sahara.*

Rio Muni or **Continental Spanish Guinea** (rē′ō moo′nē) see *Equatorial Guinea.*

Riverside City (CA) pop. 226,505, urb. 2,588,793.

Riyadh (ri-yäd′) City (cap. of Saudi Arabia) pop. 1,380,000.

Rochester (ro′ches-tər) City (NY) pop. 231,636, urb. 1,062,470.

Romania (rō-mā′nė-ə) 91,671 sq. mi., pop. 23,172,000, cap. Bucharest.

Rome [*It.* **Roma**] (rōm, rō′mä) City (cap. of Italy) pop. 2,828,692, urb. 3,033,000.

Roseau (rō-zō′) City (cap. of Dominica) pop. 22,000.

Rotterdam (rot′ər-dam″) City (Netherlands) pop. 704,858, urb. 1,037,548.

Ruanda-Urundi (roo-än′dä-û-rûn′dė) see *Rwanda* and *Burundi.*

Rumania (roo-mān′yə) see *Romania.*

Russia (rush′ə) 6,593,391 sq. mi., pop. 148,542,000, cap. Moscow.

Rwanda, Republic of (rwän′dä) 10,170 sq. mi., pop. 8,521,000, cap. Kigali.

Ryukyu Islands (rū′kū) (Japan) 1,850 sq. mi., pop. 1,245,000, cap. Naha (nä′hä).

Sabah (sä′bə) State (Malaysia) pop. 633,000, cap. Kota Kinabalu.

Sacramento (sak-rə-men′to) City (cap. of CA) pop. 369,365, urb. 1,481,102.

Saigon (sī′gon) see *Ho Chi Minh City.*

St. Croix (sānt kroi) (Virgin Islands, U.S.) 80 sq. mi., pop. 49,013, cap. Christiansted (kris′tyán-sted).

Saint-Denis (san-də-nē′) City (cap. of Réunion) pop. 117,523.

St. George's (sānt jôr′jəs) City (cap. of Grenada) pop. 30,000.

fat, fāte, fär, fāre, fâll, ȧsk; met, hē, hėr, maybė; pin, pīne; not, nōte, ôr, tool

St. Helena (sānt he-lē′nə) Island (Br.) 47 sq. mi., pop. 6,720, cap. Jamestown.

St. John (sānt jon) (Virgin Islands, U.S.) 20 sq. mi., pop. 2,360.

St. Johns City (cap. of Antigua and Barbuda) pop. 24,359.

St. John's City (cap. of Nfld.) pop. 163,300.

St. Kitts and Nevis, Federation of (kits; ne′vis) 155 sq. mi., pop. 40,211, cap. Basse-Terre.

St. Louis (sānt lū′əs) City (MO) pop. 396,685, urb. 2,492,525.

Saint Lucia (sānt loo′shē-ə) Island 233 sq. mi., pop. 154,399, cap. Castries.

St. Paul (sānt pâl) City (cap. of MN) pop. 272,235, urb. 2,538,834.

St. Petersburg (sānt pē′tərz-bərg) City (FL) pop. 238,629, urb. 2,067,959. See also *Leningrad*.

St. Pierre and Miquelon (mik″ə-lon′) (Fr.) 93 sq. mi., pop. 6,541, cap. St. Pierre (pop. 5,416).

St. Thomas (sānt tom′əs) (Virgin Islands, U.S.) 32 sq. mi., pop. 44,218, cap. Charlotte Amalie.

Saint Vincent and the Grenadines (sānt vin′sənt) 150 sq. mi., pop. 116,611, cap. Kingstown.

Sakhalin (sä-kä-lēn′) Island (Russia) 29,000 sq. mi., pop. 669,000, cap. Yuzhno Sakhalinsk (yū′zhnə suk″həl-yēnsk′).

Salem (sā′ləm) City (cap. of OR) pop. 107,786, urb. 278,024.

Salisbury (sôlz′bēr-ē) see *Harare*.

Salt Lake City (sâlt lāk) City (cap. of UT) pop. 159,936, urb. 1,072,227.

Samoa, American (sä-mō′ə) Islands (U.S.) 76 sq. mi., pop. 53,139, cap. Pago Pago (päng′gō päng′gō).

Samoa, Western, Independent State of (sä-mō′ə) Islands (C. of N.) 1,133 sq. mi., pop, 190,000, cap. Apia.

Sana'a (sä-nä′) City (cap. of Yemen) pop. 427,185.

San Antonio (san an-tō′nē-ō) City (TX) pop. 935,933, urb. 1,324,749.

San Diego (san dē-ā′gō) City (CA) pop. 1,110,549, urb. 2,498,016.

San Francisco (san fran-sis′kō) City (CA) pop. 723,959, urb. 6,253,311.

San Jose (sän″ hō-zā′) **1,** City (cap. of Costa Rica) pop. 215,441, urb. 890,000. **2,** City (CA) pop. 782,248, urb. 1,497,577.

San Juan (sän hwän) City (cap. of Puerto Rico) pop. 432,973, urb. 1,816,300.

San Marino, Most Serene Republic of (san mə-rē′nō) 38 sq. mi., pop. 23,541, cap. San Marino (pop. 4,450).

San Salvador (sän säl-vä-dôr′) City (cap. of El Salvador) pop. 471,436, urb. 1,400,000.

Santa Ana (an′ə) City (CA) pop. 293,742.

Sante Fe (san″tə fā′) City (cap. of NM) pop. 56,551, urb. 117,043.

Santiago (sän″tē-ä′gō) City (cap. of Chile) pop. 4,099,714, urb. 5,378,000.

Santo Domingo (sän′tō dō-ming′gō) City (cap. of Dominican Republic) pop. 950,000.

São Paulo (sow pow′lō) City (Brazil) pop. 10,099,086, urb. 18,701,000.

São Tome and Principe, Democratic Republic of (sowṅ tō-mā′; prēn′sē-pe) 372 sq. mi., pop. 136,276, cap. São Tome (pop. 40,000).

Sarajevo (sä-rä-yā′vō) City (cap. of Bosnia and Herzegovina) pop. 319,017.

Sarawak (sə-rä′wäk) (Malaysia) 50,000 sq. mi., pop. 977,000, cap. Kuching.

Sardinia (sär-din′yə) Island (Ital.) 9,301 sq. mi., pop. 1,468,737, cap. Cagliari (kä′lyä-rē).

Saskatchewan (sas-kach′ə-wàn) Prov. (Canada) 251,700 sq. mi., pop. 1,000,300, cap. Regina.

Saskatoon (sas″kə-toon′) City (Sask.) pop. 154,210, urb. 204,300.

Saudi Arabia, Kingdom of (sä-oo′dē) 350,000 sq. mi., pop. 17,615,000, cap. Riyadh.

Scotland (skot′lənd) (U.K.) 30,405 sq. mi., pop. 5,195,000, cap. Edinburgh.

Seattle (sē-at′əl) City (WA) pop. 516,259, urb. 2,970,328.

Senegal, Republic of (sen-ə-gâl′) 77,401 sq. mi., pop. 8,463,000, cap. Dakar.

Seoul [*Jap.* Keijo] (sōl, su′ool, kā′jō″) City (cap. of South Korea) pop. 9,639,110, urb. 16,792,000.

Serbia (sēr′bē-ə) Republic, formerly part of Yugoslavia, 34,116 sq. mi., pop. 9,721,177, cap. Belgrade.

Seychelles, Republic of (sā-shel′) Islands (C. of N.) 156 sq. mi., pop. 70,096, cap. Port Victoria.

Shanghai (shang′hi) City (China) pop. 6,292,960, urb. 11,185,100.

Shenyang [formerly Mukden] (Shung-yäng′, muk′den) City (cap. of Manchuria) pop. 3,944,240, urb. 5,054,640.

Shetland Islands (shet′lənd) (Scotland) 550 sq. mi., pop. 17,812, cap. Lerwick (lēr′wik).

Shreveport (shrēv′pôrt) City (LA) pop. 198,525.

Siam, see *Thailand*.

Sian (shē′än) see *Xian*.

Sicily (sis′ə-lē) Island (Ital.) 9,926 sq. mi., pop. 4,721,000, cap. Palermo (pə-ler′mō).

Sierra Leone, Republic of (sē-er′ə lē-ō′nē) (C. of N.) 27,295 sq. mi., pop. 4,511,000, cap. Freetown.

Sikkim (sik′im) (kingdom in NE India) 2,818 sq. mi., pop. 215,000, cap. Gangtok.

Singapore (sing-ə-pôr′) (C. of N.) 220 sq. mi., pop. 2,826,000, cap. Singapore (pop. 2,704,000).

Skopje (skop′yä) City (cap. of Macedonia), pop. 444,900.

Slovak Republic or **Slovakia** (slō′väk, slō-väk′ė-ə) 18,923 sq. mi., pop. 5,268,935, cap. Bratislava.

Slovenia, Republic of (slō-vē′nė-ə) (formerly part of Yugoslavia) 7,819 sq. mi., pop. 1,974,000, cap. Ljubljana.

Society Islands (sō-sī′ə-tė) (Fr.) (part of French Polynesia) 650 sq. mi., pop. 68,245, cap. Papeete.

Socotra (sō-kō′trə) Island (Dem. Rep. of Yemen) 1,400 sq. mi., pop. 12,000, cap. Tamridah.

Sofia (sō′fė-ə) City (cap. of Bulgaria) pop. 1,127,527.

Solomon Islands (sol′ə-mən) 11,497 sq. mi., pop. 347,000, cap. Honiara.

Somalia, Democratic Republic of (sō-mä′lė-ə) 262,000 sq. mi., pop. 6,709,000, cap. Mogadishu.

Somaliland, French (sō-mä′li-land) see *Djibouti.*

South Africa, Republic of 472,494 sq. mi., pop. 42,802,000, cap. Cape Town (legislative), Pretoria (administrative), Bloemfontein (judicial).

South America (ə-mer′i-kə) Continent, 6,814,000 sq. mi., pop. 235,444,000.

South Carolina (kar-ə-lī′nə) State (U.S.) 30,203 sq. mi., pop. 3,559,618, cap. Columbia.

South China Sea, between China, Vietnam & the Philippines, 1,148,500 sq. mi..

South Dakota (də-kō′tə) State (U.S.) 75,952 sq. mi., pop. 703,301, cap. Pierre.

South-West Africa, see *Namibia.*

Spain (spän) 195,258 sq. mi., pop. 39,384,000, cap. Madrid.

Spanish Sahara (sə-hēr′ə; -här′ə) 102,700 sq. mi., pop. 75,000.

Spitsbergen [*Nor.* **Svalbard**] (spits′bərgən, sväl′bär) Islands (Norway) 15,075 sq. mi., pop 3,431.

Spokane (spō-kan′) City (WA) pop. 177,196, urb. 361,364.

Springfield (spring′fėld) **1,** City (cap. of IL) pop. 105,227, urb. 189,550. **2,** City (MA) pop. 156,983, urb. 587,884. **3,** City (MO) pop. 140,494, urb. 264,346.

Sri Lanka, Democratic Socialist Republic of [formerly **Ceylon**] (srē läng′kə) (C. of N.) 25,332 sq. mi., pop. 17,423,000, cap. Colombo.

Stanley (stan′lē) City (cap. of Falkland Islands) pop. 1,231.

Stockholm (stok′hōm″) City (cap. of Sweden) pop. 666,810, urb. 1,461,618.

Stockton (stok′tən) City (CA) pop. 210,943, urb. 480,628.

Sucre (soo′krā) City (cap. of Bolivia) pop. 105,800.

Sudan, Republic of the (soo-dan′) 967,500 sq. mi., pop. 27,220,000, cap. Khartoum.

Sudanese Republic, see *Mali.*

Suez Canal (soo′ez) between Mediterranean & Red Seas, 107 mi.

Sulawesi (soo″lä-wä′sė) (Indonesia) 72,986 sq. mi., pop. 8,925,000, cap. Makasaar (mə-kas′ər) (pop. 384,159).

Sulu Sea (soo′loo) between Philippine Islands & Borneo.

Sumatra (sû-mä′trə) Island (Indonesia) 164,148 sq. mi., pop. 20,800,000, cap. Padang (pä′däng′).

Superior, Lake (Great Lakes) 31,810 sq. mi.

Surabaja (sûr″ə-bä′yə) City (Indonesia) pop. 1,283,000.

Suriname, Republic of [formerly **Dutch Guiana**] (soo-ri-näm′) 63,037 sq. mi., pop. 402,000, cap. Paramaribo.

Suva (soo′vä) City (cap. of Fiji) pop. 69,665, urb. 141,273.

Sverdlovsk (svûrd-lôvsk′) City (Russia) pop. 1,331,000.

Swan Islands (swän) (U.S.) 1 sq. mi., pop. 28.

Swaziland, Kingdom of (swä′zi-land) (C. of N.) 6,704 sq. mi., pop. 859,000, cap. Mbabane.

Sweden, Kingdom of (swē′dən) 173,394 sq. mi., pop. 8,564,000, cap. Stockholm.

Switzerland (swit′zər-lənd) 15,944 sq. mi., pop. 6,783,000, cap. Bern.

Sydney (sid′nė) City (Australia) pop. 3,531,000.

Syracuse (sir′ə-kyoos) City (NY) pop. 163,860.

Syria, Arab Republic of (sir′ė-ə) 71,227 sq. mi., pop. 12,965,000, cap. Damascus.

Tacoma (tə-kō′mə) City (WA) pop. 176,664.

Tahiti (tä-hē′tė) see *French Polynesia.*

Taipei (tī-pā′) City (cap. of Taiwan) pop. 1,850,000.

Taiwan or **Formosa** (tī-wän′, fôr-mō′sə) [The Republic of China] 13,885 sq. mi., pop. 20,658,000, cap. Taipei.

Taiyuan (tī-yü-än′) City (China) pop. 1,350,000.

Tajikistan, Republic of (tä-jik′ə-stan) 54,019 sq. mi., pop. 5,100,000, cap. Dushanbe.

Talien or **Dalien** (dä′lyen′) see *Dalian.*

Tallahassee (tal-ə-has′ė) City (cap. of FL) pop. 124,773, urb. 233,598.

Tallinn (täl'lin) City (cap. of Estonia), pop. 502,000.

Tampa (tam'pə) City (FL) pop. 280,015, urb. 2,067,959.

Tanganyika (tan-gən-yē'kə) see *Tanzania.*

Tanganyika, Lake (Africa) 12,700 sq. mi.

Tangier (tan-jir') City (Morocco) pop. 185,850, urb. 304,000.

Tanzania, United Republic of (tan″zə-nē'ə; tan-zā'nē-ə) (C. of N.) 362,820 sq. mi., pop. 26,869,000, cap. Dar es Salaam.

Tarawa (tar'ə-wä″) City (cap. of Kiribati) pop. 22,000.

Tashkent (tash-kent') City (cap. of Uzbekistan) pop. 2,124,000.

Tasmania (taz-mā'nē-ə) Island (Austl.) 26,215 sq. mi., pop. 389,500, cap. Hobart (hō'bərt).

Tbilisi (tə-bə-lē'sē) City (cap. of Republic of Georgia) pop. 1,194,000.

Tegucigalpa (te-goo″sē-gäl'pä) City (cap. of Honduras) pop. 597,512.

Tehran (te-rän') City (cap. of Iran) pop. 6,042,584, urb. 9,779,000.

Tel Aviv (tel a-vēv') City (seat of government of Israel, official name **Tel Aviv-Jaffa,** jaf'ə) pop. 317,800, urb. 1,663,200.

Tennessee (ten-ə-sē') State (U.S.) 41,155 sq. mi., pop. 4,952,726, cap. Nashville.

Texas (tek'səs) State (U.S.) 262,017 sq. mi., pop. 17,348,206, cap. Austin.

Thailand, Kingdom of [formerly **Siam**] (tī'land, sī-am') 200,148 sq. mi., pop. 58,814,000, cap. Bangkok.

Thimphu (tim'poo) City (cap. of Bhutan) pop. 9,000.

Thorshavn (tôrs-hown') City (cap. of Faroe Islands) pop. 15,000.

Tianjin or **Tientsin** (tyän'jin') City (China) pop. 5,152,180, urb. 7,790,160.

Tibet (ti-bet') (admin. district of China) 469,413 sq. mi., pop. 1,300,000, cap. Lhasa (lä'sə).

Timbuktu (tim-buk'too) City (Mali) pop. 12,000.

Timor (tē'môr) Island (Indonesia & Port.) 13,071 sq. mi., pop. 850,000.

Timor, Portuguese (tē'môr) eastern part of Timor (Port.) 7,330 sq. mi., pop. 465,000, cap. Dili.

Tiranë (tē-rä'nə) City (cap. of Albania) pop. 232,500.

Tobago, see *Trinidad and Tobago.*

Togo, Republic of (tō'gō) 20,733 sq. mi., pop. 3,810,000, cap. Lomé.

Togoland (tō'gō-land) former Br. Trust., now part of Ghana.

Tokelau Islands (tō″kə-low') (New Zeal.) 4 sq. mi., pop. 2,000.

Tokyo (tō'kē-ō) City (cap. of Japan) pop. 8,323,699, urb. 11,935,700.

Toledo (tə-lē'dō) City (OH) pop. 332,943, urb. 614,128.

Tonga, Kingdom of (Friendly Islands) (tong'gə) (C. of N.) 269 sq. mi., pop. 102,000, cap. Nuku'alofa.

Topeka (tə-pē'kə) City (cap. of KS) pop. 119,883, urb. 160,976.

Toronto (tə-ron'to) City (Ont.) pop. 599,217, urb. 3,666,600.

Transjordan, see *Jordan.*

Trenton (tren'tən) City (cap. of NJ) pop. 88,675, urb. 325,824..

Trieste (trē-est') (Italy) 287 sq. mi., pop. 280,017.

Trinidad and Tobago, Republic of (trin'ə-dad, tə-bä'gō) Islands (C. of N.) 1,980 sq. mi., pop. 1,285,000, cap. Port of Spain.

Tripoli (trip'ə-lē) City (cap. of Libya) pop. 551,477.

Tristan da Cunha (tris'tan dä koon'yə) Island (Br.) 40 sq. mi., pop. 262.

Tsingtao (ching'dow') City (China) pop. 1,300,000.

Tucson (too'son) City (AZ) pop. 405,390, urb. 666,880.

Tulsa (tul'sə) City (OK) pop. 367,302, urb. 708,954.

Tunis (too'nis) City (cap. of Tunisia) pop. 596,654, urb. 1,394,749.

Tunisia, Republic of (too-nizh'ə) 48,300 sq. mi., pop. 8,276,000, cap. Tunis.

Turin [*Ital.* **Torino**] (tûr'in, tō-rē'nō) City (Italy) pop. 1,177,900.

Turkey, Republic of (tēr'kē) 296,185 sq. mi., pop. 58,580,000, cap. Ankara.

Turkmenistan (tûrk-men'i-stan) 188,417 sq. mi., pop. 3,500,000, cap. Ashkhabad (pop. 325,000).

Turks and Caicos Islands (Jamaica) (tērks, kī'kōs) (Br.) 166 sq. mi., pop. 13,137, cap. Grand Turk.

Tuvalu [formerly **Ellice Islands**] (too″və-loo') (C. of N.) 10 sq. mi., pop. 9,317, cap. Funafuti.

Uganda, Republic of (ū-gan'də) (C. of N.) 80,292 sq. mi., pop. 18,690,000, cap. Kampala.

Ukraine (yū-krān') 226,687 sq. mi., pop. 51,994,000, cap. Kiev.

Ulan Bator (oo'län bä'tôr) City (cap. of Mongolia) pop. 515,100.

Union of South Africa, see *South Africa, Republic of.*

United Arab Emirates [formerly **Trucial States**] 31,992 sq. mi., pop. 2,389,000, cap. Abu Dhabi.

United Kingdom (of Great Britain and Northern Ireland) 94,279 sq. mi., pop. 55,486,800, cap. London.

United States of America 3,554,613 sq.

mi., pop. 248,709,873 (50 states), cap. Washington.

Upper Volta (vôl'tə) see Burkina Faso.

Uruguay, Republic of (yûr'ə-gwā) 72,172 sq. mi., pop. 3,121,000, cap. Montevideo.

Utah (ū'tâ″, -tä″) State (U.S.) 82,073 sq. mi., pop. 1,770,212, cap. Salt Lake City.

Uzbekistan, Republic of (ûz-bek'i-stan) 172,700 sq. mi., pop. 19,900,000, cap. Tashkent.

Vaduz (vä'dûts) City (cap. of Liechtenstein) pop. 4,904.

Valencia (və-len'shė-ə) City (Spain) pop. 718,750.

Valletta (və-let'ə) City (cap. of Malta) pop. 17,600.

Vancouver (van-koo'vər) City (B.C.) pop. 414,281, urb. 1,506,000.

Vanuatu (vä-noo-ä'too) (formerly **New Hebrides**) 57,000 sq. mi., pop. 112,600, cap. Vila.

Vatican City (vat'i-kən) 109 acres, pop. 1,025.

Venezuela, Republic of (ven-i-zwä'lə) 325,143 sq. mi., pop. 20,189,000, cap. Caracas.

Venice [*It.* **Venezia**] (ven'is, vā-nā'tsyə) City (Italy) pop. 367,327.

Vermont (vər-mont') State (U.S.) 9,273 sq. mi., pop. 566,619, cap. Montpelier.

Versailles (ver-sī') City (France) pop. 94,900.

Victoria (vik-tôr'ė-ə) **1,** City (cap. of Hong Kong) pop. 1,026,870. **2,** City (cap. of Seychelles) pop. 16,000.

Victoria Island (vik-tôr'ė-ə) (Canada) 81,930 sq. mi., pop. 61,800.

Victoria, Lake (vik-tôr'ė-ə) (Africa) 26,000 sq. mi.

Vienna [*Ger.* **Wien**] (vė-en'ə, vēn) City (cap. of Austria) pop. 1,486,963, urb. 2,044,331.

Vientiane (ven-tyen') City (cap. of Laos) pop. 173,000.

Vietnam or **Viet Nam, Socialist Republic of** (vyet-näm') 127,267 sq. mi., pop. 67,568,000. cap. Hanoi.

Vila (vē'la) City (cap. of Vanuata) pop. 15,000.

Virgin Islands (vėr'jin) **1,** (U.S.) 132 sq. mi., pop. 98,130, cap. Charlotte Amalie. **2,** (Br.) 58 sq. mi., pop. 12,707, cap. Road Town.

Virginia (vər-jin'yə) State (U.S.) 39,703 sq. mi., pop. 6,285,931, cap. Richmond.

Virginia Beach City (VA) pop. 393,069.

Vladivostok (vlad″i-və-stok') City (Russia) pop. 615,000.

Wake (wāk) Island (U.S.) 3 sq. mi., pop. 300.

Wales (wālz) (U.K.) 7,466 sq. mi., pop. 2,724,000, cap. Cardiff (kär'dif).

Wallis and Futuna Islands (wol'is; footoo'nə) Fr. Terr., 106 sq. mi., pop. 17,613, cap. Mata-Utu.

Warsaw [*Pol.* **Warszawa**] (wôr-sâ, värshä'və) City (cap. of Poland) pop. 1,673,688.

Washington (wosh'ing-tən) **1,** City (cap. of U.S.) pop. 606,900, urb. 4,223,485. **2,** State (U.S.) 66,511 sq. mi., pop. 5,017,724, cap. Olympia.

Wellington (wel'ing-tən) City (cap. of New Zealand) pop. 134,400, urb. 324,600.

Western Sahara 102,700 sq. mi., pop. 206,629, cap. El Aaiún.

West Indies (in'dėz) Archipelago, 100,000 sq. mi., pop. 9,000,000.

West Virginia (vər-jin'yə) State (U.S.) 24,119 sq. mi., pop. 1,800,936, cap. Charleston.

White Russia, see *Belarus*

White Sea, off no. Russia (Eur.), 36,680 sq. mi.

Wichita (wich'i-tâ) City (Kan.) pop. 304,011.

Willemstad (vil'əm-stät) City (cap. of Netherlands Antilles) pop. 47,000.

Wilmington (wil'ming-tən) City (DE) pop. 71,529, urb. 513,293.

Windhoek (vint'hûk) City (cap. of Namibia) pop. 114,000.

Windward Islands (wind'wərd) (Br.) 821 sq. mi., pop. 367,416, cap. St. George's.

Winnipeg (win'ə-peg) City (Manitoba) pop. 564,473, urb. 640,400.

Winnipeg, Lake (Canada) 9,398 sq. mi.

Wisconsin (wis-kon'sin) State (U.S.) 54,426 sq. mi., pop. 4,955,127, cap. Madison.

Wuhan (woo'hän') City (China) pop. 3,287,720, urb. 4,273,080.

Wyoming (wī-ō'ming) State (U.S.) 96,989 sq. mi., pop. 459,511, cap. Cheyenne.

Xian (shē'än) City (China) pop. 1,310,000.

Yangon (yang'gon) City (cap. of Myanmar) pop. 2,513,023.

Yangtze River (yang'tsē″) (China) 3,400 miles.

Yaoundé (yä-oon-dā) City (cap. of Cameroon) pop. 653,670.

Yellow Sea, between Korea & China.

Yemen, Republic of (yem'ən) 205,356 sq. mi., pop. 10,062,000, cap. Sana'a.

Yerevan [*Russ.* **Erivan**] (ye-rə-vän', er″yə-vän') City (cap. of Armenia) pop. 1,168,000.

Yokohama (yōk″ə-hä'mə) City (Japan) pop. 3,151,087.

Yonkers (yonk′ərz) City (NY) pop. 188,082.

Yucatán (ū″kə-tan′) a peninsula in SE Mexico and N Central Amer.

Yugoslavia, Federal Republic of (ū-gō-slä′vė-ə) 39,000 sq. mi., pop. 10,337,000, cap. Belgrade.

Yukon Territory (ū′kon) (Canada) 205,346 sq. mi., pop. 23,153, cap. Whitehorse.

Zagreb (zä′greb) City (cap. of Croatia) pop. 566,084.

Zaire, Republic of [formerly **Democratic Republic of the Congo; Belgian Congo**] (zī′ēr) 904,764 sq. mi., pop. 37,832,000, cap. Kinshasa.

Zambia, Republic of (zam′bė-ə) (C. of N.) 290,586 sq. mi., pop. 8,445,000, cap. Lusaka.

Zanzibar (zan-zi-bär′) see *Tanzania.*

Zetland (zet′lənd) see *Shetland Islands*

Zimbabwe, Republic of [formerly **Southern Rhodesia**] (zim-bäb′wā) 150,333 sq. mi., pop. 10,720,000, cap. Salisbury.

Zurich (zûr′ik) City (Switzerland) pop. 346,018, urb. 837,683.

LANGUAGES AND LANGUAGE FAMILIES

Afrikaans, a language of So. Afr., derived from 17th-c. Dutch.

Afro-Asiatic, the language family of No. Africa, including Semitic, Berber, and Egyptian.

Ainu, the language of the aborigines of northern Japan.

Akkadian, any of several Semitic languages spoken in ancient Mesopotamia.

Albanian, the Indo-European language of Albania.

Aleut, a language of the native peoples of the Alaskan Peninsula.

Algonquian, a family of No. Amer. Indian languages.

Altaic, a language family spoken widely in Asia, including Turkic and Mongolian.

American Spanish, Spanish dialects of So. and Central Amer. and the Caribbean.

Amharic, the Semitic language of Ethiopia.

Anatolian, a group of Indo-European languages spoken in ancient Asia Minor.

Anglo-French, the dialect of French spoken in England after the Norman invasion of 1066.

Arabic, the Semitic language of the Arabs.

Aramaic, the Semitic language of the Near East spoken from 300 B.C. to about 500 A.D.

Arawakan, a family of So. Amer. languages, once also found in southern Florida and the West Indies.

Armenian, the Indo-European language of Armenia and parts of neighboring countries.

Assyrian, the ancient Semitic language of Assyria.

Attic, a dialect of ancient Greece, the principal literary language.

Australian Aborigine, any of the languages of the aborigines of Australia, having no known relationship to any other languages.

Avestan, an ancient Iranian language, the language of the Avesta.

Baltic, the Indo-European source for languages of the eastern Baltic region.

Bantu, a branch of Niger-Congo languages found south of the African equator.

Basque, the language of the Basque peoples, unrelated to any other language.

Bengali, an Indo-European language spoken in India and Bangladesh.

Berber, a Hamitic language of No. Africa.

Breton, the Celtic language of Brittany.

Bulgarian, the Slavic language of Bulgaria.

Burmese, the Tibeto-Burman language of Burma.

Bushman, a Khoisan language spoken in So. and SW Africa.

Canadian French, a dialect of French spoken in French-speaking Canada.

Carib, a family of So. Amer. Indian languages.

Celtic, an Indo-European language family including Irish, Gaelic and Welsh.

Chinese, a catch-all term for the many dialects of China.

Coptic, a Hamitic language derived from ancient Egyptian.

Cornish, the Celtic language of Cornwall, England, until the late 1700s.

Creole, a dialect of French spoken in southern Louisiana.

Cushitic, a Hamitic language group of Ethiopia and E. Africa.

Czech, the Slavic language of the Czech Republic.

Danish, the Scandinavian language of Denmark.

Dravidian, a family of languages spoken in So. India.

Dutch, the Germanic language of the Netherlands, descended from Low German.

Egyptian, the Hamitic language of the ancient Egyptians.

English, the Germanic language of England, the United States, Australia, Canada, and many other countries.

Estonian, the Finno-Ugric language of Estonia.

Etruscan, the language of ancient Tuscany.

Finnish, the Finno-Ugric language of Finland.

Finno-Ugric, a family of languages of eastern Europe and western Asia including Finnish and Hungarian.

Flemish, the Germanic language of Flanders, related to Dutch.

Frankish, the W. Germanic language of Northern Gaul from 400 to 600 A.D.

French, the Romance language of France.

Gaelic, the Celtic language of Scotland.

Gaulish, the Celtic language of the ancient Gauls, a source for many Latin and Old French words.

German, the Germanic language of Germany, Austria, and parts of Switzerland.

Germanic, a branch of Indo-European, comprising Gothic, Scandinavian languages, English, Frisian, Dutch, and German.

Gothic, the E. Germanic language of the Goths, which largely disappeared after about 400 A.D.

Guarani, a So. Amer. Indian language spoken in Paraguay.

Gullah, an English dialect spoken by African-Americans along the Southern east coast of the U.S.

Haitian Creole, the French dialect spoken in Haiti.

Hamitic, the branch of Afro-Asiatic including ancient Egyptian and Berber.

Hawaiian, the Polynesian language of Hawaii.

Hebrew, the ancient Semitic language of the Jews.

High German, the Germanic language of Central and So. Germany, an ancestor of modern German.

Hindi, an Indic language of No. India, the literary and official language of the Republic of India.

Hungarian, the Finno-Ugric language of Hungary.

Icelandic, the Scandinavian language of Iceland.

Indo-European, the conjectural prehistoric language family comprising the Slavic, Germanic, Italic, Celtic, and Indic branches, among others.

Indonesian, a language branch including Malay, Indonesian, and Tagalog; also, the language of Indonesia.

Iranian, a branch of Indo-European including Persian and Kurdish.

Irish, the Celtic language of Ireland.

Italian, the Romance language of Italy and parts of Switzerland.

Italic, a branch of Indo-European including Latin.

Japanese, the language of Japan, not clearly related to any other language.

Khoisan, a language group of So. Africa employing click consonants.

Kwa, a branch of Niger-Congo spoken in E. Africa.

Lao, the Sino-Tibetan language of Laos.

Lapp, the Finno-Ugric language of Lapland and other northern European areas.

Late Greek, the Greek language from about 300 to 700 A.D.

Late Latin, the Latin language from about 300 to 700 A.D.

Latin, the Italic language of the ancient Romans.

Latvian, the Baltic language of Latvia.

Lithuanian, the Baltic language of Lithuania.

Low German, the German dialects of No. Germany.

Malagasy, the Indonesian language of Madagascar.

Malay, the Indonesian language of the Malay peninsula.

Malinke, a Mande language spoken in Senegal, Gambia, and other Afr. countries.

Mandarin, the standard Chinese dialect, based on Beijing speech.

Mande, a branch of Niger-Congo including the W. African languages Malinke and Kpelle.

Manx, the Celtic language spoken on the Isle of Man.

Maori, the Polynesian language spoken by the natives of New Zealand.

Mayan, a language family of Mexico and Central America, deriving from the language of the ancient Maya people.

Medieval Greek, the Greek language from about 700 to 1500 A.D.

Medieval Latin, the Latin language from about 700 to about 1500 A.D., largely in use by European intellectuals.

Mexican Spanish, the dialect of Spanish employed in Mexico.

Middle Dutch, the Dutch language from about 1100 to 1500 A.D.

Middle English, the English language from 1100 to about 1500 A.D., incorporating many words of French origin.

Middle French, the French language from about 1350 to 1600 A.D.

Middle High German, the High German language from about 1100 to 1500 A.D.

Middle Low German, the Low German language from about 1100 to about 1500 A.D.

Mongolian, the Altaic language of Mongolia.

Mon-Khmer, a language family of SE Asia, including languages spoken in Cambodia, India, Burma, and Vietnam.

Nahuatl, the language of the Indians of central Mexico and Central America, including the Aztecs.

New Latin, the Latin language after 1500, containing words formed from Greek, Latin, etc., once used in the Roman Catholic liturgy and still used for forming scientific terminology.

Niger-Congo, the major language family of Africa.

Nootka, an American Indian language spoken on Vancouver Island and in NW Washington.

Norwegian, the Scandinavian language of Norway.

Old Dutch, the Dutch language before 1100 A.D.

Old English, the Germanic language of the English people before 1100 A.D.

Old French, the French language from about 800 to about 1400 A.D.

Old High German, the German language used in southern Germany before 1100 A.D.

Old Irish, the Irish language before 1200 A.D.

Old Latin, the Latin language used before about 100 B.C.

Old Norse, the North Germanic language of Scandinavia before 1300 A.D.

Old Slavic, a Slavic language found in Eastern Orthodox religious texts of 800–900 A.D. Also, **Old Church Slavonic.**

Pennsylvania German or **Dutch,** a dialect of High German mixed with English spoken in Pennsylvania. ("Dutch" refers to the German word *Deutsch,* German.)

Persian, the Iranian language of Persia.

Pidgin English, any of a number of dialects of English having simplified grammar and a mixed vocabulary, usu. used as a language of trade or communication between foreigners and natives.

Prakrit, any of several Indic languages of ancient and medieval India (not including Sanskrit).

Polynesian, a language branch including Hawaiian, Tahitian, Samoan, and Maori.

Portuguese, the Romance language of Portugal, Brazil, and former Portuguese colonies.

Provençal, the Romance language of SE France.

Quechua, the So. Amer. Indian language of the Incas and of certain So. Amer. countries.

Romance, an Indo-European language group developed from Vulgar Latin and including French, Spanish, Italian and Portuguese.

Romanian, the Romance language of Romania.

Romany, the Indo-European language of the Gypsies.

Russian, the Slavic language of Russia.

Samoyed, a language branch of Uralic comprising languages of N Siberia and NE Russia.

Sanskrit, the ancient literary and religious language of India.

Scandinavian, the Germanic languages of the Scandinavian peninsula, Denmark, and surrounding islands.

Scots or **Scottish,** the dialect of British English spoken in Scotland.

Semitic, the branch of Afro-Asiatic languages including Hebrew, Arabic, and Aramaic.

Serbian, the Serbo-Croatian language spoken by Serbs.

Serbo-Croatian, a Slavic language spoken in parts of former Yugoslavia.

Singhalese, the Indic language of Sri Lanka.

Sino-Tibetan, a language family including Chinese, Tibeto-Burman, Thai, and Lao.

Slavic, a branch of Indo-European including Polish, Czech, Slovak, Russian, Ukrainian, Bulgarian, Serbo-Croatian, and Slovene.

Slovak, the Slavic language of Slovakia.

Slovene, the Slavic language of Slovenia.

Spanish, the Romance language of Spain and most Latin Amer. countries.

Sudanic, a language family of No. Africa.

Swahili, a Bantu language of eastern Africa.

Swedish, the Scandinavian language of Sweden and part of Finland.

Tagalog, the Indonesian language of the Philippines.

Taino, the extinct language of the W. Indian Arawakan tribe.

Tamil, a Dravidian language of So. India and Malaysia.

Telugu, a Dravidian language of SE India.

Thai, the Sino-Tibetan language of Thailand.

Tibeto-Burman, a branch of Sino-Tibetan including Tibetan and Burmese.

Tupi, a S. Amer. Indian language spoken in Brazil.

Turkic, a branch of the Altaic language family spoken in Turkey and south central Asia.

Turkish, the Turkic language of Turkey.

Uralic, a language family comprising the Finno-Ugric and Samoyed languages.

Urdu, an Indic language of Pakistan.

Uzbek, a Turkic language of central Asia.

Vulgar Latin, the spoken form of Latin used in the later Roman Empire.

Walloon, a French dialect of Belgium.

Welsh, the Celtic language of Wales.

Xhosa, a Bantu language spoken in So. Africa.

Yoruba, a Kwa language of Nigeria.

Yiddish, a Germanic language spoken by the Jews of eastern and central Europe, containing Hebrew, Slavic and Romance elements.

Zulu, a Bantu language spoken in SE Africa.

FORMS OF ADDRESS

The following are the forms of address most commonly used in correspondence.

When two different salutations are given, the first is the more formal of the two; if the forms are separated by *or*, however, they are interchangeable. A salutation of "Sir:", "Madam:", Dear Sir:", or "Dear Madam:" is acceptable in practically any situation.

If the husband or wife of a person of rank or title is to be included in the address, he or she is listed second. If the husband has the title, the form is

> *(title)* and Mrs. *(full name)*
> e.g., The Honorable and Mrs. John Doe.

If the wife has the title, the form is

> *(title)* *(wife's full name)* and Mr. *(surname)*
> e.g., The Honorable Jane Doe and Mr. Doe.

The salutation in these cases would be "Dear Mr. & Mrs. Doe:". If the person of rank has a specific title of office (as President, Attorney General, etc.) the salutation is

> Dear Mr. (Madam) *(title)* and Mrs. (Mr.) *(surname)*
> e.g., Dear Mr. President and Mrs. Doe.

In general, a complimentary close of "Sincerely yours," or "Very truly yours," is proper, with the latter being slightly the more formal of the two.

If the addressee is the holder of one or more academic degrees, these follow the name, preceded by a comma:

> *(title)* *(full name)*, *(degrees)*
> e.g., Professor John Doe, Ph.D., LL.D.

If the addressee holds a doctorate, he or she may be addressed as "Dr." instead of Mr. (Mrs., Ms., Miss).

Full addresses are given only when appropriate; otherwise, a proper local address is to be supplied.

ALDERMAN

Address
Alderman *(full name)*
Salutation
Dear Sir (Madam):
Dear Mr. (Mrs., Ms., Miss) *(surname)*:

AMBASSADOR

AMERICAN
Address
The Honorable *(full name)*
American Ambassador to *(country)*
American Embassy
Salutation
Dear Mr. (Madam) Ambassador:
FOREIGN
Address
His (Her) Excellency the Ambassador of *(country)*
Embassy of *(country)*
Salutation
Your Excellency:
Sir (Madam):

ARCHBISHOP

ANGLICAN (Great Britain)
Address
His Grace the Lord Archbishop of *(city)*
Salutation
My Lord Archbishop:
Your Grace:
ANGLICAN (Canada)

Address
The Most Reverend *(full name)*
Archbishop of *(place)*
Salutation
Most Reverend Sir:
Dear Archbishop:

ARMY OFFICERS

Be careful to use the exact rank. A qualifying adjective is not used in the salutation (e.g., Lieutenant Colonel Smith becomes "Dear Colonel:"). Warrant officers are addressed as "Mister."
Address
(rank) *(full name)*
(military unit), U.S.A.
Salutation
Sir:
Dear *(rank)* *(surname)*:

ASSEMBLYMAN
(see REPRESENTATIVE, U.S., LOCAL)

ASSOCIATE JUSTICE OF THE SUPREME COURT

FEDERAL
Address
The Honorable *(full name)*
Associate Justice of the Supreme Court
Washington, D.C. 20543
Salutation
Dear Mr. (Madam) Justice:

Dear Justice (*surname*):
STATE
Address
　The Honorable (*full name*)
　Associate Justice of the Supreme Court
　(*capital city, state, ZIP*)
Salutation
　Dear Sir (Madam):
　Dear Mr. (Madam) Justice:

ATTORNEY GENERAL

FEDERAL
Address
　The Honorable (*full name*)
　Attorney General
　Washington, D.C. 20530
Salutation
　Dear Sir (Madam): *or*
　Dear Mr. (Madam) Attorney General:
STATE
Address
　The Honorable (*full name*)
　Attorney General of (*state*)
　(*capital city, state, ZIP*)
Salutation
　Dear Sir (Madam): *or*
　Dear Mr. (Madam) Attorney General:

BARON (BARONESS)

Address
　The Right Honourable Lord (Baroness)
　(*surname*)
Salutation
　My Lord: (Madam:)

BARONET

Address
　Sir (*full name*), Bart.
Salutation
　Sir:

BISHOP

ANGLICAN (Great Britain)
Address
　The Right Reverend the Lord Bishop
　of (*place*)
Salutation
　My Lord Bishop:
ANGLICAN
(Canadian) / PROTESTANT
EPISCOPAL
Address
　The Right Reverend (*full name*)
　Bishop of (*place*)
Salutation
　Right Reverend Sir:
　Dear Bishop (*surname*):
METHODIST
Address
　Bishop (*full name*)
Salutation
　Dear Bishop (*surname*):
ROMAN CATHOLIC
Address
　The Most Reverend (*full name*)

　Bishop of (*place*)
Salutation
　Your Excellency:

BROTHER OF A RELIGIOUS ORDER

Address
　The Reverend Brother (*full or given name*)
Salutation
　Dear Brother (*given name*):

CABINET OFFICER OR MINISTER

AMERICAN
Address
　The Honorable (*full name*)
　Secretary of (*name of Dept.*)
　Washington, D.C. (*ZIP of Dept.*)
Salutation
　Dear Sir (Madam): *or*
　Dear Mr. (Madam) Secretary:
CANADIAN
Address
　The Honourable (*full name*)
　Minister of (*function*)
　House of Commons
　Parliament Buildings
　Ottawa, Ontario K1A 0A2
Salutation
　Dear Sir (Madam):
　Dear Mr. (Mrs., Ms., Miss) (*surname*):

CARDINAL

Address
　His Eminence (*given name*), Cardinal
　(*surname*)
　Archbishop of (*place*)
Salutation
　Your Eminence:

CHIEF JUSTICE

AMERICAN (Federal)
Address
　The Chief Justice of the United States
　The Supreme Court of the United States
　Washington, D.C. 20543
Salutation
　Dear Mr. (Madam) Chief Justice:
AMERICAN (State)
Address
　The Chief Justice
　Supreme Court of the State (Common-
　wealth) of (*name*)
　(*capital city, state, ZIP*)
Salutation
　Dear Mr. (Madam) Chief Justice:
CANADIAN
Address
　The Right Honourable (*full name*)
　Chief Justice of Canada
　Supreme Court Building
　Ottawa, Ontario K1A 0J1

CLERGYMAN

Address
　The Reverend (*full name*)

Salutation
Reverend Sir (Madam):
Dear Mr. (Mrs., Ms., Miss) (*surname*):

CONSUL

Address
Mr. (Mrs., Ms., Miss) (*full name*)
American Consul at (*place*)
Salutation
Dear Sir (Madam):
Dear Mr. (Mrs., Ms., Miss) (*surname*):

DEACON

Address
The Reverend Deacon (*surname*)
Salutation
Reverend Sir (Madam):

DEAN (Ecclesiastic)

Address
The Very Reverend (*full name*)
Dean of (*church or place*)
Salutation
Very Reverend Sir:
Dear Dean (*surname*):

DELEGATE
(see REPRESENTATIVE, U.S., LOCAL)

DUKE (DUCHESS)

Address
His (Her) Grace the Duke (Duchess) of (*place*)
Salutation
Your Grace:
WHEN OF ROYAL BLOOD
Address
His (Her) Royal Highness the Duke (Duchess) of (*place*)
Salutation
May it please your Royal Highness:

EARL (COUNTESS)

Address
The Right Honourable the Earl (Countess) of (*place*)
Salutation
Sir (Madam):

GOVERNOR GENERAL (Canada)

Address
His (Her) Excellency (*full name*)
Government House
Ottawa, Ontario K1A 0A1
Salutation
Sir (Madam):
Dear Governor General:

GOVERNOR
(LIEUTENANT GOVERNOR)

Address
The Honorable (*full name*)
Governor (Lieutenant Governor) of (*state*)
(*capital city, state, ZIP*)

Salutation
Governor: Dear Governor (*surname*):
Lieutenant Governor: Dear Mr. (Mrs., Ms., Miss) (*surname*):

JUDGE (JUSTICE)

Address
The Honorable (*full name*)
Judge (Justice) of the (*name of court; district, if any*)
Salutation
Dear Judge (*surname*):

KING (QUEEN)

Address
His (Her) Majesty, (*full name*), King (Queen) of (*place*)
Salutation
May it please your Majesty:
Sir (Madam):

LADY

A Lady is a peeress under the rank of Duchess; a wife of a Baronet, knight, or Lord of session; or a daughter of a Duke, Marquis, or Earl.
Address
Lady (*full name*)
Salutation
Madam: *or*
Your Ladyship:

MARINE OFFICER

Same form as Army officers, except that U.S.M.C. follows name of military unit.

MARQUIS (MARCHIONESS)

Address
The Most Honourable the Marquis (Marchioness) of (*place*)
Salutation
My Lord (*place*): (Madam:)

MAYOR

AMERICAN
Address
The Honorable (*full name*)
Mayor of (*city*)
City Hall
(*city, state, ZIP*)
Salutation
Dear Sir (Madam): *or*
Dear Mr. (Madam) Mayor:
CANADIAN
Address
His (Her) Worship Mayor (*full name*)
City Hall
(*city, province, code*)
Salutation
Dear Sir (Madam):

MINISTER (Diplomatic)

Address
His (Her) Excellency (*surname*) *or*
The Honorable (*surname*)
Minister of (*country*)

Salutation
  Your Excellency:
  Dear Mr. (Madam) Minister:

MONSIGNOR

Address
  The Right Reverend Monsignor
  (*surname*)
Salutation
  Right Reverend Monsignor:
WHEN A PAPAL CHAMBERLAIN
Address
  The Very Reverend Monsignor
  (*surname*)
Salutation
  Very Reverend Monsignor:

NAVAL OFFICER

Same form as Army officers, except: Officers under the rank of Commander are addressed as "Mister"; a naval officer regardless of rank who is in command of a ship is addressed as "Captain" for the period of his command; U.S.N. follows military unit.

POPE

Address
  His Holiness the Pope *or*
  His Holiness, Pope (*official name*)
Salutation
  Your Holiness: *or*
  Most Holy Father:

PRESIDENT OF THE UNITED STATES

Address
  The President
  The White House
  Washington, D.C. 20500
Salutation
  Sir (Madam): *or*
  Dear Mr. (Madam) President:

RABBI

Address
  Rabbi (*full name*)
Salutation
  Dear Rabbi (*surname*):

REPRESENTATIVE

U.S., FEDERAL
Address
  The Honorable (*full name*)
  The House of Representatives
  Washington, D.C. 20515
Salutation
  Sir (Madam):
  Dear Congressman (Congresswoman)
  (*surname*):
U.S., LOCAL
Address
  The Honorable (*full name*)

  (*place*) House of Representatives (*or*
  Assembly *or* House of Delegates)
  (*city, state, ZIP*)
Salutation
  Dear Mr. (Mrs., Ms., Miss) (*surname*):
CANADIAN, FEDERAL
Address
  Mr. (Mrs., Ms., Miss) (*full name*), M.P.
  House of Commons
  Parliament Buildings
  Ottawa, Ontario K1A 0A6
Salutation
  Dear Sir (Madam):
  Dear Mr. (Mrs., Ms., Miss) (*surname*):
CANADIAN, PROVINCIAL
Address
  Mr. (Mrs., Ms., Miss) (*full name*), M.L.A.
  (*Ontario*: M.P.P.; *Quebec*: M.N.A.)
  Member of Legislative Assembly
  (*city, province, code*)
Salutation
  Dear Sir (Madam):
  Dear Mr. (Mrs., Ms., Miss) (*surname*):

SENATOR

U.S., FEDERAL
Address
  The Honorable (*full name*)
  United States Senate
  Washington, D.C. 20510
Salutation
  Sir (Madam):
  Dear Senator (*surname*):
U.S., STATE
Address
  The Honorable (*full name*)
  (*place*) Senate
  (*capital, city, state, ZIP*)
Salutation
  Dear Mr. (Mrs., Ms., Miss) (*surname*):
CANADIAN
Address
  The Honourable (*full name*)
  The Senate
  Parliament Buildings
  Ottawa, Ontario K1A 0A4
Salutation
  Dear Sir (Madam):
  Dear Senator (*surname*):

SISTER OF A RELIGIOUS ORDER

Address
  The Reverend Sister (*full or given name*)
Salutation
  Dear Sister (*given name*):

VICE-PRESIDENT OF THE UNITED STATES

Address
  The Honorable (*full name*)
  Vice-President of the United States
  Washington, D.C. 20501
Salutation
  Sir (Madam):
  Dear Mr. (Madam) Vice-President:

TABLES OF WEIGHTS AND MEASURES
U.S. SYSTEM

Linear Measure

	1 inch (in)	= 2.54 centimeters (cm)
12 inches =	1 foot (ft)	0.3048 meter (m)
3 feet	1 yard (yd)	0.9144 meter
5½ yards	1 rod (rd)	5.029 meters
40 rods	1 furlong (fur)	201.168 meters
8 furlongs	1 (statute) mile (mi)	1609.344 meters
3 (statute) miles	1 (land) league	4.828 kilometers
6 feet	1 fathom	1.828 meters
1,000 fathoms or 1.1508 statute miles	1 nautical mile (knot)	1.852 kilometers

Area or Square Measure

	1 square inch (sq in)	= 6.452 square centimeters
144 square inches =	1 square foot (sq ft)	929.030 square centimeters
9 square feet	1 square yard (sq yd)	0.836 square meter
30¼ square yards	1 square rod (sq rd)	25.293 square meters
160 square rods	1 acre	0.405 hectare
640 acres	1 square mile (sq mi)	258.999 hectares
1 square mile	1 section (of land)	
36 square miles	1 township	

Volume or Cubic Measure

	1 cubic inch (cu in)	= 16.387 cubic centimeters
1,728 cubic inches =	1 cubic foot (cu ft)	0.028 cubic meter
27 cubic feet	1 cubic yard (cu yd)	0.765 cubic meter
16 cubic feet	1 cord foot	
8 cord feet	1 cord	3.625 cubic meters

Capacity Measures
Dry Measure

1 pint (pt) =	(33.60 cubic inches)	= 0.551 liter
2 pints	1 quart (qt)	1.101 liters
8 quarts	1 peck (pk)	8.810 liters
4 pecks	1 bushel (bu)	35.238 liters

Liquid Measure

1 minim =	(0.004 cubic inch)	= 0.062 milliliter
60 minims	1 fluid dram (fl dr)	3.697 milliliters
8 fluid drams	1 fluid ounce (fl oz)	0.030 liter
4 fluid ounces	1 gill	0.118 liter

8 fluid ounces	= 1 cup	=	0.236 liter
2 cups	1 pint (pt)		0.473 liter
2 pints	1 quart (qt)		0.946 liter
4 quarts	1 gallon		3.785 liters

1 teaspoon (tsp)	1⅓ fluid drams
1 tablespoon (tbsp)	3 teaspoons

Angular and Circular Measure

60 seconds (″)	=	1 minute (′)
60 minutes		1 degree (°)
90 degrees		1 right angle, or 1 quadrant of a circle
4 quadrants or 360 degrees	=	1 circle

Weights

Avoirdupois Weight

	1 grain (gr)	=	0.065 gram
27.34 grains	= 1 dram (dr)		1.772 grams
16 drams	1 ounce (oz)		28.350 grams
16 ounces	1 pound (lb)		453.592 grams
100 pounds	1 hundredweight (cwt)		45.359 kilograms
2,000 pounds	1 ton (tn)		907.18 kilograms
14 pounds	1 stone (Great Britain)		6.35 kilograms

Troy Weight

	1 grain	=	0.065 gram
3.086 grains	= 1 carat (c)		200 milligrams
24 grains	1 pennyweight (dwt)		1.555 grams
20 pennyweights	1 ounce (oz)		31.104 grams
12 ounces	1 pound (lb)		373.242 grams

Apothecaries' Weight

	1 grain	=	0.065 gram
20 grains	= 1 scruple		1.296 grams
3 scruples	1 dram		3.888 grams
8 drams or 480 grains	1 ounce		31.104 grams
12 ounces or 5,760 grains	1 pound		373.24 grams

METRIC SYSTEM

Linear Measure

	1 millimeter (mm)	=	0.039 inch
10 millimeters =	1 centimeter (cm)		0.394 inch
10 centimeters	1 decimeter (dm)		3.937 inches
10 decimeters	1 meter (m)		39.37 inches
10 meters	1 decameter (dam)		32.8 feet
10 decameters	1 hectometer (hm)		328. feet
10 hectometers	1 kilometer (km)		0.621 mile

Square Measure

	1 square millimeter (sq mm)	=	0.002 square inch
100 square millimeters =	1 square centimeter (cm²)		0.155 square inch
100 square centimeters	1 square decimeter (dm²)		15.499 square inches
100 square decimeters	1 square meter (m²)		1549. square inches
1 square meter	1 centare		10.76 square feet
100 centares	1 are (a)		119.6 square yards
100 ares	1 hectare (ha)		2.471 acres
100 hectares	1 square kilometer (km²)		0.386 square mile

Volume Measure

	1 cubic centimeter	=	.061 cubic inch
1,000 cubic centimeters =	1 cubic decimeter (dm³)		61.02 cubic inches
1,000 cubic decimeters	1 cubic meter (cm³)		35.314 cubic feet

Capacity Measure

	1 milliliter (ml)	=	.027 fluid drams
10 milliliters =	1 centiliter (cl)		.338 fluid ounce
10 centiliters	1 deciliter (dl)		3.38 fluid ounces
10 deciliters	1 liter (l)		1.057 liquid quarts or 0.908 dry quart
10 liters	1 decaliter (dal)		2.64 gallons or 0.284 bushel
10 decaliters	1 hectoliter (hl)		264.18 gallons or 2.838 bushels
10 hectoliters	1 kiloliter (kl)		264.18 gallons or 28.38 bushels

Weights

	1 milligram (mg)	=	0.015 grain
10 milligrams =	1 centigram (cg)		0.154 grain
10 centigrams	1 decigram (dg)		1.543 grains
10 decigrams	1 gram (g)		15.432 grains

10 grams	1 decagram (dag)	0.353 ounce
10 decagrams	1 hectogram (hg)	3.527 ounces
10 hectograms	1 kilogram (kg)	2.205 pounds
100 kilograms	1 quintal	220.46 pounds
10 quintals	1 metric ton (t)	2204.6 pounds

CONVERSION FACTORS

These conversion factors are provided as an aid in quickly converting selected units of weight and measure from the U.S. System to the Metric System and back. To make the opposite conversion from that given below, simply divide by the number given instead of multiplying.

TO CHANGE	TO	MULTIPLY BY
inches	centimeters	2.54
feet	meters	.305
miles	kilometers	1.609
kilometers	miles	.621
square inches	square centimeters	6.452
square yards	square meters	.836
square meters	square yards	1.196
ounces (fluid)	cubic centimeters	29.57
quarts	liters	.946
cubic inches	cubic centimeters	16.387
cubic yards	cubic meters	.765
grains	milligrams	64.799
ounces (dry)	grams	28.35
pounds	grams	454
pounds	kilograms	.454
degrees Centigrade	degrees Fahrenheit	$\frac{9}{5}$ and add 32
degrees Fahrenheit	degrees Centigrade	subtract 32, then multiply by $\frac{5}{9}$

Other conversion factors of use include:

MULTIPLY	BY	TO OBTAIN
Diameter circle	3.1416	Circumference of circle
Diameter circle	.8862	Side of equal square
Diameter circle squared	.7854	Area of circle
Diameter sphere squared	3.1416	Area of sphere
Diameter sphere cubed	.5236	Volume of sphere
U.S. gallons	.8327	Imperial gallons (British)
U.S. gallons	.1337	Cubic feet
U.S. gallons	8.330	Pounds of water at 20° C.
Cubic feet	62.427	Pounds of water at 4° C.
Feet of water at 4° C.	.4335	Pounds per square inch
Inch of mercury at 0° C.	.4912	Pounds per square inch
Knots	1.1516	Miles per hour

SIGNS AND SYMBOLS

Accents and Punctuation:

´	acute
&	ampersand
{ }	braces
[ ]	brackets
˘	breve
¸	cedilla
ˆ	circumflex
¨	dieresis
"	ditto
. . .	ellipsis
&c or etc	et cetera
!	exclamation mark
`	grave
¯	macron
¶	paragraph mark
( )	parentheses
§	section mark
~	tilde
/	virgule

Business and Finance:

a/c	account
@	at or each
B/L	bill of lading
B/S	bill of sale
¢	cent
$	dollar
L/C	letter of credit
#	number (before a figure); pound (weight) (after a figure)
%	per cent
£	pound (currency—sterling)
lb	pound (weight)

Electrical:

⇄	alternating current
⊻	antenna
battery.eps	battery
⊣⊢	capacitor
⊸	diode
⇒	direct current; or direction of flow
⊟	fuse
⏚	ground
⬚	inductor
⊸◯	lamp
⊳	microphone
Ω	ohm
–	polarity, negative
+	polarity, positive
⊸⊢	rectifier
⊸⋀⋀⊢	resistor
⟋	switch
⬚	transformer
⏀	transistor—position of arrow indicates type

Mathematical:

∥	parallel
× or ·	multiplied by
÷ or /	divided by
:	ratio; is to
∴	therefore
∵	because
>	greater than
≧	greater than or equal to
≷	greater than or less than
<	less than
≦	less than or equal to
≑	approaches
=	equal to
≠ or ≠	not equal to
≡	identical with
≢ or ≢	not identical with
~	equivalent to
∼	difference
√	radical or root
π	pi
ε	epsilon
±	plus or minus
#	number
%	per cent
⇒	approaches limit of

Σ	sum; sigma
sin	sine of angle
cos	cosine of angle
tan	tangent of angle
log	logarithm
!	factorial
∞	infinity

Medical:

*	birth
†	death
♀	female
○	female, in charts
♂ or ⚥	male
□	male, in charts
Rh–	Rhesus factor, negative
Rh+	Rhesus factor, positive

Planets and Zodiac:

☿	Mercury
♀	Venus
⊕	Earth
♂	Mars
♃	Jupiter
♄	Saturn
♅	Uranus
♆	Neptune
♇	Pluto
☌	conjunction
☍	opposition
☉	Sun
●	Moon
●	New Moon
☽	Moon: first quarter
☾	Moon: last quarter
○	full Moon
♈	Aries; Ram

♉	Taurus; Bull
♊	Gemini; Twins
♋	Cancer; Crab
♌	Leo; Lion
♍	Virgo; Virgin
♎	Libra; Balance
♏	Scorpio; Scorpion
♐	Sagittarius; Archer
♑	Capricornus; Goat
♒	Aquarius; Water Bearer
♓	Pisces; Fish

Weather:

T	thunder
Я	thunderstorm
↓	precipitate
⦀	rain
▲	hail
⊗	sleet
V	frost
*	snow
≡	fog
∞	haze
◑	cloudy
©	calm
○	clear
↺	tropical storm
▲▲▲	cold front
▬▬	warm front
∿	stationary front

Miscellaneous:

©	copyright
®	registered trademark
℞	prescription; recipe
†	dagger
‡	double dagger

FOR THE BEST IN PAPERBACKS, LOOK FOR THE

In every corner of the world, on every subject under the sun, Penguin represents quality and variety—the very best in publishing today.

For complete information about books available from Penguin—including Penguin Classics, Penguin Compass, and Puffins—and how to order them, write to us at the appropriate address below. Please note that for copyright reasons the selection of books varies from country to country.

In the United States: Please write to *Penguin Group (USA), P.O. Box 12289 Dept. B, Newark, New Jersey 07101-5289* or call 1-800-788-6262.

In the United Kingdom: Please write to *Dept. EP, Penguin Books Ltd, Bath Road, Harmondsworth, West Drayton, Middlesex UB7 0DA*.

In Canada: Please write to *Penguin Books Canada Ltd, 10 Alcorn Avenue, Suite 300, Toronto, Ontario M4V 3B2*.

In Australia: Please write to *Penguin Books Australia Ltd, P.O. Box 257, Ringwood, Victoria 3134*.

In New Zealand: Please write to *Penguin Books (NZ) Ltd, Private Bag 102902, North Shore Mail Centre, Auckland 10*.

In India: Please write to *Penguin Books India Pvt Ltd, 11 Panchsheel Shopping Centre, Panchsheel Park, New Delhi 110 017*.

In the Netherlands: Please write to *Penguin Books Netherlands bv, Postbus 3507, NL-1001 AH Amsterdam*.

In Germany: Please write to *Penguin Books Deutschland GmbH, Metzlerstrasse 26, 60594 Frankfurt am Main*.

In Spain: Please write to *Penguin Books S. A., Bravo Murillo 19, 1° B, 28015 Madrid*.

In Italy: Please write to *Penguin Italia s.r.l., Via Benedetto Croce 2, 20094 Corsico, Milano*.

In France: Please write to *Penguin France, Le Carré Wilson, 62 rue Benjamin Baillaud, 31500 Toulouse*.

In Japan: Please write to *Penguin Books Japan Ltd, Kaneko Building, 2-3-25 Koraku, Bunkyo-Ku, Tokyo 112*.

In South Africa: Please write to *Penguin Books South Africa (Pty) Ltd, Private Bag X14, Parkview, 2122 Johannesburg*.